THE
NEW
LIFE™
BIBLE

D0324596

BARBOUR
PUBLISHING

The Word (for Life)
ISBN 978-1-59789-683-2

Promise (for Life)
ISBN 978-1-59789-684-9

Truth (for Life)
ISBN 978-1-59789-685-6

Refresh (for Life)
ISBN 978-1-59789-686-3

Published by Barbour Publishing, Inc., P.O. Box 719, Uhrichsville, Ohio 44683
www.barbourbooks.com

Our mission is to publish and distribute inspirational products offering exceptional value and biblical encouragement to the masses.

Presented to

_____

By

_____

On the Occasion of

_____

Date

_____

INTRODUCTION

The idea of a very readable and yet accurate version of the scriptures came to us in an igloo in the frozen Canadian Arctic many years ago. A few of the primitive Eskimos with whom we were working then were just starting to learn English. Although it was twenty years later before the NEW LIFE Bible was published, the idea never left us. Instead, during those years, vocabulary and thought patterns were observed which helped set the course for a version that would eventually be used and appreciated in many parts of the world where English is used as a second language.

The secret of its readability is in the limited vocabulary. In most cases, each word uses only one meaning. Difficult biblical words found in other versions were broken down into simple, meaningful phrases. Other problems in Bible reading were researched, and the end result is a very readable and understandable version. Even educated adults who are familiar with the scriptures find themselves startled into new insights by its blunt simplicity.

Those of us who worked on this limited vocabulary NEW LIFE Version were constantly watching to keep it understandable without sacrificing accuracy. There was no thought to change God's holy Word to today's street language. In fact, in many places, the wording and beauty of older versions have been retained. Paraphrasing, or man's idea of what the Bible says, was ruled out. The careful and prayerful use of some basic words can be made to say what the original languages said, thus assuring the reader of an accurate text.

Two different times, the Bible speaks of the very words that were written by God and by Christ. Exodus 31:18 says, "When the Lord had finished speaking with Moses on Mount Sinai, He gave him the two stone writings of the Law, pieces of stone written on by the finger of God." And John 8:6 says, "Jesus got down and began to write in the dust with His finger." Both of these writings were soon destroyed. The pieces of stone with the written Law were broken in front of the children of Israel who were worshiping a false god, and it was not long before the people walked over what Jesus had written on the ground. But it pleased God to have His law and the good news of life that lasts forever written by men He chose for that special job.

Those early men of God who copied the words given by the Holy Spirit that make up the 66 different books of the Bible used different languages than are used today. From Genesis to Revelation forty different men were used over a period of 1600 years. Four hundred years of time separated the Old Testament from the New. The way of life of the people living in Old Testament times was much different from those living during New Testament times. Hebrew was the language of the Old Testament, and Greek was used in the New Testament.

Those men did not write the Bible, but were led or guided by the Holy Spirit as to what they wrote and the words to use. "Understand this first: No part of the Holy Writings was ever made up by any man. No part of the Holy Writings came long ago because of what men wanted to write. But holy men who belonged to God spoke (wrote) what the Holy Spirit told them" (2 Peter 1:20–21).

The first copies of the holy scriptures were perfect and without error. But man is not perfect, and because of changes in languages through the many years and translation from one language to another, no version can claim that same degree of perfection.

Since about 1900, many different versions have been printed in English—and hundreds in other major languages and tribal languages around the world. In all these languages, God's written Word is alive today. Through the years, sinful men have tried to destroy it, but this living Book can never be destroyed. "Heaven and earth will pass away, but My words will never pass away" (Matthew 24:35).

The Word of God contains many promises. This one tells what reading the Bible will do: "All the Holy Writings are God-given and are made alive by Him. Man is helped when he is taught God's Word. It shows him how to be right with God. It gives the man who belongs to God everything he needs to work well for Him" (2 Timothy 3:16–17).

We dedicate this NEW LIFE Bible to Him in whose honor it has been published. May it give all who read it a greater understanding of the scriptures and a better knowledge of Jesus Christ, who came to save from the penalty and power of sin all who will put their trust in Him.

GLEASON AND KATHRYN LEDYARD

Wherever * is seen, the words that follow are not in all the early writings of the New Testament. If part of a verse or more than one verse is missing in some of the early writings, it is marked [*].

CONTENTS

The OLD TESTAMENT

The NEW TESTAMENT

The OLD TESTAMENT

GENESIS

The Beginning

1 In the beginning God made from nothing the heavens and the earth. **2** The earth was an empty waste and darkness was over the deep waters. And the Spirit of God was moving over the top of the waters. **3** Then God said, "Let there be light," and there was light. **4** God saw that the light was good. He divided the light from the darkness. **5** Then God called the light day, and He called the darkness night. There was evening and there was morning, one day.

6 Then God said, "Let there be an open space between the waters. Let it divide waters from waters." **7** God made the open space, and divided the waters under the open space from the waters above the open space. And it was so. **8** Then God called the open space Heaven. There was evening and there was morning, the second day.

9 Then God said, "Let the waters under the heavens be gathered into one place. Let the dry land be seen." And it was so. **10** Then God called the dry land Earth. He called the gathering of the waters Seas. And God saw that it was good. **11** Then God said, "Let plants grow from the earth, plants that have seeds. Let fruit trees grow on the earth that bring their kind of fruit with their own seeds." And it was so. **12** Plants grew out of the earth, giving their own kind of seeds. Trees grew with their fruit, and their kind of seeds. And God saw that it was good. **13** There was evening and there was morning, the third day.

14 Then God said, "Let there be lights in the open space of the heavens to divide day from night. Let them tell the days and years and times of the year. **15** Let them be lights in the open space of the heavens to give light on the earth." And it was so. **16** Then God made the two great lights, the brighter light to rule the day, and the smaller light to rule the night. He made the stars also. **17** God put them in the open space of the heavens to give light on the earth, **18** to rule the day and the night. He divided the light from the darkness. And God saw that it was good. **19** There was evening and there was morning, the fourth day.

20 Then God said, "Let the waters be full of living things. Let birds fly above the earth in the open space of the heavens." **21** God made the big animals that live in the sea, and every living thing that moves through the waters by its kind, and every winged bird after its kind. And God saw

that it was good. **22** God wanted good to come to them, saying, "Give birth to many. Grow in number. Fill the waters in the seas. Let birds grow in number on the earth." **23** There was evening and there was morning, the fifth day.

24 Then God said, "Let the earth bring into being living things after their kind: Cattle and things that move upon the ground, and wild animals of the earth after their kind." And it was so. **25** Then God made the wild animals of the earth after their kind, and the cattle after their kind, and every thing that moves upon the ground after its kind. And God saw that it was good.

26 Then God said, "Let Us make man like Us and let him be head over the fish of the sea, and over the birds of the air, and over the cattle, and over all the earth, and over every thing that moves on the ground." **27** And God made man in His own likeness. In the likeness of God He made him. He made both male and female. **28** And God wanted good to come to them, saying, "Give birth to many. Grow in number. Fill the earth and rule over it. Rule over the fish of the sea, over the birds of the sky, and over every living thing that moves on the earth." **29** Then God said, "See, I have given you every plant that gives seeds that is on the earth, and every tree that has fruit that gives seeds. They will be food for you. **30** I have given every green plant for food to every animal of the earth, and to every bird of the sky, and to every thing that moves on the earth that has life." And it was so. **31** God saw all that He had made and it was very good. There was evening and there was morning, the sixth day.

2 So the heavens and the earth were completed, and all that is in them. **2** On the seventh day God ended His work which He had done. And He rested on the seventh day from all His work which He had done. **3** Then God honored the seventh day and made it holy, because in it He rested from all His work which He had done.

The Garden of Eden

4 This is the story of the heavens and the earth when they were made, in the day the Lord God made the earth and the heavens. **5** Now no bush of the field was yet on the earth. And no plant of the field had started to grow. For the Lord God had not sent rain upon the earth. And there was no man to work the ground. 6 But a fog came from the earth and watered the whole top of the ground. 7 Then the Lord God made man from the dust of the ground. And He breathed into his nose the breath of life. Man became a living being. 8 The Lord God planted a garden to the east in Eden. He put the man there whom He had made. 9 And the Lord God made to grow out of the ground every tree that is pleasing to the eyes and good for food. And He made the tree of life grow in the center of the garden, and the tree of learning of good and bad.

10 Now a river flowed out of Eden to water the garden. And from there it divided and became four rivers. 11 The name of the first is Pishon. It flows around the whole land of Havilah, where there is gold. 12 The gold of that land is good. Bdellium and onyx stone are there. 13 The name of the second river is Gihon. It flows around the whole land of Cush. 14 The name of the third river is Tigris. It flows east of Assyria. And the fourth river is the Euphrates.

15 Then the Lord God took the man and put him in the garden of Eden to work the ground and care for it. 16 The Lord God told the man, "You are free to eat from any tree of the garden. 17 But do not eat from the tree of learning of good and bad. For the day you eat from it you will die for sure."

18 Then the Lord God said, "It is not good for man to be alone. I will make a helper that is right for him." 19 Out of the ground the Lord God made every animal of the field and every bird of the sky. He brought them to the man to find out what he would call them. And whatever the man called a living thing, that was its name. 20 Adam gave names to all the cattle, and to the birds of the sky, and to every animal of the field. But there was no helper found that was right for Adam. 21 So the Lord God put the man to sleep as if he were dead. And while he was sleeping, He took one of the bones from his side and closed up the place with flesh. 22 The Lord God made woman from the bone which He had taken from the man. And He brought her to the man. 23 The man said, "This is now bone of my bones, and flesh of my flesh. She will be called Woman, because she was taken out of Man." 24 For this reason a man will leave his father and his mother, and will be joined to his wife. And they will become one flesh. 25 The man and his wife were both without clothes and were not ashamed.

Man Does Not Obey God

3 Now the snake was more able to fool others than any animal of the field which the Lord God had made. He said to the woman, "Did God say that you should not eat from any tree in the garden?" 2 Then the woman said to the snake, "We may eat the fruit of the trees of the garden. 3 But from the tree which is in the center of the garden, God has said, 'Do not eat from it or touch it, or you will die.'"

4 The snake said to the woman, "No, you for sure will not die! 5 For God knows that when you eat from it, your eyes will be opened and you will be like God, knowing good and bad." 6 The woman saw that the tree was good for food, and pleasing to the eyes, and could fill the desire of making one wise. So she took of its fruit and ate. She also gave some to her husband, and he ate. 7 Then the eyes of both of them were opened, and they knew they were without clothes. So they sewed fig leaves together and made themselves clothing.

8 Then they heard the sound of the Lord God walking in the garden in the evening. The man and his wife hid themselves from the Lord God among the trees of the garden. 9 But the Lord God called to the man. He said to him, "Where are you?" 10 And the man said, "I heard the sound of You in the garden. I was afraid because I was without clothes. So I hid myself." 11 The Lord God said, "Who told you that you were without clothes? Have you eaten from the tree of which I told you not to eat?" 12 The man said, "The woman whom You gave to be with me, she gave me fruit of the tree, and I ate." 13 Then the Lord God said to the woman, "What is this you have done?" And the woman said, "The snake fooled me, and I ate."

14 Then the Lord God said to the snake, "Because you have done this, you will be hated and will suffer more than all cattle, and more than every animal of the field. You will go on your stomach and you will eat dust all the days of your life. 15 And I will make you and the woman hate each other, and your seed and her seed will hate each other. He will crush your head, and you will crush his heel."

16 To the woman He said, "I will make your pain much worse in giving birth. You will give birth to children in pain. Yet your desire will be for your husband, and he will rule over you."

17 Then He said to Adam, "Because you have listened to the voice of your wife,

and have eaten from the tree of which I told you, 'Do not eat from it,' the ground is cursed because of you. By hard work you will eat food from it all the days of your life. 18 It will give thorns and thistles for you. You will eat the plants of the field. 19 You will eat bread by the sweat of your face because of hard work, until you return to the ground, because you were taken from the ground. You are dust, and you will return to dust."

20 The man called his wife's name Eve, because she was the mother of all living. 21 And the Lord God made clothes of skins for Adam and his wife, and dressed them.

22 Then the Lord God said, "See, the man has become like one of Us, knowing good and bad. Now then, he might put out his hand to take from the tree of life also, and eat and live forever." 23 So the Lord God sent him out from the garden of Eden, to work the ground from which he was taken. 24 So He drove the man out. And He placed cherubim east of the garden of Eden with a sword of fire that turned every way. They kept watch over the path to the tree of life.

Cain Kills Abel

4 The man lay with his wife Eve and she was going to have a child and she gave birth to Cain. She said, "I have given birth to a man with the help of the Lord." 2 Next she gave birth to his brother Abel. Now Abel was a keeper of sheep, but Cain was one who worked the ground.

3 The day came when Cain brought a gift of the fruit of the ground to the Lord. 4 But Abel brought a gift of the first-born of his flocks and of the fat parts. The Lord showed favor to Abel and his gift. 5 But He had no respect for Cain and his gift. So Cain became very angry and his face became sad. 6 Then the Lord said to Cain, "Why are you angry? And why are you looking down? 7 Will not your face be happy if you do well? If you do not do well, sin is waiting to destroy you. Its desire is to rule over you, but you must rule over it."

8 Cain told this to his brother Abel. And when they were in the field, Cain stood up against his brother Abel and killed him.

9 Then the Lord said to Cain, "Where is Abel your brother?" And he said, "I do not know. Am I my brother's keeper?" 10 The Lord said, "What have you done? The voice of your brother's blood is crying to Me from the ground. 11 Now you are cursed because of the ground, which has opened its mouth to receive your brother's blood from your hand. 12 When you work the ground, it will no longer give its strength to you. You will always travel from place to place on the earth."

13 Then Cain said to the Lord, "I am being punished more than I can take! 14 See, this day You have made me go away from the land. And I will be hidden from Your face. I will run away and move from place to place. And whoever finds me will kill me."

15 So the Lord said to him, "Whoever kills Cain will be punished by Me seven times worse." And the Lord put a mark on Cain so that any one who found him would not kill him.

16 Then Cain went away from the face of the Lord, and stayed in the land of Nod, east of Eden. 17 Cain lay with his wife and she was going to have a child and she gave birth to Enoch. Cain built a city and gave it the name of Enoch, the name of his son. 18 Now Irad was born to Enoch. And Irad became the father of Mehujael. Mehujael became the father of Methushael. And Methushael became the father of Lamech. 19 Lamech took two wives for himself. The name of one was Adah. And the name of the other was Zillah. 20 Adah gave birth to Jabal. He was the father of those who live in tents and have cattle. 21 His brother's name was Jubal. He was the father of all those who play the harp and the horn. 22 Zillah gave birth to Tubal-cain who made things from brass and iron. The sister of Tubal-cain was Naamah.

23 And Lamech said to his wives, "Adah and Zillah, listen to my voice. Hear what I say, you wives of Lamech. For I have killed a man for hurting me, and a boy for hitting me. 24 If those who hurt Cain are punished seven times worse, then those who hurt Lamech will be punished seventy-seven times worse."

25 And Adam lay with his wife again, and she gave birth to a son and gave him the name Seth. For she said, "God has let me have another son in the place of Abel, for Cain killed him." 26 A son was born to Seth also, and he gave him the name Enosh. Then men began to call upon the name of the Lord.

The Families from Adam to Noah

5 This is the book of the children of Adam and of their children's children. When God made man, He made him in the likeness of God. 2 He made them male and female, and brought good to them. And He gave them the name Man when they were made. 3 When Adam had lived 130 years, he gave birth to a son in his own likeness. And he gave him the name Seth. 4 Adam lived 800 years after he became the father of Seth. He had other sons and daughters. 5 So Adam lived 930 years, and he died.

6 When Seth had lived 105 years, he became the father of Enosh. 7 Seth lived 807 years after the birth of Enosh. He had other sons and daughters. 8 So Seth lived 912 years, and he died.

9 When Enosh had lived ninety years, he became the father of Kenan. 10 Enosh lived 815 years after the birth of Kenan. He had other sons and daughters. 11 So Enosh lived 905 years, and he died.

12 When Kenan had lived seventy years, he became the father of Mahalalel. 13 Kenan lived 840 years after the birth of Mahalalel. He had other sons and daughters. 14 So Kenan lived 910 years, and he died.

15 When Mahalalel had lived sixty-five years, he became the father of Jared. 16 Mahalalel lived 830 years after the birth of Jared. He had other sons and daughters. 17 So Mahalalel lived 895 years, and he died.

18 When Jared had lived 162 years, he became the father of Enoch. 19 Jared lived 800 years after the birth of Enoch. He had other sons and daughters. 20 So Jared lived 962 years, and he died.

21 When Enoch had lived sixty-five years, he became the father of Methuselah. 22 Enoch walked with God 300 years after the birth of Methuselah. He had other sons and daughters. 23 So Enoch lived 365 years. 24 Enoch walked with God, and he was seen no more, for God took him.

25 When Methuselah had lived 187 years, he became the father of Lamech. 26 Methuselah lived 782 years after the birth of Lamech. He had other sons and daughters. 27 So Methuselah lived 969 years, and he died.

28 When Lamech had lived 182 years, he became the father of a son. 29 He gave him the name Noah. He said, "This one will give us rest from our work, from the hard work of our hands because the ground was cursed by the Lord." 30 Lamech lived 595 years after the birth of Noah. He had other sons and daughters. 31 So Lamech lived 777 years, and he died.

32 When Noah had lived 500 years, he became the father of Shem, Ham, and Japheth.

Sinful Man

6 When men became many in number on the earth, and daughters were born to them, 2 the sons of God saw that the daughters of men were beautiful. And they took wives for themselves, whomever they chose. 3 Then the Lord said, "My Spirit will not stay in man forever, for he is flesh. But yet he will live for 120 years." 4 Very large men were on the earth in those days, and later also, when the sons of God lived with the daughters of men, who gave birth to their children. These were the powerful men of long ago, men of much strength.

5 Then the Lord saw that man was very sinful on the earth. Every plan and thought of the heart of man was sinful always. 6 The Lord was sorry that He had made man on the earth. He had sorrow in His heart. 7 So the Lord said, "I will destroy man whom I have made from the land, man and animals, things that move upon the earth and birds of the sky. For I am sorry that I have made them." 8 But Noah found favor in the eyes of the Lord.

9 This is the story of Noah and his family. Noah was right with God. He was without blame in his time. Noah walked with God. 10 And Noah became the father of three sons: Shem, Ham, and Japheth. 11 Now the earth was sinful in the eyes of God. The earth was filled with people hurting each other. 12 God looked at the earth and saw how sinful it was. For all who lived on the earth had become sinful in their ways.

13 Then God said to Noah, "I have decided to make an end to all the people on the earth. They are the cause of very much trouble. See, I will destroy them as I destroy the earth. 14 Make a large boat of gopher wood for yourself. Build rooms in the boat. And cover it inside and out with tar. 15 This is how you are to make it: The boat is to be as long as 150 long steps, as wide as twenty-five long steps, and eight times taller than a man. 16 Make a window for the boat, that goes down a cubit from the roof. Put a door in the side of the boat. And make it with first, second, and third floors. 17 See, I will bring a flood of water upon the earth, to destroy all flesh under heaven that has the breath of life. Everything on earth will be destroyed. 18 But I will make My agreement with you. You will go into the large boat, you and your sons and your

wife, and your sons' wives with you. ¹⁹ You are to bring into the large boat two of every kind of living thing of all flesh, to keep them alive with you. They will be male and female. ²⁰ Two of all the kinds of birds, and animals, and every thing that moves on the ground are to be with you to keep them alive. ²¹ And take with you every kind of food that is eaten, and store it. It will be food for you and for them." ²² Noah did just what God told him to do.

The Flood

7 Then the Lord said to Noah, "Go into the boat, you and all your family. For I have seen that you only are right and good at this time. ² Take with you seven of every clean animal of each sex, and one of each sex of the animals that are unclean. ³ And take with you seven of every kind of bird of the sky of each sex, to keep their kind alive over all the earth. ⁴ In seven days I will send rain on the earth for forty days and forty nights. I will destroy from the land every living thing that I have made." ⁵ And Noah did all that the Lord told him to do.

⁶ Noah was 600 years old when the flood of water came upon the earth. ⁷ Then Noah and his sons and his wife and his sons' wives all went into the large boat because of the water of the flood. ⁸ Clean animals and animals that were unclean and birds and every thing that moved on the ground ⁹ went into the large boat with Noah. They went two by two, male and female, just as God had told Noah. ¹⁰ After seven days the waters of the flood came upon the earth. ¹¹ In the year 600 of Noah's life, in the second month, on the seventeenth day of the month, all the wells of water under the earth broke open. The windows of the heavens were opened. ¹² And the rain fell upon the earth for forty days and forty nights.

¹³ On the very same day Noah and his sons, Shem and Ham and Japheth, and Noah's wife and the three wives of his sons with them, all went into the large boat. ¹⁴ With them went every kind of animal, and all the cattle, and every thing that moved on the earth, and every kind of bird. ¹⁵ They went into the large boat with Noah, two of every living thing. ¹⁶ Male and female of all flesh went in as God had told Noah. Then the Lord shut him in.

¹⁷ The flood came upon the earth for forty days. The water got deeper and raised up the large boat so that it was lifted above the earth. ¹⁸ The water was very deep upon the earth. And the boat stayed upon the top of the water. ¹⁹ The water got higher and higher upon the earth until all the high mountains under heaven were covered. ²⁰ But the water went about four times taller than a man above the tops of the mountains. ²¹ All flesh that moved on the earth was destroyed, birds and cattle and wild animals, and every man. ²² Every thing that had the breath of life and lived on dry land died. ²³ God destroyed every living thing upon the land, from man to animals, from things that moved upon the ground to birds of the sky. They were destroyed from the earth. Only Noah was left, and those that were with him in the large boat. ²⁴ And the water covered the earth for 150 days.

The Flood Ends

8 But God remembered Noah and all the wild animals and all the cattle that were with him in the large boat. Then God made a wind blow over the earth until the water went down. ² Also the wells of water under the earth and the windows of the heavens were shut. And it stopped raining. ³ The water kept moving away from the earth. At the end of 150 days the water was less. ⁴ And in the seventh month, on the seventeenth day of the month, the large boat came to rest on Mount Ararat. ⁵ The water kept on going down until the tenth month. In the tenth month, on the first day of the month, the tops of the mountains could be seen.

⁶ At the end of forty days, Noah opened the window of the large boat which he had made. ⁷ Then he sent out a raven, and it flew here and there until the water was dried up from the earth ⁸ Then he sent out a dove, to see if the water was gone from the ground. ⁹ But the dove found no place to set her foot, so she returned to him in the boat. For the water was still over the earth. So Noah put out his hand and took her, and brought her into the boat with him. ¹⁰ He waited another seven days, and sent the dove from the boat again. ¹¹ The dove returned to him in the evening. In her mouth was an olive leaf that had just been picked. So Noah knew that the water had gone from the earth. ¹² Then he waited another seven days, and sent out the dove. But she did not return to him again.

¹³ In the year 601, in the first month, on the first day of the month, the water was dried up from the earth. Then Noah took

the covering off the large boat, and looked out and saw that the earth was dry. 14 In the second month, on the twenty-seventh day of the month, the ground was dry. 15 Then God said to Noah, 16 "Go out of the boat, you and your wife and your sons and your sons' wives with you. 17 Bring out with you every living thing of all flesh that is with you, birds and animals and everything that moves on the earth. So they may give birth and become many upon the earth." 18 So Noah went out with his sons and his wife and his sons' wives. 19 Every animal, every bird, everything that moves on the earth, went out of the large boat by their families.

20 Then Noah built an altar to the Lord. He took of every clean animal and every clean bird, and gave burnt gifts in worship on the altar. 21 Then the Lord smelled a pleasing smell. And the Lord said to Himself, "I will never again curse the ground because of man. For the desire of man's heart is sinful from when he is young. I will never again destroy every living thing as I have done. 22 While the earth lasts, planting time and gathering time, cold and heat, summer and winter, and day and night will not end."

God's Agreement with Noah

9 God made good come to Noah and his sons, and said to them, "Have many children, and cover the earth. 2 Every animal of the earth, every bird of the sky, everything that moves on the ground, and all the fish of the sea will be afraid of you. They are given into your hand. 3 Every moving thing that lives will be food for you. I give all to you as I gave you the green plants. 4 But you must not eat meat with blood in it because that is its life. 5 For sure, I will take the life of every animal and every person for taking a life. I will punish every man's brother for taking the life of man. 6 Whoever takes the life of a man will have his life taken. For God made man to be like Him. 7 As for you, have many children. Cover the earth with many people."

8 Then God said to Noah and his sons, 9 "See, I make My agreement with you, and with your children after you, 10 and with every living thing that is with you, the birds, the cattle, and every animal of the earth, of all that came out of the large boat, every living thing on earth. 11 I make My agreement with you, that never again will all flesh be destroyed by the water of a

flood. There will never again be a flood to destroy the earth." 12 Then God said, "This is something special to see for all time, because of the agreement that I am making between Me and you and every living thing that is with you: 13 I will set My rainbow in the cloud, and it will be something special to see because of an agreement between Me and the earth. 14 When I bring clouds over the earth and the rainbow is seen in the clouds, 15 I will remember My agreement that is between Me and you and every living thing of all flesh. Never again will the water become a flood to destroy all flesh. 16 When the rainbow is in the cloud, I will look upon it to remember the agreement that will last forever between God and every living thing of all flesh that is on the earth." 17 God said to Noah, "This is the special thing to see because of the agreement I have made between Me and all flesh upon the earth."

Noah and His Sons

18 The sons of Noah who came out of the large boat were Shem, Ham and Japheth. Ham was the father of Canaan. 19 These three were the sons of Noah. And all the people of the earth came from them.

20 Then Noah became a farmer and planted a grape-field. 21 And he drank of the wine, and drank too much, and lay without covering himself in his tent. 22 Then Ham, the father of Canaan, saw that his father was without clothes. And he told his two brothers outside. 23 But Shem and Japheth took a coat and laid it upon their shoulders and walked in with their backs toward their father and covered him. Their faces were turned away, so that they did not see their father without clothes. 24 When Noah awoke from his wine, he knew what his youngest son had done to him. 25 So he said, "May Canaan be cursed! He will be a servant of servants to his brothers." 26 He also said, "Honor and thanks be to the Lord, the God of Shem. Let Canaan be his servant. 27 May God make Japheth great. Let him live in the tents of Shem. And let Canaan be his servants."

28 Noah lived 350 years after the flood. 29 So Noah lived 950 years, and he died.

The Families after Noah's Sons

10 These are the families of Shem, Ham and Japheth, the sons of Noah, and of their families. Sons were born to them after the flood.

² The sons of Japheth were Gomer, Magog, Madai, Javan, Tubal, Meshech, and Tiras. ³ The sons of Gomer were Ashkenaz, Riphath, and Togarmah. ⁴ The sons of Javan were Elishah, Tarshish, Kittim, and Dodanim. ⁵ From these the people who live beside the sea spread out into their lands, each one by his language, family, and nation.

⁶ The sons of Ham were Cush, Mizraim, Put, and Canaan. ⁷ The sons of Cush were Seba, Havilah, Sabtah, Raamah, and Sabteca. The sons of Raamah were Sheba and Dedan. ⁸ Cush became the father of Nimrod, who was the first on earth to become a powerful man. ⁹ He was a powerful animal-killer in the eyes of the Lord. So it is said, "Like Nimrod, a powerful animal-killer in the eyes of the Lord." ¹⁰ The beginning of his nation was Babel, Erech, Accad, and Calneh, in the land of Shinar. ¹¹ He went into Assyria from the land, and built Nineveh, Rehoboth-Ir, Calah ¹² and Resen between Nineveh and Calah. That is the great city. ¹³ Mizraim became the father of Ludim, Anamim, Lehabim, Naphtuhim, ¹⁴ Pathrusim, Casluhim (from which came the Philistines), and Caphtorim.

¹⁵ Canaan became the father of Sidon, his first-born, and Heth, ¹⁶ and the Jebusite, the Amorite, the Girgashite, ¹⁷ the Hivite, the Arkite, the Sinite, ¹⁸ the Arvadite, the Zemarite, and the Hamathite. Later the Canaanite families spread out. ¹⁹ So the land of the Canaanite was from Sidon toward Gerar as far as Gaza, then toward Sodom, Gomorrah, Admah and Zeboiim as far as Lasha. ²⁰ These are the sons of Ham, by their families, languages, lands and nations.

²¹ Children were born to Shem, the father of all the children of Eber, and the older brother of Japheth. ²² The sons of Shem were Elam, Asshur, Arpachshad, Lud, and Aram. ²³ The sons of Aram were Uz, Hul, Gether, and Mash. ²⁴ Arpachshad became the father of Shelah. Shelah became the father of Eber. ²⁵ Eber had two sons. The name of one was Peleg, for the earth was divided in his day. The name of his brother was Joktan. ²⁶ Joktan became the father of Almodad, Sheleph, Hazarmaveth, Jerah, ²⁷ Hadoram, Uzal, Diklah, ²⁸ Obal, Abimael, Sheba, ²⁹ Ophir, Havilah, and Jobab. All these were the sons of Joktan. ³⁰ The land where they lived was from Mesha toward Sephar to the hill country of the east. ³¹ These are the sons of Shem, by their families, languages, lands and nations.

³² These are the families of the sons of Noah. From these family groups, nations were spread over the earth after the flood.

The Tower at Babel

11 Now the whole earth used the same language and the same words. ² And as men traveled in the east, they found a valley in the land of Shinar and made their home there. ³ They said to one another, "Come, let us make blocks and burn them until they are hard." They used blocks for stone, and tar to hold them together. ⁴ Then they said, "Come, let us build a city for ourselves, with a tower that touches the heavens. Let us make a name for ourselves, or else we may be sent everywhere over the whole earth."

⁵ Then the Lord came down to see the city and the tower that the sons of men had built. ⁶ And the Lord said, "See, they are one people, and they all have the same language. This is only the beginning of what they will do. Now all they plan to do will be possible for them. ⁷ Come, let Us go down and mix up their language so they will not understand what each other says." ⁸ So the Lord sent them everywhere over the whole earth. And they stopped building the city. ⁹ So the name of the city was Babel, because there the Lord mixed up the language of the whole earth. The Lord sent the people everywhere over the whole earth.

The Families after Shem

¹⁰ These are the children of Shem. When Shem had lived 100 years, he became the father of Arpachshad, two years after the flood. ¹¹ Shem lived 500 years after the birth of Arpachshad. He had other sons and daughters.

¹² When Arpachshad had lived thirty-five years, he became the father of Shelah. ¹³ Arpachshad lived 403 years after the birth of Shelah. He had other sons and daughters.

¹⁴ When Shelah had lived thirty years, he became the father of Eber. ¹⁵ Shelah lived 403 years after the birth of Eber. He had other sons and daughters.

¹⁶ When Eber had lived thirty-four years, he became the father of Peleg. ¹⁷ Eber lived 430 years after the birth of Peleg. He had other sons and daughters.

¹⁸ When Peleg had lived thirty years, he became the father of Reu. ¹⁹ Peleg lived 209 years after the birth of Reu. He had other sons and daughters.

20 When Reu had lived thirty-two years, he became the father of Serug. 21 Reu lived 207 years after the birth of Serug. He had other sons and daughters.

22 When Serug had lived thirty years, he became the father of Nahor. 23 Serug lived 200 years after the birth of Nahor. He had other sons and daughters.

24 When Nahor had lived twenty-nine years, he became the father of Terah. 25 Nahor lived 119 years after the birth of Terah. He had other sons and daughters.

26 When Terah had lived seventy years, he became the father of Abram, Nahor and Haran.

27 Now these are the children of Terah. Terah became the father of Abram, Nahor and Haran. And Haran became the father of Lot. 28 Haran died with his father Terah beside him in the land of his birth, Ur of the Chaldeans. 29 Abram and Nahor both married. The name of Abram's wife was Sarai. The name of Nahor's wife was Milcah, the daughter of Haran. Haran was the father of Milcah and Iscah. 30 But Sarai could not give birth. She had no child. 31 Terah took his son Abram, and his grandson Lot, the son of Haran, and his daughter-in-law Sarai, the wife of his son Abram and they went together from Ur of the Chaldeans to the land of Canaan. But when they went as far as Haran, they made their home there. 32 Terah lived 205 years, and he died in Haran.

God Calls Abram

12 Now the Lord said to Abram, "Leave your country, your family and your father's house, and go to the land that I will show you. 2 And I will make you a great nation. I will bring good to you. I will make your name great, so you will be honored. 3 I will bring good to those who are good to you. And I will curse those who curse you. Good will come to all the families of the earth because of you."

4 So Abram left as the Lord told him to do, and Lot went with him. Abram was seventy-five years old when he left Haran. 5 Abram took his wife Sarai, and his brother's son Lot, and all the things they had gathered, and the people who joined them in Haran. And they left to go to the land of Canaan. So they came to the land of Canaan. 6 Abram passed through the land as far as the oak of Moreh at Shechem. The Canaanite people were living in the land at that time. 7 Then the Lord showed Himself to Abram and said,

"I will give this land to your children and to your children's children." So Abram built an altar there to the Lord Who had shown Himself to him. 8 Then he went from there to the mountain east of Bethel. He put up his tent, with Bethel on the west and Ai on the east. There he built an altar to the Lord and called upon the name of the Lord. 9 Then Abram traveled on, still going toward the Negev.

10 Now there was no food in the land. So Abram went south to Egypt to stay there, because it was very hard to live in the land with no food. 11 When he was about to go into Egypt, Abram said to his wife Sarai, "I know that you are a beautiful woman. 12 When the men of Egypt see you, they will say, 'This is his wife.' And they will kill me, but they will let you live. 13 Say that you are my sister. Then it may go well with me because of you. And because of you they will not kill me."

14 When Abram came into Egypt, the men of Egypt saw that the woman was very beautiful. 15 Pharaoh's rulers saw her and told Pharaoh of her beauty. So the woman was taken into Pharaoh's house. 16 And Pharaoh acted well toward Abram because of Sarai. He gave Abram sheep, cattle, male and female donkeys, and camels, and men and women servants. 17 But the Lord sent much sickness upon Pharaoh and his house because of Abram's wife Sarai. 18 Then Pharaoh called Abram and said, "What is this you have done to me? Why did you not tell me that she was your wife? 19 Why did you say, 'She is my sister,' so that I took her for my wife? Now then, here is your wife. Take her and go." 20 And Pharaoh told his men what to do with Abram. They led him away with his wife and all that belonged to him.

Abram and Lot Go Different Ways

13 So Abram left Egypt and went to the Negev, with his wife and all that belonged to him. And Lot went with him. 2 Now Abram was very rich in cattle, silver and gold. 3 He traveled from the Negev as far as Bethel, to the place where his tent had been at the beginning, between Bethel and Ai, 4 where he had made an altar. And there Abram called on the name of the Lord. 5 Now Lot, who went with Abram, had flocks and cattle and tents of his own. 6 There was not enough land to feed all the animals while they lived together. They owned so many things that they were not able to stay together. 7 There was fighting between those who cared for Abram's animals and those who cared for Lot's animals. The Canaanite and the Perizzite were living in the land at that time. [8] So Abram said to Lot, "Let there be no fighting between you and me or between the men who take care of our animals, for we are brothers. [9] Is not the whole land in front of you? Let each of us go a different way. If you go to the left, then I will go to the right. Or if you go to the right, then I will go to the left."

[10] Lot looked and saw that the Jordan valley was well watered everywhere like the garden of the Lord, like the land of Egypt as you go to Zoar. (This was before the Lord destroyed Sodom and Gomorrah.) [11] So Lot chose all the Jordan valley for himself. And as Lot traveled east, they went apart from each other. [12] Abram made his home in the land of Canaan. Lot made his home in the cities of the valley and moved his tents as far as Sodom, [13] whose men were sinful, sinning against the Lord.

[14] The Lord said to Abram, after Lot had left him, "Raise your eyes and look from where you are to the north and south and east and west. [15] For I will give all the land that you see to you and to your children and to your children's children forever. [16] I will make your family after you like the dust of the earth. So if anyone could number the dust of the earth, then he could number your children's children. [17] Rise up and walk far and wide upon the land. For I will give it to you." [18] Then Abram moved his tent and came to live among the oaks of Mamre in Hebron. There he built an altar to the Lord.

Abram Keeps Lot from Being Killed

14 It was in the days of Amraphel king of Shinar, Arioch king of Ellasar, Chedorlaomer king of Elam, and Tidal king of Goiim, [2] that they made war against Bera king of Sodom, Birsha king of Gomorrah, Shinab king of Admah, Shemeber king of Zeboiim, and the king of Bela (that is, Zoar). [3] All these joined together in the valley of Siddim (that is, the Salt Sea). [4] They had been ruled by Chedorlaomer for twelve years. But in the thirteenth year they went against him. [5] Then in the fourteenth year, Chedorlaomer and the kings who were with him came and won a war against the Rephaim in Ashteroth-karnaim, the Zuzim in Ham, the Emim in Shavehkiriathaim, [6] and the

Horites in their Mount Seir as far as El-paran near the desert. [7] Then they turned around and came to Enmishpat (that is, Kadesh). There they won a war against all the country of the Amalekites and the Amorites who lived in Hazazon-tamar. [8] Then the kings of Sodom, Gomorrah, Admah, Zeboiim and Bela (that is, Zoar) went out and joined in war against them in the valley of Siddim. [9] They fought against Chedorlaomer king of Elam, Tidal king of Goiim, Amraphel king of Shinar, and Arioch king of Ellasar, four kings against five. [10] Now the Siddim valley was full of deep holes with tar. The kings of Sodom and Gomorrah turned and ran, and some fell there. But the others ran away into the hill country. [11] Then those who won the war took all that belonged to Sodom and Gomorrah, and all their food, and left. [12] They also took Lot, the son of Abram's brother, who lived in Sodom, and all that belonged to him, and left.

[13] Then one who had run for his life came and told Abram the Hebrew. Abram was living by the oaks of Mamre the Amorite, brother of Eshcol and Aner, who were friends of Abram. [14] When Abram heard that one of his family had been taken away, he led 318 men who had been born in his house and whom he had taught to fight. They went after them as far as Dan. [15] Abram divided his army against them by night, he and his servants. They won the war against them, and followed them as far as Hobah, north of Damascus. [16] Then Abram returned with all the things they had taken. He also returned with his brother's son Lot and all that belonged to him, and the women and the people.

[17] After Abram returned from destroying Chedorlaomer and the kings who were with him, the king of Sodom went out to meet him at the valley of Shaveh (that is, the King's valley). [18] Melchizedek king of Salem brought out bread and wine. He was a religious leader of God Most High. [19] And Melchizedek honored Abram and said, "May good come to Abram from God Most High, Maker of heaven and earth. [20] Honor and thanks be to God Most High, Who has given into your hand those who fought against you." Then Abram gave Melchizedek a tenth of all he had taken. [21] And the king of Sodom said to Abram, "Give me the people, but take the riches and food for yourself." [22] But Abram said to the king of Sodom, "I have promised the

Lord God Most High, Maker of heaven and earth, 23 that I will not take a piece of string or piece of leather or anything that is yours. Or else you might say, 'I have made Abram rich.' 24 I will take nothing but what the young men have eaten, and the share of the men who went with me. Let Aner, Eshcol and Mamre take their share."

God's Agreement with Abram

15 After these things, the word of the Lord came to Abram in a special dream, saying, "Do not be afraid, Abram. I am your safe place. Your reward will be very great." 2 Then Abram said, "O Lord God, what will You give me? For I have no child. And the one who is to receive what belongs to me is Eliezer of Damascus." 3 Abram said, "Because You have not given me a child, one born in my house will be given all I have." 4 Then the word of the Lord came to him, saying, "This man will not be given what is yours. But he who will come from your own body will be given what is yours." 5 He took him outside and said, "Now look up into the heavens and add up the stars, if you are able to number them." Then He said to him, "Your children and your children's children will be as many as the stars." 6 Then Abram believed in the Lord, and that made him right with God.

7 God said to him, "I am the Lord Who brought you out of Ur of the Chaldeans to give you this land for your own." 8 And Abram said, "O Lord God, how may I know that it will be mine?" 9 So the Lord said to him, "Bring Me a three-year-old cow, a three-year-old female goat, a three-year-old ram, a turtle-dove and a young pigeon." 10 Then Abram brought all these to Him, and cut them in two. And he laid each half beside the other. But he did not cut the birds. 11 When the meat-eating birds came down upon the dead animals, Abram made them go away.

12 When the sun was going down, Abram went into a sleep as if he were dead. And much fear and darkness came upon him. 13 God said to Abram, "Know for sure that your children and those born after them will be strangers in a land that is not theirs. There they will be servants and suffer for 400 years. 14 But I will punish the nation they will serve. And later they will come out with many riches. 15 You will live many years, die in peace and be buried. 16 Then your great great-grandchildren will return here. For the sins of the Amorite are not yet finished."

17 When the sun had gone down and it was very dark, a fire pot of smoke and a burning fire passed between these parts of animals. 18 The Lord made an agreement with Abram on that day. He said, "I have given this land to your children and to their children's children, from the river of Egypt as far as the big Euphrates River, 19 the land of the Kenite, the Kenizzite, the Kadmonite, 20 the Hittite, the Perizzite, the Rephaim, 21 the Amorite, the Canaanite, the Girgashite and the Jebusite."

Hagar and Ishmael

16 Now Abram's wife Sarai had not given birth to any children. She had a woman servant from Egypt whose name was Hagar. 2 So Sarai said to Abram, "Now see, the Lord has kept me from having children. Go in to the woman who serves me. It may be that I will get children through her." Abram listened to what Sarai said. 3 So Abram's wife Sarai took Hagar the Egyptian, who served her, and gave her to her husband Abram as his wife. That was after Abram had lived ten years in the land of Canaan. 4 He went in to Hagar, and she was going to have a child. And when she saw that she was going to have a child, she began to hate Sarai. 5 Then Sarai said to Abram, "May the wrong done to me be upon you. I gave the woman who served me into your arms. But when she saw that she was going to have a child, she began to hate me. May the Lord judge who is guilty or not between you and me." 6 But Abram said to Sarai, "See, the woman who serves you is in your power. Do what you want with her." So Sarai made it hard for Hagar. And Hagar ran away from her.

7 The angel of the Lord found Hagar by a well of water in the desert on the way to Shur. 8 He said, "Hagar, you who serve Sarai, where have you come from and where are you going?" And she said, "I am running away from Sarai, the one I serve." 9 Then the angel of the Lord said to her, "Return to your boss. Put yourself under her power." 10 The angel of the Lord said to her, "I will give you so many people in your family through the years that they will be too many to number." 11 The angel of the Lord also said to her, "See, you are going to have a child. And you will give birth to a son. You will give him the name Ishmael, because the Lord has heard how you have suffered. 12 He will be a wild

donkey of a man. His hand will be against all people. And the hand of all people will be against him. He will live to the east of all his brothers." 13 So Hagar gave him a new name to the Lord Who spoke to her, "You are a God Who sees." For she said, "Have I even stayed alive here after seeing Him?" 14 So the well was called Beer-lahai-roi. It is between Kadesh and Bered.

15 Hagar gave birth to Abram's son. And Abram gave his son who was born of Hagar the name Ishmael. 16 Abram was eighty-six years old when Hagar gave birth to his son Ishmael.

The Special Act of the Agreement

17 When Abram was ninety-nine years old, the Lord came to him and said, "I am God All-powerful. Obey Me, and be without blame. 2 And I will keep My agreement between Me and you. I will give you many children." 3 Then Abram fell on his face. God said to him, 4 "See, My agreement is with you. You will be the father of many nations. 5 No more will your name be Abram. But your name will be Abraham. For I will make you the father of many nations. 6 Many will come from you. I will make nations of you. Kings will come from you. 7 I will make My agreement between Me and you and your children after you through their whole lives for all time. I will be God to you and to your children's children after you. 8 I will give to you and your children after you the land in which you are a stranger, all the land of Canaan for yourselves forever. And I will be their God."

9 Then God said to Abraham, "You must keep My agreement, you and your children after you for all time. 10 This is My agreement between Me and you and your children after you, which you must obey. Every man among you must have this religious act done. 11 In this religious act the skin is cut off from the end of your sex part. This will be the special act of the agreement between Me and you. 12 Every male child among you who is eight days old must have this religious act done, through all time. The same must be done to all the men born in your house or bought with your money from any stranger, who is not one of your family. 13 He that is born in your house and he that is bought with your money must have this religious act done. So will My agreement be marked in your flesh, an agreement that lasts forever. 14 But the man who has not had this

religious act done, of cutting off his piece of skin, will be cut off from his people. He has broken My agreement."

15 Then God said to Abraham, "As for Sarai your wife, do not call her name Sarai. But Sarah will be her name. 16 And I will bring good to her. I will give you a son by her. I will bring good to her. And she will be the mother of nations. Kings of many people will come from her."

17 Then Abraham fell on his face and laughed. He said to himself, "Will a child be born to a man who is one hundred years old? 18 Then Abraham said to God, "If only Ishmael might live before You!" 19 But God said, "No, but your wife Sarah will give birth to your son. And you will give him the name Isaac. I will make My agreement with him and for his children after him, an agreement that will last forever. 20 As for Ishmael, I have heard you. I will bring good to him. I will make him grow in number. He will be the father of twelve rulers. I will make him a great nation. 21 But I will make My agreement with Isaac, who will be born to Sarah at this time next year."

22 When He had finished talking with him, God went up from Abraham. 23 Then Abraham took his son Ishmael, and all who were born in his house, and all who were bought with his money, and every man and boy who lived in his house. And he cut off their piece of skin that very day, as God had told him to do. 24 Abraham was ninety-nine years old when he had the religious act done of cutting off his piece of skin. 25 His son Ishmael was thirteen years old when he had the religious act done of cutting off his piece of skin. 26 Abraham and his son Ishmael had this religious act done that very day. 27 And all the men of his house, who were born in the house or bought with money from a stranger, had this religious act done with him.

Abraham Is Promised a Son

18 The Lord showed Himself to Abraham by the oak trees of Mamre, as he sat at the tent door in the heat of the day. 2 Abraham looked up and saw three men standing in front of him. When he saw them, he ran from the tent door to meet them. He put his face to the ground 3 and said, "My lord, if I have found favor in your eyes, please do not pass by your servant. 4 Let us have a little water brought to wash your feet. Rest yourselves under the tree. 5 And I will get a piece of bread so you may eat and get strength. After that you may go on your way, since you have come to your servant."

The men said, "Do as you have said." 6 So Abraham ran into the tent to Sarah, and said, "Hurry and get three pails of fine flour, mix it well, and make bread." 7 Then Abraham ran to the cattle and took out a young and good calf. He gave it to the servant to make it ready in a hurry. 8 He took milk and cheese and the meat which he had made ready, and set it in front of them. He stood by them under the tree while they ate.

9 Then they said to him, "Where is your wife Sarah?" And he said, "There in the tent." 10 The Lord said, "I will be sure to return to you at this time next year. And your wife Sarah will have a son." Sarah was listening at the tent door behind him. 11 Now Abraham and Sarah were old. They had lived many years. The way of women had stopped for Sarah. 12 So Sarah laughed to herself, saying, "Will I have this joy after my husband and I have grown old?" 13 Then the Lord said to Abraham, "Why did Sarah laugh and say, 'How can I give birth to a child when I am so old?' 14 Is anything too hard for the Lord? I will return to you at this time next year, and Sarah will have a son." 15 But Sarah said, "I did not laugh," because she was afraid. And He said, "No, but you did laugh."

Abraham Cries Out for Sodom

16 Then the men got up from there and looked down toward Sodom. Abraham went with them to send them on their way. 17 And the Lord said, "Should I hide from Abraham what I am about to do, 18 since Abraham will become a great and powerful nation, because good will come to all the nations of the earth through him? 19 For I have chosen him, so that he may teach his children and the sons of his house after him to keep the way of the Lord by doing what is right and fair. So the Lord may bring to Abraham what He has promised him." 20 Then the Lord said, "The cry against Sodom and Gomorrah is loud. Their sin is very bad. 21 I will now go down and see if they have done as much wrong as the cry against them has told Me they have. And if not, I will know."

22 Then the men turned away from there and went toward Sodom. But Abraham still stood before the Lord. 23 Abraham came near and said, "Will You destroy the good also, with the bad? 24 What if there are fifty good people within the city? Will You destroy the place and not save it because of the fifty good people in it? 25 May You never do such a thing as to destroy the good with the bad! May the good never be punished like the bad! You would never do such a thing! Will not the Judge of all the earth do what is right?" 26 So the Lord said, "If I find fifty good people in the city of Sodom, I will save the whole place because of them." 27 Abraham said, "Now see, I have taken upon myself to speak to the Lord, I who am only dust and ashes. 28 What if five of the fifty good people are not so good. Will You destroy the whole city because of five?" The Lord said, "I will not destroy it if I find forty-five good people there." 29 Abraham spoke to Him again and said, "What if only forty are found there?" The Lord said, "I will not destroy it if there are forty." 30 Then Abraham said, "O may the Lord not be angry, and I will speak. What if only thirty are found there?" The Lord said, "I will not do it if I find thirty there." 31 Abraham said, "Now see, I have taken upon myself to speak to the Lord. What if twenty are found there?" The Lord said, "I will not destroy it because of the twenty." 32 Then Abraham said, "O may the Lord not be angry. And I may speak once more. What if ten are found there?" The Lord said, "I will not destroy it because of the ten." 33 Then the Lord went on His way when He finished speaking with Abraham, and Abraham returned to his place.

Sodom and Gomorrah Destroyed

19 The two angels came to Sodom in the evening. Lot was sitting in the gate of Sodom. When Lot saw them, he got up to meet them. He put his face to the ground 2 and said, "My lords, come into the house of your servant. Stay the night, and wash your feet. Then you may rise early and go on your way." But they said, "No, we will stay the night in the street." 3 But he begged them, so they turned aside with him and went into his house. And he made a supper for them. He made bread without yeast, and they ate.

4 Before they went to bed, all the men of the city of Sodom both young and old gathered around the house. 5 They called to Lot, saying, "Where are the men who came to you tonight? Bring them out to us so we may lie with them." 6 Lot went out the door to the men, and shut the door behind him. 7 He said, "My brothers, please do not be so sinful. 8 See, I have

two daughters who have never had a man. Let me bring them out to you. And do to them whatever you want. But do nothing to these men, for they have come to be safe under my roof." ⁹ But they said, "Get out of our way. This man came to live here from another land. And already he acts like a judge. Now we will do worse things to you than to them." So they pushed hard against Lot and almost broke down the door. ¹⁰ But the two men put out their hands and brought Lot into the house with them, and shut the door. ¹¹ Then they blinded the men who were at the door of the house, both small and big. So the men became tired trying to find the door.

Lot Leaves Sodom

¹² Then the two men asked Lot, "Do you have any others here? Sons-in-law, your sons, your daughters, anyone you have in the city, bring them out of this place. ¹³ For we are about to destroy this place. Because the cry against its people has become so loud to the Lord that the Lord has sent us to destroy it." ¹⁴ So Lot went out to speak to his sons-in-law who were to marry his daughters. He said, "Get up! Get out of this place! For the Lord will destroy the city!" But his sons-in-law thought he was only joking.

¹⁵ When morning came, the angels told Lot to hurry. They said, "Get up. Take your wife and your two daughters who are here. Or else you will be destroyed when the city is punished." ¹⁶ But Lot was slow to move. So the men took him, his wife and two daughters by the hand and brought them out of the city. For the Lord had loving pity for him. ¹⁷ When they had brought them out of the city, one of them said, "Run for your life! Do not look behind you. Do not stop until you are out of the valley. Run to the mountains or else you will be destroyed." ¹⁸ But Lot said to them, "O, no, my lords! ¹⁹ See, your servant has found favor in your eyes. You have shown me great kindness in what you have done for me by saving my life. But I cannot run to the mountains. For I will run into danger and die. ²⁰ See, this town is near enough to run to, and it is small. Let me run there (is it not small?) and my life will be saved." ²¹ The angel said to him, "See, I am doing what you ask. I will not destroy this town that you have spoken about. ²² Hurry and run there. For I cannot do anything until you get there." So the name given to the town was Zoar.

²³ The sun had moved over the earth when Lot came to Zoar. ²⁴ Then the Lord poured fire from the heavens upon Sodom and Gomorrah. ²⁵ He destroyed those cities, and all the valley, and all the people of the cities, and what grew on the ground. ²⁶ But Lot's wife behind him turned and looked toward the cities. And she was changed into salt.

²⁷ Abraham went early in the morning to the place where he had stood before the Lord. ²⁸ He looked down toward Sodom and Gomorrah and toward all the land of the valley. And he saw the smoke of the land going up like the smoke from a place where there is much fire. ²⁹ But when God destroyed the cities of the valley, He remembered Abraham. He sent Lot out of the center of the danger, when He destroyed the cities where Lot lived.

³⁰ Then Lot went up from Zoar with his two daughters, and lived in the mountains for he was afraid to stay in Zoar. He lived in a cave in the side of a mountain with his two daughters. ³¹ Then the first-born daughter said to the younger one, "Our father is old. And there is not a man on earth to marry us. ³² Come, let us make our father drink wine. Let us lie with him, so we may keep our family through our father." ³³ So they made their father drink wine that night. And the first-born went in and lay with her father. He did not know when she lay down or when she got up. ³⁴ On the next day, the first-born said to the younger, "See, I lay with my father last night. Let us make him drink wine tonight also, then you go in and lie with him. And we may keep our family through our father." ³⁵ So they made their father drink wine that night also, then the younger daughter went and lay with him. He did not know when she lay down or when she got up. ³⁶ So both the daughters of Lot were going to have a child by their father. ³⁷ The first-born daughter gave birth to a son, and gave him the name Moab. He is the father of the Moabites to this day. ³⁸ The younger daughter gave birth to a son also. She gave him the name Benammi. He is the father of the Ammonites to this day.

Abraham and Abimelech

20 Abraham traveled from there to the land of the Negev, and made his home between Kadesh and Shur. Then he lived for a time in Gerar. ² Abraham said about his wife Sarah, "She is my sister." So Abimelech king of Gerar sent for Sarah and took her for his wife. 3 But God came to Abimelech in a dream of the night, and said, "See, you are a dead man because of the woman you have taken. For she is already married." 4 But Abimelech had not come near her. He said, "Lord, will You destroy a nation who is without blame? 5 Did the man not tell me, 'She is my sister'? And she, even she herself said, 'He is my brother.' I have done this with a heart of honor and with hands that are not guilty."

6 Then God said to him in the dream, "Yes, I know that you have done this with a heart of honor. And I kept you from sinning against Me. I did not let you touch her. 7 So now return the man's wife. For he is one who speaks for Me. Then he will pray for you, and you will live. But if you do not return her, know that you and all who are yours will die for sure."

8 So Abimelech got up early in the morning. He called all his servants and told them all these things. And the men were very much afraid. 9 Then Abimelech called Abraham and said, "What have you done to us? What wrong have I done to you, that made you bring a great sin upon me and my nation? You have done to me what should not have been done." 10 Abimelech said to Abraham, "What made you do such a thing?" 11 Abraham said, "I did it because I thought there was no fear of God in this place. I thought they would kill me because of my wife. 12 And it is true she is my sister. She is the daughter of my father, but not of my mother. And she became my wife. 13 When God made me go from my father's house, I said to Sarah, 'This is the kindness you must show me. Everywhere we go, say of me, "He is my brother."'" 14 Then Abimelech gave to Abraham sheep and cattle, and men and women servants. And he returned his wife Sarah to him. 15 Abimelech said, "See, my land is in front of you. Make your home any place you want." 16 He said to Sarah, "See, I have given your brother a thousand pieces of silver. It is to pay you for all that has happened. Your honor is made right in the eyes of all men."

17 So Abraham prayed to God. And God healed Abimelech, his wife and the women who served him, so that they gave birth to children. 18 For the Lord had stopped all births in the house of Abimelech because of Abraham's wife Sarah.

The Birth of Isaac

21 Then the Lord visited Sarah as He had said and did for her as He had promised. 2 Sarah was able to have a child and she gave birth to a son when Abraham was very old. He was born at the time the Lord said it would happen. 3 Abraham gave the name Isaac to his son who was born to him by Sarah. 4 Then Abraham did the religious act of the Jews on Isaac when he was eight days old, as God had told him to do. 5 Abraham was one hundred years old when Isaac was born. 6 And Sarah said, "God has made me laugh. All who hear will laugh with me." 7 She said, "Who would have said to Abraham that Sarah would nurse children? Yet when he is so old I have given him a son." 8 When the child grew old enough to stop nursing, Abraham made a special supper on that day.

Hagar and Ishmael Are Sent Away

9 But Sarah saw the son of Hagar the Egyptian make fun of Isaac. Abraham was the father of Hagar's son. 10 So Sarah said to Abraham, "Put this woman servant and her son out of your home. The son of this woman servant will never get any of the riches of the family as will my son Isaac." 11 And the thing brought much sorrow to Abraham because of his son. 12 But God said to Abraham, "Do not be full of sorrow because of the boy and the woman who serves you. Listen to whatever Sarah tells you. For your children and all their children's children after you will be given a name through Isaac. 13 But I will also make a nation of the son of the woman who serves you, because he is your son."

14 So Abraham got up early in the morning. He took bread and a leather bag of water, and gave it to Hagar, putting it on her shoulder. He gave her the boy, and sent her away. She left, and went from place to place in the desert in Beersheba. 15 When the water was gone, she put the boy under one of the bushes. 16 Then she sat down as far away from him as an arrow flies. For she said, "Do not let me see the boy die." As she sat there, she cried a loud cry. 17 But God heard the voice of the boy. Then the angel of God called to Hagar from heaven, and said, "Why are you so troubled, Hagar? Do not be afraid. For God has heard the cry of the boy. 18 Get up. Lift up the boy and hold him by the hand. For I will make a great nation of him."

¹⁹ Then God opened Hagar's eyes. And she saw a well of water. She went and filled the leather bag with water and gave the boy a drink. ²⁰ God was with the boy and he grew. He lived in the desert, and became very good in using the bow. ²¹ While living in the desert of Paran, his mother took a wife for him from the land of Egypt.

The Agreement at Beersheba

²² At that time, Abimelech with Phicol, the head of his army, said to Abraham, "God is with you in all that you do. ²³ So promise me here by God that you will not work against me, or my son, or any children after me. I have shown you kindness. So return kindness to me and to the land where you have come." ²⁴ Abraham said, "I promise." ²⁵ But Abraham spoke to Abimelech about a well of water that the servants of Abimelech had taken. ²⁶ Abimelech said, "I do not know who did this. You never told me. And I did not hear about it until today." ²⁷ So Abraham took sheep and cattle and gave them to Abimelech. Then the two men made an agreement. ²⁸ Abraham set seven lambs of the flock away from the others. ²⁹ Abimelech said to Abraham, "What do these seven lambs that you have set apart mean?" ³⁰ Abraham said, "Take these seven lambs from me as an agreement to me that I dug this well." ³¹ So he gave that place the name Beersheba because both of them made a promise there. ³² So they made an agreement at Beersheba. Then Abimelech and Phicol, the head of his army, returned to the land of the Philistines. ³³ Abraham planted a tree at Beersheba. He called there on the name of the Lord, the God Who lives forever. ³⁴ And Abraham stayed in the land of the Philistines for many days.

Abraham Is Tested

22 Later God tested Abraham, and said to him, "Abraham!" Abraham said, "Here I am." ² God said, "Take now your son, your only son, Isaac, whom you love. And go to the land of Moriah. Give him as a burnt gift on the altar in worship, on one of the mountains I will show you." ³ So Abraham got up early in the morning and got his donkey ready. He took two of his young men with him and his son Isaac. He cut wood for the burnt gift. And he went to the place where God told him to go. ⁴ Abraham looked up on the third day and saw the place far away. ⁵ He said to his

young men, "Stay here with the donkey. I and the boy will go to that place and worship, and return to you." ⁶ Abraham took the wood for the burnt gift and had Isaac carry it. He took in his hand the fire and the knife. And the two of them walked on together. ⁷ Then Isaac said to Abraham, "My father!" Abraham answered, "Here I am, my son." Isaac said, "See, here is the fire and the wood. But where is the lamb for the burnt gift?" ⁸ Abraham said, "God will have for Himself a lamb ready for the burnt gift, my son." So the two of them walked on together.

⁹ Then they came to the place that God told them about. Abraham built the altar there, and set the wood in place. Then he tied rope around his son Isaac, and laid him upon the wood on the altar. ¹⁰ And Abraham put out his hand and took the knife to kill his son. ¹¹ But the angel of the Lord called to him from heaven, and said, "Abraham! Abraham!" And Abraham said, "Here I am." ¹² The angel of the Lord said, "Do not put out your hand against the boy. Do nothing to him. For now I know that you fear God. You have not kept from Me your son, your only son." ¹³ Then Abraham looked and saw a ram behind him, with his horns caught in the bushes. Abraham went and took the ram, and gave him as a burnt gift instead of his son. ¹⁴ Abraham gave that place the name "The Lord will give us what we need." And it is said to this day, "On the mountain of the Lord it will be given."

¹⁵ The angel of the Lord called to Abraham from heaven a second time. ¹⁶ He said, "I have promised by Myself, says the Lord, because you have done this and have not kept from Me your son, your only son, ¹⁷ I will bring good to you. I will add many to the number of your children and all who come after them, like the stars of the heavens and the sand beside the sea. They will take over the cities of those who hate them. ¹⁸ Good will come to all the nations of the earth by your children and their children's children. Because you have obeyed My voice." ¹⁹ So Abraham returned to his young men. And they got up and went with him to Beersheba. Abraham made his home there.

²⁰ Later it was told to Abraham, "Milcah also has given birth to the children of your brother Nahor: ²¹ Uz the first-born, Buz his brother, Kemuel the father of Aram, ²² Chesed, Hazo, Pildash, Jidlaph, and Bethuel." ²³ Bethuel became the father

of Rebekah. Milcah gave birth to these eight by Nahor, Abraham's brother. 24 And Reumah, the woman he kept who acted as his wife, gave birth to Tebah, Gaham, Tahash, and Maacah.

The Death of Sarah

23 Sarah lived 127 years. These were the years of Sarah's life. 2 Then Sarah died in Kiriath-arba (that is, Hebron) in the land of Canaan. And Abraham had sorrow for Sarah and cried for her. 3 Then Abraham got up from beside his dead wife, and said to the sons of Heth, 4 "I am a stranger living among you for a time. Give me some of your land so I may bury my wife." 5 The sons of Heth answered Abraham, 6 "Listen to us, my lord. You are a powerful ruler among us. Bury your wife in the best of our graves. None of us will keep his grave from you for burying your wife." 7 So Abraham stood up and bowed to the people of the land, the sons of Heth. 8 He said to them, "If you are willing to have me bury my wife, hear me, and ask Zohar's son Ephron for me. 9 Ask him to give me the grave of Machpelah which he has at the other side of his field. Let him give it to me for the full price in front of you, for a place to bury my wife."

10 Ephron was sitting among the sons of Heth. So Ephron the Hittite answered Abraham so what he said could be heard by the sons of Heth and all who came in through the gate of his city. 11 He said, "No, my lord. Listen to me. I give you the field. And I give you the grave that is in it. I give it to you in front of the sons of my people. Bury your wife."

12 Abraham bowed to the people of the land. 13 He said to Ephron so that all the people of the land heard it, "Listen to me if you will. I will give you the price of the field. Receive it from me, that I may bury my wife there."

14 Ephron answered Abraham, 15 "My lord, listen to me. The land is worth four hundred pieces of silver. What is that between me and you? So bury your wife."

16 Abraham listened to Ephron. And Abraham weighed for Ephron the silver which he had said and was heard by the sons of Heth to be the price, four hundred pieces of silver. He weighed it in the same way those who buy and sell weighed it at that time. 17 So Ephron's field in Machpelah east of Mamre, the field and grave that was in it, and all the trees within the sides of the field, were handed over 18 to Abraham for his own. It was handed over in front of the sons of Heth and all who came in through the gate of his city. 19 After this, Abraham buried his wife Sarah in the grave of the field of Machpelah east of Mamre (that is, Hebron) in the land of Canaan. 20 The field and the grave in it were handed over to Abraham by the sons of Heth for a place to bury his wife.

Isaac and Rebekah

24 Now Abraham was old. He had lived many years. And the Lord had brought good to Abraham in every way. 2 Abraham said to the oldest servant in his house and the one who took care of all that he owned, "Place your hand under my hip, 3 and I will have you promise by the Lord, the God of heaven and earth. Promise that you will not take a wife for my son from the daughters of the Canaanites, who live around me. 4 But go to my country and to those of my family. Take a wife for my son Isaac from there." 5 The servant said to Abraham, "What if the woman will not be willing to follow me to this land? Should I take your son to the land you came from?" 6 Abraham said to him, "Make sure that you do not take my son there. 7 The Lord, the God of heaven, Who took me from my father's house and from the land of my birth, spoke to me and promised me. He said, 'I will give this land to your children and out to their children's children.' He will send His angel in front of you. And you will take a wife for my son from there. 8 But if the woman is not willing to follow you, then you will be free from this promise to me. Only do not take my son there." 9 So the servant placed his hand under the hip of Abraham, and he promised to do this.

10 Then the servant took ten of Abraham's camels and left. He took with him all kinds of gifts from Abraham. Then he went to the city of Nahor in Mesopotamia. 11 He made the camels get down on their knees outside the city by the well of water in the evening. It was the time when women go out to get water. 12 He said, "O Lord, the God of my boss Abraham, let all go well for me today. Show loving-kindness to my boss Abraham. 13 See, I am standing here by the well of water. And the daughters of the men of the city are coming out to get water. 14 If I say to a girl, 'Let down your jar so that I may drink,' and she answers, 'Drink, and I will give water to your camels also,' let her be the one whom You

have chosen for your servant Isaac. I will know by this that You have shown loving-kindness to my boss."

15 Before he had finished speaking, Rebekah came out, the daughter of Bethuel, the son of Milcah and Nahor, the brother of Abraham. She had a jar on her shoulder. 16 The girl was very beautiful and had never lain with a man. She went down to the well, filled her jar and came up. 17 Then the servant ran to meet her. He said, "Let me drink a little water from your jar." 18 She said, "Drink, my lord." And she was quick to lift her jar to her hand and give him a drink. 19 When she had finished giving him a drink, she said, "I will get water for your camels also, until they have finished drinking." 20 She was quick to empty her jar into the animals' drinking place. Then she ran to the well for more water, and got enough for all his camels.

21 The man was quiet and watched her, waiting to know if the Lord had made all go well or not during his visit. 22 When the camels had finished drinking, the man took a heavy gold ring and two heavy gold objects to wear on her arms. 23 He said, "Whose daughter are you? Tell me, is there a place for us to stay in your father's house?" 24 She said to him, "I am the daughter of Bethuel, the son of Milcah and Nahor." 25 She also said, "We have both enough straw and food, and a place to stay." 26 Then the man bowed low and worshiped the Lord. 27 He said, "Honor and thanks be to the Lord, the God of my boss Abraham. He has not kept His loving-kindness and His truth from my boss. He has led me in the way to the house of my boss's brothers."

28 Then the girl ran and told about all this to those in her mother's house. 29 Rebekah had a brother whose name was Laban. And Laban ran outside to the man at the well. 30 When he saw the gold objects his sister was wearing, and heard his sister Rebekah saying, "This is what the man said to me," he went to the man. He saw him standing by the camels at the well. 31 Laban said, "Come in, you who receive good from the Lord! Why do you stand outside? I have made the house ready, and a place for the camels." 32 So the man came into the house. Laban took the load off the camels, and gave them straw and food. He got water to wash the feet of Abraham's servant and the feet of the men who were with him. 33 Then food was set in front of the man to eat. But he said, "I

will not eat until I have told you why I came here." Laban said, "Tell it." 34 So he said, "I am Abraham's servant. 35 And the Lord has brought much good to my boss. He has become rich. The Lord has given him flocks and cattle, silver and gold, men and women servants, and camels and donkeys. 36 My boss's wife Sarah gave birth to my boss's son when she was very old. And he has given him all he has.

37 "My boss made me promise, saying, 'Do not take a wife for my son from the daughters of the Canaanites, in whose land I live. 38 But go to my father's house, to those of my family, and take a wife for my son there.' 39 I said to my owner, 'What if the woman will not follow me?' 40 He said to me, 'The Lord, Whom I have always obeyed, will send His angel with you to make all go well during your visit there. You will take a wife for my son from those of my family and from my father's house. 41 Then you will be free from your promise to me. When you come to those of my family, and if they do not give her to you, then you will be free from your promise to me.'

42 "So I came to the well today. I said, 'O Lord, the God of my boss Abraham, may all go well during my visit here. 43 See, I am standing by the well of water. It I say to the girl who comes out for water, "Let me drink a little water from your jar," 44 and she says, "You drink, and I will get water for your camels also," then let her be the woman whom the Lord has chosen for my boss's son.' 45 Before I had finished speaking in my heart, Rebekah came out with her jar on her shoulder. She went down to the well and got water. I asked her, 'Let me drink.' 46 And she was quick to take down her jar from her shoulder. She said, 'Drink, and I will give water to your camels also.' So I drank and she gave water to the camels also. 47 Then I asked her, 'Whose daughter are you?' She said, 'The daughter of Bethuel the son of Milcah and Nahor.' And I put the gold objects on her nose and arms. 48 Then I bowed low and worshiped the Lord. I gave honor and thanks to the Lord, the God of my boss Abraham. For He had led me in the right way to take the daughter of my boss's brother for his son. 49 So now if you will show kindness and be true to my boss, tell me. And if not, tell me so I may know which way to turn."

50 Then Laban and Bethuel answered, "This thing comes from the Lord. We

cannot speak for or against it. 51 See, Rebekah is in front of you. Take her and go. Let her be the wife of your boss's son, as the Lord has spoken." 52 When Abraham's servant heard their words, he put his face to the ground before the Lord. 53 He brought out things made of silver and gold, and clothes, and gave them to Rebekah. He gave things of much worth to her brother and mother also. 54 Then he and the men with him ate and drank and stayed the night there. When they got up in the morning, he said, "Send me away to my boss."

55 But her brother and her mother said, "Let the girl stay with us a few days, at least ten. Then she may go." 56 But he said to them, "Do not make me stay any more days, since the Lord has made my way go well. Send me away so I may go to my boss." 57 They said, "We will call the girl and ask her what she wants to do." 58 They called Rebekah and asked her, "Will you go with this man?" And she said, "I will go." 59 So they sent away their sister Rebekah and her nurse. They went with Abraham's servant and the men who were with him. 60 They prayed that good would come to Rebekah, and said to her, "You are our sister. May you become the mother of millions. May your children and all their children's children after them take over the cities of those who hate them." 61 Then Rebekah and her servants got up on the camels and followed the man. So the servant of Abraham took Rebekah and left.

62 Now Isaac had come from Beer-lahai-roi, and was living in the Negev. 63 Isaac had gone out to pray in the field in the evening. He looked up and saw that camels were coming. 64 And Rebekah looked up and saw Isaac. She got off the camel 65 and said to Abraham's servant, "Who is that man walking in the field to meet us?" Abraham's servant said, "He is my boss." So she took a cloth and covered her face. 66 The servant told Isaac all the things he had done. 67 Then Isaac brought Rebekah into his mother Sarah's tent, and she became his wife. And he loved her. So Isaac found comfort after his mother's death.

The Death of Abraham

25 Abraham took another wife whose name was Keturah. 2 She gave birth to his sons, Zimran, Jokshan, Medan, Midian, Ishbak, and Shuah. 3 Jokshan became the father of Sheba and Dedan. The sons of Dedan were Asshurim, Letushim,

and Leummim. 4 The sons of Midian were Ephah, Epher, Hanoch, Abida, and Eldaah. All these were the sons of Keturah.

5 Abraham gave all he had to Isaac. 6 But while he was still living, Abraham gave gifts to the sons of the women he kept who acted as his wives. And he sent them to the land of the East, away from his son Isaac. 7 Abraham lived 175 years. 8 Then Abraham breathed his last and died, after living a long and full life of many good years, and was buried with his people. 9 His sons Isaac and Ishmael buried him in the grave of Machpelah, in the field of Ephron the son of Zohar the Hittite, east of Mamre. 10 This was the field that Abraham bought from the sons of Heth. Abraham was buried there with his wife Sarah. 11 After the death of Abraham, God brought good to his son Isaac. And Isaac lived at Beer-la-hai-roi.

12 These are the children and their children's children of Abraham's son Ishmael, who was born to Abraham and Hagar, who was Sarah's woman servant. 13 These are the names of the sons of Ishmael, the names of the first-born to the last: Nebaioth, Ishmael's first-born, then Kedar, Adbeel, Mibsam, 14 Mishma, Dumah, Massa, 15 Hadad, Tema, Jetur, Naphish, and Kedemah. 16 These are the sons of Ishmael and these are their names, by their towns and by their groups of tents, twelve rulers and their families.

17 Ishmael lived 137 years. Then he breathed his last and died, and was buried with his people. 18 His people lived from Havilah as far as Shur, east of Egypt on the way toward Assyria. He lived away from all his brothers.

The Birth of Esau and Jacob

19 These are the children and their children's children of Abraham's son Isaac. Abraham was the father of Isaac. 20 Isaac was forty years old when he married Rebekah, the daughter of Bethuel the Syrian of Paddan-aram, and the sister of Laban the Syrian. 21 Isaac prayed to the Lord for his wife, because she could not give birth and the Lord answered him. Rebekah was able to give birth. 22 But the babies within her fought together. And she said, "If this is so, why am I like this?" She went to ask the Lord why. 23 The Lord said to her, "Two nations are within you. Two peoples will be divided from your body. One will be stronger than the other. And the older will serve the younger."

24 When the day came for her to give birth, there were two babies to be born. 25 The first to come out was red and he had hair all over his body. They gave him the name of Esau. 26 Then the brother was born. His hand was holding Esau's heel. So he was given the name of Jacob. Isaac was sixty years old when Rebekah gave birth to them.

Esau Sells His Birth-Right

27 When the boys grew older, Esau became a good hunter, a man of the field. But Jacob was a man of peace, living in tents. 28 Isaac showed favor to Esau, because he liked to eat the meat of the animals Esau killed. But Rebekah showed favor to Jacob.

29 As Jacob was getting food ready one day, Esau came in from the field and was very hungry. 30 Esau said to Jacob, "Let me eat some of that red meat, for I am very hungry." That is why his name was called Edom. 31 But Jacob said, "First, sell me your birth-right." 32 Esau said, "See, I am about to die. So what good is my birth-right to me?" 33 Jacob said, "First give me your promise." So Esau promised, and sold his birth-right to Jacob. 34 Then Jacob gave Esau bread and vegetables, and Esau ate and drank. Then Esau stood up and went on his way. So Esau hated his birth-right.

Isaac and Abimelech

26 Now there was another time when there was no food in the land, after the time of no food in the days of Abraham. So Isaac went to Gerar, to Abimelech king of the Philistines. 2 The Lord showed Himself to Isaac, and said, "Do not go to Egypt. Stay in the land I will tell you about. 3 Live in this land and I will be with you and bring good to you. For I will give all these lands to you and your children. I will keep the promise I made to your father Abraham. 4 I will make your children and all your children's children as many as the stars of heaven. I will give these lands to them. 5 For Abraham obeyed Me. He did what I told him to do. He kept My Word and My Law."

6 So Isaac stayed in Gerar. 7 When the men of the place asked him about his wife, he said, "She is my sister." He was afraid to say, "She is my wife," because he thought to himself, "The men of this place might kill me because of Rebekah, for she is beautiful."

8 When Isaac had been there a long time, Abimelech king of the Philistines looked out of the window. And he saw Isaac loving his wife Rebekah. 9 So Abimelech called Isaac and said, "See, she is your wife! How could you say, 'She is my sister'?" Isaac said to him, "Because I thought I would die because of her." 10 Abimelech said, "What is this you have done to us? One of the men might have lain with your wife. And you would have brought guilt upon us." 11 So Abimelech told all the people, "Whoever touches this man or his wife will be put to death."

12 Isaac planted seeds in that land. And he gathered in the same year a hundred times as much as he had planted. The Lord brought good to him. 13 Isaac became rich and kept getting richer until he became a great man. 14 For he had flocks and many cattle and many people working in his house. The Philistines became jealous of him. 15 They filled all the wells with dirt that his father's servants had dug in the days of his father Abraham. 16 Then Abimelech said to Isaac, "Go away from us. For you are too powerful for us."

17 So Isaac left that place. He put up his tents in the valley of Gerar, and lived there. 18 And Isaac dug again the wells of water that had been dug in the days of his father Abraham. For the Philistines had closed them up after the death of Abraham. And he gave them the same names that his father had given them. 19 Now Isaac's servants dug in the valley and found a well of flowing water there. 20 The men who took care of the cattle of Gerar argued with the men who took care of Isaac's cattle. They said, "The water belongs to us!" So Isaac gave the well the name Esek, because they argued with him. 21 Then his servants dug another well. And they argued about it also. So he gave it the name Sitnah. 22 He moved away from there and dug another well. And they did not argue about it. So he gave it the name Rehoboth. For he said, "Now the Lord has made a large place for us. We will grow much in this land."

23 Then he went from there to Beersheba. 24 The Lord showed Himself to Isaac that same night, and said, "I am the God of your father Abraham. Do not be afraid, for I am with you. I will bring good to you, and add many to the number of your children and their children's children, because of My servant Abraham." 25 So Isaac built an altar there. And he called upon the name of the Lord. He put up his

tent there. And there Isaac's servants dug a well.

²⁶ Then Abimelech came to him from Gerar, with his friend Ahuzzath, and Phicol, the leader of his army. ²⁷ Isaac said to them, "Why have you come to me when you hate me and have sent me away from you?" ²⁸ They said, "It is easy for us to see that the Lord is with you. So we said, 'Let there now be a promise between us, between you and us. Let us make an agreement with you, ²⁹ that you will not hurt us in any way. For we have not touched you, and have done nothing to you but good. We sent you away in peace. And you now have the Lord's favor.' " ³⁰ So Isaac made a special supper for them, and they ate and drank. ³¹ They got up early in the morning and made promises to each other. Then Isaac sent them away, and they left him in peace.

³² That same day Isaac's servants came and told him about the well they had dug. They said to him, "We have found water." ³³ So he gave the well the name Shibah. So the name of the city is Beersheba to this day.

³⁴ When Esau was forty years old, he married Judith the daughter of Beeri the Hittite, and Basemath the daughter of Elon the Hittite. ³⁵ And they made life full of sorrow for Isaac and Rebekah.

Isaac Prays for Good to Come to Jacob

27 Isaac was now old, and had become blind. He called to his older son Esau, saying, "My son." And Esau answered, "Here I am." ² Isaac said, "See, I am old. I do not know when I will die. ³ Take your bow and arrows, and go out to the field to get meat for me. ⁴ Get some food ready for me that I love. Bring it to me to eat, so that before I die I will pray that good will come to you."

⁵ And Rebekah was listening while Isaac spoke to his son Esau. So when Esau went to the field to hunt for meat to bring home, ⁶ Rebekah said to her son Jacob, "I heard your father talking to your brother Esau. He said, ⁷ 'Bring me some meat. Make good-tasting food for me to eat. And before I die I will pray to the Lord for good to come to you.' ⁸ So now, my son, listen to what I tell you to do. ⁹ Go to the flock and bring me two fat young goats. I will cook them into good-tasting food, just what your father loves to eat. ¹⁰ Then you will take it to your father for him to eat. So before he dies he will pray for good to come to you."

¹¹ Jacob said to his mother Rebekah, "But my brother Esau has much hair. And my skin is smooth. ¹² If my father touches me, he will think of me as one trying to fool him. Then he will bring a curse upon me instead of good." ¹³ His mother said to him, "The curse will come upon me instead of you, my son. You do what I say, and go get them for me." ¹⁴ So Jacob went and got them, and brought them to his mother. And his mother made good-tasting food, just what his father loved to eat. ¹⁵ Then Rebekah took the best clothes that belonged to her older son Esau, that were with her in the house. And she put them on her younger son Jacob. ¹⁶ She put the skins of the young goats on his hands and on the smooth part of his neck. ¹⁷ And she gave her son Jacob the bread and the good-tasting food she had made.

¹⁸ Then he went to his father and said, "My father." Isaac said, "Here I am. Who are you, my son?" ¹⁹ Jacob said to his father, "I am Esau, your first-born. I have done as you told me. Sit up and eat the meat I brought, so you will pray that good will come to me." ²⁰ But Isaac said to his son, "How have you found it so fast, my son?" And Jacob said, "Because the Lord your God made it happen."

²¹ Then Isaac said to Jacob, "Come near so I can touch you, my son, to know for sure if you are my son Esau or not." ²² So Jacob came near his father Isaac. Isaac touched him, and said, "The voice is Jacob's voice. But the hands are Esau's hands." ²³ He did not know who he was, because his hands were covered with hair like his brother Esau's hands. So Isaac prayed that good would come to him. ²⁴ Isaac said, "Is it true that you are my son Esau?" Jacob answered, "I am." ²⁵ So Isaac said, "Bring it to me so I may eat the meat my son has made ready. And I will pray that good will come to you." He brought it to him, and he ate. He brought him wine also, and he drank.

²⁶ Then his father Isaac said to him, "Come near and kiss me, my son." ²⁷ So Jacob came near and kissed him. When Isaac smelled his clothes, he prayed that good would come to him. He said, "The smell of my son is like the smell of a field that has received good from the Lord. ²⁸ May God give you from heaven water on the grass in the early morning, and the riches of the earth, and more than enough grain and new wine. ²⁹ May nations serve you, and the people bow down in front of

you. Be the ruler of your brothers. May your mother's sons bow down in front of you. Cursed be those who curse you, and may good come to those who honor you."

30 When Isaac had finished praying that good would come to Jacob, Jacob left his father Isaac. Just then his brother Esau came in from hunting. 31 Then Esau made good-tasting food and brought it to his father, and said, "Sit up, my father, and eat the meat your son has made ready, so you will pray that good will come to me." 32 His father Isaac said to him, "Who are you?" He answered, "I am your son, your first-born, Esau." 33 Then Isaac shook all over, and he said, "Who was it then who killed an animal and brought meat to me? I ate all of it before you came! And I prayed that good would come to him! Yes, and good will come to him!"

34 When he heard what his father said, Esau cried out with a loud and sad cry. He said to his father, "Pray that good will come to me also, O my father!" 35 But Isaac said, "Your brother came in and fooled me. He has taken away the good that was to come to you."

36 Then Esau said, "Was it not right that he was given the name Jacob? Two times now he has taken what should have been mine. He took away my right as a first-born. And now he has taken away the good that was to come to me." Then he said, "Can you not pray that good will come to me also?"

37 Isaac answered Esau, "See, I have made him to rule over you. I have given him all his brothers as servants. I have given him grain and new wine to keep him alive and well. What then can I do for you, my son?"

38 Esau said to his father, "Do you have only one prayer for good to come, my father? Pray that good will come to me also, O my father." And Esau gave out a loud cry. 39 Then his father Isaac answered him: "See, the place where you live will be away from the riches of the earth, and away from the water on the grass in the early morning. 40 You will live by your sword and you will serve your brother. But when you break loose, you will throw his load off your back."

Jacob Goes to Laban

41 Esau hated Jacob because his father had prayed that good would come to Jacob. Esau said to himself, "The days when I will have sorrow for the loss of my father

are soon. Then I will kill my brother Jacob." 42 But the words of her older son Esau were told to Rebekah. She called her younger son Jacob, and said to him, "See, your brother Esau comforts himself by planning to kill you. 43 So now, my son, do what I tell you. Get ready, and go at once to my brother Laban at Haran. 44 Stay with him for a few days, until your brother's anger goes away. 45 When your brother's anger against you is gone and he forgets what you did to him, then I will send for you and have you return from there. Why should I have sorrow for both of you in one day?"

46 Then Rebekah said to Isaac, "I am tired of living because of the daughters of Heth. If Jacob marries one of the daughters of Heth, like these, from the women of the land, what good will my life be to me?"

28

So Isaac called Jacob and prayed that good would come to him. He said to him, "Do not marry one of the daughters of Canaan. 2 Get ready, and go to the house of your mother's father Bethuel in Paddan-aram. Take a wife for yourself from the daughters of your mother's brother Laban. 3 May the All-powerful God bring good to you and give you many children until you become many nations. 4 May He give you and your children after you the same gift that He gave Abraham. May He give you the land that He gave Abraham, the land where you are now a stranger." 5 Then Isaac sent Jacob away. And he went to Paddan-aram, to Laban, the son of Bethuel the Syrian, the brother of Rebekah, Jacob and Esau's mother.

6 Now Esau saw that Isaac had prayed for good to come to Jacob and that he had sent him away to Paddan-aram to find a wife. Esau knew that his father had prayed for good to come to Jacob and said, "Do not marry one of the daughters of Canaan," 7 and that Jacob had obeyed his father and mother and had gone to Paddan-aram. 8 Esau knew that the daughters of Canaan did not please his father Isaac. 9 So Esau went to Ishmael, and married Mahalath the daughter of Abraham's son Ishmael, the sister of Nebaioth. He added her to the wives he already had.

Jacob's Dream

10 Jacob left Beersheba and went toward Haran. 11 He came to a certain place and stayed the night there, because the sun had gone down. He took one of the stones

there and put it under his head for a pillow. 12 And he had a dream. He saw steps going up from the earth to heaven. He saw the angels of God going up and down these steps. 13 And he saw the Lord standing above them. He said, "I am the Lord, the God of your father Abraham, and the God of Isaac. I will give to you and your children after you the land where you are lying. 14 They will be like the dust of the earth. You will spread out to the west and the east and the north and the south. Good will come to all the families of the earth because of you and your children. 15 See, I am with you. I will care for you everywhere you go. And I will bring you again to this land. For I will not leave you until I have done all the things I promised you." 16 Then Jacob awoke from his sleep and said, "For sure the Lord is in this place and I did not know it." 17 He was afraid and said, "This place is so different! This is none other than the house of God, and this is the gate of heaven."

18 So Jacob got up early in the morning. He took the stone he had used as a pillow, and set it up as a pillar. He poured oil on the top of it. 19 He gave that place the name Bethel. Its name had been Luz before. 20 Then Jacob made a promise. He said, "If God will be with me and take care of me as I go, and if He will give me food to eat and clothes to wear, 21 so that I return in peace to my father's house, then the Lord will be my God. 22 I have set up this stone as a pillar to be God's house. And I will give You a tenth part of all You give to me."

Jacob Finds Laban

29 Then Jacob went on his way and came to the land of the people of the east. 2 He looked up and saw a well in the field where three flocks of sheep were lying beside it. The people gave water to the flocks from that well. The stone covering the top of the well was large. 3 When all the flocks were gathered there, the men would roll the stone from the top of the well. Then after giving water to the sheep, they would put the stone again in its place on top of the well.

4 Jacob said to them, "My brothers, where are you from?" They said, "We are from Haran." 5 He said to them, "Do you know Laban the son of Nahor?" They said, "We know him." 6 He asked them, "Is he well?" They said, "He is well. And see, his daughter Rachel is coming with the sheep." 7 Jacob said, "See, the sun is still high. It is not time for the flocks to be gathered. Give water to the sheep, and return them to their field." 8 But they said, "We cannot, until all the flocks are gathered and they roll the stone from the top of the well. Then we will give the sheep water."

9 He was still talking with them when Rachel came with her father's sheep, for she cared for them. 10 When Jacob saw Rachel the daughter of his mother's brother Laban, and the sheep of his mother's brother Laban, Jacob went near and rolled the stone from the top of the well. And he gave water to the flock of his mother's brother Laban. 11 Then Jacob kissed Rachel and began to cry for joy. 12 Jacob told Rachel that he was of her father's family, the son of Rebekah. And she ran and told her father.

13 When Laban heard the news of his sister's son Jacob, he ran to meet him. He put his arms around him and kissed him, and brought him to his house. Then Jacob told Laban all these things. 14 Laban said to him, "For sure you are my bone and my flesh." And Jacob stayed with him a month.

Jacob Works for Laban

15 Then Laban said to Jacob, "Because you are one of my family, should you serve me for nothing? Tell me, what do you want to be paid?" 16 Now Laban had two daughters. The name of the older one was Leah, and the name of the younger one was Rachel. 17 Leah's eyes were weak. But Rachel was beautiful in body and face. 18 Jacob loved Rachel. So he said, "I will serve you seven years for your younger daughter Rachel." 19 Laban said, "It is better that I give her to you than to another man. Stay with me." 20 So Jacob served seven years for Rachel. It was only like a few days to him, because of his love for her.

21 Then Jacob said to Laban, "Give me my wife so I may go in to her. For my time is finished." 22 And Laban gathered all the men of the place together, and made a special supper. 23 But in the evening he took his daughter Leah to him. Jacob went in to her. 24 Laban also took Zilpah, a woman who served him, and gave her to his daughter Leah, to serve her.

25 When the morning came, Jacob saw that it was Leah. He said to Laban, "What have you done to me? Did I not work for you for Rachel? Why have you fooled me?" 26 Laban said, "It is not allowed in our

country to give the younger in marriage before the first-born. ²⁷ Complete the wedding week of this one. Then we will give you the other one also if you work for me seven years more." ²⁸ Jacob did so and completed her wedding week. And Laban gave him his daughter Rachel as his wife. ²⁹ Laban also took Bilhah, a woman who served him, and gave her to his daughter Rachel, to serve her. ³⁰ So Jacob went in to Rachel also. He loved Rachel more than Leah. And he worked for Laban seven years more.

Jacob's Children

³¹ When the Lord saw that Leah was not loved, He made her able to give birth. But Rachel could not give birth. ³² Leah was able to have a child and she gave birth to a son. She gave him the name Reuben. For she said, "The Lord has seen my trouble. Now my husband will love me." ³³ Then she was going to have another child and she gave birth to a son. She said, "The Lord has given me this son also, because He has heard that I am not loved." So she gave him the name Simeon. ³⁴ She was going to have another child and she gave birth to a son. She said, "Now this time my husband will be joined to me because I have given birth to his three sons." So she gave him the name Levi. ³⁵ She was going to have another child and she gave birth to a son. And she said, "This time I will praise the Lord." So she gave him the name of Judah. Then she stopped giving birth.

30 When Rachel saw that she had not given birth to any children for Jacob, she became jealous of her sister. She said to Jacob, "Give me children, or else I am going to die!" ² Then Jacob became angry with Rachel. He said, "Am I taking God's place, Who has kept you from giving birth?" ³ Then she said, "Here is Bilhah, the woman who serves me. Go in to her, and let her give birth for me. Even I may have children through her." ⁴ So she gave Bilhah to him for a wife, the woman who served her. And Jacob went in to her, ⁵ Bilhah was going to have a child and gave birth to a son. ⁶ Then Rachel said, "God has done the right thing for me. He has heard my voice and has given me a son." So she gave him the name Dan. ⁷ Bilhah, the woman who served Rachel, was going to have another child. And she gave birth to another son for Jacob. ⁸ So Rachel said, "I have fought a hard fight with my sister,

and I have won." She gave him the name Naphtali.

⁹ Leah saw that she had stopped giving birth. So she took Zilpah, the woman who served her, and gave her to Jacob as a wife. ¹⁰ And a son was born to Jacob through Zilpah, the woman who served Leah. ¹¹ Then Leah said, "Good things have happened to me!" So she gave him the name Gad. ¹² A second son was born to Jacob through Zilpah, the woman who served Leah. ¹³ Then Leah said, "I am happy! For women will say that I am happy." So she gave him the name Asher.

¹⁴ During the time of gathering grain, Reuben went out in the field and found some fruit. He brought it to his mother Leah. Then Rachel said to Leah, "Give me some of your son's fruit." ¹⁵ But Leah said, "Is it not enough to take my husband? Would you take my son's fruit also?" So Rachel said, "Jacob may lie with you tonight if you give me your son's fruit."

¹⁶ When Jacob came in from the field in the evening, Leah went to meet him. She said, "You must sleep with me tonight. For I have paid for you with my son's fruit." So he lay with her that night. ¹⁷ And God heard Leah and she gave birth to a fifth son for Jacob. ¹⁸ Leah said, "God has given me my pay because I gave my husband the woman who serves me." So she gave him the name Issachar. ¹⁹ Leah was going to have another child and she gave birth to a sixth son for Jacob. ²⁰ Then Leah said, "God has given me a good gift. Now my husband will live with me, because I have given birth to six sons." So she gave him the name of Zebulun. ²¹ Later she gave birth to a daughter, and gave her the name Dinah.

²² Then God remembered Rachel. God listened to her, and made her able to have a child. ²³ and she gave birth to a son. Then she said, "God has taken away my shame." ²⁴ She gave him the name Joseph, saying, "May the Lord give me another son."

²⁵ When Rachel had given birth to Joseph, Jacob said to Laban, "Send me away, so I may go to my own place and my own country. ²⁶ Give me my wives and my children for whom I have served. Let me leave, for you know how much I have served you."

²⁷ But Laban said to him, "If now it pleases you, stay with me. I have learned that the Lord has brought good to me because of you." ²⁸ Then he said, "Tell me what you want to be paid, and I will pay it."

29 Jacob said to him, "You know how much I have served you and how I have cared for your cattle. 30 For you had little before I came. But now it has become very much. The Lord has brought good to you everywhere I turned. But when will I be able to give much to those of my own house also?"

31 Laban said, "What should I pay you?" Jacob said, "Do not pay me anything. If you will do this one thing for me, I will again feed and take care of your flock. 32 Let me go through your whole flock today. Let me take out of it every sheep and every goat that has spots, and every black lamb. These will be my pay. 33 So my fair actions will answer for me later, when you come to look at what I have been paid. If you find any sheep or goat without spots or any lamb that is not black, you may think of them as stolen." 34 And Laban said, "Good! Let it be done as you say." 35 That day Laban took out all the male goats with spots and all the female goats with spots, every one with white on it, and every black sheep. And he put them into the care of his sons. 36 Then he traveled three days away from Jacob. And Jacob was left to care for the rest of Laban's flocks.

37 Then Jacob took green sticks of three kinds of trees. And he cut white marks in them, showing the white which was in the sticks. 38 He took these sticks which he had cut and set them in front of the flocks, in the place where the flocks came to drink. And the animals mated when they came to drink. 39 So the flocks mated in front of the sticks. And the young that were born had spots. 40 Then Jacob divided the lambs. He made the flocks look toward Laban's flock of the animals which were black or with spots. And he put his own flocks by themselves. He did not put them with Laban's flock. 41 When the stronger animals of the flock were mating, Jacob would put the sticks in the water in front of the flock so they would mate by the sticks. 42 But when the flock was weak, Jacob did not put the sticks in. So the weaker animals went to Laban and the stronger ones went to Jacob. 43 Jacob became very rich. He had large flocks and camels and donkeys, and men and women servants.

Jacob Leaves Laban

31 Jacob heard the words of Laban's sons, saying, "Jacob has taken away all that our father had. He has become rich with what had belonged to our father." 2 Jacob saw that Laban did not show him as much favor as he did before. 3 Then the Lord said to Jacob, "Return to the land of your fathers and to those of your family. And I will be with you."

4 So Jacob called Rachel and Leah to come to his flock in the field. 5 He said to them, "I see that your father does not show me as much favor as he did before. But the God of my father has been with me. 6 You know that I have worked for your father with all my strength. 7 Yet your father has not been fair with me. He has changed my pay ten times. But God did not let him hurt me. 8 If he said, 'The animals that have spots will be your pay,' then all the flock gave birth to young ones with spots. If he said, 'The animals with black marks will be your pay,' then all the flock gave birth to young ones with black marks. 9 So God has taken away your father's animals and has given them to me. 10 I had a dream at the time the flocks were mating. I looked up and saw that the male goats which were mating with the female goats had black marks and spots. 11 Then the angel of God said to me in the dream, 'Jacob,' and I said, 'Here I am.' 12 He said, 'Look and see how all the male goats that are mating with the others have black marks and spots. For I have seen all that Laban has been doing to you. 13 I am the God of Bethel, where you set up a stone in honor to Me, and where you made a promise to Me. Now get up, leave this land, and return to the land of your birth.' "

14 Rachel and Leah answered him, "Do we still have any part or share in our father's house? 15 Does he not think of us as strangers? For he has sold us. And he has used all the money that was paid for us. 16 All the riches that God has taken away from our father belong to us and our children. So do whatever God has told you to do."

17 Then Jacob got up and put his children and his wives on camels. 18 He took away all his animals, all the riches he had gathered and all the cattle he had gathered in Paddan-aram. And he left to go to his father Isaac in the land of Canaan. 19 Laban had gone to cut the wool from his flock. And Rachel stole the gods of her father's house. 20 Jacob fooled Laban the Syrian by not telling him that he was going. 21 So he left with all he had. He went and crossed the Euphrates River, and turned toward the hill country of Gilead.

Laban Follows after Jacob

22 But Laban was told on the third day that Jacob had gone. 23 So he took the men of his family with him, and followed Jacob for seven days. He found him in the hill country of Gilead. 24 But God came to Laban the Syrian in a dream by night. He said to him, "Be careful that you do not speak good or bad to Jacob."

25 Then Laban came to Jacob. Now Jacob had put up his tent in the hill country. Laban and the men of his family put up their tents in the hill country of Gilead. 26 Laban said to Jacob, "What do you mean by fooling me and carrying away my daughters as if they were taken by the sword? 27 Why did you leave in secret and fool me? Why did you not tell me, so I would have sent you away with joy and with songs and with sounds of joy on the timbrel and harp. 28 Why did you not let me kiss my grandchildren and daughters good-bye? Now you have been foolish. 29 I have the power to hurt you. But the God of your father spoke to me last night, saying, 'Be careful not to speak good or bad to Jacob.' 30 Now you have gone away because you had a desire for your father's house. But why did you steal my gods?"

31 Jacob answered Laban, "Because I was afraid you might take your daughters from me and make them stay. 32 The one with whom you find your gods will not live. In front of those of our family, look for what I have that is yours, and take it." For Jacob did not know that Rachel had stolen them.

33 So Laban went into Jacob's tent, and into Leah's tent, and into the tent of the two women who served Rachel and Leah. But he did not find his gods. Then he went from Leah's tent into Rachel's tent. 34 Now Rachel had taken the gods of Laban's house and put them in the seat that was used on the camel's back. And she sat upon them. Laban looked through the whole tent, but did not find them. 35 She said to her father, "My lord, do not be angry that I cannot rise in front of you. For the way of women is upon me." So he looked, but could not find the gods.

36 Then Jacob became angry and argued with Laban. Jacob said to Laban, "What have I done wrong? What is my sin that made you run after me? 37 What things of your house have you found by looking through all that belongs to me? Set it here in front of my brothers and your brothers, so they may judge between us. 38 During these twenty years I have been with you, your female goats and sheep have not lost a young one. And I have not eaten the sheep of your flocks. 39 I did not bring to you those that were torn by wild animals. I took the loss upon myself. You had me pay for what was carried away during the day or during the night. 40 This is the way it was for me. I suffered from heat during the day, and from cold during the night. And I could not sleep. 41 I have been in your house twenty years. I worked for you fourteen years for your two daughters, and six years for your flock. And you changed my pay ten times. 42 If the God of my father, the God of Abraham and the fear of Isaac, had not been with me, for sure you would have sent me away with nothing. God has seen my suffering and the work of my hands. So He spoke sharp words to you last night."

43 Laban answered Jacob, "The daughters are my daughters. The children are my children. And the flocks are my flocks. All that you see is mine. But what can I do today to these my daughters or to their children who were born to them? 44 So come now, let us make an agreement, you and I. And let us do something to show we have an agreement between us."

45 So Jacob took a stone and set it up in honor of the agreement. 46 Then Jacob said to the men of his family, "Gather stones." So they took stones and put them on top of each other. And they ate there by all the stones. 47 Laban gave the stones the name of Jegar-sahadutha. But Jacob gave them the name Galeed. 48 Laban said, "These stones are to stand for the agreement between you and me today." So they were given the name Galeed. 49 They were given the name of Mizpah also. For Laban said, "May the Lord watch between you and me when we are apart from each other. 50 If you hurt my daughters, or if you take wives other than my daughters, no man may see it. But God sees what happens between you and me." 51 Laban said to Jacob, "See these stones that have been set up between you and me. 52 These stones that have been set up will stand for our agreement. I will not pass by these stones to hurt you. And you will not pass by these stones to hurt me. 53 The God of Abraham, the God of Nahor, the God of their father, judge between us." So Jacob promised by the fear of his father Isaac. 54 Then Jacob gave a gift in worship to God on the mountain. Then he called his

brothers to eat bread. And they ate bread and stayed the night on the mountain.

55 Laban got up early in the morning and kissed his grandchildren and daughters. He prayed that good would come to them. Then Laban left and returned home.

Esau Comes to Meet Jacob

32 Jacob went on his way, and God's angels met him. 2 When Jacob saw them, he said, "This is God's camp!" So he gave the place the name Mahanaim.

3 Jacob sent men to carry news before him to his brother Esau in the land of Seir, the country of Edom. 4 He told them, "Say this to my lord Esau: 'Your servant Jacob says, "I have been living with Laban, and stayed there until now. 5 I have cattle and donkeys and flocks and men and women servants. And I have sent to tell my lord, hoping to find favor in your eyes.' " 6 The men that carried the news returned to Jacob and said, "We came to your brother Esau. He is coming to meet you, and four hundred men are with him."

7 Then Jacob was afraid and troubled. And he divided the people who were with him, and the flocks and cattle and camels, into two groups. 8 For he said, "If Esau comes to the one group and destroys it, then the other group will get away." 9 Then Jacob said, "O God of my father Abraham and God of my father Isaac, O Lord, Who said to me, 'Return to your country and to those of your family, and I will bring good to you.' 10 I have not earned any of the loving-kindness and faith which You have shown to your servant. For I had crossed this Jordan with only my walking stick. And now I have become two large groups. 11 Save me, I pray, from the hand of my brother, from the power of Esau. For I am afraid of him. I am afraid he will come and kill us all, the mothers with the children. 12 But You said, 'I will bring good to you. I will make your children like the sand of the sea. There will be too many to number.' "

13 So Jacob stayed there that night. Then he chose a gift from what he had for his brother Esau: 14 Two hundred female goats, twenty male goats, two hundred female sheep, twenty rams, 15 thirty milk camels and their young ones, forty cows, ten bulls, twenty female donkeys and ten male donkeys. 16 He put them into the care of his servants, every group of animals by itself. Then he said to his servants, "Go in front of me. And keep the groups of animals apart." 17 He told the one in front, "When my brother Esau meets you and asks, 'To whom do you belong, and where are you going, and who owns these animals in front of you?' 18 then you say, 'These belong to your servant Jacob. It is a gift sent to my lord Esau. And he is coming behind us.' " 19 He also told the second and the third and all those who followed the animals, "This is what you are to say to Esau when you meet him. 20 And be sure to say, 'Your servant Jacob is coming behind us.' " For he said, "I will take away his anger with the gift that goes in front of me. Then when I meet him, he might receive me." 21 So the gift went in front of him, while he stayed that night in the tent.

Jacob's Name Is Changed to Israel

22 But he got up that same night and crossed the Jabbok River, with his two wives, the two women who served him, and his eleven children. 23 He took them and sent them to the other side of the river with all that he had. 24 Then Jacob was left alone. And a man fought with him until morning. 25 When the man saw that he was not winning he touched the joint of Jacob's thigh. And Jacob's thigh was put out of joint while he fought with him. 26 The man said, "Let me go. For the morning has come." But Jacob said, "I will not let you go unless you pray that good will come to me." 27 The man asked him, "What is your name?" He said, "Jacob." 28 And the man said, "Your name will no longer be Jacob, but Israel. For you have fought with God and with men, and have won." 29 Then Jacob asked him, "Tell me, what is your name?" But he said, "Why is it that you ask my name?" And there he prayed that good would come to Jacob. 30 So Jacob gave the place the name of Peniel. For he said, "I have seen God face to face, and yet I am still alive."

31 The sun rose upon him as he passed through Peniel. It was hard to walk on his leg. 32 So to this day the sons of Israel do not eat the meat from inside the joint of the thigh, because he touched this part of the joint on Jacob's leg.

Jacob Meets Esau

33 Then Jacob looked up and saw Esau coming with 400 men. So he divided the children among Leah and Rachel and the two women who served him. 2 He put the women who served him and their children in front, and Leah and her children behind them, and Rachel and Joseph behind them. ³ Then Jacob went before them. He bowed to the ground seven times, until he came near his brother. ⁴ But Esau ran to meet him and put his arms around him and kissed him. And they cried.

⁵ Then Esau looked up and saw the women and the children. He said, "Who are these with you?" Jacob said, "They are the children whom God, in His lovingfavor, has given your servant." ⁶ Then the women who served Jacob came near with their children, and they bowed to the ground. ⁷ Leah also came near with her children, and they bowed to the ground. Then Joseph and Rachel came near and bowed to the ground.

⁸ Esau said, "What do you mean by all these animals I have met?" And Jacob said, "They are a gift so I may find favor in the eyes of my lord." ⁹ But Esau said, "I have enough, my brother. Keep what you have for yourself." ¹⁰ But Jacob said, "No, I ask of you, if I have found favor in your eyes, then receive my gift. For I see your face as one sees the face of God. You have received me with favor. ¹¹ Take my gift that has been brought to you. For God has shown lovingkindness to me, and I have all I need." So he begged him until he took it.

¹² Then Esau said, "Let us be on our way. I will go with you." ¹³ But Jacob said to him, "My lord knows that the children are weak. And there are young ones in my flocks that need milk. If they are made to go a long way in one day, all the flocks will die. ¹⁴ Let my lord go in front of his servant. And I will be slow in coming to my lord at Seir. I will go as fast as the cattle in front of me and as the children are able." ¹⁵ So Esau said, "Let me leave with you some of the people who are with me." But Jacob said, "What need is there? Let me find favor in the eyes of my lord." ¹⁶ So Esau returned that day on his way to Seir. ¹⁷ But Jacob traveled to Succoth. He built his house there, and put up small buildings for his animals. So the name of the place is Succoth.

¹⁸ Now Jacob came in peace from Paddan-aram to the city of Shechem in the land of Canaan. And he put up his tents near the city. ¹⁹ He bought the piece of land where he had put up his tents for one hundred pieces of money from the sons of Hamor, Shechem's father. ²⁰ He built an altar there, and gave it the name El-Elohe Israel.

Dinah and Shechem

34 Now Leah's daughter Dinah, who was born to Jacob, went out to visit the women of the land. ² And she was seen by Shechem the son of Hamor the Hivite, the ruler of the land. He took her and made her lay with him, and she was put to shame. ³ He had much desire for Dinah the daughter of Jacob. He loved the girl and spoke kind words to her. ⁴ So Shechem said to his father Hamor, "Get me this young girl for a wife."

⁵ Now Jacob heard that Shechem had put his daughter Dinah to shame. But his sons were with the flocks in the field, so Jacob kept quiet until they returned. ⁶ Then Shechem's father Hamor went to speak with Jacob. ⁷ Jacob's sons returned from the field when they heard what had happened. They were full of sorrow and were angry. For Shechem had put Israel to shame by lying with Jacob's daughter. Such a thing should not be done. ⁸ But Hamor said to them, "The soul of my son Shechem has much desire for your daughter. I ask of you, give her to him in marriage. ⁹ Marry with our people. Give your daughters to us. And take our daughters for yourselves. ¹⁰ May you live with us. And the land will be open to you. Live and trade in it, and buy land in it."

¹¹ Then Shechem said to Dinah's father and brothers, "Let me find favor in your eyes. I will give you whatever you ask. ¹² Make your price and wedding gift as much as you want. I will give you as much as you ask. Only give me the girl to be my wife."

¹³ But Jacob's sons lied in their answer to Shechem and his father Hamor because he had put their sister Dinah to shame. ¹⁴ They said to them, "We cannot do this. We cannot give our sister to one who has not gone through the religious act of having his flesh cut. For that would be a shame to us. ¹⁵ We will give you our sister only if you become like us. Every man among you must have this religious act done. ¹⁶ Then we will give our daughters to you. And we will marry your daughters. We will live with you and become one people. ¹⁷ But if you will not listen to us and have this religious act done, then we will take our daughter and go."

¹⁸ Their words pleased Hamor and his son Shechem. ¹⁹ The young man did not wait to do what they asked, because he was in love with Jacob's daughter. And he was the most honored of all his family.

20 So Hamor and his son Shechem came to the gate of their city. And they said to the men of their city, 21 "These men want to be at peace with us. Let them live in the land and trade in it. For, see, the land is large enough for them. Let us take their daughters in marriage, and give our daughters to them. 22 But the men will be willing to live with us and become one people only if every man among us goes through the religious act that they have gone through. 23 Will not their cattle and all they own, all their animals, be ours? Let us just do what they ask, and they will live with us." 24 All who went out of the gate of his city listened to Hamor and his son Shechem. And every man went through the religious act of having his flesh cut, all who went out of the gate of his city.

25 But on the third day, when all the men were in pain, two of Jacob's sons, Simeon and Levi, Dinah's brothers, took their swords and went into the city in secret. And they killed every man. 26 They killed Hamor and his son Shechem with the sword. And they took Dinah from Shechem's house and went away. 27 Then Jacob's sons went over the dead men and robbed the city of its riches because its men had put their sister to shame. 28 They took their flocks and cattle and donkeys and whatever was in the city and in the field. 29 They took all their riches, their little ones, their wives, even all that was in the houses.

30 Then Jacob said to Simeon and Levi, "You have brought trouble on me by making me hated by the people of the land, the Canaanites and Perizzites. My men are few in number. And these people will gather together against me and fight me. I and those of my house will be destroyed." 31 But they said, "Should he act towards our sister as if she were a woman who sells the use of her body?"

Jacob Returns to Bethel

35 God said to Jacob, "Get ready and go to Bethel to live. Make an altar there to God, Who showed Himself to you when you ran away from your brother Esau." 2 So Jacob said to those of his house and all who were with him, "Put away the strange gods that are among you. Make yourselves clean and change your clothes. 3 Then let us get ready and go to Bethel. I will make an altar there to God, Who answered me in the day of my trouble, and was with me every place I went." 4 So they gave to Jacob all the strange gods they had, and the gold objects which they wore in their ears. And Jacob hid them under the tree near Shechem. 5 As they traveled, much fear from God came upon the cities around them. So the people of the land did not go against the sons of Jacob.

6 So Jacob and all the people who were with him came to Luz (that is, Bethel) in the land of Canaan. 7 He built an altar there, and gave the place the name El-bethel. Because God had shown Himself to him there, when Jacob ran away from his brother. 8 Then Rebekah's nurse Deborah died. She was buried below Bethel under a tree. It was given the name of Allon-bacuth.

9 When Jacob came from Paddan-aram, God showed Himself to him again and brought good to him. 10 God said to him, "Your name is Jacob. You will not be called Jacob any longer, but Israel will be your name." So his name was Israel. 11 Then God said to him, "I am the All-powerful God. Have many children and add to your number. A nation and a group of nations will come from you. Kings will come from you. 12 I will give you the land which I gave to Abraham and Isaac. This land I will give to your children and their children's children after you." 13 Then God went up from him in the place where He had spoken with him. 14 Jacob set up a pillar of stone in the place where He had spoken with him. And he poured a drink offering and also oil on it. 15 So Jacob gave the place where God had spoken with him the name Bethel.

16 Then they traveled from Bethel. When there was still a long way to go before coming to Ephrath, Rachel began to give birth. She suffered much pain. 17 And while she was suffering, the woman who was helping her said to her, "Do not be afraid. For now you have another son." 18 As Rachel's soul was leaving, for she died, she gave him the name Benoni. But his father gave him the name Benjamin. 19 So Rachel died, and was buried on the way to Ephrath (that is, Bethlehem). 20 Jacob set up a stone on her grave. And that is the stone of Rachel's grave to this day.

21 Then Israel traveled on, and put up his tent on the other side of the tall building of Eder. 22 While Israel lived in that land, Reuben went and lay with Bilhah, the woman who acted as his father's wife. And Israel heard about it.

The Sons of Jacob

There were twelve sons of Jacob. 23 The sons of Leah were Reuben, Jacob's first-born, then Simeon, Levi, Judah, Issachar, and Zebulun. 24 The sons of Rachel were Joseph and Benjamin. 25 The sons of Bilhah, the woman who served Rachel, were Dan and Naphtali. 26 The sons of Zilpah, the woman who served Leah, were Gad and Asher. These are the sons who were born to Jacob in Paddan-aram.

The Death of Isaac

27 Jacob came to his father Isaac at Mamre of Kiriath-arba (that is, Hebron), where Abraham and Isaac had been living. 28 Now Isaac had lived 180 years. 29 And Isaac breathed his last and died, and was joined to his people who died before him. He was an old man who had a long life, and his sons Esau and Jacob buried him.

The Families of Esau

36 These are the children of Esau (that is, Edom).

2 Esau took his wives from the women of Canaan: Adah the daughter of Elon the Hittite, and Oholibamah the daughter of Anah and granddaughter of Zibeon the Hivite, 3 and Ishmael's daughter Basemath, the sister of Nebaioth. 4 Adah gave birth to Esau's son Eliphaz. Basemath gave birth to Reuel. 5 And Oholibamah gave birth to Jeush, Jalam and Korah. These are the sons who were born to Esau in the land of Canaan.

6 Then Esau took his wives and sons and daughters and all those of his house, and his flocks and cattle, and all his riches from the land of Canaan. And he went to another land away from his brother Jacob. 7 For they owned too much for them to live together. The land where they were staying could not keep them alive, because of all their animals. 8 So Esau lived in the hill country of Seir. Esau is Edom.

9 These are the children, and their children, of Esau the father of the Edomites in the hill country of Seir. 10 These are the names of Esau's sons: Eliphaz the son of Esau's wife Adah, and Reuel the son of Esau's wife Basemath. 11 The sons of Eliphaz were Teman, Omar, Zepho, Gatam, and Kenaz. 12 Timna acted as the wife of Esau's son Eliphaz. And she gave birth to Eliphaz's son Amalek. These are the sons of Esau's wife Adah. 13 These are the sons of Reuel: Nahath, Zerah, Shammah, and Mizzah. They are the sons of Esau's wife Basemath.

14 These are the sons of Esau's wife Oholibamah, the daughter of Anah, the daughter of Zibeon: She gave birth to Esau's sons, Jeush, Jalam and Korah.

15 These are the leaders of the sons of Esau. The sons of Esau's first-born, Eliphaz, are leaders Teman, Omar, Zepho, Kenaz, 16 Korah, Gatam, and Amalek. These are the leaders of Eliphaz in the land of Edom. They are the sons of Adah.

17 These are the sons of Esau's son Reuel: Leaders Nahath, Zerah, Shammah, and Mizzah. These are the leaders of Reuel in the land of Edom. They are the sons of Esau's wife Basemath.

18 These are the sons of Esau's wife Oholibamah: Leaders Jeush, Jalam and Korah. These are the leaders of Esau's wife Oholibamah, the daughter of Anah. 19 These are the sons of Esau (that is, Edom), and these are their leaders.

20 These are the sons of Seir the Horite, who lived in that land: Lotan, Shobal, Zibeon, Anah, 21 Dishon, Ezer, and Dishan. These are the leaders of the Horites, the sons of Seir in the land of Edom.

22 The sons of Lotan are Hori and Hemam. Lotan's sister was Timna. 23 The sons of Shobal are Alvan, Manahath, Ebal, Shepho, and Onam. 24 The sons of Zibeon are Aiah and Anah. He is the Anah who found the hot water well in the desert when he was caring for the donkeys of his father Zibeon. 25 The children of Anah are Dishon and Oholibamah, Anah's daughter. 26 The sons of Dishon are Hemdan, Eshban, Ithran, and Cheran. 27 The sons of Ezer are Bilhan, Zaavan and Akan. 28 And the sons of Dishan are Uz and Aran.

29 These are the leaders of the Horites: Leaders Lotan, Shobal, Zibeon, Anah, 30 Dishon, Ezer, and Dishan. These are the leaders of the Horites, by their families in the land of Seir.

The Kings of Edom

31 These are the kings who ruled in the land of Edom before any king ruled the sons of Israel. 32 Bela the son of Beor ruled in Edom. The name of his city was Dinhabah. 33 Then Bela died. And Jobab the son of Zerah of Bozrah became king in his place. 34 Then Jobab died. And Husham of the land of the Temanites became king in his place. 35 Then Husham died. And Hadad the son of Bedad, who won the fight against Midian in the field of Moab, became king in his place. The name of his city was Avith. 36 Then Hadad died. And

Samlah of Masrekah became king in his place. 37 Then Samlah died. And Shaul of Rehoboth on the Euphrates River became king in his place. 38 Then Shaul died. And Achbor's son Baal-hanan became king in his place. 39 Then Achbor's son died. And Hadar became king in his place. The name of his city was Pau. His wife's name was Mehetabel, the daughter of Matred, daughter of Mezahab.

40 These are the names of the leaders of Esau, by family, place and name: Leaders Timna, Alvah, Jetheth, 41 Oholibamah, Elah, Pinon, 42 Kenaz, Teman, Mibzar, 43 Magdiel, and Iram. These are the leaders of Edom (that is, Esau, the father of the Edomites), who lived in the land that belonged to them.

Joseph's Dream

37 Jacob lived in the land where his father had lived as a stranger, in the land of Canaan. 2 This is the story of the children of Jacob and of their children.

When Joseph was seventeen years old, he was caring for the flock with his brothers. The boy was with the sons of Bilhah and Zilpah, his father's wives. And Joseph told his father about how bad they were. 3 Now Israel loved Joseph more than all his sons, because Joseph was born when he was an old man. And Israel made him a long coat of many colors. 4 His brothers saw that their father loved him more than all his brothers. So they hated Joseph and could not speak a kind word to him.

5 Then Joseph had a dream. When he told it to his brothers, they hated him even more. 6 He said to them, "Listen to the dream that I have had. 7 We were gathering grain in the field. My bundle of grain stood up. Your bundles of grain gathered around it and bowed down to my bundle." 8 Then his brothers said to him, "Are you going to be our king? Are you going to rule over us?" So they hated him even more for his dreams and for what he said.

9 Then he had another dream, and he told it to his brothers. He said, "I have had another dream. The sun and the moon and eleven stars were bowing down to me." 10 He told it to his father and to his brothers. His father spoke sharp words to him, saying, "What is this dream you have had? Will I and your mother and brothers come to bow ourselves down to the ground in front of you?" 11 Joseph's brothers were jealous of him. But his father thought about what he said.

Joseph Is Sold and Taken to Egypt

12 Then his brothers went to feed their father's flock in Shechem. 13 Israel said to Joseph, "Are not your brothers feeding the flock in Shechem? Come, I will send you to them." And Joseph said to him, "I will go." 14 Then Israel said, "Go now, see if it is well with your brothers and with the flock. Then come and tell me." So he sent him from the valley of Hebron, and he came to Shechem. 15 A man found him walking through a field, and asked him, "What are you looking for?" 16 Joseph said, "I am looking for my brothers. Tell me where they are feeding the flock." 17 And the man said, "They have moved from here. For I heard them say, 'Let us go to Dothan.' " So Joseph followed his brothers and found them at Dothan.

18 When they saw him far away, before he came near them, they made plans to kill him. 19 They said to one another, "Here comes this dreamer! 20 Now come and let us kill him and throw him into one of the deep holes. Then we will say that a wild animal ate him. And we will see what becomes of his dreams!"

21 But Reuben heard this and saved him from their hands, saying, "Let us not kill him." 22 Reuben then said, "Do not put him to death. Throw him into this hole here in the desert. But do not lay a hand on him." He wanted to be able to save Joseph and return him to his father.

23 So when Joseph came to his brothers, they tore off his coat, the coat of many colors that he was wearing. 24 And they took him and threw him into the hole. The hole was empty and had no water in it.

25 Then they sat down to eat. When they looked up, they saw a group of Ishmaelites coming from Gilead. They were taking spices and perfumes on their camels to Egypt. 26 Judah said to his brothers, "What do we get by killing our brother and covering his blood? 27 Come, let us sell him to the Ishmaelites and not lay our hands on him. For he is our brother, our own flesh." And his brothers listened to him. 28 Some Midianite traders were passing by. So the brothers pulled Joseph up out of the hole. And they sold him to the Ishmaelites for twenty pieces of silver, and they took Joseph to Egypt.

29 Then Reuben returned to the hole. When he saw that Joseph was not in the hole, he tore his clothes. 30 He returned to his brothers and said, "The boy is not there! What can I do?" 31 So they took

Joseph's coat, killed a male goat, and put the blood on the coat. ³² They sent the coat of many colors to their father. And they said, "We found this. Is it your son's coat or not?"

³³ Jacob looked at it and said, "It is my son's coat! A wild animal has eaten him! For sure Joseph has been torn to pieces!" ³⁴ So Jacob tore his clothes and dressed in clothes made from hair. He had sorrow for his son many days. ³⁵ All his sons and daughters tried to comfort him. But he would not be comforted. He said, "I will go down to the grave in sorrow for my son." And his father cried for him.

³⁶ The Midianites sold Joseph in Egypt to Potiphar, the head of the soldiers of Pharaoh's house.

Judah and Tamar

38 Judah went away from his brothers at that time. He visited a certain Adullamite whose name was Hirah. ² There Judah saw a daughter of a certain Canaanite whose name was Shua. He took her as his wife and lived with her. ³ And she was going to have a child and gave birth to a son. He gave him the name Er. ⁴ Then she was going to have another child and she gave birth to a son. She gave him the name Onan. ⁵ Then she gave birth to another son at Chezib. And she gave him the name Shelah.

⁶ Judah chose a wife for his first-born son Er. Her name was Tamar. ⁷ But Er, Judah's first born, was sinful in the eyes of the Lord. So the Lord took his life. ⁸ Then Judah said to Onan, "Go in to your brother's wife. Do your duty as her brother-in-law. Have children for your brother." ⁹ But Onan knew that the children would not be his. So when he went in to his brother's wife, he wasted his seed on the ground to keep his brother from having children. ¹⁰ What he did was sinful in the eyes of the Lord. So the Lord took his life also. ¹¹ Then Judah said to his daughter in law Tamar, "Stay in your father's house as a woman whose husband has died, until my son Shelah is grown." For he thought, "I am afraid that he also may die like his brothers." So Tamar went and lived in her father's house.

¹² Now after a long time, Shua's daughter, the wife of Judah, died. And after the time of sorrow, Judah and his friend Hirah the Adullamite went to the men who cut the wool from his sheep at Timnah. ¹³ It was told to Tamar, "Your father-in-law is

going to Timnah to cut the wool from his sheep." ¹⁴ So she took off the clothes of a woman whose husband has died and put on other clothes and covered her face with cloth. Then she sat in the gate of Enaim, which is on the road to Timnah. For she saw that Shelah was grown, and she had not been given to him for a wife. ¹⁵ When Judah saw her, he thought she was a woman who sold the use of her body. For she had covered her face. ¹⁶ He went to her at the side of the road, and said, "Here now, let me come in to you." He did not know that she was his daughter-in-law. And she said, "What will you give me to come in to me?" ¹⁷ He answered, "I will send you a young goat from the flock." She asked, "Will you give something as a promise until you send it?" ¹⁸ He said, "What should I give you as a promise?" And she said, "The ring you use to mark your name, and its string, and the stick that is in your hand." So he gave them to her and went in to her. And she was going to have a baby by him. ¹⁹ Then she got up and left. She took off the cloth that covered her, and put on the clothes worn by a woman whose husband has died.

²⁰ Judah sent his friend the Adullamite to bring the young goat to the woman and take from her the things he had given as a promise. But he did not find her. ²¹ He asked the men of the place, "Where is the woman who was selling the use of her body beside the road at Enaim?" They said, "There has been no woman selling the use of her body here." ²² So he returned to Judah, and said, "I did not find her. The men of the place said, 'There has been no woman selling the use of her body here.'" ²³ Then Judah said, "Let her keep the things, or else we will be laughed at. I sent the young goat, and you did not find her."

²⁴ About three months later, Judah was told, "Your daughter-in-law Tamar has sold the use of her body. She is going to have a baby by doing this sinful thing." Judah said, "Bring her out and let her be burned!" ²⁵ When she was brought out, she sent word to her father-in-law, "I am going to have a baby by the man who owns these things." She said, "Look and see, who owns this ring for marking a name, and this string and stick?" ²⁶ Judah saw that they belonged to him. He said, "She is more right than I, because I did not give her to my son Shelah." And he did not lie with her again.

27 When the time came for Tamar to give birth, there were two babies. 28 While she was giving birth, one put out a hand. The nurse took his hand and tied a red string around it, saying, "This one came out first." 29 But when he pulled away his hand, his brother was born. Then she said, "What an opening you have made for yourself!" So he was given the name of Perez. 30 After that, his brother came out with the red string around his hand. He was given the name Zerah.

Joseph and Potiphar's Wife

39 Now Joseph had been taken down to Egypt by the Ishmaelites. And Potiphar, an Egyptian leader, the head of the soldiers of Pharaoh's house, bought him from the Ishmaelites. 2 The Lord was with Joseph, and all went well with him. He was in the house of his boss the Egyptian. 3 Now his boss saw that the Lord was with him. He saw how the Lord made all that Joseph did go well. 4 So Joseph found favor in his eyes, and worked only for him. Potiphar made him the one to watch over his house and take care of all that he owned. 5 And from the time that he watched over his house and all he owned, the Lord brought good to the Egyptian's house because of Joseph. The Lord brought good upon all that he owned in the house and in the field. 6 So he put all he owned in Joseph's care. Having Joseph near, he did not need to think about anything but the food he ate. Now Joseph was strong and good-looking. 7 The time came when his boss's wife saw him, and she said, "Lie with me." 8 But he would not do it. He said to his boss's wife, "See, with me near, my boss does not worry about anything in the house. He has put all he owns in my care. 9 There is no one more important in this house than I. And he has held nothing from me except you, because you are his wife. How then could I do this sinful thing, and sin against God?" 10 She spoke to Joseph day after day. But he did not listen to her. He would not lie with her or be with her. 11 Then one day Joseph went into the house to do his work. None of the men of the house were inside. 12 She caught him by his coat, saying, "Lie with me!" But he ran out of the house leaving the coat in her hand. 13 When she saw that he had left his coat in her hand and had run out of the house, 14 she called the men of her house. And she said to them, "See, this Hebrew has been brought to us

to make fun of us. He came in to lie with me, and I cried out with a loud voice. 15 When he heard my loud cry, he left his coat with me and ran outside."

16 She kept his coat with her until his boss came home. 17 Then she told him the same story, saying, "The Hebrew servant whom you brought to us came to me to lie with me. 18 But when I called out in a loud voice, he left his coat with me and ran outside." 19 When his boss heard his wife's story and her words, "This is what your servant did to me," he became very angry. 20 So Joseph's boss took him and put him in prison, the place where the men who did wrong against the king were put in chains. So there he was in prison.

21 But the Lord was with Joseph, and showed him kindness. He gave him favor in the eyes of the man who watched over the prison. 22 The head of the prison put all the men who were in prison into Joseph's care. So whatever was done there was because of Joseph. 23 The head of the prison did not worry about anything under Joseph's care, because the Lord was with him. The Lord made all go well with whatever Joseph did.

Joseph Tells about Two Dreams

40 Some time later, the man who carried the king's cup and the man who made the king's bread did wrong against the king of Egypt. 2 Pharaoh was angry with these two important men, the head cup-carrier and the head bread-maker. 3 So he put them in prison under the care of the head of the soldiers, the same place where Joseph was in prison. 4 The head of the soldiers had Joseph watch over them. He took care of them, and they were in prison for a long time. 5 One night both the cup-carrier and the bread-maker of the king of Egypt had a dream while they were in prison. Each man had his own dream, and each dream had its own meaning. 6 When Joseph came in and looked at them in the morning, he saw that they were sad. 7 So he asked these men who had worked for Pharaoh and who were with him in prison in his boss's house, "Why are your faces so sad today?" 8 They said to him, "We have had a dream and there is no one to tell us what it means." Then Joseph said to them, "Do not the meanings of dreams belong to God? Tell them to me."

9 So the head cup-carrier told his dream to Joseph. He said, "In my dream, there was a vine in front of me. 10 And there

were three branches on the vine. Then its flowers grew out. From the many flowers came grapes ready to eat. ¹¹ Pharaoh's cup was in my hand. So I took the grapes and made wine from them and poured it into Pharaoh's cup. And I put the cup into Pharaoh's hand."

¹² Then Joseph said to him, "This is the meaning of it: The three branches are three days. ¹³ Before three days are over, Pharaoh will give you honor and return you to your place of work. You will put Pharaoh's cup into his hand just like you did before when you were his cup-carrier. ¹⁴ But remember me when it is well with you, and show me kindness. Say a good word about me to Pharaoh. Get me out of this prison. ¹⁵ For I was stolen from the land of the Hebrews. And here also I have done nothing for which they should put me in prison."

¹⁶ The head bread-maker saw that the meaning of the dream was good. He said to Joseph, "I had a dream also. There were three baskets of white bread on my head. ¹⁷ All kinds of food for Pharaoh were in the top basket. But the birds were eating them out of the basket on my head."

¹⁸ Then Joseph answered, "This is the meaning of it: The three baskets are three days. ¹⁹ Within three days, Pharaoh will lift up your head from you and put your body up on a tree. And the birds will eat the flesh from you."

²⁰ On the third day, Pharaoh's birthday, he made a special supper for his servants. He gave honor to the head cup-carrier and the head bread-maker among his servants. ²¹ He returned the head cup-carrier to his place of work and he put the cup into Pharaoh's hand. ²² But he killed the head bread-maker on a tree, just like Joseph had told them it would happen. ²³ Yet the head cup-carrier did not remember Joseph. He forgot him.

Joseph Tells What the King's Dreams Mean

41 After two years had passed, Pharaoh had a dream. He dreamed that he was standing by the Nile River. ² And he saw seven cows coming out of the Nile. They were good-looking and fat, and they ate the grass beside the river. ³ Then he saw seven other cows coming out of the Nile after them. They looked bad and were thin. They stood by the other cows beside the Nile. ⁴ Then the bad looking cows that were thin ate the seven good-looking, fat cows, and Pharaoh awoke.

⁵ Then he fell asleep and dreamed a second time. He saw seven heads of grain growing on one stick of grain. They were large and full. ⁶ Then he saw seven heads of grain come after them, which were small and made dry by the east wind. ⁷ And the small heads of grain ate the seven large, full heads of grain.

Then Pharaoh awoke and saw that it was a dream. ⁸ So when morning came his spirit was troubled. He called for all the wise men of Egypt. Pharaoh told them his dreams. But there was no one who could tell Pharaoh the meaning of them.

⁹ Then the head cup-carrier said to Pharaoh, "I remember today what I have done wrong. ¹⁰ Pharaoh was angry with his servants. And he put me and the head bread-maker in prison in the house of the head of the soldiers. ¹¹ He and I had a dream on the same night. Each dream had its own meaning. ¹² A young Hebrew was there with us. He worked for the head of the soldiers. We told our dreams to him. And he told us the meaning of them. He told each of us what our different dreams meant. ¹³ And it happened just like he had said it would. I was returned to my place of work. The bread-maker was killed on a tree."

¹⁴ Pharaoh then called for Joseph. And they brought him out of the prison in a hurry. He cut off the hair on his face and put on clean clothes. Then he came to Pharaoh. ¹⁵ Pharaoh said to Joseph, "I have had a dream. But no one can tell me what it means. I have heard it said that you are able to hear a dream and tell what it means." ¹⁶ Joseph answered Pharaoh, "Not by myself. God will give Pharaoh a good answer." ¹⁷ So Pharaoh said to Joseph, "In my dream, I was standing beside the Nile. ¹⁸ I saw seven cows coming out of the Nile. They were fat and good-looking, and they ate the grass beside the river. ¹⁹ Then I saw seven other cows coming after them. They looked bad and were thin. I had never seen worse cows in all the land of Egypt. ²⁰ Then the bad looking cows that were thin ate the first seven fat cows. ²¹ But after they had eaten them, it could not be seen that they had eaten them. For they were just as bad looking as before. Then I awoke. ²² I saw also in my dream seven heads of grain growing on one stick of grain. They were large and full. ²³ Then I saw seven heads of grain come after them. They were small and were dry because of the east wind. ²⁴ The

small heads of grain ate the seven good heads of grain. Then I told it to the wise men. But there was no one who could tell me what it means."

25 Joseph said to Pharaoh, "Pharaoh's dreams are one and the same. God has shown Pharaoh what He is about to do. 26 The seven good cows are seven years. And the seven good heads of grain are seven years. The dreams are one and the same. 27 The seven bad looking cows that are thin that came up after them are seven years. And the seven small heads of grain made dry by the east wind mean seven years without food. 28 It is as I have said to Pharaoh. God has shown Pharaoh what He is about to do. 29 Seven years are coming when there will be much food in all the land of Egypt. 30 But after them will come seven years when there will be no food. The time of much food will be forgotten in the land of Egypt. The time of no food will destroy the land. 31 The time without food will be so hard that no one in the land will remember when they had much. 32 That the dream was sent twice to Pharaoh shows that what will happen is planned by God. And God will make it happen soon.

33 "So now let Pharaoh look for a man who is understanding and wise. Let the land of Egypt be put into his care. 34 Let Pharaoh take action to choose men to watch over the land. And let him take a fifth part of the food of the land of Egypt during the seven years of much food. 35 Let them gather all the food of these good years that are coming. Have them store the grain under the power of Pharaoh, to be used as food in the cities. And let them keep it safe. 36 This food will be kept for the people to eat during the seven years of no food that will come upon the land of Egypt. This way the land will not be destroyed during the time without food."

Joseph Made Ruler over Egypt

37 The plan pleased Pharaoh and all his servants. 38 Then Pharaoh said to his servants, "Can we find a man like this, who has in him the Spirit of God?" 39 So Pharaoh said to Joseph, "Because God has shown you all this, there is no one as understanding and wise as you are. 40 My house will be put in your care. And all my people will do as you say. Only on the throne will I be greater than you." 41 Pharaoh said to Joseph, "See, I have put you in power over all the land of Egypt."

42 Then Pharaoh took the ring from his hand, and put it on Joseph's hand. He dressed him in clothes of fine cloth. He put a gold chain around his neck. 43 He had him travel in his second wagon of honor. And they called out in front of him, "Bow down!" Pharaoh put him in power over all the land of Egypt. 44 Pharaoh said to Joseph, "I am Pharaoh. But unless it is your will, no one will raise his hand or foot in all the land of Egypt." 45 Then Pharaoh gave Joseph the name of Zaphenath-paneah. He gave him for a wife Asenath, the daughter of Potiphera who was the religious leader of On. So Joseph went out through the land of Egypt.

46 Joseph was thirty years old when he stood in front of Pharaoh, king of Egypt. And Joseph went from Pharaoh to visit every part of Egypt. 47 During the seven good years the land brought much food. 48 So he gathered into the cities all the food of these seven years when there was much in the land of Egypt. He put into each city the food from the fields around it. 49 Joseph gathered as much grain as the sand of the sea. The time came when he stopped trying to know how much there was.

Joseph's Two Sons

50 Two sons were born to Joseph before the years without food came. Asenath, the daughter of Potiphera, the religious leader of On, gave birth to them. 51 Joseph gave the first-born the name Manasseh. "For," he said, "God has made me forget all my trouble and all those of my father's house." 52 He gave the second son the name of Ephraim. "For," he said, "God has given me children in the land of my suffering."

53 The seven good years of much food in the land of Egypt came to an end. 54 And the seven bad years of no food began, as Joseph had said. No food was growing in all the lands, but in all the land of Egypt there was food. 55 So when all the people of Egypt were hungry, they cried to Pharaoh for bread. Pharaoh said to all the Egyptians, "Go to Joseph. Do what he tells you." 56 When the hunger was spreading over all the earth, Joseph opened the store-houses. And he sold food to the Egyptians for the time without food had become hard in the land of Egypt. 57 The people of all the earth came to Egypt to buy grain from Joseph because the time without food was hard everywhere.

Joseph's Brothers Go to Egypt

42 Now Jacob learned that there was grain in Egypt. He said to his sons, "Why are you looking at one another?" 2 And he said, "I have heard that there is grain in Egypt. Go there and buy some for us, so we may live and not die." 3 So ten of Joseph's brothers went to buy grain in Egypt. 4 But Jacob did not send Joseph's brother Benjamin with his brothers. For he said, "I am afraid that something will happen to him."

Joseph's Brothers Bow before Him

5 So the sons of Israel joined those who were coming to buy grain for there was no food in Canaan. 6 Joseph was the ruler of the land. He was the one who sold grain to all the people of the land. And Joseph's brothers came and bowed to the ground in front of him. 7 When Joseph saw his brothers, he knew who they were. But he acted like a stranger and spoke sharp words to them. He said, "Where have you come from?" They answered, "From the land of Canaan, to buy food."

8 Joseph knew his brothers but they did not know him. 9 Joseph remembered the dreams he had had about them. He said to them, "You are spies. You have come to find the weak places in our land." 10 They said to him, "No, my lord. Your servants have come to buy food. 11 We are all sons of one man. We do not lie. Your servants are not working against you in secret."

12 He said to them, "No! You have come to find the weak places in our land!" 13 But they said, "Your servants are twelve brothers, the sons of one man in the land of Canaan. The youngest is now with our father. And one is no more." 14 But Joseph said to them, "It is as I said. You are spies. 15 You will be put to a test. By the life of Pharaoh, you will not leave this place unless your youngest brother comes here. 16 Send one of you to bring your brother, and the rest of you will be kept in prison. Your words will be put to a test to see if you are telling the truth. Or else, by the life of Pharaoh, you are spies for sure."

17 He put them all together in prison for three days. 18 Then Joseph said to them on the third day, "Do this and live, for I fear God. 19 If you are men who do not lie, let one of your brothers stay here in prison for all of you. But you others go and carry grain for your hungry families. 20 Then bring your youngest brother to me, so your words will be proven true. And you will live." So they did what he said. 21 They said to one another, "For sure we are guilty for what we did to our brother. We saw the suffering of his soul while he begged us. But we would not listen. So this trouble has come to us."

22 Reuben answered them, "Did I not tell you, 'Do not sin against the boy?' But you would not listen. Now we must pay for his blood." 23 They did not know that Joseph understood them. For there was a man between them to tell the meaning of each other's language. 24 Joseph went away from them and cried. Then he returned to speak with them. And he took Simeon from them and put chains on him in front of his brothers.

Joseph's Brothers Return to Canaan

25 Then Joseph had their bags filled with grain. He had each man's money returned to his bag, to buy what was needed as they traveled. So this was done for them. 26 Then they loaded their donkeys with their grain, and left. 27 When one of them opened his bag to give his donkey food at the place where they were staying the night, he saw his money. It was there at the top of his bag. 28 He said to his brothers, "My money has been returned! It is inside my bag!" Then their hearts became full of fear. They turned to each other, shaking in fear, saying, "What is this that God has done to us?"

29 When they came to their father Jacob in the land of Canaan, they told him all that had happened to them. They said, 30 "The man who is ruler of the land spoke sharp words to us. He thought that we had gone there to find the weak places in the country. 31 But we said to him, 'We do not lie. We are not working against you in secret. 32 We are twelve brothers, the sons of our father. One is no more. And the youngest is now with our father in the land of Canaan.' 33 Then the man who is ruler of the land said to us, 'I will know that you are telling the truth by this: Leave one of your brothers with me. Take grain for your hungry families and go. 34 But bring your youngest brother to me, so I will know you are not spies, but honest men telling the truth. Then I will return your brother to you. And then you may trade in the land.' "

35 When they took the grain out of their bags, they found that every man's money was in his bag. And when they and their father saw the money, they were afraid.

36 Their father Jacob said to them, "You have taken my children from me! Joseph is no more. Simeon is no more. And now you would take Benjamin! All this has come upon me!"

37 Then Reuben told his father, "You may kill my two sons if I do not return him to you. Put him in my care, and I will return him to you." 38 But Jacob said, "My son will not go with you. For his brother is dead, and only he is left. If something were to happen to him during your traveling, you would bring my white hair down to the grave in sorrow."

Joseph's Brothers Go to Egypt the Second Time

43 The time of no food was hard in the land. 2 When they had eaten all the grain they had brought from Egypt, their father said to them, "Go again and buy us a little food." 3 But Judah told him, "The man said to us with sharp words, 'You will not see my face unless your brother is with you.' 4 If you send our brother with us, we will go to Egypt and buy you food. 5 But if you do not send him, we will not go. For the man said, 'You will not see my face unless your brother is with you.'"

6 Israel said, "Why did you do me such a wrong by telling the man that you had another brother?" 7 And they said, "The man asked questions about us and our family. He said, 'Is your father still alive? Do you have another brother?' So we answered his questions. How could we know that he would say, 'Bring your brother here'?"

8 Judah said to his father Israel, "Send the boy with me. And we will get up and go, so we and you and our children may live and not die. 9 I will put myself as trust for him. You may put him in my care. If I do not return him to you and set him in front of you, then let the blame be on me forever. 10 For if we had not waited, we would have returned twice by now."

11 Then their father Israel said to them, "If it must be so, then do this: take some of the best things of the land in your bags. Carry them to the man as a gift. Give him perfume and honey and spices and special things to eat. 12 Take twice as much money with you to take the place of the money that was returned in your bags. It may be that it was a mistake. 13 Take your brother also. Get up, and return to the man. 14 May the All-powerful God give you such favor with the man that he may let your other brother and Benjamin return. If my children are taken from me, I am filled with sorrow."

15 So the men took the gift, and twice as much money, and Benjamin. They got up and went to Egypt, and stood in front of Joseph. 16 When Joseph saw Benjamin with them, he said to the man who took care of his house, "Bring the men into the house. And kill an animal and make it ready. For the men will eat with me at noon." 17 So the man did what Joseph said, and brought the men to Joseph's house. 18 The men were afraid because they were brought to Joseph's house. They said, "We are being brought in because of the money that was returned in our bags the first time we came. He is looking for something against us. He will come down on us and take us for servants with our donkeys." 19 So they came near the man who took care of Joseph's house, and spoke to him at the door of the house. 20 They said, "O, my lord, we came here the first time to buy food. 21 When we came to the place where we stayed the night, we opened our bags. And we found that the full weight of each man's money was at the top of the bag. So we have brought it again with us. 22 We have brought other money with us also to buy food. We do not know who put our money in our bags."

23 But he answered, "Peace be with you. Do not be afraid. Your God and the God of your father has given you riches in your bags. I received your money." Then he brought Simeon out to them. 24 The man brought the men into Joseph's house and gave them water to wash their feet. And he fed their donkeys. 25 So they made the gift ready to give to Joseph when he came at noon. For they had heard that they were to eat there.

26 When Joseph came home, they gave him the gift they had brought with them. They bowed to the ground in front of him. 27 Then Joseph asked them about their well-being. He said, "Is your father well, the old man you spoke about? Is he still alive?" 28 And they said, "Your servant, our father is well. He is still alive." Then they bowed their heads low in honor to Joseph.

29 As he looked up, he saw his brother Benjamin, his mother's son. He said, "Is this your youngest brother whom you told me about? May God show you loving-favor, my son." 30 Then Joseph went out in a hurry. For he had much feeling for his brother. He went in his room and cried.

31 Then he washed his face and came out. Hiding his feelings, he said, "Bring the food."

32 So they brought food to Joseph by himself, and to them by themselves, and to the Egyptians who ate with him by themselves. The Egyptians could not eat bread with the Hebrews because they thought it would be sinful. 33 Joseph's brothers were seated in front of him by the way they were born, from the oldest to the youngest. And the men looked at each other in wonder. 34 Joseph took food to them from his own table. But Benjamin's food was five times as much as any of theirs. And they were free in eating and drinking with him.

Joseph's Cup

44 Then Joseph told the man who took care of his house, "Fill the men's bags with as much food as they can carry. And put each man's money in his bag. 2 Put my silver cup in the bag of the youngest, and his money for the grain." And he did what Joseph had told him to do. 3 Early in the morning the men were sent away with their donkeys. 4 When they had left the city and were not far away, Joseph said to the man who took care of his house, "Get up and follow the men. When you come to them, say to them, 'Why have you returned bad for good? Why have you stolen the silver cup? 5 Is this not my lord's drinking cup that he uses for telling about the future? You have done wrong.'"

6 So he came to them and spoke these words to them. 7 And they said to him, "Why does my lord say these things? Your servants would never do such a thing. 8 Remember how we returned to you from the land of Canaan with the money we found in the top of our bags. Then why would we steal silver or gold from your owner's house? 9 If the cup is found with any of your servants, let him be put to death. And the others of us will be your servants."

10 He answered, "Let it be as you say. He who is found to have the cup will be my servant. But you others will be without blame." 11 Then each man put his bag down on the ground in a hurry and opened it. 12 The man looked for it, beginning with the oldest and stopping with the youngest. And the cup was found in Benjamin's bag. 13 Then they tore their clothes. After each man loaded his donkey again, they returned to the city.

14 When Judah and his brothers came to Joseph's house, he was still there. They fell to the ground in front of him. 15 Joseph said to them, "What is this that you have done? Did you not know that a man like me has power to know what is not known by others?" 16 Judah said, "We do not know what to say to my lord. How can we make ourselves right in your eyes? God has shown the guilt of your servants. See, we are your servants, both we and the one who was found with the cup." 17 But Joseph said, "No. I will do no such thing. The person who was found with the cup will be my servant. But you others may go in peace to your father."

18 Then Judah came near to him, and said, "O my lord, let your servant speak a word in my lord's ears. Do not be angry with your servant. For you are like Pharaoh himself. 19 My lord asked his servants, 'Do you have a father or a brother?' 20 We said to my lord, 'We have an old father and a young brother who was born to him when he was old. Now his brother is dead. So he is all that is left of his mother, and his father loves him.' 21 Then you said to your servants, 'Bring him here to me, so I may see him.' 22 But we said to my lord, 'The boy cannot leave his father. For if he should leave his father, his father would die.' 23 Then you said to your servants, 'Unless your youngest brother comes here with you, you will not see my face again.'

24 "When we returned to your servant my father, we told him what my lord had said. 25 Our father said, 'Go again and buy us a little food.' 26 But we said, 'We cannot go there. If our youngest brother is with us, we will go there. For we cannot see the man's face unless our youngest brother is with us.'

27 "Then your servant my father said to us, 'You know that my wife gave birth to two of my sons. 28 One left me, and I said, "For sure he is torn to pieces." I have not seen him since. 29 If you take this one also from me, and something happens to him, you will bring my white hair down to the grave in sorrow.' 30 My father's life and the boy's life are one. If I return to your servant my father, and the boy is not with us, 31 when he sees that the boy is not with us, he will die. So your servants will bring the white hair of your servant our father down to the grave in sorrow. 32 For I put myself as trust for the boy to my father. I said, 'If I do not return him to you, then let the blame be on me forever.' 33 So let your servant stay and work for my lord, instead of the boy. Let the boy go home

with his brothers. 34 For how can I return to my father if the boy is not with me? I am afraid to see the sorrow that my father would suffer."

Joseph Tells His Brothers Who He Is

45 Then Joseph could not hide his feelings in front of all who stood by him. He cried, "Send all the people away from me." So no one was with him when Joseph told his brothers who he was. 2 He cried so loud that the Egyptians heard it, and those of Pharaoh's house heard of it. 3 Joseph said to his brothers, "I am Joseph! Is my father still alive?" But his brothers could not answer him, for they were afraid in front of him.

4 Joseph said to his brothers, "Come near to me." So they came near. He said, "I am your brother Joseph, whom you sold into Egypt. 5 But do not be troubled or angry with yourselves because you sold me here. For God sent me before you to save your life. 6 For the land has been without food these two years. And there are five more years without plowing or gathering. 7 God sent me before you to make sure that your people will keep living on the earth. Now many of you will be saved. 8 So it was not you who sent me here, but God. He has made me a father to Pharaoh, and ruler of all his house, and of all the land of Egypt. 9 Hurry and go to my father. Say to him, 'Your son Joseph says to you, "God has made me ruler of all Egypt. Come to me, and do not wait. 10 You will live in the land of Goshen, you and your children and grandchildren, your flocks and cattle, and all you have. And you will be near me. 11 There I will take care of you, so that you and your family will not be in need. For there are still five years coming without food. By then you would have nothing."'

12 "Now your eyes see, and the eyes of my brother Benjamin see, that it is my mouth which is speaking to you. 13 You must tell my father of all my greatness in Egypt, and of all you have seen. You must hurry and bring my father here." 14 Then he put his arms around his brother Benjamin and cried. And Benjamin cried on his neck. 15 Joseph kissed all his brothers and cried over them. After that his brothers talked with him.

16 When the news was heard in Pharaoh's house that Joseph's brothers had come, Pharaoh and his servants were pleased. 17 Pharaoh said to Joseph, "Tell your brothers this: 'Load your animals and go to the land of Canaan. 18 Take your father and your families and come to me. I will give you the best of the land of Egypt. And you will live on the fat of the land.' 19 Also say to them, 'Take wagons from the land of Egypt for your little ones and your wives. Bring your father and come. 20 Do not worry about the things that belong to you. For the best of all the land of Egypt is yours.'"

21 The sons of Israel did as he said. Joseph gave them wagons as Pharaoh had told him. And he gave them what they would need as they traveled. 22 He gave new clothes to each of them. But to Benjamin he gave 300 pieces of silver and five times as many clothes. 23 To his father he sent ten donkeys loaded with the best things of Egypt, and ten female donkeys loaded with grain and bread and things his father would need as he traveled. 24 Then he sent his brothers away. As they left he said to them, "Do not be mad at each other on the way."

25 So they went out of Egypt and came to their father Jacob in the land of Canaan. 26 They told him, "Joseph is still alive! He is ruler of all the land of Egypt!" Jacob's heart almost stopped, because he did not believe them. 27 So they told him all the things that Joseph had said to them. And when he saw the wagons that Joseph had sent to carry him, the life of Jacob's spirit returned. 28 Israel said, "It is enough. My son Joseph is still alive. I will go and see him before I die."

Jacob and His Family Go to Egypt

46 So Israel traveled with all he had to Beersheba. There he gave gifts to the God of his father Isaac. 2 God spoke to Israel in special dreams in the night, saying, "Jacob, Jacob." And Jacob answered, "Here I am." 3 He said, "I am God, the God of your father. Do not be afraid to go to Egypt. For I will make you a great nation there. 4 I will go with you to Egypt. I will bring you out again. And Joseph's hand will close your eyes."

5 Then Jacob left Beersheba. The sons of Israel carried their father Jacob, their little ones and their wives in the wagons which Pharaoh had sent to carry him. 6 They took their animals and all the things they owned from the land of Canaan. And they came to Egypt, Jacob and all his children with him, 7 his sons and grandsons, his daughters and granddaughters. He brought all his children with him to Egypt.

8 These are the names of the sons of Israel who came to Egypt, Jacob and his sons: Reuben, Jacob's first-born, 9 and Reuben's sons Hanoch, Pallu, Hezron, and Carmi.

10 The sons of Simeon were Jemuel, Jamin, Ohad, Jachin, Zohar, and Shaul, the son of a Canaanite woman. 11 The sons of Levi were Gershon, Kohath and Merari. 12 The sons of Judah were Er, Onan, Shelah, Perez, and Zerah (but Er and Onan died in the land of Canaan). The sons of Perez were Hezron and Hamul. 13 The sons of Issachar were Tola, Puvvah, Iob, and Shimron. 14 The sons of Zebulun were Sered, Elon and Jahleel. 15 These are the sons who were born to Leah and Jacob in Paddan-aram, with his daughter Dinah. He had thirty-three sons and daughters.

16 The sons of Gad were Ziphion, Haggi, Shuni, Ezbon, Eri, Arodi, and Areli. 17 The sons of Asher were Imnah, Ishvah, Ishvi, Beriah, and their sister Serah. The sons of Beriah were Heber and Malchiel. 18 These are the sons of Jacob and Zilpah, the woman whom Laban gave to his daughter Leah. She gave birth to sixteen of Jacob's children.

19 The sons of Jacob's wife Rachel were Joseph and Benjamin. 20 The sons of Joseph in the land of Egypt were Manasseh and Ephraim. Their mother was Asenath, the daughter of Potiphera, the religious leader of On. 21 The sons of Benjamin were Bela, Becher, Ashbel, Gera, Naaman, Ehi, Rosh, Muppim, Huppim, and Ard. 22 These are the sons of Jacob and Rachel, fourteen sons in all. 23 Dan's son was Hushim. 24 The sons of Naphtali were Jahzeel, Guni, Jezer, and Shillem. 25 These are the sons of Jacob and Bilhah, the woman whom Laban gave to his daughter Rachel. There were seven sons in all.

26 All the people who came to Egypt with Jacob, the children of his own body, were sixty six people in all. Added to this were the wives of Jacob's sons. 27 Two sons were born to Joseph in Egypt. So all the people of Jacob's family when he came to Egypt were seventy.

Jacob Lives in Goshen

28 Jacob sent Judah ahead of him to Joseph to learn the way to Goshen. And they came to the land of Goshen. 29 Then Joseph made his wagon ready and went to Goshen to meet his father Israel. When he came to him, they put their arms around each other and cried for a long time. 30 Then Israel said to Joseph, "Now let me die, since I have seen your face and know that you are still alive."

31 Joseph said to his brothers and to his father's family, "I will go and tell Pharaoh, 'My brothers and my father's family have come to me from the land of Canaan. 32 And the men are shepherds, for they have taken care of animals. They have brought their flocks and cattle and all they have.' 33 When Pharaoh calls you and says, 'What is your work?' 34 you answer, 'Your servants have taken care of cattle since we were young, both we and our fathers.' Then he will let you live in the land of Goshen. For the Egyptians look down upon every shepherd."

47 Then Joseph went to Pharaoh and said, "My father and my brothers and their flocks and cattle and all they own have come from the land of Canaan. See, they are in the land of Goshen." 2 He took five men from among his brothers, and brought them to Pharaoh. 3 Then Pharaoh said to his brothers, "What is your work?" So they said to Pharaoh, "Your servants are shepherds, both we and our fathers." 4 They said to Pharaoh, "We have come to live in the land, for there is no field with food for our flocks. The time without food is hard in the land of Canaan. So now we ask of you, let your servants live in the land of Goshen.

5 Then Pharaoh said to Joseph, "Your father and your brothers have come to you. 6 The land of Egypt is in front of you. Have your father and your brothers live in the best of the land. Let them live in the land of Goshen. And if you know any able men among them, put my cattle in their care."

7 Then Joseph brought his father Jacob to Pharaoh. Jacob prayed that good would come to Pharaoh. 8 And Pharaoh said to Jacob, "How old are you?" 9 Jacob answered Pharaoh, "I have traveled on this earth for 130 years. The years of my life have been few and full of sorrow, and less than the years that my fathers lived." 10 Then Jacob prayed that good would come to Pharaoh, and went away from him.

11 So Joseph made a place for his father and his brothers. He gave them a part of the land of Egypt, in the best of the land, in the land of Rameses, as Pharaoh had told him, 12 Joseph gave food to his father and his brothers and all his father's family, for the needs of their children.

No Food Anywhere but in Egypt

13 Now there was no food in the land for the time without food was very hard. So the people in the land of both Egypt and Canaan became weak because of hunger. 14 So Joseph gathered all the money that was found in Egypt and Canaan for the grain they bought. And Joseph brought the money into Pharaoh's house. 15 When the money was gone from the lands of Egypt and Canaan, all the Egyptians came to Joseph and said, "Give us food! Why should we die in front of you? For we have no more money."

16 Then Joseph said, "Give your cattle. I will give you food in trade for your cattle, because your money is gone." 17 So they brought their animals to Joseph. And Joseph gave them food in trade for the horses and flocks and cattle and donkeys. He fed them that year in trade for their animals.

18 When that year ended, they came to him the next year. They said, "We will not hide from my lord that our money is all gone. And the cattle belong to my lord. There is nothing left for our lord except our bodies and our lands. 19 Why should we die in front of you and our lands be wasted? Buy us and our land in trade for food. We and our land will work for Pharaoh. Give us seed, so that we may live and not die, and so the land will not be wasted."

20 So Joseph bought all the land of Egypt for Pharaoh. For every Egyptian sold his field, because the time without food was hard for them. So the land became Pharaoh's. 21 He had the people move to the cities from one end of Egypt to the other, to work for Pharaoh. 22 Only the land of the religious leaders he did not buy. For the religious leaders received money from Pharaoh. They lived on the money Pharaoh gave them. So they did not sell their land.

23 Then Joseph said to the people, "See, today I have bought you and your land for Pharaoh. Now here is seed for you to plant in the fields. 24 At gathering time, you must give a fifth part to Pharaoh. Keep the rest to have seeds for the field, and to feed yourselves and your children and those of your houses."

25 So they said, "You have saved our lives! Let us find favor in the eyes of my lord. We will be Pharaoh's servants." 26 Joseph made it a law in the land of Egypt that Pharaoh should have the fifth part. It is a law to this day. Only the land of the religious leaders did not become Pharaoh's.

Jacob's Last Wish

27 Now Israel lived in the land of Egypt, in Goshen. They became richer there, and had children, and grew to a very large number. 28 Jacob lived in the land of Egypt seventeen years. So Jacob had lived 147 years in all. 29 When the time came for Israel to die, he called his son Joseph. He said to him, "If I have found favor in your eyes, give me your promise to be kind and faithful to me. I ask of you, do not bury me in Egypt. 30 But let me lie down with my fathers. Carry me out of Egypt and bury me where they are buried." And Joseph said, "I will do as you have said." 31 Jacob said, "Promise me." So Joseph gave him his promise. Then Israel bowed in worship at the head of the bed.

Jacob and Joseph's Sons

48 After this Joseph was told, "See, your father is sick." So he took his two sons Manasseh and Ephraim with him. 2 When Jacob was told, "Your son Joseph has come to you," Israel gathered his strength and sat up in bed. 3 Then Jacob said to Joseph, "The All-powerful God showed Himself to me at Luz in the land of Canaan, and He brought good to me. 4 He said to me, 'See, I will give you many children. I will make you a group of nations. And I will give this land to your children and to your children's children after you. It will belong to them forever.' 5 Now your two sons, who were born to you in Egypt before I came to you here, are mine. Ephraim and Manasseh will be mine, as Reuben and Simeon are. 6 The children born to you after them will be yours. They will be called by the names of their brothers in their share of what the family is to receive. 7 For when I came from Paddan, Rachel died by my side in the land of Canaan before we came to Ephrath. I buried her there on the way to Ephrath (that is, Bethlehem)." 8 When Israel saw Joseph's sons, he said, "Who are these?" 9 Joseph said to his father, "They are my sons, whom God has given me here." So Israel said, "Bring them to me, so I may pray that good will come to them."

10 Now Israel's eyes had become weak from being old, and he could not see. So Joseph brought them near to him. And Israel kissed them and put his arms around them. 11 Israel said to Joseph, "I never

thought I would see your face. But see, God has let me see your children also." [12] Then Joseph took them from his knees, and bowed to the ground. [13] Then taking Ephraim with his right hand, Joseph put him at Israel's left side. And with his left hand he put Manasseh at Israel's right side, placing them near him. [14] But Israel put out his right hand and laid it on the head of Ephraim, the younger son. And he put his left hand on Manasseh's head, crossing his hands. But Manasseh was the first-born. [15] Then he prayed that good would come to Joseph, and said, "The God with Whom my fathers Abraham and Isaac walked, the God Who has been my Shepherd all my life to this day, [16] the Angel Who has set me free from all sin, bring good to these boys. May my name and the names of my fathers Abraham and Isaac live on in them. May they become a great nation on the earth."

[17] When Joseph saw that his father laid his right hand on Ephraim's head, he was not pleased. He took his father's hand to move it from Ephraim's head to Manasseh's head. [18] Joseph said to his father, "Not this way, my father, for this one is the first-born. Place your right hand on his head." [19] But his father would not, and said, "I know, my son, I know. He will become a nation also, and he also will be great. But his younger brother will be greater than he. His children and their children's children will become many nations." [20] Then he prayed that day that good would come to them. He said, "By you Israel will pray that good will come, saying, 'May God make you like Ephraim and Manasseh!' " So he placed Ephraim before Manasseh.

[21] Then Israel said to Joseph, "See, I am about to die. But God will be with you. He will return you to the land of your fathers. [22] I have given you more than your brothers. I have given you the side of the mountain that I took from the Amorites with my sword and my bow."

Jacob's Last Words to His Sons

49 Then Jacob called his sons and said, "Gather yourselves together so that I may tell you what will happen to you in the days to come. [2] Gather together and hear, O sons of Jacob. Listen to your father Israel.

[3] "Reuben, you are my first-born, my power and the beginning of my strength, first in pride and first in power. [4] But because you are as wild as water, the first place will not be yours. It is because you went to your father's bed and made it unclean.

[5] "Simeon and Levi are brothers. They hurt others with their swords. [6] May my soul not have a part in their secrets, nor my shining-greatness be joined to them. Because in their anger they killed men and for no reason they hurt cattle. [7] Their anger will be punished, for it is bad. Their bad temper will be punished, for it is bad. I will divide them in Jacob and spread them apart in Israel.

[8] "Judah, your brothers will praise you. Your hand will be on the neck of those who hate you. Your father's sons will bow down to you. [9] Judah is a young lion. Like a lion full of meat, you have become great, my son. He lies down and sleeps like a lion. And as a lion, who is willing to wake him? [10] The right of a ruler will not leave Judah. The ruler's special stick will not go from between his feet, until Shiloh comes. Then the people will obey Him. [11] He ties his young donkey to the vine, his donkey's young one to the best vine. He washes his clothes in wine, his coats in the blood of grapes. [12] His eyes are darker than wine. And his teeth are whiter than milk.

[13] "Zebulun will live beside the sea and be a safe place for ships. His land will lie beside Sidon.

[14] "Issachar is a strong donkey lying down between the loads. [15] He saw that a resting place was good and that the land was pleasing. So he made his shoulder ready to carry loads. He let himself be a servant.

[16] "Dan will judge his people, as one of the families of Israel. [17] Dan will be a snake in the way, a snake in the road, that bites the horse's heels so that the man falls off. [18] I wait for Your saving power, O Lord.

[19] "A group of soldiers will go against Gad. But he will go against them at their heels.

[20] "Asher's food will be rich. He will give pleasing food to kings.

[21] "Naphtali is a female deer let loose who gives beautiful young ones.

[22] "Joseph is a branch with much fruit, a branch with much fruit by a well. It grows over the wall. [23] The men fought against him with their bows. They sent arrows toward him and made it hard for him. [24] But his bow did not shake. His arms were made strong by the hands of the Powerful One of Jacob, by the name of the

Shepherd, the Rock of Israel, 25 by the God of your father Who helps you, and by the All-powerful Who brings good to you. He brings good from heaven above, and from the deep that lies below, and from the body of a mother. 26 More good has come to your father than to my fathers before me, as lasting as the hills that last forever. May this good be on the head of Joseph, on the crown of him who was divided from his brothers. 27 "Benjamin is a hungry wolf. In the morning he eats the animals he has caught. And in the evening he divides what he has taken."

28 All these are the twelve family groups of Israel. This is what their father said to them when he prayed that good would come to them. He prayed for each of them to receive the good they should have.

The Death of Jacob

29 Then he told them, "I will soon be with my people who have died before me. Bury me with my fathers in the grave that is in the field of Ephron the Hittite, 30 in the grave that is in the field of Machpelah, east of Mamre, in the land of Canaan. Abraham bought this grave and the field from Ephron the Hittite for a burying place. 31 There they buried Abraham and his wife Sarah. There they buried Isaac and his wife Rebekah. And there I buried Leah. 32 The field and the grave that is in it were bought from the sons of Heth."

33 When Jacob finished telling his sons what to do, he lay back down on his bed and died.

50 Then Joseph threw himself upon his father, and cried over him and kissed him. 2 Joseph told his servants the doctors to make his father ready to be buried. So the doctors made Israel ready. 3 Forty days were needed for this. For this is how much time it took for making the body ready to be buried. And the Egyptians cried for him seventy days.

4 When the days of sorrow for him were past, Joseph said to those of Pharaoh's house, "If now I have found favor in your eyes, speak to Pharaoh, saying, 5 'My father had me make a promise to him. He said, "See, I am about to die. Bury me in my grave which I dug for myself in the land of Canaan." So let me go and bury my father. Then I will return.' " 6 Pharaoh answered, "Go and bury your father as he made you promise."

7 So Joseph went to bury his father. With him went all the servants of Pharaoh, the leaders of his house and all the important men of the land of Egypt, 8 and all those of the house of Joseph, and his brothers, and those of his father's house. They left only their little ones and their flocks and cattle in the land of Goshen. 9 Wagons and men on horses went with him also. It was a very large group of people.

10 They came to the grain-floor of Atad on the other side of the Jordan. There they cried with much sorrow. Joseph cried in sorrow for his father for seven days. 11 When those who lived in the land, the Canaanites, saw the people crying in sorrow at the grain-floor of Atad, they said, "This is a great sorrow for the Egyptians." So the place was given the name Abel-mizraim. It is on the other side of the Jordan.

12 Jacob's sons did as he had told them. 13 They carried him to the land of Canaan. They buried him in the grave of the field of Machpelah, east of Mamre, which Abraham had bought with the field from Ephron the Hittite for a burying place. 14 After he had buried his father, Joseph returned to Egypt with his brothers and all who had gone with him to bury his father.

Joseph Tells His Brothers Not to Be Afraid

15 When Joseph's brothers saw that their father was dead, they said, "It may be now that Joseph will hate us, and pay us in return for all the wrong that we did to him!" 16 So they sent word to Joseph, saying, "Before he died, our father told us, 17 'You say to Joseph, "Forgive the wrong-doing of your brothers and their sin. For they did a bad thing to you." ' Now we beg you, forgive the wrong-doing of the servants of the God of your father." Joseph cried when they spoke to him. 18 Then his brothers came and fell down in front of him and said, "See, we are your servants."

19 But Joseph said to them, "Do not be afraid. Am I in the place of God? 20 You planned to do a bad thing to me. But God planned it for good, to make it happen that many people should be kept alive, as they are today. 21 So do not be afraid. I will take care of you and your little ones." He gave them comfort and words of kindness.

The Death of Joseph

22 Joseph and his father's family stayed in Egypt. And Joseph lived 110 years. 23 He lived long enough to see Ephraim's

grandchildren. And the sons of Manasseh's son Machir were held on Joseph's knees. 24 Joseph said to his brothers, "I am about to die. But God will take care of you. He will bring you from this land to the land that He promised to Abraham, to Isaac and to Jacob." 25 Then Joseph made the sons of Israel promise. He said, "God will take care of you. And you will carry my bones from here." 26 So Joseph died after living 110 years. They made his body ready, and he was put in a grave in Egypt.

EXODUS

Children of Israel Suffer in Egypt

1 These are the names of the sons of Israel who came to Egypt with Jacob. Each one came with those of his house: 2 Reuben, Simeon, Levi, Judah, 3 Issachar, Zebulun, Benjamin, 4 Dan, Naphtali, Gad, and Asher. 5 There were seventy people in Jacob's family. But Joseph was already in Egypt. 6 Joseph and all his brothers died and all their families of that time. 7 But the sons of Israel had many children, and the people became many in number. There were so many that the land was filled with them.

8 Then a new king came into power over Egypt. He did not know Joseph. 9 He said to his people, "See, the people of Israel are too many and too powerful for us. 10 Come, let us be wise in how we act towards them, or they will become more in number. If there is a war, they might join with those who hate us. They might fight against us and then leave the land."

11 So they put men in power over them to make them work hard. And they built the store-cities Pithom and Raamses for Pharaoh the king. 12 But the more the Egyptians made them suffer, the more they became until they spread throughout the land. So the Egyptians were afraid of the people of Israel. 13 The Egyptians made the people of Israel work very hard. 14 They made their lives bitter with hard work building with stones and with all kinds of work in the field. They made them work very hard.

15 Then the king of Egypt spoke to the Hebrew nurses. The name of one was Shiphrah. The name of the other was Puah. 16 He said, "When you are helping the Hebrew women to give birth, and see the baby before the mother does, if it is a son, kill him. But if it is a daughter, let her live." 17 But the nurses feared God. They did not do what the king of Egypt told them. They let the boys live. 18 So the king of Egypt called the nurses and said to them, "Why have you done this, and let the boys live?" 19 The nurses answered Pharaoh, "Because the Hebrew women are not like the Egyptian women. They are strong. They give birth before the nurse comes to them." 20 So God was good to the nurses. And the people became many and strong. 21 Because the nurses feared God, He gave them families. 22 Then Pharaoh told all his people, "Throw every son who is born to the Hebrews into the Nile. But keep every daughter alive."

2 Now a man of the family of Levi married a daughter of Levi. 2 She was going to have a baby, and she gave birth to a son. When she saw that he was beautiful, she hid him for three months. 3 But the time came when she could hide him no longer. So she took a basket made from grass, and covered it with tar and put the child in it. And she set it in the grass by the side of the Nile. 4 His sister stayed to watch and find out what would happen to him.

5 Then the daughter of Pharaoh came to wash herself in the Nile. Her young women walked beside the Nile. She saw the basket in the tall grass and sent the woman who served her to get it. 6 She opened it and saw the child. The boy was crying. She had pity on him and said, "This is one of the Hebrews' children." 7 Then his sister said to Pharaoh's daughter, "Should I go and call a nurse from the Hebrew women to nurse the child for you?" 8 Pharaoh's daughter said to her, "Go." So the girl went and called the child's mother. 9 Then Pharaoh's daughter said to her, "Take this child away and nurse him for me. And I will pay you." So the woman took the child and nursed him. 10 The child grew, and she brought him to Pharaoh's daughter. And he became her son. She gave him the name Moses, saying, "Because I took him out of the water."

11 One day after Moses had grown up, he went out to his brothers and saw how hard they worked. He saw an Egyptian beating a Hebrew, one of his people, 12 so he looked this way and that way. He did

not see anyone, so he killed the Egyptian and hid him in the sand. 13 The next day he went out and saw two Hebrews fighting. He said to the man who did the wrong, "Why are you hitting your neighbor?" 14 But the man said, "Who made you a ruler and a judge among us? Do you plan to kill me like you killed the Egyptian?" Then Moses was afraid. He thought, "For sure the thing I have done is known."

15 When Pharaoh heard what had happened, he tried to kill Moses. But Moses ran away from Pharaoh and stayed in the land of Midian. He sat down there by a well. 16 Now the religious leader of Midian had seven daughters. They came to get water, and filled the barrels used to water their father's flock. 17 The shepherds came and tried to make them go away. But Moses stood up and helped them. He gave water to their flock. 18 When they came to their father Reuel, he said, "Why have you returned so soon today?" 19 They answered, "An Egyptian saved us from the shepherds. He even got the water for us and gave water to the flock." 20 He said to his daughters, "Where is he? Why have you left the man? Ask him to have something to eat with us." 21 Moses was willing to stay with the man, and he gave his daughter Zipporah to Moses. 22 She gave birth to a son. And he gave him the name Gershom. For he said, "I have been a stranger in a strange land."

23 Now after a long time, the king of Egypt died. The people of Israel were sad in their spirit because of being servants. They cried for help. And because of their hard work their cry went up to God. 24 God heard their crying and remembered His agreement with Abraham, Isaac and Jacob. 25 God saw the people of Israel and He cared about them.

Moses and the Burning Bush

3 Now Moses was taking care of the flock of his father-in-law Jethro, the religious leader of Midian. He led the flock to the west side of the desert, and came to Horeb, the mountain of God. 2 There the Angel of the Lord showed Himself to Moses in a burning fire from inside a bush. Moses looked and saw that the bush was burning with fire, but it was not being burned up. 3 So Moses said, "I must step aside and see this great thing, why the bush is not being burned up."

4 The Lord saw him step aside to look. And God called to him from inside the bush, saying, "Moses, Moses!" Moses answered, "Here I am." 5 God said, "Do not come near. Take your shoes off your feet. For the place where you are standing is holy ground." 6 He said also, "I am the God of your father, the God of Abraham, the God of Isaac, and the God of Jacob." Then Moses hid his face. For he was afraid to look at God. 7 The Lord said, "I have seen the suffering of My people in Egypt. I have heard their cry because of the men who make them work. I know how they suffer. 8 So I have come down to save them from the power of the Egyptians. I will bring them out of that land to a good big land, to a land flowing with milk and honey, to the place of the Canaanite, the Hittite, the Amorite, the Perizzite, the Hivite and the Jebusite. 9 Now the cry of the people of Israel has come to Me. I have seen what power the Egyptians use to make it hard for them. 10 Now come, and I will send you to Pharaoh so that you may bring My people, the sons of Israel, out of Egypt."

11 But Moses said to God, "Who am I to go to Pharaoh and bring the people of Israel out of Egypt?" 12 God said, "But I will be with you. And this will be something special for you to see to know that I have sent you: When you have brought the people out of Egypt, you will worship God at this mountain."

13 Then Moses said to God, "See, I am going to the people of Israel, and I will say to them, 'The God of your fathers has sent me to you.' Now they might say to me, 'What is His name?' What should I say to them?" 14 And God said to Moses, "I AM WHO I AM." And He said, "Say to the Israelites, 'I AM has sent me to you.' " 15 Again He said, "Say this to the people of Israel, 'The Lord, the God of your fathers, the God of Abraham, the God of Isaac, and the God of Jacob, has sent me to you.' This is My name forever. By this name I am to be remembered by all people for all time. 16 Go and gather together the leaders of Israel. Say to them, 'The Lord, the God of your fathers, the God of Abraham, Isaac and Jacob, has shown Himself to me. And He said, 'I have visited you and have seen what has been done to you in Egypt. 17 I promise to bring you out of the suffering of Egypt to the land of the Canaanite, the Hittite, the Amorite, the Perizzite, the Hivite, and the Jebusite, to a land flowing with milk and honey.' " 18 They will listen to what you say. Then you and the leaders of Israel will go to the king of Egypt

and say to him, 'The Lord, the God of the Hebrews, has met with us. So now we ask you to let us travel three days to the desert to give gifts on an altar in worship to the Lord our God.' ¹⁹ But I know that the king of Egypt will not let you go, except by a powerful hand. ²⁰ So I will put out My hand and trouble Egypt with all the powerful works I will do there. After that he will let you go. ²¹ And I will give these people favor in the eyes of the Egyptians. When you go, you will not go empty handed. ²² But each woman will get from her neighbor and the woman who lives in her house, things made of silver and gold, and clothes that you will put on your sons and daughters. You will take the best of things from the Egyptians."

Moses Is Given Special Power

4 Then Moses answered, "What if they will not believe me or listen to me? They might say, 'The Lord has not shown Himself to you.' " ² The Lord said to him, "What is that in your hand?" Moses said, "A stick." ³ Then the Lord said, "Throw it on the ground." So Moses threw it on the ground, and it became a snake. And Moses ran from it. ⁴ But the Lord said to Moses, "Put out your hand and take it by its tail." So Moses put out his hand and caught it. And it became a stick in his hand. ⁵ The Lord said, "By seeing this they may believe that the Lord, the God of their fathers, the God of Abraham, the God of Isaac, and the God of Jacob, has shown Himself to you."

⁶ The Lord said to him, "Put your hand inside your coat." So Moses put his hand inside his coat. When he took it out, his hand had a bad skin disease and was white as snow. ⁷ Then God said, "Put your hand inside your coat again." So Moses put his hand inside his coat again. When he took it out of his coat, he saw that it had become like his other flesh. ⁸ God said, "If they will not listen to you or believe you when they are shown the first thing, they may believe when this is shown to them. ⁹ But they might not believe even these two things or listen to what you say. So then take some water from the Nile and pour it on the dry ground. And the water you take from the Nile will become blood on the dry ground."

¹⁰ Moses said to the Lord, "Lord, I am not a man of words. I have never been. Even now since You spoke to Your servant, I still am not. For I am slow in talking and it is difficult for me to speak." ¹¹ Then

the Lord said to him, "Who has made man's mouth? Who makes a man not able to speak or hear? Who makes one blind or able to see? Is it not I, the Lord? ¹² So go now. And I will be with your mouth. I will teach you what to say."

¹³ But Moses said, "O Lord, I ask of You, send some other person."

¹⁴ Then the anger of the Lord burned against Moses. He said, "Is not Aaron the Levite your brother? I know he can speak well. Also, he is coming to meet you. And when he sees you, he will be glad in his heart. ¹⁵ You must speak to him and put the words in his mouth. I will be with your mouth and his mouth. I will teach you what you are to do. ¹⁶ He will speak to the people for you. He will be a mouth for you. And you will be as God to him. ¹⁷ You will take this special stick in your hand. And you will use it to make the special things happen for the people to see."

Moses Returns to Egypt

¹⁸ Then Moses left and returned to Jethro his father-in-law, and said to him, "I ask of you, let me return to my brothers in Egypt to see if they are still alive." And Jethro said to Moses, "Go in peace." ¹⁹ The Lord said to Moses in Midian, "Return to Egypt. For all the men who wanted to kill you are dead." ²⁰ So Moses took his wife and sons and put them on a donkey, and he returned to the land of Egypt. Moses also took the special stick of God in his hand.

²¹ The Lord said to Moses, "When you return to Egypt, make sure you show Pharaoh all the works that I have placed in your power. But I will make his heart hard so that he will not let the people go. ²² Then say to Pharaoh, 'The Lord says this: "Israel is My son, My first-born. ²³ And I say to you, 'Let My son go. Let him work for Me.' But if you will not let him go, I will kill your son, your first-born." ' "

²⁴ The Lord met Moses at a resting place on the way and would have put him to death. ²⁵ But Zipporah took a knife and cut off her son's piece of skin and threw it at Moses' feet. And she said, "For sure you are a husband of blood to me." ²⁶ Then the Lord let him alone. Zipporah said, "You are a husband of blood," because of the religious act of becoming a Jew.

²⁷ The Lord said to Aaron, "Go to meet Moses in the desert." So he went and met him at the mountain of God and kissed him. ²⁸ Moses told Aaron all the words of the Lord with which He had sent him.

And he told him about all the special works that the Lord had told him to do. 29 Then Moses and Aaron went and gathered together all the leaders of the people of Israel. 30 Aaron spoke all the words which the Lord had spoken to Moses. Then he did all the special works for the people to see. 31 So the people believed. When they heard that the Lord cared about the people of Israel and had seen their suffering, they bowed to the ground and worshiped.

Moses and Aaron Talk to Pharaoh

5 After this, Moses and Aaron went to Pharaoh and said, "The Lord, the God of Israel, says this: 'Let My people go, that they may have a special supper to honor Me in the desert.' " 2 But Pharaoh said, "Who is the Lord, that I should obey Him and let Israel go? I do not know the Lord. And I will not let Israel go." 3 Then they said, "The God of the Hebrews has met with us. We ask of you, let us travel into the desert three days, to give a gift on an altar in worship to the Lord our God. Or He may send death to us by disease or by the sword." 4 But the king of Egypt said to them, "Moses and Aaron, why do you take the people away from their work? Return to your work!" 5 Then Pharaoh said, "See, the people of the land are now many. And you would have them stop working!"

6 That same day Pharaoh told the men who made the people work, 7 "Do not give the people straw for making clay blocks any more. Let them go and gather straw for themselves. 8 But have them make the same number of clay blocks as before, and no less. They are crying, 'Let us go and give a gift in worship to our God,' because they are lazy. 9 Let more work be given to the men so they will not have time to listen to lies."

10 So the men who made the people work went out and said to the people, "This is what Pharaoh says: 'I will not give you straw. 11 You go and get straw for yourselves where you can find it. But you will not work any less than before.' " 12 So the people went out through all the land of Egypt to gather what they could use for straw. 13 The men who made them work made them hurry, saying, "Finish your full day's work as you did when there was straw." 14 And the Hebrew men who had been made to rule over the people by Pharaoh's work-leaders were beaten. They were asked, "Why have you not made as many clay blocks yesterday or today as you made before?"

15 Then the Hebrew men who made the people work went to Pharaoh and cried, "Why do you act this way toward your servants? 16 There is no straw given to your servants. Yet they still say to us, 'Make clay blocks!' See, your servants are being beaten. But your own people are to blame." 17 But Pharaoh said, "You are lazy, very lazy. So you say, 'Let us go and give a gift on an altar in worship to the Lord.' 18 Go now and work. You will be given no straw. Yet you must make the same number of clay blocks." 19 The Hebrew men who made the people work knew that they were in trouble because they were told, "You must make the same number of clay blocks each day." 20 When they came from Pharaoh, they met Moses and Aaron who were waiting for them. 21 They said to Moses and Aaron, "May the Lord look upon you and judge you. For you have caused us to be hated by Pharaoh and his servants. You have put a sword in their hand to kill us."

God's Promise to Israel

22 Then Moses returned to the Lord and said, "O Lord, why have You hurt these people? Why did you ever send me? 23 For since I went to Pharaoh to speak in Your name, he has hurt these people. You have not set Your people free at all."

6 Then the Lord said to Moses, "Now you will see what I will do to Pharaoh. For he will be made to let them go because of My strong hand. By My strong hand, he will make them go out of his land."

God Calls Moses

2 God said to Moses, "I am the Lord. 3 I showed Myself as God All-powerful to Abraham, Isaac and Jacob. But I did not make Myself known to them by My name, the Lord. 4 I also made My agreement with them, to give them the land of Canaan, the land where they were strangers. 5 I have heard the crying of the people of Israel, because they are being held by the Egyptians. And I have remembered My agreement. 6 So say to the people of Israel, 'I am the Lord. I will take you away from the hard work and suffering in Egypt. I will take you away from being their servants. I will make you free by the strength of My arm and by the great things I will do to punish the guilty. 7 Then I will take you for My people, and I will be your God. And

you will know that I am the Lord your God. I will bring you out from under the heavy loads of the Egyptians. 8 I will bring you to the land I promised to give to Abraham, Isaac and Jacob. I will give it to you for your own. I am the Lord.' " 9 So Moses said this to the people of Israel. But they did not listen to Moses because of their broken spirit and how hard they were made to work.

10 Then the Lord said to Moses, 11 "Go and tell Pharaoh king of Egypt to let the people of Israel go out of his land." 12 But Moses said to the Lord, "See, the people of Israel have not listened to me. How then will Pharaoh listen to me? I am not able to speak well." 13 But the Lord spoke to Moses and Aaron. He told them to tell the people of Israel and Pharaoh king of Egypt that they were to bring the people of Israel out of the land of Egypt.

The Family of Moses and Aaron

14 These are the leaders of their fathers' families. The sons of Reuben, Israel's first-born: Hanoch, Pallu, Hezron, and Carmi. These are the families of Reuben. 15 The sons of Simeon: Jemuel, Jamin, Ohad, Jachin, Zohar, and Shaul the son of a Canaanite woman. These are the families of Simeon. 16 These are the names of Levi's sons by their family groups: Gershon, Kohath and Merari. Levi lived 137 years. 17 The sons of Gershon by their families: Libni and Shimei. 18 The sons of Kohath: Amram, Izhar, Hebron, and Uzziel. Kohath lived 133 years. 19 The sons of Merari: Mahli and Mushi. These are the families of the Levites by their family groups. 20 Amram married his father's sister Jochebed. She gave birth to his sons, Aaron and Moses. Amram lived 137 years. 21 The sons of Izhar: Korah, Nepheg and Zichri. 22 The sons of Uzziel: Mishael, Elzaphan and Sithri.

23 Aaron married Elisheba, the daughter of Amminadab, the sister of Nahshon. She gave birth to his sons, Nadab, Abihu, Eleazar, and Ithamar. 24 The sons of Korah: Assir, Elkanah and Abiasaph. These are the families of the Korahites. 25 Aaron's son Eleazar married one of the daughters of Putiel. She gave birth to his son Phinehas. These are the heads of the fathers' houses of the Levites by their families.

26 It was the same Aaron and Moses to whom the Lord said, "Bring the people of Israel out of the land of Egypt by their family groups." 27 They were the ones who spoke to Pharaoh king of Egypt about bringing the people of Israel out of Egypt. It was the same Moses and Aaron.

28 On the day when the Lord spoke to Moses in the land of Egypt, 29 the Lord said to Moses, "I am the Lord. Tell Pharaoh king of Egypt all that I say to you." 30 But Moses said to the Lord, "See, I am not able to speak well. How then will Pharaoh listen to me?"

Aaron Speaks for Moses

7 The Lord said to Moses, "See, I have made you as God to Pharaoh. Your brother Aaron will be the one who speaks for you. 2 You will speak all that I tell you. Your brother Aaron will tell Pharaoh to let the people of Israel leave his land. 3 But I will make Pharaoh's heart hard. So I will do many powerful works for the people to see in the land of Egypt. 4 Pharaoh will not listen to you. Then I will lay My hand on Egypt. By great acts that will punish the Egyptians, I will bring out My family groups, My people, the sons of Israel, from the land of Egypt. 5 The Egyptians will know that I am the Lord when I put My hand upon Egypt and bring out the people of Israel from among them." 6 So Moses and Aaron did what the Lord told them to do. 7 Moses was eighty years old and Aaron was eighty-three years old, when they spoke to Pharaoh.

Aaron's Special Walking Stick

8 The Lord said to Moses and Aaron, 9 "When Pharaoh says to you, 'Prove yourselves by doing a powerful work,' then you say to Aaron, 'Take your special stick and throw it down in front of Pharaoh so that it will become a snake.' " 10 So Moses and Aaron went to Pharaoh. They did just as the Lord had told them. Aaron threw his stick down in front of Pharaoh and his servants and it became a snake. 11 Then Pharaoh called for his wise men and wonderworkers. They did the same thing using their secret ways. 12 For each one threw down his stick and it became a snake. But Aaron's special stick ate their sticks. 13 Yet Pharaoh's heart was hard. He did not listen to them, just as the Lord had said.

Water Becomes Blood

14 The Lord said to Moses, "Pharaoh's heart is not changed. He will not let the people go. 15 Go to Pharaoh in the morning when he is going out to the water. Wait for him beside the Nile River. Take in your

hand the special stick that became a snake. 16 And say to him, 'The Lord, the God of the Hebrews, sent me to you, saying, "Let My people go, so they may worship Me in the desert. But see, you have not yet listened." 17 So the Lord says, "By this you will know that I am the Lord. I will hit the water of the Nile with the special stick that is in my hand. And the water will be changed to blood. 18 The fish that are in the Nile will die. And the Nile will have a bad smell. The Egyptians will not be able to drink water from the Nile." ' " 19 Then the Lord said to Moses, 'Say to Aaron, 'Take your special stick and put your hand out over the waters of Egypt, over their rivers, their pools, and all their man-made lakes of water, so they will become blood. There will be blood through all the land of Egypt, even in pots of wood and pots of stone.' "

20 Moses and Aaron did what the Lord had told them. Aaron raised the special stick and hit the water of the Nile in front of Pharaoh and his servants. And all the water in the Nile was turned into blood. 21 The fish that were in the Nile died. And the Nile had a bad smell. So the Egyptians could not drink water from the Nile. The blood was through all the land of Egypt. 22 But the wonder-workers of Egypt did the same thing using their secret ways. And Pharaoh's heart was hard. He did not listen to them, just as the Lord had said. 23 Then Pharaoh turned and went into his house, without even thinking what had happened. 24 And all the Egyptians dug around the Nile for water to drink. For they could not drink the water of the Nile. 25 Seven days passed after the Lord had hit the Nile.

Frogs Cover the Land

8 Then the Lord said to Moses, "Go to Pharaoh and say to him, 'The Lord says this: "Let My people go, so they may worship Me. 2 But if you will not let them go, I will bring trouble to your whole country with frogs. 3 The Nile will be full of frogs. They will come up and go in your house and in your room and on your bed. They will come in the houses of your servants and on your people. They will come in your stoves and in your bread dough. 4 The frogs will come up on you and your people and all your servants." ' " 5 Then the Lord said to Moses, "Say to Aaron, 'Put out your hand with your special stick over the rivers and over the pools. Make frogs

come up on the land of Egypt.' " 6 So Aaron put his hand out over the waters of Egypt. And the frogs came up and covered the land of Egypt. 7 But the wonder-workers did the same thing using their secret ways. They made frogs come up on the land of Egypt.

Frogs Destroyed

8 Then Pharaoh called for Moses and Aaron and said, "You pray to the Lord to take the frogs away from me and my people. And I will let the people go, so they may give a gift in worship to the Lord." 9 Moses said to Pharaoh, "The honor is yours to tell me when I should pray for you and your servants and your people, that the frogs may be sent away from you and your houses and stay only in the Nile." 10 Pharaoh said, "Tomorrow." And Moses said, "May it be as you say. You will know that there is no one like the Lord our God. 11 The frogs will go away from you and your houses and your servants and your people. They will stay only in the Nile." 12 Then Moses and Aaron went away from Pharaoh. And Moses cried to the Lord about the frogs that He had brought against Pharaoh. 13 The Lord did as Moses said. The frogs died in and around the houses and the fields. 14 The people gathered them together, and the land had a bad smell. 15 But when Pharaoh saw that there was rest from the trouble, he made his heart hard. He did not listen to them, just as the Lord had said.

Dust Turned to Lice

16 Then the Lord said to Moses, "Say to Aaron, 'Put out your special stick and hit the dust of the earth. It will become lice through all the land of Egypt.' " 17 And they did so. Aaron put out his hand with his stick and hit the dust of the earth. And there were lice on man and animal. All the dust of the earth became lice through all the land of Egypt. 18 The wonder-workers tried to cause lice to come by using their secret ways. But they could not. So there were lice on man and animal. 19 Then the wonder-workers said to Pharaoh, "This is the finger of God." But Pharaoh's heart was hard. He did not listen to them, just as the Lord had said.

Flies Cover All the Land

20 Then the Lord said to Moses, "Get up early in the morning and wait for Pharaoh as he goes out to the water. Say to

him, 'The Lord says this: "Let My people go, so they may worship Me. 21 For if you will not let My people go, I will send many flies upon you and upon your servants and upon your people and into your houses. The houses of the Egyptians will be full of flies, and also the ground will be covered with them. 22 But on that day I will set apart the land of Goshen where My people are living so no flies will be there. Then you may know that I, the Lord, am in the land. 23 I will divide My people from your people. Tomorrow you will see this happen."' " 24 And the Lord did so. And there came a great many flies flying all over inside the house of the Pharaoh and in the houses of his servants. The land was destroyed because of the many flies in all the land of Egypt.

25 Then Pharaoh called for Moses and Aaron and said, "Go and give a gift in worship to your God here in the land." 26 But Moses said, "It is not right to do this. For the Egyptians hate what we would give in worship to the Lord our God. If the Egyptians see us giving this gift and doing what they think is sinful, will they not throw stones at us? 27 We must travel three days to the desert and give a gift in worship to the Lord our God, as He tells us to do."

28 So Pharaoh said, "I will let you go, so you may give a gift to the Lord your God. But do not go very far away. Pray for me." 29 Then Moses said, "I am leaving you. I will pray to the Lord that the many flies may leave Pharaoh and his servants and his people tomorrow. But do not let Pharaoh lie again by not letting the people go to give a gift on an altar to the Lord."

The Flies Are Destroyed

30 So Moses left Pharaoh and prayed to the Lord. 31 And the Lord did as Moses asked. He took the many flies away from Pharaoh and his servants and his people. Not one was left. 32 But Pharaoh made his heart hard this time also. He did not let the people go.

Animals Owned by Egyptians Die

9 Then the Lord said to Moses, "Go to Pharaoh and say to him, 'The Lord, the God of the Hebrews, says this: "Let My people go, so they may worship Me. 2 For if you will not let them go, and still hold them, 3 the hand of the Lord will come with a very bad disease on your animals in the field, on the horses, the donkeys, the camels, the cattle and the flocks. 4 But the

Lord will divide the animals of Israel from the animals of Egypt. So nothing will die of all that belongs to the people of Israel."' " 5 The Lord made a time for this, saying, "Tomorrow the Lord will do this in the land." 6 So the Lord did this on the next day. All the animals of Egypt died. But not one of the animals died that belonged to the people of Israel. 7 Pharaoh learned that not one of the animals of Israel was dead. But the heart of Pharaoh was hard. He did not let the people go.

Bad Sores Come on Egyptians and Their Animals

8 Then the Lord said to Moses and Aaron, "Fill your hands with ashes from a stove. Let Moses throw them toward the sky in front of Pharaoh. 9 And it will become fine dust over all the land of Egypt and will become bad sores on man and animal through all the land of Egypt." 10 So they took ashes from a stove. Moses stood in front of Pharaoh and threw the ashes toward the sky. And it became sores on man and animal. 11 The wonder-workers could not stand in front of Moses because of the sores. For the sores were on the wonder-workers and on all the Egyptians. 12 But the Lord made the heart of Pharaoh hard. He did not listen to them, just as the Lord had said to Moses.

Large Hail and Fire

13 Then the Lord said to Moses, "Get up early in the morning and stand in front of Pharaoh and say to him, 'The Lord, the God of the Hebrews, says this: "Let My people go, so they may worship Me. 14 For this time I will send all My troubles on you and your servants and your people, so you may know that there is no one like Me in all the earth. 15 For by now I could have put out My hand and hit you and your people with much trouble and great suffering. You would then have been destroyed from the earth. 16 But I have let you live so you could see My power and so My name may be honored through all the earth. 17 But you still use your power against My people by not letting them go. 18 About this time tomorrow I will send a very heavy hail such as has never been seen in Egypt from the day it began until now. 19 Have your cattle and whatever you have in the field brought to a safe place. For the hail will come down upon every man and animal that is in the field and is not brought home. And they will die."' "

20 Any of the people of Egypt who feared the word of the Lord made his servants and animals run to the houses. 21 But he who did not listen to the word of the Lord left his servants and animals in the field.

22 The Lord said to Moses, "Put out your hand toward the sky and hail will fall on all the land of Egypt. Hail will fall on man and animal and every plant of the field through all the land of Egypt." 23 Moses put out his special stick toward the sky. Then the Lord sent thunder and hail. And lightning struck the ground. The Lord poured hail on the land of Egypt. 24 So there was hail and lightning striking through the hail without stopping. It was very bad, worse than had ever been in all the land of Egypt since it became a nation. 25 The hail hit all that was in the field through all the land of Egypt, both man and animal. The hail hit every plant of the field and broke down every tree of the field. 26 Only in the land of Goshen where the people of Israel were, there was no hail.

27 Then Pharaoh sent for Moses and Aaron. He said to them, "I have sinned this time. The Lord is right. I and my people are guilty. 28 Pray to the Lord. For there has been enough of God's thunder and hail. And I will let you go. You will stay here no longer." 29 Moses said to him, "When I have gone out of the city, I will spread out my hands to the Lord. The thunder will stop. There will be no more hail. Then you may know that the earth is the Lord's. 30 But I know that you and your servants do not yet fear the Lord God." 31 The flax and the barley were destroyed. For these plants had just begun to grow. 32 But the other grains were not destroyed, because they grow later.

33 So Moses left the city and Pharaoh. He spread out his hands to the Lord. And the thunder and the hail stopped. The rain no longer poured on the earth. 34 But when Pharaoh saw that the rain and hail and thunder had stopped, he sinned again. He and his servants made their hearts hard. 35 Pharaoh's heart was not changed. He did not let the people of Israel go, just as the Lord had said by Moses.

Locusts Come

10 Then the Lord said to Moses, "Go to Pharaoh. For I have made his heart and the heart of his servants hard, so that I may do My powerful works among them. 2 You may tell your son and your grandson how I made it very hard for the Egyptians and how I did My powerful works among them. So you may know that I am the Lord." 3 Moses and Aaron went to Pharaoh. They said to him, "The Lord, the God of the Hebrews, says this: 'How long will you hold your pride before Me? Let My people go, so they may worship Me. 4 If you will not let My people go, tomorrow I will bring locusts into your country. 5 They will cover the land, so no one will be able to see the ground. They will eat what is left for you after the hail. They will eat every tree of yours that grows in the field. 6 They will fill your houses, and the houses of your servants, and the houses of all the Egyptians. Your fathers and your grandfathers have never seen such a thing from the day they were born until this day.'" Then Moses turned and left Pharaoh.

7 Pharaoh's servants said to him, "How long will this man bring trouble to us? Let the men go, so they may worship the Lord their God. Do you not yet understand that Egypt is destroyed?" 8 So Moses and Aaron were brought again to Pharaoh. He said to them, "Go and worship the Lord your God. But who will be going?" 9 Moses said, "We will go with our young and our old, our sons and our daughters, and our flocks and cattle. For we must make a special supper to the Lord." 10 Then Pharaoh said to them, "Let the Lord be with you if I ever let you go with your little ones! See, you have something bad in mind. 11 No! You men go and worship the Lord. For that is what you want." And Moses and Aaron were sent away from Pharaoh.

12 Then the Lord said to Moses, "Put out your hand over the land of Egypt for the locusts to come upon the land of Egypt. They will eat every plant of the land, all that the hail has left." 13 So Moses put out his special stick over the land of Egypt. And the Lord sent an east wind on the land all that day and all that night. When it was morning, the east wind brought the locusts. 14 The locusts came over all the land of Egypt and they stayed on the whole country of Egypt. There were very many. There had never been so many locusts. And there would never be so many again. 15 For they covered the whole land and made it dark. They ate every plant of the land, and all the fruit of the trees that the hail had left. Nothing green was left on any tree or plant of the field through all the land of Egypt.

16 Then Pharaoh called for Moses and Aaron in a hurry. He said, "I have sinned

against the Lord your God and against you. [17] So now forgive my sin only this once. Pray to the Lord your God to take this death away from me." [18] So Moses left Pharaoh and prayed to the Lord. [19] And the Lord changed the wind to a very strong west wind. It lifted the locusts and sent them into the Red Sea. Not one locust was left in all the country of Egypt. [20] But the Lord made Pharaoh's heart hard. He did not let the people of Israel go.

Darkness Covers the Land

[21] Then the Lord said to Moses, "Put out your hand toward the sky. And there will be darkness over the land of Egypt, a darkness people will feel." [22] So Moses put out his hand toward the sky. And there was darkness in all the land of Egypt for three days. [23] The Egyptians did not see each other. No one got up from his place for three days. But all the people of Israel had light in their homes. [24] Then Pharaoh called to Moses, and said, "Go and worship the Lord. Your children may go with you also. Only let your flocks and your cattle stay." [25] But Moses said, "You must let us have gifts to give in worship and gifts for burning, so we may give them to the Lord our God. [26] So our animals will go with us also. Not a foot of an animal will be left behind. For we will take some of them to use as we worship the Lord our God. And until we are there, we do not know which ones we will use in worshiping the Lord." [27] But the Lord made Pharaoh's heart hard. He was not willing to let them go. [28] Pharaoh said to Moses, "Go away from me! Make sure that you do not see my face again! For the day you see my face again, you will die!" [29] Moses said, "You are right. I will never see your face again."

The First-Born Die

11 The Lord said to Moses, "I will bring trouble upon Pharaoh and upon Egypt one more time. After that he will let you go. He will not only let you go, but he will make you leave. [2] Tell the people that each man should ask his neighbor and each woman ask her neighbor for things made of silver and gold." [3] Then the Lord gave the people favor in the eyes of the Egyptians. And the man Moses was respected in the land of Egypt, in the eyes of Pharaoh's servants and the people.

[4] Moses said, "The Lord says this: 'About midnight I will go through Egypt. [5] And

all the first-born in the land of Egypt will die, from the first-born of Pharaoh who sits on his throne to the first-born of the servant-girl grinding the grain, and even the first-born of the cattle. [6] There will be loud crying in all the land of Egypt, more than has ever been heard before or will ever be heard again. [7] Not even a dog will make a sound against those of Israel, man or animal, so you may know that the Lord divides Egypt from Israel.' [8] All these who are your servants will come to me and bow in front of me. They will say, 'Go away, you and all the people who follow you.' After that I will go." And he went away from Pharaoh very angry. [9] Then the Lord said to Moses, "Pharaoh will not listen to you. So I will do more powerful works in the land of Egypt." [10] Moses and Aaron did all these great works in front of Pharaoh. But the Lord made Pharaoh's heart hard. He did not let the people of Israel leave his land.

The Passover

12 The Lord said to Moses and Aaron in the land of Egypt, [2] "This month will be the beginning of months. It will be the first month of the year to you. [3] Speak to the people of Israel when they are gathered together. Tell them that on the tenth day of this month, every man must take a lamb for those of his father's house, a lamb for each house. [4] If those in the house are too few to eat a lamb, let him and his near est neighbor take the right amount for the number of people. Divide the lamb by how much each can eat. [5] Your lamb must be perfect, a male lamb one year old. You may take it from the sheep or the goats. [6] Keep it until the fourteenth day of the same month. Then all the people of Israel are to kill it in the evening. [7] Then they must take some of the blood and put it on the wood pieces at the sides and top of the door of each house where they will eat it. [8] They must eat the meat that same night, made ready over a fire. They will eat it with bread made without yeast and with bitter plants. [9] Do not eat any of it if it is not cooked or if it is made ready by boiling. But cook it over a fire, its head, legs and inside parts. [10] Do not save any of it until morning. Burn with fire whatever is left of it before morning.

[11] "Eat it with your shoes on your feet and your walking stick in your hand. And you must eat it in a hurry. It is the time the Lord will pass over. [12] For I will go through

the land of Egypt on that night. And I will kill all the first-born in the land of Egypt, both man and animal. I will punish all the gods of Egypt. I am the Lord. 13 But the blood will mark for you the houses where you live. When I see the blood I will pass over you. And no trouble will come upon you to destroy you when I punish the land of Egypt.

14 "This day will be for you to remember. You must remember it by having a special supper in honor to the Lord. All of you must keep it as a law forever. 15 Seven days you must eat bread without yeast. On the first day you must get all the yeast out of your houses. Whoever eats anything with yeast from the first day until the seventh day will be taken away from Israel. 16 On the first day you must have a holy meeting of the people, and another holy meeting on the seventh day. Do no work at all on these days, except to get ready what every person must eat. You may do only that. 17 You must have the special supper of bread without yeast. For on this same day I brought your family groups out of the land of Egypt. So all of you must remember this day as a law forever.

18 "In the first month, from the evening of the fourteenth day until the evening of the twenty-first day, you must eat bread made without yeast. 19 There must be no yeast found in your houses for seven days. For whoever eats anything with yeast, that person, stranger or born in the land, will be cut off from the people of Israel. 20 Do not eat anything with yeast. You must eat bread made without yeast in all your homes."

21 Then Moses called for all the leaders of Israel. He said to them, "Go and choose lambs for your families, and kill the Passover lamb. 22 Take a small branch and put it in the blood in the pot. Spread some of the blood on the wood pieces on the top and sides of the door. Then none of you go outside the door of his house until morning. 23 For the Lord will pass through to kill the Egyptians. But when He sees the blood around your door, the Lord will pass over the door. He will not let the one who destroys come into your houses to kill you. 24 You must remember this as a law for you and your children forever. 25 You must remember this special time when you go to the land that the Lord has promised to give you. 26 When your children ask you, 'What does this special time mean to you?' 27 you will say, 'It is a Passover gift to the

Lord. Because He passed over the houses of the people of Israel in Egypt. He killed the Egyptians but saved our homes.'" And the people bowed to the ground and worshiped. 28 Then the people of Israel went and did what the Lord had told Moses and Aaron.

Death of the First-Born

29 At midnight the Lord killed all the first-born in the land of Egypt, from the first-born of Pharaoh who sat on the throne to the first-born of the one who was held in prison, and all the first-born of the cattle. 30 Pharaoh got up in the night, he and his servants and all the Egyptians. And there was a loud cry in Egypt. For there was no home where there was not someone dead.

Children of Israel Leave Egypt

31 Then Pharaoh called for Moses and Aaron at night. He said, "Get up and go away from my people, both you and the people of Israel. Go and worship the Lord, as you have said. 32 Take your flocks and your cattle, as you have said, and go. And pray that good will come to me also."

33 The Egyptians were trying to make the people hurry out of the land. For they said, "We will all be dead." 34 So the people took their dough before yeast had been added. They tied their dough pots in their clothes on their shoulders. 35 The people of Israel had done what Moses had said. They had asked the Egyptians for things made of silver and gold and for clothes. 36 And the Lord had given the people favor in the eyes of the Egyptians. So the Egyptians let them have whatever they asked for. And they took the best things of Egypt.

37 The people of Israel traveled from Rameses to Succoth. There were about 600,000 men on foot, and also the women and children. 38 And a mixed group of people went with them, and very many flocks and cattle. 39 They made the dough they had brought out of Egypt into loaves of bread without yeast. Yeast was not added to the dough because they had been sent out of Egypt and could not wait. They could not make ready any food for themselves.

40 The people of Israel had lived in Egypt 430 years. 41 At the end of 430 years, on that same day, all of the Lord's people left Egypt. 42 It was a night to be remembered for the Lord for having brought them out of the land of Egypt. This night is for the

Lord, to be remembered by all the people of Israel for all time.

How the Passover Supper Should Be Eaten

43 The Lord said to Moses and Aaron, "This is the Law of the Passover. No stranger may eat of it. **44** But every servant who is bought with money may eat of it, only after he has gone through the religious act of becoming a Jew. **45** A stranger or paid servant may not eat of it. **46** It must be eaten in one house. You must not carry any of the meat outside the house. And you must not break a bone of it. **47** All the people of Israel must remember this. **48** But when a stranger staying with you wants to share in this special supper to the Lord, let all his men and boys go through the religious act of becoming a Jew. Then let him come near to share in the special supper. He will be like one who is born in the land. But no person who has not gone through the religious act may eat of it. **49** The same law is for the one who is born in the land and for the stranger who stays among you."

50 Then all the people of Israel did just as the Lord had told Moses and Aaron. **51** On that same day the Lord brought the people of Israel out of the land of Egypt by their family groups.

The First-Born Given to God

13 The Lord said to Moses, **2** "Set apart to Me every first-born male. The first-born male among the people of Israel, and the first-born male animal are Mine."

Special Supper of Bread without Yeast

3 Then Moses said to the people, "Remember this day in which you went out of Egypt, out of the land where you were made to stay and work. For the Lord brought you out of this place by a powerful hand. No bread made with yeast will be eaten. **4** This day you are about to go out, in the month of Abib. **5** And the Lord will bring you to the land of the Canaanite, the Hittite, the Amorite, the Hivite and the Jebusite, which He promised to your fathers to give you. It is a land flowing with milk and honey. There you will do this act of worship in this month. **6** For seven days you will eat bread without yeast. On the seventh day there will be a special supper to the Lord. **7** Bread without yeast will be eaten for seven days. Nothing made with yeast will be

seen among you. No yeast will be seen among you in all your country. **8** You will say to your son on that day, 'It is because of what the Lord did for me when I came out of Egypt.' **9** It will be a special mark on your hand and on your forehead to make people remember, that the Law of the Lord is to be in your mouth. For the Lord brought you out of Egypt with a powerful hand. **10** So you must keep this Law at the time given for it from year to year.

The First-Born

11 "The Lord will bring you to the land of the Canaanite. He will give it to you as He promised you and your fathers. **12** There you must give to the Lord the first male to be born. And all the first male animals born belong to the Lord. **13** But you may buy every first-born donkey by giving a lamb for it. But if you do not buy it, then you must break its neck. You must buy with a gift of money every first-born male among your sons. **14** And when the time comes when your son asks you, 'What does this mean?' then say to him, 'With a powerful hand the Lord brought us out of Egypt, from the land where we were servants. **15** When Pharaoh would not let us go, the Lord killed every first-born in the land of Egypt, both the first-born of man and of animal. So I give to the Lord every first male animal to be born. But I buy with a gift of money every first-born of my sons.' **16** So it will be like a special mark on your hand and on your forehead. For the Lord brought us out of Egypt with a powerful hand."

Cloud by Day and Fire by Night

17 When Pharaoh had let the people go, God did not lead them by the way of the land of the Philistines, even when that was nearer. For God said, "The people may change their minds when they see war, and return to Egypt." **18** So God led the people through the desert to get to the Red Sea. The people of Israel went out of the land of Egypt ready for war. **19** Moses took the bones of Joseph with him because Joseph had made the people of Israel promise. He had said, "For sure God will keep you and you will carry my bones with you from here." **20** Then they left Succoth and set up their tents at Etham, beside the desert. **21** The Lord went before them, in a pillar of cloud during the day to lead them on the way, and in a pillar of fire during the night to give them light. So they could travel day and night. ²² The pillar of cloud during the day and the pillar of fire during the night did not leave the people.

Crossing the Red Sea

14 Then the Lord said to Moses, ² "Tell the people of Israel to turn around and set up their tents in front of Pi-hahiroth, between Migdol and the sea. Set up your tents in front of Baal-zephon, beside the sea. ³ For Pharaoh will say of the people of Israel, 'They have lost their way. The desert has shut them in.' ⁴ I will make Pharaoh's heart hard. And he will try to catch them. So I will be honored through Pharaoh and his whole army. Then the Egyptians will know that I am the Lord." And they did so.

⁵ When the king of Egypt was told that the people had left, Pharaoh and his servants changed their minds about the people. They said, "What is this we have done? We have let Israel go from working for us." ⁶ So he made his war-wagon ready and took his people with him. ⁷ He took 600 of the best war-wagons, and all the other war-wagons of Egypt in the care of leaders. ⁸ The Lord made the heart of Pharaoh, king of Egypt hard. And Pharaoh went to catch the people of Israel, who were leaving without fear. ⁹ The Egyptians followed them with all the horses and war-wagons of Pharaoh, his horsemen and his army. And they came to them at their tents by the sea, beside Pi-hahiroth, in front of Baal-zephon.

¹⁰ When Pharaoh came near, the people of Israel looked and saw the Egyptians coming after them. And they were filled with fear and cried out to the Lord. ¹¹ Then they said to Moses, "Is it because there were no graves in Egypt that you have taken us away to die in the desert? What have you done to us, in bringing us out of Egypt? ¹² Did we not tell you in Egypt, 'Leave us alone and let us serve the Egyptians'? It would have been better for us to serve the Egyptians than to die here."

¹³ But Moses said to the people, "Do not be afraid! Be strong, and see how the Lord will save you today. For the Egyptians you have seen today, you will never see again. ¹⁴ The Lord will fight for you. All you have to do is keep still."

¹⁵ Then the Lord said to Moses, "Why do you cry to me? Tell the people of Israel to keep going. ¹⁶ Lift up your special stick and put out your hand over the sea, and divide it. Then the people of Israel will go through the sea on dry land. ¹⁷ I will make the Egyptians' hearts hard, so they will go after them. And I will be honored through Pharaoh and his whole army, his war-wagons and his horsemen. ¹⁸ The Egyptians will know that I am the Lord when I am honored through Pharaoh, his war-wagons and his horsemen." ¹⁹ Then the Angel of God, who had been going in front of the army of Israel, moved and went behind them. The cloud moved from the front of them and stood behind them. ²⁰ It came between the army of Egypt and the army of Israel. There was the cloud and the darkness, yet it gave light at night. And the one army did not come near the other all night. ²¹ Then Moses put out his hand over the sea. And the Lord moved the sea all night by a strong east wind. So the waters were divided. ²² And the people of Israel went through the sea on dry land. The waters were like a wall to them on their right and on their left. ²³ Then the Egyptians followed them. All Pharaoh's horses and war-wagons and horsemen went in the sea after them. ²⁴ In the morning hours, the Lord looked down on the Egyptian army through the fire and cloud. And He made the Egyptian army afraid. ²⁵ He made the wheels of their war-wagons come off, so it was hard for the wagons to be moved. So the Egyptians said, "Let us run away from Israel. For the Lord is fighting for them against the Egyptians."

²⁶ Then the Lord said to Moses, "Put out your hand over the sea. And the waters will flow over the Egyptians, and over their war-wagons and their horsemen." ²⁷ And when the morning came, the Egyptians ran into the wall of water as the sea returned to the way it was before. The Lord destroyed the Egyptians in the sea. ²⁸ The waters returned and covered the war-wagons and the horsemen and Pharaoh's whole army that had gone in the sea after them. Not even one of them was left. ²⁹ But the people of Israel walked on dry land through the sea. The waters were like a wall to them on their right and on their left.

³⁰ So the Lord saved Israel that day from the Egyptians. And Israel saw the Egyptians dead beside the sea. ³¹ Israel saw the great power which the Lord had used against the Egyptians. And the people had fear of the Lord. They believed in the Lord and in His servant Moses.

15 Then Moses and the people of Israel sang this song to the Lord, saying, "I will sing to the Lord, for He is praised for His greatness. He has thrown the horse and horseman into the sea. ² The Lord is my strength and song. He is the One Who saves me. He is my God and I will praise Him. He is my father's God and I will honor Him. ³ The Lord is a fighter. The Lord is His name. ⁴ He has thrown Pharaoh's war-wagons and army into the sea. The best of Pharaoh's leaders are under the Red Sea. ⁵ The water covers them. They went down in the deep water like a stone. ⁶ O Lord, Your right hand is great in power. O Lord, Your right hand destroys those who hate You. ⁷ In the greatness of Your power You destroy those who fight against You. You send Your burning anger and it burns them like straw. ⁸ The waters were lifted up by Your breath. The flowing waters stood up like a wall. The water became hard in the middle of the sea. ⁹ Those who hated us said, 'I will go after them. I will catch them. I will divide the riches taken from them. My soul will have its way against them. I will take out my sword and my hand will destroy them.' ¹⁰ You, Lord, blew with Your wind and the sea covered them. They went down like iron in the powerful sea. ¹¹ Who is like You among the gods, O Lord? Who is like You, great and holy, praised in fear, doing powerful works? ¹² You put out Your right hand, and the earth swallowed them. ¹³ You have led with loving-kindness the people You have made free. You have led them in Your strength to Your holy place. ¹⁴ The nations have heard of it, and they shake in fear. Pain has come upon the people of Philistia. ¹⁵ Now the leaders of Edom are afraid. The leaders of Moab shake in fear. All the people of Canaan have become weak. ¹⁶ Much fear comes upon them. They see Your strength, O Lord. They are afraid and do not move until Your people have passed by, the people You have bought and made free. ¹⁷ You will bring them in and put them on Your own mountain. It is the place, O Lord, where You have made Your house, the holy place, which Your hands have built. ¹⁸ The Lord will rule forever and ever."

¹⁹ For Pharaoh's horses and war-wagons and horsemen went in the sea. The Lord brought the waters of the sea upon them. But the people of Israel walked on dry land through the sea. ²⁰ Then Aaron's sister Miriam, the woman who spoke for

the Lord, took a timbrel in her hand. And all the women followed her, with timbrels and dancing. ²¹ Miriam said to them, "Sing to the Lord, for He is praised for His greatness. He has thrown the horse and horseman into the sea."

Bitter Water

²² Then Moses led Israel from the Red Sea. They went into the Desert of Shur. They went three days in the desert and found no water. ²³ When they came to Marah, they could not drink the water of Marah because it was bitter. So it was given the name Marah. ²⁴ The people complained to Moses, saying, "What can we drink?" ²⁵ Moses cried to the Lord, and the Lord showed him a tree. He threw it into the water, and the water became sweet.

There the Lord made a Law for them and tested them. ²⁶ He said, "Listen well to the voice of the Lord your God. Do what is right in His eyes. Listen to what He tells you, and obey all His Laws. If you do this, I will put none of the diseases on you which I have put on the Egyptians. For I am the Lord Who heals you."

²⁷ Then they came to Elim, where there were twelve wells of water and seventy trees. They set up their tents there beside the water.

Bread in the Morning, Meat in the Evening

16 All the people of Israel left Elim, and came to the Desert of Sin, between Elim and Sinai. It was the fifteenth day of the second month after they left the land of Egypt. ² And all the people of Israel complained against Moses and Aaron in the desert, ³ saying, "We should have died by the Lord's hand in the land of Egypt, when we sat by the pots of meat and ate all the bread we wanted. For you have brought us out into this desert to kill all of us with hunger."

⁴ Then the Lord said to Moses, "See, I will rain bread from heaven for you. The people will go out and gather a day's share every day, so I may test them to see if they will follow My Law or not. ⁵ On the sixth day they are to bring in twice as much as they gather each day." ⁶ So Moses and Aaron said to the people of Israel, "This evening you will know that the Lord has brought you out of the land of Egypt. ⁷ And in the morning you will see the greatness of the Lord. For He hears your complaining against the Lord. What are we, that

you complain against us?" 8 Moses said, "The Lord is giving you meat to eat in the evening and all the bread you want in the morning. For He hears how you complain against Him. What are we? You complain not against us, but against the Lord." 9 Then Moses said to Aaron, "Say to all the people of Israel, 'Come near to the Lord, for He has heard your complaining.' " 10 When Aaron spoke to all the people of Israel, they looked toward the desert. And they saw in the cloud the shining-greatness of the Lord. 11 The Lord said to Moses, 12 "I have heard the complaining of the people of Israel. Say to them, 'In the evening you will eat meat, and in the morning you will be filled with bread. Then you will know that I am the Lord your God.' "

13 In the evening quails came and covered the place where the people were staying. And in the early morning a little water was around the tents. 14 When the water had gone, there were small white pieces all over the ground of the desert. 15 When the people of Israel saw it, they said to one another, "What is it?" For they did not know what it was. Moses said to them, "It is the bread that the Lord has given you to eat. 16 This is what the Lord has told you to do: 'Every man gather as much of it as he can eat. Take a jar for every person that each of you has in his tent.' " 17 The people did so. Some gathered much and some less. 18 When they saw how much they had, he who had gathered much had no more than what was needed. And he who had gathered less had enough. Every man gathered as much as he could eat. 19 Moses said to them, "Let no one save any of it until morning." 20 But they did not listen to Moses. Some left part of it until morning. And worms grew in it and it became bad to eat. So Moses was angry with them. 21 Morning after morning they gathered it, every man as much as he could eat. But when the sun became hot, it would melt.

22 On the sixth day they gathered twice as much bread, two jars for each person. When all the leaders of the people came and told Moses, 23 he said to them, "This is what the Lord said: 'Tomorrow is a time of rest, a holy Day of Rest to the Lord. Make ready the food you will need for today. Then put aside what is left to be kept until morning.' " 24 So they put it aside until morning, as Moses told them. And it did not become bad to eat, and there were no worms in it. 25 Moses said, "Eat it today. For today is a Day of Rest to the Lord.

Today you will not find it in the field. 26 Six days you will gather it. But on the seventh day, the Day of Rest, there will be none." 27 On the seventh day some of the people went out to gather it. But they found none. 28 Then the Lord said to Moses, "How much longer will you go against My Word and My Laws? 29 See, the Lord has given you the Day of Rest. This is why He gives you bread for two days on the sixth day. Every man should stay home and not leave his place on the seventh day." 30 So the people rested on the seventh day.

31 The people of Israel called it bread from heaven. It was like coriander seed, white, and tasted like bread made with honey. 32 Moses said, "This is what the Lord has said: 'Let a jar of it be kept for your children- and grandchildren-to-come, so they may see the bread that I fed you in the desert when I brought you out of the land of Egypt.' " 33 Then Moses said to Aaron, "Take a jar full of the bread from heaven. And put it before the Lord, to be kept for all your children-to-come." 34 As the Lord told Moses, Aaron put it in front of the special box of the agreement to be kept. 35 The people of Israel ate the bread from heaven forty years, until they came to a land where other people lived. They ate the bread from heaven until they came to the land of Canaan. 36 (It took about ten jars to fill a large basket.)

Water from the Rock

17 All the people of Israel left the Desert of Sin, traveling from one place to another as the Lord told them. They set up their tents at Rephidim. But there was no water for the people to drink. 2 So the people argued with Moses, saying, "Give us water to drink." And Moses said to them, "Why do you argue with me? Why do you test the Lord?" 3 But the people were thirsty there for water. They complained against Moses, saying, "Why did you bring us out of Egypt, to kill us and our children and animals with thirst?" 4 So Moses called to the Lord, saying, "What should I do with these people? They are almost ready to throw stones at me." 5 The Lord said to Moses, "Pass in front of the people and take some of the leaders of Israel with you. Take the special stick in your hand with which you hit the Nile, and go. 6 See, I will stand before you there on the rock at Horeb. When you hit the rock, water will come out of it and the people will drink." And Moses did so, with the leaders of Israel watching. 7 He called the name of the place Massah and Meribah because of the arguing of the people of Israel, and because they tested the Lord, saying, "Is the Lord among us or not?"

War with Amalek

8 Then Amalek came and fought against Israel at Rephidim. 9 So Moses said to Joshua, "Choose men for us. And go out and fight against Amalek. Tomorrow I will stand on the top of the hill with the special stick of God in my hand." 10 Joshua did as Moses told him. He fought against Amalek. And Moses, Aaron and Hur went up to the top of the hill. 11 When Moses held up his hand, Israel would be winning. But when he let his hand down, Amalek would win. 12 Moses' hands became tired. So they took a stone and put it under him, and he sat on it. Then Aaron and Hur held up his hands, one on each side. His hands did not move until the sun went down. 13 So Joshua destroyed Amalek and his people with the sword.

14 Then the Lord said to Moses, "Write this in a book, to be remembered, and tell Joshua that I will take away everything under heaven that would help you remember Amalek." 15 Moses built an altar and gave it the name The Lord is My Banner. 16 And he said, "Because the Lord has promised to have war against Amalek through all time."

Jethro Helps Moses

18 Moses' father-in-law, Jethro, the religious leader of Midian, heard about all that God had done for Moses and for Israel His people. He heard about how the Lord had brought Israel out of Egypt. 2 Moses' father-in-law, Jethro, had taken Moses' wife, Zipporah, after Moses had sent her away. 3 And he had taken her two sons. One was given the name Gershom, for he said, "I have been a stranger in a strange land." 4 The other was given the name Eliezer, for he said, "The God of my father was my help. And He saved me from the sword of Pharaoh."

5 Then Moses' father-in-law, Jethro, came to Moses with his sons and his wife to the desert by the mountain of God where he was staying. 6 He sent the news to Moses, "I, your father-in-law, Jethro, am coming to you with your wife and her two sons with her." 7 Then Moses went to meet his father-in-law. He bowed down and kissed them. They asked each other

if all was well, and went into the tent. 8 Moses told his father-in-law all the Lord had done to Pharaoh and the Egyptians because of Israel. He told him about how they had suffered on the way, and how the Lord had saved them. 9 Jethro was glad because of all the good things the Lord had done for Israel in saving them from the hand of the Egyptians. 10 So Jethro said, "Honor and thanks be to the Lord, Who saved you from the hand of the Egyptians and from the hand of Pharaoh, and Who made you free from the power of Egypt. 11 Now I know that the Lord is greater than all the gods. It was proven when they acted in their pride against the people." 12 Then Moses' father-in-law, Jethro, gave a burnt gift in worship to God. And Aaron came with all the leaders of Israel to eat bread with Moses' father-in-law before God.

Men Who Judge

13 The next day Moses sat to judge the people. And the people stood around Moses from morning until evening. 14 When Moses' father-in-law saw all he was doing for the people, he said, "What is this that you do for the people? Why do you sit alone and judge and all the people stand around you from morning until evening?" 15 Moses said to his father-in-law, "Because the people come to me to learn God's will. 16 When they argue, they come to me. And I judge between a man and his neighbor. I teach them the Laws of God." 17 Moses' father-in-law said to him, "What you are doing is not good. 18 You and the people with you will become tired and weak. For the work is too much for you. You cannot do it alone. 19 Now listen to me. I will tell you what you should do, and God be with you. You speak for the people before God. Bring the troubles to God. 20 Then teach them the Laws. Make them know the way they must walk and the work they must do. 21 Also, you should choose from the people able men who fear God, men of truth who hate to get things by doing wrong. Have these men rule over the people, as leaders of thousands, of hundreds, of fifties and of tens. 22 Let them judge the people at all times. But have all the big troubles brought to you. But have them judge the small troubles. So it will be easier for you. They will share the work with you. 23 If you do this and God tells you to do it, then you will be able to keep your strength. And all these people will go to their place in peace."

24 Moses listened to his father-in-law, and did all that he had said. 25 Moses chose able men out of all Israel. And he made them leaders over the people, leaders of thousands, of hundreds, of fifties and of tens. 26 They judged the people at all times. They would bring the big troubles to Moses. But they would judge every small trouble themselves.27 Then Moses let his father-in-law return to his own land.

Moses Meets God on Mount Sinai

19 In the third month after the people of Israel left Egypt, they came to the Sinai Desert on the same day. 2 They had left Rephidim and had come to the Sinai Desert. There Israel set up their tents in front of the mountain. 3 And Moses went up to God. The Lord called to him from the mountain, saying, "Say this to the house of Jacob and tell the people of Israel: 4 'You have seen what I did to the Egyptians, and how I carried you on eagles' wings and brought you to Myself. 5 Now then, if you will obey My voice, and keep My agreement, you will belong to Me from among all nations. For all the earth is Mine. 6 You will be to Me a nation of religious leaders, a holy nation.' These are the words you will speak to the people of Israel."

7 So Moses came and called the leaders of the people. He told them all these words which the Lord had told him. 8 And all the people answered together and said, "We will do all that the Lord has said!" Then Moses went to tell the Lord what the people had said. 9 The Lord said to Moses, "See, I will come to you in a thick cloud. So the people may hear when I speak with you, and may believe you forever." Then Moses told the Lord what the people had said. 10 The Lord said to Moses, "Go to the people. Today and tomorrow set them apart to be holy. Have them wash their clothes. 11 And let them be ready for the third day. For on the third day the people will see the Lord come down on Mount Sinai. 12 Let the people know the places all around that they must not pass. Tell them, 'Be careful that you do not go up on the mountain or touch any place around it. Whoever touches the mountain will be put to death. 13 No hand will touch him. But he will be killed with stones or arrows. If he be animal or man, he will not live.' When a long sound from a horn is heard, they may come up to the mountain."

14 So Moses went down from the mountain to the people. He set the people apart to be holy, and they washed their clothes. 15 He said to the people, "Be ready for the third day. Do not go near a woman."

16 On the morning of the third day there was thunder and lightning. A cloud covered the mountain, and a very loud horn sounded. All the people among the tents shook with fear. 17 Then Moses brought the people from among the tents to meet God. They stood at the base of the mountain. 18 Mount Sinai was all in smoke because the Lord came down upon it in fire. Its smoke went up like the smoke of a stove. And the whole mountain shook. 19 The sound of the horn became louder and louder. Moses spoke, and God answered him with thunder. 20 Then the Lord came down upon Mount Sinai, to the top of the mountain. The Lord called Moses to the top of the mountain, and he went up. 21 Then the Lord said to Moses, "Go down and tell the people not to break through to look at the Lord. For then many of them would be destroyed. 22 Have the religious leaders who come near to the Lord set themselves apart to be holy. Or the Lord will go against them." 23 Moses said to the Lord, "The people cannot come up to Mount Sinai. For You told us, 'Set places around the mountain that must not be passed, and set it apart as holy.'" 24 Then the Lord said to him, "Go down, and then come up with Aaron. But do not let the religious leaders and the people break through to come up to the Lord, or He will go against them." 25 So Moses went down to the people and told them.

God's Ten Great Laws

20 Then God spoke all these words, saying, 2 "I am the Lord your God, Who brought you out of the land of Egypt, out of the house where you were servants.

3 "Have no gods other than Me.

4 "Do not make for yourselves a god to look like anything that is in heaven above or on the earth below or in the waters under the earth.

5 "Do not worship them or work for them. For I, the Lord your God, am a jealous God. I punish the children, even the great-grandchildren, for the sins of their fathers who hate Me. 6 But I show loving-kindness to thousands of those who love Me and keep My Laws.

7 "Do not use the name of the Lord your God in a false way. For the Lord will punish the one who uses His name in a false way.

8 "Remember the Day of Rest, to keep it holy. 9 Six days you will do all your work. 10 But the seventh day is a Day of Rest to the Lord your God. You, your son, your daughter, your male servant, your female servant, your cattle, or the traveler who stays with you, must not do any work on this day. 11 For in six days the Lord made the heavens, the earth, the sea and all that is in them. And He rested on the seventh day. So the Lord gave honor to the Day of Rest and made it holy.

12 "Honor your father and your mother, so your life may be long in the land the Lord your God gives you.

13 "Do not kill other people.

14 "Do not do sex sins.

15 "Do not steal.

16 "Do not tell a lie about your neighbor.

17 "Do not have a desire for your neighbor's house. Do not have a desire for his wife or his male servant, his female servant, or his bull or his donkey or anything that belongs to your neighbor."

18 All the people heard and saw the thunder and lightning, the sound of the horn, and the mountain smoking. And when the people saw it, they shook with fear and stood far away. 19 They said to Moses, "You speak to us and we will listen. But do not let God speak to us or we will die." 20 Moses said to the people, "Do not be afraid. God has come to test you, so you may have enough fear of Him to keep you from sinning." 21 The people stood far away, while Moses came near to the cloud where God was.

22 Then the Lord said to Moses, "Say this to the people of Israel: 'You have seen for yourselves that I have spoken to you from heaven. 23 Do not make any gods other than Me. Do not make for yourselves gods of silver or gods of gold. 24 Make an altar of earth for Me, and on it give your burnt and peace gifts in worship, your sheep and cattle. In every place where My name is to be remembered, I will come to you and bring good to you. 25 If you make an altar of stone for Me, do not build it of cut stones. For if you use an object to cut it, it will be unclean. 26 And do not go up on steps to My altar, so no part of your body may be seen without being covered.'

Laws about Servants

21

"Now these are the Laws which you are to give them. 2 If you buy a Hebrew servant, he will work for six years. In the seventh year he will go free,

paying nothing. 3 If he comes alone, he will leave by himself. If he is married, then his wife will leave with him. 4 If his owner gives him a wife and she gives birth to his sons or daughters, the wife and her children will belong to her owner, and he will leave by himself. 5 But if the servant says, 'I love my owner, my wife and my children; I do not care to go free,' 6 then his owner will bring him to the judges. And he will bring him to the door or the side of the door. There his owner will make a hole in his ear with a sharp object. And he will serve him all his life.

7 "If a man sells his daughter to be a female servant, she is not to go free as the male servants do. 8 If she does not please her owner who has taken her for himself, he will take pay for her to be set free. He does not have the right to sell her to a strange people, because he has not been fair to her. 9 If he takes her for his son, he will act toward her as with a daughter. 10 If he marries again, her food, clothing and marriage rights are to stay the same. 11 And if he will not do these three things for her, then she may go free, without paying any money.

Laws about Fighting and Killing

12 "Whoever hits a man so that he dies will be put to death. 13 But if he did not plan to hurt him, but God allowed it to happen, then I will give you a place where he may run to be safe. 14 But if a man wants to hurt his neighbor and he plans to kill him, then you take him away from My altar and put him to death.

15 "Whoever hits his father or his mother will be put to death.

16 "Whoever steals a man and sells him, or keeps him for himself, will be put to death. 17 Whoever curses his father or his mother will be put to death.

18 "When men argue and one hits the other with a stone or with his hand, and he does not die but has to stay in bed because of it, 19 then if he gets up and walks around outside using his walking stick, the one who hit him will not be punished. He will only pay for the loss of his time. And he will take care of him until he is healed.

20 "When a man hits his male or female servant with a stick so that he or she dies, he will be punished. 21 But if he or she lives a day or two, he will not be punished, for his servant belongs to him.

22 "If men fight with each other and hit a woman who is going to have a child so that

she loses her baby but no other hurt comes to her, he must pay whatever the woman's husband says he must, as agreed upon by the judges. 23 But if there is other hurt also, then it is life for life, 24 eye for eye, tooth for tooth, hand for hand, foot for foot, 25 burn for burn, cut for cut, sore for sore.

26 "If a man hits the eye of his male or female servant and destroys it, he will let the person go free because of the eye. 27 If he knocks out a tooth of his man or woman servant, he will let the person go free because of the tooth.

Laws about Owning Animals

28 "When a bull kills a man or a woman with its horns, the bull will be killed with stones. And its flesh will not be eaten. But the owner of the bull will not be punished. 29 But if a bull has tried to kill with its horns before, and the owner has been told but does not keep him shut up, and the bull kills a man or a woman, the bull will be killed with stones and the owner will be put to death. 30 But if he is allowed to pay for his life, then he will pay whatever is asked of him. 31 If the bull kills a son or a daughter, it will be punished by the same law. 32 If the bull kills a male or female servant, the bull's owner will give the servant's owner thirty pieces of silver. And the bull will be killed with stones.

33 "When a man leaves a deep hole open, or digs a deep hole and does not cover it, and a bull or donkey falls into it, 34 the owner of the hole will pay for the loss. He will give money to the animal's owner. And the dead animal will become his.

35 "If one man's bull hurts another's so that it dies, they will sell the live bull and divide the price so they will each have the same. And they will divide the dead bull. 36 Or if it is known that the bull has tried to kill with its horns in the past, but its owner has not kept it shut up, he will pay bull for bull. And the dead animal will become his.

Laws about Paying Back What Is Owed

22 "If a man steals a bull or a sheep and kills it or sells it, he will pay five bulls for the bull and four sheep for the sheep. 2 If the robber is caught while breaking in, and is hit so that he dies, the owner of the house is not guilty for his blood. 3 But if the sun has risen on him, there will be guilt for his blood. The robber must pay for the loss. If he has nothing, then he must be sold for stealing.

4 If the stolen bull or donkey or sheep is found alive with him, he must pay twice what it is worth. 5 If a man lets his cattle eat from a field or grape-field and lets his cattle loose to eat in another man's field, he will pay for the loss from the best of his own field or grape-field.

6 "When a fire starts and spreads to thorn bushes so as to burn up picked grain or standing grain or the field itself, he who started the fire will pay for the loss.

7 "If a man gives his neighbor money or things to keep for him, and it is stolen from the man's house, if the robber is caught he will pay twice as much as the loss. 8 If the robber is not caught, then the owner of the house will be brought to the judges. They will see if he stole what belongs to his neighbor. 9 For every wrong act, if it is for bull, donkey, sheep, clothing, or any lost thing about which someone says, 'This is mine,' the stories of both men will come in front of the judges. Whoever the judges say is guilty will pay his neighbor twice as much as the loss.

10 "If a man gives his neighbor a donkey, bull, sheep or any animal to keep for him, and it dies or is hurt or is driven away while no one is looking, 11 the two men will make a promise before the Lord that he has not taken what belongs to his neighbor. The owner will take his word for it. And he will not make him pay for the loss. 12 But if it is stolen from him, he will pay the owner for the loss. 13 If the animal is torn to pieces, let him bring it to prove what happened. He will not pay for what has been torn to pieces.

14 "If a man asks to use anything that belongs to his neighbor, and it gets hurt or dies while its owner is not with it, the man who was using it will pay for the loss. 15 If its owner is with it, the man who was using it will not pay for the loss. If he paid money to use it, then the loss is paid for.

Laws about Right Living

16 "If a man tempts a woman who has never had a man and is not promised in marriage, and lies with her, he must pay a wedding gift for her to be his wife. 17 If her father will not give her to him, he will pay the wedding gift that is to be paid for women who have never had a man.

18 "Do not allow a woman to live who does witchcraft. 19 Whoever does sex sins with an animal will be put to death.

20 "He who gives a gift in worship to any god other than the Lord alone will

be destroyed. 21 Do not do wrong to a stranger or make it hard for him. For you were strangers in the land of Egypt. 22 Do not bring trouble to any woman whose husband has died or any child whose parents have died. 23 If you bring them trouble, and they cry out to Me, for sure I will hear their cry. 24 My anger will burn and I will kill you with the sword. Then your wives will lose their husbands. And your children will lose their fathers.

25 "If you let any of the poor among My people use your money, do not act toward him like one who is owed money. And do not make him pay you for the use of it. 26 If you ever take your neighbor's coat to keep while he owes you money, return it to him before the sun goes down. 27 For that is his only covering. It is his clothing for his body. What else will he sleep in? When he cries out to Me, I will hear him. For I have loving-pity.

28 "Do not curse God, or a ruler of your people. 29 Do not wait before giving Me a gift from your gathered grain and the fruit of your fields. You will give to Me the first-born of your sons. 30 You will do the same with your cattle and your sheep. The first-born will be with its mother seven days. On the eighth day you will give it to Me. 31 You will be holy men to Me. So you will not eat any flesh torn to pieces in the field. You will throw it to the dogs.

Different Laws

23 "Do not tell a lie about someone else. Do not join with the sinful to say something that will hurt someone. 2 Do not follow many people in doing wrong. When telling what you know in a trial, do not agree with many people by saying what is not true. 3 And do not show favor to a poor man when he has a problem.

4 "If you meet a bull or donkey that belongs to a man who hates you, be sure to return the animal to him. 5 If you see the donkey of one who hates you falling under its load, do not leave the problem to him. Help him to free the animal. 6 Do not keep from doing what is right and fair in trying to help a poor brother when he has a problem. 7 Do not lie against someone. And do not kill those who are right and good or those who are not guilty. For I will not free the guilty. 8 Do not take pay in secret for wrong-doing. For such pay blinds the one who sees well and destroys the words of a good man. 9 Do not make it hard for a stranger because you know how

a stranger feels. You were strangers in the land of Egypt.

Seventh Year and Seventh Day

10 "You will plant seeds in your land for six years, and gather the grain. 11 But in the seventh year you will let the land rest without planting. So your people who are in need may eat. Whatever they leave, the animals may eat. You are to do the same with your grape-fields and olive trees. 12 You will work six days and rest on the seventh day. So your bull and your donkey may rest. And the son of your female servant, and the stranger, may get their strength again. 13 Be careful to do all I have said to you. Never speak the name of other gods. Do not let them be heard from your mouth.

Three Great Suppers

14 "Three times a year you will have a special supper to honor Me. 15 You will have the special supper of bread made without yeast. For seven days you are to eat bread without yeast at the time I tell you in the month of Abib. For you came out of Egypt during this month. And no one will come before Me with nothing in his hands. 16 You will have the special supper of the gathering time of the first-fruits of your work, of all you plant in the field. And you will have the special supper of gathering at the end of the year when you gather in the fruit of your work from the field. 17 Three times a year all your males will come before the Lord God.

18 "Do not give the blood of My gift of worship with bread made with yeast. And the fat of My special supper is not to be kept all night until morning. 19 Bring the best first-fruits of your land to the house of the Lord your God. Do not boil the meat of a young goat in its mother's milk.

The Angel and the Promises

20 "See, I am sending an angel before you to keep you safe on the way. He will bring you to the place I have made ready. 21 Listen to him and obey his voice. Do not turn against him, for he will not forgive your sins, because My name is in him. 22 But if you obey his voice and do all that I say, then I will hate those who hate you and fight against those who fight against you. 23 For My angel will go before you and bring you into the land of the Amorites, the Hittites, the Perizzites, the Canaanites, the Hivites and the Jebusites. And I

will destroy them. 24 Do not worship their gods, or serve them, or act like them. But you are to destroy them and break their pillars of worship to pieces. 25 Serve the Lord your God and He will give you bread and water. And I will take sickness from among you. 26 Women in your land will not lose their babies before they are born, and will be able to give birth. I will give you a full life. 27 I will send My fear before you. The people you meet will be afraid. And I will make all those who hate you run away from you. 28 I will send hornets before you. They will drive out the Hivites, the Canaanites and the Hittites before you come. 29 I will not move them out of your way in one year. So the land will not become a waste, and the animals of the field become too many for you. 30 I will drive them out a few at a time, until you become many and take the land for your own. 31 I will give you the land from the Red Sea to the sea of the Philistines, and from the desert to the Euphrates River. For I will give you power over the people of the land. And you will drive them away from you. 32 Make no agreement with them or their gods. 33 They are not to live in your land, or they will make you sin against Me. If you worship their gods, for sure it will be a trap to you."

Israel Agrees

24 Then He said to Moses, "Come up to the Lord, you and Aaron, Nadab, Abihu and seventy of the leaders of Israel and worship from far away. 2 But Moses alone may come near the Lord. The others should not come near and should not come up with him."

3 Moses came and told the people all the Lord said and all the Laws. All the people answered with one voice, saying, "We will do all that the Lord has spoken." 4 Moses wrote all the words of the Lord. He got up early the next morning and built an altar at the base of the mountain, with twelve pillars, one for each of the twelve families of Israel. 5 Then he sent young men of Israel, who gave burnt gifts and killed young bulls as gifts of peace given in worship to the Lord. 6 Moses took half of the blood and put it in pots. The other half of the blood he put upon the altar. 7 Then he took the Book of the Agreement and read it for the people to hear. They said, "We will do all that the Lord has spoken. We will obey." 8 So Moses took the blood and put some on the people. He said, "See, the blood of

the agreement, which the Lord has made with you in these words."

9 Then Moses went up with Aaron, Nadab, Abihu and seventy of the leaders of Israel. 10 And they saw the God of Israel. The ground under His feet looked like sapphire stone, as clear as the sky itself. 11 He did not let His hand come against the leaders of Israel. But they saw God, and ate and drank.

Moses on Mount Sinai

12 The Lord said to Moses, "Come up to Me on the mountain and stay there. I will give you the pieces of stone with the Law which I have written for you to teach the people." 13 Then Moses got up with his helper Joshua, and Moses went up on the mountain of God. 14 He said to the leaders, "Wait here until we return to you. See, Aaron and Hur are with you. Let whoever has a problem go to them." 15 Then Moses went up on the mountain, which was covered with a cloud. 16 The shining-greatness of the Lord rested on Mount Sinai. And the cloud covered it for six days. On the seventh day He called to Moses from the cloud. 17 To the people of Israel, the shining-greatness of the Lord looked like a fire that destroys on the mountain-top. 18 Moses went into the cloud as he went up on the mountain. And Moses was on the mountain forty days and forty nights.

Gifts Given in Worship

25 The Lord said to Moses, 2 "Tell the people of Israel to take a gift for Me. Receive the gift for Me from every person whose heart makes him willing. 3 This is the gift you are to receive from them: Gold, silver and brass, 4 blue, purple and red cloth, fine linen, goat hair, 5 rams' skins made red, badgers' skins, acacia wood, 6 lamp oil, spices for the oil used in worship and for perfumes, 7 onyx stones, and stones to be set in the clothing of the religious leaders. 8 Let them make a holy place for Me, so I may live among them. 9 Make the meeting tent and all that is in it like the plans I am going to show you.

The Special Box of the Agreement

10 "They will make a special box of acacia wood, two and a half cubits long, one and a half cubits wide, and one and a half cubits tall. 11 Cover it inside and out with pure gold. And make a piece of gold to put on it all around. 12 Make four gold rings for it and put them on its four feet. Put two rings

on one side of it and two rings on the other side. ¹³ Cut long pieces of acacia wood for carrying and cover them with gold. ¹⁴ Then put the pieces of wood through the rings on the sides of the box, for carrying the box. ¹⁵ The long pieces will stay in the rings of the box. They must not be taken out. ¹⁶ Put into the special box the Law which I will give you. ¹⁷ Then make a mercy-seat from pure gold, two and a half cubits long and one and a half cubits wide. ¹⁸ Make two cherubim out of beaten gold. Make them at the two ends of the mercy-seat. ¹⁹ Make one cherub on one end and one cherub on the other end. Make the top of the mercy-seat, with the cherubim at each end, of one piece. ²⁰ The wings of the cherubim should spread up over the mercy-seat. Their faces should be toward each other, and toward the mercy-seat. ²¹ Put the mercy-seat on top of the box. Put the Law which I will give you into the box. ²² I will meet with you there. Between the two cherubim which are upon the special box of the Law, I will speak to you about all the Laws I will give you for the people of Israel.

The Table for the Holy Bread

²³ "Make a table of acacia wood, two cubits long, one cubit wide, and one and a half cubits tall. ²⁴ Cover it with pure gold and make a gold piece around it. ²⁵ Make a piece around it as wide as a hand and put gold on the side of this piece all around. ²⁶ Make four rings of gold for it. Put them on the four corners that are on the table's four legs. ²⁷ The rings will be close to the sides, to hold the long pieces of wood used to carry the table. ²⁸ Cut the long, straight pieces of acacia wood and cover them with gold. The table will be carried with these. ²⁹ Make its plates, its pots and its jars, for pouring your gifts of drink. Make them of pure gold. ³⁰ And set the holy bread on the table before Me all the time.

³¹ "Then make a lamp-stand of pure gold. The lamp-stand and its base are to be made of beaten gold. Its cups, its buds, and its flowers will be of one piece with it. ³² Six branches will go out of its sides, three branches of the lamp-stand out of one side, and three branches out of its other side. ³³ Three cups will be made to look like almond flowers, each with bud and flower on one branch, and three on the next branch. This is to be done for all six branches going out of the lamp-stand. ³⁴ Four cups made to look like almond

flowers, with their buds and flowers, will be put on the lamp-stand's base. ³⁵ Make a bud under each of the six branches going out from the place where the lamp-stand is put. ³⁶ Their buds and their branches will all be one piece with the lamp-stand of pure, beaten gold. ³⁷ Then make the seven lamps and put them where they will give light to the space in front of it. ³⁸ The objects for putting out the light and their dishes will be of pure gold. ³⁹ Make it and all the objects for it out of a piece of gold about half the weight of a man. ⁴⁰ See that you make them by following the plan for them that was shown to you on the mountain.

The Meeting Tent

26 "Make the meeting tent with ten curtains of fine linen, blue and purple and red. Make them with cherubim sewed into them by an able workman. ² Each curtain will be as long as fourteen long steps, and as wide as two long steps, all of them the same. ³ Five curtains will be joined to one another. And the other five curtains will be joined to one another. ⁴ Take small pieces of blue cloth, longer than they are wide. Sew both ends to the side of the last curtain in the first group. Then do the same on the side of the last curtain in the second group. ⁵ Put fifty of these pieces on the one curtain. And put fifty on the side of the other curtain, so that the pieces meet each other. ⁶ Make fifty hooks of gold and join the curtains together with the hooks so the meeting tent will be as one.

⁷ "Make curtains of goat hair for a covering over the meeting tent. Make eleven curtains in all. ⁸ Each curtain will be as long as fifteen long steps, and as wide as two long steps, all of them the same. ⁹ Join five curtains by themselves and six curtains by themselves. Lay the sixth curtain over the front of the meeting tent twice. ¹⁰ Take fifty small pieces of cloth, longer than they are wide. Sew both ends of each to the side of the last curtain in the first group. Then sew fifty pieces onto the side of the last curtain in the second group. ¹¹ Make fifty hooks of brass. Put the hooks through the sewed pieces of cloth and join the tent together as one. ¹² The part that is left of the tent's curtains, the half curtain, will lie over the back of the meeting tent. ¹³ There will be parts of the tent's curtains left over on each side, about a cubit. These will hang over each side of the meeting

tent to cover it. 14 Make a covering for the tent of rams' skins made red, and a covering over that of badgers' skins.

15 "Then make the standing pieces of wood for the meeting tent out of acacia wood. 16 Each piece of wood will be as long as five long steps, and as wide as one step. 17 Make two joint-pieces in each piece of wood for joining them together. Do this for all the pieces of wood of the meeting tent. 18 Set up twenty pieces of wood for the south side of the meeting tent. 19 Make forty silver bases under the twenty pieces of wood, with two holes in each one for joining the two joint-pieces on each piece of wood. 20 Cut twenty pieces of wood for the north side of the meeting tent. 21 And make forty silver bases, two under each piece of wood. 22 Then cut six pieces of wood for the back or west side of the meeting tent. 23 Cut two pieces of wood for the back corners. 24 They will be apart at the bottom, and joined at the top with one ring. They will both be made the same and will make the two corners. 25 There will be eight special pieces of wood and their silver bases with sixteen holes, two holes under each piece of wood.

26 "Then make cross-pieces of acacia wood, five for the pieces of wood on one side of the meeting tent, 27 and five for the pieces of wood on the other side of the meeting tent. Then make five for the pieces of wood at the back of the meeting tent to the west side. 28 The long, cross-piece for the center of the standing pieces of wood will go through from end to end. 29 Cover the standing pieces of wood with gold. Make rings of gold to hold the cross-pieces and cover these pieces with gold. 30 Build the meeting tent by following the plan for it that was shown to you on the mountain.

31 "Make a curtain of blue and purple and red cloth and fine linen. It will be made with cherubim sewed into it by an able workman. 32 Hang it on four strong pillars of acacia wood covered with gold. Their hooks will be made of gold also. And the pillars will stand on four silver bases. 33 Hang the top of the curtain from the hooks. Then bring the box of the Law within the curtain. This curtain will divide the holy place from the Holiest Place of All. 34 Put the mercy-seat on the box of the Law in the Holiest Place of All. 35 Set the table outside the curtain. Put the lampstand on the south side of the meeting tent. And put the table on the north side.

36 "Make another curtain of fine linen for the door of the tent. It will be made of blue and purple and red cloth by an able workman. 37 Hang it on five pillars of acacia wood covered with gold. Make their hooks of gold. And make five brass bases for them.

The Altar

27 "Make the altar of acacia wood. It will be as long and as wide as three steps, and as tall as a man's chest. 2 Make horns for it on its four corners. They will be of one piece and covered with brass. 3 Make its pails for taking away its ashes, its tools for picking up the ashes, its pots, meat-hooks and fire-holders. Make all of these out of brass. 4 Make a net for it out of brass, with four rings of brass at its four corners. 5 Put it under the altar so that the net comes up to the center of the altar. 6 Make long, straight pieces of acacia wood for the altar. And cover them with brass. 7 Put the long pieces of wood through the rings on each side of the altar when it is carried. 8 Make the altar with pieces of wood so it is empty inside. Make it as it was shown to you on the mountain.

The Open Spaces

9 "Make the open space of the meeting tent. On the south side there will be curtains for the open space. Make them of fine linen, as long as fifty long steps. 10 They will hang from twenty pillars which are put on twenty bases of brass. The hooks of the pillars and their rings will be made of silver. 11 Do the same for the north side. There will be curtains as long as fifty long steps, and twenty pillars with twenty bases of brass. The hooks of the pillars and their rings will be made of silver. 12 On the west side of the open space there will be curtains as long as twenty-five long steps. They will have ten pillars with ten bases. 13 And the east side of the open space will be as wide as twenty-five long steps.

14 "The curtains for one side of the gate will be as long as seven steps. They will have three pillars with three bases. 15 On the other side there will be curtains as long as seven steps, with three pillars and three bases. 16 Have an able workman make a curtain out of fine linen for the gate of the open space. It will be blue, purple and red, and as long as ten long steps. It will have four pillars with four bases. 17 All the pillars around the open space will have silver hooks, silver rings, and their bases of

brass. 18 The open space will be as long as fifty long steps, as wide as twenty-five long steps, and as high as a man raises his hand. It will have curtains of fine linen and the bases will be brass. 19 All the tools used in the meeting tent, all its nails, and all the nails for the open space will be made of brass.

Care of the Lamp-Stand

20 "Tell the people of Israel to bring you clear oil of beaten olives for the light, so a lamp may burn all the time. 21 In the meeting tent, outside the curtain which is in front of the Law, Aaron and his sons take care of it from evening until morning before the Lord. It will be a law forever for the people of Israel.

Clothes for Religious Leaders

28 "Take from among the people of Israel your brother Aaron and his sons, Nadab, Abihu, Eleazar and Ithamar, to work for Me as religious leaders. 2 Make holy clothing for your brother Aaron, for honor and for beauty. 3 Tell all the able workmen, whom I have given the spirit of wisdom, to make Aaron's clothing to set him apart for My work. He will work for Me as a religious leader. 4 These are the clothes they will make: A breast-piece, a linen vest, a long piece of clothing, a long coat, a head-covering, and a wide belt. They will make holy clothing for your brother Aaron and his sons to work for Me as religious leaders. 5 They will use gold and blue and purple and red cloth and fine linen.

The Linen Vest

6 "They will use gold and blue, purple and red cloth and fine linen to make the linen vest that holds the breast-piece. It will be the work of the able workman. 7 It will have two shoulder pieces to join it at the two ends. 8 The well-made belt on it will be made of the same gold and blue, purple and red cloth and fine linen. 9 Take two onyx stones and cut on them the names of Israel's sons. 10 Put six of their names on one stone, and the six names of the others on the other stone, from the oldest to the youngest. 11 As an able workman cuts words in a ring, cut the names of Israel's sons on the two stones. Then set them into beautiful pieces of gold. 12 Put the two stones on the shoulder pieces of the linen vest, as stones for the family groups of Israel to be remembered. Aaron

will carry their names on his two shoulders before the Lord, to be remembered. 13 Make beautiful pieces of gold 14 and two chains of pure gold. Make them like ropes are made. And put the chains on the pieces of gold.

The Breast-Piece

15 "Make a breast-piece to be used when judging. It is to be made by an able workman. Make it like the work of the linen vest, of gold, and blue, purple and red cloth and fine linen. 16 It will be as long as it is wide, with one half laid over the other. Make it as long and as wide as a man's fingers can spread. 17 Put four straight rows of stones on it. The first row will be a ruby, a topaz and an emerald. 18 The second row will be a turquoise, a sapphire and a diamond. 19 The third row will be a jacinth, an agate and an amethyst. 20 And the fourth row will be a beryl, an onyx and a jasper. They will be set in beautiful pieces of gold. 21 There will be twelve stones, one for each name of the sons of Israel. The name of each family group will be cut on one of these special stones. 22 Make chains for the breast-piece, like ropes of pure gold. 23 And make two rings of gold and put them on the two ends of the breast-piece. 24 Join the two gold chains to the two rings at the ends of the breast-piece. 25 Join the other two ends of the two chains to the beautiful gold pieces that hold the two stones at the shoulders in the front. 26 Make two rings of gold to put on the two ends of the breast-piece, on the inside, next to the linen vest. 27 Then make two rings of gold and put them on the bottom of the two shoulder pieces of the linen vest in front, near where they join. They will be above the well-made belt of the linen vest. 28 Tie the rings of the breast-piece to the rings of the linen vest with a blue rope so the breast-piece may not come loose from the linen vest.

29 "Aaron will carry the names of the sons of Israel over his heart on the breast-piece of judging when he goes in the holy place, so they will be remembered before the Lord all the time.

Other Religious Leaders' Clothes

30 "Put the Urim and the Thummim into the breast-piece over Aaron's heart when he goes before the Lord. Aaron will carry the judging of the people of Israel over his heart before the Lord all the time.

31 "Make the long piece of clothing all of

blue. 32 There will be an opening at its top in the center. Around the opening it will be sewed like the opening on heavy battle-clothes, so it may not be torn. 33 Make pomegranates of blue and purple and red cloth to put all around the bottom of this clothing. And put bells of gold between them. 34 Put a gold bell and a pomegranate, then a gold bell and a pomegranate, all the way around the bottom of this clothing. 35 Aaron will wear it when he serves Me. The sound of the bells will be heard when he goes in the holy place and when he comes out so that he will not die.

36 "Make a plate of pure gold and write on it, 'Holy to the Lord.' 37 Put it to the front of the head-covering with a blue rope. 38 It will be on Aaron's forehead. Aaron will take away the sin of the holy things which the people of Israel set apart for the Lord as their holy gifts. It will always be on his forehead, so they may be received by the Lord. 39 Make the long coat of fine linen, a head-covering of fine linen, and a wide belt, the work of an able workman.

40 "Make long coats for Aaron's sons. And make belts and head-coverings for them, for honor and for beauty. 41 Dress your brother Aaron and his sons in them. Then pour oil on them, set them apart and make them holy, so they may serve Me as religious leaders. 42 Make for them linen clothing to cover their flesh from their belts to their legs. 43 Aaron and his sons will wear them when they go into the meeting tent, or when they go near the altar to serve in the holy place. Then they will not be guilty and die. It will be a law for him and for his children forever.

Aaron and His Sons Set Apart

29 "This is what you will do to set them apart to serve as religious leaders for Me. Take one young bull and two rams that are perfect. 2 Have bread without yeast, and bread mixed with oil, and hard bread made without yeast and spread with oil. Make them of fine grain flour. 3 Put them in one basket. Then bring them in the basket with the bull and the two rams. 4 Bring Aaron and his sons to the door of the meeting tent, and wash them with water. 5 Take the clothing and dress Aaron in the long coat, the clothing over the linen vest, the linen vest, and the breast-piece. Put on him the well-made belt of the linen vest. 6 Put the covering on his head, and the holy crown on the head-covering. 7 Then take the oil for holy use

and pour it on his head to set him apart for My work. 8 Bring his sons and dress them with long coats. 9 Put belts on Aaron and his sons. Tie head-coverings on them. And they will be religious leaders by law for all time. So you will set apart Aaron and his sons for My work.

10 "Then bring the bull in front of the meeting tent. Aaron and his sons will lay their hands on the head of the bull. 11 Then kill the bull before the Lord at the door of the meeting tent. 12 Take some of the blood of the bull and put it on the horns of the altar with your finger. Then pour out all the blood at the base of the altar. 13 Take all the fat that covers the inside parts, and the part that is on the liver, and the two kidneys with the fat that is on them, and burn them on the altar. 14 But the flesh of the bull, its skin, and its waste you will burn away from the tents. It is a sin gift.

15 "Then take one of the rams and have Aaron and his sons lay their hands on the head of the ram. 16 Kill the ram and take its blood and put it around the altar. 17 Cut the ram into pieces. Wash its inside parts and its legs. And put them with its pieces and its head. 18 Burn the whole ram on the altar for a burnt gift in worship to the Lord. It is a pleasing smell, a gift by fire to the Lord.

19 "Then take the other ram and have Aaron and his sons lay their hands on the ram's head. 20 Kill the ram and put some of its blood on the bottom of Aaron's right ear, on the bottom of his sons' right ears, on the thumbs of their right hands, and on the big toes of their right feet. Put the rest of the blood around the altar. 21 Take some of the blood from the altar and some of the special oil. Put some on Aaron and his sons and their clothing. So Aaron and his sons and their clothing will be set apart and made holy. 22 Take the fat from the ram, the fat tail, the fat that covers the inside parts, the part that is on the liver, the two kidneys with their fat, and the fat that is on the right thigh. For it is a ram used to set apart those who work for Me. 23 And take one loaf of bread, and one loaf of bread mixed with oil, and one piece of hard bread from the basket of bread without yeast that is set before the Lord. 24 Put all these in the hands of Aaron and his sons. They will wave them for a wave gift before the Lord. 25 Then take them from their hands and burn them on the altar for a burnt gift in worship. It is a

pleasing smell before the Lord. It is a gift by fire to the Lord.

26 "Take the breast of Aaron's ram used to set him apart. Wave it as a wave gift before the Lord. And it will be your share. 27 Then set apart the breast of the wave gift and the thigh that was waved and given from the ram used to set apart those who work for Me. One was for Aaron and one for his sons. 28 It will be for Aaron and his sons as their share forever from the people of Israel. For it is the religious leaders' share to be given by the people of Israel from their peace gifts. It is their gift to the Lord.

29 "The holy clothing of Aaron will be for his sons after him. They will wear them when the oil for holy use is poured on them and they are set apart for My work. 30 The son who takes his place as religious leader will wear them seven days as he goes into the meeting tent to serve in the holy place. 31 "Take the ram used to set apart those who work for Me and boil its flesh in a holy place. 32 Aaron and his sons will eat the flesh of the ram, and the bread that is in the basket, at the door of the meeting tent. 33 They will eat those things that were used in worship when they were forgiven of their sin and when they were set apart for My work. But one who is not a religious leader may not eat them, because they are holy. 34 If any of the meat or bread used to set apart those who work for Me is left until morning, it must be burned. It must not be eaten, because it is holy.

35 "Do to Aaron and his sons all I have told you. For seven days you will set them apart for My work. 36 Give a bull each day for a sin gift, to take away sin. Make the altar clean by taking sin away from it and pour special oil on it to set it apart for Me. 37 For seven days give gifts upon the altar to take away sin and set it apart for Me. Then the altar will be most holy. And whatever touches the altar will be holy.

The Gifts Given Each Day

38 "Now this is what you will give on the altar: Two lambs one year old, given every day. 39 Give one lamb in the morning, and the other lamb in the evening. 40 With the first lamb give a jar of fine flour mixed with a half jar of beaten oil, and a half jar of wine to be poured out. 41 Give the other lamb in the evening. Do it with a grain gift and a gift to pour out as in the morning. It has a pleasing smell, a gift by fire to the

Lord. 42 For all time to come this burnt gift is to be given at the door of the meeting tent before the Lord. There I will meet with you and speak to you. 43 I will meet there with the people of Israel. It will be set apart by My shining-greatness. 44 I will set apart the meeting tent and the altar. And I will set apart Aaron and his sons to work as religious leaders for Me. 45 I will live among the people of Israel and will be their God. 46 They will know that I am the Lord their God, Who brought them out of the land of Egypt to live among them. I am the Lord their God.

The Altar for Special Perfume

30 "Make an altar for burning special perfume. Make it of acacia wood. 2 It will be as long and as wide as a man's arm and as high as a man's waist. Its horns will be of one piece with it. 3 Cover its top, all its sides and its horns with pure gold. And make a piece of gold to go around it. 4 Then make two gold rings for the altar to put under this piece. Put one on each side of the altar so it can hold the long pieces of wood used for carrying it. 5 Make the long pieces of acacia wood and cover them with gold. 6 Put this altar in front of the curtain that is by the box of the Law, in front of the mercy-seat that is over the box of the Law. There I will meet with you. 7 Aaron will burn special perfume on it every morning when he takes care of the lamps. 8 And when Aaron takes care of the lamps in the evening, he will burn special perfume. There will be a burning of special perfume before the Lord for all your people for all time. 9 Do not give upon this altar any perfume, burnt gift or grain gift that is not holy. And do not pour out a drink gift on it. 10 Once a year Aaron will give a gift for sin on its horns to take away sin. He will give the blood of the sin gift to make it holy once a year for all your people for all time. It is most holy to the Lord."

Tax for the Meeting Tent

11 The Lord said to Moses, 12 "When you number the people of Israel, each one of them will pay a price for his life to the Lord. Then no trouble will come upon them when you number them. 13 Every one who is numbered will give one piece of silver, by the weight decided upon for the holy place. One piece of silver will be a gift to the Lord. 14 Every one who is numbered, twenty years old and older, will give the gift to the Lord. 15 The rich

will not pay more and the poor will not pay less than one piece of silver. It will be a gift to the Lord so you will be forgiven of sin. 16 Receive this money from the people of Israel and use it for the work of the meeting tent. Then it will be remembered before the Lord that the people of Israel gave a gift to take away their sin of being numbered."

The Pot of Brass for Washing

17 The Lord said to Moses, 18 "Make a pot of brass for washing. Make its base of brass also. Put it between the meeting tent and the altar, and put water in it. 19 Aaron and his sons will wash their hands and feet with water from it. 20 When they go into the meeting tent, they will wash with water, so they will not die. And they will wash when they go near the altar to give a gift made by fire to the Lord. 21 They will wash their hands and their feet, so they will not die. It will always be a law for Aaron and his children forever."

The Holy Oil for Pouring

22 The Lord said to Moses, 23 "Take the best spices: a heavy weight of flowing myrrh, half that weight of sweet-smelling cinnamon and of sweet-smelling cane, 24 and a heavy weight of cassia, the weight decided upon by the holy place, and a large jar of olive oil. 25 Mix these to make a holy oil for holy use, mixed like perfume made by an able workman. It will be a holy oil for holy use. 26 Pour it on the meeting tent and the box of the Law, 27 the table and all its objects, the lamp-stand and all its objects, the altar of special perfume, 28 the altar of burnt gifts and all its objects, and the washing pot and its base. 29 Set them apart so they may be most holy. Whatever touches them will be holy. 30 Pour oil on Aaron and his sons. Set them apart so they may serve as religious leaders for Me. 31 Say to the people of Israel, 'This will be a holy oil to Me for all your people for all time. 32 It will not be poured on the flesh of man. And you will not mix any like it. It is holy. It will be holy to you. 33 Whoever mixes any like it, or puts any of it on a man who is not a religious leader, will be cut off from his people.' "

34 The Lord said to Moses, "Take sweet spices, stacte, onycha and galbanum, spices with pure frankincense. Take the same amount of each. 35 Mix them to make a special perfume, salted, pure and holy, the work of an able workman.

36 Beat some of it very fine. And put some of it in front of the special box of the agreement in the meeting tent, where I will meet with you. It will be most holy to you. 37 Do not mix this special perfume in the same way for yourselves. It will be holy for you to the Lord. 38 Whoever makes any like it to use as perfume will be cut off from his people."

Builders of the Meeting Tent

31 The Lord said to Moses, 2 "See, I have called by name Bezalel, the son of Uri, the son of Hur, of the family of Judah. 3 I have filled him with the Spirit of God in wisdom, understanding, much learning, and all kinds of special work. 4 He will plan good work in gold, silver and brass, 5 in cutting stones to set, and in cutting wood, for all kinds of good work. 6 And see, I have given Aholiab the son of Ahisamach, of the family of Dan to help him. I have put wisdom in the hearts of all who are wise, so they may make all that I have told you: 7 the meeting tent, the box of the Law, the mercy-seat upon it, and all the objects of the tent, 8 the table and its objects, the pure gold lamp-stand with all its objects, the altar of special perfume, 9 the altar of burnt gifts with all its objects, the washing pot and its base, 10 the well-made clothing, the holy clothing for Aaron the religious leader, the clothing for his sons for their work as religious leaders, 11 the oil for holy use, and the sweet-smelling perfume for the holy place. Have them do all I have told you."

The Day of Rest

12 The Lord said to Moses, 13 "Say to the people of Israel, 'Keep My Days of Rest. For this is something special between Me and you for all your people forever. So you may know that I am the Lord Who sets you apart for Myself. 14 You will keep the Day of Rest, for it is holy to you. Every one who does what is sinful on this day will be put to death for sure. Whoever does any work on this day will be cut off from among his people. 15 Work may be done for six days. But the seventh day is a Day of Rest, holy to the Lord. Whoever does any work on the Day of Rest will be put to death for sure. 16 So the people of Israel will keep the Day of Rest as a special day for all their people for all time, as an agreement forever.' 17 It is something special between Me and the people of Israel forever. For the Lord made heaven and earth in six

days. But He stopped working and rested on the seventh day."

¹⁸ When the Lord had finished speaking with Moses on Mount Sinai, He gave him the two stone writings of the Law, pieces of stone written on by the finger of God.

The Gold Calf

32 When the people saw that Moses was staying a long time before coming down from the mountain, they gathered around Aaron, and said, "Come, make a god for us who will go in front of us. For we do not know what has become of Moses, the man who brought us out of the land of Egypt." ² Aaron said to them, "Take the objects of gold from the ears of your wives, your sons and your daughters, and bring them to me." ³ So all the people took the gold objects from their ears and brought them to Aaron. ⁴ He took the gold from their hands, worked on it with a sharp tool, and by melting it, made it into a calf. Then they said, "This is your god, O Israel, who brought you out of the land of Egypt." ⁵ When Aaron saw this, he built an altar in front of it. Aaron said to all the people, "Tomorrow will be a special supper to the Lord." ⁶ So the next day they got up early and gave burnt gifts and peace gifts. The people sat down to eat and drink, and got up to play.

⁷ Then the Lord said to Moses, "Go down. For your people, whom you brought out of the land of Egypt, have turned to sin. ⁸ They have been quick to turn aside from the way I have told them. They have melted gold and made a calf for them selves. They have worshiped it, have given gifts to it, and have said, 'This is your god, O Israel, who brought you out of the land of Egypt!' " ⁹ The Lord said to Moses, "I have seen this people, and see, they are a strong-willed people. ¹⁰ Now let Me alone, so My anger may be against them and I may destroy them. But I will make you into a great nation."

¹¹ Then Moses begged the Lord his God, saying, "O Lord, why are you very angry against Your people whom You brought out of the land of Egypt with great power and a strong hand? ¹² Why should the Egyptians say, 'He brought them out to kill them in the mountains and destroy them from the earth'? Turn from Your anger and change Your mind about destroying Your people. ¹³ Remember Abraham, Isaac and Israel, who were your servants. You promised them by Yourself, saying,

'I will make your children become as many as the stars of the heavens. And I will give all this land I have spoken about to your children. It will be theirs forever.' " ¹⁴ So the Lord changed His mind about the things He said He would do to His people.

¹⁵ Then Moses turned and went down from the mountain with the two stone writings of the Law in his hand. The stones were written on both sides, on one side and the other. ¹⁶ The stone writings were God's work. The writing was God's writing cut into the stones. ¹⁷ When Joshua heard the sound of the people as they made noise, he said to Moses, "There is a sound of war at the tents." ¹⁸ But Moses said, "It is not the sound of winning, or the sound of losing. It is the sound of singing I hear." ¹⁹ As soon as Moses came near the tents, he saw the calf and the dancing. Moses became very angry. He threw the stone writings from his hands and broke them at the base of the mountain. ²⁰ And he took the calf they had made and burned it with fire, ground it to dust, spread it over the top of the water, and made the people of Israel drink it.

²¹ Then Moses said to Aaron, "What did this people do to you to make you bring such great sin upon them?" ²² Aaron said, "Do not let my lord be angry. You know the people yourself and how sinful they are. ²³ They said to me, 'Make a god for us who will go in front of us. For we do not know what has become of Moses, the man who brought us out of the land of Egypt.' ²⁴ And I said to them, 'Whoever has any gold, let them take it off.' So they gave it to me. I threw it into the fire and out came this calf."

²⁵ Moses saw that Aaron had let the people go wild and become a shame to those who hated them. ²⁶ So Moses stood in the gate of the place where they had set up their tents and said, "Whoever is for the Lord, come to me!" And all the sons of Levi came together around him. ²⁷ He said to them, "This is what the Lord, the God of Israel, says: 'Every man put his sword on his thigh. And go from one end of the tents to the other, and each one kill his brother, his friend, and his neighbor.' " ²⁸ So the sons of Levi did as Moses said. About 3,000 men fell that day. ²⁹ Then Moses said, "Today you have set yourselves apart for the Lord. For each man has been against his son and against his brother, so the Lord may bring good to you today."

³⁰ The next day Moses said to the people,

"You have sinned. Now I am going up to the Lord. It might be that I can have your sin forgiven." 31 Then Moses returned to the Lord and said, "O, this people have sinned. They have made a god of gold for themselves. 32 But now, if You will, forgive their sin. If not, then take my name out of Your book which You have written." 33 The Lord said to Moses, "I will put out of My book whoever has sinned against Me. 34 But go now. Lead the people where I told you. See, My angel will go before you. But in the day when I punish, I will punish them for their sin." 35 Then the Lord sent trouble upon the people, because of what they did with the calf Aaron had made.

Israel Leaves Mount Sinai

33 The Lord said to Moses, "Go away from this place, you and the people you have brought out of the land of Egypt. Go to the land that I promised to Abraham, Isaac and Jacob, saying, 'I will give it to your children.' 2 I will send an angel before you. And I will drive out the Canaanite, the Amorite, the Hittite, the Perizzite, the Hivite, and the Jebusite. 3 Go up to a land flowing with milk and honey. But I will not go with you, because you are a strong-willed people and I might destroy you on the way." 4 When the people heard this bad news, they were filled with sorrow. None of them wore his objects of gold or silver. 5 For the Lord had said to Moses, "Say to the people of Israel, 'You are a strong-willed people. If I go with you even for just a little time, I would destroy you. So take off your objects of gold and silver that I may know what to do with you.'" 6 So the people of Israel took off all their objects of gold and silver at Mount Horeb.

Moses Meets with the Lord

7 Now Moses used to take the tent and set it up far away from the other tents. He called it the meeting tent. Anyone who wanted to meet with the Lord would go away from the other tents to the meeting tent. 8 When Moses went out to the tent, all the people would get up and stand at the doors of their tents. And they would watch Moses until he went into the meeting tent. 9 Whenever Moses went into the meeting tent, the cloud would come down and stand at the door of the tent. And the Lord would speak with Moses. 10 When all the people saw the cloud standing at the door of the meeting tent, they would stand up and worship, each at his tent door. 11 The Lord spoke to Moses face to face, as a man speaks to his friend. When Moses returned to the other tents, his servant Joshua, the son of Nun, a young man, would not leave the meeting tent.

God's Promise to Be with His People

12 Moses said to the Lord, "See, You say to me, 'Lead this people!' But You have not let me know whom You will send with me. Yet You said, 'I have known you by name. You have found favor in My eyes.' 13 So I pray to You, if I have found favor in Your eyes, let me know Your ways. Then I may know You and find favor in Your eyes. And keep in mind that this nation is Your people." 14 The Lord said, "I Myself will go with you. I will give you rest." 15 Then Moses said to Him, "If You Yourself do not go with us, do not have us leave this place. 16 For how will it be known that I and Your people have found favor in Your eyes, unless You go with us? Then I and Your people will be different from all the other people on the earth."

17 The Lord said to Moses, "I will do what you have said. For you have found favor in My eyes, and I have known you by name." 18 Moses said, "I pray to You, show me Your shining-greatness!" 19 And God said, "I will have My goodness pass in front of you. I will make the name of the Lord known in front of you. I will have loving-kindness and loving-pity for anyone I want to." 20 But He said, "You cannot see My face. For no man can see Me and live!" 21 Then the Lord said, "See, there is a place beside Me. You stand there on the rock. 22 While My shining-greatness is passing by, I will put you in the large crack of the rock. And I will cover you with My hand until I have passed by. 23 Then I will take My hand away and you will see My back. But My face will not be seen."

Moses Makes New Pieces of Stone

34 The Lord said to Moses, "Cut two pieces of stone like the first ones. And I will write on the stones the words that were on the first stones which you broke. 2 So be ready in the morning. Come up in the morning to Mount Sinai. And stand before Me on the top of the mountain. 3 No one is to come up with you. Do not let anyone be seen on the whole mountain. Even the sheep and the cattle may not eat in front of the mountain." 4 So Moses cut two pieces of stone like the first ones. Then he got up early in the morning and went up on Mount Sinai, as the Lord told him. And he took the two pieces of stone in his hand. 5 The Lord came down in the cloud and stood there with Moses as he called upon the name of the Lord. 6 Then the Lord passed by in front of him, saying, "The Lord, the Lord God, with loving-pity and loving-favor, slow to anger, filled with loving-kindness and truth, 7 keeping loving-kindness for thousands, forgiving wrong-doing and sin. But He will not let the guilty go without being punished. He brings the sin of fathers down upon the children, even the great-grandchildren." 8 Moses was quick to put his face to the ground and worship. 9 And Moses said, "O Lord, if I have found favor in Your eyes, I pray, let the Lord go with us, even if the people are strong-willed. Forgive our wrong-doing and our sin. And take us for Your own."

The Agreement Made Alive Again

10 Then God said, "See, I am going to make an agreement. I will do powerful works in front of all your people which have never been done on earth among any nation. All the people with whom you live will see the work of the Lord. For what I am going to do with you will fill people with fear. 11 Be sure to do what I am telling you this day. See, I am going to drive out of your way the Amorite, the Canaanite, the Hittite, the Perizzite, the Hivite, and the Jebusite. 12 Take care to make no agreement with the people of the land where you are going. It would be a trap to you. 13 Instead you are to tear down their altars, break their objects of worship, and cut down their false gods. 14 For you must not worship any other god. For the Lord, Whose name is Jealous, is a jealous God. 15 So do not make an agreement with the people of the land. Or when they follow their desire with their gods and give gifts to their gods, they would ask you to eat of their gift used in worship. 16 And you would marry your sons to their daughters who follow their gods. And they would lead your sons to follow their gods also. 17 Do not make any gods for yourself.

18 "Keep the special supper of bread without yeast. Eat bread without yeast for seven days as I told you, at the time set aside for it in the month of Abib. For you came out of Egypt in the month of Abib. 19 Every first born belongs to Me and all your male animals, the first-born from cattle and sheep. 20 But the life of a first-born donkey should be paid for with the blood of a lamb. If you do not pay for its life, you should break its neck. Pay for the life of all your first-born sons with the blood of a lamb. No one is to come before Me without a gift.

21 "Work six days, but rest on the seventh day. Rest even during plowing time and gathering time. 22 Have the special supper of weeks at the first gathering of grain. Have the special supper of gathering time at the end of the year. 23 Three times a year all your males are to come before the Lord God, the God of Israel. 24 For I will drive nations out of your way and give you more land. No man will desire to have your land when you go to show yourselves before the Lord your God.

25 "Do not give the blood of My gift together with bread made with yeast. Do not leave any of the gift of the special supper of the Passover until morning. 26 Bring the first of the first-fruits of your ground into the house of the Lord your God. Do not boil the meat of a young goat in its mother's milk."

27 The Lord said to Moses, "Write these words. For by these words I have made an agreement with you and with Israel." 28 Moses was there with the Lord forty days and forty nights. He did not eat bread or drink water. And he wrote on the stones the words of the agreement, the Ten Great Laws.

Moses Goes Down from Mount Sinai

29 Moses came down from Mount Sinai with the two stone writings in his hand. He did not know that the skin of his face was shining because of his speaking with the Lord. 30 When Aaron and all the people of Israel saw Moses, they saw that the skin of his face was shining. They were afraid to come near him. 31 But Moses called to them, and Aaron and all the leaders of the people returned to him. And Moses spoke to them. 32 After this all the people of Israel came near. Moses told them to do all the Lord had said to him on Mount Sinai. 33 When Moses had finished speaking with them, he covered his face with a piece of cloth. 34 But whenever Moses went before the Lord to speak with Him, he would take off the face-covering until he came out. Then he would tell the people of Israel what the Lord had said for them to do. 35 The people of Israel saw that the skin of Moses' face shone. So Moses would put the covering over his

face again until he went in to speak with the Lord.

The Seventh Day—a Holy Day

35 Then Moses gathered together all the people of Israel, saying, "These are the things that the Lord has told you to do. ² Work may be done for six days. But the seventh day will be a holy day for you, a Day of Rest to the Lord. Whoever does any work on this day will be put to death. ³ Do not make a fire in any of your tents on the Day of Rest."

Gifts for the Meeting Tent

⁴ Moses said to all the people of Israel, "This is what the Lord has told you to do. ⁵ Take from among you a gift to the Lord. Whoever has a willing heart, let him bring the Lord's gift: gold, silver and brass, ⁶ and blue, purple and red cloth, fine linen, cloth made from goat hair, ⁷ rams' skins made red, badgers' skins and acacia wood, ⁸ lamp oil, spices for the oil for holy use and for the sweet-smelling perfume, ⁹ onyx stones and stones to be set for the linen vest and the breast-piece.

Parts of the Meeting Tent

¹⁰ "Let every able workman among you come and make all that the Lord has told us to make: ¹¹ the meeting tent, its tent and its covering, its hooks, its wood pieces, its cross-pieces, its pillars and their bases, ¹² the special box of the agreement and the long pieces of wood for carrying it, the mercy-seat, the curtain to hang in front of it, ¹³ the table and the long pieces of wood for carrying it, all its objects, and the holy bread to set before the Lord. ¹⁴ Also the able workmen are to make: the lamp-stand for the light, and its lamps and oil for the light, ¹⁵ the altar of special perfume and the long pieces of wood for carrying it, the oil for holy use, the sweet-smelling perfume, and the curtain for the door of the meeting tent. ¹⁶ Also they are to make: the altar of burnt gifts with its brass net and long pieces of wood for carrying it, all its objects, the washing pot and its base, ¹⁷ the curtains of the open space, its pillars and its bases, and the curtain for the gate of the open space. ¹⁸ Also the able workmen are to make: the nails of the meeting tent and the nails of the open space and their ropes, ¹⁹ the well-made clothing for working in the holy place, the holy clothing for Aaron the religious leader, and the clothing for his sons as they work as religious leaders."

People Bring Their Gifts

²⁰ Then all the people of Israel went away from Moses. ²¹ And every one whose heart or spirit moved him brought the Lord's gift to be used for the meeting tent, for all its work, and for the holy clothing. ²² Then all the men and women who wanted to give brought objects of gold that had been worn on their clothing, ears, fingers and arms. Every man gave a gift of gold to the Lord. ²³ And every one who had blue, purple and red cloth, fine linen, cloth made from goats' hair, rams' skins made red, and badgers' skins, brought them. ²⁴ Every one who could give a gift of silver or brass brought it as a gift to the Lord. Every one who had acacia wood to be used for the work, brought it. ²⁵ All the able women made cloth with their hands. They brought the blue, purple and red cloth and fine linen they had made. ²⁶ All the able women whose hearts moved them made cloth from goat hair. ²⁷ The leaders brought the onyx stones and the stones to be set for the linen vest and the breast-piece, ²⁸ and the spice and the oil for the light, and the oil for holy use, and for the sweet-smelling perfume. ²⁹ The people of Israel who wanted to brought gifts to the Lord. Every man and woman, whose heart moved them, brought what the Lord had told them through Moses.

Workmen Called by God

³⁰ Then Moses said to the people of Israel, "See, the Lord has called by name Bezalel the son of Uri, the son of Hur, of the family of Judah. ³¹ The Lord has filled him with the Spirit of God, in wisdom, understanding, much learning, and in all work. ³² So he can make plans for working in gold, silver and brass, ³³ and cut stones to be set, cut wood, and do good work of every kind. ³⁴ The Lord has given him the power to teach also, both he and Oholiab, the son of Ahisamach, of the family of Dan. ³⁵ He has made them able to do every work: writing words in stone, gold, silver and brass, planning, sewing beautiful work on blue, purple and red cloth and fine linen, making cloth, and all kinds of work done by able workmen.

36 "Bezalel and Oholiab will do the work, together with every workman whom the Lord has made able and understands how to do all the work in the building of the holy place. They will do all that the Lord has said."

The People Bring More Than Enough

2 Then Moses called Bezalel and Oholiab and every workman whom the Lord had made able, every one whose heart moved him to come to do the work. **3** They received from Moses all the gifts the people of Israel had brought for the work of building the holy place. And they kept bringing gifts because they wanted to every morning. **4** All the able workmen came who were doing all the work on the holy place. Each man came from the work he had been doing. **5** They said to Moses, "The people are bringing much more than enough for the work the Lord told us to do." **6** So Moses made it be known to all the people, saying, "No man or woman is to give any more gifts for the holy place." So the people were kept from bringing any more. **7** For the things they had were enough for doing all the work. There was more than enough.

Building of the Tent

8 All the able men among those who were doing the work made the meeting tent with ten curtains. They made them of fine linen and blue, purple and red cloth, with cherubim sewed into them by an able workman. Bezalel made them. **9** Each curtain was as long as fourteen long steps and as wide as two long steps, all of them the same. **10** He joined five curtains to each other. And the other five curtains he joined to each other. **11** He took small pieces of blue cloth, longer than they were wide. He sewed both ends to the side of the last curtain in the first row. Then he did the same on the side of the last curtain in the second row. **12** He put fifty of these pieces on the one curtain. And he put fifty on the side of the other curtain, so that the pieces met each other. **13** He made fifty hooks of gold. Then he joined the curtains together with the hooks so the meeting tent was as one.

14 He made curtains of goat hair for a covering over the meeting tent. He made eleven curtains in all. **15** Each curtain was as long as fifteen long steps, and as wide as two long steps, all of them the same. **16** He joined five curtains by themselves and six curtains by themselves. **17** He took fifty small pieces of cloth, longer than they were wide. He sewed both ends of each to the side of the last curtain in the first row. Then he sewed fifty pieces onto the side of the last curtain in the second row. **18** He made fifty hooks of brass. And he put the hooks through the sewed pieces of cloth and joined the tent together as one. **19** He made a covering for the tent out of rams' skins made red, and a covering of badgers' skins over this. **20** Then he made the pillars of acacia wood for the meeting tent. **21** Each piece of wood was as long as five long steps, and as wide as one step. **22** He made two joining pieces in each piece of wood for joining them together. He did this for all the pieces of wood of the meeting tent. **23** He made twenty pieces of wood for the south side of the meeting tent. **24** He made forty silver bases under the twenty pieces of wood, two bases under each piece of wood. **25** Then he made twenty pieces of wood for the north side of the meeting tent. **26** And he made forty silver bases, with two bases under each piece of wood. **27** He made six pieces of wood for the back or west side of the meeting tent. **28** He made two pieces of wood for the back corners. **29** They were together at the bottom, and joined at the top with one ring. They were made the same for the two corners. **30** There were eight pieces of wood, with sixteen silver bases, two under each piece of wood.

31 He made long, straight pieces of acacia wood, five for the pieces of wood on one side of the meeting tent, **32** and five for the pieces of wood on the other side of the meeting tent. Then he made five for the pieces of wood at the back of the meeting tent, the west side. **33** He made the long, straight cross-piece for the center to pass through from end to end. **34** He covered the pieces of wood with gold. He made rings of gold to hold the long, straight pieces of wood. And he covered these pieces of wood with gold.

35 He made the curtain of blue and purple and red cloth and fine linen. He made it with cherubim sewed into it by an able workman. **36** He hung it on four pillars of acacia wood covered with gold. Their hooks were made of gold and he made four silver bases for it. **37** He made a curtain for the door of the meeting tent out of blue, purple and red cloth and fine linen, the work of an able workman. **38** He made five pillars with their hooks and covered their tops with gold. But he made their five bases of brass.

Making the Special Box of the Agreement

37 Bezalel made the special box of the agreement of acacia wood, two and a half cubits long, one and a half cubits wide, and one and a half cubits tall. **2** He covered it inside and out with pure gold. And he made a piece of gold to put on it all around. [3] He made four rings of gold for it and put them on its four feet. He put two rings on one side of it and two rings on the other side. [4] He made long pieces of acacia wood and covered them with gold. [5] Then he put the long pieces of wood through the rings on the sides of the special box to carry it. [6] He made a mercy-seat of pure gold, two and a half cubits long, and one and a half cubits wide. [7] He made two cherubim out of beaten gold at the two ends of the mercy-seat. [8] He made one cherub on one end and one cherub on the other end. He made the cherubim and the mercy-seat of one piece. [9] The cherubim had their wings spread up over the mercy-seat. Their faces were toward each other, and toward the mercy-seat. [10] Then he made a table of acacia wood, two cubits long, one cubit wide, and one and a half cubits tall. [11] He covered it with pure gold and made a gold piece around it. [12] He made a piece around it as wide as a hand. And he put gold on the side of this piece all around. [13] He made four rings of gold for it. He put them on the four corners that were on the table's four legs. [14] The rings were close to the sides, to hold the long pieces of wood used to carry the table. [15] He made the long pieces of acacia wood and covered them with gold. The table was carried with these. [16] He made of pure gold its plates, its pots and its jars, for pouring gifts of drink.

Making the Lamp-Stand

[17] Then he made the lamp-stand of pure gold and the base of the lamp-stand of beaten gold. Its cups, its buds and its flowers were all made of one piece with it. [18] Six branches went out of its sides, three branches of the lamp-stand out of one side, and three branches out of its other side. [19] Three cups were made to look like almond flowers, each with bud and flower, on one branch, and three on the next branch. This was done for all six branches going out of the lamp-stand. [20] In the lamp-stand there were four cups made to look like almond flowers, with their buds and flowers. [21] A bud was under each of the six branches going out of the lamp-stand. [22] Their buds and their branches were of one piece with it. All of it was one piece of pure, beaten gold. [23] He made its seven lamps, the tools for putting out the light, and its dishes of pure gold. [24] He

made it and all its objects out of a piece of gold about half the weight of a man.

Making the Altar

[25] Then he made the altar for burning special perfume of acacia wood. It was one cubit long, one cubit wide, and as high as a man's waist. Its horns were of one piece with it. [26] He covered its top, all its sides and its horns with pure gold. And he made a piece of gold to go around it. [27] Then he made two gold rings to put under this piece. He put one on the altar's left side and one on its right side to hold the long pieces of wood used for carrying it. [28] He made the long pieces of acacia wood and covered them with gold.

Making the Holy Oil and Special Perfume

[29] And he made the holy oil for pouring, and the pure, sweet-smelling perfume of spices, the work of an able workman.

Making the Altar for Burnt Gifts

38 Then he made the altar for burnt gifts of acacia wood. It was as long and as wide as three steps, and as tall as a man's chest. [2] He made horns on its four corners of one piece with it and covered it with brass. [3] He made all the objects of the altar, its pails, its tools for picking up the ashes, its pots, meat-hooks and fire-holders of brass. [4] He made a net for it of brass. It was put under the altar and it came up half-way. [5] He put four rings of brass at the four corners of the net to hold the long pieces of wood. [6] He made the long pieces of wood out of acacia wood and covered them with brass. [7] He put the long pieces of wood through the rings on each side of the altar for carrying it. He made the altar with pieces of wood so it was empty inside.

Making the Pot of Brass for Washing

[8] He made the pot for washing and its base of brass. They were made from the mirrors of the women servants who worked at the door of the meeting tent. [9] Then he made the open space for the holy tent. On the south side were curtains for the open space. They were made of fine linen, as long as fifty long steps. [10] They hung from twenty pillars with twenty brass bases. The hooks of the pillar and their rings were made of silver. [11] And on the north side there were curtains as long as fifty long steps, and twenty pillars with twenty brass bases. The hooks of the pillars and

their rings were made of silver. 12 On the west side there were curtains as long as twenty-five long steps. They had ten pillars with ten bases. The hooks of the pillars and their rings were made of silver. 13 The east side was as wide as twenty-five long steps. 14 The curtains for one side of the gate were as long as seven steps. They had three pillars with three bases. 15 And on the other side there were curtains as long as seven steps, with three pillars and three bases. 16 All the curtains around the open space were made of fine linen. 17 The bases for the pillars were made of brass. The hooks of the pillars and their rings were made of silver. Their tops were covered with silver. And the pillars were joined with silver. 18 The curtain for the gate of the open space was the work of an able workman. It was made of blue, purple and red cloth and fine linen. It was as long as ten long steps, and as high as a man raises his hand, to go with the curtains around the open space. 19 Its four pillars and their bases were made of brass. Their hooks and rings were made of silver. And their tops were covered with silver. 20 All the nails of the meeting tent and the open space were made of brass.

The Parts Are Weighed

21 This is the number of the things for the meeting tent, the meeting tent of the Law, as they were given by the mouth of Moses, for the work of the Levites, under the leading of Ithamar, the son of Aaron the religious leader. 22 Bezalel, the son of Uri, son of Hur, of the family of Judah, made all that the Lord had told Moses. 23 With him was Oholiab, the son of Ahisamach, of the family of Dan. He was an able workman who cut words in stone, gold or silver, and in sewing blue, purple and red cloth and fine linen.

24 All the gold used for the work of the holy tent, the gold given as a gift in worship, weighed as much as twelve men. 25 The silver given by the people weighed as much as forty men. 26 Each one of the men who were twenty years old and older, added up to 603,550 men, gave only a small weight of silver. 27 One hundred heavy weights of silver were used for making the bases for the holy tent and for the curtain in front of the most holy place. One hundred bases were made from the heavy weights of silver. 28 And from the heavy weights of silver he made hooks and joining parts for the pillars, and also covered

their tops. 29 The brass that was given weighed as much as thirty men. 30 With it he made the base for the door of the meeting tent, the brass altar and its brass net, and all the objects of the altar. 31 He also made bases all around the open space and the base for the gate of the open space, and all the nails of the meeting tent and all around the open space.

Making the Clothes of the Religious Leader

39 They used the blue, purple and red cloth for the well-made clothing for those working in the holy place. They made the holy clothing for Aaron, just as the Lord had told Moses.

Making the Linen Vest

2 Bezalel made the linen vest of gold and blue, purple and red cloth and fine linen. 3 They beat the gold into plates. Then they cut them into strings to be sewed in with the blue, purple and red cloth and the fine linen, the work of an able workman. 4 They made shoulder pieces for the linen vest, joined at its two top ends. 5 The well-made belt on it was made of the same gold, and blue, purple and red cloth and fine linen, just as the Lord had told Moses. 6 They set the onyx stones into beautiful pieces of gold. The names of Israel's sons were cut in the stones like the writing on a ring by an able workman. 7 They were put on the shoulder pieces of the linen vest, to help them remember the sons of Israel, just as the Lord had told Moses.

Making the Breast-Piece

8 Bezalel made the breast-piece, the work of an able workman. It was like the work of the linen vest, of gold, and blue, purple and red cloth and fine linen. 9 It was as long as it was wide, with one half laid over the other. It was made as long and as wide as a man's fingers can spread. 10 They put four rows of stones on it. The first row was a ruby, a topaz and an emerald. 11 The second row was a turquoise, a sapphire and a diamond. 12 The third row was a jacinth, an agate and an amethyst. 13 And the fourth row was a beryl, an onyx and a jasper. They were set in beautiful pieces of gold. 14 Each of the twelve stones had written on it the name of one of the sons of Israel. Each name spoke of one of the twelve family groups. 15 They made chains for the breast-piece, like ropes of pure gold. 16 And they made two gold

rings and put them on the two ends of the breast-piece. 17 They joined the two gold chains to the two rings at the ends of the breast-piece. 18 They joined the other two ends of the two chains to the beautiful gold pieces that hold the two stones at the shoulders, joining them in the front. 19 They made two gold rings to put on the two ends of the breast-piece, on the inside next to the linen vest. 20 Then they made two gold rings and put them on the bottom of the two shoulder pieces of the linen vest in front, near where they join. They were above the belt of the linen vest. 21 They tied the rings of the breast-piece to the rings of the linen vest with a blue rope. So the breast-piece could not come loose from the linen vest, just as the Lord had told Moses.

Making Other Pieces of Clothes

22 Then he made the long piece of clothing all of blue. 23 There was an opening at its top in the center. Around the opening it was sewed like the opening on heavy battle-clothes, so it could not be torn. 24 They made pomegranates of blue, purple and red cloth and fine linen, to put all around the bottom of this clothing. 25 They made bells of pure gold. And they put the bells between the pomegranates all around the bottom of the clothing. 26 They put a bell and then a pomegranate all around the bottom of this clothing. It was for the work of the Lord, and was just as the Lord had told Moses.

27 They made the long coats of fine linen for Aaron and his sons. 28 They made the beautiful head-coverings of fine linen and the clothing that covered the flesh from the belt to the legs. 29 And they made the wide belt of fine linen and blue, purple and red cloth which was the work of an able workman, just as the Lord had told Moses. 30 They made the plate of the holy crown of pure gold. And they cut in it like the writings on a ring: "Holy to the Lord." 31 They joined it to the front of the head-covering with a blue rope, just as the Lord had told Moses.

The Work Finished

32 So all the work of the holy tent, the meeting tent, was finished. The sons of Israel did all that the Lord had told Moses. 33 They brought the meeting tent to Moses, the tent and all its objects, its hooks, all kinds of pieces of wood, pillars and bases. 34 They brought the covering of rams' skins made red, the covering of badgers' skins, and the curtain to hang in front of the most holy place. 35 They brought the special box of the agreement, its long pieces of wood for carrying it and its mercy-seat, 36 the table and all its objects, the bread to be put before the Lord, 37 the pure gold lamp-stand with its lamps, all its objects and the oil for the light. 38 They brought the gold altar, the oil for holy use, the sweet-smelling perfume, and the curtain for the door of the meeting tent. 39 They brought the brass altar, its brass net, its long pieces of wood for carrying it and all its objects, the washing pot and its stand, 40 the curtains for the open space, its pillars and bases, the curtain for the gate of the open space, its ropes and nails, and all the tools for the work of the meeting tent. 41 They brought the clothing for the work in the holy place, the holy clothing for Aaron the religious leader, and the clothing of his sons for their work as religious leaders. 42 So the people of Israel did all the work just as the Lord had told Moses. 43 Moses looked at all the work and saw they had done it just as the Lord had said. So Moses gave thanks and prayed that good would come to them.

Putting Up the Meeting Tent and Setting It Apart

40 The Lord said to Moses, 2 "Set up the holy tent, the meeting tent, on the first day of the first month. 3 Put the special box of the Law there. And hang the curtain in front of it. 4 Bring in the table and set its objects on it. Bring in the lamp-stand and light its lamps. 5 Set the gold altar of special perfume in front of the box of the Law. Hang the curtain for the door of the meeting tent. 6 Set the altar of burnt gifts in front of the door of the holy tent, the meeting tent. 7 Set the washing pot between the meeting tent and the altar and put water in it. 8 Hang the curtains all around the open space and hang the curtain at the gate of the open space. 9 Then take the oil and pour it upon the meeting tent and all that is in it. Set it apart with all its objects, and it will be holy. 10 Pour the oil upon the altar of burnt gifts and all its objects. Set the altar apart, and it will be most holy. 11 Pour the oil upon the washing pot and its stand, to set it apart.

12 "Then bring Aaron and his sons to the door of the meeting tent. And wash them with water. 13 Put the holy clothing on Aaron. Then pour oil upon him and

set him apart to work for Me as a religious leader. ¹⁴ Bring his sons and put long coats on them. ¹⁵ Then pour oil upon them as you have done to their father, so they may serve Me as religious leaders. Pouring oil upon them will make them ready to be religious leaders, they and all their children-to-come."

¹⁶ Moses did all that the Lord told him to do. ¹⁷ On the first day of the first month of the second year, the meeting tent was set up. ¹⁸ Moses set up the meeting tent, laid the bases, set up its pieces of wood, put in its cross-pieces and set up its pillars. ¹⁹ He spread the covering over the meeting tent. And he put the top covering over it, just as the Lord had told Moses. ²⁰ Then he took the Law and put it into the special box. He put the long pieces of wood on the special box of the agreement. And he put the mercy-seat on top of the special box. ²¹ He brought the special box into the meeting tent and hung the curtain. He put the curtain in front of the special box of the agreement, just as the Lord had told Moses. ²² Then he put the table in the meeting tent, on the north side of the tent, outside the curtain. ²³ He set the bread in its place on the table before the Lord, just as the Lord had told Moses. ²⁴ Then he put the lamp-stand in the meeting tent, away from the table, on the south side of the tent. ²⁵ He set up the lamps before the Lord, just as the Lord had told Moses. ²⁶ He put the gold altar in the tent of meeting, in front of the curtain. ²⁷ And he burned sweet-smelling perfume on it, just as the Lord had told Moses. ²⁸ Then he hung the curtain at the door of the meeting tent. ²⁹ He set the altar of burnt gifts in front of the door of the meeting tent. And he gave the burnt gift and the grain gift on it, just as the Lord had told Moses. ³⁰ He put the washing pot between the tent of meeting and the altar, with water in it for washing. ³¹ Moses and Aaron and his sons washed their hands and feet there. ³² They washed when they came into the tent of meeting and when they came near the altar, just as the Lord had told Moses. ³³ He made the open space all around the meeting tent and the altar. And he hung the curtain for the gate of the open space. So Moses finished the work.

The Cloud over the Meeting Tent

³⁴ Then the cloud covered the meeting tent. The shining-greatness of the Lord filled the holy tent. ³⁵ Moses was not able to go into the meeting tent because the cloud had rested upon it and the shining-greatness of the Lord filled the holy tent. ³⁶ When the cloud was lifted from the meeting tent, the people of Israel would go on their way through all their traveling days. ³⁷ But when the cloud was not lifted, they did not move on until the day when it was lifted. ³⁸ For the cloud of the Lord rested on the meeting tent during the day. And fire was in the cloud during the night. It was seen by all the people of Israel as they traveled.

LEVITICUS

Burnt Gifts on the Altar

1 The Lord called to Moses and spoke to him from the meeting tent, saying, ² "Speak to the people of Israel. Tell them, 'When any of you bring a gift in worship to the Lord, bring your gift of animals from the herd or the flock. ³ If his gift is a burnt gift from the cattle, he should bring a male that is perfect. He should give it at the door of the meeting tent, so he will be pleasing to the Lord. ⁴ He will lay his hand on the head of the burnt gift and it will be received to take away his sins. ⁵ He will kill the young bull before the Lord. Then Aaron's sons, the religious leaders, will take the blood and put it around on the altar that is at the door of the meeting tent. ⁶ He will skin the burnt gift and cut it into pieces. ⁷ The sons of Aaron the religious leader will put fire on the altar and lay wood on the fire. ⁸ Then Aaron's sons, the religious leaders, will lay the pieces, the head and the fat on the wood that is on the altar fire. ⁹ But he will wash its legs and inside parts with water. Then the religious leader will burn all of it on the altar as a burnt gift. It will be a gift by fire, a pleasing smell to the Lord.

¹⁰ 'If this gift is a burnt gift from the sheep or the goats of the flock, he should give a male that is perfect. ¹¹ He should kill it on the north side of the altar before the Lord. Aaron's sons, the religious leaders, will put its blood around on the altar. ¹² Then he

will cut it into pieces with its head and its fat. And the religious leader will lay them on the wood that is on the altar fire. ¹³ But he will wash the legs and inside parts with water. The religious leader will burn all of it on the altar as a burnt gift. It will be a gift by fire, a pleasing smell to the Lord.

¹⁴ 'If his gift is a burnt gift of birds, he should bring his gift from the turtle-doves or young pigeons. ¹⁵ The religious leader will bring it to the altar and take off its head. Then he will burn it on the altar. Its blood will flow down on the side of the altar. ¹⁶ He will take the part of its body where the food it eats is kept and with its feathers throw them on the ashes on the east side of the altar. ¹⁷ Then he will tear it by its wings, but not divide it. And the religious leader will burn it on the altar as a burnt gift. It will be a gift by fire, a pleasing smell to the Lord.

Grain Gifts

2 'When anyone gives a grain gift to the Lord, it should be of fine flour. He should pour oil on it and put special perfume on it. ² Then he will take it to Aaron's sons, the religious leaders. The religious leader will fill his hand with the fine flour, oil and special perfume and will burn it on the altar as a part to be remembered. It will be a gift by fire, a pleasing smell to the Lord. ³ The rest of the grain gift will belong to Aaron and his sons. It is a most holy part of the gifts by fire to the Lord.

⁴ 'When you bring a gift of grain that has been baked, it should be loaves of fine flour without yeast and mixed with oil, or hard bread without yeast and spread with oil. ⁵ If your gift of grain has been cooked on top of the stove, it should be of fine flour without yeast and mixed with oil. ⁶ Break it into pieces and pour oil on it. It is a grain gift. ⁷ If your gift of grain has been cooked in a pot, it should be made of fine flour with oil. ⁸ Bring the grain gift that is made of these things to the Lord. It will be given to the religious leader, and he will bring it to the altar. ⁹ The religious leader will take the part to be remembered from the grain gift and burn it on the altar. It will be a gift by fire, a pleasing smell to the Lord. ¹⁰ The rest of the grain gift belongs to Aaron and his sons. It is a most holy part of the gifts by fire to the Lord.

¹¹ 'No grain gift that you bring to the Lord will be made with yeast. For you must never burn yeast or honey in any gift by fire to the Lord. ¹² You may bring them to the Lord as a gift of first-fruits, but not for a pleasing smell upon the altar. ¹³ You should add salt to all your grain gifts. The salt of the agreement of your God must be in your grain gift. Give salt with all your gifts.

¹⁴ 'If you give a grain gift of first-fruits to the Lord, give crushed new grain from new plants, dried by fire. ¹⁵ Put oil and special perfume on it. It is a grain gift. ¹⁶ The religious leader will burn part of its crushed grain and oil with all its special perfume, as its part to be remembered. It is a gift by fire to the Lord.

Peace Gifts

3 'If this gift given on the altar is a peace gift taken from the herd, male or female, he should give one to the Lord that is perfect. ² He will lay his hand on the head of his gift, and kill it at the door of the meeting tent. Aaron's sons, the religious leaders, will put the blood around on the altar. ³ And from the peace gift, a gift by fire to the Lord, he will give all the fat that covers and is upon the inside parts, ⁴ and the two kidneys with the fat that is on them, and the part that is on the liver, which he will take away with the kidneys. ⁵ Then Aaron's sons will burn it on the altar, on the burnt gift that is on the wood of the fire. It is a gift by fire, a pleasing smell to the Lord. ⁶ If his peace gift to the Lord is from the flock, male or female, he will give one that is perfect. ⁷ If he gives a lamb, then he will give it to the Lord. ⁸ He will lay his hand on the head of his gift, and kill it in front of the meeting tent. Aaron's sons will put its blood around on the altar. ⁹ And from the peace gifts he will bring as a gift by fire to the Lord, its fat, the whole fat tail, taking it off close to the backbone, and the fat that covers and is upon the inside parts, ¹⁰ and the two kidneys with the fat that is on them, and the part that is on the liver, which he will take away with the kidneys. ¹¹ Then the religious leader will burn them on the altar, a food gift by fire to the Lord.

¹² 'If his gift is a goat, then he will give it to the Lord. ¹³ He will lay his hand on its head, and kill it in front of the meeting tent. The sons of Aaron will put its blood around on the altar. ¹⁴ Then he will give from it as his gift by fire to the Lord, the fat that covers and is on the inside parts, ¹⁵ and the two kidneys with the fat that is on them, and the part that is on the liver, which he will take away with the kidneys. ¹⁶ The religious leader will burn them on the altar,

a food gift by fire for a pleasing smell. All fat is the Lord's. 17 It will be a Law forever for all your people in all your houses, that you do not eat any fat or any blood.' "

Gifts Given When a Person Sins without Meaning To

4 The Lord said to Moses, 2 "Say to the people of Israel, 'If a person sins without meaning to, by not obeying what the Lord has told us to do, these are the rules he must follow. 3 If the chosen religious leader sins and so brings guilt on the people, let him give to the Lord a bull that is perfect. It is a sin gift for the sin he has done. 4 He will bring the bull to the door of the meeting tent before the Lord. He will lay his hand on the head of the bull, and kill the bull before the Lord. 5 Then the chosen religious leader is to take some of the bull's blood and bring it to the meeting tent. 6 The religious leader will put his finger in the blood and put some of the blood seven times before the Lord and in front of the curtain of the holy place. 7 And the religious leader will put some of the blood on the horns of the altar of sweet-smelling perfume in the meeting tent before the Lord. Then he will pour out all of the bull's blood at the base of the altar of burnt gifts at the door of the meeting tent. 8 He will take from it all the fat of the bull of the sin gift, the fat that covers the inside parts, and all the fat that is on the inside parts, 9 and the two kidneys with the fat that is on them, and the part on the liver, which he will take off with the kidneys, 10 just as these are taken from the bull of the peace gift. The religious leader is to burn them on the altar of burnt gifts. 11 But the bull's skin and all its flesh, its head, legs, inside parts and its waste, 12 all the rest of the bull, he is to bring to a clean place away from the tents, where the ashes are poured out. There he will burn it on wood with fire. It will be burned where the ashes are poured out.

13 'If all the people of Israel sin and do not obey what the Lord has told them, without meaning to and without knowing about it, they are guilty. 14 When their sin becomes known, the people will give a bull from the herd for a sin gift. They will bring it in front of the meeting tent. 15 Then the leaders of the people will lay their hands on the bull's head before the Lord. And the bull will be killed before the Lord. 16 The chosen religious leader will take some of the bull's blood to the meeting tent. 17 There the religious leader will put his finger in the blood and put it seven times before the Lord and in front of the curtains. 18 He will put some of the blood on the horns of the altar before the Lord in the meeting tent. And he will pour out all the blood at the base of the altar of burnt gifts at the door of the meeting tent. 19 He will take all its fat from it and burn it on the altar. 20 He will do the same with the bull as he did with the bull of the sin gift. So the religious leader will pay for their sins. And they will be forgiven. 21 Then he will bring the bull away from the tents and burn it as he burned the first bull. It is the sin gift for all the people.

22 'When a leader sins without meaning to, by doing any of all the things the Lord God has told us not to do, he becomes guilty. 23 If his sin is made known to him, he will bring for his gift a male goat that is perfect. 24 He will lay his hand on the head of the male goat, and kill it in the place where they kill the burnt gifts before the Lord. It is a sin gift. 25 Then the religious leader will take some of the blood of the sin gift with his finger and put it on the horns of the altar of burnt gifts. He will pour out the rest of its blood at the base of the altar of burnt gifts. 26 He will burn all its fat on the altar like the fat of the peace gifts. So the religious leader will pay the price for the man's sin. And he will be forgiven.

27 'If anyone among the people of the land sins without meaning to, by doing any of the things the Lord said not to do, he becomes guilty. 28 If his sin is made known to him, he will bring for his gift a female goat that is perfect, for the sin he has done. 29 He will lay his hand on the head of the sin gift, and kill the sin gift at the place of burnt gifts. 30 The religious leader will take some of its blood with his finger and put it on the horns of the altar of burnt gifts. He will pour out all the rest of its blood at the base of the altar. 31 Then he will take all its fat, just as the fat was taken from the peace gifts. And the religious leader will burn it on the altar for a pleasing smell to the Lord. So the religious leader will pay for his sin. And he will be forgiven.

32 'If he brings a lamb for a sin gift, he will bring a female lamb that is perfect. 33 He will lay his hand on the head of the sin gift, and kill it for a sin gift in the place where they kill the burnt gifts. 34 The religious leader will take some of the blood of the sin gift with his finger and put it on the horns of the altar of burnt gifts. He

will pour out all the rest of its blood at the base of the altar. 35 Then he will take all its fat, just as the lamb's fat is taken from the peace gifts. The religious leader will burn it on the altar, on the gifts by fire to the Lord. So the religious leader will pay for him the price for the sin he has done. And he will be forgiven.

5 'If a person sins by saying nothing when he is told in court to tell what he knows or what he has seen, he will become guilty. 2 If a person touches anything that is unclean, the dead body of a wild animal, or of cattle, or of anything that moves on the earth that is unclean, even without knowing it, then he will be unclean and will be guilty. 3 Or if he touches a human who is unclean for whatever reason, without knowing it, when he learns about it, he will be guilty. 4 If a person without thinking swears he will do something, whether bad or good, any foolish promise a person may swear, when he learns about it, he will be guilty. 5 When a person is guilty in any of these, he should tell of the sin he has done. 6 He should bring his guilt gift to the Lord for the sin he has done, a female from the flock, a lamb or a goat, for a sin gift. And the religious leader will pay the price for him for his sin.

7 'But if he does not have enough money for a lamb, he should bring to the Lord as his guilt gift for his sin two turtle-doves or two young pigeons. One will be for a sin gift, and the other for a burnt gift. 8 He will bring them to the religious leader, who will give the sin gift first. He will break its neck without taking off its head. 9 Then he will put some of the blood of the sin gift on the side of the altar. He will pour out the rest of the blood at the base of the altar. It is a sin gift. 10 Then he will make the second bird ready for a burnt gift, by following the Law. So the religious leader will pay the price for him for the sin he has done. And he will be forgiven.

11 'But if he does not have enough money for two turtle-doves or two young pigeons, he should bring one-tenth part of a basket of fine flour for a sin gift. He should not put oil or special perfume on it, for it is a sin gift. 12 He will bring it to the religious leader, who will take a handful of it as a part to be remembered. And he will burn this part of the flour on the altar with the gifts made by fire to the Lord. It is a sin gift. 13 So the religious leader will pay the price for him for the sin he has done in any of

these things. And he will be forgiven. The rest of the flour will be for the religious leader, as in the grain gift.' "

Making Things Right

14 The Lord said to Moses, 15 "If a person is not faithful and sins against the holy things of the Lord without meaning to, he should bring his guilt gift to the Lord. It should be a ram that is perfect from the flock, worth money the same as the weight of silver decided upon for the holy place. It is a guilt gift. 16 He should pay for his sin against the holy thing, and add one-fifth part to it, and give it to the religious leader. Then the religious leader will give for his sin the ram of the guilt gift as the price for his sin. And he will be forgiven.

17 "If a person sins by doing any of the things the Lord has told him not to do, even without meaning to, he is guilty and must pay for his sin. 18 He will bring to the religious leader a ram that is perfect from the flock, that is decided to be the right price for a guilt gift. So the religious leader will pay the price for him for the sin he had done without meaning to. And he will be forgiven. 19 It is a guilt gift. For sure he has sinned against the Lord."

6 The Lord said to Moses, 2 "If a person is not faithful and sins against the Lord by lying to his neighbor about money given to him for safe-keeping, or by stealing, or by false ways, 3 or by finding what was lost and lying about it before God, if a man does any of the things that men sin by doing, 4 he will become guilty. Then he should return what he took by stealing, or what he got by false ways, or the money which was given to him for safe-keeping, or the lost thing which he found, 5 or anything that he lied about. He should pay for it in full, and add to it one-fifth part more. He should give it to whom it belongs on the day he gives his guilt gift. 6 Then he will bring to the religious leader his guilt gift to the Lord, a ram that is perfect from the flock, that you decide to be the right price for a guilt gift. 7 Before the Lord the religious leader will pay the price for him for whatever he did that made him guilty. And he will be forgiven."

The Law of the Burnt Gift

8 The Lord said to Moses, 9 "Tell Aaron and his sons, 'This is the Law for the burnt gift. The burnt gift should stay on the altar all night until the morning, and

the fire should be kept burning on the altar. 10 Then the religious leader will put on the clothing next to his flesh, and the long linen clothing over that. And he will take the ashes that are left from the fire of the burnt gift on the altar, and put them beside the altar. 11 Then he will change his clothes and carry the ashes to a clean place away from the tents. 12 The fire should be kept burning on the altar. It should not go out. The religious leader should burn wood on it every morning. He will lay the burnt gifts on it, and burn the fat parts of the peace gifts on it. 13 Fire should always be kept burning on the altar. It is not to go out.

The Law of the Grain Gift

14 'This is the Law of the grain gift. The sons of Aaron will give it to the Lord in front of the altar. 15 One of them will fill his hand with the fine flour of the grain gift, with its oil and all the special perfume that is on it, and burn it on the altar to be remembered as a pleasing smell to the Lord. 16 Aaron and his sons are to eat what is left of it. It will be eaten as loaves without yeast in a holy place. They will eat it in the open space of the meeting tent. 17 It will not be baked with yeast. I have given it as their share from My gifts by fire. It is most holy, like the sin gift and the guilt gift. 18 Every male among the sons of Aaron may eat it. It is a Law forever for all your people, from the gifts by fire to the Lord. Whoever touches them will become holy.' "

19 The Lord said to Moses, 20 "This is the gift which Aaron and his sons are to give to the Lord on the day when he is set apart. The tenth part of a basket of fine flour for a grain gift each day, half of it in the morning and half of it in the evening. 21 It should be cooked with oil on top of a stove. Bring it when it is mixed well, and give the grain gift in baked pieces as a pleasing smell to the Lord. 22 The religious leader among Aaron's sons, who is chosen to be in his place, will give it. By a Law forever, all of it will be burned and given to the Lord. 23 Every grain gift of the religious leader will be all burned. It will not be eaten."

The Law of the Sin Gift

24 The Lord said to Moses, 25 "Tell Aaron and his sons, 'This is the Law of the sin gift. The sin gift will be killed before the Lord in the place where the burnt gift is killed. It is most holy. 26 The religious leader who gives it for sin will eat it. It will be eaten in

a holy place, in the open space of the meeting tent. 27 Anyone who touches its flesh will become holy. When any of its blood gets on a piece of clothing, wash the blood from the clothing in a holy place. 28 The clay pot in which it was made ready should be broken. But if it was made ready in a brass pot, it should be well cleaned with water. 29 Every male among the religious leaders may eat of it. It is most holy. 30 But no sin gift should be eaten from which any blood is brought into the meeting tent to pay for sins in the holy place. It should be burned with fire.

The Law of the Guilt Gift

7 'This is the Law of the guilt gift. It is most holy. 2 They are to kill the guilt gift in the place where they kill the burnt gift. And the religious leader should put its blood around on the altar. 3 Then he will give all its fat, the fat tail, the fat that covers the inside parts, 4 the two kidneys with the fat that is on them, and the part that is on the liver which he will take away with the kidneys. 5 The religious leader will burn them on the altar as a gift by fire to the Lord. It is a guilt gift. 6 Every male among the religious leaders may eat of it. It will be eaten in a holy place. It is most holy. 7 The guilt gift is like the sin gift. There is one Law for them. It belongs to the religious leader who pays the price for sin with it. 8 And the religious leader who gives any man's burnt gift will keep for himself the skin of the burnt gift he has given. 9 Every grain gift that is baked in a stove and everything that is cooked in a pot or on top of a stove will belong to the religious leader who gives it. 10 And every grain gift, mixed with oil or dry, will belong to all the sons of Aaron, to all the same.

The Law of the Peace Gift

11 'This is the Law of giving peace gifts in worship to the Lord. 12 If he gives it because he is thankful, then with the thank gift he will give bread mixed with oil and without yeast, hard bread spread with oil and without yeast, and loaves of fine flour well mixed with oil. 13 With loaves of bread with yeast he will give his thank gift with the peace gifts. 14 Out of each gift he will give a part as a gift to the Lord. It will belong to the religious leader who puts the blood on the peace gifts.

15 'The flesh of the thank gift, given as a peace gift, will be eaten on the day it is given. None of it is to be left until morning.

16 But if his gift is for a promise or is given only because he wants to give it, it will be eaten the same day he gives his gift. And whatever is left may be eaten the next day. 17 But what is left of the flesh of the gift until the third day will be burned with fire. 18 If any of the flesh of his gift is eaten on the third day, then the one who brought it will not be received and it will not do him any good. It will be a sin. And the person who eats of it must suffer for his own sin.

19 'The flesh that touches anything that is unclean must not be eaten. It will be burned with fire. Anyone who is clean may eat other flesh. 20 But the person who is unclean, who eats the flesh of the peace gifts which belong to the Lord, will be kept away from his people. 21 And a person will be kept away from his people when he touches anything that is unclean, a human, animal or thing that is unclean, and then eats of the flesh of the peace gifts that belong to the Lord.' "

Fat and Blood Not to Be Eaten

22 The Lord said to Moses, 23 "Say to the people of Israel, 'Do not eat any fat from a bull, sheep or goat. 24 The fat of an animal that dies, and the fat of an animal torn by wild animals, may be used in other ways. But for sure you must not eat it. 25 For whoever eats the fat of the animal from which a gift is given by fire to the Lord will be kept away from his people. 26 Do not eat any blood, of bird or animal, in any of your houses. 27 Whoever eats any blood will be kept away from his people.' "

The Part for Aaron and His Sons

28 The Lord said to Moses, 29 "Say to the people of Israel, 'Whoever gives his peace gift to the Lord will bring a part of it as a special gift to the Lord. 30 With his own hands he will bring the gift given to the Lord by fire. He will bring the fat with the breast so the breast may be given as a wave gift before the Lord. 31 The religious leader will burn the fat on the altar. But the breast will belong to Aaron and his sons. 32 And you will give the right thigh to the religious leader as his part of your peace gift. 33 The son of Aaron who gives the blood and the fat of the peace gift will have the right thigh for his share. 34 For I have taken the breast of the wave gift and the right thigh out of the peace gifts given by the people of Israel. And I have given them to Aaron the religious leader and to his sons as their share forever from the people of Israel.

35 'This is the share for Aaron and his sons from the gifts made by fire to the Lord. It was set apart for them on the day they were set apart to work as religious leaders for the Lord. 36 The Lord said that this should be given to them by the people of Israel on the day they were set apart. It is their share forever.' "

37 This is the Law of the burnt gift, the grain gift, the sin gift, the guilt gift, the gift when the religious leader is set apart for the Lord's work, and the peace gift. 38 The Lord gave this Law to Moses on Mount Sinai on the day that He told the people of Israel to give their gifts to the Lord in the Desert of Sinai.

Aaron and His Sons Set Apart for Their Work

8 The Lord said to Moses, 2 "Take Aaron and his sons, and the clothing, the oil for holy use, the bull for the sin gift, the two rams and the basket of bread without yeast. 3 And gather together all the people at the door of the meeting tent." 4 So Moses did just as the Lord told him. The people were gathered together at the door of the meeting tent. 5 Moses said to the people, "This is what the Lord has said to do."

6 Moses brought Aaron and his sons, and washed them with water. 7 He dressed him with the coat, the belt, the long piece of clothing, and the linen vest. He tied the well-made rope of the linen vest, to keep his clothing in place. 8 Then he put the breast-piece on him. And he put the Urim and the Thummim into the breast-piece. 9 He put the head-covering on his head. And on the front of it he put the gold plate, the holy crown, just as the Lord had told Moses.

10 Then Moses took the oil for holy use and poured it on the meeting tent and all that was in it, and made them holy. 11 He put some of it on the altar seven times. He poured this oil on the altar and all its objects, and the washing pot and its base, to make them holy. 12 And he poured some of the oil for holy use on Aaron's head, to make him holy. 13 Then Moses had Aaron's sons come near and dressed them with coats, belts and head-coverings, just as the Lord had told Moses.

14 Moses brought the bull of the sin gift. And Aaron and his sons laid their hands on the head of the bull of the sin gift. 15 Then Moses killed it. He took some of the blood, and put it around on the horns of the altar with his finger, to make the altar clean. He

poured out the rest of the blood at the base of the altar to make it holy. 16 He took all the fat that was on the inside parts, and the part that was on the liver, and the two kidneys and their fat. And Moses burned them on the altar. 17 But the bull and its skin, its meat and its waste, he burned in the fire away from the tents, just as the Lord had told Moses.

18 Moses brought the ram of the burnt gift. And Aaron and his sons laid their hands on the head of the sheep. 19 Then Moses killed it and put the blood around on the altar. 20 He cut the ram into pieces. And Moses burned the head, the pieces, and the fat. 21 After he had washed the inside parts and the legs with water, Moses burned the whole ram on the altar. It was a burnt gift for a pleasing smell. It was a gift by fire to the Lord, just as the Lord had told Moses. 22 Then Moses brought the ram, the ram for setting them apart. Aaron and his sons laid their hands on the head of the ram. 23 And Moses killed it, took some of its blood, and put it on the bottom of Aaron's right ear, the thumb of his right hand, and the big toe of his right foot. 24 Then he had Aaron's sons come near. Moses put some of the blood on the bottom of their right ear, the thumb of their right hand, and the big toe of their right foot. Then Moses put the rest of the blood around on the altar. 25 He took the fat, the fat tail, all the fat that was on the inside parts, the part that is on the liver, the two kidneys and their fat, and the right thigh. 26 From the basket of bread made without yeast that was before the Lord, he took one loaf without yeast, and one loaf of bread mixed with oil, and one piece of hard bread. And he put them on the fat parts and the right thigh. 27 He put all these on the hands of Aaron and his sons, and waved them for a wave gift before the Lord. 28 Then Moses took these things from their hands and burned them on the altar with the burnt gift. It was a gift to set them apart. It was a pleasing smell, a gift by fire to the Lord. 29 Moses took the breast of the ram also. He gave it as a wave gift before the Lord. It was Moses' part of the ram for setting Aaron and his sons apart, just as the Lord had told Moses.

30 Moses took some of the oil for holy use and some of the blood that was on the altar. He put it on Aaron and his clothing, and on his sons and their clothing. So Aaron and his clothing and his sons and their clothing were set apart.

31 Then Moses said to Aaron and his sons, "Boil the meat at the door of the meeting tent. And eat it there with the bread which is in the basket that was set apart as an offering. Just as I said, 'Aaron and his sons will eat it.' 32 Burn in the fire what is left of the flesh and the bread. 33 Do not go outside the door of the meeting tent for seven days, until the time is over for you to be set apart. For it will take seven days to set you apart. 34 The Lord has told us to do what has been done today, to take away your sins. 35 Stay day and night at the door of the meeting tent for seven days. Do what the Lord has told you to do, so you will not die. For this is what I have been told." 36 So Aaron and his sons did all that the Lord had told them to do by Moses.

The Religious Leaders Begin Their Work

9 On the eighth day Moses called Aaron and his sons and the leaders of Israel. 2 He said to Aaron, "Take a bull calf for a sin gift and a ram for a burnt gift, both of them perfect. And give them to the Lord. 3 Then say to the people of Israel, 'Take a male goat for a sin gift, and a calf and a lamb, both a year old and perfect, for a burnt gift, 4 and a bull and a ram for peace gifts. Give them to the Lord with a grain gift mixed with oil. For today the Lord will show Himself to you.' " 5 So they brought to the front of the meeting tent what Moses had told them. All the people came near and stood before the Lord. 6 Moses said, "This is what the Lord has told you to do. And the shining-greatness of the Lord will be shown to you." 7 Then Moses said to Aaron, "Come to the altar and give your sin gift and burnt gift to pay for the sins of yourself and for the people. Then give the gift for the people, to pay for their sins, just as the Lord has said."

8 So Aaron came to the altar and killed the calf of the sin gift, which was for himself. 9 The sons of Aaron gave the blood to him. He put his finger in the blood and put some on the horns of the altar. He poured out the rest of the blood at the base of the altar. 10 But he burned on the altar the fat and the kidneys and the part that is on the liver from the sin gift, just as the Lord had told Moses. 11 He burned the flesh and the skin away from the tents.

12 Then he killed the burnt gift. Aaron's sons handed the blood to him and he put it around on the altar. 13 They gave the burnt gift to him in pieces, with the head. And he

burned them on the altar. 14 He washed the inside parts and legs and burned them on the altar with the burnt gift.

15 Then he gave the people's gift. He took the goat of the sin gift which was for the people. And he killed it and gave it for sin, like the first sin gift. 16 He gave the burnt gift. He gave it just the way the Law said. 17 Next he gave the grain gift. He filled his hand with some of the grain and burned it on the altar beside the burnt gift of the morning.

18 Then he killed the bull and the ram, the peace gifts which were for the people. Aaron's sons handed the blood to him and he put it around on the altar. 19 The fat parts from the bull and ram, the fat tail, the fat around the inside parts, the kidneys and the part that is on the liver, 20 all the fat parts they put on the breasts. And they burned the fat parts on the altar. 21 But Aaron gave the breasts and the right thigh as a wave gift before the Lord, just as Moses had said.

22 Then Aaron lifted up his hands toward the people and prayed that good would come to them. After giving the sin gift, the burnt gift and the peace gifts, he came down. 23 Moses and Aaron went into the meeting tent. When they came out and prayed that good would come to the people, the shining-greatness of the Lord was shown to all the people. 24 Then fire came from the Lord and burned up the burnt gift and the fat parts on the altar. When the people saw it, they cried out and bowed down with their faces to the ground.

The Sin of Nadab and Abihu

10 Aaron's sons, Nadab and Abihu, each took his fire pan, put fire in it, and put special perfume on it. They gave a fire that was not holy to the Lord because the Lord had not told them to do this. 2 So the Lord sent out fire that burned them up and they died before the Lord. 3 Then Moses said to Aaron, "This is what the Lord meant when He said, 'I will show Myself holy among those who are near Me. I will be honored in front of all the people.' " And Aaron said nothing. 4 Moses called Mishael and Elzaphan, the sons of Uzziel, the brother of Aaron's father. He said to them, "Come, carry your brothers away from the holy place and away from the tents." 5 So they came and carried them in their coats away from the tents, as Moses had said. 6 Then Moses said to Aaron and

his sons Eleazar and Ithamar, "Do not take the covering off your heads and do not tear your clothes, so you will not die and God will not be angry with all the people. But your brothers, the whole house of Israel, will cry in sorrow because of the burning the Lord has done. 7 Do not even go out the door of the meeting tent, so you will not die. For the holy oil of the Lord is upon you." And they did what Moses said.

How the Religious Leaders Were to Act

8 The Lord said to Aaron, 9 "Do not drink wine or strong drink, you or your sons, when you come into the meeting tent, so you will not die. It is a Law forever for all your people. 10 You are to know the difference between what is holy and what is not, and between what is clean and what is not. 11 You are to teach the people of Israel all the Laws which the Lord has told them by Moses." 12 Then Moses said to Aaron and his sons who were left, Eleazar and Ithamar, "Take the grain gift that is left from the gifts by fire to the Lord. And eat it without yeast beside the altar, for it is most holy. 13 Eat it in a holy place, because it is yours and your sons', from the gifts by fire to the Lord. For so I have been told. 14 But you and your sons and daughters may eat in a clean place the breast of the wave gift and the thigh that is given. For they are given to you as your right and your sons' right, from the peace gifts of the people of Israel. 15 They will bring the thigh that is given and the breast of the wave gift, with the gifts by fire of the fat. They will wave them before the Lord for a wave gift. They will be yours and your sons', as your right forever, as the Lord has said."

16 But Moses looked and looked for the goat of the sin gift, and found that it had been burned up! So he was angry with Aaron's sons who were left, Eleazar and Ithamar, saying, 17 "Why have you not eaten the sin gift in the holy place? For it is most holy and He gave it to you to take away the guilt of the people, to take away their sins before the Lord. 18 See, its blood has not been brought inside the holy place. You should have been sure to eat it in the holy place, as I told you." 19 But Aaron said to Moses, "See, today they have given their sin gift and their burnt gift to the Lord. When things like these happened to me, if I had eaten a sin gift today, would it have been good in the eyes of the Lord?" 20 And when Moses heard that, he was not angry any more.

Foods That Could Be Eaten

11 The Lord said to Moses and Aaron, 2 "Say to the people of Israel, 'These are the living things which you may eat among all the animals on the earth. 3 You may eat any animal that has hard and divided feet and chews its food again. 4 But among those which chew their food again or have feet that are hard and divided, do not eat the camel. For it chews its food again, but does not have feet that are hard and divided. It is unclean to you. 5 Do not eat the rock badger. For it chews its food again, but does not have feet that are hard and divided. It is unclean to you. 6 Do not eat the rabbit. For it chews its food again, but does not have feet that are hard and divided. It is unclean to you. 7 And do not eat the pig. For it has feet that are hard and divided, but it does not chew its food again. It is unclean to you. 8 Do not eat their flesh or touch their dead bodies. They are unclean to you.

9 'These you may eat, of all that are in the water. You may eat everything in the water that has fins and scales, in the seas or in the rivers. 10 But whatever is in the seas and rivers that does not have fins and scales, among all the living things moving in the water, are to be hated by you. 11 You will hate them. You may not eat their meat, and you will hate their dead bodies. 12 Whatever in the water does not have fins and scales will be hated by you.

13 'These you will hate among the birds. They are hated and not to be eaten: the eagle, the vulture, the buzzard, 14 the kite, every kind of falcon, 15 every kind of raven, 16 the ostrich, the owl, the sea gull, every kind of hawk, 17 the little owl, the cormorant, the big owl, 18 the white owl, the pelican, the vulture that eats dead flesh, 19 the stork, every kind of heron, the hoopoe and the bat.

20 'All bugs with wings and that walk on all fours are to be hated by you. 21 But you may eat, among all the bugs with wings and that walk on all fours, those which have legs above their feet that allow them to jump on the ground. 22 You may eat every kind of locust, every kind of destroying locust, every kind of cricket, and every kind of grasshopper. 23 But you are to hate all other bugs with wings and four feet.

24 'If you touch these you will be unclean. Whoever touches their dead bodies will be unclean until evening. 25 And whoever picks up any of their dead bodies will wash his clothes and be unclean until evening. 26 Every animal that has a parted foot but not a divided foot, or that does not eat its food again, is unclean to you. Whoever touches them will be unclean. 27 Whatever walks on its soft feet, among all the animals that walk on all fours, are unclean to you. Whoever touches their dead bodies will be unclean until evening. 28 And he who picks up their dead bodies will wash his clothes and be unclean until evening. They are unclean to you.

29 'These animals that move on the earth are unclean to you: the mole, the mouse, every kind of big lizard, 30 the gecko, the crocodile, the lizard, the sand lizard, and the chameleon. 31 These animals that move on the earth are unclean to you. Whoever touches their dead bodies will be unclean until evening. 32 And anything on which one of them may fall when they are dead will be unclean. Each piece of wood or clothing or skin or bag or anything used as you work, must be put in water. It will be unclean until evening. Then it will be clean. 33 If any falls into a clay pot, whatever is in the pot will be unclean. You should break the pot. 34 Any food that could be eaten but has water from such a pot on it will be unclean. And anything which could be drunk from any such pot will be unclean. 35 Everything on which part of their dead body may fall will be unclean. A stove or a place for pots must be broken. They are unclean to you. 36 But a well or a place holding water will be clean. But whoever touches a dead body will be unclean. 37 If a part of their dead body falls on any seed which is to be planted, it is clean. 38 But if water is put on the seed, and a body falls on it, it is unclean to you.

39 'If one of the animals dies which you have for food, the one who touches its dead body will be unclean until evening. 40 He who eats some of the dead body will wash his clothes and be unclean until evening. And he who picks up its dead body will wash his clothes and be unclean until evening.

41 'Anything that moves around on the ground in large numbers is hated and is not to be eaten. 42 You should not eat whatever moves on its stomach, or goes on four feet, or has many feet, among all the things that move around on the ground in large numbers. For they are hated. 43 Do not make yourselves unclean by any of the small living things that move together on the ground, so you become unclean. 44 For I am the Lord your God. So set yourselves

apart, and be holy. For I am holy. Do not make yourselves unclean with any of the small living things that move together in large numbers on the ground. 45 For I am the Lord Who brought you out of the land of Egypt to be your God. So be holy, because I am holy.' "

46 This is the Law of the animal, the bird, every living thing that moves in the water, and everything that moves on the ground. 47 It is so you know the difference between those that are clean and those that are unclean, and between the animal that may be eaten and the animal that may not be eaten.

Women after Childbirth

12 Then the Lord said to Moses, 2 "Say to the people of Israel, 'When a woman gives birth to a male child, she will be unclean for seven days as during her time each month. 3 On the eighth day the child is to go through the religious act of becoming a Jew. 4 The mother will be unclean for thirty-three days, until her blood stops flowing. She will not touch any holy thing or go into the holy place, until the days for making her clean are finished. 5 If she gives birth to a female child, she will be unclean for two weeks, as during the time she is unclean each month. She will be unclean for sixty-six days, until her blood stops flowing.

6 'When the days for making her clean are finished, for a son or for a daughter, she will bring her gifts to the religious leader at the door of the meeting tent. She will bring a one year old lamb for a burnt gift, and a young pigeon or a turtle-dove for a sin gift. 7 Then he will give it to the Lord and pay for her sins. She will be made clean from the flow of her blood. This is the Law for her who gives birth to a son or daughter. 8 But if she does not have enough money for a lamb, then she will take two turtle-doves or two young pigeons, one for a burnt gift and the other for a sin gift. The religious leader will pay for her sins and she will be clean.' "

Laws about a Bad Skin Disease

13 The Lord said to Moses and Aaron, 2 "When a man has a sore spot on his skin, an open sore or a bright spot, and it becomes a bad skin disease, he should be brought to the religious leader, to Aaron or one of his sons. 3 The religious leader will look at the mark on his skin of the body. If the hair in the spot has become white and

the disease looks deeper than his skin, it is a bad skin disease. The religious leader will look at him, and will say that he is unclean. 4 But the spot may be white on his skin, and not seem to be deeper than the skin, and the hair on it not white. Then the religious leader will keep the sick man away from other people for seven days. 5 The religious leader will look at him on the seventh day. If he finds that the disease has not changed and has not spread on the skin, the religious leader will keep him away from other people for seven more days. 6 The religious leader will look at him again on the seventh day. If the spot is not as bright and has not spread on the skin, the religious leader will say he is clean. It is only what is left of a sore. He will wash his clothes and be clean.

7 "But if what is left of the sore spreads farther on the skin, after he has been seen by the religious leader as being clean, he must show himself to the religious leader again. 8 And the religious leader will look, and if the sore has spread on the skin, the religious leader will say that he is unclean. It is a bad skin disease.

9 "When a man has a bad skin disease, he will be brought to the religious leader. 10 The religious leader will look at it. If there is a white sore on the skin that has made the hair white, and there are open sores growing on the flesh, 11 it is an old and deep skin disease on his body. The religious leader will say he is unclean. He will not keep him away from others, for he already is unclean. 12 But the disease may spread farther on the skin, and cover all the skin of him who has the disease from head to foot, everywhere the religious leader looks. 13 If the religious leader sees that the skin disease has covered all his body, he will say he is clean from the disease, because the skin has all become white and he is clean. 14 But when open sores in the flesh show on him, he will be unclean. 15 The religious leader will look at the open sores in the flesh, and he will say he is unclean. The open sores in the flesh are unclean. It is a bad skin disease. 16 If the flesh with open sores changes again and becomes white, he will come to the religious leader. 17 If the religious leader sees that the disease has become white, the religious leader will say that he who had the disease is clean; he is clean.

18 "When there is a sore on the skin of the body that has been healed, 19 and in the place of the sore there is a white, growing

spot or a light-red, bright spot, it must be shown to the religious leader. 20 If the religious leader finds that it is under the skin and that the hair on it has become white, the religious leader will say he is unclean. It is the bad skin disease. It has broken out in the sore. 21 But the religious leader may find there are no white hairs in it, and that it is not under the skin and not as dark. Then the religious leader will keep him away from other people for seven days. 22 If it spreads farther on the skin, the religious leader will say he is unclean. It is a spreading disease. 23 But if the bright spot stays in one place and does not spread, it is only what is left of the sore. The religious leader will say he is clean.

24 "If the body has a burn on its skin, and the open sore of the burned flesh becomes a bright spot, light-red or white, 25 the religious leader must look at it. If the hair in the bright spot has become white and it shows to be deeper than the skin, it is a bad skin disease. It has broken out in the burn. So the religious leader will say he is unclean. It is a bad skin disease. 26 But the religious leader may find there is no white hair in the bright spot, and that it is not under the skin and not as dark. Then the religious leader will keep him away from other people for seven days. 27 On the seventh day the religious leader will look at him. If it has spread farther in the skin, the religious leader will say he is unclean. It is a bad skin disease. 28 But if the bright spot stays in one place and has not spread in the skin and is not as dark, it is only what is left of the burn. The religious leader will say he is clean. For it is what is left of the burn.

29 "When a man or woman has a sore on the head or in the hair of the face, 30 the religious leader will look at the sore. If it looks like it is under the skin, with yellow, fine hair in it, the religious leader will say he is unclean. It is a bad skin disease of the head or hair of the face. 31 But the religious leader may find that the skin disease is not under the skin and there is no black hair in it. Then the religious leader will keep the person with the disease away from other people for seven days. 32 On the seventh day the religious leader will look at the disease. If the sore has not spread, and no yellow hair has grown in it, and it does not look like it is under the skin, 33 then the sick man will cut off his hair. But he will not cut the hair from the sore. The religious leader will keep the person with the disease away

from other people seven more days. 34 On the seventh day the religious leader will look at the disease. If the disease has not spread and looks like it is not under the skin, the religious leader will say he is clean. And he will wash his clothes and be clean. 35 But if the disease spreads farther in the skin after he was to have been clean, 36 then the religious leader will look at him. If the disease has spread in the skin, the religious leader does not need to look for yellow hair. He is unclean. 37 But if he finds that the disease has stayed in one place and black hair has grown in it, the disease has healed. He is clean. And the religious leader will say he is clean.

38 "When a man or woman has very white spots on the skin of their body, 39 then the religious leader will look at them. If the white spots on the skin are not very bright, it is not a bad disease that has broken out on the skin. He is clean.

40 "If a man's hair has fallen out and he has no hair on his head, he is clean. 41 If the hair has fallen from the front part of his head so that he has no hair there, he is clean. 42 But if a red and white sore is on the head where there is no hair, it is a bad skin disease breaking out on his head. 43 Then the religious leader will look at him. If the sore is red and white on the head where there is no hair, looking like a bad disease in the skin of the body, 44 he is a man with a bad skin disease. He is unclean. The religious leader will say he is unclean. His disease is on his head.

Laws about Clothing

45 "The person who has the bad skin disease will wear torn clothes and not cover the hair of his head. He will cover his mouth and cry out, 'Unclean! Unclean!' 46 He will be unclean as long as he has the disease. He is unclean. He will live alone. His home will be away from the tents. 47 When a mark of a bad skin disease is in a piece of clothing, wool or linen, 48 in the cloth of linen or wool, or in leather or anything made of leather, 49 if the mark is green or red in the clothing or leather, in the cloth or in anything made of leather, it is the mark of a bad skin disease. It will be shown to the religious leader. 50 The religious leader will look at the mark, and will keep the piece of clothing away from people for seven days. 51 He will look at the mark again on the seventh day. If the mark has spread in the clothing, in the cloth or leather or anything made of leather, the

mark is a bad disease. It is unclean. ⁵² So he will burn the clothing if the disease is in the cloth, in wool or linen or in anything made of leather, for it is a very bad disease. It will be burned in the fire.

⁵³ "But the religious leader may look and find that the mark has not spread in the clothing, in the cloth or anything made of leather. ⁵⁴ Then the religious leader will tell them to wash the thing that has the mark of disease. And he will keep it away from people for seven more days. ⁵⁵ After the piece of cloth or leather with the mark has been washed, the religious leader will look at it again. If the mark has not changed, even if the mark has not spread, it is unclean. You will burn it in the fire, if the mark of disease is on the back or the front.

⁵⁶ "But the religious leader may find that the mark is not as easy to see after it is washed. Then he will tear it out of the clothing, leather or cloth. ⁵⁷ If it is seen again in the clothing, in cloth or anything made of leather, it is spreading. The thing that has the mark will be burned in the fire. ⁵⁸ But if the clothing, cloth or anything made of leather, had the mark washed out of it, it will then be washed a second time. And it will be clean."

⁵⁹ This is the law for the mark of a very bad disease in clothing of wool or linen, in cloth or in anything made of leather, for deciding if it is clean or not.

Laws about Skin Diseases

14 The Lord said to Moses, ² "This is the law of the person with a bad skin disease when he is made clean. He will be brought to the religious leader. ³ The religious leader will go away from the tents and look at him. If the sick person has been healed of the bad skin disease, ⁴ the religious leader must have two live clean birds, cedar wood, a red string and hyssop brought for the one who is to be made clean. ⁵ The religious leader will have one of the birds killed in a clay pot over flowing water. ⁶ Then he will take the living bird with the cedar wood, the red string and the hyssop. He will put them and the live bird in the blood of the bird that was killed over the flowing water. ⁷ He will put blood seven times on the one who is to be made clean from the bad skin disease. And he will say he is clean. Then he will let the live bird go free over the open field. ⁸ The one to be made clean will wash his clothes, cut off all his hair, wash

himself in water, and be clean. After that he may go among the tents. But he must stay outside his tent for seven days. ⁹ On the seventh day he will cut off his hair. He will cut the hair from his head and face, all his hair. Then he will wash his clothes and wash himself in water, and be clean.

¹⁰ "On the eighth day he is to take two male lambs that are perfect, a year old female lamb that is perfect, three-tenths part of a basket of fine flour mixed with oil for a grain gift, and one jar of oil. ¹¹ The religious leader who makes him clean will set the man who is to be made clean and these things before the Lord at the door of the meeting tent. ¹² Then the religious leader will take the one male lamb and bring it for a guilt gift with the jar of oil. He will give them as a wave gift before the Lord. ¹³ He will kill the lamb in the holy place where they kill the sin gifts and the burnt gifts. For the guilt gift belongs to the religious leader like the sin gift. It is most holy. ¹⁴ Then the religious leader will take some of the blood of the guilt gift. He will put it on the bottom part of the right ear of the person to be made clean. And he will put it on the thumb of his right hand and on the big toe of his right foot. ¹⁵ Then the religious leader will take some of the oil in the jar and pour it into his left hand. ¹⁶ The religious leader will put a finger of his right hand into the oil that is in his left hand seven times before the Lord. ¹⁷ Then the religious leader will put some of the rest of the oil upon the blood of the guilt gift on the bottom part of the right ear, the thumb of the right hand and the big toe of the right foot of the person to be made clean. ¹⁸ The rest of the oil in the religious leader's hand will be put on the head of the person to be made clean. So the religious leader will pay for the person's sins before the Lord. ¹⁹ The religious leader will then give the sin gift to pay for the sins of the person to be made clean. After that he will kill the burnt gift. ²⁰ The religious leader will give the burnt gift and the grain gift on the altar. So the religious leader will pay for the person's sins, and he will be clean.

²¹ "But if he is poor and does not have enough money for so much, he will take one male lamb for a guilt gift, a wave gift, to pay for his sins. And he will take one-tenth part of a basket of fine flour mixed with oil for a grain gift, a jar of oil, ²² and two turtle-doves or two young pigeons, whatever he is able to buy. One will be a sin gift and the other a burnt gift. ²³ On

the eighth day he will bring them to the religious leader at the door of the meeting tent before the Lord so he can be made clean. 24 The religious leader will take the lamb of the guilt gift and the jar of oil. And the religious leader will wave them as the wave gift before the Lord. 25 Then he will kill the lamb of the guilt gift. The religious leader will take some of the blood of the guilt gift and put it on the bottom part of the right ear, the thumb of the right hand and the big toe of the right foot of the person to be made clean. 26 The religious leader will pour some of the oil into his left hand. 27 The religious leader will put a finger of his right hand into the oil that is in the left hand seven times before the Lord. 28 Then the religious leader will put some of the oil in his hand on the bottom part of the right ear, the thumb of the right hand and the big toe of the right foot of the person to be made clean. It will be put on the place where he has put the blood of the guilt gift. 29 The rest of the oil in the religious leader's hand will be put on the head of the person to be made clean, to pay for his sins before the Lord. 30 Then he will give one of the turtle-doves or young pigeons that he was able to buy. 31 He will give what he is able to give, one for a sin gift and the other for a burnt gift, together with the grain gift. So the religious leader will pay for the sins of the person to be made clean before the Lord. 32 This is the law for him who had a bad skin disease and is not able to buy what is needed for making him clean."

Laws about the House Where the Person with a Bad Skin Disease Lived

33 The Lord said to Moses and Aaron, 34 "When you come into the land of Canaan, which I give you for your own, and I put a mark of a bad skin disease on a house in your land, 35 then the one who owns the house will come and tell the religious leader, 'I see something like a mark of a bad skin disease in my house.' 36 Then the religious leader will tell them to empty the house before he goes in to look at the mark, so he will not say that everything in the house is unclean. After this the religious leader will go in to look at the house. 37 He will look at the mark of the disease. If the mark is in the walls of the house with green or red spots deep in the walls, 38 the religious leader will go out the door and shut up the house for seven days. 39 He will come again on the seventh

day and look. If the disease has spread in the walls of the house, 40 the religious leader will tell them to tear out the stones with the disease in them and throw them away outside the city at an unclean place. 41 He will have the walls and floors of the house cleaned inside. And they will take the pieces that are rubbed off to an unclean place outside the city. 42 Then they will take other stones to put in the place of those stones. And he will cover the walls with a new covering.

43 "If the disease comes again in the house, after he has taken out the stones, cleaned the house inside and covered the walls again, 44 then the religious leader will come and look. If the disease has spread in the house, it is a very bad disease in the house. It is unclean. 45 He will tear down the house, its stones, wood, and all the covering of the house. And he will take the pieces outside the city to an unclean place. 46 Anyone who goes into the house during the time it is shut up will be unclean until evening. 47 Whoever lies down in the house will wash his clothes. And whoever eats in the house will wash his clothes.

48 "But the religious leader may come in and find that the disease has not spread in the house after its walls have been covered again. Then the religious leader will say the house is clean, because the mark of the disease cannot be seen. 49 He will take two birds, cedar wood, a red string and hyssop to make the house clean. 50 He will kill one of the birds in a clay pot over flowing water. 51 Then he will take the cedar wood and the hyssop and the red string, with the live bird, and put them in the blood of the killed bird and in the flowing water. And he will put some of the blood and water on the house seven times. 52 He will make the house clean with the blood of the bird, the flowing water, the live bird, the cedar wood, the hyssop and the red string. 53 He will let the live bird go free outside the city into the open field. So he will take away sin from the house, and it will be clean."

54 This is the law for any very bad skin disease, even a sore, 55 and for a disease in clothing or in a house, 56 and for a growing sore, and what is left of a sore, and for a bright spot. 57 It is to teach when they are unclean, and when they are clean. This is the law of the very bad skin disease.

Laws about Flows from the Body

15 The Lord said to Moses and Aaron, [2] "Say to the people of Israel, 'When a man has something flowing from his body, what is flowing is unclean. [3] If it flows, or if it fills up and stops flowing, he will be unclean. [4] Every bed on which the person with the flow lies will be unclean. [5] Whoever touches his bed must wash his clothes and wash himself in water. And he will be unclean until evening. [6] Whoever sits where the man with the flow has been sitting must wash his clothes and wash himself with water. He will be unclean until evening. [7] Whoever touches the person with the flow must wash his clothes and wash himself in water. And he will be unclean until evening. [8] If the man with the flow spits on one who is clean, then he must wash his clothes, wash himself in water, and be unclean until evening. [9] Any leather seat on which the man with the flow is unclean has been sitting will be unclean. [10] Whoever touches anything that was under him will be unclean until evening. [11] Anyone the man with the flow touches must wash his clothes and wash himself in water. He will be unclean until evening. [12] The clay pot that the man with the flow touches must be broken. And anything made of wood must be washed in water.

[13] 'When the flow of the man stops, he will take seven days to make himself clean. Then he will wash his clothes and wash his body in running water. And he will be clean. [14] On the eighth day he will take two turtle-doves or two young pigeons, come before the Lord at the door of the meeting tent, and give them to the religious leader. [15] The religious leader will give them, one for a sin gift, and the other for a burnt gift. So the religious leader will pay for his sins before the Lord because of his flow.

[16] 'If a man's seed comes from his sex part, he must wash his whole body in water. And he will be unclean until evening. [17] Any clothing or leather on which the seed touches must be washed with water. It will be unclean until evening. [18] If a man lies with a woman so that seed goes out from him, they must both wash themselves in water and will be unclean until evening.

[19] 'When a woman has something flowing from her body, and if it is blood, she will be unclean for seven days. Whoever touches her will be unclean until evening. [20] Everything she lies on while she is unclean will be unclean. And everything she sits on will be unclean. [21] Whoever touches her bed must wash his clothes and wash himself in water and be unclean until evening. [22] Whoever touches anything she sits on must wash his clothes and wash himself in water and be unclean until evening. [23] If he touches anything on her bed or where she sat, he will be unclean until evening. [24] If a man lies with her so that her blood is on him, he will be unclean for seven days. And every bed he lies on will be unclean.

[25] 'If a woman has a flow of blood for many days, at a different time than when it happens each month, or if the blood flows longer at that time, all the days the blood flows she will be unclean. It will be as if it were the time when she is unclean each month. She will be unclean. [26] Any bed she lies on while her blood is flowing will be like the bed during the time she is unclean and whatever she sits on will be unclean. [27] Whoever touches them will be unclean. He must wash his clothes and wash himself in water and be unclean until evening. [28] When she becomes clean from her flow, she will wait seven days. After that she will be clean. [29] On the eighth day she will take two turtle-doves or two young pigeons, and bring them to the religious leader at the door of the meeting tent. [30] The religious leader will give one for a sin gift and the other for a burnt gift. In this way the woman will be clean before the Lord from the flow of blood that made her unclean.'

[31] "In this way you will keep the people of Israel away from whatever makes them unclean or they will die because of making My meeting tent unclean that is among them." [32] This is the law for him who has something flowing from his body, and for the man whose seed flows from his sex part and makes him unclean. [33] And this is the law for the woman who is sick because of her flow of blood, and for the man or woman who has something flowing from the body, and for the man who lies with a woman who is unclean.

Animals Pay the Price for Man's Sin

16 The Lord spoke to Moses after the death of Aaron's two sons, when they had come near the Lord and died. [2] The Lord said to Moses, "Tell your brother Aaron that he must not come just any time into the holy place inside the curtain, in front of the mercy-seat on the special box of the agreement or he will die. For I will show Myself in the cloud over the mercy-seat. ³ Only this way will Aaron go into the holy place, with a bull for a sin gift and a ram for a burnt gift. ⁴ He will put on the holy linen coat. And the linen under-clothing will be next to his body. He will be wearing the linen belt and the linen head-covering. These are holy clothing. He will wash his body in water and then dress himself. ⁵ He will take from the people of Israel two male goats for a sin gift and one ram for a burnt gift. ⁶ Then Aaron will give the bull as a sin gift for himself, to pay for the sins of himself and those in his house. ⁷ He will take the two goats and set them before the Lord at the door of the meeting tent. ⁸ Aaron will draw names for the two goats, choosing one for the Lord and the other to be sent away. ⁹ Then Aaron will bring the goat that was chosen for the Lord and give it as a sin gift. ¹⁰ But the goat that was chosen to be sent away will be brought alive before the Lord, for the taking away of sin. And it will be sent into the desert.

¹¹ "Then Aaron will give the bull as the sin gift for himself, to pay for the sins of himself and those in his house. He will kill the bull as the sin gift for himself. ¹² He will take a fire pan full of fire from the altar before the Lord, and enough fine, ground, sweet perfume to fill two hands. And he will bring it inside the curtain. ¹³ He will put the special perfume on the fire before the Lord so that the cloud of the special perfume covers the mercy-seat on the special box of the agreement or he will die. ¹⁴ He will take some of the bull's blood and put it with his finger on the east side of the mercy-seat. And with his finger he will put some of the blood seven times in front of the mercy-seat.

¹⁵ "Then he will kill the goat as the sin gift for the people. He will bring its blood inside the curtain, and do the same with its blood as he did with the bull's blood. He will put it on the seat and in front of the mercy-seat. ¹⁶ He will make the holy place, and also the meeting tent which is in the center of the camp, clean and pure because all the sins of the people make them unclean. ¹⁷ When he goes in to pay for sins in the holy place, no one will be in the meeting tent until he comes out. He will pay for the sins of himself, of those in his house, and of all the people of Israel. ¹⁸ Then he will go out to the altar before the Lord and make it clean and pure. He will take some of the bull's blood and goat's blood and put it on the horns of the

altar on all sides. ¹⁹ With his finger he will put some of the blood on the altar seven times so it will be clean. He will set it apart from what is unclean among the people of Israel.

²⁰ "When he finishes making the holy place, the meeting tent and the altar free from sin, he will give the live goat. ²¹ Aaron will lay both his hands on the head of the live goat, and tell of all the sins and wrong-doings of the people of Israel. He will lay them upon the head of the goat and send it away into the desert by the hand of a man ready to help. ²² The goat will carry upon itself all their sins to a land where no one lives. Then the man will let the goat go free there.

²³ "Aaron will come into the meeting tent. He will take off the linen clothing he put on when he went into the holy place. And he will leave them there. ²⁴ He will wash his body with water in a holy place and put on his clothes. Then he will come out and give his burnt gift and the people's burnt gift, to pay for the sins of himself and the people. ²⁵ He will burn the fat of the sin gift on the altar. ²⁶ The man who let the goat carry away the sins will wash his clothes and wash his body with water. Then he may come among the tents. ²⁷ The bull and the goat for the sin gift, whose blood was brought in to pay for sins in the holy place, will be taken away from the tents. Their skin, their flesh and their waste will be burned with fire. ²⁸ Whoever burns them will wash his clothes and wash his body with water. Then he may come among the tents.

²⁹ "This will be a Law forever for you. On the tenth day of the seventh month, you must get rid of your pride and not do any work, both those who live in the land and those who visit from another land. ³⁰ For on this day your sin will be taken away and you will be clean. You will be made free from all your sins before the Lord. ³¹ It is to be a special Day of Rest for you, that you may be free from pride. It is a Law forever. ³² The chosen religious leader who is set apart to work as religious leader in his father's place will pay for the sin. He will put on the holy linen clothing ³³ and make the holy place, the meeting tent and the altar free from sin. He will make the religious leaders and all the people free from sin also. ³⁴ This will be a Law forever for you. The people of Israel must be made free from all their sins once a year." And Moses did what the Lord told him to do.

Blood Must Not Be Eaten

17 The Lord said to Moses, [2] "Say to Aaron and his sons and to all the people of Israel, 'This is what the Lord has told us to do. [3] If any man of the house of Israel kills a bull, lamb or goat, among the tents or away from the tents, [4] and has not brought it to the door of the meeting tent to give it to the Lord, he will be guilty for that blood, and will not be among God's people. [5] The reason is so that the people of Israel may bring their gifts which were killed in the open field to the Lord, to the religious leader at the door of the meeting tent. Then they can be given as peace gifts to the Lord. [6] The religious leader will put the blood on the altar of the Lord at the door of the meeting tent. And he will burn the fat for a pleasing smell to the Lord. [7] So they will no longer give their gifts to the goat-like gods to whom they sell themselves. This will be a Law to them for all their people forever.'

[8] "Then say to them, 'Any man of the house of Israel, or visiting from another land, who gives a burnt gift or other gift, [9] and does not bring it to the door of the meeting tent to give it to the Lord, will be cut off from his people.

[10] 'If any man of the house of Israel, or visiting from another land, eats any blood, I will turn against that person who eats blood, and he will not be among God's people. [11] For the life of the flesh is in the blood. I have given it to you on the altar to make your souls free from sin. For the blood makes you free from sin because of the life in it.' [12] So I have said to the people of Israel, 'None of you should eat blood. And the man who visits you from another land should not eat blood.' [13] If any man from the people of Israel, or from other people living among them, catches an animal or bird which may be eaten, he should pour out its blood and cover it with dust.

[14] "For blood is the life of every living thing. So I said to the people of Israel, 'Do not eat the blood of any living thing. For the life of every living thing is its blood. Whoever eats it will be cut off.' [15] Every person, both living in the land or one who has come from another land, who eats an animal that dies or is killed by wild animals, must wash his clothes and wash himself in water. He will be unclean until evening. Then he will be clean. [16] But if he does not wash them or wash his body, he will suffer for his own sin."

Laws about Sex

18 The Lord said to Moses, [2] "Say to the people of Israel, 'I am the Lord your God. [3] Do not do what is done in the land of Egypt where you lived. And do not do what is done in the land of Canaan where I am bringing you. Do not follow their laws. [4] You are to do what I say and keep My Laws and live by them. I am the Lord your God. [5] So keep My Laws and do what I say. If a man obeys them, My Laws will be life for him. I am the Lord.

[6] 'You should not go near a person of your own family to have sex. I am the Lord. [7] Do not put your father to shame by taking the clothes off your mother. She is your mother. Do not take her clothes off. [8] Do not take the clothes off your father's wife. Her body is for your father. [9] Do not take the clothes off your sister, the daughter of your father or of your mother, if she is born at home or away from home. [10] Do not take the clothes off your son's daughter or your daughter's daughter. For they are of your own family. [11] Do not take the clothes off your father's wife's daughter, born to your father. She is your sister. [12] Do not take the clothes off your father's sister. She is of your father's own family. [13] Do not take the clothes off your mother's sister. She is of your mother's own family. [14] Do not put your father's brother to shame. Do not go near to take the clothes off his wife. She is of your family. [15] Do not take the clothes off your daughter-in-law. She is your son's wife. Do not take her clothes off. [16] Do not take the clothes off your brother's wife. Her body is for your brother. [17] Do not take the clothes off a woman and her daughter. And do not take the clothes off her son's daughter or her daughter's daughter. They are of her own family. It is sin. [18] While your wife is still living do not marry her sister making her as important to you. Do not take off her sister's clothes.

[19] 'And you are not to go near a woman to take off her clothes during the time when she has a flow of blood. [20] Do not have sex with your neighbor's wife. You would be unclean. [21] Do not give any of your children as a gift on an altar to the false god Molech. Do not put the name of your God to shame. I am the Lord. [22] Do not lie with a man as one lies with a woman. It is a sinful thing. [23] Do not have sex with any animal, or you will be unclean. And no woman should give herself to an animal to lie with it. It is a sin.

24 'Do not allow yourself to sin in any of these ways. For by doing all these things the nations that I am driving out in front of you became unclean. 25 For the land is unclean. So I have punished its sin. The land has spit out its people. 26 But as for you, you are to keep My Laws and do what I have decided. Do not do any of these sinful things, not you or the man who lives among you from another land. 27 For the men who have lived in the land before you have done all of these sinful things. The land is unclean. 28 Do none of these things or the land will spit you out when you make it sinful, as it has spit out the nation that was before you. 29 Whoever does any of these sinful things will be cut off from his people. 30 So do what I say. Do not do any of these sinful things that were done before you. Do not make yourselves sin by doing them. I am the Lord your God.' "

Laws about Right Living

19 The Lord said to Moses, 2 "Say to all the people of Israel, 'Be holy, for I the Lord your God am holy. 3 Every one of you must have respect for his mother and his father. And keep My Days of Rest. I am the Lord your God. 4 Do not turn to false gods or make gods for yourselves. I am the Lord your God.

5 'When you give the Lord a peace gift, give it so you will be pleasing Him. 6 It will be eaten the same day you give it, and the next day. But what is left until the third day will be burned with fire. 7 If it is eaten at all on the third day, it is a sin. It will not be received. 8 Every one who eats it will carry his guilt. For he has made the holy thing of the Lord sinful. That person will not be among God's people.

9 'When you pick the food of your land at gathering time, do not pick all the way to the corners of your field. And do not gather the food left on the ground there after you have picked. 10 Do not gather what is left among your vines, or gather the grapes that have fallen. Leave them for those in need and for the stranger. I am the Lord your God.

11 'Do not steal. Be honest in what you do. Do not lie to one another. 12 Do not lie when you make a promise in My name, and so put the name of your God to shame. I am the Lord.

13 'Do not make it hard for your neighbor or rob him. You should not keep the pay of a man who works for you until the next morning. 14 Do not say bad things against a man who cannot hear. Do not put something in the way of a man who cannot see. But fear your God. I am the Lord.

15 'Be fair in how you judge. Do not show favor to the poor or to the great. Be fair in how you judge your neighbor. 16 Do not go around saying things that hurt your people. Do not do things against the life of your neighbor. I am the Lord.

17 'In your heart do not hate someone from your own country. You may speak sharp words to your neighbor, but do not sin because of him. 18 Do not hurt someone who has hurt you. Do not keep on hating the sons of your people, but love your neighbor as yourself. I am the Lord.

19 'Keep My Laws. Do not let your cattle have young by a different kind. Do not plant your field with two kinds of seed. Do not wear clothing made of two kinds of cloth. 20 If a man lies with a woman who is a servant, promised to another man, but has not been paid for or made free, they must be punished. But they will not be put to death, because she was not free. 21 He will bring his guilt gift to the Lord at the door of the meeting tent. A ram will be used for the guilt gift before the Lord. 22 With it the religious leader will go through the worship of washing to take away the man's sin, and he will be forgiven for the sin he has done.

23 'When you come into the land and plant all kinds of trees for food, think of their fruit as being something you should not touch. You should not touch it for three years. It must not be eaten. 24 But in the fourth year all their fruit will be holy, a gift of praise to the Lord. 25 In the fifth year you may eat of their fruit, so they may give more food for you. I am the Lord your God.

26 'Do not eat anything with the blood in it. Do not tell the future or do witchcraft. 27 Do not cut the hair on the side of your head or face. 28 Do not make any cuts on your body for the dead. Do not burn any pictures that will stay on your body. I am the Lord.

29 'Do not put your daughter to shame by making her sell the use of her body. Or the land will become full of shame and sin. 30 Keep My Days of Rest and honor My holy place. I am the Lord.

31 'Do not ask what you should do from those who speak with bad spirits or talk to the dead. Do not find them or you will be unclean. I am the Lord your God.

32 'Show respect to the person with white

hair. Honor an older person and you will honor your God. I am the Lord.

33 'If a stranger lives with you in your land, do not do wrong to him. 34 You should act toward the stranger who lives among you as you would toward one born among you. Love him as you love yourself. For you were strangers in the land of Egypt. I am the Lord your God.

35 'Do not lie about the weight or price of anything. 36 Always tell the truth about it. I am the Lord your God, Who brought you out of the land of Egypt. 37 Keep all My Laws and do all that I tell you. I am the Lord.' "

Punishment for Those Who Do Not Obey the Law

20 The Lord said to Moses, 2 "Say to the people of Israel, 'Any man of Israel or of the strangers living in Israel, who gives any of his children to the false god Molech, must be put to death. The people of the land will kill him with stones. 3 I Myself will go against that man and he will not be numbered among God's people, because he has given some of his children to Molech, making My holy place sinful and bringing shame on My holy name. 4 If the people of the land close their eyes when a man gives any of his children to Molech, and do not put him to death, 5 then I Myself will go against that man and his family. They will not be numbered among God's people, and all who follow him to sell themselves to Molech.

6 'I will go against the person who turns to those who speak with bad spirits and talk to the dead. In doing this, he sells himself to them. He will not be numbered among God's people. 7 So you should set yourselves apart and be holy. For I am the Lord your God. 8 Keep My Laws and live by them. I am the Lord Who sets you apart.

9 'If there is anyone who curses his father or mother, he will for sure be put to death. Because he has cursed his father or mother, his blood will be on his own head.

10 'If a man does sex sins with another man's wife, even his friend's wife, both the sinful man and woman must be put to death. 11 If a man lies with his father's wife, he has put his father to shame. Both of the guilty ones must be put to death. They will suffer for their own sin. 12 If a man lies with his daughter-in-law, both of them must be put to death. They have done a bad sex sin. They will suffer for their own sin. 13 If a man lies with a male as if he were

a woman, both of them have done a very sinful act. They must be put to death. They will suffer for their own sin. 14 If a man marries a woman and her mother, it is sin. Both he and they will be burned with fire, so this kind of sin will not be among you. 15 If a man lies with an animal, he must be put to death. Kill the animal also. 16 If a woman goes near any animal to have sex with it, you must kill the woman and the animal. They must be put to death. They will suffer for their own sin.

17 'If a man takes his sister, his father's or mother's daughter, and he sees her without clothes on and she sees him, it is a shame. They will be punished in front of their people. He has taken off his sister's clothes. He will suffer for his own sin. 18 If a man lies with a woman who has a flow of blood, and takes her clothes off, he has made her flow to show. And she has shown the flow of her blood. So both of them will not be numbered among God's people. 19 Do not take the clothes off your mother's sister or father's sister. For that is putting to shame one of your own family. They will suffer for their own sin. 20 If a man lies with the wife of his father's or mother's brother, he has put to shame his father's or mother's brother. They will suffer for their own sin. They will die without children. 21 If a man takes his brother's wife, it is sin. He has put his brother to shame. They will have no children.

22 'Keep all My Laws and do what I tell you, so the land where I am bringing you to live will not spit you out. 23 Do not follow the ways of the nation which I am driving out before you. For they did all these things, and so I hated them. 24 But I have said to you, "Their land will belong to you. I Myself will give it to you for your own, a land flowing with milk and honey." I am the Lord your God, Who has set you apart from all other peoples. 25 You are to know the difference between the clean animal and the animal that is unclean, and between the clean bird and the bird that is unclean. Do not make yourselves a sinful people with animal or bird or anything that moves on the ground, which I have set apart from you as being unclean. 26 Be holy to Me, for I the Lord am holy. I have divided you from the nations, so you belong to Me.

27 'A man or woman who speaks with bad spirits or who talks to the dead must be put to death. They will be killed with stones. They will suffer for their own sin.' "

How the Religious Leaders Should Live

21 The Lord said to Moses, "Say to the religious leaders, the sons of Aaron, 'No one should make himself unclean for a dead person among his people, 2 except for his own family, his mother, father, son, daughter and brother, 3 or his young sister who is near to him because she has had no husband. For her he may make himself unclean. 4 He should not make himself unclean as a husband among his people, and so make himself sinful. 5 They should not cut all the hair from any part on their heads, or cut part of the hair off their face, or make cuts in their flesh. 6 They should be holy to their God and not put the name of their God to shame. For they give the gifts by fire to the Lord, the bread of their God. So they must be holy. 7 They should not take a woman who is unclean because of selling the use of her body. They should not take a woman who is divorced from her husband. For the religious leader is holy to his God. 8 So you must set him apart, for he gives the bread of your God. He will be holy to you. For I, the Lord Who sets you apart, am holy. 9 If the daughter of any religious leader makes herself sinful by selling the use of her body, she puts her father to shame. She will be burned with fire.

10 'The head religious leader on whose head the holy oil has been poured, and who has been set apart to wear the clothing, must not take the covering off his head or tear his clothes. 11 He must not go near any dead person or make himself unclean even for his father or mother. 12 He must not go out of the holy place or sin against the holy place of his God. For the crown of the holy oil of his God is on him. I am the Lord. 13 He should take a wife who has never had a man before. 14 He should not marry a woman whose husband has died, or a divorced woman, or one who has made herself sinful by selling the use of her body. But he should marry a woman from his own people, who has never had a man. 15 By doing this he will not sin against his children among his people. For I am the Lord Who makes him holy.'"

16 Then the Lord said to Moses, 17 "Say to Aaron, 'None of your children or their children who has something wrong with his body should go near to give the bread as a gift to his God. 18 For no one whose body is not perfect should come near, no blind man, or man who cannot walk, or one with a marked face, or a bad arm or leg, 19 or a man who has a broken foot or hand, 20 or a man with a crooked upper back from birth, or a very little man, or one who has a bad eye or skin trouble or sores, or one whose sex parts have been crushed. 21 No man among the children of Aaron the religious leader, who has something wrong with his body, should come near to give the Lord's gifts by fire. He should not come near to give the bread of his God, because he has something wrong with him. 22 He may eat the bread of his God, both of the most holy and of the holy. 23 But he should not come near the curtain or the altar, because he has something wrong with him, and so he may not sin against My holy places. For I am the Lord Who makes them holy.'" 24 So Moses spoke to Aaron and to his sons and to all the people of Israel.

22 The Lord said to Moses, 2 "Tell Aaron and his sons to be careful with the holy gifts that the people of Israel set apart for Me. So they will not sin against My holy name. I am the Lord. 3 Say to them, 'If any one of all your children comes near the holy gifts that the people of Israel set apart for the Lord, while he is unclean, he will be cut off from My holy place. I am the Lord. 4 None of the children of Aaron who has a bad skin disease or something flowing from his body may eat of the holy gifts until he is clean. If one touches anything that is unclean because of a dead body, or has had his seed come from his sex part, 5 or touches anything that is unclean that moves on the ground, or touches any man who makes him unclean, for whatever reason, 6 the man who touches any such thing will be unclean until evening. He must not eat of the holy gifts unless he has washed his body in water. 7 When the sun has gone down, he will be clean. After that he may eat of the holy gifts, for they are his food. 8 He should not eat an animal that dies of itself or is killed by wild animals. He will be unclean if he does. I am the Lord. 9 The religious leaders must obey My Law, so they will not be sinful because of it and die because they sin against My Law. I am the Lord Who makes them holy.

10 'But no one who is not a religious leader may eat the holy gift. One who is visiting the religious leader or working for him must not eat of the holy gift. 11 But a person whom the religious leader buys to work for him with his own money may eat of it. And those who are born in his house may eat of his food. 12 If a religious

leader's daughter is married to a man who is not a religious leader, she must not eat of the holy gifts. 13 But if a religious leader's daughter loses her husband by death or divorce, and has no child and returns to her father's house as when she was young, she may eat of her father's food. But no stranger may eat of it. 14 If a man eats a holy gift by mistake, he must add a fifth of its worth to it and give the holy gift to the religious leader. 15 The religious leaders must not make the holy gifts unclean that the people of Israel give to the Lord. 16 This would bring sin upon them when they eat their holy gifts. For I am the Lord Who makes them holy.' "

Gifts That Are Not Good Enough

17 Then the Lord said to Moses, 18 "Say to Aaron and to his sons and to all the people of Israel, 'When any man of the house of Israel or of the strangers in Israel gives his gift for a burnt gift to the Lord, to pay a promise or as a free-will gift 19 to please the Lord, it must be a male that is perfect from the cattle, sheep or goats. 20 Do not give anything that is not perfect, for you will not please the Lord. 21 When a man gives a peace gift to the Lord to keep a special promise or for a free-will gift from the cattle or the flock, it must be perfect to be received. It must have nothing wrong with it. 22 You must not give to the Lord or make a gift by fire on the altar to the Lord any animals that are blind or broken or hurt or have a flowing sore or a skin disease. 23 You may give for a free-will gift a bull or lamb which has some part too long or too short. But it will not be received if it is to pay a promise. 24 Do not give to the Lord any animal with its sex parts hurt or crushed or torn or cut. Do not give such animals on the altar in your land. 25 And do not receive such animals from a man from another land to give as the food of your God. For they are unclean. They are not perfect. They will not be received from you.' "

26 The Lord said to Moses, 27 "When a bull or sheep or goat is born, it must stay seven days with its mother. After that it will be received as a gift by fire to the Lord. 28 But do not kill a cow or female sheep and her young on the same day. 29 When you give thanks to the Lord by giving a gift in worship, give it the right way so you will be received. 30 It must be eaten on the same day. Do not leave any of it until morning. I am the Lord.

31 "So keep My Laws and obey them. I am the Lord. 32 Do not sin against My holy name. I will be honored among the people of Israel. I am the Lord Who makes you holy. 33 I brought you out of the land of Egypt to be your God. I am the Lord."

Religious Suppers

23 The Lord said to Moses, 2 "Say to the people of Israel, 'These are the special suppers of the Lord, which you will keep for holy meetings. These are My special suppers. 3 Work may be done for six days. But the seventh day is the Day of Rest, a holy meeting when you do no work at all. It is the Day of Rest to the Lord in all your homes.

The Supper of Bread without Yeast

4 'These are the special suppers of the Lord, the holy meetings you will keep at the right times. 5 On the fourteenth day of the first month in the evening begins the Lord's religious gathering to remember how His people left Egypt. 6 On the fifteenth day of the same month is the Lord's special supper of bread without yeast. For seven days you will eat bread made without yeast. 7 On the first day you will have a holy meeting. You will not do any hard work. 8 But you will give a gift by fire to the Lord for seven days. On the seventh day is a holy meeting. You will not do any hard work.' "

The Supper of First-Fruits

9 Then the Lord said to Moses, 10 "Say to the people of Israel, 'When you come into the land I am going to give you and gather its grain, bring some of the first-fruits of your grain to the religious leader. 11 He will wave the grain before the Lord for you to be received. The religious leader will wave it on the day after the Day of Rest. 12 On the day when you wave the grain, you will give a perfect, one year old male lamb as a burnt gift to the Lord. 13 The grain gift with it will be one-fifth part of a basket of fine flour mixed with oil. It is a gift by fire to the Lord for a pleasing smell. And the drink gift with it will be a jar of wine. 14 Do not eat bread or dry grain or new grain until this same day, when you have brought the gift to your God. It is to be a Law forever for all your people in all your homes.

The Supper of Weeks

15 'Number seven full weeks from the day after the Day of Rest, from the day when

you give the grain for the wave gift. There will be seven whole Days of Rest. 16 Number fifty days to the day after the seventh Day of Rest. Then give a new grain gift to the Lord. 17 Bring from your homes two loaves of bread for a wave gift, made of one-fifth part of a basket of fine flour. They will be made with yeast, as first-fruits to the Lord. 18 With the bread give seven one year old male lambs that are perfect, and one young bull, and two rams. They will be a burnt gift to the Lord, with their grain gift and their drink gift. It is a gift by fire with a pleasing smell to the Lord. 19 Then give one male goat for a sin gift and two male lambs one year old for a peace gift. 20 The religious leader will wave them with the bread of the first-fruits as a wave gift before the Lord, with the two lambs. They will be holy to the Lord for the religious leader. 21 On this same day call together a holy meeting. Do no hard work. It is a Law forever in all your homes for all your people.

22 'When you gather the food of your land, do not pick all the way to the corners of your field. And do not gather the food that falls. Leave it for those in need and the stranger. I am the Lord your God.' "

The Supper of Horns

23 The Lord said to Moses, 24 "Say to the people of Israel, 'On the first day of the seventh month, you will have a Day of Rest. It will be a day of remembering made known by the blowing of horns, a holy meeting. 25 Do not do any hard work. But give a gift by fire to the Lord.' "

A Day to Be Made Free from Sin

26 Then the Lord said to Moses, 27 "The tenth day of this seventh month is the day to be made free from sin. It will be a holy meeting for you. You will be without pride and give a gift by fire to the Lord. 28 'Do no work on this day. For it is a day to be made free from sin, to be made free from your sin before the Lord your God. 29 If there is any person who will not be free from his pride on this day, he will be kept away from his people. 30 Whoever does any work on this day, I will destroy from among his people. 31 Do no work at all. It is a Law forever for all your people in all your homes. 32 It will be a Day of Rest for you. And you must be without pride. You will keep your Day of Rest from evening until evening on the ninth day of the month."

The Supper of Tents

33 The Lord said to Moses, 34 "Say to the people of Israel, 'On the fifteenth day of this seventh month is the special supper of tents to the Lord. It will last seven days. 35 A holy meeting will be on the first day. Do no hard work of any kind. 36 Give a gift by fire to the Lord for seven days. On the eighth day have a holy meeting and give a gift by fire to the Lord. It is a special gathering. Do no hard work.

37 'These are the special suppers, the holy meetings you will keep at the right times. They will be for giving to the Lord gifts by fire, burnt gifts and grain gifts, gifts of animals and drink gifts, each on its own day. 38 These are to be added to the Days of Rest of the Lord, and your gifts, both those that are promised and your free-will gifts that you give to the Lord.

39 'On the fifteenth day of the seventh month, when you have gathered the food of your land, you will have the special supper of the Lord for seven days. The first day and the eighth day will be Days of Rest. 40 On the first day, you will take the leaves of beautiful trees, branches of trees with big leaves and of trees beside the river. And be full of joy before the Lord your God for seven days. 41 You will keep it as a special supper to the Lord seven days in the year. It will be a Law forever for all your people. You will have it in the seventh month. 42 You will live in tents for seven days. All who were born in Israel will live in tents. 43 So all your people-to-come may know that I had the people of Israel live in tents when I brought them out of the land of Egypt. I am the Lord your God.' " 44 So Moses made known to the people of Israel the special suppers of the Lord.

Oil for the Lamps

24 The Lord said to Moses, 2 "Tell the people of Israel to bring you pure oil from beaten olives for the light to keep a lamp burning all the time. 3 Outside the curtain of the Law in the meeting tent, Aaron will keep it burning from evening to morning before the Lord always. It will be a Law forever for all your people. 4 He will take care of the lamps on the pure gold lamp-stand before the Lord all the time.

The Bread Gift

5 "Then take fine flour and bake twelve loaves of bread. Use two jars of flour for each loaf. 6 Set them side by side in two

rows, six in each row, on the pure gold table before the Lord. 7 Put pure, sweet-smelling spices on each row to go with the bread as something to be remembered. It is a gift by fire to the Lord. 8 Every Day of Rest he will set it before the Lord all the time. It is a Law forever for the people of Israel. 9 The bread is for Aaron and his sons who will eat it in a holy place. It is a most holy part for him out of the gifts by fire to the Lord. It is his share forever."

Punishment for a Person Who Spoke against God

10 Now the son of an Israelite woman, whose father was an Egyptian, went among the people of Israel. And the Israelite woman's son and a man of Israel fought with each other among the tents. 11 The son of the Israelite woman swore against the name of the Lord. So they brought him to Moses. (His mother's name was She-lomith, the daughter of Dibri, of the family of Dan.) 12 And they kept him shut up until the will of the Lord might be made known to them.

13 Then the Lord said to Moses, 14 "Take the one who has sworn against Me away from the tents. Let all who heard him lay their hands on his head. Then let all the people kill him by throwing stones. 15 Say to the people of Israel, 'If anyone swears against his God, he will suffer for his own sin. 16 The one who speaks against the name of the Lord will be put to death for sure. All the people will kill him with stones. Both the stranger and those born in the land will be put to death when he speaks against the name of the Lord.

17 'If a man takes the life of any human being, he will be put to death for sure. 18 The one who takes the life of an animal will pay for it, a life for a life. 19 If a man hurts his neighbor, it will be done to him just as he has done, 20 broken bone for broken bone, eye for eye, tooth for tooth. Just as he has hurt a man, so he will be hurt. 21 So the one who kills an animal will pay for it with an animal. But the one who kills a man will be put to death. 22 You will have the same Law for the stranger and for the one born among you. For I am the Lord your God.' "

23 Then Moses spoke to the people of Israel. And they took the one who swore against God and brought him away from the tents and killed him with stones. So the people of Israel did as the Lord told Moses.

The Seventh Year—a Year of Rest for the Lord

25 The Lord said to Moses at Mount Sinai, 2 "Say to the people of Israel, 'When you come to the land I will give you, then the land will have a Year of Rest to the Lord. 3 Six years you will plant seeds in your field. Six years you will take care of your vines and gather their fruit. 4 But the seventh year will be a Year of Rest for the land, a Year of Rest to the Lord. You will not plant seeds in your field or take care of your vines. 5 You will not gather what grows of itself in your field. And do not gather the fruit of the vines that have not been cared for. The land will have a Year of Rest. 6 During the Year of Rest the land will give food for you, for your men and women servants, the man you pay to work for you, and the stranger who lives with you. 7 Even your cattle and the animals in your land will have food to eat.

The Fiftieth Year

8 'You are to number seven Years of Rest for yourself, seven times seven years. The time of the seven Years of Rest will be forty-nine years. 9 Then let the horn be heard on the tenth day of the seventh month. On the day to be made free from sin you will let a horn be heard all through your land. 10 You will honor the fiftieth year as holy. And let it be known in all the land that all who are living there are free. It will be a happy time for you. Each of you will return to what is his. Each will return to his family. 11 That fiftieth year will be a happy time for you. You will not plant seeds in the field, or gather the food that grows of itself, or gather fruit from the vines that are not cared for. 12 This is a happy time. It will be holy to you. You will eat from what the field gives.

13 'In this Year of Jubilee each one will have what was his. 14 If you sell anything to your neighbor, or buy from your neighbor, do not do wrong to one another. 15 You will pay your neighbor by the number of years since the Year of Jubilee. And he will sell to you by the number of years the food may be gathered. 16 You will make the price more if there are many years, and make the price less if there are few years. For he is selling you the food that is gathered each year. 17 Do not do wrong to one another, but fear your God. I am the Lord your God.

The Seventh Year

18 'So keep My Laws and do what I say, and you will be safe living in the land. 19 Then the land will give its food, so you can eat all you want and be safe living there. 20 If you say, "What will we eat in the seventh year if we do not plant seeds or gather in the food of our field?" 21 I will let My good come upon you in the sixth year, so it will give you enough food for three years. 22 When you are planting seeds in the eighth year, you can still eat from the old store of food. You can eat the old food until the food of the ninth year is gathered.

23 'The land will not be sold to be kept forever. For the land is Mine. You are only strangers staying with Me. 24 For all the land you have, you must be willing to let it go. 25 When your brother becomes poor and sells some of his land, then one in his family who is near to him is to come and buy what his brother has sold. 26 But a man may have no one to buy his land, and he himself may become able to buy it again. 27 Then he should add up the years since he sold it, and pay what is left of the price to the man to whom he sold it. So he will return to his own land. 28 But if he is not able to buy it again for himself, then what he has sold will belong to the one who bought it until the Year of Jubilee. In the Year of Jubilee it will be let go and he may return to it.

29 'If a man sells a house within the walls of a city, he has the right to buy it back for a whole year from the time he sold it. He can buy it during that year. 30 But if it is not bought back again for him within a whole year, then the house within the city walls belongs forever to the family of the one who bought it. It will not be returned to him in the Year of Jubilee. 31 But houses in towns that have no walls will be thought of as open fields. They may be let go, and will be returned in the Year of Jubilee. 32 The houses in the cities of the Levites may be returned to the Levites at any time. 33 If a house is not bought again by a Levite, then the house that was sold in one of their cities will be returned to him in the Year of Jubilee. For the houses of the Levites belong to them among the people of Israel. 34 But the open field of their cities must not be sold. It belongs to them forever.

The Poor Paying Money Back

35 'If your brother becomes poor and is not able to pay you what he owes, then you should help him as you would help a stranger or visitor. So he may live with you. 36 Do not make him pay for the use of the money he owes you. But fear your God, so your brother may live with you. 37 Do not make him pay for the use of your money or your food. 38 I am the Lord your God, Who brought you out of the land of Egypt to give you the land of Canaan and to be your God.

About Servants and Workmen

39 'If your brother becomes so poor that he sells himself to you, do not make him work as a servant. 40 He will be as a man who is paid to work for you, as one who is traveling from place to place, until the Year of Jubilee. 41 Then he will leave you, he and his children, that he may return to the land of his fathers. 42 For I brought them out of the land of Egypt as My servants. They are not to be sold as a servant. 43 Do not make it hard for him, but fear your God. 44 Those men and women you may have who are sold as servants will be from the nations around you. 45 You may buy from among the children of the strangers who live among you, and from their families that are with you and were born in your land. You may own them. 46 You may give them to your children after you, to receive as their own. You can have them as servants forever. But do not make it hard for your brothers, the people of Israel.

47 'Now a stranger or one visiting you may become rich. And your brother may become so poor that he sells himself to a stranger living among you, or to the children of a stranger's family. 48 Then he may be made free after he has been sold. One of his brothers may pay the price to free him. 49 His father's brother, the son of his father's brother, or one of his own family may pay the price to free him. Or if he becomes rich he may pay the price himself. 50 With the one who bought him he will add the years from the year he sold himself until the Year of Jubilee. The price for him to be set free will be decided upon by the number of years. The time he was with the man who owned him will be as that of a man paid to work for him. 51 If there are still many years, he will return a part of the price which was given for him. 52 If there is only a few years until the Year of Jubilee, he will decide upon the amount of money with his owner. He should pay the price to be set free, decided upon by the number of years. 53 He will be like a man paid to work for him year by year. Make sure his owner

does not make it hard for him. ⁵⁴ Even if the price is not paid for him in this way, he will go free in the Year of Jubilee, he and his children. ⁵⁵ Because the people of Israel are My servants. They are My servants whom I brought out of the land of Egypt. I am the Lord your God.

Good Comes to Those Who Obey

26 ¹ Do not make gods for yourselves. Do not set up for yourselves something to look like a god or a holy object. Do not set up something cut from stone in your land to bow down to. For I am the Lord your God. ² Keep My Days of Rest and honor My holy place. I am the Lord. ³ If you live by My Laws and do what I say, ⁴ I will give you rain at the right time. So the land will give its food and the trees will give their fruit. ⁵ The crushing of your grain will last until the grapes are gathered. The grape gathering will last until the seeds are planted. You will eat your food until you are full, and be safe living in your land. ⁶ I will give peace in the land. You will lie down and no one will make you afraid. I will make the land free from the danger of wild animals. And no sword will move through your land. ⁷ You will go after those who hate you, and they will fall in front of you by the sword. ⁸ Five of you will go after a hundred. A hundred of you will go after ten thousand. And those who hate you will fall in front of you by the sword. ⁹ I will care for you and give you many children. I will keep My agreement with you. ¹⁰ You will eat last year's food, and use it all because you will have new. ¹¹ I will make My home among you. My soul will not turn away from you. ¹² I will walk among you and be your God. And you will be My people. ¹³ I am the Lord your God Who brought you out of the land of Egypt so you would not be their servants. I have broken loose the heavy load from your back and made you walk straight.

Punishment to Those Who Do Not Obey

¹⁴ But if you do not obey Me and do not do all I say, ¹⁵ if you turn away from My Laws and do not want to do what I tell you to do, and do not do it, and so break My agreement, ¹⁶ I will do this to you: I will bring upon you much fear, disease that destroys, and sickness that will waste away the eyes and make the body weak. You will plant your seeds for nothing, for those who hate you will eat it. ¹⁷ I will turn against you so you will fall in front of those who fight you. Those who hate you will rule over you. You will run away when no one is coming after you. ¹⁸ If after all of these things you still do not obey Me, I will punish you seven times more for your sins. ¹⁹ I will break the pride you have of your power. I will make your sky like iron and your earth like brass. ²⁰ You will use your strength for nothing. For your land will not give food, and the trees of the land will not give fruit.

²¹ If you act against Me and will not obey Me, I will bring you seven times more trouble than your sins. ²² I will let the wild animals loose among you. They will rob you of your children and destroy your cattle. They will make you few in number, so that your roads will be empty.

²³ If after these things you do not turn to Me, but still go against Me, ²⁴ then I will go against you. I Myself will punish you seven times for your sins. ²⁵ I will bring a sword upon you that will punish you for breaking the agreement. I will send disease among you when you gather together in your cities. So you will be given into the hands of those who hate you. ²⁶ When I take away your bread of life, ten women will make your bread in one stove. They will give out your bread by weight. And you will eat it and not be full.

²⁷ If you still do not obey Me after all this, but go against Me, ²⁸ then I will go against you with anger. I Myself will punish you seven times for your sins. ²⁹ You will eat the flesh of your sons and daughters. ³⁰ I will destroy your high places and cut down your altars of special perfume. I will throw your dead bodies on what is left of your gods. My soul will hate you. ³¹ I will destroy your cities also, and your holy places. I will not smell your pleasing smells. ³² I will destroy the land, so those living in it who hate you will be filled with fear because of it. ³³ I will divide you among the nations and send the sword after you. Your land will be destroyed and your cities a waste.

³⁴ Then the land will be like new because of its Days of Rest while it lies waste and you are in the land of those who hate you. Then the land will rest and have new life because of the Days of Rest. ³⁵ As long as it lies waste it will have the rest it did not have on your Days of Rest, while you were living in it. ³⁶ Of those of you who are left in the lands of those who hate you, I will make their hearts weak. The sound of

a leaf blown by the wind will make them run away even when no one is going after them. They will run away as if it were a sword, and they will fall. ³⁷ They will fall over each other as if running from the sword, when no one is going after them. You will have no strength to stand up in front of those who hate you. ³⁸ You will die among the nations. The land of those who hate you will eat you up. ³⁹ So those of you who are left will waste away in the lands of those who hate you, because of their sins. Also because of the sins of their fathers, they will waste away with them.

⁴⁰ 'If they tell their sins and the sins of their fathers which they did when they were not faithful to Me and were against Me with anger, ⁴¹ (I also was angry with them and brought them into the land of those who hate them) if their sinful heart loses its pride and they are willing to turn away from their sin, ⁴² I will remember My agreement with Jacob, My agreement with Isaac, and My agreement with Abraham. And I will remember the land. ⁴³ But the land will be left behind them and become better with its Days of Rest while it lies empty without them. During this time they will turn away from their sin because they had not done what I told them to do and their soul hated My Laws. ⁴⁴ Yet even when they are in the land of those who hate them, I will not turn away from them. I will not hate them enough to destroy them and break My agreement with them. For I am the Lord their God. ⁴⁵ But because of them I will remember the agreement with their fathers, whom I brought out of the land of Egypt in the eyes of the nations, to be their God. I am the Lord.'"

⁴⁶ These are the Laws which the Lord made between Himself and the people of Israel through Moses at Mount Sinai.

Laws about Gifts to the Lord

27 Then the Lord said to Moses, ² "Say to the sons of Israel, 'When a man makes a special promise, you will decide upon the worth of this person for the Lord. ³ The price you put on a man from twenty to sixty years old will be fifty pieces of silver, by the weight of the holy place. ⁴ For a woman it will be thirty pieces of silver. ⁵ For a male from five to twenty years old it will be twenty pieces of silver. For a woman it will be ten pieces of silver. ⁶ Your price for a child from one month to five years old will be five pieces

of silver for the boy, and three pieces of silver for the girl. ⁷ Your price for a person sixty years old and older will be fifteen pieces of silver for the man, and ten pieces of silver for the woman. ⁸ But if the person is too poor to pay your price, he will be brought to the religious leader. The religious leader will decide the worth of the person by how much he who made the promise is able to pay.

⁹ 'If it is a kind of animal which men give as a gift to the Lord, any such animal that is given to the Lord will be holy. ¹⁰ He must not have another animal take its place, good for bad or bad for good. If he does trade one animal for another, then both animals will become holy. ¹¹ But if the animal is unclean and not the kind which men give to the Lord, then he will bring the animal to the religious leader. ¹² The religious leader will decide if it is good or bad. Whatever price the religious leader puts on it, so it will be. ¹³ If the man wants to buy it again, he will add a fifth to your price.

¹⁴ 'When a man sets apart his house as holy to the Lord, the religious leader will decide if it is good or bad. Whatever price the religious leader puts on it, so it will be. ¹⁵ If the man who sets it apart wants to buy his house again, he will add one-fifth part to your price. Then it will be his.

¹⁶ 'If a man sets apart to the Lord part of a field he owns, you will decide upon its price by the seed needed for it. Ten baskets of barley seed will be worth fifty pieces of silver. ¹⁷ If he sets apart his field during the Year of Jubilee, it will be worth your full price. ¹⁸ But if he sets apart his field after the Year of Jubilee, the religious leader will decide upon its worth by the years left until the next Year of Jubilee. It will be taken off your price. ¹⁹ If the man who sets it apart wants to buy his field again, he will add one-fifth part to your price. Then it will be his. ²⁰ But if he does not want to buy the field again, or has sold the field to another man, it cannot be bought again. ²¹ And when the field becomes free in the Jubilee, it will be holy to the Lord, like a field set apart. It will belong to the religious leader. ²² If a man sets apart to the Lord a field he has bought, which is not a part of the land he was given by his father, ²³ the religious leader will decide its worth until the Year of Jubilee. The man will pay that amount on that day as holy to the Lord. ²⁴ In the Year of Jubilee the field will return from him who bought it to the one who owned

it first. 25 The price of silver used in the holy place will decide its worth. One piece of silver will be worth twenty small pieces of money.

26 'But no man may set apart a first-born of the animals. A first-born of the cattle or the flock belongs to the Lord. 27 If it is an animal that is unclean, he will buy it again by paying your price and one-fifth part added to it. If it is not bought again, then it will be sold for your price.

28 'But nothing that a man sets apart to the Lord of all he has, of man or animal or his own land, will be sold or bought. Everything that has been set apart is most holy to the Lord. 29 No person who has been set apart to be destroyed from among men can be paid for. He must be put to death.

30 'The tenth part of all the land, of the seed of the land or of the fruit of the tree, is the Lord's. It is holy to the Lord. 31 If a man wants to buy any of the tenth part that belongs to the Lord, he will add one-fifth part to its price. 32 And every tenth animal of the cattle or flock, whatever passes under the shepherd's stick, the tenth one will be holy to the Lord. 33 The man will not ask if it is good or bad, or trade it for something else. If he does trade it for something else, then both will become holy. He cannot buy them again.' "

34 These are the Laws the Lord gave Moses on Mount Sinai for the sons of Israel.

NUMBERS

Israel Is Numbered by Families

1 The Lord spoke to Moses in the Sinai desert, in the meeting tent on the first day of the second month, in the second year after they had come out of the land of Egypt. The Lord said, 2 "Number all the people of Israel, by their families, by those of their fathers' houses. Write down the names of every male, head by head, 3 twenty years old and older. You and Aaron number by their armies whoever in Israel is able to go out to war. 4 A man from each family should be with you to help you. Each one should be the head of his father's house. 5 These are the names of the men who will help you: Shedeur's son Elizur from Reuben, 6 Zurishaddai's son Shelumiel from Simeon, 7 Amminadab's son Nahshon from Judah, 8 Zuar's son Nethanel from Issachar, 9 and Helon's son Eliab from Zebulun. 10 From the sons of Joseph there will be Ammihud's son Elishama from Ephraim, and Pedahzur's son Gamaliel from Manasseh. 11 There will be Gideoni's son Abidan from Benjamin, 12 Ammishaddai's son Ahiezer from Dan, 13 Ochran's son Pagiel from Asher, 14 Deuel's son Eliasaph from Gad, 15 and Enan's son Ahira from Naphtali." 16 These were the ones chosen from the people. They were the leaders of their fathers' families, the heads of thousands in Israel.

17 Moses and Aaron took these men who had been chosen by name. 18 And they gathered all the people together on the first day of the second month. The people gave their names by families, by their fathers' houses, by the number of names from twenty years old and older, head by head. 19 They did just as the Lord had told Moses. So he numbered them in the desert of Sinai.

20 The sons of Reuben, Israel's first-born, were numbered by their families, by their fathers' houses, by the number of names. Every male twenty years old and older was numbered, whoever was able to go out to war. 21 The number of the family of Reuben was 46,500.

22 The sons of Simeon were numbered by their families, by their fathers' houses, by the number of names. Every male twenty years old and older was numbered, whoever was able to go out to war. 23 The number of the family of Simeon was 59,300.

24 The sons of Gad were numbered by their families, by their fathers' houses, by the number of names. Every male twenty years old and older was numbered, whoever was able to go out to war. 25 The number of the family of Gad was 45,650.

26 The sons of Judah were numbered by their families, by their fathers' houses, by the number of names. Every male twenty years old and older was numbered, whoever was able to go out to war. 27 The number of the family of Judah was 74,600.

28 The sons of Issachar were numbered by their families, by their fathers' houses, by the number of names. Every male twenty years old and older was numbered, whoever was able to go out to war.

²⁹ The number of the family of Issachar was 54,400.

³⁰ The sons of Zebulun were numbered by their families, by their fathers' houses, by the number of names. Every male twenty years old and older was numbered, whoever was able to go out to war. ³¹ The number of the family of Zebulun was 57,400.

³² The sons of Joseph, the sons of Ephraim, were numbered by their families, by their fathers' houses, by the number of names. Every male twenty years old and older was numbered, whoever was able to go out to war. ³³ The number of the family of Ephraim was 40,500.

³⁴ The sons of Manasseh were numbered by their families, by their fathers' houses, by the number of names. Every male twenty years old and older was numbered, whoever was able to go out to war. ³⁵ The number of the family of Manasseh was 32,200.

³⁶ The sons of Benjamin were numbered by their families, by their fathers' houses, by the number of names. Every male twenty years old and older was numbered, whoever was able to go out to war. ³⁷ The number of the family of Benjamin was 35,400.

³⁸ The sons of Dan were numbered by their families, by their fathers' houses, by the number of names. Every male twenty years old and older was numbered, whoever was able to go out to war. ³⁹ The number of the family of Dan was 62,700.

⁴⁰ The sons of Asher were numbered by their families, by their fathers' houses, by the number of names. Every male twenty years old and older was numbered, whoever was able to go out to war. ⁴¹ The number of the family of Asher was 41,500.

⁴² The sons of Naphtali were numbered by their families, by their fathers' houses, by the number of names. Every male twenty years old and older was numbered, whoever was able to go out to war. ⁴³ The number of the family of Naphtali was 53,400.

⁴⁴ These were numbered by Moses and Aaron, and the leaders of Israel, twelve men, each chosen from his father's house. ⁴⁵ All the men of Israel were numbered by their fathers' houses, twenty years old and older, whoever in Israel was able to go out to war. ⁴⁶ The number of all the men was 603,550. ⁴⁷ But the Levites by their fathers' family were not numbered with them. ⁴⁸ For the Lord had told Moses, ⁴⁹ "Only the family of Levi should not be numbered. Do not add their number among the sons of Israel. ⁵⁰ But have the Levites take care of the meeting tent of the Law, and all that is in it, and all that belongs to it. They will carry the meeting tent and all that goes in it. They will take care of it, and set up their tents around it. ⁵¹ When the meeting tent is to be moved, the Levites will take it down. When the meeting tent is brought to a place to stay, the Levites will set it up. If anyone else comes near, he must be put to death. ⁵² The people of Israel will set up their tents by their own groups and armies, each man by his own flag. ⁵³ But the Levites will set up their tents around the meeting tent of the Law. Then no anger will come upon the people of Israel. The Levites must take care of the meeting tent of the Law." ⁵⁴ So the people of Israel did this. They did everything the Lord had told Moses.

The Family Groups in Camp

2 The Lord said to Moses and Aaron, ² "The people of Israel will set up their tents, each by his own flag and beside that of their fathers'. They will set up their tents to face the meeting tent on every side. ³ Those who stay in their tents on the east side toward the sunrise will have the flag of Judah by their armies. The leader of the people of Judah is Nahshon the son of Amminadab. ⁴ The number of all his army is 74,600. ⁵ The family of Issachar will set up their tents next to Judah. The leader of the people of Issachar is Nethanel the son of Zuar. ⁶ The number of his army is 54,400. ⁷ The family of Zebulun will be next. The leader of the people of Zebulun is Eliab the son of Helon. ⁸ The number of his army is 57,400. ⁹ The whole number among the tents of Judah is 186,400, by their armies. They will be first to move on.

¹⁰ "On the south side will be the tents of Reuben by their armies with their flags. The leader of the people of Reuben is Elizur the son of Shedeur. ¹¹ The number of his army is 46,500. ¹² The family of Simeon will set up their tents next to him. The leader of the people of Simeon is Shelumiel the son of Zurishaddai. ¹³ The number of his army is 59,300. ¹⁴ The family of Gad will be next. The leader of the people of Gad is Eliasaph the son of Deuel. ¹⁵ The number of his army is 45,650. ¹⁶ The whole number among the tents of Reuben is 151,450 by their armies. They will be second to move on.

17 "Then the meeting tent will go out with the Levites among the people. In the same way that they set up their tents, so they will leave to move on, every man in his place, by his flags.

18 "On the west side will be the flag of the tents of Ephraim by their armies. The leader of the people of Ephraim is Elishama the son of Ammihud. 19 The number of his army is 40,500. 20 The family of Manasseh will be next to him. The leader of the people of Manasseh is Gamaliel the son of Pedahzur. 21 The number of his army is 32,200. 22 The family of Benjamin will be next. The leader of the people of Benjamin is Abidan the son of Gideoni. 23 The number of his army is 35,400. 24 The whole number among the tents of Ephraim is 108,100, by their armies. They will be third to move on.

25 "On the north side will be the flag of the tents of Dan by their armies. The leader of the people of Dan is Ahiezer the son of Ammishaddai. 26 The number of his army is 62,700. 27 The family of Asher will set up their tents next to him. The leader of the people of Asher is Pagiel the son of Ochran. 28 The number of his army is 41,500. 29 The family of Naphtali will be next. The leader of the people of Naphtali is Ahira the son of Enan. 30 The number of his army is 53,400. 31 The whole number among the tents of Dan is 157,600. They will be last to move on with their flags."

32 These are the numbers of the men of Israel by their fathers' houses. The whole number among all the tents, by their armies, was 603,550. 33 But the Levites were not numbered with the people of Israel, just as the Lord had told Moses. 34 So the people of Israel did all that the Lord had told Moses. They set up their tents by their flags. And they left to move on in the same way, every one by his family and by his father's house.

The Sons of Aaron

3 These are the people of Aaron and Moses at the time when the Lord spoke with Moses on Mount Sinai. 2 The names of the sons of Aaron are Nadab the first-born, Abihu, Eleazar and Ithamar. 3 These are the names of the sons of Aaron, the chosen religious leaders. Aaron set them apart to work as religious leaders. 4 But Nadab and Abihu died before the Lord when they made a fire that was not holy to the Lord in the Desert of Sinai. And they had no children. So Eleazar and Ithamar worked as religious leaders during the life-time of their father Aaron.

The Levites Serve in the Meeting Tent

5 Then the Lord said to Moses, 6 "Bring the family of Levi near. Set them in front of Aaron the religious leader so they may serve him. 7 They will do the duties for him and for all the people in front of the meeting tent. They will do the work around the meeting tent, 8 and will keep all the things that belong to the meeting tent. They will take care of the duties for the people of Israel as they work around the meeting tent. 9 You will give the Levites to Aaron and his sons. They are all given to him from among the people of Israel. 10 Set apart Aaron and his sons to do the work of religious leaders. But if anyone comes near who is not a religious leader, he must be put to death."

11 The Lord said to Moses, 12 "See, I have taken the Levites from among the people of Israel instead of every first-born among the people of Israel. The Levites will be Mine. 13 For all the first-born are Mine. On the day that I killed all the first-born in the land of Egypt, I set apart for My own all the first-born in Israel, both man and animal. They will be Mine. I am the Lord."

The Levites Are Numbered

14 Then the Lord said to Moses in the Desert of Sinai, 15 "Number the sons of Levi by their fathers' houses and by their families. Number every male a month old and older." 16 So Moses numbered them just as he had been told by the word of the Lord. 17 The names of the sons of Levi are Gershon, Kohath and Merari. 18 The names of the sons of Gershon by their families are Libni and Shimei. 19 The sons of Kohath by their families are Amram, Izhar, Hebron and Uzziel. 20 The sons of Merari by their families are Mahli and Mushi. These are the families of the Levites by their fathers' houses.

21 Of Gershon were the families of the Libnites and the Shimeites. These were the families of the Gershonites. 22 The number of their men, every male a month old and older, was 7,500. 23 The families of the Gershonites were to set up their tents behind the meeting tent on the west side. 24 The leader of the fathers' houses of the Gershonites was Eliasaph the son of Lael. 25 The sons of Gershon were to take care of the meeting tent, its covering, and the curtain for the door of the meeting tent.

26 And they were to take care of the curtains for the door of the open space, and all curtains around the meeting tent and the altar and their ropes. They did all the work having to do with them.

27 Of Kohath were the families of the Amramites, the Izharites, the Hebronites and the Uzzielites. These were the families of the Kohathites. 28 The number of every male a month old and older was 8,600. They did the duties of the holy place. 29 The families of the sons of Kohath were to set up their tents on the south side of the meeting tent. 30 The leader of the fathers' houses of the Kohathite families was Elizaphan the son of Uzziel. 31 They took care of the special box with the Law, and the table, the lamp-stand, the altars, the things used in the holy place, and the curtain. They did all the work having to do with them. 32 Eleazar, the son of Aaron the religious leader, was the head of the leaders of Levi. He watched over those who did the duties of the holy place.

33 Of Merari were the families of the Mahlites and the Mushites. These were the families of Merari. 34 The number of their men, every male a month old and older, was 6,200. 35 The leader of the fathers' houses of the families of Merari was Zuriel the son of Abihail. They were to set up their tents on the north side of the meeting tent. 36 The duties given to the sons of Merari were to take care of the parts made of wood of the meeting tent, its cross-pieces, its pillars, its bases, and all the pieces that had to do with them. They took care of all these things, 37 and of the pillars around the open space and their bases and their nails and their ropes.

38 Moses and Aaron and his sons were to set up their tents on the east side in front of the meeting tent, toward the sunrise. They did the duties of the meeting tent, whatever had to be done for the people of Israel. But the one who came near who was not a religious leader was to be put to death. 39 The number of all the Levite men a month old and older, whom Moses and Aaron numbered by their families as the Lord told them, was 22,000.

Levites Take the Place of First-Born Sons

40 The Lord said to Moses, "Number every first-born male of the sons of Israel a month old and older. Write down their names. 41 Take the Levites for Me, instead of all the first-born among the sons of Israel. I am the Lord. And take the cattle

of the Levites instead of all the first-born among the cattle of the people of Israel."
42 So Moses numbered all the first-born among the sons of Israel, just as the Lord had told him. 43 The number of names of all the first-born males a month old and older was 22,273.

44 Then the Lord said to Moses, 45 "Take the Levites instead of all the first-born sons of Israel, and the cattle of the Levites. The number of the Levites will be Mine. I am the Lord. 46 There are 273 first-born of the sons of Israel, who are more in number than the Levites. You must pay the price for each of them. 47 Take five pieces of silver for each, by the weight of silver agreed upon for the meeting tent. 48 Give the money, the price of those who are more in number than the Levites, to Aaron and his sons." 49 So Moses took the money to pay for those who were more in number than the Levites. 50 He took the money from the first-born sons of Israel, by the weight agreed upon for the meeting tent. He took 1,365 pieces of silver. 51 Then Moses gave the money to Aaron and his sons, just as the Lord had told Moses by His Word.

The Work of the Sons of Kohath

4 The Lord said to Moses and Aaron, 2 "Number the sons of Kohath from among the sons of Levi. Number them by their families, by the fathers' houses, 3 from thirty years old and older, even to fifty years old. Number all who are able to do the work in the meeting tent. 4 This is the work of the sons of Kohath in the meeting tent to do with the most holy things. 5 When the people leave to move on, Aaron and his sons will go in and take down the curtain in front of the special box with the Law inside. And they will cover the special box with it. 6 Then they will lay a covering of badgers' skins on it, and spread a pure blue cloth over that. And they will put in the long pieces of wood to carry it. 7 They will spread a blue cloth over the table of the bread before the Lord. They will put on it the plates, the dishes for special perfume, the pots, and the jars for the drink gift. And the bread will be on it always. 8 They will spread a red cloth over them, and cover that with badgers' skins. And they will put in its long pieces of wood to carry it. 9 They will take a blue cloth and cover the lamp-stand for the light, with its lamps, its objects to put out the light, its dishes and all its pots of oil used for the light. 10 They will put the

lamp-stand and all its objects in a covering of badgers' skins. Then they will put it on the long pieces of wood used to carry it. [11] They will spread a blue cloth over the altar of gold, and cover it with badgers' skins. And they will put in the long pieces of wood to carry it. [12] They will take all the things used for the work done in the meeting tent. They will put them in a blue cloth and cover them with a covering of badgers' skins. And they will put them on the long pieces of wood used to carry them. [13] Then they will take away the ashes from the altar, and spread a purple cloth over it. [14] They will put on it all the things used for the work done on the altar: the fire-holders, meat-hooks, objects for picking up the ashes, and the pots. Then they will spread a covering of badgers' skins over it, and put in the long pieces of wood for carrying it. [15] Aaron and his sons will finish covering the holy objects and all the things of the meeting tent, as the people move on. After that the sons of Kohath will come to carry them. In this way they will not touch the holy objects and die. These are the things in the meeting tent which the sons of Kohath are to carry. [16] Eleazar the son of Aaron the religious leader will take care of the oil for the light, the special perfume, the grain gift which is always given, and the oil for holy use. He will watch over all the meeting tent and all that is in it, the holy place and its objects."

[17] Then the Lord said to Moses and Aaron, [18] "Do not let the family group of the Kohathites be destroyed from among the Levites. [19] But do this to them so they may live and not die when they come near the most holy objects. Aaron and his sons must go in and give each of them their work and what they are to carry. [20] But they must not go in to see the holy objects even for a short time, or they will die."

The Work of the Sons of Gershon

[21] The Lord said to Moses, [22] "Number the sons of Gershon also, by their fathers' houses, by their families. [23] Number those who are thirty years old and older, to fifty years old, all who go in to do the work in the meeting tent. [24] These are the duties of the families of the Gershonites, in working and in carrying. [25] They will carry the curtains of the meeting tent and the meeting tent with its covering and the covering of badgers' skins that is over it. They will carry the curtain for the door of the meeting tent, [26] the curtains of the open space,

and the curtain for the gate of the open space which is around the meeting tent and the altar. And they will carry the ropes for the curtains, and all the things used for their work. They will do whatever needs to be done with them. [27] All the work of the sons of the Gershonites will be what Aaron and his sons tell them to do. They will tell them what they are to carry and what work they are to do. You will tell them what things they have a duty to carry. [28] This is the work to be done by the families of the sons of the Gershonites in the meeting tent. Ithamar the son of Aaron the religious leader will watch over their duties.

The Work of the Sons of Merari

[29] "As for the sons of Merari, number them by their families and by their fathers' houses. [30] Number those who are thirty years old and older, to fifty years old, everyone who goes in to do the work of the meeting tent. [31] This is what they are to carry for their work in the meeting tent: the wood pieces of the meeting tent, its cross-pieces, pillars and its bases. [32] And they are to carry the pillars which are around the open space and their bases and their nails and ropes, with all the things used for their work. You will tell each man by name what he is to carry. [33] This is the work of the families of the sons of Merari, all their work in the meeting tent. Ithamar the son of Aaron the religious leader will watch over their duties."

The Levites Are Numbered

[34] So Moses and Aaron and the leaders of the people numbered the sons of the Kohathites by their families and by their fathers' houses. [35] They numbered those who were thirty years old and older, to fifty years old, everyone who went in to do the work in the meeting tent. [36] And their number by families was 2,750. [37] These are the numbered men of the Kohathite families, everyone who worked in the meeting tent. Moses and Aaron numbered them as the Lord told them to do through Moses.

[38] The sons of Gershon were numbered, by their families and their fathers' houses, [39] from thirty years old to fifty years old. Everyone who went in to do the work in the meeting tent was numbered. [40] And the number of their men by their families and by their fathers' houses was 2,630. [41] These are the numbered men of the families of the sons of Gershon, all who were working in the meeting tent. Moses

and Aaron numbered them as the Lord told them to do.

⁴² The men of the families of the sons of Merari were numbered, by their families and their fathers' houses, ⁴³ from thirty years old to fifty years old. Everyone who went in to do the work in the meeting tent was numbered. ⁴⁴ And the number of their men by their families was 3,200. ⁴⁵ These are the numbered men of the families of the sons of Merari. Moses and Aaron numbered them as the Lord told them to do through Moses.

⁴⁶ Moses and Aaron and the leaders of Israel numbered all the men of the Levites by their families and their fathers' houses, ⁴⁷ from thirty years old to fifty years old. Everyone who could go in to do the work and the carrying of the meeting tent was numbered. ⁴⁸ And the number of their men was 8,580. ⁴⁹ They were each given their work and load to carry, as the Lord told them to do through Moses. So these were his numbered men, just as the Lord had told Moses.

People with a Bad Skin Disease

5 The Lord said to Moses, ² "Tell the people of Israel to send away from the tents every person with a bad skin disease, every one with a flow that is unclean, and every one who is unclean because of a dead person. ³ Send away both male and female. Send them away from the tents so they will not make the place sinful where I live among them." ⁴ The people of Israel did so. They sent them away from the tents. The people of Israel did just as the Lord had said to Moses.

Paying Back for Wrongs Done

⁵ Then the Lord said to Moses, ⁶ "Say to the people of Israel, 'When a man or woman sins the way that man sins by not acting in faith toward the Lord, and that person is guilty, ⁷ then he must tell about the sins he has done. He must pay in full for his wrong-doing, and add one-fifth part to it, and give it to the one he has sinned against. ⁸ But if the man has no brother to whom pay for the wrong can be made, then it must go to the Lord for the religious leader. He must also give a ram to pay for his sins. And his sins will be forgiven. ⁹ Every gift of all the holy things of the Israelites which they bring to the religious leader will become his. ¹⁰ So every man's holy gifts will be his. Whatever any man gives to the religious leader will be his.'"

Wives Who Are Not Faithful

¹¹ The Lord said to Moses, ¹² "Say to the people of Israel, 'If a man's wife turns away and is not faithful to him, ¹³ and another man has sex with her and it is hidden from her husband's eyes, even if it is hidden, she will be unclean. And even if no one speaks against her, because she has not been caught in the act, ¹⁴ but a spirit of jealousy comes over her husband, he will be jealous of his wife when she has made herself unclean. Or if he becomes jealous of his wife when she has done nothing to make herself unclean, ¹⁵ then the man must bring his wife to the religious leader. He must bring one-tenth part of a basket of barley as the gift needed for her. He must not pour oil on it. He must not put special perfume on it. For it is a grain gift of jealousy. It is a grain gift to make the sin remembered.

¹⁶ 'Then the religious leader will bring her near and have her stand before the Lord. ¹⁷ The religious leader will take holy water in a clay pot. He will take some of the dust on the floor of the meeting tent and put it into the water. ¹⁸ Then the religious leader will have the woman stand before the Lord and let the hair of the woman's head hang loose. He will put the grain gift of remembering into her hands. It is the grain gift of jealousy. In the religious leader's hand will be the bitter water that can bring a curse to the woman, ¹⁹ Then the religious leader will have her make a promise. He will say to the woman, "If no man has lain with you and if you have not turned away into sin, while under the power of your husband, this bitter water that brings punishment will not hurt you. ²⁰ If you have turned away, while under the power of your husband, and have made yourself unclean by having another man who is not your husband," ²¹ then the religious leader will have the woman make a promise so she will be punished if she has sinned. He will say to the woman, "May the Lord make you a curse among your people. May the Lord make your leg waste away and your stomach grow bigger. ²² This water that brings a curse will go into your stomach and make it grow bigger and your leg to waste away." And the woman will say, "Let it be so. Let it be so."

²³ 'Then the religious leader will write these curses in a book. And he will wash them off into the bitter water. ²⁴ He will make the woman drink the bitter water

that brings a curse. The water that brings a curse will go into her and give her pain. ²⁵ The religious leader will take the grain gift of jealousy from the woman's hand. He will wave the grain gift before the Lord and bring it to the altar. ²⁶ The religious leader will fill his hand with the grain gift, as the part to be remembered. And he will burn it on the altar. Then he will make the woman drink the water. ²⁷ If she has not been faithful to her husband, the water that brings a curse will go into her and give her pain. Her stomach will get larger and her leg will become as dead. A curse will come upon the woman among her people. ²⁸ But if the woman has not sinned and is clean, she will be free and able to have children.

²⁹ 'This is the law of jealousy. If a wife who is under the power of her husband turns away and makes herself unclean, ³⁰ and a spirit of jealousy comes upon a man, making him jealous of his wife, then he must make the woman stand before the Lord. And the religious leader will do to her all the rules of this Law. ³¹ The husband will be free from guilt. But the woman will carry her guilt.' "

Rules for the Nazirites

6 Then the Lord said to Moses, ² "Say to the people of Israel, 'A man or woman may make a special promise, the promise of a Nazirite, to set himself apart to the Lord. ³ Then he must keep away from wine and strong drink. He will drink no sour wine, made from wine or strong drink. He will not drink any grape drink. And he will not eat new or dried grapes. ⁴ All the days he is set apart, he must not eat anything made from the grape-field, not even the seeds or the skins.

⁵ 'No hair of his head will be cut, all the days of his promise to be set apart. He must be holy until the time is finished for which he set himself apart to the Lord. He will let the hair on his head grow long.

⁶ 'All the days he is set apart to the Lord, he must not go near a dead person. ⁷ He must not allow himself to be made unclean when his father, mother, brother or sister die. For he has made a promise to be set apart to God. ⁸ He is holy to the Lord all the days he is set apart.

⁹ 'But if a man dies next to him, making his hair unclean which had been set apart to the Lord, then he must cut all the hair from his head on the day he is made clean. He will cut it off on the seventh day.

¹⁰ On the eighth day he must bring two turtle-doves or two young pigeons to the religious leader, to the door of the meeting tent. ¹¹ The religious leader will give one for a sin gift and the other for a burnt gift. He will pay for his sin because of the dead person. And he will make his head holy that same day. ¹² He will set apart to the Lord his days as a Nazirite. And he will bring a year old male lamb for a guilt gift. But the past days will be a loss, because he had become unclean during the time he was set apart.

¹³ 'This is the Law of the Nazirite when the time he is set apart is finished. He must bring the gift to the door of the meeting tent. ¹⁴ He will give his gift to the Lord. It will be a perfect male lamb a year old for a burnt gift, one perfect female lamb a year old for a sin gift, and one perfect ram for a peace gift. ¹⁵ And he will give a basket of bread made of fine flour mixed with oil, made without yeast. He will give hard bread spread with oil and made without yeast. With them he will give their grain gift and drink gifts. ¹⁶ Then the religious leader will give all these to the Lord and his sin gift and his burnt gift. ¹⁷ He will also give the ram for peace gifts to the Lord, together with the basket of bread made without yeast. Then the religious leader will give its grain gift and drink gift. ¹⁸ Then at the door of the meeting tent the Nazirite will cut off the hair that has been set apart for holy use. He is to take the hair and put it in the fire under the peace gifts. ¹⁹ The religious leader will take the shoulder of the ram when it has been boiled and a loaf of bread and a piece of hard bread, both made without yeast and put them in the hands of the Nazirite. This is done after he has cut off the hair that has been set apart. ²⁰ The religious leader will wave them for a wave gift before the Lord. They are holy and belong to the religious leader, together with the breast given as a wave gift and the thigh given by lifting it up. After that the Nazirite may drink wine.'

²¹ "This is the Law of the Nazirite who makes a promise to give to the Lord what he promised as a Nazirite, and whatever else he is able to give. He must do what he has promised by the Law of being set apart as a Nazirite."

Religious Leaders Bring Good to the People

²² Then the Lord said to Moses, ²³ "Say to Aaron and his sons, 'This is the way you

should bring good to the people of Israel. Say to them, 24 "May the Lord bring good to you and keep you. 25 May the Lord make His face shine upon you, and be kind to you. 26 May the Lord show favor toward you, and give you peace." ' 27 So they will put My name upon the people of Israel, and I will bring good to them."

Gifts Given on the Altar by the Leaders

7 Moses finished putting up the meeting tent. On that day he put oil on it and made it holy, with the things inside, the altar and all its objects. He put oil on them and made them holy. 2 Then the leaders of Israel, the heads of their fathers' houses, brought their gifts. They were the leaders of the families, the heads of those who were numbered. 3 As gifts to the Lord they brought six covered wagons and twelve bulls, a wagon for every two of the leaders and a bull for each one. Then they gave them in front of the meeting tent. 4 The Lord said to Moses, 5 "Receive these things from them, that they may be used in the work of the meeting tent. Give them to the Levites, to each man for the work he does." 6 So Moses took the wagons and the bulls, and gave them to the Levites. 7 He gave two wagons and four bulls to the sons of Gershon, for the work they were doing. 8 He gave four wagons and eight bulls to the sons of Merari, for the work they were doing under the leading of Ithamar the son of Aaron the religious leader. 9 But Moses did not give any to the sons of Kohath. They had the duty of taking care of the holy objects which had to be carried on their shoulders. 10 The leaders gave gifts to set apart the altar on the day the oil was poured on it. They gave their gifts in front of the altar. 11 Then the Lord said to Moses, "Let one leader each day give the gifts to set apart the altar."

12 The one who gave his gift on the first day was Nahshon the son of Amminadab, of the family of Judah. 13 His gift was one silver dish that weighed as much as 130 pieces of silver, and one silver dish that weighed as much as seventy pieces of silver. They were weighed by the weight of silver agreed upon for the meeting tent. Both of them were full of fine flour mixed with oil for a grain gift. 14 And he gave one gold dish weighing as much as ten pieces of silver, full of special perfume. 15 He gave one bull, one ram, and one male lamb one year old, for a burnt gift in worship. 16 He gave one male goat for a sin gift. 17 For the

peace gifts he gave two bulls, five rams, five male goats, and five male lambs one year old. This was the gift given by Nahshon the son of Amminadab.

18 On the second day Nathanel the son of Zuar, leader of Issachar, gave a gift in worship. 19 He gave for his gift one silver dish that weighed as much as 130 pieces of silver, and one silver dish weighing as much as seventy pieces of silver. They were weighed by the weight of silver agreed upon for the meeting tent. Both of them were full of fine flour mixed with oil for a grain gift. 20 And he gave one gold dish weighing as much as ten pieces of silver, full of special perfume. 21 He gave one bull, one ram, and one male lamb one year old, for a burnt gift. 22 He gave one male goat for a sin gift. 23 For the peace gifts he gave two bulls, five rams, five male goats, and five male lambs one year old. This was the gift of Nathanel the son of Zuar.

24 On the third day it was Eliab the son of Helon, leader of the sons of Zebulun. 25 His gift was one silver dish that weighed as much as 130 pieces of silver, and one silver dish weighing as much as seventy pieces of silver. They were weighed by the weight of silver agreed upon for the meeting tent. Both of them were full of fine flour mixed with oil for a grain gift. 26 And he gave one gold dish weighing as much as ten pieces of silver, full of special perfume. 27 He gave one young bull, one ram, and one male lamb one year old, for a burnt gift. 28 He gave one male goat for a sin gift. 29 For the peace gifts he gave two bulls, five rams, five male goats, and five male lambs one year old. This was the gift of Eliab the son of Helon.

30 On the fourth day it was Elizur the son of Shedeur, leader of the sons of Reuben. 31 His gift was one silver dish that weighed as much as 130 pieces of silver, and one silver dish weighing as much as seventy pieces of silver. They were weighed by the weight of silver agreed upon for the meeting tent. Both of them were full of fine flour mixed with oil for a grain gift. 32 And he gave one gold dish weighing as much as ten pieces of silver, full of special perfume. 33 He gave one bull, one ram, and one male lamb one year old, for a burnt gift. 34 He gave one male goat for a sin gift. 35 For the peace gifts he gave two bulls, five rams, five male goats, and five male lambs one year old. This was the gift of Elizur the son of Shedeur.

36 On the fifth day it was Shelumiel the

son of Zurishaddai, the leader of the sons of Simeon. 37 His gift was one silver dish that weighed as much as 130 pieces of silver, and one silver dish weighing as much as seventy pieces of silver. They were weighed by the weight of silver agreed upon for the meeting tent. Both of them were full of fine flour mixed with oil for a grain gift. 38 And he gave one gold dish weighing as much as ten pieces of silver, full of special perfume. 39 He gave one bull, one ram, and one male lamb one year old, for a burnt gift. 40 He gave one male goat for a sin gift. 41 For the peace gifts he gave two bulls, five rams, five male goats, and five male lambs one year old. This was the gift of Shelumiel the son of Zurishaddai.

42 On the sixth day it was Eliasaph the son of Deuel, the leader of the sons of Gad. 43 His gift was one silver dish that weighed as much as 130 pieces of silver, and one silver dish weighing as much as seventy pieces of silver. They were weighed by the weight of silver agreed upon for the meeting tent. Both of them were full of fine flour mixed with oil for a grain gift. 44 And he gave one gold dish weighing as much as ten pieces of silver, full of special perfume. 45 He gave one bull, one ram, and one male lamb one year old, for a burnt gift. 46 He gave one male goat for a sin gift. 47 For the peace gifts he gave two bulls, five rams, five male goats, and five male lambs one year old. This was the gift of Eliasaph the son of Deuel.

48 On the seventh day it was Elishama the son of Ammihud, the leader of the sons of Ephraim. 49 His gift was one silver dish that weighed as much as 130 pieces of silver, and one silver dish weighing as much as seventy pieces of silver. They were weighed by the weight of silver agreed upon for the meeting tent. Both of them were full of fine flour mixed with oil for a grain gift. 50 And he gave one gold dish weighing as much as ten pieces of silver, full of special perfume. 51 He gave one bull, one ram, and one male lamb one year old, for a burnt gift. 52 He gave one male goat for a sin gift. 53 For the peace gifts he gave two bulls, five rams, five male goats, and five male lambs one year old. This was the gift of Elishama the son of Ammihud.

54 On the eighth day it was Gamaliel the son of Pedahzur, the leader of the sons of Manasseh. 55 His gift was one silver dish that weighed as much as 130 pieces of silver, and one silver dish weighing as much as seventy pieces of silver. They were

weighed by the weight of silver agreed upon for the meeting tent. Both of them were full of fine flour mixed with oil for a grain gift. 56 And he gave one gold dish weighing as much as ten pieces of silver, full of special perfume. 57 He gave one bull, one ram, and one male lamb one year old, for a burnt gift. 58 He gave one male goat for a sin gift. 59 For the peace gifts he gave two bulls, five rams, five male goats, and five male lambs one year old. This was the gift of Gamaliel the son of Pedahzur.

60 On the ninth day it was Abidan the son of Gideoni, the leader of the sons of Benjamin. 61 His gift was one silver dish that weighed as much as 130 pieces of silver, and one silver dish weighing as much as seventy pieces of silver. They were weighed by the weight of silver agreed upon for the meeting tent. Both of them were full of fine flour mixed with oil for a grain gift. 62 And he gave one gold dish weighing as much as ten pieces of silver, full of special perfume. 63 He gave one bull, one ram, and one male lamb one year old, for a burnt gift. 64 He gave one male goat for a sin gift. 65 For the peace gifts he gave two bulls, five rams, five male goats, and five male lambs one year old. This was the gift of Abidan the son of Gideoni.

66 On the tenth day it was Ahiezer the son of Ammishaddai, the leader of the sons of Dan. 67 His gift was one silver dish that weighed as much as 130 pieces of silver, and one silver dish weighing as much as seventy pieces of silver. They were weighed by the weight of silver agreed upon for the meeting tent. Both of them were full of fine flour mixed with oil for a grain gift. 68 And he gave one gold dish weighing as much as ten pieces of silver, full of special perfume. 69 He gave one bull, one ram, and one male lamb one year old, for a burnt gift. 70 He gave one male goat for a sin gift. 71 For the peace gifts he gave two bulls, five rams, five male goats, and five male lambs one year old. This was the gift of Ahiezer the son of Ammishaddai.

72 On the eleventh day it was Pagiel the son of Ochran, the leader of the sons of Asher. 73 His gift was one silver dish that weighed as much as 130 pieces of silver, and one silver dish weighing as much as seventy pieces of silver. They were weighed by the weight of silver agreed upon for the meeting tent. Both of them were full of fine flour mixed with oil for a grain gift. 74 And he gave one gold dish weighing as much as ten pieces of silver,

full of special perfume. 75 He gave one bull, one ram, and one male lamb one year old, for a burnt gift. 76 He gave one male goat for a sin gift. 77 For the peace gifts he gave two bulls, five rams, five male goats, and five male lambs one year old. This was the gift of Pagiel the son of Ochran.

78 On the twelfth day it was Ahira the son of Enan, the leader of the sons of Naphtali. 79 His gift was one silver dish that weighed as much as 130 pieces of silver, and one silver dish weighing as much as seventy pieces of silver. They were weighed by the weight of silver agreed upon for the meeting tent. Both of them were full of fine flour mixed with oil for a grain gift. 80 And he gave one gold dish weighing as much as ten pieces of silver, full of special perfume. 81 He gave one bull, one ram, and one male lamb one year old, for a burnt gift. 82 He gave one male goat for a sin gift. 83 For the peace gifts he gave two bulls, five rams, five male goats, and five male lambs one year old. This was the gift of Ahira the son of Enan. 84 This was the gift to set apart the altar on the day the oil was poured on it. The leaders of Israel gave twelve silver dishes, twelve deep dishes made of silver, and twelve gold dishes. 85 Each silver dish weighed as much as 130 pieces of silver. Each deep dish weighed as much as seventy pieces of silver. All the silver of the dishes weighed as much as 2,400 pieces of silver. They were weighed by the weight of silver agreed upon for the meeting tent. 86 The twelve gold dishes full of special perfume each weighed as much as ten pieces of silver. They were weighed by the weight of silver agreed upon for the meeting tent. All the gold of the dishes weighed as much as 120 pieces of silver. 87 All the animals given for the burnt gift were twelve bulls, twelve rams, and twelve male lambs one year old with their grain gifts. Twelve male goats were given for a sin gift. 88 All the animals given for the peace gifts were twenty four bulls, sixty rams, sixty male goats, and sixty male lambs one year old. This was the gift to set apart the altar after the oil was poured on it.

89 Moses went into the meeting tent to speak with the Lord. And he heard the voice speaking to him from above the mercy-seat that was on the special box with the Law, between the two cherubim. So the Lord spoke to him.

Setting Up the Lamps

8 The Lord said to Moses, 2 "Say to Aaron, 'When you put the seven lamps on the lamp-stand, they should give light in front of the lamp-stand.' " 3 And Aaron did so. He put the lamps so they would give light in front of the lamp-stand, as the Lord had told Moses. 4 Now this is the way the lamp-stand was made. It was made of beaten gold from the base to its flowers. He made the lamp-stand the way the Lord had shown Moses.

The Levites Are Set Apart

5 Then the Lord said to Moses, 6 "Take the Levites from among the people of Israel, and make them clean. 7 To make them clean, put holy water on them that takes away sin. Let them cut all the hair from their body, and wash their clothes, and they shall be clean. 8 Then let them take a young bull and its grain gift of fine flour mixed with oil. Take another young bull for a sin gift. 9 Bring the Levites in front of the meeting tent and gather together all the people of Israel also. 10 Bring the Levites before the Lord and the people of Israel will lay their hands on the Levites. 11 Aaron will give the Levites to the Lord as a wave gift from the people of Israel so they will be able to do the work of the Lord. 12 The Levites will lay their hands on the heads of the bulls. They will give one for a sin gift and the other for a burnt gift to the Lord, to pay for the sins of the Levites. 13 Then have the Levites stand in front of Aaron and his sons, to give them as a wave gift to the Lord.

14 "So you will divide the Levites from the people of Israel. And the Levites will be Mine. 15 After that the Levites may go in to work in the meeting tent. But you must make them clean and give them as a wave gift. 16 For they are all given to Me from among the people of Israel. I have taken them for Myself instead of every first child to be born, the first-born of all the people of Israel. 17 For every first-born among the people of Israel is Mine, both of man and animal. I set them apart for Myself on the day that I killed all the first-born in the land of Egypt. 18 But I have taken the Levites instead of every first-born among the people of Israel. 19 And I have given the Levites as a gift to Aaron and his sons from among the people of Israel. They will do the work of the people of Israel at the meeting tent. By this they take away the sins of the people of Israel. So no trouble

will come upon the people of Israel if they come near the meeting tent."

20 Moses and Aaron and all the people of Israel did this to the Levites. The people of Israel did to them all the things the Lord had told Moses about the Levites. 21 The Levites made themselves pure, putting away their sin. And they washed their clothes. Aaron gave them as a wave gift before the Lord. He did what had to be done to pay for their sin so they would be clean. 22 After that the Levites went in to do their work in the meeting tent in front of Aaron and his sons. So they did to the Levites just what the Lord had told Moses to do.

23 The Lord said to Moses, 24 "This is the rule for the Levites. Those who are twenty-five years old and older will go in to do the work of the meeting tent. 25 But when they are fifty years old they will stop these duties and not work any more. 26 They may help their brothers in the meeting tent to do what needs to be done but they themselves must not do the work. These are the rules for the Levites when giving them their duties."

The Passover

9 The Lord spoke to Moses in the Sinai desert, in the first month of the second year after they had come out of the land of Egypt. The Lord said, 2 "Let the people of Israel keep the Passover at the time given for it. 3 Keep it at its given time, in the evening of the fourteenth day of this month. Keep it by obeying all its Laws." 4 So Moses told the people of Israel to keep the Passover. 5 And they kept the Passover in the evening of the fourteenth day of the first month, in the Sinai desert. The people of Israel did all that the Lord had told Moses. 6 But there were some men who were unclean because they had touched a dead person. So they could not keep the Passover on that day. They came to Moses and Aaron that day 7 and said to Moses, "We are unclean because we touched a dead person. But why are we kept from giving the Lord's gift at its given time among the people of Israel?" 8 Moses said to them, "Wait, and I will listen to what the Lord will tell me to do with you."

9 Then the Lord said to Moses, 10 "Say to the people of Israel, 'If anyone of you or your children touch a dead person and become unclean, or if you are traveling far away, even so, he may still keep the Passover to the Lord. 11 They will keep it in the evening of the fourteenth day of the second month. They will eat it with

bread without yeast and with bitter tasting plants. 12 They must not leave any of it until morning. And they must not break a bone of the lamb. They must obey all of the Law of the Passover. 13 But if a man is clean and is not away traveling, yet does not keep the Passover, he must be cut off from his people. For he did not give the Lord's gift at the time he was to do so. That man will be guilty of his sin. 14 If a stranger staying with you wants to keep the Passover to the Lord and obey the Law of the Passover, he may do so. You will have one law, both for the stranger and for the one who was born in the land.'"

The Cloud of Fire

15 On the day that the meeting tent was set up, the cloud covered the meeting tent, the tent of the law. In the evening it was over the meeting tent. It looked like fire until morning. 16 It was like this always. The cloud would cover it during the day. What looked like fire would cover it during the night. 17 When the cloud was lifted from over the meeting tent, the people of Israel would move on. Where the cloud rested, there the people of Israel would set up their tents. 18 The people of Israel would move on as the Lord told them. And they would set up their tents as the Lord told them. They stayed in one place as long as the cloud rested over the meeting tent. 19 Even when the cloud rested over the meeting tent for many days, the people of Israel would obey the Lord and not leave. 20 Sometimes the cloud stayed a few days over the meeting tent. But they obeyed the Lord and stayed in that place. Then they would leave when the Lord told them. 21 Sometimes the cloud stayed from evening until morning. When the cloud lifted in the morning, they would leave. If the cloud stayed during the day and the night, when it was lifted, they would leave that place. 22 Even when the cloud stayed over the meeting tent for two days, or a month, or a year the people of Israel would stay in that place and not leave. They would leave when it was lifted. 23 They set up their tents as the Lord told them. And they moved on as the Lord told them. They obeyed what the Lord had told them to do through Moses.

The Silver Horns

10 The Lord said to Moses, 2 "Make two silver horns of beaten silver. Use them for calling the people together and for having the people move on. 3 When both horns sound, all the people will gather in front of you at the door of the meeting tent. 4 If only one horn sounds, then the leaders, the heads of the families of Israel, will gather in front of you. 5 When you blow the horn to tell of danger, the people whose tents are on the east side will leave. 6 When you blow the horn to tell of danger a second time, the people whose tents are on the south side will leave. A horn telling of danger will be blown when they are to move on. 7 But when the people are to be gathered together, you will blow the horn without the sound of danger. 8 Aaron's sons, the religious leaders, will blow the horns. This will be a Law for all your people forever. 9 When you go to war in your land against those who fight you, then sound the horns to tell of war. That way you will be remembered before the Lord your God, and be saved from those who hate you. 10 On the days you are glad and at the time of your special suppers and on the first days of your months, blow the horns. Blow the horns over your burnt gifts and over your peace gifts. Then you will be remembered before your God. I am the Lord your God."

The Children of Israel Leave Sinai

11 On the twentieth day of the second month in the second year, the cloud was lifted from over the meeting tent of the Law. 12 The people of Israel moved on from the Desert of Sinai. Then the cloud came down and rested in the desert of Paran. 13 So they moved for the first time as the Lord had told them through Moses. 14 The flag of the people of Judah left first, by their armies. Amminadab's son Nahshon was the head of their army. 15 Zuar's son Nethanel was the head of the men of Issachar. 16 And Helon's son Eliab was the head of the men of Zebulun.

17 When the meeting tent was taken down, the sons of Gershon and Merari left carrying it. 18 Next the flag of the people of Reuben left, by their armies. Shedeur's son Elizur was the head over this army. 19 Zurishaddai's son Shelumiel was the head of the men of Simeon. 20 Deuel's son Eliasaph was the head of the men of Gad. 21 Then the Kohathites left, carrying the holy objects. The meeting tent was set up before they came to the next place. 22 Next the flag of the people of Ephraim left, by their armies. Ammihud's son Elishama was the head over this army. 23 Pedahzur's son Gamaliel was the head of the men of

Manasseh. 24 Gideoni's son Abidan was the head of the men of Benjamin.

25 Then the flag of the people of Dan left, by their armies. They followed behind all the people of Israel, to watch for danger. Ammishaddai's son Ahiezer was the head over this army. 26 Ochran's son Pagiel was the head of the men of Asher. 27 And Enan's son Ahira was the head of the men of Naphtali. 28 This was how the people of Israel moved on by their armies.

29 Then Moses said to Hobab the son of Reuel the Midianite, Moses' father-in-law, "We are going to the place the Lord said He will give to us. Come with us and we will do you good. For the Lord has promised good to Israel." 30 But Hobab said to him, "I will not come. I will go to my own land and family." 31 Moses said, "I beg you, do not leave us. For you know where we should stay in the desert. You will be like eyes for us. 32 If you go with us, we will do for you whatever good the Lord does for us."

33 So they traveled for three days from the mountain of the Lord with the special box with the Law of the Lord in front of them looking for a place for them to rest. 34 The cloud of the Lord was over them during the day, when they moved on.

35 When the special box of the Lord moved on, Moses said, "Rise up, O Lord! Let those who hate You be divided. Let those who hate You run away before You." 36 And when it rested, he said, "Return, O Lord, to the many thousands of Israel."

The Children of Israel Complain

11 Now the people complained about their troubles in the hearing of the Lord. When the Lord heard it, His anger burned. The fire of the Lord burned among them, and destroyed some around the outer parts of the tents. 2 Then the people cried to Moses and he prayed to the Lord, and the fire went out. 3 So the name of that place was called Taberah, because the fire of the Lord burned among them.

4 The mixed group of people among them had strong desires. The people of Israel cried again and said, "Who will give us meat to eat? 5 We remember all the fish we could eat free in Egypt, and all the fruit and vegetables and spices. 6 But now our strength is gone. There is nothing at all to look at except this bread from heaven." 7 Now the bread from heaven was like coriander seed, and it looked like bdellium. 8 The people would go and gather it and

beat it between stones. They boiled it in a pot or made bread with it. It tasted like bread made with oil. 9 When the grass became wet around the tents at night, the bread from heaven would fall.

10 Moses heard all the people crying in every family, each man at the door of his tent. The Lord became very angry with them and Moses was not pleased. 11 So Moses said to the Lord, "Why have You been so hard on Your servant? Why have I not found favor in Your eyes, that You have laid the troubles of all these people on me? 12 Did I give birth to all these people? Did I bring them out, that You should say to me, 'Carry them close to your heart as a nurse carries a nursing baby, to the land You promised their fathers'? 13 Where am I to get meat to give to all these people? They cry in front of me, saying, 'Give us meat so we may eat!' 14 I am not able to carry all these people alone. The load is too heavy for me. 15 So if You are going to act this way toward me, I beg You to kill me now, if I have found favor in Your eyes. Do not let me see how bad off I am."

The Seventy Leaders

16 The Lord said to Moses, "Gather for Me seventy men from the leaders of Israel, whom you know to be the leaders of the people, the men who rule over them. Bring them to the meeting tent and let them stand there with you. 17 Then I will come down and speak with you there. I will take of the Spirit Who is upon you, and will put Him upon them. Then they will carry the troubles of the people with you so you will not carry them all alone. 18 Say to the people, 'Make yourselves holy for tomorrow, and you will eat meat. The Lord heard you when you cried and said, "If only someone would give us meat to eat! For it was well with us in Egypt." So the Lord will give you meat and you will eat. 19 You will not eat it for only one day, or two days, or five days, or ten days, or twenty days. 20 But you will eat it a whole month, until it comes out of your nose and you hate it, because you have turned away from the Lord Who is among you. You have cried before Him, saying, "Why did we ever leave Egypt?" ' " 21 But Moses said, "The people whom I am among are 600,000 on foot. And You have said, 'I will give them meat so they may eat for a whole month.' 22 Will enough flocks and cattle be killed to feed them? Or will enough fish be gathered from the sea to feed them?"

23 The Lord said to Moses, "Is there an end to the Lord's power? Now you will see if My Word will come true for you or not."

24 So Moses went out and told the people the words of the Lord. And he gathered seventy men from the leaders of the people, and had them stand around the meeting tent. 25 Then the Lord came down in the cloud and spoke to him. He took of the Spirit Who was upon him and put Him upon the seventy leaders. When the Spirit rested upon them, they spoke the word of the Lord. But they did not do it again.

26 But two men had stayed among the tents. Their names were Eldad and Medad, and the Spirit rested upon them. They were among those who had been chosen, but had not gone out to the meeting tent. So they spoke the word of the Lord among the tents. 27 A young man ran and told Moses, "Eldad and Medad are speaking the word of the Lord among the tents." 28 Then Joshua the son of Nun, the helper of Moses since he was young, said, "Moses, my lord, do not let them." 29 But Moses said to him, "Are you jealous for my good? If only all the Lord's people would speak for God, that the Lord would put His Spirit upon them!" 30 Then Moses and the leaders of Israel returned to the tents.

The Lord Sends Quails

31 Now a wind went out from the Lord. It brought quail from the sea, and let them fall beside the place where the tents were set up. They fell all around the tents, about as far on each side as it takes to travel in a day. They lay on the ground as deep as two cubits. 32 The people worked all day and all night and all the next day gathering the quail. He who gathered the least gathered enough to fill 110 baskets. And they spread them out for themselves all around the tents. 33 While the meat was still between their teeth and not yet eaten, the Lord became angry with the people. The Lord sent a bad sickness upon the people. 34 So the name of that place was called Kibroth-hattaavah. Because there they buried the people who had wanted meat to eat. 35 The people left Kibroth-hattaavah and went to Hazeroth. And they stayed at Hazeroth.

Miriam and Aaron Spoke against Moses

12 Miriam and Aaron spoke against Moses because of his Cushite wife, for he had married a Cushite woman. 2 They said, "Is it true that the Lord has spoken only through Moses? Has He not spoken through us also?" And the Lord heard it. [3] Now Moses was a man with no pride, more so than any man on the earth. [4] At once the Lord said to Moses and Aaron and Miriam, "You three come out to the meeting tent." So the three of them came out. [5] Then the Lord came down in a cloud and stood at the door of the meeting tent, and called Aaron and Miriam. When both of them had come near, [6] the Lord said, "Now listen to Me. If there is a man who speaks for God among you, I the Lord will make Myself known to him in a special dream. I will speak with him in a dream. [7] Not so, with My servant Moses. He is faithful in all My house. [8] With him I speak face to face in ways he understands, and not in ways he does not understand. And he sees what the Lord is like. Why then were you not afraid to speak against My servant Moses?"

[9] The Lord was angry with them, and He left. [10] When the cloud lifted from over the meeting tent, Miriam had a very bad skin disease. She was as white as snow. Aaron turned toward Miriam and saw that she had a bad skin disease. [11] Then Aaron said to Moses, "O, my lord, I beg you. Do not punish us because we have been foolish and have sinned. [12] Let her not be like one who is dead, whose flesh is half eaten away when he is born!" [13] And Moses cried to the Lord, saying, "O God, heal her, I pray!" [14] But the Lord said to Moses, "If her father had only spit in her face, would she not carry her shame for seven days? Let her be shut up for seven days away from the tents. After that, she may be brought in again." [15] So Miriam was shut up away from the tents for seven days. And the people did not travel on until Miriam was brought in again.

[16] The people moved from Hazeroth after that. And they set up their tents in the desert of Paran.

Men Sent to Spy out the Land

13 The Lord said to Moses, [2] "Send men to spy out the land of Canaan which I am going to give to the people of Israel. Send a man from each of their fathers' families, every one a leader among them." [3] So Moses sent them from the desert of Paran, as the Lord had told him. All of the men were heads of the people of Israel. [4] These were their names. There was Shammua the son of Zaccur from the family of Reuben, [5] Shaphat the son of Hori

from the family of Simeon, [6] Caleb the son of Jephunneh from the family of Judah, [7] and Igal the son of Joseph from the family of Issachar. [8] There was Hoshea the son of Nun from the family of Ephraim, [9] Palti the son of Raphu from the family of Benjamin, [10] Gaddiel the son of Sodi from the family of Zebulun, [11] and Gaddi the son of Susi from the family of Joseph, from the family of Manasseh. [12] There was Ammiel the son of Gemalli from the family of Dan, [13] Sethur the son of Michael from the family of Asher, [14] Nahbi the son of Vophsi from the family of Naphtali, [15] and Geuel the son of Machi from the family of Gad. [16] These are the names of the men whom Moses sent to spy out the land. But Moses called Hoshea the son of Nun, Joshua.

[17] Moses sent them to spy out the land of Canaan. He said to them, "Go up there into the Negev. Then go up into the hill country. [18] See what the land is like. See if the people who live in it are strong or weak, and if they are few or many. [19] Find out if the land they live in is good or bad. See if the cities they live in are open or if they have walls. Find out if the land is rich or poor, and if there are trees in it or not. Then try to get some of the fruit of the land." Now this was the gathering time of the first grown grapes.

[21] So they went up and spied out the land from the Desert of Zin as far as Rehob, at Lebo-hamath. [22] When they had gone up into the Negev, they came to Hebron. Anak's sons Ahiman, Sheshai and Talmai were there. (Hebron was built seven years before Zoan in Egypt.)

[23] Then they came to the valley of Eshcol. They cut down a branch from there with some grapes on it. And they carried it on a long piece of wood between two men, with some pomegranates and figs. [24] That place was called the valley of Eshcol, because of much fruit the men of Israel cut down from there.

[25] They returned from looking over the land after forty days. [26] And they came to Moses and Aaron and to all the people of Israel in the desert of Paran, at Kadesh. They brought news to them and to all the people, and showed them the fruit of the land. [27] They told Moses, "We went to the land where you sent us. It does flow with milk and honey. This is its fruit. [28] But the people who live in the land are strong. The cities have walls and are very large. And we saw the children of Anak there. [29] Amalek is living in the land of

the Negev. The Hittites and Jebusites and Amorites are living in the hill country. And the Canaanites are living by the sea and by the side of the Jordan."

30 Then Caleb told the people in front of Moses to be quiet. And he said, "Let us go up at once and take the land. For we are well able to take it in battle." 31 But the men who had gone up with him said, "We are not able to go against the people. They are too strong for us." 32 So they brought the people of Israel bad news about the land they had spied out, saying, "The land we have gone to spy out is a land that destroys those who go there to live. All the people we saw in it are very large. 33 We saw the Nephilim there. (The sons of Anak are part of the Nephilim.) We looked like grasshoppers in our own eyes, and we looked the same to them."

The People Complain

14 Then all the people cried out with a loud voice, and they cried that night. 2 All the people of Israel complained against Moses and Aaron, and said to them, "If only we had died in the land of Egypt! Or if only we had died in this desert! 3 Why is the Lord bringing us into this land to be killed by the sword? Our wives and our little ones will be taken away. Would it not be better for us to return to Egypt?" 4 So they said to one another, "Let us choose a leader and return to Egypt."

5 Then Moses and Aaron fell on their faces in front of all the gathering of the people of Israel. 6 And Joshua the son of Nun and Caleb the son of Jephunneh tore their clothes. They were among those who had spied out the land. 7 They said to all the people of Israel, "The land we passed through to spy out is a very good land. 8 If the Lord is pleased with us, then He will bring us into this land and give it to us. It is a land which flows with milk and honey. 9 Only do not go against the Lord. And do not be afraid of the people of the land. For they will be our food. They have no way to keep safe, and the Lord is with us. Do not be afraid of them." 10 But all the people said to throw stones at Joshua and Caleb. Then the shining-greatness of the Lord was seen in the meeting tent by all the people of Israel.

Moses Prays for the People

11 The Lord said to Moses, "How long will this people turn away from Me? How long will they not believe in Me, even after all the great works I have done among them? 12 I will punish them with disease, and will not give them the land. And I will make you into a nation greater and stronger than they."

13 But Moses said to the Lord, "Then the Egyptians will hear of it. For You brought this people here by Your strength from among them. 14 And they will tell the people who live in this land. They have heard that You, O Lord, are with these people and that You, O Lord, are seen face to face as Your cloud is over them. You go before them in a cloud during the day, and in fire during the night. 15 Now if You kill these people as one man, the nations who have heard how great You are will say, 16 'The Lord was not able to bring these people into the land He promised to give them. So He has killed them in the desert.' 17 But now, I pray, let the power of the Lord be great as You have promised, saying, 18 'The Lord is slow to anger and filled with loving-kindness, forgiving sin and wrong-doing. But He will not let the guilty go without being punished. He brings the sin of fathers down upon the children, even the great-grandchildren.' 19 I pray that You will forgive the sin of this people by the greatness of Your loving-kindness. Forgive them as You have forgiven them from Egypt until now."

20 So the Lord said, "I have forgiven them as you asked. 21 But for sure, as I live, all the earth will be filled with the shining-greatness of the Lord. 22 All the men who have seen My greatness and My wonderful works which I did in Egypt and in the desert but have put Me to the test these ten times and have not listened to My voice, for sure, they 23 will not see the land I promised to their fathers. None of those who have turned away from Me will see it. 24 But My servant Caleb has had a different spirit and has followed Me in every way. I will bring him into the land where he went, and his children will take it for themselves. 25 Now the Amalekites and the Canaanites live in the valleys. So turn tomorrow and move on to the desert by the way of the Red Sea."

Punishment for the People Who Complained

26 Then the Lord said to Moses and Aaron, 27 "How long will these sinful people speak against Me? I have heard the people of Israel complaining against Me. 28 Say to them, 'As I live, what you have

said in My hearing I will do to you,' says the Lord. 29 'Your dead bodies will fall in this desert, all of you who were numbered from twenty years old and older, who have spoken against Me. 30 For sure, not one will go into the land where I promised to have you live, except Caleb the son of Jephunneh and Joshua the son of Nun. 31 You said that your children would be taken and killed. But I will bring them in, and they will know the land you have turned away from. 32 But as for you, your dead bodies will fall in this desert. 33 Your children will be shepherds in the desert for forty years. They will suffer because you were not faithful, until your dead bodies lie in the desert. 34 You spied out the land for forty days. For each day you will carry your guilt a year, forty years. And you will know that I am against you. 35 I the Lord have spoken. For sure I will do this to all these sinful people who are gathered together against Me. They will be destroyed in this desert. And there they will die.' " 36 Moses had sent men to spy out the land. They returned and made all the people complain against him by bringing bad news about the land. 37 These men who brought the very bad news about the land died of a disease before the Lord. 38 But Joshua the son of Nun and Caleb the son of Jephunneh stayed alive, of those men who went to spy out the land.

39 When Moses told these words to all the people of Israel, the people were filled with much sorrow. 40 They got up early in the morning and went up to the top of the hill country, saying, "Here we are. It is true we have sinned. But we will go up to the place which the Lord has promised." 41 But Moses said, "Why now do you sin against the Word of the Lord? It will not get you what you want. 42 Do not go up, or you will be killed by those who fight against you. For the Lord is not with you. 43 The Amalekites and the Canaanites will be there in front of you, and you will be killed by the sword. Because you have turned away from following the Lord, the Lord will not be with you." 44 But they would not listen and went up to the top of the hill country. The special box with the Law of the Lord, and Moses, did not leave the tents. 45 Then the Amalekites and the Canaanites who lived in that hill country came down and went against them and beat them down as far as Hormah.

Laws about Gifts Given on the Altar

15 The Lord said to Moses, 2 "Say to the people of Israel, 'When you go into the land where you are to live, which I am giving you, 3 then give a gift in worship by fire to the Lord. Give a gift from the herd or the flock, a burnt gift, or a gift to keep a special promise, or a free-will gift, or one during special suppers. This will be to make a pleasing smell to the Lord. 4 The one who brings his gift will bring to the Lord a grain gift of one-tenth part of a basket of fine flour mixed with one-fourth part of a large jar of oil. 5 And make ready one-fourth part of a large jar of wine to pour over the burnt gift or for each lamb given on the altar in worship. 6 Or for a ram, make ready a grain gift of two-tenths part of a basket of fine flour mixed with one-third part of a large jar of oil. 7 Then make one-third part of a large jar of wine for the drink gift, a pleasing smell to the Lord. 8 You may make ready a bull for a burnt gift or give an animal on the altar in worship, to keep a special promise, or give peace gifts to the Lord. 9 With the bull bring a grain gift of three-tenths part of a basket of fine flour mixed with half a large jar of oil. 10 Bring for the drink gift half a large jar of wine, as a gift by fire, a pleasing smell to the Lord.

11 'It must be done this way for each bull, or for each ram, or for each of the male lambs or young goats. 12 Whatever number you make ready, you must do for everyone. 13 All who are born in the land must do these things in this way by giving a gift by fire, a pleasing smell to the Lord. 14 A stranger staying with you, or a man living among your people, may want to give a gift by fire, a pleasing smell to the Lord. Then he must do just as you do. 15 There will be one Law for you and for the stranger who stays with you. It will be a Law forever for all your children-to-come. As you are, so will the stranger be before the Lord. 16 One Law will be for you and for the stranger who stays with you.' "

17 Then the Lord said to Moses, 18 "Say to the people of Israel, 'When you come into the land where I bring you 19 and when you eat of the food of the land, you must lift up a gift in worship to the Lord. 20 Give a loaf of bread as a gift from the first of your grain. Give it as the gift of the grain-floor. 21 From the first of your grain you and all your children-to-come must give a gift to the Lord.

22 'Without knowing it you might not

obey all these Laws which the Lord has spoken to Moses, 23 even all that the Lord has told you to do through Moses, from the day when the Lord told you and through all your children-to-come. 24 If this is done without the people knowing it, then all the people must give one bull for a burnt gift. It will be a pleasing smell to the Lord. It must be brought with its grain gift and its drink gift, by the Law, and with one male goat for a sin gift. 25 Then the religious leader will pay for the sins of all the people of Israel, and they will be forgiven. Because it was a mistake, they brought their gift, a gift by fire to the Lord, and their sin gift to the Lord, for their mistake. 26 So all the people of Israel and the stranger who stays among them will be forgiven. For it happened to all the people by mistake.

27 'If one person sins without knowing it, he must bring a one year old female goat for a sin gift. 28 And the religious leader before the Lord will pay for the sin of the person who sins without knowing it. He will pay for his sin so he may be forgiven. 29 You will have one Law for him who does anything without knowing it, for him who is one of the people of Israel and for the stranger who lives among them. 30 But if a person born in the land or a stranger does anything wrong and means to do it, he is speaking against the Lord. That person must be cut off from among his people. 31 Because he has hated the Word of the Lord and has broken His Law, that person must be cut off for sure. His guilt will be on him.' "

Punishment for Those Who Worked on the Day of Rest

32 While the people of Israel were in the desert, they found a man gathering wood on the Day of Rest. 33 Those who found him gathering wood brought him to Moses and Aaron, and to all the people. 34 They put him in chains, because they did not know what should be done to him for gathering wood on the Day of Rest. 35 Then the Lord said to Moses: "The man must be put to death. All the people must kill him with stones away from the tents." 36 So all the people took him away from the tents and killed him with stones, just as the Lord had told Moses.

37 The Lord said to Moses, 38 "Speak to the people of Israel. Tell them that they and all their children-to-come are to make tassels for themselves on the corners of their clothing. And they are to put a blue rope on the tassel of each corner. 39 It will be a tassel for you to look at and remember all the Laws of the Lord, and to do them. Do not follow your own heart and your own eyes, as you did when you acted like a woman selling the use of her body. 40 It will be so that you may remember to obey all My Laws, and be holy to your God. 41 I am the Lord your God Who brought you out from the land of Egypt to be your God. I am the Lord your God."

Korah Works against Moses

16 Now Korah the son of Izhar, the son of Kohath, the son of Levi, with Dathan and Abiram, the sons of Eliab, and On the son of Peleth, sons of Reuben, caused trouble. 2 They came in front of Moses, together with some of the sons of Israel. They had chosen 250 leaders of the people of Israel, well-known men. 3 They all gathered together against Moses and Aaron, and said to them, "You have gone too far! For all the people are holy, every one of them, and the Lord is among them. So why do you honor yourselves more than the people of the Lord?"

4 When Moses heard this, he bowed to the ground. 5 He said to Korah and all who were with him, "Tomorrow morning the Lord will show who is His, and who is holy. He will have him come near to Him. He will bring near to Himself the one whom He will choose. 6 Do this, Korah and all who are with you. Take pots for burning special perfume. 7 Put fire in them, and put special perfume upon them before the Lord tomorrow. The man whom the Lord chooses will be the one who is holy. You have gone too far, you sons of Levi!"

8 Then Moses said to Korah, "Hear now, you sons of Levi. 9 Is it not enough for you that the God of Israel has set you apart from the rest of the people of Israel? He has brought you near to Himself. He has you do the work around the meeting tent of the Lord. And He has you stand in front of the people to care for them. 10 He has brought you near to Him, Korah, and all your brothers who are the sons of Levi, with you. Would you try to be the religious leaders also? 11 So you and all who are with you are gathered together against the Lord. But as for Aaron, who is he that you complain against him?"

12 Then Moses sent to call Dathan and Abiram, the sons of Eliab. But they said, "We will not come up. 13 Is it not enough that you have brought us up out of a land

flowing with milk and honey to have us die in the desert? Must you make yourself a ruler over us also? 14 More than this, you have not brought us into a land flowing with milk and honey. You have not given us any land with fields and grape-vines. Would you put out the eyes of these men? We will not come up!"

15 Moses became very angry. He said to the Lord, "Do not respect their gift! I have not taken one donkey from them. And I have not hurt one of them." 16 Then Moses said to Korah, "You and all who are with you be before the Lord tomorrow, you and they, and Aaron. 17 Each of you take his fire pot and put special perfume on it. And each of you bring his fire pot before the Lord, 250 fire pots. Let both you and Aaron bring his fire pot also." 18 So each man took his fire pot and put fire in it and put special perfume on it. And they stood at the door of the meeting tent with Moses and Aaron. 19 Korah gathered together all the people against them at the door of the meeting tent. And the shining-greatness of the Lord was seen by all the people.

20 The Lord said to Moses and Aaron, 21 "Go away from these people, so I may destroy them at once." 22 But they fell on their faces, and said, "O God, the God of the spirits of all flesh, when one man sins, will You be angry with all the people?" 23 Then the Lord said to Moses, 24 "Say to the people, 'Get away from the tents of Korah, Dathan and Abiram.'"

25 Then Moses got up and went to Dathan and Abiram, with the leaders of Israel following him. 26 And he said to the people, "Go away now from the tents of these sinful men. Touch nothing that belongs to them, or you will be destroyed because of all their sin." 27 So they went away from the tents of Korah, Dathan and Abiram. And Dathan and Abiram came out and stood at the door of their tents, with their wives, their sons, and their little ones. 28 Moses said, "By this you will know that the Lord has sent me to do all these works. For this is not my doing. 29 If these men die in the same way all men die, or if what happens to everyone happens to them, then the Lord has not sent me. 30 But the Lord will do something new. The ground will open its mouth and take them with all that belongs to them. And they will go down alive into the place of the dead. Then you will understand that these men have turned against the Lord."

31 As soon as he stopped speaking, the ground under them opened up. 32 The earth opened its mouth and took them and all those of their house, and all Korah's men and all that belonged to them. 33 They and all that belonged to them went down alive to the place of the dead, and the earth closed over them. They were destroyed from among the people. 34 And all Israel who were around them ran away at their cry. For they said, "The earth may take us too!" 35 Then fire came from the Lord and destroyed the 250 men who had brought the special perfume.

36 The Lord said to Moses, 37 "Tell Eleazar the son of Aaron the religious leader to take the fire pots out of the fire. For they are holy. Then spread the burning pieces far apart. 38 Let the fire pots of these men who have sinned and lost their lives be made into beaten plates to cover the altar. For they did bring them to the Lord and they are holy. They will be something special for the people of Israel to see." 39 So Eleazar the religious leader took the brass fire pots which the men who were burned had brought. And they beat them into plates to cover the altar. 40 They were to make the people of Israel remember that no man who is not a religious leader and a son of Aaron should come to burn special perfume before the Lord. Or he might become like Korah and those who were with him, as the Lord said to Eleazar through Moses.

The People Complain

41 But on the next day all the people of Israel complained against Moses and Aaron, saying, "You are the ones who have caused the death of the Lord's people." 42 When the people had gathered against Moses and Aaron, they turned toward the meeting tent. There the cloud covered it and they saw the shining-greatness of the Lord. 43 Then Moses and Aaron came to the front of the meeting tent. 44 And the Lord said to Moses, 45 "Get away from these people, so I may destroy them at once." Then they fell on their faces. 46 Moses said to Aaron, "Take your fire pot and put fire in it from the altar, and lay special perfume on it. Then be quick to bring it to the people and pay for their sin. For anger has gone out from the Lord. The disease has come!" 47 So Aaron took it as Moses said, and ran to the people. The disease had already come upon them. He put on the special perfume and paid for

the sin of the people. 48 He stood between the dead and the living, and the disease was stopped. 49 But 14,700 people died by the disease, as well as those who died because of Korah. 50 Then Aaron returned to Moses at the door of the meeting tent, for the disease had been stopped.

Aaron's Stick Began to Grow

17 The Lord said to Moses, 2 "Speak to the people of Israel. Get walking sticks from them, one for each father's house. Get twelve walking sticks, from all their leaders by their fathers' houses. Write each man's name on his stick. 3 Write Aaron's name on the walking stick of Levi. For there will be one walking stick for the head of each father's house. 4 Then put them in the meeting tent before the Law, where I meet with you. 5 And the walking stick of the man I choose will begin to grow. In this way I will stop the complaining of the people of Israel, who are complaining against you." 6 So Moses spoke to the people of Israel. All their leaders each gave him a walking stick, one for each leader by their fathers' houses, twelve walking sticks. And the walking stick of Aaron was among their walking sticks. 7 Moses put the walking sticks before the Lord in the meeting tent of the Law.

8 The next day Moses went into the meeting tent of the Law. And he saw that the walking stick of Aaron for the house of Levi had begun to grow buds and flowers and almonds. 9 Moses brought out all the walking sticks from before the Lord to all the people of Israel. They looked, and each man took his stick. 10 But the Lord said to Moses, "Put the walking stick of Aaron in front of the Law again. It will be something special to see against those who go against My Word. Then you may put an end to their complaining against Me, so they will not die." 11 So Moses did this. He did just as the Lord had told him.

12 Then the people of Israel said to Moses, "See, we are being destroyed! We are dying! We are all dying! 13 Everyone who comes near, who comes near the meeting tent of the Lord, must die. Are we all to be destroyed?"

The Work of the Religious Leaders and Levites

18 The Lord said to Aaron, "You and your sons and those of your father's house will carry the guilt for any sin done in the meeting tent. And you and your

sons with you will carry the guilt of any sin of the religious leaders. 2 Bring with you your brothers also, the family of Levi, the family of your father. Then they may join you and help you while you and your sons are in front of the meeting tent of the Law. 3 They will help you and help in doing all the work of the tent. But they must not come near the objects of the meeting tent and the altar, or both they and you will die. 4 They will join you and help do all the work of the meeting tent. But no one else may come near you. 5 You must do the work of the meeting tent and the work of the altar, so there will no longer be anger on the people of Israel. 6 See, I Myself have taken your brothers the Levites from among the people of Israel. They are a gift to you, given to the Lord, to do the work for the meeting tent. 7 But you and your sons with you will do the religious work, in all that has to do with the altar and inside the curtain. I am giving you the work of being the religious leader as a gift. Anyone else who comes near the holy objects will be put to death."

Gifts for the Religious Leaders

8 Then the Lord said to Aaron, "Now see, I am giving you all the gifts brought to Me that are not burned on the altar. I am giving them to you as a share, and to your sons as a share forever. 9 This will be yours from the most holy gifts, kept from the fire: every gift of theirs, even every grain gift, every sin gift and every guilt gift, which they bring to Me. They will be most holy for you and your sons. 10 You will eat it as the most holy gifts. Every male will eat it. It will be holy to you. 11 And this is yours: their gift that is lifted up and all the wave gifts of the people of Israel. I am giving them to you and to your sons and daughters with you, as a share forever. Everyone in your house who is clean may eat it. 12 I give to you all the best of the oil and all the best of the wine and of the grain, the first-fruits of what they give to the Lord. 13 The first-fruits ready to eat of all that is in their land, which they bring to the Lord, will be yours. Everyone in your house who is clean may eat it. 14 Everything in Israel that has been set apart to the Lord will be yours. 15 Every first-born of all flesh, man or animal, which they give to the Lord, will be yours. But you must pay the price and make free the first-born of man and the first-born of animals that are unclean. 16 You must make them free when

they are one month old. The price to free them will be five large pieces of silver, the price decided upon at the meeting tent. One large piece of silver is worth twenty small pieces of silver. [17] But do not free the first-born of a bull or sheep or goat. For they are holy. You will put their blood on the altar and burn their fat as a gift by fire, a pleasing smell to the Lord. [18] But their meat will be yours, like the breast of a wave gift and like the right thigh are yours. [19] I have given to you and your sons and daughters, for a share forever, all the holy gifts which the people of Israel bring to the Lord. It is an agreement of salt forever before the Lord for you and your children with you." [20] Then the Lord said to Aaron, "You will have no share in their land. You will not own any part of land among them. I am your part and your share among the people of Israel.

[21] "See, I have given a tenth part of everything in Israel to the Levites, in return for the work they do, the work of the meeting tent. [22] The people of Israel must not come near the meeting tent again, or they will be guilty of sin and die. [23] Only the Levites may do the work around the meeting tent, and they will carry their sin. It will be a Law forever for all your children-to-come. And they will have no land among the people of Israel. [24] For I have given to the Levites one-tenth part of what the people of Israel give to the Lord. This is why I have said of them, 'They will have no land among the people of Israel.'"

[25] Then the Lord said to Moses, [26] "Say to the Levites, 'When you take from the people of Israel the tenth which I have given you from them for your share, then give a gift from it to the Lord. Give one-tenth part of the tenth. [27] And your gift will be to you as if it were the grain from the grain-floor or all the wine from the crushed grapes. [28] So you must give a gift to the Lord from the tenth of what you receive from the people of Israel. And from it you must give the Lord's gift to Aaron the religious leader. [29] Out of all the gifts to you, you must give every gift that should go to the Lord, from all the best of them. Give the holy part from them.'

[30] "And say to them, 'When you have given the best part of it, the rest of it will be to you as if it were the grain from the grain-floor and the wine from the crushed grapes. [31] You and those of your houses may eat it in any place. For it is your pay for your work in the meeting tent. [32] You will

not be guilty because of it, when you have given the best of it. But do not make unclean the holy gifts of the people of Israel, or you will die.'"

Laws for Washing

19 Now the Lord said to Moses and Aaron, [2] "This is the Law which the Lord has told you. Tell the people of Israel to bring you a young red cow that is perfect, one that has never pulled a load. [3] You will give it to Eleazar the religious leader. It will be brought away from the tents and killed in front of him. [4] Next Eleazar the religious leader will take some of its blood with his finger, and put some of it toward the front of the meeting tent seven times. [5] Then Eleazar will watch the young cow being burned. Its skin, its flesh, its blood and its waste will be burned. [6] The religious leader will take cedar wood and hyssop and red cloth, and put it on the burning cow. [7] Then the religious leader will wash his clothes and wash his body in water. After this the religious leader may come among the tents, but he will be unclean until evening. [8] The one who burns it will also wash his clothes and wash his body in water. And he will be unclean until evening. [9] Now a man who is clean will gather up the ashes of the young cow and put them in a clean place away from the tents. They will be kept for the people of Israel to mix with the water used to make things clean, to take away sin. [10] The one who gathers the ashes of the young cow must wash his clothes. He will be unclean until evening. This will be a Law forever to the people of Israel and to the stranger who lives among them.

[11] "The one who touches the dead body of any person will be unclean for seven days. [12] He must clean himself with the water on the third day and on the seventh day. Then he will be clean. But if he does not clean himself on the third day and on the seventh day, he will be unclean. [13] Whoever touches the body of any man who has died, and does not make himself clean, makes the meeting tent of the Lord unclean. That person must be cut off from Israel. Because the water for cleaning was not put upon him, he will be unclean.

[14] "This is the Law when a man dies in a tent. Everyone who comes into the tent and everyone who is in the tent will be unclean for seven days. [15] And every open pot that has no cover on it will be unclean. [16] Anyone in an open field who touches

one who has been killed with a sword, or who has died, or who touches a bone of a man, or a grave will be unclean for seven days. ¹⁷ The person who is unclean must take some of the ashes from the burning of the sin gift. Clean water must be added to them in a pot. ¹⁸ Then a clean person must take hyssop and put it in the water, and put it on the tent and on all the objects within the tent. He must put it on the persons who were there, and on the one who touched the bone or the man who was killed or the dead person or the grave. ¹⁹ The clean person must put the water on whoever is unclean, on the third day and on the seventh day. He will make him clean on the seventh day. He will wash his clothes and wash himself in water, and will be clean at evening.

²⁰ "But the man who is unclean and does not make himself clean, will no longer be one of God's people. Because he has made unclean the holy place of the Lord. The water for cleaning has not been put on him. He is unclean. ²¹ It will be a Law forever for them. He who puts the water on to be made clean must wash his clothes. And he who touches the water used to be made clean will be unclean until evening. ²² Anything that the person who is unclean touches will be unclean. And the person who touches it will be unclean until evening."

Water from the Rock

20 Then all the people of Israel came to the Desert of Zin in the first month. And the people stayed at Kadesh. Miriam died there and was buried.

² Now there was no water for the people, and they gathered together against Moses and Aaron. ³ The people complained to Moses, saying, "If only we had died when our brothers died before the Lord! ⁴ Why have you brought the Lord's people into this desert, for us and our animals to die here? ⁵ Why have you made us come up from Egypt, to bring us into this bad place? It is not a place of grain, or figs, or vines, or pomegranates. And there is no water to drink." ⁶ Then Moses and Aaron went from the people to the door of the meeting tent, and bowed to the ground. They saw the shining-greatness of the Lord. ⁷ The Lord said to Moses, ⁸ "Take the special stick. You and your brother Aaron gather the people together. Speak to the rock in front of them and it will give its water. So you will bring water out of the rock for

them. Let the people and their animals drink." ⁹ So Moses took the special stick from before the Lord, just as He had told him. ¹⁰ Moses and Aaron gathered the people in front of the rock. And he said to them, "Listen now, you people who go against the Lord. Should we bring water for you out of this rock?" ¹¹ Then Moses lifted up his hand and hit the rock twice with his stick, and more than enough water came out. The people and their animals drank. ¹² But the Lord said to Moses and Aaron, "Because you have not believed Me and honored Me as holy in the eyes of the people of Israel, you will not bring these people into the land I have given them." ¹³ These were the waters of Meribah because the people of Israel complained against the Lord, and He proved Himself holy among them.

¹⁴ Moses sent men from Kadesh to the king of Edom, saying, "This is what your brother Israel has said: 'You know all the troubles we have had. ¹⁵ Our fathers went down to Egypt, and we lived in Egypt a long time. The Egyptians were bad in the way they acted toward us. ¹⁶ But we cried out to the Lord. He heard our voice and sent an angel and brought us out from Egypt. Now look, we are at Kadesh, a town at the side of your country. ¹⁷ We ask you to let us pass through your land. We will not pass through field or vines. We will not even drink water from a well. We will go on the king's road and will not turn to the right or left, until we pass through your country.' " ¹⁸ But Edom said to him, "You must not pass through, or I will come out with the sword against you." ¹⁹ The people of Israel said to him, "We will go up by the straight road. If I and my animals do drink any of your water, then I will pay for it. Let me only pass through on my feet, nothing else." ²⁰ But Edom said, "You must not pass through." And Edom came out against him with many men and much strength. ²¹ Edom would not let Israel pass through his country. So Israel turned away from him.

²² When they traveled from Kadesh, all the people of Israel came to Mount Hor. ²³ The Lord spoke to Moses and Aaron at Mount Hor by the side of the land of Edom, saying, ²⁴ "Aaron will be buried with his people. For he will not go into the land I have given to the people of Israel, because you went against what I told you to do at the waters of Meribah. ²⁵ Take Aaron and his son Eleazar, and bring them

up to Mount Hor. 26 Take the clothing off Aaron and put them on his son Eleazar. Aaron will die there and be buried with his people." 27 Moses did just as the Lord had told him. They went up to Mount Hor before the eyes of all the people. 28 After Moses had taken the clothing off Aaron and put them on his son Eleazar, Aaron died there on the mountain-top. Then Moses and Eleazar came down from the mountain. 29 When all the people saw that Aaron had died, all the house of Israel cried in sorrow for Aaron thirty days.

Battle with the Canaanites

21 The Canaanite, the king of Arad, who lived in the Negev, heard that Israel was coming by the way of Atharim. He fought against Israel, and took some of them against their will. 2 So Israel made a promise to the Lord, and said, "If You will give this people into my hand, I will destroy every part of their cities." 3 The Lord heard the voice of Israel, and gave them the Canaanites. Then Israel destroyed all of them and their cities. So the name of the place was called Hormah.

The Brass Snake

4 Then they traveled from Mount Hor by the way of the Red Sea, to go around the land of Edom. And the people wanted to give up because of the long way. 5 They spoke against God and Moses, saying, "Why have you brought us up out of Egypt to die in the desert? For there is no food and no water. And we hate this bad food." 6 Then the Lord sent snakes with a bite of poison among the people. They bit the people, so that many people of Israel died. 7 So the people came to Moses and said, "We have sinned, because we have spoken against the Lord and you. Pray to the Lord, that He will take away the snakes from us." So Moses prayed for the people. 8 The Lord said to Moses, "Make a special snake and put it up on a long piece of wood. Everyone who is bitten will live when he looks at it." 9 So Moses made a brass snake and put it up on the long piece of wood. If a snake bit any man, he would live when he looked at the brass snake.

From Mount Hor to Moab

10 The people of Israel traveled on, and set up their tents in Oboth. 11 Then they left Oboth and stopped at Iye-abarim, in the desert beside Moab, to the east. 12 From there they traveled on to Wadi Zered.

13 And from there they traveled on and set up their tents on the other side of the Arnon. It is in the desert that goes out from the land of the Amorites. For the Arnon is the side of Moab, between Moab and the Amorites. 14 So it is said in the Book of the Wars of the Lord: "Waheb in Suphah, and the valleys of the Arnon, 15 and the hill-side of the valleys that goes to the place of Ar, and rests on the side of Moab." 16 From there they went on to Beer. That is the well where the Lord said to Moses, "Gather the people together, so I may give them water."

17 Then Israel sang this song: "Come up, O well! Sing to it! 18 The well, which the leaders dug, which the rulers of the people dug, with the special stick of power and with their walking sticks." From the desert they went on to Mattanah. 19 From Mattanah they went to Nahaliel, and from Nahaliel to Bamoth. 20 From Bamoth they went to the valley in the land of Moab, at the top of Pisgah which looks down upon the desert.

Battle with Amorites

21 Then Israel sent men to Sihon king of the Amorites, saying, 22 "Let me pass through your land. We will not turn aside into field or vines. We will not drink water from wells. We will go on the king's road until we have passed through your country." 23 But Sihon would not let Israel pass through his country. He gathered all his people and went out against Israel in the desert. He came to Jahaz and fought against Israel. 24 Then Israel killed Sihon with the sword. They took his land from the Arnon to the Jabbok, as far as the people of Ammon. For Jazer was the side of the land of the Ammonites. 25 Israel took all these cities. They lived in all the cities of the Amorites, in Heshbon, and in all its towns. 26 For Heshbon was the city of Sihon king of the Amorites. He had fought against the man who was once the king of Moab, and had taken all his land as far as the Arnon 27 So those who use wise sayings say, "Come to Heshbon! Let it be built! Let the city of Sihon be built. 28 For a fire went out from Heshbon, fire from the city of Sihon. It burned up Ar of Moab, and the lords of the high places of the Arnon. 29 It is bad for you, O Moab! You are destroyed, O people of Chemosh! His sons run for their lives. His daughters have been taken against their will by an Amorite king, Sihon. 30 But we have put them down,

Heshbon is destroyed as far as Dibon. We have destroyed even to Medeba." 31 So Israel lived in the land of the Amorites. 32 Then Moses sent men to spy out Jazer in secret. And Israel took its towns and took the place of the Amorites who were there.

King Og Killed

33 Then they turned and went up by the way of Bashan. Og the king of Bashan went out with all his people to battle at Edrei. 34 But the Lord said to Moses, "Do not be afraid of him. For I have given him into your hand, with all his people and his land. Do to him as you did to Sihon king of the Amorites who lived at Heshbon." 35 So the people of Israel killed Og and his sons and all his people, until there was not one left alive. And they took his land.

Balak Sends for Balaam

22 Then the people of Israel traveled on and set up their tents in the plains of Moab on the other side of the Jordan beside Jericho. 2 Now Balak the son of Zippor saw all that Israel had done to the Amorites. 3 So Moab was filled with much fear because of the people, for they were many. Moab was very afraid of the people of Israel. 4 And Moab said to the leaders of Midian, "Now these people will take away everything around us like the bull eats up the grass of the field." Balak the son of Zippor was king of Moab at that time. 5 So he sent men to Balaam the son of Beor, at Pethor, which is near the River in the land of the children of his people. They said to him, "See, a people came out of Egypt. See, they cover the land, and they are living beside me. 6 Now come, I beg you. Curse this people for me, because they are too strong for me. Then I may be able to win the battle against them and send them out of the land. For I know that good will come to the one you pray for, and trouble will come to the one you curse."

7 So the leaders of Moab and the leaders of Midian left with the pay in their hand for the one who tells what will happen in the future. When they came to Balaam, they told him Balak's words. 8 Balaam said to them, "Stay here tonight. I will bring word to you as the Lord may speak to me." So the leaders of Moab stayed with Balaam. 9 Then God came to Balaam and said, "Who are these men with you?" 10 Balaam said to God, "Balak the son of Zippor, king of Moab, has sent word to me, saying, 11 'See, the people who came out of Egypt cover the land. Now come, curse them for me. Then I may be able to fight against them and send them away.' " 12 God said to Balaam, "Do not go with them. Do not curse the people, for I have decided that good would come to them." 13 So Balaam got up in the morning and said to Balak's leaders, "Return to your land. For the Lord will not let me go with you." 14 So the leaders of Moab got up and went to Balak, and said, "Balaam would not come with us."

15 Balak sent leaders again, more than were sent before, and men who were more important. 16 They came to Balaam and said to him, "Balak the son of Zippor says, 'I beg you, let nothing keep you from coming to me. 17 I will give you much honor. I will do whatever you tell me. I beg you to come and curse these people for me.' " 18 Balaam answered and said to Balak's men, "Balak could give me his house full of silver and gold. But I could not do anything, small or big, against the Word of the Lord my God. 19 Now I ask you to stay here tonight. I will find out what else the Lord will say to me." 20 God came to Balaam at night and said to him, "If the men have come to call you, get up and go with them. But do only what I tell you."

Balaam's Donkey and the Angel

21 So Balaam got up in the morning and got his donkey ready, and went with the leaders of Moab. 22 But God was angry because he was going. The angel of the Lord stood in the way against him. Balaam was sitting on his donkey, and his two servants were with him. 23 When the donkey saw the angel of the Lord standing in the way with his sword in his hand, the donkey turned off the road and went into the field. But Balaam hit the donkey to turn her on the road again. 24 Then the angel of the Lord stood in a narrow path in the grape-field, with a wall on each side. 25 The donkey saw the angel of the Lord. So she pushed herself against the wall and crushed Balaam's foot against it, so he hit her again. 26 Then the angel of the Lord went farther. He stood in a narrow place where there was no way to turn to the right or the left. 27 When the donkey saw the angel of the Lord, she lay down under Balaam. So Balaam was angry and hit the donkey with his stick. 28 And the Lord opened the mouth of the donkey, and she said to Balaam, "What have I done to you?

Why have you hit me these three times?" ²⁹ Balaam said to the donkey, "Because you have made a fool of me! If there had been a sword in my hand, I would have killed you by now!" ³⁰ The donkey said to Balaam, "Am I not your donkey on which you have traveled all your life to this day? Have I ever done this to you before?" And Balaam said, "No."

³¹ Then the Lord opened Balaam's eyes, and he saw the angel of the Lord standing in the way with his sword in his hand. And he bowed to the ground. ³² The angel of the Lord said to him, "Why have you hit your donkey these three times? See, I have come out against you, because your way was against me. ³³ But the donkey saw me and turned from me these three times. If she had not turned from me, for sure I would have killed you, and let her live." ³⁴ Balaam said to the angel of the Lord, "I have sinned. For I did not know that you were standing in the way against me. But now, if it does not please you, I will turn back." ³⁵ The angel of the Lord said to Balaam, "Go with the men. But speak only what I tell you." So Balaam went with the leaders of Balak.

³⁶ Balak heard that Balaam was coming. He went out to meet him at the city of Moab, on the Arnon, at the far side of the country. ³⁷ Balak said to Balaam, "Did I not send men to tell you to come? Why did you not come to me? Am I not able to honor you?" ³⁸ Balaam said to Balak, "See, I have come to you! Am I able to speak anything at all? The Word that God puts in my mouth is what I must speak." ³⁹ Then Balaam went with Balak, and they came to Kiriathhuzoth. ⁴⁰ Balak killed bulls and sheep on the altar in worship, and sent some to Balaam and the leaders who were with him.

⁴¹ The next morning Balak took Balaam and brought him up to the high places of Baal. From there he saw part of the people of Israel.

Balaam Tells What Will Happen the First Time

23 Then Balaam said to Balak, "Build seven altars here for me. And make ready seven bulls and seven rams for me here." ² Balak did as Balaam had said. Balak and Balaam gave a bull and a ram on each altar in worship. ³ Then Balaam said to Balak, "Stand beside your burnt gift, and I will go. It might be that the Lord will come to me. And whatever He shows me I

will tell you." So he went up to a hill without trees. ⁴ God met Balaam. Balaam said to Him, "I have made seven altars. And I have given a bull and a ram on each altar in worship." ⁵ Then the Lord put words in Balaam's mouth, and said, "Return to Balak. This is what you should say." ⁶ So Balaam returned to Balak, and saw him and all the leaders of Moab standing beside his burnt gift. ⁷ Balaam began speaking and said, "Balak the king of Moab has brought me from Aram, from the mountains of the east. 'Come, curse Jacob for me,' he said. 'Come, say that Israel should be punished!' ⁸ How can I curse those whom God has not cursed? How can I say that those should be punished whom God has not said should be punished? ⁹ I see Israel from the top of the rocks. I look at them from the hills. See, the people live apart. They will not be thought of as one of the nations. ¹⁰ Who can number the dust of Jacob, or number the fourth part of Israel? Let me die the death of those who are right and good. Let my end be like theirs!"

¹¹ Balak said to Balaam, "What have you done to me? I took you to curse those who hate me. But see, you have asked that good would come to them!" ¹² Balaam answered, "Must I not be careful to speak what the Lord puts in my mouth?"

Balaam Tells What Will Happen the Second Time

¹³ Balak said to him, "I beg you, come with me to another place from where you will see them. But you will only see a part of them and not all of them. Curse them for me from there." ¹⁴ So he took him to the field of Zophim, to the top of Pisgah. He built seven altars and gave a bull and a ram on each altar. ¹⁵ Balaam said to Balak, "Stand here beside your burnt gift, while I meet the Lord over there." ¹⁶ The Lord met Balaam and put words in his mouth and said, "Return to Balak. This is what you should say." ¹⁷ So he returned to Balak, and saw him and all the leaders of Moab standing beside his burnt gift. Balak said to him, "What has the Lord said?" ¹⁸ Then Balaam began speaking and said, "Rise, O Balak, and hear! Listen to me, O son of Zippor! ¹⁹ God is not a man, that He should lie. He is not a son of man, that He should be sorry for what He has said. Has He said, and will He not do it? Has He spoken, and will He not keep His Word? ²⁰ See, I have been told to speak good of Israel. When He has spoken good of them,

I cannot change it. 21 No hard times are seen in Jacob. No trouble is seen in Israel. The Lord their God is with them. And the cry of a king is among them. 22 God brings them out of Egypt. He is for them like the horns of the wild bull. 23 For there is no special thing that has been shown against Jacob. Nothing has told of a bad future for Israel. Now it will be said of Jacob and Israel, 'Look what God has done!' 24 See, people rise like a female lion. It lifts itself like a lion. It will not lie down until it eats the food it has killed, and drinks the blood of the kill." 25 Balak said to Balaam, "Do not curse them at all or pray that good would come to them!" 26 But Balaam answered Balak, "Did I not tell you that I must do whatever the Lord says?"

Balaam Tells What Will Happen the Third Time

27 Then Balak said to Balaam, "I beg you, come. I will take you to another place. It might be that God will be pleased to have you curse them for me from there." 28 So Balak took Balaam to the top of Peor which looks over the desert. 29 Balaam said to Balak, "Build seven altars for me here. And make ready seven bulls and seven rams for me here." 30 Balak did just as Balaam had said. He gave a bull and a ram on each altar in worship.

24 Balaam saw that it pleased the Lord to speak good of Israel. So he did not go, as at other times, and look for special things to see. Instead he looked toward the desert. 2 Balaam looked up and saw Israel living in their tents by their families. And the Spirit of God came upon him. 3 He began speaking and said, "Balaam the son of Beor is the man whose eye is opened. 4 He hears the words of God. He sees what the All-powerful wants him to see. He falls down, but has his eyes open. 5 How fair are your tents, O Jacob, and your homes, O Israel! 6 They are like valleys that spread out, and like gardens beside the river. They are like aloes planted by the Lord, and like cedars beside the waters. 7 Water will flow from his pails. His seed will be by many waters. His king will be more powerful than Agag, and his nation will be honored. 8 God brings him out of Egypt. He is for him like the horns of the wild bull. He will destroy the nations who fight against him. He will crush their bones in pieces and cut through them with his arrows. 9 He bows down. He lies down like a lion. And

as a lion, who will wake him? Good will come to everyone who prays for you. And cursed is everyone who curses you."

10 Then Balak's anger burned against Balaam, and he hit his hands together. Balak said to Balaam, "I called you to curse those who hate me. But see, you have done nothing but pray that good would come to them these three times! 11 So now run away to your place. I said I would give you much honor, but the Lord has kept you from honor." 12 Then Balaam said to Balak, "Did I not tell the men you had sent to me, 13 'Even if Balak were to give me his house full of silver and gold, I cannot do anything against the Word of the Lord'? I said, 'I cannot do good or bad because I want to. What the Lord says, I will say.' 14 Now see, I am going to my people. Come, I will tell you what this people will do to your people in the days to come."

Balaam Tells What Will Happen the Fourth Time

15 Then he began speaking and said, "Balaam the son of Beor is the man whose eye is opened. 16 He hears the words of God. He knows what the Most High wants him to know. He sees what the All-powerful wants him to see. He falls down, but has his eyes open. 17 I see him, but not now. I see him, but he is not near. A star will come out of Jacob. A special stick of power will rise from Israel. It will crush the forehead of Moab, and break down all the sons of Sheth. 18 It will take the land of Edom. And it will take the land of Seir, who fights against Israel. And Israel will fight with much power. 19 One from Jacob will rule. He will destroy from the city all who are left alive." 20 Then Balaam looked at Amalek and said, "Amalek was the first of the nations. But he will be destroyed in the end." 21 Then he looked at the Kenite and said, "The place where you live is strong. Your nest is set in the rock. 22 But Kain will be destroyed. How long will Asshur keep you against your will?" 23 Then Balaam said, "Who can live when God does this? 24 But ships will come from Kittim. They will bring trouble to Asshur and Eber, but they will be destroyed also." 25 Then Balaam got up and left. He returned to his place, and Balak went on his way.

Israel Sins in Moab

25 While Israel stayed at Shittim, the people were not faithful to the Lord and began to have sex with the daughters of Moab. 2 They asked the people of Israel to bring gifts to their gods, and the people ate and bowed down to their gods. 3 So Israel joined themselves to Baal of Peor, and the Lord was angry with Israel. 4 The Lord said to Moses, "Take all the leaders of the people, kill them, and put their bodies in the bright daylight before the Lord. Then the strong anger of the Lord may turn away from Israel." 5 So Moses said to the judges of Israel, "Each of you kill his men who have joined themselves to Baal of Peor."

6 Then one of the people of Israel came and brought a Midianite woman to his family. Moses and all the people of Israel saw this while they were crying at the door of the meeting tent. 7 When Phinehas the son of Eleazar, the son of Aaron the religious leader, saw it, he rose up from among the people. He took a spear in his hand 8 and went after the man of Israel into the tent. Then he cut through the bodies of both the man of Israel and the woman. So the very bad disease that spread on the people of Israel was stopped. 9 Those who died because of this bad disease were 24,000.

10 Then the Lord said to Moses, 11 "Phinehas the son of Eleazar, the son of Aaron the religious leader, has turned My anger away from the people of Israel. He was jealous with My jealousy among them, so I did not destroy the people of Israel in My jealousy. 12 So say to them that I make My agreement of peace with Phinehas. 13 It will be an agreement for him and his children after him that they will always be religious leaders, because he was jealous for his God, and did what he was to do to pay for the sin of the people of Israel."

14 The name of the man of Israel who was killed with the Midianite woman was Zimri the son of Salu. He was a leader of a father's house among the Simeonites. 15 The name of the Midianite woman who was killed was Cozbi the daughter of Zur. Zur was the head of the people of a father's house in Midian.

16 The Lord said to Moses, 17 "Be angry at the Midianites and fight against them. 18 For they have brought trouble to you with their false ways. They have fooled you and turned you to the wrong way. They have brought you trouble at Peor with Cozbi, the daughter of the leader of Midian, their sister. She was killed on the day of the very bad disease came because of Peor."

The Second Numbering of Israel

26 After the very bad disease came on the people because of Israel's sin, the Lord said to Moses and Eleazar the son of Aaron the religious leader, 2 "Add the numbers of all the people of Israel who are twenty years old and older, by their fathers' houses. Number whoever in Israel is able to go to war." 3 So Moses and Eleazar the religious leader said to the people in the plains of Moab by the Jordan at Jericho, 4 "Number the people who are twenty years old and older, as the Lord has told Moses."

Now these were the sons of Israel who came out of the land of Egypt. 5 Reuben was the first-born son of Israel. Reuben's sons were the family of the Hanochites from Hanoch, the family of the Palluites from Pallu, 6 the family of the Hezronites from Hezron, and the family of the Carmites from Carmi. 7 These are the families of the Reubenites, and their number was 43,730. 8 Eliab was the son of Pallu. 9 The sons of Eliab were Nemuel, Dathan and Abiram. These are Dathan and Abiram who were chosen by the people and who joined with Korah to argue against Moses and Aaron. They argued against the Lord, 10 and the earth opened its mouth and took them together with Korah, when that group died. The fire destroyed 250 men, and taught others to be careful. 11 But the sons of Korah did not die.

12 The sons of Simeon by their families were the family of the Nemuelites from Nemuel, the family of the Jaminites from Jamin, the family of the Jachinites from Jachin, 13 the family of the Zerahites from Zerah, and the family of the Shaulites from Shaul. 14 These are the families of the Simeonites, 22,200 people. 15 The sons of Gad by their families were the family of the Zephonites from Zephon, the family of the Haggites from Haggi, the family of the Shunites from Shuni, 16 the family of the Oznites from Ozni, the family of the Erites from Eri, 17 the family of the Arodites from Arod, and the family of the Arelites from Areli. 18 These are the families of the sons of Gad. Their number was 40,500.

19 The sons of Judah were Er and Onan. But Er and Onan died in the land of Canaan. 20 The sons of Judah by their families were the family of the Shelanites from Shelah, the family of the Perezites from Perez, and the family of the Zerahites from Zerah. 21 The sons of Perez were the

family of the Hezronites from Hezron, and the family of the Hamulites from Hamul. ²² These are the families of Judah. Their number was 76,500.

²³ The sons of Issachar by their families were the family of the Tolaites from Tola, the family of the Punites from Puvah, ²⁴ the family of the Jashubites from Jashub, and the family of the Shimronites from Shimron. ²⁵ These are the families of Issachar. Their number was 64,300.

²⁶ The sons of Zebulun by their families were the family of the Seredites from Sered, the family of the Elonites from Elon, and the family of the Jahleelites from Jahleel. ²⁷ These are the families of the Zebulunites. Their number was 60,500.

²⁸ The sons of Joseph by their families were Manasseh and Ephraim. ²⁹ The sons of Manasseh were the family of the Machirites from Machir, and the family of the Gileadites from Gilead. Machir was the father of Gilead. ³⁰ The sons of Gilead were the family of the Iezerites from Iezer, the family of the Helekites from Helek, ³¹ the family of the Asrielites from Asriel, the family of the Shechemites from Shechem, ³² the family of the Shemidaites from Shemida, and the family of the Hepherites from Hepher. ³³ Hepher's son Zelophehad had no sons, but only daughters. The names of Zelophehad's daughters were Mahlah, Noah, Hoglah, Milcah and Tirzah. ³⁴ These were the families of Manasseh. Their number was 52,700.

³⁵ The sons of Ephraim by their families were the family of the Shuthelaites from Shuthelah, the family of the Becherites from Becher, and the family of the Tahanites from Tahan. ³⁶ The sons of Shuthelah were the family of the Eranites from Eran. ³⁷ These are the families of the sons of Ephraim. Their number was 32,500. These are the sons of Joseph by their families.

³⁸ The sons of Benjamin by their families were the family of the Belaites from Bela, the family of the Ashbelites from Ashbel, the family of the Ahiramites from Ahiram, ³⁹ the family of the Shuphamites from Shupham, and the family of the Huphamites from Hupham. ⁴⁰ The sons of Bela were Ard and Naaman, the family of the Ardites from Ard, and the family of the Naamites from Naaman. ⁴¹ These are the sons of Benjamin by their families. Their number was 45,600.

⁴² The sons of Dan by their families were the family of the Shuhamites from Shuham. These are the families of Dan by their families. ⁴³ The number of all the families of the Shuhamites was 64,400.

⁴⁴ The sons of Asher by their families were the family of the Imnites from Imnah, the family of the Ishvites from Ishvi, and the family of the Beriites from Beriah. ⁴⁵ The sons of Beriah were the family of the Heberites from Heber, and the family of the Malchielites from Malchiel. ⁴⁶ The name of Asher's daughter was Serah. ⁴⁷ These are the families of the sons of Asher. Their number was 53,400.

⁴⁸ The sons of Naphtali by their families were the family of the Jahzeelites from Jahzeel, the family of the Gunites from Guni, ⁴⁹ the family of the Jezerites from Jezer, and the family of the Shillemites from Shillem. ⁵⁰ These are the families of Naphtali by their families. Their number was 45,400.

⁵¹ Those who were numbered of the sons of Israel were 601,730.

⁵² The Lord said to Moses, ⁵³ "The land will be divided among these people by the number of names. ⁵⁴ Give more land to the larger group. Give less land to the smaller group. Each family should be given land by the number of its people. ⁵⁵ But the land should be divided by drawing names. They will receive their land by the names of the families of their fathers. ⁵⁶ The land will be divided between the larger and smaller groups by the names that are drawn."

⁵⁷ Those who were numbered of the Levites by their families were the family of the Gershonites from Gershon, the family of the Kohathites from Kohath, and the family of the Merarites from Merari. ⁵⁸ The families of Levi were the Libnites, the Hebronites, the Mahlites, the Mushites, and the Korahites. Kohath was the father of Amram. ⁵⁹ The name of Amram's wife was Jochebed, the daughter of Levi. She was born to Levi in Egypt. And she gave birth to Amram's children, Aaron and Moses and their sister Miriam. ⁶⁰ Aaron was the father of Nadab, Abihu, Eleazar and Ithamar. ⁶¹ But Nadab and Abihu died when they burned fire that was not holy before the Lord. ⁶² The number of all of their males a month old and older was 23,000. For they were not numbered among the people of Israel, because no land was given to them among the people of Israel.

⁶³ These are the people who were numbered by Moses and Eleazar the religious

leader. They numbered the sons of Israel in the plains of Moab by the Jordan at Jericho. 64 But among all these was not one of those numbered by Moses and Aaron the religious leader when the people of Israel were numbered in the Desert of Sinai. 65 For the Lord had said of them, "For sure they will die in the desert." There was not a man left of them, except Caleb the son of Jephunneh, and Joshua the son of Nun.

Zelophehad's Daughters

27 Then came the daughters of Zelophehad the son of Hepher, the son of Gilead, the son of Machir, the son of Manasseh, from the families of Manasseh the son of Joseph. The names of his daughters were Mahlah, Noah, Hoglah, Milcah and Tirzah. 2 They stood in front of Moses and Eleazar the religious leader, and the leaders, and all the people at the door of the meeting tent. The daughters said, 3 "Our father died in the desert. He was not one of those who gathered together with Korah against the Lord. But he died for his own sin, and he had no sons. 4 Why should the name of our father be taken away from his family because he had no son? Give us land among our father's brothers."

5 Moses asked the Lord what should be done. 6 Then the Lord said to Moses, 7 "The daughters of Zelophehad are right in what they say. Be sure to give them their own land among their father's brothers. Give them what would have been given to their father. 8 And say to the people of Israel, 'If a man dies and has no son, then give what belongs to him to his daughter. 9 If he has no daughter, then give what belongs to him to his brothers. 10 If he has no brothers, give what belongs to him to his father's brothers. 11 And if his father has no brothers, then you must give what belongs to him to the nearest person in his own family and it will be his. This will be a Law to the people of Israel, just as the Lord told Moses.'"

Joshua Takes over from Moses

12 Then the Lord said to Moses, "Go up to this mountain of Abarim, and see the land I have given to the people of Israel. 13 When you have seen it, you will be buried with your people as Aaron your brother was. 14 For you went against My Word when the people complained in the Desert of Zin. You should have honored Me as holy at the waters in front of their eyes." (These are the waters of Meribah of Kadesh in the Desert of Zin.)

15 Moses said to the Lord, 16 "May the Lord, the God of the spirits of all flesh, choose a man to lead the people. 17 Let this man go out and come in before them. Let him lead them out and bring them in. Then the people of the Lord may not be like sheep which have no shepherd." 18 So the Lord said to Moses, "Take Joshua the son of Nun, in whom is the Spirit, and lay your hand on him. 19 Have him stand in front of Eleazar the religious leader and in front of all the people. Let them see you give him the work he must do. 20 Give some of your power to him so all the people of Israel will obey him. 21 He will stand in front of Eleazar the religious leader, who will learn My will for him by using the Urim. At his word, both he and all the people of Israel will go out and at his word, they will come in." 22 Moses did just as the Lord told him. He took Joshua and had him stand in front of Eleazar the religious leader, and in front of all the people. 23 Then he laid his hands on him and gave him the work he must do, just as the Lord had said through Moses.

Daily Gifts on the Altar

28 The Lord said to Moses, 2 "Tell the people of Israel, 'Be careful to bring My gift, My food for My gifts by fire, as a pleasing smell to me, at the right time.' 3 And say to them, 'This is the gift by fire which you must give to the Lord. Give two perfect male lambs one year old, as a burnt gift every day. 4 Give one lamb in the morning, and the other lamb in the evening. 5 And give a tenth part of a basket of fine flour for a grain gift, mixed with a fourth part of a jar of beaten oil. 6 It is a burnt gift which was set apart at Mount Sinai as a pleasing smell, a gift by fire always to the Lord. 7 Its drink gift will be a fourth part of a jar for each lamb. Pour out a drink gift of strong drink to the Lord in the holy place. 8 Give the other lamb in the evening. Like the grain gift of the morning, and like its drink gift, you will give it as a gift by fire. It is a pleasing smell to the Lord.

Day of Rest Gifts

9 'On the Day of Rest give a gift of two perfect male lambs one year old. With it give two-tenths part of a basket of fine flour mixed with oil for a grain gift, and its drink gift. 10 The burnt gift of every Day of Rest is to be added to the burnt gift which is always given and its drink gift.

Gifts Each Month

11 'Then you must give a burnt gift to the Lord at the beginning of your months. Give two bulls, one ram, and seven male lambs one year old that are perfect. 12 Give three-tenths part of a basket of fine flour mixed with oil for a grain gift for each bull. Give two-tenths part of fine flour mixed with oil for a grain gift for the one ram. 13 And give a tenth part of a basket of fine flour mixed with oil for a grain gift for each lamb. They are to be given for a burnt gift of a pleasing smell, a gift by fire to the Lord. 14 Their drink gifts will be half a jar of wine for a bull, a third of a jar for the ram, and a fourth part of a jar for a lamb. This is the burnt gift of each month for all the months of the year. 15 And give one male goat for a sin gift to the Lord. It will be given with its drink gift, besides each day's burnt gift.

Gifts at Passover

16 'The fourteenth day of the first month will be the Lord's Passover. 17 A special supper will be on the fifteenth day of this month. Bread without yeast will be eaten for seven days. 18 On the first day will be a holy gathering. You must do no hard work. 19 You will give a gift by fire, a burnt gift to the Lord. It will be two bulls, one ram, and seven perfect male lambs one year old. 20 And give fine flour mixed with oil for their grain gift. Give three-tenths part of a basket for a bull, two-tenths part for a ram, 21 and a tenth part of a basket for each of the seven lambs. 22 Then give one male goat for a sin gift, to pay for your sins. 23 Give these besides the burnt gift of the morning, which is each day's burnt gift. 24 Give the food of the gift by fire in this way each day for seven days, as a pleasing smell to the Lord. Give it with its drink gift, besides each day's burnt gift. 25 And on the seventh day you will have a holy gathering. You must do no hard work.

Gifts at Supper of Weeks

26 'You will have a holy gathering on the day of the first-fruits also. This is when you will bring a gift of new grain to the Lord in your Special Supper of Weeks. You must do no hard work. 27 And you will give for a pleasing smell to the Lord a burnt gift of two young bulls, one ram, and seven male lambs one year old. 28 Give fine flour mixed with oil for their grain gift. Give three-tenths part of a basket for each bull, two-tenths part for the one ram, 29 and a tenth part for each of the seven lambs. 30 And give one male goat to pay for your sins. 31 These gifts should be besides each day's burnt gift and its grain gift. Give them with their drink gifts. The animals must be perfect.

Gifts at Supper of Horns

29 'You will have a holy gathering on the first day of the seventh month. You must do no hard work. It is a day for you to blow the horns. 2 Give as a pleasing smell to the Lord a burnt gift of one bull, one ram, and seven male lambs one year old, all are to be perfect. 3 And give fine flour mixed with oil for their grain gift. Give three-tenths part of a basket for the bull, two-tenths part for the ram, 4 and one-tenth part for each of the seven lambs. 5 Then give one male goat for a sin gift, to pay for your sins. 6 These gifts should be besides the burnt gift of the new moon, and its grain gift, and each day's burnt gift and its grain gift, and their drink gifts. It must be done by the Law, for a pleasing smell, a gift by fire to the Lord.

Gifts on the Day to Pay for Sins

7 'You will have a holy gathering on the tenth day of this seventh month, and be without pride. You must not do any work. 8 You will give to the Lord as a pleasing smell a burnt gift of one bull, one ram, and seven male lambs one year old, all are to be perfect. 9 And give fine flour mixed with oil for their grain gift. Give three-tenths part of a basket for the bull, two-tenths part for the one ram, 10 and a tenth part for each of the seven lambs. 11 Then give one male goat for a sin gift, besides the sin gift to pay for sins, each day's burnt gift and its grain gift, and their drink gifts.

Gifts at Supper of Tents

12 'You will have a holy gathering on the fifteenth day of the seventh month. You must do no hard work, and you will have a special supper to the Lord for seven days. 13 You will give a burnt gift of thirteen bulls, two rams, and fourteen male lambs one year old that are perfect. They will be a gift by fire, a pleasing smell to the Lord. 14 And give fine flour mixed with oil for their grain gift. Give three-tenths part of a basket for each of the thirteen bulls, two-tenths part for each of the two rams, 15 and a tenth part of a basket for each of the fourteen lambs. 16 Then give one male goat for a sin gift, besides each day's burnt gift, its grain gift and its drink gift.

¹⁷ 'Then on the second day give twelve bulls, two rams, and fourteen male lambs one year old that are perfect. ¹⁸ And give their grain gifts and drink gifts for the number of bulls, rams and lambs, by the Law. ¹⁹ Give one male goat for a sin gift, besides each day's burnt gift and its grain gift, and their drink gifts.

²⁰ 'On the third day give eleven bulls, two rams, and fourteen male lambs one year old that are perfect. ²¹ Give their grain gifts and drink gifts for the number of bulls, rams and lambs, by the Law. ²² Then give one male goat for a sin gift, besides each day's burnt gift and its grain gift and drink gift.

²³ 'On the fourth day give ten bulls, two rams, and fourteen male lambs one year old that are perfect. ²⁴ Give their grain gifts and drink gifts for the number of bulls, rams and lambs, by the Law. ²⁵ Then give one male goat for a sin gift, besides each day's burnt gift, its grain gift and drink gift.

²⁶ 'On the fifth day give nine bulls, two rams, and fourteen male lambs one year old that are perfect. ²⁷ Give their grain gifts and drink gifts for the number of bulls, rams and lambs, by the Law. ²⁸ Then give one male goat for a sin gift, besides each day's burnt gift and its grain gift and drink gift.

²⁹ 'On the sixth day give eight bulls, two rams, and fourteen male lambs one year old that are perfect. ³⁰ Give their grain gifts and drink gifts for the number of bulls, rams and lambs, by the Law. ³¹ Then give one male goat for a sin gift, besides each day's burnt gift, its grain gift and drink gift.

³² 'On the seventh day give seven bulls, two rams, and fourteen male lambs one year old that are perfect. ³³ Give their grain gifts and drink gifts for the number of bulls, rams and lambs, by the Law. ³⁴ Then give one male goat for a sin gift, besides each day's burnt gift, its grain gift and drink gift.

³⁵ 'You will have a religious gathering on the eighth day. You must do no hard work. ³⁶ But give a burnt gift of one bull, one ram, and seven male lambs one year old that are perfect. It will be a gift by fire, a pleasing smell to the Lord. ³⁷ Give their grain gifts and drink gifts for the bull, the ram and lambs, for their number, by the Law. ³⁸ Then give one male goat for a sin gift, besides each day's burnt gift and its grain gift and drink gift.

³⁹ 'Give these to the Lord at the times given, besides your promised gifts and your free-will gifts. They will be for your burnt gifts, your grain gifts, your drink gifts and for your peace gifts.' " ⁴⁰ Moses said to the people of Israel all that the Lord had told him.

Laws about Agreements

30 Then Moses said to the heads of the families of the sons of Israel, "This is what the Lord has said. ² If a man makes a promise to the Lord, or swears that he will keep his promise, he must not break his word. He must do all that he said he would do. ³ If a woman makes a promise to the Lord, and swears to keep her promise in her father's house when she is young, ⁴ and if her father hears her promise and how she has sworn to keep it, and says nothing to her, then all her promises must be kept. She must keep every promise she has sworn to keep. ⁵ But if her father does not allow her to keep her promise on the day he hears of it, then she does not need to keep any of the promises she has sworn to keep. The Lord will forgive her because her father would not allow it.

⁶ "If she gets married and has promises to keep because of what she swore without thinking, ⁷ and if her husband hears of it and says nothing to her on the day he hears, then she must keep the promises she has sworn to keep. ⁸ But if on the day he hears of it, her husband does not allow her to keep her promise, then she will not have to keep the promise that she had sworn to keep when she was not thinking. The Lord will forgive her.

⁹ "A woman whose husband has died or left her must keep the promises she has sworn to keep. ¹⁰ But if she has made a promise in her husband's house, and she has sworn to keep a promise there ¹¹ and if her husband hears of it, and does not go against her or say anything to her, then she must keep all the promises she had sworn to keep. ¹² But if her husband does not allow her to keep her promises on the day he hears of them, then she does not have to keep the promises she had sworn to keep. If her husband will not let her keep them, the Lord will forgive her.

¹³ "Her husband has the right to have her keep, or not keep, any promise she has sworn to keep. ¹⁴ But if her husband says nothing to her from day to day, then she must keep all her promises. He made her promises so they could not be changed,

because he said nothing to her on the day he heard of them. 15 But if he will not allow her to keep her promises after he has heard of them, then her guilt will be on him."

16 These are the Laws which the Lord told Moses, between a man and his wife, and between a father and his daughter, while she is young and in her father's house.

War against Midian

31 The Lord said to Moses, 2 "Punish the Midianites for the people of Israel. After that you will be buried with your people." 3 Then Moses said to the people, "Take men from among you and make them ready for war against Midian. They will punish Midian for the Lord. 4 Send to the war 1,000 men from each of all the family groups of Israel." 5 So 1,000 men came from each of the family groups of the thousands of Israel. There were 12,000 ready for war. 6 Moses sent them, 1,000 from each family group, to the war. Phinehas the son of Eleazar the religious leader went to the war with them. In his hand were the holy objects and the horns for blowing the sound of coming danger. 7 So the men made war against Midian, just as the Lord had told Moses, and they killed every male. 8 They killed the five kings of Midian with the sword also, Evi, Rekem, Zur, Hur, and Reba. And they also killed Balaam the son of Beor with the sword. 9 The people of Israel took the women of Midian and their little ones, and all their cattle, all their flocks, and all the good things that belonged to them. 10 Then they burned all their cities where they lived and all their tents. 11 They took all that was left of both man and animal. 12 And they brought the people they had taken and the animals and whatever belonged to them to Moses, and to Eleazar the religious leader, and to the people of Israel. Their tents were on the plains of Moab by the Jordan near Jericho.

13 Moses and Eleazar the religious leader and all the leaders of the people went out from the tents to meet them. 14 Moses was angry with the leaders of the army, the heads of thousands and the heads of hundreds, who had fought in the war. 15 He said to them, "Have you allowed all the women to live? 16 See, these women listened to Balaam and caused the people of Israel to sin against the Lord in what happened at Peor. So the very bad disease came to the people of the Lord. 17 Now kill every male among the little ones, and kill every woman who has had a man. 18 But keep alive for yourselves all the girls who have not had a man. 19 Stay away from the tents for seven days. If you have killed any person or have touched any dead body, you must make yourself and those you have taken clean, on the third day and on the seventh day. 20 You must clean every piece of clothing, everything made of leather, everything made of goats' hair, and everything made of wood."

21 Then Eleazar the religious leader said to the men of war who had gone to battle, "This is the Law which the Lord has told Moses. 22 Take the gold, silver, brass, iron, tin and lead, 23 everything that can last through fire. Pass it through the fire, and it will be clean. But it must be made pure with the water for cleaning. Whatever cannot last through fire you must pass through the water. 24 You must wash your clothes on the seventh day, and you will be clean. Then you may come among the tents."

25 The Lord said to Moses, 26 "You and Eleazar the religious leader and the heads of the fathers' houses of the people should number all that was taken from the battle, both of man and animal. 27 Divide what was taken between the men of war who went to battle and all the people. 28 Then take a tax for the Lord from the men of war who went out to battle. Take one out of 500 of the persons and the cattle and the donkeys and the sheep. 29 Take this from their half and give it to Eleazar the religious leader, as a gift to the Lord. 30 From the half belonging to the people of Israel, take one out of every fifty of the persons and cattle and donkeys and sheep and all the animals. Give them to the Levites who take care of the meeting tent of the Lord." 31 Moses and Eleazar the religious leader did just as the Lord had told Moses.

32 What was left from that which the men of war had taken was 675,000 sheep, 33 72,000 cattle, 34 61,000 donkeys, 35 and 32,000 persons in all, of women who had never had a man. 36 The half taken by those who went out to war was 337,500 sheep. 37 The Lord's tax was 675 sheep. 38 There were 36,000 cattle, from which the Lord's tax was seventy-two. 39 There were 30,500 donkeys, from which the Lord's tax was sixty-one. 40 And there were 16,000 persons, from whom the Lord's tax was thirty-two. 41 Moses gave the tax, which was the Lord's gift, to Eleazar the religious leader, just as the Lord had told Moses.

⁴² Moses divided the people of Israel's half from the men who had gone to war. ⁴³ The people's half was 337,500 sheep, ⁴⁴ 36,000 cattle, ⁴⁵ 30,500 donkeys, ⁴⁶ and 16,000 persons. ⁴⁷ Moses took one out of every fifty of both man and animal from the people of Israel's half. He gave them to the Levites, who took care of the meeting tent of the Lord, just as the Lord had told Moses.

⁴⁸ Then the leaders of the thousands of the army, the heads of thousands and the heads of hundreds, came to Moses. ⁴⁹ They said to him, "Your servants have numbered the men of war whom we lead. Not one man is missing from us. ⁵⁰ We have brought as a gift to the Lord what each man found, objects of gold, things to be worn on the arms and fingers and ears and necks. They are to pay for our sins before the Lord." ⁵¹ Moses and Eleazar the religious leader took the gold from them, all the objects made of beaten gold. ⁵² All the gold of the gift they gave to the Lord from the heads of thousands and the heads of hundreds was worth 16,750 gold pieces. ⁵³ For the men of war had taken things from the battle, every man for himself. ⁵⁴ So Moses and Eleazar the religious leader took the gold from the heads of thousands and of hundreds. They brought it to the meeting tent so that the people of Israel would be remembered before the Lord.

The Family Groups East of the Jordan

32 Now the sons of Reuben and the sons of Gad had very many cattle. And they saw that the land of Jazer and the land of Gilead was a good place for cattle. ² So the sons of Gad and the sons of Reuben came and said to Moses and Eleazar the religious leader and the leaders of the people, ³ "Ataroth, Dibon, Jazer, Nimrah, Heshbon, Elealeh, Sebam, Nebo and Beon, ⁴ the land which the Lord won in battle in front of the people of Israel, is a land for cattle and your servants have cattle." ⁵ And they said, "If we have found favor in your eyes, let this land be given to your servants as our own. Do not take us to the other side of the Jordan."

⁶ But Moses said to the sons of Gad and the sons of Reuben, "Should your brothers go to war while you sit here? ⁷ Why do you take from the people of Israel the desire to cross over into the land the Lord has given them? ⁸ This is what your fathers did when I sent them from Kadesh-barnea to see the land. ⁹ They went up to the valley of Eshcol

and saw the land. Then they took the desire away from the people of Israel so that they did not go into the land the Lord had given them. ¹⁰ So the Lord's anger burned on that day, and He swore, saying ¹¹ 'None of the men who came up from Egypt, twenty years old and older, will see the land I promised to Abraham, Isaac and Jacob. For they did not follow Me with all their heart. ¹² Only Caleb the son of Jephunneh the Kenizzite and Joshua the son of Nun will see it. For they have followed the Lord with all their hearts.' ¹³ So the Lord's anger burned against Israel. He made them travel in the desert forty years, until all the people of that day who had sinned in the eyes of the Lord were destroyed. ¹⁴ Now see, you have grown up in your fathers' place, children of sinful men. You add still more to the burning anger of the Lord against Israel. ¹⁵ For if you turn away from following Him, He will leave them in the desert again and you will destroy all these people."

¹⁶ Then they came near him and said, "We will build safe places for our flocks here, and cities for our little ones. ¹⁷ But we will be ready for battle and will go with the people of Israel until we have brought them to their place. Our little ones will live within the walls of the cities because of the people who live in the land. ¹⁸ We will not return to our homes until every one of the people of Israel has received his land. ¹⁹ For we will not have any land among them on the other side of the Jordan. Our land has come to us on this side of the Jordan toward the east."

²⁰ So Moses said to them, "Do as you say. Get ready for war before the Lord. ²¹ All of you men of war cross over the Jordan before the Lord until He has driven away those who fight against Him, ²² and has won the land in battle. Then after this you may return because you have done your duty to the Lord and to Israel. This land will be your land before the Lord. ²³ But if you do not do as you say, you have sinned against the Lord. And for sure you will be punished for your sin. ²⁴ Build cities for your little ones and places for your sheep. Then do what you have promised." ²⁵ The sons of Gad and the sons of Reuben said to Moses, "Your servants will do just as my lord says. ²⁶ Our little ones, our wives, our flocks and all our cattle will stay there in the cities of Gilead. ²⁷ But your servants, everyone who is ready for war, will cross over before the Lord to battle, just as my lord says."

28 So Moses gave news about them to Eleazar the religious leader, Joshua the son of Nun, and to the heads of the fathers' houses of the families of the people of Israel. 29 Moses said to them, "The sons of Gad and the sons of Reuben, every man ready for battle, are to cross with you over the Jordan before the Lord, and the land will be won. After this, you must give them the land of Gilead for their own. 30 But if they will not cross over with you ready for battle, their land must be among you in the land of Canaan." 31 The sons of Gad and the sons of Reuben answered, "We will do as the Lord has said to your servants. 32 We will cross over into the land of Canaan ready for battle before the Lord. And the land on this side of the Jordan will be ours."

33 So Moses gave the nations of Sihon king of the Amorites and Og king of Bashan to the sons of Gad and the sons of Reuben and the half-family group of Joseph's son Manasseh. He gave them the land, with its cities and the country around them. 34 Then the sons of Gad built Dibon, Ataroth, Aroer, 35 Atrothshophan, Jazer, Jogbehah, 36 Bethnimrah and Beth-haran, cities with walls around them. And they made safe places for their sheep. 37 The sons of Reuben built Heshbon, Elealeh, Kiriathaim, 38 Nebo and Baal-meon (their names to be changed), and Sibmah. And they gave other names to the cities they built. 39 The sons of Manasseh's son Machir went to Gilead and took it. They drove away the Amorites who were in it. 40 So Moses gave Gilead to Machir the son of Manasseh, and he lived in it. 41 Jair the son of Manasseh went and took its towns, and called them Havvoth-jair. 42 Nobah went and took Kenath and its towns, and called it Nobah after his own name.

From Egypt to Moab

33 These are the travels of the people of Israel, when Moses and Aaron led them out from the land of Egypt by their armies. 2 Moses wrote down the starting places of their travels, as the Lord told him. These are their travels by their starting places. 3 They traveled from Rameses on the fifteenth day of the first month. On the day after the Passover the people of Israel started out strong in heart in front of all the Egyptians. 4 The Egyptians were burying all their first-born whom the Lord had killed among them. The Lord had punished their gods also.

5 Then the people of Israel traveled from Rameses and stayed in Succoth. 6 They traveled from Succoth and stayed in Etham, beside the desert. 7 They went from Etham and turned back to Pi-hahiroth, east of Baal-zephon, and stayed at Migdol. 8 Then they traveled from Hahiroth and passed through the sea into the desert. They traveled for three days in the desert of Etham, and stayed at Marah. 9 They left Marah and came to Elim. There were twelve wells of water and seventy palm trees in Elim, and they stayed there. 10 Then they traveled from Elim and stayed by the Red Sea. 11 They left the Red Sea and stayed in the Desert of Sin. 12 They traveled from the Desert of Sin, and stayed at Dophkah. 13 Then they left Dophkah and stayed at Alush. 14 They traveled from Alush and stayed at Rephidim. It was there that the people had no water to drink. 15 They went from Rephidim and stayed in the Desert of Sinai. 16 They traveled from the Desert of Sinai, and stayed at Kibroth-hattaavah.

17 They went from Kibroth-hattaavah and stayed at Hazeroth. 18 They left Hazeroth and stayed at Rithmah. 19 Then they went from Rithmah and stayed at Rimmon-perez. 20 They traveled from Rimmon-perez, and stayed at Libnah. 21 They left Libnah, and stayed at Rissah. 22 Then they went from Rissah and stayed at Kehelathah. 23 They went from Kehelathah and stayed at Mount Shepher. 24 They traveled from Mount Shepher and stayed at Haradah. 25 They left Haradah and stayed at Makheloth. 26 Then they traveled from Makheloth, and stayed at Tahath. 27 They traveled from Tahath, and stayed at Terah. 28 They went from Terah and stayed at Mithkah. 29 They left Mithkah and stayed at Hashmonah. 30 Then they left Hashmonah and stayed at Moseroth. 31 They went from Moseroth and stayed at Benejaakan. 32 They traveled from Benejaakan, and stayed at Hor-haggidgad. 33 They went from Hor-haggidgad and stayed at Jotbathah. 34 Then they left Jotbathah and stayed at Abronah. 35 They went from Abronah and stayed at Ezion-geber. 36 They went from Ezion-geber and stayed in the Desert of Zin, that is, Kadesh. 37 And they traveled from Kadesh, and stayed at Mount Hor, beside the land of Edom.

38 Then Aaron the religious leader went up to Mount Hor, as the Lord told him. He died there, in the fortieth year after the people of Israel had left the land of Egypt, on the first day of the fifth month.

³⁹ Aaron was 123 years old when he died on Mount Hor.

⁴⁰ The Canaanite king of Arad, who lived in the Negev in the land of Canaan, heard of the coming of the people of Israel.

⁴¹ Then the people traveled from Mount Hor, and stayed at Zalmonah. ⁴² They left Zalmonah, and stayed at Punon. ⁴³ They went from Punon and stayed at Oboth. ⁴⁴ Then they left Oboth and stayed at Iye-abarim, beside Moab. ⁴⁵ They traveled from Iyim, and stayed at Dibon-gad. ⁴⁶ They went from Dibon-gad and stayed at Almon-diblathaim. ⁴⁷ They left Almon-diblathaim and stayed in the mountains of Abarim, near Nebo. ⁴⁸ They traveled from the mountains of Abarim, and stayed in the plains of Moab by the Jordan near Jericho. ⁴⁹ And they stayed by the Jordan, from Beth-jeshimoth as far as Abelshittim in the plains of Moab.

⁵⁰ Then the Lord said to Moses in the plains of Moab by the Jordan near Jericho, ⁵¹ "Say to the people of Israel, 'You will cross over the Jordan into the land of Canaan. ⁵² Then drive out all the people living in the land in front of you. Destroy all their cut stones, and all their man-made gods, and all their high places. ⁵³ Take the land for your own and live in it. For I have given the land to you. ⁵⁴ Your families will receive land by drawing names. The larger families should be given more land. The smaller families should be given less land. When a man's name is drawn, that land will be his. You will receive land by the family groups of your fathers. ⁵⁵ Drive out the people who live in the land in front of you. If you do not, then those who are allowed to stay will be like sharp pieces in your eyes and like thorns in your sides. They will trouble you in the land where you live. ⁵⁶ And I will do to you as I thought to do to them.'"

The Land of Canaan

34 Then the Lord said to Moses, ² "Tell the people of Israel, 'When you go into the land of Canaan, this is the land that will be given to you, all the land of Canaan. ³ Your south side will be from the Desert of Zin along the side of Edom. It will go east from the end of the Salt Sea. ⁴ Then the side of your land will turn from the south up to the pass of Akrabbim and on to Zin. It will go to Hazaraddar and on to Azmon. ⁵ Then it will turn from Azmon to the river of Egypt, and will end at the sea.

⁶ 'The west side of your land will be the shore of the Great Sea.

⁷ 'Your north side will be from the Great Sea to Mount Hor. ⁸ And it will go from Mount Hor to the Lebohamath, and end at Zedad. ⁹ Then it will go to Ziphron and end at Hazer-enan. This will be the north side.

¹⁰ 'The east side of your land will be from Hazer-enan to Shepham, ¹¹ then down from Shepham to Riblah on the east side of Ain. Then it will go down to the hill on the east side of the Sea of Chinnereth. ¹² It will go down to the Jordan and end at the Salt Sea. This will be the sides all around your land.'"

¹³ Moses told the people of Israel, "This is the land you will receive by drawing names, which the Lord has said should be given to the nine and a half-family groups. ¹⁴ For the sons of Reuben have received their land by their fathers' houses. The sons of Gad have received theirs by their fathers' houses. And the half-family group of Manasseh has received their land. ¹⁵ The two and a half-family groups have received their land on the other side of the Jordan from Jericho, toward the east."

¹⁶ The Lord said to Moses, ¹⁷ "Eleazar the religious leader and Joshua the son of Nun are the men who will divide the land to be given to you. ¹⁸ And take one leader of every family group to divide the land among you. ¹⁹ These are the names of the men. Take Caleb the son of Jephunneh of the family group of Judah. ²⁰ Take Samuel the son of Ammihud of the family group of the sons of Simeon. ²¹ Take Elidad the son of Chislon of the family group of Benjamin. ²² Take Bukki the son of Jogli as the leader of the family group of the sons of Dan. ²³ Of the sons of Joseph, take Hanniel the son of Ephod as the leader of the family group of the sons of Manasseh. ²⁴ Take Kemuel the son of Shiphtan as the leader of the family group of the sons of Ephraim. ²⁵ Take Elizaphan the son of Parnach as the leader of the family group of the sons of Zebulun. ²⁶ Take Paltiel the son of Azzan as the leader of the family group of the sons of Issachar. ²⁷ Take Ahihud the son of Shelomi as the leader of the family group of the sons of Asher. ²⁸ And take Pedahel the son of Ammihud as the leader of the family group of the sons of Naphtali." ²⁹ These are the men whom the Lord told to divide the land among the people of Israel in the land of Canaan.

Cities for the Levites

35 The Lord said to Moses in the plains of Moab by the Jordan near Jericho, 2 "Tell the people of Israel to give the Levites cities to live in from the land they receive. And give the Levites fields around the cities. 3 The cities will be theirs to live in. Their fields will be for their cattle and flocks and for all their animals. 4 The fields you give the Levites should be around the cities, from the city walls out 500 long steps. 5 And you should number 1,000 long steps from the city on the east side, on the south side, on the west side, and on the north side, with the city in the center. These fields around the cities will belong to them for their animals. 6 The cities you give the Levites will be the six cities where people can go to be safe. They will be where a man may run to if he has killed another person. And give them forty-two other cities, added to these. 7 Give forty-eight cities in all to the Levites, together with their fields. 8 Take more cities from the larger families of Israel to give to the Levites. And take less cities from the smaller families. Each should give some of its cities to the Levites by how much land is received."

The Cities to Be a Safe Place

9 Then the Lord said to Moses, 10 "Say to the people of Israel, 'When you cross the Jordan into the land of Canaan, 11 choose which cities are to be the ones where you can run to be safe. The man who has killed a person without meaning to may run there. 12 The cities will be a safe place for you from the one who wants to punish you. So the one who has killed a person may not die until the people decide if he is guilty or not. 13 The cities you give will be your six cities where you can go to be safe. 14 Give three cities on the east side of the Jordan and three cities in the land of Canaan. They will be the cities where you can go to be safe. 15 These six cities will be safe places for the people of Israel and for the stranger and for the one who visits them. Anyone who kills a person without meaning to may run there.

16 'But if he killed him with an iron object, then he is guilty. For sure the killer will be put to death. 17 If he knocked him down with a stone so that he died, he is guilty. For sure the killer will be put to death. 18 Or if he hit him with a piece of wood in his hand so that he died, he is guilty. For sure the killer will be put to death.

19 The man who wants to punish him for the killing will put the killer to death. He will put him to death when he meets him. 20 If the killer has pushed him because he hated him, or has thrown something at him after waiting for him, and because of this he died, 21 or if he hit him down with his hand because he hated him and killed him, for sure the one who killed him must be put to death. He is guilty. The man who wants to punish him for the killing will put him to death when he meets him.

22 'But if he pushed him without planning to and without hating him, or threw something at him without having waited for him, 23 or he threw a stone without seeing him, killing him without hating him or meaning to hurt him, 24 then the people will decide by these Laws between the killer and the one who wants to punish him. 25 The people will save the killer from the man who wants to punish him. And they will return him to his city where he had gone to be safe. He will live in it until the death of the head religious leader who was set apart with the holy oil. 26 But if the man who killed another person at sometime goes outside his city where he went to be safe, 27 then the man who wants to punish him will not be guilty of blood if he finds him outside the safe city and kills him. 28 Because the man should have stayed in his city to be safe until the death of the head religious leader. But after the head religious leader dies, the man who killed another person may return to his own land.

29 'These things will be a Law to you and to all your children-to-come in all your homes. 30 If anyone kills a person, the killer must be put to death by what is told by those who saw the killing. But no person may be put to death because of what one person says. 31 You must not take pay to save the life of a killer who is guilty of death. But he must be put to death. 32 You must not take pay for him who has run to his city to be safe, so that he may return to live in the land before the death of the religious leader. 33 You must not make the land where you live unclean. The land is not holy when people are killed. And only the blood of him who is guilty can pay to make the land free from the blood that has fallen on it. 34 Do not make the land where you live unclean, in the place where I live. For I the Lord am living among the people of Israel.' "

Married Women and What They Would Get from Their Families

36 The heads of the fathers' houses of the family group of the sons of Gilead the son of Machir, the son of Manasseh, of the families of the sons of Joseph, came near. They spoke in front of Moses and the leaders, the heads of the fathers' houses of the people of Israel. 2 They said, "The Lord told my lord to give the land to the people of Israel by drawing names. And my lord was told by the Lord to give the land of our brother Zelophehad to his daughters. 3 But if they marry one of the sons of the other family groups of Israel, then their land would be taken away from what was given to our fathers and would be added to the land of the family group they marry into. So it would be taken from the land that had been given to us. 4 When the Year of Jubilee of the people of Israel comes, their land will be added to the land of the family group into which they marry. So their land will be taken from the land of the family group of our fathers."

5 Then Moses told the people of Israel what the Lord said. He said, "The family group of the sons of Joseph are right in what they say. 6 This is what the Lord has said about the daughters of Zelophehad: 'Let them marry whom they think best. Only they must marry within the family group of their father.' 7 This way no land of the people of Israel will go from one family group to another. The people of Israel will each hold to the land of the family group of his fathers. 8 Every daughter who comes to own the land of any family group of Israel, must be the wife of one of her father's family group. So every one of the people of Israel may own the land of his fathers. 9 No land will go from one family group to another. For the families of Israel will each hold to his own land." 10 The daughters of Zelophehad did just as the Lord had told Moses. 11 Mahlah, Tirzah, Hoglah, Milcah and Noah, the daughters of Zelophehad, married sons of father's brothers. 12 They married into the families of the sons of Manasseh the son of Joseph. And their land stayed with their father's family group.

13 These are the Laws which the Lord told the people of Israel through Moses in the plains of Moab by the Jordan at Jericho.

DEUTERONOMY

Israel Told to Go to Canaan

1 These are the words which Moses spoke to all Israel on the other side of the Jordan, in the desert, in the Arabah beside Suph, between Paran and Tophel, Laban, Hazeroth and Dizahab. 2 It takes eleven days to travel from Horeb by the way of Mount Seir to Kadesh-barnea. 3 On the first day of the eleventh month in the fortieth year, Moses spoke to the children of Israel. He told them all the Lord said they must do. 4 This was after he had won the war against Sihon the king of the Amorites, who lived in Heshbon, and Og the king of Bashan, who lived in Ashtaroth and Edrei. 5 On the other side of the Jordan in the land of Moab, Moses talked to the people about this Law, He said, 6 "The Lord our God spoke to us at Mount Sinai, saying, 'You have stayed long enough at this mountain. 7 Get ready to travel now. Go to the hill country of the Amorites, and to all their neighbors in the Arabah, in the hill country and in the valley, in the Negev and by the sea, the land of the Canaanites, and Lebanon, as far as the big river, the river Euphrates. 8 See, I have set the land in front of you. Go in and take for your own the land which the Lord promised to give to your fathers, Abraham, Isaac and Jacob, and to their children after them.'

Leaders of Family Groups

9 "At that time I said to you, 'I am not able to take care of you alone. 10 The Lord your God has made you become many people. Now you are as many as the stars of heaven. 11 May the Lord, the God of your fathers, make you 1,000 times as many as you are. May He bring good to you just as He has promised you! 12 How can I alone carry the weight of your troubles? 13 Choose wise, understanding and able men from your family groups. And I will make them leaders over you.' 14 You answered me and said, 'The thing which you have spoken is good for us to do.' 15 So I took the leaders of your family groups, wise and able men. I made them leaders over you, leaders of thousands, of hundreds, of fifties and of tens, and rulers of your family groups. 16 "Then I said to your judges at that

time, 'Listen to the problems between your brothers. And be right in what you decide between a man and his brother or the stranger who is with him. ¹⁷ Do not show favor as you judge. Listen to the small and the great alike. Do not be afraid of any man, because you are judging for God. Bring to me any problem that is too hard for you, and I will hear it.' ¹⁸ I told you at that time all the things you should do.

Men Are Sent to Spy Out the Land

¹⁹ "Then we left Mount Sinai. We went through the big desert you saw which fills people with fear, on the way to the hill country of the Amorites, just as the Lord our God had told us. And we came to Kadesh-barnea. ²⁰ I said to you, 'You have come to the hill country of the Amorites, which the Lord our God will give us. ²¹ See, the Lord your God has set the land in front of you. Go and take it for your own, as the Lord, the God of your fathers, has told you. Do not be afraid or troubled.' ²² Then all of you came to me and said, 'Let us send men before us, to spy out the land for us. They will return and tell us which way we should go and which cities we will come to.' ²³ What you said pleased me. I took twelve of your men, one man for each family group. ²⁴ They went up into the hill country, came to the valley of Eshcol, and saw what was there. ²⁵ They took some of the fruit of the land in their hands and brought it down to us. And they told us that it is a good land which the Lord our God is giving us.

²⁶ "Yet you would not go up. You went against what the Lord your God told you to do. ²⁷ You complained in your tents, saying, 'Because the Lord hates us He has brought us out of the land of Egypt to give us to the Amorites to destroy us. ²⁸ Where would we be going? Our brothers have made our hearts weak with fear, saying, 'The people are bigger and taller than we. The cities are large, with walls as high as the heavens. And we have even seen the sons of the Anakim there.' " ²⁹ Then I said to you, 'Do not be afraid of them. ³⁰ The Lord your God Who goes before you will Himself fight for you. He did this for you in Egypt in front of your eyes, ³¹ and in the desert. There you saw how the Lord your God carried you, as a man carries his son, in all the way you have walked until you came to this place.' ³² But even so, you did not trust the Lord your God, ³³ Who goes before you on your way. He finds a place for you to set up your tents. He uses fire to show you the way to go during the night. During the day He uses a cloud to lead you.

Israel's Punishment

³⁴ "The Lord heard your words and was angry. He swore, ³⁵ 'Not one of these men of these sinful people will see the good land I promised to give your fathers, ³⁶ except Caleb the son of Jephunneh. He will see it. I will give the land on which he has walked to him and his children because he has always followed the Lord.' ³⁷ The Lord was angry with me because of you. He said, 'Not even you will go in there. ³⁸ Joshua the son of Nun, who stands in front of you, will go in there. Tell him to be strong, for he will bring Israel into their new land. ³⁹ And your little ones whom you said would be taken by strange hands, and your children who do not yet know the difference between good and bad, will go in there. I will give the land to them. It will be theirs. ⁴⁰ But as for you, turn around and go into the desert by way of the Red Sea.'

⁴¹ "Then you said to me, 'We have sinned against the Lord. We will go up and fight, just as the Lord our God told us.' So every man of you put on his sword and thought it an easy thing to go up into the hill country. ⁴² The Lord said to me, 'Say to them, "Do not go up or fight. For I am not among you. You would be destroyed by those who hate you." ' ⁴³ So I spoke to you but you would not listen. You went against what the Lord told you. In your pride you went up into the hill country. ⁴⁴ Then the Amorites who lived in that hill country came out against you. They came at you like bees, and crushed you from Seir to Hormah. ⁴⁵ And you returned and cried before the Lord but the Lord did not listen to you. ⁴⁶ So you stayed in Kadesh. Many days you stayed there.

Years in the Desert

2 "Then we turned and went into the desert by the way of the Red Sea, as the Lord said to me. We went around Mount Seir for many days. ² And the Lord said to me, ³ 'You have traveled around this mountain long enough. Now turn north. ⁴ Tell the people, "You will pass through the land of your brothers the sons of Esau who live in Seir. They will be afraid of you, so be very careful. ⁵ Do not make them angry. For I will not give you any of their land, not even enough for a foot to step on. I have given Mount Seir to Esau for his own. 6 You will pay them with money for the food you eat. And you will pay them with money for the water you drink. 7 For the Lord your God has brought good to you in all you have done. He knows about your traveling through this big desert. The Lord your God has been with you these forty years. You have not been without a thing." '

8 "So we moved on from our brothers the sons of Esau who live in Seir, away from the Arabah road, away from Elath and Ezion-geber. We turned and went by the way of the desert of Moab. 9 Then the Lord said to me, 'Do not bring trouble to Moab or fight them in war. For I will not give you any of their land for your own. I have given Ar to the children of Lot for their own.' 10 (The Emim had lived there before. These people were many and powerful, and as tall as the Anakim. 11 They are known as Rephaim also, like the Anakim. But the Moabites call them Emim. 12 The Horites once lived in Seir also. But the sons of Esau took their place. They destroyed them and took the land for themselves, as Israel did to the land which the Lord gave them for their own.) 13 'Now get up and go over the river Zered.' So we went over the river Zered. 14 It was thirty-eight years from the time we left Kadesh-barnea until we crossed over the river Zered. By that time all the men of war among us had died, as the Lord had said they would. 15 The hand of the Lord was against them, to destroy them within their tents until they were all dead.

16 "When all the men of war had died from among the people, 17 the Lord said to me, 18 'Today you will cross over Ar and into Moab. 19 But when you come near the land of the sons of Ammon, do not bring them trouble or make them angry. For I will not give you any of the land of the sons of Ammon for your own. Because I have given it to the sons of Lot for their own.' 20 (It is known as the land of the Rephaim also. For Rephaim once lived in it. But the Ammonites call them Zamzummin, 21 a people as great, as many and as tall as the Anakim. But the Lord destroyed them, and the sons of Ammon took their place and lived in their land. 22 It was as He did for the sons of Esau, who live in Seir. He destroyed the Horites, and the sons of Esau took their place and live in their land even to this day. 23 And the Caphtorim

who came from Caphtor destroyed the Avvim who lived in towns as far as Gaza. Then they lived in their place.) 24 'Now rise up and go on your way. Pass through the valley of Arnon. See, I have given you Sihon the Amorite, king of Heshbon, and his land. Begin to take it for your own, and fight with him in battle. 25 This day I will begin to put much fear of you upon the nations everywhere under the heavens. When they hear about you, they will shake with fear and be filled with trouble because of you.'

Battle with King Sihon

26 "So I sent men carrying news from the desert of Kedemoth to Sihon king of Heshbon with words of peace. They said, 27 'Let me pass through your land. I will travel only on the road. I will not turn to the right or to the left. 28 You will sell me food for money so I may eat, and give me water for money so I may drink. Only let me pass through on foot 29 as the sons of Esau did for us in Seir and the Moabites in Ar. Do this until I cross over the Jordan into the land the Lord our God is giving us.' 30 But Sihon king of Heshbon was not willing to let us pass through his land. For the Lord your God made his spirit and heart hard, so He might give him into your hand, as he is today. 31 Then the Lord said to me, 'See, I have begun to give Sihon and his land to you. Begin to take it for your own, so you may live in it.'

32 "Then Sihon and all his people came out to meet us in battle at Jahaz. 33 The Lord our God gave him to us. We won the fight against him, his sons and all his people. 34 So we took all his cities at that time, and destroyed every man, woman and child in them. We left no one alive. 35 We took only the animals for our own, and the things that were left behind in the cities. 36 There was no city too strong for us, from Aroer by the valley of Arnon, and from the city which is in the valley, as far as Gilead. The Lord our God gave all to us. 37 Only you did not go near the land of the sons of Ammon, all along the river Jabbok and the cities of the hill country. You did not go where the Lord our God told us not to go.

Battle with King Og

3 "Then we turned and went up the road to Bashan. Og king of Bashan and all his people came out to meet us in battle. 2 But the Lord said to me, 'Do not be afraid of him. For I have given him and

all his people and his land to you. Do to him just as you did to Sihon king of the Amorites who lived at Heshbon.' ³ So the Lord our God gave us Og king of Bashan and all his people also. We destroyed them until no one was left alive. ⁴ And we took all his cities at that time. There was not a city which we did not take from them. We took sixty cities, the whole land of Argob, the nation of Og in Bashan. ⁵ All these cities were built strong, with high walls, gates and iron. There were many towns without walls also. ⁶ We destroyed them, as we had done to Sihon king of Heshbon. We destroyed every man, woman and child in every city. ⁷ But we took for ourselves all the animals and what was left in the cities. ⁸ So we took the land at that time from the two kings of the Amorites who were on the east side of the Jordan, from the valley of Arnon to Mount Hermon ⁹ (Sidonians call Hermon Sirion, and the Amorites call it Senir). ¹⁰ We took all the cities of the plain and all Gilead and all Bashan, as far as Salecah and Edrei, cities of the nation of Og in Bashan. ¹¹ (For only Og king of Bashan was left of the children of the Rephaim. His bed was made of iron. It is in Rabbah of the sons of Ammon. It was as long as five steps, and as wide as two long steps.)

Dividing the Land East of the Jordan

¹² "So we took this land for ourselves at that time. I gave to the Reubenites and the Gadites the land from Aroer, which is by the valley of Arnon, and half the hill country of Gilead. ¹³ I gave to the half-family of Manasseh the rest of Gilead and all Bashan, the nation of Og, all the land of Argob. It is called the land of Rephaim. ¹⁴ Manasseh's son Jair took all the land of Argob as far as the land of the Geshurites and the Maacathites. He called Bashan after his own name, Havvothjair. And that is its name to this day. ¹⁵ I gave Gilead to Machir. ¹⁶ To the Reubenites and the Gadites I gave from Gilead to the valley of Arnon, from the center of the valley to the river Jabbok, beside the Ammonites. ¹⁷ I gave them the Arabah also, with the Jordan as its west side, from Chinnereth as far as the sea of the Arabah, the Salt Sea, at the bottom of the hills of Pisgah on the east.

¹⁸ "At that time I told you, 'The Lord your God has given you this land for your own. All you men with strength of heart will cross over ready to fight before your brothers, the sons of Israel. ¹⁹ But your wives, your little ones and your animals (I know you have many animals) will stay in your cities that I have given you. ²⁰ They will stay until the Lord gives rest to your brothers as He has to you, and until they own the land the Lord your God will give them on the other side of the Jordan. Then every one of you may return to what is his, which I have given you.' ²¹ And then I told Joshua, 'Your eyes have seen all the Lord your God has done to these two kings. The Lord will do the same to all the nations through which you pass. ²² Do not be afraid of them. For the Lord your God is the One fighting for you.'

Moses Not Allowed to Cross the Jordan

²³ "After that I begged the Lord, ²⁴ 'O Lord God, You have begun to show Your servant Your great power and Your strong hand. For what god is there in heaven or on earth who can do such works and powerful acts as You do? ²⁵ I ask of You, let me cross over and see the good land on the other side of the Jordan, that good hill country and Lebanon.' ²⁶ But the Lord was angry with me because of you. He would not listen to me. The Lord told me, 'Enough! Speak to Me no more about this. ²⁷ Go up to the top of Pisgah, and look to the west and north and south and east. See it with your eyes, for you will not cross over this Jordan. ²⁸ But tell Joshua what is to be done. For he will cross in front of this people. And he will give them for their own the land that you will see.' ²⁹ So we stayed in the valley beside Beth-peor.

Moses Tells Israel to Obey

4 "Now, O Israel, listen to the Laws I am teaching you. Do them so that you may live and go in to take the land for your own that the Lord, the God of your fathers, is giving you. ² Do not add to the Word that I tell you, and do not take away from it. Keep the Laws of the Lord your God which I tell you. ³ Your eyes saw what the Lord did because of Baal-peor. The Lord your God destroyed from among you all the men who followed the Baal of Peor. ⁴ But you who stayed faithful to the Lord your God are all alive today. ⁵ See, I have taught you Laws just as the Lord my God told me. So you are to live by them in the land you are going to have for your own. ⁶ Keep them and do them. For this will show how wise and understanding you are. The people who will hear all these Laws will say, 'For sure this great nation is a wise and understanding people.' 7 For what great nation is there that has a god so near as the Lord our God is to us every time we call to Him? 8 What great nation is there that has laws as right as this whole Law which I am giving you today?

9 "Only be careful. Keep watch over your life. Or you might forget the things you have seen. Do not let them leave your heart for the rest of your life. But teach them to your children and to your grandchildren. 10 Remember the day you stood before the Lord your God at Mount Sinai. The Lord said to me, 'Gather the people together before Me, so I may let them hear My words. Then they may learn to fear Me all the days they live on the earth, and they may teach their children.' 11 You came near and stood at the bottom of the mountain. And the mountain burned with fire into the heavens, which were covered with darkness and black clouds. 12 Then the Lord spoke to you from the center of the fire. You heard the sound of words, but saw no body. There was only a voice. 13 He told you His agreement which He told you to keep, the Ten Laws. And He wrote them on two pieces of stone. 14 The Lord told me at that time to teach you Laws. So you might obey them in the land that you are going to have for your own.

Israel Not to Worship False Gods

15 "So watch yourselves and be careful. For you saw no body on the day the Lord spoke to you in the fire at Mount Sinai. 16 Do not become sinful and make a false god for yourselves that looks like a body or object, like a male or female, 17 or like an animal on the earth, or a bird with wings that flies in the sky, 18 or like anything that moves on the ground, or like any fish in the water below the earth. 19 Be careful not to lift up your eyes toward heaven and see the sun and moon and stars, all the things of heaven, and be pulled away and worship them and serve them. The Lord your God has given these things to all the nations under the whole heavens. 20 But the Lord has taken you and brought you out of the iron stove, out of Egypt, to be His own people, as you are this day.

21 "The Lord was angry with me because of you. He swore that I should not cross the Jordan, and that I should not go into the good land the Lord your God is giving you for your own. 22 For I must die in this land. I will not cross the Jordan. But you

will cross and take that good land for your own. 23 So watch yourselves, so that you do not forget the agreement the Lord your God made with you, or make a false god for yourselves that looks like something which the Lord your God has told you not to do. 24 For the Lord your God is an all-burning fire, a jealous God.

25 "When you become the father of children and grandchildren and have grown old in the land, if you become sinful and make a god that looks like anything, and anger the Lord your God by doing what is bad in His eyes, 26 I call heaven and earth to speak against you this day. You will soon be destroyed from the land you are crossing the Jordan to have for your own. You will not live long on it, but will all be destroyed. 27 The Lord will spread you out among the nations. And there will not be many of you left among the nations where the Lord will drive you. 28 There you will work for gods made by man's hands out of wood and stone. They do not see or hear or eat or smell. 29 But from there you will look for the Lord your God. And you will find Him if you look for Him with all your heart and soul. 30 When you are in trouble and all these things have happened to you in later days, you will return to the Lord your God and listen to His voice. 31 For the Lord your God is a God of loving-pity. He will not leave you or destroy you or forget the agreement He promised to your fathers.

32 "Ask about the past days, the days before your time, since the day that God made man on the earth. Ask from one end of the heavens to the other. Has anything been done like this great thing? Has anything been heard like it? 33 Have any people ever heard the voice of God speaking from the center of the fire, as you have heard it, and still live? 34 Or has a god tried to go to take for himself a nation from within another nation, by trials, special things to see, great works, war, a powerful hand, a long arm, and spreading much fear? The Lord your God did this for you in Egypt in front of your eyes. 35 It was shown to you so you might know that the Lord is God. There is no other except Him. 36 He let you hear His voice from the heavens to teach you. On earth He let you see His great fire. And you heard His words from the center of the fire. 37 He loved your fathers, so He chose their children after them. He Himself brought you from Egypt by His great power. 38 He drove out from in front of

you nations greater and more powerful than you. And He brought you in and gave you their land for your own, as it is today. 39 So know this day, take it to your heart, that the Lord is God in the heavens above and on the earth below. There is no other. 40 Keep His Laws which I am giving you today. Then it may go well with you and your children after you. And you may live long in the land the Lord your God is giving you for all time."

41 Then Moses set apart three cities east of the Jordan 42 where a person may run to, if he killed his neighbor without meaning to and had not hated him in the past. He might save his life by running to one of these cities: 43 Bezer in the desert on the plain for the Reubenites, and Ramoth in Gilead for the Gadites, and Golan in Bashan for the Manassites.

44 This is the Law which Moses gave to the children of Israel. 45 These are the Laws which Moses spoke to the children of Israel when they came out of Egypt. 46 They were on the other side of the Jordan, in the valley beside Beth-peor, in the land of Sihon, king of the Amorites who lived at Heshbon. Moses and the sons of Israel won the war against him when they came out of Egypt. 47 They took for their own his land and the land of Og king of Bashan, the two kings of the Amorites, east of the Jordan, 48 from Aroer beside the valley of Arnon, as far as Mount Sion (that is, Hermon). 49 They took all the Arabah east of the Jordan, as far as the sea of the Arabah at the bottom of the hills of Pisgah.

God's Ten Great Laws

5 Then Moses called all Israel, and said to them, "Listen, O Israel, to the Laws which I speak in your hearing today. Learn them and be careful to live by them. 2 The Lord our God made an agreement with us at Mount Sinai. 3 The Lord did not make this agreement with our fathers, but with us, all those of us alive here today. 4 The Lord spoke to you face to face at the mountain from the center of the fire. 5 I was standing between the Lord and you then, to tell you the Word of the Lord. For you were afraid because of the fire and did not go up the mountain. He said:

6 'I am the Lord your God, Who brought you out of the land of Egypt, out of the house where you were servants.

7 'Have no other gods except Me.

8 'Do not make a false god for yourselves, or anything that is like what is in heaven above or on the earth below or in the water under the earth. 9 Do not bow down to them or serve them. I, the Lord your God, am a jealous God. I punish the children, the grandchildren and the great-grandchildren for the sins of their fathers who hate Me. 10 But I show loving-kindness to thousands, to those who love Me and keep My Laws.

11 'Do not use the name of the Lord your God in a bad way. For the Lord will punish the one who uses His name in a bad way.

12 'Remember the Day of Rest, to keep it holy, as the Lord your God told you. 13 Six days you will do all your work. 14 But the seventh day is a Day of Rest to the Lord your God. You, your son, your daughter, your man servant, your woman servant, your bull, donkey or any of your cattle, or the traveler who stays with you, must not do any work on this day. So your man servant and woman servant may rest as well as you. 15 Remember that you were servants in the land of Egypt. The Lord your God brought you out of there by a powerful hand and a long arm. So the Lord your God told you to keep the Day of Rest.

16 'Honor your father and your mother, as the Lord your God has told you. So your life may be long and it may go well with you in the land the Lord your God gives you.

17 'Do not kill another person.

18 'Do not do sex sins.

19 'Do not steal.

20 'Do not tell a lie about your neighbor.

21 'Do not have a desire for your neighbor's wife. Do not desire your neighbor's house, his field, his man servant, his bull, his donkey, or anything that belongs to your neighbor.'

22 "The Lord spoke these words to you while you were all gathered at the mountain. He spoke with a loud voice from the center of the fire, the cloud and the darkness. He added no more. And He wrote them on two pieces of stone and gave them to me.

The People Are Afraid

23 "When you heard the voice from the center of the darkness while the mountain burned with fire, you came to me with all the heads of your families and your leaders. 24 And you said, 'See, the Lord our God has shown us His shining-greatness. We have heard His voice from the center of the fire. Today we have seen that God speaks with man and man still lives. 25 But why should we die now? For this big fire

will burn us up. If we hear the voice of the Lord our God any more, we will die. ²⁶ For who of all flesh has ever heard the voice of the living God speaking from the center of the fire, as we have heard, and lived? ²⁷ Go near and hear all the Lord our God says. Then tell us all the Lord our God says to you, and we will listen and do it.'

²⁸ "The Lord heard what you said when you spoke to me. And the Lord said to me, 'I have heard the words which the people have spoken to you. They have done well in all that they have said. ²⁹ If only they had such a heart in them that they would fear Me and live by all My Laws always! Then it would go well with them and with their children forever. ³⁰ Go and say to them, "Return to your tents." ³¹ But you stand here by Me. And I will tell you all the Laws which you should teach them, so they may keep them in the land I give them for their own.' ³² Be careful to do just as the Lord your God has told you. Do not turn aside to the right or to the left. ³³ Walk in all the way the Lord your God has told you. Then you may live, it may be well with you, and you may live a long time in the land that will belong to you.

The Greatest Law

6 "These are the Laws which the Lord your God has told me to teach you. You are to do them in the land you are going to take for your own. ² Then you and your son and your grandson will fear the Lord your God. You will obey all His Laws that I tell you, all the days of your life. And then you will have a longer life. ³ O Israel, you should listen and be careful to do them. Then it will go well with you. And you will become many in a land flowing with milk and honey. This is what the Lord, the God of your fathers, has promised you.

⁴ "Hear, O Israel! The Lord our God is one Lord! ⁵ And you must love the Lord your God with all your heart and with all your soul and with all your strength. ⁶ Keep these words in your heart that I am telling you today. ⁷ Do your best to teach them to your children. Talk about them when you sit in your house and when you walk on the road and when you lie down and when you get up. ⁸ Tie them as something special to see on your hand and on your forehead. ⁹ Write them beside the door of your house and on your gates.

¹⁰ "The Lord your God will bring you into the land He promised to your fathers, Abraham, Isaac and Jacob, to give to you.

There will be big and beautiful cities which you did not build. ¹¹ Houses full of good things which you did not fill. There will be pools for keeping water which you did not dig, and grape-vines and olive trees which you did not plant. You will eat and be filled. ¹² But then be careful not to forget the Lord Who brought you from the land of Egypt, out of the land where you were held as servants. ¹³ You must fear the Lord your God. You must worship Him, and swear by His name. ¹⁴ Do not follow other gods, any of the gods of the people around you. ¹⁵ Or the anger of the Lord your God will burn against you. He will destroy you from the earth. For the Lord your God Who is among you is a jealous God.

¹⁶ "Do not test the Lord your God, as you put Him to the test at Massah. ¹⁷ Be careful to keep all the Laws which the Lord your God has told you. ¹⁸ Do what is right and good in the eyes of the Lord. Then it will be well with you. And you may go in and take the good land for your own which the Lord promised to give to your fathers. ¹⁹ You will drive out of your way all who hate you, as the Lord has promised.

²⁰ "In time to come your son will ask you, 'What do all the Laws mean which the Lord told you?' ²¹ Then say to your son, 'We were servants of Pharaoh in Egypt. But the Lord brought us out of Egypt with a strong hand. ²² The Lord showed us great and powerful works against Egypt, Pharaoh, and all those of his house. ²³ The Lord brought us out from there to bring us into the land He had promised to our fathers.' ²⁴ So the Lord told us to do all these Laws and to fear the Lord our God for our good always, as it is today. ²⁵ We will be right with the Lord our God if we are careful to obey all of the Law before Him, just as He told us.

God's Chosen People

7 "The Lord your God will bring you into the land you are taking for your own. He will drive away many nations in front of you, the Hittites, the Girgashites, the Amorites, the Canaanites, the Perizzites, the Hivites, and the Jebusites, seven nations bigger and stronger than you. ² When the Lord your God gives them to you and you win the battles against them, you must destroy all of them. Make no agreement with them and show no favor to them. ³ Do not take any of them in marriage. Do not give your daughters to their sons. And do not take their daughters for your sons.

4 For they will turn your sons away from following Me to serve other gods. Then the anger of the Lord will burn against you. And He will be quick to destroy you. **5** But do this to them: Break down their altars. Crush their objects of worship. Cut down their female goddess Asherim. And burn their false gods with fire.

6 "For you are a holy nation to the Lord your God. The Lord your God has chosen you out of all the nations on the earth, to be His own. **7** The Lord did not give you His love and choose you because you were more people than any of the nations. For the number of your people was less than all nations. **8** But it is because the Lord loves you and is keeping the promise He made to your fathers. So the Lord brought you out by a strong hand. He set you free from the land where you were servants, and from the power of Pharaoh king of Egypt. **9** Know then that the Lord your God is God, the faithful God. He keeps His promise and shows His loving-kindness to those who love Him and keep His Laws, even to a thousand family groups in the future. **10** But He destroys those who hate Him. He will not show kindness to the one who hates Him, but will punish him to his face. **11** So keep and obey all the Laws I am telling you today.

Good Comes to Those Who Obey

12 "If you listen to these Laws and keep and obey them, the Lord your God will keep His agreement and loving-kindness as He promised to your fathers. **13** He will love you and bring good to you and make you a nation of many. He will bring good to your children and the fruit of your land, your grain, your new wine and your oil. And He will give you many cattle and young ones in your flock, in the land He promised to your fathers to give you. **14** More good will come to you than to any other nation. There will be no male or female among you or your cattle that is not able to have young ones. **15** The Lord will take all sickness from you. He will not let any bad diseases come upon you that you have known in Egypt. But He will give them to all who hate you. **16** You will destroy all the nations the Lord your God will give to you. You will not pity them or worship their gods, for that would be a trap to you.

17 "You may say in your heart, 'These nations are stronger than I. How can I drive them out?' **18** But you will not be afraid of them. You will remember what the Lord your God did to Pharaoh and to all Egypt. **19** You will remember the hard trials you saw, the powerful works, and the strong hand and powerful arm the Lord your God used to bring you out. The Lord your God will do the same to all the nations who make you afraid. **20** And the Lord your God will send the hornet against them. Those who are left will hide themselves from you and be destroyed. **21** You will not be afraid of them. For the Lord your God is among you, a great and powerful God. **22** The Lord your God will drive away these nations in front of you one by one. You will not be able to destroy them in a short time, or the wild animals may become too many for you. **23** But the Lord your God will give them to you. He will bring much trouble upon them until they are destroyed. **24** He will give their kings into your hand. And you will destroy their name from under heaven. No man will be able to stand in front of you until you have destroyed them. **25** You must burn with fire their objects of worship. Do not want the silver or gold that is on them, or take it for yourselves. It would be a trap to you, for it is a hated thing to the Lord your God. **26** Do not bring a hated thing into your house. You would become hated also. But turn from it with fear and hate, for bad will come from it.

The Promised Land to Be Taken

8 "Be careful to do all that I am telling you today. Then you will live and have many children, and go in to own the land the Lord promised to give to your fathers. **2** You will remember all the way the Lord your God led you in the desert these forty years, so you would not have pride, and how He tested you to know what was in your heart to see if you would obey His Laws or not. **3** He let you be hungry which helped you to not have pride. Then He fed you with bread from heaven which you and your fathers had not known. He did this to make you understand that man does not live by bread alone. But man lives by everything that comes out of the mouth of the Lord. **4** Your clothes did not wear out, and your feet did not get sore during these forty years. **5** So know in your heart that the Lord your God was punishing you just as a man punishes his son. **6** Keep the Laws of the Lord your God. Walk in His ways, and fear Him. **7** For the Lord your God is bringing you into a good land, a land of rivers and wells of water, flowing into valleys from hills. 8 It is a land of grains, vines, fig trees, fruit, olive oil and honey. 9 It is a land where you will have enough food to eat and not have to do without, a land where stones are iron. And you can make brass from what you dig out of its hills. 10 When you have eaten and are filled, you will honor and thank the Lord your God for the good land He has given you.

11 "Be careful not to forget the Lord your God by not keeping all His Laws which I am telling you today. 12 When you have eaten and are filled, and have built good houses to live in, 13 and when your cattle and flocks become many, and you get much silver and gold, and have many things for your own, 14 be careful not to become proud. Do not forget the Lord your God Who brought you out of the land of Egypt, out of the house where you were servants. 15 He led you through the big desert that brought fear with its poisonous snakes and scorpions and thirsty ground where there was no water. He brought you water out of hard rock. 16 In the desert He fed you bread from heaven, which your fathers did not know about. He did this so you would not have pride and that He might test you. It was for your good in the end. 17 Be careful not to say in your heart, 'My power and strong hand have made me rich.' 18 But remember the Lord your God. For it is He Who is giving you power to become rich. By this He may keep His agreement which He promised to your fathers, as it is this day. 19 If you ever forget the Lord your God and go to other gods to worship and work for them, I tell you today that you will be destroyed for sure. 20 You will be destroyed like the nations the Lord destroys before you, because you would not listen to the voice of the Lord your God.

Israel to Remember How They Did Not Obey

9 "Hear, O Israel! You are crossing over the Jordan today to take the land that belongs to nations greater and stronger than you, with big cities with walls as high as heaven. 2 The people there are strong and tall, the sons of Anakim. You know of them and have heard it said, 'Who can stand in front of the sons of Anak?' 3 But know today that it is the Lord your God Who is crossing over before you as a fire that destroys everything. He will destroy them and bring them down before you. So you may drive them out and be quick to

destroy them, just as the Lord has told you. 4 But after the Lord your God has driven them out before you, do not say in your heart, 'The Lord has brought me in to take this land because I am right and good.' It is because of the sin of these nations that the Lord is driving them out in front of you. 5 It is not because of your being right with God that you are going to take their land. But it is because of the sin of these nations that the Lord your God is driving them out in front of you. By this the Lord is proving that He keeps the promise He made to your fathers, to Abraham, Isaac and Jacob. 6 Understand that it is not because you are right with God that the Lord your God is giving you this good land for your own, for you are a strong-willed people.

7 "Remember and do not forget how you made the Lord your God angry in the desert. You have gone against the Lord from the day you left the land of Egypt until you came to this place. 8 Even at Mount Sinai you made the Lord angry. The Lord was so angry with you that He would have destroyed you. 9 I went up the mountain to receive the pieces of stone, the Laws of the agreement which the Lord had made with you. I stayed on the mountain forty days and nights. I did not eat bread or drink water. 10 Then the Lord gave me the two pieces of stone written by the finger of God. On them were all the words the Lord had spoken with you on the mountain from the fire on the day of the meeting. 11 At the end of forty days and nights the Lord gave me the two pieces of stone, the Laws of the agreement. 12 Then the Lord said to me, 'Get up. Hurry and go down from here. For your people whom you brought out of Egypt have become very sinful. They have been quick to turn away from what I told them. They have made a false god for themselves.' 13 And the Lord said to me, 'I have seen these people. See, they are strong-willed. 14 Let Me alone, so I may destroy them and destroy their name from under heaven. I will make you into a nation that will be greater and stronger than they.' 15 So I turned and came down from the mountain while the mountain was burning with fire. The two pieces of stone of the agreement were in my hands. 16 And I saw that it was true that you had sinned against the Lord your God. You had made for yourselves a calf out of gold. You had been quick to turn away from what the Lord had told you. 17 So I took the two pieces of stone

and threw them from my hands, and broke them in front of your eyes. [18] Then again I fell down before the Lord for forty days and nights. I did not eat bread or drink water, because of all the sin you had done. You did what was sinful in the eyes of the Lord and made Him angry. [19] I was afraid of the anger of the Lord which was burning against you to destroy you. But the Lord listened to me again. [20] The Lord was angry enough with Aaron to destroy him. So I prayed for Aaron at the same time also. [21] Then I took your sinful thing, the calf you had made, and burned it with fire and crushed it. I ground it into pieces until it was as fine as dust. And I threw its dust into the river that flowed down from the mountain.

[22] "You made the Lord angry again at Taberah, Massah and Kibroth-hattaavah. [23] The Lord sent you from Kadesh-barnea, saying, 'Go and take for your own the land I have given you.' But you went against what the Lord your God told you to do. You did not believe Him or listen to His voice. [24] You have gone against the Lord from the day I first knew you.

[25] "So I fell down before the Lord and lay forty days and nights, because the Lord had said He would destroy you. [26] I prayed to the Lord, saying, 'O Lord God, do not destroy Your people, Your chosen nation, whom You have set free by Your power and brought out of Egypt with a strong hand. [27] Remember Your servants, Abraham, Isaac and Jacob. Do not look at the strong will or sin or wrong-doing of these people. [28] Or the land You brought us from may say, "The Lord was not able to bring them into the land He promised them. Because He hated them, He brought them out to kill them in the desert." [29] Yet they are Your people, Your chosen nation, whom You have brought out by Your great power and Your long arm.'

The Second Pieces of Stone

10 "At that time the Lord said to me, 'Cut out for yourself two pieces of stone like the other ones. Then come up to Me on the mountain, and make a box of wood. [2] I will write on the pieces of stone the words that were on the other pieces of stone which you broke. And you will put them in the box.' [3] So I made a box of acacia wood and cut out two pieces of stone like the other ones. Then I went up the mountain with the two stone pieces in my hand. [4] The Lord wrote the Ten Laws the same

as before on the pieces of stone which He had spoken to you on the mountain from the fire on the day of the meeting. And the Lord gave them to me. [5] Then I turned and came down from the mountain, and put the stone pieces in the box I had made. There they are, as the Lord told me."

[6] (The people of Israel traveled from the wells of the sons of Jaakan to Moserah. Aaron died there and was buried and his son Eleazar took his place as religious leader. [7] From there they traveled to Gudgodah. And from Gudgodah they went to Jotbathah, a land of rivers of water. [8] At that time the Lord set apart the family of Levi to carry the special box of the Law of the Lord, and to stand before the Lord to work for Him and honor His name to this day. [9] So Levi does not have a share of what is given to his brothers. The Lord is his share, just as the Lord your God promised him.)

[10] "Once more I stayed on the mountain forty days and forty nights, like the first time. And the Lord listened to me that time also. The Lord did not destroy you. [11] Then the Lord said to me, 'Get up. Travel in front of the people, so they may go in and take the land which I promised to give their fathers.'

What God Wants

[12] "And now, Israel, what does the Lord your God ask of you? He wants you to fear the Lord your God, to walk in all His ways and love Him. He wants you to serve the Lord your God with all your heart and all your soul. [13] He wants you to keep all the Laws of the Lord which I am telling you today for your good. [14] See, heaven and the highest heavens, the earth and all that is in it belong to the Lord your God. [15] The Lord had joy in loving your fathers more than other nations, and you are still His chosen people to this day. [16] So then, from now on, obey the Lord. Do not be strong-willed any more. [17] For the Lord your God is the God of gods and the Lord of lords. He is the great and powerful God and is to be honored with fear. He does not show favor, and cannot be bought with money. [18] He does what is right and fair for the child without parents and the woman whose husband has died. He shows His love for the stranger by giving him food and clothing. [19] So show your love for the stranger. For you were strangers in the land of Egypt. [20] Fear the Lord your God. Work for Him, hold on to Him, and swear by His

name. 21 He is your praise and He is your God. You have seen the great and powerful things He has done for you. 22 Your fathers went to Egypt, seventy people in all. And now the Lord your God has made you as many as the stars of heaven.

Love and Obey the Lord

11 "Love the Lord your God. Always do what He tells you and keep all His Laws. 2 I am not speaking to your children. They have not seen how the Lord worked and how great He is. 3 They have not seen the special things you have seen, what He did in Egypt to Pharaoh the king of Egypt and to all his land. 4 They have not seen what He did to Egypt's army, the horses and war-wagons. He made the water of the Red Sea flow over them while they were coming after you. He destroyed every one of them. 5 They have not seen what He did to you in the desert until you came to this place. 6 They do not know what He did to Dathan and Abiram, the sons of Eliab, son of Reuben. The earth opened its mouth and swallowed them, those of their house, their tents, and every living thing that followed them among Israel. 7 But your own eyes have seen all the great work the Lord has done.

8 "So keep every Law which I am telling you today. And you will be strong and go in and take the land which is to be yours. 9 You will live long in the land the Lord promised to your fathers and their children, a land flowing with milk and honey. 10 For the land you are going in to take is not like the land you came from in Egypt. There you planted your seed and watered it using your feet, like a vegetable garden. 11 But the land you are about to go into and take for your own is a land of hills and valleys. It drinks water from the rain of heaven. 12 The Lord your God cares for this land. His eyes watch over it from the beginning to the end of the year.

13 "Listen to and obey all the Laws I am telling you today. Love the Lord your God. Work for Him with all your heart and soul. If you do, 14 He will give the rain for your land at the right times, the early and late rain. So you may gather in your grain, your new wine and your oil. 15 He will give grass in your fields for your cattle. And you will eat and be filled. 16 Be careful not to let your hearts be fooled so you turn away and work for other gods and worship them. 17 Or the anger of the Lord will burn against you. He will shut the heavens

so there will be no rain and the ground will not give its fruit. Then you will be quick to die from the good land the Lord is giving you.

18 "Keep these words of mine in your heart and in your soul. Tie them as something special to see upon your hand and on your forehead between your eyes. 19 Teach them to your children. Talk about them when you sit in your house and when you walk on the road and when you lie down and when you get up. 20 Write them beside the door of your house and on your gates. 21 And your days and the days of your children will become many in the land the Lord promised to give to your fathers, as long as the heavens are above the earth. 22 Be careful to obey all this Law which I am telling you. Love the Lord your God. Walk in all His ways and hold on to Him. If you do, 23 the Lord will drive out all these nations in front of you. And you will take for your own what has belonged to nations greater and stronger than you. 24 Every place where your foot steps will be yours. Your land will be from the desert to Lebanon, and from the River Euphrates to the sea in the west. 25 There no man will be able to stand in front of you. The Lord your God will put the fear of you on all the land where you walk, as He has promised you.

26 "See, I am putting in front of you today good and a curse. 27 Good will come to you if you listen to the Laws of the Lord your God, which I am telling you today. 28 But a curse will come to you if you do not listen to the Laws of the Lord your God and turn aside from the way I am telling you today, by following other gods you have not known. 29 When the Lord your God brings you into the land which is to be yours, you are to speak on Mount Gerizim about the good and on Mount Ebal the curses. 30 You know they are on the other side of the Jordan, west of the road where the sun goes down. They are in the land of the Canaanites who live in the Arabah, beside Gilgal, next to the trees of Moreh. 31 You are about to cross the Jordan to go in to take the land the Lord your God is giving you. It will be your land and you will live in it. 32 Be careful to obey all the Laws which I am giving you today.

The One Place for Worship

12 "These are the Laws you should be careful to obey in the land which the Lord, the God of your fathers, has given you for your own as long as you live on the earth. 2 Be sure to destroy all the places of worship of the nations whose place you are taking. Destroy them on the high mountains, on the hills, and under every green tree. 3 Break down their altars and crush their pillars of worship. Burn their wooden female gods of worship named Asherim with fire. Cut down the objects made to look like their gods. And destroy their name from that place. 4 But do not act like this toward the Lord your God. 5 Look for the Lord at the place which the Lord your God will choose from all your family groups. There He will make His name known, and make His home there, and there you will come. 6 Bring to this place your burnt gifts, your gifts of worship, the tenth part of what you receive, the gifts of your hands, your promises, your free-will gifts, and the first-born of your cattle and your flock. 7 You and those of your house will eat there before the Lord your God, and have joy in all that you do, in which the Lord your God has brought good to you. 8 You will not do at all the things we are doing here today, for every man is doing whatever is right in his own eyes. 9 For you have not yet come to the resting place and the land the Lord your God is giving you. 10 You will cross the Jordan and live in the land the Lord your God is giving you. He will give you rest from all those around you who hate you, so you will be safe. 11 Then bring all I tell you to the place where the Lord your God will choose to make His name known. Bring your burnt gifts, your gifts of worship, the tenth part of what you receive, the gifts of your hands, and all the special gifts that you promised to the Lord. 12 Be full of joy before the Lord your God, you and your sons and daughters, your men and women servants, and the Levite within your town who has no share of their gift. 13 Be careful that you do not give your burnt gifts in just any place you see. 14 But give your burnt gifts in the place which the Lord chooses in the land where your families live. There you should do all that I tell you.

15 "But you may kill and eat meat within any of your towns, as much as you want, as the Lord your God has given you His good gifts. Both the clean and the unclean may eat of it, as you would of the gazelle and the deer. 16 Only do not eat the blood. You are to pour it out on the ground like water. 17 You are not allowed to eat within your towns the tenth part of your grain, or new wine, or oil, or the first-born of your cattle or flock, or any of your promised gifts, or

your free-will gifts, or the gifts of your hands. 18 But you should eat them before the Lord your God in the place which the Lord your God will choose, you and your son and daughter, your men and women servants, and the Levite who is within your towns. Be full of joy before the Lord your God in everything you do. 19 Be careful that you do not stop caring for the Levites as long as you live in your land.

20 "The Lord your God will give you more land as He has promised you. And when you say, 'I will eat meat,' because you want to eat meat, then you may eat as much meat as you want. 21 If the place where the Lord your God chooses to put His name is too far from you, then you may kill from your cattle or flock which the Lord has given you, as I have told you, and you may eat within your towns whatever you want. 22 You will eat it just as a gazelle or a deer is eaten. Both the clean and unclean may eat of it. 23 Only be sure not to eat the blood. For the blood is the life. You must not eat the life with the flesh. 24 Do not eat it, but pour it out on the ground like water. 25 Do not eat it, so it may go well with you and your children after you. For you will be doing what is right in the eyes of the Lord. 26 Take your holy things which you may have and all the special gifts you promised to give to the place which the Lord chooses. 27 Give your burnt gifts, the flesh and the blood, on the altar of the Lord your God. The blood of your gifts will be poured out on the altar of the Lord your God. And you will eat the flesh. 28 Be careful to listen to all these words I am telling you. Then it will go well with you and your children after you forever. For you will be doing what is good and right in the eyes of the Lord your God.

Israel to Watch out for False Gods

29 "The Lord your God will cut off before you the nations whose land you will take. You will take their place and live in their land. 30 But be careful that you are not fooled into following them, after they are destroyed before you. Do not ask about their gods, saying, 'How do these nations worship their gods so that I may do the same?' 31 Do not act this way toward the Lord your God. For they have done for their gods every sinful act which the Lord hates. They even burn their sons and daughters in the fire for their gods.

32 "Be careful to do whatever I tell you. Do not add to it or take away from it.

Worshiping False Gods

13 "A man who tells what is going to happen or a dreamer of dreams may come among you. He may give you something special to see or do a powerful work. 2 And what he tells you will happen might come true. But if he says to you, 'Let us follow other gods (whom you have not known) and let us worship them,' 3 do not listen to the words of that man who tells you what will happen or that dreamer of dreams. For the Lord your God is putting you to the test to see if you love the Lord your God with all your heart and with all your soul. 4 Follow the Lord your God and fear Him. Keep His Laws, and listen to His voice. Work for Him, and hold on to Him. 5 But that man who tells what is going to happen or that dreamer of dreams must be put to death, because he has talked to you about turning away from the Lord your God Who brought you from the land of Egypt and set you free from the land where you were servants. That man tried to turn you from the way the Lord your God told you to walk. You must take the sinful away from you.

6 "Your brother, your mother's son, or your son or daughter, or the wife you love, or your friend who is as your own soul, might tempt you in secret. They might say, 'Let us go and worship other gods' (whom you and your fathers have not known. 7 They might be gods of the nations who are around you, near you, or far from you, from one end of the earth to the other), 8 do not agree with him or listen to him. Do not look on him with pity. And do not show him loving-kindness or hide him. 9 You must kill him. Your hand should be first against him to put him to death, and then the hand of all the people. 10 Kill him with stones, because he has tried to turn you away from the Lord your God Who brought you out of the land of Egypt, out of the land where you were servants. 11 Then all Israel will hear and be afraid. No one will do such a sinful thing among you again.

12 "You might hear that in one of the cities the Lord your God has given you to live in 13 that some men of no worth have gone out from among you to tempt those who live in their city. They might say, 'Let us go and worship other gods,' (whom you have not known). 14 Then you should ask around and try to find out if this is true. If it is true that this sinful thing has been done among you, 15 you must be sure to go against those of that city with the sword. Destroy all of it, all that is in it, and its cattle, with the sword. 16 Then gather all that is left into the center of the city. Burn the city and all that is left in it with fire as a whole burnt gift to the Lord your God. It will be destroyed forever. It will never be built again. 17 Let nothing of the things to be destroyed be kept in your own hand so the Lord may turn from His burning anger and show loving-kindness to you. He will show you loving-pity and make you a nation of many, just as He promised your fathers. 18 But you must listen to the voice of the Lord your God. Obey all His Laws which I am telling you today. Do what is right in the eyes of the Lord your God.

Good and Bad Foods

14 "You are the sons of the Lord your God. Do not cut yourselves or cut the hair from your foreheads because of the dead. 2 For you are a holy nation to the Lord your God. The Lord has chosen you to be His own nation out of all the nations on the earth.

3 "Do not eat any hated thing. 4 These are the animals you may eat: the bull, the sheep, the goat, 5 the deer, the gazelle, the roebuck, the wild goat, the ibex, the antelope, and the mountain sheep. 6 And you may eat any animal that has a parted foot divided in two and that chews its food again. 7 But you must not eat of those that chew their food again or have a divided foot: the camel, the rabbit and the rock badger. For though they eat their food again, they do not have a divided foot. They are unclean to you. 8 And do not eat the pig, because it has a divided foot but does not chew its food again. It is unclean for you. Do not eat any of their flesh or touch their dead bodies.

9 "Of all that are in the water, you may eat anything that has fins and scales. 10 Do not eat anything that does not have fins and scales. It is unclean for you.

11 "You may eat any clean bird. 12 But these are the ones you may not eat: the eagle, the vulture, the buzzard, 13 the red kite, the falcon, every kind of kite, 14 every kind of raven, 15 the ostrich, the owl, the sea gull, every kind of hawk, 16 the little owl, the great owl, the white owl, 17 the pelican, the vulture that eats dead flesh, the cormorant, 18 the stork, every kind of heron, the hoopoe and the bat. 19 And all flying bugs are unclean for you. Do not eat them. 20 But you may eat any clean bird.

21 "Do not eat anything that dies of itself. You may give it to the stranger in your town, so he may eat it. Or you may sell it to a person from another land. For you are a holy nation to the Lord your God.

"Do not boil a young goat in its mother's milk.

The Law of the Tenth Part

22 "Be sure to give a tenth part to the Lord of all you plant that comes from your field every year. 23 Before the Lord your God, at the place He chooses to put His name, you may eat the tenth part of your grain, your new wine, your oil, and the first-born of your cattle and your flock. Then you may learn to fear the Lord your God always. 24 If the place where the Lord your God chooses to put His name is too far away for you to bring the tenth part of all the good things you have received, 25 you should trade it for money. Then tie the money in your hand and go to the place which the Lord your God chooses. 26 You may spend the money for whatever your heart may desire, for bulls, sheep, wine, strong drink, or whatever you desire. And there you and those of your house may eat before the Lord and be full of joy. 27 Do not stop caring for the Levite who is in your town for he has no share of what is given to you.

28 "At the end of every third year you should bring the tenth part of that year's grain into your towns. 29 And the Levite who has no share of what is given to you, and the stranger, and the child without parents, and the woman whose husband has died, who are in your towns, may come and eat and be filled. Then the Lord your God will bring good to you in all the work done by your hands.

The Seventh Year

15 "At the end of every seven years you must do away with debts that are owed. 2 This is the way you are to do it: Every man who has loaned money must forget the debt. He cannot make his neighbor and his brother pay it because the Lord has said that all should be forgotten. 3 You may make a stranger pay what he owes, but not your brother. 4 Yet there will be no poor among you for the Lord will be sure to bring good to you in the land the Lord your God is giving you for your own. 5 But you must listen and obey the voice of the Lord your God. Be careful to do all the Law which I am telling you today. 6 The Lord your God will bring

good to you as He has promised. You will let many nations use what belongs to you but you will not use what belongs to them. You will rule over many nations but they will not rule over you.

7 "In any of the towns in your land the Lord your God is giving you, if there is anyone poor among you, do not let your heart be hard and not be willing to help him. 8 Be free to give to him. Let him use what is yours of anything he needs. 9 Be careful that there is no sinful thought in your heart, saying, 'It is almost the seventh year, the time to do away with the debt owed to me,' so you look on your brother with hate and give him nothing. Then he may cry to the Lord against you and you may be guilty of sin. 10 Give much to him, without being sorry that you do. Because the Lord your God will bring good to you for this, in all your work and in everything you do. 11 The poor will always be in the land. So I tell you to be free in giving to your brother, to those in need, and to the poor in your land.

12 "If your brother, a Hebrew man or a Hebrew woman, is sold to you, he will work for you six years. But you must set him free in the seventh year. 13 When you set him free, do not send him away with nothing. 14 Give him much from your flock, from your grain, and from your wine. Give to him as the Lord your God has given to you. 15 Remember that you were servants in the land of Egypt, and the Lord your God set you free. And so I am telling you today to do this. 16 But he may say to you, 'I will not leave you,' because he loves you and those of your house and gets along well with you. 17 Then take a sharp tool and put it through his ear into the door. And he will be your servant forever. Do the same with your woman servant. 18 It should not be hard for you to set him free for he has worked for you six years. He has been worth twice as much as a man paid to work for you. The Lord your God will bring good to you in whatever you do.

19 "Set apart for the Lord your God all the first-born males among your cattle and your flock. Do no work with the first-born of your cattle. Do not cut the wool from the first-born of your flock. 20 You and those of your house will eat it every year before the Lord your God in the place the Lord chooses. 21 But do not kill it and give it to the Lord your God if it is not perfect, such as not being able to walk or see,

or anything else wrong with it. ²² Eat it within your towns. Both the clean and the unclean may eat it, as if it were a gazelle or deer. ²³ But do not eat its blood. You must pour it out on the ground like water.

The Passover

16 "Remember the month of Abib and keep the Passover to the Lord your God. For the Lord your God brought you out of Egypt during the night in the month of Abib. ² Give the Passover gift to the Lord your God from the flock and the cattle, in the place where the Lord chooses to put His name. ³ Do not eat bread made with yeast. For seven days eat bread made without yeast, the bread of sorrow, because you came out of the land of Egypt in a hurry. So all the days of your life you will remember the day when you came out of the land of Egypt. ⁴ For seven days there is to be no yeast around in all your land. And none of the flesh you give in worship on the evening of the first day will be kept through the night until morning. ⁵ You are not allowed to give the Passover gift in any of your towns the Lord your God gives you. ⁶ But give it at the place where the Lord your God chooses to put His name. You must kill the Passover gift in the evening when the sun goes down, at the time that you came out of Egypt. ⁷ Make it ready and eat it in the place the Lord your God chooses. Then return to your tents in the morning. ⁸ For six days eat bread made without yeast. On the seventh day there will be a holy meeting to the Lord your God. Do no work on this day.

The Supper of Weeks

⁹ "Number seven weeks. Begin to number seven weeks from the time you begin to cut the standing grain. ¹⁰ Then keep the Special Supper of Weeks to the Lord your God by giving a free-will gift. Give as the Lord your God has given to you. ¹¹ Be full of joy before the Lord your God, you and your son and daughter, your men and women servants, the Levite who is in your town, the stranger, the child whose parents have died, and the woman whose husband has died. Be full of joy in the place where the Lord your God chooses to put His name. ¹² Remember that you were servants in Egypt. And be careful to obey these Laws.

¹³ "Keep the Special Supper of Tents seven days after you have gathered your grain and wine. ¹⁴ Be full of joy during your special supper, you and your son and daughter, your men and women servants, the Levite, the stranger, the child whose parents have died, and the woman whose husband has died, who are in your towns. ¹⁵ Seven days you will have a special supper to the Lord your God in the place which the Lord chooses. You will be full of joy because the Lord your God will bring good to you in all the food you grow and in all the work you do. ¹⁶ All your males must show themselves before the Lord your God three times a year in the place He chooses, at the Special Supper of Bread Without Yeast, the Special Supper of the First-Fruits of the Land, and the Special Supper of Tents. They must not show themselves before the Lord with nothing in their hands. ¹⁷ Every man should give as he is able, as the Lord your God has given to you.

Those Who Judge

¹⁸ "Choose judges and other leaders for all your towns the Lord your God is giving you, among each of your family groups. They must be wise in judging the people. ¹⁹ Be fair and do not show favor. Do not take pay in secret for doing wrong. Such pay blinds the eyes of the wise and causes them to change the words of a good man. ²⁰ Follow what is right, and only what is right. Then you will live and receive the land the Lord your God is giving you.

²¹ "When you make an altar for the Lord your God, do not put beside it a wooden god like the false goddess Asherah. ²² Do not set up for yourself a pillar for worship that the Lord your God hates.

17 "Do not give to the Lord your God a bull or a sheep which is not perfect. For that is a hated thing to the Lord your God.

² "You may find among you, within any of your towns the Lord your God gives you, a man or a woman who does what is sinful in the eyes of the Lord your God by sinning against the Lord's agreement, ³ If he has served other gods and worshiped them, or the sun, or the moon or the stars, which I have told him not to worship, ⁴ and if someone told you about this, then you should do your best to find out if it is true. If it is true that this hated thing has been done in Israel, ⁵ then bring that man or woman who has done this sinful act to your gates, and kill the man or woman with stones. ⁶ If two or three people tell

what they know against this person, he who is to die must be put to death. But he should not be put to death if only one person speaks against him. 7 Those who speak against him should be first to put him to death. And then all the people should join them. You must get rid of all sin from among you.

8 "There may be a problem too hard for you to decide, between two kinds of killing, between two kinds of questions about the law, between two kinds of hurting, problems argued about in your courts. Then get up and go to the place which the Lord your God chooses. 9 Go to the Levite religious leader or the judge who is at work at that time. Ask them, and they will tell you what they decide. 10 Then do what should be done by what they tell you they have decided at that place which the Lord chooses. Be careful to do all they tell you. 11 Do what they teach you about the Law and about what they decide. Do not turn aside from what they tell you to do, to the right or to the left. 12 The man must die who does foolish things and will not listen to the judge or the religious leader who serves the Lord your God. You must get rid of sin from Israel. 13 Then all the people will hear and be afraid. They will not act in a foolish way again.

A King

14 "When you go into the land the Lord your God gives you, and own it and live in it, and you say, 'I will have a king rule over me like all the nations around me,' 15 then you will set a king over you whom the Lord your God chooses. Set a king over you from among your brothers. Do not give a stranger power over you if he is not your brother. 16 He must not take many horses for himself or make the people return to Egypt to get many horses. Because the Lord has told you, 'You must never again return that way.' 17 He must not take many wives for himself or his heart may turn away. And he must not gather much silver and gold for himself.

18 "When he sits on the throne of his nation, he should write this Law for himself in a book in front of the Levite religious leaders. 19 It should be kept with him and he should read it all the days of his life. Then he will learn to fear the Lord his God, by being careful to obey all the words of these Laws. 20 And he will not think he is better than his brothers. He will not turn aside from the Law, to the right or to the left, so that he and his children may live long in his nation in Israel.

What the Religious Leaders and Levites Are to Receive

18 "The Levite religious leaders of the family group of Levi will have no share of the land given to Israel. They will live on the gifts given to the Lord by fire. 2 They will have no share of the land among their brothers. The Lord is their share, as He promised them.

3 "When the people bring their gifts, a bull or a sheep, the religious leader is to be given the shoulder, the parts of the face, and the stomach. 4 Give him the first of your grain, your wine, and your oil, and the first wool of your sheep. 5 For the Lord your God has chosen him and his sons from all your families, to stand and serve in the name of the Lord forever.

6 "If a Levite comes whenever he desires from any of the towns in Israel to the place the Lord chooses, 7 then he may work in the name of the Lord his God, like all his brother Levites who stand there before the Lord. 8 They will all eat the same share of food, except what they receive from what is sold of their fathers' lands.

Stay Away from What Is Sinful

9 "When you go into the land the Lord your God gives you, do not learn to follow the hated and sinful ways of those nations. 10 There must not be found among you anyone who makes his son or daughter pass through the fire, or uses secret ways, or does witchcraft, or tells the meaning of special things, or is a witch, 11 or uses secret power on people, or helps people talk to spirits, or talks to spirits himself, or talks with the dead. 12 For the Lord hates whoever does these things. And because of these hated things, the Lord your God will drive them out from in front of you. 13 You must be without blame before the Lord your God. 14 For these nations that you are about to take listen to those who do witchcraft and use secret ways. But the Lord your God has not allowed you to do so.

A Man Who Speaks for God

15 "The Lord your God will give you a man who speaks for God like me from among your own brothers. You must listen to him. 16 This is what you asked of the Lord your God at Sinai on the day of the meeting, when you said, 'Do not let me hear the voice of the Lord my God again.

Do not let me see this fire any more, or I will die.' 17 And the Lord said to me, 'They have spoken well. 18 I will give them a man who speaks for God like you from among their brothers. I will put My words in his mouth. And he will make known to them all that I tell him. 19 He will speak in My name. And I will punish whoever will not listen to him. 20 But that man of God will die who is not careful and speaks in My name what I did not tell him to speak, or speaks in the name of other gods.' 21 You may say to yourselves, 'How can we know which words the Lord has not spoken?' 22 When a man who speaks for God speaks in the name of the Lord, and what he says does not come true, that word is not from the Lord. The man has spoken on his own. Do not be afraid of him.

The Cities to Be a Safe Place

19 "The Lord your God will destroy the nations whose land the Lord your God gives you. You will take their place and live in their cities and in their houses. At that time 2 you should set apart three cities for yourself in the land the Lord your God gives you for your own. 3 Make the roads good that lead to these cities. Divide into three parts the land the Lord your God gives you for your own. Any man who kills another may run to a city and be safe.

4 "This is the law of the person who kills another and runs to a city to save his life. He might have killed his friend without meaning to, a friend he did not hate in the past. 5 He could have gone among the trees with his friend to cut wood. As he was using his ax to cut down a tree, the ax head could have come off the stick and hit his friend, killing him. Then he may run to one of these cities and live. 6 Or else the one who is angry will want to punish him for the killing, and will catch him and kill him. But the killer should not be put to death, because he had not hated the man in the past. 7 So I tell you, 'Set apart three cities for yourself.' 8 The Lord your God will give you even more land, as He was promised your fathers. He will give you all the land which He promised to give your fathers, 9 if you are careful to obey all the Laws I tell you today. Love the Lord your God. Walk in His ways always. Then you will add three other cities to these three. 10 So the person without guilt will not be put to death in the land the Lord your God gives you as a gift. And you will not be guilty of blood.

11 "But there might be a man who hates his neighbor, lies in wait for him, goes against him, and hurts him so that he dies. After this he might run to one of these cities. 12 Then the leaders of his city should send men to take him from there and bring him to the one who wants to punish him for the killing that he may die. 13 Do not pity him. In Israel be free from the blood of those that are not guilty. Then it will go well with you.

14 "Do not move your neighbor's landmark which the fathers of long ago have set in the land the Lord your God gives you for your own.

15 "One person will not prove the guilt of a sin another man may have done. It will take two or three people who know about the sin to prove the man's guilt. 16 If an angry person speaks against a man, saying that he did something wrong, 17 then both men who are arguing should stand before the Lord, in front of the religious leaders and the judges who are at work at that time. 18 The judges will choose careful questions to ask about the problem. If the man lied who said his brother is guilty, 19 then you should do to him just what he wanted to do to his brother. In this way you will get rid of the sin among you. 20 The rest of the people will hear and be afraid. They will never do such a sinful thing among you again. 21 Do not pity him. It will be life for life, eye for eye, tooth for tooth, hand for hand, foot for foot.

About Battles

20 "When you go to battle against those who hate you and see more horses and war-wagons and soldiers than you have, do not be afraid of them. For the Lord your God, Who brought you from the land of Egypt, is with you. 2 When you are coming near the battle, the religious leader will come near and speak to the people. 3 He will say to them, 'Hear, O Israel. Today you are going into battle against those who hate you. Do not let your hearts become weak. Do not be afraid and shake in fear before them. 4 For the Lord your God is the One Who goes with you. He will fight for you against those who hate you. And He will save you.' 5 The leaders will speak to the people also, saying, 'Is there anyone among you who has built a new house and has not given it to God? Let him go and return to his house or he might die in battle and another man will give it to God. 6 Is there anyone who has planted grape-vines and has not begun to eat their fruit? Let him go and return to his house or he might die in the battle and another man will begin to eat the fruit. 7 Is there a man who is promised in marriage to a woman and has not married her? Let him go and return to his house or he might die in the battle and another man marry her.' 8 Then the leaders will say to the people, 'Is there a man here who is afraid and is weak in heart? Let him go and return to his house so he will not make his brothers' hearts afraid like his heart.' 9 When the leaders have finished speaking to the people, they will choose heads of the army to lead the people.

10 "When you come near a city to fight against it, ask the people of the city if they would rather have peace. 11 If they agree to make peace with you and open their gates to you, all the people who are found there will be made to work for you and serve you. 12 But if they do not make peace with you and fight against you, you must take the city in battle. 13 When the Lord your God gives the city to you, you must kill all the men in it with the sword. 14 Take for yourselves what is left, the women, the children, all the animals, and all that is in the city. Use what is left of those who fought against you, which the Lord your God has given you. 15 Do this to all the cities that are very far from you and are not of the cities of the nations that are near. 16 But in the cities of these nations that the Lord your God is giving you for your own, do not leave alive anything that breathes. 17 Destroy everything and everyone in them, the Hittite, the Amorite, the Canaanite, the Perizzite, the Hivite and the Jebusite, as the Lord your God has told you. 18 Then they will not teach you to do all the hated and sinful things they have done for their gods, and make you sin against the Lord your God.

19 "When you stay around a city a long time, to make war against it and take it, do not destroy its trees with the ax. You may eat from them but do not cut them down. For are trees of the field men that they should be killed? 20 You may destroy and cut down only the trees you know are not fruit trees. Then you may build walls with the trees to help you fight against the city that makes war with you, until it falls.

About Killing Someone

21 "If a person has been killed and is found lying in a field in the land the Lord your God is giving you for your own and it is not known who killed him,

2 then your leaders and judges will go out and see how far it is to the cities that are around the dead man. 3 The leaders of the city that is nearest to the dead man will take a young cow from the cattle. The cow must never have been worked or pulled a plow. 4 The leaders of that city will bring the young cow down to a valley with flowing water, which has not been plowed or planted. They will break the cow's neck there in the valley. 5 Then the religious leaders, the sons of Levi, will come near for the Lord your God has chosen them to serve Him and to bring good in the name of the Lord. Every question about what is right and every fight will be decided upon by them. 6 All the leaders of that city nearest to the dead man will wash their hands over the young cow whose neck was broken in the valley. 7 Then they will say, 'Our hands have not killed him. Our eyes have not seen it. 8 O Lord, forgive Your people Israel whom You have set free. Do not put the guilt of killing a man who did no wrong on Your people Israel.' And they will be forgiven from the guilt of the man's death. 9 So you must take away the guilt of taking the life of a good man by doing what is right in the eyes of the Lord.

Marrying a Woman Taken in Battle

10 "When you go out to battle against those who hate you, and the Lord your God gives them to you, and you make them go with you, 11 and you see a beautiful woman and have a desire for her as a wife, 12 bring her home to your house. There she will cut off all the hair from her head and cut her nails. 13 She will change the clothes she wore when you took her away, and stay in your house. She will have sorrow for her father and mother for one month. After that you may go in to her and be her husband and she will be your wife. 14 If you are not pleased with her, you should let her go wherever she wants. But do not sell her for money or act as if she were a servant because you have put her to shame.

15 "If a man has two wives, one loved and the other not loved, and both the loved and the one not loved have borne him sons, and if the first-born son belongs to the wife who is not loved, 16 on the day when the man divides what he has for his sons, he cannot make the first-born of his loved wife the first-born before the son of the wife who is not loved, who is the first-born. 17 He must respect the first-born, the

son of the wife who is not loved, by giving him twice the share of all he has. He is the beginning of his strength and the right of the first-born belongs to him.

18 "If a man has a strong-willed son who goes against him and does not obey his father or mother and when they punish him he will not even listen to them, 19 then his father and mother will take hold of him and bring him to the leaders of his city at the gate of his city. 20 They will say to the leaders of his city, 'This son of ours is strong-willed and goes against us. He will not obey us. He eats and drinks too much.' 21 Then all the men of his city will kill him with stones. You must get rid of the sin from among you. All Israel will hear about it and be afraid.

22 "If a man has sinned and should be put to death and he is put to death and you hang him on a tree, 23 his body must not hang all night on the tree. You should be sure to bury him on the same day (for he who hangs is cursed by God). So do not make your land unclean which the Lord your God is giving you.

22 "If you see your brother's bull or sheep walking away, do not pretend that you do not see them. Be sure to return them to your brother. 2 If your brother is not home, or if you do not know who he is, then bring the animal to your house. Keep it there until your brother looks for it. Then return it to him. 3 Do the same with his donkey, or his coat, or anything lost by your brother. If you find what he has lost, you must help him. 4 If you see your brother's donkey or his ox fallen down by the road, do not pretend that you do not see them. Be sure to help him lift them up again.

5 "A woman must not wear men's clothing. And a man must not put on women's clothing. For the Lord your God hates whoever does these things.

6 "You might find a bird's nest by the road, in a tree or on the ground, with young ones or eggs. If you find the mother sitting on the young or on the eggs, do not take the mother with the young. 7 Be sure to let the mother go. But you may take the young for yourself. Then it will go well with you, and you will live long.

8 "When you build a new house, you should put a short wall around your roof. Then no one will fall from it and bring the guilt of blood upon your house.

9 "Do not plant among your vines another kind of seed. All that grows from what you have planted will be unclean. 10 Do not plow with a bull and a donkey together. 11 Do not wear clothing made of both wool and linen together.

12 "Make tassels to put on the four corners of the clothing you use to cover yourself.

Law of Those Who Are Not Faithful in Marriage

13 "If a man takes a wife and goes in to her and decides he does not like her, 14 and says that she did sinful acts and puts her to shame before others and says, 'I took this woman, but when I came near her, I found that she had been with another man,' 15 then the girl's father and mother should bring what is needed to prove she has not been with another man to the leaders of the city at the gate. 16 The girl's father will say to the leaders, 'I gave my daughter to this man for a wife. But he turned against her. 17 He said she has done sinful acts, saying, "I found that your daughter has been with another man." But I brought what will prove that my daughter has not been with another man.' And they will spread the clothing in front of the leaders of the city. 18 Then the leaders of that city will take the man and punish him. 19 They will make him pay a hundred pieces of silver and give it to the girl's father, because he has put to shame the name of an Israelite girl who has not had a man. She will still be his wife. He cannot divorce her as long as he lives. 20 But if it is true that the girl was found to have had another man, 21 then they will bring the girl to the door of her father's house. There the men of her city will kill her with stones, because she has done a foolish act in Israel by acting in her father's house like a woman who sells the use of her body. So you will get rid of the sin from among you.

22 "If a man is found lying with a married woman, then both of them must die, the man who lay with the woman, and the woman. So you will get rid of the sin from Israel.

23 "If a girl who has never had a man is promised in marriage to a man, another man might find her in the city and lie with her. 24 Then you must bring them both to the gate of that city and kill them with stones. Put the girl to death because she did not cry for help in the city, and the man because he has sinned against his neighbor's wife. So you will get rid of the sin from

among you. 25 But if the man finds a girl in the field who is promised in marriage, and makes her lie with him, then only the man who lies with her will die. 26 Do nothing to the girl. There is no sin in the girl bad enough for her to be put to death. It is as if a man goes against his neighbor and kills him. 27 When he found her in the field, the girl promised in marriage cried out. But there was no one to save her.

28 "If a man finds a girl who has never had a man and is not promised in marriage, and takes her and lies with her, and they are found, 29 then the man who lay with her must give fifty pieces of silver to the girl's father. And she will become his wife, because he has put her to shame. He cannot divorce her as long as he lives.

30 "A man must not take his father's wife. He must not take the clothes off the woman who belongs to his father.

Those Who Cannot Go into the Meeting of the Lord

23 "No man who has his sex part crushed or cut off will go into the meeting of the Lord. 2 No one who was born to parents who were not married will go into the meeting of the Lord. And none of his children will go into the meeting of the Lord, even to the children's children of ten families in the future. 3 No Ammonite or Moabite will go into the meeting of the Lord. None of their children will go into the meeting of the Lord, even to the children's children of ten families of the future, 4 because they did not meet you with food and water on your way from Egypt, and they paid Balaam the son of Beor from Pethor of Mesopotamia to curse you. 5 But the Lord your God would not listen to Balaam. Instead He changed the curse into good for you, because the Lord your God loves you. 6 Do nothing for their peace or their well-being all your days.

7 "Do not hate an Edomite, for he is your brother. Do not hate an Egyptian. For you were a stranger in his land. 8 Their great-grandchildren may go into the meeting of the Lord.

The Camp Is to Be Clean

9 "When you go as an army against those who hate you, keep yourself away from every sinful thing. 10 If there is any man among you who is unclean because he had a flow from his body during the night, he must go away from the tents. He must not come among the tents. 11 When evening comes he must wash his body with water. And when the sun goes down he may return to the tents.

12 "You should have a place to go away from the tents. 13 You should have a tool there to dig with. Use it to dig a hole when you sit down outside. Then use it to cover the waste from your body. 14 Because the Lord your God walks among your tents to set you free and make you win the battle against those who hate you, the place where your tents are must be holy. He must not see anything among you that is unclean and turn away from you.

Different Laws

15 "If a servant runs away from his owner and comes to you, do not return him to his owner. 16 Let him stay with you, in the place he chooses in one of your towns, where it pleases him. Do not make it hard for him.

17 "No daughter of Israel is to sell the use of her body in worship to a strange god. And no son of Israel is to sell the use of his body for a strange god. 18 You must not bring the pay of a woman who sells the use of her body or of a man who does sex sins into the house of the Lord your God for any promised gift. For the Lord your God hates both of these. 19 Do not make your brothers pay you for the use of money, food, or anything you might give them to use. 20 You may make a stranger pay you for the use of money, but not your brother. So the Lord your God may bring good to you in all you do in the land you are going into to have for your own.

21 "When you make a promise to the Lord your God, do not be slow to pay it. It would be sin in you, for the Lord your God will be sure to ask you for it. 22 But if you do not make a promise, it would not be sin in you. 23 Be careful to do what you say you are going to do. Keep the promise you have made to the Lord your God because you want to.

24 "When you go into your neighbor's grape-field, you may eat grapes until you are full. But do not put any in your basket. 25 When you go into your neighbor's grain-field, you may pick the heads with your hand. But do not cut down any of your neighbor's standing grain.

24 "When a man takes a wife and marries her, and he does not like her because he finds something bad in her, he will write her a paper of divorce and give it to her and send her away from his house. ² When she leaves his house, she may go and become another man's wife. ³ If the second husband turns against her and gives her a paper of divorce and sends her out of his house, or if the second husband dies who took her for his wife, ⁴ then her first husband who sent her away is not allowed to take her for his wife again, because she has become unclean. It is a hated thing to the Lord and you must not bring sin on the land the Lord your God is giving you.

⁵ "When a man takes a new wife, he must not go with the army or be given any other work. He should be free to be at home one year to make the wife he has taken happy.

⁶ "No one should take a man's stones that he uses to crush grain as a promise to pay what he owes, for he would be taking away a man's living.

⁷ "If a man is found stealing one of his brothers of the sons of Israel, and makes it hard for him, or sells him, then that robber must die. You must get rid of the sin from among you.

⁸ "When there is a very bad skin disease, be careful to do all the Levite religious leaders tell you to do. Be careful to do what I have told them. ⁹ Remember what the Lord your God did to Miriam on your way out of Egypt.

¹⁰ "When you let your neighbor use anything of yours, do not go into his house to take what he would give you to make his promise sure. ¹¹ Stay outside. The man who is using something of yours will bring the object out to you. ¹² If he is a poor man, do not keep what he gives you through the night. ¹³ Return his coat to him when the sun goes down so he may sleep in it and be thankful for you. You will be doing what is right before the Lord your God.

¹⁴ "Do not make it hard for a paid servant who is poor and in need, if he is one of your brothers or one of the strangers who is living in one of your towns. ¹⁵ Give him his pay on the day he earns it before the sun goes down. He is poor and he needs it. Then he will not cry to the Lord against you and you would be guilty of sin.

¹⁶ "Fathers are not to be put to death for their children. Children are not to be put to death for their fathers. Each man will be put to death for his own sin.

¹⁷ "Do what is fair for a stranger or a child whose parents are dead. Do not take the clothing of a woman whose husband has died to make sure she will pay what she owes. ¹⁸ Remember that you were servants in Egypt, and that the Lord your God set you free. So I am telling you to do this.

¹⁹ "When you gather the grain in your field and have forgotten some of it, do not return to the field to get it. Leave it for the stranger, the child whose parents have died, and the woman whose husband has died. Then the Lord your God will bring good to you in all the work of your hands. ²⁰ When you beat your olive trees, do not beat the branches a second time. Leave the fruit for the stranger, the child whose parents have died, and the woman whose husband has died. ²¹ When you gather the grapes from your vines, do not gather a second time. Leave them for the stranger, the child whose parents have died, and the woman whose husband has died. ²² Remember that you were servants in the land of Egypt. Because of this, I am telling you to do this.

25 "Two men might argue and go to court. The judges will decide between them, saying that the right man is not guilty and that the sinful man is guilty. ² If the sinful man should be beaten, the leader will make him lie down and be beaten in front of him. The number of times he is beaten will be decided upon by how bad his sin is. ³ The number may be as much as forty, but no more. If he is beaten more than this, your brother would be put to much shame in your eyes.

⁴ "When the bull is made to walk on the grain to break it open, do not stop him from eating some.

⁵ "When brothers live together and one of them dies and has no son, the dead man's wife must not be married outside the family to a strange man. The husband's brother will take her as his wife and do what he should for her as a brother-in-law. ⁶ The first son born to her will take the name of the dead brother so his name will not be forgotten in Israel. ⁷ But the man might not want to take his brother's wife. Then his brother's wife should go to the leaders at the gate and say, 'My husband's brother will not make his brother's name to be remembered in Israel. He is not willing to do the duty of a brother-in-law to me.' ⁸ Then the leaders of his city will call him and speak to him. If he still says, 'I do not want to take her,' ⁹ then his brother's wife will come to him in front of the leaders. She will pull his shoe off his foot and spit in his face. And she will say, 'This is what is done to the man who will not

build up his brother's house.' 10 In Israel his name will be called, 'The house of him whose shoe is pulled off.'

11 "If two men are fighting together and the wife of one comes to save her husband from the one who is hitting him and if she puts out her hand and takes hold of his sex part, 12 you must cut off her hand. Do not show pity.

13 "You must not have two different weights in your bag, one large and one small. 14 You must not have in your house different ways of showing how big or small something is. 15 You must have a full and fair weight. You must have a fair way to show how big something is. Then you will live long in the land the Lord your God gives you. 16 For the Lord hates everyone who does such things, who lies and is not fair.

17 "Remember what Amalek did to you on your way out of Egypt. 18 He met you on the way when you were weak and tired. And he fought with those who were behind. He did not fear God. 19 When the Lord your God gives you rest from all those around you who hate you, in the land the Lord your God gives you for your own, you must forget all about Amalek, so no one under heaven will remember him. Do not forget to do this.

Gifts at Gathering Time

26 "When you go into the land the Lord your God gives you, it will be yours and you will live in it. 2 You must take some of the first of all the fruit of the ground, which you gather from the land the Lord your God gives you, and put it in a basket and go to the place where the Lord your God chooses to have His name. 3 Go to the religious leader who is working at that time, and say to him, 'I make known this day to the Lord my God that I have come into the land which the Lord promised to our fathers to give us.' 4 Then the religious leader will take the basket from your hand and set it down in front of the altar of the Lord your God. 5 And you will say before the Lord your God, 'My father was a traveling Aramean. He went to Egypt, few in number, and stayed there. But there he became a nation, great, powerful, and with many people. 6 The Egyptians made it hard for us. They brought us much trouble and made us work very hard. 7 Then we cried to the Lord, the God of our fathers. The Lord heard our voice and saw our troubles, our work, and

how hard our lives were. 8 And the Lord brought us out of Egypt with a strong hand and a long arm, causing much fear by doing powerful works. 9 He has brought us to this place. He has given us this land, a land flowing with milk and honey. 10 Now see, I have brought the first of the fruit of the ground that You have given me, O Lord.' Then you will set it down before the Lord your God, and worship Him. 11 You and the Levite and the stranger who is among you will be full of joy because of all the good the Lord your God has given you and those of your house.

12 "When you have finished paying all the tenth of the food you received in the third year, the year of giving a tenth, then give it to the Levite, the stranger, the child whose parents have died, and the woman whose husband has died. So they may eat it in your towns and be filled. 13 Then say before the Lord your God, 'I have taken the share for holy use from my house. I have given it to the Levite, the stranger, the child whose parents have died, and the woman whose husband has died. I have done this because of all Your Laws which You have told me to do. I have not sinned or forgotten any of Your Laws. 14 I have not eaten of it while in sorrow, or taken any of it while I was unclean, or given any of it to the dead. I have listened to the voice of the Lord my God, and have done all You have told me to do. 15 Look down from Your holy place in heaven and bring good to Your people Israel. Bring good to the ground You have given us, a land flowing with milk and honey, as You promised our fathers.'

The Lord's Special People

16 "This day the Lord your God tells you to obey these Laws. Be careful to obey them with all your heart and with all your soul. 17 Today you have said that the Lord is your God, and that you will walk in His ways, keep all His Laws, and listen to His voice. 18 And the Lord today has made it known that you are His own people, as He promised you, and that you should keep all His Laws. 19 He has told you that He will set you high above all the nations He has made. You will be praised, remembered, and honored. You will be a holy nation to the Lord your God, as He has said."

The Law Written on Stones

27 Then Moses and the leaders of Israel said to the people, "Keep all the Laws which I tell you today. 2 On the day you cross the Jordan to the land the Lord your God gives you, set up large stones and cover them with plaster. 3 Write on them all the words of this Law when you cross the river and go into the land the Lord your God gives you. It is a land flowing with milk and honey, as the Lord, the God of your fathers, promised you. 4 When you cross the Jordan, set up these stones on Mount Ebal and cover them with plaster, as I tell you today. 5 Build an altar of stones there to the Lord your God. Do not work on them with an iron tool. 6 And build the altar of the Lord your God with stones that are not cut. Then give a burnt gift on it to the Lord your God. 7 Give peace gifts and eat there. And be full of joy before the Lord your God. 8 Write all the words of this Law on the stones. Make it easy to read."

What Happens to Those Who Do Not Obey

9 Then Moses and the Levite religious leaders said to all Israel, "Be quiet and listen, O Israel! This day you have become the people of the Lord your God. 10 So obey the Lord your God. Keep all of His Laws which I tell you today."

11 Moses told the people that same day, 12 "Simeon, Levi, Judah, Issachar, Joseph and Benjamin will stand on Mount Gerizim when you cross the Jordan. They will pray that good will come to the people. 13 And Reuben, Gad, Asher, Zebulun, Dan and Naphtali will stand on Mount Ebal to tell of the curses. 14 The Levites will say with a loud voice to all the people of Israel:

15 'Cursed is every man who makes a god or something to look like a god, the work of the hands of the able workman, and sets it up in secret. It is hated by the Lord.' Then all the people will answer, 'Let it be so.'

16 'Cursed is the one who puts his father or mother to shame.' And all the people will say, 'Let it be so.'

17 'Cursed is the man who moves his neighbor's land-mark.' And all the people will say, 'Let it be so.'

18 'Cursed is the one who leads a blind person on the road the wrong way.' Then all the people will say, 'Let it be so.'

19 'Cursed is the one who is not fair to a stranger, a child whose parents have died, and the woman whose husband has died.' And all the people will say, 'Let it be so.'

20 'Cursed is the man who lies with his father's wife because he has taken off the clothes of her who belongs to his father.' And all the people will say, 'Let it be so.'

21 'Cursed is the man who lies with any animal.' And all the people will say, 'Let it be so.'

22 'Cursed is the man who lies with his sister, the daughter of his father or mother.' Then all the people will say, 'Let it be so.'

23 'Cursed is the man who lies with his mother-in-law.' And all the people will say, 'Let it be so.'

24 'Cursed is the one who hits his neighbor in secret.' And all the people will say, 'Let it be so.'

25 'Cursed is the one who receives pay to kill a person who is not guilty.' Then all the people will say, 'Let it be so.'

26 'Cursed is the one who does not obey the words of this Law.' And all the people will say, 'Let it be so.'

28 "Be faithful in obeying the Lord your God. Be careful to keep all His Laws which I tell you today. And the Lord your God will set you high above all the nations of the earth. 2 All these good things will come upon you if you will obey the Lord your God. 3 Good will come to you in the city, and good will come to you in the country. 4 Good will come to your children, and the fruit of your ground, and the young of your animals. Your cattle and flock will have many young ones. 5 Good will come to your basket and your bread pan. 6 Good will come to you when you come in, and when you go out.

7 "The Lord will cause you to win the battles against those who fight against you. They will come against you one way, and run away from you seven ways. 8 The Lord will send good upon you in your store-houses and in all your work. He will bring good to you in the land the Lord your God gives you. 9 The Lord will make you a holy nation to Himself, as He promised you. But you must keep the Laws of the Lord your God and walk in His ways. 10 Then all the nations of the earth will see that you are called by the name of the Lord and they will be afraid of you. 11 The Lord will give much to you. He will give you many children, and many young ones among your animals, and much food from the ground, in the land the Lord promised to your fathers to give you. 12 The Lord will open for you His good store-house, the heavens. He will give rain to your land at the right time. He will bring good to all the work you do. You will give to many nations. But you will not use anything that belongs to them. 13 The Lord will make

you the head and not the tail. If you listen to the Laws of the Lord your God which I tell you today and be careful to obey them, you will only be above and not below. 14 Do not turn aside from any of the words I tell you today, to the right or to the left. Do not follow other gods and work for them.

15 "If you will not obey the Lord your God or be careful to do all His Laws which I tell you today, all these curses will come upon you. 16 You will be cursed in the city, and in the country. 17 Your basket and your bread pan will be cursed. 18 Your children will be cursed, and the fruit of your ground, and the young of your cattle and flock. 19 You will be cursed when you come in and when you go out.

20 "The Lord will send upon you curses, trouble and sharp words in all you try to do, until you are destroyed. You will be quick to die, because of the sinful things you do, and because you have turned away from Me. 21 The Lord will make disease to be with you until He has destroyed you from the land you are going in to take. 22 The Lord will punish you with a wasting disease, a hot sickness, growing pain, heat like fire, the sword, and diseases that destroy your food. They will follow you until you die. 23 The heavens above your head will be brass. And the earth under you will be iron. 24 The Lord will change the rain of your land into dust. It will come down on you until you are destroyed. 25 The Lord will cause you to lose the battle against those who hate you. You will go one way against them, but run seven ways away from them. You will fill all the nations of the earth with fear. 26 Your dead bodies will be food for all the birds of the sky and the wild animals of the earth. There will be no one to make them afraid and to send them away.

27 "The Lord will punish you with the sores of Egypt, growing sores, and skin diseases, that will not be healed. 28 The Lord will punish you by making you crazy, and blind, and troubled in your mind. 29 You will have to feel for your way at noon, as the blind man feels his way in darkness. And your way will not go well. It will be made hard for you, and you will always be robbed. There will be no one to save you. 30 You will marry a wife. But another man will lie with her. You will build a house. But you will not live in it. You will plant vines. But you will not eat the fruit. 31 Your bull will be killed in front of you. But you will not eat of it. Your donkey will be taken

from you, and will not be returned. Your sheep will be given to those who hate you. No one will help you. 32 Your sons and daughters will be given to another nation. Your eyes will watch for them always and you will have much desire for them. But there will be nothing you can do. 33 A nation you have not known will eat the food of your field and of your work. You will suffer under the power of others always. 34 You will be driven crazy by what you see. 35 The Lord will make sores on your knees and legs that you cannot heal, from the bottom of your foot to the top of your head. 36 The Lord will bring you and your chosen king to a nation that you and your fathers have not known. There you will work for other gods, of wood and stone. 37 You will become a people who are hated, who are made fun of, and a shame among the people where the Lord will send you.

38 "You will sow much seed in the field, but gather little, for the locust will eat it. 39 You will plant and take care of vines, but you will not drink the wine or gather the grapes, for worms will eat them. 40 You will have olive trees everywhere. But you will not pour the oil upon yourself, for your olives will fall off. 41 You will have sons and daughters, but you will not keep them, for they will be taken away. 42 The locust will own all your trees and the food of your field. 43 The stranger among you will rise above you higher and higher, but you will become less and less. 44 He will give to you. But you will not give to him. He will be the head and you will be the tail. 45 All these curses will come upon you. They will follow you and come upon you until you are destroyed, because you would not obey the Lord your God by keeping all the Laws He gave you. 46 They will be something special to see, and a powerful work upon you and your children forever. 47 Because you did not serve the Lord your God with joy and a glad heart because of all He has given you, 48 you will serve those who hate you, whom the Lord will send against you. You will be hungry, thirsty, without clothing, and needing all things. He will put a heavy load on your neck until He has destroyed you.

49 "The Lord will bring a nation against you from far away, from the end of the earth, as fast as an eagle flies. It will be a nation whose language you will not understand, 50 a nation that shows a hard face. It will have no respect for the old, or show favor to the young. 51 It will eat the

young ones of your cattle and the food of your field until you are destroyed. It will leave you no grain, new wine, oil, or the young of your cattle or flock, until it has caused you to die. [52] Your towns will be taken over by its armies until your high strong walls that you have trusted in come down everywhere in your land. Its armies will take over all your towns everywhere in the land the Lord your God has given you. [53] During this time and because of the trouble caused by those who hate you, you will eat your own children, the flesh of your sons and daughters whom the Lord your God has given you. [54] The most gentle man among you will be against his brother, the wife he loves, and the children he still has. [55] He will not give them any of the flesh of his children whom he is eating, because it is all he has left for himself. This is how bad the trouble will be that those who hate you will bring to all your towns. [56] The most gentle woman among you may be careful not to set the bottom of her foot on the ground. But she will be hard to the husband she loves, to her son and daughter, [57] to the afterbirth which comes out of her body, and to the children who are born from her. She will eat them in secret because she has nothing else. This is how bad the trouble will be that those who hate you will bring to all your towns.

[58] "If you are not careful to obey all the words of the Law which are written in this book, to fear this honored name of the Lord your God, [59] then the Lord will bring bad diseases on you and your children, hard and lasting diseases and sicknesses. [60] He will bring all the diseases upon you that you were afraid of in Egypt. And they will stay with you. [61] The Lord will bring upon you every sickness and every trouble which is not written in the book of this Law also, until you are destroyed. [62] You will have been as many as the stars of heaven but there will be few of you left, because you did not obey the Lord your God. [63] As the Lord was happy with you and caused good to come to you and you were many, He will be happy to bring trouble upon you and destroy you. And you will be taken from the land you are going in to take. [64] The Lord will spread you out among all nations, from one end of the earth to the other. There you will serve other gods, of wood and stone, which you and your fathers have not known. [65] You will find no rest among those nations. There will

be no place of rest for the bottom of your foot. But there the Lord will give you fear in your heart, eyes that become weak, and sorrow in your soul. [66] Your life will be full of doubts. You will be afraid night and day. And you will not be sure of anything in your life. [67] In the morning you will say, 'If it were only evening!' In the evening you will say, 'If it were only morning!' because of the fear of your heart, and the things your eyes see. [68] The Lord will bring you back to Egypt in ships, in the way I said, 'You will never see it again.' There you will try to sell yourselves as men and women servants to those who hate you. But no one will buy you."

The Agreement in Moab

29 These are the words of the agreement the Lord told Moses to make with the people of Israel in the land of Moab, as well as the agreement He had made with them at Mount Sinai.

[2] Moses called all Israel and said to them, "You have seen all the Lord did in front of you in the land of Egypt to Pharaoh and all his servants and all his land. [3] You have seen great tests and powerful works. [4] Yet to this day the Lord has not given you a heart to know, or eyes to see, or ears to hear. [5] I have led you forty years in the desert. Your clothes did not wear out. And your shoes did not wear out on your feet. [6] You did not eat bread, or drink wine or strong drink, so you might know that I am the Lord your God. [7] When you came to this place, Sihon the king of Heshbon and Og the king of Bashan came to meet us to fight. But we won the fight [8] We took their land and gave it as a gift to the Reubenites, the Gadites, and the half-family group of Manasseh. [9] So be careful to keep the words of this agreement and obey them so all that you do will go well.

[10] "Today you all stand before the Lord your God, you, your rulers, your families, your leaders, all the men of Israel, [11] your children, your wives, the stranger who is among your tents, from the one who cuts your wood to the one who gets your water. [12] You are here to take part in the agreement with the Lord your God, and in His promise which the Lord your God is making with you today. [13] So today He will make you His people. He will be your God, just as He told you and as He promised your fathers, Abraham, Isaac and Jacob.

[14] "I am not making this agreement and this promise with you alone. [15] I am

making them with those who stand here with us today before the Lord our God, and with those who are not here with us today. 16 You know how we lived in the land of Egypt, and how we passed through the land of the nations on our way here. 17 You have seen their sinful things and their gods of wood, stone, silver and gold, which they had with them. 18 Be careful not to have any man or woman or family or group among you whose heart turns away from the Lord our God today to go and worship the gods of those nations. Do not let there be a root among you giving poison fruit and bad-tasting plants. 19 When one hears the words of this curse, he will say in his pride, 'I have peace even though I am strong-willed in my heart.' This will destroy the land that is watered along with the dry land. 20 The Lord will never be willing to forgive him. But the Lord will be jealous and His anger will burn against that man. Every curse written in this book will be upon him. And the Lord will take out his name from under heaven. 21 The Lord will set him apart for trouble from all the families of Israel, with all the curses of the agreement which are written in this book of the Law.

22 "The children-to-come, your sons who grow up after you, and the stranger who comes from a land far away, will see the troubles and diseases the Lord has sent upon the land. And they will say, 23 'The whole land is sulphur and salt, a burning waste, not planted and not giving any plants, and no grass grows in it. It is like Sodom and Gomorrah, Admah and Zeboiim, which the Lord destroyed in His anger.' 24 All the nations will say, 'Why has the Lord done this to this land? Why was He so angry?' 25 Then men will say, 'It is because they did not keep the agreement of the Lord, the God of their fathers, which He made with them when He brought them out of the land of Egypt. 26 They went and served other gods and worshiped them, gods they had not known and whom He had not given to them. 27 So the anger of the Lord burned against that land. Every curse was brought upon it that is written in this book. 28 The Lord drove them from their land in much anger. And He sent them into another land, as it is today.'

29 "The secret things belong to the Lord our God. But the things that are made known belong to us and to our children forever, so we may obey all the words of this Law.

Good Comes to Those Who Return to the Lord

30 "When all these things have come upon you, the good things and the curses which I have told you about, you will remember them in all the nations where the Lord your God has sent you. 2 When you and your children return to the Lord your God and obey Him with all your heart and soul by all I have told you today, 3 then the Lord your God will have you return from where you were held. He will have loving-pity for you. He will gather you again from all the nations where the Lord your God has sent you. 4 Even if you are driven to the ends of the earth, the Lord your God will gather you and bring you back. 5 The Lord your God will bring you into the land your fathers lived in and it will be yours. He will bring good to you and make you more in number than your fathers. 6 The Lord your God will take away the sin from your heart and from the heart of your children. You will love the Lord your God with all your heart and with all your soul, so you may live. 7 Then the Lord your God will send all these curses upon those who hate you and upon those who made it hard for you. 8 You will obey the Lord again, and keep all His Laws which I tell you today. 9 And the Lord your God will bring much good upon all the work you do, and upon your children, and the young of your cattle, and the food of your field. For the Lord will again be happy to bring good to you, just as He was happy with your fathers. 10 But you must obey the Lord your God to keep His Laws which are written in this book of the Law. You must turn to the Lord your God with all your heart and soul.

Life or Death

11 "For this Law I give you today is not too hard for you, or too far from you. 12 It is not in heaven. You do not need to say, 'Who will go up to heaven for us and bring it down to make us hear it, so we may obey it?' 13 It is not farther than the sea. You do not need to say, 'Who will cross the sea for us and bring it to us to make us hear it, so we may obey it?' 14 But the Word is very near you, in your mouth and in your heart, so that you may obey it.

15 "See, I have put in front of you today life and what is good, and death and what is bad. 16 I tell you today to love the Lord your God. Walk in His ways. Keep all His Laws and all that He has decided. Then

you will live and become many. And the Lord your God will bring good to you in the land you are going in to take. ¹⁷ But if your heart turns away and you will not obey, but leave to worship other gods and serve them, ¹⁸ I tell you today that you will die for sure. You will not live long in that land across the Jordan which you are about to take for your own. ¹⁹ I call heaven and earth to speak against you today. I have put in front of you life and death, the good and the curse. So choose life so you and your children after you may live. ²⁰ Love the Lord your God and obey His voice. Hold on to Him. For He is your life, and by Him your days will be long. You will be allowed to live in the land the Lord promised to give to your fathers, Abraham, Isaac and Jacob."

Joshua Is the New Leader

31 Then Moses spoke these words to all Israel. ² He said to them, "I am 120 years old today. I am no longer able to come and go. And the Lord has told me, 'You will not cross this Jordan.' ³ The Lord your God Himself will cross before you. He will destroy these nations in front of you. And you will take their place. Joshua will cross before you also, as the Lord has said. ⁴ The Lord will do the same to them that He did to Sihon and Og, the kings of the Amorites, and to their land when He destroyed them. ⁵ The Lord will give them to you. Then you will do to them as I have told you. ⁶ Be strong and have strength of heart. Do not be afraid or shake with fear because of them. For the Lord your God is the One Who goes with you. He will be faithful to you. He will not leave you alone."

⁷ Then Moses called Joshua and said to him in front of all Israel, "Be strong and have strength of heart. For you will go with this people into the land the Lord has promised to their fathers to give them. And you will bring them in to take it. ⁸ The Lord is the One Who goes before you. He will be with you. He will be faithful to you and will not leave you alone. Do not be afraid or troubled."

Reading of the Law Every Seven Years

⁹ So Moses wrote this Law and gave it to the religious leaders, the sons of Levi who carried the special box of the Law of the Lord, and to all the leaders of Israel. ¹⁰ Then Moses told them, "At the end of every seven years, at the time when money owed is done away with at the Special Supper of Tents, ¹¹ when all Israel comes to stand before the Lord your God at the place He will choose, you must read this Law so all Israel will hear it. ¹² Gather together the people in your town, the men and the women, the children, and the stranger. So they may hear and learn and fear the Lord your God. Be careful to obey all the words of this Law. ¹³ Then their children, who have not known it, will hear and learn to fear the Lord your God, as long as you live in the land you are crossing the Jordan to take."

The Lord's Last Words to Moses

¹⁴ The Lord said to Moses, "See, the time for you to die is near. Call Joshua, and go to the meeting tent, so I may tell him what to do." So Moses and Joshua went to the meeting tent. ¹⁵ The Lord showed Himself in a pillar of cloud which stayed at the door of the tent. ¹⁶ And the Lord said to Moses, "See, you will soon die and be with your fathers. Then these people will soon act like a woman who sells the use of her body. They will follow the strange gods of the land where they are going. They will turn away from Me and break My agreement which I have made with them. ¹⁷ Then My anger will burn against them. I will leave them alone and hide My face from them and they will be destroyed. Many hard things and big troubles will come upon them. So they will say in that day, 'Have not these troubles come upon us because our God is not with us?' ¹⁸ But I will hide My face in that day because of all the sinful things they will do, for they will turn to other gods and serve them. ¹⁹ So write this song for yourselves. Teach it to the people of Israel. Put it on their lips, so this song may speak for Me against all the people of Israel. ²⁰ For when I bring them into the land flowing with milk and honey, which I promised to their fathers, and they eat and are filled and have become rich, they will turn to other gods and serve them. They will turn against Me and break My agreement. ²¹ When many hard things and big troubles come upon them, this song will speak for Me against them. It will not be forgotten from the lips of their children and their children's children. I know the plans they are making today, before I have brought them into the land I promised them." ²² So Moses wrote this song the same day, and taught it to the people of Israel.

²³ Then the Lord said to Joshua the

son of Nun, "Be strong and have strength of heart. For you will bring the people of Israel into the land I promised them. And I will be with you."

24 Moses wrote the words of this Law in a book from beginning to the end. 25 Then Moses said to the Levites who carried the special box of the Law of the Lord, 26 "Take this box of the Law and put it beside the special box of the Law of the Lord your God. It will be there to speak against you. 27 For I know how strong your will is and that you do not want to obey. See, while I am still alive with you today, you have gone against the Lord. How much worse it will be after my death! 28 Gather together and bring to me all the leaders and heads of your families. I will speak these words to them and call heaven and earth to speak against them. 29 For I know that after my death you will sin and turn from the way I have told you. Much trouble will come to you in the days to come. For you will do what is sinful in the eyes of the Lord. You will make Him angry through the work of your hands."

30 Then Moses spoke all the words of this song to all the people of Israel.

The Song of Moses

32 "Listen, O heavens, and let me speak. Let the earth hear the words of my mouth. 2 Let my teaching fall as the rain, and my voice like the water on the grass in the early morning, like rain upon the new grass, and rain upon the plant. 3 For I will make known the name of the Lord. I will tell of the greatness of God! 4 The Rock! His work is perfect. All His ways are right and fair. A God Who is faithful and without sin, right and good is He. 5 They have acted in sin toward Him, but they are not His children, because the mark of sin is on them. They are a bad and sinful people. 6 Is this how you pay the Lord, you foolish people who are not wise? Is He not your Father Who has bought you? He has made you and given you your place. 7 Remember the days long ago. Think of the years of all people. Ask your father and he will show you. Ask your leaders. They will tell you. 8 When the Most High divided up the world among the nations, he divided the children of men. He set the place where each nation was to live by the number of the sons of Israel. 9 For the Lord's share is His people. He chose the people of Jacob for Himself. 10 He found him in a desert land, in the empty waste of a desert. He

came around him and cared for him. He kept him as He would His own eye. 11 Like an eagle that shakes its nest, that flies over its young, He spread His wings and caught them. He carried them on His wings. 12 The Lord alone led him. There was no strange god with him. 13 He made him sit on the high places of the earth. And he ate the food of the field. He made him eat honey from the rock, oil out of hard rock, 14 milk from cows and milk from the flock, the fat of lambs, rams of Bashan, goats, and the best of the grain. And you drank wine of the blood of grapes.

15 "But Jeshurun grew fat and would not obey. You became fat and full of food. Then he turned away from God Who made him. He hated the Rock of His saving power. 16 They made Him jealous with strange gods. They made Him angry with hated things. 17 They gave gifts to demons who were not God, to gods they have not known, new gods who came later, whom your fathers did not fear. 18 You did not think of the Rock Who gave you birth. You forgot the God Who gave you birth.

19 "The Lord saw this, and hated them. His sons and daughters made Him angry. 20 Then He said, 'I will hide My face from them. I will see what their end will be. For they are a sinful people, children who are not faithful. 21 They have made Me jealous with what is not God. They have made Me angry with their false gods. So I will make them jealous with those who are not a people. I will make them angry with a foolish nation. 22 For a fire is started by My anger. It burns to the very bottom of the place of the dead. It burns up the earth and all that grows on the earth. It burns the base of the mountains.

23 'I will send much trouble upon them. I will use My arrows against them. 24 They will be wasted with hunger. They will be destroyed by burning heat and disease. I will send the teeth of wild animals against them, with the poison of things moving in the dust. 25 The sword will bring death in the street, and bring fear in the homes. It will destroy both young man and young woman, the baby and the man with white hair. 26 I would have said, "I will cut them to pieces. I will make all people forget about them." 27 But I was afraid that those who hate them would fight in anger against them and would not understand. They would say, "We have won with our own strength. The Lord has not done this." '

28 "For they are a nation without wise teaching. There is no understanding in them. 29 If they were wise, they would understand this. They would know their future! 30 How could one run after a thousand? How could two make ten thousand run away, unless their Rock had sold them, and the Lord had given them up? 31 For their rock is not like our Rock. Even those who hate us judge this. 32 Their vine is from the vine of Sodom, and from the fields of Gomorrah. Their grapes are grapes of poison. Their fruit tastes bitter. 33 Their wine is the poison of snakes that kill.

34 'Are they not kept in store with Me, shut in with My stores of riches? 35 It is Mine to punish when their foot makes a false step. The day of their trouble is near. Their fall is coming fast upon them.' 36 For the Lord will judge His people. He will have loving-pity on His servants when He sees their strength is gone, and none are left of those who are free or of those who are not free. 37 Then He will say, 'Where are their gods? Where is the rock where they went to be safe? 38 Who ate the fat of their burnt gifts and drank the wine of their drink gifts? Let them come and help you. Let them be your hiding place! 39 See now that it is I, I am He. There is no god except Me. It is I Who kills and gives life. I hurt, and I heal. And there is no one who can take from My hand. 40 For I lift up My hand to heaven, and promise that, as I live forever, 41 I will make My shining sword sharp. My hand takes hold of what is right and fair. I will punish those who are against Me. And I will punish those who hate Me. 42 I will make My arrows drunk with blood. My sword will eat flesh with the blood of those who are killed and those who are in prison, from the long-haired leaders of those who hate Me.' 43 Be glad, O nations, with His people! For He will punish because of the blood of His servants. He will punish those who fight against Him. And He will take away the sin of His land and His people."

44 Moses came with Joshua the son of Nun and spoke all the words of this song in the ears of the people. 45 When Moses had finished speaking all these words to all Israel, 46 he said to them, "Take into your heart all the words I tell you today. Tell them to your children, so they may be careful to do all the words of this Law. 47 This word is of great worth to you. It is your very life. By this word you will live long in the land you are crossing the Jordan to take."

Moses to Die on Mount Nebo

48 The Lord said to Moses that same day, 49 "Go up to this mountain of the Abarim, Mount Nebo, in the land of Moab beside Jericho. Look at the land of Canaan, which I am giving to the people of Israel for their own. 50 Then die on the mountain you go up, and join your people, as Aaron your brother died on Mount Hor and joined his people. 51 This is because you were not faithful to Me among the people of Israel at the waters of Meribah-Kadesh, in the Desert of Zin and you did not honor Me as holy among the people of Israel. 52 You will see the land from far away, but you will not go into the land I am giving the people of Israel."

Moses' Last Words to Israel

33 Moses the man of God prayed before his death that good would come to the people of Israel. 2 He said, "The Lord came from Sinai. He came upon us from Seir. He shined from Mount Paran. He came among 10,000 holy ones. He came with fire at His right hand. 3 Yes, He loves His people. All Your holy ones are in Your hand. They followed in Your steps. They receive Your Word. 4 Moses gave us the Law, which belongs to the people of Jacob. 5 The Lord was King in Jeshurun, when the leaders of the people were gathered, all the families of Israel together.

6 "May Reuben live and not die. Do not let his men be few."

7 About Judah he said, "O Lord, hear the voice of Judah, and bring him to his people. He fought for them with his hands. Give him help against those who fight against him."

8 About Levi he said, "Let Your Thummim and Your Urim belong to Your man of God. You proved him at Massah, and at the waters of Meribah. 9 He said of his father and mother, 'I do not think of them.' He kept himself apart from his brothers, and his own children. Yes, they obeyed Your Word and kept Your agreement. 10 They will teach Your Laws to Jacob. They will teach Your Laws to Israel. They will put special perfume before You, and whole burnt gifts on Your altar. 11 O Lord, give him good things. Receive the work of his hands. Crush those who go against him and those who hate him, so they may not get up again."

12 About Benjamin he said, "May the one the Lord loves live by Him and be safe. The Lord covers him all the day long. And he lives between His shoulders."

13 About Joseph he said, "May the Lord bring good to his land, with the best gifts from heaven above, with water on the grass in the early morning, and from the deep waters below, 14 with the best things from the sun, and the best foods of the months. 15 May the Lord bring good to his land with the best things of the old mountains, and the best things of the hills that last forever, 16 with the best things of the earth and all that is in it, and the favor of Him Who lived in the bush. Let these gifts come upon the head of Joseph, upon the crown of the head of the one who is ruler among his brothers. 17 His great power is like the first-born of his bull. His horns are like the horns of the wild bull. With them he will push all the nations to the ends of the earth. They are the ten thousands of Ephraim, and the thousands of Manasseh."

18 About Zebulun he said, "Be full of joy, Zebulun, in your going out. Be full of joy, Issachar, in your tents. 19 They will call the people to the mountain. There they will give gifts that are right with God. For they will take out the riches of the seas and the hidden riches of the sand."

20 About Gad he said, "Happy is the one who gives much land to Gad! He lies down like a lion, and tears the arm and the crown of the head. 21 He chose the best part for himself, for that was the ruler's share. He came with the leaders of the people. He did what the Lord wanted him to do. And he obeyed His Law with Israel."

22 About Dan he said, "Dan is a young lion, that jumps out from Bashan."

23 About Naphtali he said, "O Naphtali, filled with favor, and full of the good things of the Lord, take the sea and the south for your own."

24 About Asher he said, "May Asher be given more than the other sons. May he be favored by his brothers. Let him put his foot in oil. 25 Your locks will be iron and brass. And your strength will last like your days.

26 "There is none like the God of Jeshurun. He comes through the heavens to help you, through the sky in His great power. 27 The God Who lives forever is your safe place. His arms are always

under you. He drove away from in front of you those who hate you, and said, 'Destroy!' 28 So Israel lives in a safe place, the well of Jacob is safe, in a land of grain and new wine. Rain falls from His heavens. 29 Happy are you, O Israel! Who is like you, a nation saved by the Lord! He is the battle-covering Who helps you. He is the sword of your great power. So those who hate you will be afraid in front of you. And you will walk upon their high places."

The Death of Moses

34 Now Moses went up from the valleys of Moab to Mount Nebo, to the top of Pisgah, beside Jericho. And the Lord showed him all the land, Gilead as far as Dan, 2 all of Naphtali, the land of Ephraim and Manasseh, all the land of Judah as far as the sea in the west, 3 the Negev and the plain in the valley of Jericho, the city of palm trees, as far as Zoar. 4 Then the Lord said to him, "This is the land I promised Abraham, Isaac and Jacob, saying, 'I will give it to your children.' I have let you see it with your eyes, but you will not go over there." 5 So Moses the servant of the Lord died there in the land of Moab, as the Word of the Lord said. 6 And He buried him in the valley in the land of Moab, beside Beth-peor. But no man knows where he is buried to this day. 7 Moses was 120 years old when he died. But his eyes were not weak, and his strength had not left him. 8 The children of Israel cried for Moses in the valley of Moab for thirty days. Then the days of crying and sorrow for Moses came to an end.

9 Now Joshua the son of Nun was filled with the spirit of wisdom, for Moses had laid his hands on him. So the people of Israel listened to him and did what the Lord had told Moses. 10 There has never been another man who speaks for God in Israel like Moses. The Lord knew him face to face. 11 There has never been another like him who has done all the powerful works the Lord sent him to do in the land of Egypt against Pharaoh, all his servants, and all his land. 12 There has never been another who has shown all the great power and all the great fear which Moses did for all Israel to see.

JOSHUA

God Tells Joshua to Go and Take the Land

1 After the death of the Lord's servant Moses, the Lord said to Moses' helper, Joshua the son of Nun, 2 "My servant Moses is dead. So you and all these people get up and cross the Jordan River to the land I am giving to the people of Israel. 3 I have given you every place where the bottom of your foot steps, as I promised Moses. 4 Your land will be from the desert and from Lebanon as far as the big Euphrates River. It will be all the land of the Hittites to the Great Sea on the west. 5 No man will be able to stand against you all the days of your life. I will be with you just as I have been with Moses. I will be faithful to you and will not leave you alone. 6 Be strong and have strength of heart. For you will bring the people in to take this land which I promised to their fathers to give them. 7 Only be strong and have much strength of heart. Be careful to obey all the Law which My servant Moses told you. Do not turn from it to the right or to the left. Then all will go well with you everywhere you go. 8 This book of the Law must not leave your mouth. Think about it day and night, so you may be careful to do all that is written in it. Then all will go well with you. You will receive many good things. 9 Have I not told you? Be strong and have strength of heart! Do not be afraid or lose faith. For the Lord your God is with you anywhere you go."

Joshua Tells the People to Go

10 Then Joshua told the leaders of the people, 11 "Go among the tents and tell the people, 'Gather together the things you will need. For within three days you will cross this Jordan to go in to take the land the Lord your God is giving you for your own.'"

12 To the Reubenites, the Gadites and the half-family group of Manasseh, Joshua said, 13 "Remember what the Lord's servant Moses told you, saying, 'The Lord your God gives you rest, and will give you this land.' 14 Your wives, your children and your cattle will stay in the land Moses gave you on this side of the Jordan. But you and all your strong-hearted soldiers will cross the river dressed for battle in front of your brothers. You will help them 15 until the Lord gives your brothers rest, as He has given you. Help them until they own the land the Lord your God is giving

them. Then you will return to your own land. You will own what the Lord's servant Moses gave you on the east side of the Jordan." 16 They answered Joshua, saying, "We will do all that you have told us. And we will go anywhere you send us. 17 We will obey you in all things just as we obeyed Moses. Only may the Lord your God be with you as He was with Moses. 18 Anyone who goes against what you say, and does not obey all that you tell him to do, will be put to death. Only be strong and have strength of heart."

Rahab and the Men Sent to Spy Out the Land

2 Then Joshua the son of Nun sent two men from Shittim to go in secret to learn about the land. He said to them, "Go and spy out the land, and Jericho." So they went and came to the house of Rahab, a woman who sold the use of her body, and they stayed there. 2 Then the king of Jericho was told, "See, men of Israel have come here to spy out the land." 3 So the king of Jericho sent word to Rahab, saying, "Bring out the men who have come to you and have gone into your house. For they have come to spy out all the land." 4 But the woman had taken the two men and hidden them. She said, "Yes, the men came to me. But I did not know where they were from. 5 When it was time for the gate to be shut after dark, the men went out. I do not know where they went. Be quick to go after them, for you will catch them." 6 But she had brought them up to the roof and had hidden them under the grain she had put up there. 7 The men went after them on the road to the Jordan as far as the river crossing. As soon as those going after them had gone out, they shut the gate.

8 Before they lay down, she came up to them on the roof. 9 And she said to the men, "I know that the Lord has given you the land. The fear of you has come upon us. All the people living in the land have become weak with fear because of you. 10 For we have heard how the Lord dried up the water of the Red Sea for you when you came out of Egypt. We have heard how you destroyed the two kings of the Amorites, Sihon and Og, on the other side of the Jordan. 11 When we heard it, our hearts became weak. No man had strength of heart any more because of you. For the Lord your God is God in heaven above

and on earth below. 12 Now I have shown you kindness. So I beg of you, promise me by the Lord that you will show kindness to those of my father's house. Give me something to show that you will be faithful. 13 Do not kill my father and mother and my brothers and sisters, and all who belong to them. Save us from death." 14 So the men said to her, "Our life for yours! If you do not tell anyone what we are doing, we will be faithful and show you kindness when the Lord gives us the land."

15 Then she let them down by a rope through the window. She lived in her house that was built on top of the city wall. 16 She said to them, "Go to the hill country, or those who are looking for you might find you. For three days hide yourselves there until those who are looking for you return. Then you may go on your way." 17 The men said to her, "We will be free from this promise you have made us swear 18 unless, when we come into the land, you tie this red rope in the window you let us down through. Bring your father and mother, your brothers and all those of your father's house into your house. 19 If anyone goes out through the doors of your house into the street, his blood will be on his own head. We will not be guilty for his death. But if a hand is laid upon anyone who is with you in the house, his blood will be on our head. 20 And we will be free from the promise you made us swear if you tell anyone what we are doing." 21 She said, "Let it be as you have said." Then she sent them away, and tied the red rope in the window.

22 They left and came to the hill country and stayed there for three days until those who were looking for them returned. The men had looked for them all along the road, but had not found them. 23 Then the two men came down from the hill country, crossed over the Jordan, and came to Joshua the son of Nun. They told him all that had happened to them. 24 They said to Joshua, "For sure the Lord has given all the land into our hands. All the people living in the land have become weak with fear because of us."

Israel Crosses over the Jordan

3 Joshua got up early in the morning. He and all the people of Israel left Shittim and came to the Jordan. And they stayed there before they crossed. 2 After three days the leaders went among the tents.

3 They told the people, "When you see the special box of the agreement of the Lord your God with the religious leaders carrying it, leave your places and follow it. 4 Then you may know the way to go, for you have not passed this way before. But stay about 1,000 long steps away from it. Do not come near it."

5 Then Joshua said to the people, "Make yourselves holy. For tomorrow the Lord will do powerful works among you." 6 Joshua said to the religious leaders, "Take up the special box of the agreement and cross over in front of the people." So they took up the special box of the agreement and went in front of the people.

7 The Lord said to Joshua, "Today I will begin to give you honor in the eyes of all Israel. Then they may know that I will be with you just as I have been with Moses. 8 Tell the religious leaders who are carrying the special box of the agreement, 'When you come to the water of the Jordan River, stand still in it.' " 9 Then Joshua said to the people of Israel, "Come here. Listen to the words of the Lord your God." 10 And Joshua said, "You will know that the living God is among you because He will be sure to drive away from in front of you the Canaanite, the Hittite, the Hivite, the Perizzite, the Girgashite, the Amorite and the Jebusite. 11 See, the special box of the agreement of the Lord of All the earth is crossing over in front of you in the Jordan. 12 Now choose twelve men from the families of Israel, one man for each family. 13 The religious leaders who carry the special box of the agreement of the Lord of All the earth, will rest their feet in the water of the Jordan. Then the water of the Jordan will be cut off. The water flowing down from above will gather together in one place."

14 So the people left their tents to cross the Jordan. The religious leaders carried the special box of the agreement in front of the people. 15 They carried it to the Jordan and put their feet in the water. (For the Jordan water floods during the time of gathering grain.) 16 Then the water flowing down from above stood and rose up in one place far away at Adam, the city beside Zarethan. The water flowing down toward the sea of the Arabah, the Salt Sea, was all cut off. So the people crossed beside Jericho. 17 The religious leaders who carried the special box of the agreement of the Lord stood on dry ground in the middle of the Jordan. And all Israel

crossed on dry ground, until all the nation had crossed the Jordan.

Stones Are Set Up

4 When all the nation had crossed the Jordan, the Lord said to Joshua, ² "Choose twelve men from the people, one man from each family. ³ Tell them, 'Take twelve stones from the middle of the Jordan. Take them from the place where the religious leaders' feet are standing. Carry them over with you, and lay them down in the place where you stay tonight.'" ⁴ So Joshua called the twelve men he had chosen from the sons of Israel, one man from each family. ⁵ And Joshua said to them, "Go into the middle of the Jordan in front of the special box of the agreement of the Lord your God. Each of you take a stone on his shoulder, one for each of the twelve family groups of Israel. ⁶ Let this be something special among you. Your children will ask you later, 'What do these stones mean to you?' ⁷ Then you will tell them that the water of the Jordan was cut off before the special box of the agreement of the Lord. When it crossed the Jordan, the water of the Jordan was cut off. So these stones will become something to be remember to the people of Israel forever."

⁸ The sons of Israel did as Joshua told them. They took up twelve stones from the middle of the Jordan, just as the Lord told Joshua. There was one stone for each family group of the sons of Israel. They carried them over with them to the place where they stayed, and put them down there. ⁹ Then Joshua set up twelve stones at the place where the feet of the religious leaders who carried the special box of the agreement were standing in the middle of the Jordan. They are there to this day. ¹⁰ The religious leaders who carried the special box of the agreement stood in the middle of the Jordan. They stood there until everything was finished that the Lord told Joshua to tell the people, all that Moses had told Joshua.

The people crossed in a hurry. ¹¹ When all the people were over, they watched the religious leaders carry the special box of the agreement to the other side. ¹² The sons of Reuben and Gad and the half-family group of Manasseh crossed over ready for battle before the people of Israel, just as Moses had told them. ¹³ About 40,000 soldiers ready for battle crossed before the Lord to the desert plains of Jericho. ¹⁴ On that day the Lord gave Joshua

honor in the eyes of all Israel. So they honored him as a great man just as they had honored Moses all the days of his life.

¹⁵ The Lord said to Joshua, ¹⁶ "Tell the religious leaders who carry the special box of the agreement to come up from the Jordan." ¹⁷ So Joshua told the religious leaders to come up from the Jordan. ¹⁸ The religious leaders who carried the special box of the agreement of the Lord came up from the middle of the Jordan. When their feet stepped on dry ground, the water of the Jordan returned to its place. It flowed over its sides as before.

¹⁹ The people came up from the Jordan on the tenth day of the first month. Then they stayed at Gilgal on the east side of Jericho. ²⁰ Joshua set up at Gilgal the twelve stones they had taken from the Jordan. ²¹ He said to the people of Israel, "Your children will ask their fathers some time in the future, 'What do these stones mean?' ²² Then let your children know that Israel crossed this Jordan on dry ground. ²³ For the Lord your God dried up the water of the Jordan before you until you had crossed. It was just as the Lord your God had done to the Red Sea, which He dried up before us until we had crossed. ²⁴ Now all the people of the earth may know that the hand of the Lord is powerful, so that you may fear the Lord your God forever."

The Religious Act at Gilgal

5 All the Amorite kings west of the Jordan and all the Canaanite kings by the sea heard how the Lord had dried up the water of the Jordan for the people of Israel until they had crossed. And their hearts became weak. There was no spirit in them any more because of the people of Israel.

² Then the Lord said to Joshua, "Make knives for yourselves out of hard stone. And cut the piece of skin from the sex part of the sons of Israel as before." ³ So Joshua made knives of hard stone. Then he had the sons of Israel go through this religious act at Gibeath-haaraloth. ⁴ This is the reason why Joshua had them go through this religious act. All the males who had come out of Egypt, all the soldiers, had died in the desert on the way from Egypt. ⁵ All the people who came out went through this religious act. But all the people who were born in the desert on the way from Egypt had not gone through this religious act. ⁶ For the people of Israel walked forty years in the desert, until all the men of war

who came out of Egypt died, because they did not listen to the voice of the Lord. The Lord had promised them that He would not let them see the land He had promised to their fathers to give us, a land flowing with milk and honey. [7] So Joshua went through the religious act on their children, whom the Lord raised up in their place. For they had not gone through this religious act along the way. [8] When the whole nation had gone through this religious act, they stayed in their places among the tents until they were healed. [9] Then the Lord said to Joshua, "Today I have rolled away from you the shame of Egypt." So the name of that place is called Gilgal to this day. [10] The people of Israel stayed at Gilgal. They kept the Passover on the evening of the fourteenth day of the month on the desert plains of Jericho. [11] On the very next day after the Passover, they ate some of the food of the land. They ate bread without yeast, and dry grain. [12] The bread from heaven stopped on the day after they had eaten some of the food of the land. So the people of Israel no longer had bread from heaven. But they ate food of the land of Canaan during that year.

The Captain of the Lord's Army

[13] When Joshua was by Jericho, he looked up and saw a man standing near him with his sword in his hand. Joshua went to him and said, "Are you for us or for those who hate us?" [14] "No," He said, "I have now come as Captain of the army of the Lord." Joshua fell on his face to the ground and worshiped, and said to Him, "What has my Lord to say to His servant?" [15] The Captain of the Lord's army said to Joshua, "Take your shoes off your feet. For the place where you are standing is holy." And Joshua did so.

Jericho Is Destroyed

6 Now the gates of Jericho were all shut because of the people of Israel. No one went out and no one came in. [2] The Lord said to Joshua, "See, I have given Jericho into your hand, with its king and soldiers. [3] Walk around the city. Have all the men of war go around the city once. Do this for six days. [4] Seven religious leaders will carry seven rams' horns. They will walk in front of the special box of the agreement. Then on the seventh day you will walk around the city seven times. And the religious leaders will blow horns. [5] When you hear the long sound of the ram's horn,

all the people should call out with a loud noise. The wall of the city will fall to the ground. And then all the people will all go in the city."

[6] So Joshua the son of Nun called the religious leaders and said to them, "Take up the special box of the agreement. And let seven religious leaders carry seven rams' horns in front of the special box of the agreement." [7] Then he said to the people, "Go and walk around the city. Let the men ready for battle go in front of the special box of the agreement." [8] When Joshua had spoken to the people, the seven religious leaders carrying the seven rams' horns before the Lord walked on and blew the horns. And the special box of the agreement of the Lord followed them. [9] The men ready for battle went in front of the religious leaders who blew the horns. The other soldiers came behind the special box of the agreement while the horns sounded without stopping. [10] But Joshua told the people, "Do not call out or let your voice be heard. Not a word should come from your mouth until the day I tell you to call out. Then you must call out." [11] So he had the special box of the agreement taken around the city once. Then they returned to the tents and stayed there through the night.

[12] Joshua got up early in the morning. And the religious leaders took up the special box of the agreement. [13] The seven religious leaders carrying the seven rams' horns in front of the special box of the agreement began walking and blew the horns without stopping. The men ready for battle went in front of them. The other soldiers came behind the special box of the agreement. And the horns sounded without stopping. [14] The second day they walked around the city once. Then they returned to the tents. They did this for six days.

[15] On the seventh day they got up early at the rising of the sun. They walked around the city in the same way, but on that day they walked around the city seven times. [16] The seventh time, when the religious leaders blew their horns, Joshua said to the people, "Call out! For the Lord has given you the city. [17] The city and all that is in it must be destroyed because everything in it belongs to the Lord. Only Rahab, the woman who sells the use of her body, and all who are with her in the house will live, because she hid the men we sent. [18] But keep yourselves from the things that are to be destroyed. Or while you give them

up to be destroyed, you might desire them. Then you would make the camp of Israel sinful also, and bring trouble on it. 19 But all the silver and gold and objects of brass and iron are holy to the Lord. They will go into the store-house of the Lord." 20 So the people called out and the religious leaders blew the horns. When the people heard the sound of the horns, they called out even louder. And the wall fell to the ground. All the people went straight in and took the city. 21 They destroyed everything in the city, both man and woman, young and old, cattle, sheep, and donkey, with the sword.

22 Joshua said to the two men who had spied out the land, "Go into the house of the woman who sells the use of her body. Bring out the woman and all who are with her, as you promised her." 23 So the young men who had spied out the land went in, and brought out Rahab and her father and mother and brothers and all she had. They brought out all of her family and took them outside the tents of Israel. 24 Then they burned the city with fire, and all that was in it. Only the silver and gold and objects of brass and iron they put into the store-house of the holy tent of the Lord. 25 Joshua saved the life of Rahab, the woman who sold the use of her body, and those of her father's house and all she had. She has lived among Israel to this day, because she hid the men Joshua had sent to spy out Jericho.

26 Then Joshua made them promise at that time, saying, "May the Lord destroy the man who gets up and builds this city of Jericho. With the loss of his first-born he will begin to build it. With the loss of his youngest son he will set up its gates." 27 So the Lord was with Joshua. He was well-known and respected in all the land.

Achan's Sin

7 But the people of Israel sinned with the things that were to be destroyed. Achan, the son of Carmi, the son of Zabdi, the son of Zerah, from the family of Judah, took some of the things that were to be destroyed. So the Lord was very angry with the people of Israel.

2 Joshua sent men from Jericho to Ai, which is near Beth-aven, east of Bethel. He said to them, "Go and spy out the land in secret." So the men went and spied out Ai. 3 When they returned to Joshua, they said, "Do not have all the people go there. Only about 2,000 or 3,000 men need to go to Ai. Do not make the whole army fight,

for the people of Ai are few." 4 So about 3,000 men of Israel went, but they ran away from the men of Ai. 5 The men of Ai killed about thirty-six of their men and ran after them from the gate as far as She-barim. And they killed more on the way down. So the hearts of the people became weak. They became like water.

6 Then Joshua and the leaders of Israel tore their clothes. They fell with their faces on the ground in front of the special box of the agreement until evening. And they put dust on their heads. 7 Joshua said, "O Lord God, why did You ever bring this nation over the Jordan, only to give us into the hand of the Amorites to be destroyed? If only we had been willing to live on the other side of the Jordan! 8 O Lord, what can I say? Israel has turned their backs in front of those who fight against them. 9 The Canaanites and all the people living in the land will hear of it. They will gather around us and destroy our name from the earth. Then what will You do for Your great name?"

10 The Lord said to Joshua, "Get up! Why have you fallen on your face? 11 Israel has sinned. They have gone against My agreement which I told them to keep. They have even taken some of the things that were to be destroyed. They have stolen and lied. And they have put them among their own things. 12 That is why the people of Israel cannot stand in front of those who fight against them. They turn their backs in front of those who hate them because they are being punished. I will not be with you any more unless you destroy the things among you that should be destroyed. 13 Get up! Set apart the people and say, 'Make yourselves holy for tomorrow. For the Lord, the God of Israel, has said, "There are things among you which should be destroyed, O Israel. You cannot stand in front of those who fight against you until you take away the things among you which should be destroyed." 14 In the morning you must come near by your family groups. Then the family group which the Lord takes must come near by families. The family which the Lord takes must come near by tents. And the tent which the Lord takes must come near man by man. 15 Then the one who is taken with the things which should have been destroyed must be burned with fire, he and all that belongs to him because he has sinned against the agreement of the Lord. He has done an act of shame in Israel.' "

16 So Joshua got up early in the morning and brought Israel near by family groups. The family group of Judah was taken. 17 He brought the family group of Judah near. And he took the family of the Zerahites. He brought the family of the Zerahites near man by man. Zabdi was taken. 18 Then he brought those of Zabdi's tent near man by man. And Achan, son of Carmi, son of Zabdi, son of Zerah, from the family of Judah, was taken. 19 Joshua said to Achan, "My son, I beg you, give honor and praise to the Lord, the God of Israel. Tell me now what you have done. Do not hide it from me." 20 Achan answered Joshua, saying, "It is true. I have sinned against the Lord, the God of Israel. This is what I did. 21 I saw among what was left of the city a beautiful coat from Shinar. I saw 200 pieces of silver, and a large piece of gold as heavy as fifty pieces of silver. I had a desire for them and took them. See, they are hidden in the ground inside my tent, with the silver under it."

22 So Joshua sent men to the tent. There they found it, with the silver under it. 23 They took these things from inside the tent and brought them to Joshua and all the people of Israel. And they laid them down before the Lord. 24 Then Joshua and all Israel took Achan the son of Zerah, the silver, the coat, the large piece of gold, his sons and daughters, his cattle, donkeys, sheep, tent and all that belonged to him. They brought them to the valley of Achor. 25 And Joshua said, "Why have you brought trouble upon us? The Lord will trouble you this day." Then all Israel threw stones at them. After that they burned them with fire. 26 They put many stones over him that stand to this day. Then the Lord was no longer angry. The name of that place has been called the Valley of Achor to this day.

Ai Is Destroyed

8 The Lord said to Joshua, "Do not be afraid. Take all the men of war with you and go up to Ai. See, I have given the king of Ai into your hand, his people, his city, and his land. 2 Do the same to Ai and its king as you did to Jericho and its king. Take only its riches and its cattle for yourselves. Hide men behind the city to fight against it."

3 So Joshua and all the men of war got ready to go up to Ai. Joshua chose 30,000 strong soldiers, and sent them out during the night. 4 He told them, "See, you are going to fight the city from behind it. Do not go very far from the city, but all of you be ready. 5 I and all the people will come near the city. When they come out to meet us as they did before, we will run from them. 6 They will come out after us until we have taken them away from the city. For they will say, 'They are running from us as they did before.' So we will run from them. 7 Then you will come out of your hiding place and take the city. The Lord will give it to you. 8 When you have taken the city, set it on fire. Do what the Lord says. See, I have told you." 9 When Joshua sent them away, they went to the hiding place. They waited between Bethel and Ai, on the west side of Ai. But Joshua stayed that night among the people.

10 Joshua got up early in the morning and gathered the people. Then he went up with the leaders of Israel in front of the people to Ai. 11 All the men of war who were with him went up and came to the front of the city. They stayed on the north side of Ai. There was a valley between him and Ai. 12 Then he took about 5,000 men and hid them between Bethel and Ai, on the west side of the city. 13 So they put the men in their places. There was the army on the north side of the city, and the secret army on the west side of the city. But Joshua stayed that night in the center of the valley. 14 The king of Ai saw this. So the men of the city were quick to get up early and go out to meet Israel in battle at the chosen place near the desert plain. But he did not know that there was an army hiding behind the city. 15 Joshua and all Israel pretended to be beaten in front of them. And they ran away into the desert. 16 All the people in the city were called together to go after them. They went after Joshua, and were taken away from the city. 17 So not a man was left in Ai or Bethel who had not gone out after Israel. They left the city open and ran after Israel.

18 Then the Lord said to Joshua, "Hold out the spear that is in your hand toward Ai. For I will give the city to you." So Joshua held out the spear that was in his hand toward the city. 19 The men who were hiding got up in a hurry from their place and ran when he held out his hand. They went into the city and took it, and were quick to set it on fire. 20 When the men of Ai looked back, they saw the smoke of the city going up to the sky. They had no place to run. Then the people of Israel who had been running away in the desert

turned against those who went after them. 21 Joshua and all Israel saw that the men who had been hiding had taken the city. They saw the smoke from the city, so they turned around and killed the men of Ai. 22 The others came out from the city to meet them. The men of Ai were caught in the center of Israel. There were some on one side and some on the other side. They killed until no one was left alive. No one got away. 23 But they took the king of Ai alive and brought him to Joshua.

24 Israel killed all the men of Ai in the field and in the desert where they had run after them. All of them were killed with the sword until they were destroyed. Then all Israel returned to Ai and destroyed it with the sword. 25 All the men and women of Ai died that day, 12,000 in all. 26 Joshua did not put down his hand he used to hold out the spear until he had destroyed all the people of Ai. 27 Israel took only the cattle and the riches of that city for themselves, as the Lord had told Joshua. 28 So Joshua burned Ai and destroyed it forever, as it is to this day. 29 He hanged the king of Ai on a tree until evening. When the sun went down, Joshua had them take his body down from the tree and throw it down at the gate of the city. They put many stones over it, and they are there to this day.

The Agreement Is Read on Mount Ebal

30 Then Joshua built an altar to the Lord, the God of Israel, at Mount Ebal. 31 It was built just as the Lord's servant Moses had told the people of Israel, as it is written in the book of the Law of Moses. It was an altar made of stones which had not been cut. No one had used an iron object on them. On the altar they gave burnt gifts in worship to the Lord. And there they gave peace gifts in worship. 32 There Joshua wrote on the stones the Law of Moses in front of the people of Israel. 33 All Israel stood on both sides of the special box, in front of the Levite religious leaders who carried the special box of the agreement of the Lord. Strangers stood there as well as those born among the people, with their leaders and heads and men who judge between what is right or wrong. Half of them stood in front of Mount Gerizim. The other half stood in front of Mount Ebal. They did just as the Lord's servant Moses had told them before. They prayed for good to come to the people of Israel. 34 After this Joshua read all the words of the Law, the good and the bad that will

happen. He read all that is written in the book of the Law. 35 There was not a word of all that Moses had said which Joshua did not read. He read it in front of all the people of Israel, with the women and children and strangers who were living among them.

The Gibeonites Lie to Joshua

9 The kings west of the Jordan, in the hill country and the valleys and beside the Great Sea toward Lebanon all heard what had happened. These kings were of the Hittites, the Amorites, the Canaanites, the Perizzites, the Hivites, and the Jebusites. 2 They gathered together as one to fight against Joshua and Israel. 3 The people of Gibeon heard what Joshua had done to Jericho and Ai. 4 So they went out to fool him, as men from another land. They took old bags on their donkeys, and skin bags of wine that were old and torn and mended. 5 They wore old and mended shoes on their feet, and old clothes on themselves. All their bread was dry and broken. 6 They went to Joshua among the tents at Gilgal. And they said to him and the men of Israel, "We have come from a far country. Now make an agreement with us." 7 The men of Israel said to the Hivites, "It may be that you are living within our land. How then can we make an agreement with you?" 8 But they said to Joshua, "We are your servants." Then Joshua said to them, "Who are you? Where do you come from?" 9 They said to him, "Your servants have come from a very far country because of the name of the Lord your God. For we have heard about Him and all He did in Egypt. 10 We heard what He did to the two kings of the Amorites east of the Jordan, to Sihon king of Heshbon and to Og king of Bashan who was at Ashtaroth. 11 So our leaders and all the people of our country said to us, 'Take what you need for traveling. Go to meet them and tell them, "We are your servants. Now make an agreement with us." ' 12 Our bread was warm when we took it along with what we needed from our houses on the day we left to come to you. But now look, it is dry and broken. 13 These skin bags that we filled with wine were new. Now look, they are torn. And our clothes and shoes have become old because of the very long way we had to travel." 14 So the men of Israel took some of their food. They did not ask the Lord what they should do. 15 Joshua made peace with them and made an agreement

with them, to let them live. And the leaders of the people made a promise to them.

16 But three days after they had made an agreement with them, they heard that they were neighbors who lived in their land. 17 Then the people of Israel left that place and came to their cities on the third day. Their cities were Gibeon, Chephirah, Beeroth and Kiriath-jearim. 18 But the people of Israel did not kill them because the leaders of the people had made a promise to them by the Lord the God of Israel. All the people complained against the leaders. 19 Then all the leaders said to all the people, "We have made a promise to them by the Lord, the God of Israel. Now we cannot touch them. 20 This is what we will do to them. We will let them live, or anger would be upon us for the promise we swore to them." 21 And the leaders said to them, "Let them live." So they cut wood and brought water for all the people, as the leaders had told them.

22 Joshua called them and said, "Why have you lied to us, saying, 'We are very far from you,' when you are living within our land? 23 Now you are cursed. You will never stop being servants, cutting wood and bringing water, for the house of my God." 24 They answered Joshua, "Because it was told to your servants that the Lord your God had told His servant Moses to give you all the land and kill all the people of the land in front of you. We were very much afraid for our lives because of you. That is why we have done this thing. 25 Now see, we are in your hands. Do to us whatever you think is good and right in your eyes." 26 So he did this to them. He saved them from the hands of the people of Israel. They did not kill them. 27 But on that day Joshua made them cut wood and bring water for the people of Israel and for the altar of the Lord, at whatever place He chooses. That was to be their work to this day.

The Sun Stands Still

10 Adoni-zedek king of Jerusalem heard that Joshua had taken Ai and had destroyed it. Joshua had done the same thing to Ai and its king that he had done to Jericho and its king. Adoni-zedek heard that the people of Gibeon had made peace with Israel and were among them. 2 He was very much afraid. Because Gibeon was a large city, like one of the cities of a king. It was larger than Ai. All its men were strong. 3 So Adoni-zedek

of Jerusalem sent word to Hoham king of Hebron, Piram king of Jarmuth, Japhia king of Lachish, and Debir king of Eglon. He said to them, 4 "Come and help me. Let us go fight against Gibeon. For it has made peace with Joshua and the people of Israel." 5 So the five kings of the Amorites, the kings of Jerusalem, Hebron, Jarmuth, Lachish and Eglon, gathered together with all their armies. And they went and set up their tents by Gibeon, to fight against it.

6 Then the men of Gibeon sent word to Joshua at the tents at Gilgal, saying, "Do not leave your servants alone. Hurry and help us. For all the kings of the Amorites who live in the hill country have gathered against us." 7 So Joshua went up from Gilgal. He took with him all the men of war and all the strong soldiers. 8 The Lord said to Joshua, "Do not be afraid of them. For I have given them into your hands. Not one of them will stand in front of you." 9 So Joshua came upon them by surprise by traveling all night from Gilgal. 10 The Lord brought trouble upon the Amorites in front of Israel. He killed many of them at Gibeon, and went after them on the way up to Beth-horon. He killed them as far as Azekah and Makkedah. 11 They ran from Israel. And while they ran from Beth-horon, the Lord made large hail-stones fall from heaven on them as far as Azekah, and they died. More died from the hail-stones than the sons of Israel killed with the sword.

12 Then Joshua spoke to the Lord on the day when the Lord made the Amorites lose the war against the sons of Israel. He said, in the eyes of Israel, "O sun, stand still at Gibeon. O moon, stand still in the valley of Aijalon." 13 So the sun stood still and the moon stopped, until the nation punished those who fought against them. Is it not written in the Book of Jashar? The sun stopped in the center of the sky. It did not hurry to go down for about a whole day. 14 There has been no day like it before or since, when the Lord listened to the voice of a man. For the Lord fought for Israel. 15 Then Joshua and all Israel returned to the tents at Gilgal.

Five Amorite Kings Are Found and Killed

16 Now these five kings had run away and hidden themselves in the cave at Makkedah. 17 Joshua was told, "The five kings have been found hiding in the cave at Makkedah." 18 And Joshua said, "Roll large stones against the opening of the cave. Then put men there to watch over them.

19 But do not stay there yourselves. Go after those who hate you. Follow after them and fight. Do not let them go into their cities. For the Lord your God has given them into your hand." 20 Joshua and the sons of Israel finished killing many of them, until they were destroyed. Those who were left alive went into their strong cities. 21 Then all the people returned to Joshua at the tents at Makkedah in peace. No one said a word against any of the people of Israel.

22 Then Joshua said, "Open the mouth of the cave and bring those five kings out to me." 23 The five kings were brought to him from the cave, the king of Jerusalem, Hebron, Jarmuth, Lachish and Eglon. 24 When they brought those kings out to Joshua, he called for all the men of Israel. He said to the leaders of the men of war who had gone with him, "Come near. Put your feet on the necks of these kings." So they came and put their feet on their necks. 25 Then Joshua said to them, "Do not be afraid or troubled. Be strong and have strength of heart. For the Lord will do this to all who hate you and fight against you." 26 After this Joshua killed the kings. He hanged them on five trees, and they hung on the trees until evening. 27 When the sun went down, Joshua had them taken down from the trees and thrown into the cave where they had hidden. Large stones were put over the opening of the cave. And they are there to this day.

Joshua Takes More Amorite Land

28 Joshua took Makkedah on that day. He destroyed it and its king with the sword. He destroyed all of it and every person in it. No one was left alive. He did the same to the king of Makkedah as he had done to the king of Jericho.

29 Then Joshua and all Israel went from Makkedah to fight against Libnah. 30 The Lord gave it and its king into the hands of Israel also. Joshua destroyed it and every person in it with the sword. He left no one alive. So he did the same to its king as he had done to the king of Jericho.

31 Joshua and all Israel went from Libnah to Lachish. They stayed beside it and fought against it. 32 And the Lord gave Lachish into the hands of Israel. Joshua took it on the second day. He destroyed it and every person in it with the sword, just as he had done to Libnah.

33 Horam king of Gezer came to help Lachish. But Joshua won the battle against him and his people. He left no one alive.

34 Joshua and all Israel went from Lachish to Eglon. They stayed beside it and fought against it. 35 And they took it on that day and destroyed it with the sword. He destroyed every person who was in it that day, just as he had done to Lachish.

36 Joshua and all Israel went from Eglon to Hebron. And they fought against it. 37 They took it and destroyed it. They destroyed its king, all its cities and all who were in it with the sword. He left no one alive, just as he had done to Eglon. He destroyed all of it and every person in it. 38 Then Joshua and all Israel returned to Debir. And they fought against it. 39 He took it, its king and all its cities. He destroyed them with the sword. Every person in it was destroyed. No one was left alive. He did the same to Debir and its king as he had done to Hebron and Libnah and their kings.

40 So Joshua won the war against the whole land, the hill country, the Negev, the valleys, the hill-sides, and all their kings. He left no one alive. He destroyed all who breathed, just as the Lord, the God of Israel, had told him. 41 Joshua killed them from Kadesh-barnea as far as Gaza. He killed them in all the country of Goshen as far as Gibeon. 42 Joshua took all these kings and their lands at the same time. Because the Lord, the God of Israel, fought for Israel. 43 Then Joshua and all Israel returned to the tents at Gilgal.

Northern Kings Are Killed

11 Jabin king of Hazor heard what had happened. He sent news to Jobab king of Madon and to the kings of Shimron and Achshaph. 2 He sent news to the kings in the hill country to the north, in the Arabah south of Chinneroth, in the valleys, and in the high land of Dor to the west. 3 He sent news to the Canaanite in the east and in the west, and the Amorite, the Hittite, the Perizzite, the Jebusite in the hill country, and the Hivite at the base of Hermon in the land of Mizpeh. 4 Then they came out, they and all their armies with them. There were as many people as the sand beside the sea. And they had very many horses and war-wagons. 5 All of these kings met and came and stayed together at the waters of Merom, to fight against Israel.

6 "Do not be afraid," the Lord said to Joshua. "For tomorrow at this time I will have killed all of them for Israel. You will cut the legs of their horses and burn

their war-wagons with fire." 7 So Joshua with all the men of war came upon them by surprise at the waters of Merom, and fought against them. 8 And the Lord gave them into the hand of Israel. They won the war against them and ran after them as far as the big city of Sidon and Misrephoth-maim and the valley of Mizpeh to the east. They killed them until no one was left alive. 9 Joshua did to them as the Lord had told him. He cut the legs of their horses and burned their war-wagons with fire.

10 Then Joshua turned back and took Hazor and killed its king with the sword. For Hazor had been the head of all these nations. 11 They killed every person in it with the sword, destroying all of them. There was no one left who breathed. Then he burned Hazor with fire. 12 Joshua took all the cities of these kings, and all their kings and killed them with the sword. He destroyed all of them, just as the Lord's servant Moses had told him. 13 But Israel did not burn any cities that stood on their hills, except Hazor, which Joshua burned. 14 The sons of Israel took for themselves all the riches of these cities and the cattle. But they killed every man with the sword until they had destroyed them. They left no one who breathed. 15 What the Lord had told His servant Moses to do, he told Joshua, and Joshua did it. He did everything the Lord had told Moses.

The Lands Taken by Joshua

16 So Joshua took all that land. He took the hill country, all the Negev, all the land of Goshen, the valleys, the Arabah, the hill country of Israel and its valleys. 17 He took the land from Mount Halak which goes up to Seir as far as Baal-gad in the valley of Lebanon at the base of Mount Hermon. He took all their kings and killed them. 18 Joshua made war against these kings for a long time. 19 There was not a city which made peace with the sons of Israel except the Hivites living in Gibeon. They took them all in battle. 20 For the Lord made their hearts hard to meet Israel in battle, so Israel might destroy all of them. They would not be shown pity but would be destroyed, just as the Lord had told Moses.

21 At that time Joshua went and killed the big powerful men in the hill country. He killed them in Hebron, Debir, Anab, and all the hill country of Judah and Israel. Joshua destroyed all of them with their cities. 22 There were no big powerful men left in the land of the people of Israel. Some were left only in Gaza, Gath and Ashdod. 23 So Joshua took the whole land, just as the Lord had told Moses. And Joshua gave it as a gift to Israel, a share for each family group. Then the land had rest from war.

The Kings Taken by Moses

12 These are the kings of the land whom the sons of Israel won the war against east of the Jordan. They took their land from the Arnon valley to Mount Hermon, and all the Arabah to the east. 2 There was Sihon king of the Amorites, who lived in Heshbon. He ruled from Aroer on the side of the Arnon valley, and from the center of the valley and half of Gilead as far as the river Jabbok, beside the Ammonites. 3 And he ruled the Arabah as far as the Sea of Chinneroth in the east, and as far as the sea of the Arabah, the Salt Sea, east toward Beth-jeshimoth and south to the bottom of the hills of Pisgah. 4 And they took the land of Og, king of Bashan, one of the Rephaim who were still living. Og lived at Ashtaroth and Edrei. 5 He ruled over Mount Hermon and Salecah and all Bashan. He ruled as far as the land of the Geshurites, the Maacathites, and half of Gilead, as far as the land of Sihon, king of Heshbon. 6 The Lord's servant Moses and the people of Israel won the war against them. Moses the Lord's servant gave their land to the Reubenites, the Gadites and the half-family group of Manasseh.

The Kings Taken by Joshua

7 These are the kings of the land whom Joshua and the sons of Israel won the war against west of the Jordan, from Baal-gad in the valley of Lebanon as far as Mount Halak which goes up to Seir. (Joshua gave their land as a gift to the family groups of Israel, by each one's share. 8 He gave them the hill country, the valleys, the Arabah, the hill-sides, the desert, and the Negev. It was the land of the Hittite, the Amorite, the Canaanite, the Perizzite, the Hivite and the Jebusite.) 9 There was the king of Jericho, the king of Ai which is beside Bethel, 10 the king of Jerusalem, the king of Hebron, 11 the king of Jarmuth, the king of Lachish, 12 the king of Eglon, and the king of Gezer. 13 There was the king of Debir, the king of Geder, 14 the king of Horman, the king of Arad, 15 the king of Libnah, the king of Adullam, 16 the king of Makkedah, and the king of Bethel. 17 There was the king of Tappuah, the king

of Hepher, 18 the king of Aphek, the king of Lasharon, 19 the king of Madon, the king of Hazor, 20 the king of Shimron-meron, and the king of Achshaph. 21 There was the king of Taanach, the king of Megiddo, 22 the king of Kedesh, the king of Jokneam in Carmel, 23 the king of Dor in the highlands of Dor, the king of Goiim in Gilgal, 24 and the king of Tirzah. There were thirty-one kings in all.

The Land to Be Taken

13 Now Joshua was old. He had lived many years. The Lord said to him, "You are old and have lived many years. And there is very much land yet to be taken. 2 This is the land that is left. There is all the land of the Philistines and the Geshurites, 3 from the Shihor east of Egypt as far as the land of Ekron in the north (it is thought of as Canaanite). There are the five rulers of the Philistines, those of Gaza, Ashdod, Ashkelon, Gath, Ekron, and those of the Avvim. 4 In the south, there is all the land of the Canaanite, and Mearah that belongs to the Sidonians, as far as Aphek, to the land of the Amorite, 5 and the land of the Gebalite. There is all of Lebanon east from Baal-gad at the base of Mount Hermon as far as Lebo-hamath. 6 I will drive out from in front of the people of Israel all those living in the hill country from Lebanon as far as Misrephoth-maim, all the Sidonians. Give the land as a gift to Israel, as I have told you. 7 Divide this land for a gift to the nine families and to the half-family group of Manasseh."

The Land East of the Jordan Is Divided

8 The other half-family group, the Reubenites and the Gadites received their gift of land which Moses gave them east of the Jordan, just as the Lord's servant Moses gave it to them. 9 It spread from Aroer, beside the Arnon valley, and the city in the center of the valley, and the plain of Medeba as far as Dibon, 10 and all the cities of Sihon king of the Amorites, who ruled in Heshbon. And it went as far as the land of the Ammonites, 11 and Gilead, and the land of the Geshurites and Maacathites. They received all Mount Hermon, all Bashan as far as Salecah, 12 and all the nation of Og in Bashan, who ruled in Ashtaroth and Edrei. (He alone was left of the Rephaim still living.) For Moses had won the war against them and had driven them out. 13 But the people of Israel did not drive out the Geshurites or the Maacathites. For Geshur and Maacath live among Israel to this day. 14 Moses did not give any land to the family of Levi. Gifts given on the altar to the Lord, the God of Israel, are their share, as He said to him.

The Land of Reuben

15 Moses gave land to the family group of the Reubenites by their families. 16 Their land was from Aroer beside the Arnon valley, and the city in the center of the valley, and all the plain by Medeba, 17 with Heshbon and all its cities on the plain. There was Dibon, Bamoth-baal, Bethbaal-meon, 18 Jahaz, Kedemoth, Mephaath, 19 Kiriathaim, Sibmah. There was Zereth-shahar on the hill of the valley, 20 Beth-peor, the hill-sides of Pishgah, and Beth-jeshimoth. 21 There were all the cities of the plain, and all the nation of Sihon king of the Amorites who ruled in Heshbon. Moses won the war against Sihon and the leaders of Midian, Evi, Rekem, Zur, Hur, and Reba, the princes of Sihon, who lived in the land. 22 The sons of Israel also killed with the sword Balaam, the son of Beor, the one who told what would happen in the future. 23 The side of the land belonging to the people of Reuben was the Jordan. This is what was given to the people of Reuben for their families with their cities and towns.

The Land of Gad

24 Moses gave land to the family group of the Gadites for their families. 25 Their land was Jazer, and all the cities of Gilead. And it was half the land of the Ammonites, as far as Aroer which is east of Rabbah. 26 It went from Heshbon as far as Ramath-mizpeh and Betonim, and from Mahanaim as far as the land of Debir. 27 In the valley there was Bethharam, Beth-nimrah, Succoth, and Zaphon. They were given the rest of the nation of Sihon king of Heshbon, with the Jordan along its side. It went up to the south end of the Sea of Chinnereth east of the Jordan. 28 This is what was given to the people of Gad for their families with their cities and towns.

The Half-Family Group of Manasseh East of the Jordan River

29 Moses gave land to the half-family group of Manasseh. It was divided among the families of the half-family group of the sons of Manasseh. 30 Their land was from Mahanaim through all Bashan, all the nation of Og king of Bashan. It was all the towns

of Jair which are in Bashan, sixty cities.
31 It was half of Gilead, and Ashtaroth and Edrei, the cities of the nation of Og in Bashan. These were given to the people of Machir the son of Manasseh, for half of the sons of Machir by their families.

32 These are the lands which Moses divided in the plains of Moab on the other side of the Jordan east of Jericho. 33 But Moses did not give any land to the family of Levi. The Lord, the God of Israel, is their share, as He had told them.

The Land West of the Jordan Is Divided

14 These are the lands which the people of Israel received in the land of Canaan. They were given to them as a gift by Eleazar the religious leader, Joshua the son of Nun, and the heads of the fathers' houses of the families of the people of Israel. 2 Their share was decided upon by drawing names, as the Lord told Moses, for the nine families and the half-family group. 3 For Moses had given land to the two families and the half-family group east of the Jordan. But he did not give land to the Levites among them. 4 Because the sons of Joseph were two families, Manasseh and Ephraim. And they did not give part of the land to the Levites. They only gave them cities to live in, with fields for their animals and whatever they had. 5 The people of Israel did just as the Lord had told Moses. They divided the land.

Caleb Gets Hebron

6 Then the sons of Judah came to Joshua in Gilgal. Caleb the son of Jephunneh the Kenizzite said to him, "You know what the Lord said to Moses the man of God about you and me in Kadesh-barnea. 7 I was forty years old when the Lord's servant Moses sent me from Kadesh-barnea to spy out the land. I returned with news for him as it was in my heart. 8 My brothers who went up with me made the heart of the people weak with fear. But I followed the Lord my God with all my heart. 9 So Moses promised on that day, 'For sure the land where your foot has stepped will be a gift to you and your children forever. Because you have followed the Lord my God with all your heart.' 10 Now see, the Lord has let me live, as He said, these forty-five years since the Lord spoke this word to Moses while Israel walked in the desert. Today I am eighty-five years old. 11 I am as strong today as I was the day Moses sent me. I am as strong now as I was then, for war,

or for anything. 12 So now give me this hill country the Lord spoke about on that day. For you heard then that big powerful men were there, with strong cities with high walls. If the Lord will be with me, I will drive them out just as the Lord said."

13 So Joshua prayed that God would favor him. And he gave Hebron to Caleb the son of Jephunneh for his share. 14 Hebron became the land of Caleb the son of Jephunneh the Kenizzite to this day. Because he followed the Lord God of Israel with all his heart. 15 The name of Hebron had been Kiriath-arba. For Arba was the most powerful among the big powerful men. Then the land had rest from war.

The Land of Judah

15 The share of land for the family group of the people of Judah by their families was south to the land of Edom. It went to the Desert of Zin at the far south. 2 The south side of their land was from the south end of the Salt Sea. 3 It went south of the hill of Akrabbim and on to Zin. Then it went up by the south of Kadesh-barnea and on to Hezron and Addar and turned to Karka. 4 It went on to Azmon and the river of Egypt and ended at the sea. This was the south side of their land. 5 The east side was the Salt Sea, as far as the end of the Jordan. The north side was from the part of the sea at the end of the Jordan. 6 It went up to Beth-hoglah, passed north of Beth-arabah, and went up to the stone of Bohan the son of Reuben. 7 It went up to Debir from the valley of Achor, then turned north to Gilgal beside the hill of Adummim which is on the south side of the valley. It went on to the waters of En-shemesh, and ended at En-rogel. 8 Then the side of their land went up the valley of Ben-Hinnom to the hill of the Jebusite on the south (that is, Jerusalem). It went on to the top of the mountain beside the valley of Hinnom on the west, at the north end of the valley of Rephaim. 9 The side of their land then went from the top of the mountain to the well of the waters of Nephtoah. It went on to the cities of Mount Ephron, then turned to Baalah (that is, Kiriath-jearim). 10 The side of their land went around west of Baalah to Mount Seir. It went on to the north side of Mount Jearim (that is, Chesalon), then down to Beth-shemesh and on through Timnah. 11 The side of their land went on to the north side of Ekron. Then it turned to Shikkeron and went on to Mount

Baalah and on to Jabneel, and ended at the sea. ¹² The west side of their land was along the side of the Great Sea. These are the sides of the land of the people of Judah by their families.

Caleb Takes Hebron and Debir

¹³ Joshua gave Caleb son of Jephunneh a share among the people of Judah, as the Lord told him. It was Kiriath-arba (that is, Hebron), named for Arba, the father of Anak. ¹⁴ Caleb drove away from there the three sons of Anak. The children of Anak were Sheshai, Ahiman and Talmai. ¹⁵ From there he went to fight against the people of Debir. The name of Debir had been Kiriath-sepher before. ¹⁶ Caleb said, "I will give my daughter Achsah as a wife to the one who fights against Kiriath-sepher and takes it." ¹⁷ Othniel the son of Kenaz, Caleb's brother, took it. So Caleb gave him his daughter Achsah as a wife. ¹⁸ When she came to Othniel, she talked him into asking her father for a field. When she got down off her donkey, Caleb said to her, "What do you want?" ¹⁹ Achsah answered, "Give me a gift. You have given me the land of the Negev. Give me wells of water also." So Caleb gave her the wells in the high-land and in the valley.

The Cities of Judah

²⁰ This is the land given to the family group of the people of Judah for their families.

²¹ The cities of the family of Judah in the far south, toward the land of Edom, were Kabzeel, Eder, Jagur, ²² Kinah, Dimonah, Adadah, ²³ Kedesh, Hazor, Ithnan, ²⁴ Ziph, Telem, Bealoth, ²⁵ Hazor-hadattah, Kerioth-hezron (that is, Hazor), ²⁶ Amam, Shema, Moladah, ²⁷ Hazar-gaddah, Heshmon, Beth-pelet, ²⁸ Hazar-shual, Beersheba, Biziothiah, ²⁹ Baalah, Iim, Ezem, ³⁰ Eltolad, Chesil, Hormah, ³¹ Ziklag, Madmannah, Sansannah, ³² Lebaoth, Shilhim, Ain, and Rimmon. There were twenty-nine cities in all, with the towns around them.

³³ Near the sea were Eshtaol, Zorah, Ashnah, ³⁴ Zanoah, En-gannim, Tappuah, Enam, ³⁵ Jarmuth, Adullam, Socoh, Azekah, ³⁶ Shaaraim, Adithaim, Gederah, and Gederothaim, fourteen cities with their towns.

³⁷ And there were Zenan, Hadashah, Migdal-gad, ³⁸ Dilean, Mizpeh, Joktheel, ³⁹ Lachish, Bozkath, Eglon, ⁴⁰ Cabbon, Lahmas, Chitlish, ⁴¹ Gederoth, Beth-dagon, Naamah, and Makkedah, sixteen

cities with their towns. ⁴² There were Libnah, Ether, Ashan, ⁴³ Iphtah, Ashnah, Nezib, ⁴⁴ Keilah, Achzib, and Mareshah, nine cities with their towns.

⁴⁵ And there was Ekron with its towns and villages, ⁴⁶ from Ekron to the sea, all that were by the side of Ashdod, with their towns and villages.

⁴⁷ There were Ashdod with its towns and villages, and Gaza with its towns and villages, as far as the river of Egypt and the side of the Great Sea.

⁴⁸ In the hill country there were Shamir, Jattir, Socoh, ⁴⁹ Dannah, Kiriath-sannah (that is, Debir), ⁵⁰ Anab, Eshtemoh, Anim, ⁵¹ Goshen, Holon, and Giloh, eleven cities with their towns.

⁵² And there were Arab, Dumah, Eshan, ⁵³ Janum, Beth-tappuah, Aphekah, ⁵⁴ Humtah, Kiriath-arba (that is, Hebron), and Zior, nine cities with the towns around them.

⁵⁵ There were Maon, Carmel, Ziph, Juttah, ⁵⁶ Jezreel, Jokdeam, Zanoah, ⁵⁷ Kain, Gilbeah, and Timnah, ten cities with the towns around them.

⁵⁸ There were Halhul, Beth-zur, Gedor, ⁵⁹ Maarath, Beth-anoth, and Eltekon, six cities with the towns around them.

⁶⁰ And there were Kiriath-baal (that is, Kiriath-jearim), and Rabbah, two cities with the towns around them.

⁶¹ In the desert there were Betharabah, Middin, Secacah, ⁶² Nibshan, the City of Salt, and Engedi, six cities with the towns around them.

⁶³ But the sons of Judah could not drive out the Jebusites, the people of Jerusalem. So the Jebusites live with the people of Judah at Jerusalem to this day.

The Land Given to Ephraim and West Manasseh

16 The share of land for the people of Joseph went from the Jordan at Jericho, east of the waters of Jericho, into the desert. It went from Jericho through the hill country to Bethel. ² It went from Bethel to Luz, and on to the land of the Archites at Ataroth. ³ Then it went west to the land of the Japhletites, as far as the land of lower Beth-horon, and to Gezer. It ended at the sea.

⁴ The people of Joseph, Manasseh and Ephraim received their land.

The Land of Ephraim

⁵ The land of the people of Ephraim by their families on the east side was Ataroth-addar,

as far as upper Beth-horon. 6 Then the side of the land went toward the sea, with Mich-methath on the north, and turned east to Taanath-shiloh, and on to the east side of Janoah. 7 From Janoah it went down to Ataroth, to Naarah, touched Jericho, and ended at the Jordan. 8 From Tappuah it went west to the river of Kanah and ended at the sea. This is the land given to the family group of the people of Ephraim for their families. 9 And there are the cities which were set apart for the people of Ephraim within the land that was given to the people of Manasseh, all the cities with the towns around them. 10 But they did not drive out the Canaanites who lived in Gezer. So the Canaanites live among Ephraim to this day. But they have been made to work for the people of Ephraim.

The Half-Family Group of Manasseh West of the Jordan River

17 This was the share of land given to the family of Manasseh, the first-born of Joseph. Gilead and Bashan were given to Machir, the first-born of Manasseh, the father of Gilead, because he was a man of war. 2 And land was given to the rest of the sons of Manasseh for their families. The sons of Joseph's son Manasseh, with their families, were Abiezer, Helek, Asriel, Shechem, Hepher, and Shemida. 3 But Zelophehad, the son of Hepher, son of Gilead, son of Machir, son of Manasseh, had no sons, only daughters. The names of his daughters were Mahlah, Noah, Hoglah, Milcah, and Tirzah. 4 They came to Eleazar the religious leader, Joshua the son of Nun, and the leaders, saying, "The Lord told Moses to give us a share of land among our brothers." So they gave them a share of land among their father's brothers, as the Lord had said. 5 Ten parts of the land were given to Manasseh, besides the land of Gilead and Bashan on the other side of the Jordan; 6 because Manasseh's daughters received a share of land among his sons. The land of Gilead belonged to the rest of the sons of Manasseh.

7 The side of the land of Manasseh went from Asher to Michmethath, east of Shechem. Then it went south to the people of En-tappuah. 8 The land of Tappuah belonged to Manasseh. But the town of Tappuah on the side of Manasseh's land belonged to the sons of Ephraim. 9 Then the side of the land went down to the river of Kanah. The cities south of

the river, among the cities of Manasseh, belonged to Ephraim. Then Manasseh's land went along the north side of the river and ended at the sea. 10 The south side belonged to Ephraim. The north side belonged to Manasseh. Their land spread from the sea to Asher on the north and to Issachar on the east. 11 In Issachar and in Asher, Manasseh had Beth-shean and its towns, Ibleam and its towns, the people of Dor and its towns, the people of En-dor and its towns, the people of Taanach and its towns, and the people of Megiddo and its towns. The third city is Napheth. 12 But the sons of Manasseh could not take these cities for their own because the Canaan-ites would not leave that land. 13 When the people of Israel became strong, they made the Canaanites work for them. But they did not drive all of them out.

Ephraim and the West Part of Manasseh Ask for More Land

14 The sons of Joseph said to Joshua, "Why have you given us only one share of the land? We have many people. And the Lord has brought good to us until now." 15 Joshua said to them, "If you have many people, go up among the trees and clear a place for yourselves in the land of the Perizzites and the Rephaim, since the hill country of Ephraim is too narrow for you." 16 The sons of Joseph said, "The hill country is not enough for us. But all the Canaanites who live in the valley have iron war-wagons. Both those in Beth-shean and those in the valley of Jezreel have them." 17 Then Joshua said to the families of Joseph, to Ephraim and Manasseh, "You have many people and much power. You will not have only one share of land. 18 The hill country will be yours. It is full of trees, but you will clear it. All of it will be yours. For you will drive out the Canaanites, even if they have iron war-wagons and much strength."

The Rest of the Land Is Divided

18 Then all the people of Israel gath-ered together at Shiloh. They set up the tent of meeting there. The land around them had been taken in battle. 2 There were still seven family groups among the people of Israel who had not received their share of land. 3 So Joshua said to the people of Israel, "How long will you wait before going in to take the land the Lord, the God of your fathers, has given you? 4 Choose three men from each of these seven family groups. I will send them to go through the land and write down what they find it to be like, to be shared by each family. Then they will return to me. ⁵ They will divide it into seven parts. Judah will stay in his land in the south. The house of Joseph will stay in their land in the north. ⁶ You will write down how the land should be divided into seven parts, then bring it to me. I will draw names for you here before the Lord our God. ⁷ The Levites have no share of land among you. Being the religious leaders for the Lord is their share. Gad and Reuben and the half-family group of Manasseh have received their land east of the Jordan. The Lord's servant Moses gave it to them."

⁸ As the men got up to go, Joshua told them, "Go and walk through the land. Write down what you find, and return to me. Then I will draw names for you here before the Lord in Shiloh." ⁹ The men went and passed through the land. They wrote in a book the cities they found and divided them into seven parts. Then they returned to Joshua among the tents at Shiloh. ¹⁰ Joshua drew names for them in Shiloh before the Lord. There he divided the land among the people of Israel, a part for each family.

The Land of Benjamin

¹¹ The first name drawn was for the families of the people of Benjamin. The share of their land was between the people of Judah and the people of Joseph. ¹² The north side of their land was from the Jordan up to the north side of Jericho. Then it went west through the hill country, ending at the desert of Beth-aven. ¹³ The side of their land went from there south to the side of Luz (that is, Bethel). Then it went down to Ataroth-addar, near the hill south of the valley land of Beth-horon. ¹⁴ The side of their land turned west from there around the south side of the hill before Beth horon. It ended at Kiriath-baal (that is, Kiriath-jearim), a city of the people of Judah. This was the west side. ¹⁵ The south side was from the side of Kiriath-jearim west to the well of the waters of Nephtoah. ¹⁶ Then the side of their land went down to the side of the hill in the valley of Ben Hinnom, at the north end of the valley of Rephaim. It went down to the valley of Hinnom, south of the side of the Jebusites, and down to En-rogel. ¹⁷ Then it went north to En-shemesh and on to Geliloth by the hill of Adummim, then down to

the stone of Bohan the son of Reuben. ¹⁸ It went on to the north side of Beth-arabah, and down to the Arabah. ¹⁹ Then the side of their land went along the north side of Beth-hoglah. And it ended at the north waters of the Salt Sea at the south end of the Jordan. This was the south side. ²⁰ The east side of their land was the Jordan. This was the land with its sides, given to the family group of Benjamin.

²¹ The cities of the people of Benjamin for their families were Jericho, Beth-hoglah, Emek-keziz, ²² Betharabah, Zemaraim, Bethel, ²³ Avvim, Parah, Ophrah, ²⁴ Chephar-ammoni, Ophni, and Geba, twelve cities with their towns. ²⁵ And there were Gibeon, Ramah, Beeroth, ²⁶ Mizpeh, Chephirah, Mozah, ²⁷ Rekem, Irpeel, Taralah, ²⁸ Zelah, Haeleph, the Jebusite (that is, Jerusalem), Gibeah, and Kiriath, fourteen cities with their towns. This is the land that was given to the families of the people of Benjamin.

The Land of Simeon

19 The second name drawn was for the families of the people of Simeon. Their land was in the center of the land of the people of Judah. ² They had in their land the cities of Beersheba, Sheba, Moladah, ³ Hazar-shual, Balah, Ezem, ⁴ Eltolad, Bethul, Hormah, ⁵ Ziklag, Beth-marcaboth, Hazar-susah, ⁶ Beth-lebaoth, and Sharuhen, thirteen cities with the towns around them. ⁷ There were Ain, Rimmon, Ether, and Ashan, four cities with their towns. ⁸ And they had all the towns around these cities as far as Baalath-beer, also known as Ramah of the Negev. This was the land given to the families of the people of Simeon. ⁹ The land of the people of Simeon was taken from the land of the people of Judah. For the share of the people of Judah was too large for them. So the people of Simeon received a share of land in the center of Judah's land.

The Land of Zebulun

¹⁰ The third name drawn was for the families of the people of Zebulun. The share of their land was as far as Sarid. ¹¹ The side of their land went from there west to Marealah, touched Dabbesheth, and on to the river by Jokneam. ¹² It turned east from Sarid toward the sunrise as far as the land of Chisloth-tabor, then on to Daberath and up to Japhia. ¹³ From there it went east toward the sunrise to Gath-hepher, Eth-kazin, and on to Rimmon,

turning toward Neah. ¹⁴ Then the side of their land turned north to Hannathon, and ended at the valley of Iphtahel. ¹⁵ In their land were Kattah, Nahalal, Shimron, Idalah, and Bethlehem. In all there were twelve cities with the towns around them. ¹⁶ This is what was given to the families of the people of Zebulun, these cities with the towns around them.

The Land of Issachar

¹⁷ The fourth name drawn was for the families of the people of Issachar. ¹⁸ Their land spread to Jezreel. In it were Chesulloth, Shunem, ¹⁹ Hapharaim, Shion, Anaharath, ²⁰ Rabbith, Kishion, Ebez, ²¹ Remeth, En-gannim, En-haddah, and Bethpazzez. ²² Their land spread to Tabor, Shahazumah, Beth-shemesh, and ended at the Jordan, with sixteen cities and their towns. ²³ This is what was given to the families of the people of Issachar, the cities with the towns around them.

The Land of Asher

²⁴ The fifth name drawn was for the families of the people of Asher. ²⁵ In their land were Helkath, Hali, Beten, Achshaph, ²⁶ Allammelech, Amad, and Mishal. It spread west to Carmel and Shihor-libnath. ²⁷ It turned east to Beth-dagon and to Zebulun along the valley of Iphtahel north to Bethemek and Neiel. Then it went on north to Cabul, ²⁸ Ebron, Rehob, Hammon, and Kanah, as far as the big city of Sidon. ²⁹ From there the side of their land turned toward Ramah and then to the strong city of Tyre, turned again to Hosah, and ended at the sea near Achzib, ³⁰ Ummah, Aphek and Rehob. There were twenty-two cities with the towns around them. ³¹ This is what was given to the families of the people of Asher, these cities with the towns around them.

The Land of Naphtali

³² The sixth name drawn was for the people of Naphtali, for the families of the people of Naphtali. ³³ Their land spread from Heleph, from the big tree in Zaanannim. It went through Adami-nekeb and Jabneel as far as Lakkum. And it ended at the Jordan. ³⁴ The side of their land turned from there west to Aznoth-tabor, and went on to Hukkok. It spread to Zebulun in the south, Asher in the west, and to Judah at the Jordan in the east. ³⁵ The strong cities were Ziddim, Zer, Hammath, Rakkath, Chinnereth, ³⁶ Adamah, Ramah,

Hazor, ³⁷ Kedesh, Edrei, En-hazor, ³⁸ Yiron, Migdal-el, Horem, Beth-anath, and Beth-shemesh. There were nineteen cities with their towns. ³⁹ This is what was given to the families of the people of Naphtali, the cities with their towns.

The Land of Dan

⁴⁰ The seventh name drawn was for the families of the people of Dan. ⁴¹ In their land were Zorah, Eshtaol, Ir-shemesh, ⁴² Shaalabbin, Aijalon, Ithlah, ⁴³ Elon, Timnah, Ekron, ⁴⁴ Eltekeh, Gibbethon, Baalath, ⁴⁵ Jehud, Bene-berak, Gath-rimmon, ⁴⁶ Me-jarkon and Rakkon, with the land near Joppa. ⁴⁷ The people of Dan needed more land. So they went up and fought with Leshem and took it with the sword. They took it for themselves and lived in it. And they gave it the name Leshem Dan after the name of Dan their father. ⁴⁸ This is what was given to the families of the people of Dan, these cities with their towns.

The Land That Joshua Received

⁴⁹ When they finished dividing the land and giving to each family group their share, then the people of Israel gave some land among them to Joshua the son of Nun. ⁵⁰ As the Lord had told them, they gave him the city he asked for. They gave him Timnath-serah in the hill country of Ephraim. So he built the city and lived in it.

⁵¹ This is the land which was given by Eleazar the religious leader, Joshua the son of Nun, and the heads of the houses of the families of the people of Israel. It was given by drawing names in Shiloh before the Lord at the door of the meeting tent. So they finished dividing the land.

The Cities Where People Could Run to Be Safe

20 The Lord said to Joshua, ² "Say to the people of Israel, 'Choose the cities where you may go and be safe when you are in trouble, as I said to you through Moses. ³ So the man who kills any person without meaning to or planning to may run to one of these cities. They will be places where you can go to be safe from the one who wants to punish you for the killing. ⁴ He will run to one of these cities and stand at the city gate. There he will tell his story to the leaders of that city. They will take him into the city and give him a place. So he may live among them. ⁵ If the one who wants to punish him comes after him, they will not give him the one who killed the person, because he killed his neighbor without planning to, and did not hate him in the past. [6] He will live in that city until he has been tried in front of the people. And he will live there until the death of the one who is the head religious leader at the time. Then the one who killed the person may return to his own city and his own house, to the city he ran away from.' "

[7] So they set apart Kedesh in Galilee in the hill country of Naphtali. They set apart Shechem in the hill country of Ephraim. And they set apart Kiriath-arba (that is, Hebron) in the hill country of Judah. [8] On the other side of the Jordan east of Jericho, they set apart Bezer in the desert plain from the family of Reuben. They set apart Ramoth in Gilead from the family of Gad. And they set apart Golan in Bashan from the family of Manasseh. [9] These were the chosen cities for all the people of Israel and for the stranger staying among them. So whoever killed any person without meaning to could run there. He could not be killed by the one who wanted to punish him, before standing trial in front of the people.

The Cities of the Levites

21 Then the family heads of the Levites came to Eleazar the religious leader, Joshua the son of Nun, and the heads of the family groups of Israel. [2] They said to them at Shiloh in Canaan, "The Lord said through Moses to give us cities to live in, as well as fields around them for our cattle." [3] So the sons of Israel gave these cities and fields of their land to the Levites, as the Lord had said. [4] The name drawn first was for the families of the Kohathites. The Levites who were children of Aaron the religious leader received thirteen cities from the families of Judah, Simeon and Benjamin. [5] The rest of the sons of Kohath by drawing names received ten cities from the families of Ephraim and Dan and the half-family group of Manasseh. [6] The sons of Gershon by drawing names received thirteen cities from the families of Issachar, Asher, Naphtali and the half-family group of Manasseh in Bashan. [7] The sons of Merari received twelve cities from the families of Reuben, Gad and Zebulun. [8] The sons of Israel by drawing names gave these cities with their fields to the Levites, as the Lord had said through Moses.

[9] They gave from the families of Judah and Simeon the cities given here by name. [10] They were for the sons of Aaron, one of the families of the Kohathites, of the sons of Levi. For their name was drawn first. [11] They gave them Kiriath-arba (that is, Hebron) with the fields around it in the hill country of Judah. (Arba was the father of Anak.) [12] But the city's fields and towns had been given to Caleb the son of Jephunneh as his own.

[13] So to the sons of Aaron the religious leader they gave Hebron and Libnah with their fields. Hebron was the city where one who killed a man could go to be safe. [14] And they gave them Jattir with its fields, Eshtemoa with its fields, [15] Holon with its fields, Debir with its fields, [16] Ain with its fields, Juttah with its fields, and Beth-shemesh with its fields. There were nine cities from these two family groups. [17] From the family of Benjamin were given Gibeon with its fields, Geba with its fields, [18] Anathoth with its fields, and Almon with its fields, four cities. [19] For the sons of Aaron, the religious leaders, there were thirteen cities in all, with their fields.

[20] Then cities from the family of Ephraim were given to the rest of the families of the people of Kohath, the Levites. [21] They gave them Shechem with its fields in the hill country of Ephraim. A man who killed another person could run to Shechem to be safe. And they gave them Gezer with its fields, [22] Kibzaim with its fields, and Beth-horon with its fields, four cities. [23] From the family of Dan were given Elteke with its fields, Gibbethon with its fields, [24] Aijalon with its fields, and Gath-rimmon with its fields, four cities. [25] From the half-family group of Manasseh were given Taanach with its fields, and Gath-rimmon with its fields, two cities. [26] There were ten cities in all, with their fields, for the rest of the families of the Kohathites.

[27] From the half-family group of Manasseh they gave Golan in Bashan and Be-eshterah and their fields to the sons of Gershon, one of the Levite families. A man who killed another person could run to Golan in Bashan to be safe. They were given two cities. [28] From the family of Issachar were given Kishion with its fields, Daberath with its fields, [29] Jarmuth with its fields, and Engannim with its fields, four cities. [30] From the family of Asher were given Mishal with its fields, Abdon with its fields, [31] Helkath with its fields, and Rehob with its fields, four cities. [32] From

the family of Naphtali were given Kedesh in Galilee with its fields, Hammoth-dor with its fields, and Kartan with its fields, three cities. A man who killed another man could run to Kedesh to be safe. 33 The cities for the families of the Gershonites were thirteen in all, with their fields.

34 They gave cities to the families of the sons of Merari, the rest of the Levites, from the family of Zebulun. They gave them Jokneam with its fields, Kartah with its fields, 35 Dimnah with its fields, and Nahalal with its fields, four cities. 36 From the family of Reuben were given Bezer with its fields, Jahaz with its fields, 37 Kedemoth with its fields, and Mephaath with its fields, four cities. 38 From the family of Gad was given Ramoth in Gilead with its fields. A man who killed another person could run to Ramoth in Gilead to be safe. And they gave them Mahanaim with its fields, 39 Heshbon with its fields, and Jazer with its fields, four cities in all. 40 There were twelve cities in all given to the families of the people of Merari, the rest of the families of the Levites.

41 The cities of the Levites among the land of the people of Israel were forty-eight cities in all, with their fields. 42 Each one of these cities had its fields around it. So it was with all these cities.

Israel Takes over the Land

43 The Lord gave Israel all the land He had promised to give to their fathers. They took it for their own, and lived in it. 44 The Lord gave them peace on every side, just as He had promised their fathers. Not one of all those who hated them could stand in front of them. The Lord gave all those who hated them into their hand. 45 Every good promise which the Lord had made to the people of Israel came true.

Joshua Sends Eastern Family Groups Home

22 Joshua called the Reubenites, the Gadites and the half-family group of Manasseh. 2 He said to them, "You have done all that the Lord's servant Moses told you to do. You have obeyed me in all I have told you to do. 3 You have not left your brothers alone even to this day. But you have been careful to do what the Lord your God has told you. 4 Now the Lord your God has given rest to your brothers, as He promised them. So go now. Return to your homes in your own land, which the Lord's servant Moses gave you on the other side

of the Jordan. 5 Only be very careful to obey the Law which the Lord's servant Moses told you. Love the Lord your God. Walk in all His ways. Obey His Laws. Stay close to Him, and work for Him with all your heart and soul." 6 Joshua prayed that good would come to them, and sent them away. Then they went to their homes.

7 Moses had given land in Bashan to the half-family group of Manasseh. But Joshua gave land west of the Jordan to the other half of the family among their brothers. Joshua prayed that good would come to them when he sent them away to their homes. 8 He said to them, "Return to your homes with much riches, many animals, silver, gold, brass, iron, and very many clothes. Share with your brothers the riches taken from those who fought against you." 9 The sons of Reuben and Gad and the half-family group of Manasseh returned home. They left the people of Israel at Shiloh in the land of Canaan and went to their own land of Gilead. They had taken this land by the word of the Lord through Moses.

An Altar beside the Jordan

10 The sons of Reuben and Gad and the half-family group of Manasseh came to the Jordan River. Before they crossed the Jordan, they built a very large altar on the Canaan side of the Jordan. 11 The people of Israel heard the news, "See, the people of Reuben and Gad and the half-family group of Manasseh have built an altar in the land of Canaan by the Jordan. It stands on the side that belongs to the people of Israel." 12 When the people of Israel heard about it, all the sons of Israel gathered at Shiloh to make war against them.

13 Then the sons of Israel sent Phinehas the son of the religious leader Eleazar into the land of Gilead to the people of Reuben and Gad and the half-family group of Manasseh. 14 With him were ten leaders, one leader from each ruling house in every family of Israel. Each one was the head of his father's house among the families of Israel. 15 They came to the people of Reuben and Gad and the half-family group of Manasseh in the land of Gilead, and said to them, 16 "All the people of the Lord say, 'What sin is this that you have done against the God of Israel? You have turned away from following the Lord this day, by building yourselves an altar. Today you have gone against the Lord. 17 Is not the sin of Peor enough for us? We have made

ourselves unclean from that to this day, and much trouble has come upon the people of the Lord. 18 Now to add to that sin, this day you have turned away from following the Lord. If you go against the Lord today, He will be angry with all the people of Israel tomorrow. 19 Now if the land you have been given is unclean, cross over into the Lord's land. Take land for yourselves among us. But do not go against the Lord, or against us, by building an altar other than the altar of the Lord our God. 20 Did not Zerah's son Achan sin by taking things that should have been destroyed? Anger came upon all the people of Israel. He did not die alone for his sin.' " 21 Then the people of Reuben and Gad and the half-family group of Manasseh answered the leaders of the families of Israel, saying, 22 "The Powerful One, the Lord, the Powerful One, God, the Lord! He knows! And may Israel itself know! If it was going against the Lord and not being faithful to Him, do not save us this day! 23 If we have built an altar to turn away from following the Lord, or to give burnt gifts, grain gifts or peace gifts on it, may the Lord Himself punish us. 24 We have done this because we were afraid that in time to come your children might say to our children, 'What have you to do with the Lord, the God of Israel? 25 For the Lord has put the Jordan between us and you people of Reuben and Gad. You have nothing to do with the Lord.' Then your children might make our children stop worshiping the Lord. 26 So we said, 'Let us build an altar. It will not be for burnt gifts or killing animals in worship.' 27 But it will be something special to be seen between us and you and our children after us. It will show that we are to serve the Lord before Him with our burnt gifts, our gifts of animals and our peace gifts. Then your children will not say to our children in the future, "You have nothing to do with the Lord." ' 28 We thought that if they say this to us or our children in the future we can say, 'See the altar we have made like the altar of the Lord which our fathers made. It is not for burnt gifts or killing animals in worship. But it is something special to see between us and you.' 29 Never let it be said that we went against the Lord and turned away from following the Lord this day by building an altar. It is not for burnt gifts or grain gifts or killing animals in worship. It is not to be used instead of the altar of the Lord our God before His meeting tent."

30 Phinehas the religious leader and the leaders of the people, the heads of the families of Israel who were with him, were pleased when they heard the words of the people of Reuben, Gad and Manasseh. 31 Phinehas the son of Eleazar the religious leader said to the people of Reuben, Gad and Manasseh, "Today we know that the Lord is among us. Because you have not done this as sin against the Lord. Now you have saved the people of Israel from the hand of the Lord." 32 Then Phinehas the son of the religious leader Eleazar and the leaders left the people of Reuben and Gad. They returned from the land of Gilead to the people of Israel in the land of Canaan. And they told them what had happened. 33 The news pleased the people of Israel, and they gave thanks to God. They said no more about going against them in war, to destroy the land where the people of Reuben and Gad were living. 34 The people of Reuben and Gad said, "This altar shows the agreement between us that the Lord is God."

Joshua's Last Words to the People

23 A long time after that, the Lord had given Israel rest from all those around them who hated them. Joshua had grown old, and had lived many years. 2 Joshua called all Israel, their leaders, their heads, and the men chosen among them who judge between what is right or wrong. Then he said to them, "I am old and have lived many years. 3 And you have seen all the Lord your God has done to all these nations because of you. The Lord your God is the One Who has fought for you. 4 See, I have given to you as land for your families those nations that are left, with all the nations I have destroyed. They lie from the Jordan to the Great Sea in the west. 5 The Lord your God will send them out from in front of you. He will send them away from you. Then their land will be yours, just as the Lord your God promised you. 6 So do not be moved by others. Keep and obey all that is written in the book of the Law of Moses. Do not turn from it to the right or to the left. 7 Do not mix with these nations that stay among you. Do not say the names of their gods or make anyone swear by them. Do not work for them or worship them. 8 But hold on to the Lord your God, as you have done to this day. 9 For the Lord has driven away large and strong nations from in front of you. No man has been able to stand in front of you to this day. 10 One of your men makes a thousand run away. For the Lord your God is the One Who fights for you, just as He promised you. 11 Be very careful to love the Lord your God. 12 For if you ever turn away and join the people of these nations left among you and marry some of their people and go among them, 13 know for sure that the Lord your God will stop driving these nations away from you. And they will be a net and a trap to you. They will be a whip on your sides and thorns in your eyes, until you are destroyed from this good land the Lord your God has given you.

14 "See, today I am going the way of all the earth. Know in all your hearts and in all your souls that not one of all the good promises the Lord your God made to you has been broken. All have come true for you. Not one of them has been broken. 15 Every good promise the Lord your God made to you has come true. But in the same way, He will keep His promises to punish you. He will punish you until He has destroyed you from this good land the Lord your God has given you. 16 If you do not keep the agreement the Lord your God made with you, and serve other gods and worship them, then the anger of the Lord will burn against you and you will be destroyed from the good land He has given you."

The Agreement at Shechem

24 Then Joshua gathered all the families of Israel to Shechem. He called for the leaders of Israel, the heads of the families and those who judged between what is right or wrong. And they showed themselves before God. 2 Joshua said to all the people, "This is what the Lord, the God of Israel, says: 'Long ago your fathers lived on the other side of the River. There was Terah, the father of Abraham and Nahor. And they worshiped other gods. 3 Then I took your father Abraham from the other side of the River. I led him through all the land of Canaan. I gave him many children, and I gave him Isaac. 4 To Isaac I gave Jacob and Esau. I gave Mount Seir to Esau for his own. But Jacob and his children went down to Egypt. 5 I sent Moses and Aaron. I had to bring trouble upon Egypt by what I did among them. Then I brought you out. 6 I brought your fathers out of Egypt to the Sea. Egypt went after your fathers to the Red Sea with war-wagons and horsemen. 7 But when they cried out to the Lord, He

put darkness between you and the Egyptians. He brought the sea upon them and covered them. Your own eyes saw what I did in Egypt. And you lived in the desert for a long time. 8 I brought you into the land of the Amorites who lived on the east side of the Jordan. They fought with you, and I gave them to you. You took their land for your own when I destroyed them in front of you.

9 Then Balak the son of Zippor, king of Moab, came and fought against Israel. He sent for Balaam the son of Beor to curse you. 10 But I would not listen to Balaam. So he had to pray for good to come to you. And I saved you from his hand.

11 'You crossed the Jordan and came to Jericho. The people of Jericho fought against you. And the Amorite, the Perizzite, the Canaanite, the Hittite, the Girgashite, the Hivite and the Jebusite fought against you. So I gave them into your hand. 12 I sent the hornets ahead of you. They drove out the people and the two kings of the Amorites from in front of you. You did not do it by your sword or bow. 13 I gave you a land you did not work for. You live in cities you did not build. You are eating from vines and olive trees you did not plant.'

14 "So fear the Lord. Serve Him in faith and truth. Put away the gods your fathers served on the other side of the river and in Egypt. Serve the Lord. 15 If you think it is wrong to serve the Lord, choose today whom you will serve. Choose the gods your fathers worshiped on the other side of the river, or choose the gods of the Amorites in whose land you are living. But as for me and my family, we will serve the Lord."

16 The people answered, "May it never be that we turn away from the Lord and serve other gods. 17 For the Lord our God is the One Who brought us and our fathers out of the land of Egypt, from the house where we were made to work. He did these powerful works in front of our eyes. He kept us safe everywhere we went, among all the nations we passed through. 18 The Lord drove away from in front of us all the nations, even the Amorites who lived in the land. So we will serve the Lord. For He is our God."

19 Then Joshua said to the people, "You will not be able to serve the Lord. For He is a holy God. He is a jealous God. He will not forgive your wrong-doing or your sins. 20 If you turn away from the Lord and serve strange gods, He will turn and

punish you. He will destroy you after He has been good to you." 21 The people said to Joshua, "Not so, for we will serve the Lord." 22 Then Joshua said to the people, "You have spoken for yourselves that you have chosen to serve the Lord." And they said, "We have spoken for ourselves." 23 Joshua said, "So put away the strange gods that are among you. Give your hearts to the Lord, the God of Israel." 24 The people said to Joshua, "We will serve the Lord our God. We will obey His voice." 25 So Joshua made an agreement with the people that day. And he made Laws for them in Shechem. 26 Joshua wrote these words in the book of the Law of God. Then he took a large stone and set it up there under the tree that was by the holy place of the Lord. 27 Joshua said to all the people, "See, this stone will be here to speak against us. For it has heard all the words the Lord spoke to us. So it will be here to speak against you, if you do not stay true to

your God." 28 Then Joshua sent the people away, each to his own land.

The Death of Joshua and Eleazar

29 After this, Joshua the son of Nun, the Lord's servant, died. He was 110 years old. 30 They buried him in the land he was given in Timnath-serah, in the hill country of Ephraim, north of Mount Gaash. 31 Israel served the Lord all the days of Joshua, and of the leaders who lived after him who had known all the works the Lord had done for Israel.

32 The people of Israel brought the bones of Joseph from Egypt. They buried them in Shechem, in the piece of ground Jacob had bought from the sons of Hamor the father of Shechem for 100 pieces of money. It became the land of Joseph's children.

33 Eleazar the son of Aaron died also. They buried him on the hill at Gibeah that was given to his son Phinehas in the hill country of Ephraim.

JUDGES

Adoni-bezek Is Taken

1 After the death of Joshua, the people of Israel asked the Lord, "Who will be first to go up and fight against the Canaanites for us?" 2 The Lord said, "Judah will go up. See, I have given the land into his hand." 3 Then Judah said to his brother Simeon, "Come with me into the land which is given to me. Let us fight against the Canaanites together. Then I will go with you into the land which is given to you." So Simeon went with him. 4 Judah went up, and the Lord gave the Canaanites and the Perizzites into their hands. They killed 10,000 men at Bezek. 5 They found Adoni-bezek in Bezek and fought against him, and they won the war against the Canaanites and the Perizzites. 6 Adoni-bezek tried to run away, but they went after him and caught him. They cut off his thumbs and big toes. 7 Adoni-bezek said, "Seventy kings with their thumbs and big toes cut off had to gather their food under my table. Now God has paid me for what I have done." So they brought him to Jerusalem and there he died.

8 Then the men of Judah fought against Jerusalem and took it. They destroyed it with the sword and set the city on fire. 9 After this the men of Judah went down to fight against the Canaanites living in the

hill country, in the Negev and in the plains. 10 Judah went against the Canaanites who lived in Hebron. (The name of Hebron was Kiriath-arba before.) They won the war against Sheshai and Ahiman and Talmai.

11 From there Judah went against the people of Debir. (The name of Debir was Kiriath-sepher before.) 12 Caleb said, "I will give my daughter Achsah as a wife to the one who fights against Kiriath-sepher and takes it." 13 Othniel the son of Kenaz, Caleb's younger brother, took the city. So Caleb gave him his daughter Achsah for a wife. 14 When she came to Othniel, she talked him into asking her father for a field. As she came down from her donkey, Caleb said to her, "What do you want?" 15 She said to him, "Give me a special gift. You have given me the land of the Negev. Give me the wells of water also." So Caleb gave her the wells in the high land and in the valley.

16 The children of the Kenite, Moses' father-in-law, went with the people of Judah from Jericho to the desert of Judah south of Arad. They went and lived with the people. 17 Then Judah went with his brother Simeon. They killed the Canaanites living in Zephath and destroyed the whole city. The name of the city was called Hormah. 18 Judah took Gaza with

its land, Ashkelon with its land, and Ekron with its land. 19 The Lord was with Judah. They took the hill country for their own. They could not drive out the people living in the valley, because they had iron war-wagons. 20 They gave Hebron to Caleb, as Moses had promised, and he drove out the three sons of Anak. 21 But the people of Benjamin did not drive out the Jebusites who lived in Jerusalem. So the Jebusites have lived with the people of Benjamin in Jerusalem to this day.

22 The men of the family of Joseph went up against Bethel. And the Lord was with them. 23 Those of the family of Joseph spied out Bethel. (The name of the city was Luz before.) 24 The men who were spying out Bethel saw a man coming out of the city. They said to him, "Show us the way into the city, and we will be kind to you." 25 So he showed them the way into the city. They destroyed the city with the sword. But they let the man and all his family go free. 26 The man went into the land of the Hittites. He built a city there and gave it the name of Luz. That is its name to this day.

Some of the People Were Not Driven Out of the Land

27 But the men of Manasseh did not take for their own Beth-shean and its towns or Taanach and its towns. They did not drive out the people of Dor and its towns, or of Ibleam and its towns, or of Megiddo and its towns. So the Canaanites stayed in that land. 28 When Israel became strong, they made the Canaanites work for them. But they did not drive all of them out.

29 Ephraim did not drive out the Canaanites who were living in Gezer. So the Canaanites lived in Gezer among them.

30 Zebulun did not drive out the people of Kitron or the people of Nahalol. So the Canaanites lived among them and were made to work.

31 Asher did not drive out the people of Acco, or the people of Sidon, Ahlab, Achzib, Helbah, Aphik, or Rehob. 32 So the Asherites lived among the Canaanites, the people of the land. For they did not drive them out.

33 Naphtali did not drive out the people of Beth-shemesh or the people of Beth-anath. But they lived among the Canaanites, the people of the land. The people of Beth-shemesh and Beth-anath were made to work for them.

34 The Amorites drove the people of Dan into the hill country. They did not let them come down to the valley. 35 The Amorites would not leave Mount Heres, Aijalon or Shaalbim. But when the family of Joseph became strong, they made the Amorites work for them. 36 The land of the Amorites was from the hill-side of Akrabbim, up from Sela.

The Angel of the Lord Speaks to Israel

2 The angel of the Lord came up from Gilgal to Bochim. And he said, "I brought you out of Egypt and led you into the land I promised your fathers. I said, 'I will never break My agreement with you. 2 Do not make any agreement with the people of this land. Tear down their altars.' But you have not obeyed Me. What is this you have done? 3 So now I say, 'I will not drive them away from you. They will be like thorns in your sides. Their gods will be a trap to you.' " 4 When the angel of the Lord spoke these words to all the people of Israel, the people cried in a loud voice. 5 So they called that place Bochim. And there they gave gifts in worship to the Lord.

The Death of Joshua

6 When Joshua sent the people of Israel away, each one went home to his own land. 7 The people served the Lord all the days of Joshua and all the days of the leaders who lived longer than Joshua and who had seen all the great works the Lord had done for Israel. 8 Joshua the son of Nun, the servant of the Lord, died when he was 110 years old. 9 They buried him within his land in Timnath-heres, in the hill country of Ephraim, north of Mount Gaash. 10 All the people of that day died. The children who came after them did not know the Lord. They did not know about the things He had done for Israel.

Israel Is No Longer Faithful to the Lord

11 Then the people of Israel sinned in the eyes of the Lord. They served the Baals, the gods of the Canaanites. 12 They turned away from the Lord, the God of their fathers, Who had brought them out of the land of Egypt. They followed other gods of the nations around them, and worshiped them. So they made the Lord angry. 13 They turned away from the Lord and served Baal and the Ashtaroth. 14 The Lord was angry with Israel. He gave them into the hands of angry men who robbed them. He sold them into the hands of those around them who hated

them. The people of Israel could no longer stand in front of those who hated them. [15] The Lord punished them everywhere they went. The Lord did what He had told them and promised them He would do. The people were very troubled.

[16] Then the Lord gave them special men to judge between what was right or wrong. These men saved them from those who robbed them. [17] But the people did not listen to those chosen to judge. The people were not faithful to the Lord and they worshiped other gods. They were quick to turn aside from the way their fathers had walked in obeying the Laws of the Lord. They did not do as their fathers had done. [18] When the Lord gave them special men to judge them, the Lord was with the judge. And He saved them from those who hated them. For the Lord showed them pity because of their pain when others made it hard for them and hurt them. [19] But when the judge died, they would turn again and act worse than their fathers. They would follow other gods and serve them and worship them. They would not give up their sinful acts or their strong wills. [20] So the anger of the Lord was against Israel. He said, "This nation has sinned against My agreement I made with their fathers. They have not listened to My voice. [21] I will stop driving away from them any of the nations Joshua left when he died. [22] I will use them to test Israel. I will see if Israel will keep the way of the Lord to walk in it like their fathers did, or not." [23] So the Lord let those nations stay. He was not quick to drive them out. And He did not give them into the power of Joshua.

The Nations That Are Still in the Land

3 These are the nations the Lord left to test Israel. They were left to test all those who had not fought in any of the wars in Canaan. [2] So the children of the people of Israel who had not fought in wars might be taught about war. [3] These nations are: the five rulers of the Philistines, all the Canaanites, the Sidonians, and the Hivites who lived on Mount Lebanon, from Mount Baal-hermon as far as Lebo-hamath. [4] They were left to test Israel, to find out if Israel would obey the Laws the Lord gave their fathers through Moses. [5] The people of Israel lived among the Canaanites, the Hittites, the Amorites, the Perizzites, the Hivites and the Jebusites. [6] They married their daughters. They gave

their own daughters to their sons, and they worshiped their gods. [7] The people of Israel did what was sinful in the eyes of the Lord. They forgot the Lord their God and served the Baals and the Asheroth. [8] So the anger of the Lord was against Israel. He sold them into the hand of Cushan-rishathaim king of Mesopotamia. The people of Israel worked for Cushan-rishathaim for eight years. [9] But the people of Israel cried to the Lord. And the Lord gave the people of Israel someone who would save them. He gave them Othniel the son of Kenaz, Caleb's younger brother. [10] The Spirit of the Lord came upon him, and he led Israel. When he went out to war, the Lord gave Cushan-rishathaim king of Mesopotamia into his hand. He was stronger than Cushan-rishathaim. [11] The land had rest for forty years. Then Othniel the son of Kenaz died.

[12] The people of Israel sinned in the eyes of the Lord again. So the Lord gave Eglon king of Moab strength against Israel, because they had sinned in the eyes of the Lord. [13] Eglon gathered together with the people of Ammon and Amalek. They went and won the war against Israel. And they took the city of Jericho. [14] The people of Israel worked for Eglon the king of Moab for eighteen years.

[15] But when the people of Israel cried to the Lord, the Lord gave them someone to save them. He gave them Ehud the son of Gera, the Benjamite, a left-handed man. The people of Israel sent taxes by him to Eglon the king of Moab. [16] Ehud made a sword for himself with two sharp sides, almost as long as an arm. He tied it to the top part of his right leg, under his coat. [17] Then he brought the taxes to Eglon king of Moab. Now Eglon was a very fat man. [18] When Ehud had finished paying the taxes, he sent away the people who had carried the taxes. [19] But he himself turned around at the stone gods of Gilgal and returned to Eglon, saying, "I have secret news for you, O king." Eglon said, "Keep quiet." And all who stood by him went away from him. [20] Ehud came to him while Eglon was sitting alone in his summer room. And Ehud said, "I have news from God for you." The king got up from his seat. [21] Ehud put out his left hand, took the sword from his right leg, and pushed it into Eglon's stomach. [22] The whole sword went into his stomach and the fat closed over it. For he did not pull the sword out of his stomach. The insides of Eglon's stomach ran out. [23] Then

Ehud went out the back way. He closed the doors of the summer room behind him, and locked them.

24 When Ehud had gone out, Eglon's servants came. They saw that the doors of the summer room were locked. So they said, "He is only resting in there away from the heat." 25 They waited until they were afraid because Eglon did not open the doors of the summer room. So they opened the lock and looked in the doors. And they found their owner lying dead on the floor.

26 Ehud got away while they were waiting. He passed the stone gods and got away to Seirah. 27 When he got there, he blew the horn in the hill country of Ephraim. Then the people of Israel went down with him from the hill country. Ehud went in front of them. 28 He said to them, "Go after them. For the Lord has given into your hands the Moabites who hate you." So they went down after him. They took over the crossing places of the Jordan beside Moab. And they did not let anyone cross. 29 At that time they killed about 10,000 Moabites, all strong men with strength of heart. No one got away. 30 So Moab was crushed under the power of Israel that day. And the land had rest for eighty years.

31 After Ehud, Shamgar the son of Anath became the leader. He killed 600 Philistines with a stick used to push cattle, and he also saved Israel.

Deborah and Barak

4 After Ehud died, the people of Israel sinned in the eyes of the Lord again. 2 So the Lord let them be taken by Jabin king of Canaan, who ruled in Hazor. The head of his army was Sisera, who lived in Harosheth-hagoyim. 3 The people of Israel cried to the Lord, for Jabin had 900 iron war-wagons. He made it very hard for the people of Israel for twenty years.

4 Now Lappidoth's wife Deborah, a woman who spoke for God, was judging Israel at that time. 5 She would sit under the tree of Deborah between Ramah and Bethel in the hill country of Ephraim. And the people of Israel came to her to find out what was right or wrong. 6 She sent for Barak the son of Abinoam from Kedesh-naphtali, and said to him, "The Lord, the God of Israel, says, 'Go to Mount Tabor. Take with you 10,000 men from the sons of Naphtali and Zebulun. 7 I will have Sisera, the head of Jabin's army, meet you at the river Kishon. He will have his war-wagons

and his many soldiers with him. But I will give him into your hand.' " 8 Then Barak said to her, "I will go if you go with me. But if you do not go with me, I will not go." 9 And she said, "For sure I will go with you. But the honor will not be yours as you go on your way. For the Lord will sell Sisera into the hands of a woman." Then Deborah got up and went with Barak to Kedesh. 10 Barak called Zebulun and Naphtali to come to Kedesh. He went up with 10,000 men. And Deborah went up with him.

11 Now Heber the Kenite had gone away from the Kenites, from the sons of Hobab the father-in-law of Moses. He had put up his tent as far away as the big tree in Zaanannim, near Kedesh.

12 They told Sisera that Barak the son of Abinoam had gone up to Mount Tabor. 13 Sisera gathered together all his 900 iron war-wagons. He gathered together all the people who were with him, from Harosheth-hagoyim to the river Kishon. 14 Deborah said to Barak, "Get up! For this is the day the Lord has given Sisera into your hands. See, the Lord has gone out before you." So Barak went down from Mount Tabor, and 10,000 men followed him. 15 The Lord brought trouble upon Sisera and all his war-wagons and all his army in front of Barak with the sword. Sisera got down from his war-wagon and ran away on foot. 16 But Barak went after the war-wagons and the army as far as Harosheth-hagoyim. All of Sisera's army fell by the sword. Not one was left.

17 Sisera ran away on foot to the tent of Jael the wife of Heber the Kenite. For there was peace between Jabin the king of Hazor and the family of Heber the Kenite. 18 Jael went out to meet Sisera, saying, "Come in, my lord. Come in to me. Do not be afraid." So he went into her tent, and she put a cover over him. 19 He said to her, "Give me a little water to drink. For I am thirsty." So she opened a skin bag of milk and gave him a drink. Then she covered him. 20 He said to her, "Stand in the door of the tent. If anyone comes and asks you, 'Is there anyone here?' you say, 'No.' " 21 But Heber's wife Jael took a big tent nail in her hand and a tool to hit it with. Because Sisera was very tired, he went into a deep sleep. She went to him in secret and hit the big nail into the side of his head. It went through and into the ground. So he died. 22 As Barak came after Sisera, Jael came out to meet him. She said to him, "Come. I will show you the man you are

looking for." So Barak went in with her, and he saw Sisera lying dead with the big tent nail in his head.

23 God put Jabin the king of Canaan under the power of the people of Israel on that day. 24 The people of Israel made it harder and harder for Jabin the king of Canaan, until they had destroyed him.

The Song of Deborah

5 That day Deborah and Barak the son of Abinoam sang this song: 2 "The leaders led in Israel. The people were willing to help them. For this we give thanks to the Lord! 3 Hear, O kings! Listen, O rulers! I will sing to the Lord. I will sing praise to the Lord, the God of Israel. 4 Lord, You went out from Seir. You walked from the field of Edom. And the earth shook. Water fell from the heavens. Yes, water fell from the clouds. 5 The mountains shook before the Lord. Mount Sinai shook before the Lord, the God of Israel.

6 "In the days of Shamgar the son of Anath, in the days of Jael, the wide roads were empty. Travelers walked on the side roads. 7 Country towns were empty. They were no more in Israel, until I, Deborah, came. I came as a mother in Israel. 8 New gods were chosen. Then war was in the gates. No battle-covering or sword was seen among 40,000 in Israel. 9 My heart is with the leaders of Israel, who were willing to help among the people. Thanks be to the Lord! 10 Tell of it, you who ride on white donkeys and you who sit on rich floor coverings. Tell of it, you who travel on the road. 11 They will tell of the right and good acts of the Lord at the sound of music beside the wells of water. They will tell of His right and good acts toward His towns people in Israel. Then the people of the Lord went down to the gates.

12 "Awake, awake, Deborah! Awake, awake, sing a song! Get up, Barak! Lead away the people you took in war, O son of Abinoam. 13 Those who were left came down to the rulers. The people of the Lord came down to me as soldiers. 14 The children of Amalek came down from Ephraim. They followed you, Benjamin, with your people. Leaders came down from Machir. Leaders came from Zebulun. 15 The rulers of Issachar came with Deborah. Issachar was faithful to Barak. They ran behind him into the valley. There was much thinking done among the families of Reuben. 16 Why did you sit among the sheep, to hear the horns blow for the

flocks? There was much thought among the families of Reuben. 17 Gilead stayed on the other side of the Jordan. Why did Dan stay in ships? Asher sat beside the sea. He stayed by its rivers. 18 Zebulun is a people who put their lives in danger even to death. Naphtali did this also, on the high places of the field.

19 "The kings came and fought. The kings of Canaan fought at Taanach near the waters of Megiddo. They did not get any silver. 20 The stars fought from heaven. From their paths they fought against Sisera. 21 The fast river of Kishon took them away, the rushing river, the river Kishon. O my soul, walk on with strength. 22 The beating of the feet of horses was loud, because the strong horses went fast. 23 'Curse Meroz,' said the angel of the Lord. 'Curse its people, because they did not come to the help of the Lord. They did not help the Lord against the powerful soldiers.'

24 "The most respected of women is Jael, the wife of Heber the Kenite. She is the most respected of women in the tent. 25 Sisera asked for water and she gave him milk. She brought him milk in a fine pot. 26 She put out her hand to the big tent nail. And she put out her right hand for the servant's heavy object. Then she hit Sisera. She crushed his head. She broke and cut through the side of his head. 27 He went down. He fell and lay without moving at her feet. He fell dead where he went down.

28 "The mother of Sisera looked out of the window. She looked through the window and cried in sorrow, 'Why is his war-wagon so long in coming? Why do the steps of his horses wait?' 29 Her wise ladies answered her. But she asked herself again and again, 30 'Are they not finding and dividing the riches? Is there not a girl or two for every man? Is there not colored cloth for Sisera to take? Is there not colored cloth with beautiful sewing on it? Are there not two pieces of colored cloth with beautiful sewing on them for the neck of the one who takes them?' 31 So let all those who hate You die, O Lord. But let those who love Him be like the sun as he rises in his power." And the land had peace for forty years.

Gideon

6 Then the people of Israel sinned in the eyes of the Lord. And the Lord gave them into the hands of Midian for seven years. 2 Midian was stronger than Israel.

Because of Midian the people of Israel made big caves in the sides of the mountains where they could live which were safe places for themselves. ³ For when Israel had planted seeds, the Midianites and Amalekites and the people of the east would come and fight against them. ⁴ They would set up their tents beside them and destroy the food of the field as far as Gaza. They would leave no food for Israel, and no sheep, cattle or donkeys. ⁵ They would come with their animals and their tents. They were like locusts, there were so many of them. There were too many of them and their camels to number. And they came into the land to destroy it. ⁶ So Israel became very poor because of Midian. The people of Israel cried to the Lord.

⁷ The people of Israel cried to the Lord because of Midian. ⁸ And the Lord sent a man to speak for Him to the people of Israel. The man said to them, "The Lord, the God of Israel, says, 'I brought you here from Egypt. I brought you out of the house where you were made to work. ⁹ I set you free from the power of the Egyptians and from the hands of all who made it hard for you. I drove them away from in front of you and gave you their land. ¹⁰ I said to you, "I am the Lord your God. Do not be afraid of the gods of the Amorites in whose land you live." But you have not obeyed Me.'"

¹¹ Then the angel of the Lord came and sat under the oak tree in Ophrah, which belonged to Joash the Abiezrite. The angel came as Abiezra's son Gideon was beating out grain where grapes are crushed, to save it from the Midianites. ¹² The angel of the Lord showed himself to Gideon and said to him, "The Lord is with you, O powerful soldier." ¹³ Gideon said to him, "O sir, if the Lord is with us, why has all this happened to us? Where are all His powerful works which our fathers told us about? They said, 'Did not the Lord bring us out of Egypt?' But now the Lord has left us alone. He has put us under the power of Midian." ¹⁴ The Lord looked at him and said, "Go in this strength of yours. And save Israel from the power of Midian. Have I not sent you?" ¹⁵ Gideon said to Him, "O Lord, how can I save Israel? See, my family is the least in Manasseh. And I am the youngest in my father's house." ¹⁶ But the Lord said to him, "For sure I will be with you. You will destroy Midian as one man." ¹⁷ Gideon said to Him, "If I have found favor in Your eyes, show me something to prove that

it is You Who speaks with me. ¹⁸ I ask of You, do not leave here until I return to You with my gift and lay it before You." And the Lord said, "I will stay until you return."

¹⁹ Then Gideon went into his house and got a young goat ready. He made bread without yeast from a basket of flour. He put the meat in a basket and the water from boiling the meat in a pot. Then he brought them out to him under the tree and set them down in front of him. ²⁰ The angel of God said to him, "Take the meat and the bread without yeast and lay them on this rock. Then pour out the water." Gideon did so. ²¹ The angel of the Lord put out the end of the stick that was in his hand and touched the meat and the bread without yeast. And fire came up from the rock and burned up the meat and the bread without yeast. Then the angel of the Lord was seen no more. ²² So Gideon knew that he was the angel of the Lord. And he said, "I am afraid, O Lord God! For now I have seen the angel of the Lord face to face." ²³ The Lord said to him, "Peace be with you. Do not be afraid. You will not die." ²⁴ Then Gideon built an altar there to the Lord. He gave it the name, The Lord is Peace. It is still in Ophrah of the Abiezrites to this day.

²⁵ That same night the Lord said to him, "Take your father's bull and a second bull seven years old. Use them to pull down the altar of Baal which belongs to your father. And cut down the tree of the false goddess Asherah that is beside it. ²⁶ Build an altar to the Lord your God on the top of this strong-place. Set the stones in the right way. Then take a second bull and give a burnt gift. Use the wood of the tree of the false goddess Asherah which you cut down." ²⁷ Gideon took ten of his servants and did what the Lord had told him to do. But he was too afraid of those of his father's house and the men of the city to do it during the day. So he did it during the night.

²⁸ When the men of the city got up early in the morning, they saw that the altar of Baal was torn down. They saw that the false goddess Asherah which was beside it was cut down. And the second bull was given on the altar which had been built. ²⁹ The men said to one another, "Who did this?" After they had looked around and asked, they were told, "Gideon the son of Joash did this thing." ³⁰ Then the men of the city said to Joash, "Bring out your son, so he may die. For he has torn down the

altar of Baal. And he has cut down our goddess Asherah which was beside it." [31] But Joash said to all who were gathered against him, "Will you fight for Baal? Will you save him? Whoever will fight for him will be put to death this morning. If he is a god, let him fight for himself because someone has torn down his altar." [32] So on that day he gave Gideon the name Jerubbaal, which means, "Let Baal fight against him." Because he tore down his altar.

[33] Then all the Midianites and Amalekites and people of the east gathered together. They crossed the Jordan and set up their tents in the valley of Jezreel. [34] But the Spirit of the Lord came upon Gideon. He blew a horn and called together the Abiezerites to follow him. [35] He sent men with news to go through Manasseh. And the Manassites were called together to follow him. He sent men with news to Asher, Zebulun and Naphtali. And they came to meet him.

[36] Then Gideon said to God, "Save Israel through me, as You have said. [37] See, I will put wool on the floor where grain is crushed. If the wool is wet, and it is dry on the ground, I will know that You will save Israel through me, as You have said." [38] It was so. Gideon got up early the next morning and took the wool in his hand. Enough water poured from the wool to fill a pot. [39] Then Gideon said to God, "Do not let Your anger burn against me for speaking to You once again. Let me make one more test with the wool. Let it be dry only on the wool. And let the ground be wet all around it." [40] God did so that night. For it was dry only on the wool. And all the ground was wet around it.

Gideon and the Three Hundred Men

7 Then Jerubbaal (that is, Gideon) and all the people who were with him got up early and set up their tents beside the well of Harod. The tents of Midian were north of them, by the hill of Moreh in the valley.

[2] The Lord said to Gideon, "The people with you are too many for Me to give Midian into their hands. Israel might say with pride, 'Our own power has saved us.' [3] So say to all the people, 'Whoever is afraid and shaking with fear may leave Mount Gilead and return home.' " So 22,000 people returned. But 10,000 stayed.

[4] Then the Lord said to Gideon, "There are still too many people. Bring them down to the water. I will test them for

you there. Whoever I say is to go with you will go. But whoever I say is not to go with you will not go." [5] So Gideon brought the people down to the water. The Lord said to Gideon, "Divide every man who drinks the water as dogs drink with their tongues from every man who gets down on his knees to drink." [6] There were 300 men who drank from their hand, putting their hand to their mouth. But all the rest of the people got down on their knees to drink water. [7] The Lord said to Gideon, "I will save you with the 300 men who drank from their hands. I will give the Midianites into your hands. Let all the others return, every man to his home." [8] So the 300 men took the people's food and their horns. Gideon sent all the other men of Israel to their tents. He kept only the 300 men. And the tents of Midian were below him in the valley.

[9] That same night the Lord said to Gideon, "Get up. Go down and fight against them at their tents. For I have given them into your hands. [10] But if you are afraid to go down, go with your servant Purah down to their tents. [11] You will hear what they say. Then your hands will become strong enough to go down and fight against them." So he went with his servant Purah down to the side of the tents where soldiers were keeping watch. [12] The Midianites and Amalekites and all the people of the east were lying in the valley. They were like locusts, there were so many. Their camels were too many to number. They were like sand beside the sea, there were so many. [13] When Gideon came, a man was telling a dream to his friend. The man said, "I had a dream. A loaf of barley bread was rolling toward the tents of Midian. It came to the tent and hit it so it fell down. It turned it up-side-down so the tent fell apart." [14] His friend answered and said, "This is nothing else but the sword of Gideon the son of Joash, a man of Israel. God has given Midian and all the army into his hand."

[15] When Gideon heard the story of the dream and what it meant, he bowed down and worshiped God. Then he returned to the tents of Israel and said, "Get up! For the Lord has given the army of Midian into your hands." [16] He divided the 300 men into three groups. He gave horns and empty pots with fire sticks inside to each of them. [17] And he said to them, "Watch me, and do what I do. When I come to the side of their tents, do as I do. [18] I and all

those with me will blow the horns. Then you blow the horns all around the tents, and say, 'For the Lord and for Gideon!'" 19 So Gideon and the one hundred men who were with him came to the side of the tents. It was late in the night. Different soldiers had just come to keep watch. Then the men blew the horns and broke the pots that were in their hands. 20 All three groups blew their horns and broke their pots. They held the sticks of fire in their left hands and horns to be blown in their right hands. And they called out, "A sword for the Lord and for Gideon!" 21 Each man stood in his place around the tents. And all the Midianite army ran. They cried out and ran away. 22 When the 300 horns were blown, the Lord made every man fight the man next to him among the tents. And the army ran away as far as Beth-shittah toward Zererah. They went as far as the land of Abel-meholah, by Tabbath. 23 The men of Israel were called out from Naphtali and Asher and all Manasseh, to go after Midian.

24 Gideon sent men through all the hill country of Ephraim, saying, "Come down against Midian. Take the waters in front of them, as far as Beth-barah and the Jordan." So all the men of Ephraim were gathered together. And they took the waters as far as Beth-barah and the Jordan. 25 They took the two leaders of Midian, Oreb and Zeeb. They killed Oreb at the rock of Oreb. And they killed Zeeb at the place of Zeeb where the grapes are crushed. They went after Midian, and brought the heads of Oreb and Zeeb to Gideon from the other side of the Jordan.

Gideon Wins over the Midianites

8 Then the men of Ephraim said to Gideon, "What is this you have done to us? Why did you not call us when you went to fight against Midian?" They were angry when they argued with him. 2 But he said to them, "What have I done to compare with you? Are not the grapes that are left of Ephraim better than all the grapes gathered of Abiezer? 3 God has given the leaders of Midian, Oreb and Zeeb, into your hands. What was I able to do to compare with you?" They were no longer angry when he said that.

4 Then Gideon and the 300 men with him came to the Jordan and crossed it. They were tired but they kept going. 5 Gideon said to the men of Succoth, "I ask of you, give loaves of bread to the people

who are following me. For they are tired and weak. I am going after Zebah and Zalmunna, the kings of Midian." 6 But the leaders of Succoth said, "Are Zebah and Zalmunna already in your hands, that we should give bread to your army?" 7 Gideon said, "The Lord will give Zebah and Zalmunna into my hand. Then I will beat your bodies with the thorns and thistles from the desert." 8 From there he went up to Penuel and spoke to them in the same way. The men of Penuel gave him the same answer as the men of Succoth. 9 So he said to the men of Penuel, "When I return safe, I will tear down this tower." 10 Now Zebah and Zalmunna were in Karkor. With them were their armies, about 15,000 men. These were all who were left of the whole army of the people of the east. For 120,000 men who fought with swords had been killed. 11 Gideon went up by the way of those who lived in tents east of Nobah and Jogbehah. And he fought against the army by surprise. 12 Zebah and Zalmunna ran away. Gideon went after them and took the two kings of Midian, Zebah and Zalmunna. The whole army was afraid.

13 Then Gideon the son of Joash returned from the battle by the way of Heres. 14 He caught a young man from Succoth and asked him questions. The young man wrote down for him the rulers and leaders of Succoth, seventy-seven men. 15 Then Gideon came to the men of Succoth and said, "See, here are Zebah and Zalmunna. You laughed at me about these men, saying, 'Are Zebah and Zalmunna already in your hand, that we should give bread to your weak and tired men?' " 16 Then he took the leaders of the city and with thorns and thistles from the desert, he punished the men of Succoth. 17 Then he tore down the tower of Penuel and killed the men of the city.

18 Gideon said to Zebah and Zalmunna, "What kind of men were they whom you killed at Tabor?" And they said, "They were like you. Each one looked like the son of a king." 19 Gideon said, "They were my brothers, the sons of my mother. As the Lord lives, if you had let them live, I would not kill you." 20 Then he said to Jether his first-born son, "Stand up and kill them." But the boy did not pick up his sword. He was afraid because he was still a boy. 21 Zebah and Zalmunna said, "Stand up yourself and kill us. For as the man is, so is his strength." So Gideon stood up and killed Zebah and Zalmunna. And he took

the religious objects that were on their camels' necks.

22 Then the men of Israel said to Gideon, "Rule over us, both you and your son, and your grandson also. For you have set us free from the power of Midian." 23 But Gideon said to them, "I will not rule over you. And my son will not rule over you. The Lord will rule over you." 24 Gideon said to them, "I only ask that each of you give me the gold objects you have taken to be worn on the ear." (They had objects to be worn on the ear because they were Ishmaelites.) 25 And they said, "For sure we will give them." So they spread out a coat, and every one of them threw into it an object he had taken. 26 The gold objects Gideon had asked for were as heavy as 1,700 pieces of gold money. He took the objects and purple clothing worn by the kings of Midian also. And he took the religious objects that were around the camels' necks. 27 Gideon made it into a holy vest and put it in his city, Ophrah. All Israel worshiped it there. So it became a trap to Gideon and those of his house. 28 Midian was put under the power of the people of Israel. They did not lift up their heads any more. And the land had peace for forty years, during the life of Gideon.

The Death of Gideon

29 Joash's son Jerubbaal (that is, Gideon) went and lived in his own house. 30 Gideon had seventy sons born to him, for he had many wives. 31 The woman in Shechem who acted as his wife gave birth to Gideon's son also. He was given the name Abimelech. 32 Gideon the son of Joash died when he was very old. He was buried in the grave of his father Joash, in Ophrah of the Abiezrites.

33 As soon as Gideon was dead, the people of Israel started again to worship the false gods of Baal. They made Baal-berith their god. 34 The people of Israel did not remember the Lord their God, Who had saved them from the power of all those around them who hated them. 35 They did not show kindness to the family of Jerubbaal (that is, Gideon). They did not remember all the good he had done to Israel.

Abimelech

9 Jerubbaal's son Abimelech went to his mother's family at Shechem. He said to them and to all those of the family of his mother's father, 2 "Speak to all the leaders of Shechem. Say to them, 'Which

is better for you? Should all seventy of Jerubbaal's sons rule over you? Or should one man rule over you? Remember that I am your own bone and flesh.'" 3 So his mother's family spoke all these words for him in the ears of the leaders of Shechem. And they decided to follow Abimelech. For they said, "He is our brother." 4 They gave him seventy pieces of silver from the family of Baal-berith. Abimelech used the money to hire wild men of no worth who followed him. 5 Then he went to his father's house at Ophrah. And he killed his brothers, the sons of Jerubbaal. He killed all seventy men upon one stone. But Jerubbaal's youngest son Jotham was left alive, because he hid himself. 6 Then all the men of Shechem and of Beth-millo gathered together. They went and made Abimelech king, by the tree that had been set up in Shechem.

7 When it was told to Jotham, he went and stood on the top of Mount Gerizim. He called out to them in a loud voice, "Listen to me, O men of Shechem. So God may listen to you. 8 One time the trees went out to choose a king to rule them. They said to the olive tree, 'Rule over us!' 9 But the olive tree said to them, 'Should I leave my riches of oil by which God and men are honored, and go to wave over the trees?' 10 Then the trees said to the fig tree, 'You come and rule over us!' 11 But the fig tree said to them, 'Should I leave my good sweet fruit, and go to wave over the trees?' 12 So the trees said to the vine, 'You come and rule over us!' 13 But the vine said to them, 'Should I leave my new wine which makes God and men happy, and go to wave over the trees?' 14 Then all the trees said to the thorn bush, 'You come and rule over us!' 15 And the thorn bush said to the trees, 'If in truth you are choosing me as king over you, come and be safe in my shadow. But if not, may fire come out of the thorn bush and burn up the tall trees of Lebanon.'

16 "Now it may be that you have acted in truth and honor in making Abimelech king. It may be that you have acted well toward Jerubbaal and his house, by paying him for what he did, 17 For my father fought for you. He put his life in danger to set you free from the power of Midian. 18 But you have gone against my father's house today. You have killed seventy of his sons on one stone. Abimelech is the son of my father's woman servant. And you have made him king over the people of Shechem, because he is your brother.

19 If you have acted in truth and honor toward Jerubbaal and his house today, then be happy with Abimelech. And let him be happy with you. 20 But if not, let fire come out from Abimelech and burn up the people of Shechem and Beth-millo. Then let it burn up Abimelech." 21 Jotham ran away from them and went to Beer. He stayed there, because he was afraid of his brother Abimelech.

22 Abimelech ruled over Israel for three years. 23 Then God sent a bad spirit between Abimelech and the men of Shechem. The men of Shechem were not faithful to Abimelech. 24 God did this to punish Abimelech and the men of Shechem, because the seventy sons of Jerubbaal were killed by their brother Abimelech. And the men of Shechem gave him the strength to do it. 25 The men of Shechem went against Abimelech by hiding men on the mountain-tops. They robbed all who passed by them on the road. Abimelech was told about it.

26 Now Gaal the son of Ebed moved with his family into Shechem. And the men of Shechem put their trust in him. 27 They went out into the field and gathered the grapes of their vines and crushed them. Then they had a special supper in the house of their god. They ate and drank and wished bad to come to Abimelech. 28 Gaal the son of Ebed said, "Who is Abimelech? And who are we of Shechem, that we should serve him? Is he not the son of Jerubbaal? Is not Zebul his leader? Serve the men of Hamor the father of Shechem, but why should we serve Abimelech? 29 If only these people were under my rule! Then I would send Abimelech away. I would say to Abimelech, 'Make your army strong, and come out.'"

30 When Zebul the ruler of the city heard the words of Gaal the son of Ebed, he was very angry. 31 He sent men to Abimelech in secret. They said, "See, Gaal the son of Ebed has come to Shechem with his family. They are turning the city against you. 32 So you and the people who are with you get up during the night and hide in the field. 33 Then get up early in the morning, as soon as the sun is up, and rush against the city. When Gaal and the people who are with him come out against you, do whatever you can to them."

34 So Abimelech and all who were with him got up during the night. They hid and waited in four groups to fight against Shechem. 35 Gaal the son of Ebed came out and stood in the city gate. And Abimelech and the people who were with him came out of their hiding places. 36 When Gaal saw the men, he said to Zebul, "See, men are coming down from the mountain-tops!" But Zebul said to him, "It is the shadow of the mountains that looks like men to you." 37 Gaal spoke again, saying, "See, men are coming down from the highest part of the land. One group is coming on the way from the oak tree of those who tell the future." 38 Then Zebul said to him, "Where is your proud talk now, you who said, 'Who is Abimelech that we should serve him?' Are these not the men whom you hated? Go out now and fight with them!" 39 So Gaal went out in front of the leaders of Shechem and fought with Abimelech. 40 Abimelech went after Gaal. And Gaal ran away from him. Many were hurt and fell all the way to the city gate. 41 Abimelech stayed at Arumah. But Zebul drove out Gaal and his family so they could not stay in Shechem.

42 The men went out to the field the next day and told Abimelech. 43 So he took his men and divided them into three groups, and they waited in the field. When he saw Gaal's people coming out of the city, Abimelech went against them and killed them. 44 Abimelech and the group with him rushed and stood in the city gate. The other two groups then rushed against all who were in the field and killed them. 45 Abimelech fought against the city all that day. He took the city and killed the people who were in it. Then he destroyed the city and covered it with salt.

46 All the leaders of the tower of Shechem heard about it. And they went into the inside room of the house of the god of El-berith. 47 Abimelech was told that all the leaders of the tower of Shechem were gathered together. 48 So Abimelech and all who were with him went up to Mount Zalmon. Abimelech took an ax in his hand and cut down a branch from the trees. Then he lifted it onto his shoulder. He said to the men who were with him, "Hurry and do what you have seen me do." 49 So each of the men cut down his branch also, and followed Abimelech. They put the branches around the inside room and set it on fire. So all the men of the tower of Shechem died. There were about 1,000 men and women in all.

50 Then Abimelech went to Thebez. He fought against it and took it. 51 But there was a strong tower in the center of the

city. All the men and women and leaders of the city ran to it and shut themselves in. And they went up on the roof of the tower. ⁵² Abimelech came to the tower and fought against it. He went near the door of the building to burn it with fire. ⁵³ But a certain woman threw a grain-crushing stone on Abimelech's head and crushed his skull. ⁵⁴ Abimelech was quick to call the young man who carried his heavy battle-clothes, saying, "Take your sword and kill me. Or else it will be said that a woman killed me." So the young man killed him with a sword. ⁵⁵ When the men of Israel saw that Abimelech was dead, each man went home. ⁵⁶ So God punished Abimelech for the sin he had done against his father by killing his seventy brothers. ⁵⁷ God punished the men of Shechem for all their sin. The words that Jotham the son of Jerubbaal spoke against them came true.

Tola

10 After Abimelech died, Tola the son of Puah, son of Dodo, a man of Issachar, came to save Israel. He lived in Shamir in the hill country of Ephraim. ² He judged Israel for twenty-three years. Then he died and was buried in Shamir.

Jair

³ Jair the Gileadite came after him. He judged Israel for twenty-two years. ⁴ He had thirty sons who traveled on thirty donkeys. They had thirty cities in the land of Gilead that are called the towns of Jair to this day. ⁵ Jair died and was buried in Kamon.

Jephthah

⁶ Then the people of Israel sinned in the eyes of the Lord. They served the male and female gods of Canaan, and the gods of Syria, Sidon, Moab, the Ammonites and of the Philistines. They turned away from the Lord and did not serve Him. ⁷ The anger of the Lord was against Israel. So He sold them into the hands of the Philistines and the people of Ammon. ⁸ They made it very hard for the people of Israel that year. For eighteen years they made it very hard for all the people of Israel in Gilead in the land of the Amorites on the other side of the Jordan. ⁹ And the sons of Ammon crossed the Jordan to fight against Judah, Benjamin and the family of Ephraim. So Israel suffered much pain. ¹⁰ The people of Israel cried out to the Lord, saying, "We have sinned against

You. We have turned away from our God and are serving the Baals." ¹¹ The Lord said to the people of Israel, "Did I not save you from the Egyptians, the Amorites, the people of Ammon and the Philistines? ¹² When the Sidonians and Amalekites and Maonites made it hard for you, you cried out to Me. And I took you away from their hands. ¹³ Yet you have turned away from Me and served other gods. So I will not take you away again. ¹⁴ Go and cry out to the gods you have chosen. Let them save you in the time of your trouble." ¹⁵ The people of Israel said to the Lord, "We have sinned. Do to us whatever You think is good. But we beg of You, take us out of this today." ¹⁶ So they put away the strange gods from among them, and served the Lord. And the Lord cared as He saw the suffering of Israel.

¹⁷ The men of Ammon were gathered together for war. They set up their tents in Gilead. The men of Israel gathered together, and set up their tents in Mizpah. ¹⁸ The leaders of Gilead said to one another, "Who is the man who will be first to fight against the men of Ammon? He will be the head of all the people of Gilead."

11 Now Jephthah the Gileadite was a powerful soldier. But he was the son of a woman who sold the use of her body. Jephthah's father was Gilead. ² Gilead's wife gave birth to his sons. And when his wife's sons grew up, they drove Jephthah away. They told him, "You will not have any share in our father's house. For you are the son of another woman." ³ So Jephthah ran away from his brothers and lived in the land of Tob. Men of no worth gathered around Jephthah and went fighting and stealing with him.

⁴ The time came when the men of Ammon fought against Israel. ⁵ When the men of Ammon fought against Israel, the leaders of Gilead went to get Jephthah from the land of Tob. ⁶ They said to Jephthah, "Come and be our leader, so we may fight against the men of Ammon." ⁷ Jephthah said to the leaders of Gilead, "Did you not hate me and drive me from my father's house? Why have you come to me now when you are in trouble?" ⁸ The leaders of Gilead said to Jephthah, "That is why we have returned to you now. So you may go with us and fight the men of Ammon. You will be the head of all the people of Gilead." ⁹ Jephthah said to the leaders of Gilead, "If you bring me home

again to fight the men of Ammon and the Lord gives them to me, will I become your head?" 10 The leaders of Gilead said to Jephthah, "The Lord is listening to what we say. For sure we will do as you have said." 11 So Jephthah went with the leaders of Gilead. And the people made him head and leader over them. Jephthah spoke all his words before the Lord at Mizpah.

12 Then Jephthah sent men to the king of the people of Ammon, saying, "What do you have against me? Why have you come to fight against my land?" 13 The king of the people of Ammon said to these men of Jephthah, "Because Israel took away my land when they came from Egypt. They took my land from the Arnon as far as the Jabbok and the Jordan. So I ask you to return this land to me in peace." 14 But Jephthah sent men to the king of the people of Ammon again, 15 saying, "Jephthah says, 'Israel did not take away the land of Moab or the land of the people of Ammon. 16 Israel came out of Egypt, went through the desert to the Red Sea, and came to Kadesh. 17 Then Israel sent men to the king of Edom, saying, "We ask you to let us pass through your land." But the king of Edom would not listen. They asked the king of Moab also. But he would not let them pass through. So Israel stayed at Kadesh. 18 Then Israel went through the desert and around the lands of Edom and Moab. They came to the east side of the land of Moab. There they set up their tents on the other side of the Arnon. But they did not go into the land of Moab. For the Arnon flowed along the side of Moab. 19 Israel sent men to Sihon king of the Amorites, the king of Heshbon, saying, "We ask you to let us pass through your land to our place." 20 But Sihon did not trust Israel. He would not let them pass through his land. Sihon gathered all his people together. They set up their tents in Jahaz, and fought with Israel. 21 The Lord, the God of Israel, gave Sihon and all his people into the hand of Israel. They won the war against Sihon. So Israel took all the land of the Amorites, the people of that country. 22 They took all the land of the Amorites, from the Arnon as far as the Jabbok, and from the desert as far as the Jordan.

23 'So the Lord, the God of Israel, drove the Amorites away from His people Israel. Now are you to take the land for your own? 24 Do you not keep for your own what your god Chemosh gives you? We will keep the land of the people the Lord our God drove away for us. 25 Are you any better than Balak the son of Zippor, king of Moab? Did he ever fight with Israel? Did he ever go to war against them? 26 While Israel lived in Heshbon and its towns and Aroer and its towns and in all the cities beside the Arnon for 300 years, why did you not take them again during that time? 27 I have not sinned against you. But you are doing wrong to me by making war against me. The Lord is the judge. May He decide today between the people of Israel and the people of Ammon.' " 28 But the king of the people of Ammon would not listen to what Jephthah said.

29 The Spirit of the Lord came upon Jephthah. So he passed through Gilead and Manasseh and through Mizpah of Gilead. He went from Mizpah of Gilead to the people of Ammon. 30 Jephthah made a promise to the Lord and said, "You give the people of Ammon into my hand. 31 And I will give to the Lord whatever comes out of the doors of my house to meet me when I return in peace from the people of Ammon. I will give it to the Lord as a burnt gift." 32 Then Jephthah crossed over to fight against the people of Ammon. And the Lord gave them into his hand. 33 He killed many of them from Aroer to Minnith, through twenty cities, as far as Abelkeramin. The people of Ammon were destroyed in front of the people of Israel.

Jephthah's Daughter

34 Then Jephthah came to his home at Mizpah. His daughter came out to meet him with music and dancing. She was his one and only child. He had no other sons or daughters. 35 When he saw her, he tore his clothes and said, "It is bad, my daughter! You have made me very sad. You have brought much trouble to me. For I have made a promise to the Lord, and I must keep it." 36 She said to him, "My father, you have made a promise to the Lord. Do to me what you have promised you would do. Because the Lord has punished the people of Ammon, who fought against you. 37 But do this for me. Let me alone for two months. So I and my friends may go to the mountains and cry because I will never have a man." 38 Jephthah said, "Go." He sent her away for two months with her friends. And they cried on the mountains because she would never have a man. 39 She returned to her father after two months. And he did what he promised the Lord and she died without having a

man. So it became the way in Israel **40** that the daughters of Israel went to have sorrow for the daughter of Jephthah for four days each year.

Jephthah and Ephraim

12 Then the men of Ephraim got ready for war. They crossed over to Zaphon and said to Jephthah, "Why did you cross over to fight the men of Ammon without calling us to go with you? With fire we will burn down your house with you in it." **2** Jephthah said to them, "I and my people were having much trouble with the people of Ammon. I did call you, but you did not take me away from them. **3** I saw that you would not help me, so I took my life in my hands. I crossed over to fight the people of Ammon. And the Lord gave them into my hand. So why have you come today to fight against me?" **4** Then Jephthah gathered all the men of Gilead and fought Ephraim. The men of Gilead won the war against Ephraim, because Ephraim said, "You people of Gilead are not respected among Ephraim and Manasseh." **5** The people of Gilead took the crossing places of the Jordan beside Ephraim. When any of the Ephraimite men ran away and said, "Let me cross over," the men of Gilead would say to him, "Are you an Ephraimite?" If he said, "No," **6** they would say to him, "Then say 'Shibboleth.' " But he would say, "Sibboleth," for he could not say it right. So they would take hold of him and kill him at the crossing places of the Jordan. At that time 42,000 men of Ephraim were killed. **7** Jephthah ruled Israel for six years. Then Jephthah the Gileadite died. He was buried in one of the cities of Gilead.

Ibzan, Elon, and Abdon

8 Ibzan of Bethlehem ruled Israel after him. **9** He had thirty sons and thirty daughters whom he gave in marriage outside the family. And he brought in thirty daughters from outside the family for his sons. He ruled Israel for seven years. **10** Then Ibzan died and was buried in Bethlehem.

11 Elon the Zebulunite ruled Israel after him. He ruled Israel for ten years. **12** Then Elon the Zebulunite died. He was buried at Aijalon in the land of Zebulun.

13 Abdon the son of Hillel the Pirathonite ruled Israel after him. **14** He had forty sons and thirty grandsons who traveled on seventy donkeys. He ruled Israel for eight years. **15** Then Abdon the son of Hillel the Pirathonite died. He was buried at Pirathon in the land of Ephraim, in the hill country of the Amalekites.

The Birth of Samson

13 The people of Israel sinned in the eyes of the Lord again. So the Lord gave them into the hands of the Philistines for forty years.

2 There was a certain man of Zorah, of the family of the Danites. His name was Manoah. His wife was not able to have children. **3** Then the angel of the Lord came to the woman and said to her, "See, you have not been able to have any children. But the Lord will make it possible for you to have a child and you will give birth to a son. **4** So be careful not to drink wine or strong drink. Do not eat anything that is unclean. **5** You will have a child and give birth to a son. His hair must never be cut. Because the boy will be a Nazirite to God from the time he is born. He will begin to take Israel away from the Philistines' power." **6** Then the woman came and told her husband. She said, "A man of God came to me. He looked like the angel of God, filling me with fear. I did not ask him where he came from. And he did not tell me his name. **7** But he said to me, 'See, it will be possible for you to have a child and give birth to a son. Do not drink wine or strong drink or eat anything that is unclean. For the boy will be a Nazirite to God from the time he is born to the time he dies.' "

8 Then Manoah asked the Lord, saying, "O Lord, let the man of God whom You have sent come to us again. Let him teach us what to do for the boy who is to be born." **9** God listened to Manoah. The angel of God came again to the woman while she was sitting in the field. But Manoah her husband was not with her. **10** So the woman ran to her husband in a hurry. She told him, "See, the man who came the other day has come to me again." **11** Manoah got up and followed his wife. When he came to the man he said to him, "Are you the man who spoke to the woman?" And he said, "I am." **12** Manoah said, "When your words come true, what will be the boy's way of life? What should he do?" **13** The angel of the Lord said to Manoah, "Let the woman be careful to do all I have said. **14** She must not eat anything from the vine or drink wine or strong drink. She must not eat anything that is unclean. Let her obey all I have told her."

15 Manoah said to the angel of the Lord,

"We ask of you, stay with us. So we may get a young goat ready for you to eat." 16 The angel of the Lord said to Manoah, "I will stay, but I will not eat your food. But if you get a burnt gift ready, then give it to the Lord." For Manoah did not know that he was the angel of the Lord. 17 Manoah said to the angel of the Lord, "What is your name? So we may honor you when your words come true." 18 But the angel of the Lord said to him, "Why do you ask my name? It is a name of wonder." 19 So Manoah took the young goat with the grain gift. And he gave it on the rock to the Lord. Then the Lord did powerful works while Manoah and his wife watched. 20 For the fire went up from the altar toward heaven. And the angel of the Lord went up in the fire of the altar. When Manoah and his wife saw this, they fell with their faces on the ground. 21 The angel of the Lord did not show himself to Manoah or his wife again. Then Manoah knew that he was the angel of the Lord. 22 So Manoah said to his wife, "We will die for sure. For we have seen God." 23 But his wife said to him, "If the Lord had wanted to kill us, He would not have received a burnt gift and grain gift from us. He would not have shown us all these things, or let us hear these things."

24 Then the woman gave birth to a son and named him Samson. The child grew up and the Lord brought good to him. 25 And the Spirit of the Lord began to work through him at the tents of Dan, between Zorah and Eshtaol.

Samson's Philistine Wife

14 Samson went down to Timnah. There he saw a woman, one of the daughters of the Philistines. 2 He returned and told his father and mother, "I saw a woman in Timnah. She is one of the daughters of the Philistines. Now get her for me as a wife." 3 But his father and mother said to him, "Is there no woman among the daughters of your family or among all our people? Must you take a wife from the Philistines who have not gone through the religious act of the Jews?" Samson said to his father, "Get her for me, for she looks good to me." 4 His father and mother did not know that it was the Lord's leading. For He was planning a way to go against the Philistines. At that time the Philistines were ruling over Israel.

5 Samson went down to Timnah with his father and mother. They came as far as the grape-fields of Timnah. There a young lion came running toward him, making a loud noise. 6 The Spirit of the Lord came upon Samson with power. Samson tore the lion apart like one tears a young goat. He had nothing in his hand. But he did not tell his father or mother what he had done. 7 Then Samson went down and talked to the woman. She looked good to him. 8 When he returned later to take her, he turned to look at the dead lion. He saw that a lot of bees and some honey were inside the lion's body. 9 So he took the honey out with his hands and went on his way, eating as he went. He came to his father and mother and gave some honey to them, and they ate it. But he did not tell them he had taken the honey out of the lion's body.

10 Then his father went down to the woman. Samson made a special supper there. The young men used to do this. 11 When the people saw him, they brought thirty friends to be with him. 12 And Samson said to them, "Let me see if you can answer this question. If you can find the answer within the seven days of the special supper, I will give you thirty linen coats and thirty pieces of clothing. 13 But if you cannot answer me, you must give me thirty linen coats and thirty pieces of clothing." And they said to him, "Ask your question. Let us hear it." 14 So Samson said to them, "Out of the eater came something to eat. Out of the strong came something sweet. Now what does this mean?" But they could not answer the question in three days.

15 On the fourth day they said to Samson's wife, "Make your husband tell us the answer. Or we will burn you and your father's house with fire. Have you asked us to come here so you can make us poor? Is it not true?" 16 So Samson's wife cried in front of Samson, saying, "You only hate me. You do not love me. You have asked my people a question. And you have not told me the answer." Samson said to her, "See, I have not told the answer to my father or mother. Should I tell it to you?" 17 But she cried in front of him for seven days while their special supper lasted. On the seventh day Samson told her the answer because she begged him so much. Then she told the answer to her people. 18 So the men of the city said to Samson before the sun went down on the seventh day, "What is more sweet than honey? What is stronger than a lion?" Samson said to them, "If you had not plowed with my young cow, you would not have found

the answer." [19] Then the Spirit of the Lord came upon him with power. Samson went down to Ashkelon and killed thirty men of the town. He took their clothing and gave it to the men who answered his question. He was very angry and returned to his father's house. [20] Samson's wife was given to his friend who had been his best man at his wedding.

Samson Wins over the Philistines

15 But later Samson visited his wife during grain gathering time with a young goat. Samson said, "I will go in to my wife in her room." But her father did not let him go in. [2] Her father said, "I thought you hated her. So I gave her to your friend. Is not her younger sister more beautiful than she? Let her be yours instead." [3] Samson said to him, "This time I will be without blame when I hurt the Philistines." [4] So Samson went and caught 300 foxes. He tied them together tail to tail. And he put a fire stick between the tails of every two foxes. [5] Then he set fire to the sticks and let the foxes go into the standing grain of the Philistines. So the standing grain and cut grain and vines and olive trees were burned up. [6] The Philistines said, "Who did this?" And they were told, "Samson, the son-in-law of the Timnite, because the Timnite took his wife and gave her to his friend." So the Philistines came and burned her and her father with fire. [7] Samson said to them, "For sure I will punish you for acting like this. After that I will stop."

[8] He killed many of them without mercy. Then Samson went down and lived in the opening of the rock of Etam.

[9] The Philistines went and set up their tents in Judah, and spread out in Lehi. [10] The men of Judah said, "Why have you come up against us?" The Philistines said, "We have come to take Samson and do to him as he did to us." [11] Then 3,000 men of Judah went down to the opening of the rock of Etam and said to Samson, "Do you not know that the Philistines rule over us? What is this that you have done to us?" Samson said to them, "I have done to them as they did to me." [12] They said to him, "We have come to take you and give you to the Philistines." Samson said to them, "Promise me that you will not kill me." [13] So they said to him, "No, we will only tie you up and give you to them. We will not kill you." So they tied him with two new ropes and brought him up from the rock.

[14] When Samson came to Lehi, the Philistines came with a loud noise to meet him. The Spirit of the Lord came upon Samson with power. The ropes on his arms became as weak as a burning plant, and fell from his hands. [15] Samson found a jawbone of a donkey and took it in his hand. He killed 1,000 men with it. [16] Then Samson said, "With the bone of a donkey there are bodies upon bodies. With the bone of a donkey I have killed 1,000 men." [17] When he was done speaking, he threw the bone from his hand. And he called that place Ramath-lehi. [18] Then Samson became very thirsty. He called to the Lord and said, "You have taken us away from trouble by the hand of Your servant. Now must I die of thirst and fall into the hands of those who have not gone through our religious act?" [19] But God broke open a place in Lehi, and water came out of it. When Samson drank, his strength returned. He received new life. So he called the place En-hakkore. It is in Lehi to this day. [20] Samson ruled Israel for twenty years in the days of the Philistines.

Samson and Delilah

16 Samson went to Gaza and saw a woman who sold the use of her body there. He went in to her. [2] The Gazites were told, "Samson has come here." So they gathered around the place and waited for him all night at the gate of the city. They were quiet all night, saying, "Let us wait until the morning light. Then we will kill him." [3] But Samson lay until late at night. Then he got up and took hold of the doors of the city gate and the pieces that held them. He pulled them up together with the locks and put them on his shoulders. And he carried them up to the top of the mountain beside Hebron.

[4] After this Samson loved a woman in the valley of Sorek. Her name was Delilah. [5] The leaders of the Philistines came to her, saying, "Tempt Samson to tell you the secret of his powerful strength. Find out how we can get power over him so we can tie him and hold him. Then we will each give you 1,100 pieces of silver." [6] So Delilah said to Samson, "I beg you. Tell me the secret of your powerful strength. Tell me how one can get power over you and tie you up and hold you." [7] Samson said to her, "They must tie me with seven new ropes that have not been dried. Then I will become weak and be like any other man." [8] So the leaders of the Philistines

brought her seven new ropes that had not been dried. And Delilah tied Samson with them. 9 She had men hiding and waiting in another room. She said to him, "The Philistines are upon you, Samson!" But he broke the ropes like a string breaks when it touches fire. So they did not find the secret of his strength.

10 Delilah said to Samson, "See, you have fooled me and told me lies. Now tell me, I beg you, how can you be tied?" 11 Samson said to her, "They must tie me with new ropes which have never been used. Then I will become weak and be like any other man." 12 So Delilah took new ropes, tied Samson with them, and said, "The Philistines are upon you, Samson!" Men were hiding and waiting in another room. But Samson broke the ropes from his arms like a string.

13 Then Delilah said to Samson, "You have fooled me and told me lies until now. Tell me how you can be tied." Samson said to her, "You must work the seven strings of my hair into the cloth you are making and hold it there with a nail. Then I will become weak and be like any other man." 14 So while Samson slept, Delilah took the seven strings of his hair and worked them into the cloth. She held it in place with the nail. Then she said to him, "The Philistines are upon you, Samson!" But he awoke from his sleep and pulled away the nail, the cloth-maker and the cloth.

15 Delilah said to Samson, "How can you say, 'I love you,' when your heart is not with me? You have lied to me these three times. You have not told me the secret of your powerful strength." 16 She asked him day after day until his soul was troubled to death. 17 So he told her all that was in his mind. He said to her, "My hair has never been cut. For I have been a Nazirite to God from the time I was born. If my hair is cut, my strength will leave me. I will become weak and be like any other man."

18 Delilah saw that Samson had told her the truth. She sent and called the leaders of the Philistines, saying, "Come once again. For he has told me all he knows." So the leaders of the Philistines came to her. And they brought the money in their hands. 19 She made Samson sleep on her knees. Then she called for a man to cut off the seven parts of Samson's hair. She began to hurt Samson, and his strength left him. 20 She said, "The Philistines are upon you, Samson!" He awoke from his sleep and said, "I will go out as I have at other times.

I will shake myself free." But he did not know that the Lord had left him. 21 The Philistines took hold of him and cut out his eyes. They brought him down to Gaza and tied him with brass chains. Samson was made to grind grain in the prison. 22 But the hair of his head started to grow again after it was cut off.

The Death of Samson

23 Now the leaders of the Philistines gathered to give a large gift to their god Dagon. They were happy, for they said, "Our god has given us Samson, the man who has fought against us." 24 The people praised their god when they saw Samson. They said, "Our god has given us the one who fought against us, destroyed our country, and killed many of us." 25 After the people had had much to drink, they said, "Bring Samson here so we can have some fun with him." So they called Samson out of prison and made fun of him. They made him stand between the stone pillars that held up the building. 26 Samson said to the boy who was holding his hand, "Let me feel the tall pillars that hold up the building. I want to rest against them." 27 Now the building was full of men and women. All the leaders of the Philistines were there, and there were about 3,000 men and women on the roof looking down and laughing at Samson.

28 Then Samson called to the Lord and said, "O Lord God, I beg You. Remember me. Give me strength only this once, O God. So I may now punish the Philistines for my two eyes." 29 Samson took hold of the two center pillars that held up the building. He pushed against them, with his right hand on one and his left hand on the other. 30 Samson said, "Let me die with the Philistines!" Then he pushed with all his strength so that the building fell on the leaders and all the people in it. He killed more at his death than he killed in his life. 31 Then his brothers and all those of his father's house came and took him. They brought him up and buried him between Zorah and Eshtaol in the grave of his father Manoah. Samson had ruled Israel for twenty years.

The False Gods of Micah

17 There was a man of the hill country of Ephraim whose name was Micah. 2 He said to his mother, "There were 1,100 pieces of silver taken from you. And I heard you pray that the robber would be cursed. See, the silver is with me. I took it." His mother said, "May the Lord bring good to you, my son." ³ He returned the 1,100 pieces of silver to his mother. And she said, "I set apart all the silver from my hand to the Lord for my son. It is to be used in making an object to look like a god. So I will return the silver to you." ⁴ When he returned the silver to his mother, she gave 200 pieces to the man who works with silver. He made them into an object to look like a god for Micah's house. ⁵ The man Micah had a special building where gods were worshiped. He made a holy vest and gods for the house. And he set apart one of his sons to be his religious leader. ⁶ There was no king in Israel in those days. Each man did what he thought was right.

⁷ Now there was a young man of Bethlehem in Judah. He was a Levite, of the family of Judah, and he was staying there. ⁸ He left the city of Bethlehem in Judah to find a place to live. As he traveled he came to the house of Micah in the hill country of Ephraim. ⁹ Micah said to him, "Where do you come from?" He answered, "I am a Levite from Bethlehem in Judah. I am going to stay where I may find a place." ¹⁰ Then Micah said to him, "Live with me. Be a father and a religious leader to me. I will give you ten pieces of silver a year, new clothes, and your living." So the Levite went in. ¹¹ The Levite agreed to live with the man. And the young man was like a son to Micah. ¹² So Micah set apart the Levite. The young man became his religious leader and lived in Micah's house. ¹³ Then Micah said, "Now I know that the Lord will bring good to me because I have a Levite as my religious leader."

Micah and the Danites

18 There was no king of Israel in those days. At that time the family of the Danites was looking for their own land to live in. For no land had been given to them yet among the families of Israel. ² So the people of Dan sent five men from all those in their family. They were men with strength of heart, from Zorah and Eshtaol, sent to look over the land. The people of Dan said to them, "Go and look over the land." And the men came to the house of Micah in the hill country of Ephraim. They stayed there. ³ When they were near the house of Micah, they heard the voice of the young man, the Levite. They knew who he was, and said to him, "Who brought you here? What are you doing in

this place? What do you have here?" ⁴ The Levite said to them, "This is what Micah has done for me. He has hired me. I have become his religious leader." ⁵ They said to him, "We beg you to ask God if all will go well for us as we travel." ⁶ The religious leader said to them, "Go in peace. The way you are going is pleasing to the Lord."

⁷ Then the five men left and came to Laish. They saw how the people lived there, quiet and feeling safe, like the Sidonians. There was no ruler in the land who would put them to shame for anything. They were far from the Sidonians and had nothing to do with anyone. ⁸ The five men returned to their brothers at Zorah and Eshtaol. Their brothers said to them, "What do you have to say?" ⁹ They answered, "Get ready. Let us go up against them. For we have seen their land and it is very good. Will you sit and do nothing? Do not wait. Go into the land and take it. ¹⁰ When you go in, you will come to people who feel very safe. They have much land, but God has given it to you. It will be a place where you will have all you need on earth."

¹¹ Then 600 men from the family of Dan, from Zorah and Eshtaol, went out ready for war. ¹² They went to Kiriath-jearim in Judah and set up their tents. They called that place Mahaneh-dan to this day. It is west of Kiriath-jearim. ¹³ They went from there to the hill country of Ephraim and came to the house of Micah.

¹⁴ Then the five men who had gone to look over the country of Laish said to their brothers, "Do you know that in these houses there are gods, a holy vest, and objects made to look like gods? So think about what you should do." ¹⁵ They turned there and came to the house of the young man, the Levite, at the home of Micah. They asked him how he was getting along. ¹⁶ The 600 men of the sons of Dan who were ready for war were standing by the gate. ¹⁷ The five men who had gone to look over the land went in the house. They took the objects made to look like gods, the holy vest and the other gods. The religious leader stood by the gate with the 600 men who were ready for war. ¹⁸ When the men went into Micah's house and took the objects made to look like gods, the holy vest and the other gods, the religious leader said to them, "What are you doing?" ¹⁹ They said to him, "Be quiet. Put your hand over your mouth and come with us. Be a father and a religious

leader to us. Is it better for you to be a religious leader to the house of one man, or to a family in Israel?" 20 The religious leader felt glad in his heart. He took the holy vest, the house gods and objects made to look like gods. And he went among the people.

21 Then they turned and left. They put the little ones, the animals and their riches in front of them. 22 They had gone a long way from the house of Micah. And the men who were in the houses near Micah's house gathered together and went after them. When they came to the sons of Dan, 23 they called out to them. The sons of Dan turned around and said to Micah, "What is wrong with us? Why have you gathered together?" 24 Micah said, "You have taken away my gods which I made. And you go away with the religious leader. What do I have left? How can you say to me, 'What is wrong with you?' " 25 The sons of Dan said to him, "Do not let your voice be heard among us. Or angry men will kill you and those of your house." 26 Then the sons of Dan went on their way. Micah saw that they were too strong for him. So he returned to his house.

27 The men of Dan took what Micah had made and the religious leader who had belonged to him. They came to Laish, to people who were quiet and felt safe. And they killed them with the sword. They burned the city with fire. 28 There was no one to take them away from their trouble, because it was far from Sidon and they had nothing to do with anyone. It was in the valley near Beth-rehob. The sons of Dan built the city again, and lived in it. 29 They called the name of the city Dan, after the name of Dan their father who was born in Israel. The name of the city had been Laish before. 30 The people of Dan set up for themselves the object made to look like a god. And Jonathan, the son of Gershom, the son of Manasseh, and his sons were religious leaders to the family of Dan until the day their land was taken. 31 They set up the false god that Micah had made, while the house of God was at Shiloh.

The Levite and Woman Who Acted as His Wife

19 There was no king in Israel in those days. And there was a certain Levite staying in a far away part of the hill country of Ephraim. He took a woman from Bethlehem in Judah to act as his wife. 2 But his woman was not faithful to him. She left him and went to her father's house in Bethlehem in Judah. She stayed there four months. 3 Then her husband got up and went after her. He was gentle in speaking to her, asking her to return with him. He brought his servant and two donkeys with him. So she brought him into her father's house. When her father saw him, he was glad to meet him. 4 His father-in-law, the girl's father, made him stay. So he stayed with him three days. They ate and drank and stayed there. 5 They got up early in the morning on the fourth day to get ready to go. The girl's father said to his son-in-law, "Eat a piece of bread to get your strength. Then you may go." 6 So both of them sat down and ate and drank together. The girl's father said to the man, "I beg you, agree to stay the night. Let your heart be happy." 7 The man stood up to go. But his father-in-law begged him so that he stayed another night there. 8 He got up to go early in the morning on the fifth day. But the girl's father said, "I beg you, get your strength first. Wait until later in the day." So both of them ate. 9 Then the man stood up to leave with his woman and his servant. His father-in-law, the girl's father, said to him, "Now see, the day is ending. I beg you, stay the night. See, the day is coming to an end. Stay here through the night so your heart may be happy. Get up early tomorrow to go on your way home."

10 But the man would not stay the night. He stood up and left and came to a place beside Jebus (that is, Jerusalem). He had his woman with him and two donkeys to carry them both. 11 The day was almost gone when they were near Jebus. The servant said to his owner, "Come, let us go in and stay the night in this city of the Jebusites." 12 But his owner said to him, "We will not go into the city of strangers who are not of the people of Israel. We will go as far as Gibeah." 13 And he said to his servant, "Come, let us go to one of these places. We will stay the night in Gibeah or Ramah." 14 So they passed Jebus and went on their way. The sun went down when they were near Gibeah, a city of Benjamin. 15 They turned to go in and stay at Gibeah. They went in and sat down outside in the center of the city. For no one took them into his house to stay the night.

16 In the evening an old man came out of the field from his work. He was from the hill country of Ephraim and was staying in Gibeah. But the men of the place were Benjamites. 17 The old man looked up and saw the traveler in the center of the city,

and said, "Where are you going? Where do you come from?" [18] The Levite said to him, "We are traveling from Bethlehem in Judah to a far away part of the hill country of Ephraim. I am from there. I went to Bethlehem in Judah, but am now returning home. But no one will take me into his house. [19] We have food for our donkeys. And we have bread and wine for me, my woman, and the young man who is with your servants. We have all we need." [20] The old man said, "Peace to you. Let me take care of all your needs. But do not stay the night in the street." [21] So he took him into his house and gave food to the donkeys. The people washed their feet and ate and drank.

[22] While they were having a happy time, certain sinful men of the city gathered around the house. They beat on the door and said to the old man, the owner of the house, "Bring out the man who came into your house so we can have sex with him." [23] The man, the owner of the house, went out to them and said, "No, my brothers. I beg you not to be so sinful. This man has come into my house. Do not do this sinful thing. [24] Here is my daughter who has never had a man. And here is the woman who belongs to the man. Let me bring them out. Put them to shame. Do to them whatever you wish. But do not do such a sinful act against this man." [25] But the men would not listen to him. So the Levite took hold of his woman and brought her out to them. The men had sex with her all night until morning. When the sun came up, they let her go. [26] The woman came early in the morning and fell down at the door of the man's house where her owner was. She lay there until it was light.

[27] Her owner got up in the morning and opened the doors of the house. He went out to go on his way and saw his woman lying at the door of the house. Her hands were on the step. [28] He said to her, "Get up. Let us be going." But there was no answer. He put her body across the donkey and started on his way home. [29] When he went into his house, he took a knife. He took hold of his woman and cut her into twelve pieces, arm by arm, leg by leg. Then he sent her out through all the land of Israel. [30] All who saw it said, "Nothing like this has happened before. Nothing like this has been seen from the day when the people of Israel came from the land of Egypt until now. Think about it. Listen to what is said about it. And say what you think."

Israel Gets Ready for War

20 Then all the people of Israel from Dan to Beersheba and from the land of Gilead came out. The people gathered together as one man to the Lord at Mizpah. [2] The leaders of all the people, all the families of Israel, showed themselves in the meeting of the people of God. There were 400,000 soldiers on foot who used the sword. [3] (The people of Benjamin heard that the people of Israel had gone up to Mizpah.) The people of Israel said, "Tell us. How did this sinful thing happen?" [4] The Levite, the husband of the woman who was killed, answered, "I came with my woman to stay the night at Gibeah, a city of Benjamin. [5] But the men of Gibeah came against me. They gathered around the house at night because of me. They wanted to kill me. But they did sex with my woman instead, so she died. [6] I took my woman and cut her into pieces. I sent her out through all the land that was given to Israel. For they have done a sinful act of shame in Israel. [7] All you people of Israel, say what should be done."

[8] All the people stood up as one man, saying, "Not one of us will go to his tent. Not one of us will return to his house. [9] But this is what we will do to Gibeah. We will go against it by drawing names. [10] We will take ten men of every 100 among the families of Israel, and 100 of every 1,000, and 1,000 of every 10,000. They will take food for the people. So when they come to Gibeah of Benjamin, they may punish them for all the acts of shame they have done in Israel." [11] All the men of Israel were gathered against the city, together as one man.

[12] The family groups of Israel sent men through the whole family group of Benjamin, saying, "What is this sin that has happened among you? [13] Now give us the sinful men of Gibeah. Then we will put them to death and take this sin away from Israel." But the people of Benjamin would not listen to the voice of their brothers, the people of Israel. [14] The people of Benjamin gathered from the cities to Gibeah. They came to go out to battle against the people of Israel. [15] Out of the sons of Benjamin, there were 26,000 men who used the sword who came from the cities on that day. And there were 700 chosen men who lived in Gibeah. [16] There were 700 chosen men of all these people who were left handed. Each one could use a sling to throw a stone at a hair and not miss.

17 Apart from Benjamin, there were 400,000 men of Israel who used the sword. All of them were men of war. 18 The people of Israel went up to Bethel. There they asked God, "Who should go first for us to fight against the people of Benjamin?" The Lord said, "Judah should go first."

19 So the people of Israel got up in the morning and went to get ready to fight against Gibeah. 20 The men of Israel went to fight against Benjamin. They dressed themselves for battle against them at Gibeah. 21 The people of Benjamin came out of Gibeah and killed 22,000 men of Israel on that day. 22 But the men of Israel made their hearts strong. They got ready for battle again in the same place they had fought the first day. 23 The people of Israel went up and cried before the Lord until evening. They asked the Lord, "Should we go again in battle against our brothers the people of Benjamin?" And the Lord said, "Go fight against them."

24 So the sons of Israel came to fight against the sons of Benjamin the second day. 25 Benjamin went out against them from Gibeah the second day. And they killed 18,000 men of Israel who used the sword. 26 Then all the people of Israel went up to Bethel and cried. They stayed that day before the Lord and would not eat until evening. They gave burnt gifts and peace gifts to the Lord. 27 The people of Israel asked the Lord what to do. (For the special box with the Law of God was there in those days. 28 Phinehas the son of Eleazar, Aaron's son, served in front of it those days.) The people said, "Should we go again in battle against our brothers the people of Benjamin? Or should we stop?" The Lord said, "Go fight against them. For tomorrow I will give them into your hand."

29 So Israel sent men to hide around Gibeah. 30 The sons of Israel went to fight against the sons of Benjamin on the third day. They dressed themselves for battle against Gibeah as they had done before. 31 The sons of Benjamin went out to fight the people and were taken away from the city. They began to fight and kill some of the people as they had done before. They killed about thirty men of Israel in the open country and on the roads. One road went up to Bethel and the other to Gibeah. 32 The sons of Benjamin said, "They are being killed in front of us as they were the first day." But the sons of Israel said, "Let us run away so we can get them away from the city and to the roads." 33 Then all the

men of Israel left their place and went to fight at Baal-tamar. And the men of Israel who were hiding rushed out of their place in the plain of Geba. 34 When 10,000 chosen men of Israel came against Gibeah, the battle was hard. But the people of Benjamin did not know that such danger was so close to them. 35 The Lord destroyed Benjamin in front of Israel. The sons of Israel destroyed 25,100 men of Benjamin that day. All these were men who used the sword. 36 So the people of Benjamin saw that they had lost the battle.

The men of Israel ran from Benjamin because they trusted in the men who were hiding and waiting to take Gibeah. 37 The men who had been hiding were quick to rush against Gibeah. They destroyed all of the city with the sword. 38 The men of Israel had agreed that the men who had been hiding should make a big cloud of smoke rise from the city. It would be something special for them to see. 39 Then the men of Israel turned around to fight in battle. Benjamin began to fight and kill about thirty men of Israel. They said, "For sure they are destroyed in front of us as in the first battle." 40 But when the cloud of smoke started to rise from the city, the men of Benjamin looked behind them. They saw the whole city going up in smoke to heaven. 41 Then the men of Israel turned around. And the men of Benjamin were filled with fear. For they saw that they were in much danger. 42 So they turned their backs to the men of Israel and ran toward the desert. But they were caught in the battle. Those who came out of the cities destroyed them. 43 They gathered around the people of Benjamin. They ran after them without stopping to rest and came upon them at the east side of Gibeah. 44 So 18,000 men of Benjamin were killed. All of them were powerful soldiers. 45 The others turned and ran toward the desert to the rock of Rimmon. But Israel killed 5,000 of them on the roads, and 2,000 at Gidom. 46 So 25,000 men of Benjamin were killed that day. All of them were powerful soldiers who used the sword. 47 But 600 men ran toward the desert to the rock of Rimmon. They stayed there for four months. 48 Then the men of Israel returned to fight the people of Benjamin. They destroyed them, their whole city, the cattle and all they found, with the sword. And they set fire to all the cities they found.

Wives for the Men of Benjamin

21 The men of Israel had made a promise in Mizpah, saying, "None of us will give his daughter in marriage to a man of Benjamin." ² So the people came to Bethel and sat there before God until evening. In loud voices they cried, ³ "O Lord, God of Israel, why has this happened in Israel? Why should there be one family group missing in Israel today?" ⁴ The people got up early the next day and built an altar there. They gave burnt gifts and peace gifts on it.

⁵ Then the people of Israel said, "Who among all the family groups of Israel did not come with the people to the Lord?" For they had made a promise about the one who did not come to the Lord at Mizpah, saying, "For sure he will be put to death." ⁶ The people of Israel were sorry for their brother Benjamin. They said, "One family is cut off from Israel today. ⁷ What will we do for wives for those who are left? We have promised by the Lord not to give them any of our daughters in marriage."

⁸ They said, "Who of the families of Israel did not come to the Lord at Mizpah?" And they found that no one had come to the meeting from Jabesh-gilead. ⁹ When the people were called, they saw that not one of the people of Jabesh-gilead was there. ¹⁰ The people sent 12,000 powerful soldiers to go there. They told them, "Go and kill the people of Jabesh-gilead with the sword. Kill the women and the children also. ¹¹ This is what you must do. Destroy every man and every woman who has had a man," ¹² They found 400 young women who had never had a man. So they brought them to the tents at Shiloh, in the land of Canaan.

¹³ Then all the people sent news to the people of Benjamin at the rock of Rimmon. They told them they wanted to have peace with them. ¹⁴ So the people of Benjamin returned. The people of Israel gave them the women they had saved alive from the women of Jabesh-gilead. But there were not enough for them. ¹⁵ The people were sorry for Benjamin because the Lord had divided the families of Israel.

¹⁶ Then the leaders of the people said, "What will we do for wives for those who are left? All the women of Benjamin were killed." ¹⁷ And they said, "There must be something that can be given to those of Benjamin who are left. Or a family will be taken out of Israel. ¹⁸ But we cannot give them our daughters for wives." For the men of Israel had promised, "A curse will come to the one who gives a wife to Benjamin."

¹⁹ So they said, "See, there is a special supper to the Lord every year in Shiloh. It is north of Bethel, east of the road that goes up from Bethel to Shechem, and south of Lebonah." ²⁰ They told the men of Benjamin, "Go and hide in the grape-fields. Wait there ²¹ and watch. The daughters of Shiloh might come out to dance. Then come out of the grape-fields. Each of you will catch his wife from the daughters of Shiloh. Then go to the land of Benjamin. ²² When their fathers or brothers come to complain to us, we will say to them, 'Give them to us of your own free will. For we did not leave a wife for each of the men of Benjamin in battle. And you did not give them any. You would have been doing wrong.' " ²³ The men of Benjamin did so. They took wives from those who danced, one for each man. They carried them away and returned to their land. Then they built the cities again and lived in them. ²⁴ The people of Israel left there at that time. Each man returned to his family in his own land.

²⁵ There was no king in Israel in those days. Each man did what he thought was right.

RUTH

Elimelech's Family Moves to Moab

1 In the days when there were judges to rule, there was a time of no food in the land. A certain man of Bethlehem in Judah went to visit the land of Moab with his wife and his two sons. ² The name of the man was Elimelech. His wife's name was Naomi. And the names of his two sons were Mahlon and Chilion. They were Ephrathites of Bethlehem in Judah. They went into the land of Moab and stayed there. ³ But Naomi's husband Elimelech died. And she was left with her two sons, ⁴ who married Moabite women. The name of one was Orpah. The name of the other was Ruth. After living there about ten years, ⁵ both Mahlon and Chilion died. Naomi was left without her two children and her husband.

Naomi and Ruth Return to Bethlehem

6 Then Naomi got ready to return from the land of Moab with her daughters-in-law. She had heard in the land of Moab that the Lord had brought food to His people. 7 So she left with her two daughters-in-law and went on the way toward the land of Judah. 8 But Naomi said to her two daughters-in-law, "Go, each one of you return to your own mother's house. May the Lord show kindness to you, as you have done with the dead and with me. 9 May the Lord help you to find a home, each in the family of her husband." Then she kissed them, and they cried in loud voices. 10 They said to her, "No, we will return with you to your people." 11 But Naomi said, "Return to your people, my daughters. Why should you go with me? Do I have more sons within me, who could become your husbands? 12 Return, my daughters. Go. For I am too old to have a husband. If I had hope, if I should have a husband tonight and give birth to sons, 13 would you wait until they were grown? Would you not marry until then? No, my daughters. It is harder for me than for you. For the hand of the Lord is against me." 14 Then they cried again in loud voices. Orpah kissed her mother-in-law. But Ruth held on to her.

15 Naomi said, "See, your sister-in-law has returned to her people and her gods. Return after your sister-in-law." 16 But Ruth said, "Do not beg me to leave you or turn away from following you. I will go where you go. I will live where you live. Your people will be my people. And your God will be my God. 17 I will die where you die, and there I will be buried. So may the Lord do the same to me, and worse, if anything but death takes me from you." 18 When Naomi saw that Ruth would do nothing but go with her, she said no more to her.

19 So they both went until they came to Bethlehem. The whole town of Bethlehem was happy because of them. The women said, "Is this Naomi?" 20 She said to them, "Do not call me Naomi. Call me Mara. For the All-powerful has brought much trouble to me. 21 I went out full. But the Lord has made me return empty. Why call me Naomi? The Lord has spoken against me. The All-powerful has allowed me to suffer."

22 So Naomi returned. And her daughter-in-law Ruth, the Moabite woman, returned with her from the land of Moab. They came to Bethlehem at the beginning of barley gathering time.

Ruth Meets Boaz

2 There was an in-law of the family of Naomi's husband there whose name was Boaz. He was a very rich man of the family of Elimelech. 2 Ruth, the Moabite woman, said to Naomi, "Let me go to the field to gather grain behind someone who might show favor to me." Naomi said to her, "Go, my daughter." 3 So Ruth went and gathered in the field behind those who picked the grain. And she happened to come to the part of the field that belonged to Boaz, who was of the family of Elimelech. 4 Now Boaz was seen coming from Bethlehem. He said to the people gathering the grain, "May the Lord be with you." And they said to him, "May the Lord bring good to you." 5 Then Boaz said to his servant who was watching over those who gathered grain, "Whose young woman is this?" 6 The servant who watched over those who gathered grain said, "She is the young Moabite woman who returned with Naomi from the land of Moab. 7 She said, 'Let me gather food behind the others who gather among the grain.' So she came and has stayed from morning until now. She has rested in the house a short time."

8 Then Boaz said to Ruth, "Be careful to listen, my daughter. Do not go to gather grain in another field. Do not leave this one. But stay here with my women who gather grain. 9 Keep your eyes upon the field where they gather grain. Go behind them. I have told the servants not to touch you. When you are thirsty, go to the water jars. Drink the water the servants have put there." 10 Then she fell with her face to the ground and said to him, "Why have I found favor in your eyes? Why do you care about me? I am a stranger from another land." 11 Boaz said to her, "I have heard about all you have done for your mother-in-law after the death of your husband. I have heard how you left your father and mother and the land of your birth to come to a people you did not know before. 12 May the Lord reward you for your work. May full pay be given to you from the Lord, the God of Israel. It is under His wings that you have come to be safe." 13 Then Ruth said, "Sir, I have found favor in your eyes. For you have brought comfort and have been kind in speaking to your woman servant. And I am not like any of your other women servants."

14 When it was time to eat, Boaz said to Ruth, "Come here. Eat of the bread and

put sour wine on it." So she sat beside the people who gathered the grain. And Boaz brought her grain made ready over a fire. She ate and was filled and had some left. [15] When she got up to gather grain, Boaz told his servants, "Let her gather even among the standing grain. Do not speak against her. [16] Pull some grain out of the grain that has been gathered together and leave it for her to gather. And do not speak sharp words to her."

[17] So Ruth gathered grain in the field until evening. Then she beat out what she had gathered. It was enough barley to fill a basket. [18] She picked it up and went into the city to show her mother-in-law what she had gathered. Ruth gave Naomi what she had left after she was filled. [19] Her mother-in-law said to her, "Where did you gather grain today? Where did you work? May good come to the man who showed you favor." So Ruth told her mother-in-law, "The name of the man I worked with today is Boaz." [20] Naomi said to her daughter-in-law, "May he receive good from the Lord, Who has not kept His kindness from the living and the dead." Then Naomi said to her, "The man is near to us. He is of our family." [21] Ruth, the Moabite woman, said, "He told me, 'You should stay close to my servants until they have finished gathering all my grain.'" [22] Naomi said to her daughter-in-law Ruth, "It is good that you go out with his women servants, my daughter. Then no danger will come upon you in another field." [23] So she stayed close to those who worked for Boaz until the end of the time of gathering grain. And she lived with her mother-in-law.

Ruth and Boaz at the Grain-Floor

3 Then Ruth's mother-in-law Naomi said to her, "My daughter, should I not look for a home for you, so all will be well with you? [2] Is not Boaz of our family, with whose women servants you were? See, he is dividing the grain from the waste at his grain floor tonight. [3] So wash yourself. Pour oil on yourself and wear your best clothes. Then go down to the grain-floor. But do not let the man know who you are until he has finished eating and drinking. [4] When he lies down, watch where he lies. Go in and take the covers off his feet and lie down. Then he will tell you what to do." [5] Ruth said to her, "I will do all that you say."

[6] So Ruth went down to the grain-floor and did all her mother-in-law had told her

to do. [7] When Boaz had finished eating and drinking and his heart was happy, he went to lie down beside the grain. Then Ruth came in secret. She took the covers off his feet and lay down. [8] The man was surprised late in the night. He turned and saw that a woman was lying at his feet. [9] He said, "Who are you?" She answered, "I am Ruth, your woman servant. Spread your covering over me. For you are of our family." [10] And Boaz said, "May the Lord bring good to you, my daughter. You have shown your last kindness to be better than your first by not going after young men, with or without riches. [11] Now my daughter, do not be afraid. I will do for you whatever you ask. For all my people in the city know that you are a good woman. [12] It is true that I am of your family. But there is one closer than I. [13] Stay this night. In the morning, if he will have you for his own, let him take you. But if he does not want to have you, then I will take you, as the Lord lives. Lie down until morning."

[14] So Ruth lay at his feet until morning. She got up before the people could see each other. For Boaz said, "Do not let it be known that the woman came to the grain-floor." [15] And he said, "Bring the coat you are wearing and hold it out." So she held it, and he loaded her with six jars full of grain. Then she went into the city. [16] When she came to her mother-in-law, Naomi said, "How did it go, my daughter?" And Ruth told her all that the man had done for her. [17] She said, "He gave me these six jars full of grain. For he said, 'Do not go to your mother-in-law with empty hands.'" [18] Naomi said, "Wait until you know what is going to happen, my daughter. For the man will not rest until the thing is decided upon today."

Boaz Marries Ruth

4 Boaz went up to the gate and sat down there. He saw the in-law of the family that he had spoken about pass by. So Boaz said, "Come here, friend, and sit down." So the man came and sat down. [2] And Boaz took ten of the leaders of the city and said, "Sit down here." So they sat down. [3] Then Boaz said to the close in-law, "Naomi has returned from the land of Moab. She is selling the piece of land which belonged to our brother Elimelech. [4] I thought I should let you know about it. Buy it in front of those who are sitting here, and in front of the leaders of my people. If you will buy it, then buy it. But if not, tell me you do not want to buy it, so I may know. For you have the right to be the first one to buy it. And I am after you." The man said, "I will buy it." ⁵ Then Boaz said, "The day you buy the field from Naomi, you must take Ruth, the Moabite woman, also. She is the wife of the dead man. You must keep alive the name of the dead man on his land." ⁶ Then the close in-law said, "I cannot buy it for myself because it might be that my own children would not be able to own my land later. Take it for yourself. I give you my right to buy it, for I cannot buy it."

⁷ This is what was done before in Israel to show that the buying or trading of land was decided upon. A man would take off his shoe and give it to another. This would make sure what was decided. ⁸ So he said to Boaz, "Buy it for yourself." And he took off his shoe. ⁹ Then Boaz said to the leaders and all the people, "You have seen today that I have bought from Naomi all that belonged to Elimelech, to Chilion and to Mahlon. ¹⁰ And I have taken Ruth, the Moabite woman who was Mahlon's wife, to be my wife. I will keep alive the name of the dead man on his land. His name will not be forgotten among his brothers or from the gate of his birth-place. You have heard this today." ¹¹ All the people in the gate and the leaders said, "We have heard it. May the Lord make the woman who is coming into your home like Rachel and Leah, who together built the house of Israel. May you become rich in Ephrathah and be known by all in Bethlehem. ¹² May your house be like the house of Perez, the son of Judah and Tamar, because of the children the Lord will give you by this young woman."

The Families to Follow Ruth and Boaz

¹³ So Boaz took Ruth. She became his wife, and he went in to her. The Lord made it possible for her to have a child and she gave birth to a son. ¹⁴ The women said to Naomi, "Thanks be to the Lord. He has not left you without a family this day. May his name become known in all of Israel. ¹⁵ May he bring you new life and strength while you are old. For your daughter-in-law who loves you, who is better to you than seven sons, has given birth to him." ¹⁶ Then Naomi took the child and held him, and became his nurse. ¹⁷ The neighbor women gave him a name. They said, "A son has been born to Naomi!" And they called him Obed. He is the father of Jesse, the father of David.

¹⁸ Now these are the children of Perez. Perez was the father of Hezron. ¹⁹ Hezron was the father of Ram. Ram was the father of Amminadab. ²⁰ Amminadab was the father of Nahshon. Nahshon was the father of Salmon. ²¹ Salmon was the father of Boaz. Boaz was the father of Obed. ²² Obed was the father of Jesse. And Jesse was the father of David.

1 SAMUEL

The Family of Elkanah at Shiloh

1 There was a certain man from Ramathaim-zophim of the hill country of Ephraim. His name was Elkanah, the son of Jeroham, the son of Elihu, the son of Tohu, the son of Zuph, an Ephraimite. ² He had two wives. The name of one was Hannah. The name of the other was Peninnah. Peninnah had children, but Hannah had no children. ³ This man would go from his city each year to worship and to give gifts on the altar in Shiloh to the Lord of All. Eli's two sons, Hophni and Phinehas, were the Lord's religious leaders there. ⁴ On the day when Elkanah killed animals on the altar in worship, he would give part of the gift to his wife Peninnah and to all her sons and daughters. ⁵ But he would give twice as much to Hannah, for he loved Hannah. But the Lord had made it so she could not have children. ⁶ Peninnah would try to make her very angry, because the Lord would not let her have children. ⁷ So it happened, year after year, each time Hannah went up to the house of the Lord, Peninnah would make her angry. Hannah cried and would not eat. ⁸ Then her husband Elkanah said to her, "Hannah, why are you crying? Why are you not eating, and why is your heart sad? Am I not better to you than ten sons?"

Hannah and Eli

⁹ Then Hannah stood up after they had eaten and drunk in Shiloh. Eli the religious leader was sitting on the seat by the door of the house of the Lord. ¹⁰ Hannah was very troubled. She prayed to the Lord and cried with sorrow. ¹¹ Then she made a promise and said, "O Lord of All, be sure to look on

the trouble of Your woman servant, and remember me. Do not forget Your woman servant, but give me a son. If You will, then I will give him to the Lord all his life. And no hair will ever be cut from his head."

12 While she kept praying to the Lord, Eli was watching her mouth. 13 Hannah was speaking in her heart. Her lips were moving, but her voice was not heard. So Eli thought she had drunk too much. 14 Eli said to her, "How long will you be drunk? Put wine away from you." 15 But Hannah answered, "No, my lord, I am a woman troubled in spirit. I have not drunk wine or strong drink, but I was pouring out my soul to the Lord. 16 Do not think of your woman servant as a woman of no worth. For I have been speaking out of much trouble and pain in my spirit." 17 Then Eli answered, "Go in peace. May the God of Israel do what you have asked of Him." 18 And Hannah said, "Let your woman servant find favor in your eyes." So she went her way and ate, and her face was no longer sad.

Samuel Is Born

19 The family got up early in the morning and worshiped before the Lord. Then they returned to their house in Ramah. Elkanah lay with his wife Hannah, and the Lord remembered her. 20 The Lord made it possible for her to have a child, and when the time came she gave birth to a son. She gave him the name Samuel, saying, "I have asked the Lord for him."

21 Then Elkanah went up with all those of his house to give the Lord the gift on the altar in worship as he did each year, and to pay what he had promised. 22 But Hannah did not go. For she said to her husband, "I will not go up until the child no longer needs to be nursed. Then I will bring him before the Lord, to stay there forever." 23 Elkanah her husband said to her, "Do what you think is best. Stay here until he no longer needs to be nursed. Only may the Lord do as He has said." So Hannah stayed and nursed her son until he no longer needed to be nursed. 24 When she had finished nursing him, she took him with her to the house of the Lord in Shiloh, and the child was young. She brought a three year old bull, one basket of flour and a jar of wine also. Then they killed the bull, and brought the boy to Eli. 26 Hannah said, "O, my lord! As you live, my lord, I am the woman who stood here beside you, praying to the Lord. 27 I prayed for this boy,

and the Lord has given me what I asked of Him. 28 So I have given him to the Lord. He is given to the Lord as long as he lives." And they worshiped the Lord there.

Hannah's Prayer

2 Then Hannah prayed and said, "My heart is happy in the Lord. My strength is honored in the Lord. My mouth speaks with strength against those who hate me, because I have joy in Your saving power. 2 There is no one holy like the Lord. For sure, there is no one other than You. There is no rock like our God. 3 Speak no more in your pride. Do not let proud talk come out of your mouth. For the Lord is a God Who knows. Actions are weighed by Him. 4 The bows of the powerful are broken. But the weak are dressed in strength. 5 Those who were full go out to work for bread. But those who were hungry are filled. She who could not give birth has given birth to seven. But she who has many children has become weak. 6 The Lord kills and brings to life. He brings down to the grave, and He raises up. 7 The Lord makes poor and makes rich. He brings low and He lifts up. 8 He lifts the poor from the dust. He lifts those in need from the ashes. He makes them sit with rulers and receive a seat of honor. For what holds the earth belongs to the Lord. He has set the world in its place. 9 He watches over the steps of His good people. But the sinful ones will be made quiet in darkness. For a man will not win by strength. 10 Those who fight with the Lord will be broken to pieces. He will thunder in heaven against them. The Lord will decide about all people to the ends of the earth. He will give strength to His king. He will give power to His chosen one."

11 Then Elkanah went home to Ramah. But the boy served the Lord with Eli the religious leader.

Eli's Sons

12 The sons of Eli were men of no worth. They did not know the Lord. 13 This is the way the religious leaders acted toward the people. When any man brought an animal to give to the Lord, the religious leader's servant would come with a meathook in his hand, while the meat was hot. 14 Then he would put it in the pot. The religious leader would take for himself all that the meat-hook brought up. They did this to all the Israelites who came there to Shiloh. 15 And before they burned the fat, the religious leader's servant would come

and say to the man who brought the gift in worship, "Give meat for the religious leader to make ready. For he will not take boiled meat from you, but only meat that has just been killed." **16** But if the man says to him, "Let them burn the fat first, then take as much as you want," then the religious leader's servant would say, "No, give it to me now; and if not, I will take it from you against your will." **17** So the sin of the young men was very bad before the Lord. For the men hated the gift of the Lord.

Samuel Serves the Lord at Shiloh

18 Now Samuel was serving the Lord, even as a boy, wearing a linen vest. **19** Each year his mother would make him a little coat. She would bring it to him when she came with her husband to bring the gift in worship each year. **20** Then Eli would pray that good would come to Elkanah and his wife, saying, "May the Lord give you children from this woman in place of the one she gave to the Lord." Then they would return to their home. **21** And the Lord visited Hannah. She gave birth to three sons and two daughters. The boy Samuel grew up to serve the Lord.

The Future of Eli's Sons

22 Now Eli was very old. He heard all that his sons were doing to all Israel, and how they lay with the women who served at the door of the meeting tent. **23** And he said to them, "Why do you do such things, the sinful things I hear from all these people? **24** No, my sons, the news is not good which I hear from the Lord's people. **25** If one man sins against another, God will help make peace for him. But if a man sins against the Lord, who can make peace for him?" Yet they would not listen to what their father said, for it was the Lord's will to kill them. **26** Now the boy Samuel grew and was in favor both with the Lord and with men.

27 Then a man of God came to Eli and said to him, "This is what the Lord says. 'Did I not let Myself be known to those of your father's family when they were in Egypt being made to work for Pharaoh's house? **28** Did I not choose them from all the families of Israel to be My religious leaders, to go up to My altar, to burn special perfume, and to wear a linen vest before Me? Did I not give all the gifts made by fire of the people of Israel to the family of your father? **29** Why do you show no respect to My gifts which I have asked for, and honor your sons more than Me? You

make yourselves fat with the best part of every gift given in worship by My people Israel.' **30** So the Lord God of Israel says, 'I did promise that those of your family and the family of your father should walk before Me forever.' But now the Lord says, 'May this be far from Me. For I will honor those who honor Me. And those who hate Me will not be honored. **31** See, the days are coming when I will break your strength and the strength of your father's family. So there will not be an old man in your family. **32** You will see the trouble of My family, even in all the good I do for Israel. And an old man will not be in your family forever. **33** But I will not destroy every man of yours from My altar. Some will be left to cry and be filled with sorrow. But all the children of your family will die in their best years. **34** This will be the special thing that you will see. Your two sons, Hophni and Phinehas, will both die on the same day. **35** I will raise up for Myself a faithful religious leader who will act by what is in My heart and mind. I will build him a family to last. And he will walk before My chosen one forever. **36** Everyone who is left in your family will come and bow down to him for a piece of silver or a loaf of bread, and say, "I beg you, put me in one of the religious leader's places so that I may eat a piece of bread." '"

Samuel's Call

3 Now the boy Samuel was working for the Lord with Eli. There were few words from the Lord given in those days, and there were not many special dreams. **2** At that time Eli was lying down in his own place. His eyes had become weak and he could not see well. **3** The lamp of God had not gone out yet. And Samuel was lying down in the house of the Lord where the special box of God was. **4** Then the Lord called Samuel, and Samuel said, "Here I am." **5** He ran to Eli and said, "Here I am, for you called me." But Eli said, "I did not call you. Lie down again." So Samuel went and lay down. **6** The Lord called again, "Samuel!" So Samuel got up and went to Eli, and said, "Here I am, for you called me." But Eli answered, "I did not call you, my son. Lie down again." **7** Now Samuel did not know the Lord yet. And the Word of the Lord had not been made known to him. **8** The Lord called Samuel again for the third time. He got up and went to Eli, and said, "Here I am, for you called me." Then Eli understood that the Lord was calling the boy. 9 Eli said to Samuel, "Go lie down. If He calls you, say, 'Speak, Lord, for Your servant is listening.' " So Samuel went and lay down in his place.

10 Then the Lord came and stood and called as He did the other times, "Samuel! Samuel!" And Samuel said, "Speak, for Your servant is listening." 11 The Lord said to Samuel, "See, I am about to do a thing in Israel which will make both ears of everyone who hears it feel strange. 12 On that day I will do all I have said I will do against the family of Eli. 13 I have told him that I will punish his family forever for the sin he knew about. Because his sons brought the sin upon themselves, and Eli did not stop them. 14 So I swear to the family of Eli that the sin of his family will not be paid for with gifts given on the altar forever."

15 Samuel lay down until morning. Then he opened the doors of the house of the Lord. But Samuel was afraid to tell Eli about the special dream. 16 Eli called Samuel and said, "Samuel, my son." And Samuel said, "Here I am." 17 Eli said, "What did the Lord tell you? Do not hide it from me. May God do so to you and more, if you hide anything from me of all He said to you." 18 So Samuel told him everything and hid nothing from him. And Eli said, "It is the Lord. Let Him do what is good in His eyes."

19 Samuel grew. And the Lord was with him and made everything he said come true. 20 All Israel from Dan to Beersheba knew that Samuel had become a man of God. 21 The Lord came again to Shiloh. For the Lord made Himself known to Samuel at Shiloh, by the Word of the Lord.

The Philistines Take the Special Box of the Agreement

4 So the news of Samuel came to all Israel. Now Israel went out to battle against the Philistines. They set up their tents beside Ebenezer while the Philistines stayed at Aphek. 2 The Philistines came dressed for battle to meet Israel. When the battle spread, Israel lost to the Philistines. The Philistines killed about 4,000 men on the battle-field. 3 When the people returned to the tents, the leaders of Israel said, "Why has the Lord made us lose today to the Philistines? Let us bring the special box that holds the Law of the Lord here from Shiloh. Then He may come among us and save us from the power of those who fight against us." 4 So the people sent men to Shiloh to take the

special box with the Law of the Lord of All Who sits above the cherubim. Eli's two sons, Hophni and Phinehas, were there with the special box with the Law of God.

5 When the box with the Law of the Lord came among the tents, all Israel called out with a loud noise, so that the earth shook. 6 When the Philistines heard the noise, they said, "What does this loud noise among the Hebrews mean?" Then they understood that the special box of the Lord had come among the Israelites. 7 The Philistines were afraid. They said, "A god has come among the tents. Trouble has come to us! Nothing like this has happened before. 8 Trouble has come to us! Who will save us from the hand of these powerful gods? These are the gods who destroyed the Egyptians with all kinds of troubles in the desert. 9 Be strong and act like men, O Philistines. Or you will be made to work for the Hebrews, as they have been made to work for you. Be men and fight." 10 So the Philistines fought, and Israel lost. Every man ran to his tent. And many were killed, for 30,000 foot soldiers of Israel fell. 11 The special box of God was taken. And Eli's two sons, Hophni and Phinehas, died.

Death of Eli

12 A man of Benjamin ran from the battle and came to Shiloh the same day. His clothes were torn and he had dust on his head. 13 When he came, Eli was sitting on his seat by the road watching, for he was very worried about the special box of God. The man told the news in the city, and all the city cried out. 14 When Eli heard the noise in the city, he said, "What does this noise mean?" Then the man came in a hurry and told Eli. 15 Now Eli was ninety-eight years old, and his eyes were weak so that he could not see. 16 The man said to Eli, "I have come from the battle. I ran from the battle today." And Eli said, "How did it go, my son?" 17 The one who brought the news answered, "Israel has run from the Philistines and there have been many people killed. Your two sons, Hophni and Phinehas, are dead. And the special box of God has been taken." 18 When he told about the special box of God, Eli fell back off the seat by the gate. His neck was broken and he died, for he was old and heavy. He had judged Israel forty years.

19 Now his daughter-in-law, Phinehas's wife, was going to have a child and about to give birth. When she heard the news that

the special box of God was taken and that her father-in-law and husband had died, she started to give birth, for her pains came upon her. 20 About the time of her death, the women who stood by her said to her, "Do not be afraid. For you have given birth to a son." But she did not answer or listen to them. 21 She gave the boy the name Ichabod, saying, "The honor has left Israel," because the special box of God was taken and because of her father-in-law and husband. 22 She said, "The honor has left Israel, for the special box of God was taken."

The Philistines and the Special Box

5 The Philistines took the special box of God and brought it from Ebenezer to Ashdod. 2 They took the special box of God into the house of Dagon, and set it beside Dagon. 3 When the Ashdodites got up early the next morning, they saw that Dagon had fallen on his face to the ground before the special box of the Lord. So they took Dagon and set him in his place again. 4 But when they got up early the next morning, they saw that Dagon had fallen on his face to the ground in front of the special box of the Lord. And Dagon's head and both his hands were cut off and lying in the doorway. Only the body of Dagon was left. 5 So the religious leaders of Dagon and all who go into Dagon's house do not step on the bottom part of the doorway in Ashdod to this day.

6 The hand of the Lord was heavy on the Ashdodites. He filled them with fear and punished them with pain and sores, both Ashdod and its lands. 7 When the men of Ashdod saw how things were, they said, "The special box of the God of Israel must not stay with us. For His hand is hard on us and on our god Dagon." 8 So they called together all the leaders of the Philistines and said, "What should we do with the special box of the God of Israel?" And they said, "Let the special box of the God of Israel be brought around to Gath." So they brought the box of the God of Israel there. 9 But after they had brought it there, the hand of the Lord was against the city, causing much fear. He punished both the young and old men of the city, so that sores broke out upon them. 10 So they sent the special box of God to Ekron. When the box of God came to Ekron, the people there cried out, "They have brought the special box of the God of Israel to us, to kill us and our people." 11 So they called together all the leaders of the Philistines and said, "Send

away the special box of the God of Israel. Let it return to its own place, that it may not kill us and our people." For the people of the city were afraid. The hand of God was very heavy there. 12 The men who did not die were punished with sores, and the cry of the city went up to heaven.

The Special Box Returned to Israel

6 The special box of the Lord had been in the country of the Philistines seven months. 2 The Philistines called for the religious leaders and those who were wise in secret ways, saying, "What should we do with the special box of the Lord? Tell us how we should send it to its place." 3 And they said, "If you send away the special box of the God of Israel, do not send it empty. But be sure to return to Him a sin gift. Then you will be healed, and it will be known to you why His hand does not turn away from you." 4 Then they said, "What should we return to Him for a sin gift?" And they said, "Five sores made of gold and five mice, as many as there are Philistine leaders. For the same trouble was upon all of you and on your leaders. 5 So make objects to look like your sores and your mice that destroyed the land, and you will give honor to the God of Israel. It may be that He will be easier on you, your gods, and your land. 6 Why do you make your hearts hard as the Egyptians and Pharaoh made their hearts hard? Do not forget how the God of Israel made it hard for them. And did they not let the people go? 7 So now take and make ready a new wagon and two milk cows that have never pulled a load. Tie the cows to the wagon and take their calves away from them. 8 Take the special box of the Lord and put it on the wagon. Put the objects of gold which you return to Him as a sin gift in a box by its side. Then send it away, and let it be gone. 9 And watch. If it goes on the way to its own land, to Beth-shemesh, then He has done this very bad thing to us. But if not, then we will know that it was not His hand that destroyed us. It will have just happened for no reason."

10 The men did so. They took two milk cows and tied them to the wagon, and shut up their calves at home. 11 They put the special box of the Lord on the wagon, and the box with the gold mice and the objects made to look like their sores. 12 And the cows went straight toward Beth-shemesh. They went along the straight road, making a sound as they went. They did not turn

aside to the right or to the left. And the leaders of the Philistines followed them to the outside of Beth-shemesh. 13 Now the people of Beth-shemesh were gathering their grain in the valley. They looked up and saw the special box of the Lord, and were glad to see it. 14 The wagon came into the field of Joshua the Bethshemite and stopped there by a big stone. They cut the wood of the wagon into pieces and gave the cows as a burnt gift to the Lord. 15 The Levites took down the special box of the Lord and the box that was with it that had the objects of gold, and put them on the big stone. The men of Beth-shemesh gave burnt gifts in worship that day to the Lord. 16 When the three leaders of the Philistines saw it, they returned that day to Ekron.

17 These are the sores made of gold which the Philistines returned for a sin gift to the Lord. There was one each for Ashdod, Gaza, Ashkelon, Gath, and Ekron. 18 And the gold mice were as many as the number of all the cities of the Philistines belonging to the five leaders, both cities with walls and country towns. The big stone where they set the special box of the Lord is there in the field of Joshua the Bethshemite to this day.

19 The Lord killed some of the men of Beth-shemesh because they had looked into the special box of the Lord. He killed 70 (50,070) men. And the people were filled with sorrow because the Lord had killed so many of them.

The Special Box at Kiriath-jearim

20 The men of Beth-shemesh said, "Who is able to stand before the Lord, this holy God? To whom can we send Him?" 21 So they sent men to the people living in Kiriath-jearim, saying, "The Philistines have returned the special box of the Lord. Come down and get it."

7 The men of Kiriath-jearim came and took the special box of the Lord and brought it to the house of Abinadab on the hill. They set apart his son Eleazar to keep the special box of the Lord.

Samuel Judges for Israel

2 The special box stayed in Kiriath-jearim a long time, for it was twenty years. And all the family of Israel cried with sorrow for the Lord. 3 Then Samuel said to all the family of Israel, "Return to the Lord with all your heart. Put away the strange gods and the false goddess Ashtaroth from among you. Turn your hearts to the Lord and worship Him alone. Then He will save you from the Philistines." 4 So the people of Israel put away from among them the false gods of Baal and Ashtaroth and worshiped the Lord alone.

5 Then Samuel said, "Gather all Israel together at Mizpah, and I will pray to the Lord for you." 6 So they gathered at Mizpah. They got water and poured it out before the Lord as a gift, and did not eat that day. They said there, "We have sinned against the Lord." And Samuel judged the people of Israel at Mizpah. 7 The Philistines heard that the people of Israel had gathered at Mizpah, so the leaders of the Philistines went to battle against them. When the people of Israel heard about it, they were afraid of the Philistines. 8 The Israelites said to Samuel, "Do not stop crying to the Lord our God for us, that He may save us from the Philistines." 9 Samuel took a young lamb and gave it as a whole burnt gift to the Lord. Samuel cried to the Lord for Israel, and the Lord answered him. 10 As Samuel was burning the gift to the Lord, the Philistines came near to battle against Israel. But the Lord made a loud thunder that day against the Philistines, making them afraid. So they lost the battle with Israel. 11 The men of Israel left Mizpah and went after the Philistines, killing them almost as far as Bethcar.

12 Then Samuel took a stone and set it between Mizpah and Shen. He gave it the name Ebenezer, saying, "The Lord has helped us this far." 13 So the Philistines were beaten. They did not come into the land of Israel again. And the hand of the Lord was against the Philistines all the days of Samuel's life. 14 The cities the Philistines had taken from Israel were returned, from Ekron to Gath. Israel saved their land from the Philistines. So there was peace between Israel and the Amorites.

15 Samuel judged Israel all the days of his life. 16 Every year he went around to Bethel, Gilgal and Mizpah, and he judged Israel in all these places. 17 Then he would return to Ramah, for his home was there. He judged Israel there also, and built an altar to the Lord.

Israel Asks for a King

8 When Samuel became old, he made his sons judges in Israel. 2 The name of his first-born son was Joel. And the name of his second son was Abijah. They were men who judged in Beersheba. ³ But his sons did not walk in his ways. They turned aside to get money. They took pay to do things that were not right and fair. ⁴ Then all the leaders of Israel gathered together and came to Samuel at Ramah. ⁵ They said to him, "See, you have grown old, and your sons do not walk in your ways. Choose a king to rule over us like all the nations." ⁶ But Samuel was not pleased when they said, "Give us a king to rule over us." And Samuel prayed to the Lord. ⁷ The Lord said to Samuel, "Listen to the voice of the people in all they say to you. For they have not turned away from you. They have turned away from Me, that I should not be king over them. ⁸ They are doing to you what they have done since the day I brought them out of Egypt until now. They have turned away from Me and worshiped other gods. ⁹ So listen to their voice. But tell them of the danger and show them the ways of the king who will rule over them."

¹⁰ So Samuel told all the words of the Lord to the people who had asked him for a king. ¹¹ He said, "This will be the way the king will rule over you. He will take your sons and make them drive his war-wagons, be his horsemen, and run in front of his war-wagons. ¹² He will choose leaders of thousands and of fifties. He will choose men to plow his ground, gather his grain, and make objects for war and for his war-wagons. ¹³ He will take your daughters to make perfume, work with the food, and make bread. ¹⁴ He will take the best of your fields and vines and olives, and give them to his servants. ¹⁵ He will take a tenth part of your grain and your vines to give to his leaders and his servants. ¹⁶ He will take your men servants and your women servants and the best of your cattle and your donkeys, and use them for his work. ¹⁷ He will take a tenth part of your flocks, and you yourselves will be made to work for him. ¹⁸ You will cry out in that day because of your king you have chosen for yourselves. But the Lord will not answer you in that day."

¹⁹ But the people would not listen to Samuel. They said, "No! We will have a king rule over us, ²⁰ so we may be like other nations. Our king may rule over us and go out before us and fight our battles." ²¹ After Samuel heard all the people's words, he told the Lord what they had said. ²² The Lord said to Samuel, "Listen to their voice, and choose a king for them."

So Samuel said to the men of Israel, "Every one of you go home to his city."

Saul Is Chosen to Be the King

9 There was a man of Benjamin whose name was Kish the son of Abiel, the son of Zeror, the son of Becorath, the son of Aphiah, a Benjamite. He was a powerful man of action. ² He had a son whose name was Saul, a good-looking young man. There was not a man among the people of Israel who was better looking than he. He was a head taller than any of the people. ³ Now the donkeys of Saul's father Kish were lost. So Kish said to his son Saul, "Take one of the servants and go look for the donkeys." ⁴ They passed through the hill country of Ephraim and the land of Shalishah, but they did not find them. They passed through the land of Shaalim, but they were not there. Then they passed through the land of the Benjamites, but they did not find them.

⁵ When they came to the land of Zuph, Saul said to his servant who was with him, "Come, let us return. My father might stop worrying about the donkeys and start worrying about us." ⁶ The servant said, "See, there is a man of God in this city, and people honor him. All that he says comes true. Let us go there. It may be that he can tell us where we should go." ⁷ Then Saul said to his servant, "But if we go, what can we bring the man? The bread in our bags is gone. There is no gift to bring to the man of God. What do we have?" ⁸ The servant answered Saul and said, "See, I have a fourth of a piece of silver in my hand. I will give it to the man of God and he will tell us the way to go." ⁹ (Before in Israel, when a man went to ask God a question, he would say, "Come, let us go to the man of God." For he who is called a man who speaks for God now, was called a seer before.) ¹⁰ Saul said to his servant, "What you said is good. Come, let us go." So they went to the city where the man of God was.

¹¹ As they went up the hill to the city, they met young women going out to get water. They said to them, "Is the man of God here?" ¹² The women answered, "He is. Look, he is up in front of you. Hurry now, for he has come to the city today because the people are giving a gift in worship on the high place today. ¹³ You will find him as you go into the city, before he goes up to the high place to eat. The people will not eat until he comes to give thanks for the gift. Then those who are asked to come

will eat. Now go up, for you will find him at once." ¹⁴ So they went up to the city. As they came into the city, they saw Samuel coming out toward them to go up to the high place.

¹⁵ Now the day before Saul came, the Lord had told Samuel, ¹⁶ "I will send you a man from the land of Benjamin about this time tomorrow. Choose him to be the leader of My people Israel. And he will save My people from the Philistines. For I have seen the trouble of My people. I have heard their cry. ¹⁷ When Samuel saw Saul, the Lord said to him, "Here is who the man I told you about. He is the one who will rule over My people." ¹⁸ Then Saul came to Samuel in the gate, and said, "Tell me, where is the man of God's house?" ¹⁹ Samuel answered Saul and said, "I am the man of God. Go up before me to the high place. For you will eat with me today, and tomorrow I will let you go. And I will tell you all that is on your mind. ²⁰ Do not worry about your donkeys which were lost three days ago, for they have been found. And for whom is all the desire of Israel? Is it not for you and for all your father's house?" ²¹ Saul answered, "Am I not a Benjamite, from the smallest of the family groups of Israel? Is not my family the least important of all the families of Benjamin? Why then do you speak to me this way?"

²² Then Samuel took Saul and his servant and brought them into the meeting room. He gave them a place at the head of those who were asked to come, about thirty men. ²³ Samuel said to the one who was making the food ready, "Bring the part I gave you and told you to set aside." ²⁴ So the man picked up the leg with what was on it and set it in front of Saul. And Samuel said, "Here is what has been saved for you. Eat. It has been kept for you until the right time, ever since I asked the people to come." So Saul ate with Samuel that day.

²⁵ When they came down from the high place into the city, Samuel spoke with Saul on the roof. ²⁶ They got up early the next day. Samuel called to Saul on the roof, saying, "Get up, that I may send you on your way." So Saul got up, and both he and Samuel went out into the street.

Saul Is Made King

²⁷ As they were going out of the city, Samuel said to Saul, "Tell the servant to go on before us, but you stand here. Then I will make the Word of God known to you."

10 Then Samuel took a bottle of oil and poured it on Saul's head. He kissed him and said, "Has not the Lord chosen you to be a ruler over His land? ² When you leave me today, you will meet two men by Rachel's grave in the land of Benjamin at Zelzah. They will say to you, 'The donkeys you went to look for have been found. Now your father has stopped worrying about the donkeys and is worried about you, saying, "What should I do about my son?" ' ³ Then you will go farther and come to the oak tree of Tabor. There three men going up to God at Bethel will meet you. One will be carrying three young goats. Another will be carrying three loaves of bread. And another will be carrying a bottle of wine. ⁴ They will greet you and give you two loaves of bread, which you will take from their hand. ⁵ Then you will come to the hill of God where there are Philistine soldiers. When you come there to the city, you will meet a group of men who speak for God coming down from the high place. They will have harps, an object to beat sounds of joy, and a horn. And they will be speaking God's Word. ⁶ Then the Spirit of the Lord will come upon you with power. You will speak God's Word with them and be changed into another man. ⁷ When you see these special things, do whatever you find that should be done. For God is with you. ⁸ You will go down before me to Gilgal. Then see, I will come down to you to give burnt gifts and peace gifts. Wait seven days until I come to you and show you what you should do."

⁹ When Saul turned his back to leave Samuel, God changed his heart. And all these special things happened on that day. ¹⁰ When they came to the hill, a group of men who speak for God met him. The Spirit of God came upon him with power, so that he spoke God's Word with them. ¹¹ People who had known him before saw him doing this and asked one another, "What has happened to the son of Kish? Is Saul one of the men who speak God's Word?" ¹² One of the men there answered, "Now, who is their father?" So it became a saying: "Is Saul one of the men who speak God's Word?" ¹³ When Saul had finished speaking the Word of God, he went to the altar at the high place.

¹⁴ The brother of Saul's father said to him and his servant, "Where have you been?" And Saul said, "To look for the donkeys. When we saw that they could not be found, we went to Samuel." ¹⁵ The

brother of Saul's father said, "Tell me, what did Samuel say to you?" [16] Saul said to his father's brother, "He told us that the donkeys had been found." But he did not tell him what Samuel had told him about being king.

[17] Then Samuel called the people together to the Lord at Mizpah. [18] He said to the people of Israel, "This is what the Lord, the God of Israel, says: 'I brought Israel out of Egypt. I saved you from the power of the Egyptians, and from the power of all the nations that made it hard for you.' [19] But today you have turned away from your God, Who saves you from all your troubles. You have said, 'No! Have a king rule over us!' So now come before the Lord, by your family groups and by your thousands." [20] When Samuel brought all the families of Israel near, the name of the family group of Benjamin was drawn. [21] Then he brought the family group of Benjamin near by its families, and the name of the Matrite family was drawn. Then the name of Saul the son of Kish was drawn. But when they looked for him, he could not be found. [22] So they asked the Lord, "Has the man come here yet?" The Lord said, "See, he is hiding among the bags." [23] They ran and brought him from there. And when he stood among the people, he was a head taller than any of them. [24] Samuel said to all the people, "Do you see him whom the Lord has chosen? For sure there is no one like him among all the people." So all the people called out and said, "Long live the king!" [25] Then Samuel told the people the rights and duties of the king and his nation. He wrote them in a book and laid it before the Lord. Then Samuel sent all the people away, each one to his home. [26] Saul went home to Gibeah. And the strong men whose hearts God had touched went with him. [27] But some men of no worth said, "How can this man save us?" They hated him and did not bring him any gift. But he kept quiet.

Saul Wins the Battle over the Ammonites

11 Then Nahash the Ammonite came and his soldiers set up their tents around Jabesh-gilead. All the men of Jabesh said to Nahash, "Make an agreement with us, and we will work for you." [2] But Nahash the Ammonite said to them, "I will make an agreement with you only if I may cut out the right eye of every one of you. This way I will put all Israel to shame."

[3] The leaders of Jabesh said to him, "Let us alone for seven days, so we may send men with news through the land of Israel. Then, if there is no one to save us, we will give ourselves up to you." [4] The men came to Gibeah of Saul and told the news to the people. And all the people cried with a loud voice.

[5] Now Saul was coming from the field behind the cattle, and he said, "What troubles the people? Why are they crying?" So they told him the news the men had brought from Jabesh. [6] The Spirit of God came upon Saul with power when he heard this news, and he became very angry. [7] He took two bulls and cut them in pieces and sent them through the land of Israel with the men who had brought the news, saying, "This will be done to the bulls of those who will not come out after Saul and Samuel." The fear of the Lord came upon the people, and they all came out together. [8] Saul numbered them at Bezek. There were 300,000 men of Israel, and 30,000 men of Judah. [9] They said to the men who had brought the news, "Tell the men of Jabesh-gilead that tomorrow, by the time the sun is hot, you will have help." So the men went and told the news to the men of Jabesh, and they were glad. [10] Then the men of Jabesh said, "Tomorrow we will give ourselves up to you. And you may do to us whatever you think is good." [11] The next morning, Saul put the people in three groups. They came among the tents early in the morning and killed the Ammonites until the heat of the day. Those who were left alive were divided, so that no two of them stayed together.

[12] Then the people said to Samuel, "Who is it that said, 'Should Saul rule over us?' Bring the men, that we may put them to death." [13] But Saul said, "No man will be put to death this day. For today the Lord has saved Israel."

[14] Samuel said to the people, "Come, let us go to Gilgal and make it the place for the king." [15] So all the people went to Gilgal. There they made Saul king before the Lord, in Gilgal. There they gave peace gifts to the Lord. And there Saul and all the men of Israel were filled with much joy.

Samuel's Last Words to Israel

12 Then Samuel said to all Israel, "See, I have listened to all you have said to me. I have chosen a king to rule over you. [2] Now see, the king walks in front of you. But I am old. My hair is growing white.

See, my sons are with you. I have walked in front of you since I was young, until this day. 3 Here I am. Speak against me to the Lord and Saul His chosen one. Whose bull have I taken? Whose donkey have I taken? To whom have I not been honest? For whom have I made it hard? From whose hand have I taken pay for closing my eyes to the truth? I will return it to you." 4 They said, "You have always been honest with us. You have not made it hard for us, or taken anything from any man's hand." 5 Samuel said to them, "The Lord has heard you. And His chosen one has heard this day that you have found nothing in my hand." And they said, "The Lord has heard." 6 Samuel said to the people, "The Lord is the One Who chose Moses and Aaron and brought your fathers out of the land of Egypt. 7 Now stand where you are, that I may argue with you before the Lord about all His saving acts which He did for you and your fathers. 8 When Jacob went into Egypt and the Egyptians made it hard for them, your fathers cried to the Lord. And the Lord sent Moses and Aaron. They brought your fathers out of Egypt, and had them live in this place. 9 But they forgot the Lord their God. So He sold them into the hand of Sisera, captain of the army of Hazor, and into the hand of the Philistines, and into the hand of the king of Moab. And they fought against them. 10 Then they cried out to the Lord and said, 'We have sinned because we have turned away from the Lord. We have worshiped the false gods, the Baals and the Ashtaroth. But now save us from the power of those who hate us, and we will worship You.' 11 The Lord sent Jerubbaal, Bedan, Jephthah and Samuel, and saved you from the power of those all around who hated you. So you were safe. 12 But then you saw that Nahash the king of the Ammonites came against you. So you said to me, 'No! A king must rule over us,' when the Lord your God was your King. 13 Now see the king you have chosen, the king you have asked for. See, the Lord has given you a king. 14 Fear the Lord and worship Him. Listen to His voice and do not go against the Word of the Lord. If both you and the king who rules over you will follow the Lord your God, it will be well. 15 But if you will not listen to the voice of the Lord, and go against the Lord's Word, then the hand of the Lord will be against you, as it was against your fathers. 16 Now stand still and see this great thing which the Lord will do

in front of your eyes. 17 Is it not the time to gather grain today? I will call to the Lord, and He will send thunder and rain. Then you will know and see that you have done a bad sin in the eyes of the Lord by asking for a king." 18 So Samuel called to the Lord, and the Lord sent thunder and rain that day. And all the people were very much afraid of the Lord and Samuel.

19 Then all the people said to Samuel, "Pray to the Lord your God for your servants, so we will not die. For we have added to all our sins this bad thing, to ask for a king." 20 Samuel said to the people, "Do not be afraid. You have done all these sins. But do not turn aside from following the Lord. Worship the Lord with all your heart. 21 Do not turn aside after things that have no worth and cannot save you, for they are nothing. 22 The Lord will not leave His people alone, because of His great name. The Lord has been pleased to make you His people. 23 And as for me, far be it from me that I should sin against the Lord by not praying for you. But I will teach you the good and the right way. 24 Only fear the Lord and be faithful to worship Him with all your heart. Think of the great things He has done for you. 25 But if you still sin, both you and your king will be destroyed."

War with the Philistines

13 Saul was forty years old when he began to rule. He ruled over Israel thirty-two years. 2 Saul chose 3,000 men of Israel. There were 2,000 of them with Saul in Michmash and in the hill country of Bethel. And 1,000 were with Jonathan at Gibeah of Benjamin. But he sent away the rest of the people, each to his tent. 3 Jonathan destroyed the place where the Philistine soldiers were in Geba, and the Philistines heard of it. Then Saul sounded the horn through all the land, saying, "Let the Hebrews hear." 4 All Israel heard the news that Saul had destroyed the place where the Philistine soldiers were. And they heard that Israel had become a hated thing to the Philistines. Then the people were called out to join Saul at Gilgal.

5 The Philistines gathered to fight against Israel, with 30,000 war-wagons, 6,000 horsemen, and people like the sand on the sea-shore. They came and set up their tents at Michmash, east of Beth-aven. 6 The men of Israel saw that they were in trouble. The people were in a place of danger. So the people hid themselves in caves,

bushes, hill-sides, graves and wells. 7 Some of the Hebrews crossed the Jordan to the land of Gad and Gilead. But as for Saul, he was still in Gilgal, and all the people followed him in fear.

8 Saul waited seven days, the time set by Samuel, but Samuel did not come to Gilgal. And the people were leaving him. 9 So Saul said, "Bring me the burnt gift and the peace gifts." And he gave the burnt gift to the Lord. 10 As soon as he finished giving the burnt gift, Samuel came. Saul went out to meet him and say hello. 11 But Samuel said, "What have you done?" Saul said, "I saw that the people were leaving me. You did not come when you said you would. And the Philistines were gathering at Michmash. 12 So I said, 'Now the Philistines will come down upon me at Gilgal, and I have not asked for the Lord's favor.' So I made myself give the burnt gift." 13 Samuel said to Saul, "You have done a foolish act. You have not kept the Law that the Lord your God gave you. For now the Lord would have made your rule over Israel last forever. 14 But now your rule will not last. The Lord has found a man who is pleasing to him in every way. He has chosen him to rule over his people, because you have not obeyed the Lord."

15 Then Samuel got up and went from Gilgal to Gibeah of Benjamin. Saul numbered the people that were left with him, about 600 men.

No Swords or Spears

16 Saul and his son Jonathan, and the people with them, stayed in Geba of Benjamin, while the Philistines stayed at Michmash. 17 Soldiers came from the tents of the Philistines in three groups. One group turned toward Ophrah, to the land of Shual. 18 Another group turned toward Beth-horon. And another group turned toward the side of the country that looks over the valley of Zeboim toward the desert. 19 Now there was no one to be found in all the land of Israel who made things of iron. For the Philistines said, "The Hebrews might make swords or spears." 20 So each one of the Israelites went down to the Philistines to get his plow, his pick, his ax, or his grain cutter sharpened. 21 He had to pay two-thirds part of a piece of silver to have the plows and picks sharpened, and one-third part of a piece of silver to have the axes and grain cutters sharpened. 22 So on the day of battle there was no sword or spear in the hands of any of the

people who were with Saul and Jonathan. But Saul and his son Jonathan had them. 23 And the Philistine soldiers went out to the pass of Michmash.

Jonathan's Battle with the Philistines

14 One day Jonathan the son of Saul said to the young man who was carrying his battle-clothes, "Come, let us go over to the place where the Philistine soldiers are on the other side." But he did not tell his father. 2 Saul was staying beside Gibeah under the pomegranate tree in Migron. There were about 600 men with him, 3 and Ahijah the son of Ahitub, Ichabod's brother, the son of Phinehas, the son of Eli, the religious leader of the Lord at Shiloh, wearing the linen vest. And the people did not know Jonathan had gone. 4 Between the passes where Jonathan went to cross over to the Philistine soldiers, there was a sharp rock on the one side, and a sharp rock on the other side. The name of one was Bozez. The name of the other was Seneh. 5 One rock stood on the north in front of Michmash. The other stood on the south in front of Geba.

6 Jonathan said to the young man who was carrying his battle-clothes, "Come, let us go over to the place where the soldiers are who have not gone through the religious act of the Jews. It may be that the Lord will work for us, for there is nothing to keep the Lord from saving by many or by few." 7 The young man who was carrying his battle-clothes said to him, "Do all that is in your mind. I am with you in whatever you think to do." 8 Jonathan said, "We will cross over to the men and show ourselves to them. 9 If they say to us, 'Wait until we come to you,' then we will stand still in our place and not go up to them. 10 But if they say, 'Come up to us,' then we will go up. For the Lord has given them into our hands. This will be the special thing for us to see." 11 So both of them showed themselves to the Philistine soldiers. The Philistines said, "See, Hebrews are coming out of the holes where they have hidden themselves." 12 The soldiers of that place said to Jonathan and the one who was carrying his battle-clothes, "Come up to us and we will tell you something." Jonathan said to the one who was carrying his battle-clothes, "Come up after me. For the Lord has given them into the hands of Israel." 13 Then Jonathan went up the hill on his hands and feet, with the one who was carrying his battle-clothes behind him. The soldiers

fell in front of Jonathan. The young man, who was carrying his battle-clothes after him, killed them. ¹⁴ In that first killing done by Jonathan and the man who carried his battle-clothes, about twenty men fell dead within a small piece of land. ¹⁵ There was fear among the Philistines, in the field, and among all the people. Even the soldiers shook with fear. And the earth shook, so there was much fear.

¹⁶ Saul's men who were watching in Gibeah of Benjamin looked and saw the people running away. They went here and there. ¹⁷ Saul said to the people who were with him, "Number them, and see who has left us." When they numbered, they found that Jonathan and the young man who carried his battle-clothes were not there. ¹⁸ Saul said to Ahijah, "Bring the special box of God here." For the special box of God was with the people of Israel at that time. ¹⁹ While Saul talked to the religious leader, the noise of the Philistines became louder. So Saul said to the religious leader, "Take your hand away." ²⁰ Then Saul and all the people with him gathered together and went into the battle. Every man's sword was against the man next to him. It was as if no one knew what to do. ²¹ The Hebrews, who had been with the Philistines and had gone up with them among the tents returned. They returned to be with the Israelites who were with Saul and Jonathan. ²² When all the men of Israel who had hidden themselves in the hill country of Ephraim heard that the Philistines had run away, they ran after them in the battle. ²³ So the Lord saved Israel that day. And the battle spread farther than Beth-aven.

²⁴ Now the men of Israel were troubled that day. For Saul made a promise and said to the people, "Cursed will be the man who eats food before evening and before I have punished those who fight against me." So none of the people tasted any food. ²⁵ And all the people came among the trees, and there was honey on the ground. ²⁶ The people went among the trees and saw honey flowing, but no man tasted it. For the people were afraid of Saul's promise. ²⁷ But Jonathan had not heard his father make the promise to the people. So he put the stick that was in his hand into the honeycomb. Then he put it to his mouth, and his eyes became bright. ²⁸ One of the men told him, "Your father put the people under a promise, saying, 'Cursed will be the man who eats food today.' " The

people were tired and weak. ²⁹ Jonathan said, "My father has troubled the land. See how my eyes have become bright because I tasted a little of this honey. ³⁰ How much better it would be if the men had been free to eat today of the food that had belonged to those who fought against them! For not many Philistines have been killed."

³¹ They killed the Philistines that day from Michmash to Aijalon. And the people were very tired and weak. ³² The people rushed upon the things that had belonged to the Philistines. They took sheep and cattle and calves, and killed them on the ground. And the people ate them with the blood. ³³ Then Saul was told, "See, the people are sinning against the Lord by eating meat with the blood in it." And Saul said, "You have not been faithful. Roll a big stone to me here." ³⁴ And he said, "Divide yourselves among the people and say to them, 'Each one of you bring me his bull or his sheep, and kill it here and eat. Do not sin against the Lord by eating with the blood.' " So every one of the people brought his bull with him that night, and killed it there. ³⁵ And Saul built an altar to the Lord. It was the first altar that he built to the Lord.

³⁶ Then Saul said, "Let us go down to the Philistines during the night and take until morning what belongs to them. Let us not leave a man of them alive." They said, "Do whatever you think is best." So the religious leader said, "Let us go to God here." ³⁷ So Saul asked God, "Should I go down to the Philistines? Will You give them into the hand of Israel?" But God did not answer him that day. ³⁸ Saul said, "Come here, all you leaders of the people. Look and see how this sin has happened today. ³⁹ For as the Lord lives Who saves Israel, even if it is in Jonathan my son, he will die for sure." But not one of all the people answered him. ⁴⁰ Then Saul said to all Israel, "You will be on one side and I and my son Jonathan will be on the other side." And the people said to Saul, "Do what you think is best." ⁴¹ So Saul said to the Lord, the God of Israel, "May the right name be drawn." And the names of Saul and Jonathan were drawn, and the people went free. ⁴² Then Saul said, "Draw names between me and my son Jonathan." And Jonathan's name was drawn.

⁴³ Saul said to Jonathan, "Tell me what you have done." So Jonathan told him, "I tasted a little honey with the end of the stick that was in my hand. Here I am.

I must die." 44 Saul said, "May God do this to me and more also, for you will die for sure, Jonathan." 45 But the people said to Saul, "Must Jonathan die, who has saved all these people of Israel? Far from it! As the Lord lives, not one hair of his head will fall to the ground. For he has worked with God this day." So the people saved Jonathan and he did not die. 46 Then Saul stopped going after the Philistines, and the Philistines went to their own place.

Saul's Family

47 When Saul had become king over Israel, he fought against all those around him who hated him. He fought against Moab, the Ammonites, Edom, the kings of Zobah, and the Philistines. He punished them in every way he turned. 48 He acted with strength of heart and destroyed the Amalekites. He saved Israel from those who came to rob them.

49 Now the sons of Saul were Jonathan, Ishvi and Malchi-shua. And he had two daughters. The name of the first-born was Merab, and the name of the younger one was Michal. 50 The name of Saul's wife was Ahinoam the daughter of Ahimaaz. The name of the captain of his army was Abner the son of Ner, the brother of Saul's father. 51 Kish was the father of Saul. And Abner's father Ner was the son of Abiel.

52 There was fighting against the Philistines all of Saul's life. When Saul saw any strong man, or any man with strength of heart, he would have the man join him.

War with the Amalekites

15 Samuel said to Saul, "The Lord sent me to choose you to be king over His people Israel. Now listen to the Words of the Lord. 2 This is what the Lord of All says. 'I will punish Amalek for what he did to Israel in standing against them on the way, when they came up from Egypt. 3 Now go and destroy Amalek. Destroy all they have, and do not let them live. Kill both man and woman, child and baby, cattle and sheep, camel and donkey.' "

4 So Saul called the people together and numbered them in Telaim. There were 200,000 foot soldiers and 10,000 men of Judah. 5 Saul came to the city of Amalek and hid, waiting in the valley. 6 Saul said to the Kenites, "Go, leave the Amalekites, or I might destroy you with them. For you showed kindness to all the people of Israel when they came up from Egypt." So the Kenites left the Amalekites. 7 Then Saul destroyed the Amalekites, from Havilah as far as Shur, east of Egypt. 8 He took Agag the king of the Amalekites alive, and destroyed all the people with the sword. 9 But Saul and the people did not kill Agag and the best of the sheep, the cattle, the fat animals ready to be killed, the lambs, and all that was good. They would not destroy them. But they destroyed everything that was hated and was of no worth.

Saul Is No Longer King

10 The Word of the Lord came to Samuel, saying, 11 "I am sorry that I have made Saul king. For he has turned away from following Me. He has not done what I told him to do." Samuel was much troubled in his heart. He cried out to the Lord all night. 12 When Samuel got up early in the morning to meet Saul, he was told, "Saul came to Carmel and set up a stone in his honor. Then he turned and went down to Gilgal." 13 Samuel came to Saul, and Saul said to him, "May the Lord bring good to you. I have done what the Lord told me to do." 14 But Samuel said, "Then why do I hear the sounds of sheep and cattle?" 15 Saul said, "They have brought them from the Amalekites. For the people saved the best of the sheep and cattle to give to the Lord your God. But we have destroyed all the rest." 16 Then Samuel said to Saul, "Stop! I will tell you what the Lord said to me last night." And Saul said to him, "Speak."

17 Samuel said, "Is it not true that even when you were not important in your own eyes, you were made the head of the families of Israel? The Lord chose you to be king over Israel. 18 And the Lord sent you to go and destroy the sinners, the Amalekites, and fight against them until they are no more. 19 Why then did you not obey the voice of the Lord? You rushed upon what was left after the battle and did what was sinful in the Lord's eyes."

20 Saul said to Samuel, "I did obey the voice of the Lord. I went where the Lord sent me. I have brought Agag the king of Amalek. And I have destroyed the Amalekites. 21 But the people took some of their things that were left. They took sheep and cattle and the best of the things to be destroyed, to give to the Lord your God at Gilgal." 22 Samuel said, "Is the Lord pleased as much with burnt gifts as He is when He is obeyed? See, it is better to obey than to give gifts. It is better to listen than to give the fat of rams. 23 To go against what you are told is like the sin of witchcraft. Not

to obey is like the sin of worshiping false gods. You have turned away from the Word of the Lord. So He has turned away from you being king."

24 Then Saul said to Samuel, "I have sinned. I have sinned against the Word of the Lord and your words, because I was afraid of the people and listened to them. 25 Now I beg you, forgive my sin and return with me, that I may worship the Lord." 26 But Samuel said to Saul, "I will not return with you. For you have turned away from the Word of the Lord. And the Lord has turned away from you being king over Israel." 27 As Samuel turned to go, Saul took hold of part of his clothing, and it tore. 28 So Samuel said to him, "Today the Lord has torn the rule of Israel away from you. He has given it to your neighbor who is better than you. 29 And the shining-greatness of Israel will not lie or change His mind. For He is not a man that He should change His mind." 30 Saul said, "I have sinned. But I beg you, honor me now in front of the leaders of my people and in front of Israel. Return with me, that I may worship the Lord your God." 31 So Samuel returned with Saul, and Saul worshiped the Lord.

32 Then Samuel said, "Bring me Agag, the king of the Amalekites." Agag was happy when he came to him. Agag said, "For sure the bad feelings of death are past." 33 But Samuel said, "As your sword has killed the children of women, so will your mother have no children." And Samuel cut Agag to pieces before the Lord at Gilgal.

34 Then Samuel went to Ramah, and Saul went up to his house at Gibeah of Saul. 35 Samuel did not see Saul again until the day of his death. But Samuel was filled with sorrow because of Saul. And the Lord was sorry that He had made Saul king over Israel.

David Becomes King

16 The Lord said to Samuel, "How long will you be filled with sorrow because of Saul, since I have turned away from him being king over Israel? Fill your horn with oil, and go. I will send you to Jesse of Bethlehem. For I have chosen a king for Myself among his sons." 2 But Samuel said, "How can I go? Saul will kill me when he hears about it." The Lord said, "Take a young cow with you, and say, 'I have come to give a gift to the Lord.' 3 Ask Jesse to come when you give the gift, and I will show you what you should do. You

will choose for Me the one I name to you." 4 So Samuel did what the Lord said, and came to Bethlehem. The leaders of the city came shaking with fear to meet him. They said, "Do you come in peace?" 5 Samuel said, "I have come in peace to give a gift to the Lord. Make yourselves holy and come with me as I give the gift." He set apart Jesse and his sons also, and asked them to come to the gift-giving. 6 When they had come, Samuel looked at Eliab and thought, "For sure he is the Lord's chosen one who is standing before Him." 7 But the Lord said to Samuel, "Do not look at the way he looks on the outside or how tall he is, because I have not chosen him. For the Lord does not look at the things man looks at. A man looks at the outside of a person, but the Lord looks at the heart." 8 Then Jesse called Abinadab and made him pass in front of Samuel. But Samuel said, "The Lord has not chosen this one." 9 Next Jesse made Shammah pass by. But Samuel said, "The Lord has not chosen this one." 10 Jesse made seven of his sons pass in front of Samuel. But Samuel said to Jesse, "The Lord has not chosen these." 11 Then Samuel said to Jesse, "Are these all the children?" And Jesse said, "There is yet the youngest one. See, he is taking care of the sheep." Samuel said to Jesse, "Send for him. We will not sit down until he comes here." 12 So he sent for him and brought him in. His youngest son had good color in his skin, beautiful eyes and was good-looking. The Lord said, "Rise up and choose him. For this is the one." 13 Then Samuel took the horn of oil and poured the oil on him in front of his brothers. The Spirit of the Lord came upon David with strength from that day on. And Samuel got up and went to Ramah.

Saul's Spirit Is Troubled

14 Now the Spirit of the Lord left Saul. And a bad spirit sent from the Lord brought trouble upon him. 15 Saul's servants said to him, "See, a bad spirit from God is bringing you trouble. 16 Let our lord now tell your servants who are in front of you to look for a man who is a good player of the harp. When the bad spirit sent from God is upon you, he will play the harp, and you will be well." 17 So Saul said to his servants, "Find me a man who can play well, and bring him to me." 18 One of the young men said, "I have seen a son of Jesse the Bethlehemite who plays music well. He is a man with strength of heart,

a man of war, wise in his speaking, and good-looking. And the Lord is with him." ¹⁹ So Saul sent men with news to Jesse, and said, "Send my son David who is with the sheep." ²⁰ Jesse took a donkey loaded with bread, a bottle of wine, and a young goat, and sent them to Saul with David his son. ²¹ David came to Saul and served him. Saul loved him very much, and he became the man who carried Saul's battle-clothes. ²² Saul sent word to Jesse, saying, "Let David serve me, for he has found favor in my eyes." ²³ When the bad spirit sent from God came upon Saul, David would take the harp and play it with his hand. And Saul would receive new strength and be well. The bad spirit would leave him.

David and Goliath

17 Now the Philistines gathered their armies for battle. They were gathered at Socoh, which belongs to Judah. They set up their tents between Socoh and Azekah, in Ephes-dammim. ² Saul and the men of Israel were gathered together, and set up their tents in the valley of Elah. They came up dressed for battle to fight against the Philistines. ³ The Philistines stood on the mountain on one side while Israel stood on the mountain on the other side, with the valley between them. ⁴ Then a strong fighter came out from the armies of the Philistines. His name was Goliath, from Gath. He was almost twice as tall as most men. ⁵ He had a head-covering of brass, and wore brass battle-clothes that weighed as much as 5,000 silver pieces. ⁶ He wore brass leg-coverings, and had a brass spear on his shoulders. ⁷ The long part of his spear was like a cross-piece used on a cloth-maker. The iron head of his spear weighed as much as 600 pieces of silver. A man walked before him to carry his shield. ⁸ Goliath stood and called out to the army of Israel, saying, "Why have you come out dressed for battle? Am I not the Philistine, and you the servants of Saul? Choose a man for yourselves, and let him come down to me. ⁹ If he is able to fight with me and kill me, then we will be your servants. But if I fight him and kill him, then you must become our servants and work for us." ¹⁰ Again the Philistine said, "I stand against the army of Israel this day. Give me a man, that we may fight together." ¹¹ When Saul and all Israel heard these words of the Philistine, they were troubled and very afraid.

¹² Now David was the son of Jesse, an Ephrathite of Bethlehem in Judah. Jesse had eight sons, and was old in the days of Saul. He had lived many years. ¹³ Jesse's three older sons had followed Saul to the battle. Their names were Eliab the first-born, next Abinadab, and third Shammah. ¹⁴ David was the youngest. The three oldest sons followed Saul. ¹⁵ But David went to and from Saul, to take care of his father's flock at Bethlehem. ¹⁶ The Philistine came out and showed himself morning and evening for forty days.

¹⁷ Then Jesse said to his son David, "Take for your brothers a basket of this baked grain and these ten loaves. Hurry and carry them to your brothers among the army. ¹⁸ And take these ten pieces of cheese to the leader of the thousand man group who is with them. See how your brothers are doing, and bring me news of them. ¹⁹ Saul and your brothers and all the men of Israel are in the valley of Elah, fighting with the Philistines."

²⁰ So David got up early in the morning and left the flock in the care of a shepherd. He took the food and went, as Jesse had told him. And he came to the tents as the army was going out dressed for battle, calling out the war cry. ²¹ Israel and the Philistines came near each other dressed for battle, army against army. ²² David left the things with the man to take care of them. He ran to the army, and went to meet with his brothers. ²³ As he talked with them, Goliath the Philistine from Gath came out of the army of the Philistines, and spoke the same words as before. And David heard him. ²⁴ When all the men of Israel saw the man, they ran away from him and were very much afraid. ²⁵ The men of Israel said, "Have you seen the man who has come out? He has come out to stand against Israel. The king will make the man who kills him rich. And he will give him his daughter, and make his father's family free from paying taxes in Israel." ²⁶ Then David said to the men standing by him, "What will be done for the man who kills this Philistine, and takes away Israel's shame? For who is this Philistine who has not gone through the religious act of the Jews? Who is he, that he should make fun of the armies of the living God?" ²⁷ And the people answered him in the same way, "This is what will be done for the man who kills him."

²⁸ His oldest brother Eliab heard what he said to the men. He became very angry with David and said, "Why have you

come here? With whom have you left those few sheep in the desert? I know of your pride and the sin of your heart. You have come to see the battle." 29 But David said, "What have I done now? Was it not just a question?" 30 Then David turned away from him to another and asked the same question. And the people gave him the same answer.

31 When David's words were heard, they were told to Saul, and Saul sent for him. 32 David said to Saul, "Let no man's heart become weak because of him. Your servant will go and fight with this Philistine." 33 Saul said to David, "You are not able to go and fight against this Philistine. You are only a young man, while he has been a man of war since he was young." 34 But David said to Saul, "Your servant was taking care of his father's sheep. When a lion or a bear came and took a lamb from the flock, 35 I went after him and fought him and saved it from his mouth. When he came against me, I took hold of him by the hair of his head and hit him and killed him. 36 Your servant has killed both the lion and the bear. And this Philistine who has not gone through our religious act will be like one of them. For he has made fun of the armies of the living God." 37 And David said, "The Lord Who saved me from the foot of the lion and from the foot of the bear, will save me from the hand of this Philistine." Saul said to David, "Go, and may the Lord be with you." 38 Then Saul dressed David with his clothes. He put a brass head-covering on his head, and dressed him with heavy battle-clothes. 39 David put on his sword over his heavy battle-clothes and tried to walk, for he was not used to them. Then David said to Saul, "I cannot go with these, for I am not used to them." And David took them off. 40 He took his stick in his hand, and chose five smooth stones from the river. He put them in his shepherd's bag. His sling was in his hand, and he went to the Philistine.

41 The Philistine came near to David, with the man carrying his shield in front of him. 42 When the Philistine looked and saw David, he thought nothing of him. For he was only a young man, with good color in his skin, and good-looking. 43 The Philistine said to David, "Am I a dog, that you come to me with sticks?" And the Philistine spoke against David by his gods. 44 The Philistine said to David, "Come to me. I will give your flesh to the birds of the sky and the animals of the field." 45 Then David

said to the Philistine, "You come to me with a sword and spears. But I come to you in the name of the Lord of All, the God of the armies of Israel, Whom you have stood against. 46 This day the Lord will give you into my hands. I will knock you down and cut off your head. This day I will give the dead bodies of the army of the Philistines to the birds of the sky and the wild animals of the earth. Then all the earth may know that there is a God in Israel. 47 All these people gathered here may know that the Lord does not save with sword and spear. For the battle is the Lord's and He will give you into our hands." 48 Then the Philistine rose up and came to meet David. And David rushed to the center of the valley to meet the Philistine. 49 David put his hand into his bag, took out a stone and threw it, and hit the Philistine on his forehead. The stone went into his forehead, so that he fell on his face to the ground.

50 So David won the fight against the Philistine with a sling and a stone. He hit the Philistine and killed him. There was no sword in David's hand. 51 Then David ran and stood over the Philistine. He took his sword out of its holder and killed him, and cut off his head with it. When the Philistines saw that their strong soldier was dead, they ran away. 52 The men of Israel and Judah rose up and called out and went after the Philistines as far as Gath and the gates of Ekron. The dead Philistines lay on the way from Shaaraim as far as Gath and Ekron. 53 Then the Israelites returned from following the Philistines and took what had belonged to them among their tents. 54 David took the Philistine's head and brought it to Jerusalem. But he put his battle-clothes in his tent.

55 When Saul saw David going out against the Philistine, he said to Abner the head of his army, "Abner, whose son is this young man?" And Abner said, "By your life, O king, I do not know." 56 The king said, "Find out whose son the young man is." 57 So when David returned from killing the Philistine, Abner brought him to Saul with the Philistine's head in his hand. 58 Saul said to him, "Whose son are you, young man?" David answered, "I am the son of your servant Jesse of Bethlehem."

King Saul Is Jealous of David

18 When David had finished speaking to Saul, the soul of Jonathan became one with the soul of David. Jonathan loved him as himself. 2 Saul took David that day, and would not let him return to his father's house. ³ Then Jonathan made an agreement with David, because he loved him as himself. ⁴ Jonathan took off his long coat and gave it to David. He gave him his battle-clothes, his sword, his bow and his belt also. ⁵ David went everywhere that Saul sent him, and did well. Saul had him lead the men of war. And it was pleasing to all the people and to Saul's servants.

⁶ When David returned from killing the Philistine, the women came out of all the cities of Israel, singing and dancing, to meet King Saul, playing songs of joy on timbrels. ⁷ The women sang as they played, and said, "Saul has killed his thousands, and David his ten thousands." ⁸ Then Saul became very angry. This saying did not please him. He said, "They have given David honor for ten thousands, but for me only thousands. Now what more can he have but to be king?" ⁹ And Saul was jealous and did not trust David from that day on.

¹⁰ The next day a bad spirit sent from God came upon Saul with power. He acted like a crazy man in his house, while David was playing the harp. Saul had a spear in his hand, ¹¹ and he threw the spear, thinking, "I will nail David to the wall." But David jumped out of his way twice. ¹² Saul was afraid of David, because the Lord was with him but had left Saul. ¹³ So Saul made David go away from him, and had him lead a thousand men. And David went out to the people. ¹⁴ David did well in all that he did, because the Lord was with him. ¹⁵ When Saul saw how well he did, he was afraid of him. ¹⁶ But all Israel and Judah loved David, for he went out and came in before them.

David Marries Saul's Daughter

¹⁷ Then Saul said to David, "Here is my older daughter Merab. I will give her to you as a wife, if you only work for me with strength of heart and fight the Lord's battles." For Saul thought, "I will not go against him. Let the Philistines go against him." ¹⁸ David said to Saul, "Who am I? What is my life or my father's family in Israel, that I should be the king's son-in-law?" ¹⁹ But at the time when Saul's daughter Merab should have been given to David, she was given to Adriel the Meholathite for a wife.

²⁰ Now Saul's daughter Michal loved David. When they told Saul, it pleased him. ²¹ Saul thought, "I will give her to

David. I will use her to trap him, and the Philistines will go against him." So Saul said to David a second time, "Now you may be my son-in-law." ²² Then Saul told his servants, "Speak to David in secret. Tell him, 'See, the king is happy with you, and all his servants love you. So now become the king's son-in-law.' " ²³ So Saul's servants said this to David. But David said, "Is it not important to you to become the king's son-in-law? I am only a poor man and am not very respected." ²⁴ Saul's servants told Saul what David had said. ²⁵ Then Saul said, "Say to David, 'The king wants no marriage gift except the pieces of skin from the sex parts of a hundred Philistines, to punish those who hate the king.' " Saul planned to have the Philistines kill David. ²⁶ When his servants told this to David, it pleased him to become the king's son-in-law. Before the time was finished, ²⁷ David and his men went and killed 200 Philistine men. Then David brought their pieces of flesh and gave all of them to the king, that he might become the king's son-in-law. So Saul gave him his daughter Michal for a wife. ²⁸ When Saul saw and knew that the Lord was with David and that his daughter Michal loved him, ²⁹ Saul was even more afraid of David. So he hated David always.

³⁰ Then the Philistine leaders went out to battle. And when they did, David acted with more wisdom than all the servants of Saul. So his name became very important.

Saul Tries to Kill David

19 Now Saul told Jonathan his son and all his servants to kill David. But Saul's son Jonathan found much joy in David. ² So Jonathan told David, "My father Saul wants to kill you. I beg you, be careful in the morning. Stay hidden in a secret place. ³ I will go out and stand beside my father in the field where you are. I will speak to my father about you. If I find out anything, I will tell you." ⁴ Then Jonathan spoke well of David to Saul his father, saying, "Do not let the king sin against his servant David. He has not sinned against you. What he has done has been good for you. ⁵ He put his life in danger and killed the Philistine. And the Lord helped all Israel with His saving power. You saw it and were glad. Why then will you sin against him who has done no wrong, by killing David for no reason?" ⁶ Saul listened to Jonathan, and promised, "As the Lord lives, David will not be killed." ⁷ Then

Jonathan called David and told him all these things. He brought David to Saul, and David stayed with Saul as before.

8 When there was war again, David went out and fought with the Philistines. He killed many of them, and the others ran away from him. 9 Then a bad spirit sent from the Lord came upon Saul as he was sitting in his house with his spear in his hand. David was playing the harp. 10 Saul tried to nail David to the wall with the spear, but David got out of the way. Saul hit the wall with the spear, and David ran away that night.

11 Then Saul sent men to David's house to watch him, that he might kill him in the morning. But David's wife Michal told him, "If you do not save your life tonight, tomorrow you will be killed." 12 So Michal let David down through a window, and he ran away. 13 Michal took a house god and laid it on the bed. She put a goat hair pillow at its head, and covered it with clothes. 14 When Saul sent men to take David, Michal said, "He is sick." 15 Then Saul sent men to see David, saying, "Bring him up to me in the bed, that I may kill him." 16 When the men came in, the house god was on the bed, with the goat hair pillow at its head. 17 So Saul said to Michal, "Why have you fooled me like this and let the man I hate go? Now he has run away to be safe." Michal said to Saul, "He said to me, 'Let me go! Why should I kill you?'"

18 Now David ran away from Saul and came to Samuel at Ramah. He told him all that Saul had done to him. Then he and Samuel went and stayed in Naioth. 19 Saul was told, "See, David is at Naioth in Ramah." 20 So Saul sent men to take David. But when they saw the men of God saying what was going to happen, with Samuel leading them, the Spirit of God came upon the men sent by Saul. And they began saying what was going to happen also. 21 When Saul heard this, he sent other men, and they began saying what was going to happen. So Saul sent men for the third time, and they began saying what was going to happen. 22 Then he himself went to Ramah, and came as far as the large well in Secu. He asked, "Where are Samuel and David?" And someone said, "See, they are at Naioth in Ramah." 23 So he went to Naioth in Ramah. And the Spirit of God came upon him also. As he traveled he said what would happen, until he came to Naioth in Ramah. 24 He took off his clothes and said what was going to

happen in front of Samuel. He lay down without clothing all that day and all that night. So they say, "Is Saul among those who say what will happen?"

Jonathan Is Good to David

20 Then David ran from Naioth in Ramah, and came and said to Jonathan, "What have I done? What is my sin? What have I done wrong to your father, that he wants to kill me?" 2 Jonathan said to him, "Far from it, you will not die. See, my father does nothing big or small without telling me about it. So why should my father hide this from me? It is not so!" 3 But David answered, "Your father knows well that I have found favor in your eyes. He has said, 'Do not let Jonathan know this, because it would fill him with sorrow.' But it is true. As the Lord lives and as your soul lives, there is only a step between me and death." 4 Then Jonathan said to David, "I will do for you whatever you say." 5 David said to Jonathan, "See, tomorrow is the new moon, and I should sit down to eat with the king. But let me go. I will hide myself in the field until the third evening. 6 If your father misses me at all, then say, 'David asked me to let him leave to run to his city Bethlehem. It is the time for the whole family to gather there for the gift given on the altar in worship each year.' 7 If he says, 'Good!' your servant will be safe. But if he is very angry, then you will know that he has decided to do what is bad. 8 So be kind to your servant. For you have brought me into an agreement of the Lord with you. But if I am guilty, kill me yourself. For why should you bring me to your father?" 9 Jonathan said, "Far be it from you! If I knew that my father has decided to do something bad to you, would I not tell you about it?" 10 Then David said to Jonathan, "Who will tell me if your father is angry when he answers you?" 11 Jonathan said to David, "Come, let us go out into the field." So both of them went out into the field.

12 Jonathan said to David, "May the Lord, the God of Israel, see it, I will speak with my father, about this time tomorrow, or the third day. If he feels good about David, will I not send news to you and let you know it? 13 But if my father wants to hurt you, may the Lord do the same to Jonathan and even more, if I do not let you know and send you away, so you may be safe. May the Lord be with you as He has been with my father. 14 If I am still alive,

show me the faithful love of the Lord, that I may not die. 15 Do not stop being faithful to my house forever, not even when the Lord destroys from the earth all who hate David. 16 Do not let the name of Jonathan be lost from the family of David. And may the Lord punish those who hate you." 17 Jonathan made David promise again, by his love for him. For he loved him as he loved his own life.

18 Then Jonathan said to David, "Tomorrow is the new moon. You will be missed because your seat will be empty. 19 On the third day hurry and come to the place where you hid yourself the other time. Stay by the stone called Ezel. 20 I will shoot three arrows to the side of it, as if I shot at a mark. 21 Then I will send the boy, saying, 'Go, find the arrows.' If I say to the boy these words, 'See, the arrows are on this side of you, get them!' then you may come. For it is safe for you and there is no danger, as the Lord lives. 22 But if I say to the boy, 'See, the arrows are farther away,' then go, for the Lord has sent you away. 23 As for the agreement you and I have spoken, see, the Lord is between us and me forever."

24 So David hid in the field. When the new moon came, the king sat down to eat food. 25 The king sat on his seat by the wall as he did other times. Jonathan sat on the other side from him, and Abner sat beside Saul. But David's place was empty. 26 But Saul did not say anything that day. For he thought, "Something has happened to him. He is not clean. For sure he is not clean." 27 But David's place was empty the next day, the second day of the new moon. So Saul said to his son Jonathan, "Why has the son of Jesse not come to the supper yesterday and today?" 28 Jonathan answered Saul, "David asked me to let him go to Bethlehem. 29 He said, 'I beg you, let me go. Our family is giving a gift on the altar in the city. And my brother has told me to be there. Now, if I have found favor in your eyes, let me leave and see my brothers.' That is why he has not come to the king's table."

30 Then Saul was very angry with Jonathan and he said to him, "You son of a sinful woman! Do I not know that you are choosing the son of Jesse to your own shame and to the shame of your mother who gave birth to you? 31 As long as the son of Jesse lives on the earth, you and the power you would have as king will not last. So send for him and bring him to me. For

he must die." 32 Jonathan answered his father Saul, "Why should he be killed? What has he done?" 33 But Saul threw his spear at Jonathan to kill him, so he knew that his father had decided to kill David. 34 Jonathan rose from the table very angry. He did not eat any food on the second day of the new moon. For he was filled with sorrow for David, because his father had brought shame upon him.

35 In the morning Jonathan went out to the field at the time he and David agreed to meet. A little boy was with him. 36 Jonathan said to his boy, "Run, find the arrows I shoot." As the boy was running, he shot an arrow past him. 37 The boy came to the place where Jonathan had shot the arrow. Jonathan called to the boy and said, "Is not the arrow farther away?" 38 Jonathan called to the boy, "Hurry, be quick, do not stay!" Then Jonathan's boy picked up the arrow and came to his owner. 39 The boy knew nothing. Only Jonathan and David knew what had happened. 40 Then Jonathan gave his bow and arrows to his boy and told him, "Go, take them to the city." 41 When the boy was gone, David rose from the south side and fell on his face to the ground. He bowed three times. Then they kissed each other and cried together, but David more. 42 Jonathan said to David, "Go in peace. For we have promised each other in the name of the Lord, saying, 'The Lord will be between me and you, and between my children and your children forever.' " Then David got up and left, and Jonathan went into the city.

David Runs from Saul

21 David came to Ahimelech the religious leader at Nob. Ahimelech came shaking in fear to meet David, and said to him, "Why are you alone? Why is no one with you?" 2 David said to Ahimelech the religious leader, "The king has given me something to do. And he has said to me, 'Let no one know anything about what I have sent you to do.' I have told the young men to meet at a certain place. 3 Now, what do you have ready? Give me five loaves of bread, or whatever you may have." 4 The religious leader answered David, "I only have bread which has been set apart as holy, if only the young men have kept themselves from women." 5 And David told the religious leader, "For sure women have been kept from us while we have traveled. The bodies of the young men are holy even on everyday trips.

How much more they are today!" 6 So the religious leader gave him holy bread. For there was no bread there but the bread before the Lord. It was taken from before the Lord, so hot bread could be put in its place. 7 Now one of Saul's servants happened to be there that day. His name was Doeg the Edomite, the head of Saul's shepherds.

8 David said to Ahimelech, "Do you have a spear or a sword? I did not bring my sword or any spears with me, because I had to hurry to do the king's work." 9 The religious leader said, "The sword is here that belonged to Goliath the Philistine, whom you killed in the valley of Elah. See, it is behind the linen vest, with a cloth around it. Take it, if you will. For it is the only one here." And David said, "There is none like it. Give it to me."

10 Then David got up and ran that day from Saul. He went to Achish king of Gath. 11 The servants of Achish said to him, "Is this not David the king of the land? Did they not sing to each other about him as they danced, saying, 'Saul has killed his thousands, and David his ten thousands?'" 12 David took these words to heart, and was very much afraid of Achish king of Gath. 13 So he changed the way he acted in front of them. He pretended to be crazy while he was with them. He made marks on the doors of the gate. He let his spit run down into the hair of his face. 14 Then Achish said to his servants, "See, you see the man is crazy. Why have you brought him to me? 15 Do I need any crazy men, that you bring this one to act crazy in front of me? Will this one come into my house?"

Religious Leaders Are Killed

22 So David left there and ran to the cave of Adullam. When his brothers and all those of his father's house heard about it, they went down there to him. 2 Then everyone who was in trouble, everyone who owed money, and everyone who was not happy with the way he was living, came together to him. He became their captain. There were about 400 men with him.

3 David went from there to Mizpah of Moab. He said to the king of Moab, "I beg of you, let my father and mother come and stay with you until I know what God will do for me." 4 Then he left them with the king of Moab. They stayed with him all the time that David was in his safe place. 5 The man who told what will happen in the future, Gad, said to David, "Do not stay in this strong-place. Leave, and go into the land of Judah." So David left and went among the trees of Hereth.

6 Now Saul heard that David and the men with him had been found. Saul was sitting in Gibeah under the tamarisk tree on the high place with his spear in his hand. All his servants were standing around him. 7 Saul said to his servants who stood around him, "Hear now, you Benjamites! Will the son of Jesse give all of you fields and grape-fields? Will he make you all leaders of thousands and hundreds? 8 For all of you have made plans against me. No one lets me know when my son makes an agreement with the son of Jesse. None of you is sorry for me or lets me know that my son has caused my servant to be against me and hide and wait, as it is this day." 9 Doeg the Edomite, who was standing by Saul's servants, said, "I saw the son of Jesse coming to Nob, to Ahimelech the son of Ahitub. 10 Ahimelech asked the Lord what David should do. He gave David food and the sword of Goliath the Philistine."

11 Then the king sent someone to call Ahimelech the religious leader, son of Ahitub, and all those of his father's family, the religious leaders who were in Nob. And all of them came to the king. 12 Saul said, "Hear now, son of Ahitub." He answered, "Here I am, my lord." 13 Saul said to him, "Why have you and the son of Jesse planned against me? Why have you given him bread and a sword, and have asked the Lord what he should do, so he could rise against me and wait in hiding, as it is this day?" 14 Ahimelech answered the king, "Who among all your servants is as faithful as David? He is the king's son-in-law. He is captain of the soldiers who keep you safe, and is honored in your house. 15 Is today the first time that I have asked things of God for him? No! Do not let the king do anything wrong to his servant or any of those of my father's family. For your servant knows nothing at all about this." 16 But the king said, "You will die for sure, Ahimelech, you and all those of your father's family!" 17 The king said to the soldiers who stood around him, "Turn and put the religious leaders of the Lord to death. Because they are on David's side. They knew he was running away, and did not tell me." But the servants of the king were not willing to go against the religious leaders of the Lord. 18 Then the king said to Doeg, "You turn and kill the

religious leaders." And Doeg the Edomite turned and killed the religious leaders. That day he killed eighty-five men who wore the linen vest. 19 Then he destroyed Nob, the city of the religious leaders, with the sword. He killed men and women, children and babies, cattle, donkeys and sheep, with the sword.

20 But Abiathar, one of the sons of Ahimelech the son of Ahitub, got away and ran after David. 21 Abiathar told David that Saul had killed the religious leaders of the Lord. 22 David said to Abiathar, "I knew that day when Doeg the Edomite was there, that he would be sure to tell Saul. I am to blame for the death of every person in your father's family. 23 Stay with me. Do not be afraid. For he who wants to kill me wants to kill you. But you are safe with me."

David Saves Keilah

23 Then they told David, "See, the Philistines are fighting against Keilah. They are taking the grain from the grain-floors." 2 So David asked the Lord, "Should I go and fight these Philistines?" And the Lord said to David, "Go, fight the Philistines, and save Keilah." 3 But David's men said to him, "See, we are afraid here in Judah. How much more then if we go to Keilah against the armies of the Philistines?" 4 Then David asked the Lord again. The Lord answered him, "Get ready and go down to Keilah. For I will give the Philistines into your hand." 5 So David and his men went to Keilah and fought with the Philistines. He killed many of them and took away their cattle. And David saved the people of Keilah.

6 When Abiathar the son of Ahimelech ran to David at Keilah, he came with a linen vest in his hand. 7 When Saul was told that David had come to Keilah, he said, "God has given him to me. For he has shut himself in by going into a city with iron gates." 8 Saul called all the men for war, to go down to Keilah to trap David and his men. 9 David knew that Saul was planning against him, so he said to Abiathar the religious leader, "Bring the linen vest here." 10 Then David said, "O Lord God of Israel, Your servant has heard for sure that Saul is planning to come to Keilah to destroy the city because of me. 11 Will the men of Keilah give me to him? Will Saul come down just as Your servant has heard? O Lord God of Israel, I pray, tell Your servant." And the Lord said, "He will come down." 12 Then David said, "Will

the men of Keilah give me and my men to Saul?" And the Lord said, "They will give you up." 13 Then David and his men, about 600, got up and left Keilah. They went where they could go. When Saul was told that David had run away from Keilah, he gave up going there.

David Stays in the Hill Country

14 David stayed in the safe places in the desert. He stayed in the hill country in the desert of Ziph. Saul looked for him every day, but God did not give David to him. 15 David saw that Saul had come out to try to kill him. David was in the desert of Ziph at Horesh. 16 Saul's son Jonathan went to David at Horesh and gave him strength in God. 17 He said to him, "Do not be afraid, because my father Saul will not find you. You will be king of Israel, and I will be next to you. My father Saul knows this also." 18 So the two of them made an agreement before the Lord. And David stayed at Horesh, and Jonathan went home.

19 Then the Ziphites came to Saul at Gibeah, saying, "Is not David hiding with us in the strong-places at Horesh, on the hill of Hachilah, south of Jeshimon? 20 Now come, O king, as you desire to come. And we will give David into the king's hand." 21 Saul said, "May the Lord bring good to you. For you have had pity on me. 22 Go and make sure. See where he is, and who has seen him there. For I am told that he is very good at fooling people. 23 Look and learn about all his hiding places, and return to me with news that is sure. Then I will go with you. If he is in the land, I will find him among all the thousands of Judah." 24 Then they got up and went to Ziph before Saul. Now David and his men were in the desert of Maon, in the Arabah, south of Jeshimon. 25 Saul and his men went to look for him, and David was told about it. So he went down to the rock in the desert of Maon. 26 Saul went on one side of the mountain, and David and his men on the other side of the mountain. David was in a hurry to get away from Saul. For Saul and his men were closing in upon David and his men to take them. 27 But a man came with news to Saul, saying, "Hurry and come, for the Philistines have come into the land by surprise to fight us." 28 So Saul returned from going after David, and went against the Philistines. So they called that place the Rock of Getting Away. 29 David went from there and stayed in the strong-places of Engedi.

David Did Not Kill Saul

24 When Saul returned from following the Philistines, he was told, "See, David is in the desert of Engedi." [2] Then Saul took 3,000 chosen men from all Israel, and went to find David and his men in front of the Rocks of the Wild Goats. [3] He came to the places where the sheep were kept on the way. There was a cave there, and Saul went in to get rid of his body waste. Now David and his men were sitting farther back in the cave. [4] David's men said to David, "See, this is the day the Lord told you, 'See, I am about to give the one who hates you into your hand. You will do to him what you think is best.' " Then David got up and cut off a piece of Saul's clothing in secret. [5] After this, David felt guilty in his heart because he had cut off a piece of Saul's clothing. [6] So he said to his men, "May the Lord not let me put out my hand against my leader, for he is the Lord's chosen one." [7] David stopped his men with these words. He did not let them go against Saul. So Saul stood up and left the cave, and went on his way.

[8] After this David got up and went out of the cave and called to Saul, saying, "My lord the king!" When Saul looked behind him, David put his face to the ground, showing much respect. [9] David said to Saul, "Why do you listen to the words of men who say, 'David wants to hurt you'? [10] See, your eyes have seen how the Lord gave you to me today in the cave. Some told me to kill you, but I had pity on you. I said, 'I will not put out my hand against my leader, for he is the Lord's chosen one.' [11] Now, my father, see the piece of your clothing in my hand. I cut off the piece of your clothing but did not kill you. So know and understand that I have no desire to do wrong to you. I have not sinned against you, yet you come wanting to kill me. [12] May the Lord judge between you and me. May He punish you for your action against me. But my hand will not be against you. [13] As the men of long ago said in their wisdom, 'Out of the sinful comes sin,' but my hand will not be against you. [14] After whom has the king come out? After whom are you running? After a dead dog? After a little bug? [15] May the Lord be the One to judge between you and me. May He see and help me, and save me from you." [16] When David had finished speaking to Saul, Saul said, "Is this your voice, my son David?" Then Saul gave a loud cry. [17] He said to David, "You are more right and good than I. For you have

brought good to me, while I have done wrong to you. [18] You have said today that you have done good to me. The Lord gave me to you and you did not kill me. [19] If a man finds the one who hates him, will he let him go away safe? May the Lord bring good to you for what you have done for me this day. [20] Now I know that you will be king for sure. The nation of Israel will be made strong under your power. [21] So promise to me by the Lord that you will not destroy my children after me. Promise that you will not destroy my name from my father's family." [22] David gave Saul his promise, and Saul went home. But David and his men went up to the safe place.

The Death of Samuel

25 Now Samuel died. All Israel gathered together and was filled with sorrow for him. They buried him at his house in Ramah.

Then David got ready and went down to the desert of Paran. [2] There was a man in Maon who worked in Carmel. The man was very rich. He had 3,000 sheep and 1,000 goats. He was cutting the wool from his sheep in Carmel. [3] The man's name was Nabal, and his wife's name was Abigail. The woman was of good understanding and beautiful. But the man was bad and sinful in his ways. He was a Calebite. [4] David heard in the desert that Nabal was cutting the wool from his sheep. [5] So David sent ten young men, saying to them, "Go up to Carmel. Visit Nabal and greet him for me. [6] Say to him, 'I have a long life. Peace be to you. Peace be to your family. And peace be to all that you have.' [7] I have heard that you have men who cut the wool from your sheep. Now your shepherds have been with us, and we have not done them any wrong. And they have not missed anything all the time they were in Carmel. [8] Ask your young men and they will tell you. So let my young men find favor in your eyes, for we have come on a special day. I ask you to give whatever you have ready to your servants and to your son David.' "

[9] When David's young men came, they said all this to Nabal in David's name. Then they waited. [10] But Nabal answered David's servants, "Who is David? Who is the son of Jesse? There are many servants these days who are leaving their owners. [11] Should I take my bread and my water and my meat that I have killed for my wool cutters, and give it to men when I do not know where they came from?"

¹² So David's young men turned away and returned to David and told him all this. ¹³ David said to his men, "Every man put on his sword!" So every man put on his sword, and David put on his sword also. About 400 men went up behind David, while 200 stayed with their things.

¹⁴ But one of the young men told Nabal's wife Abigail, "See, David sent men from the desert to greet our owner, and he spoke against them. ¹⁵ But David's men were very good to us. They did not do anything wrong to us. And we did not miss anything when we were in the fields, as long as we went with them. ¹⁶ They were a wall to us night and day, all the time we were with them taking care of the sheep. ¹⁷ So know this and think about what you should do. For bad plans have been made against our owner and all his family. He is such a sinful man that no one can speak to him."

¹⁸ In a hurry Abigail took 200 loaves of bread, two bottles of wine, five sheep ready to eat, five baskets of dry grain, 100 vines of dried grapes and 200 loaves of figs, and loaded them on donkeys. ¹⁹ She said to her young men, "Go on before me. See, I am coming after you." But she did not tell her husband Nabal. ²⁰ As she went on her donkey and came down hidden by the mountain, David and his men came down toward her, and she met them. ²¹ Now David had said, "It was for nothing that I have watched over all this man has in the desert, so that nothing was missed of all that belonged to him. He has paid me bad for good. ²² May God do the same to David and more, if I leave until morning as much as one male alive of all who belong to him."

²³ When Abigail saw David, she got off her donkey in a hurry. Then she put her face to the ground in front of David. ²⁴ She fell at his feet and said, "Let the sin be on me alone, my lord. I beg you, let your woman servant speak to you. Listen to the words of your woman servant. ²⁵ I beg you, do not let my lord think about this sinful man, Nabal. For he is like his name. Nabal is his name and he is foolish. But I your woman servant did not see my lord's young men whom you sent. ²⁶ So now, my lord, as the Lord lives, and as your soul lives, let the Lord keep you from being guilty of blood. Let Him keep you from punishing with your own hand. And let those who hate you and those who want to hurt my lord be like Nabal. ²⁷ Now let this gift which your woman servant has

brought to my lord be given to the young men who follow my lord. ²⁸ I beg you, forgive the sin of your woman servant. For the Lord will be sure to make my lord a family that will last. Because my lord is fighting the Lord's battles. Sin will not be found in you as long as you live. ²⁹ If men rise up to come after you and try to kill you, then the life of my lord will be taken care of by the Lord your God. But He will throw away the lives of those who hate you, as a rock is thrown from a sling. ³⁰ The Lord will do to my lord all the good that He has promised you. He will make you ruler over Israel. ³¹ Then my lord will have no reason to feel sorry or guilty because of killing without cause or punishing by my lord's own hand. When the Lord does good things for my lord, remember your woman servant."

³² Then David said to Abigail, "Thanks be to the Lord God of Israel, Who sent you this day to meet me. ³³ May thanks be given to you for your wisdom, and thanks be to you. You have kept me this day from being guilty of blood, and from punishing with my own hand. ³⁴ The Lord God of Israel has kept me from hurting you. And as the Lord lives, if you had not been quick to come to meet me, for sure not one male would have been left to Nabal until the morning." ³⁵ So David received what she had brought him. He said to her, "Go up to your house in peace. See, I have listened to you and have done what you asked."

³⁶ Abigail came to Nabal and saw that he was having a special supper in his house, like the special supper of a king. Nabal's heart was full of joy, because he was very drunk. So she did not tell him anything until the morning. ³⁷ But in the morning, when the wine had gone out of Nabal, his wife told him these things. And his heart died within him so that he became like a stone. ³⁸ The Lord made Nabal die about ten days later.

³⁹ When David heard that Nabal was dead, he said, "Thanks be to the Lord, Who has punished Nabal for putting me to shame. He has kept His servant from sin. And the Lord has turned the sin of Nabal upon himself." Then David sent word to Abigail, asking her to be his wife. ⁴⁰ When David's servants came to Abigail at Carmel, they said to her, "David has sent us to you, to take you as his wife." ⁴¹ She stood up and then put her face to the ground, and said, "See, your woman servant will serve you by washing the feet of my lord's servants." ⁴² Then she got ready

in a hurry and traveled on a donkey, with her five young women who followed her. She followed the men David had sent, and became his wife.

43 David had taken Ahinoam of Jezreel also. They both became his wives.

44 Saul had given his daughter Michal, David's wife, to Palti the son of Laish, who was from Gallim.

David Keeps from Killing Saul the Second Time

26 Then the Ziphites came to Saul at Gibeah, saying, "Is not David hiding on the hill of Hachilah, east of Jeshimon?" 2 So Saul got ready and went down to the desert of Ziph. He had 3,000 chosen men of Israel with him, to look for David in the desert of Ziph. 3 Saul stayed on the hill of Hachilah, beside the road east of Jeshimon. And David was staying in the desert. When he saw that Saul came after him in the desert, 4 David sent out spies and learned that Saul was coming for sure. 5 Then David got ready and came to the place where Saul was staying. He saw the place where Saul lay, with Abner the son of Ner, the captain of his army. Saul was lying in the center of the tents, and the people were sleeping around him.

6 Then David said to Ahimelech the Hittite and to Joab's brother Abishai the son of Zeruiah, "Who will go down with me to the tents of Saul?" Abishai said, "I will go down with you." 7 So David and Abishai came to the people during the night. Saul lay sleeping in the center of the tents, with his spear in the ground at his head. Abner and the people were lying around him. 8 Abishai said to David, "Today God has given the one who hates you into your hand. Now let me nail him to the earth with the spear, hitting him just once. I will not hit him a second time." 9 But David said to Abishai, "Do not destroy him. For who can put his hand out against the Lord's chosen one and not be guilty?" 10 David said, "As the Lord lives, He will destroy him. Or his day will come to die. Or he will be killed in battle. 11 May the Lord keep me from putting out my hand against the Lord's chosen one. But take the spear that is at his head and the bottle of water, and let us go." 12 So David took the spear and the bottle of water from beside Saul's head, and they went away. But no one saw it, or knew it, and no one woke, for they were all sleeping. A deep sleep from the Lord had come upon them.

13 Then David crossed over to the other side and stood far away on top of the mountain, with much land between them. 14 David called to the army and to Ner's son Abner, saying, "Will you not answer, Abner?" Abner answered, "Who are you who calls to the king?" 15 David said to Abner, "Are you not a man? Who is like you in Israel? Why have you not watched over your lord the king? For one of the people came to destroy the king your lord. 16 This thing you have done is not good. As the Lord lives, all of you must die for sure. Because you did not watch over your lord, the Lord's chosen one. Now see where the king's spear is, and the bottle of water that was beside his head."

17 Saul knew David's voice, and said, "Is this your voice, my son David?" And David said, "It is my voice, my lord the king. 18 Why is my lord coming after his servant? What have I done? What am I guilty of? 19 Now I beg you, let my lord the king listen to the words of his servant. If the Lord has made you come against me, let Him receive a gift. But if men have done this, may bad come to them before the Lord. For they have driven me out this day, that I should have no share of what the Lord has given. They say, 'Go, worship other gods.' 20 So do not let my blood fall to the ground away from the Lord. For the king of Israel has come out to look for one little bug, just as one looks for a partridge in the mountains."

21 Then Saul said, "I have sinned. Return, my son David, for I will not hurt you again. Because my life was of great worth in your eyes this day. See, I have played the fool, and have made a big mistake." 22 David answered, "See the spear of the king! Let one of the young men come over and take it. 23 The Lord will pay each man for being right and good and faithful. For the Lord gave you into my hand today. But I would not put out my hand against the Lord's chosen one. 24 Now see, as your life was of great worth in my eyes today, so may my life be of great worth in the eyes of the Lord. May He save me from all trouble." 25 Then Saul said to David, "May good come to you, my son David. You will do many things and do them well." So David went on his way, and Saul returned to his place.

David with the Philistines

27 David said to himself, "Some day Saul will kill me. There is nothing better for me than to run to the land of the Philistines. Then Saul will become tired of looking for me any more in the land of Israel. And I will get away from him." 2 So David got up and crossed over with his 600 men to Achish the son of Maoch, king of Gath. 3 David lived with Achish at Gath, he and his men. Each man had those of his family with him. David had with him his two wives, Ahinoam of Jezreel, and Abigail of Carmel, who had been Nabal's wife. 4 When Saul was told that David had run to Gath, he looked for him no more.

5 Then David said to Achish, "If I have found favor in your eyes, let me be given a place in one of the country towns, that I may live there. For why should your servant live with you in the city of the king?" 6 So Achish gave him the town of Ziklag that day. Ziklag has belonged to the kings of Judah to this day. 7 David lived in the country of the Philistines for a year and four months.

8 Now David and his men went up to fight the Geshurites, the Girzites and the Amalekites. For they had been living in the land a long time, as you come to Shur, even as far as the land of Egypt. 9 David destroyed the land and did not leave a man or a woman alive. He took away the sheep, the cattle, the donkeys, the camels, and the clothing. Then he returned and came to Achish. 10 Achish said, "Where have you gone to battle today?" And David said, "Against the Negev of Judah, the Negev of the Jerahmeelites, and the Negev of the Kenites." 11 David did not leave a man or woman alive to bring news to Gath, thinking, "They might tell about us. They might say, 'This is what David has done all the time he has lived in the country of the Philistines.' " 12 And Achish believed David, saying, "He has made the people of Israel hate him. So he will become my servant forever."

Saul and the Woman of Endor

28 In those days the Philistines gathered their armies for war against Israel. Achish said to David, "Understand that you and your men are to go out with me to battle." 2 David said to Achish, "Very well, you will know what your servant can do." And Achish said to David, "Very well, I will make you the soldier who stands by me and keeps me safe for life."

3 Now Samuel was dead, and all Israel had been filled with sorrow for him. They buried him in his own city of Ramah. And Saul had put out of the land those who spoke with spirits by using their secret ways. 4 The Philistines gathered together and came and stayed at Shunem. Saul gathered all Israel together and they stayed at Gilboa. 5 When Saul saw the Philistine army, he was afraid. His heart shook with much fear. 6 Saul asked the Lord what he should do. But the Lord did not answer him, by dreams or by Urim or by those who speak for God. 7 Then Saul said to his servants, "Find a woman for me who can speak with spirits, that I may go to her and ask her what I should do." His servants said to him, "See, there is a woman at Endor who can speak with spirits."

8 So Saul dressed up to look like somebody else and went with two other men to the woman during the night. He said, "Use your secret ways for me, I beg you, and bring up for me whom I will name to you." 9 But the woman said to him, "See, you know what Saul has done. He has put out of the land those who speak with spirits by using their secret ways. Why do you lay a trap for my life to cause my death?" 10 But Saul promised her by the Lord, saying, "As the Lord lives, you will not be punished for this." 11 Then the woman said, "Whom should I bring up for you?" And he said, "Bring up Samuel for me." 12 When the woman saw Samuel, she cried out with a loud voice. She said to Saul, "Why have you fooled me? For you are Saul!" 13 The king said to her, "Do not be afraid. What do you see?" The woman said to Saul, "I see a god coming up out of the earth." 14 He said to her, "What does he look like?" And she said, "An old man is coming up. He is dressed in a long piece of clothing." Saul knew that it was Samuel, and he put his face to the ground to show honor.

15 Then Samuel said to Saul, "Why have you troubled my rest by bringing me up?" Saul answered, "I am very troubled. The Philistines are making war against me. And God has left me and answers me no more, by those who speak for Him or by dreams. So I have called you to tell me what I should do." 16 Samuel said, "Why then do you ask me, since the Lord has left you and has turned against you? 17 The Lord has done what He said He would do through me. The Lord has torn the rule of Israel out of your hand and given it to your neighbor, David. 18 You did not obey the Lord and bring His burning anger upon Amalek. So the Lord has done this to you now. 19 What is more, the Lord will give Israel and you into the hands of the Philistines. So tomorrow you and your sons will

be with me. The Lord will give the army of Israel to the Philistines."

20 At once Saul fell to the ground with his whole body. He was very afraid because of Samuel's words. And there was no strength in him, for he had eaten no food all day and all night. 21 The woman came to Saul and saw that he was filled with fear. She said to him, "See, your woman servant has obeyed you. I have put my life in danger and have listened to what you said to me. 22 So now I beg you, let me give you a piece of bread. Eat, so you may have strength when you go on your way." 23 But he said, "I will not eat." But his servants together with the woman begged him, and he listened to them. He got up from the ground and sat on the bed. 24 The woman had a fat calf in the house and was quick to kill it. She took flour, made it into dough, and made bread without yeast. 25 She brought it to Saul and his servants, and they ate. Then they got up and went away that night.

David Is Sent Back to Ziklag

29 Now the Philistines gathered together all their armies at Aphek. The Israelites were staying by the well in Jezreel. 2 The leaders of the Philistines were moving toward them with their hundreds and their thousands. And David and his men were moving behind them with Achish. 3 Then the captains of the Philistines said, "What are these Hebrews doing here?" Achish said to the captains of the Philistines, "Is this not David, the servant of Saul the king of Israel, who has been with me now for days and years? I have found nothing wrong in him since the day he left to come to me." 4 But the Philistine captains were angry with him. They said to him, "Make the man return. Have him go again to his place which you have given him. Do not let him go down to battle with us. He might fight against us in the battle. For how could this man make his lord receive him again? Would it not be with the heads of these men? 5 Is this not David, of whom they sing in the dances, 'Saul has killed his thousands, and David his ten thousands'?" 6 Then Achish called David and said to him, "As the Lord lives, you have been honest. You go out and come in with me in the army and it is good in my eyes. I have found nothing wrong in you from the day you came to me until this day. But you are not pleasing in the eyes of the leaders. 7 So now return. Go in peace, that you may not make the Philistine leaders

angry." 8 David said to Achish, "But what have I done? What have you found in your servant from the day I came to you until now, that I may not go and fight against those who hate my lord the king?" 9 Achish answered David, "I know that you are pleasing in my eyes, like an angel of God. But the captains of the Philistines have said, 'He must not go with us to the battle.' 10 Now get up early in the morning with the servants of your lord who have come with you. Leave as soon as you are up and have light." 11 So David and his men left early in the morning to return to the land of the Philistines. But the Philistines went up to Jezreel.

David's Battle with the Amalekites

30 When David and his men came to Ziklag on the third day, the Amalekites had come to fight in the Negev and Ziklag. They had destroyed Ziklag, and burned it with fire. 2 They took the women and all who were in it, without killing anyone. They carried them out and went on their way. 3 David and his men came to the city and saw that it was burned. Their wives and sons and daughters had been taken away. 4 Then David and the people with him cried out in a loud voice until they had no more strength to cry. 5 David's two wives had been taken away, Ahinoam of Jezreel, and Abigail who had been the wife of Nabal of Carmel. 6 And David was very troubled because the people talked about killing him with stones. For all the people were very angry in their sorrow for their sons and daughters. But David got his strength from the Lord his God.

7 David said to Abiathar the religious leader, son of Ahimelech, "Bring me the linen vest." So Abiathar brought the linen vest to David. 8 Then David asked the Lord, "Should I go after this army? Should I meet them in battle?" The Lord said to him, "Go after them, for you will catch them for sure. And you will be sure to save all the people." 9 So David and the 600 men who were with him went out and came to the river of Besor. There those stayed who were left behind. 10 But David kept going after them, with 400 men. For 200 were too tired to cross the river of Besor and stayed behind.

11 They found an Egyptian in the field and brought him to David. They gave him bread and he ate, and he was given water to drink. 12 They gave him a piece of a fig loaf and two vines of dried grapes. When

he had eaten, his spirit returned to him. For he had not eaten bread or drunk water for three days and three nights. 13 David said to him, "To whom do you belong? Where are you from?" And he answered, "I am a young man of Egypt, a servant of an Amalekite. My owner left me behind when I became sick three days ago. 14 We had gone to fight in the Negev of the Cherethites, and in the land of Judah, and in the Negev of Caleb. We burned Ziklag with fire." 15 Then David said to him, "Will you take me down to his army?" And he said, "Promise me by God that you will not kill me or give me to my owner, and I will bring you down to this army."

16 When he had taken David down, he saw the soldiers spread over all the land. They were eating and drinking and dancing because of all the good things they had taken from the land of the Philistines and the land of Judah. 17 And David killed them from the evening until the evening of the next day. None of them got away, except 400 young men who ran away on camels. 18 David took back all that the Amalekites had taken, and saved his two wives. 19 Nothing was missing, small or large, sons or daughters, food or anything that had been taken. David returned with all of it. 20 And he took all the sheep and cattle. The people drove those animals in front of him, and said, "This is what belongs to David."

21 David came to the 200 men who had been too tired to follow him and had been left at the river of Besor. They went out to meet David and the people who were with him. David came near the people and said hello to them. 22 Then all the sinful men of no worth who had gone with David said, "They did not go with us. So we will not give them anything of what we have taken, except for each man's wife and children. Each man may take them and go." 23 David said, "You must not do so with what the Lord has given us, my brothers. He has kept us safe and has given us the army that came against us. 24 Who would listen to you about this? The share of those who stay by our things will be the same as the share of those who go to the battle. They will share alike." 25 He made it a law for Israel from that day to this.

26 When David came to Ziklag, he sent some of the things he had taken in battle to the leaders of Judah, his friends. He said, "See, here is a gift for you from what was taken from those who hate the Lord.

27 It is for those in Bethel, Ramoth of the Negev, Jattir, 28 Aroer, Siphmoth, Eshtemoa, 29 and Racal. It is for those in the cities of the Jerahmeelites, the cities of the Kenites, 30 Hormah, Borashan, Athach, 31 Hebron, and all the places where David and his men have gone many times."

Saul Kills Himself

31 Now the Philistines were fighting against Israel. And the men of Israel ran from the Philistines and were killed and fell on Mount Gilboa. 2 The Philistines came after Saul and his sons. They killed Saul's sons Jonathan, Abinadab and Malchi-shua. 3 The battle went against Saul. The men who used the bow hit him with arrows and hurt him very much. 4 Then Saul said to the one who carried his battle-clothes, "Take your sword and cut through me with it. Or these men who have not gone through our religious act will come and kill me with the sword and make fun of me." But the one who carried his battle-clothes would not do it, for he was filled with fear. So Saul took his sword and fell on it. 5 When the one who carried his battle-clothes saw that Saul was dead, he fell on his sword also, and died with him. 6 So Saul, his three sons, the one who carried his battle-clothes, and all his men, died that day together.

7 The men of Israel who were on the other side of the valley, on the other side of the Jordan, saw that the men of Israel had run away and that Saul and his sons were dead. So they left the cities and ran away. Then the Philistines came and lived in them. 8 When the Philistines came to rob the dead the next day, they found Saul and his three sons lying on Mount Gilboa. 9 They cut off Saul's head and took his sword and battle-clothes, and sent them through the land of the Philistines. They sent them to carry the good news to the house of their gods and to the people. 10 They put his sword and battle-clothes in the house of their god Ashtaroth. And they tied his body to the wall of Bethshan. 11 When the people of Jabesh-gilead heard what the Philistines had done to Saul, 12 all the men with strength of heart went and walked all night. They took the bodies of Saul and his sons from the wall of Beth-shan, and came to Jabesh. There they burned them. 13 They took their bones and buried them under the tamarisk tree at Jabesh. And they did not eat for seven days.

2 SAMUEL

David Hears of Saul's Death

1 Now after the death of Saul, David returned from killing the Amalekites and stayed two days in Ziklag. ² On the third day, a man came from the tents of Saul. His clothes were torn and he had dust on his head. When he came to David, he fell with his face to the ground. ³ David said to him, "Where do you come from?" And he answered, "I have run away from the tents of Israel." ⁴ David said to him, "How did it go? Tell me." And the man said, "The people have run from the battle. Many have fallen and are dead. Saul and his son Jonathan are dead also." ⁵ David said to the young man, "How do you know that Saul and his son Jonathan are dead?" ⁶ The young man said, "I happened to be on Mount Gilboa. There I saw Saul holding himself up with his spear. The war-wagons and the horsemen were coming close after him. ⁷ When he looked behind him, he saw me. He called to me and I said, 'Here I am.' ⁸ He said to me, 'Who are you?' And I answered, 'I am an Amalekite.' ⁹ Then he said to me, 'I beg you, stand beside me and kill me. I am in pain, and yet I am still alive.' ¹⁰ So I stood beside him and killed him, because I knew he could not live after he had fallen. Then I took the crown which was on his head and the beautiful gold band which he wore on his arm, and I have brought them here to my lord."

¹¹ Then David took hold of his clothes and tore them, and so did all the men who were with him. ¹² They cried in sorrow and did not eat until evening, because of Saul and his son Jonathan, and of the people of the Lord and of the family of Israel. For they had fallen by the sword ¹³ David said to the young man, "Where are you from?" And he answered, "I am the son of one from another land, an Amalekite." ¹⁴ Then David said to him, "Why were you not afraid to put out your hand to destroy the Lord's chosen one?" ¹⁵ Then David called one of the young men and said, "Go, cut him down." So he hit him and he died. ¹⁶ David said to him, "Your blood is on your head. Because your mouth has spoken against you, saying, 'I have killed the Lord's chosen one.'"

David's Song of Sorrow for Saul and Jonathan

¹⁷ Then David sang a song of sorrow for Saul and his son Jonathan. ¹⁸ He told them to teach the song of the bow to the people of Judah. See, it is written in the book of Jashar. ¹⁹ "O Israel, your beauty is destroyed on your high places! How have the powerful fallen! ²⁰ Do not tell about it in Gath. Do not tell about it in the streets of Ashkelon, or the daughters of the Philistines might be filled with joy. The daughters of those who have not gone through our religious act might be filled with joy. ²¹ O mountains of Gilboa, do not let the water that is on the grass in the early morning or rain be on you. Let not grass be grown on your fields. For there the covering of the powerful was made dirty, the covering of Saul, as if he had not been set apart with oil. ²² The bow of Jonathan did not turn away. The sword of Saul did not return empty. They did not turn from the blood of the dead and the fat of the powerful. ²³ Saul and Jonathan were loved and pleasing in their life. And they were not divided in their death. They were faster than eagles. They were stronger than lions. ²⁴ O daughters of Israel, cry for Saul. He dressed you in fine red clothing. He put on your clothing objects of gold. ²⁵ How have the powerful fallen in the center of the battle! Jonathan has been killed on your high places. ²⁶ I am troubled because of you, my brother Jonathan. You have been very pleasing to me. Your love to me was greater than the love of women. ²⁷ How have the powerful fallen, and the bows and swords of war destroyed!"

David Is Made King over Judah

2 After this, David asked the Lord, "Should I go up to one of the cities of Judah?" And the Lord said to him, "Go up." So David said, "Where should I go?" And He said, "To Hebron." ² So David went up there with his two wives, Ahinoam of Jezreel, and Abigail who had been the wife of Nabal of Carmel. ³ David brought up his men who were with him, each one with those of his family. They lived in the cities of Hebron. ⁴ Then the men of Judah came and there they chose David to be king over the family of Judah.

They told David, "It was the men of Jabesh-gilead who buried Saul." ⁵ So David sent men with news to the men of Jabesh-gilead, saying, "May the Lord bring good to you. Because you have shown kindness to your king Saul, and have buried him. ⁶ Now may the Lord show loving-kindness and truth to you. And I will do good to you, because you have done this. ⁷ So now let your hands be strong. Have strength of heart. For your king Saul is dead. And those of the family of Judah have chosen me to be their king."

Ish-bosheth Is Made King over Israel

8 But Abner the son of Ner, captain of Saul's army, had taken Saul's son Ish-bosheth to Mahanaim. 9 He made him king of Gilead, the Ashurites, Jezreel, Ephraim, Benjamin, and all Israel. 10 Saul's son Ish-bosheth was forty years old when he became king of Israel. He was king for two years. But the family of Judah followed David. 11 David was king in Hebron over the family of Judah for seven years and six months.

War between Israel and Judah

12 Now Abner the son of Ner went out from Mahanaim to Gibeon with the servants of Saul's son Ish-bosheth. 13 And Zeruiah's son Joab and the servants of David went out and met them by the pool of Gibeon. One group sat down on one side of the pool, and the other group on the other side. 14 Then Abner said to Joab, "Let the young men get up and have a test of strength in front of us." And Joab said, "Let them get up." 15 So they stood up and went over by number. There were twelve for Benjamin and Ish-bosheth the son of Saul, and twelve of the servants of David. 16 Each one of them took hold of the head of the one fighting against him, and put his sword into the other's side. So they fell down together. That is why that place was called field of swords, which is in Gibeon. 17 The battle was very bad that day. Abner and the men of Israel were beaten by the servants of David. 18 Now the three sons of Zeruiah were there, Joab and Abishai and Asahel. Asahel was as fast as a wild deer. 19 And Asahel ran after Abner. He did not turn to the right or the left from following him. 20 Then Abner looked behind him and said, "Is that you, Asahel?" And he answered, "It is I." 21 So Abner said to him, "Turn aside to your right or left. Take hold of one of the young men, and take for yourself what belongs to him." But Asahel was not willing to turn aside from following him. 22 Abner said again to Asahel, "Turn aside from following me. Why should I make you fall? How then could I lift up my face to your brother Joab?" 23 But he would not turn aside. So Abner hit him in the stomach with the end of his spear, so that the spear came out at his back. He fell there and died where he fell. And all who

came to the place where Asahel fell and died, stood still.

24 But Joab and Abishai went after Abner. When the sun was going down, they came to the hill of Ammah, which is before Giah by the way of the desert of Gibeon. 25 The sons of Benjamin gathered together behind Abner and became one army. They stood on the top of a hill. 26 Abner called to Joab and said, "Should the sword destroy forever? Do you not know that it will be bad in the end? How long will you keep from telling the people to stop following their brothers?" 27 Joab said, "As God lives, if you had not spoken, for sure the people would have stopped going after their brothers in the morning." 28 So Joab sounded the horn, and all the people stopped and went after Israel no longer. And they did not fight any more. 29 Abner and his men went all night through the Arabah. They crossed the Jordan, walked all morning, and came to Mahanaim.

30 Joab returned from following Abner, and gathered all the people together. Added to Asahel, nineteen of David's servants were missing. 31 But the servants of David had killed many of Benjamin and Abner's men, so that 360 men died. 32 They picked up Asahel and buried him in his father's grave in Bethlehem. Then Joab and his men walked all night and came to Hebron early the next morning.

3 There was a long war between the family of Saul and the family of David. David became stronger and stronger. But the family of Saul became weaker and weaker.

David's Sons

2 Sons were born to David at Hebron. His first-born was Amnon, by David's wife Ahinoam of Jezreel. 3 His second son was Chileab, by Abigail who had been the wife of Nabal of Carmel. The third was Absalom the son of Maacah, the daughter of Talmai, king of Geshur. 4 The fourth was Adonijah the son of Haggith. The fifth was Shephatiah the son of Abital. 5 And the sixth was Ithream, by David's wife Eglah. These sons were born to David at Hebron.

Abner Goes over with David

6 While there was war between the family of Saul and the family of David, Abner was making himself strong in the family of Saul. 7 Now Saul had a woman acting as his wife whose name was Rizpah, the daughter of Aiah. Ish-bosheth said

to Abner, "Why have you gone in to the woman who acted as my father's wife?" [8] Abner was very angry because of Ish-bosheth's words, and said, "Am I a dog's head that belongs to Judah? Today I show kindness to the family of your father Saul, to his brothers and to his friends. I have not given you into David's hands. Yet today you say I am guilty because of this woman. [9] May God do so to Abner, and more also, if I do not do for David what the Lord has promised him. [10] He has promised to build the throne of David over Israel and over Judah, from Dan to Beersheba." [11] And Ish-bosheth could not answer Abner, because he was afraid of him.

[12] Then Abner sent men with news to David at Hebron, saying, "Whose land is this? Make your agreement with me, and I will help you bring all Israel over to you." [13] David said, "Good! I will make an agreement with you. But you must do one thing that I say. You will not see my face unless you first bring Saul's daughter Michal when you come to see me." [14] Then David sent men to Saul's son Ish-bosheth, saying, "Give me my wife Michal. I was married to her by giving a hundred pieces of skin from the sex parts of the Philistines." [15] So Ish-bosheth sent men to take her from her husband Paltiel the son of Laish. [16] But her husband went with her, crying as he went. He followed her as far as Bahurim. Then Abner said to him, "Go, return." So he returned.

[17] Now Abner spoke with the leaders of Israel, saying, "In times past you wanted David to be your king. [18] Now make it happen! For the Lord has said of David, 'By the hand of My servant David I will save My people Israel from the Philistines and from all those who hate them.' " [19] Abner spoke to Benjamin also. Then Abner went to Hebron to tell David all that Israel and the whole family of Benjamin thought was good to do.

[20] Abner came with twenty men to David at Hebron. And David made a special supper for Abner and the men who were with him. [21] Abner said to David, "Let me go and gather all Israel to my lord the king so they may make an agreement with you. Then you may be king over all your heart desires." So David sent Abner away, and he went in peace.

Joab Kills Abner

[22] Then David's servants and Joab came from a battle and brought with them many good things they had taken. But Abner was not with David in Hebron, for David had sent him away. Abner had gone in peace. [23] When Joab and the army with him came, it was told to Joab, "Abner the son of Ner came to the king. And the king has sent him away in peace." [24] Then Joab came to the king and said, "What have you done? See, Abner came to you. Why then have you sent him away, so that he is gone? [25] You know Abner the son of Ner. He came to fool you, and to learn about your going out and coming in. He came to learn all that you are doing."

[26] When Joab left David, he sent men after Abner. They brought him back from the well of Sirah. But David did not know it. [27] When Abner returned to Hebron, Joab took him aside into the center of the gate to speak with him alone. There Joab hit him in the stomach and killed him because of the blood of his brother Asahel. [28] When David heard about it, he said, "I and my nation are forever without guilt before the Lord, from the blood of Abner the son of Ner. [29] May the guilt be on the head of Joab and all his father's family. May the family of Joab never be without one who has a flow from his body, or a bad skin disease, or the need to use a walking stick. Or may his family never be without one who falls by the sword, or who needs more bread." [30] So Joab and his brother Abishai killed Abner because he had killed their brother in the battle at Gibeon.

David Shows Sorrow for Abner

[31] Then David said to Joab and all the people who were with him, "Tear your clothes and dress in clothes made from hair. Cry in sorrow in front of Abner." And King David walked behind the box in which the dead man was carried. [32] They buried Abner in Hebron. And the king cried in a loud voice at Abner's grave. All the people cried. [33] The king sang a song of sorrow for Abner, saying, "Should Abner die as a fool dies? [34] Your hands were not tied. Your feet were not put in chains. You have fallen as one falls in front of the sinful." And all the people cried again over him. [35] Then all the people came to try to talk David into eating bread while it was still day. But David promised, saying, "May God do so to me, and more also, if I taste bread or anything else before the sun goes down." [36] All the people saw it, and it pleased them. Everything the king did pleased all the people. [37] So all the people

and all Israel understood that day that it had not been the king's will to kill Abner the son of Ner. 38 Then the king said to his servants, "Do you not know that a leader, and a great man has fallen this day in Israel? 39 And I am weak today, even if I was chosen to be king. The sons of Zeruiah are too hard for me. May the Lord pay the sinner for his sin."

Ish-bosheth Is Killed

4 When Saul's son Ish-bosheth heard that Abner had died in Hebron, he lost his strength of heart. All Israel was troubled. 2 Saul's son had two men who were captains of small armies. The name of one was Baanah, and the name of the other was Rechab. They were sons of Rimmon the Beerothite of Benjamin. (For Beeroth is thought of as part of Benjamin. 3 The people of Beeroth ran to Gittaim, and have been strangers there to this day.)

4 Now Saul's son Jonathan had a son who could not walk because of his feet. He was five years old when the news of Saul and Jonathan came from Jezreel. His nurse had picked him up and ran. In her hurry to get away, he fell and hurt his feet so he could not walk. His name was Mephibosheth.

5 The sons of Rimmon the Beerothite, Rechab and Baanah, left and came to the family of Ish-bosheth. It was during the heat of the day, while Ish-bosheth was taking his noon rest. 6 They came to the center of the house as if to get wheat, and they hit Ish-bosheth in the stomach. Then Rechab and his brother Baanah ran away. 7 They had come into the house while he was lying on his bed in his room. And they had hit him and killed him and cut off his head. They took his head and traveled by the way of Arabah all night. 8 Then they brought Ish-bosheth's head to David at Hebron, and said to the king, "See, the head of Ish-bosheth, the son of Saul, who hated you and tried to kill you. So this day the Lord has punished Saul and his children for the king."

9 David answered Rechab and Baanah his brother, sons of Rimmon the Beerothite. He said to them, "As the Lord lives, Who has saved my life from all trouble, 10 when one told me, 'See, Saul is dead,' he thought he was bringing good news. But I took hold of him and killed him in Ziklag. This was the reward I gave him for his news. 11 How much worse it is when sinful men have killed a man who is right and good, on his bed in his own house! Should I not now punish you for his blood and destroy you from the earth?" 12 Then David had the young men kill them and cut off their hands and feet. They hung them up beside the pool in Hebron. But they took the head of Ish-bosheth and buried it in Abner's grave in Hebron.

David Becomes King over All Israel

5 Then all the families of Israel came to David at Hebron and said, "See, we are your bone and your flesh. 2 When Saul was our king, you were the one who led Israel out and in. The Lord said to you, 'You will be the shepherd of My people Israel. You will be a ruler over Israel.'" 3 So all the leaders of Israel came to the king at Hebron. And there King David made an agreement with them before the Lord. Then they chose David to be the king of Israel. 4 David was thirty years old when he became king, and he ruled for forty years. 5 He ruled over Judah seven years and six months at Hebron. Then he ruled in Jerusalem thirty-three years over all Israel and Judah.

David Takes Jerusalem

6 Now the king and his men went to Jerusalem against the Jebusites, the people living in the land. They said to David, "You will not come here. Even those who cannot see or walk could stop you." They thought that David could not come here. 7 But David took the strong-place of Zion, that is, the city of David. 8 David said on that day, "Whoever would kill the Jebusites, let him go up through the hole where the water flows, to those who cannot walk or see and who are hated by David's soul." So it is said, "Those who cannot see or walk will not come to the house." 9 David lived in the strong-place and called it the city of David. He built all around it from Millo toward the center. 10 David became greater and greater, for the Lord God of All was with him.

11 Hiram king of Tyre sent men to David with cedar trees and men who build with wood and stone. And they built a house for David. 12 David understood that the Lord had made him the king of Israel, and that the Lord had given honor to David's rule because of His people Israel.

13 David took more wives from Jerusalem, after he came from Hebron. And more sons and daughters were born to him. 14 The names of those who were

born to him in Jerusalem were Shammua, Shobab, Nathan, Solomon, 15 Ibhar, Elishua, Nepheg, Japhia, 16 Elishama, Eliada and Eliphelet.

David Wins the Battle over the Philistines

17 When the Philistines heard that David had been chosen to be king of Israel, all the Philistines went up to find him. When David heard of it, he went down to the strong-place. 18 The Philistines came and spread themselves out in the valley of Rephaim. 19 Then David asked the Lord, "Should I go up against the Philistines? Will You give them into my hand?" And the Lord said to David, "Go up, for it is sure that I will give the Philistines into your hand." 20 So David came to Baal-perazim and beat them there in battle. He said, "The Lord has broken through those who hate me like the breaking through of a flood." So he gave that place the name Baal-perazim. 21 The Philistines left their false gods there, and David and his men carried them away. 22 The Philistines came up again, and spread themselves out in the valley of Rephaim. 23 David asked the Lord what he should do. And the Lord said, "Do not go up, but go around behind them and come at them in front of the balsam trees. 24 When you hear the sound of their steps in the tops of the balsam trees, then hurry to fight, for then the Lord will have gone out before you to destroy the Philistine army." 25 David did just as the Lord told him. He killed the Philistines from Geba to Gezer.

The Special Box Is Brought to Jerusalem

6 Again David gathered all the chosen men of Israel. There were 30,000 2 He got up and went with all the people who were with him to Baale-judah to bring from there the special box of God. It is called by the name of the Lord of All Who sits on His throne above the cherubim. 3 They carried the special box of God on a new wagon, and brought it out of the family of Abinadab which was on the hill. Abinadab's sons Uzzah and Ahio were leading the new wagon. 4 They brought it with the special box of God from the family of Abinadab, which was on the hill. Ahio was walking in front of the special box. 5 And David and all those of the family of Israel sang and danced before the Lord with all their strength. They played songs with harps and timbrels.

6 But the cattle pulling the wagon almost made the special box of God fall when they came to the grain-floor of Nacon. So Uzzah put out his hand and took hold of the special box so it would not fall. 7 The anger of the Lord burned against Uzzah. God killed him there for his mistake. And he died there by the special box of God. 8 David became angry because the Lord had gone against Uzzah. So that place is called Perez-uzzah to this day. 9 David was afraid of the Lord that day, and he said, "How can the special box of the Lord come to me?" 10 So David was not willing to move the special box of the Lord into the city of David. But he took it aside to the house of Obed-edom the Gittite. 11 The special box of the Lord stayed in the house of Obed-edom the Gittite for three months. And the Lord brought good to Obed-edom and all of his family.

12 Now it was told to King David, "The Lord has brought good to the house of Obed-edom and all that belongs to him, because of the special box of God." So David went and brought the special box of God from Obed-edom's family into the city of David with joy. 13 When the men who carried the special box of the Lord had gone six steps, David killed and gave to the Lord a bull and a fat calf. 14 He was dancing before the Lord with all his strength. And he was wearing a linen vest. 15 So David and all those of the family of Israel were bringing the special box of the Lord with a loud voice and the sound of the horn. 16 As the special box of the Lord came into the city of David, Saul's daughter Michal looked out of the window. She saw King David jumping and dancing before the Lord, and she hated him in her heart. 17 They brought in the special box of the Lord and put it in its place inside the tent David had set up for it. And David gave burnt gifts and peace gifts to the Lord. 18 When he had finished giving the burnt gifts and peace gifts, David prayed that good would come to the people in the name of the Lord of All. 19 Then he gave a loaf of bread, a loaf of dates and a loaf of dried grapes to each man and woman of all the people of Israel. And all the people went home.

20 David returned to pray that good would come to his family. But Saul's daughter Michal came out to meet him, and said, "How the king of Israel honored himself today! He took his clothes off today so that his servants' young women

would see him. He acted like one of the foolish ones taking his clothes off without shame!" 21 So David said to Michal, "It was before the Lord. He chose me over your father and all his family, and made me ruler over the people of the Lord, over Israel. So I will act with joy before the Lord. 22 I will be honored less than this. I will be without pride in my own eyes. But the young women you have spoken about will honor me." 23 And Saul's daughter Michal had no child to the day of her death.

God's Agreement with David

7 King David lived in his house. The Lord had given him rest from all those around him who hated him. At this time, 2 the king said to Nathan, the man who spoke for God, "See now, I live in a house of cedar wood. But the special box of God stays within tent curtains." 3 Nathan said to the king, "Go and do all that is in your mind. For the Lord is with you."

4 But that same night the word of the Lord came to Nathan, saying, 5 "Go and tell My servant David, 'This is what the Lord says, "Are you the one who should build a house for Me to live in? 6 I have not lived in a house since the day I brought the people of Israel from Egypt to this day. But I have been moving about with a tent to live in. 7 In all the places where I have moved with all the people of Israel, did I say anything about this to any of the families of Israel which I told to shepherd My people? Did I say to any of them, 'Why have you not built a house of cedar wood for Me?' " ' 8 So now tell My servant David, 'This is what the Lord of All says, "I took you from following the sheep in the field to be the ruler of My people Israel. 9 I have been with you in all the places you have gone. I have destroyed from in front of you all those who fought against you. I will make you a great name, like the names of the great men who are on the earth. 10 I will choose a place for My people Israel and will plant them, that they may live in their own place and not be troubled again. The sinful will not bring trouble to them any more, as they did before 11 since the day I told special people to rule My people Israel. I will give you rest from all those who hate you. And the Lord makes known to you that He will make a house for you. 12 When your days are done and you lie down with your fathers, I will raise up your son after you, who will be born from you. And I will build his nation. 13 He will build a house for My name, and I will build the throne of his nation to last forever. 14 I will be a Father to him and he will be a son to Me. When he sins, I will punish him with the stick of men. And I will let the sons of men hit him. 15 But My loving-kindness will not leave him, as I took it away from Saul, whom I took away from you. 16 Your house and your nation will be made sure before Me forever. Your throne will be built to last forever." ' " 17 Nathan said to David all these words of this special dream.

David's Prayer

18 Then King David went in and sat before the Lord, and said, "Who am I, O Lord God, and what is my family, that You have brought me this far? 19 Yet this was a small thing in Your eyes, O Lord God. You have spoken of Your servant's family in the future. And this is the way of man, O Lord God. 20 What more can David say to You? For You know Your servant, O Lord God. 21 Because of Your Word and Your own heart, You have done all these great things to let Your servant know. 22 For this reason You are great, O Lord God. There is none like You. And there is no God but You, by all that we have heard with our ears. 23 What other nation on earth is like Your people Israel. God went to make them free to be His people and to make a name for Himself. You did a great thing for Yourself and great things for Your land. You did them before Your people whom You have made free from Egypt, from nations and their gods. 24 For You have made for Yourself Your people Israel to be Your people forever. O Lord, You have become their God. 25 Now, O Lord God, make sure forever the word which You have spoken about Your servant and his family. Do as You have said. 26 And Your name will be honored forever. It will be said, 'The Lord of All is God over Israel.' May the family of Your servant David be made strong before You. 27 For You, O Lord of All, the God of Israel, have shown this to Your servant, saying, 'I will build a house for you.' So Your servant has found strength of heart to pray this prayer to You. 28 And now, O Lord God, You are God. Your Words are truth. And You have promised this good thing to Your servant. 29 So now may it please You to bring good to the house of Your servant, that it may last forever before You. For You have spoken, O Lord God. May Your good come to the family of Your servant forever."

David Wins Other Battles

8 After this David won the battle against the Philistines. And he took the most important city from the Philistines. ² He won the battle against Moab, and had them lie down on the ground in straight groups. Two groups were put to death, and one group was kept alive. The Moabites became servants to David and paid taxes to him.

³ Then David won the battle against Hadadezer the son of Rehob king of Zobah, as he went to get his power again at the Euphrates River. ⁴ David took 1,700 horsemen and 20,000 foot soldiers from him. He cut the legs of some of the war-wagon horses, but saved enough of them for 100 war-wagons. ⁵ When the Syrians of Damascus came to help Hadadezer king of Zobah, David killed 22,000 of them. ⁶ Then he put groups of soldiers in Damascus of Syria. The Syrians became servants to David and were made to pay taxes to him. The Lord helped David every place he went. ⁷ David took the coverings of gold which were carried by Hadadezer's army, and brought them to Jerusalem. ⁸ And he took a very large amount of brass from Hadadezer's cities, Betah and Berothai.

⁹ Now Toi king of Hamath heard that David had won the battle against the whole army of Hadadezer. ¹⁰ So Toi sent his son Joram to King David, to greet him and pray that good would come to him, because David had fought against Hadadezer and had won. Hadadezer had been at war with Toi. Joram brought with him objects of silver, gold and brass. ¹¹ David set these apart to the Lord, together with the silver and gold he had set apart from all the nations he had taken in battle. ¹² He had taken silver and gold from Syria, Moab, the sons of Ammon, the Philistines, Amalek, and from the things taken from Hadadezer the son of Rehob, king of Zobah.

¹³ So David's name was very respected when he returned from killing 18,000 Syrians in the Valley of Salt. ¹⁴ And he put groups of soldiers in Edom. In all Edom he put soldiers, and all the Edomites became servants to David. The Lord helped David every place he went.

¹⁵ So David ruled all of Israel. He did what was right and good and fair for all his people. ¹⁶ Joab the son of Zeruiah was the head of the army. Jehoshaphat the son of Ahilud wrote down the important things of the nation. ¹⁷ Ahitub's son Zadok and Abiathar's son Ahimelech were religious leaders. Seraiah was the writer. ¹⁸ Benaiah the son of Jehoiada ruled the Cherethites and the Pelethites. And David's sons were the king's helpers.

David Is Kind to Mephibosheth

9 Then David said, "Is there anyone left of the family of Saul, to whom I may show kindness because of Jonathan?" ² Now there was a servant in Saul's house whose name was Ziba. They called him to David, and the king said to him, "Are you Ziba?" And he said, "I am your servant." ³ The king said, "Is there not still someone of the family of Saul to whom I may show the kindness of God?" And Ziba said to the king, "There is still a son of Jonathan who cannot walk because of his feet." ⁴ So the king said to him, "Where is he?" Ziba answered the king, "See, he is in the family of Machir the son of Ammiel in Lo-debar." ⁵ Then King David sent men to bring him from the family of Machir the son of Ammiel, from Lodebar. ⁶ Mephibosheth the son of Saul's son Jonathan came to David and fell on his face to the ground in respect. David said, "Mephibosheth." And he answered, "Here is your servant!" ⁷ David said to him, "Do not be afraid. For I will be sure to show kindness to you because of your father Jonathan. I will return to you all the land of your grandfather Saul. And you will eat at my table always." ⁸ Again Mephibosheth put his face to the ground and said, "Who am I? Why should you care for a dead dog like me?"

⁹ Then the king called Saul's servant Ziba and said to him, "I have given to your owner's grandson all that belonged to Saul and his family. ¹⁰ You and your sons and your servants will grow food on the land for him. You will bring in the food so your owner's grandson may eat. But Mephibosheth your owner's grandson will always eat at my table." Now Ziba had fifteen sons and twenty servants. ¹¹ Then Ziba said to the king, "Your servant will do all that my lord the king tells your servant to do." So Mephibosheth ate at David's table as one of the king's sons. ¹² Mephibosheth had a young son whose name was Mica. And all who lived in Ziba's house were Mephibosheth's servants. ¹³ So Mephibosheth lived in Jerusalem, for he always ate at the king's table. Both his feet had been hurt and he could not walk.

David Wins over the Ammonites and Syrians

10 After this the king of the Ammonites died. His son Hanun became king in his place. ² Then David said, "I will show kindness to Nahash's son Hanun, just as his father showed kindness to me." So David sent some of his servants to comfort him in the loss of his father. But when David's servants came to the land of the Ammonites, ³ the Ammonite leaders said to their lord Hanun, "Do you think that David is honoring your father because he sent men to comfort you? Has he not sent his servants to you so they can spy out the city and destroy it?" ⁴ So Hanun took David's servants and cut off half the hair from their faces. Then he cut off half their clothing, almost up to the belt, and sent them away. ⁵ When David heard about it, he sent men to meet them, for they were very ashamed. The king said, "Stay at Jericho until the hair grows again on your faces. Then return."

⁶ Now when the sons of Ammon saw that they had become hated by David, they paid for the help of the Syrians of Beth-rehob and the Syrians of Zobah, 20,000 foot soldiers. And they paid for the help of the king of Maacah with 1,000 men, and 12,000 men of Tob. ⁷ When David heard about it, he sent Joab and all the army of the powerful men. ⁸ The sons of Ammon came to the city gate and got ready for battle. And the Syrians of Zobah and of Rehob, and the men of Tob and Maacah, were by themselves in the field.

⁹ Joab saw that the battle was set against him both in front and behind him. So he chose all the best men of Israel and dressed them for battle against the Syrians. ¹⁰ He put the rest of the people under the rule of his brother Abishai. He dressed them for battle against the sons of Ammon. ¹¹ Joab said, "If the Syrians are too strong for me, then help me. But if the sons of Ammon are too strong for you, then I will come and help you. ¹² Be strong. Let us show ourselves to have strength of heart because of our people and the cities of our God. And may the Lord do what is good in His eyes." ¹³ So Joab and the people who were with him came near to battle against the Syrians, and they ran away from him. ¹⁴ When the sons of Ammon saw that the Syrians had run away, they ran away from Abishai and went into the city. Then Joab returned from fighting against the sons of Ammon, and came to Jerusalem.

¹⁵ When the Syrians saw that they had lost the battle with Israel, they gathered together. ¹⁶ Hadadezer sent men and brought out the Syrians who were on the other side of the Euphrates River, and they came to Helam. They were led by Shobach, the captain of Hadadezer's army. ¹⁷ When it was told to David, he gathered all Israel together and crossed the Jordan, and came to Helam. The Syrians dressed themselves for battle against David, and fought against him. ¹⁸ But the Syrians ran away from Israel. David killed 700 drivers of the Syrian war-wagons, and 40,000 horsemen. He killed Shobach, the captain of their army, who died there. ¹⁹ When all the kings who were servants of Hadadezer saw that they had lost the battle against Israel, they made peace with Israel and served them. The Syrians were afraid to help the sons of Ammon any more.

David and Bathsheba

11 The spring of the year was the time when kings went out to battle. At that time David sent Joab and his servants and all Israel. They destroyed the sons of Ammon and gathered the army around Rabbah. But David stayed at Jerusalem.

² When evening came David got up from his bed and walked around on the roof of the king's house. From the roof he saw a woman washing herself. The woman was very beautiful. ³ So David sent someone to ask about the woman. And one said, "Is this not Eliam's daughter Bathsheba, the wife of Uriah the Hittite?" ⁴ David sent men and took her. When she came to him, he lay with her. After she had made herself clean again, she returned to her house. ⁵ She was going to have a baby, so she sent someone to tell David, "I am going to have a baby."

⁶ Then David sent men to Joab, saying, "Send me Uriah the Hittite." So Joab sent Uriah to David. ⁷ When Uriah came to him, David asked how Joab and the people were doing, and how the war was going. ⁸ Then David said to Uriah, "Go down to your house, and wash your feet." And Uriah left the king's house, and a gift from the king was sent to him. ⁹ But Uriah slept at the door of the king's house with all the servants of his lord. He did not go down to his house. ¹⁰ When they told David that Uriah did not go down to his house, David said to Uriah, "Have you not returned from traveling a long way? Why did you not go down to your house?"

11 Uriah said to David, "The special box of the Lord, and Israel and Judah, are staying in tents. My lord Joab and the servants of my lord are staying in the open field. Should I go to my house to eat and drink and lie with my wife? By your life and the life of your soul, I will not do this thing." 12 Then David said to Uriah, "Stay here today also. Tomorrow I will let you go." So Uriah stayed in Jerusalem that day and the next. 13 David called him, and he ate and drank with him, and David made him drunk. In the evening Uriah went out to lie on his bed with his lord's servants. He did not go down to his house.

14 In the morning, David wrote a letter to Joab, and sent it by Uriah. 15 He had written in the letter, "Put Uriah in the front of the hardest battle and come away from him, so that he may be killed." 16 So while Joab was watching the city, he sent Uriah to the place where he knew there were soldiers with strength of heart. 17 The men of the city went out and fought against Joab. Some of David's servants were killed. And Uriah the Hittite died also. 18 Then Joab sent a man with news to David to tell him all about the war. 19 Joab told the man, "When you have finished telling the king all about the war, 20 the king might become angry. He might say to you, 'Why did you go so near the city to fight? Did you not know that they would shoot from the wall? 21 Who killed Abimelech the son of Jerubbesheth? Did not a woman throw a grinding-stone on him from the wall so that he died at Thebez? Why did you go so near the wall?' Then you should say, 'Your servant Uriah the Hittite is dead also.' "

22 So the man left and came to David. He told him all that Joab had sent him to tell. 23 The man said to David, "The men were winning the fight against us. They came out against us in the field. But we drove them back as far as the city gate. 24 Then they shot arrows at your servants from the wall. So some of the king's servants are dead, and your servant Uriah the Hittite is dead also." 25 Then David said to the man, "Tell Joab, 'Do not let this thing trouble you. For the sword kills one as well as another. Make your battle against the city stronger and destroy it.' Comfort him with these words."

26 When Uriah's wife heard that her husband was dead, she was filled with sorrow for him. 27 When the time of sorrow was finished, David sent men and brought her to his house. She became his wife, and

gave birth to his son. But what David had done was sinful in the eyes of the Lord.

Nathan's Picture-Story about David

12 Then the Lord sent Nathan to David. He came to him and said, "There were two men in one city. One was rich and the other was poor. 2 The rich man had many flocks and cattle. 3 But the poor man had nothing except one little female lamb which he bought and fed. It grew up together with him and his children. It would eat his bread and drink from his cup and lie in his arms. It was like a daughter to him. 4 Now a traveler came to the rich man. But the rich man was not willing to take from his own flock or his own cattle, to make food for the traveler who had come to him. Instead, he took the poor man's female lamb and made it ready for the man who had come to him." 5 David was very angry at the man, and said to Nathan, "As the Lord lives, for sure the man who has done this should die. 6 And he must pay four times the worth of the lamb, because he did this thing without pity."

7 Nathan said to David, "You are the man! This is what the Lord God of Israel says: 'I chose you to be the king of Israel. I saved you from the hand of Saul. 8 I gave you Saul's family and Saul's wives into your care. I gave you the nations of Israel and Judah. And if this were too little, I would give you as much more. 9 Why have you hated the Word of the Lord by doing what is bad in His eyes? You have killed Uriah the Hittite with the sword. You have taken his wife to be your wife. You have killed him with the sword of the sons of Ammon. 10 So now some from your family, even in the future, will die by the sword, because you have turned against Me and have taken the wife of Uriah the Hittite to be your wife.' 11 This is what the Lord says: 'See, I will bring trouble against you from your own family. I will take your wives in front of your eyes and give them to your neighbor. He will lie with your wives in the light of day. 12 You did it in secret. But I will do this in front of all Israel, and under the sun.' " 13 Then David said to Nathan, "I have sinned against the Lord." And Nathan said to him, "The Lord has taken away your sin. You will not die. 14 But by this act you have given those who hate the Lord a reason to speak against the Lord. The child that is born to you will die for sure." 15 Then Nathan went home.

David's Son Dies

The Lord sent trouble upon the child of Uriah's wife and David, so that he was very sick. 16 David begged God to make the child well. He went without food and lay all night on the ground. 17 The leaders of his family stood beside him to lift him up from the ground. But David was not willing. He would not eat food with them. 18 The child died on the seventh day. And David's servants were afraid to tell him that the child was dead, for they said, "See, we spoke to him while the child was still alive, and he did not listen to us. So how can we tell him the child is dead? He might hurt himself." 19 But when David saw his servants speaking together in secret, he understood that the child was dead. He asked his servants, "Is the child dead?" And they said, "He is dead." 20 So David got up from the ground, washed, poured oil on himself, and changed his clothes. Then he came into the house of the Lord and worshiped. He returned to his own house and asked for food. So they set food in front of him, and he ate. 21 Then his servants said to him, "What is this that you have done? While the child was alive, you went without food and cried. But when the child died, you got up and ate food." 22 David said, "I went without food and cried while the child was still alive, for I said, 'Who knows? The Lord might be kind to me and let the child live.' 23 But now he has died. Why should I go without food? Can I bring him to life again? I will go to him, but he will not return to me."

Solomon Is Born

24 Then David comforted his wife Bathsheba. He went in and lay with her, and she gave birth to a son. He gave him the name Solomon. The Lord loved him, 25 and sent word through Nathan who spoke for God. And Nathan gave him the name Jedidiah because of the Lord.

David Takes Rabbah

26 Now Joab fought against Rabbah of the sons of Ammon, and took the king's city. 27 Joab sent men to David, saying, "I have fought against Rabbah. I have taken the city of waters. 28 So gather the rest of the people together. Go against the city and take it, or I will take the city myself and it will be called by my name." 29 So David gathered all the people and went to Rabbah. He fought against it, and took it. 30 Then he took the very heavy crown from their king's head. In it were beautiful stones of much worth. The crown was put on David's head. And he brought a large amount of things out of the city. 31 He brought out the people who were in it also. He made them work with saws, sharp iron tools, and iron axes. And he made them work in the heat making building stones. He did this to all the cities of the sons of Ammon. Then David and all the people returned to Jerusalem.

Amnon and Tamar

13 Now David's son Absalom had a beautiful sister whose name was Tamar. And David's son Amnon loved her. 2 Amnon was so troubled because of his sister Tamar that he became sick. She was a woman who had never had a man, and Amnon thought how hard it would be to have her. 3 But Amnon had a friend whose name was Jonadab. He was the son of David's brother Shimeah. And Jonadab was very good at making plans. 4 He said to Amnon, "O son of the king, why are you so sad from day to day? Will you not tell me?" Amnon said to him, "I am in love with Tamar, the sister of my brother Absalom." 5 Then Jonadab said to him, "Lie down on your bed and pretend to be sick. When your father comes to see you, say to him, 'I beg you, let my sister Tamar come and give me some food to eat. Let her make food ready here so I can see it and eat it from her hand.'" 6 So Amnon lay down and pretended to be sick. When the king came to see him, Amnon said to him, "I beg you, let my sister Tamar come and make two loaves beside me, that I may eat from her hand."

7 Then David sent home for Tamar, saying, "Go now to your brother Amnon's house, and make food for him." 8 So Tamar went to her brother Amnon's house. He was lying down. And she took dough and made loaves so he could watch. Then she baked them ready to eat. 9 And she took the dish and held it out in front of him. But he would not eat. Amnon said, "Have everyone leave me." So everyone left him. 10 Then Amnon said to Tamar, "Bring the food to my room, so I may eat from your hand." So Tamar took the loaves she had made and brought them to her brother Amnon in his room. 11 When she brought them to him to eat, he took hold of her and said, "Come, lie with me, my sister." 12 But she said, "No, my brother. Do not make me. For such a thing is not done in Israel.

Do not do this bad and foolish thing! 13 As for me, where could I get rid of my shame? And as for you, you would be like one of the fools in Israel. So now I beg you, speak to the king, for he will not keep me from you." 14 But Amnon would not listen to her. Being stronger than she, he made her lay with him.

15 Then Amnon hated her very much. He hated her more than he had loved her. He said to her, "Get up! Go away!" 16 But she said to him, "No! Sending me away is worse than what you have done to me!" But he would not listen to her. 17 He called the young man who helped him and said, "Throw this woman out of my house, and lock the door behind her." 18 Now she was wearing a dress which covered her arms. For this is how the king's daughters dressed when they had never had a man. The man who helped Amnon took her out and locked the door behind her. 19 Then Tamar put ashes on her head. She tore the dress she was wearing which covered her arms. And she put her hand on her head and went away with a loud cry.

20 Absalom her brother said to her, "Has your brother Amnon been with you? Be quiet now, my sister. He is your brother. Do not take this to heart." So Tamar stayed in her brother Absalom's house, sad and alone. 21 When King David heard about all this, he was very angry. 22 But Absalom did not speak good or bad to Amnon. Absalom hated Amnon because he had put his sister to shame.

Absalom Kills Amnon

23 After two full years, Absalom had men cut the wool from the sheep in Baal-hazor, near Ephraim. And Absalom asked all the king's sons to come. 24 He came to the king and said, "See, your servant has men to cut the wool from the sheep. Let the king and his men go with your servant." 25 But the king said to Absalom, "No, my son. We should not all go, or we will be trouble for you." Absalom tried to talk him into going. The king prayed that good would come to him, but he would not go with him. 26 Then Absalom said, "If you will not go, let my brother Amnon go with us." And the king said to him, "Why should he go with you?" 27 But when Absalom kept asking him, he let Amnon and all the king's sons go with him.

28 Then Absalom told his servants, "Watch when Amnon's heart is happy with wine. When I say to you, 'Kill Amnon,'

then put him to death. Do not be afraid. Have not I myself told you to do it? Have strength of heart." 29 So Absalom's servants did to Amnon just as Absalom had told them. Then all the king's sons got up on their horses and left in a hurry.

30 While they were on their way, the news came to David, saying, "Absalom has killed all the king's sons. Not one of them is left." 31 The king got up and tore his clothes, and lay on the ground. And all his servants standing beside him tore their clothes. 32 But Jonadab, the son of David's brother Shimeah, said, "Do not let my lord think they have killed all the young men, the king's sons. Only Amnon is dead. Absalom has wanted to kill him since the day he put his sister Tamar to shame. 33 So do not let my lord the king take this to heart and think that all the king's sons are dead, for only Amnon is dead."

Absalom Goes to Geshur

34 Now Absalom had run away. And the young man who kept watch looked up and saw many people coming from the road behind him by the side of the mountain. 35 Jonadab said to the king, "See, the king's sons have come. What your servant said is true." 36 As soon as he had finished speaking, the king's sons came and cried in a loud voice. The king and all his servants cried also.

37 Absalom ran away and went to Talmai the son of Ammihud, the king of Geshur. And David was filled with sorrow for his son every day. 38 So Absalom had run away to Geshur, and was there three years. 39 The spirit of King David wanted very much to go out to Absalom. For he was comforted about Amnon, since he was dead.

Absalom Returns to Jerusalem

14 Now Joab the son of Zeruiah saw that the king missed Absalom very much. 2 So Joab sent for a wise woman from Tekoa, and said to her, "Pretend to be filled with sorrow. Dress as if you were filled with sorrow, and do not pour oil on yourself. Dress like a woman who has been filled with sorrow for the dead many days. 3 Then go to the king and speak to him in this way." And Joab told her what to say.

4 When the woman of Tekoa spoke to the king, she fell on her face to the ground, showing honor, and said, "Help, O king." 5 The king said to her, "What is your trouble?" And she answered, "I am a woman whose husband has died. 6 Your

woman servant had two sons. But they fought together in the field and there was no one to pull them apart. So one hit the other and killed him. 7 Now the whole family has come against your woman servant. They say, 'Give us the one who killed his brother. We must put him to death for the life of his brother whom he killed.' So I would be without a son to receive what belonged to his parents when I die. They would put out the last of the fire which is left to me. My husband would be left without a name and with no children on the earth."

8 Then the king said to the woman, "Go to your house. I will say what should be done about your trouble." 9 The woman of Tekoa said to the king, "O my lord the king, the sin is on me and my father's family. But the king and his throne are without guilt." 10 The king said, "If anyone says anything to you, bring him to me. And he will not touch you again." 11 Then she said, "I beg the king to remember the Lord your God, that the one who punishes for blood will stop destroying. Or my son might be destroyed." And the king said, "As the Lord lives, not one hair of your son will fall to the ground."

12 Then the woman said, "Let your woman servant speak to my lord the king." And he said, "Speak." 13 The woman said, "Why then have you planned such a thing against the people of God? For in deciding in this way, the king is as one who is guilty. For the king does not bring home his son who has been driven away. 14 It is sure that we will die. We are like water poured on the ground, which cannot be picked up again. But God does not take away life. He plans ways so that the one who is driven away may not be kept away from Him. 15 I have come to say this to my lord the king because the people have made me afraid. Your woman servant thought, 'I will speak to the king. It might be that the king will do what his woman servant asks. 16 For the king will hear and save his woman servant from the man who would destroy both me and my son from the gift of God.' 17 Then your woman servant thought, 'The word of my lord the king will comfort me. For my lord the king is like the angel of God in understanding what is good and bad. May the Lord your God be with you.' "

18 Then the king said to the woman, "Do not hide anything from me that I ask you." And the woman said, "Let my lord the king speak." 19 So the king said, "Is Joab with you in all this?" The woman answered, "As your soul lives, my lord the king, no one can turn to the right or left from anything my lord the king has said. Yes, it was your servant Joab who told me to do this. It was he who put all these words in the mouth of your woman servant. 20 Your servant Joab has done this to change the way things are now. But my lord is wise like the angel of God, to know all that is on the earth."

21 Then the king said to Joab, "See now, I will do this. Go and bring back the young man Absalom." 22 And Joab fell on his face to the ground in honor and thanks to the king. Joab said, "Today your servant knows that I have found favor in your eyes, O my lord the king. Because the king has done what his servant has asked of him." 23 So Joab got up and went to Geshur, and brought Absalom to Jerusalem. 24 But the king said, "Let him go to his own house. Do not let him see my face." So Absalom went to his own house and did not see the king's face.

David Forgives Absalom

25 Now there was no one in Israel as good-looking and as much praised as Absalom. There was nothing wrong with him from the bottom of his foot to the top of his head. 26 At the end of every year he would cut the hair from his head, for it was heavy on him. When he cut it, he weighed the hair of his head. It weighed as much as 200 pieces of silver, by the king's weight. 27 Three sons were born to Absalom, and one daughter whose name was Tamar. She was a beautiful woman.

28 Absalom lived two whole years in Jerusalem, and did not see the king's face. 29 Then Absalom sent for Joab, to send him to the king. But Joab would not come to him. So he sent for him a second time. But he would not come. 30 He said to his servants, "See, Joab's field is next to mine, and he has barley there. Go and set it on fire." So Absalom's servants burned the field. 31 Then Joab got up and came to Absalom at his house, and said to him, "Why have your servants burned my field?" 32 Absalom answered Joab, "I sent for you, saying, 'Come here, that I may send you to say to the king, "Why have I come from Geshur? It would have been better for me to stay there." ' Now let me see the king's face. If there is guilt in me, let him put me to death." 33 Then Joab went to the king and told him. And he called for Absalom. So he came to the king and put his face to

the ground in front of him. And the king kissed Absalom.

Absalom Becomes Friends with Men of Israel

15 After this, Absalom got a war-wagon and horses, and fifty men to run in front of him. ² He used to get up early and stand beside the way to the gate. When any man had a problem to be decided upon by the king, Absalom would call to him and say, "What city are you from?" And he would answer, "Your servant is from one of the families of Israel." ³ Then Absalom would say to him, "Your side of the problem is good and right. But there is no man to listen to you for the king." ⁴ And Absalom would say, "If only I were chosen to be the one to be judge in the land! Then every man who has a problem could come to me. And I would do for him what is right and fair." ⁵ When a man came near to put his face to the ground in front of him, Absalom would put out his hand and take hold of him and kiss him. ⁶ He acted this way toward all those of Israel who came with a problem for the king to judge. So Absalom became friends with the men of Israel.

⁷ At the end of four years, Absalom said to the king, "I ask you, let me go to Hebron and keep my promise that I have promised to the Lord. ⁸ For your servant made a promise while I was living at Geshur in Syria, saying, 'If the Lord will bring me again to Jerusalem, then I will serve the Lord.'" ⁹ And the king said to him, "Go in peace." So he got up and went to Hebron. ¹⁰ But Absalom sent men to go in secret through all the families of Israel. He said to them, "As soon as you hear the sound of the horn, then say, 'Absalom is king at Hebron.'" ¹¹ With Absalom went 200 men from Jerusalem. They had been asked to come, and did not know what Absalom had planned. ¹² While Absalom was giving gifts on the altar in worship, he sent for Ahithophel the Gilonite, from his city Giloh. He was the man who talked with David about what to do. The plans against David became strong. For more and more people joined Absalom.

David Runs from Jerusalem

¹³ Then a man came to David with news, saying, "The hearts of the men of Israel are with Absalom." ¹⁴ David said to all his servants who were with him at Jerusalem, "Get up and let us run. Or else none of us will be safe from Absalom. Hurry and go, or he will be quick to catch us and bring trouble upon us. He would destroy the city with the sword." ¹⁵ The king's servants said to him, "See, your servants are ready to do whatever my lord the king chooses." ¹⁶ So the king left with all those of his house. But he left ten of his women to take care of the house. ¹⁷ The king left with all the people, and they stopped at the last house. ¹⁸ All his servants passed by him, and all the Cherethites, Pelethites, Gittites, and 600 men who had come with him from Gath. They all passed by the king.

¹⁹ Then the king said to Ittai the Gittite, "Why do you go with us also? Return and stay with the king. For you are from another land and have been driven from your home. ²⁰ You came only yesterday. Should I make you go with us today, when I do not know where I am going? Return with your brothers. May loving-kindness and faith be with you." ²¹ But Ittai said to the king, "As the Lord lives, and as my lord the king lives, your servant will be where my lord the king may be, in death or in life." ²² So David said to him, "Go then, pass on." And Ittai the Gittite passed on, with all his men and all the little ones who were with him. ²³ All the country was crying with a loud voice as all the people passed by. The king crossed the river Kidron, and all the people went on toward the desert.

²⁴ Zadok came also, with all the Levites who carried the special box with the Law of God. Abiathar had the special box of God put down until all the people had passed out of the city. ²⁵ The king said to Zadok, "Return the special box of God to the city. If I find favor in the eyes of the Lord, He will have me return. And He will have me see both it and His family. ²⁶ But if He says, 'I have no joy in you,' then here I am. Let Him do to me what He thinks is good." ²⁷ And the king said to Zadok the religious leader, "Are you not a man who speaks for God? Return to the city in peace with Abiathar and your two sons, your son Ahimaaz and Abiathar's son Jonathan. ²⁸ See, I will wait in the desert by the place where the river is crossed, until I hear from you." ²⁹ So Zadok and Abiathar returned the special box of God to Jerusalem and stayed there.

³⁰ David went up the Mount of Olives and cried as he went. His head was covered and he wore no shoes. And all the people who were with him covered their heads and went up crying as they went.

31 Now David was told, "Ahithophel is among those who are making plans with Absalom." And David said, "O Lord, I pray, make the words of Ahithophel foolish." **32** As David was coming to the top of the mountain, where God was worshiped, Hushai the Archite met him. His coat was torn and there was dust on his head. **33** David said to him, "If you go with me, you will be trouble for me. **34** But if you return to the city, you can bring trouble to the words of Ahithophel for me. Say to Absalom, 'I will be your servant, O king. I will work for you as I have worked for your father in the past.' Then you can make the words of Ahithophel foolish for me. **35** Will not Zadok and Abiathar the religious leaders be there with you? Tell Zadok and Abiathar whatever you hear from the king's house. **36** Their two sons are with them there, Zadok's son Ahimaaz and Abiathar's son Jonathan. By them you can send me news of all that you hear." **37** So David's friend Hushai came into Jerusalem, just as Absalom was coming into the city.

David and Ziba

16 When David had gone a short way past the mountain-top, Mephibosheth's servant Ziba met him with two donkeys ready for traveling. On them were 200 loaves of bread, 100 vines of dried grapes, 100 summer fruits, and a bottle of wine. **2** The king said to Ziba, "Why do you have these?" And Ziba said, "The donkeys are for those of the king's house to travel on. The bread and summer fruit are for the young men to eat. And the wine drink is for whoever is weak in the desert." **3** Then the king said, "Where is your owner's son?" And Ziba answered, "He is staying in Jerusalem. For he said, 'Today the family of Israel will return to me the nation of my father.'" **4** So the king said to Ziba, "See, all that belongs to Mephibosheth is yours." And Ziba said, "I bow down in honor to you. O my lord the king, let me find favor in your eyes!"

David and Shimei

5 When King David came to Bahurim, there came out a man of the family of Saul. His name was Shimei, the son of Gera. He did not stop speaking bad things as he came. **6** He threw stones at David, and at all the servants of King David. And all the people and all the strong men were at his right and at his left. **7** Shimei said as he said

bad things, "Get out! Get out, you man of blood, you man of no worth! **8** The Lord has punished you for all the blood of the family of Saul, in whose place you have ruled! The Lord has given the nation to your son Absalom! Your trouble is upon you, because you are a man of blood!" **9** Zeruiah's son Abishai said to the king, "Why should this dead dog speak against my lord the king? Let me go now and cut off his head." **10** But the king said, "What have I to do with you, O sons of Zeruiah? If he speaks against me, and if the Lord has told him, 'Speak against David,' then who should say, 'Why have you done so?'" **11** Then David said to Abishai and all his servants, "See, my own son wants to kill me. How much more now may this Benjamite? Let him alone and let him speak against me, for the Lord has told him. **12** It may be that the Lord will look upon my trouble and return good to me instead of his bad words today." **13** So David and his men went on the way. And Shimei went beside him on the hill. He spoke against David as he went, and threw stones and dust at him. **14** The king and all the people with him were tired when they came to the Jordan. There he rested and received new strength.

Absalom Goes to Jerusalem

15 Absalom and all the people, the men of Israel, came into Jerusalem. And Ahithophel was with him. **16** When David's friend Hushai the Archite came to Absalom, Hushai said to him, "Long live the king! Long live the king!" **17** And Absalom said to Hushai, "Is this your kindness to your friend? Why did you not go with your friend?" **18** Hushai said to Absalom, "No! I will belong to whoever is chosen by the Lord, this people, and all the men of Israel. **19** And whom should I serve? Should I not serve his son? As I have served your father, so I will serve you." **20** Then Absalom said to Ahithophel, "Give your wise words. What should we do?" **21** Ahithophel answered, "Go in to your father's women, whom he has left to take care of the house. Then all Israel will hear that you have made yourself hated by your father. Then the hands of all who are with you will be made stronger." **22** So they set up a tent for Absalom on the roof. And Absalom went in to his father's women so that the eyes of all Israel could see. **23** The words that Ahithophel spoke in those days were as if one had asked for the Word of God. Both David and Absalom thought of Ahithophel's words in this way.

Hushai and Absalom

17 Then Ahithophel said to Absalom, "Let me choose 12,000 men, and I will leave and go after David tonight. [2] I will come upon him while he is tired and weak. I will fill him with fear so that all the people who are with him will run away. Then I will kill the king alone [3] and return all the people to you. All will return if the man you want to kill is dead. Then all the people will be at peace." [4] The plan pleased Absalom and all the leaders of Israel

[5] Then Absalom said, "Call Hushai the Archite also. Let us hear what he has to say." [6] When Hushai had come to Absalom, Absalom said to him, "Ahithophel has said this. Should we do as he says? If not, tell us." [7] So Hushai said to Absalom, "This time what Ahithophel has said to do is not good." [8] Hushai said, "You know your father and his men. They are powerful and angry, like a bear robbed of her young ones in the field. And your father is a very able man of war. He will not stay with the people during the night. [9] He has now hidden himself in one of the caves, or in another place. When some of the people are killed in the first battle, whoever hears it will say, 'There have been many people killed who follow Absalom.' [10] Even the one who has strength of heart like the heart of a lion will be afraid. For all Israel knows that your father is a powerful man, and that those who are with him are men with strength of heart. [11] But I say that all Israel should be gathered to you, from Dan to Beersheba, as much as the sand by the sea. And you yourself should go into battle. [12] So we will find David wherever he is. We will fall on him like water falls on the ground in the early morning. And not he or any of the men with him will be left. [13] If he runs into a city, then all Israel will bring ropes to that city. We will pull it into the valley until not even a small stone is left there." [14] Then Absalom and all the men of Israel said, "The words of Hushai the Archite are better than the words of Ahithophel." In this way the Lord had planned to destroy the good leading of Ahithophel, so He might bring trouble to Absalom.

David Is Told to Leave

[15] Hushai said to Zadok and Abiathar the religious leaders, "This is what Ahithophel said that Absalom and the leaders of Israel should do. And this is what I have said they should do. [16] So be quick to send someone to tell David, 'Do not stay the night in the desert beside the place where the Jordan is crossed. But cross over, or the king and all the people with him will be destroyed.'" [17] Now Jonathan and Ahimaaz were staying at Enrogel. And a woman servant would go and tell them, and they would go and tell King David. For they could not be seen coming into the city. [18] But a boy saw them, and told Absalom. So the two of them left in a hurry and came to the house of a man in Bahurim. He had a well in the open space in the center of his house. And they went down into it. [19] Then the woman took the covering and spread it over the well's mouth, and spread grain on it, so nothing was known of it. [20] Then Absalom's servants came to the woman at the house and said, "Where are Ahimaaz and Jonathan?" The woman answered, "They have crossed the river." And after looking and not finding them, they returned to Jerusalem.

[21] When they had left, Ahimaaz and Jonathan came up out of the well and went and told King David. They said to David, "Be quick to get ready and cross over the water. For Ahithophel has told them to come against you." [22] So David and all the people with him got up and crossed the Jordan. By the light of morning, not one was left who had not crossed the Jordan. [23] When Ahithophel saw that his words were not followed, he got onto his donkey and went home to his city. He told those of his family what they must do, and he hanged himself. So he died and was buried in his father's grave.

[24] Then David came to Mahanaim. Absalom and all the men of Israel with him crossed the Jordan. [25] Absalom made Amasa captain of the army instead of Joab. Amasa was the son of a man whose name was Jithra the Israelite, who went in to Nahash's daughter Abigal, the sister of Joab's mother Zeruiah. [26] And Israel and Absalom set up their tents in the land of Gilead.

[27] When David had come to Mahanaim, he met Nahash's son Shobi from Rabbah of the sons of Ammon, Ammiel's son Machir from Lo-debar, and Barzillai the Gileadite from Rogelim. [28] They brought him beds, washing pots, dishes, grain, flour, seeds, [29] honey, sour milk, sheep, and cheese from the cattle, for David and his men to

eat. For they said, "The people are hungry and tired and thirsty in the desert."

Absalom's Death

18 Then David numbered the people who were with him. He set over them leaders of thousands and of hundreds. ² And he sent the people out. One-third of them was under the rule of Joab. One-third was under the rule of Zeruiah's son Abishai, Joab's brother. And one-third was under the rule of Ittai the Gittite. The king said to the people, "I myself will go out with you also." ³ But the people said, "You should not go out. For if we run, they will not care about us. If half of us die, they will not care about us. But you are worth 10,000 of us. So it is better that you send us help from the city." ⁴ The king said to them, "I will do whatever you think is best." So the king stood beside the gate, and all the people went out by hundreds and thousands. ⁵ The king told Joab and Abishai and Ittai, "Be gentle toward the young man Absalom because of me." And all the people heard him say this to all the leaders about Absalom.

⁶ Then the people went out into the field to fight against Israel. The battle was fought among the trees of Ephraim. ⁷ The people of Israel lost the fight there to the servants of David. Twenty thousand men were killed there that day. ⁸ The battle was spread over the whole country. Dangers from the trees destroyed more people that day than the sword.

⁹ Absalom met the servants of David. He was going on his horse, and the horse went under the many branches of a large oak tree. Absalom's hair caught in the branches of the oak. He was left hanging between heaven and earth, while the horse under him kept going. ¹⁰ When a certain man saw it, he told Joab, "I saw Absalom hanging in an oak." ¹¹ Joab said to the man, "You saw him! Why did you not kill him and let him fall to the ground? I would have given you ten pieces of silver and a belt." ¹² The man said to Joab, "Even for a thousand pieces of silver in my hand, I would not go against the king's son. For we heard the king tell you and Abishai and Ittai, 'Keep the young man Absalom safe for me.' ¹³ If I had gone against his life, there is nothing hidden from the king. And you would not have helped me." ¹⁴ Then Joab said, "I will not waste time here with you." He took three spears in his hand and threw them through Absalom's heart while he was

still alive in the oak. ¹⁵ And ten young men who carried Joab's battle-clothes gathered around and hit Absalom and killed him.

¹⁶ Then Joab sounded the horn, and all the people returned from going after Israel, for Joab stopped them. ¹⁷ They took Absalom and threw him into a deep hole among the trees, and set many stones over him. And all Israel ran away, every one to his own home. ¹⁸ While Absalom was alive, he had set up stones in his honor in the King's Valley. For he said, "I have no son to let my name be remembered." So he called the stones after his own name. And they are there to have Absalom be remembered to this day.

David Hears of Absalom's Death

¹⁹ Then Zadok's son Ahimaaz said, "Let me run and bring the king news that the Lord has saved him from those who hate him." ²⁰ But Joab said to him, "You must not carry news today, but another time. Today you should carry no news, because the king's son is dead." ²¹ Then Joab said to the Cushite, "Go and tell the king what you have seen." So the Cushite bowed to Joab and ran. ²² Zadok's son Ahimaaz said to Joab, "Whatever happens, let me run after the Cushite." Joab said, "Why would you run, my son? You would receive no reward for going." ²³ But Ahimaaz said, "Whatever happens, I will run." So Joab said to him, "Run." Then Ahimaaz ran by way of the plain and passed the Cushite.

²⁴ David was sitting between the two gates. The man who kept watch went up to the roof of the gate by the wall. He looked up and saw a man running by himself. ²⁵ The man who kept watch called and told the king. The king said, "If he is by himself, he has good news." And he came nearer and nearer. ²⁶ Then the man who kept watch saw another man running. He called to the gate-keeper and said, "See, another man is running by himself." The king said, "This one is bringing good news also." ²⁷ And the man who kept watch said, "I think the man in front runs like Ahimaaz the son of Zadok." The king said, "He is a good man, and comes with good news."

²⁸ Ahimaaz called and said to the king, "All is well." He put his face to the ground in front of the king, and said, "Thanks be to the Lord your God. He has given up the men who raised their hands against my lord the king." ²⁹ The king said, "Is it well with the young man Absalom?" And Ahimaaz answered, "When Joab sent the

king's servant, your servant, I heard noise and saw much fighting. But I did not know what it was." 30 Then the king said, "Turn aside and stand here." So he turned aside and stood still. 31 Then the Cushite came and said, "Let my lord the king receive good news. For the Lord has saved you today from all those who came against you." 32 The king said to the Cushite, "Is it well with the young man Absalom?" And the Cushite answered, "May those who hate my lord the king, all those who come to do bad things against you, be as that young man!" 33 The king filled with much sorrow. He went up to the room above the gate and cried. As he walked he said, "O my son Absalom, my son, my son Absalom! If only I had died instead of you, O Absalom, my son, my son!"

19 Then Joab was told, "See, the king is crying. He is filled with sorrow for Absalom." 2 So the happiness of winning the battle that day was changed to sorrow for all the people. For they heard that day, "The king is filled with sorrow for his son." 3 So the people were quiet as they went in secret into the city that day. They acted like people who are ashamed when they run away from a battle. 4 The king covered his face and cried out with a loud voice, "O my son Absalom, O Absalom, my son, my son!" 5 Then Joab came into the house to the king and said, "Today you have covered the faces of all your servants with shame. Today they have saved your life and the lives of your sons and daughters, your wives and the women who act as your wives. 6 But you love those who hate you, and hate those who love you. You have shown today that rulers and servants are nothing to you. For today I see that if Absalom were alive and all of us were dead, you would be pleased. 7 So now get up and go out and speak in kindness to your servants. I swear by the Lord that if you do not, for sure not a man will stay with you this night. And this will be worse for you than all the bad things that have happened to you since you were young." 8 So the king got up and sat in the gate. When they told all the people, "See, the king is sitting in the gate," then all the people came to the king.

David Returns to Jerusalem

Now every man of Israel had run to his tent. 9 And all the people in all the family groups of Israel were arguing. They said,

"The king saved us from those who hate us. He saved us from the Philistines. But now he has run from Absalom and away from the land. 10 We chose Absalom to rule over us and he has died in battle. So now why do you say nothing about bringing the king back?"

11 Then King David sent word to Zadok and Abiathar the religious leaders, saying, "Speak to the leaders of Judah. Say to them, 'Why are you the last to bring the king back to his house? I have heard from all Israel for me to return to my house. 12 You are my brothers. You are my bone and my flesh. Why should you be the last to bring back the king?' 13 And say to Amasa, 'Are you not my bone and my flesh? May God do so to me, and more also, if you will not be the captain of my army at all times instead of Joab.'" 14 He changed the hearts of all the men of Judah as if they were one man. So they sent word to the king, saying, "Return, you and all your servants." 15 So the king returned and came as far as the Jordan. Judah came to Gilgal to meet the king and bring him over the Jordan.

16 Then Gera's son Shimei, the Benjamite from Bahurim, came down in a hurry with the men of Judah to meet King David. 17 There were 1,000 men of Benjamin with him. And Ziba the servant of the family of Saul came with his fifteen sons and twenty servants. They rushed to the king at the Jordan. 18 They crossed the river to bring over those of the king's house, and to do what pleased him. Gera's son Shimei fell down in front of the king as he was about to cross the Jordan.

David Is Good to Shimei

19 He said to the king, "Let not my lord think I am guilty. Do not remember what your servant did wrong on the day when my lord the king left Jerusalem. Let not the king take it to heart. 20 For your servant knows that I have sinned. So I have come today. I am the first of all the family of Joseph to come down to meet my lord the king." 21 But Zeruiah's son Abishai answered, "Should not Shimei be put to death for this? He spoke against the Lord's chosen one." 22 But David said, "What have I to do with you, O sons of Zeruiah? Why should you be against me this day? Should any man be put to death in Israel today? For do I not know that this day I am king of Israel?" 23 The king said to Shimei, "You will not die." And the king gave him his promise.

David Is Good to Mephibosheth

24 Then Saul's grandson Mephibosheth came down to meet the king. He had not dressed his feet, trimmed the hair of his face, or washed his clothes, from the day the king left until the day he returned in peace. 25 When he came from Jerusalem to meet the king, David said to him, "Why did you not go with me, Mephibosheth?" 26 He answered, "O my lord the king, my servant lied to me. Your servant had said to him, 'Get a donkey ready for me to travel on, so I may go with the king.' Because your servant cannot walk. 27 And he has spoken against me to my lord the king. But my lord the king is like the angel of God. So do what you think is best. 28 For all those of my father's house were nothing but dead men in front of my lord the king. But you set your servant among those who ate at your own table. What right do I have to complain any more to the king?" 29 The king said to him, "Why speak any more of how things are with you? I have decided that you and Ziba should divide the land." 30 Mephibosheth said to the king, "Let him take it all, since my lord the king has come home and is safe."

David Is Good to Barzillai

31 Now Barzillai of Gilead had come down from Rogelim. He went on to the Jordan with the king, to lead him over the river. 32 Barzillai was eighty years old. He had given food to the king while he stayed at Mahanaim, for he was a very rich man. 33 The king said to Barzillai, "You cross over with me, and I will take care of you with me in Jerusalem." 34 But Barzillai said to the king, "How much longer have I to live, that I should go up with the king to Jerusalem? 35 I am now eighty years old. Can I know the difference between good and bad? Can your servant taste what I eat or what I drink? Can I hear the voice of singing men and women any more? Why should your servant be an added problem to my lord the king? 36 Your servant will only cross over the Jordan with the king. Why should the king reward me in this good way? 37 Let your servant return, that I may die in my own city near the grave of my father and mother. But here is your servant Chimham. Let him cross over with my lord the king. And do for him what is good in your eyes." 38 The king answered, "Chimham will cross over with me. And I will do for him what is pleasing to you. I will do for you whatever you ask."

39 All the people crossed over the Jordan, and the king also. Then the king kissed Barzillai and prayed that good would come to him. And Barzillai returned to his own home.

Judah and Israel Argue over the King

40 The king went on to Gilgal, and Chimham went with him. And all the people of Judah and half the people of Israel went with the king. 41 Then all the men of Israel came to the king and said to him, "Why have our brothers the men of Judah stolen you away? Why have they brought the king and those of his family over the Jordan, and all David's men with him?" 42 All the men of Judah answered the men of Israel, "Because the king is a close brother to us. Why are you angry about this? Has the king paid for our food? Has he given us any gift?" 43 But the men of Israel said to the men of Judah, "We have ten shares in the king. So we have more right to David than you. Why then did you hate us? Were we not the first to speak of bringing back our king?" But the words of the men of Judah had more anger than the words of the men of Israel.

David's Men Follow Sheba

20 A man of no worth happened to be there whose name was Sheba, the son of Bichri, a Benjamite. He sounded the horn and said, "We have no share in David! We have no share in the son of Jesse! Every man to his tents, O Israel!" 2 So all the men of Israel stopped following David, and followed Sheba the son of Bichri. But the men of Judah were not moved from following their king, from the Jordan to Jerusalem.

3 Then David came to his house at Jerusalem. The king took his ten women whom he had left to take care of the house, and had a prison soldier watch them. David gave them food, but did not go in to them. So they were shut up until the day of their death, living as women whose husbands had died.

4 Then the king said to Amasa, "Call the men of Judah to come to me within three days, and you be here yourself." 5 So Amasa went to call out the men of Judah. But he took longer than the time which had been given him. 6 David said to Abishai, "Now Bichri's son Sheba will bring us more trouble than Absalom. Take your lord's servants and go after him. Or he might

find strong cities for himself, and get away from us." 7 So Joab's men went out after him. With them went the Cherethites, the Pelethites and all the strong men. They left Jerusalem to go after Sheba the son of Bichri. 8 Amasa came to meet them at the large stone in Gibeon. Now Joab was dressed in soldier's clothing. Over his clothing was a belt with a sword in its holder tied at his side. As he walked, the sword fell out. 9 Joab said to Amasa, "Is it well with you, my brother?" And he took Amasa by the hair of his face with his right hand to kiss him. 10 But Amasa did not see the sword which was in Joab's hand. So Joab hit him in the stomach with it, and poured his inside parts out on the ground. He did not hit him again, and Amasa died.

Then Joab and his brother Abishai went after Sheba the son of Bichri. 11 Now one of Joab's young men stood by him and said, "Whoever favors Joab and whoever is for David, let him follow Joab." 12 But Amasa lay in his blood in the center of the road. When the man saw that all the people stood still, he took Amasa out of the road and into the field. And he threw a covering over him. 13 After he was taken out of the road, all the men went on and followed Joab to go after Sheba the son of Bichri.

14 Sheba passed through all the families of Israel to Abel Bethmaacah. Then all the Berites gathered together and followed him into the city. 15 And all the men who were with Joab came and gathered their armies around him in Abel Bethmaacah. They built up a hill of dirt against the wall of the city. And they were trying their best to make the wall fall down. 16 Then a wise woman called from the city, "Listen! I beg you, tell Joab to come here that I may speak with him." 17 So he came to her, and the woman said, "Are you Joab?" He answered, "I am." Then she said to him, "Listen to the words of your woman servant." And he answered, "I am listening." 18 Then she said, "In the past they used to say, 'Let them ask for words of wisdom at Abel.' And so they would stop fighting. 19 I am one of peace and faith in Israel. You want to destroy a city and a mother in Israel. Why would you swallow up the gift of the Lord?" 20 Joab answered, "Far be it from me! Far be it that I should swallow up or destroy! 21 That is not true. But a man from the hill country of Ephraim has turned against King David. His name is Sheba the son of Bichri. Give up only him, and I will leave the city." And the woman

said to Joab, "See, his head will be thrown to you over the wall." 22 Then the woman went to all the people with her plan. And they cut off the head of Sheba the son of Bichri and threw it to Joab. So he sounded the horn and they left the city, every man going to his home. Joab returned to the king at Jerusalem.

23 Now Joab was the captain of the whole army of Israel. Benaiah the son of Jehoiada was captain of the Cherethites and the Pelethites. 24 Adoram was captain of those who were made to work. Jehoshaphat the son of Ahilud wrote down the things that happened. 25 Sheva was the teacher. Zadok and Abiathar were religious leaders. 26 And Ira the Jairite was a religious leader to David also.

The Gibeonites Kill Seven of Saul's Grandsons

21 While David was king there was a time without food for three years. David went to the Lord. The Lord said, "It is because of Saul and his house of blood, for he put the Gibeonites to death." 2 So the king called the Gibeonites. (Now the Gibeonites were not of the sons of Israel, but of the people who were left of the Amorites. The sons of Israel had made an agreement with them. But Saul had wanted to kill them because he thought so much of the sons of Israel and Judah.) 3 David said to the Gibeonites, "What should I do for you? How can I pay for the sin, so you may bring good to the land of the Lord?" 4 The Gibeonites said to him, "We will take no silver or gold from Saul or his family. And it is not for us to put any man to death in Israel." David said, "I will do for you whatever you say." 5 So they said to the king, "Saul destroyed us and planned to keep us from staying in any land of Israel. 6 Let seven men from his sons be given to us. We will hang them before the Lord at Gibeon on the Lord's mountain." And the king said, "I will give them."

7 But the king kept alive Mephibosheth, the son of Saul's son Jonathan, because David had made a promise to Saul's son Jonathan before the Lord. 8 The king took the two sons of Aiah's daughter Rizpah, Armoni and Mephibosheth, whom she had born to Saul. And he took the five sons of Saul's daughter Merab, whom she had born to Adriel the son of Barzillai the Meholathite. 9 He gave them to the Gibeonites, and they hanged them on the mountain before the Lord. The seven

of them died together. They were put to death in the first days of gathering time, when the barley was ready to gather.

¹⁰ Aiah's daughter Rizpah spread cloth made from hair on the rock for herself to lie upon, from the beginning of gathering time until the rain fell from the sky upon the bodies. She would not let the birds of the sky rest on them during the day, or the animals of the field during the night. ¹¹ David was told what Aiah's daughter Rizpah, Saul's woman, had done. ¹² Then he went and took the bones of Saul and his son Jonathan from the men of Jabesh-gilead. They had stolen them from the open space in the center of Bethshan. That was where the Philistines had hanged them on the day they killed Saul in Gilboa. ¹³ David brought the bones of Saul and his son Jonathan. They gathered the bones of those who had been hanged. ¹⁴ And they buried the bones of Saul and his son Jonathan in the country of Benjamin in Zela, in the grave of Kish his father. They did all that the king told them to do. After that, God heard and answered when they prayed for the land.

¹⁵ The Philistines were at war again with Israel. David went down with his servants and they fought the Philistines. And David became tired. ¹⁶ Then Ishbi-benob wanted to kill David. He was one of the sons of the very tall and strong people. His spear weighed as much as 300 pieces of brass, and he had a new sword. ¹⁷ But Zeruiah's son Abishai helped David and killed the Philistine. Then David's men promised him, "You will not go out again with us to battle. You might put out the lamp of Israel."

¹⁸ After this there was war again with the Philistines at Gob. Then Sibbecai the Hushathite killed Saph, who was one of the sons of the very tall and strong people. ¹⁹ There was war with the Philistines again at Gob. And Elhanan the son of Jaare-oregim the Bethlehemite killed Goliath the Gittite. Goliath's spear was like the heavy piece of wood used by a cloth-maker. ²⁰ There was war at Gath again. There was a very tall man there who had six fingers on each hand and six toes on each foot, twenty-four in number. He was one of the sons of the very tall and strong people also. ²¹ When he spoke against Israel, Jonathan the son of Shimei, David's brother, killed him. ²² These four were sons of the very tall and strong people in Gath. They were killed by David and his servants.

David's Song of Praise

22 David spoke the words of this song to the Lord on the day the Lord saved him from all who hated him, and from Saul. ² He said, "The Lord is my rock, my strong-place, and the One Who sets me free. ³ He is my God, my rock, where I go to be safe. He is my covering and the horn that saves me, my strong-place where I go to be safe. You save me from being hurt. ⁴ I call upon the Lord, Who should be praised. I am saved from those who hate me.

⁵ "For the waves of death were all around me. The storm that destroys made me afraid. ⁶ The cords of the grave were around me. The nets of death came against me. ⁷ In my trouble I called upon the Lord. Yes, I cried to my God. From His house He heard my voice. My cry for help came into His ears.

⁸ "Then the earth shook. The mountains were shaking. They shook because He was angry. ⁹ Smoke went up from His nose. Fire that destroyed came from His mouth. Burnt pieces of wood were set on fire by it. ¹⁰ He tore open the heavens and came down, with darkness under His feet. ¹¹ He sat on a cherub and flew. He was seen on the wings of the wind. ¹² He made darkness around Him his tent, gathering waters, and clouds of the sky. ¹³ From the light before Him, burnt pieces of wood were set on fire. ¹⁴ "The Lord thundered from heaven. The Most High let His voice be heard. ¹⁵ He sent out arrows, and made them run. He sent lightning, and made them troubled and afraid. ¹⁶ Then the bottom of the sea was seen. The bottom of the world lost its covering, at the strong words of the Lord, at the rush of breath from His nose.

¹⁷ "He sent from above. He took me. He pulled me out of many waters. ¹⁸ He saved me from those strong ones who hated me. For they were too strong for me. ¹⁹ They came upon me in the day of my trouble. But the Lord held me up. ²⁰ He brought me into a big place. He saved me, because He was pleased with me. ²¹ "The Lord has paid me for being right with Him. He has paid me for my clean hands. ²² For I have kept the ways of the Lord. I have not acted in sin against my God. ²³ For all His Laws were in front of me, and I did not turn aside from them. ²⁴ I was without blame before Him. I kept myself from guilt. ²⁵ So the Lord has paid me for being right with Him, for being clean in His eyes.

²⁶ "With the faithful You show Yourself faithful. With the one without blame You

show Yourself without blame. 27 With the pure You show Yourself pure. But with the sinful, You show Yourself wise. 28 You save a troubled people. But Your eyes are on the proud whom You put to shame.

29 "For You are my lamp, O Lord. The Lord gives light to my darkness. 30 For by You I can run through an army. By my God I can jump over a wall. 31 As for God, His way is perfect. The Word of the Lord is proven true. He is a covering to all who go to Him to be safe.

32 "For who is God, but the Lord? Who is a Rock, except our God? 33 God is my strong-place. He has made my way safe. 34 He makes my feet like the feet of a deer. He sets me safe on high places. 35 He makes my hands ready for battle, so that my arms can use a bow of brass.

36 "You have given me the covering of Your saving power. Your help makes me strong. 37 You give me a big place for my steps. I have not fallen. 38 I went after those who hated me and destroyed them. I did not return until they were destroyed. 39 I destroyed them and cut them through, so that they did not rise. They fell under my feet. 40 For You have dressed me with strength for battle. You have put under me those who came against me. 41 You made those who fought me turn their backs to me. I destroyed those who hated me. 42 They looked, but there was no one to save them. They cried to the Lord, but He did not answer them. 43 Then I beat them as fine as the dust of the earth. I crushed and stepped on them like the mud of the streets.

44 "You have saved me from trouble with my people. You have kept me as head of the nations. People whom I have not known serve me. 45 Strangers obey me. As soon as they heard of me, they obeyed me. 46 Strangers lost their strength of heart. They came out of their secret places shaking with fear.

47 "The Lord lives. Thanks be to my Rock. May God be honored, the Rock that saves me. 48 He is the God Who punishes for me. He puts people under my rule. 49 He makes me free from those who hate me. You lift me above those who come against me. You save me from the man who wants to hurt me. 50 So I will give thanks to You among the nations, O Lord. I will sing praises to Your name. 51 With great power He saves His king. He shows loving-kindness to His chosen one, to David and his children forever."

David's Last Words

23 Now these are the last words of David. David the son of Jesse, the man who was raised on high, the chosen one of the God of Jacob, the sweet song writer of Israel, says, 2 "The Spirit of the Lord spoke by me. His Word was on my tongue. 3 The God of Israel has spoken. The Rock of Israel said to me, 'When one is right and good in ruling over men, ruling in the fear of God, 4 he shines on them like the morning light. He is like the sunshine on a morning without clouds. He is like rain that makes the new grass grow out of the earth through sunshine after rain.' 5 In truth, does not my house stand right with God? For He has made an agreement with me that lasts forever. It is planned right in all things, and sure. For will He not make all my help and my desire grow? 6 But those of no worth are all like thorns that are thrown away, because they cannot be taken with the hand. 7 The man who touches them must be covered with iron and have a spear. All of them will be burned up with fire as they sit."

David's Men of War

8 These are the names of David's men of war. There was Josheb-basshebeth a Tahchemonite, head of the three. He was called Adino the Eznite, because he had killed 800 men at one time.

9 Next to him among the three strong men was Eleazar the son of Dodo the Ahohite. He was with David when they spoke against the Philistines who were gathered there for battle, and the men of Israel had left. 10 Eleazar got up and killed the Philistines until his hand was tired from holding the sword. The Lord saved many of His people that day. The men returned after him only to take what had belonged to the dead.

11 Next to him was Shammah the son of Agee a Hararite. The Philistines were gathered together at Lehi, where there was a piece of ground full of lentil plants. The people ran from the Philistines. 12 But Shammah stood in the center of the piece of ground and fought for it. He killed the Philistines. The Lord saved many of His people that day.

13 Then three of the thirty leaders went down to David during the gathering time to the cave of Adullam. The Philistine army was staying in the valley of Rephaim. 14 David was in the strong-place, while the Philistine soldiers were in Bethlehem.

15 David had a desire and said, "If only someone would give me water to drink from the well by the gate of Bethlehem!" 16 So the three strong men broke through the Philistine army and took water from the well by the gate of Bethlehem. They brought it to David. But David would not drink it. He poured it out to the Lord, 17 and said, "O Lord, far be it from me to do this. Should I drink the blood of the men who went and put their lives in danger?" So he would not drink it. The three strong men did these things.

18 Now Abishai the brother of Joab, son of Zeruiah, was head of the thirty. He fought with his spear against 300 men and killed them. His name was respected as well as the three. 19 He was the most honored of the thirty. So he became their captain. But he was not as strong as the three.

20 Benaiah the son of Jehoiada was a man of Kabzeel with strength of heart. He had done powerful things. He killed the two sons of Ariel of Moab. And he went down and killed a lion in a hole while the snow was falling. 21 He killed an Egyptian, an important man. The Egyptian had a spear in his hand. But Benaiah went down to him with a heavy stick and took the spear from the Egyptian's hand. Then he killed him with his own spear. 22 Benaiah the son of Jehoiada did these things. His name was respected as well as the three strong men. 23 He was honored among the thirty. But he was not as strong as the three. David made him captain of the soldiers who kept him from danger.

24 Joab's brother Asahel was among the thirty. Then there was Elhanan the son of Dodo of Bethlehem, 25 Shammah the Harodite, Elika the Harodite, 26 Helez the Paltite, Ira the son of Ikkesh the Tekoite, 27 Abiezer the Anathothite, and Mebunnai the Hushathite. 28 There was Zalmon the Ahohite, Maharai the Netophathite, 29 Heleb the son of Baanah the Netophathite, and Ittai the son of Ribai of Gibeah of the sons of Benjamin. 30 There was Benaiah a Pirathonite, Hiddai of the rivers of Gaash, 31 Abialbon the Arbathite, Azmaveth the Barhumite, 32 Eliahba the Shaalbonite, the sons of Jashen, and Jonathan. 33 There was Shammah the Hararite, Ahiam the son of Sharar the Ararite, 34 Eliphelet the son of Ahasbai of Maacah, Eliam the son of Ahithophel of Gilo, 35 Hezro the Carmelite, and Paarai the Arbite. 36 There was Igal the son of Nathan of Zobah, Bani the Gadite, 37 Zelek the Ammonite, Naharai the Beerothite, the one who carried the battle-clothes of Joab the son of Zeruiah. 38 And there was Ira the Ithrite, Gareb the Ithrite, 39 and Uriah the Hittite. There were thirty-seven in all.

David Numbers Israel and Judah

24 Again the anger of the Lord burned against Israel. He moved David against them, saying, "Go, number Israel and Judah." 2 So the king said to Joab the captain of the army who was with him, "Go through all the families of Israel, from Dan to Beersheba. Number the people, so I may know how many there are." 3 But Joab said to the king, "May the Lord your God add to the people a hundred times as many as they are. And may it be while the eyes of my lord the king still see. But why does my lord the king find this thing pleasing?" 4 But the king's word was stronger than Joab and the captains of the army. So Joab and the army leaders went out from the king to number the people of Israel. 5 They crossed the Jordan and stopped at Aroer, on the south side of the city in the center of the valley of Gad. And they went on to Jazer. 6 Then they came to Gilead, and to the land of Tahtimhodshi. They came to Dan-jaan and around to Sidon. 7 They came to the strong-place of Tyre and to all the cities of the Hivites and the Canaanites. And they went out to the south of Judah, to Beersheba. 8 When they had gone through the whole land, they came to Jerusalem. They had traveled nine months and twenty days. 9 And Joab gave the number of the people to the king. There were 800,000 strong men in Israel who used the sword, and 500,000 men of Judah.

David's Sin

10 David's heart troubled him after he had numbered the people. So he said to the Lord, "I have sinned. But now I beg you, O Lord. Take away the sin of Your servant, for I have acted like a fool." 11 When David got up in the morning, the word of the Lord came to Gad, the one who spoke for God to David. The Lord said, 12 "Go and tell David, 'This is what the Lord says: "I give you three things to choose from. Choose one of them, that I may do it to you." '" 13 So Gad came to David and told him, and said, "Will you have seven years without food in your land? Or will you run from those who hate you for three months, while they come after you? Or

will there be disease in your land for three days? Now think about it. Decide what answer I should return to Him Who sent me." ¹⁴ David said to Gad, "I am in much trouble. Let us fall into the hand of the Lord, for His loving-kindness is great. But do not let me fall into the hand of man."

¹⁵ So the Lord sent a disease upon Israel from the morning until the time given. And 70,000 men died, from Dan to Beersheba. ¹⁶ The angel put out his hand to destroy Jerusalem. But the Lord had pity on them because of their trouble. He said to the angel who destroyed the people, "It is enough! Do no more!" The angel of the Lord was by the grain-floor of Araunah the Jebusite. ¹⁷ When David saw the angel who was killing the people, he said to the Lord, "See, it is I who have sinned. It is I who have done wrong. But these sheep, what have they done? I beg You, let Your hand be against me and my father's family."

David Builds an Altar

¹⁸ Then Gad came to David and said, "Go up and build an altar to the Lord on the grain-floor of Araunah the Jebusite." ¹⁹ So David went up at Gad's word, just as the Lord had told him. ²⁰ Araunah looked, and saw the king and his servants crossing over toward him. And he went out and put his face to the ground in front of the king. ²¹ Araunah said, "Why has my lord the king come to his servant?" David answered, "To buy the grain-floor from you, to build an altar to the Lord. Then the disease may be kept away from the people." ²² Araunah said to David, "Let my lord the king take whatever is good in his eyes, and make a gift of it. Look, there are the bulls for the burnt gift. The tools for cleaning the grain, and the cross-pieces the bulls wear to pull loads, can be used for the wood. ²³ Araunah gives all this to the king." And Araunah said, "May the Lord your God be pleased with your gift." ²⁴ But the king said to Araunah, "No, I will buy it from you for a price. I will not give burnt gifts to the Lord my God which I do not pay for." So David bought the grain-floor and the bulls for fifty pieces of silver. ²⁵ And David built an altar there to the Lord. He gave burnt gifts and peace gifts. So the Lord listened to the prayers for the land, and stopped the disease in Israel.

1 KINGS

Adonijah Makes Himself King

1 Now King David was old. He had lived many years. They covered him with clothes, but he could not keep warm. ² So his servants said to him, "Let a young woman who has never had a man be found for my lord the king. Let her help the king and become his nurse. And let her lie in your arms, that my lord the king may be warm." ³ So they looked through all the land of Israel for a beautiful girl, and found Abishag the Shunammite. And they brought her to the king. ⁴ The girl was very beautiful. She became the king's nurse and helped him. But the king did not have sex with her.

⁵ Now Haggith's son Adonijah honored himself, saying, "I will be king." So he made war-wagons and horsemen ready for himself, with fifty men to run in front of him. ⁶ His father had never troubled him at any time by asking, "Why have you done this?" He was a very good-looking man also, and was born next after Absalom. ⁷ He spoke with Joab the son of Zeruiah and with Abiathar the religious leader. And they followed Adonijah and helped him. ⁸ But Zadok the religious leader, Benaiah the son of Jehoiada, Nathan the man of God, Shimei, Rei, and David's strong men, were not with Adonijah.

⁹ Adonijah killed sheep and cattle and fat animals by the stone of Zoheleth, beside En-rogel. He asked all his brothers, the king's sons and all the king's men of Judah to come. ¹⁰ But he did not ask Nathan the man of God, Benaiah, the strong men or his brother Solomon to come.

¹¹ Then Nathan said to Solomon's mother Bathsheba, "Have you not heard that Adonijah the son of Haggith has become king, and our lord David does not know it? ¹² So now come, let me give you words of wisdom and save your life and the life of your son Solomon. ¹³ Go to King David and say to him, 'My lord, O king, have you not promised your woman servant, saying, "For sure your son Solomon will be king after me. He will sit on my throne"? Why then has Adonijah become king?' ¹⁴ While you are still there speaking with the king, I will come in after you and tell you your words are true."

15 So Bathsheba went to the king in his room. The king was very old, and Abishag the Shunammite was helping him. 16 Bathsheba put her face to the ground in front of the king. And the king said, "What do you wish?" 17 She said to him, "My lord, you promised your woman servant by the Lord your God, saying, 'For sure your son Solomon will be king after me. He will sit on my throne.' 18 Now, see, Adonijah is king. And my lord the king, you do not know it. 19 He has killed many cattle and sheep and fat animals. He has asked all the king's sons and Abiathar the religious leader and Joab the captain of the army to come. But he has not asked your servant Solomon to come. 20 Now, my lord the king, the eyes of all Israel are on you. They are waiting for you to tell them who should sit on the throne of my lord the king after him. 21 Or else as soon as my lord the king is dead, I and my son Solomon will be thought of as wrong-doers."

22 While she was still speaking with the king, Nathan the man of God came in. 23 They told the king, "Here is Nathan who speaks for God." When Nathan came in front of the king, he put his face to the ground. 24 Then Nathan said, "My lord the king, have you said, 'Adonijah will be king after me, and he will sit on my throne'? 25 For he has gone down today and has killed many cattle and sheep and fat animals. He has asked all the king's sons and the captains of the army and Abiathar the religious leader to come. They are eating and drinking with him, and are saying, 'Long live King Adonijah!' 26 But he has not asked me your servant, Zadok the religious leader, Benaiah the son of Jehoiada, or your servant Solomon, to come. 27 Has this been done by my lord the king? Have you not shown your servants who should sit on the throne of my lord the king after him?"

David Makes Solomon King

28 King David said, "Call Bathsheba to me." And she came and stood in front of the king. 29 The king made a promise and said, "As the Lord lives, Who has saved me from all trouble, 30 I promised you by the Lord the God of Israel, saying, 'Your son Solomon will be king after me. He will sit on my throne in my place.' And I will even do so this day." 31 Bathsheba put her face to the ground in front of the king and said, "May my lord King David live forever."

32 Then King David said, "Call to me Zadok the religious leader, Nathan the man of God, and Benaiah the son of Jehoiada." And they came to the king. 33 The king said to them, "Take the servants of your lord with you. Have my son Solomon go on my own horse. And bring him down to Gihon. 34 Let Zadok the religious leader and Nathan the man of God set him apart there as king over Israel. Sound the horn and say, 'Long live King Solomon!' 35 Then come up after him. He will come and sit on my throne and be king in my place. For I have chosen him to be ruler over Israel and Judah." 36 Benaiah the son of Jehoiada answered the king, "Let it be so! May the Lord, the God of my lord the king, say so! 37 May the Lord be with Solomon as He has been with my lord the king. May He make his throne greater than the throne of my lord King David!"

38 So Zadok the religious leader, Nathan the man of God, Benaiah the son of Jehoiada, the Cherethites, and the Pelethites went down to Gihon. And they brought Solomon with them, on King David's horse. 39 There Zadok the religious leader took the horn of oil from the tent and poured it on Solomon. Then they sounded the horn and all the people said, "Long live King Solomon!" 40 And all the people went up after him. They were playing music and were filled with joy. The earth shook with all the noise.

41 Adonijah and all who had been asked to be with him heard it as they finished eating. When Joab heard the sound of the horn, he said, "Why is there such a noise in the city?" 42 While he was still speaking, Jonathan the son of Abiathar the religious leader came. Adonijah said, "Come in, for you are a man to be trusted, and bring good news." 43 But Jonathan said to Adonijah, "No! Our lord King David has made Solomon king. 44 The king has sent with him Zadok the religious leader, Nathan the man of God, Benaiah the son of Jehoiada, the Cherethites and the Pelethites. And they have made him travel on the king's horse. 45 Zadok the religious leader and Nathan the man of God have set him apart as king in Gihon. They have come up from there filled with joy, so there is much noise in the city. This is the noise you have heard. 46 Solomon sits upon the throne of the king. 47 What is more, the king's servants came to give honor to our lord King David, saying, 'May your God make the name of Solomon better than your name and his throne greater than your throne!' And the king put his face down upon the

bed. 48 The king said, 'Thanks be to the Lord, the God of Israel. He has given one to sit on my throne today while my own eyes see it.' "

49 Then all those with Adonijah were filled with fear. Each of them got up and went his own way. 50 And Adonijah was afraid of Solomon. He got up and went and took hold of the horns of the altar. 51 Solomon was told, "See, Adonijah is afraid of King Solomon. See, he has taken hold of the horns of the altar, saying, 'Let King Solomon promise me today that he will not put his servant to death with the sword.' " 52 Solomon said, "If he will be a man of worth, not one of his hairs will fall to the ground. But if he is found to be bad, he will die." 53 So King Solomon sent men to bring him down from the altar. Adonijah came and put his face to the ground in front of King Solomon. And Solomon said to him, "Go to your house."

David's Last Words to Solomon

2 When David's time to die was near, he told his son Solomon, 2 "I am going the way of all the earth. So be strong. Show yourself to be a man. 3 Do what the Lord your God tells you. Walk in His ways. Keep all His Laws and His Word, by what is written in the Law of Moses. Then you will do well in all that you do and in every place you go. 4 Then the Lord will keep His promise to me. He has said to me, 'Your sons must be careful of their way, to walk before Me in truth with all their heart and soul. If they do, you will never be without a man on the throne of Israel.' 5 Now you know what Zeruiah's son Joab did to me. You know what he did to the two captains of the armies of Israel. He killed Abner the son of Ner, and Amasa the son of Jether in the time of peace as if it were in the time of war. He put the blood of war on his belt and on the shoes of his feet. 6 So act with wisdom. Do not let his gray hair go down to the grave in peace. 7 But show kindness to the sons of Barzillai the Gileadite. Let them be among those who eat at your table. For they helped me when I ran from your brother Absalom. 8 See, there is with you Shimei the son of Gera the Benjamite, of Bahurim. It was he who spoke bad words against me on the day I went to Mahanaim. But when he came down to me at the Jordan, I promised him by the Lord, saying, 'I will not put you to death with the sword.' 9 So do not let him go without being punished. For you are a

wise man. You will know what you should do to him. Bring his gray hair down to the grave with blood."

The Death of David

10 Then David died and was buried in the city of David. 11 He had ruled over Israel forty years. Seven years he ruled in Hebron. And thirty-three years he ruled in Jerusalem. 12 Solomon sat on the throne of his father David and things went well for the nation.

Solomon Has Adonijah Killed

13 Now Adonijah the son of Haggith came to Solomon's mother Bathsheba. She said, "Do you come in peace?" And he said, "Yes, in peace." 14 Then he said, "I have something to say to you." And she said, "Speak." 15 So he said, "You know that the nation was mine. All Israel thought I would be king. But the nation has become my brother's, for it was his from the Lord. 16 Now I have one thing to ask of you. Do not say no to me." And she said to him, "Speak." 17 He said, "I beg you, speak to Solomon the king. For he will not say no to you. Ask him to give me Abishag the Shunammite as a wife." 18 Bathsheba said, "Very well. I will speak to the king for you."

19 So Bathsheba went to speak to King Solomon for Adonijah. The king stood up to meet her, bowed in front of her, then sat on his throne. He had a seat brought in for the king's mother, and she sat on his right. 20 She said, "I am asking you for one small thing. Do not say no to me." And the king said to her, "Ask, my mother. I will not say no to you." 21 So she said, "Let Abishag the Shunammite be given to your brother Adonijah as his wife." 22 King Solomon answered his mother, "Why are you asking me to give Abishag the Shunammite to Adonijah? Ask me to give him the nation also! For he is my older brother. And Abiathar the religious leader and Joab the son of Zeruiah are on his side!" 23 Then King Solomon swore by the Lord, saying, "May God do so to me and more, if Adonijah has not asked for this against his own life. 24 The Lord has given me my place on the throne of my father David. He has made me a house as He promised. And as the Lord lives, for sure Adonijah will be put to death today." 25 So King Solomon sent Benaiah the son of Jehoiada, and he went to Adonijah and killed him.

Abiathar Sent Away and Joab Is Killed

26 Then the king said to Abiathar the religious leader, "Go to your own fields at Anathoth, for you should be put to death. But I will not have you killed at this time. Because you carried the special box of the Lord God in front of my father David. And you shared in all of my father's suffering." 27 So Solomon stopped Abiathar from being religious leader for the Lord any longer. This was done to keep the word of the Lord, which God had spoken about the family of Eli in Shiloh.

28 Now the news came to Joab. For Joab had followed Adonijah, but he had not followed Absalom. And Joab ran to the tent of the Lord and took hold of the horns of the altar. 29 King Solomon was told that Joab had run to the tent of the Lord, and was beside the altar. Then Solomon sent Benaiah the son of Jehoiada, saying, "Go and kill him." 30 Benaiah came to the tent of the Lord. He said to Joab, "The king says to come out." But Joab said, "No! I will die here." So Benaiah returned to the king and said, "This is what Joab said. This is how he answered me." 31 The king said to him, "Do as he has said. Kill him and bury him. In this way you will take away from me and my father's house the blood of those killed by Joab without a reason. 32 The Lord will return Joab's acts of killing upon his own head. Because Joab killed two men who were right and good and better than he. He killed them with the sword while my father David did not know it. He killed Abner the son of Ner, captain of the army of Israel, and Amasa the son of Jether, captain of the army of Judah. 33 So their blood will be on the head of Joab and on the head of his children forever. But may there be peace from the Lord forever to David and his children, his house and his throne." 34 Then Benaiah the son of Jehoiada went up and killed Joab. He was buried at his own house in the desert. 35 The king put Benaiah the son of Jehoiada over the army in Joab's place. And the king put Zadok the religious leader in the place of Abiathar.

The Death of Shimei

36 Then the king sent for Shimei and said to him, "Build a house for yourself in Jerusalem and live there. Do not leave there. 37 For on the day you go out and cross the river Kidron, you will know for sure that you will die. Your blood will be on your own head." 38 Shimei said to the king, "What you say is good. Your servant will do as my lord the king has said." So Shimei lived in Jerusalem many days.

39 But at the end of three years, two of Shimei's servants ran away to Achish the son of Maacah, king of Gath. Shimei was told, "See, your servants are in Gath." 40 Then Shimei got up and made his donkey ready to travel. And he went to Achish in Gath to look for his servants. Shimei went and brought his servants from Gath. 41 Solomon was told that Shimei had gone from Jerusalem to Gath and had returned. 42 So the king sent for Shimei and said to him, "Did I not make you promise by the Lord and tell you of danger, saying, 'You will know for sure that on the day you leave and go anywhere, you will die'? And you said to me, 'What you have said is good.' 43 Then why have you not kept the promise of the Lord? Why have you not done what I told you?" 44 And the king said to Shimei, "You know in your heart all the bad things you did to my father David. So the Lord will return your sin upon your own head. 45 But good will come to King Solomon. The throne of David will keep its place before the Lord forever." 46 So the king told Benaiah the son of Jehoiada, and he went out and killed Shimei. The nation was put under the rule of Solomon.

Solomon Asks for Wisdom

3 Then Solomon made a marriage agreement with Pharaoh the king of Egypt. He took Pharaoh's daughter and brought her to the city of David. She stayed there until he had finished building his own house, and the house of the Lord, and the wall around Jerusalem. 2 The people were still giving their different gifts on altars, because no house had yet been built for the name of the Lord.

3 Now Solomon loved the Lord. He walked in the Laws of his father David. But he gave gifts and burned special perfume on different altars. 4 The king went to give a gift on the altar in worship at Gibeon, for that was where the most important altar was. Solomon gave a thousand burnt gifts on that altar. 5 The Lord came to Solomon in a special dream in Gibeon during the night. God said, "Ask what you wish Me to give you." 6 Then Solomon said, "You have shown great loving-kindness to Your servant David my father because he was faithful and right and good and pure in heart before You. And You have kept for him this great and lasting love. You have

given him a son to sit on his throne this day. ⁷ Now, O Lord my God, You have made Your servant king in place of my father David. But I am only a little child. I do not know how to start or finish. ⁸ Your servant is among Your people which You have chosen. They are many people. There are too many people to number. ⁹ So give Your servant an understanding heart to judge Your people and know the difference between good and bad. For who is able to judge Your many people?"

¹⁰ It pleased the Lord that Solomon had asked this. ¹¹ God said to him, "You have asked this, and have not asked for a long life for yourself. You have not asked for riches, or for the life of those who hate you. But you have asked for understanding to know what is right. Because you have asked this, ¹² I have done what you said. See, I have given you a wise and understanding heart. No one has been like you before, and there will be no one like you in the future. ¹³ I give you what you have not asked, also. I give you both riches and honor. So there will be no king like you all your days. ¹⁴ And if you walk in My ways and keep My Laws and Word as your father David did, I will allow you to live a long time."

¹⁵ Solomon awoke, and saw it was a dream. He came to Jerusalem and stood before the Lord's special box of the agreement. There he gave burnt gifts and peace gifts, and made a special supper for all his servants.

Solomon's Wisdom

¹⁶ Then two women who sold the use of their bodies came to the king and stood in front of him. ¹⁷ One of the women said, "O my lord, this woman and I live in the same house. And I gave birth to a child while she was in the house. ¹⁸ On the third day after I gave birth, this woman gave birth to a child also. And we were alone. There was no one else with us in the house. There were only the two of us. ¹⁹ This woman's son died during the night, because she lay on him. ²⁰ So she got up in the night and took my son from my side while I was asleep. She laid him in her arms, and her dead son in my arms. ²¹ When I got up in the morning to nurse my son, I saw that he was dead. But when I came nearer and looked, I saw that he was not my son who was born to me." ²² Then the other woman said, "No! The living son is my son, and the dead one is your son." But the first woman

said, "No! The dead one is your son and the living one is my son." They spoke this way in front of the king.

²³ Then the king said, "The one says, 'This is my son who is living, and your son is the dead one.' The other says, 'No! Your son is the dead one. My son is the living one.' " ²⁴ And the king said, "Bring me a sword." So they brought a sword to the king. ²⁵ And the king said, "Divide the living child in two. Give half to the one woman and half to the other." ²⁶ Then the mother of the living child had much pity for her son and said to the king, "O, my lord, give her the living child. Do not kill him." But the other woman said, "He will not be mine or yours. Divide him." ²⁷ Then the king answered and said, "Give the first woman the living child. Do not kill him. She is his mother." ²⁸ When all Israel heard how the king had decided, they were afraid of him. For they saw that the wisdom of God was in him, to do what is right and fair.

Solomon's Leaders

4 Now King Solomon was the king of all Israel. ² These were the king's men. Azariah the son of Zadok was the religious leader. ³ Shisha's sons Elihoreph and Ahijah were the heads of meetings. Jehoshaphat the son of Ahilud was the one who wrote down the things of the nation. ⁴ Benaiah the son of Jehoiada was captain of the army. Zadok and Abiathar were religious leaders. ⁵ Azariah the son of Nathan was over the leaders. Zabud the son of Nathan was a religious leader and the king's friend. ⁶ Ahishar was head of the king's house. And Adoniram the son of Abda was head of the men who were made to work.

⁷ Solomon had twelve men over all Israel, who brought food for the king and those of his house. Each man had to bring food for one month in the year. ⁸ These were their names. There was Ben-hur, in the hill country of Ephraim, ⁹ and Ben-deker in Makaz. There were Shaalbim, Beth-shemesh, Elonbeth-hanan, ¹⁰ Ben-hesed in Arubboth (Socoh and all the land of Hepher belonged to him), ¹¹ and Ben-abinadab in all Naphath-Dor (Solomon's daughter Taphath was his wife). ¹² There was Baana the son of Ahilud, in Taanach and Megiddo and all Beth-shean which is beside Zarethan below Jezreel, from Beth-shean to Abel-meholah as far as the other side of Jokmeam. ¹³ There

was Bengeber in Ramoth-gilead. (The towns of Manasseh's son Jair which are in Gilead were his. And he had the land of Argob in Bashan, where there were sixty big cities with walls and locks of brass.) **14** There was Ahinadab the son of Iddo in Mahanaim, **15** Ahimaaz in Naphtali (who married Solomon's daughter Basemath), **16** and Baana the son of Hushai in Asher and Bealoth. **17** And there was Jehoshaphat the son of Paruah in Issachar, **18** Shimei the son of Ela in Benjamin, **19** and Geber the son of Uri in the land of Gilead, the country of Sihon king of the Amorites and of Og king of Bashan. He was the only leader in the land.

Solomon's Riches

20 There were many people in Judah and Israel, as much as the sand beside the sea. They were eating and drinking and full of joy. **21** Solomon ruled over all the nations from the Euphrates River to the land of the Philistines and to the land of Egypt. They brought taxes and worked for Solomon all the days of his life. **22** The food brought to Solomon for one day was 300 baskets of fine flour, 600 baskets of seeds, **23** ten fat bulls, twenty grass-fed bulls, 100 sheep, and deer, gazelles, roebucks and fat birds. **24** Solomon ruled over everything west of the Euphrates River, from Tiphsah to Gaza. He ruled over all the kings west of the Euphrates. And he had peace around him on all sides. **25** So Judah and Israel were safe. Every man was safe under his vine and fig tree, from Dan to Beersheba, all the days of Solomon. **26** Solomon had 40,000 rooms for his war-wagon horses, and 12,000 horsemen. **27** Those leaders brought food for King Solomon and all who came to his table, each during his month. They made sure nothing was missing. **28** They brought barley and straw for the fast horses and the war-wagon horses, where it was needed. Each man did the work he had been given to do.

29 God gave Solomon wisdom and much understanding and learning, as much as the sand beside the sea. **30** Solomon's wisdom was greater than the wisdom of all the people of the east and all the wisdom of Egypt. **31** He was wiser than all men, than Ethan the Ezrahite, Heman, Calcol, Darda, and the sons of Mahol. His name was known in all the nations around him. **32** He spoke 3,000 wise sayings and wrote 1,005 songs. **33** He spoke of trees, from the cedar in Lebanon to the hyssop that grows on the wall. He spoke of animals, birds, things that moved upon the ground, and fish. **34** Men came from all nations to hear the wisdom of Solomon. They came from all the kings of the earth who had heard of his wisdom.

Solomon Gets Ready to Build the House of God

5 Now Hiram the king of Tyre sent his servants to Solomon, when he heard that they had set him apart to be king in place of his father. Hiram had always loved David. **2** Then Solomon sent word to Hiram, saying, **3** "You know that my father David was not able to build a house for the name of the Lord his God because of the wars all around him. The Lord had not yet put those who hated him under his feet. **4** But now the Lord my God has given me rest on every side. There is no trouble or anything bad happening. **5** So I plan to build a house for the name of the Lord my God. Because the Lord said to my father David, 'I will set your son on your throne in your place. He will build the house for My name.' **6** So tell them to cut cedar trees of Lebanon for me. My servants will join yours. And I will give you whatever you say to pay your servants. For you know that there is no one among us who knows how to cut trees like the Sidonians."

7 When Hiram heard the words of Solomon, he was filled with joy and said, "Thanks be to the Lord today. He has given to David a wise son to rule this great people." **8** Hiram sent word to Solomon, saying, "I have heard the news you have sent me. I will do what you want with the cedar and cypress trees. **9** My servants will bring them down from Lebanon to the sea. I will make them ready to go on the sea to the place you choose. I will have them broken up there, and you can carry them away. Then you will do what I wish by giving food to those of my house." **10** So Hiram gave Solomon as much as he wanted of the cedar and cypress trees. **11** Then Solomon gave Hiram 200,000 baskets of grain as food for those of his house, and 200 jars of beaten oil. Solomon gave this to Hiram each year. **12** And the Lord gave wisdom to Solomon, just as He promised him. There was peace between Hiram and Solomon, and they made an agreement.

13 Now King Solomon made men work for him from all Israel. There were 30,000 men made to work for him. **14** He sent them to Lebanon, 10,000 men each month. They were in Lebanon one month and at home two months. Adoniram ruled those who were made to work. 15 Now Solomon had 70,000 men to carry loads, and 80,000 stone cutters in the mountains. 16 And he had 3,300 men who were leaders of the work, and who ruled over the people doing the work. 17 Then as the king told them, they cut out large stones of much worth for the house of God to be built on. 18 Solomon's builders and Hiram's builders and the Gebalites cut them. They made the wood and the stones ready to build the house.

Solomon Builds the House of God

6 In the 480th year after the people of Israel came out of the land of Egypt, in the fourth year of Solomon's rule over Israel, in the month of Ziv, the second month, he began to build the house of the Lord. 2 The house which King Solomon built for the Lord was as long as thirty long steps, as wide as ten long steps, and eight times taller than a man. 3 All along the front of the House of God was a porch ten long steps long and five long steps wide. It was as long as the house was wide. 4 He made windows for the house with beautiful cross-pieces. 5 He made a building of rooms against the outer walls of three sides of the house. These rooms were three floors high. 6 The bottom floor was as wide as three steps. The second floor was as wide as three long steps. And the third floor was as wide as four steps. For around the outside of the house he made places for the large wood cross-pieces to rest on. That way they would not need to be put into holes in the walls of the house. 7 The house was built of stone that was cut at the place where it was taken from the ground. There was no noise of a hammer or an ax or any iron object heard in the house while it was being built. 8 The door for the first floor room was on the right side of the house. They would go up steps to the second floor, and from the second to the third. 9 So he built the house and finished it. And he made the roof of the house of large pieces of cedar wood. 10 He built the three floors against the outside wall of the house. Each one was as high as a man could raise his hand. They were joined to the house with big pieces of cedar wood.

11 Now the word of the Lord came to Solomon, saying, 12 "If you obey My Laws and keep My Word, then I will keep My promise with you, which I spoke to your father David about this house you are building. 13 I will live among the sons of Israel. And I will not leave My people Israel alone."

14 So Solomon built the house and finished it. 15 He built the walls of the house on the inside with pieces of cedar wood. He put wood over the inside walls from the floor of the house to the roof. And he put pieces of cypress wood over the floor of the house. 16 An inside room called the most holy place was built in the back part of the house with pieces of cedar wood, from the floor to the roof and as wide as ten long steps. 17 The rest of the house, the center room in front of the most holy place, was as long as twenty long steps. 18 There was cedar on the house within, cut to look like gourds and open flowers. It was all cedar. No stone was seen. 19 Then he built the most holy place inside the house, in which to put the special box of the agreement. 20 The most holy place was as long as ten long steps, as wide as ten long steps, and more than five times taller than a man. He covered it with pure gold. And he covered the altar with cedar. 21 Solomon covered the inside of the house with pure gold. He crossed the front of the most holy place with chains of gold, and he covered it with gold. 22 He covered the whole house with gold, until all the house was finished. And he covered the whole altar by the most holy place with gold.

23 In the most holy place he made two cherubim of olive wood. Each one was almost three times taller than a man. 24 One wing of the cherub was as long as three steps. And the other wing of the cherub was as long as three steps. It was as far as five long steps from the end of one wing to the end of the other wing. 25 It was as much as five long steps between the ends of the wings of the other cherub also. Both the cherubim were the same height, length and width, and they looked alike. 26 Each of the cherubim was almost three times taller than a man. 27 He put the cherubim in the most holy place of the house. The wings of the cherubim were spread out. The wing of the one cherub was touching the one wall, and the wing of the other cherub was touching the other wall. So their wings were touching each other in the center of the house. 28 He covered the cherubim with gold.

29 Then he cut pictures in all the walls

around the house to look like cherubim, palm trees and open flowers, in the center room and the most holy place. 30 He covered the floor of the house with gold, in the center room and the most holy place. 31 He made doors of olive wood for the most holy place. The top and sides of the door had five sides. 32 He cut pictures in the two doors of olive wood, to look like cherubim, palm trees and open flowers, and covered them with gold. He spread the gold on the cherubim and on the palm trees. 33 For the doorway of the center room he made four-sided side pieces of olive wood 34 and two doors of cypress wood. Each door had two moving parts. 35 On them he cut pictures of cherubim, palm trees and open flowers. And he covered the pictures with an even covering of gold. 36 He built the inside place with three rows of cut stone and one row of large pieces of cedar wood.

37 In the fourth year the base of the house was laid in the month of Ziv. 38 In the eleventh year, in the month of Bul, the eighth month, all the parts of the house were finished just as all the plans had been made. Solomon took seven years to build it.

Solomon's House

7 Solomon was building his own house thirteen years, and he finished all of it. 2 He built the house of the trees of Lebanon. It was as long as fifty long steps, as wide as twenty-five long steps, and eight times taller than a man. It was built on four rows of cedar pillars, and large pieces of cedar wood lying on top of the pillars. 3 And it was covered with cedar above the rooms that were on the forty-five pillars, fifteen in each row. 4 There were three rows of special windows on one side, and three rows of windows on the other side. 5 All the doors and windows were as high as they were wide. And there were three rows of windows on each side. 6 Then he made a room for walking through of large pillars. It was as long as twenty-five long steps, and as wide as fifteen long steps. There was a porch in front with pillars, and an overhead covering in front of them. 7 He made a room for the throne, the room for judging. It was where he would decide between right and wrong. It was covered with cedar from the floor to the roof. 8 His own house where he was to live, in the place behind the throne room, was built the same way. Solomon made a house like

this room for Pharaoh's daughter also, whom he had married.

9 All these were made with stones of much worth, each one cut to be put into place. They were cut with saws, inside and outside, from the very base to the top of the roof, and from the outside to the largest room. 10 The base of the building was made with large stones of much worth. The stones were as long as five long steps, and four long steps. 11 Above this were stones of much worth, cut to go well into place, and cedar. 12 The largest room had three rows of cut stone around it, and a row of cedar pieces. The same was around the open space in the house of the Lord, and the porch of the house.

Hiram—the Able Workman

13 Now King Solomon brought Hiram from Tyre. 14 Hiram was the son of a woman whose husband had died, from the family of Naphtali. His father was a man of Tyre, who worked with brass. He was filled with wisdom and understanding and much learning for doing any work with brass. So he came to King Solomon, and did all his work.

The Two Brass Pillars

15 He made the two pillars of brass. One of them was five times taller than a man. And the length around each of them was as far as six long steps. 16 He made two top pieces of melted brass to set on the tops of the pillars. One piece to go on top was as tall as a man can raise his hand. And the other piece to go on top was as tall as a man can raise his hand. 17 He made nets of network and turned strings of chain-work for the pieces on top of the pillars. There were seven for one top piece, and seven for the other. 18 So Hiram made the pillars. There were two rows of pomegranates around each network, to cover the top pieces. 19 Now the top pieces on the pillars of the porch were made to look like lily flowers, as tall as a man. 20 The top pieces were upon the two pillars, and above the round part beside the network. There were 200 pomegranates in rows around both top pieces. 21 He set up the pillars at the porch of the house. He set up the right pillar and called it Jachin. And he set up the left pillar and called it Boaz. 22 The top pieces on the pillars were made to look like lily flowers. So the work of the pillars was finished.

The Brass Pool

23 Now he made a large brass water pool. It was round, and as wide as five long steps. It was as tall as a man can raise his hand. And the length around it was as far as fifteen long steps. 24 Gourds went around the top of the pool. There were ten of them for every cubit. The gourds were in two rows, and made right in with the pool. 25 The pool stood on the backs of twelve bulls made of brass. Three looked to the north. Three looked to the west. Three looked to the south. And three looked to the east. The water was set on top of them, and their back parts turned toward the center. 26 The side of the pool was as far through as the width of a man's open hand. Its round top was made like the top of a cup, like a lily flower. It could hold 2,000 bottles of water.

The Brass Stands

27 Then he made the ten stands of brass. Each stand was as long as two long steps, as wide as two long steps, and as high as a man's neck. 28 This is how the stands were made. They had sides of the same length between the cross-pieces. 29 On the side pieces between the cross-pieces were lions, bulls and cherubim. On the side pieces, both above and below the lions and bulls, there were round pieces of hanging work. 30 Each stand had four brass wheels on straight pieces of brass. At the four corners were pieces to hold up the basin. These pieces were made of melted brass with round pieces at each side. 31 Its opening inside the crown at the top was a cubit. It was round like a pillar, one and a half cubits deep. There were pictures cut on its opening. And their sides were not round, but had four sides of the same length. 32 Under the sides were the four wheels. The pieces that held the wheels were on the stand. The height of a wheel was one and a half cubit. 33 The wheels were made like the wheel of a war-wagon. The straight pieces which held the wheels, the outside of the wheels, their cross-pieces and their center pieces were all made of one piece of brass. 34 There were four pieces at the four corners of each stand to hold it up. These were of one piece with the stands. 35 A narrow piece went all the way around the top that held it up and the sides were of one piece. 36 He cut pictures of cherubim, lions and palm trees in the plates of the parts that held it up and there

were pictures all around. 37 He made the ten stands like this. All of them were made alike. They had the same length, width and height, and looked the same. 38 He made ten basins of brass. One basin held forty bottles of water. Each one was as wide as two long steps. And one basin was on each of the ten stands. 39 Then he put the stands in place. Five were on the south side of the house, and five were on the north side of the house. And he set the large basin of brass on the south-east corner of the house.

40 Hiram made the basins, and the objects for digging, and the pots. So Hiram finished doing all the work for King Solomon in the house of the Lord. 41 He made the two pillars, and the two pots of the top pieces on the top of the two pillars. And he made the two networks to cover the two pots of the pieces on top of the pillars. 42 He made the 400 pomegranates for the two networks. There were two rows of pomegranates for each network, to cover the two pots of the pieces on top of the pillars. 43 He made the ten stands with the ten basins on top of them. 44 He made the large basin and the twelve bulls under it. 45 He made the pails, the objects for digging, and the pots. All these things which Hiram made for King Solomon in the house of the Lord were made of shining brass. 46 The king made them in the plain of the Jordan, in the clay ground between Succoth and Zarethan. 47 Solomon did not weigh any of the objects, because there were too many. The weight of the brass was not known.

48 Solomon made all the holy things which were in the house of the Lord. He made the gold altar and the gold table for the bread before the Lord. 49 He made the lamp-stands of pure gold. There were five on the right side and five on the left side, in front of the most holy place. He made the flowers and the lamps and their objects out of gold. 50 He made the cups, the objects to put out the lamps, the pots, the dishes for special perfume, and the fire-holders, of pure gold. He made the hinges of gold, for the doors of the most holy place and for the doors of the house.

51 So all the work that King Solomon did in the house of the Lord was finished. And Solomon brought in the things which had been set apart by his father David, the silver and the gold and the holy things. He put them in the store-houses of the house of the Lord.

The Special Box Brought into the House of God

8 Then King Solomon gathered together the leaders of Israel in front of him in Jerusalem. He gathered together all the heads of the families and the leaders of the fathers' houses of the sons of Israel. They gathered to bring up the Lord's special box of the agreement from Zion the city of David. ² All the men of Israel gathered to King Solomon at the special supper in the seventh month, Ethanim. ³ All the leaders of Israel came, and the religious leaders took up the Lord's special box of the agreement. ⁴ They brought up the Lord's special box of the agreement, the meeting tent, and all the holy objects which were in the tent. The religious leaders and the Levites brought them up. ⁵ King Solomon and all the people of Israel, who were gathered to him, were with him in front of the special box. They killed so many sheep and cattle on the altar that their number could not be known. ⁶ Then the religious leaders brought the Lord's special box of the agreement to its place. They brought it into the most holy place of the house, under the wings of the cherubim. ⁷ The cherubim spread their wings over the place of the special box. The cherubim made a covering above the special box and its special pieces of wood used for carrying. ⁸ The carrying pieces were so long that the ends of them could be seen from the holy place in front of the most holy place. But they could not be seen from outside. They are there to this day. ⁹ There was nothing in the special box except the two stone writings which Moses put there at Horeb. There the Lord had made an agreement with the people of Israel when they came out of the land of Egypt. ¹⁰ When the religious leaders came from the holy place, the cloud filled the house of the Lord. ¹¹ So the religious leaders were not able to stand there to do their work because of the cloud. For the shining-greatness of the Lord filled the Lord's house.

¹² Then Solomon said, "The Lord has said that He would live in the thick cloud. ¹³ I have built You an honored house, a place for You to live forever."

Solomon's Words to the People

¹⁴ Then the king turned around and prayed that good would come to all the people of Israel, while all the people of Israel stood. ¹⁵ He said, "Thanks be to the Lord, the God of Israel. He spoke with His mouth to my father David. And He has kept His promise with His hand, saying, ¹⁶ 'Since the day I brought My people Israel out of Egypt, I did not choose a city of all the families of Israel in which to build a house that My name might be there. But I chose David to be king over My people Israel.' ¹⁷ Now it was in the heart of my father David to build a house for the name of the Lord, the God of Israel. ¹⁸ But the Lord said to my father David, 'Because it was in your heart to build a house for My name, you did well that it was in your heart. ¹⁹ But you will not build the house. Your son who will be born to you will build the house for My name.' ²⁰ Now the Lord has kept His promise which He made. For I have taken my father David's place and sit on the throne of Israel, as the Lord promised. And I have built the house for the name of the Lord, the God of Israel. ²¹ There I have made a place for the special box in which is the agreement of the Lord. He made it when He brought them from the land of Egypt."

Solomon's Prayer

²² Then Solomon stood before the altar of the Lord. And in front of all the people of Israel he lifted his hands toward heaven. ²³ He said, "O Lord, God of Israel, there is no God like You in heaven above or on earth below. You are keeping Your agreement and are showing loving-kindness to Your servants who walk in Your ways with all their heart. ²⁴ You have kept Your promise to Your servant, my father David. Yes, You have spoken with Your mouth, and have done it with Your hand, as it is this day. ²⁵ So now, O Lord, God of Israel, keep Your promise to my father David when You said to him, 'You will not be without a man to sit on the throne of Israel, if only your sons are careful to walk in My ways as you have walked.' ²⁶ O God of Israel, let Your Word be made sure, which You have spoken to Your servant, my father David.

²⁷ "But is it true that God will live on the earth? See, heaven and the highest heaven are not big enough to hold You. How much less this house which I have built! ²⁸ But keep in mind the prayer of Your servant, O Lord my God. Listen to the cry and to the prayer which Your servant prays to You today. ²⁹ Open Your eyes night and day toward this house, toward the place of which You have said, 'My name will be there.' Listen to the prayer Your servant

will pray toward this place. 30 Listen to the prayer of Your servant and of Your people Israel, when they pray toward this place. Hear in heaven where You live. Hear and forgive.

31 "If a man sins against his neighbor and has to make a promise, and he comes and makes a promise at Your altar in this house, 32 then hear in heaven and act. Judge Your servants. Punish the guilty forever by bringing his actions upon his own head, and free from guilt the one who is right and good, by returning his good to him.

33 "When Your people Israel do not win in battle over those who hate them, because they have sinned against You, but if they turn to You again and call on Your name and pray to You in this house, 34 then hear in heaven. Forgive the sin of Your people Israel. And return them to the land You gave to their fathers.

35 "When the heavens are shut up and give no rain because they have sinned against You, if they pray toward this place and call on Your name and turn from their sin when You bring trouble to them, 36 then hear in heaven. Forgive the sin of Your servants and of Your people Israel. Teach them the good way in which they should walk. And send rain on Your land, which You have given to Your people.

37 "If there is no food in the land, if there is a bad sickness, if there are diseases or locusts or grasshoppers that kill the plants, if the armies of those who hate Your people gather around their cities, or whatever trouble or sickness there is, 38 whatever prayer is made by any man or by all Your people Israel, each knowing the trouble of his own heart and spreading his hands toward this house, 39 then hear in heaven where You are. Forgive, and act. Give to each the pay he has earned by all his ways. You know his heart. You alone know the hearts of all the children of men. 40 May they fear You all the days they live in the land You have given to our fathers.

41 "When a stranger who is not of Your people Israel comes from a far country because of You, 42 (for they will hear of Your great name and Your powerful hand and Your long arm,) when he comes and prays toward this house, 43 hear in heaven where You are. Do all the stranger asks of You. So all the peoples of the earth may know Your name and fear You, as do Your people Israel. Then they may know that this house I have built is called by Your name

44 "When your people go out to battle against those who hate them, by whatever way You send them, when they pray to the Lord toward the city You have chosen and the house I have built for Your name, 45 then hear their prayer and their cry in heaven. See that the right thing is done to them.

46 "When they sin against You (for there is no man who does not sin), and You will be angry with them, give them to those who hate them, so they will be taken away to another land, far away or near. 47 When they do some thinking in the land where they have been taken, and pray to You in the land of those who hate them, saying, 'We have sinned and have done wrong and have done bad things,' 48 if they return to You with all their heart and soul in the land of those who hate them and have taken them there, and if they pray to You toward their land which You have given to their fathers, the city You have chosen, and the house I have built for Your name, 49 then hear their prayer in heaven where You are. See that the right thing is done to them. 50 Forgive Your people who have sinned against You and all the wrong they have done against You. Give them loving-pity in front of those who have taken them away, that they may have loving-pity on them. 51 For they are Your people and Your children whom You have brought out of Egypt, from the iron fire-place. 52 Let Your eyes be open to the prayer of Your servant and of Your people Israel. Listen to them when they call to You. 53 For You have divided them from all the peoples of the earth as Your children. You have done what You said You would do through Your servant Moses, when You brought our fathers out of Egypt, O Lord God."

Prayer for Good to Come to the People

54 When Solomon had finished praying all this prayer to the Lord, he stood up in front of the altar of the Lord. He had been on his knees with his hands lifted toward heaven. 55 He stood and prayed with a loud voice that good would come to all the people of Israel who were gathered together. He said, 56 "Thanks be to the Lord. He has given rest to His people Israel. He has done all that He promised. Every word has come true of all His good promise, which He promised through His servant Moses. 57 May the Lord our God be with us, as He was with our fathers. May He not leave us alone. 58 May He turn

our hearts to Him, to walk in all His ways, and to keep all His Word and all His Laws, which He told our fathers. 59 May these words of mine, which I have prayed to the Lord, be near to the Lord our God day and night. May He see that the right thing is done to His servant and His people Israel, day by day as we have need. 60 Then all the peoples of the earth may know that the Lord is God. There is no other. 61 So let your whole heart be true to the Lord our God. Walk in His Laws and keep His Word, just as you are doing today."

The House of God Is Set Apart

62 Then the king and all Israel with him gave a gift in worship to the Lord. 63 Solomon gave 22,000 cattle and 120,000 sheep as a peace gift to the Lord. So the king and all the people of Israel set apart the house of the Lord. 64 The same day the king set apart the center of the open space that was in front of the house of the Lord. For there he gave the burnt gift and the grain gift and the fat of the peace gifts. Because the brass altar before the Lord was too small to hold the burnt gift and the grain gift and the fat of the peace gifts. 65 So Solomon had the special supper at that time, and all Israel with him. There were many people gathered, from the way into Hamath to the river of Egypt. They were before the Lord our God for seven days and seven more days, fourteen days in all. 66 Solomon sent the people away on the eighth day, and they gave thanks to the king. Then they went to their tents full of joy and glad in their hearts for all the good things the Lord had shown to His servant David and to His people Israel.

The Lord Comes to Solomon the Second Time

9 Solomon had finished building the house of the Lord, and the king's house, and all that he wanted to build. 2 Then the Lord came to Solomon a second time, as He had come to him at Gibeon. 3 The Lord said to him, "I have heard your prayer which you have prayed to Me. I have set apart this house you have built by putting My name there forever. My eyes and My heart will be there always. 4 As for you, walk before Me as your father David walked, with a true heart doing what is right. Do all that I have told you. Obey My Laws. If you do, 5 then I will make the throne of your rule over Israel last forever. It will be just as I promised your father

David, saying, 'You will never be without a man on the throne of Israel.' 6 But if you or your sons turn away from following Me, and do not keep My Laws which I have given you, and go after other gods and worship them, if you do, 7 then I will cut off Israel from the land I have given them. And I will put away from My eyes the house which I have set apart for My name. Israel will become a word of shame among all peoples. 8 This house will be broken to pieces. Everyone who passes by will be surprised and make a sound of wonder, and say, 'Why has the Lord done this to this land and to this house?' 9 And they will say, 'Because they turned away from the Lord their God, Who brought their fathers out of the land of Egypt. They took in other gods and worshiped them and served them. So the Lord has brought all this trouble upon them.' "

Solomon and Hiram

10 At the end of twenty years, Solomon had built the two houses, the house of the Lord and the king's house. 11 Hiram king of Tyre had given Solomon all the cedar and cypress trees and gold that he wanted. Then King Solomon gave Hiram twenty cities in the land of Galilee. 12 But when Hiram came out from Tyre to see the cities Solomon had given him, they did not please him. 13 He said, "What are these cities you have given me, my brother?" So they are called the land of Cabul to this day. 14 The gold Hiram sent to the king weighed as much as 120 men.

Other Things Solomon Did

15 Now King Solomon made men work to build the house of the Lord, his own house, the Millo, the wall of Jerusalem, Hazor, Meggido and Gezer. 16 For Pharaoh king of Egypt had gone up and taken Gezer and burned it with fire. He killed the Canaanites who lived in the city, and then gave it as a wedding-gift to his daughter, Solomon's wife. 17 So Solomon built Gezer again, and the lower part of Beth-horon, 18 and Baalath and Tamar in the desert, in the land of Judah. 19 Solomon built all the store-cities that he had, the cities for his war-wagons, the cities for his horsemen, and all he wanted to build in Jerusalem, in Lebanon, and in all the land under his rule. 20 Now there were people left of the Amorites, the Hittites, the Perizzites, the Hivites and the Jebusites, who were not of the people of Israel. 21 And their children were left after

them in the land. The people of Israel were not able to destroy all of them. So Solomon made these people work for him, even to this day. 22 But Solomon did not make the people of Israel work for him. For they were men of war, his servants, his rulers, his captains, his war-wagon drivers, and his horsemen.

23 These were the heads of the captains over Solomon's work. There were 550 of them who ruled over the people doing the work.

24 But Pharaoh's daughter went up from the city of David to her own house which Solomon had built for her. Then he built the Millo.

25 Three times a year Solomon gave burnt gifts and peace gifts on the altar he built to the Lord. He burned special perfume on the altar before the Lord. So he finished the house.

26 King Solomon built a group of ships in Ezion-geber, near Eloth on the shore of the Red Sea, in the land of Edom. 27 Hiram sent his servants with the ships, sailors who knew the sea. He sent them with the servants of Solomon. 28 They went to Ophir and brought out gold weighing as much as 420 small men. And they brought it to King Solomon.

The Queen of Sheba Visits Solomon

10 When the queen of Sheba heard about the wisdom Solomon had from the Lord, she came to test him with hard questions. 2 She came to Jerusalem and many people came with her. She brought camels carrying spices and much gold and stones of much worth. When she came to Solomon, she told him all that was on her mind. 3 And Solomon answered all her questions. There was nothing hidden from the king which he could not make plain to her. 4 The queen of Sheba saw all the wisdom of Solomon, the house he had built, 5 the food on his table, and his many servants seated to eat. She saw those who brought the food and how they were dressed, and those who carried his cups. She saw the steps by which he went up to the house of the Lord. And there was no more spirit in her. 6 She said to the king, "The news was true that I heard in my own land about your words and your wisdom. 7 But I did not believe the news until I came. Now my eyes have seen it. And half of it was not told to me. You have more wisdom and riches than I heard you had. 8 How happy are your men! How happy

are these your servants who stand in front of you always and hear your wisdom! 9 Thanks be to the Lord your God Who was pleased with you and set you on the throne of Israel. Because the Lord loved Israel forever, He has made you king, to do what is fair and right and good." 10 Then she gave the king gold weighing as much as 120 small men. She gave him a very large amount of spices and stones of much worth. Never again did so much spices come in as that which the queen of Sheba gave to King Solomon.

11 The ships of Hiram brought from Ophir gold and very many almug trees and stones of much worth. 12 The king used the almug trees to make pillars for the house of the Lord and for the king's house. And he used them to make different kinds of harps for the singers. No such almug trees have come in again or have been seen to this day.

13 King Solomon gave to the queen of Sheba all she wanted, whatever she asked, as well as his gifts to her from the king's riches. Then she and her servants returned to her own land.

Solomon's Riches

14 The gold which came in to Solomon in one year weighed as much as 666 small men, 15 besides all the gold that came from the traders and all the kings of the Arabs and the leaders of the country. 16 King Solomon made 200 large body coverings for battle of beaten gold. For each covering he used 600 pieces of gold. 17 And he made 300 coverings of beaten gold, using 150 pieces of gold on each covering. The king put them in the house among the trees of Lebanon. 18 Then the king made a large throne of ivory and covered it with fine gold. 19 The throne had six steps, and a round top at its back. There were arms on each side of the seat, and two lions standing beside the arms. 20 Twelve lions stood on the six steps, one on each end. Nothing like it was made for any other king. 21 All of King Solomon's cups were made of gold. And all the cups of the house among the trees of Lebanon were made of pure gold. None of them were made of silver. Silver was not thought of as being of much worth in the days of Solomon. 22 For the king had a group of ships of Tarshish at sea with the ships of Hiram. Every three years the ships of Tarshish came bringing gold, silver, ivory, apes and peacocks.

23 So King Solomon became greater than all the kings of the earth in riches and in wisdom. 24 They came from all over the earth to see Solomon, to hear his wisdom which God had put in his heart. 25 Every one of them brought his gift. They brought objects of silver and gold, clothing, objects for fighting in battle, spices, horses and donkeys, so much year by year.

26 Solomon gathered war-wagons and horsemen. He had 1,400 war-wagons and 12,000 horsemen. He kept them in the war-wagon cities and with the king in Jerusalem. 27 The king made silver as easy to find as stones in Jerusalem. He made cedar trees as easy to find as the sycamore trees of the valley. 28 Solomon had horses brought from Egypt and Kue. The king's traders bought them from Kue, each for a price. 29 A war-wagon could be brought from Egypt for 600 pieces of silver, and a horse for 150 pieces of silver. They got them in the same way for all the kings of the Hittites and the kings of Syria.

Solomon Turns Away from the Lord

11 Now King Solomon loved many women from other nations. He loved the daughter of Pharaoh, and Moabite, Ammonite, Edomite, Sidonian and Hittite women. 2 They were from the nations about which the Lord had said to the people of Israel, "Do not take wives from them. And do not have them take wives from you. For they will be sure to turn your heart away to follow their gods." But Solomon held on to these women in love. 3 He had 700 wives, kings' daughters, and 300 women who acted as his wives. And his wives turned his heart away. 4 When Solomon was old, his wives turned his heart away to follow other gods. His whole heart was not faithful to the Lord his God, as the heart of his father David had been. 5 For Solomon followed Ashtoreth the false goddess of the Sidonians, and Milcom the hated god of the Ammonites. 6 Solomon did what was sinful in the eyes of the Lord. He did not follow the Lord with all his heart, as his father David had done. 7 Then Solomon built a high place for Chemosh the hated god of Moab, and for Molech the hated god of the sons of Ammon, on the mountain east of Jerusalem. 8 He did the same for all his wives from other nations, who burned special perfume and gave gifts to their gods.

9 Now the Lord was angry with Solomon, because Solomon's heart had turned away from the Lord, the God of Israel. The Lord had come to him twice 10 and had told him about this, that he should not follow other gods. But Solomon did not obey what the Lord had told him. 11 So the Lord said to Solomon, "Because you have done this and have not kept My agreement and My Laws which I told you, for sure I will tear the nation from you and will give it to your servant. 12 But I will not do it while you are alive, because of your father David. I will tear it out of the hand of your son. 13 But I will not tear away all the nation. I will give one family group to your son because of My servant David, and because of Jerusalem which I have chosen."

Solomon's Trouble

14 Then the Lord sent Hadad the Edomite to make trouble for Solomon. He was of the king's family in Edom. 15 For when David was in Edom, and Joab the captain of the army had gone up to bury the dead, he killed every male in Edom. 16 (For Joab and all Israel stayed there six months, until he had killed every male in Edom.) 17 But Hadad ran away to Egypt, together with certain Edomites of his father's servants, while Hadad was still a young boy. 18 They came from Midian to Paran. Then they took men with them from Paran and came to Egypt, to Pharaoh king of Egypt. Pharaoh gave Hadad a house and food and land. 19 Now Hadad found much favor in the eyes of Pharaoh. So Pharaoh gave him in marriage the sister of his own wife, the sister of Tahpenes the queen. 20 Tahpenes's sister gave birth to his son Genubath, whom Tahpenes took care of in Pharaoh's house. Genubath was in Pharaoh's house among the sons of Pharaoh. 21 But Hadad heard in Egypt that David and Joab the captain of David's army were dead. So Hadad said to Pharaoh, "Send me away, so I may return to my own country." 22 Pharaoh said to him, "But what have you been without while you stayed with me? Why do you want to go to your own country?" Hadad answered, "Nothing. But even so, let me go."

23 God sent Rezon the son of Eliada against Solomon also. Rezon had run away from his owner Hadadezer king of Zobah. 24 He gathered men around him and became the leader of a group of fighters, after David killed the men of Zobah. They went to Damascus and stayed there. Rezon was made king in Damascus. 25 So he brought trouble to Israel all the days

of Solomon, together with the trouble brought by Hadad. He hated Israel and ruled over Syria.

Jeroboam Works against the King

26 Then Jeroboam the son of Nebat turned against the king. Jeroboam was Solomon's servant, an Ephraimite of Zeredah. His mother's name was Zeruah, a woman whose husband had died. 27 Now this is the reason he turned against the king. Solomon built the Millo, and built a stronger wall around the city of his father David. 28 Now Jeroboam was a powerful soldier. When Solomon saw that the young man was a good worker, he chose him to rule over all men of the family of Joseph who were made to work. 29 When Jeroboam went out of Jerusalem, the man who spoke for God Ahijah the Shilonite found him on the road. Ahijah had dressed himself with a new coat, and both of them were alone in the field. 30 Then Ahijah took hold of his new coat and tore it into twelve pieces. 31 And he said to Jeroboam, "Take ten pieces for yourself. For the Lord, the God of Israel, says, 'See, I will tear the nation out of the hand of Solomon and give you ten family groups. 32 (But he will have one family group, because of My servant David and because of Jerusalem, the city I have chosen from all the families of Israel.) 33 Because they have turned away from Me, They have worshiped Ashtoreth the false goddess of the Sidonians, Chemosh the god of Moab, and Milcom the god of the sons of Ammon. They have not walked in My ways, doing what is right in My eyes and keeping My Laws, as his father David did. 34 But I will not take the whole nation from him. I will make him ruler all the days of his life, because of My servant David whom I chose, who kept My Word and My Laws. 35 But I will take the nation from his son, and will give to you ten family groups. 36 I will give one family group to his son, that My servant David will have a lamp always before Me in Jerusalem, the city where I have chosen for Myself to put My name. 37 And I will take you, and you will rule over whatever you want. You will be the king of Israel. 38 Listen to all I tell you to do. Walk in My ways. Do what is right in My eyes by keeping My Word and My Laws, as My servant David did. If you do, then I will be with you and build you a house that will last, as I built for David. And I will give Israel to you. 39 I will bring trouble to the children of David for this, but not forever.' " 40 So Solomon tried to put Jeroboam to death. But Jeroboam got up and ran to Egypt, to Shishak king of Egypt. And he stayed in Egypt until Solomon died.

The Death of Solomon

41 Now the rest of the acts of Solomon and whatever he did, and his wisdom, are they not written in the Book of the Acts of Solomon? 42 Solomon ruled in Jerusalem over all Israel forty years. 43 And Solomon died and was buried in the city of his father David. His son Rehoboam ruled in his place.

Israel and Rehoboam

12 Rehoboam went to Shechem. For all Israel had come to Shechem to make him king. 2 Now Jeroboam the son of Nebat was still in Egypt where he had run away from King Solomon. When Jeroboam heard the news, he returned from Egypt. 3 They sent for him. Then Jeroboam and all the people of Israel came and said to Rehoboam, 4 "Your father made our load heavy. Take away some of the hard work and heavy load your father put on us, and we will serve you." 5 Rehoboam said to them, "Leave for three days. Then return to me." So the people left.

6 King Rehoboam spoke with the leaders who had worked for his father Solomon while he was still alive. He asked them, "What answer do you think I should give to these people?" 7 They said to him, "Help these people today. Serve them. Answer them with good words. If you do, then they will be your servants forever." 8 But Rehoboam turned away from the wise words the leaders gave him. Instead he spoke with the young men who grew up with him and stood by him. 9 He said to them, "What answer do you say we should give to these people who have said to me, 'Take away some of the heavy load your father put on us?'" 10 The young men who grew up with him said, "This is what you should say to these people who said to you, 'Your father made our load heavy. Now take some of the load from us.' You should say to them, 'My little finger is bigger around than my father's body! 11 My father gave you a heavy load. I will add to your load. My father punished you with whips. But I will punish you with scorpions.'"

12 Then Jeroboam and all the people came to Rehoboam on the third day as

the king had told them, saying, "Return to me on the third day." 13 And the king was hard in his answer to them. For he turned away from the wise words the leaders had given him. 14 He spoke to them as he had been told by the young men. He said, "My father made your load heavy. I will add to your load. My father punished you with whips. But I will punish you with scorpions." 15 So the king did not listen to the people. The Lord had let this happen, that He might keep His Word, which the Lord spoke through Ahijah the Shilonite to Jeroboam the son of Nebat.

16 All Israel saw that the king did not listen to them. So they said to the king, "What share do we have in David? We have no share in the son of Jesse! To your tents, O Israel! Now look after your own house, David!" So Israel went to their tents. 17 But as for the people of Israel who lived in the cities of Judah, Rehoboam ruled over them. 18 Then King Rehoboam sent Adoram, who ruled over those who were made to work, and all Israel killed him with stones. So King Rehoboam got on his war-wagon in a hurry to go to Jerusalem. 19 So Israel turned against the family of David to this day. 20 When all Israel heard that Jeroboam had returned, they sent for him to meet with the people and made him king of all Israel. Only the family of Judah followed the family of David.

21 When Rehoboam came to Jerusalem, he gathered all the family of Judah and the family of Benjamin. He gathered together 180,000 chosen men of war to fight against the family of Israel and return the nation to Rehoboam the son of Solomon. 22 But the Word of God came to Shemaiah the man of God, saying, 23 "Speak to Solomon's son Rehoboam king of Judah, and to all the family of Judah and Benjamin, and to the rest of the people. Tell them, 24 'This is what the Lord says. "You must not go up and fight against your brothers the sons of Israel. Every man return to his house. For I have let this thing happen." ' " So they listened to the word of the Lord, and returned, as the Lord told them.

Jeroboam's Gold Calves

25 Then Jeroboam built Shechem in the hill country of Ephraim, and lived there. And he went out from there and built Penuel. 26 Jeroboam said in his heart, "Now the nation will return to the family of David. 27 If these people go up to give gifts in the house of the Lord at Jerusalem,

then their hearts will turn to their lord Rehoboam king of Judah. They will kill me and follow Rehoboam king of Judah." 28 So the king asked the leaders what he should do. And he made two calves of gold. Then he said to the people, "It is too much for you to go up to Jerusalem. Here are your gods, O Israel, that brought you up from the land of Egypt." 29 He put one in Bethel, and the other in Dan. 30 Now this thing became a sin. For the people went to worship in front of them, even as far as Dan. 31 Jeroboam made houses on high places. He made religious leaders from among all the people, who were not of the sons of Levi.

Worship of Calves at Bethel

32 He made a special supper on the fifteenth day of the eighth month, like the special supper which is in Judah. And he gave gifts on the altar. He did the same in Bethel, giving gifts to the calves he had made. And he placed in Bethel the religious leaders of the high places he made. 33 Then he went up to the altar he had made in Bethel on the fifteenth day of the eighth month, a day he chose in his own heart. He made a special supper for the people of Israel, and went up to the altar to burn special perfume.

The Man of God from Judah

13 A man of God came from Judah to Bethel by the word of the Lord. Jeroboam was standing by the altar to burn special perfume. 2 The man cried against the altar by the word of the Lord, and said, "O altar, altar, this is what the Lord says. 'See, a son will be born to the family of David. His name will be Josiah. On you he will burn the religious leaders of the high places who burn special perfume on you. Human bones will be burned on you.' " 3 He gave a special thing to be seen the same day. He said, "This is what the Lord says will be seen. 'See, the altar will be broken in two. And the ashes on it will be poured out.' " 4 When King Jeroboam heard the words the man of God cried against the altar in Bethel, he put out his hand from the altar, saying, "Take hold of him!" But his hand which he put out against him dried up. So he could not pull it back to himself. 5 The altar was broken in two and the ashes were poured out. It was the special thing to see that happened just as the man of God said it would by the word of the Lord. 6 The king said to the

man of God, "I beg you, ask for the favor of the Lord your God. Pray for me, that my hand may be made well again." So the man of God asked for the Lord's favor. And the king's hand was made well again. It became as it was before. [7] Then the king said to the man of God, "Come home with me and have something to eat to make yourself strong again. And I will pay you." [8] But the man of God said to the king, "I would not go with you if you were to give me half your house. I would not eat bread or drink water in this place. [9] For the word of the Lord said to me, 'You must not eat bread or drink water or return by the way you came.'" [10] So he went another way. He did not return by the way he came to Bethel.

The Death of the Man of God

[11] Now an old man who spoke for God was living in Bethel. His sons came and told him all the things which the man of God had done that day in Bethel. And they told their father the words which the man had spoken to the king. [12] Their father said to them, "Which way did he go?" Now his sons had seen the way which the man of God who came from Judah had gone. [13] Then he said to his sons, "Get the donkey ready for me." So they got the donkey ready for him, and he went away on it. [14] He went after the man of God and found him sitting under an oak tree. He said to him, "Are you the man of God who came from Judah?" And he said, "I am." [15] Then he said to him, "Come home with me and eat bread." [16] And he said, "I cannot return with you or go with you. I will not eat bread or drink water with you in this place. [17] For I was told by the word of the Lord, 'Do not eat bread or drink water there. Do not return by the way you came.'" [18] And he said to him, "I am a man who speaks for God like you. An angel spoke to me by the word of the Lord, saying, 'Bring him back with you to your house, that he may eat bread and drink water.'" But he lied to him. [19] So he returned with him, and ate bread in his house, and drank water.

[20] As they were sitting down at the table, the word of the Lord came to the man who spoke for God who had brought him back. [21] And he cried to the man of God who came from Judah, saying, "You have not obeyed the word of the Lord. You have not done what the Lord your God told you to do. [22] You have returned and eaten bread and

drunk water in the place the Lord said to you, "Eat no bread and drink no water." So now your body will not come to the grave of your fathers.'" [23] And after he had eaten bread and drunk, he got the donkey ready for the man of God whom he had brought back. [24] When he had gone, a lion met him on the way and killed him. His body was thrown on the road, with the donkey standing beside it. The lion stood beside the body also. [25] Then men passed by and saw the body thrown on the road, and the lion standing beside the body. So they came and told about it in the city where the old man who spoke for God lived.

[26] When the man who spoke for God who had brought him back from the way heard about it, he said, "It is the man of God. He did not obey the word of the Lord. So the Lord has given him to the lion, which has torn him and killed him. It was done as had been spoken to him by the word of the Lord." [27] Then he said to his sons, "Get the donkey ready for me." And they got it ready. [28] Then he went and found his body thrown on the road with the donkey and the lion standing beside it. The lion had not eaten the body or torn the donkey. [29] So the man who spoke for God picked up the body of the man of God and laid it on the donkey, and returned with it to the city. He had sorrow for him and buried him. [30] He laid his body in his own grave, and they had sorrow for him, saying, "O, my brother!" [31] After he had buried him, he said to his sons, "When I die, bury me in the grave where the man of God is buried. Lay my bones beside his bones. [32] For what he cried by the word of the Lord against the altar in Bethel and against all the houses of the high places in the cities of Samaria will happen for sure."

Jeroboam's Sinful Way

[33] After this, Jeroboam did not return from his sinful way. Again he made religious leaders of the high places from among all the people. He set apart any of them who were willing to be religious leaders of the high places. [34] This became the sin of the family of Jeroboam, that caused it to be cut off and destroyed from the earth.

The Death of Jeroboam's Son Abijah

14 At that time Jeroboam's son Abijah became sick. [2] And Jeroboam said to his wife, "Get ready and dress yourself so no one will know that you are the wife of Jeroboam. Then go to Shiloh. Ahijah the man who speaks for God is there. He is the one who said that I would be king over these people. 3 Take ten loaves, some sweet bread and a jar of honey with you, and go to him. He will tell you what will happen to the boy." 4 Jeroboam's wife did so. She got ready and went to Shiloh, and came to Ahijah's house. Now Ahijah could not see. His eyes were weak because he was old. 5 The Lord had said to Ahijah, "The wife of Jeroboam is coming to ask you about her son, for he is sick. This is what you should say to her. When she comes she will pretend to be another woman."

6 When Ahijah heard the sound of her feet coming to the door, he said, "Come in, wife of Jeroboam. Why do you pretend to be another woman? For I have been given news that will be hard for you. 7 Go and say to Jeroboam, 'This is what the Lord God of Israel says. "I gave you honor from among the people. I made you the leader of My people Israel. 8 I tore the nation away from the family of David and gave it to you. But you have not been like My servant David. He kept My Laws and followed Me with all his heart. He did only what was right in My eyes. 9 But you have done more sinful things than all who were before you. You have gone and made for yourself other gods and objects to look like gods to make Me angry. You have put Me behind your back. 10 So I am bringing trouble upon the family of Jeroboam. I will kill every male from Jeroboam, both owned and free in Israel. I will clean away the family of Jeroboam, as one cleans away animal waste until it is all gone. 11 The dogs will eat anyone belonging to Jeroboam who dies in the city. And the birds of the air will eat anyone who dies in the field. For the Lord has said it." ' 12 "Get up and go to your house. When your feet go into the city the child will die. 13 All Israel will have sorrow for him and bury him. For he alone of Jeroboam's family will come to the grave. Because in him there is found something good to the Lord God of Israel, in the family of Jeroboam. 14 But the Lord will send a king over Israel who will destroy the family of Jeroboam this day and from now on. 15 For the Lord will punish Israel, as a piece of grass is shaken in the water. He will send Israel out from this good land He gave to their fathers. He will spread them out on the other side of the Euphrates River, because they have their false gods, and have made the Lord angry.

16 He will give up Israel because of the sins of Jeroboam, which he sinned and made Israel to sin."

17 Then Jeroboam's wife got up and left and came to Tirzah. As she came to the door of the house, the child died. 18 And all Israel buried him and had sorrow for him, as the Word of God was spoken through His servant Ahijah the man who spoke for God.

The Death of Jeroboam

19 Now the rest of the acts of Jeroboam, how he made war and how he ruled, are written in the Book of the Chronicles of the Kings of Israel. 20 Jeroboam ruled for twenty-two years. Then he died and his son Nadab ruled in his place.

Rehoboam Rules Judah

21 Now Solomon's son Rehoboam ruled in Judah. Rehoboam was forty-one years old when he became king. And he ruled for seventeen years in Jerusalem, the city the Lord had chosen from all the families of Israel to put His name there. The name of Rehoboam's mother was Naamah of Ammon. 22 Judah did what was sinful in the eyes of the Lord. They made Him jealous with their sins, more than all their fathers had done. 23 For they built for themselves high places, holy objects and false gods on every high hill and under every green tree. 24 In their religion there were men in the land who sold the use of their bodies. They did all the hated things of the nations which the Lord drove away before the people of Israel.

25 In the fifth year of King Rehoboam, Shishak the king of Egypt came up against Jerusalem. 26 He took away the riches of the Lord's house and the riches of the king's house. He took everything. He even took all the body coverings of gold which Solomon had made. 27 So King Rehoboam made body coverings of brass in their place. He put them in the care of the captain of the soldiers who watched the door of the king's house. 28 Every time the king went into the house of the Lord, the soldiers would carry them and return them again to their room.

29 Now the rest of the acts of Rehoboam and all that he did, are they not written in the Book of the Chronicles of the Kings of Judah? 30 There was war between Rehoboam and Jeroboam always. 31 Rehoboam died and was buried with his fathers in the city of David. His mother's

name was Naamah of Ammon. And his son Abijam became king in his place.

Abijam Rules Judah

15 In the eighteenth year of King Jeroboam the son of Nabat, Abijam became king over Judah. ² He ruled for three years in Jerusalem. His mother's name was Maacah the daughter of Abishalom. ³ And he walked in all the sins which his father had done before him. He was not faithful to the Lord with all his heart, like the heart of his father David. ⁴ But the Lord his God gave him a lamp in Jerusalem because of David. He gave him a son to rule after him and to keep Jerusalem strong. ⁵ Because David did what was right in the eyes of the Lord. He did not turn away from anything the Lord told him to do all the days of his life, except in what happened with Uriah the Hittite. ⁶ And there was war between Rehoboam and Jeroboam all the days of his life.

⁷ Now the rest of the acts of Abijam and all that he did, are they not written in the Book of the Chronicles of the Kings of Judah? And there was war between Abijam and Jeroboam. ⁸ Abijam died and they buried him in the city of David. His son Asa became king in his place.

Asa Rules Judah

⁹ In the twentieth year of Jeroboam the king of Israel, Asa began to rule as king of Judah. ¹⁰ He ruled for forty-one years in Jerusalem. His mother's name was Maacah the daughter of Abishalom. ¹¹ And Asa did what was right in the eyes of the Lord, like David his father. ¹² He sent away the men from the land who sold the use of their bodies in their religion. He took away all the false gods his father had made. ¹³ He stopped his mother Maacah from being queen mother, because she had made a hated object of the false goddess Asherah. And Asa cut down her hated object and burned it at the river Kidron. ¹⁴ The high places were not taken away, But Asa was faithful to the Lord with all his heart for all his days. ¹⁵ He brought into the house of the Lord the holy things of his father and his own holy things, silver, gold, and holy objects.

¹⁶ There was war between Asa and Baasha king of Israel all their days. ¹⁷ Baasha king of Israel went up against Judah. He built walls around Ramah to stop anyone from going out or coming in to Asa king of Judah. ¹⁸ Then Asa took all the silver and the gold which were left in the storerooms of the Lord's house and the king's house, and gave them to his servants. King Asa sent them to Ben-hadad the son of Tabrimmon, the son of Hezion, king of Syria, who lived in Damascus. Asa said, ¹⁹ "Let there be an agreement of peace between me and you, as between my father and your father. See, I have sent you a gift of silver and gold. Go and break your agreement of peace with Baasha king of Israel, so that he will leave me." ²⁰ Ben-hadad listened to King Asa and sent the captains of his armies against the cities of Israel. He destroyed Ijon, Dan, Abel-bethmaacah, all Chinneroth, and all the land of Naphtali. ²¹ When Baasha heard about it, he stopped building a wall around Ramah, and stayed in Tirzah. ²² Then King Asa made the news known to all Judah. There was no one who did not hear it. They carried away the stones of Ramah and its pieces of wood with which Baasha had built. And King Asa used them to build Geba of Benjamin and Mizpah.

²³ Now the rest of all the acts of Asa and all his strength and all he did and the cities he built, are they not written in the Book of the Chronicles of the Kings of Judah? But when he was old he had a disease in his feet. ²⁴ Asa died and was buried with his fathers in the city of his father David. His son Jehoshaphat ruled in his place.

Nadab Rules Israel

²⁵ Jeroboam's son Nadab became king of Israel in the second year of Asa king of Judah. And he ruled over Israel for two years. ²⁶ He did what was sinful in the eyes of the Lord. He walked in the way of his father, and in his sin with which he made Israel sin. ²⁷ Then Baasha the son of Ahijah of the family of Issachar made plans against him. Baasha killed him at Gibbethon, which belonged to the Philistines. Nadab and all Israel had been gathering their army in battle around Gibbethon. ²⁸ So Baasha killed him in the third year of Asa king of Judah, and ruled in his place. ²⁹ As soon as he was king, Baasha killed all those of the family of Jeroboam. He did not leave to Jeroboam any person alive, destroying them all. It happened just as the word of the Lord was spoken through God's servant Ahijah the Shilonite. ³⁰ It happened because of the sins of Jeroboam, which he sinned and which he made Israel sin, He made the Lord God of Israel angry.

31 Now the rest of the acts of Nadab and all that he did, are they not written in the Book of the Chronicles of the Kings of Israel? 32 And there was war between Asa and Baasha king of Israel all their days.

Baasha Rules Israel

33 In the third year of Asa king of Judah, Baasha the son of Ahijah became king of all Israel at Tirzah. He ruled for twenty-four years. 34 He did what was sinful in the eyes of the Lord. He walked in the way of Jeroboam and in his sin which he made Israel sin.

16 Now the word of the Lord came to Jehu the son of Hanani against Baasha, saying, 2 "I took you from the dust and gave you honor. I made you leader over My people Israel. But you have walked in the way of Jeroboam and have made My people Israel sin. You have made Me angry with their sins. 3 So I will destroy Baasha and his house. I will make your house like the family of Jeroboam the son of Nebat. 4 The dogs will eat anyone of Baasha's family who dies in the city. And the birds of the air will eat anyone of his who dies in the field."

5 The rest of the acts of Baasha and what he did and his strength, are they not written in the Book of the Chronicles of the Kings of Israel? 6 Baasha died and was buried in Tirzah. His son Elah became king in his place. 7 The word of the Lord came against Baasha and his house through the man who spoke for God, Jehu the son of Hanani because Baasha had done what was sinful in the eyes of the Lord. He made the king angry with the work of his hands, in being like the family of Jeroboam, and because he destroyed it.

Elah Rules Israel

8 In the twenty-sixth year of Asa king of Judah, Elah the son of Baasha became king of Israel at Tirzah. He ruled for two years. 9 His servant Zimri, captain of half his war-wagons, made plans against him. Elah was at Tirzah drinking himself drunk in the family of Arza. Arza was the head of the house at Tirzah. 10 Zimri went in and hit him and killed him, in the twenty-seventh year of Asa king of Judah. And Zimri became king in his place. 11 When he became king, as soon as he sat on his throne, he killed all those of Baasha's house. He did not leave alive one male, of his brothers or of his friends. 12 So Zimri destroyed the whole family of Baasha, as was spoken

against Baasha by the word of the Lord through Jehu the man who spoke for God. 13 It happened because of all the sins of Baasha and his son Elah. They sinned and they made Israel sin. They made the Lord God of Israel angry with their false gods. 14 Now the rest of the acts of Elah and all that he did, are they not written in the Book of the Chronicles of the Kings of Israel?

Zimri Rules Israel

15 In the twenty-seventh year of Asa king of Judah, Zimri ruled seven days at Tirzah. Now the people were gathered against Gibbethon, which belonged to the Philistines. 16 The people who were gathered heard it said, "Zimri has made plans and has killed the king." So all Israel made Omri, the captain of the army, the king of Israel that day among the tents. 17 Then Omri went with all Israel up from Gibbethon, and they gathered in battle around Tirzah. 18 When Zimri saw that the city was taken, he went into an inside room of the king's house. And he burned the king's house over him with fire, and died. 19 He died because of his sins. He did what was sinful in the eyes of the Lord, walking in the way of Jeroboam. And in his sin, he made Israel sin. 20 The rest of the acts of Zimri and the plan he made, are they not written in the Book of the Chronicles of the Kings of Israel?

Omri Rules Israel

21 Then the people of Israel were divided into two parts. Half of the people followed Tibni the son of Ginath, to make him king. The other half followed Omri. 22 But the people who followed Omri won over the people who followed Tibni the son of Ginath. Tibni died and Omri became king. 23 In the thirty-first year of Asa king of Judah, Omri became the king of Israel. He ruled for twelve years. He ruled six years at Tirzah. 24 And he bought the hill of Samaria from Shemer for silver weighing as much as two men. He built on the hill, and gave the city he built the name of Samaria, after the name of Shemer, the owner of the hill. 25 Omri did what was sinful in the eyes of the Lord. He acted worse than all who were before him. 26 For he walked in all the way of Jeroboam the son of Nebat. And in his sin he made Israel sin. They made the Lord God of Israel angry with their false gods. 27 Now the rest of the acts of Omri and the strength that he showed, are they not written in the Book of the Chronicles of the Kings of Israel? 28 Omri

died and was buried in Samaria. His son Ahab became king in his place.

Ahab Rules Israel

29 Omri's son Ahab became king of Israel in the thirty-eighth year of Asa king of Judah. He ruled over Israel in Samaria for twenty-two years. 30 Ahab the son of Omri did what was sinful in the eyes of the Lord more than all who were before him. 31 He thought it was a small thing to walk in the sins of Jeroboam the son of Nebat. He married Jezebel the daughter of Eth-baal king of the Sidonians. Then he went to serve the false god Baal and worshiped him. 32 He built an altar for Baal in the house of Baal, which he built in Samaria. 33 Ahab made an object of wood to look like the false goddess Asherah. So Ahab did more to make the Lord God of Israel angry than all the kings of Israel before him. 34 In his days Hiel the Bethelite built Jericho. His first-born son Abiram died as he began to build the city. His youngest son Segub died as he put up its gates. It happened as it was told by the word of the Lord spoken by Joshua the son of Nun.

Elijah Fed by Ravens

17 Now Elijah the Tishbite, of the people who were staying in Gilead, said to Ahab, "As the Lord the God of Israel lives, before Whom I stand, for sure there will be no rain or water on the grass in the early morning these years, except by my word." 2 And the word of the Lord came to him, saying, 3 "Leave here and turn east. Hide yourself by the river Cherith, east of the Jordan. 4 You will drink from the river. And I have told the ravens to bring food to you there." 5 So he went and did what he was told by the word of the Lord. He went and lived by the river Cherith, east of the Jordan. 6 The ravens brought him bread and meat in the morning and in the evening. And he drank from the river. 7 But after a while, the river dried up, because there was no rain in the land.

The Woman Whose Husband Had Died

8 Then the word of the Lord came to him, saying, 9 "Get up and go to Zarephath, which belongs to Sidon, and stay there. I have told a woman there, whose husband has died, to feed you." 10 So Elijah got up and went to Zarephath. When he came to the city gate, he saw a woman there gathering sticks. He called to her and said, "I ask of you, get me a little water in a jar, that

I may drink." 11 As she was going to get it, he called to her, "I ask of you, bring me a piece of bread in your hand." 12 But she said, "As the Lord your God lives, I have no bread. I only have enough flour in the jar to fill a hand, and a little oil in the jar. See, I am gathering a few sticks so I may go in and make it ready for me and my son. Then we will eat it and die." 13 Elijah said to her, "Have no fear. Go and do as you have said. But make me a little loaf of bread from it first, and bring it out to me. Then you may make one for yourself and for your son. 14 For the Lord God of Israel says, 'The jar of flour will not be used up. And the jar of oil will not be empty, until the day the Lord sends rain upon the earth.' " 15 So she went and did what Elijah said. And she and he and those of her house ate for many days. 16 The jar of flour was not used up, and the jar of oil did not become empty. It happened as was spoken by the word of the Lord through Elijah.

Elijah and the Woman's Son

17 After this the son of the woman who owned the house became sick. His sickness was so bad that there was no breath left in him. 18 So the woman said to Elijah, "What do I have to do with you, O man of God? You have come to me to have my sin be remembered, and to kill my son!" 19 He said to her, "Give me your son." Then he took him from her arms and carried him up to the room on the second floor where he stayed. And he laid him on his own bed. 20 He called to the Lord and said, "O Lord my God, have You brought trouble to the woman I am staying with, by making her son die?" 21 Then he lay upon the child three times and called to the Lord, saying, "O Lord my God, I pray to You. Let this child's life return to him." 22 The Lord heard the voice of Elijah. And the life of the child returned to him and he became strong again. 23 Elijah took the child and brought him down from the second floor into the house and gave him to his mother. He said, "See, your son is alive." 24 Then the woman said to Elijah, "Now I know that you are a man of God. Now I know that the word of the Lord in your mouth is truth."

Elijah's Word to Ahab

18 After many days, the word of the Lord came to Elijah, in the third year, saying, "Go show yourself to Ahab. And I will send rain upon the earth." 2 So

Elijah went to show himself to Ahab. Now the time without food was very hard in Samaria. 3 And Ahab called Obadiah who was the boss over his house. (Now Obadiah had much fear of the Lord. 4 For when Jezebel destroyed the men who spoke for the Lord, Obadiah took one hundred of these men and hid them by fifties in a cave. And he fed them with bread and water.) 5 Then Ahab said to Obadiah, "Go through the land to all the wells of water and to all the valleys. It may be that we will find grass and keep the horses and donkeys alive, and not lose some of the animals. 6 So they divided the land between them to pass through it. Ahab went one way by himself. And Obadiah went another way by himself.

7 As Obadiah was on the way, Elijah met him. Obadiah knew who he was, and fell on his face and said, "Is it you, my lord Elijah?" 8 He answered, "It is I. Go and tell your owner, 'See, Elijah is here.'" 9 Obadiah said, "What sin have I done? Why are you giving your servant into the hand of Ahab to be killed? 10 As the Lord your God lives, there is no nation where the king has not sent men to look for you. And when they said, 'He is not here,' he made the nation prove that they could not find you. 11 Now you are saying, 'Go, say to your owner, "See, Elijah is here."' 12 And after I have left you, the Spirit of the Lord will carry you where I do not know. So I will go and tell Ahab, and he will not be able to find you. Then he will kill me. But I your servant have honored the Lord since I was young. 13 Have you not been told what I did when Jezebel killed the men who spoke for the Lord? I hid one hundred men of the Lord by fifties in a cave. And I gave them bread and water. 14 Now you are saying, 'Go and tell your owner, "See, Elijah is here."' He will kill me." 15 Elijah said, "As the Lord of All lives, before Whom I stand, I will show myself to Ahab today."

16 So Obadiah went to meet Ahab, and told him. And Ahab went to meet Elijah. 17 When he saw Elijah, Ahab said to him, "Is it you, the one who brings trouble to Israel?" 18 Elijah said, "I have not brought trouble to Israel. But you and your father's house have. Because you have turned away from the laws of the Lord, and have followed the false gods of Baal. 19 So now call together all Israel to me at Mount Carmel. And gather together 450 men who speak for Baal and 400 men who speak for the false goddess Asherah, who eat at Jezebel's table."

Elijah on Mount Carmel

20 So Ahab sent news among all the people of Israel. And he brought the men who speak for the false gods together at Mount Carmel. 21 Elijah came near all the people and said, "How long will you be divided between two ways of thinking? If the Lord is God, follow Him. But if Baal is God, then follow him." But the people did not answer him a word. 22 Then Elijah said to the people, "I am the only man left who speaks for God. But here are 450 men who speak for Baal. 23 Bring two bulls to us. Let them choose one bull for themselves and cut it up and put it on the wood. But put no fire under it. I will make the other bull ready and lay it on the wood. And I will put no fire under it. 24 Then you call on the name of your god, and I will call on the name of the Lord. The God Who answers by fire, He is God." All the people answered and said, "That is a good idea."

25 So Elijah said to the men who spoke for Baal, "Choose one bull for yourselves and make it ready first. For there are many of you. Then call on the name of your god, but put no fire under it." 26 So they took the bull which was given to them and made it ready. Then they called on the name of Baal from morning until noon, saying, "O Baal, answer us." But there was no voice. No one answered. They jumped and danced around the altar they had made. 27 At noon Elijah made fun of them. He said, "Call out with a loud voice, for he is a god. It might be that he is in deep thought or has turned away. He could be away traveling. Or it may be that he is asleep and needs to have someone wake him." 28 So they cried with a loud voice. They cut themselves as they had done in the past, with swords and spears until blood poured out on them. 29 When noon passed, they cried out until the time for giving the evening gift. But there was no voice. No one answered. No one listened.

30 Then Elijah said to all the people, "Come near to me." So all the people came near to him. And he built again the altar of the Lord which had been torn down. 31 Then Elijah took twelve stones, by the number of the families of Jacob's sons. The word of the Lord had come to Jacob's sons, saying, "Israel will be your name." 32 With the stones he built an altar in the name of the Lord. And he made a ditch around the altar, big enough to hold twenty-two jars of seed. 33 Then he set the wood in place. He cut the bull in pieces and laid it on the

wood. And he said, "Fill four jars with water and pour it on the burnt gift and on the wood." ³⁴ Then he said, "Do it a second time." And they did it a second time. He said, "Do it a third time." And they did it a third time. ³⁵ The water flowed around the altar, and filled the ditch also. ³⁶ Then the time came for giving the evening gift. Elijah the man who spoke for God came near and said, "O Lord, God of Abraham, Isaac and Israel, let it be known today that You are God in Israel. Let it be known that I am Your servant, and have done all these things at Your word. ³⁷ Answer me, O Lord. Answer me so these people may know that You, O Lord, are God. Turn their hearts to You again." ³⁸ Then the fire of the Lord fell. It burned up the burnt gift, the wood, the stones and the dust. And it picked up the water that was in the ditch. ³⁹ All the people fell on their faces when they saw it. They said, "The Lord, He is God. The Lord, He is God." ⁴⁰ Then Elijah said to them, "Take hold of the men who speak for Baal. Do not let one of them get away." So they took hold of them. And Elijah brought them down to the river Kishon, and killed them there.

The Rains Come

⁴¹ Then Elijah said to Ahab, "Go up, eat and drink. For there is the sound of much rain." ⁴² So Ahab went up to eat and drink. But Elijah went up to the top of Carmel. He got down on the ground and put his face between his knees. ⁴³ And he said to his servant, "Go up now and look toward the sea." So he went up and looked and said, "There is nothing." Seven times Elijah said, "Go again." ⁴⁴ The seventh time, he said, "I see a cloud as small as a man's hand coming up from the sea." Elijah said, "Go and tell Ahab, 'Make your war-wagon ready and go down, so that the rain does not stop you.'" ⁴⁵ Soon the sky became black with clouds and wind, and there was much rain. And Ahab went to Jezreel. ⁴⁶ Then the hand of the Lord was on Elijah. He pulled his clothing up under his belt and ran before Ahab to Jezreel.

Elijah Gets Away from Jezebel

19 Ahab told Jezebel all that Elijah had done. He told her how Elijah had killed with the sword all the men who spoke for Baal. ² Then Jezebel sent news to Elijah, saying, "So may the gods do to me and even more, if I do not make your life as the life of one of them by this time

tomorrow." ³ Elijah was afraid. He got up and ran for his life. When he came to Beersheba of Judah, he left his servant there. ⁴ But he himself traveled for a day into the desert. He came and sat down under a juniper tree. There he asked that he might die, saying, "It is enough now, O Lord. Take my life. For I am not better than my fathers." ⁵ When he lay down and slept under the juniper tree, an angel touched him. The angel said to him, "Get up and eat." ⁶ Then Elijah looked and saw by his head a loaf of bread made ready on hot stones, and a jar of water. So he ate and drank and lay down again. ⁷ The angel of the Lord came again a second time and touched him, and said, "Get up and eat. Because this traveling is too hard for you." ⁸ So he got up and ate and drank. And he went in the strength of that food forty days and forty nights to Horeb, the mountain of God.

⁹ He came to a cave, and stayed there. The word of the Lord came to him, and said, "What are you doing here, Elijah?" ¹⁰ Elijah said, "I have been very careful to serve the Lord, the God of All. For the people of Israel have turned away from Your agreement. They have torn down Your altars and have killed with the sword the men who speak for You. Only I am left, and they want to kill me."

God Speaks to Elijah

¹¹ So the angel said, "Go and stand on the mountain before the Lord." And the Lord passed by. A strong wind tore through the mountains and broke the rocks in pieces before the Lord. But the Lord was not in the wind. After the wind the earth shook. But the Lord was not in the shaking of the earth. ¹² After the earth shook, a fire came. But the Lord was not in the fire. And after the fire came a sound of gentle blowing. ¹³ When Elijah heard it, he put his coat over his face, and went out and stood at the opening of the hole. Then a voice came to him and said, "What are you doing here, Elijah?" ¹⁴ He said, "I have been very careful to serve the Lord, the God of All. For the people of Israel have turned away from Your agreement. They have torn down Your altars. And they have killed with the sword the men who speak for You. Only I am left, and they want to kill me."

¹⁵ The Lord said to him, "Go, return on your way to the desert of Damascus. When you get there, set apart Hazael to be

the king of Syria. 16 Set apart Nimshi's son Jehu to be the king of Israel. And set apart Elisha the son of Shaphat of Abel-meholah to speak for God in your place. 17 Jehu will kill the one who gets away from the sword of Hazael. Elisha will kill the one who gets away from the sword of Jehu. 18 But I will leave 7,000 in Israel whose knees have not bowed down in front of Baal and whose mouths have not kissed him."

God Calls Elisha

19 So Elijah left there and found Elisha the son of Shaphat. Elisha was plowing with twenty-four bulls, and was with the last two. Elijah passed by him and threw his coat on him. 20 And he left the bulls and ran after Elijah and said, "Let me kiss my father and mother. Then I will follow you." And Elijah said to him, "Return. For what have I done to you?" 21 So Elisha returned from following him. He took his two bulls and killed them. Then he boiled their flesh over a fire, burning the wood cross-pieces the bulls used to pull the load. And he gave the meat to the people, and they ate. Then Elisha got up and followed Elijah and served him.

Syria Fights Samaria

20 Ben-hadad king of Syria gathered all his army together. Thirty-two kings were with him, and horses and war-wagons. And he went up against Samaria in battle. 2 Then he sent men with news to the city of Ahab king of Israel, saying, "This is what Ben-hadad says. 3 'Your silver and gold are mine. Your most beautiful wives and children are mine also.' " 4 The king of Israel answered, "It is as you say, my lord, O king. I am yours, and all that I have." 5 Then the men returned and said, "This is what Ben-hadad says. 'I sent word to you saying, "You must give me your silver and gold and your wives and children." 6 But I will send my servants to you tomorrow about this time. They will look through your house and the houses of your servants. And they will take away all that is of worth to you.' "

7 Then the king of Israel called all the leaders of the land. He said to them, "Look and see how this man is looking for trouble. He sent to me for my wives and my children, my silver and my gold. And I did not say no to him." 8 Then all the leaders and all the people said to him, "Do not listen or agree." 9 So Ahab said to Ben-hadad's men, "Tell my lord the king, 'I will do all that you first asked of your servant, but this I cannot do.' " The men left and returned again with news for him. 10 Ben-hadad sent word to him saying, "May the gods do so to me and more also, if the dust of Samaria will be enough to fill the hands of all the people who follow me." 11 The king of Israel answered and said, "Tell him, 'Let not him who dresses in battle-clothes talk with pride like him who takes them off.' "

12 When Ben-hadad heard these words, he was drinking with the kings in the tents. He said to his servants, "Go to your places." So they went to their place of battle against the city. 13 Then a man who spoke for God came to Ahab king of Israel and said, "This is what the Lord says. 'Have you seen all these many people? See, I will give them to you today. Then you will know that I am the Lord.' " 14 Ahab said, "By whom?" So he told him, "The Lord says, 'By the young servants of the leaders of the lands you rule.' " Then Ahab said, "Who will start the battle?" And he answered, "You." 15 Then Ahab called together the young servants of the leaders of the nations, 232 men. And he called together all the people of Israel, 7,000 men.

16 They went out at noon, while Ben-hadad was drinking himself drunk in the tents with the thirty-two kings who helped him. 17 The young servants of the leaders of the lands went out first. Ben-hadad sent men out to get news, and they told him, "Men have come out from Samaria." 18 Then he said, "If they have come out for peace or for war, take them alive."

19 So the young servants of the leaders of the lands went out from the city, and the army which followed them. 20 Each one killed his man. The Syrians ran away, and Israel went after them. And Ben-hadad king of Syria got away on a horse with horsemen. 21 The king of Israel went out and destroyed the horses and war-wagons. He killed many of the Syrians. 22 Then the man who spoke for God came to the king of Israel, and said to him, "Go and make yourself strong. Look and see what you have to do. For the first of next year the king of Syria will come to fight against you."

The Syrians Lose Again

23 Now the servants of the king of Syria said to him, "Israel's gods are gods of the mountains. So they were stronger than we. But let us fight against them in the plain, and for sure we will be stronger than

they. ²⁴ And do this. Take each of the kings from his place, and put captains in their places. ²⁵ Gather together an army like the army you lost, horse for horse, and war-wagon for war-wagon. Then we will fight against Israel in the plain. For sure we will be stronger than they." And Ben-hadad listened to them and did so.

²⁶ When the new year came, Ben-hadad called together the Syrians and went up to Aphek to fight against Israel. ²⁷ The people of Israel were called together and given what they needed, and went to meet them. The people of Israel gathered in front of them like two little flocks of goats. But the Syrians filled the country. ²⁸ Then a man who spoke for God came to the king of Israel and said, "This is what the Lord says. 'The Syrians have said, "The Lord is a god of the mountains, but He is not a god of the valleys." So I will give all these many people to you. Then you will know that I am the Lord.' " ²⁹ So they stayed beside each other for seven days. On the seventh day the battle was fought. And the people of Israel killed 100,000 Syrian foot soldiers in one day. ³⁰ But the rest ran away into the city of Aphek. And the wall fell on 27,000 men who were left. Ben-hadad ran away and came to a room in the city.

³¹ His servants said to him, "Now see, we have heard that the kings of the family of Israel are kings who show kindness. Let us dress in cloth made from hair and put ropes on our heads, and go out to the king of Israel. It might be that he will save your life." ³² So they dressed in cloth made from hair and put ropes on their heads, and went to the king of Israel. They said to him, "Your servant Ben-hadad says, 'I beg you, let me live,' " Ahab said, "Is he still alive? He is my brother." ³³ Now the men were watching for something special to happen. They were quick to catch his word, and said, "Yes, your brother Ben-hadad." Then Ahab said, "Go and bring him." So Ben-hadad came out to him, and Ahab took him up into the war-wagon. ³⁴ Ben-hadad said to him, "I will return to you the cities which my father took from your father. And you will make streets for yourself in Damascus, as my father made in Samaria." Ahab said, "I will let you go with this agreement." So he made an agreement with him and let him go.

A Man of God Speaks

³⁵ Now a certain son of the men who spoke for God said to another by the word of the Lord, "Hit me." But the man would not hit him. ³⁶ Then he said to him, "Because you have not listened to the voice of the Lord, as soon as you have left me, a lion will kill you." And as soon as he had left him, a lion found him and killed him. ³⁷ Then he found another man and said, "Hit me." And the man hit him, and hurt him. ³⁸ So the man of God left, and waited for the king by the way. He tied a cloth over his eyes so no one would know him. ³⁹ As the king passed by, he cried to the king and said, "Your servant went out to the battle. A soldier turned and brought a man to me, and said, 'Keep this man. If he is missing for any reason, you will pay for his life with your own. Or else you must pay a man's weight in silver.' ⁴⁰ But while your servant was doing things here and there, the man got away." The king of Israel said to him, "So you must be punished. You yourself have decided it." ⁴¹ In a hurry the man took the cloth away from his eyes. And the king of Israel saw that he was one of the men who speak for God. ⁴² The man said to him, "This is what the Lord says. 'You have let the man go whom I had given to be destroyed. So you will pay for his life with your own. And your people will pay for his people.' " ⁴³ So the king of Israel went home sad and angry, and came to Samaria.

Naboth Is Killed in His Grape-Field

21 Now Naboth the Jezreelite had a field of grape-vines in Jezreel beside the family of Ahab king of Samaria. ² Ahab said to Naboth, "Give me your grape-field. I want it for a vegetable garden because it is near my house. I will give you a better field for it. Or I will pay for it with money, if you like." ³ But Naboth said to Ahab, "May the Lord keep me from giving you what I have received from my fathers." ⁴ Ahab went into his house sad and angry because of Naboth the Jezreelite saying to him, "I will not give you what I have received from my fathers." And Ahab lay down on his bed and turned his face away and would not eat.

⁵ His wife Jezebel came to him and said, "Why is your spirit so troubled that you are not eating food?" ⁶ He said to her, "Because I spoke to Naboth the Jezreelite. I said to him, 'Give me your grape-field for money. Or I will give you another field for it, if you like.' But he said, 'I will not give you my grape-field.' " ⁷ Jezebel his wife said to him, "Do you now rule over Israel?

Get up, eat food, and let your heart be filled with joy. I will give you the grape-field of Naboth the Jezreelite." 8 So she wrote letters in Ahab's name and put the mark of his name on them. She sent letters to the leaders and the king's sons who were living with Naboth in his city. 9 She wrote in the letters, saying, "Tell the people that it is a time when they should not eat. And put Naboth in front of the people. 10 Seat two men of no worth beside him. And have them speak against him, saying, 'You spoke against God and the king.' Then take him out and kill him with stones."

11 So the leaders and king's sons who lived in Naboth's city did just as Jezebel had written to them in the letters she had sent. 12 They told the people that it was a time when they should not eat. And they put Naboth in front of the people. 13 Then the two men of no worth came in and sat beside him. These men spoke against Naboth in front of the people, saying, "Naboth spoke against God and the king." So they took him outside the city and killed him with stones. 14 Then they sent news to Jezebel, saying, "Naboth has been killed with stones. He is dead." 15 When Jezebel heard that Naboth had been killed with stones, she said to Ahab, "Get up and take the grape-field of Naboth the Jezreelite for your own, the field he would not sell to you. For Naboth is not alive, but dead." 16 When Ahab heard that Naboth was dead, he got up to go down and take for his own the grape-field of Naboth the Jezreelite.

17 Then the word of the Lord came to Elijah the Tishbite, saying, 18 "Get ready and go down to Samaria to meet Ahab king of Israel. He is in Naboth's grape-field. He has gone down to take it for his own. 19 And you will speak to him, saying, 'This is what the Lord says, "Have you killed and also taken away?" And you will speak to him, saying, "This is what the Lord says, 'The dogs will drink up your blood in the place where the dogs drank up the blood of Naboth.' " ' " 20 Ahab said to Elijah, "Have you found me, O you who hate me?" Elijah answered, "I have found you, because you have sold yourself to do what is sinful in the eyes of the Lord. 21 See, I will bring trouble upon you. I will destroy you. I will kill every male of Ahab in Israel, both those who are servants and those who are free. 22 I will make your house like the family of Jeroboam the son of Nebat, and like the family of Baasha the son of Ahijah. Because you have made Me

angry, and have made Israel sin. 23 And the Lord has spoken about Jezebel, saying, 'The dogs will eat Jezebel in the land of Jezreel.' 24 The dogs will eat anyone belonging to Ahab who dies in the city. The birds of the air will eat anyone belonging to Ahab who dies in the field."

25 There was no one who sold himself to do what is sinful in the eyes of the Lord like Ahab did. His wife Jezebel moved him to do it. 26 He did what was hated by following false gods. He did all that the Amorites had done, whom the Lord drove out in front of the people of Israel.

27 When Ahab heard these words, he tore his clothes and dressed in cloth made from hair, and would not eat. He lay dressed in cloth made from hair, and went about very sad. 28 Then the word of the Lord came to Elijah the Tishbite, saying, 29 "Do you see how Ahab has got rid of his pride before Me? Because he has gotten rid of his pride, I will not bring trouble to him while he is alive. But I will bring trouble upon his house in his son's days."

Micaiah Speaks to Ahab

22 Three years passed without war between Syria and Israel. 2 In the third year, Jehoshaphat the king of Judah came down to the king of Israel. 3 The king of Israel said to his servants, "Do you know that Ramoth-gilead belongs to us? We are still doing nothing to take it from the king of Syria? 4 And he said to Jehoshaphat, "Will you go with me to battle at Ramoth-gilead?" Jehoshaphat said to the king of Israel, "I am as you are. My people are as your people. My horses are as your horses."

5 Jehoshaphat said to the king of Israel, "Ask first for the word of the Lord." 6 Then the king of Israel gathered together the men who spoke for God, 400 men. He said to them, "Should I go to Ramoth-gilead to battle, or should I not?" And they said, "Go. For the Lord will give it to the king." 7 But Jehoshaphat said, "Is there not another man who speaks for the Lord here, that we may ask him?" 8 The king of Israel said to Jehoshaphat, "There is only one other man whom we may ask of the Lord, but I hate him. He does not speak anything good about me, only bad. He is Micaiah the son of Imlah." But Jehoshaphat said, "Let not the king say that." 9 Then the king of Israel called a soldier and said, "Be quick to bring Micaiah the son of Imlah." 10 Now the king of Israel and Jehoshaphat

king of Judah were sitting on their thrones, dressed in their king's clothing. They sat at the grain-floor at the gate of Samaria. All the men who speak for God were speaking in front of them. 11 Then Zedekiah the son of Chenaanah made horns of iron for himself and said, "The Lord says, 'With these you will fight the Syrians until they are destroyed.' " 12 And all the men who spoke for God said so. They said, "Go up to Ramoth-gilead and do well. For the Lord will give it to the king."

13 The man who went to call Micaiah said to him, "See, the words of those who speak for God are all in the king's favor. Let your words be like theirs and speak in favor of the king." 14 But Micaiah said, "As the Lord lives, I will say what the Lord says to me." 15 Micaiah came to the king. And the king said to him, "Micaiah, should we go to Ramoth-gilead to battle, or should we not?" He answered, "Go up and do well. The Lord will give it to the king." 16 Then the king said to him, "How many times must I tell you to speak nothing but the truth in the name of the Lord?" 17 So Micaiah said, "I saw all Israel spread upon the mountains like sheep which have no shepherd. And the Lord said, 'These have no owner. Let each of them return to his house in peace.' " 18 Then the king of Israel said to Jehoshaphat, "Did I not tell you that he would not speak good of me, but bad?" 19 Micaiah said, "So hear the word of the Lord. I saw the Lord sitting on His throne. All those in heaven were standing by Him on His right and on His left. 20 The Lord said, 'Who will lead Ahab to go up and die at Ramoth-gilead?' And one said one thing, and another said another thing. 21 Then a spirit came and stood before the Lord and said, 'I will lead him.' 22 The Lord said to him, 'How?' And he said, 'I will go out and be a lying spirit in the mouth of all those who will tell what will happen in the future.' Then the Lord said, 'You are to lead him, and do well. Go and do so.' 23 Now see, the Lord has put a lying spirit in the mouth of all these who tell what will happen in the future. The Lord has said bad things against you."

24 Then Zedekiah the son of Chenaanah came and hit Micaiah on the face and said, "How did the Spirit of the Lord go from me to speak to you?" 25 Micaiah said, "See, you will see on that day when you go into a room to hide yourself." 26 Then the king of Israel said, "Take Micaiah and return him to Amon the leader of the city and

to Joash the king's son. 27 Tell them, 'The king says, "Put this man in prison and feed him with little bread and water, until I return in peace." ' " 28 Micaiah said, "If you do return in peace, then the Lord has not spoken by me." And he said, "Listen, all you people."

The Death of Ahab

29 So the king of Israel and Jehoshaphat king of Judah went up to Ramoth-gilead. 30 The king of Israel said to Jehoshaphat, "I will dress so no one will know who I am, and will go to battle. But you put on your king's clothing." So the king of Israel dressed so no one would know who he was, and went into battle. 31 Now the king of Syria had told the thirty-two captains of his war-wagons, "Do not fight with the small or strong. But only fight with the king of Israel." 32 When the captains of the war-wagons saw Jehoshaphat, they said, "For sure this is the king of Israel!" And they turned to fight against him, and Jehoshaphat cried out. 33 Then the captains of the war-wagons saw that it was not the king of Israel. So they returned from going after him.

34 But a certain man happened to shoot an arrow and hit the king of Israel between the parts of his battle-clothes. So Ahab said to the driver of his war-wagon, "Turn around and take me out of the battle. For I am hurt." 35 The battle was hard that day, and the king was set up in his war-wagon in front of the Syrians. At evening he died. The blood from the cut flowed to the bottom of the war-wagon. 36 Then a cry went through to his country!

37 So the king died and was brought to Samaria. They buried the king in Samaria. 38 And they washed the war-wagon by the pool of Samaria. The dogs drank up his blood. (The women who sold the use of their bodies washed themselves there.) It happened as the word of the Lord said it would. 39 Now the rest of the acts of Ahab and all he did, the ivory house and cities he built, are they not written in the Book of the Chronicles of the Kings of Israel? 40 Ahab died and his son Ahaziah became king in his place.

Jehoshaphat Rules Judah

41 Jehoshaphat the son of Asa became the king of Judah in the fourth year of Ahab king of Israel. 42 Jehoshaphat was thirty-five years old when he became king. And he ruled twenty-five years in Jerusalem.

His mother's name was Azubah the daughter of Shilhi. 43 He walked in all the way of Asa his father. He did not turn aside from it. He did what was right in the eyes of the Lord. But the high places were not taken away. The people still gave gifts and burned special perfume on the high places. 44 And Jehoshaphat made peace with the king of Israel.

45 The rest of the acts of Jehoshaphat, the strength he showed and how he fought, are they not written in the Book of the Chronicles of the Kings of Judah? 46 He destroyed from the land those who were left of the men who sold the use of their bodies in their religion during the days of his father Asa.

47 Now there was no king in Edom. A leader was acting as king. 48 Jehoshaphat made ships of Tarshish to go to Ophir for gold. But they did not go. For the ships were wrecked at Ezion-geber. 49 Then Ahab's son Ahaziah said to Jehoshaphat, "Let my servants go with your servants in the ships." But Jehoshaphat was not willing. 50 And Jehoshaphat died and was buried with his fathers in the city of his father David. Jehoram his son became king in his place.

Ahaziah Rules Israel

51 Ahab's son Ahaziah became the king of Israel in Samaria in the seventeenth year of Jehoshaphat king of Judah. And he ruled Israel for two years. 52 He did what was sinful in the eyes of the Lord. He walked in the way of his father and mother, and Jeroboam the son of Nebat, who caused Israel to sin. 53 He served the false god Baal and worshiped him. He made the Lord God of Israel angry in every way his father had done.

2 KINGS

The Lord Speaks to Ahaziah

1 Now Moab turned against Israel after the death of Ahab. 2 Ahaziah fell through the window of his second-floor room in Samaria, and lay sick. So he sent men with news, saying to them, "Go and ask Baalzebub the god of Ekron if I will get well again from this sickness." 3 But the angel of the Lord said to Elijah the Tishbite, "Get up and go meet the men sent from the king of Samaria. Say to them, 'Are you going to ask Baal-zebub the god of Ekron because there is no God in Israel?' 4 This is what the Lord says. 'You will not leave the bed on which you lie. You will die for sure.'" Then Elijah left.

5 When the men returned to Ahaziah, he said to them, "Why have you returned?" 6 They said, "A man came up to meet us. He said to us, 'Go and return to the king who sent you. Tell him, "This is what the Lord says. 'Are you asking Baal-zebub the god of Ekron because there is no God in Israel? So you will not leave the bed on which you lie. You will die for sure.'"'" 7 Ahaziah said to them, "What kind of man was he who came to meet you and said this to you?" 8 They answered, "He was a man with much hair. He wore a piece of leather around his body." Ahaziah said, "It is Elijah the Tishbite."

9 Then the king sent a captain with fifty of his men to take Elijah. The captain went up to him and saw Elijah sitting on the top of the hill. He said to him, "O man of God, the king says, 'Come down.'" 10 Elijah said to the captain of fifty men, "If I am a man of God, let fire come down from heaven and destroy you and your fifty men." Then fire came down from heaven and destroyed him and his fifty men. 11 So Ahaziah sent to him another captain with fifty men. The captain said to Elijah, "O man of God, the king says, 'Be quick to come down.'" 12 Elijah answered them, "If I am a man of God, let fire come down from heaven and destroy me and your fifty men." Then the fire of God came down from heaven and destroyed him and his fifty men. 13 So Ahaziah sent to him a third captain with fifty men. When the third captain of fifty men went up, he came and put his face to the ground in front of Elijah. He begged him and said, "O man of God, I beg you. Let my life and the lives of these fifty servants of yours be of great worth in your eyes. 14 Fire came down from heaven and destroyed the first two captains with their armies of fifty. But now let my life be of great worth in your eyes." 15 The angel of the Lord said to Elijah, "Go down with him. Do not be afraid of him." So Elijah got up and went with him to the king. 16 Then Elijah said to Ahaziah, "This is what the Lord says. 'You have sent men to ask of Baal-zebub

the god of Ekron. Is it because there is no God in Israel to ask of His Word? So now you will not leave the bed on which you lie. You will die for sure.' "

[17] So Ahaziah died, just as the word of the Lord had said through Elijah. Because Ahaziah had no son, Jehoram his brother became king in his place, in the second year of Jehoram the son of Jehoshaphat, king of Judah. [18] Now the rest of the acts of Ahaziah, are they not written in the Book of the Chronicles of the Kings of Israel?

Elijah Is Taken Up to Heaven

2 When the Lord was about to take Elijah up to heaven by a wind-storm, Elijah and Elisha were on their way from Gilgal. [2] Elijah said to Elisha, "Stay here, I ask you. For the Lord has sent me as far as Bethel." But Elisha said, "As the Lord lives and as you yourself live, I will not leave you." So they went down to Bethel. [3] Then the sons of the men who spoke for God at Bethel came out to Elisha. They said to him, "Do you know that the Lord will take Elijah from you today?" And he said, "Yes, I know. Say no more." [4] Elijah said to him, "Elisha, I ask you to stay here. For the Lord has sent me to Jericho." But Elisha said, "As the Lord lives and as you yourself live, I will not leave you." So they came to Jericho. [5] The sons of the men who spoke for God at Jericho came to Elisha. They said to him, "Do you know that the Lord will take Elijah from you today?" And he answered, "Yes, I know. Say no more." [6] Then Elijah said to him, "I ask you to stay here. For the Lord has sent me to the Jordan." And Elisha said, "As the Lord lives and as you yourself live, I will not leave you." So the two of them went on.

[7] Now fifty sons of the men who tell what will happen in the future went and stood on the other side of the Jordan River a long way off from the two of them who were standing by the Jordan. [8] Then Elijah took his coat and rolled it up and hit the water. And the water divided to one side and to the other, so the two of them crossed the Jordan on dry ground. [9] When they had crossed, Elijah said to Elisha, "Ask what I should do for you before I am taken from you." And Elisha said, "I ask you, let twice the share of your spirit be upon me." [10] Elijah said, "You have asked a hard thing. But if you see me when I am taken from you, it will be given to you. But if not, it will not be so." [11] As they went on and talked, a war-wagon of fire and horses of fire came

between them. And Elijah went up by a wind-storm to heaven. [12] Elisha saw it and cried out, "My father, my father, the war-wagon of Israel and its horsemen!" And he saw Elijah no more. Then he took hold of his own clothes and tore them in two pieces. [13] He picked up Elijah's coat that had fallen from him. And he returned and stood by the side of the Jordan. [14] He took Elijah's coat that fell from him, and hit the water and said, "Where is the Lord, the God of Elijah?" When he hit the water, it was divided to one side and to the other, and Elisha crossed the Jordan.

[15] The sons of the men who tell what will happen in the future at Jericho saw him. And they said, "The spirit of Elijah rests on Elisha." They came to meet him and bowed to the ground in front of him. [16] They said to him, "Now see, there are fifty strong men with your servants. Let them go and look for your teacher. It might be that the Spirit of the Lord has taken him up and put him down on some mountain or into some valley." And Elisha said, "Do not send them." [17] But they talked to him until he was ashamed, and he said, "Send them." So they sent fifty men to look for Elijah. But after three days they did not find him. [18] They returned to Elisha while he was staying at Jericho. And he said to them, "Did I not tell you, 'Do not go'?"

Powerful Works of Elisha

[19] Then the men of the city said to Elisha, "See, it is pleasing to live in this city, as my lord sees. But the water is bad. And the land does not bring fruit." [20] Elisha said, "Bring me a new jar, and put salt in it." So they brought it to him. [21] Then he went out to the well of water and threw salt into it, and said, "This is what the Lord says, 'I have made this water pure. It will not cause death or loss of fruit any more.' " [22] So the water has been pure to this day, just as Elisha said.

[23] Then he left there and went to Bethel. On the way, some young boys came out from the city and made fun of him. They said to him, "Go up, you man with no hair! Go up, you man with no hair!" [24] He looked behind him and saw them, and cursed them in the name of the Lord. Then two female bears came from among the trees and tore up forty-two of the boys. [25] Elisha went from there to Mount Carmel, then returned to Samaria.

The War between Moab and Israel

3 Ahab's son Jehoram became the king of Israel at Samaria in the eighteenth year of Jehoshaphat king of Judah. He ruled for twelve years. 2 Jehoram did what was bad in the eyes of the Lord, but not like his father and mother. For he put away the object of Baal which his father had made. 3 But he held on to the sins of Jeroboam the son of Nebat, which made Israel sin. He did not leave them.

4 Now Mesha king of Moab raised sheep. He had to pay the king of Israel 100,000 lambs and the wool of 100,000 rams each year. 5 But when Ahab died, the king of Moab turned against the king of Israel. 6 So King Jehoram went out of Samaria at that time and called all Israel together. 7 Then he went and sent word to Jehoshaphat the king of Judah, saying, "The king of Moab has turned against me. Will you go with me to fight against Moab?" And Jehoshaphat said, "I will go. I am as you are. My people are as your people. My horses are as your horses." 8 Then he said, "Which way should we go?" And he answered, "By the way of the desert of Edom." 9 So the king of Israel went with the king of Judah and the king of Edom. They traveled around for seven days, but there was no water for the army or the cattle that followed them. 10 The king of Israel said, "It is bad! For the Lord has called these three kings to give them into the hand of Moab." 11 But Jehoshaphat said, "Is there not a man who speaks for God here? Is there no one we can ask to learn what the Lord would have us do?" One of the servants of the king of Israel answered, "Elisha the son of Shaphat is here. He poured water on the hands of Elijah." 12 And Jehoshaphat said, "The word of the Lord is with him." So the king of Israel and Jehoshaphat and the king of Edom went down to him.

13 Elisha said to the king of Israel, "What have I to do with you? Go to the men who tell what will happen in the future that your father and mother have gone to." And the king of Israel said to him, "No. It is the Lord Who has called these three kings together to give them into the hand of Moab." 14 Elisha said, "As the Lord of all lives, before Whom I stand, if I did not care for Jehoshaphat the king of Judah, I would not look at you or see you. 15 But now bring me a man who plays music." And when the man played music, the power of the Lord came upon Elisha.

16 He said, "This is what the Lord says, 'Make this valley full of ditches.' 17 For the Lord says, 'You will not see wind or rain. But that valley will be filled with water so that you and your cattle and your animals will drink.' 18 This is only a small thing in the eyes of the Lord. He will give you the Moabites also. 19 Then you will destroy every strong city and cut down every good tree. You will close all the wells of water, and destroy every good piece of land with stones." 20 The next morning, about the time when the gift is given on the altar, water came by the way of Edom. The country was filled with water. 21 Now all the Moabites heard that the kings had come up to fight against them. All who were able to wear battle-clothes, young and old, were called together. And they stood at the side of the land of Moab. 22 They got up early in the morning. The sun was shining on the water. And the Moabites saw that the water beside them was as red as blood. 23 They said, "This is blood. For sure the kings have fought and killed one another. So now, Moab, let us take what is left!" 24 But when they came to the tents of Israel, the Israelites came and fought against the Moabites. The Moabites ran from them. And Israel went on into the land, killing the Moabites. 25 So they destroyed the cities. Each man threw a stone on every piece of good land until it was covered. They closed all the wells of water and cut down all the good trees. Only the stones of Kir-haraseth were left standing. But the stone-throwers went around it and fought against it. 26 The king of Moab saw that the battle was too hard for him. So he took with him 700 men who used the sword, to break through to the king of Edom. But they could not. 27 Then he took his oldest son who was to rule in his place, and gave him as a burnt gift on the wall. And many became very angry toward Israel. They left him and returned to their own land.

Elisha and the Jar of Oil

4 Now the wife of the son of one of the men who tell what will happen in the future cried out to Elisha, "Your servant, my husband, is dead. You know that your servant honored the Lord with fear. But the man to whom he owed money has come to take my two children to make them serve him." 2 Elisha said to her, "What can I do for you? Tell me, what do you have in the house?" And she said,

"Your woman servant has nothing in the house except a jar of oil." 3 Then he said, "Go around and get jars from all your neighbors. Get empty jars, many of them. 4 Then go in and shut the door behind you and your sons. Pour the oil into all these jars, and set aside each one that is full." 5 So she went from him and shut the door behind her and her sons. They took the jars to her, and she poured. 6 When the jars were full, she said to her son, "Bring me another jar." And he said to her, "There is not one jar left." Then the oil stopped flowing. 7 She came and told the man of God. And he said, "Go and sell the oil and pay what you owe. You and your sons can live on the rest."

Elisha and the Shunammite's Son

8 One day Elisha went to Shunem. An important woman was there, who talked him into eating some food. So every time he passed by, he would turn in there to eat food. 9 She said to her husband, "Now I see that this is a holy man of God who is always passing by. 10 Let us make a little room on the second floor. And let us put a bed there for him, and a table and a chair and a lamp. Then when he comes to us, he can go in there."

11 One day Elisha came there and went into the room on the second floor, and rested. 12 He said to Gehazi his servant, "Call this Shunammite." When he had called her, she came and stood in front of him. 13 Elisha said to Gehazi, "Now tell her, 'See, you have done much for us. What can I do for you? Should I speak to the king or to the captain of the army for you?' " And she answered, "I live among my own people." 14 So Elisha said, "What then is to be done for her?" Gehazi answered, "She has no son, and her husband is old." 15 Elisha said, "Call her." When he had called her, she stood at the door. 16 Then he said, "At this time next year you will hold a son in your arms." And she said, "No, my lord, O man of God. Do not lie to your woman servant." 17 Later she was going to have a child and she gave birth to a son at that time the next year, as Elisha had told her.

18 When the child was grown, he went out one day to his father who was with those gathering grain. 19 He said to his father, "O, my head, my head!" The father said to his servant, "Carry him to his mother." 20 When he was brought to his mother, he sat on her knees until noon. Then he died. 21 She went up and laid him on the bed of the man of God. She shut the door behind him, and went out. 22 Then she called to her husband and said, "Send me one of the servants and one of the donkeys, that I may run to the man of God and return." 23 Her husband said, "Why will you go to him today? It is not the time of the new moon or the Day of Rest." She said, "It will be all right." 24 Then she put a seat on a donkey and said to her servant, "Drive on. Do not slow down for me unless I tell you." 25 So she went and came to the man of God at Mount Carmel. When the man of God saw her far away, he said to Gehazi his servant, "See, there is the Shunammite. 26 Run now to meet her. Say to her, 'Is it well with you? Is it well with your husband? Is it well with the child?' " And she answered, "It is well." 27 When she came to the mountain to the man of God, she took hold of his feet. Gehazi came near to push her away, but the man of God said, "Let her alone. For her soul is troubled within her. The Lord has hidden it from me. He has not told me." 28 Then she said, "Did I ask you for a son? Did I not say, 'Do not lie to me'?"

29 Elisha said to Gehazi, "Get ready to travel. Take my walking stick and go. If you meet any man, do not greet him. If anyone greets you, do not answer him. Then lay my stick on the boy's face." 30 The mother of the boy said, "As the Lord lives and as you yourself live, I will not leave you." So Elisha got up and followed her. 31 Gehazi went on before them and laid the stick on the boy's face. But there was no sound or anything to show that the boy was alive. So Gehazi returned to meet Elisha, and told him, "The boy is not awake." 32 When Elisha came into the house, he saw the boy lying dead on his bed. 33 So he went in and shut the door behind the two of them, and prayed to the Lord. 34 He went up and lay on the child. He put his mouth on his mouth, and his eyes on his eyes, and his hands on his hands. He spread himself out on him, and the child's flesh became warm. 35 Then Elisha got up again. He walked from one end of the house to the other. Then he went up and spread himself on the child again. The boy sneezed seven times, and opened his eyes. 36 Elisha called Gehazi and said, "Call this Shunammite." So he called her. When she came to him, he said, "Take up your son." 37 She came and fell at his feet and put her face to the ground. Then she took up her son and went out.

Elisha and the Pot of Food

38 When Elisha returned to Gilgal, there was no food in the land. The sons of the men who tell what will happen in the future were sitting in front of him. Elisha said to his servant, "Put the large pot over the fire and make food ready for the sons of the men who tell what will happen in the future." 39 One of them went out into the field to gather plants. He found a wild vine, and gathered wild gourds from it. He came and cut them up in the pot of food, not knowing what they were. 40 Then they poured it out for the men to eat. As they were eating the food, they cried out, "O man of God, there is death in the pot!" And they could not eat it. 41 But he said, "Get some grain." And he threw it into the pot, and said, "Pour it out for the people to eat." Then there was no danger in the pot.

Elisha Feeds One Hundred Men

42 A man came from Baal-shalishah. He brought the man of God a gift of the first-fruits. There were twenty loaves of barley bread and new-grown grain in his bag. Elisha said, "Give them to the people, that they may eat." 43 But his servant said, "What? Should I put this in front of one hundred men?" But Elisha said, "Give them to the people to eat. For the Lord says, 'They will eat and have some left.'" 44 So he put it in front of them. And they ate and had some left, as the word of the Lord had said.

Naaman Is Healed

5 Naaman the captain of the army of the king of Syria was an important man to his king. He was much respected, because by him the Lord had made Syria win in battle. Naaman was a strong man of war, but he had a bad skin disease. 2 Now the Syrians had gone out in groups of soldiers, and had taken a little girl from the land of Israel. She served Naaman's wife. 3 And she said to her owner, "I wish that my owner's husband were with the man of God who is in Samaria! Then he would heal his bad skin disease." 4 So Naaman went in and told his king, "This is what the girl from the land of Israel said." 5 The king of Syria said, "Go now, and I will send a letter to the king of Israel." So Naaman went and took with him silver weighing as much as ten men, 6,000 pieces of gold, and ten changes of clothes. 6 He brought the letter to the king of Israel, which said, "I have sent my servant Naaman to you with this letter, that you may heal his bad

skin disease." 7 When the king of Israel read the letter, he tore his clothes and said, "Am I God, to kill and to make alive? Is this why this man sends word to me to heal a man's bad skin disease? Think about it. He wants to start a fight with me." 8 Elisha the man of God heard that the king of Israel had torn his clothes. So he sent word to the king, saying, "Why have you torn your clothes? Let him come to me. Then he will know that there is a man of God in Israel." 9 So Naaman came with his horses and his war-wagons, and stood at the door of Elisha's house. 10 Elisha sent a man to him, saying, "Go and wash in the Jordan seven times. And your flesh will be made well and you will be clean." 11 But Naaman was very angry and went away. He said, "I thought he would come out to me, and stand, and call on the name of the Lord his God. I thought he would wave his hand over the place, and heal the bad skin disease. 12 Are not Abanah and Pharpar, the rivers of Damascus, better than all the waters of Israel? Could I not wash in them and be clean?" So he turned and went away very angry. 13 Then his servants came and said to him, "My father, if the man of God had told you to do some great thing, would you not have done it? How much more then, when he says to you, 'Wash and be clean'?" 14 So Naaman went down into the Jordan River seven times, as the man of God had told him. And his flesh was made as well as the flesh of a little child. He was clean.

15 Then Naaman returned to the man of God with all those who were with him. He came and stood in front of Elisha and said, "See, now I know that there is no God in all the earth but in Israel. So I ask you now to take a gift from your servant." 16 But Elisha said, "As the Lord lives, before Whom I stand, I will take nothing." Naaman tried to talk him into taking it, but he would not. 17 Naaman said, "If not, I ask you, let your servant be given as much dirt as two horses can carry. For your servant will not give burnt gifts or kill animals on the altar in worship to other gods any more. I will only give gifts to the Lord. 18 But may the Lord forgive your servant for this. My king goes into the house of Rimmon to worship there. He rests on my arm and I put my face to the ground in the house of Rimmon. When I put my face to the ground in the house of Rimmon, may the Lord forgive your servant." 19 And Elisha said to him, "Go in peace." So Naaman went away from him a short way.

Gehazi Wants More

20 But Gehazi, the servant of Elisha the man of God, thought, "See, my owner has let Naaman the Syrian go without receiving the gift he brought. As the Lord lives, I will run after him and take something from him." **21** So Gehazi went after Naaman. When Naaman saw someone running after him, he stepped off the war-wagon to meet him, and said, "Is all well?" **22** Gehazi said, "All is well. My owner has sent me, saying, 'See, just now two young sons of the men who tell what will happen in the future have come to me from the hill country of Ephraim. I ask of you, give them a man's weight in silver and two changes of clothes.'" **23** Naaman said, "Be pleased to take silver weighing as much as two men." And he had him take two bags of silver weighing as much as two men, with two changes of clothes. He gave them to two of his servants. And they carried them before Gehazi. **24** When he came to the hill, Gehazi took them from the servants and put them in the house. Then he sent the men away, and they left. **25** And Gehazi went in and stood in front of his owner. Elisha said to him, "Where have you been, Gehazi?" And he said, "Your servant did not leave." **26** Elisha said to him, "Did I not go with you in spirit when the man turned from his war-wagon to meet you? Was it a time to receive money and clothes and olive fields and grape-fields and sheep and cattle and men servants and women servants? **27** So now the bad skin disease will be upon you and your children forever." And Gehazi went away from Elisha with a bad skin disease. He was as white as snow.

The Ax Head That Was Not Lost

6 Now the sons of the men who tell what will happen in the future said to Elisha, "See, the place where we are living under your care is too small for us. **2** Let us go to the Jordan and each of us cut down a tree there. And let us make a place for us to live there." So Elisha said, "Go." **3** Then one of them said, "Be pleased to go with your servants." And Elisha answered, "I will go." **4** So he went with them. When they came to the Jordan, they cut down trees. **5** But as one of them was cutting a tree, the ax head fell into the water. The man cried out, "It is bad, sir! The ax belongs to another man, and I was to return it." **6** The man of God said, "Where did it fall?" And when he showed him the place,

Elisha cut off a stick and threw it in, and the iron came to the top of the water. **7** He said, "Pick it up." So his servant put out his hand and took it.

Syrian Army Loses the Battle

8 Now the king of Syria was fighting a war against Israel. He had a meeting with his servants, and said, "This is the place where I will be staying." **9** The man of God sent news to the king of Israel, saying, "Be careful that you do not pass this place. For the Syrians are coming down there." **10** The king of Israel sent men to the place where the man of God said there would be danger. So he saved himself there more than once or twice. **11** The heart of the king of Syria was angry because of this. He called his servants and said to them, "Will you show me which one of us is helping the king of Israel?" **12** And one of his servants said, "None, my lord, O king. Elisha, the man of God who is in Israel, tells the king of Israel the very words you say in your bedroom." **13** So he said, "Go and see where Elisha is, that I may send men to take him." And he was told, "See, he is in Dothan." **14** So the king of Syria sent horses and war-wagons and an army of many soldiers there. They came during the night and gathered around the city.

15 The servant of the man of God got up early and went out. And he saw an army with horses and war-wagons around the city. The servant said to Elisha, "It is bad, sir! What should we do?" **16** He answered, "Do not be afraid. For those who are with us are more than those who are with them." **17** Then Elisha prayed and said, "O Lord, I pray, open his eyes, that he may see." And the Lord opened the servant's eyes, and he saw. He saw that the mountain was full of horses and war-wagons of fire all around Elisha. **18** When the Syrians came against him, Elisha prayed to the Lord, saying, "Make these people blind, I pray." So the Lord made them blind, as Elisha had said. **19** Then Elisha said to them, "This is not the way. This is not the city. Follow me and I will bring you to the man you are looking for." And he brought them to Samaria.

20 When they had come to Samaria, Elisha said, "O Lord, open the eyes of these men. Let them see." So the Lord opened their eyes, and they saw. They saw they were in the center of Samaria. **21** When the king of Israel saw them, he said to Elisha, "My father, should I kill them?

Should I kill them?" 22 He answered, "Do not kill them. Would you kill those you have taken against their will with your sword and bow? Give them bread and water. Let them eat and drink and return to their owner." 23 So he made a big supper for them. When they had eaten and drunk, he sent them away. And they went to their owner. The Syrians sent no more small groups of soldiers into the land of Israel.

Samaria's Trouble

24 After this, Ben-hadad the king of Syria gathered all his army and went up against Samaria. 25 There was a time of no food in Samaria. The Syrian army gathered around it, until a donkey's head sold for eighty pieces of silver. A half cup of dove's waste sold for five pieces of silver. 26 As the king of Israel was passing by on the wall, a woman cried out to him, "Help, my lord, O king!" 27 And he said, "If the Lord does not help you, from where can I help you? From the grain-floor, or from the grape-crusher?" 28 Then the king said to her, "What is your trouble?" And she answered, "This woman said to me, 'Give your son, so we may eat him today. And we will eat my son tomorrow.' 29 So we made my son ready to eat over the fire, and ate him. The next day I said to her, 'Give your son, so we may eat him.' But she has hidden her son." 30 When the king heard the words of the woman, he tore his clothes. He was passing by on the wall, and the people looked. They saw that he wore cloth made from hair under his clothes. 31 Then he said, "May God do so to me and more also, if the head of Elisha the son of Shaphat stays on him today."

32 Now Elisha was sitting in his house. And the leaders were sitting with him. The king sent a man, but before the man came to him, Elisha said to the leaders, "Do you see how this son of a killer has sent to take off my head? See, when the king's man comes, shut the door. Hold the door shut against him. Is not the sound of his owner's feet behind him?" 33 While he was still talking with them, the king came down to him and said, "See, this trouble is from the Lord. Why should I wait for the Lord any longer?"

7 Then Elisha said, "Listen to the word of the Lord. The Lord says, 'Tomorrow about this time, a basket of fine flour will be sold for one piece of silver in the gate of Samaria. And two baskets of barley will

be sold for a piece of silver.'" 2 The captain on whose arm the king rested said to the man of God, "See, if the Lord should make windows in heaven, could this thing be?" Elisha said, "You will see it with your own eyes. But you will not eat of it."

The Syrians Leave

3 Now there were four men at the city gate with a bad skin disease. They said to one another, "Why do we sit here until we die? 4 If we go into the city, there is no food there and we will die. And if we sit here, we will die also. So now come, let us go over to the tents of the Syrians. If they do not kill us, we will live. And if they kill us, we will die there." 5 So they got up in the evening to go to the Syrians. When they came to the tents of the Syrians, there was no one there. 6 For the Lord had made the Syrian army hear a sound of war-wagons and horses and an army of many soldiers. So they said to one another, "The king of Israel has paid the kings of the Hittites and the kings of the Egyptians to fight against us." 7 And they ran away in the evening. They left their tents and their horses and donkeys. They left everything just as it was, and ran for their lives. 8 Then the men with a bad skin disease came to the tents. They went into one tent and ate and drank. They carried away silver and gold and clothing, and hid them. Then they returned and went into another tent and carried things away from it, and hid them.

9 They said to one another, "We are not doing right. This is a day of good news, but we are keeping quiet. We will be punished if we wait until morning. So now let us go and tell those of the king's house." 10 And they came and called the men who watched the city gate. They said to them, "We went to the tents of the Syrians. But there was no one to be seen or heard there. Only the horses and donkeys were tied there. The tents were left just as they were." 11 So the men at the gate called out, and the news was heard in the king's house. 12 The king got up in the night and said to his servants, "I will tell you what the Syrians have done to us. They know that we are hungry. So they have left the tents to hide themselves in the field. They are saying, 'When they come out of the city, we will take them alive and get into the city.'" 13 One of his servants said, "Let some men take five of the horses that are left. Those who are left in the city are not

doing better than all those who have died. So let us send men out to see." [14] So they took two war-wagons with horses. And the king sent them after the Syrian army, saying, "Go and see." [15] They went after them to the Jordan. All the way was covered with clothes and objects which the Syrians had thrown away in their hurry. Then the men returned and told the king.

[16] So the people went out and took what the Syrians had left. Then a basket of fine flour was sold for a piece of silver. And two baskets of barley sold for a piece of silver, just as the word of the Lord had said. [17] Now the king chose the captain on whose arm he rested to watch the gate. But the people stepped on him at the gate. He died just as the man of God had said when the king came down to him. [18] It happened just as the man of God had told the king, saying, "About this time tomorrow at the gate of Samaria, two baskets of barley will sell for a piece of silver. And a basket of fine flour will sell for a piece of silver." [19] Then the captain had said to the man of God, "See, if the Lord should make windows in heaven, could such a thing be?" And Elisha had said, "You will see it with your own eyes. But you will not eat of it." [20] So it happened to him. The people stepped on him at the gate, and he died.

The Shunammite's Land Given Back

8 Now Elisha spoke to the woman whose son he had brought back to life. He said, "Get ready and go with those of your house. Stay in whatever country you can. For the Lord has called for a time of no food. It will come upon the land for seven years." [2] So the woman got ready as the man of God had told her. She went with those of her house and stayed in the land of the Philistines seven years. [3] At the end of seven years she returned from the land of the Philistines. And she went out to ask the king for her house and field. [4] Now the king was talking with Gehazi, the servant of the man of God, saying, "Tell me all the great things that Elisha has done." [5] Gehazi started telling the king how Elisha had brought the one who was dead to life again. Then the woman whose son he had brought back to life asked the king for her house and field. And Gehazi said, "My lord, O king, this is the woman and this is her son, whom Elisha brought back to life." [6] When the king asked the woman, she told him what had happened. So the king chose a certain captain to help her,

saying, "Give her all that was hers. And give her all the food taken from the field from the day she left the land until now."

The Death of Ben-hadad

[7] Then Elisha came to Damascus. Ben-hadad the king of Syria was sick, and he was told, "The man of God has come here." [8] The king said to Hazael, "Take a gift and go meet the man of God. Ask the Lord through him, saying, 'Will I get better from this sickness?'" [9] So Hazael went to meet Elisha and took with him a gift of every kind of good thing of Damascus. It took forty camels to carry it all. He came and stood in front of Elisha and said, "Your son Ben-hadad king of Syria has sent me to you, saying, 'Will I get better from this sickness?'" [10] Elisha said to him, "Go and tell him, 'You will get better for sure.' But the Lord has shown me that he will die for sure." [11] Then Elisha looked at Hazael until he was ashamed. And the man of God cried. [12] Hazael said, "Why are you crying, my lord?" Then Elisha answered, "Because I know the bad things that you will do to the people of Israel. You will set their strong-places on fire. You will kill their young men with the sword. You will crush their little ones against the stones. And you will cut up their women who are with child." [13] Hazael said, "What is your servant, only a dog, that he should do this bad thing?" Elisha answered, "The Lord has shown me that you will be the king of Syria." [14] Then he left Elisha and returned to his owner. Ben-hadad said to him, "What did Elisha tell you?" And Hazael answered, "He told me that you will get better for sure." [15] But the next day Hazael took the bed covering and put it in water. Then he spread it on Ben-hadad's face so that he died. And Hazael became king in his place.

Jehoram Rules Judah

[16] In the fifth year of Joram the son of Ahab, king of Israel, Jehoram the son of Jehoshaphat king of Judah began to rule. [17] He was thirty-two years old when he became king. He ruled eight years in Jerusalem. [18] He walked in the way of the kings of Israel, just as those of Ahab's house had done. Ahab's daughter became his wife. He did what was sinful in the eyes of the Lord. [19] But the Lord was not willing to destroy Judah, because of His servant David. The Lord had promised to give David one to rule through his sons always.

20 In his days Edom turned against the rule of Judah and chose a king of their own. 21 Then Joram crossed over to Zair, with all his war-wagons. He and his war-wagon captains got up during the night and fought against the Edomites who had gathered around them. But his army ran away to their tents. 22 So Edom turned against the rule of Judah's rule to this day. Libnah turned against Judah's rule at the same time. 23 The rest of the acts of Joram and all he did, are they not written in the Book of Chronicles of the Kings of Judah? 24 Then Joram died and was buried in the city of David. His son Ahaziah became king in his place.

Ahaziah Rules Judah

25 In the twelfth year of Ahab's son Joram the king of Israel, Ahaziah the son of Jehoram king of Judah began to rule. 26 Ahaziah was twenty-two years old when he became king. He ruled one year in Jerusalem. His mother's name was Athaliah the granddaughter of Omri king of Israel. 27 He walked in the way of the family of Ahab. He did what was sinful in the eyes of the Lord, like those of the family of Ahab had done, because he was a son-in-law of the family of Ahab. 28 He went with Ahab's son Joram to war against Hazael king of Syria at Ramoth-gilead. And the Syrians hurt Joram. 29 So King Joram returned to Jezreel to be healed of the cuts the Syrians had given him at Ramah when he fought against Hazael king of Syria. Then Jehoram's son Ahaziah king of Judah went down to Jezreel to see Joram the son of Ahab because he was sick.

Jehu Is Chosen to Be King of Israel

9 Now Elisha the man of God called one of the sons of those who spoke for God. He said to him, "Get ready to travel. Take this jar of oil and go to Ramothgilead. 2 When you get there, find Jehu the son of Jehoshaphat son of Nimshi. Go in and have him come away from his brothers. Bring him into a room in the house. 3 Then take the jar of oil and pour it on his head and say, 'The Lord says, "I have chosen you to be the king of Israel." ' Then open the door and run. Do not wait." 4 So the young servant of the man of God went to Ramoth-gilead. 5 When he came, he found the captains of the army sitting there. He said, "I have something to tell you, O captain." And Jehu said, "Which one of us?" And he said, "You, O captain."

6 So he got up and went into the house. He poured the oil on Jehu's head and said to him, "The Lord, the God of Israel, says, 'I have chosen you king over the people of the Lord, over Israel. 7 You are to destroy the house of your owner Ahab, so that I will punish Jezebel for the blood of My servants who speak for God, and the blood of all the Lord's servants. 8 The whole family of Ahab must be destroyed. And I will destroy every male person in Israel who belongs to Ahab, both the servants and those who are free. 9 I will make the family of Ahab like the family of Jeroboam the son of Nebat, and like the family of Baasha the son of Ahijah. 10 The dogs will eat Jezebel in the land of Jezreel. No one will bury her.' " Then he opened the door and ran away.

11 When Jehu came out to his owner's servants, one said to him, "Is all well? Why did this crazy person come to you?" Jehu said, "You know the man and his talk." 12 And they said, "That is not true. Tell us now." Jehu said, "This is how he spoke to me. He said, 'The Lord says, "I have chosen you to be the king of Israel." ' " 13 Then each man took his clothes in a hurry and put them under him on the steps. And they sounded the horn and said, "Jehu is king!"

Joram of Israel Is Killed

14 So Jehu the son of Jehoshaphat the son of Nimshi made plans against Joram. Now Joram and all Israel were fighting against Hazael king of Syria at Ramothgilead. 15 But King Joram had returned to Jezreel to be healed of the cuts the Syrians had given him, when he fought with King Hazael of Syria. So Jehu said, "If this is what you have in mind, then let no one get out of the city to tell the news in Jezreel." 16 Then Jehu went to Jezreel in a war-wagon, for Joram was lying there. And Ahaziah the king of Judah had come down to see Joram.

17 Now the man who watched for danger was standing in the tower in Jezreel. He saw the group of Jehu's men coming, and said, "I see a group of men coming." Joram said, "Send a horseman to meet them and ask, 'Do you come in peace?' " 18 So a horseman went to meet him and said, "The king asks, 'Do you come in peace?' " And Jehu said, "What have you to do with peace? Get behind me." Then the watchman told Joram, "The horseman came to them, but he did not return."

19 So he sent out a second horseman, who came to them and said, "The king asks, 'Do you come in peace?'" And Jehu answered, "What have you to do with peace? Get behind me." 20 The watchman told Joram, "He came to them, and he did not return. The leader goes in his war-wagon like a mad man, just like Jehu."

21 Then Joram said, "Get ready." And they made his war-wagon ready. Then Joram king of Israel and Ahaziah king of Judah went out, each in their war-wagon, to meet Jehu. They found him in the field of Naboth the Jezreelite. 22 When Joram saw Jehu, he said, "Do you come in peace, Jehu?" And he answered, "What peace can there be, so long as the sinful ways and witchcrafts of your mother Jezebel are so many?" 23 So Joram turned the horses around and ran away, saying to Ahaziah, "He is turning against the king, O Ahaziah!" 24 Jehu pulled his bow with all his strength and shot Joram between his arms. The arrow went through his heart, and he fell in his war-wagon. 25 Then Jehu said to Bidkar his captain, "Pick him up and throw him into the field of Naboth the Jezreelite. For I remember when you and I were going together after his father Ahab. The Lord said then that this would happen to him. 26 The Lord said, 'Yesterday I have seen the blood of Naboth and his sons. I will punish you in this field.' So now take and throw him into the field, as the word of the Lord has said."

Ahaziah of Judah Is Killed

27 When Ahaziah the king of Judah saw this, he ran away toward the garden house. Jehu went after him and said, "Shoot him in the war-wagon also." So they shot him at the hill of Gur, by Ibleam. But he got away to Megiddo and died there. 28 His servants carried him in a war-wagon to Jerusalem. They buried him in his grave with his fathers in the city of David.

29 In the eleventh year of Joram the son of Ahab, Ahaziah became the king of Judah.

Queen Jezebel Is Killed

30 When Jehu came to Jezreel, Jezebel heard about it. She colored her eyes and combed her hair, and then looked out the window. 31 As Jehu came through the gate, she said, "Is it well, Zimri, your owner's killer?" 32 Then he looked up to the window and said, "Who is on my side? Who?" And two or three men looked down at him. 33 Then he said, "Throw her down." So they threw Jezebel down. Some of her blood went on the wall and on the horses. And Jehu made his war-wagons go over her. 34 Then Jehu went in and ate and drank. And he said, "Now go out to this sinful woman and bury her, for she is a king's daughter." 35 So they went to bury her. But all they found were her skull and feet and hands. 36 When they returned and told Jehu, he said, "This is the word of the Lord, which He spoke by His servant Elijah the Tishbite. He said, 'In the land of Jezreel the dogs will eat the flesh of Jezebel. 37 Jezebel's body will be as waste on the field in the land of Jezreel. So no one will be able to say, "This is Jezebel."'"

Ahab's Seventy Sons Are Killed

10 Now Ahab had seventy sons in Samaria. So Jehu wrote letters. He sent them to Samaria, to the rulers of Jezreel, to the leaders, and to those who took care of Ahab's children. He said, 2 "Now your owner's sons are with you. And you have war-wagons, and horses, and a strong city, and things to fight with. When this letter comes to you, 3 choose the best of your owner's sons. Put him on his father's throne. And fight for your owner's house." 4 But they were filled with fear, and said, "See, the two kings could not stand in front of him. How can we stand?" 5 So the head man of the house, the head man of the city, the leaders, and those who took care of the children, sent word to Jehu, saying, "We are your servants. We will do all that you say. We will not make any man king. Do what is good in your eyes." 6 Then Jehu wrote a letter to them a second time. He said, "If you are on my side and will obey me, bring the heads of your owner's sons to me. Meet me in Jezreel about this time tomorrow." Now the king's seventy sons were with the important men of the city who were taking care of them. 7 When the letter came to them, they took the king's seventy sons and killed them. They put their heads in baskets, and sent them to Jehu at Jezreel. 8 The men who had been sent returned and told Jehu, "They have brought the heads of the king's sons." And he said, "Put them one upon the other in two places at the gate until morning." 9 In the morning Jehu went out and stood, and said to all the people, "You are without guilt. See, I made plans against my owner and killed him. But who killed all these? 10 Know now that everything the

Lord spoke about the family of Ahab will come true. For the Lord has done what He said through his servant Elijah." 11 So Jehu killed all who were left of the family of Ahab in Jezreel. He killed all of Ahab's important men, his friends, and his religious leaders. Not one person of Ahab was left alive.

Ahaziah's Forty-Two Brothers Are Killed

12 Then Jehu left and went to Samaria. On the way, while he was at Beth-eked of the shepherds, 13 Jehu met the brothers of Ahaziah king of Judah. He asked them, "Who are you?" And they answered, "We are the brothers of Ahaziah. We have come down to visit the sons of the king and the sons of the queen mother." 14 Jehu said, "Take them alive." So his men took them alive, and killed them at the hole of Beth-eked, forty-two men. He left none of them alive.

The Rest of Ahab's Family Are Killed

15 When Jehu left there, he met Jehonadab the son of Rechab coming to meet him. Jehu said to him, "Is your heart right with my heart as mine is with yours?" And Jehonadab answered, "It is." Jehu said, "If it is, give me your hand." So Jehonadab gave him his hand, and Jehu took him up into the war-wagon with him. 16 Then Jehu said, "Come with me and see how glad I am to work for the Lord." And he had him go in his war-wagon. 17 When he came to Samaria, he killed all of Ahab's people who were left in Samaria. He destroyed them, as the word of the Lord was spoken to Elijah.

The Worshipers of Baal Are Killed

18 Then Jehu gathered all the people and said to them, "Ahab worshiped Baal a little. Jehu will worship him much. 19 Now call all the men who speak for Baal, all his worshipers and all his religious leaders. Let no one be missing. For I have a big gift for Baal. Whoever is missing will not live." But Jehu did this to fool them, so that he might destroy the worshipers of Baal. 20 He said, "Set apart a special meeting for Baal." And they made the news known. 21 Then Jehu sent for all the worshipers of Baal in Israel. Every one of them came. When they went into the house of Baal, the house was filled from one end to the other. 22 Jehu said to the one who took care of the clothes, "Bring out clothing for all the worshipers of Baal." So he brought out clothing for

them. 23 Jehu went into the house of Baal with Jehonadab the son of Rechab. And he said to the worshipers of Baal, "Look and see that there are no servants of the Lord here with you, but only the worshipers of Baal." 24 Then they went in to kill animals on the altar and give burnt gifts. Now Jehu had left eighty of his men outside. He had told them, "The one who lets anyone get away, will pay for it with his life."

25 As soon as he had finished giving the burnt gift, Jehu said to the soldiers and the leaders, "Go in and kill them. Let no one come out." And they killed them with the sword. Then the soldiers and leaders threw the bodies out, and went into the inside room of the house of Baal. 26 They brought out the objects of the house of Baal, and burned them. 27 They destroyed the objects of Baal and destroyed the house of Baal. They made it a place for body waste to this day. 28 So Jehu got rid of Baal from Israel.

29 But Jehu did not turn away from the sins of Jeroboam the son of Nebat, which he made Israel sin. He kept the gold calves at Bethel and Dan. 30 The Lord said to Jehu, "You have done well what is right in My eyes. You have done to the family of Ahab all that was in My heart. So your sons, even your great great grandson, will sit on the throne of Israel." 31 But Jehu was not careful to walk in the Law of the Lord, the God of Israel, with all his heart. He did not turn away from the sins of Jeroboam, which he made Israel sin.

The Death of Jehu

32 In those days the Lord began to cut off parts of Israel. Hazael won over them in battle through the land of Israel. 33 He took the land east of the Jordan, all the land of Gilead, the Gadites, the Reubenites and the Manassites, from Aroer, by the valley of the Arnon. He took Gilead and Bashan. 34 Now the rest of the acts of Jehu, all he did and all his strength, are they not written in the Book of the Chronicles of the Kings of Israel? 35 Then Jehu died and they buried him in Samaria. And his son Jehoahaz became king in his place. 36 Jehu ruled over Israel in Samaria for twenty-eight years.

Athaliah Rules Judah

11 When Ahaziah's mother Athaliah saw that her son was dead, she got up and killed all the king's children. 2 But King Joram's daughter Jehosheba,

Ahaziah's sister, took Joash the son of Ahaziah. She stole him away from the king's sons who were being killed, and put him and his nurse in the bedroom. They hid him from Athaliah, and he was not killed. 3 Joash was hid with his nurse in the house of the Lord six years, while Athaliah was ruling over the land.

4 In the seventh year, Jehoiada sent for the captains of hundreds, men who watch over the king and the soldiers. He brought them into the house of the Lord, and made an agreement with them. He had them make a promise in the house of the Lord. Then he showed them the king's son. 5 He told them, "This is what you must do. One-third of you who come in on the Day of Rest must keep watch over the king's house. 6 One-third are to be at the gate Sur and one-third at the gate behind the soldiers. So you will keep watch over the king's house. 7 And two parts of all of you who go out on the Day of Rest must keep watch over the house of the Lord for the king. 8 You will stand around the king, with spears in your hands. Whoever comes near must be killed. Be with the king when he goes out and when he comes in."

9 The captains of hundreds did all that Jehoiada the religious leader told them to do. Each one of them brought his men to Jehoiada the religious leader. Each one brought those who were to come in on the Day of Rest, and those who were to go out on the Day of Rest. 10 The religious leader gave the captains the spears and coverings that had been King David's, which were in the house of the Lord. 11 And the soldiers stood from the right side of the house to the left side of the house. Each one held his spear. They stood by the altar and by the house, around the king. 12 Then Jehoiada brought out the king's son and put the crown on him, and gave him the Law. They made him king and poured oil on him. Then they clapped their hands and said, "Long live the king!"

13 When Athaliah heard the noise of the soldiers and the people, she came to the people in the house of the Lord. 14 She looked and saw the king standing by the pillar, as was done in those days. The captains and those who blew horns were standing beside the king. And all the people of the land were filled with joy and blew horns. Athaliah tore her clothes and cried, "They are turning against the queen!" 15 Then Jehoiada the

religious leader told the captains of the army, "Bring her out among the soldiers, and kill with the sword whoever follows her." For the religious leader said, "Do not let her be put to death in the house of the Lord." 16 So they took hold of her, and she was put to death at the horses' gate of the king's house.

17 Then Jehoiada made an agreement between the Lord and the king and the people, that they should be the Lord's people. And he made an agreement between the king and the people. 18 Then all the people of the land went to the house of Baal and tore it down. They broke to pieces all his altars and objects. And they killed Mattan the religious leader of Baal in front of the altars. Then the religious leaders chose men to watch over the house of the Lord. 19 Jehoiada took the captains and the men who watch over the king, and the soldiers and all the people of the land. They brought the king down from the house of the Lord, by the way of the soldiers' gate, to the king's house. And he sat on the throne of the kings. 20 So all the people of the land were filled with joy, and the city was quiet. For they had put Athaliah to death with the sword at the king's house.

21 Joash was seven years old when he became king.

Joash Rules Judah

12 In the seventh year of Jehu, Joash became king. He ruled for forty years in Jerusalem. His mother's name was Zibiah of Beersheba. 2 Joash did what was right in the eyes of the Lord all his days, because Jehoiada the religious leader taught him. 3 But the high places were not taken away. The people still gave gifts and burned special perfume on the high places.

4 Then Joash said to the religious leaders, "All the money of the holy things brought into the house of the Lord, money for which each man is taxed, and money that is brought in because a man wants to bring it into the house of the Lord, 5 the religious leaders may take this money. Each leader should take it from those whom he knows. And they should use it to build the house again in the places where it has been broken and destroyed."

6 But by the twenty third year of King Joash, the religious leaders had not put together the broken places of the house. 7 So King Joash called for Jehoiada the religious leader and the other religious leaders. He said to them, "Why do you

not put together the broken places of the house? Do not take any more money from those you know, but give it for the work that is needed on the house." **8** So the religious leaders agreed that they should take no more money from the people. And they agreed that they should not do the work that was needed on the house.

9 Then Jehoiada the religious leader took a box and cut a hole in its cover. He put it beside the altar, on the right side as one comes into the house of the Lord. And the religious leaders who watched the door put all the money into it that was brought into the house of the Lord. **10** When they saw that there was much money in the box, the king's writer and the head religious leader came up to the house of the Lord. They found out how much money was there, and tied it up in bags. **11** After weighing it, they gave the money to those who watched over the work that was being done on the house of the Lord. Then these men paid the wood-workers and the builders who worked on the house of the Lord. **12** They paid the stonecutters and those who laid the stones in place. And they bought the cut wood and stone and all that was needed for the work on the house of the Lord. **13** But there were no silver cups, objects to put out the lights, pots, horns, or dishes of gold or silver made for the house of the Lord. None of these were made from the money brought into the house of the Lord. **14** For they gave that to those who did the work. It was used to put together the broken places of the house of the Lord. **15** And they did not ask the men who paid those who did the work how the money was spent. For they were men of honor. **16** The money from the guilt gifts and sin gifts was not brought into the house of the Lord. It was for the religious leaders.

17 At that time King Hazael of Syria went up and fought against Gath, and took it. Then he turned to go up to Jerusalem. **18** But Joash king of Judah took all the holy things that had been set apart by his fathers, Jehoshaphat, Jehoram and Ahaziah, kings of Judah. He took his own holy things, and all the gold that was found in the store-houses of the house of the Lord and the king's house. And he sent it to Hazael king of Syria. Then Hazael went away from Jerusalem.

19 The rest of the acts of Joash and all he did are written in the Book of the Chronicles of the Kings of Judah. **20** His servants made plans against Joash, and killed him at the house of Millo on the way down to Silla. **21** He was killed by Jozacar the son of Shimeath, and Jehozabad the son of Shomer, his servants. They buried him in the city of David. His son Amaziah became king in his place.

Jehoahaz Rules Israel

13 In the twenty-third year of Ahaziah's son Joash the king of Judah, Jehoahaz the son of Jehu became the king of Israel at Samaria. He ruled for seventeen years. **2** Jehoahaz did what was sinful in the eyes of the Lord. He followed the sins of Jeroboam the son of Nebat, which made Israel sin. He did not turn from them. **3** So the anger of the Lord burned against Israel. He put them always under the power of King Hazael of Syria, and Ben-hadad the son of Hazael. **4** Then Jehoahaz begged for the Lord's favor, and the Lord listened to him. For He saw the bad power held over Israel. He saw how the king of Syria made it hard for them. **5** So the Lord gave Israel someone to save them. And they were saved from the power of the Syrians. The people of Israel lived in their tents as before. **6** But they did not turn away from the sins of the family of Jeroboam, which made Israel sin. They walked in those sins. And the object of the false goddess Asherah was left standing in Samaria. **7** The king of Syria did not leave to Jehoahaz an army of more than fifty horsemen, ten war-wagons and 10,000 foot-soldiers. For the king of Syria had destroyed them and made them like the dust of beaten grain. **8** Now the rest of the acts of Jehoahaz, all he did and his strength, are written in the Book of the Chronicles of the Kings of Israel. **9** When Jehoahaz died, they buried him in Samaria. And his son Joash became king in his place.

Jehoash Rules Israel

10 In the thirty-seventh year of Joash king of Judah, Jehoash the son of Jehoahaz became king of Israel in Samaria. He ruled for sixteen years. **11** And he did what was sinful in the eyes of the Lord. He did not turn away from all the sins of Jeroboam the son of Nebat, in which he made Israel sin. But he walked in those sins. **12** Jehoash did many things. With his strength he fought against Amaziah king of Judah. The rest of his acts are written in the Book of the Chronicles of the Kings of Israel. **13** Jehoash died, and Jeroboam sat on his throne. Jehoash was buried in Samaria with the kings of Israel.

The Death of Elisha

14 Elisha became sick with the sickness of which he was to die. And Joash the king of Israel came down to him and cried over him, saying, "My father, my father, the war-wagons of Israel and its horsemen!" 15 Elisha said to him, "Take a bow and arrows." So he took a bow and arrows. 16 Then he said to the king of Israel, "Put your hand on the bow." So he put his hand on it. Then Elisha laid his hands on the king's hands. 17 And he said, "Open the window toward the east," and he opened it. Then Elisha said, "Shoot!" And he shot. Elisha said, "The Lord's arrow of winning the battle! The arrow of winning the battle against Syria! For you will fight the Syrians at Aphek until you have destroyed them. 18 Then Elisha said, "Take the arrows," and he took them. He said to the king of Israel, "Hit the ground," and he hit it three times, and stopped. 19 So the man of God was angry with him and said, "You should have hit it five or six times. Then you would have fought Syria until you had destroyed it. But now you will win the fight against Syria only three times."

20 Elisha died, and they buried him. Now groups of Moabite soldiers would come and fight in the land in the spring of the year. 21 As a man was being buried, some Moabite soldiers were seen, so the man was thrown into Elisha's grave. When the man touched the bones of Elisha, he came alive and stood up on his feet.

The War between Israel and Syria

22 Now King Hazael of Syria had made it hard for Israel all the days of Jehoahaz. 23 But the Lord showed them kindness and loving-pity and turned to them because of His agreement with Abraham, Isaac and Jacob. He would not destroy them or put them away from Him until now. 24 When King Hazael of Syria died, his son Ben-hadad became king in his place. 25 Then Jehoash the son of Jehoahaz took back from Hazael's son Ben-hadad the cities he had taken in war from his father Jehoahaz. Three times Joash won in battle against him and took back the cities of Israel.

Amaziah Rules Judah

14 In the second year of Jehoash the son of Jehoahaz, king of Israel, Joash's son Amaziah began to rule as king of Judah. 2 He was twenty-five years old when he became king. And he ruled twenty-nine years in Jerusalem. His mother's name was Jehoaddin of Jerusalem. 3 Amaziah did what was right in the eyes of the Lord, but not like David his father. He did all that his father Joash had done. 4 But the high places were not taken away. The people still gave gifts and burned special perfume on the high places. 5 As soon as the nation was under Amaziah's power, he killed the servants who had killed his father when he was king. 6 But he did not kill the sons of the killers. Because it is written in the Book of the Law of Moses, as the Lord said, "The fathers must not be put to death for the sons. And the sons must not be put to death for the fathers. Each must be put to death for his own sin." 7 Amaziah killed 10,000 Edomites in the Valley of Salt, and took Sela by war. He gave it the name Joktheel, which is its name to this day. 8 Then Amaziah sent men with news to Jehoash, the son of Jehoahaz son of Jehu, king of Israel, saying, "Come, let us look at each other in the face." 9 Jehoash king of Israel answered Amaziah king of Judah, saying, "The thorn bush in Lebanon sent word to the cedar tree in Lebanon, saying, 'Give your daughter to my son in marriage.' But a wild animal passed by in Lebanon, and crushed the thorn bush under its feet. 10 Yes, you have won the battle against Edom. Your heart has become proud. Be happy with your greatness and stay at home. For why should you make trouble so that you fall, and Judah with you?"

11 But Amaziah would not listen. So King Jehoash of Israel went up. He and Amaziah king of Judah fought each other at Beth-shemesh, which belongs to Judah. 12 Israel won the battle against Judah, and every man of Judah ran away to his tent. 13 King Jehoash of Israel took Amaziah king of Judah, son of Jehoash the son of Ahaziah, at Beth-shemesh. Then he came to Jerusalem and tore down the city wall, from the Gate of Ephraim to the Corner Gate. He tore down the wall as far as 200 long steps. 14 He took all the gold and silver and all the objects found in the house of the Lord and in the store-rooms of the king's house. He took people against their will also, and he returned to Samaria.

15 Now the rest of the acts of Jehoash, his strength and how he fought with King Amaziah of Judah are written in the Book of the Chronicles of the Kings of Israel. 16 Jehoash died and was buried in Samaria

with the kings of Israel. His son Jeroboam became king in his place.

The Death of Amaziah

17 Amaziah the son of Joash, king of Judah, lived fifteen years after the death of Jehoash the son of Jehoahaz, king of Israel. 18 The rest of the acts of Amaziah are written in the Book of the Chronicles of the Kings of Judah. 19 They made plans against Amaziah in Jerusalem, and he ran away to Lachish. But they sent men after him to Lachish and killed him there. 20 Then they brought him on horses and buried him with his fathers at Jerusalem the city of David. 21 The people of Judah took Azariah and made him king in the place of his father Amaziah. He was sixteen years old. 22 Azariah built Elath and returned it to Judah, after the king died.

Jeroboam II Rules Israel

23 In the fifteenth year of Amaziah the son of Joash, king of Judah, Jeroboam the son of Joash, king of Israel, began to rule in Samaria and ruled forty-one years. 24 Jeroboam did what was sinful in the eyes of the Lord. He did not turn away from all the sins of Jeroboam the son of Nebat, which made Israel sin. 25 He took back the land of Israel from Hamath as far as the Sea of the Arabah, as was told by the word of the Lord, the God of Israel. The Lord spoke about this through His servant Jonah the son of Amittai. Jonah was the man from Gath-hepher who spoke for the Lord. 26 For the Lord saw that the trouble of Israel was very bitter. There was no one left of the servants or of those who were free. There was no one to help Israel. 27 The Lord did not say that He would destroy the name of Israel from under heaven. So He saved them by the hand of Jeroboam the son of Joash.

28 Jeroboam fought Judah and took back Damascus and Hamath for Israel. The rest of the acts of Jeroboam, all he did and his strength are written in the Book of the Chronicles of the Kings of Israel. 29 Jeroboam was buried with his fathers, the kings of Israel. His son Zechariah became king in his place.

Azariah Rules Judah

15 In the twenty-seventh year of King Jeroboam of Israel, Azariah the son of Amaziah, king of Judah, began to rule. 2 Azariah was sixteen years old when he became king. And he ruled for fifty-two years in Jerusalem. His mother's name was Jecoliah of Jerusalem. 3 Azariah did what was right in the eyes of the Lord, just as his father Amaziah had done. 4 But the high places were not taken away. The people still gave gifts and burned special perfume on the high places. 5 So the Lord sent trouble upon the king. Azariah had a bad skin disease to the day of his death, and he lived in a house alone. Jotham the king's son ruled over the house, and judged the people of the land. 6 Now the rest of the acts of Azariah are written in the Book of the Chronicles of the Kings of Judah. 7 Azariah died and they buried him with his fathers in the city of David. His son Jotham became king in his place.

Zechariah Rules Israel

8 In the thirty-eighth year of Azariah king of Judah, Zechariah the son of Jeroboam became the king of Israel in Samaria for six months. 9 Zechariah did what was sinful in the eyes of the Lord, as his fathers had done. He did not turn away from the sins of Jeroboam the son of Nebat, which made Israel sin. 10 Then Shallum the son of Jabesh made plans against him and killed him in front of the people. And Shallum ruled in his place. 11 The rest of the acts of Zechariah are written in the Book of the Chronicles of the Kings of Israel. 12 This is the word of the Lord which He spoke to Jehu. He said, "Your sons, even your great great-grandson, will sit on the throne of Israel." And so it was.

Shallum Rules Israel

13 Shallum the son of Jabesh became king in the thirty-ninth year of Uzziah king of Judah. He ruled for one month in Samaria. 14 Then Menahem the son of Gadi went up from Tirzah to Samaria, and killed Shallum the son of Jabesh in Samaria, and became king in his place. 15 Now the rest of the acts of Shallum and the plans he made are written in the Book of the Chronicles of the Kings of Israel. 16 Then Menahem destroyed Tiphsah and all who were in it, and its land from Tirzah, because they did not open their gates to him. So he destroyed it, and tore open all its women who were going to have babies.

Menahem Rules Israel

17 In the thirty-ninth year of Azariah king of Judah, Menahem the son of Gadi became the king of Israel. He ruled for ten years in Samaria. 18 Menahem did what

was sinful in the eyes of the Lord. All his life he did not turn away from the sins of Jeroboam the son of Nebat, which made Israel sin.

¹⁹ King Pul of Assyria came to fight against the land. And Menahem gave Pul silver weighing as much as 1,000 men, that he might help him to be a powerful king. ²⁰ Menahem took the money from all the rich men of Israel. He took fifty pieces of silver from each man to pay the king of Assyria. So the king of Assyria returned and did not stay there in the land. ²¹ Now the rest of the acts of Menahem are written in the Book of the Chronicles of the Kings of Israel. ²² Menahem died, and his son Pekahiah became king in his place.

Pekahiah Rules Israel

²³ In the fiftieth year of Azariah king of Judah, Pekahiah the son of Menahem became the king of Israel in Samaria. He ruled for two years. ²⁴ Pekahiah did what was sinful in the eyes of the Lord. He did not turn away from the sins of Jeroboam the son of Nebat, which made Israel sin. ²⁵ Then his captain Pekah the son of Remaliah made plans against him. He killed Pekahiah in Samaria, in the house of the king with Argob and Arieh. Fifty men of the Gileadites were with Pekah. He became king in his place. ²⁶ Now the rest of the acts of Pekahiah are written in the Book of the Chronicles of the Kings of Israel.

Pekah Rules Israel

²⁷ In the fifty-second year of Azariah king of Judah, Pekah the son of Remaliah became the king of Israel in Samaria. He ruled for twenty years. ²⁸ Pekah did what was sinful in the eyes of the Lord. He did not turn away from the sins of Jeroboam the son of Nebat, which made Israel sin. ²⁹ In the days of King Pekah of Israel, King Tiglath-pileser of Assyria came to fight. The king of Assyria took Ijon, Abel-beth-maacah, Janoah, Kedesh, Hazor, Gilead, Galilee, and all the land of Naphtali. And he made the people go with him to Assyria. ³⁰ Hoshea the son of Elah made plans against Pekah the son of Remaliah. He killed Pekah and became king in his place, in the twentieth year of Jotham the son of Uzziah. ³¹ Now the rest of the acts of Pekah are written in the Book of the Chronicles of the Kings of Israel.

Jotham Rules Judah

³² In the second year of Pekah the son of Remaliah king of Israel, Jotham the son of Uzziah, king of Judah, began to rule. ³³ Jotham was twenty-five years old when he became king. He ruled for sixteen years in Jerusalem. His mother's name was Jerusha the daughter of Zadok. ³⁴ Jotham did what was right in the eyes of the Lord. He did all that his father Uzziah had done. ³⁵ But the high places were not taken away. The people still gave gifts and burned special perfume on the high places. Jotham built the upper gate of the house of the Lord. ³⁶ The rest of the acts of Jotham are written in the Book of the Chronicles of the Kings of Judah. ³⁷ In those days the Lord began to send Rezin the king of Syria and Pekah the son of Remaliah against Judah. ³⁸ Jotham died, and he was buried with his fathers in the city of David his father. His son Ahaz became king in his place.

Ahaz Rules Judah

16 In the seventeenth year of Pekah the son of Remaliah, Ahaz the son of Jotham began to rule as the king of Judah. ² Ahaz was twenty years old when he became king. And he ruled for sixteen years in Jerusalem. He did not do what was right in the eyes of the Lord his God, as his father David had done. ³ But he walked in the way of the kings of Israel. He even gave his sons as a burnt gift. This was very sinful and was done by the nations which the Lord had driven out from the people of Israel. ⁴ And Ahaz gave gifts in worship and burned special perfume on the high places, on the hills, and under every green tree.

⁵ Then King Rezin of Syria and Pekah the son of Remaliah, king of Israel, came up to Jerusalem to fight a war. Their armies closed in around Ahaz, but they could not win the battle against him. ⁶ At that time King Rezin of Syria took back Elath for Syria. And he drove all the men of Judah out of Elath. The Syrians came to Elath, and have lived there to this day.

⁷ So Ahaz sent men with news to King Tiglath-pileser of Assyria, saying, "I am your servant and your son. Come up and save me from the king of Syria and the king of Israel. They are fighting against me." ⁸ And Ahaz took the silver and gold from the house of the Lord and the store-rooms of the king's house, and sent a gift to the king of Assyria. ⁹ So the king of Assyria

listened to him and went up against Damascus. He took it in battle, and took its people away against their will to Kir. And he put Rezin to death.

¹⁰ King Ahaz went to Damascus to meet King Tiglath-pileser of Assyria. He saw the altar at Damascus. And King Ahaz sent to Urijah the religious leader the plans of the altar and a small object made to look just like it. ¹¹ So Urijah the religious leader built an altar, following all the plans King Ahaz had sent from Damascus. Urijah made it before King Ahaz came from Damascus. ¹² When the king came from Damascus, he saw the altar and went up to it. ¹³ There he burned his burnt gift and his grain gift. He poured his drink gift and put the blood of his peace gift on the altar. ¹⁴ He took the brass altar which was before the Lord in front of the house, between his altar and the Lord's house, and he put it on the north side of his altar. ¹⁵ Then King Ahaz told Urijah the religious leader, "Upon the large altar, give the morning burnt gift, the evening grain gift, and the king's burnt gift and his grain gift. Give them with the burnt gifts of all the people of the land and their grain gifts and drink gifts. Put on it all the blood of the burnt gifts given in worship. But the brass altar will be for me to go to when I ask the Lord what should be done." ¹⁶ Urijah the religious leader did all that King Ahaz told him.

¹⁷ Then King Ahaz cut off the pillars and took the water pots away from them. He took the big brass pool off of the brass bulls, and put it down on stone. ¹⁸ He took from the house of the Lord the covered way they had built in the house, and the king's gate because of the king of Assyria. ¹⁹ Now the rest of the acts of Ahaz are written in the Book of the Chronicles of the Kings of Judah. ²⁰ Ahaz died, and was buried with his fathers in the city of David. And his son Hezekiah ruled in his place.

Hoshea Rules Israel

17 In the twelfth year of Ahaz king of Judah, Hoshea the son of Elah became the king of Israel in Samaria. He ruled for nine years. ² Hoshea did what was sinful in the eyes of the Lord, but not as bad as the kings of Israel before him. ³ King Shalmaneser of Assyria came up against him. And Hoshea became his servant and paid taxes to him. ⁴ But the king of Assyria found that Hoshea had been making plans against him. Hoshea had sent men to King So of Egypt, instead of

giving taxes to the king of Assyria. He had done this year after year. So the king of Assyria shut him up and put him in chains in prison.

Israel Carried Away to Assyria

⁵ Then the king of Assyria came against all the land. He went up to Samaria and kept soldiers around it for three years. ⁶ In the ninth year of Hoshea, the king of Assyria took Samaria in battle, and took the people of Israel away to Assyria. He had them live in Halah and Habor, by the river of Gozan, and in the cities of the Medes.

⁷ This happened because the people of Israel had sinned against the Lord their God. He had brought them up from the land of Egypt from under the power of Pharaoh, king of Egypt. But they worshiped other gods. ⁸ They walked in the ways of the nations the Lord had driven out from the people of Israel. And they walked in the ways the kings of Israel had started. ⁹ The people of Israel did things in secret which were not right, against the Lord their God. They built high places for themselves in all their towns, from the smallest town to the strongest city. ¹⁰ They set up holy objects of the false goddess Asherim on every high hill and under every green tree. ¹¹ There they burned special perfume on all the high places, as the nations did which the Lord carried away from them. They did what was bad and made the Lord angry. ¹² They worshiped false gods, about which the Lord had told them, "You must not do this." ¹³ The Lord told Israel and Judah of the danger, through all His men who told what would happen in the future. He said, "Turn from your sinful ways and obey My Laws. Keep all the Laws which I gave your fathers, and which I gave to you through My servants and men of God." ¹⁴ But they did not listen. They were strong-willed like their fathers, who did not believe in the Lord their God. ¹⁵ They turned away from His Laws and His agreement which He made with their fathers. They turned away when He told them of danger. They followed false gods, and became empty. They followed the nations around them. But the Lord had told them not to act like them. ¹⁶ They turned away from all the Laws of the Lord their God and made objects to look like false gods. They made two calves and an object to look like the false goddess Asherah. And they worshiped all the stars of heaven and worked for Baal. ¹⁷ Then they gave their

sons and daughters as burnt gifts. They told the future and used witchcraft. They sold themselves to do what is sinful in the eyes of the Lord. And they made Him angry. 18 The Lord was very angry with Israel, and put them away from his eyes. None was left except the family of Judah.

19 Even Judah did not keep the Laws of the Lord their God. They walked in the ways which Israel had started. 20 And the Lord turned away from all the children of Israel, and sent trouble upon them. He gave them over to those who destroyed the land, until He had put them away from His eyes. 21 When He had torn Israel from the family of David, they made Jeroboam the son of Nebat king. Then Jeroboam drove Israel away from following the Lord. He led them into sin. 22 And the people of Israel walked in all the sins of Jeroboam. They did not turn away from them, 23 until the Lord put Israel away from His eyes. He spoke through all His servants who tell what will happen in the future that He would do this. So Israel was carried away from their own land to Assyria until this day.

Assyrians Live in Israel

24 The king of Assyria brought people from Babylon, Cuthah, Avva, Hamath and Sepharvaim. He had them live in the cities of Samaria in place of the people of Israel. So they took Samaria for their own, and lived in its cities. 25 At the beginning of their living there, they did not fear the Lord. So the Lord sent lions among them, which killed some of them. 26 They said to the king of Assyria, "The nations you have carried away to the cities of Samaria do not know the way of the god of the land. So He has sent lions among them to kill them because they do not know the way of the god of the land."

27 Then the king of Assyria told them, "Take to Samaria one of the religious leaders you brought from there. Let him go and live in Samaria. And let him teach them the way of the god of the land." 28 So one of the religious leaders they had taken away from Samaria came and lived at Bethel. And he taught them how they should worship the Lord.

29 But every nation still made gods of its own. They put them in the houses of the high places which the people of Samaria had made. The people of every nation did this in the cities where they lived. 30 The men of Babylon made the false god

Succoth-benoth. The men of Cuth made the false god Nergal. The men of Hamath made the false god Ashima. 31 The Avvites made the false gods Nibhaz and Tartak. And the Sepharvites burned their children in the fire to Adram-melech and Anam-melech, the gods of Sepharvaim. 32 They feared the Lord also, and yet they chose from among themselves religious leaders of the high places. These leaders gave the gifts for them in the houses of the high places. 33 So the people feared the Lord, but they worshiped their own gods also. They followed the way of the nations from which they had been taken away.

34 To this day, they follow the ways of times past. They do not honor the Lord. They do not follow the Laws or the Word which the Lord told the sons of Jacob, whom He gave the name Israel. 35 The Lord had made an agreement and told them, "You must not fear other gods. You must not put your faces to the ground in front of them, or worship them, or give gifts to them. 36 But fear the Lord, Who brought you up from the land of Egypt with great power and with a strong arm. Put your faces to the ground before Him. And give Him your gifts. 37 Obey forever the Laws and the Word which He wrote for you. Do not fear other gods. 38 Do not forget the agreement I have made with you. And do not honor other gods with fear. 39 Fear the Lord your God and He will save you from those who hate you." 40 But they did not listen. They followed the ways of times past. 41 These nations feared the Lord, but they worshiped their false gods also. Their children and grand-children did the same, and they do as their fathers did to this day.

Hezekiah Rules Judah

18 In the third year of Hoshea the son of Elah king of Israel, Hezekiah the son of Ahaz, king of Judah, began to rule. 2 He was twenty five years old when he became king. And he ruled for twenty-nine years in Jerusalem. His mother's name was Abi the daughter of Zechariah. 3 Hezekiah did what was right in the eyes of the Lord, just as his father David had done. 4 He took away the high places. He broke down the holy pillars used in worship and cut down the Asherah. And he broke in pieces the brass snake that Moses had made. For until those days the people of Israel burned special perfume to it. It was called Nehushtan. 5 Hezekiah trusted

in the Lord, the God of Israel. There was no one like him among all the kings of Judah before him or after him. 6 For he held to the Lord and did not stop following Him. He kept His Laws which the Lord had given Moses. 7 And the Lord was with him. Hezekiah did well in every place he went. He turned against the king of Assyria and did not work for him. 8 He destroyed the Philistines as far as Gaza and its land, from the smallest town to the strongest city.

9 In the fourth year of King Hezekiah, the seventh year of Elah's son Hoshea king of Israel, King Shalmaneser of Assyria came to fight against Samaria. His army gathered around it. 10 At the end of three years they took the city. Samaria was taken by Assyria in the sixth year of Hezekiah and the ninth year of King Hoshea of Israel. 11 Then the king of Assyria carried the people of Israel away against their will to Assyria. He had them live in Halah and on the Habor, the river of Gozan, and in the cities of the Medes. 12 Because the people of Israel did not obey the voice of the Lord their God. They sinned against His agreement and even all that the Lord's servant Moses told them. They would not listen or obey.

The Assyrians Want to Take Jerusalem

13 In the fourteenth year of King Hezekiah, King Sennacherib of Assyria came and fought against all the strong cities of Judah and took them. 14 Then King Hezekiah of Judah sent word to the king of Assyria at Lachish, saying, "I have done wrong; leave me. I will pay whatever you ask." So the king of Assyria had Hezekiah king of Judah pay him silver weighing as much as 300 men, and gold weighing as much as thirty men. 15 Hezekiah gave him all the silver that was found in the house of the Lord, and in the store-rooms of the king's house. 16 Then he cut the gold off the doors of the Lord's house. He cut the gold from the sides of the door which King Hezekiah of Judah had covered with gold. And he gave it to the king of Assyria.

17 Then the king of Assyria sent Tartan, Rab-saris and Rabshakeh with a large army from Lachish to King Hezekiah at Jerusalem. So they went up and came to Jerusalem. They came and stood by the ditch of the upper pool, which is on the road to the fuller's field. 18 When they called to the king, Eliakim the son of Hilkiah, and Shebnah, and Joah the son of Asaph came out to them. Eliakim was the head of the house. Shebnah was the writer, and Joah wrote down the things of the nation. 19 Rabshakeh said to them, "Say to Hezekiah, 'This is what the great king of Assyria says. "What is this strength of heart that you have? 20 You say with empty words, 'I have wisdom and strength for war.' On whom do you trust, that you have turned against me? 21 Look, you are trusting now in Egypt. It is a walking stick like a piece of broken river-grass. It will cut into a man's hand if he rests on it. So is Pharaoh king of Egypt to all who trust in him. 22 You might tell me, 'We trust in the Lord our God.' But is it not He Whose high places and altars Hezekiah has taken away? And has he not said to Judah and Jerusalem, 'You must worship in front of this altar in Jerusalem'? 23 Come now, make an agreement with my ruler the king of Assyria. And I will give you 2,000 horses, if you are able to put horsemen on them. 24 How can you fight back one captain among the least of my ruler's servants, when you trust Egypt for war-wagons and horsemen? 25 Have I come up without the Lord against this place to destroy it? The Lord said to me, 'Go up against this land and destroy it.'"

26 Then Eliakim the son of Hilkiah, and Shebnah, and Joah, said to Rabshakeh, "Speak to your servants in the Aramaic language, for we understand it. Do not speak with us in the language of Judah. The people on the wall might hear it." 27 But Rabshakeh said to them, "Has my ruler sent me to speak these words to your ruler and to you, and not to the men sitting on the wall? They are sure to suffer with you, eating and drinking their own body waste." 28 Then Rabshakeh stood and called out with a loud voice in the language of Judah, saying, "Hear the word of the great king of Assyria. 29 The king says, 'Do not let Hezekiah lie to you. For he will not be able to save you from my power. 30 Do not let Hezekiah make you trust in the Lord, saying, "The Lord will save us for sure. And this city will not be given to the king of Assyria." 31 Do not listen to Hezekiah. For the king of Assyria says, "Make your peace with me and come out to me. Then every one of you will eat of his own vine and fig tree. And every one of you will drink the water of his own well. 32 Then I will come and take you away to a land like your own land. It is a land of grain and new wine. It is a land of bread and grape-fields and olive trees and honey. There you will

live and not die." But do not listen to Hezekiah when he lies to you, saying, "The Lord will save us." ³³ Has any one of the gods of the nations saved his land from the power of the king of Assyria? ³⁴ Where are the gods of Hamath and Arpad? Where are the gods of Sepharvaim, Hena and Ivvah? Have they saved Samaria from my power? ³⁵ Who among all the gods of the lands have saved their land from my power? So how should the Lord save Jerusalem from my power?' " ³⁶ But the people were quiet. They did not answer him a word. For Hezekiah had told them, "Do not answer him." ³⁷ Then Eliakim the son of Hilkiah who was the head of the house, and Shebna the writer, and Joah the son of Asaph who wrote down the things of the nation, came to Hezekiah. They came with their clothes torn and told him the words of Rabshakeh.

Hezekiah Talks to Isaiah

19 When King Hezekiah heard about it, he tore his clothes and covered himself with cloth made from hair. Then he went into the house of the Lord. ² He sent Eliakim who was the head of the house, Shebna the writer, and the head religious leaders, to the man of God Isaiah the son of Amoz. They were covered with cloth made from hair. ³ And they said to him, "Hezekiah says, 'This day is a day of trouble, sharp words, and shame. For children have come to be born, but there is no strength to give birth to them. ⁴ It might be that the Lord your God will hear all the words of Rabshakeh, whom his ruler the king of Assyria has sent to make fun of the living God. And the Lord your God might speak sharp words against what He has heard. So pray for them who are left of the Lord's people.' " ⁵ The servants of King Hezekiah came to Isaiah. ⁶ And Isaiah said to them, "Tell your ruler, 'This is what the Lord says: "Do not be afraid because of the words you have heard spoken against Me by the servants of the king of Assyria. ⁷ See, I will put a spirit in him so that he will hear a made-up story and he will return to his own land. And I will have him killed by the sword in his own land." ' "

Assyrians Talk of Taking Jerusalem Again

⁸ Rabshakeh returned and found the king of Assyria fighting against Libnah. For he had heard that the king had left Lachish. ⁹ The king of Assyria was told, "See, King Tirhakah of Cush has come out to fight

against you." So he sent men again to Hezekiah, saying, ¹⁰ "Tell King Hezekiah of Judah, 'Do not let your God in Whom you trust lie to you by saying that Jerusalem will not be given into the power of the king of Assyria. ¹¹ You have heard how the kings of Assyria have destroyed all the lands. And will you be saved? ¹² Did the gods of those nations which my fathers destroyed save them? Gozan, Haran, Rezeph, and the people of Eden who were in Telassar, were destroyed. ¹³ Where are the kings of Hamath, Arpad, the city of Sepharvaim, Hena and Ivvah?' "

¹⁴ Hezekiah took the letter from the hand of the men from Assyria, and read it. Then he went up to the house of the Lord, and spread the letter out before the Lord. ¹⁵ Hezekiah prayed to the Lord, saying, "O Lord the God of Israel, You sit on Your throne above the cherubim. You are the God, and You alone, of all the nations of the earth. You have made heaven and earth. ¹⁶ Turn Your ear, O Lord, and hear. Open Your eyes, O Lord, and see. Listen to the words Sennacherib has spoken against the living God. ¹⁷ O Lord, it is true that the kings of Assyria have destroyed the nations and their lands. ¹⁸ They have thrown their gods into the fire. For they were not gods, but the work of men's hands, made from wood and stone. So they have destroyed them. ¹⁹ Now, O Lord our God, I beg You to save us from his power. Then all the nations of the earth may know that You alone are God, O Lord."

Isaiah's Word to the King

²⁰ Isaiah the son of Amoz sent word to Hezekiah, saying, "The Lord, the God of Israel, says, 'I have heard your prayer to Me about Sennacherib king of Assyria.' ²¹ This is the Word that the Lord has spoken against him: 'She has hated you and made fun of you, the young daughter of Zion! She has shaken her head behind you, the daughter of Jerusalem! ²² Whom have you spoken against? Against whom have you raised your voice, and lifted your eyes in pride? Against the Holy One of Israel! ²³ You have spoken against the Lord through the men you have sent. You have said, "With my many war-wagons I have come up to the tops of the mountains, to the farthest parts of Lebanon. I cut down its tall cedar trees and its best cypress trees. I went to its highest place, where its trees are close together. ²⁴ I dug wells and drank the water of other lands. I dried up

all the rivers of Egypt with the bottom of my feet."

25 'Have you not heard that I planned this long ago? From times long ago I planned it. Now I have made it happen, that you should destroy strong cities. **26** That is why those who lived there did not have much strength. They were troubled and put to shame. They were like the plants of the field and the green grass. They were like grass on the roofs, killed by the sun before it is grown. **27** But I know when you sit down, go out, and come in. And I know how you speak in anger against Me. **28** You have spoken against Me in your anger and pride, and I have heard it. So I will put My hook in your nose, and My bit in your mouth. And I will have you return by the way you came.

29 'This will be the special thing for you to see: This year you will eat what grows of itself. In the second year you will eat what grows of the same. Then in the third year, you will plant seeds and gather food. You will plant vines and eat their fruit. **30** And those who are left of the family of Judah will again take root and give fruit. **31** For those who are left will go out of Jerusalem. Those who are still alive will go out of Mount Zion. This will be done by the power of the Lord. **32** So this is what the Lord says about the king of Assyria: He will not come to this city and shoot an arrow there. He will not come to it with a battle-covering or build a wall around it. **33** He will return by the way he came. He will not come to this city, says the Lord. **34** For I will help this city and save it, because of My honor, and because of My servant David.' "

Sennacherib's Death

35 That night the angel of the Lord went out and killed 185,000 men among the Assyrian tents. When those left alive got up early in the morning, they saw all the dead bodies. **36** Then King Sennacherib of Assyria left and returned home, and lived at Nineveh. **37** As he was worshiping in the house of his god Nisroch, Adrammelech and Sharezer killed him with the sword. Then they ran away to the land of Ararat. And his son Esarhaddon became king in his place.

Hezekiah Will Live Fifteen Years Longer

20 In those days Hezekiah became sick enough to die. The man of God, Isaiah the son of Amoz, came to him and said, "This is what the Lord says, 'Get those of your house ready. For you will die. You will not get well again.' " **2** Then Hezekiah turned his face to the wall and prayed to the Lord, saying, **3** "I beg You, O Lord, remember how I have walked before You in truth and with a whole heart. I have done what is good in Your eyes." And Hezekiah cried much. **4** Before Isaiah had gone out of the center room, the word of the Lord came to him, saying, **5** "Return to Hezekiah the leader of My people. Tell him, 'This is what the Lord, the God of your father David, says, "I have heard your prayer. I have seen your tears. See, I will heal you. On the third day you must go up to the house of the Lord. **6** And I will add fifteen years to your life. I will save you and this city from the power of the king of Assyria. And I will help this city because of My honor and because of My servant David." ' " **7** Then Isaiah said, "Bring a loaf made of figs. Have them take and lay it on the sore on Hezekiah's body. Then he will be well again." And they took and laid it on the boil and he was healed.

8 Hezekiah said to Isaiah, "What will be the special thing for me to see, that the Lord will heal me, and that I will go up to the house of the Lord on the third day?" **9** Isaiah said, "This will be the special thing for you to see from the Lord, to show that the Lord will do what He has said. Will the shadow go ten steps farther, or go back ten steps?" **10** Hezekiah answered, "It is easy for the shadow to go ten steps farther. But let the shadow turn back ten steps." **11** So Isaiah the man of God cried to the Lord, and the Lord brought the shadow back ten steps, on the steps set up by King Ahaz.

Men Come from Babylon

12 At that time Berodach-baladan, a son of Baladan, king of Babylon, sent letters and a gift to Hezekiah. For he heard that Hezekiah had been sick. **13** Hezekiah listened to them and showed them all his riches. He showed them the silver, the gold, the spices, the oil of much worth, the things used in battle, and all that was found in his store-rooms. There was nothing in his house, or in all the places of his rule, that Hezekiah did not show them. **14** Then Isaiah the man of God came to King Hezekiah and said, "What did these men say? From where have they come to you?" Hezekiah said, "They have come from a far country, from Babylon." **15** Isaiah said, "What have they seen in your house?" And Hezekiah answered, "They have seen all that is in my house. There is nothing among my riches that I have not shown them."

16 Then Isaiah said to Hezekiah, "Hear the word of the Lord. 17 'See, the days are coming when all that is in your house, all that your fathers have kept in store to this day, will be carried to Babylon. Nothing will be left,' says the Lord. 18 'And some of your sons who will be born to you will be taken away. They will be servants in the house of the king of Babylon.' " 19 Hezekiah said to Isaiah, "The word of the Lord which you have spoken is good." For he thought, "Why not, if there will be peace and people will be safe in my days?"

The Death of Hezekiah

20 Now the rest of the acts of Hezekiah and all his strength are written in the Book of the Chronicles of the Kings of Judah. He made the pool and the ditch and brought water into the city. 21 Hezekiah died, and his son Manasseh became king in his place.

Manasseh Rules Judah

21 Manasseh was twelve years old when he became king. And he ruled fifty-five years in Jerusalem. His mother's name was Hephzibah. 2 Manasseh did what was sinful in the eyes of the Lord. He did the sinful things that were done by the nations whom the Lord drove out from the people of Israel. 3 He built again the high places which his father Hezekiah had destroyed. He built altars for Baal and made an object out of wood to worship the false goddess Asherah. He did as Ahab king of Israel had done. He worshiped all the stars of heaven and served them. 4 He built altars in the house of the Lord, of which the Lord had said, "In Jerusalem I will put My name." 5 Manasseh built altars for all the stars of heaven in the two open spaces of the Lord's house. 6 He gave his son as a burnt gift, used witchcraft and told the future. He listened to those who spoke with spirits and used their secret ways. He did things that were very sinful in the eyes of the Lord, and made the Lord angry. 7 Then Manasseh put the object he had made for Asherah into the house of the Lord. But the Lord had said to David and to his son Solomon, "I have chosen this house and Jerusalem from all the families of Israel. Here I will put My name forever. 8 I will not make the feet of Israel travel any more from the land I gave to their fathers. But they must obey all that I have told them,

and all the Law that My servant Moses told to them." 9 But they did not listen. Manasseh led them to sin more than the nations whom the Lord destroyed from in front of the people of Israel.

10 Now the Lord spoke through His servants who tell what will happen in the future. He said, 11 "Manasseh king of Judah has done these sinful things. He has sinned more than all the Amorites who were before him. And he has made Judah sin with his false gods. Because he has done this, 12 the Lord, the God of Israel, says, 'See, I am bringing such trouble upon Jerusalem and Judah, that the ears of whoever hears it will be painful. 13 I will punish Jerusalem as I did Samaria and as I did the family of Ahab. I will dry Jerusalem as one dries a dish, rubbing it and turning it upside-down. 14 I will leave alone all who are left of My people, and give them to those who hate them. They will become something taken after the battle by those who fight against them. 15 Because they have done what is bad in My eyes. They have been making Me angry since the day their fathers came from Egypt until this day.'

16 Manasseh killed many who were without guilt. He filled Jerusalem with blood from one end to another. He sinned and made Judah sin, by doing what is sinful in the eyes of the Lord. 17 Now the rest of the acts of Manasseh and his sins are written in the Book of the Chronicles of the Kings of Judah. 18 Manasseh died and was buried in the garden of his own house, in the garden of Uzza. And his son Amon became king in his place.

Amon Rules Judah

19 Amon was twenty-two years old when he became king. He ruled for two years in Jerusalem. His mother's name was Meshullemeth the daughter of Haruz of Jotbah. 20 Amon did what was sinful in the eyes of the Lord, as his father Manasseh had done. 21 He walked in all the ways that his father had walked. He worshiped false gods like his father had. 22 So he turned away from the Lord, the God of his fathers. He did not walk in the way of the Lord. 23 And the servants of Amon made plans against him, and killed the king in his own house. 24 Then the people of the land killed all those who had made plans against King Amon. And they made Josiah his son king in his place. 25 Now the rest of the acts of Amon are written in the Book of the Chronicles of the Kings of Judah.

26 He was buried in his grave in the garden of Uzza. And his son Josiah became king in his place.

Josiah Rules Judah

22 Josiah was eight years old when he became king. He ruled for thirty-one years in Jerusalem. His mother's name was Jedidah the daughter of Adaiah of Bozkath. 2 Josiah did what is right in the eyes of the Lord. He walked in all the way of his father David. He did not turn aside to the right or to the left.

Hilkiah Finds the Book of the Law

3 In the eighteenth year of King Josiah, the king sent Shaphan the writer, the son of Azaliah, son of Meshullam, to the house of the Lord. He said, 4 "Go up to Hilkiah the head religious leader, that he may add up the money brought into the Lord's house which the door-keepers have gathered from the people. 5 Let the money be given to the workmen who are watching over the work on the Lord's house. And let them give it to the workmen who are doing the work on the Lord's house. 6 Have them pay the builders and the men who work with wood and with stone. Have them use it for buying wood and cut stone needed to work on the house. 7 But do not make them tell you how the money was spent that was given to them. For they are honest men."

8 Then Hilkiah the head religious leader said to Shaphan the writer, "I have found the Book of the Law in the house of the Lord." And Hilkiah gave the book to Shaphan, and he read it. 9 Then Shaphan the writer came to the king and told him, "Your servants have taken all the money found in the house. And they have given it to the workmen who are watching over the work on the Lord's house." 10 Then Shaphan the writer told the king, "Hilkiah the religious leader has given me a book." And Shaphan read it in front of the king. 11 When the king heard the words of the Book of the Law, he tore his clothes. 12 Then he told Hilkiah the religious leader, Ahikam the son of Shaphan, Achbor the son of Micaiah, Shaphan the writer, and Asaiah the king's servant, 13 "Go, ask the Lord for me and all Judah about the words of this book that has been found. For the Lord is very angry with us, because our fathers have not listened to the words of this book. They have not done all that is written for us to do."

14 So Hilkiah the religious leader, Ahikam, Achbor, Shaphan and Asaiah went to Huldah the woman who spoke for God. She was the wife of Shallum the son of Tikvah, son of Harhas, and watched over the clothes of the house. (She lived in the Second Part of Jerusalem.) They spoke to her. 15 She said to them, "This is what the Lord God of Israel says. Tell the man who sent you to me 16 that the Lord says, 'See, I will bring trouble upon this place and upon its people. All the words of the book which the king of Judah has read will come true 17 because they have turned away from Me and have burned special perfume to other gods. They have made Me angry with all the work of their hands. So My anger burns against this place, and it will not be stopped.' 18 But tell the king of Judah who sent you to ask of the Lord, 'This is what the Lord God of Israel says about the words you have heard. 19 "You heard how I spoke against this place and against its people. I said that they should be destroyed and laid waste. They should be hated and destroyed. But when you heard this, you were sorry in your heart. You put away your pride before the Lord. You have torn your clothes and cried before Me, and I have heard you," says the Lord. 20 "So I will gather you to your fathers, and you will be gathered to your grave in peace. Your eyes will not see all the trouble which I will bring upon this place." ' " So they returned to the king and told him what was said.

Josiah Brings Back True Worship

23 Then King Josiah sent men out to bring to him all the leaders of Judah and Jerusalem. 2 The king went up to the house of the Lord with all the men of Judah and all the people who lived in Jerusalem. The religious leaders, the men who speak for God, and all the people went with him, both small and great. And Josiah read in their hearing all the words of the Book of the Law which was found in the house of the Lord. 3 Then the king stood by the pillar. There he made an agreement before the Lord. He promised to follow the Lord and keep His Word and His Laws with all his heart and soul. He promised to obey the words of this agreement that were written in this book, and all the people joined him in the agreement.

4 Then the king spoke to Hilkiah the head religious leader, and the religious

leaders who were next in power, and the door-keepers. He told them to bring out of the Lord's house all the objects made for the false gods Baal and Asherah and for all the stars of heaven. He burned them outside Jerusalem in the fields of the Kidron. And he carried their ashes to Bethel. **5** He got rid of the religious leaders who worshiped false gods, whom the kings of Judah had chosen. They had been chosen to burn special perfume in the high places in the cities of Judah and in the land around Jerusalem. Josiah got rid of those who burned special perfume to Baal, to the sun and the moon, to groups of stars, and to all the stars of heaven. **6** He brought out the object of the false goddess Asherah from the Lord's house to the river Kidron outside Jerusalem. There he burned it and ground it to dust, and threw its dust on the people's graves. **7** He broke down the small rooms in the Lord's house that were used by the men who sold the use of their bodies for their false gods. The women were making special curtains for the false goddess Asherah in these rooms. **8** Then King Josiah brought all the religious leaders from the cities of Judah. And he showed how sinful the high places were where the religious leaders had burned special perfume, from Geba to Beersheba. He broke down the high places at the gate of Joshua the leader of the city, which were to the left of the city gate. **9** The religious leaders of the high places did not go up to the altar of the Lord in Jerusalem. But they ate bread without yeast among their brothers. **10** The king made Topheth unclean, which is in the valley of the sons of Hinnom. He did this so no one might give his son or daughter there as a burnt gift to the false god Molech. **11** Josiah got rid of the horses which the kings of Judah had given to the sun. They had given them at the door of the Lord's house, by the room of Nathan-melech the leader. And the king burned the war-wagons of the sun with fire. **12** King Josiah broke down the altars which were on the roof of Ahaz's room on the second floor. They had been made by the kings of Judah. And he broke down the altars which Manasseh had made in the two open spaces of the Lord's house. He broke them there and threw their dust into the river Kidron. **13** The king made the high places sinful which were east of Jerusalem and south of the Mount of Destruction. King Solomon of Israel had built them for Ashtoreth the sinful goddess of

the Sidonians, Chemosh the hated false god of Moab, and Milcom the hated god of the sons of Ammon. **14** And Josiah broke in pieces the pillars used in worship and cut down the Asherim. He filled their places with human bones.

15 The king broke down the altar at Bethel and the high place made by Jeroboam the son of Nebat, who made Israel sin, even that altar and the high place he broke down. He crushed its stones, ground them to dust, and burned the false goddess Asherah. **16** As Josiah turned, he saw the graves that were there on the mountain. He had the bones taken from the graves, and burned them on the altar. So he made the altar sinful, as the word of the Lord said would happen, through the man of God. **17** Then Josiah said, "What is this that I see?" The men of the city told him, "It is the grave of the man of God who came from Judah. He is the one who said that these things would happen which you have done against the altar of Bethel." **18** Josiah said, "Let him alone. Let no one move his bones." So they let his bones alone, with the bones of the man of God who came from Samaria. **19** Josiah took away all the houses of the high places in the cities of Samaria. The kings of Israel had made the Lord angry by building them. The king did to them just as he had done in Bethel. **20** And he killed on the altar all the religious leaders of the high places who were there. He burned human bones on them. Then he returned to Jerusalem.

Josiah Keeps the Passover

21 King Josiah told all the people, "Keep the Passover to the Lord your God, as it is written in this Book of the Law." **22** For sure no such Passover had been kept since the days of the judges who ruled Israel. It had not been kept in all the days of the kings of Israel or Judah. **23** But this Passover was kept to the Lord in Jerusalem in the eighteenth year of King Josiah.

24 Josiah put away the people who spoke with spirits, and people who used their secret ways. He put away the house gods and the false gods and all the sinful things that were seen in the land of Judah and in Jerusalem. He did this to obey the words of the Law which were written in the book that was found in the Lord's house by Hilkiah the religious leader. **25** Before Josiah there was no king like him who turned to the Lord with all his heart and soul and strength, obeying all the Law of Moses. And no one like him came after him.

26 But the Lord did not stop from being very angry against Judah. Because Manasseh had done many things to make Him angry, 27 The Lord said, "I will put Judah away from My eyes, as I have put away Israel. I will put away Jerusalem, this city I have chosen. And I will put away the family of which I said, 'My name will be there.'"

Josiah Dies in Battle

28 Now the rest of the acts of Josiah are written in the Book of the Chronicles of the Kings of Judah. 29 In his days Pharaoh Neco king of Egypt went up to the king of Assyria to the river Euphrates. King Josiah went to meet him. And Pharaoh Neco killed him at Megiddo when he saw him. 30 Josiah's servants carried his body from Megiddo in a war-wagon. They brought him to Jerusalem and buried him in his own grave. Then the people of the land took his son Jehoahaz and poured oil on him and made him king in his father's place.

Jehoahaz Rules Judah

31 Jehoahaz was twenty-three years old when he became king. He ruled for three months in Jerusalem. His mother's name was Hamutal the daughter of Jeremiah of Libnah. 32 Jehoahaz did what was sinful in the eyes of the Lord. He did all that his fathers had done. 33 Pharaoh Neco put him in prison at Riblah in the land of Hamath, that he might not rule in Jerusalem. And he made the people of the land pay a tax of silver weighing as much as one hundred men, and gold weighing as much as one man. 34 Pharaoh Neco made Josiah's son Eliakim king in the place of his father Josiah. And he changed his name to Jehoiakim. But he took Jehoahaz away to Egypt, where he died.

Jehoiakim Rules Judah

35 So Jehoiakim gave the silver and gold to Pharaoh. But he taxed the land to give Pharaoh the money he wanted. He took the silver and gold from the people of the land, from each one by the amount of tax he was made to pay. And he gave it to Pharaoh Neco. 36 Jehoiakim was twenty-five years old when he became king. He ruled for eleven years in Jerusalem. His mother's name was Zebidah the daughter of Pedaiah of Rumah. 37 Jehoiakim did what was sinful in the eyes of the Lord. He did just as his fathers had done.

24 In his days Nebuchadnezzar king of Babylon came up, and Jehoiakim became his servant for three years. Then he turned against him. 2 The Lord sent armies of Babylonians, Syrians, Moabites and Ammonites against Jehoiakim. He sent them against Judah to destroy it, just as the word of the Lord had said through His men who spoke for Him. 3 This came upon Judah at the word of the Lord, to put them away from His eyes because of the sins Manasseh had done. 4 And it happened because of the people Manasseh had killed who were not guilty. For he filled Jerusalem with their blood, and the Lord would not forgive. 5 Now the rest of the acts of Jehoiakim are written in the Book of the Chronicles of the Kings of Judah. 6 Jehoiakim died, and his son Jehoiachin became king in his place. 7 And the king of Egypt did not leave his land again. For the king of Babylon had taken all that belonged to the king of Egypt from the river of Egypt to the river Euphrates.

Jehoiachin Rules Judah

8 Jehoiachin was eighteen years old when he became king. He ruled for three months in Jerusalem. His mother's name was Nehushta the daughter of Elnathan of Jerusalem. 9 Jehoiachin did what was sinful in the eyes of the Lord. He did just as his father had done.

10 At that time the servants of Nebuchadnezzar king of Babylon went up to Jerusalem. His soldiers gathered around the city. 11 King Nebuchadnezzar of Babylon came to the city, while his soldiers were all around it trying to take it. 12 King Jehoiachin of Judah went out to the king of Babylon. He took with him his mother, his servants, his captains and his leaders. The king of Babylon took him away in the eighth year of his rule. 13 And Nebuchadnezzar carried away all the riches of the Lord's house and of the king's house. He cut in pieces all the objects of gold which King Solomon of Israel had made in the house of the Lord. It happened just as the Lord had said. 14 Then the king of Babylon led away all who lived in Jerusalem. He led away all the captains, all the powerful soldiers, and all those who were able to make things. He took 10,000 people away to Babylon. Only the very poor people of the land were left behind. 15 So he led Jehoiachin away to Babylon. He also led away the king's mother, his wives, his leaders, and the most important men of

the land. He took them from Jerusalem to Babylon. 16 He led away all the powerful soldiers, 7,000 men. And he led away 1,000 of those who were able to make things. All of them were strong and able to fight in battle. Nebuchadnezzar took them away to Babylon. 17 Then he made Mattaniah, the brother of Jehoiachin's father, king in his place, and changed his name to Zedekiah.

Zedekiah Rules Judah

18 Zedekiah was twenty-one years old when he became king. He ruled for eleven years in Jerusalem. His mother's name was Hamutal the daughter of Jeremiah of Libnah. 19 Zedekiah did what was sinful in the eyes of the Lord. He did all that Jehoiakim had done. 20 For because of the anger of the Lord, this happened in Jerusalem and Judah until the Lord put them away from Him. And Zedekiah turned against the king of Babylon.

Jerusalem Is Taken

25 On the tenth day of the tenth month in the ninth year of his rule, King Nebuchadnezzar of Babylon and all his army came against Jerusalem. His army set up their tents around the city, and built a wall all around it. 2 The city had the army of Babylon around it until the eleventh year of King Zedekiah. 3 On the ninth day of the fourth month, there was no food left in the city. There was no more food for the people of the land. 4 Then the city was broken into. All the men of war ran during the night between the two walls beside the king's garden. The Babylonians were all around the city, but the men left by the way of the Arabah. 5 Then the Babylonian army went after the king and came to him in the plains of Jericho. All his army ran away from him. 6 The Babylonians took the king and brought him to the king of Babylon at Riblah. And Nebuchadnezzar told him how he must be punished. 7 They killed Zedekiah's sons in front of his eyes. Then they put out Zedekiah's eyes and tied him up in chains, and brought him to Babylon.

The House of God Is Destroyed

8 On the seventh day of the fifth month, in the nineteenth year of King Nebuchadnezzar of Babylon, Nebuzaradan came to Jerusalem. He was the captain of the soldiers, a servant of the king of Babylon. 9 He burned the house of the Lord, the king's

house, and all the houses of Jerusalem. He burned every great house with fire. 10 And all the Babylonian army who were with the captain of the soldiers broke down the walls around Jerusalem. 11 Then Nebuzaradan the captain of the soldiers carried away to Babylon the rest of the people who were left in the city. And he carried away the soldiers who had run away from the battle. 12 But the captain of the soldiers left behind some of the very poor people of the land to take care of the vines and to plow the fields.

13 The Babylonians broke in pieces the brass pillars in the house of the Lord. And they broke in pieces the stands and the brass pool which were in the house of the Lord. Then they carried the brass to Babylon. 14 They took away the pots, the tools for digging, the things for putting out the lamps, the dishes for special perfume, and all the brass dishes used for the work of the Lord's house. 15 And they took away the fire-holders and the wash-pots. The captain of the soldiers took away what was made of fine gold and what was made of fine silver. 16 The brass of the two pillars, the one pool, and the stands which Solomon had made for the Lord's house, was too much to weigh. 17 One pillar was five times taller than a man. The brass top piece on it was three cubits tall. A network and pomegranates made of brass were all around the top piece. And the second pillar had the same, with a network.

People of Judah Are Taken to Babylon

18 Then the captain of the soldiers took Seraiah the head religious leader, and Zephaniah the religious leader next in power. And he took the three men who were keepers of the door. 19 From the city he took a captain who led the men of war, and five men found in the city who had spoken with the king about what should be done. He took the captain of the army, who called together the people of the land. And he took sixty men of the land who were found in the city. 20 Nebuzaradan the captain of the soldiers took them and brought them to the king of Babylon at Riblah. 21 Then the king of Babylon killed them. He put them to death at Riblah in the land of Hamath. So Judah was taken away from its land.

Gedaliah Is Leader of Judah

22 King Nebuchadnezzar of Babylon had left some people in the land of Judah. He

chose Gedaliah the son of Ahikam, son of Shaphan, to rule over them. 23 All the captains of the armies and their men heard that the king of Babylon had chosen Gedaliah to be leader. So they came to Gedaliah at Mizpah. The captains who came with their men were Ishmael the son of Nethaniah, Johanan the son of Kareah, Seraiah the son of Tanhumeth the Netophathite, and Jaazaniah the son of Maacathite. 24 Gedaliah made a promise to them and their men. He said to them, "Do not be afraid of the Babylonian leaders. Live in the land and work for the king of Babylon. Then it will be well with you."

25 But in the seventh month Ishmael came. He was the son of Nethaniah, son of Elishama, of the king's family. He came with ten men and killed Gedaliah and the Jews and Babylonians who were with him at Mizpah. 26 Then all the people, both small and great, and the captains of the armies left and went to Egypt. For they were afraid of the Babylonians.

27 On the twenty-seventh day of the twelfth month, in the thirty-seventh year since King Jehoiachin of Judah was taken away from his land, Evil-merodach became the king of Babylon. He showed favor to King Jehoiachin of Judah, and let him out of prison that year. 28 He spoke kind words to him, and set his throne above the thrones of the kings who were with him in Babylon. 29 Jehoiachin changed from his prison clothes. And he ate with the king all the rest of his life. 30 The King gave him a share of food every day for the rest of his life.

1 CHRONICLES

Families from Adam to Abraham

1 Adam, Seth, Enosh, 2 Kenan, Mahalalel, Jared, 3 Enoch, Methuselah, Lamech, 4 Noah and his sons: Shem, Ham and Japheth.

5 The sons of Japheth were Gomer, Magog, Madai, Javan, Tubal, Meshech, and Tiras. 6 The sons of Gomer were Ashkenaz, Diphath, and Togarmah. 7 The sons of Javan were Elishah, Tarshish, Kittim, and Rodanim.

8 The sons of Ham were Cush, Mizraim, Put, and Canaan. 9 The sons of Cush were Seba, Havilah, Sabta, Raama, and Sabteca. And the sons of Raamah were Sheba and Dedan. 10 Cush was the father of Nimrod. He began to be a powerful one on the earth. 11 Mizraim was the father of the people of Lud, Anam, Lehab, Naphtuh, 12 Pathrus, Casluh (where the Philistines came from), and Caphtor.

13 Canaan was the father of Sidon his first-born, and Heth, 14 and the Jebusites, Amorites, Girgashites, 15 Hivites, Arkites, Sinites, 16 Arvadites, Zemarites and Hamathites.

17 The sons of Shem were Elam, Asshur, Arpachshad, Lud, Aram, Uz, Hul, Gether, and Meshech. 18 Arpachshad was the father of Shelah. And Shelah was the father of Eber. 19 Two sons were born to Eber. The name of one was Peleg, for the earth was divided in his days. And his brother's name was Joktan. 20 Joktan was the father of Almodad, Sheleph, Hazarmaveth, Jerah, 21 Hadoram, Uzal, Diklah, 22 Ebal, Abimael, Sheba, 23 Ophir, Havilah, and Jobab. All these were the sons of Joktan.

24 Shem, Arpachshad, Shelah, 25 Eber, Peleg, Reu, 26 Serug, Nahor, Terah, 27 Abram, that is Abraham. 28 The sons of Abraham were Isaac and Ishmael.

The Family of Ishmael

29 These are their children. Ishmael's first-born son was Nebaioth, then Kedar, Adbeel, Mibsam, 30 Mishma, Dumah, Massa, Hadad, Tema, 31 Jetur, Naphish and Kedemah. These were the sons of Ishmael. 32 Keturah was the woman who acted as Abraham's wife. She gave birth to Abraham's sons, Zimram, Jokshan, Medan, Midian, Ishbak and Shuah. The sons of Jokshan were Sheba and Dedan. 33 The sons of Midian were Ephah, Epher, Hanoch, Abida and Eldaah. All these were the sons of Keturah.

The Family of Esau

34 Abraham was the father of Isaac. The sons of Isaac were Esau and Israel. 35 The sons of Esau were Eliphaz, Reuel, Jeush, Jalam and Korah. 36 The sons of Eliphaz were Teman, Omar, Zephi, Gatam, Kenaz, Timna and Amalek. 37 The sons of Reuel were Nahath, Zerah, Shammah and Mizzah.

The Family of Seir

38 The sons of Seir were Lotan, Shobal, Zibeon, Anah, Dishon, Ezer and Dishan.

39 The sons of Lotan were Hori and Homam. Lotan's sister was Timna. **40** The sons of Shobal were Alian, Manahath, Ebal, Shephi and Onam. The sons of Zibeon were Aiah and Anah. **41** Anah's son was Dishon. And the sons of Dishon were Hamran, Eshban, Ithran and Cheran. **42** The sons of Ezer were Bilhan, Zaavan and Jaakan. The sons of Dishan were Uz and Aran.

The Kings of Edom

43 These are the kings who ruled in the land of Edom before any kings of Israel ruled. Bela was the son of Beor. The name of his city was Dinhabah. **44** When Bela died, Jobab the son of Zerah of Bozrah became king in his place. **45** When Jobab died, Husham of the land of the Temanites became king in his place. **46** When Husham died, Hadad the son of Bedad became king in his place. Hadad won the battle against Midian in the field of Moab. The name of his city was Avith. **47** When Hadad died, Samlah of Masrekah became king in his place. **48** When Samlah died, Shaul of Rehoboth by the Euphrates River became king in his place. **49** When Shaul died, Baal-hanan the son of Achbor became king in his place. **50** When Baal-hanan died, Hadad became king in his place. The name of his city was Pai. His wife's name was Mehetabel the daughter of Matred, the daughter of Mezahab. **51** Then Hadad died. Now the leaders of Edom were Timna, Aliah, Jetheth, **52** Oholibamah, Elah, Pinon, **53** Kenaz, Teman, Mibzar, **54** Magdiel, and Iram. These were the leaders of Edom.

The Family of Israel

2 The sons of Israel were Reuben, Simeon, Levi, Judah, Issachar, Zebulun, **2** Dan, Joseph, Benjamin, Napthali, Gad, and Asher.

The Families from Judah to David

3 The sons of Judah were Er, Onan and Shelah. These three were born to him by Bath-shua of Canaan. Judah's first-born son Er was sinful in the eyes of the Lord. So the Lord put him to death. **4** Judah's daughter-in-law Tamar gave birth to Perez and Zerah. Judah had five sons in all. **5** The sons of Perez were Hezron and Hamul. **6** The sons of Zerah were Zimri, Ethan, Heman, Calcol and Dara, five in all. **7** Carmi's son was Achar, who brought trouble to Israel by sinning against what was holy. **8** The son of Ethan was Azariah.

9 The sons born to Hezron were Jerahmeel, Ram and Chelubai. **10** Ram was the father of Amminadab, and Amminadab was the father of Nahshon, the leader of the sons of Judah. **11** Nahshon was the father of Salma. Salma was the father of Boaz. **12** Boaz was the father of Obed. And Obed was the father of Jesse. **13** Jesse was the father of Eliab his first-born, then Abinadab his second son, and Shimea his third. **14** Nethanel was his fourth son, Raddai the fifth, **15** Ozem the sixth, and David the seventh. **16** Their sisters were Zeruiah and Abigail. Zeruiah's three sons were Abshai, Joab and Asahel. **17** Abigail gave birth to Amasa. And Amasa's father was Jether the Ishmaelite.

The Family of Hezron

18 Hezron's son Caleb had sons by his wives Azubah and Jerioth. Azubah's sons were Jesher, Shobab and Ardon. **19** When Azubah died, Caleb married Ephrath. She gave birth to his son Hur. **20** Hur was the father of Uri. And Uri was the father of Bezalel.

21 Later, when Hezron was sixty years old, he married the daughter of Machir the father of Gilead. She gave birth to his son Segub. **22** Segub was the father of Jair, who had twenty-three cities in the land of Gilead. **23** But Geshur and Aram took the towns of Jair from them, with Kenath and its towns. They took sixty cities in all. All these were the sons of Machir, the father of Gilead. **24** After Hezron died in Caleb-ephrathah, his wife Abijah gave birth to his son Ashhur. Ashhur was the father of Tekoa.

The Family of Jerahmeel

25 The sons of Hezron's first-born Jerahmeel were Ram the first-born, then Bunah, Oren, Ozem and Ahijah. **26** Jerahmeel had another wife, whose name was Atarah. She was the mother of Onam. **27** The sons of Jerahmeel's first-born son Ram were Maaz, Jamin and Eker. **28** The sons of Onam were Shammai and Jada. And the sons of Shammai were Nadab and Abishur. **29** The name of Abishur's wife was Abihail. She gave birth to his sons Ahban and Molid. **30** The sons of Nadab were Seled and Appaim. Seled died without sons. **31** Appaim's son was Ishi. Ishi's son was Sheshan. And Sheshan's son was Ahlai. **32** The sons of Shammai's brother Jada were Jether and Jonathan. Jether died without sons. **33** The sons of

Jonathan were Peleth and Zaza. These were the sons of Jerahmeel. 34 Now Sheshan had no sons, only daughters. And Sheshan had an Egyptian servant whose name was Jarha. 35 Sheshan gave his daughter to his servant Jarha in marriage. And she gave birth to his son Attai. 36 Attai was the father of Nathan. Nathan was the father of Zabad. 37 Zabad was the father of Ephlal. Ephlal was the father of Obed. 38 Obed was the father of Jehu. Jehu was the father of Azariah. 39 Azariah was the father of Helez. Helez was the father of Eleasah. 40 Eleasah was the father of Sismai. Sismai was the father of Shallum. 41 Shallum was the father of Jekamiah. And Jekamiah was the father of Elishama.

The Family of Caleb

42 These are the sons of Jerahmeel's brother Caleb. Mesha was his first-born and the father of Ziph. His son was Mareshah, the father of Hebron. 43 The sons of Hebron were Korah, Tappuah, Rekem and Shema. 44 Shema was the father of Raham, the father of Jorkeam. Rekem was the father of Shammai. 45 Shammai's son was Maon. Maon was the father of Bethzur. 46 Ephah was the woman who acted as Caleb's wife. She gave birth to Haran, Moza and Gazez. Haran was the father of Gazez. 47 The sons of Jahdai were Regem, Jotham, Geshan, Pelet, Ephah, and Shaaph. 48 Maacah, who acted as Caleb's wife, gave birth to Sheber and Tirhanah. 49 She also gave birth to Shaaph the father of Madmannah, and Sheva the father of Machbena and Gibea. Caleb's daughter was Achsah. 50 These were the children of Caleb.

The sons of Ephrathah's first-born son Hur were Shobal the father of Kiriath-jearim, 51 Salma the father of Bethlehem, and Hareph the father of Beth-gader. 52 Shobal the father of Kiriath-jearim had other sons. These were Haroeh, half of the Manahathites, 53 and the families of Kiriath-jearim. These families were the Ithrites, the Puthites, the Shumathites, and the Mishraites. From these came the Zorathites and the Eshtaolites. 54 The sons of Salma were Bethlehem and the Netophathites, Atroth-beth-joab, half of the Manahathites, and the Zorites. 55 The families of the writers who lived at Jabez were the Tirathites, the Shimeathites and the Sucathites. These are the Kenites who came from Hammath, the father of the house of Rechab.

The Family of David

3 These were the sons of David who were born to him in Hebron. The first-born was Amnon, whose mother was Ahinoam of Jezreel. The second was Daniel, the son of Abigail of Carmel. 2 The third was Absalom the son of Maacah, the daughter of King Talmai of Geshur. The fourth was Adonijah the son of Haggith. 3 The fifth was Shephatiah the son of Abital. And the sixth was Ithream, by David's wife Eglah. 4 Six sons were born to David in Hebron. He ruled there for seven years and six months. And he ruled in Jerusalem for thirty-three years. 5 These are the sons who were born to him in Jerusalem: Bathsheba the daughter of Ammiel gave birth to David's four sons, Shimea, Shobab, Nathan and Solomon. 6 And there were Ibhar, Elishama, Eliphelet, 7 Nogah, Nepheg, Japhia, 8 Elishama, Eliada, and Eliphelet, nine sons. 9 All these were the sons of David, added to the sons of the women who acted as David's wives. Tamar was their sister.

The Family of Solomon

10 Solomon's son was Rehoboam. Abijah was his son. Asa was his son. Jehoshaphat was his son. 11 Joram was his son. Ahaziah was his son. Joash was his son. 12 Amaziah was his son. Azariah was his son. Jotham was his son. 13 Ahaz was his son. Hezekiah was his son. Manasseh was his son. 14 Amon was his son. Josiah was his son. 15 The sons of Josiah were Johanan the first-born, Jehoiakim the second, Zedekiah the third, and Shallum the fourth. 16 The sons of Jehoiakim were Jeconiah and Zedekiah.

The Family of Jeconiah

17 Jeconiah was taken away to prison by the Babylonians. His sons were Shealtiel, 18 Malchiram, Pedaiah, Shenazzar, Jekamiah, Hoshama, and Nedabiah. 19 Pedaiah's sons were Zerubbabel and Shimei. And the sons of Zerubbabel were Meshullam and Hananiah. Shelomith was their sister. 20 Five other sons of Zerubbabel were Hashubah, Ohel, Berechiah, Hasadiah, and Jushab-hesed. 21 The sons of Hananiah were Pelatiah and Jeshaiah, whose son was Rephaiah. His son was Arnan. His son was Obadiah. And his son was Shecaniah. 22 Shecaniah's son was Shemaiah, whose sons were Hattush, Igal, Bariah, Neariah, and Shaphat, six sons. 23 The three sons of Neariah were

Elioenai, Hizkiah and Azrikam. 24 And the seven sons of Elioenai were Hodaviah, Eliashib, Pelaiah, Akkub, Johanan, Delaiah, and Anani.

The Family of Judah

4 The sons of Judah were Perez, Hezron, Carmi, Hur and Shobal. 2 Shobal's son Reaiah was the father of Jahath. And Jahath was the father of Ahumai and Lahad. These were the families of the Zorathites. 3 The sons of Etam were Jezreel, Ishma and Idbash. The name of their sister was Hazzelelponi. 4 Penuel was the father of Gedor. Ezer was the father of Hushah. These were the sons of Hur, the first-born of Ephrathah, the father of Bethlehem. 5 Tekoa's father Ashhur had two wives, Helah and Naarah. 6 Naarah gave birth to Ahuzzam, Hepher, Temeni and Haahashtari. These were the sons of Naarah. 7 The sons of Helah were Zereth, Izhar and Ethnan. 8 Koz was the father of Anub, Zobebah, and the families of Aharhel the son of Harum. 9 Jabez was more a man of honor than his brothers. His mother gave him the name Jabez, saying, "Because I gave birth to him in pain." 10 Jabez called on the God of Israel, saying, "O, if only You would bring good to me and give me more land! If only Your hand might be with me, that You would keep me from being hurt!" And God gave him what he asked for.

11 Shuhah's brother Chelub was the father of Mehir, who was the father of Eshton. 12 Eshton was the father of Bethrapha and Paseah. Tehinnah was the father of Irnahash. These are the men of Recah.

13 The sons of Kenaz were Othniel and Seraiah. Othniel's son was Hathath. 14 Meonothai was the father of Ophrah. Seraiah was the father of Joab, who was the father of Ge-harashim. They were good at making things. 15 Jephunneh's son Caleb was the father of Iru, Elah and Naam. Elah's son was Kenaz. 16 The sons of Jehallelel were Ziph, Ziphah, Tiria and Asarel. 17 The sons of Ezrah were Jether, Mered, Epher and Jalon. These are the sons of Pharaoh's daughter Bithia, whom Mered married. She gave birth to Miriam, Shammai, and Ishbah the father of Eshtemoa. 18 Mered's Jewish wife gave birth to Jered the father of Gedor, Heber the father of Soco, and Jekuthiel the father of Zanoah. 19 The sons of Hodiah's wife, the sister of Naham, were the fathers of Keilah the Garmite and Eshtemoa the Maacathite.

20 Shimon's sons were Amnon, Rinnah, Benhanan and Tilon. The sons of Ishi were Zoheth and Ben-zoheth. 21 The sons of Shelah the son of Judah were Er the father of Lecah, Laadah the father of Mareshah, and the families of the house of those who worked with linen at Bethashbea. Shelah's other sons were 22 Jokim, the men of Cozeba, Joash, Saraph who ruled in Moab, and Jaashubi-lehem. The writings of these times are old. 23 These were the people who made pots and lived in Netaim and Gederah. They lived there with the king for his work.

The Family of Simeon

24 The sons of Simeon were Nemuel, Jamin, Jarib, Zerah, and Saul. 25 Saul's son was Shallum. His son was Mibsam. And his son was Mishma. 26 Mishma's sons were Hammuel, Zaccur his son, and Shimei his son. 27 Shimei had sixteen sons and six daughters. But his brothers did not have many children. Their whole family did not have many children, like the sons of Judah. 28 They lived at Beersheba, Moladah, Hazar-shual, 29 Bilhah, Ezem, Tolad, 30 Bethuel, Hormah, Ziklag, 31 Beth-marcaboth, Hazar-susim, Bethbiri, and Shaaraim. These were their cities until David ruled. 32 Their towns were Etam, Ain, Rimmon, Tochen and Ashan, five towns. 33 And they had all the small towns that were around these towns as far as Baal. These were the places where they lived. And they wrote down all the names of their families. 34 The heads of their families were Meshobab, Jamlech, Joshah the son of Amaziah, 35 Joel, and Jehu the son of Joshibiah, the son of Seraiah, the son of Asiel. 36 And there were Elioenai, Jaakobah, Jeshohaiah, Asaiah, Adiel, Jesimiel, Benaiah, 37 and Ziza the son of Shiphi, the son of Allon, the son of Jedaiah, the son of Shimri, the son of Shemaiah. 38 These were the names of the heads of their families. And many were added to their fathers' houses. 39 They went to the gate of Gedor, to the east side of the valley, to look for fields for their flocks. 40 There they found good fields rich with grass. The land was wide and quiet, and there they had peace. For Hamites had lived there before. 41 These whose names have been written down came in the days of Hezekiah king of Judah. They destroyed their tents and the Meunites who were found there. They destroyed all of them to this day, and lived in their place because

there were fields for their flocks. **42** Then some of them, 500 sons of Simeon, went to Mount Seir. Their leaders were Pelatiah, Neariah, Rephaiah, and Uzziel, the sons of Ishi. **43** They destroyed the rest of the Amalekites who had run away to be safe. And they have lived there to this day.

The Family of Reuben

5 Reuben was the first-born son of Israel but because he sinned against his father's marriage bed, his birth-right was given to the sons of Joseph the son of Israel. Reuben is not written down in the family names by his birth-right. **2** Judah became stronger than his brothers, and a prince came from him. But the birth-right belonged to Joseph. **3** The sons of Reuben the first-born of Israel were Hanoch, Pallu, Hezron and Carmi. **4** The sons of Joel were Shemaiah, Gog his son, Shimei his son, **5** Micah his son, Reaiah his son, Baal his son, **6** and Beerah his son. Beerah was the one whom Tilgath-pilneser king of Assyria carried away to a strange land. He was a leader of the Reubenites. **7** These are his brothers by their families, from the writings of their family names. There was Jeiel the leader, then Zechariah, **8** and Bela the son of Azaz, the son of Shema, the son of Joel, who lived in Aroer as far as Nebo and Baal-meon. **9** He lived as far east as the beginning of the desert this side of the Euphrates River, because their cattle had become too many for the land of Gilead. **10** In the days of Saul they made war with the Hagrites and killed them. So they lived in their tents over all the land east of Gilead.

The Family of Gad

11 The sons of Gad lived beside them in the land of Bashan as far as Salecah. **12** Joel was the leader. Then there was Shapham, then Janai, and Shaphat in Bashan. **13** Their seven brothers of their fathers' houses were Michael, Meshullam, Sheba, Jorai, Jacan, Zia, and Eber. **14** These were the sons of Abihail, the son of Huri, the son of Jaroah, the son of Gilead, the son of Michael, the son of Jeshishai, the son of Jahdo, the son of Buz. **15** Ahi the son of Abdiel, the son of Guni, was head of their fathers' houses. **16** They lived in Gilead, in Bashan and its towns, and in all the fields of Sharon as far as they go. **17** All of these were added to the family names in the days of King Jotham of Judah and King Jeroboam of Israel.

18 The sons of Reuben, the Gadites and the half-family group of Manasseh were powerful soldiers. They carried the battle-covering and the sword, and shot with the bow. They were able men in battle. There were 44,760 of them who went to war. **19** They made war against the Hagrites, Jetur, Naphish and Nodab. **20** They were given help against them, and the Hagrites and all who were with them were given into their hand. They cried out to God in the battle. He gave them what they asked for, because they trusted in Him. **21** They took away their animals, 50,000 camels, 250,000 sheep, 2,000 donkeys, and 100,000 men. **22** Many were killed, because the war was of God. They lived in their place until they were taken away by Assyria.

The Family of Manasseh East of the Jordan River

23 The sons of the half-family group of Manasseh lived in the land. There were many of them from Bashan to Baal-hermon, Senir and Mount Hermon. **24** The heads of their fathers' houses were Epher, Ishi, Eliel, Azriel, Jeremiah, Hodaviah, and Jahdiel. They were powerful soldiers, men whose names were well-known. And they were heads of their fathers' houses.

25 But they sinned against the God of their fathers. They sold themselves to the gods of the people of the land, whom God had destroyed before them. **26** So the God of Israel moved the spirit of Pul king of Assyria, also known as Tilgath-pilneser king of Assyria. And he carried the Reubenites, the Gadites and the half-family group of Manasseh away to a strange land. He brought them to Halah, Habor, Hara, and the river of Gozan. And they are there to this day.

The Family of Levi

6 The sons of Levi were Gershon, Kohath and Merari. **2** The sons of Kohath were Amram, Izhar, Hebron and Uzziel. **3** The children of Amram were Aaron, Moses and Miriam. And the sons of Aaron were Nadab, Abihu, Eleazar and Ithamar. **4** Eleazar was the father of Phinehas. Phinehas was the father of Abishua. **5** Abishua was the father of Bukki. Bukki was the father of Uzzi. **6** Uzzi was the father of Zerahiah. Zerahiah was the father of Meraioth. **7** Meraioth was the father of Amariah. Amariah was the father of Ahitub. **8** Ahitub was the father of

Zadok. Zadok was the father of Ahimaaz. 9 Ahimaaz was the father of Azariah. Azariah was the father of Johanan. 10 Johanan was the father of Azariah. (He was the one who served as the religious leader in the house which Solomon built in Jerusalem.) 11 Azariah was the father of Amariah. Amariah was the father of Ahitub. 12 Ahitub was the father of Zadok. Zadok was the father of Shallum. 13 Shallum was the father of Hilkiah. Hilkiah was the father of Azariah. 14 Azariah was the father of Seraiah. Seraiah was the father of Jehozadak. 15 Jehozadak was taken away when the Lord carried Judah and Jerusalem away to a strange land by Nebuchadnezzar.

16 The sons of Levi were Gershom, Kohath and Merari. 17 The names of the sons of Gershom were Libni and Shimei. 18 The sons of Kohath were Amram, Izhar, Hebron and Uzziel. 19 The sons of Merari were Mahli and Mushi. These are the families of the Levites by their fathers' houses. 20 Of Gershom there were Libni his son, Jahath his son, Zimmah his son, 21 Joah his son, Iddo his son, Zerah his son, and Jeatherai his son. 22 The sons of Kohath were Amminadab, Korah his son, Assir his son, 23 Elkanah his son, Ebiasaph his son, Assir his son, 24 Tahath his son, Uriel his son, Uzziah his son, and Saul his son. 25 The sons of Elkanah were Amasai and Ahimoth, 26 Elkanah his son, Zophai his son, Nahath his son, 27 Eliab his son, Jeroham his son, and Elkanah his son. 28 The sons of Samuel were Joel the first-born, and Abijah the second. 29 The sons of Merari were Mahli, Libni his son, Shimei his son, Uzzah his son, 30 Shimea his son, Haggiah his son, and Asaiah his son.

Singers in the House of the Lord

31 David chose these men to lead the singing in the house of the Lord, after the special box with the Law of the Lord rested there. 32 They led the singing in front of the meeting tent until Solomon had built the house of the Lord in Jerusalem. And they took their places for their work at the right times. 33 These are the men who served, and their sons. From the sons of the Kohathites were Heman the singer, the son of Joel, son of Samuel, 34 son of Elkanah, son of Jeroham, son of Eliel, son of Toah, 35 son of Zuph, son of Elkanah, son of Mahath, son of Amasai, 36 son of Elkanah, son of Joel, son of Azariah, son of Zephaniah, 37 son of Tahath. Tahath was the son of Assir, son of Ebiasaph, son of Korah, 38 son

of Izhar, son of Kohath, son of Levi, son of Israel. 39 Heman's brother Asaph stood at his right hand. Asaph was the son of Berechiah, son of Shimea, 40 son of Michael, son of Baaseiah, son of Malchijah, 41 son of Ethni, son of Zerah. Zerah was the son of Adaiah, 42 son of Ethan, son of Zimmah, son of Shimei, 43 son of Jahath, son of Gershom, son of Levi. 44 On the left hand were their brothers the sons of Merari. There was Ethan the son of Kishi, son of Abdi, son of Malluch, 45 son of Hashabiah, son of Amaziah. Amaziah was the son of Hilkiah, 46 son of Amzi, son of Bani, son of Shemer, 47 son of Mahli, son of Mushi, son of Merari, son of Levi. 48 Their brothers the Levites were chosen for all the work of the house of God.

The Family of Aaron

49 But Aaron and his sons gave the gifts on the altar of burnt gifts and on the altar of special perfume. They did all the work of the most holy place, to pay for the sins of Israel. They did all that Moses the servant of God had told them to do. 50 The sons of Aaron were Eleazar, Phinehas his son, Abishua his son, 51 Bukki his son, Uzzi his son, Zerahiah his son, 52 Meraioth his son, Amariah his son, Ahitub his son, 53 Zadok his son, and Ahimaaz his son.

54 These are the places where they lived in their lands. The sons of Aaron of the families of the Kohathites were first to choose where to live. 55 They were given Hebron in the land of Judah, and the fields around it. 56 But the fields of the city and its towns were given to Caleb the son of Jephunneh. 57 The sons of Aaron were given cities where people go to be safe. These cities were Hebron, Libnah with its fields, Jatir, Eshtemoa with its fields, 58 Hilen with its fields, Debir with its fields, 59 Ashan with its fields, and Beth-shemesh with its fields. 60 From the family of Benjamin they were given Geba with its fields, Allemeth with its fields, and Anathoth with its fields. There were thirteen cities in all, by their families.

61 Ten cities were given, by drawing names, to the rest of the sons of Kohath. These cities were given from the families of the half-family group of Manasseh. 62 Thirteen cities were given to the sons of Gershom, by their families. These cities were given from the families of Issachar, Asher, Naphtali, and Manasseh. 63 Twelve cities were given, by drawing names, to the sons of Merari, by their families. These

cities were given from the families of Reuben, Gad, and Zebulun. 64 So the people of Israel gave to the Levites the cities with their fields. 65 By drawing names, they gave them these cities which are written here, from the families of the sons of Judah, Simeon and Benjamin.

66 Some of the families of the sons of Kohath had cities of their land from the family of Ephraim. 67 They were given cities where anyone could go to be safe. These cities were Shechem in the hill country of Ephraim with its fields, Gezer with its fields, 68 Jokmeam with its fields, Beth-horon with its fields, 69 Aijalon with its fields, and Gath-rimmon with its fields. 70 From the half-family group of Manasseh they were given Aner with its fields and Bileam with its fields. They were for the rest of the family of the sons of Kohath.

71 Cities were given to the sons of Gershom from the half-family group of Manasseh. These cities were Golan in Bashan with its fields and Ashtaroth with its fields. 72 From the family of Issachar they were given Kedesh with its fields, Daberath with its fields, 73 Ramoth with its fields, and Anem with its fields. 74 From the family of Asher they were given Mashal with its fields, Abdon with its fields, 75 Hukok with its fields, and Rehob with its fields. 76 From the family of Naphtali they were given Kedesh in Galilee with its fields, Hammon with its fields, and Kiriathaim with its fields.

77 The rest of the Levites, the sons of Merari were given cities from the family of Zebulun. These cities were Rimmono with its fields and Tabor with its fields. 78 On the other side of the Jordan at Jericho, on the east side of the Jordan, they were given cities from the family of Reuben. These cities were Bezer in the desert with its fields, Jahzah with its fields, 79 Kedemoth with its fields, and Mephaath with its fields. 80 From the family of Gad they were given Ramoth in Gilead with its fields, Mahanaim with its fields, 81 Heshbon with its fields, and Jazer with its fields.

The Family of Issachar

7 The four sons of Issachar were Tola, Puah, Jashub and Shimron. 2 The sons of Tola were Uzzi, Rephaiah, Jeriel, Jahmai, Ibsam and Samuel, heads of their fathers' houses. Tola's sons were powerful soldiers among the people of their day. There were 22,600 of these men in the days of David. 3 The son of Uzzi was Izrahiah. And the sons of Izrahiah were Michael, Obadiah, Joel and Isshiah. All five of them were leaders. 4 With them by their families and by their fathers' houses were 36,000 men ready to fight. For they had many wives and sons. 5 Their brothers among all the families of Issachar were powerful soldiers. There were 87,000 of them, whose names were written down by their families.

The Families of Benjamin and Naphtali

6 The three sons of Benjamin were Bela, Becher and Jediael. 7 The five sons of Bela were Ezbon, Uzzi, Uzziel, Jerimoth and Iri. They were heads of their fathers' houses and powerful soldiers. There were 22,034 of them, whose names were written down by their families. 8 The sons of Becher were Zemirah, Joash, Eliezer, Elioenai, Omri, Jeremoth, Abijah, Anathoth and Alemeth. All these were the sons of Becher. 9 Their names were written down by their families. They were heads of their fathers' houses, 20,200 powerful soldiers. 10 The son of Jediael was Bilhan. And the sons of Bilhan were Jeush, Benjamin, Ehud, Chenaanah, Zethan, Tarshish and Ahishahar. 11 All these were sons of Jediael, by the heads of their fathers' houses. They were 17,200 powerful soldiers, who were ready to go out with the army to battle. 12 Shuppim and Huppim were the sons of Ir. Hushim was the son of Aher.

13 The sons of Naphtali were Jahziel, Guni, Jezer and Shallum, the sons of Bilhah.

The Family of Manasseh West of the Jordan River

14 Manasseh's sons were Asriel and Machir the father of Gilead. Their mother was the Aramaean woman who acted as Manasseh's wife. 15 Machir took a wife of Huppim and Shuppim, whose sister's name was Maacah. The name of the second was Zelophehad. And Zelophehad had daughters. 16 Machir's wife Maacah gave birth to a son, and gave him the name Peresh. His brother's name was Sheresh. And his sons were Ulam and Rakem. 17 The son of Ulam was Bedan. These were the sons of Gilead the son of Machir, the son of Manasseh. 18 His sister Hammolecheth gave birth to Ishhod, Abiezer and Mahlah. 19 The sons of Shemida were Ahian, Shechem, Likhi and Aniam.

The Family of Ephraim

20 Ephraim's sons were Shuthelah and Bered his son, Tahath his son, Eleadah his son, Tahath his son, 21 Zabad his son, Shuthelah his son, and Ezer and Elead. The men of Gath who were born in the land killed Ezer and Elead, because they came down to take their cattle. 22 Their father Ephraim was filled with sorrow for many days. And his brothers came to comfort him. 23 Then he went in to his wife and she was able to have a child and gave birth to a son. Ephraim gave him the name Beriah, because trouble had come upon his house. 24 Beriah's daughter was Sheerah. She built both parts of Beth-horon, and Uzzen-sheerah. 25 Rephah was his son, Resheph his son, Telah his son, Tahan his son, 26 Ladan his son, Ammihud his son, Elishama his son, 27 Nun his son, and Joshua his son.

28 Their cities and their lands were Bethel with its towns, Naaran to the east, Gezer to the west with its towns, and Shechem with its towns as far as Ayyah with its towns. 29 Beside the land of the sons of Manasseh, they lived in Beth-shean with its towns, Taanach with its towns, Megiddo with its towns, and Dor with its towns. In these cities lived the sons of Joseph the son of Israel.

The Family of Asher

30 The sons of Asher were Imnah, Ishvah, Ishvi, Beriah, and Serah their sister. 31 The sons of Beriah were Heber and Malchiel, who was the father of Birzaith. 32 Heber was the father of Japhlet, Shomer, Hotham, and their sister Shua. 33 The sons of Japhlet were Pasach, Bimhal and Ashvath. These were the sons of Japhlet. 34 The sons of Shemer were Ahi, Rohgah, Jehubbah and Aram. 35 The sons of his brother Helem were Zophah, Imna, Shelesh and Amal. 36 The sons of Zophah were Suah, Harnepher, Shual, Beri, Imrah, 37 Bezer, Hod, Shamma, Shilshah, Ithran, and Beera. 38 The sons of Jether were Jephunneh, Pispa and Ara. 39 The sons of Ulla were Arah, Hanniel and Rizia. 40 All these were the sons of Asher and heads of the fathers' houses. They were chosen men and powerful soldiers, leaders of the king's sons. There were 26,000 of them, whose names were written down by their families for fighting in war.

The Family of King Saul

8 Benjamin was the father of Bela his first born, Ashbel the second, Aharah the third, 2 Nohah the fourth, and Rapha the fifth. 3 Bela's sons were Addar, Gera, Abihud, 4 Abishua, Naaman, Ahoah, 5 Gera, Shephuphan, and Huram. 6 The sons of Ehud were the heads of fathers' houses of the people of Geba. They were taken away to Manahath. 7 Their names were Naaman, Ahijah, and Gera, that is, Heglam, who was the father of Uzza and Ahihud. 8 Shaharaim had sons in the country of Moab after he had sent away Hushim and Baara his wives. 9 By his wife Hodesh he became the father of Jobab, Zibia, Mesha, Malcam, 10 Jeuz, Sachia and Mirmah. These were his sons. They were heads of fathers' houses. 11 By his wife Hushim he became the father of Abitub and Elpaal. 12 The sons of Elpaal were Eber, Misham, and Shemed, who built Ono and Lod with its towns. 13 Elpaal was the father of Beriah and Shema also. They were heads of fathers' houses of the people of Aijalon, who drove away the people of Gath. 14 Elpaal's other sons were Ahio, Shashak and Jeremoth. 15 Zebadiah, Arad, Eder, 16 Michael, Ishpah and Joha were the sons of Beriah. 17 Zebadiah, Meshullam, Hizki, Heber, 18 Ishmerai, Izliah and Jobab were the sons of Elpaal. 19 Jakim, Zichri, Zabdi, 20 Elienai, Zillethai, Eliel, 21 Adaiah, Beraiah and Shimrath were the sons of Shimei. 22 Ishpan, Eber, Eliel, 23 Abdon, Zichri, Hanan, 24 Hananiah, Elam, Anthothijah, 25 Iphdeiah and Penuel were the sons of Shashak. 26 Shamsherai, Shehariah, Athaliah, 27 Jaareshiah, Elijah and Zichri were the sons of Jeroham. 28 These were heads of the fathers' houses by their families. They were leaders who lived in Jerusalem.

29 Gibeon's father Jeiel lived in Gibeon. The name of Jeiel's wife was Maacah. 30 His sons were Abdon his first-born, then Zur, Kish, Baal, Nadab, 31 Gedor, Ahio and Zecher, 32 and Mikloth the father of Shimeah. They lived with their brothers in Jerusalem beside their other brothers. 33 Ner was the father of Kish. Kish was the father of Saul. Saul was the father of Jonathan, Malchi-shua, Abinadab and Eshbaal. 34 The son of Jonathan was Merib-baal. Merib-baal was the father of Micah. 35 The sons of Micah were Pithon, Melech, Tarea and Ahaz. 36 Ahaz was the father of Jehoaddah. Jehoaddah was the father of Alemeth, Azmaveth and Zimri. Zimri was the father of Moza. 37 Moza was the father of Binea. Raphah was his son, Eleasah his son, and Azel his son. 38 The names of Azel's six sons were Azrikam, Bocheru,

Ishmael, Sheariah, Obadiah and Hanan. All these were the sons of Azel. **39** The sons of his brother Eshek were Ulam his first-born, Jeush the second, and Eliphelet the third. **40** The sons of Ulam were powerful soldiers. They fought with the bow. And they had 150 sons and grandsons. All these were the sons of Benjamin.

9 So the names of all Israel were written down by families. See, they are written in the Book of the Kings of Israel. And Judah was carried away to Babylon because they were not faithful.

Those Who Returned to Their Land

2 The first ones to live again in their land and in their cities were Israel, the religious leaders, the Levites and the servants of the Lord's house. **3** Some of the people of Judah, Benjamin, Ephraim and Manasseh lived in Jerusalem. **4** They were Uthai the son of Ammihud, the son of Omri, the son of Imri, the son of Bani, from the sons of Perez the son of Judah. **5** From the Shilonites were Asaiah the first-born and his sons. **6** From the sons of Zerah were Jeuel and their brothers, 690 of them. **7** From the sons of Benjamin were Sallu the son of Meshullam, the son of Hodaviah, the son of Hassenuah. **8** And there were Ibneiah the son of Jeroham, Elah the son of Uzzi, son of Michri, and Meshullam the son of Shephatiah, son of Reuel, son of Ibnijah. **9** And there were their brothers by their families, 956 of them. All these were heads of fathers' houses by their fathers' houses.

The Religious Leaders for Jerusalem

10 From the religious leaders were Jedaiah, Jehoiarib, Jachin. **11** And there was Azariah the son of Hilkiah, son of Meshullam, son of Zadok, son of Meraioth, son of Ahitub. He was the head leader of the house of God. **12** And there was Adaiah the son of Jeroham, son of Pashhur, son of Malchijah. There was Maasai the son of Adiel, son of Jahzerah, son of Meshullam, son of Meshillemith, son of Immer. **13** And there were 1,760 of their brothers, who were heads of their fathers' houses. They were very able men for the work of the house of God.

The Levites in Jerusalem

14 From the Levites were Shemaiah the son of Hasshub, son of Azrikam, son of Hashabiah, of the sons of Merari. **15** There were Bakbakkar, Heresh, Galal, and Mattaniah the son of Mica, son of Zichri, son of Asaph. **16** There was Obadiah the son of Shemaiah, son of Galal, son of Jeduthun. And there was Berechiah the son of Asa, son of Elkanah, who lived in the towns of the Netophathites.

The Gate-Keepers in Jerusalem

17 The gate-keepers were Shallum, Akkub, Talmon, Ahiman and their brothers. (Shallum was the leader **18** who was at the king's gate on the east side.) These were the gate-keepers for the family group of the Levites. **19** Shallum the son of Kore, son of Ebiasaph, son of Korah, and his brothers of his father's house, were the Korahites. They led the work, and they watched the doors of the meeting tent. Their fathers had taken care of the tents of the Lord, and had watched the doors. **20** Phinehas the son of Eleazar had ruled over them before. And the Lord was with him. **21** Zechariah the son of Meshelemiah watched the gate of the meeting tent. **22** There were 212 of those who were chosen to watch the gates. Their names were written down by families in their towns. David and Samuel the man of God chose them for places of trust. **23** So they and their sons were gate-keepers of the Lord's house, the holy tent. **24** The gate-keepers were on the four sides, to the east, west, north and south. **25** Those of their family in other towns were to come in every seven days from time to time to be with them. **26** For the four head men who were gate-keepers were Levites and were in a place of trust. They watched over the rooms and the riches in the house of God. **27** They stayed during the night around the house of God. For their duty was to watch. And they were to open the house every morning.

The Other Levites

28 Some of them took care of the things used for worship. They numbered them when they were brought in and taken out. **29** Some of them were chosen to take care of the objects of the holy place, the fine flour, the wine, the oil, the special perfume, and the spices. **30** And some of the sons of the religious leaders did the work of mixing the spices. **31** Mattithiah was one of the Levites, the first-born of Shallum the Korahite. He took care of the making of bread. **32** And some of their brothers of the Kohathites took care of the making of holy bread every Day of Rest.

33 These are the singers. They were heads of fathers' houses of the Levites, who lived in the rooms of the Lord's house. They were free from other kinds of worship, for they were on duty day and night. 34 These were heads of fathers' houses of the Levites by their families. They were leaders who lived in Jerusalem.

The Family of King Saul

35 Gibeon's father Jeiel lived in Gibeon. The name of Jeiel's wife was Maacah. 36 His sons were Abdon the first-born, then Zur, Kish, Baal, Ner, Nadab, 37 Gedor, Ahio, Zechariah and Mikloth. 38 Mikloth was the father of Shimeam. They lived with their brothers in Jerusalem beside their other brothers. 39 Ner was the father of Kish. Kish was the father of Saul. Saul was the father of Jonathan, Malchi-shua, Abinadab and Eshbaal. 40 The son of Jonathan was Merib-baal. Merib-baal was the father of Micah. 41 The sons of Micah were Pithon, Melech, Tahrea and Ahaz. 42 Ahaz was the father of Jarah. Jarah was the father of Alemeth, Azmaveth and Zimri. Zimri was the father of Moza. 43 Moza was the father of Binea and Rephaiah his son, Eleasah his son, Azel his son. 44 Azel had six sons whose names were Azrikam, Bocheru, Ishmael, Sheariah, Obadiah and Hanan. These were the sons of Azel.

The Death of King Saul and His Sons

10 Now the many Philistines fought against Israel. The men of Israel ran away from the Philistines, and were killed on Mount Gilboa. 2 The Philistines went after Saul and his sons. And they killed Jonathan, Abinadab and Malchishua, Saul's sons. 3 The battle was hard for Saul. Those who fought with the bow found him, and hurt him with an arrow. 4 Then Saul said to the one who carried his battle-clothes, "Take your sword and kill me with it. Or these men who have not gone through our religious act will come and make fun of me." But the one who carried his battle-clothes would not do it. For he was very afraid. So Saul took his sword and fell on it. 5 When the one who carried his battle-clothes saw that Saul was dead, he fell on his sword and died also. 6 So Saul died with his three sons. All those of his house died together.

7 All the men of Israel who were in the valley saw that the army had run away and that Saul and his sons were dead. So they left their cities and ran away. Then the Philistines came and lived in their cities. 8 When the Philistines came the next day to take what had belonged to the dead, they found Saul and his sons dead on Mount Gilboa. 9 So they took his clothes, his head, and his battle-clothes. And they sent men around the land of the Philistines to take the good news to their false gods and to the people. 10 They put Saul's battle-clothes in the house of their gods. And they put his head in the house of Dagon. 11 All the people of Jabesh-gilead heard what the Philistines had done to Saul. 12 So all the powerful soldiers went and took the bodies of Saul and his sons. They brought them to Jabesh and buried their bones under the oak tree there. Then they went without food for seven days.

13 So Saul died for his sin against the Lord, because he did not keep the Word of the Lord. He had asked a woman who spoke with spirits what he should do. 14 He did not ask the Lord. So the Lord killed him, and gave the nation to David the son of Jesse.

David Becomes King of Israel and Judah

11 Then all Israel came to David at Hebron and said, "See, we are your bone and your flesh. 2 In times past, even when Saul was king, you were the one who led out and brought in Israel. The Lord your God said to you, 'You will be the shepherd of My people Israel. And you will be king over My people Israel.'" 3 So all the leaders of Israel came to the king at Hebron. And David made an agreement with them in Hebron before the Lord. Then they poured oil on David to be the king of Israel, just as the Lord had said through Samuel. 4 David and all Israel went to Jerusalem (that is, Jebus). And the Jebusites, the people of the land, were there. 5 The people of Jebus said to David, "You will not come in here." But David took the strong-place of Zion (that is, the city of David). 6 Now David had said, "Whoever kills a Jebusite first will be captain and leader." Joab the son of Zeruiah went up first, so he became captain. 7 Then David lived in the strong-place. So it was called the city of David. 8 He built the city all around, from the Millo and then around. And Joab built the rest of the city up again. 9 David became greater and greater, for the Lord of All was with him.

David's Strong Men

10 These are the leaders of David's strong men. They gave him much help in his

nation, together with all Israel, to make him king. It was just as the Lord had said would happen with Israel. 11 These are the names of David's strong men. There was Jashobeam the son of Hachmonite, the head of the thirty. He killed 300 men with his spear at one time. 12 Then there was Eleazar the son of Dodo, the Ahohite. He was one of the three powerful soldiers. 13 He was with David at Pasdammim when the Philistines were gathered there to battle, where there was a piece of ground full of grain. And the people ran away from the Philistines. 14 But he and his men stood on the piece of ground and fought for it, and killed the Philistines. The Lord saved them by His great power.

15 Three of the thirty leaders went down to the rock and into the cave of Adullam where David was staying. The Philistine army was staying in the valley of Rephaim. 16 David was in a strong-place, while the Philistine soldiers had their place in Bethlehem. 17 David had a strong desire. He said, "O, if only someone would give me water to drink from the well by the gate of Bethlehem!" 18 So the three men broke through the Philistine army. They took water from the well by the gate of Bethlehem, and brought it to David. But David would not drink it. He poured it out to the Lord, 19 and said, "Far be it from me that I should do this before my God. Should I drink the blood of these men? For they put their lives in danger to bring it." So he would not drink it. These things are what the three powerful soldiers did.

20 As for Abishai the brother of Joab, he was the head of the thirty. He fought and killed 300 men with his spear. And his name became well-known like the three. 21 He was the best known of the thirty. But he was not as important as the three.

22 Benaiah the son of Jehoiada, the son of a powerful soldier from Kabzeel, did great things. He killed the two sons of Ariel of Moab. He went down and killed a lion inside a deep hole on a day when there was snow. 23 And he killed an Egyptian who was very tall, five cubits tall. The Egyptian held a spear as big as the cross-piece of a cloth-maker. But Benaiah went down to him with a heavy stick and took the spear from the Egyptian's hand. Then he killed him with his own spear. 24 These are the things Benaiah the son of Johoiada did. His name was well-known like the three powerful soldiers. 25 He was respected among the thirty. But he was not as important as the three. David chose him to be the head of his house soldiers.

26 The strong men of the armies were Asahel the brother of Joab, Elhanan the son of Dodo of Bethlehem, 27 Shammoth the Harorite, and Helez the Pelonite. 28 And there were Ira the son of Ikkesh the Tekoite, Abiezer the Anathothite, 29 Sibbecai the Hushathite, and Ilai the Ahohite. 30 There were Maharai the Netophathite, Heled the son of Baanah the Netophathite, 31 Ithai the son of Ribai of Gibeah of the sons of Benjamin, and Benaiah the Pirathonite. 32 There were Hurai of the rivers of Gaash, Abiel the Arbathite, 33 Azmaveth the Baharumite, Eliahba the Shaalbonite, 34 the sons of Hashem the Gizonite. There were Jonathan the son of Shagee the Hararite, 35 Ahiam the son of Sachar the Hararite, Eliphal the son of Ur, 36 Hepher the Mecherathite, and Ahijah the Pelonite. 37 There were Hezro the Carmelite, Naarai the son of Ezbai, 38 Joel the brother of Nathan, Mibhar the son of Hagri, 39 Zelek the Ammonite, Naharai the Berothite. Naharai was the one who carried the battle-clothes of Joab the son of Zeruiah. 40 There were Ira the Ithrite, Gareb the Ithrite, 41 Uriah the Hittite, Zabad the son of Ahlai, 42 and Adina the son of Shiza the Reubenite. Adina was a leader of the Reubenites, and had thirty men with him. 43 There were Hanan the son of Maacah, Joshaphat the Mithnite, 44 Uzzia the Ashterathite, and Shama and Jeiel the sons of Hotham the Aroerite. 45 There were Jediael the son of Shimri, his brother Joha the Tizite, 46 Eliel the Mahavite, and Jeribai and Joshaviah the sons of Elnaam. And there were Ithmah the Moabite, 47 Eliel, Obed, and Jaasiel the Mezobaite.

David's Army Gets Larger

12 These are the men who came to David at Ziklag, while David was still hidden because of Saul the son of Kish. They were among the strong men who helped him in war. 2 They fought with the bow. They could also throw stones or shoot arrows with both the right and left hand. They were Saul's brothers from Benjamin. 3 The leader was Ahiezer, then Joash. Both of them were sons of Shemaah the Gibeathite. And there were Jeziel and Pelet, the sons of Azmaveth, Beracah, Jehu the Anathothite, 4 and Ishmaiah the Gibeonite. He was a strong man among the thirty, and a leader over them. There were Jeremiah, Jahaziel, Johanan,

Jozabad the Gederathite, 5 Eluzai, Jerimoth, Bealiah, Shemariah, and Shephatiah the Haruphite. 6 There were Elkanah, Isshiah, Azarel, Joezer, Jashobeam, the Korahites. 7 And there were Joelah and Zebadiah, the sons of Jeroham of Gedor.

8 Powerful soldiers came from the Gadites to David in the strong-place in the desert. They had been taught how to fight in war, and could use the battle-covering and spear. Their faces were like the faces of lions. And they were as fast as the deer on the mountains. 9 Ezer was the first. Obadiah was the second. Eliab was the third. 10 Mishmannah was the fourth. Jeremiah was the fifth. 11 Attai was the sixth. Eliel was the seventh. 12 Johanan was the eighth. Elzabad was the ninth. 13 Jeremiah was the tenth. Machbannai was the eleventh. 14 These Gadites were captains of the army. He who was least led 100. And he who was greatest led 1,000. 15 These are the ones who crossed the Jordan in the first month when the water was flowing over its sides. They drove away all those in the valleys, to the east and to the west.

16 Then some of the sons of Benjamin and Judah came to David at his strong-place. 17 David went out to meet them. He said to them, "If you come in peace to help me, my heart will be joined to you. But if you have come to hand me over to those who hate me, may the God of our fathers see it and speak strong words to you. For I have done nothing wrong." 18 Then the Spirit came upon Amasai the captain of the thirty. Amasai said, "We are yours, O David! We are with you, O son of Jesse! Peace, peace to you, and peace to those who help you! For your God helps you!" Then David received them and made them captains of his soldiers.

19 Some men from Manasseh came over to David's side when he was about to go to battle with the Philistines against Saul. But they did not help him. For after talking it over, the Philistine leaders sent him away, saying, "He might go over to Saul's side with our heads." 20 The men who came over to David's side from Manasseh as he went to Ziklag were Adnah, Jozabad, Jediael, Michael, Jozabad, Elihu and Zillethai. They were captains of thousands who belonged to Manasseh. 21 They helped David against the army of soldiers who came to fight him. For they were all powerful soldiers, and captains in the army. 22 Each day men came to David to help him. They came until there was a great army, like the army of God.

23 These are the numbers of the armies who came to David at Hebron. They came to turn the nation of Saul to him, as the Word of the Lord had said. 24 There were 6,800 sons of Judah who carried a battle-covering and spear, ready for war. 25 There were 7,100 powerful soldiers from the sons of Simeon. 26 There were 4,600 sons of Levi. 27 Jehoiada was the leader of the house of Aaron. There were 3,700 men with him. 28 And there was Zadok, a young, powerful soldier, and twenty-two captains from his own father's house. 29 There were 3,000 sons of Benjamin, Saul's brothers. For until now most of them had stayed faithful to the house of Saul. 30 There were 20,800 powerful soldiers from the sons of Ephraim. They were important men in their fathers' houses. 31 There were 18,000 men of the half-family group of Manasseh. They were chosen by name to come and make David king. 32 There were 200 captains of the sons of Issachar. They understood the times and had much understanding of what Israel should do. And all their brothers obeyed them. 33 There were 50,000 men of Zebulun who were soldiers. They could fight in battle with everything used in war. And they helped David as if they had one heart. 34 There were 1,000 captains from Naphtali. With them were 37,000 men with battle-coverings and spears. 35 There were 28,600 Danites ready for battle. 36 There were 40,000 soldiers from Asher, ready for battle. 37 And there were 120,000 sons of Reuben, Gad and the half-family group of Manasseh from the other side of the Jordan. They came with everything used in war.

38 All these were men of war, ready for battle. They came to Hebron with one desire, to make David the king of all Israel. And all the rest of Israel were of one mind to make David king. 39 They were there with David for three days, eating and drinking. For their brothers had made food ready for them. 40 And their neighbors brought food, from as far as Issachar, Zebulun and Naphtali. They brought food on donkeys, camels, horses and cattle. They brought many loaves of bread and figs, many dried grapes, wine, oil, cattle and sheep. For there was joy in Israel.

The Special Box Brought from Kiriath-Jearim

13 Then David spoke with the captains of the thousands and the hundreds and with every leader about what should be done. 2 David spoke to all the people of Israel. He said, "If you think it is good, and if it is from the Lord our God, let us send word to our brothers who are staying in all the land of Israel. Let us send word to the religious leaders and Levites who are with them in their cities that have fields. And let us ask them to meet with us. 3 Let us bring the special box with the Law of our God to us. For we did not think of it in the days of Saul." 4 Then all the people said that they would do so. For it was right in the eyes of all the people.

5 So David gathered all Israel together, from the Shihor of Egypt to the gate of Hamath, to bring the special box of God from Kiriath-jearim. 6 David and all Israel went up to Baalah, that is, to Kiriath-jearim which belongs to Judah. They went to bring the special box of God. It is called by the name of the Lord Who sits on His throne above the cherubim. 7 They carried the special box of God on a new wagon from the house of Abinadab. And Uzza and Ahio drove the wagon. 8 David and all Israel were showing their joy before God with all their strength. They were singing and playing harps and timbrels, and blowing horns.

9 When they came to the grain-floor of Chidon, the cattle pulling the wagon tripped. And Uzza put out his hand to hold the special box of God. 10 Then the anger of the Lord burned against Uzza. So He killed him because Uzza had put out his hand to the special box of God, so before God he died. 11 Then David became angry because the Lord had killed Uzza in His anger. That place is called Perez-uzza to this day. 12 David was afraid of God that day, saying, "How can I bring the special box of God home to me?" 13 So David did not take the special box of God with him to the city of David. He took it aside to the house of Obed-edom the Gittite. 14 The special box of God stayed with the family of Obed-edom in his house for three months. The Lord brought good to Obed-edom's family and all that he had.

David in Jerusalem

14 Now King Hiram of Tyre sent men with cedar trees to David. With them came men who worked with stone and wood. They came to build a house for him. 2 David understood that the Lord had made him to be king of Israel. He knew that his nation was very honored because of God's people Israel.

3 Then David took more wives at Jerusalem. He became the father of more sons and daughters. 4 The names of the children born to him in Jerusalem are Shammua, Shobab, Nathan, Solomon, 5 Ibhar, Elishua, Elpelet, 6 Nogah, Nepheg, Japhia, 7 Elishama, Beeliada and Eliphelet.

Battle with the Philistines

8 The Philistines heard that David had been chosen as king of all Israel. So they went up to look for him. David heard of it and went out against them. 9 Now the Philistines had come to fight a surprise battle in the valley of Rephaim. 10 David asked God, "Should I go fight against the Philistines? Will You give them to me?" And the Lord said to him, "Go, for I will give them to you." 11 So they came up to Baal-perazim, and David won the battle against them there. David said, "By my hand God has broken through those who hate me, like the breaking through of a flood." So they gave that place the name Baal-perazim. 12 The Philistines left their gods there. So David had them burned with fire.

13 The Philistines fought another surprise battle in the valley. 14 So David asked God again what he should do. God said to him, "Do not go after them. Go around behind them, and come upon them in front of the balsam trees. 15 When you hear the sound of their steps in the tops of the balsam trees, then go out to battle. For God will have gone out before you to destroy the Philistine army." 16 David did just as God had told him, and they destroyed the Philistine army from Gibeon as far as Gezer. 17 Then the name of David became known in all the lands. The Lord brought the fear of him upon all the nations.

The Special Box Brought to Jerusalem

15 David built houses for himself in the city of David. He made a place ready for the special box of God. And he set up a tent for it. 2 Then David said, "No one but the Levites may carry the special box of God. For the Lord chose them to carry the special box of the agreement and to serve Him forever." 3 David gathered all Israel together at Jerusalem, to bring up the special box of the Lord to the place he had made for it. 4 He gathered together the sons of Aaron and the Levites. 5 Uriel became leader of the sons of Kohath, and 120 of his brothers. 6 Asaiah became the leader of the sons of Merari, and 220 of his brothers. 7 Joel became the leader of the sons of Gershom, and 130 of his brothers. [8] Shemaiah became the leader of the sons of Elizaphan, and 200 of his brothers. [9] Eliel became the leader of the sons of Hebron, and 80 of his brothers. [10] Amminadab became the leader of the sons of Uzziel, and 112 of his brothers. [11] Then David called for Zadok and Abiathar the religious leaders. And he called for the Levites, Uriel, Asaiah, Joel, Shemaiah, Eliel and Amminadab. [12] He said to them, "You are the heads of the fathers' houses of the Levites. Make yourselves and your brothers holy, that you may bring up the special box of the Lord God of Israel to the place I have made for it. [13] The Lord our God brought trouble upon us because you did not carry it the first time. We did not care for it the way He had told us." [14] So the religious leaders and the Levites made themselves holy, to bring up the special box of the Lord God of Israel. [15] The sons of the Levites carried the special box of God on their shoulders with the long pieces of wood. They did as Moses had told them by the Word of the Lord.

[16] Then David told the heads of the Levites to choose their brothers who sing and play music. They were to play harps and timbrels and make sounds of joy. [17] So the Levites chose Heman the son of Joel. From his brothers they chose Asaph the son of Berechiah. From the sons of Merari their brothers, they chose Ethan the son of Kushaiah. [18] With them they chose their brothers of the second group. These were Zechariah, Jaaziel, Shemiramoth, Jehiel, Unni, Eliab, Benaiah, Maaseiah, Mattithiah, Eliphelehu, Mikneiah, Obed-edom, and Jeiel, the gate-keepers. [19] The singers, Heman, Asaph and Ethan were chosen to make sounds of joy with objects of brass. [20] Zechariah, Aziel, Shemiramoth, Jehiel, Unni, Eliab, Maaseiah and Benaiah were chosen to play the high sounds on harps. [21] Mattithiah, Eliphelehu, Mikneiah, Obed-edom, Jeiel and Azaziah were chosen to lead by playing the deep sounds on different kinds of harps. [22] Chenaniah, head of the Levites, was to lead the singing. He taught the singing because he was able. [23] Berechiah and Elkanah were to watch the gate for the special box. [24] Shebaniah, Joshaphat, Nethanel, Amasai, Zechariah, Benaiah and Eliezer, the religious leaders, were to blow the horns in front of the special box of God. Obed-edom and Jehiah were gate-keepers for the special box of God also.

[25] So David, the leaders of Israel and the captains of thousands went to bring up the special box with the Law of the Lord from the house of Obed-edom with joy. [26] God was helping the Levites who were carrying the special box of the agreement of the Lord. So they killed seven bulls and seven rams on the altar in worship. [27] David was dressed in a long piece of clothing of fine linen. So were all the Levites who were carrying the special box of God. And so were the singers and Chenaniah the leader of the singing. David wore a linen vest also. [28] So all Israel brought up the special box with the Law of the Lord. They brought it up with a loud voice, the sound of horns, and with loud-sounding timbrels and harps.

[29] When the special box with the Law of the Lord came to the city of David, Saul's daughter Michal looked out of the window. She saw King David dancing and jumping for joy. And she hated him in her heart.

The Special Box in the Place of Worship

16 They brought the special box of God, and put it inside the tent David had set up for it. Then they gave burnt gifts and peace gifts to God. [2] When David finished giving the burnt gifts and peace gifts, he prayed in the name of the Lord that good would come to the people. [3] He gave to every man and woman in Israel a loaf of bread, a share of meat, and a loaf of dried grapes.

[4] David chose some of the Levites to do the work in front of the special box of the Lord. They were to be glad and thank and praise the Lord God of Israel. [5] Asaph was the leader, then Zechariah, Jeiel, Shemiramoth, Jehiel, Mattithiah, Eliab, Benaiah, Obed-edom, and Jeiel. They were to play harps. And Asaph played loud-sounding timbrels. [6] The religious leaders Benaiah and Jahaziel sounded the horns all the time in front of the special box with the Law of God.

A Song of Praise

[7] Then on that day David first called upon Asaph and his brothers to give thanks to the Lord. [8] "O give thanks to the Lord. Call upon His name. Let the people know what He has done. [9] Sing to Him. Sing praises to Him. Tell of all His great works. [10] Have joy in His holy name. Let the heart of those who look to the Lord be glad. [11] Look to the Lord and ask for His strength. Look to

Him all the time. 12 Remember His great works which He has done. Remember the special things He has done and how He has judged, 13 O children of Israel His servant, sons of Jacob, His chosen ones! 14 He is the Lord our God. He is judge of all the earth. 15 Remember His agreement forever, the Word which He gave to families and a thousand of their family groups to come. 16 Remember the agreement He made with Abraham, and His promise to Isaac. 17 To Jacob He made it a Law to be kept, as an agreement forever to Israel. 18 He said, 'I will give the land of Canaan to you as the share of your birth-right,' 19 when they were few in number. They were very few, and strangers in the land. 20 They traveled from nation to nation, from the people of one king to the people of another. 21 He let no man make it hard for them. He spoke strong words to kings because of them, saying, 22 'Do not touch My chosen ones. Do not hurt those who speak for Me.' 23 Sing to the Lord, all the earth. Tell the good news of His saving power from day to day. 24 Tell of His greatness among the nations. Tell of His great works among all the people. 25 For great is the Lord. He is to be given much praise. And He is to be honored with fear more than all gods. 26 For all the gods of the people are false gods. But the Lord made the heavens. 27 Honor and great power are with Him. Strength and joy are in His place. 28 Praise the Lord, O families of the people. Praise the Lord for His greatness and strength. 29 Praise the Lord for the greatness of His name. Bring a gift and come to Him. Worship the Lord clothed in His holiness. 30 Shake with fear before Him, all the earth. Yes, the world is made to last. It will not be moved. 31 Let the heavens be glad. Let the earth be filled with joy. And let them say among the nations, 'The Lord rules!' 32 Let the sea thunder, and all that is in it. Let the field be happy, and all that is in it. 33 Then the trees of the woods will sing for joy before the Lord. For He is coming to judge the earth. 34 O give thanks to the Lord, for He is good. His loving-kindness lasts forever. 35 Then say, 'Set us free, O God Who saves us. Gather and save us from among the nations, to give thanks to Your holy name, and have joy in Your praise.' 36 Honor be to the Lord, the God of Israel forever and ever.' " Then all the people said, "Let it be so!" and they praised the Lord.

Worship at Jerusalem

37 So David left Asaph and his brothers there in front of the special box with the Law of the Lord. He left them there to do the work in front of the special box always. They were to do whatever work needed to be done each day. 38 He left Obed-edom there with his sixty-eight brothers. Obed-edom, the son of Jeduthun, and Hosah were to watch the gate. 39 David left Zadok and his brothers who were the religious leaders in front of the meeting tent of the Lord in the high place at Gibeon. 40 They were to give burnt gifts to the Lord on the altar of burnt gifts all the time, morning and evening. They were to do all that is written in the Law of the Lord which He told Israel. 41 With them were Heman, Jeduthun, and the rest who were chosen by name. They were to give thanks to the Lord, because His loving-kindness lasts forever. 42 Heman and Jeduthun had horns and timbrels for making sounds of joy as the songs of God were sung. The sons of Jeduthun were to watch the gate.

43 Then all the people left. Each one went home. And David returned to bring good to those of his house.

God's Agreement with David

17 Now when David lived in his house, he said to Nathan the special preacher, "See, I am living in a house of cedar wood. But the special box with the Law of the Lord is under a tent." 2 Nathan said to David, "Do all that is in your heart. For God is with you." 3 But that same night the Word of the Lord came to Nathan, saying, 4 "Go and tell My servant David, 'This is what the Lord says. "You will not build a house for Me to live in. 5 For I have not lived in a house since the day I brought up Israel to this day. But I have gone from tent to tent and from one place to another to live. 6 In all the places I have gone with all Israel, have I said a word to any of the judges of Israel about this? Have I said to anyone whom I told to watch over My people, 'Why have you not built a house of cedar wood for Me?' " ' 7 So now say to My servant David, 'The Lord of All says, "I took you from the field, from following the sheep, to be leader over My people Israel. 8 I have been with you in every place you have gone. I have destroyed in front of you all those who hate you. And I will make your name to be known like the name of the great ones of the earth. 9 I will choose a place for My people Israel, and will plant them. So they will live in their own place and not be moved again. Never again will they be under the power of sinful men, as they were before, ¹⁰ from the time that I told judges to rule My people Israel. I will put under your power all those who hate you. And I say to you that the Lord will build a house for you. ¹¹ When your days are over, the time will come when you must go to be with your fathers. But then I will put into power one of your sons after you. I will make him king. ¹² He will build a house for Me. And I will make his throne last forever. ¹³ I will be his father, and he will be My son. I will not take My loving-kindness away from him, as I took it from him who was before you. ¹⁴ But I will put him over My house and in My nation forever. And his throne will last forever." ' " ¹⁵ Nathan told David all these words from all this special dream.

David's Prayer of Thanks

¹⁶ Then King David went in and sat before the Lord, and said, "Who am I, O God? What is my house, that You have brought me this far? ¹⁷ This was a small thing in Your eyes, O God. You have spoken of Your servant's house for a long time to come. You have thought of me as if I were an important man, O Lord God. ¹⁸ What more can David say to You about the honor given to Your servant? For You know Your servant. ¹⁹ You have made all this greatness, O Lord. You have made known all these great things, for Your servant, and by Your own heart. ²⁰ O Lord, there is no one like You. There is no God other than You, by all that we have heard with our ears. ²¹ What other nation on earth is like Your people Israel? God went to free them to be His people. You made Yourself a name by great things which filled people with fear. You drove out the nations before Your people, whom You set free from Egypt. ²² You made Your people Israel to be Your people forever. And You, O Lord, became their God. ²³ Now, O Lord, let the Word that You have spoken about Your servant and his house be made sure forever. Do as You have said. ²⁴ Let Your name be made sure and honored forever, saying, 'The Lord of All, the God of Israel, is Israel's God. And the house of Your servant David is made to last before You.' ²⁵ For You, O my God, have made it known to Your servant that You will build a house for him. So Your servant has found strength of heart to pray to You. ²⁶ And now, O Lord, You are God.

You have promised this good thing to Your servant. ²⁷ Now it has pleased You to bring good to the house of Your servant. May it last forever before You. For when You bring good to something, O Lord, good is with it forever."

David's Battles

18 After this David won the war against the Philistines and put them under his power. He took Gath and its towns from the Philistines. ² He won the war against Moab. And the Moabites were made to work for David, bringing taxes to him. ³ David won the war against King Hadadezer of Zobah as far as Hamath, as he went to bring his power to the Euphrates River. ⁴ David took from him 1,000 war-wagons, 7,000 horsemen, and 20,000 foot soldiers. And he cut the legs of all but 100 war-wagon horses.

⁵ The Syrians of Damascus came to help King Hadadezer of Zobah. But David killed 22,000 of the Syrian men. ⁶ Then David put soldiers in Syria of Damascus. And the Syrians became servants to David, paying taxes. The Lord helped David in every place he went. ⁷ David took the battle-coverings of gold which were carried by Hadadezer's servants, and brought them to Jerusalem. ⁸ He took a very large amount of brass from Hadadezer's cities, Tibhath and Cun. This was the brass Solomon used to make the brass pool, the pillars, and the brass pots.

⁹ King Tou of Hamath heard that David had won the war against all the army of King Hadadezer of Zobah. ¹⁰ So he sent his son Hadoram to King David, to greet him and give honor to him, because David had fought against Hadadezer and won. For Hadadezer had been at war with Tou. Hadoram brought all kinds of things of gold and silver and brass. ¹¹ King David set these apart to the Lord, with the silver and gold he had carried away from all the nations. He took things from Edom, Moab, the sons of Ammon, the Philistines, and Amalek.

¹² Abishai the son of Zeruiah won the war from 18,000 Edomites in the Valley of Salt. ¹³ Then he put soldiers in Edom. And the Edomites became servants to David. The Lord helped David every place he went.

¹⁴ So David ruled over all Israel. He did what was fair and right and good for all his people. ¹⁵ Joab the son of Zeruiah was captain of the army. Jehoshaphat the son

of Ahilud wrote down the things of the nation. 16 Zadok the son of Ahitub and Abimelech the son of Abiathar were religious leaders. Shavsha was the one who writes everything down. 17 Benaiah the son of Jehoiada was over the Cherethites and the Pelethites. And the sons of David were leaders at the king's side.

David Wins over the Ammonites and Syrians

19 After this Nahash the king of the Ammonites died. And his son became king in his place. 2 David said, "I will show kindness to Hanun the son of Nahash, because his father showed kindness to me." So David sent men to bring him comfort in his sorrow for his father. David's servants came to Hanun in the land of the sons of Ammon, to bring him comfort. 3 But the princes of the sons of Ammon said to Hanun, "Do you think that David is giving honor to your father by sending men to comfort you? Have not his servants come to spy out the land and destroy it?" 4 So Hanun took David's servants and cut the hair from their faces. Then he cut off the bottom half of their clothing, and sent them away. 5 When David was told what had happened to his servants, he sent men out to meet them because the workmen were very ashamed. The king said, "Stay at Jericho until the hair grows again on your faces, and then return."

6 The sons of Ammon saw that they had made themselves to be hated by David. So Hanun and the sons of Ammon sent silver weighing as much as 1,000 men, to get war-wagons and horsemen from Mesopotamia, Aram-maacah, and Zobah. 7 They paid for 32,000 war-wagons and for the king of Maacah and his army who came and set up their tents by Medeba. Then the sons of Ammon gathered together from their cities and came to battle. 8 When David heard of it, he sent Joab and all the army of his strong men. 9 The sons of Ammon came out and were ready for battle at the city gate. The kings who had come were by themselves in the field.

10 Joab saw that the battle was set against him in front and behind. So he chose some of the best men of Israel and they made themselves ready to fight the Syrians. 11 But he had his brother Abishai lead the rest of the men. And they made themselves ready to fight the sons of Ammon. 12 Joab said, "If the Syrians are too strong for me, then help me. But if the sons of Ammon are too strong for you, then I will help you. 13 Be strong; let us show our strength of heart because of our people, and for the cities of our God. May the Lord do what is good in His eyes." 14 So Joab and the men who were with him came near to fight against the Syrians. And the Syrians ran away from him. 15 The sons of Ammon saw that the Syrians ran away. So they ran away from Joab's brother Abishai, and went into the city. Then Joab came to Jerusalem.

16 The Syrians saw that they had lost the war with Israel. So they sent men with news, and brought out the Syrians who were on the other side of the Euphrates River. Shophach the captain of Hadadezer's army was leading them. 17 When David was told about it, he gathered all Israel together and crossed the Jordan. He came to them, and made his army ready to fight against them. When David made his army ready for battle, the Syrians fought against him. 18 And the Syrians ran away from Israel. David killed 7,000 Syrians who drove war-wagons and 40,000 Syrian foot soldiers. And he killed Shophach the captain of the army. 19 Hadadezer's servants saw that they had lost the war against Israel. So they made peace with David and worked for him. The Syrians were not willing to help the sons of Ammon any more.

David Takes Rabbah

20 In the spring, at the time when kings go out to battle, Joab led out the army. He destroyed the land of the sons of Ammon. And he gathered his army around Rabbah. But David stayed at Jerusalem. Joab fought against Rabbah, and won. 2 Then David took the crown from their king's head. He found that its gold weighed as much as an older child. And there were stones of much worth in it. It was placed on David's head. He brought out the riches of the city, a very large amount. 3 He brought out the people who were in it, and made them work with saws, iron picks, and axes. David did this to all the cities of the sons of Ammon. Then he and all the people returned to Jerusalem.

Philistines' Strong Men Destroyed

4 After this there was a war with the Philistines at Gezer. Sibbecai the Hushathite killed Sippai, who was one of the sons of those who were very tall and strong.

And the Philistines were put under their power. 5 There was war with the Philistines again. Elhanan the son of Jair killed Lahmi the brother of Goliath the Gittite. Goliath's spear was as big as the crosspiece of a cloth-maker. 6 Again there was war at Gath. A very tall man was there who had six fingers on each hand and six toes on each foot, twenty-four in all. He was a son of those who were very tall and strong. 7 When he spoke against Israel, Jonathan the son of Shimea, David's brother, killed him. 8 These were sons of the people of Gath who were very tall and strong. And they were killed by David and his servants.

David Numbers Israel and Judah

21 Satan stood up against Israel, and moved David to number Israel. 2 So David said to Joab and the leaders of the people, "Go and number Israel from Beersheba to Dan. Then let me know how many people there are." 3 Joab said, "May the Lord add to His people a hundred times as many as they are! But, my lord the king, are they not all my lord's servants? Why does my lord want this thing done? Why should he bring guilt upon Israel?" 4 But the king's word was stronger than Joab. So Joab left and went through all of Israel, and returned to Jerusalem. 5 He gave the number of all the people to David. There were 1,100,000 men in all Israel who used the sword. And there were 470,000 men in Judah who used the sword. 6 But Joab did not number Levi and Benjamin among them because he did not like what the king had told him to do. 7 God was not pleased that Israel was numbered so He punished Israel. 8 David said to God, "I have sinned very much by doing this thing. But now I beg You, take away the sin of Your servant for I have done a very foolish thing."

9 The Lord said to Gad, David's man of God, 10 "Go and tell David, 'This is what the Lord says. "I give you three things to choose from. Choose one of them, that I may do it to you." ' " 11 So Gad came to David and said, "This is what the Lord says. 'Choose one of these. 12 Three years of no food in the land; three months to be destroyed by the sword of those who hate you; or three days of the sword of the Lord. This would be a disease set upon the land. The angel of the Lord would destroy with disease through all the land of Israel.' Now decide what answer I should give Him Who sent me." 13 David said to

Gad, "I am in much trouble. Let me fall into the hand of the Lord. For His lovingkindness is very great. But do not let me fall into the hand of man." 14 So the Lord sent a disease upon Israel. And 70,000 men of Israel died. 15 God sent an angel to destroy Jerusalem. But as he was about to destroy it, the Lord saw the trouble and was sorry. He said to the destroying angel, "It is enough. Now take your hand away." The angel of the Lord was standing by the grain-floor of Ornan the Jebusite. 16 Then David looked up and saw the angel of the Lord standing between earth and heaven. The angel had his sword in his hand, held out over Jerusalem. Then David and the leaders fell on their faces. They were dressed in cloth made from hair. 17 David said to God, "Was it not I who said that the people must be numbered? I am the one who has sinned and done a very bad thing. But what have these sheep done? O Lord my God, I beg You, let Your hand be against me and my father's house. But do not let the trouble be upon Your people."

18 Then the angel of the Lord told Gad to say to David, "Go up and build an altar to the Lord on the grain-floor of Ornan the Jebusite." 19 So David went up when he heard what Gad said in the name of the Lord. 20 Now Ornan was beating the grain. He turned and saw the angel. And his four sons hid themselves. 21 Ornan looked and saw David coming. So he went out from the grain-floor and put his face to the ground showing respect to David. 22 David said to him, "Give me this part of the grain-floor, that I may build an altar on it to the Lord. Give it to me for the full price. Then the disease will be turned away from the people." 23 Ornan said to David, "Take it. Let my lord the king do what is good in his eyes. See, I will give the bulls for burnt gifts. I will give the objects made of wood used for beating grain for the fire-wood. And I will give the grain for the grain gift. I will give it all." 24 But King David said to Ornan, "No, I will buy it for the full price. I will not take what is yours for the Lord. And I will not give a burnt gift for which I do not pay." 25 So David gave Ornan 600 pieces of gold by weight for the place. 26 Then David built an altar there to the Lord. He gave burnt gifts and peace gifts, and he called to the Lord. The Lord answered him with fire from heaven on the altar of burnt gifts. 27 Then the Lord told the angel to return his sword to its holder.

28 When David saw that the Lord had answered him on the grain-floor of Ornan the Jebusite, he gave his gifts there. 29 The meeting tent which Moses had made in the desert was in the high place at Gibeon then. The altar of burnt gifts was there also. 30 But David could not go in front of it to pray to God. For he was afraid of the sword of the angel of the Lord.

David Gets Ready to Build the House of God

22 Then David said, "This is the house of the Lord God. And this is the altar of burnt gifts for Israel."

2 David told his men to gather the strangers who were in the land of Israel. And he had servants cut stones to build the house of God. 3 He gave large amounts of iron to be used for making nails for the doors of the gates, and for making the parts that hold it all together. He gave more brass than could be weighed. 4 And he gave too many cedar trees to number. For the Sidonians and Tyrians brought many cut cedar trees to David. 5 David said, "My son Solomon is young and does not yet have much learning. And the house that is to be built for the Lord must be very beautiful. It must be very great, and well-known in all lands. So I will get things ready for it to be built." David made many things ready for it before his death.

6 Then he called for his son Solomon, and gave him the work of building a house for the Lord God of Israel. 7 David said to Solomon, "My son, I had planned to build a house to the name of the Lord my God. 8 But the word of the Lord came to me, saying, 'You have taken much blood, and have fought many wars. You are not to build a house to My name, because you have poured so much blood upon the earth before Me. 9 See, a son will be born to you, who will be a man of peace. I will give him peace from all those who hate him on every side. His name will be Solomon. And I will give peace and quiet to Israel in his days. 10 He will build a house for My name. He will be My son, and I will be his father. I will make his throne in Israel last forever.' 11 Now, my son, may the Lord be with you and help you to do well. May you build the house of the Lord your God just as He has said you would. 12 Only, may the Lord give you wisdom and understanding. When He has you rule over Israel, may you keep the Law of the Lord your God. 13 Then you will do well, if you are careful to obey the Laws which the Lord gave to Israel by Moses. Be strong and have strength of heart. Do not be afraid or troubled. 14 With much trouble I have made things ready for the house of the Lord. There is gold weighing as much as 100,000 men. There is silver weighing as much as 1,000,000 men. And there is too much brass and iron to weigh. I have made wood and stone ready, and you may add to them. 15 You have many servants and workmen who cut and build with stones and wood. There are men who are able to do every kind of work well. 16 Of the gold and silver and brass and iron, there is more than enough. So get ready and work, and may the Lord be with you."

17 David told all the leaders of Israel to help his son Solomon. He said to them, 18 "Is not the Lord your God with you? Has He not given you peace on every side? For He has given the people of the land into my hand. The land is put under my rule before the Lord and His people. 19 Now set your heart and soul to look to the Lord your God. Get ready and build the holy place of the Lord God. Then you may bring the special box with the Law of the Lord. You may bring the holy objects of God. And put them into the house that is to be built for the name of the Lord."

The Work of the Levites

23 When David was an old man, he made his son Solomon king of Israel. 2 He gathered together all the leaders of Israel, the religious leaders, and the Levites. 3 The Levites were numbered from thirty years old and older. Their number was 38,000. 4 Of these, 24,000 were to watch over the work of the Lord's house. There were 6,000 who were leaders and men who were to judge. 5 There were 4,000 gate-keepers. And 4,000 were praising the Lord with the things for playing music that David had made. 6 David divided them into groups by the sons of Levi, Gershon and Kohath and Merari.

7 The sons of Gershon were Ladan and Shimei. 8 The sons of Ladan were Jehiel the first, then Zetham and Joel, three in all. 9 The three sons of Shimei were Shelemoth, Haziel and Haran. These were the heads of the fathers' houses of Ladan. 10 And the sons of Shimei were Jahath, Zina, Jeush and Beriah. These four were the sons of Shimei. 11 Jahath was the first, and Zizah the second. But Jeush and Beriah did not have many sons, so they were

numbered together as one father's house.

12 The four sons of Kohath were Amram, Izhar, Hebron and Uzziel. 13 The sons of Amram were Aaron and Moses. Aaron was set apart for holy work, he and his sons forever. They were to burn special perfume before the Lord, and do His work. And they were to pray for good to come to the people in the Lord's name forever. 14 But the names of the sons of Moses the man of God were among the family of Levi. 15 The sons of Moses were Gershom and Eliezer. 16 The son of Gershom was Shebuel the leader. 17 The son of Eliezer was Rehabiah the leader. Eliezer had no other sons. But Rehabiah had many sons. 18 The son of Izhar was Shelomith the leader. 19 The sons of Hebron were Jeriah the first, Amariah the second, Jehaziel the third, and Jekameam the fourth. 20 The sons of Uzziel were Micah the first, and Isshiah the second.

21 The sons of Merari were Mahli and Mushi. The sons of Mahli were Eleazar and Kish. 22 Eleazar died and had no sons, only daughters. Their brothers the sons of Kish married them. 23 The three sons of Mushi were Mahli and Eder and Jeremoth.

24 These were the sons of Levi by their fathers' houses. They were the heads of the fathers' houses of those whose names were numbered from twenty years old and older. They were to do the work of the Lord's house. 25 For David said, "The Lord God of Israel has given peace to his people. And He lives in Jerusalem forever. 26 The Levites do not need to carry the meeting tent and all the parts for its work any longer." 27 For by the last words of David the sons of Levi were numbered, from twenty years old and older. 28 He said, "Their duties are to help Aaron's sons with the work of the Lord's house, in the open spaces and in the rooms. They are to make clean all the holy things, and do any work needed to be done in the house of God. 29 They are to take care of the holy bread, the fine flour for a grain gift, and the bread without yeast. They are to take care of what is baked, and what is well mixed, of all the right amounts. 30 They are to stand every morning and evening to thank and praise the Lord. 31 And they are to give all the burnt gifts to the Lord on the Days of Rest, the new moons, and the special days. They are to do this before the Lord all the time, by the number set by the Law. 32 In this way they are to take care of the meeting

tent, the holy place, and help their brothers the sons of Aaron, for the work of the Lord's house.

The Work of the Religious Leaders

24 These were the family groups of the sons of Aaron. The sons of Aaron were Nadab, Abihu, Eleazar and Ithamar. 2 Nadab and Abihu died before their father died. They had no sons, so Eleazar and Ithamar became the religious leaders. 3 With the help of Zadok of the sons of Eleazar and Ahimelech of the sons of Ithamar, David divided them by their given duties. 4 More leaders were found from the sons of Eleazar than the sons of Ithamar. So they were divided in this way. There were sixteen heads of families of the sons of Eleazar. And there were eight heads of families of the sons of Ithamar. 5 They were divided by drawing names, all alike. For there were leaders of the holy place and leaders of God, from both the sons of Eleazar and Ithamar. 6 The writer Shemaiah, the Levite son of Nethanel, wrote down their names. He wrote them in front of the king, the princes, Zadok the religious leader, Ahimelech the son of Abiathar, and the heads of the families of the religious leaders and of the Levites. One family was taken for Eleazar, and one for Ithamar.

7 The first name drawn was Jehoiarib, the second Jedaiah, 8 the third Harim, the fourth Seorim, 9 the fifth Malchijah, the sixth Mijamin 10 The seventh name was Hakkoz, the eighth Abijah, 11 the ninth Jeshua, the tenth Shecaniah, 12 the eleventh Eliashib, the twelfth Jakim. 13 The thirteenth name was Huppah, the fourteenth Jeshebeab, 14 the fifteenth Bilgah, the sixteenth Immer. 15 The seventeenth name was Hezir, the eighteenth Happizzez, 16 the nineteenth Pethahiah, the twentieth Jehezkel. 17 The twenty-first name was Jachin, the twenty-second Gamul, 18 the twenty-third Delaiah, and the twenty-fourth Maaziah. 19 This was the way they were to come on duty to work in the Lord's house. It was a rule given to them through their father Aaron, just as the Lord God of Israel had told him.

20 The rest of the sons of Levi were Shubael of the sons of Amram, Jehdeiah of the sons of Shubael, 21 and Isshiah was the first of the sons of Rehabiah. 22 There was Shelomoth of the Izharites, and Jahath of the sons of Shelomoth. 23 Of the sons of Hebron, there were Jeriah the first, Amariah

the second, Jahaziel the third, and Jekameam the fourth. 24 There was Micah of the sons of Uzziel, and Shamir of the sons of Micah. 25 The brother of Micah was Isshiah. There was Zechariah of the sons of Isshiah. 26 The sons of Merari were Mahli and Mushi. Jaaziah's son was Beno. 27 The sons of Merari by Jaaziah were Beno, Shoham, Zaccur and Ibri. 28 His son by Mahli was Eleazar, who had no sons. 29 His son by Kish was Jerahmeel. 30 And the sons of Mushi were Mahli, Eder and Jerimoth. These were the sons of the Levites by their families. 31 The head of each family and his younger brother drew names just as their brothers the sons of Aaron did. They drew them in front of King David, Zadok, Ahimelech, and the heads of the families of the religious leaders and of the Levites.

Songs of Joy

25 David and the captains of the army set apart for the work some of the sons of Asaph, of Heman and of Jeduthun. They were to speak God's Word with harps and timbrels were playing. These are the names of those who served in this way. 2 The sons of Asaph were: Zaccur, Joseph, Nethaniah and Asharelah. They were led by Asaph, who spoke for God under the leading of the king. 3 The six sons of Jeduthun were: Gedaliah, Zeri, Jeshaiah, Shimei, Hashabiah and Mattithiah. They were led by their father Jeduthun, who spoke God's Word using the harp, giving thanks and praising the Lord. 4 The sons of Heman were: Bukkiah, Mattaniah, Uzziel, Shebuel, Jerimoth, Hananiah, Hanani, Eliathah, Giddalti, Romamti-ezer, Joshbekashah, Mallothi, Hothir and Mahazioth. 5 All these were the sons of Heman the king's man of God, to honor him by the Words of God. God gave Heman fourteen sons and three daughters. 6 All of them were led by their father to sing in the Lord's house. They sang and played timbrels and harps, serving in the house of God. Asaph, Jeduthun and Heman were led by the king. 7 The number of those and their brothers who were taught to sing to the Lord, all who were very good singers, was 288. 8 They drew names for their work, the young and old alike, also the teacher and the one who was taught.

9 These are how the names are drawn. First was Joseph the son of Asaph. The second was Gedaliah. Together with his brothers and sons, there were twelve.

10 The third was Zaccur. With his sons and brothers there were twelve. 11 The fourth was Izri. With his sons and brothers there were twelve. 12 The fifth was Nethaniah. With his sons and brothers there were twelve. 13 The sixth was Bukkiah. With his sons and brothers there were twelve. 14 The seventh was Jesharelah. With his sons and brothers there were twelve. 15 The eighth was Jeshaiah. With his sons and brothers there were twelve. 16 The ninth was Mattaniah. With his sons and brothers there were twelve. 17 The tenth was Shimei. With his sons and brothers there were twelve. 18 The eleventh was Azarel. With his sons and brothers there were twelve. 19 The twelfth was Hashabiah. With his sons and brothers there were twelve. 20 The thirteenth was Shubael. With his sons and brothers there were twelve. 21 The fourteenth was Mattithiah. With his sons and brothers there were twelve. 22 The fifteenth was Jeremoth. With his sons and brothers there were twelve. 23 The sixteenth was Hananiah. With his sons and brothers there were twelve. 24 The seventeenth was Joshbekashah. With his sons and brothers there were twelve. 25 The eighteenth was Hanani. With his sons and brothers there were twelve. 26 The nineteenth was Mallothi. With his sons and brothers there were twelve. 27 The twentieth was Eliathah. With his sons and brothers there were twelve. 28 The twenty-first was Hothir. With his sons and brothers there were twelve. 29 The twenty-second was Giddalti. With his sons and brothers there were twelve. 30 The twenty-third was Mahazioth. With his sons and brothers there were twelve. 31 And the twenty-fourth was Romamti-ezer. With his sons and brothers there were twelve.

The Gate-Keepers

26 The gate-keepers were divided up. Of the Korahites there was Meshelemiah the son of Kore, a son of Asaph. 2 Meshelemiah's sons were Zechariah the first-born, Jediael the second, Zebadiah the third, Jathniel the fourth. 3 Elam was his fifth son, Johanan the sixth, Eliehoenai the seventh. 4 Obed-edom's sons were Shemaiah the first-born, Jehozabad the second, Joah the third, Sacar the fourth, Nethanel the fifth. 5 Ammiel was his sixth son, Issachar the seventh, and Peullethai the eighth. God had brought good to the father. 6 To his son Shemaiah sons were born who ruled over their father's house. They were strong, able men with strength of heart. 7 The sons of Shemaiah were Othni, Rephael, Obed and Elzabad. Their brothers, Elihu and Semachiah, were strong and able men. 8 All these were sons of Obed-edom. They and their sons and brothers were able men with strength for the work. There were sixty-two men from Obed-edom. 9 Meshelemiah had sons and brothers, eighteen strong and able men. 10 These are the sons of Hosah, one of Merari's sons: Shimri was the first. (He was not the first-born, but his father made him first.) 11 Hilkiah was his second, Tebaliah the third, and Zechariah the fourth. Hosah had thirteen sons and brothers in all.

12 These leaders of the families who were set apart as gate-keepers were given duties like their brothers to work in the Lord's house. 13 The families drew names by their fathers' houses, the small and the large alike, for every gate. 14 Shelemiah's name was drawn for the east gate. Then they drew the name of his son Zechariah for the north gate. Zechariah used much wisdom talking with people. 15 Obed-edom's name was drawn for the south gate. And his sons were to watch the store-house. 16 Shuppim and Hosah's names were drawn for the west gate beside the gate of Shallecheth, on the road that goes up a hill. Each one was given his duty to watch. 17 There were six Levites on the east. There were four each day on the north. There were four each day on the south. There were two at one time at the store-house. 18 There were four at the road. And there were two at the place between the west wall of the Lord's house and the wall of the open space. 19 These were the way the gate-keepers of the sons of Korah and Merari were divided.

20 Their brothers the Levites watched over the riches of the house of God and the riches of the holy gifts. 21 The sons of Ladan, who were Gershonites through the family group of Ladan were Jehielites. 22 The sons of Jehieli, Zetham and his brother Joel, watched over the riches of the house of the Lord. 23 Of the Amramites, the Izharites, the Hebronites and the Uzzielites, 24 Shebuel the son of Gershom, son of Moses, was the captain over the riches. 25 His brothers by Eliezer were Rehabiah his son, Jeshaiah his son, Joram his son, Zichri his son, and Shelomoth his son. 26 Shelomoth and his

brothers watched over all the riches of the holy gifts. These gifts had been set apart by King David and the heads of the fathers' houses, the captains of thousands and hundreds, and the captains of the army. 27 They set apart things taken in battles to do the work needed on the house of the Lord. 28 Samuel the man of God had set apart gifts. So had Saul the son of Kish, Abner the son of Ner, and Joab the son of Zeruiah, and everyone who had set apart anything. All these holy gifts were in the care of Shelomoth and his brothers.

29 Of the Izharites, Chenaniah and his sons were given outside duties for Israel. They were leaders and men who decide who is guilty or not. 30 Of the Hebronites, Hashabiah and his brothers were leaders of Israel west of the Jordan. They were 1,700 able men who did all the work of the Lord and the work of the king. 31 Of the Hebronites, Jerijah was the leader of the Hebronites by their families and fathers' houses. Very able men were found among them at Jazer in Gilead in the fortieth year of David's rule. 32 Jerijah and his brothers were 2,700 able men, heads of fathers' houses. King David chose them to take care of all the duties of God and of the king, among the Reubenites, the Gadites and the half-family group of the Manassites.

The Captains of the Army

27 These were the sons of Israel, the heads of fathers' houses. They were the leaders of thousands and of hundreds. These were the captains who worked for the king in anything to do with the armies which came in and went out every month of the year. There were 24,000 men in each army. 2 Jashobeam the son of Zabdiel was the leader of the first army for the first month. There were 24,000 in his army. 3 He was a son of Perez, and head of all the captains of the army for the first month. 4 Dodai the Ahohite was the leader of the army for the second month. Mikloth was the head captain. There were 24,000 in his army. 5 The third leader of the army for the third month was Benaiah, the son of Jehoiada the religious leader. There were 24,000 in his army. 6 This is the Benaiah who was the strong man of the thirty, and leader of the thirty. Ammizabad his son was captain of his army. 7 The fourth leader for the fourth month was Asahel the brother of Joab, and Zebadiah his son after him. There were 24,000 in his army. 8 The fifth leader for the fifth month

was Shamhuth the Izrahite. There were 24,000 in his army. 9 The sixth for the sixth month was Ira the son of Ikkesh the Tekoite. There were 24,000 in his army. 10 The seventh for the seventh month was Helez the Pelonite of the sons of Ephraim. There were 24,000 in his army. 11 The eighth for the eighth month was Sibbecai the Hushathite of the Zerahites. There were 24,000 in his army. 12 The ninth for the ninth month was Abiezer the Anathothite of the Benjamites. There were 24,000 in his army. 13 The tenth for the tenth month was Maharai the Netophathite of the Zerahites. There were 24,000 in his army. 14 The eleventh for the eleventh month was Benaiah the Pirathonite of the sons of Ephraim. There were 24,000 in his army. 15 The twelfth for the twelfth month was Heldai the Netophathite of Othniel. There were 24,000 in his army.

Leaders of Family Groups

16 The leaders of the family groups of Israel were: Eliezer the son of Zichri was the head captain of the Reubenites; Shephatiah the son of Maacah led the Simeonites. 17 Hashabiah the son of Kemuel led the sons of Levi; Zadok led the sons of Aaron. 18 Elihu, one of David's brothers, led the sons of Judah; Omri the son of Michael led the sons of Issachar; 19 Ishmaiah the son of Obadiah led the sons of Zebulun; Jeremoth the son of Azriel led the sons of Naphtali; 20 Hoshea the son of Azaziah led the sons of Ephraim; Joel the son of Pedaiah led the half-family group of Manasseh; 21 Iddo the son of Zechariah led the half-family group of Manasseh in Gilead; Jaasiel the son of Abner led the sons of Benjamin; 22 And Azarel the son of Jeroham led the sons of Dan. These were the leaders of the families of Israel. 23 But David did not number those younger than twenty years old because the Lord had promised to make Israel many, as the stars of heaven. 24 Joab the son of Zeruiah had begun to number them, but did not finish. Anger came upon Israel because of this. So the number was not put into the book of the chronicles of King David.

25 Azmaveth the son of Adiel was over the king's store-houses. Jonathan the son of Uzziah was over the store-houses in the country, in the cities, in the towns, and in the towers. 26 Ezri the son of Chelub was over those who worked in the fields, plowing and planting. 27 Shimei the Ramathite was over the grape-fields. Zabdi the Shiphmite was over the fruit of the grape-fields for the wine. 28 Baal-hanan the Gederite was over the olive and sycamore trees in the plains. Joash was captain of the stores of oil. 29 Shitrai the Sharonite was over the cattle which were eating in the fields of Sharon. Shaphat the son of Adlai was over the cattle in the valleys. 30 Obil the Ishmaelite was over the camels. Jehdeiah the Meronothite was over the donkeys. 31 And Jaziz the Hagrite was over the flocks. All these were over all that belonged to King David.

32 Jonathan, the brother of David's father, used much wisdom talking with people. And he was a writer. Jehiel the son of Hachmoni taught the king's sons. 33 Ahithophel talked about problems with the king. Hushai the Archite was the king's friend. 34 Jehoiada the son of Benaiah, and Abaiathar, talked with the king after Ahithophel. And Joab was the captain of the king's army.

Solomon to Build the House of God

28 David gathered together all the leaders of Israel. There were leaders of the family groups, and leaders of the armies that served the king. There were captains of thousands, and of hundreds. There were leaders who cared for all the things and animals belonging to the king and his sons. There were the leaders and all the powerful soldiers. 2 Then King David stood up and said, "Listen to me, my brothers and my people. I had wanted to build a house of rest for the special box with the Law of the Lord, a place for God to rest His feet, so I had made plans to build it. 3 But God said to me, 'You must not build a house for My name, because you are a man of war and blood.' 4 But the Lord, the God of Israel, chose me from all the house of my father to be the king of Israel forever. For He has chosen Judah to be a leader. And in the house of Judah, my father's house, and among my father's sons, He was pleased to make me king of all Israel. 5 The Lord has given me many sons. And of all my sons, He has chosen my son Solomon to sit on the throne of the nation of the Lord over Israel. 6 He said to me, 'Your son Solomon is the one who will build My house and My open spaces. For I have chosen him to be My son, and I will be his father. 7 I will make him king forever, if he is faithful to obey My Words and My Laws, as he is doing now.' 8 So now I say to you in front of all these people of

Israel, and in the hearing of our God: Be careful to do all the Law of the Lord your God. If you obey you will receive the good land and also leave it to your children after you forever.

9 "As for you, my son Solomon, know the God of your father. Serve Him with a whole heart and a willing mind. For the Lord looks into all hearts, and understands every plan and thought. If you look to Him, He will let you find Him. But if you turn away from Him, He will turn away from you forever. 10 Listen now, for the Lord has chosen you to build a place of worship. Be strong, and do it."

11 Then David gave his son Solomon the plan of the porch of the Lord's house, its buildings, and its store-houses. He gave him the plan of the rooms on its second floor, its inside rooms, and the room for the mercy-seat. 12 He gave him the plan of all he had in mind. It showed the open spaces of the Lord's house, and all the rooms around them. It showed the store-houses of the house of God, and the store-houses of the holy things. 13 He gave him the plan for the way the religious leaders and the Levites were to be divided up for all the work of the Lord's house. He told how all the objects were to be used in worship in the Lord's house. 14 David gave the weight of all the gold objects to be used in each part of worship. He gave the weight for all the silver objects to be used in each part of the worship. 15 The plan gave the weight of gold for the gold lamp-stands and gold lamps. It gave the weight of each lamp-stand and its lamps. It gave the weight of silver for the silver lamp-stands. It gave the weight of each lamp-stand and its lamps, by the use of each lamp-stand. 16 It gave the weight of gold for each table of holy bread, and of silver for the silver tables. 17 It gave the weight of the meat-hooks, the pots and the cups of pure gold. It gave the weight for each of the gold and silver pots. 18 It gave the weight of the fine gold of the altar of special perfume, and of the gold wagon and of the cherubim that spread out their wings and covered the special box with the Law of the Lord. 19 David said, "This is in writing because His hand was upon me. He helped me to know all the plan."

20 Then David said to his son Solomon, "Be strong. Have strength of heart, and do it. Do not be afraid or troubled, for the Lord God, my God, is with you. He will not stop helping you. He will not leave you until all the work of the house of the Lord is finished. 21 See, the religious leaders and the Levites are divided up to do all the work of the house of God. Every willing man who is able to do a special work will help you in all that is to be done. The leaders and all the people will do what you say."

Gifts for the Building of the House of God

29 Then King David said to all the people, "My son Solomon is the one God has chosen. He is still young and has not had much time to know what to do. It is a very big work because this beautiful house is not for man, but for the Lord God. 2 I have given all that I have been able to give for the house of my God. I have given the gold for the things of gold, the silver for the things of silver, and the brass for the things of brass. I have given the iron for the things of iron, and the wood for the things of wood. I have given stones of much worth, stones for setting, silver-white stones, and stones of different colors. I have given all kinds of stones of much worth, and many smooth, pure white stones. 3 The house of my God means much to me. I have much gold and silver and I give it to the house of my God, together with all I have already given for the holy house. 4 I gave gold weighing as much as 3,000 men, of the gold of Ophir. I gave fine silver weighing as much as 7,000 men, to cover the walls of the house. 5 I gave gold for the things of gold, and silver for the things of silver for all the work done by the able men. Now who is willing to give himself and be set apart today to the Lord?"

6 Then the rulers of the families gave because they wanted to. The leaders of the family groups of Israel, the captains of thousands and of hundreds, and those who watched over the king's work gave because they wanted to. 7 For the work of the house of God, they gave gold weighing as much as 5,000 men, and 10,000 gold pieces. They gave silver weighing as much as 10,000 men. They gave brass weighing as much as 18,000 men, and iron weighing as much as 100,000 men. 8 And whoever had stones of much worth gave them to the store-house of the house of the Lord, in the care of Jehiel the Gershonite. 9 Then the people were filled with joy because they had been so willing to give. They gave their gift to the Lord with a whole heart. And King David was filled with great joy.

David's Praise to God

10 So David praised the Lord in front of all the people. He said, "Honor and thanks be to You, O Lord God of Israel our father, forever and ever. **11** O Lord, You have great power, shining-greatness and strength. Yes, everything in heaven and on earth belongs to You. You are the King, O Lord. And You are honored as head over all. **12** Both riches and honor come from You. You rule over all. Power and strength are in Your hand. The power is in Your hand to make great and to give strength to all. **13** So now, our God, we thank You. We praise Your great and honored name.

14 "But who am I and who are my people, that we should be able to give so much? For all things come from You. We have given You only what already belongs to You. **15** We are strangers before You. We are just staying here for a time, as all our fathers did. Our days on the earth are like a shadow, and without hope. **16** O Lord our God, from Your hand are all these many things that we have given to build You a house for Your holy name. It all belongs to You. **17** O my God, I know that You test the heart and are pleased with what is right. I have given these things because I have wanted to with a clean heart. And now I have seen with joy how Your people who are here give gifts to You because they want to. **18** O Lord, the God of Abraham, Isaac and Israel, our fathers, keep this hope ever in the thoughts of the hearts of Your people. Lead their hearts to You. **19** Give my son Solomon a perfect heart to keep Your Words and Your Laws and to obey them all. And so let him build the beautiful house I have planned and given for."

20 Then David said to all the people, "Now praise the Lord your God." And all the people gave praise to the Lord, the God of their fathers. They bowed low to the ground before the Lord and the king. **21** On the next day they killed animals and gave burnt gifts in worship to the Lord. They gave 1,000 bulls, 1,000 rams and 1,000 lambs, with their drink gifts. They gave many gifts in worship for all Israel. **22** So they ate and drank that day with great joy before the Lord.

They made David's son Solomon king a second time. They poured oil on him to set him apart as ruler for the Lord. And they set Zadok apart as religious leader. **23** Then Solomon sat on the throne of the Lord as king instead of his father David. Everything went well for him, and all Israel obeyed him. **24** All the leaders and the powerful men and all the sons of King David promised to be faithful to King Solomon. **25** The Lord brought much honor to Solomon in the eyes of all Israel. He gave him greater power than any king before him in Israel.

26 So David the son of Jesse ruled over all Israel. **27** And he ruled over Israel for forty years. He ruled in Hebron seven years, and in Jerusalem thirty-three years. **28** Then he died as an old man. He had lived many years, had many riches and much honor. And his son Solomon ruled in his place. **29** The acts of King David, from first to last, are written in the books of Samuel, Nathan, and Gad, the men of God. **30** They tell of all his rule, his power, and of the things which happened to him, to Israel, and to all the nations of the lands.

2 CHRONICLES

Solomon Prays for Wisdom

1 Solomon the son of David became a strong king. The Lord his God was with him, and gave him much honor. **2** Solomon spoke to all Israel. He spoke to the leaders of thousands and of hundreds. He spoke to the men who judge and to every leader in all Israel, the heads of fathers' houses. **3** Then Solomon and all the people with him went to a place of worship at Gibeon where God's meeting tent was. It was the tent which Moses the servant of the Lord had made in the desert. **4** (But David had brought up the special box of God from Kiriath-jearim to the place he had made ready for it. For he had set up a tent for it in Jerusalem.) **5** Now the brass altar was there in front of the meeting tent of the Lord. It was the altar which was made by Bezalel the son of Uri, the son of Hur. Solomon and the people worshiped the Lord there. **6** Solomon went before the Lord to the brass altar at the meeting tent. And he gave a thousand burnt gifts on it.

7 That night God showed Himself to Solomon and said to him, "Ask Me for anything and I will give it to you." **8** Solomon said to God, "You have acted toward my father David with great loving-kindness. And You have made me king in his place. 9 Now, O Lord God, Your promise to my father David has come true. For You have made me king over as many people as the dust of the earth. 10 Now give me wisdom and much understanding, that I may lead these people. For who can rule this great nation of Yours?" 11 God said to Solomon, "You have not asked for riches, much money, or honor, or the life of those who hate you. And you have not asked for a long life for yourself. But you have asked for wisdom and much understanding, that you may rule My people over whom I have made you king. Because this was in your heart, 12 wisdom and much understanding have been given to you. And I will give you riches and much money and honor. You will have more than all the kings who were before you, and more than all who will come after you."

Solomon's Power and Riches

13 So Solomon went from the place of worship at Gibeon, from the meeting tent to Jerusalem. There he ruled over Israel.

14 Solomon gathered together war-wagons and horsemen. He had 1,400 war-wagons and 12,000 horsemen. And he kept some of them in the war-wagon cities, and some with him in Jerusalem. 15 The king made silver and gold as easy to find in Jerusalem as stones. He made cedar trees as easy to find as sycamore trees in the valley. 16 Solomon's horses were brought in from Egypt and Kue. The men who traded for the king received them from Kue for a special price. 17 They paid 600 pieces of silver for each war-wagon brought in from Egypt and 150 pieces of silver for each horse. They also sold them to all the kings of the Hittites and the kings of Aram.

Solomon Gets Ready to Build the House of God

2 Solomon planned to build a house for the name of the Lord, and a king's house for himself. 2 So he picked 70,000 men to carry loads, 80,000 men to cut stones in the mountains, and 3,600 men to watch over these men. 3 Then Solomon sent word to King Huram of Tyre, saying, "You sent my father David cedar trees to build him a house to live in. Do the same for me. 4 See, I am about to build a house for the name of the Lord my God. I will set it apart for Him. There special perfume will be burned before Him. The holy bread

will be there all the time. Burnt gifts will be given morning and evening, on Days of Rest, on new moons, and during the special suppers of the Lord our God. This is to be done forever in Israel. 5 The house I am about to build will be great. For our God is greater than all the gods. 6 But who is able to build a house for Him? For the heavens and the highest heavens are not big enough to hold Him. So who am I, that I should build a house for Him, except as a place to burn special perfume before Him? 7 Now send me an able man to work with gold, silver, brass, iron, and purple, red and blue cloth who knows how to cut all kinds of pictures. He will work with the able men I have in Judah and Jerusalem, whom my father David gave me. 8 Send me cedar, cypress and algum trees from Lebanon. I know you have able men who know how to do this work. My servants will work with your servants 9 to cut many trees for me. For the house I am about to build will be very great and beautiful. 10 I will give to your servants who cut trees, 200,000 baskets of crushed grain, 200,000 baskets of barley, 200,000 bottles of wine, and 200,000 bottles of oil."

11 Then King Huram of Tyre answered by letter to Solomon, "The Lord has made you king over His people because He loves them." 12 Then Huram said, "Honor and thanks be to the Lord, the God of Israel. He has made heaven and earth. And He has given King David a wise son. Wisdom and understanding have been given to David's son who will build a house for the Lord and a king's house for himself. 13 Now I am sending Huram-abi, an able man of understanding. 14 He is the son of a Danite woman and a Tyrian father. He knows how to work with gold, silver, brass, iron, stone and wood and with purple, blue, and red cloth. He knows how to cut all kinds of pictures, any kind given him to do. He is to work with your able men, and with those of my lord David your father. 15 So now let my lord send the grain, barley, oil and wine to his servant, as he has said. 16 We will cut whatever trees you need in Lebanon, and bring them to you by ship to Joppa. Then you may carry them up to Jerusalem."

17 Solomon numbered all those in Israel who were from other lands, using the number of them which his father David had taken. And 153,600 were found. 18 He picked 70,000 of them to carry loads, 80,000 to cut stones in the mountains, and 3,600 men to see that the people did their work.

Solomon Builds the House of God

3 Then Solomon began to build the Lord's house in Jerusalem on Mount Moriah. It was there that the Lord had shown Himself to his father David. It was the place that David had chosen, on the grain-floor of Ornan the Jebusite. ² Solomon began to build on the second day in the second month of the fourth year of his rule. ³ He laid the base for building the house of God. It was thirty long steps, using the old way to find the length. And it was ten long steps wide. ⁴ The porch in front of the house was as long as the house was wide, ten long steps. It was thirty-three times taller than a man. And he covered the inside with pure gold. ⁵ He covered the large room with cypress wood, and covered that with fine gold. Then he made palm trees and chains on it. ⁶ He put stones of much worth on the house for beauty. And the gold was from Parvaim. ⁷ He covered the house with gold. He covered its cross-pieces, its door-ways, its walls, and its doors. And he cut pictures of cherubim on the walls.

⁸ He made the most holy place. It was as long as the house was wide, ten long steps. And it was as wide as ten long steps. He covered it with fine gold weighing as much as 600 men. ⁹ The nails weighed as much as fifty pieces of gold. He covered the rooms on the second floor with gold also.

¹⁰ Then he made two cherubim of wood in the most holy place, and covered them with gold. ¹¹ The wings of the cherubim spread as far as ten long steps. The wing of one was as long as three steps, and touched the wall of the house. Its other wing was as long as three steps, and touched the wing of the other cherub. ¹² The wing of the other cherub was as long as three steps, and touched the wall of the house. Its other wing was as long as three steps, and was joined to the wing of the first cherub. ¹³ The wings of these cherubim spread as far as ten long steps. And they stood on their feet with their faces toward the holy place. ¹⁴ He made the curtain of blue, purple and red cloth and fine linen. And he worked cherubim on it. ¹⁵ He made two pillars in front of the house that were ten times taller than a man. The top piece of each one was as tall as a man can raise his hand. ¹⁶ For the inside holy place he made chains, and put them on the tops of the pillars. Then he made one hundred pomegranates and put them on the chains. ¹⁷ He put up the pillars in front of the house of God. One was on the right and the other was on the left. He named the one on the right Jachin, and the one on the left Boaz.

Objects for Worship

4 Then he made a brass altar. It was ten steps long, and ten steps wide, and three times taller than a man. ² He melted brass and made a pool. It was round, and five long steps from one side to the other. It was as tall as a man can raise his hand. And it took fifteen steps to walk around it. ³ There were objects that looked like oxen under the pool and all around it, (ten long steps around it). The oxen were in two rows, and were made of one piece. ⁴ The pool was put on the twelve oxen. Three had their faces toward the north, three toward the west, three toward the south, and three toward the east. The pool was put on top of them. All their tails were toward the center. ⁵ The brass of the pool was as thick as a hand is wide. Its round top was made like the top of a cup, like a lily flower. It could hold 22,000 bottles of water. ⁶ He made ten pots in which to wash. He put five on the right side and five on the left side. They were to wash what was used for the burnt gifts. But the pool was for the religious leaders to wash in.

⁷ Then he made ten gold lamp-stands, as was shown in the plan. He put them in the house of God, five on the right side and five on the left. ⁸ He made ten tables and put them in the house of God. Five were on the right side and five on the left. And he made 100 deep dishes out of gold. ⁹ Then he made the open space of the religious leaders, the large open space, and the doors for the open space. And he covered their doors with brass. ¹⁰ He set the pool at the south-east corner of the house.

¹¹ Then Huram made the pails, the tools for digging, and the pots. So Huram finished the work of God's house that he did for King Solomon. ¹² He finished making the two pillars, the pots, and the two pieces on top of the pillars. He finished the two networks to cover the two pots of the pieces on top of the pillars. ¹³ He finished the 400 pomegranates for the two networks. There were two rows of pomegranates for each network, to cover the two pots of the pieces on top of the pillars. ¹⁴ He made the stands and he made the pots on the stands. ¹⁵ He made the one pool with the twelve oxen under it. ¹⁶ Huram-abi made the pails, the tools for digging, the meat-hooks, and all their

objects. He made them of shining brass for King Solomon for the house of the Lord. 17 The king had them made on the plain of the Jordan, in the clay ground between Succoth and Zeredah. 18 Solomon made so many of these objects that the weight of the brass could not be known.

19 Solomon made all the things that were in the house of God. He made the gold altar, and the tables for the holy bread. 20 He made the lamp-stands with their lamps of pure gold, to burn in front of the most holy place in the way given. 21 He made the flowers, the lamps and their objects of pure gold. 22 He made the things to put out the lamps, the pots and the fire-holders of pure gold. And he made the front of the house, its inside doors for the most holy place, and the doors of the holy place, all of gold.

5 So all the work that Solomon did for the Lord's house was finished. He brought in the things that his father David had set apart, the silver and the gold and all the objects. He put them in the store-rooms of the house of God.

The Special Box Brought into the House of God

2 Then Solomon gathered to Jerusalem the leaders of Israel, and all the heads of the families, the leaders of the fathers' houses of the sons of Israel. He called them together to bring up the special box with the Law of the Lord out of the city of David, which is Zion. 3 All the men of Israel gathered together in front of the king at the special supper in the seventh month. 4 All the leaders of Israel came, and the Levites took up the special box of God. 5 They brought up the special box of God, the meeting tent, and all the holy objects that were in the tent. The religious leaders and the Levites brought them up. 6 Then King Solomon and all the people of Israel who were with him were in front of the special box of God. There they gave on the altar in worship so many sheep and oxen that they could not be numbered. 7 The religious leaders brought the special box of the Lord to its place. They brought it into the most holy place in the house, under the wings of the cherubim. 8 The cherubim spread their wings over the place of the special box of God. They made a covering over the special box and its long pieces of wood used for carrying. 9 The pieces of wood for the special box

of God were so long that their ends could be seen in front of the holy place. But they could not be seen outside. They are there to this day. 10 There was nothing in the special box of God except the two stone writings which Moses put there at Horeb. It was there that the Lord made an agreement with the people of Israel, when they came out of Egypt.

11 Then the religious leaders came out of the holy place. All the religious leaders who were there had set themselves apart, without thinking of how they were divided. 12 All the Levite singers, Asaph, Heman, Jeduthun and their sons and brothers, were dressed in fine linen. They stood east of the altar, with timbrels and different kinds of harps. With them were 120 religious leaders sounding horns. 13 Those who sounded the horns and the singers made themselves heard as with one voice, praising and thanking the Lord. They sang in a loud voice, with horns, and timbrels, and other objects for making music. They praised the Lord, saying, "He is good. For His loving-kindness lasts forever." Then the house of the Lord was filled with a cloud. 14 The religious leaders could not stand to do their work because of the cloud. For the shining-greatness of the Lord filled the house of God.

Solomon's Words to the People

6 Then Solomon said, "The Lord has said that He would live in the thick cloud. 2 I have built a great house for You. It is a place for You to live in forever." 3 Then the king turned around and prayed that good would come to all the people of Israel, while all the people of Israel stood.

4 Solomon said, "Honor and thanks be to the Lord, the God of Israel. He spoke with His mouth to my father David. And He has kept His promises with His hands, saying, 5 'Since the day that I brought My people from the land of Egypt, I chose no city among all the families of Israel in which to build a house for My name. I did not choose any man to be a leader over My people Israel. 6 But I have chosen Jerusalem that My name might be there. And I have chosen David to rule My people Israel.' 7 Now it was in the heart of my father David to build a house for the name of the Lord, the God of Israel. 8 But the Lord said to my father David, 'Because it was in your heart to build a house for My name, you did well that it was in your heart. 9 But you will not build the house. Your son who

will be born to you will build the house for My name.' [10] Now the Lord has kept His promise which He made. For I have taken the place of my father David and sit on the throne of Israel, as the Lord promised. And I have built the house for the name of the Lord, the God of Israel. [11] There I have put the special box with the Law of the Lord which He gave to the people of Israel."

Solomon's Prayer

[12] Then Solomon stood before the altar of the Lord, in front of all the people of Israel, and spread out his hands. [13] Solomon had made a special place to stand, out of brass. It was as long and as wide as three steps, and as high as a man's chest. And he had put it in the center of the open space. He stood on it, then got down on his knees in front of all the people of Israel, and spread out his hands toward heaven. [14] He said, "O Lord, God of Israel, there is no God like You in heaven or on earth. You keep Your promises and show loving-kindness to Your servants who walk with You with all their hearts. [15] You have kept Your promises to Your servant David my father. Yes, You have spoken with Your mouth, and have done all You said You would do, as it is today. [16] So now, O Lord, God of Israel, keep Your promise which You made to Your servant David my father, saying, 'You will never be without a man to sit on the throne of Israel. But your sons must be careful to walk in My Law, as you have done.' [17] So now, O Lord, God of Israel, let Your Word be made sure which You have spoken to Your servant David.

[18] "But is it true that God will live with man on the earth? See, heaven and the highest heaven cannot hold You. How much less can this house hold You which I have built! [19] But respect the prayer of Your servant and what he asks of You, O Lord my God. Listen to the cry and to the prayer which Your servant prays to You. [20] May Your eyes be open day and night toward this house, the place where You have promised to put Your name. Listen to the prayer which Your servant prays toward this place. [21] Listen to what Your servant and Your people Israel ask for when they pray toward this place. Hear from the place where You live, from heaven. Hear and forgive.

[22] "If a man sins against his neighbor, and has to make a promise, and he comes and makes a promise before Your altar in this house, [23] then hear from heaven, and act. Judge Your servants. Punish the sinful by bringing his actions on his own head. And make it known that the one who is right and good is not guilty. Bring good to him because he is right and good.

[24] "If Your people Israel lose a battle against those who hate them, because they have sinned against You, and they return to You and tell of Your name, and pray and ask of You in this house, [25] then listen to them from heaven and forgive the sin of Your people Israel. Bring them back to the land You have given to them and to their fathers.

[26] "When the heavens are shut up and give no rain because the people have sinned against You, and they pray toward this place and tell of Your name, and turn from their sin when You bring trouble to them, [27] then hear in heaven and forgive the sin of Your servants and Your people Israel. Teach them the good way in which they should walk. And send rain on Your land which You have given to Your people.

[28] "If there is a time of no food in the land, and if there is a disease that kills the plants, or if there are locusts or grasshoppers, if those who hate Your people send armies to trap them in their cities, whatever trouble or sickness there is, [29] hear the prayer made by any man or by all Your people Israel. Each one will know his own trouble and his own pain. And when he spreads his hands toward this house, [30] then hear from heaven where You live, and forgive. Give to each man what he should have. For You, and only You, know the hearts of men. [31] May they fear You and walk in Your ways as long as they live in the land You have given to our fathers.

[32] "If a stranger who is not from Your people Israel comes from a far country because of Your great name, Your powerful hand, and Your strong arm, when he comes and prays toward this house, [33] hear from heaven where You live. Do all that the stranger asks of You. Then all the people of the earth may know Your name and honor You with fear, as Your people Israel do. And then they may know that this house I have built is called by Your name.

[34] "When Your people go out to battle against those who hate them, by whatever way You send them, and they pray to You toward this city which You have chosen and the house I have built for Your name, [35] then hear their prayer from heaven and help them.

36 "When they sin against You, (for there is no man who does not sin), and You are angry with them and give them to those who hate them, they will be carried away against their will to a land far away or near. 37 If they think about it in the land where they have been taken, and are sorry for their sins and turn away from them and pray to You in the land where they have been taken, saying, 'We have sinned. We have been bad and have done wrong.' 38 If they come back to You with all their heart and soul in the land where they have been taken and pray toward their land which You gave to their fathers and toward the city You have chosen and toward the house I have built for Your name, 39 then hear from heaven where You live. Hear their prayer and what they ask for, and help them. Forgive Your people who have sinned against You.

40 "Now, O my God, I ask You, let Your eyes be open and let Your ears listen to the prayer given in this place. 41 Now rise up, O Lord God. Go to Your resting place, You and the special box of Your power. O Lord God, let Your religious leaders be dressed in saving power. Let those who belong to You be filled with joy in what is good. 42 O Lord God, do not turn away the face of Your chosen one. Remember Your loving-kindness to Your servant David."

The House of God Is Set Apart for God

7 When Solomon had finished praying, fire came down from heaven and burned up the burnt gift and gifts of worship. And the shining-greatness of the Lord filled the house. 2 The religious leaders could not go into the house of the Lord because it was filled with the Lord's shining-greatness. 3 All the people of Israel saw the fire come down and the shining greatness of the Lord upon the house. So they bowed their faces to the ground and worshiped. They gave thanks to the Lord, saying, "He is good. For His loving-kindness lasts forever."

4 Then the king and all the people gave gifts to the Lord. 5 King Solomon gave a gift of 22,000 cattle and 120,000 sheep. So the king and all the people set apart the house of God. 6 The religious leaders stood in their places while the Levites were praising the Lord using objects King David had made. They were playing, "For His loving-kindness lasts forever." As the religious leaders blew horns on the other side, all Israel stood.

7 Then Solomon set apart the center of the open space in front of the Lord's house. There he gave the burnt gifts and the fat of the peace gifts. The brass altar Solomon had made could not hold the burnt gift, the grain gift and the fat.

8 At that time Solomon gave the special supper for seven days, and all Israel with him. Many people were there. They had come from the gate of Hamath to the river of Egypt. 9 On the eighth day they gathered together for a special time. For seven days they had to set apart the altar, and for seven days they had the special supper. 10 On the twenty-third day of the seventh month Solomon sent the people to their tents. They were full of joy and happy in their heart for the good that the Lord had shown to David and Solomon and His people Israel.

God Comes to Solomon Again

11 Solomon finished the house of the Lord and the king's house. All that Solomon had planned to do in the Lord's house and in his own house was well done. 12 Then the Lord came to Solomon during the night and said to him, "I have heard your prayer. And I have chosen this place for Myself as a house of gifts given in worship. 13 If I shut up the heavens so that there is no rain, and if I tell the locust to destroy the land, or send disease upon My people, 14 if My people who are called by My name put away their pride and pray, and look for My face, and turn from their sinful ways, then I will hear from heaven. I will forgive their sin, and will heal their land. 15 Now My eyes will be open. And My ears will hear the prayer that is made in this place. 16 For I have chosen this house and have made it holy, that My name may be there forever. My eyes and My heart will always be there. 17 As for you, if you walk in My ways as your father David walked and do all that I have told you to do and keep My Laws, 18 then I will make your throne to last as I promised your father David. I said, 'You will never be without a man to rule Israel.'

19 "But if you turn away and leave My Laws and My Word which I have given you, if you go and serve other gods and worship them, 20 then I will take you from the land I have given you. And I will turn My eyes away from this house which I have set apart for My name. I will make it so all people speak of it in shame. 21 Everyone will look with wonder at this

house that was once honored. They will say, 'Why has the Lord done this to this land and to this house?' 22 Then they will say, 'It is because they turned away from the Lord, the God of their fathers, Who brought them out of the land of Egypt. They have taken other gods, and worshiped them and served them. So the Lord has brought all this trouble on them.'"

Some of the Things Solomon Has Done

8 It took Solomon twenty years to build the house of the Lord and his own house. At the end of that time, 2 he built again the cities which Huram had given to him. And he had the people of Israel live in them. 3 Then Solomon went to Hamath-zobah, and took it. 4 He built Tadmor in the desert and all his store-cities in Hamath. 5 He built upper Beth-horon and lower Beth-horon. He made the city strong with walls, gates, and long pieces of iron. 6 Solomon built Baalath and all the store-cities for his war-wagons, and the cities for his horsemen. He built whatever he wanted to build in Jerusalem, Lebanon, and in all the land under his rule.

7 There were people who were left of the Hittites, the Amorites, the Perizzites, the Hivites, and the Jebusites, who were not of Israel. 8 They were the children of those who were left in the land, whom the people of Israel had not destroyed. Solomon made all of these people do hard work, as they do to this day. 9 But he did not make the people of Israel do hard work. They were soldiers, leaders, captains of war-wagons, and his horsemen. 10 These were the head leaders of King Solomon. There were 250 who ruled over the people.

11 Then Solomon brought Pharaoh's daughter up from the city of David to the house he had built for her. For he said, "My wife should not live in the house of David king of Israel. Because the places are holy where the special box of the Lord has come."

12 Then Solomon gave burnt gifts to the Lord on the Lord's altar which he had built in front of the porch. 13 He gave a certain number of gifts every day, as Moses had said should be given. Gifts were given for the Days of Rest, the new moons, and the three special suppers each year. These special suppers were the Special Supper of Bread Without Yeast, the Special Supper of Weeks, and the Special Supper of Tents. 14 By the law of David his father, Solomon chose the religious leaders for their different duties. He chose the Levites for their duties of praise and helping the religious leaders for each day's needs. And he chose who should be the gate-keepers at each gate. For David the man of God had said that this must be done. 15 They did all that the king had said the religious leaders and Levites must do in every duty and with the store-houses.

16 So all the work of Solomon was done, from the day the house of the Lord was begun until it was finished. So the house of the Lord was built.

17 Then Solomon went to Ezion-geber and Eloth on the shore of the sea, in the land of Edom. 18 Huram sent his servants to him with ships and servants who knew the sea. They went to Ophir together with Solomon's servants to get gold. And they brought gold weighing as much as 450 men from there to King Solomon.

The Queen of Sheba Visits Solomon

9 The queen of Sheba heard how well Solomon was known in all the lands. So she came to Jerusalem to test him with hard questions. She came with many servants and camels carrying spices and much gold and stones of much worth. When she came to Solomon, she talked with him about all that was on her heart. 2 And Solomon answered all her questions. There was nothing hidden from him which he could not make clear to her. 3 Then the queen of Sheba saw the wisdom of Solomon and the house he had built. 4 She saw the food at his table, and all his captains sitting there. She saw all those who were bringing in the food, and how they were dressed. She saw those who carried the cups, and their clothing. And she saw the burnt gifts that Solomon gave at the house of the Lord. After that, there was no more spirit in her. 5 She said to the king, "The news was true which I heard in my own land about your words and your wisdom. 6 But I did not believe the news until I came and saw it with my own eyes. See, half the greatness of your wisdom was not told to me. You are greater than what I had heard. 7 Happy are your men! Happy are your servants who stand in front of you all the time hearing your wisdom! 8 Praise be to the Lord your God Who was pleased with you! He set you on His throne as king for the Lord your God. Your God loved Israel and would have them last forever. So He made you king over them to do what is fair and right and good." 9 Then she gave the king gold weighing as much as 120 men, a very large amount of spices, and stones of much worth. There had never been spices like what the queen of Sheba gave to King Solomon.

10 Huram's servants and Solomon's servants brought gold from Ophir. They also brought algum trees and stones of much worth. 11 The king used the algum wood to make steps for the house of the Lord and for the king's house. And he used it to make different kinds of harps for the singers. There were none like them before in the land of Judah.

12 King Solomon gave the queen of Sheba all she asked for, much more than she had brought to him. Then she returned to her own land with her servants.

King Solomon's Riches

13 The gold that came to Solomon in one year weighed as much as 666 men. 14 Traders and men who buy and sell brought gold also. And all the kings of Arabia and the leaders of the land brought gold and silver to Solomon. 15 King Solomon made 200 battle-coverings of beaten gold. The beaten gold he used to make each large covering was as much as 600 gold pieces. 16 And he made 300 battle-coverings of beaten gold, using as much as 300 gold pieces worth of gold for each covering. The king put them in the House of the Trees of Lebanon.

17 The king made a great throne of ivory and covered it with pure gold. 18 There were six steps to the throne, and a part made of gold for his feet was joined to the throne. The throne had arms on each side, and two lions standing beside the arms. 19 Twelve lions were standing on each side of the six steps. Nothing like it had ever been made for the king of any other nation. 20 All King Solomon's cups were made of gold. And all the cups of the House of the Trees of Lebanon were made of pure gold. Silver was not thought of as having much worth in the days of Solomon. 21 For the king had ships which went to Tarshish with Huram's servants. Once every three years the ships of Tarshish came bringing gold, silver, ivory, apes, and peacocks.

22 So King Solomon became greater than all the kings of the earth in riches and wisdom. 23 And all the kings of the earth wanted to be with Solomon, to hear his wisdom which God had put into his heart. 24 Every one of them brought his gift.

Objects of silver and gold, clothing, objects for battle, spices, horses and donkeys, were brought each year.

25 Solomon had 4,000 rooms for horses and war-wagons, and 12,000 horsemen. He put them in the war-wagon cities and with the king in Jerusalem. 26 He was the ruler over all the kings from the Euphrates River to the land of the Philistines, and as far as the land of Egypt. 27 And the king made silver as easy to find as stones in Jerusalem. He made cedar trees as easy to find as sycamore trees in the valley. 28 And horses were brought in for Solomon from Egypt and from all countries.

Death of Solomon

29 Now the rest of the acts of Solomon, from first to last, are written in the words of Nathan the man of God. They are written in the holy words of Ahijah the Shilonite. And they are written in the special dreams of Iddo, the man who tells what will happen in the future, about Jeroboam the son of Nebat. 30 Solomon ruled forty years in Jerusalem over all Israel. 31 When he died he was buried in the city of his father David. And his son Rehoboam ruled in his place.

Rehoboam Rules

10 Then Rehoboam went to Shechem. All Israel had come to Shechem to make him king. 2 When Jeroboam the son of Nebat heard about it, he returned from Egypt. For Jeroboam had run to Egypt to get away from King Solomon. 3 And the people sent for him. Jeroboam and all Israel came to Rehoboam and said, 4 "Your father gave us a heavy load to carry. So now make our work easier than your father made us work. Do not let our load be as heavy as the one he put on us. And we will work for you." 5 Rehoboam said to them, "Come to me again in three days." So the people left.

6 Then King Rehoboam spoke with the leaders who had served his father Solomon while he was still alive. He said, "Tell me, how do you think I should answer these people?" 7 They said to him, "If you will be kind to these people and please them and speak good words to them, they will be your servants forever." 8 But Rehoboam would not listen to the wise words of the leaders. He spoke with the young men who grew up with him and served him. 9 He said to them, "Tell me, how do you think I should answer these people who

have said to me, 'Do not let our load be as heavy as the one your father put on us'?" 10 The young men who grew up with him said to him, "Say this to the people who said to you, 'Your father made our load heavy, but you make it easier for us.' Tell them, 'My little finger is bigger around than my father's body! 11 My father gave you a heavy load. I will add to your load. My father punished you with whips. But I will punish you with scorpions.'"

12 So Jeroboam and all the people came to Rehoboam on the third day, as the king had told them, saying, "Return to me on the third day." 13 The king answered them with strong words. King Rehoboam did not listen to the wise words of the leaders. 14 Instead he listened to the words of the young men. And he said to them, "My father made your load heavy, but I will add to it. My father punished you with whips, but I will punish you with scorpions." 15 So the king did not listen to the people. God made this happen so that He might make His Word come true which He spoke through Ahijah the Shilonite to Jeroboam the son of Nebat.

16 All Israel saw that the king did not listen to them. So the people said to the king, "What share do we have in David? We have no share in the son of Jesse. Every man to your tents, O Israel! Now look to your own house, David!" So all Israel left and went to their tents. 17 But Rehoboam ruled over the people of Israel who lived in the cities of Judah. 18 Then King Rehoboam sent Hadoram, the man who made the people work. But the people of Israel killed him with stones. So King Rehoboam got on his war-wagon in a hurry, to go to Jerusalem. 19 Israel has been against the family of David to this day.

11 When Rehoboam came to Jerusalem, he gathered together the family of Judah and Benjamin. There were 180,000 chosen men of war gathered to fight against Israel to make Rehoboam their king again. 2 But the word of the Lord came to Shemaiah the man of God, saying, 3 "Speak to Rehoboam the son of Solomon, king of Judah. And speak to all Israel in Judah and Benjamin. Tell them, 4 'This is what the Lord says, "You must not go up to fight against your brothers. Every man return to his house. For I have made this happen."'" So they listened to the word of the Lord and returned. They did not go against Jeroboam.

Rehoboam Makes the Cities Strong

5 Rehoboam lived in Jerusalem and built strong cities in Judah. 6 He built Bethlehem, Etam, Tekoa, 7 Beth-zur, Soco, Adullam, 8 Gath, Mareshah, Ziph, 9 Adoraim, Lachish, Azekah, 10 Zorah, Aijalon, and Hebron. These are strong cities with walls, in Judah and in Benjamin. 11 He made the strong-places stronger. He put leaders in them, and stores of food, oil, and wine. 12 And he put battle-coverings and spears in every city and made them very strong. So he kept Judah and Benjamin.

Religious Leaders and Levites Come to Judah

13 The religious leaders and the Levites who were in all Israel joined with Rehoboam from all places where they lived. 14 The Levites left their fields and land and came to Judah and Jerusalem. For Jeroboam and his sons had stopped them from working as religious leaders for the Lord. 15 He chose religious leaders of his own for the high places, for the goat-gods and for the calves which he had made. 16 Those from all the families of Israel who set their hearts on following the Lord God of Israel came after them to Jerusalem. They came to give gifts in worship to the Lord God of their fathers. 17 They made the nation of Judah strong, and gave strength to Rehoboam the son of Solomon for three years. For they walked in the way of David and Solomon for three years.

Rehoboam's Family

18 Then Rehoboam married Mahalath. She was the daughter of Jerimoth the son of David, and of Abihail the daughter of Eliab the son of Jesse. 19 She gave birth to Rehoboam's sons: Jeush, Shemariah, and Zaham. 20 After her he married Maacah the daughter of Absalom. She gave birth to his sons: Abijah, Attai, Ziza, and Shelomith. 21 Rehoboam loved Maacah the daughter of Absalom more than all his other wives and women who acted as his wives. For he had taken eighteen wives and sixty women who acted as his wives. He was the father of twenty-eight sons and sixty daughters. 22 Rehoboam chose Maacah's son Abijah to be the head leader among his brothers. For he wanted to make him king. 23 And he acted with wisdom. He spread some of his sons to every strong city in all the lands of Judah and Benjamin. He gave them much food, and found many wives for them.

Egypt Takes Judah

12 When King Rehoboam's nation had been made strong, he and all Israel turned away from the Law of the Lord. ² After Rehoboam had been king for five years, King Shishak of Egypt came to fight against Jerusalem. This happened because they had not been faithful to the Lord. ³ Shishak came with 1,200 war-wagons and 60,000 horsemen. And the people who came with him from Egypt were too many to number. There were Libyans, Sukkites, and Ethiopians. ⁴ He took the strong cities of Judah and came as far as Jerusalem. ⁵ Then Shemaiah the man of God came to Rehoboam and the princes of Judah who had gathered at Jerusalem because of Shishak. He said to them, "The Lord says, 'You have left Me. So I have left you to Shishak.'" ⁶ So the princes of Israel and the king put away their pride and said, "The Lord is right and good."

⁷ The Lord saw that they had put away their pride. And the word of the Lord came to Shemaiah, saying, "They have put away their pride. I will not destroy them. But I will give them some help. My anger will not be poured out on Jerusalem by the power of Shishak. ⁸ But they will be made to work for him. In this way they may learn the difference between My work and the work of the kings of the countries."

⁹ So King Shishak of Egypt came and fought against Jerusalem. He took the riches of the Lord's house and the riches of the king's house. He took everything. He even took the battle-coverings of gold which Solomon had made. ¹⁰ King Rehoboam made battle-coverings of brass in their place. And he put them in the care of the captains of the soldiers who watched the door of the king's house. ¹¹ Every time the king went into the house of the Lord, the soldiers came and carried the coverings. Then they returned them to the soldiers' room. ¹² When Rehoboam put away his pride, the Lord's anger turned away from him. He was not destroyed. And things were good in Judah.

The End of Rehoboam's Rule

¹³ So King Rehoboam became strong in Jerusalem and ruled. He was forty-one years old when he began to rule. And he ruled in Jerusalem for seventeen years. This was the city the Lord had chosen from all the families of Israel to put His name there. The name of Rehoboam's mother was Naamah the Ammonitess.

¹⁴ And he did what was sinful, because he did not follow the Lord with all his heart.

¹⁵ The acts of Rehoboam, from first to last, are written in the writings of Shemaiah the man of God and of Iddo the man who told what would happen in the future. Wars were always being fought between Rehoboam and Jeroboam. ¹⁶ Rehoboam died and was buried in the city of David. His son Abijah became king in his place.

Abijah's Rule in Judah

13 Abijah became the king of Judah in the eighteenth year of King Jeroboam. ² He ruled for three years in Jerusalem. His mother's name was Micaiah the daughter of Uriel of Gibeah. And there was war between Abijah and Jeroboam. ³ Abijah began the battle with an army of powerful soldiers, 400,000 chosen men. Jeroboam came ready for battle against him with 800,000 chosen men who were powerful soldiers.

⁴ Then Abijah stood on Mount Zemaraim in the hill country of Ephraim, and said, "Listen to me, Jeroboam and all Israel! ⁵ Do you not know that the Lord God of Israel gave the rule over Israel forever to David and his sons by an agreement of salt? ⁶ But Jeroboam the son of Nebat, the servant of Solomon the son of David, went against his lord the king. ⁷ And men of no worth gathered around him. They were bad men who were too strong for Rehoboam the son of Solomon. Rehoboam was young and weak and could not stand against them. ⁸ So now you plan to stand against the power of the Lord through the sons of David. You think you can because you have many people and the gold calves Jeroboam made you for gods. ⁹ Have you not driven out the religious leaders of the Lord, the sons of Aaron and the Levites? And have you not made religious leaders for yourselves like the people of other lands? Whoever comes to make himself holy with a young bull and seven rams becomes a religious leader of false gods. ¹⁰ But as for us, the Lord is our God. We have not left Him. The sons of Aaron are working for the Lord as religious leaders. And the Levites are doing their work. ¹¹ Every morning they give burnt gifts and burn special perfume to the Lord. The holy bread is set on the clean table. And the gold lamp-stand with its lamps is ready to light every evening. For we do the work of the Lord our God. But you have left Him. ¹² Now see, God is with us at our

head. His religious leaders are ready to blow the horns, to sound the call to battle against you. O sons of Israel, do not fight against the Lord God of your fathers. For you cannot win."

13 But Jeroboam had sent soldiers to come from behind. So Israel was in front of Judah, and soldiers were behind them also. 14 When Judah looked, they saw that the battle was both in front of them and behind them. So they cried to the Lord, and the religious leaders blew the horns. 15 Then the men of Judah sounded a war cry. And when they sounded the war cry, God began destroying Jeroboam and all Israel around Abijah and Judah. 16 The men of Israel ran away from Judah. God gave them into their hand. 17 Abijah and his people killed many of them. There were 500,000 chosen men of Israel killed. 18 So the sons of Israel were set back at that time. The sons of Judah were strong because they trusted in the Lord, the God of their fathers. 19 Abijah went after Jeroboam. He took from him the cities of Bethel with its towns, Jeshanah with its towns, and Ephron with its towns. 20 Jeroboam did not become strong again in the days of Abijah. And the Lord destroyed him, and he died.

21 But Abijah became very strong. He married fourteen wives, and became the father of twenty-two sons and sixteen daughters. 22 Now the rest of the acts of Abijah, and his ways and his words, are written in the story of Iddo the man of God.

King Asa Rules in Judah

14 Abijah died and they buried him in the city of David. His son Asa became king in his place. In his days the land had peace ten years.

2 Asa did what was good and right in the eyes of the Lord his God. 3 For he put away the strange altars and high places. He tore down the pillars used in worship of false gods. And he cut down the false goddesses, the Asherim. 4 He told Judah to follow the Lord God of their fathers, and to obey the Laws. 5 He put the high places and the altars of special perfume away from all the cities of Judah. And the nation had rest under his rule. 6 He built strong cities in Judah, since the land had rest. No one fought a war with him during those years, because the Lord had given him rest. 7 So he said to the people of Judah, "Let us build these cities. And let us build walls and towers around them, with iron gates. The land is still ours, because we have followed the Lord our God. We have followed Him, and He has given us rest on every side." So they built and did well. 8 Asa had an army of 300,000 men from Judah, with large battle-coverings and spears. And he had 280,000 men from Benjamin, with battle-coverings and bows. All of them were powerful soldiers.

9 Zerah the Ethiopian came out to fight against them with an army of 1,000,000 men and 300 war-wagons. He came as far as Mareshah. 10 So Asa went out to meet him. They made themselves ready for battle in the valley of Zephathah at Mareshah. 11 Then Asa called to the Lord his God and said, "Lord, there is no one but You to help in the battle between the powerful and the weak. So help us, O Lord God. For we trust in You. In Your name we have come against these many people. O Lord, You are our God. Do not let any man win the fight against You." 12 So the Lord began to destroy the Ethiopians in front of Asa and the people of Judah, and the Ethiopians ran away. 13 Asa and the people with him went after them as far as Gerar. The Ethiopians were killed until none were left alive. They were destroyed before the Lord and His army. And they carried away many things that had belonged to the Ethiopians. 14 Then they destroyed all the cities around Gerar, for the fear of the Lord had come upon them. And they took everything of worth that was in the cities, for there was much left. 15 They destroyed the tents of the animals. And they took away many sheep and camels. Then they returned to Jerusalem.

Asa Makes Changes

15 The Spirit of God came upon Azariah the son of Oded. 2 Azariah went out to meet Asa and said to him, "Listen to me, Asa, and all Judah and Benjamin. The Lord is with you when you are with Him. If you look for Him, He will let you find Him. But if you leave Him, He will leave you. 3 For a long time Israel was without the true God, without a teaching religious leader, and without law. 4 But in their trouble they turned to the Lord God of Israel. They looked for Him, and He let them find Him. 5 In those times there was no peace for him who went out, or for him who came in. For much trouble came to all the people of the lands. 6 Nation was crushed by nation, and city by city, for

God sent every kind of trouble upon them. 7 But you be strong. Do not lose strength of heart. For you will be paid for your work."

8 When Asa heard these words and the words of Azariah the son of Oded, his heart became strong. He put away the sinful false gods from all the land of Judah and Benjamin and from the cities he had taken in the hill country of Ephraim. He built again the altar of the Lord which was in front of the porch of the Lord's house. 9 Then he gathered all Judah and Benjamin and those from Ephraim, Manasseh, and Simeon, who lived with them. For many had left Israel to come to him when they saw that the Lord his God was with him. 10 So they gathered together at Jerusalem in the third month of the fifteenth year of Asa's rule. 11 They killed animals on the altar in worship to the Lord that day. They killed and gave 700 cattle and 7,000 sheep from the animals they had taken in battle. 12 And they agreed to follow the Lord God of their fathers with all their heart and soul. 13 Whoever would not follow the Lord God of Israel should be put to death, young or old, man or woman. 14 They made a promise to the Lord with a loud voice, calling out and blowing horns. 15 All Judah was filled with joy because of the promise. For they had promised with their whole heart. They had looked for the Lord with a pure heart. And He let them find Him. So the Lord gave them rest on every side.

16 King Asa even stopped his mother from being queen mother. Because she had made a sinful object of the false goddess Asherah. Asa cut down her sinful object. He crushed it and burned it at the Kidron River. 17 But the high places were not taken away from Israel. Yet Asa's heart was without blame all his days. 18 He brought into the house of God the holy things of his father and his own holy things. He brought in silver and gold and the things used for the worship. 19 And there was no more war until the thirty-fifth year of Asa's rule.

Asa's Agreement with Syria

16 In the thirty-sixth year of Asa's rule, King Baasha of Israel came to fight against Judah. He began building a wall around Ramah to stop anyone from going out or coming in to King Asa of Judah. 2 Then Asa took silver and gold from the store-rooms of the house of the Lord and the king's house. He sent them to King

Ben-hadad of Syria, who lived in Damascus, saying, 3 "Let there be an agreement between you and me, as between my father and your father. See, I have sent you silver and gold. Go and break your agreement with King Baasha of Israel so that he will leave me." 4 Ben-hadad listened to King Asa. He sent the captains of his armies against the cities of Israel. They destroyed Ijon, Dan, Abelmaim, and all the store-cities of Naphtali. 5 When Baasha heard about it, he stopped building the wall around Ramah. 6 Then King Asa brought all the people of Judah. And they carried away the stones and wood of the wall which Baasha had been building around Ramah. Asa used them to build Geba and Mizpah.

Hanani's Words to Asa

7 At that time Hanani the man of God came to King Asa of Judah and said to him, "You have put your trust in the king of Syria and not in the Lord your God. So the army of the king of Syria got away from you. 8 Were not the Ethiopians and the Libyans a very large army with war-wagons? But because you trusted in the Lord, He gave them into your hand. 9 For the eyes of the Lord move over all the earth so that He may give strength to those whose whole heart is given to Him. You have done a foolish thing. So from now on you will have wars." 10 Then Asa was angry with the man of God. He put him in prison because he was angry at him for this. And Asa made it hard for some of the people at the same time.

The End of Asa's Rule

11 Now the acts of Asa, from first to last, are written in the Book of the Kings of Judah and Israel. 12 A disease came into Asa's feet in the thirty-ninth year of his rule. His disease was bad. But even in his disease, he did not trust in the Lord, but in the doctors. 13 So Asa slept with his fathers. He died in the forty-first year of his rule. 14 They buried him in his own grave which he had cut out for himself in the city of David. They laid him in the place of rest which he had filled with different kinds of spices mixed by those who work with perfumes. And they made a very big fire in his honor.

Jehoshaphat Becomes King in Judah

17 Jehoshaphat his son became king in his place, and made himself strong against Israel. 2 He placed soldiers in all the strong cities of Judah, and in places

built for them in the land of Judah. And he put soldiers in the cities of Ephraim which his father Asa had taken in battle. 3 The Lord was with Jehoshaphat because he followed the early ways of his father. He did not follow the false gods of Baal. 4 He looked to the God of his father, followed His Laws, and did not act as Israel did. 5 So the Lord made the nation strong under his rule. And all Judah paid taxes to Jehoshaphat. He had great riches and honor. 6 He was strong in his heart in the ways of the Lord. And he took the high places and the false goddess Asherah out of Judah again.

7 In the third year of his rule, Jehoshaphat sent his leaders to teach in the cities of Judah. He sent Ben-hail, Obadiah, Zechariah, Nethanel, and Micaiah. 8 With them he sent the Levites, Shemaiah, Nethaniah, Zebadiah, Asahel, Shemiramoth, Jehonathan, Adonijah, Tobijah, and Tobadonijah. And with them he sent the religious leaders, Elishama and Jehoram. 9 They taught in Judah, having the book of the Law of the Lord with them. They went through all the cities of Judah and taught among the people.

Jehoshaphat's Strength

10 The fear of the Lord was on all the nations of the lands around Judah. So they did not make war against Jehoshaphat. 11 Some of the Philistines brought Jehoshaphat gifts, and silver for taxes. The Arabians brought him flocks, 7,700 rams and 7,700 male goats. 12 So Jehoshaphat became greater and greater. And he built strong-places and store-cities in Judah. 13 He had many things in the cities of Judah. And he had powerful soldiers in Jerusalem. 14 This was the number of them by their fathers' houses: Adnah was the captain of thousands from Judah. He had 300,000 powerful soldiers with him. 15 Next to him was Johanan, the captain of 280,000. 16 Next to him was Amasiah the son of Zichri, who gave himself to work for the Lord. He had 200,000 powerful soldiers with him. 17 Eliada was a powerful soldier of the family of Benjamin. He had with him 200,000 men with bows and battle-coverings. 18 Next to him was Jehozabad, the captain of 180,000 ready for war. 19 These are the men who served the king, as well as those whom the king put in the strong cities through all Judah.

Micaiah Tells What Will Happen

18 Now Jehoshaphat had great riches and honor. And by a marriage he was joined with Ahab. 2 After some years he went down to visit Ahab at Samaria. Ahab killed many sheep and cattle for him and for the people who were with him. And he wanted Jehoshaphat to fight against Ramoth-gilead. 3 King Ahab of Israel said to King Jehoshaphat of Judah, "Will you go with me against Ramoth-gilead?" He answered, "I am as you are. And my people are as your people. We will be with you in the battle."

4 Then Jehoshaphat said to the king of Israel, "Ask first for word from the Lord." 5 So the king of Israel gathered together the 400 men who told what would happen in the future. He said to them, "Should we go to battle against Ramoth-gilead, or should I wait?" And they said, "Go up, for God will give it into the hand of the king." 6 But Jehoshaphat said, "Is there not another man who speaks for the Lord here whom we may ask?" 7 The king of Israel said to him, "There is yet one man whom we may ask of the Lord. But I hate him. For he never tells me anything good, only bad. He is Micaiah, the son of Imla." But Jehoshaphat said, "You should not say that." 8 Then the king of Israel called for one of his captains and said, "Hurry, bring Micaiah the son of Imla." 9 The king of Israel and King Jehoshaphat of Judah were each sitting on his throne, dressed in king's clothing. They were sitting at the grain-floor at the gate of Samaria. All the men who told what would happen in the future were speaking in front of them. 10 Zedekiah the son of Chenaanah made horns of iron for himself and said, "The Lord says that with these you will hurt the Syrians until they are destroyed." 11 All the men who told what would happen in the future were saying, "Go up to Ramoth-gilead and win the battle. For the Lord will give it into the hand of the king."

12 Then the man who was sent to call Micaiah said to him, "See, all the men who tell what will happen in the future are speaking in the king's favor. So I ask that you let your word be like one of them, and speak in the king's favor." 13 But Micaiah said, "As the Lord lives, I will speak what my God says." 14 When he came to the king, the king said to him, "Micaiah, should we go to Ramoth-gilead to battle, or should I wait?" Micaiah said, "Go up and win the battle. For they will be given into

your hand." 15 Then the king said to him, "How many times must I tell you to speak to me nothing but the truth in the name of the Lord?" 16 So he said, "I saw all Israel spread out on the mountains, like sheep without a shepherd. And the Lord said, 'These have no owner. Let each of them return to his house in peace.'" 17 Then the king of Israel said to Jehoshaphat, "Did I not tell you that he would not tell me anything good, but bad?" 18 Micaiah said, "So hear the word of the Lord. I saw the Lord sitting on His throne. All the armies of heaven were standing on His right and on His left. 19 The Lord said, 'Who will lead King Ahab of Israel to go up and fall at Ramoth-gilead?' And one said this while another said that. 20 Then a spirit came and stood before the Lord and said, 'I will lead him to do it.' And the Lord said to him, 'How?' 21 He said, 'I will go and be a lying spirit in the mouth of all Ahab's men who tell what will happen in the future.' Then the Lord said, 'You are to make him want to go, and you will do well. Go and do so.' 22 So now the Lord has put a lying spirit in the mouth of your men who speak for God. For the Lord has said that trouble will come to you."

23 Then Zedekiah the son of Chenaanah came near and hit Micaiah on the side of the face, and said, "How did the Spirit of the Lord pass from me to speak to you?" 24 Micaiah said, "See, you will see on that day when you go into a room to hide yourself." 25 Then the king of Israel said, "Take Micaiah and return him to Amon the city leader, and to Joash the king's son. 26 Tell them, 'The king says to put this man in prison. Feed him only a little bread and water until I return in peace.'" 27 Micaiah said, "If you do return in peace, the Lord has not spoken by me." And he said, "Listen, all you people."

Ahab Dies in Battle

28 So the king of Israel and King Jehoshaphat of Judah went up against Ramoth-gilead. 29 The king of Israel said to Jehoshaphat, "I will dress up to look like someone else and go into battle. But you wear your king's clothing." So the king of Israel dressed up to look like someone else, and they went into battle. 30 Now the king of Syria had told the captains of his war-wagons, "Do not fight with small or great, but only with the king of Israel." 31 So when the captains of the war-wagons saw Jehoshaphat, they said, "It is

the king of Israel." And they turned to fight against him. But Jehoshaphat cried out, and the Lord helped him. God made them go away from him. 32 When the captains of the war-wagons saw that it was not the king of Israel, they turned back from going after him. 33 But a certain man happened to shoot an arrow and hit the king of Israel in a joint of the battle-clothes. So the king said to the man on the war-wagon, "Turn around, and take me out of the battle. For I am hurt." 34 The battle was hard that day. And the king of Israel stood up against the sides of his war-wagon in front of the Syrians until the evening. When the sun went down, he died.

19

King Jehoshaphat of Judah returned in peace to his house in Jerusalem. 2 Jehu the son of Hanani the man who tells what will happen in the future went out to meet King Jehoshaphat, and said to him, "Should you help the sinful? Should you love those who hate the Lord? Because of this, the Lord is angry with you. 3 But there is some good in you. For you have destroyed from the land the false goddess Asherah. And you have set your heart to follow God."

The Changes Made by Jehoshaphat

4 So Jehoshaphat lived in Jerusalem. He went out again among the people from Beersheba to the hill country of Ephraim. And he brought them back to the Lord, the God of their fathers. 5 He chose judges in the land in all the strong cities of Judah, city by city. 6 And he said to the judges, "Think about what you do. For you do not judge for man, but for the Lord. He is with you when you judge between right and wrong. 7 So now let the fear of the Lord be upon you. Be very careful what you do. For the Lord our God will have nothing to do with what is not right and good, or with what is not fair, or with taking pay for doing what is wrong."

8 In Jerusalem also Jehoshaphat chose some of the Levites and religious leaders, and heads of families of Israel. He chose them to judge for the Lord, and to judge the troubles among the people of Jerusalem. 9 Then he told them what they must do. He said, "Do this in the fear of the Lord. Be faithful, and do your duty with your whole heart. 10 Whenever trouble comes to you between your brothers who live in the cities, between blood and blood, between one law and another, tell them

not to sin before the Lord, so God's anger may not come upon you and your brothers. Do this, and you will not be guilty. **11** See, Amariah the head religious leader will be over you in everything that has to do with the Lord. And Zebadiah the son of Ishmael, the ruler of the family of Judah, will be over you in everything that has to do with the king. The Levites will work for you as leaders. Be strong in what you do, and the Lord will be with the good."

War against Edom

20 After this the men of Moab, and Ammon, and some of the Meunites, came to make war against Jehoshaphat. **2** Some men came and told Jehoshaphat, "Very many people are coming against you from the other side of the sea, from Syria. See, they are in Hazazon-tamar (that is, Engedi)." **3** Jehoshaphat was afraid and decided to call on the Lord. He made a special time of not eating in all Judah. **4** And Judah gathered together to pray for help from the Lord. They came to the Lord from all the cities of Judah to call on the Lord.

5 Jehoshaphat stood among the people of Judah and Jerusalem, in the house of the Lord, in front of the new open space. **6** Then he said, "O Lord, the God of our fathers, are You not God in heaven? Do You not rule over all the nations? Power and strength are in Your hand, so that no one is able to stand against You. **7** O our God, did You not make the people of this land leave so that Your people Israel could have it and give it to the children of Your friend Abraham forever? **8** And they have lived in it. They have built You a holy place in it for Your name, saying, **9** 'If what is bad comes upon us, fighting, hard times, disease, or no food, we will stand in front of this house. And we will stand before You, (for Your name is in this house). We will cry to You in our trouble. And You will hear and take us out of trouble.' **10** Now see the men of Moab and Ammon and Mount Seir, whom You did not let Israel fight when they came from the land of Egypt. (They turned aside from them and did not destroy them.) **11** Look how they are paying us back. They are coming to make us leave Your land which You have given to us. **12** O our God, will You not punish them? For we have no power against all these men who are coming against us. We do not know what to do. But our eyes look to You." **13** And all the men of Judah

were standing before the Lord, with their babies, their wives, and their children.

14 Then the Spirit of the Lord came upon Jahaziel the son of Zechariah, the son of Benaiah, the son of Jeiel, the son of Mattaniah, the Levite of the sons of Asaph, as he stood among the people. **15** He said, "Listen, all Judah, the people of Jerusalem, and King Jehoshaphat. The Lord says to you, 'Do not be afraid or troubled because of these many men. For the battle is not yours but God's. **16** Go down to fight them tomorrow. See, they will come up by the hill of Ziz. You will find them at the end of the valley, in front of the desert of Jeruel. **17** You will not need to fight in this battle. Just stand still in your places and see the saving power of the Lord work for you, O Judah and Jerusalem.' Do not be afraid or troubled. Go out against them tomorrow, for the Lord is with you." **18** Then Jehoshaphat put his face to the ground. And all Judah and the people of Jerusalem fell down in worship before the Lord. **19** The Levites, of the Kohathites and Korahites, stood up to praise the Lord God of Israel, with a very loud voice.

20 They got up early in the morning and went out to the desert of Tekoa. When they went out, Jehoshaphat stood and said, "Listen to me, O Judah and people of Jerusalem. Trust in the Lord your God, and you will be made strong. Trust in the men who speak for Him, and you will do well." **21** When he had spoken with the people, he called those who sang to the Lord and those who praised Him in holy clothing. They went out in front of the army and said, "Give thanks to the Lord. For His loving-kindness lasts forever." **22** When they began to sing and praise, the Lord set traps against the men of Ammon, Moab, and Mount Seir, who had come against Judah. So they were destroyed. **23** The men of Ammon and Moab fought against the people of Mount Seir, and killed all of them. And when they finished with the people of Seir, they all helped to kill each other.

24 Judah came to the place where they could look out over the desert. When they looked toward the armies, they saw that dead bodies were lying on the ground. No one had been left alive. **25** So Jehoshaphat and his people came to take away what they wanted from them. They found cattle, many good things, clothing, and things of great worth, which they took for themselves. There was more than they could carry. It took them three days to take all the things, because there was so much. 26 They gathered together in the Valley of Beracah on the fourth day. There they praised and thanked the Lord. So the name of that place has been the Valley of Beracah to this day. 27 Then every man of Judah and Jerusalem returned, with Jehoshaphat leading them. They returned to Jerusalem with joy. For the Lord had filled them with joy by saving them from those who hated them. 28 They came to the house of the Lord in Jerusalem with horns and different kinds of harps. 29 And the fear of God came upon all the nations of the lands, when they heard that the Lord had fought against those who hate Israel. 30 So the nation of Jehoshaphat was at peace. His God gave him rest on all sides.

The End of Jehoshaphat's Rule

31 So Jehoshaphat ruled over Judah. He was thirty-five years old when he became king. And he ruled in Jerusalem for twenty-five years. His mother's name was Azubah the daughter of Shilhi. 32 Jehoshaphat walked in the way of his father Asa, and did not leave it. He did what was right in the eyes of the Lord. 33 But the high places were not taken away. The people had not yet set their hearts on the God of their fathers. 34 The rest of the acts of Jehoshaphat, from first to last, are written in the story of Jehu the son of Hanani, which is written in the Book of the Kings of Israel.

35 After this King Jehoshaphat of Judah joined with King Ahaziah of Israel who was very sinful. 36 He joined him in making ships to go to Tarshish. They made the ships in Ezion-geber. 37 Then Eliezer the son of Dodavahu of Mareshah told what would happen against Jehoshaphat, saying, "Because you have joined with Ahaziah, the Lord will destroy what you have made." So the ships were wrecked, and could not go to Tarshish.

Jehoram Rules in Judah

21 Jehoshaphat died, and was buried with his fathers in the city of David. His son Jehoram became king in his place. 2 Jehoram's brothers were Azariah, Jehiel, Zechariah, Michael, and Shephatiah. All these were the sons of King Jehoshaphat of Israel. 3 Their father gave them many gifts of silver, gold, and things of much worth. He gave them strong cities in

Judah. But he made Jehoram king, because he was the first-born.

4 Now when Jehoram had become king in the place of his father, and had made himself strong, he killed all his brothers with the sword. He killed some of the leaders of Israel also. 5 Jehoram was thirty-two years old when he became king. And he ruled for eight years in Jerusalem. 6 He walked in the way of the kings of Israel, just as those of Ahab's house did. (For Ahab's daughter was his wife.) He did what was sinful in the eyes of the Lord. 7 Yet the Lord would not destroy the family of David, because of the agreement He had made with David. He had promised to give a light to him and his sons forever.

8 In the days of Jehoram, Edom turned against the rule of Judah, and set up a king of their own. 9 Then Jehoram crossed over with his captains and all his war-wagons. He went during the night and destroyed the Edomites who had gathered around him and the captains of the war-wagons. 10 So Edom has been against the rule of Judah to this day. Libnah turned against Jehoram's rule at the same time, because he had left the Lord God of his fathers. 11 And Jehoram made high places in the mountains of Judah. He caused the people of Jerusalem to give themselves over to sin. And he made Judah sin. 12 Then a letter came to him from Elijah the man of God, saying, "The Lord God of your father David says, 'You have not walked in the ways of your father Jehoshaphat, and the ways of King Asa of Judah. 13 But you have walked in the way of the kings of Israel. You have caused Judah and the people of Israel to give themselves over to sin, as those of Ahab's house did. And you have killed your brothers, your own family, who were better than you. 14 So see, the Lord is going to send a bad disease upon your people, your sons, your wives, and all you have. 15 You yourself will suffer a bad sickness, a disease of your stomach. Your insides will come out because of the sickness, day by day.'"

16 Then the Lord made the Philistines and the Arabs who were near the Ethiopians angry against Jehoram. 17 They came and fought against Judah, and carried away all the things they found in the king's house, together with his sons and his wives. No son was left to him except Jehoahaz, his youngest. 18 After all this the Lord caused a sickness in Jehoram's stomach, which could not be cured. 19 After

that time, at the end of two years, his insides came out because of his sickness. And he died in much pain. His people made no fire for him like the fires made for his fathers. **20** Jehoram was thirty-two years old when he became king. He ruled in Jerusalem for eight years. And no one felt bad when he died. They buried him in the city of David, but not in the graves of the kings.

Ahaziah Rules in Judah

22 The people of Jerusalem made his youngest son Ahaziah king in his place. For the army of men who came with the Arabs to the tents had killed all the older sons. So Ahaziah, the son of King Jehoram of Judah, began to rule. **2** He was twenty-two years old when he became king. And he ruled for one year in Jerusalem. His mother's name was Athaliah, the granddaughter of Omri. **3** Ahaziah walked in the ways of those of Ahab's house. For his mother talked him into doing sinful things. **4** He did what was sinful in the eyes of the Lord, as those of Ahab's house had done. For after his father's death, they talked with him about what to do, and so caused him to be destroyed. **5** He did what they told him to do. He went with Jehoram the son of King Ahab of Israel to fight a war against King Hazael of Syria at Ramoth-gilead. But the Syrians hurt Jehoram. **6** So he returned to Jezreel to be healed of the cuts he had received at Ramah, when he fought against King Hazael of Syria. And Ahaziah the son of Jehoram, king of Judah, went down to see Jehoram the son of Ahab in Jezreel, because he was sick.

7 But it was planned by God that Ahaziah would be destroyed by going to Jehoram. For when he came, he went out with Jehoram against Jehu the son of Nimshi. Jehu was the one the Lord had chosen to destroy the family of Ahab. **8** When Jehu was punishing the family of Ahab, he found the sons of kings of Judah and the sons of Ahaziah's brothers. They were helping Ahaziah. And Jehu killed them. **9** Then he looked for Ahaziah, and he was found hiding in Samaria. He was brought to Jehu, and was put to death. Then they buried him, for they said, "He is the son of Jehoshaphat, who followed the Lord with all his heart." So there was no one left of Ahaziah's house who was able to rule the nation.

Athaliah Rules in Judah

10 When Athaliah, the mother of Ahaziah, saw that her son was dead, she went and destroyed all the king's children of the family of Judah. **11** But Jehoshabeath, the king's daughter, took Ahaziah's son Joash. She stole him from among the king's sons who were being killed. And she put him and his nurse in the bedroom. So Jehoshabeath, the daughter of King Jehoram, the wife of Jehoiada the religious leader, and sister of Ahaziah, hid Joash from Athaliah, so she could not kill him.

12 Joash was hidden with them in the house of God for six years, while Athaliah ruled over the land.

Joash Made King of Judah

23 In the seventh year, Jehoiada made himself strong. He made an agreement with the captains of hundreds. These captains were Azariah the son of Jeroham, Ishmael the son of Johanan, Azariah the son of Obed, Maaseiah the son of Adaiah, and Elishaphat the son of Zichri. They made an agreement with Jehoiada. **2** And they went through Judah and gathered the Levites from all the cities. They gathered the heads of the fathers' houses of Israel. And they came to Jerusalem. **3** Then all the people made an agreement with the king in the house of God. Jehoiada said to them, "See, the king's son will rule, as the Lord has spoken about the sons of David. **4** This is what you must do. One-third of you religious leaders and Levites who come in on the Day of Rest will watch the gates. **5** One-third will be at the king's house, and one-third at the Gate of the Foundation. And all the people will be in the open places of the house of the Lord. **6** But let no one come into the house of the Lord except the religious leaders and the Levite helpers. They may come in, for they are holy. But let all the other people obey the law against going into the holy place of the Lord. **7** The Levites will stand around the king. Each one will have his spear in his hand. And whoever goes into the house will be killed. Be with the king when he comes in and when he goes out."

8 The Levites and all Judah did all that Jehoiada the religious leader told them. Each one of them took his men who were to come in on the Day of Rest, with those who were to go out on the Day of Rest. For Jehoiada the religious leader did not send away any of the groups. **9** Then Jehoiada the religious leader gave the captains of hundreds the spears and the large and small battle-coverings that had been King David's, which were in the house of God. 10 And he put all the people in their places around the king. Each man had his spear in his hand. They were put in their places from the right side of the house to the left side, around the altar and the house. 11 Then they brought out the king's son and put the crown on him. They gave him the Law, and made him king. Jehoiada and his sons poured oil on him and said, "Long live the king!"

Death of Athaliah

12 When Athaliah heard the noise of the people running and praising the king, she came into the house of the Lord to the people. 13 She looked and saw the king beside his pillar at the gate. The captains and those who blew the horns were beside the king. And all the people of the land were filled with joy and blew horns. The singers were playing music and leading the praise. Athaliah tore her clothes and called out, "They are turning against the queen!" 14 Then Jehoiada the religious leader brought out the captains of hundreds who were over the army, and said to them, "Bring her out from among the groups of people. And kill with the sword whoever follows her." For the religious leader said, "Do not kill her in the house of the Lord." 15 So they took hold of her. And when she came to the Horse Gate of the king's house, they killed her there.

16 Then Jehoiada made an agreement between himself and all the people and the king, that they should be the Lord's people. 17 All the people went to the house of Baal and tore it down. They broke in pieces his altars and the objects made to look like him. And they killed Mattan the religious leader of Baal in front of the altars. 18 Then Jehoiada put the duties of the Lord's house under the care of the religious leaders and the Levites. David had chosen them to take care of the Lord's house. They were to give the burnt gifts of the Lord, as it is written in the Law of Moses. It was to be done with joy and singing, as David told them. 19 And Jehoiada put the gate-keepers in their places of the Lord's house. This was so no one would go in who was in any way unclean. 20 Then he took the captains of hundreds, the princes, the leaders of the people, and all the people of the land. And they brought the king down from the house of the Lord. They came through the high gate to the king's house. And they placed the king upon the throne of the nation. 21 So all the people of the land were filled with joy, and the city was quiet. For they had killed Athaliah with the sword.

Joash Becomes King

24 Joash was seven years old when he became king. And he ruled forty years in Jerusalem. His mother's name was Zibiah of Beersheba. 2 Joash did what was right in the eyes of the Lord all the days of Jehoiada the religious leader. 3 Jehoiada took two wives for him, and he became the father of sons and daughters.

4 After this Joash decided to do the work that was needed on the Lord's house. 5 He gathered the religious leaders and Levites, and said to them, "Go out to the cities of Judah. And gather money from all Israel to pay for the work needed to be done on the house of your God from year to year. Be quick about it." But the Levites did not hurry. 6 So the king called for Jehoiada the head religious leader, and said to him, "Why have you not made the Levites bring in from Judah and Jerusalem the tax set by Moses the Lord's servant? All the people of Israel were to pay taxes for the tent of the Law." 7 For the sons of that sinful woman Athaliah had broken into the house of God. They even used the holy things of the Lord's house for the false gods of Baal.

8 So the king had them make a box and set it outside by the gate of the Lord's house. 9 And they made it known in Judah and Jerusalem that the tax set by God's servant Moses on Israel in the desert must be brought to the Lord. 10 Then all the leaders and all the people were filled with joy. They brought in their taxes and put the money into the box until they had finished. 11 The Levites would bring the box in to the king's helper. And when they saw that there was much money, the king's writer and the head religious leader's helper would come and empty the box. They would take out the money and return the box to its place. They did this each day, and gathered much money. 12 The king and Jehoiada gave it to those who watched over the work being done on the Lord's house. They paid those who worked with stone and wood and iron and brass, for the work done on the Lord's house. 13 So the workmen worked hard

doing what needed to be done. The house of God was like new again, just as it was planned. They made it strong. 14 When they had finished, they brought the rest of the money to the king and Jehoiada. From it were made the objects used in the Lord's house. These things were made for the worship and the burnt gifts. Then dishes and pots of gold and silver were made. And they gave burnt gifts in the house of the Lord all the time, all the days of Jehoiada.

15 When Jehoiada had lived a long time, he died. He died when he was 130 years old. 16 They buried him in the city of David among the kings, because he had done well in Israel, and to God and His house. 17 But after the death of Jehoiada, the leaders of Judah came and bowed down in front of the king. And the king listened to them. 18 They left the house of the Lord the God of their fathers, and worshiped the false gods of Asherah and the objects made to look like them. So anger came upon Judah and Jerusalem because of their sin. 19 Yet God sent men who speak for God to bring them back to the Lord. These men of God spoke against them, but they would not listen. 20 Then the Spirit of God came upon Zechariah the son of Jehoiada the religious leader. He stood where he could be seen by the people and said to them, "God says, 'Why do you sin against the Laws of the Lord, and bring trouble on yourselves? Because you have left the Lord, He has left you.' " 21 So they made plans against him. At the king's word, they killed Zechariah with stones in the open space of the Lord's house. 22 So Joash the king did not remember the kindness his father Jehoiada had shown him, but he killed his son. And when Zechariah was dying, he said, "May the Lord see and punish!"

The Death of Joash

23 At the end of the year the army of the Syrians came up against Joash. They came to Judah and Jerusalem, and destroyed all the leaders of the people. And they sent all they had taken in battle to the king of Damascus. 24 The army of the Syrians came with a small number of men. But the Lord let them win against a very large army. Because the people of Judah and Jerusalem had turned away from the Lord, the God of their fathers. So the Syrians were used to punish Joash. 25 When they had left Joash, leaving him very sick, his own servants made plans against him because

of the blood of the son of Jehoiada the religious leader. And they killed him on his bed. So he died, and they buried him in the city of David. But they did not bury him in the graves of the kings. 26 The men who made plans against Joash were Zabad the son of Shimeath the Ammonitess, and Jehozabad the son of Shimrith the Moabitess. 27 Now the story of his sons, and the words spoken by wise men against him, and the work done on the house of God, are written in the Book of the Kings. His son Amaziah became king in his place.

Amaziah Rules Judah

25 Amaziah was twenty-five years old when he became king. And he ruled for twenty-nine years in Jerusalem. His mother's name was Jehoaddan of Jerusalem. 2 Amaziah did what was right in the eyes of the Lord, but not with a whole heart. 3 As soon as the nation was under his rule, he killed his servants who had killed his father the king. 4 But he did not kill their children. He did what is written in the Law in the book of Moses. The Lord had said in this Law, "Fathers must not be put to death for the children. And children must not be put to death for the fathers. Each must be put to death for his own sin." (Deuteronomy 24:16)

The War against Edom

5 Then Amaziah gathered the men of Judah together. He put them, by their fathers' houses, under the rule of captains of thousands and of hundreds for all Judah and Benjamin. He numbered those who were twenty years old and older. And he found that they were 300,000 chosen men, able to go to war and fight with spear and battle-covering. 6 He also asked for the help of 100,000 powerful soldiers from Israel and paid them with silver weighing as much as one hundred men. 7 But a man of God came to him and said, "O king, do not let the army of Israel go with you. For the Lord is not with Israel. He is not with all these sons of Ephraim. 8 But if you think that in this way you will be strong in war, God will destroy you in front of those who fight you. For God has power to help and to destroy." 9 Amaziah said to the man of God, "But what should I do about the silver weighing as much as one hundred men, which I have given to the army of Israel?" The man of God answered, "The Lord has much more to give you than this." 10 Then Amaziah sent the

army home which had come to him from Ephraim. These hired soldiers were angry at the people of Judah. As they returned home they were very angry.

11 Now Amaziah made himself strong of heart, and he led his people to the Valley of Salt and killed 10,000 men of Seir. **12** The men of Judah also took 10,000 men alive. They brought them to the top of a high rock and threw them down from it, so they were all crushed to pieces. **13** But the soldiers from Israel whom Amaziah had sent back from going with him to battle came and fought against the cities of Judah. They fought cities from Samaria to Beth-horon, and killed 3,000 people living in them. And they took many things which had belonged to the people in these cities.

14 After Amaziah came from killing the Edomites, he brought the gods of the men of Seir. He set them up as his gods. He bowed down in front of them, and burned special perfume to them. **15** Then the Lord was angry with Amaziah and sent a man who speaks for God to him, saying, "Why have you worshiped the gods of the people? These gods have not saved their own people from your hand." **16** But as he was speaking the king said to him, "Have we chosen you to give words of wisdom to the king? Stop! Or I will have you put to death." So the man who spoke for God stopped, but said, "I know that God has planned to destroy you because you have done this. And you have not listened to what I have said."

Israel Wins over Judah

17 Then King Amaziah of Judah spoke with his wise men, and sent word to Joash the son of Jehoahaz the son of Jehu, the king of Israel, saying, "Come, let us face each other." **18** King Joash of Israel sent an answer to King Amaziah of Judah, saying, "The thorn bush in Lebanon sent word to the cedar in Lebanon, saying, 'Give your daughter to my son for a wife.' But a wild animal of Lebanon passed by and crushed the thorn bush under its feet. **19** You say, 'See, I have destroyed Edom.' And your heart has become proud by what you say. Now stay at home. Why should you bring trouble so you will fall, and Judah with you?" **20** But Amaziah would not listen. God had planned that He would give Judah into the hand of Joash because Judah had worshiped the gods of Edom. **21** So King Joash of Israel met King Amaziah of Judah in battle at

Beth-shemesh of Judah. **22** And Judah lost the battle to Israel. Each man ran away to his home. **23** King Joash of Israel took King Amaziah of Judah, the son of Joash, son of Jehoahaz, at Beth-shemesh, and brought him to Jerusalem. He tore down the wall of Jerusalem from the Gate of Ephraim to the Corner Gate, as much wall as 200 long steps. **24** And he took all the gold and silver, and all the objects found in the house of God with Obed-edom. He took the riches of the king's house, and people also, and returned to Samaria.

The Death of Amaziah

25 Amaziah, the son of King Joash of Judah, lived fifteen years after the death of Joash, the son of King Jehoahaz of Israel. **26** Now the rest of the acts of Amaziah, from first to last, are written in the Book of the Kings of Judah and Israel. **27** After Amaziah turned away from the Lord, they made plans against him in Jerusalem, and he ran away to Lachish. But they sent men after him to Lachish, and killed him there. **28** Then they brought him on horses and buried him with his fathers in the city of Judah.

Uzziah Rules Judah

26 Then all the people took Uzziah, who was sixteen years old, and made him king in the place of his father Amaziah. **2** He built Eloth and returned it to Judah after the king died. **3** Uzziah was sixteen years old when he became king. And he ruled fifty two years in Jerusalem. His mother's name was Jechiliah of Jerusalem. **4** Uzziah did what was right in the eyes of the Lord. He did all that his father Amaziah had done. **5** He kept on looking to God in the days of Zechariah, who had special wisdom from God and taught him in the things of God. And as long as he looked to the Lord, God made things go well for him.

6 Uzziah went out and made war against the Philistines. He broke down the wall of Gath and the wall of Jabneh and the wall of Ashdod. And he built cities in the land of Ashdod and among the Philistines. **7** God helped him against the Philistines, and against the Arabians who lived in Gur-baal, and against the Meunites. **8** The Ammonites paid taxes to Uzziah. And his name was known as far as the land of Egypt, for he became very strong. **9** Uzziah built towers in Jerusalem at the Corner Gate, at the Valley Gate, and at the place where the walls joined. And he made them strong. [10] He built towers in the desert and dug many wells. For he had many animals, both in the valley and in the plain. He also had farmers and vine-keepers in the hill country and in the good growing fields, for he loved farming. [11] And Uzziah had an army ready for battle. It was divided by the number of names written down by Jeiel the writer and Maaseiah the captain, led by Hananiah, one of the king's leaders. [12] The whole number of the leaders of the family groups of powerful soldiers was 2,600. [13] Under their leading was an army of 307,500, who could fight with great power, to help the king against those who hated them. [14] Uzziah had battle-coverings, spears, head-coverings, strong battle-clothes, bows, and slings using arrows and large stones made for all the army. [15] In Jerusalem he made large objects of war, planned by able men, to be on the towers and the corners. They were for shooting arrows and big stones. So Uzziah's name became known in far away places. For he was helped by God in a very special way until he was strong.

Uzziah Is Punished because of His Pride

[16] But when he became strong, Uzziah's heart was so proud that his actions were sinful. He was not faithful to the Lord his God, for he went into the Lord's house to burn special perfume on the altar of special perfume. [17] Then Azariah the religious leader went in after him, with eighty religious leaders of the Lord who were men strong in heart. [18] They went against King Uzziah and said to him, "It is not for you, Uzziah, to burn special perfume to the Lord. It should be done by the religious leaders, the sons of Aaron, who are set apart to burn special perfume. Get out of the holy place, for you have not been faithful. You will have no honor from the Lord God." [19] Then Uzziah was angry, and he had a dish in his hand for burning special perfume. While he was angry with the religious leaders, a bad skin disease broke out on his forehead in front of the religious leaders in the Lord's house, beside the altar of special perfume. [20] Azariah the head religious leader and all the religious leaders looked at him and saw that he had a bad skin disease on his forehead. So they were quick to get him out of there, and he himself left in a hurry because the Lord had punished him. [21] King Uzziah had the bad skin disease to the day of his death. He lived in a separate house, suffering with the skin disease, for he was cut off from the house of the Lord. And his son Jotham was over the king's house, ruling the people of the land. [22] Now the rest of the acts of Uzziah, first to last, were written by the man of God Isaiah, the son of Amoz. [23] Uzziah died, and they buried him with his fathers in the field of the grave which belonged to the kings. For they said, "He has a bad skin disease." And Jotham his son became king in his place.

Jotham Rules Judah

27 Jotham was twenty-five years old when he became king. And he ruled for sixteen years in Jerusalem. His mother's name was Jerushah the daughter of Zadok. [2] Jotham did what was right in the eyes of the Lord. He did all that his father Uzziah had done, only he did not go into the house of the Lord. But the people still sinned much. [3] Jotham built the upper gate of the Lord's house, and did much building on the wall of Ophel. [4] He built cities in the hill country of Judah, and strong-places and towers on the tree-covered hills. [5] He fought with the king of the Ammonites and won the war against them so that the Ammonites paid taxes to him. During that year they paid him silver weighing as much as 100 men, 100,000 baskets of wheat, and 100,000 baskets of barley. The Ammonites also paid him this amount in the second and in the third year. [6] So Jotham became powerful, because he let the Lord his God lead him in all his ways. [7] Now the rest of the acts of Jotham, all his wars and his acts, are written in the Book of the Kings of Israel and Judah. [8] He was twenty-five years old when he became king, and ruled for sixteen years in Jerusalem. [9] Jotham died and they buried him in the city of David. His son Ahaz became king in his place.

Ahaz Rules Judah

28 Ahaz was twenty years old when he became king. And he ruled for sixteen years in Jerusalem. He did not do what was right in the eyes of the Lord, as his father David had done. [2] But he walked in the ways of the kings of Israel. He also made objects to look like the false gods of Baal. [3] He burned special perfume in the valley of Ben-Hinnom. And he burned his sons in fire, following the hated ways of the nations whom the Lord had driven out before the sons of Israel. [4] He gave gifts in worship and burned special perfume on the high places, on the hills, and under every green tree.

Syria and Israel Win over Judah

5 So the Lord his God gave him into the hand of the king of Syria. The Syrians won the war against Ahaz and carried away many of his people to Damascus. He was also given into the hand of the king of Israel, who killed many of his people in the war. 6 For Pekah the son of Remaliah killed 120,000 powerful soldiers of Judah in one day, because they had turned away from the Lord God of their fathers. 7 And Zichri, a strong man of Ephraim, killed the king's son Maaseiah, and Azrikam the ruler of the house, and Elkanah the second in power to the king.

Oded—the Man of God

8 The sons of Israel carried away 200,000 women and sons and daughters of Judah. They also took many good things from them to Samaria. 9 But a man who spoke for the Lord was there, whose name was Oded. He went out to meet the army that came to Samaria and said to them, "See, because the Lord, the God of your fathers, was angry with Judah, He has given them into your hand. But you have killed them in an anger which has even gone up to heaven. 10 And now you plan to make the men and women of Judah and Jerusalem work hard for you. Do you not have sins of your own against the Lord your God? 11 Now listen to me. Return the people whom you have taken from your brothers. For the burning anger of the Lord is against you." 12 Then some of the leaders of the sons of Ephraim stood up against those who were coming from the battle. These leaders were Azariah the son of Johanan, Berechiah the son of Meshillemoth, Jehizkiah the son of Shallum, and Amasa the son of Hadlai. 13 They said, "You must not bring the people in here. For you plan to bring guilt upon us against the Lord, adding to our sins and our guilt. We are already so guilty that His burning anger is against Israel." 14 So the men of war left the people and things taken from Judah in front of the leaders and all the people of Israel. 15 Then the men who were chosen by name came and took the people of Judah. And they gave clothing to all of them who had none, using the clothes found among the things taken from Judah. They gave them clothes and shoes, and food and drink, and poured oil on them. They led all their weak ones on donkeys, and brought them to their brothers at Jericho, the city of palm trees. Then they returned to Samaria.

16 At that time King Ahaz sent to the king of Assyria for help. 17 For the Edomites had come to fight Judah again, and carried people away. 18 The Philistines also had come to fight against the cities of the valley and of the Negev of Judah. They had taken Beth-shemesh, Aijalon, Gederoth, Soco with its villages, Timnah with its villages, and Gimzo with its villages. And they came to live there. 19 For the Lord brought trouble to Judah because of King Ahaz of Israel. Ahaz caused the people of Judah to sin and was not faithful to the Lord. 20 So King Tilgath-pilneser of Assyria came against him and brought him trouble instead of strength. 21 Ahaz took riches from the house of the Lord and from the house of the king and of the princes, and gave them to the king of Assyria. But it did not help him.

The Sins and Death of Ahaz

22 In the time of his trouble, this same King Ahaz became even less faithful to the Lord. 23 For he gave gifts on the altar to the gods of Damascus who had beaten him in battle. He said, "Because the gods of the kings of Syria helped them, I will give gifts to them so they may help me." But they were what destroyed him and all Israel. 24 Ahaz gathered together the objects of the house of God and cut them in pieces. Then he closed the doors of the Lord's house, and made altars for himself in every corner of Jerusalem. 25 In every city of Judah he made high places to burn special perfume to other gods. And he made the Lord, the God of his fathers, very angry. 26 Now the rest of his acts and all his ways, from first to last, are written in the Book of the Kings of Judah and Israel. 27 Ahaz died, and they buried him in the city of Jerusalem. They did not bring him into the graves of the kings of Israel. And Hezekiah his son ruled in his place.

Hezekiah Rules Judah

29 Hezekiah became king when he was twenty-five years old. And he ruled for twenty-nine years in Jerusalem. His mother's name was Abijah, the daughter of Zechariah. 2 Hezekiah did what was right in the eyes of the Lord. He did all that his father David had done.

Hezekiah Makes the House of God Holy Again

3 In the first month of the first year of his rule, he opened the doors of the Lord's house and made them like new. 4 He brought in the religious leaders and the Levites, and gathered them in the open space on the east side. 5 Then he said to them, "Listen to me, O Levites. Now make yourselves holy. And make holy the house of the Lord, the God of your fathers. Carry what is unclean out from the holy place. 6 For our fathers have not been faithful. They have done what is bad in the eyes of the Lord our God. They have left Him and turned their faces away from the house of the Lord. They have turned their backs. 7 They have also shut the doors of the porch and put out the lamps. They have not burned special perfume or given burnt gifts in the holy place to the God of Israel. 8 So the Lord was angry with Judah and Jerusalem. He has made them an object of fear and wonder and shame, as you see with your own eyes. 9 See, our fathers have fallen by the sword. And our sons, our daughters and our wives have been taken away to a strange land because of this. 10 Now it is in my heart to make an agreement with the Lord God of Israel, that His burning anger may turn away from us. 11 My sons, take care now. For the Lord has chosen you to stand before Him, to do His work and to burn special perfume."

12 Then the Levites set to work. There was Mahath the son of Amasai, and Joel the son of Azariah, from the sons of the Kohathites. From the sons of Merari there was Kish the son of Abdi, and Azariah the son of Jehallelel. From the Gershonites there was Joah the son of Zimmah, and Eden the son of Joah. 13 There were Shimri and Jeiel from the sons of Elizaphan. There were Zechariah and Mattaniah from the sons of Asaph. 14 From the sons of Heman there were Jehiel and Shimei. And from the sons of Jeduthun there were Shemaiah and Uzziel. 15 They gathered their brothers and made themselves holy, and went in to make the Lord's house clean, as the king had told them by the words of the Lord. 16 The religious leaders went in to the inside part of the Lord's house to make it clean. They brought out to the open space of the Lord's house everything they found inside which was unclean. Then the Levites took it and carried it out to the river of Kidron. 17 They began to make it holy on the first day of the first month, and on the eighth day of the month they came to the porch of the Lord. Then they made the Lord's house holy in eight days, and finished on the sixteenth day of the first month. 18 Then they went in to King Hezekiah and said, "We have made clean the whole house of the Lord, the altar of burnt gifts with all of its objects, and the table of holy bread with all of its objects. 19 And we have made all the objects holy which King Ahaz had thrown away during his rule when he was not faithful. See, they are before the altar of the Lord."

Worship in the House of God Again

20 Then King Hezekiah got up early and gathered the city rulers and went up to the house of the Lord. 21 They brought seven bulls, seven rams, seven lambs, and seven male goats, for a sin gift for the nation, the holy place, and Judah. Hezekiah told the religious leaders, the sons of Aaron, to give them on the altar of the Lord. 22 So they killed the bulls, and the religious leaders took the blood and put it on the altar. They killed the rams and put the blood on the altar. And they killed the lambs and put the blood on the altar. 23 Then they brought the male goats of the sin gift in front of the king and the people. They laid their hands on them. 24 And the religious leaders killed them and gave a sin gift with their blood, to pay for the sins of all Israel. For the king said that the burnt gift and the sin gift should be made for all Israel.

25 Then Hezekiah put the Levites in their places in the house of the Lord with timbrels and different kinds of harps. He did as David, Gad and Nathan, the men who spoke for God, had all said. For through these men the Lord said that this was to be done. 26 The Levites stood with the objects for making music which David had made. And the religious leaders stood with the horns. 27 Then Hezekiah told them to give the burnt gift on the altar. When the burnt gift began, the song to the Lord also began, with the horns and the objects for music made by David, king of Israel. 28 While all the people worshiped, the singers sang and the horns sounded. The music went on until the burnt gift was finished.

29 When the burnt gift was finished, the king and all who were with him bowed down and worshiped. 30 King Hezekiah and the rulers told the Levites to sing praises to the Lord with the words of

David and Asaph the man of God. So they sang praises with joy, and bowed down and worshiped. ³¹ Then Hezekiah said, "Now that you have made yourselves holy to the Lord, come near and bring gifts for the altar and gifts of thanks to the house of the Lord." And the people brought gifts for the altar and gifts of thanks. All those who were willing brought burnt gifts. ³² The number of the burnt gifts which the people brought was 70 bulls, 100 rams, and 200 lambs. All these were for a burnt gift to the Lord. ³³ And the holy gifts were 600 bulls and 3,000 sheep. ³⁴ But there were not enough religious leaders to skin all the burnt gifts. So their brothers the Levites helped them until the work was finished, and until all the religious leaders had made themselves holy. For the Levites put more care into making themselves holy than the religious leaders. ³⁵ There were also many burnt gifts with the fat of the peace gifts. And there were the drink gifts for the burnt gifts. So the worship was returned to the house of the Lord. ³⁶ Then Hezekiah and all the people were filled with joy because of what God had done for the people, for it was done all at once.

Hezekiah Keeps the Passover

30 Hezekiah sent word to all Israel and Judah. He wrote letters to Ephraim and Manasseh also, that they should come to the house of the Lord at Jerusalem, to keep the Passover to the Lord God of Israel. ² For the king and his rulers and all the people in Jerusalem had decided to keep the Passover in the second month. ³ For they could not keep it at the set time, because there had not been enough religious leaders who had made themselves holy. And the people had not been gathered to Jerusalem. ⁴ So the new time pleased the king and all the people. ⁵ And they made it known in all Israel, from Beersheba to Dan, that they should come to keep the Passover to the Lord God of Israel at Jerusalem. For great numbers of people had not kept it, as they were told to do. ⁶ Men were sent through all Israel and Judah with the letters from the hand of the king and his rulers, as the king had told them. The letters said, "O sons of Israel, return to the Lord God of Abraham, Isaac and Israel, that He may return to those of you who have not been taken away by the kings of Assyria. ⁷ Do not be like your fathers and your brothers. They were not faithful to the Lord God of their

fathers, so He gave them a reason to fear, as you see. ⁸ Now do not make your hearts hard like your fathers, but give yourselves to the Lord. Come to His holy place which He has set apart forever. And worship the Lord your God, that His burning anger may turn away from you. ⁹ For if you return to the Lord, your brothers and your sons will be shown pity by those who took them away, and will return to this land. For the Lord your God is kind and loving. He will not turn His face away from you if you return to Him."

¹⁰ So the men took the letters from city to city through the country of Ephraim and Manasseh, and as far as Zebulun. But the people laughed at them and made fun of them. ¹¹ Only a few men of Asher, Manasseh and Zebulun put away their pride and came to Jerusalem. ¹² The hand of God was also on Judah to give them one heart to do what the king and the rulers told them by the Word of the Lord.

The People Keep the Passover

¹³ Many people gathered together at Jerusalem to keep the Special Supper of Bread Without Yeast in the second month. There were very many people. ¹⁴ They took away the altars which were in Jerusalem. And they also took away all the special perfume altars and threw them into the river of Kidron. ¹⁵ Then they killed the Passover lambs on the fourteenth day of the second month. The religious leaders and Levites were ashamed and made themselves holy, and brought burnt gifts to the house of the Lord. ¹⁶ They stood in their places as they should, as given by the Law of Moses the man of God. The religious leaders placed the blood which they received from the hand of the Levites. ¹⁷ For there were many of the people who had not made themselves holy. So the Levites had to kill the Passover lambs for every one who was unclean, to make them holy to the Lord. ¹⁸ For many of the people, many of them from Ephraim, Manasseh, Issachar and Zebulun, had not made themselves clean. Yet they ate the Passover in a different way than had been written. For Hezekiah prayed for them, saying, "May the good Lord forgive everyone ¹⁹ who makes his heart ready to look for God, the Lord God of his fathers, even if he does not follow the rules of the holy place for making himself clean." ²⁰ And the Lord heard Hezekiah, and healed the people. ²¹ The people of Israel who were there in Jerusalem kept

the Special Supper of Bread Without Yeast for seven days with great joy. The Levites and the religious leaders praised the Lord day after day, singing with loud music to the Lord. 22 Then Hezekiah spoke comforting words to all the Levites who had good understanding in the Lord's work. So the people ate the food of the Special Supper for seven days, giving peace gifts and thanks to the Lord God of their fathers.

23 Then all the people decided to keep the Special Supper for another seven days. So they kept it for another seven days with joy. 24 For King Hezekiah of Judah had given the people 1,000 bulls and 7,000 sheep. And the rulers had given the people 1,000 bulls and 10,000 sheep. And a large number of religious leaders made themselves holy. 25 All the people of Judah were filled with joy, with the religious leaders and the Levites, and all the people who came from Israel. Both the people who came from the land of Israel and those living in Judah were filled with joy. 26 So there was great joy in Jerusalem, because there was nothing like this in Jerusalem since the days of Solomon the son of David, king of Israel. 27 Then the religious leaders and Levites stood and prayed that good would come to the people. And their voice was heard. Their prayer came to the Lord's holy place in heaven.

Changes Made by Hezekiah

31 Now when all this was finished, all the people of Israel who were there went out to the cities of Judah. They broke in pieces the pillars set up for the false gods. They cut down the objects of the false goddess Ashterah. And they pulled down the high places and the altars through all Judah and Benjamin, and in Ephraim and Manasseh. They destroyed all of them. Then all the people of Israel returned to their cities, every man to his land.

2 Hezekiah divided the religious leaders and the Levites into groups, each by the work he was to do. He chose the religious leaders and Levites for giving the burnt gifts and peace gifts, for serving and giving thanks, and for praising in the gates of the camp of the Lord. 3 He decided what the king should give of his own animals for the burnt gifts, for the morning and evening, for the Days of Rest and the New Moons and the Special Suppers, as it is written in the Law of the Lord. 4 And he told the people who lived in Jerusalem to give the share that should go to the

religious leaders and the Levites, that they might give themselves to the Law of the Lord. 5 As soon as the news spread, the people of Israel gave much of the first-fruits of grain, new wine, oil, honey, and of all the food of the field. They brought in more than a tenth part of everything. 6 The people of Israel and Judah, who lived in the cities of Judah, also brought in a tenth part of the cattle and sheep. And they brought a tenth part of the holy things which were set apart for the Lord their God. They laid them one on top of the other. 7 They began to lay them on top of each other in the third month, and finished by the seventh month.

8 And when Hezekiah and the rulers came and saw all the things, they praised the Lord and His people Israel. 9 Then Hezekiah asked the religious leaders and the Levites about all the things which had been brought. 10 Azariah the head religious leader of the family of Zadok said to him, "Since the gifts began to be brought into the Lord's house, we have had much more than enough to eat. For the Lord has brought good to His people, and we have all this much left."

11 Then Hezekiah told them to make rooms ready in the house of the Lord, and they made them ready. 12 And they were faithful to bring in the gifts and the tenth part and the holy things. Conaniah the Levite was the captain over them, and his brother Shimei was second. 13 The leaders under Conaniah and his brother Shimei were Jehiel, Azaziah, Nahath, Asahel, Jerimoth, Jozabad, Eliel, Ismachiah, Mahath, and Benaiah. They were chosen by King Hezekiah. Azariah was the head captain of the house of God. 14 Kore, the son of Imnah the Levite, who watched over the east gate, was captain of the free-will gifts to God. He divided the gifts for the Lord and the most holy things. 15 Under his rule were Eden, Miniamin, Jeshua, Shemaiah, Amariah, and Shecaniah, in the cities of the religious leaders. They were faithful to give shares to their brothers by their groups, large and small alike.

16 Also they gave to those whose names were written down by families, from three years old and older. They gave to everyone who went into the Lord's house for each day's duty, for the work each of their groups was to do. 17 The names of the religious leaders were written down by their family groups, and the Levites from twenty years old and older, by their duties and

their groups. [18] Also written down were the names of their little children, their wives, their sons and their daughters, for all the people. For they were faithful to set themselves apart to be holy. [19] Also the sons of Aaron, the religious leaders who were in the fields around their cities, or in each and every city, were taken care of. There were men chosen by name to give shares to every male among the religious leaders and to everyone whose name was written down among the Levites.

[20] Hezekiah did this through all Judah. He did what was good and right and true before the Lord his God. [21] All the work he began in the house of God, obeying the Laws and looking to his God, he did with all his heart and all went well for him.

Sennacherib Speaks against the Lord

32 After these faithful acts, King Sennacherib of Assyria came to fight against Judah. His army gathered around the strong cities. He thought he would take them for himself. [2] When Hezekiah saw that Sennacherib had come to fight against Jerusalem, [3] he planned with his captains and men of war to stop the water from the wells which were outside the city. And they helped him. [4] Many people were gathered, and they stopped all the wells and the small river which flowed through the land. They said, "Why should the kings of Assyria come and find much water?" [5] Then Hezekiah took strength of heart and built again all of the wall that had been broken down. He built towers on it, and built another outside wall. He made the Millo strong in the city of David. And he made many battle-coverings and objects to fight with. [6] He chose army captains to lead the people, and gathered them in the place by the city gate. He spoke comforting words to them, saying, [7] "Be strong and have strength of heart. Do not be afraid or troubled because of the king of Assyria and all those who are with him. For the One with us is greater than the one with him. But we have the Lord our God with us, to help us and to fight our battles." And the people trusted the words of Hezekiah king of Judah.

[9] Then King Sennacherib of Assyria, whose army was gathered around Lachish with him, sent word by his servants to Jerusalem to King Hezekiah and to all the people of Judah who were in Jerusalem. He said, [10] "King Sennacherib of Assyria says, 'On what do you trust, that you are staying in Jerusalem with my army around you? [11] Is not Hezekiah leading you the wrong way to let you die by hunger and thirst, saying, "The Lord our God will save us from the king of Assyria"? [12] Has not this same Hezekiah taken away His high places and His altars, and said to Judah and Jerusalem, "You will worship in front of one altar and burn special perfume on it"? [13] Do you not know what I and my fathers have done to all the peoples of other lands? Were the gods of the other nations able to save their lands from me? [14] Who among all the gods could save his people from me in all those nations which my fathers destroyed? Would your God be able to save you from me? [15] So now do not let Hezekiah lie to you or lead you in the wrong way like this. Do not believe him. For no god of any nation was able to save his people from me or from my fathers. How much less will your God save you from me!' "

[16] Sennacherib's men said still more against the Lord God and against His servant Hezekiah. [17] The Assyrian king also wrote letters to say things against the Lord God of Israel, saying, "As the gods of the other nations of the lands have not saved their people from me, so the God of Hezekiah will not save His people from me." [18] They called this out with a loud voice in the language of Judah to the people of Jerusalem who were on the wall. They did this to bring fear upon them, so that they might take the city. [19] They talked about the God of Jerusalem as if He were one of the gods of the people of the earth, which were made by the hands of men.

[20] But King Hezekiah and Isaiah the man of God, the son of Amoz, prayed about this and cried out to heaven. [21] And the Lord sent an angel who destroyed every powerful soldier and every captain and leader in the camp of the king of Assyria. So Sennacherib returned in shame to his own land. And when he had gone into the house of his god, some of his own children killed him there with the sword. [22] So the Lord saved Hezekiah and the people of Jerusalem from King Sennacherib of Assyria, and from all others. And He gave them rest on every side. [23] Many brought gifts to the Lord at Jerusalem, and things of much worth to King Hezekiah of Judah. So the king was honored in the eyes of all nations from that time on.

Hezekiah's Pride

24 In those days Hezekiah became very sick. He prayed to the Lord, and the Lord spoke to him and gave him something special to see. 25 But Hezekiah did not do anything in return for the good he received, because his heart was proud. So the Lord's anger came upon him and Judah and Jerusalem. 26 Then Hezekiah put away the pride of his heart, both he and the people of Jerusalem. So that the anger of the Lord did not come on them in the days of Hezekiah.

Hezekiah's Riches

27 Now Hezekiah had very great riches and honor. He made for himself store-houses for silver, gold, stones of much worth, spices, battle-coverings, and all kinds of things of much worth. 28 He made storehouses for the grain that was gathered, wine, and oil. He made places for all kinds of herds, and places for the flocks. 29 He made cities for himself, and gathered very many flocks and cattle. For God had given him very many riches. 30 It was Hezekiah who stopped the upper opening of the waters of Gihon, and made them flow to the west side of the city of David. And Hezekiah did well in all that he did. 31 It was so even when the men were sent to him from the rulers of Babylon to ask about the wonder that had happened in the land. God left Hezekiah alone to test him, that He might know all that was in his heart.

The End of Hezekiah's Rule

32 Now the rest of the acts of Hezekiah and his good works are written in the special dream of Isaiah the man of God, the son of Amoz, in the Book of the Kings of Judah and Israel. 33 Hezekiah died and they buried him in the upper graves of the sons of David. All the people of Judah and Jerusalem honored him at his death. And his son Manasseh became king in his place.

Manasseh Rules Judah

33 Manasseh was twelve years old when he became king. And he ruled for fifty-five years in Jerusalem. 2 He did what was bad in the eyes of the Lord. He did the hated things of the nations whom the Lord drove out before the sons of Israel. 3 For he built again the high places which his father Hezekiah had broken down. He built altars for the false gods of Baal and made objects of worship for the false goddess Asherah. He worshiped all the stars of heaven and served them. 4 And he built altars in the Lord's house, of which the Lord had said, "My name will be in Jerusalem forever." 5 He built altars for all the stars of heaven in the two open spaces of the house of the Lord. 6 And he burned his sons as a gift in the valley of Ben-hinnom. He did witchcraft and asked the demon world about the future. He asked the demon world to do very special things, and he talked with people who spoke with the spirits of the dead. He did what was very bad in the eyes of the Lord, and made Him angry. 7 Manasseh made an object to look like a false god, and put it in God's house, of which God had said to David and to Solomon his son, "In this house, and in Jerusalem which I have chosen from all the families of Israel, I will put My name forever. 8 And I will never again take Israel out of the land which I have chosen for your fathers, if only they will obey all that I have told them in the Laws given through Moses." 9 Manasseh led Judah and the people of Jerusalem to do more sinful things than the nations whom the Lord destroyed before the sons of Israel.

Manasseh Turns from His Sin

10 The Lord spoke to Manasseh and his people, but they would not listen. 11 So the Lord brought the captains of the army of the king of Assyria against them. And they took Manasseh with hooks and tied him with brass chains and brought him to Babylon. 12 When Manasseh was in trouble, he prayed to the Lord his God, and put away his pride before the God of his fathers. 13 When he prayed to Him, God heard his prayer and listened to him, and brought him again to Jerusalem and to his nation. Then Manasseh knew that the Lord was God.

14 After this he built the outside wall of the city of David on the west side of Gihon, in the valley, as far as the Fish Gate. He built it around the Ophel, and made it very high. Then he put army captains in all the strong cities of Judah. 15 He took away the strange gods and the false god from the house of the Lord. And he took away all the altars he had built on the mountain of the Lord's house and in Jerusalem, and threw them outside the city. 16 He set up the altar of the Lord and gave peace gifts and thank gifts in worship on it. And he told Judah to serve the Lord God of Israel. 17 But the people still killed animals in worship at the high places, but only to the Lord their God.

The End of Manasseh's Rule

18 Now the rest of the acts of Manasseh, his prayer to his God, and the words the men who spoke for God spoke to him in the name of the Lord God of Israel, are among the writings of the kings of Israel. 19 His prayer and how God heard his prayer, and of all his sin and how he was not faithful, are found in the writings of the men who spoke for God. Also it is written where he built the high places, and made the objects of the false goddess Asherah, and made objects to look like gods, before he put away his pride. 20 So Manasseh died and they buried him in his own house. And his son Amon became king in his place.

21 Amon was twenty-two years old when he became king, and ruled for two years in Jerusalem. 22 Amon did what was sinful in the eyes of the Lord, as his father Manasseh had done. He killed animals in worship to all the false gods his father Manasseh had made, and he served them. 23 He did not put away his pride before the Lord as his father Manasseh had done, but Amon added to his guilt. 24 His servants made plans against him, and killed him in his own house. 25 But the people of the land killed all those who had killed King Amon and made his son Josiah king in his place.

Josiah Rules Judah

34 Josiah was eight years old when he became king. And he ruled thirty-one years in Jerusalem. 2 He did what was right in the eyes of the Lord, and walked in the ways of his father David. He did not turn aside to the right or to the left. 3 For in the eighth year of his rule while he was still young, he began to look for the God of his father David. In the twelfth year he began to take the sinful things out of Judah and Jerusalem. He took away the high places, the objects of the false goddess Asherah, and all the objects made to look like gods. 4 They tore down the altars of the false gods of Baal in front of him. And he cut down the special perfume altars which stood above them. He broke in pieces the objects of the false goddess Asherah and all the objects made to look like gods. Then he ground them to dust and spread it on the graves of those who had given gifts in worship to them. 5 He burned the bones of their religious leaders on their altars, and made Judah and Jerusalem free from worshiping false gods. 6 And in the cities of Manasseh, Ephraim, Simeon,

and as far as Naphtali, in the broken down places around them, 7 Josiah tore down the altars and beat to dust the objects of Asherah and the objects made to look like gods. He cut down all the special perfume altars through all the land of Israel. Then he returned to Jerusalem.

The Book of the Law Is Found

8 Now it was the eighteenth year of his rule, and Josiah had made the land and the Lord's house free from worshiping false gods. At that time he sent Shaphan the son of Azaliah, Maaseiah the leader of the city, and Joah the son of Joahaz, who wrote down the things that happened, to do the work needed on the house of the Lord his God. 9 They came to Hilkiah the head religious leader and gave him the money that was brought into the house of God. The Levites who watched the door had received this money from Manasseh and Ephraim and from all those who were left of Israel, and from all Judah and Benjamin and the people of Jerusalem. 10 Then they gave the money to the workmen who watched over the work of the Lord's house. And the workmen who were working in the Lord's house used it to make the house like new. 11 They gave the money to those who work with wood and to the builders to buy cut stone and wood for joints and building-pieces for the houses. The kings of Judah had not had the needed work done on them. 12 And the men were faithful in doing the work. Watching over them were Jahath and Obadiah, the Levites of the sons of Merari, and Zechariah and Meshullam of the sons of the Kohathites. The Levites who were good at playing music 13 watched over those who carried loads and those who did work in every kind of duty. Some of the Levites were writers and leaders and gate-keepers.

14 When they were bringing out the money which had been brought into the Lord's house, Hilkiah the religious leader found the book of the Law of the Lord given by Moses. 15 Hilkiah told Shaphan the writer, "I have found the book of the Law in the Lord's house." And Hilkiah gave the book to Shaphan. 16 Then Shaphan brought the book to the king, and said to him, "Your servants are doing all the work that they have been given to do." 17 They have taken all the money that was found in the Lord's house and have given it to the leaders and the workmen."

18 Then Shaphan the writer said to the king, "Hilkiah the religious leader gave me a book." And Shaphan read it in front of the king. 19 When King Josiah heard the words of the Law, he tore his clothes. 20 Then the king called Hilkiah, Ahikam the son of Shaphan, Abdon the son of Micah, Shaphan the writer, and Asaiah the king's servant. He told them, 21 "Go, ask the Lord for me, and for those who are left in Israel and Judah, about the words of the book which have been found. For much of the Lord's anger has been poured out on us because our fathers have not obeyed the Word of the Lord. They have not done all that is written in this book."

22 So Hilkiah and those whom the king had sent went to Huldah the woman who spoke for God. She was the wife of Shallum the son of Tokhath, the son of Hasrah, who watched over the clothing. (She lived in Jerusalem in the second part of the city.) They spoke to her about this. 23 And she said to them, "The Lord, the God of Israel, says, 'Tell the man who sent you to Me 24 what I say. See, I am bringing much trouble to this place and to its people. I am allowing all the curses to come which are written in the book they have read in front of the king of Judah. 25 They have left Me and have burned special perfume to other gods, that they might make Me angry with all the work of their hands. So My anger will be poured out on this place, and it will not be stopped. 26 But tell the king of Judah who sent you to the Lord, "This is what the Lord God of Israel says about the words which you have heard: 27 'Your heart was broken and you had no pride before God when you heard His words against this place and its people. And because you came before Me with no pride, tore your clothes, and cried before Me, I have heard you,' says the Lord. 28 'Your eyes will not see all the much trouble that I will bring on this place and its people. It will come after you die. You will be taken to your grave in peace.' " ' " The men brought back this word to the king.

Josiah Brings Back True Worship

29 Then the king sent and gathered together all the leaders of Judah and Jerusalem. 30 The king went up to the house of the Lord, with all the men of Judah, the people of Jerusalem, the religious leaders, the Levites, and all the people from the greatest to the least. And he read in their hearing all the words of the book of the agreement which was found in the Lord's house. 31 Then the king stood in his place and made an agreement before the Lord. He agreed to follow the Lord, to obey His Laws with all his heart and soul, and to do what is written in the agreement in this book. 32 And he made all who were there in Jerusalem and Benjamin to stand with him. So the people of Jerusalem promised to obey the agreement of God, the God of their fathers. 33 Josiah took away all the hated false gods from all the lands belonging to the sons of Israel. He made all who were in Israel worship the Lord their God. While Josiah was alive, they did not turn from following the Lord God of their fathers.

Josiah Keeps the Passover

35 Then Josiah kept the Passover to the Lord in Jerusalem. They killed the Passover animals on the fourteenth day of the first month. 2 He gave the religious leaders their duties and gave them strength to do the work of the Lord's house. 3 And he said to the Levites who taught all Israel and who were holy to the Lord, "Put the holy box of the agreement in the house which Solomon the son of David, king of Israel, built. You do not need to carry it on your shoulders any longer. Now work for the Lord your God and His people Israel. 4 Make yourselves ready by your fathers' houses in your groups, in the way that was written by King David of Israel and his son Solomon. 5 Stand in the holy place by the family groups of your brothers who are not religious leaders. And let some of the Levites help each family group of the people. 6 Now kill the Passover animals, and make yourselves holy. Make things ready for your brothers to obey the word of the Lord by Moses."

7 Then Josiah gave flocks of lambs and young goats as Passover gifts for all the people who were there. He gave 30,000 of them, and 3,000 bulls. These were from the king's animals. 8 His leaders also gave a free-will gift to the people, the religious leaders, and the Levites. Hilkiah, Zechariah and Jehiel, the leaders of the house of God, gave 2,600 animals from the flocks and 300 bulls to the religious leaders for the Passover gifts. 9 Conaniah, and Shemaiah and Nethanel his brothers, and Hashabiah, Jeiel and Jozabad, the leaders of the Levites, gave 5,000 animals from the flocks and 500 bulls to the Levites for the Passover gifts.

10 So everything was made ready for the Passover. The religious leaders stood in their places, and the Levites stood by their groups, as the king had told them. 11 Then they killed the Passover animals. The religious leaders took the blood from them and put it on the altar. And the Levites cut the skins from the animals. 12 They set aside the burnt gifts that they might give them to the family groups of the people, to give to the Lord, as it is written in the Book of Moses. They did the same thing with the bulls. 13 So they cooked the Passover animals on the fire as the Law said. They boiled the holy things in pots and deep dishes, and carried them in a hurry to all the people. 14 After this they made everything ready for themselves and for the religious leaders because the religious leaders, the sons of Aaron, were giving in worship the burnt gifts and the fat parts until night. So the Levites made things ready for themselves and for the religious leaders, the sons of Aaron. 15 The singers, the sons of Asaph, were also in their places, as had been written by David, Asaph, Heman, and Jeduthun the king's man of God. The men who were gate-keepers did not have to leave their duty, because their brothers the Levites made things ready for them.

16 All the work of the Lord was made ready that day to keep the Passover, and to give burnt gifts on the Lord's altar, as King Josiah had said. 17 So the people of Israel who were there kept the Passover at that time. And they kept the Special Supper of Bread Without Yeast for seven days. 18 There had not been kept a Passover like it in Israel since the days of Samuel the man of God. None of the kings of Israel had kept such a Passover as Josiah did with the religious leaders, the Levites, all Judah and Israel who were there, and the people of Jerusalem. 19 This Passover was kept in the eighteenth year of Josiah's rule.

The End of Josiah's Rule

20 After all this, when Josiah had made the house of the Lord ready, King Neco of Egypt came up to make war at Carchemish on the Euphrates. And Josiah went out to fight against him. 21 But Neco sent men to him, saying, "What have we to do with each other, O King of Judah? I am not coming against you today but against the house with which I am at war, and God has told me to hurry. Do not stand in the way of God Who is with me, or He will destroy you." 22 But Josiah would not turn away from him. He made himself to look like someone else, so he could fight against him. He did not listen to the words of Neco from the mouth of God, but came to make war on the Plain of Megiddo. 23 And the bowmen shot King Josiah. The king told his servants, "Take me away, for I am hurt." 24 So his servants took him out of the war-wagon and carried him in his second war-wagon, and brought him to Jerusalem. And there he died. He was buried in the graves of his fathers. All Judah and Jerusalem were filled with sorrow for Josiah. 25 Then Jeremiah sang a song of sorrow for Josiah. And all the male and female singers speak about Josiah in their songs of sorrow to this day. They made them a law in Israel, and they are written in the Lamentations. 26 Now the rest of the acts of Josiah and his good works as written in the Law of the Lord, 27 and his acts, first to last, are written in the Book of the Kings of Israel and Judah.

Joahaz Rules Judah

36 Then the people of the land took Joahaz the son of Josiah, and made him king in place of his father in Jerusalem. 2 Joahaz was twenty-three years old when he became king. And he ruled for three months in Jerusalem. 3 Then the king of Egypt took Joahaz's power away at Jerusalem, and made the people of the land pay a tax of silver weighing as much as one hundred men, and gold weighing as much as one man. 4 The king of Egypt made Eliakim his brother king over Judah and Jerusalem, and changed his name to Jehoiakim. But Neco took Eliakim's brother Joahaz and brought him to Egypt.

Jehoiakim Rules Judah

5 Jehoiakim was twenty-five years old when he became king, and he ruled eleven years in Jerusalem. He did what was sinful in the eyes of the Lord his God. 6 King Nebuchadnezzar of Babylon came up against him and tied him with brass chains to take him to Babylon. 7 Nebuchadnezzar also brought some of the things of the Lord's house to Babylon and put them in his place of worship there. 8 Now the rest of the acts of Jehoiakim and the sinful things which he did, and what was found against him, are written in the Book of the Kings of Israel and Judah. His son Jehoiachin became king in his place.

Jehoiachin Rules Judah

9 Jehoiachin was eighteen years old when he became king, and he ruled in Jerusalem

three months and ten days. He did what was sinful in the eyes of the Lord. 10 In the spring of the year, King Nebuchadnezzar sent and brought him to Babylon with the objects of great worth from the Lord's house. He made his brother Zedekiah king over Judah and Jerusalem.

Zedekiah Rules Judah

11 Zedekiah was twenty-one years old when he became king, and he ruled eleven years in Jerusalem. 12 He did what was sinful in the eyes of the Lord his God. He had much pride in front of Jeremiah the man of God who spoke for the Lord. 13 And he turned against King Nebuchadnezzar who had made him make a promise by God. He was strong-willed and his heart hard against turning to the Lord God of Israel. 14 Also none of the rulers of the religious leaders and people were faithful. They followed all the sinful things of the nations. And they brought sinful things into the Lord's house, which the Lord had made holy in Jerusalem.

Jerusalem Is Taken

15 The Lord, the God of their fathers, sent men to speak for Him again and again, because He had loving-pity on His people and on His house. 16 But the people always made fun of the men sent by God. They hated God's words and laughed at His men who spoke for God, until the Lord was very angry with His people. And there was no way for things to be better. 17 So God brought the king of the Babylonians against them, who killed their young men with the sword in the house of God. He had no pity on anyone, young or old, men or women or the sick. He gave them all into the king's hand. 18 And he brought to Babylon all the things of the house of God, great and small, and the riches of the Lord's house, and the riches of the king and of his rulers. 19 Then they burned the house of God, and broke down the wall of Jerusalem. They burned all of its buildings built for battles, and destroyed all of its objects of great worth. 20 He carried away to Babylon those who had not been killed by the sword. They were made to work for him and his sons until the rule of the nation of Persia. 21 This was done so the word of the Lord spoken by Jeremiah came true. For the seventy years that the land was not being used, the Day of Rest was kept. So the Days of Rest were enjoyed that had not been kept before.

Cyrus Tells the Jews to Return

22 The Lord's word by the mouth of Jeremiah came true in this way also: In the first year of King Cyrus of Persia, the Lord caused the spirit of King Cyrus to send word to all his nation, and also to write it down, saying, 23 "King Cyrus of Persia says, 'The Lord, the God of heaven, has given me all the nations of the earth. He has chosen me to build Him a house in Jerusalem, which is in Judah. Whoever is among you of all His people, may the Lord his God be with him, and let him go up.' "

EZRA

Cyrus Lets the Jews Return

1 In the first year of King Cyrus of Persia, the words of the Lord spoken by Jeremiah came true. The Lord worked in the spirit of King Cyrus of Persia so that he made it known through all his nation, and also put it in writing, saying, 2 "This is what Cyrus king of Persia says: 'The Lord, the God of heaven, has given me all the nations of the earth. He has chosen me to build Him a house in Jerusalem, which is in Judah. 3 Whoever there is among you of all His people, may his God be with him! Let him go up to Jerusalem which is in Judah, the God of Israel. He is the God Who is in Jerusalem. 4 Let each one who is still alive, at whatever place he may live, be helped by the men of his place with silver and gold and with good things and cattle. Let the men also give a free-will gift for the house of God in Jerusalem.' "

5 Then the leaders of the family groups of Judah and Benjamin and the religious leaders and Levites stood up, everyone in whose spirit the Lord had worked to go up and build the Lord's house in Jerusalem again. 6 All those around them helped them with gifts of silver, gold, good things, cattle, and things worth much money, besides all that was given as a free-will gift. 7 King Cyrus brought out the objects of the house of the Lord, which Nebuchadnezzar had carried away from Jerusalem

and put in the house of his gods. **8** King Cyrus of Persia had them brought out by Mithredath, the man who took care of the nation's riches. And he numbered them as he handed them over to Sheshbazzar, the leader of Judah. **9** This was their number: 30 gold dishes, 1,000 silver dishes, 29 other dishes, **10** 30 gold pots, 410 silver pots, and 1,000 other objects. **11** There were 5,400 objects of gold and silver in all. Sheshbazzar brought all of them back when the people who had been taken away went up from Babylon to Jerusalem.

Families Who Returned

2 These are the people who left the land of Babylon and returned to Jerusalem and Judah, each to his own city. Their families had been taken away to Babylon by Nebuchadnezzar the king of Babylon. **2** These people returned with Zerubbabel, Jeshua, Nehemiah, Seraiah, Reelaiah, Mordecai, Bilshan, Mispar, Bigvai, Rehum, and Baanah.

The number of the men of Israel: **3** 2,172 sons of Parosh, **4** 372 sons of Shephatiah, **5** 775 sons of Arah, **6** 2,812 sons of Pahath-moab of the sons of Jeshua and Joab, **7** 1,254 sons of Elam, **8** 945 sons of Zattu, **9** 760 sons of Zaccai, **10** 642 sons of Bani, **11** 623 sons of Bebai, **12** 1,222 sons of Azgad, **13** 666 sons of Adonikam, **14** 2,056 sons of Bigvai, **15** 454 sons of Adin, **16** 98 sons of Ater, **17** 323 sons of Bezai, **18** 112 sons of Jorah, **19** 223 sons of Hashum, **20** 95 sons of Gibbar, **21** 123 sons of Bethlehem, **22** 56 sons of Netophah, **23** 128 sons of Anathoth, **24** 42 sons of Azmaveth, **25** 743 sons of Kiriath-arim, Chephirah, and Beeroth, **26** 621 sons of Raman and Geba, **27** 122 sons of Michmas, **28** 223 sons of Bethel and Ai, **29** 52 sons of Nebo, **30** 156 sons of Magbish, **31** 1,254 sons of the other Elam, **32** 320 sons of Harim, **33** 725 sons of Lod, Hadid, and Ono, **34** 345 sons of Jericho, **35** 3,630 sons of Senaah.

36 The religious leaders: 973 sons of Jedaiah of the house of Jeshua, **37** 1,052 sons of Immer, **38** 1,247 sons of Pashhur, **39** 1,017 sons of Harim.

40 The Levites: 74 sons of Jeshua and Kadmiel, of the sons of Hodaviah. **41** The singers: 128 sons of Asaph. **42** The sons of the gate-keepers: 139 of the sons of Shallum, Ater, Talmon, Akkub, Hatita, and Shobai.

43 The men who worked in the house of the Lord: the sons of Ziha, the sons of Hasupha, the sons of Tabbaoth, **44** the sons of Keros, the sons of Siaha, the sons of Padon, **45** the sons of Lebanah, the sons of Hagabah, the sons of Akkub, **46** the sons of Hagab, the sons of Shalmai, the sons of Hanan, **47** the sons of Giddel, the sons of Gahar, the sons of Reaiah, **48** the sons of Rezin, the sons of Nekoda, the sons of Gazzam, **49** the sons of Uzza, the sons of Paseah, the sons of Besai, **50** the sons of Asnah, the sons of Meunim, the sons of Nephisim, **51** the sons of Bakbuk, the sons of Hakupha, the sons of Harhur, **52** the sons of Bazluth, the sons of Mehida, the sons of Harsha, **53** the sons of Barkos, the sons of Sisera, the sons of Temah, **54** the sons of Neziah, the sons of Hatipha.

55 The sons of Solomon's servants: the sons of Sotai, the sons of Hassophereth, the sons of Peruda, **56** the sons of Jaalah, the sons of Darkon, the sons of Giddel, **57** the sons of Shephatiah, the sons of Hattil, the sons of Pochereth-hazzebaim, the sons of Ami. **58** All the servants of the house of the Lord, and all the sons of Solomon's servants, were 392.

59 Now these are the men who came up from Tel-melah, Tel-harsha, Cherub, Addan, and Immer. But they were not able to show that their fathers and they were children of Israel: **60** 652 sons of Delaiah, Tobiah, and Nekoda. **61** And the sons of the religious leaders: the sons of Habaiah, Hakkoz, and Barzillai, who had married one of the daughters of Barzillai the Gileadite, and was called by their name. **62** These men looked for their names among the names of all the families, but could not find them. So they were thought of as being unclean, and were not allowed to work as religious leaders. **63** And the leader told them that they should not eat from the most holy things until a religious leader learned God's will by the Urim and Thummim.

64 There were 42,360 people in all, **65** besides the 7,337 men servants and women servants, and 200 singing men and women. **66** They had 736 horses, 245 mules, **67** 435 camels, and 6,720 donkeys.

68 When they came to the house of the Lord in Jerusalem, some of the heads of the family groups gave a free-will gift for the house of God to be built again on the same place. **69** As they were able, they gave 61,000 gold pieces and 5,000 silverpieces and 100 coats for the religious leaders, for the work to be done.

70 So the religious leaders, the Levites, some of the people, the singers, the gate-keepers and the servants of the Lord's house lived in their own cities, and all Israel lived in their cities.

Worship Begins

3 When the seventh month came, and the sons of Israel were in the cities, the people gathered together as one man in Jerusalem. **2** Then Jozadak's son Jeshua and his brothers the religious leaders, and Shealtiel's son Zerubbabel and his brothers, built the altar of the God of Israel, to give burnt gifts on it. They did this as it is written in the Law of Moses, the man of God. **3** So they set up the altar in its place, for they were afraid because of the peoples of the lands. On it they gave burnt gifts in worship to the Lord morning and evening. **4** They kept the Special Supper of Tents, as it is written. They gave the right number of burnt gifts every day by the Law, as was needed for each day. **5** After that they gave the gifts to be burned day and night and for the new moons, and for all the special times of the Lord, and the gifts from every one who brought a free-will gift to the Lord. **6** From the first day of the seventh month they began to give burnt gifts to the Lord. But the house of the Lord had not begun to be built. **7** So they gave money to the men who worked with stone and wood. They gave food, drink and oil to the Sidonians and Tyrians so the cedar wood could be brought from Lebanon to the sea at Joppa, as King Cyrus of Persia had allowed them.

Work on the House of God Begins

8 In the second month of the second year of their coming to the house of God at Jerusalem, Zerubbabel the son of Shealtiel, Jeshua the son of Jozadak, and the rest of their brothers the religious leaders and Levites, and all who returned from Babylon to Jerusalem, began the work. And they chose the Levites from twenty years old and older to watch over the work of the Lord's house. **9** Then Jeshua with his sons and brothers, Kadmiel and his sons, the sons of Judah, and the sons of Henadad with their sons and brothers the Levites, together watched over the workmen in the house of God. **10** When the builders had begun building the house of the Lord, the religious leaders stood in their religious clothing blowing horns. The Levites, the sons of Asaph, stood with brass noise-makers. And they praised the Lord, as they had been told by

King David of Israel. **11** They sang, praising and giving thanks to the Lord, saying, "For He is good, for His loving-kindness is upon Israel forever." All the people called out with a loud voice when they praised the Lord because the work on the house of the Lord had begun. **12** But many of the religious leaders and Levites and heads of the family groups were old men who had seen the first house of the Lord. And they cried with a loud voice when the work of this house was begun in front of their eyes. But many called out for joy in a loud voice. **13** The people could not tell the difference between the sound of joy and the sound of crying. For the people called out with a loud voice, and the sound was heard far away.

People of the Land Try to Keep the Jews from Building

4 Now those who hated Judah and Benjamin heard that the people had returned from Babylon and were building a house of worship to the Lord God of Israel. **2** They came to Zerubbabel and the heads of the family groups and said to them, "Let us build with you. For we worship your God as you do. We have been giving gifts to Him since the days of King Esarhaddon of Assyria, who brought us here." **3** But Zerubbabel and Jeshua and the rest of the heads of the family groups of Israel said to them, "You have nothing to do with us in building a house to our God. But we alone will build to the Lord God of Israel, as King Cyrus of Persia has told us to do." **4** Then the people of the land made the hearts of the people of Judah weak, and made them afraid to go on building. **5** They paid people to speak against them and to make trouble in their plans all the days of Cyrus king of Persia, even until the rule of King Darius of Persia.

People of the Land Do Not Want Jerusalem Built Up Again

6 In the beginning of Ahasuerus's rule, people of the land wrote that the Jews in Judah and Jerusalem had done something wrong.

7 During Artaxerxes's rule, Bishlam, Mithredath, Tabeel and the rest of their friends wrote to King Artaxerxes of Persia. The letter was written in the Aramaic language. **8** Rehum the captain and Shimshai the writer wrote a letter against Jerusalem to King Artaxerxes. **9** It was written by Rehum the captain and Shimshai the writer and the rest of their friends, the judges, the leaders and important men, the men of Erech, Babylon, Shusha (that is, the Elamites), 10 and the rest of the nations. The people of these nations were sent away by the great and honored Osnappar, and made their home in the city of Samaria and in the rest of the land on the other side of the Euphrates River. Now 11 this is what they said in their letter to him: "To King Artaxerxes, your servants, the men in the land on the other side of the River, 12 let it be known to the king that the Jews who came up from you have come to Jerusalem. They are building again the sinful city that is not willing to be ruled. They are finishing the walls and beginning the work on the buildings. 13 Now let it be known to the king that, if that city is built again and the walls are finished, they will not pay what should be paid to the king. The taxes paid to the king will be less. 14 We are under the care of the king, and it is not right for us to see the king not being honored. So we have sent to let the king know. 15 Look through the books kept by your fathers. You will find from these books that Jerusalem is not willing to be ruled, and that it is a danger to kings and lands. They have turned against kings in past times, and this is why that city was laid waste. 16 We are letting the king know that, if that city is built again and the walls are finished, you will own nothing in the land on the other side of the River."

17 The king sent an answer to Rehum the captain, Shimshai the writer, and to the rest of their friends who live in Samaria and in the rest of the land on the other side of the River. He wrote: "Peace. 18 The letter you sent to us has been put into our language and read to me. 19 I have had men look through the books. And it has been found that the city has turned against kings in past times, and that plans against kings have been made in it. 20 Powerful kings have ruled over Jerusalem, who ruled over all the lands on the other side of the River, and taxes were paid to them. 21 So give word to these men to make them stop the work. This city may not be built again until I allow it. 22 Be sure that you do this. Why should more trouble be given to the kings?"

23 When the letter from King Artaxerxes was read to Rehum and Shimshai the writer and their friends, they went in a hurry to the Jews at Jerusalem and with their power made them stop. 24 Then the work on the house of God in Jerusalem

stopped. It was stopped until the second year of the rule of Darius king of Persia.

Work on the House of God Starts Again

5 Now the men who spoke for God, Haggai and Zechariah the son of Iddo, spoke for God to the Jews in Judah and Jerusalem. They spoke in the name of the God of Israel Who was over them. 2 Then Zerubbabel the son of Shealtiel and Jeshua the son of Jozadak began to build again the house of God in Jerusalem. The men who spoke for God were with them and helped them. 3 Then Tattenai, the leader over the land on the other side of the River, and Shethar-bozenai, and their friends, came to them and said, "Who told you to build on this house and to finish the building?" 4 They also asked, "What are the names of the men who are building this building?" 5 But the eye of their God was on the leaders of the Jews. They did not stop them until a letter was sent to Darius about it, and a written answer received from him.

6 This is what was said in the letter sent to King Darius from Tattenai, the leader over the land on the other side of the River, and Shethar-bozenai and his important friends. 7 It said: "To Darius the king, all peace. 8 Let it be known to the king that we have gone to the land of Judah, to the house of the great God. It is being built with very large stones, and heavy pieces of wood are being laid in the walls. This work is being done with much care and is going well in their hands. 9 We asked those leaders, 'Who told you to build this house of worship and to finish the building?' 10 We also asked them their names, that we might write down the names of their leaders and let you know. 11 They answered, 'We are the servants of the God of heaven and earth. We are building again the house of God that was built many years ago, which a great king of Israel built and finished. 12 But because our fathers had made the God of heaven angry, He gave them into the hand of Nebuchadnezzar king of Babylon, the Chaldean. Nebuchadnezzar destroyed this house of God, and carried the people away to Babylon. 13 But in the first year of Cyrus king of Babylon, King Cyrus told us to build again this house of God. 14 Nebuchadnezzar had taken the gold and silver objects of the house of God from the house in Jerusalem, and brought them to the house of worship at Babylon. But King Cyrus took them from the house of worship at Babylon and

they were given to Sheshbazzar, whom he had chosen as leader over the land. ¹⁵ He said to him, "Go, take these objects to Jerusalem and carry them into the place of worship. And let the house of God be built again in its place." ¹⁶ Then Sheshbazzar came and began building the house of God in Jerusalem. The building has been going on from then until now, and it is not yet finished.' ¹⁷ So now, if it pleases the king, have men look through the books kept there in Babylon to see if King Cyrus had told them to build again this house of God at Jerusalem. Let the king send us word on what is decided about this."

Cyrus's Book Found

6 Then King Darius had men look through the books which were kept in Babylon. ² And in Ecbatana, the most important city in the land of Media, a book was found in which was written: ³ "In the first year of King Cyrus, Cyrus the king said that this was to be done about the house of God at Jerusalem: 'Let the house of God, the place where burnt gifts are given in worship, be built again with a good base. It should be sixteen times taller than a man, and as wide as thirty long steps. ⁴ There should be three very large stones laid on the top of each other, and then one large piece of wood laid. Let it be paid for from the king's money. ⁵ Let the gold and silver objects which Nebuchadnezzar took from the house of God in Jerusalem and brought to Babylon be returned to their places in the house of God in Jerusalem. You must put them in the house of God.'

⁶ "So now, Tattenai, leader over the land on the other side of the River, Shethar-bozenai, and your friends who are leaders in the lands on the other side of the River, stay away from there. ⁷ Leave this work on the house of God alone. Let the leaders of the Jews build this house of God again where it stood before. ⁸ Also, I am making it known what you are to do for these leaders of Judah for the building of this house of God. All of it is to be paid for from the king's money out of the taxes from the lands on the other side of the River. And waste no time to get it to them. ⁹ Be sure to give them each day whatever is needed, young bulls, rams and lambs for a burnt gift to the God of heaven, and grain, salt, wine, and oil for pouring. ¹⁰ This is so they may give pleasing gifts in worship to the God of heaven and pray for

the life of the king and his sons. ¹¹ I here make it known that if anyone does not do what I say, a piece of wood will be taken from his house and he will be nailed on it. And his house will become a place to gather waste. ¹² May the God Who has caused His name to be there take away the power of any king or people who will try to change what I have said, so as to destroy this house of God in Jerusalem. I, Darius, have told this to you. Let it be done with much care."

The House of God Is Set Apart for Use

¹³ Then Tattenai, the leader over the land on the other side of the River, and Shethar-bozenai and their friends obeyed the words of the king with much care, just as King Darius had told them. ¹⁴ The leaders of the Jews did well in building, through the words spoken by Haggai the man who spoke for God and Zechariah the son of Iddo. They finished building as they had been told to do by the God of Israel, and by Cyrus, Darius, and Artaxerxes king of Persia. ¹⁵ The house of God was finished on the third day of the month of Adar, in the sixth year of the rule of King Darius.

¹⁶ The people of Israel, the religious leaders, the Levites, and the rest of the people who returned from Babylon, set apart this house of God with joy. ¹⁷ To set apart this house of God they gave 100 bulls, 200 rams, 400 lambs. For a sin gift for all Israel they gave twelve male goats, one for each number of the families of Israel. ¹⁸ Then they put the religious leaders and the Levites into groups by the work they were to do for God in Jerusalem, as it is written in the book of Moses.

The Passover

¹⁹ The people who had returned from Babylon kept the Passover on the fourteenth day of the first month. ²⁰ For the religious leaders and the Levites had made themselves holy together. All of them were clean. Then they killed the Passover lamb for all the people, for their brothers the religious leaders, and for themselves. ²¹ It was eaten by the people of Israel who returned from Babylon and all those who had separated themselves from the sin of the nations of the land to join them and to look for the Lord God of Israel. ²² They kept the Special Supper of Bread Without Yeast for seven days with joy, for the Lord had made them very happy. He had turned the heart of the king of Assyria toward

them to give them strength in the work of the house of God, the God of Israel.

Ezra Comes to Jerusalem

7 Now after this, during the rule of King Artaxerxes of Persia, Ezra went up from Babylon. Ezra was the son of Seraiah, son of Azariah, son of Hilkiah, 2 son of Shallum, son of Zadok, son of Ahitub, 3 son of Amariah, son of Azariah, son of Meraioth, 4 son of Zerahiah, son of Uzzi, son of Bukki, 5 son of Abishua, son of Phinehas, son of Eleazar, son of Aaron the head religious leader. 6 This Ezra went up from Babylon. He was a writer who knew well the Law of Moses which the Lord God of Israel had given. The king gave him everything he asked for, because the Lord his God was good to him. 7 Some of the sons of Israel and some of the religious leaders, the Levites, the singers, the gate-keepers and the servants of the house of God went up to Jerusalem in the seventh year of King Artaxerxes. 8 Ezra came to Jerusalem in the fifth month in the seventh year of the king. 9 He left Babylon on the first day of the first month, and came to Jerusalem on the first day of the fifth month, because the good hand of his God was upon him. 10 For Ezra had set his heart to learn the Law of the Lord, to live by it, and to teach His Laws in Israel.

11 This is what was written in the letter which King Artaxerxes gave to Ezra the religious leader, the writer, who had much learning in the Laws of the Lord and His Laws for Israel: 12 "Artaxerxes, king of kings, to Ezra the religious leader, the writer who knows the Law of the God of heaven: Peace. And now 13 I let it be known that if there are any people of Israel, religious leaders or Levites in my nation who are willing to go to Jerusalem, they may go with you. 14 For you are sent by the king and his seven men of wisdom to see if the Law of your God which is in your hand is being obeyed in Judah and Jerusalem. 15 Take the silver and gold which the king and his men of wisdom have given because they wanted to give to the God of Israel, Whose house is in Jerusalem. 16 Take this with all the silver and gold you will find in the whole land of Babylon. And take the gifts of the people and of the religious leaders, who have given because they have wanted to for the house of their God in Jerusalem. 17 With this money, buy bulls, rams, and lambs, with their grain gifts and their drink gifts. And give them

on the altar of the house of your God in Jerusalem. 18 Whatever you and your brothers think is best to do with the rest of the silver and gold, you may do, if it is the will of your God. 19 Also take to the God of Jerusalem all the objects given to you for the work of the house of your God. 20 Whatever else is needed for the house of your God, you may take it from the king's storehouse. 21 I, King Artaxerxes, here make this known to all those who take care of the money in the lands on the other side of the River. You should be ready and willing to give Ezra, the religious leader and writer who knows the Law of the God of heaven, whatever he needs. 22 Give silver weighing up to as much as 100 men, and as much as 1,000 baskets of grain, 1,100 jars of wine, 1,100 jars of oil, and as much salt as is needed. 23 Whatever is wanted by the God of heaven, let it be done in full for the house of the God of heaven. Or else He might be angry with the nation of the king and his sons. 24 We also let you know that it is not allowed to take any taxes from any of the religious leaders, Levites, singers, door keepers, or servants of this house of God. 25 And you, Ezra, use the wisdom of your God which is in your hand to choose leaders and judges. They are to judge all the people in the land on the other side of the River, all those who know the Laws of your God. You may teach anyone who does not know them. 26 Whoever will not obey the Law of your God and the law of the king, let his punishment be hard. Put him to death, or send him out of the land, or take what he has, or put him in prison."

Ezra Gives Praise to God

27 Honor and thanks be to the Lord, the God of our fathers, Who has put such a thing as this in the king's heart, to make the house of the Lord in Jerusalem beautiful. 28 He has shown loving-kindness to me in front of the king and his wise men, and in front of all the king's powerful leaders. I was given strength, because the hand of the Lord my God was upon me. And I gathered leaders from Israel to go up with me.

Families Who Returned

8 These are the leaders of family groups and the family names of those who went up with me from Babylon during the rule of King Artaxerxes: 2 there was Gershom of the sons of Phinehas, Daniel of the sons of Ithamar, and from the house

of David, Hattush, ³ the son of Shecaniah. There was Zechariah of the sons
of Parosh, and with him were 150 men
whose family names were written down.
⁴ Of the sons of Pahath-moab, there was
Eliehoenai the son of Zerahiah, and 200
men with him. ⁵ Of the sons of Zattu, there
was Shecaniah the son of Jahaziel, and
300 men with him. ⁶ Of the sons of Adin,
there was Ebed the son of Jonathan, and
fifty men with him. ⁷ Of the sons of Elam,
there was Jeshaiah the son of Athaliah,
and seventy men with him. ⁸ Of the sons
of Shephatiah, there was Zebadiah the son
of Michael, and eighty men with him. ⁹ Of
the sons of Joab, there was Obadiah the
son of Jehiel, and 218 men with him. ¹⁰ Of
the sons of Shelomith there was the son
of Josiphiah, and 160 men with him. ¹¹ Of
the sons of Bebai, there was Zechariah the
son of Bebai, and twenty-eight men with
him. ¹² Of the sons of Azgad, there was Johanan the son of Hakkatan, and 110 men
with him. ¹³ Of the sons of Adonikam, the
last to come, there were Eliphelet, Jeuel,
and Shemaiah, and sixty men with them.
¹⁴ Of the sons of Bigvai, there were Uthai
and Zabbud, and seventy men with them.

Ezra Finds Levites for the House of God

¹⁵ I gathered them at the river that flows to
Ahava, where we had our camp for three
days. When I saw the people and the religious leaders, I did not find any Levites
there. ¹⁶ So I sent for Eliezer, Ariel, Shemaiah, Elnathan, Jarib, Elnathan, Nathan,
Zechariah, and Meshullam, who were
leaders, and for Joiarib and Elnathan, who
were teachers. ¹⁷ I sent them to Iddo, the
leader at Casiphia. I told them what to say
to Iddo and his brothers, servants in the
house of worship at Casiphia. They were to
bring men to us to care for the house of our
God. ¹⁸ And by the good hand of our God
upon us, they brought us a man of wisdom,
of the sons of Mahli, the son of Levi, the
son of Israel. His name is Sherebiah, and
with him came his sons and brothers, eighteen men. ¹⁹ They also brought Hashabiah
and Jeshaiah of the sons of Morari, with
his brothers and their sons, twenty men.
²⁰ They brought 220 men to work in the
house of God, whom David and the leaders
had chosen to help the Levites. All of them
were chosen by name.

The People Pray

²¹ Then I set apart a time there at the
river of Ahava when we would not eat

any food. This was so we might put away
our pride before our God, and pray that
He would keep us and our children and
all our things safe as we traveled. ²² For I
was ashamed to ask the king for soldiers
and horsemen to keep us safe from those
who hate us on the way, because we had
said to the king, "The hand of our God
brings good to all who look for Him. But
His power and His anger are against all
who turn away from Him." ²³ So we did
not eat, and prayed to God about this. And
He listened to our prayer.

Gifts for the House of God

²⁴ Then I set apart twelve of the head religious leaders: Sherebiah, Hashabiah, and
ten of their brothers. ²⁵ And I weighed
and gave to them the silver, the gold and
the dishes and objects, which had been
given for the house of our God by the king
and his wise men and leaders, and all the
people of Israel who were there. ²⁶ I gave
them silver weighing as much as 650
men, silver dishes and objects weighing
as much as 100 men, and gold weighing as
much as 100 men. ²⁷ I gave them twenty
deep, gold dishes, worth 1,000 gold pieces,
and two pots of fine shining brass, worth
as much as gold. ²⁸ Then I said to them,
"You are holy to the Lord, and these objects are holy. The silver and the gold are
a free-will gift to the Lord God of your
fathers. ²⁹ Watch and keep them until you
weigh them in front of the head religious
leaders, the Levites, and the heads of the
family groups of Israel at Jerusalem, in
the house of the Lord." ³⁰ So the religious
leaders and the Levites took the weight of
silver and gold and objects, to bring them
to the house of our God at Jerusalem.

³¹ Then we left the river Ahava on the
twelfth day of the first month to go to Jerusalem. And God helped us and kept us
safe from those who hated us and from
those who hid waiting to fight us on the
way. ³² We came to Jerusalem and stayed
there for three days. ³³ On the fourth
day the silver and gold and objects were
weighed in the house of our God and
given to Meremoth the son of Uriah the
religious leader. With him was Eleazar
the son of Phinehas. And with them were
the Levites, Jozabad the son of Jeshua and
Noadiah the son of Binnui. ³⁴ Everything
was numbered and weighed, and all the
weight was written down.

³⁵ The people who had returned from
Babylon gave burnt gifts in worship to the

God of Israel. They gave 12 bulls for all Israel, 96 rams, 77 lambs, and 12 male goats for a sin gift. All this was a burnt gift to the Lord. **36** Then they let the king's rulers and leaders in the lands on the other side of the River know what the king said for them to do. And they helped the people and the house of God.

The Jews Return to Jerusalem

9 After these things had been done, the leaders came to me, saying, "The people of Israel and the religious leaders and the Levites have not separated themselves from the people of the lands. They have followed the sinful ways of the Canaanites, the Hittites, the Perizzites, the Jebusites, the Ammonites, the Moabites, the Egyptians, and the Amorites. **2** For they have taken some of their daughters as wives for themselves and for their sons. The holy people have mixed with the peoples of the lands. The leaders and rulers of the government have been the first in this sin." **3** When I heard this, I tore my clothing and my coat, and pulled hair from my head and face, and sat down filled with much trouble and fear. **4** Then everyone who shook with fear at the words of the God of Israel, because of the sin of the Jews who returned from Babylon, gathered around me. And I sat filled with trouble and fear until the time to give the evening gift in worship.

5 When the evening gift was given, I rose up from my trouble, with my clothing and coat torn. And I got down on my knees and spread out my hands to the Lord my God. **6** I said, "O my God, I am ashamed to lift up my face to You, my God, for our sins have risen above our heads. Our guilt has grown even to the heavens. **7** We have been very guilty since the days of our fathers to this day. Because of our sins, we and our kings and our religious leaders have been given into the hand of the kings of the lands. We have been killed by the sword. We have been carried away to a strange land. We have had our things taken from us, and have been put to shame, as it is this day. **8** But now for a short time loving-favor has been shown to us from the Lord our God. He has kept some of us alive to return to get a hold on His holy place, that our God may give light to our eyes, and give us some new life while we are under the power of Persia. **9** For we are servants, but our God has not left us even while we are servants of another nation. He has shown

us loving-kindness in the eyes of the kings of Persia. He has given us new life to set up the house of our God, to build again its parts that have been destroyed, and to give us a wall in Judah and Jerusalem. **10** And now, our God, what should we say after this? For we have turned away from Your Laws, **11** which You have given to us by Your servants who spoke for You, saying, 'The land which you are going in to take for your own is an unclean land. The peoples of the lands are unclean and have sinful ways, and they have filled it from end to end with their sin. **12** So do not let your daughters marry their sons, or their daughters marry your sons. Never look for their peace or their well-being, that you may be strong and eat the good things of the land, and leave it as a gift to your children forever.' **13** You, our God, have made our punishment less than our sins. You have given us these people who are left of the Jews and who have returned from a strange land. And after all that has come upon us because of our wrong-doing and much guilt, **14** should we break Your Laws again and marry the peoples who do these sinful things? Would You not be angry with us until we are destroyed and there is no one left? **15** O Lord God of Israel, You are right and good. For some of us have been left alive to return, as it is this day. See, we are guilty before You. No one can stand before You because of this."

The Jews Not to Marry People Living in the Land

10 Ezra was praying and telling their sins, and crying and lying on the ground before the house of God. Many people, men, women and children, gathered around him from Israel, for the people cried with many tears. **2** Shecaniah the son of Jehiel, one of the sons of Elam, said to Ezra, "We have not been faithful to our God. We have married strange women from the people of the land. But even so, there is hope for Israel. **3** So let us make an agreement with our God to put away all the wives and their children. Let this be done by the wise words of my lord and of those who shake with fear at the Word of our God. And let it be done by the Law. **4** Get up, for this is your duty, but we will be with you. Have strength of heart and do it." **5** So Ezra got up and made the head religious leaders, the Levites and all Israel promise that they would do as he had said, and they promised.

⁶ Then Ezra got up from before the house of God and went into the room of Jehohanan the son of Eliashib. He went there, but he did not eat bread or drink water, for he was filled with sorrow because the people who returned had not been faithful to God. ⁷ And it was made known to all the Jews who had returned to Judah and Jerusalem that they should gather together at Jerusalem. ⁸ Whoever would not come within three days, as the leaders had said, would have all he owned taken away from him. He would be sent away from the people who had returned from Babylon.

⁹ So all the men of Judah and Benjamin gathered together at Jerusalem within the three days. It was the twentieth day of the ninth month. All the people sat in the open space before the house of God, shaking because of this trouble and because of much rain. ¹⁰ Then Ezra the religious leader stood up and said to them, "You have been sinful and have married wives of strange lands, adding to the guilt of Israel. ¹¹ So now tell your sins to the Lord God of your fathers, and do His will. Separate yourselves from the people of the land and from the strange wives." ¹² Then all the people answered with a loud voice, "That is right! We must do as you have said. ¹³ But there are many people, and there is much rain. We cannot stand in the open. This cannot be done in one or two days, for we have sinned very much. ¹⁴ Let our leaders speak for all the people. Then let all those in our cities who have married strange wives come at certain times, together with the leaders and judges of each city. Let this be done until the anger of our God, because of this sin, is turned away from us." ¹⁵ Only Jonathan the son of Asahel and Jahzeiah the son of Tikvah were against this, with Meshullam and Shabbethai the Levite following them.

¹⁶ But the other people who had returned from Babylon agreed to do this. Ezra the religious leader chose men who were leaders of family groups for each of their fathers' houses. Each of them were chosen by name. So they met together on the first day of the tenth month to look into the problem. ¹⁷ And by the first day of the first month, they finished finding the names of all the men who had married wives from the other nations.

¹⁸ Of the sons of the religious leaders who had married strange wives were found the sons of Jeshua the son of Jozadak, and his brothers: Maaseiah, Eliezer, Jarib, and Gedaliah. ¹⁹ They promised to put away their wives, and because they were guilty, they gave a ram of the flock for their sin. ²⁰ And there were Hanani and Zebadiah of the sons of Immer, ²¹ and Maaseiah, Elijah, Shemaiah, Jehiel, and Uzziah, of the sons of Harim, ²² and Elionai, Maaseiah, Ishmael, Nethanel, Jozabad, and Elasah, of the sons of Pashur. ²³ Of the Levites there were Jozabad, Shimei, Kelaiah (that is, Kelita), Pethahiah, Judah, and Eliezer.

²⁴ Of the singers there was Eliashib. Of the gate-keepers there were Shallum, Telem, and Uri.

²⁵ Of Israel, there were Ramiah, Izziah, Malchijah, Mijamin, Eleazar, Malchijah, and Benaiah, of the sons of Parosh. ²⁶ There were Mattaniah, Zechariah, Jehiel, Abdi, Jeremoth, and Elijah, of the sons of Elam. ²⁷ There were Elioenai, Eliashib, Mattaniah, Jeremoth, Zabad, and Aziza, of the sons of Zattu. ²⁸ There were Jehohanan, Hananiah, Zabbai, and Athlai, of the sons of Bebai. ²⁹ There were Meshullam, Malluch, Adaiah, Jashub, Sheal, and Jeramoth, of the sons of Bani. ³⁰ There were Adna, Chelal, Benaiah, Maaseiah, Mattaniah, Bezalel, Binnui, and Manasseh, of the sons of Pahath-moab. ³¹ Of the sons of Harim, there were Eliezer, Isshijah, Malchijah, Shemaiah, Shimeon, ³² Benjamin, Malluch, and Shemariah. ³³ There were Mattenai, Mattattah, Zabad, Eliphelet, Jeremai, Manasseh, and Shimei, of the sons of Hashum. ³⁴ Of the sons of Bani, there were Maadai, Amram, Uel, ³⁵ Benaiah, Bedeiah, Cheluhi, ³⁶ Vaniah, Meremoth, Eliashib, ³⁷ Mattaniah, Mattenai, Jaasu, ³⁸ Bani, Binnui, Shimei, ³⁹ Shelemiah, Nathan, Adaiah, ⁴⁰ Machnadebai, Shashai, Sharai, ⁴¹ Azarel, Shelemiah, Shemariah, ⁴² Shallum, Amariah, and Joseph. ⁴³ And there were Jeiel, Mattithiah, Zabad, Zebina, Jaddai, Joel, and Benaiah, of the sons of Nebo. ⁴⁴ All these had married wives of the other nations, and some of the wives had given birth to children.

NEHEMIAH

Nehemiah Prays for His People

1 These are the words of Nehemiah the son of Hacaliah.

Now in the month of Chislev, in the twentieth year, while I was in the king's house in Susa, 2 Hanani, one of my brothers, and some men from Judah came. I asked them about the Jews who were still living and had gotten away from Babylon, and about Jerusalem. 3 They said to me, "The Jews who are left who have returned to the land from Babylon are in much trouble and shame. The wall of Jerusalem is broken down and its gates are destroyed by fire."

4 When I heard this, I sat down and cried and was filled with sorrow for days. I did not eat, and I prayed to the God of heaven. 5 I said, "O Lord God of heaven, the great God Who is honored with fear, Who keeps the agreement and loving-kindness for those who love Him and keep His Laws, 6 listen to me and let Your eyes be open. Hear the prayer of Your servant which I now pray to You day and night for the sons of Israel Your servants, telling the sins of the sons of Israel which we have sinned against You. I and my father's house have sinned. 7 We have sinned in our actions against You. We have not kept the Laws which You gave to Your servant Moses. 8 Remember what You told Your servant Moses, saying, 'If you are not faithful, I will make you go different places in other nations. 9 But if you return to Me and keep My Laws and obey them, I will gather you and bring you to the place where I have chosen for My name to be. I will do this even if you have been spread out to the farthest part of the heavens.' 10 They are Your servants and Your people whom You have made free by Your great power and strong hand. 11 O Lord, hear the prayer of Your servant and the prayer of Your servants who are happy to fear Your name. Make Your servant do well today, and give him loving-pity in front of this man."

Now I was the one who carried the cup for the king.

The King Sends Nehemiah to Jerusalem

2 In the month Nisan, in the twentieth year of King Artaxerxes, wine was in front of him. And I took up the wine and gave it to the king. Now I had not been sad in front of him before. 2 So the king said to me, "Why is your face so sad when you are not sick? It must be that you are sad in your heart." Then I was very much

afraid. 3 I said to the king, "Let the king live forever. Why should my face not be sad when the city, the place of my fathers' graves, lies waste and its gates destroyed by fire?" 4 Then the king said to me, "What are you asking for?" So I prayed to the God of heaven. 5 And I said to the king, "If it pleases the king, and if your servant has found favor in your eyes, send me to Judah, to the city of my fathers' graves. Let me build it again." 6 The king said to me, with the queen sitting beside him, "How long will you be gone, and when will you return?" So it pleased the king to send me, and I set him a time. 7 And I said to the king, "If it please the king, let letters be given to me for the leaders of the lands on the other side of the River, that they may allow me to pass through until I come to Judah. 8 Send a letter with me for Asaph, the keeper of the king's trees, that he may give me cut trees. These will be for making heavy wood pieces for the gates of the strong-place by the house of God, and for the city wall, and for the house where I will stay." And the king gave me what I asked for, because the good hand of my God was upon me.

9 Then I came to the leaders of the lands on the other side of the River and gave them the letters. Now the king had sent army captains and horsemen with me. 10 When Sanballat the Horonite and Tobiah the Ammonite workman heard about it, they were not pleased that someone had come to make things go well for the sons of Israel.

11 I came to Jerusalem and was there for three days. 12 Then I got up in the night, I and a few men with me. I did not tell anyone what my God was putting into my mind to do for Jerusalem. There was no animal with me except the one I was sitting on. 13 I went out at night by the Valley Gate to the Dragon's Well and to the Waste Gate. I looked at the walls of Jerusalem which were broken down and its gates which were destroyed by fire. 14 Then I went on to the Well Gate and the King's Pool, but there was no place for the animal I was on to pass. 15 So I went up in the night by the valley and looked at the wall. Then I went in through the Valley Gate again and returned. 16 The leaders did not know where I had gone or what I had done. And I had not yet told the Jews, the religious leaders, the rulers, the leaders, or the rest who did the work. 17 Then I said to them, "You see the

problem we have. Jerusalem lies waste and its gates are destroyed by fire. Come, let us build the wall of Jerusalem again, that we may no longer be put to shame." 18 I told them how the hand of my God had brought good to me, and the words that the king had spoken to me. Then they said, "Let us get up and build." So they put their hands to the good work. 19 But when Sanballat the Horonite, Tobiah the Ammonite servant, and Geshem the Arab heard about it, they made fun of us and hated us. They said, "What is this thing you are doing? Are you turning against the king?" 20 I answered them, "The God of heaven will make it go well for us. So we His servants will get up and build. But you have no share or right or anything to be remembered in Jerusalem."

Work on the Wall

3 Then Eliashib the head religious leader and his brothers the religious leaders started to work and built the Sheep Gate. They set it apart as holy, and hung its doors. They set apart as holy the wall to the Tower of the Hundred, and to the Tower of Hananel. 2 The men of Jericho built next to him. And Zaccur the son of Imri built next to them.

3 The sons of Hassenaah built the Fish Gate. They laid the long wood pieces that hold up the gate and hung its doors with its iron pieces. 4 Next to them Meremoth the son of Uriah, son of Hakkoz, did the needed work. Next to him Meshullam the son of Berechiah, son of Meshezabel, did the needed work. And next to him Zadok the son of Baana did the needed work. 5 Next to him the Tekoites did the needed work, but their rulers would not do the work they were told to do by their lords.

6 Joiada the son of Paseah and Meshullam the son of Besodeiah did the needed work on the Old Gate. They laid its long wood pieces and hung its doors with its iron pieces. 7 Next to them Melatiah the Gibeonite and Jadon the Meronothite did the needed work. They were the men of Gibeon and Mizpah, who were under the rule of the leader of the land on the other side of the River. 8 Next to them Uzziel the son of Harhaiah, who worked with gold, did the needed work. Next to him Hananiah, one of the men who made perfume, did the needed work. They made Jerusalem like new as far as the Wide Wall. 9 Next to them Rephaiah the son of Hur, the leader of half of Jerusalem, did

the needed work. 10 Next to them Jedaiah the son of Harumaph did the needed work beside his house. And next to him Hattush the son of Hashabneiah did the needed work. 11 Malchijah the son of Harim and Hasshub the son of Pahath-moab did the needed work on another part and on the Tower of the Stoves. 12 Next to him Shallum the son of Hallohesh, the leader of half of Jerusalem, did the needed work, he and his daughters. 13 Hanun and the people of Zanoah did the needed work on the Valley Gate. They built it and hung its doors with its iron pieces. And they built the wall to the Waste Gate, as far as 500 long steps. 14 Malchijah the son of Rechab, the leader of Beth-haccherem did the needed work on the Waste Gate. He built it and hung its doors with its iron pieces. 15 Shallum the son of Col-hozeh, the leader of Mizpah, did the needed work on the Well Gate. He built it, covered it, and hung its doors with its iron pieces. And he built the wall of the Pool of Shelah at the King's Garden as far as the steps that go down from the City of David. 16 After him Nehemiah the son of Azbuk, leader of half of Beth-zur, did the needed work as far as David's grave, and as far as the Man-made Pool and the House of the Powerful Men.

Levites Who Worked on the Wall

17 After him the Levites did the needed work, led by Rehum the son of Bani. Next to him Hashabiah, the leader of half of Keilah, did the needed work for his part of the city. 18 After him their brothers did the needed work, led by Bavvai the son of Henadad, leader of the other half of Keilah. 19 Next to him Ezer the son of Jeshua, the leader of Mizpah, did the needed work on another part, in front of the hill up to the place where the things for battle were kept at the turn of the wall. 20 After him Baruch the son of Zabbai did the needed work with much care on another part, from the turn of the wall to the door of the house of Eliashib the head religious leader. 21 After him Meremoth the son of Uriah, son of Hakkoz did the needed work on another part from the door of Eliashib's house to the end of the house.

Religious Leaders Who Worked on the Wall

22 After him the religious leaders, the men of the valley, did the needed work. 23 After them Benjamin and Hasshub did the needed work in front of their house.

After them Azariah the son of Maaseiah, son of Ananiah, did the needed work beside his house. 24 After him Binnui the son of Henadad did the needed work on another part, from the house of Azariah as far as the turn of the wall, and to the corner. 25 Palal the son of Uzai did the needed work in front of the turn of the wall and the tower which stands out from the upper house of the king, by the open space of the house soldiers. After him Pedaiah the son of Parosh 26 and the servants of the house of worship living in Ophel did the needed work as far as the front of the Water Gate on the east and the tall tower. 27 After him the Tekoites did the needed work on another part in front of the tall tower and as far as the wall of Ophel.

28 The religious leaders did the needed work above the Horse Gate. Each one worked in front of his house. 29 After them Zadok the son of Immer did the needed work in front of his house. And after him Shemaiah the son of Shecaniah, the keeper of the East Gate, did the needed work. 30 After him Hananiah the son of Shelemiah, and Hanun the sixth son of Zalaph, did the needed work on another part. After him Meshullam the son of Berechiah did the needed work in front of his own room. 31 After him Malchijah, one of the men who worked with gold, did the needed work as far as the house of the servants of the Lord's house and of the traders. He worked in front of the Master Gate and as far as the upper room of the corner. 32 The gold-workers and the traders did the needed work between the upper room of the corner and the Sheep Gate.

Working and Watching at the Same Time

4 When Sanballat heard that we were building the wall again, he became very angry. He was filled with anger and he made fun of the Jews. 2 He said to his brothers and the rich men of Samaria, "What are these weak Jews doing? Are they going to build things again for themselves? Will they give gifts on the altar in worship? Will they finish in a day? Will they get good stones for building from the dust, seeing they are burned?" 3 Tobiah the Ammonite was near him and said, "If a fox would jump on what they build, he would break their stone wall down!"

4 Hear, O our God, how we are hated! Return their shame on their own heads. Let them be taken as servants to a strange land. 5 Do not forgive their sin. Do not let their sin be covered from Your eyes. For they have made much fun of the builders. 6 But we built the wall, and the whole wall was joined together to half its height, for the people had a mind to work.

7 When Sanballat, Tobiah, the Arabs, the Ammonites and the Ashdodites heard that the work of building the walls of Jerusalem went on, and that the broken places began to be closed, they were very angry. 8 And all of them made plans together to come and fight against Jerusalem and cause trouble in it. 9 But we prayed to our God because of them. And we had men watching for them day and night. 10 So in Judah it was said, "Those who carry the loads are becoming weaker, and there is much dust. We are not able to work on the wall." 11 Those who hated us said, "They will not know it or see us until we are among them, kill them, and stop the work." 12 When the Jews who lived by them came, they told us ten times, "They will come up against us from all the places where they live." 13 So I put men in the lowest parts of the places behind the wall, in the open places. I put the people in place by their families with their swords, spears and bows. 14 When I saw their fear, I got up and said to the rulers and leaders and the rest of the people, "Do not be afraid of them. Remember the Lord Who is great and honored with fear. And fight for your brothers, your sons, your daughters, your wives, and your houses."

15 When those who hated us heard that it was known to us, and that God had brought trouble to their plan, then all of us returned to the wall. Each one returned to his work. 16 From that day on, half of my servants did the work while half of them held the spears, battle-coverings, bows, and battle clothes. And the captains stood behind the whole house of Judah. 17 Those who were building the wall and those who carried loads did their work with one hand, and held something to fight with in the other hand. 18 Each builder wore his sword at his side as he built. The man who blew the horn stood beside me. 19 I said to the rulers, leaders, and the rest of the people, "There is very much work to do, and we are separated on the wall far from one another. 20 In whatever place you hear the sound of the horn, gather together to us there. Our God will fight for us."

21 So we did the work with half of them holding spears from sunrise until the stars

came out. 22 At that time I also said to the people, "Let every man and his servant spend the night within Jerusalem so they may watch for us during the night and work during the day." 23 So none of us, I, my brothers, my servants, or the soldiers who followed me, took off our clothes. Each man kept something to fight with in his hand, even when he went to wash.

Help for Poor People

5 Now the people and their wives began to cry in a loud voice against their Jewish brothers. 2 For some said, "We, our sons and our daughters are many. Let us get grain, that we may eat and live." 3 And some said, "We are giving up our fields, our grape-vines and our houses, that we might get grain because of no food." 4 Others said, "We have taken money from others to pay the king's tax on our fields and our grape-vines, and we must pay back this money. 5 Our flesh is like the flesh of our brothers. Our children are like their children. Yet we are made to sell our sons and daughters to work for others. Some of our daughters have already been sold and taken away. We cannot do anything, because our fields and vines belong to others."

6 I was very angry when I heard their cry and these words. 7 I thought about it, and spoke sharp words to the rulers and leaders. I said to them, "You are making the people pay back more money than you give them to use!" So I gathered many people together against them. 8 And I said to them, "As we have been able, we have bought and freed our Jewish brothers who were sold to the nations. But you would even sell your brothers that they may be sold to us!" They were quiet and could not find a word to say. 9 So I said, "What you are doing is not good. Should you not walk in the fear of our God to stop the nations who hate us from putting us to shame? 10 I, my brothers and my servants are giving them money and grain. Let us stop making them pay back more than they are given. 11 Return to them this very day their fields, vines, olive trees, and houses. Also return to them one-hundredth part of the money, grain, new wine, and oil, that you have been making them pay." 12 Then they said, "We will give these back and will ask nothing from them. We will do just as you say." So I called the religious leaders, and had them promise that they would keep their word. 13 I shook out the front of my clothing and said, "So may God shake out

every man from his house and from all he has worked for, who does not keep this promise. So may he be shaken out and made empty." And all the people said, "Let it be so!" and praised the Lord. Then they did as they had promised.

Nehemiah Does Not Think of Himself

14 Also, in the twelve years after I was chosen to be their ruler in the land of Judah, from the twentieth year to the thirty-second year of King Artaxerxes, I and my brothers did not eat the food allowed to the ruler. 15 The rulers who were before me made the people work very hard. They took bread and wine from them, besides forty pieces of silver. Even their servants ruled over the people. But I did not do so because of the fear of God. 16 I also worked on this wall myself, and we did not buy any land. And all my servants were gathered there for the work. 17 Also, there were 150 Jews and leaders at my table, besides those who came to us from the nations that were around us. 18 One bull, six of the best sheep, and birds were made ready for me each day. All kinds of wine were brought in every ten days. Yet for all this I did not make them give me the food allowed to me as ruler, because the work was very hard for these people. 19 O my God, remember me for good for all I have done for these people.

Neighbors Do Not Want the Wall Built

6 It was told to Sanballat, Tobiah, Geshem the Arab, and to the rest of those who hated us that I had built the wall again. They were told that the wall had no more open places, but I had not yet set up the doors in the gates. 2 So Sanballat and Geshem sent word to me, saying, "Come, let us meet together in one of the villages in the plain of Ono." But they were planning to hurt or kill me. 3 So I sent men with word to them, saying, "I am doing a great work and I cannot come down. Why should the work stop while I leave it and come down to you?" 4 They sent word to me four times in this way, and I gave them the same answer. 5 Then Sanballat sent his servant to me in the same way for a fifth time, with an open letter in his hand. 6 In it was written, "It is said among the nations, and Gashmu says that you and the Jews are planning to turn against the king. This is why you are building the wall again. It is said that you wish to be their king. 7 You have also

chosen men who tell what will happen to speak to the people in Jerusalem about you, saying, 'A king is in Judah!' Now this will be told to the king. So come now, let us meet to speak with each other." 8 Then I sent word to him, saying, "No such things as you say have been done. You are making them up in your own mind." 9 For they all wanted to make us afraid, thinking, "Their hands will become weak and the work will not be done." But now, O God, strengthen my hands.

10 When I went into the house of Shemaiah the son of Delaiah, son of Mehetabel, who was at home, said, "Let us meet together inside the house of God, and close the doors of the Lord's house for they are coming to kill you. They are coming to kill you at night." 11 But I said, "Should a man like me run away? And could a man such as I go into the house of God to save his life? I will not go in." 12 Then I understood that God had not sent him. He had spoken these words against me because Tobiah and Sanballat had paid him to do it. 13 He had been paid to try to make me afraid and to do as he said and sin, so they would have sinful things to say about me and put me to shame. 14 O my God, remember Tobiah and Sanballat by these works of theirs. And remember Noadiah and the rest of the men who tell what will happen who were trying to make me afraid.

The Wall Is Finished

15 So the wall was finished on the twenty-fifth day of the month of Elul, in fifty-two days. 16 When all those who hated us heard about it, all the nations around us were afraid and troubled. For they saw that this work had been done with the help of our God. 17 In those days the rulers of Judah sent many letters to Tobiah, and Tobiah's letters came to them. 18 For many in Judah were joined by promise to him because he was the son-in-law of Shecaniah the son of Arah. And his son Jehohanan had married the daughter of Meshullam, son of Berechiah. 19 Also they spoke about Tobiah's good works in front of me, and told my words to him. Then Tobiah sent letters to make me afraid.

7 When the wall was built and I had set up the doors, and the gate-keepers and singers and Levites were chosen, 2 I gave my brother Hanani, and Hanaiah the captain of the strong-place, the work of watching over Jerusalem. For he was a faithful man and honored God with fear more than many. 3 I said to them, "Do not let the gates of Jerusalem be opened until the sun is hot. And while the soldiers are on duty watching the gates, let them shut and lock the doors. Choose soldiers from the people of Jerusalem, each one for the place he is to keep watch, and each in front of his own house."

The Jews Return to Jerusalem

4 Now the city was wide and large, but the people in it were few and the houses were not built. 5 Then my God put it into my heart to gather together the rulers, the leaders and the people to have their names written down by families. And I found the book of the family names of those who came up first. This is what I found written in it. 6 These are the people who left the land of Babylon and returned to Jerusalem and Judah, each to his own city. Their families had been taken away to Babylon by Nebuchadnezzar the king of Babylon. 7 These people returned with Zerubbabel, Jeshua, Nehemiah, Azariah, Raamiah, Nahamani, Mordecai, Bilshan, Mispereth, Bigvai, Nehum, and Baanah.

The number of the men of Israel: 8 2,172 sons of Parosh, 9 372 sons of Shephatiah, 10 652 sons of Arah, 11 2,818 sons of Pahath-moab, of the sons of Jeshua and Joab, 12 1,254 sons of Elam, 13 845 sons of Zattu, 14 760 sons of Zaccai, 15 648 sons of Binnui, 16 628 sons of Bebai, 17 2,322 sons of Azgad, 18 667 sons of Adonikam, 19 2,067 sons of Bigvai, 20 655 sons of Adin, 21 98 sons of Ater, of Hezekiah, 22 328 sons of Hashum, 23 324 sons of Bezai, 24 112 sons of Hariph, 25 95 sons of Gibeon, 26 188 sons of Bethlehem and Netophah, 27 128 sons of Anathoth, 28 42 sons of Bethazmaveth, 29 743 sons of Kiriath-jearim, Chephirah, and Beeroth, 30 621 sons of Ramah and Geba, 31 122 sons of Michmas, 32 123 sons of Bethel and Ai, 33 52 sons of the other Nebo, 34 1,254 sons of the other Elam, 35 320 sons of Harim, 36 345 sons of Jericho, 37 721 sons of Lod, Hadid, and Ono, 38 3,930 sons of Senaah.

39 The religious leaders: 973 sons of Jedaiah of the house of Jeshua, 40 1,052 sons of Immer, 41 1,247 sons of Pashhur, 42 1,017 sons of Harim.

43 The Levites: 74 sons of Jeshua, of Kadmiel, of the sons of Hodevah. 44 The singers: 148 sons of Asaph. 45 The gate-keepers: 138 sons of Shallum, of Ater, of Talmon, of Akkub, of Hatita, and of Shobai.

46 The servants of the house of God: the sons of Ziha, the sons of Hasupha, the sons of Tabbaoth, 47 the sons of Keros, the sons of Sia, the sons of Padon, 48 the sons of Lebana, the sons of Hagaba, the sons of Shalmai, 49 the sons of Hanan, the sons of Giddel, the sons of Gahar, 50 the sons of Reaiah, the sons of Rezin, the sons of Nekoda, 51 the sons of Gazzam, the sons of Uzza, the sons of Paseah, 52 the sons of Besai, the sons of Meunim, the sons of Nephushesim, 53 the sons of Bakbuk, the sons of Hakupha, the sons of Harhur, 54 the sons of Bazlith, the sons of Mehida, the sons of Harsha, 55 the sons of Barkos, the sons of Sisera, the sons of Temah, 56 the sons of Neziah, and the sons of Hatipha.

57 The sons of Solomon's servants: the sons of Sotai, the sons of Sophereth, the sons of Perida, 58 the sons of Jaala, the sons of Darkon, the sons of Giddel, 59 the sons of Shephatiah, the sons of Hattil, the sons of Pochereth-hazzebaim, and the sons of Amon. 60 All the servants in the house of God and the sons of Solomon's servants were 392.

61 Now these were the men who came up from Tel-melah, Tel-harsha, Cherub, Addon, and Immer. But they were not able to prove their fathers' houses or that they were children of Israel: 62 642 sons of Delaiah, Tobiah, and Nekoda. 63 And the sons of the religious leaders: the sons of Hobaiah, Hakkoz, and Barzillai, who had married one of the daughters of Barzillai the Gileadite, and was called by their name. 64 These men looked for their names among the names of all the families, but could not find them. So they were thought of as being unclean, and were not allowed to work as religious leaders. 65 And the leader told them that they should not eat from the most holy things until a religious leader learned God's will by the Urim and Thummin.

66 There were 42,360 people in all, 67 besides the 7,337 men and women servants, and 245 singing men and women. 68 They had 736 horses, 245 mules, 69 435 camels, and 6,720 donkeys.

70 Some from among the heads of the family groups gave to the work. The ruler gave 1,000 gold pieces, fifty deep dishes, and 530 sets of clothing for the religious leaders. 71 And some of the leaders of family groups gave 20,000 gold pieces and 2,200 silver pieces. 72 The rest of the people gave 20,000 gold pieces, 2,000 silver pieces, and 67 sets of clothing for the religious leaders.

73 Now the religious leaders, the Levites, the gate-keepers, the singers, some of the people, the servants in the house of the Lord, and all Israel, lived in their cities.

When the seventh month had come, the sons of Israel were in their cities.

Ezra Reads the Law

8 Then all the people gathered as one man at the open space in front of the Water Gate. They asked Ezra the writer to bring the book of the Law of Moses which the Lord had given to Israel. 2 And on the first day of the seventh month, Ezra the religious leader brought the Law to the gathering of men, women, and all who were able to understand. 3 He read from it in the open space by the Water Gate from early morning until noon. He read it in front of men and women and those who were able to understand and all the people listened to the book of the Law. 4 Ezra the writer stood on a raised floor of wood which they had made for this reason. Beside him stood Mattithiah, Shema, Anaiah, Uriah, Hilkiah, and Maaseiah, on his right. And Pedaiah, Mishael, Malchijah, Hashum, Hash-baddanah, Zechariah, and Meshullam stood on his left. 5 All the people saw Ezra open the book, for he was standing above all of them. And all the people stood up when he opened it. 6 Then Ezra gave honor and thanks to the Lord the great God. And all the people answered, "Let it be so!" while lifting up their hands. They bowed low with their faces to the ground and worshiped the Lord. 7 Jeshua, Bani, Sherebiah, Jamin, Akkub, Shabbethai, Hodiah, Maaseiah, Kelita, Azariah, Jozabad, Hanan, Pelaiah, and the Levites, helped the people understand the Law, while the people stayed in their places. 8 They read from the book of the Law of God, telling the meaning of it so that they understood what was read.

9 Then Nehemiah, who was the ruler, and Ezra the religious leader and writer, and the Levites who taught the people, said to all of them, "This day is holy to the Lord your God. Do not cry or be filled with sorrow." For all the people were crying when they heard the words of the Law. 10 Ezra said to them, "Go, eat and drink what you enjoy, and give some to him who has nothing ready. For this day is holy to our Lord. Do not be sad for the joy of the Lord is your strength." 11 So the Levites

made all the people quiet, saying, "Be quiet, for this is a holy day. Do not be sad." 12 And all the people went away to eat and drink, to share what they had, and to show their joy. They understood the words which had been made known to them.

13 On the second day the heads of the family groups of all the people, the religious leaders, and the Levites were gathered to Ezra the writer, that they might better understand the words of the Law. 14 They found written in the Law how the Lord had said through Moses that the sons of Israel should live in tents during the special supper of the seventh month. 15 So they made it known in all their cities and in Jerusalem, saying, "Go out to the hills and bring branches of olive, wild olive, myrtle, palm, and other trees with leaves, to make tents, as it is written." 16 So the people went out and brought them and made tents for themselves, each on his roof. And they made tents in their open spaces, in the open spaces of the house of God, in the place by the Water Gate, and in the place by the Gate of Ephraim. 17 All the people who had returned from Babylon made tents and lived in them. The sons of Israel had not done so since the days of Joshua the son of Nun. And there was much joy. 18 Every day Ezra read from the book of the Law of God, from the first day to the last day. They held the special supper seven days, and on the eighth day there was a special gathering, as it is writ ten in the Law.

The People Tell Their Sins to God

9 Now on the twenty-fourth day of this month the sons of Israel gathered together, but they did not eat. They dressed in cloth made from hair, and put dirt on their heads. 2 The children of Israel separated themselves from all those of other nations. They stood and told their sins and the sins of their fathers to God. 3 While they stood in their place, they read from the book of the Law of the Lord their God for a fourth of the day. And for another fourth they told their sins and worshiped the Lord their God. 4 Jeshua, Bani, Kadmiel, Shebaniah, Bunni, Sherebiah, Bani, and Chenani stood on the Levites' raised floor. And they cried with a loud voice to the Lord their God.

5 Then the Levites, Jeshua, Kadmiel, Bani, Hashabneiah, Sherebiah, Hodiah, Shebaniah, and Pethahiah, said, "Stand up and give honor and thanks to the Lord

your God forever and ever! O may Your great name be praised!"

The Prayer—Telling of Their Sins

6 "You alone are the Lord. You made the heavens, the heaven of heavens with all their angels. You have made the earth and all that is on it, and the seas and all that is in them. You give life to all of them, and the angels of heaven bow down to You. 7 You are the Lord God, Who chose Abram and brought him out from Ur of the Chaldees and gave him the name Abraham. 8 You found his heart faithful to You and made an agreement with him, to give his children and their children's children the land of the Canaanite, the Hittite, the Amorite, the Perizzite, the Jebusite, and the Girgashite. And You have done what You promised, for You are right and good.

9 "You saw the trouble of our fathers in Egypt. You heard their cry by the Red Sea. 10 Then You made special things to see and did powerful works against Pharaoh, against all his servants and all the people of his land. For You knew that they were proud and made it hard for our fathers. And You made a name for Yourself, as it is this day. 11 You divided the sea in front of them, so they passed through the sea on dry ground. And You threw those who went after them into the deep sea, like a stone into troubled waters. 12 You led the people during the day with a cloud, and with a pillar of fire during the night to light the way they were to go. 13 Then You came down on Mount Sinai and spoke with them from heaven. You gave them Laws that are right and true and good. 14 You made known to them Your holy Day of Rest, and gave them Laws through Your servant Moses. 15 You gave them bread from heaven for their hunger. You brought them water from a rock for their thirst. And You told them to go in to take for their own the land You promised to give them.

16 "But they, our fathers, acted with pride. They became strong-willed and would not listen to Your Words. 17 They would not listen, and did not remember Your powerful works which You had done among them. So they became strong-willed and chose a leader to return to their hard work in Egypt. But You are a forgiving God. You are kind and loving, slow to anger, and full of loving-kindness. You did not leave them. 18 They even melted gold and made a calf, and said, 'This is your God Who brought you up from Egypt.'

They spoke sinful words against You. 19 But You, in Your great loving-kindness, did not leave them in the desert. The pillar of cloud which led them on their way during the day did not leave them. And the pillar of fire which gave light to the way they were to go during the night did not leave them. 20 You gave Your good Spirit to teach them. You did not keep Your bread from heaven from their mouths. And You gave them water when they were thirsty. 21 For forty years You kept them alive in the desert and gave them everything they needed. Their clothes did not wear out, and their feet did not become sore. 22 You gave them nations and peoples, and You gave them every part. For their own they took the land of Sihon king of Heshbon and the land of Og king of Bashan. 23 You made their sons as many as the stars of heaven. And You brought them into the land which You had told their fathers to go into and take for their own. 24 So their sons went into the land and took it. You gave them power over the people of the land, the Canaanites. You gave these people into their hand, with their kings and the peoples of the land, to do with them as they would. 25 They took strong cities and a rich land. They took houses full of every good thing. They took wells that had been dug, grape-vines, olive trees, and many fruit trees. So they ate and were filled and became fat. They were glad because You were so good to them.

26 "But they would not obey and they turned against You. They put Your Law behind their backs. They killed the men who tell what will happen who had spoken sharp words to them telling them to return to You. The people spoke very sinful words against You. 27 So You gave them into the hand of those who made it hard for them. But when they cried to You in the time of their trouble, You heard from heaven. And by Your great loving-kindness You sent men to save them from those who made it hard for them. 28 But as soon as they had rest, they sinned against You again. So You left them in the hand of those who hated them, so that they ruled over them. When they cried again to You, You heard from heaven. And many times You took them away from trouble because of Your loving-kindness. 29 You spoke sharp words to them to turn them back to Your Law. Yet they acted in pride and did not listen to Your Words, but sinned against Your Laws, by which if a man obeys them he will live. They were strong-willed and made their hearts hard against You, and would not listen. 30 But You did not give up taking care of them for many years. You spoke sharp words to them by Your Spirit through the men who tell what will happen. Yet they would not listen. So You gave them into the hand of the peoples of the lands. 31 But in Your great loving-kindness, You did not make an end of them or leave them for You are a kind and loving God.

32 "So now, our God, the great and powerful God, honored with fear, Who keeps His agreement and loving-kindness, do not let all this trouble look small in Your eyes which has come upon us, our kings, our princes, our religious leaders, our men who tell what will happen, our fathers, and on all Your people since the days of the kings of Assyria to this day. 33 Yet You have been right and fair in all that has come upon us. For You have been faithful, but we have sinned. 34 Our kings, leaders, religious leaders, and fathers have not kept Your Law or listened to Your Laws and Your strong words which You have given them. 35 Even when they were in their own nation, with all the good things You gave them and with the great rich land You gave them, they did not serve You or turn from their sins. 36 See, we are servants today. We are servants in the land You gave to our fathers. You gave it to them so they could eat the fruit and have other good things. 37 The many good things the land gives are used by the kings whom You have put over us because of our sins. They also rule over our bodies and over our cattle as they please. So we are in much trouble.

The People Sign an Agreement

38 "Now because of all this we are making an agreement in writing. And our leaders, our Levites, and our religious leaders have put their mark on it."

10 Those who put their mark on the agreement were Nehemiah the ruler, the son of Hacaliah, and Zedekiah, 2 Seraiah, Azariah, Jeremiah, 3 Pashhur, Amariah, Malchijah, 4 Hattush, Shebaniah, Malluch, 5 Harim, Meremoth, Obadiah, 6 Daniel, Ginnethon, Baruch, 7 Meshullam, Abijah, Mijamin, 8 Maaziah, Bilgai, and Shemaiah. These are the religious leaders. 9 The Levites are Jeshua the son of Azaniah, Binnui of the sons of Henadad,

Kadmiel, 10 and their brothers, Shebaniah, Hodiah, Kelita, Pelaiah, Hanan, 11 Mica, Rehob, Hashabiah, 12 Zaccur, Sherebiah, Shebaniah, 13 Hodiah, Bani, and Beninuu. 14 The leaders of the people are Parosh, Pahath-moab, Elam, Zattu, Bani, 15 Bunni, Azgad, Bebai, 16 Adonijah, Bigvai, Adin, 17 Ater, Hezekiah, Azzur, 18 Hodiah, Hashum, Bezai, 19 Hariph, Anathoth, Nebai, 20 Magpiash, Meshullam, Hezir, 21 Meshezabel, Zadok, Jaddua, 22 Pelatiah, Hanan, Anaiah, 23 Hoshea, Hananiah, Hasshub, 24 Hallohesh, Pilha, Shobek, 25 Rehum, Hashabnah, Maaseiah, 26 Ahiah, Hanan, Anan, 27 Malluch, Harim, and Baanah.

The Agreement That Was Signed

28 The rest of the people, the religious leaders, Levites, gate-keepers, singers, servants in the Lord's house, and all those who had separated themselves from the peoples of the lands to the Law of God, their wives, sons, and daughters, all those who had much learning and understanding, 29 are joining with their brothers, their leaders. They all promise and swear to walk in God's Law which was given through Moses, God's servant, and to keep and obey all the Words and Laws of God our Lord. 30 We promise not to give our daughters in marriage to the people of the land, or take their daughters for our sons. 31 If the people of the land bring grain or things to sell on the Day of Rest, we will not buy from them on the Day of Rest or a holy day. During the seventh year we will not grow food in the fields and will do away with anything that is owed.

32 We also promise to give one-third part of a piece of silver each year for the work of the house of our God. 33 This will be for the holy bread, the grain and burnt gifts that must be given, for gifts on the Days of Rest, the new moon, and the special times, for the holy gifts, and for the sin gifts to pay for the sins of Israel, and for all the work of the house of our God.

34 We drew names among the religious leaders, the Levites and the people, by our family groups, for the wood to be brought to the house of our God at certain times each year. It is to be burned on the altar of the Lord our God as it is written in the Law. 35 We promise to bring the first-fruits of our ground and the first-fruits of all the fruit of every tree to the house of the Lord each year. 36 We promise to bring to the house of our God the first-born of our sons, animals, cattle and flocks, as it is written in the Law, for the religious leaders who are working in the house of our God. 37 We will bring the first of our grain, our gifts, the fruit of every tree, the new wine and the oil to the religious leaders in the rooms of the house of our God. And we will bring a tenth part of what we get from our ground to the Levites. For the Levites are the ones who receive a tenth part from all the farming towns. 38 The religious leader, the son of Aaron, will be with the Levites when they receive a tenth part. And the Levites will bring up a tenth part of all the tenth parts to the rooms of the store-house of the house of our God. 39 For the sons of Israel and the sons of Levi will bring the gifts of grain, new wine and oil to the store-rooms where the tools of the holy place are kept. The religious leaders who serve, the gate-keepers, and the singers stay here. We will not forget to take care of the house of our God.

The People Who Lived in Jerusalem

11 Now the leaders of the people lived in Jerusalem. But the rest of the people drew names to bring one out of ten to live in Jerusalem, the holy city, while nine-tenths stayed in the other cities. 2 And the people praised all the men who were willing to live in Jerusalem.

3 These are the leaders of the lands who lived in Jerusalem but in the cities of Judah every one lived on his own land there. Israel, the religious leaders, the Levites, the servants in the house of God, and the children of Solomon's servants. 4 Some of the sons of Judah and some of the sons of Benjamin lived in Jerusalem. Of the sons of Judah there was Athaiah the son of Uzziah, son of Zechariah, son of Amariah, son of Shephatiah, son of Mahalalel, of the sons of Perez, 5 and Maaseiah the son of Baruch, son of Col-hozeh, son of Hazaiah, son of Adaiah, son of Joiarib, son of Zechariah, son of the Shilonite. 6 All the sons of Perez who lived in Jerusalem were 468 able men.

7 The sons of Benjamin are Sallu the son of Meshullam, son of Joed, son of Pedaiah, son of Kolaiah, son of Maaseiah, son of Ithiel, son of Jeshaiah, 8 and after him Gabbai and Sallai, 928 men. 9 Joel the son of Zichri watched over them, and Judah the son of Hassenuah was second over the city.

10 Of the religious leaders there were Jedaiah the son of Joiarib, Jachin, 11 Seraiah

the son of Hilkiah, son of Meshullam, son of Zadok, son of Meraioth, son of Ahitub, the leader of the house of God, 12 and their brothers who did the work of the house of God, 822 men. And there was Adaiah the son of Jeroham, son of Pelaliah, son of Amzi, son of Zechariah, son of Pashhur, son of Malchijah, 13 and his brothers, heads of family groups, 242 men. And there was Amashsai the son of Azarel, son of Ahzai, son of Meshillemoth, son of Immer, 14 and their brothers, 128 men with strength of heart. Zabdiel, the son of Haggedolim, watched over them.

15 Of the Levites there was Shemaiah the son of Hasshub, son of Azrikam, son of Hashabiah, son of Bunni, 16 and Shabbethai and Jozabad, from the leaders of the Levites. They watched over the outside work of the house of God. 17 And there was Mattaniah the son of Mica, son of Zabdi, son of Asaph, who was the leader in beginning the giving of thanks at prayer, and Bakbukiah, the second among his brothers. And there was Abda the son of Shammua, son of Galal, son of Jeduthun. 18 All the Levites in the holy city were 284.

19 The gate-keepers, Akkub, Talmon, and their brothers, who kept watch at the gates, were 172. 20 The rest of Israel, of the religious leaders and of the Levites, were in all the cities of Judah, each in the land he had been given. 21 But the servants of the house of God were living in Ophel. Ziha and Gishpa were over the servants of the house of God.

22 The one who watched over the Levites in Jerusalem was Uzzi the son of Bani, son of Hashabiah, son of Mattaniah, son of Mica, from the sons of Asaph, the singers for the work of the house of God. 23 For the king had said that the singers must be given what they need each day. 24 Pethahiah the son of Meshezabel, of the sons of Zerah the son of Judah, was the king's workman in everything to do with the people.

The People Living outside Jerusalem

25 As for the villages with their fields, some of the sons of Judah lived in Kiriatharba and its villages, in Dibon and its villages, in Jekabzeel and its villages, 26 in Jeshua, Moladah, Beth-pelet, 27 Hazarshual, Beersheba and its villages, 28 Ziklag, Meconah and its villages, 29 En-rimmon, Zorah, Jarmuth, 30 Zanoah, Adullam, and their villages, Lachish and its fields, and Azekah and its villages. So they lived from

Beersheba as far as the valley of Hinnom. 31 The sons of Benjamin lived in Geba, Michmash, Aija, Bethel and its villages, 32 Anathoth, Nob, Ananiah, 33 Hazor, Ramah, Gittaim, 34 Hadid, Zeboim, Neballat, 35 Lod, and Ono, the valley of able workmen. 36 And certain groups of the Levites in Judah were joined to Benjamin.

The Religious Leaders and Levites

12 These are the religious leaders and the Levites who came up with Zerubbabel the son of Shealtiel, and Jeshua. There were Seraiah, Jeremiah, Ezra, 2 Amariah, Malluch, Hattush, 3 Shecaniah, Rehum, Meremoth, 4 Iddo, Ginnethoi, Abijah, 5 Mijamin, Maadiah, Bilgah, 6 Shemaiah, Joiarib, Jedaiah, 7 Sallu, Amok, Hilkiah, and Jedaiah. These were the heads of the religious leaders and their brothers in the days of Jeshua.

8 The Levites were Jeshua, Binnui, Kadmiel, Sherebiah, Judah, and Mattaniah, who with his brothers was over the songs of giving thanks. 9 Bakbukiah and Unni, their brothers, stood beside them in their work. 10 Jeshua was the father of Joiakim. Joiakim was the father of Eliashib. Eliashib was the father of Joiada. 11 Joiada was the father of Jonathan. Jonathan was the father of Jaddua.

12 In the days of Joiakim the religious leader, these were the heads of the family groups: Meraiah of Seraiah, Hananiah of Jeremiah, 13 Meshullam of Ezra, Jehohanan of Amariah, 14 Jonathan of Malluchi, Joseph of Shebaniah, 15 Adna of Harim, Helkai of Meraioth, 16 Zechariah of Iddo, Meshullam of Ginnethon, 17 Zichri of Abijah, Piltai of Moadiah of Miniamin, 18 Shammua of Bilgah, Jehonathan of Shemaiah, 19 Mattenai of Joiarib, Uzzi of Jedaiah, 20 Kallai of Sallai, Eber of Amok, 21 Hashabiah of Hilkiah, and Nethanel of Jedaiah.

22 As for the Levites, in the days of Eliashib, Joiada, Johanan, and Jaddua, the heads of the family groups were written down. So were the religious leaders in the rule of Darius the Persian. 23 The sons of Levi, the heads of the family groups, were written down in the Book of the Chronicles until the days of Johanan the son of Eliashib. 24 The heads of the Levites were Hashabiah, Sherebiah, and Jeshua the son of Kadmiel, with their brothers beside them. Each group praised and gave thanks, as David the man of God had told them. 25 Mattaniah, Bakbukiah, Obadiah,

Meshullam, Talmon and Akkub were gate-keepers. They watched at the store-houses of the gates. 26 These men worked in the days of Joiakim the son of Jeshua, the son of Jozadak, and in the days of Nehemiah the ruler and of Ezra the religious leader and writer.

Nehemiah Sets Apart the Jerusalem Wall for God

27 At the special time to praise God for the wall of Jerusalem, they looked for all the Levites in the places where they lived and brought them to Jerusalem so they might join them at this special time with happiness. They sang songs of thanks and other songs as timbrels and harps were played. 28 So the sons of the singers were gathered from the land around Jerusalem, from the villages of the Nethophathites, 29 from Beth-gilgal, and from their fields in Geba and Azmaveth. For the singers had built villages for themselves around Jerusalem. 30 The religious leaders and the Levites made themselves holy, and they made the people, the gates, and the wall holy.

31 Then I had the leaders of Judah come up on top of the wall. And I picked two large groups of singers to give thanks. One group was to go to the right on top of the wall to the Waste Gate. 32 Hoshaiah and half of the leaders of Judah followed them, 33 with Azariah, Ezra, Meshullam, 34 Judah, Benjamin, Shemaiah, Jeremiah, 35 and some of the sons of the religious leaders blowing horns. Then followed Zechariah the son of Jonathan, son of Shemaiah, son of Mattaniah, son of Micaiah, son of Zaccur, son of Asaph, 36 and his brothers, Shemaiah, Azarel, Milalai, Gilalai, Maai, Nethanel, Judah, and Hanani, with the objects that David the man of God had made for playing music. And Ezra the writer went before them. 37 At the Well Gate they went straight up the steps of the city of David, by the steps of the wall above the house of David, to the Water Gate on the east.

38 The second group went to the left. I followed them with half of the people on the wall, above the Tower of Stoves, to the Wide Wall. 39 They went above the Gate of Ephraim, by the Old Gate, the Fish Gate, the Tower of Hananel, and the Tower of the Hundred, as far as the Sheep Gate. And they stopped at the Gate of the Watchmen. 40 Then the two groups stood in the house of God. So did I and half of the leaders with me, 41 and the religious leaders, Eliakim,

Maaseiah, Miniamin, Micaiah, Elioenai, Zechariah, and Hananiah, with the horns, 42 and Maaseiah, Shemaiah, Eleazar, Uzzi, Jehohanan, Malchijah, Elam, and Ezer. And the singers sang with Jezrahiah as their leader. 43 On that day they gave many good gifts and were glad because God had given them great joy. Even the women and children were filled with joy, so that the joy of Jerusalem was heard from far away.

44 On that day men were chosen for the work of the store-rooms for the gifts, the first-fruits, and the tenth part for the Lord. They were to gather into them from the fields near the towns what was to be given by the Law to the religious leaders and Levites. For Judah was filled with joy because of the religious leaders and Levites who did the work. 45 They did the work of their God and the work of making everything clean from sin, together with the singers and the gate-keepers. They did as David and his son Solomon had told them. 46 For in the days of David and Asaph, long ago, there were leaders of the singers, and songs of praise and thanks to God. 47 So all Israel in the days of Zerubbabel and Nehemiah gave what was to be given to the singers and gate-keepers each day. They set apart what was for the Levites. And the Levites set apart what was for the sons of Aaron.

Nehemiah's Last Words

13 On that day they read from the book of Moses in the hearing of the people. And there was found written in it that no Ammonite or Moabite should ever gather together to worship with the people of God. 2 It was because they did not meet the sons of Israel with food and water, but paid Balaam to curse them. Yet our God turned the curse into good. 3 When the people heard the Law, they kept out all those of other nations from Israel.

4 Before this, Eliashib the religious leader, who watched over the store-rooms of the house of our God, being close to Tobiah, 5 made a room for him. They had before used the room to store the grain gifts, special perfume, dishes, and the tenth part of grain, wine and oil to be given to the Levites, the singers and the gate-keepers, and the gifts for the religious leaders. 6 But during all this time I was not in Jerusalem. For in the thirty-second year of Artaxerxes king of Babylon, I had gone to the king. Then after some time, I asked the king to let me go, 7 and came to Jerusalem. I

learned about the sinful thing Eliashib had done for Tobiah, by giving a room for him in the house of God. 8 I was very angry, and threw all the things of Tobiah's house out of the room. 9 Then I said that the rooms must be made clean, and put back the things of the house of God with the grain gifts and the special perfume.

10 I also learned that what was to be given to the Levites had not been given. So the Levites and the singers who did the work had gone back to their own fields. 11 So I spoke sharp words to the leaders and said, "Why is the house of God no longer cared for?" Then I gathered them together and returned them to their duties. 12 All the people of Judah then brought the tenth part of the grain, wine and oil into the store-houses. 13 I had Shelemiah the religious leader, Zadok the writer, and Pedaiah of the Levites, watch over the store-houses. With them was Hanan the son of Zaccur, the son of Mattaniah. For they were trusted, and it was their duty to give the needed things to their brothers. 14 Remember me for this, O my God. Do not forget my good works which I have done for the house of my God and His worship.

15 In those days I saw in Judah some who were crushing grapes to make wine on the Day of Rest. I saw them bringing in bags of grain and loading them on donkeys, as well as wine, grapes, figs, and all kinds of loads. And they brought them into Jerusalem on the Day of Rest. So I spoke sharp words to them on the day they sold food. 16 Men of Tyre were living there who brought in fish and all kinds of things to sell. They sold them to the people of Judah on the Day of Rest, even in Jerusalem. 17 Then I spoke sharp words to the leaders of Judah, saying, "What is this sinful thing you are doing by not keeping the Day of Rest holy? 18 Did not your fathers do the same, so that our God brought all this trouble to us and to this city? Yet you are bringing more anger to Israel by not keeping the Day of Rest holy."

19 Just as it became dark at the gates of Jerusalem before the Day of Rest, I had them shut the doors. And I would not let them be opened until after the Day of Rest. Then I had some of my servants watch the gates, that no load should come in on the Day of Rest. 20 Once or twice the traders and sellers stayed the night outside Jerusalem. 21 Then I spoke sharp words to them, saying, "Why do you stay the night in front of the wall? If you do so again, I will send men out to make you leave." From that time on they did not come on the Day of Rest. 22 Then I told the Levites to make themselves free from sin and come and watch the gates to keep the Day of Rest holy. Remember me for this also, O my God. Be good to me because of Your great loving-kindness.

23 In those days I saw that the Jews had married women from Ashdod, Ammon, and Moab. 24 Half of their children spoke the language of Ashdod. They could not speak the language of Judah, but the language of their own people. 25 So I fought with them and cursed them and beat some of them and pulled out their hair. And I made them promise in the name of God, saying, "You must not give your daughters to their sons, or take their daughters for your sons or for yourselves. 26 Did not King Solomon of Israel sin because of these women? Yet among the many nations there was no king like him. He was loved by his God, and God made him king over all Israel. But the women from other nations caused even him to sin. 27 Should we hear now that you also are sinning in the same way by not being faithful to our God, by marrying women from other nations?" 28 Even one of the sons of Joiada, the son of Eliashib the religious leader, was a son-in-law of Sanballat the Horonite. So I drove him away from me. 29 Remember them, O my God, because they have brought sin to the religious leaders and to the agreement of the religious leaders and the Levites.

30 So I made them free from the sin of other nations. I gave the religious leaders and the Levites their duties, each in his work. 31 And I saw to it that wood would be brought at the right times, and also the first-fruits. O my God, remember me for good.

ESTHER

Queen Vashti Is Put Aside

1 This is what happened in the days of Ahasuerus, the Ahasuerus who ruled over 127 parts of the nation from India to Ethiopia. 2 In those days King Ahasuerus sat on the king's throne in the city of Susa. 3 In the third year of his rule, he gave a special supper for all his princes and leaders. The army captains of Persia and Media, the important men and princes of the many parts of the country were there with him. 4 For 180 days he showed the great riches and honor and power that were his as king of the nation. 5 When all the days were over, the king gave a supper lasting seven days for all the people from the greatest to the least who were in the city of Susa where he ruled. The supper was given in the open space of the garden of the king's special house. 6 There were curtains of fine white and blue linen held by ropes of fine purple linen on silver rings and marble pillars. There were seats of gold and silver on a floor made of small glass-like pieces, marble, mother-of-pearl, and stones of much worth. 7 Drinks were served in different kinds of gold cups, and there was much wine, because the king was very able and willing to give it. 8 Drinking was done by the law. No one was made to drink. The king had told all the workmen of his house that they should give each person what he wanted. 9 Queen Vashti also gave a special supper for the women in the beautiful house that belonged to King Ahasuerus.

10 On the seventh day the heart of the king was happy with wine. And he told Mehuman, Biztha, Harbona, Bigtha, Abagtha, Zethar, and Carkas, the seven servants who served King Ahasuerus, 11 to bring Queen Vashti to the king with her crown. He wanted to show her beauty to the people and the princes, for she was beautiful. 12 But Queen Vashti would not come when the king sent his servants to bring her. So the king became very angry and his anger burned within him. 13 Then the king spoke to the wise men who understood the times. For it was the king's way to speak with all who knew law and what was right and fair. 14 These men next to him were Carshena, Shethar, Admatha, Tarshish, Meres, Marsena, and Memucan, the seven princes of Persia and Media. They were allowed to visit with the king and were next to the king in the nation. 15 He asked them, "By the law, what is to be done with Queen Vashti, because she did not obey what King Ahasuerus sent the servants to tell her?" 16 Then Memucan said in front of the king and the princes, "Queen Vashti has done wrong not only to the king, but to all the princes and all the people in the lands of King Ahasuerus. 17 For what the queen has done will become known to all the women, and will make them hate their husbands. They will say, 'King Ahasuerus told Queen Vashti to be brought to him, but she would not come.' 18 This very day the ladies of Persia and Media who have heard what the queen has done will speak in the same way to all the king's princes. And there will be much hate and anger. 19 If it pleases the king, let word be sent by him, and let it be written in the laws of Persia and Media which cannot be changed, that Vashti should not come again to King Ahasuerus. Let the king give the place of queen to another who is better than she. 20 Then the king's word will be heard through all his great nation, and all women will give honor to their husbands, from the greatest to the least." 21 What was said pleased the king and the princes, and the king did as Memucan said. 22 So he sent letters to all parts of the king's nation, to each land in its own writing and to every people in their own language. The letters said that every man should rule in his own house and speak there in the language of his own people.

Esther Becomes Queen

2 After these things, when King Ahasuerus was no longer angry, he remembered Vashti and what she had done, and what had been decided against her. 2 Then the king's servants who served him said, "Let beautiful young women be found for the king. 3 Let the king choose men to watch over all the parts of his nation, that they may gather every beautiful young woman who has never had a man to the city of Susa. Have them brought to the house for the king's wives, under the care of Hegai, the king's servant, who takes care of the women. And let their things for making them beautiful be given to them. 4 Then let the young lady who pleases the king be queen in place of Vashti." This pleased the king, and he did so.

5 Now in the city of Susa where the king lived there was a Jew whose name was Mordecai, the son of Jair, the son of Shimei, the son of Kish, a Benjamite. 6 He had been taken from Jerusalem with the

people who had been taken away with King Jeconiah of Judah by Nebuchadnezzar the king of Babylon. 7 He had brought up Hadassah, that is Esther, the daughter of his father's brother. For she did not have a father or mother. The young lady was beautiful in body and face. When her father and mother died, Mordecai took her as his own daughter.

8 The words of the king were made known, and many young ladies were gathered to the city of Susa and put under the care of Hegai. So Esther was taken to the king's house into the care of Hegai, who cared for the women. 9 Now the young lady pleased Hegai and she found favor with him. He was quick to give her oils and special food, and gave her seven of the best women servants from the king's special house. He moved her and her women servants to the best place in the house for the king's wives. 10 Esther had not told who her people or her family were because Mordecai had told her to say nothing. 11 And every day Mordecai walked in front of the open space of the house of the king's women to learn how Esther was and how she was getting along.

12 The time for each young lady came to go in to King Ahasuerus after the end of her twelve months of being under the rules for the women. The days of making themselves beautiful were finished after using oil from spices for six months, and perfumes and oils for making themselves beautiful for another six months. 13 When the young woman went in to the king, whatever she wanted was given to her to take from the house of the king's women to the king's special house. 14 In the evening she would go in and in the morning she would return to the second house for the king's women, into the care of Shaashgaz, the king's servant who took care of his women who acted as wives. She would not go in to the king again unless the king was pleased with her and she was called by name. 15 Now the turn came for Esther, the daughter of Abihail, the brother of the father of Mordecai who had taken her as his daughter, to go in to the king. She did not ask for anything except what Hegai, the king's servant who took care of the women, said she should take. And Esther found favor in the eyes of all who saw her.

16 So Esther was taken to the beautiful house of King Ahasuerus in the tenth month, the month of Tebeth, in the seventh year of his rule. 17 And the king loved Esther more than all the women. She found favor and kindness with him more than all the young women, so that he set the queen's crown on her head and made her queen instead of Vashti. 18 Then the king gave a great supper for all his princes and leaders. It was a special supper for Esther. He also made a special day for the nation, and gave many gifts.

Mordecai Saves the King's Life

19 When the young women were gathered together the second time, Mordecai was sitting at the king's gate. 20 Esther had not yet told who her family or her people were, as Mordecai had said. For she did what Mordecai told her just as she had done when she was under his care. 21 In those days, while Mordecai was sitting at the king's gate, Bigthan and Teresh, two of the king's servants from those who watched over the door, became angry. And they planned to kill King Ahasuerus. 22 But their plan became known to Mordecai and he told Queen Esther. And Esther told the king what Mordecai had heard. 23 When the plan was learned and found to be true, both men were hanged on a tree. It was written down in the Book of the Chronicles in front of the king.

Haman Wants to Destroy the Jews

3 After these things King Ahasuerus raised Haman, the son of Hammedatha the Agagite, to a more important duty. He was made to rule over all the princes who were with him. 2 All the king's servants who were at the king's gate bowed down and gave honor to Haman, for the king had said that this should be done. But Mordecai did not bow down or give him honor. 3 Then the king's servants who were at the king's gate said to Mordecai, "Why are you not obeying the king?" 4 They spoke to him each day, but he would not listen to them. So they told Haman to see if Mordecai's reason was good enough. For he had told them that he was a Jew. 5 When Haman saw that Mordecai did not bow down or honor him, he was very angry. 6 But he did not want to only hurt Mordecai. They had told him who the people of Mordecai were and Haman wanted to destroy all the Jews. He wanted to destroy all the people of Mordecai in the whole nation of Ahasuerus.

7 In the first month, the month of Nisan, in the twelfth year of King Ahasuerus, names were drawn in front of Haman

from day to day and from month to month, until the twelfth month, the month of Adar. [8] Then Haman said to King Ahasuerus, "There is a certain people spread out among the people in all the parts of your nation whose laws are different from those of all other people, and they do not obey the king's laws. So it is not good for the king to let them stay. [9] If it pleases the king, let it be made known that they should be destroyed. And I will pay silver weighing as much as 10,000 men to those who do the king's work, to be put into the king's store-houses." [10] Then the king took the special ring from his hand that he used for marking his name and gave it to Haman, the son of Hammedatha the Agagite, who hated the Jews. [11] And the king said to Haman, "The silver is yours, and the people also. Do with them as you please." [12] Then the king's writers were called on the thirteenth day of the first month. And all that Haman had said was written to the king's rulers who were over each part of the land, and to the princes of each people. It was written to each part in its own writing, and in the language of each people. It was written in the name of King Ahasuerus and marked with the king's special ring. [13] Men were sent with letters to all the king's lands, to destroy, to kill, and to put an end to all the Jews, both young and old, women and children, in one day. This was the thirteenth day of the twelfth month, the month of Adar. And they could take the things that belonged to the Jews. [14] The letters were to be made a law in every land to all the people so that they should be ready for this day. [15] The men went out with the letters in a hurry as the king told them. And the law was made known in the city of Susa where the king lived. While the king and Haman sat down to drink, the city of Susa was troubled.

Mordecai Asks for Esther's Help

4 When Mordecai learned all that had been done, he tore his clothes. He dressed in cloth made from hair and put on ashes, and went out into the city and cried with loud cries. [2] He went as far as the king's gate, for no one was to go through the king's gate wearing cloth made from hair. [3] There was much sorrow among the Jews in each and every part of the nation where the king's law was made known. They went without food and cried with sounds of sorrow. Many lay in cloth made from hair and in ashes.

[4] Then Esther's women and men servants came and told her, and the queen was very troubled. She sent clothes for Mordecai to wear, that he might take off his clothes made from hair. But he would not take them. [5] Then Esther called Hathach from the king's servants whom the king had chosen to help her. She told him to go to Mordecai and find out what was wrong and why. [6] So Hathach went out to Mordecai at the king's gate in the open space of the city. [7] And Mordecai told him all that had happened to him. He told him just how much money Haman had promised to pay to the king's store-houses to have the Jews destroyed. [8] He also gave him one of the letters of the law that was sent out from Susa to destroy the Jews, that he might show it to Esther and let her know. And he said that she should go in to the king and beg him to show favor to her people.

[9] Hathach went and told Esther what Mordecai had said. [10] Then Esther told Hathach to say to Mordecai, [11] "All the king's servants and the people of the king's nation know that he has one law for any man or woman who comes to him in his room who has not been called: They will be put to death, unless the king holds out his special golden stick to him so that he may live. And I have not been called to come to the king for these thirty days." [12] Then Mordecai was told what Esther had said.

[13] Mordecai answered, "Do not think that you in the king's special house will live any more than all the other Jews. [14] For if you keep quiet at this time, help will come to the Jews from another place. But you and your father's house will be destroyed. Who knows if you have not become queen for such a time as this?" [15] Then Esther told them to say to Mordecai, [16] "Go, gather together all the Jews who are in Susa, and have them all go without food so they can pray better for me. Do not eat or drink for three days, night or day. I and my women servants will go without food in the same way. Then I will go in to the king, which is against the law. And if I die, I die." [17] So Mordecai went away and did just as Esther had told him.

Esther's Special Supper

5 On the third day Esther put on her queen's clothing and stood in the open space inside the king's special house in front of his throne room. The king was sitting on his throne in the throne room looking toward the door of his house. 2 When the king saw Esther the queen standing in the open space, she found favor in his eyes. The king held his special golden stick in his hand toward Esther. So Esther came near and touched the top of the special stick. 3 Then the king said to her, "What do you want, Queen Esther? What do you ask of me? You would be given even as much as half the nation." 4 Esther said, "If it please the king, may the king and Haman come today to the special supper I have made ready for him."

5 Then the king said, "Be quick to bring Haman, that we may do as Esther wants." So the king and Haman came to the special supper that Esther had made ready. 6 As they drank their wine at the supper, the king said to Esther, "What is it that you want? For it will be given to you. What do you ask of me? You would be given as much as half the nation." 7 So Esther answered and said, "This is what I ask of you. 8 If I have found favor in the king's eyes, and if it please the king to give me what I ask of him, may the king and Haman come to the special supper that I will make ready for them. And tomorrow I will tell you what I want."

9 Then Haman went out that day glad and with joy in his heart. But when he saw Mordecai at the king's gate, and when he did not stand up or show any fear in front of him, Haman was filled with anger against Mordecai. 10 But Haman kept himself from doing anything at that time, and went home. There he sent for his friends and his wife Zeresh. 11 Haman told them about the greatness of his riches and the number of his sons. He told them how the king had raised him to a place of honor, and how he had made him more important than the princes and the king's servants. 12 Haman said, "Even Queen Esther let no one but me come with the king to the special supper that she had made ready. She has asked me to come with the king tomorrow also. 13 Yet all of this is not enough to please me every time I see Mordecai the Jew sitting at the king's gate." 14 Then Zeresh his wife and all his friends said to him, "Have a tower made ready for hanging him. Let it be thirteen times taller than a man. And in the morning ask the king to have Mordecai hanged on it. Then go with joy to the special supper with the king." These words pleased Haman, so he had the tower built.

The King Honors Mordecai

6 During that night the king could not sleep. So he had the Book of the Chronicles brought to him, and they were read to the king. 2 And it was found written what Mordecai had told him about Bigthana and Teresh, two of the king's servants who were door-keepers, who had planned to kill King Ahasuerus. 3 The king said, "What honor or reward has been given to Mordecai for this?" Then the king's servants who served him said, "Nothing has been done for him." 4 So the king said, "Who is outside?" Now Haman had just come into the garden outside the king's special house. He wanted to speak to the king about hanging Mordecai on the tower he had made ready for him. 5 The king's servants said to him, "See, Haman is standing in the garden." And the king said, "Let him come in." 6 So Haman came in and the king said to him, "What is to be done for the man whom the king wants to honor?" Haman thought to himself, "Whom would the king want to honor more than me?" 7 Then Haman said to the king, "For the man whom the king wants to honor, 8 let them bring clothing which the king wears, and the horse on which the king rides, and on whose head a crown has been placed. 9 Let the clothing and the horse be handed over to one of the king's most honored princes. Let them dress the man whom the king wants to honor and lead him on the horse through the center of the city. Have them make it known before him, 'This is being done to the man whom the king wants to honor.'"

10 Then the king said to Haman, "Be quick to take the clothing and the horse as you have said. Do this for Mordecai the Jew, who is sitting at the king's gate. Do not do any less than all that you have said." 11 So Haman took the clothing and the horse. He dressed Mordecai and led him on the horse through the center of the city. And he made known before him, "This is being done to the man whom the king wants to honor." 12 Then Mordecai returned to the king's gate. But Haman went home in a hurry with his head covered and very sad. 13 Haman told Zeresh his wife and all his friends everything that had happened to him. Then his wise men and Zeresh his wife said to him, "If Mordecai, before whom you have begun to fall, is of the Jewish people, you cannot stand against him. For sure you will fall before him." 14 While they were still talking with

him, the king's servants came and brought Haman in a hurry to the special supper that Esther had made ready.

Haman Is Put to Death

7 So the king and Haman came to eat with Esther the queen. 2 And the king said again to Esther on the second day, as they drank their wine at the special supper, "What do you want to ask of me, Queen Esther? It will be done for you. What do you want? You would be given as much as half the nation." 3 Queen Esther answered, "If I have found favor in your eyes, O king, and if it please the king, I ask that my life and the lives of my people be saved. 4 For I and my people have been sold, to be destroyed, to be killed, and to be done away with. If we had only been sold as men and women servants, I would have kept quiet. For our trouble is not to be compared with the trouble it will make for the king." 5 Then King Ahasuerus asked Queen Esther, "Who is he, and where is he, who would do such a thing?" 6 Esther said, "This sinful Haman hates us very much!" Then Haman was very afraid in front of the king and queen. 7 The king got up from drinking the wine very angry, and went into his garden, but Haman stayed to beg for his life from Queen Esther. He knew that the king planned to punish him. 8 When the king returned from his garden to the place where they were drinking wine, Haman was falling on the bed-like seat where Esther was lying. Then the king said, "Will he even trouble the queen while I am in the house?" As the king spoke the words, they covered Haman's face. 9 Then Harbonah, one of the king's servants helping the king, said, "See, there is a tower made for hanging people at Haman's house, thirteen times taller than a man. Haman had it made for hanging Mordecai who spoke good and helped the king!" And the king said, "Hang Haman on it." 10 So they hanged Haman on the tower that he had made for Mordecai. Then the king's anger became less.

The Jews Are Allowed to Fight for Their Lives

8 On that day King Ahasuerus gave everything Haman owned, the one who hated the Jews, to Queen Esther. Mordecai came to the king, for Esther had told him what he was to her. 2 The king took off the ring he used for marking his name, which he had taken away from Haman, and gave it to Mordecai. And Esther put Mordecai over everything Haman had owned.

3 Then Esther spoke again to the king. She fell at his feet and cried and begged him to stop the sinful plan of Haman the Agagite, the plan he had made against the Jews. 4 The king held out the special golden stick toward Esther. So she got up and stood in front of the king. 5 Then she said, "If it pleases the king and if I have his favor, if the king thinks it is right and if I am pleasing in his eyes, let letters be written to keep Haman's letters from being carried out. The letters Haman, the son of Hammedatha the Agagite, wrote would destroy the Jews in all the king's nation. 6 For how can I stand to see all the trouble that will come to my people? How can I keep on if I see them destroyed?" 7 So King Ahasuerus said to Queen Esther and to Mordecai the Jew, "See, I have given everything Haman owned to Esther. They have hanged him on the tower because he had wanted to destroy all the Jews. 8 Now you write whatever pleases you about the Jews, in the king's name, and mark it with the king's special ring. For what is written in the king's name and marked with the king's special ring may not be changed."

9 So the king's writers were called at that time, on the twenty-third day of the third month, the month of Sivan. All that Mordecai said was written and sent to the Jews, the rulers, the leaders, and the princes of the 127 parts of the nation from India to Ethiopia. The letters were sent to every land in its own writing and to every people in their own language. And they were sent to the Jews in their own writing and language. 10 He wrote in the name of King Ahasuerus and marked it with the king's special ring. He sent the letters by men on fast horses used in the king's work, raised from the king's best male horse. 11 In the letters the king allowed the Jews who were in every city the right to gather together to fight for their lives. He gave them the right to destroy, kill, and do away with the whole army of any people or nation which might come to fight against them. They were given the right to kill even the children and women, and to take whatever belonged to them. 12 On one day in all the nation of King Ahasuerus, the thirteenth day of the twelfth month, the month of Adar, they were to do this. 13 The letter was law in every part of the nation and was sent to all the people, so the Jews would be ready on that day

to stand against those who hated them. [14] The men went out in a hurry on the fast horses that were used for the king's work, just as the king told them. And the letter was made known in the city of Susa where the king ruled.

[15] Then Mordecai went out from the king wearing king's clothing of blue and white, with a large gold crown and a long coat of fine linen and purple cloth. The people in the city of Susa were filled with joy and called out in loud voices. [16] For the Jews it was a time of joy and happiness and honor. [17] In every part of the nation and in every city where the king's law had come, there was happiness and joy for the Jews, a special supper and a good day. And many people who had come there from other countries became Jews because they were afraid of the Jews.

The Jews Destroy Those Who Try to Kill Them

9 Now came the thirteenth day of the twelfth month, the month of Adar, when the king's law was about to be carried out. It was the day when those who hated the Jews hoped to get the rule over them. But their plan was turned around, and the Jews ruled over those who hated them. [2] The Jews gathered in their cities in all the parts of the nation of King Ahasuerus to hurt those who wanted to kill them. No one could stand in front of them, for the fear of them had come upon all the people. [3] The princes of the nation, the rulers, the leaders, and those who were doing the king's work all helped the Jews, because the fear of Mordecai had come upon them. [4] For Mordecai was great in the king's house. His name spread through all the nation, for the man Mordecai became greater and greater. [5] So the Jews killed and destroyed with sword all those who hated them. They did as they pleased to those who hated them. [6] In the city of Susa where the king ruled the Jews killed and destroyed 500 men, [7] and Parshandatha, Dalphon, Aspatha, [8] Poratha, Adalia, Aridatha, [9] Parmashta, Arisai, Aridai, and Vaizatha. [10] These were the ten sons of Haman, the son of Hammedatha, who hated the Jews. But they did not touch anything that belonged to them.

[11] On that day the number of those who were killed in the city of Susa where the king lived was told to the king. [12] And the king said to Queen Esther, "The Jews have killed and destroyed 500 men and the ten

sons of Haman in Susa. What then have they done in the rest of the king's nation! Now what do you ask of me? It will be done for you. What else do you want? It will be done." [13] Esther said, "If it pleases the king, let the Jews in Susa be allowed tomorrow also to carry out today's law. Let the bodies of Haman's ten sons be hanged on the tower." [14] So the king said that this should be done. He made it known in Susa, and the bodies of Haman's ten sons were hanged. [15] The Jews in Susa gathered also on the fourteenth day of the month of Adar and killed 300 men in Susa. But they did not touch anything that belonged to them.

[16] Now the rest of the Jews who were in the king's nation gathered to fight for their lives and get rid of those who hated them. They killed 75,000 of those who hated them. But they did not touch anything that belonged to them. [17] This was on the thirteenth day of the month of Adar. On the fourteenth day they rested and made it a day of eating and joy. [18] But the Jews in Susa gathered on the thirteenth and fourteenth days of the same month. And they rested on the fifteenth day and made it a day of eating and joy. [19] So the Jews of the villages, who lived in the small towns without walls, made the fourteenth day of the month of Adar a special day of joy and eating and sharing their food with one another.

The Special Supper of Purim

[20] Mordecai wrote down these things. And he sent letters to all the Jews who were in all the nation of King Ahasuerus, both near and far. [21] He told them to remember the fourteenth and fifteenth days of the month of Adar each year. [22] Because on those days the Jews got rid of those who hated them. It was a month which was changed from sorrow into joy, from a day of sorrow into a special day. He said that they should make them days of eating and joy and sending food to one another and gifts to the poor.

[23] So the Jews agreed to do what they had started to do, and what Mordecai had written to them. [24] For Haman the son of Hammedatha, the Agagite, the one who hated all the Jews, had planned to destroy the Jews. He had drawn names, using Pur, to trouble them and destroy them. [25] But when the king heard about it, he made it known by letter that his plan against the Jews should bring trouble upon himself.

And he had Haman and his sons hanged on the tower. 26 So they called these days Purim after the name of Pur. Because of what was written in this letter, and what they had seen and what had happened to them, 27 the Jews set apart this special time each year for themselves, for their children and their children's children, and for all who joined them. They would always remember to keep these two days special, as it was written and at the same time every year. 28 These days were to be remembered and kept as a special time for all their children-to-come, in every family, every land, and every city. These days of Purim were not to be forgotten by the Jews. Their children and their children's children were to remember them forever.

29 Then Queen Esther, the daughter of Abihail, with Mordecai the Jew, wrote with full power to make this second letter about Purim sure. 30 Letters were sent to all the Jews in the 127 parts of the nation of Ahasuerus, in words of peace and truth. 31 They made sure that these days of Purim would be kept at the right times, as Mordecai the Jew and Queen Esther had told them. These days were set apart for themselves and for their children and their children's children, with the times they were to go without food and the times they were to be sad. 32 The words of Esther made the rules for keeping Purim sure, and it was written in the book.

Mordecai Is Honored by the King

10 King Ahasuerus put a tax on the people of the nation and the parts beside the sea. 2 All the acts of his power and strength, and the whole story of the high honor given to Mordecai by the king, are written in the Book of the Chronicles of the kings of Media and Persia. 3 For Mordecai the Jew was second in power only to King Ahasuerus and great among the Jews. He found favor in the eyes of his people. He worked for the good of his people and spoke for the well-being of all the Jews.

JOB

Satan Tests Job

1 There was a man in the land of Uz whose name was Job. That man was without blame, He was right and good, he feared God, and turned away from sin. 2 Seven sons and three daughters were born to him. 3 He had 7,000 sheep, 3,000 camels, 1,000 oxen, 500 female donkeys, and many servants. He was the greatest of all the men of the east. 4 His sons used to go and make a special supper in each one's house on a special day. And they would send for their three sisters to eat and drink with them. 5 When the days of their special supper were over, Job would get up early in the morning and send for them. Then he would give burnt gifts for each of them so that they would be pure. For Job said, "It might be that my sons have sinned and cursed God in their hearts." Job always did this.

6 Now there was a day when the sons of God came to show themselves before the Lord. Satan came with them also. 7 And the Lord said to Satan, "Where have you come from?" Satan answered the Lord and said, "From traveling around on the earth and walking around on it." 8 The Lord said to Satan, "Have you thought about My servant Job? For there is no one like him on the earth. He is without blame, a man who is right and good. He honors God with fear and turns away from sin." 9 Then Satan answered the Lord, "Does Job fear God for nothing? 10 Have You not made a wall around him and his house and all that he has, on every side? You have brought good to the work of his hands, and he has received more and more in the land. 11 But put out Your hand now and touch all that he has. And for sure he will curse You to Your face." 12 Then the Lord said to Satan, "See, all that he has is in your power. Only do not put your hand on him." So Satan went out from the Lord.

Job's Children and Riches Are Destroyed

13 On a day when Job's sons and daughters were eating and drinking wine in their oldest brother's house, 14 a man came to Job with news, saying, "The oxen were pulling the plow and the donkeys were eating beside them. 15 And the Sabeans came and took them. They also killed the servants with the sword. I alone have run away from them to tell you." 16 While he was still speaking, another man came and said, "The fire of God fell from heaven and

burned up the sheep and the servants and destroyed them. I alone have gotten away to tell you." 17 While he was still speaking, another came and said, "The Babylonians divided into three groups and came to fight. They took the camels and killed the servants with the sword. I alone have gotten away to tell you." 18 While he was still speaking, another also came and said, "Your sons and daughters were eating and drinking wine in their oldest brother's house. 19 And see, a strong wind came from the desert and hit the four corners of the house. It fell on the young people and they are dead. I alone have gotten away to tell you."

20 Then Job stood up and tore his clothing and cut the hair from his head. And he fell to the ground and worshiped. 21 He said, "Without clothing I was born from my mother, and without clothing I will return. The Lord gave and the Lord has taken away. Praise the name of the Lord." 22 In all this Job did not sin or blame God.

Satan Tests Job the Second Time

2 Again there was a day when the sons of God came to show themselves before the Lord. And Satan came with them also to show himself before the Lord. 2 The Lord said to Satan, "Where have you come from?" Satan answered the Lord and said, "From traveling around the earth and walking around on it." 3 The Lord said to Satan, "Have you thought about My servant Job? For there is no one like him on the earth. He is without blame, a man who is right and good. He fears God and turns away from sin. He still holds to his good ways, even when I allowed you to go against him, and to destroy him for no reason." 4 Satan answered the Lord and said, "Skin for skin! Yes, all that a man has he will give for his life. 5 Put out Your hand now and touch his bone and his flesh, and he will curse You to Your face." 6 So the Lord said to Satan, "See, he is in your power. Only do not kill him."

7 Then Satan went out from the Lord. And he made very bad sores come on Job from the bottom of his foot to the top of his head. 8 Job took a piece of a broken pot to try to cut off the sores while he sat among the ashes. 9 Then his wife said to him, "Do you still hold on to your faith? Curse God and die!" 10 But he said to her, "You speak as one of the foolish women would speak. Should we receive good from God and not receive trouble?" In all this Job did not sin with his lips.

Job's Friends Come to Him

11 Now when Job's three friends heard of all this trouble that had come upon him, they came each from his own place. They were Eliphaz the Temanite, Bildad the Shuhite, and Zophar the Naamathite. They agreed to meet together to come to share Job's sorrow and comfort him. 12 And when they looked up from far away and saw how different he looked, they cried in loud voices. They tore their clothing and threw dust over their heads toward the sky. 13 Then they sat down on the ground with him for seven days and seven nights. No one said a word to him, for they saw that his suffering was very bad.

Job Speaks Angry Words to God

3 After this Job opened his mouth and cursed the day he was born. 2 He said, 3 "Let the day be lost on which I was born, and the night which said, 'A boy is born.' 4 May that day be darkness. May God above not care for it. May light not shine on it. 5 Let darkness and a heavy shadow take it for their own. Let a cloud come upon it. Let the darkness of the day bring fear upon it. 6 As for that night, let darkness take hold of it. Let it not have joy among the days of the year. Let it not come into the number of months. 7 Yes, let that night be alone and empty. Let no sound of joy come into it. 8 Let those curse it who curse the day, who are able to wake up the Leviathan. 9 Let the early morning stars be made dark. Let it wait for light but have none. Do not let it see the light of day. 10 Because it did not keep my mother from giving birth to me, or hide trouble from my eyes.

11 "Why did I not die at birth? Why did I not come from my mother and die? 12 Why did the knees receive me, or why the breasts, that I should have milk? 13 For now I would have lain down and been quiet. I would have slept then. I would have been at rest, 14 with kings and wise men of the earth who built cities for themselves that are now destroyed. 15 I would have been at rest with princes who had gold, who filled their houses with silver. 16 Why did I not die before I was born, hidden and put away, as babies that never see the light? 17 There the troubles of the sinful stop. There the tired are at rest. 18 Those in prison are at rest together. They do not hear the voice of the one who rules over their work. 19 The small and the great are there. And the servant is free from his owner.

20 "Why is light given to him who suffers? Why is life given to those who feel sad in their soul? 21 They wait for death, but there is none. They dig for it more than for hidden riches. 22 They are filled with much joy and are glad, when they find the grave. 23 Why is light given to a man whose way is hidden, and around whom God has built a wall? 24 For I cry inside myself in front of my food. My cries pour out like water. 25 What I was afraid of has come upon me. What filled me with fear has happened. 26 I am not at rest, and I am not quiet. I have no rest, but only trouble."

Eliphaz Talks

4 Then Eliphaz the Temanite answered, 2 "If one speaks with you, will you want him to stop? But who can keep from speaking? 3 See, you have taught many, and you have given strength to weak hands. 4 Your words have helped him stand who would have fallen. You have given strength to weak knees. 5 But now it has come to you, and you are not happy. It touches you, and you are troubled and sad. 6 Is not your fear of God what gives you strength and your good ways that give you hope?

7 "Think now, who without guilt was ever destroyed? 8 As I have seen, those who plow sin and plant trouble gather the same. 9 By the breath of God they are destroyed. They are destroyed by the wind of His anger. 10 The noise of the lion, the voice of the angry lion, and the teeth of the young lions are broken. 11 The strong lion dies because there is no food to get. And the young of the lioness are sent everywhere.

12 "Now a word was brought to me in secret. My ear heard it spoken in a quiet voice. 13 With troubled thoughts from the dreams of the night, when deep sleep comes upon men, 14 fear came to me and I shook. It made all my bones shake. 15 A spirit passed by my face. The hair of my flesh stood up. 16 The spirit stood still, but I could not understand what I saw. Something was in front of my eyes. All was quiet, then I heard a voice: 17 'Can man be right more than God? Can a man be pure more than his Maker? 18 He puts no trust even in His servants. He finds mistakes among His angels. 19 How much more those who live in houses of clay, who build upon the dust, who are crushed like the moth! 20 Between morning and evening they are destroyed. Without anyone seeing it they become lost forever. 21 Is not their tent-rope pulled up within them? They die, and have no wisdom.'

Eliphaz Keeps On Talking

5 "Call now. Is there anyone who will answer you? To which of the holy ones will you turn? 2 To be bitter kills the foolish man, and jealousy kills the child-like. 3 I have seen the fool taking root, but right away his house was cursed. 4 His sons are far from being safe. They are destroyed in the gate, and there is no one to help them. 5 The hungry eat the food of his field. They take it even out of the thorns. And the thirsty want his riches. 6 For suffering does not come from the dust. Trouble does not grow out of the ground. 7 But man is born to trouble, as fire goes up.

8 "But as for me, I would look to God. I would put my troubles before God. 9 He does great things, too great for us to understand. He does too many wonderful things for us to number. 10 He gives rain on the earth and sends water on the fields. 11 He puts those who are in low places up to high places. Those who are filled with sorrow are lifted to where they are safe. 12 He troubles the plans of those who try to fool people, so that their hands cannot do what they plan. 13 God gets them into a trap when they use their own wisdom. And the plans of the wise are brought to a quick end. 14 They meet with darkness during the day, and feel their way at noon as in the night. 15 But He saves from the sword those in need. He saves the poor from the power of the strong. 16 So those who have no hope, have hope, and what is not right and good must shut its mouth.

17 "See, happy is the man to whom God speaks strong words. So do not hate the strong teaching of the All-powerful. 18 He punishes, and He gives comfort. He hurts, but His hands heal. 19 He will take you out of six troubles. Yes, in seven, nothing will hurt you. 20 He will keep you from death in times of no food, and from the power of the sword in war. 21 You will be hidden from the punishment of the tongue. You will not be afraid of being destroyed when danger comes. 22 You will laugh at danger and times of no food. And you will not be afraid of wild animals. 23 For you will be in agreement with the stones of the field. And the animals of the field will be at peace with you. 24 You will know that your tent is safe. You will look over what you have and see that nothing is gone. 25 You will know also that your children

and children's children will be many. They will be as the grass of the earth. 26 You will come to the grave in full strength, like the grain gathered in when it is time. 27 See, this is what we have found, and it is true. Hear it, and know for yourself."

Job Speaks

6 Then Job answered, 2 "If only my trials and troubles were weighed! 3 They would weigh more than the sand of the seas. My words have been spoken fast and without thought. 4 For the arrows of the All-powerful are in me. My spirit drinks their poison. The hard things from God are like an army against me. 5 Does the wild donkey make noise when it has grass? Or does the bull make noise when it has food? 6 Can something that has no taste be eaten without salt? Is there any taste in the white of an egg? 7 My soul will not touch them. They are like hated food to me.

8 "If only I might get what I ask for, and that God would give me what I desire! 9 If only God were willing to crush me, that He would let His hand loose and destroy me! 10 But this gives me comfort even though I suffer much pain because I have not turned away from the words of the Holy One. 11 What strength have I, that I should wait? What is my end, that I should not give up? 12 Do I have the strength of stones? Is my flesh brass? 13 I have no power to help myself, and a way out is far from me.

14 "Kindness from a friend should be shown to a man without hope, or he might turn away from the fear of the All-powerful. 15 My brothers have been like rivers that are not there when needed. 16 They are dark because of ice and snow turning into water. 17 When they have no water, there is no noise. When it is hot, they are not there. 18 The people on their camels turn away from them. They go into the waste places and die. 19 The people and camels of Tema looked. The travelers of Sheba hoped for them. 20 They were troubled for they had trusted. They came there and their hope goes. 21 Yes, this is how you have been. You see my trouble and are afraid. 22 Have I said, 'Give me something,' or, 'Pay something from your riches to help me'? 23 Have I said, 'Take me out from under the power of the one who hates me,' or, 'Save me from those who make it hard for me'?

24 "Teach me, and I will be quiet. Show me where I have been wrong. 25 Honest words give pain. But what does your arguing prove? 26 Do you think you can speak against my words, and act as if the words of a man without hope are wind? 27 You would even draw names over those who have no father, and make trades over your friend. 28 Now be pleased to look at me, and see if I lie to your face. 29 I ask that you change your minds and let no wrong be done. Stop now, for I am still right and good. 30 Is there wrong-doing on my tongue? Can I not taste trouble?

Job Keeps On Talking

7 "Is not man made to work on earth? Are not his days like the days of a man paid to work? 2 Like a servant who desires to be out of the sun, and like a working man who waits for his pay, 3 I am given months of pain and nights of suffering for no reason. 4 When I lie down I say, 'When will I get up?' But the night is long, and I am always turning from side to side until morning. 5 My flesh is covered with worms and dirt. My skin becomes hard and breaks open. 6 My days are faster than a cloth-maker's tool, and come to their end without hope.

7 "Remember that my life is only a breath. My eye will not again see good. 8 The eye of him who sees me will see me no more. Your eyes will be on me, but I will be gone. 9 When a cloud goes away, it is gone. And he who goes down to the place of the dead does not come back. 10 He will not return to his house, and his place will not know him any more.

11 "So I will not keep my mouth shut. I will speak in the suffering of my spirit. I will complain because my soul is bitter. 12 Am I the sea, or a large sea animal, that You put someone to watch me? 13 When I say, 'My bed will comfort me, and there I will find rest from my complaining,' 14 then You send dreams to me which fill me with fear. 15 So a quick death by having my breath stopped would be better to me than my pains. 16 I hate my life. I will not live forever. Leave me alone, for my days are only a breath. 17 What is man, that You make so much of him? Why do You care about him, 18 that You look at him every morning, and test him all the time? 19 How long will it be until You look away from me? Will You not let me alone until I swallow my spit? 20 Have I sinned? What have I done to You, O watcher of men? Why have you made me something to shoot at, so that I am a problem to myself? 21 Why

then do You not forgive my wrong-doing and take away my sin? For now I will lie down in the dust. You will look for me, but I will not be."

Bildad Talks

8 Then Bildad the Shuhite answered, 2 "How long will you say these things, and the words of your mouth be a strong wind? 3 Does God make wrong what is fair? Does the All-powerful make wrong what is right? 4 If your children have sinned against Him, He has given them over to the power of their sin. 5 If you will look for God and pray to the All-powerful, 6 if you are pure and right and good, for sure He will help you. Because you are right and good He will put you back where you should be. 7 And even if your beginning was small, your end will be very great.

8 "Ask about those who have lived before. Think about what their fathers learned. 9 For we are only of yesterday and know nothing. Our days on earth are as a shadow. 10 Will they not teach you and tell you, and speak words of wisdom?

11 "Can the tall river-grass grow up from dry ground? Can the grass that grows in wet places grow without water? 12 While it is still green and not cut, it becomes dry and dead before any other plant. 13 So are the ways of all who forget God. The hope of the man without God is destroyed. 14 What he trusts in is easy to break, like the home of a spider. 15 The spider trusts in his house, but it falls apart. He holds on to it, but it does not hold. 16 He is full of strength in the sunshine, and his branches spread out over his garden. 17 His roots grow around rocks and they work their way among the stones. 18 If he is taken from his place, then it will turn away from him, saying, 'I have never seen you.' 19 See, this is the joy of His way. And out of the dust others will come. 20 See, God will not turn away from a man who is honest and faithful. And He will not help those who do wrong. 21 He will yet make you laugh and call out with joy. 22 Those who hate you will be dressed with shame. And the tent of the sinful will be no more."

Job Talks

9 Then Job answered, 2 "Yes, I know this is true. But how can a man be right and good before God? 3 If one wished to argue with Him, he would not be able to answer one out of a thousand of His questions. 4 He is wise in heart and powerful in strength. Who has ever stood against Him without being hurt? 5 It is He Who takes away the mountains without their knowing it, when He destroys them in His anger. 6 He shakes the earth out of its place, and its pillars shake. 7 He tells the sun not to shine, and He keeps the stars from shining. 8 He alone spreads out the heavens and walks upon the waves of the sea. 9 He makes the Bear, Orion and the Pleiades and the stars of the south. 10 He does things too great for us to understand, and more wonderful works than we can number. 11 When He passes by me, I do not see Him. When He goes by me, I do not know Him. 12 If He takes away, who can stop Him? Who could say to Him, 'What are You doing?'

13 "God will not stop His anger. The helpers of Rahab bow under Him. 14 How then can I answer Him, and choose the right words to speak with Him? 15 Even if I am right, I cannot answer Him. I must beg Him who is against me to have pity. 16 If I called and He answered me, I could not believe that He was listening to my voice. 17 For He crushes me with a storm, and hurts me more and more without a reason. 18 He will not let me get my breath, but fills me with much that is bitter. 19 If it is a question of power, see, He is the strong one! If it is a question of what is right and fair, who can call Him to a trial? 20 Even if I were right, my mouth would say that I am guilty. Even if I were without blame, He would say I am guilty. 21 Even though I am without blame, I do not care about myself. I hate my life. 22 It is all the same, so I say, 'He destroys both those who are without blame and the sinful.' 23 If death comes fast by disease, He makes fun of the trouble of those who have done no wrong. 24 The earth is given into the hand of the sinful. He covers the faces of its judges. If it is not He, then who is it?

25 "My days go faster than a runner. They fly away, and see no good. 26 They go by like fast boats, like an eagle coming down to catch its food. 27 If I say, 'I will forget my complaining. I will put off my sad face and be happy,' 28 I am still afraid of all my pains for I know You will not take away my guilt. 29 Because I am already guilty, why should I try for nothing? 30 If I wash myself with snow and clean my hands using the best soap, 31 You would still throw me down into a deep hole. And my own clothes would hate me. 32 For He is not a man, as I am, that I may answer Him, that we

might go to trial together. ³³ There is no one to decide between us, who might lay his hand upon us both. ³⁴ Let Him stop punishing me. And do not let fear of Him make me so afraid. ³⁵ Then I would speak and not be afraid of Him. But I am not like that in myself.

Job Keeps On Talking

10 "I hate my life. I will be free in my complaining. I will show how bitter I am in my soul when I speak. ² I will say to God, 'Do not say that I am guilty and punish me. Let me know why You work against me. ³ Do You think it is right for You to make it hard for me, to turn away from the work of Your hands and favor the plans of the sinful? ⁴ Do You have eyes of flesh? Do You see as a man sees? ⁵ Are Your days as the days of man, or Your years as man's years, ⁶ that You should look for my wrong-doing and my sin? ⁷ You know that I am not guilty, yet there is no one who can take me away from Your hand.

⁸ 'Your hands put me together and made me, and now would You destroy me? ⁹ Remember that You have made me as clay. Would You turn me into dust again? ¹⁰ Did You not pour me out like milk and make me become hard like cheese? ¹¹ You have given me clothing of skin and flesh, and have tied me together with bones and cord. ¹² You have given me life and loving-kindness. Your care has kept my spirit alive. ¹³ Yet You have hidden these things in Your heart. I know that this is in Your thoughts. ¹⁴ If I sin, You would see me, and would not free me from my guilt. ¹⁵ If I am sinful, it would be bad for me! If I am right and good, I cannot lift my head for I am filled with shame and see all my trouble. ¹⁶ If I would lift up my head, You would hunt me like a lion. Again You would show Your power against me. ¹⁷ You would send new ones who would speak against me, and become more angry with me. You would send me more and more trouble.

¹⁸ 'Why then did You let me be born? If only I had died and no one had seen me! ¹⁹ I should have been as if I had never lived, carried from my mother to the grave.' ²⁰ Are not my days few? Leave me alone, that I may find a little comfort ²¹ before I go to a place from which I will not return. I will go to the land of darkness and shadow. ²² It is the land of complete darkness and shadow and trouble, where the light is darkness."

Zophar Talks

11 Then Zophar the Naamathite answered, ² "Should many words go without an answer? Should a man full of talk be said to be without blame? ³ Should your words of pride make men quiet? Should you make fun of truth and no one speak sharp words to you? ⁴ For you say, 'What I believe is pure. I am without fault in Your eyes.' ⁵ If only God would speak, and open His lips against you. ⁶ He would show you the secrets of wisdom because there are two sides. Then you would know that God is punishing you less than you should get.

⁷ "Can you find out the deep things of God? Can you find out how far the All-powerful can go? ⁸ They are higher than the heavens. What can you do? They are deeper than the place of the dead. What can you know? ⁹ They are longer than the earth and wider than the sea. ¹⁰ If He passes by, puts a man in prison, or calls him to trial, who can stop Him? ¹¹ For He knows men who are no good. When He sees wrong-doing, will He not look into it? ¹² A fool cannot become wise anymore than a wild donkey can give birth to a man.

¹³ "If you set your heart right, and put out your hands to Him, ¹⁴ and if you put away the sin that is in your hand, do not let wrong-doing be in your tents. ¹⁵ Then you will be able to lift up your face without sin. You would be strong and not afraid. For you would forget your trouble, remembering it as waters that have passed by. ¹⁷ Your life would be brighter than noon. Darkness would be like the morning. ¹⁸ Then you would trust, because there is hope. You would look around and rest and be safe. ¹⁹ You would lie down and no one would make you afraid. Many would ask for your favor. ²⁰ But the eyes of the sinful will waste away. There will be no way for them to get away. And their hope is to breathe their last."

Job Talks

12 Then Job answered, ² "No doubt you are the people, and wisdom will die with you. ³ But I have understanding as well as you. I am not less than you. Who does not know such things as these? ⁴ Even my friends laugh at me. The man who called on God, and God answered him, the man who is right and without blame is laughed at. ⁵ He who lives in comfort laughs at one who has trouble and whose feet are slipping. 6 The tents of those who destroy have much. Those who make God angry are safe and have their god in their own hands.

7 "But ask the wild animals, and they will teach you. Ask the birds of the heavens, and let them tell you. 8 Or speak to the earth, and let it teach you. Let the fish of the sea make it known to you. 9 Who among all these does not know that the hand of the Lord has done this? 10 In His hand is the life of every living thing and the breath of all men. 11 Does not the ear test words as the mouth tastes food? 12 Wisdom is with old men, and understanding with long life.

13 "With God are wisdom and strength. Wise words and understanding belong to Him. 14 See, He tears down, and it cannot be built again. He puts a man in prison, and no one can free him. 15 See, He stops the waters and they dry up. He sends them out, and they cover the earth. 16 Strength and wisdom are with Him. Both the fool and the one who fools him belong to God. 17 He takes wisdom away from leaders and makes fools of judges. 18 He takes off chains put on by kings, and holds back the power of kings. 19 He makes religious leaders walk without pride, and takes the power away from those who think they are safe. 20 He stops the trusted ones from speaking and takes away the wisdom of the leaders. 21 He pours anger on rulers, and takes away the strength of the strong. 22 He makes known hidden truth from the darkness, and brings deep darkness to light. 23 He makes the nations great, and then destroys them. He helps nations to become large, then leads them away. 24 He takes away understanding from the leaders of the people of the earth, and makes them travel in a waste land with no path. 25 They feel their way in darkness with no light. And He makes them walk from side to side like a drunk man.

Job Talks

13 "See, my eye has seen all this. My ear has heard and understood it. 2 What you know I also know. I am not less than you.

3 "But I wish to speak to the All-powerful. I want to argue with God. 4 But you cover things with lies. You are doctors of no worth. 5 If only you would be quiet, and that would show your wisdom! 6 Hear what I think. Listen to the arguing of my lips. 7 Will you say what is not true

for God? Will you lie for Him? 8 Will you show favor for Him? Will you argue for God? 9 Will it be well when He tests you? Or do you lie to Him as one lies to a man? 10 For sure He will speak strong words to you if you show favor in secret. 11 Will not His great power make you afraid? Will not the fear of Him come upon you? 12 Your wise sayings are sayings of ashes. Your strength is the strength of clay.

13 "Be quiet so that I may speak. Then let come on me what will. 14 Why should I take my flesh in my teeth, and put my life in my hands? 15 Even though He would kill me, yet I will trust in Him. I will argue my ways to His face. 16 This will save me, for a sinful man may not come to Him. 17 Be careful to listen to my words. Let what I say fill your ears. 18 See, I am ready to tell everything, and all will know I am right. 19 Who will talk against me? For then I would be quiet and die.

20 "Only two things I ask of You, and then I will not hide from Your face. 21 Take Your hand from me, and do not let the fear of You make me so afraid. 22 Then call, and I will answer. Or let me speak, and You answer me. 23 How many are my sins and wrong-doings? Help me to know my wrong-doing and sin. 24 Why do You hide Your face, and think of me as one who hates You? 25 Will You make a wind-blown leaf afraid? Will You go after the dry parts of a grain-field that have no worth? 26 For You write bitter things against me. You punish me for the sins I did when I was young. 27 You put chains on my feet, and watch everything I do. You let me walk only so far. 28 I am wasting away like a piece of dead wood, like clothing eaten by the moth.

Job Keeps On Talking—Death Is Sure

14 "Man who is born of woman lives only a short time, and is full of trouble. 2 He grows up and dries like a flower. He leaves like a shadow and does not stay. 3 You open Your eyes on him and decide about him. 4 Who can make clean what is unclean? No one! 5 A man's days are numbered. You know the number of his months. He cannot live longer than the time You have set. 6 So now look away from him that he may rest, until he has lived the time set for him like a man paid to work.

7 "For there is hope for a tree, when it is cut down, that it will grow again, and that its branches will not stop growing. 8 Its

roots grow old in the ground, and the base of the tree dies in the dry ground. 9 But with water it will grow. Branches will grow from it like a plant. 10 But man dies and is laid low. Man dies, and where is he? 11 As water goes into the air from the sea, and the river wastes away and dries up, 12 so man lies down and does not get up again. Until the heavens are no more, he will not wake up or come out of his sleep.

13 "If only You would hide me in the place of the dead! If only You would hide me until Your anger is past, and set a time for me and remember me! 14 If a man dies, will he live again? I will wait all the days of my trouble until a change comes. 15 You will call and I will answer You. You will wait for the work of Your hands. 16 For now You number my steps. You do not write down my sin. 17 My sin is locked up in a bag. You cover my wrong-doing.

18 "But the mountain falls and breaks apart to nothing. The rock moves from its place. 19 Water wears away the stones. Its floods wash away the dust of the earth. So You destroy man's hope. 20 You have power over him forever, and he leaves. You change what he looks like and send him away. 21 His sons receive honor, but he does not know it. Or they lose honor, but he does not see it. 22 His body gives him pain, and he has sorrow only for himself."

Eliphaz Talks

15 Then Eliphaz the Temanite answered, 2 "Should a wise man answer with learning that is of no worth, and fill himself with the east wind? 3 Should he argue with talk that will not help, or with words that do no good? 4 For sure you are doing away with the quiet worship of God. 5 You show your sin by what you say. You are trying to hide behind your words. 6 Your own mouth says you are guilty, and not I. Your own lips speak against you.

7 "Were you the first man to be born? Or were you made before the hills? 8 Were you there to hear the secret plans of God? Are you the only one who has wisdom? 9 What do you know that we do not know? What do you understand that is not clear to us? 10 Men whose hair has grown white and those who have lived many years are among us. They are older than your father. 11 Are the gentle words spoken to you, which give comfort from God, too little for you? 12 Why does your heart carry you away? And why do your eyes shine,

13 that you turn your spirit against God and let such words go out of your mouth? 14 What is man, that he can be pure, or he who is born of a woman, that he can be right and good? 15 See, God puts no trust in His holy ones. The heavens are not pure in His eyes. 16 How much less one who is hated and sinful, a man who drinks sin like water!

17 "I will tell you, listen to me. I will make known what I have seen, 18 what wise men have told that they learned from their fathers. They have not hidden anything. 19 These were the ones to whom the land was given, and no stranger passed among them. 20 The sinful man suffers in pain all his days. His years are numbered because of all his sin. 21 Sounds of fear are in his ears. When all seems to be going well, the one who destroys will come upon him. 22 He does not believe that he will be taken away from darkness, and the sword is meant for him. 23 He goes to look for food, saying, 'Where is it?' He knows that a day of darkness is near. 24 Trouble and pain fill him with fear. They have power over him like a king ready for battle. 25 He has put out his hand against God, and is full of pride against the All-powerful. 26 He rushes in pride against Him with his big battle-covering. 27 His face is fat, and his thighs are heavy with fat. 28 He has lived in cities that have been laid waste, in houses where no one lives which will be destroyed. 29 He will no longer be rich, and what he has will not last. His grain will come to nothing. 30 He will not get away from darkness. The fire will dry up his branches, and the breath of God's mouth will drive him away. 31 Let him not lie to himself and trust in what is empty. For what is empty will be his reward. 32 It will be paid in full while he still lives, and his branch will not be green. 33 He will be like the vine that drops off its grapes before they are ready. And he will throw off his flower like the olive tree. 34 Those who visit the sinful bring no fruit. And fire destroys the tents of those who do wrong. 35 They give birth to trouble and bring sin. Their minds plan lies."

Job Talks

16 Then Job answered, 2 "I have heard many such things. All of you bring trouble instead of comfort. 3 Is there no end to your words that are full of wind? What is your problem that you keep on talking? 4 I also could speak like you, if

I were in your place. I could put words together against you, and shake my head at you. 5 I could give you strength with my mouth. I could speak words of comfort and make your pain less.

6 "If I speak, my pain is not made less. And if I keep quiet, it does not leave me. 7 But now God has taken away my strength. He has taken away all my family. 8 He has made me dry up, and this speaks against me. The wasting away of my body rises up against me. It speaks against me to my face. 9 His anger has torn me and hated me. He has ground His teeth at me. The one against me looks hard at me. 10 Men have looked at me with their mouths open. They have hit me on the face with anger. They have gathered together against me. 11 God gives me over to bad men. He throws me into the hands of the sinful. 12 I was living in comfort, but He has taken that away. He has taken hold of me by the neck and shaken me to pieces. He has set me up for something to shoot at. 13 His arrows are all around me. He cuts my kidneys open without pity. He pours the bitter insides on the ground. 14 He hurts me again and again. He runs at me like a man of war. 15 I have sewed cloth made from hair over my skin, and have laid my hope in the dust. 16 My face is red from crying, and darkness is over my eyes. 17 But my hands have done nothing bad, and my prayer is pure.

18 "O earth, do not cover my blood. Let my cry have no place to rest. 19 See, even now there is One Who sees me from heaven. The One Who speaks for me is on high. 20 My friends make fun of me. My eyes pour out tears to God. 21 If only a man could give reasons to God, as a man does for his neighbor! 22 In a few years I will go the way that I cannot return.

Job Keeps On Talking

17 "My spirit is broken. My days are gone. The grave is ready for me. 2 For sure those with me make fun of me. My eyes see how they laugh at me.

3 "Promise that You will hear me. Who is there that will trust me? 4 For You have kept their heart from understanding, so You will not honor them. 5 If one speaks against friends to get money, the eyes of his children also will become weak.

6 "But He has made me an object of shame to the people. Men spit on me. 7 My eyes have become weak with sorrow. All the parts of my body are like a shadow.

8 Men who are right and good will be surprised and afraid at this. He who is without guilt will be moved to go against the sinful. 9 But the one who is right with God will hold to his way. And he who has clean hands will become stronger and stronger. 10 But all of you try again, and I will not find a wise man among you. 11 My days are past. My plans are torn apart, even the wishes of my heart. 12 They make night into day, saying, 'The light is near,' when there is darkness. 13 If I look for the place of the dead as my home, I make my bed in the darkness. 14 If I say to the grave, 'You are my father,' and to the worm, 'My mother and my sister,' 15 then where is my hope? Who sees hope for me? 16 Will it go down with me to the place of the dead? Will we go down together into the dust?"

Bildad Talks

18 Then Bildad the Shuhite answered, 2 "How long will you keep talking? Show understanding and then we can talk. 3 Why are we thought of as animals? Why do you see us as not being able to think? 4 You who tear yourself in your anger, will the earth be left alone because of you? Or will the rocks be moved from their place?

5 "Yes, the light of the sinful is put out. His fire does not give light. 6 The light in his tent is made dark, and his lamp goes out above him. 7 His strong steps are made short, and his own plans make him fall. 8 For he is thrown down into a net by his own feet and walks on it. 9 A trap catches him by the foot and holds him. 10 A tied rope is hidden in the ground for him. A trap is set for him on the path. 11 He is filled with fear on every side. It follows him at every step. 12 His strength leaves him because trouble is waiting for him at every side. 13 His skin is eaten by disease and the beginning of death eats his legs. 14 He is taken away from his tent where he was safe, and is brought to the king of fears. 15 Fire destroys everything in his tent and sulphur is spread where he lives. 16 His roots are dried below and his branch is cut off above. 17 No one on earth will remember him. His name will not be known in the land. 18 He is sent from light into darkness, and driven away from where people live. 19 He has no children among his people to carry on his name where he lived. 20 Those in the west are surprised and afraid at what happened to him. And those in the east are filled with fear. 21 For sure, these are the houses of the

sinful. This is the place of him who does not know God."

Job Talks

19 Then Job answered, 2 "How long will you make me suffer and crush me with words? 3 Ten times you have put me to shame and are not ashamed to wrong me. 4 Even if it is true that I have done wrong, it stays with me. 5 You put yourselves up high against me, and try to prove my shame to me. 6 You will know then that God has wronged me, and has set a trap around me.

7 "See, I cry, 'Someone is hurting me!' but I get no answer. I call for help, but no one stands for what is right and fair. 8 He has built a wall in my way so that I cannot pass. And He has put darkness on my paths. 9 He has taken my honor from me, and taken the crown from my head. 10 He breaks me down on every side, and I am gone. He has pulled up my hope like a tree. 11 He has made His anger burn against me, and thinks of me as one who fights against Him. 12 His armies come together and build a path against me. They camp around my tent.

13 "He has taken my brothers far away from me and my friends have all left me. 14 My brothers have left me, and my close friends have forgotten me. 15 Those who live in my house and my women servants think of me as a stranger. I am like one from another country in their eyes. 16 I call to my servant, but he does not answer. I have to beg him. 17 My breath smells bad to my wife, and I am hated by my own brothers. 18 Even young children hate me. When I get up they speak against me. 19 All my friends hate me. Those I love have turned against me. 20 I am only skin and flesh. And I have gotten away only by the skin of my teeth. 21 Have pity on me. Have pity on me, O you my friends. For the hand of God has hit me. 22 Why do you make it hard for me as God does? Have I not suffered enough to please you?

23 "If only my words were written! If only they were written down in a book! 24 If only they were cut forever into the rock with an iron cutter and lead! 25 But as for me, I know that the One Who bought me and made me free from sin lives, and that He will stand upon the earth in the end. 26 Even after my skin is destroyed, yet in my flesh I will see God. 27 I myself will see Him. With my own eyes I will see Him and not another. My heart becomes

weak within me. 28 If you say, 'How will we make it hard for him?' and, 'The root of the problem is in him,' 29 you should be afraid of the sword for yourselves. For anger is punished by the sword, that you may know there is punishment for wrong-doing."

Zophar Talks

20 Then Zophar the Naamathite answered, 2 "My troubled thoughts make me answer, because I have no rest inside. 3 I heard the strong words that take away my honor. The spirit of my understanding makes me answer. 4 Do you not know from long ago, since man was put on earth, 5 that the honor of the sinful is short, and the joy of the sinful lasts only a short time? 6 Even if his pride is as high as the heavens and his head touches the clouds, 7 he will be gone forever, like his own waste. Those who have seen him will say, 'Where is he?' 8 He will fly away like a dream, and not be found. He will be driven away like a dream of the night. 9 The eye which saw him will see him no more. His place will no longer see him. 10 His sons will look for the favor of the poor. And his hands will give back his riches. 11 His bones are full of the strength of the young, but it will lie down with him in the dust.

12 "Sin is sweet in his mouth. He hides it under his tongue. 13 He hates to let it go, and holds it in his mouth. 14 Yet his food in his stomach is changed to the poison of snakes inside him. 15 He eats riches, but will spit them up. God will take them out of his stomach. 16 He will drink the poison of snakes. The snake's tongue will kill him. 17 He will not look at the rivers, the rivers flowing with honey and milk. 18 He must return what he has worked for, and can not eat it. He will not have joy from the riches of his trading. 19 For he has taken from the poor and left them with nothing. He has taken houses which he has not built.

20 "Because he thought he never had enough, he has nothing that gives him joy. 21 There was nothing more for him to get, so his having everything will not last. 22 Even when he has many riches, he will have trouble. Everyone who suffers will come against him. 23 When he fills his stomach, God will send His great anger on him. He will send it on him while he is eating. 24 He may get away from the iron sword, but the brass bow will shoot an arrow in him. 25 It cuts through his body and comes out of his back. The shining

arrow comes out of his liver. Much fear comes upon him. 26 Complete darkness is stored up for his riches. A fire not kept going by man will burn him up. It will destroy all that is left in his tent. 27 The heavens will make his sin known, and the earth will rise up against him. 28 The things of his house will be carried away. They will be taken away in the day of God's anger. 29 This is what God has for sinful men. It is what God chooses to give to them."

Job Talks

21 Then Job answered, 2 "Be careful to listen to my words. Let this be the comfort you give me. 3 Listen to me while I speak. Then after I have spoken, you may keep on making fun of me. 4 As for me, am I complaining against man? Why should my spirit not be troubled? 5 Look at me, and be surprised; and put your hand over your mouth. 6 When I think, I am troubled; and fear takes hold of my body. 7 Why do the sinful live, become old, and become very powerful? 8 They watch their children's children become strong in front of their eyes. 9 Their houses are safe from fear. And the punishment of God does not come upon them. 10 Their bull mates without trouble. Their cow gives birth to live calves. 11 They send out their little ones like a flock, and their children jump around. 12 They sing to the timbrel and the harp. They show their joy at the sound of the horn. 13 They spend their days with much more than they need. And all at once they go down to the place of the dead. 14 They say to God, 'Leave us alone! We do not want to know your ways 15 Who is the All-powerful, that we should serve Him? What would we have more than we have if we prayed to Him?' 16 See, their well-being is not in their own hands. The wisdom of the sinful is far from me.

17 "How many times is the lamp of the sinful put out, that their trouble comes upon them? How often does God send trouble to them in His anger? 18 Are they like straw blown by the wind? Are they like straw that the storm carries away? 19 You say, 'God stores up a man's punishment for his sons.' Let God punish him so that he may know it. 20 Let his own eyes see himself being destroyed. Let him drink the anger of the All-powerful. 21 For what does he care for his house and family after he is dead, when the number of his months is over? 22 Can anyone teach God anything, when He judges those on high?

23 One man dies while still very strong, having everything he needs and time to enjoy it. 24 His body has good food and his bones are strong. 25 Another dies with bitter feelings in his soul, never having enjoyed anything good. 26 Together they lie down in the dust, and worms cover them.

27 "See, I know your thoughts and your plans to wrong me. 28 For you say, 'Where is the house of the leader? Where are the tents where the sinful men live?' 29 Have you not asked those who travel this way? Do you listen to what they say? 30 For the sinful are kept for the day of trouble. They will be brought out on the day of anger. 31 Who will talk to him about his way to his face? And who will punish him for what he has done? 32 When he is carried to the grave, men will keep watch over his grave. 33 The earth of the valley will be sweet to him. All men will follow after him, and those who go before him are too many to number. 34 How then can you comfort me with foolish words? Your answers are full of lies."

Eliphaz Talks

22 Then Eliphaz the Temanite answered, 2 "Can a man be of use to God? Can a wise man be of use to himself? 3 Is the All-powerful pleased if you are right and good? Is it of any use to Him if your ways were perfect? 4 Is it because of how you honor God that He speaks strong words to you and punishes you? 5 Have you not done much wrong and your sins have no end? 6 For you have taken things from your brothers when they did not owe you anything. You have taken all their clothing and they have had nothing to wear. 7 To those who were tired, you have given no water to drink. And you have kept bread from the hungry. 8 But you were a powerful and respected man owning land and living on it. 9 You have sent women away with nothing, whose husbands have died. And you have crushed the strength of children who have no parents. 10 So traps are all around you, and much fear comes upon you all at once. 11 This is why it is dark and you cannot see, and a flood of water covers you.

12 "Is not God high up in heaven? See the highest stars, how high they are! 13 So you say, 'What does God know? Can He judge through the darkness?' 14 Clouds cover Him so that He cannot see. He walks on the roof of heaven.' 15 Will you keep to the old way which sinful men have walked?

16 They were taken away before their time. The ground they stood on was washed away by a river. 17 They said to God, 'Leave us!' and 'What can the All-powerful do to us?' 18 Yet He filled their houses with good things. But the wisdom of the sinful is far from me. 19 Those who are right and good see it and are glad. Those who are without guilt make fun of them, 20 saying, 'For sure those who hate us are destroyed, and fire has destroyed what they owned.'

21 "Agree with God, and be at peace with Him. Then good will come to you. 22 Receive the teaching from His mouth, and keep His words in your heart. 23 If you return to the All-powerful, things will be well with you again. Put sin far from your tent. 24 Put your gold in the dust, and gold of Ophir among the stones of the river. 25 Then the All-powerful will be your gold and silver of much worth. 26 Then you will have joy in the All-powerful, and lift up your face to God. 27 You will pray to Him, and He will hear you. And you will keep your promises to Him. 28 You will decide something, and it will be done for you. Light will shine on your path. 29 For God puts down the man who is filled with pride. But He saves the one who is not proud. 30 He will save the man who is even guilty because he will be helped by your hands that are clean."

Job Talks

23 Then Job answered, 2 "Even today my complaining is bitter. His hand is heavy even when I cry inside myself. 3 If only I knew where to find Him, that I might go where He is! 4 I would tell Him how things are with me, and my mouth would be ready to argue. 5 I would know His answer, and could think about what He would say to me. 6 Would He go against me using His great power? No, He would listen to me. 7 There a man who is right could reason with Him. And I would be set free by my Judge.

8 "See, I go east, but He is not there. I go west, but I cannot see Him. 9 When He works to the left, I cannot see Him. When He turns to the right, I cannot see Him. 10 But He knows the way that I take. When He has tried me, I will come out as gold. 11 My foot has kept close to His steps. I have kept His way and have not turned aside. 12 I have not turned away from the words of His lips. I have stored up the words of His mouth. They are worth more to me than the food I need. 13 But He cannot be

changed. Who can go against Him? He does whatever He wants. 14 For He does what He has planned for me, and many such things are in His mind. 15 So I am afraid to be with Him. When I think about it, I am very afraid of Him. 16 God has made my heart weak. The All-powerful has filled me with fear. 17 But I am not made quiet by the darkness or the deep shadow which covers my face.

Job Keeps On Talking

24 "Why are times for judging not set up by the All-powerful? And why do those who know Him not see these days? 2 Some take away the land-marks and take fields and animals. 3 They drive away the donkeys that belong to those who have no parents. They take the bull that belongs to a woman whose husband has died, as a promise that she will pay what she owes. 4 They push poor people off the road. All the poor of the land are made to hide themselves. 5 See, they go out like wild donkeys in the desert to look for food for their children. 6 They gather food in the fields, and gather what they can that is left from the grape-fields owned by the sinful. 7 They lie all night without clothing, and have no covering in the cold. 8 They are wet with the mountain rains and stay close to the rocks for cover. 9 Others take from the breast the child who has no father. They take the child from the poor as a promise that they will pay what they owe. 10 They make the poor go about without clothing, making them carry loads of cut grain while they are hungry. 11 Among the olive trees they make oil. They crush grapes but they are thirsty. 12 Men from the city cry inside themselves. The souls of those who are hurt cry out. Yet God does not listen to their prayer.

13 "Then there are those who turn against the light. They do not want to know its ways or stay in its paths. 14 The one who kills people gets up early in the morning. He kills the poor and those in need. And during the night he is like a robber. 15 The eye of the one who is not faithful in marriage waits for the evening, saying, 'No one will see me.' And he covers his face. 16 In the dark they dig into houses. They shut themselves up during the day and do not know the light. 17 For midnight is morning to them. They are not afraid of the fears of darkness.

18 "They are taken away on the top of the waters. Their part of the earth is cursed.

They do not go to their grape-fields. ¹⁹ Dry weather and heat take away the water from the snow, just as the place of the dead takes away those who have sinned. ²⁰ A mother will forget him. The worm is pleased to eat him until he is remembered no more. Sin will be broken like a tree. ²¹ He does wrong to the woman who cannot give birth. And he does no good for the woman whose husband has died. ²² But God by His power gives long life to the strong. They rise again, even when they had no hope of life. ²³ He makes them safe and gives them strength, and His eyes are on their ways. ²⁴ They are given honor for a little while, and then they are gone. They are brought low and gathered up as all others are. They are cut off like the heads of grain. ²⁵ If it is not so, who can prove me a liar, and show that what I say means nothing?"

Bildad Talks

25 Then Bildad the Shuhite answered, ² "Power and fear belong to God. He keeps peace in His high places. ³ Is there any number to His armies? Upon whom does His light not shine? ⁴ How then can a man be right and good before God? How can he who is born of woman be clean? ⁵ See, even the moon is not bright and the stars are not pure in His eyes. ⁶ How much less man, who is a bug, and the son of man, who is a worm!"

Job Talks

26 Then Job answered, ² "What a help you are to the weak! How you have saved the arm that has no strength! ³ How you have given wise words to him who has no wisdom! How much true learning you have given! ⁴ To whom have your words been said? And from whose spirit have you spoken?

⁵ The spirits of the dead shake under the waters and those living in them. ⁶ The place of the dead has no covering before God and the place that destroys has no covering. ⁷ He spreads out the north over empty waste, and hangs the earth on nothing. ⁸ He holds the waters in His clouds, and the cloud does not break under them. ⁹ He covers the face of the moon and spreads His cloud over it. ¹⁰ He has marked the sides around the waters where light and darkness are divided. ¹¹ The pillars of heaven shake with fear. They are surprised and afraid of His sharp words. ¹² He made the sea quiet by His power.

And by His understanding He destroyed Rahab. ¹³ By His breath the heavens are made beautiful. His hand cut through the snake as it tried to get away. ¹⁴ See, these are only a few of the things He does. And how quiet are the words spoken about Him! But who can understand His powerful thunder?"

Job Keeps On Talking

27 Job kept on speaking, and said, ² "As God lives, Who has taken away my right, and the All-powerful, Who has troubled my soul, ³ as long as life is in me, and the breath of God is in my nose, ⁴ my lips will not speak what is not true, and my tongue will not lie. ⁵ Far be it from me to say that you are right. Until I die I will not put away my honor. ⁶ I will hold on to what is right and good and will not let it go. My heart does not put me to shame for any of my days.

⁷ "May the one who hates me be as the sinful. And may the one who is against me be as those who are not right and good. ⁸ For what is the hope of the man without God when he dies, when God takes away his life? ⁹ Will God hear his cry when trouble comes upon him? ¹⁰ Will he be glad in the All-powerful? Will he call on God at all times? ¹¹ I will teach you about the power of God. I will not hide the ways of the All-powerful. ¹² All of you have seen it yourselves. Why then do you speak in a foolish way?

¹³ "This is what God gives to a sinful man, the gift that a man who makes it hard for others receives from the All-powerful. ¹⁴ If he has many sons, they will be killed by the sword. And his children will not have enough bread to eat. ¹⁵ Those who are left to him will be buried because of disease. And the wives who have lost their husbands will not be able to cry. ¹⁶ He may gather up silver like dust, and gather so much clothing as if they were clay. ¹⁷ He may have it, but those who are right with God will wear it. And those who are without guilt will divide the silver. ¹⁸ He builds his house like the home of a spider, or like a tent which a watchman has made. ¹⁹ He goes to bed rich, but will never again. When he opens his eyes, his riches are gone. ²⁰ Fears come over him like a flood. A storm carries him away in the night. ²¹ The east wind carries him away, and he is gone. It carries him away from his place. ²² It comes at him without pity. He tries to run from its power as fast as he can.

23 Men clap their hands at him, and drive him from his place with sounds of shame.

Where Can Wisdom Be Found?

28 "For sure there is a mine for silver, and a place where gold is made pure. 2 Iron is taken out of the earth. And copper is melted from the rock. 3 Man looks into the deepest darkness. And he goes out to the farthest part of the earth to look for rocks in the dark places. 4 Men break open deep holes far from where people live, forgotten by travelers. In the holes they hang and move from side to side far from men. 5 As for the earth, out of it comes food. But below, it is turned up as fire. 6 Sapphires come from its rocks and its dust has gold. 7 No bird who eats meat knows that path. The falcon's eye has not seen it. 8 The proud animals have not stepped on it. The strong lion has not passed over it. 9 Man puts his hand on the hard rock. He turns the mountains over at its base. 10 He makes a path through the rocks, and his eyes see everything of much worth. 11 He stops rivers from flowing. And he brings to light what is hidden.

12 "But where can wisdom be found? And where is the place of understanding? 13 Man does not know its worth, and it is not found in the land of the living. 14 The deep waters say, 'It is not in me.' The sea says, 'It is not with me.' 15 Pure gold cannot be traded for it and it cannot be bought with silver. 16 It cannot be compared in worth to the gold of Ophir, onyx of much worth, or sapphire. 17 Gold or glass cannot be compared to it in worth and it cannot be traded for objects of fine gold. 18 There is no need to say anything about coral or crystal because wisdom cannot be paid for with rubies. 19 The topaz of Ethiopia cannot be compared to it in worth and it cannot be compared with the worth of pure gold. 20 Where then does wisdom come from? Where is the place of understanding? 21 It is hidden from the eyes of all living. It is hidden from the birds of the sky. 22 The Place That Destroys and Death say, 'We have only heard about it with our ears.'

23 "God understands the way to wisdom, and He knows its place. 24 For He looks to the ends of the earth, and sees everything under the heavens. 25 He gave weight to the wind. He decided how much water would be in the sea. 26 He decided how much rain would fall, and the path for the lightning. 27 Then He saw wisdom and made it known. He made it last, and found out all about it. 28 And He said to man, 'See, the fear of the Lord, that is wisdom. And to turn away from sin is understanding.' "

Job Tells of His Past Days

29 Then Job spoke again and said, 2 "If only I could be now as I was in the months past when God watched over me! 3 His lamp shined over my head then and by His light I walked through darkness. 4 Those days were my best days when God was my friend watching over my tent. 5 The All-powerful was still with me, and my children were around me. 6 My path was washed with milk, and the rock poured out rivers of oil for me. 7 When I went to the city gate and took my place with the leaders of the city, 8 the young men saw me and let me go by. The old men rose and stood. 9 The leaders stopped talking, and put their hands on their mouths. 10 The voices of the rulers were quiet. Their tongues held to the roof of their mouths. 11 Those who heard me, honored me. Those who saw me, respected me, 12 because I helped the poor man when he cried for help and the child without parents who had no one to help him. 13 Good came to me from the man who was dying. And I made the heart of the woman whose husband had died sing for joy. 14 I put on what was right and good, and it clothed me. The right things done were my coat and head-covering. 15 I was eyes to the blind, and feet to the man who could not walk. 16 I was a father to those in need. And I helped those I did not know who had a need. 17 I broke the jaws of the sinful, and took from their teeth what they had taken. 18 Then I thought, 'I will die in my nest. My days will be as many as the sand. 19 My roots go to the water. As the water is on the grass in the early morning, it will be all night on my branches. 20 My honor is always new to me, and my bow is new in my hand.'

21 "Men listened to me and waited. They were quiet so they could hear my words of wisdom. 22 After I spoke, they did not speak again. My words stayed with them. 23 They waited for me as for rain. And they opened their mouths as for the spring rain. 24 I looked at them with joy when they were not sure of themselves, and the light of my face gave them comfort. 25 I decided the way for them and sat as their leader. I lived as a king among his army, and like one who gives comfort to those in sorrow.

Job Keeps On Talking

30 "But now those who are younger than I make fun of me. I thought so little of their fathers that I did not want them with my sheep dogs. 2 Yes, what good could I get from the strength of their hands? Their strength was gone. 3 Their bodies are thin and in need of food. At night they bite the dry ground in the waste-land. 4 They pick plants that taste of salt among the bushes, And they eat the root of the broom bush. 5 They are driven away from people. Men call out against them as if they were robbers. 6 So they live in valleys made by floods, in caves of the earth and of the rocks. 7 Among the bushes they cry out. They gather together under the thistles. 8 They are fools and they have no name. They have been driven out of the land.

9 "Now they make fun of me in song. They laugh at me. 10 They hate me and keep away from me, but they spit in my face. 11 Because God has made the string of my bow loose and has troubled me, they have thrown off their respect for me. 12 Their bad group comes to my right. They push me away and trip my feet, and make ways to destroy me. 13 They break up my path. They make trouble for me, and no one stops them. 14 They come as if through a wide hole in the wall, and roll on with much noise. 15 Fears come upon me. They go after my honor like the wind. And my well-being has passed away like a cloud.

16 "Now my soul is poured out within me. Days of trouble have taken hold of me. 17 Night cuts into my bones with pain. The pain keeps on and takes no rest. 18 My clothing is torn by a strong power. It pulls against me like the top of my coat. 19 God has thrown me into the mud, and I have become like dust and ashes. 20 I cry out to You for help, but You do not answer me. I stand up, and You turn away from me. 21 You work against me. With the power of Your hand you make it hard for me. 22 You lift me up to the wind and make it carry me. You throw me around in the storm. 23 For I know that You will bring me to death, to the place for all the living.

24 "Yet does not one in a destroyed place put out his hand, and in his trouble cry out for help? 25 Have I not cried for the one whose life is hard? Was not my soul filled with sorrow for the poor? 26 When I expected good, then trouble came. When I waited for light, darkness came. 27 My heart is troubled and does not rest. Days of trouble are before me. 28 I go about full of sorrow without comfort. I stand up where the people are gathered and cry out for help. 29 I have become a brother to wild dogs, and a friend of ostriches. 30 My skin becomes black and falls from me. My bones burn because I am sick. 31 So my harp is turned to sorrow, and my horn to the sound of crying.

Job Keeps On Talking

31 "I have made an agreement with my eyes not to look with desire at a young woman. 2 What would be my share from God above? What would my gift be from the All-powerful on high? 3 Does not trouble come to those who are not right and good? Do not hard times come to those who do wrong? 4 Does He not see my ways and number all my steps?

5 "If I have walked in ways that are false, and my foot has been quick to follow false ways, 6 let Him weigh me with a true weight. Let God know that I am honest. 7 If my step has turned from the way, and my heart has followed my eyes, or if my hands have held on to sin, 8 then let me plant and another eat. Let what grows be pulled out by the roots.

9 "If my heart has been tempted by a woman, or I have waited at my neighbor's door, 10 may my wife grind grain for another. And let others bow down upon her. 11 For that would be a very sinful thing to do. It would be a sin that would be punished by the judges. 12 For that would be a fire that burns at the Place That Destroys. It would dig out all I have planted.

13 "If I did not listen to my men servants and women servants when they complained against me, 14 what will I do when God speaks to me? When He asks me why, what will I answer Him? 15 Did not He Who made me inside my mother make him also? Did not the same One give us life from our mothers?

16 "If I have kept what the poor should have or have caused the eyes of the woman whose husband has died to be tired, 17 if I have eaten my food alone without sharing it with the child who has no parents, 18 (but from the time I was young, he grew up with me as a father, and I have helped the woman without a husband since I was born,) 19 if I have seen anyone die because he had no clothing, or left any poor person without clothes, 20 if he has not thanked me for the clothing on his body and been made warm with the wool of my sheep,

21 if I have not done these things, or if I have lifted up my hand against the child who has no parents, because I saw I had help in the gate, 22 let my shoulder fall out of place, and let my arm be broken off at the joint. 23 For trouble sent by God fills me with fear. Because of His great power I could not do these things.

24 "If I have put my faith in gold and said fine gold is my trust, 25 if I have had pride because of my many riches and have received much by my hand, 26 if I have looked at the sun shining or the bright moon going on its way, 27 and have in secret worshiped them in my heart, and have honored them by throwing them a kiss with my hand, 28 these also would be sins to be judged. It would say I did not know the God above.

29 "Have I been glad when a person who hated me was destroyed? Have I been filled with joy when trouble came to him? 30 No, I have not allowed my mouth to sin by asking his life to be cursed. 31 Have the men of my tent not said, 'Who can find one who has not been filled with his meat'? 32 The stranger has not stayed in the street, for I have opened my doors to the traveler. 33 Have I hidden my sins like Adam? Have I hidden my wrong-doing in my heart, 34 because I was afraid of all the people, and of families who hated me? Did I keep quiet and not go out of the door? 35 If only I had one to hear me! See, here my name is written. Let the All-powerful answer me! May what is against me be written down! 36 For sure I would carry it on my shoulder. I would tie it around my head like a crown. 37 I would tell Him the number of my every step. I would come near Him like a prince.

38 "If my land cries out against me and the ditches made by the plow cry together, 39 if I have eaten its fruit without paying for it, and caused its owners to die, 40 let thorns grow instead of grain. And let weeds with a bad smell grow instead of barley."

The words of Job are finished.

Elihu Talks

32 Then these three men stopped answering Job, because he was right and good in his own eyes. 2 But Elihu the son of Barachel the Buzite, of the family of Ram, became very angry. He was angry at Job because he said he was right with God. 3 And he was angry at his three friends because they had found no answer, yet they had said that Job was wrong. 4 Now Elihu had waited to speak to Job because they were older than he. 5 And when Elihu saw that there was no answer in the mouth of the three men, he was very angry. 6 So Elihu the son of Barachel the Buzite said, "I am young, and you are old. So I did not feel that I should speak. I was afraid to tell you what I think. 7 I thought the older men should speak, and that the many years should teach wisdom. 8 But it is the spirit in a man and the breath of the All-powerful that gives him understanding. 9 The old may not be wise. They may not understand what is right and fair. 10 So I say, 'Listen to me. I also will tell you what I think.'

11 "See, I waited for your words. I listened to what you said and waited to hear more from you. 12 I was careful to listen to you. There was no one who could prove that Job was wrong. None of you could answer his words. 13 Do not say, 'We have found wisdom. God will show he is wrong, not man.' 14 Now Job has not spoken his words against me. And I will not answer him with your words.

15 "They are troubled and have no more to say. Words do not come. 16 Should I wait because they do not speak, because they stand there and do not answer? 17 I also will give my answer. I will tell what I think. 18 For I am full of words. The spirit within me makes me speak. 19 See, my stomach is like wine that cannot get out. It is ready to break like new wine bottles made of skin. 20 Let me speak, that I may find comfort. Let me open my lips and answer. 21 I will not show favor to anyone, or praise any man in a false way. 22 For I do not know how to say sweet-sounding words that are not true, for then my Maker would soon take me away.

Elihu Keeps On Speaking

33 "But now, Job, hear what I say. Listen to all my words. 2 See, I open my mouth. My tongue in my mouth wants to speak. 3 My words come from my heart that is right. My lips speak in truth what I know. 4 The Spirit of God has made me. And the breath of the All-powerful gives me life. 5 Prove me wrong if you can. Get ready to answer me, and take your stand. 6 See, I belong to God like you. I also have been made from the clay. 7 See, you have no reason to be afraid of me. I should not make it hard for you.

8 "For sure you have spoken in my hearing. I have heard all you have said. 9 You

said, 'I am pure and without sin. I am not guilty, and there is no sin in me. [10] But see, God finds things against me. He thinks of me as someone who hates Him. [11] He puts my feet in chains, and watches all my paths.' [12] See, I tell you, in this you are not right. For God is greater than man.

[13] "Why do you complain against Him? He does not give a reason for all He does. [14] For God speaks once, or twice, and yet no one listens. [15] In a dream, a special dream of the night, when deep sleep comes upon men, while they sleep in their beds, [16] then He opens the ears of men. He teaches them and makes them afraid telling them of danger, [17] that He may turn man away from wrong-doing and keep him from pride. [18] He keeps his soul from going to the place of the dead. And He keeps his life from being destroyed by the sword.

[19] "Man is also punished with pain on his bed and has pain all the time in his bones. [20] So he hates bread, and has no desire for fine foods. [21] His flesh is so wasted away that it cannot be seen. His bones which were not seen stick out. [22] His soul comes close to the grave, and his life to those who bring death.

[23] "If there is an angel, one out of a thousand, to speak with God for him, and to show a man what is right for him, [24] then let him be kind to him, and say, 'Save him from going down to the grave. I have found someone to pay the price to make him free.' [25] Let his flesh become young again. Let him return to the days when he was young and strong.' [26] Then he will pray to God, and God will be pleased with him. He will see His face with joy. And God will make man right with Him again. [27] He will sing to men and say, 'I have sinned and have not done what is right, but He did not punish me. [28] He has kept my soul from going to the grave. And my life will see the light.'

[29] "See, God does all these things twice, even three times, to a man, [30] to turn back his soul from the grave, that he may see the light of life. [31] Hear what I say, O Job, listen to me. Be quiet and let me speak, [32] If you have anything to say, answer me. Speak, for I want to make you right with God. [33] If not, listen to me. Be quiet, and I will teach you wisdom."

Elihu Keeps On Speaking

34 Then Elihu said, [2] "Hear my words, you wise men. Listen to me, you who know. [3] For the ear tests words as the mouth tastes food. [4] Let us choose for ourselves what is right. Let us know among ourselves what is good. [5] For Job has said, 'I am right and good, but God has taken away my right.' [6] Would I lie about my right? I have been hurt so that I cannot be healed, but I have done no wrong.' [7] What man is like Job, who drinks up words against him like water? [8] He goes among those who do wrong, and walks with sinful men. [9] For he has said, 'A man gets nothing by trying to please God.'

[10] "So listen to me, you men of understanding. Far be it from God to do what is sinful, and from the All-powerful to do wrong. [11] For He pays a man by the work he does. He will see that a man is paid for what he does. [12] For sure God will not do wrong. The All-powerful will not turn what is right into sin. [13] Who gave Him the power over the earth? Who gave Him the whole world to take care of? [14] If He should take back His spirit and His breath, [15] all flesh would die together, and man would return to dust.

[16] "If you have understanding, hear this. Listen to what I say. [17] Should one who hates what is right be the one to rule? Will you say that He Who is right and good and strong is guilty? [18] Who says to a king, 'You are of no worth,' and to rulers, 'You are sinful'? [19] Who shows no favor to princes, or thinks of the rich as more important than the poor? They are all the work of His hands. [20] In a short time they die. At midnight the people are shaken and pass away. And the powerful are taken away by no human hand.

[21] "For God's eyes are upon the ways of a man, and He sees all his steps. [22] There is no darkness or shadow where sinners can hide themselves. [23] For God does not need to set a time for man to go before Him and be judged. [24] He breaks powerful men in pieces without asking any reason, and puts others in their place. [25] For He knows their works. He puts them down in the night, and they are crushed. [26] God punishes them for their sin where everyone can see them. [27] Because they turned aside from following Him. They did not care about any of His ways. [28] So they caused the cry of the poor to come to Him. And He heard the cry of those in need. [29] When He keeps quiet, who can say He is wrong? When He hides His face, who can see Him? But He is over both nation and man. [30] So men without God should not rule and should not be a trap for the people.

[31] "For has any one said to God, 'I have

suffered punishment, and will not cause any more trouble? 32 Teach me what I cannot see. If I have sinned, I will do it no more'? 33 Will God ask what you want to do, when you will not do what He says? You must decide, and not I. So tell what you know. 34 Men of understanding will say to me, and wise men who hear me say, 35 'Job speaks without much learning. His words are without wisdom. 36 Job should be tried to the end, because he answers like sinful men. 37 To his sin he adds a strong will against God. Making fun he claps his hands among us, and speaks many words against God.'"

Elihu Keeps On Talking

35 Then Elihu said, 2 "Do you think this is right? Do you say, 'I am more right than God'? 3 For you ask, 'What will You get by it? How will it be better for me than if I had sinned?' 4 I will answer you, and your friends with you. 5 Look at the heavens and see. See the clouds which are higher than you. 6 If you have sinned, what does that do to God? If you have done many wrongs, what does that do to Him? 7 If you are right and good, what do you give to Him? What does He receive from you? 8 Your wrong-doing may hurt another man and your being right and good may help him.

9 "People cry out because of their many hard times. They cry for help because of the arm of the powerful. 10 But no one says, 'Where is God my Maker, Who gives songs in the night, 11 Who teaches us more than the animals of the earth, and makes us wiser than the birds of the heavens?' 12 There they cry out, but He does not answer because of the pride of sinful men. 13 For sure God will not listen to an empty cry. The All-powerful will not do anything about it. 14 How much less when you say you do not see Him, that your trial is before Him, and you must wait for Him! 15 And now, because God has not punished in His anger, and does not watch for sin, 16 Job opens his mouth with empty talk. He speaks many words without much learning."

Elihu Keeps On Speaking

36 Then Elihu spoke more and said, 2 "Wait for me a little longer, and I will show you that there is yet more to be said for God. 3 I bring my learning from far away, and will tell how right and good my Maker is. 4 For sure my words are not false. One who is perfect in much learning is with you.

5 "See, God is powerful, but does not hate anyone. He is powerful in strength of understanding. 6 He does not keep the sinful alive, but gives what is right and fair to those who are troubled. 7 He does not turn His eyes away from those who are right with Him. He puts them on the throne with kings and they are honored forever. 8 If they are tied up in chains and caught in the ropes of trouble, 9 then He makes known to them their work and their sins, that they have shown pride. 10 He makes them listen to teaching, and tells them to turn away from sin. 11 If they hear and serve Him, the rest of their days will be filled with what they need and their years with peace. 12 But if they do not hear, they will die by the sword. They will die without learning.

13 "But those who do not know God keep anger in their heart. They do not cry for help when He puts them in chains. 14 They die when they are young. And their life ends among those who sell the use of their bodies in the houses of the false gods. 15 He takes those who suffer out of their suffering. He speaks to them in times of trouble. 16 He led you from being close to trouble to a wide place where you were free with your table full of food.

17 "But you wanted to punish the sinful. Punishment and being fair have taken hold of you. 18 Be careful or anger will tempt you to laugh at the truth. Do not take pay in secret for wrong-doing and be turned aside. 19 Will your riches or all your power keep you from trouble? 20 Do not desire the night, when people are taken from their place. 21 Be careful, do not turn to sin. For you have chosen this instead of suffering. 22 See, God is honored in His power. Who is a teacher like Him? 23 Who has told Him the way He should go? And who has said, 'You have done wrong'?

24 "Remember that you should honor His work, of which men have sung. 25 All men have seen it. Man sees it from far away. 26 See, God is honored, and we do not know Him. We are not able to know the number of His years. 27 For He takes up the drops of water that become rain, 28 which the clouds pour down. Much rain falls on man. 29 Can anyone understand how the clouds are spread out, or how He thunders from His tent? 30 See, He spreads His lightning around Him and covers the bottom of the sea. 31 For by

these He judges the people and He gives much food. 32 He covers His hands with the lightning, and tells it to hit the mark. 33 His thunder tells of a storm coming, and cattle also know it is coming.

Elihu Keeps On Talking

37 "At this my heart shakes with fear and jumps from its place. 2 Listen to the thunder of His voice and the noise that comes from His mouth. 3 He lets it loose under the whole heaven. He lets His lightning go to the ends of the earth. 4 His voice sounds after it. He thunders with His great and powerful voice. And He does not hold back the lightning when His voice is heard. 5 God thunders with His great voice. He does great things which we cannot understand. 6 For He says to the snow, 'Fall on the earth,' and to the rain, 'Be strong.' 7 He stops the work of every man, that all men may know His work. 8 Then the wild animals go to their holes, and stay where they live. 9 The storm comes from the south, and the cold from the north. 10 Water becomes ice by the breath of God. The wide waters become ice. 11 He loads the heavy clouds with water and they send out His lightning. 12 It changes its path and turns around by His leading, doing whatever He tells it to do on the earth where people live. 13 He causes it to happen for punishment, or for His world, or because of His love.

14 "Hear this, O Job. Stop and think about the great works of God. 15 Do you know how God does them, and makes the lightning shine from His cloud? 16 Do you know how the clouds are set in heaven, the great works of Him Who is perfect in understanding? 17 Do you know why you are hot in your clothes when the land becomes quiet because of the south wind? 18 Can you help Him spread out the sky, making it as hard as a mirror made from heated brass? 19 Teach us what we should say to Him. We cannot put words together to help us because of darkness. 20 Should He be told that I want to speak? Did a man ever wish to be swallowed up?

21 "Now men cannot look on the light when it is bright in the sky, when the wind has passed and made it clear. 22 A bright gold light is seen in the north. Around God is great power. 23 We cannot come near the All-powerful. He is lifted high with power. And He is right and fair and good and will not make it hard for us. 24 So men honor Him with fear. He has respect for any who are wise in heart."

The Lord Answers Job

38 Then the Lord answered Job out of the strong wind and said, 2 "Who is this that makes words of wisdom dark by speaking without much learning? 3 Now get ready like a man, and I will ask you some questions and you answer Me. 4 Where were you when I began building the earth? Tell Me, if you have understanding. 5 Who decided how big it was to be, since you know? Who looked to see if it was as big as it should be? 6 What was it built upon? Who laid its first stone, 7 when the morning stars sang together and all the sons of God called out for joy?

8 "Who shut up the sea with doors, when it rushed out from its secret place? 9 I made clouds its clothing, and put much darkness around it. 10 I marked the places where it could not pass, and set locks and doors. 11 And I said, 'You will come this far, and no further. Here will your proud waves stop.'

12 "Have you ever in your life told the morning when to come, and caused the first light of day to know its place, 13 that it might take hold of the ends of the earth, and the sinful be shaken out of it? 14 It is changed like clay when an object is pushed down to mark it, and they stand out like clothing. 15 The light of the sinful is held back, and the arm lifted up is broken.

16 "Have you gone into the wells of the sea? Have you walked on the bottom of the deep sea? 17 Have the gates of death been shown to you? Or have you seen the gates of the deep darkness? 18 Have you understood how great the earth is? Tell Me, if you know all this.

19 "Where does the light come from? And where is the place of darkness, 20 that you may take it to its land, and know the paths to its home? 21 You know, for you were born then. You are very old! 22 Have you gone into the store-houses of the snow? Have you seen the store-houses of the hail, 23 which I have kept for the time of trouble, for the day of war and battle? 24 What is the way to the place where the light is divided, or the east wind spread over the earth?

25 "Who has cut open a way for the flood, and a path for the thunderstorm? 26 Who brings rain on the land without people, on a desert without a man in it, 27 to fill the need of the wasted land, and to make the grass grow? 28 Does the rain have a father? Who has given birth to the drops of rain? 29 Who gave birth to ice? And who

gave birth to the snow water of heaven? [30] Water becomes hard like stone, and the top of the sea is covered with ice.

[31] "Can you tie the chains of the stars of Pleiades, or loose the ropes of Orion? [32] Can you lead the groups of stars out at the right times? Can you lead the stars of the Bear with her young? [33] Do you know the laws of the heavens? Can you make them to rule over the earth?

[34] "Can you lift up your voice to the clouds, that a flood of water may cover you? [35] Can you send out lightnings, that they may go and say to you, 'Here we are'? [36] Who has given wisdom to the heart? Who has given understanding to the mind? [37] Who can number the clouds by wisdom? Or who can push over the water jars of the heavens, [38] when the dust gathers together and becomes hard?

[39] "Can you hunt food for the lion? Can you fill the hunger of the young lions, [40] when they lie in their own place in the rock, or wait in their hiding place? [41] Who gets the food ready for the raven, when its young cry to God and go about without food?

The Lord Is Speaking to Job

39 "Do you know when the mountain goats give birth? Do you watch the deer giving birth? [2] Can you number the months that they carry their young? Or do you know the time when their young are born? [3] They get down and give birth to their young, and get rid of their pains. [4] Their young ones become strong. They grow up in the open field. They leave and do not return to them.

[5] "Who has let the wild donkey go free? Who has taken off the ropes which held the fast donkey? [6] I gave him the desert for a home, and the salt land for a place to live. [7] He hates the noise of the city. He does not hear the calls of the man who drives him. [8] He goes looking for grass to eat on the mountains. He looks for every green thing. [9] Will the wild ox be willing to serve you? Will he stay through the night by the food you give him to eat? [10] Can you tie the wild ox to a plow in the field? Will he follow you to plow the valleys? [11] Will you trust in him because he is very strong, and leave your work to him? [12] Will you trust him to return and bring your grain to your grain-floor?

[13] "The wings of the ostrich wave with joy, but are they the wings of love? [14] For she leaves her eggs to the earth and lets them get warm in the dust. [15] She forgets that a foot might crush them, or that the wild animal may step on them. [16] She is bad in the way she acts toward her young, as if they were not hers. Her work of giving birth is for nothing, for she does not care. [17] Because God has not given her wisdom or her share of understanding. [18] When she begins to run, she laughs at the horse and the horseman.

[19] "Do you give the horse his strength? Do you dress his neck with long hair? [20] Do you make him jump like the locust? The powerful noise he makes with his nostrils fills men with fear. [21] He hits his foot against the ground in the valley, and has joy in his strength. He goes out to meet the battle. [22] He laughs at fear and is not afraid. He does not turn back from the sword. [23] The arrows and spears he carries make noise as they hit together. [24] He runs fast over the ground with shaking and anger. He cannot stand still at the sound of the horn. [25] When the horn sounds, he laughs without fear. He smells the battle from far away. He hears the thunder of the captains, and the war cry.

[26] "Is it by your understanding that the hawk flies, spreading his wings toward the south? [27] Is it because the eagle is obeying you that he flies high and makes his nest in a high place? [28] He lives on a high rock. His strong-place is on the mountain-top that is hard to reach. [29] From there he looks for his food. His eyes see it from far away. [30] He is where dead bodies are and his young ones drink the blood."

The Lord Is Speaking to Job

40 Then the Lord said to Job, [2] "Will one who finds fault not agree with the All-powerful? He who speaks strong words against God, let him answer."

[3] Job answered the Lord and said, [4] "See, I am not important. What can I answer You? I put my hand on my mouth. [5] I have spoken once, and I cannot answer; even twice, and I have no more to say."

[6] Then the Lord answered out of the storm, and said, [7] "Get ready like a man. I will ask you, and you answer Me. [8] Will you say what I decide is wrong? Will you say that I have done wrong, that you may be made right? [9] Do you have an arm like God? Can you thunder with a voice like His? [10] "Dress yourself with shining-greatness and great power. Cover yourself with honor and greatness. [11] Pour out your

anger that is flowing over. Look on everyone who is proud, and put him to shame. 12 Look on everyone who is proud, and bring him down. Crush the sinful when they stand. 13 Hide them all in the dust together. Shut them up in the hidden place. 14 Then I will also tell you that your own right hand can save you.

15 "See now the hippopotamus, which I made as well as you. He eats grass like an ox. 16 See, his strength is in his body. His power is in his stomach. 17 He moves his tail like a cedar tree. His legs are made very strong. 18 His bones are like brass. His legs are like pieces of iron.

19 "He is the first of the works of God. Let his maker bring him his sword. 20 For sure the mountains bring food to him where all the animals of the field play. 21 He lies down under the lotus plants, hidden in the high river-grass. 22 He lies in the shadow of the lotus plants, with the willow trees of the river around him. 23 If a river flows over, he is not afraid. He is sure of himself even if the Jordan rushes against his mouth. 24 Can anyone take him when he is watching? Can anyone catch him and put a ring in his nose?

The Lord Is Speaking to Job

41 "Can you pull the crocodile out with a fish-hook? Can you tie his tongue down with a rope? 2 Can you put a rope in his nose, or put a hook through his jaw? 3 Will he beg you to be good to him? Will he speak soft words to you? 4 Will he make an agreement with you to take him and make him your servant forever? 5 Will you play with him as if he were a bird? Or will you put him on a rope for your young women? 6 Will traders talk about buying and selling him? Will they divide him among the store-keepers? 7 Can you fill his skin or his head with fish spears? 8 Lay your hand on him, and remember the battle. You will not do it again! 9 See, the hope of man is false. One is laid low even when seeing him. 10 No one is so powerful that he would wake him. Who then can stand before Me? 11 Who has given Me everything, that I should pay him back? Whatever is under the whole heaven is Mine.

12 "I will not keep quiet about his legs, or his powerful strength, or the good way he is made. 13 Who can take off his outside clothing? Who can get through his hard skin? 14 Who can open the doors of his mouth? Around his teeth is much fear. 15 His hard covering is his pride. He is shut

up as with a lock. 16 One piece of his hard skin is so close to another that no air can come between them. 17 They are joined one to another. They hold on to each other and cannot be separated. 18 His breath gives out light. And his eyes are like those of the first light of day. 19 Burning light goes out of his mouth. Fire comes out. 20 Smoke goes out of his nostrils, as from a boiling pot and burning grass. 21 His breath sets fire to coals. A fire goes out of his mouth. 22 Strength is in his neck, and fear jumps in front of him. 23 The folds of his flesh are joined together. They are set in place and cannot be moved. 24 His heart is as hard as a stone, even as hard as a grinding-stone. 25 When he raises himself up, the powerful are afraid. They are troubled because of his noise. 26 The sword that hits him cannot cut. And spears are of no use. 27 He thinks of iron as straw, and brass as soft wood. 28 The arrow cannot make him run away. Stones thrown at him are like dry grass to him. 29 He thinks of heavy sticks as dry grass. He laughs at the noise of the spear. 30 The parts under him are like sharp pieces of a pot. He spreads out like a grain crusher on the mud. 31 He makes the sea boil like a pot. He makes the sea like a jar of oil. 32 He makes his way shine behind him. One would think that the sea has white hair. 33 Nothing on earth is like him, one made without fear. 34 He looks on everything that is high. He is king over all that are proud."

Job Answers the Lord

42 Then Job answered the Lord, and said, 2 "I know that You can do all things. Nothing can put a stop to Your plans. 3 'Who is this that hides words of wisdom without much learning?' I have said things that I did not understand, things too great for me, which I did not know. 4 'Hear now, and I will speak. I will ask you, and you answer Me.' 5 I had heard of You only by the hearing of the ear, but now my eye sees You. 6 So I hate the things that I have said. And I put dust and ashes on myself to show how sorry I am."

Job Is Richer Now

7 After the Lord had spoken these words to Job, the Lord said to Eliphaz the Temanite, "My anger burns against you and your two friends, because you have not spoken of Me what is right, as My servant Job has. 8 So now take seven bulls and seven rams, and go to My servant Job. Give a burnt gift

for yourselves, and My servant Job will pray for you. For I will hear his prayer and not punish you for being foolish, because you have not spoken of Me what is right, as My servant Job has." 9 So Eliphaz the Temanite, Bildad the Shuhite, and Zophar the Naamathite, did what the Lord told them. And the Lord heard Job's prayer.

10 The Lord returned to Job all the things that he had lost, when he prayed for his friends. The Lord gave Job twice as much as he had before. 11 Then all his brothers and sisters and all who had known him before came to him, and ate bread with him in his house. They showed pity and comforted him for all the trouble the Lord had brought upon him. Each one gave him one piece of money and a gold ring. 12 The Lord brought more good to Job in his later years than in his beginning. He had 14,000 sheep, 6,000 camels, 2,000 oxen, and 1,000 female donkeys. 13 He had seven sons and three daughters also. 14 He gave the first name Jemimah, the second Keziah, and the third Keren-happuch. 15 No women were found in all the land who were as beautiful as Job's daughters. And their father gave them a share among their brothers. 16 After this Job lived 140 years, and saw his sons, his grandsons, and even their sons. 17 Then Job died, an old man having lived many days.

PSALMS

The Difference between Good and Sinful People

1 Happy is the man who does not walk in the way sinful men tell him to, or stand in the path of sinners, or sit with those who laugh at the truth. 2 But he finds joy in the Law of the Lord and thinks about His Law day and night. 3 This man is like a tree planted by rivers of water, which gives its fruit at the right time and its leaf never dries up. Whatever he does will work out well for him.

4 Sinful men are not like this. They are like straw blown away by the wind. 5 So the sinful will not stand. They will be told they are guilty and have to suffer for it. Sinners will not stand with those who are right with God. 6 For the Lord knows the way of those who are right with Him. But the way of the sinful will be lost from God forever.

God's Chosen One Will Rule

2 Why are the nations so shaken up and the people planning foolish things? 2 The kings of the earth stand in a line ready to fight, and all the leaders are against the Lord and against His Chosen One. 3 They say, "Let us break their chains and throw them away from us." 4 He Who sits in the heavens laughs. The Lord makes fun of them. 5 Then He will speak to them in His anger and make them afraid, saying, 6 "But as for Me, I have set My King on Zion, My holy mountain." 7 I will make known the words of the Lord. He said to Me, "You are My Son. Today I have become Your Father. 8 Ask of Me, and I will give the nations for you to own. The ends of the earth will belong to You. 9 You will break them using a piece of iron. And they will be broken in pieces like pots of clay."

10 So, kings, be wise. Listen, you rulers of the earth. 11 Serve the Lord with fear, and be full of joy as you shake in fear. 12 Kiss the Son. Be afraid that He may be angry and destroy you in the way. For His anger is quick. Happy are all who put their trust in Him.

Morning Prayer of Trust

3 O Lord, how many are they who hate me! How many rise up against me! 2 Many are saying of me, "There is no help for him in God." 3 But You, O Lord, are a covering around me, my shining-greatness, and the One Who lifts my head. 4 I was crying to the Lord with my voice. And He answered me from His holy mountain. 5 I lay down and slept, and I woke up again, for the Lord keeps me safe.

6 I will not be afraid of ten thousands of people who stand all around against me. 7 Rise up, O Lord! Save me, O my God! For You have hit on the face all those who hate me, and you have broken the teeth of the sinful. 8 It is You Who saves, O Lord. May You bring happiness to Your people.

Evening Prayer of Trust

4 Answer me when I call, O my God Who is right and good! You have made a way for me when I needed help. Be kind to me, and hear my prayer.

2 O sons of men, how long will you turn

my honor into shame? How long will you love what is of no use, and run after lies? [3] Know that the Lord has set apart him who is God-like for Himself. The Lord hears when I call to Him.

[4] Shake with anger and do not sin. When you are on your bed, look into your hearts and be quiet. [5] Give the gifts that are right and good, and trust in the Lord.

[6] Many are asking, "Who will show us any good?" Let the light of Your face shine on us, O Lord. [7] You have filled my heart with more happiness than they have when there is much grain and wine. [8] I will lie down and sleep in peace. O Lord, You alone keep me safe.

Prayer for Help

5 Hear my words, O Lord. Think about my crying. [2] Listen to my cry for help, my King and my God. For I pray to you. [3] In the morning, O Lord, You will hear my voice. In the morning I will lay my prayers before You and will look up.

[4] You are not a God Who is pleased with what is bad. The sinful cannot be with You. [5] The proud cannot stand before You. You hate all who do wrong. [6] You destroy those who tell lies. The Lord hates liars and men who kill other people.

[7] But as for me, by Your great loving-kindness, I will come into Your house. At Your holy house I will put my face to the ground before You in love and fear. [8] O Lord, lead me in what is right and good, because of the ones who hate me. Make Your way straight in front of me.

[9] For in their talk there is no truth. Their hearts destroy. Their mouths are like an open grave. With their tongues, they say sweet-sounding words that are not true. [10] Hold them guilty, O God! Let them fall by their own plans. Throw them out because of their many sins. For they have fought against You. [11] But let all who put their trust in You be glad. Let them sing with joy forever. You make a covering for them, that all who love Your name may be glad in You. [12] For You will make those happy who do what is right, O Lord. You will cover them all around with Your favor.

Prayer for Help in Time of Trouble

6 O Lord, do not speak sharp words to me in Your anger, or punish me when You are angry. [2] Be kind to me, O Lord, for I am weak. O Lord, heal me for my bones are shaken. [3] My soul is in great suffering. But You, O Lord, how long? [4] Return, O Lord. Set my soul free. Save me because of Your loving-kindness. [5] No one remembers You when he is dead. Who gives You praise from the grave? [6] I am tired of crying inside myself. All night long my pillow is wet with tears. I flood my bed with them. [7] My eye has grown weak with sorrow. It has grown old because of all who hate me. [8] Go away from me, all you who sin. For the Lord has heard the sound of my crying. [9] The Lord has heard my cry for help. The Lord receives my prayer. [10] All those who hate me will be ashamed and worried. They will turn away. They will be put to shame right away.

Prayer for Help against the Sinful

7 O Lord my God, in You I have put my trust. Save me from all those who come for me, and keep me safe. [2] Or they will tear me like a lion, carrying me away where there is no one to help. [3] O Lord my God, if I have done this, and there is guilt on my hands, [4] if I have done wrong to him who was at peace with me, or without a reason have robbed him who worked against me, [5] let him who hates me come for me and catch me. Let him break me under his feet until I die, and lay my honor in the dust.

[6] Rise up in Your anger, O Lord. Rise up against the anger of those who hate me. Awake, my God, and help me. Prove what is right. [7] Let the people gather around You, and rule over them from Your throne. [8] May the Lord judge which people are guilty or not. O Lord, judge in my favor if I am right with You, and if I am without blame. [9] Let the sins of the sinful stop. But build up those who are right with You. For the God Who is right and good tests both the hearts and the minds. [10] I am kept safe by God, Who saves those who are pure in heart.

[11] God is always right in how He judges. He is angry with the sinful every day. [12] If a man is not sorry for his sins and will not turn from them, God will make His sword sharp. He will string His bow and make it ready. [13] He takes up His sword and the bow of death. And He makes arrows of fire.

[14] See how the sinful man thinks up sins and plans trouble and lies start growing inside him. [15] He has dug out a deep hole, and has fallen into the hole he has dug. [16] The trouble he makes will return to him. When he hurts others it will come down on his own head. [17] I will give

thanks to the Lord because He is right and good. I will sing praise to the name of the Lord Most High.

God's Shining-Greatness

8 O Lord, our Lord, how great is Your name in all the earth. You have set Your shining-greatness above the heavens. 2 Out of the mouth of children and babies, You have built up strength because of those who hate You, and to quiet those who fight against You.

3 When I look up and think about Your heavens, the work of Your fingers, the moon and the stars, which You have set in their place, 4 what is man, that You think of him, the son of man that You care for him? 5 You made him a little less than the angels and gave him a crown of greatness and honor. 6 You made him to rule over the works of Your hands. You put all things under his feet: 7 All sheep and cattle, all the wild animals, 8 the birds of the air, and the fish of the sea, and all that pass through the sea. 9 O Lord, our Lord, how great is Your name in all the earth!

Thanks to God for the Way He Judges

9 I will give thanks to the Lord with all my heart. I will tell of all the great things You have done. 2 I will be glad and full of joy because of You. I will sing praise to Your name, O Most High. 3 When those who hate me turn away, they fall and are lost from You. 4 For You have stood by my right actions. You sit on Your throne, and are right in how You judge. 5 You have spoken sharp words to the nations and have destroyed the sinful. You have thrown out their name forever and ever. 6 Those who fight against You are finished forever. You have destroyed their cities. They will be remembered no more. 7 But the Lord lives forever. He has set up His throne to say who is guilty or not. 8 He will punish the world by what is right. He will be fair as He rules the people.

9 The Lord also keeps safe those who suffer. He is a safe place in times of trouble. 10 Those who know Your name will put their trust in You. For You, O Lord, have never left alone those who look for You. 11 Sing praises to the Lord, Who lives in Zion! Tell all the nations what He has done! 12 For He Who punishes for the blood of another remembers them. He does not forget the cry of those who suffer. 13 Have pity on me, O Lord! See how I suffer from those who hate me, You Who have lifted me up from the gates of death,

14 that I may tell of all Your praises in the gates of the people of Zion. There I will be full of joy because You save.

15 The nations have fallen into the hole they have dug. Their own feet have been caught in the net they have hidden. 16 The Lord has made Himself known. He is fair in His Law. The sinful trap themselves by the work of their own hands. 17 The sinful, all the nations that forget God, will be turned back into the grave.

18 But those in need will not always be forgotten. The hope of the poor will not be lost forever. 19 Rise up, O Lord! Do not let man win the fight against You. Let the nations come to You and be judged. 20 Make them afraid, O Lord. Let the nations know they are only men.

Prayer for God to Destroy the Sinful

10 Why do You stand far away, O Lord? Why do You hide Yourself in times of trouble? 2 The sinful, in their pride, try to catch the weak. Let them be caught in the plans they have made. 3 The sinful man is proud of the desires of his heart. He praises those who want everything but he speaks against the Lord. 4 The sinful man in his pride does not look for God. All his thoughts are that there is no God. 5 His ways always go well for him. Your laws are too high for him to see. He laughs at those who hate him. 6 He says to himself, "I will not be moved." For all time, I will never have trouble." 7 With his mouth he swears and lies. He makes it hard for other people. Trouble and sin are under his tongue. 8 He lies hidden in the towns, waiting to kill those who are not guilty. His eyes are always watching for the weak. 9 He lies in wait like a hidden lion. He lies in wait to catch the weak, and they become caught in his net. 10 The weak are hurt and they fall. They cannot stand under his strength. 11 He says to himself, "God has forgotten. He has hidden His face and will never see it."

12 Rise up, O Lord! Lift up Your hand, O God. Do not forget the weak. 13 Why does the sinful man turn away from God? He has said to himself, "You will not ask it of me." 14 But You have seen it. You look upon trouble and suffering, to take it into Your hands. The suffering man gives himself to You. You are the Helper of the one who has no father. 15 Break the arm of the bad and sinful man. Find out all his sins until You find no more. 16 The Lord is King forever and ever. Those who worship false gods will be taken from the land.

¹⁷ O Lord, You have heard the prayers of those who have no pride. You will give strength to their heart, and You will listen to them. ¹⁸ In this way, You will do the right thing for those without a father and those who suffer, so that man who is of the earth will no longer make them afraid.

The Lord—a Safe Place

11 In the Lord I am safe. How can you say to me, "Fly away as a bird to your mountain? ² For look, the sinful raise their bow. They make their arrow ready on the string to shoot in the dark against the pure in heart. ³ If the base of the building is destroyed, what can those who are right with God do?"

⁴ The Lord is in His holy house. The Lord's throne is in heaven. His eyes see as He tests the sons of men. ⁵ The Lord tests and proves those who are right and good and those who are sinful. And His soul hates the one who loves to hurt others. ⁶ He will send down fire upon the sinful. Fire and sulphur and burning wind will be the cup they will drink. ⁷ For the Lord is right and good. He loves what is right and good. And those who are right with Him will see His face.

God—Our Helper

12 Help, Lord! For God-like men are here no more. The faithful can no longer be seen among the sons of men. ² They lie to each other. Their lips speak with sweet-sounding words that are not true. ³ May the Lord cut off all lips of false respect, and the tongue that speaks of great things. ⁴ They say, "We can win with our tongues. Our lips are our own. Who is lord over us?"

⁵ "Because of the suffering of the weak, and because of the cries of the poor, I will now rise up," says the Lord. "I will keep him safe as he has wanted to be."

⁶ The words of the Lord are pure words. They are like silver that has been made pure seven times in a stove of earth. ⁷ O Lord, You will keep us. You will keep us safe forever from the people of this day. ⁸ The sinful walk on every side when bad actions are held in honor among the sons of men.

Prayer for Help in Time of Trouble

13 How long, O Lord? Will You forget me forever? How long will You hide Your face from me? ² How long must I plan what to do in my soul, and have sor-row in my heart all the day? How long will those who hate me rise above me?

³ Look on me and answer, O Lord, my God. Give light to my eyes, or I will sleep the sleep of death. ⁴ Or the one who hates me will say, "I have power over him." And those who hate me will be happy when I am shaken.

⁵ But I have trusted in Your loving-kindness. My heart will be full of joy because You will save me. ⁶ I will sing to the Lord, because He has been good to me.

Sinful Men

14 The fool has said in his heart, "There is no God." They are sinful and their actions are sinful. There is no one who does good. ² The Lord has looked down from heaven on the sons of men, to see if there are any who understand and look for God. ³ They have all turned aside. Together they have become bad. There is no one who does good, not even one.

⁴ Will those who sin never learn? They eat up my people like they eat bread. They do not call on the Lord. ⁵ There they are in much fear. For God is with the people of this day who do what is right and good. ⁶ You would put to shame the planning of the poor. But the Lord keeps him safe.

⁷ O, that it would come out of Zion that Israel would be saved! When the Lord returns His people to their land, Jacob will be full of joy and Israel will be glad.

Good Men

15 O Lord, who may live in Your tent? Who may live on Your holy hill? ² He who walks without blame and does what is right and good, and speaks the truth in his heart. ³ He does not hurt others with his tongue, or do wrong to his neighbor, or bring shame to his friend. ⁴ He looks down upon a sinful person, but honors those who fear the Lord. He keeps his promises even if it may hurt him. ⁵ He gives money to be used without being paid for its use. And he does not take money to hurt those who are not guilty. He who does these things will never be shaken.

The Lord—Our Safe Place in Life and Covering in Death

16 Keep me, O God, for I am safe in You. ² I said to the Lord, "You are my Lord. All the good things I have come from You." ³ As for those in the land who belong to You, they are the great ones in whom is all my joy. ⁴ Those who have traded for another god bring many troubles on themselves. I will not take part in their altar gifts of blood. And I will not take their names upon my lips.

5 The Lord is all that I am to receive, and my cup. My future is in Your hands. 6 The land given to me is good. Yes, my share is beautiful to me.

7 I will give honor and thanks to the Lord, Who has told me what to do. Yes, even at night my mind teaches me. 8 I have placed the Lord always in front of me. Because He is at my right hand, I will not be moved. 9 And so my heart is glad. My soul is full of joy. My body also will rest without fear. 10 For You will not give me over to the grave. And You will not allow Your Holy One to return to dust. 11 You will show me the way of life. Being with You is to be full of joy. In Your right hand there is happiness forever.

Prayer for Help in Time of Trouble

17 Hear what is right, O Lord. Listen to my cry. Hear my prayer, for it does not come from lying lips. 2 May You decide in my favor. May Your eyes see what is right. 3 You have tested my heart. You have visited me during the night. You have tested me and have found nothing wrong. I have decided that my mouth will not sin. 4 As for the actions of men, by the word of Your lips, I have kept myself from the paths of those who want to hurt others. 5 My steps have followed Your paths. My feet have not turned from them.

6 I have called to You, O God, for You will answer me. Listen to me and hear my words. 7 Show Your great loving-kindness. You save by Your right hand the people that come to You for help from those who hate them. 8 Keep me safe as You would Your own eye. Hide me in the shadow of Your wings, 9 from the sinful who fight against me, those who would kill me and are all around me. 10 They have closed their fat hearts to pity. And their mouths speak with pride. 11 They have followed our every step and are all around us. They are watching for a way to bring us down to the ground. 12 He is like a hungry lion, like a young lion waiting and waiting.

13 Rise up, O Lord. Stand against him. Bring him down. Save me from the sinful with Your sword. 14 O Lord, save me by Your hand from such men. Their riches are in this life. Their stomach is filled with what you have stored for them. Their children are filled. Let them leave some for their babies. 15 As for me, I will see Your face in what is right and good. I will be happy to see You when I awake.

Song of Thanks for Being Kept Safe

18 I love You, O Lord, my strength. 2 The Lord is my rock, and my safe place, and the One Who takes me out of trouble. My God is my rock, in Whom I am safe. He is my safe-covering, my saving strength, and my strong tower. 3 I call to the Lord, Who has the right to be praised. And I am saved from those who hate me.

4 The ropes of death were all around me. The floods of death make me afraid. 5 The ropes of the grave were all around me. The traps of death were set for me. 6 I called to the Lord in my trouble. I cried to God for help. He heard my voice from His holy house. My cry for help came into His ears.

7 Then the earth shook. The mountains were shaking. They shook because He was angry. 8 Smoke went out from His nose and the fire that kept coming from His mouth burned everything around it. 9 He parted the heavens and came down. Dark clouds were under His feet. 10 He sat upon a cherub and flew. He traveled on the wings of the wind. 11 He made darkness His hiding place, the covering around Him, the dark rain clouds of the sky. 12 Through the light before Him passed His dark clouds, hail stones and fire. 13 The Lord made thunder in the heavens. The voice of the Most High spoke out, hail stones and fire. 14 He sent out His arrows and divided them. He threw down lightning and sent them running. 15 Then the deep part of the sea could be seen. And the deep part of the earth was opened up, because of Your sharp words, O Lord, because of the powerful breath from Your nose.

16 He sent from above, and took me. He lifted me out of many waters. 17 He took me away from the powerful one who fights against me, and from those who hated me. They were too strong for me. 18 They stood against me in the day of my trouble. But the Lord was my strength. 19 He brought me out into a big place. He gave me a safe place, because He was pleased with me.

20 The Lord has paid me because of my being right with Him. Because of my clean hands He has paid me. 21 For I have kept the ways of the Lord. And I have not sinned by turning from my God. 22 All His Laws are in front of me. I have not set His Laws aside. 23 Before Him I was without

blame. And I have kept myself from sin. 24 So the Lord has paid me back for being right with Him, and for my hands being clean in His eyes.

25 To the faithful, You show Yourself faithful. To those without blame, You show Yourself without blame. 26 With the pure, You show Yourself pure. With the sinful You show Yourself to be against them. 27 You save those who are suffering, but You bring low those who have pride in their eyes. 28 You make my lamp bright. The Lord my God lights my darkness. 29 With Your help I can go against many soldiers. With my God I can jump over a wall.

30 As for God, His way is perfect. The Word of the Lord has stood the test. He is a covering for all who go to Him for a safe place. 31 For Who is God, but the Lord? And who is a rock except our God? 32 It is God Who covers me with strength and makes my way perfect. 33 He makes my feet like the feet of a deer. And He sets me on my high places. 34 He teaches me how to fight, so that I can use a bow of brass. 35 You have also given me the covering that saves me. Your right hand holds me up. And Your care has made me great. 36 You make the road wide for my steps, and my feet have not tripped.

37 I went after those who fight against me, and caught them. And I did not return until they were destroyed. 38 I hit them so they were not able to rise. They fell under my feet. 39 You have given me strength for war. You have put under me those who have fought against me. 40 You have made them turn their backs to me also. And I destroyed those who hated me. 41 They cried for help, but there was no one to save. They cried to the Lord, but He did not answer them. 42 Then I beat them as small as the dust in the wind. I emptied them out like mud in the streets.

43 You have taken me away from the fighting of the people. You have made me the leader of nations. People whom I have not known will serve me. 44 As soon as they hear, they obey me. Those from other lands obey me. Those people from other lands lose their strength of heart. And they come shaking from behind their walls. 46 The Lord lives! How great is my Rock! Praise be to the God Who saves me! 47 He is the God Who punishes those who have done wrong to me. He puts nations under my rule. 48 He saves me from those who hate me. Yes, You lift me above those who rise up against me. You save me from those

who want to hurt me. 49 So I will give thanks to You among the nations, O Lord. And I will sing praises to Your name. 50 He gives His king great power over trouble. And He shows loving-kindness to His chosen one, to David, and to his children after him forever.

The Works and the Word of God

19 The heavens are telling of the greatness of God and the great open spaces show the work of His hands. 2 Day to day they speak. And night to night they show much learning. 3 There is no speaking and no words where their voice is not heard. 4 Their sound has gone out through all the earth, and their words to the end of the world. In them He has placed a tent for the sun. 5 It is as a man soon to be married coming out of his room and as a strong man who is happy to run his race. 6 Its rising is from one end of the heavens, and it makes its way to the other end. Nothing is hidden from its heat.

7 The Law of the Lord is perfect, giving new strength to the soul. The Law He has made known is sure, making the child-like wise. 8 The Laws of the Lord are right, giving joy to the heart. The Word of the Lord is pure, giving light to the eyes. 9 The fear of the Lord is pure, lasting forever. The Lord is always true and right in how He judges. 10 The Word of the Lord is worth more than gold, even more than much fine gold. They are sweeter than honey, even honey straight from the comb. 11 And by them Your servant is told to be careful. In obeying them there is great reward.

12 Who can see his own mistakes? Forgive my sins that I do not see. 13 And keep Your servant from sinning by going my own way. Do not let these sins rule over me. Then I will be without blame. And I will not be found guilty of big sins. 14 Let the words of my mouth and the thoughts of my heart be pleasing in Your eyes, O Lord, my Rock and the One Who saves me.

Prayer to Be Kept Safe

20 May the Lord answer you in the day of trouble! May the name of the God of Jacob keep you safe. 2 May He send you help from the house of God, and give you strength from Zion. 3 May He remember all your gifts of grain given on the altar in worship. And may He be pleased with your burnt gifts.

4 May He give you the desire of your heart, and make all your plans go well.

5 We will sing for joy when you win. In the name of our God we will lift up our flags. May the Lord give you all the things you ask Him for.

6 Now I know that the Lord saves His chosen one. He will answer him from His holy heaven, with the saving power of His right hand. 7 Some trust in wagons and some in horses. But we will trust in the name of the Lord, our God. 8 They have fallen on their knees. But we rise up and stand straight. 9 O Lord, save! May the King answer us when we call.

Song of Praise for Being Kept Safe

21 O Lord, in Your strength the king is glad! How great is his joy in Your saving power! 2 You have given him the desire of his heart. You have not kept from him anything that he has asked for. 3 For You meet him with gifts of good things. You set a crown of pure gold on his head. 4 He asked You for life and You gave it to him, a long life forever and ever. 5 His honor is great because of Your help. You have given him greatness and power. 6 You have given him honor and respect forever. And You make him glad with the joy of being with You.

7 For the king trusts in the Lord. Because of the loving-kindness of the Most High, he will not be shaken. 8 Your hand will find all who fight against You. Your right hand will find those who hate You. 9 You will make them like a stove of fire in the time of Your anger. The Lord will eat them up in His anger. And the fire will destroy them. 10 You will destroy their children from the earth, and their sons from the children of men. 11 For they planned much trouble against You. They have made sinful plans that will come to nothing. 12 For You will make them turn their backs when You take up Your bow against them. 13 Be honored in Your strength, O Lord. We will sing and praise Your power.

A Cry of Fear and a Song of Praise

22 My God, my God, why have You left me alone? Why are You so far from helping me, and from the words I cry inside myself? 2 O my God, I cry during the day, but You do not answer. I cry during the night, but I find no rest. 3 Yet You are holy. The praises Israel gives You are Your throne. 4 Our fathers trusted in You, and You saved them. 5 They cried to You and were set free. They trusted in You and were not ashamed.

6 But I am a worm and not a man. I am put to shame by men, and am hated by the people. 7 All who see me make fun of me. They open their mouths and shake their heads, and say, 8 "He trusts in the Lord. Let the Lord help him. Let the Lord take him out of trouble, because he is happy in Him."

9 But You brought me out when I was born. You made me trust when I drank my mother's milk. 10 I was in Your care from birth. Since my mother gave birth to me, You have been my God.

11 Do not be far from me, for trouble is near. And there is no one to help. 12 Many bulls have gathered all around me. Strong bulls of Bashan stand around me. 13 They open their mouths wide against me, like a loud, hungry lion. 14 I am poured out like water. And all my bones are out of joint. My heart is like a melted candle within me. 15 My strength is dried up like a piece of a broken clay pot. My tongue sticks to the roof of my mouth. And You lay me in the dust of death. 16 For dogs have gathered around me. A group of sinful men stand around me. They have cut through my hands and feet. 17 I can tell how many bones I have. The people look at me with wide eyes. 18 They divide my clothes among them by drawing names to see who would get them.

19 But You, O Lord, be not far from me! O my Strength, hurry to help me! 20 Take me away from the sword. Save my life from the power of the dog. 21 Save me from the lion's mouth, and from the horns of the wild bulls You answer me.

22 I will make Your name known to my brothers. In the center of the meeting of worship I will praise You. 23 You who fear the Lord, give Him praise. All you children of Jacob, honor Him. Fear Him, all you children of Israel. 24 For He has not turned away from the suffering of the one in pain or trouble. He has not hidden His face from him. But He has heard his cry for help.

25 My praise will be from You in the big meeting of worship. I will keep my promises to Him in front of those who fear Him. 26 Those who suffer will eat and have enough. Those who look for the Lord will praise Him. May your heart live forever! 27 All the ends of the earth will remember and turn to the Lord. All the families of the nations will worship before Him. 28 For the holy nation is the Lord's, and He rules over the nations. 29 All the proud

ones of the earth will eat and worship. All who go down to the dust will fall to their knees before Him, even he who cannot keep his soul alive. 30 Future children will serve Him. They will tell of the Lord to their children. 31 They will come and tell about His saving power to a people yet to be born. For He has done it.

The Lord—Our Shepherd

23 The Lord is my Shepherd. I will have everything I need. 2 He lets me rest in fields of green grass. He leads me beside the quiet waters. 3 He makes me strong again. He leads me in the way of living right with Himself which brings honor to His name. 4 Yes, even if I walk through the valley of the shadow of death, I will not be afraid of anything, because You are with me. You have a walking stick with which to guide and one with which to help. These comfort me. 5 You are making a table of food ready for me in front of those who hate me. You have poured oil on my head. I have everything I need. 6 For sure, You will give me goodness and loving-kindness all the days of my life. Then I will live with You in Your house forever.

The King of Shining-Greatness

24 The earth is the Lord's, and all that is in it, the world, and all who live in it. 2 For He has built it upon the seas. He has set it upon the rivers. 3 Who may go up the mountain of the Lord? And who may stand in His holy place? 4 He who has clean hands and a pure heart. He who has not lifted up his soul to what is not true, and has not made false promises. 5 He will receive what is good from the Lord, and what is right and good from the God Who saves him. 6 Such is the family of those who look for Him, who look for Your face, O God of Jacob.

7 Lift up your heads, O gates. And be lifted up, O doors that last forever. And the King of shining-greatness will come in. 8 Who is the King of shining-greatness? The Lord strong and powerful. The Lord powerful in war. 9 Lift up your heads, O gates. Lift them up, O doors that last forever. And the King of shining-greatness will come in. 10 Who is the King of shining greatness? The Lord of All. He is the King of shining-greatness.

Prayer to Be Kept Safe from Enemies

25 I lift up my soul to You, O Lord. 2 O my God, I trust in You. Do not let me be ashamed. Do not let those who

fight against me win. 3 Yes, let no one who hopes in You be put to shame. But put to shame those who hurt others without a reason.

4 Show me Your ways, O Lord. Teach me Your paths. 5 Lead me in Your truth and teach me. For You are the God Who saves me. I wait for You all day long. 6 Remember Your loving-pity and Your loving-kindness, O Lord. For they have been from old. 7 Do not remember my sins from when I was young, or my sinful ways. By Your loving-kindness remember me for You are good, O Lord.

8 Good and right is the Lord. So He teaches sinners in His ways. 9 He leads those without pride into what is right, and teaches them His way. 10 All the paths of the Lord are loving and true for those who keep His agreement and keep His Laws. 11 For the good of Your name, O Lord, forgive my sin, even as big as it is.

12 Who is the man who fears the Lord? He will teach him in the way he should choose. 13 His soul will live a rich life. And his children will be given the land. 14 The secret of the Lord is for those who fear Him. And He will make them know His agreement. 15 My eyes are always on the Lord. For He will take my feet out of the net.

16 Turn to me and show me Your loving-kindness. For I am alone and in trouble. 17 The troubles of my heart have grown. Bring me out of my suffering. 18 Look upon my troubles and my pain, and forgive all my sins. 19 Look upon those who hate me, for they are many. And how very much they hate me! 20 Keep me safe, Lord, and set me free. Do not let me be put to shame for I put my trust in You. 21 Let what is good and what is right keep me safe, because I wait for You. 22 O God, make Israel free from all their troubles.

Prayer of a Good Man

26 O Lord, stand by me for I have lived my life without blame. I have trusted in the Lord without changing. 2 Test me and try me, O Lord. Test my mind and my heart. 3 For Your loving-kindness is always in front of my eyes. And I have walked in Your truth. 4 I do not sit with men who lie about the truth. I would not be seen with those who pretend to be someone they are not. 5 I hate the meeting of sinners, and will not sit with the sinful. 6 I will wash my hands of any guilt. And I will go around Your altar, O Lord. 7 I will speak with the voice of thanks, and tell of all Your great works.

8 O Lord, I love the house where You live, the place where Your shining-greatness lives. 9 Do not take my soul away with sinners, or my life with men who kill other people. 10 Sinful plans are in their hands. And their right hand is full of pay for hurting others. 11 But as for me, I will live a life without blame. Make me free, and show me loving-kindness. 12 My foot stands on a good place. I will give honor to the Lord, in the meeting of worship.

Prayer of Trust in God

27 The Lord is my light and the One Who saves me. Whom should I fear? The Lord is the strength of my life. Of whom should I be afraid? 2 When sinful men, and all who hated me, came against me to destroy my flesh, they tripped and fell. 3 Even if an army gathers against me, my heart will not be afraid. Even if war rises against me, I will be sure of You.

4 One thing I have asked from the Lord, that I will look for: that I may live in the house of the Lord all the days of my life, to look upon the beauty of the Lord, and to worship in His holy house. 5 For in the day of trouble He will keep me safe in His holy tent. In the secret place of His tent He will hide me. He will set me high upon a rock. 6 Then my head will be lifted up above all those around me who hate me. I will give gifts in His holy tent with a loud voice of joy. I will sing. Yes, I will sing praises to the Lord.

7 O Lord, listen to my cry. Show loving-kindness to me and answer me. 8 You have said, "Look for My face." My heart said to You, "O Lord, Your face will I look for." 9 Do not hide Your face from me. Do not turn Your servant away in anger. You have been my Helper. Do not turn away from me or leave me alone, O God Who saves me! 10 For my father and my mother have left me. But the Lord will take care of me.

11 Teach me Your way, O Lord. Lead me in a straight path, because of those who fight against me. 12 Do not give me over to the desire of those who hate me. For people who tell lies about me rise against me, and breathe a desire to hurt me. 13 I would have been without hope if I had not believed that I would see the loving-kindness of the Lord in the land of the living. 14 Wait for the Lord. Be strong. Let your heart be strong. Yes, wait for the Lord.

Prayer for Help—Praise for the Answer

28 O Lord, to You I call. O my Rock, listen to me. If You will not hear me, I will be like those who have gone down to the grave. 2 Hear my cry for loving-kindness as I call to You for help, and when I lift up my hands to Your holy place. 3 Do not drag me away with the sinful and with those who do bad things. They speak peace with their neighbors, while sin is in their hearts. 4 Pay them for their work and for the sins they do. Pay them for the works of their hands. Give them what they have earned. 5 They do not think about the works of the Lord and what His hands have done. So He will pull them down and not build them up again.

6 May honor and thanks be given to the Lord, because He has heard my prayer. 7 The Lord is my strength and my safe cover. My heart trusts in Him, and I am helped. So my heart is full of joy. I will thank Him with my song. 8 The Lord is the strength of His people. He is a safe place for His chosen one. 9 Save Your people and bring good to what is Yours. Be their shepherd and carry them forever.

The Voice of the Lord in the Storm

29 Give to the Lord, O sons of the powerful. Give to the Lord shining-greatness and strength. 2 Give to the Lord the honor that belongs to Him. Worship the Lord in the beauty of holy living.

3 The voice of the Lord is upon the waters. The God of shining-greatness thunders. The Lord is over many waters. 4 The voice of the Lord is powerful. The voice of the Lord is great. 5 The voice of the Lord breaks the cedars. Yes, the Lord breaks in pieces the tall cedars of Lebanon. 6 He makes Lebanon jump like a calf, and Sirion like a young wild bull. 7 The voice of the Lord sends out lightning. 8 The voice of the Lord shakes the desert. The Lord shakes the desert of Kadesh. 9 The voice of the Lord makes the deer give birth, and tears away the leaves of the trees. And in His holy house everything says, "Honor to God!"

10 The Lord sat as King over the flood. The Lord sits as King forever. 11 The Lord will give strength to His people. The Lord will give His people peace.

Prayer of Thanks

30 I will lift You up, O Lord, for You have lifted me up. You have not let those who hate me stand over me in joy. 2 O Lord my God, I cried to You for help and You healed me. 3 O Lord, You have brought me up from the grave. You have kept me alive, so that I will not go down into the deep. 4 Sing praise to the Lord, all you who belong to Him. Give thanks to His holy name. 5 For His anger lasts only a short time. But His favor is for life. Crying may last for a night, but joy comes with the new day.

6 As for me, when all was going well, I said, "I will never be moved." 7 O Lord, by Your favor You have made my mountain stand strong. But when You hid Your face, I was troubled. 8 I cried to You, O Lord. I begged the Lord for loving-kindness. 9 What good will come from my blood, if I go down to the grave? Will the dust thank You? Will it tell how You are faithful?

10 Hear, O Lord. And show me loving-kindness. O Lord, be my Helper. 11 You have turned my crying into dancing. You have taken off my clothes made from hair, and dressed me with joy. 12 So my soul may sing praise to You, and not be quiet. O Lord my God, I will give thanks to You forever.

Prayer of Trust in God

31 O Lord, in You I have found a safe place. Let me never be ashamed. Set me free, because You do what is right and good. 2 Turn Your ear to me, and be quick to save me. Be my rock of strength, a strong-place to keep me safe. 3 For You are my rock and my safe place. For the honor of Your name, lead me and show me the way. 4 You will free me from the net that they have hidden for me. For You are my strength. 5 I give my spirit into Your hands. You have made me free, O Lord, God of truth.

6 I hate those who worship false gods. But I trust in the Lord. 7 I will be glad and full of joy in Your loving-kindness. For You have seen my suffering. You have known the troubles of my soul. 8 You have not given me into the hand of those who hate me. You have set my feet in a large place. 9 Show me loving-kindness, O Lord, for I am in trouble. My eyes, my soul and my body are becoming weak from being sad. 10 For my life gets weaker with sorrow, and my years with crying inside myself. My strength has left me because of my sin. And my bones waste away. 11 Because of all those who hate me, I have become a shame to my neighbors. Even my friends do not want to be with me. Those who see me on the street run from me. 12 I am

forgotten like a dead man and they do not think about me. I am like a broken pot. 13 For I have heard many say things to hurt me. Fear is on every side. They planned together against me. They thought of ways to take away my life.

14 But as for me, I trust in You, O Lord. I say, "You are my God." 15 My times are in Your hands. Free me from the hands of those who hate me, and from those who try to hurt me. 16 Make Your face shine upon Your servant. Save me in Your loving-kindness. 17 Do not let me be put to shame, O Lord. For I call to You. Let the sinful be put to shame. Let them be quiet in the grave. 18 Let the lying lips be quiet. For they speak with pride and hate those who do right and good.

19 How great is Your loving-kindness! You have stored it up for those who fear You. You show it to those who trust in You in front of the sons of men. 20 You will hide them with You in secret from the sinful plans of men. You keep them in Your tent in secret from those who fight with tongues. 21 Honor and thanks be to the Lord. For He has shown His great loving-favor to me when I was in a city with armies all around. 22 In my fear I said, "You have closed Your eyes to me!" But You heard my cry for loving-kindness when I called to You.

23 Love the Lord, all you who belong to Him! The Lord keeps the faithful safe. But He gives the proud their pay in full. 24 Be strong. Be strong in heart, all you who hope in the Lord.

Joy of Being Forgiven

32 How happy he is whose wrong-doing is forgiven, and whose sin is covered! 2 How happy is the man whose sin the Lord does not hold against him, and in whose spirit there is nothing false.

3 When I kept quiet about my sin, my bones wasted away from crying all day long. 4 For day and night Your hand was heavy upon me. My strength was dried up as in the hot summer. 5 I told my sin to You, I did not hide my wrong-doing. I said, "I will tell my sins to the Lord." And You forgave the guilt of my sin. 6 So let all who are God-like pray to You while You may be found, because in the floods of much water, they will not touch him. 7 You are my hiding place. You keep me safe from trouble. All around me are your songs of being made free.

8 I will show you and teach you in the way you should go. I will tell you what

to do with My eye upon you. 9 Do not be like the horse or the donkey which have no understanding. They must be made to work by using bits and leather ropes or they will not come to you. 10 Many are the sorrows of the sinful. But loving-kindness will be all around the man who trusts in the Lord. 11 Be glad in the Lord and be full of joy, you who are right with God! Sing for joy all you who are pure in heart!

Song of Praise

33 Sing for joy in the Lord, you who are right with Him. It is right for the pure in heart to praise Him. 2 Give thanks to the Lord with harps. Sing praises to Him with a harp of ten strings. 3 Sing to Him a new song. Play well with loud sounds of joy. 4 For the Word of the Lord is right. He is faithful in all He does. 5 He loves what is right and good and what is fair. The earth is full of the loving-kindness of the Lord.

6 The heavens were made by the Word of the Lord. All the stars were made by the breath of His mouth. 7 He gathers the waters of the sea together as in a bag. He places the waters in store-houses. 8 Let all the earth fear the Lord. Let all the people of the world honor Him. 9 For He spoke, and it was done. He spoke with strong words, and it stood strong. 10 The Lord brings the plans of nations to nothing. He wrecks the plans of the people. 11 The plans of the Lord stand forever. The plans of His heart stand through the future of all people. 12 Happy is the nation whose God is the Lord. Happy are the people He has chosen for His own.

13 The Lord looks from heaven. He sees all the sons of men. 14 From where He sits He looks upon all who live on the earth. 15 He made the hearts of them all. And He understands whatever they do. 16 No king is saved by the power of his strong army. A soldier is not saved by great strength. 17 A horse cannot be trusted to win a battle. Its great strength cannot save anyone.

18 See, the eye of the Lord is on those who fear Him, and on those who hope for His loving-kindness, 19 to save their soul from death, and to keep them alive when there is nothing to eat. 20 Our soul waits for the Lord. He is our help and our safe cover. 21 For our heart is full of joy in Him, because we trust in His holy name. 22 O Lord, let Your loving-kindness be upon us as we put our hope in You.

Those Who Trust in God Are Happy

34 I will honor the Lord at all times. His praise will always be in my mouth. 2 My soul will be proud to tell about the Lord. Let those who suffer hear it and be filled with joy. 3 Give great honor to the Lord with me. Let us praise His name together.

4 I looked for the Lord, and He answered me. And He took away all my fears. 5 They looked to Him and their faces shined with joy. Their faces will never be ashamed. 6 This poor man cried, and the Lord heard him. And He saved him out of all his troubles. 7 The angel of the Lord stays close around those who fear Him, and He takes them out of trouble.

8 O taste and see that the Lord is good. How happy is the man who trusts in Him! 9 O fear the Lord, all you who belong to Him. For those who fear Him never want for anything. 10 The young lions suffer want and hunger. But they who look for the Lord will not be without any good thing. 11 Come, you children, listen to me. I will teach you the fear of the Lord. 12 Who is the man who has a desire for life, and wants to live long so that he may see good things? 13 Keep your tongue from sin and your lips from speaking lies. 14 Turn away from what is sinful. Do what is good. Look for peace and follow it.

15 The eyes of the Lord are on those who do what is right and good. His ears are open to their cry. 16 The face of the Lord is against those who sin. He will keep the people of the earth from remembering them. 17 Those who are right with the Lord cry, and He hears them. And He takes them from all their troubles. 18 The Lord is near to those who have a broken heart. And He saves those who are broken in spirit.

19 A man who does what is right and good may have many troubles. But the Lord takes him out of them all. 20 He keeps all his bones safe. Not one of them is broken. 21 Sin will kill the sinful. And those who hate God's people will be held guilty and punished forever. 22 The Lord saves the soul of those who work for Him. None of those who trust in Him will be held guilty.

Prayer for Help

35 O Lord, stand against those who stand against me. Fight those who fight me. 2 Take hold of a safe-covering and rise up to help me. 3 Take a spear and battle-ax against those who come to get me. Say to my soul, "I am the One Who saves you." **4** Let the people be ashamed and without honor who want to take my life. Let those be turned away and brought to shame who plan to hurt me. **5** Let them be like straw in the wind. May the angel of the Lord drive them away. **6** Let their way be dark and dangerous, with the angel of the Lord going to get them. **7** For without a reason they hid their net for me. Without a reason, they dug a hole for my soul. **8** Let them be destroyed before they know it. And let them be caught in their own net. May they destroy themselves as they fall into their own hole.

9 My soul will be happy in the Lord. It will be full of joy because He saves. **10** All my bones will say, "Lord, who is like You? Who saves the weak from those too strong for them? Who saves the poor from those who would rob them?" **11** People come telling lies. They ask me of things that I do not know. **12** They pay me what is bad in return for what is good. My soul is sad. **13** But when they were sick, I put on clothes made from hair. With no pride in my soul, I would not eat. And I prayed with my head on my chest. **14** I went about as if it were my friend or brother. I put my head down in sorrow, like one crying for his mother. **15** But when I would fall, they would gather together in joy. Those who say things to hurt people would gather against me. I did not know them. They spoke against me without stopping. **16** They ground their teeth at me like bad people making fun of others at a special supper.

17 Lord, how long will You look on? Save me from being destroyed by them. Save my life from the lions. **18** I will give You thanks in the big meeting. I will praise You among many people. **19** Do not let those who hate me for no reason stand over me with joy. Do not let those who hate me for no reason wink their eye. **20** They do not speak peace. But they make up lies against those who are quiet in the land. **21** And they opened their mouth wide against me. They said, "O, O, our eyes have seen it."

22 You have seen it, O Lord. Do not keep quiet. O Lord, do not be far from me. **23** Awake Yourself. Come and help me. Fight for me, my God and my Lord. **24** Say what is right or wrong with me, O Lord my God, because You are right and good. Do not let them have joy over me. **25** Do not let them say in their heart, "O, just what we wanted!" Do not let them

say, "We have swallowed him up!" **26** Let all who are happy because of my trouble be ashamed and without honor. Let those who think they are better than I, be covered with shame and without honor.

27 Let them call out for joy and be glad, who want to see the right thing done for me. Let them always say, "May the Lord be honored. He is pleased when all is going well for His servant." **28** And my tongue will tell about how right and good You are, and about Your praise all day long.

Sinful Men—Loving God

36 Sin speaks to the sinful man within his heart. There is no fear of God in his eyes. **2** For he makes much of himself in his own eyes. So his sin is not known and hated. **3** The words of his mouth are sinful and false. He has stopped being wise and doing good. **4** He plans wrong-doing upon his bed. He sets himself on a path that is not good. He does not hate what is bad.

5 O Lord, Your loving-kindness goes to the heavens. You are as faithful as the sky is high. **6** You are as right and good as mountains are big. You are as fair when You judge as a sea is deep. O Lord, You keep safe both man and animal. **7** Of what great worth is Your loving-kindness, O God! The children of men come and are safe in the shadow of Your wings. **8** They are filled with the riches of Your house. And You give them a drink from Your river of joy. **9** All life came from You. In Your light we see light.

10 Keep on giving Your loving-kindness to those who know You. Keep on being right and good to the pure in heart. **11** Do not let the foot of pride come near me. Do not let the hand of the sinful push me away. **12** There have the wrong-doers fallen. They have been thrown down, and cannot rise.

A Safe Place for Those Who Trust in the Lord

37 Do not trouble yourself because of sinful men. Do not want to be like those who do wrong. **2** For they will soon dry up like the grass. Like the green plant they will soon die. **3** Trust in the Lord, and do good. So you will live in the land and will be fed. **4** Be happy in the Lord. And He will give you the desires of your heart. **5** Give your way over to the Lord. Trust in Him also. And He will do it. **6** He will make your being right and good show as the light, and your wise actions as the noon day.

7 Rest in the Lord and be willing to wait for Him. Do not trouble yourself when all goes well with the one who carries out his sinful plans. 8 Stop being angry. Turn away from fighting. Do not trouble yourself. It leads only to wrong-doing. 9 For those who do wrong will be cut off. But those who wait for the Lord will be given the earth. 10 A little while, and the sinful man will be no more. You will look for his place, and he will not be there. 11 But those who have no pride will be given the earth. And they will be happy and have much more than they need.

12 The sinful man plans against him who is right with God. And he grinds his teeth at him. 13 The Lord laughs at him because He sees his day is coming. 14 The sinful have taken up their sword and their bow, to bring down the poor and those in need, and to kill those whose ways are right. 15 Their sword will cut into their own heart, and their bows will be broken.

16 The few things that the man right with God has is better than the riches of many sinful men. 17 For the arms of the sinful will be broken. But the Lord holds up those who are right with Him. 18 The Lord knows the days of those who are without blame. And what is theirs will last forever. 19 They will not be ashamed in the time of trouble. And in days when there is no food they will have enough. 20 But the sinful will be lost forever. Those who hate the Lord will be like the beauty of the fields. They will be gone. Like smoke they will be gone. 21 The sinful ask for something, but do not return it. But those who are right with God are kind and give. 22 For those who are made happy by Him will be given the land. But those who are being punished by Him will be cut off.

23 The steps of a good man are led by the Lord. And He is happy in his way. 24 When he falls, he will not be thrown down, because the Lord holds his hand. 25 I have been young, and now I am old. Yet I have never seen the man who is right with God left alone, or his children begging for bread. 26 All day long he is kind and lets others use what he has. And his children make him happy.

27 Turn from sin, and do good, so you will live forever. 28 For the Lord loves what is fair and right. He does not leave the people alone who belong to Him. They are kept forever. But the children of the sinful will be cut off. 29 Those who are right with God will be given the land, and live on it forever. 30 The mouth of the man who is right with God speaks wisdom. And his tongue speaks what is fair and right. 31 The Law of his God is in his heart. His steps do not leave it. 32 The sinful lie in wait for the man who is right with God, and want to kill him. 33 The Lord will not leave him in his power. He will not let him be found guilty when he is judged. 34 Wait for the Lord. Keep His way. And He will give you a high place to receive the land. When the sinful are cut off, you will see it.

35 I have seen a very sinful man spreading himself like a green tree in its home land. 36 Then he passed away and was no more. I looked for him. But he could not be found. 37 Look at the man without blame. And watch the man who is right and good. For the man of peace will have much family to follow him. 38 But all the sinners will be destroyed. The family of the sinful will be cut off. 39 But the saving of those who are right with God is from the Lord. He is their strength in time of trouble. 40 The Lord helps them and takes them out of trouble. He takes them away from the sinful, and saves them, because they go to Him for a safe place.

Prayer of a Suffering Man

38 O Lord, do not speak sharp words to me when You are angry. Do not punish me in Your burning anger. 2 For Your arrows have cut deep into me. And Your hand has come down upon me. 3 My body is in pain because of Your anger. There is no strength in my bones because of my sin. 4 For my sins are gone over my head. Like a heavy load, they weigh too much for me. 5 My sores smell and grow bigger because I do foolish things. 6 I cannot stand straight but keep my head down. I have sorrow all day long 7 for my body is filled with burning pain. There is no strength in my body. 8 I am weak and broken. I cry because of the pain in my heart. 9 Lord, all my desire is before You. And my breathing deep within is not hidden from You. 10 My heart beats fast. My strength leaves me. Even the light of my eyes has gone from me. 11 My loved ones and my friends stay away from me because of my sickness. My family stands far away. 12 Those who want to take my life set their traps. And those who want to destroy me talk about ways to do it. They make their sinful plans all day long.

13 But like a deaf man, I do not hear. I am like one who cannot speak and does not

open his mouth. 14 Yes, I am like a man who does not hear, and whose mouth does not argue. 15 For I hope in You, O Lord. You will answer, O Lord my God. 16 For I said, "Do not let them be happy and raise themselves up against me when my foot trips." 17 For I am ready to fall. And my sorrow is always with me. 18 For I tell my wrong-doings. I am full of sorrow because of my sin. 19 But those who fight against me are full of action and strength. There are many who hate me without reason. 20 They pay what is bad for what is good. They are against me because I follow what is good. 21 Do not leave me alone, O Lord! O my God, do not be far from me! 22 Hurry to help me, O Lord, Who saves me!

Prayer of a Suffering Man

39 I said, "I will watch my ways so I may not sin with my tongue. I will keep my mouth shut as if it were tied with ropes, while the sinful are near me." 2 I stayed quiet, not even saying anything good. And my sorrow grew worse. 3 My heart was hot within me. As I thought about things, the fire burned. Then I spoke with my tongue, 4 "O Lord, let me know my end and how many days I have to live. Let me know that I do not have long to stay here. 5 You have made each of my days as long as a hand is wide. My whole life is nothing in Your eyes. Every man at his best is only a breath. 6 Every man walks here and there like a shadow. He makes a noise about nothing. He stores up riches, not knowing who will gather them.

7 And now, Lord, what do I wait for? My hope is in You. 8 Save me from all my sins. Do not let me be put to shame by the foolish. 9 I cannot speak. I do not open my mouth because it is You Who has done it. 10 Do not punish me any more. I am growing weak by the beatings of Your hand. 11 With sharp words You punish a man for sin. You destroy like a moth what is worth to him. For sure, every man is only a breath.

12 O Lord, hear my prayer, and listen to my cry. Do not be quiet when You see my tears. For I am a stranger with You, a visitor like all my fathers. 13 Look away from me, so I may have joy again before I go and am no more."

God Keeps His Own

40 I did not give up waiting for the Lord. And He turned to me and heard my cry. 2 He brought me up out of

the hole of danger, out of the mud and clay. He set my feet on a rock, making my feet sure. 3 He put a new song in my mouth, a song of praise to our God. Many will see and fear and will put their trust in the Lord.

4 How happy is the man who has made the Lord his trust, and has not turned to the proud or to the followers of lies. 5 O Lord my God, many are the great works You have done, and Your thoughts toward us. No one can compare with You! If I were to speak and tell of them, there would be too many to number.

6 You have not wanted gifts given on the altar in worship. You have opened my ears. You have not wanted burnt gifts or gifts to cover sins. 7 Then I said, "Look, I have come. It is written about me in the book. 8 I am happy to do Your will, O my God. Your Law is within my heart."

9 I have told the good news about what is right and good in the big meeting with many people. You know I will not close my lips, O Lord. 10 I have not hidden what is right and good with You in my heart. I have spoken about how faithful You are and about Your saving power. I have not hidden Your loving-kindness and Your truth from the big meeting.

11 O Lord, You will not keep Your loving-pity from me. Your loving-kindness and Your truth will always keep me safe. 12 Too many troubles gather around me. My sins have taken such a hold on me that I am not able to see. There are more of them than there are hairs on my head. And the strength of my heart has left me.

13 Be pleased to save me, O Lord. Hurry, O Lord, to help me. 14 Let all who want to destroy my life be ashamed and troubled. Let those who want to hurt me be turned away without honor. 15 Let those who say to me, "O! O!" be filled with fear because of their shame. 16 But let all who look for You have joy and be glad in You. Let those who love Your saving power always say, "The Lord be honored!" 17 Because I suffer and am in need, let the Lord think of me. You are my help and the One Who sets me free. O my God, do not wait.

Prayer of a Sick Man about False Friends

41 Happy is the man who cares for the poor. The Lord will save him in times of trouble. 2 The Lord will keep him alive and safe. And he will be happy upon the earth. You will not give him over to the desire of those who hate him. 3 The Lord will give him strength on his bed of sickness. When he is sick, You will make him well again.

4 As for me, I said, "O Lord, have loving-kindness for me. Heal my soul, for I have sinned against You." 5 Those who hate me speak bad words against me, saying, "When will he die, and his name be forgotten?" 6 When one comes to see me, he speaks lies. His heart gathers up bad stories. Then he goes outside and tells them. 7 All who hate me speak in secret together against me. They make plans to hurt me, saying, 8 "A bad thing has come over him. When he lies down, he will not rise again." 9 Even a friend of mine whom I trusted, who ate my bread, has turned against me.

10 Have loving-kindness for me, O Lord. Raise me up, so that I may pay them back. 11 Then I will know that You are pleased with me, because he who hates me does not win over me. 12 As for me, You hold me up in my honesty. And You set me beside You forever.

13 Honor be to the Lord, the God of Israel, forever and ever! Let it be so!

Prayer to Be Home Safe Again

42 As the deer desires rivers of water, so my soul desires You, O God. 2 My soul is thirsty for God, for the living God. When will I come and meet with God? 3 My tears have been my food day and night, while men say to me all day long, "Where is your God?" 4 These things I remember, and I pour out my soul within me. For I used to go with many people and lead them to the house of God, with the voice of thankful joy, among the many happy people.

5 Why are you sad, O my soul? Why have you become troubled within me? Hope in God, for I will praise Him again for His help of being near me. 6 O my God, my soul is troubled within me. So I remember You from the land of the Jordan and the tops of Hermon, from Mount Mizar. 7 Sea calls to sea at the sound of Your waterfalls. All Your waves have rolled over me. 8 The Lord will send His loving-kindness in the day. And His song will be with me in the night, a prayer to the God of my life.

9 I will say to God my Rock, "Why have You forgotten me? Why do I have sorrow because those who hate me come against me with power?" 10 As a breaking of my bones, those who hate me speak sharp words to me. All day long they say to me, "Where is your God?" 11 Why are you sad, O my soul? Why have you become

troubled within me? Hope in God, for I will yet praise Him, my help and my God.

Prayer to Be Kept Safe

43 Stand by me, O God, and speak in my favor against a sinful nation. Save me from the lying and sinful man. 2 For You are the God of my strength. Why have You turned away from me? Why do I have sorrow because those who hate me come against me with power?

3 Send out Your light and Your truth. Let them lead me. Let them bring me to Your holy hill and to the places where You live. 4 Then I will go to the altar of God, the God of my joy. And I will praise You with the harp, O God, my God.

5 Why are you sad, O my soul? Why have you become troubled within me? Hope in God, for I will praise Him again, my help and my God.

Prayer because of Troubles

44 O God, we have heard with our ears. Our fathers have told us what work You did in their days, in the days long ago. 2 With Your own hand You made the nations leave, and put our fathers in the land. You brought trouble upon the nations, and You spread them out. 3 It was not by their sword that they took the land. Their own arm did not save them. But it was Your right hand, and Your arm, and the light of Your face, for You favored them.

4 You are my King, O God. Jacob wins because You say it must be so. 5 Through You we will push away those who hate us. Through Your name we will walk over those who rise up against us. 6 For I will not trust my bow, and my sword will not save me. 7 But You have saved us from those who fight against us. You have put to shame those who hate us. 8 In God we have had our pride all day long. And we will give thanks to Your name forever.

9 But now You have turned from us and have put us to shame. You do not go out with our armies. 10 You made us turn away from those who fight against us. And those who hate us have robbed us. 11 You give us up to be eaten like sheep. You have spread us out among the nations. 12 You sell Your people for nothing, and become no richer from their price. 13 You have made us a shame to our neighbors. Those around us laugh and make fun of us. 14 You have made us hated among the nations. The people laugh at us. 15 All day long my shame is with me and has become too

much for me. 16 Those who talk against me, and who hate me are around me and want to punish me.

17 All this has come upon us, but we have not forgotten You. We have not been false to Your agreement. 18 Our heart has not turned away. And our steps have not turned from Your way. 19 But You have crushed us in a place of wild dogs, and covered us with the shadow of death.

20 If we had forgotten the name of our God, or put out our hands to a strange god, 21 would not God find this out? For He knows the secrets of the heart. 22 But we are killed all day long because of You. We are thought of as sheep that are ready to be killed. 23 Awake, O Lord! Why do You sleep? Rise up! Do not turn away from us forever. 24 Why do You hide Your face? Why do You forget our troubles and our suffering? 25 For our soul is brought down to the dust. Our body holds on to the earth. 26 Rise up and help us! Save us because of Your loving-kindness.

The King's Wedding Song

45 My heart flows over with good words. I sing my songs to the King. My tongue writes the words of a good writer. 2 You are more beautiful than the children of men. Loving-favor is poured upon Your lips. So God has honored You forever.

3 Put Your sword on at Your side, O Powerful One, in Your greatness and power that can be seen. 4 And in Your great power, move on to win the fight for truth and for not having pride and for what is right and good. Let Your right hand teach You to do great things. 5 Your arrows are sharp. The people fall under You. Your arrows are in the heart of those who hate the King.

6 O God, Your throne is forever and ever. You rule Your holy nation by what is right. 7 You have loved what is right and good. You have hated what is wrong. That is why God, Your God, has chosen You. He has poured over You the oil of joy more than over anyone else. 8 All Your clothes smell of fine perfumes. Out of ivory palaces music of strings have made You glad. 9 Daughters of kings are among Your women of honor. At Your right hand stands the queen, wearing gold from Ophir.

10 Listen, O daughter, hear my words and think about them. Forget your people and your father's house. 11 Then the King will desire your beauty. Because He is

your Lord, bow down to Him. 12 And the daughter of Tyre will come with a gift. The rich people will ask for your favor.

13 The daughter of the King is beautiful within. Her clothes are made with gold. 14 She will be led to the King in clothes sewed for beauty. The young women who have never had men are her friends. They follow her and will be brought to You. 15 They will be led in with joy and happiness, because they will come into the King's palace.

16 Instead of Your fathers, it will be Your sons whom You will make rulers over all the earth. 17 I will make Your name to be remembered to all the children-to-come. So that the nations will honor You forever and ever.

God Is with Us

46 God is our safe place and our strength. He is always our help when we are in trouble. 2 So we will not be afraid, even if the earth is shaken and the mountains fall into the center of the sea, 3 and even if its waters go wild with storm and the mountains shake with its action.

4 There is a river whose waters make glad the city of God, the holy place where the Most High lives. 5 God is in the center of her. She will not be moved. God will help her when the morning comes. 6 The people made noise. The nations fell. He raised His voice and the earth melted. 7 The Lord of All is with us. The God of Jacob is our strong-place.

8 Come and see the works of the Lord. He has destroyed parts of the earth. 9 He stops wars to the ends of the earth. He breaks the bow and cuts the spear in two. He burns the war-wagons with fire. 10 Be quiet and know that I am God. I will be honored among the nations. I will be honored in the earth. 11 The Lord of All is with us. The God of Jacob is our strong-place.

God—the King of the Earth

47 Show your happiness, all peoples! Call out to God with the voice of joy! 2 For the Lord Most High is to be feared. He is a great King over all the earth. 3 He sets people under us, and nations under our feet. 4 He chooses for us what is to be ours, the pride of Jacob, whom He loves.

5 God has gone up with a loud voice, the Lord with the sound of a horn. 6 Sing praises to God. Sing praises. Sing praises to our King. Sing praises. 7 For God is the King of all the earth. Sing praises with a

well written song. 8 God rules over the nations. God sits on His holy throne. 9 The rulers of the people have gathered together as the people of the God of Abraham. For the powers of the earth belong to God. He is much honored.

It Is Foolish to Trust in Riches

48 The Lord is great and should be given much praise, in the city of our God, His holy mountain. 2 Mount Zion in the far north is beautiful and high, the joy of the whole earth, the city of the great King. 3 God has made Himself known as a safe place in that city.

4 For, see, the kings gathered themselves and went up together. 5 They saw it, then they were surprised and afraid. And they ran away fast in fear. 6 They began shaking there. And they suffered pain like a woman giving birth. 7 You wreck the ships of Tarshish with the east wind. 8 As we have heard, so we have seen in the city of the Lord of All, in the city of our God. God will make her last forever.

9 O God, we have thought about Your loving-kindness within Your holy house. 10 Like Your name, O God, Your praise is heard to the ends of the earth. Your right hand is full of what is right and good. 11 Let Mount Zion be glad! Let the people of Judah be full of joy because You are right in how You judge. 12 Walk in Zion, and go around her. See how many towers she has. 13 Give thought to her walls. Go through her beautiful houses where kings live. And tell about it to the children-to-come. 14 This is God, our God forever and ever. He will show us the way until death.

A Fool Trusts in Riches

49 Hear this, all people. Listen, all who live in the world, 2 both small and great, rich and poor together. 3 My mouth will speak wisdom. And the thoughts of my heart will be understanding. 4 I will turn my ear to a wise saying. With a harp, I will tell what is hard to understand.

5 Why should I be afraid in the days of trouble, when the sin of those who hate me is all around me? 6 They trust in their riches, and are proud of all they have. 7 No man can save his brother. No man can pay God enough to save him. 8 The cost is much for his soul to be saved. Man should stop trying 9 to live forever and not see the grave.

10 For he sees that even wise men die. The fool and those who cannot think well die alike. And they leave their riches to others. 11 They think in their hearts that their houses will last forever, and that the places where they live will last for all their children to follow. They have used their own names to name their lands. 12 But man with all his honor does not last. He is like the animals that die.

13 This is the way of the foolish, and of those after them who believe in their words. 14 Like sheep they are meant for the grave. Death will be their shepherd. And those who are right with God will rule over them in the morning. Their bodies will be eaten by the grave, so that they have no place to stay. 15 But God will free my soul from the power of the grave. For He will take me to Himself.

16 Do not be afraid when a man becomes rich and when his house grows in greatness. 17 For when he dies he will take nothing with him. His greatness will not go down with him. 18 Even if while he lives, he thinks good of himself, and even though men praise you when you do well for yourself, 19 he will go and join the family of his fathers. They will never see the light. 20 Man with all his honor, yet without understanding, is like the animals that die.

God Decides Right from Wrong

50 The Powerful One, God, the Lord, has spoken. And He calls the earth from where the sun rises to where the sun goes down. 2 God shines from Zion, perfect in beauty. 3 May our God come and not keep quiet. A fire burns before Him, and around Him is a powerful storm. 4 He calls the heavens above, and the earth, that He may judge His people: 5 "Gather My holy ones to Me, those who have made an agreement with Me by their gifts given on an altar." 6 And the heavens will tell how right and good He is, for God Himself is judge.

7 "Listen, O My people, and I will speak. O Israel, I will speak against you. I am God, your God. 8 I do not speak sharp words to you for your gifts given on an altar. And your burnt gifts are always before Me. 9 I will not take a young bull out of your house, or male goats out of your fields. 10 For every animal among the trees is Mine, and the cattle on a thousand hills. 11 I know every bird of the mountains. And all things that move in the field are Mine. 12 If I were hungry, I would not tell you. For the world is Mine, and all that is

in it. 13 Should I eat the flesh of bulls, or drink the blood of male goats? 14 Give a gift of thanks on the altar to God. And pay your promises to the Most High. 15 Call on Me in the day of trouble. I will take you out of trouble, and you will honor Me."

16 But to the sinful, God says: "What right do you have to tell of My Laws, and take My agreement in your mouth? 17 For you hate to be told what to do, and you throw My words behind you. 18 When you see a robber, you are pleased with him. And you join those who do sex sins. 19 You say bad things with your mouth, and you lie with your tongue. 20 You sit and speak against your brother. You talk against your own mother's son. 21 You have done these things, and I have kept quiet. You thought that I was just like you. But I will speak sharp words to you, and tell you who is guilty to your face.

22 "Now think about this, you who forget God, or I will tear you in pieces and there will be no one to save you. 23 He who gives a gift of thanks honors Me. And to him who makes his way right, I will show him the saving power of God."

Prayer of the Sinner

51 O God, favor me because of Your loving-kindness. Take away my wrong-doing because of the greatness of Your loving-pity. 2 Wash me inside and out from my wrong-doing and make me clean from my sin. 3 For I know my wrong-doing, and my sin is always in front of me. 4 I have sinned against You, and You only. I have done what is sinful in Your eyes. You are always right when You speak, and fair when You judge.

5 See, I was born in sin and was in sin from my very beginning. 6 See, You want truth deep within the heart. And You will make me know wisdom in the hidden part. 7 Take away my sin, and I will be clean. Wash me, and I will be whiter than snow. 8 Make me hear joy and happiness. Let the bones that You have broken be full of joy. 9 Hide Your face from my sins. And take away all my wrong-doing.

10 Make a clean heart in me, O God. Give me a new spirit that will not be moved. 11 Do not throw me away from where You are. And do not take Your Holy Spirit from me. 12 Let the joy of Your saving power return to me. And give me a willing spirit to obey you. 13 Then I will teach wrong-doers Your ways. And sinners will turn to You.

14 Save me from the guilt of blood, O God. You are the God Who saves me. Then my tongue will sing with joy about how right and good You are. 15 O Lord, open my lips, so my mouth will praise You. 16 For You are not happy with a gift given on the altar in worship, or I would give it. You are not pleased with burnt gifts. 17 The gifts on an altar that God wants are a broken spirit. O God, You will not hate a broken heart and a heart with no pride.

18 Be pleased to do good to Zion. Build the walls of Jerusalem. 19 Then You will be happy with gifts given on the altar that are right and good, with burnt gifts and whole burnt gifts. Then young bulls will be given on Your altar.

Trust in God's Love

52 Why do you take pride in wrong-doing, O powerful man? The loving-kindness of God lasts all day long. 2 Your tongue makes plans to destroy like a sharp knife, you who lie. 3 You love what is bad more than what is good, and you speak lies more than you speak the truth. 4 You love all words that destroy, O lying tongue.

5 But God will destroy you forever. He will pick you up and pull you away from your tent. He will pull up your roots from the land of the living. 6 And those who are right will see and be afraid. They will laugh at him, saying, 7 "Look, the man who would not make God his safe place, but trusted in his many riches and was strong in his sinful desire."

8 But I am like a green olive tree in the house of God. I trust in the loving kindness of God forever and ever. 9 I will give You thanks forever because of what You have done. And I will hope in Your name, for it is good to be where those who belong to You are.

Foolish Men

53 The fool has said in his heart, "There is no God." They are sinful and have done bad things. There is no one who does good. 2 God has looked down from heaven at the children of men to see if there is anyone who understands and looks for God. 3 They have all turned back. They have all turned to sin. There is no one who does good, not even one. 4 Have those who do wrong no understanding? They eat up My people like they eat bread. They have not called upon God. 5 There they were, in much fear, where there was nothing to be afraid of. For God has spread out the bones of those who come against you. You put them to shame, because God has turned away from them. 6 O, that the saving of Israel would come out of Zion! Jacob will be full of joy and Israel will be glad when God returns His people to their land.

Prayer for a Safe Place

54 Save me by Your name, O God. And stand with me by Your power. 2 Hear my prayer, O God. Listen to the words of my mouth. 3 For strangers have risen against me. And men who hurt others want to take my life. They do not think about God.

4 See, God is my Helper. The Lord is the One Who keeps my soul alive. 5 He will punish those who hate me, for the wrong they have done. He will destroy them because He is faithful.

6 I will be glad to give You a gift on the altar. I will give thanks to Your name, O Lord, for it is good. 7 For He has taken me out of all trouble. And my eyes have looked without fear upon those who hate me.

Prayer of a Man Hurt by a Friend

55 Listen to my prayer, O God. Do not hide Yourself from what I ask. 2 Hear me and answer me. My thoughts trouble me and I have no peace, 3 because of the voice of those who hate me and the power of the sinful. For they bring trouble upon me, and in anger they keep on having bad thoughts against me.

4 My heart is in pain within me. The fears of death have come upon me. 5 I have begun shaking with fear. Fear has power over me. 6 And I say, "If only I had wings like a dove, I would fly away and be at rest. 7 Yes, I would go far away. I would live in the desert. 8 I would hurry to my safe place, away from the wild wind and storm."

9 Mix them up, O Lord. Divide their tongues. For I have seen fighting and trouble in the city. 10 They go around on its walls day and night. Sin and wrong-doing are within it. 11 Destroying powers are in the city. Trouble and lies never leave its streets.

12 I would be able to take it if one who hates me were putting me to shame. I could hide from him. It is not one who hates me who has put himself up against me. 13 But it is you, a man like myself, one who has gone with me, my close friend. 14 We shared together. And we walked

with the people in the house of God. 15 Let death take them by surprise. Let them go down alive to the grave. For sin is with them where they live. 16 As for me, I will call on God and the Lord will save me. 17 I will cry out and complain in the evening and morning and noon, and He will hear my voice. 18 He will save my soul in peace from those who make war against me. For there are many who fight me. 19 God sits on His throne forever. And He will hear them and bring trouble upon them, because there has been no change in them. They do not fear God. 20 He goes against those who were at peace with him. He has broken his agreement. 21 What he says is smoother than butter, but war is in his heart. His words are softer than oil, yet they are raised swords.

22 Give all your cares to the Lord and He will give you strength. He will never let those who are right with Him be shaken. 23 But You, O God, will bring the sinful down into the hole that destroys. Men who kill and lie will not live out half their days. But I will trust in You.

Prayer of Trust in God

56 Show me Your loving-kindness, O God, for man has walked on me. All day long the one who tries to keep me down fights with me. 2 All day long those who hate me have walked on me. For there are many when fight against me with pride. 3 When I am afraid, I will trust in You. 4 I praise the Word of God. I have put my trust in God. I will not be afraid. What can only a man do to me? 5 All day long they change my words to say what I did not say. They are always thinking of ways to hurt me. 6 They go after me as in a fight. They hide themselves. They watch my steps, as they have waited to take my life. 7 Because they are bad, do not let them get away. Bring down the people in Your anger, O God.

8 You have seen how many places I have gone. Put my tears in Your bottle. Are they not in Your book? 9 Then those who hate me will turn back when I call. I know that God is for me. 10 I praise the Word of God. I praise the Word of the Lord. 11 In God I have put my trust. I will not be afraid. What can man do to me? 12 I am under an agreement with You, O God. I will give You gifts of thanks. 13 For You have set my soul free from death. You have kept my feet from falling, so I may walk with God in the light of life.

Prayer for Help

57 Show me loving-kindness, O God, show me loving-kindness. For my soul goes to You to be safe. And I will be safe in the shadow of Your wings until the trouble has passed. 2 I will cry to God Most High, to God Who finishes all things for me. 3 He will send from heaven and save me. He will put to shame him who is breaking me under his feet. God will send His loving-kindness and His truth.

4 My soul is among lions. I must lie among the sons of men who breathe fire, whose teeth are spears and arrows, and whose tongues are a sharp sword. 5 Be lifted up above the heavens, O God. Let Your shining-greatness be above all the earth. 6 They have set a net for my steps. My soul is brought down. They dug a deep hole in front of me. But they themselves have fallen into it.

7 My heart will not be moved, O God. My heart cannot be moved. I will sing, yes, I will sing praises! 8 Awake, my shining-greatness. Awake, harps. I will awake early in the morning. 9 O Lord, I will give thanks to You among the people. I will sing praises to You among the nations. 10 For Your loving-kindness is great to the heavens, and Your truth to the clouds. 11 Be lifted up above the heavens, O God. Let Your shining-greatness be above all the earth.

Prayer for God to Punish the Sinful

58 Do you speak what is right and good, O you powerful ones? Are you always right in how you judge, O sons of men? 2 No, in your heart you do what is wrong. You use your hands to hurt and destroy in the land. 3 The sinful go wrong as soon as they are born. Those who speak lies go the wrong way from birth. 4 Their poison is like the poison of a snake. They are like a cobra that cannot or will not listen. 5 It does not hear the voice of the man who has power over it, even if the man is very good in his work.

6 O God, break the teeth in their mouth. Break out the teeth of the young lions, O Lord. 7 Let them flow away like water that pours. When he uses his arrows, let them have no heads. 8 Let them be like a snail that melts away as it goes. Like a baby born dead, may they never see the sun. 9 Before your pots can feel the fire of thorns, He will blow them away with a storm, both the green and the burning ones.

10 The one who is right and good will be full of joy when he sees the sinful punished. He will wash his feet in their blood. 11 And men will say, "For sure there is pay for those who are right and good. For sure there is a God Who says who is guilty or not on the earth."

Prayer for a Safe Place

59 O my God, take me away from those who hate me. Put me up high above those who rise up against me. 2 Take me away from those who do wrong. And save me from those who kill. 3 For, look, they lie in wait for my life. Strong men are gathering together to fight me, but not because of my wrong-doing or my sin, O Lord. 4 I have done no wrong, but they get ready to fight against me. Rise up to help me. 5 You, O Lord God of All, God of Israel, rise up to punish all the nations. Show no loving-kindness to those people who cannot be trusted and plan sins. 6 They return at evening. They sound like dogs and go around the city. 7 See, they spit with their mouth. Swords are in their lips. And they say, "Who can hear us?" 8 But You laugh at them, O Lord. You laugh at all the nations.

9 O my Strength, I will watch for You. For God is my strong-place. 10 My God in His loving-kindness will meet me. God will let me look at those who come against me and know that I will win the fight. 11 Do not kill them, or my people may forget. Divide them by Your power and bring them down, O Lord, our safe-covering. 12 Let them be caught in their pride for the sin of their mouth and the words of their lips. For the lies and bad things they say, 13 destroy them so that they will be no more. Let it be known that God rules in Jacob and to the ends of the earth.

14 They return at evening. They make sounds like dogs and go around the city. 15 They go around looking for food and they show their teeth if they are not filled.

16 But as for me, I will sing of Your strength. Yes, I will sing with joy of Your loving-kindness in the morning. For You have been a strong and safe place for me in times of trouble. 17 O my Strength, I will sing praises to You. For God is my strong-place and the God Who shows me loving-kindness.

Prayer for Help

60 O God, You have turned away from us. You have broken us. You have been angry. O heal us and turn to us again. 2 You have made the land shake. You have torn it open. Heal it where it is broken, for it shakes. 3 You have made Your people suffer hard things. You have given us wine to drink that makes us not able to walk straight. 4 You have given a flag to those who fear You, so it may be seen because of the truth. 5 Save us with Your right hand, and answer us, so Your loved ones may be set free.

6 God has said in His holy place: "I will be full of joy. I will divide Shechem and the valley of Succoth. 7 Gilead is Mine. And Manasseh is Mine. Ephraim is the covering for My head. Judah is My law-giver. 8 Moab is where I wash My hands. I will throw My shoe over Edom. Call out, Philistia, because of me."

9 Who will bring me into the strong city? Who will lead me into Edom? 10 Have You not turned away from us, O God? And will You not go out with our armies, O God? 11 O give us help against those who hate us. For the help of man is worth nothing. 12 With God's help we will do well. And He will break under His feet those who fight against us.

A Safe Place in God

61 Hear my cry, O God. Listen to my prayer. 2 I call to You from the end of the earth when my heart is weak. Lead me to the rock that is higher than I. 3 For You have been a safe place for me, a tower of strength where I am safe from those who fight against me. 4 Let me live in Your tent forever. Let me be safe under the covering of Your wings. 5 For You have heard my promises, O God. You have given me that which You give to those who fear Your name. 6 You will add days to the life of the king. His years will be as long as the lives of many children and grandchildren added together. 7 He will stay forever with God. Set apart loving-kindness and truth to keep him safe. 8 So I will sing thanks to Your name forever and keep my promises day by day.

Thankful for God's Care

62 My soul is quiet and waits for God alone. He is the One Who saves me. 2 He alone is my rock and the One Who saves me. He is my strong-place. I will not be shaken.

3 How long will all of you go against a man to break him down, that you may kill him, like a wall that no longer stands straight, like a fence ready to fall? 4 They have talked only about throwing him

down from his high place. They find joy in lies. They pray with their mouth that good will come. But inside they hope that bad will come instead.

5 My soul is quiet and waits for God alone. My hope comes from Him. 6 He alone is my rock and the One Who saves me. He is my strong-place. I will not be shaken. 7 My being safe and my honor rest with God. My safe place is in God, the rock of my strength. 8 Trust in Him at all times, O people. Pour out your heart before Him. God is a safe place for us.

9 Men who are not important come to nothing. Men who are important are a lie. When weighed they go up. Together they weigh less than a breath. 10 Do not get money in a wrong way or be proud in stolen things. If you get more riches, do not set your heart on them.

11 God has spoken once. I have heard this twice: Power belongs to God. 12 And loving-kindness belongs to You, O Lord. For You pay every man by the work he has done.

Giving Thanks to God

63 O God, You are my God. I will look for You with all my heart and strength. My soul is thirsty for You. My flesh is weak wanting You in a dry and tired land where there is no water. 2 So I have seen You in the holy place. And I have seen Your power and Your shining-greatness. 3 My lips will praise You because Your loving-kindness is better than life. 4 So I will give honor to You as long as I live. I will lift up my hands in Your name. 5 My soul will be filled as with rich foods. And my mouth praises You with lips of joy.

6 On my bed I remember You. I think of You through the hours of the night. 7 For You have been my help. And I sing for joy in the shadow of Your wings. 8 My soul holds on to You. Your right hand holds me up.

9 But those who want to take my life and destroy it will go deep into the earth. 10 They will be given over to the power of the sword. They will become food for foxes. 11 But the king will be full of joy in God. All who are faithful to God will be full of joy. For the mouth of those who speak lies will be stopped.

Prayer for a Safe Place

64 O God, hear my voice when I com-plain. Keep my life safe from the fear of those who hate me. 2 Hide me from the secret plans of the sinful and from the noise of those who do bad things. 3 They have made their tongues sharp like a sword. They use poison words like arrows. 4 They shoot at the man without blame from their hiding place. They are quick to shoot at him and are not afraid. 5 They talk each other into doing sinful things. They talk about setting hidden traps. They say, "Who will see them?" 6 They think of ways to do bad things, and say, "We have made a perfect plan!" For the inside thoughts and the heart of a man are deep.

7 But God will shoot at them with an arrow. They will be hurt very soon. 8 They will be made to trip and fall. Their own tongue is against them. All who see them will shake their heads. 9 Then all men will be afraid. They will tell about the work of God. And they will think about what He has done. 10 The man who is right and good will be glad in the Lord and go to Him to be safe. All those whose hearts are right will give Him praise.

God's Favor to Earth and Man

65 All will be quiet before You, and praise belongs to You, O God, in Zion. And our promise to You will be kept. 2 O You Who hears prayer, to You all men come. 3 My sins are strong against me. But You forgive our sins. 4 Happy is the man You choose and bring near to You to live in Your holy place. We will be filled with the good things of Your house, Your holy house.

5 O God Who saves us, You answer us in the way that is right and good by Your great works that make people stand in fear. You are the hope of all the ends of the earth and of the farthest seas. 6 You have built the mountains by Your strength. You are dressed with power. 7 You quiet the storm of the seas, the sound of their waves, and the noise of the people. 8 Those who live far away are afraid of Your great works. You make morning and evening call out for joy.

9 You visit the earth and water it. You make it very rich. The river of God is full of water. You give the people grain when You have made the earth ready. 10 You water where the plow has been used. You cover the seeds with earth. You make it soft with rain. And You make the plants grow well. 11 You crown the year with Your good gifts. There is more than enough where You have been. 12 The fields of the desert are filled with water. And the hills dress

themselves with joy. 13 The grass lands are covered with birds. And the valleys are covered with grain. They call out for joy and sing.

Song of Praise and Thanks to God

66 Raise the voice of joy to God, all the earth! 2 Sing out the honor of His name! Make His praise great! 3 Say to God, "How Your great works make those who hate You afraid! They will have to obey You because of Your great power. 4 All the earth will worship You and sing praises to You. They will sing praises to Your name."

5 Come and see what God has done. There is much fear because of His great works toward the children of men. 6 He changed the sea into dry land. They passed through the river on foot. There we were full of joy in Him. 7 He rules forever by His power. His eyes keep watch over the nations. Do not let those who do not obey You honor themselves.

8 Give honor and thanks to God, O people, and let all hear how great He is! 9 He keeps us alive, and does not let our feet go out from under us. 10 For You have tested us, O God. You have made us pure like silver is made pure. 11 You brought us into the net. And You laid a heavy load on our back. 12 You made men travel over our heads. We went through fire and through water. But You brought us out into a place where we have much more than we need. 13 I will come into Your house with burnt gifts. I will give You what I promised, 14 promises made by my lips and spoken by my mouth when I was in trouble. 15 I will give You burnt gifts of fat animals with the smoke of rams. I will give You bulls with male goats.

16 Come and hear, all who fear God, and I will tell you what He has done for me. 17 I cried to Him with my mouth and praised Him with my tongue. 18 The Lord will not hear me if I hold on to sin in my heart. 19 But it is sure that God has heard. He has listened to the voice of my prayer. 20 Honor and thanks be to God! He has not turned away from my prayer or held His loving-kindness from me.

Nations Praise God

67 May God show loving-kindness toward us and bring good to us. May He make His face shine upon us. 2 May Your way be known on the earth, and Your saving power among all nations. 3 May the people praise You, O God. May all the people praise You. 4 May the nations be glad and sing for joy. For You will be fair when You judge the people and rule the nations of the earth. 5 May the people praise You, O God. May all the people praise You. 6 The earth has given its fruit. God, our God, will bring good to us. 7 God will bring good to us, and all the ends of the earth will fear Him.

The God of Israel at Sinai

68 May God rise up. May those who hate Him be divided. And may they run away from Him. 2 Drive them away like smoke in the wind. Let the sinful be destroyed before God like a candle melts by the fire. 3 But let those who are right and good be glad. Let them be happy before God. Yes, let them be full of joy. 4 Sing to God. Sing praises to His name. Make a road for Him Who goes through the deserts. The Lord is His name. Be full of joy before Him.

5 God in His holy house is a father to those who have no father. And He keeps the women safe whose husbands have died. 6 God makes a home for those who are alone. He leads men out of prison into happiness and well-being. But those who fight against Him live in an empty desert.

7 O God, when You went out before Your people, when You walked through the desert, 8 the earth shook. The heavens poured down rain before God. And Sinai shook before God, the God of Israel. 9 You sent a heavy rain, O God. You brought life back to Your promised land when it was dry. 10 Your people made it their home. O God, You gave the poor what they needed because You are good.

11 The Lord gives the Word. And the women who tell the good news are many. 12 The kings of armies run. They run away. And she who stays at home divides the riches. 13 When you lie down among the sheep, you are like the wings of a dove covered with silver, and the end of its wings with shining gold. 14 When the All-powerful divided the kings there, snow was falling in Zalmon.

15 A mountain of God is the mountain of Bashan. A mountain of many high tops is the mountain of Bashan. 16 O mountains of many high tops, why do you look with jealousy at the mountain which God has chosen for His home? For sure, the Lord will live there forever. 17 The war-wagons of God are 20,000, even thousands of thousands. The Lord is among them, as at

Sinai, in the holy place. 18 You have gone up on high. You have taken those who were held with You. You have received gifts of men, even among those who fought against You. So the Lord God may live there with them.

19 Honor and thanks be to the Lord, Who carries our heavy loads day by day. He is the God Who saves us. 20 Our God is a God Who sets us free. The way out of death belongs to God the Lord. 21 But God will break the head of those who hate Him, the hair-covered head of him who goes on in his sins. 22 The Lord said, "I will bring them back from Bashan. I will bring them back from the bottom of the sea. 23 So your feet may crush them in blood. And the tongue of your dogs may have a share of those who hate you."

24 They have seen Your people walking together, O God. They have seen the people of my God and King walking into the holy place. 25 Those who sing are in front. Those who play music are behind. And young women who beat timbrels are between. 26 Give thanks to God in the meetings of worship. Give thanks to the Lord, you who are of the family of Israel. 27 There is young Benjamin leading them. The rulers of Judah are among the people, and the rulers of Zebulun, and the rulers of Naphtali.

28 Your God has called for your strength. Show Your strength, O God, Who has acted for us. 29 Kings will bring gifts to You because of Your holy house at Jerusalem. 30 Speak sharp words to the wild animals in the tall grass by the river, the group of bulls with the calves of the people. Walk on those who desire pieces of silver. Divide the people who have joy in war. 31 Princes will come from Egypt. Ethiopia will hurry to put her hands out to God.

32 Sing to God, O nations of the earth. Sing praises to the Lord. 33 Sing to Him Who sits upon the heavens, the heavens of old. Listen, He sends out His voice, His powerful voice. 34 Tell of the power of God. His great power is over Israel and His strength is in the sky. 35 O God, You are honored with fear as You come from Your holy place. The God of Israel Himself gives strength and power to His people. Honor and thanks be to God!

A Cry for Help

69 Save me, O God, for the waters have almost taken my life. 2 I have gone down into deep mud and there is no place to put my feet. I have come into deep waters and a flood comes over me. [3] I have cried until I am tired. My mouth is dry. My eyes become weak while I wait for my God. [4] Those who hate me, without a reason, are more than the hairs on my head. Those who want to destroy me are powerful. I am made to return things that I did not steal.

[5] O God, You know how foolish I am. My sins are not hidden from You. [6] May those who wait for You not be put to shame because of me, O Lord God of All. May those who look for You not lose respect because of me, O God of Israel. [7] I have been put to shame because of You. Shame has covered my face. [8] I have become a stranger to my brothers, a stranger to my mother's sons. [9] For the strong desire for Your house has burned me up. And the bad things said about You have fallen on me. [10] When I cried and went without food, I was put to shame. [11] When I put on clothes made from hair, they made fun of me. [12] Those who sit by the gate talk about me. And I am the song of those who drink too much.

[13] But as for me, my prayer is to You at the right time, O Lord. Answer me with Your saving truth in Your great loving-kindness, O God. [14] Take me out of the mud and do not let me go down in it. Take me away from those who hate me and from the deep waters. [15] Keep the flood water from covering me. Do not let the sea swallow me up. Do not let the deep hole close its mouth over me.

[16] Answer me, O Lord, for Your loving-kindness is good. Turn to me because of Your great loving-pity. [17] Do not hide Your face from Your servant, for I am in trouble. Hurry to answer me. [18] Come near to me and save me. Pay the price to set me free from those who hate me. [19] You know how I have been put to shame by the bad things said about me. All those who hate me are before You.

[20] Being put to shame has broken my heart, and I feel very sick. I looked for pity but there was none. I looked for some-one to comfort me but there was no one. [21] They gave me bitter drink in my food. And because I was thirsty they gave me sour wine.

[22] May their table in front of them be-come a net. May it become a trap when they are in peace. [23] May their eyes grow dark so they cannot see. And may their backs always shake. [24] Pour out Your anger on them. May Your burning anger catch up with them. [25] May their place

of living be empty and may no one live in their tents. [26] For they have made it hard for the one You have punished. And they talk about the pain of those You have hurt. [27] Let their sins add up, and may they not become right with You. [28] May they be taken out of the book of life, and not be written down with those who are right with You.

[29] But I am suffering and in pain. O God, may You save me and set me up on high. [30] I will praise the name of God with song. And I will give Him great honor with much thanks. [31] This will please the Lord more than any ox or young bull with horns and hoofs. [32] Those without pride will see it and be glad. You who look for God, let your heart receive new strength. [33] For the Lord hears those who are in need, and does not hate His people in prison.

[34] Let heaven and earth and the seas and all the things that move in them give thanks to Him. [35] For God will save Zion and build the cities of Judah. Then His people may live there and have it for their own. [36] And the children of those who obey Him will have it given to them. Those who love His name will live there.

Prayer for Help

70 O God, hurry to take me out of trouble. O Lord, hurry to help me! [2] Let those who want to kill me be ashamed and brought low. Let those who want to hurt me be turned away in shame. [3] Let those who say, "O, O!" be turned back because of their shame.

[4] Let all who look for You be full of joy and be glad in You. And let those who love Your saving power always say, "Let God be honored!" [5] But I am poor and in need. Hurry to me, O God! You are my help and the One Who takes me out of trouble. O Lord, do not wait.

A Prayer of an Old Man

71 I have a safe place in you, O Lord. Let me never be ashamed. [2] Because You are right and good, take me out of trouble. Turn Your ear to me and save me. [3] Be a rock to me where I live, where I may always come and where I will be safe. For You are my rock and my safe place. [4] O my God, take me from the hand of the sinful, from the hand of the wrong-doer and the man without pity. [5] For You are my hope, O Lord God. You are my trust since I was young. [6] You have kept me safe from birth. It was You Who watched over me from the day I was born. My praise is always of You.

7 I have become a wonder and surprise to many. For You are my strong safe place. 8 My mouth is filled with Your praise and with Your honor all day long. 9 Do not let me fall by the way when I am old. Do not leave me alone when my strength is gone. 10 For those who hate me talk against me. Those who want to kill make plans together. 11 They say, "God has turned away from him. Run and catch him, for there is no one to take him out of trouble."

12 O God, do not be far from me! O my God, hurry to help me! 13 Let those who are against me be ashamed and destroyed. Let those who want to hurt me be without honor and covered with shame. 14 But as for me, I will always have hope and I will praise You more and more. 15 My mouth will tell about how right and good You are and about Your saving acts all day long. For there are more than I can know. 16 I will come in the strength of the Lord God. I will tell about how right and good You are, and You alone.

17 O God, You have taught me from when I was young. And I still tell about Your great works. 18 Even when I am old and my hair is turning white, O God, do not leave me alone. Let me tell about Your strength to all the people living now, and about Your power to all who are to come. 19 O God, You are right and good, as the heavens are high. You have done great things, O God. Who is like You? 20 You have shown me many troubles of all kinds. But You will make me strong again. And You will bring me up again from deep in the earth. 21 Add to my greatness, and turn to comfort me.

22 O my God, I will praise You with a harp. I will praise Your truth. I will sing praises to You with different kinds of harps, O Holy One of Israel. 23 My lips will call out for joy when I sing praises to You. You have set my soul free. 24 My tongue will tell about how right and good You are all day long. For those who want to hurt me are ashamed and troubled.

A Prayer for the King

72 O God, make the king right in what he decides. Make the king's son right with You. 2 May he be right when he decides who is right and who is wrong and may he be fair to the poor. 3 Let mountains and hills bring peace to the people through what is right and good. 4 May he stand by

those who are poor, save the children of those in need, and destroy the bad power over them.

5 May all the children-to-come fear You as long as the sun and the moon last. 6 May He come down like rain upon the cut grass, like rain that waters the earth. 7 In His days may all go well with those who are right and good. And may there be much peace until the moon is no more.

8 May he also rule from sea to sea, and from the river to the ends of the earth. 9 Those who live in the desert will put their faces to the ground before Him. And those who hate Him will kiss the dust. 10 Let the kings of Tarshish and of the islands bring gifts. Let the kings of Sheba and Seba bring gifts. 11 Yes, let all kings fall down at His feet, and all nations serve Him.

12 For He will take out of trouble the one in need when he cries for help, and the poor man who has no one to help. 13 He will have loving-pity on the weak and those in need. He will save the lives of those in need. 14 He will take them from the bad power that is held over them and from being hurt. Their blood will be of much worth in His eyes. 15 He will live, and the gold of Sheba will be given to Him. Prayer will be given for Him all the time. Let them honor Him all day long.

16 May there be much grain in the land on top of the mountains. May its fruit grow like the trees of Lebanon. And may those of the city grow like the grass of the earth. 17 May His name last forever. May His name become bigger as long as the sun shines. And let men respect themselves through Him. Let all nations honor Him.

18 Honor and thanks be to the Lord God, the God of Israel, Who alone does great things. 19 And honor be to His great name forever. May the whole earth be filled with His shining-greatness. Let it be so.

20 The prayers of David, the son of Jesse, are ended.

The Good and the Sinful

73 For sure God is good to Israel, to those who are pure in heart. 2 But as for me, my feet came close to falling. My steps had almost tripped. 3 For I was jealous of the proud when I saw that all was going well with the sinful. 4 For they suffer no pain in their death, and their body is fat. 5 They do not have the troubles of other men or suffer like other men. 6 So they wear pride around their neck. Fighting covers them like a coat. 7 They are so fat that their eyes are pushed out. The crazy thoughts of their hearts run wild. [8] They laugh at the truth, and speak sinful things about making it hard for others. They speak from a high place. [9] They say bad things against heaven, and their tongue walks through the earth.

[10] And so his people return to this place and drink water from a full cup. [11] They say, "How does God know? Is there much learning with the Most High?"

[12] See, this is what the sinful are like. They always have it easy and their riches grow. [13] For no good reason I have kept my heart pure and have not sinned. [14] For I have suffered all day long. I have been punished every morning.

[15] I would not have been true to Your children if I had spoken this way. [16] It was too hard for me when I tried to understand this, [17] until I went into the holy place of God. Then I understood their end. [18] For sure, You set the sinful in places where there is danger at every step. You throw them down to be destroyed. [19] How they are destroyed right away! They come to an end with much fear. [20] Like a dream when one wakes up, so You will hate what they look like when You rise up, O Lord.

[21] My heart was troubled and I was hurt inside. [22] I was without reason and did not know better. I was like an animal before You. [23] Yet I am always with You. You hold me by my right hand. [24] You will lead me by telling me what I should do. And after this, You will bring me into shining-greatness.

[25] Whom have I in heaven but You? I want nothing more on earth, but You. [26] My body and my heart may grow weak, but God is the strength of my heart and all I need forever. [27] For, see, those who are far from You will be lost from You forever. You have destroyed all those who are not faithful to You. [28] But as for me, it is good to be near God. I have made the Lord God my safe place. So I may tell of all the things You have done.

A Prayer for the Nation

74 O God, why have You turned away from us forever? Why does Your anger burn against the sheep in Your fields? [2] Remember Your people that You bought a long time ago. You made them free to be the family of Your promise, and Mount Zion, where You have lived. [3] Turn Your steps toward this place that has been destroyed forever. Those who hate You

have destroyed all that is in the holy place. [4] Those who hate You have called out in the center of Your meeting place. They have set up their flags to show that they have won. [5] They acted like men taking up axes against a group of trees. [6] All of its fine work has been broken with axes and sticks. [7] They have burned Your holy place to the dust. They have made dirty the house of Your name. [8] They said in their hearts, "Let us destroy all of these places!" They have burned all the meeting places where God was worshiped in the land. [9] We do not see any special things happening. There is no longer anyone who speaks for God. And none of us knows how long this will be. [10] O God, how long will those who hate You laugh at the truth? Will they speak against Your name forever? [11] Why do You take Your hand away, even Your right hand? Put it out and destroy them!

[12] God is still my King from long ago. He does saving works upon the earth. [13] You divided the sea by Your power. You broke the heads of the large dragons in the waters. [14] You crushed the heads of the Leviathan. And You fed him to the animals of the desert. [15] It was You Who opened up the earth for water to flow out. And You dried up rivers that flow forever. [16] The day is Yours. And the night is Yours. You have set the light and the sun in their places. [17] You have divided all the lands and seas and nations of the earth. You have made summer and winter.

[18] Remember how those who hate You have laughed at the truth, O Lord. Foolish people have spoken against Your name. [19] Do not give the life of Your dove over to the wild animal. Do not forget the lives of Your troubled people forever. [20] Think about Your agreement. For the dark places of the land are full of fighting. [21] Do not let those who suffer under a bad power return without honor. Let those who suffer and those who are in need praise Your name.

[22] Rise up, O God. Stand up for Your rights. Remember how the foolish man speaks against You all day long. [23] Do not forget the voice of those who hate You, the noise that comes without stopping from those who rise against You.

God Puts Down the Proud and Lifts Up Those Who Are Right with Himself

75 We give thanks to You, O God. We give thanks that Your name is near. Men tell about the great things You have done. [2] You say, "When the right time has come, I will be right and fair in deciding who is guilty or not. 3 When the earth and all its people shake, it is I Who will hold it together. 4 I said to the proud, 'Do not speak with pride.' And I said to the sinful, 'Do not lift up the horn. 5 Do not lift your horn up high. Do not speak in your pride.' "

6 For honor does not come from the east or the west or from the desert. 7 But God is the One Who decides. He puts down one and brings respect to another. 8 For there is a cup in the Lord's hand. It is full of strong wine that is well mixed. He pours out from it, and all the sinful people of the earth must drink all of it.

9 But as for me, I will tell of it forever. I will sing praises to the God of Jacob. 10 He will cut off all the horns of the sinful. But the horns of those who are right with God will be lifted up.

The Power That Wins

76 God is known in Judah. His name is great in Israel. 2 His holy tent of worship is in Salem. He lives in Zion. 3 There He broke the burning arrows, the iron covering and the sword, and all the things used for fighting in war.

4 You are shining with greatness, more beautiful than the mountains with many animals. 5 Strong men have been robbed. They sleep their last sleep. Not one of the soldiers can lift his hands. 6 O God of Jacob, both soldier and horse were put in a dead sleep because of Your sharp words. 7 You alone are to be feared. Who may stand before You when You are angry?

8 You said from heaven who is guilty or not. The earth was afraid and quiet 9 when God stood up to say who is guilty or not, and to save all the people of the earth who are not proud. 10 For the anger of man will praise You. And You will keep what is left of anger around You.

11 Make promises to the Lord your God and keep them. Let all who are around Him bring gifts to Him, Who is to be feared. 12 He will cut off the spirit of princes. He is feared by the kings of the earth.

Comfort in Times of Trouble

77 My voice goes up to God, and I will cry out. My voice goes up to God and He will hear me. 2 I looked to the Lord when I was in trouble. I put out my hand at night, and it did not get tired. My soul would not be comforted. 3 When I remember God, then I am troubled. When I am in deep thought, then my spirit

becomes weak. 4 You keep my eyes from closing. I am so troubled that I cannot speak. 5 I have thought about the days of old, the years of long ago. 6 I remember my song in the night. I think with my heart. And my spirit asks questions.

7 Will the Lord turn away forever? Will He never show favor again? 8 Has His loving-kindness stopped forever? Has His promise come to an end for all time? 9 Has God forgotten to be loving and kind? Has He in anger taken away His loving-pity? 10 Then I said, "It is my sorrow that the right hand of the Most High has changed."

11 I will remember the things the Lord has done. Yes, I will remember the powerful works of long ago. 12 I will think of all Your work, and keep in mind all the great things You have done. 13 O God, Your way is holy. What god is great like our God? 14 You are the God Who does great works. You have shown Your power among the people. 15 You have set free Your people, the sons of Jacob and Joseph, with Your strong arm.

16 The waters saw You, O God. The waters saw You and shook. The sea shook also. 17 The clouds poured down water. The sky sounded with thunder. Your arrows of lightning went this way and that. 18 The sound of Your thunder was in the turning wind. The lightning lit up the world. The earth shook. 19 Your way was through the sea. Your paths went through the powerful waters. And it cannot be known where You stepped. 20 You led Your people like a flock by the hand of Moses and Aaron.

God Is Good to His People

78 O my people, hear my teaching. Listen to the words of my mouth. 2 I will open my mouth in picture-stories. I will tell things which have been kept secret from long ago, 3 which we have heard and known because our fathers have told us. 4 We will not hide them from their children. But we will tell the children-to-come the praises of the Lord, and of His power and the great things He has done.

5 For He has made His will known to Jacob. He made the Law in Israel, which He told our fathers to teach their children. 6 So the children-to-come might know, even the children yet to be born. So they may rise up and tell it to their children. 7 Then they would put their trust in God and not forget the works of God. And they would keep His Law. 8 They would not be

like their fathers, who were not right with God and would not obey Him or be faithful to Him. 9 The sons of Ephraim were ready with their bows. But they turned away in the day of fighting. 10 They did not keep the agreement of God. And they would not walk in His Law. 11 They forgot what He had done and His great works that He had shown them. 12 He did powerful works in front of their fathers, in the land of Egypt, in the field of Zoan. 13 He divided the sea and made them pass through it. He made the water stand up like a wall. 14 He led them with the cloud during the day, and with a light of fire during the night. 15 He broke the rocks in the desert, and gave them water as if it flowed from the sea. 16 He made water come out of the rock. He made the water flow down like rivers.

17 But they still kept on sinning against Him. They did not obey the Most High in the desert. 18 They tested God in their hearts by asking for the food they wanted. 19 Then they spoke against God, saying, "Can God set a table in the desert? 20 See, He hit the rock and water poured out and rivers flowed over. Can He give bread also? Will He give meat to His people?"

21 The Lord was full of anger when He heard them. And a fire was set against Jacob. His anger went up against Israel, 22 because they did not believe in God. They did not trust in Him to save them. 23 Yet He spoke to the clouds above, and opened the doors of heaven. 24 He sent down bread from heaven for them to eat. He gave them food from heaven. 25 Men ate the bread of angels. He sent them all the food they could eat. 26 He made the east wind blow in the heavens. And He brought in the south wind by His power. 27 He sent meat down on them like dust, winged birds like the sand of the sea. 28 He let them fall in the place where they were staying, all around their tents. 29 So they ate until they were full. He gave them what they wanted. 30 But before they had eaten all they wanted, even while it was still in their mouths, 31 the anger of God came upon them. And He killed the strongest of them. He cut down the young men of Israel. 32 But still they kept on sinning. They did not believe in His powerful works. 33 So He made their days come to nothing. He made their years end in fear all at once.

34 When He killed some of them, the others would look for Him. They returned and looked for God. 35 They remembered that God was their rock, and that the Most High God was the One Who set them free. 36 But they gave Him false honor with their mouth. They lied to Him with their tongue. 37 For their heart was not right toward Him. They were not faithful to His agreement. 38 But He showed them loving-kindness and forgave their sins. He did not destroy them. He held back His anger many times. He did not let all of His anger loose. 39 He remembered that they were only flesh, a wind that passes and does not return.

40 How many times they went against Him in the desert, and gave Him sorrow in that empty land! 41 They put God to the test again and again, and troubled the Holy One of Israel. 42 They did not remember His power and the day He saved them from those who hated them, 43 when He did His powerful works in Egypt and showed His greatness in the field of Zoan. 44 He changed their rivers into blood. They could not drink from their rivers. 45 He sent many flies among them that ate them, and frogs that destroyed them. 46 He gave their fields of food to the grasshopper, and all they worked for to the locust. 47 He destroyed their vines with hail, and their sycamore trees with cold. 48 He killed their cattle with hail and lightning. 49 He sent them His burning anger and trouble. He sent a group of angels to bring trouble and sorrow to them. 50 He made a straight path for His anger. He did not save their soul from death. But He gave their lives over to all these troubles. 51 He killed all the first born in Egypt, the first children of their strength in the tents of Ham. 52 But He brought His people out like sheep. And He led them like a flock in the desert. 53 He led them and kept them safe, so they were not afraid. But the sea covered those who hated them.

54 He brought them to His holy land, to the hill country His right hand had taken. 55 He drove out the nations before them. He gave them parts of the land for a gift. And He made the families of Israel live in their tents.

56 But they tempted and went against the Most High God. They did not keep His Law. 57 They turned away and acted without faith like their fathers. They were like a bow that cannot be trusted. 58 They made Him angry with their sinful places of worship. And they made Him jealous with their false gods. 59 God was very angry when He

heard them, and He hated Israel. 60 He left the holy tent at Shiloh, the tent He had set up among men. 61 And He let His strength be taken. He put His greatness into the hands of those who hated Israel. 62 He allowed His people to be killed with the sword. And He was very angry with those who belong to Him. 63 Fire burned up their young men. And their young women had no wedding songs. 64 Their religious leaders fell by the sword. And the women who lost their husbands could not cry.

65 Then the Lord woke up as if from sleep, like a strong man wild with wine. 66 He beat back those who hated Him. And He put them to shame forever. 67 He turned away from the tent of Joseph. He did not choose the family of Ephraim, 68 but chose the family of Judah, Mount Zion which He loved. 69 He built His holy place like the high mountains, like the earth He has built forever. 70 He chose David, His servant and took him from the flocks of sheep. 71 He brought him from caring for the sheep and their lambs to being the shepherd of Jacob His people, and Israel who belongs to Him. 72 So David was their shepherd with a heart that was right, and led them with good hands and wisdom.

A Prayer for Jerusalem

79 O God, the nations have come into the land of Your people. They have made Your holy house dirty. They have crushed the walls and buildings of Jerusalem. 2 They have given the dead bodies of Your servants to the birds of the heavens for food. The flesh of those who belong to You has been given to the wild animals of the earth. 3 They have poured out their blood like water all around Jerusalem. And there was no one to bury them. 4 We have become a shame to our neighbors. Those around us laugh at and make fun of us. 5 How long, O Lord? Will You be angry forever? Will Your jealousy burn like fire? 6 Pour out Your anger on the nations that do not know You, and on the nations that do not call on Your name. 7 For they have destroyed Jacob. They have laid waste the place where he lived.

8 Do not hold the sins of our fathers against us. Let Your loving-pity come fast to meet us. For we are in much need. 9 O God Who saves us, help us for the honor of Your name. Take us out of trouble and forgive our sins, for the honor of Your name. 10 Why should the nations say, "Where

is their God?" Make it known among the nations, in front of our eyes, that You punish for the blood that has poured from Your servants. 11 Hear the cries of those in prison. By the greatness of Your power, save those who are being sent to death. 12 And return to our neighbors seven times the shame that they have brought You, O Lord. 13 Then we Your people, the sheep of Your field, will give thanks to You forever. We will tell of Your praise to all the people of all times.

A Prayer for the Nation

80 Hear us, O Shepherd of Israel, You Who lead Joseph like a flock! You Who sit on Your throne above the angels, let Your light shine! 2 Stir up Your power in front of Ephraim and Benjamin and Manassah, and come to save us! 3 O God, bring us back to You. Make Your face shine upon us, that we may be saved.

4 O Lord God of all, how long will You be angry with the prayers of Your people? 5 You have fed them with the bread of tears. And You have made them drink a big amount of tears. 6 You have made us an object of arguing to our neighbors. Those who hate us laugh among themselves. 7 O God of all, bring us back to You. Make Your face shine upon us, and we will be saved.

8 You brought a vine out of Egypt. You drove out the nations, and You planted it. 9 You cleared the land for it. And its roots went deep and filled the land. 10 The mountains were covered with its shadow. And the tall trees were covered with its branches. 11 It sent out its branches to the sea, and its new branches to the River. 12 Why have You broken down its walls so that all who pass by pick its fruit? 13 The wild pig from among the trees eats it away. And whatever moves in the field eats from it.

14 O God of all, we beg You to return. Look down from heaven and see. Take care of this vine. 15 Take care of the root Your right hand has planted, and the branch that You have raised up for Yourself. 16 They have burned it with fire. It is cut down. May they be lost when they hear Your strong words. 17 Let Your hand be upon the man of Your right hand, the son of man you have made strong for Yourself. 18 Then we will not turn away from You. Give us new life again, and we will call on Your name. 19 O Lord God of all, bring us back to You. Make Your face shine upon us, and we will be saved.

A Song to God's Care

81 Sing for joy to God our strength! Call out for joy to the God of Jacob! 2 Sing a song, beat the timbrel. Play the sweet-sounding harps. 3 Blow the horn at the new moon, at the full moon on the day of our special supper. 4 For this is a Law for Israel, a Law of the God of Jacob. 5 He made it a Law for Joseph, when he went through the land of Egypt. I heard a language that I did not know:

6 "I took the load off his shoulders. His hands were set free from the basket. 7 You called in your trouble, and I took you out of it. I answered you in the hiding place of thunder. I tested you at the waters of Meribah. 8 Hear, O My people, and I will tell you what to do. O Israel, if you would listen to Me! 9 Let there be no strange god among you. Do not worship any false god. 10 I, the Lord, am your God. I brought you out of the land of Egypt. Open your mouth wide and I will fill it.

11 "But My people did not listen to My voice. And Israel did not obey Me. 12 So I let them follow the desires of their sinful hearts. They followed their own plans. 13 If only My people would listen to Me! If only Israel would follow My ways! 14 I would hurry to crush those who fight against them. I would turn My hand against those who hate them. 15 Those who hate the Lord would pretend to obey Him. And their punishment would last forever. 16 But I would feed you with the best of grain, And I would fill you with honey from the rock."

God's Rule

82 God takes His stand in the great meeting of His people. He judges among the rulers. 2 How long will you rulers be wrong in how you judge? How long will you show favor to the sinful? 3 Do the right thing for the weak and those without a father. Stand up for the rights of those who are suffering and in need. 4 Save the weak and those in need. Set them free from the hand of the sinful.

5 They know nothing; they understand nothing. They walk around in the dark. All that the earth is built upon is shaking. 6 I said, "You are gods. You are all sons of the Most High. 7 But you will die like men, and fall like one of the princes."

8 Rise up, O God! Say who is guilty or not guilty upon the earth! For all the nations belong to you.

A Prayer for Israel

83 O God, do not keep quiet. Do not be quiet, O God, and do not hold Your peace. 2 For, look, those who hate You are making much noise. Those who fight against You have honored themselves. 3 They make bad plans against Your people. They plan against those You care for. 4 They say, "Come, let us destroy them as a nation. Let the name of Israel be remembered no longer." 5 For they plan together with one mind. They make an agreement against You: 6 The tents of Edom and the Ishmaelites; Moab and the Hagarites; 7 Gebal, and Ammon, and Amalek; Philistia with those who live in Tyre; 8 Assyria has joined them also. They help the children of Lot.

9 Do to them as You did to Midian, and to Sisera and Jabin at the river of Kishon. 10 They were destroyed at Endor. They were spread over the field. 11 Make their respected men like Oreb and Zeeb. Make their princes like Zebah and Zalmunna, 12 who said, "Let us take for ourselves the fields of God."

13 O my God, make them like dust turning in the wind, like parts of the grass that have no worth and are blown away. 14 As the fire that burns up the trees and spreads over the mountains, 15 so go behind them with Your storm. Make them afraid with Your storm. 16 Fill their faces with shame, so they will look to Your name, O Lord. 17 Let them be ashamed and afraid forever. Let them be put to shame and lost 18 Then they may know that You alone, Whose name is the Lord, are the Most High over all the earth.

A Desire for God's House

84 How beautiful are the places where You live, O Lord of all! 2 My soul wants and even becomes weak from wanting to be in the house of the Lord. My heart and my flesh sing for joy to the living God. 3 Even the bird has found a home. The swallow has found a nest for herself where she may lay her young at Your altars, O Lord of all, my King and my God. 4 How happy are those who live in Your house! They are always giving thanks to You.

5 How happy is the man whose strength is in You and in whose heart are the roads to Zion! 6 As they pass through the dry valley of Baca, they make it a place of good water. The early rain fills the pools with good also. 7 They go from strength to

strength. Every one of them stands before God in Zion.

8 O Lord God of all, hear my prayer. Listen, O God of Jacob. 9 Look upon our safe-covering, O God. And look upon the face of Your chosen one. 10 For a day in Your house is better than a thousand outside. I would rather be the one who opens the door of the house of my God, than to live in the tents of the sinful. 11 For the Lord God is a sun and a safe-covering. The Lord gives favor and honor. He holds back nothing good from those who walk in the way that is right. 12 O Lord of all, how happy is the man who trusts in You!

A Prayer for the Nation's Good

85 O Lord, You showed favor to Your land. You have returned those of Jacob who were taken away. 2 You have forgiven the sins of Your people. You have covered all their sin. 3 You have taken away all Your anger. You have turned away from Your burning anger.

4 O God Who saves us, give us life again. Make Your anger toward us stop. 5 Will You be angry with us forever? Will You spread out Your anger to families of all times? 6 Will You not bring us back to life again so that Your people may be happy in You? 7 Show us Your loving-kindness, O Lord, and save us.

8 I will listen to what God the Lord will say. For He will speak peace to His people, to those who are right with Him. But do not let them turn again to foolish things. 9 For sure His saving power is near those who fear Him, so His shining-greatness may live in the land. 10 Loving-kindness and truth have met together. Peace and what is right and good have kissed each other. 11 Truth comes up from the earth. And what is right and good looks down from heaven. 12 Yes, the Lord will give what is good. And our land will give its fruit. 13 What is right and good will go before Him and make a way for His steps.

A Prayer for Help

86 Hear, O Lord, and answer me. For I am suffering and in need. 2 Keep my life, for I am faithful to You. You are my God. Save Your servant who trusts in You. 3 Show me loving-kindness, O Lord. For I cry to You all day long. 4 Bring joy to Your servant. For I lift up my soul to You, O Lord. 5 For You are good and ready to forgive, O Lord. You are rich in loving-kindness to all who call to You. 6 Hear my prayer, O

Lord. Listen to my cry for help. 7 I will call to You in the day of my trouble. For You will answer me. 8 There is no one like You among the gods, O Lord. And there are no works like Yours. 9 All the nations You have made will come and worship before You, O Lord. And they will bring honor to Your name. 10 For You are great and do great things. You alone are God.

11 Teach me Your way, O Lord. I will walk in Your truth. May my heart fear Your name. 12 O Lord my God, I will give thanks to You with all my heart. I will bring honor to Your name forever. 13 For Your loving-kindness toward me is great. And You have saved my soul from the bottom of the grave.

14 O God, proud men have come up against me. A group of fighting men want to take my life. And they do not think of You. 15 But You, O Lord, are a God full of love and pity. You are slow to anger and rich in loving-kindness and truth. 16 Turn to me, and show me loving-kindness. Give Your strength to Your servant. And save the son of your woman servant. 17 Give me something special to see of Your favor. Then those who hate me may see it and be ashamed. Because You, O Lord, have helped me and comforted me.

Praise in Zion

87 The city God built stands on the holy mountains. 2 The Lord loves the gates of Zion more than all the other places of Jacob. 3 Great things are said about you, O city of God. 4 I will say that Rahab and Babylon are among those who know Me. Look, Philistia and Tyre and Ethiopia say, "This one was born there." 5 But it will be said of Zion, "This one and that one were born in her." And the Most High Himself will make her strong. 6 The Lord will write in the book of the people, "This one was born there." 7 Then those who sing and those who play music will say, "All my wells of joy are in you."

A Prayer to Be Saved from Death

88 O Lord, the God Who saves me, I have cried out before You day and night. 2 Let my prayer come to You. Listen to my cry. 3 For my soul is filled with troubles. And my life comes near the grave. 4 I am added among those who go down into the deep hole. I am like a man without strength. 5 I am left among the dead, like those who have been killed and lie in the grave, whom You remember no more.

They are cut off from Your help. 6 You have put me in the deepest hole, in a dark and deep place. 7 Your anger has rested upon me. And You have troubled me with all Your waves. 8 You have taken my good friends far from me. You have made me hated by them. I am shut in and cannot go out. 9 My eyes have become weak because of trouble. I have called to You every day, O Lord. I have spread out my hands to You.

10 Will You show Your great works to the dead? Will the dead rise and praise You? 11 Will Your loving-kindness be told about in the grave, and how faithful You are in the place that destroys? 12 Will Your great works be known in the darkness, and Your right and good works in the land where all is forgotten?

13 But I have cried to You for help, O Lord. My prayer comes to You in the morning. 14 O Lord, why do You turn away from me? Why do You hide Your face from me? 15 I have been troubled and near death since I was young. I have suffered Your punishment. And I cannot win. 16 Your burning anger has passed over me. The punishment You have sent destroys me. 17 They gather around me like water all day long. Together they close in upon me. 18 You have taken my friend and loved one far from me. Friends that were near to me are in darkness.

God's Promise to David

89 I will sing of the loving-kindness of the Lord forever. I will make known with my mouth how faithful You are to all people. 2 For I said, "Loving-kindness will be built up forever. You will make known how faithful You are in the heavens."

3 You said, "I have made an agreement with My chosen one. I have promised to David, Your servant. 4 I will make your seed last forever. I will build up your throne for all the children-to-come."

5 O Lord, the heavens will praise Your great works and how faithful You are in the meeting of the holy ones. 6 For who in the heavens is like the Lord? Who among the sons of the powerful is like the Lord? 7 God is honored with fear in the meeting of the holy ones. He is honored with fear more than all who are around Him. 8 Lord God of all, powerful Lord, who is like You? All around You we see how faithful You are. 9 You rule over the rising sea. When its waves rise, You quiet them. 10 You have crushed Rahab like one who is killed. You have destroyed those who hate You with Your powerful arm.

11 The heavens are Yours; and the earth is Yours. You have made the world and all that is in it. 12 You have made from nothing the north and the south. Tabor and Hermon call out for joy at Your name. 13 You have a strong arm. Your hand is powerful. Your right hand is honored. 14 Your throne stands on what is right and fair. Loving-kindness and truth go before You. 15 How happy are the people who know the sound of joy! They walk in the light of Your face, O Lord. 16 They are full of joy in Your name all day long. And by being right with You, they are honored. 17 For You are the shining-greatness of their strength. And our horn is lifted high by Your favor. 18 For our safe-covering belongs to the Lord. And our king belongs to the Holy One of Israel.

19 Once You spoke in a special dream to Your faithful ones, saying: "I have given help to a powerful one. I have honored a chosen one from among the people. 20 I have found David, Your servant. I have poured My holy oil upon him. 21 My hand will stay with him. And My arm will give him strength. 22 Those who hate him will not fool him. No sinful man will bring trouble to him. 23 But he will see Me crush those who fight against him. I will kill those who hate him. 24 I will be faithful and My loving-kindness will be with him. And in My name he will become great. 25 I will set his hand on the sea also, and his right hand on the rivers. 26 He will cry to Me, 'You are my Father, my God, and the rock that saves me.' 27 I will make him My first-born also, the highest of the kings of the earth. 28 I will keep My loving-kindness for him forever. And My agreement with him will be made strong. 29 I will make his seed last forever. And his throne will last as long as heaven.

30 "If his sons leave My Law and do not do what I say, 31 and if they break My Laws and do not obey My Word, 32 then I will punish their sin with the stick, and their wrong doing with the whip. 33 But I will not take my loving-kindness from him, I will always be faithful to him. 34 I will not break My agreement, or change what was spoken by My lips. 35 Once I have promised by My holy name, I will not lie to David. 36 His seed will last forever. And his throne will last before Me like the sun. 37 It will last forever like the moon, which may always be seen in the sky."

38 But You have thrown off and turned away from Your chosen one. You have

been full of anger against him. 39 You have hated the agreement with Your servant. You have made his crown dirty in the dust. 40 You have broken down all his walls. You have destroyed his strong-places. 41 All who pass on the road rob him. He has become a shame to his neighbors. 42 You have honored the right hand of those who fight against him. You have made all who hate him glad. 43 You have turned away the sharp part of his sword. And You have not made him stand in a fight. 44 You have put an end to what shows of his greatness, and have thrown his throne to the ground. 45 You have made him old before his time, and have covered him with shame.

46 How long, O Lord? Will You hide Yourself forever? Will Your anger burn like fire? 47 Remember how fast my life is passing. You have made all men for nothing. 48 What man can live and not see death? Can he save himself from the power of the grave?

49 O Lord, where is the loving-kindness You used to have, that You promised in faith to David? 50 O Lord, remember the shame of those who work for You. Remember how I carry near my heart the shame of all the nations. 51 Those who hate You have put us to shame, O Lord. They have put to shame the footsteps of Your chosen one.

52 Praise the Lord forever! Let it be so.

God Is Forever—Man's Short Life

90 Lord, You have been the place of comfort for all people of all time. 2 Before the mountains were born, before You gave birth to the earth and the world, forever and ever, You are God.

3 You change man into dust again, and say, "Return, O children of men." 4 For a thousand years in Your eyes are like yesterday when it passes by, or like the hours of the night. 5 You carry men away as with a flood. They fall asleep. In the morning they are like the new grass that grows. 6 It grows well in the morning, but dries up and dies by evening.

7 For we are burned up by Your anger. By Your anger we are troubled and afraid. 8 You have set our wrong-doing before You, our secret sins in the light of Your face. 9 For all our days pass away in Your anger. We finish our years with a quiet cry. 10 The days of our life are seventy years, or eighty if we have the strength. Yet the best of them are only hard work and sorrow. For they are soon gone and

we fly away. 11 Who understands the power of Your anger? Your anger is as great as the fear that we should have for You. 12 Teach us to understand how many days we have. Then we will have a heart of wisdom to give You.

13 Return, O Lord. How long will it be? Have pity upon those who work for You. 14 Fill us in the morning with Your loving-kindness. Let us sing for joy and be glad all our days. 15 Make us glad for as many days as You have made us suffer, and for the years we have seen trouble. 16 Let Your work be shown to Your servants. And let Your wonderful greatness be shown to their children. 17 Let the favor of the Lord our God be upon us. And make the work of our hands stand strong. Yes, make the work of our hands stand strong.

The Lord—the One We Trust

91 He who lives in the safe place of the Most High will be in the shadow of the All-powerful. 2 I will say to the Lord, "You are my safe and strong-place, my God, in Whom I trust." 3 For it is He Who takes you away from the trap, and from the killing sickness. 4 He will cover you with His wings. And under His wings you will be safe. He is faithful like a safe-covering and a strong wall.

5 You will not be afraid of trouble at night, or of the arrow that flies by day. 6 You will not be afraid of the sickness that walks in darkness, or of the trouble that destroys at noon. 7 A thousand may fall at your side, and ten thousand at your right hand. But it will not come near you. 8 You will only look on with your eyes, and see how the sinful are punished. 9 Because you have made the Lord your safe place, and the Most High the place where you live, 10 nothing will hurt you. No trouble will come near your tent.

11 For He will tell His angels to care for you and keep you in all your ways. 12 They will hold you up in their hands. So your foot will not hit against a stone. 13 You will walk upon the lion and the snake. You will crush under your feet the young lion and the snake.

14 Because he has loved Me, I will bring him out of trouble. I will set him in a safe place on high, because he has known My name. 15 He will call upon Me, and I will answer him. I will be with him in trouble. I will take him out of trouble and honor him. 16 I will please him with a long life. And I will show him My saving power.

A Song of Praise

92 It is good to give thanks to the Lord, and sing praises to Your name, O Most High. ² It is good to tell of Your loving-kindness in the morning, and of how faithful You are at night, ³ with harps, and with music of praise. ⁴ For You have made me glad by what You have done, O Lord. I will sing for joy at the works of Your hands.

⁵ How great are Your works, O Lord! How deep are Your thoughts! ⁶ A man who cannot reason does not have much learning. A fool does not understand this. ⁷ Even if the sinful grow up like grass and all goes well with wrong-doers, they will be destroyed forever. ⁸ But You, O Lord, rule from Your high place forever. ⁹ For, look, those who hate You will be lost from You forever, O Lord. All those who do wrong will be destroyed.

¹⁰ But You have lifted up my horn like that of a wild bull. New oil has been poured upon me. ¹¹ My eyes have seen those who wait to hurt me. My ears hear the bad men who rise up against me. ¹² The man who is right and good will grow like the palm tree. He will grow like a tall tree in Lebanon. ¹³ Planted in the house of the Lord, they will grow well in the home of our God. ¹⁴ They will still give fruit when they are old. They will be full of life and strength. ¹⁵ And they will show that the Lord is faithful. He is my rock. There is nothing in Him that is not right and good.

God Is King

93 The Lord rules. He is dressed with great power. The Lord has dressed Himself with strength. For sure, the world is built to last. It will not be moved. ² Your throne is set up from long ago. You have always been. ³ The floods have lifted up, O Lord. The floods have lifted up their voice. The floods lift up their beating waves. ⁴ The Lord on high is more powerful than the sound of many waters and the strong waves of the sea. ⁵ Your Word is very sure. O Lord, Your house is holy forever.

God judges

94 O Lord, the God Who punishes, God Who punishes, let Your light shine! ² Rise up, You Judge of the earth. Pay what is owed to the proud. ³ How long will the sinful, O Lord, how long will the sinful be full of joy? ⁴ They pour out proud words. All those who do wrong, talk about themselves as if they are great people.

⁵ They crush Your people, O Lord. They bring trouble upon Your chosen nation. ⁶ They kill the woman whose husband has died and the stranger. They kill the children who have no parents. ⁷ And they say, "The Lord does not see. The God of Jacob does not care."

⁸ Listen, you foolish ones among the people. You fools, when will you understand? ⁹ He Who made the ear, does He not hear? He Who made the eye, does He not see? ¹⁰ He Who punishes nations so they might give up sin, will He not speak strong words to them? Is He not the One Who teaches man all he knows? ¹¹ The Lord knows the thoughts of man. He knows that they are empty.

¹² Happy is the man who is punished until he gives up sin, O Lord, and whom You teach from Your Law. ¹³ You give him rest from days of trouble, until a hole is dug for the sinful. ¹⁴ For the Lord will not turn away from His people. He will not leave His chosen nation. ¹⁵ For what is decided will be right and good. And all those whose hearts are right will follow it. ¹⁶ Who will rise up for me against the sinful? Who will take a stand for me against those who do wrong?

¹⁷ If the Lord had not been my help, my soul would soon have been among the dead. ¹⁸ When I said, "My foot is going out from under me," Your loving-kindness held me up, O Lord. ¹⁹ When my worry is great within me, Your comfort brings joy to my soul. ²⁰ Can a sinful throne that brings trouble by its laws be a friend to You? ²¹ They join together against the life of those who are right and good. They send those who are not guilty to their death. ²² But the Lord has been my strong-place, my God, and the rock where I am safe. ²³ He has brought back their own sin upon them and will destroy them for their wrong-doing. The Lord our God will destroy them.

A Song of Praise

95 Come, let us sing with joy to the Lord. Let us sing loud with joy to the rock Who saves us. ² Let us come before Him giving thanks. Let us make a sound of joy to Him with songs. ³ For the Lord is a great God, and a great King above all gods. ⁴ The deep places of the earth are in His hand. And the tops of the mountains belong to Him. ⁵ The sea is His, for He made it. And His hands made the dry land.

6 Come, let us bow down in worship. Let us get down on our knees before the Lord Who made us. 7 For He is our God. And we are the people of His field, and the sheep of His hand. If you hear His voice today, 8 do not let your hearts become hard as you did at Meribah, as you did that day at Massah in the desert. 9 Your early fathers put Me to the test and tried Me. But they had seen the work I did. 10 I was angry with the people of that day for forty years. I said, "They always think wrong thoughts. And they do not know My ways." 11 I was angry with them and said, "They will never go into My rest."

A Call to Worship the Lord

96 Sing to the Lord a new song. Let all the earth sing to the Lord. 2 Sing to the Lord. Honor His name. Make His saving power known from day to day. 3 Tell of His shining-greatness among the nations. Tell of His wonderful works among all the people. 4 For the Lord is great and should be given much praise. He is to be honored with fear above all gods. 5 For all the gods of the nations are false gods. But the Lord made the heavens. 6 Honor and great power are with Him. Strength and beauty are in His holy place.

7 Give to the Lord, O families of the nations, give to the Lord the honor and strength that He should have. 8 Give to the Lord the honor of His name. Bring a gift and come into His holy place. 9 Worship the Lord in holy clothing. May all the earth shake in fear before Him. 10 Say among the nations that the Lord rules. The world is built to last. It will not be moved. He will be right when He says who is guilty or not.

11 Let the heavens be glad. And let the earth be full of joy. Let the sea and all that is in it make a loud noise. 12 Let the fields and all that is in them be full of joy. Then all the trees of the land will sing for joy 13 before the Lord. For He is coming. He is coming to say who is guilty or not on the earth. He will be right in what He decides about the people. And He will be faithful to the people.

God's Power over the Earth

97 The Lord rules. Let the earth be full of joy. Let the many islands be glad. 2 Clouds and darkness are all around Him. His throne is built upon what is right and fair. 3 Fire goes before Him and burns up those who hate Him on every side. 4 His lightning lights up the world. The earth sees, and shakes. 5 The mountains melt like a candle before the Lord, before the Lord of the whole earth. 6 The heavens tell about how right and good He is. And all the people see His shining-greatness.

7 Let all those who serve false gods be ashamed, those who talk about how great their gods are. Worship Him, all you gods! 8 Zion heard this and was glad. The people of Judah have been full of joy because of what You decide, O Lord. 9 For You are the Lord Most High over all the earth. You are honored above all gods.

10 Let those who love the Lord hate what is bad. For He keeps safe the souls of His faithful ones. He takes them away from the hand of the sinful. 11 Light is spread like seed for those who are right and good, and joy for the pure in heart. 12 Be glad in the Lord, you who are right and good. Give thanks to His holy name.

A Call to Praise the Lord

98 Sing a new song to the Lord. For He has done great things. His right hand and His holy arm have won the fight for Him. 2 The Lord has made His saving power known. He has shown to the nations how right and good He is. 3 He has shown His loving-kindness and how beautiful He is to the house of Israel. All the ends of the earth have seen the saving power of our God.

4 Call out for joy to the Lord, all the earth. Sing out loud songs of joy and sing praises. 5 Sing praises to the Lord with harps, with harps and the voice of singing. 6 Call out for joy with the sound of horns before the King, the Lord.

7 Let the sea and all that is in it make a loud noise, and the world and all who live in it. 8 Let the rivers clap their hands. Let the mountains sing together for joy 9 before the Lord. For He is coming to say who is guilty or not on the earth. He will be right in what He decides about the world. And He will be fair to the people.

The Lord Is Good to His People

99 The Lord rules! Let the people shake in fear! He sits on His throne above the angels. Let the earth shake! 2 The Lord is great in Zion. And He is honored above all people. 3 Let them praise Your great name. It is to be honored with fear. He is holy!

4 The strength of the King loves what is right. You have set up what is fair. You do

what is right and fair in Jacob. 5 Honor the Lord our God. Worship at His feet. For He is holy!

6 Moses and Aaron were among His religious leaders. And Samuel was among those who called on His name. They called upon the Lord, and He answered them. 7 He spoke to them from the cloud. They kept His Word and the Law that He gave them. 8 O Lord our God, You answered them. You were a forgiving God to them. But You punished them for their wrong-doing. 9 Honor the Lord our God. And worship at His holy mountain. For the Lord our God is holy!

A Song of Praise

100 Call out with joy to the Lord, all the earth. 2 Be glad as you serve the Lord. Come before Him with songs of joy. 3 Know that the Lord is God. It is He Who made us, and not we ourselves. We are His people and the sheep of His field.

4 Go into His gates giving thanks and into His holy place with praise. Give thanks to Him. Honor His name. 5 For the Lord is good. His loving-kindness lasts forever. And He is faithful to all people and to all their children-to-come.

A Song of Praise

101 I will sing of loving-kindness and of what is right and fair. I will sing praises to You, O Lord. 2 I will be careful to live a life without blame. When will You come to me? I will walk within my house with a right and good heart. 3 I will set no sinful thing in front of my eyes. I hate the work of those who are not faithful. It will not get hold of me. 4 A sinful heart will be far from me. I will have nothing to do with sin. 5 I will stop whoever talks against his neighbor in secret. I will not listen to anyone who has a proud look and a proud heart.

6 My eyes will look with favor on the faithful in the land, so they may serve me. He who walks without blame will help me. 7 He whose ways are false will not live in my house. He who tells lies will not stand in front of me. 8 I will destroy all the sinful in the land every morning. I will cut off all those who do wrong from the city of the Lord.

The Prayer of a Man in Trouble

102 Hear my prayer, O Lord! Let my cry for help come to You. 2 Do not hide Your face from me in the day of my trouble. Turn Your ear to me. Hurry to answer me in the day when I call. 3 For my days go up in smoke. And my bones are burned as with fire. 4 My heart is crushed and dried like grass. And I forget to eat my food. 5 I am nothing but skin and bones because of my loud cries. 6 I am like a pelican in the desert. I am like an owl of the waste places. 7 I lie awake. And I feel like a bird alone on the roof.

8 Those who hate me have made it hard for me all day long. Those who are angry with me curse my name. 9 For I have eaten ashes like bread and have mixed my drink with tears, 10 because of Your great anger. For You have lifted me up and thrown me away. 11 My days are like the evening shadow. I dried up like grass.

12 But You and Your name, O Lord, will always be forever and to all people for all time. 13 You will rise up and have loving-pity on Zion. For it is time to show favor to her. The set time has come. 14 For Your servants respect her stones and show pity for her dust. 15 The nations will fear the name of the Lord. All the kings of the earth will fear Your shining-greatness. 16 For the Lord has built up Zion. He will come in His shining-greatness. 17 He will answer the prayer of those in need. He will not turn from their prayer.

18 This will be written for the children-to-come. So a people not yet born may give thanks to the Lord. 19 For He looked down from His holy place. He watched the earth from heaven, 20 to hear the loud cries of those in prison and to set free those who are being sent to death. 21 So the name of the Lord will be made known in Zion and His praise in Jerusalem, 22 when the people gather together and the nations gather to serve the Lord.

23 He has taken away my strength. He has taken days from my life. 24 I said, "O my God, do not take me away when my days are only half done. Your years go on to all people of all time. 25 You made the earth in the beginning. You made the heavens with Your hands. 26 They will be destroyed but You will always live. They will all become old as clothing becomes old. You will change them like a coat. And they will be changed, 27 but You are always the same. Your years will never end. 28 The children of those who work for You will live on. And their children will be set before You."

Praise for God's Love

103 Praise the Lord, O my soul. And all that is within me, praise His holy name. [2] Praise the Lord, O my soul. And forget none of His acts of kindness. [3] He forgives all my sins. He heals all my diseases. [4] He saves my life from the grave. He crowns me with loving-kindness and pity. [5] He fills my years with good things and I am made young again like the eagle.

[6] The Lord does what is right and fair for all who suffer under a bad power. [7] He made His ways known to Moses and His acts to the people of Israel. [8] The Lord is full of loving-pity and kindness. He is slow to anger and has much loving-kindness. [9] He will not always keep after us. And He will not keep His anger back forever. [10] He has not punished us enough for all our sins. He has not paid us back for all our wrong-doings. [11] For His loving-kindness for those who fear Him is as great as the heavens are high above the earth. [12] He has taken our sins from us as far as the east is from the west. [13] The Lord has loving-pity on those who fear Him, as a father has loving-pity on his children. [14] For He knows what we are made of. He remembers that we are dust.

[15] The days of man are like grass. He grows like a flower of the field. [16] When the wind blows over it, it is gone. Its place will remember it no more. [17] But the loving-kindness of the Lord is forever and forever on those who fear Him. And what is right with God is given forever to their children's children, [18] to those who keep His agreement and remember to obey His Law.

[19] The Lord has set up His throne in the heavens. And His holy nation rules over all. [20] Praise the Lord, you powerful angels of His who do what He says, obeying His voice as He speaks! [21] Praise the Lord, all you armies of His who work for Him and do what pleases Him. [22] Praise the Lord, all His works in all places under His rule. Praise the Lord, O my soul!

The Lord Watches Over All His Works

104 Praise the Lord, O my soul! O Lord my God, You are very great. You are dressed with great honor and wonderful power. [2] He covers Himself with light as with a coat. He spreads out the heavens like a tent. [3] He makes His home on the waters. He makes the clouds His wagon. He rides on the wings of the wind. [4] He makes the winds carry His news. He makes His helpers a burning fire.

[5] He set the earth in its place so that it will stay that way forever. [6] You covered it with the sea as with a coat. The waters stood above the mountains. [7] The waters left at Your strong words. They went away in a hurry at the sound of Your thunder. [8] The mountains went up and the valleys went down to the place that You made for them. [9] You set a place that they may not pass over. The waters will never cover the earth again.

[10] He sends rivers into the valleys. They flow between the mountains. [11] They give water to all the animals of the field. The wild donkeys drink until they are no longer thirsty. [12] The birds of the sky nest beside them. They sing among the branches. [13] He waters the mountains from His home above. The earth is filled with the fruit of His works.

[14] He makes the grass grow for the cattle, and plants for man to use. So He may bring food from the earth, [15] wine that makes man's heart glad, oil to make his face shine, and food to make his heart strong. [16] The tall cedar trees that the Lord planted in Lebanon drink their fill. [17] The birds make their nests there. The stork has its nest in the green trees.

[18] The high mountains are for the wild goats. The rocks are a safe place for the badgers. [19] He made the moon to mark the time of year. And the sun knows when to go down. [20] You make darkness and it becomes night. Then all the wild animals among the trees come out. [21] The young lions make a loud noise as they go after meat. And they get their food from God. [22] They go to their homes and lie down when the sun rises. [23] Then man goes out to his work and works until evening.

[24] O Lord, how many are Your works! You made them all in wisdom. The earth is full of what You have made. [25] There is the wide sea full of both large and small animals. There are too many for us to number. [26] The ships sail there. And the very large sea animal You have made plays in it.

[27] They all wait for You to give them their food at the right time. [28] You give it to them and they gather it up. You open Your hand and they are filled with good things. [29] They are troubled and afraid when You hide Your face. And when You take away their breath, they die and return to the dust. [30] They are made when You send Your Spirit. And You make the land of the earth new again.

[31] May the shining-greatness of the Lord last forever. May the Lord be glad in

His works. ³² He looks at the earth and it shakes with fear. He touches the mountains and they smoke. ³³ I will sing to the Lord all my life. I will sing praise to my God as long as I live. ³⁴ May the words of my heart be pleasing to Him. As for me, I will be glad in the Lord. ³⁵ Let sinners be destroyed from the earth. And let the sinful be no more. Honor the Lord, O my soul! Praise the Lord!

God's Work with Israel

105 O give thanks to the Lord. Call on His name. Make His works known among the people. ² Sing to Him. Sing praises to Him. Tell of all His great works. ³ Honor His holy name. Let the heart of those who look to the Lord be glad. ⁴ Look for the Lord and His strength. Look for His face all the time. ⁵ Remember the great and powerful works that He has done. Keep in mind what He has decided and told us, ⁶ O children of His servant Abraham, O sons of Jacob, His chosen ones! ⁷ He is the Lord our God. What He has decided is in all the earth.

⁸ He has remembered His agreement forever, the promise He made to last through a thousand families-to-come, ⁹ the agreement that He made with Abraham, and His promise to Isaac. ¹⁰ He gave it to Jacob as a Law, to Israel as an agreement that will last forever. ¹¹ He said, "I will give the land of Canaan to you as your share," ¹² when they were only a few men in number and were strangers in it. ¹³ They went from nation to nation, from the people under one king to the people under another. ¹⁴ He did not allow anyone to hold power over them. And He spoke sharp words to kings because of them. ¹⁵ He said, "Do not touch My chosen ones. And do not hurt those who speak for Me."

¹⁶ Then He called for a time of no food on the land. He cut off all their bread. ¹⁷ He sent a man, Joseph, before them who was sold as a servant. He hurt his feet with chains. He was put in irons, ¹⁹ until what he had said would happen came to pass. The Word of the Lord tested him. ²⁰ The king sent and had him taken out of prison. The ruler of many people set him free. ²¹ He made him the lord of his house and ruler over all he had. ²² He could punish the rulers as he pleased. And he taught wisdom to the wise. ²³ Then Israel also came into Egypt. So Jacob stayed in the land of Ham. ²⁴ And He made the number of His people grow until they were stronger than those who held power over them.

²⁵ He turned their hearts to hate His people and to make plans against His servants. ²⁶ He sent Moses, His servant, and Aaron whom He had chosen. ²⁷ They did His great works for them to see, powerful works in the land of Ham. ²⁸ He sent darkness and made the land dark. They did not fight against what He told them to do. ²⁹ He changed their water into blood, so their fish died. ³⁰ Their land became covered with frogs, even in the rooms of their kings. ³¹ He spoke and there came many flies all over their land. ³² He gave them hail instead of rain, and lightning like fire in their land. ³³ He destroyed their vines and fig trees and the trees of their country. ³⁴ He spoke and the locusts came. There were too many to number. ³⁵ They ate up all the plants in their country. They ate all the fruit of their land. ³⁶ He killed all the first-born in their land, the first-fruits of all their strength.

³⁷ Then He brought Israel out with silver and gold. And there was not one weak person among their families. ³⁸ Egypt was glad when they left. For they had become afraid of Israel. ³⁹ He spread a cloud for a covering, and fire to give light at night. ⁴⁰ They asked, and He brought them quails for meat. And He filled them with the bread of heaven. ⁴¹ He opened the rock and water flowed out. It flowed in the desert like a river. ⁴² For He remembered His holy Word with Abraham His servant. ⁴³ And He brought His people out with joy, His chosen ones with singing. ⁴⁴ He gave them the lands of the nations. They were given what others had worked for, ⁴⁵ so that they might do what He told them and keep His Law. Praise the Lord!

The Lord Is Good to His People

106 Praise the Lord! O give thanks to the Lord for He is good. His loving-kindness lasts forever. ² Who can put into words the great works of the Lord? Who can make known all His praise? ³ Happy are those who are faithful in being fair and who always do what is right and good!

⁴ O Lord, remember me when You show favor to Your people. Visit me also when You save them. ⁵ So I may share in the well-being of Your chosen ones. So I may share in the joy of Your nation, and be proud of Your people.

⁶ We have sinned like our fathers. We have done wrong. We have been sinful

in our actions. 7 Our fathers in Egypt did not understand Your powerful works. They did not remember how many times You showed Your loving-kindness. But they turned against You by the sea, the Red Sea. 8 Yet He saved them because of the honor of His name, and to make His great power known. 9 So He spoke sharp words to the Red Sea and it dried up. And He led them through the sea as through a desert. 10 He saved them from the hand of those who hated them. He set them free from the hand of those who went against them. 11 And the waters covered those who hated them. Not one of them was left. 12 Then they believed His promises. They sang His praise.

13 But they soon forgot His works. They did not wait to hear what He wanted them to do. 14 They wanted many things in the desert, and they tempted God there. 15 So He gave them what they wanted, but He allowed their souls to become weak because of it.

16 They were jealous of Moses in the place where they set up their tents. And they were jealous of Aaron, the holy one of the Lord. 17 So the earth opened up and swallowed Dathan. It closed over the group of Abiram. 18 And a fire came among their followers. It burned up the sinful people.

19 They made a calf at Horeb and worshiped a god of gold. 20 They traded their shining-greatness for something that looked like a bull that eats grass. 21 They forgot the God Who saved them, Who had done great things in Egypt, 22 powerful works in the land of Ham, and works that brought fear by the Red Sea. 23 So He said that He would destroy them. But Moses, His chosen one, stood in the way to keep His anger from destroying them. 24 Then they hated the good land. They did not believe in His Word. 25 They did not listen to the voice of the Lord. 26 So He swore to them that He would let them die in the desert. 27 And He would spread out their children among the nations and divide them over all the earth.

28 They joined themselves to Baal of Peor and ate gifts given to the dead. 29 They made the Lord angry by their actions and a sickness broke out among them. 30 Then Phinehas stood up and came between them, and the sickness was stopped. 31 And this made him right with God to all people forever.

32 They also made the Lord angry at the waters of Meribah. And trouble came to Moses because of them. 33 He spoke from his lips without thinking because they went against the Spirit of God.

34 They did not destroy the people as the Lord told them to do. 35 But they mixed with the nations and learned their ways. 36 They served their gods, which became a trap to them. 37 They even gave their sons and daughters as gifts on an altar to the demons. 38 They poured out the blood of those who were not guilty, the blood of their sons and daughters, whom they gave on an altar to the gods of Canaan. And the land was poisoned with blood. 39 They made themselves unclean by what they did. They were not true to God in what they did.

40 So the Lord was angry with His people. He hated His people. 41 So He handed them over to the nations. And those who hated them ruled over them. 42 Those who hated them held a strong power over them. And they were made to obey them. 43 God set them free many times. But they always turned against Him and went deeper into sin.

44 But He looked upon their trouble when He heard their cry. 45 He remembered His agreement because of them, and took pity on them by the greatness of His loving-kindness. 46 Those who held them also saw how God took pity on them.

47 O Lord our God, save us! Gather us from among the nations. And we will give thanks to Your holy name and find honor in Your praise. 48 Honor and thanks be to the Lord, the God of Israel, forever and ever. Let all the people say, "Let it be so!" Praise the Lord!

God Helps Men in Trouble

107 Give thanks to the Lord for He is good! His loving-kindness lasts forever! 2 Let the people who have been saved say so. He has bought them and set them free from the hand of those who hated them. 3 He gathered them from the lands, from east and west, from north and south.

4 Some traveled through the desert wastes. They did not find a way to a city where they could live. 5 They were hungry and thirsty. Their souls became weak within them. 6 Then they cried out to the Lord in their trouble. And He took them out of their suffering. 7 He led them by a straight path to a city where they could

live. 8 Let them give thanks to the Lord for His loving-kindness and His great works to the children of men! 9 For He fills the thirsty soul. And He fills the hungry soul with good things.

10 Some sat in darkness and in the shadow of death. They suffered in prison in iron chains. 11 Because they had turned against the Words of God. They hated what the Most High told them to do. 12 So He loaded them down with hard work. They fell and there was no one to help. 13 Then they cried out to the Lord in their trouble. And He saved them from their suffering. 14 He brought them out of darkness and the shadow of death. And He broke their chains. 15 Let them give thanks to the Lord for His loving-kindness and His great works to the children of men! 16 For He has broken gates of brass and cut through walls of iron.

17 Some were fools because of their wrong-doing. They had troubles because of their sins. 18 They hated all kinds of food. And they came near the gates of death. 19 Then they cried out to the Lord in their trouble. And He saved them from their suffering. 20 He sent His Word and healed them. And He saved them from the grave. 21 Let them give thanks to the Lord for His loving-kindness and His great works to the children of men! 22 Let them give Him gifts of thanks and tell of His works with songs of joy.

23 Some went out to sea in ships to buy and sell on the great waters. 24 They have seen what the Lord can do and His great works on the sea. 25 For He spoke and raised up a storm that lifted up the waves of the sea. 26 They went up to the heavens and down to the deep. Their strength of heart left them in their danger. 27 They could not walk straight but went from side to side like a drunk man. They did not know what to do. 28 Then they cried out to the Lord in their trouble. And He took them out of all their problems. 29 He stopped the storm, and the waves of the sea became quiet. 30 Then they were glad because the sea became quiet. And He led them to the safe place they wanted. 31 Let them give thanks to the Lord for His loving-kindness and His great works to the children of men! 32 Let them honor Him in the meeting of the people and praise Him in the meeting of the leaders.

33 He changes rivers into a desert and wells of water into a thirsty ground. 34 He changes a land of much fruit into a salt

waste because of the sin of those who live in it. 35 He changes a desert into a pool of water and makes water flow out of dry ground. 36 And He makes the hungry go there so they may build a city to live in. 37 They plant seeds in the fields and plant grape-vines and gather much fruit. 38 He lets good come to them and they become many in number. And He does not let the number of their cattle become less.

39 When the number of people becomes less and they are put to shame under a bad power and trouble and sorrow, 40 He pours anger on rulers. He makes them walk in the waste places where there is no path. 41 But He lifts those in need out of their troubles. He makes their families grow like flocks. 42 Those who are right see it and are glad. But all the sinful shut their mouths. 43 Let the wise man think about these things. And may he think about the loving-kindness of the Lord.

A Song of Praise

108 My heart will not be moved, O God. I will sing. Yes, I will sing praises with my soul. 2 Wake up, different kinds of harps. I will wake up the new day. 3 I will give thanks to You among the people, O Lord. I will sing praises to You among the nations. 4 For Your loving-kindness is great above the heavens. And Your truth can touch the sky. 5 Be lifted up high above the heavens, O God. Let Your shining-greatness be over all the earth. 6 Save us with Your right hand and answer me. Let Your loved ones be set free.

7 God has said in His holy place: "I will be full of joy. I will divide Shechem and the valley of Succoth. 8 Gilead is Mine. Manasseh is Mine. Ephraim is the covering for My head. Judah is My law-giver. 9 Moab is where I wash My hands. I will throw My shoe over Edom. I will call out over Philistia that I have won."

10 Who will bring me into the strong city? Who will lead me into Edom? 11 Have You not turned away from us, O God? And will You not go out with our armies, O God? 12 O give us help against those who hate us. For the help of man is worth nothing. 13 With God's help we will do great things. And He will break under His feet those who fight against us.

A Man in Trouble

109 I give praise to You, O God. Do not be quiet. 2 For sinners and liars have opened their mouths against me. They have spoken against me with lying tongues. 3 They have gathered around me with words of hate. They fought against me for no reason. 4 I give them my love but they speak against me in return. But I am in prayer. 5 They pay me what is bad for what is good. They give me hate for my love.

6 Let a sinful man have power over him. Let one who speaks against him stand at his right hand. 7 When he is tried, let him be found guilty. And may his prayer become sin. 8 Let his days be few. Let another person take over his work. 9 Let his children be without a father. And let his wife be without a husband. 10 May his children go around begging. And may they look for food far from their destroyed homes. 11 Let the one to whom he owes money take all that he has. May strangers take away all he has worked for. 12 May no one show him kindness. Let no one pity his children who have no father. 13 Let his children be cut off. Do not let their family name be remembered by the people-to-come.

14 Let the sins of his fathers be remembered by the Lord, and do not let the sins of his mother be forgotten. 15 May these sins always be before the Lord. So He may not let them be remembered on the earth. 16 Because he did not remember to show loving-kindness. Instead he made it hard for the poor and those in need and those with a broken heart. He even put them to death. 17 He loved to curse others, so may it come to him. He did not like to have good come to others, so good was far from him. 18 He dressed himself with cursing as with a coat. They came into his body like water and into his bones like oil. 19 May they be like clothing that covers him and like a belt that he always wears. 20 Let this be what the Lord pays to those who speak against me and wish bad things would happen to me.

21 But You, O God, the Lord, be kind to me because of Your name. Take me out of trouble because Your loving-kindness is good. 22 For I am in trouble and in need. And my heart is hurt within me. 23 I am passing like an evening shadow. I am shaken off like a locust. 24 My knees are weak from going without food. And my body has lost all its fat. 25 Others laugh at me. They look at me and shake their heads.

26 Help me, O Lord my God! Save me by Your loving-kindness. 27 Let them know that this is Your hand and that You, O Lord, have done it. 28 Let them hope that bad things will happen. But You make good things happen. Let them be ashamed when they rise up against me. But let Your servant be full of joy. 29 Let those who speak against me be dressed with shame. Let them cover themselves with shame as with a coat. 30 I will give thanks to the Lord in a loud voice. I will praise Him among many people. 31 For He stands at the right hand of the one in need to save him from those who judge his soul.

The King Rules

110 The Lord says to my Lord, "Sit at My right side, for those who hate You will be a place to rest Your feet." 2 The Lord will send out Your strength from Zion, saying, "Rule in front of those who hate You." 3 Your people will be willing to help in the day of Your power. Your young men will be dressed in holy clothes. They will come to You like water on the grass in the early morning.

4 The Lord has sworn and will not change His mind: "You are a Religious Leader forever, in the same way as Melchizedek." 5 The Lord is at Your right hand. He will crush kings in the day of His anger. 6 He will say who is guilty or not among the nations. He will fill them with dead bodies. He will crush the leaders of many lands. 7 He will drink from the river on the way. And so He will lift up His head.

The Lord Be Praised

111 Praise the Lord! I will give thanks to the Lord with all my heart where those who are right with God gather together and in the meeting of the people. 2 The works of the Lord are great. All who find joy in them try to understand them. 3 His work is great and powerful. And He is right and good forever. 4 He has made His great works to be remembered. The Lord shows loving-favor and pity. 5 He gives food to those who fear Him. He will remember His agreement forever. 6 He has shown His people the power of His works by giving them the land of other nations.

7 The works of His hands are faithful and right. All His Laws are true. 8 They stand strong forever and ever. They are done by what is true and right. 9 He has made a way for His people to be free. He has set up His agreement forever. His holy name is to be honored with fear. 10 The fear of the Lord is the beginning of wisdom. All who obey

His Laws have good understanding. His praise lasts forever.

Good Comes to the Person Who Honors the Lord

112 Praise the Lord! How happy is the man who honors the Lord with fear and finds joy in His Law! **2** His children will be powerful in the land. Each family who is right will be happy. **3** Riches and well-being are in his house. And his right-standing with God will last forever. **4** Light rises even in darkness for the one who is right. He is kind and has loving-pity and does what is right. **5** Good will come to the man who is ready to give much, and fair in what he does. **6** He will never be shaken. The man who is right and good will be remembered forever. **7** He will not be afraid of bad news. His heart is strong because he trusts in the Lord. **8** His heart will not be shaken. He will not be afraid and will watch those who fight against him. **9** He has given much to the poor. His right-standing with God lasts forever. His horn will be lifted high in honor.

10 The sinful man will see it and be troubled and angry. He will grind his teeth and waste away. The desire of the sinful will come to nothing.

The Lord Helps the Poor

113 Praise the Lord! Praise Him, O you who serve the Lord. Praise the name of the Lord. **2** Let the name of the Lord be honored, now and forever. **3** The name of the Lord is to be praised from the time the sun rises to when it sets. **4** The Lord is high above all nations. His shining-greatness is above the heavens.

5 Who is like the Lord our God? He sits on His throne on high. **6** He looks down upon the heavens and the earth. **7** He raises the poor from the dust. He lifts those in need from the ashes. **8** He makes them sit with rulers, with the rulers of His people. **9** He gives a home to the woman who could not give birth and makes her the mother of children. Praise the Lord!

God Takes Israel from Egypt

114 Israel came out of Egypt. The house of Jacob came from a people who spoke a strange language. **2** Then Judah became His holy place, and Israel became the place of His rule.

3 The sea looked and ran away. The Jordan turned back. **4** The mountains jumped like sheep, the hills like lambs. **5** Why did

you try to get away, O sea? Why did you turn back, O Jordan? **6** O mountains, why did you jump like sheep? O hills, why did you jump like lambs?

7 Shake in fear before the Lord, O earth, before the God of Jacob. **8** He changed the rock into a pool of water. He made water flow out of hard rock.

One True God

115 Let honor be given to Your name and not to us, O Lord, not to us. Because You are loving and kind and faithful. **2** Why should the nations say, "Where is their God now?" **3** But our God is in the heavens. He does whatever He wants to do. **4** Their gods are silver and gold, the work of human hands. **5** They have mouths but they cannot speak. They have eyes but they cannot see. **6** They have ears but they cannot hear. They have noses but they cannot smell. **7** They have hands but they cannot feel. They have feet but they cannot walk. They cannot make a sound come out of their mouths. **8** Those who make them and trust them will be like them.

9 O Israel, trust in the Lord. He is their help and safe-covering. **10** O house of Aaron, trust in the Lord. He is their help and safe-covering. **11** You who fear the Lord, trust in the Lord. He is their help and safe-covering. **12** The Lord has remembered us and will make good come to us. He will make good come to the house of Israel. He will make good come to the house of Aaron. **13** He will make good come to those who fear the Lord, both the small and the great. **14** May the Lord make your numbers grow, both you and your children. **15** May you be given good things by the Lord, the Maker of heaven and earth.

16 The heavens belong to the Lord. But He has given the earth to the children of men. **17** The dead do not praise the Lord. Neither do those who go down into the quiet place. **18** But we will give honor and thanks to the Lord, now and forever. Praise the Lord!

Praises to God for Being Saved from Death

116 I love the Lord, because He hears my voice and my prayers. **2** I will call on Him as long as I live, because He has turned His ear to me. **3** The strings of death are all around me. And the fear of the grave came upon me. I suffered with trouble and sorrow. **4** Then I called on the name of the Lord: "O Lord, I beg You, save my life!"

5 The Lord is loving and right. Yes, our God is full of loving-kindness. **6** The Lord takes care of the child-like. I was brought down, and He saved me. **7** Return to your rest, O my soul. For the Lord has been good to you. **8** For You, O Lord, have saved my soul from death, my eyes from tears, and my feet from falling. **9** I will walk with the Lord in the land of the living. **10** I believed when I said, "I am very troubled." **11** I said in my fear, "All men are liars."

12 What should I give to the Lord for all the good things He has done for me? **13** I will show Him my thanks for saving me with a gift of wine and praise His name. **14** I will keep my promises to the Lord before all His people. **15** The death of His holy ones is of great worth in the eyes of the Lord. **16** For sure I am Your servant, O Lord. I am Your servant, the son of the woman who served You. You have set me free from my chains. **17** I will give a gift of thanks to You and call on the name of the Lord. **18** I will keep my promises to the Lord before all His people, **19** in the holy place of the Lord, and in the center of you, O Jerusalem. Praise the Lord!

A Psalm of Praise

117 Praise the Lord, all nations! Praise Him, all people! **2** For His loving-kindness toward us is great. And the truth of the Lord lasts forever. Praise the Lord!

A Prayer of Thanks

118 Give thanks to the Lord, for He is good. His loving-kindness lasts forever. **2** Let Israel say, "His loving-kindness lasts forever." **3** Let the house of Aaron say, "His loving-kindness lasts forever." **4** Let those who fear the Lord say, "His loving-kindness lasts forever."

5 I cried to the Lord in my trouble, and He answered me and put me in a good place. **6** The Lord is with me. I will not be afraid of what man can do to me. **7** The Lord is with me. He is my Helper. I will watch those lose who fight against me. **8** It is better to trust in the Lord than to trust in man. **9** It is better to trust in the Lord than to trust in rulers.

10 All nations gathered around me. But I cut them off in the name of the Lord. **11** They gathered around me. Yes, they were on every side. But I cut them off in the name of the Lord. **12** They were all around me like bees and they died out fast like burning thorns. I will destroy them in the name of the Lord. **13** You pushed me back so that I was falling, but the Lord helped me. **14** The Lord is my strength and my song. He is the One Who saves me.

15 The joy of being saved is being heard in the tents of those who are right and good. The right hand of the Lord does powerful things. **16** The Lord's right hand is lifted high. The right hand of the Lord does powerful things. **17** I will not die but live. And I will tell of what the Lord has done. **18** The Lord has punished me but He has not given me over to death.

19 Open to me the gates of what is right and good. I will go through them and give thanks to the Lord. **20** This is the gate of the Lord. Those who are right with God will pass through it. **21** I will give thanks to You, for You have answered me. And You are the One Who saves me.

22 The stone that was put aside by the workmen has become the most important stone in the building. **23** The Lord has done this. We think it is great! **24** This is the day that the Lord has made. Let us be full of joy and be glad in it. **25** O Lord, we beg You to save us! O Lord, we ask that You let everything go well for us! **26** Great and honored is he who comes in the name of the Lord. We honor you from the house of the Lord. **27** The Lord is God. He has given us light. Tie the gift with rope to the horns of the altar on this special day. **28** You are my God and I will give You thanks. You are my God and I will praise You. **29** Give thanks to the Lord, for He is good. His loving-kindness lasts forever.

The Law of the Lord

119 Happy are those whose way is without blame, who walk in the Law of the Lord. **2** Happy are those who keep His Law and look for Him with all their heart. **3** They also do not sin, but walk in His ways. **4** You have set down Laws that we should always obey. **5** O, that my ways may be always in keeping with Your Law! **6** Then I will not be put to shame when I respect Your Word. **7** I will praise You with a heart that is right when I learn how right You judge. **8** I will obey Your Law. Do not leave me all alone.

9 How can a young man keep his way pure? By living by Your Word. **10** I have looked for You with all my heart. Do not let me turn from Your Law. **11** Your Word have I hid in my heart, that I may not sin against You. 12 Great and honored are You, O Lord. Teach me Your Law. 13 I have told with my lips of all the Laws of Your mouth. 14 I have found as much joy in following Your Law as one finds in much riches. 15 I will think about Your Law and have respect for Your ways. 16 I will be glad in Your Law. I will not forget Your Word.

17 Do good to Your servant so I may live and obey Your Word. 18 Open my eyes so that I may see great things from Your Law. 19 I am a stranger on the earth. Do not hide Your Word from me. 20 My soul is crushed with a desire for Your Law at all times. 21 You speak sharp words to the proud, the hated ones, because they turn from Your Word. 22 Take away shame and bad feelings from me, for I have kept Your Law. 23 Even if rulers sit together and speak against me, Your servant thinks about Your Law. 24 Your Law is my joy and it tells me what to do.

25 My soul is laid in the dust. Give me new life because of Your Word. 26 I have told about my ways, and You have answered me. Teach me Your Law. 27 Make me understand the way of Your Law so I will talk about Your great works. 28 My soul cries because of sorrow. Give me strength because of Your Word. 29 Take the false way from me. Show Your loving-favor by giving me Your Law. 30 I have chosen the faithful way. I have set Your Law in front of me. 31 I hold on to Your Law, O Lord. Do not put me to shame. 32 I will run the way of Your Law, for You will give me a willing heart.

33 O Lord, teach me the way of Your Law and I will obey it to the end. 34 Give me understanding. Then I will listen to Your Word and obey it with all my heart. 35 Make me walk in the path of Your Word, for I find joy in it. 36 Turn my heart toward Your Law, so I will not earn money in a wrong way. 37 Turn my eyes away from things that have no worth, and give me new life because of Your ways. 38 Keep Your promise to Your servant, the promise You made to those who fear and worship You. 39 Turn away the shame that I do not want to come to me, for Your Law is good. 40 O, how I desire Your Law! Give me new life because of Your right and good way.

41 May Your loving-kindness also come to me, O Lord. May You save me as Your Word says. 42 Then I will have an answer for the one who puts me to shame, for I trust in Your Word. 43 Do not take the word of truth out of my mouth, for I hope in Your Law. 44 I will always obey Your Law, forever and ever. 45 I will walk as a free man, for I look for Your Law. 46 I will speak of Your Law in front of kings and will not be ashamed. 47 I will be glad in Your Law, which I love. 48 I will lift up my hands to Your Word, which I love, and I will think about Your Law.

49 Remember Your Word to Your servant, for You have given me hope. 50 Your Word has given me new life. This is my comfort in my suffering. 51 The proud always laugh at me, but I do not turn away from Your Law. 52 I have remembered Your Law from a long time ago, O Lord, and I am comforted. 53 Burning anger comes upon me because of the sinful who turn away from Your Law. 54 Your Laws are my songs in whatever house I stay. 55 I remember Your name in the night, O Lord, and I have kept Your Law. 56 It has become my way to obey Your Law.

57 The Lord is my share. I have promised to obey Your Word. 58 I begged for Your favor with all my heart. Show me Your love because of Your Word. 59 I thought about my ways and turned my steps to Your Law. 60 I hurried and did not wait to obey Your Law. 61 The ropes of the sinful are all around me, but I have not forgotten Your Law. 62 I will rise late in the night to give thanks to You because Your Law is right and good. 63 I am a friend to all who fear You and of those who keep Your Law. 64 The earth is full of Your loving-kindness, O Lord. Teach me Your Law.

65 You have done good to Your servant, O Lord, because of Your Word. 66 Teach me what I should know to be right and fair for I believe in Your Law. 67 Before I suffered I went the wrong way, but now I obey Your Word. 68 You are good and You do good. Teach me Your Law. 69 The proud have put together a lie against me. I will keep Your Law with all my heart. 70 Their heart is covered with fat, but I find joy in Your Law. 71 It is good for me that I was troubled, so that I might learn Your Law. 72 The Law of Your mouth is better to me than thousands of gold and silver pieces.

73 Your hands made me and put me together. Give me understanding to learn Your Law. 74 May those who fear You see me and be glad, for I have put my hope in Your Word. 75 O Lord, I know that what You decide is right and good. You punish me because You are faithful. 76 May Your loving-kindness comfort me because of Your promise to Your servant. 77 Let Your

loving-pity come to me so I may live. For Your Law is my joy. 78 May the proud be ashamed, because they do wrong to me for no reason, but I will think about Your Law. 79 May those who fear You and those who know Your Law turn to me. 80 Let my heart be without blame in Your Law. Do not let me be put to shame.

81 My soul becomes weak with desire for Your saving power, but I have put my hope in Your Word. 82 My eyes become weak with desire for Your Word. I say, "When will You comfort me?" 83 I have become like a wineskin in the smoke, but I do not forget Your Law. 84 How long must Your servant wait? When will You punish those who make it hard for me? 85 The proud have dug deep holes for me. They do not obey Your Law. 86 All of Your Word is faithful. Help me! For they have made it hard for me with a lie. 87 They almost destroyed me on the earth, but I did not turn away from Your Law. 88 Give me life again by Your loving-kindness, and I will keep the Word of Your mouth.

89 Forever, O Lord, Your Word will never change in heaven. 90 You are faithful to all people for all time. You have made the earth, and it stands. 91 They stand today by Your Law, for all things serve You. 92 I would have been lost in my troubles if Your Law had not been my joy. 93 I will never forget Your Word for by it You have given me new life. 94 I am Yours. Save me, for I have looked to Your Law. 95 The sinful wait to destroy me, but I will think about Your Word. 96 I have seen that all things have an end, even if they are perfect, but Your Word is without end.

97 O, how I love Your Law! It is what I think about all through the day. 98 Your Word makes me wiser than those who hate me, for it is always with me. 99 I have better understanding than all my teachers because I think about Your Law. 100 I have a better understanding than those who are old because I obey Your Word. 101 I have kept my feet from every sinful way so that I may keep Your Word. 102 I have not turned away from Your Law, for You Yourself have taught me. 103 How sweet is Your Word to my taste! It is sweeter than honey to my mouth! 104 I get understanding from Your Law and so I hate every false way.

105 Your Word is a lamp to my feet and a light to my path. 106 I have promised that I will keep Your Law. And I will add strength to this promise. 107 I am in much suffering. O Lord, give me life again by Your Word. 108 Take my willing gift of thanks, O Lord, and teach me Your Law. 109 My life is always in my hand, yet I do not forget Your Law. 110 The sinful have set a trap for me, yet I have not turned from Your Law. 111 I have been given Your Law forever. It is the joy of my heart. 112 I have set my heart on obeying Your Law forever, even to the end.

113 I hate those who have two ways of thinking, but I love Your Law. 114 You are my hiding place and my battle-covering. I put my hope in Your Word. 115 Go away from me, you who do wrong, so I may keep the Word of my God. 116 Hold me up by Your Word and I will live. Do not let me be ashamed of my hope. 117 Hold me up so I will be safe, and I will always have respect for Your Law. 118 You turn away from all those who turn from Your Law. They fool themselves with their own lying. 119 You put away like waste all the sinful of the earth, so I love Your Law. 120 My flesh shakes in fear of You, and I am afraid of how You may punish.

121 I have done what is fair and right. Do not leave me to those who would make it hard for me. 122 Promise that You will bring good to Your servant. Do not let the proud make it hard for me. 123 My eyes become weak with desire for Your saving power and for Your Word that is right and good. 124 Act in Your loving-kindness toward Your servant, and teach me Your Laws. 125 I am Your servant. Give me understanding so I may know Your Law. 126 It is time for You to work, Lord, for they have broken Your Law. 127 I love Your Word more than gold, more than pure gold. 128 And so I look upon all of Your Law as right. I hate every false way.

129 Your Laws are wonderful, and so I obey them. 130 The opening up of Your Word gives light. It gives understanding to the child-like. 131 I opened my mouth wide, breathing with desire for Your Law. 132 Turn to me and show me loving-favor, as You always do to those who love Your name. 133 Set my steps in Your Word. Do not let sin rule over me. 134 Set me free from the power of man, and I will obey Your Law. 135 Make Your face shine upon Your servant and teach me Your Law. 136 Tears flow from my eyes because of those who do not keep Your Law.

137 You are right and good, O Lord, and Your Law is right. 138 The Law You have made is right and good and very faithful. 139 I feel weak because those who hate

me have forgotten Your Word. **140** Your Word is very pure and Your servant loves it. **141** I am not important and I am hated but I do not forget Your Law. **142** You are right forever, and Your Law is truth. **143** Trouble and suffering have come upon me, yet Your Word is my joy. **144** Your Law is right forever. Give me understanding and I will live.

145 I cried with all my heart. Answer me, O Lord! I will keep Your Law. **146** I cried to You. Save me, and I will keep Your Word. **147** I rise before the morning comes and cry for help. I have put my hope in Your Word. **148** My eyes wait for the night hours, so I may think about Your Word. **149** Hear my voice because of Your loving-kindness. O Lord, give me new life again because of Your Law. **150** Those who follow sinful ways come near. But they are far from Your Law. **151** You are near, O Lord. And all of Your Word is truth. **152** I learned from Your Law long ago that You made it to last forever.

153 Look upon my suffering and take me from it. For I do not forget Your Law. **154** Stand by me and set me free. Give me life again because of Your Word. **155** Your saving help is far from the sinful, for they do not look to Your Law. **156** Your loving-kindness is great, O Lord. Give me life again because of Your Law. **157** There are many who hate me and make it hard for me. Yet I do not turn from Your Law. **158** I look with hate on those who cannot be trusted, because they do not keep Your Word. **159** Think about how I love Your Law. Give me life again, O Lord, because of Your loving-kindness. **160** All of Your Word is truth, and every one of Your laws, which are always right, will last forever.

161 Rulers make it hard for me for no reason, but my heart honors Your Words with fear. **162** I am made happy by Your Word, like one who finds great riches. **163** I hate what is false, but I love Your Law. **164** I praise You seven times a day, because Your Law is right. **165** Those who love Your Law have great peace, and nothing will cause them to be hurt in their spirit. **166** I hope for Your saving power, O Lord, and I follow Your Word. **167** I obey Your Law, for I love it very much. **168** I obey Your Word and Laws, for You know all my ways.

169 Let my cry come to You, O Lord. Give me understanding because of Your Word. **170** Let my prayer come to You. Help me because of Your Word. **171** May praise come from my lips, for You teach me Your Law. **172** May my tongue sing about Your Word, for all of Your Word is right and good. **173** May Your hand be ready to help me, for I have chosen Your Law. **174** I have much desire for Your saving power, O Lord. Your Law is my joy. **175** Let me live so I may praise You, and let Your Law help me. **176** I have gone from the way like a lost sheep. Look for Your servant, for I do not forget Your Word.

A Prayer for Help

120 I cried to the Lord in my trouble, and He answered me. **2** O Lord, save me from lying lips and a false tongue. **3** What will be given to you and what more will be done to you, you false tongue? **4** He will punish you with sharp arrows of the soldier, and with the hot fire of the broom tree.

5 It is bad for me, for I travel in Meshech and live among the tents of Kedar! **6** I have lived too long with those who hate peace. **7** I am for peace. But when I speak, they are for war.

The Lord—Our Helper

121 I will lift up my eyes to the mountains. Where will my help come from? **2** My help comes from the Lord, Who made heaven and earth. **3** He will not let your feet go out from under you. He Who watches over you will not sleep. **4** Listen, He Who watches over Israel will not close his eyes or sleep.

5 The Lord watches over you. The Lord is your safe cover at your right hand. **6** The sun will not hurt you during the day and the moon will not hurt you during the night. **7** The Lord will keep you from all that is sinful. He will watch over your soul. **8** The Lord will watch over your coming and going, now and forever.

A Prayer for the Peace of Jerusalem

122 I was glad when they said to me, "Let us go to the house of the Lord." **2** Our feet are standing inside your gates, O Jerusalem. **3** Jerusalem is built as a city where people come together. **4** That is where the different families go, the families of the Lord. There they give thanks to the name of the Lord, by the Law that was given to Israel. **5** For thrones were set there for telling who is guilty or not, the thrones of the house of David.

6 Pray for the peace of Jerusalem. May all go well for those who love you. **7** May there be peace within your walls. May all go well within your houses. 8 I will now say, "May peace be within you," for the good of my brothers and my friends. 9 Because of the house of the Lord our God, I will pray for your good.

A Prayer for the Lord's Help

123 I lift up my eyes to You, O You Whose throne is in the heavens. 2 See, the eyes of servants look to the hand of their owner. The eyes of a woman servant look to the hand of her owner. So our eyes look to the Lord our God, until He shows us loving-kindness.

3 Show loving-kindness to us, O Lord. Show loving-kindness to us. For we have had our fill of hate. 4 The proud have laughed at us too long. We have had more than enough of their hate.

God Watches Over His People

124 "If the Lord had not been on our side," let Israel say, 2 "If the Lord had not been on our side when men came against us, 3 they would have eaten us up alive. Because their anger burned against us. 4 The waters would have covered us. The river would have passed over our soul. 5 The angry waters would have passed over our soul."

6 Honor and thanks be to the Lord! He has not let us be torn by their teeth. 7 We have become free like a bird out of a trap. The net is broken and now we are free. 8 Our help is in the name of the Lord, Who made heaven and earth.

God's People Are Safe

125 Those who trust in the Lord are like Mount Zion, which cannot be moved but stands forever. 2 The Lord is around His people like the mountains are around Jerusalem, now and forever. 3 For the sinful will not rule over the land of those who are right with God. So those who are right and good may not use their hands to do wrong.

4 O Lord, do good to those who are good, and to those who are right in their hearts. 5 But the Lord will let all those who turn aside to their sinful ways go with those who are sinners. Peace be upon Israel.

A Prayer for Help

126 It was like a dream when the Lord brought back to Zion those who had been held in another land. 2 Then we laughed with our mouths, and we sang with our tongues. Then it was said among the nations, "The Lord has done great

things for them." 3 The Lord has done great things for us and we are glad.

4 Bring back our people, O Lord, like the rivers in the South. 5 Those who plant with tears will gather fruit with songs of joy. 6 He who goes out crying as he carries his bag of seed will return with songs of joy as he brings much grain with him.

God Is Good to His People

127 Unless the Lord builds the house, its builders work for nothing. Unless the Lord watches over the city, the men who watch over it stay awake for nothing. 2 You rise up early, and go to bed late, and work hard for your food, all for nothing. For the Lord gives to His loved ones even while they sleep.

3 See, children are a gift from the Lord. The children born to us are our special reward. 4 The children of a young man are like arrows in the hand of a soldier. 5 Happy is the man who has many of them. They will not be put to shame when they speak in the gate with those who hate them.

The Joy of Obeying

128 Happy are all who honor the Lord with fear, and who walk in His ways. 2 For you will eat the fruit of your hands. You will be happy and it will be well with you. 3 Your wife will be like a vine with much fruit within your house. Your children will be like olive plants around your table. 4 This is the good that will come to the man who honors the Lord with fear.

5 May the Lord do good things for you from Zion. And may you see good come to Jerusalem all the days of your life. 6 Yes, may you see your children's children. Peace be upon Israel.

A Prayer against All Who Hate Zion

129 "They have made it hard for me many times since I was young," let Israel now say. 2 "They have made it hard for me many times since I was young. But they have not won over me. 3 Those who plow have plowed my back. And they have made their ditches long." 4 The Lord is right and good. He has cut in two the ropes of the sinful.

5 May all who hate Zion be put to shame and turned away. 6 Let them be like grass on the roof, which dries up before it grows. 7 No one can pick it and fill his hand. No one can gather it and fill his arms. 8 And those who pass by do not say, "May the

Lord be good to you. We pray that good will come to you in the name of the Lord."

A Prayer for Help

130 O Lord, I have cried to You out of the deep places. 2 Lord, hear my voice! Let Your ears hear the voice of my prayers. 3 If you, Lord, should write down our sins, O Lord, who could stand? 4 But You are the One Who forgives, so You are honored with fear.

5 I wait for the Lord. My soul waits and I hope in His Word. 6 My soul waits for the Lord more than one who watches for the morning; yes, more than one who watches for the morning. 7 O Israel, hope in the Lord! For there is loving-kindness with the Lord. With Him we are saved for sure. 8 And He will save Israel from all their sins.

Child-Like Trust in the Lord

131 O Lord, my heart is not proud. My eyes are not filled with pride. And I do not trouble myself with important things or in things too great for me. 2 For sure I have made my soul quiet like a child who no longer nurses while he is with his mother. My soul within me is like a child who no longer nurses. 3 O Israel, hope in the Lord, now and forever.

A Prayer for the House of God

132 O Lord, remember David and all of his suffering. 2 Remember how he swore to the Lord, and how he made a promise to the Powerful One of Jacob: 3 "For sure I will not go into my house or lie on my bed, 4 or let sleep come and close my eyes, 5 until I find a place for the Lord, a house of worship for the Powerful One of Jacob."

6 See, we heard about it in Ephrathah. We found it in the field of Jaar. 7 Let us go into the House of God. Let us worship at His feet. 8 Rise up, O Lord. Go to the place where You can rest, You and the special box of the Way of Worship which is Your strength. 9 Let Your religious leaders be dressed with what is right and good. And let those who belong to You sing for joy.

10 Because of David Your servant, do not turn away from Your chosen one. 11 The Lord has made a sure promise to David that He will never break: "I will set upon your throne your own children. 12 If your sons will keep My Law and My Word which I will teach them, then their sons will sit upon your throne forever."

13 For the Lord has chosen Zion. He has wanted it for a place to live: 14 "This is the place where I can rest forever. Here I will live, for I have wanted it. 15 I will give her many good things. I will give her poor people much bread. 16 I will dress her religious leaders with saving power. And those in her that belong to Me will sing for joy. 17 There I will make the horn of David grow and will make a lamp ready for My chosen one. 18 I will dress those who hate him with shame. But the crown on him will shine."

A Song of Praise

133 See, how good and how pleasing it is for brothers to live together as one! 2 It is like oil of great worth poured on the head, flowing down through the hair on the face, even the face of Aaron, and flowing down to his coat. 3 It is like the morning water of Hermon coming down upon the hills of Zion. For there the Lord has given the gift of life that lasts forever.

A Call to Praise

134 See, give honor and thanks to the Lord, all who work for the Lord, who stand during the night in the house of the Lord. 2 Lift up your hands to the holy place and give thanks to the Lord. 3 May the Lord bring good to you from Zion. He is the One Who made heaven and earth.

A Song of Praise

135 Praise the Lord! Praise the name of the Lord! Praise Him, O servants of the Lord, 2 you who stand in the house of the Lord, within the walls of the house of our God. 3 Praise the Lord, for the Lord is good. Sing praises to His name, for it is sweet. 4 For the Lord has chosen Jacob for Himself. Israel belongs to Him.

5 I know that the Lord is great. He is greater than all gods. 6 The Lord does whatever is pleasing to Him, in heaven and on earth, in the seas and in all waters. 7 He makes the clouds rise from the ends of the earth. He makes lightning come with the rain. He brings the wind out from where He stores His riches.

8 He killed the first-born of Egypt, both man and animal. 9 He sent special things to see and did great works among you, O Egypt, against Pharaoh and all his servants. 10 He crushed many nations and killed powerful kings. 11 King Sihon of the Amorites, King Og of Bashan, and all the kings of Canaan. 12 And He gave their land

as a gift, a gift to Israel His people. ¹³ O Lord, Your name lasts forever. O Lord, You will be remembered for all time. ¹⁴ For the Lord will decide in favor of His people. He will have loving-pity on His servants. ¹⁵ The gods of the nations are silver and gold, made by the hands of men. ¹⁶ They have mouths but they do not speak. They have eyes but they do not see. ¹⁷ They have ears but they do not hear. And there is no breath in their mouths. ¹⁸ Those who make them and those who trust in them will be like them.

¹⁹ O house of Israel, give honor and thanks to the Lord. O house of Aaron, give honor and thanks to the Lord. ²⁰ O house of Levi, give honor and thanks to the Lord. You who fear the Lord, give honor and thanks to the Lord. ²¹ Honor and thanks be to the Lord from Zion, Who lives in Jerusalem. Praise the Lord!

A Song of Thanks

136 Give thanks to the Lord, for He is good, for His loving-kindness lasts forever. ² Give thanks to the God of gods, for His loving-kindness lasts forever. ³ Give thanks to the Lord of lords, for His loving-kindness lasts forever. ⁴ Give thanks to Him Who alone does great works, for His loving-kindness lasts forever. ⁵ Give thanks to Him Who by wisdom made the heavens, for His loving-kindness lasts forever. ⁶ Give thanks to Him Who spread out the earth upon the waters, for His loving-kindness lasts forever. ⁷ Give thanks to Him Who made the great lights, for His loving-kindness lasts forever. ⁸ He made the sun to rule during the day, for His loving-kindness lasts forever. ⁹ He made the moon and stars to rule during the night, for His loving-kindness lasts forever.

¹⁰ Give thanks to Him Who killed the first-born of Egypt, for His loving-kindness lasts forever. ¹¹ He brought Israel out from among them, for His loving-kindness lasts forever. ¹² He put out His arm and brought them out with a strong hand, for His loving-kindness lasts forever. ¹³ Give thanks to Him Who divided the Red Sea in two, for His loving-kindness lasts forever. ¹⁴ He led Israel through, for His loving-kindness lasts forever. ¹⁵ But He caused the death of Pharaoh and his army in the Red Sea, for His loving-kindness lasts forever. ¹⁶ Give thanks to Him Who led His people through the desert, for His loving-kindness lasts forever. ¹⁷ Give thanks to Him Who destroyed great kings, for His loving-kindness lasts forever. ¹⁸ He killed powerful kings, for His loving-kindness lasts forever. ¹⁹ He put to death Sihon, king of the Amorites, for His loving-kindness lasts forever. ²⁰ He put to death Og, king of Bashan, for His loving-kindness lasts forever. ²¹ He gave their land as a gift, for His loving-kindness lasts forever. ²² He gave it as a gift to Israel His servant, for His loving-kindness lasts forever.

²³ Give thanks to Him Who remembered us when we had nothing, for His loving-kindness lasts forever. ²⁴ He took us away from those who hated us, for His loving-kindness lasts forever. ²⁵ He gives food to all men, for His loving-kindness lasts forever. ²⁶ Give thanks to the God of heaven, for His loving-kindness lasts forever.

Israel in a Strange Land

137 We sat down and cried by the rivers of Babylon when we remembered Zion. ² There upon the trees we put our harps. ³ For those who held us there made us sing. And those who made it hard for us asked for joy. They said, "Sing us one of the songs of Zion."

⁴ How can we sing the song of the Lord in a strange land? ⁵ If I forget you, O Jerusalem, may my right hand forget what it is able to do. ⁶ May my tongue hold to the roof of my mouth if I do not remember you, if I do not honor Jerusalem above my highest joy.

⁷ O Lord, remember what the sons of Edom did on the day Jerusalem fell. "Knock it down," they said, "Knock it down to the ground." ⁸ O daughter of Babylon, you who will be destroyed, how honored will be the one who pays you back for what you have done to us! ⁹ How honored will be the one who catches your children and throws them against the rock!

A Song of Praise

138 I will give You thanks with all my heart. I will sing praises to You in front of the gods. ² I will bow down toward Your holy house. And I will give thanks to Your name for Your loving-kindness and Your truth. For You have honored Your Word because of what Your name is. ³ You answered me on the day I called. You gave me strength in my soul.

⁴ O Lord, all the kings of the earth will give thanks to You when they have heard the words of Your mouth. ⁵ And they will sing of the ways of the Lord. For the shining beauty of the Lord is great. ⁶ For even

if the Lord is honored, He thinks about those who have no pride. But He knows the proud from far away. 7 Even if I walk into trouble, You will keep my life safe. You will put out Your hand against the anger of those who hate me. And Your right hand will save me. 8 The Lord will finish the work He started for me. O Lord, Your loving-kindness lasts forever. Do not turn away from the works of Your hands.

God Cares for His People

139 O Lord, You have looked through me and have known me. 2 You know when I sit down and when I get up. You understand my thoughts from far away. 3 You look over my path and my lying down. You know all my ways very well. 4 Even before I speak a word, O Lord, You know it all. 5 You have closed me in from behind and in front. And You have laid Your hand upon me. 6 All You know is too great for me. It is too much for me to understand.

7 Where can I go from Your Spirit? Or where can I run away from where You are? 8 If I go up to heaven, You are there! If I make my bed in the place of the dead, You are there! 9 If I take the wings of the morning or live in the farthest part of the sea, 10 even there Your hand will lead me and Your right hand will hold me. 11 If I say, "For sure the darkness will cover me and the light around me will be night," 12 even the darkness is not dark to You. And the night is as bright as the day. Darkness and light are the same to You.

13 For You made the parts inside me. You put me together inside my mother. 14 I will give thanks to You, for the greatness of the way I was made brings fear. Your works are great and my soul knows it very well. 15 My bones were not hidden from You when I was made in secret and put together with care in the deep part of the earth. 16 Your eyes saw me before I was put together. And all the days of my life were written in Your book before any of them came to be.

17 Your thoughts are of great worth to me, O God. How many there are! 18 If I could number them, there would be more than the sand. When I awake, I am still with You.

19 If only You would kill the sinful, O God, and the men of blood would go away from me! 20 For they speak against You in sin. Those who hate You use Your name in a wrong way. 21 Do I not hate those who hate You, O Lord? And do I not hate those who rise up against You? 22 I hate them with the strongest hate. They have become men who hate me.

23 Look through me, O God, and know my heart. Try me and know my thoughts. 24 See if there is any sinful way in me and lead me in the way that lasts forever.

A Prayer for Help

140 O Lord, take me away from sinful men. Keep me safe from men who want to hurt others. 2 They make sinful plans in their hearts. They always start wars. 3 They make their tongues sharp like a snake's. And the poison of a snake is under their lips.

4 O Lord, keep me from the hands of the sinful. Keep me safe from men who want to hurt others and have planned to trip my feet. 5 The proud have hidden a trap for me. With ropes they have spread a net. They have set traps for me beside the road. 6 I said to the Lord, "You are my God. Listen to the voice of my prayers, O Lord. 7 O God the Lord, the strength that saves me, You have covered my head in the day of battle. 8 O Lord, do not give the sinful what they want. Do not let their plans work, or they will be honored.

9 "As for those who gather around me, may the wrong-doing of their lips come upon their heads. 10 May burning coals fall upon them. May they be thrown into the fire, into deep holes, and rise no more. 11 Do not let the man whose talking hurts people stand in the land. May trouble hurry to catch and destroy the man who wants to hurt others."

12 I know that the Lord will stand by those who suffer and do what is right for the poor. 13 For sure those who are right and good will give thanks to Your name. Those who are right will live with You.

An Evening Prayer

141 I call upon You, O Lord. Hurry to me! Hear my voice when I call to You! 2 May my prayer be like special perfume before You. May the lifting up of my hands be like the evening gift given on the altar in worship. 3 O Lord, put a watch over my mouth. Keep watch over the door of my lips. 4 Do not let my heart turn to any sinful thing, to do wrong with men who sin. And do not let me eat their fine food.

5 Let those who are right with God punish me and speak strong words to me in kindness. It is oil upon my head. Do not let

my head turn away from it. Yet my prayer is always against the sinful works of those who sin. 6 When their rulers are thrown down from high rocks, they will hear my words, for they are true. 7 Our bones have been spread around the mouth of the grave like the broken ground behind the plow.

8 For my eyes are toward You, O God the Lord. In You I have a safe place. Do not leave me without help. 9 Keep me from the trap they have set for me. Keep me from the nets of those who do wrong. 10 Let the sinful fall into their own nets, while I pass by and am safe.

A Prayer for Help

142 I cry with a loud voice to the Lord. I pray with my voice to the Lord. 2 I talk and complain to Him. I tell Him all my trouble. 3 When my spirit had grown weak within me, You knew my path. They have hidden a trap for me in the way where I walk. 4 Look to the right and see. For there is no one who thinks about me. There is no place for me to go to be safe. No one cares about my soul.

5 I cried out to You, O Lord. I said, "You are my safe place, my share in the land of the living. 6 Listen to my cry, for I am brought down. Save me from those who make it hard for me. For they are too strong for me. 7 Bring my soul out of prison, so that I may give thanks to Your name. Those who are right and good will gather around me. For You will give much to me."

A Prayer for Help

143 Hear my prayer, O Lord. Listen when I ask for help. Answer me because You are faithful and right. 2 Do not find Your servant guilty, for no man living is right and good in Your eyes. 3 For the one who hates me has made it hard for my soul. He has crushed my life to the ground. He has made me live in dark places, like those who have been dead for a long time. 4 So my spirit grows weak within me. My heart within me is afraid.

5 I remember the days long ago. I think about all You have done. I think about the work of Your hands. 6 I put out my hands to You. My soul is thirsty for You like a dry land.

7 Hurry to answer me, O Lord! My spirit is becoming weak! Do not hide Your face from me, or I will become like those who go down to the grave. 8 Let me hear Your loving-kindness in the morning, for I trust in You. Teach me the way I should go for I lift up my soul to You. 9 O Lord, take me away from those who hate me. I run to You to be safe.

10 Teach me to do Your will, for You are my God. Let Your good Spirit lead me on a straight path. 11 Give me new life, O Lord, because of Your name. Bring me out of trouble because You are right and good. 12 In Your loving-kindness cut off those who hate me. Destroy all those who make it hard for my soul, for I am Your servant.

A Song of Thanks

144 Praise and thanks be to the Lord, my rock. He makes my hands ready for war, and my fingers for battle. 2 He is my loving-kindness and my walls of strength, my strong-place and the One Who sets me free, my safe-covering and the One in Whom I trust. He brings my people under my rule. 3 O Lord, what is man that You think of him, the son of man that You remember him? 4 Man is like a breath. His days are like a passing shadow. 5 O Lord, divide Your heavens and come down. Touch the mountains so they will smoke. 6 Send out lightning and divide them. Send out Your arrows and trouble them. 7 Put out Your hand from above. Take me out of trouble and away from the many waters, from the power of those from other lands. 8 Their mouths speak lies. And their right hand is a right hand that is false.

9 I will sing a new song to You, O God. I will sing praises to You on a harp of ten strings. 10 You save kings. You take Your servant David away from the sharp sword. 11 Take me out of trouble and away from the power of those from other lands. Their mouths speak lies. And their right hand is a right hand that is false.

12 May our young sons be like plants that are full-grown. And may our daughters be like the corner pieces of a great house. 13 May our store-houses be full of all kinds of food. And may our sheep grow by the thousands and ten thousands in our fields. 14 Let our cattle give birth without trouble and without loss. And may there be no cry of trouble in our streets. 15 Happy are the people who have all this. Yes, happy are the people whose God is the Lord!

A Song of Praise

145 I will praise You, my God and King. I will honor Your name forever and ever. 2 I will honor You every day, and praise Your name forever and ever. 3 The Lord is great and our praise to Him should be great. He is too great for anyone to understand. 4 Families of this time will praise Your works to the families-to-come. They will tell about Your powerful acts. 5 I will think about the shining-greatness of Your power and about Your great works. 6 Men will speak of Your powerful acts that fill us with fear. And I will tell of Your greatness. 7 Many words will come from their mouths about how good You are. They will sing for joy about how right You are.

8 The Lord is full of loving-favor and pity, slow to anger and great in loving-kindness. 9 The Lord is good to all. And His loving-kindness is over all His works. 10 All Your works will give thanks to You, O Lord. And all those who belong to You will honor You. 11 They will speak of the shining-greatness of Your holy nation, and talk of Your power. 12 They will make Your powerful acts and the great power of Your holy nation known to the sons of men. 13 Your holy nation is a nation that lasts forever. And Your rule lasts for all time.

14 The Lord holds up all who fall. He raises up all who are brought down. 15 The eyes of all look to You. And You give them their food at the right time. 16 You open Your hand and fill the desire of every living thing.

17 The Lord is right and good in all His ways, and kind in all His works. 18 The Lord is near to all who call on Him, to all who call on Him in truth. 19 He will fill the desire of those who fear Him. He will also hear their cry and will save them. 20 The Lord takes care of all who love Him. But He will destroy all the sinful. 21 My mouth will speak the praise of the Lord. And all flesh will honor His holy name forever and ever.

The Lord—Our Helper

146 Praise the Lord! Praise the Lord, O my soul! 2 I will praise the Lord as long as I live. I will sing praises to my God as long as I live. 3 Do not put your trust in princes, in a son of a man, who cannot save us. 4 When his spirit leaves, he returns to the earth. His thoughts end on that day. 5 Happy is he whose help is the God of Jacob, and whose hope is in the Lord his God. 6 The Lord made heaven and earth, the sea and all that is in them. He is faithful forever. 7 He helps those who have a bad power over them. He gives food to the hungry. And He sets those in prison free.

8 The Lord opens the eyes of the blind. The Lord raises up those who are brought down. The Lord loves those who are right and good. 9 The Lord keeps the strangers safe. He takes care of the children who have no father and the woman whose husband has died. But He destroys the way of the sinful. 10 The Lord will rule forever. Your God, O Zion, will rule over all people for all time. Praise the Lord!

Praise for God's Goodness

147 Praise the Lord! For it is good to sing praises to our God. For it is pleasing and praise is right. 2 The Lord builds up Jerusalem. He gathers those of Israel who had been taken away. 3 He heals those who have a broken heart. He heals their sorrows. 4 He knows the number of the stars. He gives names to all of them. 5 Great is our Lord, and great in power. His understanding has no end. 6 The Lord lifts up those who are suffering, and He brings the sinful down to the ground.

7 Sing to the Lord with thanks. Sing praises to our God on the harp. 8 He covers the heavens with clouds. He gives rain for the earth. He makes grass grow on the mountains. 9 He gives food to the animals, and to the young ravens that cry. 10 His joy is not in the strength of a horse. He does not find joy in the legs of a man. 11 But the Lord favors those who fear Him and those who wait for His loving-kindness.

12 Praise the Lord, O Jerusalem! Praise your God, O Zion! 13 For He has made your gates strong. He has made good come to your children within you. 14 He makes peace within your walls. He fills you with the best grain. 15 He sends His Word to the earth. And His Word runs fast. 16 He gives snow like wool. He spreads ice like ashes. 17 He throws down His ice as hail stones. Who can stand before His cold? 18 He sends out His Word and melts them. He makes His wind blow and the waters flow. 19 He speaks His Word to Jacob, and His Law to Israel. 20 He has not done this with any other nation. They do not know His Law. Praise the Lord!

The Whole World Should Praise the Lord

148 Praise the Lord! Praise the Lord from the heavens! Praise Him on high! 2 Praise Him, all His angels! Praise Him, all His army! 3 Praise Him, sun and moon! Praise Him, all you shining stars! 4 Praise Him, you highest heavens, and you waters above the heavens! 5 Let them praise the name of the Lord! For He spoke and they came into being. 6 He has made them last forever and ever. He has set a Law which will not pass away.

7 Praise the Lord from the earth, you large sea animals and all seas, 8 fire and hail, snow and clouds, and wind storms, obeying His Word. 9 Praise the Lord, you mountains and all hills, fruit trees and all tall trees, 10 wild animals and all cattle, small animals that move on the ground and birds that fly, 11 kings of the earth and all people, princes and all leaders of the earth, 12 both young men and women who have never had men, and old men and children.

13 Let them praise the name of the Lord. For His name alone is honored. His shining-greatness is above earth and heaven. 14 He has raised up a horn for His people, praise for all who belong to Him, for the people of Israel, who are near to Him. Praise the Lord!

A Call to Praise God

149 Praise the Lord! Sing a new song to the Lord! Praise Him in the meeting of His people. 2 Let Israel be glad in his Maker. Let the sons of Zion be full of joy in their King. 3 Let them praise His name with dancing. Let them sing praises to Him with timbrels and a harp. 4 For the Lord is happy with His people. He saves those who have no pride and makes them beautiful.

5 Let those who are God-like be full of joy and honor. Let them sing for joy on their beds. 6 Let the high praises of God be in their mouth, and in their hand a sword that cuts both ways. 7 Let it be used to punish the nations and the people. 8 Let their kings be tied in chains, and their rulers with ropes of iron. 9 Let the punishment that is written be given to them. This is an honor for all His faithful ones. Praise the Lord!

A Song of Praise

150 Praise the Lord! Praise God in His holy place! Praise Him in the heavens of His power! 2 Praise Him for His great works! Praise Him for all His greatness!

3 Praise Him with the sound of a horn. Praise Him with harps. 4 Praise Him with timbrels and dancing. Praise Him with strings and horns. 5 Praise Him with loud sounds. Praise Him with loud and clear sounds. 6 Let everything that has breath praise the Lord. Praise the Lord!

PROVERBS

Wise Sayings for Good Use

1 These are the wise sayings of Solomon, son of David, king of Israel: 2 They show you how to know wisdom and teaching, to find the words of understanding. 3 They help you learn about the ways of wisdom and what is right and fair. 4 They give wisdom to the child-like, and much learning and wisdom to those who are young. 5 A wise man will hear and grow in learning. A man of understanding will become able 6 to understand a saying and a picture-story, the words of the wise and what they mean.

7 The fear of the Lord is the beginning of much learning. Fools hate wisdom and teaching.

8 Hear your father's teaching, my son, and do not turn away from your mother's teaching. 9 For they are a glory to your head and a chain of beauty around your neck. 10 My son, if sinners try to lead you into sin, do not go with them. 11 If they

say, "Come with us. Let us lie in wait to kill someone. Let us set a trap for those who are without blame. 12 Let us swallow them alive like death, as those who go down to the grave. 13 We will find all kinds of things of great worth. We will fill our houses with the stolen riches. 14 Throw in your share with us. We will all have one money bag."

15 My son, do not walk in the way with them. Keep your feet from their path. 16 For their feet run to sin and hurry to kill. 17 Yes, the net is spread for nothing if the bird is watching. 18 They set traps for their own lives and wait to die. 19 Such are the ways of all who get things by hurting others. Their desire for stolen riches takes away their own lives.

20 Wisdom calls out in the street. She lifts her voice in the center of town. 21 There she cries out in the noisy streets. At the open gates of the city she speaks: 22 "O foolish ones, how long will you love being foolish? How long will those who

laugh at others be happy in their laughing? How long will fools hate much learning? [23] Listen to my strong words! See, I will pour out my spirit on you. I will make my words known to you. [24] I called but you would not listen. I put out my hand and no one gave it a thought. [25] You did not listen when I told you what you should do, and you would not hear any of my strong words. [26] So I will laugh at your trouble. I will laugh when you are afraid. [27] Fear will come to you like a storm. Hard times will come like a strong wind. When trouble and suffering come upon you, [28] then they will call on me, but I will not answer. They will look for me, but they will not find me. [29] Because they hated much learning, and did not choose the fear of the Lord. [30] They would not listen when I told them what they should do. They laughed at all my strong words. [31] So they will eat the fruit of their own way, and be filled with their own plans. [32] For the foolish will be killed by their turning away. The trust that fools put in themselves will destroy them. [33] But he who listens to me will live free from danger, and he will rest easy from the fear of what is sinful."

Wisdom Brings Safety

2 My son, if you receive my sayings and store up my teachings within you, [2] make your ear open to wisdom. Turn your heart to understanding. [3] If you cry out to know right from wrong, and lift your voice for understanding; [4] if you look for her as silver, and look for her as hidden riches; [5] then you will understand the fear of the Lord, and find what is known of God. [6] For the Lord gives wisdom. Much learning and understanding come from His mouth. [7] He stores up perfect wisdom for those who are right with Him. He is a safe-covering to those who are right in their walk. [8] He watches over the right way, and He keeps safe the way of those who belong to Him. [9] Then you will understand what is right and good, and right from wrong, and you will know what you should do. [10] For wisdom will come into your heart. And much learning will be pleasing to your soul. [11] Good thinking will keep you safe. Understanding will watch over you. [12] You will be kept from the sinful man, and from the man who causes much trouble by what he says. [13] You will be kept from the man who leaves the right way to walk in the ways of darkness, [14] from the one who is happy doing wrong, and who finds joy in the way of sin. [15] His ways are not straight and are not good.

[16] You will be saved from the strange woman, from the sinful woman with her smooth words. [17] She leaves the husband she had when she was young, and forgets the agreement with her God. [18] For her house goes down to death, and her steps lead to the dead. [19] None who go to her return again, and they do not find the paths of life.

[20] So may you walk in the way of good men, and keep to the paths of those who are right and good. [21] For those who are right with God will live in the land. The men without blame will stay in it, [22] but the sinful will be destroyed from the land, and those who are not faithful will be taken away from it.

The Reward That Comes from Following Wisdom

3 My son, do not forget my teaching. Let your heart keep my words. [2] For they will add to you many days and years of life and peace. [3] Do not let kindness and truth leave you. Tie them around your neck. Write them upon your heart. [4] So you will find favor and good understanding in the eyes of God and man. [5] Trust in the Lord with all your heart, and do not trust in your own understanding. [6] Agree with Him in all your ways, and He will make your paths straight. [7] Do not be wise in your own eyes. Fear the Lord and turn away from what is sinful. [8] It will be healing to your body and medicine to your bones. [9] Honor the Lord with your riches, and with the first of all you grow. [10] Then your store-houses will be filled with many good things and your barrels will flow over with new wine. [11] My son, listen when the Lord punishes you. Do not give up when He tells you what you must do. [12] The Lord punishes everyone He loves. He whips every son He receives.

[13] Happy is the man who finds wisdom, and the man who gets understanding. [14] For it is better than getting silver and fine gold. [15] She is worth more than stones of great worth. Nothing you can wish for compares with her. [16] Long life is in her right hand. Riches and honor are in her left hand. [17] Her ways are pleasing and all her paths are peace. [18] She is a tree of life to those who take hold of her. Happy are all who hold her near. [19] The Lord built the earth by wisdom. He built the heavens

by understanding. 20 By what He knows, the seas were broken up and water falls from the sky.

21 My son, do not allow them to leave your eyes. Keep perfect wisdom and careful thinking. 22 And they will be life to your soul and a chain of beauty to your neck. 23 Then you will be safe as you walk on your way, and your foot will not trip. 24 You will not be afraid when you lie down. When you lie down, your sleep will be sweet. 25 Do not be afraid of fear that comes all at once. And do not be afraid of the storm of the sinful when it comes. 26 For the Lord will be your trust. He will keep your foot from being caught.

27 Do not keep good from those who should have it, when it is in your power to do it. 28 Do not say to your neighbor, "Go, and return tomorrow, and I will give it," when you have it with you. 29 Do not plan for your neighbor to be hurt, while he trusts you enough to live beside you. 30 Do not fight with a man for no reason, when he has done you no wrong. 31 Do not be jealous of a man who hurts others, and do not choose any of his ways. 32 For the bad man is hated by the Lord, but He is near to those who are right with Him. 33 The punishment of the Lord is on the house of the sinful, but He makes good come to the house of those who are right with Him. 34 God makes fun of those who make fun of the truth but gives loving-favor to those who have no pride. 35 Honor will be given to the wise, but shame will be given to fools.

A Father's Teaching

4 O sons, hear the teaching of a father. Listen so you may get understanding. 2 For I give you good teaching. Do not turn away from it. 3 When I was a much-loved and only son of my mother and father, 4 he taught me, saying, "Hold my words close to your heart. Keep my teachings and live. 5 Get wisdom and understanding. Do not forget or turn away from the words of my mouth. 6 Do not leave her alone, and she will keep you safe. Love her, and she will watch over you. 7 The beginning of wisdom is: Get wisdom! And with all you have gotten, get understanding. 8 Honor her and she will honor you. She will honor you if you hold her to your heart. 9 She will put on your head a crown of loving-favor and beauty."

10 Hear, my son, and receive my sayings, and the years of your life will be many.

11 I have taught you in the way of wisdom. I have led you on the right paths. 12 When you walk, your steps will not be stopped. If you run, you will not trip. 13 Take hold of teaching. Do not let go. Watch over her, for she is your life. 14 Do not go on the path of the sinful. Do not walk in the way of bad men. 15 Stay away from it. Do not pass by it. Turn from it, and pass on. 16 For they cannot sleep unless they do wrong. They are robbed of sleep unless they make someone fall. 17 For they eat the bread of sin, and drink the wine of wrong-doing. 18 But the way of those who are right is like the early morning light. It shines brighter and brighter until the perfect day. 19 The way of the sinful is like darkness. They do not know what they trip over.

20 My son, listen to my words. Turn your ear to my sayings. 21 Do not let them leave your eyes. Keep them in the center of your heart. 22 For they are life to those who find them, and healing to their whole body. 23 Keep your heart pure for out of it are the important things of life. 24 Put false speaking away from you. Put bad talk far from you. 25 Let your eyes look straight in front of you, and keep looking at what is in front of you. 26 Watch the path of your feet, and all your ways will be sure. 27 Do not turn to the right or to the left. Turn your foot away from sin.

Being Led into Sex Sins

5 My son, listen to my wisdom. Turn your ear to my understanding. 2 So you may know what is good thinking, and your lips may keep much learning. 3 For the lips of a strange woman are as sweet as honey. Her talk is as smooth as oil. 4 But in the end she is as bitter tasting as wormwood, and as sharp as a sword that cuts both ways. 5 Her feet go down to death. Her steps take hold of hell. 6 She does not think about the path of life. Her ways go this way and that, and she does not know it.

7 Now then, my sons, listen to me. Do not turn away from the words of my mouth. 8 Keep far away from her. Do not go near the door of her house. 9 If you do, you would give your strength to others, and your years to those without loving-kindness. 10 Strangers would be filled with your strength, and the fruits of your work would go to a strange house. 11 You would cry inside yourself when your end comes, when your flesh and body are wasted away. 12 You would say, "How I have hated teaching! My heart hated strong words!

¹³ I have not listened to the voice of my teachers. I have not turned my ear to those who would teach me. ¹⁴ Now I have a bad name in the meeting place of the people."

¹⁵ Drink water from your own pool, flowing water from your own well. ¹⁶ Should the waters from your well flow away, rivers of water in the streets? ¹⁷ Let them be yours alone, and not for strangers with you. ¹⁸ Let your well be honored, and be happy with the wife you married when you were young. ¹⁹ Let her be like a loving, female deer. Let her breasts please you at all times. Be filled with great joy always because of her love. ²⁰ My son, why should you be carried away with a sinful woman and fall into the arms of a strange woman? ²¹ For the ways of a man are seen by the eyes of the Lord, and He watches all his paths. ²² His own sins will trap the sinful. He will be held with the ropes of his sin. ²³ He will die for want of teaching, and will go the wrong way because of the greatness of his foolish ways.

A Father Talks to His Son

6 My son, if you have put yourself as a trust for what your neighbor owes to another, or if you have made a promise for a stranger, ² you have been trapped with the words of your lips. You have been caught with the words of your mouth. ³ Do this now, my son, and get yourself out of trouble, for you have come into the hand of your neighbor. Go without pride and beg your neighbor to let you go. ⁴ Do not let your eyes sleep. Do not let your eyes close. ⁵ Take yourself away like a deer from the man who kills animals, and like a bird from the hand of the man who catches birds.

⁶ Go to the ant, O lazy person. Watch and think about her ways, and be wise. ⁷ She has no leader, head or ruler, ⁸ but she gets her food ready in the summer, and gathers her food at the right time. ⁹ How long will you lie down, O lazy person? When will you rise up from your sleep? ¹⁰ A little sleep, a little rest, a little folding of the hands to rest, ¹¹ and being poor will come upon you like a robber, and your need like a man ready to fight.

¹² A person of no worth, a sinful man, is he who goes about telling lies. ¹³ He winks with his eyes, makes signs with his feet, and makes certain moves with his fingers. ¹⁴ He always plans to do sinful things because of his sinful heart. He causes arguing among people. ¹⁵ So trouble will come upon him all at once. Right then he will be broken, and there will be no healing.

¹⁶ There are six things which the Lord hates, yes, seven that are hated by Him: ¹⁷ A proud look, a lying tongue, and hands that kill those who are without guilt, ¹⁸ a heart that makes sinful plans, feet that run fast to sin, ¹⁹ a person who tells lies about someone else, and one who starts fights among brothers.

²⁰ My son, keep the teaching of your father, and do not turn away from the teaching of your mother. ²¹ Hold them always to your heart. Tie them around your neck. ²² They will lead you when you walk. They will watch over you when you sleep, and they will talk with you when you wake up. ²³ For the word is a lamp. The teaching is a light, and strong words that punish are the way of life. ²⁴ They keep you from the sinful woman, from the smooth tongue of a sinful woman. ²⁵ Do not desire her beauty in your heart. Do not let her catch you with her eyes. ²⁶ For because of a woman who sells the use of her body, one is brought down to a loaf of bread. A sinful woman hunts to take a man's very life. ²⁷ Can a man carry fire in his arms, and his clothes not be burned? ²⁸ Can a man walk on hot coals, and his feet not be burned? ²⁹ So is he who goes in to his neighbor's wife. Whoever touches her will be punished. ³⁰ Men do not hate a robber who steals food for himself when he is hungry. ³¹ But if he is caught, he must pay seven times what he took. He must give up all the things in his house. ³² He who does sex sins with a woman does not think well. He who does it is destroying himself. ³³ He will be hurt and ashamed, and his shame will not be taken away. ³⁴ Jealousy makes a man angry. He will show no pity for the wrong that was done to him. ³⁵ He will not take pay, and he will not be happy even if you give him many gifts.

The Talk of a Sinful Woman

7 My son, keep my words, and hold together my teachings within you. ² Keep my words and live. Keep my teachings as you would your own eye. ³ Tie them upon your fingers. Write them upon your heart. ⁴ Say to wisdom, "You are my sister." Call understanding your special friend. ⁵ They will keep you from the strange woman, from the stranger with her smooth words.

⁶ For I looked out through the woodwork at the window of my house. ⁷ And I saw among the child-like and among

the young people a young man without wisdom and understanding. 8 He passed through the street near her corner and took the path to her house, 9 in the light of the evening, after it was dark. 10 See, a woman comes to meet him. She is dressed like a woman who sells the use of her body, and with a heart that wants to fool and trap someone. 11 She is loud and has a strong self-will. Her feet do not stay at home. 12 She is now in the street, now in the center of town where people gather. She lies in wait at every corner. 13 So she catches him and kisses him. With a hard face she says to him, 14 "It was time for me to give gifts on the altar in worship, and today I have paid what I promised. 15 So I have come out to meet you, to look for you, and I have found you. 16 I have spread my bed with coverings of linen cloth from Egypt. 17 I have perfumed my bed with fine perfumes and spices. 18 Come, let us take our fill of love until morning. Let us make ourselves happy with love. 19 For my husband is not at home. He has gone on a long trip. 20 He has taken a bag of money with him, and he will come home at full moon."

21 She leads him away with her tempting talk. She tempts him with the smooth words of her lips. 22 All at once he follows her, like a bull going to be killed, like a wild animal goes into a trap, 23 until an arrow cuts through him. Like a bird that hurries into the net, he does not know that he will lose his life.

24 So, my sons, listen to me. Listen to the words of my mouth. 25 Do not let your heart turn aside to her ways. Do not turn aside into her paths. 26 For she has hurt many and destroyed many others. She has killed a great number. 27 Her house is the way to hell, going down to the rooms of death.

Praising Wisdom

8 Does not wisdom call? Does not understanding raise her voice? 2 She takes her stand on the top of the hill beside the way, where the paths meet. 3 Beside the gates in front of the town, at the open doors, she cries out, 4 "I call to you, O men. My voice is to the sons of men. 5 O child-like ones, learn to use wisdom. O fools, make your mind understand. 6 Listen, for I will speak great things. What is right will come from my lips. 7 For my mouth will speak the truth. My lips hate wrong-doing. 8 All the words

of my mouth are right and good. There is nothing in them that is against the truth. 9 They are all clear to him who understands, and right to those who find much learning. 10 Take my teaching instead of silver. Take much learning instead of fine gold. 11 For wisdom is better than stones of great worth. All that you may desire cannot compare with her.

12 "I, wisdom, live with understanding, and I find much learning and careful thinking. 13 The fear of the Lord is to hate what is sinful. I hate pride, self-love, the way of sin, and lies. 14 I have teaching and wisdom. I have understanding and power. 15 By me kings rule and rulers make laws that are fair. 16 By me rulers rule, and all the princes rule on the earth. 17 I love those who love me, and those who look for me with much desire will find me. 18 Riches and honor are mine, lasting riches and being right with God. 19 My fruit is better than gold, even pure gold. What I give is better than fine silver. 20 I walk in the way that is right with God, in the center of the ways that are fair. 21 I give riches to those who love me, and fill their store-houses.

22 "The Lord made me at the beginning of His work, before His first works long ago. 23 I was set apart long ago, from the beginning, before the earth was. 24 I was born when there were no seas, when there were no pools full of water. 25 I was born before the mountains and hills were in their places. 26 It was before He had made the earth or the fields, or the first dust of the world. 27 I was there when He made the heavens, and when He drew a mark around the top of the sea. 28 I was there when He put the skies above, and when He put the wells of the waters in their place. 29 I was there when He marked out the places for the sea, so that the waters would not go farther than what He said. I was there when He marked out the ground for the earth. 30 I was beside Him as the leading workman. I was His joy every day. I was always happy when I was near Him. 31 I was happy in the world, His earth, and found joy in the sons of men.

32 "So now, O sons, listen to me, for happy are they who keep my ways. 33 Hear my teaching and be wise. Do not turn away from it. 34 Happy is the man who listens to me, watching every day at my gates, waiting beside my doors. 35 For he who finds me finds life, and gets favor from the Lord. 36 But he who misses me hurts himself. All those who hate me love death."

Wisdom—or the Way to Hell

9 Wisdom has built her house. She has made seven pillars to hold it up. 2 She has cooked her food, and has mixed her wine, and she has set her table. 3 She has sent out the young women who work for her. She calls from the highest places of the city, 4 "Whoever is easy to fool, let him turn in here!" She says to the one without understanding, 5 "Come and eat my food, and drink the wine I have mixed. 6 Turn from your foolish way, and live. Walk in the way of understanding."

7 He who speaks strong words to the man who laughs at the truth brings shame upon himself. He who speaks strong words to a sinful man gets hurt. 8 Do not speak strong words to a man who laughs at the truth, or he will hate you. Speak strong words to a wise man, and he will love you. 9 Give teaching to a wise man and he will be even wiser. Teach a man who is right and good, and he will grow in learning. 10 The fear of the Lord is the beginning of wisdom. To learn about the Holy One is understanding. 11 For by me your days will grow in number, and years will be added to your life. 12 If you are wise, your wisdom is a help to you. If you laugh at the truth, you alone will suffer for it.

13 A foolish woman makes much noise. She is open to sin, and knows nothing. 14 She sits at the door of her house or on a seat in the high places of the city. 15 She calls to those who pass by and are making their paths straight, 16 "Whoever is easy to fool, let him turn in here!" She says to the one without understanding, 17 "Stolen water is sweet. And bread eaten in secret is pleasing." 18 But he does not know that the dead are there, and that the ones who visit her are in the bottom of hell.

The Wise Sayings of Solomon, Chapters 10 through 29

10 The sayings of Solomon:
A wise son makes a father glad, but a foolish son is a sorrow to his mother.

2 Riches taken by wrong-doing do no good, but doing what is right and good saves from death.

3 The Lord will not let those who are right with Him go hungry, but He puts to one side the desire of the sinful.

4 He who works with a lazy hand is poor, but the hand of the hard worker brings riches.

5 A son who gathers in summer is wise but a son who sleeps during gathering time brings shame.

6 Good things are given to those who are right with God, but the mouth of the sinful hides trouble.

7 Those who are right with God are remembered with honor, but the name of the sinful will waste away.

8 The wise in heart will receive teaching, but a fast talking fool will become nothing.

9 He who is right in his walk is sure in his steps, but he who takes the wrong way will be found out.

10 He who winks the eye causes trouble, and a fast talking fool will become nothing.

11 The mouth of the one who is right with God is a well of life, but the mouth of the sinful hides trouble.

12 Hate starts fights, but love covers all sins.

13 Wisdom is found on the lips of him who has understanding, but a stick is for the back of him who has no understanding.

14 Wise men store up learning, but the foolish will be destroyed with their mouths.

15 The riches of a rich man are his strength, but the need of the poor is what destroys them.

16 The pay earned by those who are right with God is life, but the sinful are paid by being punished.

17 He who listens to teaching is on the path of life, but he who will not listen to strong words goes the wrong way.

18 He who hides hate has lying lips, and he who talks to hurt people is a fool.

19 The one who talks much will for sure sin, but he who is careful what he says is wise.

20 The tongue of those who are right with God is like fine silver, but the heart of the sinful is not worth much.

21 The lips of those who are right with God feed many, but fools die for want of understanding.

22 The good that comes from the Lord makes one rich, and He adds no sorrow to it.

23 Doing wrong is like play to a fool, but a man of understanding has wisdom.

24 What the sinful man is afraid of will come upon him, and what is wanted by the man who is right with God will be given to him.

25 When the storm passes, the sinful man is no more, but the man who is right with God has a place to stand forever.

26 Like sour wine to the teeth and smoke

to the eyes, so is the lazy one to those who send him.

²⁷ The fear of the Lord makes life longer, but the years of the sinful will be cut off.

²⁸ The hope of those who are right with God is joy, but the hope of the sinful comes to nothing.

²⁹ The way of the Lord is a strong-place to those who are faithful, but it destroys those who do wrong.

³⁰ Those who are right with God will never be shaken, but the sinful will not live in the land.

³¹ The mouth of those who are right with God flows with wisdom, but the sinful tongue will be stopped.

³² The lips of those who are right with God speak what is pleasing to others, but the mouth of the sinful speaks only what is bad.

11
The Lord hates a false weight, but a true weight is His joy.

² When pride comes, then comes shame, but wisdom is with those who have no pride.

³ The honor of good people will lead them, but those who hurt others will be destroyed by their own false ways.

⁴ Riches are of no use in the day of God's anger, but being right with God saves from death.

⁵ Those right with God, who are without blame, make a straight way for themselves, but the sinful will fall by their own wrong-doing.

⁶ Being right with God will save the honest man, but those who hurt others will be trapped by their wrong desires.

⁷ When a sinful man dies, his hope dies with him, and all his power comes to nothing.

⁸ The one who is right with God is kept from trouble, but the sinful get into trouble instead.

⁹ The sinful man destroys his neighbor with his mouth, but those who are fair will be saved through knowing God.

¹⁰ The city is glad when everything goes well with those who are right with God, and there are shouts of joy when the sinful are destroyed.

¹¹ A city is honored by the good things that come to the faithful, but it is torn down by the mouth of the sinful.

¹² He who hates his neighbor does not think well, but a man of understanding keeps quiet.

¹³ He who is always telling stories makes secrets known, but he who can be trusted keeps a thing hidden.

¹⁴ A nation falls where there is no wise leading, but it is safe where there are many wise men who know what to do.

¹⁵ He who puts himself as trust for what a stranger owes to another will suffer for it, but he who hates to be trusted for what another owes is safe.

¹⁶ A kind woman gets honor, and bad men get riches.

¹⁷ The man who shows loving-kindness does himself good, but the man without pity hurts himself.

¹⁸ The sinful man earns false pay, but he who spreads what is right and good gets pay that is sure.

¹⁹ He who will not be moved from being right with God will live, but he who goes for what is bad will bring about his own death.

²⁰ The Lord hates those who are sinful in heart, but those who walk without blame are His joy.

²¹ Know for sure that the sinful man will not go without being punished, but the children of those who are right with God will be saved.

²² A beautiful woman who does not think well is like a gold ring in the nose of a pig.

²³ The desire of those who are right with God is only good, but the hope of the sinful is anger.

²⁴ There is one who is free in giving, and yet he grows richer. And there is one who keeps what he should give, but he ends up needing more.

²⁵ The man who gives much will have much, and he who helps others will be helped himself.

²⁶ The people curse him who keeps grain for himself, but good comes to him who sells it.

²⁷ He who looks for good finds favor, but he who looks for wrong-doing will have bad come to him.

²⁸ He who trusts in his riches will fall, but those who are right with God will grow like a green leaf.

²⁹ He who troubles his own house will be given the wind, and the foolish will serve those with a wise heart.

³⁰ The fruit of those who are right with God is a tree of life, and he who wins souls is wise.

³¹ If those who are right with God will be paid on earth, how much more the sinful and the wrong-doer!

12 Whoever loves strong teaching loves much learning, but he who hates strong words is foolish.

2 A good man will get favor from the Lord, but He will punish a man who makes sinful plans.

3 A man will not stand by doing what is wrong, but the root of those who are right with God will not be moved.

4 A good wife is the pride and joy of her husband, but she who brings shame is like cancer to his bones.

5 The thoughts of those who are right with God can be trusted, but the words of the sinful are false.

6 The words of the sinful lie in wait for blood, but the mouth of the faithful will take them away from trouble.

7 The sinful are destroyed and are no more, but the house of those who are right with God will stand.

8 A man will be praised for his wisdom, but a man with a sinful mind will be hated.

9 A man who has only a little honor and has a servant is better than one who honors himself and does not have bread.

10 A man who is right with God cares for his animal, but the sinful man is hard and has no pity.

11 He who works his land will have all the bread he needs, but he who follows what is of no worth has no wisdom.

12 The sinful man wants what sinful men have, but the root of those who are right with God gives fruit.

13 A sinful man is trapped by the sin of his lips, but those who are right with God will get away from trouble.

14 A man will be filled with good from the fruit of his words, and the work of a man's hands will return to him.

15 The way of a fool is right in his own eyes, but a wise man listens to good teaching.

16 The anger of a fool is known at once, but a wise man does not speak when he is spoken against.

17 He who speaks the truth tells what is right, but a liar tells lies.

18 There is one whose foolish words cut like a sword, but the tongue of the wise brings healing.

19 Lips that tell the truth will last forever, but a lying tongue lasts only for a little while.

20 Lying is in the heart of those who plan what is bad, but those who plan peace have joy.

21 No trouble comes upon those who are right with God, but the sinful are filled with trouble.

22 The Lord hates lying lips, but those who speak the truth are His joy.

23 A wise man hides how much learning he has, but the heart of fools makes known their foolish way.

24 The hand of those who do their best will rule, but the lazy hand will be made to work.

25 Worry in the heart of a man weighs it down, but a good word makes it glad.

26 The man who is right with God is a teacher to his neighbor, but the way of the sinful leads them the wrong way.

27 The lazy man will not cook the food he has caught, but the man who does his best has what is of great worth.

28 Life is in the way of those who are right with God, and in its path there is no death.

13 A wise son listens when his father tells him the right way, but one who laughs at the truth does not listen when strong words are spoken to him.

2 The one who is careful what he says will have good come to him, but the one who wants to hurt others will have trouble.

3 He who watches over his mouth keeps his life. He who opens his lips wide will be destroyed.

4 The soul of the lazy person has strong desires but gets nothing, but the soul of the one who does his best gets more than he needs.

5 A man who is right with God hates lies, but the actions of a sinful man are hated and he is put to shame.

6 What is right and good watches over the one whose way is without blame, but sin destroys the sinful.

7 There is one who pretends to be rich, but has nothing. Another pretends to be poor, but has many riches.

8 A rich man can use his riches to save his life, but the poor man does not hear strong words spoken to him.

9 Those who are right with God are full of light, but the lamp of the sinful will be put out.

10 Fighting comes only from pride, but wisdom is with those who listen when told what they should do.

11 Riches taken by false ways become less and less, but riches grow for the one who gathers by hard work.

12 Hope that is put off makes the heart

sick, but a desire that comes into being is a tree of life.

13 He who hates the Word is under its power, but he who fears the Word will be well paid.

14 The teaching of the wise is a well of life, to save one from the nets of death.

15 Good understanding wins favor, but the way of the sinful is hard.

16 Every wise man acts with much learning, but a fool makes his foolish way known.

17 A sinful helper falls into trouble, but a faithful helper brings healing.

18 He who will not listen to strong teaching will become poor and ashamed, but he who listens when strong words are spoken will be honored.

19 A desire that is filled is sweet to the soul, but fools hate to give up what is sinful.

20 He who walks with wise men will be wise, but the one who walks with fools will be destroyed.

21 Trouble follows sinners, but good things will be given to those who are right with God.

22 A good man leaves what he owns for his children's children. The riches of the sinner are stored up for those who are right with God.

23 Much food is in the plowed land of the poor, but it is taken away because of wrong-doing.

24 He who does not punish his son when he needs it hates him, but he who loves him will punish him when he needs it.

25 The man who is right with God has all the food he needs, but the stomach of the sinful man never has enough.

14 The wise woman builds her house, but the foolish woman tears it down with her own hands.

2 He who walks in honor fears the Lord, but he who is sinful in his ways hates Him.

3 A foolish man's talk brings a stick to his back, but the lips of the wise will keep them safe.

4 There is no grain where there are no oxen, but much grain comes by the strength of the ox.

5 A faithful man who tells what he knows will not lie, but the man who is not faithful will lie.

6 One who laughs at the truth looks for wisdom and does not find it, but much learning is easy to him who has understanding.

7 Go away from a foolish man, for you will not find words of much learning.

8 The wisdom of the wise is to understand what to do, but lying is the foolish way of fools.

9 Fools laugh at sin, but the favor of God is among the faithful.

10 The heart knows when it is bitter, and a stranger cannot share its joy.

11 The house of the sinful will be destroyed, but all will go well in the tent of the faithful.

12 There is a way which looks right to a man, but its end is the way of death.

13 Even while laughing the heart may be in pain, and the end of joy may be sorrow.

14 The man who has gone back into sin will get the fruit of his ways, and a good man will get the fruit of what he does.

15 The one who is easy to fool believes everything, but the wise man looks where he goes.

16 A wise man fears God and turns away from what is sinful, but a fool is full of pride and is not careful.

17 He who has a quick temper acts in a foolish way, and a man who makes sinful plans is hated.

18 Those who are easy to fool are foolish, but the wise have much learning.

19 Sinful men will bow in front of the good, and at the gates of those who are right with God.

20 The poor man is hated even by his neighbor, but the rich man has many friends.

21 He who hates his neighbor sins, but happy is he who shows loving-favor to the poor.

22 Do not those who make sinful plans go the wrong way? Kindness and truth are for those who plan good.

23 Some good comes from all work. Nothing but talk leads only to being poor.

24 What the wise receive is their riches, but fools are known by their foolish ways.

25 A faithful man who tells what he knows saves lives, but he who tells lies hurts others.

26 There is strong trust in the fear of the Lord, and His children will have a safe place.

27 The fear of the Lord is a well of life. Its waters keep a man from death.

28 The shining-greatness of a king is in many people, but without people a prince has nothing.

29 He who is slow to get angry has great understanding, but he who has a quick temper makes his foolish way look right.

30 A heart that has peace is life to the body, but wrong desires are like the wasting away of the bones.

31 He who makes it hard for the poor brings shame to his Maker, but he who shows loving-favor to those in need honors Him.

32 The sinful is thrown down by his wrong-doing, but the man who is right with God has a safe place when he dies.

33 Wisdom rests in the heart of one who has understanding, but what is in the heart of fools is made known.

34 Being right with God makes a nation great, but sin is a shame to any people.

35 The king's favor is toward a wise servant, but his anger is toward the one who brings shame by what he does.

15 A gentle answer turns away anger, but a sharp word causes anger.

2 The tongue of the wise uses much learning in a good way, but the mouth of fools speaks in a foolish way.

3 The eyes of the Lord are in every place, watching the bad and the good.

4 A gentle tongue is a tree of life, but a sinful tongue crushes the spirit.

5 A fool turns away from the strong teaching of his father, but he who remembers the strong words spoken to him is wise.

6 Great riches are in the house of those who are right with God, but trouble is what the sinful will receive.

7 The lips of the wise spread much learning, but the minds of fools do not.

8 The Lord hates the gifts of the sinful, but the prayer of the faithful is His joy.

9 The Lord hates the way of the sinful, but He loves him who follows what is right and good.

10 He who turns from the right way will be punished. He who hates strong words spoken to him will die.

11 The world of the dead lies open before the Lord. How much more the hearts of men!

12 A man who laughs at the truth has no love for the one who speaks strong words to him. He will not go to the wise.

13 A glad heart makes a happy face, but when the heart is sad, the spirit is broken.

14 The mind of him who has understanding looks for much learning, but the mouth of fools feeds on foolish ways.

15 All the days of the suffering are hard, but a glad heart has a special supper all the time.

16 A little with the fear of the Lord is better than great riches with trouble.

17 A dish of vegetables with love is better than eating the best meat with hate.

18 A man with a bad temper starts fights, but he who is slow to anger quiets fighting.

19 The path of the lazy man is grown over with thorns, but the path of the faithful is a good road.

20 A wise son makes a father glad, but a foolish man hates his mother.

21 A foolish way is joy to him who has no wisdom, but a man of understanding walks straight.

22 Plans go wrong without talking together, but they will go well when many wise men talk about what to do.

23 To give a good answer is a joy to a man, and how pleasing is a word given at the right time!

24 The path of life leads up for the wise, so he may keep away from hell below.

25 The Lord will tear down the house of the proud, but He will make a place for the woman whose husband has died.

26 The Lord hates the plans of the sinful, but the words of the pure are pleasing to Him.

27 He who gets things by doing wrong brings trouble to his family, but he who will not be paid in secret for wrong-doing will live.

28 The mind of the one who is right with God thinks about how to answer, but the mouth of the sinful pours out sinful things.

29 The Lord is far from the sinful, but He hears the prayer of those who are right with Him.

30 The light of the eyes makes the heart glad. Good news puts fat on the bones.

31 He whose ear listens to careful words spoken will live among the wise.

32 He who does not listen to strong teaching hates himself, but he who listens when strong words are spoken gets understanding.

33 The fear of the Lord is the teaching for wisdom, and having no pride comes before honor.

16 The plans of the heart belong to man, but the answer of the tongue is from the Lord.

2 All the ways of a man are pure in his own eyes, but the Lord weighs the thoughts of the heart.

3 Trust your work to the Lord, and your plans will work out well.

⁴ The Lord has made all things for His own plans, even the sinful for the day of trouble.

⁵ Everyone who is proud in heart is a shame to the Lord. For sure, that one will be punished.

⁶ Sin has been paid for by loving-kindness and truth. The fear of the Lord keeps one away from sin.

⁷ When the ways of a man are pleasing to the Lord, He makes even those who hate him to be at peace with him.

⁸ A little earned in a right way is better than much earned in a wrong way.

⁹ The mind of a man plans his way, but the Lord shows him what to do.

¹⁰ The lips of the king should decide as God would. His mouth should not sin in deciding what is right or wrong.

¹¹ What is fair in telling the weight of something belongs to the Lord. He cares about all the weights of the bag.

¹² It is a hated thing for kings to do what is wrong. For a throne is built on what is right.

¹³ Lips that speak what is right and good are the joy of kings, and he who speaks the truth is loved.

¹⁴ The anger of a king carries death, but a wise man will quiet it.

¹⁵ Life is in the light of a king's face, and his favor is like a cloud bringing the spring rain.

¹⁶ To get wisdom is much better than getting gold. To get understanding should be chosen instead of silver.

¹⁷ The road of the faithful turns away from sin. He who watches his way keeps his life.

¹⁸ Pride comes before being destroyed and a proud spirit comes before a fall.

¹⁹ It is better to be poor in spirit among poor people, than to divide the riches that were taken with the proud.

²⁰ He who listens to the Word will find good, and happy is he who trusts in the Lord.

²¹ The wise in heart will be called understanding. And to speak in a pleasing way helps people know what you say is right.

²² Understanding is a well of life to him who has it, but to speak strong words to fools is of no use.

²³ The heart of the wise has power over his mouth and adds learning to his lips.

²⁴ Pleasing words are like honey. They are sweet to the soul and healing to the bones.

²⁵ There is a way that looks right to a man, but its end is the way of death.

²⁶ A workman's hunger works for him. The need of his mouth pushes him on.

²⁷ A man of no worth looks for wrong-doing. His words are like burning fire.

²⁸ A bad man spreads trouble. One who hurts people with bad talk separates good friends.

²⁹ A man who hurts people tempts his neighbor to do the same, and leads him in a way that is not good.

³⁰ He who winks his eyes plans to do bad things. He who closes his lips allows sinful things to happen.

³¹ Hair that is turning white is like a crown of honor. It is found in the way of being right with God.

³² He who is slow to anger is better than the powerful. And he who rules his spirit is better than he who takes a city.

³³ Man decides by throwing an object into the lap, but it is the Lord only who decides.

17 A dry piece of food with peace and quiet is better than a house full of food with fighting.

² A servant who is wise in what he does will rule over a son who acts in shame. He will share in what is given as one of the brothers.

³ The melting-pot is for silver and the hot fire is for gold, but the Lord tests hearts.

⁴ A wrong-doer listens to sinful lips. A liar listens to a tongue that destroys.

⁵ He who laughs at the poor brings shame to his Maker. He who is glad at trouble will be punished.

⁶ Grandchildren are the pride and joy of old men and a son is proud of his father.

⁷ Fine speaking is not right for a fool. Even worse are lying lips to a ruler.

⁸ Being paid in secret for wrong-doing is like a stone of much worth to the one who has it. Wherever he turns, he does well.

⁹ He who covers a sin looks for love. He who tells of trouble separates good friends.

¹⁰ A man of understanding learns more from being told the right thing to do than a fool learns from being beaten a hundred times.

¹¹ A man who will not obey looks only for what is bad. So one who has no loving-pity will be sent against him.

¹² A man meeting a bear robbed of her little ones is better than meeting a fool in his foolish way.

¹³ If a man returns bad for good, trouble will not leave his house.

14 The beginning of trouble is like letting out water. So stop arguing before fighting breaks out.

15 He who says that the sinful are right, and he who says those who do right are wrong, both are hated by the Lord.

16 It does a fool no good to try to buy wisdom, when he has no understanding.

17 A friend loves at all times. A brother is born to share troubles.

18 A man without good thinking makes promises, and becomes a trust for what another man owes his neighbor.

19 He who loves sin loves making trouble. He who opens his door wide for trouble is looking for a way to be destroyed.

20 He who has a sinful heart finds no good. He who has a sinful tongue falls into sin.

21 A foolish son is a sorrow to his father, and the father of a fool has no joy.

22 A glad heart is good medicine, but a broken spirit dries up the bones.

23 A sinful man receives pay in secret to change the right way into wrong-doing.

24 Wisdom is with the one who has understanding, but the eyes of a fool are on the ends of the earth.

25 A foolish son is a sorrow to his father, and trouble to her who gave birth to him.

26 It is not good to punish those who are right with God, and it is wrong to beat men of honor for being faithful.

27 He who is careful in what he says has much learning, and he who has a quiet spirit is a man of understanding.

28 Even a fool, when he keeps quiet, is thought to be wise. When he closes his lips, he is thought of as a man of understanding.

18 He who stays away from others cares only about himself. He argues against all good wisdom.

2 A fool does not find joy in understanding, but only in letting his own mind be known.

3 When a sinful man comes, hate comes also, and where there is no honor, there is shame.

4 The words of a man's mouth are deep waters. Wisdom comes like a flowing river making a pleasant noise.

5 It is not good to favor the sinful, or to keep what is fair from one who is right with God.

6 The lips of a fool bring fighting, and his mouth calls for a beating.

7 The mouth of a fool is what destroys him, and his lips are a trap to his soul.

8 The words of one who speaks about others in secret are like tempting bites of food. They go down into the inside parts of the body.

9 He who is lazy in his work is a brother to him who destroys.

10 The name of the Lord is a strong tower. The man who does what is right runs to it and is safe.

11 The rich man's money is his strong city, and he thinks it is like a high wall.

12 The heart of a man is proud before he is destroyed, but having no pride goes before honor.

13 If one gives an answer before he hears, it makes him foolish and ashamed.

14 The spirit of a man can help him through his sickness, but who can carry a broken spirit?

15 An understanding mind gets much learning, and the ear of the wise listens for much learning.

16 A man's gift makes room for him, and brings him in front of great men.

17 He who tells his story first makes people think he is right, until the other comes to test him.

18 Throwing an object to decide puts an end to arguing. It keeps powerful men from fighting.

19 A brother who has been hurt in his spirit is harder to be won than a strong city, and arguing is like the iron gates of a king's house.

20 A man's stomach will be filled with the fruit of his mouth. He will be filled with what his lips speak.

21 Death and life are in the power of the tongue, and those who love it will eat its fruit.

22 He who finds a wife finds a good thing, and gets favor from the Lord.

23 The poor man asks for loving-kindness, but the rich man is hard in his answers.

24 A man who has friends must be a friend, but there is a friend who stays nearer than a brother.

19 A poor man who walks with honor is better than a fool who is sinful in his speaking.

2 It is not good for a person to be without much learning, and he who hurries with his feet rushes into sin.

3 The foolish acts of man make his way bad, and his heart is angry toward the Lord.

4 Riches add many friends, but a poor man is separated from his friend.

5 A man who tells lies about someone will be punished. He who tells lies will not get away.

6 Many will ask for the favor of a man who gives much, and every man is a friend to him who gives gifts.

7 All the brothers of a poor man hate him. How much more do his friends go far from him! He runs to them with words, but they are gone.

8 He who gets wisdom loves his own soul. He who keeps understanding will find good.

9 A man who tells lies about someone will be punished. He who tells lies will be lost.

10 It is not right for a fool to live in great comfort, and for sure, for a servant to rule over rulers.

11 A man's understanding makes him slow to anger. It is to his honor to forgive and forget a wrong done to him.

12 The king's anger is like the noise of a lion, but his favor is like morning water upon the grass.

13 A foolish son destroys his father. The arguing of a wife is like water falling drop by drop all the time.

14 House and riches are handed down from fathers, but an understanding wife is from the Lord.

15 Being lazy makes one go into a deep sleep, and a lazy man will suffer from being hungry.

16 He who keeps God's Word keeps his soul, but he who is not careful of his ways will die.

17 He who shows kindness to a poor man gives to the Lord and He will pay him in return for his good act.

18 Punish your son if he needs it while there is hope, and do not worry about his crying.

19 An angry man will suffer punishment. For if you save him from his trouble, you will only have to do it again.

20 Listen to words about what you should do, and take your punishment if you need it, so that you may be wise the rest of your days.

21 There are many plans in a man's heart, but it is the Lord's plan that will stand.

22 What is desired in a man is his kindness, and it is better to be a poor man than a liar.

23 The fear of the Lord leads to life, and he who has it will sleep well, and will not be touched by sin.

24 The lazy man buries his hand in the dish, and will not even bring it to his mouth again.

25 Hit a man who laughs at the truth, and the foolish may become wise. But speak strong words to one who has understanding, and he will get more learning.

26 He who hurts his father and puts his mother out of the house is a son who causes much shame.

27 My son, stop listening to teaching that will cause you to turn away from the words of much learning.

28 A man without worth who tells all he knows laughs at what is right and fair, and the mouth of the sinful spreads wrong-doing.

29 Ways of punishing are made ready for those who laugh at the truth, and beatings are for the back of fools.

20

Wine makes people act in a foolish way. Strong drink starts fights. Whoever is fooled by it is not wise.

2 The anger of a king is like the noise of a lion. He who makes him angry gives up his own life.

3 It is an honor for a man to keep away from fighting, but any fool will argue.

4 The lazy man does not plow before winter. So he begs during gathering time and has nothing.

5 The plan in a man's heart is like water in a deep well, but a man of understanding gets it out.

6 Many men tell about their own loving-kindness and good ways but who can find a faithful man?

7 How happy are the sons of a man who is right with God and walks in honor!

8 A king who sits on his throne to judge finds out all sin with his eyes.

9 Who can say, "I have made my heart clean, and I am pure from my sin?"

10 The Lord hates the use of tools that lie about how heavy or how long something is.

11 A young man makes himself known by his actions and proves if his ways are pure and right.

12 The hearing ear and the seeing eye were both made by the Lord.

13 Do not love sleep, or you will become poor. Open your eyes, and you will be filled with food.

14 "It is bad, it is bad," says the one who buys, but when he goes away, he talks much about his good buy.

15 There is gold and many stones of great worth, but the lips of much learning are worth more.

¹⁶ Take a man's coat when he has given himself as trust for what a stranger owes. And hold him to his promise when he gives himself as trust for what the people from other lands owe.

¹⁷ Bread a man gets by lying is sweet to him, but later his mouth will be filled with sand.

¹⁸ Make plans by listening to what others have to say, and make war by listening to the leading of wise men.

¹⁹ He who goes about talking to hurt people makes secrets known. So do not be with those who talk about others.

²⁰ If a son talks against his father or his mother, his lamp will be put out in the time of darkness.

²¹ A large gift received at one time in a hurry will not bring good in the end.

²² Do not say, "I will punish wrong-doing." Wait on the Lord, and He will take care of it.

²³ Giving the wrong weight is hated by the Lord. And weighing something wrong is not good.

²⁴ A man's steps are decided by the Lord. How can anyone understand his own way?

²⁵ It is a trap for a man to say without thinking, "It is holy," and then later think more about what he has promised.

²⁶ A wise king puts the sinful aside and crushes the grain over them.

²⁷ The spirit of man is the lamp of the Lord. It shows all the inside parts of his heart.

²⁸ A king will stay in power as long as he is faithful and true. He can stay on his throne if he does what is right and good.

²⁹ The honor of young men is their strength. And the honor of old men is their hair turning white.

³⁰ Beatings that hurt clean away sin. And beatings make even the inside parts clean.

21

The heart of the king is like rivers of water in the hand of the Lord. He turns it where He wishes.

² Every man's way is right in his own eyes, but the Lord knows the hearts.

³ To do what is right and good and fair is more pleasing to the Lord than gifts given on the altar in worship.

⁴ Eyes lifted high and a proud heart is sin and is the lamp of the sinful.

⁵ The plans of those who do their best lead only to having all they need, but all who are in a hurry come only to want.

⁶ Getting riches by a lying tongue is like a passing cloud, and leads to death.

⁷ The way the sinful hurt others will draw them away, because they will not do what is right and fair.

⁸ The way of a guilty man is sinful, but the actions of the pure man are right.

⁹ It is better to live in a corner of a roof than in a house shared with an arguing woman.

¹⁰ The soul of the sinful has a desire for what is bad. His neighbor finds no favor in his eyes.

¹¹ When the man who laughs at the truth is punished, the fool becomes wise. When a wise man is taught, he gets much learning.

¹² The One Who is right and good thinks about the house of the sinful, and the sinful are thrown down to be destroyed.

¹³ He who shuts his ears to the cry of the poor will also cry himself and not be answered.

¹⁴ A gift in secret quiets anger. A gift from the heart quiets strong anger.

¹⁵ When what is right and fair is done, it is a joy for those who are right with God. But it fills the sinful with fear.

¹⁶ A man who goes away from the way of understanding will rest in the gathering of the dead.

¹⁷ He who loves only fun will become a poor man. He who loves wine and oil will not become rich.

¹⁸ The sinful man is the price given for the man who is right with God, the man who is not faithful for the faithful man.

¹⁹ It is better to live in a desert land than with a woman who argues and causes trouble.

²⁰ There are riches and oil of great worth in the house of the wise, but a foolish man swallows them up.

²¹ He who follows what is right and loving and kind finds life, right-standing with God and honor.

²² A wise man goes over the city walls of the powerful, and brings down the strong-place in which they trust.

²³ He who watches over his mouth and his tongue keeps his soul from troubles.

²⁴ "Proud," "Self-important" and "One who laughs at the truth" are the names of the man who acts without respect and is proud.

²⁵ The desire of the lazy man kills him, for his hands will not work.

²⁶ He is filled with desire all day long, but the man who is right with God gives all he can.

²⁷ The gift given on an altar in worship

by the sinful is a hated thing. How much more when he brings it for the wrong reason!

28 A person who tells a lie about someone else will be lost, but the man who listens to the truth will speak forever.

29 A sinful man's face shows he is pretending, but a good man is sure of himself.

30 There is no wisdom and no understanding and no words that can stand against the Lord.

31 The horse is made ready for war, but winning the fight belongs to the Lord.

22

A good name is to be chosen instead of many riches. Favor is better than silver and gold.

2 The rich and the poor meet together. The Lord is the maker of them all. 3 A wise man sees sin and hides himself, but the foolish go on, and are punished for it.

4 The reward for not having pride and having the fear of the Lord is riches, honor and life.

5 Thorns and traps are in the way of the sinful. He who watches himself will stay far from them.

6 Bring up a child by teaching him the way he should go, and when he is old he will not turn away from it.

7 The rich rules over the poor. The man who uses something that belongs to someone else is ruled by the one who let him use it.

8 He who plants sin will gather trouble, and the heavy stick of his anger will break.

9 He who gives much will be honored, for he gives some of his food to the poor.

10 Send away the man who laughs at the truth, and arguing, fighting and shame will stop.

11 He who loves a pure heart and is kind in his speaking has the king as his friend.

12 The eyes of the Lord keep watch over much learning, but He destroys the words of the man who is not faithful.

13 The lazy man says, "There is a lion outside! I will be killed in the streets!"

14 The mouth of a sinful woman is a deep hole. He with whom the Lord is angry will fall into it.

15 A foolish way is held in the heart of a child, but the punishing stick will send it far from him.

16 He who makes it hard for the poor by getting more for himself, or who gives to the rich, will become poor himself.

17 Turn your ear and hear the words of the wise, and open your mind to what they teach. 18 For it will be pleasing if you keep them in your heart, so they may be ready on your lips. 19 I have taught you today, even you, so that your trust may be in the Lord. 20 Have I not written to you great things of wise teaching and much learning 21 to show you that the words of truth are sure, so you may give a true answer to him who sent you?

22 Do not rob the poor because he is poor, or crush those who suffer at the gate. 23 For the Lord will stand by them and help them, and take the life of those who rob them.

24 Do not have anything to do with a man given to anger, or go with a man who has a bad temper. 25 Or you might learn his ways and get yourself into a trap.

26 Do not be among those who make promises and put themselves up as trust for what others owe. 27 If you have nothing with which to pay, why should he take your bed from under you?

28 Do not take away the old land-mark which your fathers have set.

29 Do you see a man who is good at his work? He will stand in front of kings. He will not stand in front of men who are not important.

23

When you sit down to eat with a ruler, think about what is in front of you. 2 Put a knife to your neck if you are a man who is given to much eating. 3 Do not desire his special foods, for they are put there for no good reason.

4 Do not work hard to be rich. Stop trying to get things for yourself. 5 When you set your eyes upon it, it is gone. For sure, riches make themselves wings like an eagle that flies toward the heavens.

6 Do not eat the bread of a man who thinks only about himself. Do not have a desire for his fine food. 7 For as he thinks in his heart, so is he. He says to you, "Eat and drink!" But his heart is not with you. 8 You will spit up the piece of food you have eaten, and waste your good words.

9 Do not speak in the hearing of a fool, for he will hate the wisdom of your words.

10 Do not take away the old land-mark, or go into the fields of those without a father. 11 For the One Who saves them is strong. He will stand by them and give them help against you. 12 Open your heart to teaching, and your ears to words of much learning.

13 Do not keep from punishing the child if he needs it. If you beat him with the

stick, he will not die. ¹⁴ Beat him with the stick, and save his soul from hell.

¹⁵ My son, if your heart is wise, my own heart will be glad also. ¹⁶ My heart will be full of joy when your lips speak what is right.

¹⁷ Do not let your heart be jealous of sinners, but live in the fear of the Lord always. ¹⁸ For sure there is a future and your hope will not be cut off. ¹⁹ Listen, my son, and be wise. Lead your heart in the way. ²⁰ Do not be with those who drink too much wine or eat too much meat. ²¹ For the man who drinks too much or eats too much will become poor, and much sleep will dress a man in torn clothes.

²² Listen to your father who gave you life, and do not hate your mother when she is old. ²³ Buy truth, and do not sell it. Get wisdom and teaching and understanding.

²⁴ The father of one who is right with God will have much joy. He who has a wise son will be glad in him. ²⁵ Let your father and mother be glad, and let her who gave birth to you be full of joy.

²⁶ Give me your heart, my son. Let your eyes find joy in my ways. ²⁷ For a woman who sells the use of her body is like a deep hole. A sinful woman is a narrow well. ²⁸ She lies in wait as a robber, and makes many more men not faithful.

²⁹ Who has trouble? Who has sorrow? Who is fighting? Who is complaining? Who is hurt without a reason? Who has eyes that have become red? ³⁰ Those who stay a long time over wine. Those who go to taste mixed wine. ³¹ Do not look at wine when it is red, when it shines in the cup, when it is smooth in going down. ³² In the end it bites like a snake. It stings like the bite of a snake with poison. ³³ Your eyes will see strange things. Your mind will say the wrong things. ³⁴ And you will be like one who lies down in the center of the sea, or like one who lies above a ship's sail. ³⁵ "They hit me, but I was not hurt. They beat me, but I did not know it. When will I wake up? I will look for another drink."

24

Do not be jealous of sinful men. Do not want to be with them. ² For their hearts make plans to hurt others and their lips talk about trouble.

³ A house is built by wisdom. It is made strong by understanding, ⁴ and by much learning the rooms are filled with all riches that are pleasing and of great worth.

⁵ A wise man is strong. A man of much learning adds to his strength. ⁶ For by wise leading you will make war, and the fight is won when there are many wise men to help you make the plans.

⁷ Wisdom is too hard for a fool to understand. He does not open his mouth in the gate. ⁸ He who plans to do wrong will be called a trouble-maker. ⁹ Planning to do foolish things is sin, and the man who laughs at the truth is hated by men.

¹⁰ If you are weak in the day of trouble, your strength is small.

¹¹ Save those who are being taken away to death. Keep them from being killed. ¹² If you say, "See, we did not know this," does not He Who knows what is in hearts see it? Does not He Who keeps watch over your soul know it? And will He not pay each man for his work?

¹³ My son, eat honey, for it is good. Yes, the honey from the comb is sweet to your taste. ¹⁴ Know that wisdom is like this to your soul. If you find it, there will be a future, and your hope will not be cut off.

¹⁵ O sinful man, do not lie in wait against the house of the man who is right with God. Do not destroy his resting place. ¹⁶ For a man who is right with God falls seven times, and rises again, but the sinful fall in time of trouble.

¹⁷ Do not be full of joy when the one who hates you falls. Do not let your heart be glad when he trips. ¹⁸ The Lord will see it and will not be pleased, and He will turn away His anger from him.

¹⁹ Do not worry yourself because of those who do wrong and do not be jealous of the sinful. ²⁰ For there will be no future for the sinful man. The lamp of the sinful will be put out.

²¹ My son, fear the Lord and the king. Have nothing to do with those who are given to change. ²² For their trouble will rise up all at once, and who knows how much both of them will destroy?

²³ These also are sayings of the wise. It is not good to show favor in judging. ²⁴ He who says to the sinful, "You are right and good," will be spoken against by people and hated by nations. ²⁵ But those who speak strong words to the sinful will find joy and good will come upon them. ²⁶ To give the right answer is like a kiss on the lips.

²⁷ Get your work done outside. Make your fields ready. Then after that, build your house.

²⁸ Do not speak against your neighbor without a reason, and do not lie with your lips. ²⁹ Do not say, "I will do to him as he

has done to me. I will pay the man for what he has done."

30 I passed by the field of the lazy man, by the grape-vines of the man without understanding. 31 And see, it was all grown over with thorns. The ground was covered with weeds, and its stone wall was broken down. 32 When I saw it, I thought about it. I looked and received teaching. 33 "A little sleep, a little rest, a little folding of the hands to rest," 34 and your being poor will come as a robber, and your need like a man ready to fight.

25 These also are wise sayings of Solomon, which were written down by the men of Hezekiah, king of Judah.

2 It is the greatness of God to keep things hidden, but it is the greatness of kings to find things out. 3 As the heavens are high and the earth is deep, so the heart of kings is more than can be known. 4 Take away the waste from the silver, and a silver pot comes out for the workman. 5 Take the sinful away from the king, and his throne will stand on what is right and good. 6 Do not honor yourself in front of the king, and do not stand in the place of great men. 7 For it is better to be told, "Come up here," than to be put down in front of the ruler whom your eyes have seen.

8 Do not go out in a hurry to argue. Or what will you do in the end, when your neighbor puts you to shame? 9 Argue your side of the problem with your neighbor, but do not tell the secret of another. 10 Or he who hears you may put you to shame, and bad things will be said about you forever.

11 A word spoken at the right time is like fruit of gold set in silver.

12 A wise man speaking strong words to a listening ear is like a piece of gold for the ear and a beautiful object of fine gold.

13 A faithful man who carries news is like the cold of snow at gathering time to those who send him, for he makes the spirit of his owners feel new again.

14 A man who talks much of a gift he never gives is like clouds and wind without rain. 15 When one is slow to anger, a ruler may be won over. A gentle tongue will break a bone.

16 Have you found honey? Eat only what you need, or you may become filled with it and spit it up.

17 Do not let your foot be in your neighbor's house too much, or he may become tired of you and hate you.

18 A man who tells a lie against his neighbor is like a heavy stick or a sword or a sharp arrow.

19 In time of trouble, trusting in a man who is not faithful is like a bad tooth or a foot out of joint.

20 He who sings songs to a heavy heart is like one who takes off a coat on a cold day, or like sour wine poured on soda.

21 If the one who hates you is hungry, feed him. If he is thirsty, give him water. 22 If you do that, you will be making him more ashamed of himself, and the Lord will reward you.

23 The north wind brings rain, and a tongue that hurts people brings angry looks.

24 It is better to live in a corner of the roof than in a house shared with an arguing woman.

25 Good news from a land far away is like cold water to a tired soul.

26 A man who does what is right but gives way in front of the sinful, is like a well of mud or poisoned water.

27 It is not good to eat much honey, and looking for honor is not good.

28 A man who cannot rule his own spirit is like a city whose walls are broken down.

26 Like snow in summer and like rain at gathering time, so honor is not right for a fool.

2 Like a sparrow in its traveling, like a swallow in its flying, so bad words said against someone without reason do not come to rest.

3 A whip is for the horse, leather ropes are for the donkey, and a stick is for the back of fools.

4 Do not answer a fool by his foolish ways, or you will be like him.

5 Answer a fool in the way he has earned by his foolish acts, so he will not be wise in his own eyes.

6 He who sends a letter by the hand of a fool cuts off his own feet and brings trouble upon himself.

7 A wise saying in the mouth of fools is like the legs on a man who cannot walk.

8 He who gives honor to a fool is like one who ties a stone in a sling.

9 A wise saying in the mouth of fools is like a thorn that goes into the hand of a man who drinks too much.

10 He who hires a fool or hires those who pass by is like a man who uses a bow to hurt everyone.

¹¹ A fool who does his foolish act again is like a dog that turns back to what he has thrown up.

¹² Do you see a man who is wise in his own eyes? There is more hope for a fool than for him.

¹³ The lazy man says, "There is a lion in the way! There is a lion in the streets!"

¹⁴ As a door turns, so does the lazy man on his bed.

¹⁵ The lazy man buries his hand in the dish. It makes him tired to bring it to his mouth again.

¹⁶ The lazy man is wiser in his own eyes than seven men who can give a wise answer.

¹⁷ He who passes by and has a part in someone else's fight is like one who takes a dog by the ears.

¹⁸ Like a crazy man who throws pieces of burning wood and arrows of death, ¹⁹ so is the man who fools his neighbor with a lie, and says, "I was only joking."

²⁰ When there is no wood, the fire goes out. Where there is no one telling secret stories about people, arguing stops.

²¹ An arguing man makes fights worse. He is like coals to burning wood and wood to a fire.

²² The words of one who tells secret things about people are like good-tasting bites of food. They go down into the inside parts of the body.

²³ Burning lips and a sinful heart are like a pot covered with silver waste.

²⁴ He who hates covers it up with his lips, but stores up false ways in his heart. ²⁵ When he speaks with kindness, do not believe him, for there are seven things that are hated in his heart. ²⁶ Even if his hate is covered with false ways, his sin will be found out in front of the great meeting.

²⁷ He who digs a deep hole will fall into it, and he who rolls a stone will have it return upon him.

²⁸ A lying tongue hates those it crushes, and a mouth that speaks false words destroys.

27

Do not talk much about tomorrow, for you do not know what a day will bring.

² Let another man praise you, and not your own mouth. Let a stranger, and not your own lips.

³ A stone is heavy, and sand is heavy, but to be made angry by a fool weighs more than both of them.

⁴ Anger causes trouble and a bad temper is like a flood, but who can stand when there is jealousy?

⁵ Sharp words spoken in the open are better than love that is hidden.

⁶ The pains given by a friend are faithful, but the kisses of one who hates you are false.

⁷ He who is full hates honey, but any bitter thing is sweet to a hungry man.

⁸ Like a bird that goes away from her nest, so is a man who goes away from his home.

⁹ Oil and perfume make the heart glad, so are a man's words sweet to his friend.

¹⁰ Do not leave your own friend or your father's friend alone, and do not go to your brother's house in the day of your trouble. A neighbor who is near is better than a brother who is far away.

¹¹ Be wise, my son, and make my heart glad, so I may answer him who puts me to shame.

¹² A wise man sees sin and hides himself, but the fool goes on and suffers for it.

¹³ Take the man's coat who has given himself as trust for what a stranger owes. And hold him to his promise who has given it as trust for a sinful woman.

¹⁴ He who praises his neighbor with a loud voice early in the morning will be thought of as saying bad things against him.

¹⁵ An arguing woman is like water falling drop by drop on a day it is raining. ¹⁶ To try to stop her is like trying to stop the wind, or like trying to catch oil in his right hand.

¹⁷ Iron is made sharp with iron, and one man is made sharp by a friend.

¹⁸ He who cares for the fig tree will eat its fruit, and he who cares for the one he works for will be honored.

¹⁹ As water acts as a mirror to a face, so the heart of man acts as a mirror to a man.

²⁰ The place of the dead is never filled, and the eyes of man are never filled.

²¹ The melting-pot is for silver and the fire for gold, and a man is tested by the praise he receives.

²² Even if you crush a fool in a pot used for crushing grain, his foolish way will not leave him.

²³ Know well how your flocks are doing, and keep your mind on your cattle. ²⁴ Riches do not last forever, and a crown does not pass from family to family. ²⁵ When the grass is gone, the new plants are seen, and the plants of the mountains are gathered in. ²⁶ The lambs will be for your clothes, and the goats will bring the

price of a field. 27 There will be enough goats' milk for your food, for the food of all your house, and a living for your young women.

28 The sinful run away when no one is trying to catch them, but those who are right with God have as much strength of heart as a lion.

2 When a nation sins, it has many rulers, but with a man of understanding and much learning, it will last a long time.

3 A poor man who makes it hard for the poor is like a heavy rain which leaves no food.

4 Those who turn away from the law praise the sinful, but those who keep the law fight against them.

5 Sinful men do not understand what is right and fair, but those who look to the Lord understand all things.

6 A poor man who walks in his honor is better than a rich man who is sinful in his ways.

7 He who keeps the law is a wise son, but a friend of men who eat too much puts his father to shame.

8 He who gets money by being paid much for the use of it, gathers it for him who will be kind to the poor.

9 He who turns his ear away from listening to the law, even his prayer is a hated thing.

10 He who leads good people into a sinful way will fall into his own deep hole, but good will come to those without blame.

11 The rich man is wise in his own eyes, but the poor man who has understanding sees through him.

12 When those who are right with God win, there is great honor, but when the sinful rule, men hide themselves.

13 It will not go well for the man who hides his sins, but he who tells his sins and turns from them will be given loving-pity.

14 Happy is the man who always fears the Lord, but he who makes his heart hard will fall into trouble.

15 A sinful ruler over poor people is like a lion making noise or a bear running to fight.

16 A ruler who takes much from the people who have little does not have understanding. But he who hates wanting something that belongs to someone else will live a long time.

17 A man who is loaded down with the guilt of human blood will run in fear until death. Let no one help him.

18 He who walks without blame will be kept safe, but he who is sinful will fall all at once.

19 He who works his land will have more than enough food, but he who wastes his time will become very poor.

20 A faithful man will have many good things, but he who hurries to be rich will be punished for it.

21 To show favor is not good, because a man will sin for a piece of bread.

22 A man with a sinful eye hurries to be rich. He does not know that he will be in need.

23 He who speaks strong words to a man will later find more favor than he who gives false respect with his tongue.

24 He who robs his father or his mother, and says, "It is not a sin," is the friend of a man who destroys.

25 A proud man starts fights, but all will go well for the man who trusts in the Lord.

26 He who trusts in his own heart is a fool, but he who walks in wisdom will be kept safe.

27 He who gives to the poor will never want, but many bad things will happen to the man who shuts his eyes to the poor.

28 When the sinful rule, men hide themselves, but when they pass away, those who do what is right become many.

29 A man who does not listen after many strong words are spoken to him will be destroyed all at once and without help.

2 When those who are right with God rule, the people are glad, but when a sinful man rules, the people have sorrow.

3 A man who loves wisdom makes his father glad, but he who goes with women who sell the use of their bodies wastes his money.

4 The king makes the land strong by doing what is right and fair, but the one who takes pay for doing wrong, destroys it.

5 A man who gives his neighbor sweet-sounding words that are not true spreads a net for his own feet.

6 A sinful man is trapped by his sins, but a man who is right with God sings for joy.

7 The man who is right with God cares about the rights of poor people, but the sinful man does not understand such things.

8 Men who speak against others set a city on fire, but wise men turn away anger.

9 When a wise man argues with a foolish man, the fool only gets angry or laughs, and there is no peace and quiet.

¹⁰ Men who kill hate him without blame, but a good man cares for his life.

¹¹ A fool always loses his temper, but a wise man keeps quiet.

¹² If a ruler listens to lies, all who work for him will become sinful.

¹³ The Lord gives light to the eyes of both the poor man and the man who makes it hard for others.

¹⁴ If the king is fair as he judges the poor, his throne will stand forever.

¹⁵ The stick and strong words give wisdom, but a child who gets his own way brings shame to his mother.

¹⁶ When the sinful are many, sins become many, but those who are right with God will see their fall.

¹⁷ Punish your son when he does wrong and he will give you comfort. Yes, he will give joy to your soul.

¹⁸ Where there is no understanding of the Word of the Lord, the people do whatever they want to, but happy is he who keeps the law.

¹⁹ A servant will not be taught by words alone. For even if he understands, he will not answer.

²⁰ Do you see a man who is quick with his words? There is more hope for a fool than for him.

²¹ He who gives good care to his servant from the time he is young, will in the end find him to be a son.

²² A man of anger starts fights, and a man with a bad temper is full of wrong doing.

²³ A man's pride will bring him down, but he whose spirit is without pride will receive honor.

²⁴ He who works with a robber hates his own life. He knows about the bad that will come, but can tell nothing.

²⁵ The fear of man brings a trap, but he who trusts in the Lord will be honored.

²⁶ Many look for the ruler's favor, but what is right and fair comes from the Lord.

²⁷ A sinful man is a shame to those who are right with God, and he who is right with God is a shame to the sinful.

The Wisdom of Agur

30 The words of Agur the son of Jakeh of Massa. The man says to Ithiel and Ucal:

² For sure, I am more foolish than any man, and I do not have the understanding of a man. ³ I have not learned wisdom, and I do not know much about the Holy One. ⁴ Who has gone up into heaven and come down? Who has gathered the wind in His hands? Who has gathered the waters in His coat? Who has put in place all the ends of the earth? What is His name, and what is His Son's name? For sure you know!

⁵ Every word of God has been proven true. He is a safe-covering to those who trust in Him. ⁶ Do not add to His words, or He will speak strong words to you and prove you to be a liar.

⁷ Two things I have asked of You. Do not keep me from having them before I die: ⁸ Take lies and what is false far from me. Do not let me be poor or rich. Feed me with the food that I need. ⁹ Then I will not be afraid that I will be full and turn my back against You and say, "Who is the Lord?" And I will not be afraid that I will be poor and steal, and bring shame on the name of my God.

¹⁰ Do not speak against a slave while talking with his owner, or he may curse you and you will be found guilty.

¹¹ There are those who curse their fathers, and do not honor their mothers. ¹² There are people who are pure in their own eyes, but are not washed from their own dirt. ¹³ There is a kind, O how proud are his eyes! His eyes are opened wide with pride. ¹⁴ There is a kind of man whose teeth are swords, whose jaws are like knives, who eat up those who are suffering from the earth, and those in need from among men.

¹⁵ The one who lives by the blood of another has two daughters, "Give," "Give." There are three things that are never filled, four that never say, "Enough": ¹⁶ The place of the dead, the woman who cannot have children, the earth that is always thirsty for water, and fire that never says, "Enough."

¹⁷ The eye that makes fun of a father and hates to obey a mother will be picked out by the ravens of the valley and eaten by the young eagles.

¹⁸ There are three things which are too great for me, four which I do not understand: ¹⁹ The way of an eagle in the sky, the way of a snake on a rock, the way of a ship out at sea, and the way of a man with a woman.

²⁰ This is the way of a woman who is not faithful in marriage: She eats and washes her mouth, and says, "I have done no wrong."

²¹ Under three things the earth shakes, and under four it cannot stand: ²² Under a servant when he becomes king, under a fool when he is filled with food, ²³ under

a woman who is not loved when she gets a husband, and under a woman servant when she takes the place of the woman of the house.

24 There are four things that are small on the earth, but they are very wise: 25 The ants are not a strong people, but they store up their food in the summer. 26 The badgers are not a strong people, but they make their houses in the rocks. 27 The locusts have no king, but they go as an army. 28 You can take the lizard in your hands, but it is found in kings' houses.

29 There are three things which have honor in their steps, even four which show honor in their walk: 30 The lion, which is powerful among wild animals and does not turn away from any, 31 the proud rooster, the male goat, and a king when his army is with him.

32 If you have been foolish in honoring yourself, or if you have planned wrongdoing, put your hand on your mouth. 33 Shaking milk makes butter, and hitting the nose brings blood. So fighting comes because of anger.

The Wisdom of King Lemuel's Mother

31 The words of Lemuel king of Massa, which his mother taught him:

2 What, my son? What, son who came from within me? What, son of my promises? 3 Do not give your strength to women, or your ways to that which destroys kings. 4 It is not for kings, O Lemuel, it is not for kings to drink wine, or for rulers to desire strong drink. 5 Or they might drink and forget the law, and go against the rights of all who are suffering. 6 Give strong drink to him who is about to die, and wine to him whose life is full of trouble. 7 Let him drink and forget how poor he is, and remember his trouble no more. 8 Open your mouth for those who cannot speak, and for the rights of those who are left without help. 9 Open your mouth. Be right and fair in what you decide. Stand up for the rights of those who are suffering and in need.

10 Who can find a good wife? For she is worth far more than rubies that make one rich. 11 The heart of her husband trusts in her, and he will never stop getting good things. 12 She does him good and not bad all the days of her life. 13 She looks for wool and flax, and works with willing hands. 14 She is like ships that trade. She brings her food from far away. 15 She rises while it is still night and makes food for all those in her house. She gives work for the young women to do. 16 She gives careful thought to a field and buys it. She plants grapevines from what she has earned. 17 She makes herself ready with strength, and makes her arms strong. 18 She sees that what she has earned is good. Her lamp does not go out at night. 19 She puts her hands to the wheel to make cloth. 20 She opens her hand to the poor, and holds out her hands to those in need. 21 She is not afraid of the snow for those in her house, for all of them are dressed in red. 22 She makes coverings for herself. Her clothes are linen cloth and purple. 23 Her husband is known in the gates, when he sits among the leaders of the land. 24 She makes linen clothes and sells them. She brings belts to those who trade. 25 Her clothes are strength and honor. She is full of joy about the future. 26 She opens her mouth with wisdom. The teaching of kindness is on her tongue. 27 She looks well to the ways of those in her house, and does not eat the bread of doing nothing. 28 Her children rise up and honor her. Her husband does also, and he praises her, saying: 29 "Many daughters have done well, but you have done better than all of them." 30 Pleasing ways lie and beauty comes to nothing, but a woman who fears the Lord will be praised. 31 Give her the fruit of her hands, and let her works praise her in the gates.

ECCLESIASTES

Life Is of No Worth

1 These are the words of the Preacher, the son of David, king in Jerusalem. 2 "It is of no use," says the Preacher. "It is of no use! All is for nothing."

3 What does a man get for all his work which he does under the sun? 4 People die and people are born, but the earth stays forever. 5 The sun rises and the sun sets, and travels in a hurry to the place where it rises. 6 The wind blows to the south and goes around to the north. It goes around and around, and returns again on its way. 7 All the rivers flow into the sea, yet the sea is not full. And they return again to the place from which the rivers flow. 8 All

things are tiring. Man is not able to tell about them. The eye never has enough to see, and the ear is never filled with what it hears. 9 What has been is what will be. And what has been done is what will be done. So there is nothing new under the sun. 10 Is there anything of which one might say, "See, this is new"? It has already been there since long before us. 11 No one remembers the things that happened before. And no one will remember the things that will happen in the future among those who will come later.

Looking for Wisdom Is like Trying to Catch the Wind

12 I, the Preacher, have been king over Israel in Jerusalem. 13 And I set my mind to look for wisdom to learn about all that has been done under heaven. It is a hard work which God has given to the sons of men to be troubled with. 14 I have seen all the works which have been done under the sun. And see, it is all for nothing. It is like trying to catch the wind. 15 What is not straight cannot be made straight. What is not there cannot be numbered. 16 I said to myself, "I have received more wisdom than all who were over Jerusalem before me. My mind has seen much wisdom and much learning." 17 And I set my mind to know wisdom and to know what is crazy and foolish. I saw that this also is like trying to catch the wind. 18 Because in much wisdom there is much trouble. And he who gets much learning gets much sorrow.

Fun Is of No Worth

2 I said to myself, "Come now, I will test you with things that are fun. So have a good time." But see, this also was for nothing. 2 I said of laughing, "It is crazy," and of fun, "What use is it?" 3 I tried to find in my mind how to make my body happy with wine, yet at the same time having my mind lead me with wisdom. I tried to find how to take hold of what is foolish, until I could see what good there is for the sons of men to do under heaven during the few years of their lives. 4 I did great things. I built houses for myself. I planted grape-fields for myself. 5 I made gardens and beautiful places for myself, and planted in them all kinds of fruit trees. 6 I made pools of water for myself from which to water many new trees. 7 I bought men and women servants, and had other servants who were born in my house. I had more flocks and cattle than anyone before me

in Jerusalem. 8 I gathered for myself silver and gold and the riches of kings and lands. I got for myself male and female singers, and kept many women who acted as my wives, the joy of man. 9 Then I became great, greater than all who lived before me in Jerusalem. And my wisdom stayed with me. 10 Whatever my eyes wanted I did not keep away from them. I did not keep my heart from anything that was pleasing, for my heart was pleased with all my work. This was my reward for all my work. 11 Then I thought about all that my hands had done, and the work I had done. I saw that it was all for nothing. It was like trying to catch the wind, and there was nothing to get for it under the sun.

The End of the Wise Man or Fool

12 So I turned to think about wisdom and what is crazy and foolish. For what can the man do who comes after the king, except what has already been done? 13 And I saw that wisdom is better than what is foolish, as light is better than darkness. 14 The wise man's eyes are in his head, but the fool walks in darkness. Yet I know that one thing will happen to both of them. 15 Then I said to myself, "What happens to the fool will happen to me also. Why then have I been so very wise?" So I said to myself, "This also is for nothing." 16 For the wise man will not be remembered forever any more than the fool. All will be forgotten in the days to come. The wise man dies just like the fool! 17 So I hated life. For the work which had been done under the sun brought sorrow to me. Because everything is for nothing and is like trying to catch the wind.

18 I hated what came from all my work which I had done under the sun. For I must leave it to the man who will come after me. 19 And who knows if he will be a wise man or a fool? Yet he will rule over all that I have worked for by acting with wisdom under the sun. This also is for nothing. 20 So I was filled with sorrow for all I had worked for under the sun. 21 For here is a man who has worked with wisdom, much learning, and an able hand. Yet he must give this to one who has not worked for it. This also is for nothing, and very wrong. 22 For what does a man get from all his work and trouble under the sun? 23 For his work brings pain and sorrow all his days. Even during the night his mind does not rest. This also is for nothing.

24 There is nothing better for a man than

to eat and drink and find joy in his work. I have seen that this also is from the hand of God. 25 For who can eat and who can find joy without Him? 26 For God has given wisdom and much learning and joy to the person who is good in God's eyes. But to the sinner He has given the work of gathering and getting many riches together to give to the one who pleases God. This also is for nothing, like trying to catch the wind.

A Time for Everything

3 There is a special time for everything. There is a time for everything that happens under heaven. 2 There is a time to be born, and a time to die; a time to plant, and a time to pick what is planted. 3 There is a time to kill, and a time to heal; a time to break down, and a time to build up. 4 There is a time to cry, and a time to laugh; a time to have sorrow, and a time to dance. 5 There is a time to throw stones, and a time to gather stones; a time to kiss, and a time to turn from kissing. 6 There is a time to try to find, and a time to lose; a time to keep, and a time to throw away. 7 There is a time to tear apart, and a time to sew together; a time to be quiet, and a time to speak. 8 There is a time to love, and a time to hate; a time for war, and a time for peace.

The God-Given Work

9 What does the worker get for his work? 10 I have seen the work which God has given the sons of men to do. 11 He has made everything beautiful in its time. He has put thoughts of the forever in man's mind, yet man cannot understand the work God has done from the beginning to the end. 12 I know that there is nothing better for men than to be happy and to do good as long as they live. 13 And I know that every man who eats and drinks sees good in all his work. It is the gift of God. 14 I know that everything God does will last forever. There is nothing to add to it, and nothing to take from it. God works so that men will honor Him with fear. 15 That which is, already has been. And that which will be, has already been. For God allows the same things to happen again.

Sin Is Everywhere

16 Also I have seen under the sun that in the place of what is right and fair there is sin. And in the place of what is right and good there is wrong-doing. 17 I said to myself, "God will judge both the man who is right and good, and the sinful man." For there is a time for everything to be done and a time for every work. 18 I said to myself about the sons of men, "God is testing them to show them that they are like animals." 19 For the same thing is to happen to both the sons of men and animals. As one dies, so dies the other. They all have the same breath, and to be a man is no better than to be an animal. Because all is for nothing. 20 All go to the same place. All came from the dust and all return to the dust. 21 Who knows that the spirit of man goes up and the spirit of the animal goes down to the earth? 22 So I have seen that nothing is better than that man should be happy in his work, for that is all he can do. Who can bring him to see what will happen after him?

4 Then I saw all the bad powers that were ruling under the sun. I saw the tears of the people who were suffering under these powers, with no one to comfort them. Those who made it hard for them had the power. But the people had no one to comfort them. 2 So I thought that those who are already dead are better off than those who are still living. 3 But better than both is the one who has never been, who has never seen the wrong that is done under the sun.

4 I have seen that all the work done is because a man wants what his neighbor has. This also is for nothing, like trying to catch the wind. 5 The fool folds his hands and has no food to eat. 6 One hand full of rest is better than two hands full of work and trying to catch the wind.

7 Then I looked again at what is of no use under the sun. 8 There was a certain man who lived alone. He did not have a son or a brother. Yet he worked all the time. His eyes were never happy with the riches he had, and he never asked, "For whom am I working and why am I keeping myself from happiness?" This also is for nothing. It is work that brings sorrow.

A True Friend

9 Two are better than one, because they have good pay for their work. 10 For if one of them falls, the other can help him up. But it is hard for the one who falls when there is no one to lift him up. 11 And if two lie down together, they keep warm. But how can one be warm alone? 12 One

man is able to have power over him who is alone, but two can stand against him. It is not easy to break a rope made of three strings.

¹³ A poor and wise boy is better than an old and foolish king who will no longer listen to words of wisdom. ¹⁴ A man can come out of prison to become king, even if he was born poor in his nation. ¹⁵ I have seen all the living under the sun gather to the side of the boy who becomes king in his place. ¹⁶ There was no end to all the people. He ruled over all of them. Yet those who come later will not be happy with him. For this also is for nothing, like trying to catch the wind.

Do What You Promise

5 Watch your steps as you go to the house of God. Go near and listen but do not give the gift of fools. For they do not know they are sinning. ² Do not hurry to speak or be in a hurry as you think what to tell God. For God is in heaven and you are on the earth. So let your words be few. ³ For a dream comes with much work, and the voice of a fool comes with many words. ⁴ When you make a promise to God, do not be late in paying it, for He is not pleased with fools. Pay what you promise to pay! ⁵ It is better not to make a promise, than to make a promise and not pay it. ⁶ Do not let your mouth cause you to sin. And do not say to the one sent from God that it was a mistake. Why should God be angry because of what you said, and destroy the work of your hands? ⁷ For when there are many dreams, there are many empty words. Instead of this, honor God with fear.

Money and Honor Are of Little Worth

⁸ In one part of a land if you see a bad power held over the poor, and what is right and fair and good taken away, do not be surprised by what you see. For one leader watches over another leader, and more important leaders watch over them. ⁹ After all, a country does better with a king in power.

¹⁰ He who loves money will never have enough money to make him happy. It is the same for the one who loves to get many things. This also is for nothing. ¹¹ When there are more good things, there are also more people to eat them. So what does their owner get except to see them with his eyes? ¹² The sleep of the working man is pleasing, if he eats little or much.

But the full stomach of the rich man does not let him sleep.

¹³ There is something very wrong which I have seen under the sun: Riches being kept by the owner and he is hurt by them. ¹⁴ When those riches are lost because he used them in a wrong way, and he had become the father of a son, there was nothing left for him. ¹⁵ A man comes from his mother without clothing, and he will go as he came. He will take nothing from his work that he can carry in his hand. ¹⁶ This also is very wrong: As a man is born, this is the way he will leave. So what does the man get who works for the wind? ¹⁷ All his life he eats in darkness with much sorrow, sickness and anger.

¹⁸ This is what I have seen to be good and right: to eat and to drink and be happy in all the work one does under the sun during the few years of his life which God has given him. For this is his reward. ¹⁹ As for every man to whom God has given riches and many good things, He has also given him the power to eat from them, receive his reward and be happy in his work. This is the gift of God. ²⁰ For he will not think much about the years of his life, because God keeps him happy in his heart.

6 There is another bad thing which I have seen under the sun, and it is hard for men: ² God gives a man riches and many good things and honor, so that he has everything he wants. But He does not allow him to have joy from them, for a stranger has joy from them. This is for nothing, and is very bad. ³ If a man becomes the father of a hundred children and lives many years until he is very old, but he is not happy with good things, and is not buried as he should be, then I say that the child who dies before it is born is shown more favor than he. ⁴ For this child comes for nothing and goes into darkness, and in darkness its name is covered. ⁵ It never sees the sun and it never knows anything. It is better off than he. ⁶ Even if the other man lives a thousand years twice and does not find joy in good things, do not all go to the same place?

⁷ All a man's work is for his mouth, and yet his hunger is not filled. ⁸ For what is better for the wise man than for the fool? And what good does the poor man have who knows how to walk among the living? ⁹ What the eyes see is better than what there is a desire for. This also is for nothing, like trying to catch the wind.

¹⁰ Whatever has come to be has already been given a name. It is known what man is, and that he cannot argue with one who is stronger than he. ¹¹ The more words there are, the more they are worth nothing. What good is that to anyone? ¹² For who knows what is good for a man during his life, during the few years of his living for nothing? He will spend them like a shadow. For who can tell a man what will happen after he is gone under the sun?

Wisdom Is Worth a Lot

7 A good name is better than oil of much worth. And the day of one's death is better than the day of one's birth. ² It is better to go to a house of sorrow than to go to a house of much eating. For this is the end of all men, and the living takes it to heart. ³ To have sorrow is better than to laugh because when a face is sad, the heart may become strong. ⁴ The heart of the wise is in the house of sorrow, while the heart of fools is in the house where there is fun. ⁵ It is better to listen to the sharp words of a wise man than to listen to the song of fools. ⁶ For the laughing of a fool is like the sound of a thorn bush burning under a pot. This also is for nothing. ⁷ For sure a bad power makes the wise man angry. And to get paid in secret for wrong-doing destroys the heart. ⁸ The end of something is better than its beginning. Not giving up in spirit is better than being proud in spirit. ⁹ Do not be quick in spirit to be angry. For anger is in the heart of fools. ¹⁰ Do not say, "Why were the days of the past better than these?" For it is not wise to ask this. ¹¹ Wisdom with a gift passed down from father to son is good and a help to those who see the sun. ¹² For wisdom keeps one from danger just as money keeps one from danger. But the good thing about much learning is that wisdom keeps alive those who have it. ¹³ Think of the work of God, for who is able to make straight what He has not made straight? ¹⁴ In the day of well-being be happy. But in the day of trouble, think about this: God has made the one as well as the other, so that man can never know what is going to happen.

¹⁵ In the days of my life I have seen everything, but my life has been worth nothing. There is a right and good man who is destroyed while he is right and good. And there is a sinful man who lives long in his wrong-doing. ¹⁶ Do not be too right and good, and do not be too wise. Why should you destroy yourself? ¹⁷ Do not be too sinful, and do not be a fool. Why should you die before your time? ¹⁸ It is good that you take hold of one thing, and do not let go of the other. For the one who fears God will have both of them.

¹⁹ Wisdom gives more strength to a wise man than ten rulers have in a city. ²⁰ For sure there is not a right and good man on earth who always does good and never sins. ²¹ Do not listen to all the things that are said, or you might hear your servant cursing you. ²² For you know in your heart that many times you have cursed others.

²³ I tested all this with wisdom, and I said, "I will be wise," but it was far from me. ²⁴ Wisdom has been far away and hidden. Who can find it? ²⁵ I turned my mind to know, to find out, and to look for wisdom and the reason of things, and to know how sinful it is to be foolish, and that being mad is foolish. ²⁶ And I found that the woman whose heart is traps and nets, and whose hands are chains is more bitter than death. He who pleases God will get away from her. But the sinner will be taken in by her.

²⁷ "See, I have found this out," says the Preacher. "I have added one thing to another to find the reason, ²⁸ which I am still looking for but have not found. I have found one man among a thousand, but I have not found a woman among all these. ²⁹ See, I have found only this, that God made men right, but they have found many sinful ways."

8 Who is like the wise man? And who understands the meaning of anything? A man's wisdom makes his face shine. The hard look on his face is changed.

Obey the King

² I say, "Obey the words of the king because of the promise you made to God. ³ Do not be in a hurry to leave him. Do not join in wrong-doing, for he will do whatever he pleases." ⁴ Since the king's word is powerful, who will say to him, "What are you doing?"

⁵ He who obeys the king's law will have no trouble, for a wise heart knows the right time and way. ⁶ For there is a right time and way for everything, even if a man's trouble is heavy upon him. ⁷ If no one knows what will happen, who can tell him when it will happen? ⁸ No man has the right and power to hold back the wind with the wind, or power over the day of his death. No man is free to leave in

the time of war. And sin will not take the sinner out of trouble. 9 All this I have seen while thinking about every work that has been done under the sun. There is a time when one man has power over another man and makes him suffer.

Death Comes to Everyone

10 Then I saw the sinful buried, who used to go in and out of the holy place. They are soon forgotten in the city where they did this. This also is for nothing. 11 Because a sinful act is not punished in a hurry, so the hearts of the sons of men are given completely over to sin. 12 Even though a sinner does sinful things a hundred times and lives a long time, still I know that it will be well for those who fear God, and let others know they fear God. 13 But it will not go well for the sinful man. His days will not be long like a shadow, because he does not fear God. 14 There is something that is of no use on the earth: There are right and good men who have the same thing happen to them that happens to those who do sinful things. And there are sinful men who have the same thing happen to them that happens to those who are right and good. I say this also is for nothing. 15 So I say a man should enjoy himself. For there is nothing good for a man under the sun except to eat and drink and be happy. For this will be with him in his work through the days of his life which God has given him under the sun.

16 I gave my heart to know wisdom and to see the work which has been done on the earth, not sleeping day or night. 17 And I saw all the work of God and knew that man cannot even think of all that is done under the sun. Even if man tries hard to find out, he will not be able to. Even if a wise man says he knows, he does not.

9 For I have thought of all this, how good and wise men and their works are in the hand of God. Man does not know if love or hate is waiting for them.

2 It is the same for all. The same thing will happen to both the man who is good and the man who is sinful. The same thing will happen to the clean and the unclean, and to the man who gives a gift on the altar and to the man who does not. As the good man is, so is the sinner. As the man who swears, so is the one who is afraid to swear. 3 This is a bad thing in all that is done under the sun, that the same thing happens to all men. Also the hearts of men

are sinful and crazy all their lives. Then they join the dead. 4 But there is hope for the one who is among the living. For sure a live dog is better off than a dead lion. 5 For the living know they will die. But the dead know nothing, and they will receive nothing further, for they are forgotten. 6 Their love and hate and desire have already died. They will no longer have a part in what is done under the sun.

7 Go and eat your bread in happiness. Drink your wine with a happy heart. For God has already been pleased with your works. 8 Let your clothes be white all the time. And let there always be oil on your head. 9 Enjoy life with the woman you love all the days of your life that will soon be over. God has given you these days under the sun. This is the good you will get in life and in your work which you have done under the sun.

10 Whatever your hand finds to do, do it with all your strength. For there is no work or planning or learning or wisdom in the place of the dead where you are going. 11 Again I saw under the sun that the race is not to the fast and the battle to the men of war. Bread is not to the wise and riches are not to the men of understanding. Favor is not to able workers. Time comes and goes and things happen for no reason to them all. 12 Man does not know his time. Like fish caught in a bad net, and birds caught in a trap, so men are trapped at a bad time when trouble comes upon them when they do not expect it.

Wisdom Is Better Than Being Foolish

13 I have also seen this as wisdom under the sun, and it made me think. 14 There was a small city with few men in it, and a great king came to it. His army gathered around it and built a large wall to help them in battle against it. 15 But a poor wise man was found in the city, and he brought the city out of its trouble by his wisdom. Yet no one remembered that poor man. 16 So I said, "Wisdom is better than strength." But the wisdom of the poor man is hated and his words are not carried out. 17 The words of the wise heard in quiet are better than the loud words of a ruler among fools. 18 Wisdom is better than objects used in war, but one sinner destroys much good.

10 Dead flies make a perfume maker's oil smell bad. So does acting a little foolish weigh more than wisdom and honor. 2 A wise man's heart leads him toward the right. But the foolish man's heart leads him toward the left. ³ Even when the fool walks on the road, he has little understanding and shows everyone that he is a fool. ⁴ If the ruler becomes angry with you, do not back away. If you are quiet, much wrong-doing may be put aside.

⁵ There is a sin I have seen under the sun, like a mistake done by a ruler: ⁶ Fools are put in many places of honor, while rich men sit in places that are not important. ⁷ I have seen servants riding on horses, and princes walking like servants on the land.

⁸ He who digs a deep hole may fall into it. And a snake may bite him who breaks through a wall. ⁹ He who cuts stones may be hurt by them. And he who cuts trees may be in danger by them. ¹⁰ If the ax is not sharp and he does not make it sharp, then he must use more strength. Wisdom helps one to do well. ¹¹ If the snake bites before it is put under a man's power, it will not be of help to the man who would have power over it. ¹² The words of a wise man's mouth are kind, but the lips of a fool destroy him. ¹³ The beginning of his talking is foolish, and the end of it is sinful and crazy. ¹⁴ Yet the fool speaks many words. No man knows what will happen. And who can tell him what will come after him? ¹⁵ The work of a fool makes him so tired that he does not even know the way to a city. ¹⁶ It is bad for you, O land, when your king is a child and your princes eat too much in the morning. ¹⁷ Happy are you, O land, when your king is from parents who have ruled, and your princes eat at the right time, for strength and not to get drunk. ¹⁸ When men are lazy, the roof begins to fall in. When they will do no work, the rain comes into the house. ¹⁹ Food is made ready to be enjoyed, wine makes life happy, but money is the answer to everything. ²⁰ Do not curse a king even in your thoughts, and do not curse a rich man in your bedroom because a bird of the heavens will carry your voice and an animal with wings will make it known.

The Ways of a Wise Man

11 Throw your bread upon the waters, for you will find it after many days. ² Share what you have with seven, or even with eight, for you do not know what trouble may come on the earth. ³ If the clouds are full, they pour out rain upon the earth. And if a tree falls to the south or to the north, wherever the tree falls, there it lies. ⁴ He who watches the wind will not plant his seeds. And he who looks at the clouds will not gather the food. ⁵ Just as you do not know the path of the wind or how the bones are made of a child yet to be born, so you do not know the work of God Who makes all things. ⁶ Plant your seeds in the morning, and do not be lazy in the evening. You do not know which will grow well, the morning or evening planting, or if both of them will do well.

⁷ Light is pleasing. It is good for the eyes to see the sun. ⁸ If a man should live many years, let him have joy in them all. Yet let him remember the days of darkness, for they will be many. All that comes is for nothing.

What Young People Should Do

⁹ Young man, be filled with joy while you are young. And let your heart be happy while you are a young man. Follow the ways of your heart and the desires of your eyes. But know that God will judge you for all these things. ¹⁰ So put away trouble from your heart, and put away pain from your body. Because the years when you were a child and the best years of your life are going by fast.

12 Remember also your Maker while you are young, before the days of trouble come and the years when you will say, "I have no joy in them," ² before the sun, the light, the moon and the stars are made dark, and clouds return after the rain. ³ This will be the day when the men who watch the house shake in fear. Strong men bow. Those who grind will stop because they are few. And the eyes of those who look through windows will not see well. ⁴ The doors on the street will be shut when the sound of the grinding is no more. One will rise up at the sound of a bird. All the daughters of song will sing very low. ⁵ Men will be afraid of a high place and of fears on the road. Flowers will grow on the almond tree. The grasshopper will pull himself along. And desire will be at an end. For man will go to his home that lasts forever, while people filled with sorrow go about in the street. ⁶ Remember Him before the silver rope of life is broken and the gold dish is crushed. Remember Him before the pot by the well is broken and the wheel by the water-hole is crushed. ⁷ Then the dust will return to the earth as it was. And the spirit will return to God Who gave it. ⁸ "It is of no use," says the Preacher, "It is all for nothing!"

The Preacher's Last Words

9 Besides being a wise man, the Preacher also taught the people much learning. He thought about, and looked for, and put together many wise sayings. 10 The Preacher looked to find pleasing words and to write words of truth in the right way.

11 The words of wise men are like a stick. Their gathered sayings are like well-driven nails given by one Shepherd. 12 But more than this, my son, be careful. There is no end to the writing of many books and reading many of them makes the body tired.

13 The last word, after all has been heard, is: Honor God and obey His Laws. This is all that every person must do. 14 For God will judge every act, even everything which is hidden, both good and bad.

SONG OF SOLOMON

1 The Song of Songs, the most beautiful of them all, which is Solomon's.

The First Song

The Woman

2 "May he kiss me with the kisses of his mouth! For your love is better than wine. 3 Your oils have a pleasing smell. Your name is like oil poured out. So the young women love you. 4 Take me away with you, and let us run together. The king has brought me into his room.

"We will have joy and be glad because of you. We will praise your love more than wine. They are right to love you.

5 "I am dark but beautiful, O people of Jerusalem, like the tents of Kedar, like the curtains of Solomon. 6 Do not look hard at me because I am dark, for the sun has burned me. My mother's sons were angry with me, and made me take care of the grape-fields. But I have not taken care of my own grape-field. 7 Tell me, O you whom my soul loves. In what field do you feed your flock? Where do your sheep lie down at noon? Why should I need to look for you beside the flocks of your friends?"

King Solomon

8 "If you do not know, most beautiful among women, follow the path of the flock. And let your young goats eat in the field beside the tents of the shepherds.

9 "To me, my love, you are like my horse among the war-wagons of Pharaoh. 10 Your face is beautiful with the objects you wear, and your neck with the beautiful chain around it. 11 We will make objects of gold and silver for you."

The Woman

12 "While the king was at his table, my perfume gave out its smell. 13 My loved one is like a jar of perfume to me, who lies all night between my breasts. 14 My loved one is to me like many henna flowers, in the grape-fields of Engedi."

King Solomon

15 "How beautiful you are, my love! How beautiful you are! Your eyes are like doves."

The Woman

16 "How beautiful you are, my love, and so pleasing! Our bed is green. 17 The pillars of our house are cedars. The pieces on our roof are pine.

2 "I am the rose of Sharon, the lily of the valleys."

King Solomon

2 "Like a lily among the thorns, so is my loved one among the young women."

The Woman

3 "Like a fruit tree among many trees, so is my loved one among the young men. With much joy I sat down in his shadow And his fruit was sweet to my taste. 4 He brought me to his special large room for eating, and his colors over me were love. 5 Make me strong with cakes of dried grapes. Make me strong again with fruit, because I am sick with love. 6 Let his left hand be under my head and his right hand hold me close."

King Solomon

7 "I tell you, O daughters of Jerusalem, by the gazelles and deer of the field, you must not wake up my love until it is pleasing to her."

The Second Song

The Woman

8 "Listen, it is the voice of my loved one! See, he is coming! He is running over the

mountains, jumping across the hills. 9 My love is like a gazelle or a young deer. See, he is standing behind our wall. He is looking through the windows, through the wood cross-pieces.

10 "My love speaks and says to me, 'Get up, my love, my beautiful one, and come with me. 11 For see, the winter is past. The rain is over and gone. 12 The flowers are coming through the ground. The time for singing has come. The voice of the turtle-dove has been heard in our land. 13 The fig tree has its fruits. The flowers on the vines spread their sweet smell. Get up, my love, my beautiful one, and come with me! 14 O my dove, hidden in the rock, in the secret place in the mountain-side, let me see you. Let me hear your voice. For your voice is sweet, and you are beautiful.

15 'Catch the foxes for us, the little foxes that are destroying our grape-fields, for the flowers are on the vines. 16 My love is mine, and I am his. He lets his flock eat among the lilies. 17 Until the morning comes and the shadows hurry away, turn, my love. Be like a gazelle or a young deer on the mountains of Bether.' "

The Woman

3 "On my bed night after night I looked for him whom my soul loves. I looked for him but did not find him. 2 'I must get up now and go about the city, in the streets and in the open places. I must look for him whom my soul loves.' I looked for him but did not find him. 3 The men who watch over the city found me, and I said, 'Have you seen him whom my soul loves?' 4 I had just passed them when I found him whom my soul loves. I held on to him and would not let him go, until I had brought him to my mother's house, and into the room of her who gave birth to me."

King Solomon

5 "I tell you, O daughters of Jerusalem, by the gazelles or the deer of the field, you must not wake up my love until it is pleasing to her."

The Third Song

The Woman

6 "What is this coming up from the desert like smoke? It has the smell of special perfumes, with all the perfumes of the traders. 7 See, it is the traveling wagon of Solomon. Sixty of the strong men of Israel are around it. 8 All of them use the sword

and are very able in war. Each man has his sword at his side, keeping watch against trouble in the night. 9 King Solomon has made for himself a beautiful wagon from the wood of Lebanon. 10 He made its long pieces of silver, its back of gold, and its seat of purple cloth. The inside of it was made beautiful by the daughters of Jerusalem. 11 Go out, O daughters of Zion, and look at King Solomon as he wears the crown his mother put on his head on the day of his wedding, on the day his heart was glad."

King Solomon

4 "How beautiful you are, my love! How beautiful you are! Your eyes are like doves behind your face-covering. Your hair is like a flock of goats coming down from Mount Gilead. 2 Your teeth are like a flock of sheep that have just had their wool cut and have come up from their washing. All have given birth to two lambs, and not one among them has lost her young. 3 Your lips are like a bright red string. Your mouth is beautiful. The sides of your face are like a piece of a pomegranate under your covering. 4 Your neck is like the tower of David, built with beauty. On it hang a thousand battle-coverings, the coverings of men of war. 5 Your two breasts are like two young deer, the two young ones of a gazelle, that eat among the lilies. 6 Until the morning comes and the shadows hurry away, I will go to the mountain of perfume plants, to the hill of special perfume.

7 "You are all beautiful, my love. You are perfect. 8 Come with me from Lebanon, my bride. May you come with me from Lebanon. Travel down from the top of Amana, from the top of Senir and Hermon, from the homes of lions, from the mountain homes of leopards. 9 You have made my heart beat faster, my sister, my bride. You have made my heart beat faster with one look from your eyes, with one piece of the beautiful chain around your neck. 10 How beautiful is your love, my sister, my bride! How much better is your love than wine, and the sweet smell of your oils than all kinds of spices! 11 Honey comes from your lips, my bride. Honey and milk are under your tongue. And the sweet smell of your clothing is like the smell of Lebanon. 12 A garden closed and locked is my sister, my bride, a garden shut up and covered over. 13 Your young branches are a garden of pomegranates with all the best fruits, henna with nard plants. 14 There is nard and saffron, calamus and cinnamon,

with all the trees of frankincense, myrrh and aloes, with all the best spices. 15 You are a garden well, a well of flowing water, and rivers coming from Lebanon."

The Woman

16 "Wake up, O north wind! Come, south wind! Blow upon my garden so the sweet smells will spread far. May my loved one come into his garden and eat its best fruits."

King Solomon

5 "I have come into my garden, my sister, my bride. I have gathered my perfume with my spice. I have eaten my honey and the comb. I have drunk my wine and my milk. Eat and drink, friends. Drink much, O lovers."

The Fourth Song

The Woman

2 "I was asleep, but my heart was awake. A voice! My love was knocking: 'Open to me, my sister, my love, my dove, my perfect one! For my head is wet from the water on the grass in the early morning. My hair is wet from the night.' 3 I have taken off my dress. How can I put it on again? I have washed my feet. Should I get them dirty again? 4 My love put his hand through the opening, and joy filled my heart. 5 I got up to let my love in, and perfume fell from my hands. Wet perfume fell from my fingers onto the lock. 6 I opened the door to my love, but he had already gone! My heart went out to him as he spoke. I looked for him, but did not find him. I called him, but he did not answer me. 7 The watchmen of the city found me. They beat me and hurt me. The watchmen of the walls took my coat from me. 8 I tell you, O daughters of Jerusalem, if you find my loved one, you must tell him that I am weak with love."

Women of Jerusalem

9 "What is your loved one more than another loved one, O most beautiful among women? What is your loved one more than another loved one, that you tell us to do this?"

The Woman

10 "My loved one is bright and red, the best among 10,000. 11 His head is like gold, pure gold. His hair has waves and is black as a raven. 12 His eyes are like doves beside rivers of water, washed in milk, and resting

in their places. 13 His cheeks are like beds of spices, with sweet-smelling plants. His lips are like lily flowers giving off drops of perfume. 14 His hands are strong pieces of gold set with stones of much worth. His body is made of ivory set with stones of much worth. 15 His legs are pillars of clay put on bases of pure gold. He looks like Lebanon, as beautiful as the cedar trees. 16 His mouth is very sweet, everything about him is pleasing. This is my loved one and this is my friend, O daughters of Jerusalem."

Women of Jerusalem

6 "Where has your loved one gone, O most beautiful among women? Where has your loved one turned, that we may look for him with you?"

The Woman

2 "My love has gone down to his garden, to the beds of spices. He has gone to feed his flock in the gardens and to gather lilies. 3 I am my love's, and my love is mine, he who feeds his flock among the lilies."

The Fifth Song

King Solomon

4 "You are as beautiful as Tirzah, my love, as beautiful as Jerusalem. You are to be feared as an army with flags. 5 Turn your eyes away from me, for they trouble me. Your hair is like a flock of goats that has come down from Gilead. 6 Your teeth are like a flock of sheep which has come up from the washing. All of them give birth to two lambs at a time, and not one of them has lost her young. 7 The sides of your forehead are like a piece of a pomegranate behind your face-covering. 8 There are sixty queens, and eighty women kept who act like wives, and there are too many young women to number who have never had a man. 9 But my dove, my perfect one, is special. She is her mother's only daughter. She is the pure child of the one who gave birth to her. The young women saw her and knew she was honored. The queens and the women who act as wives praised her, saying, 10 'Who is this that looks out like the first light of day? She is as beautiful as the full moon, as pure as the sun. She is to be feared as an army with flags.'"

The Woman

11 "I went down to the field of nut trees to see the flowers of the valley, to see if the

vines or the pomegranates had flowers.
12 Before I knew it, I wanted to be over the
war-wagons of the princes of my people."

Women of Jerusalem

13 "Return, return, O Shulammite! Return,
return, that we may look upon you!"

The Woman

"Why should you look upon the Shulammite, as upon a dance in front of two
armies?"

King Solomon

7 "How beautiful are your feet in their
shoes, O daughter! Your legs are like
stones of much worth, the work of an able
workman. 2 Your navel is like a beautiful
glass full of wine. Your stomach is like
gathered grain with lilies around it. 3 Your
two breasts are like two young deer, the
two young ones of a gazelle. 4 Your neck
is like a tower of ivory. Your eyes are like
the pools in Heshbon by the gate of Bath-
rabbim. Your nose is like the tower of
Lebanon, which looks toward Damascus.
5 Your head crowns you like Carmel. Your
flowing hair is like strings of purple. The
king is held by the beauty of your hair.
6 How beautiful and how pleasing you are,
my love! How happy you make me! 7 You
stand like a palm tree. And your breasts
are like its fruit. 8 I said, 'I will go to the
top of the palm tree. I will take hold of its
branches.' O, may your breasts be like the
fruit of the vine, and the sweet smell of
your breath like pleasing fruit. 9 And may
your mouth be like the best wine."

The Woman

"For my love, it is smooth going down,
flowing through the lips while sleeping.

10 "I am my love's, and he wants me.
11 Come, my love, let us go to the country.
Let us spend the night in the villages. 12 Let
us get up early and go to the grape-fields.
Let us see if the buds are on the vines, and
if its flowers have opened. Let us see if the
pomegranates have flowers. There I will
give you my love. 13 The mandrakes have
given out their sweet smell. And over our
doors are all the best fruits, both new and
old, which I have saved for you, my love.

8 "O that you were like a brother to me,
who nursed from my mother's breasts!
If I found you outside, I would kiss you,
and no one would hate me. 2 I would lead
you and bring you into the house of my

mother, who used to teach me. I would
give you wine with spices to drink, made
from my pomegranates. 3 Let his left hand
be under my head, and his right hand hold
me close."

King Solomon

4 "I tell you, O daughters of Jerusalem.
You must not wake up my love, until it is
pleasing to her."

The Sixth Song

Women of Jerusalem

5 "Who is this coming up from the desert,
resting on her loved one?"

The Woman

"I woke you up under the fruit tree. There
your mother suffered and gave birth to
you. 6 Put me over your heart and on your
arm, never to be taken off. For love is as
strong as death. Jealousy is as hard as the
grave. Its bright light is like the light of fire,
the very fire of the Lord. 7 Many waters
cannot put out love. Rivers cannot cover it.
If a man were to give all the riches of his
house for love, it would all be hated."

The Woman's Brothers

8 "We have a little sister, and she has no
breasts. What should we do for our sister
on the day when she is promised in marriage? 9 If she is a wall, we should build on
her a tower of silver. But if she is a door,
we should cover her with strong pieces of
cedar wood."

The Woman

10 "I was a wall, and my breasts were like
towers. Then I was in his eyes as one who
finds peace."

The Woman's Brothers

11 "Solomon has a grape-field at Baal-
hamon. He put the grape-field into the
care of certain men. Each one was to bring
1,000 pieces of silver for its fruit. 12 My own
grape-field is for myself. The 1,000 pieces
of silver are for you, Solomon. And 200 are
for those who take care of its fruit."

13 "O you who sit in the gardens, my
friends are listening for your voice. Let me
hear it."

The Woman

14 "Hurry, my love. Be like a gazelle or a
young deer on the mountains of spices."

ISAIAH

The Sinful Nation of Judah

1 This is the special dream of Isaiah the son of Amoz, about Judah and Jerusalem, which he saw during the rule of Uzziah, Jotham, Ahaz, and Hezekiah, kings of Judah.

2 Listen, O heavens, and hear, O earth, for the Lord has spoken: "I have brought up and have taken care of sons, but they have turned against Me. 3 An ox knows its owner. A donkey knows where to find the food its owner gives it. But Israel does not know. My people do not understand." 4 O sinful nation, people weighed down with sin, children of those who do wrong, sons who act in a sinful way! They have left the Lord. They have hated the Holy One of Israel. They have turned away from Him.

5 Where will you be punished again, since you still fight against the Lord? Your whole head is sick, and your whole heart is weak. 6 From the bottom of the foot even to the head, there is no good part. There are only sores from beatings and open sores. They are not taken care of or covered or made soft with oil.

7 Your land lies waste. Your cities are burned with fire. Strangers are eating the food of your fields in front of you. It lies waste, as destroyed by strangers. 8 The people of Zion are left like a tent in a grape-field, like a watchman's house in a vegetable field, like a city closed in by armies. 9 If the Lord of All had not left some people, we would have all been destroyed like those who lived in the cities of Sodom and Gomorrah.

10 Hear the Word of the Lord, you rulers of Sodom. Listen to the teaching of our God, you people of Gomorrah. 11 What are your many gifts given in worship to Me?" says the Lord. "I have had enough burnt gifts of rams and the fat of cattle. And I am not pleased with the blood of bulls, lambs, or goats. 12 When you come to show yourselves before Me, who says you must walk and walk around My open spaces? 13 Do not bring your gifts of no worth any more. Your special perfume is a hated thing to Me. The new moon and Day of Rest, this calling together of the people, I cannot put up with. I cannot put up with your sin and your meetings of worship. 14 I hate your new moons and your special suppers. They have become heavy upon Me. I am tired of carrying them. 15 So when you spread out your hands in prayer, I will hide My eyes from you. Even if you pray many times, I will not listen. Your hands are full of blood.

16 "Wash yourselves. Make yourselves clean. Take your sinful actions from My eyes. Stop doing sinful things. 17 Learn to do good. Look for what is right and fair. Speak strong words to those who make it hard for people. Stand up for the rights of those who have no parents. Help the woman whose husband has died. 18 "Come now, let us think about this together," says the Lord. "Even though your sins are bright red, they will be as white as snow. Even though they are dark red, they will be like wool. 19 If you are willing and obey, you will eat the best of the land. 20 But if you are not willing and turn against Me, you will be destroyed by the sword." For the mouth of the Lord has spoken.

The Sinful City

21 The faithful city has become like a woman who sells the use of her body. At one time she was full of what was right and fair! Those who are right and good lived in her, but now those who kill. 22 Your silver has lost its worth. Your wine is mixed with water. 23 Your rulers have turned against what is right. They are the friends of robbers. Every one loves to get pay in secret for wrong-doing, and they run after gifts. They do not stand for the rights of those who have no parents. And they never hear the cry for help of the woman whose husband has died.

24 So the Lord God of All, the Powerful One of Israel, says, "I will put an end to those who fight against Me. I will punish those who hate Me. 25 I will turn My hand against you and burn what is of no worth in you. And I will take away from you all that is not pure. 26 Then I will give you judges as at the first, and your wise men as at the beginning. After that you will be called the city that is right and good, a faithful city."

27 Zion will be saved by being fair. Those who are sorry for their sins and turn from them will be saved by being right and good. 28 But wrong-doers and sinners will be crushed together. Those who turn away from the Lord will come to an end. 29 For you will be ashamed of the oaks where you worshiped. You will be ashamed of the gardens you have chosen. 30 For you will be like an oak tree whose leaf dries up, or like a garden that has no water. 31 The strong man will become easy to burn, and his work also a fire. They will burn together, and there will be no one to put the fire out.

The Mountain of the House of God

2 This is what Isaiah the son of Amoz saw about Judah and Jerusalem that was coming: 2 In the last days, the mountain of the house of the Lord will be the most important of the mountains. It will be raised above the hills. All the nations will come to it. 3 Many people will come and say, "Come, let us go up to the mountain of the Lord, to the house of the God of Jacob. Then He will teach us about His ways, that we may walk in His paths. For the Law will go out from Zion, and the Word of the Lord from Jerusalem." 4 He will judge between the nations, and will decide for many people. And they will beat their swords into plows, and their spears into knives for cutting vines. Nation will not lift up sword against nation, and they will not learn about war anymore.

The Day of the Lord

5 Come, people of Jacob. Let us walk in the light of the Lord. 6 For You have left Your people, the family of Jacob, because they are filled with the sinful ways of the East. They use secret ways to tell the future like the Philistines. And they make agreements with the children of strangers. 7 Their land is filled with silver and gold. There is no end to their riches. Their land is filled with horses also. And there is no end to their war-wagons. 8 Their land is filled with false gods. They worship the work of their hands, that which their fingers have made. 9 So pride has been taken away from the poor man, and important men have been put to shame. Do not forgive them. 10 Go into the rock and hide in the dust from the anger of the Lord and from the shining-greatness of His power. 11 The proud look of man will be put to shame. The pride of men will be taken away. And the Lord alone will be honored in that day.

12 On that day the Lord of All will be against everyone who is proud and feels important, and against all who are honored. They will be put to shame. 13 He will be against all the cedar trees of Lebanon that are tall and honored, and against all the oak trees of Bashan. 14 He will be against all the high mountains, against all the high hills, 15 against every high tower, and against every strong wall. 16 He will be against all the ships of Tarshish, and against all the beautiful boats. 17 The pride of man will be taken away. What men honor will be put to shame. The Lord alone will be honored in that day. 18 All the

false gods will be gone. 19 Men will go into the caves of the rocks and into holes of the earth because of the anger of the Lord and the shining-greatness of His power when He rises up to shake the earth. 20 In that day men will take their false gods of silver and gold which they made for themselves to worship and will throw them away to the moles and the bats. 21 They will go into the caves of the rocks and mountains. They will try to hide from the anger of the Lord and from the shining-greatness of His power, when He rises up to shake the earth. 22 Stop trusting in man. He has only a breath in his nose. Why should he be honored?

God Will Remove the Leaders of Judah

3 See, the Lord, the Lord God of All, is going to take away from Jerusalem and Judah all they have to keep themselves alive and safe, all the bread and all the water. 2 He will take away the strong man, the man of war, the man who judges, the man who tells what will happen in the future, the man who uses secret ways, and the leader. 3 He will take away the captain of fifty, the man of honor, the wise man, the able workman, and the one who uses secret powers. 4 I will make boys their rulers. Foolish children will rule over them. 5 The people will make it hard for each other. Each one will hurt the other, and each one will be hurt by his neighbor. The younger will show anger toward the older. And the man who is not respected will show anger toward the man of honor.

6 A man will take hold of his brother in his father's house, saying, "You have a coat. You will be our ruler. This destroyed city will be under your rule." 7 In that day he will call out, "I can not be of help to you. For in my house there is no bread or coat. You should not choose me to be ruler of the people." 8 For Jerusalem has no strength, and Judah has fallen, because their speaking and their actions are against the Lord. They have turned against His shining-greatness. 9 The look on their faces speaks against them. They show their sin like Sodom. They do not even hide it. It is bad for them! For they have brought trouble upon themselves. 10 Tell those who are right and good that it will go well for them. For they will enjoy the fruit of what they do. 11 It will be bad for the sinful man! It will not go well for him, for what he has done will be done to him. 12 O My people! Children make

it hard for them. And women rule over them. O My people! Your leaders lead you in the wrong way. You do not know which path to take.

The Lord Will Judge His People

13 The Lord is ready to say what He thinks and stands to judge the people. 14 The Lord judges the leaders and rulers of His people: "It is you who have destroyed the grape-field. What had belonged to the poor is in your houses. 15 What do you mean by crushing My people, and grinding the faces of the poor?" says the Lord God of All.

Women of Jerusalem Will Suffer

16 The Lord said, "The daughters of Zion are proud. They walk with heads held high and a wrong desire in their eyes. They walk with short steps, making noise with the chains on their ankles. 17 So the Lord will make sores come upon the heads of the daughters of Zion, and take the hair from their head. 18 In that day the Lord will take away the beauty of their ankle chains, headbands, moon-like objects, 19 rings worn on their ears and arms, face-coverings, 20 head-dresses, leg-chains, wide belts, perfume boxes, objects with secret powers, 21 finger rings, nose rings, 22 bright clothing, coats, money-bags, 23 hand mirrors, underclothes, head-coverings, and face-coverings. 24 Instead of sweet perfume there will be a bad smell. Instead of a belt there will be a rope. Instead of well set hair there will be no hair. Instead of fine clothes they will wear cloth made from hair. And there will be burnt marks instead of beauty. 25 Your men will fall by the sword. Your strong ones will fall in battle. 26 Jerusalem's gates will be filled with sorrow. She will sit on the ground, laid waste and empty.

Jerusalem to Have Its Shining-Greatness Again

4 Seven women will take hold of one man in that day, saying, "We will eat our own bread and wear our own clothes. Only let us be called by your name. Take away our shame!"

2 In that day the Branch of the Lord will be beautiful and shining with greatness. The fruit of the earth will be the pride and the beauty of those of Israel who are still alive. 3 He who is left in Zion and stays in Jerusalem will be called holy, everyone who has been written down among the living in Jerusalem. 4 The Lord will wash away the sin of the daughters of Zion. He will wash away the blood that was shed in Jerusalem, by the spirit of punishment and the spirit of fire. 5 Then the Lord will cover the whole land of Mount Zion and her people with a cloud of smoke during the day, and a bright fire that shines during the night. The Lord's shining-greatness will cover everything. 6 It will be a covering from the heat during the day and it will keep the people safe from the storm and the rain.

The Song of the Grape-Field

5 Let me sing for my loved one a love song about His grape-field: My loved one had a grape-field on a hill that grows much fruit. 2 He dug all around it and took away its stones, and planted it with the best vine. He built a tower in the center of it, and cut out a place in it for crushing grapes. Then He expected it to give good grapes, but it gave only wild grapes.

3 "And now, O people living in Jerusalem and men of Judah, judge between Me and My grape-field. 4 What more was there to do for My grape-field that I have not done for it? When I expected it to give good grapes, why did it give wild grapes? 5 Now I will tell you what I am going to do to My grape-field. I will take away its fence and it will be destroyed. I will break down its wall and it will be crushed under foot. 6 I will make it a waste. It will not be taken care of, and thistles and thorns will come up. I will also tell the clouds not to rain on it."

7 For the grape-field of the Lord of All is the people of Israel, and the men of Judah are the vines He planted. So He looked for what is right and fair, but He saw blood poured out. He looked for what is right and good, but He heard a cry of those in trouble.

It Is Bad for the Sinful

8 It is bad for those who join house to house and field to field until there is no empty space, and you have to live alone in the land. 9 The Lord of All has sworn in my ears, "For sure, many houses will be laid waste. Large and beautiful houses will be empty. 10 For ten fields of vines will give only eleven large bottles of wine. And 110 jars of seed will give only eleven jars of grain." 11 It is bad for those who get up early in the morning to run after strong drink! It is bad for those who stay

up late in the evening that they may get drunk! 12 They have harps, a noise-maker, a horn, and wine at their special suppers. But they do not think about the works of the Lord. They do not think of the work of His hands.

13 So My people are taken away to strange lands because they have not been wise. Their men of honor are dying because they are hungry. Their people are dried up because they are thirsty. 14 So the grave has become larger and has opened its mouth wide. And Jerusalem's greatness, her people, her sounds of wild joy, and those who are happy with sin go down into it. 15 Man's pride will be taken away. Important men will be put to shame. The eyes of the proud also will be put to shame. 16 But the Lord of All will be honored in what is right and fair. The holy God will show Himself holy in what is right and good. 17 Then the lambs will eat as in their field. And strangers will eat in the waste places of the rich.

18 It is bad for those who pull sin along with ropes of lies, who pull wrong-doing as with a wagon rope, 19 who say, "Let Him hurry. Let Him be quick to do His work, that we may see it. Let the plan of the Holy One of Israel be done, that we may know it!" 20 It is bad for those who call what is sinful good, and good sinful, who say dark is light and light is dark, who make bitter sweet, and sweet bitter! 21 It is bad for those who are wise in their own eyes, and who think they know a lot! 22 It is bad for those who are good at drinking wine, and are proud as they mix strong drink! 23 They take money in secret for saying that bad people are good. And they take away the rights of those who are not guilty.

24 So, as fire destroys what is left of the cut grain and dry grass falls into the fire, so their root will waste away and their flower blow away like dust. For they have turned away from the Law of the Lord of All. They have hated the Word of the Holy One of Israel. 25 Because of this the anger of the Lord has burned against His people. He has put out His hand against them and destroyed them. The mountains shook. Their dead bodies lay like waste in the center of the streets. For all this His anger is not turned away but His hand is still put out.

26 He will raise up flags as a sign to the nations far away. He will call for them from the ends of the earth, and they will hurry to come. 27 Not one of them is tired or falls. No one sleeps. Not a belt is loosened at the waist, or a shoe string broken. 28 Their arrows are sharp, and their bows are ready. The feet of their horses are like hard stone. And the wheels of their war-wagons are like a strong wind. 29 Their noise is like that of a female lion. They sound like young lions. They make an angry noise as they take their food, and carry it away where no one can take it from them. 30 In that day they will make an angry noise over it like the noise of the sea. If one looks to the land, he will see darkness and trouble. Even the light is made dark by its clouds.

Isaiah Called to Be a Man Who Speaks for God

6 In the year of King Uzziah's death, I saw the Lord sitting on a throne, high and honored. His long clothing spread out and filled the house of God. 2 Seraphim stood above Him, each having six wings. With two he covered his face, and with two he covered his feet, and with two he flew. 3 One called out to another and said, "Holy, holy, holy, is the Lord of All. The whole earth is full of His shining-greatness." 4 And the base of the doorways shook at the voice of him who called out, while the house of God was filled with smoke. 5 Then I said, "It is bad for me, for I am destroyed! Because I am a man whose lips are unclean. And I live among a people whose lips are unclean. For my eyes have seen the King, the Lord of All."

6 Then one of the seraphim flew to me, with a burning coal which he had taken from the altar using a special tool. 7 He touched my mouth with it, and said, "See, this has touched your lips, and your guilt is taken away. Your sin is forgiven." 8 Then I heard the voice of the Lord, saying, "Whom should I send? Who will go for Us?" Then I said, "Here am I. Send me!" 9 He said, "Go, and tell these people, 'You hear and hear but do not understand. You look and look but do not see.' 10 Make the hearts of these people hard. May their ears hear little and their eyes see little. Or they will see with their eyes and hear with their ears and understand with their hearts, and turn again and be healed." 11 Then I said, "Lord, how long?" And He answered, "Until cities are destroyed and empty, and until houses are without people and the land is laid waste. 12 Until the Lord has taken men far away, and there are many

places with no people in the land. 13 Yet one-tenth part of the people will stay in it. But it will be burned again, like an oak tree whose roots are still there when it is cut down. The holy seed is all that will be left (of Israel)."

Isaiah Is Sent to King Ahaz

7 In the days of Ahaz the son of Jotham, son of Uzziah, king of Judah, King Rezin of Syria and Pekah the son of Remaliah, king of Israel, went up to make war against Jerusalem. But they could not win the battle. 2 When the family of David was told, "Syria has joined with Ephraim," his heart and the hearts of his people shook as trees shake with the wind.

3 Then the Lord said to Isaiah, "Now you and your son Shear-jashub go out to meet Ahaz at the end of the ditch of the upper pool on the road to the Fuller's Field. 4 Say to him, 'Be careful and quiet. Do not be afraid or weak in your heart because of these two pieces of burnt and smoking wood. Do not be afraid of the burning anger of Rezin and Syria and the son of Remaliah. 5 Syria, with Ephraim and the son of Remaliah, have made sinful plans against you, saying, 6 "Let us go up against Judah and make the people very afraid. Let us break open its walls, and make the son of Tabeel its king." 7 But the Lord God says, "This plan will not work. It will not happen. 8 For the head of Syria is Damascus and the head of Damascus is Rezin. (Within another sixty-five years Ephraim will be destroyed so that it is no longer a people.) 9 The head of Ephraim is Samaria. And the head of Samaria is the son of Remaliah. If you will not believe, for sure you will not last." ' "

Word about Immanuel

10 Then the Lord spoke again to Ahaz, saying, 11 "Ask for something special to see from the Lord your God. Ask for it to be as deep as the place of the dead or as high as heaven." 12 But Ahaz said, "I will not ask. I will not test the Lord." 13 Then Isaiah said, "Listen now, O people of David! Is it too small a thing for you to test men, that you will test my God as well? 14 So the Lord Himself will give you a special thing to see: A young woman, who has never had a man, will give birth to a son. She will give Him the name Immanuel. 15 He will eat milk and honey when He knows enough to have nothing to do with wrong-doing and chooses good. 16 For before the boy

knows to turn away from what is bad and choose good, the land whose two kings you are afraid of will be left empty." 17 The Lord will bring upon you and your people and your father's house such days as have never come since the day that Ephraim was divided from Judah. He is going to bring the king of Assyria on you. 18 In that day the Lord will call for flies that are in the farthest part of the rivers of Egypt, and for bees that are in the land of Assyria. 19 They will all come and stay in the narrow valleys, on the hill-sides, on the thorn bushes, and in the fields.

20 In that day the Lord will use the king of Assyria from the other side of the Euphrates to cut off the hair from your head, your legs, and your face.

21 In that day a man will keep alive a young cow and two sheep. 22 And because they give much milk, he will have all he can use. For everyone who is left in the land will have milk and honey to eat. 23 In that day, every place where there used to be a thousand vines, worth a thousand pieces of silver, will be thistles and thorns. 24 Men will go there with bows and arrows because all the land will be covered with thistles and thorns. 25 As for all the hills which used to be cared for as a garden, you will not go there for fear of thistles and thorns. They will become a place where cattle feed and where sheep will run.

Assyria Will Take the Land

8 Then the Lord said to me, "Take a large piece of stone and write on it in easy-to-read letters: 'They hurry to get what they can. They run to pick up what is left.' " 2 And I took men who could be trusted to watch the writing, Uriah the religious leader and Zechariah the son of Jeberechiah. 3 Then I went to the woman who spoke for God, and she was able to have a child, and gave birth to a son. Then the Lord said to me, "Name him Maher-shalal-hashbaz. 4 For before the boy knows how to cry out 'My father' or 'My mother,' the riches of Damascus and everything of any worth in Samaria will be carried away by the king of Assyria."

5 The Lord spoke to me again, saying, 6 "These people have turned away from the gentle, flowing waters of Shiloah, and find joy in Rezin and the son of Remaliah. 7 So now, see, the Lord is ready to bring on them the strong and powerful waters of the Euphrates, the king of Assyria and all his greatness. It will rise up high and cause

a flood. 8 Then it will flow into Judah. It will flood and pass through, and come up even to the neck. And the spread of its wings will cover the width of your land, O Immanuel.

9 "Be broken, O people, and be afraid. Listen, all you far places of the earth. Get ready, yet be afraid. Get ready, yet be afraid. 10 Make a plan, but it will come to nothing. Give your plan, but it will not be done. For God is with us."

The People Are Told to Obey

11 For the Lord said this to me with great power, and told me not to walk in the way of these people. He said, 12 "Do not call holy all that these people call holy. Do not fear what they fear, or be afraid of it. 13 It is the Lord of All Whom you should think of as holy. Let Him be the One you fear. He is the One to be afraid of. 14 Then He will become a holy place. But He will be a stone of trouble and a rock to fall over for both houses of Israel. He will be a net and a trap for the people of Jerusalem. 15 Many will fall over them. They will fall and be broken. They will be trapped and caught."

16 Put together what I have said. Hold to my teachings among my followers. 17 I will wait for the Lord Who is hiding His face from the family of Jacob. I trust Him and hope in Him. 18 See, I and the children the Lord has given me are something special to see and a wonder in Israel from the Lord of All, Who lives on Mount Zion.

19 When they say to you, "Ask those who speak in secret with the spirits of the dead and who use their secret ways," should not a people ask their God? Should they speak to the dead for the living? 20 Tell them to put their faith in the teaching and the Law. If they do not speak what this word says, it is because they have no light in them. 21 They will pass through the land troubled and hungry. And when they are hungry, they will be angry and curse their king and their God as they look up. 22 Then they will look to the earth and see trouble and darkness and suffering and will be driven out into darkness.

Birth and Rule of the Prince of Peace

9 But there will be no more heavy hearts for those who were suffering. In the past God allowed the lands of Zebulun and Naphtali to be put to shame. In the future He will honor Galilee where those who are not Jews live and where the road to the sea is. It is on the other side of the Jordan. 2 The people who walk in darkness will see a great light. The light will shine on those living in the land of dark shadows. 3 You will make the nation great. You will give them great joy. They will be glad before You, as with the joy of gathering time, and as men have joy when they divide the riches taken after a battle. 4 For You will break the heavy load from their neck and shoulders. You will break the power of those who made it hard for them, as at the battle of Midian. 5 For every shoe of the soldiers in the battle, and every coat rolled in blood, will be burned in the fire. 6 For to us a Child will be born. To us a Son will be given. And the rule of the nations will be on His shoulders. His name will be called Wonderful, Teacher, Powerful God, Father Who Lives Forever, Prince of Peace. 7 There will be no end to His rule and His peace, upon the throne of David and over his nation. He will build it to last and keep it strong with what is right and fair and good from that time and forever. The work of the Lord of All will do this.

Punishment against Israel

8 The Lord sends word against Jacob, and it falls on Israel. 9 And all the people will know it, that is, Ephraim and the people of Samaria. They say with a proud spirit in their hearts, 10 "The clay blocks have fallen down, but we will build again with smooth stones. The sycamore trees have been cut down, but we will put cedar trees in their place." 11 So the Lord brings men from Rezin to fight against them. He makes those who hate them move to action. 12 The Syrians on the east and the Philistines on the west swallow Israel with an open mouth. Even with this, the Lord's anger does not turn away. His hand is still held out.

13 Yet the people do not return to Him Who punished them. They do not look to the Lord of All. 14 So the Lord will cut off the head and tail from Israel, both palm branch and river-grass in one day. 15 The leaders and men of honor are the head, and the tail is the false preachers who teach lies. 16 For those who lead these people are leading them from the right way, and those who are led by them are going the wrong way. 17 So the Lord is not pleased with their young men. He does not have pity on their children who have no parents or on their women whose husbands have died. Every one of them is without God and does sinful things. Every

mouth speaks foolish words. Even with all this, His anger does not turn away. His hand is still held out.

18 For sin burns like a fire. It burns thistles and thorns. It sets the woods on fire, and they go up in smoke. 19 The land is burned up by the anger of the Lord, and the people are like wood for the fire. No man shows pity on his brother. 20 They take what is on the right hand but still are hungry. They eat what is in the left hand but are not filled. Each of them eats the flesh of his own children. 21 Manasseh goes against Ephraim, and Ephraim goes against Manasseh. And together they are against Judah. Even with all this, the Lord's anger does not turn away. His hand is still held out.

10 It is bad for those who make laws that are not fair. It is bad for those who make it hard for people. 2 They keep what is right and fair from those in need. They take away the rights of the poor of My people. They take from wives after their husbands die, and take what belongs to those who have no parents. 3 Now what will you do in the day of punishment, when the destroying power comes from far away? To whom will you run for help? Where will you leave your riches? 4 Nothing will be left to do but to bow down among those who are being taken to prison, or fall among those who are killed. Even with all this, His anger does not turn away. His hand is still held out.

Assyria Used to Punish Israel

5 It is bad for Assyria. I use Assyria like a stick to punish Israel. 6 I sent it against a nation without God, against the people of My anger. I sent it to take away the riches of battle, and to step hard on the people like dirt in the streets. 7 But this is not what is in Assyria's mind. It does not plan this in its heart. It plans to destroy and to cut off many nations. 8 For it says, "Are not my princes all kings? 9 Is not Calno like Carchemish, or Hamath like Arpad, or Samaria like Damascus? 10 My hand took the nations of the false gods, whose false gods were greater than those of Jerusalem and Samaria. 11 Should I not do to Jerusalem and her gods just as I have done to Samaria and her gods?"

12 So when the Lord has completed all His work on Mount Zion and on Jerusalem, He will punish the proud heart of the king of Assyria and his proud spirit. 13 For

the king has said, "I did this by the power of my hand and by my wisdom, for I have understanding. I moved the land-marks of the people and took their riches. Like a strong man I have brought down those who sat on thrones. 14 My hand has taken the riches of the people like one taken from a nest. I gathered all the earth as one gathers eggs that have been left. And there was not one that moved its wing or opened its mouth or made a sound."

15 Can an ax say it is more important than the one who uses it? Is the saw more important than the one who saws with it? A stick of wood does not lift up a man. A man lifts up a stick. 16 So the Lord, the Lord of All, will send a wasting disease among the strong Assyrian soldiers. Under the king's greatness a fire will be started that will burn and burn. 17 The light of Israel and his Holy One will become a fire. And it will burn and destroy his thorns and thistles in one day. 18 The Lord will destroy the greatness of the trees and the fields that give much fruit, both soul and body. It will be as when a sick man wastes away. 19 And the rest of his trees will be so few that a child could write them down.

A Few of Israel Will Return

20 In that day those of Israel and of the family of Jacob who are still alive will never again trust in the one who destroyed them. But they will trust in the Lord, the Holy One of Israel. 21 Some people, those who are left of Jacob, will return to the powerful God. 22 Even if there are as many Jews as the sand by the sea, only a few of them will return. The plan is to destroy them and it will be right and complete. 23 For the Lord of All will destroy everything in the whole land and do what He planned.

Assyria Will Be Punished

24 So the Lord, the Lord of All, says, "O My people who live in Zion, do not be afraid of the Assyrians when they come to fight against you as the Egyptians did. 25 For in a very little while My anger against you will come to an end and it will be turned to destroy them." 26 The Lord of All will punish them like He punished Midian at the rock of Oreb. His special stick will be over the sea and He will lift it up the way He did in Egypt. 27 In that day the Assyrian's load will be taken from your shoulders and neck, and it will be broken because you are so fat. 28 He has come against

Aiath. He has passed through Migron. At Michmash he left his bags. **29** They have gone through a narrow path. They stayed in Geba during the night. Ramah is afraid, and Gibeah of Saul has run away. **30** Cry out with your voice, O people of Gallim! See, Laishah! Answer her, O Anathoth! **31** Madmenah has run away. The people of Gebim have looked for a safe place. **32** Yet today he will stop at Nob. He shakes his hand at the mountain of the people of Zion, the hill of Jerusalem.

33 See, the Lord, the Lord of All, will cut off the branches with a great noise. Those who stand tall will be cut down. And those who are high will be brought low. **34** He will cut down the many trees with an iron ax. And Lebanon will fall by the Powerful One.

Peace through the One from the Family of Jesse

11 Then One will come from the family of Jesse. A branch will grow out of his roots. **2** And the Spirit of the Lord will rest on Him, the spirit of wisdom and understanding, the spirit of wise words and strength, the spirit of much learning and the fear of the Lord. **3** He will be glad in the fear of the Lord. He will not judge by what His eyes see, or decide by what His ears hear. **4** But He will judge the poor in a right and good way. He will be fair in what He decides for the people of the earth who have much trouble. He will punish the earth with His powerful mouth, and kill the sinful with the breath of His lips. **5** He will wear a belt of what is right and good and faithful around His body.

6 The wolf will live with the lamb. The leopard will lie down with the baby goat. The calf and the young lion and the young fat animal will lie down together. And a little boy will lead them. **7** The cow and the bear will eat side by side. And their young will lie down together. The lion will eat straw like the ox. **8** The nursing child will play by the hole of the cobra. And another child will put his hand in the hole of a snake whose bite is poison. **9** They will not hurt or destroy in all My holy mountain. For the earth will be as full of much learning from the Lord as the seas are full of water.

The People of Israel and Judah Return

10 In that day the nations will turn to the One from the family of Jesse. He will be honored by the people as someone special

to see. And His place of rest will be full of His shining-greatness. **11** In that day the Lord will put out His hand a second time to bring back His people who are left. He will bring them back from Assyria, Egypt, Pathros, Cush, Elam, Shinar, Hamath, and from the islands of the sea. **12** He will lift up flags for the nations, and will gather together the people of Israel and of Judah who had been sent away. He will bring them back from the four corners of the earth. **13** Ephraim will not be jealous. Those who made it hard for Judah will be cut off. Ephraim will not be jealous of Judah, and Judah will not make it hard for Ephraim. **14** But they will go down against the Philistines in the west. Together they will take what belongs to the sons of the east. They will go against Edom and Moab. And they will rule the sons of Ammon. **15** The Lord will dry up all the tongue of the Sea of Egypt. He will wave His hand over the Euphrates River with His burning wind, and will break it into seven rivers. Men will be able to walk over it with dry feet. **16** And there will be a road from Assyria for those of His people who will be left just as it was for Israel when they came up from the land of Egypt.

A Song of Thanks

12 You will say on that day, "I will give thanks to You, O Lord. Even though You were angry with me, Your anger is turned away and You comfort me. **2** See, God saves me. I will trust and not be afraid. For the Lord God is my strength and song. And He has become the One Who saves me." **3** As water from a well brings joy to the thirsty, so people have joy when He saves them. **4** In that day you will say, "Give thanks to the Lord. Call on His name. Make known His works among the people. Help them remember that His name is honored." **5** Sing praises to the Lord, for He has done great things. Let this be known in all the earth. **6** Call out and sing for joy, O people of Zion. For the Holy One of Israel is great among you.

Babylon Will Be Punished

13 The special word about Babylon which Isaiah the son of Amoz saw: **2** Lift up a flag on the hill without trees. Call out to the people. Wave the hand for them to go into the gates of the princes. **3** I have told My holy ones, and My powerful soldiers who take pride in their strength, to carry out My anger. **4** Listen to the noise on the mountains, like that of many people! Listen to the loud sound of the many people, of nations gathered together! The Lord of All is gathering an army for battle. 5 They are coming from a far country, from the end of the heavens. The Lord and all He is using to show His anger are coming to destroy the whole land. 6 Cry out in sorrow, for the day of the Lord is near! It will come as a destroying power from the All-powerful. 7 So all hands will become weak, and every man's heart will melt. 8 They will be filled with fear. Pain and suffering will take hold of them. They will suffer like a woman giving birth. They will look surprised at one another, their faces burning. 9 See, the day of the Lord is coming, without pity and with much anger. He is coming to destroy the land and its sinners from it. 10 The stars of heaven and every group of stars will not give out their light. The sun will be dark when it comes up, and the moon will not give its light. 11 This is how I will punish the world for its sin, and the sinful for their wrong-doing. I will also put an end to those who are proud. And I will put to shame those who make it hard for others and show no pity. 12 I will make men so few that they will be of more worth than pure gold, even the gold of Ophir. 13 I will make the heavens shake. And the earth will be shaken from its place with the anger of the Lord of All in the day of His burning anger. 14 Every man will turn to his own people and run to his own land like a hunted gazelle or like sheep with no shepherd. 15 Anyone who is found will have a spear put through him. And anyone who is caught will fall by the sword. 16 Their little ones will be broken in pieces in front of their eyes. Their things will be taken from their houses. And their wives will be carried away.

17 See, I am going to make the Medes go against them, who will not want silver or be happy with gold. 18 Their bows will cut down the young men. They will have no pity on babies. Their eyes will not pity children. 19 And Babylon, the beauty of nations, the shining-greatness and pride of the Babylonians, will be as when God destroyed Sodom and Gomorrah. 20 People will never live in it again, even all the people-to-come. No Arab will set up his tent there. No shepherds will make their flocks lie down there. 21 But wild animals of the desert will lie down there. Their houses will be full of owls. Ostriches will live there, and wild goats will play there.

22 Hyenas will make noise in their strong towers, and wild dogs in their beautiful houses. The end of her time is near. Her days will be few.

Loving-Pity on Jacob

14 The Lord will have loving-pity on Jacob and will again choose Israel. He will have them return to live in their own land. Then people from other countries will come and be with them, and will join themselves to the family of Jacob. 2 Nations will take them and bring them to their place. The family of Israel will own them in the Lord's land as men and women servants. They will take those who had taken them away and they will rule over those who had made it hard for them.

Babylon's King in the World of the Dead

3 When the Lord gives you rest from your pain and trouble and the hard work which you were made to do, 4 you will speak against the king of Babylon, and say, "How the one who made it hard for us has been stopped! How his anger has been stopped! 5 The Lord has broken the walking stick of the sinful, the power of rulers, 6 which used to beat the people in anger without stopping. The nations were ruled in anger. It was very hard for the people and there was no pity shown to them.

7 "Now the whole earth is at rest and quiet. They sing out with joy. 8 Even the cypress trees and the cedars of Lebanon are glad over you, and say, 'Since you were cut down no one comes to cut us down.' 9 The world of the dead below wants to meet you when you come. It wakes up the spirits of the dead for you, all the leaders of the earth. It raises all the kings of the nations from their thrones. 10 All of them will speak and say to you, 'Even you have become as weak as we. You have become like us. 11 Your honor and power along with the music of your harps have been brought down to the place of the dead. Worms are spread out as your bed under you and worms cover you.'

12 "How you have fallen from heaven, O shining one, son of the morning! you have been cut down to the earth, you who have made the nations weak! 13 You said in your heart, 'I will go up to heaven. I will raise my throne above the stars of God. And I will sit on the mount of meeting in the far north 14 I will go much higher than the clouds. I will make myself like the Most High.' 15 But you will be brought down

to the place of the dead, to the bottom of the grave. 16 Those who see you will look hard at you and think about you, and say, 'Is this the man who made the earth shake with fear, who shook nations? 17 Is this the man who made the world like a desert and destroyed its cities, who did not let those whom he had put in prison go home?'

18 "All the kings of the nations lie in greatness, each in his own grave. 19 But you have been thrown out of your grave like a hated part of the family. You are clothed with the dead who were killed with a sword, who go down to the stones of the grave, like a dead body crushed under foot. 20 You will not be joined with them when you are buried, because you have destroyed your country. You have killed your people. May the children of sinners never be spoken about again! 21 Make a place ready for his sons to be killed because of the sin of their fathers. They must not come into power and take the earth, and fill the world with cities."

God Will Destroy Babylon

22 "I will come against them," says the Lord of All. "And I will cut off from Babylon its name and people, its children and their children," says the Lord. 23 "I will turn it into a place for hedgehogs, full of pools of water. And I will go over it and destroy it," says the Lord of All.

God Will Destroy the Assyrians

24 The Lord of All has promised, "It will happen just as I have planned it. As I have planned, so will it be. 25 I will break Assyria in My land. I will crush him under foot on My mountains. Then his load will be taken from My people. His load will be taken from their shoulder." 26 This is the plan made against the whole earth and this is the hand that is put out against all the nations. 27 For the Lord of All has planned, and who can keep it from happening? Who can turn His hand back?

God Will Destroy the Philistines

28 In the year that King Ahaz died this special word came: 29 "Do not be glad, O Philistia, all of you, because the special stick that made it hard for you is broken. One snake dies and a worse one comes, a snake that can fly. 30 The poor will eat. Those in need will lie down and be safe. I will destroy all of you with hunger and it will kill those who are left. 31 Cry out, O gate. Cry, O city. All you Philistines are

weak in heart. For smoke comes from the north, and everyone keeps his place in his army. 32 What answer will be given to the men sent by the nation? That the Lord is the builder of Zion, and it will be a safe place for His people who are poor and troubled."

God Will Destroy Moab

15 The special word against Moab: Ar of Moab is destroyed and laid waste in a night. And in a night Kir of Moab is destroyed and laid waste. 2 They have gone up to the house of worship and to Dibon. They have gone to the high places to cry. Moab cries over Nebo and Medeba. The hair has been cut from everyone's head and face. 3 In their streets they have dressed themselves with cloth made from hair. On the tops of their houses and in their open spaces everyone is crying with many tears. 4 Heshbon and Elealeh cry out also. Their voice is heard as far as Jahaz. So the soldiers of Moab cry out. Moab's soul shakes within him. 5 My heart cries out for Moab. His men have run away as far as Zoar and Eglath-shelishiyah. For they go up the hill of Luhith crying. On the road to Horonaim they cry in sorrow over their being destroyed. 6 For the waters of Nimrim have been laid waste. The grass is dried up. The new grass died out. There is no green thing. 7 So the many things they have gathered and stored up they carry away over the river of Arabim. 8 The cry of sorrow has gone around the land of Moab. Its noise is heard as far as Eglaim and Beer-elim. 9 The waters of Dimon are full of blood. Yet I will bring more troubles to Dimon. I will bring a lion upon those of Moab who have run away, and upon the people of the land who are still alive.

Moab Is without Hope

16 Send lambs as taxes to the ruler of the land, from Sela by the way of the desert to the mountain of the people of Zion. 2 Then, like birds driven from their nest, the people of Moab will be where the Arnon River can be crossed. 3 "Give us words of wisdom. Do what is right for us. Make your shadow like night at noonday. Hide those who have been sent away. Do not go against those who are running for their lives. 4 Let those of Moab who have been sent away stay with you. Hide them from the one who destroys." For the one who uses sinful power has come to an end, and trouble has stopped. Those who make

it hard for the people have gone from the land. 5 A throne will be set up in loving-kindness. A faithful judge will sit on it from the family of David. He will be fair as he judges, and will be quick to do what is right and good.

6 We have heard of the pride of Moab, how very proud he is. We have heard of how proud he is of himself and of his anger. His proud words are false. 7 So Moab will cry out. Everyone of Moab will cry out. You will cry for the dried-grape cakes of Kir-hareseth, as if you were in the worst trouble. 8 The fields of Heshbon and the vines of Sibmah have dried up. The lords of the nations have crushed under foot its best vines, which went as far as Jazer and the desert. They spread themselves out and passed over the sea. 9 So I will cry with much sorrow for Jazer and for the vines of Sibmah. I will make you wet with my tears, O Heshbon and Elealeh, because there is nothing to gather from your summer fruits. 10 Happiness and joy are taken away from the field that gives much fruit. No songs are sung in the grape-fields. No one crushes grapes to make wine, for I have stopped the cry of joy. 11 So my heart cries with sorrow for Moab like a harp. Inside myself I cry for Kir-hareseth. 12 When Moab goes to his high place, he will only become tired. When he goes to his holy place to pray, it will do him no good.

13 This is the word which the Lord spoke before about Moab. 14 But now the Lord says, "In three years, as a servant would count them, the shining-greatness of Moab and all his many people will be hated. And those left alive will be very few and weak."

God Will Destroy Damascus

17 The special word about Damascus: "See, Damascus will no longer be a city. It will be destroyed and laid waste. 2 The cities of Aroer are left empty. They will be for the flocks to lie down in, and no one will make them afraid. 3 The strong city will be gone from Ephraim. Damascus will no longer rule. And those of Syria who are left alive will be like the shining-greatness of the sons of Israel," says the Lord of All.

4 In that day Jacob will lose his shining-greatness. And he will lose the fat of his flesh. 5 It will be like one who gathers the standing grain, taking the ears of grain with his arm or like one who gathers the ears of grain in the valley of Rephaim.

6 Yet some good will be left in it, as when an olive tree is shaken. There will still be two or three olives on the highest branch, and four or five on the branches of a tree that gives much fruit, says the Lord God of Israel.

7 In that day man will turn to his Maker. His eyes will look to the Holy One of Israel. 8 He will not look to the altars, the work of his hands. He will not look to what his fingers have made, or to the false goddess Asherah and the altars of special perfume.

9 In that day their strong cities will be like places left empty among the trees, or like high branches which they left behind because of the sons of Israel. The land will be laid waste. 10 For you have forgotten the God Who saves you. You have not remembered the rock where you are safe. So you plant beautiful plants, and put them with the vine-cuttings of a strange god. 11 In the day that you plant it you fence it in, and in the morning your seed is growing. But its fruit will waste away in a day of sickness and pain which cannot be healed.

Other Nations Are Like Grain Worth Nothing

12 Listen to the cry of sorrow of many people. They sound like the noise of the seas and the noise of nations! They sound like the rushing of powerful waters. 13 The nations move on like the noise of many waters. But God will speak sharp words to them and they will run far away. They will be blown away like the part of grain that is of no worth by the wind in the mountains. They will be like dust blown around in a storm. 14 At evening time there is much fear! Before morning, they are gone. This will be what will come to those who take what belongs to us. It will be what happens to those who rob us.

Word about Cush

18 Trouble will come to the land on the other side of the rivers of Cush where the sound of wings is heard. 2 From that land men are sent by the sea in boats made from tall river-grass. Go, you fast men, to a nation tall and smooth, to a people who fill others with fear both near and far. Go to the powerful nation that rules over those who hate it, whose land is divided by rivers. 3 All you people of the world, you who live on the earth, as soon as a flag is raised on the mountain, you will see it. As soon as the horn is sounded, you will hear it. 4 For the Lord has said to me, "I will be quiet and watch from the place where I live, like shining heat in the sunshine, like a cloud of fog in the heat of gathering time." 5 For before the gathering time, as soon as the bud blossoms and the grape is ready to eat, He will cut off the new branches with knives and will cut away the spreading branches. 6 They will be left for the birds of the mountains and for the wild animals of the earth. The birds will spend the summer eating them. And all the wild animals of the earth will eat them during the winter. 7 At that time tall people with smooth skin will bring gifts to the Lord of All. These people make others afraid both near and far. They are a strong and powerful nation who rule over others, whose land is divided by rivers. And they will go to Mount Zion, the place of the Name of the Lord of All.

Word about Egypt

19 The special word about Egypt: See, the Lord is traveling on a fast cloud and is coming to Egypt. The false gods of Egypt shake in fear before Him. The hearts of the Egyptians become weak. 2 "I will make Egyptians go against Egyptians. Each of them will fight against his brother, and each against his neighbor. City will fight against city, and nation against nation. 3 Then the spirit of the Egyptians will become weak within them. And I will bring their plans to nothing. They will go to false gods and spirits of the dead for help, and to those who speak with spirits of the dead and use their secret ways. 4 Then I will give the Egyptians into the hand of a bad ruler. An angry king will rule over them," says the Lord God of All.

5 The waters of the sea will dry up. The river will become dry. 6 Man-made rivers will smell bad. The small rivers of Egypt will dry up. And the plants by the rivers will waste away. 7 The grass by the side of the Nile and all that is planted by the Nile will become dry, will be driven away, and be no more. 8 The fishermen will cry in sorrow. All those who fish for a living in the Nile River will be filled with sorrow. And those who put out nets on its waters will become weak. 9 Those who make linen and white cloth will be very troubled. 10 The pillars of Egypt will be crushed. All the able workmen will be filled with sorrow.

11 The king's sons of Zoan are very foolish. The words of Pharaoh's wisest men are foolish words. How can you men say to Pharaoh, "I am a son of the wise, a son of early kings"? 12 Where then are your wise men? Let them tell you. And let them understand what the Lord of All has planned against Egypt. 13 The king's sons of Zoan have become fools. The king's sons of Memphis have been fooled. The heads of her family groups have led Egypt from the right way. 14 The Lord has mixed a troubled spirit within her. They have led Egypt the wrong way in all that it does, as a drunk man walks from side to side in what he has spit up. 15 And there will be no work in Egypt and nothing can be done by anyone, its head or tail, its palm branch or river-grass.

Good Will Come to Egypt, Assyria and Israel

16 In that day the Egyptians will be like women. They will shake with fear because of the hand which the Lord of All is going to wave over them. 17 The land of Judah will fill Egypt with fear. Whoever hears its name will be afraid of it, because of the plan which the Lord of All is making against them.

18 In that day five cities in the land of Egypt will be speaking the language of Canaan and promising to follow the Lord of All. One will be called the City of Destruction.

19 In that day there will be an altar to the Lord in the center of the land of Egypt, and an altar to the Lord by the side of its land. 20 It will be something special to see, to make the Lord of All known in the land of Egypt. For they will cry to the Lord because of those who make it hard for them. And He will send a Powerful One to save them, and He will take them out of trouble. 21 The Lord will make Himself known to Egypt, and in that day the Egyptians will know the Lord. They will even worship with gifts on the altar. They will make promises to the Lord and keep them. 22 And the Lord will punish Egypt, but then He will heal them. So they will return to the Lord, and He will answer their prayers and heal them.

23 In that day there will be a road from Egypt to Assyria. The Assyrians will go to Egypt, and the Egyptians will go to Assyria. The Egyptians will worship with the Assyrians.

24 In that day Israel will be the third country with Egypt and Assyria, a good and respected nation on the earth, 25 to whom the Lord of All has brought good,

saying, "Good will come to Egypt My people, and Assyria the work of My hands, and Israel My chosen people."

Word about Egypt and Cush

20 In the year that Sargon the king of Assyria sent his head captain to fight against Ashdod, he took it in battle. ² At that time the Lord spoke through Isaiah the son of Amoz, saying, "Go and take off the clothes made from hair, and take your shoes off your feet." And he did so, going without clothes and shoes. ³ The Lord said, "My servant Isaiah has gone without clothing and shoes for three years as something special to be seen against Egypt and Cush. ⁴ So the king of Assyria will take away the people of Egypt and Cush, young and old, without clothes or shoes. Their bodies will not be covered, to the shame of Egypt. ⁵ Then they will be ashamed and troubled because of Cush their hope and Egypt their pride. ⁶ The people living on this island will say in that day, 'See, this is what has happened to those in whom we hoped, and to whom we ran for help to be saved from the king of Assyria. Now how can we get away?'"

Babylon to Be Destroyed

21 The special word about the place by the sea where no people live: As wind-storms in the Negev go rushing through, it comes from the desert, from a bad land. ² A hard special dream has been shown to me. The one who hurts still goes on hurting others, and the destroyer still destroys. Go up, Elam. Gather your armies around, Media. I will bring an end to all the crying she has caused. ³ For this reason my body is full of suffering. Pains have taken hold of me like the pains of a woman giving birth. I am so troubled that I cannot hear. I am so afraid that I cannot see. ⁴ My mind turns. Fear has come over me. The evening I have waited so long for has been turned into a time of shaking with fear. ⁵ They set the tables. They spread out the cloth. They eat and drink. Rise up, captains, oil the battle-coverings! ⁶ For the Lord says to me, "Go, set a man to keep watch. Let him tell what he sees. ⁷ When he sees men riding on horses, two by two, and men on donkeys, and men on camels, let him be very careful to watch." ⁸ Then the watchman called out like a lion, "O Lord, I stand watching from the watch-tower at all times during the day. And I stand there every night. ⁹ Now see, here comes an army of men riding on horses, two by two." One answered and said, "Fallen, fallen is Babylon. All the objects of her gods are broken to pieces on the ground." ¹⁰ O my people of Israel, you were beaten and crushed like grain! What I have heard from the Lord of All, the God of Israel, I make known to you.

Word about Edom

¹¹ The special word about Edom: One is calling to me from Seir, "Watchman, what is the time of night? Watchman, what is the time of night?" ¹² The watchman says, "The morning comes, but also the night. If you have questions to ask, ask them, and come back again."

Word about Arabia

¹³ The special word about Arabia: You must stay the night among the trees of Arabia, O traveling people of Dedanim. ¹⁴ Bring water for the thirsty. O people of the land of Tema, give bread to the one who is running from trouble. ¹⁵ They are running from swords, from lifted swords, from bows that are ready to shoot, and from the trouble of battle. ¹⁶ For the Lord said to me, "In a year, as the servant would count it, all the greatness of Kedar will come to an end. ¹⁷ And the rest of the men who use the bow, the strong men of the sons of Kedar, will be few. For the Lord God of Israel has spoken."

Word about Jerusalem

22 The special word about the Valley of Visions: What is wrong, that you have all gone up to the house tops, ² you who were full of noise, you loud town, you joy-filled city? Your dead were not killed with the sword. They did not die in battle. ³ All your rulers have run away together, and were taken without using the bow. All of you who were found were taken away together, even though you had run far away. ⁴ So I said, "Turn your eyes away from me. Let me cry with much sorrow. Do not try to comfort me about my people being destroyed." ⁵ For the Lord God of All has a day of fear, crushing down, and trouble in the Valley of Vision. There is a breaking down of walls and a crying out to the mountain. ⁶ Elam took up the arrows with the war-wagons, soldiers and horsemen. And Kir let the battle-covering be seen. ⁷ Your best valleys were full of war-wagons, and the horsemen took their places at the gate. ⁸ Then God took away the safe-covering of Judah. In that day you trusted in the objects you had to fight with that were stored in the house among the trees. 9 You saw that there were many broken places in the wall of the city of David. You stored water in the lower pool. 10 Then you numbered the houses of Jerusalem, and tore down houses to make the wall stronger. 11 You made a place to store water between the two walls for the waters of the old pool. But you did not trust in God Who made it. You did not think about Him Who planned it long ago.

12 So in that day the Lord God of All called you to cry in sorrow, to cut off the hair from your head, and to wear cloth made from hair. 13 But instead, there is joy and happiness, killing of cattle and sheep, eating of meat, and drinking of wine. You say, "Let us eat and drink, for tomorrow we die." 14 But the Lord of All has made Himself known to me. The Lord God of All says, "For sure you will not be forgiven for this sin until you die."

Word about Shebna

15 The Lord God of All says, "Come, go to this person in Shebna who is taking care of the king's house. Say to him, 16 'What right do you have here? Who told you that you could cut out a grave for yourself here? You cut out a grave on a high place! You cut a resting place for yourself in the rock! 17 See, the Lord will throw you away without pity, O you strong man. He will take a strong hold of you 18 and roll you up like a ball to be thrown into a wide land. There you will die, and there your great warwagons will be. You are a shame to your king's house.' 19 I will throw you out of your place of power. I will take you down from your place. 20 In that day I will call My servant Eliakim, the son of Hilkiah. 21 I will clothe him with your coat, and tie your belt around him. I will give him the power you had. He will become a father to the people of Jerusalem and to the family of Judah. 22 Then I will put on his shoulder the rule of the family of David. What he opens, no one will shut. What he shuts, no one will open. 23 I will drive him like a nail in a hard place. He will become a throne of honor to his father's house. 24 So they will put on him all the honor of his father's house, and of his children, and every little dish, from the cups to all the jars. 25 "In that day," says the Lord of All, "the nail driven in a hard place will give way. It will break off and fall, and the load

hanging on it will be cut off. For the Lord has spoken."

Word about Tyre

23 The special word about Tyre: Cry out in sorrow, O ships of Tarshish. For Tyre is destroyed, so that there is no house or safe place for ships. It is made known to them from the land of Cyprus. 2 Be quiet, you people who live on the islands, you traders of Sidon. You sent men to cross the sea 3 and go on many waters. The grain of the Nile, that was gathered beside that River, made money for Tyre who was the trader of the nations. 4 Be ashamed, O Sidon, the strong-place of the sea. The sea speaks and says, "I have not suffered or given birth. I have not brought up young men or young women." 5 When the news comes to Egypt, they will be in pain when they hear about Tyre. 6 Pass over to Tarshish. Cry out in sorrow, O people of the islands. 7 Is this your joy-filled city, whose beginning was long ago, whose feet have taken her to live in places far away?

8 Who has planned this against Tyre, the giver of crowns, whose traders were princes and the honored of the earth? 9 The Lord of All has planned it, to put to shame the pride of all beauty, and to take honor away from all the honored of the earth. 10 Flow over your land like the Nile, O people of Tarshish. There is nothing holding you back any more. 11 He has put out His hand over the sea. He has made the nations shake with fear. The Lord has said that the strong-places of Canaan must be destroyed. 12 He has said, "You will not be filled with joy anymore, O pure crushed daughters of Sidon. Get up and go over to Cyprus. Even there you will not find any rest."

13 It was the Babylonians, not the Assyrians, who let the wild animals come upon Tyre. They built towers for their armies. They tore down her beautiful houses. They destroyed her. 14 Cry out in sorrow, O ships of Tarshish, for your strong-place is destroyed. 15 In that day Tyre will be forgotten for seventy years like the days of one king. At the end of seventy years it will happen to Tyre as in the song of the woman who sells the use of her body: 16 "Take your harp and walk through the city, O forgotten woman who sells the use of her body. Play the strings well. Sing many songs, that you may be remembered." 17 At the end of seventy years, the

Lord will visit Tyre. Then she will return to her sinful woman's pay. She will be as a woman who sells the use of her body to all the nations on the earth. [18] Her riches and her pay for selling the use of her body will be set apart to the Lord. It will not be stored up or saved. But what she receives will give much food and good clothes to those who live for the Lord.

The Earth Will Be Punished

24 See, the Lord will lay the earth waste. He will destroy it, turn its ground up-side-down, and send its people everywhere. [2] What happens to the people will happen to the religious leader. What happens to the man servant will happen to his owner. The woman servant will be like her owner. The buyer will be like the seller. The giver will be like the receiver. The one who lets another use his money will be like the one who uses it. [3] All the earth will be laid waste and destroyed, for the Lord has said this.

[4] The earth cries in sorrow and wastes away. The world becomes weak with sorrow and wastes away, together with the honored people of the earth. [5] The earth has been made unclean by its people. They have sinned and not obeyed the laws, and have broken the agreement that was to be forever. [6] So the earth is cursed and those who live in it suffer for their guilt. So the people of the earth are burned, and few men are left.

[7] The new wine dries up and the vine wastes away. All the glad in heart are in sorrow. [8] The happiness of the music makers stops. The noise of those filled with joy stops. The happiness of the harp stops. [9] They do not drink wine with singing. Strong drink tastes bad to those who drink it. [10] The city of trouble is broken down. Every house is shut up so no one may go in. [11] There is a crying out in the streets about the wine. All joy turns to darkness. The happiness of the earth is gone. [12] The city is laid waste. The gate is broken to pieces. [13] For this is how it will be on the earth among the nations. It will be like the shaking of an olive tree, and like what is left after the grapes have been gathered. [14] They raise their voices. They call out for joy. They cry out from the west about the wonderful power of the Lord. [15] So honor the Lord in the east. Honor the name of the Lord God of Israel in the islands of the sea. [16] From the ends of the earth we hear songs: "Praise the One

Who is right and good." But I say, "I waste away! I waste away! It is bad for me! The false ones are not faithful. Yes, their way is very false." [17] Fear and the deep hole and the trap are before you, O people of the earth. [18] He who runs from the news of trouble will fall into a deep hole. And he who comes out of the hole will be caught in a trap. For the windows of heaven are opened, and the earth shakes. [19] The earth is broken in pieces. The earth is torn apart. The earth is very shaken. [20] The earth turns from one side to the other side like a drunk man. It shakes like a tent because its sin is heavy upon it. It will fall, never to rise again. [21] In that day the Lord will punish the powers of heaven above, and the kings of the earth below. [22] They will be gathered together like those in a prison. They will be kept in a deep, dark prison, and after many days they will be punished. [23] Then the moon will be dark and the sun will not shine, for the Lord of All will rule on Mount Zion and in Jerusalem. And in front of His leaders, He will let His shining-greatness be seen.

A Song of Praise

25 O Lord, You are my God. I will praise You. I will give thanks to Your name. For You have been faithful to do great things, plans that You made long ago. [2] For You have laid waste a city. The beautiful house of strangers is a city no more. And it will never be built again. [3] So strong people will honor You. Cities of nations that show no pity will fear You. [4] For You have been a strong-place for those who could not help themselves and for those in need because of much trouble. You have been a safe place from the storm and a shadow from the heat. For the breath of the ones who shows no pity is like a storm against a wall. [5] Like heat in a dry place, You quiet the noise of the strangers. Like heat by the shadow of a cloud, the song of the one who shows no pity is made quiet.

A Supper for All People

[6] On this mountain the Lord of All will make a supper of good things ready for all people. It will be a supper of good wine, of the best foods, and of fine wine. [7] And on this mountain He will destroy the covering which is over all people, the covering which is spread over all nations. [8] He will take away death for all time. The Lord God will dry tears from all faces. He will take

away the shame of His people from all the earth. For the Lord has spoken. 9 It will be said in that day, "See, this is our God. We have waited for Him, that He might save us. This is the Lord for Whom we have waited. Let us be glad and full of joy because He saves us."

Moab Will Be Punished

10 For the hand of the Lord will rest on this mountain. And Moab will be crushed in his place, as straw is crushed down in animal waste. 11 Moab will spread out his hands in it, as a man spreads out his hands to swim. But the Lord will put his pride to shame, together with the sinful work of his hands. 12 And the Lord will bring down your high walls built for war and lay them low. He will throw them to the ground, even to the dust.

A Song of Trust in God

26 In that day this song will be sung in the land of Judah: "We have a strong city. The Lord saves us and puts up walls to keep us safe. 2 Open the gates, that the nation that is right with God may come in, the one that keeps faithful. 3 You will keep the man in perfect peace whose mind is kept on You, because he trusts in You. 4 Trust in the Lord forever. For the Lord God is a Rock that lasts forever. 5 For He has brought down low those who live on a high place, the high city. He lays it low. He lays it low to the ground. He throws it to the dust. 6 It will be crushed under foot, under the feet of those who have suffered and the steps of those who cannot help themselves."

7 The way of the man who is right with God is smooth. O Upright One, make the path straight of those who are right with You. 8 While following in Your ways, O Lord, we have waited for You. To remember You and Your name is the desire of our souls. 9 My soul has a desire for You in the night. Yes, my spirit within me looks for You in the morning. For when you punish the earth, the people of the world learn what is right and good. 10 When favor is shown to the sinful, he does not learn what is right and good. He goes on doing what is wrong in the land of those who are right. He does not see the wonderful power of the Lord.

11 O Lord, Your hand is lifted up but they do not see it. Let them see Your care for Your people and be ashamed. Let fire destroy those who hate You. 12 O Lord, You will give us peace, for You have done all our works for us. 13 O Lord our God, other lords than You have ruled us, but Your name alone is the One we honor. 14 They are dead, and will not live. Their spirits will not return. So You have punished and destroyed them. You have caused them all to be forgotten. 15 You have made the nation great, O Lord. You have made the nation great. You have received much praise. You have made the land larger. 16 O Lord, they looked for You in their trouble. They could only say a quiet prayer while You were punishing them. 17 As the woman who is going to have a baby comes close to the time to give birth, she suffers and cries out in her pains. This is how we were before You, O Lord. 18 We suffered in pain. We gave birth, as it were, only to wind. We could not bring the world out of its trouble. And no people of the earth were born. 19 Your dead will live. Their dead bodies will rise. You who lie in the dust, wake up and call out for joy. For as the water on the grass in the morning brings new life, the earth will bring back to life those who have been dead.

Punishment of Sinners

20 Come, my people, go into your rooms. Close your doors behind you. Hide for a little while until God's anger is past. 21 For see, the Lord is about to come out from His place to punish the people of the earth for their sin. And the earth will let the blood be seen that has poured on her. She will no longer cover her dead.

Israel Set Free

27 In that day the Lord will punish Leviathan, the large snake-like sea animal, with His sharp and great and powerful sword. He will punish Leviathan the turning snake, and kill the big dragon that lives in the sea.

2 In that day it will be said: "Sing about a grape-field of wine! 3 I, the Lord, am its keeper. I water it all the time. I watch over it day and night so no one will hurt it. 4 I am not angry. If someone were to give Me thistles and thorns in battle, I would step on them. I would burn them together. 5 Or let him trust in Me to keep him safe. Let him make peace with Me. Yes, let him make peace with Me." 6 In the days to come Jacob will take root. Israel will flower and begin to grow, and fill the whole world with fruit.

7 Has the Lord punished Israel as He

punished those who went against Israel? Or have as many people of Israel been killed as their killers were killed? **8** You showed Your anger towards them by driving them out of the land. You moved them out with Your strong wind on the day of the east wind. **9** So by this Jacob's sin will be forgiven. This will be the full price of taking his sin away: When he crushes all the altar stones into fine pieces, so the wooden female goddess Asherah and the altars of special perfume will not stand. **10** The city made strong for battle is empty and alone, a place left alone like the desert. The calves eat there, and they lie down and eat from its branches. **11** When its branches are dry, they are broken off. Women come and make a fire with them. They are not a people of understanding, so their Maker will not have pity on them. The One Who made them will not show kindness to them.

12 In that day the Lord will beat out His grain from the flowing river of the Euphrates to the river of Egypt. And you will be gathered up one by one, O sons of Israel. **13** In that day a great horn will be blown. Those who were dying in the land of Assyria and those who were sent everywhere through the land of Egypt will come and worship the Lord on the holy mountain at Jerusalem.

Time of Trouble for Ephraim and Jerusalem

28 It is a time of trouble to the crown of pride and to the drunk men of Ephraim, whose shining beauty is a dying flower. It is at the head of the rich valley of those who have taken too much wine! **2** See, the Lord has one who is strong and powerful, like a storm of hail, a destroying storm. As with a flood of powerful waters flowing over, He will bring them down to the earth with His hand. **3** The crown of pride, the drunk men of Ephraim, will be crushed under foot. **4** The dying flower of its shining beauty which is at the head of the rich valley will be like the first fig grown before the summer. When one sees it, he takes it in his hand and eats it. **5** In that day the Lord of All will be a crown of shining-greatness, a beautiful crown to those who are left of His people. **6** He will be a spirit of what is fair to him who judges the people. He will be a strength to those who turn back the battle at the gate. **7** These also walk from one side to the other because of wine and strong

drink. The religious leaders and the men who tell what will happen in the future make mistakes because of strong drink. They are troubled by wine. They walk from side to side because of strong drink. They make mistakes as they have special dreams. And they make mistakes when judging between right and wrong. **8** All the tables are covered with what they have spit up. There is no place that is clean.

9 "Who is it He is trying to teach? To whom will He tell what He has to say? Children finished with their nursing and just taken from the breast? **10** For He says, 'Law on law, law on law, rule on rule, rule on rule, a little here, a little there.' " **11** The Lord will speak to these people through men from other lands and in strange languages. **12** He Who said to them, "This is rest, give rest to the tired and weak." And, "This is the place to rest," but they would not listen. **13** So the Word of the Lord to them will be, "Law on law, law on law, rule on rule, rule on rule, a little here, a little there," that they may go and fall back, be broken, trapped, and taken away by those who hate them.

A Stone of Great Worth in Jerusalem

14 So hear the Word of the Lord, you who laugh at the truth, who rule the people in Jerusalem! **15** You have said, "We have made an agreement with death. With the place of the dead we have made an agreement. The destroying flood will not touch us when it passes by. We have made lies our safe place. We have made ourselves with what is false." **16** So the Lord God says, "See, I lay in Jerusalem a Stone of great worth to build upon, a tested Stone. Anyone who puts his trust in Him will not be afraid of what will happen. **17** And I will use what is fair to decide about the base. And I will use what is right and good to make it straight. Then hail will take away all the lies you depend on, and the waters will flow over the place where you hide. **18** Your agreement with death will come to an end. Your agreement with the place of the dead will be stopped. When a flood of trouble passes through, you will be beaten down by it. **19** As often as it passes through, it will take you. And it will pass through morning after morning, anytime during the day or night. To understand what it means will bring much fear." **20** The bed is too short to lie on in comfort. And the covering is too small to put around yourself. **21** For the Lord will rise up as at Mount

Perazim. He will be angry as in the valley of Gibeon, to do what He needs to do, His strange act, and to do His work, His different kind of work. 22 So now do not laugh, or your chains will be made stronger. I have heard that the Lord God of All plans to destroy the whole earth.

The Wisdom of God

23 Listen and hear my voice. Listen and hear my words. 24 Does the farmer plow all the time to plant seed? Does he keep on turning and digging up the ground? 25 When he gets the ground ready to plant, does he not sow dill seeds and cummin seeds and wheat in rows? Does he not put barley in its place, and rye in the right place? 26 For his God tells him what to do and teaches him the right way. 27 Dill is not crushed with a crushing object. And the wagon wheel is not rolled over cummin. But dill is beaten out with a stick, and cummin with a heavy stick. 28 Grain for bread is crushed. He does not keep on crushing it forever. When he drives his wagon wheel over it with his horses, it does not crush it. 29 This also comes from the Lord of All, Who has given wonderful wise words and great wisdom.

Trouble for Jerusalem

29 It is bad for Ariel, Ariel the city where David once set up his tents! Add year to year. Keep your special suppers at the right times. 2 I will bring trouble to Ariel. She will be a city of sorrow and crying. She will be like an altar covered with blood to me. 3 I will camp against you, all around you. And I will build battle-walls against you, and towers from which to fight you. 4 Then you will be brought low. From the earth you will speak. Your words will come from the dust. Your voice will be like that of a spirit from the ground. Your quiet speaking will come from the dust.

5 But the many who hate you will become like fine dust. The many who show no pity will be like the part of the grain that is of no worth and blows away. It will happen all at once. 6 You will be visited by the Lord of All, with thunder and earth-shaking and loud noise, and with wind and storm and a destroying fire. 7 And the many nations that fight against Ariel, all who fight against her and her strong-place and bring trouble to her, will be like a dream. They will be like a special dream of the night. 8 It will be as when a hungry man dreams

he is eating, but when he wakes up, he is not filled. It will be as when a thirsty man dreams he is drinking, but when he wakes up, he is weak and still thirsty. This is how the many nations will be that fight against Mount Zion.

The Locked Book

9 Stop and wait. Blind yourselves and be blind. They are drunk, but not with wine. They walk from side to side, but not because of strong drink. 10 For the Lord has given you a deep sleep. He has shut your eyes, you who speak for God. He has covered your heads, men of God. 11 And the special dream of all this will be to you like the words of a locked book. When they give it to one who can read, saying, "Read this," he says, "I cannot, for it is locked." 12 Then they will give the book to one who cannot read, saying, "Read this." And he will say, "I cannot read."

13 The Lord said, "These people show respect to Me with their mouth, and honor Me with their lips, but their heart is far from Me. Their worship of Me is worth nothing. They teach rules that men have made. 14 So see, I will once again do great things with these people, great and wonderful things. And the wisdom of their wise men will be gone. The understanding of their wise men will be hidden."

Hope for the Future

15 It is bad for those who try to hide their plans from the Lord, and whose works are done in a dark place. They say, "Who sees us?" or, "Who knows us?" 16 You turn things up-side-down! Is the pot-maker the same as the clay? Should what is made say to its maker, "He did not make me"? Should what is made say to him who made it, "He has no understanding"?

17 Is it not yet a very little while before Lebanon will be turned into a rich good field? The rich good field will be thought of as being full of many trees. 18 In that day those who cannot hear will hear the words of a book. And the eyes of the blind will see out of the darkness. 19 Those who have suffered will be happier in the Lord. Those who are in need will have joy in the Holy One of Israel. 20 For those who show no pity will come to an end. And those who laugh at the truth will be stopped. All who want to be sinful will be cut off. 21 Those who say something to make a man seem to be in the wrong, and who trap the one who acts as a judge at the gate,

and who tell lies to cause a good man to be punished, will be cut off.

22 So this is what the Lord, Who made Abraham free, said about the family of Jacob: "Jacob will not be ashamed. No more will their faces become white with fear. 23 But when they see their children with them, the work of My hands, they will keep My Name holy, and will give honor to the Holy One of Jacob. They will stand in wonder of the God of Israel. 24 Those who do wrong in spirit will understand the truth. And those who complain will receive teaching."

Israel Cannot Depend on Egypt

30 "It is bad for the children who will not obey!" says the Lord, "They act on a plan that is not Mine, and make an agreement that is not of My Spirit, and so add sin to sin. 2 They go down to Egypt without asking Me. They want Pharaoh to keep them safe and they look for a safe place in the shadow of Egypt. 3 So the safe place of Pharaoh will be your shame. You will be brought low in the safe place in the shadow of Egypt. 4 For their rulers are at Zoan, and leaders come to Hanes. 5 Everyone will be ashamed because of a people who cannot be of help to them. They do not bring help or riches, but only shame."

6 The special word about the wild animals of the Negev: They go through a land of trouble and suffering, where there are male and female lions, deadly snakes and flying snakes. They carry their riches on the backs of young donkeys and camels, to a people who cannot be of help to them. 7 Egypt's help is of no worth and is empty. So I have called her Rahab who has done nothing.

The People Who Do Not Obey

8 Now go and write it down in front of them. And write it in a book, that it may be seen for all time to come. 9 For these people will not obey. They are not true sons. They will not listen to the teaching of the Lord. 10 They say to the men who tell what will happen in the future, "Do not see special dreams." They say to those who speak for God, "You must not tell to us what is right. Speak pleasing things to us, tell us what we like to hear. 11 Get out of the way. Turn aside from the path. We do not want to hear any more about the Holy One of Israel." 12 So the Holy One of Israel says, "Because you have turned away from this Word, and have put your trust in a power that makes it hard for others and fools them, 13 this sin will be to you like a high wall, ready to break and fall apart. It will fall all at once. 14 Its fall is like the breaking of a pot-maker's jar. It is broken in so many pieces that a piece will not be found big enough to pick up hot coals from the fire or to get water from the well." 15 The Lord God, the Holy One of Israel, has said, "In turning away from sin and in rest, you will be saved. Your strength will come by being quiet and by trusting." But you would not. 16 You said, "No, we will go away fast on horses." So you will go away in a hurry! You say, "We will go on fast horses." So those who come to take you will be fast. 17 One thousand will run away as one man stands up against them. You will all run away when five stand up against them, until you are like flags lifted up on a mountain-top, like something special to see on a hill.

Good Will Come to God's People

18 So the Lord wants to show you kindness. He waits on high to have loving-pity on you. For the Lord is a God of what is right and fair. And good will come to all those who hope in Him. 19 O people in Zion who live in Jerusalem, you will cry no more. For sure He will show loving-kindness to you at the sound of your cry. When He hears it, He will answer you. 20 The Lord has given you the bread of trouble and water of suffering. But He, your Teacher, will not hide Himself any more. Your eyes will see your Teacher. 21 Your ears will hear a word behind you, saying, "This is the way, walk in it," whenever you turn to the right or to the left. 22 You will take your sinful objects of worship, covered with silver and gold and will throw them away as an unclean cloth, and say to them, "Be gone!"

23 Then He will give you rain for the seed you will plant in the ground. And He will give you bread from the grain from the ground. It will be good, and more than you need. In that day your cattle will eat in a large field. 24 The oxen and the donkeys which work the ground will eat salted grain, which has been spread out with certain tools. 25 On every high mountain and on every high hill there will be rivers flowing with water in the day when many will be killed, when the towers fall. 26 The light of the moon will be like the light of the sun, the light of the sun will be seven times brighter, like the light of seven days, on the day the Lord takes care of the hurts

of His people and heals the sores He has given them.

God Will Punish Assyria

27 See, the name of the Lord comes from a far away place, with His anger burning, and with dark smoke rising. His lips are full of anger and His tongue is like a destroying fire. 28 His breath is like a river flowing over, that comes up to the neck. It shakes the nations back and forth putting them through a test of pride. And it puts a piece of iron in the mouths of the people to lead them the wrong way.

29 You will have a song as in the night when you have a special holy supper. You will be glad in your heart as when one steps to the sound of the horn going to the mountain of the Lord, to the Rock of Israel. 30 The Lord will make His voice of great power heard. And He will let His arm be seen coming down in the destroying fire, hard rain, storm, and hailstones. 31 The Assyrians will be filled with fear at the voice of the Lord, when He punishes them with His power. 32 Every beat from the special stick of punishment which the Lord will give them will be to the sound of timbrels and of harps. He will fight them in battle with a strong arm. 33 For a place of fire has long been ready. Yes, it has been made ready for the king. It has been made deep and wide, with fire and much wood. The breath of the Lord starts the fire and it is like a river of sulphur.

Help Comes from the Lord, Not Egypt

31 It is bad for those who go down to Egypt for help, and trust in the many horses and war-wagons, and in the much strength of their horsemen. They do not look to the Holy One of Israel or ask the Lord for help. 2 Yet He is wise and brings trouble, and does not take back His words. He will go against the house of wrong-doers, and against the helpers of those who sin. 3 The Egyptians are men, and not God. Their horses are flesh and not spirit. The Lord puts out His hand, and the helper and the one who is helped will fall. All of them will be destroyed together.

4 For the Lord has said to me, "As the lion or the young lion makes noise over the food he has killed, and when a group of shepherds go against him, he will not be afraid of their voice, or troubled by their noise. In the same way, the Lord of All will come down to fight on Mount Zion and on its hill." 5 Like flying birds, the Lord of All will keep Jerusalem safe. He will keep it safe and bring it out of trouble. He will pass over and save it. 6 O sons of Israel, return to Him against Whom you have sinned much. 7 For in that day every man will throw away his silver and gold objects of worship, which his sinful hands have made. 8 And the Assyrian will fall by a sword that is not of man, a sword that man has had no part of will destroy him. He will run from the sword, and his young men will be made to work hard. 9 "His safe place will pass away because of fear. And his rulers will be afraid of the flags lifted up," says the Lord, Whose fire is in Zion and Whose place of burning is in Jerusalem.

A Nation of Right Living

32 See, a king will rule by what is right and good and princes will be fair. 2 Each will be like a safe place from the wind, and a covering from the storm. Each will be like rivers of water in a dry country, and like the shadow of a large rock in a waste-land. 3 Then the eyes of those who see will be able to see. And the ears of those who hear will listen. 4 The mind of those who act in a hurry will understand the truth. And the tongue of those who have trouble speaking will hurry to speak well. 5 The fool will no more be called great. The bad man will no more be called a man of honor. 6 For a fool speaks foolish things. His mind plans wrong-doing, to sin and to say false things against the Lord, to keep the hungry person hungry, and to keep drink from the thirsty. 7 The ways of the bad man are sinful. He makes sinful plans to destroy the suffering with lies, even when the one in need asks for what is right. 8 But the man of honor makes good plans, and he stands for what is good.

The Women of Jerusalem

9 Rise up, you women who live an easy life, and hear my voice. Listen to what I say, you daughters. 10 In a little more than a year, you will be troubled. There will be no grapes to gather, the wine will not be made. 11 Shake with fear, you women who live an easy life. Be troubled, you daughters, who feel safe. Take off your clothes and cover your bodies with cloth made from hair. 12 Beat your breasts for the good fields, for the vine full of fruit, 13 and for the land of my people in which thorns and thistles will come up. Yes, be sorry for all the houses of joy, and for the

happy city, 14 because the king's house will be empty. The city full of people will be left empty. The hill and the watch-tower will become a place for wild animals forever, a happy place for wild donkeys, a field for flocks. 15 It will be this way until the Spirit is poured out upon us from heaven, and the desert becomes a field giving so much fruit, that it seems as if it has many trees. 16 Then what is right and fair will be in the desert. What is right and good will be in the field of much fruit. 17 The work of being right and good will give peace. From the right and good work will come quiet trust forever. 18 Then my people will live in a place of peace, in safe homes, and in quiet resting places. 19 But it will hail when the many trees come down and all the city will be laid waste. 20 How happy will you be, you who plant seeds beside all waters, and let the cattle and donkeys eat in any field.

A Prayer for Help

33 It is bad for you, O destroyer, you who were not destroyed yourself! You cannot be trusted, but others have trusted you. As soon as you finish destroying, you will be destroyed. As soon as you stop lying, others will lie to you. 2 O Lord, be kind to us. We have waited for You. Be our strength every morning. Save us in the time of trouble. 3 At the loud noise of battle, the people run. When You lift Yourself up, nations divide and run. 4 The things taken in war will be gathered as the caterpillar gathers. Men rush upon it like locusts. 5 The Lord is honored, for He lives on high. He has filled Zion with what is right and fair and good. 6 He will be for you what is sure and faithful for your times, with much saving power, wisdom and learning. The fear of the Lord is worth much. 7 See, their men with strength of heart cry in the streets. The men sent to bring peace cry many tears. 8 The roads are empty. The traveler does not travel. He has broken the agreement. He has hated the cities. He does not care for man. 9 The land is filled with sorrow and wastes away. Lebanon is put to shame and wastes away. Sharon is like a desert. And Bashan and Carmel shake off their leaves.

10 "Now I will rise up," says the Lord. "Now I will be honored. Now I will be lifted up. 11 You bring life to what is of no worth. You give birth to what is of no use. My breath will destroy you like a fire. 12 The people will be burned to white dust, like thorns cut down and burned in the fire.

13 "You who are far away, hear what I have done. And you who are near, speak of My power." 14 Sinners in Zion are filled with fear. The sinful shake with fear. They cry, "Who among us can live with the fire that destroys? Who among us can live with the fire that burns forever?" 15 He who walks with God, and whose words are good and honest, he who will not take money received from wrong-doing, and will not receive money given in secret for wrong-doing, he who stops his ears from hearing about killing, and shuts his eyes from looking at what is sinful, 16 he will have a place on high. His safe place will be a rock that cannot be taken over. He will be given food and will have water for sure.

17 Your eyes will see the King in His beauty. They will see a land that is far away. 18 Your heart will think about fear, asking, "Where is he who numbers? Where is he who weighs? Where is he who numbers the towers?" 19 You will not see people who show no pity, people whose language no one knows, whose strange tongue you cannot understand. 20 Look upon Zion, the city of our special suppers! Your eyes will see Jerusalem, a quiet resting place, a tent that will not be moved. Its tie-downs will never be pulled up, and none of its ropes will be broken. 21 But there the Lord in His great power will be for us. It will be a place of rivers and wide waterways, where no rowboats can go, and where no powerful ships can pass. 22 For the Lord is our judge. The Lord is our law-giver. The Lord is our king. He will save us. 23 Your ropes are loose. They cannot hold the sail up in its place or spread it out. Then the many riches taken in battle will be divided. Even those who cannot walk will take the riches. 24 And no one living there will say, "I am sick." The people who live there will be forgiven of their sin.

God Will Punish the Nations

34 Come near, O nations, to hear! Listen, O people! Let the earth and all that is in it listen, the world and all that comes from it. 2 For the Lord's anger is against all the nations. And His anger is against all their armies. He has destroyed all of them. He has given them over to be killed. 3 Their dead will be thrown out. Their dead bodies will give off a bad smell. The mountains will flow with their blood. 4 All the stars of the heavens will waste away. And the sky will be rolled up like writings. All that are in them will waste away also, as a leaf dries up from the vine, or as one dries up from the fig tree. 5 For My sword has drunk its fill in heaven. See, it will come down to punish Edom. It will come down upon the people whom I have given over to be destroyed. 6 The sword of the Lord is covered with blood. It is filled with fat, with the blood of lambs and goats, and with the fat of the kidneys of rams. For the Lord has a killing in Bozrah, and much killing in the land of Edom. 7 Wild oxen will fall with them, and young bulls with strong ones. So their land will be filled with blood, and their dust will become rich with fat. 8 For the Lord has a day when He will punish, a year when He pays back which will help Zion. 9 Edom's rivers will be turned into tar, and its dust into sulphur. Her land will become burning tar. 10 Its fire will not be put out night or day. Its smoke will go up forever. From one family to their children's children and on into the future, it will lie waste. No one will pass through it forever and ever. 11 But the pelican and hedgehog will have it for their own. The owl and raven will live in it. The Lord will make it into an empty waste-land. 12 Its rulers will be gone. And no kings will be named there. All their rulers will be no more. 13 Thorns will grow in its strong towers. Thistles grow in cities where battles were fought. It will be a place for wild dogs, and a home for ostriches. 14 The desert animals will meet with the wolves. The wild goats will cry to its kind. Yes, the night-demon will stop there and find a resting place. 15 The snake will make its nest and lay eggs there. Her young will be born from the eggs and she will gather them under her shadow. Yes, the hawks will be gathered there, every one with its kind.

16 Look in the book of the Lord, and read: Not one of these will be missing. None will be without its mate. For the mouth of the Lord has said so, and His Spirit has gathered them. 17 He will divide the land among them and give each of them a share. It will be theirs forever. From one family to their children's children and on into the future, they will live in it.

The Future Greatness of Zion

35 The waste-land and the dry land will be glad. The desert will be full of joy and become like a rose. 2 Many flowers will grow in it, and it will be filled with joy and singing. The greatness of Lebanon will be given to it, and the beauty of Carmel and Sharon. They will see the shining-greatness of the Lord, the wonderful power of our God. 3 Give strength to weak hands and to weak knees. 4 Say to those whose heart is afraid, "Have strength of heart, and do not be afraid. See, your God will come ready to punish. He will come to make sinners pay for their sins, but He will save you." 5 Then the eyes of the blind will be opened. And the ears of those who cannot hear will be opened. 6 Then those who cannot walk will jump like a deer. And the tongue of those who cannot speak will call out for joy. For waters will break out in the wilderness, and rivers in the desert. 7 The burning sand will become a pool. The thirsty ground will become wells of water. The resting place of the wild dog will be filled with river-grasses. 8 And a road will be there. It will be called the Holy Way. Those who are unclean will not travel on it. But it will be for those who walk in that way. Fools will not walk on it. 9 No lion will be there. No angry and hungry animal will go up on it. They will not be found there. But those whose sin has been paid for will walk there. 10 Those whom the Lord has paid for and set free will return. They will come to Zion with singing. Joy that lasts forever will crown their heads. They will be glad and full of joy. Sorrow and sad voices will be gone.

Assyria Takes Cities of Judah

36 In the fourteenth year of King Hezekiah, Sennacherib king of Assyria came up against all the strong cities of Judah and took them. 2 The king of Assyria sent Rabshakeh from Lachish to King Hezekiah at Jerusalem with a large army. And he stood by the ditch of the upper pool on the road of the Fuller's Field. 3 Then Eliakim the son of Hilkiah, who was the head of the house, and Shebna the writer, and Joah the son of Asaph, who wrote down the things that happened, came out to him.

4 Rabshakeh said to them, "Tell Hezekiah, 'The great king, the king of Syria, says, "What is the reason for this hope you have? 5 Do you think that empty words are plans and strength for war? In whom do you trust, that you have turned against me? 6 See, you are trusting in Egypt, whose power is like a broken piece of grass. If a man rests against it, it will cut into his hand. So is Pharaoh king of Egypt to all

who trust in him. 7 But if you tell me, 'We trust in the Lord our God,' is it not He whose high places and altars Hezekiah has taken away, saying to Judah and Jerusalem, 'You must worship at this altar'? 8 So now come and make an agreement with my leader, the king of Assyria. And I will give you 2,000 horses, if you are able to put horsemen on them. 9 How then can you turn away from one captain of the least of my king's servants, and trust in Egypt for war-wagons and horsemen? 10 Have I now come up to destroy the land against the Lord's will? The Lord said to me, 'Go up against this land, and destroy it.' " ' "

11 Then Eliakim and Shebna and Joah said to Rabshakeh, "Speak to your servants in the Aramaic language, for we understand it. Do not speak with us in the language of Judah so the people who are on the wall will hear." 12 But Rabshakeh said, "Has my king sent me only to speak to your leader and to you, and not to the men who sit on the wall? They will have to eat and drink their own body waste with you."

13 Then Rabshakeh stood and called out with a loud voice in the language of Judah, and said, "Hear the words of the great king, the king of Assyria. 14 The king says, 'Do not let Hezekiah lie to you. For he will not be able to bring you out of your trouble. 15 And do not let Hezekiah make you trust in the Lord, saying, "For sure the Lord will bring us out of our trouble. This city will not be given into the hand of the king of Assyria." 16 Do not listen to Hezekiah.' For the king of Assyria says, 'Make your peace with me and come out to me. Each one of you should eat of his own vine and fig tree, and drink the water of his own well, 17 until I come and take you away to a land like your own land. It is a land of grain and new wine, a land of bread and grape-fields. 18 Be careful not to let Hezekiah lead you the wrong way, saying, "The Lord will bring us out of our trouble." Has any of the gods of the nations saved his land from the power of the king of Assyria? 19 Where are the gods of Hamath and Arpad? Where are the gods of Sepharvaim? When have they taken Samaria out of my hand? 20 Who among all the gods of these lands have taken their land out of my hand? So why should the Lord save Jerusalem from my hand?' "

21 But they were quiet and did not answer him. For the king had told them, "Do not answer him." 22 Then Eliakim the son of Hilkiah, who was the head of the house,

and Shebna the writer, and Joah the son of Asaph, who wrote down the things that happened, came to Hezekiah with their clothes torn. They told him the words of Rabshakeh.

Jerusalem Will Be Free

37 When King Hezekiah heard it, he tore his clothes. He covered himself with cloth made from hair, and went into the house of the Lord. 2 Then he sent Eliakim, the head of the house, and Shebna the writer, and the head religious leaders, covered with cloth made from hair, to Isaiah the man of God, the son of Amoz. 3 They said to him, "Hezekiah says, 'This day is a day of trouble, pain, and shame. For children have come to birth, and there is no strength for them to be born. 4 It may be that the Lord your God will hear the words of Rabshakeh, whom his leader the king of Assyria has sent to try to bring shame upon the living God. The Lord your God may speak sharp words against what He has heard. So say a prayer for those who are left of His people.' " 5 So the servants of King Hezekiah came to Isaiah. 6 And Isaiah said to them, "Tell your king, 'This is what the Lord says. "Do not be afraid because of the words that you have heard, with which the servants of the king of Assyria have spoken against Me. 7 See, I will put a spirit in him so that he will hear some news and return to his own land. And I will make him fall by the sword in his own land." ' "

8 Then Rabshakeh returned and found the king of Assyria fighting against Libnah, for he had heard that the king had left Lachish. 9 Now the king had heard them say about King Tirhakah of Cush, "He has come out to fight against you." When he heard it, he sent men to Hezekiah, saying, 10 "Tell Hezekiah king of Judah, 'Do not let your God in Whom you trust fool you, saying, "Jerusalem will not be given into the hand of the king of Assyria." 11 See, you have heard what the kings of Assyria have done to all the lands. They have destroyed them all. So will you be kept from trouble? 12 Did the gods of those nations which my fathers have destroyed take them out of trouble? Did they save Gozan, Haran, Rezeph, and the sons of Eden who were in Telassar? 13 Where is the king of Hamath, the king of Arpad, the king of the city of Sepharvaim, the king of Hena, or the king of Ivvah?' "

Hezekiah's Prayer

14 Then Hezekiah took the letter from the hand of the men from Assyria, and read it. He went up to the house of the Lord and spread it out before the Lord. 15 And Hezekiah prayed to the Lord, 16 "O Lord of All, the God of Israel, Who sits on the throne above the cherubim, You are the God, You alone, of all the nations of the earth. You have made heaven and earth. 17 Listen, O Lord, and hear. Open Your eyes, O Lord, and see. Listen to all the words of Sennacherib, which he has sent to speak against the living God. 18 It is true, O Lord, the kings of Assyria have destroyed all the nations and their lands. 19 They have thrown their gods into the fire, for they were not gods but the work of men's hands, made of wood and stone. So they have destroyed them. 20 Now, O Lord our God, take us out of his hand, that all the nations of the earth may know that You alone are the Lord."

The Word of the Lord to the King

21 Then Isaiah the son of Amoz sent word to Hezekiah, saying, "This is what the Lord, the God of Israel, says, 'Because you have prayed to Me about Sennacherib king of Assyria, 22 this is the word the Lord has spoken against him: "She has hated you and made fun of you, the young daughter of Zion who has never had a man! She has shaken her head behind you, the people of Jerusalem! 23 Whom have you put to shame and spoken against? Against whom have you raised your voice and lifted up your eyes in pride? Against the Holy One of Israel! 24 Through your servants you have spoken against the Lord. You have said, 'I came up to the high mountains with my many war-wagons, to the farthest parts of Lebanon. I cut down its tall cedar trees and its best cypress trees. I came to its highest mountain-top, and to the place that has the most trees. 25 I dug wells in strange lands and drank water there. With the bottom of my feet I dried up all the rivers of Egypt.' 26 Have you not heard that I planned this long ago? From days of old I planned it. Now I have made it happen, that you should turn strong cities built for battles into waste-lands. 27 So their people did not have any more strength. They were troubled and put to shame. They were like the grass of the field and like the green plant. They were like grass on the housetops, dried up before it is grown. 28 But I know your sitting down,

and your going out and your coming in, and your anger against Me. 29 Because of your anger against Me, and because I have heard of your pride, I will put My hook in your nose, and My bit in your mouth. And I will make you return the way you came.

30 "This will be the special thing for you to see: You will eat this year what grows of itself. In the second year you will eat what grows up from the same. Then in the third year you will plant and gather. You will plant grape-fields and eat their fruit. 31 And those who are left of the family of Judah will again have their roots grow down and grow their fruit above. 32 For My people who are left will go out from Jerusalem and from Mount Zion. This will be done by the work of the Lord of All." ' " 33 So the Lord says about the king of Assyria, 'He will not come to this city or shoot an arrow there. He will not come before it with a battle-covering, or build a battle-wall against it. 34 He will return by the same way he came, and he will not come to this city,' says the Lord. 35 'For I will fight for this city to save it for My own good, and for the good of My servant David.' "

36 Then the angel of the Lord went out and killed 185,000 men in the Assyrian camp. And when men got up early in the morning, they saw all these dead bodies. 37 So Sennacherib king of Assyria left and returned home, and lived at Nineveh. 38 When he was worshiping in the house of his god Nisroch, his sons Adrammelech and Sharezer killed him with the sword. Then they ran away to the land of Ararat. And his son Esarhaddon became king in his place.

Hezekiah Will Live Fifteen More Years

38 In those days Hezekiah became sick and was near death. Isaiah the man of God, the son of Amoz, came to him and said, "The Lord says, 'Make those of your house ready, for you will die and not live.' " 2 Then Hezekiah turned his face to the wall, and prayed to the Lord, 3 and said, "O Lord, I ask you from my heart to remember now how I have walked with You in truth and with a whole heart. I have done what is good in Your eyes." And Hezekiah cried with a bitter cry. 4 Then the Word of the Lord came to Isaiah, saying, 5 "Go and tell Hezekiah, 'The Lord, the God of your father David, says, "I have heard your prayer. I have seen your tears. See, I will add fifteen years to your life. 6 And I will take you and this city out of the hand of the king of Assyria. I will fight for this city." ' " 7 "This is the special thing for you to see from the Lord, that the Lord will do what He has said: 8 See the shadow on the steps, which has gone down with the sun on the steps of Ahaz. I will make it go back ten steps." So the sun's shadow went back the ten steps it had gone down.

9 This is the writing of King Hezekiah of Judah, after he had been sick and became well again: 10 I said, "Half-way through my life I am to go through the gates of the place of the dead. The rest of my years have been kept from me." 11 I said, "I will not see the Lord, the Lord in the land of the living. I will not look upon man any more among the people of the world. 12 My house is pulled up like a shepherd's tent and taken from me. I have rolled up my life like a cloth-maker. He cuts me off from the cloth He is making. From day to night You make an end of me. 13 I waited for help until morning. Like a lion He breaks all my bones. From day to night You make an end of me. 14 I make noise like the birds. I cry like a dove. My eyes are tired from looking up. O Lord, I am having a hard time. Keep me safe.

15 "But what can I say? For He has spoken to me, and He Himself has done it. I will walk with care all my years because my soul is bitter. 16 O Lord, by these things men live. And in all these is the life of my spirit. O heal me, and let me live! 17 See, it was for my own well-being that I was bitter. But You have kept my soul from the grave that destroys. You have put all my sins behind Your back. 18 The place of the dead cannot thank You. Death cannot praise You. Those who go down to the grave cannot hope that You will be faithful. 19 It is the living who give thanks to You, as I do today. A father tells his sons about how faithful You are. 20 The Lord will save me. And we will sing my songs with harps all the days of our life in the house of the Lord."

21 Now Isaiah had said, "Let them take a cake of figs and put it on the sore, that he may get well." 22 Then Hezekiah had said, "What is the special thing to see, that I will go up to the house of the Lord?"

Men Come from Babylon

39 At that time Merodach-baladan son of Baladan, king of Babylon, sent letters and a gift to Hezekiah. He heard that he had been sick and had become well. 2 Hezekiah was pleased and showed them all his store-house of riches. He showed them the silver, the gold, the spices, the oil of much worth, and all his objects used in battle. He showed them everything that was in his store-houses. There was nothing in his house or under his rule that Hezekiah did not show them. 3 Then Isaiah the man of God came to King Hezekiah and said to him, "What did these men say? From where have they come to you?" And Hezekiah said, "They have come to me from a far country, from Babylon." 4 Isaiah said, "What have they seen in your house?" Hezekiah answered, "They have seen everything in my house. There is nothing among my riches that I have not shown them."

5 Then Isaiah said to Hezekiah, "Hear the Word of the Lord of All: 6 'See, the days are coming when everything in your house, and everything your fathers have stored up to this day, will be carried to Babylon. Nothing will be left,' says the Lord. 7 'And some of your own sons who are born to you will be taken away. They will work in the house of the king of Babylon.'" 8 Then Hezekiah said to Isaiah, "The Word of the Lord which you have spoken is good." For he thought, "There will be peace and truth in my days."

God's People Have Hope

40 "Comfort, comfort My people," says your God. 2 "Speak kind words to Jerusalem. Call out to her that her time of war has ended, that her sin has been taken away, and that she has received from the Lord's hand twice as much for all her sins."

3 A voice is calling, "Make the way ready for the Lord in the desert. Make the road in the desert straight for our God. 4 Every valley will be lifted up and every mountain and hill will be brought down. The turns in the road will be made straight and the bad places will be made smooth. 5 Then the shining-greatness of the Lord will be seen. All flesh together will see it, for the mouth of the Lord has spoken." 6 A voice says, "Cry." And he said, "What should I cry?" All flesh is grass. All its beauty is like the flower of the field. 7 The grass dries up and the flower loses its color when the breath of the Lord blows upon it. For sure the people are grass. 8 The grass dries up. The flower loses its color. But the Word of our God stands forever.

9 O Zion, you who bring good news, go up on the high mountain! Lift up your

voice with strength, O Jerusalem, you who bring good news. Lift it up, do not be afraid. Say to the cities of Judah, "Here is your God!" 10 See, the Lord God will come with power, and His arm will rule for Him. See, He is bringing the reward He will give to everyone for what he has done. 11 He will feed His flock like a shepherd. He will gather the lambs in His arms and carry them close to His heart. He will be gentle in leading those that are with young.

12 Who knows how much water is in His hand? Who has used his hand to know how far the heavens reach? Who knows what the dust of the earth would fill? Who has weighed the mountains and the hills? 13 Who has led the Spirit of the Lord? Who has taught Him words of wisdom? 14 From whom did He ask for wisdom, and who gave Him understanding? Who taught Him the right way, and taught Him much learning? Who showed Him the way of understanding? 15 See, the nations are like a drop in a pail. Their weight is like a little piece of dust. See, He lifts up the islands like fine dust. 16 Even Lebanon is not enough to burn. Its animals are not enough for a burnt gift in worship. 17 All the nations are as nothing before Him. He thinks of them as less than nothing and of no worth.

18 To Whom then is God like? What will you compare Him with? 19 An able workman makes a false god. A man who works with gold covers it with gold. And a man who works with silver makes silver chains for it. 20 He who is too poor to give such a gift, picks out a tree that will not waste away. He finds an able workman to set up a false god that will not be moved.

21 Do you not know? Have you not heard? Has it not been told to you from the beginning? Have you not understood from the beginning of the earth? 22 It is God Who sits on the throne above the earth. The people living on the earth are like grasshoppers. He spreads out the heavens like a curtain. He spreads them out like a tent to live in. 23 It is He Who brings rulers down to nothing. He makes the judges of the earth as nothing. 24 They have just been planted, and have begun to take root in the earth. But He only blows on them and they dry up, and the storm carries them away like dry grass. 25 "To whom will you compare Me, that I should be like him?" says the Holy One. 26 Lift up your eyes and see. Who has made these stars? It is the One Who leads them out

by number. He calls them all by name. Because of the greatness of His strength, and because He is strong in power, not one of them is missing.

27 O Jacob and Israel, why do you say, "My way is hidden from the Lord. My God does not think about my cause"? 28 Have you not known? Have you not heard? The God Who lives forever is the Lord, the One Who made the ends of the earth. He will not become weak or tired. His understanding is too great for us to begin to know. 29 He gives strength to the weak. And He gives power to him who has little strength. 30 Even very young men get tired and become weak and strong young men trip and fall. 31 But they who wait upon the Lord will get new strength. They will rise up with wings like eagles. They will run and not get tired. They will walk and not become weak.

God Will Help Israel

41 "Islands, be quiet and listen to Me. Let the people get new strength. Let them come near, then let them speak. Let us come together to be judged. 2 Who has called this one from the east, one who is right at every step? He gives up nations in front of him and makes him ruler over kings. He makes them like dust with his sword, and like wind-blown dry grass with his bow. 3 He goes after them and is safe as he passes, on paths he has not gone on before. 4 Who has done this, calling out all the people from the beginning? I, the Lord, am the first, and with the last. I am He."

5 The islands have seen and are afraid. The ends of the earth shake in fear and they have come. 6 Every one helps each other, and says to his brother, "Be strong!" 7 The able workman gives strength of heart to the one who works with gold. He who makes iron smooth gives strength of heart to the one who beats the iron, saying of his work, "It is good." And he puts it in its place with nails so that it cannot be moved.

8 "But you, Israel, My servant, Jacob, whom I have chosen, son of My friend Abraham, 9 I have taken you from the ends of the earth. I have called you from its farthest parts, and said to you, 'You are My servant. I have chosen you and have not turned away from you.' 10 Do not fear, for I am with you. Do not be afraid, for I am your God. I will give you strength, and for sure I will help you. Yes, I will hold you up with My right hand that is right and

good. ¹¹ See, all those who are angry with you will be put to shame and troubled. Those who fight against you will be as nothing and will be lost. ¹² You will look for those who argue with you, but will not find them. Those who war against you will be as nothing, as nothing at all. ¹³ For I am the Lord your God Who holds your right hand, and Who says to you, 'Do not be afraid. I will help you.' ¹⁴ Do not fear, you worm Jacob, you men of Israel. I will help you," says the Lord. "The One Who bought you and sets you free is the Holy One of Israel. ¹⁵ See, I have made you a new, sharp, crushing tool with teeth. You will beat the mountains and crush them. You will make the hills like dry grass. ¹⁶ You will make the wind blow over them, and it will carry them away. The storm will send them everywhere. But you will have joy in the Lord. You will be glad in the Holy One of Israel.

¹⁷ "The suffering and those in need look for water, but there is none. Their tongue is dry with thirst. I the Lord will answer them. I the God of Israel will not leave them alone. ¹⁸ I will open rivers on the dry mountain-tops, and give water in the valleys. I will make the desert a pool of water, and the dry land wells of water. ¹⁹ I will put in the desert the cedar, the acacia, the myrtle, and the olive tree. I will put the juniper tree in the desert, together with the box tree and the cypress. ²⁰ Then men will see and know and think about and understand that the hand of the Lord has done this, that the Holy One of Israel has made it happen.

²¹ "Let your cause be known," says the Lord. "Bring what you have to prove it," says the King of Jacob. ²² Let them bring what they have, and tell us what is going to happen. Let them tell us what has happened in the past, that we may think about it and know what will happen in the future. ²³ Tell us what will happen after this, that we may know that you are gods. Yes, do good or bad, that we may together be afraid and fear. ²⁴ See, you are nothing. And your work is nothing. He who chooses you is hated and sinful.

²⁵ "I have called one from the north, and he has come. From the rising of the sun he will call on My name. He will step hard on rulers as on builder's clay, as the pot-maker steps hard on clay." ²⁶ Who has said this from the beginning, that we might know, or from times long ago, that we might say, "He is right"? There was no one who said it, no one who made it known, no one who heard your words. ²⁷ "Before I had said to Zion, 'See, here they are,' and to Jerusalem, 'I will send someone to bring good news.' ²⁸ But I see that there is no one, even no wise man among them, who can answer My questions. ²⁹ See, all of them are false. Their works are nothing. Their objects of worship are empty wind.

The Servant of the Lord

42 "See! My servant, My chosen one! My much-Loved, in Whom My soul is well pleased! I will put My Spirit on Him. He will say to the nations what is right from wrong. ² He will not cry out or speak with a loud voice. His voice will not be heard in the streets. ³ He will not break a broken branch or put out a little fire. He will be faithful to make everything fair. ⁴ He will not lose hope or be crushed, until He has made things right on the earth. And the islands will wait with hope in His Law."

⁵ This is what God the Lord Who made the heavens and spread them out and Who spread out the earth and what comes from it, Who gives breath to the people on it, and spirit to those who walk in it, says, ⁶ "I am the Lord. I have called you to be right and good. I will hold you by the hand and watch over you. And I will give you as an agreement to the people, as a light to the nations. ⁷ You will open blind eyes. You will bring people out of prison, out of the prison where they live in darkness. ⁸ I am the Lord. That is My name. I will not give My shining-greatness to another, or My praise to false gods. ⁹ See, the things told about in the past have happened. Now I speak about new things. Before they happen I will tell you about them."

A Song of Praise to the Lord

¹⁰ Sing a new song to the Lord! Sing His praise from the end of the earth, you who go down to the sea, and all that is in it, you islands and those who live on them. ¹¹ Let the desert and its cities lift up their voice, the towns where Kedar lives. Let the people of Sela sing. Let them call out for joy from the tops of the mountains. ¹² Let them give honor to the Lord, and praise Him in the islands. ¹³ The Lord will go out like a powerful soldier. He will be ready like a man of war. He will call out, yes, He will call out a war cry. He will be strong against those who hate Him

God Promises to Help His People

14 "I have been quiet for a long time. I have been quiet and have held Myself back. Now I will cry out like a woman giving birth. I will breathe hard and fast. 15 I will lay waste the mountains and hills, and dry up all their plants. I will make the rivers into islands, and dry up the pools. 16 I will lead the blind by a way that they do not know. I will lead them in paths they do not know. I will turn darkness into light in front of them. And I will make the bad places smooth. These are the things I will do and I will not leave them." 17 They will be turned back and be put to shame who trust in false gods, who say to these objects of worship, "You are our gods."

Israel Is Blind and Cannot Hear

18 Listen, you who do not hear! And look, you blind, that you may see. 19 Who is blind but My servant? Who does not hear, as the one whom I send with news? Who is so blind as he who is at peace with Me, or so blind as the servant of the Lord? 20 You see many things, but you cannot tell what you see. Your ears are open, but you do not hear. 21 Because He is right and good, the Lord was pleased to make the Law great and give it honor. 22 But this is a people robbed of what they owned. All of them are trapped in deep holes, or hidden in prisons. They have been robbed of what they have, with no one to help them. They have been taken away, with no one to say, "Give them back!"

23 Who among you will hear this? Who will listen and hear in the future? 24 Who let Jacob be taken? Who gave Israel to robbers? Was it not the Lord, Whom we have sinned against, in Whose ways we were not willing to walk, and Whose Law we did not obey? 25 So He poured out upon Israel the heat of His anger and the power of battle. It set him on fire all around. Yet he did not understand. It burned him, but he did not think about it.

God Promises to Save Israel

43 But now the Lord Who made you, O Jacob, and He Who made you, O Israel, says, "Do not be afraid. For I have bought you and made you free. I have called you by name. You are Mine! 2 When you pass through the waters, I will be with you. When you pass through the rivers, they will not flow over you. When you walk through the fire, you will not be burned. The fire will not destroy you. 3 For I am the Lord your God, the Holy One of Israel, Who saves you. I have given Egypt as pay for your life, and have traded Cush and Seba for you. 4 You are of great worth in My eyes. You are honored and I love you. I will give other men in your place. I will trade other people for your life. 5 Do not fear, for I am with you. I will bring your children from the east, and I will gather you from the west. 6 I will say to the north, 'Give them up!' and to the south, 'Do not hold them back.' Bring My sons from far away, and My daughters from the ends of the earth. 7 Bring every one who is called by My name, for I have made him for My honor, yes, I made him."

8 Bring out the people who are blind, even though they have eyes, and those who cannot hear, even though they have ears. 9 All the nations have gathered together so the people may be together. Who among them can make this known, and tell us what has happened before? Let them bring people who can show us that they are right. Let them hear and say, "It is true." 10 "You can speak for Me," says the Lord. "You are My servant whom I have chosen so that you may know and believe Me, and understand that I am He. No God was made before Me, and there will be none after Me. 11 I, even I, am the Lord. There is no one who saves except Me. 12 I have spoken and saved and have made things known, and there was no strange god among you. You can speak for Me," says the Lord, "and I am God. 13 I am God and always will be. No one is able to take anything out of My hand. I do something, and who can change it?"

God's Loving-Kindness—Israel Not Faithful

14 The Lord Who bought you and sets you free, the Holy One of Israel, says, "Because of you I have sent to Babylon, and will bring down all their leaders, even the Babylonians, into the ships in which they find joy. 15 I am the Lord, your Holy One, the Maker of Israel, your King." 16 This is what the Lord says, Who makes a way through the sea and a path through the powerful waters, 17 Who brings out the war-wagon and the horse, the army and the strong man, (They will lie down together and will not rise again. They are destroyed, put out like the fire of a little light): 18 "Do not remember the things that have happened before. Do not think about the things of the past. 19 See, I will do a new

thing. It will begin happening now. Will you not know about it? I will even make a road in the wilderness, and rivers in the desert. 20 The wild animals will honor Me, the wild dogs and the ostriches. For I give waters in the wilderness, and rivers in the desert, to give drink to My chosen people. 21 The people whom I made for Myself will make known My praise.

22 "Yet you have not called on Me, O Jacob! You have become tired of Me, O Israel! 23 You have not brought the sheep of your burnt gifts to Me in worship. You have not honored Me with your gifts on the altar. I have not made you bring gifts or special perfume to Me. 24 You have not bought Me any sweet-smelling plants with money. And you have not given Me the fat of your gifts on the altar. Instead you have put the weight of your sins upon Me. You have made Me tired with your wrong-doing.

25 "I, even I, am the One Who takes away your sins because of Who I am. And I will not remember your sins. 26 Make Me remember, and let us talk together. Make your cause known, that you may be shown not to be guilty. 27 Your first father sinned, and those who have spoken for you have sinned against Me. 28 So I will make unclean the leaders of the holy place. I will give Jacob over to be destroyed, and Israel to sharp words of shame.

Good Will Come to Israel

44 "But now listen, O Jacob My servant, and Israel whom I have chosen. 2 This is what the Lord Who made you, Who put you together before you were born, Who will help you, says, 'Do not be afraid, O Jacob My servant, and you Jeshurun whom I have chosen. 3 For I will pour water on the thirsty land and rivers on the dry ground. I will pour out My Spirit on your children, and will bring good to your children's children. 4 They will grow like grass in the fields, and like poplar trees by the rivers.' 5 This one will say, 'I am the Lord's.' And that one will call on the name of Jacob. Another will write on his hand, 'I belong to the Lord,' and will name Israel's name with honor."

Only One God

6 The Lord, the King of Israel and the One Who saves and frees from sin, the Lord of All, says, "I am the first and I am the last. There is no God besides Me. 7 Who is like Me? Let him make it known. Yes, let him tell Me what happened from the time I made people long ago. And let him tell the things that are coming and what is going to happen. 8 Do not fear. Do not be afraid. Have I not made it known to you from long ago? And you have heard Me. Is there a God besides Me? No, there is no other Rock. I know of none."

Following False Gods Is Sinful

9 All who make objects to worship are for nothing. The things they think are worth much are worth nothing. Those who speak for them do not see or know, so they will be put to shame. 10 Who has made a false god or an object of worship that is of no worth? 11 See, all his friends will be put to shame, for the workmen themselves are only men. Let them all gather, let them stand up, let them shake with fear, and let them together be put to shame.

12 The one who works with iron makes a sharp tool for cutting, working over a fire. He makes it by beating it with his strong arm. He becomes hungry and has no strength. He drinks no water and becomes tired. 13 One works with wood, he marks it, and draws on it with a red marker. He makes it smooth and makes it like a man, like the beauty of a man, so that it may sit in a house. 14 He cuts down cedar trees, and takes a cypress or an oak, and lets it grow strong among the trees. He plants a fir tree, and the rain makes it grow. 15 Then it becomes something for a man to burn, so he takes one of them and warms himself. He makes a fire to bake bread. He also makes a god and worships it. He makes an object of worship and bows down in front of it. 16 He burns half of it in the fire. Over this half he cuts meat as he makes it ready, and is filled. He also warms himself and says, "O, I am warm. I see the fire." 17 But he makes the rest of it into a god, his object of worship. He bows down in front of it and worships. He prays to it and says, "Bring me out of my trouble, for you are my god."

18 They do not know, and they do not understand. For the Lord has covered their eyes so that they cannot see and their hearts so that they cannot understand. 19 And no one remembers about it, or knows or understands enough to say, "I have burned half of it in the fire, and have baked bread over the fire. I have cooked the meat over a fire and have eaten it. Should I make the rest of it into an object the Lord hates? Should I bow down in

front of a block of wood?" 20 He eats ashes!
A false idea in his heart has led him the
wrong way. And he cannot save himself
or say, "Is not what I have here in my right
hand a lie?"

The Lord Does Not Forget Israel
21 "Remember these things, O Jacob and
Israel, for you are My servant. I have
made you, you are My servant. O Israel, I
will not forget you. 22 I have taken away
your wrong-doing like a dark cloud, and
your sins like a fog. Return to Me, for I
have bought you and set you free." 23 Call
out for joy, O heavens, for the Lord has
done it! Call out for joy, you deep places
of the earth. Break out into singing, you
mountains and every tree. For the Lord
has bought Jacob and set him free and has
shown His shining-greatness in Israel!

People Will Live in Jerusalem Again
24 The Lord, Who makes you, bought
you and saves you, and the One Who put
you together before you were born, says,
"I am the Lord, Who made all things. I
alone spread out the heavens, and I alone
spread out the earth. 25 I allow trouble to
come on the special things done by men
who lie and speak in pride. I make fools
out of those who tell the future using their
secret ways. I turn back wise men, and
make their learning foolish. 26 I make the
word of My servant sure, and act upon the
words of the men who speak for Me. It is
I Who says of Jerusalem, 'She will have
people living in her,' and of the cities of
Judah, 'They will be built.' And I will build
her up again. 27 It is I Who says to the
deep sea, 'Dry up!' And I will dry up your
rivers. 28 It is I Who says of Cyrus, 'He is
My shepherd, and he will do all that I
want him to do,' even saying of Jerusalem,
'She will be built,' and of the house of God,
'Your first stones will be laid again.' "

Cyrus to Lead
45 This is what the Lord says to Cyrus,
whom He has chosen, whose right
hand He has held, "I send him to put nations under his power, and to take away
the power of kings. And I will open doors
in front of him so that gates will not be
shut. 2 I will go before you and make the
hard places smooth. I will break the brass
doors to pieces, and cut through their iron
gates. 3 I will give you riches hidden in the
darkness and things of great worth that
are hidden in secret places. Then you may

know that it is I, the Lord, the God of Israel, who calls you by name. 4 For the good
of Jacob My servant and Israel My chosen
one, I called you by your name. I gave you
a name of honor, when you had not known
Me. 5 I am the Lord, and there is no other.
There is no God besides Me. I will give
you strength, even though you have not
known Me. 6 Then men may know from
sunrise to sunset that there is no God besides Me. I am the Lord, and there is no
other. 7 I make light and I make darkness.
I bring good and I make trouble. I am the
Lord Who does all these things.

8 "Send down, O heavens, from above,
and let the clouds pour down what is right
and good. Let the earth open up and bring
the fruit of saving power. And let what is
right and good grow with it. I the Lord
have made it.

9 "It is bad for the one who works against
His Maker. He is just a clay pot among the
other pots of earth. Will the clay say to the
pot-maker, 'What are you doing?' or, your
work say, 'He has no hands?' 10 It is bad for
him who says to his father, 'To what are
you giving life?' or to a woman, 'To what
are you giving birth?' "

11 The Lord, the Holy One of Israel, and
his Maker, says, "Will you ask Me about
the things to come for My children? Will
you tell Me about the work of My hands?
12 I made the earth, and made man upon
it. I spread out the heavens with My
hands, and put all the stars in their places.
13 I have sent Cyrus to do what is right and
good. And I will make all his ways smooth.
He will build My city and without any
money will set My people free who were
taken away," says the Lord of All.

14 The Lord says, "The riches of Egypt
and the good things of Cush and the tall
Sabeans will come over to you and be
yours. They will walk behind you in chains
and bow down to you. They will beg you,
saying, 'For sure God is with you, and
there is no other God. There is none other.' "
15 It is true that You are a God Who hides
Himself, O God of Israel, the One Who
saves! 16 All of them will be put to shame
and troubled. Those who make false gods
will go away together in shame. 17 Israel
has been saved forever by the Lord. You
will never be put to shame for all time.

18 This is what the Lord Who made the
heavens, the God Who planned and made
the earth, and everything in it and did not
make it a waste place, but made it a place
for people to live in, says, "I am the Lord,

and there is no other. 19 I have not spoken in secret in some dark land. I did not say to the children of Jacob, 'Look for Me for nothing.' I the Lord speak the truth. I say what is right.

20 "Gather together and come. Come near together, you who are left of the nations. They have no learning, who carry around their false god made of wood and pray to a god who cannot save. 21 Make your need known. Yes, let them talk it over together. Who said this would happen from long ago? Who has been saying it for a long time? Is it not I, the Lord? There is no other God besides Me, a God Who is right and good, a God Who saves. There is none except Me. 22 Look to Me and be saved, all the ends of the earth. For I am God, and there is no other. 23 By Myself I have sworn. The Word has gone out from My mouth in truth, and will not turn back: 'Every knee will bow down before Me. And every tongue will say that I am God.' 24 They will say of Me, 'Strength and what is right and good are only found in the Lord.' Men will come to Him, and all who were angry at Him will be put to shame. 25 In the Lord all the children of Israel be made right, and will give praise."

False Gods and the Living God

46 The false gods, Bel and Nebo, bow down. Their objects of worship were put on animals and cattle and the wagons had heavy loads making it hard for the tired animals. 2 They get down, they bow down together. They could not save the heavy load, but are themselves carried away to another land.

3 "Listen to Me, O family of Jacob, and all who are left of the family of Israel. You have been helped by Me before you were born and carried since you were born. 4 Even when you are old I will be the same. And even when your hair turns white, I will help you. I will take care of what I have made. I will carry you, and will save you.

5 "To whom will you compare Me? With whom will you make Me the same and compare Me, that we should be alike? 6 Those who take much gold from the money bag and weigh silver hire one who works with gold, and he makes it into a god. Then they bow down and worship it. 7 They lift it upon their shoulders and carry it. They set it in its place and it stands there. It does not move from its place. When one cries to it, it cannot answer. It cannot take him away from his trouble.

8 "Remember this and be men. Bring it to mind again, you sinners. 9 Remember the things of long ago. For I am God, and there is no other. I am God, and there is no one like Me. 10 I tell from the beginning what will happen in the end. And from times long ago I tell of things which have not been done, saying, 'My Word will stand. And I will do all that pleases Me.' 11 I call a strong and hungry bird from the east, the man from a far country who will do what I have planned. I have spoken, and I will make it happen. I have planned it, and I will do it.

12 "Listen to Me, you strong-willed people who are far from being right and good. 13 I bring near what is right and good. It is not far away. And My saving power is ready now. I will save Zion, and will bring My great power to Israel.

Babylon Is Punished

47 "Come down and sit in the dust, O pure daughter of Babylon. Sit on the ground without a throne, O people of the Babylonians. For you will no longer be called soft and gentle. 2 Take the heavy stones and grind grain. Take off your face-covering and your clothing. Take the covering off your legs, and cross the rivers. 3 Your body will not be covered, and your shame will be seen. I will punish, and will not show pity to any man." 4 The One Who bought us and saves us, the Lord of All is His name, the Holy One of Israel. 5 "Sit and be quiet, and go into darkness, O people of the Babylonians. For you will no more be called the queen of nations. 6 I was angry with My people. I made My chosen nation unclean, and gave them into your hand. You did not show loving-kindness to them. On the older people you made your load very heavy. 7 You said, 'I will be a queen forever.' So you did not think about these things, or remember what might happen.

8 "So now hear this, you who love the desires of the body, who live without fear of danger. You say in your heart, 'I am, and there is no one besides me. I will not sit as a woman whose husband has died, and I will not lose my children.' 9 But these two things will come upon you all at once in one day. You will lose your children and your husband. All this trouble will come to you, even with all your witchcraft and the strong power of your sinful secret ways. 10 You trusted in your sin and said, 'No one sees me.' Your wisdom and learning have

led you the wrong way, for you have said in your heart, 'I am, and there is no one besides me.' 11 Much trouble will come upon you, and you will not know how to get away from it. Trouble will fall on you, and there will be no way for you to pay that it might go away. You will not know it but all at once you will be destroyed.

12 "Keep on with your sinful secret ways and all your witchcraft that you have used since you were young. It might be that you will get something from it. Maybe you can cause fear. 13 You are tired with your many wise men. Now call the star watchers, those who tell by the stars what will happen in the future, those who tell the future by the new moons. Have them stand up and save you from what will come upon you. 14 See, they have become like dry grass. Fire burns them. They cannot save themselves away from the power of the fire. This is no fire for making one warm, or fire to sit by! 15 This is how those are to you, with whom you have worked since you were young. Each one has gone on in his own wrong way. There is no one who can save you.

Israel Is Not Faithful in Following the Lord

48 "Hear this, O family of Jacob, who are called by the name of Israel, and who come from the seed of Judah. They make promises in the name of the Lord, and call upon the God of Israel, but not in truth or by what is right and good. 2 For they call themselves people of the holy city, and trust in the God of Israel. The Lord of All is His name. 3 I made known the things that would happen long ago. From My mouth My words went out. Then all at once I did what I said I would, and they came to pass. 4 I know that your heart is hard. Your neck is like iron, and your forehead is like brass. 5 So I made them known to you long ago. I told you before they happened, or else you might say, 'My false god has done them. My objects of worship have made them happen.' 6 You have heard, now look at all this. And will you say that you will not tell about it? I tell you new things from this time on, even hidden things which you have not known. 7 They are made now, not long ago. Before today you have never heard of them, or you would say, 'See, I knew them.' 8 You have not heard. You have not known. Even from long ago your ear has not been open, because I knew that

you could not be trusted. You have been known to fight against the law and not obey from birth. 9 Because of My name I hold back My anger. For My praise I keep Myself from cutting you off. 10 See, I have tested you, but not as silver. I have tested you in the fire of suffering. 11 For My own good, for My own good, I will do this. For why should I allow My name to be put to shame? I will not give My shining-greatness to another.

God Will Take Israel Out of Trouble

12 "Listen to Me, O Jacob, and Israel whom I called. I am He. I am the first, and I am the last. 13 My hand put the earth in its place. And My right hand spread out the heavens. When I call to them, they stand together. 14 Gather together, all of you, and listen! Who among them has made these things known? The Lord loves him. He will do to Babylon what pleases him, and his arm will be against the Babylonians. 15 I, even I, have spoken. Yes, I have called him, I have brought him, and he will do well. 16 Come near to Me and listen to this: From the beginning I have not spoken in secret. From the time it came to be, I was there. And now the Lord God has sent me and His Spirit."

17 The Lord Who bought you and saves you, the Holy One of Israel, says, "I am the Lord your God, Who teaches you to do well, Who leads you in the way you should go. 18 If only you had listened to My Laws! Then your peace would have been like a river and your right-standing with God would have been like the waves of the sea. 19 Your children's children would have been like the sand. Those born to you would have been like the sand. Their name would never be cut off or destroyed from before Me."

20 Go out from Babylon! Run from the Babylonians! Call out for joy and let this be known to the end of the earth, saying, "The Lord has bought and set free His servant Jacob!" 21 They were not thirsty when He led them through the deserts. He made water flow out of the rock for them. He broke the rock, and the water flowed out. 22 "There is no peace for the sinful," says the Lord.

The Servant of the Lord

49 Listen to Me, O islands. Listen, you people from far away. The Lord called Me before I was born. From the body of My mother he said My name. ² He has made My mouth like a sharp sword. He has hidden Me in the shadow of His hand. He has made Me a shining arrow, keeping Me in His secret place. ³ And He said to Me, "You are My Servant Israel, in Whom I will show My shining-greatness." ⁴ But I said, "My work has been for nothing. I have spent My strength for nothing. Yet for sure what should come to Me is with the Lord, and My reward is with My God."

⁵ And now the Lord speaks, Who made Me before I was born to be His Servant, to bring Jacob back to Him, that Israel might be gathered to Him. For I am honored in the eyes of the Lord, and My God is My strength. ⁶ He says, "It is too small a thing that You should be My Servant to raise up the family groups of Jacob, and to bring back those of Israel I have kept safe. I will also make You a light to the nations, so that men over all the earth can be saved from the punishment of their sins." ⁷ This is what the Lord, the One Who saves Israel, and its Holy One, says to the hated One, to the One hated by the nations, to the Servant of rulers: "Kings will see and rise up. Rulers will also bow down, because of the Lord Who is faithful, the Holy One of Israel Who has chosen You."

Israel as a Nation

⁸ The Lord says, "I have answered You at the right time. I have helped You in a day when people are saved. I will keep You and give You for an agreement to the people, to make the land good again, and to give them their land which had been destroyed. ⁹ I will say to those in prison, 'Come out,' and to those who are in darkness, 'Show yourselves.' They will eat along the roads, and find grass on all the hills. ¹⁰ They will not be hungry or thirsty. The burning heat of the sun will not trouble them. For He Who has loving-pity on them will lead them. He will lead them to wells of water. ¹¹ And I will make all My mountains a road. My straight roads will be raised up. ¹² See, these will come from far away. See, these will come from the north and from the west, and from the land of Sinim." ¹³ Sing for joy, O heavens! Be glad, O earth! Break out into songs of joy, O mountains! For the Lord has comforted His people. He will have loving-pity on His suffering people.

God Remembers Zion

¹⁴ But Zion said, "The Lord has left me alone. The Lord has forgotten me." ¹⁵ "Can

a woman forget her nursing child? Can she have no pity on the son to whom she gave birth? Even these may forget, but I will not forget you. ¹⁶ See, I have marked your names on My hands. Your walls are always before Me. ¹⁷ Your builders hurry. And those who destroy you will leave you. ¹⁸ Lift up your eyes and look around. All of them gather together and come to you. As I live," says the Lord, "you will put them on like objects of beauty. You will tie them on as a bride does. ¹⁹ For your waste places and your destroyed land will now be too small for the people. And those who destroyed you will be far away. ²⁰ The children born to you during the time of your sorrow will say for you to hear, 'The place is too small for us. Make a bigger place for us to live in.' ²¹ Then you will say in your heart, 'Who has given birth to these for me? My children were taken from me, and I could not give birth. I was sent away and had no place of my own. Who has brought up these children? See, I was left alone. Where have these come from?' "

²² The Lord God says, "See, I will lift up My hand to the nations. I will raise My flag to the people. And they will bring your sons in their arms, and your daughters will be carried on their shoulders. ²³ Kings will take care of you as fathers. And their queens will be your nursing mothers. They will bow down to you with their faces to the ground, and kiss the dust of your feet. Then you will know that I am the Lord. Those who wait for Me with hope will not be put to shame. ²⁴ "Can that which was taken by a strong man in battle be taken from him? Can those taken away to prison by a powerful ruler be saved?" ²⁵ The Lord says, "Even those taken away by the strong man will be taken from him. Those taken by the powerful ruler will be saved. For I will fight with the one who fights with you, and I will save your sons. ²⁶ I will feed those who make it hard for you with their own flesh. They will become drunk with their own blood as with sweet wine. Then all flesh will know that I, the Lord, am the One Who saves you, and the One Who bought you, the Powerful One of Jacob."

Israel's Hope

50 The Lord says, "Where is the writing of your mother's divorce, by which I have sent her away? To whom of those who owed Me money did I sell you? See, you were sold for your sins. For your wrong-doing your mother was sent away. 2 Why was there no man when I came? When I called, why was there no one to answer? Is My hand so short that it cannot pay for your life? Have I no power to take you out of trouble? See, I dry up the sea with My sharp words. I make the rivers a desert. Their fish smell bad because they do not have enough water, and die of thirst. 3 I clothe the heavens with darkness. I make cloth made from hair its covering."

4 The Lord God has given Me the tongue of those who follow Him, that I may know how to give strength when I speak to one who is tired. He wakes Me up morning by morning. He wakes up My ear to listen as a follower. 5 The Lord God has opened My ear, and I obeyed Him. I did not turn back. 6 I gave My back to those who hit Me, and My face to those who pull out the hair on my face. I did not cover My face from shame and spit. 7 For the Lord God helps Me, so I am not put to shame. I have set My face like hard stone, and know that I will not be ashamed. 8 He Who shows I am right is near. Who will fight with Me? Let us stand up to each other. Who has something against Me? Let him come near to Me. 9 See, the Lord God helps Me. Who will say that I am guilty? See, they will all wear out like a piece of clothing. The moth will eat them. 10 Who among you fears the Lord and obeys the voice of His Servant, yet walks in darkness and has no light? Let him trust in the name of the Lord and have faith in his God. 11 See, all you who start a fire and put fire all around you! Walk in the light of your fire and among the pieces of wood you have started to burn. You will receive this from My hand: You will lie down in much suffering.

Comfort for Zion

51 "Listen to me, you who are following what is right and good, and who are looking for the Lord. Look to the rock from which you were cut out, and to the hole from which you were dug. 2 Look to Abraham your father, and to Sarah who gave birth to you in pain. When he was but one, I called him. Then I brought good to him and made him many." 3 For the Lord will comfort Zion. He will comfort all her waste places. He will make her desert like Eden, like the garden of the Lord. Joy and happiness will be found in her. There will be much giving of thanks and much singing.

4 "Listen to Me, O My people. Hear Me, O My nation. The Law will go out from Me and My Law will be a light to the people. 5 My being right and good is near. My saving power has gone out, and My arms will judge the people. The islands will wait for Me. They will trust with hope for My arm. 6 Lift up your eyes to the sky, and look to the earth below. For the sky will go away like smoke. And the earth will wear out like a piece of clothing and those who live in it will die like flies. But My saving power will be forever. My being right and good will not come to an end. 7 Listen to Me, you who know what is right and good, you people who have My Law in your hearts. Do not fear the shame of strong words from man. Do not be troubled when they speak against you. 8 For the moth will eat them like a piece of clothing. And the worm will eat them like wool. But My being right and good will be forever. My saving power will be to all children's children-to-come."

9 Awake, awake, put on strength, O arm of the Lord. Awake as in the days of old, as You did with the people who lived long ago. Was it not You Who cut Rahab in pieces, and Who cut through the big dragon? 10 Was it not You Who dried up the sea, the deep waters, and Who made a path through the deep sea for Your saved people to cross over? 11 So the people, for whom the Lord paid the price to be saved, will return. They will come with songs of joy to Zion. Joy that lasts forever will be on their heads. They will receive joy and happiness, and sorrow and sad voices will hurry away.

12 "I, even I, am He Who comforts you. Who are you that you are afraid of a man who dies? Why are you afraid of the sons of men who are made like grass, 13 that you have forgotten the Lord Who made you? He spread out the heavens and put the earth in its place. Why do you live in fear all day long because of the anger of the one who makes it hard for you as he makes ready to destroy? But where is his anger? 14 The one in chains will soon be set free, and will not die in prison. And he will always have enough bread. 15 For I am the Lord your God, Who fills the sea with action so that its waves sound: The Lord of All is His name. 16 I have put My words in your mouth, and have covered you with the shadow of My hand. I spread out the heavens and put the earth in its place, and say to Zion, 'You are My people.'"

No More Suffering for Jerusalem

17 Awake! awake! Stand up, O Jerusalem, you who have drunk from the Lord's hand the cup of His anger. You drank it down, and you had trouble walking. **18** There is no one to lead her among all the sons born of her. There is no one to take her by the hand among all the sons she has brought up. **19** These two things have come upon you: Being laid waste and destroyed, hunger and the sword. Who will have sorrow for you? How can I comfort you? **20** Your sons have become weak and have fallen down. They cannot help themselves and they lie at the top of every street, like a deer in a net. The Lord has poured out His anger and sharp words upon them.

21 So hear this, you who are suffering, who are drunk, but not with wine. **22** Your Lord, the Lord your God Who fights for His people, says, "See, I have taken out of your hand the cup that makes you have trouble walking. You will never drink from the cup of My anger again. **23** I will put it into the hand of those who make it hard for you, who have said to you, 'Lie down that we may walk over you.' You have made your back like the ground and like the street for them to walk over."

God Saves Israel

52 Awake, awake, put on your strength, O Zion. Put on your beautiful clothes, O Jerusalem, the holy city. For those who have not gone through the religious act of becoming a Jew and those who are unclean will not come into you any more. **2** Shake off the dust. Rise up, O Jerusalem, who has been taken into prison. Loose yourself from the chains around your neck, O chained people of Zion who are in prison. **3** For the Lord says, "You were sold for nothing, and you will be bought without money and made free." **4** For the Lord God says, "My people went down at first to Egypt to live there. Then the Assyrian made it hard for them without a reason. **5** So now what do I have here," says the Lord, "Seeing that My people have been taken away for no reason?" The Lord says, "Those who rule over them call out in a loud voice and My name is spoken against all day long. **6** So My people will know My name. In that day they will know that it is I Who says, 'Here I am.' "

7 How beautiful on the mountains are the feet of him who brings good news, who tells of peace and brings good news of

happiness, who tells of saving power, and says to Zion, "Your God rules!" **8** Listen! Your watchmen lift up their voices. They call out together for joy, for they will see with their own eyes the return of the Lord to Zion. **9** Break out together into singing, you waste places of Jerusalem. For the Lord has comforted His people. He has saved Jerusalem. **10** The Lord has shown His holy arm in the eyes of all the nations, that all the ends of the earth may see that our God saves.

11 Leave, leave, go from them. Touch nothing that is unclean. Leave and make yourselves pure, you who carry the holy objects of the Lord. **12** But you will not go out in a hurry. You will not leave as if you were running for your lives. For the Lord will go before you. And the God of Israel will keep watch behind you.

The Suffering Servant

13 See, My Servant will do well. He will be high and lifted up and honored very much. **14** Just as many looked in wonder at you, My people, so His face was marked worse than any man, and His body more than the sons of men. **15** He will surprise many nations. Kings will shut their mouths because of Him. What they had never been told about Him, they will see. And what they had never heard about Him, they will understand.

53 Who has believed what we told them? And to whom has the arm of the Lord been shown? **2** He grew up before Him like a young plant, and like a root out of dry ground. He has no beautiful body and when we see Him there is no beauty that we should desire Him. **3** He was hated and men would have nothing to do with Him, a man of sorrows and suffering, knowing sadness well. We hid, as it were, our faces from Him. He was hated, and we did not think well of Him.

4 For sure He took on Himself our troubles and carried our sorrows. Yet we thought of Him as being punished and hurt by God, and made to suffer. **5** But He was hurt for our wrong-doing. He was crushed for our sins. He was punished so we would have peace. He was beaten so we would be healed. **6** All of us like sheep have gone the wrong way. Each of us has turned to his own way. And the Lord has put on Him the sin of us all.

7 Men made it very hard for Him and caused Him to suffer, yet He did not open

His mouth. He was taken like a lamb to be put to death. A sheep does not make a sound while its wool is cut and He did not open His mouth. ⁸ He was taken away as a prisoner and then judged. Who among the people of that day cared that His life was taken away from the earth? He was hurt because of the sin of the people who should have been punished. ⁹ They gave Him a grave with the sinful, but with the rich at His death, for He had done no wrong, and there was nothing false in His mouth.

¹⁰ But it was the will of the Lord to crush Him, causing Him to suffer. Because He gives His life as a gift on the altar for sin, He will see His children. Days will be added to His life, and the will of the Lord will do well in His hand. ¹¹ He will see what the suffering of His soul brings, and will be pleased. By what He knows, the One Who is right and good, My Servant, will carry the punishment of many and He will carry their sins. ¹² So I will give Him a share among the great. He will divide the riches with the strong, because He gave up His life. They thought of Him as One Who broke the Law. Yet He Himself carried the sin of many, and prayed for the sinners.

The Lord Loves Israel

54 "Woman, be happy, you who have had no children. Cry for joy, you who have never had the pains of having a child, for you will have many children. Yes, you will have more children than the one who has a husband," says the Lord. ² "Make your tent bigger. Spread out the curtains of your home, and do not hold back. Make your ropes longer and your tie-downs stronger. ³ For you will spread out to the right and to the left. Your children will own nations, and they will fill the destroyed cities with people.

⁴ "Fear not, for you will not be ashamed. Do not be troubled, for you will not be put to shame. You will forget how you were ashamed when you were young. You will not remember the sorrow of being without a husband any more. ⁵ Your Maker is your husband. His name is the Lord of All. And the One Who saves you is the Holy One of Israel. He is called the God of All the earth. ⁶ For the Lord has called you like a wife left alone and filled with sorrow, like a wife who married when young and is left," says your God. ⁷ "For a short time I left you, but with much loving-pity I will take you back. ⁸ When I was very angry I hid My face from you for a short time. But

with loving-kindness that lasts forever I will have pity on you," says the Lord Who bought you and saves you.

⁹ "For this is like the days of Noah to Me. As I promised that the waters of Noah should not flood the earth again, so I have promised that I will not be angry with you or speak sharp words to you. ¹⁰ The mountains may be taken away and the hills may shake, but My loving-kindness will not be taken from you. And My agreement of peace will not be shaken," says the Lord who has loving-pity on you.

¹¹ "O suffering one, shaken by the storm and not comforted, see, I will set your stones in beautiful colors. You will stand upon blue stones of much worth. ¹² I will make your towers of bright red stones. Your gates will be made of shining stones, and all your walls will be made of stones of great worth. ¹³ All your sons will be taught by the Lord, and the well-being of your children will be great. ¹⁴ All will be right and good for you. No one over you will make it hard for you, and you will not be afraid. You will be far from trouble, for it will not come near you. ¹⁵ If anyone brings trouble against you, it will not be from Me. Whoever comes against you will fall because of you. ¹⁶ See, I Myself have made the workman who blows on the fire to give it more heat and makes a sword for its work. I have made the destroyer to destroy. ¹⁷ No tool that is made to fight against you will do well. And you will prove wrong every tongue that says you are guilty. This is the gift given to the servants of the Lord. I take away their guilt and make them right," says the Lord.

A Great Full Life

55 "Listen! Every one who is thirsty, come to the waters. And you who have no money, come, buy and eat. Come, buy wine and milk without money and without price. ² Why do you spend money for what is not bread? Why spend your pay for what you do not enjoy? Listen well to Me, and eat what is good. Find joy in the best food. ³ Listen and come to Me. Hear, so you may live. And I will make an agreement with you that lasts forever, because of the faithful love promised to David. ⁴ See, I made him one who told of what he had seen and heard to the nations, a leader and ruler of the people. ⁵ See, you will call nations that you do not know. And nations that did not know you will run to you, because of the Lord your God, the Holy

One of Israel. For He has given shining-greatness to you."

6 Look for the Lord while He may be found. Call upon Him while He is near. 7 Let the sinful turn from his way, and the one who does not know God turn from his thoughts. Let him turn to the Lord, and He will have loving-pity on him. Let him turn to our God, for He will for sure forgive all his sins. 8 "For My thoughts are not your thoughts, and My ways are not your ways," says the Lord. 9 "For as the heavens are higher than the earth, so are My ways higher than your ways, and My thoughts than your thoughts. 10 The rain and snow come down from heaven and do not return there without giving water to the earth. This makes plants grow on the earth, and gives seeds to the planter and bread to the eater. 11 So My Word which goes from My mouth will not return to Me empty. It will do what I want it to do, and will carry out My plan well. 12 You will go out with joy, and be led out in peace. The mountains and the hills will break out into sounds of joy before you. And all the trees of the field will clap their hands. 13 Instead of the thorn bush, the cypress tree will come up. Instead of the thistle, the myrtle tree will come up. It will cause you to remember the Lord, something special to see that will last forever."

All Nations Can Be Saved

56 The Lord says, "Hold on to what is right and fair. Do what is right and good. My saving power will soon come, and I will show what is right. 2 How happy is the man who does this, and the son of man who takes hold of it! How happy is he who keeps the Day of Rest holy, and keeps his hand from doing wrong." 3 Let not the man from a strange land who has joined the Lord say, "For sure the Lord will keep me away from His people." Let not the man who had been made so that he could not have children say, "See, I am a dry tree." 4 To these the Lord says, "If these servants keep My Days of Rest and choose what pleases Me, and hold on to My agreement, 5 I will give them something in My house and within My walls to be remembered. I will give them a name better than that of sons and daughters, a name that will be forever and never be cut off.

6 "And those from a strange land who join themselves to the Lord, to serve Him and to love His name, to be His servants, and keep the Day of Rest holy, and keep

My agreement, 7 even those I will bring to My holy mountain and give them joy in My house of prayer. Their burnt offerings and gifts will be received on My altar. For My house will be called a house of prayer for all people." 8 The Lord God Who gathers the people of Israel from other lands says, "I will gather yet others to them, besides those already gathered."

Israel's Sinful Leaders

9 All you animals of the field, all you animals among the trees, come to eat. 10 The men of Israel who keep watch are blind to trouble. They know very little. They are all dogs that cannot make noise. They dream and lie down, and love to sleep. 11 The dogs are hungry and never have enough. The shepherds have no understanding. They have all turned to their own way, each one wanting to get things for himself that are not his. 12 "Come," they say, "let us get wine. Let us drink much strong drink. And tomorrow will be even better than today."

False Gods Must Be Put Away

57 "The man who is right and good dies, and no one cares. Very good men are taken away, while no one understands. But the man who is right with God is taken away from what is sinful, 2 and goes where there is peace. They have rest in their graves, each one who walked in the right way. 3 But come here, you sons of a witch, children of a man who does sex sins and a woman who sells the use of her body. 4 Against whom are you making fun? Against whom do you open your mouth wide and put out your tongue? Are you not children of sin, the young ones of lies? 5 You burn with desire with your false gods under every green tree. You put your children on the altar of your false gods in the valleys under high rocks that hang over. 6 Your part is among the smooth stones of the valley. They are what you get. You have poured out drink gifts to them and given grain gifts. Should I be pleased about these things? 7 You have made your bed on a high mountain. And you went up there to give your gifts in worship. 8 You have put up your false gods behind the door on the other side. You have turned away from Me and have taken the covering off yourself. You have gone up and made your bed wide. You have made an agreement for yourselves with them. You have loved their bed, and have looked upon their bodies. **9** You have traveled to the king with oil and much perfume. You have sent your men with gifts a very long way, and made them go down to the place of the dead. **10** You were tired because your road was so long, yet you did not say, 'There is no hope.' You found new strength, so you did not become weak.

11 "Of whom were you afraid, when you lied, and did not remember Me or think about Me? Have I not been quiet for a long time, so you are not afraid of Me? **12** I will make known how right you are and what you have done, but it will not help you. **13** When you cry out, let the false gods that you have take you out of trouble. The wind will carry them away. A breath will take them away. But he who comes to Me to be safe will receive the land. My holy mountain will be his."

God's Promise for Help

14 It will be said, "Build up, build up, make the way ready. Take everything out of the way of My people." **15** For the high and honored One Who lives forever, Whose name is Holy, says, "I live in the high and holy place. And I also live with those who are sorry for their sins and have turned from them and are not proud. I give new strength to the spirit of those without pride, and also to those whose hearts are sorry for their sins. **16** I will keep on fighting against you, and will not always be angry, for then your spirit would become weak before Me, the ones to whom I gave life. **17** Because of the sin of his desire to get more of everything, I was angry. I punished him and hid My face in anger. He went on sinning, following the way of his own heart. **18** I have seen his ways and will heal him. I will lead him and give comfort to him and to those who have sorrow for him. **19** I will make the lips to praise. Peace, peace to him who is far and to him who is near," says the Lord, "and I will heal him." **20** But the sinful are like the troubled sea, for it cannot rest. Its waters throw up mud and dirt. **21** "There is no peace," says my God, "for the sinful."

Going without Food Pleases God

58 "Cry with a loud voice. Do not hold back. Raise your voice like a horn, and show My people their wrong-doing and the family of Jacob their sins. **2** Yet they look for Me day by day, and are happy to know My ways, as a nation that has done what is right and good, and has not

turned away from the Law of their God. They ask Me to be fair in what I decide, and they are happy to come near to God. **3** They say, 'Why have we gone without food, and You do not see it? Why have we put away our pride, and You do not know it?' See, on the day you do not eat, you do what you want to do, and make it hard for all your workers. **4** See, while you go without food you argue and fight and hit with a sinful hand. Going without food as you do today will not help your voice to be heard on high. **5** Is it a time without eating like this that I choose, a day for a man to put away his pride? Is it for bowing his head like a piece of grass, and to spread ashes and cloth made from hair for his bed? Will you call this time without eating a day that pleases the Lord? **6** Is not the time without eating which I choose, a time to take off the chains of sin, and to take the heavy load of sin off the neck? Is it not a time to let those who suffer under a sinful power go free, and to break every load from their neck? **7** Is it not a time to share your food with the hungry, and bring the poor man into your house who has no home of his own? Is it not a time to give clothes to the person you see who has no clothes, and a time not to hide yourself from your own family? **8** Then your light will break out like the early morning, and you will soon be healed. Your right and good works will go before you. And the shining-greatness of the Lord will keep watch behind you. **9** Then you will call, and the Lord will answer. You will cry, and He will say, 'Here I am.' If you take the weight of sin away, and stop putting the blame on others and stop speaking sinful things, **10** and if you give what you have to the hungry, and fill the needs of those who suffer, then your light will rise in the darkness, and your darkness will be like the brightest time of day. **11** The Lord will always lead you. He will meet the needs of your soul in the dry times and give strength to your body. You will be like a garden that has enough water, like a well of water that never dries up. **12** And your cities which were destroyed long ago will be built again. You will set up the stones of the bases of the old buildings. You will be called the one who builds again the broken walls, and who makes the streets on which people live like new.

13 "If you keep from doing what pleases you on the Day of Rest, on My holy day and call the Day of Rest a happy time, and respect the holy day of the Lord, and if you honor it by turning from your own ways, and from following your own desire and by not talking in a foolish way, [14] then you will have joy in the Lord. I will cause you to ride on the high places of the earth. And I will feed you with the best from the land given to your father Jacob. The mouth of the Lord has spoken."

Sin Keeps One from God

59 See, the Lord's hand is not so short that it cannot save, and His ear is not closed that it cannot hear. [2] But your wrong-doings have kept you away from your God. Your sins have hidden His face from you, so that He does not hear. [3] For your hands are sinful with blood, your fingers with wrong-doing, your lips have lied, and your tongue talks about sin. [4] No one wants what is right and fair in court. And no one argues his cause with the truth. They trust in what is false, and speak lies. They plan to make trouble and do what is sinful. [5] They bring young ones from the eggs of deadly snakes and make traps as a spider does. He who eats of their eggs dies, and a snake comes out of the egg that is crushed. [6] Clothing cannot be made from the work of the spider, so they cannot cover themselves with what they make. Their works are works of sin. They hurt others with their hands. [7] And they are quick to sin and to kill people who are not guilty. Their thoughts are thoughts of sin. Wherever they go, they destroy and cause suffering. [8] They know nothing about peace, and there is nothing fair in their paths. Their roads are not straight. Whoever walks on them does not know peace.

[9] So what is right and fair is far from us. What is right and good does not come to us. We hope for light, but see darkness. We hope for bright light, but we walk in the dark. [10] We feel for the wall like blind men. We feel our way like those who have no eyes. We trip at noon as in the night. Among those who are strong, we are like dead men. [11] All of us make noise like bears, and cry inside ourselves like doves. We hope for what is right and fair, but it is not there. We hope to be saved, but it is far from us. [12] For we have done much wrong before You, and our sins speak against us. Our wrong-doing is with us, and we know our sins. [13] We have gone against the Lord and have acted as if we do not know Him. We have turned away from our God. We have made it hard for others. We have thought and spoken lying words from the

heart. [14] What is right and fair is turned back. What is right and good stands far away. Truth has fallen in the street, and what is right cannot come in. [15] Yes, truth is not there. And he who turns away from sin comes under the anger of sinners.

Now the Lord saw this, and it did not please Him to see that what is right and fair was not being done. [16] He saw and wondered that there was no man to speak up for what is right. Then His own arm brought saving power, and what is right with Him gave Him strength. [17] Being right and good was His covering for His breast, saving power was His head covering, clothing of anger was His covering, and His strong desires were like a coat. [18] He will pay them back for their works. He will send anger upon those who are against Him, and will punish those who hate Him. He will send punishment on the islands. [19] They will fear the name of the Lord from the west, and His shining-greatness from the rising of the sun. When the one who hates us comes in like a flood, the Spirit of the Lord will lift up a wall against him. [20] "The One Who saves from the punishment of sin will come to Zion, and He will come to those of Jacob who turn from their sinful ways," says the Lord. [21] "And as for Me, this is My agreement with them," says the Lord. "My Spirit which is upon you, and My Words which I have put in your mouth, will not leave your mouth, or the mouth of your children, or the mouth of your children's children," say the Lord, "from now and forever."

60 "Rise up and shine, for your light has come. The shining-greatness of the Lord has risen upon you. [2] For see, darkness will cover the earth. Much darkness will cover the people. But the Lord will rise upon you, and His shining-greatness will be seen upon you. [3] Nations will come to your light. And kings will see the shining-greatness of the Lord on you.

[4] "Lift up your eyes and look around you, and see. They all gather together. They come to you. Your sons will come from far away, and your daughters will be carried in the arms. [5] Then you will see and shine with joy. Your heart will be glad and full of joy, because the riches of the sea will be turned to you. And the riches of the nations will come to you. [6] Many camels will cover your land, the young camels of Midian and Ephah. All those from Sheba will come. They will bring gold and

special perfume, and will carry good news of the praises of the Lord. 7 All the flocks of Kedar will be gathered to you. The male sheep of Nebaioth will be ready for your need. They will be received on My altar. And I will make My house beautiful. 8 Who are these who fly like a cloud, and like doves to their windows? 9 For sure the islands will wait for Me. And the ships of Tarshish will come first, to bring your sons from far away, and their silver and gold with them. They will come because of the name of the Lord your God, and for the Holy One of Israel, for He has brought great honor to you.

10 "People from strange lands will build up your walls, and their kings will help you. For I destroyed you in My anger, but in My favor I have had loving-pity on you. 11 Your gates will always be open. They will not be closed day or night, so that men may bring the riches of the nations to you with the kings leading the way. 12 For the nation which does not serve you will be destroyed. Those nations will all be destroyed. 13 The beauty of Lebanon will come to you. The juniper, the box tree and the cypress will be brought to make My holy place beautiful. I will make the place of My feet a beautiful place. 14 The sons of those who made it hard for you will come bowing to you. All those who hated you will bow down at your feet. And they will call you the City of the Lord, the Zion of the Holy One of Israel.

15 "You have been left and hated, with no one passing through. But I will make you a pride forever, a joy for all your children's children. 16 You will drink the milk of nations. You will drink from the breast of kings. Then you will know that I, the Lord, am the One Who saves you, and the One Who bought you and made you free, the Powerful One of Jacob. 17 Instead of brass, I will bring gold. Instead of iron, I will bring silver. Instead of wood, I will bring brass. And instead of stones, I will bring iron. I will make peace your leader, and what is right and good will be your boss. 18 Fighting will not be heard again in your land. Nothing within your land will be destroyed. You will call your walls Saving Power and your gates Praise. 19 No more will the sun be your light during the day, and the moon during the night. But the Lord will be your light forever and your God will be your shining-greatness. 20 Your sun will set no more, and your moon will not become less. For the Lord will be your light forever and ever, and the days of your sorrow will end. 21 Then all your people will be right with God. They will have the land forever. They are the branch I planted, the work of My hands, that I may be honored. 22 The smallest one will become a family of a thousand. And the least one will become a powerful nation. I, the Lord, will make it happen in its time."

The Good News

61 The Spirit of the Lord God is on me, because the Lord has chosen me to bring good news to poor people. He has sent me to heal those with a sad heart. He has sent me to tell those who are being held and those in prison that they can go free. 2 He has sent me to tell about the year of the Lord's favor, and the day our God will bring punishment. He has sent me to comfort all who are filled with sorrow. 3 To those who have sorrow in Zion I will give them a crown of beauty instead of ashes. I will give them the oil of joy instead of sorrow, and a spirit of praise instead of a spirit of no hope. Then they will be called oaks that are right with God, planted by the Lord, that He may be honored.

4 They will build the cities again that were destroyed long ago. They will raise up what had been torn down, and will build the cities that were destroyed, and have lain waste through the years of many families and their children's children. 5 Strangers will stand and feed your flocks. Men from other lands will be your farmers and care for your vines. 6 But you will be called the religious leaders of the Lord. Men will speak of you as servants of our God. You will eat the riches of the nations, and in their riches you will speak with pride. 7 Instead of your shame you will have a share that is twice as much. Instead of being without honor, they will sing for joy over all you receive. So they will have twice as much in their land, and joy that lasts forever will be theirs. 8 For I, the Lord, love what is right and fair. I hate stealing and what is wrong. I will be faithful to pay them what they should have. And I will make an agreement with them that will last forever. 9 Their children will be known among the nations. Their children's children will be known among the people. All who see them will know them, because they are the people to whom the Lord has brought honor.

¹⁰ I will have much joy in the Lord. My soul will have joy in my God, for He has clothed me with the clothes of His saving power. He has put around me a coat of what is right and good, as a man at his own wedding wears something special on his head, and as a bride makes herself beautiful with stones of great worth. ¹¹ As the earth lets its new plants grow, and as a garden causes the things planted in it to grow, in the same way, the Lord God will cause what is right and good and words of praise to grow up in front of all the nations.

Something New for Zion

62 Because of Zion I will not keep quiet. Because of Jerusalem I will not rest, until her being right with God shines like a bright light, and her being saved shines like fire. ² The nations will see that you are right and good. All kings will see your shining-greatness. And you will be called by a new name which the mouth of the Lord will give. ³ You will be a crown of beauty in the hand of the Lord, a king's crown in the hand of your God. ⁴ You will no longer be called "Left Alone." Your land will no longer be called "Forgotten." But you will be called "My joy is in her," and your land "Married." For the Lord finds joy in you, and to Him your land will be married. ⁵ For as a young man marries a young woman who has never had a man, your sons will marry you. And as the man to be married finds joy in his bride, so your God will find joy in you.

⁶ On your walls, O Jerusalem, I have put men to keep watch. All day and all night they will never be quiet. You who help the Lord remember, do not rest. ⁷ And give Him no rest until He builds Jerusalem and makes it a praise in the earth. ⁸ The Lord has sworn by His right hand and by His strong arm, "I will never again give your grain to be food for those who hate you. And strangers will never again drink your new wine that you have worked hard to make. ⁹ But those who have worked on it will eat it and praise the Lord. And those who gather it will drink it in the open spaces inside My holy house."

¹⁰ Go through, go through the gates. Open the way for the people. Build up, build up the road. Take away the stones, and raise the flag over the people. ¹¹ See, the Lord has made it known to the end of the earth: Say to the people of Zion, "Look, the One Who saves you is coming! See, He is bringing His Reward that He will give." ¹² And they will call them "The holy people, the people who have been saved and set free by the Lord." And you will be called "A city looked for, a city that God has not forgotten."

The Lord Wins over the Nations

63 Who is this Who comes from Edom, with dark red clothing from Bozrah? Who is this One Who is beautiful in His clothing, walking in the greatness of His strength? "It is I, Who speaks what is right and good, powerful to save." ² Why is Your clothing red? Why is Your clothing like his who crushes the grapes? ³ "I have crushed the grapes alone. From the people there was no man with Me. I crushed them in My anger. I was angry as I stepped on them. And their life blood is on My clothing, and all My clothing is red. ⁴ For the day of punishment was in My heart. And My year to save My people and make them free has come. ⁵ I looked, and there was no one to help. I wondered that there was no one to help. So My own arm brought saving power to Me, and My anger helped Me. ⁶ I crushed the nations in My anger and I made them drunk in My anger. I poured out their life blood on the earth."

Israel Remembers God's Loving-Kindness

⁷ I will tell of the loving-kindness of the Lord, and praise Him for all He has done. I will tell of all the Lord has given us, the great goodness He has shown to the family of Israel and given to them because of His loving-pity and His great loving-kindness. ⁸ For He said, "For sure they are My people, sons who will not be false to Me." So He saved them from the punishment of sin. ⁹ He suffered with them in all their troubles, and the angel of the Lord saved them. In His loving-kindness He paid the price and made them free. He lifted them up and carried them all the days of long ago. ¹⁰ But they turned against Him and made His Holy Spirit have sorrow. So He turned Himself and hated them, and fought against them. ¹¹ Then His people remembered the days long ago, the days of Moses. Where is He Who brought them through the sea with the shepherd of His flock? Where is He Who put His Holy Spirit among them? ¹² Where is He Who caused His great arm to be at the right hand of Moses? Where is He Who divided the waters in front of them to make for

Himself a name that lasts forever. [13] Who led them through the sea? Like a horse in the desert, they did not lose their step. [14] Like cattle that go down into the valley, the Spirit of the Lord gave them rest. So You led Your people, to make for Yourself a great and honored name.

A Prayer for Help

[15] Look down from heaven, and see from Your holy and beautiful house. Where are Your strong desires and Your powerful works? Your kindness and Your loving-pity are kept from me. [16] For You are our Father. Even though Abraham does not know us, and Israel does not see who we are, You, O Lord, are our Father. The One Who bought us and made us free from long ago is Your name. [17] O Lord, why do You make us turn aside from Your ways and make our hearts hard so we do not fear You? Return because of Your servants, the families of Your promised land. [18] Your holy people kept Your holy house for a little while. But those who hate us have broken it under their feet. [19] We have become like those over whom You have never ruled, like those who were not called by Your name.

64 If only You would tear open the heavens and come down! The mountains would shake before You, [2] as when fire burns the wood and causes the water to boil. Come and make Your name known to those who are against you, that the nations may shake in fear before You! [3] When You did powerful things which we did not expect, You came down, and the mountains shook before You. [4] From long ago no ear has heard and no eye has seen any God besides You, Who works for those who wait for Him. [5] You meet him who finds joy in doing what is right and good, and remembers You in Your ways. See, You were angry because we sinned. We have been sinning for a long time, and will we be saved? [6] All of us have become like one who is unclean. All our right and good works are like dirty pieces of cloth. And all of us dry up like a leaf. Our sins take us away like the wind. [7] There is no one who calls on Your name, who stirs himself up to take hold of You. For You have hidden Your face from us, and have given us over to the power of our sins.

[8] But now, O Lord, You are our Father. We are the clay, and You are our pot-maker. All of us are the work of Your hand.

[9] Do not be so angry, O Lord. Do not remember our sin forever. Look now, all of us are Your people. [10] Your holy cities have become a waste place. Zion has become a waste place. Jerusalem lies destroyed. [11] Our holy and beautiful house, where our fathers praised You, has been burned by fire. And all our things of great worth have been destroyed. [12] Will You do nothing after seeing these things, O Lord? Will You keep quiet and make us suffer even more?

God's Ways Are Right and Good

65 "I let Myself be looked for by those who did not ask for Me. I let Myself be found by those who did not look for Me. I said, 'Here I am, here I am,' to a nation that did not call on My name. [2] All day long I held out My hand to a people who would not obey Me and who worked against Me. They walk in a way that is not good, following their own thoughts. [3] These people always make Me angry, giving gifts of worship in gardens and burning special perfume on altars of clay blocks. [4] They sit among graves, and spend the night in secret places. They eat the flesh of pigs, and have boiled meat that is unclean in their pots. [5] They say, 'Keep to yourself. Do not come near me. For I am holier than you.' These are smoke in My nose, a fire that burns all the day. [6] See, it is written before Me: 'I will not keep quiet, but I will pay them back. I will pay them back into their breast, [7] for both their own sins and the sins of their fathers,' " says the Lord. "Because they have burned special perfume on the mountains and have spoken against Me on the hills, I will give them into their breasts the full pay for what they have done."

[8] The Lord says, "New wine is found in the grapes, and one says, 'Do not destroy them, for there is still some good in them.' I will act in the same way for My servants, and not destroy them all. [9] I will bring children from Jacob, and one out of Judah who will have My mountains for a gift. They will be given to My chosen ones, and My servants will live there. [10] Sharon will become a field for flocks. And the valley of Achor will be a resting place for herds, for My people who look for Me. [11] But you who turn away from the Lord, who forget My holy mountain, who set a table for the false god, Gad, and who fill cups of mixed wine for the false female goddess, Meni, [12] I will have your future be the sword. All

of you will bow down to be killed. Because when I called, you did not answer. I spoke, but you did not hear. You did what was sinful in My eyes, and chose what did not please Me."

13 So the Lord God says, "See, My servants will eat, but you will be hungry. See, My servants will drink, but you will be thirsty. See, My servants will be glad, but you will be put to shame. 14 See, My servants will call out for joy with a glad heart. But you will cry out with pain in your heart and with a broken spirit. 15 And you will leave your name as a curse for My chosen ones. The Lord God will kill you, but My servants will be called by another name. 16 Anyone who has good things come to him in the land will have good things come to him by the God of truth. And he who makes a promise in the land will promise by the God of truth. The troubles of the past are forgotten, and are hidden from My eyes.

New Heavens and a New Earth

17 "For, see, I will make new heavens and a new earth. The past things will not be remembered or come to mind. 18 But be glad and have joy forever in what I make. For see, I make Jerusalem for joy, and her people for happiness. 19 I will have joy in Jerusalem and be glad in My people. The voice of crying will no longer be heard in it, or the cry of trouble. 20 No more will there be in it a child who lives only a few days, or an old man who does not live many years. For the child will live to be a hundred years old. And the one who does not live a hundred years will be thought to be cursed. 21 They will build houses and live in them. They will plant grapes and eat their fruit 22 They will not build a house and another live in it. They will not plant and another eat. For My people will live a long time, like the days of a tree. And for a long time My chosen ones will enjoy the work of their hands. 23 They will not work for nothing, or give birth to children and have trouble. For they will be the children of those who receive good from the Lord, and their children with them. 24 And it will be before they call, I will answer. While they are still speaking, I will hear. 25 The wolf and the lamb will eat together, and the lion will eat straw like the ox. And dust will be the snake's food. They will not hurt or destroy in all My holy mountain," says the Lord.

The Lord Judges

66 The Lord says, "Heaven is My throne, and the earth is the place where I rest My feet. Where then is a house you could build for Me? And where is a place that I may rest? 2 My hands made all these things, and so all these things came into being," says the Lord. "But I will look to the one who has no pride and is broken in spirit, and who shakes with fear at My Word.

3 "He who kills an ox is like one who kills a man. He who kills a lamb on the altar in worship is like one who breaks a dog's neck. He who gives a grain gift is like one who gives pig's blood. He who burns special perfume is like the one who gives honor and thanks to a false god. They have chosen their own ways, and their soul finds joy in the sinful things they do. 4 So I will choose their punishments, and will bring on them what they are most afraid of. I called, but no one answered, and spoke, but they did not listen. They did what was sinful in My eyes, and chose what did not please Me." 5 Hear the word of the Lord, you who shake in fear at His word; "Your brothers who hate you and have nothing to do with you because of Me have said, 'Let the Lord be honored, that we may see your joy.' But they will be put to shame. 6 Listen! A noise from the city! A voice from the house of God! It is the voice of the Lord Who is giving punishment to those who hate Him.

7 "Before she suffered, she gave birth. Before her pain came, a son was born to her. 8 Who has heard such a thing? Who has seen such things? Can a land be born in one day? Can a nation be born all at once? As soon as Zion's pains came, she gave birth to her sons. 9 Will I bring a child to birth, and not let him be born?" says the Lord. "Will I, Who gives birth, stop it?" says your God. 10 Be glad with Jerusalem and have joy in her, all you who love her. Be filled with joy for her, all you who have sorrow for her. 11 Then you will nurse and be filled with her comforting breasts. You will drink and be happy with her greatness." 12 For the Lord says, "See, I will give peace to her like a river, and the greatness of the nations like a river flowing over. And you will be nursed. You will be carried at the side and given loving-kindness on the knees. 13 I will comfort you as one is comforted by his mother. And you will be comforted in Jerusalem." 14 When you see this, your heart will be glad. Your

bones will get new strength like the new grass. And the hand of the Lord will be made known to His servants. But He will be angry with those who hate Him. 15 For see, the Lord will come in fire. His war-wagons will be like a very strong wind. And He will show His anger with fire. 16 The Lord will punish by fire and by His sword on all flesh. And those killed by the Lord will be many. 17 Those who set themselves apart and make themselves pure to go to the gardens, following one in the center, who eat pig's flesh, hated things, and mice, will come to an end together," says the Lord. 18 "For I know their works and their thoughts. The time is coming to gather all nations and tongues. And they will come and see My shining-greatness. 19 I will put something special among them. And I will send some of them who are left alive to the nations: Tarshish, Put, Lud, Mashech, Rosh, Tubal, and Javan, to the far islands that have not heard of My name or seen My greatness. And they will make My greatness known among the nations. 20 Then they will bring all your brothers from all the nations as a grain gift to the Lord, on horses, in war-wagons, on beds pulled by animals, on donkeys, and on camels. They will be brought to My holy mountain Jerusalem," says the Lord, "just as the sons of Israel bring their grain gift in a clean pot to the house of the Lord. 21 I will take some of them for religious leaders and for Levites," says the Lord. 22 "As the new heavens and the new earth which I make will last before Me," says the Lord, "in the same way, your children's children and your name will last. 23 From a new moon to another new moon, and from one Day of Rest to another Day of Rest, all people will come to bow down before Me," says the Lord. 24 "Then they will go out and look on the dead bodies of the men who have sinned against Me. For their worm will not die, and their fire will not be put out. And they will be a hated thing to all people."

JEREMIAH

The Call of Jeremiah

1 These are the words of Jeremiah, the son of Hilkiah, one of the religious leaders at Anathoth in the land of Benjamin. 2 The Word of the Lord came to Jeremiah in the days of Josiah, the son of Amon, king of Judah, in the thirteenth year of his rule. 3 It came also in the days of Jehoiakim, the son of Josiah, king of Judah, until the fifth month of the eleventh year of Zedekiah, the son of Josiah, king of Judah, when the people of Jerusalem were taken away.

4 Now the Word of the Lord came to me saying, 5 "Before I started to put you together in your mother, I knew you. Before you were born, I set you apart as holy. I chose you to speak to the nations for Me." 6 Then I said, "O, Lord God! I do not know how to speak. I am only a boy." 7 But the Lord said to me, "Do not say, 'I am only a boy.' You must go everywhere I send you. And you must say whatever I tell you. 8 Do not be afraid of them. For I am with you to take you out of trouble," says the Lord. 9 Then the Lord put out His hand and touched my mouth, and said to me, "See, I have put My words in your mouth. 10 I have chosen you this day to be over the nations and the kings, to dig up and to pull down, to destroy and to throw down, to build and to plant."

11 And the Word of the Lord came to me saying, "What do you see, Jeremiah?" I said, "I see a branch of an almond tree." 12 Then the Lord said to me, "You have seen well, for I am watching to see that My Word is completed."

13 The Word of the Lord came to me a second time saying, "What do you see?" And I said, "I see a boiling pot, with its face turned away from the north." 14 Then the Lord said to me, "Out of the north trouble will come upon all the people of the land. 15 For, see, I am calling all the families of the nations of the north," says the Lord. "And they will come. Then every one will set up his throne at the gates of Jerusalem, and against all the walls around it, and against all the cities of Judah. 16 And I will tell how they are to be punished for all their sin. For they have turned away from Me and have given gifts to other gods, and worshiped the works of their own hands. 17 Now get ready. Stand up and tell them everything that I tell you. Do not be afraid of them, or I will make trouble for you in front of them. 18 Today I have made you as a strong city ready for war, as a pillar of iron and as walls of brass against the

whole land, against the kings of Judah, the rulers, its religious leaders, and the people of the land. 19 And they will fight against you. But they will not have power over you, for I am with you to take you out of trouble," says the Lord.

Israel Turns Away from God

2 The Word of the Lord came to me saying, 2 "Go and speak so those in Jerusalem will hear, 'This is what the Lord says: "I remember how you loved Me when you were young. Your love was as a bride. I remember how you followed Me in the desert, through a land that had not been planted. 3 Israel was holy to the Lord, the first-fruits of His gathering. All who ate of it (Israel) were guilty, and trouble came upon them," says the Lord.' "

The Sin of Israel's Early Families

4 Hear the Word of the Lord, O family of Jacob, and all the families of the people of Israel. 5 The Lord says, "What wrong did your fathers find in Me, that they turned so far from Me and followed false gods? 6 They did not say, 'Where is the Lord Who brought us up from the land of Egypt? Where is He Who led us through the wilderness, through a land of deserts and deep holes, through a land without water and with much trouble, through a land that no one traveled and where no man lived?' 7 And I brought you into a rich land to eat its fruit and its good things. But you came and made My land unclean. You made the land I gave you sinful and hated. 8 The religious leaders did not say, 'Where is the Lord?' And those who worked with the Law did not know Me. The rulers sinned against Me. And the men of God spoke by the false god of Baal, and went after things that did not help.

The Lord Speaks against His People

9 "So I will still fight with you," says the Lord. "And I will fight your children's children. 10 Go over to the land of Cyprus and see. Or send men to Kedar to watch with care. And see if there has been such a thing as this! 11 Has a nation changed its gods, even when they are not gods? But My people have changed their greatness for that which does not help them. 12 Be full of wonder at this, O heavens. Shake with fear and waste away," says the Lord. 13 "For My people have done two sinful things: They have turned away from Me, the well of living waters. And they have

cut out of the rock wells for water for themselves. They are broken wells that cannot hold water.

What Happens When Israel Is Not Faithful

14 "Is Israel a servant? Is he born as a servant? Why can he be taken away? 15 The young lions have made noise against him. They have made a loud noise. And they have made his land a waste. His cities have been destroyed, and have no people. 16 The men of Memphis and Tahpanhes have broken the crown of your head. 17 Have you not brought this upon yourself, by turning away from the Lord your God, when He led you in the way? 18 Now why are you going to Egypt to drink water from the Nile? Or why are you going to Assyria to drink water from the Euphrates? 19 Your own sin will punish you. Your turning away from the Lord will punish you. So know and see that it is sinful and bitter for you to leave the Lord your God. You have no fear of Me," says the Lord God of All.

Israel Turns Its Back on God

20 "Long ago I broke the load from your neck and tore off your chains. But you said, 'I will not serve!' For on every high hill and under every green tree you have lain down as a woman who sells the use of her body. 21 Yet I planted you as a vine of much worth, in every way a true seed. How then have you turned away from Me and become a wild vine? 22 Even when you wash yourself with much strong soap, the mark of your sin is still before Me," says the Lord God. 23 "How can you say, 'I am clean. I have not gone after the false gods of Baal'? Look at what you did in the valley! Know what you have done! You are like a wild young camel wanting to mate. 24 You are a wild donkey used to the desert, that smells the wind in her desire. In the time of her mating who can turn her away? All who look for her will not become tired. In her month of mating they will find her. 25 Do not run until your shoes wear out or until your mouth is dry. But you said, 'It is of no use, for I love strange gods, and I will go after them.'

Israel Should Be Punished

26 "As a robber is put to shame when he is caught, so the family of Israel is put to shame: they, their kings, their rulers, their religious leaders, and their men of God.

27 They say to a tree, 'You are my father,' and to a stone, 'You gave me birth.' For they have turned their back to Me, and not their face. But in the time of their trouble they will say, 'Rise up and save us.' 28 But where are your gods that you made for yourself? Let them come if they can save you when you are in trouble. For you have as many gods as cities, O Judah.

29 "Why do you complain against Me? You have all sinned against Me," says the Lord. 30 "I have punished your children for nothing, for they would not learn from it. Your sword has destroyed your men of God like a destroying lion. 31 O people of this day, listen to the Word of the Lord. Have I been a desert to Israel, or a land of much darkness? Why do My people say, 'We are free to go, and we will come to You no more'? 32 Can a young woman forget the beautiful objects she wears? Can a bride forget her clothing? Yet My people have forgotten Me too many days to number. 33 How you dress yourself and go after lovers! You have taught your ways even to the sinful women. 34 On your clothing is found the blood of the poor who could not be blamed. You did not find them breaking in. But even with all these things, 35 you say, 'I am not guilty. For sure He has turned His anger away from me.' See, I will punish you because you say, 'I have not sinned.' 36 Why do you go around so much changing your way? You will be put to shame by Egypt as you were put to shame by Assyria. 37 From Egypt also you will go out with your hands on your head. For the Lord has turned against those in whom you trust, and as you are with them, it will not go well for you."

Israel Is Not Faithful

3 God says, "If a husband divorces his wife and she leaves him and marries another man, should he return to her again? Would not the land be made unclean? But you are like a sinful woman with many lovers, yet would you return to Me?" says the Lord. 2 "Lift up your eyes to the open hill-tops and see. Is there any place you have not lain with your lovers? You have sat by the roads waiting for them like an Arab in the desert. And you have made the land unclean with your sinful ways and your wrong-doing. 3 So the rains have been held back. There has been no spring rain. You look like a woman who sells the use of her body, and would not be ashamed. 4 Have you not just now called

to Me? You said, 'My Father, You have been my friend since I was young. 5 Will You be angry forever? Will You be angry to the end?' See, this is how you talk, but you do all the sinful things you can."

Israel and Judah Must Turn Away from Their Sins

6 The Lord said to me in the days of King Josiah, "Have you seen what Israel did, and what little faith she has? She went up on every high hill and under every green tree, like one who sells the use of her body. 7 And I thought, 'After she has done all these things, she will return to Me.' But she did not return, and her sister Judah, who has not been faithful, saw it. 8 She saw that for all of Israel's sins and how she had not been faithful, I had sent her away and given her a paper of divorce. Yet her sister Judah had no fear, but she went and sold the use of her body also. 9 And because this sin was so easy for her, she sinned by worshiping stones and trees. 10 Even with all this, her sister Judah did not return to Me with all her heart, but in a false way," says the Lord.

11 And the Lord said to me, "Israel, who has not been faithful, has shown herself more right and good than Judah who could not be trusted. 12 Go and make these words known to the north, saying, 'Return, Israel, who has not been faithful,' says the Lord. 'I will not look on you in anger. For I show loving-kindness,' says the Lord. 'I will not be angry forever. 13 Only know and tell of your guilt, that you have sinned against the Lord your God and have given your favors to the strangers under every green tree. Know that you have not obeyed My voice,' says the Lord. 14 'Return, O sons who are not faithful,' says the Lord. 'For you belong to Me. I will take you, one from a city and two from a family, and I will bring you to Zion.' 15 Then I will give you shepherds after My own heart, who will feed you with much learning and understanding. 16 And in those days when you have become many in the land," says the Lord, "they will no more say, 'The special box with the Law of the Lord.' It will not come to mind, and they will not remember it. They will not miss it, and it will not be made again. 17 At that time they will call Jerusalem 'The throne of the Lord.' And all the nations will gather in Jerusalem to honor the name of the Lord. They will not follow the strong-will of their sinful heart any more. 18 In those days the people of

Judah will walk with the people of Israel. They will come together from the land of the north to the land that I gave your fathers as a gift.

God's People Worship False Gods

19 "Then I said, 'How I would like to make you My sons and give you a pleasing land, the most beautiful land of the nations!' And I said, 'You will call Me, "My Father," and not turn away from following Me.' 20 For sure, as a woman is not faithful and leaves her husband, so you have not been faithful to Me, O people of Israel," says the Lord.

21 A voice is heard on the open hill-tops, the cries and prayers of the sons of Israel, because they have made their way sinful. They have forgotten the Lord their God. 22 "Return, O sons who are not faithful. I will heal you and make you faithful." "See, we come to You, for You are the Lord our God. 23 For sure the hills are a false hope, a noise on the mountains. In truth, the saving of Israel is in the Lord our God. 24 But false gods have brought us shame and have destroyed what our fathers worked for since we were young, their flocks and cattle, their sons and their daughters. 25 Let us lie down in our shame, and let our shame cover us. For we and our fathers have sinned against the Lord our God ever since we were young. We have not obeyed the voice of the Lord our God."

God Asks Israel to Turn from Its Sins

4 "If you will return, O Israel," says the Lord, "return to Me. If you will put away your false gods from Me and be faithful to Me, 2 and promise, 'As the Lord lives,' by what is true and right and good, then the nations will be happy in Him. And in Him they will have honor."

3 For the Lord says to the men of Judah and Jerusalem, "Break up your ground which has not been planted, and do not plant seeds among thorns. 4 Set yourselves apart to the Lord, and put away the flesh from your heart, men of Judah and people of Jerusalem. Or My anger will go out like fire and burn with no one to stop it, because of the sinful things you do."

Armies from the North Are Coming

5 Make it known in Judah and Jerusalem, and say, "Sound the horns in the land." Cry out and say, "Gather together, and let us go into the strong cities made ready for battle." 6 Lift up a flag toward Zion! Run

to a safe place, do not stand still. For I am bringing much trouble from the north that will destroy much. 7 A lion has gone up from his secret place. A destroyer of nations has begun to move. He has gone out from his place to make your land a waste. Your cities will be destroyed and no people will live in them. 8 Cover yourselves with cloth made from hair because of this. Cry out in sorrow. For the burning anger of the Lord has not turned away from us. 9 "In that day," says the Lord, "the heart of the king and the hearts of the rulers will become weak. The religious leaders will be filled with fear. And the men of God will be troubled and filled with wonder."

10 Then I said, "O Lord God, for sure You have fooled these people and Jerusalem, saying, 'You will have peace,' when in truth a sword brings danger to their lives."

11 At that time it will be said to these people and Jerusalem, "A hot wind from the open hill-tops in the desert will come toward My people, but not to blow away what is of no worth, and not to make clean. 12 A wind too strong for this will come at My word. Now I will bring punishment against them."

Armies Are All Around Judah

13 See, he comes up like clouds. His warwagons come like the strong wind. His horses are faster than eagles. It is bad for us, for we are destroyed!

14 Wash your heart from sin, O Jerusalem, that you may be saved. How long will your sinful thoughts stay within you? 15 For a voice calls out from Dan, and tells of sin from Mount Ephraim. 16 "Tell it to the nations now! Make it known over all Jerusalem, saying, 'An army is coming from a far country, and they lift up their voices against the cities of Judah.' 17 They are against her all around, like watchmen of a field, because she has turned against Me,' says the Lord. 18 "Your ways and what you do have brought these things to you. This is your sin. How bitter it is! It has touched your very heart!"

Jeremiah Feels Pain for His People

19 My soul, my soul! I am in pain! O, my heart! My heart is beating so hard! It cannot be quiet, for I hear the sound of the horn, telling of the coming war. 20 News of much trouble comes again and again, for the whole land is laid waste. All at once my tents and my curtains are destroyed. 21 How long must I see the flag and hear

the sound of the horn? 22 "For My people are foolish. They do not know Me. They are children who do not think, and they have no understanding. They know a lot about how to do sinful things, but they do not know how to do good."

Jeremiah Saw What the Future Would Be Like

23 I looked on the earth and saw that it was an empty waste. I looked to the heavens, and they had no light. 24 I looked on the mountains and saw they were shaking, and all the hills moved this way and that. 25 I looked and saw that there were no people. And all the birds of the heavens had left. 26 I looked and saw that the rich land was a desert. All its cities were laid waste before the Lord and His burning anger.

27 For the Lord says, "The whole land will be laid waste, yet I will not destroy everything. 28 For the earth will be filled with sorrow and the heavens above will be dark, because I have spoken. I have planned it, and will not change My mind or turn back." 29 Every city runs as they hear the sound of the horseman and the one who fights with arrows. They go among the trees and the rocks. Every city is left empty, and no one lives in them. 30 And you, O destroyed one, what will you do? Even when you dress in red, and wear objects of gold, and color your eyes to make them look bigger, you make yourself beautiful for nothing. Your lovers hate you, and want to kill you. 31 I heard a cry as of a woman in pain, as if she were giving birth to her first child. It was the cry of the people of Zion, working hard to breathe, holding out hands, and saying, "O, it is bad for me! I am losing strength in front of those who want to kill me."

Jerusalem's Sin

5 "Go up and down through the streets of Jerusalem, and look and learn. Look in her open places to see if you can find just one man who does what is right and looks for the truth. Then I will forgive this city. 2 Even if they say, 'As the Lord lives,' for sure their promises are false." 3 O Lord, do not Your eyes look for truth? You have punished them, but they were not sorry. You have destroyed them, but they would not change. They have made their faces harder than rock. They would not be sorry for their sins and turn from them.

4 Then I said, "They are only the poor. They are foolish. For they do not know the way of the Lord or the Law of their God. 5 I will go to the great men and will speak to them, for they know the way of the Lord, and the Law of their God." But they too have broken the load from their neck and have broken the chains. 6 So a lion from among the trees will kill them. A wolf of the deserts will destroy them. A leopard is watching their cities. Every one who goes out of them will be torn in pieces, because they have done many sins. They have turned away from the Lord in many ways.

7 "Why should I forgive you? Your sons have left Me and have sworn by those who are not gods. When I gave them everything they needed, they did sex sins and met at the house of the woman who sells the use of her body. 8 They were like well-fed horses full of sinful desire, each one wanting his neighbor's wife. 9 Should I not punish these people?" says the Lord. "Should I not make a nation such as this pay for its sins?

10 "Go up through her grape-fields and destroy, but do not destroy all of them. Cut away her branches, for they are not the Lord's. 11 For the people of Israel and the people of Judah have not been faithful to Me," says the Lord.

Jerusalem Will Be Destroyed

12 "They have lied about the Lord and said, 'He will do nothing. Nothing bad will happen to us, and we will not see sword or hunger. 13 The men who speak for God are only wind. The word is not in them. So let what they say be done to them!' "

14 So the Lord, the God of All, says, "Because you have said this, I am making My words in your mouth a fire and I am making these people wood so they will be burned up. 15 See, I am bringing a nation that is far away against you, O people of Israel," says the Lord. "It is a strong nation and an old nation, a nation whose language you do not know. You cannot understand what they say. 16 Their arrow-holder is like an open grave. All of them are powerful men. 17 They will eat up your food that you gather from your fields. They will eat the food your sons and your daughters should eat. They will eat up your flocks and your cattle. They will destroy your grape-fields and your fig trees. They will destroy with the sword your strong cities in which you trust.

18 "Yet even in those days I will not make a complete end of you," says the Lord. 19 "When your people say, 'Why has the

Lord our God done all these things to us?' then you will say to them, 'As you have left Me and served strange gods in your land, so you will serve strangers in a land that is not yours.'

20 "Make this known in the family of Jacob and in Judah, saying, 21 'Hear this, O foolish people without understanding, who have eyes but do not see, who have ears but do not hear. 22 Do you not fear Me?' says the Lord. 'Do you not shake in fear before Me? For I have placed the sand to be on one side of the sea, a lasting wall that it cannot cross. Even if there are waves, they cannot pass. Even if they make much noise, they cannot cross over it. 23 But these people have a strong-will and a heart that has turned against Me. They have turned aside and gone away. 24 They do not say in their heart, "Let us fear the Lord our God, Who gives rain in its time, both the fall rain and the spring rain, Who keeps for us the weeks for gathering food." 25 Your wrong-doing has kept these good things away. Your sins have kept good from you. 26 For sinful men are found among My people. They watch like men lying in wait watching for birds. They set a trap, and they catch men. 27 Like a basket full of birds, their houses are full of lies and false ways. So they have become important and rich. 28 They are fat and smooth, and have done many sinful acts. They do not do what is right for those whose parents have died so that they may do well. And they do not help fight for the rights of the poor. 29 Should I not punish these people?' says the Lord. 'Should I not punish a nation such as this?'

30 "A very bad and surprising thing has happened in the land. 31 The men of God say things that are not true, and the religious leaders rule by their own thoughts. And My people love to have it this way! But what will you do in the end?

Armies around Jerusalem

6 "Run away to be safe, O sons of Benjamin! Run from Jerusalem! Blow the horn in Tekoa, and light a fire in Beth-haccerem. For a sinful power is coming down from the north, that will destroy much. 2 I will cut off the beautiful and fine ones, the people of Zion. 3 Shepherds and their flocks will come to her. They will set up their tents around her and feed their flocks there, each in his place. 4 Make war against her. Rise up, let us go and fight her at noon. It is bad for us, for the day is

passing! The shadows of the evening are longer! 5 Rise up, let us go and fight in the night and destroy her strong houses!" 6 For the Lord of All says, "Cut down her trees, and build a battle-wall against Jerusalem. This is the city to be punished. There is nothing but a sinful power that makes hard times for others within her. 7 As a well keeps its water good for drinking, so Jerusalem keeps going on in her sin. The sounds of those who fight and those who destroy are heard in her. Sickness and sorrow are always before Me. 8 Listen about the danger, O Jerusalem, or I will become a stranger to you. I will make you a waste, a land with no people."

Israel Will Not Listen

9 The Lord of All says, "They will gather all the people of Israel who are left like gathering from the vine. Pass your hand over the branches again like one who gathers grapes." 10 Whom should I tell of the danger, that they may hear? See, their ears are closed and they cannot listen. They have become ashamed of the Word of the Lord. They have no joy in it. 11 But I am full of the anger of the Lord. I am tired of holding it in. "Pour it out on the children in the street, and on the young men gathered together. For both husband and wife will be taken, the old and those who have lived a very long time. 12 Their houses, their fields and their wives will be given to others. I will put out My hand against the people of the land," says the Lord. 13 "For from the least to the greatest of them, every one is always wanting something. And from the man of God to the religious leader, every one lies to get what he wants. 14 They have healed the hurt of My people only a little, saying, 'Peace, peace,' when there is no peace. 15 Were they ashamed because of the sinful things they had done? No, they were not ashamed at all. They did not even know how to turn red. So they will fall among those who fall. When I punish them, they will be brought down," says the Lord.

Israel Will Not Go God's Way

16 The Lord says, "Stand by where the roads cross, and look. Ask for the old paths, where the good way is, and walk in it. And you will find rest for your souls. But they said, 'We will not walk in it.' 17 I set watchmen over you, saying, 'Listen to the sound of the horn!' But they said, 'We will not listen.' 18 So hear, O nations, and know,

O people, what will happen to them. ¹⁹ Hear, O earth. See, I am bringing much trouble upon these people. It is the fruit of their plans, because they have not listened to My words. And they have turned away from My law. ²⁰ Why does special perfume come to Me from Sheba, or sweet spices from a far away land? I will not receive your burnt gifts on the altar in worship. The gifts you give on the altar are not pleasing to Me." ²¹ So the Lord says, "See, I am laying things in front of these people, and they will fall over them. Fathers and sons will fall together, and neighbor and friend will die."

Armies from the North

²² The Lord says, "See, a people is coming from the north country. A great nation is being raised up from the farthest parts of the earth. ²³ They take hold of bow and spear. They are hard on people and have no pity. Their voice sounds like the sea. They ride on horses, dressed as a man for battle against you, O people of Zion!" ²⁴ We have heard about it. Our hands fall weak. Suffering has taken hold of us, like the pain of a woman giving birth. ²⁵ Do not go out into the field, and do not walk on the road. For the one who hates us has a sword. Fear is all around us. ²⁶ O daughter of my people, dress in cloth made from hair and roll in ashes. Have sorrow as if you lost your only son. Cry with a bitter cry. For all at once the destroyer will come upon us.

²⁷ "I have asked you to test My people, that you may know and test their ways." ²⁸ All of them are strong-willed in turning to their own way, going about telling stories to hurt people. They are brass and iron. All of them are sinful. ²⁹ Air is blown hard on the fire to burn up the lead. It is of no use because the sinful ones are not taken away. ³⁰ They are called waste silver, because the Lord has turned away from them.

Israel Must Not Trust in Lying Words

7 This word came to Jeremiah from the Lord, saying, ² "Stand in the gate of the Lord's house and make this word known: 'Hear the Word of the Lord, all you men of Judah who go through these gates to worship the Lord!' " ³ The Lord of All, the God of Israel, says, "Change your ways and your works for the better, and I will let you live in this place. ⁴ Do not trust the lies that say, 'This is the house of the Lord, the house of the Lord, the house of

the Lord.' ⁵ For if you for sure change your ways and what you do for the better, if you are fair as you judge between a man and his neighbor, ⁶ if you do not make it hard for the stranger from another land, or the child whose parents have died, or the woman whose husband has died, and do not kill those who are not guilty in this place, and stop going after other gods, for that will destroy you, ⁷ then I will let you live in this place, in the land that I gave to your fathers forever and ever.

⁸ "See, you are trusting in lies which cannot help you. ⁹ Will you steal, kill, do sex sins, make false promises, give gifts to the false god Baal, and go after other gods that you have not known, ¹⁰ and then come and stand before Me in this house which is called by My name, and say, 'We are safe and free!' and still do all these hated sins? ¹¹ Has this house which is called by My name become a place of robbers in your eyes? See, I Myself have seen it," says the Lord.

¹² "But go now to the place in Shiloh where I first made a place for My name. And see what I did to it because of the sin of My people Israel. ¹³ Now you have done all these things," says the Lord. "I spoke to you again and again, but you did not hear. I called you but you did not answer. ¹⁴ So as I did to Shiloh, I will do to the house that is called by My name and in which you trust, and to the place that I gave you and your fathers. ¹⁵ I will send you away from My eyes, as I have sent away all your brothers, all the children of Ephraim.

Israel Does Not Obey

¹⁶ "As for you, do not pray for these people. Do not lift up a cry or prayer for them. Do not speak with Me about them, for I do not hear you. ¹⁷ Do you not see what they are doing in the cities of Judah and in the streets of Jerusalem? ¹⁸ The children gather wood. The fathers make the fire. And the women make bread and cakes for the queen of heaven. They pour out drink gifts to other gods to make Me angry. ¹⁹ Do they make Me angry?" says the Lord. "Is it not themselves they hurt, to their own shame?" ²⁰ So the Lord God says, "See, My anger will be poured out on this place, on man and animal, on the trees of the field and on the fruit of the ground. It will burn and not be stopped."

²¹ The Lord of All, the God of Israel, says, "Add your burnt gifts to the animals you kill on the altar, and eat the flesh. ²² For

when I brought your fathers out of the land of Egypt, I did not speak to them or tell them what to do about burnt gifts and animals killed on the altar. 23 But I did tell them, 'Obey My voice, and I will be your God, and you will be My people. Walk in all the way that I tell you, that it may be well with you.' 24 Yet they did not obey or listen, but walked in the way they wanted to and in the strong-will of their sinful heart. They only stepped back and did not go on. 25 Since the day that your fathers came out of the land of Egypt until this day, I have sent you all My servants who speak for Me. I have risen up early and sent them day after day. 26 Yet they did not listen to Me or turn their ear to Me, but made their neck hard. They sinned more than their fathers.

Israel's Sinful Actions

27 "You will speak all these words to them, but they will not listen to you. You will call to them, but they will not answer you. 28 And you will say to them, 'This is the nation that did not obey the voice of the Lord their God or receive His strong teaching. They have lost the truth. It has been cut off from their mouth. 29 Cut off your hair and throw it away. And cry in sorrow on the open hill-tops. For the Lord has turned away and left the people who made Him angry.' 30 For the sons of Judah have done what is sinful in My eyes," says the Lord. "They have put their hated things in the house that is called by My name, to make it unclean. 31 And they have built the high places of Topheth, in the valley of the son of Hinnom, to burn their sons and daughters in the fire. I did not tell them to do this. It did not come into My mind. 32 So the days are coming," says the Lord, "when it will not be called Topheth any more, or the valley of the son of Hinnom. But it will be called the valley of Killing. For they will bury in Topheth because there is no other place. 33 The dead bodies of these people will be food for the birds of the sky and for the wild animals of the earth. And no one will send them away in fear. 34 Then in the cities of Judah and in the streets of Jerusalem, I will put an end to the voice of joy and the voice of happiness, the voice of the man to be married and the voice of the bride. For the land will become a waste.

8 "At that time," says the Lord, "they will bring out the bones of the kings and leaders of Judah, the bones of the religious leaders, the bones of the men of God, and the bones of the people of Jerusalem from their graves. 2 And they will spread them out to the sun, the moon, and to all the stars of heaven. For these they have loved, and served, and followed, and looked for, and worshiped. The bones will not be gathered or buried. They will be as animal waste on top of the ground. 3 And death will be chosen instead of life by all those who are left of this sinful family in all the places where I have driven them," says the Lord of All.

Sin and Its Punishment

4 "You will say to them, 'This is what the Lord says: "Do men fall and not get up again? Does one turn away and not return? 5 Why then have the people of Jerusalem always turned away from Me? They hold on to what is false, and will not return. 6 I have listened and heard, but they have not said what is right. No man turned from his sinful way, saying, 'What have I done?' Every one turns to his own way like a horse running into battle. 7 Even the stork in the sky knows her times. And the turtle-dove, crane, and swallow keep the time of their coming. But My people do not know the Law of the Lord.

8 "How can you say, 'We are wise, and the Law of the Lord is with us'? See, the lying hand of the writers has made it into a lie. 9 The wise men are put to shame. They are troubled and taken. See, they have turned away from the Word of the Lord, and what kind of wisdom do they have? 10 So I will give their wives to others, and their fields to new owners. Because from the least to the greatest, every one is always wanting much. From the man of God to the religious leader, no one can be trusted in what he does. 11 They have healed the hurt of My people very little, saying, 'Peace, peace,' when there is no peace. 12 Were they ashamed because of the hated sin they had done? They were not ashamed at all. They did not even know how to turn red. So they will fall among those who fall. When I punish them, they will be put down," says the Lord.

13 "For sure I will take them away," says the Lord. "There will be no grapes on the vine, and no figs on the fig tree, and the leaves will dry up. What I have given them will pass away." 14 Why are we sitting here? Gather together, and let us go into the strong cities and die there. For the Lord our God has given us up to die. He

has given us poison in our water to drink, for we have sinned against Him. ¹⁵ We waited for peace, but no good came. We waited for a time of healing, but see, there is much trouble. ¹⁶ The noise of his horses is heard from Dan. The whole land shakes at the sound of his war horses. For they come and destroy the land and everything that is in it, the city and those who live in it. ¹⁷ "For see, I am sending the worst of snakes against you, poison snakes which cannot be stopped. And they will bite you," says the Lord.

¹⁸ My sorrow is too much to heal. My heart is weak within me. ¹⁹ Listen! It is the cry of my people from a far away land: "Is the Lord not in Zion? Is her King not in her?" "Why have they made Me angry with their objects of worship, and with strange gods?" ²⁰ "Gathering time is past, summer is ended, and we are not saved." ²¹ I am hurt because my people are hurt. I am filled with sorrow, and fear has taken hold of me. ²² Is there no healing oil in Gilead? Is there no doctor there? Why then have my people not been healed?

9 If only my head were a well of water, and my eyes a well of tears, that I might cry day and night for my people who have been killed! ² If only I had a place in the desert for travelers to stay, that I might leave my people, and go away from them! For none of them are faithful. They are a gathering of men who cannot be trusted. ³ "They use their tongue like their bow. Lies, and not truth, rule the land. For they go from sin to sin, and they do not know Me," says the Lord. ⁴ "Let every one watch his neighbor. Do not trust any brother. Because every brother sets traps, and every neighbor goes about hurting people with his talk. ⁵ Every one fools his neighbor, and does not tell the truth. They have taught their tongue to tell lies. They become tired doing so many sins. ⁶ You live in the center of false ways. In their false ways they are not willing to know Me," says the Lord.

⁷ So the Lord of All says, "See, I will make them pure and test them. For what else can I do with My people? ⁸ Their tongue is an arrow that kills. It lies. A man speaks peace to his neighbor with his mouth, but in his heart he plans to trap him. ⁹ Should I not punish them for these things?" says the Lord. "Should I not make a nation such as this pay for its sins?

¹⁰ "I will cry with a loud voice for the mountains. I will cry out in sorrow for the fields, because they are laid waste. No one passes through them. The sound of the cattle is not heard. The birds of the sky and the wild animals have run away. They are gone. ¹¹ I will break down Jerusalem into pieces, a place where wild dogs live. And I will lay waste the cities of Judah. No people will live there."

¹² Who is the man wise enough to understand this? To whom has the mouth of the Lord spoken, that he may make it known? Why is the land destroyed and laid waste like a desert, so that no one passes through? ¹³ And the Lord said, "They have turned away from My Law that I have given them. They have not obeyed My voice and would not be led by it. ¹⁴ But they have followed the strongwill of their own hearts, and have gone after the false gods of Baal, as their fathers taught them." ¹⁵ So the Lord of All, the God of Israel, says, "See, I will feed these people with wormwood and put poison in their drinking water. ¹⁶ I will spread them out among the nations whom they and their fathers have not known. And I will go after them with the sword until I have put an end to them."

Jerusalem Cries for Help

¹⁷ The Lord of All says, "Take thought and call for the women who are filled with sorrow, that they may come. Call for the women who cry for the dead, that they may come. ¹⁸ Let them hurry and cry in a loud voice for us, that tears may come from our eyes, and that our eyes will flow with water. ¹⁹ For a sound of loud crying is heard from Zion: 'How we are destroyed! We are filled with shame, for we have left the land because they have broken down our houses.' " ²⁰ Now hear the Word of the Lord, O you women. Let your ear receive the Word of His mouth. Teach your daughters a song of sorrow. Every one teach her neighbor a song for the dead. ²¹ For death has come in through our windows. It has come into our beautiful houses of kings. It has cut off the children from the streets, and the young men from the open spaces of the city. ²² Say, "This is what the Lord says: 'The dead bodies of men will fall like animal waste on the open field, and like grain after the gatherer. But no one will gather them.' "

²³ The Lord says, "Let not a wise man speak with pride about his wisdom. Let not the strong man speak with pride about his strength. And let not a rich man speak

with pride about his riches. 24 But let him who speaks with pride speak about this, that he understands and knows Me, that I am the Lord who shows loving-kindness and does what is fair and right and good on earth. For I find joy in these things," says the Lord.

25 "See, the days are coming," says the Lord, "when I will punish all who have gone through the religious act of the Jews, but have not had the sin cut from their heart. 26 I will punish Egypt, Judah, Edom, the sons of Ammon, Moab, and all those who live in the desert. For none of these nations have had their flesh cut. And none of the people of Israel have had the sin cut from their heart."

True Worship and False Gods

10 Hear the word which the Lord speaks to you, O people of Israel. 2 The Lord says, "Do not learn the way of the nations. And do not be afraid of the things seen in the heavens, even if the nations are afraid of them. 3 For the ways of the people are of no use. They cut wood from the trees. A workman cuts it with an ax. 4 They make it beautiful with silver and gold. They put it together with nails so that it cannot fall apart. 5 Their false gods are like a wooden man set up in a vegetable field to make birds be afraid and stay away. They cannot speak. They must be carried, because they cannot walk. Do not be afraid of them, for they cannot hurt you. And they cannot help you."

6 There is no one like You, O Lord. You are great, and Your name is great in power. 7 Who would not fear You, O King of the nations? For You should be honored with fear. Among all the wise men of the nations, and in all their lands, there is no one like You. 8 They are all poor thinkers and foolish. What can they learn from a false god of wood? 9 Beaten silver is brought from Tarshish, and gold from Uphaz. They are the work of an able workman and of one who works with gold. Their clothing is blue and purple. They are all the work of able workmen. 10 But the Lord is the true God. He is the living God and the King Who lives forever. The earth shakes at His anger. And the nations cannot last when He is angry.

11 This is what you should say to them: "The gods that did not make the heavens and the earth will be destroyed from the earth and from under the heavens."

A Song of Praise

12 It is He Who made the earth by His power, and the world by His wisdom. By His understanding He has spread out the heavens. 13 When He speaks, there is a storm of waters in the heavens. He makes the clouds rise from the ends of the earth. He makes lightning for the rain, and brings out the wind from His store-houses. 14 Every man is a poor thinker and without learning. Every one who works with gold is put to shame by his false gods. For his objects of worship fool people. There is no breath in them. 15 They are without worth, and make fun of the truth. In the time of their punishment, they will be destroyed. 16 He Who is the God of Jacob is not like these, for He has made all things. And Israel is His chosen family. The Lord of All is His name.

People of Jerusalem Will Be Taken Away

17 Pick up your load from the ground, you who are shut in by armies! 18 For the Lord says, "See, I am throwing out the people of the land at this time. And I will trouble them, that they may feel it."

19 It is bad for me because I am hurt! My sore cannot be healed. But I said, "For sure this sickness is mine, and I must suffer with it." 20 My tent is destroyed and all my ropes are broken. My sons have gone from me and are no more. There is no one to put up my tent again or to set up my curtains. 21 For the shepherds are poor thinkers and have not asked for the Lord's help. So they have not done well, and all their flock is sent different places. 22 Listen, the sound of news! See, it comes! Much noise of moving is coming out of the land of the north to destroy the cities of Judah, and to make it a place where wild dogs live.

Jeremiah's Prayer

23 O Lord, I know that a man's way is not known by himself. It is not in man to lead his own steps. 24 Punish me when I need it, O Lord, but be fair. Do not punish me in Your anger, or You will bring me to nothing. 25 Pour out Your anger on the nations that do not know You, and on the families that do not call on Your name. For they have destroyed Jacob. They have destroyed him and have laid waste his land.

The Agreement Is Broken

11 The word that came to Jeremiah from the Lord, saying, 2 "Hear the words of this agreement, and speak to the men of Judah and the people of Jerusalem.

3 Say to them, 'This is what the Lord, the God of Israel, says: "Cursed is the man who does not listen to the words of this agreement 4 which I told to your fathers before you when I brought them out of the land of Egypt. I brought them from the land that was like an iron stove. I said to them, 'Listen to My voice, and do all that I tell you. Then you will be My people and I will be your God.' 5 And so I will keep the promise I made to your fathers before you, to give them a land flowing with milk and honey, as it is this day.'"' Then I answered and said, "Let it be so, O Lord."

6 The Lord said to me, "Make these words known in the cities of Judah and in the streets of Jerusalem, saying, 'Hear the words of this agreement and do them. 7 For by My strong words I told your fathers of the danger when I brought them up from the land of Egypt. I kept telling them even to this day, saying, "Listen to My voice." 8 Yet they did not obey or listen. Every one walked in his own strong-will because of his sinful heart. So I brought upon them all the words of this agreement, which I told them to do, but they did not.'"

9 Then the Lord said to me, "Sinful plans have been made by the men of Judah and the people of Jerusalem. 10 They have returned to the sins of their fathers before them who would not listen to My words. And they have gone to serve other gods. The people of Israel and Judah have broken the agreement I made with their fathers." 11 So the Lord says, "See, I am bringing much trouble on them. They will not be able to get away from it. Even when they cry to Me, I will not listen to them. 12 Then the cities of Judah and the people of Jerusalem will go and cry to the gods to whom they burn special perfume. But they cannot save them in the time of their trouble. 13 For your gods are as many as your cities, O Judah. And your altars you have set up to burn special perfume to the false god Baal are as many as the streets of Jerusalem.

14 "So do not pray for these people. Do not lift up a cry or prayer for them. For I will not listen when they call to Me because of their trouble. 15 What right has My loved one to be in My house when she has done many sinful acts? Can animals killed on My altar take your trouble away from you? Can you then find joy?" 16 The Lord called you, "A green olive tree, beautiful and with good fruit." But with a noise like thunder He set fire to it, and its branches were destroyed. 17 The Lord of All, Who planted you, has said that bad will come to you because of the sin of the people of Israel and of the people of Judah. They have done wrong to make Me angry by burning special perfume to the false god Baal.

Men of Anathoth Want to Kill Jeremiah

18 The Lord made it known to me and I knew it. You showed me the sinful things they did. 19 But I was like a gentle lamb led to be killed. I did not know that they had made plans against me, saying, "Let us destroy the tree with its fruit. Let us cut him off from the land of the living, that his name be remembered no more." 20 But, O Lord of All, Who is right as He judges, Who tests the heart and the mind, let me see You punish them. For I have put my cause before You.

21 So the Lord speaks about the men of Anathoth who want to kill you. These men say, "Do not speak in the name of the Lord, or you will die by our hand." 22 So the Lord of All says, "See, I am about to punish them! The young men will die by the sword. And their sons and daughters will die from hunger. 23 None of them will be left. For I will bring much trouble to the men of Anathoth, in the year of their punishment."

Jeremiah's Question

12 You are right and good, O Lord, when I complain to You about my trouble. Yet I would like to talk with You about what is fair. Why does the way of the sinful go well? Why do all those who cannot be trusted have it so easy? 2 You have planted them, and they have taken root. They grow and have given fruit. You are near on their lips but far from their heart. 3 But You know me, O Lord. You see me. And You test how my heart is with You. Take them off like sheep to be killed. Set them apart for the day of killing. 4 How long will the land be filled with sorrow? How long will the grass of every field dry up? For the sin of those who live in it, animals and birds have been taken away, because men have said, "He will not see what happens to us."

God's Answer

5 "If you have run with men on foot and they have made you tired, then how can you run as fast as horses? If you fall down in a land of peace, how will you do among

all the trees beside the Jordan? 6 For even your brothers and those of your father's house have not been faithful to you. They have cried to you in a loud voice. Do not believe them, even if they say pleasing things to you."

The Lord's Sorrow for Israel

7 "I have left My house. I have left My chosen nation. I have given the loved one of My soul into the hand of those who hate her. 8 My chosen nation has become to Me like a lion among the trees. She has raised her voice against Me, so I hate her. 9 Is My chosen nation like a spot-covered, flesh-eating bird to Me? Are the flesh-eating birds against her on every side? Go, gather all the wild animals of the field, and bring them to eat. 10 Many shepherds have destroyed My grape-field. They have crushed My field under foot. They have turned My good field to an empty desert. 11 It has been laid waste. Destroyed and empty, it cries with sorrow before Me. The whole land has been laid waste, because no one cares. 12 On all the open hill-tops in the desert, destroyers have come. For the sword of the Lord destroys from one end of the land to the other. There is no peace for anyone. 13 They have planted grain and have gathered thorns. They have worked hard, but have nothing. Be ashamed of what you gather because of the burning anger of the Lord."

Israel's Neighbors

14 This is what the Lord says about all My sinful neighbors who take the gift I have given to My people Israel: "See, I am about to pull them up by the roots from their land. And I will pull up the people of Judah by the roots from among them. 15 But after I have pulled them up by the roots, I will have loving-pity on them again, and will bring them back. I will return each one to what he has been given and to his land. 16 Then if they will for sure learn the ways of My people, and promise by My name, 'As the Lord lives,' even as they taught My people to promise by Baal, then they will be built up among My people. 17 But if they will not listen, then I will pull that nation up by the roots and destroy it," says the Lord.

The Linen Belt

13 The Lord said to me, "Go and buy a linen belt, and put it around yourself. But do not put it in water." 2 So I bought the belt as the Lord had said and put it around

me. 3 Then the Word of the Lord came to me a second time, saying, 4 "Take the belt that you have bought and are wearing, get up, and go to the Euphrates. Hide it there in a hole in the rock." 5 So I went and hid it by the Euphrates, as the Lord had told me. 6 After many days the Lord said to me, "Get up and go to the Euphrates and get the belt which I told you to hide there." 7 Then I went to the Euphrates and dug, and I took the belt from the place where I had hidden it. And I saw that the belt was worth nothing.

8 Then the Word of the Lord came to me, saying, 9 "This is what the Lord says: 'In this way I will destroy the pride of Judah and the great pride of Jerusalem. 10 These sinful people would not listen to My words. They walk in the strong-will of their own hearts and have gone to serve and worship other gods. So let them be just like this linen belt, which is good for nothing. 11 For as the belt holds on to a man's body, so I made the whole family of Israel and the whole family of Judah hold on to Me,' says the Lord. 'This was so that they might be for Me a people, a name, a praise, and an honor. But they would not listen.'

The Wine Bottles

12 "So you are to tell this to them: 'The Lord, the God of Israel, says, "Every jar is to be filled with wine." ' And when they say to you, 'Do we not know very well that every jar is to be filled with wine?' 13 then tell them, 'The Lord says, "I am about to fill all the people of this land, the kings who sit on David's throne, the religious leaders, the men of God, and all the people of Jerusalem with too much drink. 14 And I will throw them against each other, both the fathers and sons together," says the Lord. "I will not let pity or sorrow or loving-kindness keep Me from destroying them." ' "

Pride Comes before Punishment

15 Listen and hear. Do not be proud, for the Lord has spoken. 16 Give honor to the Lord your God before He brings darkness and before you slip and fall on the dark mountains. You hope for light, but He will turn it into darkness and it will be very dark. 17 But if you will not listen, my soul will cry in secret because of your pride. My eyes will cry with a bitter cry and tears will flow down, because the Lord's people have been taken away in chains. 18 Say to the king and the queen mother, "Come

down from your throne. Your beautiful crown has been taken from your head." [19] The cities of the Negev have been locked up, and there is no one to open them. All Judah has been taken away. All the people of Judah have been taken to another land.

[20] "Look up and see those who are coming from the north. Where is the flock that was given to you, your beautiful sheep? [21] What will you say when He sets over you those whom you have taught and who were your friends? Will not pain take hold of you, like a woman giving birth? [22] And if you say in your heart, 'Why have these things happened to me?' It is because of your many sins that your clothing has been torn off and you suffer punishment. [23] Can the Ethiopian change his skin or the leopard his spots? Then you also can do good who are used to doing wrong. [24] I will cause you to go everywhere like straw blown by the desert wind. [25] This is what you get, the share given to you from Me," says the Lord, "because you have forgotten Me and trusted in lies. [26] So I will pull your clothing up over your face, that your shame may be seen. [27] As for your sex sins and cries of desire, your sinful sex acts on the hills in the field, I have seen your hated sins. It is bad for you, O Jerusalem! How long will you be unclean?"

No Water—No Food

14 The Word of the Lord which came to Jeremiah when there was no water: [2] "Judah is full of sorrow and her gates are weak. Her people sit on the ground in sorrow, and a cry goes up from Jerusalem. [3] Their men of honor have sent their servants for water. They have come to the wells and found no water, and returned with their jars empty. They have been put to shame and troubled, and covered their heads. [4] The ground is dried up because there has been no rain on the land. The farmers have been put to shame and have covered their heads. [5] Even the deer in the field leaves her young one which has just been born, because there is no grass. [6] The wild donkeys stand on the open hill-tops. They breathe hard for air like wild dogs. Their eyes become weak because there is nothing to eat.

[7] "Even when our sins speak against us, O Lord, do something for the good of Your name. For we have fallen away from You many times. We have sinned against You. [8] You are the Hope of Israel, the One Who saves it in time of trouble. Why are You like a stranger in the land? Why are You like a traveler who has set up his tent for the night? [9] Why are You like a man surprised, like a strong man who cannot save? Yet You are among us, O Lord, and we are called by Your name. Do not leave us!"

[10] The Lord says this about these people, "They have loved to go their own way. They have not held their feet back. So the Lord is not pleased with them. Now He will remember their wrong-doing and punish their sins." [11] The Lord said to me, "Do not pray for the well-being of these people. [12] When they go without food, I will not listen to their cry. And when they give burnt gifts and grain gifts, I will not receive them. But I will destroy them by the sword, hunger and disease."

[13] Then I said, "O Lord God, the ones who speak in Your name are telling them, 'You will not see the sword and you will not go hungry. But I will give you lasting peace in this place.' " [14] Then the Lord said to me, "Those men are speaking lies in My name. I have not sent them, or told them, or spoken to them. They are telling you a false dream of a false future that means nothing. They are speaking the lies of their own hearts. [15] So this is what the Lord says about those men who tell what is going to happen in the future using My name. I did not send them, yet they keep saying, 'There will be no sword or hunger in this land.' So by the sword and by hunger those false teachers will be destroyed! [16] And the people they tell these things to will be thrown out into the streets of Jerusalem because of hunger and the sword. There will be no one to bury them, or their wives, or their sons, or their daughters. For I will pour out their own sin upon them. [17] You will say to them, 'Let my eyes flow with tears without stopping night and day. For my people have been crushed with a very hard beating. [18] If I go out to the country, I see those killed by the sword! Or if I go into the city, I see diseases because of hunger! For both the man who speaks for God and the religious leader have gone around and around in the land they do not know.' "

The People Cry to the Lord

[19] Have You nothing at all to do with Judah any more? Do You hate Zion? Why have You punished us so that we cannot be healed? We waited for peace, but nothing good came. We waited for a time of healing, but there is much trouble. [20] We know that we are sinful, O Lord, and we

know the sin of our fathers. For we have sinned against You. 21 For the good of Your name do not hate us. Do not put to shame the throne of Your shining-greatness. Remember and do not break Your agreement with us. 22 Are there any among the false gods of the nations who give rain? Or can the heavens give rain? Is it not You, O Lord our God? So we hope in You. For You are the One Who has done all these things.

Troubles for Judah

15 Then the Lord said to me, "Even if Moses and Samuel were to stand before Me, My heart would not be with these people. Send them away from Me and let them go! 2 And when they ask you, 'Where should we go?' then tell them, 'The Lord says, "Those who are to die, to death, and those who are to be killed by the sword, to the sword. Those who are to go hungry, to hunger, and those who are to be taken away as prisoners, to be taken away.' 3 I will set over them four kinds of destroyers," says the Lord: "The sword to kill, the dogs to take away, and the birds of the sky and the wild animals of the earth to eat and destroy. 4 I will make them an object of much fear and hate among all the nations of the earth because of Manasseh, the son of Hezekiah, king of Judah, for what he did in Jerusalem.

5 "Who will have pity on you, O Jerusalem, or who will have sorrow for you? Who will turn aside to ask about your well-being? 6 You have turned away from Me," says the Lord. "You keep going back into sin. So I will put out My hand against you and destroy you. I am tired of having pity on you! 7 I will throw them to the wind like straw at the gates of the land. I will take their children from them. I will destroy My people. For they did not turn from their ways. 8 Their women whose husbands have died will be as many as the sand of the seas. At noon I will bring a destroyer against the mothers of young men. I will bring suffering and fear to them all at once. 9 She who gave birth to seven sons will become weak and die. Her sun will set while it is still day, and she will be put to shame. I will give the rest of them to the sword in front of those who hate them," says the Lord.

Jeremiah Complains

10 It is bad for me, my mother, that you have given birth to me! I am a man of trouble and fighting to all the land. No one owes money to me, and I do not owe money to others, yet every one curses me. 11 The Lord said, "For sure I will set you free for a good reason. For sure I will make those who hate you ask of you in times of trouble and suffering.

12 "Can anyone crush iron, iron from the north, or brass? 13 I will give your money and riches to those who fight against you, without a price, because of all your sins in all your land. 14 I will make those who hate you bring your riches into a land you do not know. For My anger has started a fire that will burn you."

15 O Lord, You understand. Remember me and visit me. And punish those who make it hard for me. Do not take me away, for You are slow to be angry. Know that because of You I suffer and am put to shame. 16 Your words were found and I ate them. And Your words became a joy to me and the happiness of my heart. For I have been called by Your name, O Lord God of All. 17 I did not sit with those who were having fun, and I was not full of joy. I sat alone because Your hand was upon me. For You had filled me with hate for their sin. 18 Why is there no end to my pain? And why will my hurt not be healed? Will You be to me like a river that flows with water some of the time and is dry at other times?

The Lord's Answer

19 So the Lord says, "If you return, then I will let you take your place again, standing before Me. And if you take out what is of worth from what is of no worth, then you will speak for Me. Let these people turn to you, but you must not turn to them. 20 Then I will make you like a strong wall of brass to these people. Even if they fight against you, they will not get power over you. For I am with you to save you and bring you out of trouble," says the Lord. 21 "I will take you from the hand of the sinful. And I will free you from the hand of those who would hurt you."

16 The Word of the Lord came to me, saying, 2 "Do not get married or have sons or daughters in this place." 3 For this is what the Lord says about the sons and daughters born in this land, and about their mothers who give birth to them, and their fathers who gave them life in this land: 4 "They will die of bad diseases. No one will cry for them or bury them. They will be as animal waste on the ground, destroyed by sword and hunger. Their dead bodies will become food for the birds of the sky and for the wild animals of the earth."

5 For the Lord says, "Do not go into a house where the people have lost a loved one. Do not go to cry or to comfort them. For I have taken My peace, My loving-kindness and My pity from these people," says the Lord. 6 "Both great men and small will die in this land. They will not be buried. No one will cry for them. And no one will cut himself or cut off his hair for them. 7 No one will give food to comfort those who sorrow for the dead. And no one will give them the cup of comfort to drink even for the death of their father or mother. 8 Do not go into a house where they are eating much and sit with them to eat and drink." 9 For the Lord of All, the God of Israel, says, "Before your eyes and in your time, I am going to bring an end to the voice of joy, the voice of happiness, the voice of the man to be married and the voice of the bride in this place.

10 "When you tell these people all these words, they will say to you, 'Why has the Lord said all these bad things will happen to us? What wrong have we done? What sin have we done against the Lord our God?' 11 Then you tell them, 'It is because your fathers before you have turned away from Me,' says the Lord. 'They have followed other gods and served them and worshiped them. But they have left Me and have not kept My Law. 12 And you have sinned even more than your fathers before you. For see, each one of you is following the strong-will of his own sinful heart instead of listening to Me. 13 So I will throw you out of this land into a land which you and your fathers have not known. There you will serve other gods day and night, for I will show you no favor.'

God Will Bring Israel Back

14 "So the days are coming," says the Lord, "when it will no longer be said, 'As the Lord lives, Who brought up the sons of Israel out of the land of Egypt.' 15 But it will be said, 'As the Lord lives, Who brought the sons of Israel from the land of the north and from all the countries where He had sent them.' For I will return them to their own land which I gave to their fathers.

The Punishment That Is Coming

16 "See, I am going to send for many fishermen," says the Lord, "and they will fish

for them. After this I will send for many men who hunt. And they will hunt them from every mountain and every hill, and out of the holes in the rocks. 17 For I see all their ways. They are not hidden from My face, and their sin is not hidden from My eyes. 18 And I will pay them back twice as much for their wrong-doing and their sin, because they have made My land unclean. They have filled My land with the bodies of their hated false gods and with sinful things offered to them."

Jeremiah's Prayer

19 O Lord, my strength and my strong-place, my safe place in the day of trouble, nations will come to You from the ends of the earth and say, "Our fathers have received nothing but lies, only things that have no worth and do not help them." 20 Can man make his own gods? What man makes is not gods!

21 "So I am going to make them know. This time I will make them know My power and My strength. And they will know that My name is the Lord."

Judah's Sin and the Punishment

17 The sin of Judah is written down with pen of iron and with a sharp diamond. It is written on their hearts and on the horns of their altars. 2 Even their children remember their altars and their wooden female goddesses of Asherah by green trees and on the high hills. 3 O My mountain in the country, I will give your money and all your riches to those who fight against you. I will give your high places as the price of your sin through all your land. 4 And you yourself will let your land go that I gave you. I will make you serve those who hate you in a land which you do not know. For you have made My anger start a fire which will burn forever.

5 The Lord says, "Cursed is the man who trusts in man, who trusts in the flesh for his strength, and whose heart turns away from the Lord. 6 For he will be like a bush in the desert and will not see when good comes. He will live in dry wastes in the desert, in a land of salt where no other people live. 7 Good will come to the man who trusts in the Lord, and whose hope is in the Lord. 8 He will be like a tree planted by the water, that sends out its roots to the river. It will not be afraid when the heat comes but its leaves will be green. It will not be troubled in a dry year, or stop giving fruit.

9 "The heart is fooled more than anything else, and is very sinful. Who can know how bad it is? 10 I the Lord look into the heart, and test the mind. I give to each man what he should have because of his ways and because of the fruit that comes from his works. 11 As a bird that sits on eggs which it has not laid, so is he who gets rich by doing wrong. When his life is half over, they will leave him, and in the end he will be a fool."

12 A beautiful throne on high from the beginning is our holy place. 13 O Lord, the hope of Israel, all who leave You will be put to shame. Those who turn away from You will be written in the earth, because they have left the Lord, the well of living water.

Jeremiah Prays for Help

14 Heal me, O Lord, and I will be healed. Save me and I will be saved. For You are my praise. 15 They say to me, "Where is the Word of the Lord? Let it come now!" 16 But as for me, I have not run away from being a shepherd who follows You. And I have not been hoping for the day of trouble. You know what I said was spoken in front of You. 17 Do not make me afraid of You. You are my safe place in the day of trouble. 18 Let those who make it hard for me be put to shame, but do not let me be put to shame. Let them be afraid, but do not let me be afraid. Bring on them a day of trouble, and destroy them with twice as much!

Keeping the Day of Rest Holy

19 The Lord said to me, "Go and stand in the people's gate, through which the kings of Judah come in and go out, and also in all the gates of Jerusalem. 20 And say to them, 'Listen to the Word of the Lord, kings of Judah, and all Judah, and all people of Jerusalem who come in through these gates. 21 The Lord says, "Be careful for your lives. Do not carry any load on the Day of Rest or bring anything in through the gates of Jerusalem. 22 Do not bring a load out of your houses on the Day of Rest or do any work. But keep the Day of Rest holy, as I told your fathers before you. 23 Yet they did not listen or hear, but made their necks hard and would not change their ways.

24 "Listen to Me," says the Lord, "and bring no load through the city gates on the Day of Rest. Keep the Day of Rest holy by doing no work on it. 25 Then kings and their sons will come through the city gates who will sit on the throne of David. They will come in war-wagons and on horses, with the men of Judah and the people of Jerusalem. And people will live in this city forever. 26 People will come in from the cities of Judah and from the places around Jerusalem. They will come from the land of Benjamin, from the valleys, from the hill country, and from the Negev. They will bring burnt gifts, animals to kill on the altar in worship, grain gifts, special perfume, and gifts of thanks to the house of the Lord. 27 But if you do not listen to Me, to keep the Day of Rest holy by not carrying a load when coming through the gates of Jerusalem on the Day of Rest, then I will start a fire in its gates. And it will burn up the beautiful houses of the kings of Jerusalem and will not be stopped."'"

The Pot-Maker and the Clay

18 The word which came to Jeremiah from the Lord saying, 2 "Go down to the pot-maker's house, and there I will let you hear My words." 3 So I went down to the pot-maker's house, and saw him making one on the wheel. 4 But the pot he was making of clay did not come out like he wanted it. So the pot-maker used the clay to make another pot that pleased him.

5 Then the Word of the Lord came to me saying, 6 "O people of Israel, can I not do with you as this pot-maker has done?" says the Lord. "Like the clay in the pot-maker's hand, so are you in My hand, O people of Israel. 7 If at any time I speak about a nation, to pull up, and to break down and to destroy, 8 and if that nation I spoke against turns from its sin, then I will change My mind about the trouble I planned to bring upon it. 9 If at another time I speak about a nation, that I will build and plant it, 10 and if it does what is sinful in My eyes by not obeying My voice, then I will change My mind about the good I had promised to bring to it. 11 So now speak to the men of Judah and the people of Jerusalem. Tell them, 'The Lord says, "See, I am making trouble for you and making a plan against you. So each of you turn from your sinful way. Change your ways and your works." ' 12 But they will say, 'There is no hope! For we are going to follow our own plans. Each of us will act in the strong-will of his sinful heart.'

The People Turn from the Lord

13 "So the Lord says, 'Ask now among the nations: Who has heard such things? Pure Israel has done a very sinful thing. 14 Does the snow of Lebanon ever leave its

rocky mountains? Does the cold flowing water of other lands ever dry up? 15 But My people have forgotten Me. They burn special perfume to false gods of no worth. They have fallen in their ways, from the old paths, and have gone on side roads, not on the straight road. 16 They make their land a waste, a thing that is spoken against forever. Everyone who passes by it will be surprised and shake his head. 17 I will send them out everywhere like an east wind in front of those who hate them. I will show them My back and not My face in the day of their trouble.' "

Plans to Kill Jeremiah

18 They said, "Come and let us make plans against Jeremiah. For the Law is not going to be lost to the religious leader, or wise words to the wise man, or the Word of God to the man of God! Come and let us hurt him with our tongue, and let us not listen to any of his words."

19 Think of me, O Lord, and listen to what those who hate me are saying! 20 Should bad be given in return for good? Yet they have dug a deep hole for me. Remember how I stood before You to speak good for them, to turn Your anger away from them. 21 So give their children over to hunger. Give them up to the power of the sword. Let their wives lose their children and husbands. Let their men be put to death. And let their young men be killed by the sword in battle. 22 May a cry be heard from their houses when You bring an army upon them by surprise. For they have dug a deep hole to take me, and have hidden traps for my feet. 23 Yet You, O Lord, know all their plans to kill me. Do not forgive their wrong-doing or cover their sin from Your eyes. Let them be taken down before You. Punish them in the time of Your anger.

The Broken Jar

19 The Lord says, "Go and buy a pot-maker's clay jar, and take some of the leaders of the people and some of the older religious leaders. 2 Then go out to the valley of Ben-hinnom, by the Potsherd Gate, and there say the words that I will tell you. 3 Say, 'Hear the Word of the Lord, O kings of Judah and people of Jerusalem. The Lord of All, the God of Israel, says, "See, I am about to bring much trouble to this place. The ears of everyone that hears of it will hurt. 4 The people have left Me and have made this a strange place. They have burned special perfume in it to other gods that they and their fathers

and the kings of Judah had never known. They have filled this place with the blood of those who were not guilty. 5 They have built the high places of the false god Baal to burn their sons in the fire as burnt gifts to Baal. This is a thing which I never told them to do or spoke of. It did not even come to My mind. 6 So see, the days are coming," says the Lord, "when this place will no longer be called Topheth or the valley of Ben-hinnom. Instead it will be called the Valley of Killing. 7 I will make the plans of Judah and Jerusalem come to nothing in this place. I will cause them to fall by the sword in front of those who hate them and by the hand of those who want to kill them. And I will feed their dead bodies to the birds of the sky and the wild animals of the earth. 8 I will make this city a waste place, and people will make sounds of hate. Everyone who passes by it will be surprised and make strange noises because of all its troubles. 9 I will make them eat the flesh of their sons and daughters. And they will eat each other's flesh when the armies shut them in, and when those who want to kill them bring much trouble to them." '

10 "Then you are to break the jar in front of the men who go with you. 11 And say to them, 'The Lord of All says, "In this way I will break these people and this city, even as one breaks a pot-maker's jar, which cannot be put back together. Men will bury the dead in Topheth until there is no place left to bury. 12 This is what I will do to this place and its people," says the Lord. "I will make this city like Topheth. 13 The houses of Jerusalem and the houses of the kings of Judah will be made unclean like Topheth. This will be because of all the houses on whose roofs they burned special perfume to all the false gods of the heavens and poured out drink gifts to other gods." ' "

14 Then Jeremiah came from Topheth, where the Lord had sent him to tell what would happen. And he stood in the open space of the Lord's house and said to all the people, 15 "The Lord of All, the God of Israel, says, 'See, I am about to bring to this city and to all its towns all the trouble that I have spoken about, because they have made their necks hard and would not listen to My Words.' "

Jeremiah and the Religious Leader Pashhur

20 Now Pashhur the religious leader, the son of Immer, was the head leader in the house of the Lord. When he heard Jeremiah saying these things,

2 Pashhur had Jeremiah the man of God beaten. Then he put him in chains at the upper Benjamin Gate by the house of the Lord. 3 On the next day, when Pashhur set Jeremiah free from the chains, Jeremiah said to him, "The Lord does not call you Pashhur, but Fear Everywhere. 4 For the Lord says, 'See, I am going to make you a fear to yourself and to all your friends. They will fall by the sword of those who hate them while you look on. I will give all Judah into the hand of the king of Babylon. And he will carry them away in chains to Babylon and kill them with the sword. 5 I will give over all the riches of this city, all that its people have worked for, and all its things of much worth. Even all the riches of the kings of Judah I will give to those who hate them. They will take their things, and take hold of them, and carry them to Babylon. 6 And you, Pashhur, and all who live in your house will be taken away in chains. You will go to Babylon, and there you will die, and there you will be buried, you and all your friends to whom you have told lies.' "

Jeremiah's Complaint to the Lord

7 O Lord, You have lied to me and I was fooled. You are stronger than I, and have had power over me. I have been laughed at all day. Everyone makes fun of me. 8 For whenever I speak, I cry out. I tell of fighters and destroyers. For the Word of the Lord has become a shame and a cause of laughing at me all day long. 9 But if I say, "I will not remember Him or speak any more in His name," then in my heart it is like a burning fire shut up in my bones. I am tired of holding it in, and I cannot do that. 10 For I have heard many speaking in secret, saying, "Fear and trouble is on every side! Speak against him! Yes, let us speak against him!" All my trusted friends, watching for my fall, say, "It may be that he will be fooled. Then we can get power over him and punish him." 11 But the Lord is with me like a powerful one who causes fear. So those who make it hard for me will fall and not have power over me. They will be put to much shame, because their plans have not gone well. Their shame will last forever and will not be forgotten. 12 O Lord of All, You test those who are right and good. You see the mind and the heart. Let me see You punish them, for I have given my cause to You. 13 Sing to the Lord! Praise the Lord! For He has taken the soul of the one in need from the hand of the sinful.

14 Cursed is the day when I was born! Let the day not be honored when my mother gave birth to me! 15 Cursed be the man who brought the news to my father, saying, "A baby boy has been born to you!" and made him very happy. 16 Let that man be like the cities which the Lord destroyed without pity. Let him hear a cry in the morning and a call of danger at noon. 17 For he did not kill me before I was born, so that my mother's body would have been my grave. 18 Why was I ever born to see trouble and sorrow, and spend my days in shame?

Jerusalem to Be Taken

21 This is the word which came to Jeremiah from the Lord when King Zedekiah sent to him Pashhur the son of Malchijah, and Zephaniah the religious leader, the son of Maaseiah, saying, 2 "Will you speak to the Lord about us? For King Nebuchadnezzar of Babylon is making war against us. It may be that the Lord will do something for us like He did in times past, and make him leave us."

3 Then Jeremiah said to them, "Say this to Zedekiah: 4 'The Lord God of Israel says, "See, I will turn against you the objects of war you are using to fight with against the king of Babylon and the Babylonians who are gathered outside the wall to shut you in. And I will bring them into the center of this city. 5 I Myself will fight against you with My hand out and with a strong arm, in much anger. 6 I will kill both man and animal in this city. They will die of a bad disease. 7 After this" says the Lord, "I will give over Zedekiah king of Judah, his servants, and the people who were not killed in this city by the disease, the sword, and hunger. I will give them into the hand of Nebuchadnezzar king of Babylon, and into the hand of those who hate them, and into the hand of those who want to kill them. And he will kill them with the sword. He will not let them live or have pity for them." '

8 "Also tell the people, 'The Lord says, "See, I set before you the way of life and the way of death. 9 He who lives in this city will die by the sword and by hunger and by disease. But he who goes out and gives himself up to the Babylonians whose armies shut you in will live, he will at least have his life. 10 For I have set My face against this city for trouble and not for good," says the Lord. "It will be given to the king of Babylon, and he will burn it with fire." '

Words against Judah

11 "Then say to those of the house of the king of Judah, 'Hear the Word of the Lord, 12 O house of David, the Lord says, "Do what is right every morning. Take the person who has been robbed away from the one who has made it hard for him. So My anger will not go out like fire and burn with no one to put it out, because of the sinful things you have done.

13 "See, I am against you, O you who live in the valley, O rock of the plain," says the Lord, "you who say, 'Who will come down against us? Or who will come into our houses?' 14 I will punish you for what has come of what you have done," says the Lord. "I will start a fire among your trees, and it will destroy all that is around it."'"

Jeremiah's Words to the Kings of Judah

22 The Lord says, "Go down to the house of the king of Judah, and speak this word there. 2 Say, 'Hear the Word of the Lord, O king of Judah, who sits on David's throne, you and your servants and your people who come through these gates. 3 The Lord says, "Do what is right and fair and good, and take the one who has been robbed away from the power of the one who has made it hard for him. Do not hurt or do wrong to the stranger, the one whose parents have died, or the woman whose husband has died. And do not kill those who are not guilty in this place. 4 For if you will obey this word, then kings will come through the gates of this house and sit on the throne of David. They will be in war-wagons and on horses, together with their servants and their people. 5 But if you will not obey these words, I promise by Myself," says the Lord, "that this house will be destroyed."'" 6 For the Lord says about the house of the king of Judah: "You are like Gilead to Me, or like the top of Lebanon. Yet I will be sure to make you like a desert, like cities without people. 7 I will send destroyers against you, each with his things for fighting. And they will cut down your best cedar trees and throw them on the fire. 8 Many nations will pass by this city, and they will say to one another, 'Why has the Lord done such a thing to this great city?' 9 And they will answer, 'Because they did not keep the agreement of the Lord their God. They worshiped other gods and served them.'"

Words about Shallum

10 Do not cry for the one who is dead or have sorrow for him. But cry all the time for the one who goes away, for he will never return or see the land of his birth again. 11 For the Lord says about Shallum the son of Josiah, king of Judah, who ruled in the place of Josiah his father, and who left this place: "He will never return. 12 He will die in the place where they took him, and he will not see this land again."

Words about Jehoiakim

13 "It is bad for him who builds his house by wrong-doing, and his upper rooms by not being fair, who has his neighbor serve him for nothing and does not pay him, 14 who says, 'I will build myself a big house with large upper rooms. I will cut out its windows, cover it with cedar and color it bright red.' 15 Do you become a king by trying to build better houses of cedar? Did not your father eat and drink? He did what was right and fair and good, so all went well with him. 16 He spoke strong words in the cause of the poor and those in need, and so all went well. Is not that what it means to know Me?" says the Lord. 17 "But your eyes and heart are set only on what you can get by wrong-doing, and on killing those who are not guilty, and on making it hard for people and on hurting others." 18 So the Lord says about Jehoiakim the son of Josiah, king of Judah, "They will not cry in sorrow for him, saying, 'It is bad, my brother!' or, 'It is bad, my sister!' They will not cry in sorrow for him, saying, 'O lord!' or, 'O, how great he was!' 19 He will be buried like they bury a donkey, pulled away and thrown out on the other side of the gates of Jerusalem.

The Future of Jerusalem

20 "Go up to Lebanon and cry out. And let your voice be heard in Bashan. Cry out from Abarim also. For all your lovers have been destroyed. 21 I spoke to you when things were going well for you, but you said, 'I will not listen!' This has been your way since you were young. You have not obeyed My voice. 22 The wind will take away all your shepherds, and your lovers will be taken away in chains. Then you will be ashamed and troubled because of all your sin. 23 O you people of Lebanon, who make your nest among the cedars, how you will cry inside yourselves when pain comes upon you! It will be pain like a woman giving birth."

Words against Coniah

24 "As I live," says the Lord, "even if Coniah the son of Jehoiakim, king of Judah, were a marking ring on My right hand, I would still pull you off. 25 I will give you over to those who want to kill you, to those whom you fear. I will give you to Nebuchadnezzar king of Babylon, and to the Babylonians. 26 I will throw you and your mother who gave birth to you into another country where you were not born, and there you will die. 27 You will want to return to this land again but you will not return." 28 Is this man Coniah a hated, broken jar? Is he a pot that no one cares for? Why have he and his children been thrown out into a land that they had not known? 29 O land, land, land, hear the Word of the Lord! 30 The Lord says, "Write this man down as one who has no children, a man who will not do well in his days. For none of his children or children's children will do well sitting on the throne of David or ruling again in Judah."

The Right and Good Branch

23 "It is bad for the shepherds who are destroying and dividing the sheep of My field!" says the Lord. 2 The Lord God of Israel says this about the shepherds who are caring for My people, "You have made My flock go everywhere and have driven them away, and have not cared for them. See, I am about to punish you for your sinful things you have done," says the Lord. 3 "Then I Myself will gather those who are left of My flock out of all the countries where I have driven them, and will bring them back to their field. And they will have many children. 4 I will have shepherds over them who will care for them. And they will not be afraid any longer, or filled with fear, and none of them will be missing," says the Lord.

5 "See, the days are coming," says the Lord, "when I will raise up for David a right and good Branch. He will rule as king and be wise and do what is right and fair and good in the land. 6 In His days Judah will be saved, and Israel will be safe. And this is the name He will be called by: 'The Lord Who makes us right and good.' 7 So see, the days are coming," says the Lord, "when they will no longer say, 'As the Lord lives, Who brought the sons of Israel up from the land of Egypt.' 8 But they will say, 'As the Lord lives, Who brought up and led the children of the people of Israel back from the north country and from all the countries where He had driven them.' Then they will live in their own land."

False Preachers and Empty Words

9 As for the men who speak for God, my heart is broken within me. All my bones shake. I have become like a drunk man, like a man who has had too much wine, because of the Lord and because of His holy words. 10 For the land is full of people who are not faithful. Because of the bad things that have come upon it, the land is filled with sorrow, and the fields of the desert have dried up. Their way is sinful, and they use their power in a wrong way. 11 "For both the men of God and the religious leaders are sinful. I have found their sin even in My house," says the Lord. 12 "So their way will be a danger to them. They will be driven away into the darkness and fall down in it. For I will bring much trouble upon them in the year of their punishment," says the Lord.

13 "In Samaria I have seen a very bad thing among the men of Samaria who tell what is going to happen in the future. They speak for the false god Baal, and have led My people into sin. 14 In Jerusalem I have seen a very sinful thing among the men of Jerusalem who tell what is going to happen in the future. They do sex sins and tell lies, and give help to those who do sinful things, so that no one turns from his sin. All of them have become like Sodom to Me. The people of Jerusalem have become like Gomorrah." 15 So the Lord of All says about the men who tell what is going to happen in the future, "See, I will make them eat bitter food and drink water with poison. For from these men of Jerusalem sin has gone out into all the land."

16 The Lord of All says, "Do not listen to the words of those who are telling you what will happen in the future. They are filling you with empty hopes. They tell of dreams from their own thoughts, not from the mouth of the Lord. 17 They keep saying to those who hate Me, 'The Lord has said, "You will have peace."' To every one who walks in the strong-will of his own heart, they say, 'Trouble will not come to you.' 18 But who among them has listened to the Lord, that he should see and hear His Word? Who has given thought to His Word and listened? 19 See, the strong wind storm of the Lord has gone out in anger. It will come down upon the head of the sinful. 20 The anger of the Lord will not turn back until He has done all that

He has planned in His heart. In the last days you will understand. ²¹ I did not send these men who say they speak for God, yet they ran to tell their news. I did not speak to them, yet they spoke in My name. ²² But if they had listened to Me, then they would have made My words known to My people. And they would have turned them back from their sinful way and from the sinful things they did."

²³ "Am I a God Who is near," says the Lord, "and not a God Who is far away? ²⁴ Can a man hide himself in secret places so that I cannot see him?" says the Lord. "Do I not fill heaven and earth?" says the Lord.

²⁵ "I have heard what the men say who speak false words in My name. They say, 'I had a dream, I had a dream!' ²⁶ How long will there be lies in the hearts of those who speak false words in My name, who speak the lies of their own heart? ²⁷ They plan to make My people forget My name by their dreams which they tell one another, just as their fathers forgot My name because of Baal. ²⁸ The one who has a dream may tell about his dream, but let him who has My Word speak My Word in truth. How can straw be compared with grain?" says the Lord. ²⁹ "Is not My Word like fire," says the Lord, "and like iron that breaks a rock in pieces? ³⁰ So I am against those who tell what is going to happen in the future," says the Lord, "who steal My words from each other. ³¹ See, I am against these men," says the Lord, "who use their tongues and say, 'This is what the Lord says.' ³² I am against those who have told false dreams," says the Lord, "and have led My people the wrong way by their lies and foolish words of pride. I did not send them or tell them what to say, so they do not help these people at all," says the Lord.

³³ "When these people, or the one who speaks in My name, or a religious leader asks you, 'What heavy load has the Lord placed on us?' then you say to them, 'You are the heavy load. And I will throw you off, says the Lord.' ³⁴ As for the man who speaks in My name, or the religious leader, or anyone of the people, who say, 'The heavy load of the Lord,' I will punish that man and those of his house. ³⁵ Each of you say to his neighbor and to his brother, 'What has the Lord answered?' or, 'What has the Lord said?' ³⁶ But you must not say, 'The heavy load of the Lord,' any more. For every man's own word will be the weight upon himself. And you have made sinful

the words of the living God, the Lord of All, our God. ³⁷ This is what you should say to the man who speaks in My name: 'What answer has the Lord given you?' and, 'What has the Lord said?' ³⁸ But if you say, 'The heavy load of the Lord,' then the Lord says, 'You have said, "The heavy load of the Lord," when I told you not to say it.' ³⁹ So I will pick you up and throw you away from Me, together with the city which I gave to you and your fathers. ⁴⁰ I will put you to shame forever. You will always be ashamed, and it will not be forgotten."

The Two Baskets of Figs

24 After King Nebuchadnezzar of Babylon took away Jeconiah the son of Jehoiakim, king of Judah, and the leaders of Judah, together with the able workmen from Jerusalem, and brought them to Babylon, the Lord showed me two baskets of figs set in front of the house of the Lord. ² One basket had very good figs, like figs just ready to eat. And the other basket had very bad figs, so bad that they could not be eaten. ³ Then the Lord said to me, "What do you see, Jeremiah?" And I said, "Figs, the good figs very good, and the bad figs very bad, so bad that they cannot be eaten."

⁴ Then the Word of the Lord came to me, saying, ⁵ "This is what the Lord God of Israel says: 'Like these good figs, so will I think of the people of Judah as being good, whom I have sent away from this place into the land of the Babylonians. ⁶ For I will keep My eyes on them for their good, and I will return them to this land. I will build them up and not tear them down. I will plant them and not pull them up by the roots. ⁷ And I will give them a heart to know Me, for I am the Lord. They will be My people and I will be their God, for they will return to Me with their whole heart.'

⁸ "But the Lord says, 'Like the bad figs which are so bad they cannot be eaten, so I will give up Zedekiah king of Judah and his captains. And I will give up those left of Jerusalem who stay in this land, and those who live in the land of Egypt. ⁹ I will make them a cause of fear and trouble for all the nations of the earth. They will be a shame and a curse and spoken against in all the places where I will make them go. ¹⁰ And I will send the sword and hunger and disease upon them until they are destroyed from the land which I gave to them and their fathers.' "

Seventy Years of Not Being Free

25 This is the word that came to Jeremiah about all the people of Judah, in the fourth year of Jehoiakim the son of Josiah, king of Judah. (That was the first year of Nebuchadnezzar king of Babylon.) ² Jeremiah the man of God spoke this word to all the people of Judah and Jerusalem, saying, ³ "These twenty-three years, from the thirteenth year of Josiah the son of Amon, king of Judah, until this day, the Word of the Lord has come to me. And I have spoken to you again and again, but you have not listened. ⁴ The Lord has sent to you all his servants who have spoken for Him again and again, but you have not listened or turned your ear to hear. ⁵ They have said, 'Every one of you turn now from your sinful way and the sinful things you do, and live on the land which the Lord has given to you and your fathers forever and ever. ⁶ Do not go after other gods to serve and worship them. Do not make Me angry with the work you do, and I will not hurt you.' ⁷ Yet you have not listened to Me," says the Lord. "You have made Me angry with the work of your hands to your own hurt. ⁸ "So the Lord of All says, 'Because you have not obeyed My words, ⁹ I will send for all the families of the north. And I will send for Nebuchadnezzar king of Babylon, My servant, and will bring them against this land, against its people, and against all these nations around you. I will make a complete end of them. I will destroy them all and make them an object of fear and hate, and a waste place forever. ¹⁰ I will also take from them the voice of joy, the voice of happiness, the voice of the man to be married and the voice of the bride. I will take from them the sound of the grinding-stones and the light of the lamp. ¹¹ This whole land will be a waste and a cause of fear. And these nations will serve the king of Babylon for seventy years.

¹² 'Then when seventy years have past, I will punish the king of Babylon and that nation, and the land of the Babylonians, for their sin,' says the Lord. 'And I will make that land a waste forever. ¹³ I will bring upon that land all My words which I have spoken against it, all that is written in this book, which Jeremiah has spoken against all the nations. ¹⁴ They themselves will be made to serve many nations and great kings. I will pay them for what they have done, and for the work of their hands.' "

The Cup of God's Anger

¹⁵ For the Lord, the God of Israel, says to me, "Take this cup of the wine of anger from My hand. And make all the nations to whom I send you drink it. ¹⁶ They will drink and have trouble walking and become crazy because of the sword that I will send among them." ¹⁷ So I took the cup from the Lord's hand, and made all the nations to whom the Lord sent me drink it. ¹⁸ I was sent to Jerusalem and to the cities of Judah, to its kings and its leaders, to make them a waste, an object of fear and hate, and a curse, as it is this day. ¹⁹ I was sent to Pharaoh king of Egypt, his servants, his sons, and to all his people. ²⁰ I was sent to all the people from different countries, all the kings of the land of Uz, and to all the kings of the land of the Philistines (Ashkelon, Gaza, Ekron, and those left of Ashdod). ²¹ I was sent to Edom, Moab, the sons of Ammon, ²² and to all the kings of Tyre, all the kings of Sidon, and to the kings of the lands across the sea. ²³ I was sent to Dedan, Tema, Buz, to all who are far away in their lands, ²⁴ to the kings of Arabia, and to all the kings of the different people who live in the desert. ²⁵ I was sent to all the kings of Zimri, all the kings of Elam, all the kings of Media, ²⁶ and to all the kings of the north, near and far, one after another. I was sent to all the nations on the earth. And after them the king of Sheshach will drink.

²⁷ "Then you will say to them, 'The Lord of All, the God of Israel, says, "Drink, be drunk, throw up, fall, and get up no more, because of the sword which I will send among you." ' ²⁸ And if they will not take the cup from your hand to drink, then say to them, 'The Lord of All says, "You must drink! ²⁹ See, I am beginning to make trouble in this city which is called by My name. And will you not be free from punishment, for I am bringing a sword against all the people of the earth," says the Lord of All.'

³⁰ "So you should speak all these words against them. Tell them, 'The Lord will sound from on high. His voice will be heard from His holy place. He will call out in a loud voice against his flock. He will call out like those who crush the grapes, against all the people of the earth. ³¹ The noise will go to the ends of the earth, because the Lord has something against the nations. He is deciding what should be done with all flesh. As for the sinful, He has given them to the sword,' " says the Lord.

32 The Lord of All says, "See, sinful ways are spreading from nation to nation. A powerful storm is moving from the farthest parts of the earth. 33 Those killed by the Lord on that day will be from one end of the earth to the other. No one will cry for them or gather up the bodies and bury them. They will be like animal waste on the ground. 34 Cry in a loud voice, you shepherds. And roll in ashes, you leaders of the flock. For the days for you to be killed and sent everywhere have come, and you will fall and be broken like a fine pot. 35 The shepherds will have no place to run. And the leaders of the flock will have no place to get away. 36 Listen to the cry of the shepherds and the loud cry of the leaders of the flock! For the Lord is destroying their field. 37 The fields of peace are laid waste because of the burning anger of the Lord. 38 He has left His hiding place like a lion. For their land has become a cause of much fear because of the sword of the one who makes it hard for them, and because of the Lord's burning anger."

Jeremiah's Trial

26 In the beginning of the rule of Jehoiakim the son of Josiah, king of Judah, this word came from the Lord, saying, 2 "This is what the Lord says: 'Stand in the open space of the Lord's house, and speak to all the cities of Judah who have come to worship in the Lord's house. Tell them all the words that I have told you to say to them. Do not leave out one word! 3 It may be they will listen and everyone will turn from his sinful way. Then I may change My mind about the trouble I plan to put on them because of the sinful things they have done.' 4 And tell them, 'This is what the Lord says: "If you will not listen to Me and follow My Law which I have set before you, 5 and if you do not listen to the words of My servants who speak for Me, whom I have been sending to you again and again, but you have not listened, 6 then I will make this House of God like Shiloh. And I will make this city a curse to all the nations of the earth." ' "

7 The religious leaders and the men of God and all the people heard Jeremiah speaking these words in the house of the Lord. 8 And when Jeremiah had finished speaking all that the Lord had told him to speak to all the people, the religious leaders and men of God and all the people took hold of him, saying, "You must die! 9 Why have you spoken in the name of

the Lord saying, 'This house will be like Shiloh, and this city will be laid waste with no one living in it'?" And all the people gathered around Jeremiah in the house of the Lord.

10 When the leaders of Judah heard these things, they came up from the king's house to the house of the Lord and sat beside the New Gate of the Lord's house. 11 Then the religious leaders and men of God said to the leaders and to all the people, "This man must die! For he has spoken against this city, as you have heard with your own ears." 12 Then Jeremiah said to all the leaders and to all the people, "The Lord sent me to speak against this house and against this city all the words that you have heard. 13 So now change your ways and your works, and obey the voice of the Lord your God. Then the Lord will change His mind about the trouble He has said would come to you. 14 But as for me, see, I am in your hands. Do with me what is good and right in your eyes. 15 Only know for sure that if you put me to death, you will bring the sin of killing a man who is not guilty on yourselves, on this city, and on its people. For it is true that the Lord has sent me to you to speak all these words for you to hear."

16 Then the leaders and all the people said to the religious leaders and men of God, "No, this man should not be put to death! For he has spoken to us in the name of the Lord our God." 17 Then some of the leaders of the land stood up and said to all the people who had gathered, 18 "Micah of Moresheth spoke in God's name in the days of King Hezekiah of Judah. He said to all the people of Judah, 'This is what the Lord of All has said: Zion will be plowed as a field, and Jerusalem will be destroyed. And trees will cover the mountain where the Lord's house is.' 19 Did King Hezekiah of Judah and all the people of Judah put him to death? Did he not fear the Lord and pray for the Lord's favor? And the Lord changed His mind about the trouble He had said would come to them. But we are about to bring a very bad thing on ourselves."

20 There was another man who spoke in the name of the Lord. He was Uriah the son of Shemaiah from Kiriath-jearim. He spoke against this city and against this land in words like those of Jeremiah. 21 When King Jehoiakim and all his powerful men and all his leaders heard his words, the king wanted to put Uriah to death. But

Uriah heard about it, and he was afraid and ran away to Egypt. 22 Then King Jehoiakim sent Elnathan the son of Achbor and certain men with him to Egypt. 23 And they took Uriah from Egypt and brought him to King Jehoiakim, who killed him with a sword. Then he threw his dead body where most people are buried.

24 But Ahikam the son of Shaphan helped Jeremiah, so that he was not given over to the people to be put to death.

Judah Will Serve Nebuchadnezzar

27 In the beginning of the rule of Zedekiah the son of Josiah, king of Judah, this word came to Jeremiah from the Lord. 2 The Lord said to me, "Make ropes and a cross-bar for carrying a load, and put them on your neck. 3 Then send word to the king of Edom, to the king of Moab, to the king of the sons of Ammon, to the king of Tyre, and to the king of Sidon. Send them with the men who bring news to Jerusalem to King Zedekiah of Judah. 4 Tell them to go to their leaders, saying, 'This is what the Lord of All, the God of Israel, says, and this is what you should say to your leaders: 5 "I have made the earth, and the men and the animals that are on it by My great power and by My long arm. And I will give it to the one who is right in My eyes. 6 Now I have given all these lands to Nebuchadnezzar king of Babylon, My servant. And I have given him the wild animals of the field to serve him. 7 All the nations will serve him and his son and his grandson, until the time for his land comes. Then many nations and great kings will make him their servant. 8 But if any nation will not serve Nebuchadnezzar king of Babylon, and will not put its neck under the load of the king of Babylon, I will punish that nation with the sword, hunger, and disease," says the Lord, "until I have destroyed it by his hand. 9 So do not listen to your men who tell of their special dreams, your men who tell what is going to happen in the future, or your wonder-workers who use their secret ways. They say to you, 'You must not serve the king of Babylon.' 10 But they are lying to you, and will cause you to be taken far from your land. I will drive you out, and you will die. 11 But the nation that brings its neck under the cross-bar of the king of Babylon and serves him, I will let stay on its own land," says the Lord. "And its people will take care of the fields and live there." ' "

12 I spoke to King Zedekiah of Judah in the same way, saying, "Bring your necks under the cross-bar of the king of Babylon. Serve him and his people, and live! 13 Why will you and your people die by the sword, hunger, and disease, as the Lord has said would happen to that nation which will not serve the king of Babylon? 14 Do not listen to the men who tell of their dreams and say to you, 'You will not serve the king of Babylon.' For they are telling you a lie. 15 I have not sent them," says the Lord. "They speak false words in My name, so that I may drive you out, and that you may die, both you and the men who tell these things to you."

16 Then I said to the religious leaders and to all these people, "The Lord says: Do not listen to the men who speak in God's name saying, 'See, the objects of the Lord's house will soon be returned from Babylon,' for they are telling you a lie. 17 Do not listen to them. Serve the king of Babylon and live! Why should this city be destroyed? 18 But if they are true men of God, and if the Word of the Lord is with them, let them now pray to the Lord of All. Let them ask that the objects which are left in the house of the Lord, in the house of the king of Judah, and in Jerusalem, may not go to Babylon. 19 For this is what the Lord of All says about the pillars, the brass pool, the stands, and the rest of the objects that are left in this city. 20 Nebuchadnezzar king of Babylon did not take these things from Jerusalem to Babylon when he took Jeconiah the son of Jehoiakim, king of Judah, and all the leaders of Judah and Jerusalem. 21 So this is what the Lord of All, the God of Israel, says about the objects that are left in the house of the Lord, and in the house of the king of Judah, and in Jerusalem. He says, 22 "They will be carried to Babylon, and they will be there until the day I visit them,' says the Lord. 'Then I will bring them back to this place.' "

Jeremiah and the False Preacher Hananiah

28 In that same year, in the beginning of the rule of King Zedekiah of Judah, in the fifth month of the fourth year, Hananiah the son of Azzur, the man from Gibeon who told what would happen in the future, spoke to me in the house of the Lord. He said to me in front of the religious leaders and all the people, 2 "This is what the Lord of All, the God of Israel, says: 'I have broken the crossbar across the shoulders of the king of Babylon. 3 Within two years I will bring back to this place all the objects of the Lord's house, which Nebuchadnezzar king of Babylon took away from here and carried to Babylon. 4 I will also bring back to this place Jeconiah the son of Jehoiakim, king of Judah, and all the people of Judah who were taken to Babylon,' says the Lord. 'For I will break the cross-bar of the king of Babylon.' "

5 Then Jeremiah, the man of God, spoke to Hananiah, the man who told what would happen, in front of the religious leaders and all the people who were standing in the house of the Lord. 6 And Jeremiah, the man who spoke for God, said, "Let it be so! May the Lord do so. May the Lord make the words you have spoken come true, and bring back to this place from Babylon the objects of the Lord's house and all the people of Judah. 7 Yet listen now to what I am about to say in your hearing and in the hearing of all the people. 8 The men who spoke for God before us from long ago spoke of war and trouble and disease coming to many lands and great nations. 9 As for the man who told that peace would come, when his word comes to pass, then that man will be known as the one that the Lord has sent." 10 Then Hananiah, the man who told what would happen, took the cross-bar from the neck of Jeremiah the man of God and broke it. 11 And Hananiah said in front of all the people, "The Lord says, 'In this way I will break the cross-bar of Nebuchadnezzar king of Babylon from the neck of all the nations within two years.' " Then Jeremiah the man of God went his way.

12 Some time after Hananiah had broken the cross-bar from off the neck of Jeremiah, the Word of the Lord came to Jeremiah, saying, 13 "Go and tell Hananiah, 'The Lord says, "You have broken the cross-bars of wood, but you have made bars of iron in their place." 14 For the Lord of All, the God of Israel, says, "I have put the cross-bar of iron on the neck of all these nations, that they may serve Nebuchadnezzar king of Babylon. And they will serve him. I have given him the animals of the field also." ' " 15 Then Jeremiah who spoke for God said to Hananiah who told what would happen, "Listen, Hananiah, the Lord has not sent you. And you have made these people trust in a lie. 16 So the Lord says, 'See, I am about to take you from the earth. This year you are going to die, because you have spoken against the right and power of the Lord.' " 17 So

Hananiah, who had said these things in God's name, died in the seventh month of the same year.

Jeremiah's Letter to Those Taken to Babylon

29 These are the words of the letter which Jeremiah the man of God sent from Jerusalem to the leaders, the religious leaders, the men of God, and all the people whom Nebuchadnezzar had taken away from Jerusalem to Babylon. 2 (This was after King Jeconiah and the queen mother, the king's servants, the rulers of Judah and Jerusalem, and the able workmen had left Jerusalem.) 3 The letter was sent with Elasah the son of Shaphan, and Gemariah the son of Hilkiah, whom King Zedekiah of Judah sent to King Nebuchadnezzar in Babylon. It said, 4 "This is what the Lord of All, the God of Israel, says to all of His people who have been sent from Jerusalem to Babylon: 5 'Build houses and live in them. Plant gardens and eat their fruit. 6 Take wives and become the fathers of sons and daughters. And take wives for your sons and give your daughters in marriage, that they may give birth to sons and daughters. Become many there, and do not let your number become less. 7 Work for the well-being of the city where I have sent you to and pray to the Lord for this. For if it is well with the city you live in, it will be well with you.' 8 For the Lord of All, the God of Israel, says, 'Do not let the people among you who tell what is going to happen in the future and those who use their secret ways fool you. Do not listen to their dreams. 9 For they speak false words to you in My name. I have not sent them,' says the Lord.

10 "For the Lord says, 'When seventy years are completed for Babylon, I will visit you and keep My promise to you. I will bring you back to this place. 11 For I know the plans I have for you,' says the Lord, 'plans for well-being and not for trouble, to give you a future and a hope. 12 Then you will call upon Me and come and pray to Me, and I will listen to you. 13 You will look for Me and find Me, when you look for Me with all your heart. 14 I will be found by you,' says the Lord. 'And I will bring you back and gather you from all the nations and all the places where I have made you go,' says the Lord. 'I will bring you back to the place from where I sent you away.'

15 "You have said that the Lord has given men who speak for Him in Babylon.

16 This is what the Lord says about the king who sits on the throne of David, and about all the people who live in this city, your brothers who were not taken with you to Babylon. 17 The Lord of All says, 'I am sending the sword, hunger, and disease upon them. I will make them like bad figs which are so bad they cannot be eaten. 18 I will go after them with the sword, hunger, and disease, and will make them a cause of trouble to all the nations of the earth. They will be a curse, an object of much shame and hate among all the nations where I have made them go. 19 This is because they have not listened to My words,' says the Lord, 'which I sent to them again and again by My servants who spoke for Me. And you did not listen,' says the Lord. 20 So hear the Word of the Lord, all you people who have been sent away from Jerusalem to Babylon.

21 "This is what the Lord of All, the God of Israel, says about Ahab the son of Kolaiah and about Zedekiah the son of Maaseiah, who are speaking false words to you in My name: 'See, I will give them over to Nebuchadnezzar king of Babylon. And he will kill them in front of your eyes. 22 Because of them a curse will be used by all the people who are from Judah but are in Babylon: "May the Lord make you like Zedekiah and like Ahab, whom the king of Babylon burned in the fire." 23 This is because they have done what is foolish in Israel. They have done sex sins with their neighbors' wives. And they have spoken false words in My name, which I did not tell them to speak. I am He Who knows, and I see what they have done,' says the Lord."

The Letter to Shemaiah

24 And say to Shemaiah the Nehelamite, 25 "This is what the Lord of All, the God of Israel, says. 'You have sent letters in your own name to all the people in Jerusalem and to Zephaniah the son of Maaseiah, the religious leader, and to all the religious leaders. You said to Zephaniah, 26 "The Lord has made you the religious leader over the house of the Lord instead of Jehoiada. You are to take every crazy man who says he speaks in God's name and put him in chains with iron around his neck. 27 So why have you not spoken sharp words to Jeremiah of Anathoth who is speaking in God's name? 28 For he has sent word to us in Babylon, saying, 'You will be held there for a long time. So

build houses and live in them. And plant gardens and eat their fruit.' " ' "

29 Zephaniah the religious leader read this letter to Jeremiah the man of God. 30 Then the Word of the Lord came to Jeremiah, saying, 31 "Send word to all My people held in Babylon, saying, 'This is what the Lord says about Shemaiah the Nehelamite: Shemaiah has spoken to you in My name, but I did not send him. He has made you trust in a lie.' 32 So the Lord says, 'I am about to punish Shemaiah the Nehelamite and his children after him. He will not have anyone living among these people. And he will not see the good that I am about to do to My people,' says the Lord, 'because he has spoken against Me.' "

Israel and Judah to Be Free Again

30 The word which came to Jeremiah from the Lord, saying, 2 "This is what the Lord, the God of Israel, says: 'Write in a book all the words which I have spoken to you. 3 For the days are coming,' says the Lord, 'when I will bring back My people Israel and Judah from where they are held.' The Lord says, 'I will bring them back to the land that I gave to their fathers before them, and it will be theirs.' "

4 These are the words which the Lord spoke about Israel and Judah: 5 "The Lord says, 'I have heard cries of much trouble, of being afraid, and there is no peace. 6 Ask now and see, can a man give birth to a child? Why do I see every man with his hands on his body like a woman giving birth? Why have all faces turned white? 7 That day will be very bad! There is none like it. It is the time of Jacob's trouble, but he will be saved out of it. 8 On that day,' says the Lord of All, 'I will break the cross-bar off from their neck, and will tear off their chains. Strangers will no longer make them their servants. 9 But they will serve the Lord their God and David their king, whom I will raise up for them. 10 So do not be afraid, O Jacob My servant,' says the Lord, 'and do not be troubled, O Israel, for see, from far away I will save you and your children from the land where they are being held. Jacob will return and have quiet rest, and no one will make him afraid. 11 For I am with you to save you,' says the Lord. 'I will make a complete end of all the nations where I have sent you. I will not make a complete end of you, but I will give you the right punishment. I will not let you go without being punished.'

12 "For the Lord says, 'Your hurt cannot be healed. Your hurt is very bad. 13 There is no one to ask for you in your cause, no help for your hurt, no healing for you. 14 All your lovers have forgotten you. They do not care about you. For I have hurt you as if you were hurt by one who hates you. You have been punished without pity, because you have much guilt. You have done many sins. 15 Why do you cry out because of your hurt? Your pain cannot be healed. Because you have much guilt and have done many sins, I have done these things to you. 16 But all who destroy you will be destroyed. Every one of those who hate you will be taken away against their will. Those who rob you will be robbed, and all who hurt you will be hurt. 17 For I will heal you. I will heal you where you have been hurt,' says the Lord, 'because they have said that you are not wanted. They have said, "It is Zion. No one cares for her." '

18 "The Lord says, 'I will bring the tents of Jacob back from Babylon, and will have pity on his houses. The city will be built up again on its broken walls. And the king's house will stand where it used to be. 19 The people who live there will give much thanks and happy voices will be heard. And I will add to their numbers. They will not be made less. I will honor them, and they will be important. 20 Their children will be as they were before. They will be a strong people before Me. And I will punish all those who make it hard for them. 21 Their leader will be one of them. Their ruler will come from among them. I will bring him near, and he will come close to Me. For who would have the strength of heart to come near Me on his own?' says the Lord. 22 'And you will be My people, and I will be your God.' '

23 See the storm of the Lord! Anger has gone out, a very bad storm. It will break upon the heads of the sinful. 24 The burning anger of the Lord will not turn back until He has done what He has planned in His heart to do. In days to come you will understand this.

Israel Returns Home

31 "At that time," says the Lord, "I will be the God of all the families of Israel, and they will be My people." 2 The Lord says, "The people who were not killed by the sword found loving-favor in the desert, when Israel looked for rest." 3 The Lord came to us from far away, saying, "I have loved you with a love that lasts forever. So I have helped you come to Me with loving-kindness. 4 Again I will build you, and you will be built, O pure Israel! Again you will take up your brass noise-makers and go to the dances of the happy people. 5 Again you will plant grape-fields on the hills of Samaria. The planters will plant and find joy in the fruit. 6 For there will be a day when watchmen on the hills of Ephraim will call out, 'Get up, and let us go up to Zion, to the Lord our God.' "

7 For the Lord says, "Sing loud with joy for Jacob, and call out among the heads of the nations. Make it known, give praise, and say, 'O Lord, save Your people. Save those who are left of Israel.' 8 See, I am bringing them from the north country. And I will gather them from the farthest parts of the earth. Among them will be the blind and those who cannot walk, the woman with child and she who is giving birth, together. Many people will return here. 9 They will come crying, and in answer to their prayers, I will lead them. I will make them walk by rivers of waters on a straight path where they will not fall. For I am a father to Israel, and Ephraim is My first-born."

10 Hear the Word of the Lord, O nations, and make it known in the lands far across the sea. Say, "He Who sent Israel everywhere will gather them, and will watch over His flock like a shepherd." 11 For the Lord has paid the price to make Jacob free. He has made him free from the one who was stronger than he. 12 And they will come and call out for joy on the height of Zion. They will shine with joy over the goodness of the Lord, over the grain, the new wine, and the oil, and over the young of the flock and the cattle. Their life will be like a well-watered garden. They will never have sorrow again. 13 Then the young women who have never had a man will dance for joy, and the young men and old as well. For I will change their sorrow to joy, and will comfort them. I will give them joy for their sorrow. 14 I will fill the soul of the religious leaders with more than they need. My people will be filled with My goodness," says the Lord.

The Lord Shows His Loving-Kindness on Israel

15 The Lord says, "The sound of crying and much sorrow is heard in Ramah. Rachel is crying for her children. She will not be comforted because they are dead." 16 The Lord says, "Keep your voice from

crying and your eyes from tears. For you will receive pay for your work," says the Lord. "They will return from the land of those who hate them. ¹⁷ There is hope for your future," says the Lord, "and your children will return to their own land. ¹⁸ I have heard Ephraim crying in sorrow, 'You have punished me, and I was punished, like a calf that has not learned. Bring me back that I may return to my place, for You are the Lord my God. ¹⁹ For after I turned back, I was sorry for my sins. And after I was taught, I hit my upper leg in sorrow. I was ashamed and troubled, because I suffered the shame from what I did when I was young.' ²⁰ Is Ephraim My loved son? Is he the child of My joy? Yes, as many times as I have spoken against him, I still remember him. So My heart has a desire for him. For sure I will have loving-pity on him," says the Lord.

²¹ "Set up marks on the road for yourself. Set up marks to lead you the right way. Remember the way you went, and return, O pure Israel. Return to your cities. ²² How long will you go here and there, O daughter without faith? For the Lord has made a new thing on the earth: A woman will keep a man safe."

Good Will Come to God's People

²³ The Lord of All, the God of Israel, says, "When I bring them back to their own land, once again the people in the land of Judah and in its cities will speak these words: 'May the Lord bring good to you, O place that is right with God, O holy hill!' ²⁴ The people of Judah and all its cities will live there together, the farmer and they who go about with flocks. ²⁵ For I will help the tired ones and give strength to everyone who is weak." ²⁶ At this I woke up and looked, and my sleep was pleasing to me.

²⁷ "See, the days are coming," says the Lord, "when I will plant the people of Israel and the people of Judah with the seed of man and the seed of animal. ²⁸ And as I have watched over them to pull up, to break down, to take power away, to destroy, and to bring trouble, so I will watch over them to build and to plant," says the Lord. ²⁹ "In those days they will no longer say, 'The fathers have eaten sour grapes, and the children got the sour taste.' ³⁰ But every one will die for his own sin. Each man who eats the sour grapes will get the sour taste. ³¹ The days are coming," says the Lord, "when I will make a New Way

of Worship for the Jews and those of the family group of Judah. ³² The New Way of Worship will not be like the Old Way of Worship I gave to their early fathers. That was when I took them by the hand and led them out of Egypt. But they did not follow the Old Way of Worship, even when I was a husband to them," says the Lord. ³³ "This is the New Way of Worship that I will give to the Jews. When that day comes," says the Lord, "I will put My Law into their minds. And I will write it on their hearts. I will be their God, and they will be My people. ³⁴ No one will need to teach his neighbor or his brother to know the Lord. All of them will already know Me from the least to the greatest," says the Lord. "I will forgive their sins. I will remember their sins no more."

³⁵ The Lord, the Lord of All is His name, Who gives the sun for light during the day, and put the moon and the stars in place to give light during the night, Who causes the waves of the sea to make a loud noise, says, ³⁶ "If these laws change before Me, then the children of Israel will stop being a nation before Me forever." ³⁷ The Lord says, "If one can find out how wide the heavens are, and look through the deepest places of the earth, then I will send all the children of Israel away from Me for all that they have done," says the Lord.

³⁸ "See, the days are coming," says the Lord, "when the city will be built again for the Lord from the tower of Hananel to the Corner Gate. ³⁹ And its wall will go out farther, straight on to the hill of Gareb. Then it will turn to Goah. ⁴⁰ The whole valley of the dead bodies and of the ashes, and all the fields as far as the river Kidron, to the corner of the Horse Gate toward the east, will be holy to the Lord. It will never again be pulled up by the roots or destroyed."

Jeremiah Buys a Field

32 This is the word that came to Jeremiah from the Lord in the tenth year of Zedekiah king of Judah, which was the eighteenth year of Nebuchadnezzar. ² At that time the army of the king of Babylon was around Jerusalem. And Jeremiah the man of God was shut up in the open space of the prison, in the house of the king of Judah. ³ For King Zedekiah of Judah had shut him up, saying, "Why do you speak these things in the Lord's name? You have said, 'This is what the Lord says: "I am giving this city to the king of Babylon, and he will take it. ⁴ King Zedekiah of

Judah will not get away from the Babylonians. For sure he will be given into the hand of the king of Babylon. He will speak with him face to face and see him eye to eye. 5 He will take Zedekiah to Babylon, and he will be there until I visit him," says the Lord. "If you fight against the Babylonians, you will not win." ' "

6 Jeremiah said, "The Word of the Lord came to me, saying, 7 'Hanamel, the son of your father's brother Shallum, will come to you and say, "Buy my field at Anathoth. For because of your place in the family you have the right to buy it." ' 8 Then Hanamel, the son of my father's brother, came to me in the open space of the prison, as the Word of the Lord had said. And he said to me, 'Buy my field at Anathoth in the land of Benjamin. For you have the right to own it. Because of your place in the family you have the right, so buy it for yourself.' Then I knew that this was the Word of the Lord. 9 So I bought the field at Anathoth from Hanamel, the son of my father's brother. And I weighed out seventeen pieces of silver for him. 10 I wrote my name and put my mark on the agreement, and called in people to watch. And I weighed the silver. 11 Then I took the agreement which showed that I had bought the field, both the agreement which was not to be opened, and the open one. 12 And I gave the written agreement to Baruch the son of Neriah, the son of Mahseiah. This was seen by Hanamel, the son of my father's brother, and by those who watched me write my name on the agreement, and by all the Jews who were sitting in the open space of the prison. 13 I said to Baruch in front of them, 14 'This is what the Lord of All, the God of Israel, says: "Take these agreements, both the closed and open one, and put them in a clay jar so they may last a long time." 15 For the Lord of All, the God of Israel, says, "Houses and fields and grape-fields will again be bought in this land." '

Jeremiah's Prayer

16 "After I had given the agreement showing I had bought the field to Baruch the son of Neriah, I prayed to the Lord, saying, 17 'O Lord God! See, You have made the heavens and the earth by Your great power and by Your long arm! Nothing is too hard for You! 18 You show loving-kindness to thousands, but put punishment for the sins of fathers on their children after them. O great and powerful God, the Lord of All

is Your name. 19 You are great in wisdom and powerful in Your works. Your eyes are open to all the ways of men. You pay every one for what he does and for the fruit of what he does. 20 You have made special things to see and have done wonders in the land of Egypt, and are still doing them even to this day both in Israel and among all men. You have made a name for Yourself as it is today. 21 You brought Your people Israel out of the land of Egypt with special things to see and with wonders, and with a strong hand and a long arm, and with much trouble. 22 And You gave them this land which You promised their fathers to give them, a land flowing with milk and honey. 23 They came in and took it for their own. But they did not obey Your voice or walk in Your Law. They did not do anything that You told them to do. So You have made all this trouble come upon them. 24 See, a battle-wall has been built up against the city to take it. And the city is given to the Babylonians who fight against it, because of the sword, hunger, and disease. What You have said would happen has now happened, as You see. 25 O Lord God, You have said to me, "Buy the field with money, and call in people to see you buy it," even though the city will be given over to the Babylonians." ' "

26 Then the Word of the Lord came to Jeremiah, saying, 27 "I am the Lord, the God of all flesh. Is anything too hard for Me? 28 So this is what the Lord says: 'See, I am giving this city to the Babylonians and to Nebuchadnezzar king of Babylon, and he will take it. 29 The Babylonians who are fighting against this city will come into it and set this city on fire and burn it. And the houses will burn where people have given special perfume to Baal on their roofs and poured out drink gifts to other gods to make Me angry. 30 For the sons of Israel and the sons of Judah have been doing only what is sinful in My eyes since they were young. The sons of Israel have been only making Me angry by the work of their hands," says the Lord. 31 'This city has made Me very angry since the day they built it until now. So I will put it away from before My face 32 because of all the sin of the sons of Israel and the sons of Judah, which they have done to make Me angry. They have sinned together with their kings, their leaders, their religious leaders, their men who speak in My name, the men of Judah, and the people of Jerusalem. 33 They have turned their back

to Me, and not their face. I taught them again and again, but they would not listen and learn. 34 They put their things that I hate in the house which is called by My name, and made it unclean. 35 They built the high places of the false god Baal in the valley of Ben-Hinnom, to give their sons and daughters as burnt gifts to Molech. I did not tell them to do this hated thing that made Judah sin. It did not even come into My mind.

A Promise for the Future

36 "So now this is what the Lord God of Israel says about this city of which you say, 'It is given over to the king of Babylon because of the sword, hunger, and disease.' 37 I will gather them out of all the lands to which I have driven them in My strong anger. And I will bring them back to this place to live where they will be safe. 38 They will be My people, and I will be their God. 39 I will give them one heart and one way, that they may fear Me always, for their own good and for the good of their children after them. 40 I will make an agreement with them that I will not turn away from them. I will do good to them, an agreement that will last forever. And I will help them fear Me in their hearts so they will not turn away from Me. 41 I will have joy in doing good to them. And I will be faithful to plant them in this land with all My heart and with all My soul. 42 For the Lord says, 'Just as I brought all this trouble on these people, so I am going to bring all the good on them that I have promised them. 43 Fields will be bought in this land of which you say, "It is a waste, without man or animal. It is given over to the Babylonians." 44 Men will buy fields for money, write their names and put their marks on agreements while people watch them do this in the land of Benjamin and in the places around Jerusalem. Also they will do this in the cities of Judah, in the cities of the hill country, in the cities of the valley, and in the cities of the Negev. For I will bring them back to their own land,' says the Lord."

A Promise of Hope

33 While Jeremiah was still shut up in the open space of the prison, the Word of the Lord came to him a second time, saying, 2 "This is what the Lord says Who made the earth. The Lord made it to last. The Lord is His name. 3 'Call to Me, and I will answer you. And I will show you great and wonderful things which you do not know.' 4 For this is what the Lord God of Israel says about the houses of this city and about the houses of the kings of Judah which have been torn down to make a strong wall to help in the battle against the Babylonians. 5 Some will come to fight with the Babylonians, and they will fill the houses with the dead bodies of men whom I have killed in My anger. I will hide My face from this city because of all their sin. 6 See, I will make it well again, and I will heal them. I will let them have much peace and truth. 7 I will return the land to Judah and to Israel, and I will help them to become as they were before. 8 I will make them clean from all the sins they have done against Me. I will forgive all their sins against Me. 9 This city will make My name known. It will be to Me joy, praise and shining-greatness before all the nations of the earth that hear of all the good that I do for them. And they will fear and shake because of all the good and all the peace that I give it.'

10 "This is what the Lord says: 'You say of this place, "It is a waste, without man or animal." Yet in the cities of Judah and in the streets of Jerusalem that are laid waste, with no man or animal living in them, there will again be heard 11 the voice of joy and the voice of happiness. In this place will be heard the voice of the man to be married and the voice of the bride, and the voice of those who say, "Give thanks to the Lord of All, for the Lord is good. His loving-kindness lasts forever." And here will be heard the voice of those who bring a gift of thanks into the house of the Lord. For I will bring them back to the land as they were before,' says the Lord.

12 "The Lord of All says, 'This place is now a waste, without man or animal. Yet there will again be shepherds living in this place and in all its cities who can care for their sheep. 13 In the cities of the hill country, in the cities of the valley, in the cities of the Negev, in the land of Benjamin, in the land around Jerusalem, and in the cities of Judah, the flocks will again pass under the hands of the one who numbers them,' says the Lord.

14 'See, the days are coming,' says the Lord, 'when I will do what I promised to the people of Israel and the people of Judah. 15 In those days and at that time I will cause a right and good Branch of David to rise up. And He will do what is fair and right and good on the earth. 16 In those

days Judah will be saved, and Jerusalem will be safe. And this is the name it will be called: The Lord makes us right and good.' ¹⁷ For the Lord says, 'David will never be without a man to sit on the throne of the people of Israel. ¹⁸ And the Levite religious leaders will never be without a man before Me to give burnt gifts, to burn grain gifts, and to make gifts ready on the altar all the time.' "

¹⁹ The Word of the Lord came to Jeremiah, saying, ²⁰ "This is what the Lord says: 'If you can break My agreement with the day and night, so that day and night will not come at their set time, ²¹ then My agreement may also be broken with David My servant, that he will not have a son to rule on his throne. And then My agreement may be broken with My servants, the Levite religious leaders. ²² The stars of heaven cannot be numbered, and the sand of the sea cannot be weighed. In the same way I will make the children of David My servant many, as well as the Levites who serve Me.' "

²³ The Word of the Lord came to Jeremiah, saying, ²⁴ "Have you not heard what these people are saying? They say, 'The Lord has turned away from the two families He had chosen.' So they hate My people. They are no longer a nation in their eyes. ²⁵ This is what the Lord says: 'If I do not keep My agreement with day and night and the laws of heaven and earth, ²⁶ then I will turn away from the children of Jacob and David My servant. Then I will not choose one of his children to rule over the children of Abraham, Isaac, and Jacob. For I will bring them back to their land and will have loving-pity on them.' "

God Speaks to Zedekiah

34 This is the word which came to Jeremiah from the Lord, when Nebuchadnezzar king of Babylon and all his army and all the nations of the earth that were under his rule, and all the people, were fighting against Jerusalem and all its cities: ² "The Lord God of Israel says, 'Go and say to Zedekiah king of Judah, "This is what the Lord says: 'See, I am giving this city to the king of Babylon, and he will burn it with fire. ³ And you will not get away from him. You will be taken and given into his hand. You will see the king of Babylon eye to eye, and he will speak with you face to face. And you will go to Babylon.' " ' ⁴ Yet hear the Word of the Lord, O Zedekiah king of Judah! The

Lord says this about you: 'You will not die by the sword. ⁵ You will die in peace. And as spices were burned for your fathers, the kings who were before you, so they will burn spices for you and cry in sorrow for you, "It is bad, lord!" ' I Myself have said this," says the Lord.

⁶ Then Jeremiah the man of God told all this to King Zedekiah of Judah in Jerusalem, ⁷ when the army of the king of Babylon was fighting against Jerusalem and all the cities that were left of Judah. These cities were Lachish and Azekah. They were the only strong cities left in Judah that were ready for war.

Servants Were to Be Free

⁸ This is the word which came to Jeremiah from the Lord, after King Zedekiah had made an agreement to set free ⁹ their Hebrew male and female servants so that no one would have a Hebrew servant work for him. ¹⁰ And all the leaders and all the people obeyed, who had joined in the agreement that every man should set his male and female servants free. No one was to keep them working any longer for him. So they obeyed and set them free. ¹¹ But after this they turned around and took back the male and female servants whom they had set free. They brought them back and made them work for them again as male and female servants.

¹² Then the Word of the Lord came to Jeremiah, saying, ¹³ "This is what the Lord God of Israel says: 'I made an agreement with your fathers when I brought them out of the land of Egypt, from the house where they were made to work. I said to them, ¹⁴ "At the end of seven years each of you must set free his Hebrew brother, who has been sold to you and has served you for six years. You must send him away from you as a free man." But your fathers did not obey Me, or listen to Me. ¹⁵ Not long ago you had turned and done what is right in My eyes. Each man told his neighbor that he was free. And you had made an agreement before Me in the house which is called by My name. ¹⁶ Yet you turned and sinned against My name. Each man took back his male and female servant whom you had set free to go where they wished. And you brought them under your power again to be your male and female servants.'

¹⁷ "So the Lord says, 'You have not obeyed Me. Each man has not set his brother or his neighbor free. So I am letting you free,'

says the Lord, 'free to fall by the sword, by disease, and by hunger. I will cause you to be hated and feared by all the nations of the earth. ¹⁸ I will take the men who have sinned against My agreement, who have not kept the words of the agreement they made before Me when they cut the calf in two and passed between its parts. ¹⁹ I will take these leaders of Judah, and leaders of Jerusalem, the king's servants, the religious leaders, and all the people of the land who passed between the parts of the calf. ²⁰ And I will give them over to those who hate them and to those who want to kill them. Their dead bodies will be food for the birds of the sky and the wild animals of the earth. ²¹ I will give Zedekiah king of Judah and his captains over to those who hate them and to those who want to kill them. I will give them to the army of the king of Babylon which has left from you. ²² See,' says the Lord, 'I will tell them to come back to this city. And they will fight against it and take it and burn it with fire. I will make the cities of Judah a waste place where no people live.'"

The Rechabites

35 This is the word which came to Jeremiah from the Lord in the days of Jehoiakim the son of Josiah, king of Judah: ² "Go to the house of the Rechabites and speak to them. Then bring them to one of the rooms of the house of the Lord, and give them wine to drink." ³ So I took Jaazaniah the son of Jeremiah, son of Habazziniah, and his brothers and all his sons, and all those of the Rechabite family. ⁴ And I brought them into the house of the Lord, into the room of the sons of Hanan, the son of Igdaliah, the man of God. This room was near the room of the leaders and above the room of Maaseiah the son of Shallum, the doorkeeper. ⁵ Then I set jars full of wine and some cups in front of the men of the Rechabite family. And I said to them, "Drink wine." ⁶ But they said, "We will not drink wine. For Jonadab the son of Rechab, our father, told us, 'You and your sons must never drink wine. ⁷ You must never build a house. You must never plant seeds. And you must never plant a grape-field or own one. But you must always live in tents. Then you will live many days in the land where you have come to.' ⁸ We have obeyed the voice of Jonadab the son of Rechab, our father, in all that he told us. We, our wives, our sons, and our daughters, never drink wine. ⁹ We have

never built houses to live in, and we do not have grape-fields or fields or seeds to plant. ¹⁰ We have only lived in tents. We have obeyed, and have done all that our father Jonadab told us. ¹¹ But when Nebuchadnezzar king of Babylon came up against the land, we said, 'Come and let us go to Jerusalem to get away from the armies of the Chaldeans and the Syrians.' So we are living in Jerusalem."

¹² Then the Word of the Lord came to Jeremiah, saying, ¹³ "This is what the Lord of All, the God of Israel, says: 'Go and say to the men of Judah and the people of Jerusalem, "Will you not learn by listening to My words?" says the Lord. ¹⁴ "The words of Jonadab the son of Rechab, telling his sons not to drink wine, are obeyed. They do not drink wine to this day, for they have obeyed their father. But I have spoken to you again and again, yet you have not listened to Me. ¹⁵ And again and again I have sent you all My servants who spoke for Me, saying, 'Everyone turn now from your sinful way, and do what I tell you to do. Do not go after other gods to worship them. Then you will live in the land I have given to you and to your fathers before you. But you have not turned your ear to listen to Me. ¹⁶ The sons of Jonadab, the son of Rechab, have obeyed what their father told them, but these people have not listened to Me.' " ' ¹⁷ So the Lord, the God of All, the God of Israel, says, 'I am bringing on Judah and on all the people of Jerusalem all the trouble I have said would come upon them. For I spoke to them but they did not listen. I have called them but they did not answer.' "

¹⁸ Then Jeremiah said to those of the Rechabite family, "This is what the Lord of All, the God of Israel, says: 'You have obeyed everything that Jonadab your father told you to do.' ¹⁹ And so the Lord of All, the God of Israel, says, 'Jonadab the son of Rechab will never be without a man to stand before Me.' "

Baruch Reads the Book in the House of God

36 In the fourth year of Jehoiakim the son of Josiah, king of Judah, this word came to Jeremiah from the Lord, saying, ² "Take a book and write in it all the words which I have said to you about Israel, Judah, and all the nations. Write all I have said since the day I first spoke to you, from the days of Josiah until today. ³ It may be that the house of Judah will hear all the trouble I am planning to bring on them, so that everyone will turn from his sinful way. Then I will forgive their wrong-doing and their sin."

4 So Jeremiah called Baruch, the son of Neriah. And Baruch wrote in the book all the words which Jeremiah told him that the Lord had said to him. 5 Then Jeremiah said to Baruch, "I am shut up here and cannot go into the house of the Lord. 6 So you go to the Lord's house on the special day of no food, and read to the people the words of the Lord which you have written down as I told them to you. And also read them to all the people of Judah who come from their cities. 7 It may be that their prayer will come before the Lord, and everyone will turn from his sinful way. For the punishment that the Lord said would come to these people because of His anger is very bad." 8 Baruch the son of Neriah did all that Jeremiah the man of God told him. He read from the book the words of the Lord in the Lord's house.

9 In the ninth month of the fifth year of Jehoiakim the son of Josiah, king of Judah, all the people in Jerusalem and all those from the cities of Judah set apart to the Lord a day when they would not eat. 10 Then Baruch read from the book the words of Jeremiah to all the people in the house of the Lord, in the room of Gemariah the son of Shaphan the writer, in the upper place by the New Gate of the Lord's house.

The Book Is Read to the Leaders

11 When Micaiah the son of Gemariah, the son of Shaphan, had heard all the words of the Lord from the book, 12 he went down to the king's house, into the writer's room. And he saw that all the leaders were sitting there. There was Elishama the writer, and Delaiah the son of Shemaiah, and Elnathan the son of Achbor, and Gemariah the son of Shaphan, and Zedekiah the son of Hananiah, and all the other leaders. 13 And Micaiah told them all that he had heard Baruch read to the people from the book. 14 Then all the leaders sent Jehudi the son of Nethaniah, the son of Shelemiah, the son of Cushi, to Baruch, saying, "Take the book you have read to the people, and come." So Baruch the son of Neriah took the book in his hand and went to them. 15 They told him, "Sit down and read it to us." So Baruch read it to them. 16 When they had heard all the words, they turned in fear to one another and said to Baruch, "For sure we will tell all these words to the

king." 17 And they asked Baruch, "Tell us, how did you write all this? Did Jeremiah tell it to you?" 18 Baruch said to them, "He told me all these words, and I wrote them down in the book." 19 Then the leaders said to Baruch, "Go and hide, both you and Jeremiah. And do not let anyone know where you are."

The King Burns Jeremiah's Book

20 So they went to the king in the open space, but they had put the book in the room of Elishama the writer. And they told all the words to the king. 21 Then the king sent Jehudi to get the book, and he took it out of the room of Elishama the writer. And Jehudi read it to the king and to all the leaders who stood beside him. 22 It was the ninth month, and the king was sitting in the winter house with a fire burning in the fireplace in front of him. 23 When Jehudi had read three or four parts, the king cut them with a small knife and threw them into the fire in the fireplace. He did this until the book was destroyed in the fire. 24 The king and all his servants who heard all these words were not afraid, and they did not tear their clothes. 25 Elnathan and Delaiah and Gemariah begged the king not to burn the book, but he would not listen to them. 26 And the king told Jerahmeel the king's son, Seraiah the son of Azriel, and Shelemiah the son of Abdeel to take hold of Baruch the writer and Jeremiah the man of God. But the Lord had hidden them.

Jeremiah Writes Another Book

27 Now the Word of the Lord came to Jeremiah after the king had burned the book with the words Jeremiah had told Baruch to write down. The Lord said, 28 "Take another book and write in it all the words that were in the first book which Jehoiakim the king of Judah burned. 29 And about Jehoiakim the king of Judah you will say, 'This is what the Lord says: "You have burned this book, saying, 'Why have you written in it that the king of Babylon will be sure to come and destroy this land and put an end to every man and animal in it?'" 30 So this is what the Lord says about Jehoiakim king of Judah: "He will have no one to sit on the throne of David. And his dead body will be thrown out to the heat of the day and the cold of the night. 31 I will punish him and his children and his servants for their sin. And I will bring on them and the people of Jerusalem and the

men of Judah all the trouble that I have said would come to them, because they would not listen." ' " 32 Then Jeremiah took another book and gave it to Baruch the son of Neraiah, the writer. And as Jeremiah told them to him, he wrote down all the words of the book which Jehoiakim king of Judah had burned in the fire. And many words of the same kind were added to them.

Jeremiah in Prison

37 Zedekiah the son of Josiah, whom Nebuchadnezzar king of Babylon had made king in the land of Judah, ruled in place of Coniah the son of Jehoiakim. 2 But he and his servants and the people of the land would not listen to what the Lord said through Jeremiah the man of God.

3 King Zedekiah sent Jehucal the son of Shelemiah, and Zephaniah the son of Maaseiah, the religious leader, to Jeremiah the man of God, saying, "Pray to the Lord our God for us." 4 Now Jeremiah was still free to come and go among the people, for they had not yet put him in prison. 5 The army of Pharaoh had come out of Egypt. And when the Babylonian army which had been around Jerusalem heard the news about them, they left Jerusalem.

6 Then the Word of the Lord came to Jeremiah the man of God, saying, 7 "This is what the Lord God of Israel says: 'Tell the king of Judah, who sent you to ask Me what will happen, "See, Pharaoh's army which has come to help you is going to return to its own land of Egypt. 8 Then the Babylonians will return and fight against this city. They will take it and burn it with fire." ' 9 The Lord says, 'Do not fool yourselves, saying, "For sure the Babylonians will go away from us." For they will not go. 10 Even if you had won the battle against the whole Babylonian army fighting with you, and only men who were hurt were left in their tents, they would rise up and burn this city with fire.' "

11 Now the Babylonian army had left Jerusalem because of Pharaoh's army. 12 And so Jeremiah left Jerusalem to go to the land of Benjamin to take his land there among the people. 13 While he was at the Gate of Benjamin, a soldier was there watching. His name was Irijah, the son of Shelemiah, the son of Hananiah. He took hold of Jeremiah the man of God, saying, "You are going over to the Babylonians!" 14 But Jeremiah said, "It is a lie! I am not going over to the Babylonians." But Irijah

would not listen to him. He took hold of Jeremiah and brought him to the leaders. 15 The leaders were angry with Jeremiah and beat him. They put him in prison in the house of Jonathan the writer, which they had made into a prison.

16 After Jeremiah had been in an underground prison many days, 17 King Zedekiah sent for him and had him brought to his house. The king asked him in secret, "Is there any word from the Lord?" And Jeremiah said, "There is!" Then he said, "You will be given over to the king of Babylon!" 18 Jeremiah also said to King Zedekiah, "In what way have I sinned against you or your servants, or against these people? Why have you put me in prison? 19 Where are your men who spoke to you in God's name, saying, 'The king of Babylon will not come against you or against this land'? 20 But now I ask you to listen, O my lord the king. Hear what I ask, and do not make me return to the house of Jonathan the writer, or I will die there." 21 So King Zedekiah had them put Jeremiah in the open space of the prison. And a loaf of bread was given to him every day from the bread-makers' street, until all the bread in the city was gone. So Jeremiah stayed in the open space of the prison.

Jeremiah in a Dry Water Well

38 Now Shaphatiah the son of Mattan, Gedaliah the son of Pashhur, Jucal the son of Shelemiah, and Pashhur the son of Malchijah heard Jeremiah telling all the people, 2 "The Lord says, 'He who stays in this city will die by the sword and by hunger and by disease. But he who goes over to the Babylonians will live. He will get away with his life and live.' 3 The Lord says, 'For sure this city will be given to the army of the king of Babylon, and he will take it.' " 4 Then the leaders said to the king, "Now let this man be put to death. For he is making the hearts of the men of war weak who are left in this city, and of all the people, by saying such words to them. This man does not care about the wellbeing of these people, but instead wants them hurt." 5 So King Zedekiah said, "He is in your hands. The king can do nothing against you." 6 So they took Jeremiah and put him into the well of Malchijah the king's son, in the open space of the prison, letting him down with ropes. There was no water in the well, but only mud. And Jeremiah went down into the mud. 7 But Ebed-melech, an Ethiopian servant of the king who had been made so he could not have children, heard in the king's house that they had put Jeremiah into the well. Now the king was sitting in the Gate of Benjamin. 8 And Ebed-melech went from the king's house and said to him, 9 "My lord the king, these men have been very sinful in all they have done to Jeremiah the man of God. They have put him in the well. And he will die there of hunger, for there is no more bread in the city." 10 Then the king told Ebed-melech the Ethiopian, "I am giving you the power to take thirty men with you, and bring Jeremiah the man of God up from the well before he dies." 11 So Ebed-melech as the leader took the men with him and went into the king's house to a place under the store-room. He took from there old pieces of cloth and worn-out clothes and let them down by ropes to Jeremiah in the well. 12 Then Ebed-melech the Ethiopian said to Jeremiah, "Put the clothes and pieces of cloth between your arms and the ropes," and Jeremiah did so. 13 Then they pulled Jeremiah up with the ropes and lifted him out of the well. And Jeremiah stayed in the open space of the prison.

Zedekiah Asks Jeremiah about Future Happenings

14 King Zedekiah sent for Jeremiah the man of God and had him brought to him at the third door of the house of the Lord. And the king said to him, "I am going to ask you something. Do not hide anything from me." 15 Then Jeremiah said to Zedekiah, "If I tell you, will you not kill me? Even if I speak wise words to you, you will not listen to me." 16 But King Zedekiah promised Jeremiah in secret, "As the Lord lives, Who gave us life, for sure I will not kill you or give you over to these men who want to kill you."

17 Then Jeremiah said to Zedekiah, "This is what the Lord God of All, the God of Israel, says: 'If you will go out to the captains of the king of Babylon, then you will live. This city will not be burned with fire, and you and those of your house will live. 18 But if you will not go out to the captains of the king of Babylon, then this city will be given to the Babylonians. They will burn it with fire, and you will not get away from them.' " 19 King Zedekiah said to Jeremiah, "I am afraid of the Jews who have gone over to the Babylonians. I am afraid I will be given over to them, and that they will make it hard for me." 20 But Jeremiah said, "They will not give you to them. Obey the Lord by doing what I tell you. Then it will go well with you and you will live. 21 But if you will not go out, this is the word which the Lord has shown me: 22 'All of the women left in the house of the king of Judah are going to be brought out to the captains of the king of Babylon. And these women will say, "Your trusted friends have lied to you and have become stronger than you. Now when your feet have gone down into the mud, they turn away from you." 23 All your wives and your sons will be led out to the Babylonians. And you yourself will not get away from them. The king of Babylon will take hold of you, and this city will be burned with fire.' "

24 Then Zedekiah said to Jeremiah, "Let no one know about these words and you will not die. 25 The leaders might hear that I have talked with you, and come and say to you, 'Tell us what you said to the king, and what the king said to you. Do not hide it from us, and we will not kill you.' 26 Then you must tell them, 'I was asking the king not to make me return to the house of Jonathan to die there.' " 27 All the leaders did come to Jeremiah to ask him questions. So he said to them everything the king had told him to say. And they stopped speaking with him, because the words he and the king had spoken together had not been heard by anyone else. 28 So Jeremiah stayed in the open space of the prison until the day Jerusalem was taken.

Jerusalem Taken by the Babylonians

39 In the tenth month of the ninth year of Zedekiah king of Judah, Nebuchadnezzar king of Babylon and all his army came and gathered around Jerusalem. 2 And on the ninth day of the fourth month of the eleventh year of Zedekiah, the city wall was broken open. 3 Then all the captains of the king of Babylon came in and sat down at the Middle Gate: Nergal-sar-ezer, Samgar-nebu, Sarsekim, the Rab-saris, Nergal-sar-ezer the Rab-mag, and all the rest of the captains of the king of Babylon. 4 When King Zedekiah of Judah and all his men of war saw them, they ran out of the city at night by way of the king's garden through the gate between the two walls. They went out toward the Jordan Valley. 5 But the Babylonian army went after them and came to Zedekiah in the plains of Jericho. They took hold of him and brought him up to Nebuchadnezzar king of Babylon at Riblah in the land of

Hamath. And Nebuchadnezzar decided how he should be punished. 6 The king of Babylon killed Zedekiah's sons in front of his eyes at Riblah. He killed all the leaders of Judah also. 7 Then he put out Zedekiah's eyes and put him in chains of brass to take him to Babylon. 8 The Babylonians burned the king's house and the houses of the people with fire. And they broke down the walls of Jerusalem. 9 Then Nebuzaradan, the captain of the soldiers, carried the rest of the people who were left in the city away to Babylon, those who went over with him, and the people who stayed. 10 But Nebuzaradan, the captain of the prison soldiers, left behind in the land of Judah some of the poorest people who had nothing. He gave them grape-fields and fields at the same time.

Jeremiah Is Not Held

11 Now Nebuchadnezzar king of Babylon said what must be done about Jeremiah through Nebuzaradan the captain of the prison soldiers. He said, 12 "Take him and watch over him. Do not hurt him, but do with him as he tells you." 13 So Nebuzaradan the captain of the prison soldiers, Nebushazban the Rab-saris, Nergal-sarezer the Rab-mag, and all the leading captains of the king of Babylon 14 sent for Jeremiah and took him out of the open space of the prison. And they put him in the care of Gedaliah, the son of Ahikam, the son of Shaphan, to take him home. So Jeremiah stayed among the people.

Ebed-melech's Future

15 The Word of the Lord had come to Jeremiah while he was being kept in the open space of the prison, saying, 16 "Go and tell Ebed-melech the Ethiopian, 'This is what the Lord of All, the God of Israel says: "I will bring My words on this city for bad and not for good. And they will happen in front of you at that time. 17 I will save you on that day," says the Lord. "You will not be given over to the men you are afraid of. 18 For I will be sure to take you away, and you will not be killed by the sword. You will have your life because you trusted in Me." ' " says the Lord.

Jeremiah Free to Go

40 This is the word which came to Jeremiah from the Lord after Nebuzaradan, captain of the prison soldiers, had let him go from Ramah. He had taken him there in chains with all the other people of Jerusalem and Judah who were being taken to Babylon. 2 The captain of the prison soldiers took Jeremiah and said to him, "The Lord your God promised this trouble against this place. 3 The Lord has brought it about, and has done just as He promised. This thing has happened to you because you people sinned against the Lord and did not listen to Him. 4 But now I am setting you free today from the chains on your hands. If you would like to come with me to Babylon, then come, and I will see that it goes well with you. But if you do not want to come with me to Babylon, do not come. See, the whole land is before you. Go where you think it is good and right for you to go. 5 If you stay, then go back to Gedaliah the son of Ahikam, the son of Shaphan, whom the king of Babylon has set over the cities of Judah. Stay with him among the people. Or go where you think it is right to go." Then the captain of the prison soldiers gave him a share of food and a gift, and let him go. 6 So Jeremiah went to Mizpah, to Gedaliah the son of Ahikam. And he stayed with him among the people who were left in the land.

Gedaliah Is Ruler of Judah

7 Now all the captains of the armies that were in the field and their men heard that the king of Babylon had chosen Gedaliah the son of Ahikam to rule over the land. The king had put him over the men, women and children who were the poorest of the land and had not been taken to Babylon. 8 So they came to Gedaliah at Mizpah. With them were Ishmael the son of Nethaniah, Johanan and Jonathan the sons of Kareah, Seraiah the son of Tanhumeth, the sons of Ephai the Netophathite, and Jezaniah the son of the Maacathite, together with their men. 9 Then Gedaliah the son of Ahikam, the son of Shaphan, made a promise to them and their men, saying, "Do not be afraid of serving the Babylonians. Stay in the land and serve the king of Babylon. Then it will go well with you. 10 As for me, I will stay at Mizpah to stand for you in front of the Babylonians who come to us. But as for you, gather wine and summer fruit and oil, and store them in your jars. And live in your cities that you have taken." 11 All the Jews in Moab and Ammon and Edom, and in all the other countries, heard that the king of Babylon had left some of the people in Judah. They heard that he had chosen Gedaliah the son of Ahikam, the son of Shaphan, to rule

over them. 12 Then all the Jews returned from all the places where they had been driven, and came to the land of Judah, to Gedaliah at Mizpah. And they gathered much wine and summer fruit.

Gedaliah Is Killed

13 Now Johanan the son of Kareah and all the captains of the armies that were in the field came to Gedaliah at Mizpah. 14 They said to him, "Do you know that Baalis, the king of the sons of Ammon, has sent Ishmael the son of Nethaniah to kill you?" But Gedaliah the son of Ahikam did not believe them. 15 Then Johanan the son of Kareah said in secret to Gedaliah in Mizpah, "Let me go and kill Ishmael the son of Nethaniah, and no one will know about it. Why should he kill you? Then all the Jews who are gathered to you would go everywhere. And those of Judah who are left here would die." 16 But Gedaliah the son of Ahikam said to Johanan the son of Kareah, "Do not do this. For you are telling a lie about Ishmael."

41 In the seventh month, Ishmael the son of Nethaniah, the son of Elishama, of the king's family, came to Gedaliah the son of Ahikam at Mizpah. He came with one of the head captains of the king, and ten other men. While they were eating bread together there in Mizpah, 2 Ishmael the son of Nethaniah and the ten men who were with him rose up and killed Gedaliah the son of Ahikam, the son of Shaphan, with the sword. They killed the one whom the king of Babylon had chosen to rule the land. 3 Ishmael also killed all the Jews who were with Gedaliah at Mizpah, and the Babylonian soldiers who were found there.

4 The next day, before anyone knew that Gedaliah had been killed, 5 eighty men came from Shechem, from Shiloh, and from Samaria. Their hair was cut from their faces, their clothes were torn, and their bodies were cut. They came with grain gifts and special perfume in their hands to bring to the house of the Lord. 6 Then Ishmael the son of Nethaniah went out from Mizpah to meet them, crying as he went. As he met them he said, "Come to Gedaliah the son of Ahikam." 7 When they came inside the city, Ishmael the son of Nethaniah and the men who were with him killed them, and threw them into the well. 8 But there were ten men among them who said to Ishmael, "Do not kill us!

For we have stores of grain, barley, oil and honey hidden in the field." So he did not kill them with their friends.

9 The well where Ishmael had thrown all the bodies of the men he had killed because of Gedaliah was the one that King Asa had made because of his fear of Baasha, king of Israel. Ishmael the son of Nethaniah filled it with the dead. 10 Then he put all the rest of the Jews in chains who were in Mizpah, the king's daughters and all the people left in Mizpah, whom Nebuzaradan, the captain of the prison soldiers, had put under the rule of Gedaliah the son of Ahikam. Then Ishmael the son of Nethaniah took them and started to cross over to the sons of Ammon.

11 But Johanan the son of Kareah, and all the captains of the armies that were with him, heard about all the bad things that Ishmael the son of Nethaniah had done. 12 So they took all the men and went to fight with Ishmael the son of Nethaniah. They found him by the large pool in Gibeon. 13 When all the people who were with Ishmael saw Johanan the son of Kareah and the captains of the armies with him, they were glad. 14 So all the people Ishmael had taken from Mizpah turned around and came back, and went to Johanan the son of Kareah. 15 But Ishmael the son of Nethaniah got away from Johanan with eight men and went to the sons of Ammon. 16 Then Johanan the son of Kareah and all the captains of the armies that were with him took all the rest of the people whom Ishmael the son of Nethaniah had taken away from Mizpah after he had killed Gedaliah the son of Ahikam. They took the soldiers, the women, the children, and the servants, whom Johanan had brought back from Gibeon, 17 and they went and stayed in GeruthChimham near Bethlehem. They were on their way to Egypt 18 because of the Babylonians. For they were afraid of them, because Ishmael the son of Nethaniah had killed Gedaliah the son of Ahikam, whom the king of Babylon had chosen to rule the land.

The People Want to Go to Egypt

42 Then all the captains of the armies, Johanan the son of Kareah, Jezaniah the son of Hoshaiah, and all the people both small and great, came near 2 and said to Jeremiah the man of God, "Hear what we ask of you. Pray to the Lord your God for us, for all these people who are left.

As you see, only a few of us are left out of many. ³ Pray that the Lord your God may show us the way we should go and what we should do." ⁴ Then Jeremiah the man of God said to them, "I have heard you. I will pray to the Lord your God as you ask. And I will tell you the whole answer that the Lord gives. I will not keep anything from you." ⁵ Then they said to Jeremiah, "May the Lord be true and faithful to speak against us if we do not do all that the Lord your God tells you we must do. ⁶ If it is good or bad, we will listen to the voice of the Lord our God to Whom we are sending you. It will go well with us if we listen to the voice of the Lord our God."

⁷ At the end of ten days the Word of the Lord came to Jeremiah. ⁸ Then he called for Johanan the son of Kareah, and all the captains of the armies that were with him, and for all the people both small and great. ⁹ And he said to them, "This is what the Lord the God of Israel says, to Whom you sent me to bring Him what you asked for: ¹⁰ 'If you will stay in this land, then I will build you up and not tear you down. I will plant you and not pull you up by the roots. For I will change My mind about the trouble that I have given you. ¹¹ Do not be afraid of the king of Babylon, who now fills you with fear. Do not be afraid of him,' says the Lord. 'For I am with you to save you and take you from his hands. ¹² I will show you loving pity, so that he will have pity on you and let you stay in your own land. ¹³ But if you say, "We will not stay in this land," and will not listen to the voice of the Lord your God, ¹⁴ and if you say, "No, we will go to the land of Egypt, where we will not see war or hear the sound of a horn or be hungry for bread, and we will stay there," ¹⁵ then listen to the Word of the Lord, O you who are left of Judah. This is what the Lord of All, the God of Israel, says: "If you set your mind to go into Egypt, and go to live there, ¹⁶ then the sword which you are afraid of will come to you there in the land of Egypt. The hunger you are worried about will follow after you there in Egypt. And there you will die. ¹⁷ So all the men who set their mind to go and live in Egypt will die by the sword and hunger and disease. They will have no one left alive and no one who will get away from the trouble that I will bring to them.'"

¹⁸ "For the Lord of All, the God of Israel, says, 'As My anger has been poured out on the people of Jerusalem, so My anger will be poured out on you when you go into Egypt. You will become a curse, and object of hate. People will say bad things against you. You will be put to shame. And you will never see this place again.' ¹⁹ O people who are left of Judah, the Lord has said to you, 'Do not go into Egypt!' Know for sure that I have told you of the danger today. ²⁰ You have fooled yourselves. You sent me to the Lord your God, saying, 'Pray to the Lord our God for us. Whatever the Lord our God says, tell us and we will do it.' ²¹ So I have told you today, but you have not obeyed the Lord your God in anything that He told me to tell you. ²² So now be sure and know that you will die by the sword and hunger and disease, in the place where you want to go to live."

Jeremiah Is Taken to Egypt

43 Jeremiah, whom the Lord their God had sent, finished telling all the people all these words of the Lord their God. ² Then Azariah the son of Hoshaiah, and Johanan the son of Kareah, and all the proud men said to Jeremiah, "You are lying! The Lord our God has not sent you to say, 'You must not go into Egypt to live.' ³ But Baruch the son of Neriah is leading you against us to give us over to the Babylonians, so they may kill us or take us away to Babylon." ⁴ So Johanan the son of Kareah and all the captains of the armies, and all the people, did not obey the voice of the Lord to stay in the land of Judah. ⁵ Johanan the son of Kareah and all the captains of the armies took all the people left of Judah, who had returned to live in the land of Judah from all the nations where they had been driven. ⁶ They took the men, women, children, the king's daughters, and every person that Nebuzaradan the captain of the prison soldiers had left with Gedaliah the son of Ahikam and grandson of Shaphan. They also took Jeremiah the man of God and Baruch the son of Neriah. ⁷ And they went into the land of Egypt, for they did not obey the voice of the Lord. They went in as far as Tahpanhes.

⁸ Then the Word of the Lord came to Jeremiah in Tahpanhes, saying, ⁹ "Take some large stones in your hands. And hide them among the stone blocks by the door of Pharaoh's house in Tahpanhes. Let some of the Jews see you do this. ¹⁰ Tell them, 'The Lord of All, the God of Israel, says, "See, I will send for Nebuchadnezzar the king of Babylon, My servant. And I will

set his throne over these stones that I have hidden. He will spread his covering over them. [11] He will come and fight against the land of Egypt. Those who are meant to die will die. Those who are to be taken away will be taken away. And those who are to be killed by the sword will be killed by the sword. [12] I will set fire to the houses of worship where the gods of Egypt are worshiped. He will burn them and take them away. So he will dress himself with the land of Egypt as a shepherd puts on his coat. And he will go away from there in peace. [13] He will break to pieces the objects of worship in the house of the Sun god in Egypt. And he will burn the houses of the gods of Egypt with fire.' "

The People Will Be Punished in Egypt

44 This word came to Jeremiah for the Jews living in the land of Egypt, at Migdol, Tahpanhes, Memphis, and in the land of Pathros, saying, [2] "This is what the Lord of All, the God of Israel, says: 'You have seen all the trouble I have brought to Jerusalem and to all the cities of Judah. See, today they are a waste. No one lives in them. [3] This is because of the sins they did that made Me angry. They kept burning special perfume and worshiping other gods whom they, you, and your fathers had not known. [4] Yet I sent you all My servants who spoke for Me again and again, saying, "O, do not do this very sinful thing which I hate!" [5] But they did not listen and would not turn from their sinful ways. They would not stop burning special perfume to other gods. [6] So My anger was poured out and burned in the cities of Judah and in the streets of Jerusalem. And they have been destroyed and laid waste, as they are today. [7] Now this is what the Lord God of All, the God of Israel, says: "Why are you hurting yourselves so much? Why are you cutting off from Judah man and woman, child and baby, and leaving yourselves without anyone? [8] You are making Me angry with the works of your hands. You burn special perfume to other gods in the land of Egypt, where you have gone to live. And so you will be cut off and become a curse and a shame among all the nations of the earth. [9] Have you forgotten the sins of your fathers, the sins of the kings of Judah, the sins of their wives, your own sins, and the sins of your wives? They sinned in the land of Judah and in the streets of Jerusalem. [10] They have not been sorry for their sins even to this day. They have not feared

Me or walked in My Laws which I have given you and your fathers." '

[11] "So the Lord of All, the God of Israel, says, 'I will turn against you and destroy all Judah. [12] I will take away those left of Judah who have set their mind on going into the land of Egypt to live. They will come to an end in the land of Egypt. They will fall by the sword or die from hunger. Both the small and the great will die by the sword or hunger. They will be a curse and a cause of fear. They will be spoken against and put to shame. [13] I will punish those who live in the land of Egypt as I have punished Jerusalem, with the sword and hunger and disease. [14] So none of those left of Judah who have come to live in the land of Egypt will be able to leave and go to the land of Judah, where they want to return and live. None will return except a few who run for their lives.' "

[15] Then all the men who knew that their wives were burning special perfume to other gods, and all the many women who stood by, and all the people who were living in Pathros in the land of Egypt, said to Jeremiah, [16] "We will not listen to what you have said to us in the name of the Lord! [17] But we will do everything that we have said we would do. We will burn special perfume to the queen of heaven and pour out drink gifts to her. We will do just as we ourselves, our fathers, our kings and our leaders did in the cities of Judah and in the streets of Jerusalem. For then we had much food, and got along well, and had no trouble. [18] But since we stopped burning special perfume to the queen of heaven and pouring out drink gifts to her, we have been without everything. We have been destroyed by the sword and by hunger." [19] And the women said, "When we baked cakes which looked like the queen of heaven, burned special perfume, and poured out our drink gifts, did not our husbands know about it?"

[20] Then Jeremiah said to all the people, both the men and women, who had given him this answer, [21] "As for the special perfume that you and your fathers, your kings and your leaders, and the people of the land burned in the cities of Judah and in the streets of Jerusalem, did not the Lord remember it? Did it not come into His mind? [22] The Lord could no longer stand by while you did such sinful things. You have done very sinful acts. So your land has been laid waste. It has become a hated and cursed land, a place without

people, as it is today. 23 Because you have burned special perfume and have sinned against the Lord and have not obeyed the voice of the Lord or walked in His Laws or done what He said to do, this trouble has come upon you, as it has this day." 24 Then Jeremiah said to all the people and all the women, "Hear the Word of the Lord, all you of Judah who are in the land of Egypt. 25 This is what the Lord of All, the God of Israel, says: 'You and your wives have said with your mouths and have done it with your hands, saying, "For sure we will keep our promises to burn special perfume to the queen of heaven and pour out drink gifts to her." Then keep your promises! Do what you have promised!' 26 But hear the Word of the Lord, all you of Judah who are living in the land of Egypt: 'I have sworn by My great name,' says the Lord, 'that My name will no more be named in the mouth of any man of Judah in all the land of Egypt, saying, "The Lord God lives." 27 For I am watching over them for trouble and not for good. All the men of Judah who are in the land of Egypt will be destroyed by the sword and hunger until there is an end of them. 28 And those who get away from the sword and return from Egypt to the land of Judah will be few. Then all those left of Judah who have gone to the land of Egypt to live will know whose word will stand, Mine or theirs. 29 This will be the special thing for you to see,' says the Lord. 'I am going to punish you in this place, so that you may know that My words will be sure to stand against you for your hurt.' 30 The Lord says, 'I will give Pharaoh Hophra king of Egypt over to those who hate him and want to kill him. It will be just as I gave Zedekiah king of Judah over to Nebuchadnezzar king of Babylon, who hated him and wanted to kill him.'"

God Speaks through Jeremiah to Baruch

45 This is the word which Jeremiah the man of God said to Baruch the son of Neriah, when he had written down in a book what Jeremiah told him. This was in the fourth year of Jehoiakim the son of Josiah, king of Judah. 2 "This is what the Lord, the God of Israel, says to you, O Baruch: 3 'You said, "O, it is bad for me! For the Lord has added sorrow to my pain. I am tired from crying inside myself, and have found no rest." ' " 4 "So you are to tell him, 'The Lord says, "I am breaking down what I have built. And I am pulling up by the roots what I have planted, that

is, the whole land." 5 Are you looking for great things for yourself? Do not look for them. For I am bringing trouble to all flesh,' says the Lord. 'But I will give you life in all the places you go.' "

God Speaks through Jeremiah about Egypt

46 This is the Word of the Lord which came to Jeremiah the man of God about the nations. 2 This is what He said about Egypt, and about the army of Pharaoh Necho king of Egypt, which was by the Euphrates River at Carchemish. Nebuchadnezzar king of Babylon had won the battle against Pharaoh's army in the fourth year of Jehoiakim the son of Josiah, king of Judah. 3 "Get your coverings ready and go out to the battle! 4 Get the horses ready and get on them! Take your places with your head-coverings on! Make your spears shine, and put on your heavy battle-clothes! 5 What do I see? They are filled with fear and are turning back. Their strong men are beaten and are running away without looking back. Much fear is on every side," says the Lord. 6 Do not let the fast man run away. Do not let the strong man get away. In the north by the River Euphrates they have lost their step and have fallen. 7 Who is this that rises like the Nile, like rivers of rising waters? 8 Egypt rises like the Nile, like the rivers of rising waters. He has said, "I will rise and cover that land. I will destroy the city and its people." 9 Go up, you horses! Drive hard, you war-wagons! Let the men of war go up, Ethiopia and Put who use the battle-covering, and the Lydians who are able men with the bow. 10 That day is the day of the Lord God of All, a day of punishment, when He will punish those who hate Him. The sword will destroy until it is filled. It will drink its fill of their blood. For there will be many killed for the Lord, the God of All, in the land of the north by the River Euphrates. 11 Go up to Gilead and get healing oil, O young daughter of Egypt! You have used many medicines for nothing. There is no healing for you. 12 The nations have heard of your shame, and the earth is full of your cry. For one soldier has fallen over another, They have both fallen together.

Nebuchadnezzar and Egypt

13 This is the word which the Lord spoke to Jeremiah the man of God about the coming of Nebuchadnezzar king of Babylon

to punish the land of Egypt: 14 "Make it known in Egypt. Make it known in Migdol, in Memphis, and in Tahpanhes. Say, 'Take your places and get ready, for the sword has destroyed those around you.' 15 Why have your strong ones gone away? They did not stand because the Lord has thrown them down. 16 The Lord made many fall. They have fallen on each other. And they said, 'Get up! Let us return to our own people and our own land, away from the sword of the one who makes it hard for us.' 17 There they cried, 'Pharaoh king of Egypt is but a noise. He has passed by the time he was to have!' 18 "As I live," says the King, Whose name is the Lord of All, "one will come who is like Tabor among the mountains, or like Carmel by the sea. 19 Get your things ready for when you are taken away, you who are living in Egypt. For Memphis will become a waste. It will be burned down and will have no people. 20 Egypt is like a beautiful young cow. But a horsefly has come upon her from the north. 21 Her hired soldiers among her are like calves, ready to eat. For they also have turned back and have run away together. They did not stay in their places. For the day of their trouble has come upon them, the time of their punishment. 22 Egypt will sound like a snake moving away. For an army will come against her with axes, like those who cut down trees. 23 They will cut down all her trees," says the Lord, "even though there are so many. There are more trees than locusts, too many to number. 24 The people of Egypt will be put to shame. She will be given over to the people of the north." 25 The Lord of All, the God of Israel, says, "I am going to punish Amon of Thebes, and Pharaoh, and Egypt and her gods and her kings. I will punish Pharaoh and those who trust in him. 26 I will give them over to those who want to kill them, to Nebuchadnezzar king of Babylon and his captains. After that, Egypt will be filled with people as it was long ago," says the Lord.

God Will Save Israel

27 "But do not be afraid, O Jacob My servant. Do not be troubled, O Israel. For I am going to save you from far away. I will bring your children back from the land where they are held. Jacob will return and have quiet and rest. And no one will make him afraid. 28 O Jacob My servant, do not be afraid," says the Lord, "for I am with you. I will make a complete end of all

the nations where I have driven you. But I will not make a complete end of you. I will punish you so you will go the right way. I will not leave you without punishment."

God Speaks through Jeremiah about the Philistines

47 This is the Word of the Lord which came to Jeremiah the man of God about the Philistines, before Pharaoh won the war against Gaza. 2 The Lord says, "Waters are going to rise from the north and become a flood. They will flow over the land and everything in it, the cities and all who live in them. The men will cry out. Every person living in the land will cry in a loud voice. 3 Because of the noise of the feet of horses running, the noise of war-wagons and the sound of wheels, fathers have not turned back for their children. Their hands have become too weak, 4 because of the day that is coming to destroy all the Philistines. And all those who helped Tyre and Sidon will be destroyed. For the Lord is going to destroy the Philistines, those who are left of the land of Caphtor by the sea. 5 All the hair is gone from the head of Gaza. Ashkelon has been destroyed. O you who are left of their valley, how long will you cut yourselves? 6 O, sword of the Lord, how long will it be before you are quiet? Return to your holder. Be at rest and do not move. 7 How can it be quiet, when the Lord has given it work to do? He has sent it against Ashkelon and against the land by the sea."

Moab Is Destroyed

48 About Moab, the Lord of All, the God of Israel, says, "It is bad for Nebo, for it has been destroyed. Kiriathaim has been put to shame and taken. The high, strong-place has been put to shame and crushed. 2 The praise for Moab has come to an end. In Heshbon they have planned trouble against her, saying, 'Come, let us destroy her from being a nation!' You, O Madmen, will be made quiet also. The sword will follow you. 3 Listen, the sound of a cry from Horonaim, saying, 'Laid waste and all destroyed!' 4 Moab is destroyed. The cry of her little ones is heard. 5 They go up the hill of Luhith crying all the time. For at the hill of Horonaim they have heard the troubled cry of those who are being destroyed. 6 Run fast! Run for your lives! You will be like a bush in the desert. 7 Because you have trusted in your own works and riches, you also will be taken. And Chemosh will go away to a strange land together with his religious leaders and important men. **8** The destroyer will come to every city. No city will be free from him. The valley and the plain will be destroyed also, as the Lord has said. **9** Give wings to Moab, for she will fly away. Her cities will become a waste, with no people living in them. **10** The one who does the Lord's work without care is cursed. Cursed is the one who keeps his sword from blood.

11 "Moab has been at rest since he was young. He has been like wine which sits a long time, not being poured from jar to jar. He has not gone away to a strange land. So he keeps his taste, and his smell is not changed. **12** The days are coming," says the Lord, "when I will send to him those who turn over jars, and they will turn him over. They will empty his jars and break them in pieces. **13** Then Moab will be ashamed of Chemosh, as the house of Israel was ashamed of Bethel that they trusted. **14** How can you say, 'We are strong soldiers and powerful men of war'? **15** Moab has been destroyed, and men have gone up to his cities. His best young men have gone down to be killed," says the King, Whose name is the Lord of All. **16** The trouble of Moab will soon come. His suffering comes in a hurry. **17** Have sorrow for him, all you who live around him, and all who know his name. Say, 'How his power has been broken, the greatness of his power!' **18** Come down from your greatness and sit on the hot ground, O you who live in Dibon. For the destroyer of Moab has come up against you. He has destroyed your strong-places built for battle. **19** Stand by the road and keep watch, O you who live in Aroer. Ask the man or woman who runs away, 'What has happened?' **20** Moab has been put to shame, for it is broken down. Cry out. Let it be known by the Arnon that Moab has been destroyed. **21** Punishment has come upon the plain, against Holon, Jahzah, Mephaath, **22** Dibon, Nebo, Beth-diblathaim, **23** Kiriathaim, Beth-gamul, Beth-meon, **24** Kerioth, Bozrah, and all the cities of the land of Moab, far and near. **25** Moab's strength has been cut off, and his arm broken," says the Lord. **26** "Make him drunk, for he has become proud before the Lord. So Moab will roll in the food he has thrown up, and he will be laughed at. **27** Did you not laugh at Israel? Or was he found among robbers? For each time you speak about him you laugh and shake your

head. **28** Leave the cities and live among the rocks, O people of Moab. Be like a dove that has its nest in a hole in the side of the rock. **29** We have heard of the pride of Moab. He is very proud. We have heard of all his pride and how he honors himself. **30** I know his anger," says the Lord, "but it is of no use. His proud words have done nothing. **31** So I will cry in a loud voice for Moab. I will cry out for all Moab. I will have sorrow for the men of Kir-heres. **32** I will cry for you more than for Jazer, O vine of Sibmah! Your branches have gone over the sea, even to the sea of Jazer. The destroyer has fallen upon your summer fruits and your grapes. **33** Happiness and joy have been taken away from the land of Moab with all its fruit. I have stopped the crushing of the grapes to make wine. No one crushes them under foot. The noise they make is not the sound of joy. **34** They cry out from Heshbon even to Elealeh, even to Jahaz, and from Zoar even to Horonaim and to Eglath-shelishiyah. Even the waters of Nimrim have become a waste. **35** And I will make an end of Moab," says the Lord. "I will destroy the one who gives gifts of worship on the high place and burns special perfume to his gods.

36 "So My heart cries out for Moab like a horn. My heart cries like a horn also for the men of Kir-heres. The riches they had for themselves have been lost. **37** The hair has been cut from every head, and the hair has been cut short on every face. There are cuts on all the hands, and they wear clothes made from hair. **38** On all the roofs of Moab and in its streets there are cries of sorrow everywhere. For I have broken Moab like a pot that is not wanted," says the Lord. **39** "How broken it is! How they cry! How Moab has turned his back in shame! So Moab has become something to laugh at and hate to all those around him." **40** For the Lord says, "One will fly fast like an eagle, and spread out his wings against Moab. **41** Kerioth has been taken, and the strong-places built for battle have been taken. In that day the hearts of the strong men of Moab will be like the heart of a woman giving birth. **42** Moab will be destroyed and will no longer be a nation, because he was proud before the Lord. **43** Fear, traps and nets are coming upon you, O you who live in Moab," says the Lord. **44** "The one who runs from trouble will fall into the trap. And the one who comes up out of the trap will be caught in the net. For I will bring these things upon

Moab in the year of their punishment," says the Lord.

45 "In the shadow of Heshbon, those who have run for their lives stand without strength. For a fire has gone out from Heshbon and from Sihon. It has destroyed the forehead of Moab and the top of the heads of the trouble-makers. 46 It is bad for you, Moab! The people of Chemosh have been destroyed. Your sons and daughters have been taken away in chains. 47 Yet I will return the people of Moab to their land in the last days," says the Lord. This is the punishment of Moab.

God Speaks through Jeremiah about Ammon

49 About the sons of Ammon, the Lord says, "Does Israel have no sons? Does she have no one to receive what she leaves? Why then has Malcam taken Gad as his own? Why do his people live in its cities? 2 But the days are coming," says the Lord, "when I will blow a horn giving the sound of war against Rabbah of the sons of Ammon. And it will become a waste. Its towns will be set on fire. Then Israel will take the land from those who had taken it from her," says the Lord.

3 "Cry out, O Heshbon, for Ai has been destroyed! Cry out, O people of Rabbah. Put on clothes made from hair and cry in sorrow. And run this way and that way inside the walls. For Malcam will go to a strange land, together with his religious leaders and his important men. 4 How you speak in pride about the valleys! Your valley is flowing away, O daughter without faith who trusts in her riches, saying, 'Who will come against me?' 5 I will bring much trouble upon you," says the Lord God of All. "It will come from all around you, and each of you will be driven away. There will be no one to gather together those who run for their lives. 6 But after this I will return the sons of Ammon to their land," says the Lord.

God Speaks through Jeremiah about Edom

7 About Edom, the Lord of All says, "Is there no longer any wisdom in Teman? Have wise words been lost from the wise? Is their wisdom all gone? 8 Run away! Turn back and live in the deep places, O people of Dedan. For I will bring the trouble of Esau upon him when I punish him. 9 If those who gather grapes came to you, would they not leave some grapes behind? If robbers came during the night, would they not take only what was enough for them? 10 But I have taken all that Esau has. I have taken the covering from his hiding places so that he will not be able to hide himself. His children, his brothers, and his neighbors are destroyed. And he is no more. 11 Leave your children behind, who have lost their parents, and I will keep them alive. And let your women whose husbands have died trust in Me." 12 For the Lord says, "If those who were not to drink the cup must drink it, will you go without being punished? You will not go without being punished, but you must drink it. 13 For I have promised by Myself," says the Lord, "that Bozrah will become an object of trouble, a shame, a waste, and a curse. All its cities will be destroyed forever."

14 I have heard word from the Lord. A man with news is sent among the nations, saying, "Gather together and come against her! Rise up for battle! 15 For I have made you small among the nations, hated among men. 16 As for the fear you have caused, the pride of your heart has fooled you, O you who live in the holes of rocks, who live on the top of the hill. Even if you make your nest as high as an eagle's, I will bring you down from there," says the Lord. 17 'Edom will become an object of trouble. Everyone who passes by will be surprised and will make fun of all its suffering. 18 As when Sodom and Gomorrah and their neighbors were destroyed, no one will live there," says the Lord. "No man will live there. 19 One will come up like a lion from the trees by the Jordan to rich grass fields. All at once I will make him run away from Edom. And I will make whoever I choose rule over it. For who is like Me? Who will call Me into court? What shepherd can stand against Me?"

20 So hear the plan the Lord has made against Edom. Listen to His plans which He has made against the people of Teman. Even the little ones of the flock will be pulled away. For sure He will make their fields an empty waste because of them. 21 The earth will shake at the sound of their fall. The sound of their cry will be heard at the Red Sea. 22 See, one will come and fly down in a hurry like an eagle. He will spread out his wings against Bozrah. In that day the hearts of the strong men of Edom will be like the heart of a woman giving birth.

God Speaks through Jeremiah about Damascus

23 About Damascus, He says, "Hamath and Arpad are troubled, for they have heard bad news. Their hearts have become weak. They are troubled like the sea which cannot be quiet. 24 Damascus has become weak. She has turned to run away. Fear has taken hold of her. Pain and sorrows have taken hold of her like a woman giving birth. 25 Why does the city of praise, the town of My joy, still have people in it? 26 For sure her young men will fall in her streets. And all the men of war will be destroyed in that day," says the Lord of All. 27 "I will set fire to the wall of Damascus. And it will burn up the strong towers of Ben-hadad."

God Speaks through Jeremiah about Kedar and Hazor

28 About Kedar and the nations of Hazor, which were beaten in battle by Nebuchadnezzar king of Babylon, the Lord says, "Get up and go to Kedar, and destroy the men of the east. 29 Their tents and their flocks will be taken. Their tent curtains, and all their good things, and their camels will be carried away for themselves. And men will call out to them, 'Trouble is on every side!' 30 Run! Run far away! Live in the deep places, O people of Hazor," says the Lord. "For Nebuchadnezzar king of Babylon has made a plan against you. He has thought of a way to hurt you. 31 Get up and go to fight against a nation which is at rest and lives without fear," says the Lord. "It has no gates with pieces of iron. And its people live alone. 32 Their camels and their many cattle will become a prize of war. I will send everywhere to the winds those who are in the farthest places. I will bring trouble to them from every side," says the Lord. 33 "Hazor will become a place where wild dogs live, a waste place forever. No man will live there, and no man will stay there."

God Speaks through Jeremiah about Elam

34 This is the Word of the Lord which came to Jeremiah the man of God about Elam, at the beginning of the rule of King Zedekiah of Judah, saying, 35 "The Lord of All says, 'I will break the bow of Elam, the best of their strength. 36 I will bring the four winds to Elam from the four ends of heaven. And I will have these winds send them everywhere. There will not be a nation to which

the people sent out of Elam will not go. 37 I will fill Elam with fear in front of those who hate them and want to kill them. I will bring much trouble upon them, even My burning anger,' says the Lord. 'I will send the sword after them until I have destroyed them. 38 Then I will set My throne in Elam, and will destroy their kings and leaders,' says the Lord. 39 'But in the last days I will return the people of Elam to their land,' " says the Lord.

God Speaks through Jeremiah about Babylon

50 The word which the Lord spoke about Babylon, the land of the Babylonians, through Jeremiah the man of God: 2 "Make it known among the nations. Lift up a flag and make it known. Do not hide it, but say, 'Babylon has been taken. Bel has been put to shame. Marduk has been broken down. Her objects of worship have been put to shame. Her false gods have been broken down.' 3 For a nation has come up against her from the north. It will make her land an empty waste, and no one will live in it. Both man and animal will run away.

4 "In those days and at that time," says the Lord, "the sons of Israel will come, together with the sons of Judah. They will cry as they come, and will be looking for the Lord their God. 5 They will ask the way to Zion, with faces turned toward it, saying, 'Come, let us join ourselves to the Lord in an agreement that lasts forever, one that will never be forgotten.'

6 "My people have become lost sheep. Their shepherds have led them the wrong way. They have made them turn away on the mountains. They have gone from mountain to hill and have forgotten their resting place. 7 All who found them have destroyed them. Those who hate them have said, 'We are not guilty, for they have sinned against the Lord, their true resting place Who is right and good, the hope of their fathers.' 8 Run out of Babylon. Go from the land of the Babylonians. Be like male goats that go before the flock. 9 For I am going to raise up and bring against Babylon a group of great nations from the land of the north. They will come ready for battle against her, and she will be taken. Their arrows will be like an able soldier who does not return with empty hands. 10 Babylon will become a prize of war. All who take things from her will have enough," says the Lord.

Babylon Is Punished

11 "You are glad and full of joy, O you who take what belongs to My people. You play around like a young cow in grain, and sound like strong horses. Because of this, 12 your mother will be very ashamed. She who gave birth to you will be put to shame. She will be the least of the nations, a wilderness, a waste, and a desert. 13 Because of the Lord's anger no people will live there. She will be left with no people. Everyone who passes by Babylon will be surprised, and will make fun of her because of her sores. 14 Come up for battle against Babylon on every side, all you who use the bow. Shoot at her. Do not save any of your arrows, for she has sinned against the Lord. 15 Raise your battle cry against her on every side. She has given herself up. Her strong pillars have fallen. Her walls have been torn down. Since this is the punishment of the Lord, punish her. Do to her as she has done to others. 16 Cut off from Babylon the one who plants seeds and the one who cuts the grain at gathering time. Because of the sword of the one who makes it hard for them, everyone will return to his own people. Each one will run to his own land.

Israel Is Like a Flock of Sheep

17 "Israel is like sheep sent everywhere, driven away by lions. The first one who destroyed Israel was the king of Assyria. And the last one who has broken his bones is Nebuchadnezzar king of Babylon. 18 So the Lord of All, the God of Israel, says: 'I am going to punish the king of Babylon and his land, just as I punished the king of Assyria. 19 I will return Israel to his field, and he will feed on Carmel and Bashan. And his desire will be filled in the hill country of Ephraim and Gilead. 20 In those days and at that time,' says the Lord, 'sin will be looked for in Israel, but there will be none. And sin will be looked for in Judah, but it will not be found. For I will forgive those whom I allow to return.'

Words about Babylon

21 "Go up against the land of Merathaim, and against the people of Pekod. Kill and destroy all of them," says the Lord, "and do all that I have told you. 22 The noise of battle is in the land, and much is destroyed. 23 How the strong one of the whole earth has been cut off and broken! Babylon has become a complete waste among the nations! 24 I set a trap for you, and you were caught, O Babylon, and you did not know it. You have been found and caught, because you have fought against the Lord." 25 The Lord has opened His store-house and has brought out the swords of His anger. For the Lord, the God of All, has work to do in the land of the Babylonians. 26 Come to her from the farthest land. Open her store-houses. Gather her up like grain, and destroy all of her. Let nothing be left of her. 27 Kill all her young bulls. Let them go down to be killed. It is bad for them, for their day has come, the time of their punishment. 28 Listen! They are running from the land of Babylon to tell in Zion about the punishment of the Lord our God. They are telling how the Lord punishes those who destroyed His house of worship.

29 "Call all those who use the bow to fight against Babylon. Gather around her on every side. Let no one get away. Pay her back for what she did. Do to her all that she has done. For she has been proud against the Lord, against the Holy One of Israel. 30 So her young men will fall in her streets. And all her men of war will be made quiet in that day," says the Lord. 31 "See, I am against you, O proud one," says the Lord God of All. "For your day has come, the time when I will punish you. 32 The proud one will trip and fall with no one to help him up. I will set fire to his cities, and it will burn up all that is around him." 33 The Lord of All says, "The sons of Israel and the sons of Judah are troubled and are held under a bad power. All who took them away in chains have held on to them. They have not been willing to let them go. 34 The One Who saves and makes them free is strong. The Lord of All is His name. He will work hard for their cause, so that He may give rest to the land. But He will not give rest to the people of Babylon. 35 A sword is against the Babylonians," says the Lord, "and against the people of Babylon, and against her leaders and her wise men! 36 A sword is against her religious leaders who are false and lie. They will become fools! A sword is against her strong men, and they will be filled with fear! 37 A sword is against her horses and war-wagons, and against all the soldiers from other lands who are with her! They will become like women! A sword is against her riches, and they will be taken! 38 A time of no rain and her waters will be dried up! For it is a land of false gods. They are wild over false gods. 39 So the desert

animals will live there together with the wild dogs. And ostriches also will live in it. Never again will people live there. 40 As when God destroyed Sodom and Gomorrah and their neighboring cities," says the Lord, "no man will live there. And no man will stay there.

41 "See, a nation is coming from the north. A great nation and many kings are moving from the farthest parts of the earth. 42 They take hold of their bow and spear. They fight without pity. Their voice sounds like the sea. And they ride on horses, dressed ready for battle against you, O people of Babylon. 43 The king of Babylon has heard the news about them, and his hands hang without strength. Suffering has taken hold of him, like the pain of a woman giving birth.

44 "One will come up like a lion from the trees by the Jordan to rich grass fields. All at once I will make the people run away from Babylon. And I will make whoever I choose to rule over it. For who is like Me? Who will call Me into court? What shepherd can stand before Me?" 45 So hear the plan which the Lord has made against Babylon. Listen to His plans which He has made against the land of the Babylonians. Even the little ones of the flock will be taken away. He will make their fields an empty waste because of them. 46 At the cry, "Babylon has been taken!" the earth will shake, and the cry will be heard among the nations.

Babylon Is Destroyed

51 The Lord says, "See, I will raise up the spirit of a destroyer against Babylon and against the people of Chaldea. 2 I will send strangers to destroy Babylon like a wind that blows straw away. For they will be against her on every side and leave her land empty in the day of her trouble. 3 Do not let the bow-man use his bow. Do not let him stand up in his heavy battle-clothes. Do not leave her young men alive, but destroy all of her army. 4 They will fall down dead in the land of Babylon and be killed in their streets.

5 For Israel and Judah have not been left alone by their God, the Lord of All, even though their land is full of guilt against the Holy One of Israel. 6 Run away from Babylon! Let every man save his life! Do not be destroyed in her punishment, for it is time for the Lord to punish her. He will make her pay for her sins. 7 Babylon has been a gold cup in the Lord's hand, making all the earth drunk. The nations have drunk her wine, and so the nations have gone wild. 8 All at once Babylon has fallen and been broken. Cry over her with a loud voice. Bring healing oil for her pain. It may be that she will be healed. 9 We would have healed Babylon, but she was not healed. Leave her alone, and let each of us go to his own country. For she is being judged from as far as heaven and lifted even to the skies. 10 The Lord has taken our guilt away. Come and let us make the work of the Lord our God known in Zion.

11 Make the arrows sharp! Take the body-coverings! The Lord has moved the spirit of the kings of the Medes, because He is planning to destroy Babylon. It is the punishment of the Lord, the punishment for what was done to His house of worship. 12 Lift up a flag on the walls of Babylon. Have many keep watch. Put the watchmen in their places. And get men ready to fight against her by surprise. For the Lord has both planned and done what He said about the people of Babylon. 13 O you who live by many waters and have many riches, your end has come. Your life is being cut off. 14 The Lord of All has promised to Himself, saying, "For sure I will fill you with men, as with many locusts. And they will call out that they have won the war against you."

A Song of Praise

15 He made the earth by His power. He made the world by His wisdom. And by His understanding He spread out the heavens. 16 When He speaks, there is a storm of waters in the heavens. He makes the clouds rise from the ends of the earth. He makes lightning for the rain, and brings the wind from His store-houses. 17 No man thinks well, and he is without learning. Every man who works with gold is put to shame by his false gods. For the objects of worship that he makes are false, and there is no breath in them. 18 They are of no worth, a false show. At the time of their punishment they will be destroyed. 19 He Who is the Share of Jacob is not like these. For He is the Maker of All. And Israel is the family who receives His gifts. The Lord of All is His name.

20 He says, "You are My battle-ax which I use in war. With you I destroy countries. With you I destroy nations. 21 With you I break in pieces the horse and its rider. 22 With you I destroy the war-wagon and its driver. With you I destroy man and

woman. With you I destroy old man and boy. With you I destroy young man and young woman. 23 With you I destroy the shepherd and his flock. With you I destroy the farmer and his oxen. And with you I destroy rulers and captains.

Babylon Is Punished

24 "I will punish Babylon and all the people of Chaldea for all their sins that they have done in Zion in front of your eyes," says the Lord. 25 "See, I am against you, O destroying mountain, who destroys the whole earth," says the Lord. "I will put out My hand against you and roll you down from the high rocks. I will make you a burned-out mountain. 26 Not even a stone will be taken from you for a corner stone, or a stone to be used to build upon. But you will be a waste forever," says the Lord.

27 Lift up a flag in the land! Sound the horn among the nations! Make the nations ready to fight against Babylon. Call against her the nations of Ararat, Minni, and Ashkenaz. Choose a captain to go against her. Bring up the horses like many locusts. 28 Make the nations ready to fight against her. Make ready the kings of the Medes, their rulers and captains, and every land under their rule. 29 The land shakes and moves in its pain. For the Lord's plans against Babylon stand, to make the land of Babylon a waste-land without people. 30 The powerful soldiers of Babylon have stopped fighting. They stay in their strong-places. Their strength is gone. They have become like women. Their houses are set on fire, and the iron parts of her gates are broken. 31 One man with news runs to meet another, and he runs to meet another. They run to tell the king of Babylon that his city has been taken from end to end. 32 The ways to cross the river have been stopped. The water grass has been burned with fire. And the soldiers are filled with fear.

33 The Lord of All, the God of Israel, says, "The daughter of Babylon is like the grain-floor when it is being stepped on and made hard. In a little while her gathering time will come."

34 "Nebuchadnezzar king of Babylon has destroyed me, and has crushed me. He has made me like an empty pot. He has eaten me up like a large, angry animal. He has filled his stomach with my good food, and he has washed me away. 35 May the hurt done to me and to my flesh be upon Babylon," the person living in Zion will say. "May my blood be upon the people of Babylon," Jerusalem will say.

36 So the Lord says, "See, I will help you in your cause and punish Babylon for you. I will dry up her sea, and make her well dry. 37 Babylon will become a waste place, a place where wild dogs live. She will be an object of trouble and hate, where no people live. 38 Together the people of Babylon make noise like young lions. They sound like a lion's young ones. 39 But when they are hot, I will give them a special supper and make them drunk. Then they will be happy and fall asleep, and will never wake up," says the Lord. 40 "I will bring them down like lambs to be killed, like rams and male goats.

Babylon Is Destroyed

41 "How Babylon has been taken, the praise of the whole earth taken! How Babylon has become an object of trouble among the nations! 42 The sea has come up over Babylon. She has been covered with its many big waves. 43 Her cities have become an object of trouble, a dry land and a desert. It is a land where no man lives, and where no man passes through. 44 And I will punish the false god of Bel in Babylon. I will make what he has eaten come out of his mouth. The nations will no longer come to him. The wall of Babylon will fall.

45 "Come out of her, My people. Save yourselves from the burning anger of the Lord. 46 Do not let your heart become weak. Do not be afraid at the news that will be heard in the land. For news will come this year, and other news will come the next. There will be fighting in the land, with ruler against ruler. 47 So the days are coming when I will punish the false gods of Babylon. Her whole land will be put to shame, and all her dead will fall within her. 48 Then heaven and earth and all that is in them will call out for joy over Babylon. For the destroyers will come to her from the north," says the Lord.

49 "Babylon must fall because of the dead of Israel, just as the dead of all the earth have fallen because of Babylon. 50 You who have not been killed by the sword, go! Do not stay! Remember the Lord from far away, and think of Jerusalem. 51 We are ashamed because much has been said against us. Our faces are covered with shame, for strangers have gone into the holy places of the Lord's house.

52 "But the days are coming," says the Lord, "when I will punish her false gods.

And those who are hurt will cry in pain through all her land. 53 Even if Babylon rises to the heavens and makes her high place strong, I will send destroyers against her," says the Lord.

54 The sound of a cry comes from Babylon! A noise comes from the land of the Babylonians because much is being destroyed! 55 For the Lord will destroy Babylon. He will quiet her loud voice. Their waves will sound like many waters, and the noise of their voices is loud. 56 For the destroyer is coming against Babylon, and her strong men will be taken. Their bows are broken. For the Lord is a God Who makes the sinner pay for his sin, and He will be sure to punish. 57 "I will make her leaders and her wise men, her rulers, her captains, and her strong men of war drunk. Then they will fall asleep and never wake up," says the King, Whose name is the Lord of All. 58 The Lord of All says, "The wide wall of Babylon will be broken to the ground. Her high gates will be set on fire. So the people will work hard for nothing, and because of the fire nations become tired."

Jeremiah's Word Gets to Babylon

59 This is the word which Jeremiah the man of God told Seraiah the son of Neriah, the grandson of Mahseiah, when he went with Zedekiah the king of Judah to Babylon in the fourth year of his rule. Seraiah was the head captain of the house. 60 Jeremiah wrote in a book all the trouble that would come upon Babylon. He wrote down all these words which have been written about Babylon. 61 Then Jeremiah said to Seraiah, "As soon as you come to Babylon, see that you read all these words out loud. 62 And say, 'O Lord, You have said that this place will be destroyed, so that there will be nothing living in it, not man or animal. It is to be a waste place forever.' 63 When you have finished reading this book, tie a stone to it and throw it into the Euphrates River. 64 And say, 'In this way Babylon will go down and not rise again, because of the trouble I am going to bring upon her. And her people will fall.' " The words of Jeremiah end here.

Jerusalem Destroyed

52 Zedekiah was twenty-one years old when he became king, and he ruled for eleven years in Jerusalem. His mother's name was Hamutal, the daughter of Jeremiah of Libnah. 2 Zedekiah did what was sinful in the eyes of the Lord, like all that Jehoiakim had done. 3 The Lord became so angry with Jerusalem and Judah that He had them sent away from Him. And Zedekiah turned against the king of Babylon.

4 On the tenth day of the tenth month in the ninth year of his rule, King Nebuchadnezzar of Babylon came with all his army to fight against Jerusalem. His soldiers gathered outside the city and built a battle-wall all around it. 5 So the city was shut in by the army of the Babylonians until the eleventh year of King Zedekiah. 6 On the ninth day of the fourth month, the hunger became very bad in the city. There was no food for the people of the land. 7 Then the city was broken into, and all the men of war ran away. They left the city at night by way of the gate between the two walls, by the king's garden, while the Babylonians were all around the city. They went by way of the Arabah. 8 But the Babylonian army went after King Zedekiah and came to him in the plains of Jericho, and all his army was divided and ran away from him. 9 They took the king and brought him up to the king of Babylon at Riblah in the land of Hamath. And he decided what Zedekiah's punishment would be. 10 The king of Babylon killed the sons of Zedekiah in front of his eyes. He killed all the leaders of Judah in Riblah. 11 Then he put out Zedekiah's eyes, put him in chains of brass, and took him to Babylon. There he was put in prison until the day of his death.

The House of God Destroyed

12 On the tenth day of the fifth month in the nineteenth year of King Nebuchadnezzar of Babylon, Nebuzaradan came to Jerusalem. Nebuzaradan was the captain of the prison soldiers and served the king of Babylon. 13 And he burned the house of the Lord, the king's house, and all the houses of Jerusalem. He burned down every great house. 14 The whole Babylonian army that was with the captain of the prison soldiers broke down all the walls around Jerusalem. 15 Then Nebuzaradan, captain of the prison soldiers, carried away to Babylon some of the poorest of the people, the rest of the people who were left in the city, those who had joined the king of Babylon, and the rest of the able workmen. 16 But Nebuzaradan left some of the poorest people of the land to take care of the vines and fields.

17 The Babylonians broke in pieces the brass pillars which belonged to the house of the Lord, and the stands and the brass pool which were in the Lord's house. And they carried all the brass to Babylon. 18 They also took away the pots, the tools, the objects for putting out the lamps, the washing pots, the dishes for special perfume, and all the brass objects used in the work of the Lord's house. 19 The captain of the prison soldiers also took away the deep dishes, the fire-holders, the washing pots, the other pots, the lamp-stands, the dishes for special perfume, and the dishes for drink gifts, that were made of fine gold and fine silver. 20 He took the two pillars, the brass pool, the twelve brass bulls that were under the pool, and the stands, which King Solomon had made for the house of the Lord. The brass of all these objects was too heavy to weigh. 21 Each pillar was five times taller than a man, as long around as six long steps, as wide as four fingers, and empty inside. 22 Its top part was brass and as tall as a man can raise his hand, with a network and pomegranates all around the top part, all made of brass. The second pillar with its pomegranates was the same. 23 There were ninety-six pomegranates on the sides. There were one hundred pomegranates on the network all around.

The People Taken to Babylon

24 Then the captain of the prison soldiers took Seraiah, the head religious leader, and Zephaniah, the second religious leader, and the three door-keepers of the Lord's house. 25 He also took from the city one captain who had been over the men of war, and seven of the king's wise men who were found in the city. He took the writer who worked for the captain of the army, who called together the people of the land. And he took sixty men of the land who were found in the city. 26 Nebuzaradan the captain of the prison soldiers took them and brought them to the king of Babylon at Riblah, 27 and the king of Babylon killed them. He put them to death at Riblah in the land of Hamath. So Judah was led out of its land in chains.

28 These are the people whom Nebuchadnezzar carried away to Babylon: In the seventh year he took 3,023 Jews. 29 In the eighteenth year of Nebuchadnezzar he took 832 people from Jerusalem. 30 In the twenty-third year of Nebuchadnezzar, Nebuzaradan the captain of the prison soldiers took away 745 Jews. There were 4,600 people taken away in all.

31 On the twenty-fifth day of the twelfth month in the thirty-seventh year since King Jehoiachin of Judah was taken away to Babylon, Evilmerodach king of Babylon showed favor to Jehoiachin king of Judah. It was the first year of his rule, and he brought Jehoiachin out of prison. 32 He spoke to him with kindness, and gave him a seat of honor higher than the other kings who were with him in Babylon. 33 So Jehoiachin changed from his prison clothes, and ate with the king every day for the rest of his life. 34 And a share of money was given to him by the king of Babylon every day as long as he lived, until the day of his death.

LAMENTATIONS

Jerusalem's Sorrows

1 How empty is the city that was once full of people! She was once great among the nations. But now she has become like a woman whose husband has died. She who was once a queen among the cities has become a servant made to work. 2 She cries hard in the night, with tears on her face. She has no one to comfort her among all her lovers. All her friends have not been faithful to her. They have turned against her. 3 Judah has been taken away to a strange land where she suffers much and is made to work hard as a servant. She lives among the nations, but has no rest. All those who went after her have taken her in her trouble. 4 The roads of Zion are filled with sorrow, because no one comes to the special suppers. All her gates are laid waste. Her religious leaders are crying in sorrow. Her pure young women are troubled, and she herself is in bitter suffering. 5 Those who hate her have power over her, and all goes well for them. For the Lord has made her suffer for her many sins. Her children have been taken away in front of those who hate her. 6 The people of Zion have lost all her great power. Her princes are like deer that find no field where they can eat. They are weak as they run away from those who are after them. 7 In the days of her trouble

and when she had no home, Jerusalem remembers all the things of much worth that were hers in days long ago, when her people fell into the hands of those who hated her. No one helped her. Those who hated her saw her and made fun of her when she was destroyed. 8 Jerusalem sinned very much, so she is unclean. All who honored her hate her, because they have seen her put to shame. Even she herself cries in sorrow and turns away. 9 She was unclean in her clothing. She did not think about her future. She came to nothing. She had no one to comfort her. "O Lord, see my suffering, for those who hate me have won!" 10 Those who hate her have laid their hands on all her things of much worth. For she has seen the nations go into her holy place, those whom You said must not gather with Your people. 11 All her people cry inside themselves as they look for bread. They have traded their things of much worth for food to have strength. "Look and see, O Lord, for I am hated. 12 Is it nothing to all you who pass this way? Look and see if there is any sorrow like my sorrow given me, which the Lord put on me in the day of His burning anger. 13 He sent fire from on high into my bones. He has spread a net for my feet and has turned me back. He has left me destroyed, and weak all day long. 14 The weight of my sins is put upon me. He tied them together and put them upon my neck. He has taken away my strength. The Lord has given me over to those I cannot stand against. 15 The Lord has turned away from all my strong soldiers. He has sent an army against me to crush my young men. The Lord has crushed the pure daughters of Judah like grapes are crushed to make wine. 16 This is why I cry. Tears flow from my eyes, because a comforter is far from me who would give strength to my soul. My children are destroyed, because those who hate me have won." 17 Zion has put out her hands, but there is no one to comfort her. The Lord has spoken against Jacob, that his neighbors should fight against him. Jerusalem has become unclean to them. 18 "The Lord is right and good, yet I have not wanted to obey His Word. Listen now, all you people, and see my suffering. My pure young women and young men have been taken away to a strange land. 19 I called to my lovers, but they were not faithful to me. My religious leaders and leaders of the people died in the city, while they looked for food to get

their strength back. 20 See how I suffer, O Lord. My spirit is very troubled. My heart has no rest within me, for I have not obeyed. The sword kills in the street. In the house there is only death. 21 They have heard how I cry in sorrow. There is no one to comfort me. All those who hate me have heard of my trouble. They are glad for what You did. Bring the day that You have told us about, and let them become like me. 22 Let their sin come before You, and do to them what You have done to me because of all my sin. My cries are many, and my heart is weak."

Jerusalem Is Punished

2 How the Lord has covered Zion with a cloud in His anger! He has thrown the shining-greatness of Israel from heaven to earth. In the day of His anger He has not remembered the place where He rests His feet. 2 The Lord has destroyed all the places of Jacob. In His anger He has broken down the strong-places of Judah. He has brought the nation and its leaders down to the ground in shame. 3 In burning anger He has cut off all the strength of Israel. He would not help us fight against those who hate us. He has burned like a hot fire in Jacob, destroying everything around it. 4 He has pulled back His bow string like one who fights against us. He has set His right hand like one who hates us, and has killed all that we liked to see. He has poured out His anger like fire on the tent of Zion. 5 The Lord has become like one who hates us. He has destroyed Israel. He has destroyed all its beautiful houses. He has destroyed its strong places, and has caused much sorrow and crying for the people of Judah. 6 He has broken down His house like a garden tent. He has destroyed His chosen meeting place. The Lord has caused the special suppers and Day of Rest to be forgotten in Zion. And He has hated the king and the religious leader in His anger. 7 The Lord has had nothing to do with His altar. He has left His holy place. He has given the walls of her beautiful houses over to those who hate us. They have made a noise in the house of the Lord as on the day of a special supper. 8 The Lord plans to destroy the wall of the people of Zion. He marked how long it was, and has not kept His hand from destroying. He has caused tower and wall to cry in sorrow. They suffer together. 9 Her gates have gone down into the ground. He has destroyed and broken her iron pieces.

Her king and leaders have been sent among the nations. The Law is no more. And her men who spoke for God have no more special dreams from the Lord. 10 The leaders of the people of Zion sit quietly on the ground. They have thrown dust on their heads, and have dressed themselves in cloth made from hair. The pure young women of Jerusalem have bowed their heads to the ground. 11 My eyes become weak from crying. My spirit is very troubled. My heart is poured out in sorrow, because my people have been destroyed, and because children and babies fall down weak in the city streets. 12 They cry to their mothers, "Where is bread and wine?" as they fall down weak in the city streets like a man hurt in battle, and as they die in their mothers' arms. 13 What can I say for you? What can I compare you with, O people of Jerusalem? What can I compare you with, that I may comfort you, O pure daughter of Zion? For you have been destroyed as much as the sea is large. And who can heal you? 14 Your men who speak in God's name have given you false and foolish dreams. They have not made your sin known, so you could return from where you are held. But they have told you false dreams that have led you the wrong way. 15 All who pass by clap their hands at you. They make fun of you and shake their heads at the people of Jerusalem, saying, "Is this the city which was called perfect in beauty, the joy of all the earth?" 16 All who hate you have opened their mouths wide against you. They make fun of you and grind their teeth and say, "We have destroyed her! For sure this is the day we have waited for! We have lived to see it!" 17 The Lord has done what He planned. He has done what He had said He would do long ago. He has destroyed without pity. He has caused those who hate you to have joy over you. He has given strength to those who fight against you. 18 Let your heart cry out to the Lord. O wall of the people of Zion, let your tears flow down like a river day and night. Give yourself no rest. Do not let your eyes stop crying. 19 Get up and cry out in the night, at the beginning of the night hours. Pour out your heart like water before the Lord. Lift up your hands to Him for the lives of your children who are weak with hunger on every street." 20 See, O Lord, and look! To whom have You done this? Should women eat their children, the little ones they have cared for? Should religious leaders and

men of God be killed in the Lord's holy place? 21 The young and the old lie in the dust of the streets. My pure young women and young men have been killed by the sword. You have killed them in the day of Your anger. You have killed without pity. 22 As people are asked to come to a special supper, You have sent trouble on every side. And no one got away or stayed alive in the day of the Lord's anger. Those I have cared for and brought up have been destroyed by those who hate me.

Jerusalem's Hope

3 I am the man who has been suffering because of the power of God's anger. 2 He has led me and brought me into darkness and not into light. 3 For sure He has turned His hand against me again and again all day long. 4 He has made my flesh and my skin waste away. He has broken my bones. 5 He has shut me in with trouble and suffering. 6 He has made me live in dark places, like those who have been dead a long time. 7 He has put a wall around me so that I cannot go out. He has put heavy chains on me. 8 Even when I cry and call for help, he shuts out my prayer. 9 He has stopped me with blocks of stone. He has made my paths no longer straight. 10 He is like a bear lying in wait, like a lion hiding in secret places. 11 He has turned me from the path and torn me to pieces. He has destroyed me. 12 He used His bow, and set me as a mark for His arrow. 13 He has taken out His arrows and sent them into my heart. 14 All my people laugh at me. They sing songs that make fun of me all day long. 15 He has filled me with bitter feelings. He has made me drunk with wormwood. 16 He has broken my teeth with rocks, and has covered me with dust. 17 Peace has left my soul. I have forgotten what it is like to be happy. 18 So I say, "My strength is gone, and so has my hope from the Lord."

19 Remember my trouble and my traveling from place to place, the wormwood and bitter feelings. 20 I remember it always, and my soul bows down within me. 21 But this I remember, and so I have hope. 22 It is because of the Lord's loving-kindness that we are not destroyed for His loving-pity never ends. 23 It is new every morning. He is so very faithful. 24 "The Lord is my share." says my soul, "so I have hope in Him." 25 The Lord is good to those who wait for Him, to the one who looks for Him. 26 It is good that

one should be quiet and wait for the saving power of the Lord. 27 It is good for a man to carry the load while he is young. 28 Let him sit alone and be quiet when God has laid the load on him. 29 Let him put his mouth in the dust. There may be hope yet. 30 Let him give his face to the one who hits him, and be filled with shame. 31 For the Lord will not turn away from a man forever. 32 For if He causes sorrow, He will have loving-pity because of His great loving-kindness. 33 He does not want to cause trouble or sorrow for the children of men. 34 He is not pleased when all those on earth who are in prison are crushed under foot. 35 The Most High is not pleased when the rights are kept away from a man who is before Him, 36 and when wrong is done to him in his cause. The Lord is not pleased with these things. 37 Who has said that something would happen and then it did happen, unless the Lord has said that it should be? 38 Is it not from the mouth of the Most High that both good and bad come?

39 Why should any living man complain about the punishment of his sins? 40 Let us test and look over our ways, and return to the Lord. 41 Let us lift up our heart and hands to God in heaven, saying, 42 "We have sinned and would not obey You, and You have not forgiven us. 43 You have covered Yourself with anger and have followed us, killing without pity. 44 You have covered Yourself with a cloud so that no prayer can get through. 45 You have made us a waste and something that is not wanted among the nations. 46 All those who hate us have spoken against us. 47 Fear and a trap have come upon us. We are laid waste and destroyed. 48 My eyes flow with rivers of tears because my people are destroyed. 49 Tears flow from my eyes all the time without stopping, 50 until the Lord looks down from heaven and sees. 51 My eyes bring me suffering because of what is happening to all the women of my city. 52 I have been hunted like a bird by those who hate me for no reason. 53 They threw me alive into the deep hole and have put a stone on me. 54 Water flowed over my head, and I said, "I am cut off!" 55 I called on Your name, O Lord, out of the deep hole. 56 You have heard my voice. Do not close Your ears to my cry for help. 57 You came near when I called You, and You said, "Do not be afraid!" 58 You have helped me in my cause, O Lord. You have saved my life. 59 O Lord, You have seen the wrong

done to me. Judge in my favor. 60 You have seen how much they hate me and plan against me. 61 O Lord, You have heard how they put me to shame and how they work against me. 62 The lips and thoughts of those who hurt me are against me all day long. 63 Watch their sitting down and standing up. I am their song as they make fun of me. 64 O Lord, You will punish them for what they have done. 65 You will give them hard hearts, and curse them. 66 Go after them in anger and destroy them from under Your heavens, O Lord.

Jerusalem's Sinful Leaders

4 How dark the gold has become! How the pure gold has changed! The stones from the house of God are poured out at the corner of every street. 2 The sons of Zion are worth their weight in fine gold. But they are thought of as clay pots, the work of a pot-maker's hands! 3 Even wild dogs give their breast to feed their young, but my people show no pity. They are like ostriches in the desert. 4 The baby's tongue sticks to the roof of its mouth because of thirst. The children beg for bread, but no one gives it to them. 5 Those who ate fine foods are dying in the streets. Those who were brought up dressed in purple now lie in ashes. 6 For the sin of the daughter of my people is worse than the sin of Sodom, which was destroyed all at once without a hand turned to help her. 7 Her religious leaders were more pure than snow. They were more white than milk. Their bodies were more red than coral. They were more beautiful than sapphire. 8 Now they look more black than dark ashes. No one knows who they are in the streets. Their skin has dried up on their bones. It has become as dry as wood. 9 Those who are killed with the sword are better off than those killed with hunger. For they waste away, suffering because they have no fruits of the field. 10 Women who had shown loving-kindness have boiled their own children for food, because my people are destroyed. 11 The Lord has acted in His anger. He has poured out His burning anger, and has set a fire in Zion which has burned it to the ground. 12 The kings of the earth and all the people of the world did not believe that those who hated them could come into the gates of Jerusalem. 13 This was because of the sins of her men who spoke in God's name, and the sins of her religious leaders, who killed those within her who were right and good. 14 They walked

as blind men through the streets. They were made unclean with blood so that no one could touch their clothing. 15 People cried to them, "Go away! You are unclean! Leave! Go away! Do not touch!" So they ran away and traveled from place to place. Men among the nations said, "They must not stay with us any longer." 16 The Lord Himself has sent them everywhere. He will not care about them any more. They did not honor the religious leaders or favor the leaders of the people. 17 Our eyes have become weak in looking for help that did not come. In our watching we have waited for a nation that was not able to save us. 18 They kept following after our steps so that we could not walk in our streets. Our end came near. Our days were finished, for our end had come. 19 Those who came after us were faster than the eagles of the sky. They came after us on the mountains. They hid and waited for us in the desert. 20 The Lord's chosen one, our very breath, was caught in their traps. We had said about him, "Under his shadow we will live among the nations." 21 Be filled with joy and be glad, O people of Edom, who live in the land of Uz. But the cup will be passed to you also. You will become drunk and your shame will be seen. 22 The punishment of your sin is completed, O people of Zion. The Lord will not keep you away any longer. But He will punish your sin, Edom. He will let your sins be seen!

Jerusalem's Prayer for God's Loving-Kindness

5 O Lord, remember what has happened to us. Look, and see our shame! 2 The land we received from You has been given over to strangers. Our homes have been given to people from other lands. 3 We have lost our fathers. Our mothers are like those who have lost their husbands. 4 We have to pay for our drinking water, and we must buy our wood. 5 Those who come after us are at our necks. We are tired and cannot rest. 6 We have put out our hands to Egypt and Assyria to get enough bread. 7 Our fathers sinned, and are no more, and we have suffered for their sins. 8 Servants rule over us. There is no one to save us from their hand. 9 We put our lives in danger to get our bread, because of the sword in the desert. 10 Our skin has become as hot as fire because of the burning heat of hunger. 11 They have taken and sinned against the women in Zion, and the young women who have never had a man in the cities of Judah. 12 Rulers were hung by their hands. Leaders were not respected. 13 Young men worked to grind the grain, and boys fell under loads of wood. 14 The old men have left the city gate. Young men have stopped playing their music. 15 The joy of our hearts has come to an end. Our dancing has been turned into sorrow. 16 The crown has fallen from our head. It is bad for us, for we have sinned! 17 Because of this our heart is weak. Because of these things our eyes are weak. 18 Mount Zion lies in waste, so foxes run all over it.

19 O Lord, You rule forever. Your throne will last for all people-to-come. 20 Why do You forget us forever? Why do You leave us alone for so long? 21 Return us to You, O Lord. Bring us back. Make our days as they were before. 22 Or have You turned away from us forever? Is there no end to Your anger?

EZEKIEL

Ezekiel Sees God's Throne

1 On the fifth day of the fourth month in the thirtieth year, while I was by the Chebar River with the Jews who had been taken away from their land, the heavens were opened and I saw God in a special way. 2 (On the fifth day of the month in the fifth year that King Jehoiachin had been living in a strange land, 3 the Word of the Lord came to Ezekiel the religious leader, son of Buzi, in the land of the Babylonians by the Chebar River. There the hand of the Lord came upon him.)

4 I looked and saw a wind storm coming from the north. There was a big cloud with lightning coming from it and with a bright light around it. Inside the fire was something like shining brass, 5 and in the fire was what looked like four living beings. They looked like men, 6 but each of them had four faces and four wings. 7 Their legs were straight, and their feet were like those of a calf. They shined like bright brass. 8 Under their wings on their four sides were hands like a man's. As for the faces and wings of the four of them, 9 their wings touched one another. Their faces did not turn when they moved. Each

one moved straight ahead. 10 As for what their faces looked like, each of the four had the face of a man, the face of a lion on the right side, the face of a bull on the left side, and the face of an eagle. 11 Such were their faces. Their wings were spread out above. Each had two wings touching the wings of another, and two covering their bodies. 12 And each one went straight ahead. Every place where the spirit would go, they would go, without turning as they went. 13 Between the living beings there was something that looked like burning coals of fire, like fire lamps moving from side to side among the living beings. The fire was bright, and lightning was coming out of the fire. 14 And the living beings ran this way and that, like lightning.

15 As I looked at the living beings, I saw one wheel on the earth beside each of the living beings with its four faces. 16 The way the wheels were made, they looked like shining chrysolite stone. All four of them looked the same. They were made to look as if one wheel were within another. 17 When they moved, they went in one of their four ways, without turning as they went. 18 The wheels were so high that they caused fear. And all four of them were full of eyes all around. 19 When the living beings moved, the wheels moved with them. And when the living beings rose from the earth, the wheels rose also. 20 Whatever way the spirit would go, they would go that way. And the wheels rose close beside them, for the spirit of the living beings was in the wheels. 21 When the living beings moved, they moved. When the beings stood still, they stood still. And when the beings rose up from the earth, the wheels rose close beside them. For the spirit of the living beings was in the wheels.

22 Over the heads of the living beings there was something that looked like the sky. It shined like crystal and spread over their heads. 23 Under this covering their wings were spread out straight, one toward the other. Each one also had two wings covering their bodies on one side and on the other. 24 When they went, I heard the sound of their wings. They sounded like many waters, like the voice of the All-powerful. They sounded like the noise of an army camp. Whenever they stood still, they let down their wings. 25 A voice came from above the large covering over their heads. Whenever they stood still, they let down their wings.

26 Above the large covering that was

over their heads there was something that looked like a throne, and looked like it was made of sapphire. Sitting on the throne was what looked like a man. 27 Then I saw that there was something like shining brass from the center of his body and up to his head. It looked like fire all around within it. And from the center of his body and down to his feet I saw something like fire. There was a bright light shining all around Him.

28 This light shining around Him looked like the rainbow in the clouds on a day of rain.

This was what the shining-greatness of the Lord looked like. And when I saw it, I fell on my face and heard a voice speaking.

God Calls Ezekiel to Speak for Him

2 He said to me, "Son of man, stand on your feet, and I will speak with you." 2 And when He spoke to me, the Spirit came into me and set me on my feet. I heard Him speaking to me. 3 He said, "Son of man, I am sending you to the sons of Israel, to sinful people who have turned against Me. They and their fathers have sinned against Me to this very day. 4 I am sending you to these strong-willed children who show no respect. And you must say to them, 'This is what the Lord God says.' 5 If they listen or not (for they are sinful people) they will know that a man of God has been among them. 6 And you, son of man, do not be afraid of them or of what they say, even if thistles and thorns are with you and you sit on scorpions. Do not be afraid of what they say or lose strength of heart by their looks, for they will not obey Me. 7 You must speak My words to them if they listen or not, for they do not obey Me.

8 "As for you, son of man, listen to what I am telling you. Do not be sinful like these sinful people. Open your mouth and eat what I am giving you." 9 Then I looked and saw that a hand was held out to me, and there was a book in it. 10 He held it out in front of me, and it had writing on the front and back. Words of trouble and sorrow were written on it.

3 Then He said to me, "Son of man, eat what is in front of you. Eat this book, then go and speak to the people of Israel." 2 So I opened my mouth, and He fed me this book. 3 And He said to me, "Son of man, eat this book that I give you and fill your stomach with it." So I ate it, and it was as sweet as honey in my mouth.

4 Then He said to me, "Son of man, go to the people of Israel, and speak My words to them. 5 For you are not being sent to people of strange speech and a hard language, but to the people of Israel. 6 You are not being sent to many people of strange speech and a hard language whom you cannot understand. If I had sent you to them, they would have listened to you. 7 But the people of Israel will not listen to you, for they are not willing to listen to Me. All the people of Israel are strong-willed and show no respect. 8 See, I have made you as strong-willed and as hard as they are. 9 I have made your forehead harder than the hardest stone. Do not be afraid of them. Do not be afraid of how they look, even if they do not obey Me." 10 He said to me, "Son of man, take all My words that I say to you into your heart, and hear with your ears. 11 Then go to the Jews who have been taken away from their land. Go to the sons of your people. And if they listen or not, tell them, 'This is what the Lord God says.'"

12 Then the Spirit lifted me up, and I heard a loud sounding voice behind me say, "Great is the shining-greatness of the Lord from His place." 13 I heard the sound of the wings of the living beings touching one another, and the sound of the wheels beside them. It was a loud rushing sound. 14 The Spirit lifted me up and took me away. And I went with a bitter and angry spirit. The hand of the Lord was strong upon me. 15 Then I came to the Jews who had been taken from their land and who lived by the Chebar River at Tel-abib. I sat among them seven days where they were living, and I was filled with fear.

Ezekiel to Watch Over Israel

16 At the end of seven days the Word of the Lord came to me, saying, 17 "Son of man, I have chosen you to be a watchman over the people of Israel. Whenever you hear a word from My mouth, tell them of the danger. 18 If I say to the sinful man, 'You will die for sure,' and you do not tell him of the danger, and try to turn him from his sinful way so that he may live, that sinful man will die in his sin. But you will be guilty for his blood. 19 But if you tell a sinful man of the danger he is in, and he does not turn from his sins or from his sinful way, then he will die in his sin. But you will have saved yourself. 20 Again, if a right and good man turns away from his right and good way and sins, and I put a cause of falling in his way, he will die. Because you have not told him of the danger, he will die in his sin, and the right and good things he has done will not be remembered. But you will be guilty for his blood. 21 Yet if you have told the right and good man of the danger of his sinning, and he does not sin, he will live for sure because he listened to you. And you will have saved yourself."

Ezekiel Is Not Able to Speak

22 The hand of the Lord was upon me there, and He said to me, "Get up, go out to the plain, and I will speak to you there." 23 So I got up and went out to the plain, and saw the shining-greatness of the Lord standing there. It was like the shining-greatness which I saw by the Chebar River, and I fell on my face. 24 Then the Spirit came into me and made me stand on my feet. And He spoke and said to me, "Go, shut yourself up in your house. 25 As for you, son of man, they will put ropes on you and tie you up with them, so that you cannot go out among the people. 26 And I will make your tongue stick to the roof of your mouth so that you cannot speak. You will not be able to speak sharp words to them, for they will not obey Me. 27 But when I speak to you, I will open your mouth, and you will tell them, 'This is what the Lord God says.' He who hears, let him hear. And he who is not willing to hear, let him not be willing. For they are a sinful people.

Ezekiel Shows How Jerusalem Will Be Taken

4 "Now, son of man, get a hard clay block. Set it down in front of you and draw the city of Jerusalem on it. 2 Then build a battle-wall around it to shut it in, and build a hill of dirt against the wall. Cut down trees and lay them on wheels all around the city, to use for breaking down the walls. 3 Then get an iron plate and set it up as an iron wall between you and the city, and turn your face toward it. It will be shut in, and you will fight a battle against it. This will be something special for the people of Israel to see.

4 "Then lie on your left side, and I will lay the sin of the people of Israel upon you. You will be under the weight of their sin for the number of days that you lie on your side. 5 I have set a number of days for you which is the same as the number of years of their sin, 390 days. This is how long you must be under the weight of the sin of the people of Israel. 6 When you

have completed these, you must lie down a second time, but on your right side. And you must be under the weight of the sin of the people of Judah. I have set a time of forty days for you to do this, one day for each year. [7] Then you must turn your face toward the battle against Jerusalem with no covering on your arm, and tell what will happen against the city. [8] I will tie you up with ropes so that you cannot turn from one side to the other, until you have completed the days of your battle.

[9] "Take wheat, barley, beans, lentils, millet and spelt and put them in one pot, and make them into bread for yourself. Eat it during the 390 days that you lie on your side. [10] The food you eat each day will weigh as much as twenty pieces of silver, and will have to last until the next day. [11] And the water you drink each day will be enough to fill a bottle. You will drink it from time to time. [12] Eat your food as you would barley cakes, making it ready in front of their eyes over a fire burning human waste." [13] The Lord said, "In this way the people of Israel will eat unclean food among the nations where I will drive them." [14] But I said, "O Lord God! See, I have never been unclean. Since I was young until now, I have never eaten what died of itself or what was torn by wild animals. No unclean meat has ever come into my mouth." [15] So He said to me, "Then I will let you make your bread over cow's waste instead of human waste." [16] And He said to me, "Son of man, I am going to take away the bread that is needed in Jerusalem. They will weigh the bread they eat and they will drink water from small cups, and be afraid [17] because there will not be enough bread and water. They will look at one another in fear, and waste away in their sin.

Ezekiel Cuts His Hair with a Sword

5 "As for you, son of man, take a sharp sword. Use it to cut the hair from your head and face. Then weigh and divide the hair. [2] A third part you must burn in the fire in the center of the city, when the days of the battle are completed. Then take a third part and cut it up with your sword as you move around the city. And a third part you must throw to the wind. For I will pull out a sword behind them. [3] Take a small number of the hairs and tie them in the cloth of your coat. [4] Take some more of them and throw them into the fire, and burn them up. A fire will spread from there to all the

people of Israel. [5] The Lord God says, 'This is Jerusalem. I have set her in the center of the nations, with lands around her. [6] But she has turned against My Laws worse than the nations and the lands around her. The people of Jerusalem have turned away from My Laws and have not obeyed them.' [7] So the Lord God says, 'You have been more sinful than the nations around you. You have not walked in My Laws or kept them. You have not even kept Laws like the nations around you have. Because you have acted this way,' [8] the Lord God says, 'I Myself am against you, and I will punish you in the eyes of the nations. [9] Because of all the things you have done which I hate, I will do with you what I have never done before, and what I will never do again. [10] Fathers will eat their sons among you, and sons will eat their fathers. I will punish you and divide you, and spread to every wind those of you who are left. [11] You have made My holy place unclean with all your hated objects of worship and sinful ways. So as I live,' says the Lord, 'for sure I will turn away from you. My eye will have no pity and I will punish all of you. [12] One-third of you will die by disease or be destroyed by hunger among you. A third will be killed by the sword around you. And a third I will spread to every wind, and go after them with a sword.

[13] 'This is how My anger will stop. I will cause My anger to be upon them, and I will be comforted. Then they will know that I, the Lord, have spoken in My jealousy when I have sent My anger upon them. [14] I will make you a waste and a shame among the nations around you, in the eyes of all who pass by. [15] You will be a shame, and people will speak against you. You will show people the danger of sinning and fill the nations around you with fear, when I punish you in anger and with angry words. I, the Lord, have spoken. [16] I will keep you from getting food. I will make your hunger worse, and take away the bread you need. [17] I will send hunger and wild animals against you, and they will take away your children. Disease and death will pass through you, and I will bring the sword against you. I, the Lord, have spoken.' "

The Lord Judges Israel for Worshiping False Gods

6 The Word of the Lord came to me, saying, [2] "Son of man, turn your face toward the mountains of Israel, and tell what is going to happen against them.

3 Say, 'Mountains of Israel, listen to the Word of the Lord God! This is what the Lord God says to the mountains, the hills, the deep and wide valleys: "I Myself am going to bring a sword against you. And I will destroy your high places. 4 So your altars will be laid waste. Your altars for special perfume will be broken. And I will kill your people in front of your false gods. 5 I will lay the dead bodies of the sons of Israel in front of their false gods, and spread your bones around your altars. 6 In every place you live, cities will be laid waste and the high places will be destroyed. Your altars will be laid waste and destroyed. Your false gods will be broken and destroyed. Your altars for special perfume will come to an end. 7 Your people will fall dead among you, and you will know that I am the Lord.

8 "But I will leave some of you alive. For some of you will get away from the sword when you are spread among the lands and nations. 9 Then those who get away will remember Me in the nations where they have been taken. They will remember how I have been hurt by their sinful hearts which turned away from Me, and by their sinful eyes which followed after their false gods. And they will hate themselves in their own eyes for the sins they have done, for all their sinful ways. 10 Then they will know that I am the Lord. I have not spoken with empty words that I would bring this trouble upon them." '

11 "The Lord God says, 'Clap your hands, and step hard with your feet, and say, "It is bad because of all the hated sins of the people of Israel! They will fall by the sword, hunger, and disease. 12 He who is far away will die by disease. And he who is near will be killed by the sword. He who stays and is shut in by armies will die by hunger. This is how I will send My anger upon them. 13 Then you will know that I am the Lord, when their dead lie among their false gods around their altars. They will lie on every high hill, on all the mountain-tops, under every green tree, and under every oak tree with many leaves. Their dead will be in all the places where they burned special perfume to all their false gods. 14 I will put out My hand against them in every place they live. I will make the land more of a waste than the desert toward Diblah. Then they will know that I am the Lord.' "

The End Has Come for Israel

7 The Word of the Lord came to me saying, 2 "Son of man, this is what the Lord God says to the land of Israel: 'The end! The end has come upon the four corners of the land. 3 Now the end is upon you. I will send My anger against you and punish you because of your ways. I will make you pay for all your sinful actions. 4 My eye will have no pity on you. And I will not let you go without punishment. I will punish you for your ways, and for the hated sins that are among you. Then you will know that I am the Lord!'

5 "The Lord God says, 'See, much trouble is coming! 6 An end has come! The end has come! It has come up against you. See, it has come! 7 Your punishment has come upon you, O you who live in the land. The time has come. The day is near. The sound of trouble and not of joy is upon the mountains. 8 Now I will soon pour out My anger upon you. I will send My anger against you. I will punish you for your ways and for the hated sins that are among you. 9 My eye will show no pity, and I will not let you go without punishment. I will make you pay for your ways, and for the hated sins that are among you. Then you will know that it is I, the Lord, Who punishes you.

10 'See, the day! See, it is coming! The time for your punishment has come. The power against you has started to grow. Pride has begun to grow. 11 Angry action has grown into a power of sin. None of them will be left. None of their people, none of their riches, or anything of honor, will be left among them. 12 The time has come. The day has come. Let not the one who buys have joy, or the one who sells have sorrow. For anger is against all their people. 13 For the one who sells will not get back what he has sold as long as both of them live. For the punishment of all their people will not be turned back. Because of their sins, not one of them will keep his life.

14 'They have sounded the horn and made everything ready, but no one is going to the battle. For My anger is against all their people. 15 The sword is outside, and disease and hunger are inside. He who is in the field will die by the sword. And he who is in the city will be destroyed by disease and hunger. 16 Whoever gets away alive will be on the mountains like doves of the valleys. Each of them will be crying in sorrow because of his sin. 17 All hands will hang without strength, and all knees

will be as weak as water. 18 They will dress themselves in cloth made from hair. Much fear will cover them. Shame will be upon all faces, and the hair will be cut from all their heads. 19 They will throw their silver into the streets, and their gold will become an unclean thing. Their silver and gold will not be able to help them in the day of the Lord's anger. They cannot stop their hunger or fill their stomachs with it. For riches have been the cause of their falling into sin. 20 They turned the beauty of gold into objects of pride, and made their hated objects of worship with it. So I will make it an unclean thing to them. 21 I will give it to the strangers and to the sinful people of the earth as a prize of war, and they will make it sinful. 22 I will turn My face from them, and they will make My secret place sinful. Robbers will go into it and make it sinful.

23 'Make chains, for the land is guilty of blood and the city is full of angry actions. 24 So I will bring the worst of the nations to take their houses for their own. I will put an end to the pride of the strong ones, and their holy places will become unclean. 25 When suffering comes, they will look for peace, but there will be none. 26 Trouble will come upon trouble, and one story will come after another. They will look for a special dream from a man of God, but the Law will be lost from the religious leader. And wisdom will be lost from the leaders. 27 The king will be full of sorrow. The king's son will be covered with fear. And the hands of the people of the land will shake in fear. I will punish them for their ways. I will give them the punishment they have earned. And they will know that I am the Lord.'"

False Gods in the House of God

8 On the fifth day of the sixth month in the sixth year, I was sitting in my house with the leaders of Judah sitting in front of me. And the hand of the Lord God came upon me there. 2 Then I saw what looked like a man. From the center of His body and down to his feet, there was what looked like fire. And from the center of His body and up to his head, there was a bright light which looked like shining brass. 3 He put out what looked like a hand and caught me by the hair on my head. Then the Spirit lifted me up between earth and heaven and brought me to see Jerusalem in a special way. He brought me to the north gate of the open space within its walls, and there was the seat of the false god which causes jealousy. 4 And I saw that the shining-greatness of the God of Israel was there, like what I had seen in the plain.

5 He said to me, "Son of man, look toward the north." So I looked toward the north, and saw that to the north of the altar gate was this false god of jealousy in the doorway. 6 And the Spirit said to me, "Son of man, do you see what the people of Israel are doing? Do you see the hated sins that they are doing here to drive Me far from My holy place? But you will see even worse sins."

7 Then He brought me to the gate of the open space, and I looked and saw a hole in the wall. 8 And He said to me, "Son of man, now dig through the wall." So I dug through the wall and saw a door. 9 He said to me, "Go in and see the hated sins that they are doing here." 10 So I went in and looked. And I saw that on the wall all around were pictures of every kind of thing which moves along the ground, and wild animals, and hated things, and all the false gods of the people of Israel. 11 Standing in front of these pictures were seventy leaders of the people of Israel, with Jaazaniah the son of Shaphan standing among them. Each man held a dish in his hand from which the smell of special perfume rose up in a cloud. 12 Then He said to me, "Son of man, do you see what the leaders of the people of Israel are doing without anyone seeing them? They are worshiping in a room full of false gods. For they say, 'The Lord does not see us. The Lord has left the land.'" 13 And He said to me, "You will see even worse sins which they are doing."

14 Then He brought me to the north gate of the Lord's house. And I saw women sitting there crying for the false god Tammuz. 15 Then He said to me, "Do you see this, son of man? You will see even worse sins than this."

16 He brought me into the open space of the Lord's house. And I saw about twenty-five men at the gate to the house of the Lord, between the porch and the altar. Their backs were toward the Lord's house, and their faces were toward the east. They were bowing toward the east worshiping the sun. 17 And He said to me, "Do you see this, son of man? Is it a little thing for the people of Judah to do the hated sins which they have done here? They have filled the land with sinful actions and have

made Me angry again and again. See, they are doing what I hate. 18 So I will act in My anger. My eye will have no pity, and I will not let any go without punishment. Even if they cry in My ears with a loud voice, I will not listen to them."

The Sinful Are Killed

9 Then I heard Him call out in a loud voice, "Come near, you who punish the city, each with a destroying ax in his hand." 2 And I saw six men coming from the upper gate on the north side. Each man had his battle-ax in his hand. Among them was a certain man dressed in linen, with things for writing at his side. And the men went in and stood by the brass altar.

3 Then the shining-greatness of the God of Israel went up from the cherub where it had been, to the door of the Lord's house. And He called to the man dressed in linen with the things for writing at his side. 4 The Lord said to him, "Go through the city of Jerusalem and put a mark on the foreheads of the men who cry inside themselves over all the hated sins which are being done among them." 5 But to the others I heard Him say, "Go through the city after him, and destroy. Do not let your eye have pity. And do not let any sinner go without punishment. 6 Kill and destroy old men, young men, young women, little children, and women. But do not touch anyone who has the mark. Begin at My holy house." So they started with the leaders who were in front of the Lord's house. 7 He said to them, "Make the house of worship unclean and fill the open spaces with the dead. Go out!" So they went out and killed the people in the city. 8 As they were killing, I alone was left, and I fell on my face and cried out, "It is bad, O Lord God! Are You destroying all the people of Israel who are left, by pouring out Your anger on Jerusalem?"

9 Then He said to me, "The sin of the people of Israel and Judah is very, very bad. The land is filled with blood, and the city is full of wrong-doing. For they say, 'The Lord has left the land, and the Lord does not see.' 10 But as for Me, My eye will have no pity, and I will not leave any sinner without punishment. I will bring their wrong-doing upon their own heads."

11 Then I saw the man dressed in linen, who had the things for writing at his side, come and say, "I have done just as You have told me."

God's Shining-Greatness Leaves the House of God

10 Then I looked and saw something like a sapphire stone in the open space that was over the cherubim's heads. It looked like a throne above them. 2 And the Lord said to the man dressed in linen, "Go in between the wheels under the cherubim. Fill your hands with coals of fire from between the cherubim and throw them over the city." And as I watched, he went in.

3 Now the cherubim were standing on the right side of the house of the Lord when the man went in. And the cloud filled the open space inside. 4 Then the shining-greatness of the Lord went up from above the cherubim to the door of the Lord's house. The house of the Lord was filled with the cloud. And the open space was filled with the bright and shining-greatness of the Lord. 5 The sound of the wings of the cherubim was heard as far as the outside open space. It was like the voice of God All-powerful when He speaks.

6 When He told the man dressed in linen, "Take fire from between the wheels, from between the cherubim," the man went in and stood beside a wheel. 7 Then one of the cherubim put out his hand to the fire which was among them. He took some and put it into the hands of the one dressed in linen, who took it and went out. 8 (The cherubim had what looked like a man's hands under their wings.)

9 Then I looked and saw four wheels beside the cherubim, one wheel beside each cherub. The wheels looked like they were made of shining chrysolite stone. 10 All four of them looked the same. Each looked like they had one wheel inside another wheel. 11 When they moved, they went in any of their four ways without turning as they went, but followed the way the head was facing without turning as they went. 12 And their whole body, their backs, their hands, their wings, and the wheels were full of eyes all around, the wheels belonging to all four of them. 13 The wheels were called in my hearing, "the turning wheels." 14 Each one of the cherubim had four faces. The first face was the face of a cherub. The second face was the face of a man. The third was the face of a lion. And the fourth was the face of an eagle.

15 Then the cherubim rose up. They were the living beings that I saw by the Chebar River. 16 Now when the cherubim moved, the wheels went beside them. And

when the cherubim lifted up their wings to rise from the ground, the wheels did not leave their side. 17 When the cherubim stood still, the wheels stood still. When they rose up, the wheels rose with them. For the spirit of the living beings was in them.

18 Then the shining-greatness of the Lord left the door of the Lord's house and stood over the cherubim. 19 When the cherubim left, they lifted their wings and rose up from the earth in front of my eyes, with the wheels beside them. And they stood still at the door of the east gate of the Lord's house. The shining-greatness of the God of Israel was over them.

20 These are the living beings that I saw under the God of Israel by the Chebar River, so I knew that they were cherubim. 21 Each one had four faces and four wings, and under their wings were what looked like human hands. 22 Their faces looked the same as those I had seen by the Chebar River. Each one went straight ahead.

Israel's Leaders Are Judged

11 The Spirit lifted me up and brought me to the east gate of the Lord's house which faces eastward. There I saw twenty-five men at the door of the gate. Among them I saw Jaazaniah the son of Azzur, and Pelatiah the son of Benaiah, leaders of the people. 2 Then He said to me, "Son of man, these are the men who make sinful plans and tell others in this city to do what is wrong. 3 They say, 'Will it not soon be time to build houses? This city is the pot and we are the meat.' 4 So tell what will happen against them, son of man. Speak the Word of God!"

5 Then the Spirit of the Lord came upon me, and He said to me, "Tell them, 'This is what the Lord says: "This is what you thought, O people of Israel. For I know the things that come into your mind. 6 You have made many more of your people die in this city. You have filled its streets with them." 7 So the Lord God says, "Your dead whom you have laid in the city are the meat, and this city is the pot. But I will bring you out of it. 8 You have been afraid of the sword, so I will bring a sword upon you," the Lord God says. 9 "And I will bring you out of the city, and give you over to strangers and punish you. 10 You will be killed by the sword all the way to the land of Israel, so you will know that I am the Lord. 11 This city will not be a pot for you, and you will not be the meat inside it. But

I will punish you all the way to the land of Israel. 12 And you will know that I am the Lord. For you have not walked in my Laws or obeyed them, but have followed the ways of the nations around you."' "

13 While I was saying what was going to happen, Pelatiah the son of Benaiah died. Then I fell on my face and cried out with a loud voice, "It is bad, Lord God! Will You bring a complete end to those of Israel who are left?"

God Will Bring Israel Back

14 Then the Word of the Lord came to me, saying, 15 "Son of man, your brothers, your family, those who were driven out of the land, and all the people of Israel are those of whom the people of Jerusalem have said, 'They have gone far away from the Lord. This land has been given to us for our own.' 16 So tell them, 'This is what the Lord God says: "I sent them far away among the nations. I divided them among the countries. But still I was a holy place for them a little while in the countries where they had gone." ' 17 So tell them, 'This is what the Lord God says: "I will gather you from the nations. I will gather you together out of the countries where you have been divided. And I will give you the land of Israel." ' 18 When they return to it, they will take away all its hated and sinful things. 19 I will give them one heart, and put a new spirit within them. I will take the heart of stone out of their flesh and give them a heart of flesh. 20 Then they will walk in My Laws and keep them, and obey them. They will be My people, and I will be their God. 21 But as for those whose hearts go after their hated and sinful things, I will bring their actions upon their own heads," says the Lord God.

22 Then the cherubim lifted up their wings with the wheels beside them. And the shining-greatness of the God of Israel was over them. 23 The shining-greatness of the Lord went up from the city and stood over the mountain east of it. 24 The Spirit lifted me up and brought me in a special dream by the Spirit of God to the Jews who had been taken to Babylon. Then the special dream that I had seen left me. 25 And I told the Jews in Babylon all the things that the Lord had shown me.

The Man of God Leaves

12 The Word of the Lord came to me, saying, 2 "Son of man, you live among sinful people. They have eyes to see but do not see, and ears to hear but do

not hear. For they are sinful people. ³ So, son of man, get your things ready to take with you to another land, and let them see you leave during the day. Let them see you leave to go to another place. It may be that they will understand even if they are sinful people. ⁴ Take your things with you during the day, with them watching you. Take the things you will need for going to another land. Then let them see you go out at evening, like those who go to another land. ⁵ While they watch, dig a hole through the wall and go out through it. ⁶ Load your things on your shoulder while they watch, and carry the load out in the dark. Cover your face so that you cannot see the land. For I have made you as something special for the people of Israel to see."

⁷ I did as I was told. During the day I brought out my things that I would need to go to another land. Then in the evening I dug through the wall with my hands. I went out in the dark and carried the load on my shoulder while they watched.

⁸ In the morning the Word of the Lord came to me, saying, ⁹ "Son of man, have not the sinful people of Israel said to you, 'What are you doing?' ¹⁰ Tell them, 'This is what the Lord God says: "This word is about the leader in Jerusalem, as well as all the people of Israel who are in it." ' ¹¹ Tell them, 'I am something special for you to see. As I have done, so it will be done to them. They will be taken to another land and held there.' ¹² The leader among them will load his things on his shoulder in the dark and go out. A hole will be dug through the wall for him to go through. He will cover his face so that he cannot see the land with his eyes. ¹³ I will spread My net over him, and he will be caught in My trap. I will bring him to Babylon in the land of the Babylonians, yet he will not see it. And he will die there. ¹⁴ I will divide all his helpers and all his army who are around him to the four winds and have the sword follow them. ¹⁵ Then they will know that I am the Lord when I divide them among the nations, and spread them among the countries. ¹⁶ But I will let a few of them get away from the sword, hunger and disease. They will tell about all their sinful ways to the nations where they go. And they will know that I am the Lord."

¹⁷ The Word of the Lord came to me, saying, ¹⁸ "Son of man, shake in fear as you eat your bread and drink your water. ¹⁹ Then tell the people of the land, 'This is what the Lord God says about the people of Jerusalem in the land of Israel: "They will be afraid as they eat their bread, and drink their water in fear. For their land will lay waste because of the fighting of all who live in it. ²⁰ The cities where people live will be laid waste, and the land will be destroyed. Then you will know that I am the Lord." ' "

²¹ The Word of the Lord came to me, saying, ²² "Son of man, what is this saying you people have about the land of Israel, which says, 'The days are long and every special dream comes to nothing'? ²³ Tell them, 'The Lord God says, "I will make this saying come to an end, so that they will no longer use it as a saying in Israel." ' But tell them, 'The days are near when all the special dreams from God will come true. ²⁴ For there will be no more false dreams or good sounding words that do not come true. ²⁵ For I the Lord will speak, and whatever I say will be done. It will no longer be held back. For in your days, O sinful people, I will speak the word and do it,' says the Lord God."

²⁶ Again the Word of the Lord came to me, saying, ²⁷ "Son of man, the people of Israel are saying, 'The special dream he sees will not come to pass for many years. He is speaking of times far in the future.' ²⁸ So tell them, 'The Lord God says, "None of My words will be held back any longer. Whatever I say will be done,' " says the Lord God."

Word against False Preachers

13 Then the Word of the Lord came to me saying, ² "Son of man, speak against those of Israel who speak false words in My name. Say to those who tell what is going to happen in the future out of their own minds, 'Listen to the Word of the Lord! ³ The Lord God says, "It is bad for the foolish people who tell what is going to happen by following their own spirit and have seen nothing. ⁴ O Israel, your men who speak in My name are of no more worth than foxes in destroyed cities. ⁵ You have not gone up to the broken places to build the wall around the people of Israel so that it will stand in the battle on the day of the Lord. ⁶ They have lied and have spoken false words using their secret ways, saying, 'This is what the Lord says,' when the Lord has not sent them. Yet they hope that what they say will come true. ⁷ Did you not see a false dream and tell a lie using your secret ways when you said, 'This is what the Lord says,' when I have not spoken?' ' "

8 So the Lord God says: "Because you have spoken false words and seen a lie, I am against you," says the Lord God. 9 "My hand will be against those who see false dreams and speak false words. They will have no place in the gathering of My wise people. Their names will not be written down with the people of Israel. And they will not go into the land of Israel. Then you will know that I am the Lord God. 10 Because they have led My people the wrong way by saying, 'Peace,' when there is no peace, and because, when anyone builds a bad wall, they cover it with whitewash, 11 tell those who cover it with whitewash that it will fall! A flood of rain will come, and large hailstones will fall. And a strong wind will break out. 12 When the wall has fallen, will you not be asked, 'Where is the covering you used to cover the wall?' " 13 So the Lord God says, "I will make a strong wind break out in My anger. There will also be a flood of rain in My anger, and large hailstones to destroy that wall. 14 I will break down the wall that you covered with whitewash. I will bring it down to the ground so that its base will be showing. And when it falls, you will be destroyed with it. Then you will know that I am the Lord. 15 I will send My anger upon the wall and upon those who have covered it with whitewash. And I will say to you, 'The wall is gone and the ones who covered it are gone. 16 There are no more people of Israel who speak false words to Jerusalem in My name, and who see dreams of peace for her when there is no peace,' says the Lord God.

17 "Now, son of man, set your face against the daughters of your people who are telling what will happen from their own minds. Speak against them, 18 and tell them, 'This is what the Lord God says: "It is bad for the women who sew objects with secret powers to wear on their arms, and make coverings for the heads to trap people. Will you go after the lives of My people, but save the lives of others for yourselves? 19 You have used Me in a sinful way among My people for hands full of barley and for pieces of bread. You have killed people who should not die, and have kept others alive who should not live, by your lying to My people who listen to lies." '

20 So the Lord God says, "I am against your objects with secret powers that you wear on your arms with which you trap people like birds. I will tear them from your arms. And I will let the people go that you trap like birds. 21 I will also tear off your head-coverings and save My people from you. They will no longer be trapped by your hands. Then you will know that I am the Lord. 22 You have made My good people sad because of your lies whom I did not want to hurt. But you have helped the sinful man, so that he does not turn from his sinful way and save his life. 23 So you women will no longer see false dreams or use your secret ways to learn the future. I will save My people from your hands. And then you will know that I am the Lord."

Worshipers of False Gods

14 Then some leaders of Israel came and sat down in front of me. 2 And the Word of the Lord came to me saying, 3 "Son of man, these men have taken false gods into their hearts. They have put in front of their faces the cause of their fall. Should I let Myself be asked questions by them at all? 4 So speak to them and tell them, 'The Lord God says, "Every man of Israel who has given his heart to false gods and lets them lead him into sin and then comes to the man of God, I the Lord will answer him, the answer that his many false gods should get, 5 that I may again have the hearts of the people of Israel who have left Me for their false gods." '

6 "So tell the people of Israel, 'The Lord God says, "Be sorry for your sins and turn away from your false gods. Turn your faces away from all your sinful ways. 7 If a man of Israel or a stranger living in Israel who turns away from Me and gives his heart to false gods, and worships them, and if he then comes to the man of God to get answers from Me, I the Lord will answer him Myself. 8 I will set My face against that man and make him something special to see and to speak against. I will cut him off from among My people. And you will know that I am the Lord. 9 But if the man who speaks in My name is given a false answer, it is I, the Lord, Who has caused him to speak. And I will put out My hand against him and destroy him from among My people Israel. 10 They will suffer the punishment of their sin. The man who asks the question and the man who speaks to him in My name will both be punished in the same way. 11 This is so that the people of Israel may no longer turn away from Me, and no longer make themselves sinful with all their wrong-doing. They will be

My people and I will be their God," ' says the Lord God."

Those Not Faithful Are Judged

12 Then the Word of the Lord came to me saying, 13 "Son of man, if a country sins against Me by not being faithful, I will put out My hand against it. I will destroy its store of bread, and send hunger against it, and take away both man and animal from it. 14 For even if these three men, Noah, Daniel and Job, were in this country, they would save only their own lives by being right and good," says the Lord God. 15 "If I sent wild animals to pass through the land to kill its people and destroy it so that no one would go through it because of the wild animals, 16 even if these three men were in the land, as I live," says the Lord God, "they could not save their sons or their daughters. They alone would be saved, but the country would be laid waste. 17 If I bring a sword against that country and say, 'Let the sword pass through the country and cut off man and animal from it,' 18 even if these three men were in the land, as I live," says the Lord God, "they could not save their sons or their daughters. They alone would be saved. 19 Or if I send a disease against that country and show My anger by killing, to take away man and animal from it, 20 even if Noah, Daniel and Job were in the land, as I live," says the Lord God, "they could not save their son or daughter. They would save only themselves by being right and good.

21 "For the Lord God says, 'How much worse will it be when I send my four worst punishments against Jerusalem! I will send the sword, hunger, wild animals, and disease, to take away man and animal from it! 22 Yet there will be some people and their children left alive in it who will be brought out. When they come to you, see how sinful they are. Then you will know that all the trouble I brought upon Jerusalem was right. 23 It will help you when you see how they act. Then you will know that there was a good reason for everything I did,' says the Lord God."

Jerusalem—a Vine of No Worth

15 Then the Word of the Lord came to me saying, 2 "Son of man, how is the wood of the vine better than any wood of a branch among the trees? 3 Can wood be taken from it to make anything? Or can men take a piece of wood from it on which to hang a pot? 4 If it has been put into the fire to burn, and the fire has burned up both of its ends, and the center of it is black from the fire, can it then be used for anything? 5 See, if it is not used for anything while it is whole, how much less can it ever be used for anything when the fire has burned it up and it has turned black! 6 So the Lord God says, 'Like the wood of the vine among the trees, which I have given to be burned in the fire, so will I give up the people of Jerusalem. 7 I will set My face against them. Even if they get away from the fire, the fire will yet destroy them. Then you will know that I am the Lord, when I set My face against them. 8 I will lay waste the land, because they have not been faithful,' " says the Lord God.

Jerusalem—Not Faithful

16 The Word of the Lord came to me, saying, 2 "Son of man, make known to Jerusalem her hated sins. 3 Tell them, 'This is what the Lord God says to Jerusalem: "Your beginning and your birth are from the land of the Canaanite. Your father was an Amorite and your mother was a Hittite. 4 On the day you were born the cord between you and your mother was not cut. You were not washed with water to make you clean. You were not rubbed with salt or even covered with cloth. 5 No one looked with pity on you or did any of these things for you out of loving-kindness. Instead you were thrown out into the open field, for you were hated on the day you were born.

6 "When I passed by you and saw you rolling about in your blood, I said to you in your blood, 'Live!' Yes, I said to you while you were in your blood, 'Live!' 7 I made you become many, like plants of the field. Then you grew up and became tall. You grew into a beautiful woman. You had breasts and your hair had grown. Yet you were not covered and your body could be seen. 8 Then I passed by you and saw that you were old enough for love. So I spread my clothing over you and covered your body. I gave you my promise and made an agreement with you so that you became Mine," says the Lord God. 9 "Then I washed you with water, washed the blood from you, and poured oil on you. 10 I dressed you with beautiful cloth, and put leather shoes on your feet. I dressed you with fine linen and covered you with silk. 11 I put on you objects of beauty. I put beautiful objects on your arms and around your neck. 12 I put rings in your nose and in your ears, and a

beautiful crown on your head. 13 So you were dressed with gold and silver. Your clothing was of fine linen, silk, and beautiful cloth. You ate fine flour, honey, and oil. So you were very beautiful, and became a queen. 14 Your name became known among the nations because of your beauty. For it was perfect because of My shining-greatness which I had given to you," says the Lord God.

15 "But you trusted in your beauty. Because your name was well-known, you acted like a woman who sells the use of her body. And you did sex sins with anyone who passed by. 16 You took some of your clothes of many colors and made for yourself places of worship. There you acted like a woman who sells the use of her body. Such things should never happen or come to pass. 17 You also took your objects of beauty made of My gold and silver, which I had given you. And you used them to make things that looked like men, that you might play with them as a woman who sells the use of her body. 18 Then you took your beautiful cloth and covered them, and set My oil and My special perfume in front of them. 19 You also set in front of them My bread which I gave you, the fine flour, oil and honey I gave you to eat. You gave it all to them as a special perfume. So it was," says the Lord God. 20 "You even took your sons and daughters whom you had given birth for Me, and gave them to the false gods to be destroyed. Were your sex sins too little? 21 You killed My children and gave them as burnt gifts to false gods. 22 And in all your hated acts and sex sins you did not remember the days when you were young. You did not remember when you were without clothing or covering, and when you rolled about in your blood.

23 "It is bad for you!" says the Lord God. "After all your sinful acts, 24 you built a place of worship for yourself, and a high place in every street. 25 You built yourself a high place at the beginning of every street and made your beauty a hated thing. You gave yourself to anyone who passed by, to make your sex sins many. 26 You also gave the use of your body to the Egyptians, your neighbors who have much desire for sex sins. And you sinned many times to make Me angry. 27 So I have raised My hand to punish you and have made your share smaller. I have given you over to the desire of those who hate you, the daughters of the Philistines, who were ashamed of your

sinful actions. 28 You also gave the use of your body to the Assyrians because you had not had enough. Yes, you even gave the use of your body to them and still thought you had not had enough. 29 You did many sex sins with Babylon, the land of those who trade. Yet even this was not enough for you.

30 "How sinful your heart is," says the Lord God, "that you do all these things, the actions of a sinful woman, and show no shame. 31 You built your places of worship at the beginning of every street and made your high place at every crossing. But you were not like a woman who sells the use of her body, because you did not want pay. 32 You are like a wife who is not faithful and has strangers instead of her husband! 33 Men give gifts to all women who sell the use of their body. But you give your gifts to all your lovers. You pay them to come to you from everywhere for your sex sins. 34 You are different from other women in your sex sins. You go after men; they do not come to you. You pay men instead of them giving pay to you. Yes, you are different."

God Judges Jerusalem

35 So, sinful woman, hear the Word of the Lord. 36 The Lord God says, "Your shame was poured out and your clothing was taken off because of your sex sins with your lovers and with all your hated false gods. And you killed your children and gave them to false gods. Because of these things, 37 I will gather all your lovers who pleased you. I will gather all those whom you loved and all those whom you hated. I will gather them against you from every side, and take off your covering so that they may see all your shame. 38 I will punish you as I punish women who are not faithful in marriage, or women who kill. I will do it in My anger and jealousy. 39 And I will give you over to your lovers. They will tear down your places of worship and destroy your high places. They will take all of your clothes and your beautiful objects, and will leave you without any covering. 40 They will bring up a group of people against you, and they will kill you with stones and cut you to pieces with their swords. 41 They will burn your houses with fire and punish you as many women watch. Then I will stop you from acting like a woman who sells the use of her body, and you will no longer pay your lovers. 42 Then I will take away My anger

from you, and My jealousy will leave you. I will be at peace, and will not be angry any more. 43 You have not remembered the days when you were young, but have made Me angry with all these things. So I will punish you for what you have done," says the Lord God. "Did you not add these sex sins to all your other hated sins?

More Sinful Than Samaria and Sodom

44 "Every one who uses sayings will use this saying about you: 'Like mother, like daughter.' 45 You are the daughter of your mother, who hated her husband and her children. You are also a sister of your sisters who hated their husbands and children. Your mother was a Hittite and your father was an Amorite. 46 Your older sister is Samaria, who lives north of you with her daughters. And your younger sister is Sodom, who lives south of you with her daughters. 47 Yet you have walked in their ways and done their hated acts. As if that were too little, you acted worse in all your ways than they. 48 As I live," says the Lord God, "your sister Sodom and her daughters have not done as you and your daughters have done. 49 Now this was the sin of your sister Sodom: She and her daughters had pride, much food, and too much rest, but she did not help those who were poor and in need. 50 They were proud and did hated sins in front of Me. So I took them away when I saw it. 51 Samaria has not done half of your sins. You have done more sins than they. So you have made your sisters look right and good by all the hated sins which you have done. 52 Take your shame upon you, for you have made Me show favor to them in their punishment. Because of your sins in which you acted worse than they, they are more in the right than you. So then be ashamed and take your shame upon you, for you have made your sisters look right and good.

53 "I will return them to their land, both Sodom and her daughters, and Samaria and her daughters. With them I will return you to your land. 54 This is so you will take your shame upon you, and feel ashamed for all that you have done in becoming a comfort to them. 55 Your sisters, Sodom with her daughters and Samaria with her daughters, will return to the land they had before. And you with your daughters will return to your land also. 56 You did not speak against your sister Sodom in the days of your pride, 57 before your sinful acts were seen. Now you have

become like her, an object of shame for the daughters of Edom and all her neighbors, and for the daughters of the Philistines. All those around you who hate you now look on you with shame. 58 The penalty of your sex sins and other hated sins has come upon you," says the Lord. 59 For the Lord God says, "I will do with you as you have done, because you have hated your promise by breaking the agreement.

An Agreement That Lasts Forever

60 "But I will remember My agreement which I made with you when you were young. And I will make an agreement with you that lasts forever. 61 Then you will remember your ways and be ashamed when you receive your sisters, both your older one and younger one. I will give them to you as daughters, but not because of your agreement with Me. 62 So I will make My agreement with you, and you will know that I am the Lord. 63 Then you will remember and be ashamed. You will never open your mouth again because of your shame, when I have forgiven you for all that you have done," says the Lord God.

The Picture-Story of the Eagles and the Vine

17 The Word of the Lord came to me saying, 2 "Son of man, give the people of Israel this picture-story to think about. 3 Tell them, 'The Lord God says, "A large eagle with big wings and long feathers of many colors came to Lebanon and took away the top of the cedar tree. 4 He broke off the very top of its young branches and brought it to a land of traders. He placed it in a city of people who buy and sell. 5 Then he took some of the seed of the land and planted it in good ground for growing. He planted it like a willow tree where there was much water to make it grow. 6 And it grew and became a low spreading vine. Its branches grew toward him, but its roots stayed under it. So it became a vine, and branches and leaves grew out from it.

7 "But there was another large eagle with big wings and many feathers. And the vine turned its roots and branches toward him from where it was planted, that he might water it. 8 It had been planted in good ground beside much water, that it might grow branches and give fruit and become a beautiful vine." ' 9 Tell them, 'The Lord God says, "Will it live and grow? Will not its roots be pulled up and

its fruit be cut off so that its leaves that started to grow dry up? It will not take a strong arm or many people to pull it up by the roots. 10 Even if it is planted again, will it live and grow? Will it not dry up when the east wind hits it? Will it not dry up in the place where it grew?" ' "

11 Then the Word of the Lord came to me saying, 12 "Now tell these sinful people, 'Do you not know what these things mean?' Tell them, 'See, the king of Babylon came to Jerusalem. He took its king and the king's sons, and brought them back with him to Babylon. 13 He took one of the king's family and made an agreement with him. And he made him promise to keep it. He also took away the strong leaders of the land, 14 so that the nation would be under his power and not become strong again. It could only last by keeping his agreement. 15 But the king of Judah turned against him by sending his men to Egypt to get horses and a large army for him. Will it go well for him? Can he get away with that? Can he break the agreement and not be punished? 16 As I live," says the Lord God, 'he will die in the land of the king who put him on the throne, whose promise he hated, and whose agreement he broke. He will die in Babylon. 17 Pharaoh with his powerful army of many men will not help him in the war, when battle-walls are put up so that many people are killed. 18 He hated the promise and broke the agreement. Because he had given his promise and then did all these things, he will not get away from being punished.' " 19 So the Lord God says, "As I live, I will punish him for hating My promise and for breaking My agreement. 20 I will spread My net over him and he will be caught in My trap. Then I will bring him to Babylon and punish him there for not being faithful to Me. 21 And all the best of his soldiers will be killed by the sword, and those left alive will be thrown to the wind. Then you will know that I, the Lord, have spoken."

God's Promise of Hope

22 The Lord God says, "I will also take a young branch from the very top of the cedar tree and plant it. I will break a soft new one from the very top of its young branches, and plant it on a high mountain. 23 I will plant it on the high mountain of Israel. It will grow branches and give fruit and become a beautiful cedar. Birds of every kind will nest in it. They will nest in the shadow of its branches. 24 Then all the trees of the field will know that I am the Lord. I bring down the high tree and make the low tree grow tall. I dry up the green tree, and make the dry tree become green. I, the Lord, have spoken, and I will do what I say."

18 The Word of the Lord came to me saying, 2 "What do you mean by using this saying about the land of Israel: The fathers eat the sour grapes, but the children get the sour taste'? 3 As I live," says the Lord God, "you will never use this saying in Israel again. 4 For all souls belong to Me. Both the soul of the father and the soul of the son are Mine. The soul who sins will die. 5 But if a man is right and good and does what is right and good, 6 he does not eat at the altars on the mountains or look up to the false gods of Israel. He does not sin with his neighbor's wife or go near a woman during the time she is unclean. 7 He does not make it hard for anyone. He keeps his promise to pay back what he owes. He does not steal, but gives his bread to the hungry, and gives clothing to those who have none. 8 He does not make others pay back more than they owe him. He keeps away from sin, and is an honest judge when men argue. He walks in My Laws and is careful to obey them. This man is right and good, and will live for sure," says the Lord God.

10 "But he may have a son who acts in anger and kills another man, or does any of these other things 11 that the father never did. He eats at the altars on the mountains, and sins with his neighbor's wife. 12 He makes it hard for the poor and those in need, and he steals. He does not keep his promise to pay back what he owes. He looks up to false gods, and does sinful acts. 13 And he makes people pay back more than they owe him. Will this man live? He will not live! He has done all these sinful acts, and for sure he will die. He will be guilty for his own death.

14 "Now this man may have a son who has seen all the sins his father has done, but does not do the same. 15 He does not eat at the altars on the mountains or look to the false gods of Israel. He does not sin with his neighbor's wife, 16 or make it hard for anyone. He does not keep what another man has given him in trust for a promise. He does not steal, but he gives his bread to the hungry and clothing to those who have none. 17 He keeps away from sin. He does not make a person pay back

more than he owes him. But he walks in My Laws and obeys them. This man will not die for his father's sin. He will live for sure. 18 As for his father, because he used his power to rob his brother, and did what was wrong among his people, he will die for his sin.

19 "Yet you say, 'Why should the son not suffer for the father's sin?' Since the son has done what is right and good, and has kept and obeyed all My Laws, he will live for sure. 20 The person who sins will die. The son will not be punished for the father's sin. And the father will not be punished for the son's sin. The right and good man will receive good, and the sinful man will suffer for his sin.

21 "But if the sinful man turns from all the sins he has done and obeys all My Laws and does what is right and good, he will live for sure. He will not die. 22 None of the sins he has done will be remembered against him. Because of the right and good things he has done, he will live. 23 Am I pleased with the death of a sinful man?" says the Lord God. "No, instead I would like him to turn from his sinful ways and live.

24 "But when a right and good man turns away from doing what is right and good, and sins, doing all the bad things that a sinful man does, will he live? None of the right and good things he has done will be remembered. Because he has not been faithful and has sinned, he will die. 25 Yet you say, 'The Lord is not doing what is right.' Listen, O people of Israel! Is My way not right? Is it not your ways that are not right? 26 When a right and good man turns away from doing what is right and good, and sins, and dies because of it, he dies because of the sin he has done. 27 But when a sinful man turns away from his sin and does what is right and good, he will save his life. 28 Because he thought about it and turned away from all the sins he had done, he will live for sure. He will not die. 29 But the people of Israel say, 'The Lord is not doing what is right.' Are My ways not right, O people of Israel? Is it not your ways that are not right?

30 "So I will judge you, O people of Israel, each of you by what he has done," says the Lord God. "Be sorry for all your sins and turn away from them, so sin will not destroy you. 31 Turn away from all the sins you have done, and get a new heart and a new spirit! Why will you die, O people of Israel? 32 For I am not pleased with the death of anyone who dies," says the Lord God. "So be sorry for your sins and turn away from them, and live."

A Song of Sorrow for Israel's Leaders

19 "As for you, sing a song of sorrow for the leaders of Israel, 2 and say: 'What was your mother? A female lion among lions! She lay down with young lions. She raised her young ones. 3 She brought up one of her little ones, and he became a lion. He learned to catch his food. He ate men. 4 The nations heard about him, and he was caught in their trap. And they brought him with hooks to the land of Egypt. 5 Your mother waited until she saw that her hope was lost. Then she took another of her little ones and made him a young lion. 6 He walked up and down among the lions. He became a young lion and learned to catch his food. He ate men. 7 He wrecked their strong towers and destroyed their cities. The land and all who were in it were filled with fear because of the loud noise he made. 8 Then the nations came against him from their lands all around. They spread their net over him, and he was caught in their trap. 9 They put him in a prison with chains and brought him to the king of Babylon. They put him in prison so that his voice would never be heard again on the mountains of Israel.

10 Your mother was like a vine in your grape-field, planted by the water. It gave much fruit and was full of branches because there was much water. 11 Its branches were strong enough to be made into sticks held by rulers to show their power. It grew as high as the clouds. Everyone saw how high it was and that it had many branches. 12 But it was pulled up by the roots in anger and thrown down to the ground. The east wind dried up its fruit. Its strong branch was torn off so that it dried up. And fire destroyed it. 13 Now it is planted in the desert, in a dry and thirsty land. 14 Fire has spread from its largest branch and has destroyed its young branches and its fruit. No strong branch is left on it to be made into a stick for a ruler.' This is a song of sorrow, and is to be used as a death song."

Israel Fights against God

20 On the tenth day of the fifth month in the seventh year, some of the leaders of Israel came to ask the Lord's will, and they sat down in front of me.

2 The Word of the Lord came to me saying, 3 "Son of man, speak to the leaders of Israel. Tell them, 'The Lord God says, "Have you come to ask My will? As I live," says the Lord God, "I will not let you ask me anything." ' 4 Will you judge them, son of man? Will you judge them? Make known to them the sinful things their fathers did. 5 Tell them, 'The Lord God says, "On the day I chose Israel, I raised My hand and made a promise to the children of the family of Jacob and made Myself known to them in the land of Egypt. I made a promise to them, saying, 'I am the Lord your God.' 6 On that day I promised to bring them out of the land of Egypt to a land I had chosen for them, a land flowing with milk and honey, the most beautiful of all lands. 7 I said to them, 'Each of you get rid of the sinful things you have looked upon. Do not make yourselves sinful with the false gods of Egypt. I am the Lord your God.' 8 But they turned against Me and would not listen to Me. They did not get rid of the sinful things they had looked upon. And they did not turn away from the false gods of Egypt.

"Then I said that I would be angry with them. I would send My anger against them in the land of Egypt. 9 But I acted for the good of My name. I did what would keep My name clean in the eyes of the nations they lived among, in whose eyes I made Myself known to them by bringing My people out of Egypt. 10 So I led them out of the land of Egypt and brought them into the desert. 11 I gave them My Laws and made known to them My Words, which bring life to anyone who obeys them. 12 I gave them My Days of Rest to be something special to see between Me and them, so they would know that I am the Lord Who makes them holy. 13 But the people of Israel turned against Me in the desert. They did not obey My Laws, and they turned away from My Words which bring life to anyone who obeys them. They made My Days of Rest very sinful. Then I said that I would be angry with them in the desert and destroy them. 14 But I acted for the good of My name. I did what would keep My name clean in the eyes of the nations who saw Me bring them out of Egypt. 15 So I promised them in the desert that I would not bring them into the land I had given them, the land flowing with milk and honey, the most beautiful of all lands. 16 This was because they turned away from My Laws and did not obey My Words. They did not keep My Days of Rest holy, for they followed after their false gods with all their heart. 17 Yet I looked on them with pity and did not destroy them. I did not make an end of them in the desert.

18 "And I said to their children in the desert, 'Do not keep the laws of your fathers, or follow their ways, or make yourselves sinful with their false gods. 19 I am the Lord your God. Keep My Laws and obey My Words. 20 Keep My Days of Rest holy, and they will be something special to see between Me and you. Then you will know that I am the Lord your God.' 21 But the children turned against Me. They did not keep My Laws or obey My Words which bring life to anyone who obeys them. They did not keep My Days of Rest holy. So I said I would be angry with them. I would send My anger against them in the desert. 22 But I held My hand back, and acted for the good of My name, to keep it clean in the eyes of the nations who saw Me bring them out of Egypt. 23 And I promised them in the desert that I would send them everywhere among the nations and spread them out among the lands. 24 This is because they had not obeyed My Words. They had turned away from My Laws and did not keep My Days of Rest holy. And they worshiped the false gods of their fathers. 25 Then I gave them laws that were not good, and words they could not live by. 26 And I let them become sinful because of their gifts. I let them give all their first-born sons as burnt gifts. This was to punish them and show them that I am the Lord." '

27 "So, son of man, speak to the people of Israel. Tell them, 'The Lord God says, "This is another way that your fathers have brought shame to My name by not being faithful to Me. 28 I brought them into the land I promised to give them. And when they saw all the high hills and trees with many leaves, they gave their gifts on all of them and made Me angry. They also burned special perfume there, and poured out their drink gifts. 29 Then I said to them, 'What is this high place you go to?' So it is called Bamah to this day." ' 30 So tell the people of Israel, 'The Lord God says, "Will you make yourselves sinful in the same way your fathers did, and go after their sinful things? 31 When you give your gifts and make your sons go through the fire, you are making yourselves sinful with all your false gods to this day. Am I to let you question Me, O people of Israel? As I live,"

says the Lord God, "I will not let you ask Me anything. ³² You say, 'We will be like the nations, like the people of the lands, who serve wood and stone.' But what you have in mind will never happen.

Israel Will Come Back to God

³³ "As I live," says the Lord God, "I will be King over you, and will rule with a powerful hand, a strong arm, and with anger. ³⁴ I will bring you out of the nations and countries where you have been divided. I will gather you together with a powerful hand, a strong arm, and with anger. ³⁵ I will bring you into the desert of the nations, and there I will punish you face to face. ³⁶ As I punished your fathers in the desert of Egypt, so I will punish you," says the Lord God. ³⁷ "I will hold power over you and make you obey the agreement. ³⁸ I will take away from among you all those who sin or who turn against Me. I will bring them out of the land where they are living, but they will not go into the land of Israel. Then you will know that I am the Lord. ³⁹ As for you, O people of Israel," the Lord God says, "Go and serve your false gods, every one of you, now and later if you will not listen to Me. Do not ever again bring shame to My holy name with your gifts and your false gods. ⁴⁰ For on My holy mountain, the high mountain of Israel," says the Lord God, "all the people of Israel will serve Me in the land. There I will receive them. And there I will ask for the best of your gifts, with all your holy things. ⁴¹ I will receive you as the pleasing smell of special perfume, when I bring you out of the nations and gather you from the different lands where you have been sent. And I will prove Myself holy among you in the eyes of the nations. ⁴² Then you will know that I am the Lord, when I bring you into the land of Israel, the land I promised to give to your fathers. ⁴³ There you will remember your ways and all the bad things you did to make yourselves sinful. And you will hate yourselves in your own eyes for all the sinful things you have done. ⁴⁴ You will know that I am the Lord when I honor My name by being good to you even though your ways have been sinful and you have done many sinful things, O people of Israel," says the Lord God.' "

Words against the South

⁴⁵ The Word of the Lord came to me saying, ⁴⁶ "Son of man, look toward the south. And speak out against the south and against the land of many trees in the Negev. ⁴⁷ Say to the land of trees in the Negev, 'Hear the Word of the Lord. The Lord God says, "See, I am about to start a fire that will destroy all of your green trees and all of your dry trees. The hot fire will not be put out, and every face from south to north will be burned by it. ⁴⁸ Everyone will see that I, the Lord, have made the fire. It will not be put out." ' " ⁴⁹ Then I said, "O Lord God! They are saying of me, 'Is he not just telling picture-stories?' "

Babylon Is God's Sword

21 The Word of the Lord came to me saying, ² "Son of man, look toward Jerusalem and speak against the holy places. Speak against the land of Israel. ³ Tell the land of Israel, 'The Lord says, "See, I am against you. I will take My sword out of its holder and destroy from you both the good and the sinful. ⁴ Because I will destroy from you both the good and the sinful, My sword will go out against everyone from south to north. ⁵ Then all people will know that I, the Lord, have taken out My sword. It will not be put back into its holder again." ' ⁶ As for you, son of man, cry in sorrow in front of them, as if your heart is breaking. ⁷ And when they ask you, 'Why are you crying?' tell them, 'Because of the news that is coming, every heart will melt and all hands will be weak. Every spirit will lose its strength, and all knees will be as weak as water. It is coming, and it will happen,' says the Lord God."

⁸ Again the Word of the Lord came to me saying, ⁹ "Son of man, speak in My name and tell them, 'The Lord says, "A sword, a sharp and shining sword! ¹⁰ It is made sharp to kill, and shined to look like lightning! Shall we have joy? It hates the special stick of My son, as it does all wood. ¹¹ The sword is being shined to make it ready to use. It is made sharp and shiny, to be put into the hand of the killer. ¹² Cry out in a loud voice, son of man, for the sword is against My people. It is against all the leaders of Israel. They are going to be killed with My people, so beat your upper leg in sorrow. ¹³ They will be put to the test. If they do not turn from their sinful ways, these things will happen," says the Lord God.'

¹⁴ "So speak in My name, son of man, and clap your hands together. Let the sword that kills hit two, even three times. It is the sword that kills and is all around

them, 15 so that they will lose their strength of heart, and many will be killed at all their gates. I have sent the shining sword. It is made to shine like lightning, and is ready to kill. 16 O sharp sword, cut to the left and to the right. Cut wherever you have been sent. 17 I will also clap My hands, and My anger will be gone. I, the Lord, have spoken.'

18 The Word of the Lord came to me saying, 19 "Son of man, make two ways for the king of Babylon to come with his sword. Both of them will come from the same land. Mark the way where the road divides and goes to the city. 20 Mark a way for the sword to go to Rabbah of the Ammonites, and to Judah into the strong city of Jerusalem. 21 For the king of Babylon stands where the road divides in two to use strange secret powers. He shakes the arrows and speaks with false gods, and looks at the liver. 22 In his right hand is the arrow marked for Jerusalem. It tells him to set up objects to knock down the city walls, to call out the battle cry, to set up objects to break down the gates, and to build a wall of dirt and battle towers. 23 The people who promised to obey him will not believe this. But he will make them remember their guilt so that they may be taken. 24 So the Lord God says, 'You have made your guilt to be remembered. Your sins are no longer covered, and everyone has seen the bad things you have done and remembers them. So you will be taken in battle. 25 And you, O bad and sinful one, the leader of Israel, the day of your punishment has come. Your sin will end.' 26 The Lord God says, 'Take off the head-covering. Take off the crown. Things will not stay as they are. Honor that which is low. And bring down that which is honored. 27 A waste, a waste. I will lay the city waste. It will be no more, until He comes whose right it is, and I will give it to Him.'

28 "And you, son of man, speak in My name and tell them, 'This is what the Lord God says about the sons of Ammon and about their shame.' Tell them, 'A sword is pulled out ready to kill! It is made to shine like lightning! 29 Even with the false dreams about you, and the lies spoken about you by using secret ways, you will be laid on the necks of the sinful who are killed, whose day has come for their last punishment. 30 Put your sword back into its holder. I will punish you in the place where you were made, in the land of your birth. 31 I will be angry with you. I will

blow on you with the fire of My anger. And I will give you over to men who show no pity, who have been taught to destroy. 32 You will be destroyed by fire. You will be killed in your land, and you will not be remembered. For I, the Lord, have spoken.' "

Jerusalem's Sins

22 The Word of the Lord came to me saying, 2 "Son of man, will you judge? Will you judge this city of blood? Then tell the people about all their sinful acts. 3 Tell them, 'The Lord God says, "O city, because you have killed your own people and have made yourselves false gods to add to your sins, your time will come! 4 You have become guilty by killing your people, and sinful by the false gods you have made. You have brought the day of your punishment near. The end of your years has come. So I have made you a shame to the nations. All the countries laugh at you. 5 People from near and far will make fun of you, you who are full of shame and trouble. 6 See, each of the rulers of Israel who are in you has used his power to kill. 7 They have not honored father and mother within you. They have made it hard for the stranger living among you. They have done wrong to those in you who have lost their father or husband. 8 You have hated My holy things and have not kept My Days of Rest holy. 9 There are men in you who have lied about others to cause them to be put to death. Some have eaten at the altars on the mountains, and have done sex sins there. 10 Men have done sex sins with their fathers' wives. Men have put women to shame during their time of the month when they are unclean. 11 One has done sex sins with his neighbor's wife. Another has done sex sins with his daughter-in-law. And another has put his own sister to shame, his father's daughter. 12 In you they have taken pay to kill people. You have made others pay back more than they owe you. You have hurt your neighbors by making it hard for them to pay you. And you have forgotten Me," says the Lord God.

13 "I will bring My hand down hard upon the money you have made by your sinful ways, and for the blood of those you have killed among you. 14 Can your strength of heart last? Or can your hands be strong, in the days that I punish you? I, the Lord, have spoken, and I will do what I say. 15 I will divide you among the

nations and spread you out through the lands. I will take away from you all that is unclean. 16 You will become sinful in the eyes of the nations, and you will know that I am the Lord.' '"

17 The Word of the Lord came to me saying, 18 "Son of man, the people of Israel have become waste to Me. They are like brass, tin, iron, and lead in the fire and have become waste that is left after silver has gone through the fire. 19 So the Lord God says, 'Because you have all become waste, I am going to gather you together in Jerusalem. 20 As men gather silver and brass and iron and lead and tin into the stove to blow fire on it and melt it, so I will gather you in My anger. I will put you in the city and melt you. 21 I will gather you and blow on you with the fire of My anger, and you will be melted within it. 22 As silver is melted in the hot stove, so you will be melted in Jerusalem. Then you will know that I, the Lord, have poured out My anger upon you.' "

23 The Word of the Lord came to me saying, 24 "Son of man, tell Israel, 'You are a land that is not made clean or rained on in the day of anger.' 25 Israel's false religious leaders are making plans within her. They are like a lion making noise over the food it has killed. They have taken human lives and also riches and things of much worth. They have made many women in Israel lose their husbands. 26 Her religious leaders have broken My Law, and have made My holy things unclean. It makes no difference to them if something is holy or unclean. They have not taught the difference between what is clean and unclean. They hide their eyes from My Days of Rest, and I am not honored among them. 27 Her leaders are like wolves tearing apart the animals they have killed. They kill and destroy lives to get things by doing wrong. 28 Her men who speak in My name have covered these sins with whitewash for the people. They see false dreams and lie to them using their secret ways, saying, 'This is what the Lord God says,' when the Lord has not spoken. 29 The people of the land have made it hard for others and have stolen. They have done wrong to the poor and those in need. And they have made it hard for the stranger who lives among them, taking away his rights. 30 I looked for a man among them who would build up the wall and stand before Me in the place where it is broken, to stop Me from destroying the land, but I found no one.

31 So I have become angry with them. I have destroyed them with the fire of My anger. I am punishing them for what they have done," says the Lord God.

Two Sinful Sisters

23 The Word of the Lord came to me saying, 2 "Son of man, there were two women, daughters of the same mother. 3 They sold the use of their bodies in Egypt, and did so when they were young. Their breasts were lain upon in that land. Their breasts, which had never before been held by a man, were held. 4 The name of the older sister was Oholah, and her younger sister was Oholibah. They became Mine and gave birth to sons and daughters. Oholah is Samaria, and Oholibah is Jerusalem.

The Older Sister—Samaria

5 "Oholah sold the use of her body while she was Mine. She was full of desire for her lovers, the Assyrians who lived near her 6 who were dressed in purple. They were rulers and leaders, all of them good-looking young men who rode on horses. 7 She gave her body to them for sex. They were all the best men of Assyria. And she also sinned by worshiping the false gods of all the men she desired. 8 She did not turn away from her sex sins she had begun in Egypt. Men had lain with her since she was young. They had held her young breasts and used her to fill their desire. 9 So I gave her over to her lovers the Assyrians whom she desired. 10 They took off her clothes. They took her sons and daughters. But they killed her with the sword. So she became a saying among women, because she was punished.

The Younger Sister—Jerusalem

11 "Her sister Oholibah saw this, but she was more sinful in her desire for sex than Oholah. Her sex sins were worse than those of her sister. 12 She wanted to have the Assyrians, rulers and leaders, men who were well dressed, those who rode on horses, all those good-looking young men. 13 And I saw that she was sinful. Both sisters went the same way. 14 But she did even more sex sins. She saw pictures of men on the wall, pictures of Babylonians drawn in bright red. 15 They had belts around them, and flowing head-coverings. All of them looked like Babylonian captains who were born in Chaldea. 16 And when she saw them, she had a desire for

sex with them, and sent word to them in Chaldea. 17 The Babylonians came to her, to the bed of love. They made her sinful with their desire. And after she had had sex with them, she became sick of them. 18 When she let her sins and her body be seen, I turned away from her in anger, as I had turned from her sister. 19 Yet she did even more sex sins. She remembered when she was young, when she sold the use of her body in the land of Egypt. 20 She was full of desire for lovers whose flesh was like those of donkeys, and whose flow was like that of horses. 21 Oholibah, you were filled with desire for the sex sins you did when you were young, when the Egyptians held your breasts.

Jerusalem Is Judged

22 "So, Oholibah, the Lord God says, 'I will bring your lovers against you, those you turned away from. I will bring them against you from every side: 23 Babylonians and all the Chaldeans, Pekod, Shoa, Koa, and all the Assyrians with them, good-looking young men, all of them rulers, leaders, captains, and men who are well-known, all of them riding on horses. 24 They will come against you from the north, with war-wagons and an army of people. They will come against you on every side with battle-coverings and head-coverings. And I will let them punish you. They will punish you in their own way. 25 Because of My jealous anger, I will let them act toward you in anger. They will cut off your nose and ears, and any people who are left will be killed by the sword. They will take your sons and daughters, and any yet left will be burned in the fire. 26 They will take away your clothes and take away the beautiful objects you wear. 27 So I will put an end to the sex sins you brought from the land of Egypt. You will never again look at these things with desire or remember Egypt.' 28 For the Lord God says, 'I will give you over to those you hate, to the men you turned away from. 29 And because they hate you, they will take away everything you own and leave you without clothing. Then your body without clothes will be seen as a sinful woman. 30 These things will be done to you because you have sold the use of your body to the nations, and because you have made yourself sinful with their false gods. 31 You have followed the way of your sister, so I will give you the same cup of punishment to drink.' 32 The Lord God says, 'You will drink your sister's

cup, which is deep and wide. You will be laughed at and made fun of, for it holds much. 33 You will become drunk and filled with sorrow, with the cup of fear and waste, with the cup of your sister Samaria. 34 You will drink it until it is empty. Then you will chew its pieces and tear your breasts, for I have spoken,' says the Lord God. 35 So the Lord God says, 'Because you have forgotten Me and put Me behind your back, now suffer the punishment of your sex sins.' "

Both Sisters Are Judged

36 The Lord said to me, "Son of man, will you judge Oholah and Oholibah? Make them know their sinful acts. 37 For they have not been faithful to Me, and blood is on their hands. They have left Me for their false gods. And they gave their sons to these false gods as burnt gifts, the sons they had given to Me at birth. 38 That is not all they did. At that same time they have not kept My holy place and My Days of Rest holy. 39 When they had killed their children for their false gods, they went into My holy place on the same day to make it unclean. This is what they did within My house. 40 They even sent for men who came from far away. And when they came, you washed yourselves, colored your eyes, and put on beautiful objects for them. 41 You sat on a beautiful seat with a table made ready in front of it on which you had set My special perfume and My oil. 42 The sound of a group free of care was around you. Men who drank too much were brought from the desert with men who were not important. They put beautiful objects on the women's hands and beautiful crowns on their heads. 43 Then I said about the one who was worn out by sex sins, 'Will they now lie with her when she is this way?' 44 But they went in to her as they would go in to a woman who sells the use of her body. So they went in to Oholah and Oholibah, the sinful women. 45 But men who are right and good will punish them as women are punished who do sex sins and kill, because they are sinful women and blood is on their hands.

46 "The Lord God says, 'Bring up a group against them to fill them with fear and to rob them. 47 The group will kill them with stones and with swords. They will kill their sons and daughters and burn down their houses. 48 So I will put an end to sex sins in the land, that all women will learn of the danger and not sin as you

have done. 49 You will suffer the penalty for your sex sins and for worshiping your false gods. Then you will know that I am the Lord God.' "

The Boiling Pot

24 The Word of the Lord came to me on the tenth day of the tenth month in the ninth year, saying, 2 "Son of man, put down in writing this day, this very day. The king of Babylon has shut Jerusalem in with his army this very day. 3 And tell a picture-story to these sinful people of Israel. Tell them, 'The Lord God says, "Put the pot on the fire. Put it on, and pour water in it. 4 Put all the good pieces of meat in it, the thigh, the shoulder. And fill it with the best bones. 5 Take the best of the flock. Put more and more wood under the pot to make it boil, and boil the bones in it."

6 'For the Lord God says, "It is bad for the city of blood, for the rusted pot whose rust has not been cleaned out of it! Take the pieces of meat out of it without choosing them. 7 For the blood of the city has been poured on the rock. It was not poured on the ground where the dust would cover it. 8 I have put the blood on the rock where it could not be covered, so that it would cause anger and punishment." 9 So the Lord God says, "It is bad for the city of blood! I will put much wood on the fire. 10 Put on more and more wood, and make the fire burn. Boil the meat well. Mix in the spices, and let the bones be burned up. 11 Now set the empty pot on the coals until it becomes hot and its brass becomes bright with the heat. Then what is not clean in it will melt away. Its rust will be destroyed. 12 But it has been all for nothing. Its rust has not left it, not even by fire. 13 It is sin that makes you unclean. I have tried to make you clean, but you would not be made clean from your sins. So you will not be clean again until My anger against you is finished. 14 I, the Lord, have spoken. The time has come for Me to act. I will not hold back, I will not pity, and I will not be sorry. I will punish you for your ways and for what you have done," says the Lord God.' "

Ezekiel's Wife Dies

15 The Word of the Lord came to me saying, 16 "Son of man, with one blow I am about to take away from you the desire of your eyes. But do not have sorrow or loud crying or any tears. 17 Cry inside yourself. Do not show sorrow for the dead. Put your head-covering on. Put your shoes on your feet. Do not cover your face or eat the bread of those in sorrow." 18 So I spoke to the people in the morning, and in the evening my wife died. The next morning I did as I was told. 19 And the people said to me, "Will you not tell us what these things you are doing mean for us?" 20 So I said to them, "The Word of the Lord came to me saying, 21 'Tell the people of Israel, "The Lord God says, 'I am about to let sin fill My holy place, the pride of your power, the desire of your eyes, and the happiness of your soul. And your sons and daughters you have left behind will be killed by the sword. 22 Then you will do as I have done. You will not cover your face or eat the bread of those in sorrow. 23 Your heads will be covered and your shoes will be on your feet. You will not have sorrow or cry. But you will waste away in your sins and cry in pain to one another. 24 So Ezekiel will be something special for you to see. You will do just as he has done. When this happens, you will know that I am the Lord God.' "

25 'Son of man, I will take away their strong-place that was their joy and pride, the desire of their eyes and the things their hearts wanted most. And I will take away their sons and their daughters. 26 On that day, one who gets away will come to you with the news. 27 That same day your mouth will be opened. You will speak with him and no longer be quiet. So you will be something special for them to see, and they will know that I am the Lord.' "

Word against Ammon

25 The Word of the Lord came to me saying, 2 "Son of man, look toward the Ammonites and speak against them. 3 Tell them, 'Hear the Word of the Lord God! The Lord God says, "Because you were happy when My holy place was made unclean, and when the land of Israel was made waste, and when the people of Judah were taken away, 4 I am going to give you to the people of the east. They will put up their tents among you and live among you. They will eat your fruit and drink your milk. 5 I will turn the city of Rabbah into a field for camels, and Ammon into a resting place for flocks. Then you will know that I am the Lord." 6 For the Lord God says, "Because you have clapped your hands and crushed under your feet and showed your joy because of your hate for Israel, 7 I have put out My hand against you. I will give you away to the nations.

And I will destroy you from the nations and from the lands. Then you will know that I am the Lord."

Word against Moab

8 The Lord God says, "Because Moab and Seir say, 'See, Judah is like all the nations,' 9 I will lay waste the side of Moab, beginning with these cities there, Beth-jeshimoth, Baal-meon, and Kiriathaim, the best of the country. 10 I will give it to the people of the east, as I did with Ammon, so that the Ammonites will not be remembered among the nations. 11 I will punish Moab, and they will know that I am the Lord."

Word against Edom

12 The Lord God says, "Because Edom has fought against Judah in its anger, and has become very guilty by doing so," 13 the Lord God says, "I will put out My hand against Edom and kill its men and their animals. I will destroy it and they will fall by the sword from Teman to Dedan. 14 I will punish Edom by the hand of My people Israel. They will act in My anger against Edom, and Edom will know My anger," says the Lord God.

Word against Philistia

15 The Lord God says, "Because the Philistines have fought to destroy Judah with the lasting anger that is in their hearts," 16 the Lord God says, "I will put out My hand against the Philistines. And I will destroy the Cherethites and those left beside the sea. 17 I will punish them in My anger, and they will know that I am the Lord when I punish them.'"

Word against Tyre

26 In the eleventh year, on the first day of the month, the Word of the Lord came to me saying, 2 "Son of man, Tyre has said this about Jerusalem, 'O, the gate to the nations is broken. It has opened to me. I will do well, now that she is laid waste.' 3 So the Lord God says, 'I am against you, O Tyre. And I will bring up many nations against you, as the sea brings up its waves. 4 They will destroy the walls of Tyre and break down her towers. Then I will clean away what is left from her and make her nothing but rock. 5 She will be a place to spread fish nets out in the sea, for I have spoken,' says the Lord God. 'The nations will take her riches. 6 And her villages on the land across the sea from her will be destroyed by the sword. Then they will know that I am the Lord.'"

7 For the Lord God says, "I will bring Nebuchadnezzar king of Babylon, king of kings, against Tyre from the north. He will come with horses, war-wagons, horsemen, and a large army. 8 And he will kill with the sword those in your villages. He will build battle-walls around you. He will build up earth so they can go over your walls. He will build walls and make battle-coverings around you. 9 He will roll down large objects to knock down your walls, and will break down your towers with axes. 10 There will be so many horses that you will be covered by their dust. Your walls will shake at the noise of the horsemen and wheels and war-wagons, when he comes through your gates as men come into a city that has been broken open. 11 The feet of his horses will run all over your streets. He will kill your people with the sword, and your strong pillars will fall to the ground. 12 They will take your riches and good things as prizes of war. They will break down your walls and destroy your beautiful houses. And they will throw your stones and wood into the sea. 13 I will put an end to the music of your songs. And the sound of your harps will be heard no more. 14 I will make you nothing but rock. You will be a place for nets to spread. You will never be built again, for I the Lord have spoken," says the Lord God.

15 The Lord God says to Tyre, "Will not the lands beside the sea shake at the sound of your fall, when those who have been hurt cry in pain, when your people are killed? 16 Then all the leaders of the sea will step down from their thrones and take off their beautiful clothing. They will clothe themselves with fear. They will sit on the ground and not be able to stop shaking, full of fear and wonder because of you. 17 They will cry in sorrow for you and say, 'How you have been destroyed from the seas, O well-known city where many people once lived! You were powerful on the sea. You and all your people who lived here were filled with fear. 18 Now the islands shake in fear on the day of your fall. Yes, the lands which are by the sea are afraid because of how you are destroyed.'"

19 The Lord God says, "I will lay waste your city and make you like a destroyed city where no one lives. I will bring up the deep sea over you, and the many waters will cover you. 20 Then I will send you down with those who go down to the grave, to the people of long ago. I will make you stay in the lower parts of the earth, like

in waste places of long ago, with those who go down to the grave. So you will not have people living in you, and you will not have a place in the land of the living. ²¹ I will fill you with fear and destroy you. People will look for you, but you will never be found again," says the Lord God.

A Song of Sorrow for Tyre

27 The Word of the Lord came to me saying, ² "Son of man, sing a song of sorrow over Tyre. ³ Say to Tyre, whose people live at the gateway to the sea and trade with people from many lands, 'The Lord God says, "O Tyre, you have said, 'I am perfect in beauty.' ⁴ Your home is on the sea. Your builders have made you perfect in beauty. ⁵ They made your pieces of wood from the fir trees from Senir. They made the wood that holds your sail out of a cedar from Lebanon. ⁶ They made your oars out of oak trees from Bashan. They made your floor of ivory and boxwood from the land of Cyprus. ⁷ Your sail was made of fine and beautiful linen from Egypt, to show all people who you are. Your covering was made of blue and purple cloth from the land of Elishah. ⁸ The people of Sidon and Arvad were your rowers. Your own wise and able men were your sailors. ⁹ The leaders and wise men of Gebal were with you, putting tar where it was needed to keep the water out. All the ships of the sea and their sailors were with you to trade for your good things.

¹⁰ "Soldiers from Persia and Lud and Put were in your army. They hung battle-coverings and head-coverings in you, and made you beautiful. ¹¹ The men of Arvad and Helech were on your walls all around. And men of Gammad were in your towers. They hung their battle-coverings all around your walls, and made you perfect in beauty.

¹² "Tarshish traded with you because of all your riches of every kind. They paid for your good things with silver, iron, tin, and lead. ¹³ Javan, Tubal, and Meshech traded with you. They paid for your good things with servants and objects of brass. ¹⁴ Men of Beth-togarmah paid for your good things with horses, war horses, and mules. ¹⁵ The men of Dedan traded with you. Many lands beside the sea traded with you, paying you with ivory horns and beautiful dark wood. ¹⁶ Syria traded with you because of all your good things. They bought them with stones of great worth, purple cloth, cloth with beautiful sewing, fine linen, and coral. ¹⁷ Judah and the land of Israel traded with you. They paid for your good things with the grain of Minnith, cakes, honey, oil, and medicine. ¹⁸ Damascus traded with you because of all your good things and riches of all kinds. They paid for them with the wine of Helbon and white wool. ¹⁹ Vedan and Javan traded with you from Uzal. They paid you with pure iron and spices. ²⁰ Dedan paid you with horse coverings. ²¹ Arabia and all the leaders of Kedar traded with you. They paid you with lambs, rams, and goats. ²² Sheba and Raamah traded with you. They paid for your good things with the best of all kinds of spices, stones of great worth, and gold. ²³ Haran, Canneh, Eden, Sheba, Asshur, and Chilmad traded with you. ²⁴ They paid you with the best clothing, clothes of blue cloth and beautiful sewing, floor coverings of many colors, and strong ropes. ²⁵ The ships of Tarshish carried your good things for you. You were filled and honored in the middle of the seas.

²⁶ "Your rowers have brought you into deep waters. The east wind has wrecked you far out in the sea. ²⁷ Your riches, your good things, the things you trade, your sailors, your pilots, your builders, your traders, all your soldiers, and all your people will fall into the sea on the day you are destroyed. ²⁸ The lands by the sea will shake at the sound of your sailors' cry. ²⁹ All the rowers and sailors of the sea will leave their ships. They will stand on the land ³⁰ and cry in a loud voice of sorrow over you. They will throw dust on their heads and roll in ashes. ³¹ They will cut off their hair because of you, and dress themselves in cloth made from hair. They will cry over you with much sorrow in their soul. ³² In their crying they will sing a song of sorrow for you, saying, 'Who is like Tyre, destroyed and quiet in the sea? ³³ When your good things went out on the sea, you pleased many nations. With all your riches and good things you made the kings of the earth rich. ³⁴ Now you are wrecked by the sea, in the deep waters. Your good things and all your people have gone down with you. ³⁵ All the people who live on the islands are full of fear and wonder because of you. Their kings are very afraid. Their faces are troubled. ³⁶ The traders among the nations make sounds of surprise at you. You have come to an end and you will be no more.' " '"

Words against the King of Tyre

28 The Word of the Lord came to me saying, 2 "Son of man, tell the leader of Tyre, 'The Lord God says, "Because your heart is proud, you have said, 'I am a god. I sit in the seat of gods, with the seas around me.' Yet you are a man and not God, even if you think you are as wise as God. 3 You are wiser than Daniel. There is no secret that is hidden from you. 4 By your wisdom and understanding you have gathered riches for yourself. You have gathered gold and silver for your store-houses. 5 By all your wisdom in trade you have added to your riches, and your heart has become proud because of them. 6 So the Lord God says, 'Because you think you are as wise as God, 7 I will bring strangers against you, those who have the hardest hearts of all the nations. With their swords they will destroy the beauty of your wisdom and your greatness. 8 They will bring you down to the grave. You will die the death of those who are killed on the sea. 9 Will you still say, "I am a god," in front of those who kill you? You will be only a man and not a god in the hands of those who kill you. 10 You will be killed by strangers, and will die the death of one who has not gone through the religious act of My people. For I have spoken,' says the Lord God.' "

Song of Sorrow for the King of Tyre

11 The Word of the Lord came to me saying, 12 "Son of man, sing a song of sorrow for the king of Tyre, and tell him, 'The Lord God says, "You were once the mark of what is perfect, full of wisdom and perfect in beauty. 13 You were in Eden, the garden of God. Every stone of great worth covered you: ruby, topaz, diamond, beryl, onyx, jasper, chrysolite, turquoise, and emerald. And you had beautiful objects of gold. They were made for you when you were made. 14 You were the cherub who kept watch, and I placed you there. You were on the holy mountain of God. You walked among the stones of fire. 15 You were without blame in your ways from the day you were made until sin was found in you. 16 Through all your trading you were filled with bad ways, and you sinned. So I have sent you away in shame from the mountain of God and I have destroyed you and driven you out from the stones of fire, O cherub who kept watch. 17 Your heart was proud because of your beauty. You made your wisdom sinful because of your beauty. So I threw you to the ground. I laid

you in front of kings for them to see you. 18 By all your wrong-doing and sinful trading you made your holy places sinful. So I made a fire come out from you, and it has destroyed you. I have turned you to ashes on the earth in the eyes of all who see you. 19 All the nations who know you are filled with wonder and fear because of you. You have come to a bad end, and you will be no more forever.' "

Words against Sidon

20 The Word of the Lord came to me saying, 21 "Son of man, look toward Sidon and speak against her. 22 Tell her, 'The Lord God says, "I am against you, O Sidon, and My greatness will be honored among you. They will know that I am the Lord when I punish Sidon. I will show Myself holy within her. 23 For I will send disease upon her, and blood into her streets. People will be killed by the sword from every side. Then they will know that I am the Lord. 24 No longer will the people of Israel have neighbors like a sharp thistle or thorn who hate them. Then they will know that I am the Lord God.

25 "The Lord God says, 'I will gather the people of Israel from the different nations where they have been sent. And I will show Myself holy among them in the eyes of the nations. Then they will live in their own land which I gave to My servant Jacob. 26 They will live there and be safe. They will build houses, plant grape-fields and be safe, when I punish all those around them who speak against them. Then they will know that I am the Lord their God.' "

Word against Egypt

29 On the twelfth day of the tenth month in the tenth year, the Word of the Lord came to me saying, 2 "Son of man, look toward Pharaoh king of Egypt, and speak against him and against all Egypt, 3 Tell them, 'The Lord God says, "I am against you, Pharaoh king of Egypt. You are the big animal that lies in his rivers and says, 'The Nile is mine. I made it.' 4 I will put hooks in your mouth. I will make the fish of your rivers stick to your hard skin. And I will pull you up out of your rivers, with the fish that stick to your hard skin. 5 Then I will leave you in the desert, you and all the fish of your rivers. You will fall on the open field, and not be gathered or buried. I will feed you to the wild animals of the earth and to the birds of the sky.

6 Then all the people of Egypt will know that I am the Lord. They have been only a weak piece of river-grass to the people of Israel. 7 When they took hold of you with their hands, you broke and tore all their shoulders. When they rested on you, you broke and hurt their backs." 8 So the Lord God says, "I will bring a sword against you and kill your people and animals. 9 And the land of Egypt will be destroyed and laid waste. Then they will know that I am the Lord.

"Because you said, 'The Nile is mine, and I made it,' 10 I am against you and against your rivers. I will destroy Egypt and make it nothing but waste from Migdol to Syene and even to the land of Ethiopia. 11 No foot of man or animal will pass through it, and no one will live there for forty years. 12 I will make the land of Egypt a waste among the lands which are laid waste. Her cities will be a waste for forty years among cities that are laid waste. I will divide the Egyptians among the nations and spread them out among the lands."

13 For the Lord God says, "At the end of forty years I will gather the Egyptians from the nations where they were divided. 14 I will bring them back to Egypt and let them live in Pathros, the land they came from. And there they will be a small nation. 15 It will be the least of the nations, and will never lift itself up above other nations again. I will make them so small that they will never rule over the nations. 16 It will never again be a hope for the people of Israel. They will remember their sin in turning to Egypt for help in the past. Then they will know that I am the Lord God." ' "

King Nebuchadnezzar Will Take Egypt

17 On the first day of the first month in the twenty-seventh year, the Word of the Lord came to me saying, 18 "Son of man, Nebuchadnezzar king of Babylon made his army work hard against Tyre. Every head lost its hair, and skin was rubbed off every shoulder. But he and his army did not receive anything from Tyre to pay for the work he had done against it." 19 So the Lord God says, "I will give the land of Egypt to Nebuchadnezzar king of Babylon. And he will carry away her riches. He will take all her good things, and they will be pay for his army. 20 I have given him the land of Egypt for the work he has done, because he and his army worked for Me," says the Lord God.

21 "On that day I will make the people of Israel strong, and give you the power to speak among them. Then they will know that I am the Lord."

The Lord Will Punish Egypt

30 The Word of the Lord came to me saying, 2 "Son of man, speak in My name and say, 'This is what the Lord God says: "Cry in a loud voice, 'It is bad for that day!' 3 For the day is near. The day of the Lord is near. It will be a day of clouds, a time of trouble for the nations. A sword will come against Egypt, and Ethiopia will be very troubled. When the people are killed in Egypt, her riches will be taken away, and her country destroyed. 5 Ethiopia, Put, Lud, all of Arabia, Libya, and the people of Israel living there, all who have an agreement with Egypt will be killed by the sword." ' "

6 'The Lord says, "Those who help Egypt will be killed in battle. The pride of her power will come down. From Migdol to Syene they will be killed by the sword," says the Lord God. 7 "They will be a waste among the lands that are laid waste. And her cities will be among the destroyed cities. 8 Then they will know that I am the Lord, when I start a fire in Egypt and all those who help her are destroyed. 9 On that day I will send men in ships to bring fear to Ethiopians who think they are safe. They will be troubled and afraid as when Egypt is destroyed, for their day is coming!" 10 The Lord God says, "I will put an end to Egypt's riches by the hand of Nebuchadnezzar king of Babylon. 11 He and his people show the least pity of all the nations, and they will be brought in to destroy the land. They will use their swords against Egypt and fill the land with dead bodies. 12 And I will dry up the Nile River and sell the land to sinful men. I will destroy the land and everything in it, by the hand of strangers. I, the Lord, have spoken."

13 'The Lord God says, "I will also destroy the false gods and put an end to the objects of worship in Memphis. There will no longer be a leader in the land of Egypt, so I will put fear in the land. 14 I will destroy Pathros, start a fire in Zoan, and punish Thebes. 15 I will be angry with Pelusium, the strong city of Egypt. And I will destroy the riches of Thebes. 16 I will start a fire in Egypt. Pelusium will suffer much. Thebes will be broken open. And Memphis will not have rest from troubles and fear. 17 The young men of On and Pi-beseth

will be killed in battle, and the women will be taken away. [18] At Tehaphnehes the day will be dark when I break the power of Egypt. The pride of her strength will come to an end. A cloud will cover her, and her daughters will be taken away. [19] So I will punish Egypt, and they will know that I am the Lord.' "

Word against Pharaoh

[20] On the seventh day of the first month in the eleventh year, the Word of the Lord came to me saying, [21] "Son of man, I have broken the arm of Pharaoh king of Egypt. And it has not been wrapped so that it could heal and be strong enough to hold the sword. [22] So the Lord God says, 'I am against Pharaoh king of Egypt and will break his arms, both the strong one and the one already broken. And I will make the sword fall from his hand. [23] I will divide the Egyptians among the nations and spread them out among the lands. [24] For I will give strength to the arms of the king of Babylon and put My sword in his hand, and I will break the arms of Pharaoh, so that he will cry in pain in front of him like a dying man in battle. [25] I will give strength to the arms of the king of Babylon, but Pharaoh's arms will fall. Then they will know that I am the Lord, when I give My sword to the king of Babylon and he uses it against the land of Egypt. [26] I will make the Egyptians go to the different nations and spread them out among the lands. Then they will know that I am the Lord.' "

Egypt Is Like a Cedar Tree

31 On the first day of the third month in the eleventh year, the Word of the Lord came to me saying, [2] "Son of man, say to Pharaoh king of Egypt and to his people, 'Who can be compared with you in greatness? [3] Look at Assyria, once a cedar in Lebanon with beautiful branches and many leaves. It was very high, and its top was among the heavy branches. [4] The waters made it grow, and the water under the ground made it grow high. Its rivers flowed all around its base, and spread water to all the trees of the field. [5] So it was higher than all the trees of the field. And it grew many long and spreading branches because it had so much water. [6] All the birds of the air made their nests in its branches. And under its branches all the animals of the field gave birth. All great nations lived in its shadow. [7] It was beautiful in its greatness with its spreading

branches, for its roots went down to much water. [8] The cedars in God's garden could not compare with it. The fir trees and the chestnut trees could not compare with its branches. No tree in God's garden was like it in beauty. [9] I made it beautiful with its many branches. And all the trees that were in Eden were jealous of it.

[10] 'So the Lord God says, "Because it has grown high with its top among the heavy branches, its heart has become proud, [11] I will give it over to a powerful ruler of the nations, and he will punish it. Because of its sin, I will drive it out. [12] Rulers from other nations will cut it down and leave it. Its branches will fall on the mountains and in all the valleys. Its spreading branches will be broken in all the deep valleys of the land. All the people of the earth will go away from its shadow and leave it. [13] All the birds of the air will live on its broken pieces. And all the animals of the field will be on its fallen branches. [14] This will be so that no trees by the water will grow high with their tops among the heavy branches. No trees that drink water will ever grow so high. For they have all been given over to death. They will go to the earth below, among men who die and go down to the grave."

[15] 'The Lord God says, "When it goes down to the place of the dead, I will make the waters under the ground cover it in sorrow. I will stop its rivers of water and fill Lebanon with sorrow over it. All the trees of the field will waste away because of it. [16] I will make the nations shake in fear at the sound of its fall when I send it to the place of the dead with those who go down to the grave. Then all the well-watered trees of Eden, the best of Lebanon, will be comforted in the earth below. [17] And those who lived under its shadow among the nations will go down to the place of the dead with it, to those who were killed by the sword.

[18] "Which of the trees of Eden can be compared with you in beauty and greatness? Yet you will be brought down with the trees of Eden to the earth below. You will lie among the sinful, with those who were killed by the sword. This is Pharaoh and all his people!" says the Lord God.'

King of Egypt Is Like a Dragon

32 On the first day of the twelfth month in the twelfth year, the Word of the Lord came to me saying, [2] "Son of man, sing a song of sorrow for Pharaoh king of Egypt, and say to him, 'You compared yourself to a young lion among the nations, yet you are like the big dragon in the seas. You go through your rivers, troubling the water with your feet and making the rivers muddy.' " ³ The Lord God says, "Now I will throw My net over you with an army of many nations. They will lift you up in My net. ⁴ And I will leave you on the land. I will throw you on the open field. I will have all the birds of the air live on you. And I will feed you to the wild animals of the earth. ⁵ I will lay your flesh on the mountains, and fill the valleys with what is left of you. ⁶ I will make the land drink your flowing blood as far as the mountains, and the deep valleys will be full of you. ⁷ When I destroy you, I will cover the heavens and make the stars dark. I will cover the sun with a cloud, and the moon will not give its light. ⁸ I will make all the shining lights in the heavens dark over you, and bring darkness upon your land," says the Lord God. ⁹ "I will trouble the hearts of many people when I destroy you among the nations, among lands you have not known. ¹⁰ I will fill many nations with fear and wonder because of you. Their kings will shake in fear for you when I wave My sword in front of them. Every man will keep shaking in fear for his own life, on the day you are destroyed."

¹¹ For the Lord God says, "The sword of the king of Babylon will come against you. ¹² I will cause your people to be killed by the swords of powerful men who will have no pity, all of them strong rulers of the nations. They will destroy the pride of Egypt and kill all its people. ¹³ I will also destroy all its cattle from beside many waters. No foot of man or animal will fill them with mud any more. ¹⁴ I will make their waters clear and make their rivers flow like oil," says the Lord God. ¹⁵ "When I destroy the land of Egypt and take from the land everything that was in it, and when I punish all who live there, then they will know that I am the Lord. ¹⁶ This is the song of sorrow they will sing. The women of the nations will sing it. They will sing it over Egypt and all her people," says the Lord God.

The Place of the Dead

¹⁷ In the twelfth year, on the fifteenth of the month, the Word of the Lord came to me saying, ¹⁸ "Son of man, cry in a loud voice for the people of Egypt. Send them down with the powerful nations to the place of the dead, with those who go down to the grave. ¹⁹ Say to them, 'Do you think you are more favored than anyone else? Go down and make your bed with the sinful.' ²⁰ They will fall among those who are killed by the sword. The sword is ready to kill all of Egypt's people. ²¹ From the place of the dead the powerful leaders will say of Egypt and her helpers, 'They have come down. They lie with the sinful, with those killed by the sword.'

²² "Assyria is there, with all of her army. All around her are the graves of her dead, who have been killed by the sword. ²³ Their graves lie in the farthest parts of the place of the dead. Her army is around her grave. All who had spread fear in the land of the living are dead, killed by the sword.

²⁴ "Elam is there, with all of her people around her grave. All of them are dead, killed by the sword. They have gone to the lower parts of the earth having not gone through the religious act of the Jews. They filled the land of the living with fear, and carried their shame with those who went down to the place of the dead. ²⁵ A bed is made for her among the dead with all her people. Their graves are around her. They are all sinful people, killed by the sword. They spread fear in the land of the living, and were put to shame with those who go down to the place of the dead and are among the dead.

²⁶ "Meshech and Tubal are there, with all their people. Their graves are around them. All of them are sinful, killed by the sword, for they had spread fear in the land of the living. ²⁷ They do not lie beside the graves of the powerful men of long ago, who went down to the place of the dead with their swords of war, whose swords were laid under their heads. But the punishment for their sin rested on their bones. For the fear of these powerful men was once in the land of the living. ²⁸ You too, O Pharaoh, will be broken and lie among the sinful, with those killed by the sword.

²⁹ "Edom is there, with its kings and all its leaders. Even with all their power they are laid with those killed by the sword. They lie with the sinful, with those who go down to the place of the dead.

³⁰ "All the leaders of the north and all the Sidonians are there. Even with the fear they caused by their power, they went down with the dead in shame. They lie as sinful people with those killed by the sword. They carried their shame with those who go down to the place of the dead.

31 "When Pharaoh and his army see them, they will be comforted for all his people who were killed by the sword," says the Lord God. 32 "I spread fear of him in the land of the living, yet Pharaoh and all his people will be laid among the sinful, with those killed by the sword," says the Lord God.

The Words of the Watchman

33 The Word of the Lord came to me saying, 2 "Son of man, speak to the children of your people. Say to them, 'If I bring a sword upon a land, and the people of the land choose one of their men to keep watch for them, 3 and he sees the sword coming upon the land and sounds the horn to tell the people of the danger, 4 then if anyone hears the horn and does not take care, and a sword comes and kills him, he will be to blame for his own death. 5 He heard the sound of the horn, but did not worry about the danger. He will be to blame for his own death. If he had been careful, he would have saved his life. 6 But if the watchman sees the sword coming and does not blow the horn, and the people are not told of the danger, and a sword comes and kills one of them, that man will be taken away because of his sin. But the blood of the watchman must be given.'

7 "Son of man, I have chosen you as a watchman for the people of Israel. So when I give you the word, you must tell them of the danger. 8 When I tell a sinful man that he will die for sure, and you do not speak to him about the danger of his way, that sinful man will die in his sin. But your blood must be given. 9 But if you tell a sinful man to turn from his way, and he does not turn from his way, he will die in his sin. But you have saved your life.

God Judges Well

10 "Son of man, say to the people of Israel, 'You have said, "Our sins are upon us, and we are wasting away in them. How then can we live?" ' 11 Say to them, 'As I live,' says the Lord God, 'I am not pleased when sinful people die. But I am pleased when the sinful turn from their way and live. Turn! Turn from your sinful ways! Why will you die, O people of Israel?' 12 Now, son of man, tell the children of your people, 'If a man does what is right and good, it will not save him when he sins.' And the sins of a sinful man will not make him fall when he turns from his sinful way. But the man who is right and good will not

be able to live by his good ways when he sins. 13 When I tell the man who is right and good that he will live, and he trusts in his good ways so much that he sins, none of his good works will be remembered. He will die for the sin he has done. 14 But when I tell the sinful man that he will die, and he turns from his sin and does what is right and good, 15 if he gives back what a person gave him as trust for a promise, pays back what he had stolen, follows the Laws that give life and does not sin, he will live for sure. He will not die. 16 None of the sins he has done will be remembered against him. He has done what is right and good, and he will live for sure.

17 "Yet the children of your people say, 'The way of the Lord is not right.' But it is their way that is not right. 18 When the right and good man turns from his good way and sins, he will die for it. 19 But when the sinful man turns from his sin and does what is right and good, he will live because of it. 20 Yet you say, 'The way of the Lord is not right.' O people of Israel, I will judge each of you by his ways."

Jerusalem Is Taken

21 On the fifth day of the tenth month in the twelfth year since we had been taken to a strange land, a man who got away from Jerusalem came and said to me, "The city has been taken." 22 Now the hand of the Lord had been upon me in the evening before the man came. And He opened my mouth so that when the man came to me in the morning, I was able to speak.

The Sins of the People

23 Then the Word of the Lord came to me saying, 24 "Son of man, the people who live in these waste places in the land of Israel are saying, 'Abraham was only one man, yet he owned the land. But we are many, and for sure the land has been given to us.' 25 So tell them, 'The Lord God says, "You eat meat with the blood in it, and worship your false gods as you kill. Should the land belong to you? 26 You trust in your sword, and keep on sinning. Each of you does sex sins with his neighbor's wife. Should the land belong to you?" ' 27 Tell them, 'The Lord God says, "As I live, those who are in the waste places will be killed by the sword. Whoever is in the open field, I will feed to the wild animals. And those who are in the strong-places and in the caves will die of disease. 28 I will destroy the land and make it a waste. The pride of her

power will come to an end. The mountains of Israel will be laid waste, so that no one will pass through. ²⁹ Then they will know that I am the Lord, when I destroy the land and make it a waste because of all the hated sins they have done." '

³⁰ "As for you, son of man, your people are talking to each other about you by the walls and at the doors of the houses. They are saying, 'Come and hear the word that has come from the Lord.' ³¹ They come and sit in front of you as My people, and listen to the words you say. But they do not do them. With their mouth they speak of love, but their hearts are full of sinful desire. ³² They think of you as nothing more than one who sings love songs with a beautiful voice and plays music well. For they hear what you say, but they will not do it. ³³ When all this comes true, and it will, then they will know that a man of God has been among them."

The Shepherds of Israel

34 The Word of the Lord came to me saying. ² "Son of man, speak against the shepherds of Israel. Speak in My name and tell those shepherds, 'The Lord God says, "It is bad for the shepherds of Israel who have been feeding themselves! Should not the shepherds feed the flock? ³ You eat the fat and clothe yourselves with the wool. You kill the fat sheep without feeding the flock. ⁴ You have not given strength to the weak ones. You have not healed the sick. You have not helped the ones that are hurt. You have not brought back those that have gone away. And you have not looked for the lost. But you have ruled them with power and without pity. ⁵ They went everywhere because they had no shepherd. And they became food for every animal of the field. ⁶ My flock went many different ways through all the mountains and on every high hill. My sheep were spread over all the earth, and there was no one looking for them." ' "

⁷ So, you shepherds, hear the Word of the Lord. ⁸ "As I live," says the Lord God, "My flock has been killed and become food for wild animals because they had no shepherd. My shepherds did not look for My flock. They fed themselves, but have not fed My flock." ⁹ So, you shepherds, hear the Word of the Lord. ¹⁰ The Lord God says, "I am against the shepherds, and I will ask them for My sheep. I will stop them from feeding the sheep, so they will no longer be able to feed themselves. I will

save my sheep from their mouths, so that they will no longer be food for them."

The Good Shepherd

¹¹ For the Lord God says, "I Myself will look for My sheep and find them. ¹² As a shepherd looks for his sheep when they are not together, so I will look for My sheep. And I will save them from all the places where they were spread out on a day of clouds and darkness. ¹³ I will bring them out from the people and gather them from the countries, and bring them to their own land. I will feed them on the mountains of Israel, by the rivers, and in all the places of the land where people live. ¹⁴ I will feed them in a good field. The ground they eat upon will be on the mountains of Israel. There they will lie down in a good field and feed on good grass on the mountains of Israel. ¹⁵ I will feed My sheep, and give them rest," says the Lord God. ¹⁶ "I will look for the lost, bring back those that have gone away, help those who have been hurt, and give strength to the sick. But I will destroy the fat and the strong. I will feed them with punishment.

¹⁷ "As for you, My flock, the Lord God says, 'I will judge between one sheep and another, between the rams and the male goats. ¹⁸ Is it not enough for you to eat in the good field? Must you crush under foot the rest of your fields? Is it not enough for you to drink of the clear waters? Must your feet fill the rest with mud? ¹⁹ Must My flock eat what you have crushed with your feet, and drink what you have made dirty with your feet?' "

²⁰ So the Lord God says to them, "I Myself will judge between the fat sheep and the weak sheep. ²¹ Because you push with your side and shoulder and run against all the weak with your horns until you have driven them away, ²² I will save My flock. They will no longer be hurt. And I will judge between one sheep and another. ²³ Then I will set over them one shepherd, My servant David, and he will feed them. He will feed them and be their shepherd. ²⁴ I, the Lord, will be their God, and My servant David will be their leader. I, the Lord, have spoken.

²⁵ "I will make a peace agreement with them and take away wild animals from the land. Then they will be safe as they live in the desert and sleep in the woods. ²⁶ I will bring good to them and to the places around My hill. I will give them rain when they need it. Good will rain down

upon them. 27 The trees of the field will give their fruit and the earth will give its food. They will be safe in their land. Then they will know that I am the Lord, when I have broken the load from their backs and have saved them from those who made servants of them. 28 They will no longer be under the power of the nations. And the wild animals of the earth will not eat them. But they will be safe, and no one will make them afraid. 29 I will give them a land well-known for its fields of food. They will never suffer with hunger again, and will no longer be put to shame by the nations. 30 Then they will know that I, the Lord their God, am with them, and that they, the people of Israel, are My people," says the Lord God. 31 "You, My sheep, the sheep of My field, are people, and I am your God," says the Lord God.

God Judges Edom

35 The Word of the Lord came to me saying, 2 "Son of man, look toward Mount Seir and speak against it, 3 saying, 'The Lord God says, "I am against you, Mount Seir. I will put out My hand against you and make you a waste-land. 4 I will destroy your cities, and you will become a waste. Then you will know that I am the Lord. 5 You have always hated the people of Israel and have given them over to be killed at the time of their trouble, at the time of the punishment of the end. 6 So as I live," says the Lord God, "I will give you over to death, and you will not get away from death. Since you have not hated killing, death will come after you. 7 I will destroy Mount Seir and make it a waste. And I will kill all who travel through it. 8 I will fill its mountains with its dead. Those killed by the sword will fall on your hills and in your valleys. 9 I will destroy you forever, and no one will live in your cities. Then you will know that I am the Lord.

10 "You have said, 'These two nations and these two lands will be mine, and we will own them,' even when the Lord was there. 11 So as I live," says the Lord God, "I will punish you for your anger and the jealousy you showed because of your hate toward them. And I will make Myself known among them when I judge you. 12 Then you will know that I, the Lord, have heard all the bad things you have said against the mountains of Israel. You have said, 'They are destroyed. They are given to us for food.' 13 You have spoken in pride against Me, with many words and I have heard you." 14 The Lord God says, "While the whole earth is filled with joy, I will destroy you. 15 As you had joy because the land of Israel was destroyed, so I will do to you. You will be destroyed, O Mount Seir, and all Edom, all of it. Then they will know that I am the Lord." '

Good Comes to Israel

36 "Son of man, speak in My name to the mountains of Israel. Say, 'O mountains of Israel, hear the Word of the Lord. 2 The Lord God says, "Those who hate you have laughed and spoken against you, saying, 'The old hills now belong to us.' 3 So tell the mountains of Israel, 'The Lord God says, "They have made you a waste-land, and destroyed you from every side. You were taken by the rest of the nations for their own. And the people have been saying bad things about you." ' "

4 So, mountains of Israel, hear the Word of the Lord God. This is what the Lord God says to the mountains, the hills, the valleys, the destroyed places and empty cities, which have been robbed and made fun of by the rest of the nations around them. 5 The Lord God says, "I speak in the fire of My jealousy against the rest of the nations and against all Edom. They have taken My land for themselves with hearts full of joy and hate, that they might rob its good things."

6 'So speak about the land of Israel, and tell the mountains, the hills, and valleys, "The Lord God says, 'I speak in My jealousy and anger because you have been put to shame by the nations.' 7 So the Lord God says, 'I promise that the nations around you will also suffer shame. 8 But you, O mountains of Israel, will put out your branches and give your fruit for My people Israel. For they will come home soon. 9 See, I care for you and will show you favor. You will be plowed and planted. 10 I will cause the people to become many, all the people of Israel. People will live in the cities, and the places that have been destroyed will be built again. 11 I will give you many people and animals, and they will have many young ones. You will be full of people as you were before. And I will do more good to you than ever before. Then you will know that I am the Lord. 12 I will have people, My people Israel, walk on you and own you. You will belong to them, and you will never again take their children from them.'

13 "The Lord God says, 'People say to

you, "You destroy men and have taken children from your nation. ¹⁴ But you will no longer destroy men and take away your nation's children," says the Lord God. ¹⁵ "I will not let you hear words of shame from the nations any more. You will not be put to shame by the nations any longer. And you will no longer make your nation fall," says the Lord God.' "

New Life for Israel

¹⁶ The Word of the Lord came to me saying, ¹⁷ "Son of man, when the people of Israel were living in their own land, they made it sinful by their ways and their works. The way they acted before Me was unclean, like a woman is unclean during her time each month. ¹⁸ So I poured out My anger upon them because of the blood they had poured on the land, and because they had made it sinful with their false gods. ¹⁹ I sent them among the different nations and spread them out among the lands. I judged them for their ways and their works. ²⁰ But in every place they went among the nations, they brought shame upon My holy name, because it was said of them, 'These are the people of the Lord, yet they had to leave His land.' ²¹ But I cared about My holy name, which the people of Israel had put to shame among the nations where they had gone.

²² "So tell the people of Israel, 'The Lord God says, "It is not because of you, O people of Israel, that I am about to act. It is because of My holy name, which you have put to shame among the nations where you have gone. ²³ I will show how holy My great name is, which you have put to shame among the nations. Then the nations will know that I am the Lord," says the Lord God, "when I use you to show them that I am holy. ²⁴ For I will take you from the nations and gather you from all the lands, and bring you into your own land. ²⁵ Then I will put clean water on you, and you will be clean. I will make you clean from all your unclean ways and from all your false gods. ²⁶ I will give you a new heart and put a new spirit within you. I will take away your heart of stone and give you a heart of flesh. ²⁷ And I will put My Spirit within you and cause you to follow My Laws and be careful to do what I tell you. ²⁸ And you will live in the land that I gave to your fathers. You will be My people, and I will be your God. ²⁹ I will save you from all your unclean ways. I will give you much grain, and you will not have

to go without food. ³⁰ I will have the trees give much fruit and the fields give much food. So you will never again suffer the shame of going hungry among the nations. ³¹ Then you will remember your sinful ways and your sinful works, and you will hate yourselves because of your sins and wrong-doing. ³² I want you to know that I am not doing this because of you," says the Lord God. "Be ashamed and troubled because of your ways, O people of Israel!"

³³ 'The Lord God says, "On the day that I make you clean from all your sins, I will fill the cities with people, and the destroyed places will be built again. ³⁴ And the waste-land will be planted, instead of being a waste in the eyes of all who pass by. ³⁵ They will say, 'This waste-land has become like the garden of Eden. And the destroyed cities now have strong walls and many people.' ³⁶ Then the nations that are left around you will know that I, the Lord, have built again the places that were destroyed, and planted what had been waste-land. I, the Lord, have spoken, and I will do what I say."

³⁷ 'The Lord God says, "I will also let the people of Israel ask Me to do this for them: I will give them many people, like the sheep of a flock. ³⁸ The empty cities will be filled with flocks of people, like the flock kept for burnt gifts, like the flock at Jerusalem during her special suppers. Then they will know that I am the Lord." ' "

The Valley of Dry Bones

37 The hand of the Lord was upon me. He brought me out by His Spirit and set me down in the center of the valley. It was full of bones. ² He led me around the valley. I saw there were very many bones, and they were very dry. ³ He said to me, "Son of man, can these bones live?" I answered, "O Lord God, only You know that." ⁴ He said to me, "Speak in My name over these bones. Say to them, 'O dry bones, hear the Word of the Lord.' ⁵ This is what the Lord God says to these bones: 'I will make breath come into you, and you will come to life. ⁶ I will join you together, make flesh grow back on you, cover you with skin, and put breath in you to make you come to life. Then you will know that I am the Lord.' "

⁷ So I spoke as I was told. And as I spoke, there was a noise, the sound of bones hitting against each other. The bones came together, bone to bone. ⁸ I looked and saw that parts had grown to hold them

together. Flesh had grown, and they were covered with skin. But there was no breath in them. 9 Then He said to me, "Speak to the breath in My name, son of man. Tell the breath, 'The Lord God says, "Come from the four winds, O breath, and breathe on these dead bodies to make them come to life." ' " 10 So I spoke as I had been told. The breath came into them, and they came to life and stood on their feet. They were a large army.

11 Then He said to me, "Son of man, these bones are all the people of Israel. They say, 'Our bones are dried up, and our hope is gone. We are all destroyed.' 12 So speak in My name and tell them, 'The Lord God says, "I will open your graves, My people, and make you come out of them. And I will bring you into the land of Israel. 13 Then, My people, you will know that I am the Lord, when I have opened your graves and brought you up. 14 I will put My Spirit within you, and you will come to life. I will place you in your own land. Then you will know that I, the Lord, have spoken and have done it," says the Lord.' "

Judah and Israel under One King

15 The Word of the Lord came to me saying, 16 "Son of man, take one stick of wood and write on it, 'For Judah and for the people of Israel with him.' Then take another stick of wood and write on it, 'For Joseph, the stick of Ephraim, and for all the people of Israel with him.' 17 Then join them together into one stick so that they will become one in your hand. 18 And when your people say to you, 'Will you not let us know what you mean by these?' 19 tell them, 'The Lord God says, "I will take the stick of Joseph, which is in the hand of Ephraim, and the people of Israel who are with him. And I will put it with the stick of Judah, and make them one stick. They will be one in My hand." ' 20 Hold in front of them the sticks you write on, 21 and tell them, 'The Lord God says, "I will take the people of Israel from the nations where they have gone. I will gather them from every side and bring them into their own land. 22 I will make them one nation in the land, on the mountains of Israel. And one king will rule over all of them. They will no longer be two nations, and they will no longer be divided under two kings. 23 They will no longer make themselves unclean with their false gods, or with their hated objects of worship, or with any of their sins. I will keep them from turning again to these sins, and will make them clean. They will be My people, and I will be their God.

24 "My servant David will be their king, and they will have one shepherd. They will follow and keep My Laws, and obey them. 25 And they will live in the land that I gave to My servant Jacob, where your fathers lived. They and their children and their children's children will live in it forever. And My servant David will be their leader forever. 26 I will make a peace agreement with them, one that lasts forever. I will bring good to them and make them many in number. And I will set My holy place among them forever. 27 I will live with them, and will be their God, and they will be My people. 28 Then the nations will know that I am the Lord Who makes Israel holy, when My holy place is among them forever." ' "

Words against Gog

38 The Word of the Lord came to me saying, 2 "Son of man, look toward Gog of the land of Magog, the leader of Rosh, Meshech, and Tubal, and speak against him. 3 Tell him, 'The Lord God says, "I am against you, O Gog, leader of Rosh, Meshech, and Tubal. 4 I will turn you around, put hooks into your mouth, and bring you out with your whole army. Your horses and horsemen will be dressed for battle. The army will be very large, with all the men holding battle-coverings and waving swords. 5 Persia, Ethiopia, and Put will be with you, all with battle-coverings and head-coverings. 6 There will be Gomer with all its army, and Beth togarmah from the farthest parts of the north with all its army. Many nations will be with you.

7 "Get ready and keep ready, you and all the armies gathered around you, and watch over them. 8 After many days you will be called. In future years you will come into the land where people have been gathered from many nations and have lived without fear of war. You will come to the mountains of Israel, which had been a waste-land for a long time. But its people were brought out from the nations, and all of them are living without fear. 9 You and all your army will come up against them like a storm. You will be like a cloud covering the land. Many nations will be with you."

10 'The Lord God says, "On that day, thoughts will come into your mind, and you will make a sinful plan. 11 You will say, 'I will go up against the open country,

where people are quiet and live in peace. They live in villages without walls and have no iron pieces or gates.' 12 You will go to rob the land and fight in the waste places where people now live. You will go up against the people who were gathered from the nations and are rich with cattle and good things and who live at the center of the land. 13 Sheba and Dedan and the traders of Tarshish and all its villages will say to you, 'Have you come to take prizes of war? Have you gathered your army to carry away silver and gold, cattle, good things, and many prizes of war?' "'

14 "So, son of man, speak in My name and tell Gog, 'The Lord God says, "On that day when My people Israel are living in peace and without fear, will you not know it? 15 You will come from your place in the far north, and many nations will be with you. All of them will be riding on horses, a large and powerful army. 16 You will come up against My people Israel like a cloud covering the land. In the last days, O Gog, I will bring you against My land, so that the nations may know Me when I show Myself holy through you in front of their eyes." 17 The Lord God says, "Are you the one I spoke of in the past, through My servants of Israel who spoke in My name? At that time they said for many years that I would bring you against them.

18 "On the day when Gog comes against the land of Israel, I will become very angry," says the Lord God. 19 "In My jealousy and in My burning anger I have said that on that day the earth will shake in the land of Israel. 20 The fish of the sea, the birds of the air, the wild animals of the field, all the animals that move upon the earth, and all the men on the earth will shake before Me. Mountains will be thrown down, the mountain-sides will fall, and every wall will fall to the ground. 21 I will call for a sword against Gog on all My mountains," says the Lord God. "His men will turn their swords against one another. 22 I will punish each with disease and with blood. I will send down a hard rain, hailstones, fire and sulphur upon him and his army and the many nations with him. 23 I will show the many nations that I am great and holy. And they will know that I am the Lord."

Gog's Armies Are Destroyed

39 "Son of man, speak against Gog, and tell him, 'The Lord God says, "I am against you, O Gog, leader of Rosh, Meshech, and Tubal. 2 I will turn you

around and drive you on. I will bring you from the farthest parts of the north and lead you against the mountains of Israel. 3 I will knock your bow out of your left hand, and knock your arrows out of your right hand. 4 You will fall dead on the mountains of Israel, you and all your army and the nations who are with you. I will feed you to every kind of meat-eating bird and wild animal of the field. 5 You will fall dead in the open field, for I have spoken," says the Lord God. 6 "I will send fire upon Magog and upon those who think they are safe in the islands. Then they will know that I am the Lord.

7 "I will make My holy name known among My people Israel. I will not let My holy name be made unclean any more. And the nations will know that I am the Lord, the Holy One in Israel. 8 It is coming, and it will be done," says the Lord God. "This is the day I have spoken of.

9 "Then those who live in the cities of Israel will go out and make fires to burn up the objects of war. They will burn battle-coverings, bows and arrows, heavy sticks, and spears. For seven years they will use them to make fires. 10 They will not take wood from the field or from among the trees to burn. For they will make fires with the objects of war. And they will rob those who robbed them," says the Lord God.

Gog Is Buried

11 "On that day I will give Gog a place in Israel for burying his dead. It will be the valley of those who travel east of the sea. And it will close that road to travelers, for Gog and all his people will be buried there. They will call it the Valley of Hamon-Gog. 12 It will take the people of Israel seven months to bury the dead and make the land clean again. 13 All the people of the land will bury them, and they will be honored for this on the day that I show My greatness," says the Lord God. 14 "At the end of seven months, they will choose men to pass through the land to look for bodies that may be left on the ground. And the bodies will be buried to make the land clean. 15 Those who pass through and see a man's bone will set up something to mark the place, until it is buried in the valley of Hamon-Gog. 16 (There will be a city called Hamonah there also.) And so they will make the land clean." '"

17 "Son of man, the Lord God says, 'Speak to every kind of bird and to every wild animal of the field. Say to them, "Gather

together and come. Come together from
every side to the special supper I have
made for you. Much food has been killed
for you on the mountains of Israel. You
will eat flesh and drink blood. **18** You will
eat the flesh of powerful men, and drink
the blood of the leaders of the earth. It will
be as if they were rams, lambs, goats, and
bulls, all of them fat animals of Bashan.
19 You will eat fat until you are filled, and
drink blood until you are drunk, at the
special supper I have killed and made
ready for you. **20** You will be filled at My
table with horses and horsemen, with
powerful men and all the men of war,"
says the Lord God.

The Land Is Given Back to Israel

21 "I will show My greatness among the
nations. All the nations will see how I
have punished Israel and My hand which
I have laid on them. **22** Then the people of
Israel will know that I am the Lord their
God from that day on. **23** The nations will
know that the people of Israel were taken
from their land because of their sin, because they were not faithful to Me. So I hid
My face from them and gave them over to
those who hated them, and they died in
battle. **24** I punished them because they
were unclean and sinful, and I hid My face
from them.' "

25 So the Lord God says, "Now I will return the people of Jacob to their land and
show loving-kindness to all the people of
Israel. And I will be jealous for My holy
name. **26** They will forget their shame and
how unfaithful they were to Me, when
they live in peace on their own land with
no one to make them afraid. **27** I will bring
them back from the nations and gather
them from the lands of those who hate
them. In this way I will show the many
nations that I am holy. **28** Then they will
know that I am the Lord their God, because I sent them away into the other
nations and then gathered them again to
their own land. And I will not leave any of
them there any longer. **29** I will not hide
My face from them again, for I will pour
out My Spirit on the people of Israel," says
the Lord God.

A New House of God

40 It was the twenty-fifth year since
the people of Israel were taken
away to a strange land, at the beginning
of the year, on the tenth of the month, and
fourteen years since Jerusalem was taken

in battle. On that day the hand of the Lord
was upon me and He brought me there.
2 In a special way God brought me into
the land of Israel and set me on a very
high mountain. There were some buildings on its south side that looked like a city.
3 He took me there, and I saw a man who
looked like he was made of brass. In his
hand was a linen rope and a stick to find
how long something is. He was standing
at the gate. **4** And the man said to me, "Son
of man, look with your eyes, hear with
your ears, and think about all I am going
to show you. For you have been brought
here so that I may show it to you. Tell the
people of Israel everything you see."

The East Gate

5 I saw a wall all around the outside of the
house of the Lord. The stick in the man's
hand was six cubits long (with the width
of a hand being added to the length of each
arm). And with it he showed that the wall
was one stick wide and one stick high.
6 Then he went up the steps of the east
gate, and showed me with his stick that the
gateway was one stick wide, and the other
gate was also one stick wide. **7** The rooms
for the watchmen were each one stick
long and one stick wide, and they were
five cubits apart. And the gateway next
to the porch toward the Lord's house was
one stick wide. **8** Then he showed me with
his stick that the porch of the inside gate
was one-tenth stick wide. **9** The porch of
the gate was eight cubits and its side pillars
two cubits wide. The porch of the gate was
on the inside. **10** There were three rooms
for the watchmen on each side of the east
gate. They all had the same length and
width. And the pillars on each side were
the same in width. **11** Then he showed
me that the opening of the gateway was
ten cubits wide and thirteen cubits long.
12 There was a wall one-tenth cubit wide
in front of the watchmen's rooms on each
side. And the watchmen's rooms were six
cubits wide and six cubits long. **13** Then he
showed me that it was twenty-five cubits
from the roof of one room to the roof of
the room across from it. **14** He showed me
that it was twenty cubits around the walls
inside the gateway, up to the porch facing
the open space. **15** It was fifteen cubits
from the front of the outer gate to the front
of the porch of the inner gate. **16** There
were narrow windows looking toward the
watchmen's rooms and toward their side
pillars, all around inside the gate and also

in the porches. And pictures of palm trees were cut on each side pillar.

The Outside Open Space

17 Then he brought me into the outer open space, and I saw rooms and a stone floor all around it. Thirty rooms were around the stone floor. 18 The lower stone floor was beside the gates, and was as wide as the gates. 19 Then he showed me how far it was from the inside of the lower gate to the outside of the inner open space. Both east and north sides were 100 cubits each.

The North Gate

20 He then showed me the length and width of the north gate of the outer open space. 21 It had three rooms on each side for the watchmen. Its side pillars and porches were as long and as wide as the first gate. It was as long as fifty cubits, and as wide as twenty-five cubits. 22 Its windows, its porches, and palm tree pictures were the same length and width as those of the east gate. Seven steps led up to it, and its porch was in front of them. 23 Across from the north gate was another gate leading to the inner open space, just as there was for the east gate. He showed me that it was 100 cubits from gate to gate.

The South Gate

24 Then he led me to the south, and I saw a gate toward the south. He showed me the length and width of its side pillars and its porches, and they were the same as the others. 25 The gate and its porches had windows like the others all around and was as long as fifty cubits and as wide as twenty-five cubits. 26 Seven steps led up to it, and its porches were in front of them. And it had pictures of palm trees on its side pillars, one on each side. 27 The open space had a gate toward the south. He showed me that it was 100 cubits from gate to gate toward the south.

The Inside Open Space

28 Then he brought me to the inner open space by the south gate, and showed me that this gate had the same width as the others. 29 Its watchmen's rooms, side pillars and porches were also the same as the others and had windows all around. It was as long as fifty cubits and as wide as twenty-five cubits. 30 (There were porches all around, as long as twenty-five cubits and five cubits wide) 31 and its porches were toward the outer open space. Pictures of palm trees were on its side pillars, and leading up to it were eight steps.

32 Then he brought me to the inner open space toward the east. He showed me that it was as wide as the others. 33 Its watchmen's rooms, side pillars and porches were also the same as the others and, there were windows all around which were as long as fifty cubits and as wide as twenty-five cubits. 34 Its gateway was toward the outer open space. Pictures of palm trees were on its side pillars, on each side. And going up to it were eight steps.

35 Then he brought me to the north gate, and showed me that it was the same width as the others. 36 Its watchmen's rooms, side pillars and porches were also the same as the others. There were windows all around and it was as long as fifty cubits and as wide as twenty-five cubits. 37 Its side pillars were toward the outer open space. Pictures of palm trees were on its side pillars, on each side. And going up to it were eight steps.

Where the Burnt Gifts Were Made Ready

38 There was a room with its door by the side pillars, where the burnt gifts were washed. 39 And there were two tables on each side of the porch. On these tables the animals were killed for the burnt gifts, the sin gifts, and the guilt gifts. 40 On the outer side of the gateway, by the north gate, were two tables. And there were two tables on the other side of the gate. 41 So there were four tables on each side of the gateway, eight tables in all, where they killed the animals for the altar. 42 There were four tables for the burnt gifts. They were made of cut stone, and were one and a half cubits long, one and a half cubits wide, and one cubit high. The objects used for killing the animals for the burnt gifts were kept on these stone tables. 43 Hooks as long as a man's hand hung on the wall all around. The tables were for the meat of the burnt gifts.

44 Then he brought me from the outside into the inner open space and there were two rooms for the singers. One was at the side of the north gate which faced the south, and the other was at the side of the south gate which faced the north. 45 And he said to me, "This room which faces the south is for the religious leaders who take care of the Lord's house. 46 The room which faces the north is for the religious leaders who take care of the altar. These are the sons of Zadok, who are the only Levites who may come near the Lord to do His work."

The Inside Open Space and the House of God

47 He showed me that the inner open space was as long as one hundred cubits and as wide as one hundred cubits, the same on all four sides. And the altar was in front of the Lord's house.

48 Then he brought me to the porch of the Lord's house. He showed me that each side pillar of the porch was five cubits wide. And each side of the gate was three cubits wide. **49** The porch was as long as twenty cubits, and six steps wide. Ten steps led up to it, and there was one pillar on each side.

41 Then he brought me into the center room, and showed me the width of the side pillars. They were six cubits wide on each side. **2** The doorway was ten cubits wide, and the side walls on each side of it were five cubits wide. The center room was as long as forty cubits and as wide as twenty cubits. **3** Then he went into a smaller room. Each side pillar of the doorway was two cubits wide, and the doorway was six cubits high and seven cubits wide. **4** The room was as long as twenty cubits and as wide as twenty cubits, at the far end of the center room. He said to me, "This is the most holy place."

5 Then he showed me that the wall of the Lord's house was six cubits in width. And the side rooms all around the house on every side were four cubits wide. **6** The side rooms were on three floors, one above the other, and thirty on each floor. The outside wall on each floor was not as wide as the one below it, so the side rooms could sit upon the wall without being nailed to it. **7** The side rooms at the top were larger than the ones at the bottom, all around the Lord's house. The house became wider as it went higher. There were steps leading up from the first floor all the way to the third floor. **8** I saw that the house had a raised base all around it, which made the base for the side rooms six cubits high. **9** The width of the outside wall of the side rooms was five cubits. But the open space between the side rooms **10** and the center rooms was as wide as twenty cubits all around the house on every side. **11** There were doorways to the side rooms from this open space, one on the north and another on the south. The width of this open space was five cubits wide all around.

12 The building in front of the open space of the Lord's house, on the west side, was as wide as seventy cubits. The width of the building wall was five cubits, and it was as long as ninety cubits.

13 Then he showed me that the Lord's house was as long as 100 cubits. The open space and the other building and its walls were also as long as 100 cubits. **14** And the front of the Lord's house and its grounds on the east side were as wide as 100 cubits.

15 He showed me the length of the building to the west, with its walkways on each side. It was as long as one hundred cubits. The center room, the most holy place, and the outer porch, **16** all had roofs of wood. And all three had windows with wooden cross-pieces all around. The inside walls of the house were covered with wood from the floor up to the windows, and from the windows to the roof. **17** There was wood covering the wall above the door, and all the way to the most holy place, and all the walls both inside and out. **18** Pictures of cherubim and palm trees were cut into the wood. A palm tree was between every two cherubim, and each cherub had two faces. **19** The face of a man looked toward the palm tree on one side, and the face of a young lion looked toward the palm tree on the other side. These pictures were cut into the wood all around the Lord's house. **20** There were cherubim and palm trees from the floor to above the door, and on the wall of the center room.

21 The pillars beside the door of the center room were the same width on all four sides, and they looked alike. **22** There was an altar of wood three cubits high and two cubits long. Its corners, base, and sides were made of wood. And he said to me, "This is the table that is before the Lord." **23** The center room and the most holy place each had two doors. **24** And each of these doors had two parts that opened and closed. **25** Pictures of cherubim and palm trees were made on the doors of the center room, like the pictures on the walls. And there was a roof of wood over the front of the porch outside. **26** There were windows with wooden cross-pieces and palm trees cut on each side wall of the house porch. It was the same on the side rooms of the house and their roofs.

Rooms for the Religious Leaders

42 Then he brought me to the outside open space toward the north. He brought me to the rooms which were on the other side of the open space and the building to the north. 2 The building whose door faced north was as long as one hundred cubits and as wide as fifty cubits. 3 Over from the place in the inner open space which was as wide as twenty cubits, and over from the stone floor in the outer open space, was a walkway on the three floors, one above the other. 4 In front of the rooms was an inside walkway as wide as ten cubits and as long as 100 cubits. Their doors were on the north. 5 The upper rooms were smaller because the walkways took more away from them than from the rooms on the first and second floors of the building. 6 For the rooms on all three floors had no pillars like the other buildings on the grounds. So the upper rooms were smaller than the ones on the first and second floors. 7 There was an outside wall built beside the rooms toward the outer open space. It was in front of the rooms for fifty cubits. 8 The rooms next to the outer open space were as long as fifty cubits, and those over from the Lord's house were as long as 100 cubits. 9 Below these rooms was a door on the east side, as one goes into them from the outer open space.

10 There were rooms in the width of the wall of the open space toward the east, over from the other open space and the other building. 11 These rooms had a walkway in front of them, and they were like the rooms on the north. They had the same length and width. The ways out of them were the same, and the doors were made the same way. 12 And like the doors of the rooms on the south side, there was a door at the beginning of the walkway in front of the wall toward the east, as one goes into them.

13 Then he said to me, "The north rooms and the south rooms, over from the other open space, are the holy rooms where the religious leaders who go near the Lord eat the most holy things. There they will lay the most holy things, the grain gift, the sin gift, and the guilt gift. For the place is holy. 14 When the religious leaders go in, they are not to go out into the outer open space from the holy place without leaving behind the clothes they wear while they do the Lord's work, for these are holy. They must put on other clothes before they go near the places that are for the people."

15 When he had finished showing me the lengths and widths of the inner house, he brought me out through the east gate. And he showed me the lengths of all the open space around the house.

16 He showed me with his stick that the east side was as long as 500 sticks. 17 The north side was as long as 500 sticks. 18 The south side was as long as 500 sticks. 19 And the west side was as long as 500 sticks. 20 He showed me the length of the four sides. It had a wall all around it, as long as 500 sticks and as wide as 500 sticks. This wall divided what was holy from what was not.

The Lord Returns to the House of God

43 Then he brought me to the east gate, 2 and I saw the shining-greatness of the God of Israel coming from the east. His voice was like the sound of many waters, and the earth was shining because of His greatness. 3 It was like the special dream that I saw when He came to destroy the city. It was like the special dream that I saw by the Chebar River. I fell with my face to the ground. 4 As the shining-greatness of the Lord came into the house through the east gate, 5 the Spirit lifted me up and brought me into the inner open space. And the shining-greatness of the Lord filled the house.

6 While the man was standing beside me, I heard Someone speaking to me from inside the house. 7 And He said to me, "Son of man, this is the place for My throne and for the bottom of My feet, where I will live among the people of Israel forever. No longer will the people of Israel or their kings make My holy name unclean, by worshiping other gods or by the dead bodies of their kings. 8 They put their doorways by My doorways, and their door pillars beside My door pillars, with only a wall between Me and them. In doing so, they have made My holy name unclean by the hated sins they have done. So I have destroyed them in My anger. 9 Now let them put their worship of other gods and the dead bodies of their kings far from Me. And I will live among them forever.

10 "Son of man, tell the people of Israel about the house of the Lord, that they may be ashamed of their sins. Let them look over the plan. 11 And if they are ashamed of all that they have done, let them know how the house is built, the house with its doors and gateways, and its whole plan. Let them know all its laws. Write it down in front of them, so that they will see its whole plan and obey all its laws. 12 This is the law of the house: All the ground around it on top of the mountain will be most holy. This is the law of the house.

The Altar

13 "This is the length, width, and height of the altar by cubits (with the length of the hand being added to the length of each arm). The base will be one cubit long and one cubit wide, with a side piece going around it as wide as a man's spread hand. This will be the height of the altar: 14 The base will be two cubits long from the base on the ground to its top, and one cubit wide. And it will be four cubits from the smaller part up to its larger top part, and one cubit wide. 15 The altar fireplace will be four cubits high, and four horns will go up from the top four corners of the altar one cubit high. 16 This top part of the altar will be twelve cubits long and twelve cubits wide, the same on each of the four sides. 17 The side of it will be fourteen cubits long and fourteen cubits wide, the same on each of the four sides. And a side piece half a cubit will be around that. Its base will be a cubit wide all around, and its steps will be on the east side."

18 And He said to me, "Son of man, the Lord God says, 'These are the laws for giving burnt gifts and for putting blood on the altar on the day it is built: 19 You must give a young bull for a sin gift to the Levite religious leaders of the sons of Zadok. They are the ones who come near Me to do My work,' says the Lord God. 20 'You must take some of the bull's blood and put it on the four horns of the altar, and on the four corners of the top of the altar, and on the side piece that goes around it. In this way you will make it clean and free from sin. 21 You must also take the bull for the sin gift, and burn it in the chosen place of the house, outside the holy place. 22 On the second day you must give a male goat that is perfect for a sin gift. And the altar will be made clean, as it was made clean with the bull. 23 When you have finished making it clean, you must give a young bull that is perfect, and a ram from the flock that is perfect. 24 You must bring them before the Lord. The religious leaders will throw salt on them, and burn them on the altar as a gift to the Lord. 25 You must make ready a goat for a sin gift each day for seven days. Also make ready a young bull and a ram from the flock. They must be perfect. 26 For seven days they must make the altar free from sin and make it pure, so it will be set apart for Me. 27 At the end of these days, from the eighth day on, the religious leaders will give your burnt gifts and peace gifts on the altar. And I will receive you,' says the Lord God."

The Use of the East Gate

44 Then he brought me back to the outer gate of the holy place, toward the east, and it was shut. 2 The Lord said to me, "This gate must stay shut. It must not be opened. No one may come in through it, for the Lord God of Israel has come in through it. So it must stay shut. 3 Only the ruler may sit at the gate to eat bread before the Lord. He must come in through the porch of the gate, and go out the same way."

Those Who Could Go In to the House of God

4 Then he brought me by way of the north gate to the front of the house. There I saw the shining-greatness of the Lord filling the Lord's house, and I fell with my face to the ground. 5 The Lord said to me, "Son of man, be careful to see with your eyes and to hear with your ears everything that I say to you about all the rules and laws of the Lord's house. Be careful to learn which persons are allowed to go in and out of the Lord's house, and which persons are not allowed. 6 Tell the sinful people of Israel, 'The Lord God says, "Enough of your hated sins, O people of Israel! 7 You have brought in strangers, who had not gone through the religious act of becoming a Jew, and who were sinful in their heart. You brought them into My holy place to make it unclean, when you brought My food of the fat and the blood. You have broken My agreement by all your hated sins. 8 And you have not taken care of My holy things yourselves. You have let strangers take care of My holy place." 9 So the Lord God says, "No stranger among the people of Israel who has not gone through the religious act of becoming a Jew, and is sinful in his heart, may come into My holy place,

Levites Cannot Be Religious Leaders

10 "The Levites who went far from Me when Israel left Me to follow their false gods, will be punished for their sin. 11 They may do the work in My holy place. They may watch over the gates of the house and do the work in the house. They may kill the burnt gifts and the gifts brought by the people. And they may stand in front of the people to serve them. 12 But because they served them in front of their false gods and caused the people of Israel to sin, I have promised," says the Lord God, "that they will be punished for their sin. 13 They must not come near Me to serve Me as a

religious leader. They must not come near any of My holy things and the things that are most holy. But they must suffer their shame because of the hated sins they have done. 14 Yet I will have them take care of the house and do all the work that is needed to be done in it.

Zadok's Sons to Serve in the House of God

15 "But the Levite religious leaders of the sons of Zadok took care of My holy place when the people of Israel left Me. So they will come near Me to serve Me. They will stand before Me to give Me the fat and the blood," says the Lord God. 16 "They will come into My holy place and come near My table, to serve Me and to do My work. 17 When they come through the gates of the inner open space, they will be dressed in linen clothing. They must not wear any wool while they are serving inside the gates of the inner open space or in the house. 18 They will wear linen head-coverings and linen underclothes. They must not dress in anything that makes their bodies wet with heat. 19 When they go out to the people in the outer open space, they must take off the clothes they wear while they serve Me, and lay them in the holy rooms. Then they will put on other clothes, so that they do not make the people holy because of their clothing. 20 And they must not cut all the hair from their heads, yet they must not let their hair grow long. They must only cut their hair shorter. 21 None of the religious leaders may drink wine when they come into the inner open space. 22 They must not marry a woman whose husband has died, or who has been divorced. But they may marry women of Israel who have never had a man, or a woman whose husband was a religious leader before he died. 23 They will teach My people the difference between what is holy and what is not. And they will teach them to know what is unclean and what is clean. 24 In an argument, the religious leaders will serve as judges, and will judge by My Laws. They will also keep My Laws in all My special suppers. And they will keep My Day of Rest holy. 25 They must not make themselves unclean by going near a dead person. But they may make themselves unclean if the dead person is their father or mother, son or daughter, brother, or sister who was not married. 26 After a religious leader has become clean again, he must wait seven days. 27 And on the day he goes into the holy place, into the inner open space to serve in the holy place, he must bring his sin gift," says the Lord God.

28 "I am to be the only part that the religious leaders have. You must not give them any land in Israel for their own. I am their part. 29 They will eat the grain gift, the sin gift, and the guilt gift. Everything in Israel that is set apart to Me will be theirs. 30 The first of all the first-fruits of every kind, and every kind of gift you bring, will be for the religious leaders. And you must give them the first of your grain, so that good will come to your house. 31 The religious leaders must not eat any bird or animal that has died of itself or has been torn to pieces.

The Land Is Divided

45 "When the land is divided and each family receives its part, you must give a part to the Lord. This will be a holy piece of land, as long as 12,500 long steps and as wide as 5,000 long steps. This whole piece of land will be holy. 2 Of this, there will be a piece of land for the holy place, as long as 250 long steps and as wide as 250 long steps. It will have four sides of the same length. And there will be an open space around it as wide as fifty cubits. 3 In the holy piece of land, number a length of 12,500 long steps and a width of 5,000 long steps. And in it will be the most holy place. 4 It will be the holy part of the land. It will be for the religious leaders, those who do the work in the holy place, who come near to serve the Lord. It will also be a place for their houses, and a holy place for the Lord's House. 5 Another piece of land as long as 12,500 long steps and as wide as 5,000 long steps will be for the Levites who serve in the house. It will be land to build their houses on. 6 Next to the holy piece of land, another piece as wide as 2,500 long steps and as long as 12,500 long steps will be set aside for a city belonging to all the people of Israel. 7 The ruler will have land on both sides of the holy piece of land and the place for the city. His land will be next to these two pieces of land, on the west side and on the east side. It will be as long as one of the shares of land, from the west side of the whole land to the east side. 8 This land in Israel will belong to him. So My rulers will no longer make it hard for My people. They will give the rest of the land to the people of Israel by their family groups."

9 'The Lord God says, "Enough, you rulers of Israel! Stop ruling in bad ways with your power and do what is right and good. Stop driving My people off their land," says the Lord God. 10 "Be honest in your weights. 11 One barrel of grain must be the same amount as one barrel of water. And one-tenth part of a barrel of grain must be the same amount as one-tenth part of a barrel of water. 12 The silver piece of money must be worth the same as twenty small silver pieces. And sixty silver pieces of money must be worth the same as the heavy silver weight.

13 "This is the gift that you must bring: One-sixtieth part of a barrel of wheat, one-sixtieth part of a barrel of barley, 14 and one-hundredth part of a barrel of oil. 15 Also bring one lamb from each flock of 200 sheep from the well-watered fields of Israel. Bring them for a grain gift, a burnt gift, and a peace gift, to pay for the people's sins," says the Lord God. 16 "All the people of the land must take these gifts to the ruler in Israel. 17 It will be the ruler's duty to bring the burnt gifts, the grain gifts, and the drink gifts, to the special suppers on the new moons and on the Days of Rest, and to all the special suppers of the people of Israel. He must bring the sin gift, the grain gift, the burnt gift, and the peace gifts, to pay for the sins of the people of Israel."

The Special Suppers

10 "The Lord God says, "On the first day of the first month, you must take a young bull that is perfect and make the holy place clean. 19 The religious leader will take some of the blood from the sin gift and put it on the door pillars of the house, on the four corners of the altar, and on the pillars of the gate of the inner open space. 20 You must do the same on the seventh day of the month for every one who sins by mistake or because he does not know any better. In this way you will keep the Lord's house holy.

21 "On the fourteenth day of the first month, you will have the Passover, a special supper that lasts for seven days. Every one will eat bread made without yeast. 22 On that day the ruler is to bring a bull as a sin gift for himself and all the people of the land. 23 During the seven days of the special supper he will bring as a burnt gift to the Lord seven bulls and seven rams that are perfect, on each of the seven days. And he will bring a male

goat each day for a sin gift. 24 For a grain gift he will bring a tenth part of a barrel of grain for each bull, a tenth part of a barrel for each ram. And he will bring a large jar of oil for each tenth part of a barrel of grain. 25 On the fifteenth day of the seventh month, and for the seven days of the special supper, he is to bring the same amount for the sin gift, the burnt gift, the grain gift, and the oil."

The Way of Worship

46 'The Lord God says, "The east gate of the inner open space must stay shut during the six working days. But it may be opened on the Day of Rest and on the day of the new moon. 2 The ruler will come in through the porch of the gate from outside and stand by the pillar of the gate. The religious leaders will make ready his burnt gift and his peace gifts, and he will worship at the gate and then go out. But the gate will not be shut until evening. 3 The people of the land will also worship at the gate before the Lord on the Days of Rest and on the new moons. 4 The burnt gift the ruler gives to the Lord on the Day of Rest will be six lambs that are perfect and a ram that is perfect. 5 The grain gift will be one-tenth part of a barrel of grain with the ram, and as much grain as he is able to give with the lambs. And he will give a large jar of oil with each tenth part of a barrel of grain. 6 On the day of the new moon he will give a young bull that is perfect, and six lambs and a ram that are perfect. 7 He will give a grain gift, one-tenth part of a barrel of grain with the bull, one-tenth part of a barrel of grain with the ram, and as much grain as he is able to give with the lambs. And he will give a large jar of oil with each tenth part of a barrel of grain. 8 When the ruler comes in, he must come in through this gateway, and go out the same way. 9 But when the people of the land come before the Lord at the special suppers, he who comes in through the north gate to worship must go out through the south gate. And he who comes in through the south gate must go out through the north gate. No one should leave through the same gate that he came in. Each person must go out the gate on the other side from where he came in. 10 The ruler should come in when the people come in, and leave when they come. 11 At the special times and special suppers, the grain gift will be one-tenth part of a barrel of grain with a

bull, and one-tenth part of a barrel with a ram. A person should give as much grain as he is able to give with the lambs. And he will give a large jar of oil with each tenth part of a barrel of grain. 12 When the ruler brings a free-will gift to the Lord, a burnt gift or a peace gift, the east gate must be opened for him. He will bring his burnt gift and his peace gifts as he does on the Day of Rest. Then he will leave, and the gate will be shut after he goes out.

13 "You must bring a one-year-old lamb that is perfect for a burnt gift to the Lord each day. Morning by morning you must bring it. 14 And you must bring a grain gift with it each morning. Bring one-sixtieth part of a barrel of grain, and one-third part of a large jar of oil to mix with the flour. This is the law for the grain gift to the Lord forever. 15 In this way the lamb, the grain gift and the oil will be brought each morning for a burnt gift forever."

16 The Lord God says, "If the ruler gives some of his land to any of his sons, it will belong to his sons. They will own the land for their families. 17 But if he gives some of his land to one of his servants, it will be his until the year he is set free. Then it will be returned to the ruler. His land may be kept only by his sons. It will belong to them. 18 The ruler must not take any land from the people, driving them away from what belongs to them. He must give only his own land to his sons, so that My people will not be divided from what belongs to them." ' "

19 Then he brought me through the door beside the gate into the holy rooms for the religious leaders, toward the north. And I saw a place at the far west end. 20 He said to me, "This is the place where the religious leaders will boil the guilt gift and the sin gift, and make the grain gift ready. This is so they will not bring them into the outer open space and make the people holy." 21 Then he brought me into the outer open space and led me to its four corners. And in every corner I saw a small open space. 22 In the four corners there were open spaces with walls around them, as long as twenty long steps and as wide as fifteen long steps. All four spaces in the corners were the same in length and width. 23 There was a fireplace of stone all around in each of them. 24 Then he said to me, "These are the places where those who serve in the house will boil the gifts brought by the people."

The River Coming from the House of God

47 Then he brought me back to the door of the house. And I saw water flowing from under the doorway toward the east, for the house looked toward the east. The water was flowing from under the right side of the house, from south of the altar. 2 He brought me out through the north gate and led me around on the outside to the east gate. And I saw water coming from the south side.

3 Going toward the east, the man numbered 500 long steps, and he led me through the water, which covered my feet. 4 He numbered another 500 long steps and led me through the water, which came up to my knees. He numbered another 500 long steps and led me through the water. This time it came above my legs. 5 Again he numbered 500 long steps, and it was a river that I could not walk through. The water had risen. It was deep enough to swim in, and no one could cross it. 6 He said to me, "Son of man, do you see this?"

Then he brought me back to the side of the river. 7 As I returned, I saw that there were very many trees on both sides of the river. 8 He said to me, "These waters go out toward the east country and down into the Arabah, then flow into the Dead sea. When they flow into the sea, the waters there become clean again. 9 Every living thing that gathers where the river goes will live. There will be very many fish, because these waters go there and make the salt water clean. So everything will live where the river goes. 10 Fishermen will stand beside it. They will have places to spread their nets from Engedi to Eneglaim. The fish will be of many kinds, like the fish of the Great Sea. 11 But its wet places and pools will not be good for animal life. They will be left for salt. 12 All kinds of fruit trees will grow on both sides of the river. Their leaves will not dry up, and they will never stop giving fruit. They will give fruit every month because their water flows from the holy place. Their fruit will be for food and their leaves for healing."

13 The Lord God says, "This is how you should divide the land among the twelve family groups of Israel. Joseph will have two parts. 14 You must divide the land so each family receives the same amount. For I promised to give this land to your fathers, and it will be your land to own.

15 "This will be the side of the land: The north side will go from the Great Sea by

way of Hethlon, and on to Zedad, 16 Hamath, Berothah, Sibraim (between the lands of Damascus and Hamath), and to Hazer-hatticon, by the land of Hauran. 17 So the land will spread from the sea to Hazarenan on the north side of Damascus, with the land of Hamath toward the north. This will be the north side. 18 The east side of the land will go from between Hauran and Damascus along the Jordan between Gilead and the land of Israel, to the sea in the east. This will be the east side. 19 The south side of the land will go from Tamar as far as the waters of Meribath-kadesh, then to the River of Egypt and to the Great Sea. This will be the south side. 20 The west side of the land will be the Great Sea, to a place beside Lebo-hamath. This will be the west side.

21 "So divide this land among your family groups of Israel. 22 Divide it by drawing names for yourselves and for the people from other lands who live with you and raise their children among you. You are to think of them as if they were born Israelites. They must be given a share of land with you among the families of Israel. 23 The man from another country must be given a share of land among the family group he lives with," says the Lord God.

The Land Divided among the Family Groups

48 "These are the names of the family groups. Dan will have one share of land at the far north. His land will follow the Hethlon road to Lebo-hamath, as far as Hazar-enan beside the land of Damascus, toward the north beside Hamath, going from east to west. 2 Asher will have one share of land beside Dan, from the east side to the west side. 3 Naphtali will have one share beside Asher, from the east side to the west side. 4 Manasseh will have one share beside Naphtali, from the east side to the west side. 5 Ephraim will have one share beside Manasseh, from the east side to the west side. 6 Reuben will have one share beside Ephraim, from the east side to the west side. 7 Judah will have one share beside Reuben, from the east side to the west side.

8 "Beside Judah, from the east side to the west side, will be the share of land you must set apart as a special gift. It will be as wide as 12,500 long steps, and as long as one of the other shares of land, from the east side to the west side. And the holy place will be in the center of it. 9 The gift of land that you will set apart to the Lord will be as long as 12,500 long steps and as wide as 5,000 long steps. 10 There will be a holy part for the religious leaders. It will be as long as 12,500 long steps on the north side, 5,000 long steps on the west side, 5,000 long steps on the east side, and 12,500 long steps on the south side. The holy house of the Lord will be in the center of it. 11 It will be for the religious leaders who are set apart of the sons of Zadok, who have been faithful in serving Me. They did not sin as the Levites did when the people of Israel went the wrong way. 12 It will belong to them as a special gift from part of the land, a most holy place, beside the land of the Levites. 13 The Levites will have land beside the religious leaders, as long as 12,500 long steps and as wide as 5,000 long steps. The whole length will be 12,500 long steps, and the width 5,000 long steps. 14 They must not sell or trade any of it. This is the best part of the land, and it must not pass into other hands. For it is holy to the Lord.

15 "The rest of the land, 2,500 long steps in width and 12,500 long steps in length, will be for all the people. It will be for houses and for open fields, and the city will be in the center of it. 16 The city will be 2,250 long steps on each of its four sides. 17 And it will have open fields, 125 long steps in width, all around the city. 18 The rest of the length beside the holy part of the land will be 5,000 long steps toward the east and 5,000 long steps toward the west. This will be where food is grown for those who work in the city. 19 And the workers of the city, from all the family groups of Israel, will work the ground. 20 The whole piece of land will be as long as 12,500 long steps on each of its four sides. You will set apart the holy piece of land, together with the land for the city.

21 "The rest of the land will be for the ruler, on both sides of the holy piece of land and of the land for the city. It will go from the 12,500 long steps of the holy piece of land all the way to the east side, and from the 12,500 long steps all the way to the west side, along the shares for the family groups. It will belong to the ruler. The holy piece of land and the house of the Lord will be in the center of it. 22 So the land of the Levites and the land of the city will be in the center of the ruler's land. And the ruler's land will be between the land of Judah and the land of Benjamin.

23 "As for the rest of the family groups, Benjamin will have one share of land,

It will spread from the east side to the west side. 24 Simeon will have one share beside Benjamin, from the east side to the west side. 25 Issachar will have one share beside Simeon, from the east side to the west side. 26 Zebulun will have one share beside Issachar, from the east side to the west side. 27 Gad will have one share beside Zebulun, from the east side to the west side. 28 The south side of Gad's share will be from Tamar to the waters of Meribath-kadesh, then to the River of Egypt and to the Great Sea. 29 This is the land you will give by drawing names to the family groups of Israel for their own. And these are their shares," says the Lord God.

The Gates of Jerusalem

30 "These are the gates of the city: Beginning on the north side, which is as long as 2,250 long steps, 31 the gates of the city will be given the names of the family groups of Israel. The three gates on the north side will be the gate of Reuben, the gate of Judah, and the gate of Levi. 32 The east side is as long as 2,250 long steps. The three gates on this side will be the gate of Joseph, the gate of Benjamin, and the gate of Dan. 33 The south side is as long as 2,250 long steps. The three gates on this side will be the gate of Simeon, the gate of Issachar, and the gate of Zebulun. 34 And the west side is as long as 2,250 long steps. The three gates on this side will be the gate of Gad, the gate of Asher, and the gate of Naphtali. 35 It will be 9,000 long steps around the city. And the name of the city from that time on will be: 'The Lord is there.' "

DANIEL

Daniel Obeys God

1 In the third year that Jehoiakim was king of Judah, King Nebuchadnezzar of Babylon came against Jerusalem. His army was all around the city. 2 The Lord let him take King Jehoiakim of Judah, with some of the objects of the house of God. He brought them to the house of his god in the land of Shinar, and put the objects into the store-room of his god. 3 Then the king told Ashpenaz, his head ruler, to bring in some of the sons of Israel, both those of the king's family and of the important leaders. 4 They were to be young men, perfect in body, good-looking, with wisdom, understanding, much learning, and able to serve in the king's house. The king told Ashpenaz to teach them the writings and language of the Babylonians. 5 And the king gave them a share of his best food and wine every day. They were to be taught for three years, and after that they were to serve the king. 6 Among these were Daniel, Hananiah, Mishael, and Azariah from the sons of Judah. 7 The king's head ruler gave them new names. To Daniel he gave the name Belteshazzar. To Hananiah he gave the name Shadrach. To Mishael he gave the name Meshach. And to Azariah he gave the name Abed-nego.

8 But Daniel made up his mind that he would not make himself unclean with the king's best food and wine. So he asked the head ruler to allow him not to make himself unclean. 9 Now God gave Daniel favor and pity in the eyes of the head ruler. 10 The head ruler said to him, "I am afraid of my lord the king, who has said you were to have so much and he would see that you were not looking as good as the other young men who are as old as you. The king would cut off my head because of you." 11 Then Daniel said to the man whom the head ruler had chosen to watch over Daniel, Hananiah, Mishael, and Azariah, 12 "Test your servants for ten days. Give us only vegetables to eat and water to drink. 13 Then compare how we look with the young men who are eating the king's best food. And do with us what you think is best by what you see."

14 So he listened to them, and tested them for ten days. 15 At the end of ten days they looked even better. They were fatter than all the young men who had been eating the king's best food. 16 So the man who watched over them took away the best food and the wine they were to drink, and kept giving them vegetables.

17 God gave these four young men much learning and understanding in all kinds of writings and wisdom. Daniel even had understanding in all kinds of special dreams. 18 At the end of the time set by the king to bring them in, the head ruler brought them to Nebuchadnezzar. 19 The king talked with them, and found no one like Daniel, Hananiah, Mishael, and Azariah.

So they became the king's own helpers. ²⁰ Every time the king asked them questions that needed wise and understanding answers, he found that they knew ten times more than all the wonder-workers under his rule who used their secret ways. ²¹ And Daniel was there until the first year of King Cyrus.

Nebuchadnezzar's Dream

2 In the second year that Nebuchadnezzar was king, he had a dream. His spirit was troubled and he could not sleep. ² Then the king called for the wonder-workers, those who used secret ways, those who learned from stars, to tell the king what he had dreamed. So they came in and stood in front of the king. ³ The king said to them, "I had a dream that troubles me, and I want to know what the dream means."

⁴ Then those who learn from stars said to the king in the Aramaic language, "O king, live forever! Tell the dream to your servants, and we will tell you what it means." ⁵ The king answered, saying, "My word is sure. If you do not tell me what my dream was and what it means, you will be torn apart and your houses will be laid waste. ⁶ But if you tell me the dream and what it means, I will give you gifts and riches and great honor. So tell me the dream and what it means." ⁷ They answered the king a second time, saying, "Let the king tell the dream to his servants, and we will tell you what it means." ⁸ The king said, "I am sure that you are trying to get more time, because you see that my word is sure. ⁹ You know that if you do not tell me what I dreamed, there is only one penalty for you. You have agreed among yourselves to keep telling me lies until things change. So tell me the dream. Then I will know that you can tell me what it means." ¹⁰ Those who learn from stars answered the king and said, "There is not a man on earth who can do this for the king. For no great king or ruler has ever asked anything like this of any wonder-worker or one who learns from stars. ¹¹ What the king asks is too hard. No one can do it for you except the gods, who do not live among men." ¹² Because of this the king became very angry and said that all the wise men of Babylon must be destroyed. ¹³ So the law was sent out that the wise men must be killed. They looked for Daniel and his friends, to kill them also.

God Shows Daniel the Meaning of the Dream

¹⁴ Then Daniel spoke with wisdom and understanding to Arioch, the captain of the soldiers who watched over the king, who had gone out to kill the wise men of Babylon. ¹⁵ He said to Arioch, the king's captain, "Why is the king's law so hard?" Then Arioch told him what had happened. ¹⁶ So Daniel went in and asked the king for time, so that he could tell the king what the dream meant.

¹⁷ Then Daniel went to his house and told his friends, Hananiah, Mishael and Azariah, what had happened. ¹⁸ He told them to ask for loving-pity from the God of heaven about this secret, so that Daniel and his friends might not be killed with the other wise men of Babylon. ¹⁹ Then the secret was made known to Daniel in a special dream during the night. He gave honor and thanks to the God of heaven. ²⁰ Daniel said, "Let the name of God be honored forever and ever, for wisdom and power belong to Him. ²¹ He changes the times and the years. He takes kings away, and puts kings in power. He gives wisdom to wise men and much learning to men of understanding. ²² He makes known secret and hidden things. He knows what is in the darkness. Light is with Him. ²³ I give thanks and praise to You, O God of my fathers. For You have given me wisdom and power. Even now You have made known what we asked of You. You have made the king's dream known to us."

Daniel Tells the Meaning to the King

²⁴ So Daniel went in to Arioch, whom the king had told to kill the wise men of Babylon. He went and said to him, "Do not kill the wise men of Babylon! Take me to the king, and I will tell him what his dream means."

²⁵ Then Arioch brought Daniel to the king in a hurry, and said to him, "I have found a man among those brought out of Judah who can tell the king what his dream means!" ²⁶ The king said to Daniel (also called Belteshazzar), "Are you able to tell me the dream I had, and what it means?" ²⁷ Daniel answered the king and said, "No wise men, wonder-workers, or men who use secret ways can make this dream known to the king. ²⁸ But there is a God in heaven who makes secrets known. And He has made known to King Nebuchadnezzar what will happen in the future. This was the special dream you

had while you were on your bed. ²⁹ O king, while on your bed your thoughts turned to what would happen in the future. And He Who makes secrets known has let you know what will happen. ³⁰ But this secret has not been made known to me because I am wiser than any other living man. It was made known to me so that I can make it known to the king, and that you may understand the thoughts of your mind.

³¹ "O king, you were looking and saw a great object. The object was large and very bright, and it was standing in front of you. It filled you with fear and wonder as you looked at it. ³² The object's head was made of fine gold. Its breast and arms were made of silver. Its stomach and thighs were made of brass. ³³ Its legs were made of iron, and its feet were part iron and part clay. ³⁴ While you were watching, a rock was cut out, but not by human hands. It fell and hit the large object on its feet of iron and clay, and crushed them. ³⁵ Then the iron, the clay, the brass, the silver and the gold were broken to pieces at the same time and became like dust on the grain-floor in the summer. The wind carried the dust away so nothing was to be found. But the stone that hit the large object became a large mountain and filled the whole earth.

³⁶ "This was the dream. Now we will tell the king what it means. ³⁷ You, O king, are the king of kings. The God of heaven has given you the nation, the power, the strength, and the honor. ³⁸ In every place where people live, or the animals of the field, or the birds of the air, He has given them to you and has caused you to rule over them all. You are the head of gold. ³⁹ After you there will be another nation that is not as great as yours. A third nation of brass will come, which will rule over all the earth. ⁴⁰ Then there will be a fourth nation, as strong as iron. Iron crushes and breaks all things. So, like iron breaks things to pieces, this nation will crush and break all the others. ⁴¹ Just as you saw the feet and toes made of part clay and part iron, it will be a divided nation. But it will have some of the strength of iron, just as you saw the iron mixed with the clay. ⁴² As the toes of the feet were made of part iron and part clay, so some of the nation will be strong and part of it will be weak. ⁴³ As you saw the iron mixed with clay, they will try to join with one another. But they will not stay together any more than iron mixes with clay. ⁴⁴ In the days of those kings the

God of heaven will set up a nation which will never be destroyed. And it will never be taken by another people. It will crush and put an end to all these nations, but it will last forever. ⁴⁵ You saw how a stone was cut out of the mountain by no human hands, and how it crushed the iron, the brass, the clay, the silver, and the gold. The great God has shown the king what will happen in the future. The dream is true. And I have given you its true meaning."

Daniel Becomes Ruler of Babylon

⁴⁶ Then King Nebuchadnezzar fell on his face and gave honor to Daniel. He had a gift and special perfume brought to him. ⁴⁷ The king said to Daniel, "For sure your God is God of gods and Lord of kings, and He makes hidden things known. For you have been able to make known this secret." ⁴⁸ Then the king gave Daniel much power and gave him many great gifts. He made him ruler over the whole land of Babylon and the head of all the wise men of Babylon. ⁴⁹ And Daniel asked the king to put Shadrach, Meshach and Abed-nego as leaders over the land of Babylon, while Daniel stayed near the king.

The False God Made of Gold

3 King Nebuchadnezzar made an object of gold which looked like a god. It was fifteen times taller than a man, and as wide as three long steps. He set it up on the plain of Dura in the land of Babylon. ² Then Nebuchadnezzar called together all the captains, leaders, rulers, wise men, money-keepers, judges, and law-keepers of Babylon's lands. He called them to come to the first showing of the object that he had set up. ³ So all the captains, leaders, rulers, wise men, money-keepers, judges, and law-keepers of Babylon's lands were gathered together for the special time of setting apart this object Nebuchadnezzar had set up. And they stood in front of it. ⁴ Then the man who spread news for the king said in a loud voice, "This is what you must do, O people of every nation and language: ⁵ When you hear the sound of the horns and harps, and all kinds of music, you are to get down on your knees and worship the object of gold that King Nebuchadnezzar has set up. ⁶ Whoever does not get down and worship will be thrown at once into the big and hot fire." ⁷ Then all the people heard the sound of the horns and harps and all kinds of music. All the people of every nation and language got

down and worshiped the object of gold that King Nebuchadnezzar had set up.

Daniel's Friends Do Not Obey the King

8 At this time certain ones who learned from stars came up and spoke against the Jews. 9 They said to King Nebuchadnezzar, "O king, live forever! 10 You yourself, O king, have made a law that every man who hears the sound of the horns and harps and all kinds of music is to get down on his knees and worship the object of gold. 11 And whoever does not get down and worship must be thrown into the big and hot fire. 12 There are certain Jews whom you have chosen as leaders over the land of Babylon. Their names are Shadrach, Meshach, and Abed-nego. These men have not listened to you, O king. They do not serve your gods or worship the object of gold which you have set up."

13 Then Nebuchadnezzar became very angry and called for Shadrach, Meshach, and Abed-nego. And they were brought to the king. 14 Nebuchadnezzar said to them, "Is it true, Shadrach, Meshach and Abed-nego, that you do not serve my gods or worship the object of gold that I have set up? 15 Now if you are ready to get down on your knees and worship the object I have made when you hear the sound of the horns and harps and all kinds of music, very well. But if you will not worship, you will be thrown at once into the fire. And what god is able to save you from my hands?" 16 Shadrach, Meshach and Abed-nego answered and said to the king, "O Nebuchadnezzar, we do not need to give you an answer to this question. 17 If we are thrown into the fire, our God Whom we serve is able to save us from it. And He will save us from your hand, O king. 18 But even if He does not, we want you to know, O king, that we will not serve your gods or worship the object of gold that you have set up."

Daniel's Friends Come Out of the Fire Alive

19 Then Nebuchadnezzar was filled with anger, and he looked at Shadrach, Meshach and Abed-nego with an angry face. He had the fire made seven times hotter than it was. 20 And he told certain powerful soldiers in his army to tie up Shadrach, Meshach and Abed-nego, and to throw them into the fire. 21 So the men were tied up in their coats and head-coverings and their other clothes, and were thrown into

the fire. 22 Because the king had spoken that the fire was to be very hot, those men who put Shadrach, Meshach and Abed-nego into the fire were killed by the fire. 23 The three men were still tied up when they fell into the fire.

24 Then King Nebuchadnezzar was very surprised and stood up in a hurry. He said to his leaders, "Did we not throw three men who were tied up into the fire?" They answered, "That is true, O king." 25 He said, "Look! I see four men loose and walking about in the fire without being hurt! And the fourth one looks like a son of the gods (or the Son of God)!"

Nebuchadnezzar Praises God

26 Then Nebuchadnezzar came near the door where the fire was burning, and said, "Shadrach, Meshach and Abed-nego, servants of the Most High God, come out! Come here!" So Shadrach, Meshach and Abed-nego came out of the fire. 27 The captains, leaders, rulers, and the king's important men gathered around and saw that the fire had not hurt the bodies of these three men. Their hair was not burned. Their clothes were not burned. They did not even smell like fire.

28 Nebuchadnezzar said, "Praise be to the God of Shadrach, Meshach, and Abed-nego. He has sent His angel and saved His servants who put their trust in Him. They changed the king's word and were ready to give up their lives instead of serving or worshiping any god except their own God. 29 So I now make a law that if any people of any nation or language say anything against the God of Shadrach, Meshach and Abed-nego, they will be torn apart and their houses will be laid waste. For there is no other god who is able to save in this way." 30 Then the king made Shadrach, Meshach and Abed-nego very important in the land of Babylon.

Nebuchadnezzar's Second Dream

4 King Nebuchadnezzar sent this letter to all the people of every nation and language who live in all the world: "May you have much peace! 2 I am pleased to tell you about the wonderful things which the Most High God has done for me. 3 How great are the special things He shows us! How powerful are His wonderful works! His nation lasts forever, and His rule is for all people for all time.

4 "I, Nebuchadnezzar, was at rest in my house. Everything was going well for me

there. 5 But I had a dream that made me afraid. As I lay on my bed the pictures that passed through my mind filled me with fear. 6 So I called for all the wise men of Babylon to come and tell me the meaning of my dream. 7 Then the wonder-workers, those who learn from stars, and those who use their secret ways, came in. I told them about the dream, but they could not tell me what it meant. 8 At last Daniel came to me, who was given the name Belteshazzar after the name of my god. A spirit of the holy gods is in him, and I told him about my dream. I said, 9 'O Belteshazzar, head of the wonder-workers, I know that the spirit of the holy gods is in you and that no secret is hidden from you. So tell me what dream I had, and what it means. 10 This is what I saw in my mind as I lay on my bed: I saw a tree in the center of the land. It was very tall. 11 The tree grew and became strong. Its top went up to the sky, and it could be seen to the end of the whole earth. 12 Its leaves were beautiful and it had much fruit. It had enough food for everyone. The wild animals of the field rested in its shadow. The birds of the air lived in its branches. And every living thing was fed from it.

13 'In the dreams I had as I lay on my bed, I looked and saw an angel who kept watch. He was a holy one who came down from heaven. 14 He said in a loud voice, "Cut down the tree and cut off its branches. Tear off its leaves and throw away its fruit. Let the animals run from under it and the birds fly from its branches. 15 Yet leave the base of the tree with its roots in the ground, and tie a chain of iron and brass around it. Leave it there in the new grass of the field. Let him be wet with the water from heaven on the grass in the early morning. Let him share with the wild animals in the grass of the earth. 16 Let his mind be changed from that of a man, and for seven years let him have the mind of an animal. 17 This penalty is by the law of the angels who keep watch. This is what the holy ones have decided, so that the living may know that the Most High is ruler over the nation of all people. He gives it to whomever He wants, and lets the least important of men rule over it." 18 This is the dream that I, King Nebuchadnezzar, have seen. Now, Belteshazzar, tell me what it means. None of the wise men in my nation can tell me what it means, but you can. For the spirit of the holy gods is in you.'

Daniel Tells the Meaning of the Second Dream

19 "Then Daniel (also called Belteshazzar) was afraid for a while. His thoughts filled him with fear. The king said, 'Belteshazzar, do not be afraid of the dream or its meaning.' Belteshazzar answered, 'My lord, if only the dream and its meaning had to do with those who hate you and fight against you! 20 You saw the tree which grew large and strong, whose top went up to the sky and could be seen over all the earth. 21 Its leaves were beautiful and it had much fruit, enough food for all. Wild animals of the field rested under it, and birds of the air lived in its branches. 22 This tree is you, O king! For you have become great and strong. Your power has become great and has gone up to the sky, and your rule has gone to the end of the earth. 23 The king saw an angel who kept watch, a holy one coming down from heaven and saying, "Cut down the tree and destroy it. Yet leave its base with its roots in the ground. Put a chain of iron and brass around it and leave it in the new grass of the field. And let him be wet with the water from heaven on the grass in the early morning. Let him share with the wild animals of the field for seven years." 24 This is what it means, O king. This is what the Most High said would happen to my lord the king: 25 'You will be driven away from all people and will live with the wild animals of the field. You will eat grass like cattle and become wet with the water from heaven. Seven years will pass until you understand that the Most High is ruler over the nations of men, and gives them to whomever He wants. 26 It was said that the base of the tree and its roots must be left. This means that your nation will be returned to you after you understand that it is Heaven that rules. 27 So, O king, may my words be pleasing to you. Turn away from your sins by doing what is right and good. Turn away from your wrong-doing by being kind to the poor. Then it may be that things will keep going well for you.'

The King Loses Everything

28 "All this happened to King Nebuchadnezzar. 29 Twelve months later he was walking on the roof of his beautiful house in Babylon. 30 And he said, 'Is not this the great Babylon which I have built as a beautiful place for the king? I have built it by my great strength and for the greatness of my power.' 31 Before the king was finished speaking, a voice came from heaven,

saying, 'King Nebuchadnezzar, to you it is said: Your power over the nation has been taken from you. 32 You will be driven away from all people and will live with the wild animals of the field. You will eat grass like cattle. And seven years will pass until you understand that the Most High is ruler over the nations of men, and gives them to whomever He wants.' 33 At once these words about Nebuchadnezzar came true. He was driven away from all people and began eating grass like cattle. His body became wet with the water from heaven, until his hair grew as long as eagles' feathers and his nails like those of birds.

Nebuchadnezzar Praises God

34 "But at the end of that time I, Nebuchadnezzar, looked up toward heaven and my understanding returned to me. And I gave thanks to the Most High and praised and honored Him Who lives forever. For His nation lasts forever, and His rule is for all people for all time. 35 All the people of the earth are thought of as nothing. He does as He pleases with the angels of heaven and the people of the earth. No one can hold back His hand or say to Him, 'What have You done?' 36 At that time my understanding returned to me. And my honor and power were returned to me for the greatness of my nation. My wise men and my leaders began looking for me, and I was made king again, with even more greatness added to me. 37 Now I, Nebuchadnezzar, praise and honor the King of heaven. For all His works are true and His ways are right. And He is able to bring down those who walk in pride."

Belshazzar's Special Supper

5 King Belshazzar gave a special supper for a thousand of his important men, and drank wine with them. 2 When Belshazzar tasted the wine, he had all the gold and silver cups brought which his father Nebuchadnezzar had taken out of the Lord's house in Jerusalem. The king sent for them so that he and his important men and all his wives could drink from them. 3 So they brought the gold cups that had been taken from the house of God in Jerusalem. And the king and his important men and all his wives drank from them. 4 They drank wine and praised the gods of gold and silver, brass, iron, wood, and stone.

5 All at once the fingers of a man's hand were seen writing on the wall near the lamp-stand of the king's house. And the king saw the back of the hand as it wrote. 6 Then the king's face turned white, and his thoughts turned to fear. His legs became weak and his knees began shaking. 7 The king called in a loud voice for the wonder-workers, the men who learned from stars and those who used their secret ways. He said to the wise men of Babylon, "Any man who can read this writing and tell me what it means will be dressed with purple clothing and have a chain of gold around his neck. And he will be the third in power in the nation." 8 Then all the king's wise men came in. But they could not read the writing or tell the king what it meant. 9 Then King Belshazzar was very afraid. His face lost even more of its color, and his important men did not know what to do.

10 The queen heard the words of the king and his men, and came into the room where they were eating. She said, "O king, live forever! Do not let your thoughts make you afraid or your face turn white. 11 There is a man in your nation who has the spirit of the holy gods in him. In your father's time light and understanding and wisdom, like the wisdom of the gods, were found in him. And King Nebuchadnezzar, your father, made him the head of the wonder-workers, the men who learned from stars, and those who use their secret ways. 12 This was because a special spirit was found in this Daniel whom the king called Belteshazzar. He had much learning and understanding to tell the meaning of dreams and secrets and to give answers to problems. Call for Daniel, and he will tell you what this means."

Daniel Tells What the Writing Means

13 So Daniel was brought to the king. And the king said to him, "Are you that Daniel who is one of the people whom my father the king brought from Judah? 14 I have heard that the spirit of the gods is in you. Light and understanding and special wisdom have been found in you also. 15 The wise men and wonder-workers were brought in to me so that they might read this writing and tell me what it means. But they could not tell me its meaning. 16 Now I have heard that you are able to tell the meaning of such things and give answers to hard problems. If you are able to read the writing and tell me what it means, you will be dressed in purple and wear a chain of gold around your neck. And you will be the third in power in the nation."

17 Then Daniel answered the king, saying, "Keep your gifts for yourself, or give them to someone else. But I will read the writing to the king and tell him what it means. 18 O king, the Most High made your father Nebuchadnezzar king, and gave him greatness, honor, and power. 19 Because of the greatness He gave to him, all the people of every nation and language shook in fear in front of him. He killed whomever he wanted. And he let live whomever he wanted. He gave honor to whomever he wanted. And he put down whomever he wanted. 20 But when his heart and spirit became proud and he acted in pride, he was taken from his throne and his greatness was taken from him. 21 He was driven away from people, and his mind became like that of an animal. He lived with the wild donkeys. He ate grass like cattle, and his body became wet with the water from heaven. It was like this for him until he understood that the Most High God is ruler over the nation of all men, and that He lets whomever He wants rule it. 22 Yet you, his son Belshazzar, have not put away the pride from your heart, even though you knew all this. 23 You have honored yourself more than the Lord of heaven. The cups of His house have been brought to you. And you and your important men and all your wives have been drinking wine from them. You have praised the gods of silver, gold, brass, iron, wood, and stone, which do not see, hear or understand. But you have not honored the God Who holds your life and your ways in His hand. 24 So the hand was sent from Him to write on your wall. 25 "This is what was written: 'MENE, MENE, TEKEL, and PARSIN.' 26 And this is what it means: 'MENE' means that God has numbered the days of your rule and has brought it to an end. 27 'TEKEL' means that you have been weighed and found to be too light. 28 'PERES' means that your nation has been divided and given to the Medes and Persians."

29 Then Belshazzar had them dress Daniel in purple and put a chain of gold around his neck. And he made it known that Daniel was the third most powerful ruler in the nation.

Belshazzar Is Killed

30 That very night Belshazzar the king of Babylon was killed. 31 So Darius the Mede became the king when he was sixty-two years old.

Daniel Is Thrown to the Lions

6 It pleased Darius to choose 120 captains to rule over the people. They would rule over the whole nation. 2 And three leaders were to rule over them, and Daniel was one. The captains were to answer to them, so that the king might suffer no loss. 3 Then Daniel showed that he could do better work than the other leaders and captains because a special spirit was in him. So the king planned to give him power over the whole nation. 4 Then the leaders and captains tried to find a reason to complain against Daniel about his duties over the nation. But they could not find any reason to complain or anything to blame him for, because he was faithful and honest and did not do anything wrong. 5 Then these men said, "We will not find anything to say against Daniel unless it has to do with the Law of his God." 6 So these leaders and captains came as a group to the king and said, "King Darius, live forever! 7 All the leaders of the nation, the captains, the important men and the rulers have spoken with each other and have agreed that a new law should be made. The king should make a law that must be obeyed, saying that anyone who asks something of any god or man besides you, O king, for thirty days, must be thrown to the lions. 8 O king, make this law now and write your name on it so that it may not be changed. It will be by the law of the Medes and Persians, and cannot be changed." 9 So King Darius made the law and wrote his name on it.

10 When Daniel knew that the king had written his name on this law, he went into his house where, in his upper room, he had windows open toward Jerusalem. There he got down on his knees three times each day, praying and giving thanks to his God, as he had done before. 11 Then these men came as a group and found Daniel praying and asking favor from his God. 12 So they went to the king and spoke to him about his law, saying, "Did you not write your name on a law which says that anyone who asks something of any god or man besides you, O king, for thirty days, is to be thrown to the lions?" The king answered, "This is true. It is by the law of the Medes and Persians, which cannot be changed." 13 Then they said to the king, "Daniel, who is one of the people brought from Judah, does not listen to you, O king. He is not obeying the law that you wrote your name on. He is still asking things of

his God three times a day." 14 When the king heard this, he was very troubled and tried to think of a way to save Daniel. Even until sunset he was trying to find a way to save him. 15 Then these men came as a group to the king and said, "Understand, O king, that it is a law of the Medes and Persians that any law the king makes cannot be changed."

16 So the king had Daniel brought in and thrown into the place where lions were kept. The king said to Daniel, "May your God, Whom you are faithful to serve, save you." 17 And a stone was brought and laid over the mouth of the hole. The king marked it with his own special ring and with the rings of his important men, so that no one could save Daniel. 18 Then the king went to his beautiful house and spent the night without food and sleep. And nothing was brought to make him feel better.

Daniel Is Saved from the Lions

19 The king got up at sunrise and went in a hurry to the place where lions were kept. 20 When he came to the hole in the ground where Daniel was, he called to him with a troubled voice, "Daniel, servant of the living God, has your God, Whom you always serve, been able to save you from the lions?" 21 Then Daniel said to the king, "O king, live forever! 22 My God sent His angel and shut the lions' mouths. They have not hurt me, because He knows that I am not guilty, and because I have done nothing wrong to you, O king." 23 Then the king was very pleased and had Daniel taken up out of the hole in the ground. So they took Daniel out of the hole and saw that he had not been hurt at all, because he had trusted in his God. 24 Then the king had those men brought to him who had spoken against Daniel. And they threw them with their wives and children into the hole with the lions. Even before they hit the bottom of the hole, the lions went after them and crushed all their bones.

25 Then King Darius wrote to all the people of every nation and language who were living on the earth. He wrote, "May you have much peace! 26 I make a law that all those under my rule are to fear and shake before the God of Daniel. For He is the living God and He lives forever. His nation will never be destroyed and His rule will last forever. 27 He saves and brings men out of danger, and shows His great power in heaven and on earth. And

He has saved Daniel from the power of the lions."

28 So things went well for Daniel during the rule of Darius and during the rule of Cyrus the Persian.

Daniel's Special Dream of the Four Animals

7 In the first year that Belshazzar was king of Babylon, Daniel had a special dream in his mind as he lay on his bed. And he wrote the dream down, telling what he saw. 2 Daniel said, "In my dream at night I looked and saw the four winds of heaven causing waves in the great sea. 3 And four large animals were coming up from the sea, different from one another. 4 The first was like a lion and it had the wings of an eagle. I watched until its wings were pulled off, and it was lifted up from the ground and made to stand on two feet like a man. A man's heart was given to it also. 5 Then I saw a second animal, which looked like a bear. It was raised up on one of its sides, and three ribs were in its mouth between its teeth. And it was told, 'Get up, and eat much meat!' 6 Then I looked and saw another animal, which looked like a leopard. It had four wings of a bird on its back, and four heads. And it was given the power to rule. 7 After this I looked in my dream in the night and saw a fourth animal. It filled me with a very great fear. It was very strong and it had large, iron teeth. It ate and crushed, and whatever was left, it crushed with its feet. It was different from all the animals that were before it, and it had ten horns. 8 While I was thinking about the horns, I saw another horn, a little one, come up among them. And three of the first horns were pulled out by the roots in front of it. This horn had eyes like the eyes of a man, and a mouth which spoke in pride.

The Special Dream of the One Who Has Always Lived

9 "As I kept looking, thrones were set up and the One Who has lived forever took His seat. His clothing was as white as snow and the hair of His head was like pure wool. His throne and its wheels were a burning fire. 10 A river of fire was flowing and coming out from before Him. Many thousands were serving Him, and many millions were standing before Him. The Judge was seated, and The Books were opened. 11 I kept looking because of the sound of the proud words which the

horn was speaking. I watched until the fourth animal was killed, and its body was destroyed and thrown into the burning fire. 12 The other three animals had their power taken away, but they were allowed to live for a time.

13 "I kept looking in the night dream and saw One like a Son of Man coming with the clouds of heaven. He came to the One Who has lived forever, and was brought before Him. 14 And He was given power and shining-greatness, and was made King, so that all the people of every nation and language would serve Him. His rule lasts forever. It will never pass away. And His nation will never be destroyed.

Daniel Tells the Meaning of His Dream

15 "As for me, Daniel, my spirit was troubled within me. The things I saw in my dream made me afraid. 16 I went to one of those who were standing near and asked him the true meaning of all this. So he told me what these things meant. 17 'These four large animals are four kings who will rise from the earth. 18 But the holy ones of the Most High will receive the nation and keep it forever and ever.' 19 Then I wanted to know the true meaning of the fourth animal which was different from all the others. It filled me with fear, with its iron teeth and sharp nails of brass. It ate and crushed, and whatever was left it crushed with its feet. 20 I wanted to know about the ten horns on its head, and the other horn which came up. I wanted to know about the three horns that fell in front of this larger horn which had eyes and a mouth which spoke proud words. 21 As I watched, this horn was fighting a war against the holy ones and winning the battle, 22 until the One came Who has lived forever. This One judged in favor of the holy ones of the Most High. And the time came when the holy ones took the nation for their own.

23 "He told me, 'The fourth animal will be a fourth nation on the earth. It will be different from all the other nations. It will destroy the whole earth. And it will crush under foot whatever is left. 24 The ten horns are ten kings who will come from this nation. And another will come after them who will be different from the ones before. He will put three kings under his power. 25 He will speak against the Most High and make it hard for His holy ones. And he will try to make changes in times and in law. The holy ones will be given

into his hand for a time, times, and half a time (three and a half years). 26 But the Judge will decide against him. And his ruling power will be taken away and destroyed forever. 27 Then the ruling power and greatness of all the nations under the whole heaven will be given to the holy people of the Most High. His nation will last forever, and all rulers will serve and obey Him.' 28 This is the end of the special dream. As for me, Daniel, my thoughts filled me with fear and my face turned white. But I kept everything to myself."

Daniel's Special Dream of a Ram and Goat

8 In the third year that Belshazzar was king, I, Daniel, had another special dream. 2 In the dream I looked and saw that I was in the strong city of Susa, in the land of Elam. I saw that I was beside the Ulai River. 3 Then I looked up and saw a ram with two horns standing by the river. The two horns were long, but one was longer than the other. And the longer one came up last. 4 I saw the ram pushing to the west, to the north, and to the south. No other animals could stop him or be saved from his power. He did as he pleased and made himself great.

5 While I was watching, a male goat came from the west across the whole earth without touching the ground. And the goat had a horn between his eyes that was very easy to see. 6 He came up to the ram with the two horns, which I had seen standing by the river, and rushed at him in his strong anger. 7 I saw him come at the ram in his anger. He hit the ram and broke his two horns to pieces. The ram was not strong enough to fight against him. So the goat threw him to the ground and crushed him under foot. And there was no one to save the ram from his power. 8 Then the male goat became very great. But as soon as he was powerful, the large horn was broken. And four large horns came up in its place, toward the four winds of heaven.

9 Out of them came a little horn which grew toward the south, toward the east, and toward the Beautiful Land. 10 It grew to be as great as the army of heaven and made some of them fall to the earth, and it crushed them into the ground. 11 It thought itself to be as great as the Ruler of the army of heaven. It took away the burnt gifts which were given to Him each day, and destroyed His holy place. 12 Because of sin, the army

of heaven and the burnt gifts were given over to the horn. It did well in whatever it wanted to do, and truth was thrown to the ground. 13 Then I heard a holy one speaking. And another holy one said to the one that spoke, "How long will it take for the things seen in the dream to happen? How long will the burnt gifts be taken, and sin allowed to destroy, so that the holy place and the army of heaven are crushed under foot?" 14 He said to me, "For 2,300 evenings and mornings. Then the holy place will be put to use again."

Gabriel Tells the Meaning of the Dream

15 When I, Daniel, had seen the special dream, I tried to understand it. Then I saw one standing in front of me who looked like a man. 16 And I heard a man's voice from the Ulai River. He called out and said, "Gabriel, help this man to understand the special dream." 17 When he came near the place where I was standing, I was afraid and fell on my face to the ground. But he said to me, "Son of man, understand that the special dream is about the time of the end." 18 While he was talking to me, I fell into a deep sleep with my face to the ground. But he touched me and made me stand up. 19 He said, "I am going to let you know what the end of God's anger will be. For the special dream is about the time of the end. 20 The ram you saw had two horns which are the kings of Media and Persia. 21 The male goat is the king of Greece, and the large horn between his eyes is the first king. 22 The broken horn and the four horns that grew in its place are the four nations which will come from his nation. But they will not be as powerful. 23 In the later part of their rule, when they have become as sinful as they can be, a king will rise to power. This king will be very proud and will understand secret things. 24 He will become very strong, but not by his own power. He will destroy much, and do well in whatever he wants done. He will destroy powerful men and the holy people 25 He will do well by using his false ways and lies, and will think of himself as great. He will destroy many who are taking it easy. He will even go against the Prince of princes. Yet he will be destroyed, but not by a human hand. 26 The special dream of the evenings and mornings that has been given to you is true. But keep the dream secret, for it has to do with things far into the future."

27 I, Daniel, was tired and sick for days. Then I got up again and did the work that the king had given me. But I was filled with wonder because of the special dream, and did not understand it.

Daniel's Prayer for the People

9 Darius the son of Ahasuerus, who was born a Mede, was made king over the nation of the Babylonians. 2 In the first year of his rule, I, Daniel, understood the books which were given by the Lord through Jeremiah that Jerusalem would lie waste for seventy years. 3 So I turned to the Lord God in prayer and did not eat. I dressed in cloth made from hair, and threw ashes on myself. 4 I prayed to the Lord my God and told him the sins of my people, saying, "O Lord, you are great and we fear You. You keep Your agreement and show loving-kindness to those who love You and keep Your Laws.

5 "But we have sinned. We have done wrong and have acted in sin. We have turned against You and against Your Laws. 6 We have not listened to Your servants who spoke for You, who spoke in Your name to our kings, our leaders, our fathers, and all the people of the land. 7 You are right and good, O Lord. But we are all covered with shame, all the men of Judah, the people of Jerusalem, and all Israel. The people both near and far away in all the countries where You have driven us are covered with shame because they have not been faithful to You. 8 We, our kings, our leaders and our fathers are all covered with shame, O Lord, because we have sinned against You. 9 O Lord our God, You are kind and forgiving, even when we would not obey You. 10 We have not obeyed the voice of the Lord our God by following the Laws He gave us through His servants who spoke for Him. 11 All Israel has sinned against Your Law and turned away, not obeying Your voice. So the curses and punishments have been poured out on us, which were written about in the Law of God's servant Moses. For we have sinned against Him. 12 He has done what He said He would do against us and our leaders, and has brought much trouble upon us. For under the whole heaven nothing has ever been done like what has been done to Jerusalem. 13 All this trouble has come upon us just as it is written in the Law of Moses. Yet we have not looked for the favor of the Lord our God by turning from our sin and following

Your truth. 14 So the Lord brought trouble upon us. For the Lord our God is right and good in all He does, but we have not obeyed His voice.

15 "O Lord our God, You have brought Your people out of the land of Egypt with a powerful hand. And You have made a name for Yourself that is known to this day. Now we have sinned. We have done sinful things. 16 O Lord, because You are right and good in what You do, do not be angry any longer with Your city Jerusalem, Your holy mountain. For because of our sins and the sins of our fathers, Jerusalem and Your people have been put to shame by everyone around us. 17 So now, our God, listen to Your servant's prayer and what he is asking. And for Your good, O Lord, look with favor upon the House of God which now lies waste. 18 O my God, turn Your ear and hear! Open Your eyes and see our trouble and the city that is called by Your name. We are not asking this of You because we are right or good, but because of Your great loving-pity. 19 O Lord, hear! O Lord, forgive! O Lord, listen and act! For Your own good, O my God, do not wait, because Your city and Your people are called by Your name."

Daniel Tells about the Future

20 I was speaking and praying, and telling the Lord my sin and the sin of my people Israel. I was asking the Lord my God to show favor to His holy mountain. 21 And while I was still praying, the man Gabriel, whom I had seen before in the dream, flew to me in a hurry at about the time when the evening gift is given in worship. 22 He talked to me and told me things, saying, "O Daniel, I have now come to give you wisdom and understanding. 23 As soon as you began to pray, an answer was given, which I have come to tell you. For you are loved very much. So listen to what I say and understand the special dream.

24 "Seventy weeks are given for your people and your holy city to finish the wrong-doing and put an end to sin. By the end of this time, you must pay for your sins and follow what is right and good forever. You must finish what was shown in the special dream and what has been spoken in My name, and set apart the most holy place. 25 Know and understand that seven weeks and sixty-two weeks will pass from the time the people are told to build Jerusalem again until the Chosen One comes. It will be built again, with streets and with a ditch of water around it. But that will be a troubled time. 26 After the sixty-two weeks, the Chosen One will be killed and have nothing. And the people of the ruler who is to come will destroy the city and the holy place. The end will come like a flood. Even to the end there will be war. For the Lord has said that much will be destroyed. 27 That ruler will make a strong agreement with many for one week. But when half that time is past, he will put a stop to burnt gifts and grain gifts. And a very sinful man-made god will be put there. It will stay there until the one who put it there is destroyed."

Daniel's Special Dream by the Tigris River

10 In the third year that Cyrus was the king of Persia, some news was made known to Daniel (who was called Belteshazzar). The news was true and it was about a battle. He received understanding of the news in a special dream.

2 In those days, I, Daniel, had been full of sorrow for three weeks. 3 I did not eat any fine food, and no meat or wine came into my mouth. And I did not use any oil at all, until the three weeks were finished. 4 On the twenty-fourth day of the first month, I was standing by the side of the wide Tigris River. 5 I looked up and saw a certain man dressed in linen. Around him was a belt of fine gold. 6 His body was like shining stone. His face looked like lightning. His eyes were like fire. His arms and feet were like shining brass. And his voice was like the noise of many people. 7 I, Daniel, was the only one who saw the special dream. The men who were with me did not see it. But they were filled with much fear, and ran away to hide themselves. 8 So I was left alone and saw this special dream. I had no strength left. My skin color turned white as if I were dead, and there was no strength left in me. 9 Then I heard the sound of his words. And as soon as I heard him speak, I fell into a deep sleep with my face to the ground.

The Future for Persia and Greece

10 Then a hand touched me and I shook with fear on my hands and knees. 11 And he said to me, "O Daniel, you who are loved very much, understand what I am about to tell you, and stand up. For I have now been sent to you." When he said this to me, I stood up shaking in fear. 12 Then he said to me, "Do not be afraid, Daniel.

Since the first day that you set your mind on understanding and getting rid of your pride before your God, your words were heard. And I have come because of your words. ¹³ But the ruler of Persia stood against me for twenty-one days. Then Michael, one of the leading princes of honor, came to help me, because I had been left there with the king of Persia. ¹⁴ Now I have come to help you understand what will happen to your people in the last days. For the special dream is about the days yet to come." ¹⁵ When he had said this to me, I turned my face toward the ground and could not speak. ¹⁶ Then one who looked like a man touched my lips, and I opened my mouth and spoke. I said to him who was standing in front of me, "O my lord, pain has come to me because of the special dream, and I have no strength left. ¹⁷ How can I, your servant, talk with you, my lord? My strength is gone and no breath is left in me."

¹⁸ Then the one who looked like a man touched me again and gave me strength. ¹⁹ He said, "O man who is loved very much, do not be afraid. May peace be with you. Be strong and have strength of heart." And when he had spoken to me, I received strength, and said, "May my lord speak, for you have given me strength." ²⁰ He said, "Do you understand why I have come to you? Soon I will return to fight against the ruler of Persia. And when I go, the ruler of Greece will come. ²¹ But first I will tell you what is written in the Book of Truth. (No one helps me against these rulers except Michael, your leading angel.

11 "And in the first year of Darius the Mede, I stood up to help him and give him strength.) ² I tell you the truth. Three more kings will rule over Persia. Then a fourth will become much richer than all of them. As soon as he becomes strong because of his riches, he will move everyone against the nation of Greece. ³ Then a powerful king will rise up, and he will rule with power and do as he pleases. ⁴ But as soon as he has risen to power, his nation will be broken and divided to the four winds of heaven. It will not be divided among his own children, or because of his own power. For his power will be taken and given to others besides these.

The Nations of Egypt and Syria

⁵ "Then the king of the South will become strong. But one of his leaders will become stronger than he and will rule with much power. ⁶ After some years they will join together. The daughter of the king of the South will come to the king of the North to make an agreement. But she will not keep her power, and he will not keep his. She will be killed, together with those who brought her, and her father, and the one who helped her. ⁷ But one of her family will become king in his place. He will fight against the army and go into the strong city of the king of the North. He will fight against them and win. ⁸ And he will carry their false gods and objects of silver and gold away to Egypt. For some years he will leave the king of the North alone. ⁹ Then the king of the North will go to fight against the king of the South, but will return to his own land.

¹⁰ "His sons will get ready for war and gather together a very large army. They will come like a flood and pass through, and fight in battle as far as his strong city. ¹¹ The king of the South will be very angry and will go and fight with the king of the North, who will have a very large army. But his army will be given over to the king of the South. ¹² When the army is taken away, the king of the South will become very proud, and he will kill tens of thousands. But his strength will not last. ¹³ For the king of the North will gather together a larger army than before. And after some years he will come with a large army ready to do battle.

¹⁴ "In those times many will fight against the king of the South. Angry men among your people will also go against the king to do what was shown in the special dream, but they will not win. ¹⁵ Then the king of the North will come and build a battle-wall, and take a very strong city. The army of the South will not be able to stand against him, not even their best soldiers. They will not have enough strength. ¹⁶ The king of North will do as he pleases. No one will be able to stand against him. He will stay for awhile in the Beautiful Land with the power to destroy it. ¹⁷ He will plan to come with the strength of his whole nation and will make a peace agreement with the king of the South. He will give him a daughter in marriage to try to destroy his nation. But she will not help him or be on his side. ¹⁸ Then he will turn to the lands beside the sea and take many in battle. But a captain will stop him (king of the North) in his pride, and cause trouble to be put on him. ¹⁹ So he will turn to the strong cities of his

own land. But he will lose his step and fall, and will not be seen again.

The Sinful King of Syria

20 "Then one will become king in his place, who will send a man through his great nation to make the people pay taxes. Yet within a short time that king will be killed, but not in anger or in battle. 21 A very sinful person will rise to power in his place. He will not be given the honor of being king, but he will come in a time of peace and take over the nation using smooth sounding words and false ways. 22 Armies will be driven away and destroyed in front of him, and also the ruler of the agreement. 23 And after a peace agreement is made with him, he will use false ways and become strong with a small army. 24 In a time of peace he will go into the richest parts of the land, and do what his fathers and his fathers' fathers never did. He will divide the things taken in war and make plans against strong cities, but only for a time. 25 He will gather all his strength against the king of the South with a large army. So the king of the South will gather together a very large and powerful army for war, but he will not win the battle. Secret plans will be made against him. 26 Those who eat his best food will destroy him. And his army will be driven away and many will be killed. 27 The hearts of both kings will be sinful. They will lie to each other at the same table. But nothing will come of it, for the end will still come at the chosen time. 28 Then the king of the North will return to his land with many things of much worth. But his heart will be set against the holy agreement. He will work against it and then return to his own land.

29 "At the chosen time he will return to the South, but this time it will not be as it was before. 30 For ships of Kittim will come against him, and he will be afraid and turn back. He will return in anger and go against the holy agreement. He will come back and show favor to those who have turned away from the holy agreement. 31 His armies will come and make the house of God unclean, and put an end to the burnt gifts. Then they will set up the very sinful man-made god. 32 He will speak well of those who sin against the agreement. But the people who know their God will show their strength and stand against him. 33 Those people who are wise will make many understand. But

for many days they will be killed by the sword or by fire, or be taken to prison or robbed. 34 When they fall, they will receive a little help. And many will pretend to be their friends. 35 Some of the wise people will be hurt, but this is so they will be made pure through punishment until the time of the end. For the end will still come at the chosen time.

36 "Then the king will do as he pleases. He will honor himself more than every god, and will say very bad things against the God of gods. Everything will go well for him until the time of anger is finished. For what has been planned will be done. 37 He will not care about the gods of his fathers or for the one that women like. He will not care about any other god, for he will honor himself more than any of them. 38 Instead he will honor a god of strong cities, a god his fathers did not know. He will honor him with gold, silver, stones of much worth, and riches. 39 And he will fight against the strongest cities with the help of a strange god. He will give great honor to those who follow him, and will let them rule over many people. And he will divide the land for a price.

40 "At the time of the end the king of the South will go against him. And the king of the North will fight against him with war-wagons, horsemen, and many ships. He will come into countries like a flood and pass through. 41 He will also come into the Beautiful Land and many countries will be taken. But Edom, Moab and the leaders of Ammon will be saved from his power. 42 Then he will fight against other countries, and Egypt will be taken. 43 He will get the hidden riches of gold and silver and all the things of great worth in Egypt. And the people of Libya and Ethiopia will follow behind him. 44 But news from the East and from the North will trouble him, and he will go with much anger to kill and destroy many people. 45 He will set up his tents made for kings between the sea and the beautiful holy mountain. Yet he will come to his end, and no one will help him.

The Future End Time

12 "At that time the great angel Michael, who watches over your people, will rise up. And there will be a time of trouble, the worst since there was a nation. But at that time, every one whose name is written in the Book will be taken out of the trouble. 2 Many of those who sleep in the dust of the earth will wake up. Some will have life that lasts forever, but others will have shame and will suffer much forever. ³ Those who are wise will shine like the bright heavens. And those who lead many to do what is right and good will shine like the stars forever and ever. ⁴ But as for you, Daniel, keep these words hidden and lock up the Book until the end of time. Many will travel here and there and knowledge will be more and more."

⁵ Then I, Daniel, looked and saw two others. One was standing on this side of the river, and the other was standing on that side. ⁶ And one said to the man dressed in linen, who was above the waters of the river, "How long will it be until the end of these wonders?" ⁷ The man dressed in linen, who was above the waters of the river, raised his right hand and his left hand toward heaven. And I heard him promise by Him Who lives forever that it would be for a time, times, and a half a time (three and a half years). As soon as the power of the holy people is broken, all these things will be completed. ⁸ I heard, but I did not understand. So I said, "My lord, how will it all end?" ⁹ And he said, "Go your way, Daniel. For these words are hidden and locked up until the end of time. ¹⁰ Many will be made pure and made white and tried, but the sinners will be very sinful. None of the sinful will understand, but those who are wise will understand. ¹¹ From the time the burnt gifts are stopped and the very sinful man-made god is set up, there will be 1,290 days. ¹² How happy is he who waits and comes to the end of the 1,335 days! ¹³ But go your way until the end. Then you will have rest, and will rise again to take your place at the end of time."

HOSEA

1 The Word of the Lord came to Hosea the son of Beeri during the time that Uzziah, Jotham, Ahaz and Hezekiah were kings of Judah, and Jeroboam the son of Joash was king of Israel.

Hosea's Family

² When the Lord first spoke through Hosea, the Lord said to him, "Go and marry a wife who is not faithful in marriage, and have children from that woman. For the land is guilty of not being faithful to the Lord." ³ So he married Gomer the daughter of Diblaim and she gave birth to his son. ⁴ And the Lord said to Hosea, "Name him Jezreel, because I will soon punish the people of Jehu for the killing at Jezreel. And I will put an end to the ruling power of the people of Israel. ⁵ On that day, I will break the power of Israel in the valley of Jezreel." ⁶ Then Gomer gave birth to a daughter. And the Lord said to Hosea, "Name her Lo-ruhamah, for I will no longer have loving-pity on the people of Israel and forgive them. ⁷ But I will have loving-pity on the people of Judah. I, the Lord their God, will save them. But I will not save them by bow, sword, war, horses, or horsemen." ⁸ When Gomer had finished nursing Lo-ruhamah, she gave birth to a son. ⁹ And the Lord said, "Name him Lo-ammi, for you are not My people and I am not your God

The Gathering of Israel and Judah

¹⁰ "Yet the number of the people of Israel will be like the sand of the sea, which cannot be numbered. And in the place where it was said to them, 'You are not My people,' it will be said to them, 'You are the sons of the living God.' ¹¹ The people of Judah and the people of Israel will be gathered together, and they will choose one leader for themselves. And they will go up from the land, for the day of Jezreel will be a great day.

2 "Say to your brothers, 'My people,' and to your sisters, 'My loved one.'

God's People Who Are Not Faithful

² "Speak with strong words to your mother. Speak with strong words, for she is not My wife and I am not her husband. Tell her to stop selling the use of her body and giving herself to other men. ³ If she does not, I will put her to shame by taking off her clothes and show her as when she was born. I will make her like a desert, like a hot and dry land, and will kill her with thirst. ⁴ I will have no loving-pity on her children, for they are children of her sinful ways. ⁵ Their mother has not been faithful. She who gave birth to them has acted in shame. For she said, 'I will go after my lovers. They give me my bread and water, my wool and linen, my oil and my drink.'

6 So I will put thorn bushes in her way. I will build a wall so that she cannot find her way. 7 She will go after her lovers but will not catch up with them. She will look for them but will not find them. Then she will say, 'I will return to my first husband. For it was better for me then than now.'

8 "She does not know that it was I Who gave her the grain, the new wine, the oil, and all the silver and gold, which they used for the false god Baal. 9 So I will take back My grain during the gathering time, and My new wine during its time. And I will take away My wool and My linen, which were given to cover her. 10 So I will take away the covering of her shame in the eyes of her lovers. And no one will take her out of My hand. 11 I will put an end to all her fun, her special suppers, her new moons, her Days of Rest, and all her special times for gathering together. 12 I will destroy her vines and fig trees, which she said were her pay from her lovers. I will make many trees grow wild among them, and the animals of the field will eat them. 13 I will punish her for the days she gave gifts in worship to the false gods of Baal. I will punish her for the times she forgot Me, and put on rings and other beautiful objects and went after her lovers" says the Lord.

God's Loving-Kindness for His People

14 "So I will lead her into the desert and speak words of comfort to her. 15 I will give her grape-fields there, and make the Valley of Achor a door of hope. And she will sing there as she did when she was young, as in the day she came out of the land of Egypt. 16 In that day" says the Lord, "you will call Me, 'My Husband.' And you will no longer call Me, 'My Baal.' 17 For I will take the names of the Baals from her mouth. The names of these false gods will never be spoken again. 18 In that day I will make an agreement for them with the wild animals of the field, the birds of the sky, and the things which move upon the ground. I will put an end to the bow, the sword, and war in all the land. And I will let My people lie down in peace and be safe. 19 I will promise to make you Mine forever. Yes, I will take you as My bride in what is right and good and fair, and in loving-kindness and in loving-pity. 20 I will keep My promise and make you Mine. Then you will know the Lord.

21 "In that day" says the Lord, "I will give an answer to the heavens, and they

will give an answer to the earth. 22 The earth will give an answer to the grain, the new wine, and the oil. And they will give an answer to Jezreel. 23 I will plant her for Myself in the land. Those who were not loved, I will call, 'My loved ones.' Those who were not My people, I will call, 'My people.' And they will say, 'You are my God!' "

Israel Will Return to the Lord Their God

3 Then the Lord said to me, "Go again and love your wife, even when she is loved by another and is not faithful. Love her as the Lord loves the people of Israel, even when they turn to other gods and love cakes of dried grapes." 2 So I bought her for fifteen pieces of silver money and ten baskets of barley. 3 Then I said to her, "You must stay with me for many days, and be faithful to me. Do not have another man, and I will also be faithful to you." 4 For the sons of Israel will live many days without a king or leader, without holy gifts or holy stone pillars, and without linen vests or false gods. 5 After this the sons of Israel will return and look for the Lord their God and for David their king. And they will come shaking before the Lord and receive His goodness in the last days.

God Speaks against Israel

4 Listen to the Word of the Lord, O people of Israel, because He has something against the people of the land. "They are not faithful or kind, and no one in the land knows God. 2 There is swearing, lying, killing, stealing, and sex sins. They are always hurting others, and there is one killing after another. 3 The land is filled with sorrow. Everyone who lives on it wastes away, together with the animals of the field and the birds of the sky. Even the fish of the sea are taken away.

4 "Yet let no one put blame or guilt upon another. For your people are like those who argue with the religious leader. 5 You will fall during the day, and the religious leaders will fall with you during the night. And I will destroy your mother. 6 My people are destroyed because they have not learned. You were not willing to learn. So I am not willing to have you be My religious leader. Since you have forgotten the Law of your God, I also will forget your children.

7 "The more there were, the more they sinned against Me. I will change their shining-greatness into shame. 8 They feed on the sin of My people, and so they want

them to sin more. 9 The religious leaders will be punished the same as the people. I will punish them for what they have done. 10 They will eat, but not have enough. They will do sex sins, but the number of their children will not grow because they have not been faithful to the Lord.

The Worship of False Gods

11 "Their sinful ways and both old and new wine take away My people's understanding. 12 They ask things of a wooden god and are answered by a stick of wood. A false spirit has led them the wrong way. They have not been faithful, and they have left their God. 13 They give gifts in worship on the tops of the mountains and burn special perfume on the hills. They do this under oak, poplar and terebinth trees, because their shadow is pleasing. So your daughters are like women who sell the use of their bodies, and your brides sin sex sins. 14 I will not punish your daughters when they are like women who sell the use of their bodies, or your brides when they do sex sins. For the men themselves go with the sinful women to give gifts in worship to false gods. And people without understanding will be destroyed.

15 "Even if you, Israel, are like women who sell the use of their bodies, do not let Judah become guilty. Do not go to Gilgal or up to Beth-aven. And do not swear, 'As the Lord lives!' 16 The people of Israel are strong-willed like a young cow. How then can the Lord feed them like a lamb in a large field? 17 Ephraim is joined to false gods. Let him alone. 18 Their strong drink is gone. They are like women who sell the use of their bodies all the time. Their rulers love shame. 19 The wind will carry them away, and they will be ashamed because they gave gifts to false gods.

The Lord Will Judge Israel and Judah

5 "Hear this, O religious leaders! Listen, O people of Israel! Listen, O family of the king! For you are to be judged. You have been a trap at Mizpah, and a net spread out on Tabor. 2 Those who will not obey have gone deep into sin, but I will punish all of them. 3 I know all about Ephraim. Israel is not hidden from Me. O Ephraim, you have acted like a woman who sells the use of her body. Israel has made itself unclean. 4 Their wrong-doing will not allow them to return to their God. For a spirit of a woman who sells the use of her body is within them, and they do

not know the Lord. 5 The pride of Israel speaks against them. Israel and Ephraim fall in their sin, and Judah has fallen with them. 6 They will go with their flocks and cattle to look for the Lord, but they will not find Him. He has gone away from them. 7 They have not been faithful to the Lord, for they have given birth to children who are not His. Now the new moon will destroy them with their land.

War between Judah and Israel

8 "Blow the horn in Gibeah and in Ramah! Let the sound of danger be heard at Beth-aven! Look behind you, Benjamin! 9 Ephraim will be laid waste in the day of punishment. Among the family groups of Israel I make known what is sure. 10 The leaders of Judah are like those who take away the land-marks. I will pour out My anger on them like water. 11 It is hard for Ephraim. He is crushed by punishment, because he wanted to follow what is of no worth. 12 So I am like a moth to Ephraim, and like a wasting disease to the people of Judah. 13 When Ephraim saw his sickness and Judah saw his sore, then Ephraim went to Assyria and sent to King Jareb for help. But he is not able to cure you, or heal your sore. 14 For I will be like a lion to Ephraim, and like a young lion to the people of Judah. I will tear them to pieces and go away. I will carry them away, with no one to take them. 15 I will go away and return to My place until they know they are guilty and look for Me. In their suffering they will try to find Me."

The People Are to Turn from Their Sin

6 "Come, let us return to the Lord. He has hurt us but He will heal us. He has cut us but He will cover the sore. 2 After two days He will give us new life. He will raise us up on the third day, that we may live before Him. 3 So keep on trying to know the Lord. His coming to us is as sure as the rising of the sun. He will come to us like the rain, like the spring rain giving water to the earth."

4 "What should I do with you, Ephraim? What should I do with you, Judah? Your loving-kindness is like a morning cloud, and like the water on the grass in the early morning. 5 So I have cut them in pieces by the men who speak for Me. I have killed them by the words of My mouth. My punishments come upon you like lightning. 6 I want loving-kindness and not a gift to be given in worship. I want people

to know God instead of giving burnt gifts. 7 But like Adam they have sinned against the agreement. They were not faithful to Me there. 8 Gilead is a city of wrong-doers, with blood in every footstep. 9 Like robbers lie in wait for a man, a group of religious leaders kill on the way to Shechem. For sure they have done a sin-ful thing. 10 I have seen a very bad thing among the people of Israel. Ephraim has left Me to worship false gods. Israel has made itself unclean. 11 Also, Judah, there is a time coming for you, when I give back the riches of My people.

7 "Whenever I would heal Israel, I see the sin of Ephraim and the wrong-doing of Samaria. They are false in their ways. The robber breaks into houses, and sinful men rob in the streets. 2 They do not think about how I remember all the sinful things they do. Their sins are all around them, and are always before Me. 3 They make the king glad with their wrong-doing, and the leaders with their lies. 4 None of them are faithful. They are like a hot stove whose fire the bread-maker leaves alone from the time he makes the dough until the bread rises. 5 On the special day of our king the leaders became drunk with wine. He joined hands with those who laughed at the truth. 6 Their hearts are like a hot stove as they make their plans. Their anger smokes all night, and in the morning it burns like a hot fire. 7 All of them are hot like a stove, and they destroy their leaders. All their kings have fallen, and none of them calls to Me for help.

Israel Cannot Depend on the Nations

8 "Ephraim mixes with the nations. Ephraim is a cake not turned. 9 Strangers destroy his strength, yet he does not know it. White hairs come upon him, yet he does not know it. 10 Israel's pride speaks against him, yet they do not return to the Lord their God. Even for all this, they do not look for Him. 11 Ephraim is like a foolish dove that is not able to think. They call to Egypt. They go to Assyria. 12 When they go, I will spread My net over them. I will bring them down like the birds of the sky. I will punish them for the sinful things they have done. 13 It is bad for them, for they have turned away from Me! They will be destroyed, for they would not obey Me! I would save them and make them free, but they speak lies against Me. 14 They do not cry out to Me from their heart

when they cry on their beds. They come together for grain and new wine, but turn away from Me. 15 I taught them and gave strength to their arms, yet they make sin-ful plans against Me. 16 They do not turn to the Most High. They are like a bow that does not work right. Their leaders will be killed by the sword because of their proud words. And those in the land of Egypt will laugh at them.

Israel Worships False Gods

8 "Put the horn to your lips! Men who hate us are coming like an eagle to fight against the house of the Lord, because the people of Israel have sinned against My agreement and would not obey My Law. 2 They cry out to Me, 'My God, we of Is-rael know You!' 3 Israel has turned away from the good, and those who hate him will come after him. 4 They have set up kings, but not by Me. They have chosen leaders, but I did not know it. They have made false gods for themselves out of sil-ver and gold, so they will be destroyed. 5 O Samaria, I will have nothing to do with the calf you worship. My anger burns against them! How long will it be before they are pure 6 in Israel? A workman made this calf, so it is not God. The calf of Samaria will be broken to pieces. 7 They plant the wind and they will gather the storm. The standing grain has no heads, and will give no food. If it were to give food, strangers would eat it.

8 "Israel is eaten up. They are now among the nations like a pot that is of no worth. 9 They have gone up to Assyria like a wild donkey all alone. Ephraim has hired lovers. 10 Even when they hire people among the nations to help them, I will now gather them together. And they will begin to waste away because the powerful king will make it hard for them.

11 "Because Ephraim has made many altars for sin gifts, they have become altars for sinning. 12 I wrote 10,000 of My Laws for him, but they think of them as some-thing strange. 13 They give gifts to Me and eat the meat of the gifts, but the Lord is not pleased with them. Now He will remem-ber their wrong-doing and punish them for their sins. They will return to Egypt. 14 Israel has forgotten his Maker and built great houses. And Judah has built many strong cities ready for battle. But I will send a fire upon its cities that will destroy its beautiful houses."

Israel Is Judged for Its Sin

9 Do not be happy, O Israel! Do not be glad like the nations! For you have sinned like a woman who sells the use of her body, turning away from your God. You have loved selling yourselves on every grain-floor. 2 The grain-floor and the place where the grapes are crushed will not feed them. And they will not have enough new wine. 3 They will not stay in the Lord's land, but Ephraim will return to Egypt. And in Assyria they will eat unclean food. 4 They will not pour out drink gifts of wine to the Lord. Their gifts of worship will not please Him. Their bread will be like the bread of those in sorrow. Everyone who eats it will be unclean, for their bread will be for themselves alone. It will not come into the house of the Lord. 5 What will you do on the days set to have a special supper for the Lord? 6 When trouble comes and the people try to get away, Egypt will gather them up. Memphis will bury them. Their riches of silver will be grown over by weeds, and thorns will be in their tents.

7 The days of punishment have come, the days when the people must pay for their sins. Let Israel know this. The man who tells what will happen in the future is a fool. The man who is led by the spirit is crazy. This is because of all your sin and anger. 8 Ephraim was meant to be a watchman who would speak for God. Yet there is a net in all his ways, and only anger in the house of his God. 9 They have gone deep into sin, as in the days of Gibeah. The Lord will remember their wrong doing, and will punish their sins.

10 "I found Israel like grapes in the desert. I saw your fathers like the first-fruit on the fig tree in its first year. But they came to Baal-peor and gave themselves to that false god of shame. They became as sinful as the thing they loved. 11 Ephraim's greatness will fly away like a bird. There will be no more children born to them, and they will not be able to have children. 12 Even if they raise children, I will take them away and not leave anyone alive. It will be bad for them when I leave them! 13 I have seen Ephraim planted in a good field like Tyre. But Ephraim will bring his children out to be killed." 14 O Lord, what will You give them? Give them children who die before they are born, and make them not able to nurse their babies.

15 "Because of all their sin at Gilgal, I hated them there. Because of the sinful things they did, I will drive them out of My house. I will not love them any more. All their leaders would not obey Me. 16 Ephraim is destroyed. Their root is dried up and they will give no fruit. Even if they give birth, I will kill the children they love." 17 My God will send them away because they have not listened to Him. And they will travel from nation to nation.

Israel's Sin

10 Israel is a spreading vine full of fruit. The more fruit he had, the more altars he made. As his land became richer, he made his pillars for worship better. 2 Their heart is not faithful, and now they must suffer for their sins. The Lord will break down their altars and destroy their pillars for worship.

3 Then they will say, "We have no king because we do not fear the Lord. And what could a king do for us?" 4 They speak empty words and make false promises, so punishment grows like weeds of poison in a plowed field. 5 The people of Samaria will be afraid for the calf of Beth-aven. Its people will have sorrow for it. Its religious leaders who worship false gods will cry over it in a loud voice. They will cry because its greatness has gone. 6 The thing itself will be carried to Assyria and given to King Jareb. Ephraim will be put to shame, and Israel will be ashamed of its false god. 7 Samaria and its king will be lost like a piece of wood on the water. 8 The high places of Aven, the sin of Israel, will be destroyed. Thorns and thistles will grow on their altars. Then they will say to the mountains, "Cover us!" and to the hills, "Fall on us!"

9 "You have sinned since the days of Gibeah, O Israel, and there you have stayed. Will not the sinners be destroyed in battle in Gibeah? 10 I will punish them when I please. And the nations will be gathered against them when they are punished for their many sins.

11 "Ephraim is a well-taught young cow that loves to crush the grain. But I will put a load on her beautiful neck. I will drive Ephraim. Judah must plow. And Jacob must break up the ground. 12 Plant what is right and good for yourselves. Gather the fruit of lasting love. Break up your ground that has not been plowed. For it is time to look for the Lord, until He comes and pours His saving power on you. 13 You have plowed wrong-doing and have gathered sin. You have eaten the fruit of lies. You have trusted in your own strength

and in your many soldiers. 14 The noise of battle will rise up among your people. All your strong cities will be destroyed, as Shalman destroyed Beth-arbel on the day of battle. Mothers were crushed in pieces with their children. 15 This will be done to you at Bethel because of your many sins. When the day begins, the king of Israel will be destroyed.

God's Love for His Sinful People

11 "When Israel was a child, I loved him. And I called My son out of Egypt. 2 The more I called them, the more they went from Me. They kept giving gifts in worship to the Baals and burning special perfume to false gods. 3 Yet it was I who taught Ephraim to walk. I took them in My arms. But they did not know that I healed them. 4 I led them with ropes of human kindness, with ties of love. I lifted the load from their neck and went down to feed them.

5 "They will not return to the land of Egypt, and Assyria will be their king, because they would not return to Me. 6 The sword will come upon their cities and destroy their gates. And it will destroy them because of their plans. 7 My people are always turning from Me. Even when those who speak for the Lord call them to the Most High, no one honors Him.

8 "How can I give you up, O Ephraim? How can I give you up, O Israel? How can I make you like Admah? How can I make you like Zeboiim? My heart will not let Me do it. I love you very much. 9 I will not do anything in My burning anger. I will not destroy Ephraim again. For I am God and not man. I am the Holy One among you, and I will not come in anger. 10 They will follow the Lord, and He will make noise like a lion. Yes, He will make noise like a lion, and His children will come from the west shaking with fear. 11 They will come shaking like birds from Egypt, and like doves from the land of Assyria. And I will return them to their homes," says the Lord.

Israel and Judah Are Judged

12 "The lies of Ephraim and the lies of the people of Israel are all around Me. And Judah will not obey God, the One Who is holy and faithful."

12 Ephraim's food is the wind, he goes after the east wind all day long. He tells many lies and does much in his anger. He makes an agreement with Assyria and takes oil to Egypt. 2 The Lord has a cause against Judah, and will punish Jacob for his ways. He will make him pay for what he has done. 3 Before he was born he took his brother by the heel. And when he was grown he fought with God. 4 He fought with the angel and won. He cried and begged for His favor. He met God at Bethel, and God spoke with him there. 5 This was the Lord, the God of All. The Lord is His name. 6 So return to your God. Show kindness and do what is fair, and wait for your God all the time. 7 One who buys and sells and who lies about the weight of things loves to make it hard for others. 8 Ephraim has said, "I have become rich. I have found riches for myself. With all my riches they will not find any sin in me."

9 "I am the Lord your God Who brought you out of Egypt. I will make you live in tents again, as in the days of your special suppers. 10 I have spoken to the men who speak for Me. I have given many special dreams. And I gave picture-stories through the men who speak for Me."

11 Is there sin in Gilead? For sure its people are of no worth. In Gilgal they kill people in worship. Their altars are like the many stones laid beside a plowed field. 12 Jacob ran away to the land of Aram. There he worked for a wife, and for a wife he kept sheep. 13 By a man who spoke for Him, the Lord brought Israel from Egypt. And by a man who spoke for Him, the Lord cared for him. 14 But Ephraim has made the Lord very angry. So the Lord will leave on him the guilt of his blood, and make his shame return to him.

Israel Judged the Last Time

13 When Ephraim spoke, men shook in fear. He was honored in Israel. But he sinned by worshipping Baal, and died. 2 And now they sin more and more. They make false gods for themselves. Their able workmen make them out of silver. And they say, "Let the men who give gifts in worship kiss the calf-gods!" 3 So they will be like the morning cloud, and like the water on the grass in the early morning which is soon gone. They will be like the dust of the grain that is blown away from the grain-floor, and like smoke from a fire.

4 "I am the Lord your God Who brought you out of Egypt. You were not to know any god but Me, for there is no one who can save you but Me. 5 I cared for you in the desert, in the land where there was

no water. 6 When I fed them, they were filled. And when they were filled, their heart became proud and they forgot Me. 7 So I will be like a lion to them. I will lie in wait by the road like a leopard. 8 I will fight them like a bear robbed of her young ones. I will tear open their chests. I will eat them there like a female lion, and tear them like a wild animal.

9 "I will destroy you, O Israel, because you are against Me, against your Helper. 10 Where is your king, that he may save you? Where are your rulers in all your cities, of whom you said, 'Give me a king and leaders'? 11 I gave you a king in My anger, and in My anger I took him away.

12 "The wrong-doing of Ephraim is being kept. His sin is being stored up. 13 The pains like a woman giving birth will come upon him, but he is not a wise son. He is not willing to be born. 14 I will pay the price to free them from the power of the grave. I will save them from death. O Death, where are your thorns? O Grave, where is your power to destroy? I will have no loving-pity.

15 "Even if he grows among his brothers, an east wind will come. The wind of the Lord will come from the desert. And his well will dry up. His water will be gone. It will take away everything of much worth. 16 Samaria will suffer for her guilt, for she has not wanted to obey her God. They will be killed by the sword. Their little ones will be crushed in pieces. And their women who are soon to give birth will be torn open."

Hosea's Last Words to Israel

14 Return to the Lord your God, O Israel, for you have fallen because of your sin. 2 Take words with you and return to the Lord. Say to Him, "Take away all sin, and receive us in kindness, that we may praise You with our lips. 3 Assyria will not save us. We will not ride on horses. And we will never say again, 'Our god,' to what we have made with our hands. For those who have no father find loving-kindness in You."

New Life for Israel

4 "I will bring My people back to Me. I will not hold back My love from them, for I am no longer angry with them. 5 I will be to Israel like the water on the grass in the early morning. He will grow like the lily, and have roots like the cedars of Lebanon. 6 His young branches will spread out and his beauty will be like the olive tree. His smell will be like the cedars of Lebanon. 7 Those who live in his shadow will grow like grain and like flowers of the vine. He will be known like the wine of Lebanon.

8 "O Ephraim, what have I to do with false gods? It is I Who answer and take care of you. I am like a green cypress tree. Your fruit comes from Me."

9 Whoever is wise, let him understand these things and know them. For the ways of the Lord are right, and those who are right and good will follow them, but sinners will not follow them.

JOEL

1 This is the word of the Lord that came to Joel, the son of Pethuel.

The Land Is Destroyed

2 Hear this, you old men. Listen, all who live in the land. Has anything like this happened in your days or in your fathers' days? 3 Tell your sons about it, and let your sons tell their sons, and their sons tell the next son-to-come.

4 What the chewing locust has left, the flying locust has eaten. What the flying locust has left, the jumping locust has eaten. And what the jumping locust has left, the destroying locust has eaten. 5 Wake up and cry, you who drink too much. Cry in a loud voice, all you who drink wine, for

the sweet wine has been taken from your lips. 6 A nation has come to fight against my land. Its army is powerful, with too many to number. Its teeth are the teeth of a lion. It has the long, sharp teeth of a female lion. 7 It has made my vine a waste, and has broken my fig tree to pieces. It has torn off their covering and thrown it away. Their branches have become white.

8 Cry in sorrow like a young, pure woman dressed in cloth made from hair because the man she was going to marry is dead. 9 The grain gifts and drink gifts have been cut off from the house of the Lord. The religious leaders who served the Lord are full of sorrow. 10 The fields are laid waste and the land is full of sorrow. The grain

is destroyed, the new wine dries up, and the oil wastes away. **11** Be troubled, you farmers! Cry in a loud voice, you who take care of the vines! Cry for the wheat and the barley, because what was gathered from the field is destroyed. **12** The vine dries up and the fig tree wastes away. The pomegranate, the palm, the apple tree, and all the trees of the field dry up. And the people's joy dries up.

13 Dress in cloth made from hair, and cry in sorrow, you religious leaders! Cry in a loud voice, you who serve at the altar! Come, spend the night in cloth made from hair, you who serve my God. For the grain gifts and drink gifts are kept from the house of your God. **14** Set apart a time when no food will be eaten. Call together a holy meeting. Gather the leaders and all the people of the land to the house of the Lord your God, and cry out to the Lord. **15** What a bad day it will be! The day of the Lord is near, when the All-powerful God will come to destroy. **16** Do you see how our food has been taken from us? Has not happiness and joy been cut off from the house of our God? **17** The seeds dry up under the ground. The store-houses are laid waste. The buildings where the grain was kept are torn down, for the grain is destroyed. **18** How the animals cry inside themselves! The cattle go from place to place because there is no food for them. Even the flocks of sheep suffer. **19** I cry to You, O Lord. For fire has destroyed the fields of the desert. All the trees of the field have burned up. **20** Even the animals of the field cry to You. For the rivers are dried up, and fire has burned up the fields of the desert.

The Day of the Lord

2 Blow a horn in Zion! Give the sound of danger on My holy mountain! Let all the people of the land shake in fear, for the day of the Lord is coming. The day is near. **2** It will be a day of darkness, a day of clouds and much darkness. A large and powerful army will come like darkness spreading over the mountains. There has never been anything like it, and there will never be anything like it again for all time to come. **3** Fire destroys in front of them and behind them. The land is like the garden of Eden in front of them, but a desert waste is left behind them. Nothing gets away from them. **4** They look like horses. They run like war horses. **5** As they jump on the tops of the mountains they sound like war-wagons. They sound like a fire

burning up the dry grass, like a powerful army ready for battle. **6** Nations suffer in front of them. All faces turn white. **7** They run like strong men. They go over the wall like soldiers. They each walk straight on, and do not turn from their paths. **8** They do not push each other. Each one walks in his path. When they break through those who fight against them, their path is not changed. **9** They rush upon the city. They run on the wall. They go into the houses through the windows like a robber. **10** The earth shakes in front of them. The heavens shake. The sun and the moon become dark, and the stars stop shining. **11** The Lord thunders in front of His army. His army has too many to number. Those who obey His Word are powerful. The day of the Lord is very great and fills people with fear and wonder. Who can live through it?

A Call to Turn from Sin

12 "Yet even now," says the Lord, "return to Me with all your heart, crying in sorrow and eating no food. **13** Tear your heart and not your clothes." Return to the Lord your God, for He is full of loving-kindness and loving-pity. He is slow to anger, full of love, and ready to keep His punishment from you. **14** It may be that He will turn and have pity, and leave good behind for you. He may leave you a grain gift and a drink gift for the Lord your God. **15** Blow a horn in Zion. Set apart a time when no food will be eaten. Call together a holy meeting. **16** Gather the people and make them holy. Gather together the leaders, the children, and the nursing babies. Let the man to be married come out of his room, and the bride come out of her room. **17** Let the religious leaders who serve the Lord cry between the porch and the altar. Let them say, "Have pity on Your people, O Lord. Do not put your people to shame. And do not make the nations speak against them. Why should the people of the nations say, 'Where is their God?'"

The Lord Gives Food Again

18 Then the Lord will be jealous for His land and have pity on His people. **19** The Lord will say to His people, "I am going to send you grain, new wine, and oil, and you will be filled with them. I will never again put you to shame among the nations. **20** I will take the army from the north far from you, and will drive it into a hot and dry land. The ones in front will be driven into the sea in the east. The ones in the back will be driven into the sea in the west. And a bad smell will rise up from their dead bodies. For He has done great things."

21 Do not be afraid, O land. Have joy and be glad, for the Lord has done great things. 22 Do not be afraid, you animals of the field. For the fields of the desert have turned green and there is fruit on the trees. The fig trees and vines are full of fruit. 23 Be glad, O sons of Zion. Be happy in the Lord your God. For He has given the early rain to help you. He has poured down much rain for you, both fall and spring rains, as before. 24 The grain-floors will be full of grain, and the crushing-places will flow over with new wine and oil. 25 "I will pay you back for the years that your food was eaten by the flying locust, the jumping locust, the destroying locust, and the chewing locust, My large army which I sent among you. 26 You will have much to eat and be filled. And you will praise the name of the Lord your God, Who has done wonderful things for you. Then My people will never be put to shame. 27 You will know that I am in Israel. You will know that I am the Lord your God, and that there is no other. And My people will never be put to shame.

God Sends His Spirit

28 "In the last days I will send My Spirit on all men. Then your sons and daughters will speak God's Word. Your old men will dream dreams. Your young men will see special dreams. 29 Yes, on My servants, both men and women, I will pour out My Spirit in those days. 30 I will show powerful works in the heavens and on the earth, like blood and fire and clouds of smoke. 31 The sun will turn dark and the moon will turn to blood before the day of the Lord. His coming will be a great and troubled day. 32 It will be that whoever calls on the name of the Lord will be saved from the punishment of sin. For on Mount Zion and in Jerusalem some will be taken out of trouble, as the Lord has said. Those whom the Lord calls will be kept alive.

The Nations Will Be Judged

3 "In those days and at that time, I will return the riches of Judah and Jerusalem. 2 I will gather all the nations and bring them down to the valley of Jehoshaphat. There I will judge them for what they did to My people Israel. They have sent My people out among the different nations, and have divided up My land. 3 They

have drawn names to see who would get My people. They have traded a boy for a woman who sells the use of her body. And they have sold a girl for wine to drink. 4 What are you to Me, O Tyre, Sidon, and all the lands of Philistia? Are you paying Me back for something? If you are, I will be quick to pay you back! 5 You have taken My silver and My gold, and brought My riches to your places of worship. 6 You have sold the sons of Judah and Jerusalem to the Greeks, sending them far from their land. 7 So I am going to move them from the place where you have sold them, and do to you what you have done to them. 8 I will sell your sons and daughters to the sons of Judah. And they will sell them to the Sabeans, to a nation far away." The Lord has spoken.

9 Make this known among the nations: Get ready for war! Call your strong men! Gather all the soldiers and let them come up! 10 Beat your plows into swords, and your vine hooks into spears. Let the weak say, "I am a powerful soldier." 11 Hurry and come, all you nations on every side, and gather yourselves there. Bring down Your men of war, O Lord. 12 Let the nations get ready and come to the valley of Jehoshaphat. For there I will sit to judge all the nations on every side. 13 Use the long, sharp knife, for the fruit is full-grown. Come and crush the grapes, for the crushing-place is full. They flow over, for their sins are many. 14 Thousands and thousands are in the valley of God's punishment. For the day of the Lord is near in the valley of God's punishment. 15 The sun and moon become dark, and the stars stop shining. 16 The Lord makes a loud noise from Zion. He lets His voice be heard from Jerusalem, and the heavens and the earth shake. But the Lord is a safe place for His people, a strong-place to the sons of Israel.

17 "Then you will know that I am the Lord your God, living in Zion My holy mountain. Jerusalem will be holy, and strangers will never pass through it again.

God Brings Good to His People

18 "In that day the mountains will drip with sweet wine and the hills will flow with milk. All the rivers of Judah will flow with water. And a river will go out from the house of the Lord to water the valley of Shittim. 19 Egypt will be destroyed and Edom will become a desert waste, because of the bad things done to the sons of

Judah. They have killed people in the land of Judah who were not guilty of wrong-doing. **20** But people will live in Judah and Jerusalem forever. **21** I will punish the ones who killed them, whom I have not yet punished, for the Lord lives in Zion."

AMOS

1 These are the words of Amos, a shep-herd of Tekoa, which he received in special dreams about Israel two years be-fore the earth shook. Uzziah was king of Judah then, and Jeroboam the son of Joash was the king of Israel. **2** He said, "The Lord makes a loud noise from Zion. He lets His voice be heard from Jerusalem. And the shepherds' fields are filled with sorrow, and the top of Carmel dries up."

God Judges Israel's Neighbors—Syria

3 The Lord says, "For three sins of Da-mascus and for four, I will not hold back punishment. They have crushed Gilead with tools of sharp iron. **4** So I will send fire upon the people of Hazael, and it will destroy the strong-places of Ben-hadad. **5** I will break down the gate of Damascus, and destroy the people from the Valley of Aven and the king from Beth-Eden. The people of Syria will be taken away to Kir," says the Lord.

Philistia

6 The Lord says, "For three sins of Gaza and for four, I will not hold back punish-ment. They took a nation of people away and sold them to Edom. **7** So I will send fire upon the wall of Gaza, and it will de-stroy her strong-places. **8** I will destroy the people from Ashdod and the king from Ashkelon. I will send My power against Ekron, and the rest of the Philistines will die," says the Lord God.

Tyre

9 The Lord says, "For three sins of Tyre and for four, I will not hold back punish-ment. They took a nation of people and sold them to Edom. They did not remem-ber the agreement between brothers. **10** So I will send fire upon the wall of Tyre, and it will destroy her strong-places."

Edom

11 The Lord says, "For three sins of Edom and for four, I will not hold back punish-ment. He went after his brother with the sword and would not have loving-pity. He was always angry, and he held on to his anger forever. **12** So I will send fire upon Teman, and it will destroy the strong-places of Bozrah."

Ammon

13 The Lord says, "For three sins of Ammon and for four, I will not hold back punishment. They tore open the women of Gilead who were going to have a baby, so that they would get more land. **14** So I will set a fire on the wall of Rabbah, and it will destroy her strong-places. Then there will be cries of war on the day of battle, and strong winds on the day of the storm. **15** And their king and his sons will be taken away to a strange land," says the Lord.

Moab

2 The Lord says, "For three sins of Moab and for four, I will not hold back pun-ishment. He burned the bones of the king of Edom to ashes. **2** So I will send fire upon Moab, and it will destroy the strong-places of Kerioth. Moab will die among much noise, with cries of war and the sound of a horn. **3** I will kill the ruler of Moab and all his sons with him," says the Lord.

Judah

4 The Lord says, "For three sins of Judah and for four, I will not hold back punish-ment. They turned away from the Law of the Lord. They have not obeyed His Laws. They have gone the wrong way, following the lies of their fathers. **5** So I will send fire upon Judah, and it will destroy the strong-places of Jerusalem."

God Judges Israel

6 The Lord says, "For three sins of Israel and for four, I will not hold back punish-ment. They sell those who are right and good for money. To get shoes, they sell people who are in need. **7** They crush those who are poor in the dust of the earth with their feet. They push the poor out of the way. A man and his father go to the same girl and sin against My holy name. **8** They lie down beside every altar on clothing taken as trust for promises. And in the house of their God they drink the wine which was paid by those who have done wrong.

9 "I destroyed the Amorite before them, who was as tall as the cedar trees and as strong as the oaks. I destroyed his fruit above and his root below. 10 I brought you up from the land of Egypt and led you in the desert for forty years to give you the land of the Amorite. 11 Then I raised up some of your sons to speak for Me, and some of your young men to be Nazirites. Is this not true, you sons of Israel?" says the Lord. 12 "But you made the Nazirites drink wine. And you told the men who speak for Me not to speak. 13 Now I will crush you down like a wagon is crushed under a heavy load of grain. 14 Even the fast man will not get away. The strong man will not keep his strength. And the powerful man will not save his life. 15 He who uses the bow will not stand. The fast runner will not get away. The horseman will not save his life. 16 Even the strongest of heart among the men of war will run away without clothes on that day," says the Lord.

Word from the Man of God

3 O people of Israel, hear this word which the Lord has spoken against you and against the whole family which He brought up from the land of Egypt. 2 "You are the only ones I have chosen among all the families of the earth. So I must punish you for all your sins." 3 Do two men walk together unless they have made an agreement? 4 Does a lion make noise among the trees when he has no food? Does a young lion cry out from his home if he has not caught anything? 5 Does a bird fall into a trap on the ground when there is no food to tempt it? Does a trap jump up from the ground when it does not catch anything? 6 Are not the people afraid when a horn is blown in a city? When trouble comes to a city, has not the Lord caused it? 7 For sure the Lord does not do anything without making His plan known to His servants who speak for Him. 8 The lion has made a noise! Who will not be afraid? The Lord God has spoken! Who can keep from speaking His Word?

Israel Will Be Punished for Its Sin

9 Say to the people who live in the strong cities of Ashdod and Egypt, "Gather together on the mountains of Samaria. See all the trouble within her and how her people suffer. 10 They do not know how to do what is right," says the Lord. "They store up in their strong cities what they have fought for and robbed."

11 So the Lord God says, "Those who hate you will gather around the land. They will pull down your strong-places and rob your strong cities." 12 The Lord says, "As the shepherd saves from the lion's mouth just two legs or a piece of an ear, so will the people of Israel living in Samaria be saved, with the corner of a bed and a part of a cover. 13 Hear and speak against the family of Jacob," says the Lord God, the God of All. 14 "On the day I punish Israel for her sins, I will punish the altars of Bethel. The horns of the altar will be cut off and fall to the ground. 15 I will destroy the winter house together with the summer house. The houses of ivory will be destroyed, and the beautiful houses will come to an end," says the Lord.

4 Listen to this, you fat cows of Bashan who are on the mountain of Samaria. You make it hard for the poor. You crush those in need. You say to your husbands, "Bring us something to drink!" 2 As the Lord God is holy, He has promised, "The days are coming when they will take you away with meat-hooks. And the last of you will be taken with fish hooks. 3 You will go out through breaks in the walls. Each of you will go straight out. And you will be sent to Harmon," says the Lord.

4 "Go to Bethel and sin! Go and sin much more in Gilgal! Bring your gifts in worship every morning. Every three days give a tenth part of what you receive. 5 Give a thank gift of bread made with yeast. And make your free-will gifts known. For this is what you love to do, O people of Israel," says the Lord God.

Israel Did Not Learn

6 "I kept food from your teeth in all your cities. I did not let you have enough bread in all your places. Yet you have not returned to Me," says the Lord. 7 "I kept the rain from you while there were still three months until gathering time. Then I would send rain on one city, but would send no rain on another city. One part would receive rain, while the part which did not receive rain would dry up. 8 People would go from city to city to drink water, but would not get enough. Yet you have not returned to Me," says the Lord. 9 "I sent hot wind to dry up your fields. The locust destroyed your many gardens and grape-fields, fig trees and olive trees. Yet you have not

returned to Me," says the Lord. ¹⁰ "I sent a very bad disease upon you as I had done to Egypt. I killed your young men with the sword and took your horses away. I filled your nose with the bad smell of your camp. Yet you have not returned to Me," says the Lord. ¹¹ "I destroyed some of you as I destroyed Sodom and Gomorrah. You were like a burning stick pulled out of the fire. Yet you have not returned to Me," says the Lord. ¹² "So I will do this to you, O Israel. And because I will do this to you, get ready to meet your God, O Israel." ¹³ He is the One Who makes the mountains and the wind. He makes His thoughts known to man. He turns the morning into darkness, and walks on the high places of the earth. The Lord God of All is His name.

A Call to Turn from Sin

5 Hear this word, O people of Israel, this song of sorrow which I sing for you: ² "The young pure woman Israel has fallen, and she will not rise again. She is left alone on her land. There is no one to raise her up." ³ For the Lord God says, "The city of Israel that sends out a thousand soldiers will have a hundred left. And the one that sends out a hundred will have ten left."

⁴ The Lord says to the people of Israel, "Look for Me and live. ⁵ But do not look for Bethel. Do not go to Gilgal or cross over to Beersheba. For the people of Gilgal will be taken away to a strange land, and Bethel will come to nothing." ⁶ Look for the Lord and live, or He will break out like fire in the family of Joseph. It will destroy, and no one in Bethel will be able to stop it. ⁷ You turn what is right into something bitter. You throw what is right and good down to the earth.

⁸ The Lord made the stars of Pleiades and Orion. He changes darkness into morning, and turns day into night. He calls for the waters of the sea and pours them out on the earth. The Lord is His name. ⁹ He destroys the strong, so that the strong city is laid waste.

¹⁰ They hate him who speaks strong words in the gate. They hate him who speaks the truth. ¹¹ You crush the poor under foot and make them pay taxes with their grain. Because of this, even though you have built houses of cut stone, you will not live in them and even though you have planted beautiful grape-fields, you will not drink their wine. ¹² For I know that you have done much wrong and your sins are many. You make trouble for those who are

right and good, and you take pay in secret for wrong-doing. You will not be fair to the poor. ¹³ The wise man keeps quiet at such a time, for it is a sinful time.

¹⁴ Look for good and not sin, that you may live. Then the Lord God of All will be with you, just as you have said. ¹⁵ Hate sin, and love good. And let what is fair be done at the gate. It may be that the Lord God of All will show kindness to those left of Joseph.

The Day of the Lord

¹⁶ So the Lord, the Lord God of All, says, "There is a loud crying in the city. In all the streets they say, 'It is bad! It is bad!' They call the farmers to cry in sorrow. They call those whose work is to cry over the dead to sing songs of sorrow. ¹⁷ And there are cries of sorrow in all the grape-fields, because I will pass among you," says the Lord.

¹⁸ It is bad for you who want the day of the Lord to come. For what will the day of the Lord be to you? It will be darkness and not light. ¹⁹ It will be as when a man runs away from a lion and is met by a bear. It will be as when a man goes home and rests with his hand against the wall, and gets bitten by a snake. ²⁰ Will not the day of the Lord be darkness instead of light, very dark with nothing bright in it?

²¹ "I hate your special suppers. I will have nothing to do with them. And I am not pleased with your religious meetings. ²² Even if you give Me burnt gifts and grain gifts in worship, I will not receive them. I will not even look at the peace gifts of your fat animals. ²³ Take the noise of your songs away from Me. I will not listen to the sound of your harps. ²⁴ But let what is fair roll down like waters. Let what is right and good flow forever like a river.

²⁵ "O people of Israel, was it to Me you gave gifts of animals and grain on the altar for forty years in the desert? ²⁶ You also carried with you Sikkuth your king and Kiyyun your star god, the false gods you made for yourselves. ²⁷ So I will make you go as prisoners to the other side of Damascus," says the Lord, Whose name is the God of All.

Israel to Be Destroyed

6 It is bad for those who are taking it easy in Zion, and for those who feel safe on the mountain of Samaria, you great men of the most important nation, to whom the people of Israel come! ² Go over to Calneh and look. And go from there to great Hamath. Then go down to Gath of the Philistines. Are they better than these nations? Is their land better than yours? [3] You put off the day of trouble, and bring near the seat of anger.

[4] How bad it will be for you who lie on beds of ivory and spread out upon your long seats! You eat lambs from the flock and calves from the cattle-house. [5] You sing songs to the sound of the harp. Like David you write songs for yourselves. [6] You drink wine from the holy dishes, and pour the best oil on yourselves. Yet you are not filled with sorrow because Joseph has been destroyed! [7] You will be among the first to be taken away as prisoners to a strange land, and your happy times of rest will pass away.

[8] The Lord God has promised by Himself. The Lord God of All has said, "I hate the pride of Jacob, and I hate his strong-places, so I will give up the city and everything in it." [9] If ten men are left in one house, they will die. [10] The dead man's brother, who is to take care of the body, will lift him up to carry his bones from the house. And he will say to the one inside the house, "Is anyone else with you?" That one will say, "No." Then he will say, "Keep quiet! For the name of the Lord must not be spoken." [11] For the Lord is going to say that the great house must be broken apart and the small house into pieces.

[12] Do horses run on rocks? Does one plow them with oxen? Yet you have turned what is fair into poison. You have turned what is right and good into something bitter. [13] You who have joy in Lo-debar, and say, "Did we not take Karnaim by our own strength?" [14] The Lord God of All says, "I am going to raise up a nation against you, O people of Israel. And they will bring much suffering upon you from the gate of Hamath to the river of the Arabah."

Special Dream about Locusts

7 This is what the Lord God showed me: He was making a gathering of locusts when the spring grain began to grow. The spring grain was after the king's share had been cut. [2] When they had finished eating the grass I said, "Lord God, forgive! O that Jacob may stay alive for he is so small!" [3] So the Lord changed His mind about this. "It will not be," said the Lord.

Special Dream about Fire

[4] This is what the Lord God showed me: The Lord God was calling for a punishment by fire. It dried up the deep waters and began to destroy the farm land. [5] Then I said, "Lord God, I beg You to stop! How can Jacob stay alive, for he is so small?" [6] So the Lord changed His mind about this. "This also will not be," said the Lord God.

Special Dream about a String

[7] This is what He showed me: The Lord was standing by a wall made straight by a string held in His hand. [8] The Lord said to me, "What do you see, Amos?" And I said, "A string." Then the Lord said, "See, I am about to put a straight string among my people Israel. I will not change My mind again about punishing them. [9] The high places of Isaac will be destroyed. The holy places of Israel will be laid waste. Then I will rise up against the people of Jeroboam with the sword."

Amos and Amaziah

[10] Then Amaziah, the religious leader of Bethel, sent word to King Jeroboam of Israel, saying, "Amos has made plans against you among the people of Israel. His words will destroy the land. [11] For this is what Amos is saying: 'Jeroboam will die by the sword, and the people of Israel will be taken away from their own land to a strange land.'" [12] Then Amaziah said to Amos, "Go, you who tell what is going to happen in the future! Run away to the land of Judah! There eat your bread, and there speak your words! [13] But never speak about your special dreams again at Bethel. For it is a holy place of the king, a place where the nation worships."

[14] Amos answered Amaziah, saying, "I am not a man who tells what is going to happen in the future, or the son of such a man. I take care of sheep and cattle, and grow fig trees. [15] But the Lord took me from following the flock and said to me, 'Go and speak in My name to My people Israel.' [16] So now hear the Word of the Lord. You are saying, 'Do not speak against Israel or preach against the people of Isaac.' [17] So this is what the Lord says: 'Your wife will sell the use of her body in the city. Your sons and daughters will be killed by the sword. Your land will be divided and given to others. You yourself will die in an unclean land. And Israel will be driven away from this land to a strange country.'"

Special Dream of a Basket of Fruit

8 This is what the Lord God showed me: There was a basket of summer fruit. [2] And the Lord said, "What do you see, Amos?" I said, "A basket of summer fruit." Then the Lord said to me, "The end has come for My people Israel. I will not change My mind again about punishing them. 3 The songs of the king's house will become loud cries of sorrow on that day," says the Lord God. "There will be many dead bodies. In every place they will be thrown out without a word."

4 Hear this, you who crush under foot those who are in need, to put an end to the poor of the land. 5 You say, "When will the New Moon be over, so that we may buy grain? When will the Day of Rest be over, so that we may open the store and sell grain? Then we will make the basket smaller and the weight bigger, and we will lie about the weight. 6 We will buy the poor for money, and those in need for shoes. And we will sell the part of the grain that is of no worth."

7 The Lord has promised by the pride of Jacob, "For sure I will never forget anything they have done. 8 Will not the land shake because of this? Will not everyone who lives in it be filled with sorrow? All of it will rise up like the Nile. It will be troubled, and will fall like the Nile River of Egypt. 9 On that day," says the Lord God, "I will make the sun go down at noon. I will make the earth dark in the daytime. 10 I will turn your special suppers into times of sorrow, and all your songs into songs of sorrow. I will make all of you wear cloth made from hair, and cut all the hair from your heads. I will fill that time with sorrow, as if an only son had died. And the end of it will be like a bitter day.

11 "The days are coming," says the Lord God, "when I will send a time upon the land when the people will be very hungry. They will not be hungry for bread or thirsty for water, but they will be hungry to hear the Words of the Lord. 12 People will go from sea to sea, and from the north to the east. They will go from place to place to look for the Word of the Lord, but they will not find it. 13 On that day the beautiful, pure, young women and the young men will lose their strength and fall because of thirst. 14 As for those who swear by the false gods of Samaria, saying, 'As your god lives, O Dan,' and 'As the way of Beersheba lives,' they will fall and never rise again."

The Lord Judges Israel

9 I saw the Lord standing beside the altar, and He said, "Break the tops of the pillars so that the bases shake! Break them to pieces on the heads of all the people! Then I will kill the rest of them with the sword. Not one of them will get away. 2 Even if they dig into the place of the dead, My hand will take them from there. Even if they go up to heaven, I will bring them down from there. 3 Even if they hide on the top of Mount Carmel, I will find them and take them from there. Even if they hide themselves from My eyes on the bottom of the sea, there I will tell the large sea-snake to bite them. 4 Even if they are taken away to a strange land by those who hate them, there I will have the sword kill them. I will set My eyes against them to hurt them, and not to bring good to them."

5 The Lord God of All is the One Who touches the land and it melts. All those who live in it are filled with sorrow. All of it rises and falls like the Nile River of Egypt. 6 The Lord builds His upper rooms in the heavens and sets His sky over the earth. He calls for the waters of the sea and pours them out on the earth. The Lord is His name.

7 "Are you not like the Ethiopians to Me, you people of Israel?" says the Lord. "Did I not bring up Israel from the land of Egypt, and the Philistines from Caphtor, and the Syrians from Kir? 8 See, the eyes of the Lord God are on the sinful nation, and I will destroy it from the earth. But I will not destroy all the people of Jacob," says the Lord.

9 "I will say what must be done. I will shake the people of Jacob among all the nations, as grain is shaken on a fine net. But not the smallest seed will fall to the ground. 10 All the sinners among My people who say, 'The trouble will not catch up to us or come to us,' will die by the sword.

Israel to Have New Life

11 "In that day I will build again the tent of David that fell down. Yes, I will build it again from the stones that fell down. I will set it up again as it used to be. 12 And so the people of Israel will own what is left of the land of Edom and all the nations that are called by My name," says the Lord who does this.

13 "The days are coming," says the Lord, "when the man who plows will catch up with the man who gathers. The man who crushes the grapes will catch up with the man who plants the seed. The mountains will drip sweet wine, and all the hills will flow with it. 14 And I will return My people Israel to their riches. They will

build again the cities that have been destroyed, and live in them. They will plant grape-fields and drink their wine. And they will make gardens and eat their fruit.

¹⁵ I will plant My people on their land. And they will never again be pulled up from the land I gave them," says the Lord your God.

OBADIAH

Edom to Be Judged

This is the special dream of Obadiah, what the Lord God says about Edom. We have heard this news from the Lord. And a man has been sent among the nations to say, "Get ready! Let us go fight a war against Edom." ² "I will make you small among the nations. Everyone will hate you. ³ The pride of your heart has fooled you. You live in the holes of the rock. Your home is high in the mountains. And so you say in your heart, 'Who will bring me down to the ground?' ⁴ Even when you build your home as high as the eagle, and make your nest among the stars, I will bring you down from there," says the Lord. ⁵ "If robbers came to you during the night, O how you will be destroyed! Would they not steal only enough for themselves? If those who gather grapes came to you, would they not leave some behind? ⁶ O how Esau will be robbed! His hidden riches will be looked for until they are found. ⁷ All the men you have made an agreement with will drive you from the country. The men at peace with you will lie to you and get power over you. Those who eat your bread will set a trap for you, but you will not know it." ⁸ The Lord says, "On that day I will destroy the wise men from Edom and understanding from Mount Esau. ⁹ Then your powerful soldiers will be troubled, O Teman, and every one from Mount Esau will be killed.

Edom Hurt His Brother

¹⁰ "Because you have hurt your brother Jacob, you will be covered with shame and destroyed forever. ¹¹ You stood aside on that day when strangers carried his riches away. Men from another land went in through his gate and divided Jerusalem among themselves. And you were like one of them. ¹² Do not look down on your brother in the day of his trouble. Do not be happy about the sons of Judah in the day they are destroyed. Yes, do not speak with pride in the day of their trouble. ¹³ Do not go in through the gate of My people in the day of their trouble. Do not speak with pride about their suffering in the day of their trouble. And do not rob their riches in the day of their trouble. ¹⁴ Do not stand at the cross-roads to kill their people who get away. And do not put into prison those who are left alive in the day of their trouble.

¹⁵ "For the day of the Lord is near for all nations. As you have done, it will be done to you. What you do will come back to you on your own head. ¹⁶ Just as you drank on My holy mountain, so all the nations will drink all the time. They will drink and drink, and be as if they had never been.

Israel Will Win

¹⁷ "But on Mount Zion there will be a way to be set free, and it will be holy. The people of Jacob will own what belongs to them. ¹⁸ The people of Jacob will be a fire. The people of Joseph will be burning. But the people of Esau will be like dry grass. They will set them on fire and destroy them. None of the people of Esau will be left alive," for the Lord has spoken. ¹⁹ People of the Negev will live on Mount Esau. And those in the lower land will live in the land of the Philistines. They will live in the land of Ephraim and Samaria, and Benjamin will own Gilead. ²⁰ The people of Israel who are living among the Canaanites as far as Zarephath, and the people of Jerusalem who are in Sephared, will own the cities of the Negev. ²¹ The men of Jerusalem who fight and win the battle will go up Mount Zion to rule over Mount Esau. And the nation will belong to the Lord.

JONAH

Jonah Does Not Obey the Lord

1 The Word of the Lord came to Jonah the son of Amittai, saying, 2 "Get up and go to the large city of Nineveh, and preach against it. For their sin has come up before Me." 3 But Jonah ran away from the Lord going toward Tarshish. He went down to Joppa and found a ship which was going to Tarshish. Jonah paid money, and got on the ship to go with them, to get away from the Lord.

4 Then the Lord sent a powerful wind upon the sea, and there was such a big storm that the ship was about to break up. 5 The sailors became afraid, and every man cried to his god. They threw the things that were in the ship into the sea so that it would not be so heavy. But Jonah had gone below in the ship and had lain down and fallen asleep. 6 So the captain went to him and said, "How can you sleep? Get up and call on your god. It may be that your god will care about us, and we will not die." 7 Then the sailors said to each other, "Come, let us draw names so we can find out who is to blame for this trouble." So they drew names, and Jonah's name was drawn. 8 Then they said to him, "Now tell us! Who is to blame for this? What is your work? Where do you come from? What is your country? From what people are you?" 9 Jonah said to them, "I am a Hebrew, and I worship the Lord God of heaven Who made the sea and the dry land."

10 Then the men were filled with fear and said to him, "How could you do this?" For the men knew that he was running away from the Lord, because he had told them. 11 So they said to him, "What should we do to you to make the sea quiet down for us?" For the storm was getting worse. 12 Jonah said to them, "Pick me up and throw me into the sea. Then the sea will quiet down for you. For I know that this bad storm has come upon you because of me." 13 The men rowed hard to return to land, but they could not, for the wind was blowing even worse against them. 14 Then they called on the Lord and said, "We beg You, O Lord, do not let us die for what this man has done. And do not let us become guilty for killing someone who is not to blame. For You, O Lord, have done as You have pleased."

15 So they picked up Jonah and threw him into the sea, and the storm stopped. 16 Then the men feared the Lord very much. They gave a gift in worship to the Lord and made promises to Him.

17 The Lord sent a big fish to swallow Jonah, and he was in the stomach of the fish for three days and three nights.

Jonah's Prayer

2 Then Jonah prayed to the Lord his God while in the stomach of the fish, 2 saying, "I called out to the Lord because of my trouble, and He answered me. I cried for help from the place of the dead, and You heard my voice. 3 You threw me into the deep waters, to the very bottom of the sea. A flood was all around me and all Your waves passed over me. 4 Then I said, 'I have been sent away from Your eyes. But I will look again toward Your holy house.' 5 Waters closed in over me. The sea was all around me. Weeds were around my head. 6 I went down to the roots of the mountains. The walls of the earth were around me forever. But You have brought me up from the grave, O Lord my God. 7 While I was losing all my strength, I remembered the Lord. And my prayer came to You, into Your holy house. 8 Those who worship false gods have given up their faith in You. 9 But I will give gifts in worship to You with a thankful voice. I will give You what I have promised. The Lord is the One Who saves."

10 Then the Lord spoke to the fish, and it spit Jonah out onto the dry land.

Jonah Obeys the Lord

3 The Word of the Lord came to Jonah a second time, saying, 2 "Get up and go to the large city of Nineveh, and tell the people there the news which I am going to tell you." 3 So Jonah got up and went to Nineveh, as the Lord had told him. Now Nineveh was a very large city. It took three days to walk through it. 4 Jonah started into the city, for a day's walk, and he cried out, "In forty days Nineveh will be destroyed!"

5 Then the people of Nineveh believed in God. They called for a time when no food was to be eaten. And all the people, from the greatest to the least, put on clothes made from hair. 6 When the news came to the king of Nineveh, he got up from his throne and laid aside his beautiful clothing. Then he covered himself with cloth made from hair, and sat in ashes. 7 And he sent word through all of Nineveh, saying, "By the law of the king and his leaders, do not let man or animal, cattle or flock, taste anything. Do not let them eat or drink water. 8 Both man and animal

must be covered with cloth made from hair. Everyone must pray to God with all his heart, so each person may turn from his sinful way and from the bad things he has done. 9 Who knows? God may change His mind and stop being angry so that we will not die."

10 When God saw what they did, and that they turned from their sinful way, He changed His mind about the trouble He said He would bring upon them, and He did not destroy Nineveh.

Jonah's Anger and the Lord's Loving-Pity

4 But Jonah was not pleased at all, and he became angry. 2 He prayed to the Lord and said, "O Lord, is this not what I said You would do while still in my own country? That is why I ran away to Tarshish. For I knew that You are a kind and loving God Who shows pity. I knew that You are slow to anger and are filled with loving-kindness, always ready to change Your mind and not punish. 3 So now, O Lord, take my life from me. For death is better to me than life." 4 And the Lord said, "Have you any reason to be angry?"

5 Then Jonah left the city and sat to the east of the city. There he made a tent for himself, and sat in its shadow until he could see what would happen in the city. 6 Then the Lord God made a plant grow up over Jonah to cover him from the hot sun and to stop his suffering. Jonah was very happy about the plant. 7 But at the beginning of the next day, God sent a worm to destroy the plant and it dried up. 8 When the sun came up, God sent a hot east wind. And the sun's heat came upon Jonah's head so that he became weak and begged with all his heart to die. He said, "Death is better to me than life."

9 Then God said to Jonah, "Do you have a good reason to be angry about the plant?" And Jonah said, "I have a good reason to be angry, angry enough to die." 10 The Lord said, "You had loving-pity on the plant which you did not work for. You did not cause it to grow. It came up during the night and died during the night 11 And should I not have loving-pity for Nineveh, the large city where more than 120,000 people live who do not know the difference between their right and left hand, as well as many animals?"

MICAH

1 This is the Word of the Lord which came to Micah of Moresheth about Samaria and Jerusalem in the days of Jotham, Ahaz, and Hezekiah, kings of Judah.

Israel Is Judged

2 Hear, O people, all of you. Listen, O earth and all who are in it. The Lord God will speak against you from His holy house. 3 See, the Lord is coming from His place. He will come down and walk on the high places of the earth. 4 The mountains will melt under Him and the valleys will break open, like a candle in front of the fire, like water poured down a hill. 5 All this is because Jacob would not obey and because of the sins of the people of Israel. What is Jacob's sin? Is it not Samaria? What is the high place of Judah? Is it not Jerusalem? 6 So I will make Samaria a waste in the open country, a place to plant grape-fields. I will pour her stones down into the valley, and lay open the base of the city. 7 All of her false gods will be broken to pieces. Everything given in the place

of worship will be burned with fire. I will destroy all her objects of worship, for she gathered them from the pay of a woman who sells the use of her body. They will return to pay a woman who sells the use of her body.

Jerusalem Will Be Taken

8 Because of this I must cry out in sorrow. I must go without shoes and clothing. I must cry out like the wild dogs, and cry in sorrow like the ostriches. 9 For her hurt cannot be cured. It has come to Judah. It has come to the gate of my people, even to Jerusalem. 10 Do not tell about it in Gath. Do not cry at all. Roll in the dust in Beth-leaphrah. 11 Go on your way, people of Shaphir, without clothing and in shame. The people of Zaanan do not come out. Cries of sorrow come from Beth-ezel. Its help is taken from you. 12 Those who live in Maroth become weak waiting for good, because trouble has come down from the Lord to the gate of Jerusalem. 13 Tie the war-wagons to the horses, you people of Lachish. You were the beginning of sin

to the people of Zion, for the sins of Israel were found in you. 14 So give gifts to Moresheth-gath. The people of Achzib will fool the kings of Israel. 15 I will bring one who will beat you in battle, O people of Mareshah. The shining-greatness of Israel will come to Adullam. 16 Cut off all your hair in sorrow for the children you love. Let no hair be on your head like the eagle, for your children will be taken away from you.

It Is Bad for Wrong-Doers

2 It is bad for those who make plans to do wrong, who lie on their beds thinking of something sinful to do! When morning comes, they do it, because it is in their power. 2 They want fields that belong to someone else, and take them. They want houses, and take them. They rob a man and his house, a man and what has been given to him. 3 So the Lord says, "I am planning trouble against this family, from which you cannot save yourselves. You will no longer walk in pride, for it will be a time of much trouble. 4 On that day they will make fun of you and sing a bitter song of sorrow, saying, 'We are destroyed and everything is gone! My people's land is divided. He takes it from me! He gives our fields to those who turned against us.' " 5 So you will have no one among the Lord's people to divide the land in a right way for you.

Men Who Lie

6 "The people say to me, 'Do not speak about these things, because we will not be put to shame.' 7 Should it be said, O people of Jacob: "Is the Spirit of the Lord angry? Would He do such things? Do not My Words do good to the one whose way is right and good? 8 My people have begun to hate those who are at peace with them. You pull the coat off from a brother Israelite, from those who pass by in peace like men returning from war. 9 You drive the women of My people away from their beautiful houses. You take My greatness away from their children forever. 10 Get up and go away, for this is no place of rest, because it is made unclean. It is destroyed with much suffering. 11 If a man comes speaking lies and says, 'I will speak to you about wine and strong drink,' he would be the one for these people!

Israel Is Gathered Together

12 "I will gather all of you together, Jacob. I will gather all those left of Israel. I will put them together like sheep within a fence, like a flock in its field. The land will be filled with the noise of many people. 13 The One Who breaks open the way will go out before them. They will break through the gate and go out. Their king will pass through before them, and the Lord will lead them."

Sinful Leaders and Rulers

3 And I said, "Hear now, leaders of Jacob and rulers of the people of Israel! Should you not know what is fair? 2 Yet you hate good and love sin. You tear off the skin from my people and the flesh from their bones. 3 You eat my people's flesh, pull their skin off, break their bones, and cut them up like meat for the pot." 4 Then they will cry to the Lord, but He will not answer them. He will hide His face from them at that time, because they have done sinful things.

5 This is what the Lord says about the men who speak in God's name and lead my people the wrong way. When they have something to eat, they speak of peace. But they make holy war against him who does not feed them. 6 So night will come to you without a special dream. Darkness will come to you without any word about the future. The sun will go down on those who speak about special dreams, and the day will become dark over them. 7 Those who tell what is going to happen in the future will be ashamed. Those who learn about the future using their secret ways will be ashamed. They will all cover their mouths because there is no answer from God. 8 But as for me, I am filled with power, with the Spirit of the Lord, with what is fair, and with strength. I am able to make known to Jacob his wrong-doing, and to Israel his sin. 9 Now listen to this, you leaders of Jacob and rulers of the people of Israel. You hate what is fair, and turn everything around that is right. 10 You built Zion with blood and Jerusalem with much wrong-doing. 11 Her leaders take pay in secret for doing wrong. Her religious leaders teach for a price. Her men who tell what is going to happen in the future do it for money. Yet they rest upon the Lord and say, "Is not the Lord among us? No trouble will come to us." 12 So because of you Zion will be plowed as a field. Jerusalem will be laid waste. And the mountain of the Lord's house will be covered with trees.

The Lord Rules in Jerusalem

4 In the last days the mountain of the Lord's house will be the highest one of all. It will be raised above the hills, and the people will flow to it. ² Many nations will come and say, "Come, let us go up to the mountain of the Lord and to the house of the God of Jacob. He will teach us about His ways, so that we may walk in His paths." For the Law will go out from Zion, and the Word of the Lord from Jerusalem. ³ He will judge between many people. He will decide for strong nations that are far away. Then they will beat their swords into plows, and their spears into cutting hooks. Nation will not lift up sword against nation, and they will never learn war any more. ⁴ Every man will sit under his vine and under his fig tree, with no one to make him afraid. For the mouth of the Lord of All has spoken. ⁵ All the nations may walk in the name of their god. But we will walk in the name of the Lord our God forever and ever.

Israel Will Return from the Strange Land

⁶ "In that day," says the Lord, "I will gather together those who cannot walk and those who have been driven away, even those whom I have made to suffer. ⁷ I will make a new beginning with those who cannot walk. I will make a strong nation of those who have been driven away. And the Lord will rule over them in Mount Zion from that day and forever. ⁸ As for you, O watchtower of the flock, the strong place of the people of Zion, the power you had to rule will come to you again. The nation will come to Jerusalem.

⁹ "Now why do you cry out in a loud voice? Is there no king among you? Has your wise man died, so that you have pains like a woman giving birth? ¹⁰ Suffer in pain, O people of Zion, like a woman giving birth. For now you will go out of the city and live in the field, and go to Babylon. There you will be saved and He will make you free from the power of those who hate you.

¹¹ "Now many nations are gathered against you. They say, 'Let her be unclean. Let our eyes look on Zion.' ¹² But they do not know the thoughts of the Lord. They do not understand His plan. For He has gathered them like grain to the crushing-floor. ¹³ Get up and crush the grain, O people of Zion. For I will give you horns of iron and feet of brass, and you will break many nations to pieces. You will give to

the Lord what they received by hurting others. You will give their riches to the Lord of all the earth.

5 "Now gather yourselves into armies, people of Israel. They are all around us with their army. They will hit the judge of Israel on the face.

God's Chosen One Will Come from Bethlehem

² "Bethlehem Ephrathah, you are too little to be among the family groups of Judah. But from you One will come who will rule for Me in Israel. His coming was planned long ago, from the beginning." ³ He will give them up until the time when the woman in pain gives birth to a child. Then the rest of His brothers will return to the people of Israel. ⁴ And He will come and feed His flock in the strength of the Lord, in the great power of the name of the Lord His God. His people will live there and be safe, because at that time He will be great to the ends of the earth. ⁵ And He will be their peace.

Those Who Fight Israel Are Judged

When the Assyrian comes into our land and crushes under foot our strong-places, we will fight against him with seven shepherds and eight leaders. ⁶ They will rule the land of Assyria, the land of Nimrod, with the sword. And He will take us from the Assyrians when they come into our country and crush under foot our land.

⁷ Then the people who are left of Jacob will be among many people like water on the ground in the early morning from the Lord, like rain on the grass, which does not wait for man. ⁸ Those who are left of Jacob will be among the nations, among many people, like a lion among the animals in the woods, like a young lion among flocks of sheep. When he passes through, he crushes them and tears them to pieces, and there is no one to help them. ⁹ Your hand will be lifted up against those who hate you, and all of them will be destroyed.

¹⁰ "In that day," says the Lord, "I will destroy your horses and your war wagons from among you. ¹¹ I will destroy the cities of your land and tear down all your strong-places. ¹² I will put an end to your witchcraft, and you will not have people telling your future any more. ¹³ I will destroy your false gods and your pillars of worship, so that you will no longer bow down to the work of your hands. ¹⁴ I will

pull up your wooden, female goddesses Asherah, and destroy your cities. ¹⁵ And in My anger I will punish the nations that have not obeyed."

The Lord Speaks against Israel

6 Listen to what the Lord says: "Stand up and make your cause known in front of the mountains. Let the hills hear your voice. ² Listen to the Lord's cause, you mountains and bases of the earth that last forever. The Lord has something against His people, and will speak against Israel. ³ My people, what have I done to you? How have I made it hard for you? Answer Me. ⁴ I brought you out of the land of Egypt. I took you out of the land where you were servants. And I sent Moses, Aaron and Miriam to lead you. ⁵ My people, remember what Balak king of Moab said, and what Balaam son of Beor answered him. Remember what happened from Shittim to Gilgal, so that you may know the good things the Lord has done."

What the Lord Wants

⁶ What should I bring to the Lord when I bow down before the God on high? Should I come to Him with burnt gifts, with calves a year old? ⁷ Will the Lord be pleased with thousands of rams, or with 10,000 rivers of oil? Should I give my first-born to pay for not obeying? Should I give the fruit of my body for the sin of my soul? ⁸ O man, He has told you what is good. What does the Lord ask of you but to do what is fair and to love kindness, and to walk without pride with your God?

Israel Is Punished

⁹ The voice of the Lord is calling to the city, and it is wise to fear Your name: "Listen, O family of Judah, you who are gathered in the city. ¹⁰ O sinful house, can I forget the riches you got by wrong-doing? You lied about the weight of things, which I hate. ¹¹ Can I make a man not guilty who lies and has false weights in his bag? ¹² The rich men of the city have hurt many people. Her people are liars. Their tongues in their mouths speak false words. ¹³ So I have begun to punish you, to destroy you because of your sins. ¹⁴ You will eat, but you will not be filled. Your stomachs will still be empty. You will store up, but save nothing. And what you save I will give to the sword. ¹⁵ You will plant, but you will not gather. You will crush the olive, but you will not pour oil on yourself. You will

crush the grapes, but you will not drink wine. ¹⁶ You have kept the laws of Omri and all the works of the people of Ahab. You have followed their ways. So I will give you up to be destroyed, and your people will be made fun of. You, My people, will be put to shame."

Sorrow for Israel's Sins

7 It is bad for me! For I am like those who pick fruit and gather grapes. There are no grapes to eat, or any of the early figs that I want so much. ² There is not a God-like person left in the land. There is no good person among men. All of them lie in wait to kill. Each one hunts the other with a net. ³ Both hands are very able in doing sinful things. The ruler and the judge ask for pay in secret to do what is wrong. The powerful man tells what he wants, and they all make plans together. ⁴ The best of them is like a thistle. The most honest of them is like a thorn bush. The day you have a watchman, you will be punished. Then their trouble will come. ⁵ Do not trust a neighbor. Do not put trust in a friend. Be careful what you say even with her who lies in your arms. ⁶ For a son does not honor his father. A daughter rises up against her mother. And a daughter-in-law turns against her mother-in-law. Those of a man's own house hate him.

⁷ But as for me, I will watch for the Lord. I will wait for the God Who saves me. My God will hear me.

The Lord Saves

⁸ Do not have joy over me, you who hate me. When I fall, I will rise. Even though I am in darkness, the Lord will be my light. ⁹ I will suffer under the Lord's anger, because I have sinned against Him, until He speaks for me and does what is fair for me. He will bring me out to the light, and I will see His saving power. ¹⁰ Then the one who hated me will see, and shame will cover her who said to me, "Where is the Lord your God?" My eyes will look on her, and she will be crushed under foot like mud in the streets. ¹¹ It will be a day for building your walls. At that time your land will be made larger. ¹² In that day people will come to you from Assyria and the cities of Egypt, from Egypt to the Euphrates River, from sea to sea and from mountain to mountain. ¹³ The earth will be laid waste because of its people and the things they have done.

The Lord's Loving-Kindness for Israel

14 Shepherd Your people with Your power. Take care of Your chosen flock which lives by itself in the woods, in a field of much fruit. Let them eat in Bashan and Gilead as in days long ago. 15 "As in the days when you came out of the land of Egypt, I will show you powerful works." 16 Nations will see and be ashamed of all their power. They will put their hands on their mouths, and will not be able to hear with their ears. 17 They will eat the dust like a snake, like animals that move along the ground. They

will come out of their strong-places shaking with fear. They will come in much fear to the Lord our God, and they will be afraid of You. 18 Who is a God like You, Who forgives sin and the wrong-doing of Your chosen people who are left? He does not stay angry forever because He is happy to show loving-kindness. 19 He will again have loving-pity on us. He will crush our sins under foot. Yes, You will throw all our sins into the deep sea. 20 You will be true to Jacob and show loving-kindness to Abraham, as You promised our fathers in days long ago.

NAHUM

1 This is the word about Nineveh, the book of the special dream of Nahum the Elkoshite.

God's Anger against Nineveh

2 The Lord is a jealous God and One Who punishes. The Lord punishes and is angry. The Lord punishes those who fight against Him. He is angry with those who hate Him. 3 The Lord is slow to anger and great in power. The Lord will be sure to punish the guilty. The way He punishes is in the strong wind and storm. The clouds are the dust under His feet. 4 He speaks sharp words to the sea and makes it dry. He dries up all the rivers. Bashan and Carmel dry up. The flowers of Lebanon dry up. 5 Mountains shake because of Him, and the hills melt. The earth is laid waste before Him, the world and everyone in it. 6 Who can stand before His anger? Who can live through the burning of His anger? His anger is poured out like fire, and the rocks are broken up by Him. 7 The Lord is good, a safe place in times of trouble. And He knows those who come to Him to be safe. 8 But He will put an end to Nineveh by making a flood flow over it. And He will drive those who hate Him into darkness. 9 Whatever plan you make against the Lord, He will destroy it. Trouble will not come a second time. 10 They are like thorns that tie themselves together, like those who are drunk with strong drink. They are destroyed like dry grass. 11 From you one has come who makes sinful plans against the Lord, one who talks about sinful things to do. 12 The Lord says, "Even if they are strong and many, they will be destroyed and pass away. I have brought trouble to you, O Judah, but I will not

bring you trouble any more. 13 Now I will break his load off your shoulders and tear off your chains."

14 The Lord has said this about you: "You will have no one to carry on your name. I will destroy the false gods and objects of worship from the house of your gods. I will make your grave ready, for you are very sinful."

15 See, on the mountains are the feet of him who brings good news and speaks of peace! Keep your special suppers, O Judah. Keep your promises. For the sinful one will never come against you again. He is destroyed.

Nineveh Is Destroyed

2 The one who destroys has come against you, O Nineveh. Put men on the battle-walls. Watch the road. Be strong. Be ready for battle. 2 For the Lord will make Jacob great again, like the greatness of Israel, even when destroyers have destroyed them and their vine branches.

3 The battle-coverings of his strong men are red. His men of war are dressed in red. The war-wagons shine like fire when they are made ready. The cypress spears are waved. 4 The war-wagons race in the streets. They rush through the city. They look like fire and move like lightning. 5 The leaders are called. They lose their step as they go, and hurry to the wall. The battle-covering is set up. 6 The river gates are opened and the king's house falls down. 7 The city is laid waste and the people are carried away. Her women servants are crying like doves, beating on their breasts.

8 Nineveh is like a pool, where water runs away. "Stop! Stop!" they cry. But no

one turns back. 9 Take the silver! Take the gold! For there is no end of the riches, every kind of thing of great worth. 10 Everything has been taken from her! Yes, she is an empty waste! Hearts are melting in fear and knees are knocking! All bodies suffer, and all their faces turn white! 11 Where is the home of the lions, the place where they feed their young, where the male and female and young lions went, with nothing to be afraid of? 12 The lion killed enough for his young, and for his female lions. He filled his home with food, with torn flesh. 13 "I am against you," says the Lord of All. "I will burn up your war-wagons in smoke. A sword will destroy your young lions. I will cut off your food from the land. And the voice of your men who came with news will never be heard again."

It Is Bad for Nineveh

3 It is bad for the city of blood, full of lies and stolen riches! There is no end of her prizes of war! 2 The noise of the whip, the noise of the wheel, running horses and rolling war-wagons! 3 Horsemen rushing to battle, swords and spears shining, many dead, too many dead bodies to number! They fall over the dead bodies! 4 All this is because of the many sins of the woman who sells the use of her body. She tempts with her beauty and uses witchcraft. She sells nations by her sinful acts, and families by her witchcraft. 5 "I am against you," says the Lord of All. "I will lift up your clothing over your face and let the nations see your body. The nations will see your shame. 6 I will throw dirt on you and make you unclean. People will look at you and see how bad you are. 7 All who see you will leave you and say, 'Nineveh is destroyed! Who will have sorrow for her?' Where can I find anyone to comfort you?"

8 Are you better than Thebes, which is

by the Nile River? Water was all around her. The sea kept her safe, for the water was her wall. 9 Ethiopia and Egypt were her strength, with too many to number. Put and Lubim were among her helpers. 10 Yet she was taken away to a strange land. She was taken away in chains. Her small children were beaten to death at every street corner. They drew names to see who would get her men of honor. And all her great men were put in chains. 11 You also will become drunk. You will be hidden. You will look for a safe place from those who hate you. 12 All your strong towers are like fig trees with first-fruits. When they are shaken, they fall into the mouth of the one who eats them. 13 Your soldiers are all women. The gates of your land are opened wide to those who hate you. Fire destroys your gates. 14 Store up water to drink when you are shut in by armies! Make your walls stronger! Go into the clay to make more clay blocks for building! 15 There the fire will destroy you. The sword will kill you. It will destroy you like the locust.

Make yourselves as many as the locusts, as many as the flying locusts. 16 You have more traders than the stars of heaven. The locust destroys everything from the land and flies away. 17 Your watchmen are like the flying locusts. Your leaders are like clouds of locusts. They stay in the stone walls on a cold day. When the sun rises they fly away and no one knows where they are. 18 Your shepherds are sleeping, O king of Assyria. Your leaders are lying down. Your people have gone everywhere on the mountains. And there is no one to gather them together again. 19 Nothing can heal your hurt. Your sore cannot be cured. All who hear about you will clap their hands over you. For who has not suffered under your sinful ways again and again?

HABAKKUK

Habakkuk's Question

1 This is the special word which Habakkuk the man of God saw. 2 O Lord, how long must I call for help before You will hear? I cry out to You, "We are being hurt!" But You do not save us. 3 Why do you make me see sins and wrong-doing? People are being destroyed in anger in front of me. There is arguing and fighting.

4 The Law is not followed. What is right is never done. For the sinful are all around those who are right and good, so what is right looks like sin.

The Lord's Answer

5 "Look among the nations, and see! Be surprised and full of wonder! For I am doing something in your days that you

would not believe if you were told. 6 I am bringing the Babylonians to power. They are people filled with anger who go across the whole earth to take homes that are not theirs. 7 They fill others with fear. They make their own law about what is fair and honored. 8 Their horses are faster than leopards, and show less pity than wolves in the evening. Their horsemen come on running horses from far away. They fly like an eagle coming down to get food. 9 They all come in anger. Their armies move like the desert wind. They gather prisoners like sand. 10 They make fun of kings and laugh at rulers. They laugh at every strong city and build a battle-wall to take it. 11 Then they move through like the wind and keep going. They are guilty men, whose strength is their god."

Habakkuk's Second Question

12 Have You not lived forever, O Lord, my God, my Holy One? We will not die. O Lord, You have chosen them to judge. You, O Rock, have chosen them to punish us. 13 Your eyes are too pure to look at sin. You cannot look on wrong. Why then do You look with favor on those who do wrong? Why are You quiet when the sinful destroy those who are more right and good than they? 14 Why have You made men like the fish of the sea, like things which move along the ground that have no ruler? 15 The Babylonians bring all of them up with a hook, and pull them away with their net. They gather them together in their fishing net, and so they have joy and are glad. 16 So they give gifts in worship to their net. They burn special perfume to their fishing net, because their net catches all the good things and good food they need. 17 Will they empty their net forever and keep on destroying nations without pity?

2 I will take my stand and keep watch. I will take my place on the tower. And I will keep watch to see what the Lord will say, and how I should answer when He speaks strong words to me.

The Lord's Answer to Habakkuk

2 Then the Lord answered me and said, "Write down the special dream on stone so that one may read it in a hurry. 3 For it is not yet time for it to come true. The time is coming in a hurry, and it will come true. If you think it is slow in coming, wait for it. For it will happen for sure, and it will not wait. 4 As for the proud one, his soul is not

right in him. But the one who is right and good will live by his faith.

It Is Bad for the Wrong-Doers

5 "Also, wine fools the proud man, so he does not stay at home. He is like the grave who always wants more. Like death, he never has enough. He gathers all nations for himself, and gathers all people for his own. 6 "Will not all these people make fun of him and say, 'It is bad for him who gathers what is not his and makes himself rich with other people's money. How long will this go on?' 7 Will not those to whom you owe money rise up all at once? Will they not wake up and make you afraid? Then they will take what belongs to you. 8 Because you have robbed many nations, the rest of them will rob you. For you have killed men. You have destroyed lands and cities and everyone in them.

9 "It is bad for him who builds his house by sinful ways, to put his nest in a high place to be safe from trouble! 10 You have brought shame upon your house by destroying many nations. You are sinning against yourself. 11 The stone will cry out from the wall, and the roof will answer it from the wood.

12 "It is bad for him who builds a city with blood, and builds a town with wrong-doing! 13 Is it not the will of the All-powerful Lord that people work for what will burn up and nations make themselves tired for nothing? 14 For the earth will be filled with knowing of the Lord's shining-greatness, as the waters cover the sea.

15 "It is bad for him who makes his neighbors drink, mixing in his poison to make them drunk, so he can look on their shame! 16 You will be filled with shame instead of honor. Now you yourself drink and let your own shame be seen. The cup in the Lord's right hand will come around to you, and your greatness will turn to shame. 17 The bad things you have done to Lebanon will come back to you. Because you have killed its animals, now they will make you afraid. This will happen because of all the killing you have done. You have destroyed lands and cities and everyone in them.

18 "Of what worth is a false god when a workman has made it? Of what worth is an object of worship, a teacher of lies? For the workman trusts in his own work when he makes these false gods that cannot speak. 19 It is bad for him who says to a piece of wood, 'Wake up!' or to a stone

that cannot speak, 'Get up!' Can this teach you? See, it is covered with gold and silver. There is no breath in it. ²⁰ But the Lord is in His holy house. Let all the earth be quiet before Him."

Habakkuk's Prayer

3 Shigionoth tells of this prayer of Habakkuk, the man of God.

² O Lord, I have heard of what You have done, and I am filled with fear. O Lord, do again in our times the great things which You have done before. Remember to show loving-kindness, even when You are angry.

³ God comes from Teman. The Holy One comes from Mount Paran. His shining-greatness covers the heavens, and the earth is full of His praise. ⁴ He is as bright as the sun. He has light shining from His hand, where His power is hidden. ⁵ Disease goes before Him, and much trouble comes after Him. ⁶ He stood and looked over the earth. He looked and shook the nations. The lasting mountains were broken to pieces, and the old hills fell down. His ways last forever. ⁷ I saw the tents of Cushan in trouble. The tent curtains of the land of Midian were shaking.

⁸ Were You angry with the rivers, O Lord? Was Your anger against the rivers? Or were You angry with the sea? You rode on Your horses. You rode on Your war-wagons saving people. ⁹ You took the covering off Your bow and put the arrows to the string.

You divided the earth with rivers. ¹⁰ The mountains saw You and shook. The flood of waters flowed by. The sea made its noise and its waves rose high. ¹¹ The sun and moon stood still in the heavens at the light of Your arrows, at the shining of Your spear. ¹² You walked over the earth in Your anger. In anger You crushed the nations under foot. ¹³ You went to save Your people, to save Your chosen ones. You crushed the leader of the land of the sinful and laid him open from thighs to neck. ¹⁴ With his own spear You cut through the head of his soldiers. They came like a storm to send us everywhere, finding joy as if they were destroying in secret those who had it very hard. ¹⁵ You stepped on the sea with Your horses, on the waves of many waters.

¹⁶ I heard and my body shook. My lips shook at the sound. My bones began to waste away and my legs shook. Yet I will be quiet and wait for the day of trouble to come upon the people who fight against us. ¹⁷ Even if the fig tree does not grow figs and there is no fruit on the vines, even if the olives do not grow and the fields give no food, even if there are no sheep within the fence and no cattle in the cattle-building, ¹⁸ yet I will have joy in the Lord. I will be glad in the God Who saves me. ¹⁹ The Lord God is my strength. He has made my feet like the feet of a deer, and He makes me walk on high places.

This is for the song leader, on my different kinds of harps.

ZEPHANIAH

1 This is the Word of the Lord which came to Zephaniah the son of Cushi, son of Godaliah, son of Amariah, son of Hezekiah, in the days of Josiah son of Amon, king of Judah.

The Day of the Lord Is Near

² "I will take away everything from the earth," says the Lord. ³ "I will take away man and animal. I will take away the birds of the sky and the fish of the sea. I will destroy the sinful. And I will take man from off the earth," says the Lord. ⁴ "I will put out My hand against Judah and against all the people of Jerusalem. I will destroy from this place the rest of the people who worship Baal, and the names of the religious leaders who worship false gods. ⁵ I will destroy those who bow down on the

roofs to the stars of heaven, and those who bow down and make promises to the Lord and yet promise in the name of Milcom. ⁶ I will destroy those who have turned back from following the Lord, and those who have not looked for the Lord or prayed to Him."

⁷ Be quiet before the Lord God! For the day of the Lord is near. The Lord has made a gift ready for the altar. He has made holy those whom He has asked to come. ⁸ "On the day of the Lord's gift, I will punish the leaders, the king's sons, and all who dress themselves with strange clothes. ⁹ On that day I will punish everyone who is quick to jump through the door, who fill the house of their owner with angry actions and lies. ¹⁰ On that day," says the Lord, "a cry will be heard from the Fish Gate. A cry of sorrow

will be heard from the new part of the city, and a loud noise from the hills. **11** Cry in a loud voice, you people who live in the part of the city where people buy and sell. For all the traders of Canaan will be destroyed. All who weigh out silver will be cut off. **12** At that time I will look through Jerusalem with a light and will punish those who take it easy and do not care what happens. They say in their hearts, 'The Lord will not do good or bad.' **13** Their riches will be taken from them and their houses will be laid waste. They will build houses but not live in them. They will plant grape-fields but not drink their wine."

14 The great day of the Lord is near. It is near and coming soon. Listen! The cry on the day of the Lord! The man of war will cry out with a bitter cry. **15** That day is a day of anger, a day of trouble and suffering, a day when much will be destroyed, a day of darkness, a day of clouds and much darkness. **16** It is a day of the sound of a horn and the cry of battle against the strong cities and the high towers. **17** I will bring trouble to men so that they will walk like the blind, because they have sinned against the Lord. Their blood will be poured out like dust, and their flesh like body waste. **18** Their silver and gold will not be able to save them on the day of the Lord's anger. All the earth will be destroyed in the fire of His jealousy. For all at once He will make an end of all the people of the earth.

A Call to Turn from Sin

2 Gather together. Gather together, O nation without shame, **2** before you are driven away like the waste from the grain. Gather together before the burning anger of the Lord comes upon you, before the day of the Lord's anger, **3** Look for the Lord, all you people of the earth who are not proud, and who have obeyed His Laws. Look for what is right and good. Have no pride. You may be kept safe on the day of the Lord's anger.

The Nations around Israel Are Judged

4 For Gaza will be left empty. Ashkelon will be laid waste. Ashdod's people will be driven out at noon, and Ekron will be pulled up by the roots. **5** It is bad for the people who live by the sea, the nation of the Cherethites! The Word of the Lord is against you, O Canaan, land of the Philistines. I will destroy you so that no people will be left living in you. **6** The land by the

sea will be open fields, a place for shepherds and fences for sheep. **7** The land by the sea will be for those left of the people of Judah. They will let their flocks eat there. In the evening they will lie down in the houses of Ashkelon. For the Lord their God will care for them and return their riches.

8 "I have heard how Moab has made fun of My people and the sons of Ammon have spoken strong words against them. They have spoken in pride against My people's land. **9** So as I live," says the Lord of All, the God of Israel, "Moab will be like Sodom, and the sons of Ammon will be like Gomorrah, a land taken over by thistles and salt, a waste-land forever. Those left of My people will rob them. Those left of My nation will take their land." **10** This will happen to them because of their pride, because they have made fun of the people of the Lord of All. **11** They will be filled with fear because of the Lord. He will destroy all the gods of the earth. All the nations beside the sea will worship Him, every one in his own land. **12** "You also, O Ethiopians, will be killed by My sword." **13** He will put out His hand against the north and destroy Assyria. And He will destroy Nineveh, making it a waste-land like the desert. **14** Flocks will lie down in it, all the animals of the field. The pelican and the hedgehog will live in the tops of its pillars. Birds will sing in the window. And the doorways will be broken down. The pieces of cedar will not be covered. **15** This is the city that is full of joy and takes it easy and thinks it is safe. It says to itself, "I am, and there is no one else." How it has become a waste, a resting place for animals! All who pass by will make fun of her and laugh at her shaking their hands.

Jerusalem's Sin

3 It is bad for her who does not obey and is unclean, the city who makes it hard for the people! **2** She does not listen to anyone and will not be taught. She did not trust in the Lord. She does not come near to her God. **3** Her leaders are lions that make a loud noise. Her judges are wolves at evening. They leave nothing for the morning. **4** Her men who tell what is going to happen in the future are proud and cannot be trusted. Her religious leaders have made the holy place unclean. They have turned in anger against the Law. **5** The Lord within her is right and good. He will be fair and do nothing wrong. Every morning He brings to light what is fair. Every new day He is faithful. But the one who does wrong knows no shame. 6 "I have cut off nations. Their towers are destroyed. I have laid waste their streets so that no one walks in them. Their cities are laid waste, and no one lives in them. 7 I said, 'For sure you will honor Me with fear and receive teaching.' Then her place would not be destroyed and she would not be punished as I had planned. But they were quick to make all their works sinful.

8 "So wait for Me," says the Lord, "for the day when I stand up to speak. I have decided to gather nations together to pour My burning anger upon them. All the earth will be destroyed by the fire of My jealous anger. 9 Then I will make the lips of the people pure. And all of them will call on the name of the Lord, to serve Him shoulder to shoulder. 10 Those who worship Me and have been driven away will bring My gifts in worship from the other side of the rivers of Ethiopia. 11 On that day you will not be put to shame because of all the works you have done against Me. For then I will take away all your people who find joy in their pride. And you will never be proud again on My holy mountain. 12 But I will leave among you people who are not proud, and they will be safe in the name of the Lord. 13 The people of Israel who are left

will do no wrong and tell no lies. A lying tongue will not be found in their mouths. They will eat and lie down with no one to make them afraid."

A Song of Joy

14 Sing, O people of Zion! Call out, O Israel! Have joy and be happy with all your heart, O people of Jerusalem! 15 The Lord has taken away your punishment. He has taken away those who hate you. The King of Israel, the Lord, is with you. You will not be afraid of trouble any more. 16 On that day it will be said to Jerusalem: "Do not be afraid, O Zion. Do not let your hands lose their strength. 17 The Lord your God is with you, a Powerful One Who wins the battle. He will have much joy over you. With His love He will give you new life. He will have joy over you with loud singing. 18 I will gather those who have sorrow for the special days, and take away their shame. 19 At that time I will punish all those who made it hard for you. I will save those who cannot walk and gather those who have been driven away. And I will turn their shame into praise. They will be known all over the earth. 20 At that time I will bring you home, at the time when I gather you together. I will make you known all over the earth, and all the nations will praise you, when I return your riches before your eyes," says the Lord.

HAGGAI

Word Is Given to Build the House of God

1 On the first day of the sixth month in the second year of Darius the king, the Word of the Lord came to Haggai. The Word was for Zerubbabel the son of Shealtiel, ruler of Judah, and to Joshua the son of Jehozadak, the head religious leader, saying, 2 "This is what the Lord of All says: 'These people say, "The time has not yet come to build again the house of the Lord." ' " 3 Then the Word of the Lord came by Haggai the man of God, saying, 4 "Is it a time for you yourselves to live in your houses with walls covered with wood, while this house lies waste?" 5 Now the Lord of All says, "Think about your ways! 6 You have planted much, but gather little. You eat, but there is not enough to fill you. You drink, but never have your fill.

You put on clothing, but no one is warm enough. You earn money, but put it into a bag with holes."

7 The Lord of All says, "Think about your ways! 8 Go up to the mountains and bring wood and build again the house of God, that I may be pleased with it and worshiped as I should be," says the Lord. 9 "You look for much, but it turns out to be little. When you bring it home, I blow it away. Why?" says the Lord of All. "Because My house lies waste, while each of you takes care of his own house. 10 So the sky has held back the water on the grass in the early morning because of you, and the earth has held back its food. 11 I have called for a time without rain on the land, on the mountains, on the grain, on the new wine, on the oil, on the vegetables, on men, on cattle, and on all the work of your hands."

The People Obey

12 Then Zerubbabel the son of Shealtiel, and Joshua the son of Jehozadak, the head religious leader, and all the rest of the people of Israel, obeyed the voice of the Lord their God. They obeyed the words of Haggai the man of God, as the Lord their God had sent him. And the people honored the Lord with fear. 13 Then Haggai the man of God spoke for the Lord to the people, saying, "I am with you," says the Lord. 14 So the Lord moved the spirit of Zerubbabel the son of Shealtiel, ruler of Judah, and the spirit of Joshua the son of Jehozadak, the head religious leader, and the spirit of all the rest of the people. And they came and worked on the house of the Lord of All, their God. 15 This was on the twenty-fourth day of the sixth month in the second year of Darius the king.

The Great New House of God

2 On the twenty-first day of the seventh month, the Word of the Lord came by Haggai the man of God, saying, 2 "Speak now to Zerubbabel the son of Shealtiel, ruler of Judah, and to Joshua the son of Jehozadak, the head religious leader, and to the rest of the people. Say to them, 3 'Who is left among you who saw this house of God as it was before in its greatness? And how does it look to you now? Is it anything like it was? 4 But now be strong, Zerubbabel,' says the Lord. 'Be strong, Joshua son of Jehozadak, head religious leader. And be strong, all you people of the land,' says the Lord. 'Do the work, for I am with you,' says the Lord of All. 5 'As I promised you when you came out of Egypt, My Spirit is with you. Do not be afraid.' 6 For the Lord of All says, 'Once again, in a little while, I am going to shake the heavens and the earth, the sea and the dry land. 7 I will shake all the nations so that the riches of all nations will come in. And I will fill this house with greatness,' says the Lord of All. 8 'The silver is Mine, and the gold is Mine,' says the Lord of All. 9 'This house will be even greater than it was before,' says the Lord of All. 'And in this place I will give peace,' says the Lord of All."

The People Are Unclean

10 On the twenty-fourth day of the ninth month in the second year of Darius, the Word of the Lord came to Haggai the man of God, saying, 11 "The Lord of All says, 'Ask the religious leaders to decide about this: 12 If a man carries holy meat in the fold of his clothing, and this fold touches bread or hot food, or wine, oil, or any other food, will it become holy?' " The religious leaders answered and said, "No." 13 Then Haggai said, "If a man is unclean because he touched a dead body and touches any of these, will it become unclean?" And the religious leaders answered and said, "It will become unclean."

The Lord Promises Good to Come to His People

14 Then Haggai said, " 'So are these people, and so is this nation before Me,' says the Lord. 'And so is everything they have made. What they give there is unclean. 15 Now think about this from this day on. Think about how things were before one stone was placed on another in the house of the Lord. 16 When anyone came to a place where there were twenty baskets of grain, there would be only ten. When anyone came to a place to get fifty bottles of wine, there would be only twenty. 17 I destroyed you and everything you did with a strong wind, disease, and hail. Yet you did not return to Me,' says the Lord. 18 'Think about this from this day on, from the twenty-fourth day of the ninth month. Since the day when the base of the Lord's house was laid, think about this: 19 Is the seed still in the store-house? The vine, the fig tree, the pomegranate and the olive tree have not given any fruit. Yet from this day on I will bring good to you.' "

The Lord's Promise to Zerubbabel

20 The Word of the Lord came a second time to Haggai on the twenty-fourth day of the month, saying, 21 "Tell Zerubbabel, ruler of Judah, 'I am going to shake the heavens and the earth. 22 I will take the power away from kings and destroy the power of the nations. I will destroy war-wagons and their drivers. Horses and their horsemen will fall, every one by the sword of another. 23 On that day,' says the Lord of All, 'I will take you, Zerubbabel, son of Shealtiel, My servant,' says the Lord, 'And I will make you like a ring for marking My name. For I have chosen you,' says the Lord of All."

ZECHARIAH

The Lord Calls His People to Turn from Sin

1 In the eighth month of the second year of Darius, the Word of the Lord came to Zechariah the man of God, the son of Berechiah, the son of Iddo, saying, 2 "The Lord was very angry with your fathers. 3 So tell them, 'The Lord of All says, "Return to Me, that I may return to you. 4 Do not be like your fathers. The men who spoke for Me in the past told them, 'The Lord of All says, "Return from your sinful ways and from your sinful works." ' But they did not listen to Me," says the Lord. 5 "Where are your fathers now? And the men who spoke for Me, do they live forever? 6 I gave My Words and My Laws to your fathers through My servants who spoke for Me. But they would not listen and so they were punished. Then they were sorry for their sins and said, 'The Lord of All has punished us for our ways and our works, as He said He would.' " ' "

Zechariah Sees Horses during the Night

7 On the twenty-fourth day of the eleventh month, the month of Shebat, in the second year of Darius, the Word of the Lord came to Zechariah the man of God, the son of Berechiah, the son of Iddo. 8 During the night while I was sleeping I saw a man traveling on a red horse. He was standing among the myrtle trees in the narrow valley, with red, brown, and white horses behind him. 9 I asked, "My lord, what are these?" And the angel who was speaking with me said, "I will show you what these are." 10 So the man who was standing among the myrtle trees said, "These are the ones whom the Lord has sent to travel all over the earth to keep watch." 11 And they said to the angel of the Lord who was standing among the myrtle trees, "We have looked over all the earth, and saw that the whole earth is at rest and in peace."

The Lord Comforts Jerusalem

12 Then the angel of the Lord said, "O Lord of All, how long will You have no loving-pity for Jerusalem and the cities of Judah? You have been angry with them for seventy years now." 13 And the Lord spoke kind and comforting words to the angel who was speaking with me. 14 So the angel who was speaking with me said to me, "Make this known: 'The Lord of All says, "I am very jealous for Jerusalem and Zion. 15 But I am very angry with the nations who take it easy. When I was only a little angry, they added to the trouble." 16 So the Lord says, "I will return to Jerusalem with loving-pity. My house will be built in it and all Jerusalem will be built again," says the Lord of All. 17 Also make this known: 'The Lord of All says, "My cities will again be filled with riches. The Lord will again comfort Zion and again choose Jerusalem." ' "

Zechariah Sees Horns

18 Then I looked up and saw four horns. 19 So I said to the angel who was speaking with me, "What are these?" And he said, "These are the horns which have divided the people of Judah, Israel, and Jerusalem." 20 Then the Lord showed me four workmen. 21 I said, "What are these coming to do?" And he said, "These are the horns which have sent the people of Judah everywhere, so that no man raised his head. But these workmen have come to make them afraid and to throw down the horns of the nations who have lifted up their horns against the land of Judah so the people would be sent everywhere."

Zechariah Sees a String

2 Then I looked up and saw a man holding a string used to find the length of things. 2 So I said, "Where are you going?" And he said to me, "To see how long and how wide Jerusalem is." 3 Then the angel who was speaking with me was going out, and another angel was coming out to meet him, 4 and said to him, "Run, say to that young man, 'Jerusalem will be a city without walls because of the many men and cattle in it. 5 For I will be a wall of fire around her," says the Lord. 'And I will be the shining-greatness of her.' "

Joy to Come for Jerusalem

6 "Come, come, run from the land of the north!" says the Lord. "For I have sent you to the four winds of the heavens," says the Lord. 7 "O Zion! Run away, you who are living with the people of Babylon." 8 For the Lord of All says, "The Lord of shining-greatness has sent Me against the nations which have robbed you in battle. For whoever touches you, touches what is of great worth to Him. 9 I will wave My hand over them, and they will be taken by those who were made to serve them. Then you will know that the Lord of All has sent Me. 10 Sing for joy and be glad, O people of Zion. For I am coming and I will live among you," says the Lord. 11 "Many

nations will be joined to the Lord in that day and will become My people. I will live among you, and you will know that the Lord of All has sent Me to you. 12 The Lord will receive Judah as His share in the holy land, and will again choose Jerusalem. 13 All of you be quiet before the Lord. For He is coming from His holy place."

Zechariah Sees a Religious Leader

3 Then he showed me Joshua the head religious leader standing before the angel of the Lord. And Satan was standing at his right side to blame him. 2 The Lord said to Satan, "May the Lord's Word be sharp against you, Satan! May the Lord who has chosen Jerusalem speak sharp words against you! Is not this a burning stick saved from the fire?" 3 Now Joshua was dressed in dirty clothes and standing in front of the angel. 4 The angel said to those who were standing in front of him, "Take off his dirty clothes." And he said to him, "See, I have taken your sin away from you, and will dress you in beautiful clothes." 5 Then I said, "Let them put a clean covering on his head." So they put a clean covering on his head and dressed him in clothes, while the angel of the Lord was standing by.

6 The angel of the Lord told Joshua in strong words, 7 "The Lord of All says, 'If you will walk in My ways and do My work, then you will rule My house and everything around it. And I will give you a place among these who are standing here. 8 Now listen, Joshua the head religious leader, and your friends who are sitting in front of you are men who show a part of the good things to come in the future. See, I am going to bring My Servant the Branch. 9 See the stone that I have set in front of Joshua. There are seven eyes on that one stone, and I will cut writings on it,' says the Lord of All. 'And I will take away the sin of that land in one day. 10 In that day,' says the Lord of All, 'every one of you will ask his neighbor to come sit under his vine and under his fig tree.' "

Zechariah Sees a Lamp-Stand

4 Then the angel who was speaking with me returned and woke me up like a man would be made to wake up from his sleep. 2 He said to me, "What do you see?" And I said, "I see a gold lamp-stand with a cup at the top and seven lamps on it. And there are seven places to hold oil, one on the top of each of the lamps. 3 There are

two olive trees by it, one on the right side of the cup and the other on its left side." 4 Then I said to the angel who was speaking with me, "What are these, my lord?" 5 So the angel who was speaking with me said, "Do you not know what these are?" And I said, "No, my lord."

God's Promise to Zechariah

6 Then he said to me, "This is the Word of the Lord to Zerubbabel saying, 'Not by strength nor by power, but by My Spirit,' says the Lord of All. 7 'What are you, O great mountain? In front of Zerubbabel you will become a plain. Then he will bring out the top stone and call out, "May God give it loving-favor!" ' " 8 Also the Word of the Lord came to me saying, 9 "Zerubbabel's hands have laid the first stones of this house, and his hands will finish it. Then you will know that the Lord of All has sent me to you. 10 Who has hated the day of small things? Men will be glad when they see Zerubbabel building the walls of the Lord's house. These seven are the eyes of the Lord which travel over all the earth."

11 Then I said to him, "What are these two olive trees on the right and left sides of the lamp-stand?" 12 A second time I said to him, "What are the two olive branches beside the two gold places that hold the oil to be poured out?" 13 He answered me saying, "Do you not know what these are?" And I said, "No, my lord." 14 Then he said, "These are the two who are set apart to serve the Lord of All the earth."

Zechariah Sees a Flying Book

5 I looked up again and saw a flying book. 2 And the angel said to me, "What do you see?" I said, "I see a flying book, as long as ten long steps and as wide as five long steps." 3 Then he said to me, "This is the curse that is going out over all the land. Everyone who steals will be cut off by what is written on one side. And everyone who swears will be cut off by what is written on the other side. 4 I will send it out," says the Lord of All, "and it will go into the house of the robber and the house of the one who makes false promises using My name. It will spend the night in that house and destroy it, both its wood and stones."

Zechariah Sees a Woman in a Basket

5 Then the angel who was speaking with me came out and said to me, "Look up and

see what this is that is going out." 6 And I said, "What is it?" He said, "This is the large basket going out." And he said, "This is the sin of all the people in all the land." 7 Then the lead cover was lifted up, and there was a woman sitting in the large basket. 8 The angel said, "This is Sin!" And he threw her back into the basket and threw the lead weight on its opening. 9 Then I looked up and saw two women coming out with the wind in their wings. They had wings like the wings of a stork. And they lifted up the large basket between earth and heaven. 10 I said to the angel who was speaking with me, "Where are they taking the basket?" 11 He said to me, "To build a house for it in the land of Shinar. When it is ready, it will be put in its place."

Zechariah Sees Four War-Wagons

6 I looked up again and saw four war-wagons coming out from between the two mountains. The mountains were made of brass. 2 The first war-wagon had red horses. The second war-wagon had black horses. 3 The third war-wagon had white horses, and the fourth war-wagon had strong horses with spots. 4 Then I said to the angel who was speaking with me, "What are these, my lord?" 5 The angel said to me, "These are the four spirits of heaven, going away from standing before the Lord of All the earth. 6 The war-wagon with the black horses is going toward the north country. The white ones follow them. And the horses with spots go toward the south country. 7 When the strong horses went out, they were in a hurry to look over all the earth." And he said, "Go, look over all the earth." So they went over the whole earth. 8 Then he called to me, "See, those who are going to the land of the north have given My Spirit rest in the north country."

The Crown on Joshua

9 The Word of the Lord came to me saying, 10 "Take the gifts from Heldai, Tobijah, and Jedaiah, who have returned from Babylon. And go the same day to the house of Josiah the son of Zephaniah. 11 Take the silver and gold and make a crown, and set it on the head of Joshua the son of Jehozadak, the head religious leader. 12 Then tell him, 'The Lord of All says, "See, the man whose name is the Branch, for He will branch out from where He is. And He will build the house of the Lord. 13 Yes, He is the One Who will build the house of the

Lord. He will be honored as King, and sit and rule on His throne. And He will be a religious leader on His throne, and there will be peace between the two." ' 14 The crown will be in the Lord's house, that people may remember Helem, Tobijah, Jedaiah, and Hen the son of Zephaniah. 15 Those who are far away will come to build the house of the Lord. Then you will know that the Lord of All has sent me to you. This will happen if you are careful to obey the Lord your God."

It Is Better to Obey Than Go without Food

7 In the fourth year of King Darius, the Word of the Lord came to Zechariah. This was on the fourth day of the ninth month, the month of Chislev. 2 Now the people of Bethel had sent Sharezer and Regemmelech and their men to ask for the Lord's favor. 3 They asked the religious leaders of the house of the Lord of All, and the men who speak for God, "Should I cry and go without food in the fifth month, as I have done these many years?" 4 Then the Word of the Lord of All came to me saying, 5 "Say to all the people of the land and to the religious leaders, 'When you went without food and cried in sorrow in the fifth and seventh months these seventy years, was it to honor Me? 6 When you eat and drink, do you not eat and drink for yourselves? 7 Are not these the words the Lord made known through the men who spoke for Him in the past? They spoke these words when Jerusalem was full of people and riches, together with the cities around it, and when the Negev and the lower hills were full of people.' "

People Taken Away Because of Not Obeying

8 Then the Word of the Lord came to Zechariah saying, 9 "The Lord of All said, 'Do what is right and be kind and show loving-pity to one another. 10 Do not make it hard for the woman whose husband has died, or the child who has no parents, or the stranger, or the poor. Do not make sinful plans in your hearts against one another.' 11 But they would not listen. They turned away and stopped their ears from hearing. 12 They made their hearts like hard stone, so that they could not hear the Law and the words which the Lord of All had sent by His Spirit through the men who spoke for Him in the past. So the Lord of All became very angry. 13 When I

called, they would not listen. So when they called, I would not listen," says the Lord of All. 14 "With the wind of a storm I sent them everywhere among all the nations that they had not known. The land was laid waste behind them, so that no one could come or go. They turned the good land into an empty waste."

The Lord Promises to Build Jerusalem Again

8 Then the Word of the Lord came to me saying, 2 "The Lord of All says, 'I am very jealous for Zion. I am jealous for her with much anger.' 3 The Lord says, 'I will return to Zion and live in Jerusalem. Then Jerusalem will be called the City of Truth, and the mountain of the Lord of All will be called the Holy Mountain.' 4 The Lord of All says, 'Old men and old women will sit in the streets of Jerusalem again. Each man will have a walking stick in his hand because he will be old. 5 And the city will be filled with boys and girls playing in the streets.' 6 The Lord of All says, 'It may be wonderful to the few people here in those days, but will it be wonderful to Me also?' says the Lord of All. 7 The Lord of All says, 'I am going to save My people from the land of the east and from the land of the west. 8 I will bring them back and they will live in Jerusalem. They will be My people and I will be their God. I will be faithful and do what is right and good for them.'

9 "The Lord of All says, 'You who are now listening to these words spoken through the men of God who were there when the Lord's house was started, let your hands be strong for building the Lord's house. 10 Before that time there was no pay for man or animal. No one could come in or go out in peace because of those who hated him. I turned people against one another. 11 But now I will not do to the rest of these people as I did in the past,' says the Lord of All. 12 'The seed will grow in peace. The vine will give its fruit. The land will give its food. The heavens will give water on the grass in the early morning. And I will let the rest of this people have all these things. 13 O people of Judah and Israel, just as you were a curse among the nations, I will save you and make you something good. Do not be afraid. Let your hands be strong.'

14 "The Lord of All says, 'I wanted to hurt you because your fathers made Me angry. 15 But now I want to do good to Jerusalem and to the people of Judah. Do not be afraid. 16 These are the things you

are to do: Speak the truth to one another. Judge with truth so there will be peace within your gates. 17 Do not make sinful plans against one another in your hearts. And do not love to make false promises. For I hate all these things,' says the Lord."

18 Then the Word of the Lord came to me saying, 19 "The Lord of All says, 'The times when you do not eat in the fourth, fifth, seventh and tenth months will become glad times of joy. They will become happy, special suppers for the people of Judah. So love truth and peace.' 20 The Lord of All says, 'Many people will yet come from many cities. 21 The people of one city will say to another, "Let us go at once and pray to the Lord and ask for His favor. I will go also." 22 'So many people and powerful nations will come to look for the Lord of All in Jerusalem and to ask for the Lord's favor.' 23 The Lord of All says, 'In those days ten men from the nations of every language will take hold of the coat of a Jew, saying, "Let us go with you, for we have heard that God is with you." ' "

Other Nations Are Judged

9 The Word of the Lord is against the land of Hadrach and will rest upon Damascus. For the eyes of men and all the family groups of Israel are on the Lord. 2 The Word of the Lord is against Hamath also, which is beside Hadrach, and against Tyre and Sidon, even though they are very wise. 3 For Tyre built a strong tower for herself. She gathered silver like dust, and gold like the dirt of the streets. 4 But the Lord will take away her riches and throw them into the sea. And she will be destroyed by fire. 5 Ashkelon will see it and be afraid. Gaza will suffer with much pain. So will Ekron, for her hope will be destroyed. Gaza will lose her king, and no one will live in Ashkelon. 6 A mixed people will live in Ashdod, and I will destroy the pride of the Philistines. 7 I will take the blood from their mouths, and the unclean food from between their teeth. Those who are left will belong to our God, and be like a family in Judah. Ekron will be like the Jebusites. 8 Then I will camp around My land and keep armies from going through it. No one will make it hard for them again, for now I am keeping watch.

The Future King

9 Be full of joy, O people of Zion! Call out in a loud voice, O people of Jerusalem! See, your King is coming to you. He is fair and

good and has the power to save. He is not proud and sits on a donkey, on the son of a female donkey. 10 I will destroy the war-wagon from Ephraim, and the horse from Jerusalem. The battle-bow will be broken. He will make peace among the nations and rule from sea to sea, and from the Euphrates River to the ends of the earth.

The Lord Will Save His People

11 As for you, because of the blood of My agreement with you, I have set your people free from the deep hole that has no water. 12 Return to the strong city, you prisoners who have hope. Today I am telling you that I will give you twice as much as you had before. 13 I will use Judah as My bow, and Ephraim as My arrow. I will move your sons, O Zion, against your sons, O Greece, and make you like a soldier's sword. 14 Then the Lord will be seen over them, and His arrow will go out like lightning. The Lord God will blow the horn and go in the storm winds of the south. 15 The Lord of All will fight for them, and they will destroy, and walk on the stones that were to be thrown at them. They will drink and make much noise as with wine. They will be filled like a cup used for putting blood on the corners of the altar. 16 The Lord their God will save them on that day as the flock of His people. For they are like the stones of a crown, shining in His land. 17 How good and how beautiful they will be! Grain will make the young men grow strong. And the young, pure women will grow strong with new wine.

Israel Will Be Brought Home

10 Ask the Lord for rain in the spring time. It is the Lord Who makes the storm clouds. He gives rain to men, and gives vegetables in the field to every one. 2 The false gods say what is not true. Those who use their secret ways tell lies about the false dreams they have seen. Their comfort means nothing. So the people go from place to place like sheep and are troubled because they have no shepherd. 3 "My anger burns against the shepherds, and I will punish the leaders. For the Lord of All has visited His flock, the people of Judah, and will make them like His proud horse in battle. 4 From them will come the cornerstone. From them will come the tent nail. From them will come the bow of battle. And from them will come every ruler. 5 Together they will be like powerful men, crushing under foot those who hate

them into the mud of the streets. They will fight and win the battle against the horsemen because the Lord is with them. 6 I will give strength to the family of Judah. I will save the family of Joseph, and I will bring them back, because I have loving-pity on them. They will be as if I had not turned away from them. For I am the Lord their God, and I will answer them. 7 Ephraim will be like a powerful man. Their hearts will be glad as with wine. And their children will see it and be glad. Their hearts will have joy in the Lord. 8 I will call them together, for I have saved them and set them free. And they will be as many as they were before. 9 Even when I send them everywhere among the nations, they will remember Me in far countries. They and their children will live and return. 10 I will bring them back from the land of Egypt and gather them from Assyria. I will bring them into the land of Gilead and Lebanon until there is no more room for them. 11 When they pass through the sea of trouble, I will hold back the waves in the sea. The whole Nile River will dry up. The pride of Assyria will be brought down, and Egypt will lose its power. 12 I will make My people Israel strong in the Lord, and they will walk in His name," says the Lord.

Strong Men Are Destroyed

11 Open your doors, O Lebanon, so that fire may destroy your cedars! 2 Cry in sorrow, O cypress, for the cedar has fallen. The beautiful trees have been destroyed. Cry in sorrow, O oaks of Bashan, for the many trees have fallen. 3 Listen to the cry of the shepherds, for their great land is laid waste. Listen to the sound of the young lions, for the trees along the valley of the Jordan River lay waste.

The Two Shepherds

4 The Lord my God said, "Take care of the flock that is to be killed. 5 Those who buy them kill them and are not punished. And those who sell them say, 'Thanks and honor be to the Lord, for I have become rich!' Their own shepherds have no pity on them. 6 For I will no longer have pity on the people who live in this land," says the Lord. "I will give everyone over to the power of his neighbor and his king. They will bring trouble to the land, and I will not save them from their power."

7 So I took care of the flock that was to be killed, and those of the flock who suffered. I took two walking sticks. One I

called Favor, and the other I called Agreement. I took care of the flock. 8 I destroyed the three shepherds in one month. I was angry with them, and they hated me. 9 Then I said, "I will not take care of you. Let those die who are to die. And what is to be destroyed, let it be destroyed. Let those who are left eat each other's flesh." 10 And I took my walking stick Favor and cut it in pieces, to break the agreement I had made with all the people. 11 So it was broken on that day. And those of the flock who suffered and were watching me knew that it was the Word of the Lord. 12 I said to them, "If you think it is right, give me my pay. But if not, keep it." So they weighed out thirty pieces of silver as my pay. 13 Then the Lord said to me, "Throw it to the one who makes pots—the great price they thought I was worth." So I took the thirty pieces of silver and threw them to the pot-maker in the house of the Lord. 14 Then I cut my second walking stick, Agreement, in pieces, to break the agreement between Judah and Israel.

15 Then the Lord said to me, "Take again the tools of a foolish shepherd. 16 For I am going to have a shepherd rule over the land who will not care for the dying. He will not look for those who were sent everywhere or heal the hurt, or feed those who are well. But he will eat the flesh of the fat sheep and tear off their feet. 17 It is bad for the shepherd who has no worth and who leaves the flock! A sword will destroy his arm and his right eye! His arm will be all dried up, and his right eye will be blind."

Judah to Be Saved

12 The Word of the Lord about Israel: The Lord, Who spread out the heavens, who put the earth in its place, and made the spirit of man within him says this about Israel: 2 "I am going to make Jerusalem like a cup that makes all the people around it seem to be drunk. Judah will be shut in by armies as well as Jerusalem. 3 On that day I will make Jerusalem a heavy stone for all the people. All who lift it will be hurt. And all the nations of the earth will be gathered against it. 4 On that day," says the Lord, "I will put fear in every horse, and make the horsemen crazy. But I will watch over the people of Judah, while I make every horse of the nations blind. 5 Then the leaders of Judah will say in their hearts, 'The people of Jerusalem are strong because of the

Lord of All, their God.' 6 On that day I will make the leaders of Judah like a pot of fire among pieces of wood, like fire among cut grain. They will destroy all the people around them, on the right and on the left. And the people of Jerusalem will again live on their own land in Jerusalem. 7 The Lord will save the tents of Judah first, so that the shining-greatness of the family of David and of the people of Jerusalem may not be greater than that of Judah. 8 On that day the Lord will fight for the people of Jerusalem. The one who is weak among them on that day will be like David. And the family of David will be like God, like the angel of the Lord leading them. 9 On that day I will destroy every nation that comes against Jerusalem.

Sorrow in Jerusalem

10 "I will pour out the Spirit of loving-favor and prayer on the family of David and on those who live in Jerusalem. They will look on Him Whose side they cut. They will cry in sorrow for Him, as one cries for an only son. They will cry much over Him, like those who have lost their first-born son. 11 On that day there will be much crying in Jerusalem, like the cries of Hadadrimmon in the plain of Megiddo. 12 The land will be filled with sorrow, each family by itself. The families of David and their wives, and the family of Nathan and their wives, will each be filled with sorrow. 13 The family of Levi and their wives will cry in sorrow, and the family of the Shime-ites and their wives, 14 and all the families that are left, and their wives.

False Gods and False Preachers

13 "On that day a well of water will be opened for the family of David and for the people of Jerusalem to make them clean from their sin.

2 "On that day," says the Lord of All, "I will destroy the names of the false gods from the land. They will no longer be remembered. And I will take away from the land those who tell what will happen in the future and the unclean spirit. 3 If anyone still tells what will happen in the future, his father and mother who gave birth to him will tell him, 'You must not live, because you have lied in the name of the Lord.' And his father and mother who gave birth to him will kill him when he speaks false words. 4 On that day those who tell what will happen in the future will each be ashamed of his special dream when he

speaks. He will not put on clothing made from hair to fool the people. 5 But he will say, 'I am not a man who speaks for God. I am a farmer. A man sold me as a servant when I was young.' 6 If someone asks him, 'What are these sores on your back?' he will answer, 'They are the sores I received in the house of my friends.'

The Shepherd Who Saves

7 "Wake up, O sword, against My shepherd and against the man who is close to Me," says the Lord of All. "Kill the shepherd, and the sheep will go everywhere. And I will turn My hand against the little ones. 8 In the whole land," says the Lord, "two-thirds will die, but one-third will be left alive. 9 And I will bring the third part through the fire. I will make them pure like silver is made pure. I will test them as gold is tested. They will call on My name, and I will answer them. I will say, 'They are My people,' and they will say, 'The Lord is my God.'"

The Day of the Lord

14 A day of the Lord is coming when the things of much worth taken from you will be divided among you. 2 For I will gather all the nations against Jerusalem to battle. The city will be taken. The houses will be robbed. The women will be taken against their will. And half of the city will be taken away to a strange land. But the rest of the people will not be taken away from the city. 3 Then the Lord will go out and fight against those nations, as when He fights on a day of battle. 4 On that day His feet will stand on the Mount of Olives, in front of Jerusalem on the east. And the Mount of Olives will be divided in two from east to west by a very large valley. Half the mountain will move toward the north and the other half toward the south. 5 You will run away by the valley of My mountains, for it will go as far as Azel. You will run away just as you did when the earth shook in the days of Uzziah king of Judah. Then the Lord my God will come, and all the holy ones with Him. 6 On that day there will be no light. The stars of heaven will be made dark. 7 It will be a special day which is known to the Lord. It will not be day or night. For when evening comes, there will be light. 8 On that day living waters will flow out of Jerusalem. Half of them will flow toward the sea in the east. The other half will flow toward the

sea in the west. They will flow in summer and in winter.

9 The Lord will be King over all the earth. On that day the Lord will be the only one, and His name the only one. 10 The whole land will be changed into a plain from Geba to Rimmon south of Jerusalem. But Jerusalem will rise and stay on its land from the Gate of Benjamin to the place of the First Gate, to the Corner Gate, and from the Tower of Hananel to where the king's wine is made. 11 People will live in it, and there will be no more curse. The people of Jerusalem will live without fear.

12 Now this is how the Lord will punish all the people who have gone to war against Jerusalem. Their flesh will waste away while they stand on their feet. Their eyes will waste away in their faces, and their tongues will waste away in their mouths. 13 On that day the Lord will send much fear upon them. They will take hold of one another's hand, and the hand of one will be raised against the hand of another. 14 Judah also will fight at Jerusalem. And the riches of all the nations around will be gathered, much gold and silver and clothing. 15 The same kind of punishment will come upon the horse, the mule, the camel, the donkey, and all the cattle in those camps.

The Nations Worship the King

16 Then everyone who is left of all the nations that went against Jerusalem will go each year to worship the King, the Lord of All, and to keep the Special Supper of Tents. 17 If any of the families of the earth do not go up to Jerusalem to worship the King, the Lord of All, they will have no rain. 18 If the family of Egypt does not go up to worship, then they will have no rain. The Lord will punish them as He punishes the nations that do not go up to keep the Special Supper of Tents. 19 This will be the punishment of Egypt, and the punishment of all the nations that do not go up to keep the Special Supper of Tents. 20 On that day, "Holy to the Lord," will be written on the bells of the horses. And the cooking pots in the house of the Lord will be like the holy dishes in front of the altar. 21 Every cooking pot in Jerusalem and in Judah will be holy to the Lord of All. And all who come bringing gifts in worship will take some of the pots and cook in them. On that day there will no longer be one who buys and sells in the house of the Lord of All.

MALACHI

1 This is the Word of the Lord spoken to Israel through Malachi.

God's Love for Israel

2 "I have loved you," says the Lord. But you say, "How have You loved us?" "Was not Esau Jacob's brother?" says the Lord. "Yet I have loved Jacob, 3 but I have hated Esau. I have laid waste his mountains and have given his riches to the wild dogs of the desert." 4 Edom may say, "We have been destroyed, but we will return and build our cities again." But the Lord of All says, "They may build, but I will tear down. They will be called the sinful land, the people with whom the Lord is angry forever." 5 You will see this with your own eyes and say, "The Lord is great even outside the land of Israel!"

Unclean Gifts Given on the Altar

6 "A son honors his father. A servant honors his owner. Then if I am a father, where is My honor? If I am a boss, where is My respect? says the Lord of All to you, O religious leaders who hate My name. But you say, 'How have we hated Your name?' 7 You are bringing unclean food to My altar. But you say, 'How have we made Your altar unclean?' "Because you say the Lord's table is to be hated. 8 When you bring a blind animal to the altar as My gift, is it not sinful? When you bring one that cannot walk, or one that is sick, is it not sinful? Why not bring it to your ruler? Would he be pleased with you? Would he receive it?" says the Lord of All. 9 "Now pray for God's favor, that He may be kind to us. With such gifts from your hands, will He receive any of you in kindness?" says the Lord of All. 10 "If only there were one among you who would shut the gates and stop you from burning a fire on My altar for nothing! I am not pleased with you," says the Lord of All. "And I will not receive a gift in worship from you. 11 From sunrise to sunset My name will be great among the nations. Special perfume will be given to My name everywhere, and a grain gift that is pure. For My name will be great among the nations," says the Lord of All. 12 "But you are making it unclean when you say that the table of the Lord is unclean, and that its food is to be hated. 13 You say, 'How tired it makes us!' And you turn your nose away from it," says the Lord of All. "You bring what was stolen, and what cannot walk, and what is sick. You bring this as your gift! Should I receive that from your

hands?" says the Lord. 14 "A curse will come upon the sinful man who promises to give a male from his flock, but gives an animal that is not perfect to the Lord. For I am a great King," says the Lord of All. "And My name is feared among the nations.

Sinful Religious Leaders

2 "And now, this word is for you, O religious leaders. 2 If you do not listen, and if you do not set your heart to honor My name," says the Lord of All, "then I will send the curse on you. I will destroy the good things you have been given. Yes, I have cursed them already, because you have not set your heart to honor Me. 3 I will speak sharp words to your children. I will spread animal waste on your faces, the waste of your special suppers. And you will be taken away with it. 4 Then you will know that I have sent this word to you, so that My agreement with Levi may be kept," says the Lord of All. 5 "My agreement with him was one of life and peace, and I gave them to him, that he might honor Me with fear. So he honored Me with fear. My name filled him with fear and wonder. 6 True teaching was in his mouth, and no wrong was found on his lips. He walked with Me in peace and was right and good. And he turned many from sin. 7 For the lips of a religious leader should have much learning. Men should listen for teaching from his mouth, for he is sent by the Lord of All. 8 But you have turned aside from the way. You have made many fall by your teaching. You have sinned against the agreement of Levi," says the Lord of All. 9 "So I have made you hated and ashamed in front of all the people, for you are not keeping My ways. You have shown favor to certain people when you teach them."

The People Are Not Faithful to God

10 "Do we not all have one Father? Has not one God made us? Why can we not be trusted by one another? Why do we sin against the agreement of our fathers? 11 Judah has not been faithful. A very sinful thing has been done in Israel and in Jerusalem. For Judah has made unclean the holy place of the Lord, which He loves. And he has married the daughter of a strange god. 12 May the Lord cut off from the tents of Jacob every man who does this, even if he brings a gift in worship to the Lord of All. 13 This is another thing you do: You cover the altar of the Lord with tears from much crying, because He

no longer cares about the gift or receives it with favor from your hands. 14 You ask, "Why?" It is because the Lord has seen how you have not been faithful to the wife you married when you were young, even when she stays with you and is your wife by agreement. 15 Has not the Lord made them one in flesh and spirit? And what does He desire but God-like children? Be careful then in your spirit, and stay faithful to the wife you married when you were young. 16 "For I hate divorce," says the Lord, the God of Israel. "And I hate the man who does wrong to his wife," says the Lord of All. "So be careful in your spirit, and be one who can be trusted."

17 You have made the Lord tired with your words. Yet you say, "How have we made Him tired?" By saying, "Everyone who sins is good in the eyes of the Lord, and He is pleased with them." Or by asking, "Where is the God Who is fair?"

The One to Come

3 "See, I am going to send one with news, and he will make the way ready before Me. Then all at once the Lord you are looking for will come to His house. The one with the news of the agreement, whom you desire, is coming," says the Lord of All. 2 "But who can live through the day of His coming? Who can stand when He shows Himself? For He is like a fire for making gold pure, and like a strong cleaner. 3 He will sit as one who melts silver and makes it pure. He will make the sons of Levi pure. He will make them pure like gold and silver, so that they may bring the right gifts to the Lord. 4 Then the gifts of Judah and Jerusalem will be pleasing to the Lord, as they were in the past. 5 Then I will come to judge you. I will be quick to speak against those who use witchcraft, and those who do sex sins, and those who make false promises. I will speak against those who do not pay a man what he has earned, and who make it hard for the woman whose husband has died and for children who have no parents. And I will speak against those who turn away the stranger and do not fear Me," says the Lord of All.

6 "For I, the Lord, do not change. So you, O children of Jacob, are not destroyed.

Giving to God a Tenth Part

7 "From the days of your fathers you have turned aside from My Laws and have not obeyed them. Return to Me, and I will return to you," says the Lord of All. "But you say, 'How are we to return?' 8 Will a man rob God? Yet you are robbing Me! But you say, 'How have we robbed You?' You have not given Me the tenth part of what you receive and your gifts. 9 You are cursed, for you are robbing Me, the whole nation of you! 10 Bring the tenth part into the store-house, so that there may be food in My house. Test Me in this," says the Lord of All. "See if I will not then open the windows of heaven and pour out good things for you until there is no more need. 11 I will speak sharp words to the destroyer for you, so that it may not destroy the fruits of the ground. And your vine in the field will be sure to give its grapes," says the Lord of All. 12 "All the nations will say that much good has come to you, for you will be a happy land," says the Lord of All.

The People Complain

13 "Your words have been spoken in pride against Me," says the Lord. "Yet you say, 'What have we said against You?' 14 You have said, 'It is of no worth to serve God. What do we get by doing what He says, or by walking in sorrow before the Lord of All? 15 So now we say that it is good to be proud. Not only are sinners doing well, but they put God to the test and get away with it.' "

The Book to Be Remembered

16 Then those who feared the Lord spoke often to one another, and the Lord listened to them. And the names of those who worshiped the Lord and honored Him were written down before Him in a Book to be remembered. 17 "They will be Mine says the Lord of All, "on that day that I gather My special people. I will have loving-pity on them as a man has loving-pity on his own son who serves him." 18 Then you will again see the difference between those who are right and good, and those who are sinful. You will see the difference between one who serves God and one who does not serve Him.

The Great Day of the Lord

4 "See, the day is coming. It is burning like a hot fire. And all those who are proud and those who do wrong will be like dry grass. The day that is coming will set them on fire," says the Lord of All. "Not a root or branch will be left to them. 2 But for you who fear My name, the sun of what is right and good will rise with healing in its wings. And you will go out and dance like calves from the cattle-house. ³ You will crush the sinful under foot. They will be ashes under your feet on the day when I do these things," says the Lord of All.

⁴ "Remember the Law of My servant Moses. Remember all the Laws I gave him in Horeb for all Israel. ⁵ See, I will send you Elijah the man of God before the day of the Lord comes, that great day that will be full of much trouble. ⁶ And he will turn the hearts of the fathers to their children, and the hearts of the children to their fathers. Or else I will come and destroy the land with a curse."

The NEW TESTAMENT

The NEW TESTAMENT

MATTHEW

The Families Jesus Came Through
(Luke 3:23–38)

1 These are the families through which Jesus Christ came. He came through David and Abraham. ² Abraham was the father of Isaac. Isaac was the father of Jacob. Jacob was the father of Judah and his brothers. ³ Judah was the father of Perez and Zerah. Their mother was Tamar. Perez was the father of Hezron. Hezron was the father of Aram. ⁴ Aram was the father of Amminadab. Amminadab was the father of Nahshon. Nahshon was the father of Salmon. ⁵ Salmon was the father of Boaz. The mother of Boaz was Rahab. Boaz was the father of Obed. The mother of Obed was Ruth. Obed was the father of Jesse. ⁶ Jesse was the father of David the king.

King David was the father of Solomon. His mother had been the wife of Uriah. ⁷ Solomon was the father of Rehoboam. Rehoboam was the father of Abijah. Abijah was the father of Asa. ⁸ Asa was the father of Jehoshaphat. Jehoshaphat was the father of Joram. Joram was the father of Uzziah. ⁹ Uzziah was the father of Jotham. Jotham was the father of Ahaz. Ahaz was the father of Hezekiah. ¹⁰ Hezekiah was the father of Manasseh. Manasseh was the father of Amon. Amon was the father of Josiah. ¹¹ Josiah was the father of Jeconiah and his brothers at the time the people were taken to Babylon.

¹² After they were taken to the city of Babylon, Jeconiah was the father of Shealtiel. Shealtiel was the father of Zerubbabel. ¹³ Zerubbabel was the father of Abiud. Abiud was the father of Eliakim. Eliakim was the father of Azor. ¹⁴ Azor was the father of Zadok. Zadok was the father of Achim. Achim was the father of Eliud. ¹⁵ Eliud was the father of Eleazar. Eleazar was the father of Matthan. Matthan was the father of Jacob. ¹⁶ Jacob was the father of Joseph. Joseph was the husband of Mary. She was the mother of Jesus Who is called the Christ. ¹⁷ So the number of families from Abraham to David was fourteen. The number of families from David to the time the people were taken to Babylon was fourteen. The number of families after they were taken to Babylon to the birth of Jesus Christ was fourteen.

The Birth of Jesus
(Luke 2:1–7)

¹⁸ The birth of Jesus Christ was like this: Mary His mother had been promised in marriage to Joseph. Before they were married, it was learned that she was to have a baby by the Holy Spirit. ¹⁹ Joseph was her promised husband. He was a good man and did not want to make it hard for Mary in front of people. He thought it would be good to break the promised marriage without people knowing it. ²⁰ While he was thinking about this, an angel of the Lord came to him in a dream. The angel said, "Joseph, son of David, do not be afraid to take Mary as your wife. She is to become a mother by the Holy Spirit. ²¹ A Son will be born to her. You will give Him the name Jesus because He will save His people from the punishment of their sins."

²² This happened as the Lord said it would happen through the early preacher. ²³ He said, "The young woman, who has never had a man, will give birth to a Son. They will give Him the name Immanuel. This means God with us." (Isaiah 7:14) ²⁴ Joseph awoke from his sleep. He did what the angel of the Lord told him to do. He took Mary as his wife. ²⁵ But he did not have her, as a husband has a wife, until she gave birth to a Son. Joseph gave Him the name Jesus.

Wise Men Visit the Young Child Jesus

2 Jesus was born in the town of Bethlehem in the country of Judea. It was the time when Herod was king of that part of the country. Soon after Jesus was born, some wise men who learned things from stars came to Jerusalem from the East. ² They asked, "Where is the King of the Jews Who has been born? We have seen His star in the East. We have come to worship Him."

³ King Herod heard this. He and all the people of Jerusalem were worried. ⁴ He called together all the religious leaders of the Jews and the teachers of the Law. Herod asked them where Christ was to be born. ⁵ They said to him, "In Bethlehem of Judea. The early preacher wrote, ⁶ 'You, Bethlehem of Judah, are not the least of the leaders of Judah. Out of you will come a King Who will lead My people the Jews.'" (Micah 5:2)

⁷ Then Herod had a secret meeting with the men who learned things from stars. He asked them about what time the star had been seen. ⁸ He sent them to Bethlehem and said, "Go and find the young Child. When you find Him, let me know. Then I can go and worship Him also."

⁹ After the king had spoken, they went

on their way. The star they had seen in the East went before them. It came and stopped over the place where the young Child was. 10 When they saw the star, they were filled with much joy.

11 They went into the house and found the young Child with Mary, His mother. Then they got down before Him and worshiped Him. They opened their bags of riches and gave Him gifts of gold and perfume and spices. 12 Then God spoke to them in a dream. He told them not to go back to Herod. So they went to their own country by another road.

Joseph Goes to Egypt

13 When they had gone, an angel of the Lord came to Joseph in a dream. He said, "Get up. Take the young Child and His mother to the country of Egypt. Go as fast as you can! Stay there until you hear from Me. Herod is going to look for the young Child to kill Him." 14 During the night he got up and left with the young Child and His mother for Egypt. 15 He stayed there until Herod died. This happened as the Lord had said through an early preacher, "I called My Son out of Egypt." (Hosea 11:1)

Herod Had All the Young Boys Killed

16 Herod learned that the wise men had fooled him. He was very angry. He sent men to kill all the young boys two years old and under in Bethlehem and in all the country near by. He decided to do this from what he had heard from the wise men as to the time when the star was seen. 17 Then it happened as the early preacher Jeremiah said it would happen. 18 He said, "The sound of crying and much sorrow was heard in Ramah. Rachel was crying for her children. She would not be comforted because they were dead." (Jeremiah 31:15)

Joseph Goes from Egypt to Nazareth
(Luke 2:39–40)

19 After Herod died, an angel of the Lord came to Joseph in a dream while he was in Egypt. 20 He said, "Get up. Take the young Child and His mother and go into the land of the Jews. Those who tried to kill the young Child are dead." 21 Joseph got up. He took the young Child and His mother and came into the land of the Jews. 22 Joseph heard that Archelaus was the king of the country of Judea. Herod, the father of Archelaus, had died. Joseph was afraid to go there. God told him in a dream to go to

the country of Galilee and he went. 23 Joseph stayed in a town called Nazareth. It happened as the early preachers said it would happen. They said, "Jesus will be called a Nazarene."

John the Baptist Makes the Way Ready for Jesus
(Mark 1:1–8; Luke 3:1–18; John 1:15–28)

3 In those days John the Baptist came preaching in the desert in the country of Judea. 2 He said, "Be sorry for your sins and turn from them! The holy nation of heaven is near." 3 The early preacher Isaiah spoke of this man. He said, "Listen! His voice calls out in the desert! 'Make the way ready for the Lord. Make the road straight for Him!' " (Isaiah 40:3)

4 John wore clothes made of hair from camels. He had a leather belt around him. His food was locusts and wild honey.

5 Then the people of Jerusalem and of all the country of Judea and those from near the Jordan River went to him. 6 Those who told of their sins were baptized by him in the Jordan River. 7 He saw many proud religious law-keepers and other people of the religious group who believe no one will be raised from the dead. They were coming to him to be baptized. He said to them, "You family of snakes! Who told you how to keep from God's anger that is coming? 8 Do something to show me that your hearts are changed. 9 Do not think you can say to yourselves, 'We have Abraham as our father.' For I tell you, God can make children for Abraham out of these stones.

10 "Even now the ax is on the root of the trees. Every tree that does not give good fruit is cut down and thrown into the fire. 11 For sure, I baptize with water those who are sorry for their sins and turn from them. The One Who comes after me will baptize you with the Holy Spirit and with fire. He is greater than I. I am not good enough to take off His shoes. 12 He comes ready to clean the grain. He will gather the grain and clean it all. The clean grain He will put into a building. He will burn that which is no good with a fire that cannot be put out."

The Baptism of Jesus
(Mark 1:9–11; Luke 3:21–22; John 1:29–34)

13 Jesus came from Galilee. He went to John at the Jordan River to be baptized by him. 14 John tried to stop Him. He said,

"I need to be baptized by You. Do You come to me?" 15 Jesus said to him, "Let it be done now. We should do what is right." John agreed and baptized Jesus. 16 When Jesus came up out of the water, the heavens opened. He saw the Spirit of God coming down and resting on Jesus like a dove. 17 A voice was heard from heaven. It said, "This is My much-loved Son. I am very happy with Him."

Jesus Was Tempted
(Mark 1:12–13; Luke 4:1–13)

4 Jesus was led by the Holy Spirit to a desert. There He was tempted by the devil. 2 Jesus went without food for forty days and forty nights. After that He was hungry. 3 The devil came tempting Him and said, "If You are the Son of God, tell these stones to be made into bread." 4 But Jesus said, "It is written, 'Man is not to live on bread only. Man is to live by every word that God speaks.' " (Deuteronomy 8:3)

5 Then the devil took Jesus up to Jerusalem, the holy city. He had Jesus stand on the highest part of the house of God. 6 The devil said to Him, "If You are the Son of God, throw Yourself down. It is written, 'He has told His angels to look after You. In their hands they will hold You up. Then Your foot will not hit against a stone.' " (Psalm 91:11–12) 7 Jesus said to the devil, "It is written also, 'You must not tempt the Lord your God.' " (Deuteronomy 6:16)

8 Again the devil took Jesus to a very high mountain. He had Jesus look at all the nations of the world to see how great they were. 9 He said to Jesus, "I will give You all these nations if You will get down at my feet and worship me." 10 Jesus said to the devil, "Get away, Satan. It is written, 'You must worship the Lord your God. You must obey Him only.' " (Deuteronomy 6:13) 11 Then the devil went away from Jesus. Angels came and cared for Him.

Jesus Preaches in Galilee
(Mark 1:14–15; Luke 4:14–15)

12 When Jesus heard that John the Baptist had been put in prison, He went to the country of Galilee. 13 He left Nazareth and went to live in the city of Capernaum. It is by the lake in the land of Zebulun and Naphtali.

14 This happened as the early preacher Isaiah said it would happen. He said, 15 "The land of Zebulun and Naphtali is along the road to the lake. It is on the other side of the Jordan River in Galilee. These people are not Jews. 16 The people who sat in darkness saw a great light. Light did shine on those in the land who were near death." (Isaiah 9:1–2)

17 From that time on, Jesus went about preaching. He said, "Be sorry for your sins and turn from them. The holy nation of heaven is near."

Jesus Calls Peter and Andrew
(Mark 1:16–20; Luke 5:1–11)

18 Jesus was walking by the Sea of Galilee. He saw two brothers. They were Simon (his other name was Peter) and Andrew, his brother. They were putting a net into the sea for they were fishermen. 19 Jesus said to them, "Follow Me. I will make you fish for men!" 20 At once they left their nets and followed Him.

21 Going from there, Jesus saw two other brothers. They were James and John, the sons of Zebedee. They were sitting in a boat with their father, mending their nets. Jesus called them. 22 At once they left the boat and their father and followed Jesus.

Jesus Keeps On Preaching in Galilee
(Mark 1:35–39; Luke 4:42–44)

23 Jesus went over all Galilee. He taught in their places of worship and preached the Good News of the holy nation. He healed all kinds of sickness and disease among the people. 24 The news about Him went over all the country of Syria. They brought all the sick people to Him with many kinds of diseases and pains. They brought to Him those who had demons. They brought those who at times lose the use of their minds. They brought those who could not use their hands and legs. He healed them. 25 Many people followed Him from Galilee and Judea. They followed Him from the cities of Decapolis and Jerusalem. They followed Him from Judea and from the other side of the Jordan River.

Jesus Teaches on the Mountain
(Luke 6:20–49)

5 Jesus saw many people. He went up on the mountain and sat down. His followers came to Him. 2 He began to teach them, saying, 3 "Those who know there is nothing good in themselves are happy, because the holy nation of heaven is theirs. 4 Those who have sorrow are happy, because they will be comforted. 5 Those who have no pride in their hearts are happy, because the earth will be given to them. 6 Those who are hungry and

thirsty to be right with God are happy, because they will be filled. 7 Those who show loving-kindness are happy, because they will have loving-kindness shown to them. 8 Those who have a pure heart are happy, because they will see God. 9 Those who make peace are happy, because they will be called the sons of God. 10 Those who have it very hard for doing right are happy, because the holy nation of heaven is theirs. 11 You are happy when people act and talk in a bad way to you and make it very hard for you and tell bad things and lies about you because you trust in Me. 12 Be glad and full of joy because your reward will be much in heaven. They made it very hard for the early preachers who lived a long time before you.

Jesus Teaches about Salt and Light

13 "You are the salt of the earth. If salt loses its taste, how can it be made to taste like salt again? It is no good. It is thrown away and people walk on it. 14 You are the light of the world. You cannot hide a city that is on a mountain. 15 Men do not light a lamp and put it under a basket. They put it on a table so it gives light to all in the house. 16 Let your light shine in front of men. Then they will see the good things you do and will honor your Father Who is in heaven.

Jesus Teaches about the Law

17 "Do not think that I have come to do away with the Law of Moses or the writings of the early preachers. I have not come to do away with them but to complete them. 18 I tell you, as long as heaven and earth last, not one small mark or part of a word will pass away of the Law of Moses until it has all been done. 19 Anyone who breaks even the least of the Law of Moses and teaches people not to do what it says, will be called the least in the holy nation of heaven. He who obeys and teaches others to obey what the Law of Moses says, will be called great in the holy nation of heaven. 20 I tell you, unless you are more right with God than the teachers of the Law and the proud religious law-keepers, you will never get into the holy nation of heaven.

Jesus Teaches about Anger and Killing

21 "You have heard that men were told long ago, 'You must not kill another person. If someone does kill, he will be guilty and will be punished for his wrong-doing.'

22 But I tell you that whoever is angry with his brother will be guilty and have to suffer for his wrong-doing. Whoever says to his brother, 'You have no brains,' will have to stand in front of the court. Whoever says, 'You fool,' will be sent to the fire of hell. 23 If you take your gift to the altar and remember your brother has something against you, 24 leave your gift on the altar. Go and make right what is wrong between you and him. Then come back and give your gift. 25 Agree with the one who is against you while you are talking together, or he might take you to court. The court will hand you over to the police. You will be put in prison. 26 For sure, I tell you, you will not be let out of prison until you have paid every piece of money of the fine.

Jesus Teaches about Husband and Wife

27 "You have heard that it was said long ago, 'You must not do sex sins.' 28 But I tell you, anyone who even looks at a woman with a sinful desire of wanting her has already sinned in his heart. 29 If your right eye is the reason you sin, take it out and throw it away. It is better to lose one part of your body than for your whole body to be thrown into hell. 30 If your right hand is the reason you sin, cut it off and throw it away. It is better to lose one part of your body than for your whole body to go to hell.

Jesus Teaches about Marriage

31 "It has been said, 'Whoever wants to divorce his wife should have it put in writing, telling her he is leaving her.' 32 But I tell you, whoever divorces his wife except if she has not been faithful to him, makes her guilty of a sex sin. Whoever marries a woman who has been divorced is guilty of a sex sin.

Jesus Teaches about What to Say

33 "You have heard that it was said long ago, 'You must not make a promise you cannot keep. You must carry out your promises to the Lord.' 34 I tell you, do not use strong words when you make a promise. Do not promise by heaven. It is the place where God is. 35 Do not promise by earth. It is where He rests His feet. Do not promise by Jerusalem. It is the city of the great King. 36 Do not promise by your head. You are not able to make one hair white or black. 37 Let your yes be YES. Let your no be NO. Anything more than this comes from the devil.

Jesus Teaches about Fighting

38 "You have heard that it has been said, 'An eye for an eye and a tooth for a tooth.' 39 But I tell you, do not fight with the man who wants to fight. Whoever hits you on the right side of the face, turn to he can hit the other side also. 40 If any person takes you to court to get your shirt, give him your coat also. 41 Whoever makes you walk a short way, go with him twice as far. 42 Give to any person who asks you for something. Do not say no to the man who wants to use something of yours.

Jesus Teaches about Loving Those Who Hate You

43 "You have heard that it has been said, 'You must love your neighbor and hate those who hate you.' 44 But I tell you, love those who hate you. (*Respect and give thanks for those who say bad things to you. Do good to those who hate you.) Pray for those who do bad things to you and who make it hard for you. 45 Then you may be the sons of your Father Who is in heaven. His sun shines on bad people and on good people. He sends rain on those who are right with God and on those who are not right with God. 46 If you love those who love you, what reward can you expect from that? Do not even the tax-gatherers do that? 47 If you say hello only to the people you like, are you doing any more than others? The people who do not know God do that much. 48 You must be perfect as your Father in heaven is perfect.

Jesus Teaches on the Mountain about Helping Others

6 "Be sure you do not do good things in front of others just to be seen by them. If you do, you have no reward from your Father in heaven. 2 When you give to the poor, do not be as those who pretend to be someone they are not. They blow a horn in the places of worship and in the streets so people may respect them. For sure, I tell you, they have all the reward they are going to get. 3 When you give, do not let your left hand know what your right hand gives. 4 Your giving should be in secret. Then your Father Who sees in secret will reward you.

Jesus Teaches about Prayer

5 "When you pray, do not be as those who pretend to be someone they are not. They love to stand and pray in the places of worship or in the streets so people can see them. For sure, I tell you, they have all the reward they are going to get. 6 When you pray, go into a room by yourself. After you have shut the door, pray to your Father Who is in secret. Then your Father Who sees in secret will reward you. 7 When you pray, do not say the same thing over and over again making long prayers like the people who do not know God. They think they are heard because their prayers are long. 8 Do not be like them. Your Father knows what you need before you ask Him.

9 "Pray like this: 'Our Father in heaven, Your name is holy. 10 May Your holy nation come. What You want done, may it be done on earth as it is in heaven. 11 Give us the bread we need today. 12 Forgive us our sins as we forgive those who sin against us.

13 'Do not let us be tempted, but keep us from sin. *Your nation is holy. You have power and shining-greatness forever. Let it be so.'

Jesus Teaches about Forgiveness

14 "If you forgive people their sins, your Father in heaven will forgive your sins also. 15 If you do not forgive people their sins, your Father will not forgive your sins.

Jesus Teaches about Not Eating So You Can Pray Better

16 "When you go without food so you can pray better, do not be as those who pretend to be someone they are not. They make themselves look sad so people will see they are going without food. For sure, I tell you, they have all the reward they are going to get. 17 When you go without food so you can pray better, put oil on your head and wash your face. 18 Then nobody knows you are going without food. Then your Father Who sees in secret will reward you.

Jesus Teaches about Having Riches

19 "Do not gather together for yourself riches of this earth. They will be eaten by bugs and become rusted. Men can break in and steal them. 20 Gather together riches in heaven where they will not be eaten by bugs or become rusted. Men cannot break in and steal them. 21 For wherever your riches are, your heart will be there also. 22 The eye is the light of the body. If your eye is good, your whole body will be full of light. 23 If your eye is bad, your whole body will be dark. If the light in you is dark, how dark it will be! 24 No one can

have two bosses. He will hate the one and love the other. Or he will listen to the one and work against the other. You cannot have both God and riches as your boss at the same time.

Jesus Teaches about Cares of Life

25 "I tell you this: Do not worry about your life. Do not worry about what you are going to eat and drink. Do not worry about what you are going to wear. Is not life more important than food? Is not the body more important than clothes? 26 Look at the birds in the sky. They do not plant seeds. They do not gather grain. They do not put grain into a building to keep. Yet your Father in heaven feeds them! Are you not more important than the birds? 27 Which of you can make himself a little taller by worrying? 28 Why should you worry about clothes? Think how the flowers grow. They do not work or make cloth. 29 But I tell you that Solomon in all his greatness was not dressed as well as one of these flowers. 30 God clothes the grass of the field. It lives today and is burned in the stove tomorrow. How much more will He give you clothes? You have so little faith! 31 Do not worry. Do not keep saying, 'What will we eat?' or, 'What will we drink?' or, 'What will we wear?' 32 The people who do not know God are looking for all these things. Your Father in heaven knows you need all these things. 33 First of all, look for the holy nation of God. Be right with Him. All these other things will be given to you also. 34 Do not worry about tomorrow. Tomorrow will have its own worries. The troubles we have in a day are enough for one day.

Jesus Teaches on the Mountain about Saying What Is Wrong in Others

7 "Do not say what is wrong in other people's lives. Then other people will not say what is wrong in your life. 2 You will be guilty of the same things you find in others. When you say what is wrong in others, your words will be used to say what is wrong in you. 3 Why do you look at the small piece of wood in your brother's eye, and do not see the big piece of wood in your own eye? 4 How can you say to your brother, 'Let me take that small piece of wood out of your eye,' when there is a big piece of wood in your own eye? 5 You who pretend to be someone you are not, first take the big piece of wood out of your own eye. Then you can see better to

take the small piece of wood out of your brother's eye.

6 "Do not give that which belongs to God to dogs. Do not throw your pearls in front of pigs. They will break them under their feet. Then they will turn and tear you to pieces.

Jesus Teaches about Prayer

7 "Ask, and what you are asking for will be given to you. Look, and what you are looking for you will find. Knock, and the door you are knocking on will be opened to you. 8 Everyone who asks receives what he asks for. Everyone who looks finds what he is looking for. Everyone who knocks has the door opened to him. 9 What man among you would give his son a stone if he should ask for bread? 10 Or if he asks for a fish, would he give him a snake? 11 You are bad and you know how to give good things to your children. How much more will your Father in heaven give good things to those who ask Him?

Jesus Teaches about Others

12 "Do for other people whatever you would like to have them do for you. This is what the Jewish Law and the early preachers said.

Jesus Teaches about Two Roads

13 "Go in through the narrow door. The door is wide and the road is easy that leads to hell. Many people are going through that door. 14 But the door is narrow and the road is hard that leads to life that lasts forever. Few people are finding it.

Jesus Teaches about False Teachers

15 "Watch out for false teachers. They come to you dressed as if they were sheep. On the inside they are hungry wolves. 16 You will know them by their fruit. Do men pick grapes from thorns? Do men pick figs from thistles? 17 It is true, every good tree has good fruit. Every bad tree has bad fruit. 18 A good tree cannot have bad fruit. A bad tree cannot have good fruit. 19 Every tree that does not have good fruit is cut down and thrown into the fire. 20 So you will know them by their fruit. 21 Not everyone who says to me, 'Lord, Lord,' will go into the holy nation of heaven. The one who does the things My Father in heaven wants him to do will go into the holy nation of heaven. 22 Many people will say to Me on that day, 'Lord, Lord, did we not preach in Your Name? Did we not put out demons in Your Name? Did we not

do many powerful works in Your Name?' 23 Then I will say to them in plain words, 'I never knew you. Go away from Me, you who do wrong!'

Jesus Teaches about Houses Built on Rock or Sand

24 "Whoever hears these words of Mine and does them, will be like a wise man who built his house on rock. 25 The rain came down. The water came up. The wind blew and hit the house. The house did not fall because it was built on rock. 26 Whoever hears these words of Mine and does not do them, will be like a foolish man who built his house on sand. 27 The rain came down. The water came up. The wind blew and hit the house. The house fell and broke apart." 28 Then Jesus finished talking. The people were surprised and wondered about His teaching. 29 He was teaching them as One Who has the right and the power to teach. He did not teach as the teachers of the Law.

The Healing of a Man with a Bad Skin Disease
(Mark 1:40–45; Luke 5:12–16)

8 Jesus came down from the mountain. Many people followed Him. 2 A man with a bad skin disease came and got down before Jesus and worshiped Him. He said, "Lord, if You will, You can heal me!" 3 Then Jesus put His hand on him and said, "I will. You are healed!" At once the man was healed. 4 Jesus said to him, "Go now, but tell no one. Let the religious leader see you. Give the gift in worship that Moses told you to give. This will show them you have been healed." (Leviticus 13:49)

Healing of the Captain's Servant
(Luke 7:1–10)

5 Jesus came to the city of Capernaum. A captain of the army came to Him. He asked for help, 6 saying, "Lord, my servant is sick in bed. He is not able to move his body. He is in much pain." 7 Jesus said to the captain, "I will come and heal him." 8 The captain said, "Lord, I am not good enough for You to come to my house. Only speak the word, and my servant will be healed. 9 I am a man who works for some one else and I have men working under me. I say to this man, 'Go!' and he goes. I say to another, 'Come!' and he comes. I say to my servant, 'Do this!' and he does it." 10 When Jesus heard this, He was surprised and wondered about it. He said to

those who followed Him, "For sure, I tell you, I have not found so much faith in the Jewish nation. 11 I say to you, many people will come from the east and from the west. They will sit down with Abraham and with Isaac and with Jacob in the holy nation of heaven. 12 But those who should have belonged to the holy nation of heaven will be thrown out into outer darkness, where there will be crying and grinding of teeth." 13 Jesus said to the captain, "Go your way. It is done for you even as you had faith to believe." The servant was healed at that time.

Peter's Mother-in-Law Healed
(Mark 1:29–31; Luke 4:38–39)

14 Jesus came to Peter's house. He saw Peter's wife's mother in bed. She was very sick. 15 He touched her hand and the sickness left her. She got up and cared for Jesus.

Many People Are Healed
(Mark 1:32–34; Luke 4:40–41)

16 That evening they brought to Jesus many people who had demons in them. The demons were put out when Jesus spoke to them. All the sick people were healed. 17 It happened as the early preacher Isaiah said it would happen. He said, "He took on Himself our sickness and carried away our diseases." (Isaiah 53:4)

Testing Some Followers
(Luke 9:57–62)

18 Jesus saw many people and told them to go to the other side of the lake. 19 A teacher of the Law came to Jesus. He said, "Lord, I will follow You wherever You go." 20 Jesus said to him, "Foxes have holes. Birds have nests. But the Son of Man has no place to lay His head."

21 Another of His followers said to Him, "Lord, let me go first and bury my father." 22 Jesus said to him, "Follow Me. Let the people who are dead bury their own dead."

The Wind and Waves Obey Jesus
(Mark 4:35–41; Luke 8:22–25)

23 Jesus got into a boat. His followers followed Him. 24 At once a bad storm came over the lake. The waves were covering the boat. Jesus was sleeping. 25 His followers went to Him and called, "Help us, Lord, or we will die!" 26 He said to them, "Why are you afraid? You have so little faith!" Then He stood up. He spoke sharp words to the wind and the waves. Then the wind stopped blowing. 27 Then men

were surprised and wondered about it. They said, "What kind of a man is He? Even the winds and the waves obey Him."

Demons Ask Jesus to Let Them Live in Pigs
(Mark 5:1–20; Luke 8:26–39)

28 Jesus came to the other side of the lake into the country of the Gadarenes. Two men came to Him from among the graves. They had demons in them and were very wild men. They were so bad that no one would go near them. 29 They called out, saying, "What do You want of us, You Son of God? Have You come here to make us suffer before it is our time to suffer?"

30 A long way from there many pigs were eating. 31 The demons begged Jesus, saying, "If You put us out, send us into the pigs." 32 Jesus said to the demons, "Go!" They came out of the men and went into the pigs. At once the pigs ran down the mountain-side. They fell into the water and died.

33 The men who cared for the pigs ran fast into the city and told everything. They told what happened to the men who had the demons. 34 Every person in the city came to meet Jesus. When they saw Jesus, they asked Him to leave their country.

The Healing of a Man Who Could Not Move His Body
(Mark 2:1–12; Luke 5:17–26)

9 Jesus got into a boat. He crossed over to the other side and came into His own city. 2 They took a man to Him who was on his bed. This man was not able to move his body. Jesus saw their faith. He said, "Son, take hope. Your sins are forgiven." 3 Some of the teachers of the Law said to themselves, "This man speaks as if He is God, but He is not!" 4 Jesus knew what they were thinking. He said, "Why do you think bad thoughts in your hearts? 5 Which is easier to say, 'Your sins are forgiven,' or to say, 'Get up and walk?' 6 But this is to show you that the Son of Man has power on earth to forgive sins." He said to the sick man, "Get up! Take your bed and go home." 7 He got up and went to his home. 8 All the people saw this. They were surprised and wondered about it. Then they gave thanks to God because He had given such power to men.

Jesus Calls Matthew
(Mark 2:13–17; Luke 5:27–32)

9 As Jesus went from there, He saw a man called Matthew. Matthew was sitting at his work gathering taxes. Jesus said to him, "Follow Me." Matthew got up and followed Jesus. 10 Jesus ate in Matthew's house. Many men who gathered taxes and many who were sinners came to Matthew's house and sat down with Jesus and His followers. 11 The proud religious law-keepers saw this. They said to the followers of Jesus, "Why does your Teacher eat with men who gather taxes and with sinners?" 12 Jesus heard them and said, "People who are well do not need a doctor. 13 But go and understand these words, 'I want loving-kindness and not a gift to be given.' (Hosea 6:6) For I have not come to call good people. I have come to call those who are sinners."

Jesus Teaches about Going without Food So You Can Pray Better
(Mark 2:18–22; Luke 5:33–35)

14 Then the followers of John the Baptist came to Jesus. They asked, "Why do we and the proud religious law-keepers many times go without food so we can pray better? But Your followers never go without food so they can pray better." 15 Jesus said, "Can the friends at a wedding be sorry when the man just married is with them? But the days will come when the man just married will be taken from them. Then they will not eat food so they can pray better.

16 "No one sews a piece of new cloth on an old coat, because if the new piece pulls away, it makes the hole bigger. 17 Men do not put new wine into old skin bags. If they did, the skins would break and the wine would run out. The bags would be no good. They put new wine into new skin bags and both can be used."

Two Healed Through Faith
(Mark 5:21–43; Luke 8:40–56)

18 While Jesus talked to them, a leader of the people came and got down before Him, and worshiped Him. He said, "My daughter has just died. But come, lay Your hand on her and she will live." 19 Jesus got up and followed him. His followers went also. 20 Just then a woman who had been sick with a flow of blood for twelve years came from behind. She touched the bottom of His coat. 21 She said to herself, "If I only touch the bottom of His coat, I will be healed." 22 Then Jesus turned around. He saw her and said, "Daughter, take hope! Your faith has healed you." At once the woman was healed.

23 Jesus came into the leader's house. He saw the people playing music and making much noise. 24 He said to them, "Go now! For the girl is not dead, but is sleeping." But they laughed at Him. 25 He sent the people outside. Then He went in and took the girl's hand. She was raised up. 26 News of this went out into all the country.

The Healing of Two Blind Men

27 Jesus went on from there. Two blind men followed Him. They called out, "Take pity on us, Son of David." 28 Jesus went into the house. The blind men came to Him. Then Jesus said to them, "Do you have faith that I can do this?" They said to Him, "Yes, Sir!" 29 Then Jesus put His hands on their eyes and said, "You will have what you want because you have faith." 30 Their eyes were opened. Jesus told them to tell no one. 31 But when they had gone, they told about Him everywhere in the country.

32 As they went on their way, a man who had a demon and could not talk was brought to Jesus. 33 When the demon was put out of him, the man was able to talk. Many people were surprised and wondered about it. They said, "We have never seen in the nation of the Jews like this." 34 But the proud religious law-keepers said, "He puts out demons by the help of the leader of the demons."

35 Jesus went on to all the towns and cities. He taught in their places of worship. He preached the Good News of the holy nation of God. He healed every sickness and disease the people had. 36 As He saw many people, He had loving-pity on them. They were troubled and were walking around everywhere. They were like sheep without a shepherd. 37 Then He said to His followers, "There is much grain ready to gather. But the workmen are few. 38 Pray then to the Lord Who is the Owner of the grain-fields that He will send work men to gather His grain."

Jesus Calls Twelve Followers and Sends Them Out
(Mark 6:7-13; Luke 9:1-6)

10 Jesus called His twelve followers to Him. He gave them power to put out demons and to heal all kinds of sickness and disease. 2 These are the names of the twelve followers. There were Simon who was called Peter, and Andrew his brother, and James and John who were the sons of Zebedee. 3 There were Philip and Bartholomew and Thomas. There was Matthew, the man who gathered taxes. There were James the son of Alphaeus, and Thaddaeus, and 4 Simon the Canaanite. There was Judas Iscariot who handed Jesus over to be killed.

5 Jesus sent out these twelve followers. He told them to go, saying, "Stay away from people who are not Jews. And do not go to any town in the country of Samaria. 6 But go to the Jewish people who are lost. 7 As you go, preach. Say, 'The holy nation of heaven is near.' 8 Heal the sick and those with bad skin diseases. Raise the dead. Put out demons. You have received much, now give much. 9 Do not take gold or silver or brass money with you. 10 Do not take a bag of things for the trip. Do not take two coats or shoes or a walking stick. A workman should receive his food and what he needs.

11 "When you come to a city or town, find a home that is respected and stay there until you leave. 12 As you go into a house, tell them you hope good comes to them. 13 And if the house is respected, give them your good wishes. If it is not respected, let your good wishes come back to you. 14 Whoever does not receive you or does not listen to what you say, as you leave that house or city, shake off the dust from your feet. 15 For sure, I tell you, it will be easier for the land of Sodom and Gomorrah on the day men stand before God and are told they are guilty, than for that city.

16 "I am sending you out like sheep with wolves all around you. Be wise like snakes and gentle like doves. 17 But look out for men. They will take you up to their courts and they will hurt you in their places of worship. 18 They will take you in front of the leaders of the people and of the kings because of Me. You will tell them and the people who do not know God about Me. 19 When you are put into their hands, do not worry what you will say or how you will say it. The words will be given you when the time comes. 20 It will not be you who will speak the words. The Spirit of your Father will speak through you.

21 "A brother will hand over a brother to be put to death. A father will hand over his child to be put to death. Children will hand over their parents to be put to death. 22 You will be hated by all people because of Me. But he who stays true to the end will be saved. 23 When they make it hard for you in one town, go to another. For sure, I tell you, before you have gone

through the Jewish cities, the Son of Man will come.

24 "A follower is not greater than his teacher. A servant who is owned by someone is not greater than his owner. 25 A follower should be happy to be as his teacher, and a servant who is owned by someone should be happy to be as his owner. If they have called the head of the house Satan, how much more will they speak against those of the house. 26 Then do not be afraid of them. For nothing is covered up that will not be brought out into the light. There is nothing hid that will not be made known. 27 You tell in the light what I tell you in the dark. You must speak with a loud voice from the roofs of houses what you have heard. 28 Do not be afraid of them who kill the body. They are not able to kill the soul. But fear Him Who is able to destroy both soul and body in hell. 29 Are not two small birds sold for a very small piece of money? And yet not one of the birds falls to the earth without your Father knowing it. 30 God knows how many hairs you have on your head. 31 So do not be afraid. You are more important than many small birds.

32 "Whoever makes Me known in front of men, I will make him known to My Father in heaven. 33 But whoever does not make Me known in front of men and acts as if he does not know Me, I will not make him known to My Father in heaven.

34 "Do not think I came to bring peace on the earth. I did not come to bring peace, but a sword. 35 I came to turn a man against his father. I came to turn a daughter against her mother. I came to turn a daughter-in-law against her mother-in-law. 36 A man will be hated by his own family.

Giving Up Things of This Earth
(Luke 14:25–35)

37 "He who loves his father and mother more than Me is not good enough for Me. He who loves son or daughter more than Me is not good enough for Me. 38 He who does not take his cross and follow Me is not good enough for Me. 39 He who wants to keep his life will have it taken away from him. He who loses his life because of Me will have it given back to him.

40 "Whoever receives you, receives Me. Whoever receives Me, receives Him Who sent Me. 41 Whoever receives a preacher who speaks for God because he is a preacher, will get the reward of a preacher who speaks for God. Whoever receives a man right with God, because he is a man right with God, will get the reward of a man right with God. 42 For sure, I tell you, anyone who gives a cup of cold water to one of these little ones because he follows Me, will not lose his reward."

John the Baptist Asks about Jesus
(Luke 7:18–23)

11 When Jesus finished telling His twelve followers what to do, He went away from there to teach and preach in their towns.

2 When John the Baptist was in prison, he heard what Jesus was doing. He sent his followers. 3 They asked, "Are You the One Who was to come, or should we look for another?" 4 Jesus said to them, "Go and tell John what you see and hear. 5 The blind are made to see. Those who could not walk are walking. Those who have had bad skin diseases are healed. Those who could not hear are hearing. The dead are raised up to life and the Good News is preached to poor people. 6 He is happy who is not ashamed of Me and does not turn away because of Me."

Jesus Tells about John the Baptist
(Luke 7:24–35)

7 As the followers of John the Baptist went away, Jesus began to tell the people about John. He said, "What did you go out to see in the desert? A small tree shaking in the wind? 8 But what did you go out to see? A man dressed in good clothes? Those who are dressed in good clothes are in the houses of kings. 9 What did you go out to see? One who speaks for God? Yes, I tell you, he is more than one who speaks for God. 10 This is the man the Holy Writings spoke of when they said, 'See! I will send My helper to carry news ahead of You. He will make Your way ready for You!' **(Malachi 3:1)** 11 For sure, I tell you, of those born of women, there is no one greater than John the Baptist. The least in the holy nation of heaven is greater than he. 12 From the days of John the Baptist until now, the holy nation of heaven has suffered very much. Fighting men try to take it. 13 All the early preachers and the Law told about it until the time of John. 14 And if you will believe it, he is Elijah who was to come. **(Malachi 4:5)** 15 You have ears, then listen!

Jesus Speaks against Cities in Galilee

16 "What are the people of this day like? They are like children playing in the

center of town where people gather. They call to their friends. 17 They say, 'We played music for you, but you did not dance. We showed sorrow in front of you, but you did not show sorrow.' 18 John came and did not eat or drink. They said, 'He has a demon.' 19 Then the Son of Man came and ate and drank. They said, 'See! He eats too much and likes wine. He is a friend of men who gather taxes and of sinners!' But wisdom shows itself to be right by what it does."

20 Then He began to say strong words against the cities where most of His powerful works were done. He spoke to them because they were not sorry for their sins and did not turn from them. 21 "It is bad for you, city of Chorazin! It is bad for you, town of Bethsaida! For if the powerful works which were done in you had been done in the cities of Tyre and Sidon, they would have turned from their sins long ago. They would have shown their sorrow by putting on clothes made from hair and would have sat in ashes. 22 I tell you, it will be better for Tyre and Sidon on the day men stand before God and are told they are guilty, than for you.

23 "And Capernaum, are you to be lifted up into heaven? You will be taken down to hell. If the powerful works which were done in you had been done in the city of Sodom, it would be here to this day. 24 But I say to you that it will be better for the land of Sodom on the day men stand before God and are told they are guilty, than for you."

Jesus Prays to His Father

25 At that time Jesus said, "Thank You, Father, Lord of heaven and earth, because You hid these things from the wise and from those who have much learning. You have shown them to little children. 26 Yes, Father, it was good in Your sight.

27 "Everything has been given to Me by My Father. No one knows the Son but the Father. No one knows the Father but the Son, and those to whom the Son wants to make the Father known.

Jesus Calls People to Follow Him

28 "Come to Me, all of you who work and have heavy loads. I will give you rest. 29 Follow My teachings and learn from Me. I am gentle and do not have pride. You will have rest for your souls. 30 For My way of carrying a load is easy and My load is not heavy."

Jesus Teaches about the Day of Rest
(Mark 2:23–28; Luke 6:1–5)

12 At that time Jesus walked through the grain-fields on the Day of Rest. His followers were hungry and began to pick off grain to eat. 2 The proud religious law-keepers saw this. They said to Jesus, "See! Your followers do what the Law says not to do on the Day of Rest." 3 He said to them, "Have you not read what David did when he and his men were hungry? 4 He went into the house of God and ate the special bread used in worship which was against the Law for him or those with him to eat! Only the Jewish religious leaders were to eat that special bread. 5 Have you not read in the Law how the religious leaders do that which is not right to do on the Day of Rest, and yet they are not guilty? 6 I tell you that Someone greater than the house of God is here. 7 If you had understood what the words mean, 'I want loving-kindness and not a gift to be given,' (Hosea 6:6) you would not say a person is guilty who has done no wrong. 8 For the Son of Man is Lord of the Day of Rest."

Jesus Heals on the Day of Rest
(Mark 3:1–6; Luke 6:6–11)

9 From there Jesus went into their place of worship. 10 A man was there with a dried-up hand. The proud religious law-keepers asked Jesus, "Does the Law say it is right to heal on the Day of Rest?" They wanted something to say against Him. 11 He said to them, "If one of you has a sheep which falls into a hole on the Day of Rest, will you not take hold of it and pull it out? 12 How much better is a man than a sheep! So it is right to do good on the Day of Rest." 13 Then He said to the man, "Put out your hand." He held it out and it was made as well as the other. 14 The proud religious law-keepers went out and made plans against Him. They planned how they might kill Him.

Jesus Heals Many People
(Mark 3:7–12; Luke 6:17–19)

15 Jesus knew this and went away from there. Many people followed Him and He healed all of them. 16 He told them to tell no one of Him. 17 It happened as the early preacher Isaiah said it would happen, saying, 18 "See! My Servant Whom I have chosen! My much-Loved, in Whom My soul is well pleased! I will put My Spirit in Him. He will say to the nations what is right from wrong. 19 He will not

fight or speak with a loud voice. No man will hear His voice in the streets. 20 He will not break a broken branch. He will not put out a little fire until He makes things right. 21 In His name the nations will have hope." (Isaiah 42:1–4)

A Nation That Cannot Stand
(Mark 3:22–30; Luke 11:14–23)

22 Then they brought to Him a man who had a demon. He was blind and could not speak. Jesus healed him and he could talk and see. 23 All the people were surprised and said, "Can this Man be the Son of David?" 24 But when the proud religious law-keepers heard it, they said, "This Man puts out demons only by Satan, the leader of demons."

25 Jesus knew their thoughts and said to them, "Every nation divided into groups that fight each other is going to be destroyed. Every city or family divided into groups that fight each other will not stand. 26 If the devil puts out the devil, he is divided against himself. How will his nation stand? 27 If I put out demons by Satan, by whom do your followers put them out? So your followers will say if you are guilty. 28 But if I put out demons by the Spirit of God, then the holy nation of God is come to you. 29 How can anyone go into a strong man's house and take away his things, unless he ties up the strong man first? Only then can he take things from his house.

The Sin That Cannot Be Forgiven

30 "Whoever is not with Me is against Me. Whoever is not gathering with Me is sending everywhere. 31 I tell you, every sin and every bad word men speak against God will be forgiven, but bad words spoken against the Holy Spirit will not be forgiven. 32 Whoever speaks a word against the Son of Man will be forgiven, but whoever speaks against the Holy Spirit will not be forgiven in this life or in the life to come.

The Sin of Saying Bad Things

33 "A good tree gives good fruit. A bad tree gives bad fruit. A tree is known by its fruit. 34 You family of snakes! How can you say good things when you are sinful? The mouth speaks what the heart is full of. 35 A good man will speak good things because of the good in him. A bad man will speak bad things because of the sin in him. 36 I say to you, on the day men stand before God, they will have to give an answer for every word they have spoken that was

not important. 37 For it is by your words that you will not be guilty and it is by your words that you will be guilty."

Jesus Tells about Jonah
(Luke 11:29–32)

38 Then some of the teachers of the Law and the proud religious law-keepers said to Jesus, "Teacher, we would like to have you do something special for us to see." 39 He said to them, "The sinful people of this day look for something special to see. There will be nothing special to see but the powerful works of the early preacher Jonah. 40 Jonah was three days and three nights in the stomach of a big fish. The Son of Man will be three days and three nights in the grave also. 41 The men of the city of Nineveh will stand up with the people of this day on the day men stand before God. Those men will say these people are guilty because the men of Nineveh were sorry for their sins and turned from them when Jonah preached. And see, Someone greater than Jonah is here!

42 "The queen of the south will stand up with the people of this day on the day men stand before God. She will say that these people are guilty because she came from the ends of the earth to listen to the wise sayings of Solomon. And see, Someone greater than Solomon is here!

A Person Filled with Bad or Good
(Luke 11:24–26)

43 "When a demon is gone out of a man, it goes through dry places to find rest. It finds none. 44 Then it says, 'I will go back into my house from which I came.' When it goes back, it sees that it is empty. But it sees that the house has been cleaned and looks good. 45 Then it goes out and comes back bringing with it seven demons more sinful than itself. They go in and live there. In the end that man is worse than at first. It will be like this with the sinful people of this day."

The New Kind of Family
(Mark 3:31–35; Luke 8:19–21)

46 While Jesus was still talking to the people, His mother and His brothers came and stood outside. They wanted to talk to Him. 47 Someone said to Him, "Your mother and brothers are outside and want to talk to you." 48 Jesus said, "Who is My mother? And who are My brothers?" 49 He put out His hand to His followers and said, "See, these are My mother and

My brothers! 50 Whoever does what My father in heaven wants him to do is My brother and My sister and My mother."

Jesus Teaches with Picture-Stories
(Mark 4:1–34; Luke 8:4–18)

13 That same day Jesus went out of the house and sat down by the shore of the lake. 2 Then He got in a boat and sat down because so many people had gathered around Him. Many people were standing on the shore.

The Picture-Story of the Man Who Planted Seeds

3 Jesus taught them many things by using picture-stories. He said, "A man went out to plant seeds. 4 As he planted the seeds, some fell by the side of the road. The birds came and ate the seeds. 5 Some seeds fell between rocks. Some seeds came up at once because there was so little ground. 6 When the sun was high in the sky, they dried up and died because they had no root. 7 Some seeds fell among thorns. The thorns grew and did not give the seeds room to grow. 8 Some seeds fell on good ground and gave much grain. Some gave one hundred times as much grain. Some gave sixty times as much grain. Some gave thirty times as much grain. 9 You have ears, then listen."

Why Jesus Used Picture-Stories

10 The followers of Jesus came to Him and said, "Why do You speak to them in picture-stories?" 11 He said to the followers, "You were given the secrets about the holy nation of heaven. The secrets were not given to the others. 12 He who has will have more given to him. He will have even more than enough. But he who has little will have even that taken away from him.

13 "This is why I speak to them in picture-stories. They have eyes but they do not see. They have ears but they do not hear and they do not understand. 14 It happened in their lives as Isaiah said it would happen. He said, 'You hear and hear but do not understand. You look and look but do not see. 15 The hearts of these people have become fat. They hear very little with their ears. They have closed their eyes. If they did not do this, they would see with their eyes and hear with their ears and understand with their hearts. Then they would be changed in their ways, and I would heal them.' (Isaiah 6:9–10) 16 But how great are your eyes because they see. How great are your ears because they hear. 17 For sure, I tell you,

that many early preachers and men right with God have wanted to see the things you see, but they did not see them. They wanted to hear the things you hear, but they did not hear them.

Jesus Tells about the Man Who Planted Seeds

18 "Listen to the picture-story of the man who planted seeds in the ground. 19 When anyone hears the Word about the holy nation and does not understand it, the devil comes and takes away what was put in his heart. He is like the seed that fell by the side of the road. 20 The seed which fell between rocks is like the person who receives the Word with joy as soon as he hears it. 21 Its root is not deep and it does not last long. When troubles and suffering come because of the Word, he gives up and falls away. 22 The seed which fell among thorns is like the person who hears the Word but the cares of this life, and the love for money let the thorns come up and do not give the seed room to grow and give grain. 23 The seed which fell on good ground is like the one who hears the Word and understands it. He gives much grain. Some seed gives one hundred times as much grain. Some gives sixty times as much grain. Some gives thirty times as much grain."

The Picture-Story of the Good Seed and the Weed Seed

24 Jesus told them another picture-story. He said, "The holy nation of heaven is like a man who planted good seed in his field. 25 During the night someone who hated him came and planted weed seed with the good seed in his field and went away. 26 When the good seed started to grow and give grain, weeds came up also. 27 "The servants of the man who planted the seed came and said to him, 'Sir, did you not plant good seed in your field? Why does it have weeds also?' 28 The man who planted the seed said, 'Someone who hates me has done this.' The servants asked him, 'Should we go and pull the weeds out from among the good grain?' 29 He said, 'No, because if you pull out the weeds, the good grain will come up also. 30 Let them grow together until the time to gather the grain. Then I will say to the workmen, "Gather the weeds first and put them together to be burned. Then gather the good grain into my building." ' "

The Picture-Story of the Mustard Seed

31 Jesus told them another picture-story. He said, "The holy nation of heaven is like mustard seed which a man planted in his field. 32 It is the smallest of seeds. But when it is full-grown, it is larger than the grain of the fields and it becomes a tree. The birds of the sky come and stay in its branches."

The Picture-Story of the Yeast

33 Jesus gave them another picture-story. He said, "The holy nation of heaven is like yeast that a woman put into three pails of flour until it had become much more than at first."

34 Jesus told all these things using picture-stories to the many people. He did not speak to them without using picture-stories. 35 It happened as the early preacher said it would happen, "I will open My mouth in picture-stories. I will tell things which have been kept secret from the beginning of the world." (Psalm 78:2)

Jesus Tells about the Weed Seed

36 After Jesus sent the people away, He went into the house. His followers came to Him and said, "Tell us what You mean by the picture-story of the weeds in the field." 37 Jesus said, "He Who plants the good seed is the Son of Man. 38 The field is the world. The good seeds are the children of the holy nation. The weeds are the children of the devil. 39 The devil is the one who got in and planted the weeds. The time to gather is the end of the world. The men who gather are the angels. 40 As the weeds are gathered together and burned in the fire, so will it be in the end of the world. 41 The Son of Man will send His angels. They will gather out of His holy nation all things that cause people to sin and those who do sin. 42 They will put them into a stove of fire. There will be loud crying and grinding of teeth. 43 Then the ones right with God will shine as the sun in the holy nation of their Father. You have ears, then listen!"

The Picture-Stories of the Gold Buried in the Field and of Buying a Pearl

44 "The holy nation of heaven is like a box of riches buried in a field. A man found it and then hid it again. In his joy he goes and sells all that he has and buys that field.

45 "Again, the holy nation of heaven is like a man who buys and sells. He is looking for good pearls. 46 When he finds one good pearl worth much money, he goes and sells all that he has and buys it.

The Picture-Story of the Fish Net

47 "The holy nation of heaven is like a big net which was let down into the sea. It gathered fish of every kind. 48 When it was full, they took it to the shore. They sat down and put the good fish into pails. They threw the bad fish away. 49 It will be like this in the end of the world. Angels will come and take the sinful people from among those who are right with God. 50 They will put the sinful people into a stove of fire where there will be loud crying and grinding of teeth.

51 Jesus asked them, "Have you understood all these picture-stories?" They said, "Yes, Lord!" 52 He said to them, "Every teacher of the Law who has become a follower of the holy nation of heaven is like a man who owns his house. He takes new and old riches from his house."

They Do Not Believe in Jesus in Nazareth
(Mark 6:1–6)

53 When Jesus had finished these picture-stories, He went away from there. 54 He came to His own town and taught them in their places of worship. They were surprised and wondered, saying, "Where did this Man get this wisdom? How can He do these powerful works? 55 Is not this the son of the man who makes things from wood? Is not Mary His mother? Are not James and Joseph and Simon and Judas His brothers? 56 And are not all His sisters here? Then where did He get all these things?" 57 And they were ashamed of Him and turned away because of Him. Jesus said to them, "One who speaks for God is shown no respect in his own town and in his own house."

58 He did not do many powerful works there because they did not put their trust in Him.

John the Baptist Is Put in Prison
(Mark 6:14–20; Luke 3:18–20)

14 At that time King Herod heard much about Jesus. 2 He said to his helpers, "This must be John the Baptist. He has risen from the dead. That is why these powerful works are done by him." 3 For Herod had taken John and put him in prison. It was because of Herodias, the wife of his brother Philip. 4 For John had said to him, "It is against the Law for you to have her." 5 He would have killed John but he was afraid of the people. The people thought John was one who spoke for God.

John the Baptist Is Killed
(Mark 6:21–29; Luke 9:7–9)

6 On Herod's birthday the daughter of Herodias danced in front of them. Herod was made happy by her. 7 He promised he would give her anything she asked. 8 Because her mother told her to do it, she said, "Give me the head of John the Baptist on a plate." 9 The king was sorry. But he said for it to be given because he had promised and because of those who were eating with him. 10 He sent to the prison and had John's head cut off. 11 It was brought in on a plate and given to the girl. She brought it to her mother. 12 Then the followers of John came and took his body and buried it. They went and told Jesus.

The Feeding of the Five Thousand
(Mark 6:30–44; Luke 9:10–17; John 6:1–14)

13 When Jesus heard that John had been killed, He went from there by boat to a desert. He wanted to be alone. When the people knew it, they followed after Him by land from the cities. 14 When He got out of the boat, He saw many people. He had loving-pity for them and healed those who were sick.

15 When it was evening, His followers came to Him. They said, "This is a desert. The day is past. Send the people away so they may go into the towns and buy food for themselves." 16 Jesus said to them, "They do not have to go away. Give them something to eat." 17 They said to Him, "We have only five loaves of bread and two fish." 18 Jesus said, "Bring them to Me." 19 He told the people to sit down on the grass. Then He took the five loaves of bread and two fish. He looked up to heaven and gave thanks. He broke the loaves in pieces and gave them to His followers. The followers gave them to the people. 20 They all ate and were filled. They picked up twelve baskets full of pieces of bread and fish after the people were finished eating. 21 About five thousand men ate. Women and children ate also.

Jesus Walks on the Water
(Mark 6:45–52; John 6:15–21)

22 At once Jesus had His followers get into the boat. He told them to go ahead of Him to the other side while He sent the people away. 23 After He had sent them away, He went up the mountain by Himself to pray. When evening came, He was there alone. 24 By this time the boat was far from land and was being thrown around by the waves. The wind was strong against them.

25 Just before the light of day, Jesus went to them walking on the water. 26 When the followers saw Him walking on the water, they were afraid. They said, "It is a spirit." They cried out with fear. 27 At once Jesus spoke to them and said, "Take hope. It is I. Do not be afraid!"

28 Peter said to Jesus, "If it is You, Lord, tell me to come to You on the water." 29 Jesus said, "Come!" Peter got out of the boat and walked on the water to Jesus. 30 But when he saw the strong wind, he was afraid. He began to go down in the water. He cried out, "Lord, save me!" 31 At once Jesus put out His hand and took hold of him. Jesus said to Peter, "You have so little faith! Why did you doubt?"

32 When Jesus and Peter got into the boat, the wind stopped blowing. 33 Those in the boat worshiped Jesus. They said, "For sure, You are the Son of God!"

People Are Healed at Gennesaret
(Mark 6:53–56)

34 When they had gone over to the other side, they came to the land of Gennesaret. 35 When the men of that land saw it was Jesus, they sent word into all the country around. They brought all who were sick to Jesus. 36 They begged Him that they might touch the bottom of His coat. As many as touched the bottom of His coat were healed.

Jesus Speaks Sharp Words to the Leaders
(Mark 7:1–23)

15 Some of the teachers of the Law and the proud religious law-keepers from Jerusalem came to Jesus. They asked, 2 "Why do Your followers not obey the teaching that was given to them by our fathers? They do not wash their hands before they eat." 3 Jesus said to them, "Why do you break the Law of God by trying to keep their teaching? 4 For God said, 'Show respect to your father and mother.' (Exodus 20:12) And, 'He who curses his father or mother will be put to death.' (Exodus 21:17) 5 But you say that if a man says to his parents that anything he has, that might have been of help to them, is already given to God, 6 he does not have to show respect by helping his father and mother. You are putting aside the Word of God to keep their teaching. 7 You who pretend to be someone you are not, Isaiah told about you. He said, 8 "These people show respect to Me with their mouth, but their heart is far from Me. 9 Their worship of Me is worth nothing. They teach what men have made up.'" (Isaiah 29:13)

10 Jesus called the people to Him and said to them, "Listen and understand this! 11 It is not what goes into a man's mouth that makes his mind and heart sinful. It is what comes out of a man's mouth that makes him sinful."

12 His followers came to Him. They said, "Did You know the proud religious law-keepers were ashamed and turned away because of You when they heard this?" 13 He said, "Every plant that My Father in heaven did not plant will be pulled up by the roots. 14 Let them alone. They are blind leaders of the blind. If one blind man leads another blind man, they will both fall into a hole."

15 Then Peter said to Jesus, "Tell us this picture-story so we can understand it." 16 Jesus said, "Do you not understand yet? 17 Do you not understand that whatever goes into the mouth goes into the stomach and then out of the body? 18 But whatever comes from the mouth has come out of the heart. These things make the man unclean inside. 19 For out of the heart come bad thoughts, killing other people, sex sins of a married person, sex sins of a person not married, stealing, lying, speaking against God. 20 These are the things that make the man unclean inside. It does not make a man sinful to eat with hands that have not been washed."

Jesus Puts a Demon Out of a Girl
(Mark 7:24–30)

21 Jesus went from there to the cities of Tyre and Sidon. 22 A woman came from the land of Canaan. She cried out to Jesus and said, "Take pity on me, Lord, Son of David! My daughter has a demon and is much troubled." 23 But Jesus did not speak a word to her. His followers kept asking, saying, "Send her away for she keeps calling us." 24 He said, "I was sent only to the Jewish people who are lost." 25 Then she came and got down before Jesus and worshiped Him. She said, "Lord, help me!" 26 But He said, "It is not right to take children's food and throw it to

the dogs." 27 She said, "Yes, Lord, but even the dogs eat the pieces that fall from the table of their owners." 28 Jesus said to her, "Woman, you have much faith. You will have what you asked for." Her daughter was healed at that very time.

Jesus Heals All Who Come to Him

29 Jesus went from there and came to the Sea of Galilee. Then He went up the mountain and sat down. 30 Many people came to Him. They brought with them those who were not able to walk. They brought those who were not able to see. They brought those who were not able to hear or speak and many others. Then they put them at the feet of Jesus and He healed them. 31 All the people wondered. They saw how those who could not speak were now talking. They saw how those who could not walk were now walking. They saw how those who could not see were now seeing, and they gave thanks to the God of the Jews.

The Feeding of the Four Thousand
(Mark 8:1–9)

32 Then Jesus called His followers to Him. He said, "I pity these people because they have been with Me three days and they have no food. I do not want to send them home without food. They might get too weak as they go." 33 The followers said to Jesus, "Where can we get enough bread to feed them all in this desert?" 34 Jesus said to them, "How many loaves of bread do you have?" They said, "Seven loaves and a few small fish." 35 He told the people to sit down on the ground. 36 Then He took the seven loaves of bread and the fish and gave thanks. He broke them and gave them to His followers. The followers gave them to the people. 37 They all ate and were filled. They picked up seven baskets full of pieces of bread and fish after the people finished eating. 38 Four thousand men ate. Women and children ate also. 39 After this Jesus sent the people away. Then He got into a boat and came to a place called Magadan.

Jesus Speaks Sharp Words to the Proud Religious Law-Keepers
(Mark 8:10–13)

16 The proud religious law-keepers and a religious group of people who believe no one will be raised from the dead came to Jesus. They asked Him to show something special from heaven. They wanted to trap Jesus. 2 (*He said to them,

"In the evening you say, 'The weather will be good tomorrow because the sky is red.' 3 And in the morning you say, 'We will have a storm today because the sky is red and the clouds are low.' You understand the things you see in the sky, but you cannot understand the special things you see these days!) 4 The sinful people of this day go after something special to see. There will be nothing special for them to see but the early preacher Jonah." Then He went away from them.

Jesus Shows That the Teaching of the Proud Religious Law-Keepers Is Wrong
(Mark 8:14–21)

5 The followers came to the other side of the lake. They remembered they had forgotten to bring bread. 6 Jesus said to them, "See! Have nothing to do with the yeast of the proud religious law-keepers and the religious group of people who believe no one will be raised from the dead." 7 They started to think about it among themselves and said, "He said this because we forgot to bring bread." 8 Jesus knew this and said, "You have very little faith! Why are you talking among yourselves about not bringing bread? 9 Do you not yet understand or remember the five loaves of bread that fed five thousand men? And how many baskets full were gathered up? 10 Or do you not even remember the seven loaves of bread that fed the four thousand men? And how many baskets full were gathered up? 11 Why is it that you do not see that I was not talking to you about bread? I was talking to you about keeping away from the yeast of the proud religious law-keepers and the religious group of people who believe no one will be raised from the dead." 12 Then they understood that it was not the yeast of bread that He was talking about. But He was talking about the teaching of the proud religious law-keepers and of the other religious group of people.

Peter Says Jesus Is the Christ
(Mark 8:27–30; Luke 9:18–20)

13 Jesus came into the country of Caesarea Philippi. He asked His followers, "Who do people say that I, the Son of Man, am?" 14 They said, "Some say You are John the Baptist and some say Elijah and others say Jeremiah or one of the early preachers." 15 He said to them, "But who do you say that I am?" 16 Simon Peter said, "You are the Christ, the Son of the living God." 17 Jesus said to him, "Simon, son of

Jonah, you are happy because you did not learn this from man. My Father in heaven has shown you this.

18 "And I tell you that you are Peter. On this rock I will build My church. The powers of hell will not be able to have power over My church. 19 I will give you the keys of the holy nation of heaven. Whatever you do not allow on earth will not have been allowed in heaven. Whatever you allow on earth will have been allowed in heaven." 20 Then with strong words He told His followers to tell no one that He was the Christ.

Jesus Tells of His Death for the First Time
(Mark 8:31–38; Luke 9:21–27)

21 From that time on Jesus began to tell His followers that He had to go to Jerusalem and suffer many things. These hard things would come from the leaders and from the head religious leaders of the Jews and from the teachers of the Law. He told them He would be killed and three days later He would be raised from the dead. 22 Peter took Jesus away from the others and spoke sharp words to Him. He said, "Never, Lord! This must not happen to You!" 23 Then Jesus turned to Peter and said, "Get behind Me, Satan! You are standing in My way. You are not thinking how God thinks. You are thinking how man thinks."

Giving Up Riches

24 Jesus said to His followers, "If anyone wants to be My follower, he must forget about himself. He must take up his cross and follow Me. 25 If anyone wants to keep his life safe, he will lose it. If anyone gives up his life because of Me, he will save it. 26 For what does a man have if he gets all the world and loses his own soul? What can a man give to buy back his soul? 27 The Son of Man will come in the greatness of His Father with His angels. Then He will give to every man his pay as he has worked. 28 For sure, I tell you, there are some standing here that will not die until they see the Son of Man coming as King."

A Look at What Jesus Will Be Like
(Mark 9:1–13; Luke 9:28–36)

17 Six days later Jesus took with Him Peter and James and his brother John. He led them up to a high mountain by themselves. 2 He was changed in looks before them. His face was as bright as the sun. His clothes looked as white as light. 3 Moses and Elijah were seen talking with Jesus. 4 Then Peter said to Jesus, "Lord, it is good for us to be here. If You will let us, we will build three altars here. One will be for You and one for Moses and one for Elijah."

5 While Peter was speaking, a bright cloud came over them. A voice from the cloud said, "This is My much-loved Son, I am very happy with Him. Listen to Him!" 6 When the followers heard this, they got down on the ground on their faces and were very much afraid. 7 Jesus came and put His hand on them. He said, "Get up! Do not be afraid." 8 When they looked up, they saw no one there but Jesus only. 9 As they came down from the mountain, Jesus told them in strong words, saying, "Do not tell anyone what you have seen until the Son of Man is raised from the dead."

The Followers Ask about Elijah

10 The followers asked Jesus, "Then why do the teachers of the Law say that Elijah must come first?" 11 He said, "For sure, Elijah will come first and get things ready. 12 But I tell you, Elijah has already come and they did not know him. They did to him whatever they wanted to do. In the same way the Son of Man will suffer from them also." 13 Then the followers understood He was talking about John the Baptist.

A Boy with a Demon Is Healed
(Mark 9:14–29; Luke 9:37–42)

14 When they came to many people, a man came up to Jesus and got on his knees. He said, 15 "Lord, have pity on my son. He is very sick and at times loses the use of his mind. Many times he falls into the fire or into the water. 16 I took him to Your followers but they were not able to heal him."

17 Then Jesus said, "You people of this day have no faith and are going the wrong way. How long must I be with you? How long must I put up with you? Bring him here to Me." 18 Jesus spoke sharp words to the demon and the demon came out of him. At once the boy was healed.

19 The followers came to Jesus when He was alone. They said, "Why were we not able to put the demon out?" 20 Jesus said to them, "Because you have so little faith. For sure, I tell you, if you have faith as a mustard seed, you will say to this mountain, 'Move from here to over there,' and it would move over. You will be able

to do anything. 21 *But this kind of demon does not go out but by prayer and by going without food so you can pray better."

Jesus Tells of His Death the Second Time
(Mark 9:30–32; Luke 9:43–45)

22 While they were still in Galilee, Jesus said to the followers, "The Son of Man will be handed over to men. 23 They will kill Him, but He will be raised from the dead three days later." The followers were very sad.

24 They came to the city of Capernaum. Those who gathered the tax for the house of God came to Peter. They said, "Does not your Teacher pay tax money for the house of God?" 25 Peter said, "Yes." When Peter came into the house, Jesus spoke to him first. He said, "What do you think, Simon? From whom do the kings of this earth get their money or taxes, from their own people or from those of another country?" 26 Peter said to Him, "From those of another country." Then Jesus said, "Then their own people do not pay taxes. 27 But so we will not make them to be troubled, go down to the lake and throw in a hook. Take the first fish that comes up. In its mouth you will find a piece of money. Take that and pay the tax for Me and yourself."

Jesus Teaches about the Faith of a Child
(Mark 9:33–50; Luke 9:46–50)

18 At that time the followers came to Jesus. They said, "Who is the greatest in the holy nation of heaven?" 2 Jesus took a little child and put him among them. 3 He said, "For sure, I tell you, unless you have a change of heart and become like a little child, you will not get into the holy nation of heaven. 4 Whoever is without pride as this little child is the greatest in the holy nation of heaven. 5 Whoever receives a little child because of Me receives Me. 6 But whoever is the reason for one of these little children who believe in Me to fall into sin, it would be better for him to have a large rock put around his neck and to be thrown into the sea.

7 "It is bad for the world because of that which makes people sin. Men will be tempted to sin. But it is bad for the one who is the reason for someone to sin. 8 If your hand or your foot is the reason you sin, cut it off and throw it away. It is better for you to go into life without a hand or a foot, than to have two hands or two feet and to be thrown into the fire of hell. 9 If your eye is the reason you sin, take it out

and throw it away. It is better for you to go into life with one eye, than to have two eyes and be thrown into the fire of hell. 10 Be sure you do not hate one of these little children. I tell you, they have angels who are always looking into the face of My Father in heaven.

The Lost Sheep

11 "For the Son of Man has come to save that which was lost. 12 What do you think about this? A man has one hundred sheep and one of them is lost. Will he not leave the ninety-nine and go to the mountains to look for that one lost sheep? 13 If he finds it, for sure, I tell you, he will have more joy over that one, than over the ninety-nine that were not lost. 14 I tell you, My Father in heaven does not want one of these little children to be lost.

What to Do with a Brother Who Sins against You

15 "If your brother sins against you, go and tell him what he did without other people hearing it. If he listens to you, you have won your brother back again. 16 But if he will not listen to you, take one or two other people with you. Every word may be remembered by the two or three who heard. 17 If he will not listen to them, tell the trouble to the church. If he does not listen to the church, think of him as a person who is as bad as one who does not know God and a person who gathers taxes.

18 "For sure, I tell you, whatever you do not allow on earth will not have been allowed in heaven. Whatever you allow on earth will have been allowed in heaven. 19 Again I tell you this: If two of you agree on earth about anything you pray for, it will be done for you by My Father in heaven. 20 For where two or three are gathered together in My name, there I am with them."

True Forgiveness

21 Then Peter came to Jesus and said, "Lord, how many times may my brother sin against me and I forgive him, up to seven times?" 22 Jesus said to him, "I tell you, not seven times but seventy times seven!

23 "The holy nation of heaven is like a king who wanted to find out how much money his servants owed him. 24 As he began, one of the servants was brought to him who owed him very much money. 25 He could pay nothing that he owed. So the king spoke the word that he and

his wife and his children and all that he had should be sold to pay what he owed. 26 The servant got down on his face in front of the king. He said, 'Give me time, and I will pay you all the money.' 27 Then the king took pity on his servant and let him go. He told him he did not have to pay the money back.

28 "But that servant went out and found one of the other servants who owed him very little money. He took hold of his neck and said, 'Pay me the money you owe me!' 29 The other servant got down at his feet and said, 'Give me time, and I will pay you all the money.' 30 But he would not. He had him put in prison until he could pay the money.

31 "When his other servants saw what had happened, they were very sorry. They came and told the king all that was done. 32 Then the king called for the first one. He said, 'You bad servant! I forgave you. I said that you would not have to pay back any of the money you owed me because you asked me. 33 Should you not have had pity on the other servant, even as I had pity on you?' 34 The king was very angry. He handed him over to men who would beat and hurt him until he paid all the money he owed. 35 So will My Father in heaven do to you, if each one of you does not forgive his brother from his heart."

What Jesus Taught about Marriage and Divorce
(Mark 10:1–12)

19 When Jesus had finished talking, He went from the country of Galilee. He came to the part of the country of Judea which is on the other side of the Jordan River. 2 Many people followed Him and He healed them there.

3 The proud religious law-keepers came to Jesus. They tried to trap Him by saying, "Does the Law say a man can divorce his wife for any reason?" 4 He said to them, "Have you not read that He Who made them in the first place made them man and woman? 5 It says, 'For this reason a man will leave his father and his mother and will live with his wife. The two will become one.' 6 So they are no longer two but one. Let no man divide what God has put together."

7 The proud religious law-keepers said to Jesus, "Then why did the Law of Moses allow a man to divorce his wife if he put it down in writing and gave it to her?" 8 Jesus said to them, "Because of your hard

hearts Moses allowed you to divorce your wives. It was not like that from the beginning. 9 And I say to you, whoever divorces his wife, except for sex sins, and marries another, is guilty of sex sins in marriage. Whoever marries her that is divorced is guilty of sex sins in marriage."

10 His followers said to Him, "If that is the way of a man with his wife, it is better not to be married." 11 But Jesus said to them, "Not all men are able to do this, but only those to whom it has been given. 12 For there are some men who from birth will never be able to have children. There are some men who have been made so by men. There are some men who have had themselves made that way because of the holy nation of heaven. The one who is able to do this, let him do it."

Jesus Gives Thanks for Little Children
(Mark 10:13–16; Luke 18:15–17)

13 Then little children were brought to Him that He might put His hands on them and pray for them. The followers spoke sharp words to them. 14 But Jesus said, "Let the little children come to Me. Do not stop them. The holy nation of heaven is made up of ones like these." 15 He put His hands on them and went away.

Jesus Teaches about Keeping the Law
(Mark 10:17–31; Luke 18:18–30)

16 A man came to Jesus and asked, "Good Teacher, what good work must I do to have life that lasts forever?" 17 Jesus said to him, "Why are you asking Me about what is good? There is only One Who is good. If you want to have life that lasts forever, you must obey the Laws." 18 The man said to Him, "What kind of laws?" Jesus said, "You must not kill another person. You must not be guilty of sex sins. You must not steal. You must not lie. 19 Show respect to your father and your mother. And love your neighbor as you love yourself." 20 The young man said to Jesus, "I have obeyed all these Laws. What more should I do?" 21 Jesus said to him, "If you want to be perfect, go and sell everything you have and give the money to poor people. Then you will have riches in heaven. Come and follow Me." 22 When the young man heard these words, he went away sad for he had many riches.

The Danger of Riches

23 Jesus said to His followers, "For sure, I tell you, it will be hard for a rich man to get into the holy nation of heaven. 24 Again I tell you, it is easier for a camel to go through the eye of a needle than for a rich man to get into the holy nation of heaven." 25 When His followers heard this, they could not understand it. They said, "Then who can be saved from the punishment of sin?" 26 Jesus looked at them and said, "This cannot be done by men. But with God all things can be done."

27 Then Peter said to Him, "We have given up everything and have followed You. Then what will we have?" 28 Jesus said to them, "For sure, I tell you, when all the earth will be new and the Son of Man will sit on His throne in His shining-greatness, you who have followed Me will also sit on twelve thrones, and judge the twelve family groups of the Jewish nation. 29 Everyone who has given up houses or brothers or sisters or father or mother or wife or children or lands because of Me, will get a hundred times more. And you will get life that lasts forever. 30 Many who are first will be last. Many who are last will be first.

The Picture-Story of the Workmen in the Grape-Field

20 "For the holy nation of heaven is like the owner of a grape-field. He went out early in the morning to hire workmen to work in his grape-field. 2 He promised to give them a day's pay and then sent them to his grape-field. 3 Later in the morning he went to the center of the town where people gather. He saw men standing there doing nothing. 4 He said to them, 'You go to my grape-field and work also. Whatever is right, I will pay you.' And they went. 5 Again he went out about noon and at three o'clock and did the same thing. 6 About five o'clock he went out and still found others doing nothing. He asked them, 'Why do you stand here all day and do nothing?' 7 They said to him, 'Because no one has hired us.' He said, 'Go to my grape-field and work. Whatever is right, I will pay you.'

8 "When evening came, the owner of the grape-field said to the boss of the workmen, 'Call the workmen. Give them their pay. Start with the last ones hired and go on to the first ones hired.' 9 The workmen who had been hired at five o'clock came up. Each one of them got a day's pay for his work. 10 When the workmen who had been hired the first thing in the morning came, they thought they would get more.

But each one got a day's pay. ¹¹ After they received it, they talked against the owner. ¹² They said, 'The last workmen hired have only worked one hour. You have given to them the same as to us. We have worked hard through the heat of the day.' ¹³ But he said to one of them, 'Friend, I am doing you no wrong. Did you not agree with me when I promised to pay you a day's pay? ¹⁴ Take your pay and go. I want to give the last ones hired the same as I have given you. ¹⁵ Do I not have the right to do what I want to do with my own money? Does your eye make you want more because I am good?' ¹⁶ So those who are last will be first and the first will be last."

Jesus Tells of His Death the Third Time
(Mark 10:32–34; Luke 18:31–34)

¹⁷ As Jesus was going up to Jerusalem, He talked also to the twelve followers by the side of the road. He said, ¹⁸ "Listen! We are going up to Jerusalem. The Son of Man will be handed over to the religious leaders and to the teachers of the Law. They will say that He must be put to death. ¹⁹ They will hand Him over to the people who do not know God. They will make fun of Him and will beat Him. They will nail Him to a cross. Three days later He will be raised to life."

The Mother of James and John Asks Jesus Something Hard
(Mark 10:35–45)

²⁰ The mother of Zebedee's children (James and John) came to Jesus with her sons. She got down on her knees before Jesus to ask something of Him. ²¹ He said to her, "What do you want?" She said, "Say that my two sons may sit, one at Your right side and one at Your left side, when You are King." ²² Jesus said to her, "You do not know what you are asking. Are you able to take the suffering that I am about to take? (Are you able to be baptized with the baptism that I am baptized with?)" They said, "Yes, we are able." ²³ He said to them, "You will suffer as I will suffer. But the places at My right side and at My left side are not Mine to give. Whoever My Father says will have those places."

²⁴ The other ten followers heard this. They were angry with the two brothers. ²⁵ Jesus called them to Him and said, "You know how the kings of the nations show their power to the people. Important leaders use their power over the people. ²⁶ It must not be that way with you. But

whoever wants to be great among you, let him care for you. ²⁷ Whoever wants to be first among you, let him be your servant. ²⁸ For the Son of Man came not to be cared for. He came to care for others. He came to give His life so that many could be bought by His blood and made free from the punishment of sin."

The Healing of the Blind Men
(Mark 10:46–52; Luke 18:35–43)

²⁹ As they went away from the city of Jericho, many people followed Him. ³⁰ Two blind men were sitting by the side of the road. They called out when they heard that Jesus was going by. They said, "Lord, take pity on us, Son of David!" ³¹ Many people spoke sharp words to them. They told the blind men not to call out. But they called all the more, "Lord! Take pity on us, Son of David!" ³² Jesus stopped and called them. He asked, "What do you want Me to do for you?" ³³ The blind men said to Jesus, "Lord, we want our eyes opened!" ³⁴ Jesus had loving-pity on them and put His hands on their eyes. At once they could see, and they followed Jesus.

The Last Time Jesus Goes into Jerusalem
(Mark 11:1–11; Luke 19:29–44; John 12:12–19)

21 They were near Jerusalem and had come to the town of Bethphage at the Mount of Olives. Jesus sent two followers on ahead. ² He said to them, "Go to the town over there. You will find a donkey tied and her young with her. Let them loose and bring them to Me. ³ If anyone says something to you, say, 'The Lord needs them.' He will send them at once."

⁴ It happened as the early preacher said it would happen, saying, ⁵ "Say to the people in Jerusalem, 'See! Your King is coming to you. He is gentle. He is riding on a young donkey.'" (Zechariah 9:9, Isaiah 62:11)

⁶ The followers went and did as Jesus told them. ⁷ They brought the donkey and her young one. They put their clothes on the donkey and Jesus sat on them. ⁸ Many people put their coats down on the road. Other people cut branches from the trees and put them along the way. ⁹ The people who went in front and those who followed Jesus called out, "Greatest One! The Son of David! Great and honored is He Who comes in the name of the Lord! Greatest One in the highest heaven."

¹⁰ When Jesus came into Jerusalem, all the people of the city were troubled.

They said, "Who is this?" **11** Many people said, "This is Jesus, the One Who speaks for God from the town of Nazareth in the country of Galilee."

Jesus Stops the Buying and the Selling in the House of God
(Mark 11:15–19; Luke 19:45–48; John 2:13–17)

12 Then Jesus went into the house of God and made all those leave who were buying and selling there. He turned over the tables of the men who changed money. He turned over the seats of those who sold doves. **13** He said to them, "It is written, 'My house is to be called a house of prayer.' You have made it a place of robbers." (Isaiah 56:7; Jeremiah 7:11)

14 The blind and those who could not walk came to Jesus in the house of God and He healed them. **15** The religious leaders of the Jews and the teachers of the Law saw the great things He did. They heard the children calling in the house of God and saying, "Greatest One! Son of David!" The leaders were very angry. **16** They said to Jesus, "Do you hear what these children are saying?" Jesus said to them, "Yes, have you not read the writings, 'Even little children and babies will honor Him'?" **17** Jesus left them and went out of the city to the town of Bethany. He stayed there that night.

The Fig Tree Dries Up
(Mark 11:20–26)

18 In the morning as He was coming back to the city, He was hungry. **19** He saw a fig tree by the side of the road and went to it. There was nothing on it but leaves. He said to the tree, "No fruit will ever grow on you again." At once the fig tree dried up. **20** The followers saw it and were surprised and wondered. They said, "How did the fig tree dry up so fast?" **21** Jesus said to them, "For sure, I tell you this: If you have faith and do not doubt, you will not only be able to do what was done to the fig tree. You will also be able to say to this mountain, 'Move from here and be thrown into the sea,' and it will be done. **22** All things you ask for in prayer, you will receive if you have faith."

They Ask Jesus Who Gave Him the Power to Do These Things
(Mark 11:27–33; Luke 20:1–8)

23 Jesus came into the house of God. The religious leaders and the other leaders of the people came up to Him as He was teaching. They said, "By what right and power are You doing these things? Who gave You the right and the power to do them?" **24** Jesus said to them, "I will ask you one thing also. If you tell Me, then I will tell you by what right and power I do these things. **25** Was the baptism of John from heaven or from men?" They thought among themselves, "If we say, 'From heaven,' then He will say, 'Then why did you not believe him?' **26** But if we say, 'From men,' we are afraid of the people, because they all think John was one who spoke for God." **27** They said to Jesus, "We do not know." He said to them, "Then I will not tell you by what right and power I do these things.

The Picture-Story of the Two Sons

28 "What do you think about this? There was a man who had two sons. He came to the first son and said, 'My son, go to my grape-field and work today.' **29** He said, 'I will go.' But he did not go. **30** The father came to the second son and asked the same thing. The son said, 'No, I will not go.' Later he was sorry and went. **31** Which one of the two sons did what his father wanted?" They said to Jesus, "The second son." Jesus said to them, "For sure, I tell you this: Tax-gatherers and women who sell the use of their bodies will get into the holy nation of heaven before you. **32** For John came to you preaching about being right with God. You did not believe him. But tax-gatherers and women who sell the use of their bodies did believe him. When you saw this, you were not sorry for your sins and did not turn from them and believe him.

The Picture-Story of the Grape-Field
(Mark 12:1–12; Luke 20:9–18)

33 "Listen to another picture-story. A man who owned land planted grapes in a field and put a fence around it. He made a place for making wine. He built a tower to look over the grape-field. He let farmers rent it and then he went into another country. **34** The time came for gathering the grapes. He sent his servants to the farmers to get the grapes. **35** The farmers took his servants and hit one. They killed another and threw stones at another. **36** Again he sent other servants. He sent more than the first time. The farmers did the same to those servants. **37** After this he sent his son to them. He said to himself, 'They will respect my son.' **38** When the farmers saw the son, they said to themselves, 'This is the one who will get everything when the owner dies. Let us kill him and we will get it all.' **39** They took him and threw him out of the grape-field and killed him. **40** When the owner of the grape-field comes, what will he do to those farmers?" **41** They said to Him, "He will put those bad men to death. Then he will rent the grape-field to other farmers who will give him the grapes when they are ready." **42** Jesus said to them, "Have you not read in the Holy Writings, 'The Stone that was put aside by the workmen has become the most important Stone in the building? The Lord has done this. We think it is great!' (Psalm 118:22–23) **43** I say to you, because of this, the holy nation of God will be taken from you. It will be given to a nation that will give fruit. **44** Whoever falls on this Stone will be broken. And on the one it falls, it will make him like dust."

45 When the religious leaders and the proud religious law-keepers heard this picture-story, they knew He spoke of them. **46** When they tried to put their hands on Him, they were afraid of the many people. The people thought He was One Who spoke for God.

The Picture-Story of the Marriage Supper

22 Again Jesus spoke to them in picture-stories. He said, **2** "The holy nation of heaven is like a king who gave a wedding supper for his son. **3** He sent his servants to tell the people, who had been asked, to come to the supper. But the people did not want to come.

4 "He sent other servants, saying to them, 'Tell those who have been asked to come, "See! My supper is ready. My cows and fat calves are killed. Everything is ready. Come to the wedding supper!"' **5** But they did not listen and went on working. One went to his farm. Another went to his store **6** The others took hold of his servants, and hurt them and killed them.

7 "When the king heard this, he was very angry. He sent his soldiers to put those to death who had killed his servants. He burned their city. **8** Then he said to his servants, 'The wedding supper is ready. Those who were asked to come to the supper were not good enough. **9** Go out into the roads and as many people as you can find, ask them to come to the wedding supper.'

10 "The servants went out into the roads and brought all they could find, both bad

and good. The wedding supper room was full of people. **11** The king came in to see those who had come. He saw one man who did not have on wedding supper clothes. **12** He said to him, 'Friend, how did you get in here without wedding supper clothes?' The man could not speak! **13** Then the king said to his servants, 'Tie his hands and feet, and throw him out into the darkness. In that place there will be loud crying and grinding of teeth.' **14** For many are called but few are chosen."

The Proud Religious Law-Keepers Try to Trap Jesus
(Mark 12:13–17; Luke 20:19–26)

15 Then the proud religious law-keepers got together to think how they could trap Jesus in His talk. **16** They sent their followers to Jesus with some of King Herod's men. They asked, "Teacher, we know that You are true. We know that You are teaching the truth about God. We know You are not afraid of what men think or say about You. **17** Tell us what You think of this. Is it right to pay taxes to Caesar, or not?" **18** Jesus knew their sinful thoughts and said, "You pretend to be someone you are not! Why do you try to trap Me? **19** Show Me a piece of money." They brought Him a piece. **20** Jesus said to them, "Whose picture is this? Whose name is on it?" **21** They said to Him, "Caesar's." Then He said to them, "Pay to Caesar the things that belong to Caesar. Pay to God the things that belong to God." **22** When they heard this, they were surprised and wondered about it. Then they went away from Him.

They Ask about Being Raised from the Dead
(Mark 12:18–27; Luke 20:27–40)

23 The same day some people from the religious group who believe no one will be raised from the dead came to Jesus. They asked, **24** "Teacher, Moses said, 'If a man should die without having children, then his brother must marry his wife. He should have children for his brother.' (Deuteronomy 25:5) **25** There were seven brothers with us. The first was married but died before he had any children. The second brother then married the first brother's wife. **26** The second brother died and the same with the third and on to the seventh. **27** Then the woman died also. **28** When people are raised from the dead, whose wife will she be of the seven? They all had her for a wife."

29 Jesus said to them, "You are wrong because you do not know the Holy Writings or the power of God. 30 After people are raised from the dead, they do not marry. They are like the angels in heaven. 31 Have you not read what God said to you about those who are raised from the dead? He said, 32 'I am the God of Abraham and the God of Isaac and the God of Jacob.' He is not the God of the dead but of the living!" (Exodus 3:6) 33 When the people heard this, they were surprised and wondered about His teaching.

The Great Law
(Mark 12:28–34)

34 The proud religious law-keepers got together when they heard that the religious group of people who believe no one will be raised from the dead were not able to talk anymore to Jesus. 35 A proud religious law-keeper who knew the Law tried to trap Jesus. He said, 36 "Teacher, which one is the greatest of the Laws?" 37 Jesus said to him, " 'You must love the Lord your God with all your heart and with all your soul and with all your mind.' 38 This is the first and greatest of the Laws. 39 The second is like it, 'You must love your neighbor as you love yourself.' 40 All the Laws and the writings of the early preachers depend on these two most important Laws."

41 The proud religious law-keepers were gathered together. Then Jesus asked, 42 "What do you think about the Christ? Whose Son is He?" They said to Him, "The Son of David." 43 Jesus said to them, "Then how is it that David, being led by the Holy Spirit, calls Him 'Lord'? He said, 44 'The Lord said to my Lord, "Sit at My right side until I make those who hate You a place to rest Your feet." ' (Psalm 110:1) 45 If David calls Him 'Lord,' then how can He be the Son of David?" 46 No one could answer a word, and after that day no one asked Him anything.

The Teachers of the Law and the Proud Religious Law-Keepers
(Mark 12:38–40; Luke 20:45–47)

23 Then Jesus talked to the many people and to His followers. 2 He said, "The teachers of the Law and the proud religious law-keepers have put themselves in Moses' place as teachers. 3 Do what they tell you to do and keep on doing it. But do not follow what they do. They preach but do not obey their own preaching. 4 They make heavy loads and

put them on the shoulders of men. But they will not help lift them with a finger. 5 Everything they do, they do to be seen of men. They have words from the Holy Writings written in large letters on their left arm and forehead and they make wide trimming for their clothes. 6 They like to have the important places at big suppers and the best seats in the Jewish places of worship. 7 They like to have people show respect to them as they stand in the center of town where people gather. They like to be called teacher.

8 "But you are not to be called teacher. There is only one Teacher, and all of you are brothers. 9 Do not call any man here on earth your father. There is only one Father and He is in heaven. 10 You are not to be called leader. There is only one Leader and He is Christ.

11 "He who is greatest among you will be the one to care for you. 12 The person who thinks he is important will find out how little he is worth. The person who is not trying to honor himself will be made important.

Jesus Speaks Sharp Words to the Proud Religious Law-Keepers

13 "It is bad for you, teachers of the Law and proud religious law-keepers, you who pretend to be someone you are not! You keep men from going into the holy nation of heaven. You are not going in yourselves, and you do not allow those to go in who are about to go in. 14 It is bad for you, teachers of the Law and proud religious law-keepers, you who pretend to be someone you are not! (*You take houses from poor women whose husbands have died. Then you try to cover it up by making long prayers. You will be punished all the more because of this.) 15 It is bad for you, teachers of the Law and proud religious law-keepers, you who pretend to be someone you are not! You go over land and sea to win one follower. When you have him, you make him twice as much a child of hell as you are.

16 "It is bad for you, blind leaders! You say, 'Whoever makes a promise by the house of God, his promise is worth nothing. But whoever makes a promise by the gold of the house of God, then his promise has to be kept.' 17 You fools and blind men! Which is greater, the gold or the house of God that makes the gold holy? 18 You say, 'Whoever will promise by the altar, his promise does not have to be kept. But

whoever makes a promise by the gift on the altar, then his promise has to be kept.' 19 You fools and blind men! Which is greater, the gift, or the altar that makes the gift holy? 20 Whoever makes a promise by the altar, promises by it and by everything on it. 21 Whoever makes a promise by the house of God, promises by it and by Him Who is in it. 22 Whoever makes a promise by heaven, promises by the throne of God and by Him Who sits there.

23 "It is bad for you, teachers of the Law and proud religious law-keepers, you who pretend to be someone you are not! You give one-tenth part of your spices, and have not done the most important things of the Law, such as thinking what is right and wrong, and having pity and faith. These you should have done and still have done the other things also. 24 You blind leaders, you take a small bug out of your cup but you swallow a camel!

25 "It is bad for you, teachers of the Law and proud religious law-keepers, you who pretend to be someone you are not! You clean the outside of the cup and plate, but leave the inside full of strong bad desires and are not able to keep from doing sinful things. 26 You blind proud religious law-keepers! Clean the inside of the cup and plate, then the outside will be clean also.

27 "It is bad for you, teachers of the Law and proud religious law-keepers, you who pretend to be someone you are not! You are like graves that have been made white and look beautiful on the outside. But inside you are full of the bones of dead men and of every sinful thing. 28 As men look at you, you seem to be good and right but inside you are full of sin. You pretend to be someone you are not.

29 "It is bad for you, teachers of the Law and proud religious law-keepers, you who pretend to be someone you are not! You make buildings for the graves of the early preachers, and you make the graves beautiful of those who are right with God. 30 You say, 'If we had lived in the days of our early fathers, we would not have helped kill the early preachers.' 31 In this way, you are showing that you are the sons of those who killed the early preachers. 32 You might as well finish what your early fathers did. 33 You snakes! You family of snakes! How can you be kept from hell?

34 "Because of this, I am going to keep on sending to you men who speak for God and wise men and teachers of the Law. Some of them you will kill and nail to a cross. Some of them you will beat in your places of worship. You will make it very hard for them as they go from city to city. 35 Because of this, you will be guilty of the blood of all those right with God on the earth. It will be from the blood of Abel who was right with God to the blood of Zachariah son of Barachias. He was the one you killed between the house of God and the altar. 36 For sure, I tell you, all these things will come on the people of this day.

Jesus Sorrows Over Jerusalem

37 "O Jerusalem, Jerusalem! You kill the men who speak for God and throw stones at those who were sent to you. How many times I wanted to gather your children around Me, as a chicken gathers her young ones under her wings. But you would not let Me. 38 See! Your house is empty. 39 I say to you, you will not see Me again until you will say, 'Great is He Who comes in the name of the Lord!' "

Jesus Tells of the House of God
(Mark 13:1–37; Luke 21:5–36)

24 Jesus went out of the house of God. On the way His followers came to Him to show Him the buildings of the house of God. 2 Jesus said to them, "Do you see all these things? For sure, I tell you, all these stones will be thrown down. Not one will be left standing on another."

Jesus Teaches on the Mount of Olives

3 Jesus sat on the Mount of Olives. The followers came to Him when He was alone and said, "Tell us, when will this happen? What can we look for to show us of Your coming and of the end of the world?"

4 Jesus said to them, "Be careful that no one leads you the wrong way. 5 Many people will come using My name. They will say, 'I am Christ.' They will fool many people and will turn them to the wrong way. 6 You will hear of wars and lots of talk about wars, but do not be afraid. These things must happen, but it is not the end yet. 7 Nations will have wars with other nations. Countries will fight against countries. There will be no food for people. The earth will shake and break apart in different places. 8 These things are the beginning of sorrows and pains.

9 "Then they will hand you over to be hurt. They will kill you. You will be hated by all the world because of My name. 10 Many people will give up and turn away at this time. People will hand over each

other. They will hate each other. 11 Many false religious teachers will come. They will fool many people and will turn them to the wrong way. 12 Because of people breaking the laws and sin being everywhere, the love in the hearts of many people will become cold. 13 But the one who stays true to the end will be saved.

14 "This Good News about the holy nation of God must be preached over all the earth. It must be told to all nations and then the end will come.

Days of Trouble and Pain and Sorrow

15 "You will see a sinful man-made god standing in the house of God in Jerusalem. It was spoken of by the early preacher Daniel. (Daniel 9:27; 12:11) The one who reads this should understand it. 16 Then those in the country of Judea should run to the mountains. 17 The man who is on the top of his house should not come down to take anything out of his house. 18 The man who is in the field should not go back to get his coat. 19 It will be hard for a woman who will soon be a mother. It will be hard for the ones feeding babies in those days! 20 Pray that you will not have to go in the winter or on the Day of Rest. 21 In those days there will be very much trouble and pain and sorrow. It has never been this bad from the beginning of the world and never will be again. 22 If the time had not been made short, no life would have been saved. Because of God's people, the time will be made short.

The False Religious Teachers

23 "If anyone says to you, 'See! Here is the Christ!' or 'There He is!' do not believe it. 24 People who say they are Christ and false preachers will come. They will do special things for people to see. They will do great things, so that if it can be done, God's people will be fooled to believe something wrong. 25 Listen! I have told you before it comes. 26 If they tell you, 'See! He is in the desert,' do not go to see. Or if they say, 'See! He is in the inside room,' do not believe them. 27 The Son of Man will come as fast as lightning shines across the sky from east to west. 28 Birds gather wherever there is a dead body.

Jesus Will Come Again in His Shining-Greatness

29 "As soon as those days of trouble and pain and sorrow are over, the sun will get dark. The moon will not give light. The stars will

fall from the sky. The powers in the heavens will be shaken. 30 Then something special will be seen in the sky telling of the Son of Man. All nations of the earth will have sorrow. They will see the Son of Man coming in the clouds of the sky with power and shining-greatness. 31 He will send His angels with the loud sound of a horn. They will gather God's people together from the four winds. They will come from one end of the heavens to the other.

The Picture-Story of the Fig Tree

32 "Now learn something from the fig tree. When the branch begins to grow and puts out its leaves, you know that summer is near. 33 In the same way, when you see all these things happen, you know the Son of Man is near, even at the door. 34 For sure, I tell you, the people of this day will not pass away before all these things have happened.

No One Knows When Jesus Will Come Again

35 "Heaven and earth will pass away, but My words will not pass away. 36 But no one knows the day or the hour. No! Not even the angels in heaven know. The Son does not know. Only the Father knows.

37 "When the Son of Man comes, it will be the same as when Noah lived. 38 In the days before the flood, people were eating and drinking. They were marrying and being given in marriage. This kept on until the day Noah went into the large boat. 39 They did not know what was happening until the flood came and the water carried them all away. It will be like this when the Son of Man comes.

40 "Two men will be working in a field. One will be taken and the other will be left. 41 Two women will be grinding grain. One will be taken and the other will be left.

42 "Because of this, watch! You do not know on what day your Lord is coming. 43 But understand this: If the owner of a house had known when the robber was coming, he would have watched. He would not have allowed his house to have been broken into. 44 You must be ready also. The Son of Man is coming at a time when you do not think He will come.

Faithful Servants and Servants Who Are Not Faithful

45 "Who is the faithful and wise servant whom his owner has made boss over the other servants? He is to have food ready for

them at the right time. 46 That servant is happy who is doing what his owner wants him to do when he comes back. 47 For sure, I tell you, he will make him boss over all that he has. 48 But if that servant is bad, he will think, 'The owner will not come soon.' 49 He will beat the others. He will eat and drink with those who are drunk. 50 The owner will come on a day and at an hour when the servant is not looking for him. 51 The owner will punish the servant and will give him his place with those who pretend to be someone they are not. There will be loud crying and grinding of teeth.

The Picture-Story of Ten Young Women

25 "At that time the holy nation of heaven will be like ten women who have never had men. They took their lamps and went out to meet the man soon to be married. 2 Five of them were wise and five were foolish. 3 The foolish women took their lamps but did not take oil with them. 4 The wise women took oil in a jar with their lamps. 5 They all went to sleep because the man to be married did not come for a long time.

6 "At twelve o'clock in the night there was a loud call, 'See! The man soon to be married is coming! Go out to meet him!' 7 Then all the women got up and made their lamps brighter. 8 The foolish women said to the wise women, 'Give us some of your oil because our lamps are going out.' 9 But the wise women said, 'No! There will not be enough for us and you. Go to the store and buy oil for yourselves.' 10 While they were gone to buy oil, the man soon to be married came. Those who were ready went in with him to the marriage. The door was shut.

11 "Later the foolish women came. They said, 'Sir, Sir, open the door for us!' 12 But he said to them, 'For sure, I tell you, I do not know you!' 13 So watch! You do not know what day or what hour the Son of Man is coming.

The Picture-Story of the Three Servants and the Money

14 "For the holy nation of heaven is like a man who was going to a country far away. He called together the servants he owned and gave them his money to use. 15 He gave to one servant five pieces of money worth much. He gave to another servant two pieces of money worth much. He gave to another servant one piece of money worth much. He gave to each one as he was able

to use it. Then he went on his trip. 16 The servant who had the five pieces of money went out to the stores and traded until he made five more pieces. 17 The servant who had two pieces of money did the same thing. He made two more pieces. 18 The servant who had received the one piece of money went and hid the money in a hole in the ground. He hid his owner's money.

19 "After a long time the owner of those servants came back. He wanted to know what had been done with his money. 20 The one who had received the five pieces of money worth much came and handed him five pieces more. He said, 'Sir, you gave me five pieces of money. See! I used it and made five more pieces.' 21 His owner said to him, 'You have done well. You have been faithful over a few things. I will put many things in your care. Come and share my joy.' 22 The one who received two pieces of money worth much came also. He said, 'Sir, you gave me two pieces of money. See! I used it and made two more pieces.' 23 His owner said to him, 'You have done well. You are a good and faithful servant. You have been faithful over a few things. I will put many things in your care. Come and share my joy.' 24 The one who had received one piece of money worth much came. He said, 'Sir, I know that you are a hard man. You gather grain where you have not planted. You take up where you have not spread out. 25 I was afraid and I hid your money in the ground. See! Here is your money.' 26 His owner said to him, 'You bad and lazy servant. You knew that I gather grain where I have not planted. You knew that I take up where I have not spread out. 27 You should have taken my money to the bank. When I came back, I could have had my own money and what the bank paid for using it. 28 Take the one piece of money from him. Give it to the one who has ten pieces of money.' 29 For the man who has will have more given to him. He will have more than enough. The man who has nothing, even what he has will be taken away. 30 Throw the bad servant out into the darkness. There will be loud crying and grinding of teeth.

The Sheep and the Goats

31 "When the Son of Man comes in His shining-greatness, He will sit down on His throne of greatness. All the angels will be with Him. 32 All the nations of the earth will be gathered before Him. He will

divide them from each other as a shepherd divides the sheep from the goats. 33 He will put the sheep on His right side, but the goats He will put on His left side.

34 "Then the King will say to those on His right side, 'Come, you who have been called by My Father. Come into the holy nation that has been made ready for you before the world was made. 35 For I was hungry and you gave Me food to eat. I was thirsty and you gave Me water to drink. I was a stranger and you gave Me a room. 36 I had no clothes and you gave Me clothes to wear. I was sick and you cared for Me. I was in prison and you came to see Me.'

37 "Then those that are right with God will say, 'Lord, when did we see You hungry and feed You? When did we see You thirsty and give You a drink? 38 When did we see You a stranger and give You a room? When did we see You had no clothes and we gave You clothes? 39 And when did we see You sick or in prison and we came to You?' 40 Then the King will say, 'For sure, I tell you, because you did it to one of the least of My brothers, you have done it to Me.'

41 "Then the King will say to those on His left side, 'Go away from Me! You are guilty! Go into the fire that lasts forever. It has been made ready for the devil and his angels. 42 For I was hungry but you did not give Me food to eat. I was thirsty but you did not give Me water to drink. 43 I was a stranger but you did not give Me a room. I had no clothes but you did not give Me clothes. I was sick and in prison but you did not come to see Me.'

44 "Then they will ask, 'Lord, when did we see You hungry or thirsty or a stranger? When did we see You without clothes or sick or in prison and did not care for You?' 45 Then He will say to them, 'For sure, I tell you, because you did not do it to one of the least of these, you did not do it to Me.' 46 These will go to the place where they will be punished forever. But those right with God will have life that lasts forever."

Jesus Tells of His Death the Fourth Time
(Mark 14:1–2; Luke 22:1–6)

26 When Jesus had finished all this teaching, He said to His followers, 2 "You know that the special religious supper to remember how the Jews left Egypt is in two days. The Son of Man will be handed over to be nailed to a cross."

3 The religious leaders and the leaders of the people gathered at the house of the head religious leader. His name was Caiaphas. 4 They talked together how they might trap Jesus and kill Him. 5 But they said, "This must not happen on the day of the special supper. The people would be against it. They would make much trouble."

Mary of Bethany Puts Special Perfume on Jesus
(Mark 14:3–9; John 12:1–11)

6 Jesus was in the town of Bethany in the house of Simon. Simon had a very bad skin disease. 7 A woman came with a jar of perfume. She had given much money for this. As Jesus ate, she poured the perfume on His head. 8 When the followers saw it, they were angry. They said, "Why was this wasted? 9 This perfume could have been sold for much money and given to poor people."

10 Jesus knew what they were saying. He said to them, "Why are you giving this woman trouble? She has done a good thing to Me. 11 You will have poor people with you all the time. But you will not have Me with you all the time. 12 She put this perfume on My body to make it ready for the grave. 13 For sure, I tell you, wherever this Good News is preached in all the world, this woman will be remembered for what she has done."

Judas Hands Jesus Over to Be Killed
(Mark 14:10–11)

14 Judas Iscariot was one of the twelve followers. He went to the religious leaders of the Jews. 15 He said, "What will you pay me if I hand Jesus over to you?" They promised to pay him thirty pieces of silver. 16 From that time on Judas looked for a way to hand Jesus over to them.

Getting Ready for the Special Supper
(Mark 14:12–16; Luke 22:7–13)

17 On the first day of the supper of bread without yeast the followers came to Jesus. They said, "What place do You want us to make ready for You to eat the supper of the special religious gathering to remember how the Jews left Egypt?" 18 He said, "Go into the city to a certain man and say to him, 'The Teacher says, "My time is near. I will eat the special supper at your house with My followers." ' " 19 The followers did as Jesus told them. They made things ready for this special supper.

The Last Special Supper
(Mark 14:17–21; Luke 22:14–18;
John 13:21–35)

20 When evening came, Jesus sat with the twelve followers. 21 As they were eating, Jesus said, "For sure, I tell you, one of you will hand Me over." 22 They were very sad. They said to Him one after the other, "Lord, is it I?" 23 He said, "The one who will hand Me over is the one who has just put his hand with Mine in the dish. 24 The Son of Man is going away as it is written of Him. It is bad for that man who hands the Son of Man over! It would have been better if he had not been born!" 25 Judas was the one who was handing Jesus over. He said, "Teacher, am I the one?" Jesus said to him, "You have said it."

The First Lord's Supper
(Mark 14:22–26; Luke 22:19–20)

26 As they were eating, Jesus took a loaf of bread. He gave thanks and broke it in pieces. He gave it to His followers and said, "Take, eat, this is My body." 27 Then He took the cup and gave thanks. He gave it to them and said, "You must all drink from it. 28 This is My blood of the New Way of Worship which is given for many. It is given so the sins of many can be forgiven. 29 I tell you that I will not drink of the fruit of the vine again until that day when I will drink it new with you in the holy nation of My Father." 30 After they sang a song they went out to the Mount of Olives.

Jesus Tells How Peter Will Lie about Him
(Mark 14:27–31; Luke 22:31–34;
John 13:36–38)

31 Jesus said to them, "All of you will be ashamed of Me and leave Me tonight. For it is written, 'I will kill the shepherd and the sheep of the flock will be spread everywhere.' (Zechariah 13:7) 32 After I am raised from the dead, I will go before you to the country of Galilee."

33 Peter said to Jesus, "Even if all men give up and turn away because of You, I will never." 34 Jesus said to him, "For sure, I tell you, before a rooster crows this night, you will say three times you do not know Me." 35 Peter said to Him, "Even if I have to die with You, I will never say I do not know You." And all the followers said the same thing.

Jesus Prays in Gethsemane
(Mark 14:32–42; Luke 22:39–46)

36 Jesus came with them to a place called Gethsemane. He said to them, "You sit here while I go over there to pray." 37 He took Peter and the two sons of Zebedee with Him. He began to have much sorrow and a heavy heart. 38 Then He said to them, "My soul is very sad. My soul is so full of sorrow I am ready to die. You stay here and watch with Me."

39 He went on a little farther and got down with His face on the ground. He prayed, "My Father, if it can be done, take away what is before Me. Even so, not what I want but what You want."

40 Then He came to the followers and found them sleeping. He said to Peter, "Were you not able to watch with Me one hour? 41 Watch and pray so that you will not be tempted. Man's spirit is willing, but the body does not have the power to do it."

42 He went away again the second time. He prayed, saying, "My Father, if this must happen to Me, may whatever You want be done." 43 He came and found them asleep again. Their eyes were heavy. 44 He went away from them the third time and prayed the same prayer.

45 Then He came to His followers and asked them, "Are you still sleeping and getting your rest? As I speak, the time has come when the Son of Man will be handed over to sinners. 46 Get up and let us go. See! The man who will hand Me over is near."

Jesus Handed Over to Sinners
(Mark 14:43–52; Luke 22:47–51;
John 18:1–11)

47 Judas, one of the twelve followers, came while Jesus was talking. He came with many others who had swords and sticks. They came from the religious leaders of the Jews and the leaders of the people. 48 The man who handed Jesus over gave the men something to look for. He said, "The One I kiss is the One you want. Take Him!" 49 At once Judas went up to Jesus and said, "Hello, Teacher," and kissed Him. 50 Jesus said to him, "Friend, do what you came to do." Then they came and put their hands on Jesus and took Him.

51 One of those with Jesus took his sword. He hit the servant who was owned by the religious leader and cut off his ear. 52 Jesus said to him, "Put your sword back where it belongs. Everyone who uses a sword will die with a sword. 53 Do you

not think that I can pray to My Father? At once He would send Me more than 70,000 angels. 54 If I did, how could it happen as the Holy Writings said it would happen? It must be this way."

55 Then Jesus said to the many people, "Have you come with swords and sticks to take Me as if I were a robber? I have been with you every day teaching in the house of God. You never put your hands on Me then. 56 But this has happened as the early preachers said in the Holy Writings it would happen." Then all the followers left Him and ran away.

Jesus Stands in Front of the Religious Leaders
(Mark 14:53–54; Luke 22:52–54; John 18:19–24)

57 Those who had taken Jesus led Him away to Caiaphas. He was the head religious leader. The teachers of the Law and the other leaders were gathered there. 58 But Peter followed Him a long way behind while going to the house of the head religious leader. Then he went in and sat with the helpers to see what would happen.

59 The religious leaders and the other leaders and all the court were looking for false things to say against Jesus. They wanted some reason to kill Him. 60 They found none, but many came and told false things about Him. At last two came to the front. 61 They said, "This Man said, 'I am able to destroy the house of God and build it up again in three days.'"

62 Then the head religious leader stood up. He said to Jesus, "Have You nothing to say? What about the things these men are saying against You?" 63 Jesus said nothing. Then the head religious leader said to Him, "In the name of the living God, I tell You to say the truth. Tell us if You are the Christ, the Son of God." 64 Jesus said to him, "What you said is true. I say to you, from now on you will see the Son of Man seated on the right hand of the All-powerful God. You will see Him coming on the clouds of the sky."

65 Then the head religious leader tore his clothes apart. He said, "He has spoken as if He were God! Do we need other people to speak against Jesus yet? You have heard Him speak as if He were God! 66 What do you think?" They said, "He is guilty of death!"

67 Then they spit on His face. They hit Him with their hands. Others beat Him.

68 They said, "Tell us, Christ, You Who can tell what is going to happen, who hit You?"

Peter Says He Does Not Know Jesus
(Mark 14:66–72; Luke 22:55–62; John 18:15–18, 25–27)

69 Peter sat outside in the yard. A young servant-girl came to him. She said, "You were also with Jesus Who is from the country of Galilee!" 70 But Peter lied in front of all of them, saying, "I do not know what you are talking about." 71 After he had gone out, another young servant-girl saw him. She said to those standing around, "This man was with Jesus of Nazareth." 72 Again he lied and swore, "I do not know this Man!" 73 After a little while some of the people standing around came up to Peter and said, "For sure, you are one of them. You talk like they do." 74 Then he began to say bad words and swear. He said, "I do not know the Man!" At once a rooster crowed.

75 Peter remembered the words Jesus had said to him, "Before a rooster crows, you will say three times you do not know Me." Peter went outside and cried with loud cries.

Jesus Stands in Front of Pilate
(Mark 15:1–5; Luke 23:1–5; John 18:28–37)

27 Early in the morning all the head religious leaders of the Jews and the leaders of the people gathered together and talked about how they could put Jesus to death. 2 They tied Him and took Him away. Then they handed Him over to Pilate who was the leader of the country.

3 Then Judas was sorry he had handed Jesus over when he saw that Jesus was going to be killed. He took back the thirty pieces of silver and gave it to the head religious leaders and the other leaders. 4 He said, "I have sinned because I handed over a Man Who has done no wrong." And they said, "What is that to us? That is your own doing." 5 He threw the money down in the house of God and went outside. Then he went away and killed himself by hanging from a rope.

6 The head religious leaders took the money. They said, "It is against the Law to put this money in the house of God. This money has bought blood." 7 They talked about what to do with the money. Then they decided to buy land to bury strangers in. 8 Because of this, that land is called the

Field of Blood to this day. 9 It happened as the early preacher Jeremiah said it would happen. He said, "And they took the thirty pieces of silver which was the price the Jews said they would pay for Him. 10 And they bought land to bury strangers in, as the Lord told me." (Zechariah 11:12–13)

11 Then Jesus stood in front of the leader of the country. The leader asked Jesus, "Are You the King of the Jews?" Jesus said to him, "What you say is true." 12 When the head religious leaders and the other leaders spoke against Him, He said nothing. 13 Then Pilate said to Him, "Do You not hear all these things they are saying against You?" 14 Jesus did not say a word. The leader was much surprised and wondered about it.

Jesus or Barabbas Is to Go Free
(Mark 15:6–14; Luke 23:17–25; John 18:38–40)

15 At the special supper each year the leader of the country would always let one person who was in prison go free. It would be the one the people wanted. 16 They had a man who was known by all the people whose name was Barabbas. 17 When they were gathered together, Pilate said to them, "Whom do you want me to let go free? Should it be Barabbas or Jesus Who is called Christ?" 18 For the leader of the country knew the religious leaders had given Jesus over to him because they were jealous.

19 While Pilate was sitting in the place where he judges, his wife sent him this word, "Have nothing to do with that good Man. I have been troubled today in a dream about Him."

20 The head religious leaders and the other leaders talked the many people into asking for Barabbas to go free and for Jesus to be put to death. 21 The leader of the country said to them, "Which one of the two do you want me to let go free?" They said, "Barabbas." 22 Pilate said to them, "Then what am I to do with Jesus Who is called Christ?" They all said to him, "Nail Him to a cross!" 23 Then Pilate said, "Why, what bad thing has He done?" But they cried out all the more, "Nail Him to a cross!"

24 Pilate saw that he could do nothing. The people were making loud calls and there was much pushing around. He took water and washed his hands in front of the many people. He said, "I am not guilty of the blood of this good Man. This is your own doing." 25 Then all the people said, "Let His blood be on us and on our children!" 26 Pilate let Barabbas go free but he had men whip Jesus. Then he handed Him over to be nailed to a cross.

The Crown of Thorns
(Mark 15:15–21; John 19:1–5)

27 Then the soldiers of Pilate took Jesus into a large room. A big group of soldiers gathered around Him. 28 They took off His clothes and put a purple coat on Him. 29 They put a crown of thorns on His head. They put a stick in His right hand. They got on their knees before Him and made fun of Him. They said, "Hello, King of the Jews!" 30 They spit on Him. They took a stick and hit Him on the head. 31 After they had made fun of Him, they took the coat off and put His own clothes on Him. Then they led Him away to be nailed to a cross. 32 As they were on the way, they came to a man called Simon from the country of Cyrene. They made him carry the cross for Jesus.

Jesus on the Cross
(Mark 15:22–26; Luke 23:26–38; John 19:17–22)

33 They came to a place called Golgotha. This name means the place of a skull. 34 They gave Him wine with something in it to take away the pain. After tasting it, He took no more. 35 When they had nailed Him to the cross, they divided His clothes by drawing names. *It happened as the early preacher said it would happen. He said, "They divided My clothes among them by drawing names to see who would get My coat." (Psalm 22:18) 36 Then they sat down and watched Him. 37 Over His head they put in writing what they had against Him, THIS IS JESUS THE KING OF THE JEWS.

The Two Robbers
(Mark 15:27–32; Luke 23:39–43)

38 They nailed two robbers to crosses beside Him. One was on His right side. The other was on His left side. 39 Those who walked by shook their heads and laughed at Him. 40 They said, "You are the One Who could destroy the house of God and build it up again in three days. Now save Yourself. If You are the Son of God, come down from the cross."

41 The head religious leaders and the teachers of the Law and the other leaders made fun of Him also. They said, 42 "He

saved others but He cannot save Himself. If He is the King of the Jews, let Him come down from the cross. Then we will believe in Him. 43 He trusts God. Let God save Him now, if God cares for Him. He has said, 'I am the Son of God.' " 44 And the robbers who were nailed to crosses beside Him made fun of Him the same way also.

Jesus Dies on the Cross
(Mark 15:33–36; Luke 23:44–49; John 19:28–37)

45 From noon until three o'clock it was dark over all the land. 46 About three o'clock Jesus cried with a loud voice, "My God, My God, why have You left Me alone?" 47 When some of those who stood by heard that, they said, "This Man is calling for Elijah." 48 At once one of them ran and took a sponge and filled it with sour wine. He put it on a stick and gave it to Him to drink. 49 The others said, "Let Him alone. Let us see if Elijah will come and save Him." 50 Then Jesus gave another loud cry and gave up His spirit and died.

The Powerful Works at the Time of His Death
(Mark 15:37–39)

51 At once the curtain in the house of God was torn in two from top to bottom. The earth shook and the rocks fell apart. 52 Graves were opened. Bodies of many of God's people who were dead were raised. 53 After Jesus was raised from the grave, these arose from their graves and went into Jerusalem, the Holy City. These'were seen by many people.

54 The captain of the soldiers and those with him who were watching Jesus, saw all the things that were happening. They saw the earth shake and they were very much afraid. They said, "For sure, this Man was the Son of God."

The Women at the Cross
(Mark 15:40–41; John 19:25–27)

55 Many women were looking on from far away. These had followed Jesus from the country of Galilee. They had cared for Him. 56 Among them was Mary Magdalene and Mary the mother of James and Joseph and the mother of Zebedee's sons.

Jesus Is Buried
(Mark 15:42–47; Luke 23:50–56; John 19:38–42)

57 When it was evening, a rich man came from the city of Arimathea. His name was Joseph. He was a follower of Jesus also. 58 He went to Pilate and asked for the body of Jesus. Then Pilate said that the body should be given to him. 59 Joseph took the body and put clean linen cloth around it. 60 He laid it in his own new grave. This grave had been cut out in the side of a rock. He pushed a big stone over the door of the grave and went away. 61 Mary Magdalene and the other Mary stayed there. They were sitting near the grave.

62 The next day, the day after Jesus was killed, the head religious leaders and the proud religious law-keepers gathered together in front of Pilate. 63 They said, "Sir, we remember what that Man Who fooled people said when He was living, 'After three days I am to rise from the dead.' 64 Speak the word to have the grave watched for three days. Then His followers cannot come at night and take Him away and say to the people, 'He has been raised from the dead.' The last mistake would be worse than the first." 65 Pilate said to them, "Take the soldiers. Go and watch the grave." 66 Then they went and made the soldiers stand by the grave. They put a lock on the big stone door.

Jesus Is Raised from the Dead
(Mark 16:1–8; Luke 24:1–12; John 20:1–18)

28 The Day of Rest was over. The sun was coming up on the first day of the week. Mary Magdalene and the other Mary came to see the grave. 2 At once the earth shook and an angel of the Lord came down from heaven. He came and pushed back the stone from the door and sat on it. 3 His face was bright like lightning. His clothes were white as snow. 4 The soldiers were shaking with fear and became as dead men.

5 The angel said to the women, "Do not be afraid. I know you are looking for Jesus Who was nailed to the cross. 6 He is not here! He has risen from the dead as He said He would. Come and see the place where the Lord lay. 7 Run fast and tell His followers that He is risen from the dead. He is going before you to the country of Galilee. You will see Him there as I have told you." 8 They went away from the grave in a hurry. They were afraid and yet had much joy. They ran to tell the news to His followers.

9 As they went to tell the followers, Jesus met them and said hello to them. They came and held His feet and worshiped

Him. 10 Then Jesus said to them, "Do not be afraid. Go and tell My followers to go to Galilee. They will see Me there."

11 While they were on their way, some of the soldiers who were to watch the grave came into the city. They told the head religious leaders everything that had happened. 12 The soldiers gathered together with the other leaders and talked about what to do. The leaders gave much money to the soldiers. 13 They said, "Tell the people, 'His followers came at night and took His body while we were sleeping.' 14 We will see that you do not get into trouble over this if Pilate hears about it." 15 They took the money and did as they were told. This story was told among the Jews and is still told today.

Jesus Sends His Followers to Teach
(Mark 16:15–18; Luke 24:44–49; John 20:21–23)

16 Then the eleven followers went to Galilee. They went to the mountain where Jesus had told them to go.

17 When they saw Jesus, they worshiped Him. But some did not believe.

18 Jesus came and said to them, "All power has been given to Me in heaven and on earth. 19 Go and make followers of all the nations. Baptize them in the name of the Father and of the Son and of the Holy Spirit. 20 Teach them to do all the things I have told you. And I am with you always, even to the end of the world."

MARK

John the Baptist Makes the Way Ready for the Coming of Jesus
(Matthew 3:1–12; Luke 3:1–18; John 1:15–28)

1 The Good News of Jesus Christ, the Son of God, 2 begins with the words of the early preachers: "Listen! I will send My helper to carry the news ahead of you. He will make the way ready. 3 His voice calls out in the desert, 'Make the way ready for the Lord. Make the road straight for Him!' " (Isaiah 40:3)

4 John the Baptist preached in the desert. He preached that people should be baptized because they were sorry for their sins and had turned from them. And they would be forgiven. 5 People from over all the country of Judea and from Jerusalem came to him. They told of their sins and were baptized by John in the Jordan River.

6 John wore clothes made of hair from camels. He had a leather belt around him. His food was locusts and wild honey. 7 He preached, saying, "One is coming after me Who is greater than I. I am not good enough to get down and help Him take off His shoes. 8 I have baptized you with water. But He will baptize you with the Holy Spirit."

The Baptism of Jesus
(Matthew 3:13–17; Luke 3:21–22; John 1:29–34)

9 Jesus came to the Jordan River from the town of Nazareth in the country of Galilee.

He was baptized by John. 10 As soon as Jesus came up out of the water, He saw heaven open up. The Holy Spirit came down on Him like a dove. 11 A voice came from heaven and said, "You are My much-loved Son. I am very happy with You."

Jesus Is Tempted
(Matthew 4:1–11; Luke 4:1–13)

12 At once the Holy Spirit sent Jesus to a desert. 13 He was tempted by Satan for forty days there. He was with wild animals but angels took care of Him.

Jesus Preaches in Galilee
(Matthew 4:12–17; Luke 4:14–15)

14 After John the Baptist was put in prison, Jesus came to the country of Galilee. He preached the Good News of God. 15 He said, "The time has come. The holy nation of God is near. Be sorry for your sins, turn from them, and believe the Good News."

Jesus Calls Simon and Andrew
(Matthew 4:18–22; Luke 5:1–11)

16 Jesus was walking by the Sea of Galilee. He saw Simon and his brother Andrew putting a net into the sea. They were fishermen. 17 Jesus said to them, "Follow Me. I will make you fish for men!" 18 At once they left their nets and followed Him.

Jesus Calls James and John

19 Jesus went on a little farther. He saw James and his brother John who were sons of Zebedee. They were in a boat

mending their nets. 20 Jesus called them and they left their father Zebedee. He was in the boat with men who were working for him.

Jesus Heals a Man with a Demon
(Luke 4:31–37)

21 Jesus and His followers went to the city of Capernaum on the Day of Rest. They went to the Jewish place of worship where Jesus taught the people. 22 The people were surprised and wondered about His teaching. He taught them as One Who had the right and the power to teach and not as the teachers of the Law.

23 There was a man in the Jewish place of worship who had a demon. The demon cried out, 24 "What do You want of us, Jesus of Nazareth? Have You come to destroy us? I know Who You are. You are the Holy One of God." 25 Jesus spoke sharp words to the demon and said, "Do not talk! Come out of the man!" 26 The demon threw the man down and gave a loud cry. Then he came out of him. 27 The people were all surprised and wondered. They asked each other, "What is this? Is this a new teaching? He speaks with power even to the demons and they obey Him!" 28 At once the news about Jesus went through all the country around Galilee.

Peter's Mother-in-Law Healed
(Matthew 8:14–15; Luke 4:38–39)

29 Jesus and His followers came out of the Jewish place of worship. Then they went to the house of Simon and Andrew. James and John went with them. 30 They told Jesus about Simon's mother-in-law who was in bed, very sick. 31 He went and took her by the hand and raised her up. At once her sickness was gone. She got up and cared for them.

Jesus Heals in Galilee
(Matthew 8:16–17; Luke 4:40–41)

32 In the evening as the sun went down, the people took all who were sick to Jesus. They took those who had demons to Him. 33 All the town gathered at the door. 34 Jesus healed those who were sick of many kinds of diseases. He put out many demons. Jesus would not allow the demons to speak because they knew Who He was.

Jesus Keeps On Preaching in Galilee
(Matthew 4:23–25; Luke 4:42–44)

35 In the morning before the sun was up, Jesus went to a place where He could be alone. He prayed there. 36 Simon and the others looked for Jesus. 37 They found Him and said, "All the people are looking for You." 38 Jesus said to the followers, "Let us go to the towns near here so I can preach there also. That is why I came." 39 He went through Galilee. He preached in their places of worship and put out demons.

Jesus Heals a Man with a Bad Skin Disease
(Matthew 8:1–4; Luke 5:12–16)

40 A man came to Jesus with a bad skin disease. This man got down on his knees and begged Jesus, saying, "If You want to, You can heal me." 41 Jesus put His hand on him with loving-pity. He said, "I want to. Be healed." 42 At once the disease was gone and the man was healed. 43 Jesus spoke strong words to the man before He sent him away. 44 He said to him, "Tell no one about this. Go and let the religious leader of the Jews see you. Give the gifts Moses has told you to give when a man is healed of a disease. Let the leaders know you have been healed." 45 But the man went out and talked about it everywhere. After this Jesus could not go to any town if people knew He was there. He had to stay in the desert. People came to Him from everywhere.

Jesus Heals a Man Who Was Let Down through the Roof of a House
(Matthew 9:1–8; Luke 5:17–26)

2 After some days Jesus went back to the city of Capernaum. Then news got around that He was home. 2 Soon many people gathered there. There was no more room, not even at the door. He spoke the Word of God to them. 3 Four men came to Jesus carrying a man who could not move his body. 4 These men could not get near Jesus because of so many people. They made a hole in the roof of the house over where Jesus stood. Then they let down the bed with the sick man on it.

5 When Jesus saw their faith, He said to the sick man, "Son, your sins are forgiven." 6 Some teachers of the Law were sitting there. They thought to themselves, 7 "Why does this Man talk like this? He is speaking as if He is God! Who can forgive sins? Only One can forgive sins and that is God!"

8 At once Jesus knew the teachers of the Law were thinking this. He said to them, "Why do you think this in your hearts? 9 Which is easier to say to the sick man, 'Your sins are forgiven,' or to say, 'Get up,

take your bed, and start to walk?' 10 I am doing this so you may know the Son of Man has power on earth to forgive sins." He said to the sick man who could not move his body, 11 "I say to you, 'Get up. Take your bed and go to your home.' " 12 At once the sick man got up and took his bed and went away. Everybody saw him. They were all surprised and wondered about it. They thanked God, saying, "We have never seen anything like this!"

Jesus Calls Matthew
(Matthew 9:9–13; Luke 5:27–32)

13 Jesus walked along the sea-shore again. Many people came together and He taught them. 14 He walked farther and saw Levi (Matthew) the son of Alphaeus. Levi was sitting at his work gathering taxes. Jesus said to him, "Follow Me." Levi got up and followed Him.

Jesus Eats with Tax-Gatherers and Sinners

15 Jesus ate in Levi's house. Many men who gather taxes and others who were sinners came and sat down with Jesus and His followers. There were many following Him. 16 The teachers of the Law and the proud religious law-keepers saw Jesus eat with men who gather taxes and others who were sinners. They said to His followers, "Why does He eat and drink with men who gather taxes and with sinners?" 17 Jesus heard it and said to them, "People who are well do not need a doctor. Only those who are sick need a doctor. I have not come to call those who are right with God. I have come to call those who are sinners."

Jesus Teaches about Going without Food So You Can Pray Better
(Matthew 9:14–17; Luke 5:33–35)

18 The followers of John and the proud religious law-keepers were not eating food so they could pray better. Some people came to Jesus and said, "Why do the followers of John and the proud religious law-keepers go without food so they can pray better, but Your followers do not?" 19 Jesus said to them, "Can the friends at a wedding go without food when the man just married is with them? As long as they have him with them, they will not go without food. 20 The days will come when the man just married will be taken from them. Then they will not eat food so they can pray better. 21 No man sews a piece of new

cloth on an old coat. If it comes off, it will make the hole bigger. 22 No man puts new wine into old skin bags. The skin would break and the wine would run out. The bags would be no good. New wine must be put into new skin bags."

Jesus Teaches about the Day of Rest
(Matthew 12:1–8; Luke 6:1–5)

23 At that time Jesus walked through the grain-fields on the Day of Rest. As they went, His followers began to take some of the grain. 24 The proud religious law-keepers said to Jesus, "See! Why are they doing what the Law says should not be done on the Day of Rest?" 25 He said to them, "Have you not read what David did when he and his men were hungry? 26 He went into the house of God when Abiathar was head religious leader of the Jews. He ate the special bread used in the religious worship. The Law says only the Jewish religious leaders may eat that. David gave some to those who were with him also." 27 Jesus said to them, "The Day of Rest was made for the good of man. Man was not made for the Day of Rest. 28 The Son of Man is Lord of the Day of Rest also."

Jesus Heals on the Day of Rest
(Matthew 12:9–14; Luke 6:6–11)

3 Jesus went into the Jewish place of worship again. A man was there with a dried-up hand. 2 The proud religious law-keepers watched Jesus to see if He would heal the man on the Day of Rest. They wanted to have something to say against Jesus. 3 Jesus said to the man with the dried-up hand, "Stand up." 4 Then Jesus said to the proud religious law-keepers, "Does the Law say to do good on the Day of Rest or to do bad, to save life or to kill?" But they said nothing. 5 Jesus looked around at them with anger. He was sad because of their hard hearts. Then He said to the man, "Put out your hand." He put it out and his hand was healed. It was as good as the other. 6 The proud religious law-keepers went out and made plans with the followers of King Herod how they might kill Jesus.

Jesus Heals by the Sea-Shore
(Matthew 12:15–21; Luke 6:17–19)

7 Jesus went with His followers to the sea. Many people followed Him from the countries of Galilee and Judea. 8 They followed from Jerusalem and from the country of Idumea. They came from the

other side of the Jordan River and from the cities of Tyre and Sidon. Many people heard all that Jesus was doing and came to Him. 9 He told His followers to have a small boat ready for Him because so many people might push Him down. 10 He had healed so many that the sick people were pushing in on Him. They were trying to put their hands on Him. 11 When demons saw Him, they got down at His feet and cried out, "You are the Son of God!" 12 He spoke strong words that the demons should tell no one Who He was.

Jesus Calls His Twelve Followers
(Matthew 10:1–4; Luke 6:12–16)

13 He went up on a mountain and called those He wanted. They followed Him. 14 He picked out twelve followers to be with Him so He might send them out to preach. 15 They would have the right and the power to heal diseases and to put out demons. 16 Jesus gave Simon another name, Peter. 17 James and John were brothers. They were the sons of Zebedee. He named them Boanerges, which means, The Sons of Thunder. 18 The others were Andrew, Philip, Bartholomew, Matthew, Thomas, James the son of Alphaeus, Thaddaeus, Simon the Canaanite, 19 and Judas Iscariot. Judas was the one who handed Jesus over to be killed.

The Family of Jesus Holds Him Back

20 When Jesus came into a house, many people gathered around Him again. Jesus and His followers could not even eat. 21 When His family heard of it, they went to take Him. They said, "He must be crazy."

A Nation That Cannot Stand
(Matthew 12:22–37; Luke 11:14–23)

22 Teachers of the Law came down from Jerusalem. They said, "Jesus has Satan in Him. This Man puts out demons by the king of demons." 23 Jesus called them to Him and spoke to them in picture-stories. He said, "How can the devil put out the devil? 24 A nation cannot last if it is divided against itself. 25 A family cannot last if it is divided against itself. 26 If the devil fights against himself and is divided, he cannot last. He will come to an end. 27 No man can go into a strong man's house and take away his things, unless he ties up the strong man first. Only then can he take things from his house. 28 For sure, I tell you, all sins will be forgiven people, and bad things they speak against God. 29 But if anyone speaks bad things against the Holy Spirit, he will never be forgiven. He is guilty of a sin that lasts forever." 30 Jesus told them this because they said, "He has a demon."

The New Kind of Family
(Matthew 12:46–50; Luke 8:19–21)

31 Then His mother and brothers came and stood outside. They sent for Jesus. 32 Many people were sitting around Him. They said, "See! Your mother and brothers are outside looking for You." 33 He said to them, "Who is My mother or My brothers?" 34 He turned to those sitting around Him and said, "See! My mother and My brothers! 35 Whoever does what My Father wants is My brother and My sister and My mother."

The Picture-Story of the Man Who Planted Seed
(Matthew 13:1–52; Luke 8:4–18)

4 Jesus began to teach by the sea-shore again. Many people gathered around Him. There were so many He had to get into a boat and sit down. The people were on the shore. 2 He taught them many things by using picture-stories. As He taught, He said, 3 "Listen! A man went out to plant seed. 4 As he planted the seed, some fell by the side of the road. Birds came and ate them. 5 Some seed fell among rocks. It came up at once because there was so little ground. 6 But it dried up when the sun was high in the sky because it had no root. 7 Some seed fell among thorns. The thorns grew and did not give the seed room to grow. This seed gave no grain. 8 Some seed fell on good ground. It came up and grew and gave much grain. Some gave thirty times as much grain. Some gave sixty times as much grain. Some gave one hundred times as much grain." 9 He said to them, "You have ears, then listen!" 10 Those who were with Jesus and the twelve followers came to Him when He was alone. They asked about the picture-story. 11 He said to them, "You were given the secrets about the holy nation of God. Everything is told in picture-stories to those who are outside the holy nation of God. 12 They see, but do not know what it means. They hear, but do not understand. If they did, they might turn to God and have their sins forgiven." (Isaiah 6:9–10)

Jesus Tells about the Man Who Planted the Seed

13 Jesus said to them, "Do you not understand this picture-story? Then how will you understand any of the picture-stories? 14 What the man plants is the Word of God. 15 Those by the side of the road are the ones who hear the Word. As soon as they hear it, the devil comes and takes away the Word that is planted in their hearts. 16 The seed that fell among rocks is like people who receive the Word with joy when they hear it. 17 Their roots are not deep so they live only a short time. When sorrow and trouble come because of the Word, they give up and fall away. 18 The seed that was planted among thorns is like some people who listen to the Word. 19 But the cares of this life let thorns come up. A love for riches and always wanting other things let thorns grow. These things do not give the Word room to grow so it does not give grain. 20 The seed that fell on good ground is like people who hear the Word and understand it. They give much grain. Some give thirty times as much grain. Some give sixty times as much grain. Some give one hundred times as much grain."

The Picture-Story of the Lamp

21 He said to them, "Is a lamp to be put under a pail or under a bed? Should it not be put on a lamp-stand? 22 Everything that is hidden will be brought into the light. Everything that is a secret will be made known. 23 You have ears, then listen!"

24 Jesus said to them, "Be careful what you listen to. The same amount you give will be given to you, and even more. 25 He who has, to him will be given. To him who does not have, even the little he has will be taken from him."

The Picture-Story of the Grain

26 He said, "The holy nation of God is like a man who plants seed in the ground. 27 He goes to sleep every night and gets up every day. The seed grows, but he does not know how. 28 The earth gives fruit by itself. The leaf comes first and then the young grain can be seen. And last, the grain is ready to gather. 29 As soon as the grain is ready, he cuts it. The time of gathering the grain has come."

The Picture-Story of the Mustard Seed

30 Jesus said, "In what way can we show what the holy nation of God is like? Or what picture-story can we use to help you understand? 31 It is like a grain of mustard seed that is planted in the ground. It is the smallest of all seeds. 32 After it is put in the ground, it grows and becomes the largest of the spices. It puts out long branches so birds of the sky can live in it." 33 As they were able to understand, He spoke the Word to them by using many picture-stories. 34 Jesus helped His followers understand everything when He was alone with them.

The Wind and Waves Obey Jesus
(Matthew 8:23–27; Luke 8:22–25)

35 It was evening of that same day. Jesus said to them, "Let us go over to the other side." 36 After sending the people away, they took Jesus with them in a boat. It was the same boat He used when He taught them. Other little boats went along with them. 37 A bad wind storm came up. The waves were coming over the side of the boat. It was filling up with water. 38 Jesus was in the back part of the boat sleeping on a pillow. They woke Him up, crying out, "Teacher, do You not care that we are about to die?" 39 He got up and spoke sharp words to the wind. He said to the sea, "Be quiet! Be still." At once the wind stopped blowing. There were no more waves. 40 He said to His followers, "Why are you so full of fear? Do you not have faith?" 41 They were very much afraid and said to each other, "Who is this? Even the wind and waves obey Him!"

Demons Ask Jesus to Let Them Live in Pigs
(Matthew 8:28–34; Luke 8:26–39)

5 Jesus and His followers came to the other side of the sea to the country of the Gerasenes. 2 He got out of the boat. At once a man came to Him from among the graves. This man had a demon. 3 He lived among the graves. No man could tie him, even with chains. 4 Many times he had been tied with chains on his feet. He had broken the chains as well as the irons from his hands and legs. No man was strong enough to keep him tied. 5 Night and day he was among the graves and in the mountains. He would cry out and cut himself with stones.

6 When the man with the demon saw Jesus a long way off, he ran and worshiped Him. 7 The man spoke with a loud voice and said, "What do You want with me, Jesus, Son of the Most High God? I ask You, in the name of God, do not hurt

me!" **8** At the same time, Jesus was saying, "Come out of the man, you demon!" **9** Jesus asked the demon, "What is your name?" He said, "My name is Many, for there are many of us." **10** The demons asked Jesus not to send them out of the country. **11** There were many pigs feeding on the mountain-side. **12** The demons asked Him saying, "Send us to the pigs that we may go into them." **13** Then Jesus let them do what they wanted to do. So they went into the pigs. The pigs ran fast down the side of the mountain and into the sea and died. There were about 2,000. **14** The men who cared for the pigs ran fast to the town and out to the country telling what had been done. People came to see what had happened. **15** They came to Jesus and saw the man who had had the demons. He was sitting with clothes on and in his right mind. The men were afraid. **16** Those who had seen it told what had happened to the man who had had the demons. They told what had happened to the pigs. **17** Then they asked Jesus to leave their country.

18 Jesus got into the boat. The man who had had the demons asked to go with Him. **19** Jesus would not let him go but said to him, "Go home to your own people. Tell them what great things the Lord has done for you. Tell them how He had pity on you." **20** The man went his way and told everyone in the land of Decapolis what great things Jesus had done for him. All the people were surprised and wondered.

Two Are Healed through Faith
(Matthew 9:18–26; Luke 8:40–56)

21 Then Jesus went by boat over to the other side of the sea. Many people gathered around Him. He stayed by the seashore. **22** Jairus was one of the leaders of the Jewish place of worship. As Jairus came to Jesus, he got down at His feet. **23** He cried out to Jesus and said, "My little daughter is almost dead. Come and put Your hand on her that she may be healed and live." **24** Jesus went with him. Many people followed and pushed around Jesus.

25 A woman had been sick for twelve years with a flow of blood. **26** She had suffered much because of having many doctors. She had spent all the money she had. She had received no help, but became worse. **27** She heard about Jesus and went among the people who were following Him. She touched His coat. **28** For she said to herself, "If I can only touch His coat, I will be healed." **29** At once the flow of blood stopped. She felt in her body that she was healed of her sickness.

30 At the same time Jesus knew that power had gone from Him. He turned and said to the people following Him, "Who touched My coat?" **31** His followers said to Him, "You see the many people pushing on every side. Why do You ask, 'Who touched My coat?' " **32** He looked around to see who had done it. **33** The woman was filled with fear when she knew what had happened to her. She came and got down before Jesus and told Him the truth. **34** He said to her, "Daughter, your faith has healed you. Go in peace and be free from your sickness."

35 While Jesus spoke, men came from the house of the leader of the place of worship. They said, "Your daughter is dead. Why trouble the Teacher anymore?" **36** Jesus heard this. He said to the leader of the Jewish place of worship, "Do not be afraid, just believe." **37** He allowed no one to go with Him but Peter and James and John, the brother of James. **38** They came to the house where the leader of the place of worship lived. Jesus found many people making much noise and crying. **39** He went in and asked them, "Why is there so much noise and crying? The girl is not dead. She is sleeping."

40 They laughed at Jesus. But He sent them all out of the room. Then He took the girl's father and mother and those who were with Him. They went into the room where the girl was. **41** He took the girl by the hand and said, "Little girl, I say to you, get up!" **42** At once the girl got up and walked. She was twelve years old. They were very much surprised and wondered about it. **43** He spoke sharp words to them that they should not tell anyone. He told them to give her something to eat.

Jesus Visits His Own Town, Nazareth
(Matthew 13:53–58)

6 Jesus went from the house of Jairus and came to His home town. His followers came after Him. **2** On the Day of Rest He began to teach in the Jewish place of worship. Many people heard Him. They were surprised and wondered, saying, "Where did this Man get all this? What wisdom is this that has been given to Him? How can He do these powerful works with His hands? **3** Is He not a Man Who makes things from wood? Is He not the Son of Mary and the brother of James and Joses and Judas and Simon? Do not His sisters live here with us?" The people were ashamed of Him and turned away from Him. **4** Jesus said to them, "One who speaks for God is respected everywhere but in his own country and among his own family and in his own house."

5 So Jesus could do no powerful works there. But He did put His hands on a few sick people and healed them. **6** He wondered because they had no faith. But He went around to the towns and taught as He went.

Jesus Calls Twelve Followers and Sends Them Out
(Matthew 10:1–42; Luke 9:1–6)

7 Jesus called the twelve followers to Him and began to send them out two by two. He gave them power over demons. **8** He told them to take nothing along with them but a walking stick. They were not to take a bag or food or money in their belts. **9** They were to wear shoes. They were not to take two coats.

10 He said to them, "Whatever house you go into, stay there until you leave that town. **11** Whoever does not take you in or listen to you, when you leave there, shake the dust off your feet. By doing that, you will speak against them. For sure, I tell you, it will be easier for the cities of Sodom and Gomorrah on the day men stand before God and are judged than for that city."

12 Then they left. They preached that men should be sorry for their sins and turn from them. **13** They put out many demons. They poured oil on many people that were sick and healed them.

John the Baptist Is Put in Prison
(Matthew 14:1–5; Luke 3:18–20)

14 King Herod heard about Jesus because everyone was talking about Him. Some people said, "John the Baptist has been raised from the dead. That is why he is doing such powerful works." **15** Other people said, "He is Elijah." Others said, "He is one who speaks for God like one of the early preachers." **16** When Herod heard this, he said, "It is John the Baptist, whose head I cut off. He has been raised from the dead." **17** For Herod had sent men to take John and put him into prison. He did this because of his wife, Herodias. She had been the wife of his brother Philip. **18** John the Baptist had said to Herod, "It is wrong for you to have your brother's wife." **19** Herodias became angry

with him. She wanted to have John the Baptist killed but she could not. **20** Herod was afraid of John. He knew he was a good man and right with God, and he kept John from being hurt or killed. He liked to listen to John preach. But when he did, he became troubled.

John the Baptist Is Killed
(Matthew 14:6–12; Luke 9:7–9)

21 Then Herodias found a way to have John killed. Herod gave a big supper on his birthday. He asked the leaders of the country and army captains and the leaders of Galilee to come. **22** The daughter of Herodias came in and danced before them. This made Herod and his friends happy. The king said to the girl, "Ask me for whatever you want and I will give it to you." **23** Then he made a promise to her, "Whatever you ask for, I will give it to you. I will give you even half of my nation." **24** She went to her mother and asked, "What should I ask for?" The mother answered, "I want the head of John the Baptist." **25** At once the girl went to Herod. She said, "I want you to give me the head of John the Baptist on a plate now."

26 Herod was very sorry. He had to do it because of his promise and because of those who ate with him. **27** At once he sent one of his soldiers and told him to bring the head of John the Baptist. The soldier went to the prison and cut off John's head. **28** He took John's head in on a plate and gave it to the girl. The girl gave it to her mother. **29** John's followers heard this. They went and took his body and buried it.

The Feeding of the Five Thousand
(Matthew 14:13–21; Luke 9:10–17; John 6:1–14)

30 The followers of Jesus came back to Him. They told Jesus all they had done and taught. **31** He said to them, "Come away from the people. Be by yourselves and rest." There were many people coming and going. They had no time even to eat. **32** They went by themselves in a boat to a desert. **33** Many people saw them leave and knew who they were. People ran fast from all the cities and got there first. **34** When Jesus got out of the boat, He saw many people gathered together. He had loving-pity for them. They were like sheep without a shepherd. He began to teach them many things.

35 The day was almost gone. The followers of Jesus came to Him. They said,

"This is a desert. It is getting late. 36 Tell the people to go to the towns and villages and buy food for themselves." 37 He said to them, "Give them something to eat." They said to Him, "Are we to go and buy many loaves of bread and give it to them?" 38 He said to them, "How many loaves of bread do you have here? Go and see." When they knew, they said, "Five loaves of bread and two fish." 39 Then He told them to have all the people sit down together in groups on the green grass. 40 They sat down in groups of fifty people and in groups of one hundred people. 41 Jesus took the five loaves of bread and two fish. He looked up to heaven and gave thanks. He broke the loaves in pieces and gave them to the followers to set before the people. He divided the two fish among them all. 42 They all ate and were filled. 43 After that the followers picked up twelve baskets full of pieces of bread and fish. 44 About five thousand men ate the bread.

Jesus Walks on the Water
(Matthew 14:22–33; John 6:15–21)

45 At once Jesus had His followers get into the boat and go ahead of Him to the other side to the town of Bethsaida. He sent the people away. 46 When they were all gone, He went up to the mountain to pray. 47 It was evening. The boat was halfway across the sea. Jesus was alone on the land. 48 He saw His followers were in trouble. The wind was against them. They were working very hard rowing the boat. About three o'clock in the morning Jesus came to them walking on the sea. He would have gone past them. 49 When the followers saw Him walking on the water, they thought it was a spirit and cried out with fear. 50 For they all saw Him and were afraid. At once Jesus talked to them. He said, "Take hope. It is I, do not be afraid." 51 He came over to them and got into the boat. The wind stopped. They were very much surprised and wondered about it. 52 They had not learned what they should have learned from the loaves because their hearts were hard.

People Are Healed at Gennesaret
(Matthew 14:34–36)

53 Then they crossed the sea and came to the land of Gennesaret and went to shore. 54 When Jesus got out of the boat, the people knew Him at once. 55 They ran through all the country bringing people who were sick on their beds to Jesus. 56 Wherever He went, they would lay the sick people in the streets in the center of town where people gather. They begged Him that they might touch the bottom of His coat. Everyone who did was healed. This happened in the towns and in the cities and in the country where He went.

Jesus Speaks Sharp Words to the Leaders
(Matthew 15:1–20)

7 The proud religious law-keepers and some of the teachers of the Law had come from Jerusalem. They gathered around Jesus. 2 They had seen some of His followers eat bread without washing their hands. 3 The proud religious law-keepers and all the Jews never eat until they wash their hands. They keep the teaching that was given to them by their early fathers. 4 When they come from the stores, they never eat until they wash. There are many other teachings they keep. Some are the washing of cups and pots and pans in a special way.

5 Then the proud religious law-keepers and the teachers of the Law asked Jesus, "Why do Your followers not obey the teaching given to them by their early fathers? They eat bread without washing their hands." 6 He said to them, "Isaiah told about you who pretend to be someone you are not. Isaiah wrote, 'These people honor Me with their lips, but their hearts are far from Me. 7 Their worship of Me is worth nothing. They teach what men say must be done.' (Isaiah 29:13) 8 You put away the Laws of God and obey the laws made by men."

9 Jesus said to them, "You put away the Laws of God but keep your own teaching. 10 Moses said, 'Respect your father and mother.' (Exodus 20:12) 'He who curses his father and mother will be put to death!' (Exodus 21:17) 11 But you say that it is right if a man does not help his father and mother because he says he has given to God what he could have given to them. 12 You are not making him do anything for his father and mother. 13 You are putting away the Word of God to keep your own teaching. You are doing many other things like this."

14 Jesus called the people to Him again. He said, "Listen to Me, all of you, and understand this. 15 It is not what goes into a man's mouth from the outside that makes his mind and heart sinful. It is what comes out from the inside that makes him sinful. 16 You have ears, then listen!"

17 He went into the house away from all the people. His followers began to ask about the picture-story. 18 He said to them, "Do you not understand yet? Do you not understand that whatever goes into a man cannot make him sinful? 19 It does not go into his heart, but into his stomach and then on out of his body." In this way, He was saying that all food is clean. 20 He said, "Whatever comes out of a man is what makes the man sinful. 21 From the inside, out of the heart of men come bad thoughts, sex sins of a married person, sex sins of a person not married, killing other people, 22 stealing, wanting something that belongs to someone else, doing wrong, lying, having a desire for sex sins, having a mind that is always looking for sin, speaking against God, thinking you are better than you are and doing foolish things. 23 All these bad things come from the inside and make the man sinful."

Jesus Puts a Demon out of a Girl
(Matthew 15:21–28)

24 Jesus went from their towns and cities to the cities of Tyre and Sidon. He went into a house and wanted to stay there without people knowing where He was. But He could not hide Himself. 25 A woman who had a daughter with a demon heard of Him. She came and got down at His feet. 26 The woman was not a Jew. She was from the country of Syrophenicia. She asked Jesus if He would put the demon out of her daughter. 27 Jesus said to her, "Let the children have what they want first. It is wrong to take children's food and throw it to the dogs." 28 She said to Him, "Yes, Lord, but even the dogs eat the pieces that fall from the children's table." 29 He said to her, "Because of what you have said, go your way. The demon is gone out of your daughter." 30 So she went to her house and found the demon was gone and her daughter was lying on the bed.

Jesus Heals the Man Who Could Not Hear or Speak Well

31 Then Jesus left the cities of Tyre and Sidon. He came back to the Sea of Galilee by way of the land of Decapolis. 32 They took a man to Him who could not hear or speak well. They asked Jesus to put His hand on him. 33 Jesus took him away from the other people. He put His fingers into the man's ears. He spit and put His finger on the man's tongue. 34 Then Jesus looked up to heaven and breathed deep within. He said to the man, "Be opened!" 35 At once his ears were opened. His tongue was made loose and he spoke as other people. 36 Then Jesus told them they should tell no one. The more He told them this, the more they told what He had done. 37 They were very much surprised and wondered about it. They said, "He has done all things well. He makes those who could not hear so they can hear. He makes those who could not speak so they can speak."

The Feeding of the Four Thousand
(Matthew 15:32–39)

8 In those days many people were gathered together. They had nothing to eat. Jesus called His followers to Him and said, 2 "I pity these people because they have been with Me three days and have nothing to eat. 3 If I send them home without food, they may be too weak as they go. Many of them have come a long way."

4 His followers said to Him, "Where can anyone get enough bread for them here in this desert?" 5 He asked them, "How many loaves of bread do you have?" They said, "Seven." 6 Then He told the people to sit down on the ground. Jesus took the seven loaves of bread and gave thanks to God. He broke the loaves and gave them to His followers to give to the people. The followers gave the bread to them. 7 They had a few small fish also. He gave thanks to God and told the followers to give the fish to them. 8 They all ate and were filled. They picked up seven baskets full of pieces of bread and fish after the people were finished eating. 9 About four thousand ate. Then Jesus sent the people away.

The Proud Religious Law-Keepers Ask for Something Special to See
(Matthew 16:1–4)

10 At once Jesus got in a boat with His followers and came to the country of Dalmanutha. 11 The proud religious law-keepers came and began to ask Him for something special to see from heaven. They wanted to trap Jesus. 12 He breathed deep within and said, "Why do the people of this day look for something special to see? For sure, I tell you, the people of this day will have nothing special to see from heaven." 13 Then He left them. He got in the boat and went to the other side of the sea.

Jesus Shows That the Teaching of the Proud Religious Law-Keepers Is Wrong
(Matthew 16:5–12)

14 The followers had forgotten to take bread, only one loaf was in the boat. 15 He said to them, "Look out! Have nothing to do with the yeast of the proud religious law-keepers and of Herod." 16 They talked about it among themselves. They said, "He said this because we forgot to bring bread." 17 Jesus knew what they were thinking. He said to them, "Why are you talking among yourselves about forgetting to bring bread? Do you not understand? Is it not plain to you? Are your hearts still hard? 18 You have eyes, do you not see? You have ears, do you not hear? Do you not remember? 19 When I divided the five loaves of bread among the five thousand, how many baskets full of pieces did you pick up?" They said, "Twelve." 20 "When I divided the seven loaves of bread among the four thousand, how many baskets full of pieces did you pick up?" They said, "Seven." 21 Then He asked, "Why do you not understand yet?"

Jesus Heals a Blind Man

22 Then they came to the town of Bethsaida. Some people brought a blind man to Jesus. They asked if He would touch him. 23 He took the blind man by the hand out of town. Then He spit on the eyes of the blind man and put His hands on him. He asked, "Do you see anything?" 24 The blind man looked up and said, "I see some men. They look like trees, walking." 25 Jesus put His hands on the man's eyes again and told him to look up. Then he was healed and saw everything well. 26 Jesus sent him to his home and said, "Do not go into the town, *or tell it to anyone there."

Peter Says Jesus Is the Christ
(Matthew 16:13–20; Luke 9:18–20)

27 Jesus and His followers went from there to the towns of Caesarea Philippi. As they went, He asked His followers, "Who do people say that I am?" 28 They answered, "Some say John the Baptist and some say Elijah and others say one of the early preachers." 29 He said to them, "But who do you say that I am?" Peter said, "You are the Christ." 30 He told them with strong words that they should tell no one about Him.

Jesus Tells of His Death for the First Time
(Matthew 16:21–28; Luke 9:21–27)

31 He began to teach them that the Son of Man must suffer many things. He told them that the leaders and the religious leaders of the Jews and the teachers of the Law would have nothing to do with Him. He told them He would be killed and three days later He would be raised from the dead.

32 He had said this in plain words. Peter took Him away from the others and began to speak sharp words to Him. 33 Jesus turned around. He looked at His followers and spoke sharp words to Peter. He said, "Get behind Me, Satan! Your thoughts are not thoughts from God but from men."

Giving Up Self and One's Own Desires

34 Jesus called the people and His followers to Him. He said to them, "If anyone wants to be My follower, he must give up himself and his own desires. He must take up his cross and follow Me. 35 If anyone wants to keep his own life safe, he will lose it. If anyone gives up his life because of Me and because of the Good News, he will save it. 36 For what does a man have if he gets all the world and loses his own soul? 37 What can a man give to buy back his soul? 38 Whoever is ashamed of Me and My Words among the sinful people of this day, the Son of Man will be ashamed of him when He comes in the shining-greatness of His Father and His holy angels."

A Look at What Jesus Will Be Like
(Matthew 17:1–13; Luke 9:28–36)

9 Jesus said to them, "For sure I tell you, some standing here will not die until they see the holy nation of God come with power!"

2 Six days later Jesus took Peter and James and John with Him. He led them up to a high mountain by themselves. Jesus was changed as they looked at Him. 3 His clothes did shine. They were as white as snow. No one on earth could clean them so white. 4 Moses and Elijah were seen talking to Jesus.

5 Peter said to Jesus, "Teacher, it is good for us to be here. Let us make three tents to worship in. One will be for You and one for Moses and one for Elijah." 6 Peter did not know what to say. They were very much afraid.

7 A cloud came over them and a voice from the cloud said, "This is My much-loved Son. Listen to Him." 8 At once they looked around but saw no one there but Jesus.

9 They came down from the mountain. Then Jesus said with strong words that

they should tell no one what they had seen. They should wait until the Son of Man had risen from the dead. 10 So they kept those words to themselves, talking to each other about what He meant by being raised from the dead.

11 They asked Jesus, "Why do the teachers of the Law say that Elijah must come first?" 12 He said to them, "For sure, Elijah will come first and get things ready. Is it not written that the Son of Man must suffer many things and that men will have nothing to do with Him? (Isaiah 53:3) 13 But I say to you, Elijah has already come. They did to him whatever they wanted to do. It is written that they would."

A Boy with a Demon Is Healed
(Matthew 17:14–21; Luke 9:37–42)

14 When Jesus came back to His followers, He saw many people standing around them. The teachers of the Law were arguing with them. 15 The people saw Jesus and were surprised and ran to greet Him. 16 Jesus asked the teachers of the Law, "What are you arguing about with them?" 17 One of the people said, "Teacher, I brought my son to You. He has a demon in him and cannot talk. 18 Wherever the demon takes him, it throws him down. Spit runs from his mouth. He grinds his teeth. He is getting weaker. I asked Your followers to put the demon out but they could not."

19 He said, "You people of this day have no faith. How long must I be with you? How long must I put up with you? Bring the boy to Me." 20 They brought the boy to Jesus. The demon saw Jesus and at once held the boy in his power. The boy fell to the ground with spit running from his mouth. 21 Jesus asked the boy's father, "How long has he been like this?" The father said, "From the time he was a child. 22 Many times it throws him into the fire and into the water to kill him. If You can do anything to help us, take pity on us!" 23 Jesus said to him, "Why do you ask Me that? The one who has faith can do all things." 24 At once the father cried out. He said with tears in his eyes, "Lord, I have faith. Help my weak faith to be stronger!" 25 Jesus saw that many people were gathering together in a hurry. He spoke sharp words to the demon. He said, "Demon! You who cannot speak or hear, I say to you, come out of him! Do not ever go into him again." 26 The demon gave a cry. It threw the boy down and came out

of him. The boy was so much like a dead man that people said, "He is dead!" 27 But Jesus took him by the hand and helped him and he stood up.

28 When Jesus went into the house, His followers asked Him when He was alone, "Why could we not put out the demon?" 29 He said to them, "The only way this kind of demon is put out is by prayer and by going without food so you can pray better."

Jesus Tells of His Death the Second Time
(Matthew 17:22–23; Luke 9:43–45)

30 From there Jesus and His followers went through the country of Galilee. He did not want anyone to know where He was. 31 He taught His followers, saying, "The Son of Man will be handed over to men. They will kill Him. Three days after He is killed, He will be raised from the dead." 32 They did not understand what He said and were afraid to ask Him.

Jesus Teaches about the Faith of a Child
(Matthew 18:1–35; Luke 9:46–50)

33 They came to the city of Capernaum and were in the house. Jesus asked His followers, "What were you arguing about along the road?" 34 They did not answer. They had been arguing along the road about who was the greatest. 35 Jesus sat down and called the followers to Him. He said, "If anyone wants to be first, he must be last of all. He will be the one to care for all."

36 Jesus took a child and stood it among them. Then He took the child up in His arms and said to the followers, 37 "Whoever receives one of these little children in My name, receives Me. Whoever will receive Me, receives not Me, but Him Who sent Me."

Jesus Speaks Sharp Words against the Followers

38 John said to Him, "Teacher, we saw someone putting out demons in Your name. We told him to stop because he was not following us." 39 Jesus said, "Do not stop him. No one who does a powerful work in My name can say anything bad about Me soon after. 40 The person who is not against us is for us. 41 For sure, I tell you, whoever gives you a cup of water to drink in My name because you belong to Christ will not lose his reward from God. 42 Whoever is the reason for one of these little ones who believes in Me to

sin, it would be better for him to have a large stone put around his neck and to be thrown into the sea. 43 If your hand is the reason you fall into sin, cut it off. It is better to go into life without a hand, than to have two hands and go into the fire of hell that cannot be put out. 44 *There is where their worm never dies and the fire cannot be put out. 45 If your foot is the reason you fall into sin, cut it off. It is better to go into life with only one foot, than to have two feet and go into the fire of hell that cannot be put out. 46 *There is where their worm never dies and the fire cannot be put out. 47 If your eye is the reason you fall into sin, take it out. It is better to go into the holy nation of God with only one eye, than to have two eyes and be thrown into the fire of hell. 48 There is where their worm never dies and the fire is never put out.

49 "Everyone will be made cleaner and stronger with fire. 50 Salt is good. But if salt loses its taste, how can it be made to taste like salt again? Have salt in yourselves and be at peace with each other."

Jesus Teaches about Divorce
(Matthew 19:1–12)

10 Jesus went away from the city of Capernaum. He came to the country of Judea and to the other side of the Jordan River. Again the people gathered around Him. He began to teach them as He had been doing.

2 The proud religious law-keepers came to Him. They tried to trap Him and asked, "Does the Law say a man can divorce his wife?" 3 He said to them, "What did the Law of Moses say?" 4 They said, "Moses allowed a man to divorce his wife, if he put it in writing and gave it to her." 5 Jesus said to them, "Because of your hard hearts, Moses gave you this Law. 6 From the beginning of the world, God made them man and woman. 7 Because of this, a man is to leave his father and mother and is to live with his wife. 8 The two will become one. So they are no longer two, but one. 9 Let no man divide what God has put together."

10 In the house the followers asked Jesus about this again. 11 He said to them, "Whoever divorces his wife and marries another is not faithful to her and is guilty of a sex sin. 12 If a woman divorces her husband and marries another, she is not faithful to her husband and is guilty of a sex sin."

Jesus Gives Thanks for Little Children
(Matthew 19:13–15; Luke 18:15–17)

13 They brought little children to Jesus that He might put His hand on them. The followers spoke sharp words to those who brought them. 14 Jesus saw this and was angry with the followers. He said, "Let the little children come to Me. Do not stop them. The holy nation of God is made up of ones like these. 15 For sure, I tell you, whoever does not receive the holy nation of God as a little child does not go into it." 16 He took the children in His arms. He put His hands on them and prayed that good would come to them.

Jesus Teaches about Keeping the Law
(Matthew 19:16–30; Luke 18:18–30)

17 Jesus was going on His way. A man ran to Him and got down on his knees. He said, "Good Teacher, what must I do to have life that lasts forever?" 18 Jesus said to him, "Why do you call Me good? There is only One Who is good. That is God. 19 You know the Laws, 'Do not be guilty of sex sins in marriage. Do not kill another person. Do not take things from people in wrong ways. Do not steal. Do not lie. Respect your father and mother.' " 20 The man said to Jesus, "Teacher, I have obeyed all these Laws since I was a boy." 21 Jesus looked at him with love and said, "There is one thing for you to do yet. Go and sell everything you have and give the money to poor people. You will have riches in heaven. Then come and follow Me." 22 When the man heard these words, he was sad. He walked away with sorrow because he had many riches here on earth.

The Danger of Riches

23 Jesus looked around Him. He said to His followers, "How hard it is for rich people to get into the holy nation of God!" 24 The followers were surprised and wondered about His words. But Jesus said to them again, "Children! How hard it is for those who put their trust in riches to get into the holy nation of God! 25 It is easier for a camel to go through the eye of a needle than for a rich man to go to heaven."

26 They were very surprised and wondered, saying to themselves, "Then who can be saved from the punishment of sin?" 27 Jesus looked at them and said, "This cannot be done by men but God can do anything."

28 Then Peter began to say to Him, "We have given up everything we had and have

followed You." 29 Jesus said, "For sure, I tell you, there are those who have given up houses or brothers or sisters or father or mother or wife or children or lands because of Me, and the Good News. 30 They will get back one hundred times as much now at this time in houses and brothers and sisters and mothers and children and lands. Along with this, they will have very much trouble. And they will have life that lasts forever in the world to come. 31 Many who are first will be last. Many who are last will be first."

Jesus Tells of His Death the Third Time
(Matthew 20:17–19; Luke 18:31–34)

32 They were on their way to Jerusalem. Jesus walked in front of them. Those who followed were surprised and afraid. Then Jesus took the twelve followers by themselves. He told them what would happen to Him. 33 He said, "Listen, we are going to Jerusalem. The Son of Man will be handed over to the religious leaders of the Jews and to the teachers of the Law. They will say that He must be put to death. They will hand Him over to the people who are not Jews. 34 They will make fun of Him and will beat Him. They will spit on Him and will kill Him. But three days later He will be raised from the dead."

James and John Ask Jesus Something Hard
(Matthew 20:20–28)

35 James and John, the sons of Zebedee, came to Jesus. They said, "Teacher, we would like to have You do for us whatever we ask You." 36 He said to them, "What would you like to have Me do for you?" 37 They said to Him, "Let one of us sit by Your right side and the other by Your left side when You receive Your great honor in heaven." 38 Jesus said to them, "You do not know what you ask. Can you take the suffering I am about to take? Can you be baptized with the baptism that I am baptized with?" 39 They said to Him, "Yes, we can." Jesus said to Him, "You will, for sure, suffer the way I will suffer. You will be baptized with the baptism that I am baptized with. 40 But to sit on My right side or on My left side is not for Me to give. It will be given to those for whom it has been made ready." 41 The other ten followers heard it. They were angry with James and John. 42 Jesus called them to Him and said, "You know that those who are made leaders over the nations show their power

over the people. Important leaders use their power over the people. 43 It must not be that way with you. Whoever wants to be great among you, let him care for you. 44 Whoever wants to be first among you, must be the one who is owned and cares for all. 45 For the Son of Man did not come to be cared for. He came to care for others. He came to give His life so that many could be bought by His blood and be made free from sin."

Healing of the Blind Man
(Matthew 20:29–34; Luke 18:35–43)

46 Then they came to the city of Jericho. When He was leaving the city with His followers and many people, a blind man was sitting by the road. He was asking people for food or money as they passed by. His name was Bartimaeus, the son of Timaeus. 47 He heard that Jesus of Nazareth was passing by. He began to speak with a loud voice, saying, "Jesus, Son of David, take pity on me!" 48 Many people spoke sharp words to the blind man telling him not to call out like that. But he spoke all the more. He said, "Son of David, take pity on me." 49 Jesus stopped and told them to call the blind man. They called to him and said, "Take hope! Stand up. He is calling for you!" 50 As he jumped up, he threw off his coat and came to Jesus. 51 Jesus said to him, "What do you want Me to do for you?" The blind man said to Him, "Lord, I want to see!" 52 Jesus said, "Go! Your faith has healed you." At once he could see and he followed Jesus down the road.

The Last Time Jesus Goes to Jerusalem
(Matthew 21:1–11; Luke 19:29–44; John 12:12–19)

11 Jesus and His followers were near Jerusalem at the Mount of Olives. They were in the towns of Bethphage and Bethany. Jesus sent two of His followers on ahead. 2 He said to them, "Go into the town over there. As soon as you get there, you will find a young donkey tied. No man has ever sat on it. Let the donkey loose and bring it here. 3 If anyone asks you, 'Why are you doing that?' say, 'The Lord needs it. He will send it back again soon.'"

4 The two followers went on their way. They found the young donkey tied by the door where two streets crossed. They took the rope off its neck. 5 Some men were standing there. They said to the two followers, "Why are you taking the rope off that young donkey?" 6 The two followers

told them what Jesus had said and the men let them take the donkey. 7 They brought it to Jesus and put their coats over it. Jesus sat on the donkey. 8 Many people put their clothes down on the road. Others cut branches off the trees and put them down on the road. 9 Those who went in front and those who followed spoke with loud voices, "Greatest One! Great and honored is He Who comes in the name of the Lord! 10 Great is the coming holy nation of our father David. It will come in the name of the Lord, Greatest One in the highest heaven."

11 Jesus came to Jerusalem and went into the house of God. He looked around at everything. Then He went with the twelve followers to the town of Bethany because it was late.

The Fig Tree with No Fruit

12 They came from Bethany the next morning. Jesus was hungry. 13 Along the road He saw a fig tree with leaves on it. He went over to see if it had any fruit. He saw nothing but leaves. It was not the right time for figs. 14 Jesus said to the tree, "Let no one ever again eat fruit from you." His followers heard Him say it.

Jesus Stops the Buying and the Selling in the House of God
(Matthew 21:12–17; Luke 19:45–48; John 2:13–17)

15 Then they came to Jerusalem. Jesus went into the house of God. He began to make the people leave who were selling and buying in the house of God. He turned over the tables of the men who changed money. He turned over the seats of those who sold doves. 16 He would not allow anyone to carry a pot or pan through the house of God. 17 He taught them saying, "Is it not written, 'My house is to be called a house of prayer for all the nations'? (Isaiah 56:7; Jeremiah 7:11) You have made it a place of robbers."

18 The teachers of the Law and the religious leaders of the Jews heard this. They tried to find some way to put Jesus to death. But they were afraid of Him because all the people were surprised and wondered about His teaching. 19 When evening came, Jesus and His followers went out of the city.

The Fig Tree Dries Up
(Matthew 21:18–22)

20 In the morning they passed by the fig tree. They saw it was dried up from the roots. 21 Peter remembered what had happened the day before and said to Jesus, "Teacher, see! The fig tree which You spoke to has dried up!" 22 Jesus said to them, "Have faith in God. 23 For sure, I tell you, a person may say to this mountain, 'Move from here into the sea.' And if he does not doubt, but believes that what he says will be done, it will happen. 24 Because of this, I say to you, whatever you ask for when you pray, have faith that you will receive it. Then you will get it. 25 When you stand to pray, if you have anything against anyone, forgive him. Then your Father in heaven will forgive your sins also. 26 *If you do not forgive them their sins, your Father in heaven will not forgive your sins."

27 They came again to Jerusalem. Jesus was walking around in the house of God. The religious leaders and the teachers of the Law and other leaders came to Him. 28 They asked, "How do You have the right and the power to do these things? Who gave You the right and the power to do them?" 29 Jesus said to them, "I will ask you one thing also. If you tell Me, then I will tell you by what right and power I do these things. 30 Was the baptism of John from heaven or from men? Tell Me." 31 They talked among themselves. They said, "If we say from heaven, He will say, 'Why did you not believe him?' 32 But how can we say, 'From men'?" They were afraid of the people because everyone believed that John was one who spoke for God. 33 So they said, "We do not know." Then Jesus said, "Then I will not tell you by what right and power I do these things."

The Picture-Story of the Grape-Field
(Matthew 21:33–46; Luke 20:9–18)

12 Jesus began to teach them by using picture-stories, saying, "There was a man who planted grapes in a field. He put a fence around it and made a place for making wine. He built a tower to look over the field. Then he let farmers rent it and went into another country.

2 "The time came for gathering the grapes. He sent his servant to the farmers to get some of the grapes. 3 The farmers took him and beat him. They sent him back with nothing. 4 The owner sent another servant. The farmers threw stones at him and hit him on the head and did other bad things to him. 5 Again the owner sent another servant. The farmers killed that one. Many other servants were sent. They beat some and they killed others.

6 "He had a much-loved son to send yet. So last of all he sent him to them, saying, 'They will respect my son.' 7 The farmers said to themselves, 'This is the one who will get everything when the owner dies. Let us kill him and we will get everything.' 8 They took him and killed him. They threw his body outside the field. 9 What will the owner of the field do? He will come and kill the farmers. He will give the field to other farmers.

10 "Have you not read what the Holy Writings say? 'The Stone that was put aside by the workmen has become the most important Stone in the corner of the building. 11 The Lord has done this. It is great in our eyes.' " (Psalm 118:22–23) 12 The leaders wanted to take Him but they were afraid of the people. They knew He had told the picture-story against them. They left Him and went away.

They Try to Trap Jesus
(Matthew 22:15–22; Luke 20:19–26)

13 Some of the proud religious law-keepers and Herod's men were sent to trap Jesus in His talk. 14 They came to Him and said, "Teacher, we know You are true. We know You are not afraid of what men think or say about You. You teach the way of God in truth. Is it right to pay taxes to Caesar or not? 15 Should we pay or not pay?" Jesus knew how they pretended to be someone they were not. He said to them, "Why do you try to trap Me? Bring Me a small piece of money so I may look at it." 16 They brought Him one. He asked them, "Whose picture is this? Whose name is on it?" They answered, "Caesar's." 17 Then Jesus said to them, "Pay to Caesar the things that belong to Caesar. Pay to God the things that belong to God." They were surprised and wondered at Him.

They Ask about Being Raised from the Dead
(Matthew 22:23–33; Luke 20:27–40)

18 Some people from the religious group who believe no one will be raised from the dead came to Jesus. They asked Him, 19 "Teacher, Moses gave us a Law. It said, 'If a man's brother dies and leaves his wife behind, but no children, then his brother should marry his wife and raise children for his brother.' (Deuteronomy 25:5) 20 There were seven brothers. The first was married. He died before he had any children. 21 The second married her and died. He had no children. The same

happened with the third. 22 All seven had her for a wife. All died without children. Last of all the woman died. 23 When people are raised from the dead, whose wife will she be? All seven had her for a wife." 24 Jesus said to them, "Is this not the reason you are wrong, because you do not know the Holy Writings or the power of God? 25 When people are raised from the dead, they do not marry and are not given in marriage. They are like angels in heaven. 26 As for the dead being raised, have you not read in the book of Moses how God spoke to him in the burning bush? He said, 'I am the God of Abraham and the God of Isaac and the God of Jacob.' (Exodus 3:2–6) 27 He is not the God of the dead, He is the God of the living. So you are very much wrong."

The Great Law
(Matthew 22:34–40)

20 Then one of the teachers of the Law heard them arguing. He thought Jesus had spoken well. He asked Him, "Which Law is the greatest of all?" 29 Jesus said to him, "The greatest Law is this, 'Listen, Jewish people, The Lord our God is one Lord! 30 You must love the Lord your God with all your heart and with all your soul and with all your mind and with all your strength.' (Deuteronomy 6:4–5) This is the first Law.

31 "The second Law is this: 'You must love your neighbor as yourself.' (Leviticus 19:18) No other Law is greater than these."

32 Then the teacher of the Law said, "Teacher, You have told the truth. There is one God. There is no other God but Him. 33 A man should love Him with all his heart and with all his understanding. He should love Him with all his soul and with all his strength and love his neighbor as himself. This is more important than to bring animals to be burned on the altar or to give God other gifts on the altar in worship." 34 Jesus saw he had spoken with understanding. He said to him, "You are not far from the holy nation of God." After that no one thought they could ask Him anything.

Jesus Asks the Proud Religious Law-Keepers about the Christ
(Matthew 22:41–46; Luke 20:41–44)

35 Jesus was in the house of God teaching. He asked, "How do the teachers of the Law say that Christ is the Son of David? 36 For David himself, led by the Holy Spirit, said, 'The Lord said to my Lord, sit

at my right side until I make those who hate You a place to rest Your feet.' (Psalm 110:1) 37 David himself calls Him Lord. Then how can He be his son?" Many people were glad to hear Him.

False Teachers
(Matthew 23:1–36; Luke 20:45–47)

38 Jesus taught them, saying, "Look out for the teachers of the Law. They like to walk around in long coats. They like to have the respect of men as they stand in the center of town where people gather. 39 They like to have the important seats in the places of worship and the important places at big suppers. 40 They take houses from poor women whose husbands have died. They cover up the bad they do by saying long prayers. They will be punished all the more."

The Woman Whose Husband Had Died Gives All She Has
(Luke 21:1–4)

41 Jesus sat near the money box in the house of God. He watched the people putting in money. Many of them were rich and gave much money. 42 A poor woman whose husband had died came by and gave two very small pieces of money.

43 Jesus called His followers to Him. He said, "For sure, I tell you, this poor woman whose husband has died has given more money than all the others. 44 They all gave of that which was more than they needed for their own living. She is poor and yet she gave all she had, even what she needed for her own living."

Jesus Tells of the House of God
(Matthew 24:1–51; Luke 21:5–36)

13 Jesus went out of the house of God. One of His followers said to Him, "Teacher, look at the big stones and these great buildings!" 2 Jesus said, "Do you see these great buildings? All these stones will be thrown down. Not one will be left standing on another."

Jesus Teaches on the Mount Of Olives

3 Jesus sat down on the Mount of Olives at a place where He could see the house of God. Peter and James and John and Andrew came to Him. They asked without anyone else hearing, 4 "Tell us when this will be. What are we to look for when these things are to happen?"

What to Look for Before Jesus Returns

5 Jesus began to say to them, "Be careful that no one leads you the wrong way.

6 Many people will come using My name. They will say, 'I am Christ.' They will turn many to the wrong way. 7 When you hear of wars and much talk about wars, do not be surprised. These things have to happen. But the end is not yet. 8 Nations will have wars with other nations. Countries will fight against countries. The earth will shake and break apart in different places. There will be no food for people. There will be much trouble. These things are the beginning of much sorrow and pain.

It Will Be Hard for Those Who Believe

9 "Watch out for yourselves. They will take you to the courts. In the places of worship they will beat you. You will be taken in front of rulers and in front of kings because of Me. You will be there to tell them about Me. 10 The Good News must first be preached to all the nations.

11 "When you are put into their hands, do not be afraid of what you are to say or how you are to say it. Whatever is given to you to say at that time, say it. It will not be you who speaks, but the Holy Spirit. 12 A brother will hand over a brother to death. A father will hand over his son. Children will turn against their parents and have them put to death. 13 You will be hated by all people because of Me. But he who stays true to the end will be saved.

Days of Trouble and Pain and Sorrow

14 "You will see a very sinful man-made god standing in the house of God where it has no right to stand. Then those in the country of Judea should run to the mountains. It was spoken of by the early preacher Daniel. (Daniel 9:27; 12:11) The one who reads this should understand. 15 He that is on the top of the house should not take the time to get anything out of his house. 16 He that is in the field should not go back to get his coat. 17 It will be hard for women who will soon be mothers. It will be hard for those feeding babies in those days! 18 Pray that it will not be during the winter. 19 In those days there will be much trouble and pain and sorrow. It has never been this bad from the beginning of time and never will be again. 20 If the Lord had not made those days short, no life would have been saved. Because of God's people whom He has chosen, He made the days short.

The False Religious Teachers

21 "If anyone says to you, 'See! Here is the Christ.' or, 'There He is!' do not believe it.

²² Some will come who will say they are Christ. False preachers will come. These people will do special things for people to see. They will do surprising things, so that if it can be, God's people will be led to believe something wrong. ²³ See! I have told you about these things before they happen.

Jesus Will Come Again in His Greatness

²⁴ "After those days of much trouble and pain and sorrow are over, the sun will get dark. The moon will not give light. ²⁵ The stars will fall from the sky. The powers in the heavens will be shaken. ²⁶ Then they will see the Son of Man coming in the clouds with great power and shining-greatness. ²⁷ He will send His angels. They will gather together God's people from the four winds. They will come from one end of the earth to the other end of heaven.

The Picture-Story of the Fig Tree

²⁸ "Now learn something from the fig tree. When the branch begins to grow and puts out its leaves, you know summer is near. ²⁹ In the same way, when you see all these things happen, you know the Son of Man is near. He is even at the door. ³⁰ For sure, I tell you, the people of this day will not pass away before all these things have happened.

³¹ "Heaven and earth will pass away, but My Words will not pass away. ³² But no one knows the day or the hour. No! Not even the angels in heaven know. The Son does not know. Only the Father knows.

³³ "Be careful! Watch and pray. You do not know when it will happen. ³⁴ The coming of the Son of Man is as a man who went from his house to a far country. He gave each one of his servants some work to do. He told the one standing at the door to watch. ³⁵ In the same way, you are to watch also! You do not know when the Owner of the house will be coming. It may be in the evening or in the night or when the sun comes up or in the morning. ³⁶ He may come when you are sleeping. ³⁷ What I say to you, I say to all. Watch!"

They Look for a Way to Put Jesus to Death

(Matthew 26:1–5; Luke 22:1–6)

14 It was now two days before the supper of the special religious gathering to remember how the Jews left Egypt and the supper of bread without yeast.

The religious leaders and the teachers of the Law tried to trap Jesus. They tried to take Him so they could put Him to death. ² These men said, "This must not happen on the day of the special supper. The people would be against it and make much trouble."

Mary of Bethany Puts Special Perfume on Jesus

(Matthew 26:6–13; John 12:1–11)

³ Jesus was in the town of Bethany eating in the house of Simon. Simon was a man with a very bad skin disease. A woman came with a jar of special perfume. She had given much money for this. She broke the jar and poured the special perfume on the head of Jesus. ⁴ Some of them were angry. They said, "Why was this special perfume wasted? ⁵ This perfume could have been sold for much money and given to poor people." They spoke against her.

⁶ Jesus said, "Let her alone. Why are you giving her trouble? She has done a good thing to Me. ⁷ You will have poor people with you all the time. Whenever you want, you can do something good for them. You will not have Me all the time. ⁸ She did what she could. She put this perfume on My body to make Me ready for the grave. ⁹ For sure, I tell you, wherever this Good News is preached in all the world, this woman will be remembered for what she has done."

Judas Hands Jesus Over to Be Killed

(Matthew 26:14–16)

¹⁰ Judas Iscariot was one of the twelve followers. He went to the head religious leaders of the Jews to talk about how he might hand Jesus over to them. ¹¹ When the leaders heard it, they were glad. They promised to give Judas money. Then he looked for a way to hand Jesus over.

Getting Ready for the Special Supper

(Matthew 26:17–19; Luke 22:7–13)

¹² The first day of the supper of bread without yeast was the day to kill an animal. It was for the special religious gathering to remember how the Jews left Egypt. His followers said to Jesus, "What place do You want us to make ready for You to eat this special supper?" ¹³ Jesus sent two of His followers on ahead and said to them, "Go into the city. There a man carrying a jar of water will meet you. Follow him. ¹⁴ He will go into a house. You say to the owner of the house, 'The Teacher asks,

"Where is the room you keep for friends, where I can eat this special supper with My followers?' ' 15 He will take you to a large room on the second floor with everything in it. Make it ready for us."

16 The followers went from there and came into the city. They found everything as Jesus had said. They made things ready for the special supper.

17 In the evening He came with the twelve followers. 18 They sat at the table and ate. Jesus said, "For sure, I tell you, one of you will hand Me over to be killed. He is eating with Me." 19 They were very sad. They said to Him one after the other, "Is it I?" 20 He said to them, "It is one of the twelve followers. It is the one who is putting his hand with mine into the same dish. 21 The Son of Man is going away as it is written of Him. But it will be bad for that man who hands the Son of Man over to be killed! It would have been better if he had not been born!"

The First Lord's Supper
(Matthew 26:26–30; Luke 22:19–20)

22 As they were eating, Jesus took a loaf of bread. He gave thanks and broke it in pieces. He gave it to them and said, "Take, eat, this is My body." 23 Then He took the cup and gave thanks. He gave it to them and they all drank from it. 24 He said to them, "This is My blood of the New Way of Worship which is given for many. 25 For sure, I tell you, that I will not drink of the fruit of the vine until that day when I drink it new in the holy nation of God." 26 After they sang a song, they went out to the Mount of Olives.

Jesus Tells How Peter Will Lie about Him
(Matthew 26:31–35; Luke 22:31–34; John 13:36–38)

27 Jesus said to them, "All of you will be ashamed of Me and leave Me tonight. For it is written, 'I will kill the shepherd and the sheep of the flock will spread everywhere.' (Zechariah 13:7) 28 After I am raised from the dead, I will go before you into the country of Galilee." 29 Peter said to Him, "Even if all men are ashamed of You and leave Me, I never will." 30 Jesus said to him, "For sure, I tell you, that today, even tonight, before a rooster crows two times, you will say three times you do not know Me." 31 Peter spoke with strong words, "Even if I have to die with You, I will never say that I do not know You." All the followers said the same thing.

Jesus Prays in Gethsemane
(Matthew 26:36–46; Luke 22:39–46)

32 They came to a place called Gethsemane. Jesus said to His followers, "You sit here while I pray." 33 He took Peter and James and John with Him. He began to have much sorrow and a heavy heart. 34 He said to them, "My soul is very sad. My soul is so full of sorrow I am ready to die. You stay here and watch." 35 He went a little farther and got down with His face on the ground. He prayed that this time of suffering might pass from Him if it could. 36 He said, "Father, You can do all things. Take away what must happen to Me. Even so, not what I want, but what You want."

37 Then Jesus came to the followers and found them sleeping. He said to Peter, "Simon, are you sleeping? Were you not able to watch one hour? 38 Watch and pray so that you will not be tempted. Man's spirit wants to do this, but the body does not have the power to do it."

39 Again Jesus went away and prayed saying the same words. 40 He came back and found them sleeping again. Their eyes were heavy. They did not know what to say to Him. 41 He came the third time and said to them, "Are you still sleeping and resting? It is enough! Listen, the time has come when the Son of Man will be handed over to sinners. 42 Get up and let us go. See! The man who will hand Me over to the head religious leader is near."

Jesus Is Handed Over to Sinners
(Matthew 26:47–56; Luke 22:47–51; John 18:1–11)

43 At once, while Jesus was talking, Judas came. He was one of the twelve followers. He came with many other men who had swords and sticks. They came from the head religious leaders of the Jews and the teachers of the Law and the leaders of the people. 44 The man who was going to hand Jesus over gave the men something to look for. He said, "The Man I kiss is the One. Take hold of Him and take Him away."

45 At once Judas went straight to Jesus and said, "Teacher!" and kissed Him. 46 Then they put their hands on Him and took Him.

47 One of the followers of Jesus who stood watching took his sword. He hit the servant owned by the head religious leader and cut off his ear. 48 Jesus said to them, "Have you come with swords and sticks to take Me as if I were a robber? 49 I have been with you every day teaching in

the house of God. You never took hold of Me. But this has happened as the Holy Writings said it would happen." **50** Then all His followers left Him and ran away.

51 A young man was following Him with only a piece of cloth around his body. They put their hands on the young man. **52** Leaving the cloth behind, he ran away with no clothes on.

Jesus Stands in Front of the Head Religious Leaders
(Matthew 26:57–58; Luke 22:52–54; John 18:19–24)

53 They led Jesus away to the head religious leader. All the religious leaders and other leaders and the teachers of the Law were gathered there. **54** But Peter followed a long way behind as they went to the house of the head religious leader. He sat with the helpers and got warm by the fire.

Jesus Stands in Front of the Court
(Matthew 26:59–68)

55 The religious leaders and all the court were looking for something against Jesus. They wanted to find something so they could kill Him. But they could find nothing. **56** Many came and told false things about Him, but their words did not agree. **57** Some got up and said false things against Him. They said, **58** "We have heard Him say, 'I will destroy the house of God that was made with hands. In three days I will build another that is not made with hands.' " Even these who spoke against Him were not able to agree.

60 The head religious leader stood up in front of the people. He asked Jesus, "Have You nothing to say? What about the things these men are saying against You?" **61** Jesus said nothing. Again the head religious leader asked Him, "Are You the Christ, the Son of the Holy One?" **62** Jesus said, "I am! And you will see the Son of Man seated on the right side of the All-powerful God. You will see Him coming again in the clouds of the sky."

63 Then the head religious leader tore his clothes apart. He said, "Do we need other people to speak against Him? **64** You have heard Him speak as if He were God! What do you think?" They all said He was guilty of death. **65** Some began to spit on Him. They covered Jesus' face, and they hit Him. They said, "Tell us what is going to happen." Soldiers hit Him with their hands.

Peter Says He Does Not Know Jesus
(Matthew 26:69–75; Luke 22:55–62; John 18:15–18, 25–27)

66 Peter was outside in the yard. One of the servant-girls of the head religious leader came. **67** She saw Peter getting warm. She looked at him and said, "You were with Jesus of Nazareth." **68** Peter lied, saying, "I do not know Jesus and do not understand what you are talking about." As he went out, a rooster crowed.

69 The servant-girl saw him again. She said to the people standing around, "This man is one of them." **70** He lied again saying that he did not know Jesus. Later, those who stood around said to Peter again, "For sure you are one of them. You are from the country of Galilee. You talk like they do." **71** He began to say strong words and to swear. He said, "I do not know the Man you are talking about!"

72 At once a rooster crowed the second time. Peter remembered what Jesus had said to him, "Before a rooster crows two times, you will say three times you do not know Me." When he thought about it, he cried.

Jesus Stands Before Pilate
(Matthew 27:1–2, 11–14; Luke 23:1–5; John 18:28–37)

15 Early in the morning the head religious leaders of the Jews and other leaders and the teachers of the Law and all the court gathered together to talk about Jesus. Then they tied up Jesus and led Him away. They handed Him over to Pilate. **2** Pilate asked Jesus, "Are You the King of the Jews?" He said to Pilate, "What you say is true."

3 The religious leaders spoke many things against Him. Jesus did not say a word. **4** Pilate asked Him again, "Have You nothing to say? Listen to the things they are saying against You!" **5** Jesus did not say a word. Pilate was much surprised and wondered about it.

Jesus or Barabbas Is to Go Free
(Matthew 27:15–26; Luke 23:17–25; John 18:38–40)

6 Each year at the special supper Pilate would let one person who was in prison go free. It would be the one the people asked for. **7** The name of one of those in prison was Barabbas. He, together with others, had killed people while working against the leaders of the country. **8** All the people went to Pilate and asked him to do as he had done before. 9 Pilate said, "Do you want me to let the King of the Jews go free?" 10 He knew the religious leaders had handed Jesus over to him because they were jealous. 11 The religious leaders talked the people into thinking that Pilate should let Barabbas go free. 12 Pilate said to them again, "What do you want me to do with the Man you call the King of the Jews?" 13 They spoke with loud voices again, "Nail Him to a cross." 14 Then Pilate said to them, "Why? What bad thing has He done?" They spoke with loud voices all the more, "Nail Him to a cross!"

The Crown of Thorns
(Matthew 27:27–32; John 19:1–5)

15 Pilate wanted to please the people. He gave Barabbas to them and had Jesus beaten. Then he handed Him over to be nailed to a cross. 16 The soldiers led Jesus away to a large room in the court. They called all the soldiers together. 17 The soldiers put a purple coat on Him. They put a crown of thorns on His head, 18 and said to Him, "Hello, King of the Jews!" 19 They hit Him on the head with a stick and spit on Him. They got down on their knees and worshiped Him. 20 After they had made fun of Him, they took the purple coat off of Him and put His own clothes back on Him. Then they led Him away to be nailed to a cross.

21 They came to a man called Simon who was coming from the country of Cyrene. He was the father of Alexander and Rufus. They made Simon carry the cross of Jesus.

Jesus on the Cross
(Matthew 27:33–37; Luke 23:26–38; John 19:17–22)

22 They led Jesus to a place called Golgotha. This name means the place of the skull. 23 They gave Him wine with something in it to take away the pain, but He would not drink it. 24 When they had nailed Jesus to the cross, they divided His clothes by drawing names to see what each man should take. 25 It was about nine o'clock in the morning when they nailed Him to the cross. 26 Over Jesus' head they put in writing what they had against Him, THE KING OF THE JEWS.

The Two Robbers
(Matthew 27:38–44; Luke 23:39–43)

27 They nailed two robbers on crosses beside Jesus. One was on His right side and the other was on His left side. 28 *It happened as the Holy Writings said it would happen, "They thought of Him as One Who broke the Law." (Isaiah 53:12)

29 Those who walked by shook their heads and laughed at Jesus. They said, "You were the One Who could destroy the house of God and build it again in three days. 30 Save Yourself and come down from the cross." 31 The head religious leaders and the teachers of the Law made fun of Him also. They said to each other, "He saved others but He cannot save Himself. 32 Let Christ, the King of the Jews, come down from the cross. We want to see it and then we will believe." Those who were on the crosses beside Jesus spoke bad things to Him.

The Death of Jesus
(Matthew 27:45–50; Luke 23:44–49; John 19:28–37)

33 From noon until three o'clock it was dark over all the land. 34 At three o'clock Jesus cried with a loud voice, "My God, My God, why have You left Me alone?"

35 When some of those who stood by heard that, they said, "Listen! He is calling for Elijah." 36 One of them ran and took a sponge and filled it with sour wine. He put it on a stick and gave it to Him to drink. He said, "Let Him alone. Let us see if Elijah will come and take Him down."

The Powerful Works at the Time of His Death
(Matthew 27:51–54)

37 Then Jesus gave a loud cry. He gave up His spirit and died. 38 The curtain in the house of God was torn in two from top to bottom. 39 The captain of the soldiers was looking at Jesus when He cried out. He saw Him die and said, "For sure, this Man was the Son of God."

The Women at the Cross
(Matthew 27:55–56; John 19:25–27)

40 Women were looking on from far away. Among them was Mary Magdalene and Mary the mother of the younger James and of Joses, and Salome. 41 These cared for Him when He was in the country of Galilee. There were many other women there who had followed Him to Jerusalem.

Jesus Is Buried
(Matthew 27:57–66; Luke 23:50–56; John 19:38–42)

42 It was the day to get ready for the Day of Rest and it was now evening. 43 Joseph,

who was from the city of Arimathea, was an important man in the court. He was looking for the holy nation of God. Without being afraid, he went to Pilate and asked for the body of Jesus. **44** Pilate was surprised and wondered if Jesus was dead so soon. He called the captain of the soldiers and asked if Jesus was already dead.

45 After the captain said that Jesus was dead, Pilate let Joseph take the body. **46** Joseph took the body of Jesus down from the cross. He put the linen cloth he had bought around the body. Then he laid the body in a grave which had been cut out in the side of a rock. He pushed a stone over to cover the door of the grave. **47** Mary Magdalene and Mary the mother of Joses saw where He was laid.

Jesus Is Raised from the Dead
(Matthew 28:1–10; Luke 24:1–12; John 20:1–18)

16 The Day of Rest was over. Mary Magdalene and Mary the mother of James, and Salome bought spices. They wanted to put the spices on Jesus' body. **2** Very early in the morning on the first day of the week, they came to the grave. The sun had come up. **3** They said to themselves, "Who will roll the stone away from the door of the grave for us?" **4** But when they looked, they saw the very large stone had been rolled away.

5 They went into the grave. There they saw a young man with a long white coat sitting on the right side. They were afraid. **6** He said, "Do not be afraid. You are looking for Jesus of Nazareth Who was nailed to a cross. He is risen! He is not here! See, here is the place where they laid Him. **7** Go and tell His followers and Peter that He is going ahead of you into Galilee. You will see Him there as He told you." **8** They ran from the grave shaking and were surprised. They did not say anything to anyone because they were afraid.

The Followers of Jesus Do Not Believe He Was Raised from the Dead
(Luke 24:13–43; John 20:24–29)

9 (*It was early on the first day of the week when Jesus was raised from the dead. Mary Magdalene saw Him first. He had put seven demons out of her. **10** She went and told His followers. They were crying because of much sorrow. **11** But they did not believe her when she said she had seen Him alive.

12 After that He was seen again by two of His followers as they walked into the country. He did not look like He had looked before to these two people. **13** They went and told it to the others. The others did not believe them.

14 Later He was seen by the eleven followers as they were eating. He spoke to them with sharp words because they did not believe and their hearts were hard. And they did not believe the others who had seen Him since He had been raised from the dead.

Jesus Sends His Followers to Preach
(Matthew 28:16–20; Luke 24:44–49; John 20:21–23)

15 He said to them, "You are to go to all the world and preach the Good News to every person. **16** He who puts his trust in Me and is baptized will be saved from the punishment of sin. But he who does not put his trust in Me is guilty and will be punished forever. **17** These special powerful works will be done by those who have put their trust in Me. In My name they will put out demons. They will speak with languages they have never learned. **18** They will pick up snakes. If they drink any poison, it will not hurt them. They will put their hands on the sick and they will be healed."

19 After Jesus had talked to them, He was taken up into heaven. He sat down on the right side of God.

20 The followers went from there and preached everywhere. The Lord worked with them. The Lord showed that the Word of God was true by the special works they had power to do.)

LUKE

Luke Writes to Theophilus

1 Many people have written about the things that have happened among us. **2** Those who saw everything from the first and helped teach the Good News have passed these things on to us. **3** Dear Theophilus, I have looked with care into these things from the beginning. I have decided it would be good to write them to you one after the other the way they happened. 4 Then you can be sure you know the truth about the things you have been taught.

An Angel Tells of the Birth of John the Baptist

5 When Herod was king of the country of Judea, there was a Jewish religious leader named Zacharias. He worked for Abijah. His wife was of the family group of Aaron. Her name was Elizabeth. 6 They were right with God and obeyed the Jewish Law and did what the Lord said to do. 7 They had no children because Elizabeth was not able to have a child. Both of them were older people.

8 Zacharias was doing his work as a religious leader for God. 9 The religious leaders were given certain kinds of work to do. Zacharias was chosen to go to the house of God to burn special perfume. 10 Many people stood outside praying during the time the special perfume was burning.

11 Zacharias saw an angel of the Lord standing on the right side of the altar where the special perfume was burning. 12 When he saw the angel, Zacharias was troubled and afraid. 13 The angel said to him, "Zacharias, do not be afraid. Your prayer has been heard. Your wife Elizabeth will give birth to a son. You are to name him John. 14 You will be glad and have much joy. Many people will be happy because he is born. 15 He will be great in the sight of the Lord and will never drink wine or any strong drink. Even from his birth, he will be filled with the Holy Spirit. 16 Many of the Jews will be turned to the Lord their God by him. 17 He will be the one to go in the spirit and power of Elijah before Christ comes. He will turn the hearts of the fathers back to their children. He will teach those who do not obey to be right with God. He will get people ready for the Lord." (Malachi 4:5–6)

Zacharias Does Not Believe the Angel

18 Zacharias said to the angel, "How can I know this for sure? I am old and my wife is old also." 19 The angel said to him, "My name is Gabriel. I stand near God. He sent me to talk to you and bring to you this good news. 20 See! You will not be able to talk until the day this happens. It is because you did not believe my words. What I said will happen at the right time."

21 The people outside were waiting. They were surprised and wondered why Zacharias stayed so long in the house of God. 22 When he came out, he could not talk to them. They knew he had seen something special from God while he was in the house of God. He tried to talk to them with his hands but could say nothing. 23 When his days of working in the house of God were over, he went to his home.

The Lord Does What He Promised

24 Some time later Elizabeth knew she was to become a mother. She kept herself hidden for five months. She said, 25 "This is what the Lord has done for me. He has looked on me and has taken away my shame from among men."

Gabriel Speaks to Mary

26 Six months after Elizabeth knew she was to become a mother, Gabriel was sent from God to Nazareth. Nazareth was a town in the country of Galilee. 27 He went to a woman who had never had a man. Her name was Mary. She was promised in marriage to a man named Joseph. Joseph was of the family of David. 28 The angel came to her and said, "You are honored very much. You are a favored woman. The Lord is with you. *You are chosen from among many women."

29 When she saw the angel, she was troubled at his words. She thought about what had been said. 30 The angel said to her, "Mary, do not be afraid. You have found favor with God. 31 See! You are to become a mother and have a Son. You are to give Him the name Jesus. 32 He will be great. He will be called the Son of the Most High. The Lord God will give Him the place where His early father David sat. 33 He will be King over the family of Jacob forever and His nation will have no end."

34 Mary said to the angel, "How will this happen? I have never had a man." 35 The angel said to her, "The Holy Spirit will come on you. The power of the Most High will cover you. The holy Child you give birth to will be called the Son of God. 36 "See, your cousin Elizabeth, as old as she is, is going to give birth to a child. She was not able to have children before, but now she is in her sixth month. 37 For God can do all things." 38 Then Mary said, "I am willing to be used of the Lord. Let it happen to me as you have said." Then the angel went away from her.

Mary Visits Elizabeth

39 At once Mary went from there to a town in the hill country of Judea. 40 She went to

the house of Zacharias to see Elizabeth.
41 When Elizabeth heard Mary speak, the
baby moved in her body. At the same time
Elizabeth was filled with the Holy Spirit.
42 Elizabeth spoke in a loud voice, "You
are honored among women! Your Child
is honored! 43 Why has this happened
to me? Why has the mother of my Lord
come to me? 44 As soon as I heard your
voice, the baby in my body moved for joy.
45 You are happy because you believed.
Everything will happen as the Lord told
you it would happen."

Mary's Song of Thanks

46 Then Mary said, "My heart sings with
thanks for my Lord. 47 And my spirit is
happy in God, the One Who saves from
the punishment of sin. 48 The Lord has
looked on me, His servant-girl and one
who is not important. But from now on
all people will honor me. 49 He Who is
powerful has done great things for me. His
name is holy. 50 The loving-kindness of
the Lord is given to the people of all times
who honor Him. 51 He has done powerful
works with His arm. He has divided from
each other those who have pride in their
hearts. 52 He has taken rulers down from
their thrones. He has put those who are in
a place that is not important to a place that
is important. 53 He has filled those who
are hungry with good things. He has sent
the rich people away with nothing. 54 He
has helped Israel His servant. This was
done to remember His loving-kindness.
55 He promised He would do this to our
early fathers and to Abraham and to his
family forever." 56 Mary stayed with Elizabeth about three months. Then she went
to her own home.

The Birth of John the Baptist

57 When the time came, Elizabeth gave
birth to a son. 58 Her neighbors and family
heard how the Lord had shown loving-
kindness to her. They were happy for her.
59 On the eighth day they did the religious
act of the Jews on the child. They named
him Zacharias, after his father. 60 But
his mother said, "No! His name is John."
61 They said to her, "No one in your family
has that name."

62 Then they talked to his father with
their hands to find out what he would
name the child. 63 He asked for something
to write on. He wrote, "His name is John."
They were all surprised and wondered
about it. 64 Zacharias was able to talk from
that time on and he gave thanks to God.

65 All those who lived near them were
afraid. The news of what had happened
was told through all the hill country of
Judea. 66 And all who heard those words
remembered them and said, "What is this
child going to be?" For the hand of the
Lord was on him.

Zacharias's Song of Thanks to God

67 Zacharias, the father of John, was filled
with the Holy Spirit. He told what was
going to happen, saying, 68 "Let us thank
the Lord God of Israel. He has bought
His people and made them free. 69 He has
raised up from the family of David One
Who saves people from the punishment
of their sins. 70 His holy early preachers
told us this long ago. 71 God told us that
we should be saved from those who hate
us and from all those who work against us.
72 He would show loving-kindness to our
early fathers. He would remember His
holy promise. 73 God promised this to our
early father Abraham. 74 He promised that
we would be saved from those who hate
us and that we might worship Him without being afraid. 75 We can be holy and
right with God all the days of our life.

76 "And you, my son, will be the one who
speaks for the Most High. For you will go
before the Lord to make the way ready for
Him. 77 You will tell His people how to be
saved from the punishment of sin by being
forgiven of their sins. 78 Because the heart
of our God is full of loving-kindness for us,
a light from heaven will shine on us. 79 It
will give light to those who live in darkness and are under the shadow of death. It
will lead our feet in the way of peace."

80 The child grew and became strong in
spirit. He lived in a desert until the day he
started to preach to the Jews.

The Birth of Jesus
(Matthew 1:18–25)

2 In those days Caesar Augustus sent
out word that the name of every person in the Roman nation must be written
in the books of the nation. 2 This first writing took place while Quirinius was ruler
of Syria.

3 So all the people went to their own
cities to have their names written in the
books of the nation. 4 Joseph went up
from the town of Nazareth in the country
of Galilee to the town of Bethlehem. It was
known as the city of David. He went there
because he was from the family of David.
5 Joseph went to have his and Mary's

names written in the books of the nation. Mary was his promised wife and soon to become a mother.

6 While they were there in Bethlehem, the time came for Mary to give birth to her baby. 7 Her first son was born. She put cloth around Him and laid Him in a place where cattle are fed. There was no room for them in the place where people stay for the night.

The Shepherds Learn of the Birth of Jesus

8 In the same country there were shepherds in the fields. They were watching their flocks of sheep at night. 9 The angel of the Lord came to them. The shining-greatness of the Lord shone around them. They were very much afraid. 10 The angel said to them, "Do not be afraid. See! I bring you good news of great joy which is for all people. 11 Today, One Who saves from the punishment of sin has been born in the city of David. He is Christ the Lord. 12 There will be something special for you to see. This is the way you will know Him. You will find the Baby with cloth around Him, lying in a place where cattle are fed." 13 At once many angels from heaven were seen, along with the angel, giving thanks to God. They were saying, 14 "Greatness and honor to our God in the highest heaven and peace on earth among men who please Him."

The Shepherds Go to Bethlehem

15 The angels went from the shepherds back to heaven. The shepherds said to each other, "Let us go now to Bethlehem and see what has happened. The Lord has told us about this." 16 They went fast and found Mary and Joseph. They found the Baby lying in a place where cattle are fed. 17 When they saw the Child, they told what the angel said about Him. 18 All who heard it were surprised at what the shepherds told them. 19 But Mary hid all these words in her heart. She thought about them much. 20 The shepherds went back full of joy. They thanked God for all they had heard and seen. It happened as the angel had told them.

Jesus Is Taken to the House of God

21 When eight days were over, they did the religious act of becoming a Jew on the Child. He was named Jesus. This name was given to Him by the angel when Mary was told He was to be born. 22 When the days were over for her to be made pure

as it was written in the Law of Moses, they took Jesus to Jerusalem to give Him to the Lord. 23 It is written in the Law of the Lord, "The first-born male born of a woman will be called holy to the Lord." 24 They were to give a gift of two turtle-doves or two young birds on the altar in worship to the Lord. This was written in the Law of the Lord.

Simeon's Song of Thanks

25 There was a man in Jerusalem by the name of Simeon. He was a good man and very religious. He was looking for the time when the Jewish nation would be saved. The Holy Spirit was on him. 26 The Holy Spirit made it known to Simeon that he would not die before he had seen God's Chosen One. 27 He came to the house of God being led by the Holy Spirit. The parents took Jesus to the house of God. They came to do what the Law said must be done. 28 Then Simeon took Jesus in his arms. He gave honor to Him and thanked God, saying,

29 "Lord, now let me die in peace, as You have said. 30 My eyes have seen the One Who will save men from the punishment of their sins. 31 You have made Him ready in the sight of all nations. 32 He will be a light to shine on the people who are not Jews. He will be the shining-greatness of Your people the Jews." 33 Joseph and the mother of Jesus were surprised and wondered about these words which were said about Jesus. 34 Simeon honored them and said to Mary the mother of Jesus, "See! This Child will make many people fall and many people rise in the Jewish nation. He will be spoken against. 35 A sword will cut through your soul. By this the thoughts of many hearts will be understood."

Anna Gives Thanks for Jesus

36 Anna was a woman who spoke God's Word. She was the daughter of Phanuel of the family group of Asher. Anna was many years old. She had lived with her husband seven years after she was married. 37 Her husband had died and she had lived without a husband eighty-four years. Yet she did not go away from the house of God. She served God day and night, praying and going without food so she could pray better. 38 At that time she came and gave thanks to God. She told the people in Jerusalem about Jesus. They were looking for the One to save them from the punishment of their sins and to set them free.

They Return to Nazareth
(Matthew 2:19–23)

39 When Joseph and Mary had done everything the Law said to do, they went back to Nazareth in Galilee. 40 The Child grew and became strong in spirit. He was filled with wisdom and the loving-favor of God was on Him.

41 His parents went to Jerusalem every year for the special religious gathering to remember how the Jews left Egypt. 42 When He was twelve years old, they went up to Jerusalem as they had done before. 43 When the days of the special supper were over, they started back to their town. But the boy Jesus was still in Jerusalem. His parents did not know it. 44 They thought Jesus was with the others of the group. They walked for one day. Then they looked for Him among their family and friends.

45 When they could not find Jesus, they turned back to Jerusalem to look for Him. 46 Three days later they found Him in the house of God. He was sitting among the teachers. He was hearing what they said and asking questions. 47 All those who heard Him were surprised and wondered about His understanding and at what He said. 48 When His parents saw Him, they were surprised. His mother said to Him, "My Son, why have You done this to us? See! Your father and I have had much sorrow looking for You." 49 He said to them, "Why were you looking for Me? Do you not know that I must be in My Father's house?" 50 They did not understand the things He said to them.

51 He went with them to Nazareth and obeyed them. But His mother kept all these words in her heart. 52 Jesus grew strong in mind and body. He grew in favor with God and men.

John the Baptist Makes the Way Ready for Jesus
(Matthew 3:1–12; Mark 1:1–8; John 1:15–28)

3 Tiberius Caesar had been ruler for fifteen years. Pontius Pilate was ruler of the country of Judea. Herod was the ruler of the country of Galilee. His brother Philip was the ruler of the countries of Ituraea and Trachonitis. Lysanias was the ruler of the country of Abilene. 2 Annas and Caiaphas were the head religious leaders.

The Word of God came to John the Baptist, the son of Zacharias. John was in the desert. 3 He went into all the country around the Jordan River. He preached that people should be baptized because they were sorry for their sins and had turned from them, and they would be forgiven. 4 The early preacher Isaiah wrote these words: "His voice calls out in the desert. 'Make the way ready for the Lord. Make the road straight for Him! 5 Every valley will be filled and every mountain and hill will be brought down. The turns in the road will be made straight and the rough places will be made smooth. 6 And all men will see God saving people from the punishment of their sins.'" (Isaiah 40:3–5)

7 John said to the people who came to be baptized by him, "You family of snakes! Who told you how to keep from the anger of God that is coming? 8 Do something to let me see that you have turned from your sins. Do not begin to say to yourselves, 'We have Abraham as our father.' I tell you, God can make children for Abraham out of these stones. 9 Even now the ax is on the root of the trees. Every tree that does not give good fruit is cut down and thrown into the fire." 10 The people asked him, "Then what should we do?" 11 He answered them, "If you have two coats, give one to him who has none. If you have food, you must share some." 12 Tax-gatherers came to be baptized also. They asked him, "Teacher, what are we to do?" 13 He said to them, "Do not take more money from people than you should." 14 Also soldiers asked him, "What are we to do?" He answered them, "Take no money from anyone by using your own strength. Do not lie about anyone. Be happy with the pay you get."

15 The people were looking for something to happen. They were thinking in their hearts about John the Baptist. They wondered if he might be the Christ. 16 But John said to all of them, "I baptize you with water. There is One coming Who is greater than I. I am not good enough to get down and help Him take off His shoes. He will baptize you with the Holy Spirit and with fire. 17 He comes ready to clean the grain. He will gather the grain and clean it all. He will put the clean grain into a building. But He will burn that which is no good with a fire that cannot be put out."

John the Baptist Is Put in Prison
(Matthew 14:1–5; Mark 6:14–20)

18 John spoke much more as he preached the Good News to the people. 19 He had also spoken sharp words to Herod the

ruler because of Herodias. She was his brother Philip's wife. And John spoke to Herod about all the wrongs he had done. 20 To all these, Herod added another sin by putting John in prison.

The Baptism of Jesus
Matthew 3:13–17; Mark 1:9–11; John 1:29–34)

21 When all the people were being baptized, Jesus was baptized also. As He prayed, the heaven opened. 22 The Holy Spirit came down on Him in a body like a dove. A voice came from heaven and said, "You are My much-loved Son. I am very happy with You."

The Family of Jesus through Mary
(Matthew 1:1–17)

23 Jesus was about thirty years old when He began His work. People thought Jesus was the son of Joseph, the son of Heli. 24 Heli was the son of Matthat. Matthat was the son of Levi. Levi was the son of Melchi. Melchi was the son of Jannai. Jannai was the son of Joseph. 25 Joseph was the son of Mattathias. Mattathias was the son of Amos. Amos was the son of Nahum. Nahum was the son of Esli. Esli was the son of Naggai. 26 Naggai was the son of Maath. Maath was the son of Mattathias. Mattathias was the son of Semein. Semein was the son of Josech. Josech was the son of Juda. 27 Juda was the son of Johanan. Johanan was the son of Rhesa. Rhesa was the son of Zerubbabel. Zerubbabel was the son of Salathiel. Salathiel was the son of Neri. 28 Neri was the son of Melchi. Melchi was the son of Addi. Addi was the son of Cosam. Cosam was the son of Elmadam. Elmadam was the son of Er. 29 Er was the son of Joshua. Joshua was the son of Eliezer. Eliezer was the son of Jorim. Jorim was the son of Matthat. Matthat was the son of Levi. 30 Levi was the son of Simeon. Simeon was the son of Judah. Judah was the son of Joseph. Joseph was the son of Janam. Janam was the son of Eliakim. 31 Eliakim was the son of Melea. Melea was the son of Menna. Menna was the son of Mattatha. Mattatha was the son of Nathan. Nathan was the son of David. 32 David was the son of Jesse. Jesse was the son of Obed. Obed was the son of Boaz. Boaz was the son of Salmon. Salmon was the son of Nahshon. 33 Nahshon was the son of Amminadab. Amminadab was the son of Admin. Admin was the son of Ram.

Ram was the son of Hezron. Hezron was the son of Perez. Perez was the son of Judah. 34 Judah was the son of Jacob. Jacob was the son of Isaac. Isaac was the son of Abraham. Abraham was the son of Terah. Terah was the son of Nahor. 35 Nahor was the son of Serug. Serug was the son of Ragau. Ragau was the son of Peleg. Peleg was the son of Eber. Eber was the son of Shelah. 36 Shelah was the son of Cainan. Cainan was the son of Arphaxad. Arphaxad was the son of Shem. Shem was the son of Noah. Noah was the son of Lamech. 37 Lamech was the son of Methuselah. Methuselah was the son of Enoch. Enoch was the son of Jared. Jared was the son of Mahalaleel. Mahalaleel was the son of Cainan. 38 Cainan was the son of Enos. Enos was the son of Seth. Seth was the son of Adam. Adam was the son of God.

Jesus Is Tempted
(Matthew 4:1–11; Mark 1:12–13)

4 Jesus was full of the Holy Spirit when He returned from the Jordan River. Then He was led by the Holy Spirit to a desert. 2 He was tempted by the devil for forty days and He ate nothing during that time. After that He was hungry. 3 The devil said to Him, "If You are the Son of God, tell this stone to be made into bread." 4 Jesus said to him, "It is written, 'Man is not to live by bread alone.' " (Deuteronomy 8:3) 5 The devil took Jesus up on a high mountain. He had Jesus look at all the nations of the world at one time. 6 The devil said to Jesus, "I will give You all this power and greatness. It has been given to me. I can give it to anyone I want to. 7 If You will worship me, all this will be Yours." 8 Jesus said to the devil, "Get behind Me, Satan! For it is written, 'You must worship the Lord your God. You must obey Him only.' " (Deuteronomy 6:13) 9 Then the devil took Jesus up to Jerusalem. He had Jesus stand on the highest part of the house of God. The devil said to Jesus, "If You are the Son of God, throw Yourself down from here. 10 For it is written, 'He has told His angels to care for You and to keep You. 11 In their hands they will hold You up. Then Your foot will not hit against a stone.' " (Psalm 91:11–12) 12 Jesus said to the devil, "It is written, 'You must not tempt the Lord your God.' " (Deuteronomy 6:16) 13 When the devil finished tempting Jesus in every way, he went away from Jesus for awhile.

Jesus Preaches in Galilee
(Matthew 4:12–17; Mark 1:14–15)

14 Jesus went back to Galilee in the power of the Holy Spirit. People talked about Him so much that He was well-known through all the country. **15** Jesus taught in their places of worship and was honored by all people.

In Nazareth They Do Not Believe in Jesus

16 Jesus came to Nazareth where He had grown up. As He had done before, He went into the Jewish place of worship on the Day of Rest. Then He stood up to read. **17** Someone handed Him the book of the early preacher Isaiah. He opened it and found the place where it was written, **18** "The Spirit of the Lord is on Me. He has put His hand on Me to preach the Good News to poor people. He has sent Me to heal those with a sad heart. He has sent Me to tell those who are being held that they can go free. He has sent Me to make the blind to see and to free those who are held because of trouble. **19** He sent Me to tell of the time when men can receive favor with the Lord." (Isaiah 61:1–2)

20 Jesus closed the book. Then He gave it back to the leader and sat down. All those in the Jewish place of worship kept their eyes on Him. **21** Then He began to say to them, "The Holy Writings you have just heard have been completed today."

22 They all spoke well of Jesus and agreed with the words He spoke. They said, "Is not this the son of Joseph?" **23** He said to them, "I wonder if you will tell this old saying to Me, 'Doctor, heal Yourself. What You did in the city of Capernaum, do in Your own country'." **24** He said, "A man who speaks for God is not respected in his own country. **25** It is true that there were many women whose husbands had died in the Jewish land when Elijah lived. For three and a half years there was no rain and there was very little food in the land. **26** Elijah was sent to none of them, but he was sent to a woman in the city of Zarephath in the land of Sidon. This woman's husband had died. **27** There were many people in the Jewish land who had a bad skin disease when the early preacher Elisha lived. None of them was healed. But Naaman from the country of Syria was healed."

28 All those in the Jewish place of worship were angry when they heard His words. **29** They got up and took Jesus out of town to the top of a high hill. They wanted to throw Him over the side. **30** But Jesus got away from among them and went on His way.

Jesus Heals a Man with a Demon
(Mark 1:21–28)

31 Jesus went down to Capernaum in Galilee. He taught them on the Days of Rest. **32** The people were surprised and wondered about His teaching. His words had power. **33** A man in the Jewish place of worship had a demon. He cried with a loud voice, **34** "What do You want of us, Jesus of Nazareth? I know Who You are. You are the Holy One of God." **35** Jesus spoke sharp words to the demon and said, "Do not talk! Come out of him!" When the demon had thrown the man down, he came out without hurting the man.

36 The people were all surprised. They asked each other, "What kind of word is this? He speaks to the demons with power and they come out!" **37** The news about Jesus went through all the country.

Peter's Mother-in-Law Is Healed
(Matthew 8:14–15; Mark 1:29–31)

38 Jesus went away from the Jewish place of worship and went into Simon's house. Simon's mother-in-law was in bed, very sick. They asked Jesus to help her. **39** He stood by her and told the disease to leave. It went from her. At once she got up and cared for them.

Jesus Heals in Galilee
(Matthew 8:16–17; Mark 1:32–34)

40 As the sun went down, the people took all that were sick with many kinds of diseases to Jesus. He put His hands on all of them and they were healed. **41** Also demons came out of many people. The demons cried out and said, "You are Christ, the Son of God." Jesus spoke strong words to them and would not let them speak. They knew He was the Christ.

Jesus Keeps On Preaching in Galilee
(Matthew 4:23–25; Mark 1:35–39)

42 In the morning He went out to a desert. The people looked for Him. When they found Him, they were trying to keep Him from going away from them. **43** He said to them, "I must preach about the holy nation of God in other cities also. This is why I was sent." **44** And He kept on preaching in the Jewish places of worship in Galilee.

Jesus Calls Simon and James and John
(Matthew 4:18–22; Mark 1:16–20)

5 While Jesus was standing by the lake of Gennesaret, many people pushed to get near Him. They wanted to hear the Word of God. 2 Jesus saw two boats on the shore. The fishermen were not there because they were washing their nets. 3 Jesus got into a boat which belonged to Simon. Jesus asked him to push it out a little way from land. Then He sat down and taught the people from the boat.

4 When He had finished speaking, He said to Simon, "Push out into the deep water. Let down your nets for some fish." 5 Simon said to Him, "Teacher, we have worked all night and we have caught nothing. But because You told me to, I will let the net down." 6 When they had done this, they caught so many fish, their net started to break. 7 They called to their friends working in the other boat to come and help them. They came and both boats were so full of fish they began to sink. 8 When Simon Peter saw it, he got down at the feet of Jesus. He said, "Go away from me, Lord, because I am a sinful man." 9 He and all those with him were surprised and wondered about the many fish. 10 James and John, the sons of Zebedee, were surprised also. They were working together with Simon. Then Jesus said to Simon, "Do not be afraid. From now on you will fish for men." 11 When they came to land with their boats, they left everything and followed Jesus.

Jesus Heals a Man with a Bad Skin Disease
(Matthew 8:1–4; Mark 1:40–45)

12 While Jesus was in one of the towns, a man came to Him with a bad skin disease over all his body. When he saw Jesus, he got down on his face before Him. He begged Him, saying, "Lord, if You are willing, You can heal me." 13 Jesus put His hand on him and said, "I will, be healed." At once the disease went away from him. 14 Then Jesus told him to tell no one. He said, "Go and let the religious leader of the Jews see you. Give the gift on the altar in worship that Moses told you to give when a man is healed of a disease. This will show the leaders you have been healed." 15 The news about Jesus went out all the more. Many people came to hear Jesus and to be healed of their diseases. 16 Then He went away by Himself to pray in a desert.

Jesus Heals a Man Let Down through the Roof of a House
(Matthew 9:1–8; Mark 2:1–12)

17 On one of the days while Jesus was teaching, some proud religious law-keepers and teachers of the Law were sitting by Him. They had come from every town in the countries of Galilee and Judea and from Jerusalem. The power of the Lord was there to heal them. 18 Some men took a man who was not able to move his body to Jesus. He was carried on a bed. They looked for a way to take the man into the house where Jesus was. 19 But they could not find a way to take him in because of so many people. They made a hole in the roof over where Jesus stood. Then they let the bed with the sick man on it down before Jesus. 20 When Jesus saw their faith, He said to the man, "Friend, your sins are forgiven."

21 The teachers of the Law and the proud religious law-keepers thought to themselves, "Who is this Man Who speaks as if He is God? Who can forgive sins but God only?" 22 Jesus knew what they were thinking. He said to them, "Why do you think this way in your hearts? 23 Which is easier to say, 'Your sins are forgiven,' or, 'Get up and walk'?

24 "So that you may know the Son of Man has the right and the power on earth to forgive sins," He said to the man who could not move his body, "I say to you, get up. Take your bed and go to your home." 25 At once the sick man got up in front of them. He took his bed and went to his home thanking God. 26 All those who were there were surprised and gave thanks to God, saying, "We have seen very special things today."

Jesus Calls Matthew
(Matthew 9:9–13; Mark 2:13–17)

27 After this Jesus went out and saw a man who gathered taxes. His name was Levi (Matthew). Levi was sitting at his work. Jesus said to him, "Follow Me." 28 Levi got up, left everything and followed Jesus. 29 Levi made a big supper for Jesus in his house. Many men who gathered taxes and other people sat down with them. 30 The teachers of the Law and the proud religious law-keepers talked against the followers of Jesus. They said, "Why do You eat and drink with men who gather taxes and with sinners?" 31 Jesus said to them, "People who are well do not need a doctor. Only those who are sick need a doctor. 32 I

have not come to call good people. I have come to call sinners to be sorry for their sins and to turn from them."

Jesus Teaches about Going without Food So You Can Pray Better
(Matthew 9:14–17; Mark 2:18–22)

33 They asked Jesus, "Why do the followers of John and of the proud religious law-keepers go without food so they can pray better, but Your followers keep on eating and drinking?" 34 Jesus answered them, "Can the friends at a wedding be sorry when the man just married is with them? 35 The days will come when the man just married will be taken from them. Then they will not eat food so they can pray better in those days."

The Picture-Story of the Cloth and the Bags

36 Then Jesus told them a picture-story. He said, "No one sews a piece of cloth from a new coat on an old coat. If he does, the new coat will have a hole. The new piece and the old coat will not be the same. 37 No man puts new wine into old skin bags. If they did, the skins would break and the wine would run out. The bags would be no good. 38 New wine must be put into new bags and both are kept safe. 39 No one wants new wine after drinking old wine. He says, 'The old wine is better.'"

Jesus Teaches about the Day of Rest
(Matthew 12:1–8; Mark 2:23–28)

6 On the next Day of Rest Jesus was walking through the grain-fields. His followers picked grain. They rubbed it in their hands and ate it. 2 Some of the proud religious law-keepers said to them, "Why are you doing what the Law says should not be done on the Day of Rest?" 3 Jesus answered them, "Have you not read what David did when he and his men were hungry? 4 He went into the house of God and ate the special bread used in the religious worship. He gave some to those who were with him also. The Law says only the religious leaders may eat that bread. 5 The Son of Man is Lord of the Day of Rest also."

Jesus Heals on the Day of Rest
(Matthew 12:9–14; Mark 3:1–6)

6 On another Day of Rest Jesus went into the Jewish place of worship and taught. A man with a dried-up hand was there. 7 The teachers of the Law and the proud religious law-keepers watched to see if He would heal on the Day of Rest. They wanted to have something to say against Him. 8 Jesus knew what they were thinking. He said to the man with the dried-up hand, "Stand up and come here." The man stood up and went to Jesus. 9 Then Jesus said to them, "I will ask you one thing. Does the Law say to do good on the Day of Rest or to do bad? To save life or to kill?" 10 Jesus looked around at them all and said to the man, "Put out your hand." He put it out and his hand was healed. It was as good as his other hand. 11 The teachers of the Law and the proud religious law-keepers were filled with anger. They talked with each other about what they might do to Jesus.

Jesus Calls His Twelve Followers
(Matthew 10:1–4; Mark 3:13–19)

12 One day Jesus went up on a mountain to pray. He prayed all night to God. 13 In the morning He called His followers to Him. He chose twelve of them and called them. 14 There were Simon, whom He also named Peter, and his brother Andrew. There were James and John, Philip and Bartholomew, 15 Matthew and Thomas. There were James the son of Alphaeus, and Simon the Canaanite. 16 There were Judas, who was the brother of James, and Judas Iscariot who would hand Jesus over to be killed.

Jesus Heals Many People
(Matthew 12:15–21; Mark 3:7–12)

17 Then Jesus came down and stood on a plain with many of His followers. Many people came from the country of Judea and from Jerusalem and from the cities of Tyre and Sidon. They came to hear Him and to be healed of their diseases. 18 Those who were troubled with demons came and were healed. 19 All the people tried to put their hands on Jesus. Power came from Him and He healed them all.

Jesus Teaches on the Mountain
(Matthew 5:1–7:29)

20 He looked at His followers and said, "Those of you who are poor are happy, because the holy nation of God is yours. 21 Those of you who are hungry now are happy, because you will be filled. Those of you who have sorrow now are happy, because you will laugh. 22 You are happy when men hate you and do not want you around and put shame on you because you trust in Me. 23 Be glad in that day. Be full of joy for your reward is much in heaven.

Their fathers did these things to the early preachers.

24 "It is bad for you who are rich. You are receiving all that you will get. 25 It is bad for you who are full. You will be hungry. It is bad for you who laugh now. You will have sorrow and you will cry. 26 It is bad for you when everyone speaks well of you. In the same way, their fathers spoke well of the false teachers.

Jesus Teaches What the Law Says about Love

27 "I say to you who hear Me, love those who work against you. Do good to those who hate you. 28 Respect and give thanks for those who try to bring bad to you. Pray for those who make it very hard for you. 29 Whoever hits you on one side of the face, turn so he can hit the other side also. Whoever takes your coat, give him your shirt also. 30 Give to any person who asks you for something. If a person takes something from you, do not ask for it back. 31 Do for other people what you would like to have them do for you.

32 "If you love those who love you, what pay can you expect from that? Sinners also love those who love them. 33 If you do good to those who do good to you, what pay can you expect from that? Sinners also do good to those who do good to them. 34 If you let people use your things and expect to get something back, what pay can you expect from that? Even sinners let sinners use things and they expect to get something back. 35 But love those who hate you. Do good to them. Let them use your things and do not expect something back. Your reward will be much. You will be the children of the Most High. He is kind to those who are not thankful and to those who are full of sin.

Jesus Teaches about Finding Bad in Others

36 "You must have loving-kindness just as your Father has loving-kindness. 37 Do not say what is wrong in other people's lives. Then other people will not say what is wrong in your life. Do not say someone is guilty. Then other people will not say you are guilty. Forgive other people and other people will forgive you.

38 "Give, and it will be given to you. You will have more than enough. It can be pushed down and shaken together and it will still run over as it is given to you. The way you give to others is the way you will receive in return."

39 Jesus used a picture-story as He spoke to them. He said, "Can one blind man lead another blind man? Will they not fall into the ditch together? 40 The follower is not more important than his teacher. But everyone who learns well will be like his teacher.

Jesus Teaches about Saying What Is Wrong in Others

41 "Why do you look at the small piece of wood in your brother's eye and do not see the big piece of wood in your own eye? 42 How can you say to your brother, 'Let me take that small piece of wood out of your eye,' when you do not see the big piece of wood in your own eye? You pretend to be someone you are not. First, take the big piece of wood out of your own eye. Then you can see better to take the small piece of wood out of your brother's eye.

Jesus Teaches about False Teachers

43 "A good tree cannot have bad fruit. A bad tree cannot have good fruit. 44 For every tree is known by its own fruit. Men do not gather figs from thorns. They do not gather grapes from thistles. 45 Good comes from a good man because of the riches he has in his heart. Sin comes from a sinful man because of the sin he has in his heart. The mouth speaks of what the heart is full of.

Jesus Teaches about Houses Built on Rock and Sand

46 "And why do you call Me, 'Lord, Lord,' but do not do what I say? 47 Whoever comes to Me and hears and does what I say, I will show you who he is like. 48 He is like a man who built a house. He dug deep to put the building on rock. When the water came up and the river beat against the house, the building could not be shaken because it was built on rock. 49 But he who hears and does not do what I say, is like a man who built a house on nothing but earth. The water beat against the house. At once it fell and was destroyed."

The Healing of the Captain's Helper
(Matthew 8:5–13)

7 When Jesus had finished teaching the people, He went back to Capernaum. 2 A captain of the army had a servant whom he thought much of. This servant was very sick and was about to die. 3 When the captain heard of Jesus, he sent some Jewish leaders to Him. They were to ask if He would come and heal this

servant. 4 They came to Jesus and begged Him, saying, "The man is respected and should have this done for him. 5 He loves our nation and has built our Jewish place of worship."

6 Jesus went with them. When He was not far from the house, the captain told some friends to tell this to Jesus, "Lord, do not take the time to come to my house, because I am not good enough. 7 And I am not good enough to come to You. But just say the word and my servant will be healed. 8 For I am a man who works for someone else also, and I have soldiers who work for me. I say to this man, 'Go!' and he goes. I say to another, 'Come!' and he comes. I say to my workman, 'Do this!' and he does it."

9 Jesus was surprised when He heard this. He turned to the people following Him and said, "I tell you, I have not found so much faith even in the Jewish nation." 10 Those who had been sent went back to the captain's house and found the servant well again.

The Son of a Woman Whose Husband Had Died Is Raised from the Dead

11 The next day Jesus went to a city called Nain. His followers and many other people went with Him. 12 When they came near the city gate, a dead man was being carried out. He was the only son of a woman whose husband had died. Many people of the city were with her. 13 When the Lord saw her, He had loving-pity for her and said, "Do not cry." 14 He went and put His hand on the box in which the dead man was carried. The men who were carrying it, stopped. Jesus said, "Young man, I say to you, get up!" 15 The man who was dead sat up and began to talk. Then Jesus gave him to his mother. 16 Everyone was afraid and they gave thanks to God. They said, "A great Man Who speaks for God has come among us! God has cared for His people!" 17 The news about Jesus went through all the country of Judea and over all the land.

John the Baptist Asks about Jesus
(Matthew 11:1-6)

18 The followers of John the Baptist told him about all these things. 19 John called two of his followers and sent them to Jesus to ask, "Are You the One Who is to come? Or are we to look for another?" 20 The men came to Jesus and said, "John the Baptist sent us to ask You, 'Are You the One Who is to come? Or are we to look for another?'"

21 At that time Jesus was healing many people of all kinds of sickness and disease and was putting out demons. Many that were blind were able to see. 22 Jesus said to John's followers, "Go back to John the Baptist and tell him what you have seen and heard. Tell him the blind are made to see. Those who could not walk, are walking. Those with a bad skin disease are healed. Those who could not hear, are hearing. The dead are raised to life and poor people have the Good News preached to them. 23 The person who is not ashamed of Me and does not turn away from Me is happy."

Jesus Tells about John the Baptist
(Matthew 11:7-19)

24 As John's followers were going away, Jesus began to tell the people about John the Baptist. He said, "Why did you go out to the desert? Did you go out to see a small tree moving in the wind? 25 What did you go out to see? A man dressed in good clothes? Those who are dressed in good clothes are in the houses of kings. 26 But what did you go to see? One who speaks for God? Yes, I tell you, he is more than one who speaks for God. 27 This is the man the Holy Writings spoke of when they said, 'See! I will send My helper to carry news ahead of You. He will make Your way ready for You!' (Malachi 3:1; Isaiah 40:3) 28 "I tell you, of those born of women, there is no one greater than John the Baptist. The least in the holy nation of God is greater than he."

29 All the people who heard Jesus and those who gathered taxes showed they knew God was right and were baptized by John. 30 But the proud religious law-keepers and the men who knew the Law would not listen. They would not be baptized by John and they did not receive what God had for them.

Jesus Speaks against the People of This Day

31 Then the Lord said, "What are the people of this day like? 32 They are like children playing in front of stores. They call to their friends, 'We have played music for you, but you did not dance. We have had sorrow for you, but you did not have sorrow.' 33 John the Baptist did not come eating bread or drinking wine and you say, 'He has a demon.' 34 The Son of Man came eating and drinking and you say, 'See! He likes food and wine. He is a

friend of men who gather taxes and of sinners!' 35 Wisdom is shown to be right by those who are wise."

A Woman Puts Special Perfume on the Feet of Jesus

36 One of the proud religious law-keepers wanted Jesus to eat with him. Jesus went to his house and sat down to eat. 37 There was a woman in the city who was a sinner. She knew Jesus was eating in the house of the proud religious law-keeper. She brought a jar of special perfume. 38 Then she stood behind Him by His feet and cried. Her tears wet His feet and she dried them with her hair. She kissed His feet and put the special perfume on them.

39 The proud religious law-keeper who had asked Jesus to eat with him saw this. He said to himself, "If this Man were One Who speaks for God, He would know who and what kind of a woman put her hands on Him. She is a sinner." 40 Jesus said to him, "I have something to say to you, Simon." And Simon said, "Teacher, say it."

41 "There were two men who owed a certain man some money. The one man owed 500 pieces of silver money. The other man owed 50 pieces of silver money. 42 Neither one of them had any money, so he told them they did not have to pay him back. Tell Me, which one would love him the most?" 43 Simon said, "I think it would be the one who owed the most." And Jesus said to him, "You have said the right thing."

44 He turned to the woman and said to Simon, "Do you see this woman? I came into your house and you gave Me no water to wash My feet. She washed My feet with her tears and dried them with the hairs of her head. 45 You gave me no kiss, but this woman has kissed my feet from the time I came in. 46 You did not put even oil on My head but this woman has put special perfume on My feet. 47 I tell you, her many sins are forgiven because she loves much. But the one who has been forgiven little, loves little." 48 Then He said to the woman, "Your sins are forgiven." 49 Those who were eating with Him began to say to themselves, "Who is this Man Who even forgives sins?" 50 He said to the woman, "Your faith has saved you from the punishment of sin. Go in peace."

Jesus Teaches in Galilee

8 After this Jesus went to all the cities and towns preaching and telling the Good News about the holy nation of God. The twelve followers were with Him. 2 Some women who had been healed of demons and diseases were with Him. Mary Magdalene, who had had seven demons put out of her, was one of them. 3 Joanna, the wife of Chuza who was one of Herod's helpers, was another one. Susanna and many others also cared for Jesus by using what they had.

The Picture-Story of the Man Who Planted Seed
(Matthew 13:1–52; Mark 4:1–34)

4 Many people came together from every town to Jesus. He told them a picture-story.

5 "A man went out to plant seed. As he planted the seed, some fell by the side of the road. It was walked on and birds came and ate it. 6 Some seed fell between rocks. As soon as it started to grow, it dried up because it had no water. 7 Some seed fell among thorns. The thorns grew and did not give the seed room to grow. 8 Some seed fell on good ground. It grew and gave one hundred times as much grain." When Jesus had finished saying this, He cried out, "You have ears, then listen!"

9 His followers asked Him what this picture-story meant. 10 Jesus said, "You were given the secrets about the holy nation of God. Others are told picture-stories. As they look, they do not see. As they hear, they do not understand.

Jesus Tells about the Man Who Planted Seed

11 "This is what the picture-story means. The seed is the Word of God. 12 Those by the side of the road hear the Word. Then the devil comes and takes the Word from their hearts. He does not want them to believe and be saved from the punishment of sin. 13 Those which fell among rocks are those who when they hear the Word receive it with joy. These have no root. For awhile they believe, but when they are tempted they give up. 14 Those which fell among thorns hear the Word but go their own way. The cares of this life let the thorns grow. A love for money lets the thorns grow also. And the fun of this life lets the thorns grow. Their grain never becomes full-grown. 15 But those which fell on good ground have heard the Word. They keep it in a good and true heart and they keep on giving good grain.

The Picture-Story of the Lamp

16 "No man lights a lamp and puts it under a pail or under a bed. He puts it on a lampstand so all who come into the room may see it. 17 Nothing is secret but what will be known. Anything that is hidden will be brought into the light. 18 Be careful how you listen! Whoever has, to him will be given. Whoever does not have, even the little he has will be taken from him."

The New Kind of Family
(Matthew 12:46–50; Mark 3:31–35)

19 The mother of Jesus and His brothers came to Him. They could not get near Him because of so many people. 20 Someone said to Jesus, "Your mother and brothers are standing outside. They want to see You." 21 Jesus said to them, "My mother and brothers are these who hear the Word of God and do it."

The Wind and Waves Obey Jesus
(Matthew 8:23–27; Mark 4:35–41)

22 On one of those days Jesus and His followers got into a boat. Jesus said to them, "Let us go over to the other side of the lake." Then they pushed out into the water. 23 As they were going, Jesus fell asleep. A wind storm came over the lake. The boat was filling with water and they were in danger. 24 The followers came to awake Jesus. They said, "Teacher! Teacher! We are going to die!" Then Jesus got up and spoke sharp words to the wind and the high waves. The wind stopped blowing and there were no more waves. 25 He said to them, "Where is your faith?" The followers were surprised and afraid. They said to each other, "What kind of a man is He? He speaks to the wind and the waves and they obey Him."

Demons Ask Jesus to Let Them Live in Pigs
(Matthew 8:28–34; Mark 5:1–20)

26 They came to the land of the Gadarenes, which is on the other side of the country of Galilee. 27 As Jesus stepped out on land, a man met Him who had come from the city. This man had demons in him. For a long time he had worn no clothes. He did not live in a house, but lived among the graves. 28 When he saw Jesus, he got down before Him and cried with a loud voice, "What do You want with me, Jesus, Son of the Most High? I beg of You not to hurt me!" 29 For Jesus had spoken to the demon to come out of the man. Many

times the demon had taken hold of him. The man had to be tied with chains. But he would break the chains and be taken by the demon into the desert.

30 Jesus asked him, "What is your name?" And the demon answered, "Many," because many demons had gone into him. 31 The demons asked Jesus not to send them to the hole without a bottom in the earth. 32 There were many pigs feeding on the side of the mountain. The demons begged Jesus to let them go into the pigs. Jesus said they could. 33 The demons came out of the man and went into the pigs. Then the many pigs ran down the side of the mountain into the water and died.

34 The men who cared for the pigs ran fast and told what had happened in the town and in the country. 35 People came to see what had happened. They came to Jesus and saw the man from whom the demons had been sent. He was sitting at the feet of Jesus with clothes on and had the right use of his mind. The people were afraid. 36 Those who had seen it told how the man who had had the demons was healed. 37 Then all the people of the country of the Gadarenes begged Jesus to go away from them. They were very much afraid. Jesus got into the boat and went back to the other side.

38 The man out of whom the demons had gone begged to go with Jesus. But Jesus sent him away and said, 39 "Go back to your house and tell everything God has done for you." He went back and told all the people of the city what great things Jesus had done for him.

Two Are Healed through Faith
(Matthew 9:18–26; Mark 5:21–43)

40 Many people were glad to see Jesus when He got back. They were waiting for Him. 41 A man named Jairus was a leader of the Jewish place of worship. As he came to Jesus, he got down at His feet. He asked Jesus if He would come to his house. 42 He had only one daughter and she was dying. This girl was about twelve years old. As Jesus went, the people pushed Him from every side.

43 A woman had been sick for twelve years with a flow of blood. (*She had spent all the money she had on doctors.) But she could not be healed by anyone. 44 She came behind Jesus and touched the bottom of His coat. At once the flow of blood stopped. 45 Jesus said, "Who

touched Me?" Everyone said that they had not touched Him. Peter said, "Teacher, so many people are pushing You from every side and You say, 'Who touched Me?'" 46 Then Jesus said, "Someone touched Me because I know power has gone from Me." 47 When the woman saw she could not hide it, she came shaking. She got down before Jesus. Then she told Jesus in front of all the people why she had touched Him. She told how she was healed at once. 48 Jesus said to her, "Daughter, your faith has healed you. Go in peace."

49 While Jesus was yet talking, a man came from the house of the leader of the place of worship. This man said to Jairus, "Your daughter is dead. Do not make the Teacher use anymore of His time." 50 Jesus heard it and said to Jairus, "Do not be afraid, only believe. She will be made well."

51 Jesus went into the house. He let only Peter and James and John and the father and mother of the girl go in with Him. 52 Everyone was crying and full of sorrow because of her. Jesus said, "Do not cry. She is not dead, but is sleeping." 53 Then they laughed at Jesus because they knew she was dead. 54 Jesus sent them all out. He took the girl by the hand and said, "Child, get up!" 55 Her spirit came back and she got up at once. Jesus told them to bring her food. 56 Her parents were surprised and wondered about it. Then Jesus told them they should tell no one what had happened.

Jesus Sends His Twelve Followers Out
(Matthew 10:1–42; Mark 6:7–13)

9 Jesus called His twelve followers to Him. He gave them the right and the power over all demons and to heal diseases. 2 He sent them to preach about the holy nation of God and to heal the sick. 3 Then He said to them, "Take nothing along for the trip. Do not take a walking stick or a bag or bread or money. Do not take two coats. 4 Whatever house you go into, stay there until you are ready to go on. 5 If anyone will not take you in, as you leave that city, shake its dust off your feet. That will speak against you."

6 They went out, going from town to town. They preached the Good News and healed the sick everywhere.

John the Baptist Is Killed
(Matthew 14:6–12; Mark 6:21–29)

7 Now Herod the leader heard of all that had been done by Jesus. He was troubled because some people said that John the Baptist had been raised from the dead. 8 Some people said that Elijah had come back. Others thought one of the early preachers had been raised from the dead. 9 Then Herod said, "I had John's head cut off. But who is this Man that I hear these things about?" He wanted to see Jesus.

The Feeding of the Five Thousand
(Matthew 14:13–21; Mark 6:30–44; John 6:1–14)

10 The twelve followers came back. They told Jesus what they had done. Jesus took them to a desert near the town of Bethsaida. There they could be alone. 11 When the people knew where Jesus was, they followed Him. Jesus was happy to see them and talked to them about the holy nation of God. He healed all who were sick.

12 When the day was about over, the twelve followers came to Jesus. They said, "Send these many people away so they can go to the towns and country near here. There they can find a place to sleep and get food. We are here in a desert." 13 But Jesus said to them, "Give them something to eat." They said, "We have only five loaves of bread and two fish. Are we to go and buy food for all these people?" 14 There were about five thousand men. Jesus said to His followers, "Have them sit down in groups of fifty people." 15 They did as He told them. They made all of the people sit down. 16 As Jesus took the five loaves of bread and two fish, He looked up to heaven and gave thanks. He broke them in pieces and gave them to His followers to give to the people. 17 They all ate and were filled. They picked up twelve baskets full of pieces of bread and fish after the people finished eating.

Peter Says Jesus Is the Christ
(Matthew 16:13–20; Mark 8:27–30)

18 While Jesus was praying alone, His followers were with Him. Jesus asked them, "Who do people say that I am?" 19 They said, "John the Baptist, but some say Elijah. Others say that one of the early preachers has been raised from the dead." 20 Jesus said to them, "But who do you say that I am?" Peter said, "You are the Christ of God."

Jesus Tells of His Death for the First Time
(Matthew 16:21–28; Mark 8:31–38)

21 Then Jesus spoke to them and told them to tell no one. 22 He said, "The Son of

Man must suffer many things. The leaders and the religious leaders and the teachers of the Law will have nothing to do with Him. He must be killed and be raised from the dead three days later."

Giving Up Self and One's Own Desires

23 Then Jesus said to them all, "If anyone wants to follow Me, he must give up himself and his own desires. He must take up his cross everyday and follow Me. 24 If anyone wants to keep his own life safe, he must lose it. If anyone gives up his life because of Me, he will save it. 25 For what does a man have if he gets all the world and loses or gives up his life? 26 Whoever is ashamed of Me and My Words, the Son of Man will be ashamed of him when He comes in His own shining-greatness and of the Father's and of the holy angels. 27 I tell you the truth, some standing here will not die until they see the holy nation of God."

A Look at What Jesus Will Be Like
(Matthew 17:1–13; Mark 9:1–13)

28 About eight days after Jesus had said these things, He took Peter and James and John with Him. They went up on a mountain to pray. 29 As Jesus prayed, He was changed in looks before them. His clothes became white and shining bright. 30 Two men talked with Jesus. They were Moses and Elijah. 31 They looked like the shining-greatness of heaven as they talked about His death in Jerusalem which was soon to happen.

32 But Peter and those with him had gone to sleep. When they woke up, they saw His shining-greatness and the two men who stood with Him. 33 As the two men went from Jesus, Peter said to Him, "Teacher, it is good for us to be here. Let us build three tents to worship in. One will be for You. One will be for Moses. One will be for Elijah." He did not know what he was saying. 34 While he was talking, a cloud came over them. They were afraid as the cloud came in around them.

35 A voice came out of the cloud, saying, "This is My Son, the One I have chosen. Listen to Him!" 36 When the voice was gone, Jesus was standing there alone. From that time on, they kept these things to themselves. They told no one what they had seen.

A Boy with a Demon Is Healed
(Matthew 17:14–21; Mark 9:14–29)

37 The next day they came down from the mountain and many people met Jesus.

38 A man from among the people cried out, "Teacher, I beg of You to look at my son. He is my only child. 39 See, a demon takes him and makes him cry out. It takes hold of him and makes him shake. Spit runs from his mouth. He has marks on his body from being hurt. The demon does not want to go from him. 40 I begged Your followers to put the demon out, but they could not."

41 Then Jesus said, "You people of this day do not have faith. You turn from what is right! How long must I be with you? How long must I put up with you? Bring your son to Me." 42 While the boy was coming, the demon threw him down and made him lose the use of his mind for awhile. Jesus spoke sharp words to the demon. He healed the child and gave him back to his father.

Jesus Tells of His Death the Second Time
(Matthew 17:22–23; Mark 9:30–32)

43 They were all surprised at the great power of God. They all were thinking about the special things Jesus had done. And Jesus said to His followers, 44 "Remember these words. For the Son of Man will be given over into the hands of men." 45 They did not understand these words because it was hidden from them. They did not know what Jesus meant and were afraid to ask Him.

Jesus Teaches about the Faith of a Child
(Matthew 18:1–35; Mark 9:33–50)

46 The followers argued among themselves about which of them would be the greatest. 47 Jesus knew what they were thinking. He put a child beside Him. 48 He said to the followers, "Whoever receives this child in My name, receives Me. Whoever receives Me, receives Him Who sent Me. The one who is least among you is the one who is great."

The Sharp Words against the Followers

49 John said, "Teacher, we saw someone putting out demons in Your name. We told him to stop because he was not following us." 50 Jesus said to him, "Do not stop him. He who is not against us is for us."

Jesus and His Followers Leave Galilee

51 It was about time for Jesus to be taken up into heaven. He turned toward Jerusalem and was sure that nothing would stop Him from going. 52 He sent men on ahead of Him. They came to a town in Samaria. There they got things ready for Jesus.

53 The people did not want Him there because they knew He was on His way to Jerusalem. 54 James and John, His followers, saw this. They said, "Lord, do You want us to speak so fire will come down from heaven and burn them up as Elijah did?" 55 Jesus turned and spoke sharp words to them. (*He said, "You do not know what kind of spirit you have. 56 The Son of Man did not come to destroy men's lives. He came to save them from the punishment of sin." They went on their way to another town.)

The Testing of Some Followers
(Matthew 8:18–22)

57 As they were going on their way, a man said to Jesus, "Lord, I will follow You wherever You go." 58 Jesus said to him, "Foxes have holes. Birds of the sky have nests. The Son of Man has no place to put His head." 59 He said to another, "Follow Me." But the man said, "Lord, let me go first and bury my father." 60 Jesus said to him, "Let the people who are dead bury their own dead. You go and preach about the holy nation of God." 61 And another one said, "Lord, I will follow You, but first let me go and say good-bye to those at home." 62 Jesus said to him, "Anyone who puts his hand on a plow and looks back at the things behind is of no use in the holy nation of God."

Seventy Are Sent Out

10 After this the Lord chose seventy others. He sent them out two together to every city and place where He would be going later. 2 Jesus said to them, "There is much grain ready to gather. But the workmen are few. Pray then to the Lord Who is the Owner of the grain-fields that He will send workmen to gather His grain. 3 Go on your way. Listen! I send you out like lambs among wolves. 4 Take no money. Do not take a bag or shoes. Speak to no one along the way. 5 When you go into a house, say that you hope peace will come to them. 6 If a man who loves peace lives there, your good wishes will come to him. If your good wishes are not received, they will come back to you. 7 Stay in the same house. Eat and drink what they give you. The workman should have his thanks. Do not move from house to house.

8 "Whenever a city receives you, eat the things that are put before you there. 9 Heal the sick. Say to them, 'The holy nation of God is near.' 10 Whatever city does not receive you, go into its streets and say, 11 'Even the dust of your city that is on our feet we are cleaning off against you. But understand this, the holy nation of God has come near you.' 12 I tell you, on the day men stand before God, it will be easier for the city of Sodom than for that city.

13 "It is bad for you, city of Chorazin! It is bad for you, town of Bethsaida! For if the powerful works which were done in the cities of Tyre and Sidon they would have turned from their sins long ago. They would have shown their sorrow by putting on clothes made from hair and would have sat in ashes. 14 It will be better for Tyre and Sidon on the day men stand before God and be told they are guilty than for you. 15 And you, Capernaum, are you to be lifted up into heaven? You will be taken down to hell. 16 Whoever listens to you, listens to Me. Whoever has nothing to do with you, has nothing to do with Me. Whoever has nothing to do with Me, has nothing to do with the One Who sent Me."

The Seventy Come Back

17 The seventy came back full of joy. They said, "Lord, even the demons obeyed us when we used Your name." 18 Jesus said to them, "I saw Satan fall from heaven like lightning. 19 Listen! I have given you power to walk on snakes. I have given you power over small animals with a sting of poison. I have given you power over all the power of the one who works against you. Nothing will hurt you. 20 Even so, you should not be happy because the demons obey you but be happy because your names are written in heaven."

The Joy of the Holy Spirit

21 At this time Jesus was full of the joy of the Holy Spirit. He said, "I thank You, Father, Lord of heaven and earth. You have kept these things hidden from the wise and from those who have much learning. You have shown them to little children. Yes, Father, it was what you wanted done. 22 "Everything has been given to Me by My Father. No one knows the Son but the Father. No one knows the Father but the Son and the Son makes the Father known to those He chooses."

23 Then He turned to His followers and said without anyone else hearing, "Happy are those who see what you see! 24 I tell you, many early preachers and kings have wanted to see the things you are seeing,

but they did not see them. They have wanted to hear the things you are hearing, but they did not hear them."

Jesus Talks to the Man Who Knew the Law

25 A man stood up who knew the Law and tried to trap Jesus. He said, "Teacher, what must I do to have life that lasts forever?" 26 Jesus said to him, "What is written in the Law? What does the Law say?" 27 The man said, "You must love the Lord your God with all your heart. You must love Him with all your soul. You must love Him with all your strength. You must love Him with all your mind. You must love your neighbor as you love yourself." 28 Jesus said to him, "You have said the right thing. Do this and you will have life." The man tried to make himself look good. He asked Jesus, "Who is my neighbor?"

The Picture-Story of the Good Samaritan

30 Jesus said, "A man was going down from Jerusalem to the city of Jericho. Robbers came out after him. They took his clothes off and beat him. Then they went away, leaving him almost dead. 31 A religious leader was walking down that road and saw the man. But he went by on the other side. 32 In the same way, a man from the family group of Levi was walking down that road. When he saw the man who was hurt, he came near to him but kept on going on the other side of the road. 33 Then a man from the country of Samaria came by. He went up to the man. As he saw him, he had loving-pity on him. 34 He got down and put oil and wine on the places where he was hurt and put cloth around them. Then the man from Samaria put this man on his own donkey. He took him to a place where people stay for the night and cared for him. 35 The next day the man from Samaria was ready to leave. He gave the owner of that place two pieces of money to care for him. He said to him, 'Take care of this man. If you use more than this, I will give it to you when I come again.'

36 "Which of these three do you think was a neighbor to the man who was beaten by the robbers?" 37 The man who knew the Law said, "The one who showed loving-pity on him." Then Jesus said, "Go and do the same."

Mary and Martha Care for Jesus

38 As they went on their way, they came to a town where a woman named Martha lived. She cared for Jesus in her home. 39 Martha had a sister named Mary. Mary sat at the feet of Jesus and listened to all He said. 40 Martha was working hard getting the supper ready. She came to Jesus and said, "Do You see that my sister is not helping me? Tell her to help me." 41 Jesus said to her, "Martha, Martha, you are worried and troubled about many things. 42 Only a few things are important, even just one. Mary has chosen the good thing. It will not be taken away from her."

Jesus Teaches His Followers to Pray

11 Jesus had been praying. One of His followers said to Him, "Lord, teach us to pray as John the Baptist taught his followers." 2 Jesus said to them, "When you pray, say, 'Our Father in heaven, Your name is holy. May Your holy nation come. *What You want done, may it be done on earth as it is in heaven. 3 Give us the bread we need everyday. 4 Forgive us our sins, as we forgive those who sin against us. Do not let us be tempted.'"

A Picture-Story about How to Ask

5 Jesus said to them, "If one of you has a friend and goes to him in the night and says, 'Friend, give me three loaves of bread, 6 for a friend of mine is on a trip and has stopped at my house. I have no food to give him.' 7 The man inside the house will say, 'Do not trouble me. The door is shut. My children and I are in bed. I cannot get up and give you bread.' 8 I say to you, he may not get up and give him bread because he is a friend. Yet, if he keeps on asking, he will get up and give him as much as he needs. 9 I say to you, ask, and what you ask for will be given to you. Look, and what you are looking for you will find. Knock, and the door you are knocking on will be opened to you. 10 For everyone who asks, will receive what he asks for. Everyone who looks, will find what he is looking for. Everyone who knocks, will have the door opened to him.

11 "Would any of you fathers give your son a stone if he asked for bread? Or would you give a snake if he asked for a fish? 12 Or if he asked for an egg, would you give him a small animal with a sting of poison? 13 You are sinful and you know how to give good things to your children. How much more will your Father in heaven give the Holy Spirit to those who ask Him?"

A Nation That Cannot Stand
(Matthew 12:22–37; Mark 3:22–30)

14 Jesus was putting a demon out of a man who could not speak. When the demon was gone, the man could speak. All the people were surprised and wondered about it. 15 Some of them said, "He puts out demons through Satan, the king of demons." 16 Others tried to trap Jesus. They asked for something special to see from heaven. 17 But He knew their thoughts and said to them, "Every nation divided into groups that fight each other will be destroyed. Every family divided into groups that fight each other will not stand. 18 If Satan is divided against himself, how will his nation stand? And yet you say I put out demons through Satan! 19 If I put out demons through Satan, by whose help do your sons put them out? Your own sons will say if you are guilty or not. 20 But if I put out demons by the power of God, then the holy nation of God has come to you.

21 "When a strong man watches his house and is ready to fight, his things are safe. 22 When a stronger man comes along, he wins the fight. He takes away all the things to fight with that the man of the house had put his trust in. Then the stronger man takes anything he wants from the house. 23 Whoever is not with Me is against Me. Whoever does not gather with Me is sending them everywhere.

A Person Filled with Bad or Good
(Matthew 12:43–45)

24 "When a demon is gone out of a man, it goes through dry places to find rest. If it finds none, it says, 'I will go back to my house I came from.' 25 When the demon comes back, it finds the house cleaned and looking good. 26 Then the demon goes out and comes back bringing seven demons worse than itself. They go in and live there. In the end that man is worse than at the first." 27 As Jesus was talking, a woman of the group said with a loud voice, "The woman is happy who gave You birth and who fed You." 28 But He said, "Yes, but those who hear the Word of God and obey it are happy."

Jesus Tells about Jonah
(Matthew 12:38–42)

29 When the people were gathered near Jesus, He said, "The people of this day are sinful. They are looking for something special to see. They will get nothing special to see, except what Jonah the early preacher did. 30 As Jonah was something special to the people of the city of Nineveh, the Son of Man will be to the people of this day also. 31 The queen of the south will stand up on the day men stand before God. She will say the people of this day are guilty because she came from the ends of the earth to listen to the wise sayings of Solomon. And look, Someone greater than Solomon is here! 32 The men of Nineveh will stand up on the day men stand before God. They will say the people of this day are guilty because the men of Nineveh were sorry for their sins and turned from them when Jonah preached. And look, Someone greater than Jonah is here!

Jesus Teaches about Light

33 "No man lights a lamp and then hides it under a pail. He puts the light on a lampstand so those who come in can see it. 34 The eye is the light of the body. When your eye is good, your whole body is full of light. When your eye is sinful, your whole body is full of darkness. 35 Be careful that the light in you is not dark. 36 If your whole body is full of light, with no dark part, then it will shine. It will be as a lamp that gives light."

Jesus Speaks Sharp Words to the Proud Religious Law-Keepers

37 As Jesus was talking, a proud religious law-keeper asked Him to eat with him. Jesus went to the man's house and took His place at the table. 38 The proud religious law-keeper was surprised and wondered why Jesus had not washed before He ate. 39 But the Lord said to him, "You proud religious law-keepers make the outside of the cup and plate clean, but inside you are full of stealing and sinning. 40 You are foolish. Did not He that made the outside make the inside also? 41 Give yourself as a gift and then you will be clean.

42 "It is bad for you, proud religious law-keepers! You give one-tenth part of your spices. But you give no thought to what is right and to the love of God. You should do both of these.

43 "It is bad for you, proud religious law-keepers! For you like to have the important seats in the places of worship. You like to have people speak good-sounding words to you as you are in the center of town where people gather. 44 It is bad for you, teachers of the Law and proud religious law-keepers and you who pretend to be someone you are not! For you are

like graves that are hidden. Men walk on graves without knowing they are there."

Jesus Speaks Sharp Words to the Men Who Knew the Law

45 One of the men who knew the Law said to Jesus, "Teacher, You are making us look bad when You speak like this." 46 Jesus said, "It is bad for you also, you men who know the Law! For you put heavy loads on the shoulders of men. But you will not even put your finger on one of these loads to help them. 47 It is bad for you! For you make beautiful buildings for the graves of the early preachers your fathers killed. 48 You are saying what your fathers did was good, because they killed the early preachers and you are making their graves.

49 "For this reason the wisdom of God has said, 'I will send them early preachers and missionaries. Some they will kill and some they will make it very hard for.' 50 The blood of all the early preachers from the beginning of the world is on the people of this day. 51 It will be from the blood of Abel to the blood of Zacharias, the one who died between the altar and the house of God. For sure, I tell you, the people of this day will be guilty for this.

52 "It is bad for you men who know the Law! For you have locked the door to the house of learning. You are not going in yourselves and you do not allow those to go in who are about to go in."

53 As Jesus went away from there, the teachers of the Law and the proud religious law-keepers were very angry and tried to make Him say many things. 54 They planned against Jesus and tried to trap Him with something He might say.

Jesus Teaches His Followers and Thousands of Other People

12 At that time thousands of people gathered together. There were so many that they walked on each other. Jesus spoke to His twelve followers first, saying, "Look out! Have nothing to do with the yeast of the proud religious law-keepers which is pretending to be something it is not. 2 For there is nothing covered up that will not be seen. There is nothing hidden that will not be known. 3 What you have said in the dark will be heard in the light. What you have said in a low voice in a closed room will be spoken with a loud voice from the top of houses.

4 "I say to you, My friends, do not be afraid of those who kill the body and then can do no more. 5 I will tell you the one to be afraid of. Be afraid of Him Who has power to put you into hell after He has killed you. Yes, I say to you, be afraid of Him!

6 "Are not five small birds sold for two small pieces of money? God does not forget even one of the birds. 7 God knows how many hairs you have on your head. Do not be afraid. You are worth more than many small birds.

8 "Also, I tell you, everyone who makes Me known to men, the Son of Man will make him known to the angels of God. 9 But whoever acts as if he does not know Me and does not make Me known to men, he will not be spoken of to the angels of God.

The Sin That Cannot Be Forgiven

10 "Whoever speaks a word against the Son of Man will be forgiven. Whoever speaks against the Holy Spirit will not be forgiven. 11 When they take you to the places of worship and to the courts and to the leaders of the country, do not be worried about what you should say or how to say it. 12 The Holy Spirit will tell you what you should say at that time."

13 One of the people said to Jesus, "Teacher, tell my brother to divide the riches that our father left us." 14 Jesus said to him, "Friend, who has said to Me to say who should get what?" 15 Then Jesus said to them all, "Watch yourselves! Keep from wanting all kinds of things you should not have. A man's life is not made up of things, even if he has many riches."

The Picture-Story of the Rich Fool

16 Then He told them a picture-story, saying, "The fields of a rich man gave much grain. 17 The rich man thought to himself, 'What will I do? I have no place to put the grain.' 18 Then he said, 'I know what I will do. I will take down my grain building and I will build a bigger one. I will put all my grain and other things I own into it. 19 And I will say to my soul, "Soul, you have many good things put away in your building. It will be all you need for many years to come. Now rest and eat and drink and have lots of fun." ' 20 But God said to him, 'You fool! Tonight your soul will be taken from you. Then who will have all the things you have put away?' 21 It is the same with a man who puts away riches for himself and does not have the riches of God."

Jesus Teaches about the Cares of This Life

22 Jesus said to His followers, "Because of this, I say to you, do not worry about your life, what you are going to eat. Do not worry about your body, what you are going to wear. 23 Life is worth more than food. The body is worth more than clothes. 24 Look at the birds. They do not plant seeds. They do not gather grain. They have no grain buildings for keeping grain. Yet God feeds them. Are you not worth more than the birds?

25 "Which of you can make yourself a little taller by worrying? 26 If you cannot do that which is so little, why do you worry about other things? 27 Think how the flowers grow. They do not work or make cloth. Yet, I tell you, that King Solomon in all his greatness was not dressed as well as one of these flowers. 28 God puts these clothes on the grass of the field. The grass is in the field today and put into the fire tomorrow. How much more would He want to give you clothing? You have so little faith! 29 Do not give so much thought to what you will eat or drink. Do not be worried about it. 30 For all the nations of the world go after these things. Your Father knows you need these things. 31 Instead, go after the holy nation of God. Then all these other things will be given to you. 32 Do not be afraid, little flock. Your Father wants to give you the holy nation of God. 33 Sell what you have and give the money to poor people. Have money-bags for yourselves that will never wear out. These money-bags are riches in heaven that will always be there. No robber can take them and no bugs can eat them there. 34 Your heart will be wherever your riches are.

Jesus Says to Watch and Be Ready for His Second Coming

35 "Be ready and dressed. Have your lights burning. 36 Be like men who are waiting for their owner to come home from a wedding supper. When he comes and knocks on the door, they will open it for him at once. 37 Those servants are happy when their owner finds them watching when he comes. For sure, I tell you, he will be dressed and ready to care for them. He will have them seated at the table. 38 The owner might come late at night or early in the morning. Those servants are happy if their owner finds them watching whenever he comes. 39 But understand this, that if the owner of a house had known when the robber was coming, he would have been watching. He would not have allowed his house to be broken into. 40 You must be ready also. The Son of Man is coming at a time when you do not think He will come."

Faithful Servants and Servants Who Are Not Faithful

41 Peter said, "Lord, are You telling this picture-story to us or to all the people?" 42 The Lord said, "Who is the faithful and wise servant his owner made boss over the others? He is the one who is to have food ready at the right time. 43 That servant is happy who is doing his work when the owner comes. 44 For sure, I tell you, he will make him boss over all he has.

45 "But what if that servant says to himself, 'The owner will not be coming soon,' and then beats the other servants and eats and drinks and gets drunk? 46 The owner of that servant will come on a day and at an hour when he is not looking for him. He will cut him in pieces and will put him with those who do not believe.

47 "The servant who knew what the owner wanted done, but did not get ready for him, or did not do what he wanted done, will be beaten many times. 48 But the servant who did not know what his owner wanted done, but did things that would be reason to be beaten, will be beaten only a few times. The man who receives much will have to give much. If much is given to a man to take care of, men will expect to get more from him.

Men Are Divided When They Follow Christ

49 "I have come to bring fire down to the earth. I wish it were already started! 50 I have a baptism to go through. How troubled I am until it is over! 51 Do you think I came to bring peace on the earth? I tell you, no! I came to divide. 52 From now on there will be five in one house divided. Three will be against two and two will be against three. 53 The father will be against the son. The son will be against the father. The mother will be against the daughter. The daughter will be against the mother. The mother-in-law will be against the daughter-in-law. The daughter-in-law will be against the mother-in-law."

54 Then Jesus also said to the people, "When you see a cloud coming in the west, you say at once, 'It is going to rain.'

And it does. 55 When you see the wind blow from the south, you say, 'It will be a hot day.' And it is. 56 You who pretend to be someone you are not, you know all about the sky and the earth. But why do you not know what is happening these days? 57 Why do you not know for yourselves what is right? 58 When a person says you are wrong and takes you to court, try to make it right with him as you go, or he will take you to the head of the court. Then he will take you to the police and you will be put in prison. 59 I tell you, you will not be let out of prison until you have paid the last piece of money of the fine."

Everyone Should Be Sorry for Their Sins and Turn from Them

13 At this time some people came to Jesus. They told Him that Pilate had killed some people from the country of Galilee. It was while they were giving gifts of animals on the altar in worship to God. 2 Pilate put their blood together with the blood of the animals. Jesus said to them, "What about these people from Galilee? Were they worse sinners than all the other people from Galilee because they suffered these things? 3 No, I tell you. But unless you are sorry for your sins and turn from them, you too will all die. 4 What about those eighteen men who were killed when the high building in Siloam fell on them? Do you think they were the worst sinners living in Jerusalem? 5 No, I tell you. But unless you are sorry for your sins and turn from them, you too will all die."

The Picture-Story of the Fig Tree Which Had No Fruit

6 Then He told them this picture-story: "A man had a fig tree in his grape-field. He looked for fruit on it but found none. 7 He said to his servant, 'See! For three years I have been coming here looking for fruit on this fig tree. I never find any. Cut it down. Why does it even waste the ground?' 8 The servant said, 'Sir! Leave it here one more year. I will dig around it and put plant food on it. 9 It may be that it will give fruit next year. If it does not, then cut it down.' "

Jesus Heals on the Day of Rest

10 Jesus was teaching in one of the Jewish places of worship on the Day of Rest. 11 A woman was there who had suffered for eighteen years because of a demon. She was not able to stand up straight. 12 Jesus saw her and said, "Woman, you are now

free from your trouble!" 13 Then He put His hand on her. At once she stood up straight and gave thanks to God.

14 The leader of the Jewish place of worship was angry because Jesus healed on the Day of Rest. The leader said to the people, "There are six days in which work should be done. Come on those days and get healed. Do not come to be healed on the Day of Rest." 15 The Lord said to him, "You pretend to be someone you are not! Do not each of you let his cow or his donkey out and lead them to water on the Day of Rest? 16 Should not this Jewish woman be made free from this trouble on the Day of Rest? She has been chained by Satan for eighteen years." 17 When He said this, all those who were against Him were ashamed. All the many people were glad for the great things being done by Him.

The Picture-Stories of the Mustard Seed and the Yeast
(Matthew 13:1-52; Mark 4:1-34)

18 Then Jesus asked, "What is the holy nation of God like? What can I use to show you? 19 It is like a mustard seed which a man took and planted in his field. It grew and became a tree. The birds of the sky stayed in its branches." 20 Again Jesus said, "What can I use to show you what the holy nation of God is like? 21 It is like yeast that a woman put into three pails of flour until it was all full of yeast."

Jesus Teaches on the Way to Jerusalem

22 Jesus taught the people as He went through the cities and towns on His way to Jerusalem. 23 Someone asked Jesus, "Lord, will only a few people be saved from the punishment of sin?" Jesus said to them, 24 "Work hard to go in through the narrow door. I tell you, many will try to go in but will not be able to go in. 25 The owner of the house will get up and shut the door. You who are on the outside will knock on the door and say, 'Lord, let us in.' Then He will say, 'I do not know you.' 26 Then you will say, 'We ate and drank with You when You taught in our streets.' 27 But He will say, 'I tell you, I do not know you. Go away from Me. You are sinful.' 28 "There will be loud crying and grinding of teeth when you see Abraham and Isaac and Jacob and all the early preachers in the holy nation of God, but you will be put out. 29 Those who sit at the table in the holy nation of God will come from the east and west and from the north and south.

30 Listen! Some are last who will be first. Some are first who will be last."

31 That same day some of the proud religious law-keepers came to Jesus. They said, "Go away from here! Herod wants to kill You." 32 Jesus said to them, "Go and tell that fox, 'See. I put out demons and heal the sick. I will do these things today and tomorrow. And the third day My work will be finished.' 33 But I must go on My way today and tomorrow and the day after. One who speaks for God cannot die except at Jerusalem.

Jesus Sorrows Over Jerusalem

34 "Jerusalem, Jerusalem, you kill the early preachers and throw stones on those sent to you. How many times I wanted to gather your children around me, as a bird gathers her young under her wings, but you would not let Me. 35 See! Your house is empty. And I tell you, you will not see Me again until the time comes when you will say, 'Great and honored is the One Who comes in the name of the Lord.' "

Another Man Is Healed on the Day of Rest

14 On the Day of Rest Jesus went into the house of one of the leaders of the proud religious law-keepers to eat. They all watched Jesus to see what He would do. 2 A man who had very large arms and legs because of a sickness was put before Jesus. 3 Jesus asked the teachers of the Law and the proud religious law-keepers, "Does the Law say it is right to heal on the Day of Rest, or not?" 4 They did not answer. Jesus took hold of the man and healed him and sent him away. 5 Then Jesus said to the leaders, "If one of you had a cow or donkey that fell into a hole, would you not go at once and pull it out on the Day of Rest?" 6 And they were not able to answer His questions.

Jesus Teaches about How to Live with Others

7 Jesus had been watching those who were asked to come to supper. They were all trying to get the important seats. He told them a picture-story, saying, 8 "When you are asked by someone to a wedding supper, do not take the important seat. Someone more important than you may have been asked to come also. 9 The one who asked both of you to come may say to you, 'The important seat is for this man.' Then you will be ashamed as you take the last place.

10 But when you are asked to come to the table, sit down on the last seat. Then the one who asked you may come and say to you, 'Friend, go to a more important place.' Then you will be shown respect in front of all who are at the table with you. 11 Whoever makes himself look more important than he is will find out how little he is worth. Whoever does not try to honor himself will be made important."

12 Then Jesus said to the man who asked Him to eat in his house, "When you have a supper, do not ask your friends or your brothers or your family or your rich neighbors. They will ask you to come to their place for a supper. That way you will be paid back for what you have done. 13 When you have a supper, ask poor people. Ask those who cannot walk and those who are blind. 14 You will be happy if you do this. They cannot pay you back. You will get your pay when the people who are right with God are raised from the dead."

15 When one of those eating at the table with Jesus heard this, he said, "Everyone is happy who will eat in the holy nation of God."

The Picture-Story of the Big Supper
(Matthew 22:1–14)

16 Then Jesus said to the leader of the proud religious law-keepers, "There was a man who was giving a big supper. He asked many people to come to eat. 17 When it was about time to eat, he sent one of the servants he owned to tell those he had asked, saying, 'Come, everything is ready now.' 18 They all gave different reasons why they could not come. The first said, 'I have bought some land and I must go and see it. Do not expect me to come.' 19 Another one said, 'I have bought ten cows to use for working in my fields. I must go and try them out. Do not expect me to come.' 20 And another one said, 'I have just been married and I cannot come.'

21 "The servant went back to his owner and told him these things. Then his owner became angry. He said to his servant, 'Hurry into the streets and narrow roads of the city and bring poor people here. Bring those whose bodies are diseased. Bring those who cannot walk and those who are blind.' 22 The servant came back and said, 'Sir, what you told me to do has been done. But there are still some empty places.' 23 Then the owner said to his servant, 'Go out along the roads leading away from the city and into the fields. Tell them

they must come. Do this so my house will be filled. 24 I tell you, not one of those I had asked will eat of my supper.' "

Giving Up Things of This Earth
(Matthew 10:37–39)

25 Many people followed Jesus. Then He turned around and said to them, 26 "If any man comes to Me and does not have much more love for Me than for his father and mother, wife and children, brothers and sisters, and even his own life, he cannot be My follower. 27 If he does not carry his cross and follow Me, he cannot be My follower.

28 "If one of you wanted to build a large building, you would sit down first and think of how much money it would take to build it. You would see if you had enough money to finish it, 29 or when the base of the building is finished, you might see that you do not have enough money to finish it. Then all who would see it would make fun of you. 30 They would say, 'This man began to build and was not able to finish.'

31 "What if a king is going to war with another king? Will he not sit down first and decide if he is able to go with 10,000 men against the other king who is coming with 20,000 men? 32 Or, he will send a soldier to the other king while he is still a long way off. He will ask what can be done to have peace. 33 In the same way, whoever does not give up all that he has, cannot be My follower.

34 "Salt is good. But if salt has lost its taste, how can it be made to taste like salt again? 35 It is no good for the field or the waste place. Men throw it away. You have ears, then listen!"

The Picture-Story of the Lost Sheep

15 All the tax-gatherers and sinners were coming to hear Jesus. 2 The proud religious law-keepers and the teachers of the Law began to speak against Him. They said, "This man receives sinners and eats with them."

3 Then Jesus told them a picture-story, saying, 4 "What if one of you had one hundred sheep and you lost one of them? Would you not leave the ninety-nine in the country and go back and look for the one which was lost until you find it? 5 When you find it, you are happy as you carry it back on your shoulders. 6 Then you would go to your house and call your friends and neighbors. You would say to them, 'Be happy with me because I have found

my sheep that was lost.' 7 I tell you, there will be more joy in heaven because of one sinner who is sorry for his sins and turns from them, than for ninety-nine people right with God who do not have sins to be sorry for.

The Picture-Story of the Lost Piece of Money

8 "What if a woman has ten silver pieces of money and loses one of them? Does she not light a lamp and sweep the floor and look until she finds it? 9 When she finds it, she calls her friends and neighbors together. She says to them, 'Be happy with me. I have found the piece of money I had lost.' 10 I tell you, it is the same way among the angels of God. If one sinner is sorry for his sins and turns from them, the angels are very happy."

The Picture-Story of the Foolish Son Who Spent All His Money

11 And Jesus said, "There was a man who had two sons. 12 The younger son said to his father, 'Father, let me have the part of the family riches that will be coming to me.' Then the father divided all that he owned between his two sons. 13 Soon after that the younger son took all that had been given to him and went to another country far away. There he spent all he had on wild and foolish living. 14 When all his money was spent, he was hungry. There was no food in the land. 15 He went to work for a man in this far away country. His work was to feed pigs. 16 He was so hungry he was ready to eat the outside part of the ears of the corn the pigs ate because no one gave him anything.

17 "He began to think about what he had done. He said to himself, 'My father pays many men who work for him. They have all the food they want and more than enough. I am about dead because I am so hungry. 18 I will get up and go to my father. I will say to him, "Father, I have sinned against heaven and against you. 19 I am not good enough to be called your son. But may I be as one of the workmen you pay to work?" '

20 "The son got up and went to his father. While he was yet a long way off, his father saw him. The father was full of loving-pity for him. He ran and threw his arms around him and kissed him. 21 The son said to him, 'Father, I have sinned against heaven and against you. I am not good enough to be called your son.' 22 But the father said to

the workmen he owned, 'Hurry! Get the best coat and put it on him. Put a ring on his hand and shoes on his feet. 23 Bring the calf that is fat and kill it. Let us eat and be glad. 24 For my son was dead and now he is alive again. He was lost and now he is found. Let us eat and have a good time.'

25 "The older son was out in the field. As he was coming near the house, he heard music and dancing. 26 He called one of the servants and asked what was happening. 27 The servant answered, 'Your brother has come back and your father has killed the fat calf. Your brother is in the house and is well.' 28 The older brother was angry and would not go into the house. His father went outside and asked him to come in. 29 The older son said to his father, 'All these many years I have served you. I have always obeyed what you said. But you never gave me a young goat so I could have a supper and a good time with my friends. 30 But as soon as this son of yours came back, you killed the fat calf. And yet he wasted your money with bad women.'

31 "The father said to him, 'My son, you are with me all the time. All that I have is yours. 32 It is right and good that we should have a good time and be glad. Your brother was dead and now he is alive again. He was lost and now he is found.' "

The Picture-Story of the Boss Who Stole

16 Jesus said to His followers, "There was a rich man who put a boss over his houses and lands. Someone told him that his boss was not using his riches in a right way. 2 The rich man sent for the boss and said, 'What is this I hear about you? Tell me what you have done with my things. You are not to be the boss of my houses and lands anymore.'

3 "The boss said to himself, 'What will I do now? The owner of the houses and lands is taking my work away from me. I cannot dig in the ground for a living. I am too proud to ask for help. 4 I know what I will do. I will make it so that when I lose this work I will be able to go to the homes of my friends.'

5 "He sent for the people who owed the rich man. He asked the first one, 'How much do you owe the owner?' 6 The first man said, 'One hundred barrels of oil.' The boss said to him, 'Take your bill. Sit down at once and change it to fifty.' 7 He asked another one, 'How much do you owe?' He said, 'One hundred bags of wheat.' He said to him, 'Take your bill and change it

to eighty.' 8 Then the rich man said that this sinful boss had been wise to plan for himself for the days ahead. For the people of the world are wiser in their day than the children of light.

9 "I tell you, make friends for yourselves by using the riches of the world that are so often used in wrong ways. So when riches are a thing of the past, friends may receive you into a home that will be forever. 10 He that is faithful with little things is faithful with big things also. He that is not honest with little things is not honest with big things. 11 If you have not been faithful with riches of this world, who will trust you with true riches? 12 If you have not been faithful in that which belongs to another person, who will give you things to have as your own? 13 No servant can have two bosses. He will hate the one and love the other. Or, he will be faithful to one and not faithful to the other. You cannot be faithful to God and to riches at the same time."

Jesus Teaches That the Law Is Not Finished

14 The proud religious law-keepers heard all these things. They loved money so they made fun of Jesus. 15 Jesus said to them, "You are the kind of people who make yourselves look good before other people. God knows your hearts. What men think is good is hated in the eyes of God. 16 Until John came, you had the writings of the Law and of the early preachers. From that time until now the Good News of the holy nation of God has been preached. Everyone is pushing his way in. 17 But it is easier for heaven and earth to pass away than for one small part of a word in the Law to be of no more use.

18 "Whoever divorces his wife and marries another woman is not faithful in marriage and is guilty of sex sins.

The Rich Man and the Man Who Begged for Food

19 "There was a rich man who dressed in purple linen clothes everyday. He lived like a king would live with the best of food. 20 There was a poor man named Lazarus who had many bad sores. He was put by the door of the rich man. 21 He wanted the pieces of food that fell from the table of the rich man. Even dogs came and licked his sores.

22 "The poor man who asked for food died. He was taken by the angels into the arms of Abraham. The rich man died also

and was buried. 23 In hell the rich man was in much pain. He looked up and saw Abraham far away and Lazarus beside him. 24 He cried out and said, 'Father Abraham, take pity on me. Send Lazarus. Let him put the end of his finger in water and cool my tongue. I am in much pain in this fire.' 25 Abraham said, 'My son, do not forget that when you were living you had your good things. Lazarus had bad things. Now he is well cared for. You are in pain. 26 And more than all this, there is a big deep place between us. No one from here can go there even if he wanted to go. No one can come from there.'

27 "Then the rich man said, 'Father, then I beg you to send Lazarus to my father's house. 28 I have five brothers. Let him tell them of these things, or they will come to this place of much pain also.' 29 Abraham said, 'They have the Writings of Moses and of the early preachers. Let them hear what they say.' 30 But the rich man said, 'No, Father Abraham. If someone goes to them from the dead, they will be sorry for their sins and turn from them.' 31 Abraham said to him, 'If they do not listen to Moses and to the early preachers, they will not listen even if someone is raised from the dead.' "

Jesus Teaches about Forgiving

17 Jesus said to His followers, "For sure, things will come that will make people sin. But it is bad for the person who makes someone else sin. 2 It would be better for him to have a large rock put around his neck and be thrown into the sea, than that he should cause one of these little ones to sin.

3 "Watch yourselves! If your brother sins, speak sharp words to him. If he is sorry and turns from his sin, forgive him. 4 What if he sins against you seven times in one day? If he comes to you and says he is sorry and turns from his sin, forgive him."

5 The followers said to the Lord, "Give us more faith." 6 The Lord said, "If your faith was as a mustard seed, you could say to this tree, 'Be pulled out of the ground and planted in the sea,' and it would obey you.

Jesus Teaches about Being Faithful

7 "What if you owned a servant who was working in the field or taking care of sheep? Would you say to him when he came in from his work, 'Come and sit down to eat?' 8 No, instead you would say, 'Get my supper ready. Dress yourself and care for me until I am through eating and

drinking. Then you can eat and drink.' 9 Does the servant get thanks for doing what he was told to do? I am sure he does not. 10 It is the same with you also. When you do everything you have been told to do, you must say, 'We are not any special servants. We have done only what we should have done.' "

Jesus Heals Ten Men with a Bad Skin Disease

11 Jesus went on His way to Jerusalem. He was passing between the countries of Samaria and Galilee. 12 As He was going into one of the towns, ten men with a bad skin disease came to Him. They stood a little way off. 13 They called to Him, "Jesus! Teacher! Take pity on us!" 14 When Jesus saw them, He said, "Go and show yourselves to the religious leaders." As they went, they were healed. 15 One of them turned back when he saw he was healed. He thanked God with a loud voice. 16 He got down on his face at the feet of Jesus and thanked Him. He was from the country of Samaria. 17 Jesus asked, "Were there not ten men who were healed? Where are the other nine? 18 Is this stranger from another country the only one who turned back to give thanks to God?" 19 Then Jesus said to him, "Get up and go on your way. Your trust in God has healed you."

Jesus Teaches about the Holy Nation of God

20 The proud religious law-keepers asked when the holy nation of God would come. Jesus said to them, "The holy nation of God is not coming in such a way that can be seen with the eyes. 21 It will not be said, 'See, here it is!' or, 'There it is!' For the holy nation of God is in you."

Jesus Tells of His Second Coming

22 Jesus said to His followers, "The time will come when you will wish you could see the Son of Man for one day. But you will not be able to. 23 They will say to you, 'He is here,' or, 'He is there,' but do not follow them. 24 When the Son of Man comes, He will be as lightning that shines from one part of the sky to the other. 25 But before that, He must suffer many hard things. The people of this day will have nothing to do with Him.

26 "As it was in the time of Noah, so will it be when the Son of Man comes back. 27 People ate and drank. They married and were given in marriage. They did

these things until the day Noah went into the large boat. Then the flood came and killed all the people on earth. 28 It was the same in the time of Lot. People ate and drank. They bought and sold. They planted and built. 29 But the day Lot left the city of Sodom, fire and sulphur came down from heaven like rain. It killed all the people of Sodom.

30 "It will be the same on the day when the Son of Man comes again. 31 In that day the man who is on top of a house should not come down to take his things out of the house. In the same way, the man who is in the field should not go back to his house. 32 Remember Lot's wife!

33 "He who wants to keep his life will have it taken away from him. He who loses his life will have it given back to him. 34 I tell you, on that night there will be two men in the same bed. One of them will be taken. The other will be left. 35 Two women will be grinding grain together. One of them will be taken. The other will be left. 36 *Two men will be working in a field. One will be taken. The other will be left."

37 Then they asked Jesus, "Where will this happen?" He said to them, "Birds also gather where there is a dead body."

The Picture-Story of the Woman Whose Husband Had Died

18 Jesus told them a picture-story to show that men should always pray and not give up. 2 He said, "There was a man in one of the cities who was head of the court. His work was to say if a person was guilty or not. This man was not afraid of God. He did not respect any man. 3 In that city there was a woman whose husband had died. She kept coming to him and saying, 'Help me! There is someone who is working against me.' 4 For awhile he would not help her. Then he began to think, 'I am not afraid of God and I do not respect any man. 5 But I will see that this woman whose husband has died gets her rights because I get tired of her coming all the time.' " 6 Then the Lord said, "Listen to the words of the sinful man who is head of the court. 7 Will not God make the things that are right come to His chosen people who cry day and night to Him? Will He wait a long time to help them? 8 I tell you, He will be quick to help them. But when the Son of Man comes, will He find faith on the earth?"

The Picture-Story of the Proud Religious Law-Keepers and the Tax-Gatherers

9 Jesus told another picture-story to some people who trusted in themselves and thought they were right with God. These people did not think well of other men. 10 Jesus said, "Two men went up to the house of God to pray. One of them was a proud religious law-keeper. The other was a man who gathered taxes. 11 The proud religious law-keeper stood and prayed to himself like this, 'God, I thank You that I am not like other men. I am not like those who steal. I am not like those who do things that are wrong. I am not like those who do sex sins. I am not even like this tax-gatherer. 12 I go without food two times a week so I can pray better. I give one-tenth part of the money I earn.' 13 But the man who gathered taxes stood a long way off. He would not even lift his eyes to heaven. But he hit himself on his chest and said, 'God, have pity on me! I am a sinner!' 14 I tell you, this man went back to his house forgiven, and not the other man. For whoever makes himself look more important than he is will find out how little he is worth. Whoever does not try to honor himself will be made important."

Jesus Gives Thanks for Little Children
(Matthew 19:13–15; Mark 10:13–16)

15 People took their little children to Jesus so He could put His hand on them. When His followers saw it, they spoke sharp words to the people. 16 Jesus called the followers to Him and said, "Let the little children come to Me. Do not try to stop them. The holy nation of God is made up of ones like these. 17 For sure, I tell you, whoever does not receive the holy nation of God as a child will not go into the holy nation."

Jesus Teaches about Keeping the Law
(Matthew 19:16–30; Mark 10:17–31)

18 A leader of the people asked Jesus, "Good Teacher, what must I do to have life that lasts forever?" 19 Jesus said to him, "Why do you call Me good? There is only One Who is good. That is God. 20 You know the Laws. You must not do any sex sins. You must not kill another person. You must not steal. You must not tell a lie about someone else. Respect your father and your mother." 21 The leader said, "I have obeyed all these Laws since I was a boy." 22 When Jesus heard this, He said to the leader of the people, "There is still

one thing you need to do. Sell everything you have. Give the money to poor people. Then you will have riches in heaven. Come and follow Me." 23 When the leader heard this, he was very sad because he had many riches. 24 When Jesus saw that he was very sad, He said, "It is hard for those with riches to go into the holy nation of God! 25 It is easier for a camel to go through the eye of a needle than for a rich man to go into the holy nation of God."

26 Those who heard this, said, "Then who can be saved from the punishment of sin?" 27 Jesus said, "God can do things men cannot do." 28 Then Peter said, "See, we have left everything and have followed You." 29 Jesus said to them, "For sure, I tell you, anyone who has left his house or parents or brothers or wife or children because of the holy nation of God 30 will receive much more now. In the time to come he will have life that lasts forever."

Jesus Tells of His Death the Third Time
(Matthew 20:17–19; Mark 10:32–34)

31 Then Jesus took the twelve followers to one side and said, "See! We are going up to Jerusalem. All the things the early preachers wrote about the Son of Man are going to happen. 32 He will be given over to the people who are not Jews. He will be made fun of. He will be hurt. He will be spit on. 33 They will beat Him and kill Him. After three days He will be raised again."

34 The followers did not understand these words. The meaning of these words was hidden from them. They did not know what He said.

The Healing of the Blind Man
(Matthew 20:29–34; Mark 10:46–52)

35 Jesus was coming near Jericho. A blind man was sitting by the side of the road, begging. 36 He heard many people going by and asked what was happening. 37 They told him that Jesus of Nazareth was going by. 38 Then he cried out and said, "Jesus, Son of David, have pity on me." 39 The people spoke sharp words to him and told him not to call out. But he cried out all the more, "Son of David, have pity on me."

40 Jesus stopped and told the people to bring the blind man to Him. When the man was near, Jesus asked, 41 "What do you want Me to do for you?" He answered, "Lord, I want to see." 42 Jesus said to him, "Then see! Your faith has healed you." 43 At once he could see. He followed Jesus and gave thanks to God. All the people gave thanks to God when they saw it.

The Changed Life of Zaccheus

19 Jesus went on to the city of Jericho and was passing through it. 2 There was a rich man named Zaccheus. He was a leader of those who gathered taxes. 3 Zaccheus wanted to see Jesus but he could not because so many people were there and he was a short man. 4 He ran ahead and got up into a sycamore tree to see Him. Jesus was going by that way.

5 When Jesus came to the place, He looked up and saw Zaccheus. He said, "Zaccheus, come down at once. I must stay in your house today." 6 At once he came down and was glad to have Jesus come to his house. 7 When the people saw it, they began to complain among themselves. They said, "He is going to stay with a man who is known to be a sinner."

8 Zaccheus stood up and said to the Lord, "Lord, see! Half of what I own I will give to poor people. And if I have taken money from anyone in a wrong way, I will pay him back four times as much." 9 Jesus said to him, "Today, a person has been saved in this house. This man is a Jew also. 10 For the Son of Man came to look for and to save from the punishment of sin those who are lost."

The Picture-Story of the Ten Servants and the Money

11 As they heard these things, Jesus told them a picture-story. Because He was near Jerusalem, they thought the holy nation of God would come at once. 12 So Jesus said, "A leader of a country went to another country far away. A nation was to be given to him, then he would return home. 13 He called ten of the servants he owned. He gave them ten pieces of money and said to them, 'Put this money to use until I return.' 14 But other men in his country hated him. They sent men after him to tell him they did not want him as their king. 15 After he had been given the other nation, he returned as king. He asked for his servants who had received the money to come to him. He wanted to know how much more they had after putting it to use. 16 The first one came and said, 'Lord, the piece of money you gave me has made ten more pieces of money.' 17 He said to him, 'You are a good servant. You have been faithful in using a little. Now you will be leader over ten cities.'

18 "The second man came to him and said, 'Lord, the piece of money you gave me has made five more pieces of money.'

19 He said to him, 'You are to be leader over five cities.'

20 "Another one came saying, 'Lord, look! Here is your piece of money. I have kept it hid in a piece of cloth. 21 I was afraid of you. You are a hard man. You take what you have not put down. You gather where you have not planted.' 22 The king said to him, 'By the words from your own mouth I must say that you are guilty. You knew I was a hard man. You knew I take what I have not put down. You knew I gather where I have not planted. 23 Why did you not put my money in the bank? Then when I came back I could have had my own money and what the bank paid for using it.'

24 "Then he said to those who were standing by, 'Take the piece of money from him and give it to the one who has ten pieces of money.' 25 And they said to him, 'Lord, he already has ten pieces of money.'

26 Jesus said, "I tell you, he who has, to him will be given more. To him who does not have, even the little he has will be taken from him. 27 'Bring here those who hated me and did not want me to be king and kill them in front of me.' " 28 When He had finished the picture-story, He went on ahead of them up to Jerusalem.

The Last Time Jesus Goes into Jerusalem
(Matthew 21:1–11; Mark 11:1–11; John 12:12–19)

29 When Jesus was coming near the towns of Bethphage and Bethany by the Mount of Olives, He sent two of His followers on ahead. 30 He said, "Go into the town ahead of you. There you will find a young donkey tied. No man has ever sat on it. Let it loose and bring it to Me. 31 If anyone asks you, 'Why are you letting it loose?' say to him, 'Because the Lord needs it.' "

32 Those who were sent found everything as Jesus had told them. 33 As they were letting the young donkey loose, the owners said to them, "Why are you letting the young donkey loose?" 34 They answered, "The Lord needs it." 35 Then they brought it to Jesus. They put their coats on the donkey and they put Jesus on it.

36 As Jesus was going, they put their coats down on the road. 37 Jesus was near the city and ready to go down the Mount of Olives. The many people who were following Him began to sing with loud voices and give thanks for all the powerful

works they had seen. 38 They said, "Great and honored is the King Who comes in the name of the Lord. There is peace and greatness in the highest heaven."

39 Some of the proud religious law-keepers who were in among the people said to Jesus, "Teacher, speak sharp words to Your followers." 40 Jesus said to them, "I tell you that if these did not speak, the very stones would call out."

Jesus Cries as He Sees Jerusalem

41 When Jesus came near the city, He cried as He saw it. 42 He said, "If you had only known on this great day the things that make peace! But now they are hidden from your eyes. 43 The time is coming when those who hate you will dig earth and throw it up around you making a wall. They will shut you in from every side. 44 They will destroy you and your children with you. There will not be one stone on another. It is because you did not know when God visited you."

Jesus Stops the Buying and Selling in the House of God
(Matthew 21:12–17; Mark 11:15–19; John 2:13–17)

45 Jesus went into the house of God. He made those leave who were buying and selling there. 46 He said to them, "It is written, 'My house is a house of prayer.' But you have made it a place of robbers." (Isaiah 56:7; Jeremiah 7:11)

47 Jesus taught each day in the house of God. But the religious leaders and the teachers of the Law and other leaders of the people tried to think of some way they could kill Him. 48 They could not find a way because the people were always near Him listening to Him teach.

They Ask Jesus Who Gave Him the Power to Do These Things
(Matthew 21:23–32; Mark 11:27–33)

20 As He was teaching and preaching the Good News, the religious leaders and the teachers of the Law and the elders came. 2 They said to Him, "Tell us, by what right and power are You doing these things? Who gave You the right and the power?" 3 Jesus said to them, "I will ask you one question also. You answer Me. 4 Was the baptism of John from heaven or from men?"

5 They said to themselves, "If we say, 'From heaven,' He will say, 'Then why did you not believe him?' 6 But if we say, 'From

men,' then all the people will throw stones at us because they believe John was one who spoke for God." 7 They said that they did not know where John's baptism came from. 8 Jesus said to them, "And I will not tell you where I get the right and the power to do these things."

The Picture-Story of the Grape-Field
(Matthew 21:33–46; Mark 12:1–12)

9 Jesus began to tell the people a picture-story, saying, "There was a man who planted a grape-field. He rented it to farmers. Then he went to a country far away for a long time. 10 At the time of gathering fruit he sent one of his servants to the farmers to get some of the fruit. But the farmers beat him and sent him away without fruit. 11 He sent another servant. The farmers beat him also. They made it very hard for him and sent him away without fruit. 12 He sent a third servant. They hurt him and threw him out of the grape-field.

13 "Then the owner of the grape-field said, 'What should I do? I will send my much-loved son. They might respect him.' 14 The farmers saw the son. They said to themselves, 'This is the one who will get everything when the owner dies. Let us kill him, and we will get everything.' 15 They put him out of the grape-field and killed him. Now what will the owner of the grape-field do to them? 16 He will come and kill those farmers. Then he will rent the grape-field to other farmers."

When they heard this, they said, "May this never be done!" 17 Jesus looked at them and said, "What does this writing mean, 'The Stone that was put aside by the workmen has become the most important Stone in the building'? (Psalm 118:22) 18 Whoever falls on this Stone will be broken. And on the one it falls, it will make him like dust." (Isaiah 8:14–15)

They Try to Trap Jesus
(Matthew 22:15–22; Mark 12:13–17)

19 At this time the religious leaders and the teachers of the Law tried to take Jesus, but they were afraid of the people. These leaders knew Jesus had told this picture-story against them. 20 They watched Jesus and they sent men who pretended to be good people to watch Him. They wanted to trap Him in something He said. Then they could give Him over to the leader of the people who had the right and the power to say what to do with Him.

21 These men who were sent asked Jesus, "Teacher, we know what You say and teach is right. We know You do not show more respect to one person than to another. We know You teach the truth about God. 22 Is it right for us to pay taxes to Caesar or not?" 23 Jesus knew they were trying to trap Him. He said, 24 "Show Me a piece of money. Whose picture is this? Whose name is on it?" And they said, "Caesar's." 25 Jesus said to them, "Pay to Caesar the things that belong to Caesar. Pay to God the things that belong to God." 26 They could find nothing wrong with what He taught. They were surprised and wondered about what He told the people, so they said nothing more.

They Ask about Being Raised from the Dead
(Matthew 22:23–33; Mark 12:10–27)

27 Some people from the religious group who believe no one will be raised from the dead came to Jesus. They asked Him, 28 "Teacher, Moses wrote to us in the Law, 'If a man's brother dies and leaves a wife but no children, then his brother must marry her. He should have children for his brother who died.' (Deuteronomy 25:5) 29 There were seven brothers. The first had a wife but died without children. 30 The second brother took her for his wife. He died without children. 31 The third brother took her for his wife. In the same way all seven took her for a wife. They all died without children. 32 Then the woman died also. 33 When people are raised from the dead, whose wife will she be? All seven brothers had her for a wife."

34 Jesus said to them, "People of this earth marry and are given in marriage. 35 But those who have the right to have that life and are raised from the dead do not marry and are not given in marriage. 36 They cannot die anymore. They are as the angels and are sons of God. They are children who have been raised from the dead. 37 As for the dead being raised, even Moses spoke of that when he told of the burning bush. There he calls the Lord, the God of Abraham and the God of Isaac and the God of Jacob. 38 For He is not the God of the dead. He is the God of the living. All live for Him."

39 One of the teachers of the Law said, "Teacher, You have spoken well." 40 After that they were afraid to ask Him anything.

Jesus Asks the Teachers of the Law about the Christ

(Matthew 22:41–46; Mark 12:35–37)

41 Jesus said to them, "How do they say that Christ is the Son of David? 42 For David himself said in the Book of Psalms, 'The Lord said to My Lord, "Sit at my right side 43 until I make those who hate You a place to rest Your feet." ' (Psalm 110:1) 44 David calls Him, 'Lord!' Then how can He be his son?"

False Teachers

(Matthew 23:1–36; Mark 12:38–40)

45 All the people were listening. He said to His followers, 46 "Look out for the teachers of the Law. They like to walk around in long coats. They like to have people speak words of respect to them in the center of town where people gather. They like the important seats in the places of worship. They like the important places at big suppers. 47 They take houses from poor women whose husbands have died. They cover up their actions by making long prayers. They will be punished all the more."

A Woman Whose Husband Had Died Gives All She Has

(Mark 12:41–44)

21 Jesus looked up and saw rich men putting their money into the money box in the house of God. 2 He saw a poor woman whose husband had died. She put in two very small pieces of money. 3 He said, "I tell you the truth, this poor woman has put in more than all of them. 4 For they have put in a little of the money they had no need for. She is very poor and has put in all she had. She has put in what she needed for her own living."

Jesus Tells of the House of God

(Matthew 24:1–51; Mark 13:11–37)

5 Some people were talking about the house of God. They were saying that the stones were beautiful and that many gifts had been given. Jesus said, 6 "As for these things you see, all these stones will be thrown down. Not one will be left on another." 7 They asked Jesus, "Teacher, when will this take place? What are we to look for to show us these things are about to happen?" 8 He said, "Be careful that no one leads you the wrong way. For many people will come in My name. They will say, 'I am the Christ.' The time is near. Do not follow them. 9 When you hear of wars

and fighting in different places, do not be afraid. These things have to happen first, but the end is not yet."

10 Then Jesus said to them, "Nations will have wars with other nations. Countries will fight against countries. 11 The earth will shake and break apart in different places. There will be no food. There will be bad diseases among many people. Very special things will be seen in the sky that will make people much afraid.

12 "But before all this happens, men will take hold of you and make it very hard for you. They will give you over to the places of worship and to the prisons. They will bring you in front of kings and the leaders of the people. This will all be done to you because of Me. 13 This will be a time for you to tell about Me. 14 Do not think about what you will say ahead of time. 15 For I will give you wisdom in what to say and I will help you say it. Those who are against you will not be able to stop you or say you are wrong.

16 "You will be handed over by your parents and your brothers and your family and your friends. They will kill some of you. 17 All men will hate you because of Me. 18 Yet not one hair of your head will be lost. 19 But stay true and your souls will have life.

Days of Trouble and Pain and Sorrow

20 "When you see armies all around Jerusalem, know that it will soon be destroyed. 21 Those in the country of Judea must run to the mountains. Those in the city must leave at once. Those in the country must not go into the city. 22 People will be punished in these hard days. All things will happen as it is written. 23 "It will be hard for women who will soon be mothers. It will be hard for those feeding babies in those days. It will be very hard for the people in the land and anger will be brought down on them. 24 People will be killed by the sword. They will be held in prison by all nations. Jerusalem will be walked over by the people who are not Jews until their time is finished.

Jesus Will Come Again in His Shining-Greatness

25 "There will be special things to look for in the sun and moon and stars. The nations of the earth will be troubled and will not know what to do. They will be troubled at the angry sea and waves. 26 The hearts of men will give up because of being afraid

of what is coming on the earth. The powers of the heavens will be shaken. 27 Then they will see the Son of Man coming in the clouds with power and much greatness. 28 When these things begin to happen, lift up your heads because you have been bought by the blood of Christ and will soon be free."

The Picture-Story of the Fig Tree

29 Jesus told them a picture-story. He said, "Look at the fig tree and all the other trees. 30 When you see their leaves coming out, you know summer is near. 31 In the same way, when you see these things happening, you will know the holy nation of God is near. 32 For sure, I tell you, that the people of this day will not die before all these things happen.

33 "Heaven and earth will pass away, but My Words will not pass away. 34 Watch yourselves! Do not let yourselves be loaded down with too much eating and strong drink. Do not be troubled with the cares of this life. If you do, that day will come on you without you knowing it. 35 It will come on all people over all the earth. 36 Be sure you watch. Pray all the time so that you may be able to keep from going through all these things that will happen and be able to stand before the Son of Man."

37 Every day Jesus taught in the house of God. At night He went to the Mount of Olives and stayed there. 38 Early in the morning all the people came to the house of God to hear Him.

They Look for a Way to Put Jesus to Death
(Matthew 26:1–5; Mark 14:1–2)

22 The time for the supper of bread without yeast was near. It was the special religious gathering to remember how the Jews left Egypt. 2 The religious leaders and the teachers of the Law looked for a way to kill Jesus. But they were afraid of the people.

3 Then Satan came into the heart of Judas who was called Iscariot. He was one of the twelve followers. 4 Judas went away and talked with the religious leaders and the leaders of the people. He talked about how he might hand Jesus over to them. 5 They were glad and promised to pay him money. 6 Judas promised to do this and then looked for a way to hand Jesus over when there were no people around.

Getting Ready for the Special Supper
(Matthew 26:17–19; Mark 14:12–16)

7 The day of bread without yeast came. It was the day when the lamb had to be killed and given on the altar in worship in the house of God. It was the special religious gathering to remember how the Jews left Egypt. 8 Jesus sent Peter and John and said, "Go and get this special supper ready for us that we may eat." 9 They said to Him, "Where do You want us to get it ready?" 10 He answered, "See, when you go into the city, you will meet a man carrying a jar of water. Follow him into the house where he goes. 11 Say to the owner of the house, 'The Teacher asks you, "Where is the room you keep for friends where I may eat this special supper with My followers?" ' 12 He will take you to a large room on the second floor with everything in it. Make it ready for us."

13 They went and found everything as Jesus had said. They got ready for the special supper.

The First Lord's Supper
(Matthew 26:26–30; Mark 14:22–26)

14 When the time came, Jesus sat down with the twelve followers. 15 He said to them, "I have wanted very much to eat this special supper with you to remember how the Jews left Egypt. I have wanted to eat this with you before I suffer. 16 I say to you, I will not eat this special supper again until its true meaning is completed in the holy nation of God."

17 Then Jesus took the cup and gave thanks. He said, "Take this and pass it to each one. 18 I say to you that I will not drink of the fruit of the vine until the holy nation of God comes."

19 Then Jesus took bread and gave thanks and broke it in pieces. He gave it to them, saying, "This is My body which is given for you. Do this to remember Me." 20 In the same way, after they had finished the bread, He took the cup. He said, "This cup is My blood of the New Way of Worship which is given for you.

Jesus Tells of the One Who Will Hand Him Over

21 "See, the hand of the one who will give Me over to the leaders of the country is on the table with Me. 22 The Son of Man will be taken this way because it has been in God's plan. But it is bad for that man who hands Him over!" 23 They began to ask each other which of them would do this.

Arguing about Who Is the Greatest

24 They started to argue among themselves about who was thought to be the greatest. 25 Jesus said to them, "The kings of the nations show their power to the people. Those who have power over the people are given names of honor. 26 But you will not be like that. Let the greatest among you be the least. Let the leader be as the one who cares for others. 27 Who is greater, the one who is eating at the table, or the one who is caring for him? Is it not the one who is eating at the table? But I am here with you as One Who cares for you.

The Followers Will Be Honored

28 "You have stayed with Me through all the hard things that have come to Me. 29 As My Father has given Me a holy nation, I will give you the right 30 to eat and drink at My table in My holy nation. You will sit on thrones and judge the twelve family groups of the Jewish nation."

Jesus Tells How Peter Will Lie about Him

(Matthew 26:31–35; Mark 14:27–31; John 13:36–38)

31 The Lord said, "Simon, Simon, listen! Satan has wanted to have you. He will divide you as wheat is divided from that which is no good. 32 But I have prayed for you. I have prayed that your faith will be strong and that you will not give up. When you return, you must help to make your brothers strong." 33 Peter said to Jesus, "Lord, I am ready to go to prison and to die with You!" 34 Jesus said, "I tell you, Peter, a rooster will not crow today before you will say three times that you do not know Me."

The Followers Are Told of Trouble to Come

35 Jesus said to them, "I sent you without money or bag or shoes. Did you need anything?" They said, "Nothing." 36 Then He said to them, "But now whoever has a money-bag and a bag for food should take it. Whoever does not have a sword should sell his coat and buy one. 37 I tell you, that what has been written about Me must happen. It says, 'They thought of Him as One Who broke the Law.' (Isaiah 53:12) What is told about Me must happen."

38 They said, "Lord, look, we have two swords." He answered, "That is enough."

Jesus Prays in the Garden

(Matthew 26:36–46; Mark 14:32–42)

39 Jesus came out of the room. Then He went to the Mount of Olives as He had been doing. The followers went with Him. 40 When He got there, He said to them, "Pray that you will not be tempted." 41 He walked away from them about as far as a stone can be thrown. There He got down with His face on the ground and prayed. 42 He said, "Father, if it can be done, take away what must happen to Me. Even so, not what I want, but what You want." 43 An angel from heaven came and gave Him strength. 44 His heart was much troubled and He prayed all the more. Water ran from His face like blood and fell to the ground.

45 When Jesus got up after praying, He went back to the followers. He found them sleeping because of so much sorrow. 46 He said to them, "Why are you sleeping? Get up and pray that you will not be tempted."

Jesus Is Handed Over to Sinners

(Matthew 26:47–56; Mark 14:43–52; John 18:1–11)

47 While Jesus was speaking, Judas came walking ahead of many people. He was one of the twelve followers. He came near to Jesus to kiss Him. 48 But Jesus said to him, "Judas, are you handing over the Son of Man with a kiss?" 49 Those around Jesus saw what was going to happen and asked, "Lord, should we fight with our swords?" 50 One of them hit a servant who was owned by the head religious leader and cut off his right ear. 51 Jesus said, "Stop! This is enough." And He put His hand on his ear and healed him.

Jesus Stands in Front of the Religious Leaders

(Matthew 26:57–58; Mark 14:53–54; John 18:19–24)

52 Jesus said to the religious leaders and the leaders of the house of God and the other leaders who came to Him, "Have you come with swords and sticks to take Me, as if I were a robber? 53 While I was with you everyday in the house of God, you never took hold of Me. But now is the time you are to come and you have come in the dark."

54 Then they led Jesus away to the house of the head religious leader. Peter followed a long way behind Him.

Peter Says He Does Not Know Jesus
(Matthew 26:69–75; Mark 14:66–72; John 18:15–18, 25–27)

55 They built a fire in the yard and sat down. Peter sat down with them. 56 One of the servant-girls saw Peter as he sat by the fire and looked right at him. She said, "This man was with Jesus also." 57 Peter lied and said, "Woman, I do not know Him." 58 After awhile another person saw him and said, "You are one of them also." Peter said, "No, sir, I am not." 59 About an hour later another person said the same thing, "For sure, this man was with Jesus also because he is from Galilee." 60 But Peter said, "Sir, I do not know what you are saying." And at once, while he was talking, a rooster crowed. 61 The Lord turned and looked at Peter. He remembered the Lord had said, "Before a rooster crows, you will say three times that you do not know Me." 62 Peter went outside and cried with a troubled heart.

63 Those who watched Jesus so He could not get away made fun of Him and beat Him. 64 They covered His eyes with a cloth and asked Him, "Tell us who hit You!" 65 They said many other bad things against Jesus.

66 When it was morning the leaders of the people and the religious leaders and the teachers of the Law got together. They took Jesus to the court of the religious leader. They said, 67 "Tell us if you are the Christ." He said to them, "If I tell you, you will not believe Me. 68 If I ask you something, you will not tell Me. 69 From now on, the Son of Man will be seated at the right hand of the All-powerful God." 70 They all said, "Then are You the Son of God?" He said, "You say that I am." 71 Then they said, "What other word do we need against Him? We have heard Him say this with His own mouth."

Jesus Stands in Front of Pilate
(Matthew 27:1–2, 11–14; Mark 15:1–5; John 18:28–37)

23 Then all the many people got up and took Jesus to Pilate. 2 They began to tell things against Him, saying, "We have found this Man leading the people of our nation in a wrong way. He has been telling them not to pay taxes to Caesar. He has been saying He is Christ, a King."

3 Pilate asked Jesus, "Are You the King of the Jews?" He said, "What you said is true." 4 Then Pilate said to the religious leaders and to the people, "I find nothing wrong in this Man." 5 They became more angry. They said, "He makes trouble among the people. He has been teaching over all the country of Judea, starting in Galilee and now here."

Jesus Is Sent to Herod

6 When Pilate heard the word, Galilee, he asked, "Is the Man from Galilee?" 7 As soon as Pilate knew Jesus belonged in the country where Herod was king, he sent Him to Herod. Herod was in Jerusalem at that time also.

8 Herod was very glad when he saw Jesus because he had wanted to see Him for a long time. He had heard many things about Him and had hoped to see Him do some powerful work. 9 Herod talked to Jesus and asked many things. But Jesus said nothing. 10 The religious leaders and the teachers of the Law were standing there. They said many false things against Him.

11 Then Herod and his soldiers were very bad to Jesus and made fun of Him. They put a beautiful coat on Him and sent Him back to Pilate. 12 That day Pilate and Herod became friends. Before that they had worked against each other.

13 Pilate called the religious leaders and the leaders of the people and the people together. 14 He said to them, "You brought this Man to me as one that leads the people in the wrong way. I have asked Him about these things in front of you. I do not find Him guilty of the things you say against Him. 15 Herod found nothing wrong with Him because he sent Him back to us. There is no reason to have Him put to death. 16 I will punish Him and let Him go free."

Jesus or Barabbas Is to Go Free
(Matthew 27:15–26; Mark 15:6–14; John 18:38–40)

17 *Every year at the time of the special supper, Pilate would let one person who was in prison go free. 18 They all cried out together with a loud voice, "Take this Man away! Let Barabbas go free." 19 Barabbas had killed some people and had made trouble against the leaders of the country. He had been put in prison.

20 Pilate wanted to let Jesus go free so he talked to them again. 21 But they cried out, "Nail Him to a cross! Nail Him to a cross!" 22 Pilate said to them the third time, "Why, what bad thing has He done? I have found

no reason to put Him to death. I will punish Him and let Him go free."

23 But they kept on crying out with loud voices saying that He must be nailed to a cross. Their loud voices got what they wanted. 24 Then Pilate said that it should be done as they wanted. 25 Pilate let the man go free who had made trouble against the leaders of the country and who had killed people. He gave Jesus over to them to do with as they wanted.

Jesus on the Cross
(Matthew 27:33–37; Mark 15:22–26; John 19:17–22)

26 They led Jesus away. A man named Simon was coming in from the country of Cyrene and they made him carry the cross following behind Jesus.

27 Many people followed Jesus. There were women who cried and had sorrow for Him. 28 Jesus turned to them and said, "Daughters of Jerusalem do not cry for Me. Cry for yourselves and your children. 29 Listen! The days are coming when they will say, 'Those who have never had children are happy. Those whose bodies have never given birth are happy. Those who have never fed babies are happy.' 30 They will begin to say to the mountains, 'Fall on us.' They will say to the hills, 'Cover us.' 31 If they do these things to a green tree, what will they do when it is dry?"

32 Two other men were led away with Jesus to be put to death also. These men had done things making them guilty of death. 33 When they came to the place called Calvary, they nailed Jesus to a cross. The other two men were nailed to crosses also. One was on the right side of Jesus and the other was on His left side. 34 Then Jesus said, "Father, forgive them. They do not know what they are doing." And they divided His clothes by drawing names.

35 The people stood around looking on. The leaders were there with them making fun of Jesus. They said, "He saved others, let Him save Himself if He is the Christ, the Chosen One of God!" 36 The soldiers made fun of Him also. They put sour wine before Him. 37 They said, "If You are the King of the Jews, save Yourself." 38 These words were written in the Greek and Latin and Hebrew languages above His head: "THIS IS THE KING OF THE JEWS."

The Two Robbers
(Matthew 27:38–44; Mark 15:27–32)

39 One of the men who was guilty of death who was on a cross beside Jesus spoke bad words to Him. He said, "If You are the Christ, save Yourself and us." 40 But the other man on a cross spoke sharp words to the one who made fun of Jesus. He said, "Are you not afraid of God? You are also guilty and will be punished. 41 We are suffering and we should, because of the wrong we have done. But this Man has done nothing wrong." 42 And he said to Jesus, "Lord, remember me when You come into Your holy nation." 43 Jesus said to him, "For sure, I tell you, today you will be with Me in Paradise."

Jesus Dies on the Cross
(Matthew 27:45–50; Mark 15:33–36; John 19:28–37)

44 It was dark over all the earth from noon until three o'clock. 45 The sun did not shine. In the house of God the curtain was torn in two pieces.

46 Then Jesus cried out with a loud voice, "Father, into Your hands I give My spirit." When He said this, He died.

47 When the soldier saw what had happened, he thanked God. He said, "For sure, He was a good man." 48 All the many people who came together to see the things that were done, went away beating themselves on their chests. 49 All His friends and the women who had come with Him from Galilee stood a long way off watching these things.

Jesus Is Buried
(Matthew 27:57–66; Mark 15:42–47; John 19:38–42)

50 There was a man named Joseph who belonged to the court. He was a good man and one who did right. 51 This man did not agree with what the court did. He was from Arimathea, a city of the Jews. He was looking for the holy nation of God to come. 52 Joseph went to Pilate and asked for the body of Jesus.

53 Then he took it down and put it in linen cloth. It was laid in a grave which had been cut out in the side of a rock. This grave had never been used. 54 It was time to get ready for the Day of Rest which was about to begin. 55 The women who had come with Jesus from Galilee followed behind. They saw the grave and how His body was laid. 56 They went back and got some spices and perfumes ready. But they rested on the Day of Rest as the Law said to do.

Jesus Is Raised from the Dead

(Matthew 28:1–10; Mark 16:1–8; John 20:1–18)

24 Early in the morning on the first day of the week, the women went to the grave taking the spices they had made ready. 2 They found the stone had been pushed away from the grave. 3 They went in but they did not find the body of the Lord Jesus.

4 While they wondered about what had happened, they saw two men standing by them in shining clothes. 5 They were very much afraid and got down with their faces to the ground. The men said to them, "Why do you look for the living One among those who are dead? 6 He is not here. He is risen. Do you not remember what He said to you when He was yet in Galilee? 7 He said, 'The Son of Man must be given over into the hands of sinful men. He must be nailed to a cross. He will rise again three days later.' " 8 They remembered what He had said.

9 When they came back from the grave, they told all these things to the eleven followers and to all the others. 10 They were Mary Magdalene and Joanna and Mary the mother of James. Other women who were with them told these things to the followers also. 11 Their words sounded like foolish talk. The followers did not believe them. 12 But Peter got up and ran to the grave. He got down to look in and saw only the linen clothes. Then he went away, surprised about what had happened.

The Followers of Jesus Do Not Believe He Is Risen

(Mark 16:9–14; John 20:24–29)

13 That same day two of His followers were going to the town of Emmaus. It was about a two-hour walk from Jerusalem. 14 They talked of all these things that had happened. 15 While they were talking together, Jesus Himself came and walked along with them. 16 Something kept their eyes from seeing Who He was.

17 He said to them, "What are you talking about as you walk?" They stood still and looked sad. 18 One of them, whose name was Cleopas, said to Him, "Are you the only one visiting Jerusalem who has not heard of the things that have happened here these days?" 19 Jesus said to them, "What things?" They answered, "The things about Jesus of Nazareth. He was the great One Who spoke for God. He did powerful things and spoke pow-

erful words in the sight of God and the people. 20 And the religious leaders and the leaders of the people gave Him over to be killed and nailed Him to a cross. 21 We were hoping He was the One Who was going to make the Jewish people free. But it was three days ago when these things happened.

22 "Some of the women of our group have surprised us and made us wonder. They went to the grave early this morning. 23 They did not find His body. They came back saying they had seen angels in a special dream who said that He was alive. 24 Some of those who were with us went to the grave and found it as the women had said. But they did not see Him."

25 Then Jesus said to them, "You foolish men. How slow you are to believe what the early preachers have said. 26 Did not Christ have to go through these hard things to come into His shining-greatness?" 27 Jesus kept on telling them what Moses and all the early preachers had said about Him in the Holy Writings.

28 When they came to the town where they were going, Jesus acted as if He were going farther. 29 But they said to Him, "Stay with us. It will soon be evening. The day is about over." He went in to stay with them. 30 As He sat at the table with them, He took the bread and gave thanks and broke it. Then He gave it to them. 31 And their eyes were opened and they knew Him. Then He left them and could not be seen. 32 They said to each other, "Were not our hearts filled with joy when He talked to us on the road about what the Holy Writings said?"

33 Then they got up at once and went back to Jerusalem. They found the eleven followers together and others with them. 34 They said, "For sure the Lord is risen and was seen by Simon." 35 Then they told what had happened on the road and how they came to know Him when He broke the bread.

Jesus Is Seen by the Other Ten Followers

36 As they talked, Jesus Himself stood among them. He said, "May you have peace." 37 But they were afraid and full of fear. They thought they saw a spirit. 38 Jesus said to them, "Why are you afraid? Why do you have doubts in your hearts? 39 Look at My hands and My feet. See! It is I, Myself! Touch Me and see for yourself. A spirit does not have flesh and bones as I have." 40 When Jesus had said this, He showed them His hands and feet.

41 They still wondered. It was hard for them to believe it and yet it made them happy. Then He said to them, "Do you have anything here to eat?" 42 They gave Jesus a piece of fish that had been cooked and some honey. 43 He took it and ate it in front of them.

Jesus Sends His Followers to Teach
(Matthew 28:16–20; Mark 16:15–18; John 20:21–23)

44 Jesus said to them, "These are the things I told you while I was yet with you. All things written about Me in the Law of Moses and in the Books of the early preachers and in the Psalms must happen as they said they would happen." 45 Then He opened their minds to understand the Holy Writings. 46 He said to them, "It is written that Christ should suffer and be raised from the dead after three days. 47 It must be preached that men must be

sorry for their sins and turn from them. Then they will be forgiven. This must be preached in His name to all nations beginning in Jerusalem. 48 You are to tell what you have seen. 49 See! I will send you what My Father promised. But you are to stay in Jerusalem until you have received power from above."

Jesus Goes to Be Beside His Father
(Mark 16:19–20)

50 Jesus led them out as far as Bethany. Then He lifted up His hands and prayed that good would come to them. 51 And while He was praying that good would come to them, He went from them (*and was taken up to heaven and 52 they worshiped Him). Then they went back to Jerusalem with great joy. 53 They spent all their time in the house of God honoring and giving thanks to God.

JOHN

Christ Lived Before the World Was Made

1 The Word (Christ) was in the beginning. The Word was with God. The Word was God. 2 He was with God in the beginning. 3 He made all things. Nothing was made without Him making it. 4 Life began by Him. His Life was the Light for men. 5 The Light shines in the darkness. The darkness has never been able to put out the Light.

John the Baptist Tells of the Coming of Christ

6 There was a man sent from God whose name was John. 7 He came to tell what he knew about the Light so that all men might believe through him. 8 John was not the Light, but he was sent to tell about the Light.

9 This true Light, coming into the world, gives light to every man. 10 He came into the world. The world was made by Him, but it did not know Him. 11 He came to His own, but His own did not receive Him. 12 He gave the right and the power to become children of God to those who received Him. He gave this to those who put their trust in His name. 13 These children of God were not born of blood and of flesh and of man's desires, but they were born of God. 14 Christ became human flesh

and lived among us. We saw His shining-greatness. This greatness is given only to a much-loved Son from His Father. He was full of loving-favor and truth.

John the Baptist Makes the Way Ready for Jesus Christ
(Matthew 3:1–12; Mark 1:1–8; Luke 3:1–18)

15 John told about Christ and said, "I have been telling you about this One. I said, 'He is coming after me. He is more important than I because He lived before me.'" 16 From Him Who has so much we have all received loving-favor, one loving-favor after another. 17 The Law was given through Moses, but loving-favor and truth came through Jesus Christ. 18 The much-loved Son is beside the Father. No man has ever seen God. But Christ has made God known to us.

19 The Jews sent their religious leaders and men from the family group of Levi to ask John, "Who are you?" 20 He told them without holding back any words, "I am not the Christ." 21 They asked him, "Then who are you? Are you Elijah?" He said, "I am not!" Then they asked, "Are you the special One Who was to come to speak for God?" John said, "No." 22 Then they asked him, "Who are you? We must tell those who sent us. What do you say about yourself?"

23 John said, "I am the voice of one crying in the desert. 'Make the road straight for the Lord,' as the early preacher Isaiah said." (Isaiah 40:3)

24 Those who had been sent were from the proud religious law-keepers. 25 They asked John again, "Then why do you baptize if you are not the Christ or Elijah or that special One Who was to come to speak for God?" 26 John answered, "I baptize with water. But there is One standing among you Whom you do not know. 27 He is the One Who is coming after me. I am not good enough to get down and help Him take off His shoes." 28 All this happened when John was baptizing in the town of Bethany. He was on the other side of the Jordan River.

The Baptism of Jesus
(Matthew 3:13–17; Mark 1:9–11; Luke 3:21–22)

29 The next day John the Baptist saw Jesus coming to him. He said, "See! The Lamb of God Who takes away the sin of the world! 30 I have been talking about Him. I said, 'One is coming after me Who is more important than I am, because He lived before I was born.' 31 I did not know who He was, but I have come to baptize with water so the Jews might know about Him."

32 Then John said, "I saw the Holy Spirit come down on Jesus as a dove from heaven. The Holy Spirit stayed on Him. 33 I did not know Him then. But God sent me to baptize with water. God said to me, 'The Holy Spirit will come down and stay on Him. He is the One Who baptizes with the Holy Spirit.' 34 I saw this happen. I am now saying that Jesus is the Son of God."

Jesus Calls Andrew and Peter

35 The next day John the Baptist was standing with two of his own followers. 36 Jesus walked by. John looked at Him and said, "See! The Lamb of God." 37 John's two followers heard him say this and followed Jesus. 38 Jesus turned around and saw them following. He said to them, "What are you looking for?" They answered, "Teacher, where are you staying?" 39 He said to them, "Come and see." They followed Him and saw where He lived. They stayed with Him that day. It was about four o'clock in the afternoon.

40 Andrew, Simon Peter's brother, was one of the two who had heard John's words and had followed Jesus. 41 The first thing he did was to find his brother Simon. He said to him, "We have found the Christ!" 42 Andrew took Simon to Jesus. When Jesus saw Simon, He said, "You are Simon, the son of John. Your name will be Cephas." The name Cephas means Peter, or a rock.

Jesus Calls Philip And Nathanael

43 The next day Jesus wanted to go to the country of Galilee. He found Philip and said to him, "Follow Me." 44 Philip was from the town of Bethsaida. Andrew and Peter were from this town also. 45 Philip found Nathanael and said to him, "We have found the One Moses wrote about in the Law. He is the One the early preachers wrote about. He is Jesus of Nazareth, the Son of Joseph." 46 Nathanael said, "Can anything good come out of the town of Nazareth?" Philip said, "Come and see."

47 Jesus saw Nathanael coming to Him and said, "See! There is a true Jew. There is nothing false in him." 48 Nathanael said to Jesus, "How do you know me?" Jesus answered him, "Before Philip talked to you, I saw you under the fig tree." 49 Nathanael said to Him, "Teacher, You are the Son of God. You are the King of the Jews." 50 Jesus said to him, "Do you believe because I said I saw you under the fig tree? You will see greater things than that. 51 For sure, I tell you, you will see heaven opened and God's angels going up and coming and down on the Son of Man."

The Powerful Work at the Wedding of Cana

2 Three days later there was a wedding in the town of Cana in the country of Galilee. The mother of Jesus was there. 2 Jesus and His followers were asked to come to the wedding. 3 When the wine was all gone, the mother of Jesus said to Him, "They have no more wine." 4 Jesus said to her, "Woman, what is that to you and to Me? It is not time for Me to work yet." 5 His mother said to the helpers, "Do whatever He says."

6 Six stone water jars were there. Each one held about one half barrel of water. These water jars were used in the Jewish worship of washing. 7 Jesus said to the helpers, "Fill the jars with water." They filled them to the top. 8 Then He said, "Take some out and give it to the head man who is caring for the people." They took some to him. 9 The head man tasted the water that had become wine. He did not

know where it came from but the helpers who took it to him knew. He called the man who had just been married. ¹⁰ The head man said to him, "Everyone puts out his best wine first. After people have had much to drink, he puts out the wine that is not so good. You have kept the good wine until now!"

¹¹ This was the first powerful work Jesus did. It was done in Cana of Galilee where He showed His power. His followers put their trust in Him. ¹² After this He went down to the city of Capernaum. His mother and brothers and followers went with Him. They stayed there a few days.

Jesus Stops the Buying and the Selling in the House of God

(Matthew 21:12–17; Mark 11:15–19; Luke 19:45–48)

¹³ It was time for the special religious gathering to remember how the Jews left Egypt. Jesus went up to Jerusalem. ¹⁴ He went into the house of God and found cattle and sheep and doves being sold. Men were sitting there changing money. ¹⁵ Jesus made a whip of small ropes. He used it to make them all leave the house of God along with the sheep and cattle. He pushed their money off the tables and turned the tables over. ¹⁶ He said to those who sold doves, "Take these things out of here! You must not make My Father's house a place for buying and selling!" ¹⁷ Then His followers remembered that it was written in the Holy Writings, "I am jealous for the honor of Your house." (Psalm 69:9)

The Jews Ask for Something Special to See

¹⁸ Then the Jews asked Him, "What can You do to show us You have the right and the power to do these things?" ¹⁹ Jesus answered them, "Destroy this house of God and in three days I will build it again." ²⁰ Then the Jews said, "It took forty-six years to build this house of God. Will You build it up in three days?" ²¹ Jesus was speaking of His body as the house of God. ²² After Jesus had been raised from the dead, His followers remembered He said this. They believed the Holy Writings and what He had said.

²³ Jesus was in Jerusalem at the time of the special religious gathering to remember how the Jews left Egypt. Many people put their trust in Him when they saw the powerful works He did. ²⁴ But Jesus did not trust them because He knew all men. ²⁵ He did not need anyone to tell Him about man. He knew what was in man.

Nicodemus Asks Jesus about Life

3 There was a man named Nicodemus. He was a proud religious law-keeper and a leader of the Jews. ² He came to Jesus at night and said, "Teacher, we know You have come from God to teach us. No one can do these powerful works You do unless God is with Him."

Jesus Tells of the New Kind of Birth

³ Jesus said to him, "For sure, I tell you, unless a man is born again, he cannot see the holy nation of God." ⁴ Nicodemus said to Him, "How can a man be born when he is old? How can he get into his mother's body and be born the second time?" ⁵ Jesus answered, "For sure, I tell you, unless a man is born of water and of the Spirit of God, he cannot get into the holy nation of God. ⁶ Whatever is born of the flesh is flesh. Whatever is born of the Spirit is spirit.

⁷ "Do not be surprised that I said to you, 'You must be born again.' ⁸ The wind blows where it wants to and you hear its sound. You do not know where it comes from or where it goes. It is the same with everyone who is born of the Spirit of God."

⁹ Nicodemus said to Him, "How can this be?" ¹⁰ Jesus said, "Are you a teacher among the Jews and do not know these things? ¹¹ For sure, I tell you, We are talking about things We know. We tell of what We have seen. Yet you do not take Our words to be true. ¹² I tell you about things of the earth and you do not believe them. How will you believe if I tell you things about heaven?

¹³ "No one has gone up into heaven except the One Who came down from heaven. That One is the Son of Man *Who is in heaven. ¹⁴ As Moses lifted up the snake in the desert, so the Son of Man must be lifted up. ¹⁵ Then whoever puts his trust in Him will have life that lasts forever. ¹⁶ For God so loved the world that He gave His only Son. Whoever puts his trust in God's Son will not be lost but will have life that lasts forever. ¹⁷ For God did not send His Son into the world to say it is guilty. He sent His Son so the world might be saved from the punishment of sin by Him. ¹⁸ Whoever puts his trust in His Son is not guilty. Whoever does not put his trust in Him is guilty already. It is because

he does not put his trust in the name of the only Son of God.

19 "The Light has come into the world. And the Light is the test by which men are guilty or not. People love darkness more than the Light because the things they do are sinful. 20 Everyone who sins hates the Light. He stays away from the Light because his sin would be found out. 21 The man who does what is right comes to the Light. What he does will be seen because he has done what God wanted him to do."

Jesus Preaches in Judea

22 After this, Jesus and His followers came into the country of Judea. He stayed with them there and baptized people.

John the Baptist Tells More about Jesus

23 John was baptizing in the town of Aenon near Salim. There was much water there and people were coming to be baptized. 24 John had not been put in prison yet.

25 Then some of the followers of John and a Jew started to argue about the religious washing of the Jewish worship. 26 They came to John and said to him, "Teacher, the One with you on the other side of the Jordan River is baptizing also. He is the One you told of. Everyone is going to Him."

27 John said, "A man can receive nothing unless it has been given to him from heaven. 28 You heard the words that I said, 'I am not the Christ, but I have been sent before Him.' 29 The man who has just been married has the bride. The friend of the man just married stands at his side and listens to him. He has joy when he hears the voice of the man just married. I am full of this joy. 30 He must become more important. I must become less important.

31 "He Who comes from above is above all. He who comes from the earth is of the earth and speaks of the earth. He Who comes from heaven is above all. 32 He tells of what He has seen and heard. But no one believes what He says. 33 Whoever receives His words proves that God is true. 34 He was sent by God and He speaks God's Word. God gives Him all of His Spirit. 35 The Father loves the Son and has given all things into His hand. 36 He who puts his trust in the Son has life that lasts forever. He who does not put his trust in the Son will not have life, but the anger of God is on him."

A Woman of Samaria at the Well

4 Jesus knew the proud religious law-keepers had heard He was making and baptizing more followers than John. 2 Jesus did not baptize anyone Himself but His followers did. 3 Then Jesus went from the country of Judea to the country of Galilee. 4 He had to go through the country of Samaria. 5 So He came to a town in Samaria called Sychar. It was near the piece of ground that Jacob gave to his son Joseph. 6 Jacob's well was there. Jesus was tired from traveling so He sat down just as He was by the well. It was about noon.

7 A woman of Samaria came to get water. Jesus said to her, "Give Me a drink." 8 His followers had gone to the town to buy food. 9 The woman of Samaria said to Him, "You are a Jew. I am of Samaria. Why do You ask me for a drink when the Jews have nothing to do with the people of Samaria?"

10 Jesus said to her, "You do not know what God has to give. You do not know Who said to you, 'Give Me a drink.' If you knew, you would have asked Him. He would have given you living water." 11 The woman said to Him, "Sir, the well is deep. You have nothing to get water with. Where will You get the living water? 12 Are You greater than our early father Jacob? He gave us the well. He and his children and his cattle drank from it."

Jesus Tells of the Living Water

13 Jesus said to her, "Whoever drinks this water will be thirsty again. 14 Whoever drinks the water that I will give him will never be thirsty. The water that I will give him will become in him a well of life that lasts forever."

15 The woman said, "Sir, give me this water so I will never be thirsty. Then I will not have to come all this way for water."

The True Kind of Worship

16 Jesus said to her, "Go call your husband and come back." 17 The woman said, "I have no husband." Jesus said, "You told the truth when you said, 'I have no husband.' 18 You have had five husbands. The one you have now is not your husband. You told the truth."

19 The woman said to Him, "Sir, I think You are a person Who speaks for God. 20 Our early fathers worshiped on this mountain. You Jews say Jerusalem is the place where men should worship."

21 Jesus said to her, "Woman, believe

Me. The time is coming when you will not worship the Father on this mountain or in Jerusalem. 22 You people do not know what you worship. We Jews know what we worship. It is through the Jews that men are saved from the punishment of their sins. 23 The time is coming, yes, it is here now, when the true worshipers will worship the Father in spirit and in truth. The Father wants that kind of worshipers. 24 God is Spirit. Those who worship Him must worship Him in spirit and in truth.

Jesus Is the One the Jews Are Looking For

25 The woman said to Him, "I know the Jews are looking for One Who is coming. He is called the Christ. When He comes, He will tell us everything." 26 Jesus said to her, "I am the Christ, the One talking with you!"

27 Right then the followers came back and were surprised and wondered about finding Him talking with a woman. But no one said, "What do You want?" or, "Why are You talking with her?"

28 The woman left her water jar and went into the town. She said to the men, 29 "Come and see a Man Who told me everything I ever did! Can this be the Christ?" 30 They went out of town and came to Him.

Jesus Tells Them of a New Kind of Food

31 During this time His followers were saying to Him, "Teacher, eat something." 32 He said, "I have food to eat that you do not know of." 33 The followers said to each other, "Has someone taken food to Him?" 34 Jesus said, "My food is to do what God wants Me to do and to finish His work. 35 Do you not say, 'It is four months yet until the time to gather grain'? Listen! I say to you, open your eyes and look at the fields. They are white now and waiting for the grain to be gathered in. 36 The one who gathers gets his pay. He gathers fruit that lasts forever. The one who plants and the one who gathers will have joy together. 37 These words are true, 'One man plants and another man gathers.' 38 I sent you to gather where you have not planted. Others have planted and you have come along to gather in their fruit."

The People of Samaria Believe in Jesus

39 Many people in that town of Samaria believed in Jesus because of what the woman said about Him. She said, "He told me everything I ever did." 40 So the people of Samaria came to Him. They asked Him to stay with them. Jesus stayed there two days. 41 Many more people believed because of what He said. 42 They said to the woman, "Now we believe! It is no longer because of what you said about Jesus but we have heard Him ourselves. We know, for sure, that He is the Christ, the One Who saves men of this world from the punishment of their sins."

Jesus Goes to Galilee

43 Two days later He went from there and came to the country of Galilee. 44 Jesus Himself said that no one who speaks for God is respected in his own country. 45 When He came to Galilee, the people there were glad. They had seen all the things He did in Jerusalem. It was at the time of the special religious gathering to remember how the Jews left Egypt. They had been there also.

Jesus Heals the Dying Boy in Capernaum

46 Jesus came again to the town of Cana of Galilee where He had made water into wine. A man who worked with the king had a son who was sick in the city of Capernaum. 47 This man went to Jesus. He had heard that Jesus had come from the country of Judea to Galilee. The man asked Jesus if He would go to Capernaum and heal his son who was dying. 48 Then Jesus said to him, "Unless you see special things and powerful works done, you will not believe." 49 The man said to Him, "Sir, come with me before my son dies." 50 Jesus said to him, "Go your way. Your son will live." The man put his trust in what Jesus said and left.

51 As he was on his way home, his servants met him. They said to him, "Your son is living!" 52 He asked them what time his boy began to get well. They said to him, "Yesterday at one o'clock the sickness left." 53 The father knew it was the time Jesus had said to him, "Your son will live." He and everyone in his house put their trust in Jesus. 54 This was the second powerful work that Jesus did after He came from the country of Judea to the country of Galilee.

Jesus Heals the Man at the Pool of Bethesda

5 Some time later, there was a religious gathering of the Jews. Jesus went up to Jerusalem. 2 In Jerusalem there is a pool with five porches called Bethesda

near the sheep gate. 3 Inside these porches lay many sick people. Some were blind. Some could not walk. Some could not move their bodies. 4 (*An angel of the Lord came at certain times and made the water move. All of them were waiting for it to move. Whoever got in the water first after it was moving was healed of whatever sickness he had.)

5 A man was there who had been sick for thirty-eight years. 6 Jesus saw him lying there and knew the man had been sick a long time. Jesus said to him, "Would you like to be healed?" 7 The sick man said, "Sir, I have no one to put me in the pool when the water is moving. While I am coming, another one gets in first." 8 Jesus said to him, "Get up! Pick up your bed and walk." 9 At once the man was healed and picked up his bed and walked. This happened on the Day of Rest.

10 The Jews said to the man who had been healed, "This is the Day of Rest. It is against the Law for you to carry your bed." 11 He said to them, "The Man Who healed me said to me, 'Pick up your bed and walk.'" 12 Then the Jews asked him, "What man said to you, 'Pick up your bed and walk'?" 13 The man who had been healed did not know Who He was. Jesus had gone away while many people were there.

14 Later Jesus found the man who had been healed in the house of God. He said to him, "Listen! You have been healed. Stop sinning or something worse will come to you." 15 The man went away and told the Jews that it was Jesus Who had healed him.

The Jews Want to Kill Jesus

16 Because Jesus did these things on the Day of Rest, the Jews made it very hard for Him. 17 Jesus said to them, "My Father is still working all the time so I am working also." 18 The Jews tried all the more to kill Him, not only because He had worked on the Day of Rest, but because He had also called God His Own Father. This made Him the same as God.

Jesus Tells How He Works

19 Then Jesus said to them, "For sure, I tell you, the Son can do nothing by Himself. He does what He sees the Father doing. Whatever the Father does, the Son does also. 20 The Father loves the Son and shows the Son everything He does. The Father will show Him greater works than these. They will surprise you. 21 The

Father raises up the dead and makes them live. The Son also gives life to anyone He chooses. 22 The Father does not say who is guilty. He gives this to the Son to do. 23 He does this so that all people will honor the Son as they honor the Father. He who does not honor the Son does not honor the Father Who sent Him.

24 "For sure, I tell you, anyone who hears My Word and puts his trust in Him Who sent Me has life that lasts forever. He will not be guilty. He has already passed from death into life.

The Good People and the Sinful People Are Raised from the Dead

25 "For sure, I tell you, the time is coming. Yes, the time is here when the dead will hear the voice of the Son of God. Those who hear will live. 26 The Father has life in Himself. He has given power to the Son to have life in Himself. 27 God has given Him the right and the power to say if people are guilty, because He is the Son of Man. 28 Do not be surprised at this. The time is coming when all who are in their graves will hear His voice. 29 They will come out. Those who have done good will be raised again and will have new life. Those who have been sinful will be raised again and will be told they are guilty and will be punished.

Jesus Tells of John and of Himself

30 "I can do nothing by Myself. I say who is guilty only as My Father tells Me. That way, what I say is right, because I am not trying to do what I want to do. I am doing what the Father, Who sent Me, wants Me to do. 31 If I tell about Myself, My words are worth nothing. 32 There is another One Who tells about Me. I know the words He says about Me are true.

33 "You sent to John the Baptist and he told you the truth. 34 I do not need words from men to say I am right. I say this that you might be saved from the punishment of sin. 35 John the Baptist was a burning and shining light. You were willing for awhile to be glad in his light. 36 I have something greater than John which tells of Me. I am doing works the Father has given Me to do and they are proving that the Father has sent Me. 37 The Father has told of Me and has sent Me. You have never heard His voice. You have never seen Him. 38 You do not have His Word living in your hearts because you do not put your trust in the One He sent.

39 "You do read the Holy Writings. You think you have life that lasts forever just because you read them. They do tell of Me. 40 But you do not want to come to Me so you might have life. 41 I do not take any honor from men. 42 I know you and you do not have the love of God in your hearts. 43 I have come in the name of My Father. You do not receive Me. If another person comes in his own name, you will receive him. 44 How can you believe when you are always wanting honor from each other? And yet you do not look for the honor that comes from the only God.

45 "Do not think that I will tell the Father you are guilty. The one who says you are guilty is Moses. You trust him. 46 If you had believed Moses, you would believe Me. For Moses wrote about Me. 47 If you do not believe what he wrote, how will you believe My Words?"

The Feeding of the Five Thousand
(Matthew 14:13–21; Mark 6:30–44; Luke 9:10–17)

6 After this Jesus went over to the other side of the Sea of Galilee. It is sometimes called Tiberias. 2 Many people followed Him. They saw the powerful works He did on those who were sick. 3 Jesus went up on a mountain and sat down with His followers. 4 The special religious supper to remember how the Jews left Egypt was soon.

5 Jesus looked up and saw many people coming to Him. He said to Philip, "Where can we buy bread to feed these people?" 6 He said this to see what Philip would do. Jesus knew what He would do. 7 Philip said to Him, "The money we have is not enough to buy bread to give each one a little."

8 One of His followers was Andrew, Simon Peter's brother. He said to Jesus, 9 "There is a boy here who has five loaves of barley bread and two small fish. What is that for so many people?" 10 Jesus said, "Have the people sit down." There was much grass in that place. About five thousand men sat down.

11 Jesus took the loaves and gave thanks. Then He gave the bread to those who were sitting down. The fish were given out the same way. The people had as much as they wanted. 12 When they were filled, Jesus said to His followers, "Gather up the pieces that are left. None will be wasted." 13 The followers gathered the pieces together. Twelve baskets were filled with pieces of barley bread. These were left after all the people had eaten.

14 The people saw the powerful work Jesus had done. They said, "It is true! This is the One Who speaks for God Who is to come into the world."

Jesus Walks on the Water
(Matthew 14:22–33; Mark 6:45–52)

15 Jesus knew they were about to come and take Him to make Him king, so He went to the mountain by Himself. 16 When evening had come, His followers went down to the lake. 17 They got into a boat and started to cross the lake to go to the city of Capernaum. By this time it was dark. Jesus had not come back to them yet. 18 A strong wind was making high waves on the lake. 19 They were about half-way across the lake when they saw Jesus walking on the water. As He got near the boat, they were afraid. 20 But Jesus called to them, "It is I. Do not be afraid." 21 They were glad to take Him into the boat. At once they got to the other side where they wanted to go.

Jesus Teaches Many People

22 The next day the people on the other side of the lake saw no other boat there but the one His followers had been in. The people knew Jesus had not gone with His followers in the boat because they had gone alone. 23 There were other boats from Tiberias that had come near the place where they had eaten the bread after the Lord had given thanks. 24 The people saw that Jesus and His followers were not there. They got into boats and went to Capernaum looking for Jesus.

25 The people found Him on the other side of the lake. They said to Him, "Teacher, when did You come here?" 26 Jesus said to them, "For sure, I tell you, you are not looking for Me because of the powerful works. You are looking for Me because you ate bread and were filled. 27 Do not work for food that does not last. Work for food that lasts forever. The Son of Man will give you that kind of food. God the Father has shown He will do this."

Jesus Teaches about Doing the Work of God

28 Then the people said to Him, "What are the works God wants us to do?" 29 Jesus said to them, "This is the work of God, that you put your trust in the One He has sent." 30 They said to Him, "Can You show us some powerful work? Then we can

see it and believe You. What will You do? 31 Our early fathers ate bread that came from heaven in the desert. This happened as it is written, 'He gave them bread from heaven to eat.' " (Exodus 16:15)

Jesus Is the Bread of Life

32 Then Jesus said to the people, "For sure, I tell you, it was not Moses who gave you bread from heaven. My Father gives you the true Bread from heaven. 33 The Bread of God is He Who comes down from heaven and gives life to the world." 34 They said to Him, "Sir, give us this Bread all the time."

35 Jesus said to them, "I am the Bread of Life. He who comes to Me will never be hungry. He who puts his trust in Me will never be thirsty. 36 I said to you that you have seen Me and yet you do not put your trust in Me. 37 All whom My Father has given to Me will come to Me. I will never turn away anyone who comes to Me. 38 I came down from heaven. I did not come to do what I wanted to do. I came to do what My Father wanted Me to do. He is the One Who sent Me.

39 "The Father sent Me. He did not want Me to lose any of all those He gave Me. He wants Me to raise them to life on the last day. 40 He wants everyone who sees the Son to put his trust in Him and have life that lasts forever. I will raise that one up on the last day."

41 The Jews talked among themselves against Him. They did not like it because He said, "I am the Bread that came down from heaven." 42 They asked each other, "Is not this Jesus, the son of Joseph? We know His father and mother. How can He say, 'I came down from heaven'?"

43 Jesus said to them, "Do not talk among yourselves against Me. 44 The Father sent Me. No man can come to Me unless the Father gives him the desire to come to Me. Then I will raise him to life on the last day. 45 The early preachers wrote, 'They will all be taught of God.' (Isaiah 54:13) Everyone who listens to the Father and learns from Him comes to Me. 46 No one has seen the Father. I am the only One Who has seen Him. 47 For sure, I tell you, he who puts his trust in Me has life that lasts forever. 48 I am the Bread of Life. 49 Your early fathers ate bread that came from heaven in the desert. They died. 50 But this is the Bread that comes down from heaven. The one who eats it never dies. 51 I am the Living Bread that came down from heaven. If anyone eats this Bread, he will live forever. The Bread which I will give is My flesh. I will give this for the life of the world." 52 The Jews argued among themselves, saying, "How can this Man give us His flesh to eat?"

53 Jesus said to them, "For sure, I tell you, unless you eat the flesh of the Son of Man and drink My blood, you do not have life in you. 54 Whoever eats My flesh and drinks My blood has life that lasts forever. I will raise him up on the last day. 55 My flesh is true food and My blood is true drink. 56 Whoever eats My flesh and drinks My blood lives in Me and I live in him. 57 The living Father sent Me and I live because of Him. In the same way, the one who eats Me will live because of Me. 58 I am this Bread that came down from heaven. It is not like the bread that your early fathers ate and they died. Whoever eats this Bread will live forever." 59 Jesus said these things in the Jewish place of worship while He was teaching in the city of Capernaum.

The Troubled Followers Leave Jesus

60 After hearing this, many of His followers said, "This teaching is too hard! Who can listen to it?" 61 Jesus knew His followers talked against what He had said. He said to them, "Does this trouble you? 62 Then what would you say if you saw the Son of Man going up where He was before? 63 It is the Spirit that gives life. The flesh is of no help. The words I speak to you are spirit and life. 64 But some of you do not believe." Jesus knew from the beginning who would not put their trust in Him. He knew who would hand Him over to the leaders of the country. 65 He said, "That is why I told you no one can come to Me unless the Father allows it." 66 From that time on, many of His followers turned back to their old ways of living. They would not go along with Him after that.

Peter Knows Who Jesus Is

67 Then Jesus said to the twelve followers, "Will you leave Me also?" 68 Simon Peter said to Him, "Lord, who else can we go to? You have words that give life that lasts forever. 69 We believe and know You are the Christ. You are the Son of the Living God." 70 Jesus said to them, "I chose you twelve as My followers. And one of you is a devil." 71 He was speaking of Judas Iscariot, Simon's son, who was one of the twelve followers. He was ready to hand Jesus over to the leaders of the country.

The Brothers of Jesus Argue with Him

7 Jesus did not stay in the country of Judea because the Jews were trying to kill Him. After this He went from place to place in the country of Galilee. 2 A religious gathering of the Jews was near. This gathering was called the Supper of Tents. 3 The brothers of Jesus said to Him, "Leave here and go to the country of Judea. Let Your followers there see the things You do. 4 If a person wants others to know what he is doing, he does things to be seen. Since You are doing such things, show Yourself to the world." 5 Not even His brothers were putting their trust in Him.

6 Jesus said to them, "My time has not yet come. But any time is good for you. 7 The world cannot hate you but it hates Me. I speak against the world because of its sinful works. 8 You go to the religious gathering. I am not going yet. My time has not yet come."

9 Jesus told His brothers this and then stayed in Galilee. 10 His brothers went to the religious gathering. He went later by Himself so He would not be seen there.

11 At the religious gathering the Jews were looking for Jesus. They were saying, "Where is He?" 12 There was much talk among the people about Him. Some said, "He is a good Man." Others said, "No, He leads the people in the wrong way." 13 No one spoke about Him in front of other people. They were afraid of the Jews.

Jesus Tells Where His Teaching Is From

14 The religious gathering was half over when Jesus went to the house of God and taught. 15 The Jews were surprised and wondered, saying, "How can this Man know so much when He has never been to school?"

16 Jesus said to them, "What I teach is not Mine. It is from God Who sent Me. 17 If anyone will do what God wants, he will know if My teaching is from God, or if I am speaking of Myself. 18 The man who speaks of himself is looking for greatness for himself. But He Who is looking for the greatness of the One Who sent Him is true. There is nothing false in Him. 19 Did not Moses give you the Law? And yet not one of you keeps the Law. Why do you try to kill me?"

20 The people said, "You have a demon in You. Who is trying to kill You?"

21 Jesus said to them, "I did one work and you are surprised. 22 Moses gave you the religious act of becoming a Jew. (Yet it was not from Moses but from the early fathers.) You do this religious act on a man on the Day of Rest. 23 Now if you can do that, why are you angry with Me for healing a man on the Day of Rest? 24 Do not say a person is guilty by what you see. Be sure you know when you say what is right or wrong."

25 Some of the people of Jerusalem said, "Is not this the Man the Jews want to kill? 26 But see! This Man is speaking out in the open. They are saying nothing to Him. Do the leaders know this is the true Christ? 27 We know where this Man came from. When the Christ comes, no one will know where He comes from."

28 Then Jesus spoke with a loud voice as He taught in the house of God. He said, "You know Me. You know where I came from. I have not come on My own. The One Who sent Me is true but you do not know Him. 29 I know Him because I am from Him and He sent Me."

30 Then they wanted to take Jesus but no one put his hands on Him. His time had not yet come. 31 Many of the people believed in Him. They said, "When Christ comes, will He do more powerful works than this Man?"

32 The proud religious law-keepers heard the people talking about Jesus. The religious leaders of the Jews and the proud religious law-keepers sent soldiers to take Him. 33 Jesus said to them, "I will be with you a little while yet. Then I will go back to Him Who sent Me. 34 You will look for Me but you will not find Me. Where I go, you cannot come."

35 The Jews said to themselves, "Where can He go that we will not find Him? Will He go to our people who live among the Greeks and teach the Greeks? 36 What does He mean when He says, 'You will look for Me but you will not find Me, and where I go, you cannot come'?"

Jesus Promises to Give the Holy Spirit

37 It was the last and great day of the religious gathering. Jesus stood up and spoke with a loud voice, "If anyone is thirsty, let him come to Me and drink. 38 The Holy Writings say that rivers of living water will flow from the heart of the one who puts his trust in Me." 39 Jesus said this about the Holy Spirit Who would come to those who put their trust in Him. The Holy Spirit had not yet been given. Jesus had not yet been raised to the place of honor.

The People Cannot Make Up Their Minds Who He Is

40 When many of the people heard His words, they said, "For sure, this is the One Who speaks for God." 41 Others said, "He is the Christ!" Some said, "The Christ would not come from the country of Galilee, would He? 42 Do not the Holy Writings say that the Christ will come from the family of David? Will He not come from the town of Bethlehem where David lived?" 43 The people were divided in what they thought about Him. 44 Some of them wanted to take Him. But no one put their hands on Him.

45 The soldiers came back to the religious leaders of the Jews and to the proud religious law-keepers. They said to the soldiers, "Why did you not bring Him?" 46 The soldiers answered, "No man has ever spoken like this Man speaks." 47 The proud religious law-keepers said, "Have you been led the wrong way also? 48 Has anyone of the leaders or anyone from our group believed in Him? 49 As for all these people, they do not know the Law. They are guilty and will be punished by God."

50 (Nicodemus was one of the proud religious law-keepers. He had come to Jesus at another time.) Nicodemus said to them, 51 "Our Law does not say a man is guilty before he has been in court and before we know what he has done." 52 They said to him, "Are you from Galilee also? Look into the Word of God yourself. You will see that no one who speaks for God comes from Galilee." 53 *Then everyone went home.

Jesus Speaks to the Teachers of the Law and the Proud Religious Law-Keepers

8 (*Jesus went to the Mount of Olives. 2 Early in the morning He went back to the house of God and all the people came to Him. He sat down and taught them.

3 The teachers of the Law and the proud religious law-keepers came to Him. They brought a woman who had been caught doing a sex sin. They made her stand in front of them all. 4 Then they said to Jesus, "Teacher, this woman was caught in the act of doing a sex sin. 5 Moses told us in the Law to throw stones and kill a woman like this. What do You say about it?"

6 They were trying to set a trap to find something against Him. Jesus got down and began to write in the dust with His finger. 7 They kept on asking Him. Then He stood up and said, "Anyone of you who is without sin can throw the first stone

at her." 8 Again He got down and wrote in the dust. 9 When they heard what He said, they went away one by one, beginning with the older ones until they were all gone. Then Jesus was left alone with the woman.

10 Jesus stood up and said to her, "Woman, where are those who spoke against you? Has no man said you are guilty?" 11 She said, "No one, Sir." Jesus said to her, "Neither do I say you are guilty. Go on your way and do not sin again.")

Jesus Teaches about the Light of the World

12 Jesus spoke to all the people, saying, "I am the Light of the world. Anyone who follows Me will not walk in darkness. He will have the Light of Life."

13 The proud religious law-keepers said to Him, "You are talking about Yourself. What You say about Yourself is not true."

14 Jesus said, "Even if I speak of Myself, what I am saying is true. I know where I came from and where I am going. You do not know where I came from or where I am going. 15 You say as a man would say if people are guilty or not guilty. I am not saying anyone is guilty. 16 But even if I did, it would be true. I am not alone. The Father Who sent Me is with Me. 17 It is written in your Law that when two men agree about something, it proves it is true. (Deuteronomy 19:15) 18 I speak for Myself and the Father Who sent Me speaks for Me."

19 The proud religious law-keepers asked Him, "Where is Your Father?" Jesus said, "You do not know Me or My Father. If you had known Me, you would have known My Father also."

20 Jesus spoke these words near the money box while He taught in the house of God. No one put his hands on Jesus because His time had not yet come.

Jesus Tells of His Going Away

21 Jesus spoke to the Jews again, saying, "I am going away. You will look for Me but you will die in your sins. Where I am going, you cannot come." 22 The Jews said, "Will He kill Himself because He said, 'Where I am going you cannot come'?"

23 He answered them, "You are from below. I am from above. You are of this world. I am not of this world. 24 That is why I said that you will die in your sins. If you do not believe that I am the Christ, you will die in your sins."

25 Then they said to Him, "Who are You?"

Jesus answered, "The answer is the same as I told you from the beginning. 26 I have much to say about you. I must say if you are guilty. But He Who sent Me is true. I tell the world the things I have heard from Him."

27 They did not understand that Jesus was speaking to them about the Father. 28 Jesus said to them, "When you have lifted up the Son of Man, you will know that I am the Christ. I do nothing of Myself. I say these things as My Father has taught Me. 29 He that sent Me is with Me. The Father has not left Me alone. I always do what He wants Me to do." 30 As Jesus said these things, many people put their trust in Him. 31 He said to the Jews who believed, "If you keep and obey My Word, then you are My followers for sure. 32 You will know the truth and the truth will make you free."

Jesus Teaches What It Means to Be Free

33 They said to Jesus, "We are children of Abraham. We have never been servants to anyone. What do you mean when You say, 'You will be free'?" 34 Jesus answered them, "For sure, I tell you, everyone who sins is the servant of sin because sin has a hold on him. 35 And the servant does not belong in the house. The son belongs in the house. 36 So if the Son makes you free, you will be free for sure.

37 "I know that you are the children of Abraham. But you want to kill Me because My Word is not in your hearts. 38 I speak of what I saw when I was with My Father. You do what you have seen your father do."

39 They said to Him, "Abraham is our father." Jesus said, "If you were children of Abraham, you would do what he did. 40 I am a Man Who has told you the truth as I heard it from God. Now you are trying to kill Me. Abraham never did anything like that. 41 You are doing the works of your father." They said to Him, "We were born of parents who were faithful in marriage. We have one Father. He is God."

42 Jesus said to them, "If God were your father, you would love Me. I came from God. I did not come on My own, but God sent Me. 43 Why do you not understand what I say? It is because you do not want to hear My teaching. 44 The devil is your father. You are from him. You want to do the sinful things your father, the devil, wants you to do. He has been a killer from the beginning. The devil has nothing to do

with the truth. There is no truth in him. It is expected of the devil to lie, for he is a liar and the father of lies. 45 I tell you the truth and that is why you do not put your trust in Me. 46 Which one of you can say I am guilty of sin? If I tell you the truth, why do you not believe Me? 47 Whoever is born of God listens to God's Word. You do not hear His Word because you are not born of God."

The Jews Say Jesus Has a Demon

48 The Jews said to Jesus, "Are we not right when we say You are from the country of Samaria, and You have a demon?" 49 Jesus said, "No, I do not have a demon. I honor My Father. You do not honor Me. 50 I am not looking for honor for Myself. There is One Who is looking for it. He says what is right from wrong. 51 For sure, I tell you, if anyone keeps My Word, that one will never die."

52 Then the Jews said to Him, "Now we know You have a demon. Abraham died. The early preachers died. You say, 'If anyone keeps My Word, that one will never die.' 53 Are you greater than our father Abraham? He died and the early preachers died. Who do You think You are?" 54 Jesus said, "If I honor Myself, My honor would be worth nothing. My Father honors Me. You say He is your God. 55 You have never known Him, but I know Him. If I said I did not know Him, I would be a liar like you. But I do know the Father and obey His Word. 56 Your father Abraham was glad that he was to see My coming. He saw it and was happy."

57 The Jews said to Jesus, "You are not even fifty years old. How could you have seen Abraham?" 58 Jesus said to them, "For sure, I tell you, before Abraham was born, I was and am and always will be!"

59 Then they picked up stones to throw at Him. Jesus hid Himself *and left the house of God.

Jesus Heals a Man Who Was Born Blind

9 As Jesus went on His way, He saw a man who had been born blind. 2 His followers asked Him, "Teacher, whose sin made this man to be born blind? Was it the sin of this man or the sin of his parents?" 3 Jesus answered, "The sin of this man or the sin of his parents did not make him to be born blind. He was born blind so the work of God would be seen in him. 4 We must keep on doing the work of Him Who sent Me while it is day. Night is coming

when no man can work. 5 While I am in the world, I am the Light of the world."

6 After Jesus had said this, He spit on the ground. He mixed it with dust and put that mud on the eyes of the blind man. 7 Then Jesus said to him, "Go and wash in the pool of Siloam." (Siloam means Sent.) The man went away and washed. When he came back, he could see.

8 Neighbors and others had seen him begging. They said, "Is not this the man who sat and begged?" 9 Some said, "This is the one." Others said, "No, but he looks like him." But the man who had been blind said, "I am the man." 10 They said to him, "How were your eyes opened?" 11 He answered, "A Man called Jesus made mud and put it on my eyes. Then He said to me, 'Go and wash in the pool of Siloam.' I went and washed and I can see." 12 Then they asked him, "Where is He?" He answered, "I do not know."

The Proud Religious Law-Keepers Are Troubled about This Healing

13 They took the man who had been born blind to the proud religious law-keepers. 14 It was the Day of Rest when Jesus had made mud and opened his eyes. 15 Again the proud religious law-keepers asked the man who had been born blind how he had been made to see. He answered them, "Jesus put mud on my eyes. I washed and now I see!" 16 Some of the proud religious law-keepers said, "The Man Who did this is not from God because He worked on the Day of Rest." Others said, "How can a sinful man do powerful works?" They could not agree about Jesus. 17 They spoke again to the blind man, saying, "What do you say about Him since He opened your eyes?" He answered, "He is One Who speaks for God."

18 The Jews did not believe this man had been blind and had been made to see. They called his parents 19 and asked them, "Is this your son? Do you say he was born blind? How does he see now?" 20 They answered, "We know this is our son and we know he was born blind. 21 But we do not know how it is that he can see now. We do not know who opened his eyes. He is old enough, ask him. He can tell you himself." 22 His parents said this because they were afraid of the Jews. The Jews had talked among themselves. They had agreed that the person who said that Jesus was the Christ would be put out of the Jewish place of worship. 23 That is

why his parents said, "He is old enough, ask him."

24 The proud religious law-keepers asked the man again, who had been blind, to come. They said to him, "Give thanks to God. We know this man is a sinner." 25 The man who had been blind said to them, "I do not know if He is a sinner or not. One thing I know. I was blind, but now I can see." 26 They asked him again, "What did He do to you? How did He open your eyes?" 27 He answered, "I have told you already. You did not listen. Why do you want to hear it again? Do you want to become His followers also?"

28 The proud religious law-keepers became angry at him and said, "You are a follower of Jesus. We are followers of Moses. 29 We know God spoke to Moses. We do not know where this Man is from." 30 The man said to them, "This is strange! You do not know where He came from and yet He opened my eyes. 31 We know that God does not listen to sinners. We know if anyone loves and worships God, and does what He wants, God listens to him. 32 From the beginning of the world no one has ever heard of anyone opening the eyes of a man born blind. 33 If this Man were not from God, He would not be able to do anything like this."

34 They said to him, "You were born in sin. Are you trying to teach us?" Then they put him out of the place of worship.

Jesus Speaks Sharp Words to the Proud Religious Law-Keepers

35 Jesus heard that the proud religious law-keepers had put the man who had been healed out of the place of worship. He found the man and said to him, "Do you put your trust in the Son of God?" 36 He said, "Who is He, Sir? Tell me so that I can put my trust in Him." 37 Jesus said to him, "You have seen Him. He is talking with you." 38 He said, "I do put my trust in You, Lord." Then he bowed down before Jesus and worshiped Him.

39 Jesus said, "I came into this world to say what is right from wrong. I came so those who do not see might see, and those who do see might be made blind." 40 Some of the proud religious law-keepers who were with Him heard this. They said to Him, "Are we blind also?" 41 Jesus said to them, "If you were blind, you would not be guilty of sin. But because you say, 'We see,' you still are guilty of your sin.

The Shepherd and the Door

10 "For sure, I tell you, the man who goes into the sheep-pen some other way than through the door is one who steals and robs. 2 The shepherd of the sheep goes in through the door. 3 The one who watches the door opens it for him. The sheep listen to the voice of the shepherd. He calls his own sheep by name and he leads them out. 4 When the shepherd walks ahead of them, they follow him because they know his voice. 5 They will not follow someone they do not know because they do not know his voice. They will run away from him." 6 Jesus told this picture-story to them. Yet they did not understand what He said.

Jesus Is the Door

7 Again Jesus said to them, "For sure, I tell you, I am the Door of the sheep. 8 All others who came ahead of Me are men who steal and rob. The sheep did not obey them. 9 I am the Door. Anyone who goes in through Me will be saved from the punishment of sin. He will go in and out and find food. 10 The robber comes only to steal and to kill and to destroy. I came so they might have life, a great full life.

Jesus Teaches about the Good Shepherd

11 "I am the Good Shepherd. The Good Shepherd gives His life for the sheep. 12 One who is hired to watch the sheep is not the shepherd. He does not own the sheep. He sees the wolf coming and leaves the sheep. He runs away while the wolf gets the sheep and makes them run everywhere. 13 The hired man runs away because he is hired. He does not care about the sheep.

14 "I am the Good Shepherd. I know My sheep and My sheep know Me. 15 I know My Father as My Father knows Me. I give My life for the sheep. 16 I have other sheep which are not from this sheep-pen. I must bring them also. They will listen to My voice. Then there will be one flock with one shepherd.

17 "For this reason My Father loves Me. It is because I give My life that I might take it back again. 18 No one takes my life from Me. I give it by Myself. I have the right and the power to take it back again. My Father has given Me this right and power."

19 Because of what He said, the Jews did not agree in their thinking. 20 Many of them said, "He has a demon and is crazy. Why listen to Him?" 21 Others said, "A man who has a demon does not talk this way. Can a demon open the eyes of a blind man?"

Jesus Tells Who He Is

22 It was time for the religious gathering of remembering how the house of God was opened in Jerusalem. 23 It was winter and Jesus was there. He was walking in Solomon's porch in the house of God. 24 The Jews gathered around Him. They said, "How long are You going to keep us in doubt? If You are the Christ, tell us." 25 Jesus answered, "I told you and you do not believe. The works I do in My Father's name speak of Me. 26 You do not believe because you are not My sheep. 27 My sheep hear My voice and I know them. They follow Me. 28 I give them life that lasts forever. They will never be punished. No one is able to take them out of My hand. 29 My Father Who gave them to Me is greater than all. No one is able to take them out of My Father's hand. 30 My Father and I are one!"

Jesus Talks to Angry Men

31 Again the Jews picked up stones to throw at Him. 32 Jesus said to them, "Many good things have I shown you from My Father. For which of these things are you going to throw stones at Me?" 33 They said, "We are not going to throw stones at You for any good work. It is because of the way You talk against God. It is because You make Yourself to be God when You are only a man." 34 Jesus said to them, "Is it not written in your Law, 'I said, you are gods'? (Psalm 82:6) 35 The Holy Writings were given to them and God called them gods. (The Word of God cannot be put aside.) 36 But God has set Me apart for Himself. He sent Me into the world. Then how can you say that I am speaking against God because I said, 'I am the Son of God'? 37 If I am not doing the works of My Father, do not believe Me. 38 But if I do them, even if you do not believe Me, believe the works that I do. Then you will know the Father is in Me and I am in Him." 39 They tried again to take Him but He got out of their hands.

Jesus Goes to the Other Side of the Jordan River

40 Jesus went away to the other side of the Jordan River to the place where John was baptizing people. Jesus stayed there. 41 Many people came to Him and said,

"John did no powerful work, but what John said about this Man is true." ⁴² Many people put their trust in Jesus there.

Jesus Hears about Lazarus

11 A man named Lazarus was sick. He lived in the town of Bethany with his sisters, Mary and Martha. ² This was the Mary who put perfume on the Lord and dried His feet with her hair. It was her brother Lazarus who was sick. ³ The sisters sent word to Jesus, saying, "Lord, your friend is sick!" ⁴ When Jesus heard this, He said, "This sickness will not end in death. It has happened so that it will bring honor to God. And the Son of God will be honored by it also."

Jesus Tells of the Death of Lazarus

⁵ Jesus loved Martha and her sister and Lazarus. ⁶ But when He heard that Lazarus was sick, He stayed where He was two more days. ⁷ Then He said to His followers, "Let us go into the country of Judea again." ⁸ The followers said to Him, "Teacher, the Jews tried to throw stones at You to kill You not long ago. Are You going there again?" ⁹ Jesus said, "Are there not twelve hours in the day? If a man walks during the day, he will not fall. He sees the light of this world. ¹⁰ If a man walks during the night, he will fall. The light is not in him."

¹¹ After Jesus had said this, He spoke again and said, "Our friend Lazarus is sleeping. I will go and wake him up." ¹² The followers said to Him, "If he is sleeping, he will get well." ¹³ But Jesus meant Lazarus was dead. They thought He meant Lazarus was resting in sleep. ¹⁴ Then Jesus said to them, "Lazarus is dead. ¹⁵ Because of you I am glad I was not there so that you may believe. Come, let us go to him."

¹⁶ Thomas, who was called the Twin, said to the other followers, "Let us go also so we may die with Jesus."

Jesus Tells That the Grave Will Not Hold the Dead

¹⁷ When Jesus got there, He heard that Lazarus had been in the grave four days. ¹⁸ Bethany was about one-half hour walk from Jerusalem. ¹⁹ Many Jews had come to Martha and Mary to give words of comfort about their brother. ²⁰ Martha heard that Jesus was coming and went to meet Him. Mary stayed in the house. ²¹ Martha said to Jesus, "Lord,

if You had been here, my brother would not have died. ²² I know even now God will give You whatever You ask." ²³ Jesus said to her, "Your brother will rise again." ²⁴ Martha said to Him, "I know that he will rise again when the dead are raised from the grave on the last day."

²⁵ Jesus said to her, "I am the One Who raises the dead and gives them life. Anyone who puts his trust in Me will live again, even if he dies. ²⁶ Anyone who lives and has put his trust in Me will never die. Do you believe this?" ²⁷ She answered, "Yes, Lord, I believe that You are the Christ, the Son of God. You are the One Who was to come into the world."

Lazarus Is Raised from the Dead

²⁸ After Martha said this, she went and called her sister Mary. She said without anyone else hearing, "The Teacher is here and has sent for you." ²⁹ When Mary heard this, she got up and went to Him. ³⁰ Jesus had not yet come into their town. He was still where Martha had met Him.

³¹ The Jews had been in the house comforting Mary. They saw her get up and hurry out. They followed her and said, "She is going to the grave to cry there." ³² Mary went to the place where Jesus was. When she saw Him, she got down at His feet. She said to Him, "Lord, if You had been here, my brother would not have died." ³³ Jesus saw her crying. The Jews who came with her were crying also. His heart was very sad and He was troubled. ³⁴ He said, "Where did you lay Lazarus?" They said, "Lord, come and see." ³⁵ Then Jesus cried. ³⁶ The Jews said, "See how much He loved Lazarus." ³⁷ Some of them said, "This Man opened the eyes of the blind man. Could He not have kept this man from dying?"

³⁸ Jesus went to the grave with a sad heart. The grave was a hole in the side of a hill. A stone covered the door. ³⁹ Jesus said, "Take the stone away." The dead man's sister, Martha, said to Him, "Lord, by now his body has a bad smell. He has been dead four days." ⁴⁰ Jesus said to her, "Did I not say that if you would believe, you would see the shining greatness of God?"

⁴¹ They took the stone away. Jesus looked up and said, "Father, I thank You for hearing Me. ⁴² I know You always hear Me. But I have said this for the people standing here, so they may believe You have sent Me."

⁴³ When He had said this, He called with

a loud voice, "Lazarus, come out!" 44 The man who had been dead came out. His hands and feet were tied in grave clothes. A white cloth was tied around his face. Jesus said to the people, "Take off the grave clothes and let him go!"

The Proud Religious Law-Keepers Try to Think of a Way to Kill Jesus

45 Many of the Jews who had come to visit Mary and had seen what Jesus had done put their trust in Him. 46 Some of them went to the proud religious law-keepers and told them what Jesus had done. 47 The religious leaders of the Jews and the proud religious law-keepers gathered a court together. They said, "What will we do? This Man is doing many powerful works. 48 If we let Him keep doing these things, all men will put their trust in Him. The Romans will come and take away the house of God and our nation." 49 Caiaphas was the head religious leader that year. He said to them, "You know nothing about this. 50 Do you not see it is better for one man to die for the people than for the whole nation to be destroyed?"

51 Caiaphas did not think of these words himself. He spoke what God had said would happen. He was telling before it happened that Jesus must die for the nation. 52 He must die not only for the nation, but also to bring together into one group the children of God who were living in many places.

53 From that day on they talked together about how they might kill Jesus. 54 For this reason Jesus did not walk out in the open among the Jews. He went to a town called Ephraim. It was near a desert. He stayed there with His followers.

The Proud Religious Law-Keepers Look for Jesus

55 The special religious gathering to remember how the Jews left Egypt was soon. Many people from around the country came up to Jerusalem to go through the religious washing before the special supper. 56 They looked for Jesus. They stood together in the house of God and asked each other, "What do you think? Will He come to the special supper?" 57 The religious leaders of the Jews and the proud religious law-keepers had said that if any man knew where Jesus was, he should tell them. They wanted to take Him.

Mary of Bethany Puts Special Perfume on Jesus
(Matthew 26:6–13; Mark 14:3–9)

12 It was six days before the special religious gathering to remember how the Jews left Egypt. Jesus came to Bethany where Lazarus lived. Jesus had raised Lazarus from the dead. 2 They made supper for Him. Martha put the food on the table. Lazarus was at the table with Him.

3 Mary took a jar of special perfume that cost much money and poured it on the feet of Jesus. She dried His feet with her hair. The house was filled with the smell of the special perfume.

4 Judas Iscariot was one of the followers. He was about to hand Jesus over to the leaders of the country. He said, 5 "Why was not this special perfume sold for much money and given to poor people?" 6 He did not say this because he cared for poor people. He said this because he was a robber. He carried the bag of money and would steal some of it for himself. 7 Jesus said, "Let her alone. She has kept it for the time when I will be buried. 8 You will always have poor people with you. You will not always have Me."

The Jews Talk about Having Lazarus Killed

9 Many Jews came to the place because they knew Jesus was there. They came not only to see Jesus, but to see Lazarus also. Jesus had raised Lazarus from the dead. 10 The religious leaders of the Jews talked together about having Lazarus killed also. 11 Because of Lazarus, many Jews were leaving their own religion. They were putting their trust in Jesus.

The Last Time Jesus Goes to Jerusalem
(Matthew 21:1–11; Mark 11:1–11; Luke 19:29–44)

12 The next day many people were in Jerusalem for the religious gathering. They heard Jesus was coming. 13 They took branches of trees and went to meet Him. They spoke with a loud voice, "Greatest One! Great and honored is He Who comes in the name of the Lord, the King of the Jews!" 14 Jesus found a young donkey and sat on it. The Holy Writings say, 15 "Do not be afraid, people of Jerusalem. See! Your King comes sitting on a young donkey!" (Zechariah 9:9) 16 His followers did not understand what this meant at first. When Jesus had gone back to heaven to receive

great honor, they remembered these things were written about Him. They remembered they had done this to Him.

17 The people who had been with Jesus when He had called Lazarus from the grave kept telling of this powerful work to others. They had seen Lazarus raised from the dead. 18 Because of this the people went to meet Jesus. They had heard He had done this powerful work. 19 The proud religious law-keepers said among themselves, "Look, we are losing followers. Everyone is following Jesus!"

The Greek People Want to See Jesus

20 Some Greek people had come to worship at the religious gathering. They were among the others who had come to worship. 21 These Greek people came to Philip. He was from the city of Bethsaida in the country of Galilee. They said to him, "Sir, we want to see Jesus!" 22 Philip went and told Andrew. Then Andrew and Philip told Jesus.

The Law of Life

23 Jesus said to them, "The hour is near for the Son of Man to be taken to heaven to receive great honor. 24 For sure, I tell you, unless a seed falls into the ground and dies, it will only be a seed. If it dies, it will give much grain. 25 Anyone who loves his life will lose it. Anyone who hates his life in this world will keep it forever. 26 If anyone wants to serve Me, he must follow Me. So where I am, the one who wants to serve Me will be there also. If anyone serves Me, My Father will honor him.

27 "Now My soul is troubled. Should I say, 'Father, save Me from this time of trouble and pain'? No, this is why I came to this time. 28 Father, honor Your name!"

The People Hear the Voice of God

Then a voice from heaven came, saying, "I have already honored My name. I will honor it again!" 29 The people heard the voice. Some who stood there said, "It was thunder." Others said, "An angel spoke to Him." 30 Jesus said, "The voice did not come for Me, but it came to be a help to you.

Jesus Tells How He Will Die

31 "Now this world is being told it is guilty. Now the leader of this world will be thrown out. 32 And when I am lifted up from the earth, I will attract all people toward Me." 33 He said this to tell the kind of death He was going to die.

34 The people said to Him, "The Law of Moses says that the Christ is to live forever. Why do you say, 'The Son of Man must be lifted up'? Who is this Son of Man?"

35 Jesus said to them, "The Light will be with you for a little while yet. Go on your way while you have the Light so you will not be in the dark. When a man is walking in the dark, he does not know where he is going. 36 While you have the Light, put your trust in the Light. Then you will be the sons of the Light." Jesus said these things and then went away. He hid Himself from them.

The People Do Not Believe

37 Jesus had done many powerful works in front of them, but they did not put their trust in Him. 38 This happened as the words of the early preacher Isaiah said it would happen. He had said, "Lord, has anyone believed our preaching? Has the Lord shown His power to anyone?" 39 The reason they could not believe is written again in Isaiah. 40 It says, "He has blinded their eyes and made their hearts hard. Then they would not see with their eyes. They would not understand with their heart. They would not turn to Me. I could not heal them." (Isaiah 6:9–10) 41 This is what Isaiah said when he saw the shining-greatness of Jesus and spoke of Him.

42 Even among the leaders of the people there were many who believed in Jesus. But because of the proud religious law-keepers, they did not tell about it. If they had, they would have been put out of the Jewish place of worship. 43 They loved to have the respect from men more than honor from God.

Jesus and His Father Are One

44 Then Jesus spoke with a loud voice, "Anyone who puts his trust in Me, puts his trust not only in Me, but in Him Who sent Me. 45 Anyone who sees Me, sees Him Who sent Me. 46 I came to the world to be a Light. Anyone who puts his trust in Me will not be in darkness. 47 If anyone hears My Words but does not believe them, I do not say he is guilty. I did not come to say the world is guilty. I came to save the world from the punishment of sin. 48 Anyone who does not receive Me and does not receive My teaching has One Who will say he is guilty. The Word that I have spoken will say he is guilty on the last day. 49 I have not spoken by My own power. The Father Who sent Me has told Me what to say and

speak. 50 I know that His Word is life that lasts forever. I speak the things the Father has told Me to speak."

Jesus Washes the Feet of His Followers

13 It was before the special religious gathering to remember how the Jews left Egypt. Jesus knew the time had come for Him to leave this world and go to the Father. He had loved His own who were in the world. He loved them to the end. 2 He and His followers were having supper. Satan had put the thought into the heart of Judas Iscariot of handing Jesus over to the leaders of the country. 3 Jesus knew the Father had put everything into His hands. He knew He had come from God and was going back to God. 4 Jesus got up from the supper and took off His coat. He picked up a cloth and put it around Him. 5 Then He put water into a wash pan and began to wash the feet of His followers. He dried their feet with the cloth He had put around Himself.

Peter Speaks Out against Jesus Washing His Feet

6 Jesus came to Simon Peter. Peter said to Him, "Lord, are You going to wash my feet?" 7 Jesus answered him, "You do not understand now what I am doing but you will later." 8 Peter said to Him, "I will never let You wash my feet." Jesus said, "Unless I wash you, you will not be a part of Me." 9 Simon Peter said to Him, "Lord, do not wash only my feet, but wash my hands and my head also." 10 Jesus said to him, "Anyone who has washed his body needs only to wash his feet. Then he is clean all over. You are all clean except one." 11 Jesus knew who was going to hand Him over to the leaders. That is why He said, "You are all clean except one."

Jesus Tells Why He Washed Their Feet

12 Jesus washed their feet and put on His coat. Then He sat down again and said to them, "Do you understand what I have done to you? 13 You call Me Teacher and Lord. You are right because that is what I am. 14 I am your Teacher and Lord. I have washed your feet. You should wash each other's feet also. 15 I have done this to show you what should be done. You should do as I have done to you. 16 For sure, I tell you, a workman who is owned by someone is not greater than his owner. One who is sent is not greater than the one who sent him. 17 If you know these things, you will be happy if you do them.

18 "I am not speaking about all of you. I know the ones I have chosen. What is written in the Holy Writings must happen. It says, 'The man who eats bread with Me has turned against Me.' (Psalm 41:9) 19 I tell you this now before it happens. After it happens, you will believe that I am Who I say I am, the Christ. 20 For sure, I tell you, he who receives the one I send out, receives Me. He who receives Me receives Him who sent Me."

Jesus Tells of the One Who Will Hand Him Over to the Leaders

(Matthew 26:20–25; Mark 14:17–21; Luke 22:14–18)

21 When Jesus had said this, He was troubled in heart. He told them in very plain words, saying, "For sure, I tell you, one of you is going to hand Me over to the leaders of the country."

22 The followers began to look at each other. They did not know which one He was speaking of. 23 One follower, whom Jesus loved, was beside Jesus. 24 Simon Peter got this follower to look his way. He wanted him to ask Jesus which one He was speaking of. 25 While close beside Jesus, he asked, "Lord, who is it?" 26 Jesus answered, "It is the one I give this piece of bread to after I have put it in the dish." Then He put the bread in the dish and gave it to Judas Iscariot, the son of Simon. 27 After Judas had eaten the piece of bread, Satan went into him. Jesus said to Judas, "What you are going to do, do in a hurry."

28 No one at the supper knew why Jesus had said this to Judas. 29 They thought it was because Judas carried the bag of money, and Jesus had said that Judas should buy what they needed for the religious gathering. Or they thought Judas should give something to poor people. 30 As soon as Judas had taken the piece of bread, he went out. It was night.

Love—the Greatest Law

31 After Judas went out, Jesus said, "The Son of Man is now honored and God has been honored in Him. 32 If God is honored in Him, God will also honor Him in Himself right now. 33 Little children, I will be with you only a little while. You will look for Me. I say to you what I said to the Jews, 'Where I am going, you cannot come!' 34 I give you a new Law. You are to love each other. You must love each other as I have loved you. 35 If you love each other, all men will know you are My followers."

Jesus Tells How Peter Will Lie about Him

(Matthew 26:31–35; Mark 14:27–31; Luke 22:31–34)

36 Simon Peter said to Jesus, "Lord, where are You going?" Jesus answered, "You cannot follow Me now where I am going. Later you will follow Me." 37 Peter said to Jesus, "Why can I not follow You now? I will die for You." 38 Jesus answered Peter, "Will you die for Me? For sure, I tell you, before a rooster crows, you will have said three times that you do not know Me."

Jesus Comforts His Followers

14 "Do not let your heart be troubled. You have put your trust in God, put your trust in Me also. 2 There are many rooms in My Father's house. If it were not so, I would have told you. I am going away to make a place for you. 3 After I go and make a place for you, I will come back and take you with Me. Then you may be where I am. 4 You know where I am going and you know how to get there."

5 Thomas said to Jesus, "Lord, we do not know where You are going. How can we know the way to get there?" 6 Jesus said, "I am the Way and the Truth and the Life. No one can go to the Father except by Me. 7 If you had known Me, you would know My Father also. From now on you know Him and have seen Him."

Jesus and His Father Are One

8 Philip said to Jesus, "Lord, show us the Father. That is all we ask." 9 Jesus said to him, "Have I been with you all this time and you do not know Me yet? Whoever has seen Me, has seen the Father. How can you say, 'Show us the Father'? 10 Do you not believe that I am in the Father and that the Father is in Me? What I say to you, I do not say by My own power. The Father Who lives in Me does His work through Me.

11 "Believe Me that I am in the Father and that the Father is in Me. Or else believe Me because of the things I do. 12 For sure, I tell you, whoever puts his trust in Me can do the things I am doing. He will do even greater things than these because I am going to the Father. 13 Whatever you ask in My name, I will do it so the shining-greatness of the Father may be seen in the Son. 14 Yes, if you ask anything in My name, I will do it.

Jesus Promises to Give the Holy Spirit

15 "If you love Me, you will do what I say. 16 Then I will ask My Father and He will give you another Helper. He will be with you forever. 17 He is the Spirit of Truth. The world cannot receive Him. It does not see Him or know Him. You know Him because He lives with you and will be in you.

Jesus Tells of His Death

18 "I will not leave you without help as children without parents. I will come to you. 19 In a little while the world will see Me no more. You will see Me. Because I live, you will live also. 20 When that day comes, you will know that I am in My Father. You will know that you are in Me. You will know that I am in you. 21 The one who loves Me is the one who has My teaching and obeys it. My Father will love whoever loves Me. I will love him and will show Myself to him."

22 The other Judas (not Iscariot) said to Him, "Why is it You are going to show Yourself to us followers and not to the world?" 23 Jesus said, "The one who loves Me will obey My teaching. My Father will love him. We will come to him and live with him. 24 The one who does not love Me does not obey My teaching. The teaching you are now hearing is not My teaching but it is from My Father Who sent Me.

25 "I have told you these things while I am still with you. 26 The Helper is the Holy Spirit. The Father will send Him in My place. He will teach you everything and help you remember everything I have told you.

Jesus Gives His Followers Peace

27 "Peace I leave with you. My peace I give to you. I do not give peace to you as the world gives. Do not let your hearts be troubled or afraid. 28 You heard Me say that I am going away. But I am coming back to you. If you love Me, you would be glad that I am going to the Father. The Father is greater than I. 29 I have told you this before it happens. Then when it does happen, you will believe.

30 "I will not talk much more with you. The leader of this world is coming. He has no power over Me. 31 I am doing what the Father told Me to do so the world may know I love the Father. Come, let us be on our way.

The Vine and the Branches

15 "I am the true Vine. My Father is the One Who cares for the Vine. [2] He takes away any branch in Me that does not give fruit. Any branch that gives fruit, He cuts it back so it will give more fruit. [3] You are made clean by the words I have spoken to you. [4] Get your life from Me and I will live in you. No branch can give fruit by itself. It has to get life from the vine. You are able to give fruit only when you have life from Me. [5] I am the Vine and you are the branches. Get your life from Me. Then I will live in you and you will give much fruit. You can do nothing without Me.

[6] "If anyone does not get his life from Me, he is cut off like a branch and dries up. Such branches are gathered and thrown into the fire and are burned. [7] If you get your life from Me and My Words live in you, ask whatever you want. It will be done for you.

[8] "When you give much fruit, My Father is honored. This shows you are My followers. [9] I have loved you just as My Father has loved Me. Stay in My love. [10] If you obey My teaching, you will live in My love. In this way, I have obeyed My Father's teaching and live in His love. [11] I have told you these things so My joy may be in you and your joy may be full.

The Christian with Other Christians

[12] "This is what I tell you to do: Love each other just as I have loved you. [13] No one can have greater love than to give his life for his friends. [14] You are My friends if you do what I tell you. [15] I do not call you servants that I own anymore. A servant does not know what his owner is doing. I call you friends, because I have told you everything I have heard from My Father. [16] You have not chosen Me, I have chosen you. I have set you apart for the work of bringing in fruit. Your fruit should last. And whatever you ask the Father in My name, He will give it to you.

The Christian and the World

[17] "This is what I tell you to do: Love each other. [18] If the world hates you, you know it hated Me before it hated you. [19] If you belonged to the world, the world would love you as its own. You do not belong to the world. I have chosen you out of the world and the world hates you. [20] Remember I said to you, 'A servant is not greater than his owner.' If they made it very hard for Me, they will make it very hard for you

also. If they obeyed My teachings, they will obey your teachings also. [21] They will do all these things to you because you belong to Me. They do not know My Father Who sent Me.

[22] "I have come and have spoken to them so they are guilty of sin. But now they have no reason to give for keeping their sin any longer. [23] Whoever hates Me, hates My Father also. [24] I have done things among them which no one else has done so they are guilty of sin. But now they have seen these things and have hated Me and My Father. [25] This happened as their Law said it would happen, 'They hated Me without a reason.'

[26] "The Helper (Holy Spirit) will tell about Me when He comes. I will send Him to you from the Father. He is the Spirit of Truth and comes from the Father. [27] You will also tell of Me because you have been with Me from the beginning.

Jesus Tells His Followers It Will Be Very Hard for Them

16 "I have told you these things so you will not be ashamed of Me and leave Me. [2] They will put you out of the places of worship. The time will come when anyone who kills you will think he is helping God. [3] They will do these things to you because they do not know the Father or Me.

[4] "When these things happen, you will remember I told you they would happen. That is why I am telling you about these things now. I did not tell you these things before, because I was with you. [5] But now I am going to Him Who sent Me. Yet none of you asks Me, 'Where are You going?'

The Three Kinds of Work of the Holy Spirit

[6] "Your hearts are full of sorrow because I am telling you these things. [7] I tell you the truth. It is better for you that I go away. If I do not go, the Helper will not come to you. If I go, I will send Him to you. [8] When the Helper comes, He will show the world the truth about sin. He will show the world about being right with God. And He will show the world what it is to be guilty. [9] He will show the world about sin, because they do not put their trust in Me. [10] He will show the world about being right with God, because I go to My Father and you will see Me no more. [11] He will show the world what it is to be guilty because the leader of this world (Satan) is guilty.

The Holy Spirit Will Give Honor to the Son

12 "I still have many things to say to you. You are not strong enough to understand them now. 13 The Holy Spirit is coming. He will lead you into all truth. He will not speak His Own words. He will speak what He hears. He will tell you of things to come. 14 He will honor Me. He will receive what is Mine and will tell it to you. 15 Everything the Father has is Mine. That is why I said to you, 'He will receive what is Mine and will tell it to you.'

Jesus Tells of His Death

16 "In a little while you will not see Me. Then in a little while you will see Me again." 17 Some of His followers said to each other, "What is He trying to tell us when He says, 'In a little while you will not see Me, and in a little while you will see Me again,' and 'Because I go to My Father'?" 18 So they said, "What is He trying to tell us by saying, 'A little while'? We do not know what He is talking about."

19 Jesus knew they wanted to ask Him something. He said to them, "Are you asking each other why I said, 'In a little while you will not see Me, and in a little while you will see Me again'? 20 For sure, I tell you, you will cry and have sorrow, but the world will have joy. You will have sorrow, but your sorrow will turn into joy. 21 When a woman gives birth to a child, she has sorrow because her time has come. After the child is born, she forgets her pain. She is full of joy because a child has been born into the world. 22 You are sad now. I will see you again and then your hearts will be full of joy. No one can take your joy from you.

Asking and Receiving

23 "When the time comes that you see Me again, you will ask Me no question. For sure, I tell you, My Father will give you whatever you ask in My name. 24 Until now you have not asked for anything in My name. Ask and you will receive. Then your joy will be full.

25 "I have told you these things in picture stories. The time is coming when I will not use picture-stories. I will talk about My Father in plain words. 26 In that day you will ask in My name. I will not ask the Father for you 27 because the Father loves you. He loves you because you love Me and believe that I came from the Father.

Jesus Tells of His Going

28 "I came from the Father and have come into the world. I am leaving the world and going to the Father." 29 His followers said to Him, "Now You are talking in plain words. You are not using picture-stories. 30 Now we are sure You know everything. You do not need anyone to tell You anything. Because of this we believe that You came from God."

31 Jesus said to them, "Do you believe now? 32 The time is coming, yes, it is already here when you will be going your own way. Everyone will go to his own house and leave Me alone. Yet I am not alone because the Father is with Me. 33 I have told you these things so you may have peace in Me. In the world you will have much trouble. But take hope! I have power over the world!"

Jesus Prays for Himself

17 When Jesus had said these things, He looked up to heaven and said, "Father, the time has come! Honor Your Son so Your Son may honor You. 2 You have given Him power over all men. He is to give life that lasts forever to all You have given to Him. 3 This is life that lasts forever. It is to know You, the only true God, and to know Jesus Christ Whom You have sent. 4 I honored You on earth. I did the work You gave Me to do. 5 Now, Father, honor Me with the honor I had with You before the world was made.

Jesus Prays for His Followers

6 "I have made Your name known to the people You have given Me from the world. They were Yours but You gave them to Me. They have obeyed Your Word. 7 Now they know that everything You have given Me came from You. 8 I gave them the Word which You gave Me. They received it. They know I came from You and they believe You sent Me.

9 "I pray for them. I do not pray for the world. I pray for those You gave Me. They are Yours. 10 All that is Mine is Yours. All that is Yours is Mine. I have been honored through them. 11 I am no longer in the world. I am coming to You. But these are still in the world. Holy Father, keep those You have given to Me in the power of Your name. Then they will be one, even as We are One. 12 While I have been with them in the world, I have kept them in the power of Your name. I have kept watch over those You gave Me. Not one of them has been lost except the one who is going

to be destroyed, which is the son of death. The Holy Writings said it would happen. (Psalm 41:9; John 6:70) ¹³ But now I come to You, Father. I say these things while I am in the world. In this way, My followers may have My joy in their hearts.

¹⁴ "I have given Your Word to My followers. The world hated them because they do not belong to the world, even as I do not belong to the world. ¹⁵ I do not ask You to take them out of the world. I ask You to keep them from the devil. ¹⁶ My followers do not belong to the world just as I do not belong to the world. ¹⁷ Make them holy for Yourself by the truth. Your Word is truth.

¹⁸ "As You sent Me into the world so I have sent them into the world also. ¹⁹ I set Myself apart to be holy for them. Then they may be made holy by the truth.

Jesus Prays for All Christians

²⁰ "I do not pray for these followers only. I pray for those who will put their trust in Me through the teaching they have heard. ²¹ May they all be as one, Father, as You are in Me and I am in You. May they belong to Us. Then the world will believe that You sent Me. ²² I gave them the honor You gave Me that they may be one as We are One. ²³ I am in them and You are in Me so they may be one and be made perfect. Then the world may know that You sent Me and that You love them as You love Me.

²⁴ "Father, I want My followers You gave Me to be with Me where I am. Then they may see My shining-greatness which You gave Me because You loved Me before the world was made. ²⁵ Holy Father, the world has not known You. I have known You. These have known You sent Me. ²⁶ I have made Your name known to them and will make it known. So then the love You have for Me may be in them and I may be in them."

Jesus Handed Over to Sinners
(Matthew 26:47–56; Mark 14:43–52)

18 When Jesus had said these things, He went with His followers across the small river Kidron. He and His followers went to a garden there. ² Judas, who was handing Him over to the leaders, knew the place also. Jesus and His followers had met there many times. ³ Judas led some soldiers and some men who had been sent by the head religious leaders of the Jews and the proud religious lawkeepers to the garden. They carried lamps and sticks that were burning and swords.

⁴ Jesus knew what was going to happen to Him. He went out and asked them, "Who are you looking for?" ⁵ The soldiers answered Him, "Jesus of Nazareth." Jesus said, "I am Jesus." Judas, who was handing Him over, was with them also.

⁶ When He said to them, "I am Jesus," they stepped back and fell to the ground. ⁷ He asked them again, "Who are you looking for?" They said again, "Jesus of Nazareth." ⁸ He said, "I have told you that I am Jesus. If you are looking for Me, let these men go their way." ⁹ He said this so the words He spoke might happen, "I have not lost one of those You gave Me."

¹⁰ Simon Peter had a sword. He took it and hit a servant who was owned by the head religious leader and cut off his right ear. The servant's name was Malchus. ¹¹ Then Jesus said to Peter, "Put your sword back where it belongs. Am I not to go through what My Father has given Me to go through?"

Jesus Stands in Front of Annas

¹² Then the soldiers and their captain and the men sent by the Jewish religious leaders took Jesus and tied Him. ¹³ They took Him to Annas first. He was the father-in-law of Caiaphas. Caiaphas was the head religious leader that year. ¹⁴ Caiaphas had talked to the Jews. He told them it would be a good thing if one man should die for the people.

Peter Lies about Jesus
(Matthew 26:69–75; Mark 14:66–72; Luke 22:55–62)

¹⁵ Simon Peter and another follower came behind Jesus. This other follower was known to the head religious leader. He went with Jesus to the head religious leader's house. ¹⁶ Peter stood outside at the gate. The other follower, who was known by the head religious leader, went out and talked to the servant-girl who watched the gate. Then he took Peter inside. ¹⁷ The servant-girl who watched the door said to Peter, "Are you not a follower of this Man?" He said, "I am not!" ¹⁸ The servants who were owned by someone and the soldiers had made a fire because it was cold. They were getting warm by the fire. Peter was standing with them getting warm.

Jesus Stands in Front of Caiaphas
(Matthew 26:57–58; Mark 14:53–54; Luke 22:52–54)

¹⁹ The head religious leader of the Jews asked Jesus about His followers. He asked

Jesus about His teaching. 20 Jesus said, "I have spoken very plain words to the world. I have always taught in the Jewish place of worship and in the house of God. It is where the Jews go all the time. My words have not been said in secret. 21 Why do you ask Me? Ask those who have heard what I said to them. They know what I said."

22 Then one of the soldiers standing there hit Jesus with his hand. He said, "Is that how You talk to the head religious leaders?" 23 Jesus said, "If I said anything wrong, tell Me what was wrong. If I said what was right, why did you hit Me?" 24 Then Annas sent Jesus to Caiaphas, the head religious leader. Jesus was still tied up.

25 Simon Peter was standing there and getting warm. They said to him, "Are you not one of His followers also?" He lied and said he did not know Jesus and answered, "I am not!" 26 A servant who was owned by the head religious leader was there. He was of the family of the man whose ear Peter cut off. The man said, "Did I not see you in the garden with Him?" 27 Again Peter lied and said he did not know Jesus. At once a rooster crowed.

Jesus Stands in Front of Pilate
(Matthew 27:1–2, 11–14; Mark 15:1–5; Luke 23:1–5)

28 They led Jesus from Caiaphas into the court room. It was early in the morning. They did not go inside because their Law said if they did they would become dirty with sin. Then they would not be able to eat the religious supper to remember how the Jews left Egypt. 29 So Pilate came out to them. He asked, "What have you to say against the Man?" 30 The Jews said, "If He had not done wrong, we would not have brought Him to you."

31 Then Pilate said to them, "Take Him yourselves and give Him a trial by your Law." The Jews said to him, "It is against our Law to put anyone to death." 32 This happened as Jesus said it would happen. He had told what kind of death He would die.

33 Then Pilate went back into the court room. He called for Jesus and said to Him, "Are You the King of the Jews?" 34 Jesus said, "Do you ask Me this yourself, or did others say this to you about Me?" 35 Pilate said, "Do you think I am a Jew? Your own people and religious leaders have handed You over to me. What have You done?" 36 Jesus said, "My holy nation does not

belong to this world. If My holy nation were of this world, My helpers would fight so I would not be handed over to the Jews. My holy nation is not of this world." 37 Pilate said to Him, "So You are a King?" Jesus said, "You are right when you say that I am a King. I was born for this reason. I came into the world for this reason. I came to speak about the truth. Everyone who is of the truth hears My voice."

Jesus or Barabbas Is to Go Free
(Matthew 27:15–26; Mark 15:6–14; Luke 23:17–25)

38 Pilate said to Jesus, "What is truth?" After Pilate said this, he went out again to the Jews. He said, "I do not find Him guilty. 39 But every year a man who is in prison is allowed to go free at the special religious gathering to remember how the Jews left Egypt. Do you want the King of the Jews to go free?" 40 Then they spoke with loud voices, "Not this Man, but Barabbas!" Now Barabbas was a robber.

The Crown of Thorns
(Matthew 27:27–32; Mark 15:15–21)

19 Then Pilate took Jesus and had Him beaten. 2 The soldiers put a crown of thorns on His head. They put a purple coat on Him. 3 Then they said, "Hello, King of the Jews!" and hit Him with their hands.

4 Pilate went out again and said to the people, "See, I bring Him out to you so you will know I do not find Him guilty." 5 Jesus came out. He had on the crown of thorns and a purple coat. Pilate said to the people, "See! This is the Man!"

Pilate Tries to Let Jesus Go Free

6 The religious leaders and the soldiers saw Him. They spoke with loud voices, "Nail Him to a cross! Nail Him to a cross!" Pilate said, "Take Him yourselves and nail Him to a cross. As for me, I do not find Him guilty." 7 The Jews said to Pilate, "We have a Law that says He should die because He has said He is the Son of God."

8 When Pilate heard them say this, he was more afraid. 9 He went into the court room again. He said to Jesus, "Where do You come from?" Jesus did not say a word. 10 Pilate said, "Will You not speak to me? Do You not know that I have the right and the power to nail You to a cross? I have the right and the power to let You go free also." 11 Jesus said, "You would not have any right or power over Me if it were not

given you from above. For this reason the one who handed Me over to you has the worse sin."

12 When Pilate heard this, he wanted to let Jesus go free. But the Jews kept saying, "If you let this Man go free, you are not a friend of Caesar! Whoever makes himself as a king is working against Caesar." 13 When Pilate heard this, he had Jesus brought in front of him. Pilate sat down at the place where men stand in front of him if they are thought to be guilty. The place is called the Stone Floor.

14 It was the day to get ready for the special religious gathering to remember how the Jews left Egypt. It was about noon. Pilate said to the Jews, "See, your King!" 15 They spoke with a loud voice, "Take Him away! Nail Him to a cross!" Pilate said to them, "Do you want me to nail your King to a cross?" The head religious leaders said, "We have no king but Caesar!" 16 Then Pilate handed Him over to be nailed to a cross. They took Jesus and led Him away.

Jesus on the Cross
(Matthew 27:33–37; Mark 15:22–26; Luke 23:26–38)

17 Jesus carried His own cross to a hill called the Place of the Skull. 18 There they nailed Him to the cross. With Him were two others. There was one on each side of Jesus. 19 Then Pilate put a writing on the cross which said, JESUS OF NAZARETH, THE KING OF THE JEWS. 20 This was read by many of the Jews. The place where Jesus was nailed to the cross was near the city. The writing was written in the Hebrew and the Latin and the Greek languages. 21 Then the head religious leaders of the Jews said to Pilate, "Do not write, 'The King of the Jews'! Write, 'He said, I am the King of the Jews.' " 22 Pilate said, "What I have written is to stay just as it is!"

They Divide His Clothes
(Matthew 27:35; Mark 15:24)

23 The soldiers who nailed Jesus to the cross took His clothes and divided them in four parts, each soldier getting one part. But His coat which was not sewed was made in one piece. 24 They said to each other, "Let us not cut it up. Let us draw names to see whose it should be." This happened as the Holy Writings said it would happen, "They divided My clothes among them and they drew names for My coat." (Psalm 22:18) 25 This is what the soldiers did.

The Women at the Cross
(Matthew 27:55–56; Mark 15:40–41)

The mother of Jesus and her sister Mary, the wife of Cleophas, were standing near the cross. Mary Magdalene was there also. 26 Jesus saw His mother and the follower whom He loved standing near. He said to His mother, "Woman, look at your son." 27 Then Jesus said to the follower, "Look at your mother." From that time the follower took her to his own house.

Jesus Dies on the Cross
(Matthew 27:45–50; Mark 15:33–36; Luke 23:44–49)

28 Jesus knew that everything was now finished. Everything happened as the Holy Writings said it would happen. He said, "I am thirsty." (Psalm 69:21) 29 There was a jar full of sour wine near. They filled a sponge and put it on a stick and put it to His mouth. 30 Jesus took the sour wine and said, "It is finished." He put His head down and gave up His spirit and died.

His Bones Are Not Broken

31 This was the day before the special religious gathering to remember how the Jews left Egypt. The next day was the Day of Rest and the great day of the religious gathering. The Jews went to Pilate and asked to have the legs of the men broken. They wanted their bodies taken away so they would not be hanging on the crosses on the Day of Rest. 32 Then the soldiers came and broke the legs of the first man and of the other one who had been nailed to crosses beside Jesus. 33 They came to Jesus. They saw He was already dead so they did not break His legs. 34 But one of the soldiers pushed a spear into His side. Blood and water ran out.

35 The one who saw it is writing this and what he says is true. He knows he is telling the truth so you may believe. 36 These things happened as the Holy Writings said they would happen, "Not one of His bones will be broken." (Exodus 12:46) 37 And in another place the Holy Writings say, "They will look at Him Whose side they cut." (Zechariah 12:10)

Jesus Is Buried
(Matthew 27:57–66; Mark 15:42–47; Luke 23:50–56)

38 Joseph was from the town of Arimathea. He was a follower of Jesus but was afraid

of the Jews. So he worshiped without anyone knowing it. He asked Pilate if he could take away the body of Jesus. Pilate said he could. Then Joseph came and took it away. **39** Nicodemus came also. The first time he had come to Jesus had been at night. He brought with him a large box of spices. **40** Then they took the body of Jesus with the spices and put it in linen cloths. This was the way the Jews made a body ready for the grave.

41 There was a garden near the place where He had been nailed to the cross. In the garden there was a new grave in the side of the hill. No one had ever been laid there. **42** This place was near by. Because it was the day the Jews got ready for the special religious gathering, they laid Jesus in it.

Jesus Is Raised from the Grave
(Matthew 28:1–10; Mark 16:1–8; Luke 24:1–12)

20 It was the first day of the week. Mary Magdalene came to the grave early in the morning while it was still dark. She saw that the stone had been pushed away from the grave. **2** She ran to Simon Peter and the other follower whom Jesus loved. She said to them, "They have taken the Lord out of the grave. We do not know where they have put Him."

3 Then Peter and the other follower went to the grave. **4** They ran but the other follower ran faster than Peter and came to the grave first. **5** He got down and looked in and saw the linen cloths but did not go in. **6** Then Simon Peter came and went into the grave. He saw the linen cloths lying there. **7** The white cloth that had been around the head of Jesus was not lying with the other linen cloths. It was rolled up and lying apart by itself. **8** Then the other follower, who had come first, went in also. He saw and believed. **9** They still did not understand what the Holy Writings meant when they said that He must rise again from the dead. **10** Then the followers went back again to their homes.

11 Mary stood outside the grave crying. As she cried, she got down and looked inside the grave. **12** She saw two angels dressed in white clothes. They were sitting where the body of Jesus had lain. One angel was where His head had lain and one angel was where His feet had lain. **13** They said to her, "Woman, why are you crying?" She said to them, "Because they have taken away my Lord. I do not know where they have put Him."

14 After saying this, she turned around and saw Jesus standing there. But she did not know that it was Jesus. **15** He said to her, "Woman, why are you crying? Who are you looking for?" She thought He was the man who cared for the garden. She said to Him, "Sir, if you have taken Jesus from here, tell me where you have put Him. I will take Him away." **16** Jesus said to her, "Mary!" She turned around and said to Him, "Teacher!" **17** Jesus said to her, "Do not hold on to Me. I have not yet gone up to My Father. But go to My brothers. Tell them that I will go up to My Father and your Father, and to My God and your God!" **18** Mary Magdalene went and told the followers that she had seen the Lord. She told them the things He had said to her.

Jesus Is Seen by His Followers— Thomas Is Not There

19 It was evening of the first day of the week. The followers had gathered together with the doors locked because they were afraid of the Jews. Jesus came and stood among them. He said, "May you have peace." **20** When He had said this, He showed them His hands and His side. When the followers saw the Lord, they were filled with joy.

Jesus Sends His Followers to Preach
(Matthew 28:16–20; Mark 16:15–18; Luke 24:44–49)

21 Then Jesus said to them again, "May you have peace. As the Father has sent Me, I also am sending you." **22** When Jesus had said this, He breathed on them. He said, "Receive the Holy Spirit. **23** If you say that people are free of sins, they are free of them. If you say that people are not free of sins, they still have them."

Thomas Does Not Believe Jesus Is Raised from the Dead
(Mark 16:9–14; Luke 24:13–43)

24 Thomas was not with them when Jesus came. He was one of the twelve followers and was called the Twin. **25** The other followers told him, "We have seen the Lord!" He said to them, "I will not believe until I see the marks made by the nails in His hands. I will not believe until I put my finger into the marks of the nails. I will not believe until I put my hand into His side."

Jesus Is Seen Again by His Followers— Thomas Is There

26 Eight days later the followers were again inside a house. Thomas was with them. The doors were locked. Jesus came and stood among them. He said, "May you have peace!" 27 He said to Thomas, "Put your finger into My hands. Put your hand into My side. Do not doubt, believe!" 28 Thomas said to Him, "My Lord and my God!" 29 Jesus said to him, "Thomas, because you have seen Me, you believe. Those are happy who have never seen Me and yet believe!" 30 Jesus did many other powerful works in front of His followers. They are not written in this book. 31 But these are written so you may believe that Jesus is the Christ, the Son of God. When you put your trust in Him, you will have life that lasts forever through His name.

The Risen Christ Talks to His Followers

21 After this, Jesus again showed Himself to His followers at the lake of Tiberias. It happened like this: 2 Simon Peter and Thomas who was called the Twin and Nathanael from the town of Cana in the country of Galilee and the sons of Zebedee and two other followers were all together. 3 Simon Peter said to them, "I am going fishing." The others said, "We will go with you." They went out and got into a boat. That night they caught no fish.

4 Early in the morning Jesus stood on the shore of the lake. The followers did not know it was Jesus. 5 Then Jesus said to them, "Children, do you have any fish?" They said, "No." 6 He said to them, "Put your net over the right side of the boat. Then you will catch some fish." They put out the net. They were not able to pull it in because it was so full of fish.

7 Then the follower whom Jesus loved said to Peter, "It is the Lord!" When Peter heard it was the Lord, he put on his fisherman's coat. (He had taken it off.) Then he jumped into the water. 8 The other followers came in the boat. They were pulling the net with the fish. They were not far from land, only a little way out.

9 When they came to land they saw fish and bread on a fire. 10 Jesus said to them, "Bring some of the fish you have just caught." 11 Simon Peter went out and pulled the net to land. There were 153 big fish. The net was not broken even with so many.

12 Jesus said to them, "Come and eat." Not one of the followers would ask, "Who are You?" They knew it was the Lord.

13 Jesus came and took bread and fish and gave it to them. 14 This was the third time Jesus had shown Himself to His followers after He had risen from the dead.

The Risen Christ Talks to Peter

15 When they were finished eating, Jesus said to Simon Peter, "Simon, son of John, do you love Me more than these?" Peter answered Jesus, "Yes, Lord, You know that I love You." Jesus said to him, "Feed My lambs."

16 Jesus said to Peter the second time, "Simon, son of John, do you love Me?" He answered Jesus, "Yes, Lord, You know that I love You." Jesus said to him, "Take care of My sheep."

17 Jesus said to Peter the third time, "Simon, son of John, do you love Me?" Peter felt bad because Jesus asked him the third time, "Do you love Me?" He answered Jesus, "Lord, You know everything. You know I love You." Jesus said to him, "Feed My sheep. 18 For sure, I tell you, when you were young, you put on your belt and went wherever you wanted to go. When you get old, you will put out your hands and someone else will put on your belt and take you away where you do not want to go." 19 He said this to tell Peter what kind of death he would die to honor God. After Jesus said this, He said to Peter, "Follow Me."

20 Peter turned around. He saw the follower whom Jesus loved, following. This one had been beside Jesus at the supper. This is the one who had asked Jesus, "Lord, who will hand You over?" 21 Peter saw him and said to Jesus, "But Lord, what about this one?" 22 Jesus said, "If I want this one to wait until I come, what is that to you? You follow Me." 23 So the news spread among the followers that this follower would not die. But Jesus did not say to him that he would not die. He said, "If I want him to wait until I come, what is that to you?"

John Tells That He Wrote This Book

24 This is the follower who is telling of these things and who has written them. We know that his word is true. 25 There are many other things which Jesus did also. If they were all written down, I do not think the world itself could hold the books that would be written.

ACTS

Luke Writes to Theophilus

1 Dear Theophilus, in my first writings I wrote about all the things Jesus did and taught from the beginning 2 until the day He went to heaven. He spoke to the missionaries through the Holy Spirit. He told those whom He had chosen what they should do. 3 After He had suffered much and then died, He showed Himself alive in many sure ways for forty days. He told them many things about the holy nation of God.

Jesus Speaks Before He Goes to Be with the Father

4 As they were gathered together with Him, He told them, "Do not leave Jerusalem. Wait for what the Father has promised. You heard Me speak of this. 5 For John the Baptist baptized with water but in a few days you will be baptized with the Holy Spirit."

6 Those who were with Him asked, "Lord, is this the time for You to give the nation back to the Jews?" 7 He said, "It is not for you to know the special days or the special times which the Father has put in His own power.

8 "But you will receive power when the Holy Spirit comes into your life. You will tell about Me in the city of Jerusalem and over all the countries of Judea and Samaria and to the ends of the earth."

Jesus Goes to Be with the Father

9 When Jesus had said this and while they were still looking at Him, He was taken up. A cloud carried Him away so they could not see Him. 10 They were still looking up to heaven, watching Him go. All at once two men dressed in white stood beside them. 11 They said, "You men of the country of Galilee, why do you stand looking up into heaven? This same Jesus Who was taken from you into heaven will return in the same way you saw Him go up into heaven."

Matthias Is Chosen to Take the Place of Judas

12 The followers went back to Jerusalem from the Mount of Olives, which is close to Jerusalem. 13 When they came into the city, they went up to a room on the second floor where they stayed. The followers were Peter and John, James and Andrew, Philip and Thomas, Bartholomew and Matthew, James the son of Alphaeus, Simon the Canaanite, and Judas the brother of James.

14 These all agreed as they prayed together. The women and Mary the mother of Jesus and His brothers were there.

15 On one of those days Peter got up in front of the followers. (There were about 120 people there.) He said, 16 "Men and brothers, it happened as the Holy Writings said it would happen which the Holy Spirit spoke through David. They told about Judas who would hand Jesus over to those who wanted to take Him. 17 Judas was one of our group and had a part in our work. 18 This man bought a field with the money he received for his sin. And falling down head first, his body broke open and his insides ran out. 19 All the people of Jerusalem knew about this. They called the place Field of Blood. 20 For it is written in the Book of Psalms, 'Let his place of living be empty and let no one live there,' and, 'Let another person take over his work.' (Psalm 69:25; 109:8)

21 "The man to take the place of Judas should be one of these men who walked along with us when the Lord Jesus was with us. 22 He must have been with Jesus from the day He was baptized by John to the day He was taken up from us. So one of these should be added to our group who will tell others that he saw Jesus raised from the dead."

23 They brought two men in front of them. They were Joseph, also called Barsabbas Justus, and Matthias. 24 Then the followers prayed, saying, "Lord, You know the hearts of all men. Show us which of these two men You have chosen. 25 He is to take the place of Judas in this work and be a missionary. Judas lost his place and went where he belonged because of sin." 26 Then they drew names and the name of Matthias was chosen. He became one with the eleven missionaries.

The Holy Spirit Comes On the Followers of Jesus

2 The followers of Jesus were all together in one place fifty days after the special religious gathering to remember how the Jews left Egypt. 2 All at once there was a sound from heaven like a powerful wind. It filled the house where they were sitting. 3 Then they saw tongues which were divided that looked like fire. These came down on each one of them. 4 They were all filled with the Holy Spirit. Then they began to speak in other languages which the Holy Spirit made them able to speak.

5 There were many religious Jews staying in Jerusalem. They were from every country of the world. 6 When they heard this strange sound, they gathered together. They all listened! It was hard for them to believe they were hearing words in their own language. 7 They were surprised and wondered about it. They said to each other, "Are not these Galileans who are speaking? 8 How is it that each one of us can hear his own language? 9 We are Parthians and Medes, Elamites and from the countries of Mesopotamia, Judea and Cappadocia, Pontus and in the countries of Asia, 10 Phrygia and Pamphylia, Egypt and the parts of Libya near Cyrene. Some have come from the city of Rome. Some are Jews by birth and others have become Jews. 11 Some are also men of the countries of Crete and Arabia. They are speaking of the powerful works of God to all of us in our own language!" 12 They were all surprised and wondered about this. They said to each other, "What can this mean?" 13 But others laughed and made fun, saying, "These men are full of new wine."

Peter Preaches—What Joel Said Would Happen Has Happened

14 Then Peter stood up with the eleven missionaries and spoke with a loud voice, "Men of the country of Judea and all of you who are living in Jerusalem, I want you to know what is happening. So listen to what I am going to say. 15 These men are not drunk as you think. It is only nine o'clock in the morning. 16 The early preacher Joel said this would happen. 17 God says, 'In the last days I will send My Spirit on all men. Then your sons and daughters will speak God's Word. Your young men will see what God has given them to see. Your old men will dream dreams. 18 Yes, on those I own, both men and women, I will send My Spirit in those days. They will speak God's Word. 19 I will show powerful works in the sky above. There will be things to see in the earth below like blood and fire and clouds of smoke. 20 The sun will turn dark and the moon will turn to blood before the day of the Lord. His coming will be a great and special day. 21 It will be that whoever calls on the name of the Lord will be saved from the punishment of sin.' (Joel 2:28-32)

Peter Preaches—Jesus Shows Who He is by What He Did

22 "Jewish men, listen to what I have to say! You knew Jesus of the town of Nazareth by the powerful works He did. God worked through Jesus while He was with you. You all know this. 23 Jesus was handed over to sinful men. God knew this and planned for it to happen. You had sinful men take Him and nail Him to a cross. 24 But God raised Him up. He allowed Him to be set free from the pain of death. Death could not hold its power over Him.

Peter Preaches—Jesus Shows Who He Is by What He Said

25 "David said this about Him, 'I can see the Lord before me all the time. He is at my right side so that I do not need to be troubled. 26 I am glad and my tongue is full of joy. My body rests in hope. 27 You will not leave my soul in death. You will not allow Your Holy One to be destroyed. 28 You have shown me the ways of life. I will be full of joy when I see Your face.' (Psalm 16)

29 "Brothers, I can tell you in plain words that our early father David not only died but was buried. We know where his grave is today. 30 He was one who spoke for God. He knew God had made a promise to him. From his family Christ would come and take His place as King. 31 He knew this before and spoke of Christ being raised from the dead. Christ's soul would not be left in hell. His body would not be destroyed. 32 Jesus is this One! God has raised Him up and we have all seen Him.

33 "This Jesus has been lifted up to God's right side. The Holy Spirit was promised by the Father. God has given Him to us. That is what you are seeing and hearing now! 34 It was not David who was taken up to heaven, because he said, 'The Lord said to my Lord, "Sit at My right side, 35 for those who hate You will be a place to rest Your feet." ' (Psalm 110:1) 36 The whole Jewish nation must know for sure that God has made this Jesus, both Lord and Christ. He is the One you nailed to a cross!"

They Ask Peter What They Should Do

37 When the Jews heard this, their hearts were troubled. They said to Peter and to the other missionaries, "Brothers, what should we do?" 38 Peter said to them, "Be sorry for your sins and turn from them and be baptized in the name of Jesus Christ, and your sins will be forgiven. You will receive the gift of the Holy Spirit. 39 This promise is to you and your children. It is to all people everywhere. It is to as many as the Lord our God will call."

40 He said many other things. He helped them understand that they should keep themselves from the sinful people of this day. **41** Those who believed what he said were baptized. There were about 3,000 more followers added that day.

The First Church

42 They were faithful in listening to the teaching of the missionaries. They worshiped and prayed and ate the Lord's supper together. **43** Many powerful works were done by the missionaries. Surprise and fear came on them all. **44** All those who put their trust in Christ were together and shared what they owned. **45** As anyone had need, they sold what they owned and shared with everyone. **46** Day after day they went to the house of God together. In their houses they ate their food together. Their hearts were happy. **47** They gave thanks to God and all the people respected them. The Lord added to the group each day those who were being saved from the punishment of sin.

Peter and John Heal a Man at the Gate of the House of God

3 Peter and John were going to the house of God about three o'clock. It was the time for prayer. **2** Each day a certain man was carried to the Beautiful Gate of the house of God. This man had never been able to walk. He was there begging for money from those who were going in. **3** He asked Peter and John for money when he saw them going in. **4** Peter and John looked at him. Then Peter said, "Look at us!" **5** The man who could not walk looked at them. He thought he would get something from them. **6** Peter said, "I have no money, but what I have I will give you! In the name of Jesus Christ of Nazareth, get up and walk!" **7** Peter took the man by the right hand and lifted him up. At once his feet and the bones in his legs became strong. **8** He jumped up on his feet and walked. Then he went into the house of God with them. He gave thanks to God as he walked.

9 All the people saw him walking and giving thanks to God. **10** They knew it was the man who had been sitting and begging at the Beautiful Gate. They were surprised he was walking. **11** The man who was healed held on to Peter and John. All the people who were surprised gathered together around them in a place called Solomon's Porch.

Peter Preaches the Second Time

12 When Peter saw this, he said to them, "Jewish men, why are you surprised at this? Why do you look at us as if we had made this man walk by our own power or holy lives? **13** The God of our fathers, the God of Abraham and Isaac and Jacob, has done this. He has honored His Son Jesus. He is the One you handed over to Pilate. You turned your backs on Him after Pilate had decided to let Him go free. **14** But you turned your backs against the Holy and Right One. Then you asked for a man who had killed someone to go free. **15** You killed the very One Who made all life. But God raised Him from the dead. We saw Him alive. **16** You see and know this man here. He has been made strong through faith in Jesus' name. Yes, it is faith in Christ that has made this man well and strong. This man is standing here in front of you all.

17 "Brothers, I know you and your leaders did this without knowing what you were doing. **18** In this way, God did what He said He would do through all the early preachers. He said that Christ must suffer many hard things. **19** But you must be sorry for your sins and turn from them. You must turn to God and have your sins taken away. Then many times your soul will receive new strength from the Lord. **20** He will send Jesus back to the world. He is the Christ Who long ago was chosen for you. **21** But for awhile He must stay in heaven until the time when all things are made right. God said these things would happen through His holy early preachers. **22** "Moses said, 'The Lord God will raise up from among your brothers One Who speaks for God, as He raised me. You must listen to everything He says. **23** Everyone among the people who will not listen to that One Who speaks for God will be put to death.' (Deuteronomy 18:18-19) **24** All the early preachers who have spoken from Samuel until now have told of these days. **25** You are of the family of the early preachers and of the promise that God made with our early fathers. He said to Abraham, 'All the families of the earth will receive God's favor through your children.' **26** God has raised up His Son Jesus and has sent Him to you first to give God's favor to each of you who will turn away from his sinful ways."

Peter and John Are Put in Prison

4 The religious leaders and the leader of the house of God and some of the religious group who believe no one will be raised from the dead came to Peter and John while they were talking to the people. 2 They were angry because Peter and John had been teaching the people and preaching that Jesus had been raised from the dead. 3 So they took them and put them in prison until the next day because it was evening. 4 But many of those who heard what Peter and John said put their trust in Christ. The group of followers was now about 5,000 men.

Peter Speaks to the Religious Leaders' Court

5 The next day the leaders of the court and the leaders of the people and the teachers of the Law came together in Jerusalem. 6 Annas the head religious leader was there. Caiaphas and John and Alexander were there also and all who were in the family of the head religious leader. 7 They put the missionaries in front of them and asked, "By what power or in whose name have you done this?"

8 Then Peter, having been filled with the Holy Spirit, said, "You who are leaders of the people, 9 are you asking us today about the good work we did to a man who needed help? Are you asking how he was healed? 10 You and all the Jews must know that it was by the name of Jesus Christ of Nazareth, the One you nailed to a cross and God raised from the dead. It is through Him that this man stands in front of you well and strong. 11 Christ is the Stone that was put aside by you workmen. But He has become the most important Stone in the building. (Psalm 118:22) 12 There is no way to be saved from the punishment of sin through anyone else. For there is no other name under heaven given to men by which we can be saved."

Peter and John Are Free to Go but Are Told Not to Preach

13 They were surprised and wondered how easy it was for Peter and John to speak. They could tell they were men who had not gone to school. But they knew they had been with Jesus. 14 They were not able to argue about what Peter and John had said because the man who had been healed was standing with them.

15 The religious leaders told Peter and John to leave the court so the leaders could talk together. 16 They said, "What should we do with these men? Everyone living in Jerusalem knows a powerful work has been done by them. We cannot say that it did not happen. 17 Let us tell

them with strong words that they must not speak again to anyone in this name. This will keep the news from going out among the people."

18 Then they called them in and told them they must not speak or teach anymore in the name of Jesus. 19 Peter and John said, "If it is right to you to listen to you more than to God, you decide about that. 20 For we must tell what we have seen and heard."

21 After they had spoken sharp words to them, they let them go. They could not beat them because the people were giving thanks to God for what had happened. 22 The man on whom this powerful work of healing had been done was more than forty years old.

The Prayer of the Young Church

23 As soon as the missionaries were free to go, they went back to their own group. They told them everything the religious leaders had said. 24 When they heard it, they all prayed to God, saying, "Lord God, You made the heaven and the earth and the sea and everything that is in them. 25 You said through the Holy Spirit by the mouth of our father David, 'Why are the nations so shaken up and the people planning foolish things? 26 The kings of the earth stood in a line ready to fight, and the leaders were all against the Lord and against His Christ.' (Psalm 2:1–2) 27 You know that Herod and Pilate and the Jews and the people who are not Jews gathered together here against Jesus. He was Your Holy Son and the One You had chosen 28 to do everything You planned and said would happen. 29 And now, Lord, listen to their sharp words. Make it easy for your servants to preach Your Word with power. 30 May You heal and do powerful works and special things to see through the name of Jesus, Your Holy Son!"

The Christians Are Filled with the Holy Spirit

31 When they had finished praying, the place where they were gathered was shaken. They were all filled with the Holy Spirit. It was easy for them to speak the Word of God.

The New Way of Life

32 The many followers acted and thought the same way. None of them said that any of their things were their own, but they shared all things. 33 The missionaries told with much power how Jesus was raised

from the dead. God's favor was on them all. 34 No one was in need. All who owned houses or pieces of land sold them and brought the money from what was sold. 35 They gave it to the missionaries. It was divided to each one as he had need.

36 Joseph was among them. The missionaries called him Barnabas. His name means Son of Comfort. He was from the family group of Levi and from the country of Cyprus. 37 He had some land which he sold and brought the money to the missionaries.

The Sin of Ananias and Sapphira

5 A man by the name of Ananias and his wife, Sapphira, sold some land. 2 He kept back part of the money for himself. His wife knew it also. The other part he took to the missionaries. 3 Peter said to Ananias, "Why did you let Satan fill your heart? He made you lie to the Holy Spirit. You kept back part of the money you got from your land. 4 Was not the land yours before you sold it? After it was sold, you could have done what you wanted to do with the money. Why did you allow your heart to do this? You have lied to God, not to men."

5 When Ananias heard these words, he fell down dead. Much fear came on all those who heard what was done. 6 The young men got up and covered his body and carried him out and buried him.

7 About three hours later his wife came in. She did not know what had happened. 8 Peter said to her, "Tell me, did you sell the land for this amount of money?" She said, "Yes." 9 Then Peter said to her, "How could you two have talked together about lying to the Holy Spirit? See! Those who buried your husband are standing at the door and they will carry you out also." 10 At once she fell down at his feet and died. When the young men came in, they found that she was dead. They took her out and buried her beside her husband. 11 Much fear came on all the church and on all who heard it.

The First Church Grows

12 The missionaries did many powerful works among the people. They gathered together on Solomon's Porch. 13 No one from outside the church came in with them because they were afraid. But those outside the church had respect for the followers. 14 Many more men and women put their trust in Christ and were added to the group. 15 They brought the sick people and laid them on the streets hoping that if Peter walked by, his shadow would fall on some of them. 16 Many people went into Jerusalem from towns nearby. They took with them their sick people and all who were troubled with demons. All of them were healed.

The Missionaries Are Put in Prison

17 The head religious leader heard this. Some of the religious group who believe no one will be raised from the dead also heard of the people being healed. They became very jealous. 18 They took hold of the missionaries and put them in prison. 19 An angel of the Lord opened the doors of the prison in the night and let them out. The angel said to them, 20 "Go, stand where you have been standing in the house of God. Keep on telling the people about this new life."

21 When Peter and John heard this, they went in the house of God early in the morning and began to teach. When the head religious leader and those with him had come, they gathered the men of the court and the leaders of the Jews together. Then they sent to have the missionaries brought to them from the prison. 22 When the soldiers got there, they did not find them in prison. They went back and told the court. 23 The soldiers said, "We found the door of the prison locked and the soldiers watching the doors. When we opened the door, we found no one inside."

24 When the religious leaders and the leader of the house of God heard this, they were much troubled as to what might happen. 25 Then someone came and told them, "The men you put in prison are now standing in the house of God and teaching the people." 26 The leader of the house of God took his men and got them. They did not hurt the missionaries because they were afraid the people would throw stones at them.

27 They brought the missionaries in and made them stand in front of the court. The head religious leader said, 28 "We told you not to teach about Christ! See! You are spreading this teaching over all Jerusalem. Now you are making it look as if we are guilty of killing this Man."

The Missionaries Speak the Truth

29 Then Peter and the missionaries said, "We must obey God instead of men! 30 The God of our early fathers raised up Jesus,

the One you killed and nailed to a cross.
31 God raised this Man to His own right side as a leader and as the One Who saves from the punishment of sin. He makes it possible for the Jews to be sorry for their sins. Then they can turn from them and be forgiven. 32 We have seen these things and are telling about them. The Holy Spirit makes these things known also. God gives His Spirit to those who obey Him."

Gamaliel Speaks in Court

33 The religious leaders became angry when they heard this. They planned to kill the missionaries. 34 Gamaliel was a man of the religious leaders' court. He was a proud religious law-keeper and a teacher of the Law. He was respected by all the people. He stood up and said that the missionaries should be sent outside for a short time.

35 Then Gamaliel said to the court, "Jewish men, be careful what you plan to do with these men. 36 Remember that many years ago a man called Theudas made himself out to be someone great. He had about 400 followers. He was killed. His followers were divided and nothing came of his teaching. 37 After him, Judas of the country of Galilee gathered many followers. It was the time for every person to have his name written in the books of the nation. This Judas was killed also. All his followers were divided and went away. 38 I say to you now, stay away from these men and leave them alone. If this teaching and work is from men, it will come to nothing. 39 If it is from God, you will not be able to stop it. You may even find yourselves fighting against God."

40 The court agreed with Gamaliel. So they called the missionaries in and beat them. They told them they must not speak in the name of Jesus. Then they were sent away.

41 So the missionaries went away from the court happy that they could suffer shame because of His Name. 42 Every day in the house of God and in the homes, they kept teaching and preaching about Jesus Christ.

Church Leaders Are Chosen

6 In those days the group of followers was getting larger. Greek-speaking Jews in the group complained against the Jews living in the country around Jerusalem. The Greek-speaking Jews said that their women whose husbands had died were not taken care of when the food was given out each day. 2 So the twelve missionaries called a meeting of the many followers and said, "It is not right that we should give up preaching the Word of God to hand out food. 3 Brothers, choose from among you seven men who are respected and who are full of the Holy Spirit and wisdom. We will have them take care of this work. 4 Then we will use all of our time to pray and to teach the Word of God."

5 These words pleased all of them. They chose Stephen who was a man full of faith and full of the Holy Spirit. They also chose Philip, Prochorus, Nicanor, Timon, Parmenas and Nicholas of Antioch who had become a Jew. 6 These men were taken to the missionaries. After praying, the missionaries laid their hands on them.

7 The Word of God spread further. The group of followers became much larger in Jerusalem. Many of the religious leaders believed in the faith of the Christians.

Stephen Is Brought in Front of the Religious Leaders' Court

8 Stephen was a man full of faith and power. He did many great things among the people. 9 But some men came from their place of worship who were known as the Free people. They started to argue with Stephen. These men were from the countries of Cyrene and Alexandria and Cilicia and Asia. 10 Stephen spoke with wisdom and power given by the Holy Spirit. They were not able to say anything against what he said. 11 So they told other men to say, "We have heard him say things against Moses and God." 12 In this way they got the people talking against Stephen. The leaders of the people and the teachers of the Law came and took him to the religious leaders' court. 13 The people were told to lie and say, "This man keeps on talking against this place of worship and the Law of Moses. 14 We have heard him say, 'Jesus of Nazareth is going to pull down this place. He is going to change what Moses taught us.'"

15 The men sitting in the religious leaders' court were looking at Stephen. They all saw that his face looked like the face of an angel.

Stephen Speaks about the God of Abraham

7 The head religious leader asked Stephen, "Are these things true?" 2 Stephen said, "My brothers and fathers, listen to me. The great God showed Himself to

our early father Abraham while he lived in the country of Mesopotamia. This was before he moved to the country of Haran. [3] God said to him, 'Leave your family and this land where you were born. Go to a land that I will show you.' [4] He went from the land of the Chaldeans and lived in Haran. After his father died, he came to this country where you now live. [5] God did not give him any land to own, not even enough to put his feet on. But He promised that the land would be his and his children's after him. At that time he had no children. [6] This is what God said, 'Your children's children will be living in a strange land. They will live there 400 years. They will be made to work without pay and will suffer many hard things. [7] I will say to that nation that it is guilty for holding them and making them work without pay. After that they will go free. They will leave that country and worship Me in this place.'

[8] "He made a promise with Abraham. It was kept by a religious act of becoming a Jew. Abraham had a son, Isaac. On the eighth day Abraham took Isaac and had this religious act done to him. Isaac was the father of Jacob. Jacob was the father of our twelve early fathers.

[9] "The sons of Jacob sold Joseph to people from the country of Egypt because they were jealous of him. But God was with Joseph. [10] He helped him in all his troubles. He gave him wisdom and favor with Pharaoh, the king of Egypt. This king made Joseph leader over Egypt and over all the king's house.

[11] "The time came when there was no food to eat in all the land of Egypt and Canaan. The people suffered much. Our early fathers were not able to get food. [12] Then Jacob heard there was food in Egypt. He sent our early fathers there the first time.

[13] "The second time they went to the country of Egypt, Joseph made himself known to his brothers. The family of Joseph became known to Pharaoh. [14] Joseph asked his father Jacob and all his family to come. There were seventy-five people in the family. [15] Jacob moved down to Egypt and died there. Our early fathers died there also. [16] They were brought back to the city of Shechem where they were buried. Abraham paid money for the grave from the sons of Hamor in Shechem.

Stephen Speaks about the God of Moses

[17] "The promise God had given Abraham was about to happen. At this time many more of our people were in the country of Egypt. [18] Then another man became king in Egypt. He was a king who did not know Joseph. [19] He was hard on our people and nation. He worked against our early fathers. He made them put their babies outside so they would die.

[20] "At that time Moses was born. He was beautiful in God's sight. He was fed in his father's house for three months. [21] Then he was put outside. Pharaoh's daughter took him and cared for him as her own son. [22] Moses was taught in all the wisdom of the Egyptians. He became a powerful man in words and in the things he did. [23] When he was forty years old, he thought he should visit his brothers, the Jews. [24] He saw one of the Jews being hurt. Moses helped the Jew and killed the man from Egypt. [25] He thought his people would understand. He thought they knew God would let them go free by his help. But the people did not understand.

[26] "The next day Moses came to some Jews who were fighting. He tried to get them to stop. Moses said to the Jews, 'Sirs, you are brothers. Why do you hurt each other?' [27] One was beating his neighbor. He pushed Moses away and said, 'Who made you a leader over us? Who said you could say who is guilty? [28] Do you want to kill me as you killed the man from Egypt yesterday?' [29] When Moses heard that, he went as fast as he could to the country of Midian where he was a stranger. While he was there, he became the father of two sons. [30] Forty years passed and Moses was near Mount Sinai where no people live. There he saw an angel in the fire of a burning bush. [31] He was surprised and wondered when he saw it. He went up close to see it better. Then he heard the voice of the Lord speak to him. [32] 'I am the God of your fathers, the God of Abraham and of Isaac and of Jacob.' Moses shook! He was so afraid he did not look at the bush.

[33] "Then the Lord said to him, 'Take your shoes off your feet! The place where you are standing is holy ground. [34] I have seen My people suffer in the country of Egypt and I have heard their cries. I have come down to let them go free. So come now, I will send you back to Egypt.'

[35] "The people had put Moses aside. They said, 'Who made you a leader over us? Who said you are the one to say what is right or wrong?' But God made this man a leader. Moses was the one who brought them out of the country of Egypt. This was

done by the help of the angel who was in the burning bush. 36 This man led them. He did powerful works in Egypt and at the Red Sea. For forty years he led them in the desert.

37 "Moses said to the Jews, 'God will give you one who speaks for Him like me from among your brothers.' 38 This is the man who was with the Jewish nation in the desert. The angel talked to him on Mount Sinai. Moses told it to our early fathers. He also received the living Words of God to give to us.

39 "Our early fathers would not listen to him. They did not obey him. In their hearts they wanted to go back to the country of Egypt. 40 They said to Aaron, 'Make us gods to go before us. We do not know what has happened to this Moses who led us out of Egypt.'

41 "In those days they made a calf of gold. They put gifts down in front of their god in worship. They were happy with what they had made with their hands. 42 But God turned from them and let them worship the stars of heaven. This is written in the book of the early preachers, 'Nation of Jews, was it to Me you gave gifts of sheep and cattle on the altar for forty years in the desert? 43 No, you set up the tent to worship the god of Molock and the star of your god Rompha. You made gods to worship them. I will carry you away to the other side of the country of Babylon.' (Amos 5:25–27)

The Place of Worship and the House of God

44 "Our early fathers had the tent to worship in. They used it in the desert. God told Moses to make it like the plan which he had seen. 45 This was received by our early fathers. They brought it here when they won the wars with the people who were not Jews. It was when Joshua was our leader. God made those people leave as our early fathers took the land. The tent was here until the time of David. 46 David pleased God and wanted to build a house for worship for the God of Jacob. 47 But Solomon was the one who built the house of God for Him. 48 But the Most High does not live in buildings made by hands. The early preacher said, 49 'Heaven is the place where I sit and the earth is the place where I rest My feet. What house will you build Me?' says the Lord. 'Or what is My place of rest? 50 Did not My hands make all these things?' (Isaiah 66:1–2)

The Jews Are Hurt

51 "You have hard hearts and ears that will not listen to me! You are always working against the Holy Spirit. Your early fathers did. You do too. 52 Which of the early preachers was not beaten and hurt by your early fathers? They killed those who told of the coming of the One Right with God. Now you have handed Him over and killed Him. 53 You had the Law given to you by angels. Yet you have not kept it."

Stephen Is Killed

54 The Jews and religious leaders listened to Stephen. Then they became angry and began to grind their teeth at him. 55 He was filled with the Holy Spirit. As he looked up to heaven, he saw the shining-greatness of God and Jesus standing at the right side of God. 56 He said, "See! I see heaven open and the Son of Man standing at the right side of God!" 57 They cried out with loud voices. They put their hands over their ears and they all pushed on him. 58 Then they took him out of the city and threw stones at him. The men who were throwing the stones laid their coats down in front of a young man named Saul. 59 While they threw stones at Stephen, he prayed, "Lord Jesus, receive my spirit." 60 After that he fell on his knees and cried out with a loud voice, "Lord, do not hold this sin against them." When he had said this, he died.

It Is Hard for the Christians in Jerusalem

8 Saul thought it was all right that Stephen was killed. On that day people started to work very hard against the church in Jerusalem. All the followers, except the missionaries, were made to leave. They went to parts of the countries of Judea and Samaria. 2 Good men put Stephen in a grave. There was much sorrow because of him. 3 During this time Saul was making it very hard for the church. He went into every house of the followers of Jesus and took men and women and put them in prison.

Philip Preaches in Samaria

4 Those who had been made to go to other places preached the Word as they went. 5 Philip went down to a city in Samaria and preached about Christ. 6 The people all listened to what Philip said. As they listened, they watched him do powerful works. 7 There were many people who

had demons in their bodies. The demons cried with loud voices when they went out of the people. Many of the people could not move their bodies or arms and legs. They were all healed. 8 There was much joy in that city.

Simon the Witch Doctor

9 A man by the name of Simon had done witchcraft there. The people of Samaria were surprised at the things he did. He pretended that he was a great man. 10 All the people watched and listened to him. They said, "This man must be that great power of God." 11 They kept running after him. For a long time he fooled them with his witchcraft.

12 Philip told the Good News of the holy nation of God and of Jesus Christ. Both men and women put their trust in Christ and were baptized. 13 Even Simon believed in Christ and was baptized. He went along with Philip everywhere. He was surprised when he saw the powerful works that were being done.

14 The missionaries in Jerusalem heard that the people of Samaria had received the Word of God. They sent Peter and John to them. 15 When Peter and John got there, they prayed that the new followers might receive the Holy Spirit. 16 He had not yet come on any of them. They had only been baptized in the name of the Lord Jesus. 17 They laid their hands on them and the followers received the Holy Spirit.

18 When Simon saw that the Holy Spirit was given when the missionaries laid their hands on the people, he wanted to give money to the missionaries. 19 He said, "Let me also have this power. Then I can give the Holy Spirit to anyone I lay my hands on." 20 Peter said to him, "May your money be destroyed with you because you thought you could buy the gift of God with money! 21 You have no part or place in this work. Your heart is not right in God's sight. 22 You must be sorry for this sin of yours and turn from it. Pray to the Lord that He will forgive you for having such a thought in your heart. 23 I see that you are full of jealousy and chained by your sin." 24 Simon said, "Pray to the Lord for me that nothing you have said will come to me."

25 Peter and John went back to Jerusalem after telling what they had seen and heard. They had preached the Word of the Lord also. On the way they preached the Good News in many other towns in the country of Samaria.

Philip and the Man from Ethiopia

26 An angel of the Lord spoke to Philip saying, "Get up and go south. Take the road that goes down from Jerusalem to the country of Gaza. It goes through the desert." 27 Philip got up and went. A man from the country of Ethiopia had come to Jerusalem to worship. He had been made so he could not have children. He cared for all the riches that belonged to Candace who was Queen of Ethiopia. 28 As he was going back home, he was sitting in his wagon reading about the early preacher Isaiah. 29 The Holy Spirit said to Philip, "Go over to that wagon and get on it." 30 Philip ran up to him. He saw that the man from Ethiopia was reading from the writings of the early preacher Isaiah and said, "Do you understand what you are reading?" 31 The man from Ethiopia said, "How can I, unless someone teaches me?" Then he asked Philip to come up and sit beside him.

32 He was reading the part in the Holy Writings which says He was taken like a lamb to be put to death. A sheep does not make a sound while its wool is cut. So He made no sound. 33 No one listened to Him because of His shame. Who will tell the story of His day? For His life was taken away from the earth. (Isaiah 53:7-8)

34 The man from Ethiopia said to Philip, "Who is the early preacher talking about, himself, or someone else?" 35 So Philip started with this part of the Holy Writings and preached the Good News of Jesus to him.

36 As they went on their way, they came to some water. The man from Ethiopia said, "See! Here is water. What is to stop me from being baptized?" 37 (*Philip said, "If you believe with all your heart, you may." The man said, "I believe that Jesus Christ is the Son of God.") 38 He stopped the wagon. Then both Philip and the man from Ethiopia went down into the water and Philip baptized him.

39 When they came up out of the water, the Holy Spirit took Philip away. The man from Ethiopia did not see Philip again. He went on his way full of joy. 40 Philip found himself at the city of Azotus. Then Philip went through all the towns as far as the city of Caesarea preaching the Good News at each place.

Saul Becomes a Christian on the Way to Damascus

(Acts 22:6–16; 26:12–18)

9 Saul was still talking much about how he would like to kill the followers of the Lord. He went to the head religious leader. [2] He asked for letters to be written to the Jewish places of worship in the city of Damascus. The letters were to say that if he found any men or women following the Way of Christ he might bring them to Jerusalem in chains.

[3] He went on his way until he came near Damascus. All at once he saw a light from heaven shining around him. [4] He fell to the ground. Then he heard a voice say, "Saul, Saul, why are you working so hard against Me?" [5] Saul answered, "Who are You, Lord?" He said, "I am Jesus, the One Whom you are working against. You hurt yourself by trying to hurt Me." [6] Saul was shaken and surprised. Then he said, "What do You want me to do, Lord?" The Lord said to him, "Get up! Go into the city and you will be told what to do."

[7] Those with Saul were not able to say anything. They heard a voice but saw no one. [8] Saul got up from the ground. When he opened his eyes, he saw nothing. They took him by the hand and led him to Damascus. [9] He could not see for three days. During that time he did not eat or drink.

[10] In Damascus there was a follower by the name of Ananias. The Lord showed him in a dream what He wanted him to see. He said, "Ananias!" And Ananias answered, "Yes, Lord, I am here." [11] The Lord said, "Get up! Go over to Straight Street to Judas's house and ask for a man from the city of Tarsus. His name is Saul. You will find him praying there. [12] Saul has seen a man called Ananias in a dream. He is to come and put his hands on Saul so he might see again."

[13] Ananias said, "But Lord, many people have told me about this man. He is the reason many of Your followers in Jerusalem have had to suffer much. [14] He came here with the right and the power from the head religious leaders to put everyone in chains who call on Your name." [15] The Lord said to him, "Go! This man is the one I have chosen to carry My name among the people who are not Jews and to their kings and to Jews. [16] I will show him how much he will have to suffer because of Me."

Saul Is Baptized

[17] So Ananias went to that house. He put his hands on Saul and said, "Brother Saul, the Lord Jesus has sent me to you. You saw the Lord along the road as you came here. The Lord has sent me so you might be able to see again and be filled with the Holy Spirit." [18] At once something like a covering fell from the eyes of Saul and he could see. He got up and was baptized. [19] After that he ate some food and received strength. For some days he stayed with the followers in Damascus.

Saul Preaches the Good News

[20] At once Saul began to preach in the Jewish places of worship that Jesus is the Son of God. [21] All who heard him were surprised and wondered. They said, "This is the man who beat and killed the followers in Jerusalem. He came here to tie the followers in chains and take them to the head religious leaders." [22] But Saul kept on growing in power. The Jews living in Damascus wondered about Saul's preaching. He was proving that Jesus was the Christ.

[23] After some days the Jews talked together and made plans how they might kill Saul. [24] He heard of their plans. Day and night they watched for him at the city gates to kill him. [25] So the followers helped him get away at night. They let him down over the wall in a basket.

Saul Comes to Jerusalem

[26] When Saul had come to Jerusalem, he tried to join the followers. But they were afraid of him. They did not believe he was a true follower of Jesus. [27] Then Barnabas took him to the missionaries. He told them that Saul had seen the Lord on the road. He told them also how the Lord had spoken to Saul and how he had preached without fear in Damascus in the name of Jesus. [28] After that he was with them going in and out of Jerusalem. [29] He preached without fear in the name of the Lord. He talked and argued with the Jews who spoke the Greek language. They kept trying to kill him. [30] When the followers heard this, they took him down to the city of Caesarea. From there they sent him to the city of Tarsus.

[31] Then the church through all the countries of Judea and Galilee and Samaria had peace for awhile. The church was made strong and it was given comfort by the Holy Spirit. It honored the Lord. More people were added to the church.

Aeneas Is Healed

32 When Peter was visiting all parts of the country, he came to the faithful followers who were living in the city of Lydda. 33 A man there named Aeneas could not move his body. He had been in bed eight years. 34 Peter said to him, "Aeneas, Jesus Christ heals you. Get up and roll up your bed." He got up at once. 35 All the people who lived in Lydda and in the city of Sharon saw Aeneas and they turned to the Lord.

Dorcas Is Raised from the Dead

36 A woman who was a follower lived in the city of Joppa. Her name was Tabitha, or Dorcas. She did many good things and many acts of kindness. 37 One day she became sick and died. After they had washed her body, they laid her in a room on the second floor. 38 The city of Lydda was near Joppa. The followers heard that Peter was at Lydda and sent two men to ask him to come at once. 39 Peter went back with them. When he came, they took him to the room. All the women whose husbands had died were standing around crying. They were showing the clothes Dorcas had made while she was with them.

40 Peter made them all leave the room. Then he got down on his knees and prayed. He turned to her body and said, "Tabitha, get up!" She opened her eyes and looked at Peter and sat up. 41 He took her by the hand and lifted her up. Then he called in the faithful followers and the women whose husbands had died. He gave her to them, a living person.

42 News of this went through all Joppa. Many people put their trust in the Lord. 43 After this, Peter stayed in Joppa many days in the house of Simon who worked with leather.

God Speaks to a Man Who Is Not a Jew

10 There was a man in the city of Caesarea by the name of Cornelius. He was a captain of an Italian group of the army. 2 He and his family were good people and honored God. He gave much money to the people and prayed always to God.

3 One afternoon about three o'clock he saw in a dream what God wanted him to see. An angel of God came to him and said, "Cornelius." 4 He was afraid as he looked at the angel. He said, "What is it, Lord?" The angel said, "Your prayers and your gifts of money have gone up to God. He

has remembered them. 5 Send some men to the city of Joppa and ask Simon Peter to come here. 6 He is living with Simon, the man who works with leather. His house is by the sea-shore. He will tell you what you must do." 7 The angel left him. Then Cornelius called two of his servants and a religious soldier who took care of him. 8 He told what had happened. Then he sent them to Joppa.

Peter's Dream

9 The next day they went on their way. About noon they were coming near the town. At this time Peter went up on the roof to pray. 10 He became very hungry and wanted something to eat. While they were getting food ready to eat, he saw in a dream things God wanted him to see. 11 He saw heaven open up and something like a large linen cloth being let down to earth by the four corners. 12 On the cloth were all kinds of four-footed animals and snakes of the earth and birds of the sky. 13 A voice came to him, "Get up, Peter, kill something and eat it." 14 Peter said, "No, Lord! I have never eaten anything that our Law says is unclean." 15 The voice said the second time, "What God has made clean you must not say is unclean." 16 This happened three times. Then it was taken back to heaven.

Cornelius's Men Find Peter

17 Peter thought about the meaning of the dream. The men that Cornelius had sent came. They were standing by the gate asking about Simon's house. 18 They called to ask if Simon Peter was staying there.

19 Peter was still thinking about the dream when the Holy Spirit said to him, "See, three men are looking for you. 20 Get up. Go down and go with them. Do not doubt if you should go, because I sent them." 21 Peter went down to the men who had been sent by Cornelius. He said, "I am the one you are looking for. Why have you come?" 22 They said, "Cornelius sent us. He is a captain and a good man and he honors God. The whole Jewish nation can say this is true. An angel from God told him to send for you. He asks you to come to his house. He wants to hear what you have to say."

Peter Goes to Cornelius

23 Peter asked them to come in and stay with him for the night. The next day he went with them. Some of the brothers

from Joppa went along. 24 The next day they came to Caesarea. Cornelius was looking for them. He had gathered all his family and close friends at his house. 25 When Peter came, Cornelius got down at his feet and worshiped him. 26 But Peter raised him up and said, "Get up! I am just a man like you." 27 As Peter spoke with Cornelius, he went into the house and found a large group of people gathered together. 28 Peter said to them, "You know it is against our Law for a Jew to visit a person of another nation. But God has shown me I should not say that any man is unclean. 29 For this reason I came as soon as you sent for me. But I want to ask you why you sent for me?"

30 Cornelius said, "Four days ago at three o'clock in the afternoon I was praying here in my house. All at once, I saw a man standing in front of me. He had on bright clothes. 31 He said to me, 'Cornelius, God has heard your prayers and has remembered your gifts of love. 32 You must send to Joppa and ask Simon Peter to come here. He is staying at the house of Simon, the man who works with leather. His house is by the sea-shore.' 33 I sent for you at once. You have done well to come. We are all here and God is with us. We are ready to hear whatever the Lord has told you to say."

Peter Preaches in Cornelius's House

34 Then Peter said, "I can see, for sure, that God does not respect one person more than another. 35 He is pleased with any man in any nation who honors Him and does what is right. 36 He has sent His Word to the Jews. He told them the Good News of peace through Jesus Christ. Jesus is Lord of All. 37 You know the story yourselves. It was told in all the country of Judea. It began in the country of Galilee after the preaching of John the Baptist. 38 God gave Jesus of Nazareth the Holy Spirit and power. He went around doing good and healing all who were troubled by the devil because God was with Him. 39 We have seen and heard everything He did in the land of the Jews and in Jerusalem. And yet they killed Him by nailing Him to a cross. 40 God raised Him to life on the third day and made Him to be seen. 41 Not all the people saw Him but those who were chosen to see Him. We saw Him. We ate and drank with Him after He was raised from the dead. 42 He told us to preach to the people and tell them that

God gave Christ the right to be the One Who says who is guilty of the living and the dead. 43 All the early preachers spoke of this. Everyone who puts his trust in Christ will have his sins forgiven through His name."

The Holy Spirit Comes to the Family of Cornelius

44 While Peter was speaking, the Holy Spirit came on all who were hearing his words. 45 The Jewish followers who had come along with Peter were surprised and wondered because the gift of the Holy Spirit was also given to the people who were not Jews. 46 They heard them speak in special sounds and give thanks to God. Then Peter said, 47 "Will anyone say that these people may not be baptized? They have received the Holy Spirit just as we have." 48 He gave the word that they should be baptized in the name of the Lord. Then they asked Peter to stay with them for some days.

Peter Tells Why He Preached to the People Who Are Not Jews

11 The missionaries and followers who were in the country of Judea heard that the people who were not Jews also had received the Word of God. 2 When Peter went up to Jerusalem, the Jewish followers argued with him. 3 They said, "Why did you visit those people who are not Jews and eat with them?"

4 Then Peter began to tell all that had happened from the beginning to the end. He said, 5 "While I was praying in the city of Joppa, I saw in a dream something coming down from heaven. It was like a large linen cloth let down by the four corners until it came to me. 6 As I looked at it, I saw four-footed animals and snakes of the earth and birds of the sky. 7 I heard a voice saying to me, 'Get up, Peter, kill something and eat it.' 8 But I said, 'No, Lord! Nothing that is unclean has ever gone into my mouth.' 9 The voice from heaven said the second time, 'What God has made clean you must not say is unclean.' 10 This happened three times and then it was taken up again to heaven.

11 "Three men had already come to the house where I was staying. They had been sent to me from the city of Caesarea. 12 The Holy Spirit told me to go with them and not doubt about going. These six men also went with me to this man's house. 13 He told us how he had seen an angel

in his own home. The angel had stood in front of him and said, 'Send men to Joppa to ask for Simon Peter. 14 He will tell you and all your family how you can be saved from the punishment of sin.'

15 "As I began to talk to them, the Holy Spirit came down on them just as He did on us at the beginning. 16 Then I remembered the Lord had said, 'John baptized with water but you will be baptized with the Holy Spirit.' 17 If God gave to them the same gift He gave to us after we put our trust in the Lord Jesus Christ, how could I stand against God?"

18 When they heard these words, they said nothing more. They thanked God, saying, "Then God has given life also to the people who are not Jews. They have this new life by being sorry for their sins and turning from them."

The Followers Are Called Christians First in Antioch

19 Those who went different places because of the trouble that started over Stephen had gone as far as the cities of Phoenicia and Cyprus and Antioch. They had preached the Word, but only to the Jews. 20 Some of the men from Cyprus and Cyrene returned to Antioch. They preached the Good News of Jesus Christ to the Greek people there. 21 The Lord gave them power. Many people put their trust in the Lord and turned to Him.

22 The news of this came to the church in Jerusalem. They sent Barnabas to Antioch. 23 When he got there and saw how good God had been to them, he was full of joy. He told them to be true and faithful to the Lord. 24 Barnabas was a good man and full of the Holy Spirit and faith. And many people became followers of the Lord.

25 From there Barnabas went on to the city of Tarsus to look for Saul. 26 When he found Saul, he brought him back with him to Antioch. For a year they taught many people in the church. The followers were first called Christians in Antioch.

The Antioch Church Helps the Jerusalem Church

27 At that time some men who preached God's Word came to Antioch and told what was going to happen. They were from Jerusalem. 28 One of them was Agabus. The Holy Spirit told him to stand up and speak. He told them there would be very little food to eat over all the world. This happened when Claudius was leader

of the country. 29 The Christians agreed that each one should give what money he could to help the Christians living in Judea. 30 They did this and sent it to the church leaders with Barnabas and Saul.

The King Makes It Hard for the Church

12 At that time King Herod used his power to make it hard for the Christians in the church. 2 He killed James, the brother of John, with a sword. 3 When he saw that it made the Jews happy, he took hold of Peter also. This was during the special religious gathering to remember how the Jews left Egypt. 4 Herod took Peter and put him in prison and had sixteen soldiers watch him. After the special religious gathering was over, he planned to bring Peter out to the people.

Peter Goes Free

5 So Peter was held in prison. But the church kept praying to God for him. 6 The night before Herod was to bring him out for his trial, Peter was sleeping between two soldiers. He was tied with two chains. Soldiers stood by the door and watched the prison.

7 All at once an angel of the Lord was seen standing beside him. A light shone in the building. The angel hit Peter on the side and said, "Get up!" Then the chains fell off his hands. 8 The angel said, "Put on your belt and shoes!" He did. The angel said to Peter, "Put on your coat and follow me." 9 Peter followed him out. He was not sure what was happening as the angel helped him. He thought it was a dream.

10 They passed one soldier, then another one. They came to the big iron door that leads to the city and it opened by itself and they went through. As soon as they had gone up one street, the angel left him.

The Christians Find It Hard to Believe Peter Is Free

11 As Peter began to see what was happening, he said to himself, "Now I am sure the Lord has sent His angel and has taken me out of the hands of Herod. He has taken me also from all the things the Jews wanted to do to me." 12 After thinking about all this, he went to Mary's house. She was the mother of John Mark. Many Christians were gathered there praying.

13 When Peter knocked at the gate, a girl named Rhoda went to see who it was. 14 She knew Peter's voice, but in her joy she forgot to open the gate. She ran in and

told them that Peter was standing outside the gate.

15 They said to her, "You are crazy." But she said again that it was so. They kept saying, "It is his angel." 16 Peter kept knocking. When they opened the gate and saw him, they were surprised and wondered about it. 17 He raised his hand and told them not to talk but to listen to him. He told them how the Lord had brought him out of prison. He said, "Tell all these things to James and to the other Christian brothers." Then he went to another place.

The Death of Herod

18 In the morning the soldiers were very troubled about what had happened to Peter. 19 Herod looked for him but could not find him. He asked the soldiers who watched the prison about Peter. Herod said that the soldiers must be killed because Peter got away. Then Herod went down from the country of Judea to the city of Caesarea to stay for awhile.

20 Herod was very angry with the people of the cities of Tyre and Sidon. They went to him and asked for peace to be made between them and the king. They asked this because their country got food from the king's country. The people made friends with Blastus, the king's helper. 21 A day was set aside. On that day Herod put on purple clothes a king wears. He sat on his throne and spoke to the people. 22 They all started to speak with a loud voice, "This is the voice of a god, not of a man." 23 The angel of the Lord knocked him down because he did not give honor to God. He was eaten by worms and died.

24 The Word of God was heard by many people and went into more places. 25 Saul and Barnabas went back to Jerusalem after they had finished their work. They took John Mark with them.

Saul and Barnabas Are Called to Be Missionaries

13 In the church in the city of Antioch there were preachers and teachers. They were Barnabas, Simeon Niger, Lucius of the country of Cyrene, Manaen of Herod's family, and Saul. 2 While they were worshiping the Lord and eating no food so they could pray better, the Holy Spirit said, "Let Barnabas and Saul be given to Me for the work I have called them to."

Paul and Barnabas Go to Antioch

3 These preachers and teachers went without food during that time and prayed. Then they laid their hands on Barnabas and Saul and sent them away. 4 They were sent by the Holy Spirit to the city of Seleucia. From there they went by ship to the island of Cyprus. 5 When they went to shore at the city of Salamis, they preached the Word of God in the Jewish place of worship. John Mark was with them as their helper.

6 They went over Cyprus as far as the city of Paphos. While there, they found a Jew who did witchcraft. He was a false preacher named Barjesus. 7 Sergius Paulus was the leader of the country and a man who knew much. Barjesus was with Sergius Paulus. Sergius Paulus asked Barnabas and Saul to come to him so he might hear the Word of God. 8 But Elymas (as he called himself), the man who did witchcraft, worked against Barnabas and Saul. He tried to keep the leader of the country from putting his trust in the Lord.

9 Saul, whose other name was Paul, was full of the Holy Spirit. He looked at Elymas. 10 Then Saul said, "You false preacher and trouble-maker! You son of the devil! You hate what is right! Will you always be turning people from the right ways of the Lord? 11 And now look! The hand of the Lord is on you. You will become blind. For a time you will not be able to see the sun." At once it became dark to Elymas, and he could not see. He asked people to take him by the hand to lead him from place to place.

12 The leader of the country put his trust in the Lord because he saw what had happened. He was surprised and wondered about the teaching of the Lord. 13 Paul and those with him went by ship from Paphos to the city of Perga in the country of Pamphylia. John Mark did not go with them but went back to Jerusalem.

Paul Preaches in Antioch

14 From Perga they went on to the city of Antioch in the country of Pisidia. On the Day of Rest they went into the Jewish place of worship and sat down. 15 After the leaders had read from the Jewish Law and the writings of the early preachers, they sent to them saying, "Brothers, if you have any word of comfort and help for the people, say it now." 16 Paul got up. He raised his hand and said, "Jewish men and you who honor God, listen! 17 The God of

the Jews chose our early fathers and made them a great people during the time they lived in the land of Egypt. With a strong hand He took them out from there. 18 For about forty years He took care of them in the desert. 19 He destroyed the people of seven nations in the land of Canaan. Then He divided the land and gave it to them as their own. 20 For about 450 years He let them have special leaders. They had these leaders until the time of Samuel.

21 "Then they wanted a king. God gave them Saul who was the son of Kish from the family group of Benjamin. He was king forty years. 22 When God took Saul as king from them, He made David to be their king. He said, 'David, Jesse's son, will please My heart. He will do all I want done.'

23 "From this man's family, God gave to the Jews the One Who saves from the punishment of sin as He had promised. He is Jesus. 24 Before Jesus came, John had preached to all the Jews that they should be baptized because they were sorry for their sins and turned from them. 25 When John was near the end of his work, he asked, 'Who do you think I am? I am not the Christ. No, but He is coming later and I am not good enough to get down and help Him take off His shoes!'

26 "Men and brothers, sons of the family of Abraham, and all of you who honor God, listen! This news of being able to be saved from the punishment of sin has been sent to you. 27 The people of Jerusalem and their leaders did not know Him. They did not understand the words from the early preachers. These words were read to them every Day of Rest. But they did the very thing the early preachers had said they would do by handing Him over to die. 28 They could find no reason that He should die, but they asked Pilate to have Him killed. 29 When everything was done that had been written about Him, they took Him down from the cross and laid Him in a grave. 30 But God raised Him from the dead. 31 For many days He was seen by those who came up with Him from Galilee to Jerusalem. These are the ones who tell the people about Him.

32 "We bring you the Good News about the promise made to our early fathers. 33 God has finished this for us who are their children. He did this by raising Jesus from the dead. It is written in the second Psalm, 'You are My Son. Today I have become Your Father.' (Psalm 2:7) 34 God proved that Jesus was His Son by

raising Him from the dead. He will never die again. He has said, 'I will complete the promises made to David.' (Isaiah 55:3)

35 "In another Psalm He says, 'You will not allow Your Holy One to go back to dust!' (Psalm 16:10) 36 David was a good leader for the people of his day. He did what God wanted. Then he died and was put into a grave close to his father's grave. His body went back to dust. 37 But God raised this One (Christ) to life. He did not go back to dust.

38 "Men and brothers, listen to this. You may be forgiven of your sins by this One I am telling you about. 39 Everyone who puts his trust in Christ will be made right with God. You will be made free from those things the Law of Moses could not make you free from. 40 But look out! The writings of the early preachers tell of many things that you do not want to happen to you. 41 'Listen, you who doubt and laugh at the truth will die. I will do a work during your days. It will be a work that you will not believe even if someone tells you about it.' " (Habakkuk 1:5)

42 As Paul and Barnabas went out of the Jewish place of worship, the people asked them to talk about these things on the next Day of Rest. 43 The people went from the place of worship. Many Jews and others who had become Jews followed Paul and Barnabas as they talked to the Jews. They told them to keep on trusting in the loving-favor of God.

Paul and Barnabas Go to the People Who Are Not Jews

44 Almost all of the people of the town came to hear the Word of God on the next Day of Rest. 45 The Jews were filled with jealousy when they saw so many people. They spoke against the things Paul said by saying he was wrong. They also spoke against God. 46 Paul and Barnabas said to the people in plain words, "We must preach the Word of God to you first. But because you put it aside, you are not good enough for life that lasts forever. So we will go to the people who are not Jews. 47 The Lord gave us a work to do. He said, 'You are to be a light to the people who are not Jews. You are to preach so that men over all the earth can be saved from the punishment of their sins.' " (Isaiah 49:6)

48 The people who were not Jews were glad when they heard this. They were thankful for the Word of God. Those who were chosen for life that lasts

forever believed. 49 The Word of God was preached over all that land.

50 The Jews worked on the feelings of the women who were religious and respected. They worked on the leading men of the city also. They worked against Paul and Barnabas and made them leave their city. 51 But Paul and Barnabas shook the dust off from their feet against them and went to the city of Iconium. 52 The missionaries were filled with joy and with the Holy Spirit.

Paul and Barnabas Preach in Iconium

14 In the city of Iconium, Paul and Barnabas went into the Jewish place of worship. They preached with power and many people became Christians. These people were Jews and Greeks. 2 But the Jews who did not want to believe worked against those who were not Jews. They made them turn against the Christians. 3 Paul and Barnabas stayed there a long time preaching with the strength the Lord gave. God helped them to do powerful works when they preached which showed He was with them. 4 The people of the city were divided. Some were on the side of the Jews. Some were on the side of the missionaries. 5 All the people and the leaders tried to hurt them and throw stones at them.

Paul and Barnabas Go to Lystra

6 When Paul and Barnabas heard this, they got away and went to the cities of Lystra and Derbe in Lycaonia and to the country close by. 7 They stayed there and kept on preaching the Good News. 8 There was a man in Lystra who had never walked from the time he was born. 9 This man listened as Paul spoke. Paul watched him. He saw that the man believed he could be healed. 10 Calling to him with a loud voice, Paul said, "Stand up on your feet!" The man jumped up and walked around.

Paul and Barnabas Are Called Gods, Then Stoned

11 The people saw what Paul did. They called with loud voices in the language of the people of Lycaonia, "The gods have become like men and have come down to us." 12 They said that Barnabas was Jupiter. Paul was called Mercury because he spoke more than Barnabas. 13 The god of Jupiter was in a building near the gate leading into the city. The religious leader of that place brought cattle and flowers

to the gate. He and many other people wanted to burn these as gifts in an act of worship to Paul and Barnabas.

14 When Paul and Barnabas heard this, they ran among the people. They tore their clothes and cried out, 15 "Why are you doing this? We are only men with feelings like yours. We preach the Good News that you should turn from these empty things to the living God. He made the heavens and the earth and the sea and everything in them. 16 Long ago He allowed all people to live the way they wanted to. 17 Even then God did not leave you without something to see of Him. He did good. He gave you rain from heaven and much food. He made you happy." 18 Even with these words it was hard for Paul and Barnabas to keep the people from burning cattle in an act of worship to them.

19 By this time some Jews from the cities of Antioch and Iconium came. They turned the minds of the people against Paul and Barnabas and told them to throw stones at Paul. After they threw stones at him, they dragged him out of the city thinking he was dead.

Paul and Barnabas Preach to the Christians on Their Return Trip to Antioch

20 As the Christians gathered around Paul, he got up and went back into the city. The next day he went with Barnabas to Derbe. 21 In that city they preached the Good News and taught many people. Then they returned to the cities of Lystra and Iconium and Antioch. 22 In each city they helped the Christians to be strong and true to the faith. They told them, "We must suffer many hard things to get into the holy nation of God."

23 In every church they chose leaders for them. They went without food during that time so they could pray better. Paul and Barnabas prayed for the leaders, giving them over to the Lord in Whom they believed.

24 When they had gone through the city of Pisidia, they came to the city of Pamphylia. 25 Then they preached the Good News in the city of Perga. After this they went down to the city of Attalia. 26 From there they went by ship to Antioch where they had been given to the Lord for His work. The work of this trip was done.

27 When they got there, they called the church together. They told them everything God had done for them. They told

how God had opened the door for the people who were not Jews to have faith. 28 They stayed there with the followers a long time.

A Meeting of Church Leaders in Jerusalem

15 Some men came down from the country of Judea and started to teach the Christians. They said, "Unless you go through the religious act of becoming a Jew as Moses taught, you cannot be saved from the punishment of sin." 2 Paul and Barnabas argued with them. Then Paul and Barnabas and some other men were chosen to go up to Jerusalem. They were to talk to the missionaries and church leaders about this teaching. 3 The church sent them on their way. They went through the countries of Phoenicia and Samaria and told how those who were not Jews were turning to God. This made the Christians very happy.

4 When they got to Jerusalem, the church and the missionaries and the church leaders were glad to see them. Paul and Barnabas told them what God had done through them.

5 Some of the Christians there had been proud religious law-keepers. They got up and said, "Doing the religious act of becoming a Jew and keeping the Law of Moses are two things that must be done." 6 The missionaries and church leaders got together to talk about this. 7 After a long time of much talking, Peter got up and said to them, "Brothers, you know in the early days God was pleased to use me to preach the Good News to the people who are not Jews so they might put their trust in Christ. 8 God knows the hearts of all men. He showed them they were to have His loving-favor by giving them the Holy Spirit the same as He gave to us. 9 He has made no difference between them and us. They had their hearts made clean when they put their trust in Him also. 10 Why do you test God by putting too heavy a load on the back of the followers? It was too heavy for our fathers or for us to carry. 11 We believe it is by the loving-favor of the Lord Jesus that we are saved. They are saved from the punishment of sin the same way."

12 All those who were gathered together said nothing. They listened to Paul and Barnabas who told of the powerful works God had done through them among the people who are not Jews.

God's Call Is Also for the People Who Are Not Jews

13 When they finished speaking, James said, "Brothers, listen to me. 14 Simon Peter has told how God first visited the people who are not Jews. He was getting a people for Himself. 15 This agrees with what the early preacher said, 16 'After this I will come back and build again the building of David that fell down. Yes, I will build it again from the stones that fell down. I will set it up again. 17 Then all the nations may look for the Lord, even all the people who are not Jews who are called by My name. The Lord said this. He does all these things. 18 God has made all His works known from the beginning of time.' (Amos 9:11-12)

The People Who Are Not Jews Are Not Under the Law

19 "So we should not trouble these people who are not Jews who are turning to God. 20 We should write to them that they should keep away from everything that is given to gods. They should keep away from sex sins and not eat blood or meat from animals that have been killed in ways against the Law. 21 For the Law of Moses has been read in every city from the early days. It has been read in the Jewish places of worship on every Day of Rest."

22 Then the missionaries and the church leaders and the whole church chose some men from among them. They were to be sent to the city of Antioch with Paul and Barnabas. They chose Judas Barsabbas and Silas. These men were leaders among the Christians.

23 They sent them with this letter: "The missionaries and church leaders and Christians greet the brothers who are not Jews in Antioch and Syria and Cilicia. 24 We have heard that some from our group have troubled you and have put doubt in your minds. They said that you must go through the religious act of becoming a Jew and you must keep the Law of Moses. We did not tell them to say these things. 25 All of us have wanted to send men to you with our much-loved Paul and Barnabas. 26 Their lives have been in danger for the name of our Lord Jesus Christ. 27 So now we send Judas and Silas to you. They will tell you the same things. 28 It pleased the Holy Spirit and us to ask you to do nothing more than these things that have to be done. 29 You are to keep away from everything that is given to

gods. Do not eat blood or meat from animals that have been killed in ways against the Law. Keep away from sex sins. If you keep yourselves free from these things you will do well. Good-bye."

The Missionaries Go Back to Antioch

30 When the meeting was finished, they went to Antioch. As soon as they gathered the people together, they gave them the letter. 31 When they read it, they were glad for the comfort and strength it brought them. 32 Judas and Silas were preachers also. They preached to the Christians and helped them to become stronger in the faith.

33 They were there for some time. Then they were sent back in peace to the missionaries who had sent them. 34 But Silas thought he should stay there. 35 Paul and Barnabas stayed in Antioch. With the help of many others, they preached and taught the Word of God.

Paul Starts Out the Second Time

36 After awhile, Paul said to Barnabas, "Let us go back and visit the Christians in every city where we have preached the Word of God. Let us see how they are doing." 37 Barnabas wanted to take John Mark with them. 38 Paul did not think it was good to take him because he had left them while they were in Pamphylia. He had not helped them in the work. 39 They argued so much that they left each other. Barnabas took John Mark with him and went by ship to the island of Cyprus. 40 Paul chose Silas. After the Christians asked for the Lord's favor to be on Paul and Silas, they went on their way. 41 They went through Syria and Cilicia making the churches stronger in the faith.

Timothy Starts to Work with Paul

16 Paul went down to the cities of Derbe and Lystra. There was a follower there named Timothy. His mother was a Jewish Christian and his father was a Greek. 2 The Christians in the city of Lystra and Iconium respected Timothy. 3 Paul wanted Timothy to go with him as a missionary. He took him and had Timothy go through the religious act of becoming a Jew because of the Jews who were in those places. Everyone knew his father was a Greek.

4 They went from city to city and told the Christians what the missionaries and the church leaders in Jerusalem had written for the Christians to do. 5 The churches were made stronger in the faith. More people were added each day.

Paul Is Called to Macedonia in a Dream

6 They went through the countries of Phrygia and Galatia. The Holy Spirit kept them from preaching the Word of God in the countries of Asia. 7 When they came to the city of Mysia, they tried to go on to the city of Bithynia but the Holy Spirit would not let them go. 8 From Mysia they went down to the city of Troas.

9 That night Paul had a dream. A man was standing in front of him crying out, "Come over to the country of Macedonia and help us!" 10 After he had seen this, we agreed that God told us to go to Macedonia to tell them the Good News.

Lydia, the First Christian in Europe

11 We took a ship from the city of Troas to the city of Samothracia. The next day we went to the city of Neapolis. 12 From there we went to the city of Philippi. This was an important city in Macedonia. It was ruled by the leaders of the country of Rome. We stayed here for some days. 13 On the Day of Rest we went outside the city to a place down by the river. We thought people would be gathering there for prayer. Some women came and we sat down and talked to them. 14 One of the women who listened sold purple cloth. She was from the city of Thyatira. Her name was Lydia and she was a worshiper of God. The Lord opened her heart to hear what Paul said. 15 When she and her family had been baptized, she said to us, "If you think I am faithful to the Lord, come and stay at my house." She kept on asking. Then we went with her.

Paul Heals a Girl with a Demon

16 One day as we were going to the place to pray, we met a servant-girl who could tell what was going to happen in the future by a demon she had. Her owner made much money from her power. 17 She followed Paul and us crying out, "These are servants of the Highest God. They are telling you how to be saved from the punishment of sin." 18 She did this many days. Paul was troubled. Then he turned and said to the demon in her, "In the name of Jesus Christ, I speak to you. Come out of her!" At once it left her.

Paul and Silas Are Put in Jail

19 The girl's owners saw that they could not make money with her anymore. Then they

took hold of Paul and Silas and dragged them to the leaders. This happened in the center of town where people gather. **20** After they brought them in front of the leaders, they said, "These men are Jews and are making a lot of trouble in our city. **21** They are teaching a religion that we Romans are not allowed to follow."

22 Many people had gathered around Paul and Silas. They were calling out things against them. The leaders had the clothes of Paul and Silas taken off and had them beaten with sticks. **23** After they had hit them many times, they put Paul and Silas in prison. The soldiers told the man who watched the prison to be sure to keep them from getting away. **24** Because of this, they were put in the inside room of the prison and their feet were put in pieces of wood that held them.

25 About midnight Paul and Silas were praying and singing songs of thanks to God. The other men in prison were listening to them. **26** All at once the earth started to shake. The stones under the prison shook and the doors opened. The chains fell off from everyone.

27 The man who watched the prison woke up. He saw the prison doors wide open and thought the men in prison had gotten away. At once he pulled out his sword to kill himself. **28** But Paul called to him, "Do not hurt yourself. We are all here!" **29** The man who watched the prison called for a light. Then he ran in and got down in front of Paul and Silas. He was shaking with fear. **30** As he took them outside, he said, "Sirs, what must I do to be saved?"

31 They said, "Put your trust in the Lord Jesus Christ and you and your family will be saved from the punishment of sin."

32 Then Paul spoke the Word of God to him and his family. **33** It was late at night, but the man who watched the prison took Paul and Silas in and washed the places on their bodies where they were hurt. Right then he and his family were baptized. **34** He took Paul and Silas to his house and gave them food. He and all his family were full of joy for having put their trust in God.

Paul and Silas Are Allowed to Go Free

35 When it was day, the leaders sent a soldier to say, "Let these men go free." **36** The man who watched the prison told this to Paul. He said, "The leaders have sent word to let you go free. Come out now and go without any trouble."

37 Paul said, "No! They have beaten us in front of many people without a trial. We are Roman citizens and they have put us in prison. Now do they think they can send us away without anyone knowing? No! They must come themselves and take us out." **38** The soldiers told this to the leaders. Then the leaders were afraid when they heard that Paul and Silas were Roman citizens. **39** They went themselves and told Paul and Silas they were sorry. Then they took them out and asked them to leave their city. **40** Paul and Silas went to Lydia's house after they left the prison. They met with the Christians and gave them comfort. Then they went away from the city.

Paul and Silas Start a Church in Thessalonica

17 After Paul and Silas had gone through the cities of Amphipolis and Apollonia, they came to the city of Thessalonica. The Jews had a place of worship there. **2** Paul went in as he always did. They gathered together each Day of Rest for three weeks and he taught them from the Holy Writings. **3** He showed them that Christ had to suffer and rise again from the dead. He said, "I preach this Jesus to you. He is the Christ." **4** Some of them put their trust in Christ and followed Paul and Silas. There were many Greek people and some leading women who honored God among those who had become Christians.

The Jews Make It Hard for Paul and Silas

5 The Jews who did not put their trust in Christ became jealous. They took along some sinful men from the center of town where people gather and brought them out on the street. These angry men started all the people in the city to cry out with loud voices. They went to the house of Jason hoping to find Paul and Silas there and bring them out to the people. **6** But they did not find them there. Then they dragged Jason and some other Christians out in front of the leaders and cried out, "These men who have been making trouble over all the world have come here also. **7** And Jason has taken them in. They say there is another King called Jesus. They are working against the laws made by Caesar."

8 When the people and city leaders heard this, they were troubled. **9** Then they made Jason and the others pay some money and let them go.

Paul and Silas Go to Berea

10 At once the Christians sent Paul and Silas away at night to the city of Berea. When they got there, they went to the Jewish place of worship. 11 These Jews were more willing to understand than those in the city of Thessalonica. They were very glad to hear the Word of God, and they looked into the Holy Writings to see if those things were true. 12 Many of them became Christians. Some of them were respected Greek women and men. 13 The Jews of Thessalonica heard that Paul was preaching the Word of God in Berea. They went there and worked against the missionaries by talking to the people. 14 At once the Christians sent Paul away to the sea-shore. But Silas and Timothy stayed there.

Paul Preaches on Mars' Hill in Athens

15 Those who took Paul brought him to the city of Athens. Paul sent word with them that Silas and Timothy should come to him as soon as they could. Then they left. 16 While Paul was waiting for Silas and Timothy in Athens, his spirit was troubled as he saw the whole city worshiping false gods. 17 He talked to the Jews and other people who were worshiping in the Jewish place of worship. Every day he talked with people who gathered in the center of town.

18 Some men from two different groups were arguing with Paul. The one group thought that men might as well get all the fun out of life that they can. The other group thought that wisdom alone makes men happy. Some of them said, "This man has lots of little things to talk about. They are not important. What is he trying to say?" Others said, "He preaches about strange gods." It was because he preached of Jesus and of His being raised from the dead.

19 Then they took him to Mars' Hill and said, "We want to hear of this new teaching of yours. 20 Some of the things you are telling us are strange to our ears. We want to know what these things mean." 21 The people of Athens and those visiting from far countries used all their time in talking or hearing some new thing. 22 Then Paul stood up on Mars' Hill and said, "Men of Athens, I see how very religious you are in every way. 23 As I was walking around and looking at the things you worship, I found an altar where you worship with the words written on it, TO THE GOD WHO IS NOT KNOWN. You are worshiping Him without knowing Him. He is the One I will tell you about.

24 "The God Who made the world and everything in it is the Lord of heaven and earth. He does not live in buildings made by hands. 25 No one needs to care for Him as if He needed anything. He is the One who gives life and breath and everything to everyone. 26 He made from one blood all nations who live on the earth. He set the times and places where they should live.

27 "They were to look for God. Then they might feel after Him and find Him because He is not far from each one of us. 28 It is in Him that we live and move and keep on living. Some of your own men have written, 'We are God's children.' 29 If we are God's children, we should not think of Him as being like gold or silver or stone. Such gods made of gold or silver or stone are planned by men and are made by them.

30 "God did not remember these times when people did not know better. But now He tells all men everywhere to be sorry for their sins and to turn from them. 31 He has set a day when He will say in the right way if the people of the world are guilty. This will be done by Jesus Christ, the One He has chosen. God has proven this to all men by raising Jesus Christ from the dead."

32 Some people laughed and made fun when they heard Paul speak of Christ being raised from the dead. Others said, "We want to listen to you again about this." 33 So Paul went away from the people. 34 Some people followed him and became Christians. One was Dionysius, a leader in the city. A woman named Damaris believed. And there were others also.

Paul Goes to Corinth

18 After that Paul went from the city of Athens and came to the city of Corinth. 2 He met a Jew there named Aquila who was born in the country of Pontus. He had lived in the country of Italy a short time. His wife Priscilla was with him. Claudius, who was the leader of the country, had told all the Jews to leave Rome. Paul went to see Aquila and Priscilla. 3 They made tents for a living. Paul did the same kind of work so he stayed with them and they worked together.

4 Every Day of Rest he would go to the Jewish place of worship and teach both Jews and Greeks. 5 Silas and Timothy came down from the country of Macedonia. Then Paul used all his time preaching to the Jews. He taught that Jesus was the Christ. 6 But they worked against Paul and said bad things about him. He shook his clothes and said, "Whatever happens to you is your own doing. I am free from your guilt. From now on I will go to the people who are not Jews."

7 Paul went from there and came to the house of a man named Titus Justus who worshiped God. His house was next to the Jewish place of worship. 8 Crispus was the leader of the Jewish place of worship. He and his family believed in the Lord. Many of the people of Corinth who heard Paul became Christians and were baptized.

9 Paul saw the Lord in a dream one night. He said to Paul, "Do not be afraid. Keep speaking. Do not close your mouth. 10 I am with you. No one will hurt you. I have many people in this city who belong to Me." 11 For a year and a half Paul stayed there and taught them the Word of God.

12 Gallio was leader of the country of Greece. All the Jews worked against Paul and brought him in front of the court. 13 They said, "This man is trying to get people to worship God against the Law." 14 Paul was ready to speak, but Gallio said to the Jews, "If this were something bad or a wrong-doing, I would listen to you. 15 But because it is about words and names and your own Law, you will have to take care of it yourselves. I do not want to judge who is right or wrong in things like this." 16 And he sent them out of his court.

17 Then all the Greek people took Sosthenes, the leader of the Jewish place of worship, and beat him in front of the court. But Gallio did not let this trouble him.

Paul Goes Back to Antioch

18 Paul stayed in Corinth many days longer. Then he said good-bye and left the followers. He went by ship to the country of Syria with Priscilla and Aquila going with him. In the city of Cenchrea he had his hair cut short because of a promise he had made to God. 19 They came to the city of Ephesus. Priscilla and Aquila stayed there. Paul went to the Jewish place of worship and argued with the Jews. 20 They wanted him to stay longer but he would not. 21 As he left them, he said,

(*"I must go to the special supper at Jerusalem.") I will return again to you if God wants me to." Then he got on a ship and left Ephesus. 22 He stopped in the city of Caesarea to greet the people in the church. Then he went down to the city of Antioch. 23 Paul stayed there for some time. Then he went from city to city through the countries of Galatia and Phrygia. In each place he helped the Christians become strong in the faith.

Aquila and Priscilla Help Apollos in Ephesus

24 A Jew by the name of Apollos had come to Ephesus. He was from the city of Alexandria. He could talk to people about the Holy Writings very well. 25 He had been taught in the way of the Lord. And with a strong desire in his heart, he taught about Jesus. What he said was true, but he knew only about the baptism of John.

26 He began to speak without fear in the Jewish place of worship. Aquila and Priscilla heard him. They took him to their house and taught him much more about the things of God. 27 Apollos wanted to cross over to Greece. The Christians wrote a letter to the followers there asking them to be good to him. When he got there, he was much help to those who had put their trust in Christ. 28 In front of everyone he proved with great power that the Jews were wrong. He showed from the Holy Writings that Jesus was the Christ.

Christians in Ephesus Are Filled with the Holy Spirit

19 While Apollos was in the city of Corinth, Paul went through the hill country to get to the city of Ephesus. He found a few followers there. 2 He asked them, "Did you receive the Holy Spirit when you put your trust in Christ?" They said, "No, we have not even heard that there is a Holy Spirit." 3 He asked them, "How were you baptized?" They answered, "The way John baptized." 4 Paul said, "John baptized those who were sorry for their sins and turned from them. He told the people to put their trust in Jesus Who was coming later."

5 The people there were baptized in the name of the Lord Jesus when they heard this. 6 When Paul laid his hands on them, the Holy Spirit came on them. They started to talk in special sounds and to speak God's Word. 7 There were about twelve men.

Paul Preaches in a Place of Worship and in a School in Ephesus

8 For three months Paul went into the Jewish place of worship and spoke without fear. He taught them things about the holy nation of God. 9 Some let their hearts grow hard. They would not put their trust in Christ. These spoke against the Christian religion in front of other people. Then Paul took the followers away from the others. He taught them each day in the school of Tyrannus. 10 He did this for two years. All the Jews and the Greeks in the countries of Asia heard the Word of the Lord.

Paul Does Powerful Works

11 God used Paul to do powerful special works. 12 Pieces of cloth and parts of his clothes that had been next to his body were put on sick people. Then they were healed of their diseases and demons came out of them.

13 There were Jews who went from city to city trying to put demons out of people. Some of these tried to use the name of the Lord Jesus on those who had demons. They said, "I speak to you in the name of Jesus, the One Paul preaches about." 14 A Jewish leader of the people by the name of Sceva had seven sons. These sons were trying to do this. 15 The demon said, "I know Jesus. I know about Paul. But who are you?" 16 Then the man with the demon jumped on the sons. He had power over them and beat them. They ran out of the house with no clothes on and they were hurt.

17 All the Jews and Greeks living in Ephesus heard about it. Because of this all the people became afraid. And the name of the Lord Jesus was held in great honor. 18 Many Christians came and told of the wrong things they were doing. 19 Many of those who did witchcraft gathered their books together and burned them in front of everyone. These books were worth 50,000 pieces of silver money. 20 The Word of the Lord became well-known.

21 After this, Paul thought he would go through the countries of Macedonia and Greece. Then he would go to Jerusalem. He said, "After I have been there, I must go to the city of Rome also." 22 He sent two of his helpers, Timothy and Erastus, to Macedonia. Paul stayed in the countries of Asia awhile longer.

The Meeting of the Silver Workmen in Ephesus

23 During that time there was much trouble about the Christians. 24 A man named Demetrius made small silver buildings for the worship of Diana. His workmen received much money for their work. 25 He called his workmen together and other men who made these small silver buildings. He said to them, "Men, you know we make much money from this work. 26 Now you hear that Paul has turned away many people in Ephesus as well as in Asia. He tells them that gods made with hands are not gods. 27 It could be that our work will not be respected. Not only that, the house of worship for the god of Diana will be worth nothing and her greatness will be destroyed. All the countries of Asia and the world worship her."

28 They became angry when they heard this and cried out, "Great is Diana of Ephesus." 29 The whole city was filled with loud cries. They caught Gaius and Aristarchus. These two men from Macedonia were with Paul. They gathered around them at the meeting place in the city.

30 Paul wanted to stand in front of all the people but his followers would not let him. 31 Some of the city leaders who were his friends told him not to go to the meeting. 32 All this time some were crying out one thing and some another. The meeting was all noise. Most of the people did not know why they had come together. 33 Then the Jews pushed Alexander to the front. Alexander held his hand up and was going to speak. 34 As soon as they saw he was a Jew, they cried out with a loud voice for two hours, "Great is Diana of Ephesus!"

35 One of the city leaders stopped the noise. He spoke, "Men of Ephesus, everyone knows our city is where the god of Diana is kept. That is the stone god that fell from the sky. 36 Everyone knows this is true, so you must not cry out or do anything foolish. 37 The men you brought here do not rob houses of worship or talk against our god. 38 If Demetrius and his workmen have something against anyone, we have special days for courts. Let them go to court. 39 If you want anything else, it should be done in another meeting. 40 We are in danger of being asked about this trouble today. There is no good reason we can give for this meeting." 41 When he had said this, he told them to leave.

Paul Goes to Greece and Macedonia

20 When the noise had come to an end, Paul called the followers to him. He spoke words of comfort and then said good-bye. He left to go to the country of Macedonia. 2 As he went through those parts of the country, he spoke words of comfort and help to the Christians. Then he went on to the country of Greece. 3 He stayed there three months. As he was about to get on a ship for the country of Syria, he learned that the Jews had made a plan to take him. He changed his plans and went back through Macedonia. 4 Some men were going along with him. They were Sopater of the city of Berea, Aristarchus and Secundus of the city of Thessalonica, Gaius of the city of Derbe, and Timothy and Tychicus and Trophimus of the countries of Asia. 5 They went on to the city of Troas and waited there for us. 6 After the supper of bread without yeast we got on a ship in the city of Philippi. We met these men at Troas. It took five days to get there and we stayed one week.

Eutychus Falls from a Building While Paul Preaches

7 On the first day of the week we met together to eat the Lord's supper. Paul talked to them. He thought he would leave the next day, so he kept on talking until twelve o'clock at night. 8 There were many lights in the room on the third floor where we had our meeting. 9 A young man named Eutychus sat in the window. As Paul kept on preaching, this man started to go to sleep. At last he went to sleep. He fell from the third floor to the ground and was picked up dead. 10 Paul went down and stood over him. Then he took him in his arms and said, "Do not be worried. He is alive!" 11 Paul went up again to the meeting and ate with them. He talked with them until the sun came up. Then he left. 12 They were happy they could take the young man home alive.

13 We went on ahead by ship to the city of Assos. There we were to pick up Paul. He had planned it that way. He wanted to walk by land that far. 14 We got to Assos and met him there. We picked him up and went on to the city of Mitylene. 15 The next day we went by ship to a place beside the island of Chios. The next day we crossed over to the island of Samos. Then the next day we came to the city of Miletus. 16 Paul planned to pass by the city of Ephesus so he would not lose more time in Asia. He wanted to be in Jerusalem if he could be on the day to remember how the Holy Spirit came on the church.

Paul Meets with the Leaders of the Church of Ephesus

17 From Miletus he sent word to Ephesus. He asked the leaders of the church to come to him. 18 When they got there, he said to them, "From the first day that I came to Asia you have seen what my life has been like. 19 I worked for the Lord without pride. Because of the trouble the Jews gave me, I have had many tears. 20 I always told you everything that would be a help to you. I taught you in open meetings and from house to house. 21 I preached to the Jews and to the Greeks. I told them to turn from their sin to God and to put their trust in our Lord Jesus Christ.

22 "As you see, I am on my way to Jerusalem. The Holy Spirit makes me go. I do not know what will happen to me there. 23 But in every city I have been, the Holy Spirit tells me that trouble and chains will be waiting for me there. 24 But I am not worried about this. I do not think of my life as worth much, but I do want to finish the work the Lord Jesus gave me to do. My work is to preach the Good News of God's loving-favor.

25 "All of you have heard me preach the Good News. I am sure that none of you will ever see my face again. 26 I tell you this day that I am clean and free from the blood of all men. 27 I told you all the truth about God. 28 Keep a careful watch over yourselves and over the church. The Holy Spirit has made you its leaders. Feed and care for the church of God. He bought it with His own blood.

29 "Yes, I know that when I am gone, hungry wolves will come in among you. They will try to destroy the church. 30 Also men from your own group will begin to teach things that are not true. They will get men to follow them. 31 I say again, keep watching! Remember that for three years I taught everyone of you night and day, even with tears.

32 "And now, my brothers, I give you over to God and to the word of His love. It is able to make you strong and to give you what you are to have, along with all those who are set apart for God. 33 I have not tried to get anyone's money or clothes. 34 You all know that these hands worked for what I needed and for what those with me needed. 35 In every way I

showed you that by working hard like this we can help those who are weak. We must remember what the Lord Jesus said, 'We are more happy when we give than when we receive.'"

36 As he finished talking, he got down on his knees and prayed with them all. 37 They cried and put their arms around Paul and kissed him. 38 What made them sad most of all was he said that they would never see his face again. Then they went with him to the ship.

Paul Goes from Miletus to Tyre

21 After we left them, we got on a ship and came straight down to the island of Cos. The next day we came to the island of Rhodes and from there to the city of Patara. 2 There we found a ship that was going over to the country of Phoenicia. We got on it and went along. 3 We saw the island of Cyprus to our left but went on to the country of Syria. We came to land at the city of Tyre. The ship was to leave its load of freight there.

4 We looked for the Christians and stayed with them seven days. The Christians had been told by the Holy Spirit to tell Paul not to go to Jerusalem. 5 When our time was up, we left there and went on our way. All of them with their wives and children went with us out of town. They got down on their knees on the shore and prayed. 6 After we said good-bye, we got on the ship and they went back to their houses.

Paul Goes from Tyre to Jerusalem

7 The same ship took us from Tyre to the city of Ptolemais. We stayed with the Christians there one day. 8 The next day we left and came to the city of Caesarea. We went to the house of Philip and stayed with him. He was a preacher who goes from town to town and was one of the seven church leaders. 9 Philip had four daughters who were not married. They spoke the Word of God.

10 While we were there a few days, a man who speaks for God named Agabus came down from the country of Judea. 11 He came to see us. Then he took Paul's belt and used it to tie his own feet and hands. He said, "This is what the Holy Spirit says, 'The Jews at Jerusalem will tie the man who owns this belt. Then they will hand him over to the people who are not Jews.'"

12 When we heard this, we and all the people living there begged Paul not to go up to Jerusalem. 13 Then Paul said, "What do you mean by crying and breaking my heart? I am ready to be put in chains in Jerusalem. I am also ready to die for the name of the Lord Jesus." 14 Paul would not listen to us. So we stopped begging him and said, "May whatever God wants be done."

Paul Is in Jerusalem

15 After this, we got ready and started up to Jerusalem. 16 Some of the followers in Caesarea went with us. They took us to Mnason's house. He was one of the first followers from Cyprus. We stayed with him.

17 When we got to Jerusalem, the Christians were glad to see us. 18 The next day we went with Paul to see James. All the church leaders came also. 19 After saying hello to them, Paul told of what God had done through his work for the people who were not Jews.

20 When they heard this, they thanked the Lord. Then they said to him, "You see, brother, how many thousands of Christians there are among the Jews. They all obey the Law of Moses. 21 They have heard about you. They have heard you teach the Jews who live among people who are not Jews. They have heard you teach them to break away from the Law of Moses. They say you are telling them not to do the religious act of becoming a Jew and not to follow old religious ways of worship. 22 What should we do about it? They will hear that you have come. 23 You must do what we tell you. We have four men with us who have made a promise to God. 24 Take these four men and go through the religious worship of washing with them. You pay to have their hair cut off. Then everybody will know what they have heard about you is not true. They will know you are careful to obey the Law of Moses. 25 As for the people who are not Jews, we wrote to them. We said that they must keep away from everything that has been given to gods. They must not eat blood or meat from animals that have been killed in ways against the Law. They must keep away from sex sins."

26 The next day Paul took the men. He went through the religious worship of washing with them. They went into the house of God to tell when their religious worship of washing would be finished. Then the gift for each one of them would be given as an act of worship.

27 The seven days were almost finished.

Jews from the countries of Asia saw Paul in the house of God. They made the people turn against him. Then they took hold of him. **28** They cried out, "You who are Jews, help us! This is the man who is teaching against our people and our Law and this house of God. Also he has brought Greek people into the house of God. This has made this holy place unclean." **29** They had seen him before in the city with Trophimus who was from the city of Ephesus. They thought Paul had brought him into the house of God also.

30 All the people in the city were crying out with loud voices. The people pushed and moved together. They took Paul and dragged him out of the house of God. Then the doors were shut. **31** They were getting ready to kill him. The captain of the soldiers heard there was trouble over all Jerusalem. **32** At once the captain called his soldiers and they ran down to the people. When the people saw the captain and his soldiers, they stopped beating Paul.

Paul Is Tied with Chains

33 The captain came and took hold of Paul. He told his soldiers to tie Paul with two chains. Then he asked who he was and what he had done. **34** Some of the people called out one thing and some another. The captain was not able to find out what had happened. He told his men to take Paul into the soldiers' building. **35** The people cried out so loud and pushed so hard that Paul had to be carried up the steps by the soldiers. **36** All the people kept pushing and calling out, "Kill him!"

37 Paul was brought into the soldiers' building. He said to the captain, "May I say something to you?" The captain said, "Can you speak the Greek language? **38** Are you not the man from the country of Egypt who made trouble against our country? That man led 4,000 fighting men into the desert." **39** Paul said, "No! I am a Jew and a citizen of a large city. I am from Tarsus in the country of Cilicia. I ask you to let me speak to the people." **40** The captain told Paul to speak. So Paul stood on the steps and held up his hand. When there was no more noise, he spoke to them in the language of the Jews.

Paul Tells of His Past Life

22 Paul said, "Brothers and fathers, listen to what I have to say to you." **2** When they heard him speak to them in their own language, they stopped making noise. Then he said,

3 "I am a Jew. I was born in the city of Tarsus in the country of Cilicia. When I was a young man, I lived here in Jerusalem. I went to Gamaliel's school and learned all about the Law of our early fathers. I worked hard for God as you all do today.

4 "I worked hard and killed men and women who believed as I believe today. I put them in chains and sent them to prison. **5** The head religious leader and the leaders of the people can tell you this is true. I got letters from them to take to our Jewish brothers in the city of Damascus. I was going there to put the Christians in chains and bring them to Jerusalem where they would be beaten.

The Change in Paul's Life on the Damascus Road

6 "I was near Damascus. All at once, about noon, I saw a bright light from heaven shining around me. **7** I fell to the ground. A voice said to me, 'Saul, Saul, why do you work so hard against Me?' **8** I said, 'Who are You, Lord?' He said to me, 'I am Jesus of Nazareth, the One you are working against.' **9** Those who were with me saw the light. But they did not hear Him speaking to me. **10** I asked, 'Lord, what should I do?' The Lord said to me, 'Get up! Go to Damascus. You will be told what to do there.'

11 "I could not see because of the bright light. Those who were with me had to lead me by the hand until we came to Damascus. **12** Ananias lived there. He obeyed the Law and was respected by all the Jews. **13** He came and stood near me and said, 'Brother Saul, receive your sight.' At once I was able to see him. **14** Then Ananias said, 'The God of our fathers chose you to know what He wants done. He chose you to see Jesus Christ, the One Right with God, and to hear His voice. **15** You are to tell all men what you have seen and heard. **16** What are you waiting for? Get up! Be baptized. Have your sins washed away by calling on His name.'

Paul Is Called to Work with the People Who Are Not Jews

17 "I came back to Jerusalem. When I was praying in the house of God, I had a dream. **18** I saw Him as He said to me, 'Get out of Jerusalem! They will not listen to you when you tell them about Me!' **19** I said, 'Lord, they know I took Christians out of every Jewish place of worship.

I had them beaten and put in prison. 20 Also when Stephen was killed, I stood there and watched them throw stones at him. Those who threw the stones had me watch their coats.' 21 The Lord said to me, 'Go! I will send you far away to the people who are not Jews.' " 22 They listened to him until he said that. Then they all cried out with loud voices, "Kill him! Take such a man from the earth! He should not live!" 23 They kept on calling out. Then they pulled off their coats and threw dust in the air.

Paul Tells Who He Is

24 The captain told them to bring Paul into the soldiers' building. He told his soldiers to find out from Paul, by beating him, why the people were crying out against him. 25 As they tied him up, Paul said to the soldier, "Does the law say that you can beat a Roman citizen when no one has said he is guilty?"

26 When the soldier heard this, he told it to the captain. He said, "Listen! What are you doing? This man is a Roman citizen." 27 The captain came and asked Paul, "Tell me, are you a Roman citizen?" Paul said, "Yes!" 28 The captain said, "I had to pay a lot of money to be a citizen." Paul said, "But I was born a Roman." 29 Those who were going to beat him left him at once. The captain was also afraid when he heard that Paul was a Roman citizen because he had him tied.

Paul Stands in Front of the Religious Leaders' Court

30 The next day they took off the chains that were holding Paul. The captain wanted to know why the Jews wanted to kill him. So the captain told the head religious leaders to gather for their court. They brought Paul and put him in front of them.

Paul Speaks to the Religious Leaders' Court

23 Paul looked straight at the court and said, "Brother Jews, I have lived for God with a heart that has said I am not guilty to this day." 2 Then Ananias, the head religious leader, told those standing near him to hit him on the mouth. 3 Paul said, "God will hit you, you white-washed wall! Do you sit there and say I am guilty by the Law when you break the Law by having me hit?"

4 Those standing near said, "Do you talk like that to God's head religious leader?" 5 Paul said, "Brother Jews, I did not know that he was God's head religious leader. I know the Holy Writings say, 'You must not speak against the leader of your people.' " (Exodus 22:28)

6 Paul saw that part of the court was made up of the religious group who believe no one is raised from the dead. The other part were proud religious law-keepers. Then he cried out, "Brother Jews, I am a proud religious law-keeper and from a family of proud religious law-keepers. I have been brought in front of this court because of the hope of being raised from the dead."

7 When they heard this, both religious groups started to argue and the people of the court were divided in what they thought. 8 The one religious group believes that no one is raised from the dead. Also, they do not believe in angels or spirits. But the other religious group, the proud religious law-keepers, believe that people are raised from the dead and that there are angels and spirits. 9 The courtroom was filled with noise. Some of the teachers of the Law working with the proud religious law-keepers stood up and said, "We find nothing wrong with this man. What if an angel or spirit has spoken to him?"

10 They argued all the more. Then the captain was afraid they would pull Paul to pieces. He told his men to get Paul out of there and take him back to the soldiers' building. 11 The next night the Lord came to Paul and said, "Paul, do not be afraid! You will tell about Me in the city of Rome the same as you have told about Me in Jerusalem."

The Plan to Kill Paul

12 In the morning some of the Jews gathered together and made a plan to kill Paul. They promised each other that they would not eat or drink until they had killed him. 13 There were more than forty of them who had made this promise. 14 These people came to the head religious leader and to the leaders of the people and said, "We have made a promise not to eat any food until we have killed Paul. 15 We ask you and the court to have the captain bring Paul down to you tomorrow. It will look as if you want to ask him some things. Before he gets near you, we will be waiting to kill him."

16 Paul's nephew heard about the plan. He went to the soldiers' building and told Paul. 17 Paul called one of the soldiers and

said, "Take this young man to the captain. He has something to tell him." 18 The soldiers brought the young man to the captain and said, "Paul asked me to bring this young man to you. He has something to tell you." 19 The captain took him by the hand and they walked over where they could be alone. He said, "What is it that you have to tell me?" 20 The young man said, "The Jews have made a plan to ask you to bring Paul to the courtroom tomorrow. It would look as if they were going to ask him some things. 21 Do not let them talk you into it. More than forty men are waiting in secret to kill him. They have promised each other not to eat or drink anything until they have killed him. They are all waiting for you to say the word." 22 The captain told the young man to go. He said, "Do not tell anyone you have told me this."

Paul Is Sent to Felix in Caesarea

23 Then the captain called two soldiers and said, "Get 200 men ready to go to the city of Caesarea by nine o'clock tonight. Also have seventy men ride on horses and 200 men carry spears. 24 Get horses ready for Paul to ride. Take him to Felix, the leader of the people."

25 He wrote a letter which said, 26 "Claudius Lysias greets Felix, the best leader of the people. 27 This man Paul was taken by the Jews. He was about to be killed by them. But I came along with my soldiers and kept him from being killed. I did this when I learned that he was a Roman citizen. 28 I wanted to know what they had against him. So I took him to the religious leaders' court. 29 I learned they were holding him because of something about their Law. There was no reason for him to be killed or to be put in prison. 30 I was told that the Jews had a plan to kill this man. At once I sent him to you. I told the Jews who wanted to kill him to tell you what they have against him. Good bye."

31 The soldiers took Paul as they were told. They brought him during the night to Antipatris. 32 The next day they went back to their building in Jerusalem. The men riding horses went on with Paul. 33 When they came to Caesarea, they gave the letter to the leader of the people. They also handed Paul over to him. 34 After he read the letter, he asked what part of the country Paul was from. He was told that Paul was from the city of Cilicia. 35 He said, "I will listen to all of this when the men come who want to kill you." He had Paul kept in King Herod's building.

Paul Stands in Front of Felix

24 Five days later Ananias came to the city of Caesarea. He was the head religious leader. Some other religious leaders and a man whose name was Tertullus came also. This man worked in courts and knew all about the laws. He told Felix what the Jews had against Paul. 2 They brought in Paul. Then Tertullus started to tell what the Jews had against him, saying,

"Most respected Felix, because of you, we are living in peace. Wrong-doings have been made right in this nation. 3 In every way and in every place, we thank you for all of this. 4 We do not want to keep you here too long. I ask you to listen to our few words. You are known to be kind in this way. 5 We have found this man to be a trouble-maker among all the Jews in the world. He is a leader of a religious group called the Nazarenes. 6 He even tried to make the house of God unclean by taking people into it who were not Jews. But we took hold of him. (*We could have said he was guilty by our Law. 7 But Lysias, the captain, came and took him out of our hands. 8 He told those who wanted to kill him to tell you what they had against him.) When you ask him about these things, you will be able to learn everything we have against him." 9 The Jews agreed to what he said against Paul.

Paul Speaks for Himself the First Time

10 Then Felix, the leader of the people, told Paul to speak. Paul said, "I know that you have been a leader of this nation for many years. I am happy to be able to speak for myself. 11 Not more than twelve days ago I went up to Jerusalem to worship. You can find out about this yourself. 12 I did not argue with anyone in the house of God or in the Jewish places of worship or in the city. I was not making trouble. 13 They cannot prove any of these things they say against me.

14 "I will say this, I worship the God of our fathers in the new Way. They say it is a false way. But I believe everything that has been written in the Law and by the early preachers. 15 I trust God for the same things they are looking for. I am looking for the dead to rise, both those right with God and the sinful. 16 I always try to live so my own heart tells me I am not guilty before God or man.

17 "After a few years I came to bring gifts of money to the people of my country (Jerusalem). 18 Some Jews from the countries of Asia found me in the house of God after I had gone through the worship of washing. There were no people around me and there was no noise or fighting. 19 They should be here if they have anything against me. 20 Or let these men tell what wrong they found in me as I stood in front of their court, 21 unless it was the words I cried out as I stood in front of them. I said, 'I have been brought in front of this court because of the hope of being raised from the dead.'"

Felix Waits for Lysias to Come

22 Felix knew about the Christian religion. He stopped the court, saying, "When Lysias the captain comes down, I will decide about this." 23 He told the soldier to watch Paul, but to let him come and go as much as he wanted to. Paul's friends were to be able to come and care for him.

Paul Speaks for Himself the Second Time

24 Some days later Felix came again. His Jewish wife Drusilla was with him. He sent for Paul and heard him talk about faith in Christ Jesus. 25 Paul spoke about being right with God. He spoke about being the boss over our own desires. He spoke about standing before One Who will tell us if we are guilty. When Felix heard this, he became afraid and said, "Go now. I will send for you when it is a better time." 26 He was hoping that Paul would give him money so he could go free. For that reason he kept sending for Paul and talking to him.

27 After two years Porcius Festus became leader of the people instead of Felix. Felix wanted to please the Jews so he kept Paul in prison.

Paul Stands in Front of Festus

25 Three days after Festus had become leader in the country, he went from the city of Caesarea to Jerusalem. 2 The head religious leaders and the leaders of the Jews told Festus what they had against Paul. 3 They asked Festus for a favor. They wanted Paul to be brought to Jerusalem because they had plans to kill him on the way. 4 Festus told them that Paul was to be kept in Caesarea and that he would be going there soon. 5 Festus said, "If Paul has done anything wrong, let your leaders go along with me and say what they have against him."

6 After staying with them about ten days, Festus went down to Caesarea. The next day he sat in the courtroom and asked for Paul to be brought in. 7 Paul came into the courtroom. The Jews who had come down from Jerusalem stood around him. They said many bad things against him. But they could not prove any of the things they said. 8 Paul spoke for himself, saying, "I have done nothing wrong against the Law of the Jews or against the house of God or against Caesar."

9 Festus was hoping to get the respect of the Jews. He asked Paul, "Will you go to the court in Jerusalem and let me say if you are guilty or not about these things?" 10 Paul said, "I am standing in front of Caesar's court where I should be told I am right or wrong. I have done no wrong to the Jews. You know that. 11 If I have done wrong and should die, I am not trying to keep from dying. But if these things they say against me are not true, no one can give me over to them. I ask to be taken to Caesar." 12 Festus talked to the leaders of the court. Then he said to Paul, "You have asked to be taken to Caesar. You will go to him."

Festus Tells King Agrippa about Paul

13 After a few days, King Agrippa and his wife, Bernice, came down to Caesarea. They went to Festus to greet him. 14 They stayed there a few days. Festus told them about Paul. He said, "There is a man here who was left in prison by Felix. 15 When I was at Jerusalem, the head religious leaders and the leaders of the people told me about him and asked me to say that he is guilty. 16 I told them it was against the Roman law to hand over a man to be put to death before he stood face to face with those who had something against him and could speak for himself. 17 When they came here, I took my seat in the courtroom at once. I had the man brought in. 18 When the others spoke, they had nothing against him that I thought they had. 19 They did not agree with him about their own religion, and they argued about someone called Jesus. He had died but Paul kept saying He was alive. 20 I did not know what to do. Then I asked him if he would go on trial about these things at Jerusalem. 21 But Paul asked to go on trial in front of Caesar. I said that he should be kept in prison until he could be sent to Caesar." 22 Agrippa said to Festus, "I would like to hear this man." Festus said, "Tomorrow you will hear him."

Paul Stands in Front of King Agrippa

23 The next day Agrippa and Bernice came into the courtroom. They were dressed to show their greatness as king and queen. Army leaders and leading men of the city came in with them. Festus had Paul brought in.

24 Festus said, "King Agrippa and all of you who are here with us, you see this man. All of the Jews both here and at Jerusalem are saying that Paul should be put to death. 25 I have heard nothing against him that would be reason to put him to death. But he asked for a trial in front of Caesar. I have agreed to send Paul to him. 26 When I write to Caesar, I have nothing to say against him. For this reason, I brought him in front of you all and in front of you, King Agrippa. After we ask him questions, I may have something to write about. 27 It is foolish for me to send a man up for trial without writing what is against him."

Paul Speaks to King Agrippa

26 Agrippa said to Paul, "You may now speak for yourself." Paul lifted his hand and started to talk, 2 "King Agrippa, the Jews have said many things against me. I am happy to be able to tell you my side of the story. 3 You know all about the Jewish ways and problems. So I ask you to listen to me until I have finished.

4 "All the Jews know about my life from the time I was a boy until now. I lived among my own people in Jerusalem. 5 If they would tell what they know, they would say that I lived the life of a proud religious law-keeper. I was in the group of proud religious law-keepers who tried to obey every law.

6 "And now I am on trial here because I trust the promise God made to our fathers. 7 This promise is what our twelve family groups of the Jewish nation hope to see happen. They worship God day and night. King Agrippa, it is because of this hope that they are saying things against me. 8 Why do you think it is hard to believe that God raises people from the dead?

9 "I used to think I should work hard against the name of Jesus of Nazareth. 10 I did that in Jerusalem. I put many of the followers in prison. The head religious leaders gave me the right and the power to do it. Then when the followers were killed, I said it was all right. 11 I beat them and tried to make them speak against God in all the Jewish places of worship. In my fight against them, I kept going after them even into cities in other countries.

12 "When I was going to Damascus to do this, I had the right and the power from the head religious leaders to make it hard for the followers. 13 I was on the road at noon. King Agrippa, I saw a light from heaven brighter than the sun. It was shining around me and the men with me. 14 We all fell to the ground. Then I heard a voice speaking to me in the Jewish language, 'Saul, Saul, why are you working so hard against Me? You hurt yourself by trying to hurt Me.' 15 I said, 'Who are You, Lord?' And He said, 'I am Jesus, the One you are working against. 16 Get up. Stand on your feet. I have chosen you to work for Me. You will tell what you have seen and you will say what I want you to say. This is the reason I have allowed you to see Me. 17 I will keep you safe from the Jews and from the people who are not Jews. I am sending you to these people. 18 You are to open their eyes. You are to turn them from darkness to light. You are to turn them from the power of Satan to the power of God. In this way, they may have their sins forgiven. They may have what is given to them, along with all those who are set apart for God by having faith in Me.'

19 "King Agrippa, I obeyed what I saw from heaven. 20 First I told what I saw to those in Damascus and then in Jerusalem. I told it through all the country of Judea. I even preached to the people who are not Jews that they should be sorry for their sins and turn from them to God. I told them they should do things to show they are sorry for their sins. 21 That is why the Jews took hold of me in the house of God and tried to kill me. 22 God has helped me. To this day I have told these things to the people who are well-known and to those not known. I have told only what the early preachers and Moses said would happen. 23 It was that Christ must suffer and be the first to rise from the dead. He would give light to the Jews and to the other nations."

24 As Paul was speaking for himself, Festus cried out in a loud voice, "Paul, you are crazy! All your learning keeps you from thinking right?" 25 Paul said, "Most respected Festus, I am not crazy. I am speaking the truth! 26 The king knows about all this. I am free to speak to him in plain words. Nothing I have said is new to him. These things happened where everyone saw them. 27 King Agrippa, do you believe the writings of the early preachers? I know that you believe them."

28 Then Agrippa said to Paul, "In this short time you have almost proven to me that I should become a Christian!" 29 Paul said, "My prayer to God is that you and all who hear me today would be a Christian as I am, only not have these chains!" 30 King Agrippa and Festus and Bernice and those who sat with them got up. 31 As they left the courtroom, they said to each other, "This man has done nothing for which he should be kept in prison or be put to death." 32 Agrippa told Festus, "This man could go free if he had not asked to be sent to Caesar."

Paul Is Sent to Rome

27 It was decided that we should go to the country of Italy by ship. Then they put Paul and some other men in chains. Julius, a captain of Caesar's army, was to watch them. 2 We went on a ship that was from the city of Adramyttian. It was going to stop at the towns along the sea-shore of Asia. Aristarchus was with us. He was a man from the city of Thessalonica in the country of Macedonia. 3 The next day we stopped in the city of Sidon. Julius was kind to Paul. He let him visit friends who cared for him.

4 After leaving Sidon we were blown by the wind along the south side of the island of Cyprus. The wind was against us. 5 We crossed the sea along the countries of Cilicia and Pamphylia and got to the city of Myra in the country of Lycia. 6 The captain found a ship from the city of Alexandria that was going to the country of Italy. He put us on it. 7 For many days the ship did not move fast. It was hard to get to the city of Cnidus. The wind would not let us go on. So we went along the south shore of the island of Crete and passed the end of the island called Salome. 8 The wind was against us, and we did not sail very fast. Then we came to a place called Fair Havens. It was near the city of Lasea.

9 Much time had been lost. To keep going that late in the year would mean danger. Paul spoke with strong words, 10 "Sirs, it looks to me as if this ship and its freight will be lost. We are in danger of being lost also."

11 The captain of the soldiers listened to what the captain of the ship said and not to what Paul said. 12 It was not a good place to spend the winter. Most of those on the ship wanted to go on and try to get to Phoenix. Crete was a good place to tie up the ship. They wanted to spend the winter

there. 13 When a south wind started to blow, they thought their plan was right. They pulled up the anchor and went close to the shore of Crete.

14 Later a bad wind storm came down from the land. It was called a northeaster. 15 The ship was stopped by the wind. After awhile we gave up and let it go with the wind. 16 We went behind a small island called Claudia. It was hard work but we were able to make the ship's boat safe. 17 They pulled it up and tied ropes around it and the ship. They were afraid of going on the Syrtis sands. So they took the sail down and let the ship go with the wind.

18 The storm was so bad the high waves were beating against the ship. The next day the men threw some of the freight over into the sea. 19 On the third day, with their own hands, they threw part of the sails and ropes into the sea. 20 We did not see the sun or stars for many days. A very bad storm kept beating against us. We lost all hope of being saved.

Paul Shows His Faith

21 No one had eaten for a long time. Then Paul stood up and said to them, "Men, you should have listened to me and not left Crete. You would not have had this trouble and loss. 22 But now I want you to take hope. No one will lose his life. Only the ship will be lost. 23 I belong to God and I work for Him. Last night an angel of God stood by me 24 and said, 'Do not be afraid, Paul. You must stand in front of Caesar. God has given you the lives of all the men on this ship.' 25 So take hope, men. I believe my God will do what He has told me. 26 But the ship will be lost on some island."

27 It was now the fourteenth night. We were going with the wind on the Adriatic Sea. At midnight the sailors thought land was near. 28 They let down the lead weight and found the water was not very deep. After they had gone a little farther, they found there was not as much water. 29 They were afraid we might be thrown against the rocks on the shore. So they put out four anchors from the back of the ship. Then they waited for morning to come.

30 The sailors were thinking of leaving the ship. They let down a boat as if they were going to put out anchors from the front of the ship. 31 But Paul said to the captain and the soldiers, "These men must stay on the ship or you cannot be safe!" 32 Then the soldiers cut the ropes and let the boat fall into the sea.

33 Just before the light of day came, Paul told all of them to eat. He said, "Today is the fourteenth day you have not eaten. 34 You must eat. It will give you strength. Not one of you will lose a hair from your head."

35 After he said this, he took some bread. He gave thanks to God in front of them all. He broke it in pieces and started to eat. 36 They all were comforted. Each one ate some food. 37 All together there were 276 of us on the ship. 38 After they had eaten, they threw the wheat into the sea so the ship would not be as heavy.

39 In the morning they could not see what land they were near. Later they could see a river. Near its mouth there was a shore of sand. They planned to run the ship onto the sand if they could. 40 The anchors were cut loose and left in the sea. Then they took the ropes off that were holding the rudder. When they put up the sail, the wind took the ship toward shore. 41 But the ship hit a place where the water was low. It was made from where two seas meet. The front of the ship did not move but the back part broke in pieces by the high waves.

42 The soldiers planned to kill the men in chains. They were afraid they would swim to shore and get away, 43 but the captain wanted to save Paul. He kept them from their plan. Calling out to those who could swim, he told them to jump into the sea and swim to shore. 44 The others should use wood or anything from the ship. In this way, they all got to shore without getting hurt.

The Powerful Work of Paul

28 After we were safe on the island, we knew that it was Malta. 2 The people on the island were very kind to us. It was raining and cold. They made a fire so we could get warm. 3 Paul had gathered some wood. As he laid it on the fire, a snake came out because of the heat. It held fast to Paul's hand. 4 When the people of the island saw the snake holding to his hand, they said to each other, "This man is a killer. He was saved from the sea and yet it is not right for him to live." 5 Paul shook off the snake into the fire. He was not hurt in any way. 6 The people waited. They thought his hand would get large and he would fall over dead. After watching for a long time, they saw nothing happen to him. Then they changed their minds and said that Paul was a god.

The Father of Publius Is Healed

7 Publius was the head man of the island. He owned land around there. For three days he took us in and gave us everything we needed. 8 The father of Publius was sick with a stomach sickness. Paul went to see him. He prayed and laid his hands on him and the man was healed. 9 Because of this, other people of the island who were sick came to Paul and were healed. 10 They had great respect for us. When we got into a ship to leave, they gave us everything we needed.

11 We had stayed on the island three months. Then we left on a ship that had stayed there during the winter. It was from the city of Alexandria. This ship was called the Twin Brothers. 12 We came to Syracuse and stayed there three days. 13 From there we went by ship around to the city of Rhegium. After a day a south wind started to blow. On the second day we came to the city of Puteoli. 14 We found some Christians there, and they asked us to stay with them. We were there seven days and then went on to the city of Rome.

15 When the Christians heard of our coming, they came to meet us. They came as far as the town of Appius and to a place to stay called the Three Stores. When Paul saw them, he thanked God and took courage.

Paul Tells Why and How He Has Come

16 When we got to Rome, Paul was allowed to live where he wanted to. But a soldier was always by his side to watch him. 17 Three days later Paul asked the leaders of the Jews to come to him. When they had gathered together, he said, "Brothers, I have done nothing against our people or the way our early fathers lived. And yet, I was tied with chains in Jerusalem and handed over to the Romans. 18 I was put on trial, but they found no reason to put me to death. They would have let me go free. 19 But the Jews did not like this. So I had to ask to be sent to Caesar. It was not because I had anything against my people. 20 The reason I have asked you to come is to tell you this. It is because of the hope of the Jewish nation that I am tied in these chains."

21 They said to Paul, "We have had no letters from Judea about you. No Jew who has come here has ever said anything bad about you. 22 We would like to hear from you what you believe. As for this new religion, all we know is that everyone is talking against it."

23 They planned to meet him on a certain

day. Many people came to the place where he stayed. He preached to them about the holy nation of God. He tried to get them to put their trust in Jesus Christ by preaching from the Law of Moses and from the writings of the early preachers. From morning until night he spoke to them. 24 Some of them believed his teaching. Others did not believe.

25 As they left, they did not agree with each other. Then Paul said, "The Holy Spirit spoke the truth to your early fathers through the early preacher Isaiah. 26 He said, 'Go to these people and say, "You will hear and never understand, you will look and never see, 27 because these people have hearts that have become fat. They do not hear well with their ears.

They have closed their eyes so their eyes do not see and their ears do not hear and their minds do not understand and they do not turn to Me and let Me heal them." ' (Isaiah 6:9–10)

28 "I want you to know that the Good News of God of knowing how to be saved from the punishment of sin has been sent to the people who are not Jews. And they will listen to it!" 29 *After he had said these things, the Jews went away and argued with each other.

30 Paul paid money to live in a house by himself for two years. He was happy for all who came to see him. 31 He kept on preaching about the holy nation of God. He taught about the Lord Jesus Christ without fear. No one stopped him.

ROMANS

1 This letter is from Paul. I am a servant owned by Jesus Christ and a missionary chosen by God to preach His Good News. 2 The Good News was promised long ago by God's early preachers in His Holy Writings. 3 It tells of His Son, our Lord Jesus Christ, Who was born as a person in the flesh through the family of King David. 4 The Holy Spirit proved by a powerful act that Jesus our Lord is the Son of God because He was raised from the dead. 5 Jesus has given us His loving-favor and has made us His missionaries. We are to preach to the people of all nations that they should obey Him and put their trust in Him. 6 You have been chosen to belong to Jesus Christ also. 7 So I write to all of you in the city of Rome. God loves you and has chosen you to be set apart for Himself. May God our Father and the Lord Jesus Christ give you His loving-favor and peace.

Prayer of Thanks

8 First of all, I keep thanking my God, through Jesus Christ, for all of you. This is because the whole world knows of your faith in Christ. 9 God knows how I work for Him. He knows how I preach with all my heart the Good News about His Son. He knows how I always pray for you. 10 I pray that I might be able to visit you, if God wants me to. 11 I want to see you so I can share some special gift of the Holy Spirit with you. It will make you strong. 12 Both of us need help. I can help make your faith

strong and you can do the same for me. We need each other.

Sinful Man

13 Christian brothers, many times I have wanted to visit you. Something has kept me from going until now. I have wanted to lead some of you to Christ also, as I have done in other places where they did not know God. 14 I must help the people who have had a chance to hear the Good News and those who have not. I must help those with much learning and those who have never learned from books. 15 So I want to preach the Good News to you who live in Rome also.

16 I am not ashamed of the Good News. It is the power of God. It is the way He saves men from the punishment of their sins if they put their trust in Him. It is for the Jew first and for all other people also. 17 The Good News tells us we are made right with God by faith in Him. Then, by faith we live that new life through Him. The Holy Writings say, "A man right with God lives by faith." (Habakkuk 2:4)

The Sinful World

18 We see the anger of God coming down from heaven against all the sins of men. These sinful men keep the truth from being known. 19 Men know about God. He has made it plain to them. 20 Men cannot say they do not know about God. From the beginning of the world, men could see what God is like through the things He

has made. This shows His power that lasts forever. It shows that He is God. 21 They did know God, but they did not honor Him as God. They were not thankful to Him and thought only of foolish things. Their foolish minds became dark. 22 They said that they were wise, but they showed how foolish they were. 23 They gave honor to false gods that looked like people who can die and to birds and animals and snakes. This honor belongs to God Who can never die.

24 So God let them follow the desires of their sinful hearts. They did sinful things among themselves with their bodies. 25 They traded the truth of God for a lie. They worshiped and cared for what God made instead of worshiping the God Who made it. He is the One Who is to receive honor and thanks forever. Let it be so.

26 Because of this, God let them follow their sinful desires which lead to shame. Women used their bodies in ways God had not planned. 27 In the same way, men left the right use of women's bodies. They did sex sins with other men. They received for themselves the punishment that was coming to them for their sin.

28 Because they would not keep God in their thoughts anymore, He gave them up. Their minds were sinful and they wanted only to do things they should not do. 29 They are full of everything that is sinful and want things that belong to others. They hate people and are jealous. They kill other people. They fight and lie. They do not like other people and talk against them. 30 They talk about people, and they hate God. They are filled with pride and tell of all the good they do. They think of new ways to sin. They do not obey their parents. 31 They are not able to understand. They do not do what they say they will do. They have no love and no lovingpity. 32 They know God has said that all who do such things should die. But they keep on doing these things and are happy when others do them also.

All Men Are Sinners

2 So you can say nothing because you are guilty when you say someone else is guilty. While you say someone is guilty, you are doing the same things he does. 2 We know that God will say those who do such things are guilty. 3 Do you think God will punish others for doing wrong and let you keep sinning? 4 Do you forget about His loving-kindness to you? Do you forget how long He is waiting for you? You know that God is kind. He is trying to get you to be sorry for your sins and turn from them. 5 Because you are not sorry for your sins and will not turn from them, you will be punished even more on the day of God's anger. God will be right in saying you are guilty. 6 He will give to every man what he should get for the things he has done. 7 Those who keep on doing good and are looking for His greatness and honor will receive life that lasts forever. 8 Those who love only themselves and do not obey the truth, but do what is wrong, will be punished by God. His anger will be on them. 9 Every Jew and every person who is not a Jew who sins will suffer and have great sorrow. 10 But God will give His greatness and honor and peace to all those who obey the truth. Both Jews and those who are not Jews will receive this. 11 God does not show favor to one man more than to another.

God Does What Is Right to All Men

12 Those who have sinned without having the Law will be lost without the Law being used. Those who have the Law and have sinned will be judged by the Law. 13 Just to hear the Law does not make a man right with God. The man right with God is the one who obeys the Law. 14 The people who are not Jews do not have the Law. When they do what the Law tells them to do, even if they do not have the Law, it shows they know what they should do. 15 They show that what the Law wants them to do is written in their hearts. Their own hearts tell them if they are guilty. 16 There will be a day when God will judge because He knows the secret thoughts of men. He will do this through Jesus Christ. This is part of the Good News I preach.

17 You are a Jew and think you are safe because of the Law. You tell others about how you know God. 18 You know what He wants you to do. You understand how the Law works. You know right from wrong. 19 You think you can lead a blind man. You think you can give light to those in darkness. 20 You think you can teach foolish people and children about God. You have in the Law the plan of truth and wisdom. 21 You teach others. Why do you not teach yourselves? You tell others not to steal. Do you steal? 22 You say that no one should do sex sins. Do you do sex sins? You hate false gods. Do you rob the houses where they are kept? 23 You are proud of the Law.

Do you take honor away from God when you do not obey the Law? 24 The Holy Writings say, "God's name is hated by the people who are not Jews because of you." (Isaiah 52:5)

25 Going through the religious act of becoming a Jew is worth something if you obey the Law. If you do not obey the Law, it is worth nothing to you. 26 If a person who is not a Jew and has not gone through the act of becoming a Jew, obeys the Law, God will think of him as a Jew. 27 You Jews have the Law but do not obey it. You have gone through the religious act also. At the same time those who are not Jews obey the Law even if they have not gone through the religious act of becoming a Jew. In this way, these people show you are guilty. 28 A man is not a Jew just because he goes through the religious act of becoming a Jew. 29 The true Jew is one whose heart is right with God. The religious act of becoming a Jew must be done in the heart. That is the work of the Holy Spirit. The Law does not do that kind of work. The true Jew gets his thanks from God, not from men.

Jews Are Sinners Also

3 Do the Jews have anything that those who are not Jews do not have? What good does it do to go through the religious act of becoming a Jew? 2 Yes, the Jews have much more in every way. First of all, God gave the Jews His Law. 3 If some of them were not faithful, does it mean that God will not be faithful? 4 No, not at all! God is always true even if every man lies. The Holy Writings say, "Speak the truth and you will not be proven guilty." (Psalm 51:4)

5 If our sins show how right God is, what can we say? Is it wrong for God to punish us for it? (I am speaking as men do.) 6 No, not at all! If it were wrong for God to punish us, how could He judge the world? 7 If my lies honor God by showing how true He is, why am I still being judged as a sinner? 8 Why not say, "Let us sin that good will come from it." (Some people have said I talk like this!) They will be punished as they should be.

The Whole World Is Guilty of Sin

9 What about it then? Are we Jews better than the people who are not Jews? Not at all! I have already said that Jews and the people who are not Jews are all sinners. 10 The Holy Writings say, "There is not one person who is right with God. No, not even one! 11 There is not one who understands. There is not one who tries to find God." (Psalm 14:2) 12 Everyone has turned away from God. They have all done wrong. Not one of them does what is good. No, not even one! 13 Their mouth is like an open grave. They tell lies with their tongues. (Psalm 5:9; 140:3) Whatever they say is like the poison of snakes. 14 Their mouths speak bad things against God. They say bad things about other people. (Psalm 10:7) 15 They are quick to hurt and kill people. 16 Wherever they go, they destroy and make people suffer. 17 They know nothing about peace. (Isaiah 59:7–8) 18 They do not honor God with love and fear." (Psalm 36:1)

19 Now we know that the Law speaks to those who live under the Law. No one can say that he does not know what sin is. Yes, every person in the world stands guilty before God. 20 No person will be made right with God by doing what the Law says. The Law shows us how sinful we are.

21 But now God has made another way to make men right with Himself. It is not by the Law. The Law and the early preachers tell about it. 22 Men become right with God by putting their trust in Jesus Christ. God will accept men if they come this way. All men are the same to God. 23 For all men have sinned and have missed the shining-greatness of God. 24 Anyone can be made right with God by the free gift of His loving-favor. It is Jesus Christ Who bought them with His blood and made them free from their sins. 25 God gave Jesus Christ to the world. Men's sins can be forgiven through the blood of Christ when they put their trust in Him. God gave His Son Jesus Christ to show how right He is. Before this, God did not look on the sins that were done. 26 But now God proves that He is right in saving men from sin. He shows that He is the One Who has no sin. God makes anyone right with Himself who puts his trust in Jesus.

27 What then do we have to be proud of? Nothing at all! Why? Is it because men obey the Law? No! It is because men put their trust in Christ. 28 This is what we have come to know. A man is made right with God by putting his trust in Christ. It is not by his doing what the Law says. 29 Is God the God of the Jews only? Is He not the God of the people who are not Jews also? He is for sure. 30 He is one God. He will make Jews and the people who are

not Jews right with Himself if they put their trust in Christ. 31 Does this mean that we do away with the Law when we put our trust in Christ? No, not at all. It means we know the Law is important.

Abraham Was Saved from Sin by His Trust in God

4 What about Abraham, our early father? What did he learn? 2 If Abraham was made right with God by what he did, he would have had something to be proud of. But he could not be proud before God. 3 The Holy Writings say, "Abraham put his trust in God and that made him right with God." (Genesis 15:6) 4 If a man works, his pay is not a gift. It is something he has earned. 5 If a man has not worked to be saved, but has put his trust in God Who saves men from the punishment of their sins, that man is made right with God because of his trust in God. 6 David tells of this. He spoke of how happy the man is who puts his trust in God without working to be saved from the punishment of sin. 7 "Those people are happy whose sinful acts are forgiven and whose sins are covered. 8 Those people are happy whose sins the Lord will not remember." (Psalm 32:1–2)

9 Is this happiness given to the Jews only? Or is it given also to the people who are not Jews? We say again, "Abraham put his trust in God and that made him right with God." (Genesis 15:6) 10 When did this happen? Was it before or after Abraham went through the religious act of becoming a Jew? It was before. 11 He went through the religious act after he had put his trust in God. That religious act proved that his trust in God made him right with God even before he went through the religious act of becoming a Jew. In that way, it made him the early father of all those who believe. It showed that those who did not go through the religious act of becoming a Jew could be right with God. 12 He is also the early father of all those who have gone through the religious act of becoming a Jew. It is not because they went through the act. It is because they put their trust in God the same as Abraham did before he went through the religious act of becoming a Jew. 13 God promised to give the world to him and to all his family after him. He did not make this promise because Abraham obeyed the Law. He promised to give the world to Abraham because he put his

trust in God. This made him right with God. 14 If those who obey the Law are to get the world, then a person putting his trust in God means nothing. God's promise to Abraham would be worth nothing. 15 God's anger comes on a man when he does not obey the Law. But if there were no Law, then no one could break it.

16 So God's promise is given to us because we put our trust in Him. We can be sure of it. It is because of His loving-favor to us. It is for all the family of Abraham. It is for those who obey the Law. It is for those who put their trust in God as Abraham did. In this way, he is the father of all Christians. 17 The Holy Writings say, "I have made you a father of many nations." This promise is good because of Who God is. He makes the dead live again. He speaks, and something is made out of nothing. 18 Abraham believed he would be the father of many nations. He had no reason to hope for this, but he had been told, "Your children will become many nations." (Genesis 15:5) 19 Abraham was about one hundred years old. His body was about dead, but his faith in God was not weak when he thought of his body. His faith was not weak when he thought of his wife Sarah being past the age of having children. 20 Abraham did not doubt God's promise. His faith in God was strong, and he gave thanks to God. 21 He was sure God was able to do what He had promised. 22 Abraham put his trust in God and was made right with Him. 23 The words, "He was made right with God," were not for Abraham only. 24 They were for us also. God will make us right with Himself the same way He did Abraham, if we put our trust in God Who raised Jesus our Lord from the dead. 25 Jesus died for our sins. He was raised from the dead to make us right with God.

The Joy of Being Right with God

5 Now that we have been made right with God by putting our trust in Him, we have peace with Him. It is because of what our Lord Jesus Christ did for us. 2 By putting our trust in God, He has given us His loving-favor and has received us. We are happy for the hope we have of sharing the shining-greatness of God. 3 We are glad for our troubles also. We know that troubles help us learn not to give up. 4 When we have learned not to give up, it shows we have stood the test. When we have stood the test, it gives us hope. 5 Hope never makes us ashamed because the love of God has come into our hearts through the Holy Spirit Who was given to us.

6 We were weak and could not help ourselves. Then Christ came at the right time and gave His life for all sinners. 7 No one is willing to die for another person, but for a good man someone might be willing to die. 8 But God showed His love to us. While we were still sinners, Christ died for us. 9 Now that we have been saved from the punishment of sin by the blood of Christ, He will save us from God's anger also. 10 We hated God. But we were saved from the punishment of sin by the death of Christ. He has brought us back to God and we will be saved by His life. 11 Not only that, we give thanks to God through our Lord Jesus Christ. Through Him we have been brought back to God.

Adam and Christ

12 This is what happened: Sin came into the world by one man, Adam. Sin brought death with it. Death spread to all men because all have sinned. 13 Sin was in the world before the Law was given. But sin is not held against a person when there is no Law. 14 And yet death had power over men from the time of Adam until the time of Moses. Even the power of death was over those who had not sinned in the same way Adam sinned. Adam was like the One Who was to come.

15 God's free gift is not like the sin of Adam. Many people died because of the sin of this one man, Adam. But the loving-favor of God came to many people also. This gift came also by one Man Jesus Christ, God's Son. 16 The free gift of God is not like Adam's sin. God told Adam he was guilty because of his sin and through this one came sin and guilt. But the free gift makes men right with God. Through One, Christ, men's sins are forgiven. 17 The power of death was over all men because of the sin of one man, Adam. But many people will receive His loving-favor and the gift of being made right with God. They will have power in life by Jesus Christ. 18 Through Adam's sin, death and hell came to all men. But another Man, Christ, by His right act makes men free and gives them life. 19 Adam did not obey God, and many people become sinners through him. Christ obeyed God and makes many people right with Himself.

God's Loving-Favor Is Greater Than the Jewish Law

20 Sin spread when the Law was given. But where sin spread, God's loving-favor spread all the more. 21 Sin had power that ended in death. Now, God's loving-favor has power to make men right with Himself. It gives life that lasts forever. Our Lord Jesus Christ did this for us.

Being Right with God

6 What does this mean? Are we to keep on sinning so that God will give us more of His loving-favor? 2 No, not at all! We are dead to sin. How then can we keep on living in sin? 3 All of us were baptized to show we belong to Christ. We were baptized first of all to show His death. 4 We were buried in baptism as Christ was buried in death. As Christ was raised from the dead by the great power of God, so we will have new life also. 5 If we have become one with Christ in His death, we will be one with Him in being raised from the dead to new life.

6 We know that our old life, our old sinful self, was nailed to the cross with Christ. And so the power of sin that held us was destroyed. Sin is no longer our boss. 7 When a man is dead, he is free from the power of sin. 8 And if we have died with Christ, we believe we will live with Him also. 9 We know that Christ was raised from the dead. He will never die again. Death has no more power over Him. 10 He died once but now lives. He died to break the power of sin, and the life He now lives is for God. 11 You must do the same thing! Think of yourselves as dead to the power of sin. But now you have new life because of Jesus Christ our Lord. You are living this new life for God.

12 So do not let sin have power over your body here on earth. You must not obey the body and let it do what it wants to do. 13 Do not give any part of your body for sinful use. Instead, give yourself to God as a living person who has been raised from the dead. Give every part of your body to God to do what is right. 14 Sin must not have power over you. You are not living by the Law. You have life because of God's loving-favor.

15 What are we to do then? Are we to sin because we have God's loving-favor and are not living by the Law? No, not at all! 16 Do you not know that when you give yourself as a servant to be owned by someone, that one becomes your owner?

If you give yourself to sin, the end is death. If you give yourself to God, the end is being right with Him. 17 At one time you were held by the power of sin. But now you obey with all your heart the teaching that was given to you. Thank God for this! 18 You were made free from the power of sin. Being right with God has power over you now. 19 I speak with words easy to understand because your human thinking is weak. At one time you gave yourselves over to the power of sin. You kept on sinning all the more. Now give yourselves over to being right with God. Set yourself apart for God-like living and to do His work.

20 When sin had power over your life, you were not right with God. 21 What good did you get from the things you are ashamed of now? Those things bring death. 22 But now you are free from the power of sin. You have become a servant for God. Your life is set apart for God-like living. The end is life that lasts forever. 23 You get what is coming to you when you sin. It is death! But God's free gift is life that lasts forever. It is given to us by our Lord Jesus Christ.

The Law Shows What Sin Is

7 Christian brothers, I am sure you understand what I am going to say. You know all about the Law. The Law has power over a man as long as he lives. 2 A married woman is joined by law to her husband as long as he lives. But if he dies, she is free from the law that joined her to him. 3 If she marries another man while her husband is still alive, she is sinning by not being faithful in marriage. If her husband dies, she is free from the law that joined her to him. After that she can marry someone else. She does not sin if she marries another man.

4 My Christian brothers, that is the way it is with you. You were under the power of the Law. But now you are dead to it because you are joined to another. You are joined to Christ Who was raised from the dead. This is so we may be what God wants us to be. Our lives are to give fruit for Him. 5 When we lived to please our bodies, those sinful desires were pulling at us all the time. We always wanted to do what the Law said not to do. Living that kind of life brings death, 6 but now we are free from the Law. We are dead to sin that once held us in its power. No longer do we follow the Law which is the old way. We now follow the new way, the way of the Spirit.

The Law and Sin

7 Then what are we saying? Is the Law sinful? No, not at all! But it was the Law that showed me what sin is. I did not know it was sin to follow wrong desires, but the Law said, "You must not follow wrong desires." 8 The Law made me know how much I was sinning. It showed me how I had a desire for all kinds of things. For without the Law, sin is dead. 9 I was once alive. That was when I did not know what the Law said I had to do. Then I found that I had broken the Law. I knew I was a sinner. Death was mine because of the Law. 10 The Law was supposed to give me new life. Instead, it gave me death. 11 Sin found a way to trap me by working through the Law. Then sin killed me by using the Law.

12 The Law is holy. Each one of the Laws is holy and right and good. 13 Then does it mean that the Law, which is good, brought death to me? No, not at all! It was sin that did it. Sin brought death to me by the Law that is good. In that way, sin was shown to be what it is. So because of the Law, sin becomes much more sinful.

The Two Kinds of Men

14 We know that the Law is right and good, but I am a person who does what is wrong and bad. I am not my own boss. Sin is my boss. 15 I do not understand myself. I want to do what is right but I do not do it. Instead, I do the very thing I hate. 16 When I do the thing I do not want to do, it shows me that the Law is right and good. 17 So I am not doing it. Sin living in me is doing it. 18 I know there is nothing good in me, that is, in my flesh. For I want to do good but I do not. 19 I do not do the good I want to do. Instead, I am always doing the sinful things I do not want to do. 20 If I am always doing the very thing I do not want to do, it means I am no longer the one who does it. It is sin that lives in me. 21 This has become my way of life: When I want to do what is right, I always do what is wrong. 22 My mind and heart agree with the Law of God. 23 But there is a different law at work deep inside of me that fights with my mind. This law of sin holds me in its power because sin is still in me. 24 There is no happiness in me! Who can set me free from my sinful old self? 25 God's Law has power over my mind, but sin still has power over my sinful old self. I thank God I can be free through Jesus Christ our Lord!

The Holy Spirit Makes Us Free

8 Now, because of this, those who belong to Christ will not suffer the punishment of sin. 2 The power of the Holy Spirit has made me free from the power of sin and death. This power is mine because I belong to Christ Jesus. 3 The Law could not make me free from the power of sin and death. It was weak because it had to work with weak human beings. But God sent His own Son. He came to earth in a body of flesh which could be tempted to sin as we in our bodies can be. He gave Himself to take away sin. By doing that, He took away the power sin had over us. 4 In that way, Jesus did for us what the Law said had to be done. We do not do what our sinful old selves tell us to do anymore. Now we do what the Holy Spirit wants us to do. 5 Those who let their sinful old selves tell them what to do live under that power of their sinful old selves. But those who let the Holy Spirit tell them what to do are under His power. 6 If your sinful old self is the boss over your mind, it leads to death. But if the Holy Spirit is the boss over your mind, it leads to life and peace. 7 The mind that thinks only of ways to please the sinful old self is fighting against God. It is not able to obey God's Laws. It never can. 8 Those who do what their sinful old selves want to do cannot please God.

9 But you are not doing what your sinful old selves want you to do. You are doing what the Holy Spirit tells you to do, if you have God's Spirit living in you. No one belongs to Christ if he does not have Christ's Spirit in him. 10 If Christ is in you, your spirit lives because you are right with God, and yet your body is dead because of sin. 11 The Holy Spirit raised Jesus from the dead. If the same Holy Spirit lives in you, He will give life to your bodies in the same way.

12 So then, Christian brothers, we are not to do what our sinful old selves want us to do. 13 If you do what your sinful old selves want you to do, you will die in sin. But if, through the power of the Holy Spirit, you destroy those actions to which the body can be led, you will have life. 14 All those who are led by the Holy Spirit are sons of God. 15 You should not act like people who are owned by someone. They are always afraid. Instead, the Holy Spirit makes us His sons, and we can call to Him, "My Father." 16 For the Holy Spirit speaks to us and tells our spirit that we are children of God. 17 If we are children of God, we will receive everything He has promised us. We will share with Christ all the things God has given to Him. But we must share His suffering if we are to share His shining-greatness.

Another Picture of the Future

18 I am sure that our suffering now cannot be compared to the shining-greatness that He is going to give us. 19 Everything that has been made in the world is waiting for the day when God will make His sons known. 20 Everything that has been made in the world is weak. It is not that the world wanted it to be that way. God allowed it to be that way. Yet there is hope. 21 Everything that has been made in the world will be set free from the power that can destroy. These will become free just as the children of God become free. 22 We know that everything on the earth cries out with pain the same as a woman giving birth to a child. 23 We also cry inside ourselves, even we who have received the Holy Spirit. The Holy Spirit is the first of God's gifts to us. We are waiting to become His complete sons when our bodies are made free. 24 We were saved with this hope ahead of us. Now hope means we are waiting for something we do not have. How can a man hope for something he already has? 25 But if we hope for something we do not yet see, we must learn how to wait for it.

26 In the same way, the Holy Spirit helps us where we are weak. We do not know how to pray or what we should pray for, but the Holy Spirit prays to God for us with sounds that cannot be put into words. 27 God knows the hearts of men. He knows what the Holy Spirit is thinking. The Holy Spirit prays for those who belong to Christ the way God wants Him to pray.

God Gives Us His Greatness

28 We know that God makes all things work together for the good of those who love Him and are chosen to be a part of His plan. 29 God knew from the beginning who would put their trust in Him. So He chose them and made them to be like His Son. Christ was first and all those who belong to God are His brothers. 30 He called to Himself also those He chose. Those He called, He made right with Himself. Then He shared His shining-greatness with those He made right with Himself.

31 What can we say about all these things? Since God is for us, who can be

against us? 32 God did not keep His own Son for Himself but gave Him for us all. Then with His Son, will He not give us all things? 33 Who can say anything against the people God has chosen? It is God Who says they are right with Himself. 34 Who then can say we are guilty? It was Christ Jesus Who died. He was raised from the dead. He is on the right side of God praying to Him for us. 35 Who can keep us away from the love of Christ? Can trouble or problems? Can suffering wrong from others or having no food? Can it be because of no clothes or because of danger or war? 36 The Holy Writings say, "Because of belonging to Jesus, we are in danger of being killed all day long. We are thought of as sheep that are ready to be killed." (Psalm 44:22) 37 But we have power over all these things through Jesus Who loves us so much. 38 For I know that nothing can keep us from the love of God. Death cannot! Life cannot! Angels cannot! Leaders cannot! Any other power cannot! Hard things now or in the future cannot! 39 The world above or the world below cannot! Any other living thing cannot keep us away from the love of God which is ours through Christ Jesus our Lord.

The People God Chose for Himself

9 I am telling the truth because I belong to Christ. The Holy Spirit tells my heart that I am not lying. 2 I have much sorrow. The pain in my heart never leaves. 3 I could even wish that I might be kept from being with Christ if that would help my people to be saved from the punishment of sin. They are of my own flesh and blood. 4 They are Jews and are the people God chose for Himself. He shared His shining-greatness with them and gave them His Law and a way to worship. They have His promises. 5 The early preachers came from this family. Christ Himself was born of flesh from this family and He is over all things. May God be honored and thanked forever. Let it be so.

6 I am not saying that God did not keep His promises. Not all the Jews are people God chose for Himself. 7 Not all of Abraham's family are children of God. God told Abraham, "Only the family of Isaac will be called your family."(Genesis 21:9–12) 8 This means that children born to Abraham are not all children of God. Only those that are born because of God's promise to Abraham are His children. 9 This was the promise God made: "About this time next year I will come, and Sarah will have a son." (Genesis 18:10) 10 Not only this, but there was Rebecca also. Rebecca gave birth to two sons at the same time. Both of them were sons of Isaac. 11 Even before the two sons were born, we see God's plan of choosing. God could choose whom He wanted. It could not be changed because of anything the older son tried to do about it. It was before either one had done anything good or bad. 12 Rebecca was told, "The older son will work for the younger son." 13 The Holy Writings say, "I loved Jacob, but hated Esau." (Malachi 1:2)

14 What about it then? Can we say that God is not fair? No, not at all! 15 God said to Moses, "I will have loving-kindness and loving-pity for anyone I want to." (Exodus 33:19) 16 These good things from God are not given to someone because he wants them or works to get them. They are given because of His loving-kindness. 17 The Holy Writings say to Pharaoh, "I made you leader for this reason: I used you to show My power. I used you to make My name known over all the world." (Exodus 9:16) 18 So God has loving-kindness for those He wants to. He makes some have hard hearts if He wants to.

19 But you will ask me, "Why does God blame men for what they do? Who can go against what God wants?" 20 Who are you to talk back to God? A pot being made from clay does not talk to the man making it and say, "Why did you make me like this?" 21 The man making the pots has the right to use the clay as he wants to. He can make two pots from the same piece of clay. One can have an important use. The other one can be of little use. 22 It may be that God wants to show His power and His anger against sin. He waits a long time on some men who are ready to be destroyed. 23 God also wanted to show His shining-greatness to those He has given His loving-kindness. He made them ready for His shining greatness from the beginning. 24 We are the ones He chose. He did not only choose Jews. He also chose some from among the people who are not Jews. 25 In the Book of Hosea He says, "Those who are not My people, I will call, 'My people.' Those who are not loved, I will call, 'My loved ones.' " (Hosea 2:23) 26 "And where it said, 'You are not my people,' they will be called sons of the living God." (Hosea 1:10) 27 Isaiah says this about the Jews, "Even if there are as many Jews as the sand by the sea, only a few of them

will be saved from the punishment of sin. 28 For the Lord will do on earth what He says in His Word. He will work fast when He says what will happen here." (Isaiah 10:22–23) 29 Isaiah said also, "If God had not left some of the Jews, we would have all been destroyed like the people who lived in the cities of Sodom and Gomorrah." (Isaiah 1:9)

The Jews and the Good News

30 What are we to say about these things? The people who are not Jews were not made right with God by the Law. They were made right with God because they put their trust in Him. 31 The Jews tried to be right with God by obeying the Law, but they did not become right with God. 32 Why? Because they did not put their trust in God. They tried to be right with God by working for it. They tripped over the most important Stone (Christ). 33 The Holy Writings say, "See! I put in Jerusalem a Stone that people will trip over. It is a Rock that will make them fall. But the person who puts his trust in the Rock (Christ) will not be put to shame." (Isaiah 28:16)

The Jews Have Tried to Make Their Own Way

10 Christian brothers, the desire of my heart and my prayer to God is that the Jews might be saved from the punishment of sin. 2 I know about them. They have a strong desire for God, but they do not know what they should about Him. 3 They have not known how God makes men right with Himself. Instead, they have tried to make their own way. They have not become right with God because they have not done what God said to do. 4 For Christ has put an end to the Law, so everyone who has put his trust in Christ is made right with God.

5 Moses writes that the man who obeys the Law has to live by it. 6 But when a man puts his trust in Christ, he is made right with God. You do not need to ask yourself, "Who will go up to heaven to bring Christ down?" 7 And you do not need to ask, "Who will go below and bring Christ up from the dead?" 8 This is what it says, "The Good News is near you. It is in your mouth and in your heart." (Deuteronomy 30:14) This Good News tells about putting your trust in Christ. This is what we preach to you. 9 If you say with your mouth that Jesus is Lord, and believe in your heart that God raised Him from the

dead, you will be saved from the punishment of sin. 10 When we believe in our hearts, we are made right with God. We tell with our mouth how we were saved from the punishment of sin. 11 The Holy Writings say, "No one who puts his trust in Christ will ever be put to shame." (Isaiah 28:16) 12 There is no difference between the Jews and the people who are not Jews. They are all the same to the Lord. And He is Lord over all of them. He gives of His greatness to all who call on Him for help. 13 For everyone who calls on the name of the Lord will be saved from the punishment of sin.

14 But how can they call on Him if they have not put their trust in Him? And how can they put their trust in Him if they have not heard of Him? And how can they hear of Him unless someone tells them? 15 And how can someone tell them if he is not sent? The Holy Writings say, "The feet of those who bring the Good News are beautiful." (Isaiah 52:7)

16 But they have not all listened to the Good News. Isaiah says, "Lord, who believed what we told them?" (Isaiah 53:1) 17 So then, faith comes to us by hearing the Good News. And the Good News comes by someone preaching it. 18 And so I ask, "Did they not hear?" For sure they did. The Holy Writings say, "Their voice was heard over all the earth. The Good News was told to the ends of the earth." (Psalm 19:4) 19 Again I ask, "Did the Jews not understand?" First of all, Moses says, "I will make you jealous of those who are not a nation. I will make you angry with a foolish nation of people who do not understand." (Deuteronomy 32:21) 20 Isaiah says even stronger words, "I have been found by men who did not look for Me. I have shown Myself to those who were not asking for Me." (Isaiah 65:1) 21 This is what God says about the Jews, "All day long I held out my hand to a people who would not obey Me and who worked against Me." (Isaiah 65:2)

God's Loving-Kindness for the Jews

11 I ask then, "Has God put His people, the Jews, aside?" No, not at all! I myself am a Jew. Abraham was my early father. I am from the family group of Benjamin. 2 God has not put His people aside. He chose them from the beginning. Do you know what the Holy Writings say about Elijah? Do you know what Elijah said to God against the Jews? 3 He said,

"Lord, they have killed Your early preachers. They have destroyed the places where You are worshiped. I am the only one left. They are trying to kill me." [4] But what did God say to him? God said, "I still have 7,000 men. None of them have worshiped the false god Baal." [5] It is the same now. A few of the Jews are being chosen because of God's loving-favor. [6] If they are saved from the punishment of sin because of God's loving-favor, it is nothing men have done to earn it. If men had earned it, then His loving-favor would not be a free gift. [7] This is the way it was. Many Jews did not get what they were looking for. Only those God chose received it. The hearts of the others were made hard. They could not understand it. [8] The Holy Writings say this about them, "God gave them hearts and minds that want to sleep. He gave them eyes that could not see. To this very day He gave them ears that could not hear." (Isaiah 29:10) [9] David said, "Let their table of food become a trap to hold them. Let it be a hole into which they fall and will suffer. [10] Let their eyes be closed so they cannot see. Keep their backs from being straight always because of their troubles." (Psalm 69:23)

[11] I ask then, "Did the Jews fall so they would be lost forever?" No, not at all! It means the people who are not Jews are able to be saved from the punishment of sin because the Jews sinned by not putting their trust in Christ. This made the Jews jealous of those who are not Jews. [12] The world received good things from God because of the sin of the Jews. Because the Jews did not receive God's free gift, the people who are not Jews received good things from Him. Think how much more the world will receive when the Jews finish God's plan by putting their trust in Christ!

The People Who Are Not Jews Can Be Saved Too

[13] I am speaking to you people who are not Jews. As long as I am a missionary to you, I want you to know how important my job is. [14] I do this so it will make my own people, the Jews, jealous. Then it may be that some will be saved from the punishment of sin. [15] Because the Jews have been put aside, many other people in the world have been saved from the punishment of sin. Think what it will be like when they are also gathered in. It will be like the dead coming back to life!

[16] If the first loaf is holy, all the bread is holy. If the root is holy, all the branches are holy.

[17] But some of the branches (who are the Jews) were broken off. You who are not Jews were put in the place where the branches had been broken off. Now you are sharing the rich root of the olive tree. [18] Do not be proud. Do not think you are better than the branches that were broken off. If you are proud, remember that you do not hold the root. It is the root that holds you. [19] You may say, "Branches were broken off to make room for me." [20] It is true. They were broken off because they did not put their trust in Christ. And you are there only because of your faith. Do not be proud. Instead, be afraid. [21] God did not keep the first branches (who are the Jews) on the tree. Then watch, or He will not keep you on the tree. [22] We see how kind God is. It shows how hard He is also. He is hard on those who fall away. But He is kind to you if you keep on trusting Him. If you do not, He will cut you off. [23] If the Jews would put their trust in Christ, God would put them back into the tree. He has power to do that. [24] You people who are not Jews were cut off from a wild olive tree. Instead of being there, you were put into a garden olive tree which is not the right place for you to grow. It would be easy for God to put the Jews back onto their own olive tree because they are the branches that belong there.

God's Loving-Kindness to All

[25] Christian brothers, I want you to understand this truth which is no longer a secret. It will keep you from thinking you are so wise. Some Jews have become hard until the right amount of people who are not Jews come to God. [26] Then all the Jews will be saved, as the Holy Writings say, "The One Who saves from the punishment of sin will come out of Jerusalem. He will turn the Jews from doing sinful things." (Isaiah 59:20-21) [27] "And this is My promise to them when I take away their sins." (Isaiah 27:9)

[28] The Jews are fighting against the Good News. Because they hate the Good News, it has helped you who are not Jews. But God still loves the Jews because He has chosen them and because of His promise to their early fathers. [29] God does not change His mind when He chooses men and gives them His gifts. [30] At one time you did not obey God. But when the

Jews did not receive God's gift, you did. It was because they did not obey. **31** The Jews will not obey now. God's loving-kindness to you will some day turn them to Him. Then the Jews may have His loving-kindness also. **32** God has said that all men have broken His Law. But He will show loving-kindness on all of them.

33 God's riches are so great! The things He knows and His wisdom are so deep! No one can understand His thoughts. No one can understand His ways. **34** The Holy Writings say, "Who knows the mind of the Lord? Who is able to tell Him what to do?" (Isaiah 40:13-14) **35** "Who has given first to God, that God should pay him back?" (Job 35:7; 41:11) **36** Everything comes from Him. His power keeps all things together. All things are made for Him. May He be honored forever. Let it be so.

Our Bodies Are to Be a Living Gift

12 Christian brothers, I ask you from my heart to give your bodies to God because of His loving-kindness to us. Let your bodies be a living and holy gift given to God. He is pleased with this kind of gift. This is the true worship that you should give Him. **2** Do not act like the sinful people of the world. Let God change your life. First of all, let Him give you a new mind. Then you will know what God wants you to do. And the things you do will be good and pleasing and perfect.

God's Church and the Gifts He Uses

3 God has given me His loving-favor. This helps me write these things to you. I ask each one of you not to think more of himself than he should think. Instead, think in the right way toward yourself by the faith God has given you. **4** Our bodies are made up of many parts. None of these parts have the same use. **5** There are many people who belong to Christ. And yet, we are one body which is Christ's. We are all different but we depend on each other. **6** We all have different gifts that God has given to us by His loving-favor. We are to use them. If someone has the gift of preaching the Good News, he should preach. He should use the faith God has given him. **7** If someone has the gift of helping others, then he should help. If someone has the gift of teaching, he should teach. **8** If someone has the gift of speaking words of comfort and help, he should speak. If someone has the gift of sharing what he has, he should give from a willing heart. If someone has

the gift of leading other people, he should lead them. If someone has the gift of showing kindness to others, he should be happy as he does it.

Ways Christians Can Help Other Christians

9 Be sure your love is true love. Hate what is sinful. Hold on to whatever is good. **10** Love each other as Christian brothers. Show respect for each other. **11** Do not be lazy but always work hard. Work for the Lord with a heart full of love for Him. **12** Be happy in your hope. Do not give up when trouble comes. Do not let anything stop you from praying. **13** Share what you have with Christian brothers who are in need. Give meals and a place to stay to those who need it. **14** Pray and give thanks for those who make trouble for you. Yes, pray for them instead of talking against them. **15** Be happy with those who are happy. Be sad with those who are sad. **16** Live in peace with each other. Do not act or think with pride. Be happy to be with poor people. Keep yourself from thinking you are so wise. **17** When someone does something bad to you, do not pay him back with something bad. Try to do what all men know is right and good. **18** As much as you can, live in peace with all men. **19** Christian brothers, never pay back someone for the bad he has done to you. Let the anger of God take care of the other person. The Holy Writings say, "I will pay back to them what they should get, says the Lord." (Deuteronomy 32:35) **20** "If the one who hates you is hungry, feed him. If he is thirsty, give him water. If you do that, you will be making him more ashamed of himself." (Proverbs 25:21-22) **21** Do not let sin have power over you. Let good have power over sin!

Obey the Leaders of the Land

13 Every person must obey the leaders of the land. There is no power given but from God, and all leaders are allowed by God. **2** The person who does not obey the leaders of the land is working against what God has done. Anyone who does that will be punished.

3 Those who do right do not have to be afraid of the leaders. Those who do wrong are afraid of them. Do you want to be free from fear of them? Then do what is right. You will be respected instead. **4** Leaders are God's servants to help you. If you do wrong, you should be afraid. They have the power to punish you. They work for

God. They do what God wants done to those who do wrong.

5 You must obey the leaders of the land, not only to keep from God's anger, but so your own heart will have peace. 6 It is right for you to pay taxes because the leaders of the land are servants for God who care for these things. 7 Pay taxes to whom taxes are to be paid. Be afraid of those you should fear. Respect those you should respect.

How a Christian Should Live with His Neighbor

8 Do not owe anyone anything, but love each other. Whoever loves his neighbor has done what the Law says to do. 9 The Law says, "You must not do any sex sin. You must not kill another person. You must not steal. You must not tell a lie about another person. You must not want something someone else has." The Law also says that these and many other Laws are brought together in one Law, "You must love your neighbor as yourself." 10 Anyone who loves his neighbor will do no wrong to him. You keep the Law with love.

11 There is another reason for doing what is right. You know what time it is. It is time for you to wake up from your sleep. The time when we will be taken up to be with Christ is not as far off as when we first put our trust in Him. 12 Night is almost gone. Day is almost here. We must stop doing the sinful things that are done in the dark. We must put on all the things God gives us to fight with for the day. 13 We must act all the time as if it were day. Keep away from wild parties and do not be drunk. Keep yourself free from sex sins and bad actions. Do not fight or be jealous. 14 Let every part of you belong to the Lord Jesus Christ. Do not allow your weak thoughts to lead you into sinful actions.

Help Weak Christians

14 If there is someone whose faith is weak, be kind and receive him. Do not argue about what he thinks. 2 One man believes he may eat everything. Another man with weak faith eats only vegetables. 3 The man who eats everything should not think he is better than the one who eats only vegetables. The man who eats only vegetables should not say the other man is wrong, because God has received him. 4 Who are you to tell another person's servant if he is right or wrong? It is to his owner that he does good or bad. The Lord is able to help him.

5 One man thinks one day is more important than another. Another man thinks every day is the same. Every man must be sure in his own mind. 6 The man who worships on a special day does it to honor the Lord. The man who eats meat does it to honor the Lord. He gives thanks to God for what he eats. The other man does not eat meat. In this way, he honors the Lord. He gives thanks to God also.

7 No one lives for himself alone. No one dies for himself alone. 8 If we live, it is for the Lord. If we die, it is for the Lord. If we live or die, we belong to the Lord. 9 Christ died and lived again. This is why He is the Lord of the living and of the dead. 10 Why do you try to say your Christian brother is right or wrong? Why do you hate your Christian brother? We will all stand before God to be judged by Him. 11 The Holy Writings say, "As I live, says the Lord, every knee will bow before Me. And every tongue will say that I am God." 12 Everyone of us will give an answer to God about himself.

Your Christian Brother

13 So you should stop saying that you think other people are wrong. Instead, decide to live so that your Christian brother will not have a reason to trip or fall into sin because of you. 14 Christ has made me know that everything in itself is clean. But if a person thinks something is not clean, then to him it is not clean. 15 If your Christian brother is hurt because of some foods you eat, then you are no longer living by love. Do not destroy the man for whom Christ died by the food you eat. 16 Do not let what is good for you be talked about as bad. 17 For the holy nation of God is not food and drink. It is being right with God. It is peace and joy given by the Holy Spirit. 18 If you follow Christ in these things, God will be happy with you. Men will think well of you also.

19 Work for the things that make peace and help each other become stronger Christians. 20 Do not destroy what God has done just because of some food. All food is good to eat. But it is wrong to eat anything that will make someone fall into sin. 21 Do not eat meat or drink wine or do anything else if it would make your Christian brother fall into sin. 22 Keep the faith you have between yourself and God. A man is happy if he knows he is doing right. 23 But if he has doubts about the food he eats, God says he is guilty when he eats it. It is because he is eating without faith. Anything that is not done in faith is sin.

Live to Please Your Neighbor

15 We who have strong faith should help those who are weak. We should not live to please ourselves. [2] Each of us should live to please his neighbor. This will help him grow in faith. [3] Even Christ did not please Himself. The Holy Writings say, "The sharp words spoken against you fell on Me." (Psalm 69:9) [4] Everything that was written in the Holy Writings long ago was written to teach us. By not giving up, God's Word gives us strength and hope. [5] Now the God Who helps you not to give up and gives you strength will help you think so you can please each other as Christ Jesus did. [6] Then all of you together can thank the God and Father of our Lord Jesus Christ.

The Good News Is for the People Who Are Not Jews

[7] Receive each other as Christ received you. This will honor God. [8] Christ came to help the Jews. This proved that God had told the truth to their early fathers. This proved that God would do what He promised. [9] This was done so the people who are not Jews can thank God for His loving-kindness. The Holy Writings say, "This is why I will give thanks to you among the people who are not Jews. I will sing to Your name." (Psalm 18:49) [10] It says also, "You who are not Jews, be happy with His people, the Jews." (Deuteronomy 32:43) [11] And, "Honor and give thanks to the Lord, you who are not Jews. Let everyone honor Him." (Psalm 117:1) [12] And Isaiah says, "There will be One from the family of Jesse Who will be a leader over the people who are not Jews. Their hope will be in Him." (Isaiah 11:10) [13] Our hope comes from God. May He fill you with joy and peace because of your trust in Him. May your hope grow stronger by the power of the Holy Spirit.

Paul's Reason for Visiting

[14] I am sure you are wise in all things and full of much good. You are able to help and teach each other. [15] I have written to you with strong words about some things. I have written so you would remember. God helped me write like this. [16] I am able to write these things because God made me a missionary to the people who are not Jews. I work as a servant of Jesus Christ. I preach the Good News of God so the people who are not Jews may be as a gift to God. The Holy Spirit will set them apart so God will be pleased with them. [17] I have reason to be proud of my work for God. It is because I belong to Christ Jesus. [18] I can only speak of what Christ has done through me. I have helped the people who are not Jews to obey Him. I have done it by words and by living with them. [19] God showed them His power through me. The Holy Spirit did powerful works through me in front of them. From Jerusalem to the country of Illyricum I have preached the Good News of Christ. [20] It is my desire to preach the Good News where it has never been preached. I want to preach only where Christ is not known. [21] The Holy Writings say, "Those who have never known about Him will see. And those who have never heard about Him will understand." (Isaiah 52:15)

Paul Hopes to Visit the Christians in Rome

[22] This is why I have been kept many times from coming to you. [23] But now I am finished with my work here. I have been wanting to come and visit you for many years. [24] I hope I can now. I am making plans to go to the country of Spain. On my way there I will stop and visit you. After I have had the joy of visiting you for awhile, you can help me on my way again. [25] But now I am going to Jerusalem to hand the Christians the gift of money. [26] The churches in the countries of Macedonia and Greece have decided to give money to help some of the poor Christians in Jerusalem. [27] They wanted to do it. They should help them in this way because they owe much to the Christians in Jerusalem. The Jews shared the Good News with the people who are not Jews. For this reason, they should share what they can with the Jews. [28] I will hand this gift of money to them. Then I will stop to see you on my way to the country of Spain. [29] I know that when I come to you, Christ will give me much good to share with you.

[30] I ask you from my heart, Christian brothers, to pray much for me. I ask this in the name of our Lord Jesus Christ. [31] Pray that God will keep me safe from the people in the country of Judea who are not Christians. Pray also that the work I am to do for the Christians in Jerusalem will help them. [32] Then I will be coming to you if God wants me to come. I will be full of joy, and together we can have some rest. [33] May our God Who gives us peace, be with you all. Let it be so.

Paul Greets Many Friends

16 I want to let you know about our Christian sister Phoebe. She is a helper in the church in the city of Cenchrea. 2 The Christians should receive her as a sister who belongs to the Lord. Help her any way you can. She has helped many people and has helped me also.

3 Greet Priscilla and Aquila. They worked with me for Christ. 4 They almost died for me. I am thankful for them. All the churches that were started among the people who are not Jews are thankful for them also. 5 Greet the church that worships in their house. Greet Epaenetus, my much-loved friend. He was the first Christian in the countries of Asia. 6 Greet Mary. She worked hard for you. 7 Greet Andronicus and Junias. They are from my family and were in prison with me. They put their trust in Christ before I did. They have been respected missionaries. 8 Greet Ampliatus. He is a much-loved Christian brother. 9 Greet Urbanus. He worked with us for Christ. Greet Stachys, my much-loved friend. 10 Greet Apelles. He proved he was faithful to Christ. Greet all the family of Aristobulus. 11 Greet Herodian. He is one of my family. Greet the Christians in the family of Narcissus. 12 Greet Tryphaena and Tryphosa and Persis. They are all much-loved workmen for the Lord. 13 Greet Rufus and his mother. She was like a mother to me. Rufus is a good Christian. 14 Greet Asyncritus and Phlegon and Hermes and Patrobas and Hermas and all the Christians with them. 15 Greet Philologus and Julia and Nereus and his sister and Olympas and all the Christians with them.

16 Greet each other with a kiss of holy love. All the churches here greet you.

17 I ask you, Christian brothers, watch out for those who make trouble and start fights. Keep your eye on those who work against the teaching you received. Keep away from them. 18 Men like that are not working for our Lord Jesus Christ. They are chained to their own desires. With soft words they say things people want to hear. People are fooled by them. 19 Everyone knows you have obeyed the teaching you received. I am happy with you because of this. But I want you to be wise about good things and pure about sinful things. 20 God, Who is our peace, will soon crush Satan under your feet. May the loving-favor of our Lord Jesus be yours. 21 Timothy, my helper, greets you. Lucius and Jason and Sosipater from my family say hello also. 22 I, Tertius, who am writing this letter for Paul, greet you as a Christian brother. 23 Gaius is the man taking care of me. The church meets here in his house. He greets you. Erastus, the man who takes care of the money for the city, greets you and Quartus does also. He is a Christian brother. 24 *May you have loving-favor from our Lord Jesus Christ. Let it be so.

25 We give honor to God. He is able to make you strong as I preach from the Holy Writings about Jesus Christ. It was a secret hidden from the beginning of the world. 26 But now it is for us to know. The early preachers wrote about it. God says it is to be preached to all the people of the world so men can put their trust in God and obey Him.

27 May God, Who only is wise, be honored forever through our Lord Jesus Christ. Let it be so.

1 CORINTHIANS

1 This letter is from Paul. I have been chosen by God to be a missionary of Jesus Christ. Sosthenes, a Christian brother, writes also. 2 I write to God's church in the city of Corinth. I write to those who belong to Christ Jesus and to those who are set apart for Him and made holy. I write to all the Christians everywhere who call on the name of Jesus Christ. He is our Lord and their Lord also. 3 May you have loving-favor and peace from God our Father and from the Lord Jesus Christ.

Paul Gives Thanks for Their Faith

4 I am thankful to God all the time for you. I am thankful for the loving-favor God has given to you because you belong to Christ Jesus. 5 He has made your lives rich in every way. Now you have power to speak for Him. He gave you good understanding. 6 This shows that what I told you about Christ and what He could do for you has been done in your lives. 7 You have the gifts of the Holy Spirit that you need while you wait for the Lord Jesus Christ to come again. 8 Christ will keep you strong until

He comes again. No blame will be held against you. 9 God is faithful. He chose you to be joined together with His Son, Jesus Christ our Lord.

The Church in Corinth Is Divided

10 Christian brothers, I ask you with all my heart in the name of the Lord Jesus Christ to agree among yourselves. Do not be divided into little groups. Think and act as if you all had the same mind. 11 My Christian brothers, I have heard from some of Chloe's family that you are arguing among yourselves. 12 I hear that some of you are saying, "I am a follower of Paul," and "I am a follower of Apollos," and "I am a follower of Peter," and "I am a follower of Christ." 13 Has Christ been divided? Was Paul put on a cross to die for your sins? Were you baptized in the name of Paul? 14 I am thankful to God that I baptized Crispus and Gaius only. 15 No one can say that you were baptized in the name of Paul. 16 I remember that I did baptize the family of Stephanas, but I do not remember baptizing any others. 17 Christ did not send me to baptize. He sent me to preach the Good News. I did not use big sounding words when I preached. If I had, the power of the cross of Christ would be taken away.

Christ Is the Power and Wisdom of God

18 Preaching about the cross sounds foolish to those who are dying in sin. But it is the power of God to those of us who are being saved from the punishment of sin. 19 The Holy Writings say, "I will destroy the wisdom of the wise people. I will put aside the learning of those who think they know a lot." (Isaiah 29:14) 20 Where is the man who is wise? Where is the man who thinks he knows a lot? Where is the man who thinks he has all the answers? God has made the wisdom of this world look foolish. 21 In His wisdom, He did not allow man to come to know Him through the wisdom of this world. It pleased God to save men from the punishment of their sins through preaching the Good News. This preaching sounds foolish. 22 The Jews are looking for something special to see. The Greek people are looking for the answer in wisdom. 23 But we preach that Christ died on a cross to save them from their sins. These words are hard for the Jews to listen to. The Greek people think it is foolish. 24 Christ is the power and wisdom of God to those who are chosen to be saved from the punishment of sin

for both Jews and Greeks. 25 God's plan looked foolish to men, but it is wiser than the best plans of men. God's plan which may look weak is stronger than the strongest plans of men.

God's Wisdom—Human Wisdom

26 Christian brothers, think who you were when the Lord called you. Not many of you were wise or powerful or born into the family of leaders of a country. 27 But God has chosen what the world calls foolish to shame the wise. He has chosen what the world calls weak to shame what is strong. 28 God has chosen what is weak and foolish of the world, what is hated and not known, to destroy the things the world trusts in. 29 In that way, no man can be proud as he stands before God. 30 God Himself made the way so you can have new life through Christ Jesus. God gave us Christ to be our wisdom. Christ made us right with God and set us apart for God and made us holy. Christ bought us with His blood and made us free from our sins. 31 It is as the Holy Writings say, "If anyone is going to be proud of anything, he should be proud of the Lord."

Paul Received the Good News from God

2 Christian brothers, when I came to you, I did not preach the secrets of God with big sounding words or make it sound as if I were so wise. 2 I made up my mind that while I was with you I would speak of nothing except Jesus Christ and of His death on the cross. 3 When I was with you, I was weak. I was afraid and I shook. 4 What I had to say when I preached was not in big sounding words of man's wisdom. But it was given in the power of the Holy Spirit. 5 In this way, you do not have faith in Christ because of the wisdom of men. You have faith in Christ because of the power of God.

True Wisdom Comes from God

6 We speak wisdom to full-grown Christians. This wisdom is not from this world or from the leaders of today. They die and their wisdom dies with them. 7 What we preach is God's wisdom. It was a secret until now. God planned for us to have this honor before the world began. 8 None of the world leaders understood this wisdom. If they had, they would not have put Christ up on a cross to die. He is the Lord of shining-greatness. 9 The Holy Writings say, "No eye has ever seen or no ear has

ever heard or no mind has ever thought of the wonderful things God has made ready for those who love Him." (Isaiah 64:4; 65:17) [10] God has shown these things to us through His Holy Spirit. It is the Holy Spirit Who looks into all things, even the secrets of God, and shows them to us. [11] Who can know the things about a man, except a man's own spirit that is in him? It is the same with God. Who can understand Him except the Holy Spirit? [12] We have not received the spirit of the world. God has given us His Holy Spirit that we may know about the things given to us by Him. [13] We speak about these things also. We do not use words of man's wisdom. We use words given to us by the Holy Spirit. We use these words to tell what the Holy Spirit wants to say to those who put their trust in Him. [14] But the person who is not a Christian does not understand these words from the Holy Spirit. He thinks they are foolish. He cannot understand them because he does not have the Holy Spirit to help him understand. [15] The full-grown Christian understands all things, and yet he is not understood. [16] For who has the thoughts of the Lord? Who can tell Him what to do? But we have the thoughts of Christ.

3 Christian brothers, I could not speak to you as to full-grown Christians. I spoke to you as men who have not obeyed the things you have been taught. I spoke to you as if you were baby Christians. [2] My teaching was as if I were giving you milk to drink. I could not give you meat because you were not ready for it. Even yet you are not able to have anything but milk. [3] You still live as men who are not Christians. When you are jealous and fight with each other, you are still living in sin and acting like sinful men in the world. [4] When one says, "I am a follower of Paul," and another says, "I am a follower of Apollos," does not this sound like the talk of baby Christians? [5] Who is Apollos? Who is Paul? We are only servants owned by God. He gave us gifts to preach His Word. And because of that, you put your trust in Christ. [6] I planted the seed. Apollos watered it, but it was God Who kept it growing. [7] This shows that the one who plants or the one who waters is not the important one. God is the important One. He makes it grow. [8] The one who plants and the one who waters are alike. Each one will receive his own reward. [9] For we work together with God. You are God's field.

You are God's building also. [10] Through God's loving-favor to me, I laid the stones on which the building was to be built. I did it like one who knew what he was doing. Now another person is building on it. Each person who builds must be careful how he builds on it. [11] Jesus Christ is the Stone on which other stones for the building must be laid. It can be only Christ. [12] Now if a man builds on the Stone with gold or silver or beautiful stones, or if he builds with wood or grass or straw, [13] each man's work will become known. There will be a day when it will be tested by fire. The fire will show what kind of work it is. [14] If a man builds on work that lasts, he will receive his reward. [15] If his work is burned up, he will lose it. Yet he himself will be saved as if he were going through a fire.

[16] Do you not know that you are a house of God and that the Holy Spirit lives in you? [17] If any man destroys the house of God, God will destroy him. God's house is holy. You are the place where He lives.

[18] Do not fool yourself. If anyone thinks he knows a lot about the things of this world, he had better become a fool. Then he may become wise. [19] The wisdom of this world is foolish to God. The Holy Writings say, "He is the One Who gets them in a trap when they use their own wisdom." (Job 5:13) [20] They also say, "The Lord knows how the wise man thinks. His thinking is worth nothing." (Psalm 94:11) [21] As a Christian, do not be proud of men and of what they can do. All things belong to you. [22] Paul and Apollos and Peter belong to you. The world and life and death belong to you. Things now and things to come belong to you. [23] You belong to Christ, and Christ belongs to God.

Servants of Christ

4 Think of us as servants who are owned by Christ. It is our job to share the secrets of God. [2] A servant must be faithful to his owner. This is expected of him. [3] It is not the most important thing to me what you or any other people think of me. Even what I think of myself does not mean much. [4] As for me, my heart tells me I am not guilty of anything. But that does not prove I am free from guilt. It is the Lord Who looks into my life and says what is wrong. [5] Do not be quick to say who is right or wrong. Wait until the Lord comes. He will bring into the light the things that are hidden in men's hearts. He will show why men have done these things. Every man will receive from God the thanks he should have.

6 Christian brothers, I have used Apollos and myself to show you what I am talking about. This is to help you so you will not think more of men than what God's Word will allow. Never think more of one of God's servants than another. 7 Who made you better than your brother? Or what do you have that has not been given to you? If God has given you everything, why do you have pride? Why do you act as if He did not give it to you? 8 You are full. You are rich. You live like kings and we do not. I wish you were kings and we could be leaders with you. 9 I think that God has made a show of us missionaries. We are the last and the least among men. We are like men waiting to be put to death. The whole world, men and angels alike, are watching us. 10 We are thought of as fools because of Christ. But you are thought of as wise Christians! We are weak. You are strong. People respect you. They have no respect for us. 11 To this hour we are hungry and thirsty, and our clothes are worn out. People hurt us. We have no homes.

12 We work with our hands to make a living. We speak kind words to those who speak against us. When people hurt us, we say nothing. 13 When people say bad things about us, we answer with kind words. People think of us as dirt that is worth nothing and as the worst thing on earth to this day.

Follow Paul's Way of Life

14 I do not write these things to shame you. I am doing this to help you know what you should do. You are my much-loved children. 15 You may have 10,000 Christian teachers. But remember, I am the only father you have. You became Christians when I preached the Good News to you. 16 So I ask you with all my heart to follow the way I live. 17 For this reason I have sent Timothy to you. He is my much-loved child and a faithful Christian. He will tell you how I act as a Christian. This is the kind of life I teach in the churches wherever I go.

18 Some of you are full of pride. You think that I am not coming to visit you. 19 If the Lord wants me to, I will come soon. I will find out when I come if these proud people have God's power, or if they just use a lot of big words. 20 The holy nation of God is not made up of words. It is made up of power. 21 What do you want? Do you want me to come with a stick to whip you? Or do you want me to come with love and a gentle spirit?

Sin in the Church

5 Someone has told me about a sex sin among you. It is so bad that even the people who do not know God would not do it. I have been told that one of the men is living with his father's wife as if she were his wife. 2 Instead of being sorry, you are proud of yourselves. The man who is living like that should be sent away from you. 3 I am far from you. Even if I am not there, my spirit is with you. I have already said that the man is guilty of this sin. I am saying this as if I were there with you. 4 Call a meeting of the church. I will be with you in spirit. In the name of the Lord Jesus Christ, and by His power, 5 hand this person over to the devil. His body is to be destroyed and his spirit may be saved on the day the Lord comes again.

6 It is not good for you to be proud of the way things are going in your church. You know a little yeast makes the whole loaf of bread rise. 7 Clean out the old yeast. Then you will be new bread with none of the old yeast in you. The Jews killed lambs when they left Egypt. Christ is our lamb. He has already been killed as a gift on the altar to God for us. 8 Bread with yeast in it is like being full of sin and hate. Let us eat this supper together with bread that has no yeast in it. This bread is pure and true.

9 I told you in my letter not to keep on being with people who do any kind of sex sins. 10 I was not talking about people doing sex sins who are bad people of this world. I was not talking about people of this world who always want to get more or those who get things in a wrong way or those who worship false gods. To get away from people like that you would have to leave this world! 11 What I wrote was that you should not keep on being with a person who calls himself a Christian if he does any kind of sex sins. You should not even eat with a person who says he is a Christian but always wants to get more of everything or uses bad language or who gets drunk or gets things in a wrong way. 12 It is not for me to judge those outside the church. You are to judge those who belong to the church. 13 God will judge those outside the church. So you must put that sinful person out of your church.

Going to Court against Christians

6 Why do you go to court when you have something against another Christian? You are asking people who are not Christians to judge who is guilty. You should go to those who belong to Christ and ask them. 2 Did you not know that those who belong to Christ will someday judge this world? If you judge the people of the world as guilty, are you not able to do this in small things? 3 Did you not know that we are to judge angels? So you should be able to take care of your problem here in this world without any trouble.

4 When you have things to decide about this life, why do you go to men in courts who are not even Christians? 5 You should be ashamed! Is it true that there is not one person wise enough in your church to decide who is right when people argue? 6 Instead, one Christian takes another Christian to court. And that court is made up of people who are not Christians! 7 This shows you are wrong when you have to go to court against each other. Would it not be better to let someone do something against you that is wrong? Would it not be better to let them rob you? 8 Instead, you rob and do wrong to other Christians.

The Body Is to Be Holy

9 Do you not know that sinful men will have no place in the holy nation of God? Do not be fooled. A person who does sex sins, or who worships false gods, or who is not faithful in marriage, or men who act like women, or people who do sex sins with their own sex, will have no place in the holy nation of God. 10 Also those who steal, or those who always want to get more of everything, or who get drunk, or who say bad things about others, or take things that are not theirs, will have no place in the holy nation of God. 11 Some of you were like that. But now your sins are washed away. You were set apart for God-like living to do His work. You were made right with God through our Lord Jesus Christ by the Spirit of our God.

12 I am allowed to do all things, but not everything is good for me to do! Even if I am free to do all things, I will not do them if I think it would be hard for me to stop when I know I should. 13 Food was meant for the stomach. The stomach needs food, but God will bring to an end both food and the stomach. The body was not meant for sex sins. It was meant to work for the Lord. The Lord is for our body. 14 God raised the Lord from death. He will raise us from death by His power also.

The Body Belongs to the Lord

15 Do you not know that your bodies are a part of Christ Himself? Am I to take a part of Christ and make it a part of a woman who sells the use of her body? No! Never! 16 Do you not know that a man who joins himself to a woman who sells the use of her body becomes a part of her? The Holy Writings say, "The two will become one." 17 But if you join yourself to the Lord, you are one with Him in spirit.

18 Have nothing to do with sex sins! Any other sin that a man does, does not hurt his own body. But the man who does a sex sin sins against his own body. 19 Do you not know that your body is a house of God where the Holy Spirit lives? God gave you His Holy Spirit. Now you belong to God. You do not belong to yourselves. 20 God bought you with a great price. So honor God with your body. You belong to Him.

How a Husband and Wife Should Live

7 You asked me some questions in your letter. This is my answer. It is good if a man does not get married. 2 But because of being tempted to sex sins, each man should get married and have his own wife. Each woman should get married and have her own husband. 3 The husband should please his wife as a husband. The wife should please her husband as a wife. 4 The wife is not the boss of her own body. It belongs to the husband. And in the same way, the husband is not the boss of his own body. It belongs to the wife.

5 Do not keep from each other that which belongs to each other in marriage unless you agree for awhile so you can use your time to pray. Then come together again or the devil will tempt you to do that which you know you should not do.

6 This is what I think. I am not saying you must do it. 7 I wish everyone were as I am, but each has his own gift from God. One has one gift. Another has another gift.

8 This is what I say to those who are not married and to women whose husbands have died. It is good if you do not get married. I am not married. 9 But if you are not able to keep from doing that which you know is wrong, get married. It is better to get married than to have such strong sex desires.

10 I have this to say to those who are married. These words are from the Lord.

A wife should not leave her husband, 11 but if she does leave him, she should not get married to another man. It would be better for her to go back to her husband. The husband should not divorce his wife. 12 I have this to say. These words are not from the Lord. If a Christian husband has a wife who is not a Christian, and she wants to live with him, he must not divorce her. 13 If a Christian wife has a husband who is not a Christian, and he wants to live with her, she must not divorce him. 14 The husband who is not a Christian is set apart from the sin of the world because of his Christian wife. The wife who is not a Christian is set apart from the sin of the world because of her Christian husband. In this way, the lives of the children are not unclean because of sin, they are clean. 15 If the one who is not a Christian wants to leave, let that one go. The Christian husband or wife should not try to make the other one stay. God wants you to live in peace. 16 Christian wife, how do you know you will not help your husband to become a Christian? Or Christian husband, how do you know you will not help your wife to become a Christian?

Stay as You Were When God Chose You

17 Everyone should live the life the Lord gave to him. He should live as he was when he became a Christian. This is what I teach in all the churches. 18 If a man became a Christian after he had gone through the religious act of becoming a Jew, he should do nothing about it. If a man became a Christian before, he should not go through the religious act of becoming a Jew. 19 If it is done or not done, it means nothing. What is important is to obey God's Word. 20 Everyone should stay the same way he was when he became a Christian. 21 Were you a servant who was owned by someone when you became a Christian? Do not worry about it. But if you are able to become free, do that. 22 A servant who is owned by someone and who has become a Christian is the Lord's free man. A free man who has become a Christian is a servant owned by Christ. 23 He paid a great price for you when He bought you. Do not let yourselves become servants owned by men. 24 Christian brothers, each one should stay as he was when he became a Christian.

25 I have no word from the Lord about women or men who have never been married. I will tell you what I think. You can trust me because the Lord has given me His loving-kindness. 26 I think, because of the troubles that are coming, it is a good thing for a person not to get married. 27 Are you married to a wife? Do not try to get a divorce. If you are not married, do not look for a wife. 28 If you do get married, you have not sinned. If a woman who is not married gets married, it is no sin. But being married will add problems. I would like to have you free from such problems.

29 I mean this, Christian brothers. The time is short. A married man should use his time as if he did not have a wife. 30 Those who have sorrow should keep on working as if they had no sorrow. Those who have joy should keep on working as if there was no time for joy. Those who buy should have no time to get joy from what they have. 31 While you live in this world, live as if the world has no hold on you. The way of this world will soon be gone.

32 I want you to be free from the cares of this world. The man who is not married can spend his time working for the Lord and pleasing Him. 33 The man who is married cares for the things of the world. He wants to please his wife. 34 Married women and women who have never been married are different. The woman who has never been married can spend her time working for the Lord. She wants to please the Lord with her body and spirit. The woman who is married cares for the things of the world. She wants to please her husband. 35 I am saying these things to help you. I am not trying to keep you from getting married. I want you to do what is best. You should work for Him without other things taking your time.

36 If a man and woman expect to get married, and he thinks his desires to marry her are getting too strong, and she is getting older, they should get married. It is no sin. 37 But if a man has the power to keep from getting married and knows in his mind that he should not, he is wise if he does not get married. 38 The man who gets married does well, but the man who does not get married does better.

39 A wife is not free as long as her husband lives. If her husband dies, she is free to marry anyone she wants, if he is a Christian. 40 I think she will be much more happy if she does not get married again. This is what I think. I believe it is what the Holy Spirit is saying.

Food Given to False Gods

8 I want to write about food that has been given as a gift in worship to a false god. We all know something about it. Knowing about it makes one feel important. But love makes one strong. 2 The person who thinks he knows all the answers still has a lot to learn. 3 But if he loves God, he is known by God also.

4 What about food that has been given as a gift to a false god in worship? Is it right? We know that a false god is not a god at all. There is only one God! There is no other. 5 Men have thought there are many such gods and lords in the sky and on the earth. 6 But we know there is only one God. He is the Father. All things are from Him. He made us for Himself. There is one Lord. He is Jesus Christ. He made all things. He keeps us alive.

7 Not all men know this. They have given food as a gift in worship to a god as if the god were alive. Some men have done this all their lives. If they eat such food, their hearts tell them it is wrong. 8 Food will not bring us near to God. We are no worse if we do not eat it, or we are no better if we eat it. 9 Since you are free to do as you please, be careful that this does not hurt a weak Christian. 10 A Christian who is weak may see you eat food in a place where it has been given as a gift to false gods in worship. Since he sees you eat it, he will eat it also. 11 You may make the weak Christian fall into sin by what you have done. Remember, he is a Christian brother for whom Christ died. 12 When you sin against a weak Christian by making him do what is wrong, you sin against Christ. 13 So then, if eating meat makes my Christian brother trip and fall, I will never eat it again. I do not want to make my Christian brother sin.

A Missionary's Rights

9 Am I not a missionary? Am I not free? Have I not seen Jesus our Lord? Are you not Christians because of the work I have done for the Lord? 2 Other people may not think of me as a missionary, but you do. It proves I am a missionary because you are Christians now. 3 When people ask questions about me, I say this: 4 Do we not have the right to have food and drink when we are working for the Lord? 5 Do we not have the right to take a Christian wife along with us? The other missionaries do. The Lord's brothers do and Peter does. 6 Are Barnabas and I the only ones who should keep working for a living so we can preach?

7 Have you ever heard of a soldier who goes to war and pays for what he needs himself? Have you ever heard of a man planting a field of grapes and not eating some of the fruit? Have you ever heard of a farmer who feeds cattle and does not drink some of the milk? 8 These things are not just what men think are right to do. God's Law speaks about this. 9 God gave Moses the Law. It says, "When the cow is made to walk on the grain to break it open, do not stop it from eating some." (Deuteronomy 25:4) Does God care about the cow? 10 Did not God speak about this because of us. For sure, this was written for us. The man who gets the fields ready and the man who gathers in the grain should expect some of the grain. 11 We have planted God's Word among you. Is it too much to expect you to give us what we need to live each day? 12 If other people have the right to expect this from you, do we not have more right? But we have not asked this of you. We have suffered many things. We did this so the Good News of Christ would not be held back.

13 You must know that those who work in the house of God get their food there. Those who work at the altar in the house of God get a part of the food that is given there. 14 The Lord has said also that those who preach the Good News should get their living from those who hear it.

15 I have not used any of these things. I am not writing now to get anything. I would rather die than lose the joy of preaching to you without you paying me. 16 I cannot be proud because I preach the Good News. I have been told to do it. It would be bad for me if I do not preach the Good News. 17 If I do this because I want to, I will get my reward. If I do not want to do it, I am still expected to do it. 18 Then what is my reward? It is when I preach the Good News without you paying me. I do not ask you to pay me as I could.

Learning to Get Along

19 No man has any hold on me, but I have made myself a workman owned by all. I do this so I might lead more people to Christ. 20 I became as a Jew to the Jews so I might lead them to Christ. There are some who live by obeying the Jewish Law. I became as one who lives by obeying the Jewish Law so I might lead them to Christ. 21 There are some who live by not

obeying the Jewish law. I became as one who lives by not obeying the Jewish law so I might lead them to Christ. This does not mean that I do not obey God's Law. I obey the teachings of Christ. 22 Some are weak. I have become weak so I might lead them to Christ. I have become like every person so in every way I might lead some to Christ. 23 Everything I do, I do to get the Good News to men. I want to have a part in this work.

Live a Life That Pleases Christ

24 You know that only one person gets a crown for being in a race even if many people run. You must run so you will win the crown. 25 Everyone who runs in a race does many things so his body will be strong. He does it to get a crown that will soon be worth nothing, but we work for a crown that will last forever. 26 In the same way, I run straight for the place at the end of the race. I fight to win. I do not beat the air. 27 I keep working over my body. I make it obey me. I do this because I am afraid that after I have preached the Good News to others, I myself might be put aside.

The Danger of Worshiping False Gods

10 Christian brothers, I want you to know what happened to our early fathers. They all walked from the country of Egypt under the cloud that showed them the way, and they all passed through the waters of the Red Sea. 2 They were all baptized as they followed Moses in the cloud and in the sea. 3 All of them ate the same holy food. 4 They all drank the same holy drink. They drank from a holy Rock that went along with them. That holy Rock was Christ. 5 Even then most of them did not please God. He destroyed them in the desert.

6 These things show us something. They teach us not to want things that are bad for us like those people did. 7 We must not worship false gods as some of them did. The Holy Writings tell us, "The people sat down to eat and drink. Then they got up to play." (Exodus 32:6) 8 We must not do sex sins as some of them did. In one day 23,000 died. 9 We must not test the Lord as some of them did. They were destroyed by snakes. 10 We must not complain against God as some of them did. That is why they were destroyed.

11 All these things happened to show us something. They were written to teach us that the end of the world is near. 12 So watch yourself! The person who thinks he can stand against sin had better watch that he does not fall into sin. 13 You have never been tempted to sin in any different way than other people. God is faithful. He will not allow you to be tempted more than you can take. But when you are tempted, He will make a way for you to keep from falling into sin.

Teaching About the Lord's Supper

14 My dear friends, keep away from the worship of false gods. 15 I am speaking to you who are able to understand. See if what I am saying is true. 16 When we give thanks for the fruit of the vine at the Lord's supper, are we not sharing in the blood of Christ? The bread we eat at the Lord's supper, are we not sharing in the body of Christ? 17 There is one bread, and many of us Christians make up the body of Christ. All of us eat from that bread.

18 Look at the Jews. They ate the animals that were brought to God as gifts in worship and put on the altar. Did this not show they were sharing with God? 19 What do I mean? Am I saying that a false god or the food brought to it in worship is worth anything? 20 No, not at all! I am saying that the people who do not know God bring gifts of animals in worship. But they have given them to demons, not to God. You do not want to have any share with demons. 21 You cannot drink from the cup of the Lord and from the cup of demons. You cannot eat at the Lord's table and at the demon's table. 22 Are we trying to make the Lord jealous? Do we think we are stronger than the Lord?

23 We are allowed to do anything, but not everything is good for us to do. We are allowed to do anything, but not all things help us grow strong as Christians. 24 Do not work only for your own good. Think of what you can do for others. 25 Eat any meat that is sold in the stores. Ask no questions about it. Then your heart will not say it is wrong. 26 The Holy Writings say, "The earth and everything in it belongs to the Lord." (Psalm 24:1) 27 If a person who is not a Christian wants you to eat with him, and you want to go, eat anything that is on the table. Ask no questions about the food. Then your heart will not say it is wrong. 28 But if someone says, "This meat has been given as a gift to false gods in worship," do not eat it. In that way, it will not hurt the faith of the one who told you and his heart will have peace. 29 How the other

person feels is important. We are not free to do things that will hurt another person. [30] If I can give thanks to God for my food, why should anyone say that I am wrong about eating food I can give thanks for? [31] So if you eat or drink or whatever you do, do everything to honor God. [32] Do nothing that would make trouble for a Greek or for a Jew or for the church of God. [33] I want to please everyone in all that I do. I am not thinking of myself. I want to do what is best for them so they may be saved from the punishment of sin.

11 Follow my way of thinking as I follow Christ.

How Christian Women Should Live

[2] I think you have done well because you always remember me and have followed the things I taught you. [3] I want you to know that Christ is the head of every man. The husband is the head of his wife. God is the head of Christ. [4] If any man prays or preaches with his head covered, he does not give honor to Christ. [5] Every woman who prays or preaches without her head covered does not respect her head. It is the same as if she had her hair cut off. [6] If a woman does not cover her head, she might as well cut off her hair also. If a woman is ashamed to have her hair cut off, she should cover her head. [7] Man is made like God and His shining-greatness. For this reason a man should not have his head covered when he prays or preaches, but the woman respects the man. [8] Man was not made from woman. Woman was made from man, [9] and man was not made for woman. Woman was made for man. [10] For this reason a woman should have a covering on her head. This shows she respects man. This is for the angels to see also. [11] In God's plan women need men and men need women. [12] Woman was made from man, but man is born of woman. God made all things.

[13] Think this over yourselves. Does it look right for a woman to pray with no covering on her head? [14] Have we not already learned that it is a shame for a man to have long hair? [15] But a woman can be proud to have long hair. Her hair is given to her for a covering. [16] If anyone wants to argue about this, my answer is that this is what we teach, and all the churches agree with me.

How the Lord's Supper Should Be Eaten

[17] While writing about these things, let me tell you what I think. Nothing good

is coming from your meeting together. [18] First of all, I hear that when you meet together in the church you are divided into groups and you argue. I almost believe this is true. [19] For there must be different groups among you. In that way, those who are right will be seen from those who are wrong. [20] When you gather together for your meetings, it is not to eat the Lord's supper. [21] Each one is in a hurry to eat his own food first. He does not wait for others. In this way, one does not get enough food and drink. Others get too much and get drunk. [22] You have your own homes to eat and drink in. Or do you hate the church of God and shame those who are poor? What am I to say to you? Am I to say you are right? No! I cannot say you are right in this.

The Meaning of the Lord's Supper

[23] I have given you the teaching I received from the Lord. The night Jesus was handed over to the soldiers, He took bread. [24] When He had given thanks, He broke it and said, "Take this bread and eat it. This is My body which is broken for you. Do this to remember Me."

[25] In the same way after supper, He took the cup. He said, "This cup is the New Way of Worship made between God and you by My blood. Whenever you drink it, do it to remember Me."

[26] Every time you eat this bread and drink from this cup you are telling of the Lord's death until He comes again. [27] Anyone who eats the bread or drinks from the cup, if his spirit is not right with the Lord, will be guilty of sinning against the body and the blood of the Lord. [28] This is why a man should look into his own heart and life before eating the bread and drinking from the cup. [29] Anyone who eats the bread and drinks from the cup, if his spirit is not right with the Lord, will be guilty as he eats and drinks. He does not understand the meaning of the Lord's body. [30] This is why some of you are sick and weak, and some have died. [31] But if we would look into our own lives and see if we are guilty, then God would not have to say we are guilty. [32] When we are guilty, we are punished by the Lord so we will not be told we are guilty with the rest of the world.

[33] Christian brothers, when you come together to eat, wait for each other. [34] If anyone is hungry, he should eat at home. Then he will not be guilty as you meet together. I will talk about the other things when I come.

The Gifts of the Holy Spirit

12 Christian brothers, I want you to know about the gifts of the Holy Spirit. You need to understand the truth about this. 2 You know that before you were Christians you were led to worship false gods. None of these gods could speak. 3 So I tell you that no one speaking by the help of the Holy Spirit can say that he hates Jesus. No one can say, "Jesus is Lord," except by the help of the Holy Spirit.

The Kinds of Gifts

4 There are different kinds of gifts. But it is the same Holy Spirit Who gives them. 5 There are different kinds of work to be done for Him. But the work is for the same Lord. 6 There are different ways of doing His work. But it is the same God who uses all these ways in all people. 7 The Holy Spirit works in each person in one way or another for the good of all. 8 One person is given the gift of teaching words of wisdom. Another person is given the gift of teaching what he has learned and knows. These gifts are by the same Holy Spirit. 9 One person receives the gift of faith. Another person receives the gifts of healing. These gifts are given by the same Holy Spirit. 10 One person is given the gift of doing powerful works. Another person is given the gift of speaking God's Word. Another person is given the gift of telling the difference between the Holy Spirit and false spirits. Another person is given the gift of speaking in special sounds. Another person is given the gift of telling what these special sounds mean. 11 But it is the same Holy Spirit, the Spirit of God, Who does all these things. He gives to each person as He wants to give.

Our Body Is Like the Body of Christ

12 Our own body has many parts. When all these many parts are put together, they are only one body. The body of Christ is like this. 13 It is the same way with us. Jews or those who are not Jews, men who are owned by someone or men who are free to do what they want to do, have all been baptized into the one body by the same Holy Spirit. We have all received the one Spirit.

14 The body is not one part, but many parts. 15 If the foot should say, "I am not a part of the body because I am not a hand," that would not stop it from being a part of the body. 16 If the ear should say, "I am not a part of the body because I am not an eye," that would not stop it from being a part of

the body. 17 If the whole body were an eye how would it hear? If the whole body were an ear, how would it smell? 18 But God has put all the parts into the body just as He wants to have them. 19 If all the parts were the same, it could not be a body. 20 But now there are many parts, but one body.

21 The eye cannot say to the hand, "I do not need you." Or the head cannot say to the feet, "I do not need you." 22 Some of the parts we think are weak and not important are very important. 23 We take good care of and cover with clothes the parts of the body that look less important. The parts which do not look beautiful have an important work to do. 24 The parts that can be seen do not need as much care. God has made the body so more care is given to the parts that need it most. 25 This is so the body will not be divided into parts. All the parts care for each other. 26 If one part of the body suffers, all the other parts suffer with it. If one part is given special care, the other parts are happy.

The Body of Christ

27 You are all a part of the body of Christ. 28 God has chosen different ones in the church to do His work. First, there are missionaries. Second, there are preachers or those who speak for God. And third, there are teachers. He has also chosen those who do powerful works and those who have the gifts of healing. And He has chosen those who help others who are in need and those who are able to lead others in work and those who speak in special sounds. 29 Are they all missionaries? No. Are they all preachers or those who speak for God? No. Do they all do powerful works? No. 30 Do they all have the gifts of healing? No. Do they all speak in special sounds? No. Are they all able to tell what the special sounds mean? No. 31 But from your heart you should want the best gifts. Now I will show you even a better way.

Love—the Greatest of All

13 I may be able to speak the languages of men and even of angels, but if I do not have love, it will sound like noisy brass. 2 If I have the gift of speaking God's Word and if I understand all secrets, but do not have love, I am nothing. If I know all things and if I have the gift of faith so I can move mountains, but do not have love, I am nothing. 3 If I give everything I have to feed poor people and if I give my body to be burned, but do not have love, it will not help me.

4 Love does not give up. Love is kind. Love is not jealous. Love does not put itself up as being important. Love has no pride. 5 Love does not do the wrong thing. Love never thinks of itself. Love does not get angry. Love does not remember the suffering that comes from being hurt by someone. 6 Love is not happy with sin. Love is happy with the truth. 7 Love takes everything that comes without giving up. Love believes all things. Love hopes for all things. Love keeps on in all things.

8 Love never comes to an end. The gift of speaking God's Word will come to an end. The gift of speaking in special sounds will be stopped. The gift of understanding will come to an end. 9 For we only know a part now, and we speak only a part. 10 When everything is perfect, then we will not need these gifts that are not perfect.

11 When I was a child, I spoke like a child. I thought like a child. I understood like a child. Now I am a man. I do not act like a child anymore. 12 Now that which we see is as if we were looking in a broken mirror. But then we will see everything. Now I know only a part. But then I will know everything in a perfect way. That is how God knows me right now. 13 And now we have these three: faith and hope and love, but the greatest of these is love.

Speaking in Special Sounds Is Not the Greatest Gift

14 You should want to have this love. You should want the gifts of the Holy Spirit and most of all to be able to speak God's Word. 2 The man who speaks in special sounds speaks to God. He is not speaking to men. No one understands. He is speaking secret things through the power of the Holy Spirit. 3 The man who speaks God's Word speaks to men. It helps them to learn and understand. It gives them comfort. 4 The man who speaks in special sounds receives strength. The man who speaks God's Word gives strength to the church. 5 I wish all of you spoke in special sounds. But more than that, I wish all of you spoke God's Word. The one who speaks God's Word has a more important gift than the one who speaks in special sounds. But if he can tell what he is speaking, the church will be helped. 6 Christian brothers, if I come to you speaking in special sounds, what good is it to you? But if I tell you something God has shown me or something I have learned or what God's Word says will happen in the

future or teach you God's Word, it will be for your good.

7 There are things on which people play music. If strange sounds are made on these, how will others know which one is played? 8 If a horn does not make a good sound, how will men know they are to get ready to fight? 9 It is the same if you speak to a person in special sounds. How will he know what you say? Your sounds will be lost in the air. 10 There are many languages in the world. All of them have meaning to the people who understand them. 11 But if I do not understand the language someone uses to speak to me, the man who speaks is a stranger to me. I am a stranger to him. 12 Since you want gifts from the Holy Spirit, ask for those that will build up the whole church. 13 So the man who speaks in special sounds should pray for the gift to be able to tell what they mean.

14 If I pray in special sounds, my spirit is doing the praying. My mind does not understand. 15 What should I do? I will pray with my spirit and I will pray with my mind also. I will sing with my spirit and I will sing with my mind also. 16 If you honor and give thanks to God with your spirit in sounds nobody understands, how can others honor and give thanks also if they do not know what you are saying? 17 You are honoring and giving thanks to God, but it is not helping other people.

18 I thank God that I speak in special sounds more than all of you. 19 But in a meeting of the church, it is better if I say five words that others can understand and be helped by than 10,000 words in special sounds.

20 Christian brothers, do not be like children in your thinking. Be full-grown, but be like children in not knowing how to sin. 21 God says in the Holy Writings, "I will speak to My people. I will speak through men from other lands in other languages. Even then My people will not listen to Me." (Isaiah 28:11-12) 22 So then speaking in special sounds is for those who do not believe. It is not for those who believe. But speaking God's Word is for those who believe. It is not for those who do not believe.

Church Meetings

23 If some people who are not Christians come to your church meeting while all the people are speaking in special sounds, they will think you are crazy. 24 But if a man who is not a Christian comes to your

church meeting while you are all speaking God's Word, he will understand that he is a sinner by what he hears. He will know he is guilty. 25 The secrets of his heart will be brought into the open. He will get on his knees and worship God. He will say, "For sure, God is here with you!"

26 What am I saying, Christian brothers? When you meet together for worship, some of you have a song to sing. Some of you want to teach and some have special words from God. Some of you speak in special sounds and some of you tell what they mean. Everything should be done to help those who are meeting together to grow strong as Christians. 27 No more than two or three people should speak in special sounds. Only one should speak at a time. Someone must tell the meaning of the special sounds. 28 If no one is there who can tell the meaning of the special sounds, he should not speak in the church. He should speak only to himself and to God. 29 Two or three should speak God's Word. The other people should listen and decide if they are speaking right. 30 If someone sitting in the meeting gets some special word from God, the one who is speaking should stop. 31 All of you can speak God's Word, but only one person at a time. In that way, all of you can learn and be helped. 32 Men who speak God's Word are able to stop when they should. 33 God does not want everyone speaking at the same time in church meetings. He wants peace. All the churches of God's people worship this way.

34 Women should not be allowed to speak in church meetings. They are to obey this teaching. The Law says this also. 35 If they want to find out about something, they should ask their husbands at home. It is a shame for a woman to speak in a church meeting.

36 Did the Word of God come from you Christians in the city of Corinth? Or are you the only people who received it? 37 Some of you may think you have the gift of speaking God's Word or some other gift from the Holy Spirit. If you do, you should know that what I am writing to you is what God has told us we must obey. 38 If any man does not listen to this, have nothing to do with him.

39 So then, my Christian brothers, you should want to speak God's Word. Do not stop anyone from speaking in special sounds. 40 All things should be done in the right way, one after the other.

Jesus Christ Was Raised from the Dead

15 Christian brothers, I want to tell the Good News to you again. It is the same as I preached to you before. You received it and your faith has been made strong by it. 2 This is what I preached to you. You are saved from the punishment of sin by the Good News if you keep hold of it, unless your faith was worth nothing.

3 First of all, I taught you what I had received. It was this: Christ died for our sins as the Holy Writings said He would. (Isaiah 53:5–12) 4 Christ was buried. He was raised from the dead three days later as the Holy Writings said He would. (Psalm 16:9–10) 5 Christ was seen by Peter. After that, the twelve followers saw Him. 6 After that, more than 500 of His followers saw Him at one time. Most of them are still here, but some have died. 7 After that, James saw Christ. Then all the missionaries saw Him. 8 Last of all, Christ showed Himself to me as if I had been born too late. 9 For I am the least important of all the missionaries. I should not be called a missionary because I made it so hard for God's church. 10 I am different now. It is all because of what God did for me by His loving-favor. His loving-favor was not wasted. I worked harder than all the other missionaries. But it was not I who worked. It was God's loving-favor working through me. 11 It makes no difference how you heard the Good News. It could have been through the other missionaries or through me. The important thing is this: We preached the Good News to you and you believed it.

We Will Be Raised from the Dead Also

12 We preached to you that Christ has been raised from the dead. But some of you say that people are not raised from the dead. Why do you say this? 13 If the dead are not raised, then Christ was not raised from the dead. 14 If Christ was not raised from the dead, then what we preach to you is worth nothing. Your faith in Christ is worth nothing. 15 That makes us all liars because we said that God raised Christ from the dead. But God did not raise Christ from the dead if the dead do not come to life again. 16 If the dead are not raised, then not even Christ was raised from the dead. 17 If Christ was not raised from the dead, your faith is worth nothing and you are still living in your sins. 18 Then the Christians who have already died are lost in sin. 19 If we have hope in

Christ in this life only, we are more sad than anyone else.

20 But it is true! Christ has been raised from the dead! He was the first One to be raised from the dead and all those who are in graves will follow. 21 Death came because of a man, Adam. Being raised from the dead also came because of a Man, Christ. 22 All men will die as Adam died. But all those who belong to Christ will be raised to new life. 23 This is the way it is: Christ was raised from the dead first. Then all those who belong to Christ will be raised from the dead when He comes again. 24 Next, at the end of the world, Christ will give His holy nation over to God the Father. Christ will have destroyed every nation and power. 25 Christ must be King until He has destroyed all those who hate Him and work against Him. 26 The last thing that will be destroyed is death. 27 The Holy Writings say that God has put all things under Christ's feet except Himself. 28 When Christ is over all things, He will put Himself under God Who put all things under Christ. And God will be over all things.

29 What good will it do people if they are baptized for the dead? If the dead are not raised, why are people baptized for them? 30 Why are we also in danger every hour? 31 I say this, Christian brothers, I have joy in what Jesus Christ our Lord has done for you. That is why I face death every day. 32 As men look at it, what good has it done for me in the city of Ephesus to fight with men who act like wild animals? If the dead are not raised, we might as well be like those who say, "Let us eat and drink, for tomorrow we die."

33 Do not let anyone fool you. Bad people can make those who want to live good become bad. 34 Keep your minds awake! Stop sinning. Some do not know God at all. I say this to your shame.

The Body That Will Be Raised

35 Someone will say, "How are the dead raised? What kind of bodies will they have?" 36 What a foolish question! When you plant a seed, it must die before it starts new life. 37 When you put it in the earth, you are not planting the body which it will become. You put in only a seed. 38 It is God Who gives it a body just as He wants it to have. Each kind of seed becomes a different kind of body.

39 All flesh is not the same. Men have one kind of flesh. Animals have another kind.

Fish have another kind, and birds have another kind. 40 There are bodies in the heavens. There are bodies on earth. Their greatness is not the same. 41 The sun has its greatness. The moon has its greatness. Stars have their greatness. One star is different from another star in greatness.

42 It is the same with people who are raised from the dead. The body will turn back to dust when it is put in a grave. When the body is raised from the grave, it will never die. 43 It has no greatness when it is put in a grave, but it is raised with shining-greatness. It is weak when it is put in a grave, but it is raised with power. 44 It is a human body when it dies, but it is a God-like body when it is raised from the dead. There are human bodies and there are God-like bodies. 45 The Holy Writings say, "The first man, Adam, became a living soul." But the last Adam (Christ) is a life-giving Spirit.

46 We have these human bodies first. Then we are given God-like bodies that are ready for heaven. 47 Adam was the first man. He was made from the dust of the earth. Christ was the second man. He came down from heaven. 48 All men of the earth are made like Adam. But those who belong to Christ will have a body like the body of Christ Who came from heaven. 49 Now, our bodies are like Adam's body. But in heaven, our bodies will be like the body of Christ.

50 Christian brothers, our bodies which are made of flesh and blood will not go into the holy nation of God. That which dies can have no part in that which will never die. 51 For sure, I am telling you a secret. We will not all die, but we will all be changed. 52 In a very short time, no longer than it takes for the eye to close and open, the Christians who have died will be raised. It will happen when the last horn sounds. The dead will be raised never to die again. Then the rest of us who are alive will be changed. 53 Our human bodies made from dust must be changed into a body that cannot be destroyed. Our human bodies that can die must be changed into bodies that will never die. 54 When this that can be destroyed has been changed into that which cannot be destroyed, and when this that does die has been changed into that which cannot die, then it will happen as the Holy Writings said it would happen. They said, "Death has no more power over life." (Isaiah 25:8) 55 O death, where is your power? O death,

where are your pains? 56 The pain in death is sin. Sin has power over those under the Law. 57 But God is the One Who gives us power over sin through Jesus Christ our Lord. We give thanks to Him for this.

58 So then, Christian brothers, because of all this, be strong. Do not allow anyone to change your mind. Always do your work well for the Lord. You know that whatever you do for Him will not be wasted.

Gifts for the Poor

16 I want to tell you what to do about the money you are gathering for the Christians. Do the same as I told the churches in the country of Galatia to do. 2 On the first day of every week each of you should put aside some of your money. Give a certain part of what you have earned. Keep it there because I do not want money gathered when I come. 3 When I get there, I will give letters to the men you want to send. They will take your gift to Jerusalem. 4 If I can go, they can go with me.

Plans for a Visit

5 I want to visit you after I have gone through the country of Macedonia for I am going through there. 6 I may be staying with you and even spend the winter with you. Then you can send me on my way to the next place. 7 I do not want to stop now. I want to spend some time with you when I can stay longer, if that is what the Lord wants. 8 I will stay in the city of Ephesus until the special day to remember how the Holy Spirit came on the church. 9 A wide door has been opened to me here

to preach the Good News. But there are many who work against me.

10 If Timothy comes, receive him and help him so he will not be afraid. He is working for the Lord as I am. 11 Everyone should respect him. Send him on his way to me in peace. I expect to see him and some of the other Christians soon. 12 I wanted brother Apollos to go with the other Christians to visit you. But he is not sure he should go now. He will come when he can.

13 Watch and keep awake! Stand true to the Lord. Keep on acting like men and be strong. 14 Everything you do should be done in love.

15 You know that the families of Stephanas were the first Christians in the country of Greece. They are working for the Lord in helping His people. 16 I ask you to listen to leaders like these and work with them as well as others like them. 17 I am happy that Stephanas and Fortunatus and Achaicus came here. They have helped me and you would have also if you had been here. 18 They have made me happy. They would have made you happy also. Show them you are thankful for their help.

19 The churches in the countries of Asia greet you. Aquila and Priscilla and the Christians who meet in their house greet you with Christian love. 20 All the Christians here greet you. Greet each other with a kiss of holy love. 21 I, Paul, am writing the last part of this letter with my own hand. 22 If anyone does not love the Lord, let him be kept from being with Christ. The Lord is coming soon! 23 May you have the loving-favor of our Lord Jesus. 24 I love you all through Christ Jesus. Let it be so.

2 CORINTHIANS

1 This letter is from Paul. I have been chosen by God to be a missionary for Jesus Christ. Timothy is here with me and is writing to you also. We are writing to God's church in the city of Corinth and to all of God's people in the country of Greece. 2 May you have loving-favor and peace from God our Father and the Lord Jesus Christ.

3 We give thanks to the God and Father of our Lord Jesus Christ. He is our Father Who shows us loving-kindness and our God Who gives us comfort. 4 He gives us comfort in all our troubles. Then we can comfort other people who have the same

troubles. We give the same kind of comfort God gives us. 5 As we have suffered much for Christ and have shared in His pain, we also share His great comfort.

6 But if we are in trouble, it is for your good. And it is so you will be saved from the punishment of sin. If God comforts us, it is for your good also. You too will be given strength not to give up when you have the same kind of trouble we have. 7 Our hope for you is the same all the time. We know you are sharing our troubles. And so you will share the comfort we receive.

8 We want you to know, Christian brothers, of the trouble we had in the countries

of Asia. The load was so heavy we did not have the strength to keep going. At times we did not think we could live. **9** We thought we would die. This happened so we would not put our trust in ourselves, but in God Who raises the dead. **10** Yes, God kept us from what looked like sure death and He is keeping us. As we trust Him, He will keep us in the future. **11** You also help us by praying for us. Many people thank God for His favor to us. This is an answer to the prayers of many people.

Paul Wants to Visit Corinth

12 I am happy to say this. Whatever we did in this world, and for sure when we were with you, we were honest and had pure desires. We did not trust in human wisdom. Our power came from God's loving-favor. **13** We write to you only what we know you can understand. I hope you will understand everything. **14** When the Lord Jesus comes again, you can be as proud of us as we will be proud of you. Right now you do not understand us real well.

15 It was because of this, I wanted to visit you first. In that way, you would be helped two times. **16** I wanted to stop to visit you on my way to the country of Macedonia. I would stop again as I came from there. Then you could help me on my way to the country of Judea. **17** Yes, I changed my mind. Does that show that I change my mind a lot? Do I plan things as people of the world who say yes when they mean no? You know I am not like that! **18** As God is true, my yes means yes. I am not the kind of person who says one thing and means another. **19** Timothy and Silvanus and I have preached to you about Jesus Christ, the Son of God. In Him there is no yes and no. In Him is yes. **20** Jesus says yes to all of God's many promises. It is through Jesus that we say, "Let it be so," when we give thanks to God. **21** God is the One Who makes our faith and your faith strong in Christ. He has set us apart for Himself. **22** He has put His mark on us to show we belong to Him. His Spirit is in our hearts to prove this.

23 I call on God to look into my heart. The reason I did not come to the city of Corinth was because I did not want my strong words to hurt you. **24** We are not the boss of your faith but we are working with you to make you happy. Your faith is strong.

2 As I thought about it, I decided I would not come to you again. It would only make you sad. **2** If I make you sad, who is going to make me happy? How can you

make me happy if I make you sad? **3** That is why I wrote that letter to you. I did not want to visit you and be made sad by the ones who should be making me happy. I am sure when I am happy, you are happy also. **4** I wrote you with a troubled heart. Tears were coming from my eyes. I did not want to make you sad. I wanted you to know how much I loved you.

Forgiving a Christian

5 If someone among you has brought sorrow, he has not made me as sad as he has all of you. I say this so I may not make it hard for you. **6** Most of you have punished him. That is enough for such a person. **7** Now you should forgive him and comfort him. If you do not, he will be so sad that he will want to give up. **8** I ask you to show him you do love him. **9** This is why I wrote to you. I wanted to test you to see if you were willing to obey in all things. **10** If you forgive a man, I forgive him also. If I have forgiven anything, I have done it because of you. Christ sees me as I forgive. **11** We forgive so that Satan will not win. We know how he works!

12 When I arrived in the city of Troas, the Lord opened the door for me to preach the Good News of Christ. **13** I was worried because I could not find our brother Titus. After saying good-bye, I went on my way to the country of Macedonia. **14** We thank God for the power Christ has given us. He leads us and makes us win in everything. He speaks through us wherever we go. The Good News is like a sweet smell to those who hear it. **15** We are a sweet smell of Christ that reaches up to God. It reaches out to those who are being saved from the punishment of sin and to those who are still lost in sin. **16** It is the smell of death to those who are lost in sin. It is the smell of life to those who are being saved from the punishment of sin. Who is able for such a work? **17** We are not like others. They preach God's Word to make money. We are men of truth and have been sent by God. We speak God's Word with Christ's power. All the time God sees us.

The Old and the New Way

3 Are we making it sound as if we think we are so important? Other people write letters about themselves. Do we need to write such a letter to you? **2** You are our letter. You are written in our hearts. You are known and read by all men. **3** You are as a letter from Christ written by us.

You are not written as other letters are written with ink, or on pieces of stone. You are written in human hearts by the Spirit of the living God. 4 We can say these things because of our faith in God through Christ. 5 We know we are not able in ourselves to do any of this work. God makes us able to do these things. 6 God is the One Who made us preachers of a New Way of Worship. This New Way of Worship is not of the Law. It is of the Holy Spirit. The Law brings death, but the Holy Spirit gives life.

7 The Law of Moses was written on stone and it brought death. But God's shining-greatness was seen when it was given. When Moses took it to the Jews, they could not look at his face because of the bright light. But that bright light in his face began to pass away. 8 The new way of life through the Holy Spirit comes with much more shining-greatness. 9 If the Law of Moses, that leads to death, came in shining-greatness, how much greater and brighter is the light that makes us right with God? 10 The Law of Moses came with shining-greatness long ago. But that light is no longer bright. The shining-greatness of the New Way of Worship that brings us life is so much brighter. 11 The shining light that came with the Law of Moses soon passed away. But the new way of life is much brighter. It will never pass away.

12 We speak without fear because our trust is in Christ. 13 We are not like Moses. He put a covering over his face so the Jews would not see that the bright light was passing away. 14 Their minds were not able to understand. Even to this day when the Law is read, there is a covering over their minds. They do not see that Christ is the only One Who can take the covering away. 15 Yes, to this day, there is a covering over their hearts whenever the Law of Moses is read. 16 But whenever a man turns to the Lord, the covering is taken away. 17 The heart is free where the Spirit of the Lord is. The Lord is the Spirit. 18 All of us, with no covering on our faces, show the shining-greatness of the Lord as in a mirror. All the time we are being changed to look like Him, with more and more of His shining-greatness. This change is from the Lord Who is the Spirit.

Paul Is Faithful in Preaching the Good News

4 Through God's loving-kindness, He has given us this job to do. So we do not give up. 2 We have put away all things that are done in secret and in shame. We do not play with the Word of God or use it in a false way. Because we are telling the truth, we want men's hearts to listen to us. God knows our desires. 3 If the Good News we preach is hidden, it is hidden to those who are lost in sin. 4 The eyes of those who do not believe are made blind by Satan who is the god of this world. He does not want the light of the Good News to shine in their hearts. This Good News shines as the shining-greatness of Christ. Christ is as God is. 5 We do not preach about ourselves. We preach Christ Jesus the Lord. We are your servants because of Jesus. 6 It was God Who said, "The light will shine in darkness." (Genesis 1:3) He is the One Who made His light shine in our hearts. This brings us the light of knowing God's shining-greatness which is seen in Christ's face.

7 We have this light from God in our human bodies. This shows that the power is from God. It is not from ourselves. 8 We are pressed on every side, but we still have room to move. We are often in much trouble, but we never give up. 9 People make it hard for us, but we are not left alone. We are knocked down, but we are not destroyed. 10 We carry marks on our bodies that show the death of Jesus. This is how Jesus makes His life seen in our bodies. 11 Every day of our life we face death because of Jesus. In this way, His life is seen in our bodies. 12 Death is working in us because we work for the Lord, but His life is working in you.

13 The Holy Writings say, "I believed, so I spoke." (Psalm 116:10) We have the same kind of faith as David had. We also believe, so we speak. 14 We know that God raised the Lord Jesus from the dead. He will raise us up also. God will take us to Himself and He will take you. 15 These things happened for your good. As more people receive God's favor, they will give thanks for the shining-greatness of God.

Life Now—Life in Heaven

16 This is the reason we do not give up. Our human body is wearing out. But our spirits are getting stronger every day. 17 The little troubles we suffer now for a short time are making us ready for the great things God is going to give us forever. 18 We do not look at the things that can be seen. We look at the things that cannot be seen. The things that can be seen will come to an end. But the things that cannot be seen will last forever.

Our Weak Human Bodies

5 Our body is like a house we live in here on earth. When it is destroyed, we know that God has another body for us in heaven. The new one will not be made by human hands as a house is made. This body will last forever. 2 Right now we cry inside ourselves because we wish we could have our new body which we will have in heaven. 3 We will not be without a body. We will live in a new body. 4 While we are in this body, we cry inside ourselves because things are hard for us. It is not that we want to die. Instead, we want to live in our new bodies. We want this dying body to be changed into a living body that lasts forever. 5 It is God Who has made us ready for this change. He has given us His Spirit to show us what He has for us.

6 We are sure of this. We know that while we are at home in this body we are not with the Lord. 7 Our life is lived by faith. We do not live by what we see in front of us. 8 We are sure we will be glad to be free of these bodies. It will be good to be at home with the Lord. 9 So if we stay here on earth or go home to Him, we always want to please Him. 10 For all of us must stand before Christ when He says who is guilty or not guilty. Each one will receive pay for what he has done. He will be paid for the good or the bad done while he lived in this body.

11 Because of this, we know the fear of God. So we try to get men to put their trust in Christ. God knows us. I hope that your hearts know me well also. 12 We do not want to sound as if we think we are so important. Instead, we are making it easy for you to be proud of us. In that way, you will be able to tell them about us. They always talk about the way people look, but do not care about their hearts. 13 Are we crazy to talk like this? It is all because of what God has done. If we are using our minds well, it is for you. 14 For the love of Christ puts us into action. We are sure that Christ died for everyone. So, because of that, everyone has a part in His death. 15 Christ died for everyone so that they would live for Him. They should not live to please themselves but for Christ Who died on a cross and was raised from the dead for them.

16 So from now on, we do not think about what people are like by looking at them. We even thought about Christ that way one time. But we do not think of Him that way anymore. 17 For if a man belongs to Christ, he is a new person. The old life is gone. New life has begun. 18 All this comes from God. He is the One Who brought us to Himself when we hated Him. He did this through Christ. Then He gave us the work of bringing others to Him. 19 God was in Christ. He was working through Christ to bring the whole world back to Himself. God no longer held men's sins against them. And He gave us the work of telling and showing men this. 20 We are Christ's missionaries. God is speaking to you through us. We are speaking for Christ and we ask you from our hearts to turn from your sins and come to God. 21 Christ never sinned but God put our sin on Him. Then we are made right with God because of what Christ has done for us.

Our Job to Do

6 We are working together with God. We ask you from our hearts not to receive God's loving-favor and then waste it. 2 The Holy Writings say, "I heard you at the right time. I helped you on that day to be saved from the punishment of sin. Now is the right time! See! Now is the day to be saved." (Isaiah 49:8) 3 We do not want to put anything in the way that would keep people from God. We do not want to be blamed. 4 Everything we do shows we are God's servants. We have had to wait and suffer. We have needed things. We have been in many hard places and have had many troubles. 5 We have been beaten. We have been put in prison. We have been in fights. We have worked hard. We have stayed awake watching. We have gone without food. 6 We have been pure. We have known what to do. We have suffered long. We have been kind. The Holy Spirit has worked in us. We have had true love. 7 We have spoken the truth. We have God's power. We have the sword of being right with God in the right hand and in the left hand. 8 Some men respect us and some do not. Some men speak bad against us and some thank us. They say we lie, but we speak the truth. 9 Some men act as if they do not know us. And yet we are known by everyone. They act as if we were dead, but we are alive. They try to hurt and destroy us, but they are not able to kill us. 10 We are full of sorrow and yet we are always happy. We are poor and yet we make many people rich. We have nothing and yet we have everything.

11 We have spoken to you who are in the city of Corinth with plain words. Our hearts are wide open. 12 Our hearts are

not closed to you. But you have closed your hearts to us. 13 I am speaking to you now as if you were my own children. Open your hearts wide to us! That will pay us back for what we have done for you.

14 Do not be joined together with those who do not belong to Christ. How can that which is good get along with that which is bad? How can light be in the same place with darkness? 15 How can Christ get along with the devil? How can one who has put his trust in Christ get along with one who has not put his trust in Christ? 16 How can the house of God get along with false gods? We are the house of the living God. God has said, "I will live in them and will walk among them. I will be their God and they will be My people." (Leviticus 26:12) 17 The Lord has said, "So come out from among them. Do not be joined to them. Touch nothing that is sinful. And I will receive you. 18 I will be a Father to you. You will be My sons and daughters, says the All-powerful God."

7 Since we have these great promises, dear friends, let us turn away from every sin of the body or of the spirit. Let us honor God with love and fear by giving ourselves to Him in every way.

His Love for the Corinthians

2 Receive us into your hearts. We have done no wrong to anyone. We have not led anyone in the wrong way. We have not used anyone for our good. 3 I do not say this to tell you that you are wrong. As I have said before, you have a place in our hearts and always will. If we live or die, we will be together. 4 I trust you and am proud of you. You give me much comfort and joy even when I suffer.

5 When we arrived in the country of Macedonia, we had no rest. We had all kinds of trouble. There was fighting all around us. Our hearts were afraid. 6 But God gives comfort to those whose hearts are heavy. He gave us comfort when Titus came. 7 Not only did his coming comfort us, but the comfort you had given him made me happy also. He told us how much you wanted to see us. He said that you were sad because of my trouble and that you wanted to help me. This made me happy.

8 I am not sorry now if my letter made you sad. I know it made you sad, but it was only for awhile. 9 I am happy now. It is not because you were hurt by my letter, but because it turned you from sin to God. God used it and you were not hurt by what we did. 10 The sorrow that God uses makes people sorry for their sin and leads them to turn from sin so they can be saved from the punishment of sin. We should be happy for that kind of sorrow, but the sorrow of this world brings death. 11 See how this sorrow God allowed you to have has worked in you. You had a desire to be free of that sin I wrote about. You were angry about it. You were afraid. You wanted to do something about it. In every way you did what you could to make it right. 12 I sent this. It was not written only because of the man who did the wrong or because of the one who suffered. 13 All this has given us comfort. More than this, we are happy for the joy Titus has. His spirit has been made stronger by all of you. 14 I told him how proud I was of you. You did not make me ashamed. What we said to Titus proved to be true. 15 He loves you all the more. He remembers how all of you were ready to obey him and how you respected him. 16 I am happy that I can have complete trust in you.

The Christian Way to Give

8 Christian brothers, we want you to know how the loving-favor of God has been shown in the churches in the country of Macedonia. 2 They have been put to the test by much trouble, but they have much joy. They have given much even though they were very poor. 3 They gave as much as they could because they wanted to. 4 They asked from their hearts if they could help the Christians in Jerusalem. 5 It was more than we expected. They gave themselves to the Lord first. Then they gave themselves to us to be used as the Lord wanted. 6 We asked Titus to keep on helping you finish this act of love. He was the one to begin this. 7 You are rich in everything. You have faith. You can preach. You have much learning. You have a strong desire to help. And you have love for us. Now do what you should about giving also. 8 I am not saying that you must do this, but I have told you how others have helped. This is a way to prove how true your love is. 9 You know of the loving-favor shown by our Lord Jesus Christ. He was rich, but He became poor for your good. In that way, because He became poor, you might become rich.

10 This is what I think. You had better finish what you started a year ago. You were

the first to want to give a gift of money.
[11] Now do it with the same strong desires you had when you started. [12] If a man is ready and willing to give, he should give of what he has, not of what he does not have. [13] This does not mean that others do not have to give and you have to give much. You should share alike. [14] You have more than you need now. When you have need, then they can help you. You should share alike. [15] The Holy Writings say, "The man who gathered much did not have too much. The man who did not gather much had enough." (Exodus 16:18)

Titus Will Be Coming

[16] I thank God that He gave Titus the same desire to help you. [17] He was glad when we asked him to help you. He decided himself to go to you. [18] We are sending the Christian brother along. He is respected in the churches for his preaching. [19] Not only that, but he has been asked by the churches to travel with me to Jerusalem. He will help in giving them the gift. The Lord will be honored by it because it shows how we want to help each other.

[20] We want everyone to trust us with the way we take this large gift of money to them. [21] We want to do the right thing. We want God and men to know we are honest. [22] We are sending another Christian brother with them. We have tested him many times. His faith has proven to be true. He wants very much to help because he trusts you. [23] Titus works with me to help you. The other two Christian brothers have been sent by the churches. Their lives honor Christ. [24] Show these men you love them and let the churches see your love. Show them the reason I am proud of you.

Giving to Help Other Christians

9 I do not need to write to you about helping those who belong to Christ. [2] I know you want to do it. I have told the people in the country of Macedonia that you were ready to send money last year. Your desire has started most of them to give. [3] I am sending these Christian brothers so the words I said about you will prove to be true and you will be ready to help. [4] What if some of the people of Macedonia came with me and found you were not ready to send your gift of money? We would all be ashamed since we have talked of you so much. [5] That is why I asked these men to go ahead of me. They can see that the gift

you promised is ready. In that way, it will be a true gift and not something you were made to do.

[6] Remember, the man who plants only a few seeds will not have much grain to gather. The man who plants many seeds will have much grain to gather. [7] Each man should give as he has decided in his heart. He should not give, wishing he could keep it. Or he should not give if he feels he has to give. God loves a man who gives because he wants to give. [8] God can give you all you need. He will give you more than enough. You will have everything you need for yourselves. And you will have enough left over to give when there is a need. [9] The Holy Writings say, "He has given much to the poor. His right-standing with God lasts forever." (Psalm 112:9) [10] It is God Who gives seed to the man to plant. He also gives the bread to eat. Then we know He will give you more seed to plant and make it grow so you will have more to give away. [11] God will give you enough so you can always give to others. Then many will give thanks to God for sending gifts through us. [12] This gift you give not only helps Christians who are in need, but it also helps them give thanks to God. [13] You are proving by this act of love what you are. They will give thanks to God for your gift to them and to others. This proves you obey the Good News of Christ. [14] They will pray for you with great love because God has given you His loving-favor. [15] Thank God for His great Gift.

Paul Proves He Is a Missionary

10 I, Paul, ask you this myself. I do it through Christ Who is so gentle and kind. Some people say that I am gentle and quiet when I am with you, but that I have no fear and that my language is strong when I am away from you. [2] Do not make me speak strong words to you when I come. Some people think we want the things of the world because of what we do and say. I have decided to talk to these people if I have to. [3] It is true, we live in a body of flesh. But we do not fight like people of the world. [4] We do not use those things to fight with that the world uses. We use the things God gives to fight with and they have power. Those things God gives to fight with destroy the strong-places of the devil. [5] We break down every thought and proud thing that puts itself up against the wisdom of God. We take hold of every thought and make it obey Christ. [6] We are ready to punish those who will not obey as soon as you obey in everything.

7 You are seeing things only as men see them. If anyone feels sure he belongs to Christ, he should remember that we belong to Christ also. 8 I am not ashamed if I say this of myself. The Lord gave me the right and the power to help you become stronger, not to break you down. 9 I do not want you to think I am trying to make you afraid with my letters. 10 They say, "His letters are strong and they make us think. When he is here with us, he is weak and he is hard to listen to." 11 What we say in our letters we will do when we get there. They should understand this. 12 We do not compare ourselves with those who think they are good. They compare themselves with themselves. They decide what they think is good or bad and compare themselves with those ideas. They are foolish. 13 But we will not talk with pride more than God allows us to. We will follow the plan of the work He has given us to do and you are a part of that work. 14 We did not go farther than we were supposed to go when we came to you. But we did come to you with the Good News of Christ. 15 We take no pride in the work others have done there. But we hope your faith will keep growing because of help from others. Then we will grow because of you. 16 We hope to preach the Good News in the countries on the other side of you. Then we would take no pride in work done by another person in another country. 17 If anyone wants to be proud, he should be proud of what the Lord has done. 18 It is not what a man thinks and says of himself that is important. It is what God thinks of him.

Paul—the True Missionary

11 I wish you would listen to a little foolish talk from me. Now listen. 2 I am jealous for you with a God-like jealousy. I have given you, as a woman who has never had a man, to one Husband, Who is Christ. 3 Eve was fooled by the snake in the garden of Eden. In the same way, I am afraid that you will be fooled and led away from your pure love for Christ. 4 You listen when someone comes and preaches a different Jesus than the One we preached. You believe what you hear about a different spirit and different good news than that which we preached.

5 I do not think I am less than those special missionaries who are coming to you. 6 Even if it is hard for me to speak, I know

what I am talking about. You know this by now. 7 Did I do wrong? I did not ask you for anything when I preached the Good News to you. I made myself poor so you would be made rich. 8 I did take money from other churches. I used it while I worked with you so you would not have to pay me. 9 Some of the time I had no money when I was with you. But I did not ask you for money. The Christians from the country of Macedonia brought me what I needed. I did not ask you and I will not ask you for anything. 10 As sure as the truth of Christ is in me, I will not stop telling those in the country of Greece that I am proud of this. 11 Does it mean I do not love you? God knows I do.

12 What I am doing now, I will keep on doing. I will do it to stop those who say they work as we do. 13 Those men are false missionaries. They lie about their work. But they make themselves look like true missionaries of Christ. 14 It is no surprise! The devil makes himself look like an angel of light. 15 And so it is no surprise if his servants also make themselves look like preachers of the Good News. They and their work will come to the same end.

What Paul Suffered as a Missionary

16 Let me say it again. Do not think of me as a fool. But if you do, then let this foolish man speak a little about himself. 17 The Lord has not told me to talk about myself. I am foolish when I do talk about myself like this. 18 Since the other men tell you all about themselves, I will talk about myself also. 19 You are so wise! You put up with fools! 20 You listen to anyone who tells you what to do or makes money off of you or sets a trap for you. You will listen to anyone who makes himself bigger than you or hits you in the face. 21 I am ashamed to say that I am weak! But I do not do as they do. Whatever they say about themselves, I can say about myself also. (I know what I am saying sounds foolish.)

22 Are they Jews? So am I. Are they from the family of Israel? So am I. Are they from the family of Abraham? So am I. 23 Do they work for Christ? I have worked for Him much more than they have. (I speak as if I am crazy.) I have done much more work. I have been in prison more times. I cannot remember how many times I have been whipped. Many times I have been in danger of death. 24 Five different times the Jews whipped me across my back thirty-nine times. 25 Three times they beat me

with sticks. One time they threw stones at me. Three times I was on ships that were wrecked. I spent a day and a night in the water. 26 I have made many hard trips. I have been in danger from high water on rivers. I have been in danger from robbers. I have been in danger from the Jews. I have been in danger from people who do not know God. I have been in danger in cities and in the desert. I have been in danger on the sea. I have been in danger among people who say they belong to Christ but do not. 27 I have worked hard and have been tired and have had pain. I have gone many times without sleep. I have been hungry and thirsty. I have gone without food and clothes. I have been out in the cold. 28 More than all these things that have happened to my body, the care of all the churches is heavy on me. 29 When someone is weak, I feel weak also. When someone is led into sin, I have a strong desire to help him. 30 If I must talk about myself, I will do it about the things that show how weak I am. 31 The God and Father of our Lord Jesus Christ is to be honored and thanked forever. He knows I am telling the truth. 32 In the city of Damascus the leader of the people under King Aretas put soldiers at the gates to take me. 33 But I was let down in a basket through a window in the wall and I got away.

Paul Sees Something True in a Special Dream

12 I have to talk about myself, even if it does no good. But I will keep on telling about some things I saw in a special dream and that which the Lord has shown me. 2 I know a man who belongs to Christ. Fourteen years ago he was taken up to the highest heaven. (I do not know if his body was taken up or just his spirit. Only God knows.) 3 I say it again, I know this man was taken up. But I do not know if his body or just his spirit was taken up. Only God knows. 4 When he was in the highest heaven, he heard things that cannot be told with words. No man is allowed to tell them. 5 I will be proud about this man, but I will not be proud about myself except to say things which show how weak I am. 6 Even if I talk about myself, I would not be a fool because it is the truth. But I will say no more because I want no one to think better of me than he does when he sees or hears me.

7 The things God showed me were so great. But to keep me from being too full of pride because of seeing these things, I have been given trouble in my body. It was sent from Satan to hurt me. It keeps me from being proud. 8 I asked the Lord three times to take it away from me. 9 He answered me, "I am all you need. I give you My loving-favor. My power works best in weak people." I am happy to be weak and have troubles so I can have Christ's power in me. 10 I receive joy when I am weak. I receive joy when people talk against me and make it hard for me and try to hurt me and make trouble for me. I receive joy when all these things come to me because of Christ. For when I am weak, then I am strong.

11 I have been making a fool of myself talking like this. But you made me do it. You should be telling what I have done. Even if I am nothing at all, I am not less important than those false missionaries of yours. 12 When I was with you, I proved to you that I was a true missionary. I did powerful works and there were special things to see. These things were done in the strength and power from God. 13 What makes you feel less important than the other churches? Is it because I did not let you give me food and clothing? Forgive me for this wrong!

14 This is the third time I am ready to come to you. I want nothing from you. I want you, not your money. You are my children. Children should not have to help care for their parents. Parents should help their children. 15 I am glad to give anything I have, even myself, to help you. When I love you more, it looks as if you love me less.

16 It is true that I was not a heavy load to you. But some say I set a trap for you. 17 How could I have done that? Did I get anything from you through the men I sent to you? 18 I asked Titus and the other Christian brother to visit you. Did Titus get anything from you? Did we not do things that showed we had the same desires and followed the same plan?

19 It may look to you as if we had been trying to make everything look right for ourselves all this time. God knows and so does Christ that all this is done to help you. 20 I am afraid that when I visit you I will not find you as I would like you to be. And you will not find me as you would like me to be. I am afraid I will find you fighting and jealous and angry and arguing and talking about each other and thinking of yourselves as being too important and making trouble. 21 I am afraid when I get

there God will take all the pride away from me that I had for you. I will not be happy about many who have lived in sin and done sex sins and have had a desire for such things and have not been sorry for their sins and turned from them.

13 This is my third visit to you. The Holy Writings tell us that when people think someone has done wrong, it must be proven by two or three people who saw the wrong being done. 2 During my second visit I talked to you who have been sinning and to all the others. While I am away, I tell you this again. The next time I come I will be hard on those who sin. 3 Since you want to know, I will prove to you that Christ speaks through me. Christ is not weak when He works in your hearts. He uses His power in you. 4 Christ's weak human body died on a cross. It is by God's power that Christ lives today. We are weak. We are as He was. But we will be alive with Christ through the power God has for us.

5 Put yourselves through a test. See if you belong to Christ. Then you will know you belong to Christ, unless you do not pass the test. 6 I trust you see that we belong to Him and have passed the test. 7 We pray to God that you do no wrong. We do not pray this to show that our teaching is so great, but that you will keep on doing what is right, even if it looks as if we have done much wrong. 8 We cannot work against the truth of God. We only work for it. 9 We are glad when we are weak and you are strong. We pray that you will become strong Christians. 10 This is why I am writing these things while I am away from you. Then when I get there, I will not have to use strong words or punish you to show you that the Lord gives me this power. This power is to be used to make you stronger Christians, not to make you weak by hurting your faith.

11 Last of all, Christian brothers, good-bye. Do that which makes you complete. Be comforted. Work to get along with others. Live in peace. The God of love and peace will be with you. 12 Greet each other with a kiss of holy love. 13 All those here who belong to Christ greet you. 14 May you have loving-favor from our Lord Jesus Christ. May you have the love of God. May you be joined together by the Holy Spirit.

GALATIANS

1 This letter is from Paul. I am a missionary sent by Jesus Christ and God the Father Who raised Jesus from the dead. I am not sent by men or by any one man. 2 All the Christians join me in writing to you who are in the churches in the country of Galatia. 3 May you have loving-favor and peace from God our Father and from the Lord Jesus Christ. 4 He gave Himself to die for our sins. He did this so we could be saved from this sinful world. This is what God wanted Him to do. 5 May He have all the honor forever. Let it be so.

Men Must Not Change the Good News

6 I am surprised you are leaving Christ so soon. You were chosen through His loving-favor. But now you are turning and listening to another kind of good news. 7 No! There is not another kind of good news. There are some who would like to lead you in the wrong way. They want to change the Good News about Christ. 8 Even if we or an angel from heaven should preach another kind of good news to you that is not the one we preached, let him be cursed. 9 As we said before, I will say it again. If any man is preaching another good news to you which is not the one you have received, let him be cursed.

This Good News Is from God

10 Do you think I am trying to get the favor of men, or of God? If I were still trying to please men, I would not be a servant owned by Christ.

11 Christian brothers, I want you to know the Good News I preached to you was not made by man. 12 I did not receive it from man. No one taught it to me. I received it from Jesus Christ as He showed it to me.

13 You have heard of my old life when I followed the Jewish religion. I made it as hard as I could for the Christians and did everything I could to destroy the Christian church. 14 I had learned more about the Jewish religion than many of the Jews my age. I had a much stronger desire than they to follow the ways of our early fathers. 15 But God chose me before I was born. By His loving-favor He called me to work for Him. 16 His Son was to be seen

in me. He did this so I could preach about Christ to the people who are not Jews. When this happened, I did not talk to men. [17] I did not even go to Jerusalem to talk to those who were missionaries before me. Instead, I went to the country of Arabia. Later I returned to the city of Damascus.

[18] Three years later I went to Jerusalem to meet Peter. I stayed with him fifteen days. [19] I did not see any of the other missionaries except James, the Lord's brother. [20] I am writing the truth. God knows I am not lying.

[21] I went from Jerusalem to the countries of Syria and Cilicia. [22] None of the Christians in the churches in the country of Judea had ever seen me. [23] The only thing they heard was, "The one who tried to destroy the Christian church is now preaching the Good News!" [24] And they gave thanks to God because of me.

The Church Leaders in Jerusalem Say Paul Is a True Missionary

2 Fourteen years later I went again to Jerusalem. This time I took Barnabas. Titus went with us also. [2] God showed me in a special way I should go. I spoke to them about the Good News that I preach among the people who are not Jews. First of all, I talked alone to the important church leaders. I wanted them to know what I was preaching. I did not want that which I was doing or would be doing to be wasted.

[3] Titus was with me. Even being a Greek, he did not have to go through the religious act of becoming a Jew. [4] Some men who called themselves Christians asked about this. They got in our meeting without being asked. They came there to find out how free we are who belong to Christ. They tried to get us to be chained to the Law. [5] But we did not listen to them or do what they wanted us to do so the truth of the Good News might be yours.

[6] Those who seemed to be important church leaders did not help me. They did not teach me anything new. What they were, I do not care. God looks on us all as being the same. [7] Anyway, they saw how I had been given the work of preaching the Good News to the people who are not Jews, as Peter had been given the work of preaching the Good News to the Jews. [8] For God helped Peter work with the Jews. He also helped me work with those who are not Jews. [9] James and Peter and John were thought of as being the head church leaders. They could see that God's

loving-favor had been given to me. Barnabas and I were joined together with them by shaking hands. Then we were sent off to work with the people who are not Jews. They were to work with the Jews. [10] They asked us to do only one thing. We were to remember to help poor people. I think this is important also.

[11] But when Peter came to Antioch, I had to stand up against him because he was guilty. [12] Peter had been eating with the people who are not Jews. But after some men came who had been with James, he kept away from them. He was afraid of those who believe in the religious act of becoming a Jew. [13] Then the rest of the Jews followed him because they were afraid to do what they knew they should do. Even Barnabas was fooled by those who pretended to be someone they were not. [14] When I saw they were not honest about the truth of the Good News, I spoke to Peter in front of them all. I said, "If you are a Jew, but live like the people who are not Jews, why do you make the people who are not Jews live like the Jews?" [15] You and I were born Jews. We were not sinners from among the people who are not Jews. [16] Even so, we know we cannot become right with God by obeying the Law. A man is made right with God by putting his trust in Jesus Christ. For that reason, we have put our trust in Jesus Christ also. We have been made right with God because of our faith in Christ and not by obeying the Law. No man can be made right with God by obeying the Law. [17] As we try to become right with God by what Christ has done for us, what if we find we are sinners also? Does that mean Christ makes us sinners? No! Never! [18] But if I work toward being made right with God by keeping the Law, then I make myself a sinner. [19] The Law has no power over me. I am dead to the Law. Now I can live for God. [20] I have been put up on the cross to die with Christ. I no longer live. Christ lives in me. The life I now live in this body, I live by putting my trust in the Son of God. He was the One Who loved me and gave Himself for me. [21] I say that we are not to put aside the loving-favor of God. If we could be made right with God by keeping the Law, then Christ died for nothing.

3 You foolish Galatians! What strange powers are trying to lead you from the way of faith in Christ? We made it plain for you to see that Jesus Christ was put on a cross to die. 2 There is one thing I want to know. Did you receive the Holy Spirit by keeping the Law? Or did you receive Him by hearing about Christ? 3 How foolish can you be? You started the Christian life by the Holy Spirit. Do you think you are going to become better Christians by your old way of worship? 4 You suffered so much because of the Good News you received. Was this all of no use? 5 He gave you the Holy Spirit and did powerful works among you. Does He do it because you do what the Law says or because you hear and believe the truth?

6 It was the same with Abraham. He put his trust in God. This made Abraham right with God. 7 Be sure to remember that all men who put their trust in God are the sons of Abraham. 8 The Holy Writings said long ago that God would save the people who are not Jews from the punishment of sin also. Before this time the Holy Writings gave the Good News to Abraham in these words, "All nations will be happy because of you." (Genesis 12:3) 9 So then, all those who have faith will be happy, along with Abraham who had faith.

10 All those who expect the Law to save them from the punishment of sin will be punished. Because it is written, "Everyone who does not keep on doing all the things written in the Book of the Law will be punished." (Deuteronomy 27:26) 11 No one is made right with God by doing what the Law says. For, "The man right with God will live by faith." (Habakkuk 2:4) 12 The Law does not use faith. It says, "You must obey all the Law or you will die." (Leviticus 18:5) 13 Christ bought us with His blood and made us free from the Law. In that way, the Law could not punish us. Christ did this by carrying the load and by being punished instead of us. It is written, "Anyone who hangs on a cross is hated and punished." (Deuteronomy 21:23) 14 Because of the price Christ Jesus paid, the good things that came to Abraham might come to the people who are not Jews. And by putting our trust in Christ, we receive the Holy Spirit He has promised.

15 Christian brothers, let me show you what this means. If two men agree to something and sign their names on a paper promising to stay true to what they agree, it cannot be changed. 16 Now the promise was made to Abraham and to his son. He does not say, "And to sons," speaking of many. But instead, "And to your Son," which means Christ. 17 This is what

I am saying: The Law which came 430 years later could not change the promise. The promise had already been made by God. The Law could not put that promise aside. 18 If it had been possible to be saved from the punishment of sin by obeying the Law, the promise God gave Abraham would be worth nothing. But since it is not possible to be saved by obeying the Law, the promise God gave Abraham is worth everything.

19 Then why do we have the Law? It was given because of sin. It was to be used until Christ came. The promise had been made looking toward Christ. The Law was given by angels through Moses who stood between God and man. 20 But when the promise was given to Abraham, God gave it without anyone standing between them. 21 Is the Law against the promise of God? No! Never! If it had been possible to be saved from the punishment of sin by obeying the Law, then being right with God would have come by obeying the Law. 22 But the Holy Writings say that all men are guilty of sin. Then that which was promised might be given to those who put their trust in Christ. It will be because their faith is in Him.

23 Before it was possible to be saved from the punishment of sin by putting our trust in Christ, we were held under the Law. It was as if we were being kept in prison. We were kept this way until Christ came. 24 The Law was used to lead us to Christ. It was our teacher, and so we were made right with God by putting our trust in Christ. 25 Now that our faith is in Christ, we do not need the Law to lead us. 26 You are now children of God because you have put your trust in Christ Jesus. 27 All of you who have been baptized to show you belong to Christ have become like Christ. 28 God does not see you as a Jew or as a Greek. He does not see you as a servant or as a person free to work. He does not see you as a man or as a woman. You are all one in Christ. 29 If you belong to Christ, then you have become the true children of Abraham. What God promised to him is now yours.

Sons of God

4 Let me say this another way. A young child who will get all the riches of his family is not different from a servant who is owned by the family. And yet the young child owns everything. 2 While he is young, he is cared for by men his father

trusts. These men tell the child what he can and cannot do. The child cannot do what he wants to do until he has become a certain age. 3 We were as children also held by the Law. We obeyed the Law in our religious worship. 4 But at the right time, God sent His Son. A woman gave birth to Him under the Law. 5 This all happened so He could buy with His blood and make free all those who were held by the Law. Then we might become the sons of God. 6 Because you are the sons of God, He has sent the Spirit of His Son into our hearts. The Spirit cries, "Father!" 7 So now you are no longer a servant who is owned by someone. You are a son. If you are a son, then you will receive what God has promised through Christ.

8 During the time when you did not know God, you worshiped false gods. 9 But now that you know God, or should I say that you are known by God, why do you turn back again to the weak old Law? Why do you want to do those religious acts of worship that will keep you from being free? Why do you want to be held under the power of the Law again? 10 You do special things on certain days and months and years and times of the year. 11 I am afraid my work with you was wasted.

Living by the Law or Being Free

12 I ask you, Christian brothers, stay free from the Law as I am. Even if I am a Jew, I became free from the Law, just as you who are not Jews. You did no wrong to me. 13 You know I preached the Good News to you the first time because of my sickness. 14 Even though I was hard to look at because of my sickness, you did not turn away from me. You took me in as an angel from God. You took me in as you would have taken in Christ Jesus Himself. 15 What has become of the happiness you once had? You would have taken out your own eyes if you could have and given them to me. 16 Do you hate me because I have told you the truth? 17 Those false teachers are trying to turn your eyes toward them. They do not want you to follow my teaching. What they are doing is not good. 18 It is good when people help you if they do not hope to get something from it. They should help you all the time, not only when I am with you. 19 My children, I am suffering birth pain for you again. I will suffer until Christ's life is in your life. 20 I wish I could be with you now. I wish I could speak to you in a more gentle voice, but I am troubled about you.

21 Listen! If you want to be under the Law, why do you not listen to what it says? 22 The Holy Writings say that Abraham had two sons. One was born from a woman servant (Hagar) who was owned by someone. She had to do what she was told. The other son was born from a woman (Sarah) who was free to work and live as she desired. (Genesis 16:15; 21:2–9) 23 The son born from the woman servant who was owned by someone was like any other birth. The son born from the free woman was different. That son had been promised by God. 24 Think of it like this: These two women show God's two ways of working with His people. The children born from Hagar are under the Law given on Mount Sinai. They will be servants who are owned by someone and will always be told what to do! 25 Hagar is known as Mount Sinai in the country of Arabia. She is as Jerusalem is today, because she and her children are not free to do what they want to do. 26 But the Jerusalem of heaven is the free woman, and she is our mother. 27 The Holy Writings say, "Woman, be happy, you who have had no children. Cry for joy, you who have never had the pains of having a child, for you will have many children. Yes, you will have more children than the one who has a husband." (Isaiah 54:1) 28 Christian brothers, we are like Isaac. We are the children God promised. 29 At that time the son born as other children are born made it hard for the son born by the Holy Spirit. It is the same way now. 30 But what do the Holy Writings say? They say, "Put the woman servant who is owned by someone and her son out of your home. The son of that woman servant will never get any of the riches of the family. It will all be given to the son of the free woman." (Genesis 21:10) 31 Christian brothers, we are not children of the woman servant who was owned by someone (Hagar). We are children of the free woman (Sarah).

Christ Made Us Free

5 Christ made us free. Stay that way. Do not get chained all over again in the Law and its kind of religious worship.

2 Listen to me! I, Paul, tell you that if you have the religious act of becoming a Jew done on you, Christ will be of no use to you at all. 3 I say it again. Every man who has the religious act of becoming a Jew done on him must obey every Law. 4 If you expect to be made right with God by obeying the Law, then you have turned away from

Christ and His loving-favor. 5 We are waiting for the hope of being made right with God. This will come through the Holy Spirit and by faith. 6 If we belong to Jesus Christ, it means nothing to have or not to have gone through the religious act of becoming a Jew. But faith working through love is important.

7 You were doing well. Who stopped you from obeying the truth? 8 Whatever he used did not come from the One Who chose you to have life. 9 It only takes a little yeast to make the whole loaf of bread rise. 10 I feel I can trust you because of what the Lord has done in your life. I believe you will not follow another way. Whoever is trying to lead you in the wrong way will suffer for it. 11 Christian brothers, if I would still preach that people must go through the religious act of becoming a Jew to be a Christian, I would not be suffering from those who are making it hard for me. If I preached like that, the Jews would have no reason to be against the cross of Christ. 12 I wish those who are so willing to cut your bodies would complete the job by cutting themselves off from you.

13 Christian brother, you were chosen to be free. Be careful that you do not please your old selves by sinning because you are free. Live this free life by loving and helping others. 14 You obey the whole Law when you do this one thing. "Love your neighbor as you love yourself." (Leviticus 19:18) 15 But if you hurt and make it hard for each other, watch out or you may be destroyed by each other.

16 I say this to you: Let the Holy Spirit lead you in each step. Then you will not please your sinful old selves. 17 The things our old selves want to do are against what the Holy Spirit wants. The Holy Spirit does not agree with what our sinful old selves want. These two are against each other. So you cannot do what you want to do. 18 If you let the Holy Spirit lead you, the Law no longer has power over you. 19 The things your sinful old self wants to do are: sex sins, sinful desires, wild living, 20 worshiping false gods, witchcraft, hating, fighting, being jealous, being angry, arguing, dividing into little groups and thinking the other groups are wrong, false teaching, 21 wanting something someone else has, killing other people, using strong drink, wild parties, and all things like these. I told you before and I am telling you again that those who do these things will have no place in the holy nation of God. 22 But the fruit that comes from having the Holy Spirit in our lives is: love, joy, peace, not giving up, being kind, being good, having faith, 23 being gentle, and being the boss over our own desires. The Law is not against these things. 24 Those of us who belong to Christ have nailed our sinful old selves on His cross. Our sinful desires are now dead.

25 If the Holy Spirit is living in us, let us be led by Him in all things. 26 Let us not become proud in ways in which we should not. We must not make hard feelings among ourselves as Christians or make anyone jealous.

Help Other Christians

6 Christian brothers, if a person is found doing some sin, you who are stronger Christians should lead that one back into the right way. Do not be proud as you do it. Watch yourself, because you may be tempted also. 2 Help each other in troubles and problems. This is the kind of law Christ asks us to obey. 3 If anyone thinks he is important when he is nothing, he is fooling himself. 4 Everyone should look at himself and see how he does his own work. Then he can be happy in what he has done. He should not compare himself with his neighbor. 5 Everyone must do his own work.

6 He who is taught God's Word should share the good things he has with his teacher. 7 Do not be fooled. You cannot fool God. A man will get back whatever he plants! 8 If a man does things to please his sinful old self, his soul will be lost. If a man does things to please the Holy Spirit, he will have life that lasts forever. 9 Do not let yourselves get tired of doing good. If we do not give up, we will get what is coming to us at the right time. 10 Because of this, we should do good to everyone. For sure, we should do good to those who belong to Christ.

The Christian's Pride Should Be in the Cross

11 See what big letters I make when I write to you with my own hand. 12 Those men who say you must go through the religious act of becoming a Jew are doing it because they want to make a good show in front of the world. They do this so they will not have to suffer because of following the way of the cross of Christ. 13 Those who have gone through the religious act of becoming a Jew do not

even keep the Law themselves. But they want you to go through that religious act so they can be proud that you are their followers. 14 I do not want to be proud of anything except in the cross of our Lord Jesus Christ. Because of the cross, the ways of this world are dead to me, and I am dead to them. 15 If a person does or does not go through the religious act of becoming a Jew, it is worth nothing. The important thing is to become a new person. 16 Those who follow this way will have God's peace and loving-kindness. They are the people of God.

17 Let no one make trouble for me from now on. For I have on my body the whip marks of one who has been a servant owned by Jesus. 18 Christian brothers, may the loving-favor of our Lord Jesus Christ be with your spirit. Let it be so.

EPHESIANS

1 This letter is from Paul. I am a missionary for Jesus Christ. God wanted me to work for Him. This letter is to those who belong to Christ in the city of Ephesus and to you who are faithful followers of Christ Jesus. 2 May you have loving-favor and peace from God our Father and from our Lord Jesus Christ.

3 Let us honor and thank the God and Father of our Lord Jesus Christ. He has already given us a taste of what heaven is like. 4 Even before the world was made, God chose us for Himself because of His love. He planned that we should be holy and without blame as He sees us. 5 God already planned to have us as His own children. This was done by Jesus Christ, In His plan God wanted this done.

6 We thank God for His loving-favor to us. He gave this loving-favor to us through His much-loved Son. 7 Because of the blood of Christ, we are bought and made free from the punishment of sin. And because of His blood, our sins are forgiven. His loving-favor to us is so rich. 8 He was so willing to give all of this to us. He did this with wisdom and understanding. 9 God told us the secret of what He wanted to do. It is this: In loving thought He planned long ago to send Christ into the world. 10 The plan was for Christ to gather us all together at the right time. If we are in heaven or still on earth, He will bring us together and will be head over all.

11 We were already chosen to be God's own children by Christ. This was done just like the plan He had. 12 We who were the first to put our trust in Christ should thank Him for His greatness. 13 The truth is the Good News. When you heard the truth, you put your trust in Christ. Then God marked you by giving you His Holy Spirit as a promise. 14 The Holy Spirit was given to us as a promise that we will receive everything God has for us. God's Spirit will be with us until God finishes His work of making us complete. God does this to show His shining-greatness.

Paul's Prayer for the Christians in Ephesus

15 I have heard of your faith in the Lord Jesus and your love for all Christians. 16 Since then, I always give thanks for you and pray for you. 17 I pray that the great God and Father of our Lord Jesus Christ may give you the wisdom of His Spirit. Then you will be able to understand the secrets about Him as you know Him better. 18 I pray that your hearts will be able to understand. I pray that you will know about the hope given by God's call. I pray that you will see how great the things are that He has promised to those who belong to Him. 19 I pray that you will know how great His power is for those who have put their trust in Him. 20 It is the same power that raised Christ from the dead. This same power put Christ at God's right side in heaven. 21 This place was given to Christ. It is much greater than any king or leader can have. No one else can have this place of honor and power. No one in this world or in the world to come can have such honor and power. 22 God has put all things under Christ's power and has made Him to be the head leader over all things of the church. 23 The church is the body of Christ. It is filled by Him Who fills all things everywhere with Himself.

God Saved Us from Sin

2 At one time you were dead because of your sins. 2 You followed the sinful ways of the world and obeyed the leader of the power of darkness. He is the devil who is now working in the people who do not obey God. 3 At one time all of us lived to please our old selves. We gave in to what our bodies and minds wanted. We were sinful from birth like all other people and would suffer from the anger of God.

4 But God had so much loving-kindness. He loved us with such a great love. **5** Even when we were dead because of our sins, He made us alive by what Christ did for us. You have been saved from the punishment of sin by His loving-favor. **6** God raised us up from death when He raised up Christ Jesus. He has given us a place with Christ in the heavens. **7** He did this to show us through all the time to come the great riches of His loving-favor. He has shown us His kindness through Christ Jesus.

8 For by His loving-favor you have been saved from the punishment of sin through faith. It is not by anything you have done. It is a gift of God. **9** It is not given to you because you worked for it. If you could work for it, you would be proud. **10** We are His work. He has made us to belong to Christ Jesus so we can work for Him. He planned that we should do this.

Followers Now Become the Body of Christ

11 Do not forget that at one time you did not know God. The Jews, who had gone through the religious act of becoming a Jew by man's hands, said you were people who do not know God. **12** You were living without Christ then. The Jewish people who belonged to God had nothing to do with you. The promises He gave to them were not for you. You had nothing in this world to hope for. You were without God.

13 But now you belong to Christ Jesus. At one time you were far away from God. Now you have been brought close to Him. Christ did this for you when He gave His blood on the cross. **14** We have peace because of Christ. He has made the Jews and those who are not Jews one people. He broke down the wall that divided them. **15** He stopped the fighting between them by His death on the cross. He put an end to the Law. Then He made of the two people one new kind of people like Himself. In this way, He made peace. **16** He brought both groups together to God. Christ finished the fighting between them by His death on the cross. **17** Then Christ came and preached the Good News of peace to you who were far away from God. And He preached it to us who were near God. **18** Now all of us can go to the Father through Christ by way of the one

Holy Spirit. **19** From now on you are not strangers and people who are not citizens. You are citizens together with those who belong to God. You belong in God's family. **20** This family is built on the teachings of the missionaries and the early preachers. Jesus Christ Himself is the cornerstone, which is the most important part of the building. **21** Christ keeps this building together and it is growing into a holy building for the Lord. **22** You are also being put together as a part of this building because God lives in you by His Spirit.

3 I, Paul, am in prison because I am a missionary for Jesus Christ to you who are not Jews. **2** I am sure you have heard that God trusted me with His loving-favor. **3** I wrote a little about this to you before. In a special way, God showed me His secret plan. **4** When you read this, you will understand how I know about the things that are not easy to understand about Christ. **5** Long ago men did not know these things. But now they have been shown to His missionaries and to the early preachers by the Holy Spirit. **6** Let me tell you that the Good News is for the people who are not Jews also. They are able to have life that lasts forever. They are to be a part of His church and family, together with the Jews. And together they are to receive all that God has promised through Christ.

7 God asked me to preach this Good News. He gave me the gift of His loving-favor. He gave me His power to preach it. **8** Of all those who belong to Christ, I am the least important. But this loving-favor was given to me to preach to the people who are not Jews. I was to tell them of the great riches in Christ which do not come to an end. **9** I was to make all men understand the meaning of this secret. God kept this secret to Himself from the beginning of the world. And He is the One Who made all things. **10** This was done so the great wisdom of God might be shown now to the leaders and powers in the heavenly places. It is being done through the church. **11** This was the plan God had for all time. He did this through Christ Jesus our Lord. **12** We can come to God without fear because we have put our trust in Christ. **13** So I ask you not to lose heart because of my suffering for you. It is to help you.

Paul's Prayer for the Church

14 For this reason, I bow my knees and pray to the Father. **15** It is from Him that every family in heaven and on earth has its name. 16 I pray that because of the riches of His shining-greatness, He will make you strong with power in your hearts through the Holy Spirit. 17 I pray that Christ may live in your hearts by faith. I pray that you will be filled with love. 18 I pray that you will be able to understand how wide and how long and how high and how deep His love is. 19 I pray that you will know the love of Christ. His love goes beyond anything we can understand. I pray that you will be filled with God Himself.

20 God is able to do much more than we ask or think through His power working in us. 21 May we see His shining-greatness in the church. May all people in all time honor Christ Jesus. Let it be so.

Full-Grown Christians

4 I am being held in prison because of working for the Lord. I ask you from my heart to live and work the way the Lord expected you to live and work. 2 Live and work without pride. Be gentle and kind. Do not be hard on others. Let love keep you from doing that. 3 Work hard to live together as one by the help of the Holy Spirit. Then there will be peace. 4 There is one body and one Spirit. There is one hope in which you were called. 5 There is one Lord and one faith and one baptism. 6 There is one God. He is the Father of us all. He is over us all. He is the One working through us all. He is the One living in us all.

7 Loving-favor has been given to each one of us. We can see how great it is by the gift of Christ. 8 The Holy Writings say, "When Christ went up to heaven, He took those who were held with Him. He gave gifts to men." (Psalm 68:18) 9 When they say, "He went up," what does it mean but that He had first gone down to the deep parts of the earth? 10 Christ Who went down into the deep also went up far above the heavens. He did this to fill all the world with Himself.

11 Christ gave gifts to men. He gave to some the gift to be missionaries, some to be preachers, others to be preachers who go from town to town. He gave others the gift to be church leaders and teachers. 12 These gifts help His people work well for Him. And then the church which is the body of Christ will be made strong. 13 All of us are to be as one in the faith and in knowing the Son of God. We are to be full-grown Christians standing as high and complete

as Christ is Himself. 14 Then we will not be as children any longer. Children are like boats thrown up and down on big waves. They are blown with the wind. False teaching is like the wind. False teachers try everything possible to make people believe a lie, 15 but we are to hold to the truth with love in our hearts. We are to grow up and be more like Christ. He is the leader of the church. 16 Christ has put each part of the church in its right place. Each part helps other parts. This is what is needed to keep the whole body together. In this way, the whole body grows strong in love.

The Old and the New Life

17 I tell you this in the name of the Lord. You must not live any longer like the people of the world who do not know God. Their thoughts are foolish. 18 Their minds are in darkness. They are strangers to the life of God. This is because they have closed their minds to Him and have turned their hearts away from Him. 19 They do not care anymore about what is right or wrong. They have turned themselves over to the sinful ways of the world and are always wanting to do every kind of sinful act they can think of.

20 But you did not learn anything like this from Christ. 21 If you have heard of Him and have learned from Him, 22 put away the old person you used to be. Have nothing to do with your old sinful life. It was sinful because of being fooled into following bad desires. 23 Let your minds and hearts be made new. 24 You must become a new person and be God-like. Then you will be made right with God and have a true holy life.

25 So stop lying to each other. Tell the truth to your neighbor. We all belong to the same body. 26 If you are angry, do not let it become sin. Get over your anger before the day is finished. 27 Do not let the devil start working in your life. 28 Anyone who steals must stop it! He must work with his hands so he will have what he needs and can give to those who need help. 29 Watch your talk! No bad words should be coming from your mouth. Say what is good. Your words should help others grow as Christians. 30 Do not make God's Holy Spirit have sorrow for the way you live. The Holy Spirit has put a mark on you for the day you will be set free. 31 Put out of your life all these things: bad feelings about other people, anger, temper, loud talk, bad talk which hurts other people, and bad

feelings which hurt other people. 32 You must be kind to each other. Think of the other person. Forgive other people just as God forgave you because of Christ's death on the cross.

5 Do as God would do. Much-loved children want to do as their fathers do. 2 Live with love as Christ loved you. He gave Himself for us, a gift on the altar to God which was as a sweet smell to God.

3 Do not let sex sins or anything sinful be even talked about among those who belong to Christ. Do not always want everything. 4 Do not be guilty of telling bad stories and of foolish talk. These things are not for you to do. Instead, you are to give thanks for what God has done for you. 5 Be sure of this! No person who does sex sins or who is not pure will have any part in the holy nation of Christ and of God. The same is true for the person who always wants what other people have. This becomes a god to him. 6 Do not let anyone lead you in the wrong way with foolish talk. The anger of God comes on such people because they choose to not obey Him. 7 Have nothing to do with them. 8 At one time you lived in darkness. Now you are living in the light that comes from the Lord. Live as children who have the light of the Lord in them. 9 This light gives us truth. It makes us right with God and makes us good. 10 Learn how to please the Lord. 11 Have nothing to do with the bad things done in darkness. Instead, show that these things are wrong. 12 It is a shame even to talk about these things done in secret. 13 All things can be seen when they are in the light. Everything that can be seen is in the light. 14 The Holy Writings say, "Wake up, you who are sleeping. Rise from the dead and Christ will give you light." (Isaiah 60:1)

Be Filled with the Spirit of God

15 So be careful how you live. Live as men who are wise and not foolish. 16 Make the best use of your time. These are sinful days. 17 Do not be foolish. Understand what the Lord wants you to do. 18 Do not get drunk with wine. That leads to wild living. Instead, be filled with the Holy Spirit. 19 Tell of your joy to each other by singing the Songs of David and church songs. Sing in your heart to the Lord. 20 Always give thanks for all things to God the Father in the name of our Lord Jesus Christ.

How Wives Must Live

21 Be willing to help and care for each other because of Christ. By doing this, you honor Christ. 22 Wives, obey your own husbands. In doing this, you obey the Lord. 23 For a husband is the head of his wife as Christ is the head of the church. It is His body (the church) that He saves. 24 As the church is to obey Christ, wives are to obey their own husbands in everything.

How Husbands Must Live

25 Husbands, love your wives. You must love them as Christ loved the church. He gave His life for it. 26 Christ did this so He could set the church apart for Himself. He made it clean by the washing of water with the Word. 27 Christ did this so the church might stand before Him in shining-greatness. There is to be no sin of any kind in it. It is to be holy and without blame. 28 So men should love their wives as they love their own bodies. He who loves his wife loves himself. 29 No man hates himself. He takes care of his own body. That is the way Christ does. He cares for His body which is the church. 30 We are all a part of His body, the church. 31 For this reason, a man must leave his father and mother when he gets married and be joined to his wife. The two become one. 32 This is hard to understand, but it shows that the church is the body of Christ. 33 So every man must love his wife as he loves himself. Every wife must respect her husband.

How Children Must Live

6 Children, as Christians, obey your parents. This is the right thing to do. 2 Respect your father and mother. This is the first Law given that had a promise. 3 The promise is this: If you respect your father and mother, you will live a long time and your life will be full of many good things.

4 Fathers, do not be too hard on your children so they will become angry. Teach them in their growing years with Christian teaching.

5 You servants who are owned by someone must obey your owners. Work for them as hard as you can. Work for them the same as if you were working for Christ. 6 Do not work hard only when your owner sees you. You would be doing this just to please men. Work as you would work for Christ. Do what God wants you to do with all your heart. 7 Be happy as you work. Do your work as for the Lord, not for men. 8 Remember this, whatever good thing

you do, the Lord will pay you for it. It is the same to the Lord if you are a servant owned by someone or if you work for pay.

9 Owners, do the right thing for those who work for you. Stop saying that you are going to be hard on them. Remember that your Owner and their Owner is in heaven. God does not respect one person more than another.

Things God Gives the Christian to Fight With

10 This is the last thing I want to say: Be strong with the Lord's strength. 11 Put on the things God gives you to fight with. Then you will not fall into the traps of the devil. 12 Our fight is not with people. It is against the leaders and the powers and the spirits of darkness in this world. It is against the demon world that works in the heavens. 13 Because of this, put on all the things God gives you to fight with. Then you will be able to stand in that sinful day. When it is all over, you will still be standing. 14 So stand up and do not be moved. Wear a belt of truth around your body. Wear a piece of iron over your chest which is being right with God. 15 Wear shoes on your feet which are the Good News of peace. 16 Most important of all, you need a covering of faith in front of you. This is to put out the fire-arrows of the devil. 17 The covering for your head is that you have been saved from the punishment of sin. Take the sword of the Spirit which is the Word of God.

How and What to Pray For

18 You must pray at all times as the Holy Spirit leads you to pray. Pray for the things that are needed. You must watch and keep on praying. Remember to pray for all Christians. 19 Pray for me also. Pray that I might open my mouth without fear. Pray that I will use the right words to preach that which is hard to understand in the Good News. 20 This is the reason I was sent out. But now I am in chains for preaching the Good News. I want to keep on speaking for Christ without fear the way I should.

21 Tychicus will tell you how I am getting along. He is a much-loved brother and a faithful preacher. 22 I have sent him to you because I want him to tell you about us. He will comfort you. 23 May all the Christian brothers have peace and love with faith from God the Father and the Lord Jesus Christ. 24 May God give loving-favor to all who love our Lord Jesus Christ with a love that never gets weak.

PHILIPPIANS

1 This letter is from Paul and Timothy. We are servants owned by Jesus Christ. This letter is to all who belong to Christ Jesus who are living in the city of Philippi and to the church leaders and their helpers also. 2 May you have loving-favor and peace from God our Father and the Lord Jesus Christ.

Paul Gives Thanks for the True Christians

3 I thank God for you whenever I think of you. 4 I always have joy as I pray for all of you. 5 It is because you have told others the Good News from the first day you heard it until now. 6 I am sure that God Who began the good work in you will keep on working in you until the day Jesus Christ comes again. 7 It is right for me to feel like this about all of you. It is because you are very dear to me. While I was in prison and when I was proving that the Good News is true, you all shared God's loving-favor with me. 8 God knows what I am saying. He knows how much I love you all with a love that comes from Christ Jesus. 9 And this is my prayer: I pray that your love will grow more and more. I pray that you will have better understanding and be wise in all things. 10 I pray that you will know what is the very best. I pray that you will be true and without blame until the day Christ comes again. 11 And I pray that you will be filled with the fruits of right living. These come from Jesus Christ, with honor and thanks to God.

Paul's Being in Prison Has Turned Out to Be a Good Thing

12 Christian brothers, I want you to know that what has happened to me has helped spread the Good News. 13 Everyone around here knows why I am in prison. It is because I preached about Jesus Christ. All the soldiers who work for the leader of the country know why I am here.

14 Because of this, most of my Christian brothers have had their faith in the Lord made stronger. They have more power to preach the Word of God without fear.

15 Some are preaching because they are jealous and want to make trouble. Others are doing it for the right reason. 16 These do it because of love. They know that I am put here to prove the Good News is true. 17 The others preach about Christ for what they get out of it. Their hearts are not right. They want to make me suffer while I am in prison. 18 What difference does it make if they pretend or if they are true? I am happy, yes, and I will keep on being happy that Christ is preached.

19 Because of your prayers and the help the Holy Spirit gives me, all of this will turn out for good. 20 I hope very much that I will have no reason to be ashamed. I hope to honor Christ with my body if it be by my life or by my death. I want to honor Him without fear, now and always. 21 To me, living means having Christ. To die means that I would have more of Him. 22 If I keep on living here in this body, it means that I can lead more people to Christ. I do not know which is better. 23 There is a strong pull from both sides. I have a desire to leave this world to be with Christ, which is much better. 24 But it is more important for you that I stay. 25 I am sure I will live to help you grow and be happy in your faith. 26 This will give you reason to give more thanks to Christ Jesus when I come to visit you again.

Fight for the Faith

27 Live your lives as the Good News of Christ says you should. If I come to you or not, I want to hear that you are standing true as one. I want to hear that you are working together as one, preaching the Good News. 28 Do not be afraid of those who hate you. Their hate for you proves they will be destroyed. It proves you have life from God that lasts forever. 29 You are not only to put your trust in Him, but you are to suffer for Him also. 30 You know what the fight is like. Now it is time for you to have a part in it as I have.

A Christian Should Not Be Proud

2 Are you strong because you belong to Christ? Does His love comfort you? Do you have joy by being as one in sharing the Holy Spirit? Do you have loving-kindness and pity for each other? 2 Then give me true joy by thinking the same thoughts.

Keep having the same love. Be as one in thoughts and actions. 3 Nothing should be done because of pride or thinking about yourself. Think of other people as more important than yourself. 4 Do not always be thinking about your own plans only. Be happy to know what other people are doing.

Christ Was Not Proud

5 Think as Christ Jesus thought. 6 Jesus has always been as God is. But He did not hold to His rights as God. 7 He put aside everything that belonged to Him and made Himself the same as a servant who is owned by someone. He became human by being born as a man. 8 After He became a man, He gave up His important place and obeyed by dying on a cross. 9 Because of this, God lifted Jesus high above everything else. He gave Him a name that is greater than any other name. 10 So when the name of Jesus is spoken, everyone in heaven and on earth and under the earth will bow down before Him. 11 And every tongue will say Jesus Christ is Lord. Everyone will give honor to God the Father.

12 My Christian friends, you have obeyed me when I was with you. You have obeyed even more when I have been away. You must keep on working to show you have been saved from the punishment of sin. Be afraid that you may not please God. 13 He is working in you. God is helping you obey Him. God is doing what He wants done in you. 14 Be glad you can do the things you should be doing. Do all things without arguing and talking about how you wish you did not have to do them. 15 In that way, you can prove yourselves to be without blame. You are God's children and no one can talk against you, even in a sin-loving and sin-sick world. You are to shine as lights among the sinful people of this world. 16 Take a strong hold on the Word of Life. Then when Christ comes again, I will be happy that I did not work with you for nothing. 17 Even if I give my life as a gift on the altar to God for you, I am glad and share this joy with you. 18 You must be happy and share your joy with me also.

Timothy Is Being Sent to You

19 I hope by the help of the Lord Jesus that I can send Timothy to you soon. It will comfort me when he brings news about you. 20 I have no one else who is as interested in you as Timothy. 21 Everyone else thinks of himself instead of Jesus

Christ. 22 You know how Timothy proved to be such a true friend to me when we preached the Good News. He was like a son helping his father. 23 I hope to send Timothy as soon as I know what they are going to do to me. 24 I hope by the help of the Lord that I can come soon also.

25 I thought it was right that I send Epaphroditus back to you. You helped me by sending him to me. We have worked together like brothers. He was like a soldier fighting beside me. 26 He has been wanting to see all of you and was troubled because you heard he was sick. 27 It is true, he was sick. Yes, he almost died, but God showed loving-kindness to him and to me. If he had died, I would have had even more sorrow. 28 This is all the more reason I have sent him to you. When you see him, you will be glad and I will have less sorrow. 29 Take him into your church with joy. Show respect for men like him. 30 He came close to death while working for Christ. He almost died doing things for me that you could not do.

It Is Christ Only—Not the Things You Do

3 So now, my Christian brothers, be happy because you belong to Christ. It is not hard for me to write the same things to you. It is good for you. 2 Watch out for false teachers. Watch out for sinful men. They want you to depend on the religious act of becoming a Jew for your hope. 3 The act of becoming a Jew has nothing to do with us becoming Christians. We worship God through His Spirit and are proud of Jesus Christ. We have no faith in what we ourselves can do. 4 I could have reason to trust in the flesh. If anyone could feel that the flesh could do something for him, I could. 5 I went through the religious act of becoming a Jew when I was eight days old. I was born a Jew and came from the family group of Benjamin. I was a Jewish son of Jewish parents. I belonged to the group of the proud religious law-keepers. 6 I followed my religion with all my heart and did everything I could to make it hard for the church. No one could say anything against the way I obeyed the Law.

Christ Must Be Lord of Our Lives

7 But I gave up those things that were so important to me for Christ. 8 Even more than that, I think of everything as worth nothing. It is so much better to know Christ Jesus my Lord. I have lost everything for

Him. And I think of these things as worth nothing so that I can have Christ. 9 I want to be as one with Him. I could not be right with God by what the Law said I must do. I was made right with God by faith in Christ. 10 I want to know Him. I want to have the same power in my life that raised Jesus from the dead. I want to understand and have a share in His sufferings and be like Christ in His death. 11 Then I may be raised up from among the dead.

12 I do not say that I have received this or have already become perfect. But I keep going on to make that life my own as Christ Jesus made me His own. 13 No, Christian brothers, I do not have that life yet. But I do one thing. I forget everything that is behind me and look forward to that which is ahead of me. 14 My eyes are on the crown. I want to win the race and get the crown of God's call from heaven through Christ Jesus. 15 All of us who are full-grown Christians should think this way. If you do not think this way, God will show it to you. 16 So let us keep on obeying the same truth we have already been following.

17 Christian brothers, live your lives as I have lived mine. Watch those who live as I have taught you to live. 18 There are many whose lives show they hate the cross of Christ. I have told you this before. Now I tell you again with tears in my eyes. 19 Their god is their stomach. They take pride in things they should be ashamed of. All they think about are the things of this world. In the end they will be destroyed. 20 But we are citizens of heaven. Christ, the One Who saves from the punishment of sin, will be coming down from heaven again. We are waiting for Him to return. 21 He will change these bodies of ours of the earth and make them new. He will make them like His body of shining-greatness. He has the power to do this because He can make all things obey Him.

4 So, my dear Christian brothers, you are my joy and crown. I want to see you. Keep on staying true to the Lord, my dear friends.

2 I ask Euodias and Syntyche to agree as Christians should. 3 My true helper, I ask you to help these women who have worked with me so much in preaching the Good News to others. Clement helped also. There are others who worked with me. Their names are in the book of life.

4 Be full of joy always because you belong to the Lord. Again I say, be full of joy!

5 Let all people see how gentle you are. The Lord is coming again soon. 6 Do not worry. Learn to pray about everything. Give thanks to God as you ask Him for what you need. 7 The peace of God is much greater than the human mind can understand. This peace will keep your hearts and minds through Christ Jesus.

8 Christian brothers, keep your minds thinking about whatever is true, whatever is respected, whatever is right, whatever is pure, whatever can be loved, and whatever is well thought of. If there is anything good and worth giving thanks for, think about these things. 9 Keep on doing all the things you learned and received and heard from me. Do the things you saw me do. Then the God Who gives peace will be with you.

10 The Lord gives me a reason to be full of joy. It is because you are able to care for me again. I know you wanted to before but you did not have a way to help me. 11 I am not saying I need anything. I have learned to be happy with whatever I have. 12 I know how to get along with little and how to live when I have much. I have learned the secret of being happy at all times. If I am full of food and have all I need, I am happy. If I am hungry and need more, I am happy. 13 I can do all things because Christ gives me the strength.

14 It was kind of you to help me when I was in trouble. 15 You Philippians also know that when I first preached the Good News, you were the only church that helped me. It was when I left for the country of Macedonia. 16 Even while I was in the city of Thessalonica you helped me more than once. 17 It is not that I want to receive the gift. I want you to get the pay that is coming to you later. 18 I have everything I need and more than enough. I am taken care of because Epaphroditus brought your gift. It is a sweet gift. It is a gift that cost you something. It is the kind of gift God is so pleased with. 19 And my God will give you everything you need because of His great riches in Christ Jesus. 20 Now may our God and Father be honored forever. Let it be so.

21 Greet all those who belong to Christ Jesus. The Christian brothers here with me greet you. 22 All those who belong to Christ greet you and most of all, those who live in Caesar's house. 23 May your spirit have the loving-favor of the Lord Jesus Christ.

COLOSSIANS

Paul Gives Thanks for the Christians in Colossae

1 This letter is from Paul, a missionary for Jesus Christ. God wanted me to work for Him. This letter is from brother Timothy also. 2 I am writing to you who belong to Christ in the city of Colossae. May all the Christian brothers there have loving-favor and peace from God our Father.

3 We always pray and give thanks to God for you. He is the Father of our Lord Jesus Christ. 4 We give thanks to God for you because we heard of your faith in Christ Jesus. We thank God for your love for all those who belong to Christ. 5 We thank God for the hope that is being kept for you in heaven. You first heard about this hope through the Good News which is the Word of Truth. 6 The Good News came to you the same as it is now going out to all the world. Lives are being changed, just as your life was changed the day you heard the Good News. You understood the truth about God's loving-kindness. 7 You heard the Good News through our much-loved brother Epaphras who is taking my place.

He is a faithful servant of Christ. 8 He told us that the Holy Spirit had given you much love.

9 This is why I have never stopped praying for you since I heard about you. I ask God that you may know what He wants you to do. I ask God to fill you with the wisdom and understanding the Holy Spirit gives. 10 Then your lives will please the Lord. You will do every kind of good work, and you will know more about God. 11 I pray that God's great power will make you strong, and that you will have joy as you wait and do not give up. 12 I pray that you will be giving thanks to the Father. He has made it so you could share the good things given to those who belong to Christ who are in the light. 13 God took us out of a life of darkness. He has put us in the holy nation of His much-loved Son. 14 We have been bought by His blood and made free. Our sins are forgiven through Him.

15 Christ is as God is. God cannot be seen. Christ lived before anything was made. 16 Christ made everything in the heavens and on the earth. He made everything that

is seen and things that are not seen. He made all the powers of heaven. Everything was made by Him and for Him. 17 Christ was before all things. All things are held together by Him. 18 Christ is the head of the church which is His body. He is the beginning of all things. He is the first to be raised from the dead. He is to have first place in everything. 19 God the Father was pleased to have everything made perfect by Christ, His Son. 20 Everything in heaven and on earth can come to God because of Christ's death on the cross. Christ's blood has made peace. 21 At one time you were strangers to God and your minds were at war with Him. Your thoughts and actions were wrong. 22 But Christ has brought you back to God by His death on the cross. In this way, Christ can bring you to God, holy and pure and without blame. 23 This is for you if you keep the faith. You must not change from what you believe now. You must not leave the hope of the Good News you received. The Good News was preached to you and to all the world. And I, Paul, am one of Christ's missionaries.

Paul Is Sent by God to Preach

24 Now I am full of joy to be suffering for you. In my own body I am doing my share of what has to be done to make Christ's sufferings complete. This is for His body which is the Church. 25 I became a preacher in His church for your good. In the plan of God I am to preach the Good News. 26 This great secret was hidden to the people of times past, but it is now made known to those who belong to Christ. 27 God wants these great riches of the hidden truth to be made known to the people who are not Jews. The secret is this: Christ in you brings hope of all the great things to come. 28 We preach Christ. We tell every man how he must live. We use wisdom in teaching every man. We do this so every man will be complete in Christ. 29 This is the reason I am working. God's great power is working in me.

The Christian Is Complete in Christ

2 I want you to know how hard I have worked for you and for the Christians in the city of Laodicea and for those who have never seen me. 2 May their hearts be given comfort. May they be brought close together in Christian love. May they be rich in understanding and know God's secret. It is Christ Himself. 3 In Christ are hidden all the riches of wisdom and understanding. 4 I tell you this so no one will

try to change your mind with big sounding talk. 5 Even if I am far away from you in body, I am with you in spirit. I am happy to learn how well you are getting along. It is good to hear that your faith is so strong in Christ. 6 As you have put your trust in Christ Jesus the Lord to save you from the punishment of sin, now let Him lead you in every step. 7 Have your roots planted deep in Christ. Grow in Him. Get your strength from Him. Let Him make you strong in the faith as you have been taught. Your life should be full of thanks to Him.

Wisdom of the World Is Empty

8 Be careful that no one changes your mind and faith by much learning and big sounding ideas. Those things are what men dream up. They are always trying to make new religions. These leave out Christ. 9 For Christ is not only God-like, He is God in human flesh. 10 When you have Christ, you are complete. He is the head over all leaders and powers. 11 When you became a Christian, you were set free from the sinful things of the world. This was not done by human hands. You were set free from the sins of your old self by what was done in Christ's body. 12 When you were baptized, you were buried as Christ was buried. When you were raised up in baptism, you were raised as Christ was raised. You were raised to a new life by putting your trust in God. It was God Who raised Jesus from the dead. 13 When you were dead in your sins, you were not set free from the sinful things of the world. But God forgave your sins and gave you new life through Christ. 14 We had broken the Law many ways. Those sins were held against us by the Law. That Law had writings which said we were sinners. But now He has destroyed that writing by nailing it to the cross. 15 God took away the power of the leaders of this world and the powers of darkness. He showed them to the world. The battle was won over them through Christ.

Watch for Those Who Want to Keep the Law

16 Do not let anyone tell you what you should or should not eat or drink. They have no right to say if it is right or wrong to eat certain foods or if you are to go to religious suppers. They have no right to say what you are to do at the time of the new moon or on the Day of Rest. 17 These things are a picture of what is coming. The

important thing is Christ Himself. 18 Do not let anyone rob you of your crown. They will try to get you to bow down in worship of angels. They think this shows you are not proud. They say they were told to do this in a dream. These people are proud because of their sinful minds. 19 Such people are not a part of Christ. Christ is the Head. We Christians make up His body. We are joined together as a body is held together. Our strength to grow comes from Christ.

20 You have died with Christ and become dead to those old ways. Then why do you follow the old ways of worship? Why do you obey man-made rules? 21 These rules say, "You must not put your hand on this." "Do not put this into your mouth." "You must not put your finger on that." 22 All these things come to an end when they are used. You are following only man-made rules. 23 It looks as if it is wise to follow these rules in an act of worship, because they are hard on the body. It looks as if they are done without pride, but they are worth nothing. They do not take away a man's desire to sin.

The New Life Lived by the Power of Christ

3 If then you have been raised with Christ, keep looking for the good things of heaven. This is where Christ is seated on the right side of God. 2 Keep your minds thinking about things in heaven. Do not think about things on the earth. 3 You are dead to the things of this world. Your new life is now hidden in God through Christ. 4 Christ is our life. When He comes again, you will also be with Him to share His shining-greatness.

The Old Person Put Aside

5 Destroy the desires to sin that are in you. These desires are: sex sins, anything that is not clean, a desire for sex sins, and wanting something someone else has. This is worshiping a god. 6 It is because of these sins that the anger of God comes down on those who do not obey Him. 7 You used to do these sins when you lived that kind of life. 8 Put out of your life these things also: anger, bad temper, bad feelings toward others, talk that hurts people, speaking against God, and dirty talk. 9 Do not lie to each other. You have put out of your life your old ways. 10 You have now become a new person and are always learning more about Christ. You are being

made more like Christ. He is the One Who made you. 11 There is no difference in men in this new life. Greeks and Jews are the same. The man who has gone through the religious act of becoming a Jew and the one who has not are the same. There is no difference between nations. Men who are servants and those who are free are the same. Christ is everything. He is in all of us.

12 God has chosen you. You are holy and loved by Him. Because of this, your new life should be full of loving-pity. You should be kind to others and have no pride. Be gentle and be willing to wait for others. 13 Try to understand other people. Forgive each other. If you have something against someone, forgive him. That is the way the Lord forgave you. 14 And to all these things, you must add love. Love holds everything and everybody together and makes all these good things perfect. 15 Let the peace of Christ have power over your hearts. You were chosen as a part of His body. Always be thankful.

16 Let the teaching of Christ and His words keep on living in you. These make your lives rich and full of wisdom. Keep on teaching and helping each other. Sing the Songs of David and the church songs and the songs of heaven with hearts full of thanks to God. 17 Whatever you say or do, do it in the name of the Lord Jesus. Give thanks to God the Father through the Lord Jesus.

How Families Should Live

18 Wives, obey your husbands. This is what the Lord wants you to do. 19 Husbands, love your wives. Do not hold hard feelings against them. 20 Children, obey your parents in everything. The Lord is pleased when you do. 21 Fathers, do not be so hard on your children that they will give up trying to do what is right.

22 You who are servants who are owned by someone, obey your owners. Work hard for them all the time, not just when they are watching you. Work for them as you would for the Lord because you honor God. 23 Whatever work you do, do it with all your heart. Do it for the Lord and not for men. 24 Remember that you will get your reward from the Lord. He will give you what you should receive. You are working for the Lord Christ. 25 If anyone does wrong, he will suffer for it. God does not respect one person more than another.

4 Owners, give your servants what is right. Do the same for all. Remember that your Owner is in heaven.

Some Things to Do

2 You must keep praying. Keep watching! Be thankful always. 3 As you pray, be sure to pray for us also. Pray that God will open the door for us to preach the Word. We want to tell the secret of Christ. And this is the reason I am in prison. 4 Pray that I will be able to preach so everyone can understand. This is the way I should speak. 5 Be wise in the way you live around those who are not Christians. Make good use of your time. 6 Speak with them in such a way they will want to listen to you. Do not let your talk sound foolish. Know how to give the right answer to anyone.

7 Tychicus will tell you how I am getting along. He is a much-loved brother and faithful helper. Both of us are owned by the Lord. 8 This is the reason I have sent him to you. It is so you can know about us. He can also bring joy to your hearts. 9 Onesimus is going with Tychicus. He is one of your own people. He is faithful and we love him very much. They will tell you about everything here.

10 One of the men here in prison with me is Aristarchus. He greets you. Mark, the cousin of Barnabas, greets you. (You have heard before that if he comes to you, you are to receive him and make him happy.) 11 Jesus Justus greets you also. These are the only Jewish workers helping me teach about the holy nation of God. What a help they have been to me!

12 Epaphras greets you. He is one of your people and a servant of Jesus Christ. As he prays for you, he asks God to help you to be strong and to make you perfect. He prays that you will know what God wants you to do in all things. 13 I can tell you for sure that he works hard for you and for the Christians in the cities of Laodicea and Hierapolis. 14 Luke, the dear doctor, and Demas greet you. 15 Greet all the Christians in Laodicea. Greet Nympha and the Christians who gather for church in her house.

16 When this letter has been read to you, have it read in the church in Laodicea also. Be sure you read the letter that is coming from Laodicea. 17 Tell Archippus to be sure to finish the work the Lord called him to do.

18 I, Paul, am writing this last part with my own hand. Do not forget that I am in prison. May you have God's loving-favor.

1 THESSALONIANS

Paul Gives Thanks for Their Faith

1 This letter is from Paul and Silas and Timothy. It is to you, the church, in the city of Thessalonica. You belong to God the Father and the Lord Jesus Christ. May you have His loving-favor and His peace.

2 We thank God for you all the time and pray for you. 3 While praying to God our Father, we always remember your work of faith and your acts of love and your hope that never gives up in our Lord Jesus Christ. 4 Christian brothers, we know God loves you and that He has chosen you. 5 The Good News did not come to you by word only, but with power and through the Holy Spirit. You knew it was true. You also knew how we lived among you. It was for your good. 6 You followed our way of life and the life of the Lord. You suffered from others because of listening to us. But you had the joy that came from the Holy Spirit. 7 Because of your good lives, you are showing all the Christians in the countries of Macedonia and Greece how to live. 8 The Word of the Lord has been spoken by you in the countries of Macedonia and Greece. People everywhere know of your faith in God without our telling them. 9 The people themselves tell us how you received us when we came to you. They talk of how you turned to God from worshiping false gods. Now you worship the true and living God. 10 They tell us how you are waiting for His Son Jesus to come down from heaven. God raised Him from the dead. It is Jesus Who will save us from the anger of God that is coming.

2 Christian brothers, you know that my visit with you was not wasted. 2 Just before we came to you, we had been in the city of Philippi. You know how they worked against us and made us suffer. But God helped us preach the Good News to you without fear, even while many people hated us and made it hard for us.

3 You remember what we said to you was true. We had no wrong desire in teaching you. We did not try to fool you. 4 God has allowed us to be trusted with the Good News. Because of this, we preach it to please God, not man. God tests and proves our hearts. 5 You know we never used smooth-sounding words. God knows we never tried to get money from you by preaching. 6 We never looked for thanks from men, not from you or from anyone else. But because we were missionaries of Christ, we could have asked you to do much for us. 7 Instead, we were gentle when we came to you. We were like a mother caring for her children. 8 We had such a strong desire to help you that we were happy to give you the Good News. Because we loved you so much, we were ready to give you our own lives also. 9 You remember, Christian brothers, we worked night and day for our food and clothes while we preached the Good News to you. We did not want to make it hard for you. 10 You know, and so does God, how pure and right and without blame we were among you who believe. 11 As a father helps his children, you know how we wanted to help you and give you comfort. We told you with strong words 12 that you should live to please God. He is the One Who chose you to come into His holy nation and to share His shining-greatness.

13 We always thank God that when you heard the Word of God from us, you believed it. You did not receive it as from men, but you received it as the Word of God. That is what it is. It is at work in the lives of you who believe. 14 Christian brothers, you became just like the churches in the country of Judea. You had to suffer from the men in your country as those churches had to suffer from the Jews. 15 It was the Jews who killed the Lord Jesus and the early preachers. The Jews made it hard for us and made us leave. They do not please God and are working against all men. 16 They tried to keep us from preaching the Good News to the people who are not Jews. The Jews do not want them saved from the punishment of sin. The lives of the Jews are full of more sin all the time. But now God's anger has come to them at last.

17 Christian brothers, because we have not been able to be with you, our hearts have been with you. We have wanted very much to see you. 18 We wanted to come to you. I, Paul, have tried to come to you more

than once but Satan kept us from coming. 19 Who is our hope or joy or crown of happiness? It is you, when you stand before our Lord Jesus Christ when He comes again. 20 You are our pride and joy.

3 When we could wait no longer, we decided it was best to stay in the city of Athens alone. 2 And we sent Timothy to you. He works with us for God, teaching the Good News of Christ. We sent him to give strength and comfort to your faith. 3 We do not want anyone to give up because of troubles. You know that we can expect troubles. 4 Even when we were with you, we told you that much trouble would come to us. It has come as you can see. 5 For this reason, I could wait no longer. I sent Timothy to find out about your faith. I was afraid the devil had tempted you. Then our work with you would be wasted.

6 But Timothy has come to us from you. He brought good news about your faith and love. It is good to know that you think well of us and that you would like to see us. We would like to see you also. 7 Christian brothers, word about your faith has made us happy even while we are suffering and are in much trouble. 8 It is life to us to know that your faith in the Lord is strong. 9 How can we give God enough thanks for you for all the joy you give us? 10 We keep on praying night and day that we may see you again. We want to help your faith to be complete. 11 May our God and Father Himself and our Lord Jesus Christ take us on our way to you. 12 May the Lord make you grow in love for each other and for everyone. We have this kind of love for you. 13 May our God and Father make your hearts strong and without blame. May your hearts be without sin in God's sight when our Lord Jesus comes again with all those who belong to Him.

Paul Tells Them to Live Holy Lives

4 Christian brothers, we ask you, because of the Lord Jesus, to keep on living in a way that will please God. I have already told you how to grow in the Christian life. 2 The Lord Jesus gave us the right and the power to tell you what to do. 3 God wants you to be holy. You must keep away from sex sins. 4 God wants each of you to use his body in the right way by keeping it holy and by respecting it. 5 You should not use it to please your own desires like the people who do not know God. 6 No man should do wrong to his Christian brother in anything. The Lord will punish a person who does. I have told you this before. [7] For God has not called us to live in sin. He has called us to live a holy life. [8] The one who turns away from this teaching does not turn away from man, but from God. It is God Who has given us His Holy Spirit.

[9] You do not need anyone to write to you about loving your Christian brothers. God has taught you to love each other. [10] You love all the Christians in all the country of Macedonia. But we ask you to love them even more. [11] Do your best to live a quiet life. Learn to do your own work well. We told you about this before. [12] By doing this, you will be respected by those who are not Christians. Then you will not be in need and others will not have to help you.

The Lord Is Coming Again

[13] Christian brothers, we want you to know for sure about those who have died. You have no reason to have sorrow as those who have no hope. [14] We believe that Jesus died and then came to life again. Because we believe this, we know that God will bring to life again all those who belong to Jesus. [15] We tell you this as it came from the Lord. Those of us who are alive when the Lord comes again will not go ahead of those who have died. [16] For the Lord Himself will come down from heaven with a loud call. The head angel will speak with a loud voice. God's horn will give its sounds. First, those who belong to Christ will come out of their graves to meet the Lord. [17] Then, those of us who are still living here on earth will be gathered together with them in the clouds. We will meet the Lord in the sky and be with Him forever. [18] Because of this, comfort each other with these words.

Watch for the Lord to Come Again

5 You do not need anyone to write to tell you when and at what kind of times these things will happen. [2] You know for sure that the day the Lord comes back to earth will be as a robber coming in the night. [3] When they say, "Everything is fine and safe," then all at once they will be destroyed. It will be like pain that comes on a woman when a child is born. They will not be able to get away from it. [4] But you are not in darkness, Christian brothers.

That day will not surprise you as a robber would. [5] For you are children of the light and of the day. We are not of darkness or of night. [6] Keep awake! Do not sleep like others. Watch and keep your minds awake to what is happening. [7] People sleep at night. Those who get drunk do it at night. [8] Because we are men of the day, let us keep our minds awake. Let us cover our chests with faith and love. Let us cover our heads with the hope of being saved. [9] God planned to save us from the punishment of sin through our Lord Jesus Christ. He did not plan for us to suffer from His anger. [10] He died for us so that, dead or alive, we will be with Him. [11] So comfort each other and make each other strong as they are already doing.

Christian Living

[12] We ask you, Christian brothers, to respect those who work among you. The Lord has placed them over you and they are your teachers. [13] You must think much of them and love them because of their work. Live in peace with each other.

[14] We ask you, Christian brothers, speak to those who do not want to work. Comfort those who feel they cannot keep going on. Help the weak. Understand and be willing to wait for all men. [15] Do not let anyone pay back for the bad he received. But look for ways to do good to each other and to all people.

[16] Be full of joy all the time. [17] Never stop praying. [18] In everything give thanks. This is what God wants you to do because of Christ Jesus. [19] Do not try to stop the work of the Holy Spirit. [20] Do not laugh at those who speak for God. [21] Test everything and do not let good things get away from you. [22] Keep away from everything that even looks like sin.

[23] May the God of peace set you apart for Himself. May every part of you be set apart for God. May your spirit and your soul and your body be kept complete. May you be without blame when our Lord Jesus Christ comes again. [24] The One Who called you is faithful and will do what He promised. [25] Christian brothers, pray for us. [26] Greet all the Christians with a kiss of holy love. [27] I tell you to have this letter read to all the Christians. [28] May you have loving-favor from our Lord Jesus Christ.

2 THESSALONIANS

1 This letter is from Paul and Silas and Timothy. It is to the church in the city of Thessalonica that belongs to God the Father and the Lord Jesus Christ. 2 May you have loving-favor and peace from God the Father and the Lord Jesus Christ.

3 We must give thanks to God for you always, Christian brothers. It is the right thing to do because your faith is growing so much. Your love for each other is stronger all the time. 4 We are proud of you and tell the other churches about you. We tell them how your faith stays so strong even when people make it hard for you and make you suffer. 5 God wants you to prove yourselves to be worth being in His holy nation by suffering for Him. 6 He does what is right and will allow trouble to come to those who are making it hard for you. 7 He will help you and us who are suffering. This will happen when the Lord Jesus comes down from heaven with His powerful angels in a bright fire. 8 He will punish those who do not know God and those who do not obey the Good News of our Lord Jesus Christ. 9 They will be punished forever and taken away from the Lord and from the shining-greatness of His power. 10 On the day He comes, His shining-greatness will be seen in those who belong to Him. On that day, He will receive honor from all those who put their trust in Him. You believed what we had to say to you. 11 For this reason, we always pray for you. We pray that our God will make you worth being chosen. We pray that His power will help you do the good things you want to do. We pray that your work of faith will be complete. 12 In this way, the name of the Lord Jesus Christ will be honored by you and you will be honored by Him. It is through the loving-favor of our God and of the Lord Jesus Christ.

Some People Will Believe a Lie

2 Our Lord Jesus Christ is coming again. We will be gathered together to meet Him. But we ask you, Christian brothers, 2 do not be troubled in mind or worried by the talk you hear. Some say that the Lord has already come. People may say that I wrote this in a letter or that a spirit told them. 3 Do not let anyone fool you. For the Lord will not come again until many people turn away from God. Then the leader of those who break the law will come. He is the man of sin. 4 He works against and puts himself above every kind of god that is worshiped. He will take his

seat in the house of God and say that he himself is God. 5 Do you not remember that while I was with you, I told you this? 6 You know the power that is keeping the man of sin back now. The man of sin will come only when his time is ready. 7 For the secret power of breaking the law is already at work in the world. But that secret power can only do so much until the One Who keeps back the man of sin is taken out of the way. 8 Then this man of sin will come. The Lord Jesus will kill him with the breath of His mouth. The coming of Christ will put an end to him. 9 Satan will use this man of sin. He will have Satan's power. He will do strange things and many powerful works that will be false. 10 Those who are lost in sin will be fooled by the things he can do. They are lost in sin because they did not love the truth that would save them. 11 For this reason, God will allow them to follow false teaching so they will believe a lie. 12 They will all be guilty as they stand before God because they wanted to do what was wrong.

You Belong to Those Who Believe the Truth

13 Christian brothers, the Lord loves you. We always thank God for you. It is because God has chosen you from the beginning to save you from the punishment of sin. He chose to make you holy by the Holy Spirit and to give you faith to believe the truth. 14 It was by our preaching the Good News that you were chosen. He chose you to share the shining-greatness of our Lord Jesus Christ. 15 So then, Christian brothers, keep a strong hold on what we have taught you by what we have said and by what we have written.

16 Our Lord Jesus Christ and God our Father loves us. Through His loving-favor He gives us comfort and hope that lasts forever. 17 May He give your hearts comfort and strength to say and do every good thing.

Christian Brothers, Pray for Us

3 My last words to you, Christian brothers, are that you pray for us. Pray that the Word of the Lord will go out over all the land and prove its power just as it did with you. 2 Pray that we will be kept from sinful men, because not all men are Christians. 3 But the Lord is faithful. He will give you strength and keep you safe from the devil. 4 We have faith in the Lord for you. We believe you are doing and will keep on doing the things we told you. 5 May the Lord lead your hearts into the love of God. May He help you as you wait for Christ.

6 Now this is what we tell you to do, Christian brothers. In the name of the Lord Jesus, keep away from any Christian who is lazy and who does not do what we taught you. 7 You know you should follow the way of life we lived when we were with you. We worked hard while we were there. 8 We did not eat anyone's food without paying for it. We worked hard night and day so none of you would have to give us anything. 9 We could have asked you to give us food. But we did not so that you might follow our way of living. 10 When we were with you, we told you that if a man does not work, he should not eat. 11 We hear that some are not working.

But they are spending their time trying to see what others are doing. 12 Our words to such people are that they should be quiet and go to work. They should eat their own food. In the name of the Lord Jesus Christ we say this. 13 But you, Christian brothers, do not get tired of doing good. 14 If anyone does not want to listen to what we say in this letter, remember who he is and stay away from him. In that way, he will be put to shame. 15 Do not think of him as one who hates you. But talk to him as a Christian brother.

16 May the Lord of peace give you His peace at all times. The Lord be with you all. 17 I, Paul, write this last part with my own hand. It is the way I finish all my letters. 18 May all of you have loving-favor from our Lord Jesus Christ.

1 TIMOTHY

1 This letter is from Paul, a missionary of Jesus Christ. I am sent by God, the One Who saves, and by our Lord Jesus Christ Who is our hope. 2 I write to you, Timothy. You are my son in the Christian faith. May God the Father and Jesus Christ our Lord give you His loving-favor and loving-kindness and peace.

Watch for False Teachers

3 When I left for the country of Macedonia, I asked you to stay in the city of Ephesus. I wanted you to stay there so you could tell those who are teaching what is not true to stop. 4 They should not listen to stories that are not true. It is foolish for them to try to learn more about their early fathers. These only bring more questions to their minds and do not make their faith in God stronger. 5 We want to see our teaching help you have a true love that comes from a pure heart. Such love comes from a heart that says we are not guilty and from a faith that does not pretend. 6 But some have turned away from these things. They have turned to foolish talking. 7 Some of them want to be teachers of the Law. But they do not know what they are talking about even if they act as if they do.

The Law Is Good

8 We know the Law is good when it is used the way God meant it to be used. 9 We must remember the Law is not for the person who is right with God. It is for those

who do not obey anybody or anything. It is for the sinners who hate God and speak against Him. It is for those who kill their fathers and mothers and for those who kill other people. 10 It is for those who do sex sins and for people who do sex sins with their own sex. It is for people who steal other people and for those who lie and for those who promise not to lie, but do. It is for everything that is against right teaching. 11 The great Good News of our honored God is right teaching. God has trusted me to preach this Good News.

Paul Gives Thanks to God

12 I thank Christ Jesus our Lord for the power and strength He has given me. He trusted me and gave me His work to do. 13 Before He chose me, I talked bad about Christ. I made His followers suffer. I hurt them every way I could. But God had loving-kindness for me. I did not understand what I was doing for I was not a Christian then. 14 Then our Lord gave me much of His loving-favor and faith and love which are found in Christ Jesus.

15 What I say is true and all the world should receive it. Christ Jesus came into the world to save sinners from their sin and I am the worst sinner. 16 And yet God had loving-kindness for me. Jesus Christ used me to show how long He will wait for even the worst sinners. In that way, others will know they can have life that lasts forever also. 17 We give honor and thanks to

the King Who lives forever. He is the One Who never dies and Who is never seen. He is the One Who knows all things. He is the only God. Let it be so.

The Good Fight of Faith

18 Timothy, my son, here is my word to you. Fight well for the Lord! God's preachers told us you would. 19 Keep a strong hold on your faith in Christ. May your heart always say you are right. Some people have not listened to what their hearts say. They have done what they knew was wrong. Because of this, their faith in Christ was wrecked. 20 This happened to Hymenaeus and Alexander. I gave them over to Satan to teach them not to speak against God.

2 First of all, I ask you to pray much for all men and to give thanks for them. 2 Pray for kings and all others who are in power over us so we might live quiet God-like lives in peace. 3 It is good when you pray like this. It pleases God Who is the One Who saves. 4 He wants all people to be saved from the punishment of sin. He wants them to come to know the truth. 5 There is one God. There is one Man standing between God and men. That Man is Christ Jesus. 6 He gave His life for all men so they could go free and not be held by the power of sin. God made this known to the world at the right time. 7 This is why I was chosen to be a teacher and a missionary. I am to teach faith and truth to the people who do not know God. I am not lying but telling the truth.

Women in the Church

8 I want men everywhere to pray. They should lift up holy hands as they pray. They should not be angry or argue. 9 Christian women should not be dressed in the kind of clothes and their hair should not be combed in a way that will make people look at them. They should not wear much gold or pearls or clothes that cost much money. 10 Instead of these things, Christian women should be known for doing good things and living good lives.

11 Women should be quiet when they learn. They should listen to what men have to say. 12 I never let women teach men or be leaders over men. They should be quiet. 13 Adam was made first, then Eve. 14 Adam was not fooled by Satan; it was the woman who was fooled and sinned. 15 But women will be saved through the

giving of birth to children if they keep on in faith and live loving and holy lives.

What a Church Leader Must Be Like

3 It is true that if a man wants to be a church leader, he wants to do a good work. 2 A church leader must be a good man. His life must be so no one can say anything against him. He must have only one wife and must be respected for his good living. He must be willing to take people into his home. He must be willing to learn and able to teach the Word of God. 3 He must not get drunk or want to fight. Instead, he must be gentle. He must not have a love for money. 4 He should be a good leader in his own home. His children must obey and respect him. 5 If a man cannot be a good leader in his own home, how can he lead the church? 6 A church leader must not be a new Christian. A new Christian might become proud and fall into sin which is brought on by the devil. 7 A church leader must be respected by people who are not Christians so nothing can be said against him. In that way, he will not be trapped by the devil.

What the Church Helpers Must Be Like

8 Church helpers must also be good men and act so people will respect them. They must speak the truth. They must not get drunk. They must not have a love for money. 9 They must have their faith in Christ and be His follower with a heart that says they are right. 10 They must first be tested to see if they are ready for the work as church helpers. Then if they do well, they may be chosen as church helpers. 11 The wives of church helpers must be careful how they act. They must not carry stories from one person to another. They must be wise and faithful in all they do. 12 Church helpers must have only one wife. They must lead their home well and their children must obey them. 13 Those who work well as church helpers will be respected by others and their own faith in Christ Jesus will grow.

Why Paul Writes to Timothy

14 I hope to come to you soon. I am writing these things 15 because it may be awhile before I get there. I wanted you to know how you should act among people in the church which is the house of the living God. The church holds up the truth. 16 It is important to know the secret of God-like living, which is: Christ came to earth as a Man. He was pure in His Spirit. He was

seen by angels. The nations heard about Him. Men everywhere put their trust in Him. He was taken up into heaven.

False Teaching in the Last Days

4 The Holy Spirit tells us in plain words that in the last days some people will turn away from the faith. They will listen to what is said about spirits and follow the teaching about demons. 2 Those who teach this tell it as the truth when they know it is a lie. They do it so much that their own hearts no longer say it is wrong. 3 They will say, "Do not get married. Do not eat some kinds of food." But God gave these things to Christians who know the truth. We are to thank God for them. 4 Everything God made is good. We should not put anything aside if we can take it and thank God for it. 5 It is made holy by the Word of God and prayer.

Christians Are to Grow

6 If you keep telling these things to the Christians, you will be a good worker for Jesus Christ. You will feed your own soul on these words of faith and on this good teaching which you have followed. 7 Have nothing to do with foolish stories old women tell. Keep yourself growing in God-like living. 8 Growing strong in body is all right but growing in God-like living is more important. It will not only help you in this life now but in the next life also. 9 These words are true and they can be trusted. 10 Because of this, we work hard and do our best because our hope is in the living God, the One Who would save all men. He saves those who believe in Him.

Paul's Helpful Words to Young Timothy

11 Tell people that this is what they must do. 12 Let no one show little respect for you because you are young. Show other Christians how to live by your life. They should be able to follow you in the way you talk and in what you do. Show them how to live in faith and in love and in holy living. 13 Until I come, read and preach and teach the Word of God to the church. 14 Be sure to use the gift God gave you. The leaders saw this in you when they laid their hands on you and said what you should do. 15 Think about all this. Work at it so everyone may see you are growing as a Christian. 16 Watch yourself how you act and what you teach. Stay true to what is right. If you do, you and those who hear you will be saved from the punishment of sin.

Teaching About Women Whose Husbands Have Died

5 Do not speak sharp words to an older man. Talk with him as if he were a father. Talk to younger men as brothers. 2 Talk to older women as mothers. Talk to younger women as sisters, keeping yourself pure. 3 Help women whose husbands have died. 4 If a woman whose husband has died has children or grandchildren, they are the ones to care for her. In that way, they can pay back to their parents the kindness that has been shown to them. God is pleased when this is done. 5 Women whose husbands have died are alone in this world. Their trust is in the Lord. They pray day and night. 6 But the one who lives only for the joy she can receive from this world is the same as dead even if she is alive.

7 Teach these things so they will do what is right. 8 Anyone who does not take care of his family and those in his house has turned away from the faith. He is worse than a person who has never put his trust in Christ. 9 A woman over sixty years old whose husband has died may receive help from the church. To receive this help, she must have been the wife of one man. 10 She must be known for doing good things for people and for being a good mother. She must be known for taking strangers into her home and for washing the feet of Christians. She must be known for helping those who suffer and for showing kindness.

11 Do not write the names of younger women whose husbands have died together with the names of others who need help. They will turn away from Christ because of wanting to get married again. 12 Then they would be thought of as guilty of breaking their first promise. 13 They will waste their time. They will go from house to house carrying stories. They will find fault with people and say things they should not talk about. 14 I think it is best for younger women whose husbands have died to get married. They should have children and care for their own homes. Then no one can speak against them. 15 Some of these women have already turned away to follow Satan. 16 If you have any women whose husbands have died in your family, you must care for them. The church should not have to help them. The church can help women whose husbands have died who are all alone in this world and have no one else to help them.

Teaching About Leaders

17 Leaders who do their work well should be given twice as much pay, and for sure, those who work hard preaching and teaching. 18 The Holy Writings say, "When a cow is walking on the grain to break it open, do not stop it from eating some" (Deuteronomy 25:4), and "A person who works should be paid." (Matthew 10:10)

19 Do not listen to what someone says against a church leader unless two or three persons say the same thing. 20 Show those who keep on sinning where they are wrong in front of the whole church. Then others will be afraid of sinning. 21 I tell you from my heart that you must follow these rules without deciding before the truth is known. God and Jesus Christ and the chosen angels know what I am saying. Show favors to no one. 22 Do not be in a hurry about choosing a church leader. You do not want to have any part in other men's sins. Keep yourself pure.

23 Do not drink water only. Use a little wine because of your stomach and because you are sick so often.

24 The sins of some men can be seen. Their sins go before them and make them guilty. The sins of other men will be seen later. 25 In the same way, good works are easy to see now. But some that are not easy to be seen cannot always be hid.

Teaching About Christians Who Were Servants

6 All you Christians who are servants must respect your owners and work hard for them. Do not let the name of God and our teaching be spoken against because of poor work. 2 Those who have Christian owners must respect their owners because they are Christian brothers. They should work hard for them because much-loved Christian brothers are being helped by their work. Teach and preach these things.

Live Like God Wants You to Live

3 Someone may teach something else. He may not agree with the teaching of our Lord Jesus Christ. He may not teach you to live God-like lives. 4 Such a person is full of pride and knows nothing. He wastes time on questions and argues about things that are not important. This makes those he teaches jealous and they want to fight. They talk bad and have bad ideas about others. 5 Men who are not able to use their minds in the right way because of sin

argue all the time. They do not have the truth. They think religion is a way to get much for themselves.

6 A God-like life gives us much when we are happy for what we have. 7 We came into this world with nothing. For sure, when we die, we will take nothing with us. 8 If we have food and clothing, let us be happy. 9 But men who want lots of money are tempted. They are trapped into doing all kinds of foolish things and things which hurt them. These things drag them into sin and will destroy them. 10 The love of money is the beginning of all kinds of sin. Some people have turned from the faith because of their love for money. They have made much pain for themselves because of this.

Fight the Good Fight of Faith

11 But you, man of God, turn away from all these sinful things. Work at being right with God. Live a God-like life. Have faith and love. Be willing to wait. Have a kind heart. 12 Fight the good fight of faith. Take hold of the life that lasts forever. You were chosen to receive it. You have spoken well about this life in front of many people.

13 I tell you this before God Who gives life to all people and before Jesus Christ Who spoke well in front of Pontius Pilate. 14 You must do all our Lord Jesus Christ said so no one can speak against you. Do this until He comes again. 15 At the right time, we will be shown that God is the One Who has all power. He is the King of kings and Lord of lords. 16 He can never die. He lives in a light so bright that no man can go near Him. No man has ever seen God or can see Him. Honor and power belong to Him forever. Let it be so.

Paul's Last Words to Timothy

17 Tell those who are rich in this world not to be proud and not to trust in their money. Money cannot be trusted. They should put their trust in God. He gives us all we need for our happiness. 18 Tell them to do good and be rich in good works. They should give much to those in need and be ready to share. 19 Then they will be gathering together riches for themselves. These good things are what they will build on for the future. Then they will have the only true life!

20 Timothy, keep safe what God has trusted you with. Turn away from foolish talk. Do not argue with those who

think they know so much. They know less than they think they do. 21 Some people have gone after much learning. It has proved to be false and they have turned away from the faith. May you have God's loving-favor.

2 TIMOTHY

1 This letter is from Paul, a missionary of Jesus Christ. God has sent me to tell that He has promised life that lasts forever through Christ Jesus. 2 I am writing to you, Timothy. You are my much-loved son. May God the Father and Christ Jesus our Lord give you His loving-favor and loving-kindness and peace.

Timothy's Special Gift

3 I thank God for you. I pray for you night and day. I am working for God the way my early fathers worked. My heart says I am free from sin. 4 When I remember your tears, it makes me want to see you. That would fill me with joy. 5 I remember your true faith. It is the same faith your grandmother Lois had and your mother Eunice had. I am sure you have that same faith also.

6 For this reason, I ask you to keep using the gift God gave you. It came to you when I laid my hands on you and prayed that God would use you. 7 For God did not give us a spirit of fear. He gave us a spirit of power and of love and of a good mind. 8 Do not be ashamed to tell others about what our Lord said, or of me here in prison. I am here because of Jesus Christ. Be ready to suffer for preaching the Good News and God will give you the strength you need. 9 He is the One Who saved us from the punishment of sin. He is the One Who chose us to do His work. It is not because of anything we have done. But it was His plan from the beginning that He would give us His loving-favor through Christ Jesus. 10 We know about it now because of the coming of Jesus Christ, the One Who saves. He put a stop to the power of death and brought life that never dies which is seen through the Good News. 11 I have been chosen to be a missionary and a preacher and a teacher of this Good News. 12 For this reason, I am suffering. But I am not ashamed. I know the One in Whom I have put my trust. I am sure He is able to keep safe that which I have trusted to Him until the day He comes again. 13 Keep all the things I taught you. They were given to you in the faith and love of Jesus Christ.

14 Keep safe that which He has trusted you with by the Holy Spirit Who lives in us.

Onesiphorus Was Faithful

15 I am sure you have heard that all the Christians in the countries of Asia have turned away from me. Phygelus and Hermogenes turned away also. 16 Onesiphorus was not ashamed of me in prison. He came often to comfort me. May the Lord show loving-kindness to his family. 17 When he came to Rome, he looked everywhere until he found me. 18 You know what a help he was to me in Ephesus. When the Lord comes again, may He show loving-kindness to Onesiphorus.

Be a Good Soldier

2 So you, my son, be strong in the loving-favor of Christ Jesus. 2 What you have heard me say in front of many people, you must teach to faithful men. Then they will be able to teach others also. 3 Take your share of suffering as a good soldier of Jesus Christ. 4 No soldier fighting in a war can take time to make a living. He must please the one who made him a soldier. 5 Anyone who runs in a race must follow the rules to get the crown. 6 A hard-working farmer should receive first some of what he gathers from the field. 7 Think about these things and the Lord will help you understand them.

8 Remember this! Jesus Christ, Who was born from the early family of David, was raised from the dead! This is the Good News I preach. 9 I suffer much and am in prison as one who has done something very bad. I am in chains, but the Word of God is not chained. 10 I suffer all things so the people that God has chosen can be saved from the punishment of their sin through Jesus Christ. Then they will have God's shining-greatness that lasts forever. 11 These things are true. If we die with Him, we will live with Him also. 12 If we suffer and stay true to Him, then we will be a leader with Him. If we say we do not know Him, He will say He does not know us. 13 If we have no faith, He will still be faithful for He cannot go against what He is.

Foolish Talk

14 Tell your people about these things again. In the name of the Lord, tell them not to argue over words that are not important. It helps no one and it hurts the faith of those who are listening. 15 Do your best to know that God is pleased with you. Be as a workman who has nothing to be ashamed of. Teach the words of truth in the right way. 16 Do not listen to foolish talk about things that mean nothing. It only leads people farther away from God. 17 Such talk will spread like cancer. Hymenaeus and Philetus are like this. 18 They have turned from the truth. They say the dead have already been raised. The faith of some people has been made weak because of such foolish talk. 19 But the truth of God cannot be changed. It says, "The Lord knows those who are His." And, "Everyone who says he is a Christian must turn away from sin!"

20 In a big house there are not only things made of gold and silver, but also of wood and clay. Some are of more use than others. Some are used every day. 21 If a man lives a clean life, he will be like a dish made of gold. He will be respected and set apart for good use by the owner of the house.

22 Turn away from the sinful things young people want to do. Go after what is right. Have a desire for faith and love and peace. Do this with those who pray to God from a clean heart. 23 Let me say it again. Have nothing to do with foolish talk and those who want to argue. It can only lead to trouble. 24 A servant owned by God must not make trouble. He must be kind to everyone. He must be able to teach. He must be willing to suffer when hurt for doing good. 25 Be gentle when you try to teach those who are against what you say. God may change their hearts so they will turn to the truth. 26 Then they will know they had been held in a trap by the devil to do what he wanted them to do. But now they are able to get out of it.

Things That Will Happen in the Last Days

3 You must understand that in the last days there will come times of much trouble. 2 People will love themselves and money. They will have pride and tell of all the things they have done. They will speak against God. Children and young people will not obey their parents. People will not be thankful and they will not be holy. 3 They will not love each other. No one can get along with them. They will tell lies about others. They will not be able to keep from doing things they know they should not do. They will be wild and want to beat and hurt those who are good. 4 They will not stay true to their friends. They will act without thinking. They will think too much of themselves. They will love fun instead of loving God. 5 They will do things to make it look as if they are Christians. But they will not receive the power that is for a Christian. Keep away from such people.

6 These are the kind of people who go from house to house. They talk to foolish women who are loaded down with sins and all kinds of sinful desires. 7 Such women are always listening to new teaching. But they are never able to understand the truth. 8 Jannes and Jambres fought against Moses. So do these teachers fight against the truth today. Their minds think only of sinful things. They have turned against the Christian teaching. 9 They will not get very far. Their foolish teaching will be seen by everyone. That was the way it was with the two who worked against Moses.

Teach the Truth

10 But you know what I teach and how I live. You know what I want to do. You know about my faith and my love. You know how long I am willing to wait for something. You know how I keep on working for God even when it is hard for me. 11 You know about all the troubles and hard times I have had. You have seen how I suffered in the cities of Antioch and Iconium and Lystra. Yet the Lord brought me out of all those troubles. 12 Yes! All who want to live a God-like life who belong to Christ Jesus will suffer from others. 13 Sinful men and false teachers will go from bad to worse. They will lead others the wrong way and will be led the wrong way themselves.

14 But as for you, hold on to what you have learned and know to be true. Remember where you learned them. 15 You have known the Holy Writings since you were a child. They are able to give you wisdom that leads to being saved from the punishment of sin by putting your trust in Christ Jesus. 16 All the Holy Writings are God-given and are made alive by Him. Man is helped when he is taught God's Word. It shows what is wrong. It changes the way of a man's life. It shows him how to be right with God. 17 It gives the man who belongs to God everything he needs to work well for Him.

Paul's Work Is Finished—Timothy Must Carry On

4 These words are from my heart to you. I say this before God and Jesus Christ. Some day He will judge those who are living and those who are dead. It will be when Christ comes to bring His holy nation. 2 Preach the Word of God. Preach it when it is easy and people want to listen and when it is hard and people do not want to listen. Preach it all the time. Use the Word of God to show people they are wrong. Use the Word of God to help them do right. You must be willing to wait for people to understand what you teach as you teach them.

3 The time will come when people will not listen to the truth. They will look for teachers who will tell them only what they want to hear. 4 They will not listen to the truth. Instead, they will listen to stories made up by men. 5 You must watch for all these things. Do not be afraid to suffer for our Lord. Preach the Good News from place to place. Do all the work you are to do.

6 It will soon be time for me to leave this life. 7 I have fought a good fight. I have finished the work I was to do. I have kept the faith. 8 There is a crown which comes from being right with God. The Lord, the One Who will judge, will give it to me on that great day when He comes again. I will not be the only one to receive a crown. All those who love to think of His coming and are looking for Him will receive one also.

Paul Sends Word About Some Friends

9 Come to me here as soon as you can. 10 Demas left me. He loved the things of this world and has gone to the city of Thessalonica. Crescens has gone to the city of Galatia. Titus has gone to the city of Dalmatia. 11 Luke is the only one with me here. Bring Mark when you come. He is a help to me in this work. 12 I sent Tychicus to the city of Ephesus. 13 When you come, bring the coat I left with Carpus in the city of Troas. Bring the books and for sure do not forget the writings written on sheepskin. 14 Alexander, the man who makes things out of copper, has worked hard against me. The Lord will give him the pay that is coming to him. 15 Watch him! He fought against every word we preached.

16 At my first trial no one helped me. Everyone left me. I hope this will not be held against them. 17 But the Lord was with me. He gave me power to preach the Good News so all the people who do not know God might hear. I was taken from the mouth of the lion. 18 The Lord will look after me and will keep me from every sinful plan they have. He will bring me safe into His holy nation of heaven. May He have all the shining-greatness forever. Let it be so.

19 Greet Priscilla and Aquila for me and to all the family of Onesiphorus. 20 Erastus stayed in the city of Corinth. I left Trophimus sick in the city of Miletus. 21 Try to come before winter. Eubulus, Pudens, Linus, Claudia, and all the Christian brothers greet you. 22 May the Lord Jesus Christ be with your spirit. May you have God's loving-favor.

TITUS

1 This letter is from Paul, a servant owned by God, and a missionary of Jesus Christ. I have been sent to those God has chosen for Himself. I am to teach them the truth that leads to God-like living. 2 This truth also gives hope of life that lasts forever. God promised this before the world began. He cannot lie. 3 He made this known at the right time through His Word. God, the One Who saves, told me I should preach it. 4 I am writing to you, Titus. You are my true son in the faith which we both have. May you have loving-favor and peace from God the Father and Jesus Christ, the One Who saves.

What a Church Leader Must Be Like

5 I left you on the island of Crete so you could do some things that needed to be done. I asked you to choose church leaders in every city. 6 Their lives must be so that no one can talk against them. They must have only one wife. Their children must be Christians and known to be good. They must obey their parents. They must not be wild. 7 A church leader is God's servant. His life must be so that no one can say anything against him. He should not try to please himself and not be quick to get angry over little things. He must not get drunk or want to fight. He must not always want more money for himself.

8 He must like to take people into his home. He must love what is good. He must be able to think well and do all things in the right way. He must live a holy life and be the boss over his own desires. 9 He must hold to the words of truth which he was taught. He must be able to teach the truth and show those who are against the truth that they are wrong.

False Teachers

10 There are many men who will not listen or will not obey the truth. Their teaching is foolish and they lead people to believe a lie. Some Jews believe their lies. 11 This must be stopped. It turns whole families from the truth. They teach these things to make money. 12 One of their own teachers said, "People of the island of Crete always lie. They are like wild animals. They are lazy. All they want to do is eat." 13 This is true of them. Speak sharp words to them because it is true. Lead them in the right way so they will have strong faith. 14 Do not let them listen to Jewish stories made up by men. Do not let them listen to man-made rules which lead them away from the truth. 15 All things are pure to the man with a pure heart. But to sinful people nothing is pure. Both their minds and their hearts are bad. 16 They say they know God, but by the way they act, they show that they do not. They are sinful people. They will not obey and are of no use for any good work.

Right Teaching

2 You must teach what is right and true. 2 Older men are to be quiet and to be careful how they act. They are to be the boss over their own desires. Their faith and love are to stay strong and they are not to give up. 3 Teach older women to be quiet and to be careful how they act also. They are not to go around speaking bad things about others or things that are not true. They are not to be chained by strong drink. They should teach what is good.

4 Older women are to teach the young women to love their husbands and children. 5 They are to teach them to think before they act, to be pure, to be workers at home, to be kind, and to obey their own husbands. In this way, the Word of God is honored. 6 Also teach young men to be wise. 7 In all things show them how to live by your life and by right teaching. 8 You should be wise in what you say. Then the one who is against you will be ashamed and will not be able to say anything bad about you.

9 Those who are servants owned by someone must obey their owners and please them in everything. They must not argue. 10 They must not steal from their owners but prove they can be trusted in every way. In this way, their lives will honor the teaching of God Who saves us.

11 God's free gift of being saved is being given to everyone. 12 We are taught to have nothing to do with that which is against God. We are to have nothing to do with the desires of this world. We are to be wise and to be right with God. We are to live God-like lives in this world. 13 We are to be looking for the great hope and the coming of our great God and the One Who saves, Christ Jesus. 14 He gave Himself for us. He did this by buying us with His blood and making us free from all sin. He gave Himself so His people could be clean and want to do good. 15 Teach all these things and give words of help. Show them if they are wrong. You have the right and the power to do this. Do not let anyone think little of you.

The Work of a Leader

3 Teach your people to obey the leaders of their country. They should be ready to do any good work. 2 They must not speak bad of anyone, and they must not argue. They should be gentle and kind to all people.

God Saved Us from All These Things

3 There was a time when we were foolish and did not obey. We were fooled in many ways. Strong desires held us in their power. We wanted only to please ourselves. We wanted what others had and were angry when we could not have them. We hated others and they hated us.

4 But God, the One Who saves, showed how kind He was and how He loved us 5 by saving us from the punishment of sin. It was not because we worked to be right with God. It was because of His loving-kindness that He washed our sins away. At the same time He gave us new life when the Holy Spirit came into our lives. 6 God gave the Holy Spirit to fill our lives through Jesus Christ, the One Who saves. 7 Because of this, we are made right with God by His loving-favor. Now we can have life that lasts forever as He has promised.

8 What I have told you is true. Teach these things all the time so those who have

put their trust in God will be careful to do good things. These things are good and will help all men.

9 Do not argue with people about foolish questions and about the Law. Do not spend time talking about all of your early fathers. This does not help anyone and it is of no use. **10** Talk once or twice to a person who tries to divide people into groups against each other. If he does not stop, have nothing to do with him. **11** You can be sure he is going the wrong way. He is sinning and he knows it.

12 I will send Artemas or Tychicus to you. As soon as one of them gets there, try to come to me in the city of Nicopolis. I have decided to spend the winter there. **13** Zenas, the man who knows the law, and Apollos are going on a trip. Do everything you can to help them. **14** Our people must learn to work hard. They must work for what they need and be able to give to others who need help. Then their lives will not be wasted. **15** All those with me here greet you. Greet my Christian friends there. May you have God's loving-favor.

PHILEMON

This letter is from Paul. I am in prison because of Jesus Christ. Brother Timothy is also writing to you, Philemon. You are a much-loved workman together with us. **2** We are also writing to the church that meets in your home. This letter is also for our Christian sister Apphia and it is for Archippus who is a soldier together with us. **3** May God our Father and the Lord Jesus Christ give you His loving-favor and peace.

4 I always thank God when I speak of you in my prayers. **5** It is because I hear of your love and trust in the Lord Jesus and in all the Christians. **6** I pray that our faith together will help you know all the good things you have through Christ Jesus. **7** Your love has given me much joy and comfort. The hearts of the Christians have been made happy by you, Christian brother.

8 So now, through Christ, I am free to tell you what you must do. **9** But because I love you, I will only ask you. I am Paul, an old man, here in prison because of Jesus Christ. **10** I am asking you for my son, Onesimus. He has become my son in the Christian life while I have been here in prison. **11** At one time he was of no use to you. But now he is of use to you and to me. **12** I am sending him back to you. It is like

sending you my own heart. **13** I would like to keep him with me. He could have helped me in your place while I am in prison for preaching the Good News. **14** But I did not want to keep him without word from you. I did not want you to be kind to me because you had to but because you wanted to. **15** He ran away from you for awhile. But now he is yours forever. **16** Do not think of him any longer as a servant you own. He is more than that to you. He is a much-loved Christian brother to you and to me.

17 If you think of me as a true friend, take him back as you would take me. **18** If he has done anything wrong or owes you anything, send me the bill. **19** I will pay it. I, Paul, am writing this with my own hand. I will not talk about how much you owe me because you owe me your life. **20** Yes, Christian brother, I want you to be of use to me as a Christian. Give my heart new joy in Christ. **21** I write this letter knowing you will do what I ask and even more.

22 Please have a room ready for me. I trust God will answer your prayers and let me come to you soon. **23** Epaphras greets you. He is a brother in Christ in prison with me. **24** Mark and Aristarchus and Demas and Luke who are workers with me greet you. **25** May the loving-favor of the Lord Jesus Christ be with your spirit.

HEBREWS

God Speaks Through His Son

1 Long ago God spoke to our early fathers in many different ways. He spoke through the early preachers. **2** But in these last days He has spoken to us through His

Son. God gave His Son everything. It was by His Son that God made the world. **3** The Son shines with the shining-greatness of the Father. The Son is as God is in every way. It is the Son Who holds up the whole world by the power of His Word. The Son gave His own life so we could be clean from all sin. After He had done that, He sat down on the right side of God in heaven.

The Son Was Greater Than the Angels

4 The Son of God was made greater and better than the angels. God gave Him a greater name than theirs. 5 God did not say to any of His angels, "You are My Son. Today I have become Your Father." (Psalm 2:7) And He did not say to any angel, "I will be a Father to Him. He will be a Son to Me." (2 Samuel 7:14) 6 But when God brought His first-born Son, Jesus, into the world, He said, "Let all the angels of God worship Him." 7 He said this about the angels, "He makes His angels to be winds. He makes His servants a burning fire." (Psalm 104:4) 8 But about His Son, He says, "O God, Your throne will last forever. Whatever You say in Your nation is right and good. 9 You have loved what is right. You have hated what is wrong. That is why God, Your God, has chosen You. He has poured over You the oil of joy more than over anyone else." (Psalm 45:6–7) 10 He said also, "Lord, You made the earth in the beginning. You made the heavens with Your hands. 11 They will be destroyed but You will always be here. They will all become old just as clothes become old. 12 You will roll up the heavens like a coat. They will be changed. But You are always the same. You will never grow old." (Psalm 102:25–27) 13 God never said to any angel, "Sit at My right side, until I make those who hate You a place to rest Your feet." (Psalm 110:1) 14 Are not all the angels spirits who work for God? They are sent out to help those who are to be saved from the punishment of sin.

Do Not Wait to Be Saved from the Punishment of Sin

2 That is why we must listen all the more to the truths we have been told. If we do not, we may slip away from them. 2 These truths given by the angels proved to be true. People were punished when they did not obey them. 3 God was so good to make a way for us to be saved from the punishment of sin. What makes us think we will not go to hell if we do not take the way to heaven that He has made for us? The Lord was the first to tell us of this. Then those who heard Him told it later. 4 God proved what they said was true by

showing us special things to see and by doing powerful works. He gave the gifts of the Holy Spirit as He wanted to.

Jesus, the Way to Heaven

5 God did not make angels to be the leaders of that world to come which we have been speaking about. 6 Instead, the Holy Writings say, "What is man that You think of him and the son of man that You should remember him?" (Psalm 8:4) 7 "You made him so he took a place that was not as important as the angels for a little while. You gave him the crown of honor and shining-greatness. *You made him the head over everything You have made. 8 You have put everything under his feet." (Psalm 8:4–6) There is nothing that does not obey him, but we do not see all things obey him yet. 9 But we do see Jesus. For a little while He took a place that was not as important as the angels. But God had loving-favor for everyone. He had Jesus suffer death on a cross for all of us. Then, because of Christ's death on a cross, God gave Him the crown of honor and shining-greatness.

10 God made all things. He made all things for Himself. It was right for God to make Jesus a perfect Leader by having Him suffer for men's sins. In this way, He is bringing many men to share His shining-greatness. 11 Jesus makes men holy. He takes away their sins. Both Jesus and the ones being made holy have the same Father. That is why Jesus is not ashamed to call them His brothers. 12 Jesus is saying to His Father, "I will tell My brothers Your name. I will sing songs of thanks for You among the people." (Psalm 22:22) 13 And again He says, "I will put My trust in God." At another time He said, "Here I am with the children God gave Me." (Isaiah 8:17–18)

14 It is true that we share the same Father with Jesus. And it is true that we share the same kind of flesh and blood because Jesus became a man like us. He died as we must die. Through His death He destroyed the power of the devil who has the power of death. 15 Jesus did this to make us free from the fear of death. We no longer need to be chained to this fear. 16 Jesus did not come to help angels. Instead, He came to help men who are of Abraham's family. 17 So Jesus had to become like His brothers in every way. He had to be one of us to be our Religious Leader to go between God and us. He had loving-pity on us and He was faithful. He gave Himself as a gift

to die on a cross for our sins so that God would not hold these sins against us any longer. 18 Because Jesus was tempted as we are and suffered as we do, He understands us and He is able to help us when we are tempted.

Jesus Was Greater Than Moses

3 Christian brothers, you have been chosen and set apart by God. So let us think about Jesus. He is the One God sent and He is the Religious Leader of our Christian faith. 2 Jesus was faithful in God's house just as Moses was faithful in all of God's house. 3 The man who builds a house gets more honor than the house. That is why Jesus gets more honor than Moses. 4 Every house is built by someone. And God is the One Who has built everything. 5 Moses was a faithful servant owned by God in God's house. He spoke of the things that would be told about later on. 6 But Christ was faithful as a Son Who is Head of God's house. We are of God's house if we keep our trust in the Lord until the end. This is our hope. 7 The Holy Spirit says, "If you hear His voice today, 8 do not let your hearts become hard as your early fathers did when they turned against Me. It was at that time in the desert when they put Me to the test. 9 Your early fathers tempted Me and tried Me. They saw the work I did for forty years. 10 For this reason, I was angry with the people of this day. And I said to them, 'They always think wrong thoughts. They have never understood what I have tried to do for them.' 11 I was angry with them and said to Myself, 'They will never go into My rest.' " (Psalm 95:7-11)

12 Christian brothers, be careful that not one of you has a heart so bad that it will not believe and will turn away from the living God. 13 Help each other. Speak day after day to each other while it is still today so your heart will not become hard by being fooled by sin. 14 For we belong to Christ if we keep on trusting Him to the end just as we trusted Him at first. 15 The Holy Writings say, "If you hear His voice today, do not let your hearts become hard as your early fathers did when they turned against Me." (Psalm 95:7-8)

16 Who heard God's voice and turned against Him? Did not all those who were led out of the country of Egypt by Moses? 17 Who made God angry for forty years? Was it not those people who had sinned in the desert? Was it not those who died

and were buried there? 18 Who did He say could never go into His rest? Was it not those who did not obey Him? 19 So we can see that they were not able to go into His rest because they did not put their trust in Him.

The Christian's Rest

4 The same promise of going into God's rest is still for us. But we should be afraid that some of us may not be able to go in. 2 We have heard the Good News even as they did, but it did them no good because it was not mixed with faith. 3 We who have put our trust in God go into His rest. God said this of our early fathers, "I was angry and said, 'They will not go into My rest.' " (Psalm 95:11) And yet God's work was finished after He made the world.

God's Rest

4 In the Holy Writings He said this about the seventh day when He made the whole world, "God rested on the seventh day from all He had made." (Genesis 2:2) 5 But God said this about those who turned against Him, "They will not go into My rest." (Psalm 95:11) 6 Those who heard the Good News first did not go into His rest. It was because they had not obeyed Him. But the promise is still good and some are going into His rest. 7 God has again set a certain day for people to go into His rest. He says through David many years later as He had said before, "If you hear His voice today, do not let your hearts become hard." (Psalm 95:7-8)

8 If Joshua had led those people into God's rest, He would not have told of another day after that. 9 And so God's people have a complete rest waiting for them. 10 The man who goes into God's rest, rests from his own work the same as God rested from His work. 11 Let us do our best to go into that rest or we will be like the people who did not go in.

12 God's Word is living and powerful. It is sharper than a sword that cuts both ways. It cuts straight into where the soul and spirit meet and it divides them. It cuts into the joints and bones. It tells what the heart is thinking about and what it wants to do. 13 No one can hide from God. His eyes see everything we do. We must give an answer to God for what we have done.

Jesus—Our Great Religious Leader

14 We have a great Religious Leader Who has made the way for man to go to God.

He is Jesus, the Son of God, Who has gone to heaven to be with God. Let us keep our trust in Jesus Christ. 15 Our Religious Leader understands how weak we are. Christ was tempted in every way we are tempted, but He did not sin. 16 Let us go with complete trust to the throne of God. We will receive His loving-kindness and have His loving-favor to help us whenever we need it.

The Job of a Religious Leader

5 Every Jewish religious leader is chosen from among men. He is a helper standing between God and men. He gives gifts on the altar in worship to God from the people. He gives blood from animals for the sins of the people. 2 A Jewish religious leader is weak in many ways because he is just a man himself. He knows how to be gentle with those who know little. He knows how to help those who are doing wrong. 3 Because he is weak himself, he must give gifts to God for his own sins as well as for the sins of the people. 4 A Jewish religious leader does not choose this honor for himself. God chooses a man for this work. Aaron was chosen this way.

Christ Is Our Religious Leader Who Has Made the Way for Man to Go to God

5 It is the same way with Christ. He did not choose the honor of being a Religious Leader Who has made the way for man to go to God. Instead, God said to Christ, "You are My Son. Today I have become Your Father." (Psalm 2:7) 6 God says in another part of His Word, "You will be a Religious Leader forever. You will be like Melchizedek." (Psalm 110:4) 7 During the time Jesus lived on earth, He prayed and asked God with loud cries and tears. Jesus' prayer was to God Who was able to save Him from death. God heard Christ because God honored God. 8 Even being God's Son, He learned to obey by the things He suffered. 9 And having been made perfect, He planned and made it possible for all those who obey Him to be saved from the punishment of sin. 10 In God's plan He was to be a Religious Leader Who made the way for man to go to God. He was like Melchizedek.

Do Not Fall Back Into Sin

11 There is much we could say about this, but it is hard to make you understand. It is because you do not want to hear well. 12 By now you should be teachers. Instead, you need someone to teach you again the first things you need to know from God's Word. You still need milk instead of solid food. 13 Anyone who lives on milk cannot understand the teaching about being right with God. He is a baby. 14 Solid food is for full-grown men. They have learned to use their minds to tell the difference between good and bad.

Going Ahead

6 So let us leave the first things you need to know about Christ. Let us go on to the teaching that full-grown Christians should understand. We do not need to teach these first truths again. You already know that you must be sorry for your sins and turn from them. You know that you must have faith in God. 2 You know about being baptized and about putting hands on people. You know about being raised from the dead and about being punished forever. 3 We will go on, if God lets us.

4 There are those who have known the truth. They have received the gift from heaven. They have shared the Holy Spirit. 5 They know how good the Word of God is. They know of the powers of the world to come. 6 But if they turn away, they cannot be sorry for their sins and turn from them again. It is because they are nailing the Son of God on a cross again. They are holding Him up in shame in front of all people. 7 It is the same with a piece of ground that has had many rains fall on it. God makes it possible for that ground to give good fruits and vegetables. 8 But if it gives nothing but weeds, it is worth nothing. It will be hated and destroyed by fire.

9 Dear friends, even as we tell you this, we are sure of better things for you. These things go along with being saved from the punishment of sin. 10 God always does what is right. He will not forget the work you did to help the Christians and the work you are still doing to help them. This shows your love for Christ. 11 We want each one of you to keep on working to the end. Then what you hope for, will happen. 12 Do not be lazy. Be like those who have faith and have not given up. They will receive what God has promised them.

God's Promise

13 When God made a promise to Abraham, He made that promise in His own name because no one was greater. 14 He said, "I will make you happy in so many ways. For sure, I will give you many children."

(Genesis 22:16–17) 15 Abraham was willing to wait and God gave to him what He had promised.

16 When men make a promise, they use a name greater than themselves. They do this to make sure they will do what they promise. In this way, no one argues about it. 17 And so God made a promise. He wanted to show Abraham that He would never change His mind. So He made the promise in His own name. 18 God gave these two things that cannot be changed and God cannot lie. We who have turned to Him can have great comfort knowing that He will do what He has promised. 19 This hope is a safe anchor for our souls. It will never move. This hope goes into the Holiest Place of All behind the curtain of heaven. 20 Jesus has already gone there. He has become our Religious Leader forever and has made the way for man to go to God. He is like Melchizedek.

Melchizedek—Like Christ

7 Melchizedek was king of Salem. He was a religious leader for God. When Abraham was coming back from the war where many kings were killed, Melchizedek met Abraham and showed respect to him. 2 Abraham gave Melchizedek one-tenth part of all he had. Melchizedek's name means king of what is right. Salem means peace. So he is king of peace. 3 Melchizedek was without a father or mother or any family. He had no beginning of life or end of life. He is a religious leader forever like the Son of God.

4 We can see how great Melchizedek was. Abraham gave him one-tenth part of all he had taken in the war. 5 The Law made the family of Levi the Jewish religious leaders. The Law said that the religious leaders were to take one-tenth part of everything from their own people. 6 Melchizedek was not even from the family group of Levi but Abraham paid him. Melchizedek showed respect to Abraham who was the one who had received God's promises. 7 The one who shows respect is always greater than the one who receives it. 8 Jewish religious leaders receive one-tenth part. They are men and they all die. But here Melchizedek received one-tenth part and is alive. 9 We might say that Levi, who receives one-tenth part, paid one-tenth part through Abraham. 10 Levi was not yet born. He was still inside Abraham's body when Abraham paid Melchizedek.

11 The Law was given during the time when Levi and his sons were the religious leaders. If the work of those religious leaders had been perfect in taking away the sins of the people, there would have been no need for another religious leader. But one like Melchizedek was needed and not one from the family group of Aaron. 12 For when the family group of religious leaders changed, the Law had to be changed also. 13 These things speak of Christ Who is from another family group. That family group never had a religious leader who killed animals and gave gifts at the altar for the sins of the people. 14 Our Lord came from the family group of Judah. Moses did not write anything about religious leaders coming from that family group.

A Different Religious Leader Has Come

15 We can see that a different Religious Leader has come. This One is like Melchizedek. 16 Christ did not become a Religious Leader by coming from the family group of Levi as the Law said had to be. He became the Religious Leader by the power of a life that never ends. 17 The Holy Writings say this about Christ, "You are a Religious Leader forever like Melchizedek." (Psalm 110:4)

18 God put the Law of Moses aside. It was weak and could not be used. 19 For the Law of Moses could not make men right with God. Now there is a better hope through which we can come near to God.

20 God made a promise when Christ became the Religious Leader Who made the way for man to go to God. 21 God did not make such a promise when Levi's family group became religious leaders. But when Christ became a Religious Leader, this is the promise God made, "The Lord has made a promise. He will never change His mind. You will be a Religious Leader forever." (Psalm 110:4) 22 Christ makes this New Way of Worship sure for us because of God's promise. 23 There had to be many religious leaders during the time of the Old Way of Worship. They died and others had to keep on in their work. 24 But Jesus lives forever. He is the Religious Leader forever. It will never change. 25 And so Jesus is able, now and forever, to save from the punishment of sin all who come to God through Him because He lives forever to pray for them.

26 We need such a Religious Leader Who made the way for man to go to God. Jesus is holy and has no guilt. He has

never sinned and is different from sinful men. He has the place of honor above the heavens. 27 Christ is not like other religious leaders. They had to give gifts every day on the altar in worship for their own sins first and then for the sins of the people. Christ did not have to do that. He gave one gift on the altar and that gift was Himself. It was done once and it was for all time. 28 The Law makes religious leaders of men. These men are not perfect. After the Law was given, God spoke with a promise. He made His Son a perfect Religious Leader forever.

8 Now the important thing is this: We have such a Religious Leader Who has made the way for man to go to God. He is the One Who sits at the right side of the All-powerful God in the heavens. 2 He is the Religious Leader of that holy place in heaven which is the true place of worship. It was built by the Lord and not by men's hands. 3 Every religious leader of the Old Way of Worship had the work of killing animals and of giving gifts on the altar to God. So Christ had to have something to give also. 4 If Christ were on the earth, He would not be a religious leader such as these. The religious leaders on earth give gifts like the Law says. 5 Their work shows us only a picture of the things in heaven. When Moses was putting up the tent to worship in, God told him, "Be sure you make the tent for worship like I showed you on Mount Sinai." (Exodus 25:40)

6 But Christ has a more perfect work. He is the One Who goes between God and man in this new and better way. The New Way of Worship promises better things. 7 If the Old Way of Worship had been perfect, there would have been no need for another one. 8 God was not happy how the people lived by the Old Way of Worship. He said, "The day will come when I will make a New Way of Worship for the Jews and those of the family group of Judah. 9 The New Way of Worship will not be like the Old Way of Worship I gave to their early fathers. That was when I took them by the hand and led them out of Egypt. But they did not follow the Old Way of Worship. And so I turned away from them. 10 This is the New Way of Worship that I will give to the Jews. When that day comes, says the Lord, I will put My Laws into their minds. And I will write them in their hearts. I will be their God, and they will be My people. 11 No one will need to teach his neighbor or his brother to know the Lord. All of them will already know Me from the least to the greatest. 12 I will show loving-kindness to them and forgive their sins. I will remember their sins no more." (Jeremiah 31:31–34)

13 When God spoke about a New Way of Worship, He showed that the Old Way of Worship was finished and of no use now. It will never be used again.

The New Way of Worship Is Better

9 There were special ways of worship and a special holy place made by man for the Old Way of Worship. 2 A big tent was built and set up. It was called the holy place. It had a light and a table, and the holy bread was on the table. 3 Behind the second curtain there was another tent. This was called the Holiest Place of All. 4 In the inside tent there was an altar where special perfume was burned. There was also a large box made of wood called the box of the Way of Worship. Both of these were covered with gold inside and out. Inside the box was a pot made of gold with the bread from heaven. It also had in it Aaron's stick that once started to grow. The stones on which the Law of Moses was written were in it. 5 Above the box were the cherubim of honor. Their wings were spread up and over and met in the center. On the top of the box and under the shadow of their wings was the mercy-seat. We cannot tell anymore about these things now.

6 When everything was finished, the Jewish religious leaders went in and out of the outside tent to do the things which had to be done to worship God. 7 Once each year the head religious leader would go into the inside tent alone. He would not go in without blood. He gave this blood to God as a gift in worship for his own sins and for the sins of all the people who sinned without knowing it.

8 And so the Holy Spirit is teaching that, with the Old Way of Worship, the people could not go into the Holiest Place of All as long as the outside tent and its Old Way of Worship were being used. 9 The outside tent is a picture of that day. With the Old Way of Worship, animals killed and gifts given in worship to God could not take away the guilty feeling of sin. 10 The Old Way of Worship was made up of Laws about what to eat and drink. These Laws told how to wash and other things to do with the body. These things had to be done until Christ came to bring a better way of worship.

The New Way of Worship Has a Better Gift

11 But Christ came as the Head Religious Leader of the good things God promised. He made the way for man to go to God. He was a greater and more perfect tent. He was not made by human hands and was not a part of this earth. **12** Christ went into the Holiest Place of All one time for all people. He did not take the blood of goats and young cows to give to God as a gift in worship. He gave His own blood. By doing this, He bought us with His own blood and made us free from sin forever. **13** With the Old Way of Worship, the blood and ashes of animals could make men clean after they had sinned. **14** How much more the blood of Christ will do! He gave Himself as a perfect gift to God through the Spirit that lives forever. Now your heart can be free from the guilty feeling of doing work that is nothing. Now you can work for the living God.

15 Christ is the One Who gave us this New Way of Worship. All those who have been called by God may receive life that lasts forever just as He promised them. Christ bought us with His blood when He died for us. This made us free from our sins which we did under the Old Way of Worship.

16 When a man wants to give his money to someone after he dies, he writes it all down on paper. But that paper is worth nothing until the man is dead. **17** That piece of paper means nothing as long as he is alive. It is good only when he dies. **18** The Old Way of Worship had to have a death to make it good. The blood of an animal was used. **19** Moses told the people all the things they had to obey in the Law. Then he took the blood of animals together with water and put it on the Book of the Law and on all the people. He used special branches and red wool as he put it on them. **20** Moses said, "This is the blood of the Way of Worship which God said you must obey." (Exodus 24:8) **21** In the same way, Moses put the blood on the tent and on all the things used in worship. **22** The Law says that almost everything is made clean by blood. Sins are not forgiven unless blood is given.

One Perfect Gift

23 The tent to worship in and the things inside to worship with were like the things in heaven. They were made clean by putting blood on them. But the things in heaven were made clean by a much better gift of worship. **24** For Christ did not go into the Holiest Place of All that was made by men, even if it was like the true one in heaven. He went to heaven itself and He is before God for us. **25** Christ has not given Himself many times, as the head religious leader here on earth went into the Holiest Place of All each year with blood that was not his own. **26** For then Christ would have had to die many times since the world began. But He came once at the end of the Old Way of Worship. He gave Himself once for all time. He gave Himself to destroy sin. **27** It is in the plan that all men die once. After that, they will stand before God and be judged. **28** It is the same with Christ. He gave Himself once to take away the sins of many. When He comes the second time, He will not need to give Himself again for sin. He will save all those who are waiting for Him.

In the Old Way of Worship Many Gifts Were Given

10 The Law is like a picture of the good things to come. The Jewish religious leaders gave gifts on the altar in worship to God all the time year after year. Those gifts could not make the people who came to worship perfect. **2** If those gifts given to God could take away sins, the people who came to worship would no longer feel guilty of sin. They would have given no more gifts. **3** When they gave the gifts year after year, it made them remember that they still had their sins. **4** The blood of animals cannot take away the sins of men.

In the New Way of Worship One Gift Was Given

5 When Christ came to the world, He said to God, "You do not want animals killed or gifts given in worship. You have made My body ready to give as a gift. **6** You are not pleased with animals that have been killed or burned and given as gifts on the altar to take away sin. **7** Then I said, 'I have come to do what You want, O God. It is written in the Law that I would.'"

8 Then Christ said, "You do not want animals killed or gifts given in worship to you for sin. You are not pleased with them." These things are done because the Law says they should be done. **9** Then He said, "I have come to do what You want Me to do." And this is what He did when He died on a cross. God did away with the Old Way of Worship and made a New Way of Worship. **10** Our sins are washed away and we are made clean because Christ gave His own body as a gift to God. He did this once for all time.

11 All Jewish religious leaders stand every day killing animals and giving gifts on the altar. They give the same gifts over and over again. These gifts cannot take away sins. **12** But Christ gave Himself once for sins and that is good forever. After that He sat down at the right side of God. **13** He is waiting there for God to make of those who have hated Him a place to rest His feet. **14** And by one gift He has made perfect forever all those who are being set apart for God-like living.

15 The Holy Spirit tells us this: First He says, **16** "This is the New Way of Worship that I will give them. When that day comes, says the Lord, I will put My Laws in their hearts. And I will write them in their minds." Then He says, **17** "I will not remember their sins and wrong-doings anymore." (Jeremiah 31:33–34) **18** No more gifts on the altar in worship are needed when our sins are forgiven.

We Can Go to God Through Christ

19 Christian brothers, now we know we can go into the Holiest Place of All because the blood of Jesus was given. **20** We now come to God by the new and living way. Christ made this way for us. He opened the curtain, which was His own body. **21** We have a great Religious Leader over the house of God. **22** And so let us come near to God with a true heart full of faith. Our hearts must be made clean from guilty feelings and our bodies washed with pure water. **23** Let us hold on to the hope we say we have and not be changed. We can trust God that He will do what He promised. **24** Let us help each other to love others and to do good. **25** Let us not stay away from church meetings. Some people are doing this all the time. Comfort each other as you see the day of His return coming near.

Do Not Fall Back Into Sin

26 If we keep on sinning because we want to after we have received and know the truth, there is no gift that will take away sins then. **27** Instead, we will stand before God and on that day He will judge us. And the hot fires of hell will burn up those who work against God. **28** Anyone who did not obey the Old Way of Worship died without

loving-kindness when two or three men spoke against him. **29** How much more will a man have to be punished if he walks on and hates the Son of God? How much more will he be punished if he acts as if the blood of God's New Way of Worship is worth nothing? This New Way of Worship is God's way of making him holy. How much more will he be punished if he laughs at the Holy Spirit Who wanted to show him loving-favor? **30** For we know God said, "I will pay back what is coming to them." And, "The Lord will judge His people." (Deuteronomy 32:35–36) **31** The very worst thing that can happen to a man is to fall into the hands of the living God!

32 Remember how it was in those days after you heard the truth. You suffered much. **33** People laughed at you and beat you. When others suffered, you suffered with them. **34** You had loving-pity for those who were in prison. You had joy when your things were taken away from you. For you knew you would have something better in heaven which would last forever.

35 Do not throw away your trust, for your reward will be great. **36** You must be willing to wait without giving up. After you have done what God wants you to do, God will give you what He promised. **37** The Holy Writings say, "In a little while, the One you are looking for will come. It will not be a long time now. **38** For the one right with God lives by faith. If anyone turns back, I will not be pleased with him." (Habakkuk 2:3–4) **39** We are not of those people who turn back and are lost. Instead, we have faith to be saved from the punishment of sin.

Faith

11 Now faith is being sure we will get what we hope for. It is being sure of what we cannot see. **2** God was pleased with the men who had faith who lived long ago.

3 Through faith we understand that the world was made by the Word of God. Things we see were made from what could not be seen.

4 Because Abel had faith, he gave a better gift in worship to God than Cain. His gift pleased God. Abel was right with God. Abel died, but by faith he is still speaking to us.

5 Because Enoch had faith, he was taken up from the earth without dying. He could not be found because God had taken him. The Holy Writings tell how he pleased God before he was taken up. ⁶ A man cannot please God unless he has faith. Anyone who comes to God must believe that He is. That one must also know that God gives what is promised to the one who keeps on looking for Him.

⁷ Because Noah had faith, he built a large boat for his family. God told him what was going to happen. His faith made him hear God speak and he obeyed. His family was saved from death because he built the boat. In this way, Noah showed the world how sinful it was. Noah became right with God because of his faith in God.

⁸ Because Abraham had faith, he obeyed God when God called him to leave his home. He was to go to another country that God promised to give him. He left his home without knowing where he was going. ⁹ His faith in God kept him living as a stranger in the country God had promised to him. Isaac and Jacob had received the same promise. They all lived in tents together. ¹⁰ Abraham was looking to God and waiting for a city that could not be moved. It was a city planned and built by God.

¹¹ Because Sarah had faith, she was able to have a child long after she was past the age to have children. She had faith to believe that God would do what He promised. ¹² Abraham was too old to have children. But from this one man came a family with as many in it as the stars in the sky and as many as the sand by the sea.

¹³ These people all died having faith in God. They did not receive what God had promised to them. But they could see far ahead to all the things God promised and they were glad for them. They knew they were strangers here. This earth was not their home. ¹⁴ People who say these things show they are looking for a country of their own. ¹⁵ They did not think about the country they had come from. If they had, they might have gone back. ¹⁶ But they wanted a better country. And so God is not ashamed to be called their God. He has made a city for them.

¹⁷ Because Abraham had faith, when he was tested, he gave his son Isaac as a gift on the altar in worship. God had made a promise to Abraham that He would give him a son. And yet Abraham was willing to give his only son as a gift on the altar in worship. ¹⁸ God had said to Abraham, "Your family will come from Isaac." (Genesis 21:12) ¹⁹ Abraham believed God was able to bring Isaac back to life again. And

so it may be said that Abraham did receive him back from death.

²⁰ Because Isaac had faith, he said that good would come to Jacob and Esau in the future. ²¹ Because Jacob had faith, he said that good would come to each of Joseph's sons as he was dying. He used his walking stick to hold him up as he prayed to God.

²² Because Joseph had faith, he spoke of the Jews leaving the country of Egypt. He was going to die soon, and he told them to bury his body in the country where they were going.

²³ Because of faith, Moses, after he was born, was hidden by his parents for three months. They saw that he was a beautiful child. They were not afraid of the king when he said that all baby boys should be killed.

²⁴ Because Moses had faith, he would not be called the son of Pharaoh's daughter when he grew up. ²⁵ He chose to suffer with God's people instead of having fun doing sinful things for awhile. ²⁶ Any shame that he suffered for Christ was worth more than all the riches in Egypt. He kept his eyes on the reward God was going to give him.

²⁷ Because Moses had faith, he left Egypt. He was not afraid of the king's anger. Moses did not turn from the right way but kept seeing God in front of him. ²⁸ Because Moses had faith, he told all the Jews to put blood over their doors. Then the angel of death would pass over their houses and not kill their oldest sons.

²⁹ Because the Jews had faith, they went through the Red Sea as if they were on dry ground. But when the people of Egypt tried to go through, they were all killed by the water.

³⁰ Because the Jews had faith, the walls of the city of Jericho fell down after the Jews had walked around the city for seven days. ³¹ Because Rahab had faith, she was kept from being killed along with those who did not obey God. She was a woman who sold the use of her body. But she helped the men who had come in secret to look over the country.

There Were Many More Who Had Faith in God

³² What more should I say? There is not enough time to tell of Gideon and of Barak and of Samson and of Jephthah and of David and of Samuel and of the early preachers. ³³ It was because these people had faith that they won wars over other

countries. They were good leaders. They received what God promised to them. They closed the mouths of lions 34 and stopped fire that was burning. They got away from being killed with swords. They were made strong again after they had been weak and sick. They were strong in war. They made fighting men from other countries run home. 35 It was because some women had faith that they received their dead back to life. Others chose to be beaten instead of being set free, because they would not turn against God. In this way, they would be raised to a better life. 36 Others were talked against. Some were beaten. Some were put in chains and in prison. 37 They were killed by stones being thrown at them. People were cut in pieces. They were tested. They were killed with swords. They wore skins of sheep and goats and had nothing they could call their own. They were hungry and sick. Everyone was bad to them. 38 They walked around in deserts and in mountains. They looked for caves and holes in the earth to live in. They were too good for this world. 39 It was because of their faith that God was pleased with them. But they did not receive what God had promised. 40 God had planned something better for us. These men could not be made perfect without us.

Christ the Perfect One

12 All these many people who have had faith in God are around us like a cloud. Let us put every thing out of our lives that keeps us from doing what we should. Let us keep running in the race that God has planned for us. 2 Let us keep looking to Jesus. Our faith comes from Him and He is the One Who makes it perfect. He did not give up when He had to suffer shame and die on a cross. He knew of the joy that would be His later. Now He is sitting at the right side of God.

3 Sinful men spoke words of hate against Christ. He was willing to take such shame from sinners. Think of this so you will not get tired and give up. 4 In your fight against sin, you have not yet had to stand against sin with your blood. 5 Do you remember what God said to you when He called you His sons? "My son, listen when the Lord punishes you. Do not give up when He tells you what you must do. 6 The Lord punishes everyone He loves. He whips every son He receives." (Proverbs 3:11–12) 7 Do not give up when you are punished

by God. Be willing to take it, knowing that God is teaching you as a son. Is there a father who does not punish his son sometimes? 8 If you are not punished as all sons are, it means that you are not a true son of God. You are not a part of His family and He is not your Father. 9 Remember that our fathers on earth punished us. We had respect for them. How much more should we obey our Father in heaven and live? 10 For a little while our fathers on earth punished us when they thought they should. But God punishes us for our good so we will be holy as He is holy. 11 There is no joy while we are being punished. It is hard to take, but later we can see that good came from it. And it gives us the peace of being right with God.

12 So lift up your hands that have been weak. Stand up on your weak legs. 13 Walk straight ahead so the weak leg will not be turned aside, but will be healed.

14 Be at peace with all men. Live a holy life. No one will see the Lord without having that kind of life. 15 See that no one misses God's loving-favor. Do not let wrong thoughts about others get started among you. If you do, many people will be turned to a life of sin. 16 None of you should fall into sex sins or forget God like Esau did. He had a right to get all Isaac had because he was the oldest son. But for one plate of food he sold this right to his brother. 17 You know that later he would have received everything. But he did not get it even when he asked for it with tears. It was too late to make right the wrong he had done.

18 For you have not come close to a mountain that you can touch. You have not come to worship where there is burning fire and darkness and storm and wind. 19 The sound of a horn was heard and God's voice spoke. The people cried out to Moses to have God stop speaking to them. 20 They could not stand to listen to His strong words, "Even if an animal comes to the mountain, it must be killed." (Exodus 19:12) 21 What Moses saw was so hard to look at that he said, "I am full of fear and am shaking." (Deuteronomy 9:19)

22 But instead, you have come to the mountain of Jerusalem. It is the city of the living God. It is the Jerusalem of heaven with its thousands of angels. 23 You have gathered there with God's children who were born long ago. They are citizens of heaven. God is there. He will judge all men. The spirits of all those right with

God are there. They have been made perfect. 24 Jesus is there. He has made a way for man to go to God. He gave His blood that men might worship God the New Way. The blood of Jesus tells of better things than that which Abel used.

25 Be sure you listen to the One Who is speaking to you. The Jews did not obey when God's Law was given to them on earth. They did not go free. They were punished. We will be punished more if we do not listen to God as He speaks from heaven. 26 On Mount Sinai, God's voice shook the earth. But now He has promised, saying, "Once more I will shake the earth and the heavens." (Exodus 19:18)

27 When God says, "Once more," He means He will take away everything of this world that can be shaken so the things that cannot be shaken will be left.

28 Since we have received a holy nation that cannot be moved, let us be thankful. Let us please God and worship Him with honor and fear. 29 For our God is a fire that destroys everything.

Christian Living

13 Keep on loving each other as Christian brothers. 2 Do not forget to be kind to strangers and let them stay in your home. Some people have had angels in their homes without knowing it. 3 Remember those in prison. Think of them as if you were in prison with them. Remember those who are suffering because of what others have done to them. You may suffer in the same way.

4 Marriage should be respected by everyone. God will punish those who do sex sins and are not faithful in marriage.

5 Keep your lives free from the love of money. Be happy with what you have. God has said, "I will never leave you or let you be alone." (Deuteronomy 31:6) 6 So we can say for sure, "The Lord is my Helper. I am not afraid of anything man can do to me." (Psalm 118:6)

7 Remember your leaders who first spoke God's Word to you. Think of how they lived, and trust God as they did. 8 Jesus Christ is the same yesterday and today and forever.

9 Do not let the many strange teachings lead you in the wrong way. Our hearts are made strong by God's loving-favor. Food does not make our hearts strong. Those who obey laws about eating certain foods are not helped by them. 10 We have an altar from which those who work in the place of worship have no right to eat.

11 The head religious leader takes the blood of animals into the holy place to give it on the altar for sins. But the bodies of the animals are burned outside the city. 12 It was the same with Jesus. He suffered and died outside the city so His blood would make the people clean from sin. 13 So let us go to Him outside the city to share His shame. 14 For there is no city here on earth that will last forever. We are looking for the one that is coming. 15 Let us give thanks all the time to God through Jesus Christ. Our gift to Him is to give thanks. Our lips should always give thanks to His name. 16 Remember to do good and help each other. Gifts like this please God.

17 Obey your leaders and do what they say. They keep watch over your souls. They have to tell God what they have done. They should have joy in this and not be sad. If they are sad, it is no help to you.

18 Pray for us. Our hearts tell us we are right. We want to do the right thing always. 19 Pray for me all the more so that I will be able to come to you soon.

20 God is a God of peace. He raised our Lord Jesus from the dead. Jesus is the Good Shepherd of the sheep. His blood made the New Way of Worship which will last forever. 21 May God give you every good thing you need so you can do what He wants. May He do in us what pleases Him through Jesus Christ. May Christ have all the shining-greatness forever! Let it be so. 22 Christian brothers, I beg of you to listen to these words that will help you. This has been a short letter. 23 I want you to know that Timothy is out of prison. If he comes soon, I will bring him with me when I come to see you. 24 Greet all of your leaders and to all those who belong to Christ. The Christians from the country of Italy greet you. 25 May all of you have God's loving-favor. Let it be so.

1 This letter is from James. I am a servant owned by God and the Lord Jesus Christ. I greet the twelve family groups of the Jewish nation living in many parts of the world.

Take Hope When Tests Come

2 My Christian brothers, you should be happy when you have all kinds of tests. 3 You know these prove your faith. It helps you not to give up. 4 Learn well how to wait so you will be strong and complete and in need of nothing.

5 If you do not have wisdom, ask God for it. He is always ready to give it to you and will never say you are wrong for asking. 6 You must have faith as you ask Him. You must not doubt. Anyone who doubts is like a wave which is pushed around by the sea. 7 Such a man will get nothing from the Lord. 8 The man who has two ways of thinking changes in everything he does.

9 A Christian brother who has few riches of this world should be happy for what he has. He is great in the eyes of God. 10 But a rich man should be happy even if he loses everything. He is like a flower that will die. 11 The sun comes up with burning heat. The grass dries up and the flower falls off. It is no longer beautiful. The rich man will die also and all his riches will be gone. 12 The man who does not give up when tests come is happy. After the test is over, he will receive the crown of life. God has promised this to those who love Him.

God Does Not Tempt Us

13 When you are tempted to do wrong, do not say, "God is tempting me." God cannot be tempted. He will never tempt anyone. 14 A man is tempted to do wrong when he lets himself be led by what his bad thoughts tell him to do. 15 When he does what his bad thoughts tell him to do, he sins. When sin completes its work, it brings death.

16 My Christian brothers, do not be fooled about this. 17 Whatever is good and perfect comes to us from God. He is the One Who made all light. He does not change. No shadow is made by His turning. 18 He gave us our new lives through the truth of His Word only because He wanted to. We are the first children in His family.

19 My Christian brothers, you know everyone should listen much and speak little. He should be slow to become angry. 20 A man's anger does not allow him to be right with God. 21 Put out of your life all that is unclean and wrong. Receive with a gentle spirit the Word that was taught. It has the power to save your souls from the punishment of sin.

22 Obey the Word of God. If you hear only and do not act, you are only fooling yourself. 23 Anyone who hears the Word of God and does not obey is like a man looking at his face in a mirror. 24 After he sees himself and goes away, he forgets what he looks like. 25 But the one who keeps looking into God's perfect Law and does not forget it will do what it says and be happy as he does it. God's Word makes men free.

26 If a person thinks he is religious, but does not keep his tongue from speaking bad things, he is fooling himself. His religion is worth nothing. 27 Religion that is pure and good before God the Father is to help children who have no parents and to care for women whose husbands have died who have troubles. Pure religion is also to keep yourself clean from the sinful things of the world.

The Rich and the Poor

2 My Christian brothers, our Lord Jesus Christ is the Lord of shining-greatness. Since your trust is in Him, do not look on one person as more important than another. 2 What if a man comes into your church wearing a gold ring and good clothes? And at the same time a poor man comes wearing old clothes. 3 What if you show respect to the man in good clothes and say, "Come and sit in this good place"? But if you say to the poor man, "Stand up over there," or "Sit on the floor by my feet," 4 are you not thinking that one is more important than the other? This kind of thinking is sinful. 5 Listen, my dear Christian brothers, God has chosen those who are poor in the things of this world to be rich in faith. The holy nation of heaven is theirs. That is what God promised to those who love Him. 6 You have not shown respect to the poor man. Is it not the rich men who make it hard for you and take you to court? 7 They speak against the name of Christ. And it was Christ Who called you. 8 You do well when you obey the Holy Writings which say, "You must love your neighbor as you love yourself." (Leviticus 19:18) 9 But if you look on one man as more important than another, you are sinning. And the Law says you are sinning.

Keep the Whole Law

10 If you obey all the Laws but one, you are as guilty as the one who has broken them all. 11 The One Who said, "You must not do any sex sins," also said, "You must not kill another person." If you do no sex sins but kill someone, you are guilty of breaking the Law. 12 Keep on talking and acting as people who will be told they are guilty or not by the Law that makes men free. 13 Anyone who shows no loving-kindness will have no loving-kindness shown to him when he is told he is guilty. But if you show loving-kindness, God will show loving-kindness to you when you are told you are guilty.

Faith Without Works Is Dead

14 My Christian brothers, what good does it do if you say you have faith but do not do things that prove you have faith? Can that kind of faith save you from the punishment of sin? 15 What if a Christian does not have clothes or food? 16 And one of you says to him, "Good-bye, keep yourself warm and eat well." But if you do not give him what he needs, how does that help him? 17 A faith that does not do things is a dead faith.

18 Someone may say, "You have faith, and I do things. Prove to me you have faith when you are doing nothing. I will prove to you I have faith by doing things." 19 You believe there is one God. That is good! But even the demons believe that, and because they do, they shake.

20 You foolish man! Do I have to prove to you that faith without doing things is of no use? 21 Was not our early father Abraham right with God by what he did? He obeyed God and put his son Isaac on the altar to die. 22 You see his faith working by what he did and his faith was made perfect by what he did. 23 It happened as the Holy Writings said it would happen. They say, "Abraham put his trust in God and he became right with God." (Genesis 15:6) He was called the friend of God. 24 A man becomes right with God by what he does and not by faith only. 25 The same was true with Rahab, the woman who sold the use of her body. She became right with God by what she did in helping the men who had been sent to look through the country and sent them away by another road. 26 The body is dead when there is no spirit in it. It is the same with faith. Faith is dead when nothing is done.

The Power of the Tongue

3 My Christian brothers, not many of you should become teachers. If we do wrong, it will be held against us more than other people who are not teachers. 2 We all make many mistakes. If anyone does not make a mistake with his tongue by saying the wrong things, he is a perfect man. It shows he is able to make his body do what he wants it to do. 3 We make a horse go wherever we want it to go by a small bit in its mouth. We turn its whole body by this. 4 Sailing ships are driven by strong winds. But a small rudder turns a large ship whatever way the man at the wheel wants the ship to go.

5 The tongue is also a small part of the body, but it can speak big things. See how a very small fire can set many trees on fire. 6 The tongue is a fire. It is full of wrong. It poisons the whole body. The tongue sets our whole lives on fire with a fire that comes from hell. 7 Men can make all kinds of animals and birds and fish and snakes do what they want them to do. 8 But no man can make his tongue say what he wants it to say. It is sinful and does not rest. It is full of poison that kills. 9 With our tongue we give thanks to our Father in heaven. And with our tongue we speak bad words against men who are made like God. 10 Giving thanks and speaking bad words come from the same mouth. My Christian brothers, this is not right! 11 Does a well of water give good water and bad water from the same place? 12 Can a fig tree give olives or can a grape-vine give figs? A well does not give both good water and bad water.

Wisdom from Above

13 Who among you is wise and understands? Let that one show from a good life by the things he does that he is wise and gentle. 14 If you have jealousy in your heart and fight to have many things, do not be proud of it. Do not lie against the truth. 15 This is not the kind of wisdom that comes from God. But this wisdom comes from the world and from that which is not Christian and from the devil. 16 Wherever you find jealousy and fighting, there will be trouble and every other kind of wrong-doing. 17 But the wisdom that comes from heaven is first of all pure. Then it gives peace. It is gentle and willing to obey. It is full of loving-kindness and of doing good. It has no doubts and does not pretend to be something it is not. 18 Those who plant seeds of peace will gather what is right and good

4 What starts wars and fights among you? Is it not because you want many things and are fighting to have them? ² You want something you do not have, so you kill. You want something but cannot get it, so you fight for it. You do not get things because you do not ask for them. ³ Or if you do ask, you do not receive because your reasons for asking are wrong. You want these things only to please yourselves.

⁴ You are as wives and husbands who are not faithful in marriage and do sex sins. Do you not know that to love the sinful things of the world and to be a friend to them is to be against God? Yes, I say it again, if you are a friend of the world, you are against God. ⁵ Do you think the Holy Writings mean nothing when they said, "The Holy Spirit Whom God has given to live in us has a strong desire for us to be faithful to Him"?

⁶ But He gives us more loving-favor. For the Holy Writings say, "God works against the proud but gives loving-favor to those who have no pride." (Proverbs 3:34) ⁷ So give yourselves to God. Stand against the devil and he will run away from you. ⁸ Come close to God and He will come close to you. Wash your hands, you sinners. Clean up your hearts, you who want to follow the sinful ways of the world and God at the same time. ⁹ Be sorry for your sins and cry because of them. Be sad and do not laugh. Let your joy be turned to sorrow. ¹⁰ Let yourself be brought low before the Lord. Then He will lift you up and help you.

Do Not Talk against Each Other

¹¹ Christian brothers, do not talk against anyone or speak bad things about each other. If a person says bad things about his brother, he is speaking against him. And he will be speaking against God's Law. If you say the Law is wrong, and do not obey it, you are saying you are better than the Law. ¹² Only God can say what is right or wrong. He made the Law. He can save or put to death. How can we say if our brother is right or wrong?

¹³ Listen! You who say, "Today or tomorrow we will go to this city and stay a year and make money." ¹⁴ You do not know about tomorrow. What is your life? It is like fog. You see it and soon it is gone. ¹⁵ What you should say is, "If the Lord wants us to, we will live and do this or that." ¹⁶ But instead you are proud. You talk loud and big about yourselves. All such pride is sin.

¹⁷ If you know what is right to do but you do not do it, you sin.

5 Listen, you rich men! Cry about the troubles that will come to you. ² Your riches are worth nothing. Your fine clothes are full of moth holes. ³ Your gold and silver have rusted. Their rust will speak against you and eat your flesh like fire. You have saved riches for yourselves for the last days. ⁴ See! The men working in your fields are crying against you because you have kept back part of their pay. Their cries have been heard by the Lord Who hears His people. ⁵ You have had everything while you lived on the earth and have enjoyed its fun. You have made your hearts fat and are ready to be killed as an animal is killed. ⁶ You have killed men who are right with God who were not making it hard for you.

The Lord Will Come Again

⁷ Christian brothers, be willing to wait for the Lord to come again. Learn from the farmer. He waits for the good fruit from the earth until the early and late rains come. ⁸ You must be willing to wait also. Be strong in your hearts because the Lord is coming again soon. ⁹ Do not complain about each other, Christian brothers. Then you will not be judged. See! The Judge is standing at the door. ¹⁰ See how the early preachers spoke for the Lord by their suffering and by being willing to wait. ¹¹ We think of those who stayed true to Him as happy even though they suffered. You have heard how long Job waited. You have seen what the Lord did for him in the end. The Lord is full of loving-kindness and pity.

¹² My Christian brothers, do not swear. Do not use heaven or earth or anything else to swear by. If you mean yes, say yes. If you mean no, say no. You will be guilty for saying anything more.

The Power of Prayer in Healing

¹³ Is anyone among you suffering? He should pray. Is anyone happy? He should sing songs of thanks to God. ¹⁴ Is anyone among you sick? He should send for the church leaders and they should pray for him. They should pour oil on him in the name of the Lord. ¹⁵ The prayer given in faith will heal the sick man, and the Lord will raise him up. If he has sinned, he will be forgiven. ¹⁶ Tell your sins to each other. And pray for each other so you may

be healed. The prayer from the heart of a man right with God has much power. 17 Elijah was a man as we are. He prayed that it might not rain. It did not rain on the earth for three and one-half years. 18 Then he prayed again that it would rain. It rained much and the fields of the earth gave fruit.

Bring Back Those Who Are Lost in Sin

19 My Christian brothers, if any of you should be led away from the truth, let someone turn him back again. 20 That person should know that if he turns a sinner from the wrong way, he will save the sinner's soul from death and many sins will be forgiven.

1 PETER

The Living Hope

1 This letter is from Peter, a missionary of Jesus Christ. I am writing to those who were taken away from their homeland and are living in the countries of Pontus and Galatia and Cappadocia and Asia and Bithynia. 2 You were chosen by God the Father long ago. He knew you were to become His children. You were set apart for holy living by the Holy Spirit. May you obey Jesus Christ and be made clean by His blood. May you be full of His loving-favor and peace.

3 Let us thank the God and Father of our Lord Jesus Christ. It was through His loving-kindness that we were born again to a new life and have a hope that never dies. This hope is ours because Jesus was raised from the dead. 4 We will receive the great things that we have been promised. They are being kept safe in heaven for us. They are pure and will not pass away. They will never be lost. 5 You are being kept by the power of God because you put your trust in Him and you will be saved from the punishment of sin at the end of the world.

6 With this hope you can be happy even if you need to have sorrow and all kinds of tests for awhile. 7 These tests have come to prove your faith and to show that it is good. Gold, which can be destroyed, is tested by fire. Your faith is worth much more than gold and it must be tested also. Then your faith will bring thanks and shining greatness and honor to Jesus Christ when He comes again. 8 You have never seen Him but you love Him. You cannot see Him now but you are putting your trust in Him. And you have joy so great that words cannot tell about it. 9 You will get what your faith is looking for, which is to be saved from the punishment of sin.

10 The early preachers tried to find out how to be saved. They told of the loving-favor that would come to you. 11 The early preachers wondered at what time or to what person this would happen. The Spirit of Christ in them was talking to them and told them to write about how Christ would suffer and about His shining-greatness later on. 12 They knew these things would not happen during the time they lived but while you are living many years later. These are the very things that were told to you by those who preached the Good News. The Holy Spirit Who was sent from heaven gave them power and they told of things that even the angels would like to know about.

Holy Living

13 Get your minds ready for good use. Keep awake. Set your hope now and forever on the loving-favor to be given you when Jesus Christ comes again. 14 Be like children who obey. Do not desire to sin like you used to when you did not know any better. 15 Be holy in every part of your life. Be like the Holy One Who chose you. 16 The Holy Writings say, "You must be holy, for I am holy." (Leviticus 11:44–45) 17 The Father is the One Who judges you by what you do. He does not respect one person more than another. If you call Him Father, be sure you honor Him with love and fear all the days of your life here on earth. 18 You know you were not bought and made free from sin by paying gold or silver which comes to an end. And you know you were not saved from the punishment of sin by the way of life that you were given from your early fathers. That way of life was worth nothing. 19 The blood of Christ saved you. This blood is of great worth and no amount of money can buy it. Christ was given as a lamb without sin and without spot. 20 Long before the world was made, God chose Christ to be given to you in these last days. 21 Because of Christ, you have put your trust in God. He raised Christ from the dead and gave Him great honor. So now your faith and hope are in God.

The Living Word

22 You have made your souls pure by obeying the truth through the Holy Spirit. This has given you a true love for the Christians. Let it be a true love from the heart. 23 You have been given a new birth. It was from a seed that cannot die. This new life is from the Word of God which lives forever. 24 All people are like grass. Their greatness is like the flowers. The grass dries up and the flowers fall off. 25 But the Word of the Lord will last forever. That Word is the Good News which was preached to you.

Food for Christians

2 Put out of your life hate and lying. Do not pretend to be someone you are not. Do not always want something someone else has. Do not say bad things about other people. 2 As new babies want milk, you should want to drink the pure milk which is God's Word so you will grow up and be saved from the punishment of sin. 3 If you have tasted of the Lord, you know how good He is.

The Living Stone

4 Come to Christ as to a living stone. Men have put Him aside, but He was chosen by God and is of great worth in the sight of God. 5 You are to be as living stones in the building God is making also. You are His religious leaders giving yourselves to God through Jesus Christ. This kind of gift pleases God. 6 The Holy Writings say, "See, I lay down in Jerusalem a Stone of great worth, worth far more than any amount of money. Anyone who puts his trust in Him will not be ashamed." (Isaiah 28:16) 7 This Stone is of great worth to you who have your trust in Him. But to those who have not put their trust in Him, the Holy Writings say, "The Stone which the workmen put aside has become the most important part of the building." (Psalm 118:22) 8 The Holy Writings say, also, "Christ is the Stone that some men will trip over and the Rock over which they will fall." (Isaiah 8:14) When they do not obey the Word of God, they trip over it. This is what happens to such men. 9 But you are a chosen group of people. You are the King's religious leaders. You are a holy nation. You belong to God. He has done this for you so you can tell others how God has called you out of darkness into His great light. 10 At one time you were a people of no use. Now you are the people of God. At one time you did not have loving-kindness. Now you have God's loving-kindness.

11 Dear friends, your real home is not here on earth. You are strangers here. I ask you to keep away from all the sinful desires of the flesh. These things fight to get hold of your soul. 12 When you are around people who do not know God, be careful how you act. Even if they talk against you as wrong-doers, in the end they will give thanks to God for your good works when Christ comes again.

Obey the Leaders

13 Obey the head leader of the country and all other leaders over you. This pleases the Lord. 14 Obey the men who work for them. God sends them to punish those who do wrong and to show respect to those who do right. 15 This is what God wants. When you do right, you stop foolish men from saying bad things. 16 Obey as men who are free but do not use this to cover up sin. Live as servants owned by God at all times. 17 Show respect to all men. Love the Christians. Honor God with love and fear. Respect the head leader of the country.

Servants

18 Servants, you are to respect your owners and do what they say. Do this if you have a good and kind owner. You must do it even if your owner is hard to work for. 19 This shows you have received loving-favor when you are even punished for doing what is right because of your trust in God. 20 What good is it if, when you are beaten for doing something wrong, you do not try to get out of it? But if you are beaten when you have done what is right, and do not try to get out of it, God is pleased. 21 These things are all a part of the Christian life to which you have been called. Christ suffered for us. This shows us we are to follow in His steps. 22 He never sinned. No lie or bad talk ever came from His lips. 23 When people spoke against Him, He never spoke back. When He suffered from what people did to Him, He did not try to pay them back. He left it in the hands of the One Who is always right in judging. 24 He carried our sins in His own body when He died on a cross. In doing this, we may be dead to sin and alive to all that is right and good. His wounds have healed you! 25 You were like lost sheep. But now you have come back to Him Who is your Shepherd and the One Who cares for your soul.

Teaching for Married Christians

3 Wives, obey your own husbands. Some of your husbands may not obey the Word of God. By obeying your husbands, they may become Christians by the life you live without you saying anything. 2 They will see how you love God and how your lives are pure. 3 Do not let your beauty come from the outside. It should not be the way you comb your hair or the wearing of gold or the wearing of fine clothes. 4 Your beauty should come from the inside. It should come from the heart. This is the kind that lasts. Your beauty should be a gentle and quiet spirit. In God's sight this is of great worth and no amount of money can buy it. 5 This was the kind of beauty seen in the holy women who lived many years ago. They put their hope in God. They also obeyed their husbands. 6 Sarah obeyed her husband Abraham. She respected him as the head of the house. You are her children if you do what is right and do not have fear.

7 In the same way, husbands should understand and respect their wives, because women are weaker than men. Remember, both husband and wife are to share together the gift of life that lasts forever. If this is not done, you will find it hard to pray.

Teaching for All Christians

8 Last of all, you must share the same thoughts and the same feelings. Love each other with a kind heart and with a mind that has no pride. 9 When someone does something bad to you, do not do the same thing to him. When someone talks about you, do not talk about him. Instead, pray that good will come to him. You were called to do this so you might receive good things from God. 10 For "If you want joy in your life and have happy days, keep your tongue from saying bad things and your lips from talking bad about others. 11 Turn away from what is sinful. Do what is good. Look for peace and go after it. 12 The Lord watches over those who are right with Him. He hears their prayers. But the Lord is against those who sin." (Psalm 34:12–16) 13 Who will hurt you if you do what is right? 14 But even if you suffer for doing what is right, you will be happy. Do not be afraid or troubled by what they may do to make it hard for you. 15 Your heart should be holy and set apart for the Lord God. Always be ready to tell everyone who asks you why you believe as you do. Be gentle as you speak and show respect. 16 Keep your heart telling you that you have done what is right. If men speak against you, they will be ashamed when they see the good way you have lived as a Christian. 17 If God wants you to suffer, it is better to suffer for doing what is right than for doing what is wrong.

Christ Suffered for Us

18 Christ suffered and died for sins once for all. He never sinned and yet He died for us who have sinned. He died so He might bring us to God. His body died but His spirit was made alive. 19 Christ went and preached to the spirits in prison. 20 Those were the spirits of the people who would not obey in the days of Noah. God waited a long time for them while Noah was building the big boat. But only eight people were saved from dying when the earth was covered with water. 21 This is like baptism to us. Baptism does not mean we wash our bodies clean. It means we are saved from the punishment of sin and go to God in prayer with a heart that says we are right. This can be done because Christ was raised from the dead. 22 Christ has gone to heaven and is on the right side of God. Angels and powers of heaven are obeying Him.

Following Christ Will Mean Suffering

4 Since Christ has suffered in His body, we must be ready to suffer also. Suffering puts an end to sin. 2 You should no longer spend the rest of your life giving in to the sinful desires of the flesh. But do what God wants as long as you live in this world. 3 In the past you gave enough of your life over to living like the people who do not know God. You gave your life to sex sins and to sinful desires. You got drunk and went to wild parties and to drinking parties and you worshiped false gods. 4 Those who do not know God are surprised you do not join them in the sinful things they do. They laugh at you and say bad things against you. 5 Remember, they will give an answer to Him Who judges all who are living or dead. 6 For this reason, the Good News was preached to the dead. They stood in the flesh before the One Who judges so they might live in the Spirit as God wants.

Love Each Other

7 The end of the world is near. You must be the boss over your mind. Keep awake so

you can pray. 8 Most of all, have a true love for each other. Love covers many sins. 9 Be happy to have people stay for the night and eat with you. 10 God has given each of you a gift. Use it to help each other. This will show God's loving-favor. 11 If a man preaches, let him do it with God speaking through him. If a man helps others, let him do it with the strength God gives. So in all things God may be honored through Jesus Christ. Shining-greatness and power belong to Him forever. Let it be so.

Stay True During Suffering

12 Dear friends, your faith is going to be tested as if it were going through fire. Do not be surprised at this. 13 Be happy that you are able to share some of the suffering of Christ. When His shining-greatness is shown, you will be filled with much joy. 14 If men speak bad of you because you are a Christian, you will be happy because the Spirit of shining-greatness and of God is in you. 15 None of you should suffer as one who kills another person or as one who steals or as one who makes trouble or as one who tries to be the boss of other peoples' lives. 16 But if a man suffers as a Christian, he should not be ashamed. He should thank God that he is a Christian. 17 The time has come for Christians to stand before God and He will judge. If this happens to us, what will happen to those who do not obey the Good News of God? 18 If it is hard for a man who is right with God to be saved, what will happen to the sinner? 19 So if God wants you to suffer, give yourself to Him. He will do what is right for you. He made you and He is faithful.

5 I want to speak to the church leaders among you. I am a church leader also. I saw Christ suffer and die on a cross. I will also share His shining-greatness when He comes again. 2 Be good shepherds of the flock God has put in your care. Do not care for the flock as if you were made to. Do not care for the flock for money, but do it because you want to. 3 Do not be bosses over the people you lead. Live as you would like to have them live. 4 When the Head Shepherd comes again, you will get the crown of shining-greatness that will not come to an end.

5 In the same way, you younger men must obey the church leaders. Be gentle as you care for each other. God works against those who have pride. He gives His loving-favor to those who do not try to honor themselves. 6 So put away all pride from yourselves. You are standing under the powerful hand of God. At the right time He will lift you up. 7 Give all your worries to Him because He cares for you.

8 Keep awake! Watch at all times. The devil is working against you. He is walking around like a hungry lion with his mouth open. He is looking for someone to eat. 9 Stand against him and be strong in your faith. Remember, other Christians all over the world are suffering the same as you are. 10 After you have suffered for awhile, God Himself will make you perfect. He will keep you in the right way. He will give you strength. He is the God of all loving-favor and has called you through Christ Jesus to share His shining-greatness forever. 11 God has power over all things forever. Let it be so.

12 I have known Silvanus as a faithful Christian brother and it is by him I have written this short letter to help you. It tells you of the true loving-favor of God. Stay true in His loving-favor. 13 The church which is in the city of Babylon greets you. It has been chosen by God the same as you have been. My son, Mark, greets you also. 14 Greet each other with a kiss of holy love. May all of you Christians have peace.

2 PETER

1 This letter is from Simon Peter. I am a missionary of Jesus Christ and a servant owned by Him. I am writing to those who have received the same faith as ours which is of great worth and which no amount of money can buy. This faith comes from our God and Jesus Christ, the One Who saves. 2 May you have more and more of His loving-favor and peace as you come to know God and our Lord Jesus Christ better.

Christians Are to Grow

3 He gives us everything we need for life and for holy living. He gives it through His great power. As we come to know Him better, we learn that He called us to share His own shining-greatness and perfect

life. 4 Through His shining-greatness and perfect life, He has given us promises. These promises are of great worth and no amount of money can buy them. Through these promises you can have God's own life in you now that you have gotten away from the sinful things of the world which came from wrong desires of the flesh.

5 Do your best to add holy living to your faith. Then add to this a better understanding. 6 As you have a better understanding, be able to say no when you need to. Do not give up. And as you wait and do not give up, live God-like. 7 As you live God-like, be kind to Christian brothers and love them. 8 If you have all these things and keep growing in them, they will keep you from being of no use and from having no fruit when it comes to knowing our Lord Jesus Christ. 9 But if you do not have these things, you are blind and cannot see far. You forget God saved you from your old life of sin. 10 Christian brothers, make sure you are among those He has chosen and called out for His own. As long as you do these things, you will never trip and fall. 11 In this way, the road will be made wide open for you. And you will go into the holy nation that lasts forever of our Lord Jesus Christ, the One Who saves.

12 You already know about these things but I want to keep telling you about them. You are strong in the faith now. 13 I think it is right as long as I am alive to keep you thinking about these things. 14 I know that I will soon be leaving this body. Our Lord Jesus Christ has told me this. 15 I will try to make a way for you to remember these things after I am gone.

16 We had nothing to do with man-made stories when we told you about the power of our Lord Jesus Christ and of His coming again. We have seen His great power with our own eyes. 17 When He received honor and shining-greatness from God the Father, a voice came to Him from the All-powerful God, saying, "This is My much-loved Son. I am very happy with Him." 18 We heard this voice come from heaven when we were with Christ on the holy mountain.

19 All this helps us know that what the early preachers said was true. You will do well to listen to what they have said. Their words are as lights that shine in a dark place. Listen until you understand what they have said. Then it will be like the morning light which takes away the darkness. And the Morning Star (Christ) will rise to shine in your hearts.

20 Understand this first: No part of the Holy Writings was ever made up by any man. 21 No part of the Holy Writings came long ago because of what man wanted to write. But holy men who belonged to God spoke what the Holy Spirit told them.

Watch for False Teachers

2 But there were false teachers among the people. And there will be false teachers among you also. These people will work in secret ways to bring false teaching to you. They will turn against Christ Who bought them with His blood. They bring fast death on themselves. 2 Many people will follow their wrong ways. Because of what they do, people will speak bad things against the way of truth. 3 They will tell lies and false stories so they can use you to get things for themselves. But God judged them long ago and their death is on the way.

4 God did not hold back from punishing the angels who sinned, but sent them down to hell. They are to be kept there in the deep hole of darkness until they stand before Him Who judges them. 5 God did not hold back from punishing the people of the world who sinned long ago. He brought the flood on the world of sinners. But Noah was a preacher of right living. He and his family of seven were the only ones God saved. 6 God said that the cities of Sodom and Gomorrah were guilty, and He destroyed them with fire. This was to show people who did not worship God what would happen to them. 7 Lot was taken away from Sodom because he was right with God. He had been troubled by the sins that bad men did in wild living. 8 He saw and heard how the people around him broke the Law. Everyday his own soul which was right with God was troubled because of their sinful ways. 9 But the Lord knows how to help men who are right with God when they are tempted. He also knows how to keep the sinners suffering for their wrong-doing until the day they stand before God Who will judge them. 10 This is true about those who keep on wanting to please their own bodies in sinful desires and those who will not obey laws. They want to please themselves and are not afraid when they laugh and say bad things about the powers in heaven. 11 Angels are greater in strength and power than they. But angels do not speak against these powers before the Lord.

12 Men like this are like animals who are not able to think but are born to be caught and killed. They speak bad words against

that which they do not understand. They will die in their own sinful ways. 13 This is the pay they will suffer for their sinful lives. They are not ashamed when they sin in the daylight. They are sores and dirty spots among you while they eat and drink big meals with you. 14 Their eyes are full of sex sins. They never have enough sin. They get weak people to go along with them. Their hearts are always wanting something. They are people who will end up in hell because 15 they have left the right way and have gone the wrong way. They have followed the way of Balaam, who was the son of Beor. He loved the money he got for his sin. 16 But he was stopped in his sin. A donkey spoke to him with a man's voice. It stopped this early preacher from going on in his crazy way.

17 Such people are like wells without water. They are like clouds before a storm. The darkest place below has been kept for them. 18 They speak big-sounding words which show they are proud. They get men who are trying to keep away from sinful men to give in to the sinful desires of the flesh. 19 They promise that these men will be free. But they themselves are chained to sin. For a man is chained to anything that has power over him.

20 There are men who have been made free from the sins of the world by learning to know the Lord Jesus Christ, the One Who saves. But if they do these sins again, and are not able to keep from doing them, they are worse than they were before. 21 After knowing the holy Law that was given to them, they turned from it. It would have been better for them if they had not known how to be right with God. 22 They are like the wise saying, "A dog turns back to what he has thrown up." (Proverbs 26:11) And, "A pig that has been washed goes back to roll in the mud."

The World Will Be Destroyed

3 Dear friends, this is the second letter I have written to you. In both of them I have tried to get you to remember some things. 2 You should remember the words that were spoken before by the holy early preachers. Do not forget the teaching of the Lord, the One Who saves. This was given to you by your missionaries.

3 First of all, I want you to know that in the last days men will laugh at the truth. They will follow their own sinful desires. 4 They will say, "He promised to come again. Where is He? Since our early fathers died, everything is the same from the beginning

of the world." 5 But they want to forget that God spoke and the heavens were made long ago. The earth was made out of water and water was all around it. 6 Long ago the earth was covered with water and it was destroyed. 7 But the heaven we see now and the earth we live on now have been kept by His word. They will be kept until they are to be destroyed by fire. They will be kept until the day men stand before God and sinners will be destroyed.

8 Dear friends, remember this one thing, with the Lord one day is as 1,000 years, and 1,000 years are as one day. 9 The Lord is not slow about keeping His promise as some people think. He is waiting for you. The Lord does not want any person to be punished forever. He wants all people to be sorry for their sins and turn from them. 10 The day of the Lord will come as a robber comes. The heavens will pass away with a loud noise. The sun and moon and stars will burn up. The earth and all that is in it will be burned up.

11 Since all these things are to be destroyed in this way, you should think about the kind of life you are living. It should be holy and God-like. 12 You should look for the day of God to come. You should do what you can to make it come soon. At that time the heavens will be destroyed by fire. And the sun and moon and stars will melt away with much heat. 13 We are looking for what God has promised, which are new heavens and a new earth. Only what is right and good will be there.

14 Dear friends, since you are waiting for these things to happen, do all you can to be found by Him in peace. Be clean and free from sin. 15 You can be sure the long waiting of our Lord is part of His plan to save men from the punishment of sin. God gave our dear brother Paul the wisdom to write about this also. 16 He wrote about these things in all of his writings. Some of these things are hard to understand. People who do not have much understanding and some who are not strong in the faith change the meaning of his letters. They do this to the other parts of the Holy Writings also. They are destroying themselves as they do this.

17 And so, dear friends, now that you know this, watch so you will not be led away by the mistakes of these sinful people. Do not be moved by them. 18 Grow in the loving-favor that Christ gives you. Learn to know our Lord Jesus Christ better. He is the One Who saves. May He have all the shining-greatness now and forever. Let it be so.

1 JOHN

Christ—the Word of Life

1 Christ is the Word of Life. He was from the beginning. We have heard Him and have seen Him with our own eyes. We have looked at Him and put our hands on Him. 2 Christ Who is Life was shown to us. We saw Him. We tell you and preach about the Life that lasts forever. He was with the Father and He has come down to us. 3 We are preaching what we have heard and seen. We want you to share together with us what we have with the Father and with His Son, Jesus Christ. 4 We are writing this to you so our joy may be full.

Christians Are to Live in the Light

5 This is what we heard Him tell us. We are passing it on to you. God is light. There is no darkness in Him. 6 If we say we are joined together with Him but live in darkness, we are telling a lie. We are not living the truth. 7 If we live in the light as He is in the light, we share what we have in God with each other. And the blood of Jesus Christ, His Son, makes our lives clean from all sin. 8 If we say that we have no sin, we lie to ourselves and the truth is not in us. 9 If we tell Him our sins, He is faithful and we can depend on Him to forgive us of our sins. He will make our lives clean from all sin. 10 If we say we have not sinned, we make God a liar. And His Word is not in our hearts.

Christ Is Our Helper

2 My dear children, I am writing this to you so you will not sin. But if anyone does sin, there is One Who will go between him and the Father. He is Jesus Christ, the One Who is right with God. 2 He paid for our sins with His own blood. He did not pay for ours only, but for the sins of the whole world.

3 We can be sure that we know Him if we obey His teaching. 4 Anyone who says, "I know Him," but does not obey His teaching is a liar. There is no truth in him. 5 But whoever obeys His Word has the love of God made perfect in him. This is the way to know if you belong to Christ. 6 The one who says he belongs to Christ should live the same kind of life Christ lived.

7 Dear friends, I am not writing a new Law for you to obey. It is an old Law you have had from the beginning. The old Law is the Word that you have heard. 8 And yet it is a new Law that I am writing to you. It is truth. It was seen in Christ and it is seen in you also. The darkness is passing away and the true Light shines instead. 9 Whoever says he is in the light but hates his brother is still in darkness. 10 But whoever loves his brother is in the light. And there will be no reason to sin because of him. 11 Whoever hates his brother is not in the light but lives in darkness. He does not know where he is going because the darkness has blinded his eyes.

Do Not Love the World

12 I am writing to you, my children, for your sins have been forgiven because of Christ's name. 13 I am writing to you, fathers, because you know Him Who has been from the beginning. I am writing to you, young men, because you have power over the devil. I have written to you, young boys and girls, because you have learned to know the Father. 14 I have written to you, fathers, because you know Him Who has been from the beginning. I have written to you, young men, because you are strong. You have kept God's Word in your hearts. You have power over the devil.

15 Do not love the world or anything in the world. If anyone loves the world, the Father's love is not in him. 16 For everything that is in the world does not come from the Father. The desires of our flesh and the things our eyes see and want and the pride of this life come from the world. 17 The world and all its desires will pass away. But the man who obeys God and does what He wants done will live forever.

18 My children, we are near the end of the world. You have heard that the false-christ is coming. Many false-christs have already come. This is how we know the end of the world is near. 19 These left us. But they never belonged to us. If they had been a part of us, they would have stayed with us. Because they left, it is known they did not belong to us. 20 The Holy Spirit has been given to you and you all know the truth. 21 I have not written to you because you do not know the truth. I have written because you do know the truth and you know that no lie comes from the truth.

22 Who is a liar? He is a person who says that Jesus is not the Christ. The false-christ will have nothing to do with the Father and the Son and he will turn away from Them. 23 A person who will have nothing to do with the Son and turns against Him does not have the Father. The one who says he knows the Son has the Father also.

24 Keep in your heart what you have heard from the beginning. Then you will

belong to the Son and to the Father if what you have heard from the beginning is in you. 25 And He has promised us life that lasts forever! 26 I have written to you about those who are trying to lead you in the wrong way. 27 Christ gave you the Holy Spirit and He lives in you. You do not need anyone to teach you. The Holy Spirit is able to teach you all things. What He teaches you is truth and not a lie. Live by the help of Christ as the Holy Spirit has taught you. 28 And now, my children, live by the help of Him. Then when He comes again, we will be glad to see Him and not be ashamed. 29 You know that Christ is right with God. Then you should know that everyone who is right with God is a child of His.

We Are God's Children

3 See what great love the Father has for us that He would call us His children. And that is what we are. For this reason the people of the world do not know who we are because they did not know Him. 2 Dear friends, we are God's children now. But it has not yet been shown to us what we are going to be. We know that when He comes again, we will be like Him because we will see Him as He is. 3 The person who is looking for this to happen will keep himself pure because Christ is pure.

4 The person who keeps on sinning is guilty of not obeying the Law of God. For sin is breaking the Law of God. 5 You know that Christ came to take away our sins. There is no sin in Him. 6 The person who lives by the help of Christ does not keep on sinning. The person who keeps on sinning has not seen Him or has not known Him. 7 My children, let no one lead you in the wrong way. The man who does what is right, is right with God in the same way as Christ is right with God. 8 The person who keeps on sinning belongs to the devil. The devil has sinned from the beginning. But the Son of God came to destroy the works of the devil. 9 No person who has become a child of God keeps on sinning. This is because the Holy Spirit is in him. He cannot keep on sinning because God is his Father. 10 This is the way you can know who are the children of God and who are the children of the devil. The person who does not keep on doing what is right and does not love his brother does not belong to God. 11 This is what you have heard from the beginning, that we should love each other. 12 Do not be like Cain. He was a child of the devil and killed his brother. Why did he kill him? It was because he did what was sinful and his brother did what was right.

13 Do not be surprised if the world hates you, Christian brothers. 14 We know we have passed from death into life. We know this because we love the Christians. The person who does not love has not passed from death into life. 15 A man who hates his brother is a killer in his heart. You know that life which lasts forever is not in one who kills.

16 We know what love is because Christ gave His life for us. We should give our lives for our brothers. 17 What if a person has enough money to live on and sees his brother in need of food and clothing? If he does not help him, how can the love of God be in him? 18 My children, let us not love with words or in talk only. Let us love by what we do and in truth. 19 This is how we know we are Christians. It will give our heart comfort for sure when we stand before Him. 20 Our heart may say that we have done wrong. But remember, God is greater than our heart. He knows everything. 21 Dear friends, if our heart does not say that we are wrong, we will have no fear as we stand before Him. 22 We will receive from Him whatever we ask if we obey Him and do what He wants. 23 This is what He said we must do: Put your trust in the name of His Son, Jesus Christ, and love each other. Christ told us to do this. 24 The person who obeys Christ lives by the help of God and God lives in him. We know He lives in us by the Holy Spirit He has given us.

The Spirits Must Be Tested

4 Dear Christian friends, do not believe every spirit. But test the spirits to see if they are from God for there are many false preachers in the world. 2 You can tell if the spirit is from God in this way: Every spirit that says Jesus Christ has come in a human body is from God. 3 And every spirit that does not say Jesus has come in a human body is not from God. It is the teaching of the false-christ. You have heard that this teaching is coming. It is already here in the world. 4 My children, you are a part of God's family. You have stood against these false preachers and had power over them. You had power over them because the One Who lives in you is stronger than the one who is in the world. 5 Those false teachers are a part of the world. They speak about the things of the world. The world listens to them. 6 We are a part of God's family. The person who knows God will listen to

us. The person who is not a part of God's family will not listen to us. In this way, we can tell what is the spirit of truth and what is the spirit of false teaching.

Loving God Makes Us Love Our Christian Brothers

7 Dear friends, let us love each other, because love comes from God. Those who love are God's children and they know God. 8 Those who do not love do not know God because God is love. 9 God has shown His love to us by sending His only Son into the world. God did this so we might have life through Christ. 10 This is love! It is not that we loved God but that He loved us. For God sent His Son to pay for our sins with His own blood.

11 Dear friends, if God loved us that much, then we should love each other. 12 No person has ever seen God at any time. If we love each other, God lives in us. His love is made perfect in us. 13 He has given us His Spirit. This is how we live by His help and He lives in us.

Love Gives Us More Faith in Christ

14 We have seen and are able to say that the Father sent His Son to save the world from the punishment of sin. 15 The person who tells of Him in front of men and says that Jesus is the Son of God, God is living in that one and that one is living by the help of God. 16 We have come to know and believe the love God has for us. God is love. If you live in love, you live by the help of God and God lives in you.

The Love of God Has Power Over Fear and Hate

17 Love is made perfect in us when we are not ashamed as we stand before Him on the day He judges. For we know that our life in this world is His life lived in us. 18 There is no fear in love. Perfect love puts fear out of our hearts. People have fear when they are afraid of being punished. The man who is afraid does not have perfect love. 19 We love Him because He loved us first. 20 If a person says, "I love God," but hates his brother, he is a liar. If a person does not love his brother whom he has seen, how can he love God Whom he has not seen? 21 We have these words from Him. If you love God, love your brother also.

5 The person who believes that Jesus is the Christ is a child of God. The person who loves the Father loves His children also. 2 This is the way we know we love

God's children. It is when we love God and obey His Word. 3 Loving God means to obey His Word, and His Word is not hard to obey. 4 Every child of God has power over the sins of the world. The way we have power over the sins of the world is by our faith. 5 Who could have power over the world except by believing that Jesus is the Son of God? 6 Jesus Christ came by water and blood. He did not come by water only, but by water and blood. The Holy Spirit speaks about this and He is truth. 7 There are three Who speak of this in heaven: the Father and the Word and the Holy Spirit. These three are one. 8 There are three who speak of this on the earth: the Holy Spirit and the water and the blood. These three speak the same thing. 9 If we believe what men say, we can be sure what God says is more important. God has spoken as He has told us about His Son. 10 The person who puts his trust in God's Son knows in his own heart that Jesus is the Son of God. The person who does not have his trust in God's Son makes God a liar. It is because he has not believed the word God spoke about His Son. 11 This is the word He spoke: God gave us life that lasts forever, and this life is in His Son. 12 He that has the Son has life. He that does not have the Son of God does not have life.

13 I have written these things to you who believe in the name of the Son of God. Now you can know you have life that lasts forever. 14 We are sure that if we ask anything that He wants us to have, He will hear us. 15 If we are sure He hears us when we ask, we can be sure He will give us what we ask for. 16 You may see a Christian brother sinning in a way that does not lead to death. You should pray for him. God will give him life unless he has done that sin that leads to death. There is a sin that leads to death. There is no reason to pray for him if he has done that sin. 17 Every kind of wrong-doing is sin. But there is a sin that does not lead to death. 18 We know that no child of God keeps on sinning. The Son of God watches over him and the devil cannot get near him. 19 We know that we belong to God, but the whole world is under the power of the devil. 20 We know God's Son has come. He has given us the understanding to know Him Who is the true God. We are joined together with the true God through His Son, Jesus Christ. He is the true God and the life that lasts forever. 21 My children, keep yourselves from false gods.

2 JOHN

The church leader writes to the chosen lady and to her children. I love you because of the truth. I am not the only one who loves you. All who know the truth love you. 2 It is because the truth is in us and will be with us forever. 3 Loving-favor and loving-kindness and peace are ours as we live in truth and love. These come from God the Father and from the Lord Jesus Christ, Who is the Son of the Father.

4 I am happy to find some of your children living in the truth as the Father has said we should. 5 And now I ask you, lady, that we have love one for the other. I am not writing to you about a new Law but an old one we have had from the beginning. 6 Love means that we should live by obeying His Word. From the beginning He has said in His Word that our hearts should be full of love.

7 There are many false teachers in the world. They do not say that Jesus Christ came in a human body. Such a person does not tell the truth. He is the false-christ. 8 Watch yourselves! You do not want to lose what we have worked for. You want to get what has been promised to you.

9 Anyone who goes too far and does not live by the teachings of Christ does not have God. If you live by what Christ taught, you have both the Father and the Son. 10 If a person comes to you with some other kind of teaching, do not take him into your home. Do not even greet him. 11 The person who does has a share in his sins.

12 I have many things to write to you. I do not want to write them in this letter. But I hope to come to you soon. Then we can talk about these things together that your joy may be full. 13 The children of your chosen sister greet you.

3 JOHN

The church leader writes to the much-loved Gaius. I love you because of the truth. 2 Dear friend, I pray that you are doing well in every way. I pray that your body is strong and well even as your soul is. 3 I was very happy when some Christians came and told me about how you are following the truth. 4 I can have no greater joy than to hear that my children are following the truth.

5 Dear friend, you are doing a good work by being kind to the Christians, and for sure, to the strangers. 6 They have told the church about your love. It will be good for you to help them on their way as God would have you. 7 These people are working for the Lord. They are taking nothing from the people who do not know God. 8 So we should help such people. That way we will be working with them as they teach the truth.

9 I wrote a letter to the church. But Diotrephes wants to be the leader and put himself first. He will have nothing to do with us. 10 So if I come, I will show what he is doing by the bad things he is saying about us. Not only that, he will not take the Christian brothers into his home. He keeps others from doing it also. When they do, he puts them out of the church. 11 Dear friend, do not follow what is sinful, but follow what is good. The person who does what is good belongs to God. The person who does what is sinful has not seen God. 12 Everyone speaks good things about Demetrius. The truth itself speaks for him. We say the same thing also and you know we are speaking the truth. 13 I have much to write about but I do not want to write it in this letter. 14 I hope to see you soon and then we can talk together. May you have peace. The friends here greet you. Greet each friend there by name.

JUDE

This letter is from Jude, a brother of James. I am a servant owned by Jesus Christ. I am writing to you who have been chosen by God the Father. You are kept for Jesus Christ. 2 May you have much of God's loving-kindness and peace and love.

3 Dear friends, I have been trying to write to you about what God did for us when He saved us from the punishment of sin. Now I must write to you and tell

you to fight hard for the faith which was once and for all given to the holy people of God. 4 Some sinful men have come into your church without anyone knowing it. They are living in sin and they speak of the loving-favor of God to cover up their sins. They have turned against our only Leader and Lord, Jesus Christ. Long ago it was written that these people would die in their sins.

5 You already know all this, but think about it again. The Lord saved His people out of the land of Egypt. Later He destroyed all those who did not put their trust in Him. 6 Angels who did not stay in their place of power, but left the place where they were given to stay, are chained in a dark place. They will be there until the day they stand before God to be judged. 7 Do you remember about the cities of Sodom and Gomorrah and the towns around them? The people in those cities did the same things. They were full of sex sins and strong desires for sinful acts of the body. Those cities were destroyed by fire. They still speak to us of the fire of hell that lasts forever.

What False Teachers Are Like

8 In the same way, these men go on dreaming and sinning against their bodies. They respect no leaders. They speak bad against those who live in the heavens. 9 Michael was one of the head angels. He argued with the devil about the body of Moses. But Michael would not speak sharp words to the devil, saying he was guilty. He said, "The Lord speaks sharp words to you." 10 But these men speak against things they do not understand. They are like animals in the way they act. By these things they destroy themselves. 11 It is bad for them! They have followed the way of Cain who killed his brother. They have chosen the way of Balaam and think only about making money. They were destroyed as Korah was destroyed who would not show respect to leaders. 12 When you come together to eat the Christians' love suppers, these people are like hidden rocks that wreck a ship. They only think of themselves. They are like clouds without rain carried along by the wind and like trees without fruit in the fall of the year. They are pulled out by

the roots and are dead now and never can live again. 13 They are like the waves of a wild sea. Their sins are like the dirty water along the shore. They look like stars moving here and there. But the darkest place has been kept for them forever.

14 Enoch was the head of the seventh family born after Adam. He said this about such people, "The Lord comes with many thousands of His holy ones. 15 He comes to say that all are guilty for all the sin they have done and all the sinful things these sinners have spoken against God." 16 These men complain and are never happy with anything. They let their desires lead them into sin. When they talk about themselves, they make it sound as if they are great people. They show respect to people only to get something out of them.

17 Dear friends, you must remember the words spoken by the missionaries of our Lord Jesus Christ. 18 They said, "In the last days there will be men who will laugh at the truth and will be led by their own sinful desires." 19 They are men who will make trouble by dividing people into groups against each other. Their minds are on the things of the world because they do not have the Holy Spirit.

20 Dear friends, you must become strong in your most holy faith. Let the Holy Spirit lead you as you pray. 21 Keep yourselves in the love of God. Wait for life that lasts forever through the loving-kindness of our Lord Jesus Christ. 22 Have loving-kindness for those who doubt. 23 Save some by pulling them out of the fire. Have loving-kindness for others but also fear them. Be afraid of being led into doing their sins. Hate even the clothes that have touched sinful bodies.

24 There is One Who can keep you from falling and can bring you before Himself free from all sin. He can give you great joy as you stand before Him in His shining-greatness. 25 He is the only God. He is the One Who saves from the punishment of sin through Jesus Christ our Lord. May He have shining-greatness and honor and power and the right to do all things. He had this before the world began, He has it now, and He will have this forever. Let it be so.

REVELATION

1 The things that are written in the Book are made known by Jesus Christ. God gave these things to Christ so He could show them to the servants He owns. These are things which must happen very soon. Christ sent His angel to John who is a servant owned by Him. Christ made these things known to John. **2** John tells that the Word of God is true. He tells of Jesus Christ and all that he saw and heard of Him. **3** The man who reads this Book and listens to it being read and obeys what it says will be happy. For all these things will happen soon.

John Writes to the Seven Churches in Asia

4 This is John writing to the seven churches in the country of Asia. May you have loving-favor and peace from God Who was and Who is and Who is to come. May you have loving-favor and peace from the seven Spirits who are before His throne. **5** May you have loving-favor and peace from Jesus Christ Who is faithful in telling the truth. Jesus Christ is the first to be raised from the dead. He is the head over all the kings of the earth. He is the One Who loves us and has set us free from our sins by His blood. **6** Christ has made us a holy nation of religious leaders who can go to His God and Father. He is the One to receive honor and power forever! Let it be so. **7** See! He is coming in the clouds. Every eye will see Him. Even the men who killed Him will see Him. All the people on the earth will cry out in sorrow because of Him. Yes, let it be so.

8 The Lord God says, "I am the First and the Last, the beginning and the end of all things. I am the All-powerful One Who was and Who is and Who is to come."

What God Wanted to Show John of Christ

9 I, John, am your Christian brother. I have shared with you in suffering because of Jesus Christ. I have also shared with you His holy nation and we have not given up. I was put on the island called Patmos because I preached the Word of God and told about Jesus Christ. **10** I was under the Spirit's power on the Lord's Day when I heard a loud voice behind me like the loud sound of a horn. **11** It said, "(*I am the First and the Last.) Write in a book what you see and send it to the seven churches. They are in the cities of Ephesus and Smyrna and Pergamum and Thyatira and Sardis and Philadelphia and Laodicea."

12 I turned around to see who was speaking to me. As I turned, I saw seven lights made of gold. **13** Among the lights stood One Who looked like the Son of Man. He had on a long coat that came to His feet. A belt of gold was around His chest. **14** His head and His hair were white like white wool. They were as white as snow. His eyes were like fire. **15** His feet were like shining brass as bright as if it were in a fire. His voice sounded like powerful rushing water. **16** He held seven stars in His right hand. A sharp sword that cuts both ways came out of His mouth. His face was shining as bright as the sun shines at noon. **17** When I saw Him, I fell down at His feet like a dead man. He laid His right hand on me and said, "Do not be afraid. I am the First and the Last. **18** I am the Living One. I was dead, but look, I am alive forever. I have power over death and hell. **19** So write the things you have seen and the things that are and the things that will happen later. **20** This is what the seven stars and the seven lights made of gold mean that you saw in My right hand. The seven stars are the angels of the seven churches. The seven lights are the seven churches.

Words to the Church in Ephesus

2 "Write this to the angel of the church in the city of Ephesus: 'The One Who holds the seven stars in His right hand and the One Who walks among the seven lights made of gold, says this: **2** I know what you have done and how hard you have worked. I know how long you can wait and not give up. I know that you cannot put up with sinful men. I know that you have put men to the test who call themselves missionaries. You have found they are not missionaries but are false. **3** You have waited long and have not given up. You have suffered because of Me. You have kept going on and have not become tired. **4** But I have this one thing against you. You do not love Me as you did at first. **5** Remember how you once loved Me. Be sorry for your sin and love Me again as you did at first. If you do not, I will come to you and take your light out of its place. I will do this unless you are sorry for your sin and turn from it. **6** But you have this: You hate what the Nicolaitans do. I hate what they do also. **7** You have ears! Then listen to what the Spirit says to the churches. I will give the fruit of the tree of life in the garden of God to everyone who has power and wins.'

Words to the Church in Smyrna

8 "Write this to the angel of the church in the city of Smyrna: 'The One Who is First and Last, the One Who died and came to life again, says this: 9 I know of your troubles. I know you are poor. But still you are rich! I know the bad things spoken against you by those who say they are Jews. But they are not Jews. They belong to the devil. 10 Do not be afraid of what you will suffer. Listen! The devil will throw some of you into prison to test you. You will be in trouble for ten days. Be faithful even to death. Then I will give you the crown of life. 11 You have ears! Then listen to what the Spirit says to the churches. The person who has power and wins will not be hurt by the second death!'

Words to the Church in Pergamum

12 "Write this to the angel of the church in the city of Pergamum: 'The One Who has the sharp sword that cuts both ways, says this: 13 I know where you live. It is the place where Satan sits. I know that you are true to Me. You did not give up and turn away from your faith in Me, even when Antipas was killed. He was faithful in speaking for Me. He was killed in front of you where Satan sits. 14 But I have a few things against you. You have some people who follow the teaching of Balaam. He taught Balak to set a trap for the Jews. He taught them to eat food that had been given as a gift in worship to false gods and to do sex sins. 15 You also have some who follow the teaching of the Nicolaitans in the same way. 16 Be sorry for your sins and turn from them. If you do not, I will come to you right away. I will fight against them with the sword of My mouth. 17 You have ears! Then listen to what the Spirit says to the churches. I will give the hidden bread from heaven to everyone who has power and wins. I will give each of them a white stone also. A new name will be written on it. No one will know the name except the one who receives it!'

Words to the Church in Thyatira

18 "Write this to the angel of the church in the city of Thyatira: 'The Son of God Who has eyes like fire and Whose feet are like shining brass, says this: 19 I know what you are doing. I know of your love and faith. I know how you have worked and how you have waited long and have not given up. I know that you are working harder now than you did at first. 20 But I have this against you: You are allowing Jezebel who calls herself a preacher to teach my servants. She is leading them in the wrong way and they are doing sex sins. And they are eating food that has been given as a gift in worship to false gods. 21 I gave her time to be sorry for her sins and turn from them. She does not want to turn from her sex sins. 22 See! I will throw her on a bed. Those who do sex sins with her will suffer much trouble and pain. I will let them suffer unless they are sorry for the sins they have done with her and turn from them. 23 And I will kill her children. All the churches will know that I am the One Who looks deep into the hearts and minds. I will give you whatever is coming to you because of your work. 24 But the rest of you there in the city of Thyatira have not followed this false teaching. You have not learned what they call the secrets of Satan. So I will put no other load on you. 25 But hold on to what you have until I come. 26 To the one who has power and wins and does what I want him to do, I will give the right and the power over the nations. 27 He will be leader over them using a piece of iron. And they will be broken in pieces like pots of clay. My Father has given Me this right and power. 28 And I will give him the Morning Star. 29 You have ears! Then listen to what the Spirit says to the churches!'

Words to the Church in Sardis

3 "Write this to the angel of the church in the city of Sardis: 'The One Who has the seven Spirits of God and the seven stars, says this: I know what you are doing. I know people think you are alive, but you are dead. 2 Wake up! Make stronger what you have before it dies. I have not found your work complete in God's sight. 3 So remember what you have received and heard. Keep it. Be sorry for your sins and turn from them. If you will not wake up, I will come as a robber. You will not know at what time I will come. 4 But there are a few people in the church in the city of Sardis whose clothes are not dirty with sins. They will walk with Me wearing white clothes. They have done what they should. 5 Everyone who has power and wins will wear white clothes. I will not take his name from the book of life. I will speak of his name before My Father and His angels. 6 You have ears! Then listen to what the Spirit says to the churches.'

Words to the Church in Philadelphia

7 "Write this to the angel of the church in the city of Philadelphia: 'He Who is holy and true, Who holds the key of David, Who opens and no man can shut, Who shuts and no man can open, says this: 8 I know what you are doing. See! You do not have much power, but you have obeyed My Word. You have not turned against Me. So I have given you an open door that no man can shut. 9 See! There are some who belong to Satan. They say they are Jews, but they are not. They are liars. See! I will make them come to you and get down at your feet. Then they will know that I love you. 10 I will keep you from the time of trouble. The time to test everyone is about to come to the whole world. I will do this because you have listened to Me and have waited long and have not given up. 11 I am coming very soon. Hold on to what you have so no one can take your crown. 12 I will make the one who has power and wins an important part that holds up the house of God. He will never leave it again. I will write on him the name of My God and the name of the city of My God. It is the new Jerusalem. The new Jerusalem will come down from My God out of heaven. I will write My new name on him. 13 You have ears! Then listen to what the Spirit says to the churches.'

Words to the Church in Laodicea

14 "Write this to the angel of the church in the city of Laodicea: 'The One Who says, Let it be so, the One Who is faithful, the One Who tells what is true, the One Who made everything in God's world, says this: 15 I know what you are doing. You are not cold or hot. I wish you were one or the other. 16 But because you are warm, and not hot or cold, I will spit you out of My mouth. 17 You say that you are rich and that you need nothing, but you do not know that you are so troubled in mind and heart. You are poor and blind and without clothes. 18 You should buy gold from Me that has been tested by fire that you may be rich. Buy white clothes to dress yourself so the shame of not wearing clothes will be taken away. Buy medicine to put on your eyes so you can see. 19 I speak strong words to those I love and I punish them. Have a strong desire to please the Lord. Be sorry for your sins and turn from them. 20 See! I stand at the door and knock. If anyone hears My voice and opens the door, I will come in to him and we will eat together. 21 I will allow the one who has power and wins to sit with Me on My throne, as I also had power and won and sat down with My Father on His throne. 22 You have ears! Then listen to what the Spirit says to the churches.'"

The King's Place of Power in Heaven

4 After this, I looked and saw a door standing open in heaven. The first voice I heard was like the loud sound of a horn. It said, "Come up here. I will show you what must happen after these things." 2 At once I was under the Spirit's power. See! The throne was in heaven, and One was sitting on it. 3 The One Who sat there looked as bright as jasper and sardius stones. The colors like those of an emerald stone were all around the throne. 4 There were twenty-four smaller thrones around the throne. And on these thrones twenty-four leaders were sitting dressed in white clothes. They had crowns of gold on their heads. 5 Lightning and noise and thunder came from the throne. Seven lights of fire were burning before the throne. These were the seven Spirits of God.

6 Before the throne there was what looked like a sea of glass, shining and clear. Around the throne and on each side there were four living beings that were full of eyes in front and in back. 7 The first living being was like a lion. The second one was like a young cow. The third one had a face like a man. The fourth one was like a very large bird with its wings spread. 8 Each one of the four living beings had six wings. They had eyes all over them, inside and out. Day and night they never stop saying, "Holy, holy, holy is the Lord God, the All-powerful One. He is the One Who was and Who is and Who is to come."

9 The four living beings speak of His shining-greatness and give honor and thanks to Him Who sits on His throne as King. It is He Who lives forever. 10 The twenty-four leaders get down before Him and worship Him Who lives forever. They lay their crowns before Him and say, 11 "Our Lord and our God, it is right for You to have the shining-greatness and the honor and the power. You made all things. They were made and have life because You wanted it that way."

The Book in Heaven

5 I saw a book in the right hand of the One Who sat on the a throne. It had writing on the inside and on the back side. It was locked with seven locks. ² I saw a powerful angel calling with a loud voice, "Who is able to open the book and to break its locks?" ³ No one in heaven or on the earth or under the earth was able to open the book or to look in it. ⁴ Then I began to cry with loud cries. I cried because no one was good enough to open the book or to look in it.

⁵ One of the leaders said to me, "Stop crying. See! The Lion from the family group of Judah has power and has won. He can open the book and break its seven locks. He is of the family of David."

⁶ I saw a Lamb standing in front of the twenty-four leaders. He was before the throne and in front of the four living beings. He looked as if He had been killed. He had seven horns and seven eyes. These are the seven Spirits of God. They have been sent out into all the world. ⁷ The Lamb came and took the book from the right hand of the One Who sat on the throne. ⁸ When the Lamb had taken the book, the four living beings and the twenty four leaders got down before Him. Each one had a harp. They all had pots made of gold, full of special perfume, which are the prayers of the people who belong to God. ⁹ They sang a new song, saying, "It is right for You to take the book and break its locks. It is because You were killed. Your blood has bought men for God from every family and from every language and from every kind of people and from every nation. ¹⁰ You have made them to be a holy nation of religious leaders to work for our God. They will be the leaders on the earth."

¹¹ I looked again. I heard the voices of many thousands of angels. They stood around the throne and around the four living beings and the leaders. ¹² They said with a loud voice, "The Lamb Who was killed has the right to receive power and riches and wisdom and strength and honor and shining-greatness and thanks."

¹³ Then I heard every living thing in heaven and on the earth and under the earth and in the sea and all that are in them. They were saying, "Thanks and honor and shining-greatness and all power are to the One Who sits on the throne and to the Lamb forever." ¹⁴ The four living beings kept saying, "Let it be so!" And the twenty-four leaders fell down and worshiped.

The Seven Locks: the First Lock— Power to Win

6 I saw the Lamb break open the first of the seven locks. I heard one of the four living beings cry out like the sound of thunder, "Come and see!" ² I looked and saw a white horse. The one who sat on it had a bow. A crown was given to him. He went out to win and he won.

The Second Lock—Fighting

³ He broke open the second lock. Then I heard the second living being say, "Come and see!" ⁴ Another horse came out. This one was red. The one who sat on it was given a long sword. He was given power to take peace from the earth so men would kill each other.

The Third Lock—No Food

⁵ He broke open the third lock. Then I heard the third living being say, "Come and see!" I looked and saw a black horse. The one who sat on it had something in his hand with which to weigh things. ⁶ I heard a voice from among the four living beings saying, "A small jar of wheat for a day's pay. Three small jars of barley for a day's pay. Do not hurt the olive oil and wine."

The Fourth Lock—Death

⁷ He broke open the fourth lock. Then I heard the fourth living being say, "Come and see!" ⁸ I looked and saw a light colored horse. The one who sat on it had the name of Death. Hell followed close behind him. They were given the right and the power to kill one-fourth part of everything on the earth. They were to kill with the sword and by people having no food and by sickness and by the wild animals of the earth.

The Fifth Lock—Killed for Telling of Jesus

⁹ He broke open the fifth lock. Then I saw under the altar all the souls of those who had been killed for telling the Word of God. They had also been killed for being faithful in telling about Christ. ¹⁰ All those who had been killed cried out with a loud voice saying, "How long will it be yet before You will punish those on the earth for killing us? Lord, You are holy and true." ¹¹ White clothes were given to each one of them. They were told to rest a little longer. They were to wait until all the other servants owned by God and their Christian brothers would be killed as they had been. Then the group would be complete.

The Sixth Lock—God's Anger on the Earth

12 I looked as the Lamb broke the sixth lock. The earth shook as if it would break apart. The sun became black like dark cloth. The moon became like blood. 13 The stars of the sky fell to the earth. They were like figs falling from a tree that is shaken by a strong wind. 14 The sky passed away like paper being rolled up. Every mountain and island moved from its place. 15 The kings and the leaders of the earth hid themselves in caves and among the rocks of the mountains. All the head soldiers and rich men and strong men and men who were free and those who were owned by someone hid themselves also. 16 They called to the mountains and to the rocks, "Fall on us! Hide us from the face of the One Who sits on the throne. Hide us from the anger of the Lamb, 17 because the special day of Their anger has come! Who is able to stand against it?"

The Servants God Owns Are Marked

7 After this I saw four angels. They were standing at the four corners of the earth. They were holding back the four winds of the earth so no wind would blow on the earth or the sea or on any tree. 2 I saw another angel coming from the east. He was carrying the mark of the living God. He called with a loud voice to the four angels who had been given power to hurt the earth and sea. 3 The angel from the east said, "Do not hurt the earth or the sea or the trees until we have put the mark of God on the foreheads of the servants He owns."

4 I heard how many there were who received the mark of God. There were 144,000 people of the twelve family groups of Israel. 5 These received the mark of God: 12,000 from the family group of Judah, 12,000 from the family group of Reuben, 12,000 from the family group of Gad, 6 12,000 from the family group of Asher, 12,000 from the family group of Naphtali, 12,000 from the family group of Manasseh, 7 12,000 from the family group of Simeon, 12,000 from the family group of Levi, 12,000 from the family group of Issachar, 8 12,000 from the family group of Zebulun, 12,000 from the family group of Joseph, and 12,000 from the family group of Benjamin.

The Many People Who Belonged to God

9 After this I saw many people. No one could tell how many there were. They were from every nation and from every family and from every kind of people and from every language. They were standing before the throne and before the Lamb. They were wearing white clothes and they held branches in their hands. 10 And they were crying out with a loud voice, "We are saved from the punishment of sin by our God Who sits on the throne and by the Lamb!" 11 Then all of the angels standing around the throne and around the leaders and the four living beings got down on their faces before God and worshiped Him. 12 They said, "Let it be so! May our God have worship and shining-greatness and wisdom and thanks and honor and power and strength forever. Let it be so!"

13 Then one of the twenty-four leaders asked me, "Who are these people dressed in white clothes? Where did they come from?" 14 I answered him, "Sir, you know." Then he said to me, "These are the ones who came out of the time of much trouble. They have washed their clothes and have made them white in the blood of the Lamb. 15 For this reason they are before the throne of God. They help Him day and night in the house of God. And He Who sits on the throne will care for them as He is among them. 16 They will never be hungry or thirsty again. The sun or any burning heat will not shine down on them. 17 For the Lamb Who is in the center of the throne will be their Shepherd. He will lead them to wells of the water of life. God will take away all tears from their eyes."

The Seventh Lock—No Sound in Heaven

8 When the Lamb broke the seventh lock, there was not a sound in heaven for about one-half hour.

2 Then I saw the seven angels standing before God. They were given seven horns. 3 Another angel came and stood at the altar. He held a cup made of gold full of special perfume. He was given much perfume so he could mix it in with the prayers of those who belonged to God. Their prayers were put on the altar made of gold before the throne. 4 Smoke from burning the special perfume and the prayers of those who belong to God went up before God out of the angel's hand. 5 Then the angel took the cup of gold. He filled it with fire from the altar and threw it down on the earth. There was thunder and noise and lightning and the earth shook.

6 The seven angels that had the seven horns got ready to blow them.

The First Horn—Hail and Fire

7 So the first angel blew his horn. Hail and fire mixed with blood came down on the earth. One-third part of the earth was burned up. One-third part of the trees were burned up. All the green grass was burned up.

The Second Horn—the Burning Mountain

8 The second angel blew his horn. Something like a large mountain was burning with fire. It was thrown into the sea. One-third part of the sea turned into blood. 9 One-third part of all sea life died. One-third part of all the ships were destroyed.

The Third Horn—the Star of Poison

10 The third angel blew his horn. A large star fell from heaven. It was burning with a fire that kept burning like a bright light. It fell on one-third part of the rivers and on the places where water comes out of the earth. 11 The name of the star is Wormwood. One-third part of the water became poison. Many men died from drinking the water because it had become poison.

The Fourth Horn—Not As Much Light

12 The fourth angel blew his horn. One-third part of the sun and one-third part of the moon and one-third part of the stars were hurt. One-third part of them was made dark so that one-third part of the day and night had no light.

13 Then I looked and saw a very large bird flying in the sky. It said with a loud voice, "It is bad! It is bad! It is bad for those who live on the earth when the sound comes from the horns that the other three angels will blow!"

The Fifth Horn—the Hole Without a Bottom

9 The fifth angel blew his horn. I saw a star from heaven which had fallen to earth. The key to the hole without a bottom was given to the angel. 2 He opened the hole and smoke came out like the smoke from a place where there is much fire. The sun and the air became dark because of the smoke from the hole. 3 Locusts came down to the earth out of the smoke. They were given power to hurt like small animals that sting. 4 They were told not to hurt the grass or any green plant or any tree. They were to hurt only the men who did not have the mark of God on their foreheads. 5 The locusts were not allowed to kill these men. They

were to give them much pain for five months like the pain that comes from a small animal that stings. 6 Men will look for ways to die during those days, but they will not find any way. They will want to die, but death will be kept from them. 7 The locusts looked like horses ready for war. They had on their heads what looked like crowns of gold. Their faces were like men's faces. 8 Their hair was like the hair of women. Their teeth were like the teeth of lions. 9 Their chests were covered with what looked like pieces of iron. The sound their wings made was like the sound of many wagons rushing to war. 10 They had tails like a small animal that stings. The sting came from their tails. They were given power to hurt men for five months. 11 These locusts have a king over them. He is the head angel of the hole that has no bottom. His name in the Hebrew language is Abaddon. In the Greek language it is Apollyon. (It means the one who destroys.)

12 The first time of trouble is past. But see, there are two more times of trouble coming after this.

The Sixth Horn—the Angels That Kill

13 The sixth angel blew his horn. I heard a voice coming from the four corners of the altar made of gold that is before God. 14 The voice said to the sixth angel who had the horn, "Let the four angels loose that have been chained at the big river Euphrates." 15 They had been kept ready for that hour and day and month and year. They were let loose so they could kill one-third part of all men that were living. 16 The army had 200 million soldiers on horses. I heard them say how many there were.

17 I saw, as God wanted to show me, the horses and the men on them. The men had pieces of iron over their chests. These were red like fire and blue like the sky and yellow like sulphur. The heads of the horses looked like the heads of lions. Fire and smoke and sulphur came out of their mouths. 18 One-third part of all men was killed by the fire and smoke and sulphur that came out of their mouths. 19 The power of the horses was in their mouths and in their tails. Their tails were like the heads of snakes and with them they could bite and kill. 20 The men that were still living after these troubles were past would not turn away from worshiping demons. They would not turn away from false gods

made from gold and silver and brass and stone and wood. None of these false gods can see or hear or walk. ²¹ These men were not sorry for their sins and would not turn away from all their killing and their witchcraft. They would not stop their sex sins and their stealing.

The Angel and the Little Book

10 Then I saw another strong angel coming down from heaven covered with a cloud. He had many colors around his head. His face was like the sun. His feet were like long flames of fire. ² He had in his hand a little book that was open. The angel put his right foot on the sea. He put his left foot on the land. ³ He cried with a loud voice like the sound of a lion. The seven thunders sounded. ⁴ I was ready to write when the seven thunders had spoken. Then I heard the voice from heaven saying, "Lock up the things which the seven thunders have spoken. Do not write them!"

⁵ Then the strong angel that I saw standing on the sea and on the land lifted his right hand to heaven. ⁶ He made a promise in the name of God Who lives forever, Who made the heaven and the earth and the sea and everything in them. He promised that there will be no more waiting. ⁷ And when the seventh angel blows his horn, God will put His secret plan into action. It will be done just as He told it to the early preachers, His servants.

⁸ Then the voice I heard from heaven spoke to me again. It said, "Go and take the little book that is open. It is in the hand of the angel who is standing on the sea and on the land."

⁹ I went to the angel and asked him to give me the little book. He said, "Take it and eat it. It will taste like honey in your mouth. But after you have eaten it, it will make your stomach sour." ¹⁰ Then I took it from the angel's hand and ate it. It was sweet as honey in my mouth, but it made my stomach sour after I had eaten it.

¹¹ Then they said to me, "You must tell what will happen again in front of many people and nations and families and kings."

The House of God

11 I was given a stick that is used to see how big things are. Someone said, "Go up to the house of God and find out how big it is. Find out about the altar also. See how many people are worshiping. ² Do not find out about the porch of the house of God. It has been given over to the nations who do not know God. They will walk over all the Holy City to wreck it for forty-two months. ³ I will give power to my two men who tell what they know. They will speak for God for 1,260 days (forty-two months). They will be dressed in clothes made from the hair of animals."

The Two Men Who Tell What They Know

⁴ These two men who tell what they know are the two olive trees and the two lights that stand before the Lord of the earth. ⁵ If anyone hates them and tries to hurt them, fire comes out of the mouths of these two men. The fire kills those who try to hurt them. ⁶ They have power to shut up the sky. During the time they speak for God, there will be no rain. They have power to change all waters into blood. They can send every kind of trouble to the earth whenever they want to.

The Death of the Two Men Who Speak for God

⁷ When they have finished speaking for God, the wild animal will make war with them. It will come up out of the hole without a bottom. This wild animal will have power over them and kill them. ⁸ Their dead bodies will lie in the street of Jerusalem. It is where their Lord was nailed to a cross. The city is sometimes called Sodom and Egypt. ⁹ For three and one-half days those from every people and from every family and from every language and from every nation will look at their dead bodies. People will not allow the dead bodies of these two men to be put in a grave. ¹⁰ Those who are living on the earth will be happy because of the death of these two men. They will do things to show they are happy. They will send gifts to each other. They will do this because these two men brought much trouble and suffering to the people of the earth.

The Two Men Come to Life Again

¹¹ After three and one-half days, life from God came into them again. They stood on their feet. Those who saw them were very much afraid.

¹² Then the two men who told what they knew heard a loud voice from heaven. It said, "Come up here." And they went up to heaven in a cloud. All those who hated them watched them go. ¹³ At the same time the earth shook. One-tenth part of

the buildings of the city fell down. Seven thousand people were killed. The rest of the people were afraid and gave honor to the God of heaven.

14 The second time of trouble is past. But look, the third time of trouble is coming soon.

The Seventh Horn—Worship in Heaven

15 The seventh angel blew his horn. There were loud voices in heaven saying, "The nations of the world have become the holy nation of our Lord and of His Christ. He will be the Leader forever." 16 Then the twenty-four leaders who sat on their thrones before God fell on their faces and worshiped God. 17 They said, "All-powerful Lord God, the One Who is and Who was and Who is to come, we thank You because You are using Your great power and have become Leader. 18 The people who do not know God have become angry with You. Now it is time for You to be angry with them. It is time for the dead to stand before You and to be judged. It is time for the servants You own who are the early preachers and those who belong to You to get the reward that is coming to them. It is time for the important people and those not important who honor Your name to get the pay that is coming to them. It is time to destroy those who have made every kind of trouble on the earth."

19 God's house in heaven was opened. The special box which held the Old Way of Worship was seen in the house of God. There was lightning and thunder and noise. The earth shook and large hail stones fell.

The Woman and the Dragon

12 Something very special was seen in heaven. A woman was there dressed with the sun. The moon was under her feet. A crown with twelve stars in it was on her head. 2 She was about to become a mother. She cried out with pain waiting for the child to be born. 3 Something else special was seen in heaven. A large dragon was there. It was red and had seven heads and ten horns. There was a crown on each head. 4 With his tail he pulled one-third part of the stars out of heaven. He threw them down to the earth. This dragon stood in front of the woman as she was about to give birth to her child. He was waiting to eat her child as soon as it was born. 5 Then the woman gave birth

to a son. He is to be the leader of the world using a piece of iron. But this child was taken away to God and His throne. 6 The woman ran away into the desert. God had made the place ready for her. He will care for her there 1,260 days.

War in Heaven

7 Then there was war in heaven. Michael and his angels fought against this dragon. This animal and his angels fought back. 8 But the dragon was not strong enough to win. There was no more room in heaven for them. 9 The dragon was thrown down to earth from heaven. This animal is the old snake. He is also called the Devil or Satan. He is the one who has fooled the whole world. He was thrown down to earth and his angels were thrown down with him.

10 Then I heard a loud voice in heaven saying, "Now God has saved from the punishment of sin! God's power as King has come! God's holy nation has come! God's Christ is here with power! The one who spoke against our Christian brothers has been thrown down to earth. He stood before God speaking against them day and night. 11 They had power over him and won because of the blood of the Lamb and by telling what He had done for them. They did not love their lives but were willing to die. 12 For this reason, O heavens and you who are there, be full of joy. It is bad for you, O earth and sea. For the devil has come down to you. He is very angry because he knows he has only a short time."

War on Earth

13 When the dragon which is the devil saw that he had been thrown down to the earth, he began to hunt for the woman who had given birth to the boy baby. 14 The woman was given two wings like the wings of a very large bird so she could fly to her place in the desert. She was to be cared for there and kept safe from the snake, which is the devil, for three and one-half years. 15 Then the snake spit water from his mouth so the woman might be carried away with a flood. 16 The earth helped the woman by opening its mouth. It drank from the flood of water that this dragon spit from his mouth. 17 This dragon was very angry with the woman. He went off to fight with the rest of her children. They are the ones who obey the Laws of God and are faithful to the teachings of Jesus.

The Two Animals—the First One from the Sea

13 I stood on the sand by the sea-shore. There I saw a wild animal coming up out of the sea. It had seven heads and ten horns with a crown on each horn. There were names on each head that spoke bad words against God. 2 The wild animal I saw was covered with spots. It had feet like those of a bear. It had a mouth like that of a lion. The dragon gave this wild animal his own power and his own throne as king. The wild animal was given much power. 3 One of the heads of the wild animal looked as if it had been killed. But the bad cut given to kill him was healed. The whole world was surprised and wondered about this, and they followed after the wild animal. 4 They worshiped the dragon for giving this wild animal such power. And they worshiped this wild animal. They said, "Who is like this wild animal? Who can fight against it?"

5 The animal was given a mouth which spoke words full of pride and it spoke very bad things against the Lord. It was given much power for forty-two months. 6 And it opened its mouth speaking very bad things against God. It spoke against God's name and His house and against those living in heaven. 7 It was allowed to fight against the people who belong to God, and it had power to win over them. It had power over every family and every group of people and over people of every language and every nation. 8 Every person on the earth from the beginning of the world whose name has not been written in the book of life of the Lamb Who was killed will worship this animal.

9 You have ears! Then listen. 10 Whoever is to be tied and held will be held. Whoever kills with a sword must himself be killed with a sword. Now is when God's people must have faith and not give up.

The Second Animal—from the Land

11 Then I saw another wild animal coming out of the earth. He had two horns like those of a lamb. His voice was like that of the dragon. 12 He used the power of the first wild animal who was there with him. He made all the people on earth worship the first wild animal who had received the bad cut to kill him but was healed. 13 The second wild animal did great powerful works. It spoke and made those who did not worship the first wild animal to be killed. 14 He fooled the men of the earth by

doing powerful works. He did these things in front of the first wild animal. He told those who live on the earth to make a god that looks like the first wild animal. The first wild animal was the one that was cut by the sword but lived. 15 The second wild animal was given power to give life to the false god. This false god was the one that was made to look like the first wild animal. It was given power to talk. All those who did not worship it would die. 16 The second wild animal made every person have a mark on their right hand or on their forehead. It was given to important men and to those not important, to rich men and poor men, to those who are free and to those who are servants. 17 No one could buy or sell anything unless he had the mark on him. This mark was the name of the first wild animal or another way to write his name. 18 This is wisdom. Let the person who has good understanding learn the meaning of the other way to write the name of the first wild animal. This name is a man's name. It is 666.

The Lamb Stands in Jerusalem

14 Then I looked and saw the Lamb standing on Mount Zion. There were 144,000 people with Him. These people had His name and His Father's name written on their foreheads. 2 I heard a voice coming from heaven. It was like the sound of rushing water and of loud thunder. The voice I heard was like people playing music on their harps. 3 This large group sang a new song. They sang before the throne and in front of the four living beings and the twenty-four leaders. Only the 144,000 could learn this song. They had been bought by the blood of Christ and made free from the earth. 4 These are men who have kept themselves pure by not being married. They follow the Lamb wherever He goes. They have been bought by the blood of Christ and have been made free from among men. They are the first ones to be given to God and to the Lamb. 5 No lie has come from their mouths. They are without blame.

The Three Angels

6 Then I saw another angel flying in the heavens. He was carrying the Good News that lasts forever. He was preaching to every nation and to every family group and to the people of every language and to all the people of the earth. 7 He said with a loud voice, "Honor God with love and

fear. The time has come for Him to judge all men. Worship Him Who made heaven and earth and the sea and the places where water comes out of the earth."

⁸ A second angel followed, saying, "Babylon has fallen! The great city Babylon has fallen! She made all the nations drink of the wine of her sinful sex life."

⁹ A third angel followed, saying with a loud voice, "If anyone worships the wild animal and his false god and receives a mark on his forehead or hand, ¹⁰ he will drink of the wine of the anger of God. It is mixed in full strength in the cup of God's anger. They will be punished with fire and burning sulphur in front of the holy angels and before the Lamb. ¹¹ The smoke of those who are being punished will go up forever. They have no rest day or night. It is because they have worshiped the wild animal and his false god and have received the mark of his name. ¹² This is why God's people need to keep true to God's Word and stay faithful to Jesus.

¹³ Then I heard a voice from heaven, saying, "Write these words: 'From now on those who are dead who died belonging to the Lord will be happy.'" "Yes," says the Spirit, "they will have rest from all their work. All the good things they have done will follow them."

The War of Armageddon

¹⁴ I looked and saw a white cloud. Sitting on the cloud was One like the Son of Man. He had a crown of gold on His head. In His hand He had a sharp knife for cutting grain. ¹⁵ Then another angel came out from the house of God and called to Him with a loud voice. He said, "Use Your knife and gather in the grain. The time has come to gather the grain because the earth is ready." ¹⁶ He Who sat on the cloud raised His knife over the earth. And the grain was gathered in.

¹⁷ Then another angel came out from the house of God in heaven. He had a sharp knife for cutting grain also. ¹⁸ Another angel who has power over fire came out from the altar. He said with a loud voice to the angel who had the sharp knife, "Use your knife and gather in the grapes from the vine of the earth, for they are ready to gather." ¹⁹ The angel used his sickle on the earth. He gathered from the vine of the earth and put the fruit into the large place for making wine. It was full of God's anger. ²⁰ They walked on it outside the city and blood came out of the place where wine is made. The blood ran as far as a man could walk in seven days. It came up as high as a horse's head.

Seven Angels with Seven Troubles

15 Then I saw something else special in heaven that was great and made me wonder. There were seven angels with the seven last kinds of trouble. With these, God's anger is finished.

² Then I saw something that looked like a sea of glass mixed with fire. I saw many standing on the sea of glass. They were those who had won their fight with the wild animal and his false god and with his mark. All of them were holding harps that God had given to them. ³ They were singing the song of Moses, who was a servant owned by God, and the song of the Lamb, saying, "The things You do are great and powerful. You are the All-powerful Lord God. You are always right and true in everything You do. You are King of all nations. ⁴ Who will not honor You, Lord, with love and fear? Who will not tell of the greatness of Your name? For You are the only One Who is holy. All nations will come and worship before You. Everyone sees that You do the right things."

⁵ After this I looked and saw that the Holiest Place of All in the house of God was opened. ⁶ The seven angels who had the seven last kinds of trouble came out of the house of God. They were wearing clothes made of clean white linen. They were wearing belts made of gold around their chests. ⁷ Then one of the four living beings gave to each of the seven angels a jar made of gold. These jars were filled with the anger of God Who lives forever. ⁸ The house of God was filled with smoke from the shining-greatness and power of God. No one was able to go into the house of God until the seven angels had completed the seven kinds of trouble.

The First Jar—Painful Sores

16 Then I heard a loud voice coming from the house of God. The voice told to the seven angels, "Go and pour out the seven jars of God's anger onto the earth."

² The first angel poured out his jar of God's anger onto the earth. Painful sores were given to everyone who had the mark of the wild animal and who worshiped his god.

The Second Jar—Death in the Sea

³ The second angel poured out his jar of God's anger onto the sea. The water

became like the blood of a dead man. Every living thing in the sea died.

The Third Jar—Water Turns to Blood

4 The third angel poured out his jar of God's anger onto the rivers and places where water comes out of the earth. The water turned to blood. 5 I heard the angel of the waters saying, "You are right in punishing by sending this trouble. You are the Holy One Who was and is and will be. 6 They have poured out the blood of God's people and of the early preachers. You have given them blood to drink. They are getting the pay that is coming to them." 7 I heard a voice from the altar saying, "Lord God, the All-powerful One! What You decide about people is right and true."

The Fourth Jar—Burning Heat

8 The fourth angel poured out his jar of God's anger onto the sun. It was allowed to burn men with its fire. 9 Men were burned with the heat of this fire and they called God bad names even when He had the power over these kinds of trouble. They were not sorry for their sins and did not turn from them and honor Him.

The Fifth Jar—Darkness

10 The fifth angel poured out his jar of God's anger upon the throne of the wild animal. The whole nation of the wild animal was turned into darkness. Those who worshiped him bit their tongues because of the pain. 11 They called the God of heaven bad names because of their pain and their sores. They were not sorry for what they had done.

The Sixth Jar—the Euphrates River Dries Up

12 The sixth angel poured out his jar of God's anger onto the great Euphrates River. The water dried up. In this way, the kings of the countries of the east could cross over. 13 Then I saw three demons that looked like frogs. They came out of the mouths of the dragon and the second wild animal and the false preacher. 14 These are demons that do powerful works. These demons go to all the kings of all the earth. They bring them together for the war of the great day of the All-powerful God.

15 (See! I will come like a robber. The man is happy who stays awake and keeps his clothes ready. He will not be walking around without clothes and be ashamed.) 16 Then the demons brought the kings together in the place called Armageddon in the Hebrew language.

The Seventh Jar—the Earth Shakes and Hail Falls

17 The seventh angel poured out his jar of God's anger into the air. A loud voice came from the throne in the house of God, saying, "It is all done!" 18 Then there were voices and lightning and thunder and the earth shook. The earth shook much more than it had ever shaken before. 19 The big and strong city of Babylon was split in three parts. The cities of other nations fell to the ground. Then God remembered the strong city of Babylon. He made her drink the wine from His cup of much anger. 20 Every island went down into the sea. No mountain could be found. 21 Large pieces of hail fell from heaven on men. These pieces were about as heavy as an older child. But men called God bad names because of so much trouble from the hail.

The Sinful Woman

17 Then one of the seven angels who had the seven jars came to me. He said, "Come! I will show you how the powerful woman who sells the use of her body will be punished. She sits on the many waters of the world. 2 The kings of the earth have done sex sins with her. People of the world have been made drunk with the wine of her sex sins."

3 I was carried away in the Spirit by the angel to a desert. I saw a woman sitting on a red wild animal. It had seven heads and ten horns. All over the red wild animal was written bad names which spoke against God. 4 The woman was wearing purple and red clothes. She was wearing gold and pearls and stones worth much money. She had in her hand a gold cup full of sinful things from her sex sins. 5 There was a name written on her forehead which had a secret meaning. It said, "The big and powerful Babylon, mother of all women who sell the use of their bodies and mother of everything sinful of the earth." 6 I looked at the woman. She was drunk with the blood of God's people and those who had been killed for telling about Jesus. When I saw her, I wondered very much.

7 The angel asked me, "Why do you wonder? I will tell you the secret about this woman and the red wild animal that carries her. It is the red wild animal with seven heads and ten horns. 8 The red wild animal you saw was alive but is now dead.

He will come up from the hole without a bottom and be destroyed. The people of the earth, whose names have not been written in the book of life from the beginning of the world, will be surprised as they look at the red wild animal. He was alive, but not now, but will yet come.

9 "Here is where we need wisdom. The seven heads of the animal are mountains where the woman sits. 10 They are seven kings also. Five of them are no longer kings. The sixth one is now king. The seventh one will be king, but only for a little while. 11 The red wild animal that died is the eighth king. He belongs to the first seven kings, but he will be destroyed also.

12 "The ten horns of the red wild animal which you saw are ten kings. They have not become leaders yet. But they will be given the right and the power to lead their nations for one hour with the red wild animal. 13 They agree to give the right and the power to the red wild animal. 14 These kings will fight and make war with the Lamb. But the Lamb will win the war because He is Lord of lords and King of kings. His people are the called and chosen and faithful ones."

15 Then the angel said to me, "You saw the waters where the woman who sold the use of her body is sitting. The waters are people and large groups of people and nations and languages. 16 The ten horns you saw and the red wild animal will hate the woman who sold the use of her body. They will take everything from her and even her clothes. They will eat her flesh and burn her with fire. 17 God put in their minds a plan that would carry out His desire. They will agree to give their nation to the red wild animal until the words of God have been completed. 18 The woman you saw is the big and powerful city that has power over the kings of the earth."

Babylon Is Destroyed

18 Then I saw another angel coming down from heaven. He had much power. The earth was made bright with his shining-greatness. 2 He cried out with a loud voice, "The big and powerful city of Babylon is destroyed. Demons and every kind of unclean spirit live there. Unclean birds that are hated are there. 3 For she gave her wine to the nations of the world. It was the wine of her desire for sex sins. The kings of the earth have done these sex sins with her. The men of the earth who buy and sell have become

rich from the riches she received while living in sin."

4 I heard another voice from heaven saying, "Come out from her, my people. Do not be a part of her sins so you will not share her troubles. 5 For her sins are as high as heaven. God is ready to punish her for her sins. 6 Pay her back for what she has paid you. Give back to her twice as much for what she has done. In her own cup give her twice as much as she gave. 7 Give her as much trouble and suffering as the fun and the rich living she chose for herself. In her heart she says, 'I sit here like a queen. I am not a woman whose husband has died. I will never have sorrow.' 8 Because of this, troubles of death and sorrow and no food will come to her in one day. She will be burned with fire. For the Lord God is powerful. He is the One Who says she is guilty.

Kings Cry Because of Babylon

9 "Then the kings of the earth will cry for her and be sorry when they see the smoke of her burning. They are the ones who did sex sins with her and lived as rich people. 10 They stand a long way from her because they are afraid of her sufferings. They say, 'It is bad! It is bad for the big and powerful city of Babylon. For in one hour she is destroyed.' 11 The men of the earth who buy and sell are sorry for her and cry. They cry because there is no one to buy their things anymore. 12 They sold gold and silver and stones worth much money and pearls. They sold fine linen and purple and red silk cloth. They sold all kinds of perfumed wood. They sold things made from the teeth of animals and things made from wood that cost much money. They sold brass and iron and stone. 13 They sold spices and perfumes of all kinds. They sold wine and olive oil and fine flour and wheat. They sold cows and sheep and horses and wagons. They sold men who are not free and they sold the lives of men. 14 They buy to her, 'All the good things you wanted so much are gone from you. Your riches are gone. The things you liked so much are gone. You will never have them again.' 15 The men of the earth who became rich by buying and selling in that city will stand a long way back because they are afraid of her sufferings. They will cry and have sorrow. 16 They will say, 'It is bad! It is bad for that powerful city. She dressed in fine linen of purple and red. She covered herself with gold and pearls and

stones worth much money. 17 For in one hour her riches are destroyed.' The captain of every ship and all who traveled on ships and all who worked on ships stood a long way back. 18 They cried out as they saw the smoke of her burning, saying, 'Has there ever been such a city as powerful as this one?' 19 They threw dirt on their heads. They cried out with much sorrow and said, 'It is bad! It is bad for the powerful city! She is the place where all those who owned ships on the sea became rich from all her riches. For in one hour everything is gone!'

20 "Be full of joy because of her, O heaven! Be full of joy, you who belong to God and missionaries and early preachers! For God has punished her for what she did to you."

21 Then a strong angel picked up a large stone like those used for grinding wheat. He threw it into the sea, saying, "The big and strong city of Babylon will be thrown down like this. It will never be found again. 22 The sound of those playing on harps and on flutes and on horns will not be heard in you again. No workman doing any kind of work will be found in you again. The sound of the grinding-stone will not be heard in you again. 23 No light will ever shine in you again. There will be no more happy voices from a wedding heard in you. Your men who bought and sold were the most powerful on earth. You fooled people over all the world by your witchcraft. 24 And in this city was found the blood of the early preachers and of those who belonged to God and of all those who had been killed on the earth."

Giving Thanks in Heaven

19 After this I heard what sounded like the voices of many people in heaven, saying, "Thanks to our God, the One Who saves. Honor and power belong to Him. 2 For the way He punishes people is right and true. He has punished the powerful woman who sold the use of her body. She was making the earth sinful with her sex sins. She killed those who worked for God. He has punished her for it." 3 Again they said, "Thanks to our God. The smoke from her burning goes up forever." 4 The twenty-four leaders and the four living beings got down and worshiped God Who was sitting on the throne. They said, "Let it be so. Thanks to our God!"

5 A voice came from the throne, saying, "Give thanks to our God, you servants who are owned by Him. Give thanks to our God, you who honor Him with love and fear, both small and great."

The Wedding Supper of the Lamb

6 Then I heard what sounded like the voices of many people. It was like the sound of powerful rushing water. And it was like loud thunder. It said, "Thanks to our God. For the Lord our God is King. He is the All-powerful One. 7 Let us be full of joy and be glad. Let us honor Him, for the time has come for the wedding supper of the Lamb. His bride has made herself ready. 8 She was given clean, white, fine linen clothes to wear. The fine linen is the right living of God's people."

9 The angel said to me, "Write this: 'Those who are asked to the wedding supper of the Lamb are happy.' " And he said, "These are the true words of God." 10 Then I fell at his feet to worship him. But he said to me, "No! Do not worship me. I am a servant together with you and your Christian brothers who tell of their trust in Christ. Worship God. For those who speak for Jesus are led in what to say as the early preachers were led."

The King of Kings on the White Horse

11 Then I saw heaven opened. A white horse was standing there. The One Who was sitting on the horse is called Faithful and True. He is the One Who punishes in the right way. He makes war. 12 His eyes are a flame of fire. He has many crowns on His head. His name is written on Him but He is the only One Who knows what it says. 13 The coat He wears has been put in blood. His name is The Word of God. 14 The armies in heaven were dressed in clean, white, fine linen. They were following Him on white horses. 15 Out of His mouth comes a sharp sword to punish the nations. He will be the Leader over them using a piece of iron. He walks on the grapes where wine is made, pressing out the anger of God, the All-powerful One. 16 On His coat and on His leg is the name written, "KING OF KINGS AND LORD OF LORDS."

17 Then I saw an angel standing in the sun. He cried out with a loud voice to all the birds flying in the sky, "Come and gather together for the great supper of God! 18 Come and eat the flesh of kings and of captains of soldiers and of strong men and of the flesh of horses and of those sitting on them. Come and eat the flesh of

all men, small and great. Some are free and some are not free."

19 Then I saw the wild animal and the kings of the earth and their armies gather together. They were ready to fight against the One Who is sitting on the white horse and against His army. 20 The wild animal was taken. The false preacher was taken with it. It was the false preacher who had done powerful works in front of the wild animal. In this way, he fooled those who had received the mark of the wild animal and those who worshiped his false god. These two were thrown alive into the lake of fire that burns with sulphur. 21 The rest were killed with the sword that came out of the mouth of the One Who sat on the horse. All the birds were filled by eating the flesh of these who were killed.

Satan Is Chained for One Thousand Years

20 Then I saw an angel coming down from heaven. He had in his hand a key to the hole without a bottom. He also had a strong chain. 2 He took hold of the dragon, that old snake, who is the Devil, or Satan, and chained him for 1,000 years. 3 The angel threw the devil into the hole without a bottom. He shut it and locked him in it. He could not fool the nations anymore until the 1,000 years were completed. After this he must be free for awhile.

4 Then I saw thrones. Those who were sitting there were given the power to judge. I saw the souls of those who had been killed because they told about Jesus and preached the Word of God. They had not worshiped the wild animal or his false god. They had not received his mark on their foreheads or hands. They lived again and were leaders along with Christ for 1,000 years. 5 The rest of the dead did not come to life again until the 1,000 years were finished. This is the first time many people are raised from the dead at the same time. 6 Those who are raised from the dead during this first time are happy and holy. The second death has no power over them. They will be religious leaders of God and of Christ. They will be leaders with Him for 1,000 years.

Satan Is Destroyed Forever

7 When the 1,000 years are finished, Satan will be free to leave his prison. 8 He will go out and fool the nations who are over all the world. They are Gog and Magog.

He will gather them all together for war. There will be as many as the sand along the sea-shore. 9 They will spread out over the earth and all around the place where God's people are and around the city that is loved. Fire will come down from God out of heaven and destroy them. 10 Then the devil who fooled them will be thrown into the lake of fire burning with sulphur. The wild animal and the false preacher are already there. They will all be punished day and night forever.

The Guilty Will Be Punished

11 Then I saw a great white throne. I saw the One Who sat on it. The earth and the heaven left Him in a hurry and they could be found no more. 12 I saw all the dead people standing before God. There were great people and small people. The books were opened. Then another book was opened. It was the book of life. The dead people were judged by what they had done as it was written in the books. 13 The sea gave up the dead people who were in it. Death and hell gave up the dead people who were in them. Each one was judged by what he had done. 14 Then death and hell were thrown into the lake of fire. The lake of fire is the second death. 15 If anyone's name was not written in the book of life, he was thrown into the lake of fire.

All Things New

21 Then I saw a new heaven and a new earth. The first heaven and the first earth had passed away. There was no more sea. 2 I saw the Holy City, the new Jerusalem. It was coming down out of heaven from God. It was made ready like a bride is made ready for her husband. 3 I heard a loud voice coming from heaven. It said, "See! God's home is with men. He will live with them. They will be His people. God Himself will be with them. He will be their God. 4 God will take away all their tears. There will be no more death or sorrow or crying or pain. All the old things have passed away." 5 Then the One sitting on the throne said, "See! I am making all things new. Write, for these words are true and faithful." 6 Then He said to me, "These things have happened! I am the First and the Last. I am the beginning and the end. To anyone who is thirsty, I will give the water of life. It is a free gift. 7 He who has power and wins will receive these things. I will be his God and he will be My son. 8 But those who are afraid and those who do not have faith and the sinful-minded people and those who kill other people and those who do sex sins and those who follow witchcraft and those who worship false gods and all those who tell lies will be put into the lake of fire and sulphur. This is the second death."

The New Jerusalem

9 Then one of the seven angels who had the seven jars full of the seven last troubles came to me and said, "Come! I will show you the bride, the wife of the Lamb." 10 I was carried away in the Spirit by the angel to a very high mountain. He showed me the Holy City of Jerusalem. It was coming out of heaven from God. 11 It was filled with the shining-greatness of God. It shone like a stone worth much money, like a jasper stone. It was clear like glass. 12 It had a very high wall, and there were twelve gates. Twelve angels stood by the gates. The names of the twelve family groups of the Jewish nation were written on the gates. 13 There were three gates on each side. There were three on the east side and three on the north side and three on the south side and three on the west side. 14 The walls were on twelve stones. The names of the twelve missionaries of the Lamb were written on the stones.

15 The angel had a stick in his hand. It was used to find out how big the city and its gates and the walls were. 16 He found out that the city was as wide as it was long and it was as high as it was wide. It was as long as a man could walk in fifty days. It was the same each way. 17 The angel found out that the walls were the same as a man taking seventy-two long steps. The angel used the same way to find out about the city as a man would have used. 18 The wall was made of jasper. The city was made of pure gold. This gold was as clear as glass. 19 The city was built on every kind of stone that was worth much money. The first stone was jasper. The second was sapphire. The third was chalcedony. The fourth was emerald. 20 The fifth was sardonyx. The sixth was sardius. The seventh was chrysolite. The eighth was beryl. The ninth was topaz. The tenth was chrysoprase. The eleventh was jacinth and the twelfth was amethyst. 21 The twelve gates were twelve pearls. Each gate was made from one pearl. The street of the city was pure gold. It was as clear as glass.

22 I did not see a house of God in the city. The All-powerful Lord God and the Lamb are the house of God in this city. 23 There is no need for the sun and moon to shine in the city. The shining-greatness of God makes it full of light. The Lamb is its light. 24 The nations will walk by its light. The kings of the earth will bring their greatness into it. 25 The gates are open all day. They will never be shut. There will be no night there. 26 The greatness and honor of all the nations will be brought into it. 27 Nothing sinful will go into the city. No one who is sinful-minded or tells lies can go in. Only those whose names are written in the Lamb's book of life can go in.

More About the New Jerusalem

22 Then the angel showed me the river of the water of life. It was as clear as glass and came from the throne of God and of the Lamb. 2 It runs down the center of the street in the city. On each side of the river was the tree of life. It gives this fruit twelve times a year, new fruit each month. Its leaves are used to heal the nations.

3 There will be nothing in the city that is sinful. The place where God and the Lamb sit will be there. The servants He owns will serve Him. 4 They will see His face and His name will be written on their foreheads. 5 There will be no night there. There will be no need for a light or for the sun. Because the Lord God will be their light. They will be leaders forever.

Jesus Is Coming Soon

6 Then the angel said to me, "These words are faithful and true. The Lord God of the early preachers has sent His angel to show the servants He owns what must happen soon." 7 "See! I am coming soon. The one who obeys what is written in this Book is happy!"

8 It was I, John, who heard and saw these things. Then I got down at the feet of the angel who showed me these things. I was going to worship him. 9 But he said to me, "No! You must not do that. I am a servant together with you and with your Christian brothers and the early preachers and with all those who obey the words in this Book. You must worship God!" 10 Then he said to me, "Do not lock up the words of this Book. These things will happen soon. 11 And let the sinful people keep on being sinful. Let the dirty-minded people keep on being dirty-minded. And let those right with God keep on being right with God. Let the holy people keep on being holy.

12 "See! I am coming soon. I am bringing with Me the reward I will give to everyone for what he has done. 13 I am the First and the Last. I am the beginning and the end. 14 Those who wash their clothes clean are happy (who are washed by the blood of the Lamb). They will have the right to go into the city through the gates. They will have the right to eat the fruit of the tree of life. 15 Outside the city are the dogs. They are people who follow witchcraft and those who do sex sins and those who kill other people and those who worship false gods and those who like lies and tell them.

16 "I am Jesus. I have sent My angel to you with these words to the churches. I am the beginning of David and of his family. I am the bright Morning Star."

17 The Holy Spirit and the Bride say, "Come!" Let the one who hears, say, "Come!" Let the one who is thirsty, come. Let the one who wants to drink of the water of life, drink it. It is a free gift.

18 I am telling everyone who hears the words that are written in this book: If anyone adds anything to what is written in this book, God will add to him the kinds of trouble that this book tells about. 19 If anyone takes away any part of this book that tells what will happen in the future, God will take away his part from the tree of life and from the Holy City, which are told about in this book.

20 He Who tells these things says, "Yes, I am coming soon!" Let it be so. Come, Lord Jesus. 21 May all of you have the loving-favor of the Lord Jesus Christ. Let it be so.